# Rand McNally
## Cosmopolitan
# World Atlas

# Rand McNally
# Cosmopolitan
# World Atlas

**Rand McNally & Company**
Chicago • New York • San Francisco

# Contents

**Cosmopolitan World Atlas**
*Rand McNally Staff*
**Cartography**
Michael W. Dobson, V. Patrick Healy, Winifred V. Farbman,
Susan K. Hudson, Mel Pofahl, Ronald F. Peters
**Design**
Gordon Hartshorne, Mary Jo Schrader
**Editorial**
Jon M. Leverenz, Rita Stevens

**Photo and map credits**
Title page photograph by David Muench: Haena Point,
Na Pali Coast, Kauai, Hawaii

© westermann Sat Map® and maps on pages I • 1; I • 6
(right); I • 7: I • 8 (right); I • 9 (upper left and below); I • 10
(upper left and lower left); I • 11; I • 12; I • 13; I • 14; I • 15;
I • 16; I • 17; I • 18 (below); I • 19 (upper right); I • 20; I • 21
(center); I • 22; I • 23; I • 24; I • 25 (below); I • 26; I • 27; I • 28;
I • 29; I • 30; I • 31; I • 32; from *Images of the World* © 1983 by
Rand McNally & Company. Originally published in German
under the title of DIERCKE WELTRAUMBILD-ATLAS.
Copyright © 1981 by Georg Westermann Verlag,
Braunschweig/Fed. Rep. of Germany.

Diagrams on pages I • 2-I • 4 from *The Great Geographical
Atlas,* Copyright © 1982 by Istituto Geografico De Agostini,
S.p.A., Novara, Italy.

Pages I • 34 – I • 40 from *The New International Atlas,*
Copyright © 1987 by Rand McNally & Company

Using the Atlas _____ vi–viii

**Satellite Portrait of a
Changing Earth** _____ I·1–I·32
Forces of Change _____ I·2
High Mountains _____ I·6
Earthquakes _____ I·8
Volcanoes _____ I·10
Coastlines _____ I·12
Rivers _____ I·14
Floods _____ I·16
Glaciers _____ I·18
Vegetation _____ I·20
Agriculture _____ I·22
Land Reclamation _____ I·24
Dams and Reservoirs _____ I·26
Urbanization _____ I·28
Cities _____ I·30

**World Patterns: Thematic
Maps of the World** _____ I·33–I·48
Population _____ I·34
Religions and Languages _____ I·36
Agriculture and Fisheries _____ I·38
Energy _____ I·40
Climate _____ I·42
Surface Configuration _____ I·44
Vegetation and Soils _____ I·46
Time Zones _____ I·48

**Reference Maps** _____ 1–128
Map Symbols _____ 1

**The World and
Special Regions** _____ 2–7
The World _____ 2
Polar Map of the World _____ 4
Atlantic Ocean _____ 5
Pacific Ocean _____ 6
Antarctica _____ 7

**Europe** _____ 8–29
Europe and Western Asia _____ 8
British Isles _____ 10
Ireland _____ 11
England and Wales _____ 12
Scotland and Northern England _____ 13
Norway, Sweden and Finland _____ 14
Denmark and Northern Germany _____ 15
France and the Low Countries _____ 16
Belgium, Netherlands, Luxembourg
  and Western Germany _____ 17
Germany, Austria and Switzerland _____ 18
Central Germany _____ 19
Alpine Regions _____ 20
Switzerland _____ 21
Spain and Portugal _____ 22
Italy _____ 23
Yugoslavia, Hungary, Romania
  and Bulgaria _____ 24
Greece, Albania and Western Turkey _____ 25
Poland and Czechoslovakia _____ 26
Western Soviet Union _____ 27
South Central Soviet Union _____ 28
Soviet Union _____ 29

**Asia** _____ 30–41
Asia _____ 30
China, Mongolia, Korea,
  Japan and Taiwan _____ 31
Northeastern China _____ 32
Japan and Korea _____ 33
Indonesia and the Philippines _____ 34
Kampuchea (Cambodia), Laos, Vietnam,
  Thailand and Malaysia _____ 35
India, Pakistan, Bangladesh, Burma
  and Sri Lanka _____ 36
Central India and Nepal _____ 37
Middle East _____ 38
Iran and Afghanistan _____ 39
Turkey, Cyprus, Syria, Jordan,
  Israel and Lebanon _____ 40
Israel and Northern Egypt _____ 41

## Africa — 42–49

Africa — 42
Northeast Africa — 43
Northwest Africa — 44
West Africa — 45
Equatorial Africa — 46
East Africa — 47
Central Africa — 48
Southern Africa — 49

## Australia and Oceania — 50–52

Australia — 50
Southeastern Australia
and New Zealand — 51
Pacific Islands — 52

## South America — 53–60

South America — 53
Central and Southern Argentina
and Chile — 54
Bolivia, Paraguay, Northern Argentina
and Chile — 55
Uruguay and Southern Brazil — 56
Eastern Brazil — 57
Peru and Ecuador — 58
Guyana, Suriname, French Guiana
and Northern Brazil — 59
Colombia and Venezuela — 60

## North America — 61–127

North America — 61
Central America — 62
Mexico — 63
West Indies — 64
Caribbean Islands — 65

## Canada — 66

Alberta — 68
British
Columbia — 69
Manitoba — 70
Maritime
Provinces — 71
Newfoundland — 72
Ontario — 73
Quebec — 74
Saskatchewan — 75

## United States of America — 76

Alabama — 78
Alaska — 79
Arizona — 80
Arkansas — 81
California — 82
Colorado — 83
Connecticut — 84
Delaware — 85
Florida — 86
Georgia — 87
Hawaii — 88
Idaho — 89
Illinois — 90
Indiana — 91
Iowa — 92
Kansas — 93
Kentucky — 94
Louisiana — 95
Maine — 96
Maryland — 97
Massachusetts — 98
Michigan — 99
Minnesota — 100
Mississippi — 101
Missouri — 102
Montana — 103
Nebraska — 104
Nevada — 105
New Hampshire — 106
New Jersey — 107
New Mexico — 108
New York — 109
North Carolina — 110
North Dakota — 111
Ohio — 112
Oklahoma — 113
Oregon — 114
Pennsylvania — 115
Rhode Island — 116
South Carolina — 117
South Dakota — 118
Tennessee — 119
Texas — 120
Utah — 121
Vermont — 122
Virginia — 123
Washington — 124
West Virginia — 125
Wisconsin — 126
Wyoming — 127

## North Polar Regions — 128

## Index to World Reference Maps — 129–224

Introduction to the Index
and List of Abbreviations — 129
Index to World Reference Maps — 130

## World Geographical Information — 225–256

World Political Information — 225
General: The Continents;
Historical Populations;
Largest Countries: Population;
Largest Countries: Area — 229
Principal Mountains — 230
Oceans, Seas, and Gulfs;
Principal Lakes; Principal
Rivers; Principal Islands — 231
World Metropolitan Areas — 232
World Populations — 233

## United States Geographical Information — 257–288

General: Territorial Acquisition
and Population Movement
State Areas and Populations — 257
United States General Information — 258
United States Historical Populations — 259
United States Metropolitan Areas — 260
United States Populations
and ZIP Codes — 261

# Using the Atlas

## Maps and Atlases

Mapmaking appears to have had its origins in the earliest ages of human history. People of all cultures have needed maps, and artifacts show they possessed the skill to draw them. The ease with which almost anyone can sketch simple directions lends credibility to the assumption that maps have been around a long time. They have always played an important and unique role in presenting information about the world — its routes, territories, and the lay of the land.

Some of the earliest maps are those defining territory and ownership. Dating from the second and first millenia B.C., the rock carving map of the Val Camonica, Italy, in figure 1 shows stepped square fields, paths, rivers, and houses. Elegant as well as useful maps have been produced by many cultures. In figure 2, the Mexican map of the Tepetlaoztoc Valley, drawn in 1583, marks hills with wavy lines and roads with footprints between parallel lines. The methods and materials used to create these maps were dependent upon the technology available, and their accuracy suffered considerably, whereas modern maps are highly accurate, benefiting from our ever-increasing technological knowledge. Satellite imagery, shown in figure 3, now furnishes current, highly precise material from which maps such as that in figure 4 may be created or updated.

In the 1500s Gerardus Mercator, a Flemish cartographer, coined the word *atlas* to describe a collection of maps. The atlas is unique among reference publications because only it, with its maps, actually shows *where* things are located in the world. As a dictionary defines words, as an encyclopedia defines things, an atlas graphically defines the world. Only on a map can the countries, cities, roads, rivers, and lakes covering a vast area be simultaneously viewed in their relative locations. Routes between places can be traced, trips planned, boundaries of neighboring states and countries examined, distances between places measured, the meandering of rivers and streams and the sizes of lakes visualized — and remote places imagined.

figure 1

figure 2

figure 3

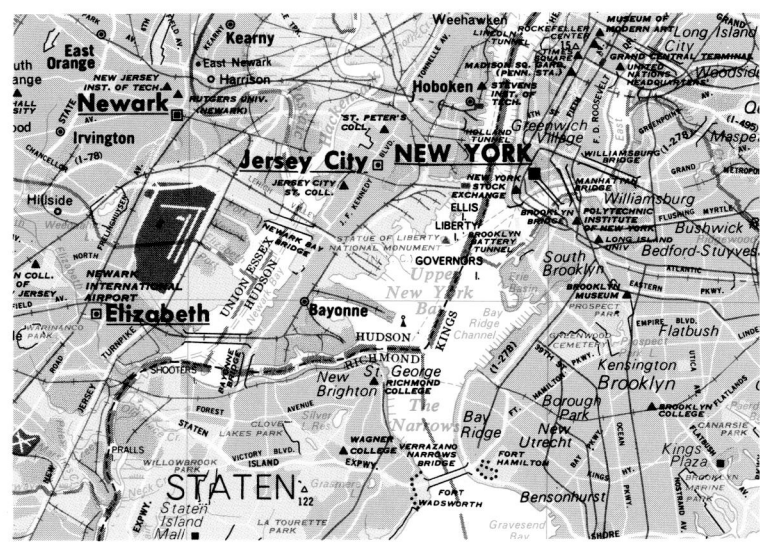

figure 4

## Sequence of the Maps

The world is made up of seven major landmasses: the continents of Europe, Asia, Africa, Australia, South America, North America, and Antarctica (figure 5). To allow for the inclusion of detail, each continent is broken down into a series of maps, and this grouping is arranged so that as consecutive pages are turned, a continuous and successive part of the continent is shown. Larger-scale maps are used for regions of greater detail (having many cities, for example) or for areas of global significance.

The continental sequence of the maps is as follows: Europe (traditionally first in atlases), Asia (connected to Europe and forming the Eurasian landmass), Africa, Australia and Oceania, South America, and North America.

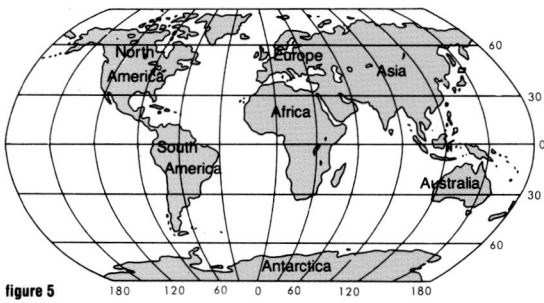

figure 5

## Getting the Information

An atlas can be used for many purposes, from planning a trip to finding hot spots in the news and supplementing world knowledge. But to realize the full potential of an atlas, the user must be able to:

1. Find places on the maps
2. Measure distances
3. Determine directions
4. Understand map symbols

### Finding Places

One of the most common and important tasks facilitated by an atlas is finding the *location* of a place in the world. A river's name in a book, a city mentioned in the news, or a vacation spot may prompt your need to know where the place is located. The illustrations and text below explain how to find Benguela, Angola.

**1.** Look up the place-name in the index at the back of the atlas. Benguela, Angola, can be found on the map on page 48, and it can be located on the map by the letter-number key *D1* (figure 6).

| | | | |
|---|---|---|---|
| Benevento, Italy | D5 | 23 | Benzonia, Mi., U.S. |
| Benevolence, Ga., U.S. | E2 | 87 | Beo, Indon. |
| *Benewah, co., Id., U.S.* | B2 | 89 | Béoumi, I.C. |
| Benezett, Pa., U.S. | D5 | 115 | Beowawe, Nv., U.S. |
| Benfeld, Fr. | A3 | 20 | Beppu, Japan |
| Bengal, Ok., U.S. | C6 | 113 | *Beqa, i., Fiji* |
| *Bengal, hist reg., Asia* | D8 | 36 | *Beqa Passage, strt., Fiji* |
| *Bengal, Bay of, b., Asia* | F8 | 36 | *Bequia, i., St. Vin.* |
| Ben Gardane, Tun. | C7 | 44 | *Berach, stm., India* |
| Bengbu, China | E8 | 31 | Berati, Alb. |
| Benghazi (Banghāzī), Libya | C4 | 43 | Berau, F.R.Ger. |
| Bengkalis, Indon. | E2 | 34 | *Berau Bay, b., Indon.* |
| *Bengkalis, i., Indon.* | L5 | 35 | Berbera, Som. |
| Bengkulu, Indon. | F2 | 34 | Berbérati, Cen. Afr. Rep. |
| *Bengo, dept., Ang.* | C1 | 48 | *Berbice, stm., Guy.* |
| Bengough, Sk., Can. | H3 | 75 | Berceto, Italy |
| Benguela, Ang. | D1 | 48 | Bercher, Switz. |
| *Benguela, dept., Ang.* | D1 | 48 | Berchogur, Sov. Un. |
| Benham, Ky., U.S. | D7 | 94 | Berchtesgaden, F.R.Ger. |
| *Ben Hill, co., Ga., U.S.* | E3 | 87 | Berck, Fr. |
| Beni, Nig. | D7 | 45 | Berclair, Tx., U.S. |
| Beni, Zaire | A4 | 48 | Berdichev, Sov. Un. |
| *Beni, dept., Bol.* | B2 | 55 | Berdsk, Sov. Un. |
| *Beni, stm., Bol.* | B2 | 55 | Berdyansk, Sov. Un. |
| Béni Abbas, Alg. | C4 | 44 | Berea, Ky., U.S. |

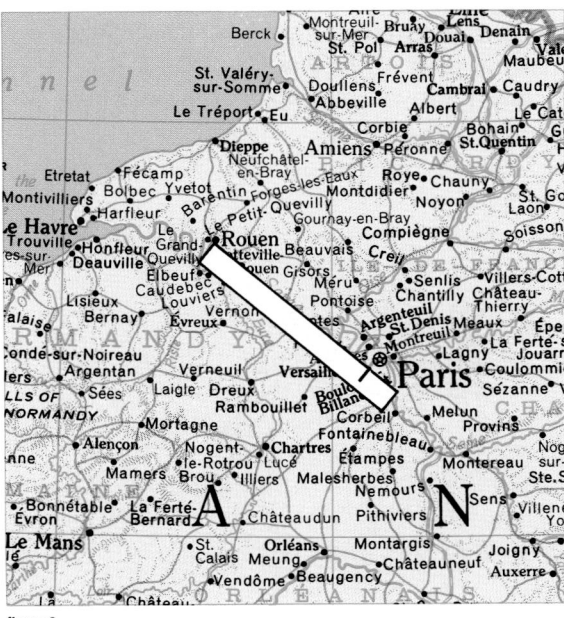

figure 6

**2.** Turn to the map of Central Africa on page 48. Note that the letters A through E and the numbers 1 through 7 appear in the margins of the maps.

**3.** To find Benguela on the map, place your left index finger on D and your right index finger on 1. Move your left finger across the map and your right finger into the map. Your fingers will meet in the area in which Benguela is located (figure 7).

figure 7

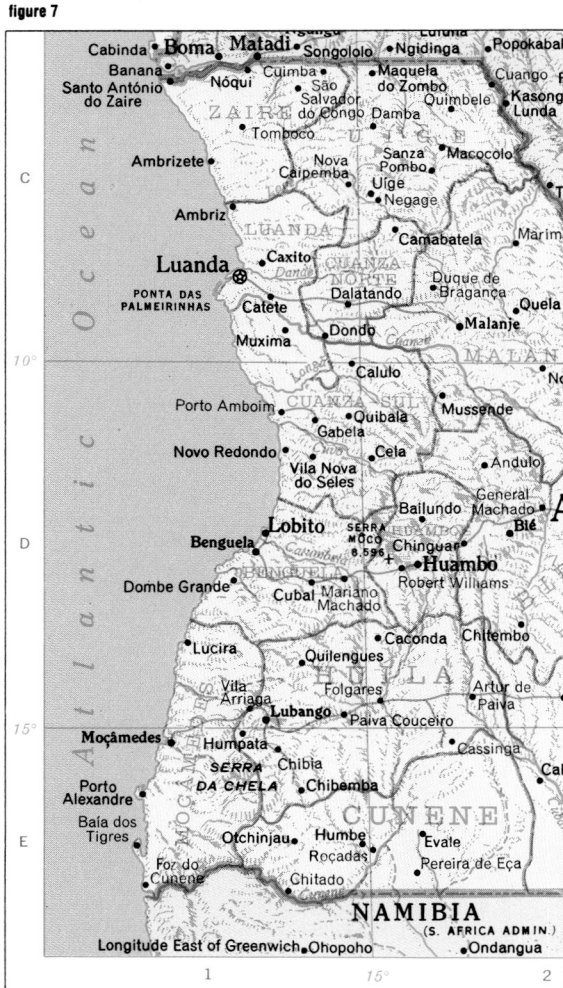

## Measuring Distances

In planning trips, determining the distance between two places is essential, and an atlas can help in travel preparation. For instance, to determine the approximate distance between Paris and Rouen, France, follow these three steps:

**1.** Lay a slip of paper on the map on page 16 so that its edge touches the two cities. Adjust the paper so one corner touches Rouen. Mark the paper directly at the spot where Paris is located (figure 8).

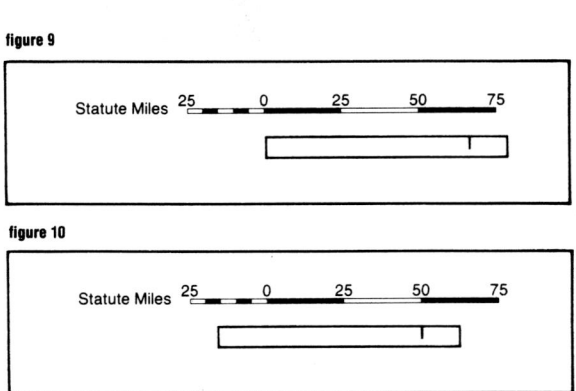

figure 8

**2.** Place the paper along the scale of statute miles beneath the map. Position the corner at 0 and line up the edge of the paper along the scale. The pencil mark on the paper indicates Rouen is between 50 and 75 miles from Paris (figure 9).

**3.** To find the exact distance, move the paper to the left so that the pencil mark is at 50 on the scale. The corner of the paper stands in the fourth 5-mile unit on the scale. This means that the two towns are 50 miles plus 15 miles plus 2 miles, or 67 miles, apart (figure 10).

figure 9

figure 10

The scale relationship of the map to the earth may also be expressed as a ratio, for example, 1:1,000,000 (one to one million). The map unit in the ratio is always given as one, and the number of similar units the map unit represents on the earth's surface is written after the colon. Thus for a 1:1,000,000 map, 1 inch on the map represents 1,000,000 inches on the earth's surface. In order to determine how many miles on the earth 1 inch on the map represents, divide 63,360 (the number of inches in one mile) into 1,000,000. This results in the written scale for a 1:1,000,000 map being stated as, 1 inch (on the map) = 16 miles (on the earth).

## Determining Directions

Most of the maps in the atlas are drawn so that when oriented for normal reading north is at the top of the map, south is at the bottom, west is at the left, and east is at the right. Most maps have a series of lines drawn across them — the lines of latitude and longitude. Lines of latitude, or parallels of latitude, are drawn east and west. Lines of longitude, or meridians of longitude, are drawn north and south (figure 11).

Parallels and meridians appear as either curved or straight lines. For example, in the section of the map of Europe in figure 12, the parallels of latitude appear as curved lines. The meridians of longitude are straight lines that come together toward the top of the map.

Latitude and longitude lines help locate places on maps. Parallels of latitude are numbered in degrees north and south of the *Equator.* Meridians of longitude are numbered in degrees east and west of a line called the *Prime Meridian,* running through Greenwich, England, near London. Any place on earth can be located by the latitude and longitude lines running through it.

To determine directions or locations on maps, you must use the parallels and meridians. For example, suppose you want to know which city is farther north, Bergen, Norway, or Stockholm, Sweden. The map in figure 12 shows that Stockholm is south of the 60° parallel of latitude and Bergen is north of it. This means that Bergen is farther north than Stockholm. By looking at the meridians of longitude, you can determine which city is farther east. Bergen is approximately 5° east of the 0° meridian (Prime Meridian), and Stockholm is almost 20° east of it. This means that Stockholm is farther east than Bergen.

## Understanding Map Symbols

In a very real sense, the whole map is a symbol, representing the world or a part of it. It is a reduced representation of the earth; each of the world's features — cities, rivers, etc. — is represented on the map by a symbol. Map symbols may take the form of points, such as dots or stars (often used for cities, capital cities, or points of interest), or lines (roads, rivers, railroads). Symbols may also occupy an area, showing extent of coverage (states, forests, deserts). They seldom look like the feature they represent and therefore must be identified and interpreted. For instance, the maps in this atlas show and differentiate political units (countries, states) with color. The political units are further defined by a heavy line depicting their boundaries. Neither the colors nor the boundary lines are actually found on the surface of the earth, but because countries and states are such important political components of the world, strong symbols are used to represent them.

The legend on page 1 identifies the symbols used in this atlas.

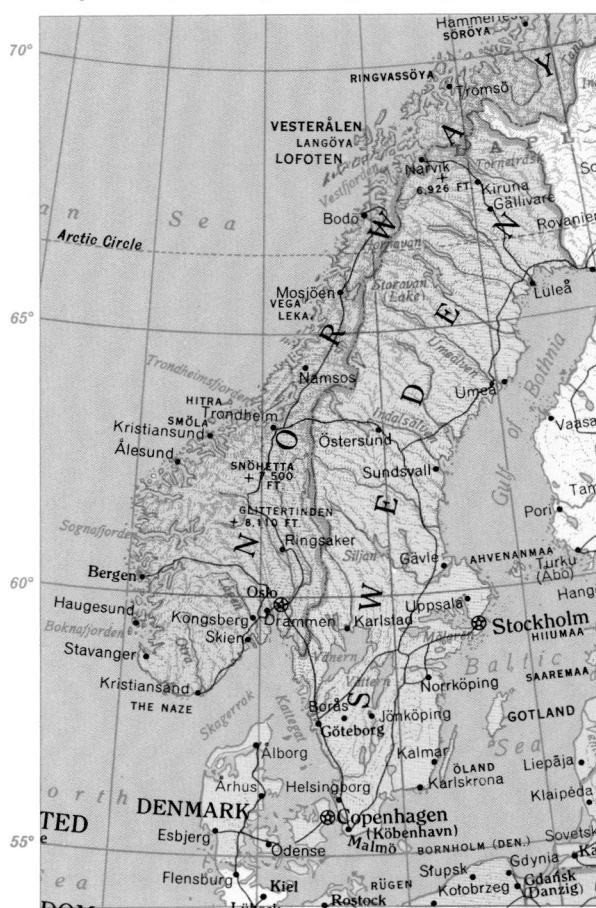

figure 12

figure 11

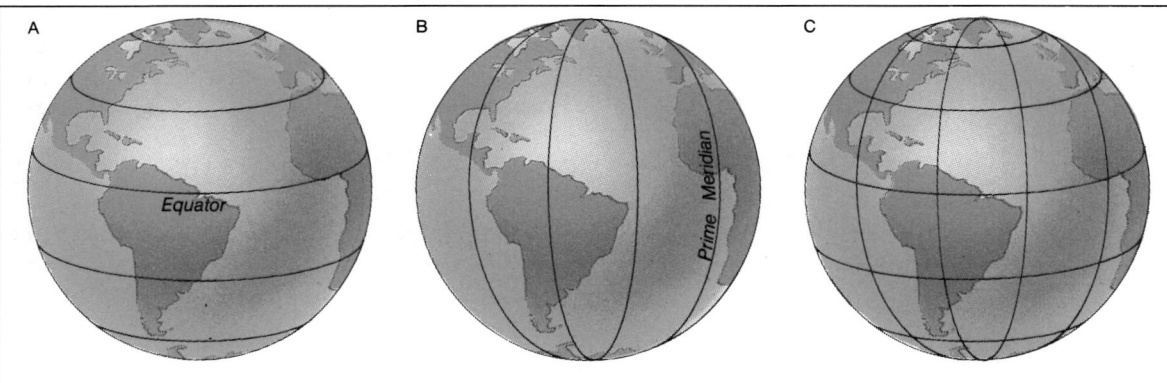

# Satellite Portrait of a Changing Earth

**" Nothing is permanent except change. "**

*Heraclitus, Greek philosopher*

*Author and Consultant:* MICHAL L. LEVASSEUR
*Department of Geography, University of South Florida*

Heraclitus' brief saying captures a fundamental truth about the persistence of change. From the primordial explosion of light and heat that created the known universe to the continual evolution of our small world, change is the one constant that runs through all of life. Yet the task of recognizing and understanding the forces of change and their effects on our lives, our environment, and our planet is as complex as Heraclitus' statement is simple.

We usually connect change to some immediate cause we can see, touch, or understand: an earthquake, a storm, a rise in prices, an abundance or scarcity of food. We seldom look deeper to the underlying forces that indirectly control these causes: the movement of the earth's crust, global atmospheric patterns, worldwide economics, and agricultural cycles around the world. These forces are the relentless, interrelated natural and human phenomena that continually shape and change our lives and our planet.

Natural forces of land, water and wind are generally beyond our control, even if we act collectively. We may be able to predict an earthquake or a hurricane but as yet we cannot prevent it or stop its destructive effects on human life and property. Human forces, on the other hand, such as agriculture and urban development, are strongly influenced by our individual or collective decisions and actions. We can destroy the land's fertility or preserve it, degrade the atmosphere or improve it, pollute our rivers, lakes, and seas or restore their diversity of life.

Within earth's closed system, natural and human forces of change continually affect one another. A change in even a small part of this complex web of life triggers a chain reaction throughout the system that eventually affects all other parts. The more we understand the interrelationship of our planet's many features, phenomena, environments, forces, and controls, the more we can learn to deal intelligently with the opportunities offered by the "permanence of change."

In the next section, we seek to build the reader's understanding and knowledge of our evolving world by briefly discussing the major controlling forces at work on earth: movement of the crust, the force of water, the changing atmosphere, and the impact of human activity. In the articles that follow, we highlight major features or phenomena of our world and concentrate on the most fundamental forces that created them and continue to shape their appearance. The reader should keep in mind, however, that over time all earth's forces interact upon these features and environments, molding and changing them.

Dramatic satellite images of the earth's surface portray the various features in each article and vividly illustrate the effects of major natural and human forces acting on those features. Most of the satellite images were recorded during the growing season and have been processed and printed in colors that closely approximate the ground vegetation. Accompanying maps locate areas covered by the images and help pinpoint interesting features and settlements. Elevations on all maps are in meters.

The map on this page shows which areas of the world are represented by the images used in the articles.

**S** ATELLITE IMAGE LOCATOR MAP
Numbers on the map refer to the atlas pages which display the satellite images.
▼

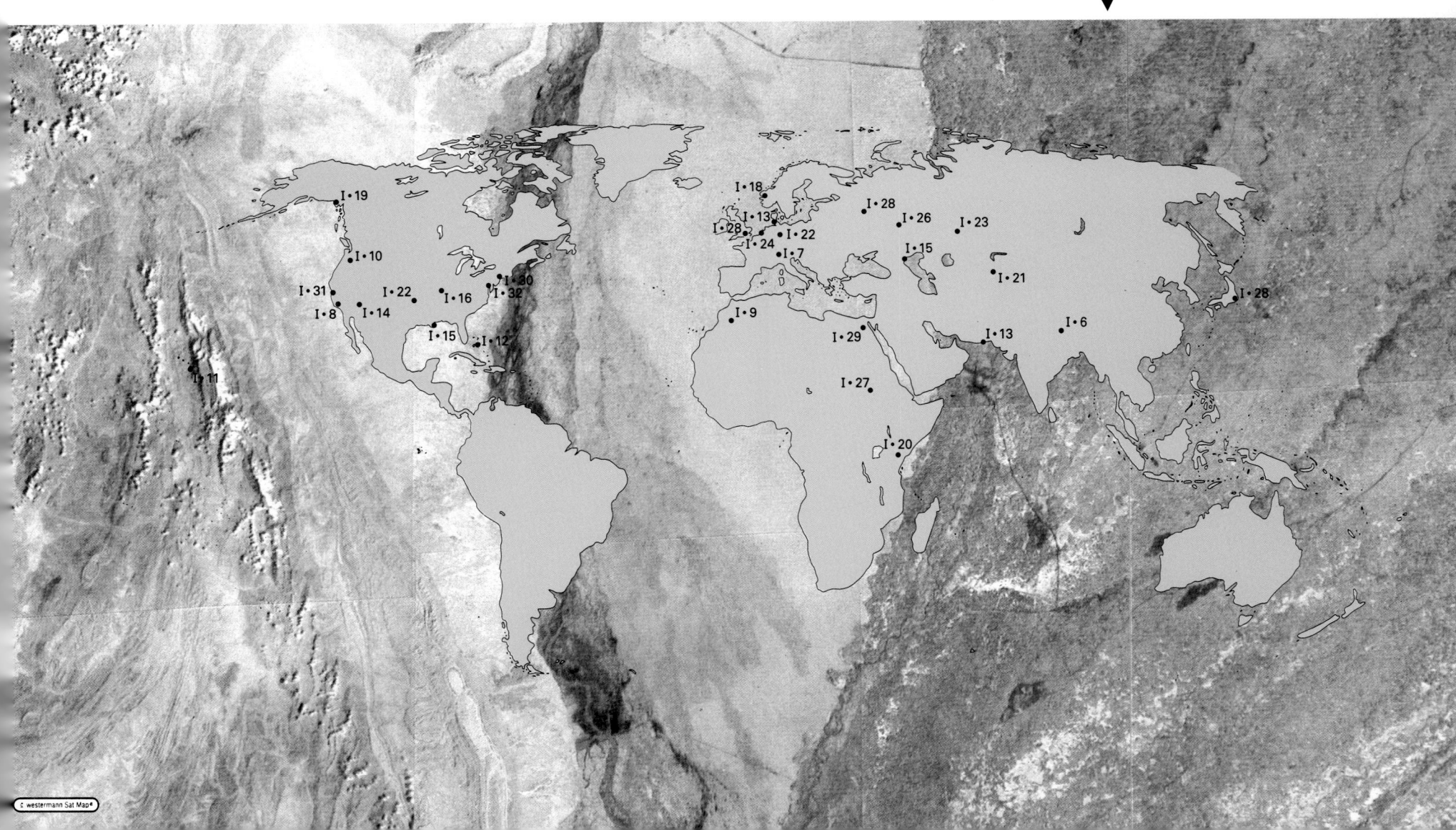

# Forces of Change

The fiery maelstrom that gave birth to the universe endowed our embryonic planet with all the elements it needed to evolve into the world we know today. Over millennia, the gradually cooling earth developed a fragile, shifting crust; oceans that encircle the globe; and an atmosphere capable of supporting life. These three forces – land, water, and air – continue to evolve and to reshape our world. The most recent force – human activity – has an equally powerful effect on the planet's evolution.

**Land**   The earth's apparently solid structure is actually composed of several layers in different physical states. (See A) The top solid layer, known as the lithosphere, is formed of the earth's crust and uppermost mantle. The lithosphere's six major plates and several platelets float on the asthenosphere – the denser fluid portion of the upper mantle. The lithosphere and asthenosphere rest on the lower mantle, which surrounds the fiery core.

The earth's plates and platelets shift constantly relative to one another. (See B) They are driven by movements that originate deep in the earth's lower mantle. (See C) Temperature differences in the mantle create slow convection currents that circulate molten rock to the surface. Where two of these currents converge and move upward, they separate, causing the crustal plates to bulge and move apart in midoceanic regions. As the plates drift, they collide with one another at their continental margins. This irresistible force causes earthquakes and, over eons of time, raises moun-

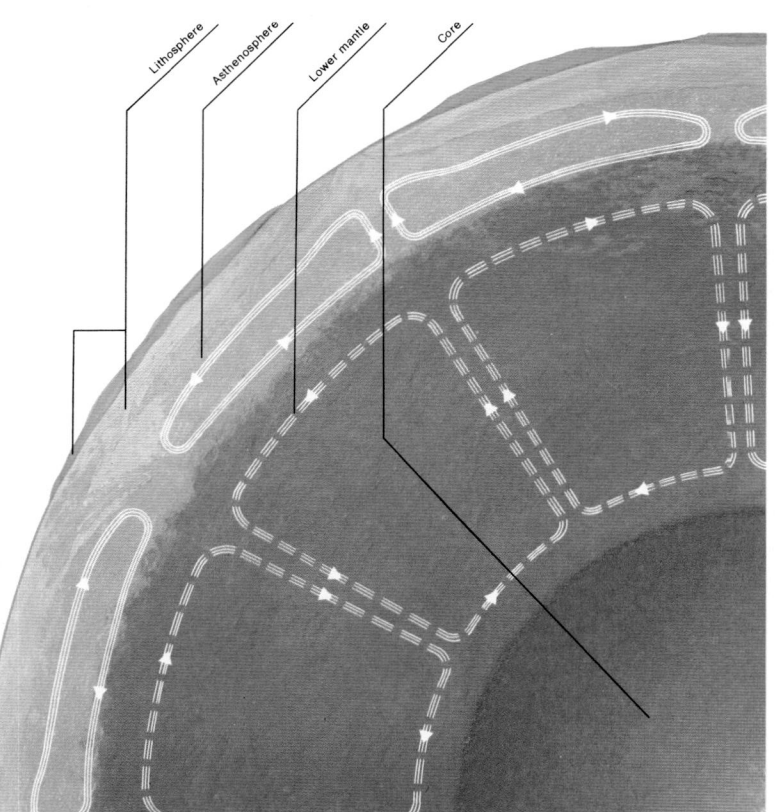

**A** ◀ **E**ARTH'S INTERNAL STRUCTURE   In its simplest form, the earth is composed of a solid crust 10-25 miles thick; a mantle 1,800 miles thick; a molten outer core 1,320 miles thick; and a solid inner core 780 miles in diameter. The solid upper mantle combines with the crust to form the lithosphere. The asthenosphere is distinguished from the lower solid mantle by its semifluid nature. The temperature at the center of the earth is believed to be between 4,000 and 5,000 degrees Fahrenheit.

Subduction Zone

Ocean Ridge Zone

**C** ▶ **C**ONSTRUCTION AND DESTRUCTION OF THE EARTH'S CRUST   The crust is thinner over midoceanic regions than over the continents. This allows molten magma from the mantle to force its way to the surface and form ridges and new crust. Growth at the midoceanic ridges slowly forces the plates apart. As they spread their outer edges collide with other plates. One plate is forced beneath the other in a subduction zone, and its crust is melted back into the mantle.

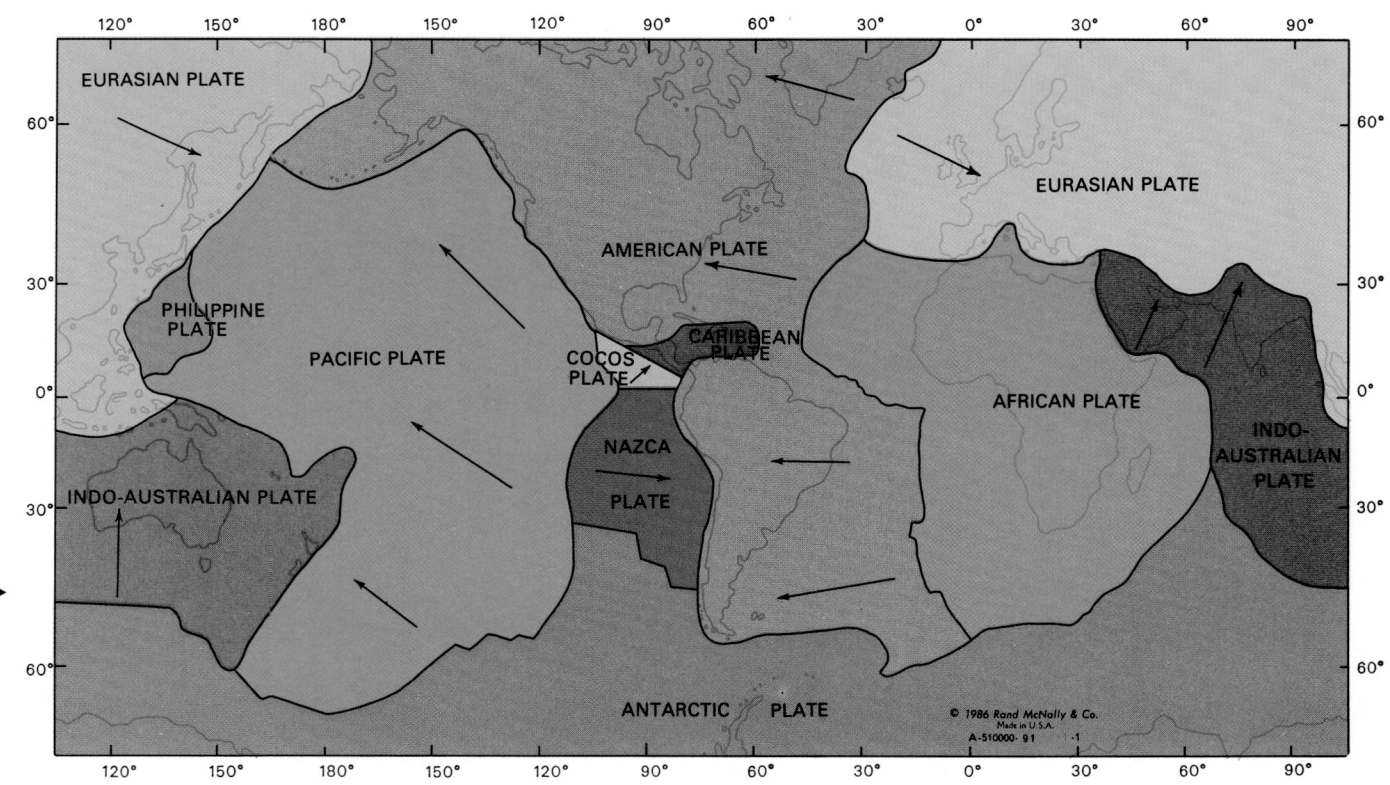

**B** ▶ **W**ORLDWIDE DISTRIBUTION OF TECTONIC PLATES   The map shows the position, names, and general movement of the lithosphere's six major plates.

EURASIAN PLATE

EURASIAN PLATE

AMERICAN PLATE

PHILIPPINE PLATE

PACIFIC PLATE

COCOS PLATE

CARIBBEAN PLATE

AFRICAN PLATE

INDO-AUSTRALIAN PLATE

INDO-AUSTRALIAN PLATE

NAZCA PLATE

ANTARCTIC PLATE

© 1986 Rand McNally & Co.
Made in U.S.A.
A-510000-91

tain ranges, alters coastlines, and moves entire continents.

**Water** Alone of all the sun's planets, earth has an abundance of water in a free or liquid state. Over two-thirds of the planet's surface is covered by water: 97 percent in the oceans and seas, 2 percent locked in glaciers, and 1 percent on land in the form of rivers, streams, ponds, reservoirs, and lakes.

The oceans and seas move in ceaseless rhythms, from the steady beat of waves and rising and falling tides to the seasonal movements of vast ocean currents. These currents, driven by prevailing winds, form huge whirlpools spanning entire seas. Below the ocean's surface flow great "rivers" of cold and warm currents that vary from salt water to fresh. (See D) The constant motion of

water, where it meets land masses or undersea features, wears against the earth and continually refashions it.

Our planet's great oceans and seas serve as a reservoir for the fresh-water rivers, streams, and lakes that enrich and erode the lands around them. Powered by the sun's energy, water evaporates from the oceans, circulates in the atmosphere, and falls to earth as rain or snow. Eventually, through countless lakes and rivers, the water finds its way back to the sea. This vast, never-ending cycle reuses an abundant water supply that has remained relatively constant for some 3 billion years. (See E)

**Air** Our atmosphere is the third vital force creating and shaping the earth. The protective atmospheric layers around our planet

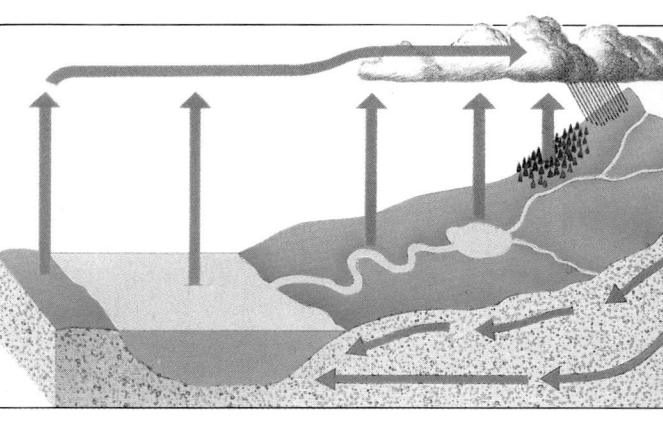

**T**HE CYCLING OF WATER Water evaporates from the world's oceans and is carried by air masses over the land, where it is precipitated in the form of rain or snow. Some of this water then evaporates; drains off the surface or seeps into rivers, lakes, or seas; or is taken up by vegetation from the soil and transpired into the air again. Throughout this cycle, water acts as an element for erosion and deposition of sediment, and it is a major force in shaping the earth.

**O**CEAN SURFACE CURRENTS AND DRAINAGE BASINS Prevailing winds together with the spinning motion of the earth drive the oceans' surface waters into massive whirlpools called gyres. The 5 major gyres are made up of 38 major currents shown on the map. Although warm currents form in the equatorial regions and cold currents near the poles, all regions have a permanent layer of cold water beneath them. Created eons ago in the polar regions, this cold layer sank to the ocean floor as the waters chilled and spread out into all other major ocean basins. The drainage basins, outlined on the map, show the relationship between the oceans and the major river systems which recycle water into the seas. Currents and tides, together with surface water flowing into the oceans, continually reshape earth's landmasses.

D ▼

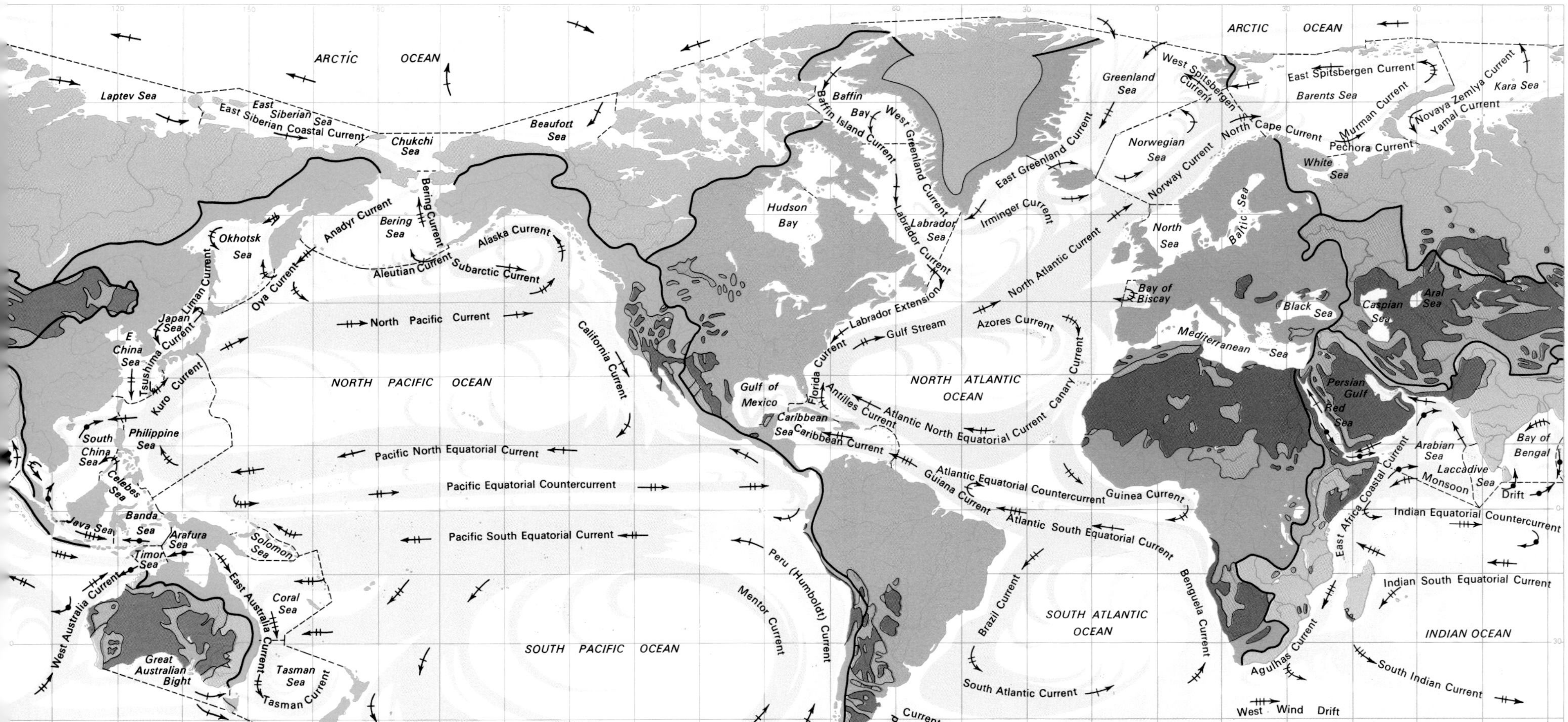

**Drainage Regions and Ocean Currents**

| Currents during Northern Hemisphere winter | Speed of current (1 knot=1 nautical mile[6,076 ft.] per hour) | Drainage regions Surface drainage reaching an Ocean | |
|---|---|---|---|
| Cold current | +−+ Less than 0.5 knots | Outline of oceanic drainage regions | Surface drainage not reaching an ocean |
| Warm current | +++ 0.5—0.8 knots | Atlantic Ocean | Arid regions |
| −+−+ Indicates a current that reverses direction during Northern Hemisphere summer | +++ Greater than 0.8 knots | Pacific Ocean | Ice cap |
| | − − − Limits of seas | Indian Ocean | |
| | | Arctic Ocean | |

Miller Cylindrical Projection
True scale only on the Equator
Encyclopaedia Britannica, Inc. 086
Drainage regions originally compiled by American Geographical Society; revised by Robert D. Hodgson

© 1987 RM©N

I·3

are proportionately no thicker than the skin of an apple. Gravity compresses the air so that half of its mass lies within 3.5 miles of the earth's surface and all climatic changes occur within an average depth of 12 miles.

Like land masses and oceans, the air is in constant motion as it circulates around the globe. (See F) The scale of this movement varies from global patterns of winds and large air masses to local breezes, from violent storms to more subtle atmospheric changes. Constant circulation of the air transfers heat and moisture throughout the planet. This action mixes warm and cool air masses, producing variations in climate and weather.

Over the millenia, atmospheric forces have created an immensely complicated and evolving pattern of climatic zones and local weather conditions. Current climatic zones range from polar to temperate to tropical, extending in bands around the globe. (See G) These established climates influence patterns of plant and animal life, create varied surface conditions, and help define the limits of human activity and settlement.

**Human Activity**  Humanity has done much to reshape the face of the planet since its first appearance on earth a scant few million years ago. Although early humans did little to alter their natural surroundings, the development of agriculture slowly began to change the landscape. Nothing in humanity's brief history, however, can match the impact on our planet of the past 200 years of industrialization and urbanization. These aspects of human activity have affected land, water, and air on a global scale. Our constant search for and exploitation of earth's resources has helped transform the natural landscape in many parts of the world and has created totally new and artificial environments. (See H)

Yet we do not have complete dominion over the earth. Although we have explored every corner of the globe, nature imposes limits on where we can live. The uneven distribution of human settlements over the

**A**TMOSPHERIC AIR MASSES  Air masses **F** ▶ are extensive portions of the atmosphere in which, at any given altitude, the moisture and temperature are almost uniform. Much of the world's weather and its climatic regions result from the movement of these huge masses of air, which are warm or cold, moist or dry, depending on the land or water over which they were formed. The boundaries and movement of air masses are also altered by other factors such as the air's vertical movement, surface friction, land topography, and the earth's rotation. The map depicts the earth's major air masses. The pattern shown creates a rough framework for the world's weather and climate.

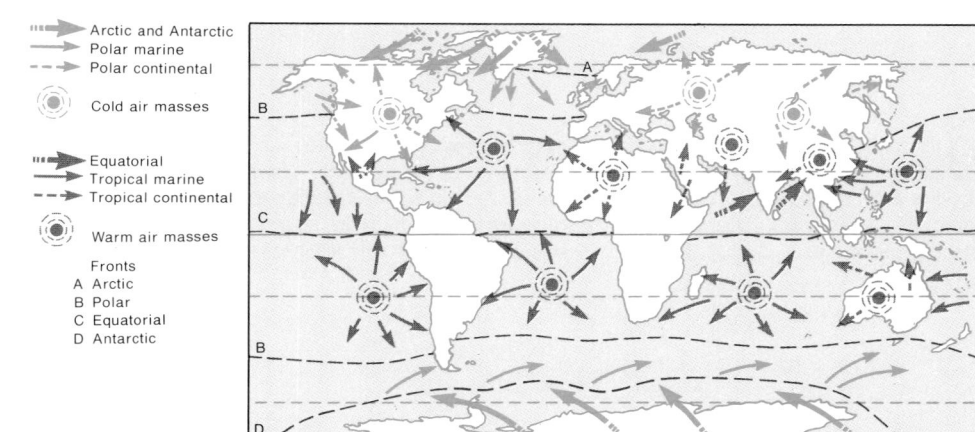

Arctic and Antarctic
Polar marine
Polar continental
Cold air masses

Equatorial
Tropical marine
Tropical continental
Warm air masses

Fronts
A  Arctic
B  Polar
C  Equatorial
D  Antarctic

**C**LIMATES OF THE WORLD  The climate of a region is the characteristic weather recorded over a long period. It is usually described in terms of monthly and yearly temperatures, precipitation, air pressures, winds, and many other elements affecting a region. Thirteen major climatic zones shown on the map are caused largely by the air movement in the atmosphere. Climatic forces play a principal role in the distribution and variation of soil, plant and animal life, and human activity in the world.

**Types of Climate**

**TROPICAL**
Hot and rainy all year
Hot, with rainy and dry seasons

**DRY**
Desert, with some rain
Desert

**TEMPERATE**
(Mild and rainy winter)
Hot and dry summer
Warm and humid summer
Mild and rainy summer

**TEMPERATE**
(Cold and snowy winter)
Long, warm, humid summer
Short, warm, humid summer
Very short, cool, humid summer

**POLAR**
Tundra (very cold and dry)
Ice cap

**HIGHLAND**
Varies with height and latitude

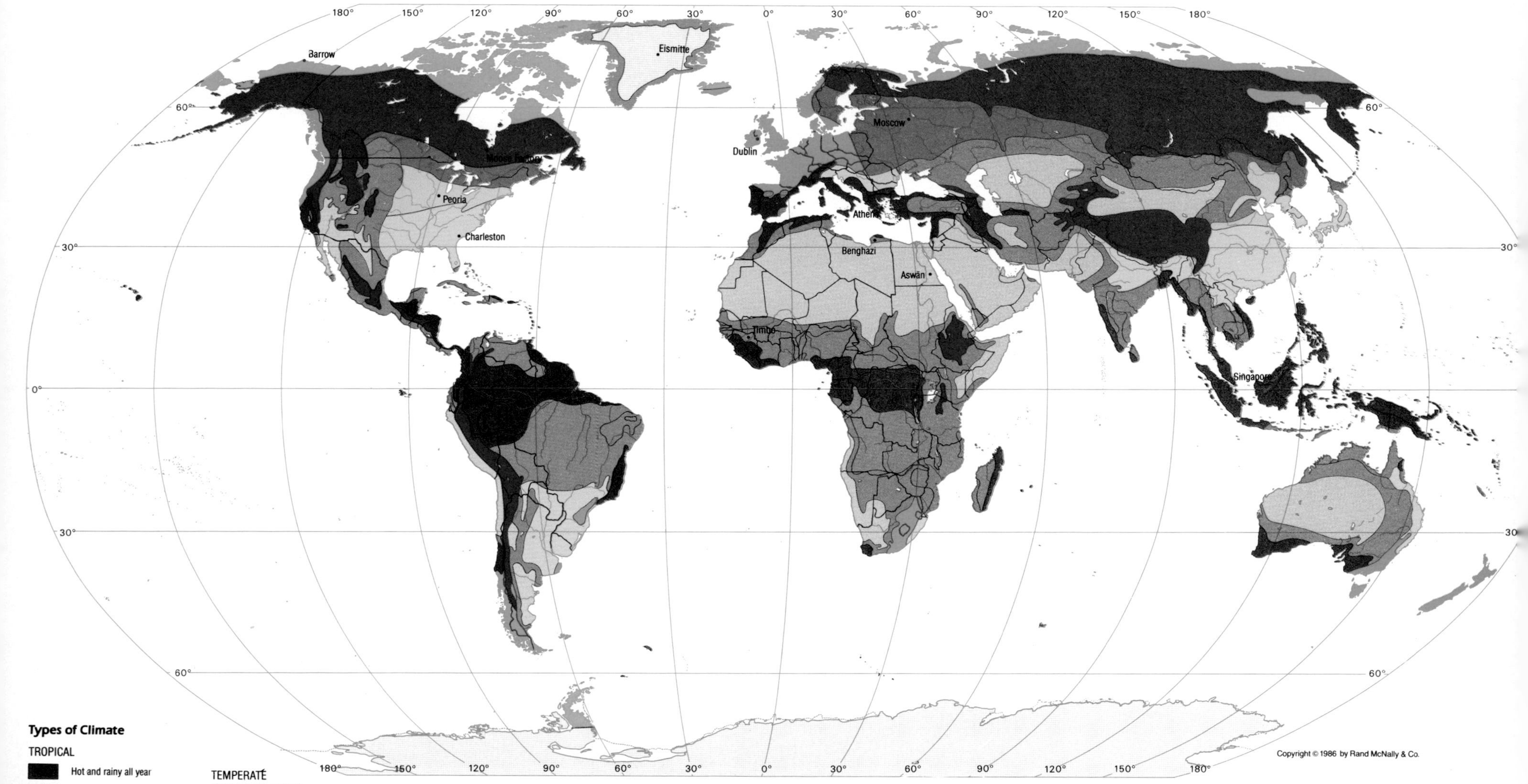

Copyright © 1986 by Rand McNally & Co.

**G**

world's surface is largely explained by the abundance or lack of agricultural development. (See I) Many areas of the world are too dry or too mountainous, or have growing seasons too short to support a large, stable population. For the most part, we can mark off the earth's rich and fertile regions as the effective limits of the habitable world.

The earth's closed system is intricately balanced and often highly vulnerable to human activity. Thus, humanity – along with land, water, and air – represents a powerful force capable of modifying the world's environment in many ways.

**M**AJOR HUMAN ACTIVITIES  People have an impressive ability to change the world in which they live. On the map, the small red portions, corresponding to dense urban populations, indicate areas of manufacturing and trade. The impact of human force upon these regions is dramatic and indirectly influences other parts of the earth. Olive-green areas indicate highly fertile sectors, such as those in Asia, where irrigation systems and terracing of the land have changed the landscape for the better. Population pressures for more space, however, have promoted deforestation and resultant soil erosion. Where population is low, commercial farming methods have made marginal land fertile, though the danger of drought and wind erosion is always present. Human influence is evident even in the tropics, deserts, and arctic regions, though not as strongly as in the densely populated areas of the world.

H
▼

**S**ETTLEMENTS OF THE WORLD  This map illustrates where humanity, represented by small red dots, has chosen to settle on the earth. These settlement areas combine adequate rainfall and growing seasons with terrain that is not too mountainous nor isolated. Some regions were chosen for their abundant mineral deposits and

I ▼

natural resources, easy access to transportation, and attraction to human laborers. In contrast, regions with less hospitable climates, such as deserts, equatorial tropics, and the poles, have discouraged heavy settlement. The density of human population is one of the forces that determines the amount and variation of change in a region.

Copyright © 1987 Rand McNally & Company

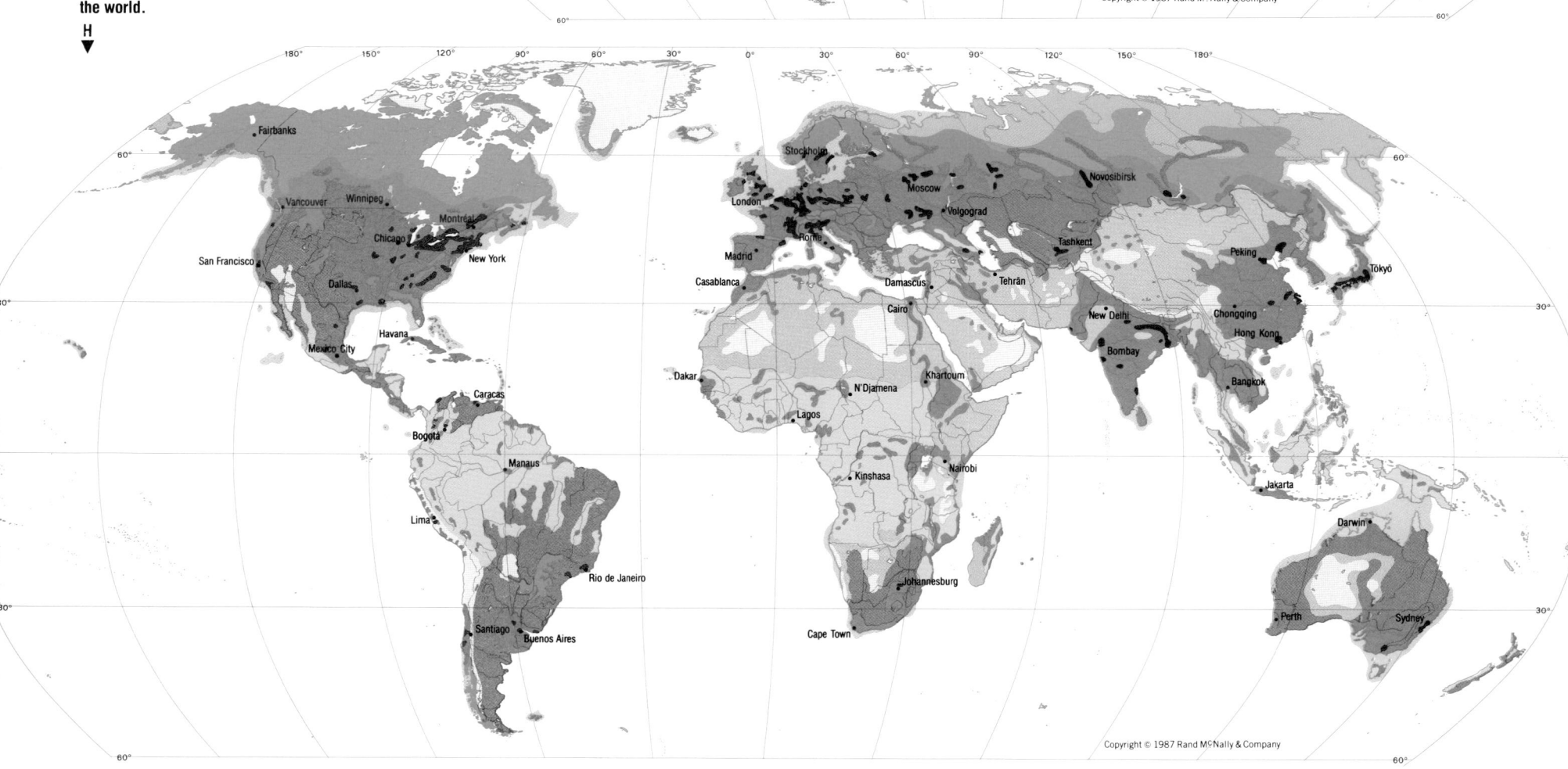

Copyright © 1987 Rand McNally & Company

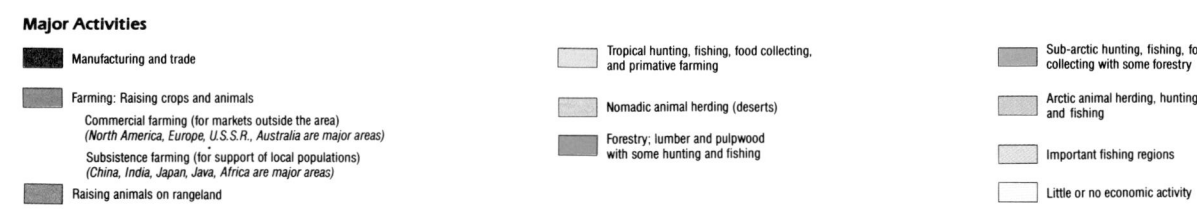

**Major Activities**

- Manufacturing and trade

- Farming: Raising crops and animals
  - Commercial farming (for markets outside the area)
    *(North America, Europe, U.S.S.R., Australia are major areas)*
  - Subsistence farming (for support of local populations)
    *(China, India, Japan, Java, Africa are major areas)*

- Raising animals on rangeland

- Tropical hunting, fishing, food collecting, and primative farming

- Nomadic animal herding (deserts)

- Forestry; lumber and pulpwood with some hunting and fishing

- Sub-arctic hunting, fishing, food collecting with some forestry

- Arctic animal herding, hunting and fishing

- Important fishing regions

- Little or no economic activity

# High Mountains

*"As the sun dries the morning dew, so are the sins of man dissipated at the sight of the Himalayas."*

*Indian Purana*

Within a human life span, mountains seem unchanging, even eternal. But in terms of geological time, high mountains go through their own cycles of change. Arising millions of years ago from the immense collision of drifting continents, the world's mountains are continually shaped by forces of nature.

High mountain ranges form long, linear belts along the unstable continental margins. The greatest of these belts include the perimeter of the Pacific Ocean and the towering ranges of southern Eurasia. The distribution of mountains closely follows other features associated with tectonic plate movement: volcanic activity, fault zones, earthquakes, and ocean trenches.

Where these massive plates collide, continental rocks are compressed and forced upward into mountains. Eventually one

**H**IMALAYA SATELLITE IMAGE   The Himalayas, formed 55 to 40 million years ago, were carved by stream flow, glaciers, and wind into their present spectacular shapes. As the Indo-Australian plate pushes against the landmass of Asia, these giants continue to rise ever higher. The Himalayas have changed the climate and vegetation zones of the regions around them. The lofty ranges act as a climatic barrier, preventing the southeast summer monsoon winds from reaching the northern plains. The satellite image shows green vegetation in Nepal, south of the mountain range, where forested slopes and fertile valleys support dense populations and cultivated terraces. In the north are the arid, largely unpopulated high grasslands of Tibet, revealed as tan areas on the image. The boxed area on the image corresponds to the boxed area on the map.

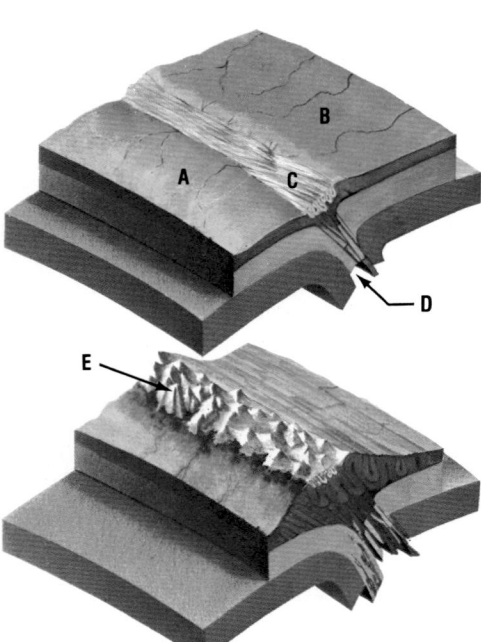

**C**RUSTAL CONVERGENCE   High mountains often form when two tectonic plates such as the Indian (A) and Asian (B) landmasses converge. Sediments and crust trapped between the plates are crushed and thrust upward (C), while the mantle is pushed downward or subducted (D). As landmasses continue to grind against each other, high mountains such as the giant Himalayas (E) are thrust up along the collision zone.

Photo scale 1 : 750,000

© westermann Sat Map®

plate is subducted or pushed under the other plate and is absorbed back into the earth's mantle. The world's major mountain chains are thrust up by the faulting and folding of pre-existing rocks along these subduction zones. Faulted mountains are created by the displacement of rock along fractures, while folding compresses the rock into a series of troughs and ridges without breaking the rock layers. Over time, these processes, alone or together, push the mountain ranges ever higher above the surrounding landscape.

High mountains require support to maintain their exalted elevations. The ranges have "roots" of lighter density rock that extend into the earth and displace heavier substrata, enabling mountain ranges to float on the earth's surface like an iceberg at sea.

Some massive systems, such as the Himalayas, do not have roots deep enough to balance their elevations and are supported instead by the extremely thick and strong tectonic plates upon which they rest.

From the moment high mountains are created, the forces of water and wind begin to wear them away. Flowing water and great sheets of ice carve out valleys and carry sediment to lower elevations, forming flood plains. Wind slowly abrades, scours, and lifts away the sediment, eroding mountain faces over the centuries. The result is a high mountain system of elevated landforms, high local relief, steep slopes, and distinct climatic and ecological zones from base to summit. As mountains wear away, their debris serves as building material for a new mountain system in an ancient cycle of change.

## WORLD'S MAJOR MOUNTAINS*

| Mountain Name | Height in Feet | Part of: | Country |
|---|---|---|---|
| Mt. Everest | 29,028 | Himalayas | China — Nepal |
| K-2 | 28,250 | Karakoram Range | China — Pakistan |
| Communism Peak | 24,590 | Pamir | Soviet Union |
| Aconcagua | 22,831 | Andes | Argentina |
| Mt. McKinley | 20,320 | Alaska Range | U.S.A. |
| Mt. Logan | 19,524 | Saint Elias Mts. | Canada |
| Citlaltepetl | 18,701 | Sierra Madre | Mexico |
| Mt. Elbrus | 18,510 | Caucasus Mts. | Soviet Union |
| Demavend | 18,386 | Elburz Mts. | Iran |
| Jaya Peak | 16,503 | Maoke Mts. | Indonesia |
| Vinson Massif | 16,067 | Ellsworth Mts. | Antarctica |
| Mt. Blanc | 15,771 | Alps | France-Italy |
| Mt. Whitney | 14,494 | Sierra Nevada | U.S.A. |
| Mt. Elbert | 14,433 | Rocky Mts. | U.S.A. |
| Mt. Rainier | 14,410 | Cascade Range | U.S.A. |
| Mt. Toubkal | 13,665 | Atlas Mts. | Morocco |
| Mt. Cook | 12,349 | Southern Alps | New Zealand |
| Aneto Peak | 11,168 | Pyrenees | Spain |
| Mt. Kosciusko | 7,310 | Snowy Mts. | Australia |
| Mt. Mitchell | 6,684 | Appalachian Mts. | U.S.A. |

*The selection has been made so that all areas of the world are represented.

Map scale 1 : 1,500,000    Photo scale 1 : 500,000

**H**IMALAYA MAP    High mountains generally provide an effective barrier to human movement, which makes them useful as political boundaries. Their elevation, rugged terrain, and harsh climate discourage settlement and travel. The Himalayas historically have served as a boundary between Nepal and Tibet (since 1965 the Tibet Autonomous Region of the People's Republic of China) and for centuries isolated Tibet from the rest of the world.

**A**LPS SATELLITE IMAGE    The Alps of Europe, smaller than the Himalayas but as majestic, are a young mountain range formed by the same force of colliding plates as their Asian counterpart. The Eurasian plate supporting the Alps is only half as thick as the Indo-Australian plate and cannot uphold the mass of a range as high as the Himalayas. Although the Alps are scored with glaciers, shown as blue streamers on the image, and the high altitude terrain is difficult to traverse, travel is not as limited as in the Asian range. Lower passes and an elaborate system of tunnels connect the regions of Switzerland, France, and Italy covered by this image. The Alps are an important source of water for lowland valleys where human settlement is concentrated, shown as red and tan areas on the image. These settlements extend along the Rhone River Valley from Lake Geneva (shown as black area at the top left of the image) to Brig (upper right).

# Earthquakes

**" Here the earth...torn with furious convulsions, opened in huge trenches...everywhere nature itself seemed tottering on the verge of dissolution. "**

*Account of the New Madrid, Missouri, earthquake, 1811.*

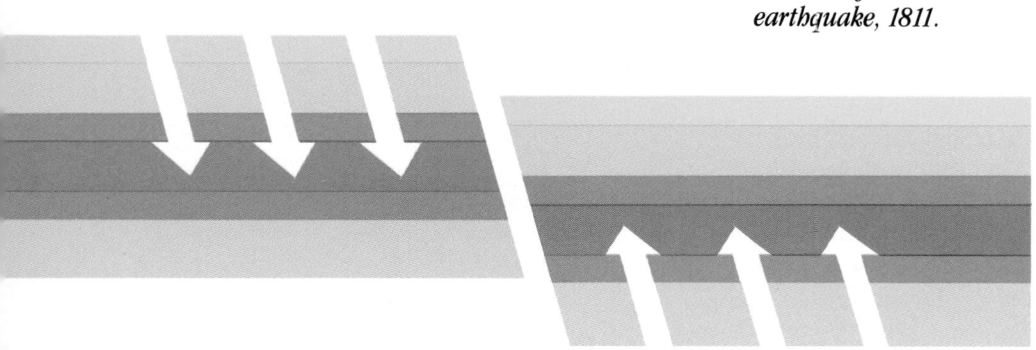

Earthquakes are one of nature's more spectacular and violent forces of change. The very ground beneath our feet ripples and cracks open. Gases released from fissures change the atmosphere, and eerie lights dance in the sky. It's no wonder that some ancient peoples described earthquakes as "great waves moving through the earth."

While the changes we see are sudden, the processes leading to them can take millions of years. Earthquakes are movements of the earth's crust that occur when stress, accumulating in the subsurface over long periods of time, is suddenly released. The ruptures created are known as faults and generally happen near the surface where rocks are brittle and break under stress. At depths greater than 12 miles, rocks are more plastic and tend to fold rather than snap under pressure.

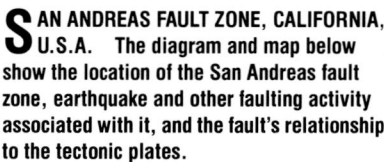

**S**AN ANDREAS FAULT ZONE, CALIFORNIA, U.S.A. The diagram and map below show the location of the San Andreas fault zone, earthquake and other faulting activity associated with it, and the fault's relationship to the tectonic plates.

Along the main fault zone, the Pacific Plate moves northwest past the North American Plate, carrying with it a slice of the California coast. Movement along this fault zone proceeds at about 1.4 inches per year and causes about ten thousand earthquakes. Fortunately, only four major quakes have occurred in California over the past 125 years. Observation stations in the area monitor earth movements in an attempt to predict when another significant adjustment along the fault will occur, bringing on the next major earthquake. ▼

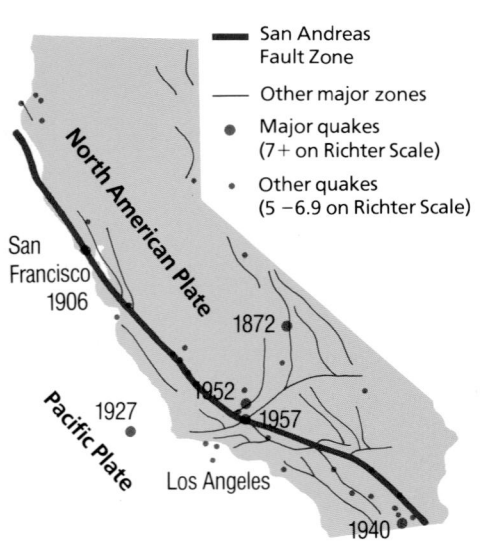

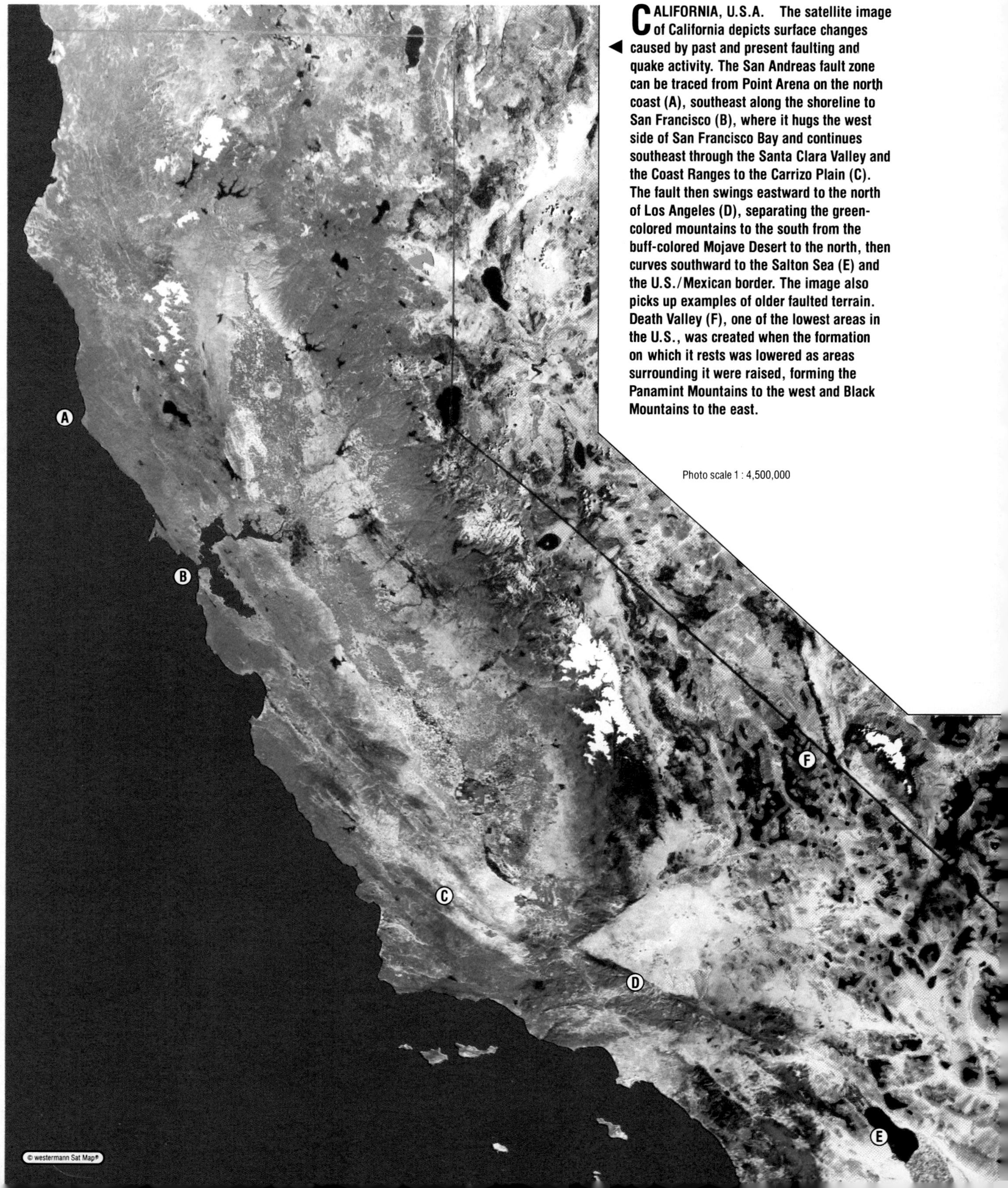

— San Andreas Fault Zone

— Other major zones

• Major quakes (7+ on Richter Scale)

· Other quakes (5 –6.9 on Richter Scale)

**C**ALIFORNIA, U.S.A. The satellite image of California depicts surface changes caused by past and present faulting and quake activity. The San Andreas fault zone can be traced from Point Arena on the north coast (A), southeast along the shoreline to San Francisco (B), where it hugs the west side of San Francisco Bay and continues southeast through the Santa Clara Valley and the Coast Ranges to the Carrizo Plain (C). The fault then swings eastward to the north of Los Angeles (D), separating the green-colored mountains to the south from the buff-colored Mojave Desert to the north, then curves southward to the Salton Sea (E) and the U.S./Mexican border. The image also picks up examples of older faulted terrain. Death Valley (F), one of the lowest areas in the U.S., was created when the formation on which it rests was lowered as areas surrounding it were raised, forming the Panamint Mountains to the west and Black Mountains to the east.

Photo scale 1 : 4,500,000

Most stress occurs where there is movement at tectonic plate boundaries, such as those ringing the Pacific Ocean. As plates push under one another, they fracture vertically. The sudden release of energy generates shock or seismic waves that ripple outward toward the surface. If strong enough, the waves cause instant, often dramatic changes in the landscape. Scientists have been carefully watching earthquake activity on the Pacific-American plate boundary along the San Andreas Fault in California, and the Pacific and Eurasian plate boundary near Japan. Because of the concentration of people and urban development in these areas, even mild tremors can cause property damage and loss of life.

Although most earthquakes occur along plate boundaries, intraplate quakes in the middle of continents can be more severe.

The worst earthquakes in United States history took place in 1811-1812 near New Madrid, Missouri. Over two months, the landscape was completely changed. The quakes destroyed New Madrid; flattened forests; caused landslides, fissures, and sand blows over an immense area; changed the course of the Mississippi River; and created the extensive lowlands of northeast Arkansas, southeast Missouri, and northwest Tennessee.

We cannot prevent the changes that plate movement, faulting, and quakes bring. But we can use ground observation stations, satellite images, and historical records to predict when and where quakes are likely to happen. Such tools can help us avoid the extreme loss of life and property that result when earthquakes strike densely settled areas.

### SIGNIFICANT EARTHQUAKES

| Place | Year |
| --- | --- |
| Shaanxi Province, China | 1556 |
| Lisbon, Portugal | 1755 |
| Naples, Italy | 1805 |
| New Madrid, Missouri | 1811 |
| San Francisco, California | 1906 |
| Tokyo-Yokohama, Japan | 1923 |
| Erzincan, Turkey | 1939 |
| Agadir, Morocco | 1960 |
| Anchorage, Alaska | 1964 |
| Guatemala City, Guatemala | 1967 |
| Chimbote, Peru | 1970 |
| Managua, Nicaragua | 1972 |
| Tangshan, China | 1976 |
| Mexico City, Mexico | 1985 |

© westermann    Map scale 1 : 750,000

oto scale 1 : 500,000

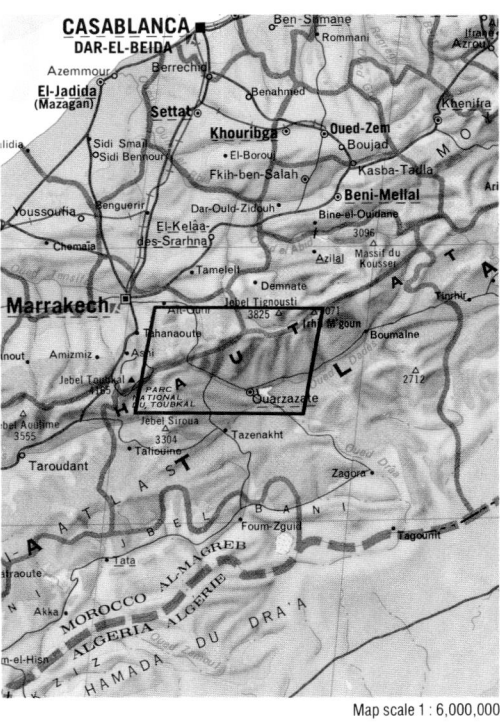

Map scale 1 : 6,000,000

**H**IGH ATLAS MOUNTAINS, MOROCCO
The satellite image covers only a portion of this massive mountain system in northwestern Africa. The map above left marks some of the major faults and folded rock formations shown in the satellite record. The map above right depicts the area represented in the image, along with major settlements in the region.

The terrain shown in the satellite image is composed of lofty ranges, high plateaus, and rugged mountains, the result of 20 million years of complex faulting and folding activity. Movements in the earth's crust gave rise to these mountains and continue to send occasional tremors through the area. The snow-capped peaks in the southwest portion of the image tower above the surrounding landscape, while more gentle slopes in the southeast spill out of the Atlas Range and disappear into the dry Sahara Desert.

The imposing Atlas form an effective barrier to human settlement and travel, and prevent moisture-laden air from reaching the less-rugged southeast. Air that rises to cross the Atlas falls as rain or snow on the north slopes, leaving little moisture for the southern slopes. To support human settlements in this desert region, water must be captured and funneled into reservoirs. The reservoir shown as a black formation in the lower right-hand corner of the image supports the town of Quarzazate and its famous date palm trees.

# Volcanoes

*"There is smoke and ash pouring out of it. There is no doubt the eruption is starting."*

*Report on Mount St. Helens' eruption, 1980*

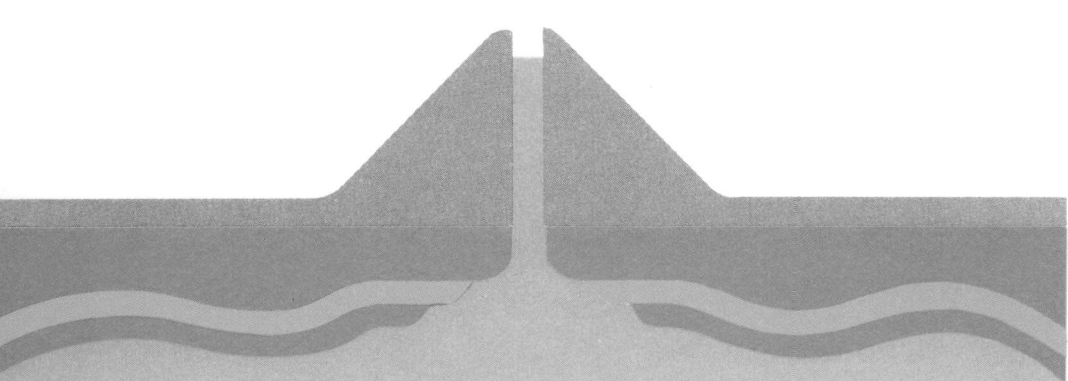

The word *volcano* is derived from Vulcan, the Roman god of fire and metalcraft. Volcanoes are dramatic evidence of the fire within the earth's interior that forces its way up to "craft" – reshape and change – our world.

Volcanic activity occurs when molten rock or magma from within the earth's mantle reaches the surface as lava. Some magmas, filled with water and gases, erupt with explosive force through central vents in the earth, spewing gas, ash, and lava into the air. Gradually, alternating layers of lava and ash build the classic, conical-shaped volcano. In 1980 this type of volcanic explosion devastated Mount St. Helens in Washington state. Other magmas with less water and gas push through numerous openings in the earth's crust. These quieter flows

Photo scale 1 : 400,000

© westermann Sat Map®

**MOUNT ST. HELENS, U.S.A.** Mount St. Helens, with its perfect, conical shape; snow-capped summit, and majestic presence once mirrored the perfection of Japan's Mount Fuji. But on May 18, 1980, after three months of ominous rumbling, the mountain erupted in a thunderous volcanic explosion heard as far away as Vancouver, British Columbia.

The satellite image (left) vividly depicts the eruption's startling changes. The blast tore 1,300 feet off Mount St. Helens' summit (to the right of the image center) and carved out a large crater (dark shadow north of the summit). Tons of hot debris and ash flowed out of the opening and mixed with mud in a vast torrent that changed the shape of river valleys and lakes in the area. The blue tongues of major flows can be seen in the image extending outward from the summit.

The map below the satellite image shows the area of devastation north of Mount St. Helens where superheated gases from the explosion uprooted and burned vegetation. All life within a six-mile radius was destroyed, while ash coated the land clear to western Idaho.

**SUBDUCTION, VOLCANISM, AND CASCADE RANGE** The first diagram below shows where the Juan de Fuca and North American Plates are colliding. Volcanic activity along this zone created the Cascade Range, a chain of volcanic peaks that extends from Lassen Peak in northern California to Mount Garibaldi in southern British Columbia.

The second diagram shows what happens as the Juan de Fuca, pushed or subducted under the North American Plate, is partly converted to molten rock or magma. As the magma rises, it erupts through volcanic vents. The Cascades have been the site of such volcanic activity for 50 million years, forming part of the "Ring of Fire" that is associated with subduction zones that rim the Pacific Ocean.

▼

Legend:
- Mud avalanche flow
- Pyroclastic (debris) flow
- Lahar (mud flow)
- Ash flow
- Area of complete devastation (blowdown zone: uprooted, shredded trees)
- Area of severe fire damage (seared zone: scorched trees)
- 30 Depth of ash layer in cm
- Preeruption shoreline of Spirit Lake
- Posteruption shoreline
- Grazing land mixed with scrub forest
- Coniferous forest
- Road
- Dam with reservoir

Map scale 1 : 400,000

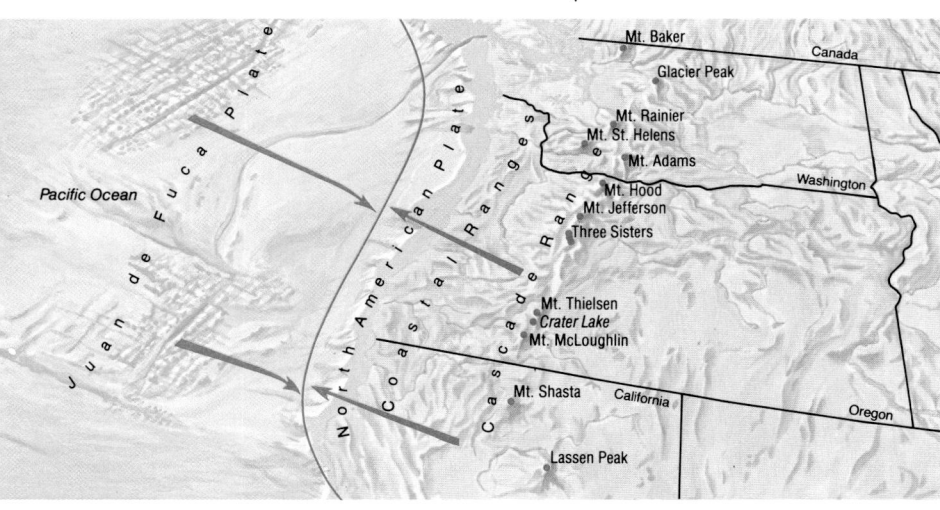

© westermann

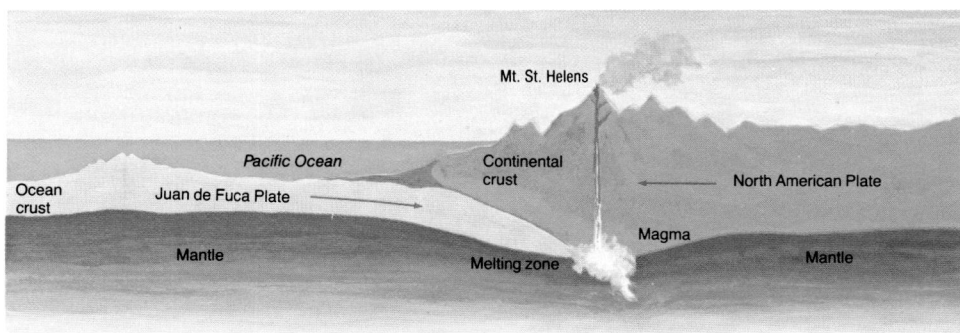

form vast lava plateaus or gently arched, shield volcanoes that merge into the landscape.

The distribution of volcanic activity follows the movement of tectonic plates. As one plate is forced under another (see second diagram on facing page), magma is released. The island arcs of the western Pacific, high volcanic ranges of western North and South America, and a zone from the Mediterranean Sea through Asia to Indonesia mark these subduction zones. Other volcanic activity takes place in continental or suboceanic rift zones where tectonic plates are pulling apart. The isolated mountains of East Africa, notably Kilimanjaro, are products of continental rifting. Iceland was created by volcanism along the rifting Mid-Atlantic Ocean Ridge, which separates the North American and European Plates.

Other volcanic change to the earth's surface occurs when crustal plates pass over "hot spots" where magma is close to the surface. Hot spots in oceanic regions ooze lava onto the sea floor and build up shield volcanoes that gradually emerge as islands. Many of the Pacific Island chains were formed in this way. Continental hot spots may cause more violent eruptions, producing large craters such as the one in Wyoming that cradles Yellowstone National Park.

In this century, volcanic activity has increased, drastically reshaping landforms in many parts of the world. Ash spewed into the atmosphere has changed climates and vegetation has been altered around volcanic sites. Vulcan as master forger truly lives on in his fiery namesake.

## MAJOR VOLCANOES OF THE WORLD

| Volcano | Country | Last Major Eruption |
|---|---|---|
| Mt. Ararat | Turkey | Dormant |
| Chimborazo | Ecuador | Dormant |
| El Chichon | Mexico | 1982 |
| Mt. Erebus | Antarctica | Dormant |
| Mt. Etna | Italy | 1980 |
| Mt. Fuji | Japan | 1701 |
| Mt. Hekla | Iceland | 1947 |
| Volcán Irazú | Costa Rica | 1965 |
| Mt. Katmai | U.S.A. | 1962 |
| Mt. Kilauea | U.S.A. | 1987 |
| Mt. Kilimanjaro | Tanzania | Dormant |
| Vulkan Klyuchevskaya Sopka | U.S.S.R. | Dormant |
| Krakatoa | Indonesia | 1883 |
| Lassen Peak | U.S.A. | 1914 |
| Paricutín | Mexico | 1943 |
| Mt. Pelée | Martinique | 1902 |
| Nevado de Ruiz | Colombia | 1985 |
| Surtsey | Iceland | 1963 |
| Mt. St. Helens | U.S.A. | 1980 |
| Mt. Vesuvius | Italy | 1944 |

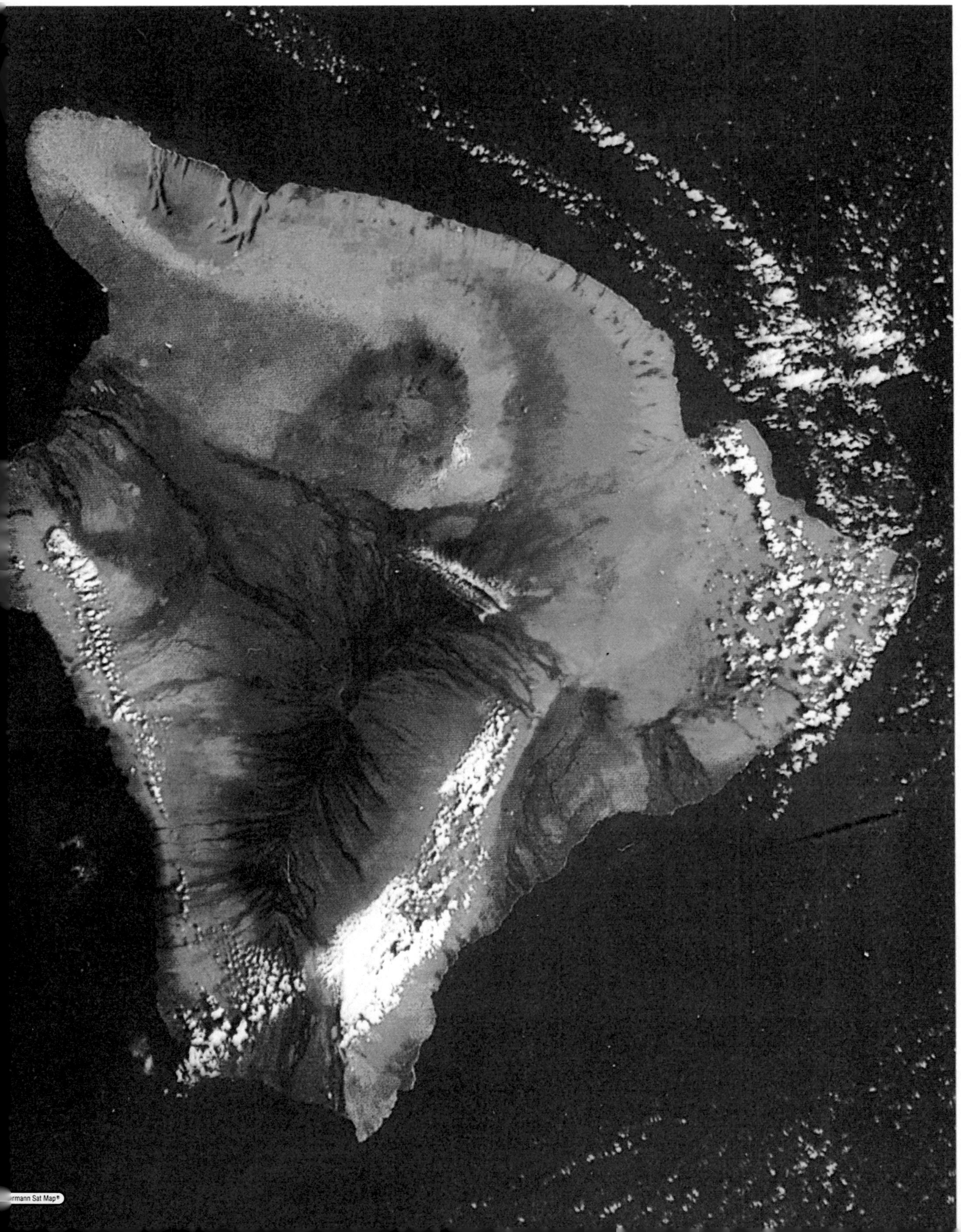

Map scale 1 : 10,000,000

### HAWAII AND THE HAWAIIAN ISLAND CHAIN

The map above depicts the Hawaiian Island chain, formed by the outpouring of magma as the Pacific Plate moves across a stationary hot spot within the earth's mantle. Kauai, oldest of the larger islands, was created almost 6 million years ago.

The island of Hawaii, shown in the satellite image to the left, is the youngest and largest in this chain. Its highest point, the summit of Mauna Loa (south of the image center) rises 30,000 feet above the ocean floor – higher than Mount Everest.

Three major volcanoes on the island represent different stages of change in volcanic landscapes. Mauna Kea, the brown circular volcano north of the island's center, is the oldest and most dormant. Pounding surf and rainfall have carved deep valleys in the volcano's sides. Mauna Loa, an intermediate stage volcano, still erupts periodically. Lava flows from Mauna Loa show up as dark brown streaks extending outward from the crater's center. Kilauea (dark green shape to the right of Mauna Loa) is the island's youngest volcano and the world's most active and closely studied volcanic site. Kilauea's growth is blocked by Mauna Kea to the north and Mauna Loa to the west, so more recent lava flows have extended the land on the southeast coast of the island.

Outpourings from these three major volcanos created the distinctive triangular shape of the island and its rich soils. The light green and brown northeast, southeast, and west coastal areas reveal soil that has developed over older volcanic deposits. Sugarcane, macadamia nuts, and coffee are some of the crops grown in these areas. The darker green and light brown regions on higher slopes, closer to the island's interior, represent grazing lands and forested areas.

As the Pacific Plate continues to move northwestward, a new undersea volcano, Loihi, is forming 19 miles southeast of Kilauea.

Photo scale 1 : 750,000

# Coastlines

*"The quintessence of the coast is restlessness. It is forever moving, changing its shape."*

*Anne W. Simon*

The boundary between land and water is one of the most prominent geographical features on the planet. The constant motion of the world's oceans reshapes and modifies the shores of all continents and islands.

The cycles of this motion may cover a single day or thousands, even millions, of years. Daily motions include tides that pull in and out along the coastlines, sifting and moving sand and sediment. Over the years, waves and currents carve out headlands and fill in bays. During countless millenia, coastlines emerge or sink as sea levels rise and fall or as the land itself is uplifted.

As the earth rotates, the gravitational pull of the sun and moon on the planet produces two bulges of water around the globe, which create the morning and evening tides. This daily rising and falling of the

**B**ERRY ISLANDS, BAHAMAS   The Berry ▶ Islands consist of a 50-mile curve of cays on the northeast edge of the Great Bahama Bank directly south of Northwest Providence Channel (see map below). As part of the Bahamas, these islands rest on a vast submerged limestone platform – the spectacular light blue area on the satellite image. The platform rises 1,500 feet from the depths of the Florida Straits and plunges over 12,000 feet below on the Atlantic Ocean side.

Cays are low islands built from coral, sand, and algae reefs that lie a little above high tide and dry out at low tide. They appear green on the image since they support a scrub forest mixed with pine and mangrove along the shores.

Behind the cays, the prevailing northeast trade winds and ocean and tidal currents distribute lime muds and sands westward along the Great Bahama Bank. Coral and other marine organisms produce much of the building material for the platform and cays. The area's warm, clear waters plus a subtropical climate, vivid scenery, and fine beaches make this a prominent winter resort.

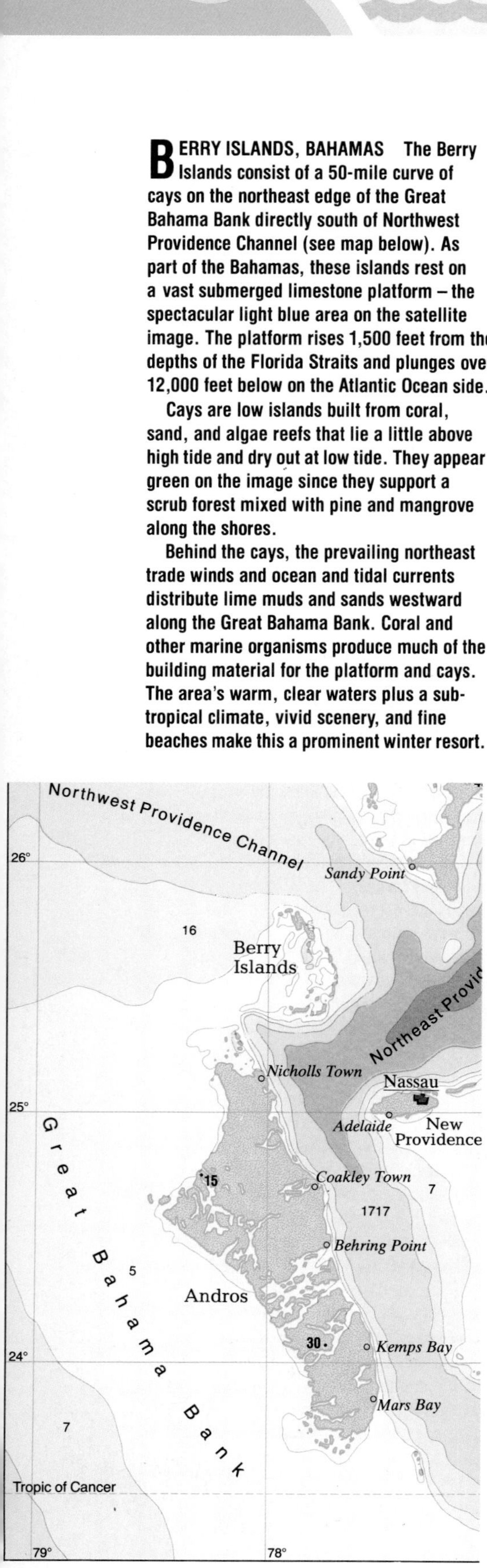

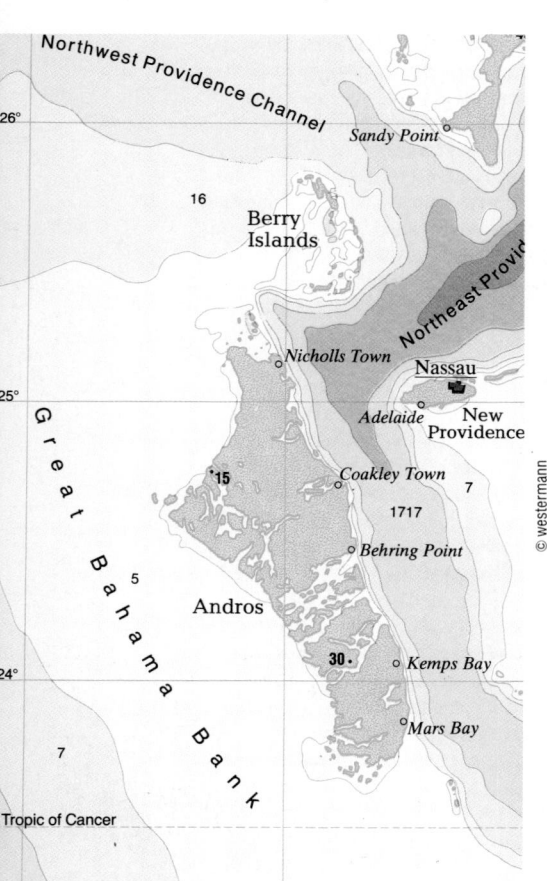

Map scale 1 : 3,000,000

© westermann

© westermann Sat Map®

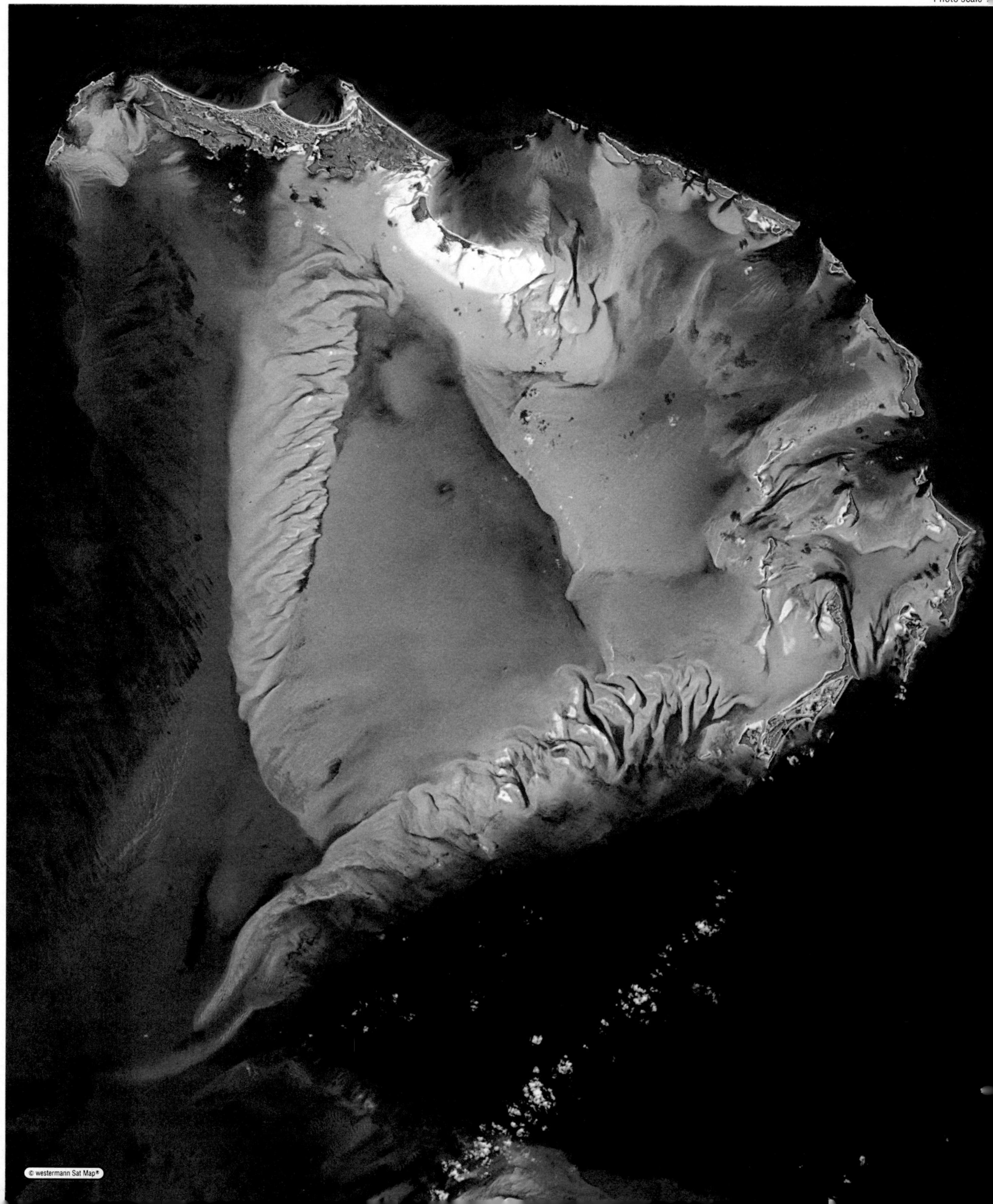

oceans refashions the coastline and carries sediment along the shore and over the adjacent shallow sea floor.

The action of tides is gentle compared to the power of wind-generated waves, created by wind moving across open ocean and disturbing the surface. Waves bend as they approach the coastlines, which concentrates their erosive energy on headlands and disperses it into bays. When a wave breaks on shore, its surge and backwash move and deposit sediment along the coastline.

Longshore currents generated by waves run parallel to the coast and transport enormous amounts of sand and sediment. The combined force of longshore currents and waves over time carves sea cliffs, platforms, and sea caves and sea stacks. The eroded material is mixed with sediment from rivers

and nearshore coral reefs and deposited as beaches, spits, sandbars, and barrier islands.

Over much longer geological eras, coastlines may be modified by tectonic activity, which can change land configuration, or by changes in sea level. During glacial epochs, for example, sea levels often fluctuate several hundred feet, exposing new coastlines then submerging them again as the glaciers melt.

The interplay of land, water, and wind creates varied, often spectacular coastlines. These range from ria coasts with their deep bays, to glacial fjords, barrier islands, tidal marshland coasts, river deltas, and coral reefs in shallow tropical seas. Many of these sculpted landforms support large populations of plant, fish, and animal life and are attractive sites for human settlement.

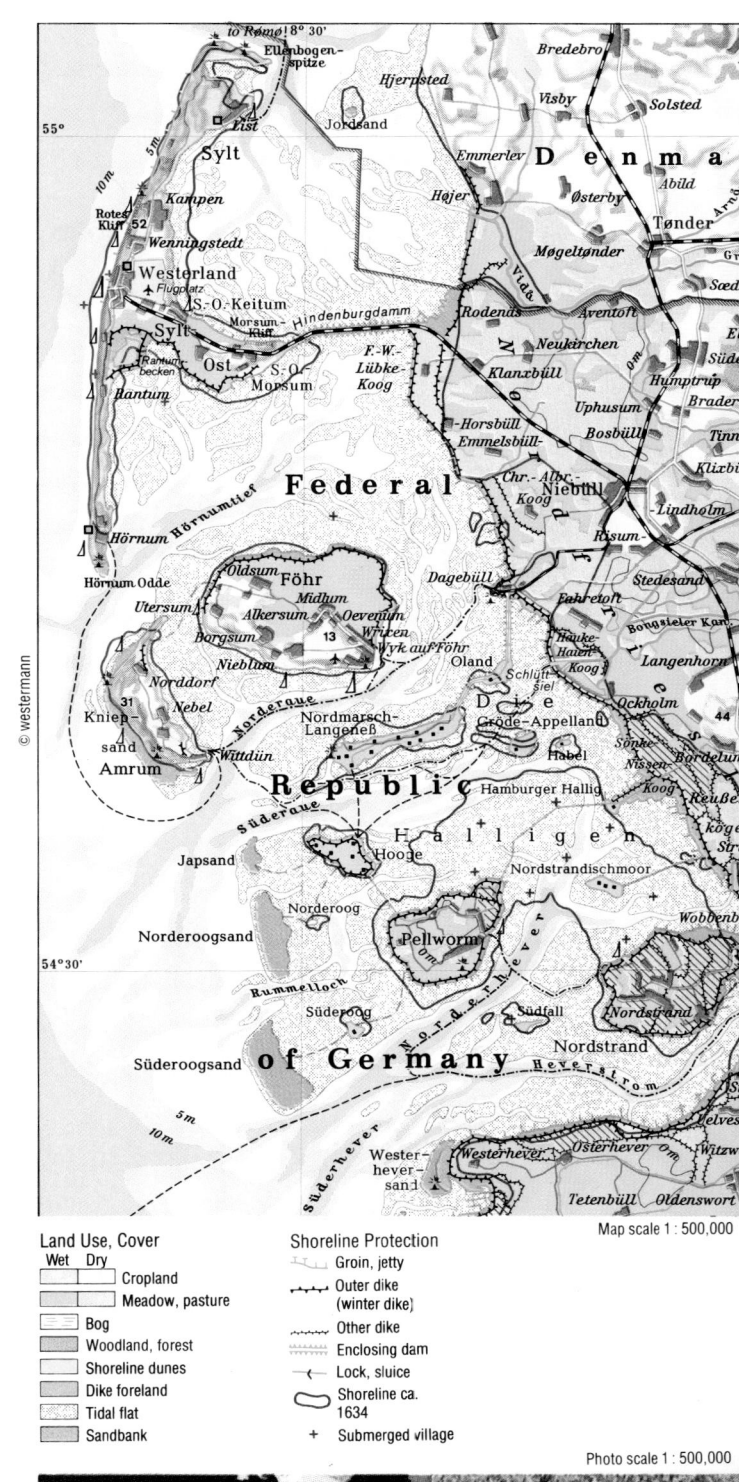

Map scale 1 : 500,000

**Land Use, Cover**

| Wet | Dry | |
|---|---|---|
| | | Cropland |
| | | Meadow, pasture |
| | | Bog |
| | | Woodland, forest |
| | | Shoreline dunes |
| | | Dike foreland |
| | | Tidal flat |
| | | Sandbank |

**Shoreline Protection**

- Groin, jetty
- Outer dike (winter dike)
- Other dike
- Enclosing dam
- Lock, sluice
- Shoreline ca. 1634
- + Submerged village

Photo scale 1 : 500,000

**N**ORTH SEA TIDAL FLATS, DENMARK AND WEST GERMANY   Tidal flats exist where low coastal lands are protected from direct wave action and are subject to salt water flooding during high tides. These areas are truly transitional between land and sea since the tides cover and uncover them daily.

The tidal flats along the coast of Denmark and West Germany appear as light blue on the image (lower right). Tidal currents – darker blue patterns within the flats – carry fine silt and clay, which is deposited on the sea bottom where salt water and fresh water mix. The North Frisian Islands on the image shelter the tidal flats but are subject to constant wave erosion and tidal floods. The red line on the map (upper right) indicates

the islands' shorelines before the severe flood of 1634. Today, Nordstrand and Pellworm, remainders of a larger island partly flooded in 1634, are barely above sea level.

The light orange and tan croplands on the image reveal the area's high population density. To protect and enlarge this coastal region, dams, jetties, dikes, and other barriers are used to reduce erosion and reclaim submerged lands. The Hindenburgdamm (top of the image) can be seen as a thin line connecting Sylt Island to the mainland. Meadowland and pastures show as light green on the image, while a few remnant woodlands appear as dark green areas. ▶

**M**AKRAN REGION, IRAN, PAKISTAN Makran is the coastal region of Baluchistan in southeastern Iran and southwestern Pakistan (see map right). This desert plateau consists of barren hills and intervening hot, dry valleys bordered by a coastal desert.

The Central Makran and Makran Coastal ranges support sparse alpine vegetation, shown as dark tan lines running southwest to northeast. Light tan areas are desert regions devoid of vegetation. Annual rainfall averages three to five inches, and rivers flow only during the seasonal rains. Dry river beds can be seen as light tan lines twisting through the ranges to empty into Gwatar Bay and the sea.

In this region of low precipitation and high evaporation, wind and waves are the principal agents for transporting sand and dust and shaping the coastline. Winter monsoon winds create driving sandstorms that billow out over the Arabian Sea, as vividly depicted on the image below. Along the coast, loose desert sands are carried by waves and currents eastward to shape a series of spits that jut out into the darker water. The shallow light blue waters (far right of the image) indicate sediments that are slowly filling in the bay where waters are calmer.

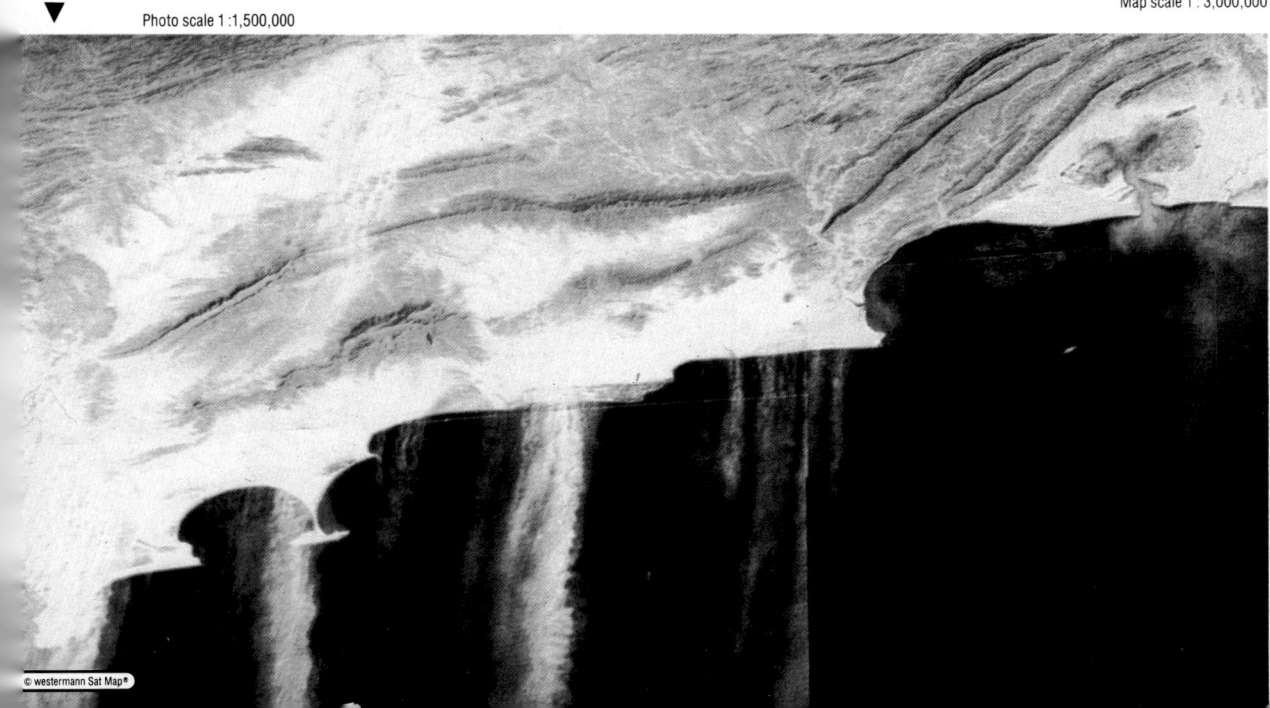

Map scale 1 : 3,000,000

▼ Photo scale 1 : 1,500,000

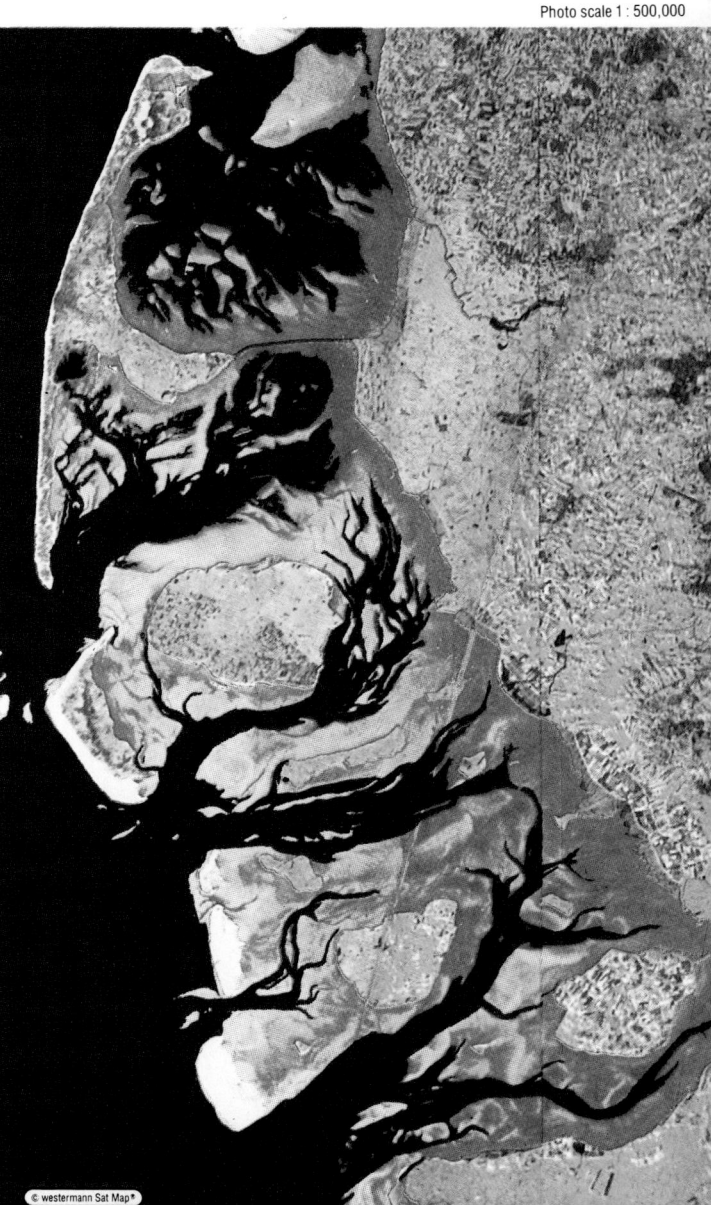

# Rivers

" Every valley shall be lifted up,
and every mountain and hill
made low… "

*Isaiah, 40:4*

Flowing water in the form of rivers and streams is one of nature's most powerful agents of change and part of the earth's immense water cycle. All continents except Antarctica have felt the force of these moving waters, which continually erode and deposit materials in a perpetual cycle of change.

Along the course of most rivers we find a sequence of developing landforms. Many rivers begin in mountainous terrain where the waters rush down steep gradients, gradually carving the channel bed into a deep, narrow valley. Along the gentler middle course, the river begins to widen its valley through lateral erosion, which eventually carves out a flat valley floor. Periodically, the river overflows its channel and forms a rich, fertile floodplain. The river's lower course

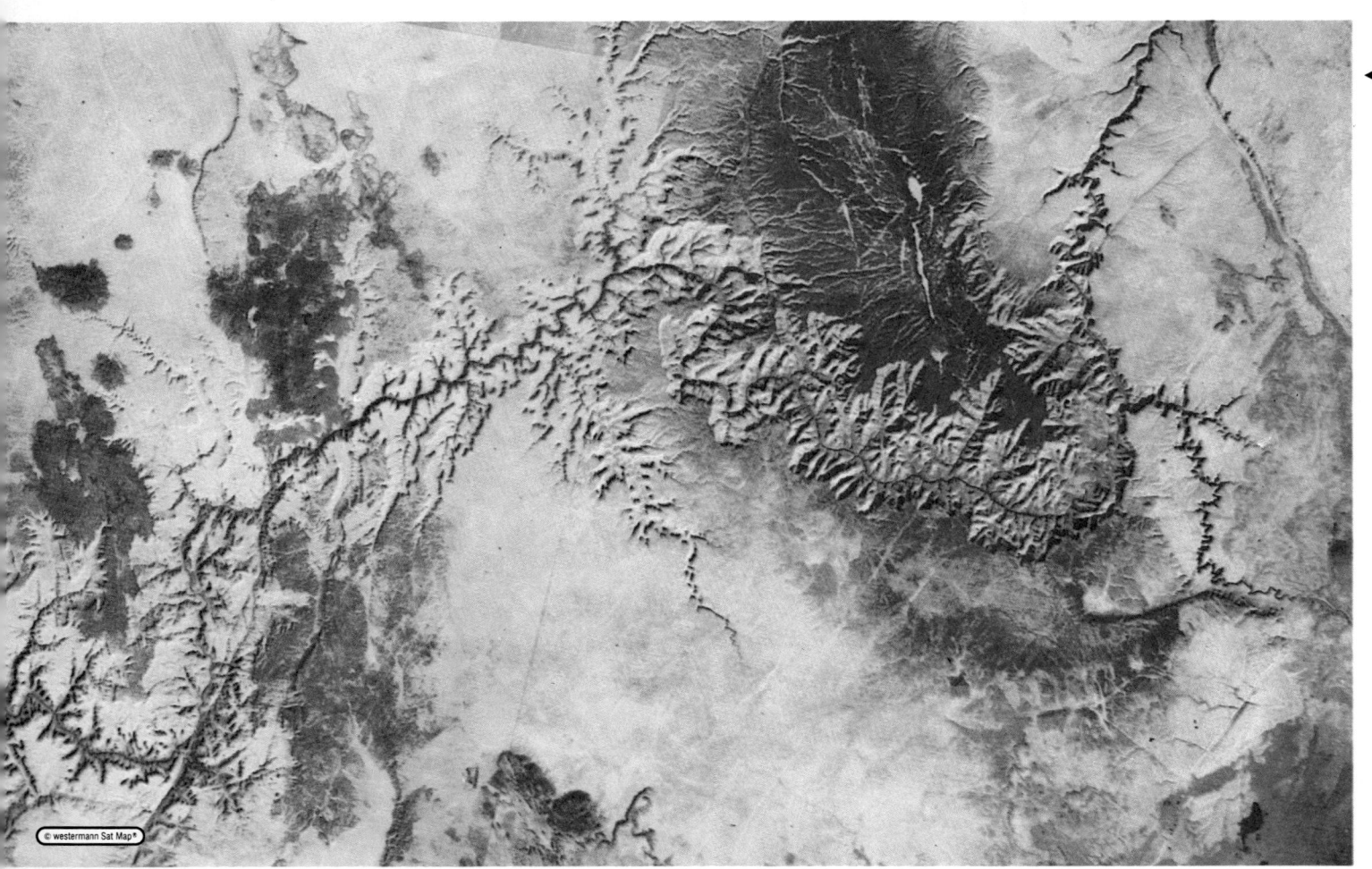

Photo scale 1 : 1,000,000

Map scale 1 : 1,000,000

**G**RAND CANYON, ARIZONA, U.S.A.
The Grand Canyon of Arizona, shown in the satellite image and the map below it, is the world's most stunning exhibition of the erosive power of flowing water. This spectacular formation was carved over a period of 10 million years.

During the millenia, as the region was slowly raised, the meandering predecessor of the Colorado River gradually cut downward through the land on its journey to the sea. The exposed canyon walls revealed an unequaled geological record covering nearly 700 million years of earth's history. As the river gained in size and force, it eroded away sediment and rock in ever more fantastic shapes, combining with wind and rain to carve spurs, pinnacles, spires, and buttes. In its present form, the Grand Canyon is 277 miles long, 600 feet to 18 miles wide, with a maximum depth of 6,000 feet.

The entire length of the canyon is displayed in the satellite image and accompanying map. One of the more noticeable features on the image include the plateaus surrounding the canyon. Kaibab Plateau, north of the canyon and to the right of the image center, is a broad, uplifted plain reaching elevations of over 9,000 feet. The higher elevations capture more moisture, which in turn supports substantial vegetation, primarily spruce and fir bordered by pine. These forested areas, depicted as dark brown and olive green on the image, are also found on the Kanab Plateau to the northwest and parts of the Coconino Plateau south of the canyon. The lighter, buff-colored areas indicate sparse woodlands of pine, juniper, and scrub oak.

While the region is composed of flat-lying, sedimentary rocks, there is one volcanic formation on the image. It is centered around Mount Trumbull north of the canyon and to the left of the image center. This area is dormant but provides vivid reminders of the violent forces of change that once affected this region. Today, the Colorado River is the most powerful force that continues to shape the Grand Canyon's immense formations.

is usually marked by a meandering channel bed which changes location over time. Lakes, swamps, or meander scars that remain on the land are mute testimony to the force of flowing water as it reshapes the landscape.

Where river waters enter the ocean or large lakes, silt deposits gradually build up to form deltas. The level land and generally rich soil of floodplains and deltas offer a perfect site for agriculture and human settlement, although the hazard of floods and shifting channel beds always exists.

The power of rivers to build new land from the erosion of mountains and rocks gives added importance to their role as a force for change. Their flowing waters also play a vital role in the complex system that recirculates the earth's moisture.

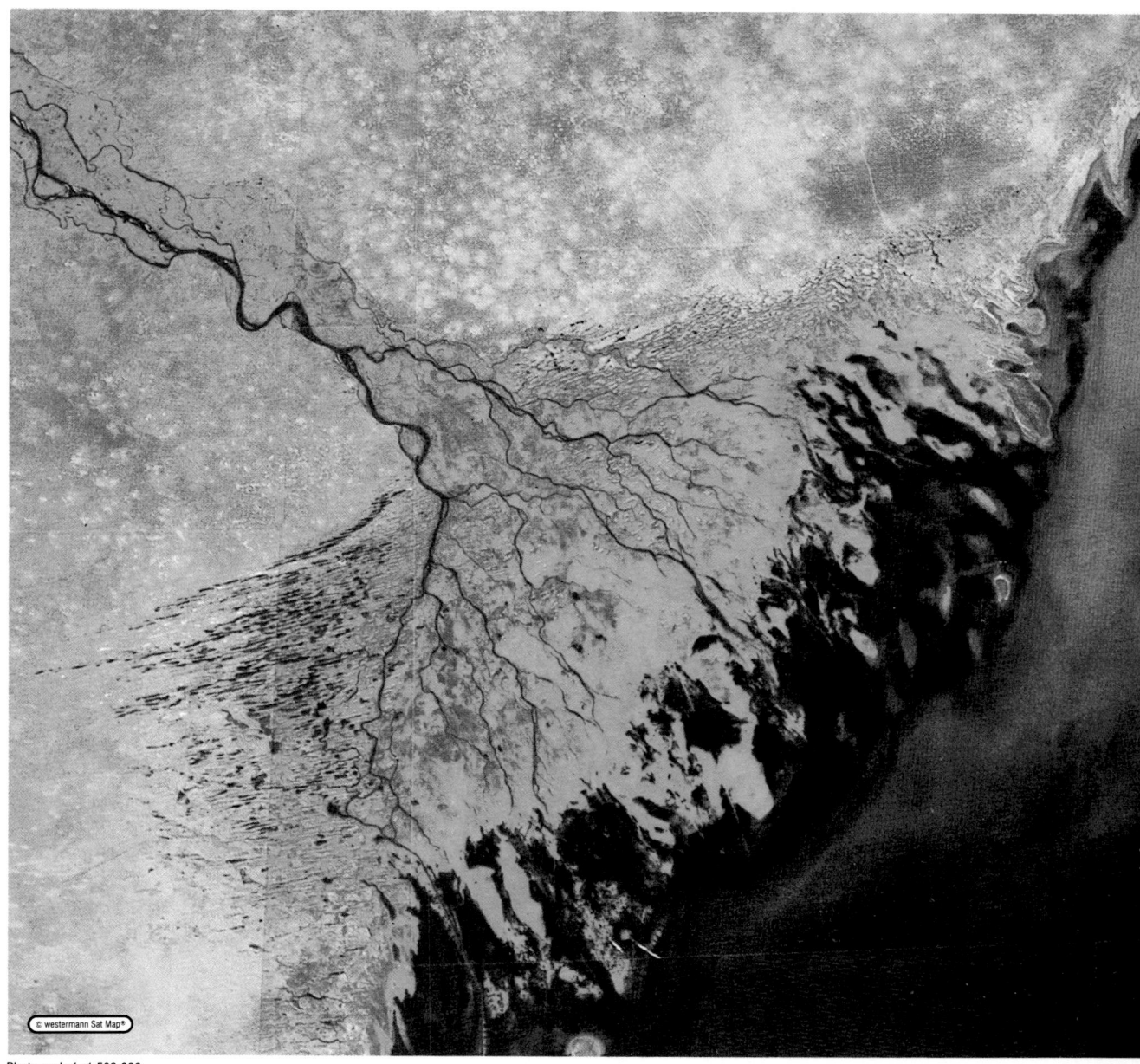

Photo scale 1 : 1,500,000

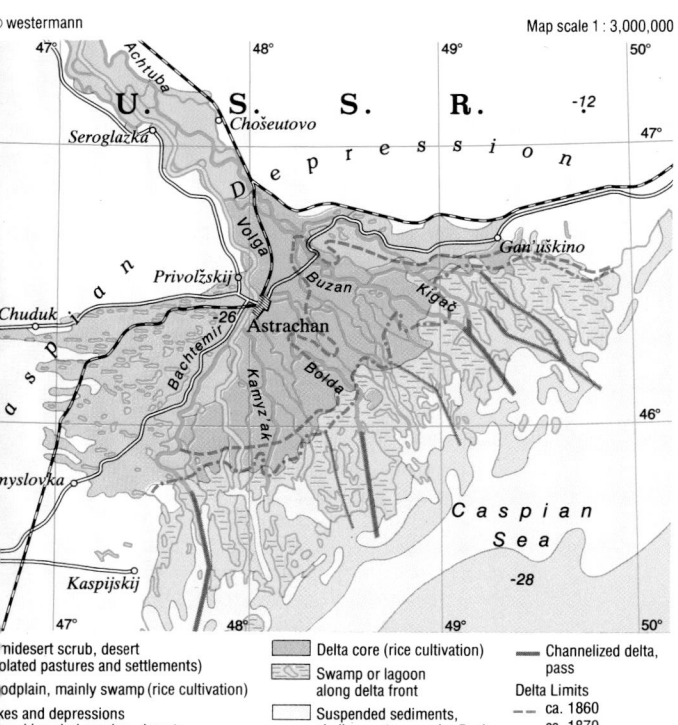

© westermann                                    Map scale 1 : 3,000,000

| | | |
|---|---|---|
| ...midesert scrub, desert (isolated pastures and settlements) | ▨ Delta core (rice cultivation) | — Channelized delta, pass |
| ...odplain, mainly swamp (rice cultivation) | ▨ Swamp or lagoon along delta front | Delta Limits |
| ...kes and depressions ...med by wind erosion, desert | ☐ Suspended sediments, shallow water area (< 5 m) | – – ca. 1860<br>– ·– ca. 1870 |

**V**OLGA RIVER DELTA, U.S.S.R.   The map above depicts the 1860, 1870 (dashed red lines), and present boundaries of the Volga River Delta. The delta was created by the Volga and Achtuba Rivers as they empty into the Caspian Sea, and continues to expand at an average rate of 3 square miles per year. In the satellite image (above right), bright green vegetation of the river floodplains and the delta stand in sharp contrast to the buff-colored, semidesert regions. Sediments from the rivers wash into the Caspian Sea where they create a shallow area shown as lighter blue on the image. This area yields about 35 percent of the Soviet fishing catch.

**M**ISSISSIPPI RIVER FLOODPLAIN AND DELTA, LOUISIANA, U.S.A.   The Mississippi River, shown as a blue line twisting across the left side of the satellite image, meanders through a wide floodplain and curves past New Orleans (seen as the light blue-gray area to the right of the image center). The river then crosses a thin bridge of land to the end of the Mississippi Delta, which fans out into the Gulf of Mexico. Clouds of silt and mud, shown as lighter blue water around the river mouth, are gradually extending the delta banks into the Gulf. However, the main river channel, choked with sediments, is shifting to the Atchafalaya River. A new part of the delta is now forming at the mouth of the Atchafalaya.

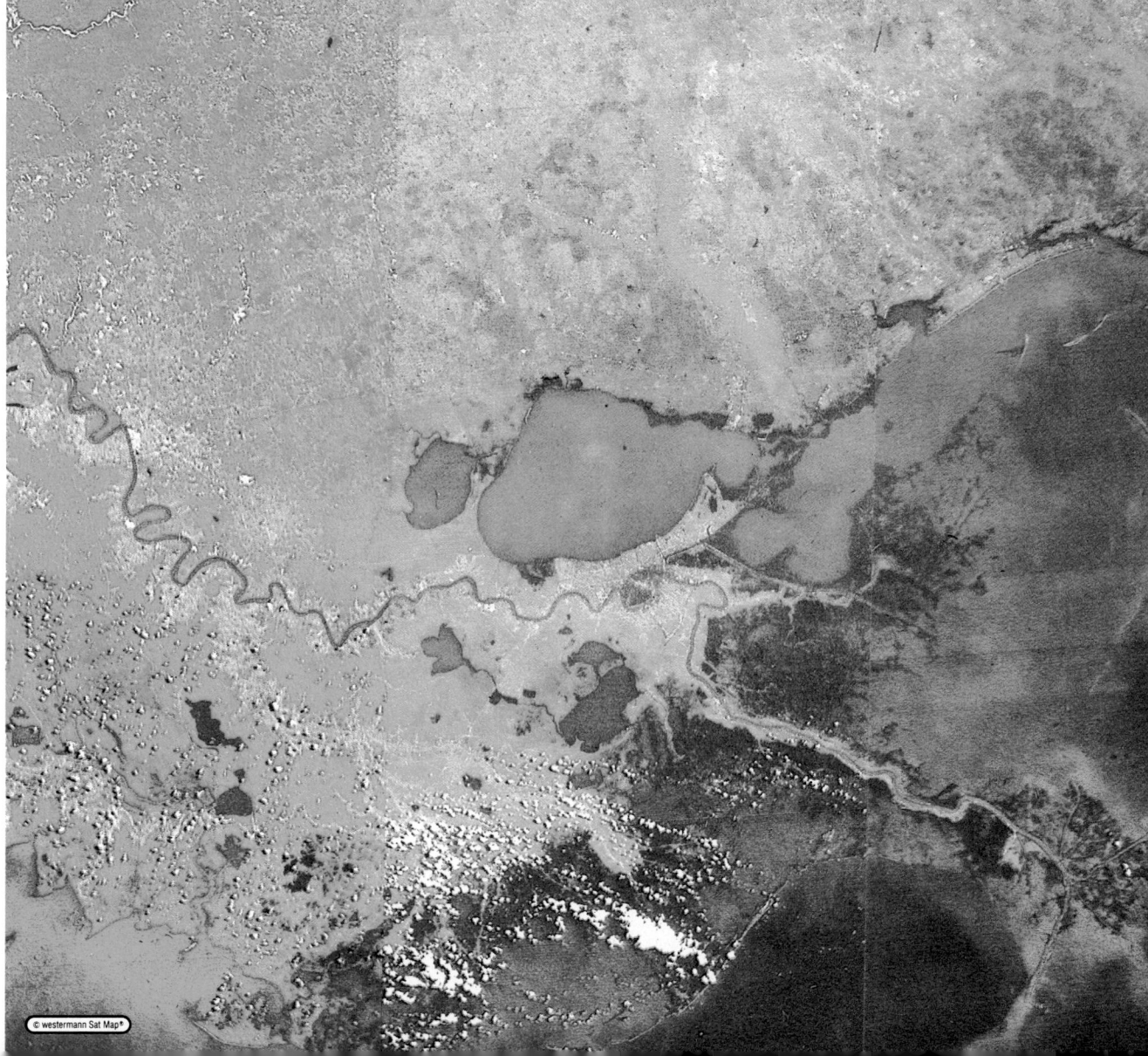

# Floods

❝ Mankind cannot tame that lawless stream, cannot curb it or confine it, cannot say to it, Go here or go there, and make it obey… ❞

*Mark Twain*

Major floods occur each year throughout the world and have been recorded in history for thousands of years. Despite all of our records on these natural disasters, some of the most flood-prone areas — coastal regions, river valleys, floodplains, and deltas — are also the most densely populated. People seem willing to accept the risks of living in regions where this awesome force of nature strikes over and over again.

Coastal flooding, caused by unusually high tides, tidal waves, and storms that push waves onto the coast, is an almost totally destructive force. It can erode seawalls, destroy beaches, change coastal outlines, and damage piers, docks, and shipping lanes. River flooding, on the other hand, can bring

**S**T. LOUIS, MISSOURI AREA, 1972   The ▶ satellite image on the immediate right was recorded in October, 1972, five months before the flooding in March, 1973.

The image shows the normal courses of the Mississippi, Missouri, and Illinois rivers at this time of year. The Illinois River parallels the Mississippi in a north-south flow before joining it, as shown on the left side of the image. Twenty miles further to the east, the Missouri River, flowing northeast, joins the Mississippi River above the city of St. Louis. St. Louis is the orange-red area roughly twenty miles south of the "meeting of the waters."

The broad floodplain formed by the merging of these three rivers represents fertile agricultural land, depicted as beige and light green on the image. Numerous towns on the floodplain show as dark red and light gray areas.

**S**T. LOUIS, MISSOURI AREA, 1973   The image in the middle was recorded in March 1973 when flooding began. Clouds appear as white clusters, mainly to the north. Bright blue flood waters show the extent of the rivers' overflow.

Flooding continued for 77 consecutive days, cresting on April 28, when the rising waters topped a 189-year record. Though the crest was only two feet higher than in the flood in 1844, the channel carried 35 percent less water than during the 1844 peak flow.

The reduced volume was attributed to extensive modification of the rivers, especially narrowing their channels and erecting levees to control the flow of water through the area. These measures, meant to protect the floodplain and surrounding communities, inadvertently made the flooding worse after unusually heavy precipitation and snowmelt swelled the rivers.

Photo scale 1 : 500,000

Photo scale 1 : 500,000

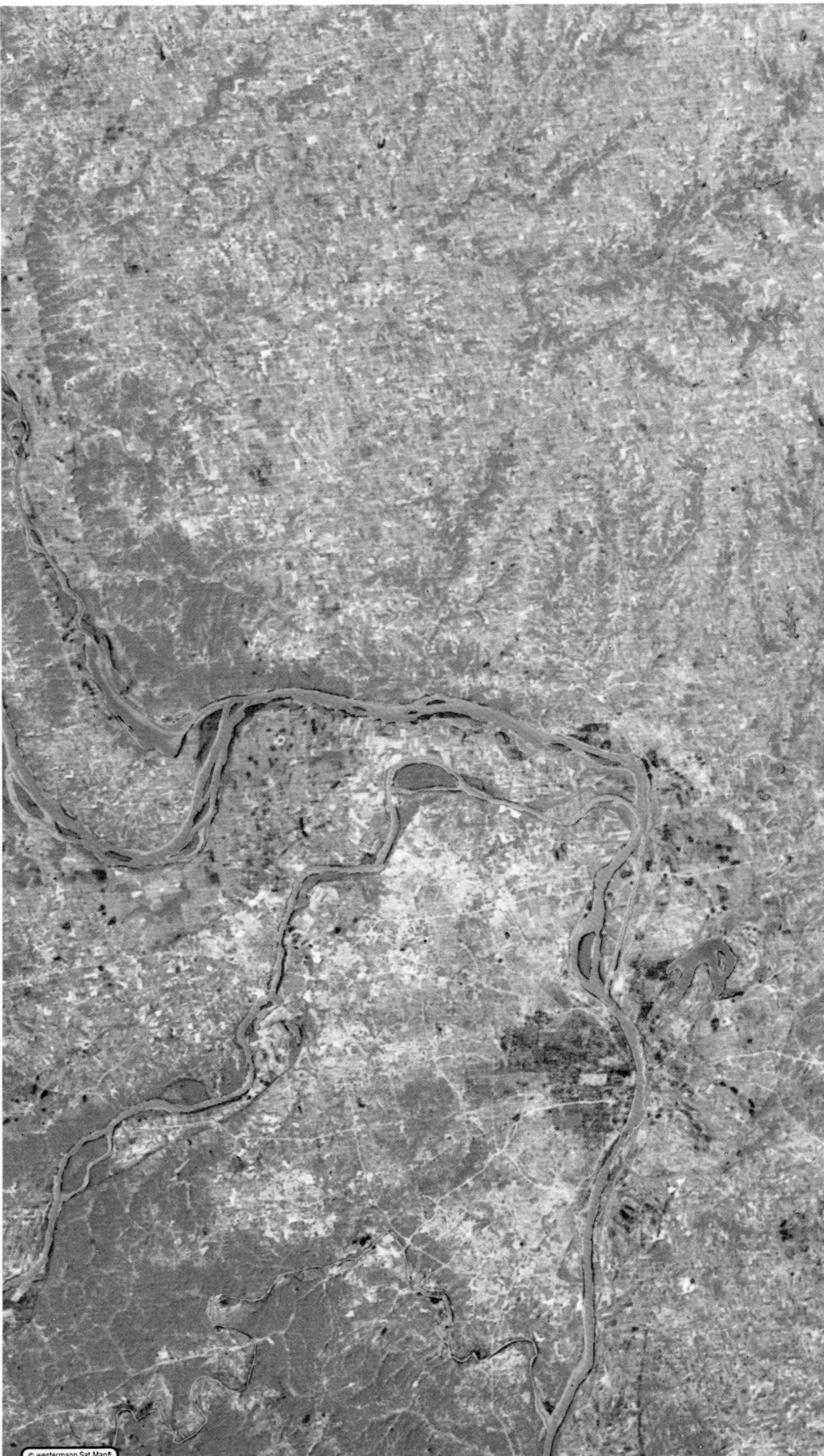

© westermann Sat Map®

© westermann Sat Map®

both destruction and new life in its wake. While exacting a toll in life, property, and soil erosion, these flood waters also deposit sediment and nutrients that replenish the land's fertility.

Some of the great river systems of the world such as the Nile (Egypt), Mississippi (U.S.), Yellow (China), Mekong (Vietnam), and Ganges (Bangladesh) have been prone to flooding throughout history. The waters of these and other major rivers overflow as the result of heavy rainfall or snowmelt over a broad stretch of the rivers' course. In mountainous terrain, excess water drains quickly into streams and small river beds, causing flash floods. As the torrent moves downstream, it gathers more water from tributaries, causing the river to rise higher and higher. Once it reaches the broad plains of its lower course, the river overflows its banks, flooding crops, roadways, even entire towns and cities.

To protect these areas from floods, people have constructed dams, levees, and channels on major river systems. Ironically, our attempts to control flooding have often compounded this destructive natural force. The more a river is channeled and bound in by levees or straightened and deepened, the less volume of water it can carry and the faster it runs. Though flooding is controlled in normal, high-water times, when abnormally high runoff occurs, the river is less able to handle the volume and breaks over its banks with more erosive force. Such floods are especially devastating to those who trusted in man-made controls and ventured farther out onto the floodplain or settled closer to the river.

It is the nature of rivers to overflow, and it seems to be the nature of people to settle in flood-prone areas where they find level acreage, rich soil, and abundant water. As long as these two forces exist, rivers will be modified in an attempt to control their flow. Satellite images like those below (taken before and after the 1973 Mississippi River flood) and the maps that are made from the images can be used to assess regional flood conditions and help plan more effective control systems.

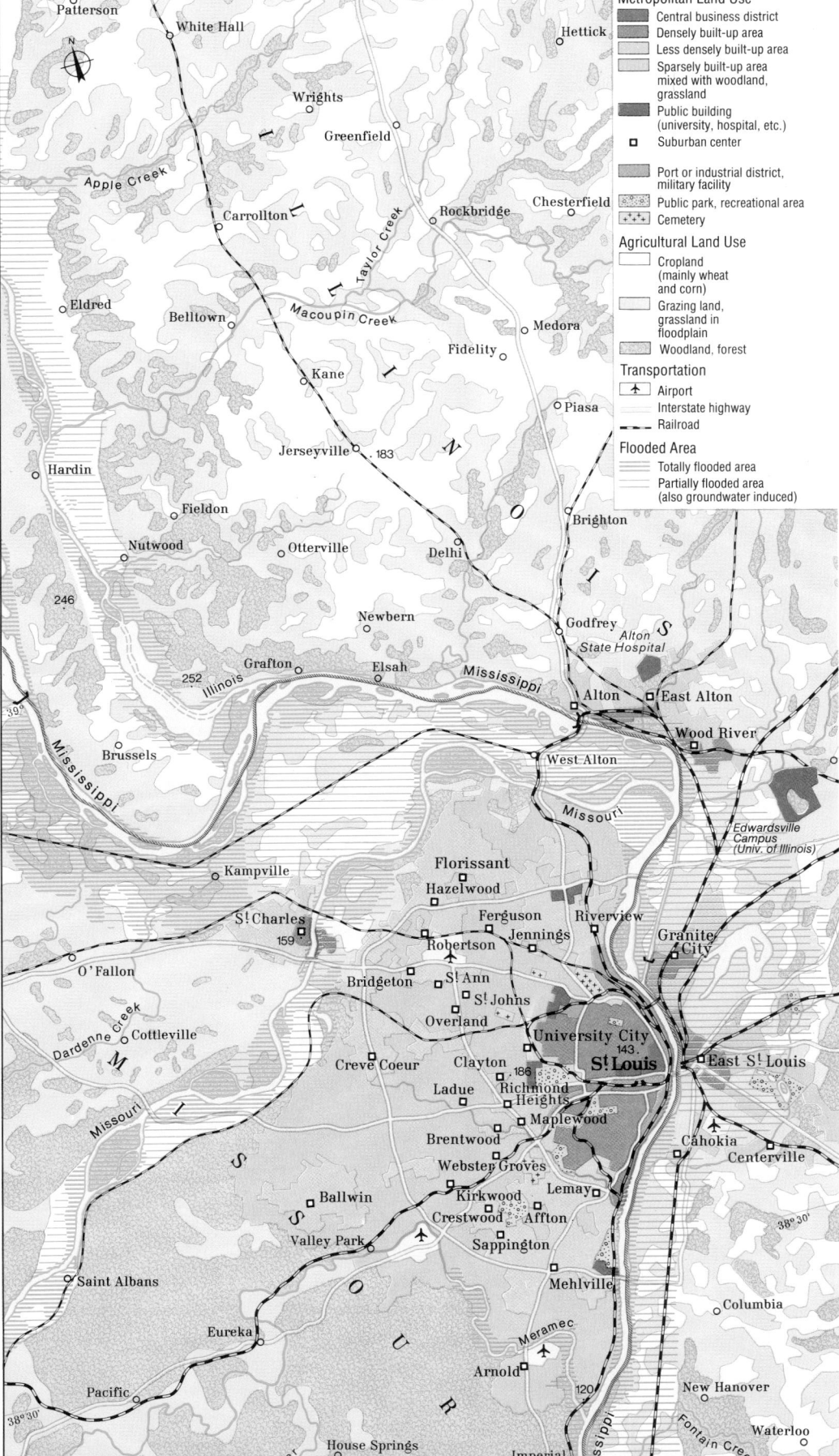

Map scale 1 : 500,000

**Metropolitan Land Use**
- Central business district
- Densely built-up area
- Less densely built-up area
- Sparsely built-up area mixed with woodland, grassland
- Public building (university, hospital, etc.)
- Suburban center
- Port or industrial district, military facility
- Public park, recreational area
- Cemetery

**Agricultural Land Use**
- Cropland (mainly wheat and corn)
- Grazing land, grassland in floodplain
- Woodland, forest

**Transportation**
- Airport
- Interstate highway
- Railroad

**Flooded Area**
- Totally flooded area
- Partially flooded area (also groundwater induced)

**S**T. LOUIS, MISSOURI AREA MAP  The map on the left was constructed using the two satellite images and shows the extent of the flooding. As the map's shaded areas reveal, the worst flooding occurred along the Mississippi River where it is joined by the Illinois and Missouri rivers, and throughout the east side of St. Louis. Other extensive flooding took place along the western bank of the Mississippi, shown on the far left of the map, and the eastern bank of the Mississippi south of St. Louis.

Satellite images can help in flood control by pinpointing precise areas affected by flood waters. State and federal governments can then modify their controls on the rivers or plan new projects for containing and channeling water flow during times of abnormally high precipitation.

**MAJOR RIVERS**

| Name | Country | Length in Miles |
| --- | --- | --- |
| Nile | Egypt | 4,145 |
| Amazon | Brazil | 4,000 |
| Yangtze (Chang) | China | 3,915 |
| Mississippi-Missouri | U.S.A. | 3,740 |
| Huang (Yellow) | China | 3,395 |
| Ob-Irtysh | Soviet Union | 3,362 |
| Congo | Zaire | 2,900 |
| Paraná | Brazil | 2,796 |
| Lena | Soviet Union | 2,734 |
| Mekong | Vietnam | 2,600 |
| Niger | Nigeria | 2,600 |
| Murray-Darling | Australia | 2,330 |
| Volga | Soviet Union | 2,194 |
| Yukon | U.S.A. | 1,979 |
| Indus | Pakistan | 1,800 |
| Danube | Romania | 1,776 |
| Brahmaputra | India/Bangladesh | 1,770 |
| Zambezi | Mozambique | 1,700 |
| Ganges | India/Bangladesh | 1,560 |
| Euphrates | Iraq | 1,510 |
| Colorado | U.S.A. | 1,450 |

I·17

# Glaciers

*"Nature chose for a tool the tender snowflakes noiselessly falling through unnumbered centuries."*

*John Muir*

During the glacial periods that punctuated earth's history, huge ice sheets advanced and retreated over many parts of the world. The most recent period started about two million years ago. Geologic evidence indicates that climatic conditions caused immense glaciers to spread across regions of North America and northern Europe. Today glaciers cover only about one-third of their former area. Almost 97 percent of glacial activity is restricted to Antarctica and Greenland, while the rest is in Iceland and the world's high mountainous regions. These glaciers are changing the landscape today as they did in the past.

Glaciers are formed when snow, accumulating year after year, compacts and eventually turns into glacial ice. As the buildup of snow and ice exceeds melting,

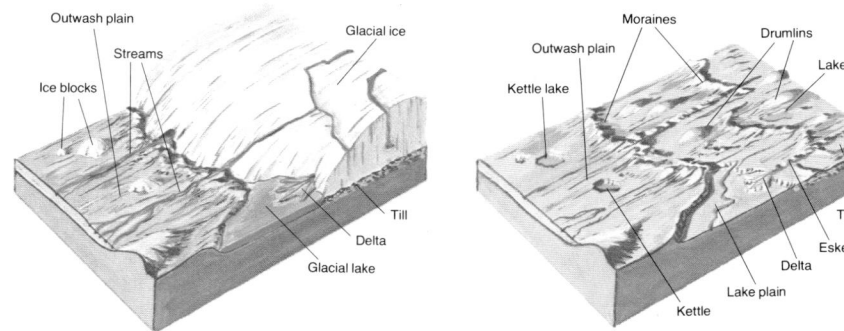

**L**ANDFORMS CREATED BY RETREATING GLACIERS   The diagram on the far left shows the initial landforms created as a glacier begins to melt and retreat. Melting ice runs off in streams and fills land depressions to form lakes. The diagram to the immediate left depicts a typical glacial landscape after the ice has receded completely. Ice blocks create kettles and kettle lakes, and underground streams form eskers. Outwash plains are deposits of fine sediment, while moraines, drumlins, and till plains are created from debris deposited as the glacier retreated.

Photo scale 1 : 750,000

Map scale 1 : 3,000,000

**G**LACIAL COAST, NORWAY   The map above shows the western coast of Norway, a classic example of past glacial activity. Moving ice carved the coastline into thousands of *fjords*. The satellite image (right) focuses on Sognafjorden, the black fjord stretching across the image center. It is 120 miles long, rising 4,000 feet above sea level and plunging as far under water. Jostedalsbreen, in the upper right (see map), is the only remnant of a massive ice sheet which once covered northern Europe. The rocky glacial landscape has little agricultural land. Communities are isolated by the fjords and are economically dependent on forest and fishing industries.

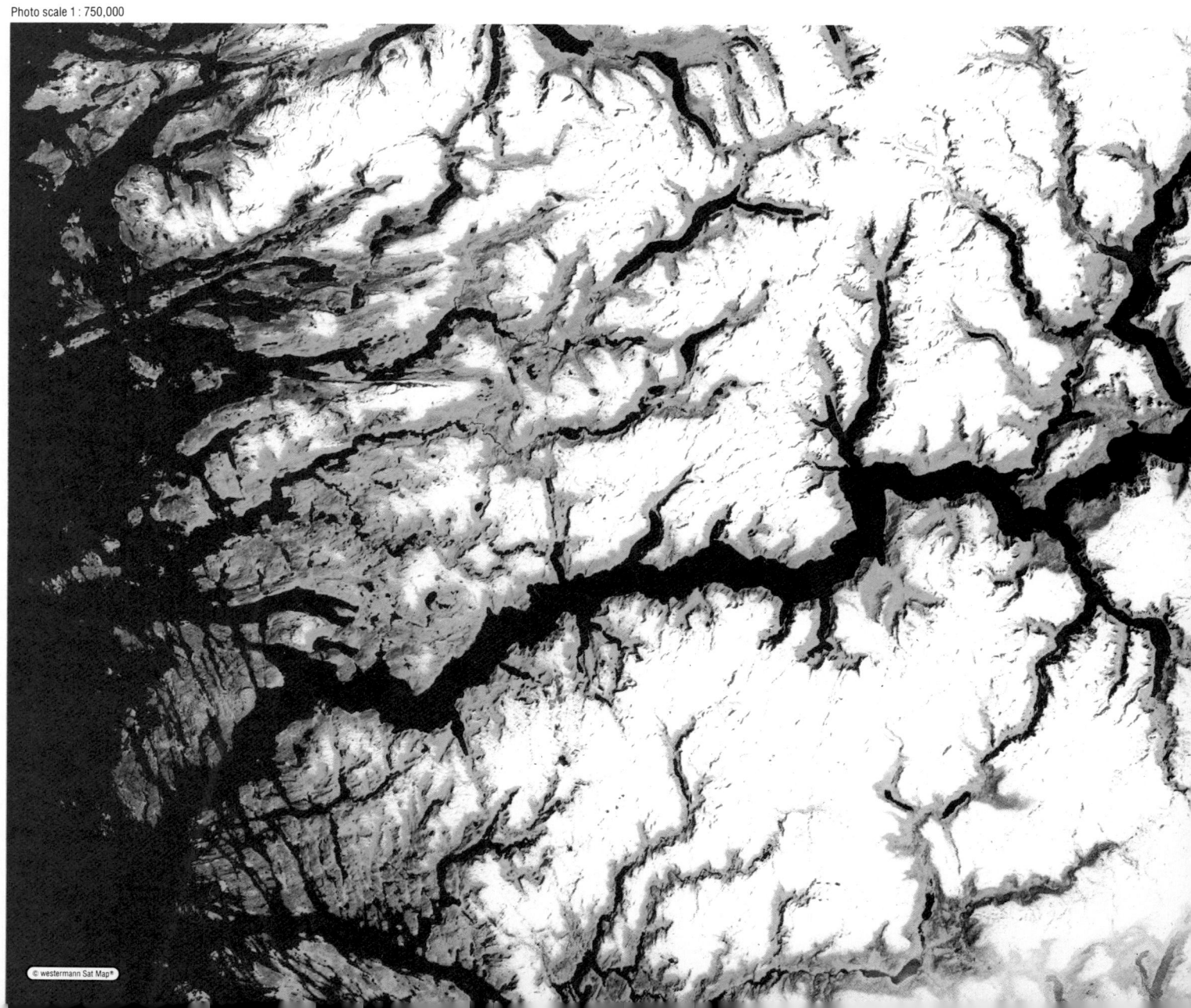

the glacier grows. In the center of the ice sheets where the most accumulation occurs there is virtually no glacial movement. The mass in this area, together with the force of gravity, causes the outer edges to expand into valleys and lower elevations. Movement varies from fractions of an inch to several feet per day, although some alpine glaciers have moved up to 330 feet in a single day.

As glaciers advance, rock fragments embedded in their ice grind the surface over which they pass. This relentless force changes "V"-shaped valleys into "U"-shaped valleys and scours the land and rock. When the climate warms up so that melting exceeds the accumulation of ice and snow, the glaciers retreat, depositing rocks, fine silt, and other debris carried in the ice. Some of the more common landforms created from

glacial deposits include moraines, eskers, lakes, outwash plains, and kettles (see diagram on the opposite page). The material deposited serves as the basis for some of the world's most fertile agricultural land.

The continental glaciers of the past altered extensive land areas as they advanced and retreated. They reshaped coastlines and created new bodies of water as their enormous ice sheets melted and raised the world's sea levels. In some areas the glaciers' weight depressed the land, and with their retreat, the land began to rebound. Areas along the Finnish coast are still rising at about three feet every 100 years.

Glaciers remaining today are actually remnants of older glaciers and continue to alter the landscape, though the change is less widespread than in the past.

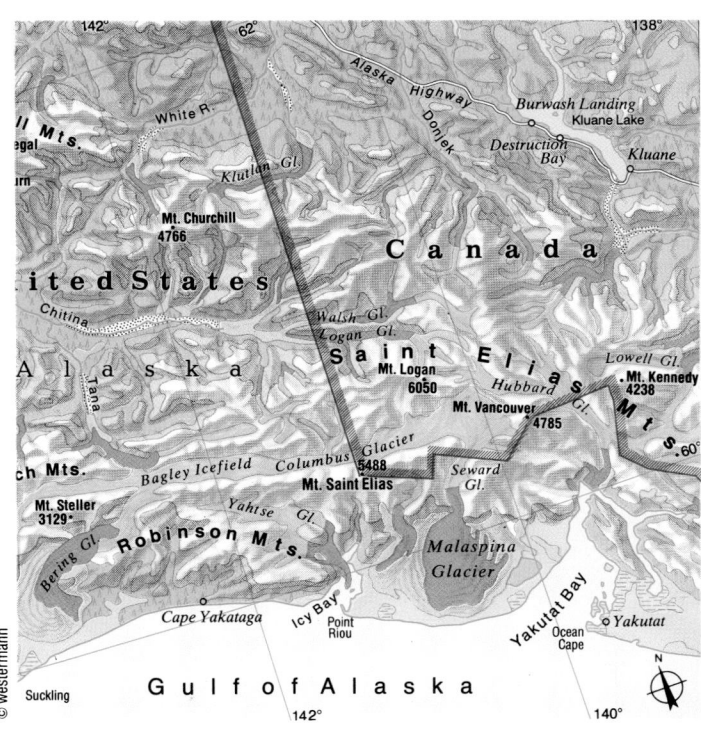

Map scale 1 : 3,000,000

oto scale 1 : 1,500,000

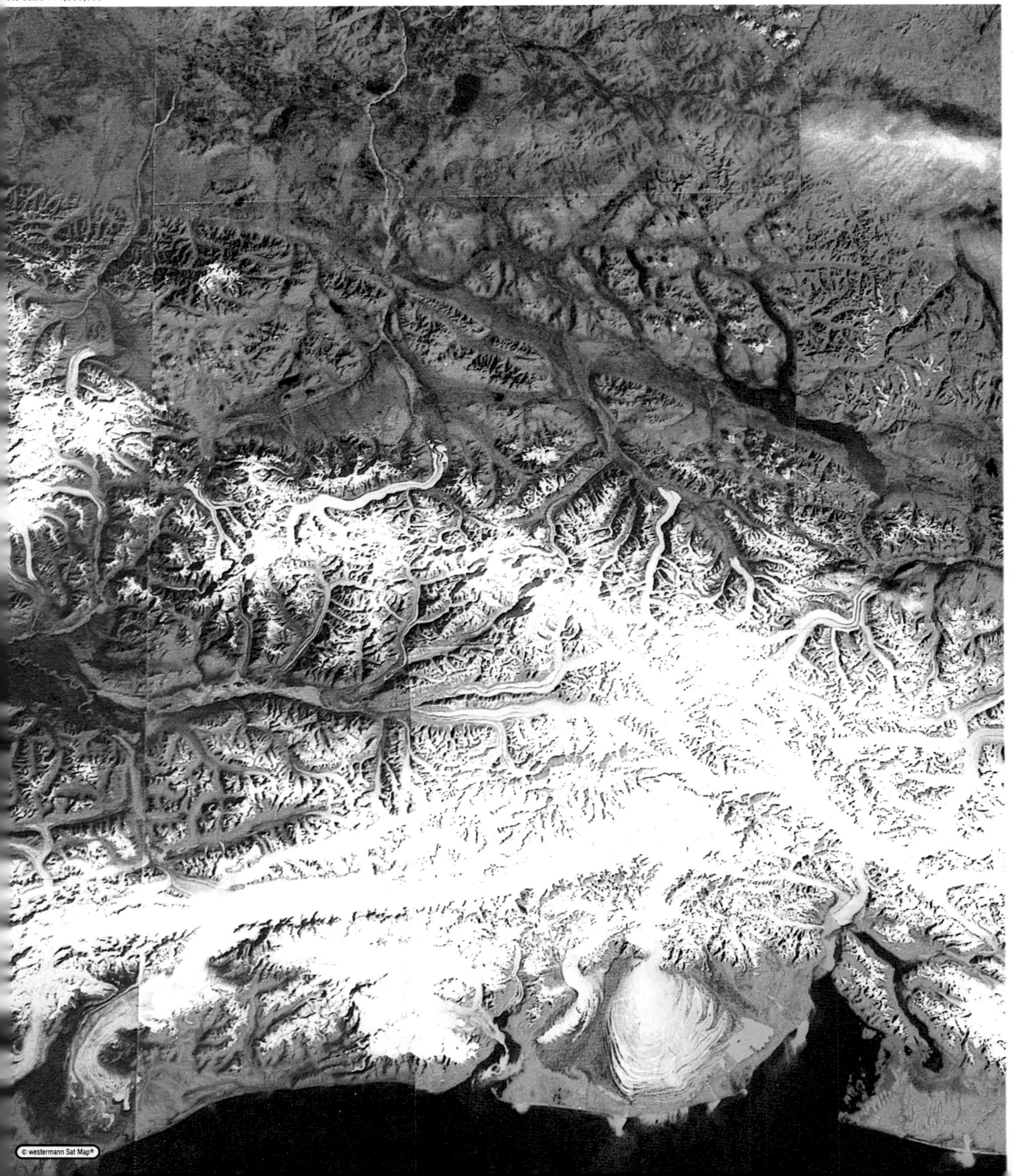

## ICEFIELDS AND GLACIERS, CANADA AND U.S.

The system of glaciers in southern Alaska and southwestern Yukon is the largest in the world outside of Greenland and Antarctica. The St. Elias Mountains, shown in the map above, contain a system of highland icefields and alpine glaciers covering the ground so completely that little is known about the underlying rock structures. These glaciers advance and retreat with the seasons, continually changing the landscape around them.

Most prominent of the ice sheets is Malaspina Glacier, which is shown as the light blue-gray triangle to the left of Yakutat Bay (lower right-hand portion of the image). Larger than the state of Rhode Island, the glacier extends beyond the ice field which spawned it and forms an ice plateau up to 1,500 feet high. Moraines of till at the edges of the Malaspina and other glaciers show as shades of gray on the image. As the glacier melts, light-blue fresh water runs off along the coast.

In 1986, the Hubbard Glacier, near the tip of Yakutat Bay, advanced suddenly, blocking the mouth of the fjord that runs parallel to the bay. The fjord turned into a fast-rising freshwater lake 80 feet above sea level. Within five months, the glacial dam broke, sending out a torrent of ice, water, and debris that rearranged the landscape once again. Other glaciers on the image can be located by referring to the map above.

### PROMINENT GLACIERS

| Continental Glaciers or Ice Sheets | Country | Area in Square Miles |
|---|---|---|
| Antarctica | | 5,000,000 |
| Greenland | | 700,000 |
| Vatna | Iceland | 3,200 |
| Jostedal | Norway | 300 |
| Columbia Icefield | Canada | 200 |
| **Mountain and Valley Glaciers** | | |
| Hubbard | U.S.A., Canada | 80 |
| Seward | U.S.A., Canada | 50 |
| Bering | U.S.A. | 50 |
| Fedchenko | Soviet Union | 40 |
| Malaspina | U.S.A. | 28 |
| Susitna | U.S.A. | 22 |
| Aletsch | Switzerland | 15 |
| Mendenhall | U.S.A. | 10 |
| Mer de Glace | France | 3 |

# Vegetation

> " The forest is so dense that for a day the sun could not be seen, . . . "
>
> *Description of Pennsylvania, 1745*

The daily temperature, precipitation, pressures, wind, and other atmospheric elements we call "weather" over time establish the climate of a region. The earth's major climatic zones, and their associated weather, set the limits and global patterns of natural vegetation zones.

These generalized zones – forests, grasslands, deserts, etc. – provide habitats for all living things. The vegetation zones shown in the diagram on the next page (upper right) give us a broad, idealized picture of this aspect of the world's geography. However, many local variations exist within each zone.

Along with natural forces, human activity also has an immense impact on the natural vegetation in each area. We cut down forests, develop and use cultivated plants, domesticate animals, develop sophisticated

Photo scale 1 : 500,000

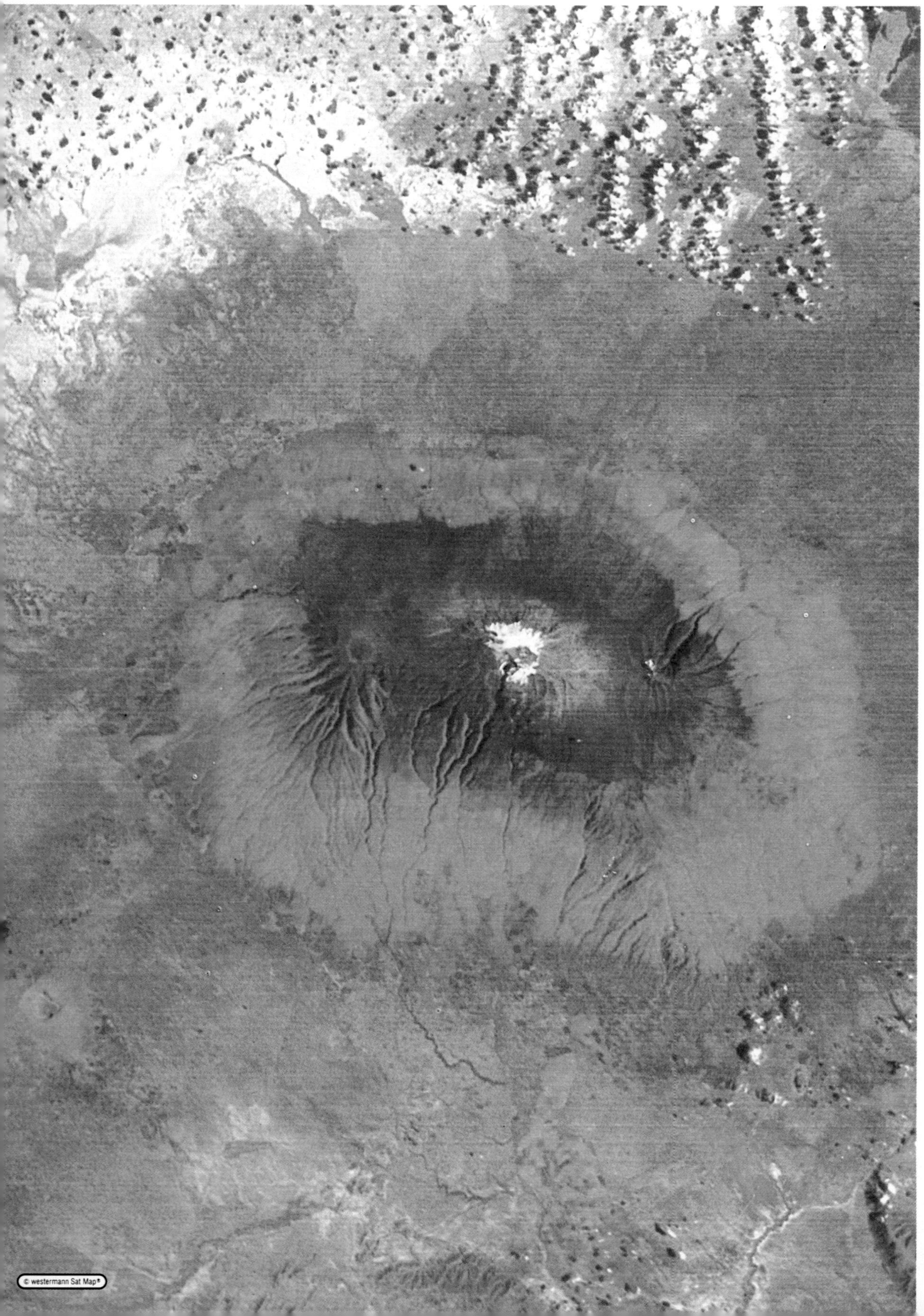

**M**OUNTAIN VEGETATION ZONES, MT. KILIMANJARO, TANZANIA   The satellite image to the left and map below illustrate distinct banding of vegetation zones as the land rises steeply from the flat savanna surrounding Kilimanjaro to the mountain's summit at 19,340 feet (5895 meters).

The savanna belt with its tufted grasses and sparse trees appears as light brown on the image. The heaviest rainfall occurs on the southeast slopes at roughly 5,000 feet (1500 meters) elevation. These slopes (lighter green areas on the image) support most of the population and a system of plantation agriculture.

With increasing elevation, grasses give way to tropical montane forests, portrayed as a narrow, darker green band above the wetter slopes. This mossy forest consists of a single layer of stunted and gnarled trees.

At about 10,000 feet (3000 meters), the colder, drier climate permits only evergreen shrubs and trees with leathery leaves to grow. This vegetation quickly gives way to tussock grasslands, shown as the dark brown area above the treeline. At higher elevations, the climate and terrain no longer support vegetation, leaving only beige-colored rocks and lava beds and, finally, the snowcapped summit of Africa's highest peak.

Map scale 1 : 500,000

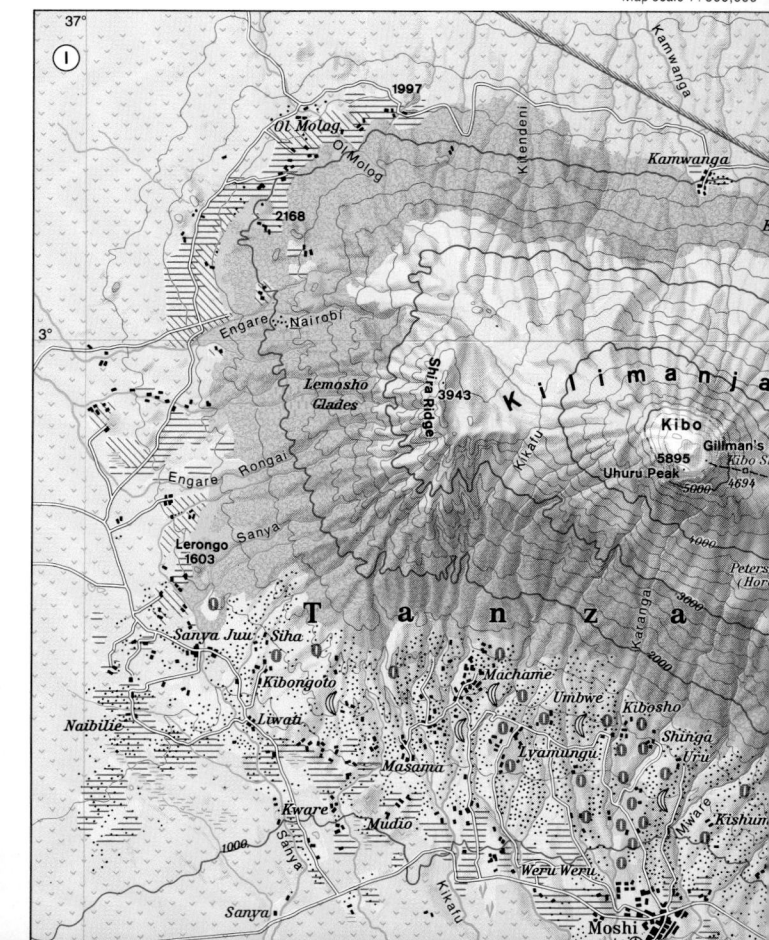

© westermann Sat Map®

systems of agriculture, and build large urban and industrial centers. These and other actions create landscapes that are more human-made than natural.

Yet vegetation within any region is a stabilizing influence, and changes to it have far-reaching effects on all life. For example, many scientists believe that the world's rainforests contribute half of our oxygen supply. Extensive deforestation in these regions not only affects the roughly two million species inhabiting the forests but could deplete the world's oxygen.

We must learn to recognize the major forces influencing vegetation throughout the world. Satellite images help us evaluate changes to vegetation zones. The two images below show dramatic alterations in plant life resulting from climate changes.

**REGIONAL VEGETATION CHANGE, FERGANA BASIN, SOVIET UNION**

The Fergana Basin (image and map below) shows how moisture and human settlement affect vegetation patterns. The basin is surrounded by the Alajskij and Kirgizskij mountains, where annual precipitation averages 60 inches.

Since the basin floor receives less than eight inches of annual rainfall, water from the mountains (shown as dark blue lines) is distributed throughout the basin by the Syrdarya River and the Great Fergana Canal. Irrigated land (olive-green areas) supports crops such as cotton and fruit. Nonirrigated regions (lighter green areas) serve as grazing lands for livestock.

Precipitation increases with the elevation, enabling the brown-toned middle slopes to support a heavier grassland cover. Near the summits, most precipitation falls as snow. At these elevations only alpine glassland and sparse fir and spruce forests survive, while dark blue-green areas on the middle and upper slopes represent barren rocks.

▼

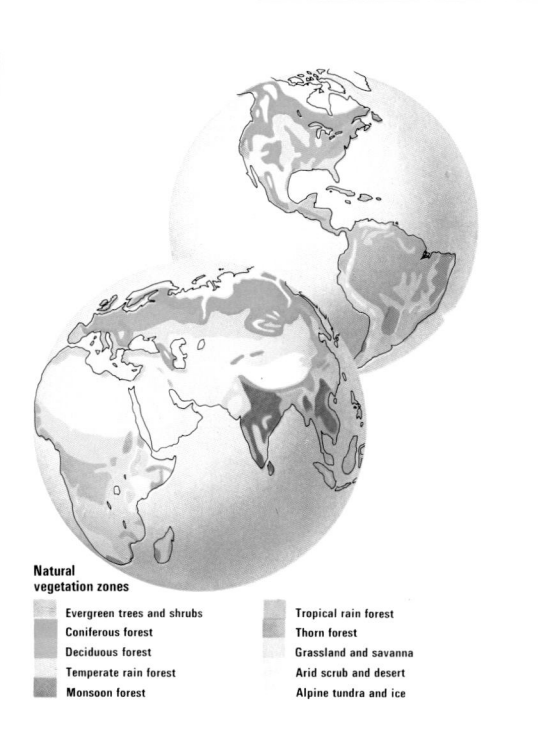

Natural vegetation zones

- Evergreen trees and shrubs
- Coniferous forest
- Deciduous forest
- Temperate rain forest
- Monsoon forest
- Tropical rain forest
- Thorn forest
- Grassland and savanna
- Arid scrub and desert
- Alpine tundra and ice

# Vegetation and Climate
### (Natural Vegetation Zones)

***Mediterranean*** Once covered with evergreen trees, these regions today support only scrub vegetation because of continual agricultural development.

***Coniferous forest*** These forests are the world's largest, continuous zone of vegetation and circle the upper northern hemisphere. They are composed primarily of spruce, pine, fir, and larch trees.

***Deciduous forest*** Deciduous forests in colder, northern climates are characterized by trees such as oak, while in milder, wetter regions evergreen forests thrive. Most of the original forest areas have been replanted.

***Temperate rain forests*** These forests of giant conifers and pines are found in temperate climates where there is high humidity and year-round rainfall.

***Monsoon forest*** Monsoon forests flourish in areas of extremely wet and dry seasons. They adapt to seasonal droughts and have fewer plants species than tropical rain forests.

***Tropical rain forests*** This vegetation is located in hot, humid equatorial lands of Latin America, West Africa, and Asia. Layers of vegetation overlap from the humid forest floor to the dense main canopy overhead.

***Thorn forest*** Found mainly in Africa and South America, forests of thorn trees are adapted to dry conditions and seasonal rains.

***Grasslands and savanna*** Grasslands flourish in semiarid regions where rain is too sparse for trees. Savannas – broad tropical grasslands – grow on each side of the equator between tropical rain forests and deserts.

***Arid scrub and desert*** Deserts exist where rainfall is low and quickly evaporates. Succulent plants dominate the landscape, although trees and shrubs with shallow, extensive roots systems can also thrive.

***Tundra*** These treeless areas in polar and alpine regions support a cover of lichen and moss. Plants grow only when the frozen ground thaws slightly during short summers.

Photo scale 1 : 1,500,000

Map scale 1 : 3,000,000

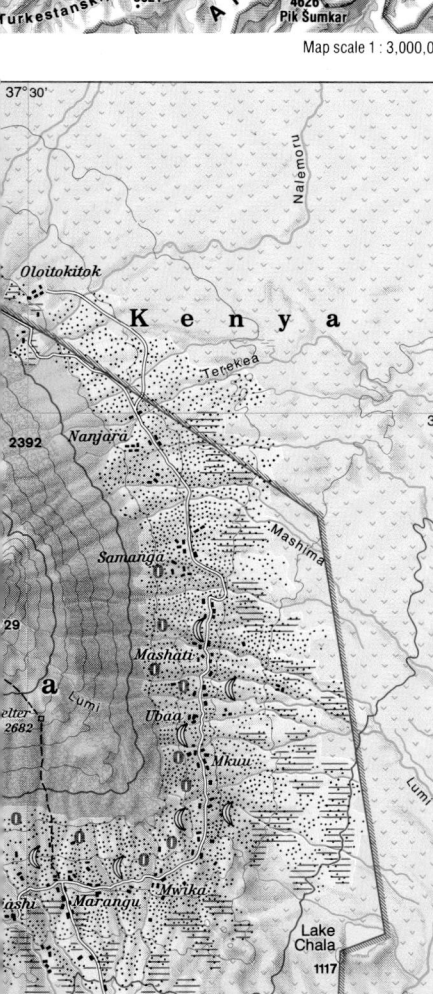

© westermann

© westermann Sat Map

# Agriculture

*" It took...so very long to [invent] ... agriculture that we may well doubt that the idea came easily... "*

*Carl O. Sauer*

Natural forces of climate, land, and water establish the broad limits for human agricultural development. Since we first began domesticating plants and animals some 10,000 years ago, we have cleared thousands of acres and patterned the earth with a variety of agricultural systems. Agricultural development increased significantly throughout the world after A.D. 1500. European expansion encouraged dramatically different patterns of land use from those existing before Columbus's time.

These patterns evolved into two distinct systems of agriculture – commercial farming and subsistence farming – used to raise crops and livestock today. Commercial farming is practiced in areas such as North America, Europe, parts of the Soviet Union, and Australia where relatively low popula-

Photo scale 1 : 75,000

© westermann Sat Map®

**WESTERN OKLAHOMA, U.S.A.** Oklahoma's pattern of rectangular fields bordered by country roads and highways (map and satellite image to the left) is typical of the agricultural landscape of many midwestern states. This geometric design is the result of a rectangular survey system first established in 1785 to ensure orderly settlement of the land.

Generations of farmers and townspeople have followed the basic survey grid to scribe each property with neat, straight boundaries. Two circular field patterns, just to the southwest of the Canadian River (see map), are the only exceptions to the grid. They are created by "center-pivot" irrigation systems whose water pipes rotate around a central pumping station.

The satellite image, recorded in late summer, clearly illustrates the different uses of the land. Beige-colored fields are planted with wheat, which has just been harvested. Lighter green pasturelands support livestock, while the dark green areas represent woodlands.

**NORTH GERMAN PLAINS, EAST AND WEST GERMANY** In most agricultural regions, settlement patterns are determined by culture and terrain. But the satellite image below illustrates how the national policies of two neighboring countries affect land use.

Larger fields in the right-hand side of the image are in the German Democratic Republic (East Germany). They reflect the collective farming system imposed by the central government. Farming state-controlled land with cooperative groups

(continued on facing page)

Map scale 1 : 75,000

Photo scale 1 : 500,000

## Legend

| | |
|---|---|
| | Scrub, woodland |
| | Meadow, pasture (incl. land not in use) |
| | Cropland (harvested at time of scan) |
| | Contour farming, terracing |
| | Windbreak |
| | Irrigated area |
| | Edge of alluvial terrace |
| | Severe soil erosion |
| | Gullies |
| | Land-partitioning system |
| | Road |
| | Unimproved road |

1 quarter section = 160 acres = 64.6 ha

1 section (1 Square Mile) = 640 acres = 258 ha

1 statute mile = 1609 m

Canadian River

457

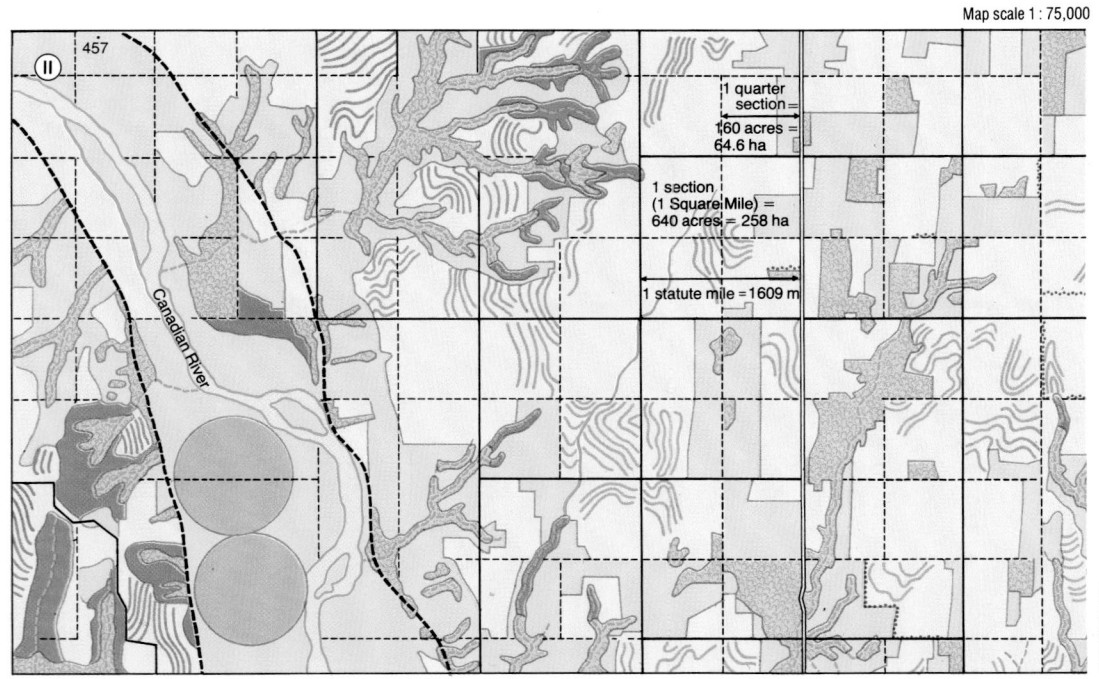

© westermann

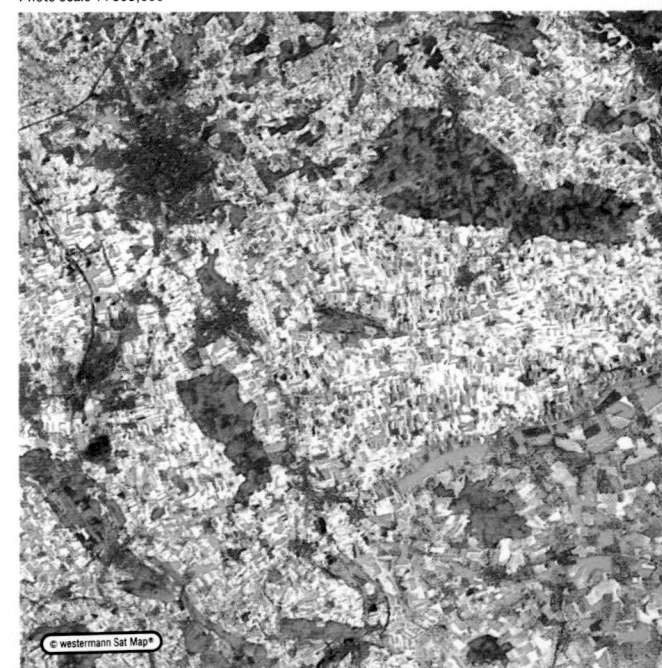

© westermann Sat Map®

I·22

tions enable growers to produce a surplus sold to outside markets. In some regions, notably the United States, industrialization has transformed crop raising. Countless small, family-owned farms have given way to huge agri-business firms. By using advanced methods of fertilization and mechanized harvesting, these agri-businesses can raise enough food to feed the U. S. population and still export surpluses to other countries.

In subsistence farming, on the other hand, farmers generally produce only enough food to feed the local population. This form of agriculture is still the main system in much of Africa, Latin America, and Asia. Even with smaller yields, farmers may practice a certain amount of specialization in raising particular kinds of livestock or crops. They can then trade their surplus for a variety of products raised by other farmers.

Whatever system of agriculture is practiced, the patterns of rural settlement and cultivation imposed on the land are distinctive for each culture, as shown in the images below and to the right. Settlements may be tightly clustered near a water source, dispersed along roads or rivers, or scattered over the countryside – which may reflect hilly terrain, methods of land subdivision, or governmental farm policies. Seen from the air, these patterns often appear in neat checkerboard squares or in a haphazard mosaic of cultivated and fallow land.

However, natural forces and governmental policies alone do not explain the world's patterns of rural settlement and agriculture. Perhaps the most enduring force is culture, the particular style and preferences of a people, which establishes how the land is used. Governments often play an important role in agricultural development by setting quotas, subsidies, and land-division systems.

allows larger field sizes than if the land were farmed by individuals.

On the left side of the image, the smaller fields and more dispersed settlement in the Federal Republic of Germany (West Germany) depict an entirely different agricultural and political system. Here farms are individually owned and operated, following the more traditional customs of land use. Prior to the Second World War, this agricultural pattern could be found in both East and West Germany.

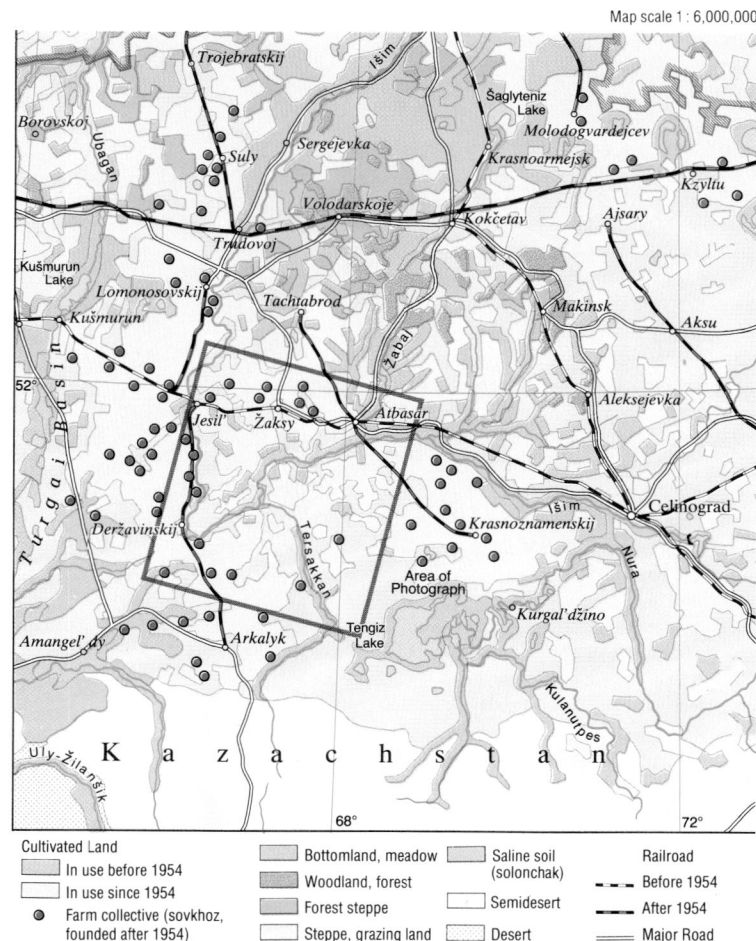

Photo scale 1 : 500,000

**NORTHERN KAZACHSTAN, SOVIET UNION** ▲ The satellite image above shows the results of the Soviet Union's recent policy to increase wheat production by extending the limits of cultivation into dry lands. The box on the map (right) outlines the area in the image. These regions have short growing seasons and are only marginally suited for crops.

Before 1954, agriculture in this area was limited to raising livestock on river bottomlands (larger areas of bright green) and on land adjacent to the rivers. Since then, the government has cultivated the hillier regions away from the rivers and planted wheat in rectangular fields, shown as various shades of green. The black squares among them, and dark strips within fields, are unplanted areas cultivated in alternate years.

The government establishes the field size (about 1,000 acres), the type of crops raised, and the collective farm settlements to work the land. By using faster-maturing, drought-resistant varieties of wheat; alternating fallow and planted fields; and farming with mechanized equipment, it has been possible to cultivate this semiarid land.

Yet, such techniques do not always ensure success. The red-brown, beige, and green-brown fields in the lower part of the image have been taken out of production because of low crop yields. They underscore the fact that farming on marginal land is risky even with government support and improved agricultural methods.

Map scale 1 : 6,000,000

Cultivated Land
- In use before 1954
- In use since 1954
- Farm collective (sovkhoz, founded after 1954)

- Bottomland, meadow
- Woodland, forest
- Forest steppe
- Steppe, grazing land

- Saline soil (solonchak)
- Semidesert
- Desert

Railroad
- Before 1954
- After 1954
- Major Road

# Land Reclamation

" But it is certain that man has done much to mould the form of the earth's surface, ... "

*George Perkins Marsh*

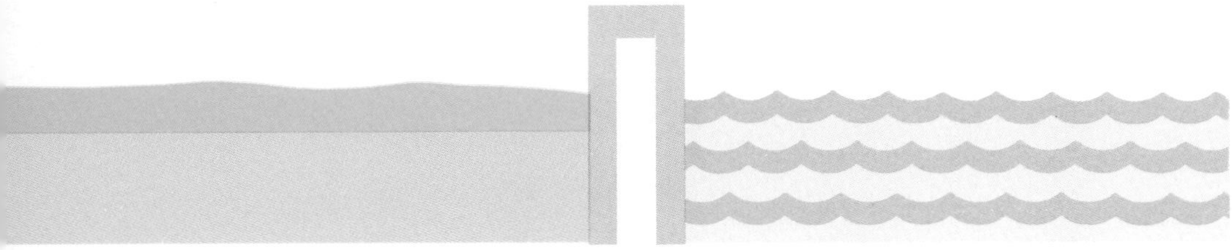

The history of human agricultural development and settlement is the story of land reclamation – people changing the natural environment to suit their needs. Over thousands of years, nearly all of the most desirable land has been developed. Today, land reclamation projects seek to create new agricultural land in marginal areas and to reclaim once productive acreage spoiled by industrial pollution and overuse.

More than in the past, the modern quest for new land has pushed agriculture into areas once considered too dry, too wet, too cold, or too mountainous. Elaborate irrigation systems built around reservoirs, deep wells, and desalinization plants converting salt water to fresh have created about 160 million acres of fertile land out of arid and semiarid regions in the past 25 years. Colder

Photo scale 1 : 500,000

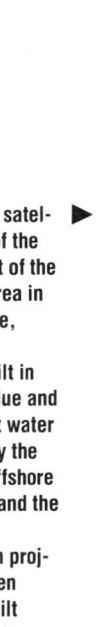

IJSSELMEER, NETHERLANDS   The satellite image (right) covers a section of the Netherlands in which about 80 percent of the land has been reclaimed. The black area in the image center is the freshwater lake, IJsselmeer, created when an 18-mile dam (top left of the lake) was built in 1932 to hold back the sea. The light blue and white area north of the dam is the salt water tidal flats of Waddenzee, restrained by the dam. The West Frisians, a series of offshore islands, stand between the tidal flats and the North Sea.

The Netherlands' major reclamation projects of the twentieth century have taken place within IJsselmeer. Engineers built a system of dikes (see diagram on facing page) and pumped out water to reclaim nearly 360,000 new acres. Thousands of fields, built on these new acres, show as light brown and yellow on the image and clearly define Flevoland and the Northeast Polder, both of which appear on the southeast side of IJsselmeer.

The satellite image, captured in spring, depicts newly planted agricultural land in tones of light brown and yellow. Light green areas represent mainly pasturelands, while woodlands are shown as the dark green region in the southeast. Cities are deeper rust-colored clusters, with most of Amsterdam appearing in the bottom left of the image. The everpresent canal systems crisscross the land in a fine network of dark lines. They continually drain this area of the Netherlands, which is almost entirely below sea level.

© westermann Sat Map®

areas have long supported agriculture in the form of livestock, but crop farming has been possible only since the development of plants that mature in the short growing seasons.

Perhaps the greatest land reclamation frontier lies in the unsettled tropics. Here, governments and private farmers have combined resources to carve permanent settlements. In settled humid, tropical areas, farmers cope with mountainous terrain and torrential rainfall by constructing elaborate terraces to increase arable land and control water. Soil is improved with mud from river valleys and various fertilizers. In parts of Southeast Asia, these tropical lands support some of the world's largest populations.

Other targets for land reclamation include swamplands and seacoasts. Draining swamplands over the past 100 years has added significantly to the agricultural lands in areas already heavily cultivated. Along some coastlines, engineers are pushing back the sea to make more arable land available. The Netherlands has constructed some of the most ambitious reclamation projects (see the maps and satellite images below).

The total arable cropland of the world is estimated to be 3.4 billion acres. About 350 million acres of new land were added in the past 40 years. This contribution is a relatively small increase; but for each country, the land reclaimed often makes a crucial difference in the country's economy and in feeding an ever increasing population.

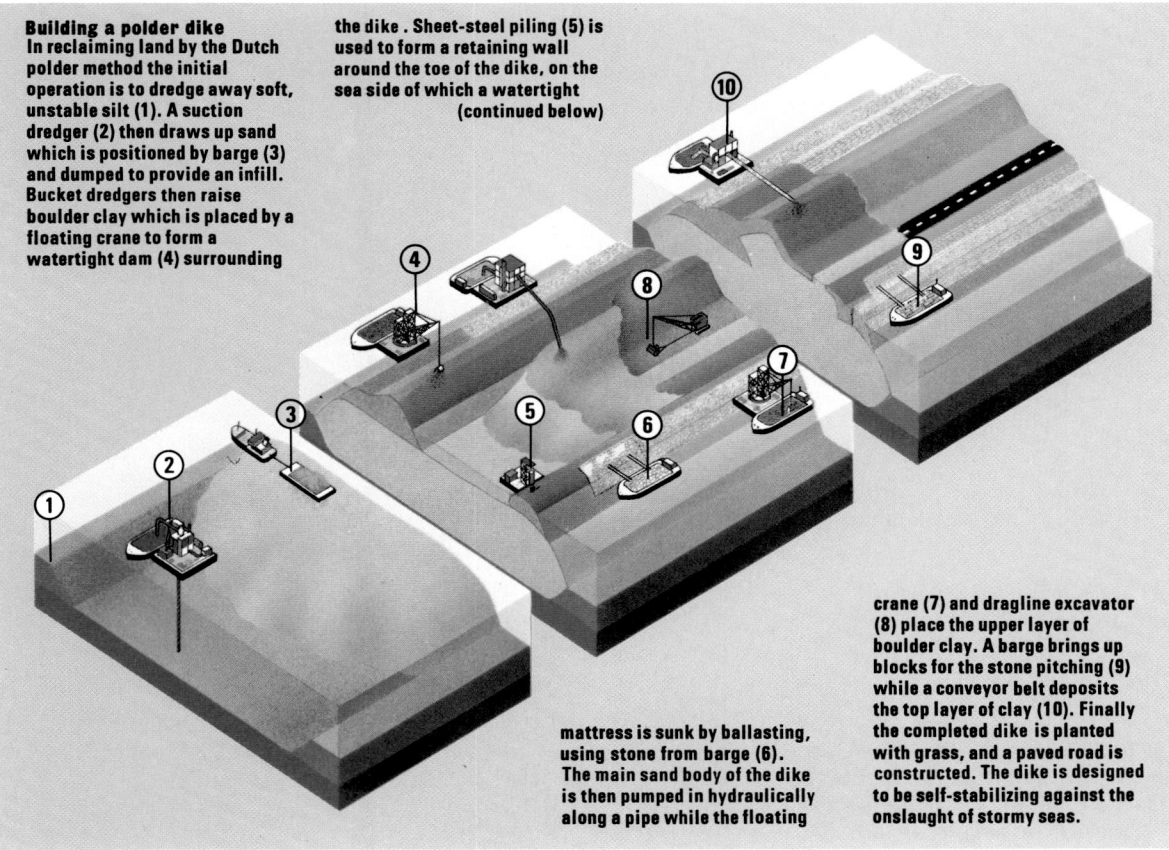

**Building a polder dike** In reclaiming land by the Dutch polder method the initial operation is to dredge away soft, unstable silt (1). A suction dredger (2) then draws up sand which is positioned by barge (3) and dumped to provide an infill. Bucket dredgers then raise boulder clay which is placed by a floating crane to form a watertight dam (4) surrounding the dike. Sheet-steel piling (5) is used to form a retaining wall around the toe of the dike, on the sea side of which a watertight (continued below)

mattress is sunk by ballasting, using stone from barge (6). The main sand body of the dike is then pumped in hydraulically along a pipe while the floating crane (7) and dragline excavator (8) place the upper layer of boulder clay. A barge brings up blocks for the stone pitching (9) while a conveyor belt deposits the top layer of clay (10). Finally the completed dike is planted with grass, and a paved road is constructed. The dike is designed to be self-stabilizing against the onslaught of stormy seas.

**P**OLDER DIKE BUILDING, NETHER-LANDS   The diagram on the right illustrates the complex set of engineering steps required in building dikes to reclaim land (polders) from the sea. The elaborate process establishes an impressive barrier that can withstand heavy gales and winter storms. After the flooding of 1953 (see the small inset in the map below) such dikes were constructed in the southern coastal areas in the 1960s, 1970s, and 1980s to prevent a repeat of the disaster.

Land Reclamation
- 14th - 16th century
- 17th century
- 18th century
- 19th century
- 20th century
- Reclamation until the year 2000

1968   Year of completion
Shoreline dunes
Enclosing dike
Shoreline dike
Lock, sluice

Map scale 1 : 1,750,000

Flood of 1953
- Flooded area
- Fresh water
- Salt water
- International boundary

Map scale 1 : 2,000,000

**N**ETHERLANDS MAP – For centuries the Dutch have pushed back the sea, dramatically changing the landscape to claim new living space and cropland. The map on the left shows the history of the country's land reclamation projects, which started in the fourteenth century. During the 1500s, the Dutch developed new methods of building secure embankments to keep out the sea and pump the water away, thus recovering additional acres of land. Reclamation projects since that time have enabled the small nation to reclaim a total of over 400,000 acres. Today, roughly 1,300 miles of dikes and other retaining walls keep the sea out of the Netherlands. The country has 25 percent of its land below sea level and one of the highest population densities in the world.

© westermann

# Dams and Reservoirs

**❝ At the foot of the main dam, all is bustle. But on top... only the wind [races] across the vast artificial lake... ❞**

*Visitor's account of Itaipu Dam, Brazil*

The earth's abundant water is unevenly distributed on the planet's surface, a problem humanity has attempted to solve through water resource management projects. The most dramatic changes to the landscape have been brought about by the construction of reservoirs and dams, which store water and release it when needed.

Dams have been in use since ancient times, but projects built to control all the waters of a river basin are a modern concept. Today, huge dams tame most of the world's great rivers, store about 15 trillion gallons of water in reservoirs, produce nearly one-fourth of the world's electricity, and, through irrigation, open up new croplands. In regions where water is scarce, irrigation is vital to the local economy and a growing population.

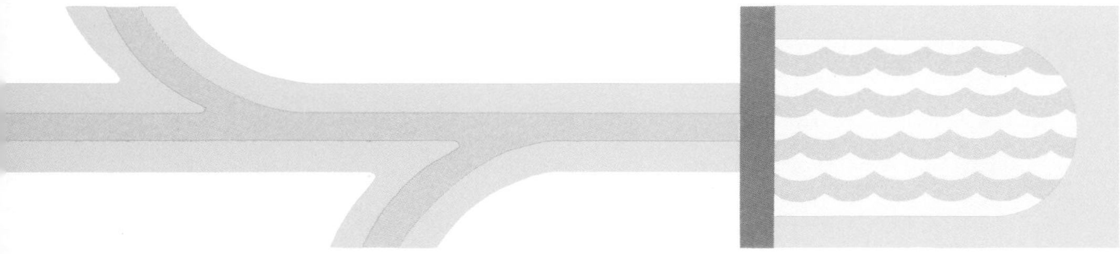

Photo scale 1 : 1,500,000

**L**OWER VOLGA RIVER RESERVOIR Since 1917, the Soviet Union has developed a series of dams, reservoirs, and hydroelectric stations along its most vital waterway, the Volga River (see map on facing page). ▶

This system regulates the Volga's seasonal flow and has improved navigation, created new transportation links, irrigated the semi-arid middle and lower reaches of the Volga, and generated electricity for the entire region. The first small-scale projects were Ivan'kovo and Uglic Reservoirs, providing power to Moscow and creating the Moscow Canal.

The Kujbyšev Dam was the first large-scale project, while the next, Volgograd Dam, gave rise to a 500-mile long trunk canal irrigating the northern Caspian lowlands. The smaller Saratov Reservoir raised the water 40 feet and extended a reservoir around Kujbyšev to the Kujbyšev Dam. The last large project built was the Čeboksary Dam at the northern end of the Kujbyšev Reservoir.

The satellite image centers on the Kujbyšev Reservoir south of Čeboksary and north of Balakovo (see map). The reservoir is built on a prominent bend in the Volga, shown toward the bottom of the image.

When the reservoir was filled in 1956, it raised the Volga waters 80 feet, created a reservoir 380 miles up the river, and forced the relocation of 280 villages. Irrigation water from the reservoir has increased cropland (mottled gray-green areas on the image) along that section of the Volga. The solid green represents coniferous and deciduous forest.

Unfortunately, Kujbyšev Reservoir, along with the rest of the water management system, is gradually lowering the level of the Caspian Sea. To alleviate the problem, the Soviet government has designed an ambitious project to transport European and Siberian waters into the Volga Basin.

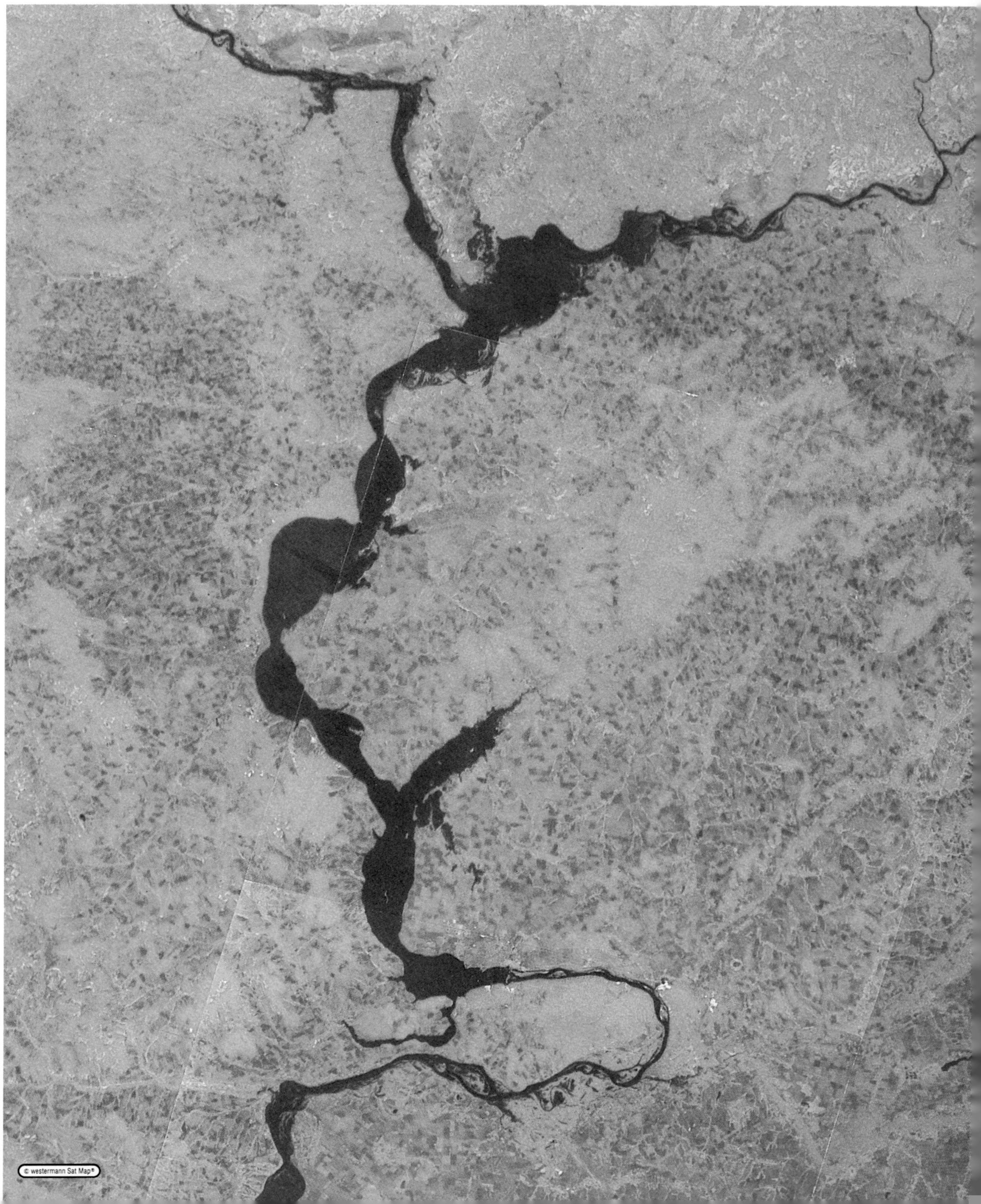

Not all the effects of these giant water projects are beneficial, however. Dams often stop the movement of silt and diminish soil fertility below the dam, slow the growth of deltas, and force the resettlement of entire communities. When Egypt's High Aswan Dam was completed in 1970, some 100,000 Egyptians and Sudanese had to be relocated as Lake Nasser flooded their former homeland. Irrigation, while opening new acreage, also can destroy the land if salts or other contaminants in the water reach toxic levels in the soil.

Despite these hazards, large-scale projects have not been abandoned. Although Itaipu Dam in Brazil is currently the world's largest, other nations are planning even greater projects to manage the earth's precious water resources.

**E**L GEZIRA PROVINCE, SUDAN   The map and satellite image (right) show the White Nile and Blue Nile flowing northward through arid thorn savanna and grassland. The area receives only eight inches of rainfall annually. Without irrigation, agricultural development would not be possible.

The Gezira irrigation scheme and its extension into Al Manaqil in 1962 (see map) opened over a million acres to agriculture, primarily cotton. The orderly green of the Gezira and Manaqil schemes between the White and Blue Niles is in stark contrast to the light tan and mottled gray-green of the more arid grassland. The Sannar Dam on the Blue Nile feeds the irrigation schemes through an elaborate system of canals.

Sudan's canal irrigation is augmented by pump irrigation along the White Nile. The White Nile Dam south of Khartoum, where the river widens into light blue silty waters, powers a pump irrigation system that supports crops (green areas) along the river.

These large-scale water management schemes have been cited as a model for agricultural improvement in Africa. They have had a vital effect on the economy of Sudan by changing an arid landscape into a fertile one.

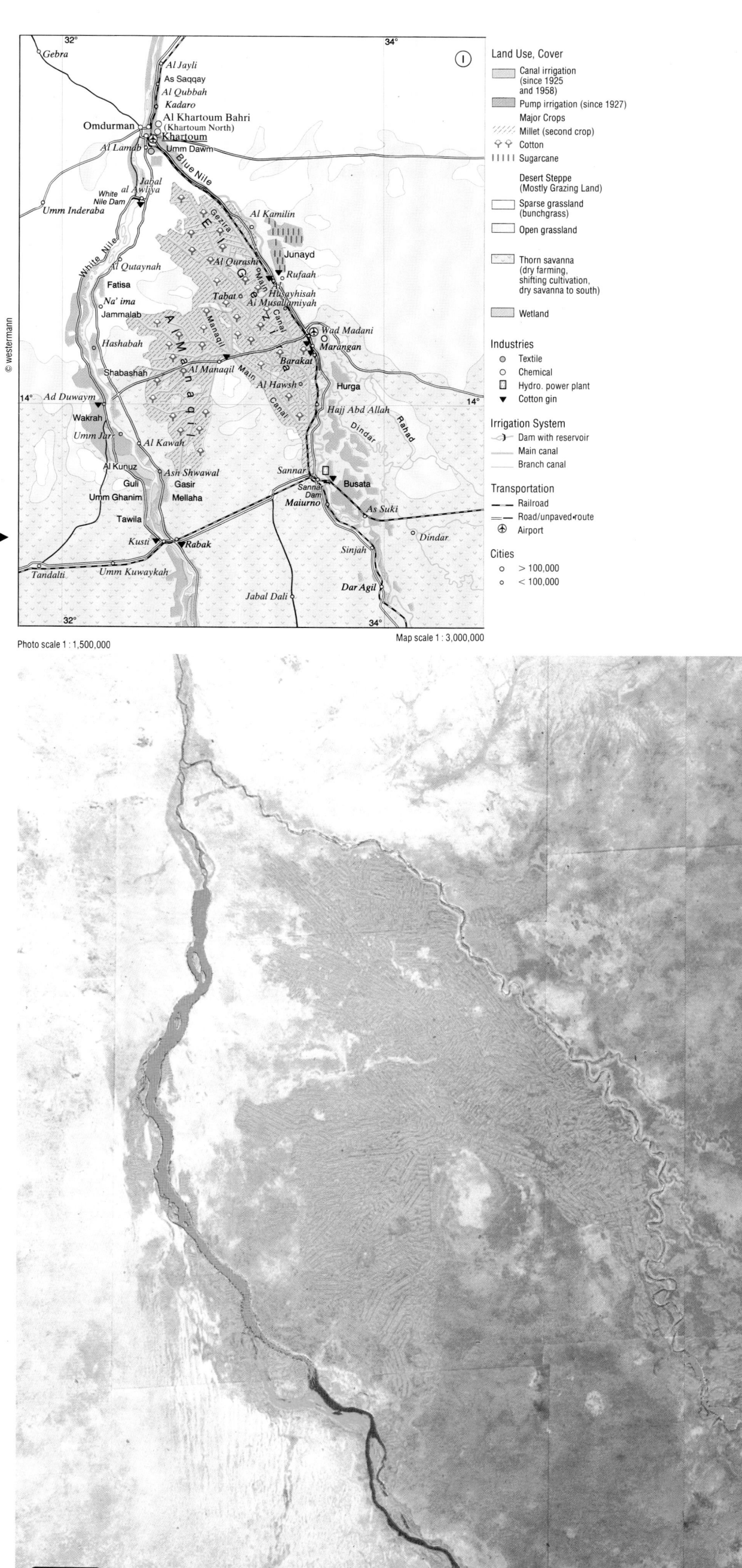

© westermann

Photo scale 1 : 1,500,000

Map scale 1 : 3,000,000

### Land Use, Cover

- Canal irrigation (since 1925 and 1958)
- Pump irrigation (since 1927)

Major Crops
- //// Millet (second crop)
- ♀ ♀ Cotton
- |||| Sugarcane

- Desert Steppe (Mostly Grazing Land)
- Sparse grassland (bunchgrass)
- Open grassland
- Thorn savanna (dry farming, shifting cultivation, dry savanna to south)
- Wetland

### Industries
- ◉ Textile
- ○ Chemical
- ▢ Hydro. power plant
- ▼ Cotton gin

### Irrigation System
- ⌐◡ Dam with reservoir
- —— Main canal
- —— Branch canal

### Transportation
- –·– Railroad
- –·– Road/unpaved route
- ⊕ Airport

### Cities
- ○ > 100,000
- ○ < 100,000

### Towns
- ⬡ > 1,000,000
- ○ 100,000 – 1,000,000
- ○ < 100,000

### Transportation
- –·– Railroad
- —— Major road
- —+— Canal
- ⌐◡ Dam with reservoir
- **358** Elevations in meters
  15

### Reservoirs
- ▢ Surface area
  249 (km²)
- ▢ Capacity (km³)
  1.2
- ▬ Dam

Map scale 1 : 15,000,000

© westermann Sat Map

# Urbanization

"Urban land utilization is indeed [rapidly] devouring land... "

*Jean Gottmann*

The movement of people from rural areas to cities – urbanization – and from inner cities to outlying suburbs – suburbanization – is one of the most important chapters in the history of human settlement of our planet. This aspect of human activity continues to impact the earth's environment as much as any natural force.

Modern urbanization had its birth in the mid-1800s during an era of rapid scientific and commercial innovation that ushered in the Industrial Revolution. As industry and commerce grew, rural people migrated to the cities by the thousands, drawn by the varied economic opportunities offered in these urban centers.

By the mid-1900s, a new phenomenon had appeared – expansion out of the cities to the suburbs. Suburbanization is especially

Map scale 1 : 590,000

Photo scale 1 : 500,000

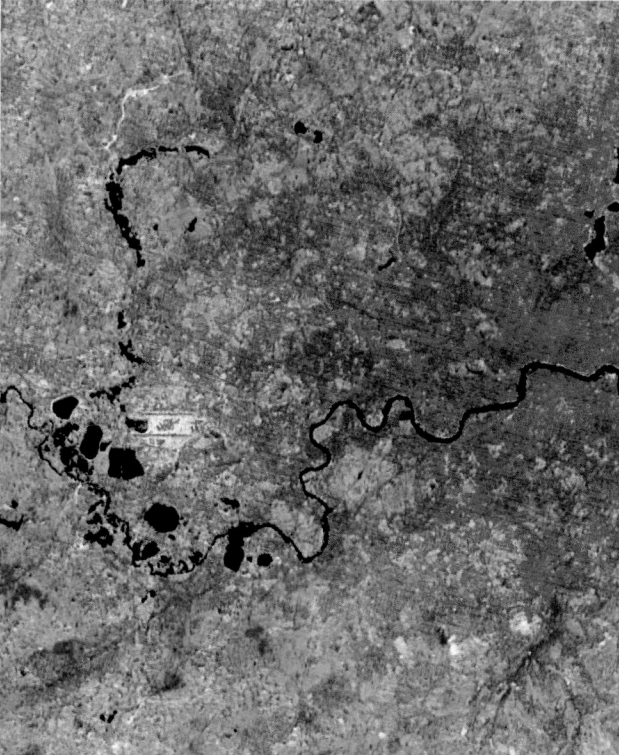

**LONDON, UNITED KINGDOM** The satellite image of London and its environs (right) shows the River Thames winding through the city. The original site of London chosen by the Romans is located on the river near the image center (close to dark center area on map). The heart of the city houses the government, financial institutions, and commercial businesses. Growth in this area is highlighted by bright red and orange tones on the image.

London and its picturesque suburbs are characterized by low buildings, parks, and open land in some sections. The mix of built-up and open areas is illustrated by dark red-green patches on the image. In the late 1940s, as the city began to expand, an extensive Green Belt was planned to surround the settled region and buffer the rural countryside from London's sprawl.

Still, the city and suburbs continue to grow. The gentle, rolling terrain offers few barriers to housing construction or transportation lines into the city. Many people prefer living in these less crowded areas where they can find single-family houses or apartment dwellings.

Photo scale 1 : 500,000

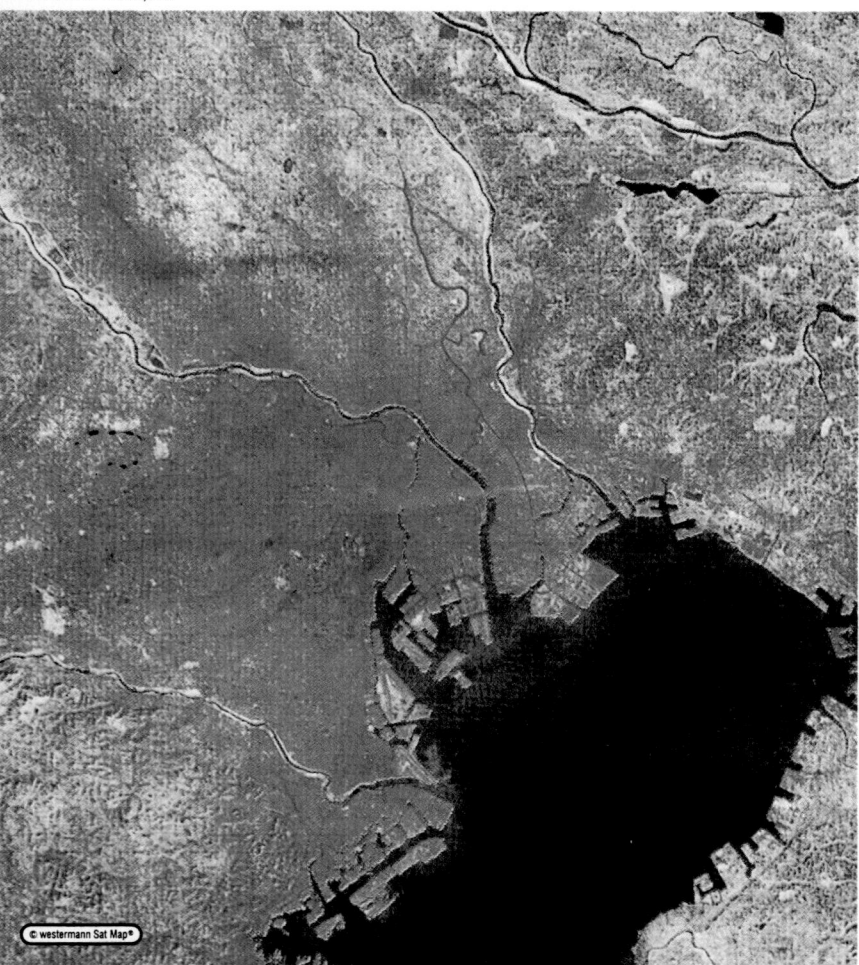

**TOKYO, JAPAN** Japan's mountainous interior makes its small coastal lowlands the most desireable areas for agricultural and urban development. The Tokyo-Kawasaki-Yokohama region, shown on the map and image to the left, highlights the problem of balancing urban growth and agricultural needs. The urban sprawl of the cities is taking over land that was once used for farming.

Tokyo, established in 1456, is young by Japanese standards. Its explosive growth came in the 1900s as people began migrating from rural areas to the city for jobs and education. Business, commercial, and financial districts are clustered around the original palace. Together with industrial works and shipping, they form the basis for many urban job opportunities.

Suburban growth, shown as red areas branching out from main urban centers, has expanded to the west into what was formerly agricultural land (light-brown and green areas in the upper left of the picture). The rapid growth of these urban sectors has been aided by efficient rail transportation and an earthquake hazard that limits the height and occupancy of each building. Since these cities cannot build up, they have grown by building out.

Photo scale 1 : 500,000

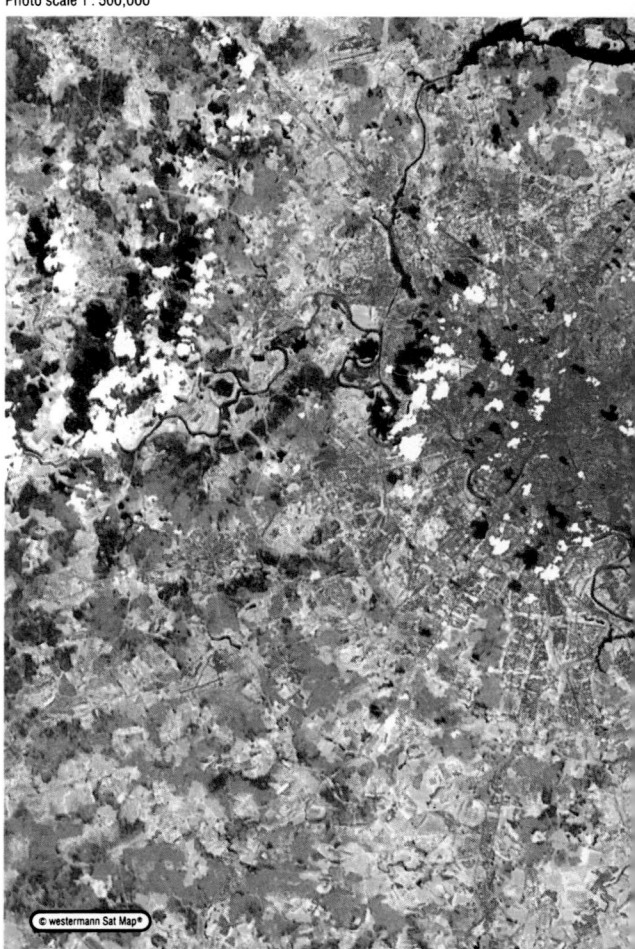

**Legend**

- Central city, major business and banking district
- Densely built-up residential area
- Industrial district

**Land Reclamation since 1945**

- Industrial and warehouse district
- ⊕ Airport on reclaimed land
- Future reclamation project

**Land Use, Cover**

- Cropland (mostly vegetables)
- Rice cultivation
- Mulberry plantations
- Orchards
- Woodland, mixed with scrub
- Heavily polluted water

prominent in North America, Europe, and Australia. Its rapid growth began when railways and roads were extended from the heart of the cities. These lines enabled people to live beyond the city limits and commute to their workplaces. Within a short time, entire communities had grown up around expressways and commuter rail transport.

Though suburbanization is still increasing in the more industrialized nations, it is not a worldwide phenomenon. Most people in African and Asian countries live close to where they work or combine their shops and homes. However, the urban-suburban trend is coming in these nations as more people converge on cities and the surrounding areas. Like their North American and European counterparts, these rural people are seeking greater economic security and better medical care, education, food supplies, and services.

Suburban growth is not without its dark side. It has often meant inner city decay, a problem facing most major cities today as residents and businesses leave downtown areas for the suburbs. The development of shopping centers, malls, and industrial districts in widely scattered suburban areas has created serious traffic congestion as people travel from suburb to suburb. Further, suburban sprawl often encroaches on valuable agricultural land.

As transportation facilities expand and cheaper sources of energy are developed, it is likely the trend of urban-suburban growth will continue – and in some developing countries may even accelerate.

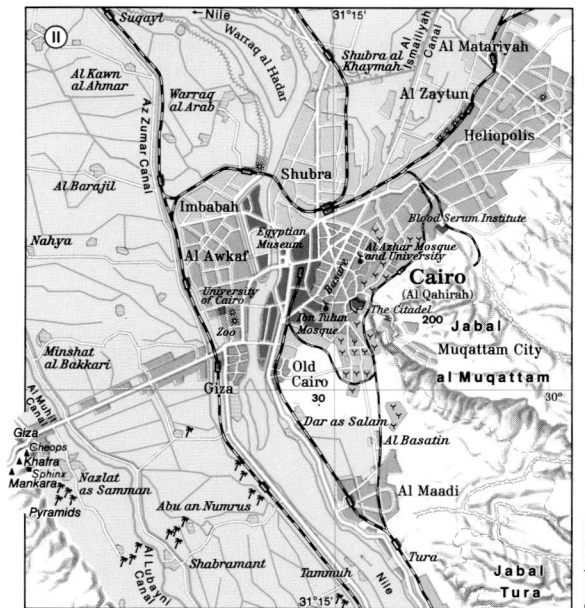

**Legend**

- Old Islamic city
- Modern city center (government quarter, shopping and business districts, hotels)
- Upper- and middle-class neighborhood
- Working-class neighborh.
- Rural settlement (fellaheen village)
- Cultivated land
- Date-palm groves
- Irrigation canal
- Cemetery
- Desert
- Railroad
- Expressway
- Major road

Map scale 1 : 295,000

**C**AIRO, EGYPT   The Arabs founded Cairo in A.D. 969 as the capital of Egypt. The city is located where the Nile River valley broadens into the green, triangular Nile Delta (see image below). Since its founding, Cairo has remained a major urban center in Egypt. The city went through a period of decline until the 1800s when it began its present era of rapid growth.

Cairo was originally settled on the east bank of the Nile then spread westward toward the pyramids. Mountains to the east, the river delta to the north, and endless stretches of desert flanking the Nile have placed limits on the city's expansion. As a result, population densities are high, causing a chronic shortage of housing. The older sections of Cairo appear as rust-colored areas on the image, while more recent sections are shown in lighter reds and yellows extending outward from the city and south along the Nile.

Cairo not only serves as the center of Egypt's government, industry, and commerce but is also the cultural center of Islam for the nation. The city has lost none of its strategic importance. Because the desert restricts transportation to the narrow band of the Nile, all traffic and trade must pass through Cairo – a vital link that connects Upper Egypt with Lower Egypt.

Photo scale 1 : 500,000 ▼

Map scale 1 : 590,000

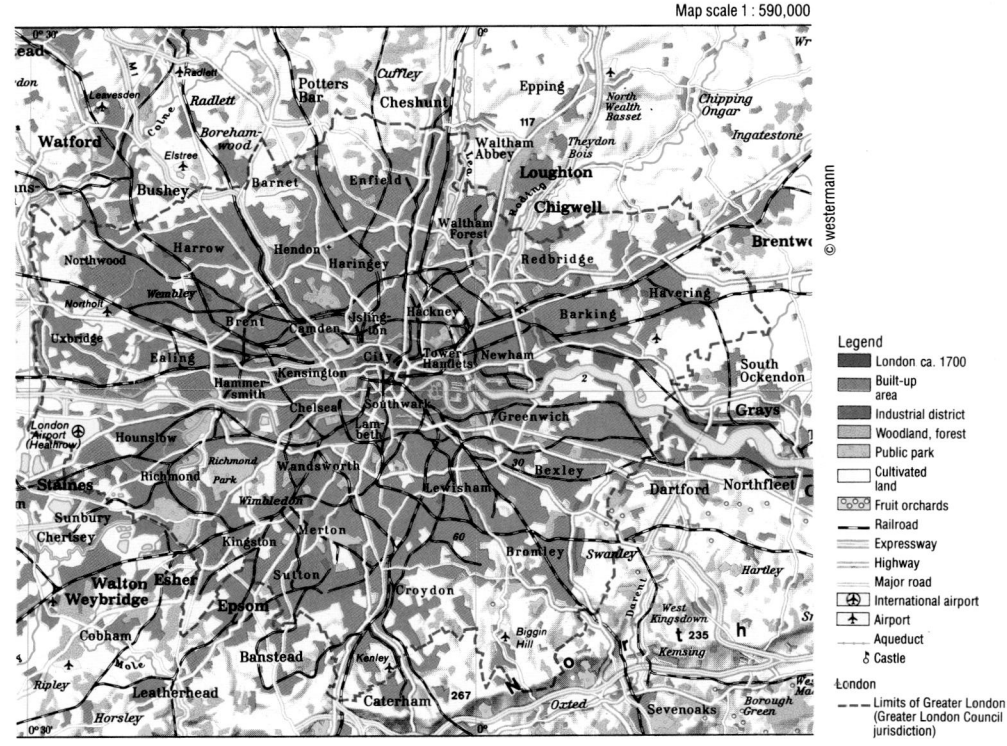

**Legend**
London

- London ca. 1700
- Built-up area
- Industrial district
- Woodland, forest
- Public park
- Cultivated land
- Fruit orchards
- Railroad
- Expressway
- Highway
- Major road
- International airport
- Airport
- Aqueduct
- Castle

- Limits of Greater London (Greater London Council jurisdiction)

**M**OSCOW, SOVIET UNION   The map (right) and satellite image (left) reveal Moscow's distinctive pattern of urban development. Its growth has been influenced both by the flat terrain and by the historical processes of city building used throughout much of old Russia. As depicted in the map and image, Moscow radiates out from a central region, its transportation lines constructed like spokes in a wheel. Settlement areas are shown in bright red, branching out from the city into light green farmland and darker green woodlands.

The original Kremlin was built as a walled city in 1147 and housed the government, religious institutions, and residences. As it grew, new walls were constructed to enclose the larger city. The walls remained until 1943 when they were demolished and boulevards built in their place. Beyond the last of the boulevards, railways and a superhighway ring the city.

The flat terrain encouraged the symmetrical development of Moscow, with transportation lines and settlement extending outward from the city's hub. The many satellite cities are connected to Moscow primarily by rail, since good roads were not built until the 1950s.

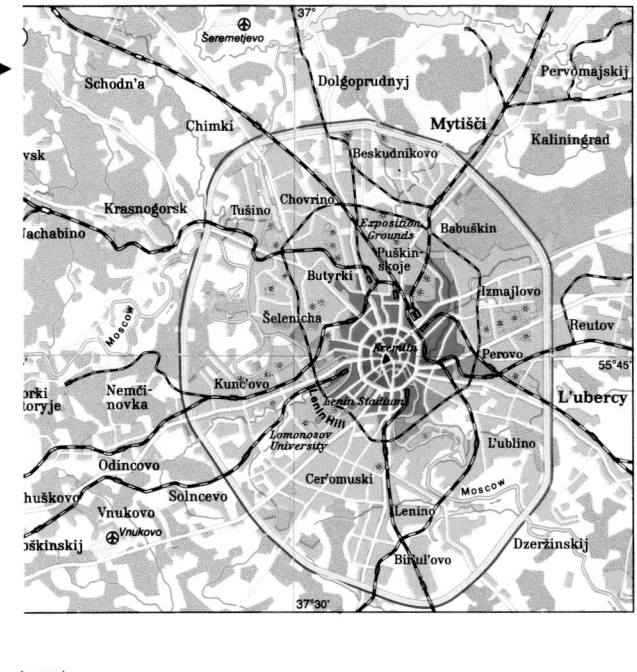

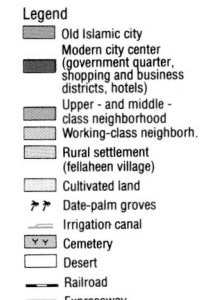

**Legend**

- Kreml ca. 1500
- Moscow ca. 1600
- Moscow ca. 1800
- Growth since 1800
- Present city limits
- Industrial district
- Railroad
- Expressway
- Highway
- Road
- International airport
- Forest, woodland
- Public park
- Cropland

Map scale 1 : 590,000

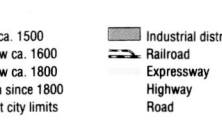

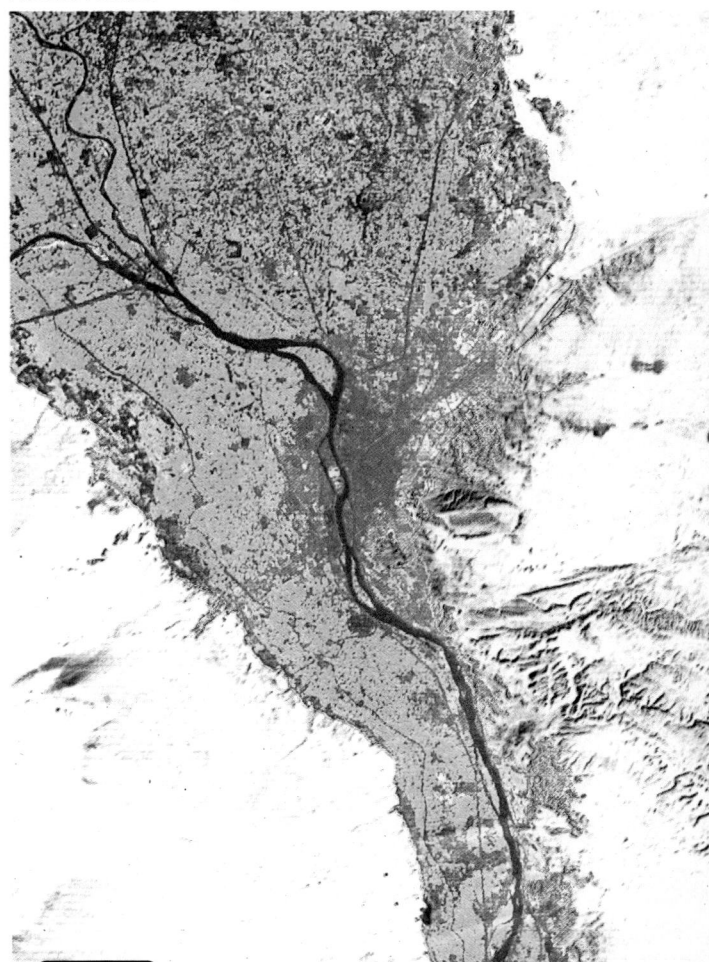

# Cities

❝ The city has always been the fireplace of civilization, whence light and heat radiated out into the dark. ❞

*Theodore Parker*

Each culture has created its own distinctive pattern of city development. In North America, most cities are built on a rectangular grid where streets, laid out in straight lines, intersect one another at right angles. Their clear-cut profiles range from skyscrapers clustered in the heart of the city to smaller commercial buildings and residences further out. These cities usually have well-defined industrial, commercial, and residential zones. The photographs on these pages illustrate three distinct city types: New York, San Francisco, and Washington, D. C.

City development in Europe is more complex. Whatever geometric pattern is evident usually has been imposed on an older, more haphazard design established long before the automotive age. Streets tend

Photo scale 1 : 50,000

© westermann Sat Map®

Map scale 1 : 50,000

© westermann

| | Park | | Railroad (trunk line) | | Subway |
| --- | --- | --- | --- | --- | --- |
| | Cemetery | | Branch line | | Ferry |
| | Car tunnel | | Railroad tunnel | | State/municipal |

**Residential Areas**

Low density (2 to 20 dwelling units per acre), mostly single-family homes and town houses with yards, also retail businesses and public and private institutions

Moderate-to-high density (20 to 90 dwelling units per acre), mostly multistory buildings and high rises, also retail businesses and public and private institutions

Highest density (90 to 275 dwelling units per acre), mostly high rises, retail businesses and public and private institutions

Major commercial center, mostly department stores and retail businesses

Central Business District, department stores, shops, public buildings (mostly skyscrapers)

Prominent skyscraper

University

Theater, concert hall, museum

U. N. mission, consulate

Hotel

Financial District, stock market, major bank, insurance company

Shopping area includes entertainment, nightclub district

Manufacturing and industrial area, warehouse, railroad yard

Urban-renewal area

Land-reclamation project

to be more irregular and narrow, housing specialty shops and fewer well-defined central business districts or "downtown" areas. Instead, these cities are usually built around a religious or government institution such as a cathedral or palace. There tends to be a sharper distinction between urban and rural landscapes, and urban sprawl is less evident. Since the skyscraper does not yet dominate European cities, the urban profile is less clearly outlined than in the United States.

Other regions of the world display a variety of city patterns. In the Middle East, cities are often walled, beginning and ending abruptly. They have low buildings, narrow streets – often with no outlets – and few clear divisions between residential and commercial or industrial districts.

Small shops and trade activities are grouped together along one or two lanes. There is no "downtown" section like those found in North American and some European cities. The city's focal point is generally a large mosque containing the tomb of the local patron saint.

In parts of the Middle East and Asia where European colonial influence has been strong, two different cities often exist side by side. Old Calcutta, for example, follows the traditional patterns of Asian cities, while New Calcutta is built in the European style. In time, such contrasting styles may blend into a unique style of its own. Until then, we can still speak of "Western" and "Eastern" patterns of city development – illustrating the power of each culture to change the landscape in its own way.

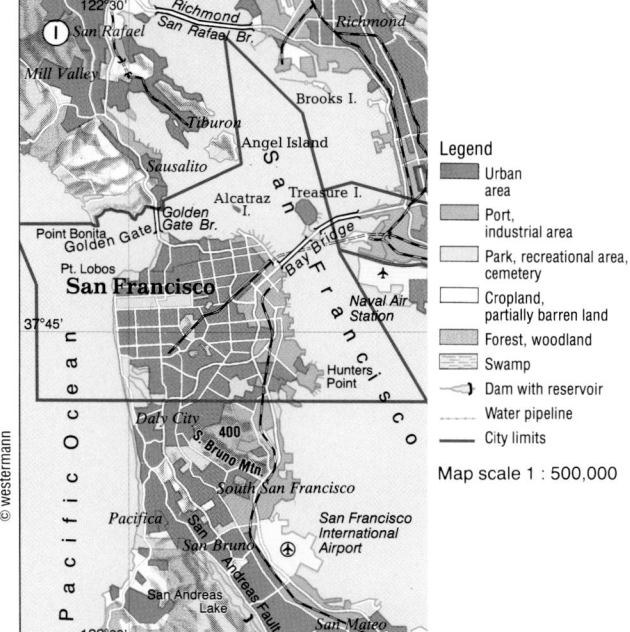

Legend

Urban area

Port, industrial area

Park, recreational area, cemetery

Cropland, partially barren land

Forest, woodland

Swamp

Dam with reservoir

Water pipeline

City limits

Map scale 1 : 500,000

© westermann

Photo scale 1 : 50,000

**SAN FRANCISCO, U.S.A.** One of the world's most beautiful cities, San Francisco boasts some of the hilliest terrain of any urban center in the United States. Nonetheless, the city still follows the standard grid pattern, as seen in the image and map.

Like New York, San Francisco is built around exceptional harbor and port facilities. Its variety of commercial and cultural activities have made it a small but energetic rival of the larger eastern city. San Francisco is considered a gateway to the Pacific just as New York is a gateway to the Atlantic. The city's distinctive profile is highlighted by only a small cluster of taller buildings, since the threat of earthquakes restricts building height. The picturesque architecture of the city gives it a unique and charming appearance.

The Presidio of San Francisco, shown as the large open area at the end of the peninsula, houses the military presence in the city. Only the Presidio and Golden Gate Park – the dark, rectangular area south of the Presidio – provide any sizeable open space within the city itself. However, the Golden Gate Bridge to the north and Bay Bridge to the east connect San Francisco to its suburbs and to nearby mountains, seacoasts, and national parks.

**NEW YORK, U.S.A.** The satellite image and map (left) of Manhattan Island in New York show the grid pattern typical of North American cities. One of the great cities of the world, New York houses a variety of industrial and commercial businesses and the headquarters of countless corporations.

The southern tip of Manhattan was first settled by the Dutch in 1615, who were attracted by the island's unsurpassed port facilities. To a large extent, the warehousing, wholesale trade, and financial activities that sprang up in the area still remain along the waterfront today.

The dark blue and black area of Manhattan near Battery Park represents the skyscraper-dominated "downtown" financial district centered on Wall Street. The other major business district – "midtown" – is located north of 34th street (see map). Although there are fewer skyscrapers, this district houses a host of professional and retail businesses.

In the past decade, some companies have moved from Manhattan to the suburbs. However, the uniform blue-gray of city blocks and lack of open space attest to Manhattan's drawing power as a place to live and work.

© westermann Sat Map*

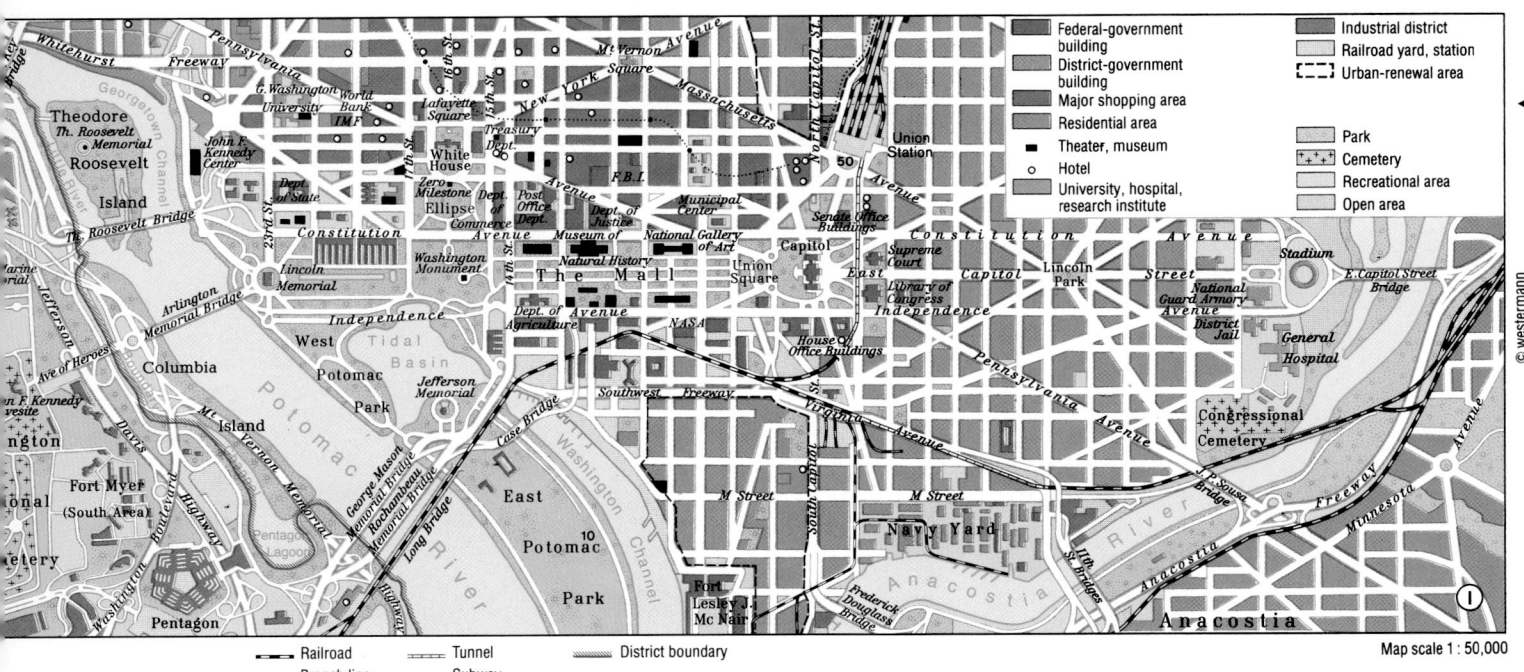

**Legend:**
- Federal-government building
- District-government building
- Major shopping area
- Residential area
- Theater, museum
- Hotel
- University, hospital, research institute
- Industrial district
- Railroad yard, station
- Urban-renewal area
- Park
- Cemetery
- Recreational area
- Open area

Railroad — Tunnel — District boundary
Branch line — Subway

Map scale 1 : 50,000

Photo scale 1 : 50,000

## WASHINGTON, D.C., U.S.A.

Washington, D.C. represents one of the first modern cities to be developed along a prescribed plan. A new capital for a new nation, the city was envisioned as a symbol of American pride. The French architect, L'Enfant, developed an innovative radial design for the capital, which was later used for the renovation of Paris in the 1800s.

The city was founded on a triangle of land flanked by the Potomac and Anacostia rivers. Washington's major streets radiate from the capitol building (above and slightly to the right of the image center), forming the basic pattern on which the city grew. Throughout Washington, monuments and parks serve as secondary hubs for other radiating streets (see map). Unfortunately, while this pattern lends charm to the city, it is not an efficient design for moving automobile traffic. In the 1700s, L'Enfant could not have known how the nation around his city would change.

The central Mall serves as the focus for the entire metropolitan area, and includes The Lincoln Memorial, Washington Monument, Museum of Natural History, National Gallery of Art, and Capitol Building within its boundaries. Other government buildings and retail and service businesses are clustered around the Mall. As shown in the image, the bridges, highways, railways, and even airports facilitate access to this downtown region.

Suburbs surrounding the nation's capital have grown in response to the economic and employment opportunities offered by the city. Over the years, many have developed their own economic base independent of Washington, D.C. Even within these suburbs, however, a federal government facility generally provides the basis for employment opportunities.

# World Patterns
## Thematic Maps of the World

This section of the atlas consists of thematic maps presenting world patterns and distributions. Together with accompanying graphs, these maps communicate basic information about selected aspects of the natural and human geographical environment.

A thematic map uses symbols to show certain characteristics of, generally, one class of geographical information. For instance, the population distribution map shows the pattern of where people live. This "theme" of a thematic map is presented upon a background of basic locational information — coastline, country boundaries, major drainage, etc. The map's primary concern is to communicate basic impressions of the distribution of the subject. Another important use of the *World Patterns* section is to compare and note the relationships between the distributions of various geographical information. For example, the relationship of the distribution of population to the various climatic regions.

The thematic maps of the world along with the satellite portrait section, reference maps, tables, and index make the atlas an indispensable aid to understanding the many facets of our complex earth and the general course of world events.

# Population

**Extent of urbanization**
Percent of total population urban

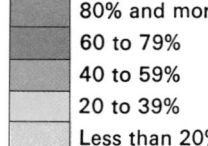

- 80% and more
- 60 to 79%
- 40 to 59%
- 20 to 39%
- Less than 20%

**Major metropolitan areas**

- ⬭ 5,000,000 and more persons
- ○ 3,000,000 to 4,999,999
- ○ 2,000,000 to 2,999,999

The increase in the proportion of urban to total population reflects the change from a dispersed pattern of human settlement to a concentrated one. In industrialized countries the proportion of people living in cities increases mainly through movement from country to city, due to the attraction of higher wages and greater opportunities, a process which in most cases started about 100 years ago. In the underdeveloped countries, where in recent years the number of people living in cities has risen sharply, the proportion of urban population has not increased appreciably; here the urban growth is generally due not so much to rural-urban migration as it is to the natural population increase in both urban and rural areas, and to the decline in the urban mortality rate.

In population studies the definitions of "urban" differ from country to country, but generally take into account the total number of people in a settlement and the percent of the population engaged in nonagricultural activities. The map shows the degree of urbanization (the proportion of urban to total population), considering as urban those communities having no fewer than 2,000 inhabitants, more than half of them dependent on nonfarm occupations. Also indicated are selected metropolitan areas where cities have expanded beyond their boundaries into the surrounding regions in patterns of continuous settlement oriented toward the central cities.

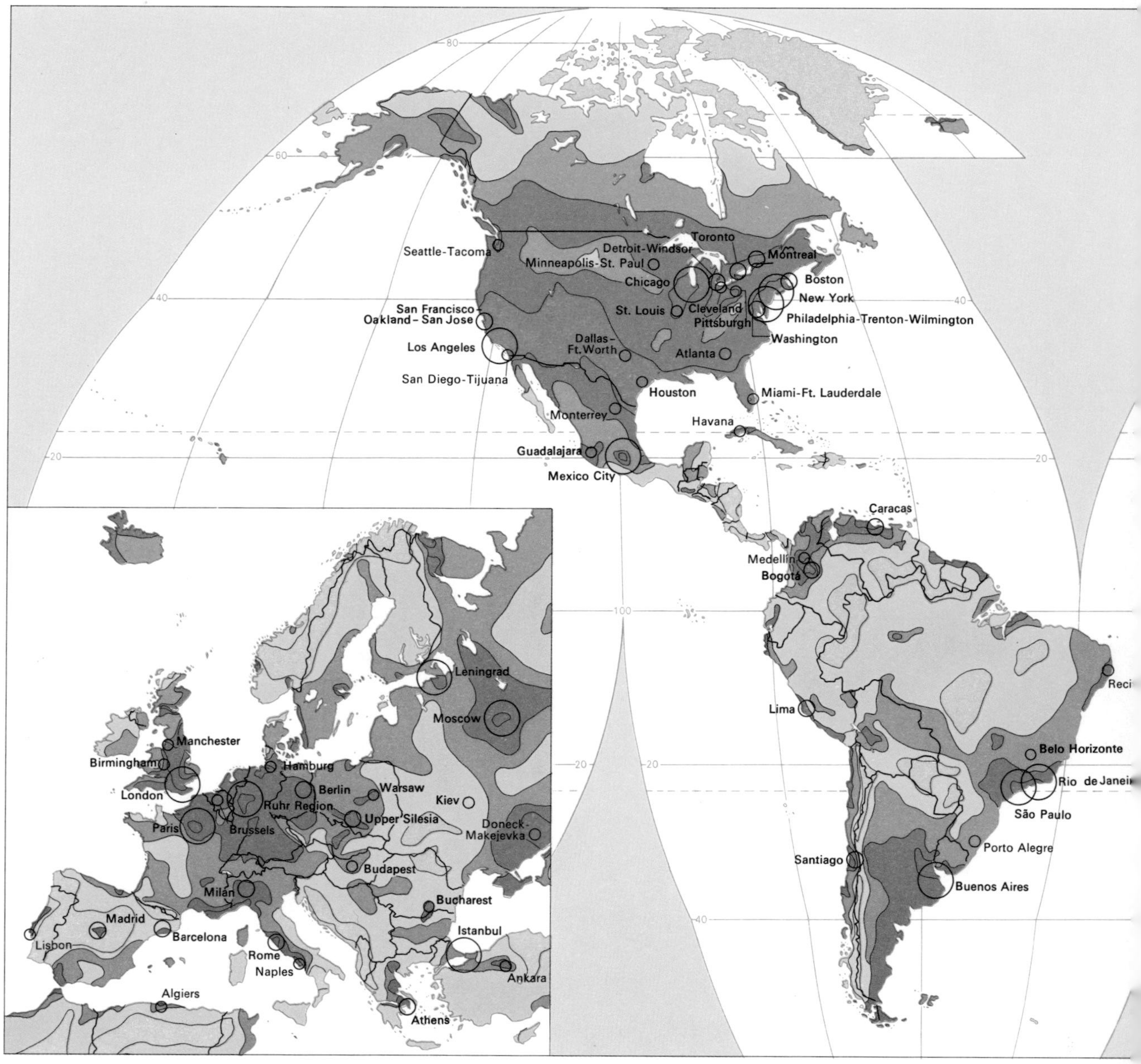

## Age and sex composition

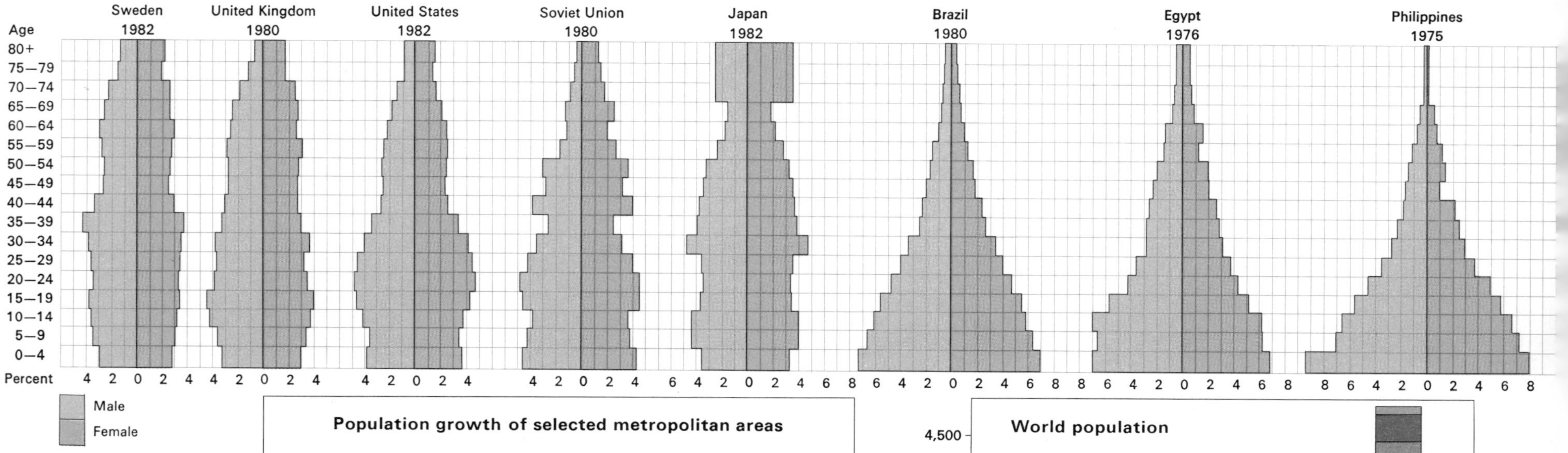

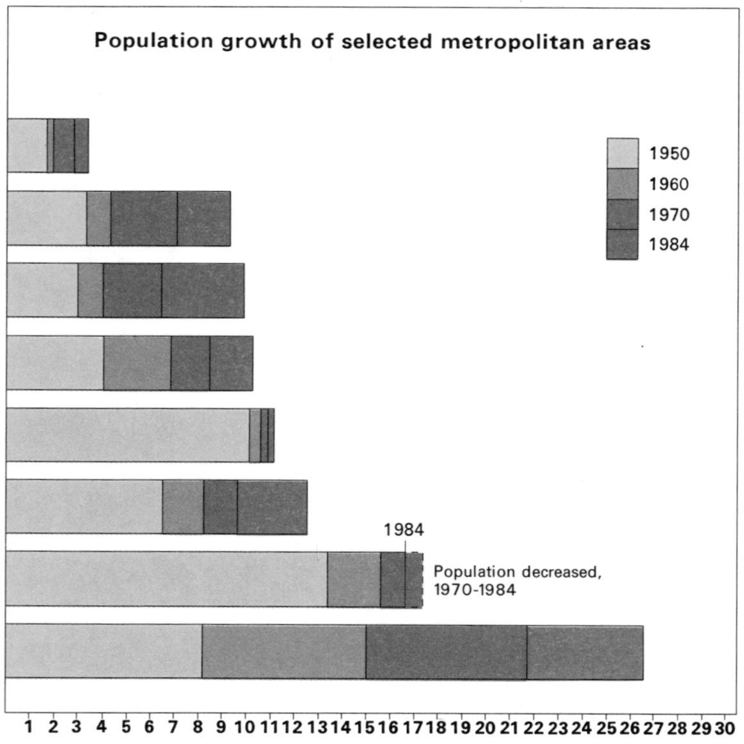

| Sweden 1982 | United Kingdom 1980 | United States 1982 | Soviet Union 1980 | Japan 1982 | Brazil 1980 | Egypt 1976 | Philippines 1975 |

Age: 80+, 75—79, 70—74, 65—69, 60—64, 55—59, 50—54, 45—49, 40—44, 35—39, 30—34, 25—29, 20—24, 15—19, 10—14, 5—9, 0—4

- Male
- Female

### Population growth of selected metropolitan areas

- Sydney, Australia
- Rio de Janeiro, Brazil
- Cairo, Egypt
- Los Angeles, United States
- London, United Kingdom
- Moscow, Soviet Union
- New York, United States — 1984 — Population decreased, 1970-1984
- Tokyo—Yokohama, Japan

- 1950
- 1960
- 1970
- 1984

Population in millions 1 2 3 4 5 6 7 8 9 10 11 12 13 14 15 16 17 18 19 20 21 22 23 24 25 26 27 28 29 30

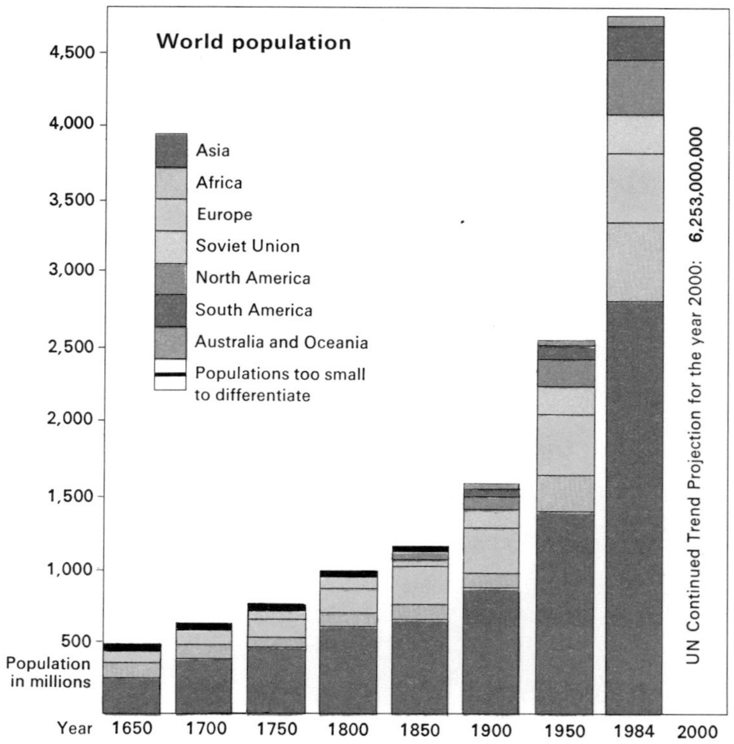

### World population

- Asia
- Africa
- Europe
- Soviet Union
- North America
- South America
- Australia and Oceania
- Populations too small to differentiate

UN Continued Trend Projection for the year 2000: 6,253,000,000

Population in millions

Year 1650 1700 1750 1800 1850 1900 1950 1984 2000

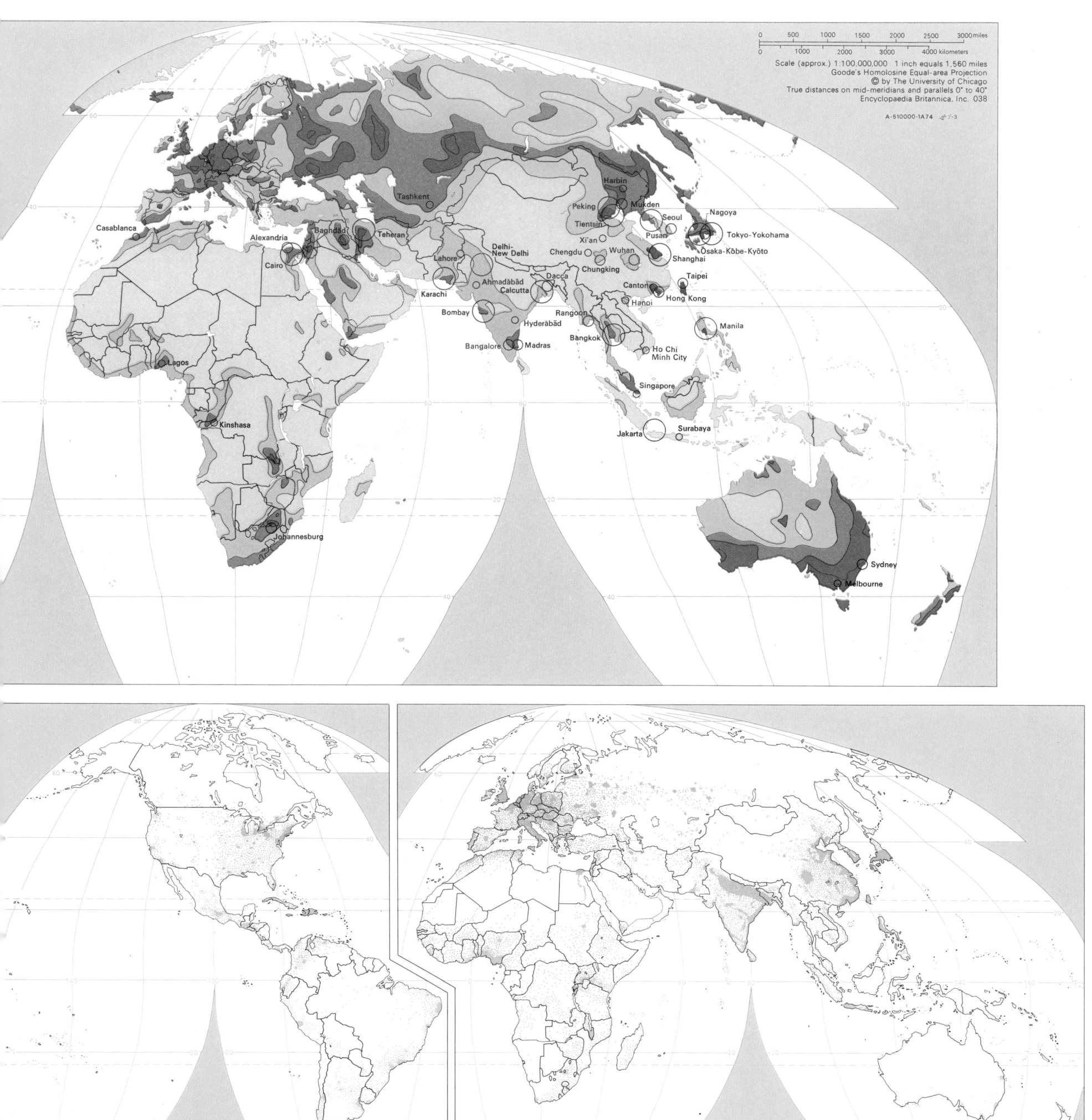

Casablanca
Alexandria
Baghdād
Teheran
Tashkent
Cairo
Harbin
Peking
Mukden
Tientsin
Seoul
Nagoya
Xi'an
Pusan
Tokyo-Yokohama
Lahore
Delhi-New Delhi
Chengdu
Wuhan
Ōsaka-Kōbe-Kyōto
Karachi
Ahmadābād
Calcutta
Chungking
Shanghai
Dacca
Taipei
Bombay
Canton
Hong Kong
Hyderābād
Hanoi
Rangoon
Bangalore
Madras
Bangkok
Manila
Ho Chi Minh City
Lagos
Singapore
Kinshasa
Jakarta
Surabaya
Johannesburg
Sydney
Melbourne

Scale (approx.) 1:100,000,000   1 inch equals 1,560 miles
Goode's Homolosine Equal-area Projection
© by The University of Chicago
True distances on mid-meridians and parallels 0° to 40°
Encyclopaedia Britannica, Inc. 038

A-510000-1A74

0   500   1000   1500   2000   2500   3000 miles
0   1000   2000   3000   4000 kilometers

Encyclopaedia Britannica, Inc. 038

## Distribution

Each dot represents 100,000 persons. The dots show the location of concentrated areas of population rather than the location of cities.

## Religions

The majority of the inhabitants in each of the areas colored on the map share the religious tradition indicated. Letter symbols show religious traditions shared by at least 25% of the inhabitants within areal units no smaller than one thousand square miles. Therefore minority religions of city-dwellers have generally not been represented.

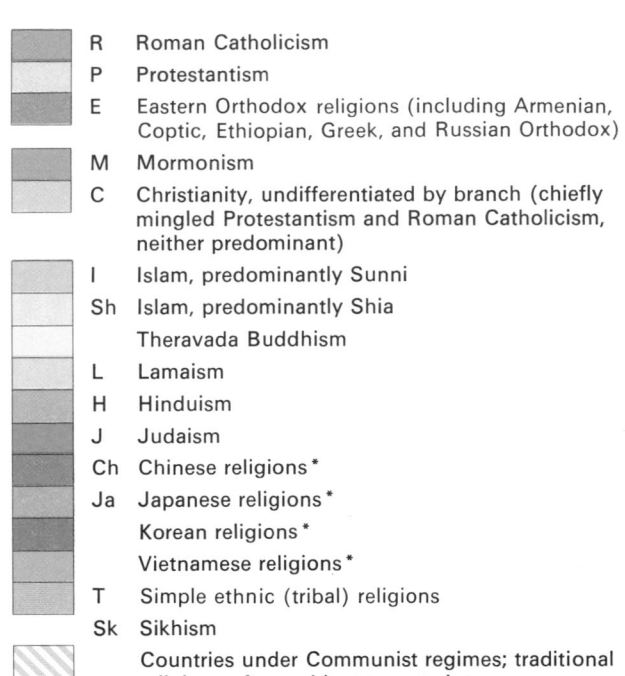

| | |
|---|---|
| R | Roman Catholicism |
| P | Protestantism |
| E | Eastern Orthodox religions (including Armenian, Coptic, Ethiopian, Greek, and Russian Orthodox) |
| M | Mormonism |
| C | Christianity, undifferentiated by branch (chiefly mingled Protestantism and Roman Catholicism, neither predominant) |
| I | Islam, predominantly Sunni |
| Sh | Islam, predominantly Shia |
| | Theravada Buddhism |
| L | Lamaism |
| H | Hinduism |
| J | Judaism |
| Ch | Chinese religions * |
| Ja | Japanese religions * |
| | Korean religions * |
| | Vietnamese religions * |
| T | Simple ethnic (tribal) religions |
| Sk | Sikhism |
| | Countries under Communist regimes; traditional religions often subject to restraint |
| | Uninhabited |

*In certain Eastern Asian areas, most of the people have plural religious affiliations. Chinese, Korean, and Vietnamese religions include Mahayana Buddhism, Taoism, Confucianism, and folk cults. The Japanese religions include Shinto and Mahayana Buddhism.

New World religions copyright by Encyclopaedia Britannica, Inc. Old World religions adapted by permission from *Geography of Religions*, D. E. Sopher, copyright, 1967, by Prentice-Hall, Inc.

## Languages

### Languages of Europe

The following languages are ranked in descending order by number of speakers. Languages spoken by more than 4.5 million people are indicated by color. Others listed, spoken by fewer than 4.5 million persons, are named on the map.

| | | | |
|---|---|---|---|
| Russian | Norwegian | Basque | Karelian |
| German | Lithuanian | Irish-Gaelic | Icelandic |
| Italian | Chuvash | Mari | Adyge |
| English | Slovenian | Welsh | Scots-Gaelic |
| French | Macedonian | Friulian | Romansh |
| Ukrainian | Latvian | Komi | Lappish |
| Polish | Mordvinian | Frisian | Lusatian |
| Spanish | Estonian | Sardinian | Ladin |
| Romanian | Breton | Maltese | |
| Serbo-Croatian | | | |
| Dutch-Flemish | | | |
| Hungarian | | | |
| Portuguese | | | |
| Czech | | | |
| Belorussian | | | |
| Greek | | | |
| Bulgarian | | | |
| Swedish | | | |
| Catalan | | | |
| Danish | | | |
| Turkish | | | |
| Slovak | | | |
| Albanian | | | |
| Finnish | | | |
| All others | | | |

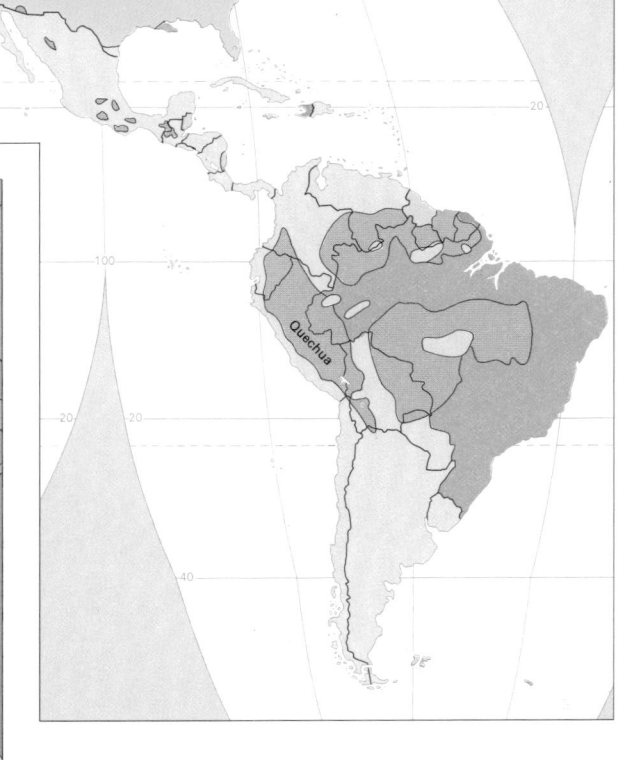

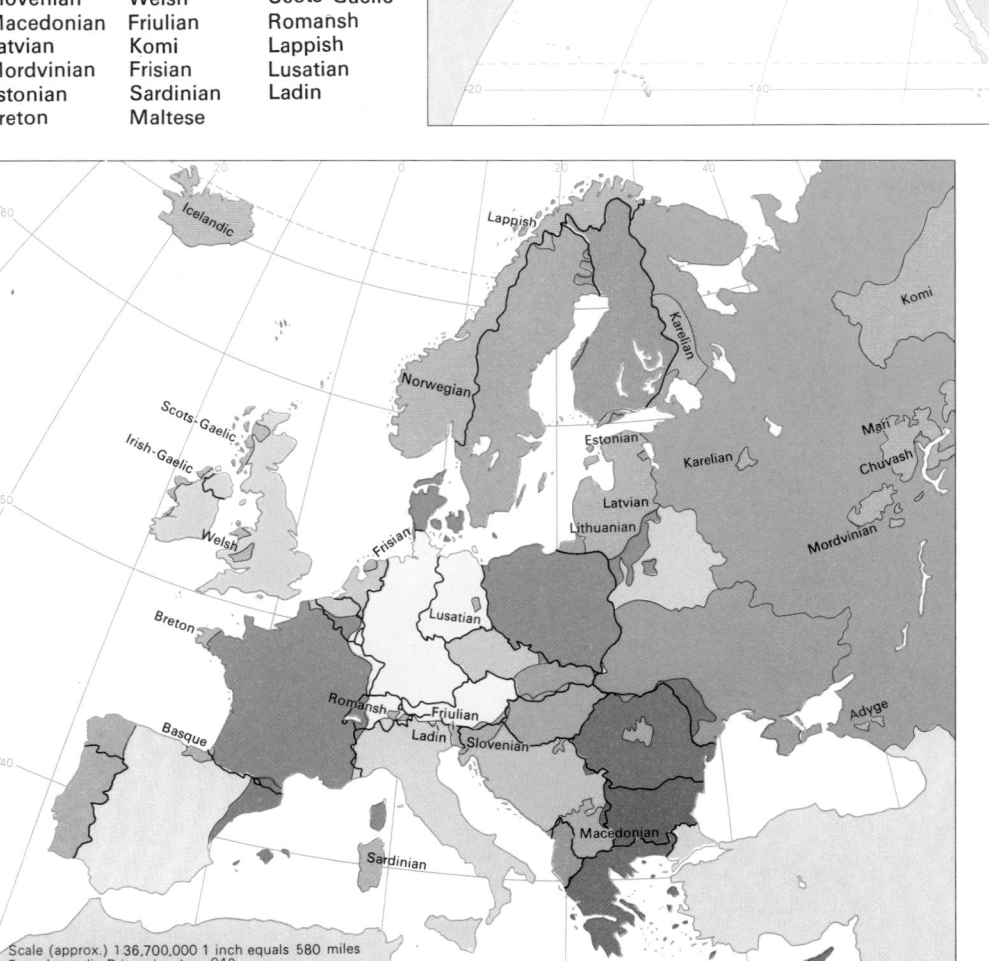

Scale (approx.) 1:36,700,000  1 inch equals 580 miles
Encyclopaedia Britannica, Inc. 048
Compiled by Philip L. Wagner

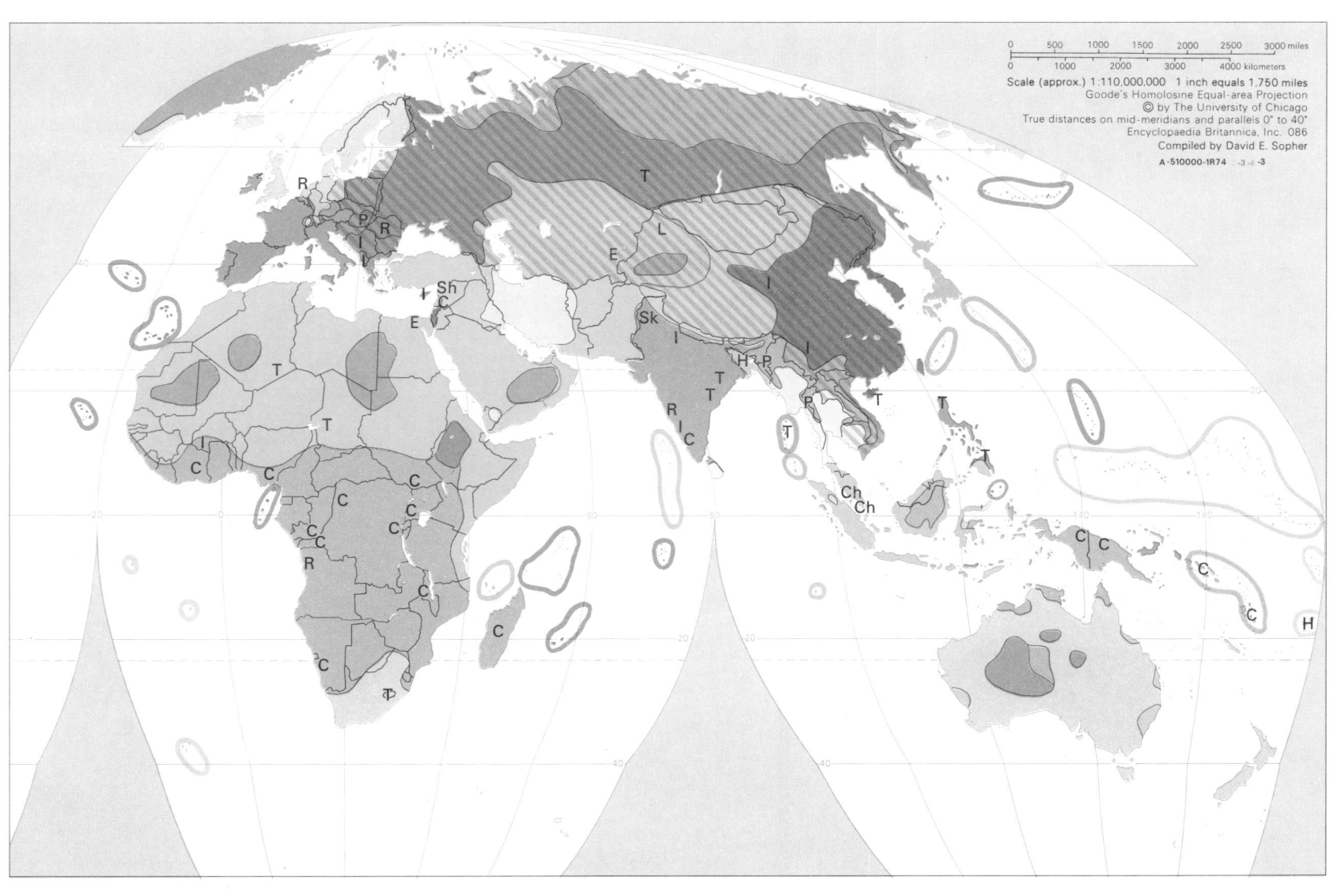

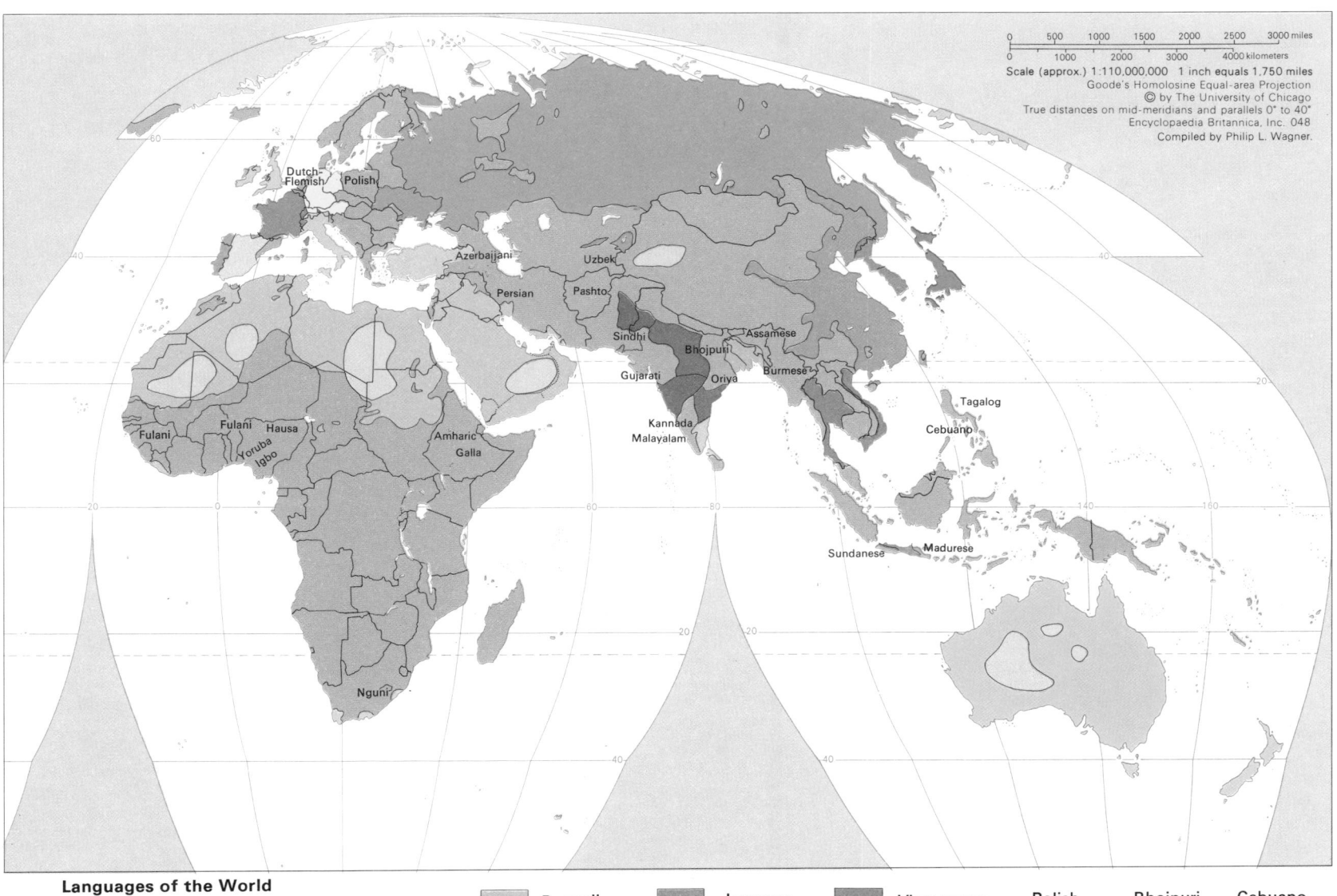

**Languages of the World**

The following languages are ranked in descending order by number of speakers. Languages spoken by more than 40 million persons are indicated by color. Others listed, spoken by 10-40 million persons, are named on the map.

Chinese    English
Spanish    Hindi

Bengali
Arabic
Russian
Portuguese
Japanese
German
Punjabi

Javanese
Korean
Telugu
Marathi
French
Italian
Tamil

Vietnamese
Urdu
Turkish
Ukrainian
Thai
All others
Uninhabited

Polish
Gujarati
Malayalam
Kannada
Oriya
Burmese
Persian
Hausa
Sundanese
Galla

Bhojpuri
Yoruba
Dutch-Flemish
Pashtu
Fulani
Igbo
Uzbek

Cebuano
Azerbaijani
Nguni
Tagalog
Assamese
Sindhi
Amharic
Madurese

## Agricultural Regions

- Cash crop and livestock farming
- Cash crop farming, grain or cotton dominant
- Crop and livestock farming with cash products minor
- Livestock ranching
- Dairying
- Mediterranean agriculture
- Specialized horticulture
- Plantation agriculture
- Intensive subsistence tillage, rice dominant
- Intensive subsistence tillage, with no dominant crop
- Rudimental sedentary farming
- Shifting cultivation
- Nomadic herding
- No agriculture

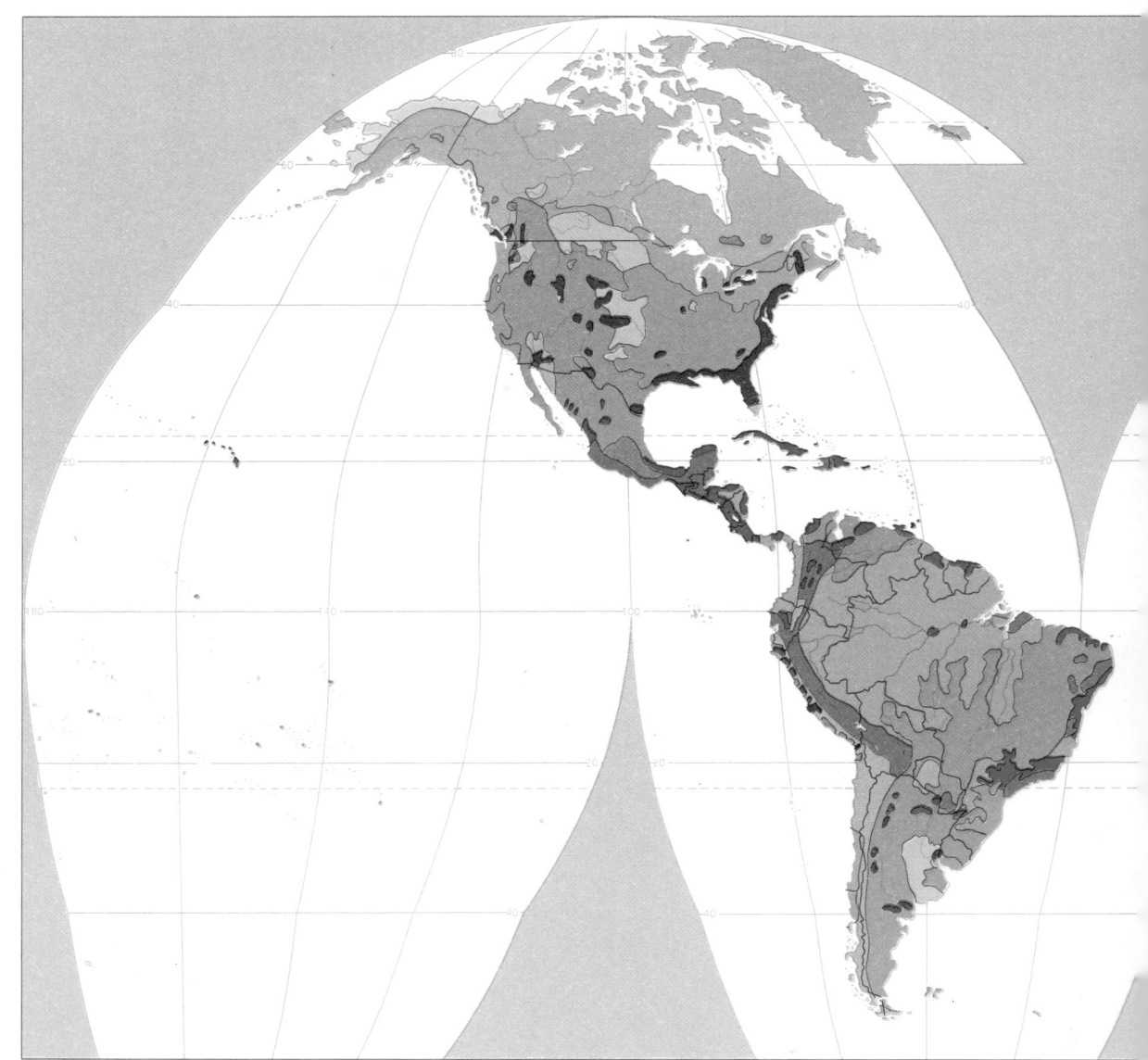

## Forests and Fisheries

### Forests

- Conifers: cedar, fir, hemlock, pine, redwood, spruce
  Regions of exploitation
- Tropical hardwoods: ebony, mahogany, rosewood, teak
  Regions of exploitation
- Temperate hardwoods: hickory, maple, oak, poplar, walnut, and some mixed hardwoods and conifers
  Regions of exploitation

### Fisheries

- Pelagic fishing regions: anchoveta, anchovy, herring, menhaden, pilchard, sardine, sprat, tuna
- Ground fishing regions: cod, haddock, hake, horse mackerel, mackerel, pollack, redfish
- Mixed ground and pelagic fishing regions
- Shellfish: clam, crab, lobster, mussel, oyster, scallop, shrimp, squid
- Whales: blue, fin, minke, pilot, sei, sperm
  Each ⊷ represents an average annual catch of about 300 whales; Each ⊷ represents an average annual catch of less than 200 whales
- Fishing regions showing percentage of world catch (excluding whales)

### Fishing catch (live weight) 1971-75 average

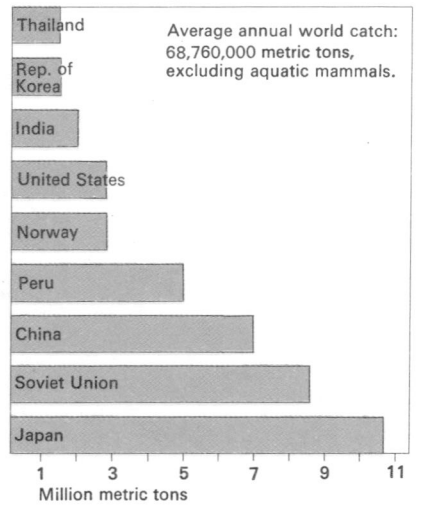

Thailand
Rep. of Korea
India
United States
Norway
Peru
China
Soviet Union
Japan

Average annual world catch: 68,760,000 metric tons, excluding aquatic mammals.

1  3  5  7  9  11
Million metric tons

### Forest removals 1971-75 average

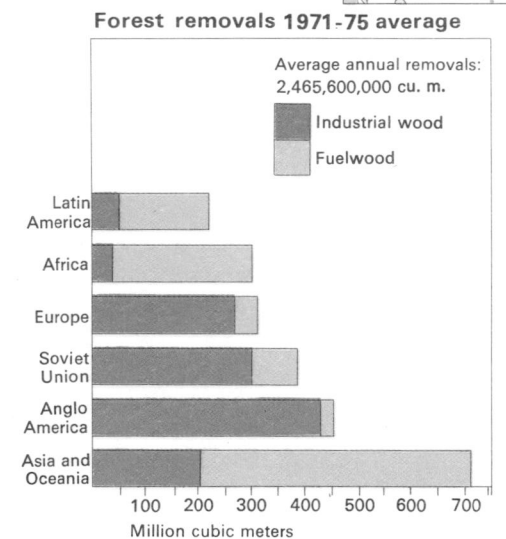

Average annual removals: 2,465,600,000 cu. m.

- Industrial wood
- Fuelwood

Latin America
Africa
Europe
Soviet Union
Anglo America
Asia and Oceania

100  200  300  400  500  600  700
Million cubic meters

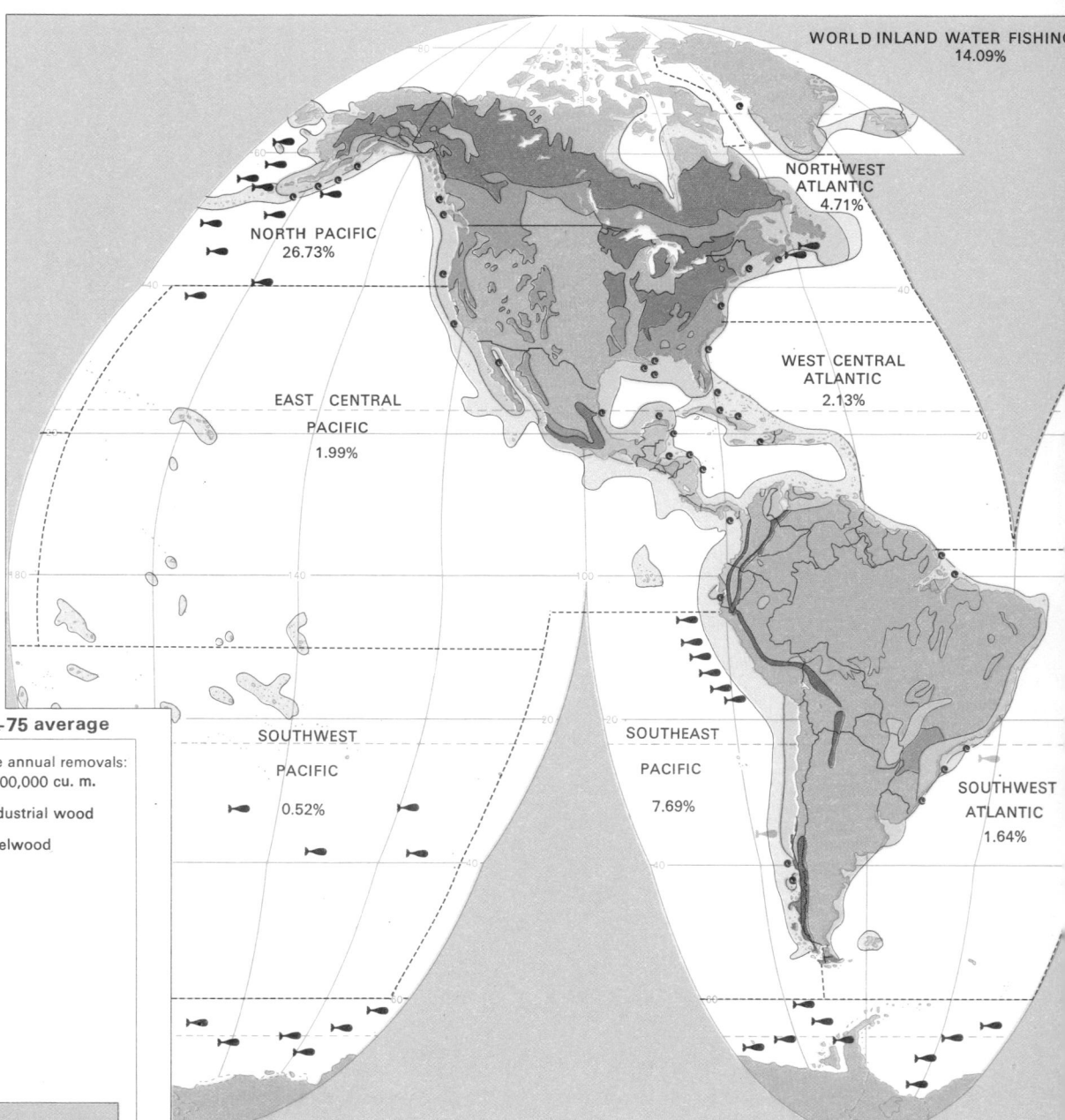

WORLD INLAND WATER FISHING 14.09%

NORTHWEST ATLANTIC 4.71%

NORTH PACIFIC 26.73%

WEST CENTRAL ATLANTIC 2.13%

EAST CENTRAL PACIFIC 1.99%

SOUTHWEST PACIFIC 0.52%

SOUTHEAST PACIFIC 7.69%

SOUTHWEST ATLANTIC 1.64%

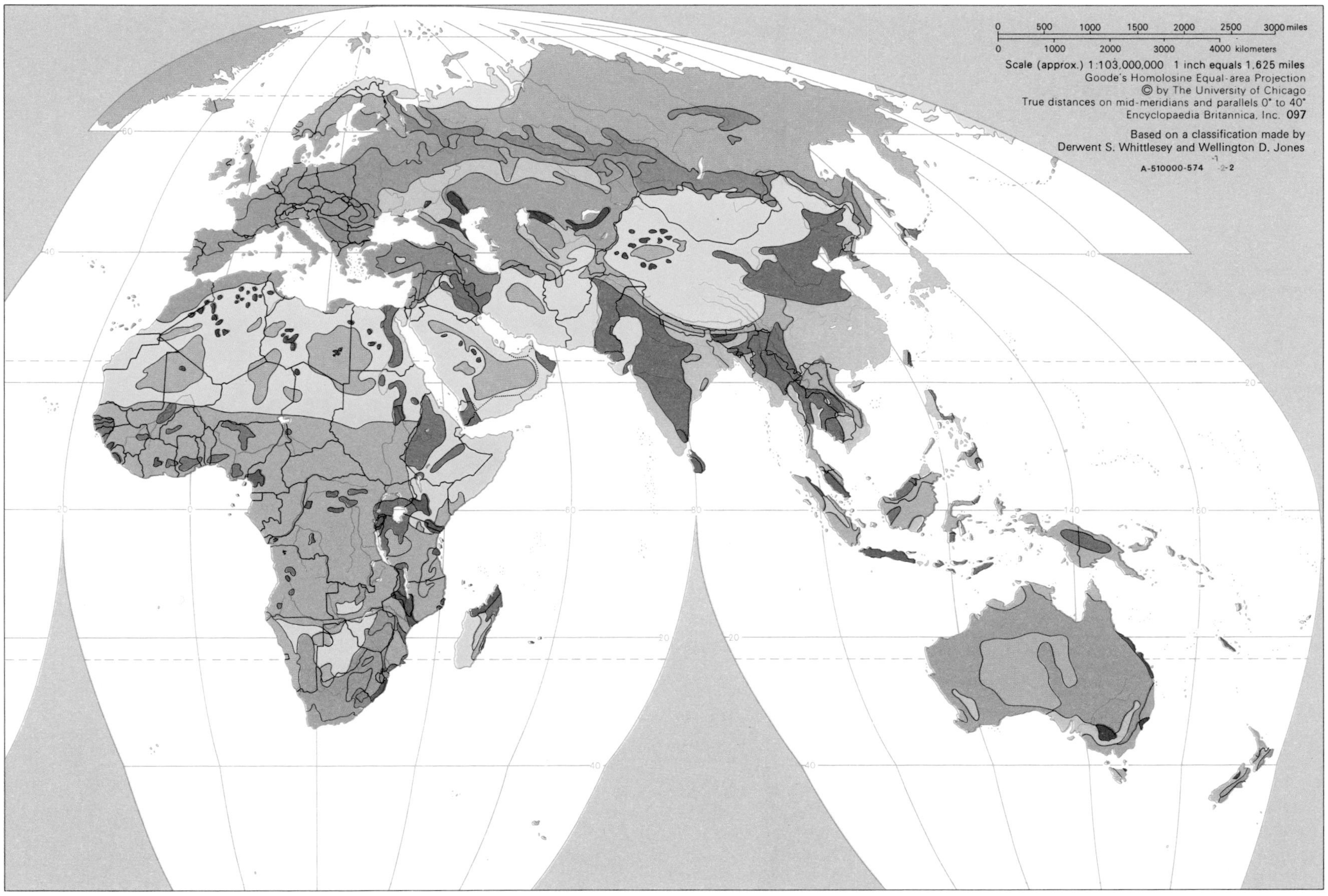
0 500 1000 1500 2000 2500 3000 miles
0 1000 2000 3000 4000 kilometers
Scale (approx.) 1:103,000,000 1 inch equals 1,625 miles
Goode's Homolosine Equal-area Projection
© by The University of Chicago
True distances on mid-meridians and parallels 0° to 40°
Encyclopaedia Britannica, Inc. 097
Based on a classification made by
Derwent S. Whittlesey and Wellington D. Jones
A-510000-574 -2-2

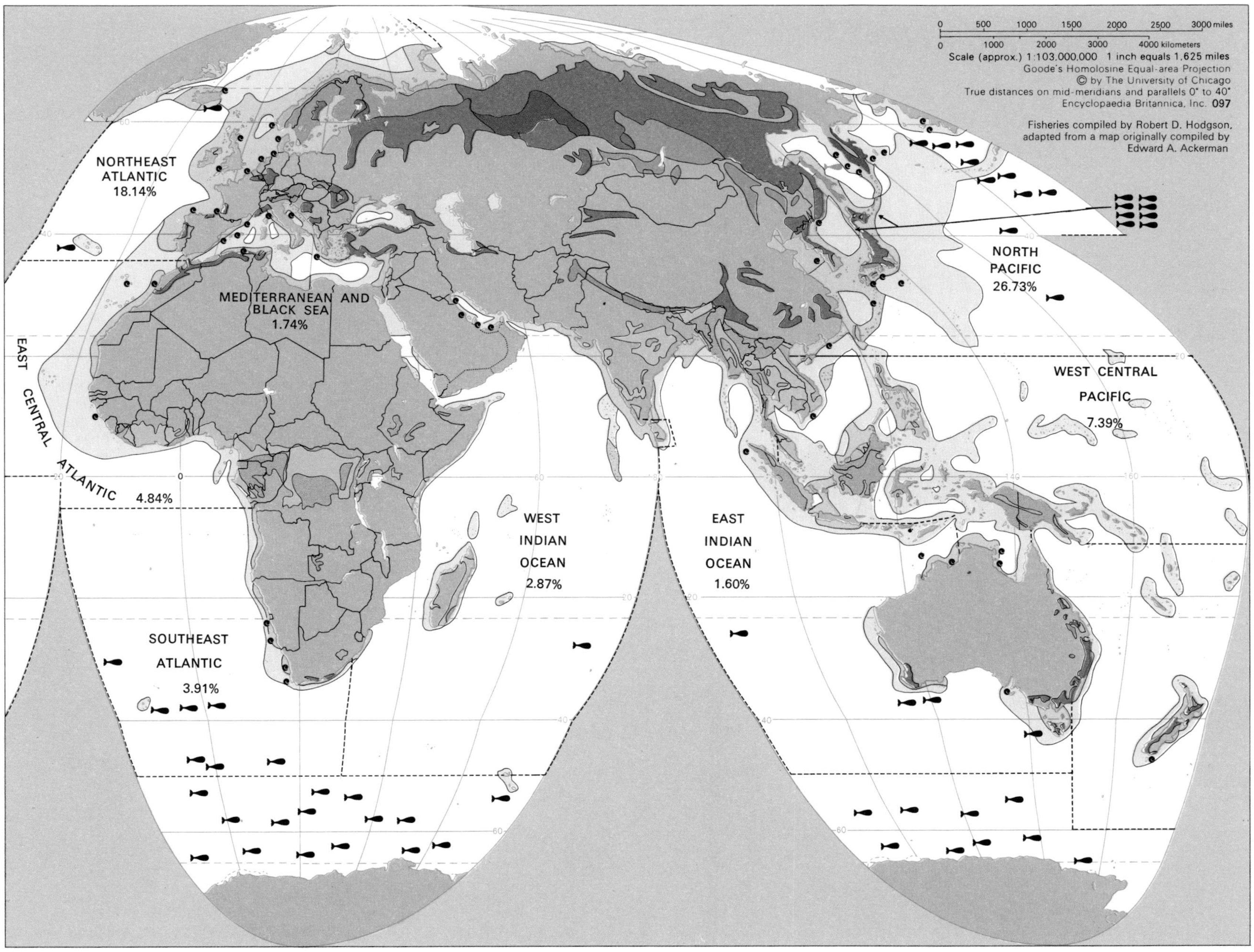
0 500 1000 1500 2000 2500 3000 miles
0 1000 2000 3000 4000 kilometers
Scale (approx.) 1:103,000,000 1 inch equals 1,625 miles
Goode's Homolosine Equal-area Projection
© by The University of Chicago
True distances on mid-meridians and parallels 0° to 40°
Encyclopaedia Britannica, Inc. 097
Fisheries compiled by Robert D. Hodgson,
adapted from a map originally compiled by
Edward A. Ackerman
NORTHEAST ATLANTIC 18.14%
MEDITERRANEAN AND BLACK SEA 1.74%
NORTH PACIFIC 26.73%
WEST CENTRAL PACIFIC 7.39%
EAST CENTRAL ATLANTIC 4.84%
WEST INDIAN OCEAN 2.87%
EAST INDIAN OCEAN 1.60%
SOUTHEAST ATLANTIC 3.91%

# Energy Production and Consumption
Unit of measure is metric tons coal equivalent (m.t.c.e.)

## Production

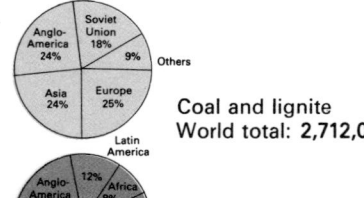

Coal and lignite
World total: 2,712,000,000

Anglo-America 24%, Soviet Union 18%, 9%, Others, Asia 24%, Europe 25%

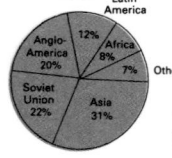

Crude petroleum
World total: 4,035,000,000

Anglo-America 12%, Africa 8%, 7% Others, Soviet Union 22%, Asia 31%, Latin America 20%

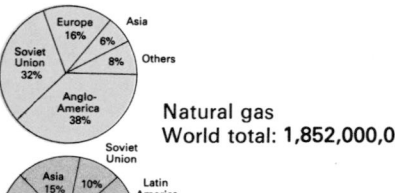

Natural gas
World total: 1,852,000,000

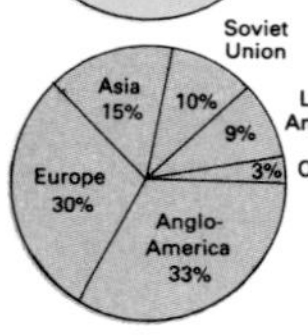

Europe 16%, Asia 6%, 8% Others, Soviet Union 32%, Anglo-America 38%

Primary electricity (hydro-, geothermal, and nuclear)
World total: 334,000,000

Asia 15%, 10%, Latin America 9%, 3% Others, Europe 30%, Anglo-America 33%, Soviet Union

## Table of equivalents

| | |
|---|---|
| Coal, anthracite and bituminous | 1 metric ton = 1.0 m.t.c.e. |
| Lignite | 1 metric ton = 0.3 – 0.6 m.t.c.e. |
| Petroleum | 1 metric ton = 1.5 m.t.c.e. |
| Natural gas | 1,000 cubic meters = 1.33 m.t.c.e. |
| Hydro-, geothermal, and nuclear electricity | 1.0 megawatt-hour = 0.125 m.t.c.e. |

Potential energy of 1 metric ton of coal equals 28,000,000 B.T.U.

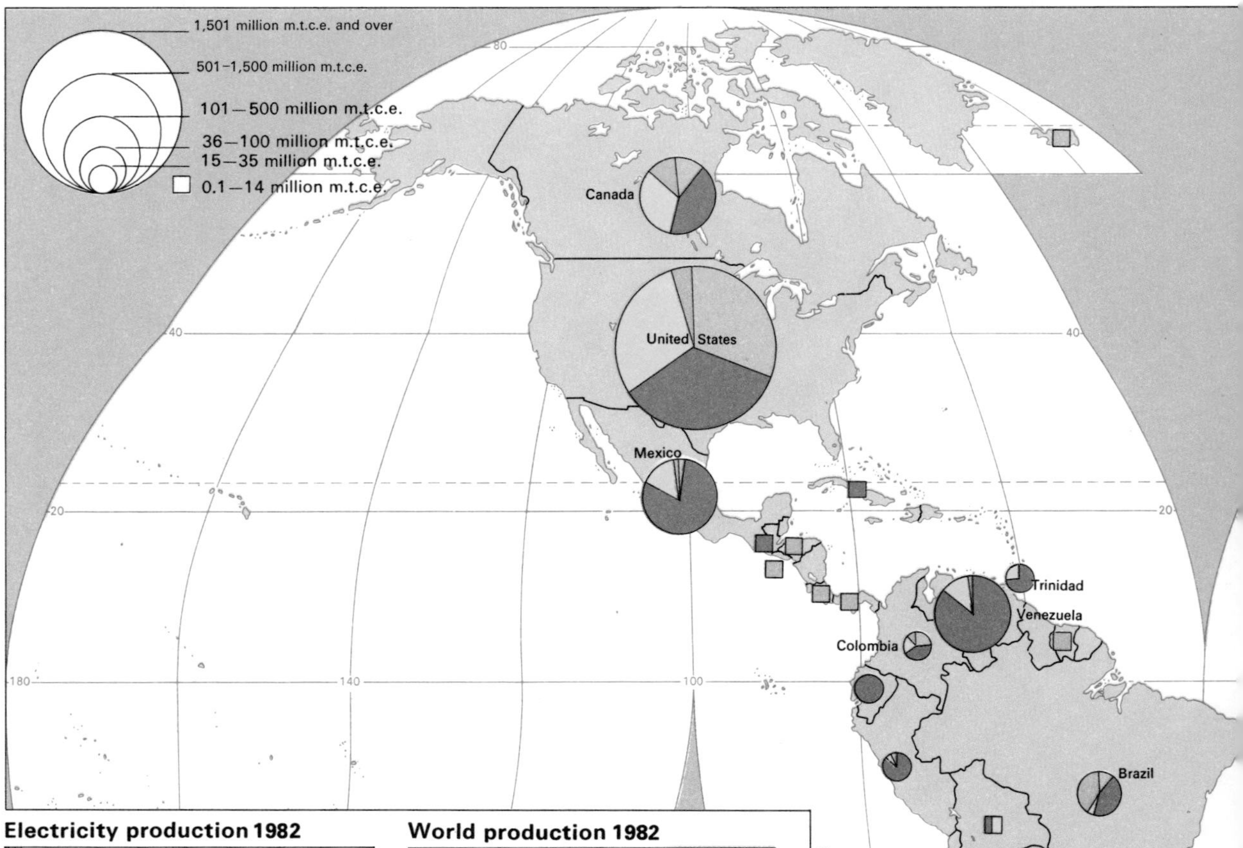

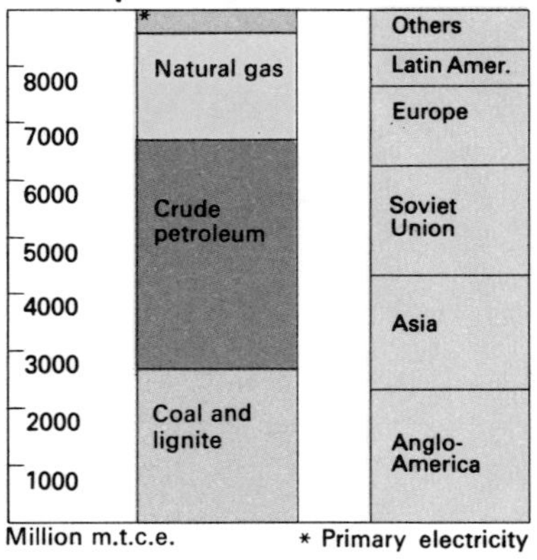

## Consumption

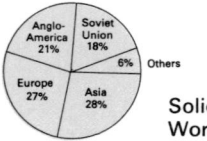

Solid fuels
World total: 2,693,000,000

Anglo-America 21%, Soviet Union 18%, 6% Others, Europe 27%, Asia 28%

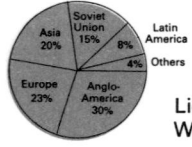

Liquid fuels
World total: 3,543,000,000

Asia 20%, Soviet Union 15%, Latin America 8%, 4% Others, Europe 23%, Anglo-America 30%

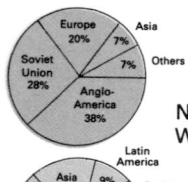

Natural and manufactured gas
World total: 1,836,000,000

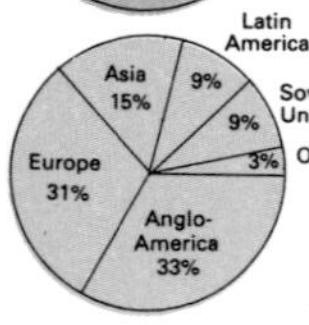

Europe 20%, Asia 7%, 7% Others, Soviet Union 28%, Anglo-America 38%, Latin America

Primary electricity (hydro-, geothermal, and nuclear)
World total: 334,000,000

Asia 15%, Latin America 9%, Soviet Union 9%, 3% Others, Europe 31%, Anglo-America 33%

Consumption totals exclude noncommercial fuels, fuels consumed by vessels engaged in international trade, and nonfuel petroleum products.

## Per capita consumption

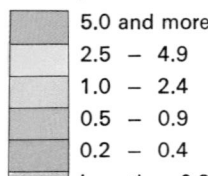

| | |
|---|---|
| | 5.0 and more |
| | 2.5 – 4.9 |
| | 1.0 – 2.4 |
| | 0.5 – 0.9 |
| | 0.2 – 0.4 |
| | Less than 0.2 |

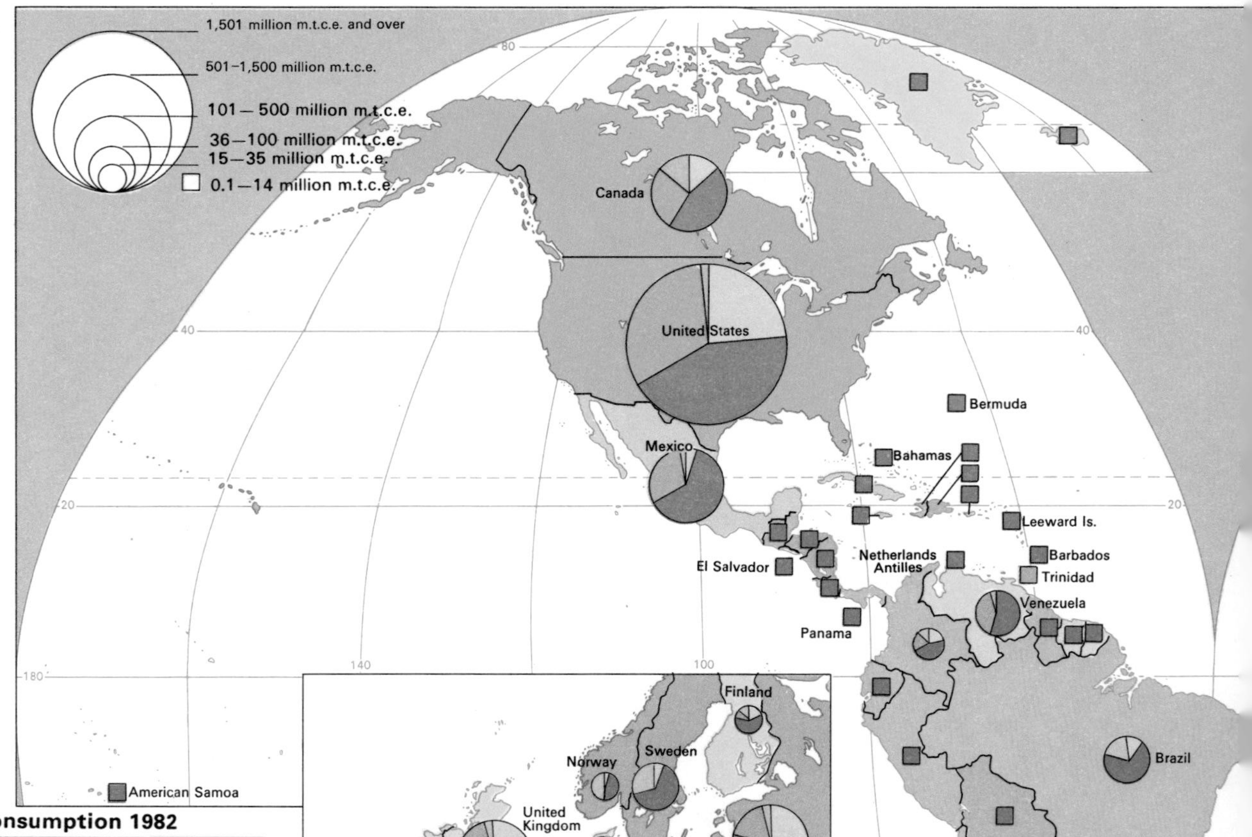

## Map legend (top)

1,501 million m.t.c.e. and over
501–1,500 million m.t.c.e.
101–500 million m.t.c.e.
36–100 million m.t.c.e.
15–35 million m.t.c.e.
0.1–14 million m.t.c.e.

Canada, United States, Mexico, Colombia, Venezuela, Trinidad, Brazil, Argentina

## Electricity production 1982

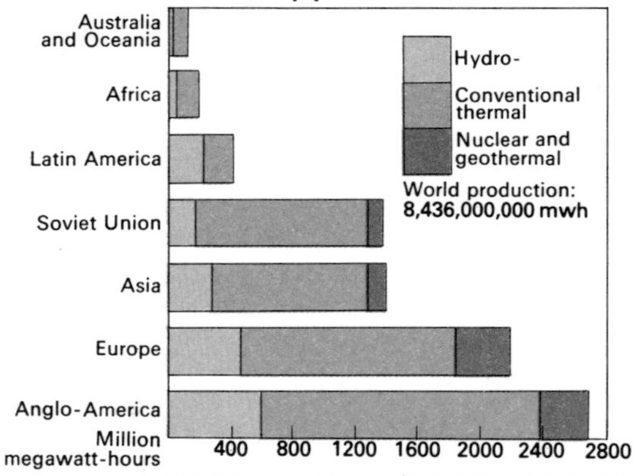

Australia and Oceania, Africa, Latin America, Soviet Union, Asia, Europe, Anglo-America

Hydro-
Conventional thermal
Nuclear and geothermal

World production: 8,436,000,000 mwh

Million megawatt-hours 400 800 1200 1600 2000 2400 2800

## World production 1982

Natural gas, Crude petroleum, Coal and lignite

Others, Latin Amer., Europe, Soviet Union, Asia, Anglo-America

Million m.t.c.e.   * Primary electricity

## Map legend (bottom)

1,501 million m.t.c.e. and over
501–1,500 million m.t.c.e.
101–500 million m.t.c.e.
36–100 million m.t.c.e.
15–35 million m.t.c.e.
0.1–14 million m.t.c.e.

Canada, United States, Mexico, Bermuda, Bahamas, Leeward Is., El Salvador, Netherlands Antilles, Barbados, Trinidad, Venezuela, Panama, Brazil, Argentina, American Samoa

Finland, Norway, Sweden, United Kingdom, Neth., Denmark, Fed. Rep. of Ger., Belgium-Luxembourg, Ger. D.R., Poland, France, Austria, Czechoslovakia, Romania, Switz., Hungary, Yugoslavia, Spain, Italy, Bulgaria, Malta

## World consumption 1982

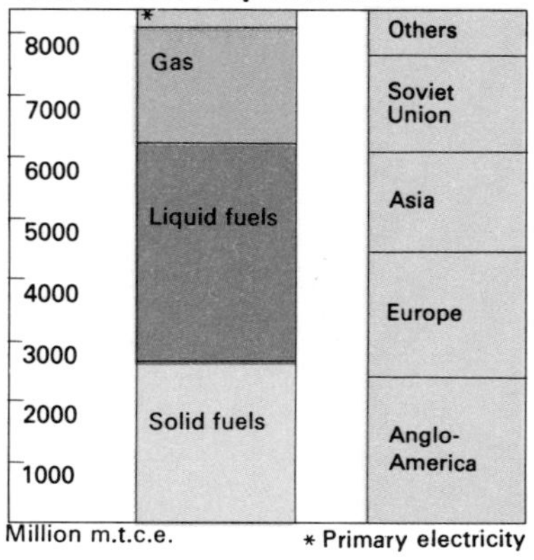

Gas, Liquid fuels, Solid fuels

Others, Soviet Union, Asia, Europe, Anglo-America

Million m.t.c.e.   * Primary electricity

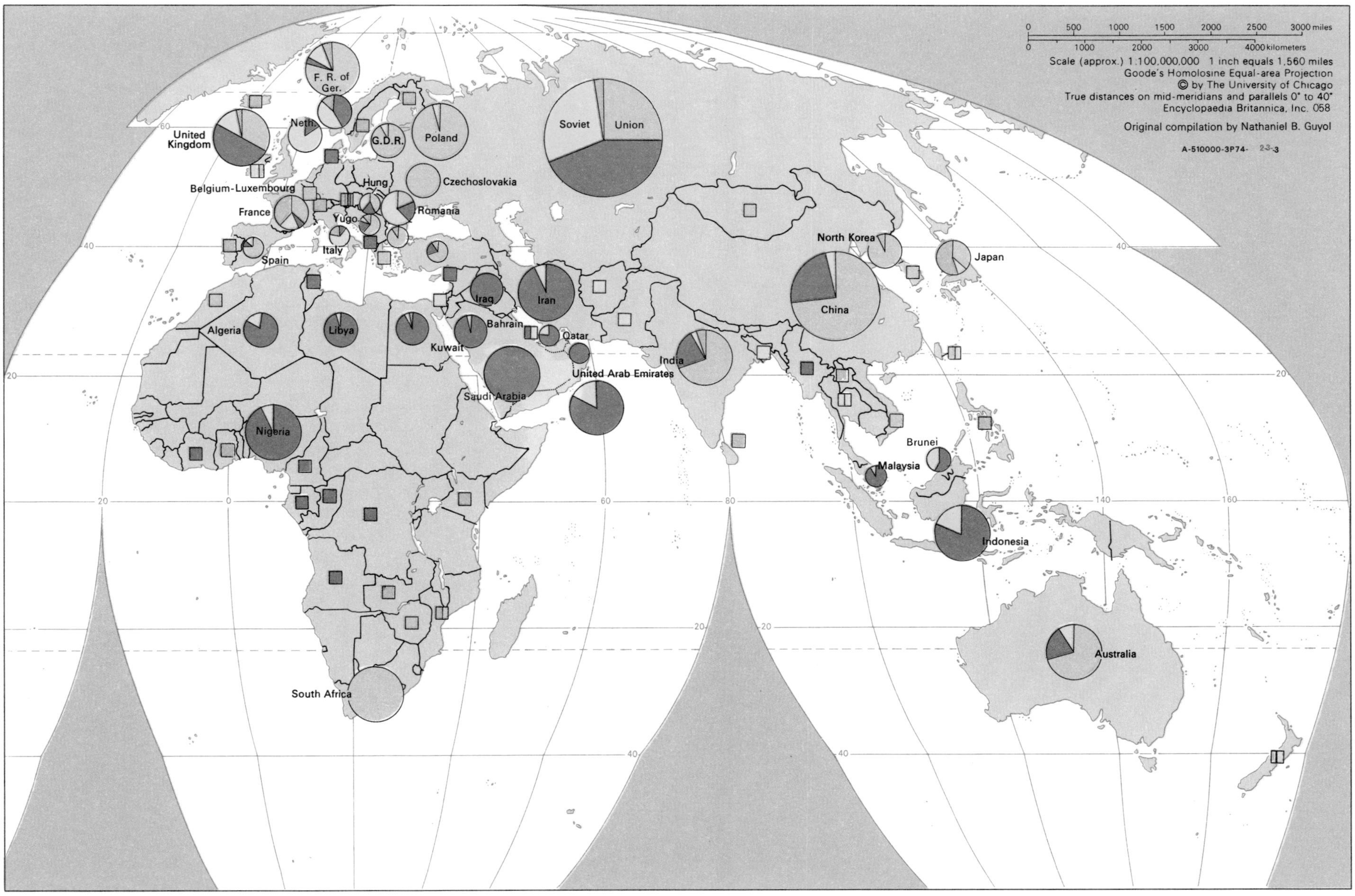

Scale (approx.) 1:100,000,000  1 inch equals 1,560 miles
Goode's Homolosine Equal-area Projection
© by The University of Chicago
True distances on mid-meridians and parallels 0° to 40°
Encyclopaedia Britannica, Inc. 058

Original compilation by Nathaniel B. Guyol

A-510000-3P74-  23-3

United Kingdom
F. R. of Ger.
Neth.
G.D.R.
Poland
Soviet Union
Belgium-Luxembourg
Hung.
Czechoslovakia
France
Yugo.
Romania
Italy
Spain
North Korea
Japan
China
Algeria
Libya
Iraq
Iran
Bahrain
Kuwait
Qatar
India
Saudi Arabia
United Arab Emirates
Nigeria
Brunei
Malaysia
Indonesia
South Africa
Australia

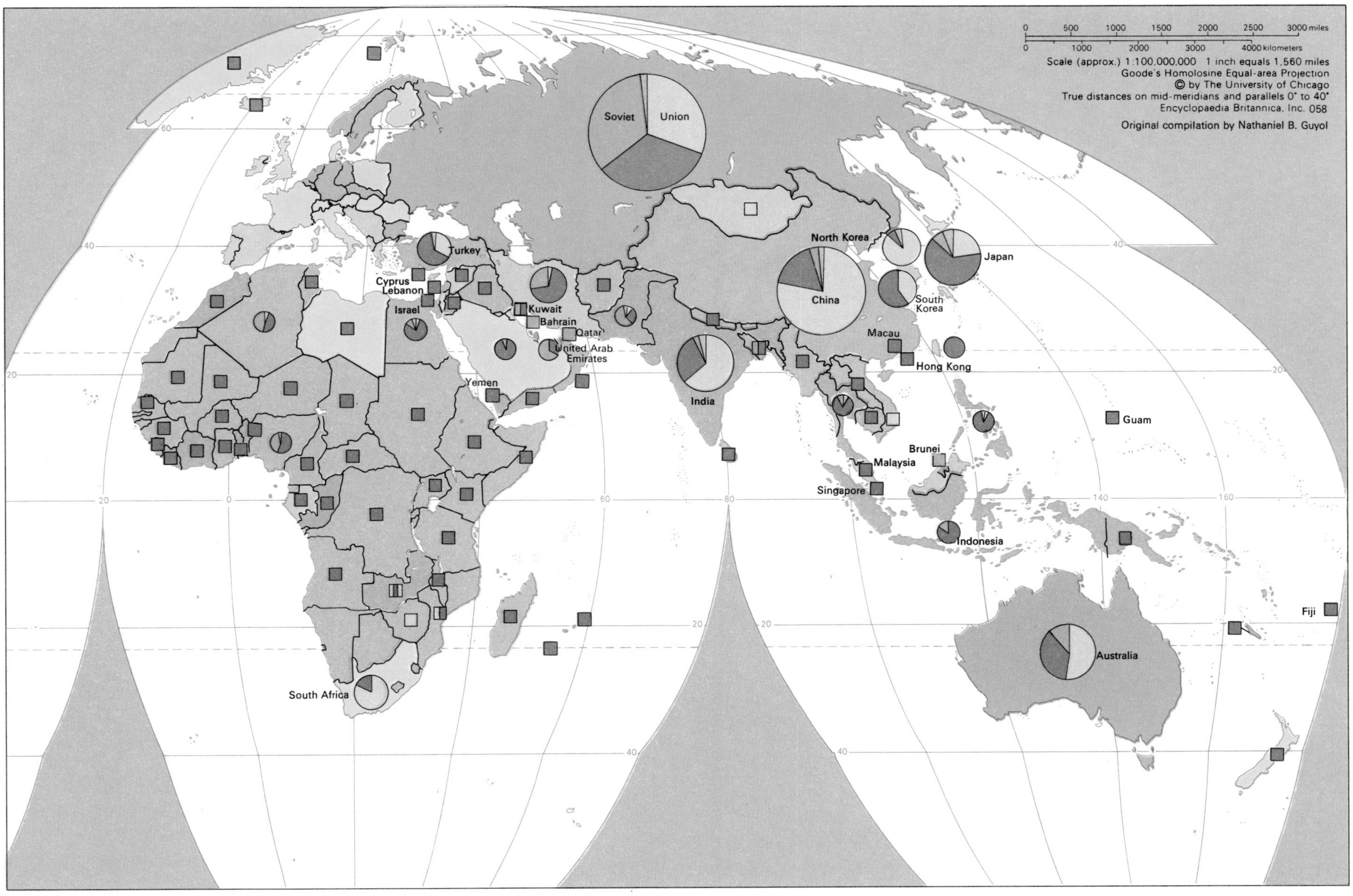

Scale (approx.) 1:100,000,000  1 inch equals 1,560 miles
Goode's Homolosine Equal-area Projection
© by The University of Chicago
True distances on mid-meridians and parallels 0° to 40°
Encyclopaedia Britannica, Inc. 058

Original compilation by Nathaniel B. Guyol

Soviet Union
Turkey
Cyprus
Lebanon
Israel
Kuwait
Bahrain
Qatar
United Arab Emirates
Yemen
North Korea
China
Japan
South Korea
Macau
Hong Kong
India
Guam
Brunei
Malaysia
Singapore
Indonesia
South Africa
Australia
Fiji

# Climate Graphs

Each graph below shows temperature and rainfall at a weather station that was selected to illustrate one of the climate regions described in the legend at the right. The weather stations are keyed by number to the maps. The elements of the graphs are identified in the sample graph at the top, with a temperature scale in degrees Fahrenheit and Celsius (Centigrade), and a precipitation scale in inches and millimeters.

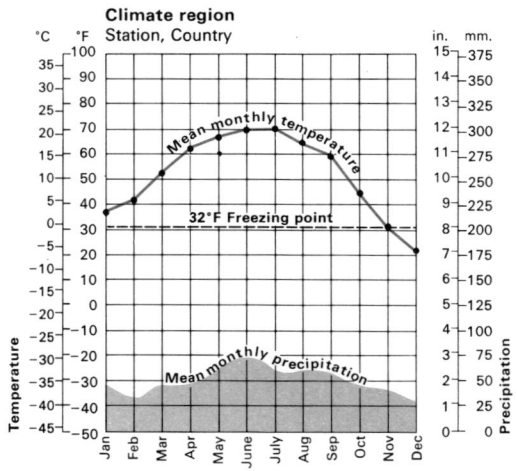

Climate region
Station, Country

## Climate Regions

**Rainy tropical** At most, one or two dry months; all months warm or hot

**Wet and dry tropical** A well-developed dry season with one or two rainy seasons; all months warm or hot

**Semiarid tropical** Light precipitation, rapid evaporation; all months warm or hot

**Hot arid** Negligible precipitation, rapid evaporation; all months warm or hot

**Humid subtropical** Precipitation in all seasons with maximum in summer; long warm summers, cool winters

**Dry subtropical** Hot dry summers; cool, moderately rainy winters

**Humid mid-latitude** Precipitation in all seasons with maximum in summer; warm or hot summers, cold winters

**Temperate marine** Numerous rainy days in all seasons with moderate total precipitation, higher precipitation in highland areas; warm summers, cool winters

**Semiarid mid-latitude** Light precipitation; warm or hot summers, cool or cold winters

**Arid mid-latitude** Extremely light precipitation; warm or hot summers, cool or cold winters

**Subarctic** Light precipitation; short cool summers, long very cold winters

**Arctic margin** Extremely light precipitation; very short cold summers, extremely long cold winters

**High altitude** Climate varies with elevation, latitude, and exposure

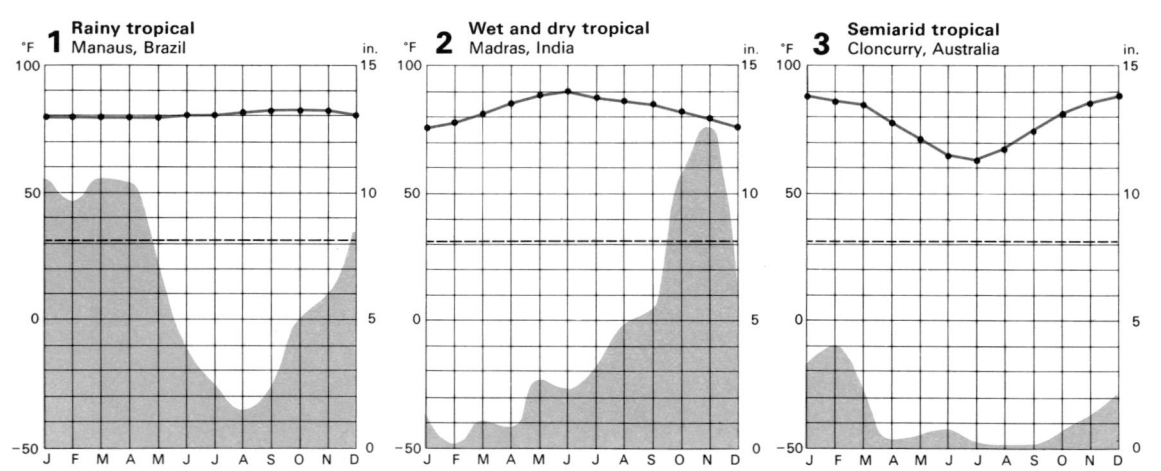

**1 Rainy tropical** Manaus, Brazil

**2 Wet and dry tropical** Madras, India

**3 Semiarid tropical** Cloncurry, Australia

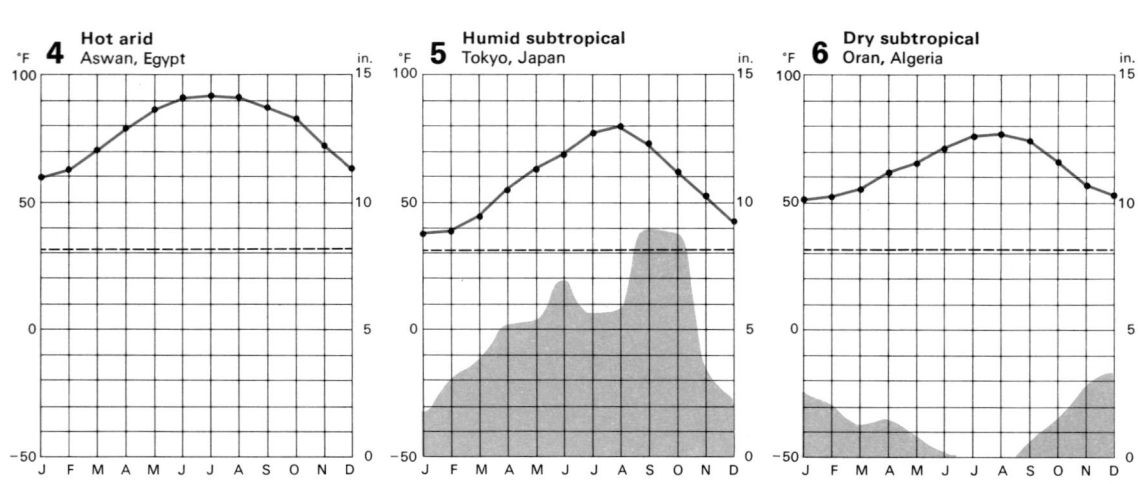

**4 Hot arid** Aswan, Egypt

**5 Humid subtropical** Tokyo, Japan

**6 Dry subtropical** Oran, Algeria

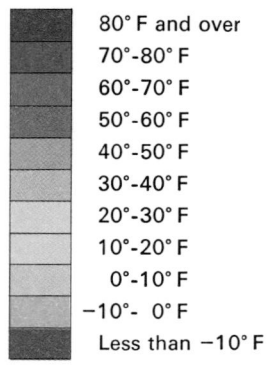

## Mean Annual Temperature

80° F and over
70°-80° F
60°-70° F
50°-60° F
40°-50° F
30°-40° F
20°-30° F
10°-20° F
0°-10° F
−10°- 0° F
Less than −10° F

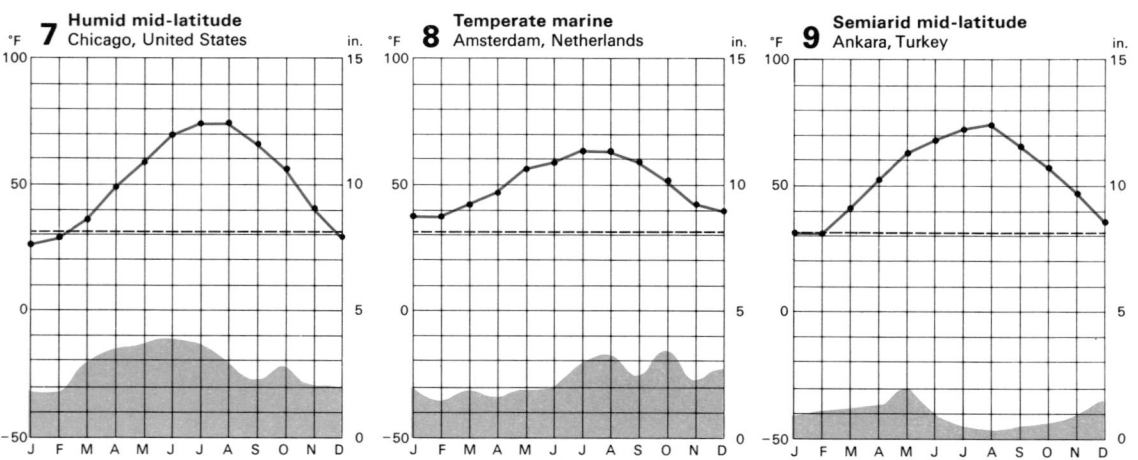

**7 Humid mid-latitude** Chicago, United States

**8 Temperate marine** Amsterdam, Netherlands

**9 Semiarid mid-latitude** Ankara, Turkey

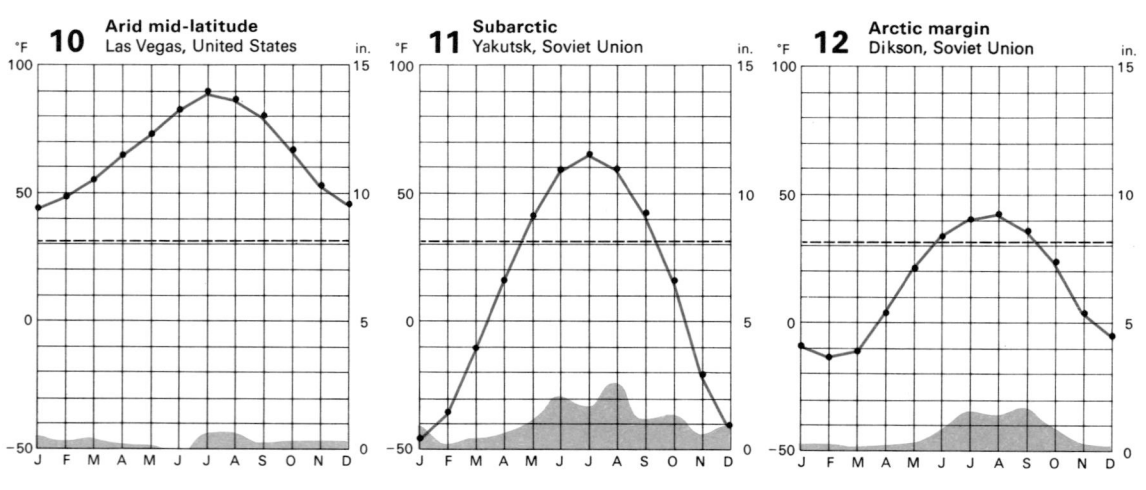

**10 Arid mid-latitude** Las Vegas, United States

**11 Subarctic** Yakutsk, Soviet Union

**12 Arctic margin** Dikson, Soviet Union

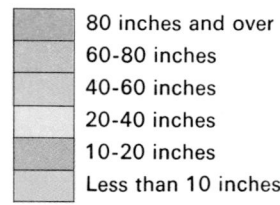

## Mean Annual Precipitation

80 inches and over
60-80 inches
40-60 inches
20-40 inches
10-20 inches
Less than 10 inches

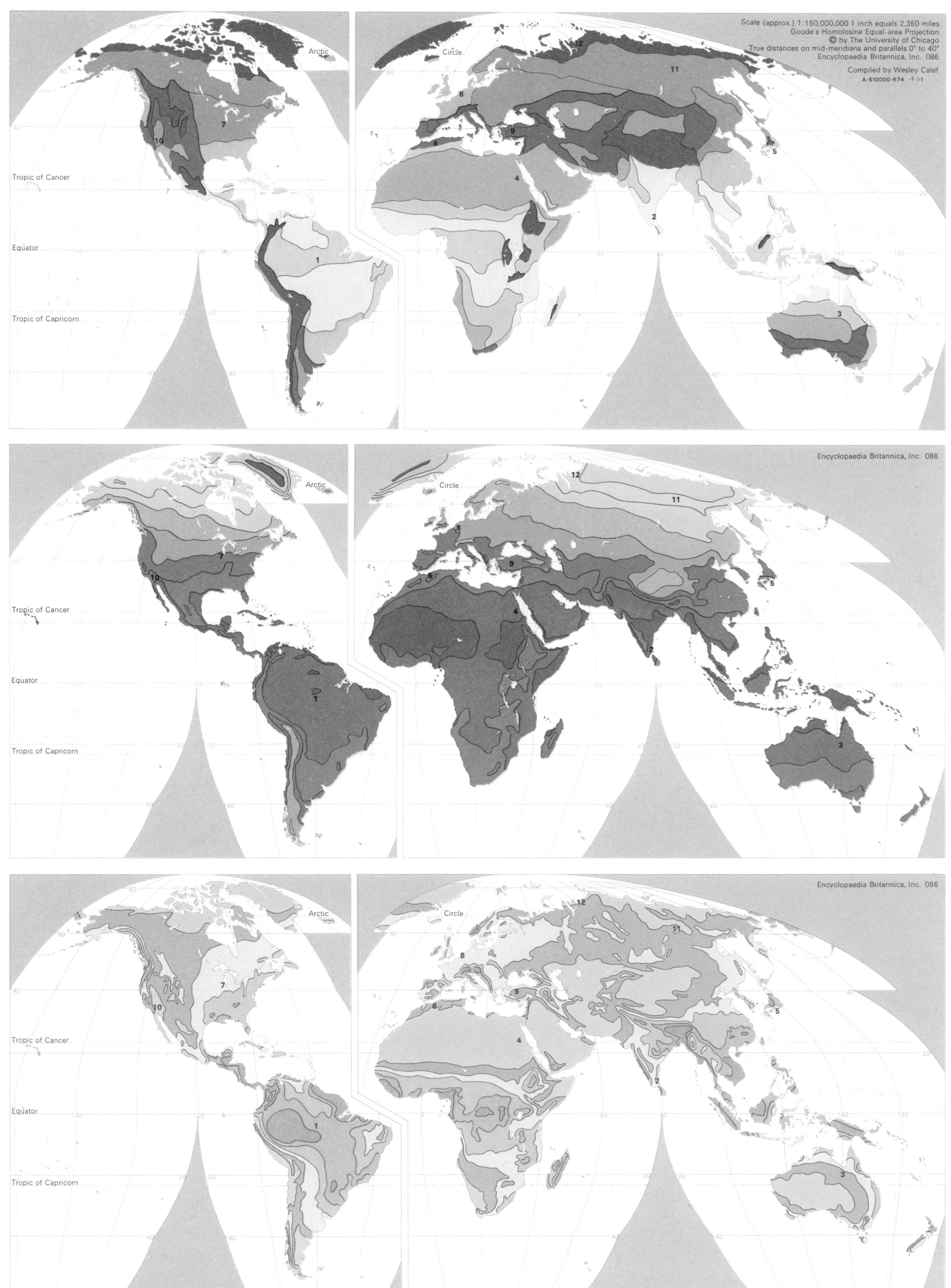

Scale (approx.) 1:150,000,000 1 inch equals 2,350 miles
Goode's Homolosine Equal-area Projection
© by The University of Chicago
True distances on mid-meridians and parallels 0° to 40°
Encyclopaedia Britannica, Inc.

Compiled by Wesley Calef

A-510000-674 -1-1-1

Arctic

Tropic of Cancer

Equator

Tropic of Capricorn

Circle

Encyclopaedia Britannica, Inc. 086

Encyclopaedia Britannica, Inc. 086

## Surface Configuration

### Smooth lands

Level plains: nearly all slopes gentle; local relief less than 100 ft. (30 m.)

Irregular plains: majority of slopes gentle; local relief 100-300 ft. (30-90 m.)

### Broken lands

Tablelands and plateaus: majority of slopes gentle, with the gentler slopes on the uplands; local relief more than 300 ft. (90 m.)

Hill-studded plains: majority of slopes gentle, with the gentler slopes in the lowlands; local relief 300-1,000 ft. (90-300 m.)

Mountain-studded plains: majority of slopes gentle, with the gentler slopes in the lowlands; local relief more than 1,000 ft. (300 m.)

### Rough lands

Hill lands: steeper slopes predominate; local relief less than 1,000 ft. (300 m.)

Mountains: steeper slopes predominate; local relief 1,000-5,000 ft. (300-1,500 m.)

Mountains of great relief: steeper slopes predominate; local relief more than 5,000 ft. (1,500 m.)

### Other surfaces

Ice caps: permanent ice

Maximum extent of glaciation

## Earth Structure and Tectonics

Precambrian stable shield areas

Exposed Precambrian rock

Paleozoic and Mesozoic flat-lying sedimentary rocks

Principal Paleozoic and Mesozoic folded areas

Cenozoic sedimentary rocks

Principal Cenozoic folded areas

Lava plateaus

Major trends of folding

### Geologic time chart

Precambrian—from formation of the earth (at least 4 billion years ago) to 600 million years ago

Paleozoic—from 600 million to 200 million years ago

Mesozoic—from 200 million to 70 million years ago

Cenozoic—from 70 million years ago to present time

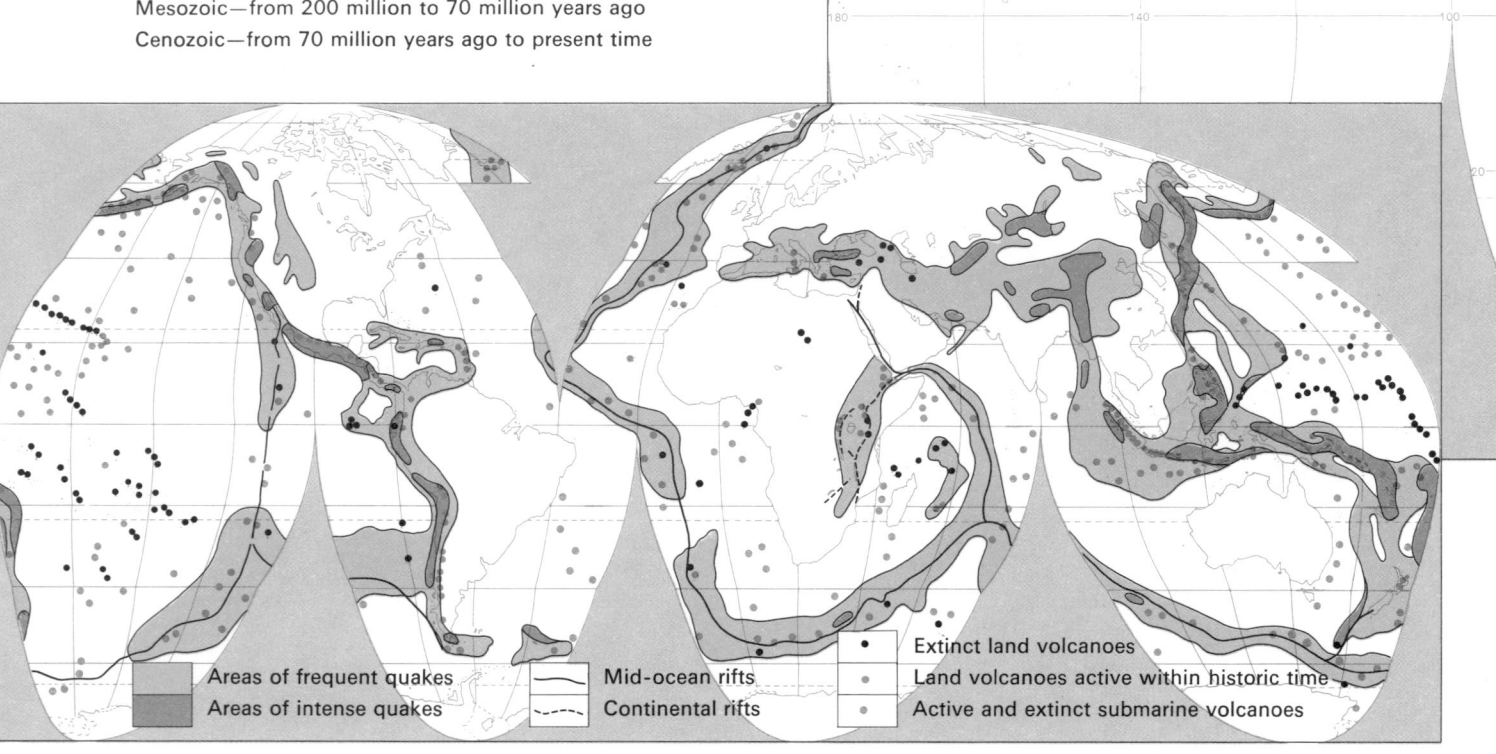

Areas of frequent quakes

Areas of intense quakes

Mid-ocean rifts

Continental rifts

Extinct land volcanoes

Land volcanoes active within historic time

Active and extinct submarine volcanoes

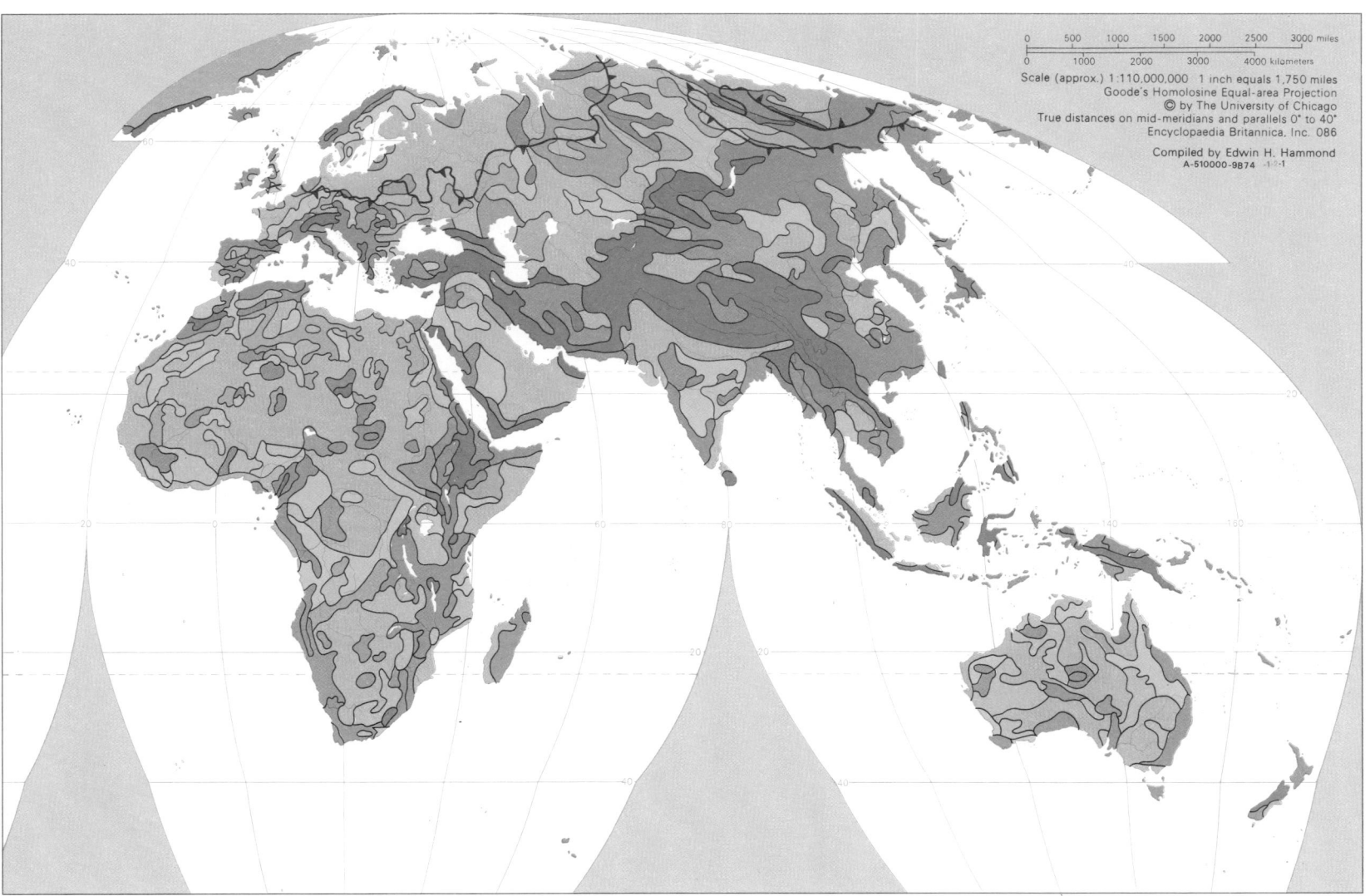

Scale (approx.) 1:110,000,000  1 inch equals 1,750 miles
Goode's Homolosine Equal-area Projection
© by The University of Chicago
True distances on mid-meridians and parallels 0° to 40°
Encyclopaedia Britannica, Inc. 086

Compiled by Edwin H. Hammond
A-510000-9874 -1-7-1

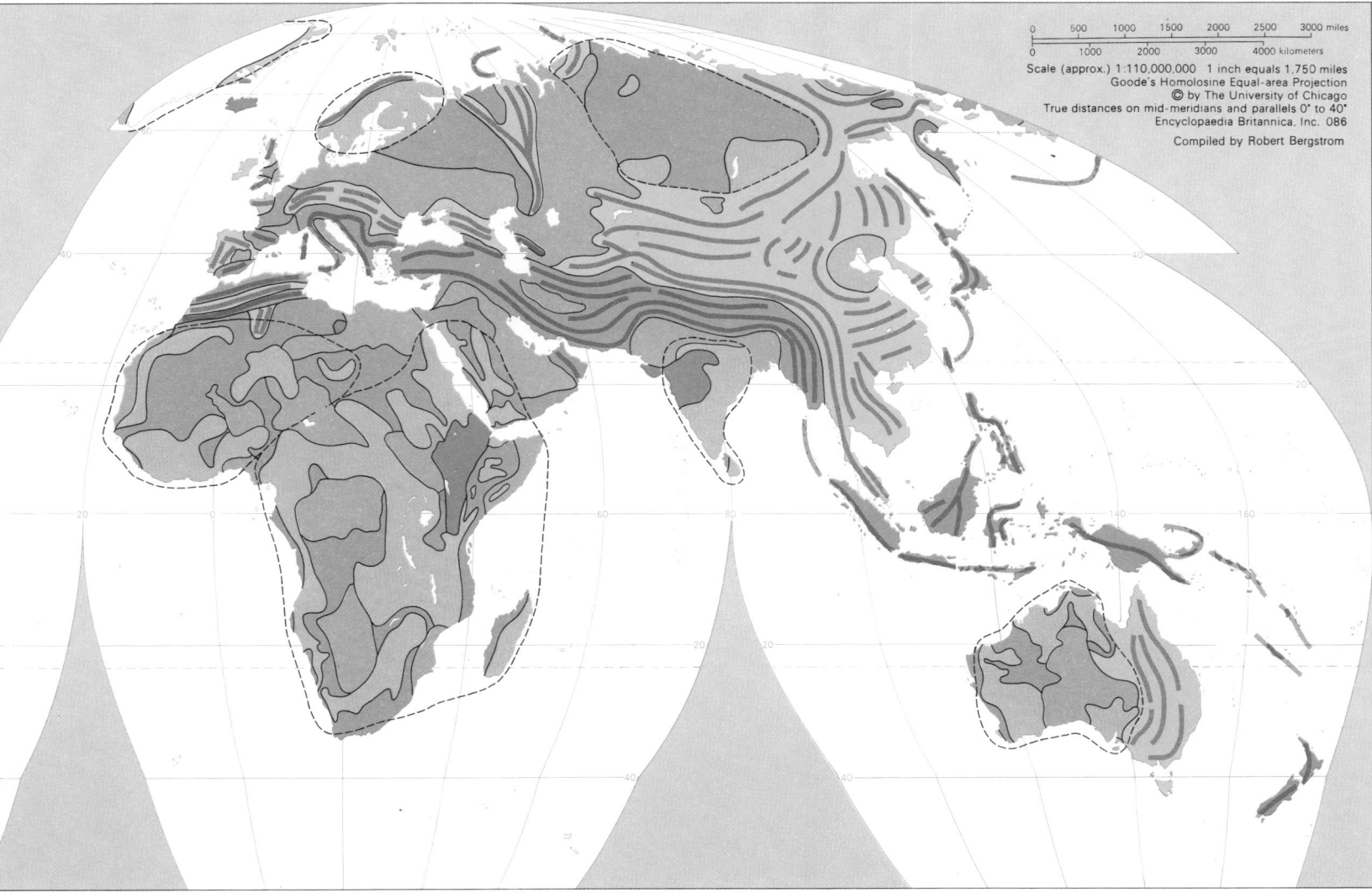

Scale (approx.) 1:110,000,000  1 inch equals 1,750 miles
Goode's Homolosine Equal-area Projection
© by The University of Chicago
True distances on mid-meridians and parallels 0° to 40°
Encyclopaedia Britannica, Inc. 086

Compiled by Robert Bergstrom

## Development of the earth's structure

The earth is in process of constant transformation.
Movements in the hot, dense interior of the earth result
in folding and fracture of the crust and transfer of molten
material to the surface. As a result, large structures
such as mountain ranges, volcanoes, lava plateaus, and
rift valleys are created. The forces that bring about these
structural changes are called *tectonic forces.*

The present continents have developed from stable
nuclei, or *shields*, of ancient (Precambrian) rock.
Erosive forces such as water, wind, and ice have worn

away particles of the rock, depositing them at the edges
of the shields, where they have accumulated and
ultimately become sedimentary rock. Subsequently,
in plaees, these extensive areas of flat-lying rock have
been elevated, folded, or warped, by the action of tectonic
forces, to form mountains. The shape of these mountains
has been altered by later erosion. Where the forces of
erosion have been at work for a long time, the mountains
tend to have a low relief and rounded contours, like the
Appalachians. Mountains more recently formed are high

and rugged, like the Himalayas.

The map above depicts some of the major geologic
structures of the earth and identifies them according to the
period of their formation. A geologic time chart is included in
the legend. The inset map shows the most important areas
of earthquakes, rifts, and volcanic activity. Comparison of
all the maps will show the close correlation between
present-day mountain systems, recent (Cenozoic)
mountain-building, and the areas of frequent earthquakes
and active volcanoes.

## Natural Vegetation

### Broad-leaved evergreen vegetation
Broad-leaved evergreen forest
Broad-leaved evergreen shrub formation
Scattered broad-leaved evergreen shrubs
Scattered broad-leaved evergreen dwarf shrubs

### Broad-leaved deciduous vegetation
Broad-leaved deciduous forest
Broad-leaved deciduous shrub formation
Scattered broad-leaved deciduous shrubs
Scattered broad-leaved deciduous dwarf shrubs

### Coniferous vegetation
Needle-leaved evergreen forest
Scattered needle-leaved evergreen trees
Needle-leaved deciduous forest

### Mixed vegetation without grass
Forest of broad-leaved evergreen and deciduous trees
Forest of broad-leaved and needle-leaved evergreen trees
Broad-leaved deciduous forests with broad-leaved evergreen shrubs
Forest of broad-leaved deciduous and needle-leaved evergreen trees

### Mixed vegetation with grass
Grassland with scattered broad-leaved evergreen trees
Grassland with broad-leaved evergreen shrubs
Grassland with scattered broad-leaved deciduous trees
Grassland with broad-leaved deciduous shrubs

### Grassland, tundra, barren
Grassland
Patches of grass
Lichens and grasses
Lichens and mosses
Barren

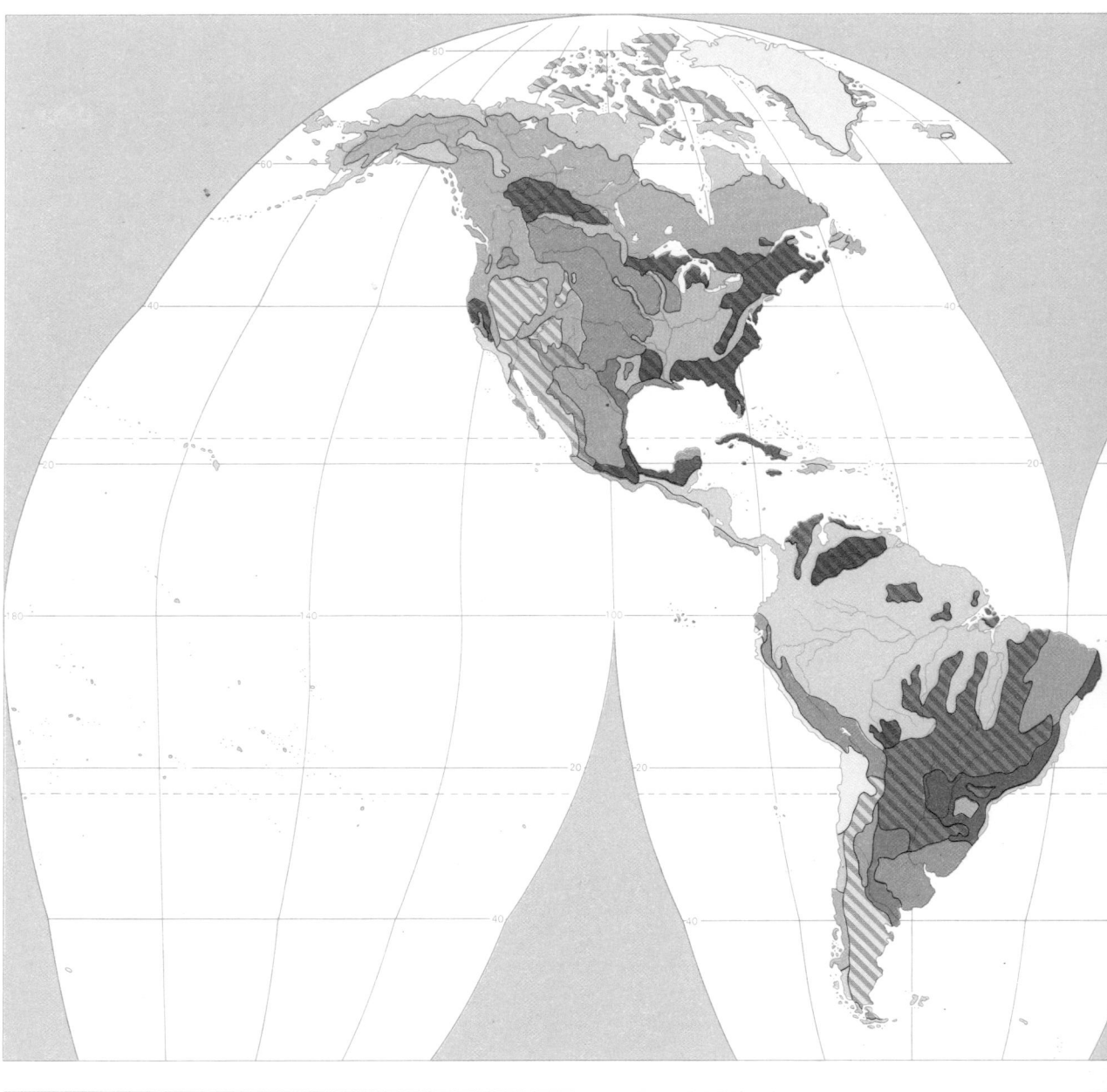

## Soils

Tundra soils of frigid climates; commonly with permanently frozen subsoil; supports dwarf shrubs, mosses, and lichens; some used for reindeer pasture

Podzolic soils of humid, cool climates; covered with predominantly coniferous forest; some farming, mainly subsistence

Podzolic soils of humid, temperate climates; originally covered with predominantly deciduous forest, much of it removed to accommodate extensive general farming, industry, and cities

Podzolic soils of humid, warm climates; covered with coniferous or mixed forest; general farming

Chernozemic soils of subhumid and semiarid, cool to tropical climates; supports mainly grasslands; extensive grain and livestock farming

Latosolic soils of humid or wet-dry tropical and subtropical climates; supports forest or savanna; shifting cultivation with some plantation agriculture

Grumusolic soils of humid to semiarid and temperate to tropical climates, with distinct wet and dry seasons; mainly grass-covered; livestock and grain farming

Desertic soils of arid climates; includes many areas of shallow, stony soils; sparse cover of shrubs and grass, some suitable for grazing; fertile if irrigated; dry farming possible in some areas

Mountain soils of all climates; shallow, stony; barren, grass-covered, or forested, depending on climate; includes many areas of other soils

Alluvial soils of all climates; deposited by water in flood plains and deltas of rivers; intensive farming in most temperate and some tropical regions (many smaller areas not shown)

Ice cap of polar regions

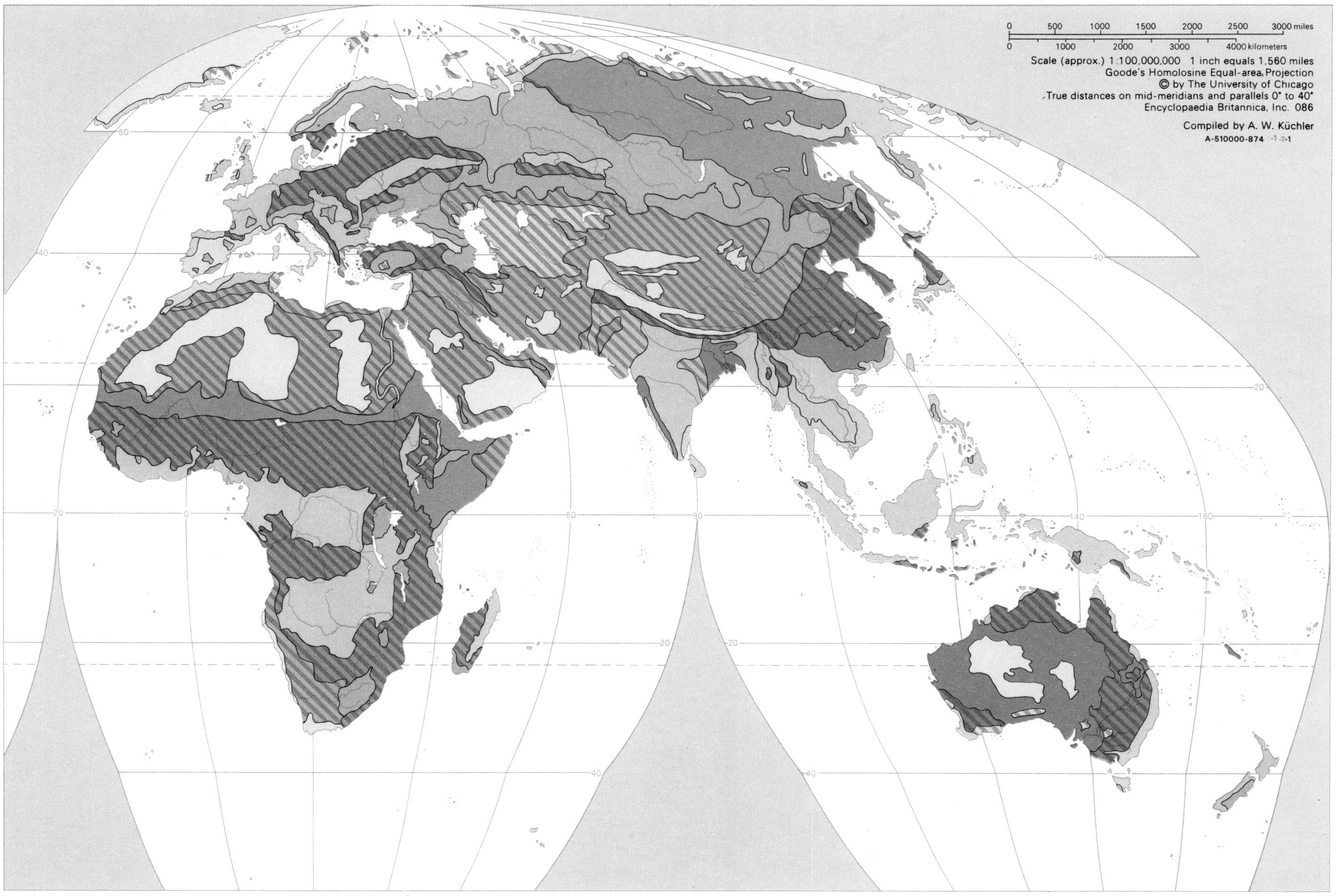
0 500 1000 1500 2000 2500 3000 miles
0 1000 2000 3000 4000 kilometers
Scale (approx.) 1:100,000,000 1 inch equals 1,560 miles
Goode's Homolosine Equal-area Projection
© by The University of Chicago
True distances on mid-meridians and parallels 0° to 40°
Encyclopaedia Britannica, Inc. 086
Compiled by A. W. Küchler
A-510000-874 -1-2-1

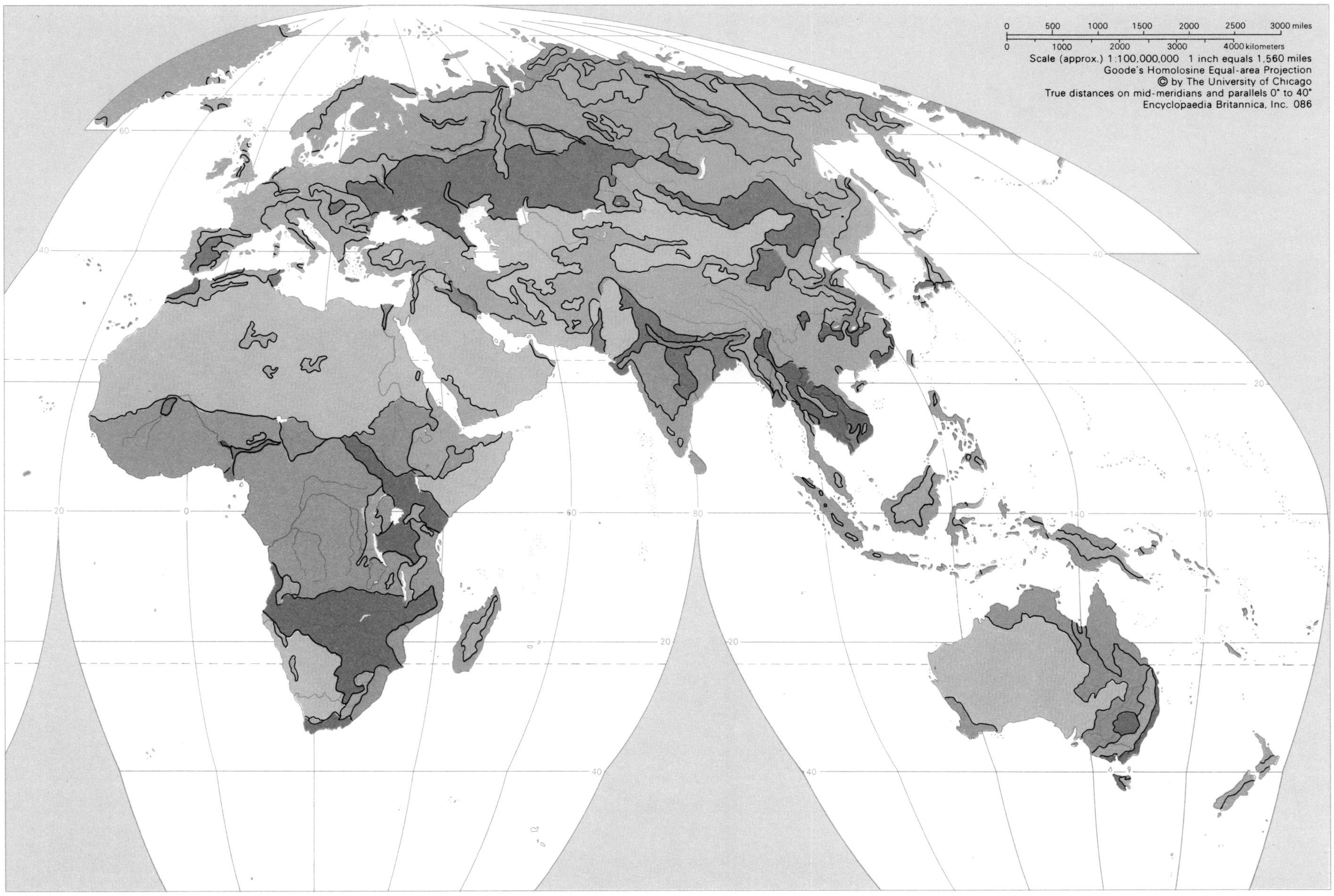
0 500 1000 1500 2000 2500 3000 miles
0 1000 2000 3000 4000 kilometers
Scale (approx.) 1:100,000,000 1 inch equals 1,560 miles
Goode's Homolosine Equal-area Projection
© by The University of Chicago
True distances on mid-meridians and parallels 0° to 40°
Encyclopaedia Britannica, Inc. 086

# Time Zones

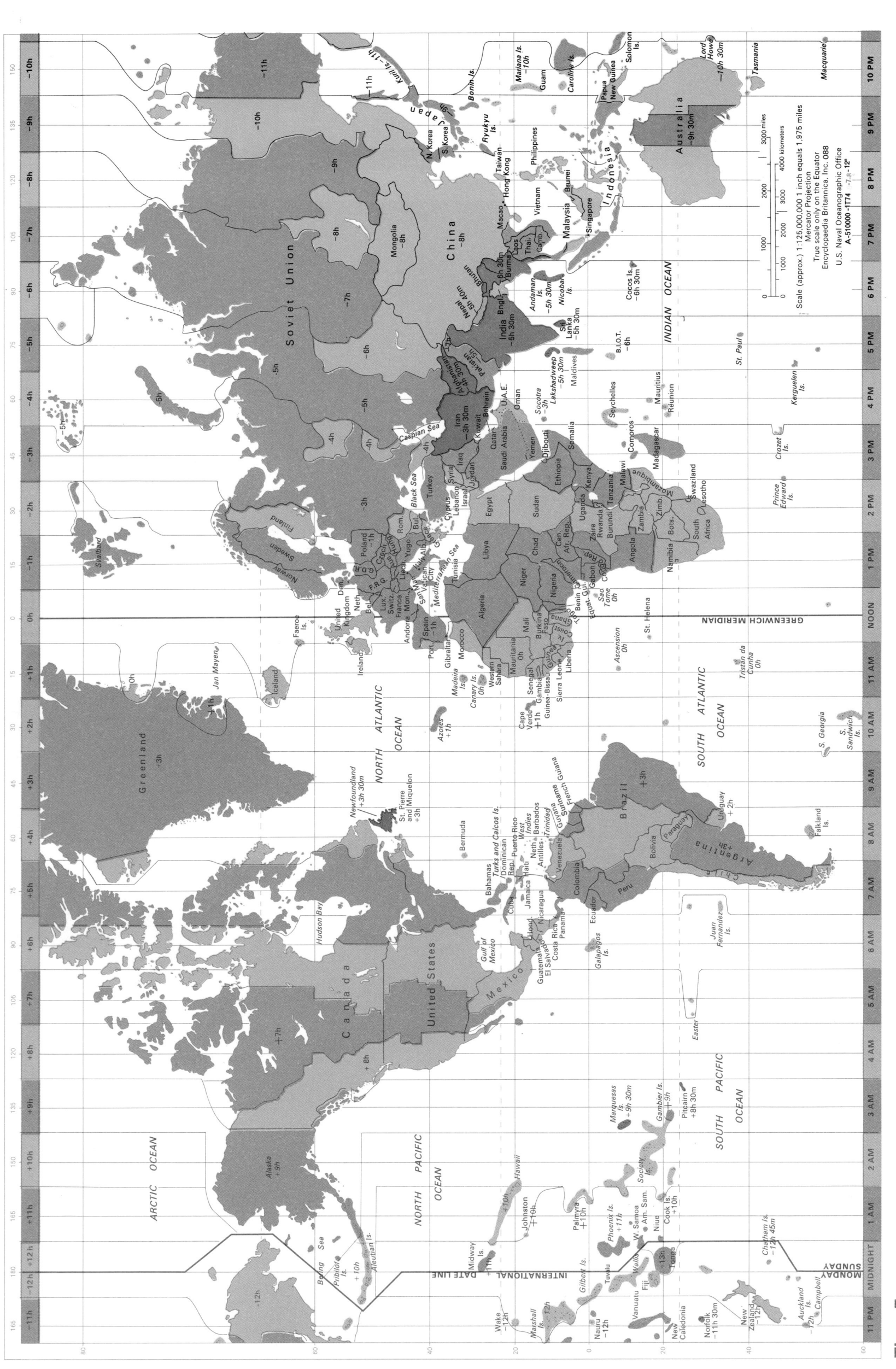

The standard time zone system, fixed by international agreement and by law in each country, is based on a theoretical division of the globe into 24 zones of 15° longitude each. The mid-meridian of each zone fixes the hour for the entire zone. The zero time zone extends 7½° east and 7½° west of the Greenwich meridian, 0° longitude. Since the earth rotates toward the east, time zones to the west of Greenwich are earlier, to the east, later. Plus and minus hours at the top of the map are added to or subtracted from local time to find Greenwich time. Local standard time can be determined for any area in the world by adding one hour for each time zone counted in an easterly direction from one's own, or by subtracting one hour for each zone counted in a westerly direction. To separate one day from the next, the 180th meridian has been designated as the international date line. On both sides of the line the time of day is the same, but west of the line it is one day later than it is to the east. Countries that adhere to the international zone system adopt the zone applicable to their location. Some countries, however, establish time zones based on political boundaries, or adopt the time zone of a neighboring unit. For all or part of the year some countries also advance their time by one hour, thereby utilizing more daylight hours each day.

|  | h m | hours, minutes |

Standard time zone of even-numbered hours from Greenwich time

Standard time zone of odd-numbered hours from Greenwich time

Time varies from the standard time zone by half an hour

Time varies from the standard time zone by other than half an hour

# Reference Maps

## MAP SYMBOLS

### CULTURAL FEATURES

**Political Boundaries**

- International
- Secondary (State, province, etc.)
- County

**Populated Places**

Cities, towns, and villages

Symbol size represents population of the place

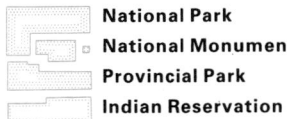

Chicago
Gary
Racine
Glenview
Edgewood

Type size represents relative importance of the place.

- Corporate area of large U.S. and Canadian cities and urban area of other foreign cities
- Major Urban Area
  Area of continuous commercial, industrial, and residential development in and around a major city
- Community within a city
- Capital of major political unit
- Capital of secondary political unit
- Capital of U.S. state or Canadian province
- County Seat
- Military Installation
- Scientific Station

**Miscellaneous**

- National Park
- National Monument
- Provincial Park
- Indian Reservation
- Point of Interest
- Ruins
- Buildings
- Race Track
- Railroad – International Maps
- Tunnel
- Underground or Subway
- Dam
- Bridge
- Dike
- Highway – U.S. and Canadian Maps
- Railroad – U.S. and Canadian Maps

### LAND FEATURES

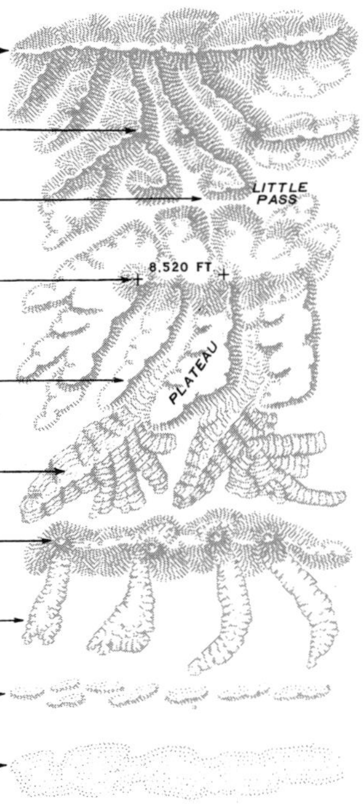


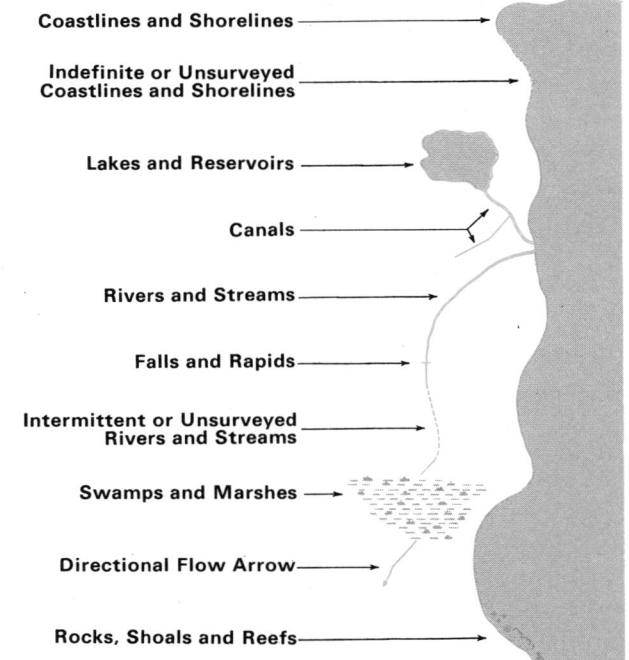

- Ranges
- Peaks
- Passes
- Point of Elevation above sea level
- Escarpments, Bluffs, Cliffs, and Plateaus
- Glaciers
- Volcanoes
- Lava Flows
- Sand Dunes
- Deserts

### WATER FEATURES

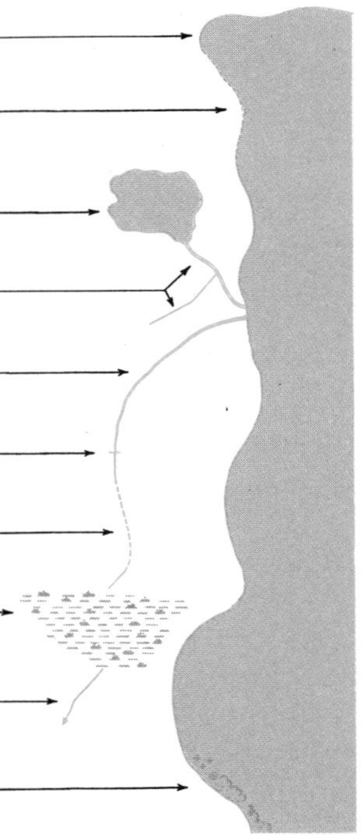

- Coastlines and Shorelines
- Indefinite or Unsurveyed Coastlines and Shorelines
- Lakes and Reservoirs
- Canals
- Rivers and Streams
- Falls and Rapids
- Intermittent or Unsurveyed Rivers and Streams
- Swamps and Marshes
- Directional Flow Arrow
- Rocks, Shoals and Reefs

### TYPE STYLES USED TO NAME FEATURES

| | | | | | |
|---|---|---|---|---|---|
| A S I A | Continent | PANTELLERIA (ITALY) | Country of which unit is a dependency in parentheses | UINTA DESERT | Major Terrain Features |
| DENMARK CANADA | Country, State, or Province | SRI LANKA (CEYLON) | Former or alternate name | MT. MORIAH | Individual Mountain |
| | | Rome (Roma) | Local or alternate city name | STROMBOLI NUNIVAK | Island or Coastal Feature |
| BÉARN | Region, Province, or Historical Region | Naval Air Station | Military Installation | Ocean Lake River Canal | Hydrographic Features |
| CROCKETT | County | MESA VERDE SAN XAVIER | National Park or Monument, Provincial Park, Indian Res., | | |

**Note: Size of type varies according to importance and available space. Letters for names of major features are spread across the extent of the feature.**

## THE INDEX REFERENCE SYSTEM

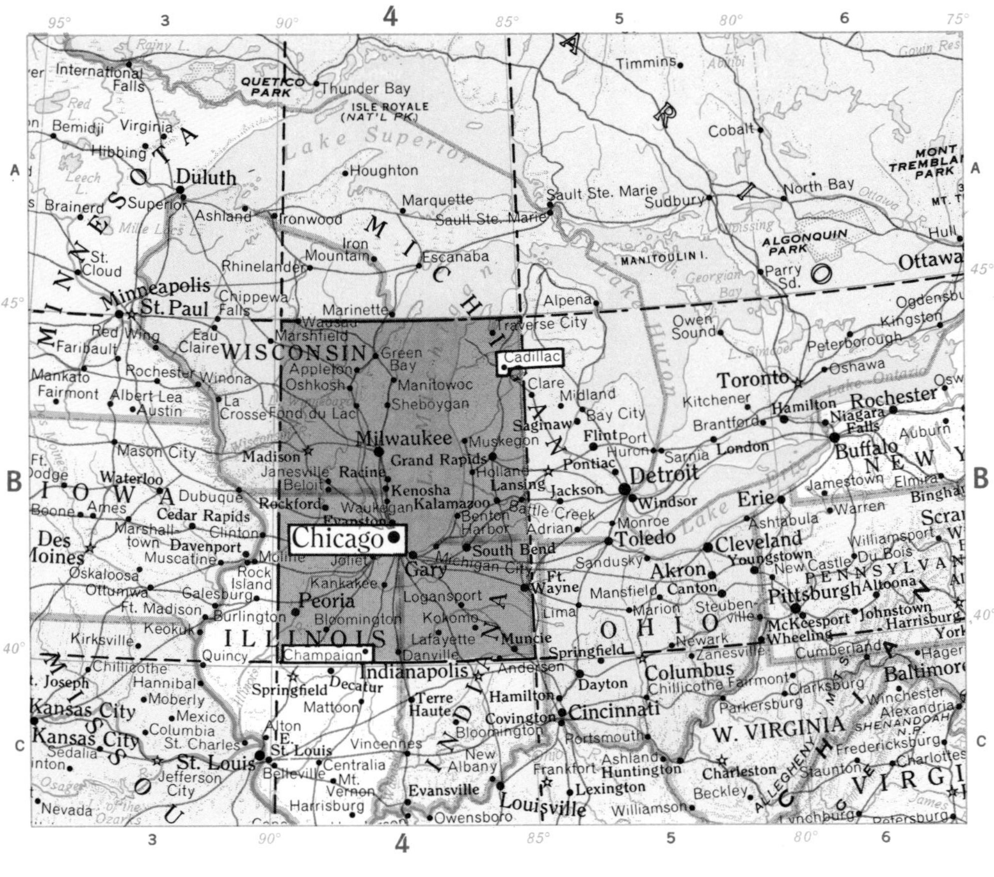


| Place Location | Index Key | Page |
|---|---|---|
| Cadillac, Que., Can | *h11 | 73 |
| Cadillac, Sask., Can | H2 | 70 |
| Cadillac, Fr | E3 | 14 |
| Cadillac, Wexford, Mich | B4 | 90 |
| Cadiz, San Bernardino, Calif | E6 | 82 |
| Cadiz, Trigg, Ky | D2 | 94 |
| *Cadron, creek, Ark* | B3 | 81 |
| Caen, Fr | C3 | 14 |
| Caetité, Braz | D2 | 57 |
| Calcutta, India | D8 | 39 |
| Cambridge, Eng | B8 | 12 |
| Catania, It | F5 | 21 |
| Ceará, state, Braz | C3 | 57 |
| Chamblee, DeKalb, Ga | h8 | 87 |
| Chambly, Que., Can | D4 | 73 |
| Chambord, Que., Can | A5 | 73 |
| Champagne, former prov., Fr | C5 | 14 |
| Champaign, Champaign, Ill | B4 | 90 |
| *Champdore, lake, Que., Can* | g8 | 75 |
| Champerico, Guat | C2 | 62 |
| Champéry, Switz | D2 | 19 |
| Champex, Switz | D3 | 19 |
| Champigneulles, Fr | F6 | 15 |
| Champion, Chase, Nebr | D4 | 103 |
| Champlain, co., Que., Can | B4 | 73 |
| *Champlain, lake, N.Y., Vt* | B2 | 120 |
| Champotón, Mex | D6 | 63 |
| Changchou, China | E8 | 34 |
| Chanthaburi, Thai | F5 | 38 |
| Chaparral, Col | C2 | 60 |
| Charleville-Mézières, Fr | C6 | 14 |
| Chatham, Eng | C8 | 12 |
| Chiapa de Corzo, Mex | D6 | 63 |
| Chiapas, state, Mex | D6 | 63 |
| Chiba, Jap | I10, n19 | 37 |
| Chiba, pref., Jap | *I10 | 37 |
| Chibemba, Ang | E1 | 48 |
| Chibougamau, Que., Can | k12 | 73 |
| Chicago, Cook, Ill | B4 | 90 |
| Chichaoua, Mor | C3 | 44 |
| *Chichen Itzá, ruins, Mex* | C7 | 63 |
| Chichester, Eng | D7 | 12 |
| Chickasaw, co., Iowa | A5 | 92 |
| Chiclana, Sp | D2 | 20 |
| Chiclayo, Peru | C2 | 58 |
| Columbus, Franklin, Ohio | C3 | 111 |

The indexing system used in this atlas is based upon the conventional pattern of parallels and meridians used to indicate latitude and longitude. The index samples beside the map indicate that the cities of *Chicago*, *Cadillac*, and *Champaign* are all located in *B4*. Each index key letter, *in this case "B,"* is placed between corresponding degree numbers of latitude in the vertical borders of the map. Each index key number, *in this case "4,"* is placed between corresponding degree numbers of longitude in the horizontal borders of the map. Crossing of the parallels above and below the index letter with the meridians on each side of the index number forms a confining "box" in which the given place is certain to be located. It is important to note that location of the place may be anywhere in this confining "box."

Insets on many foreign maps are indexed independently of the main maps by separate index key letters and figures. All places indexed to these insets are identified by the lower case reference letter in the index key. A diamond-shaped symbol in the margin of the map is used to separate the insets from the main map and also to separate key letters and numbers where the spacing of the parallels and meridians is great.

Place-names are indexed to the location of the city symbol. Political divisions and physical features are indexed to the location of their names on the map.

**COMPARATIVE WORLD TIME**
(Legal Clock Time)

In comparing the time of one zone with another, consider the zone numbers as hours, then by subtracting find the difference in time. The lower zone number represents the earlier hour and the higher zone number the later hour. (If the difference is greater than 12 hours, subtract this difference from 24 hours to find the nearest time difference.)

Antarctica has no legal time.

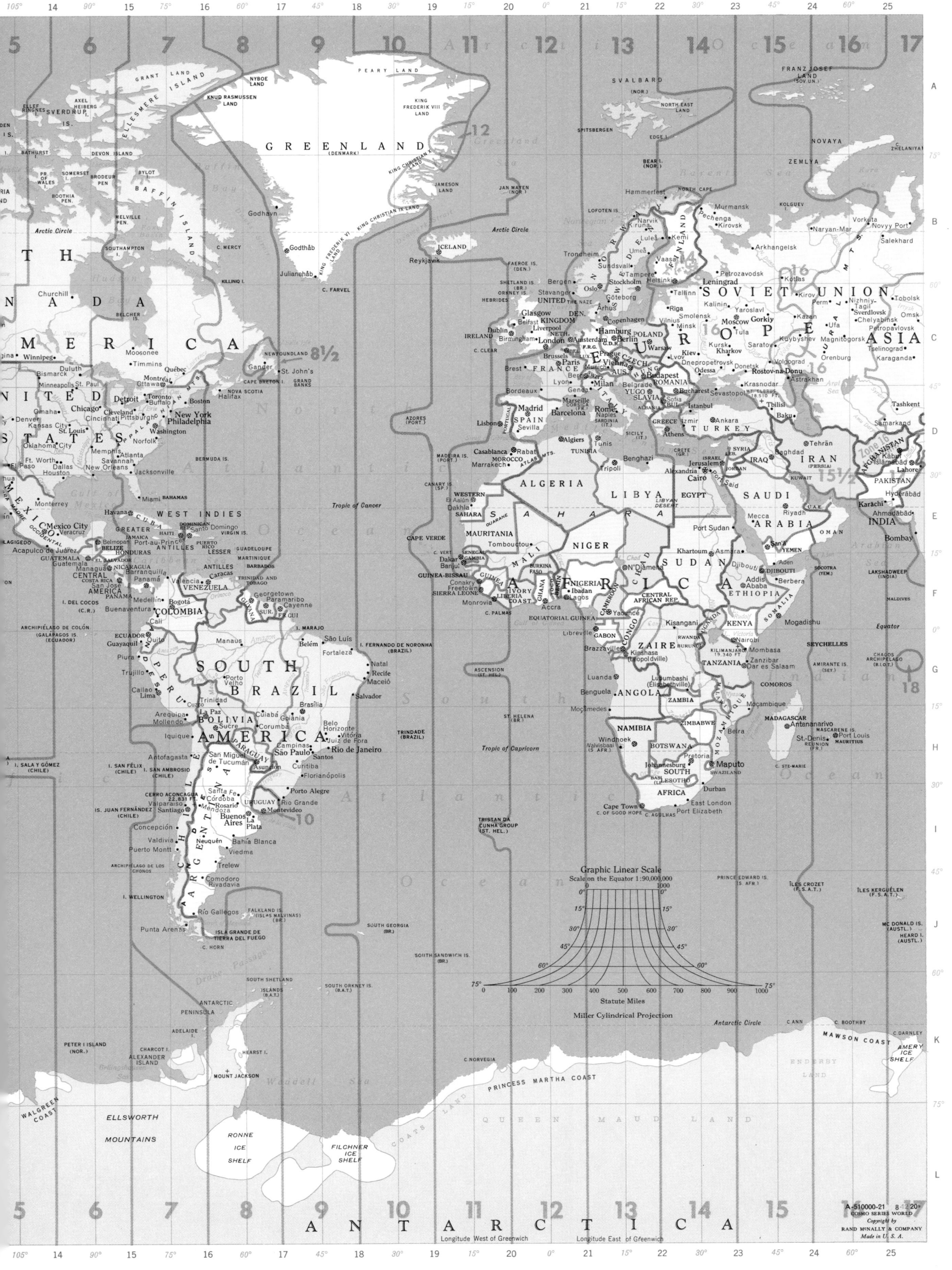

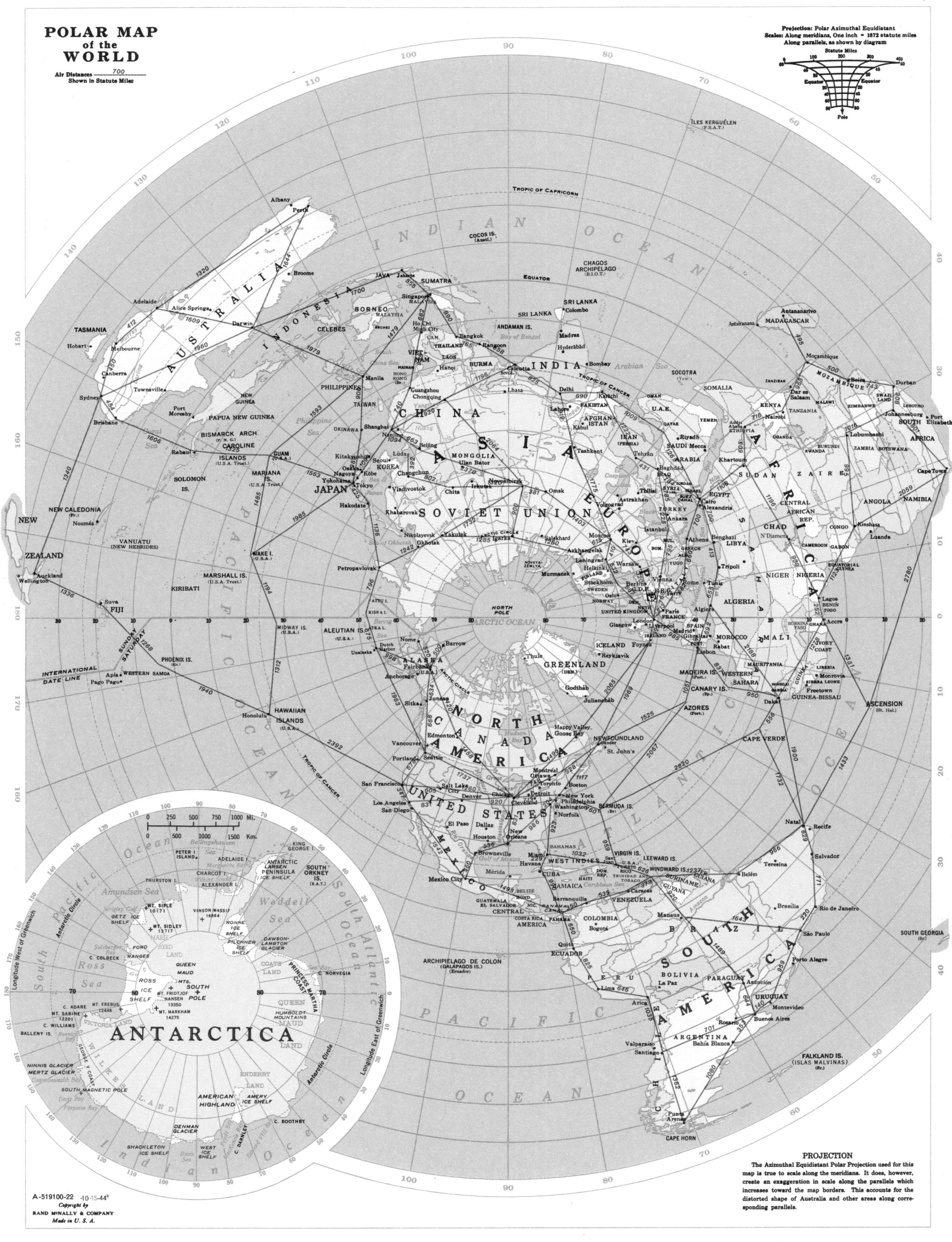

# POLAR MAP of the WORLD

Air Distances — 700 — Shown in Statute Miles

**Projection:** Polar Azimuthal Equidistant
**Scales:** Along meridians, One inch = 1872 statute miles
Along parallels, as shown by diagram

## PROJECTION

The Azimuthal Equidistant Polar Projection used for this map is true to scale along the meridians. It does, however, create an exaggeration in scale along the parallels which increases toward the map borders. This accounts for the distorted shape of Australia and other areas along corresponding parallels.

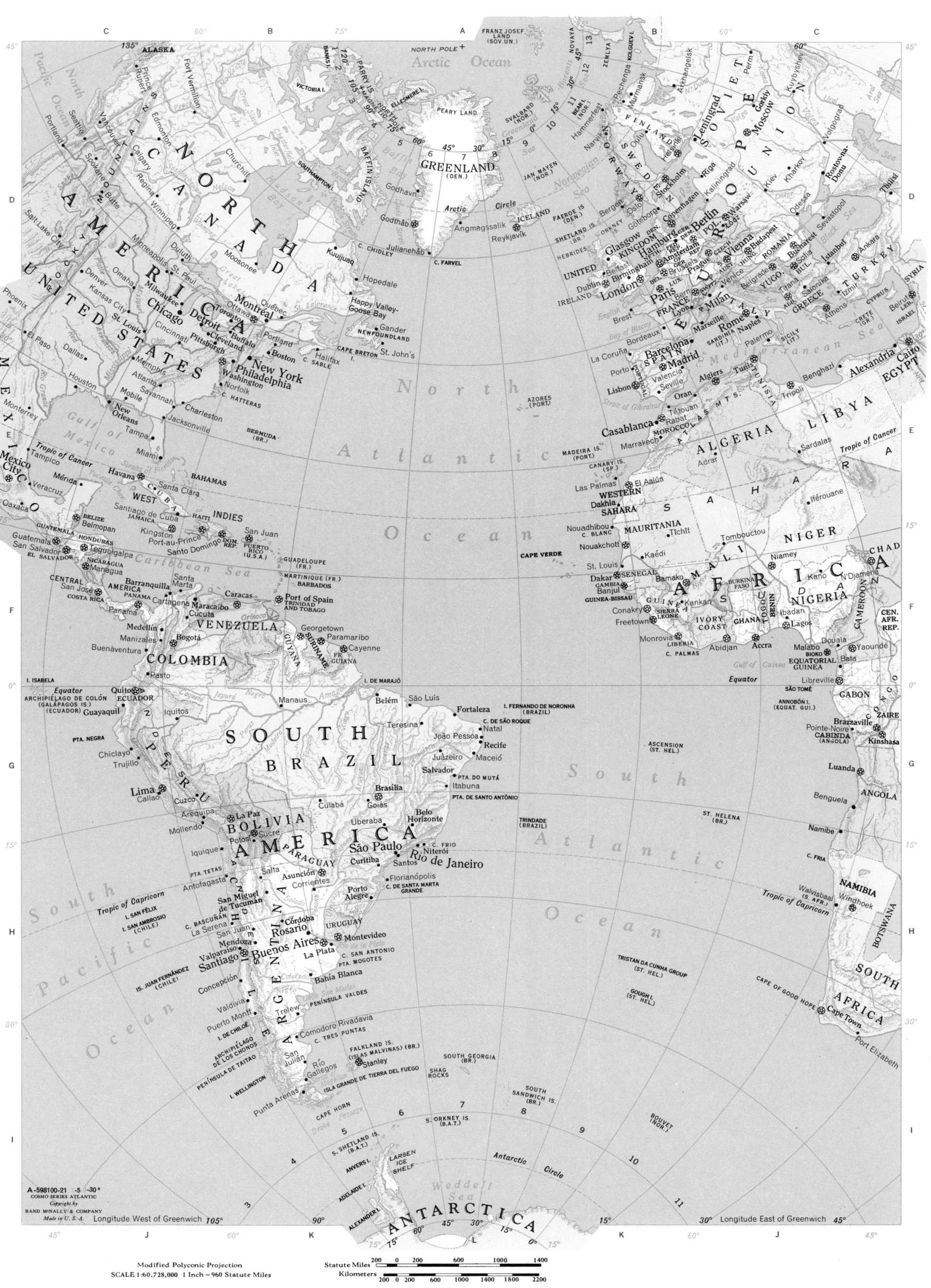

Modified Polyconic Projection
SCALE 1:60,728,000  1 Inch = 960 Statute Miles

Statute Miles
Kilometers

A-598100-21  -5  -30°
COSMO SERIES ATLANTIC
Copyright by
RAND McNALLY & COMPANY
Made in U.S.A.

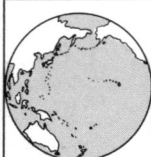

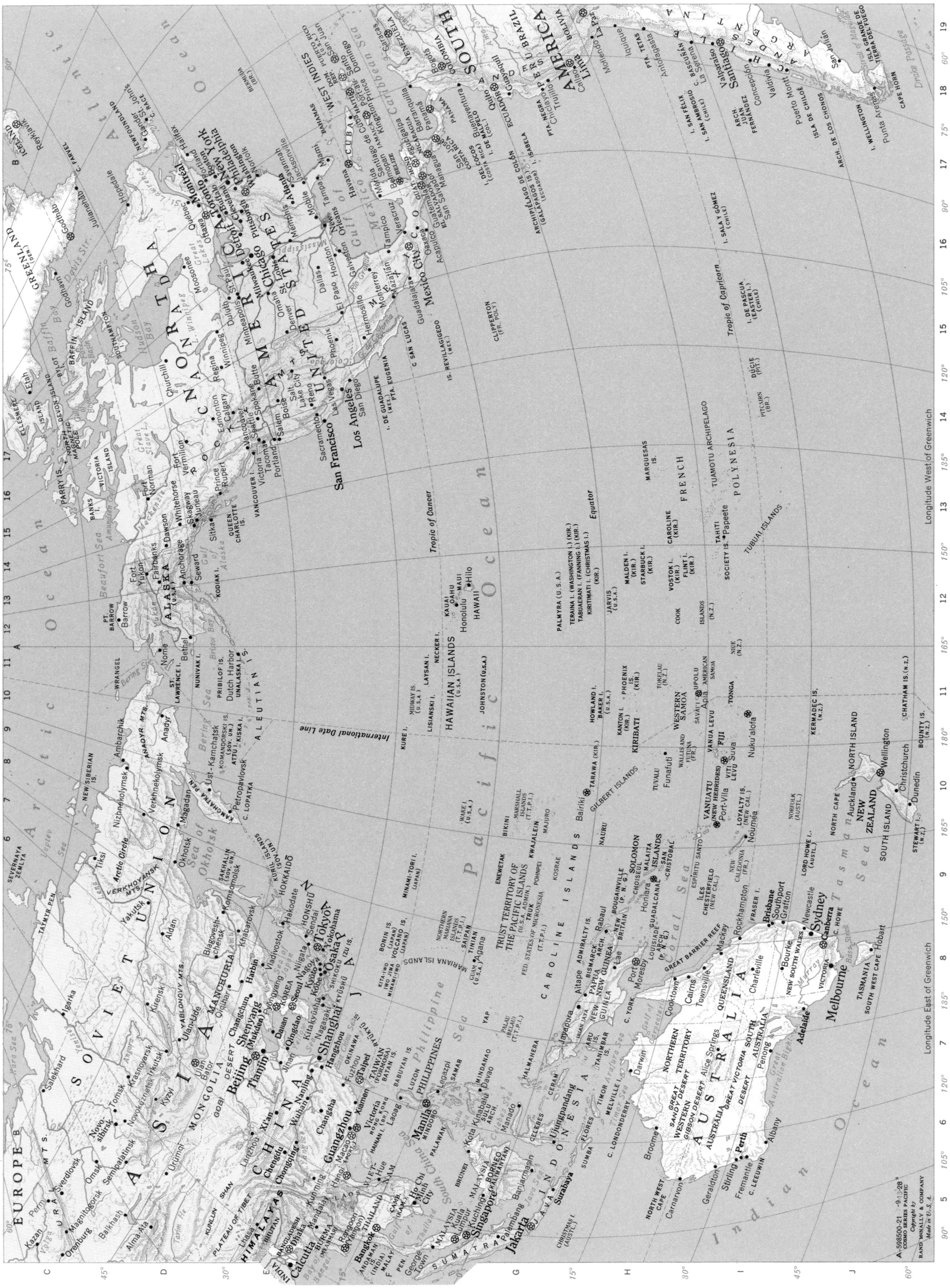

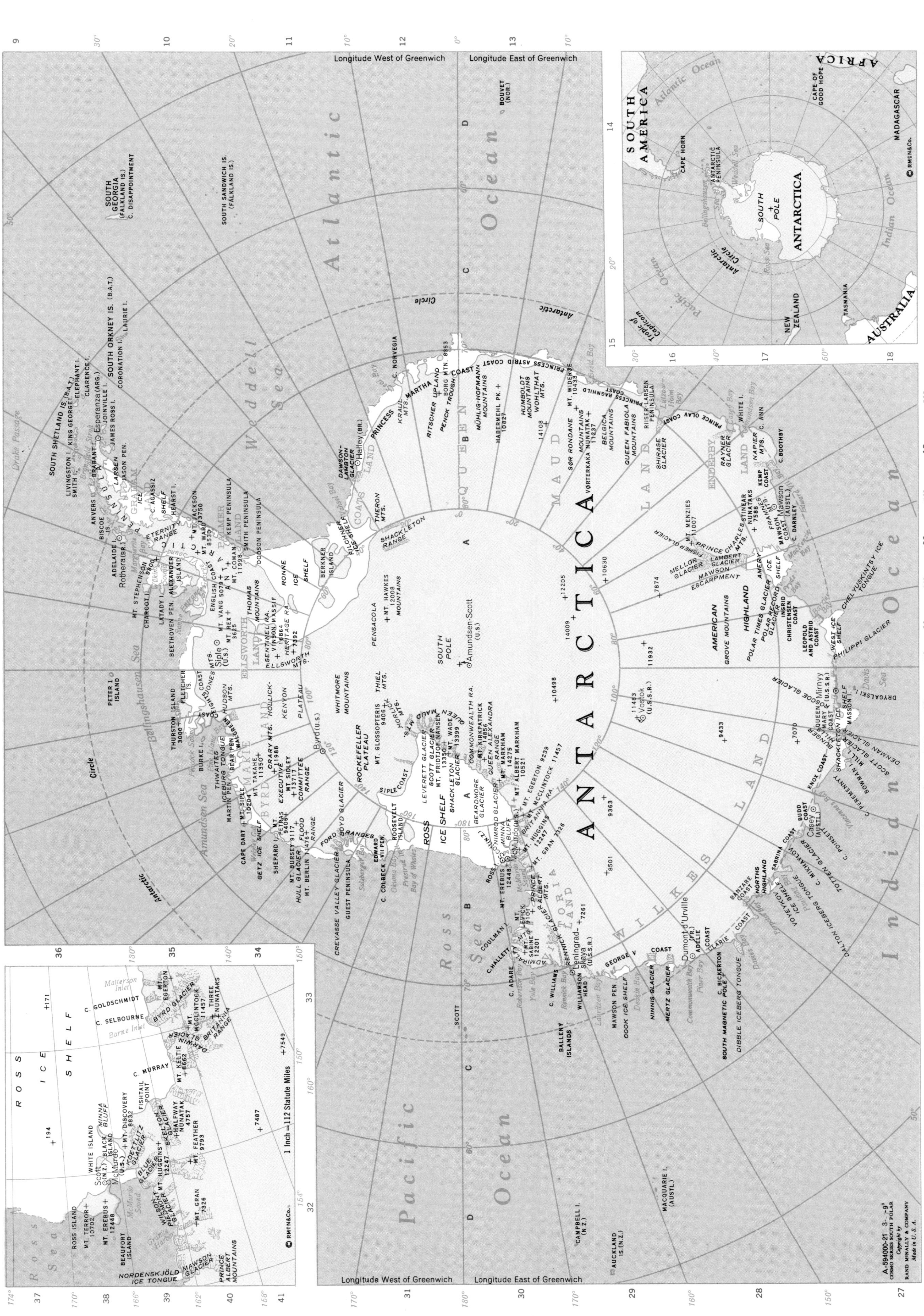

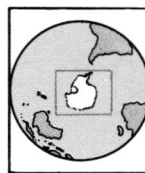

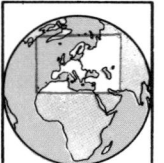

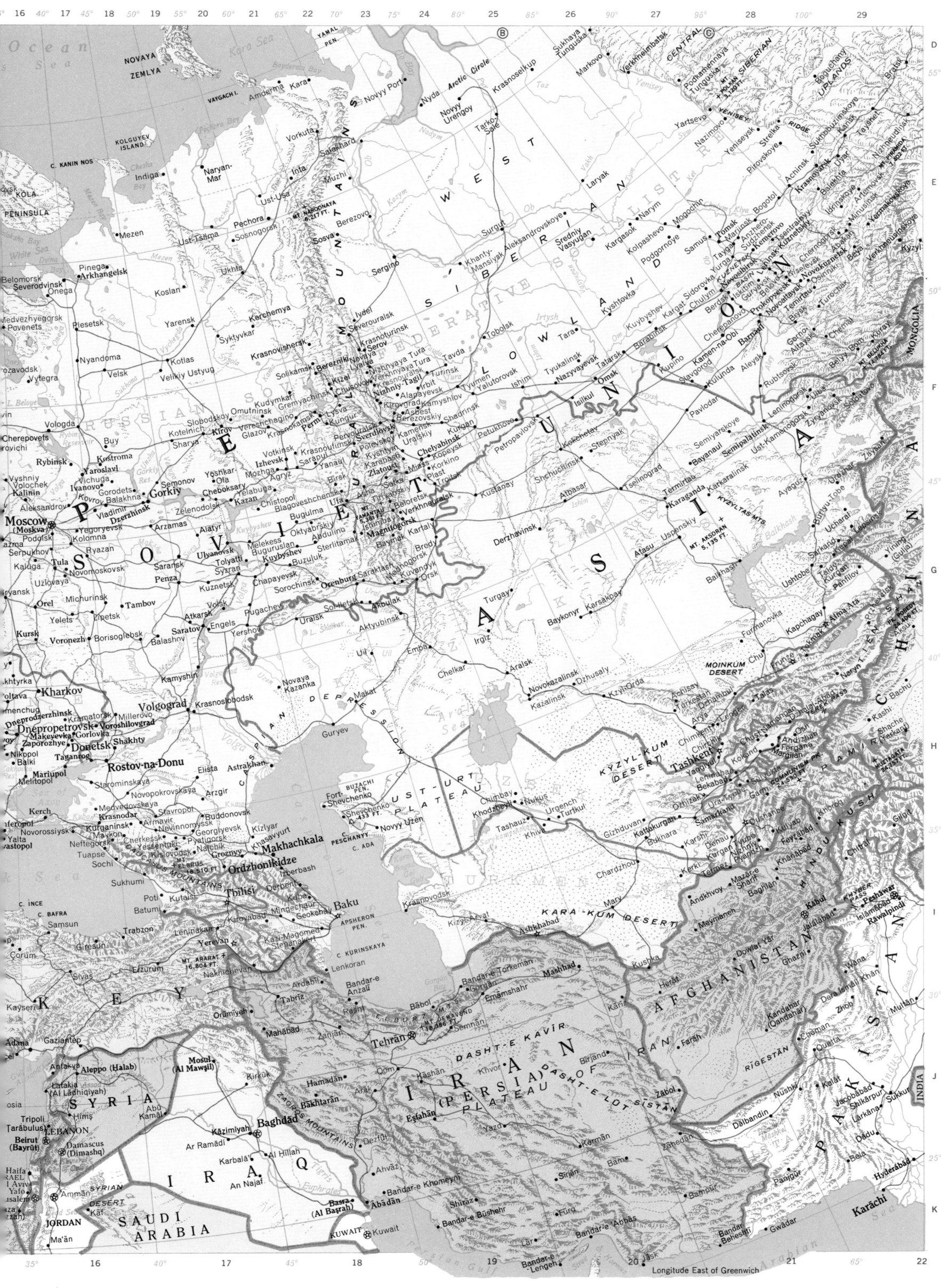

Conic Projection
SCALE 1:16,000,000   1 Inch = 252 Statute Miles

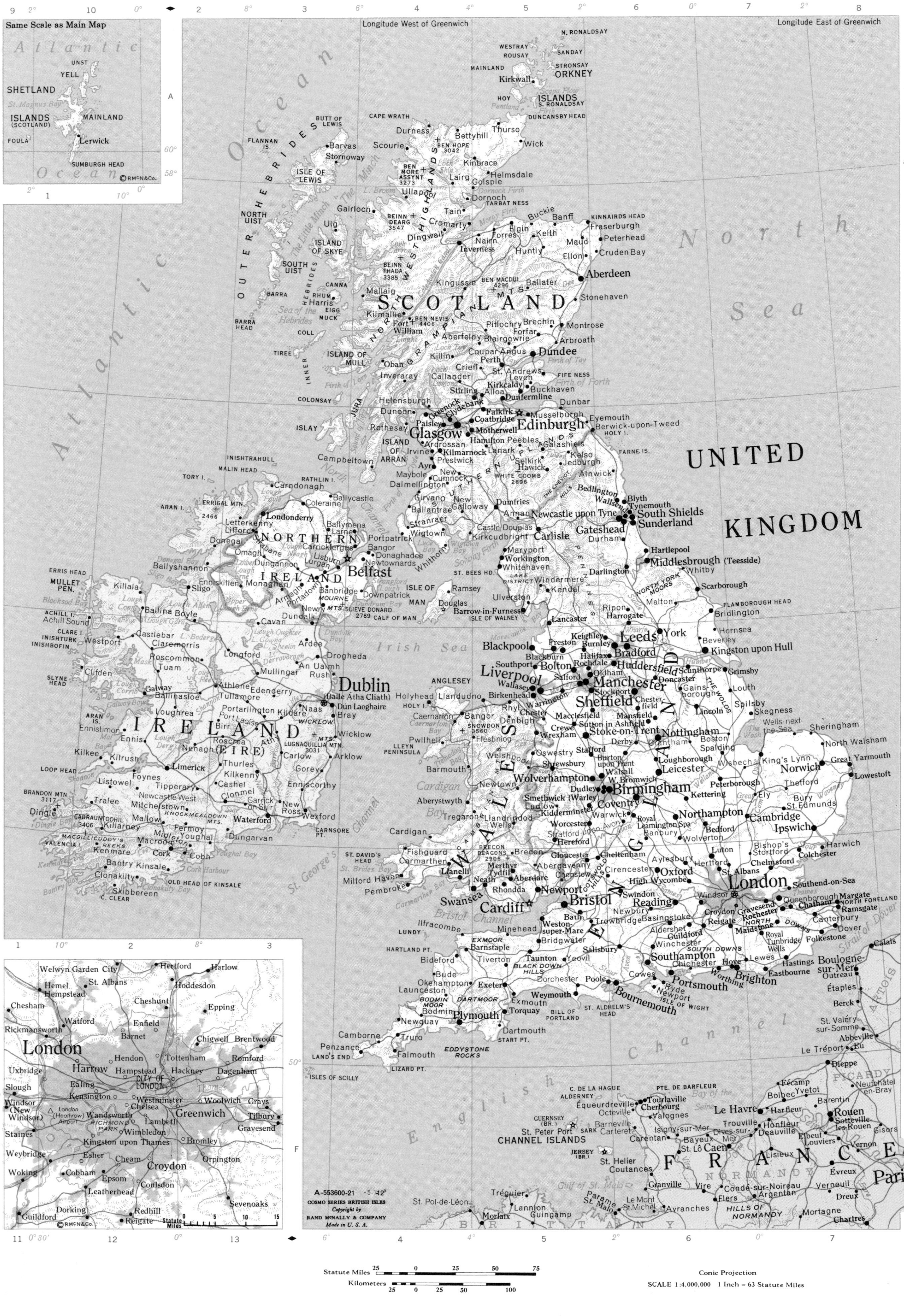

Lambert Conformal Conic Projection
SCALE 1 : 2,000,000  1 Inch = 32 Statute Miles

Statute Miles 5 0 5 10 20 30 40 50
Kilometers 5 0 5 10 20 30 40 50 60

Longitude West of Greenwich

A-551700-21 -4 -8-7°
COSMO SERIES IRELAND
Copyright by
RAND McNALLY & COMPANY
Made in U. S. A.

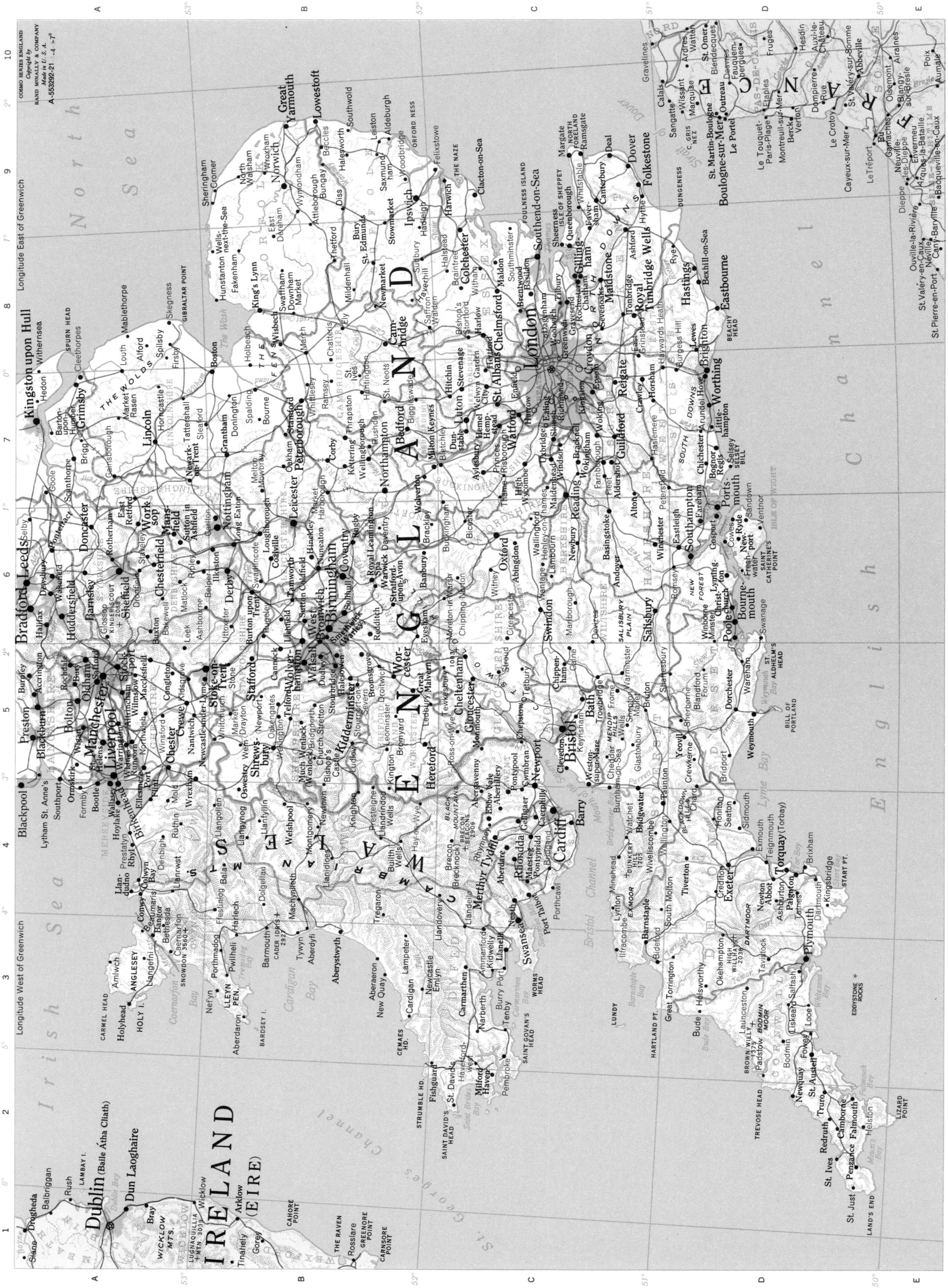

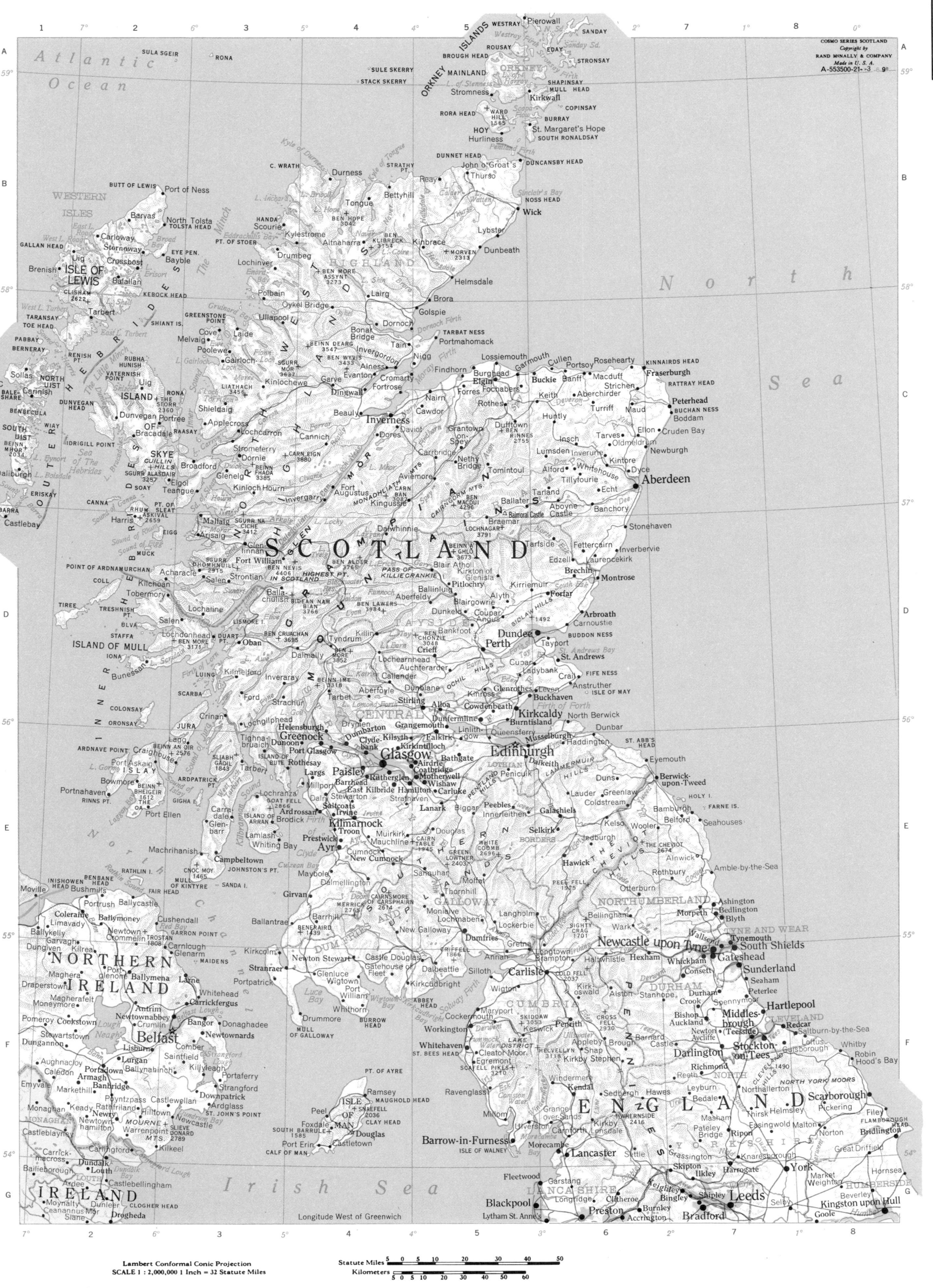

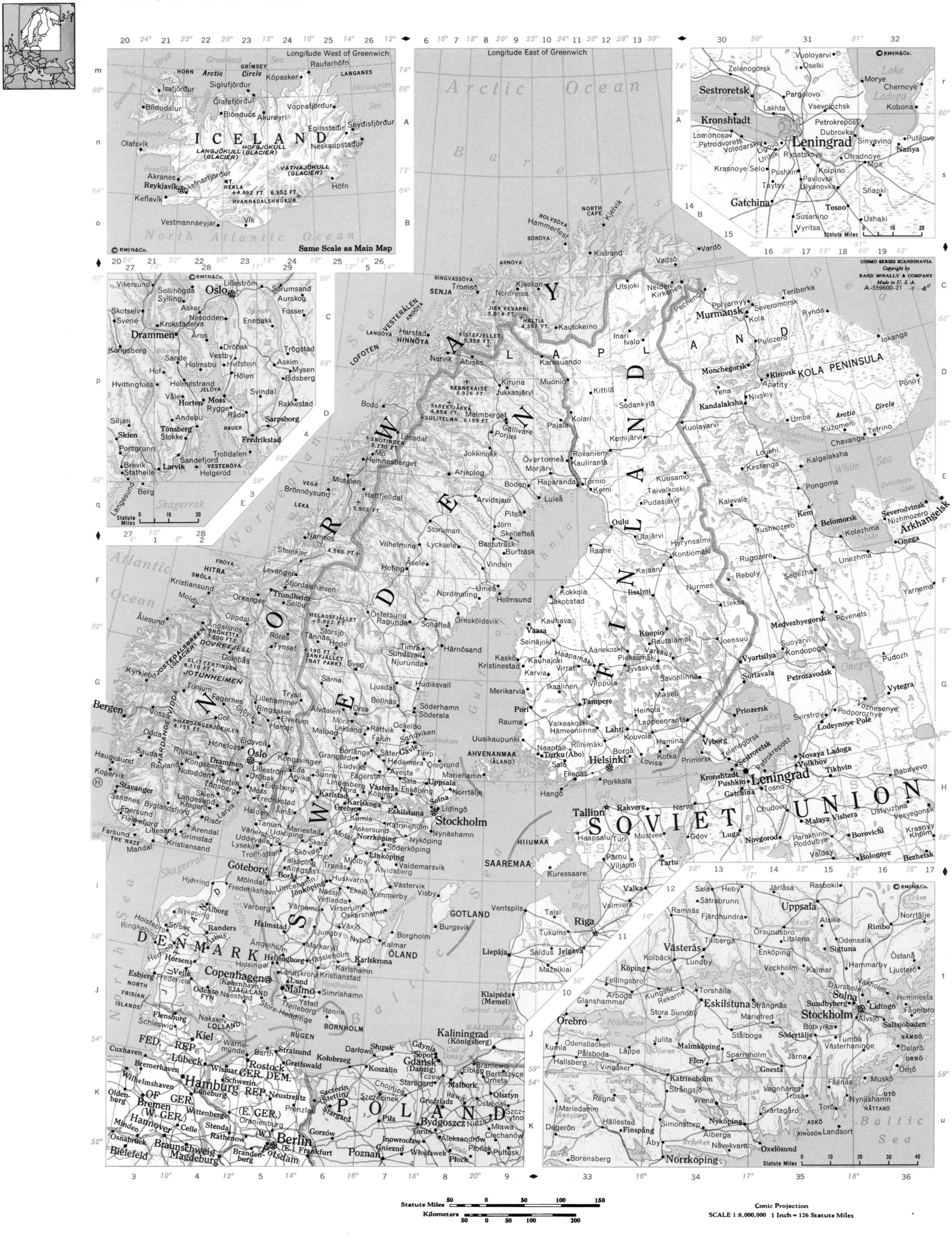

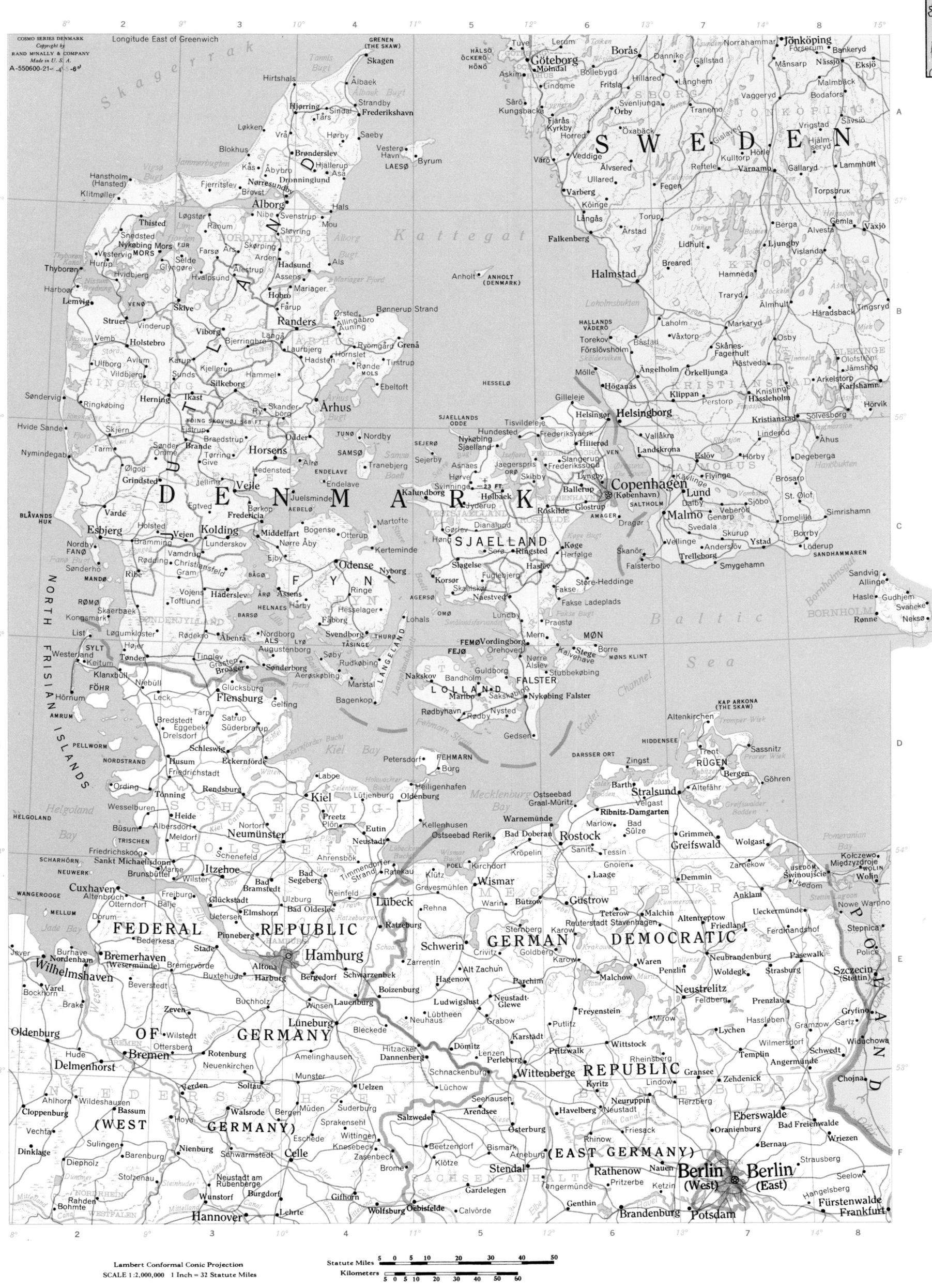

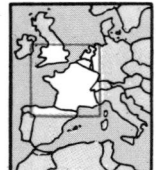

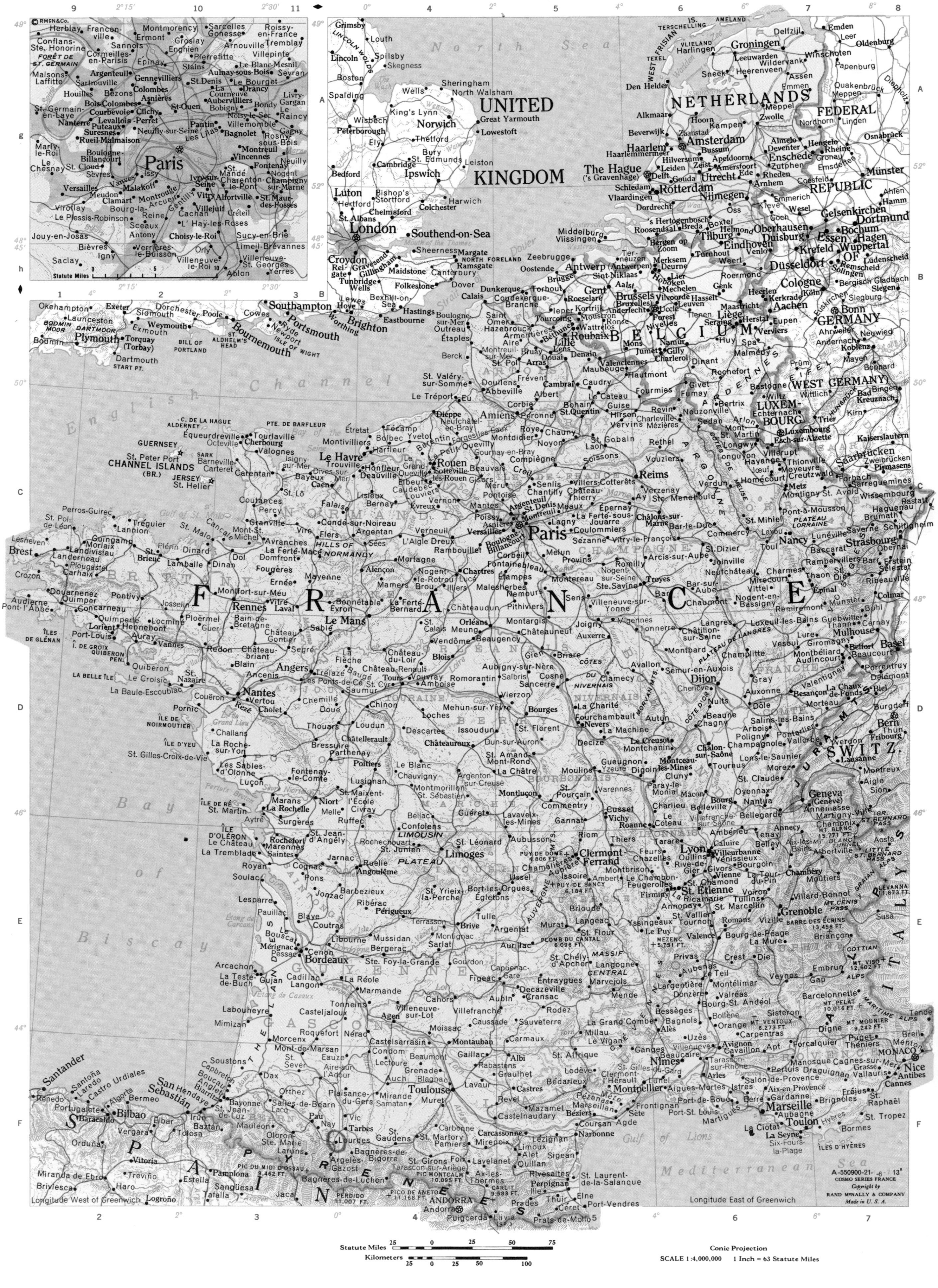

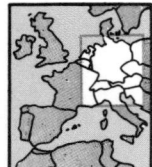

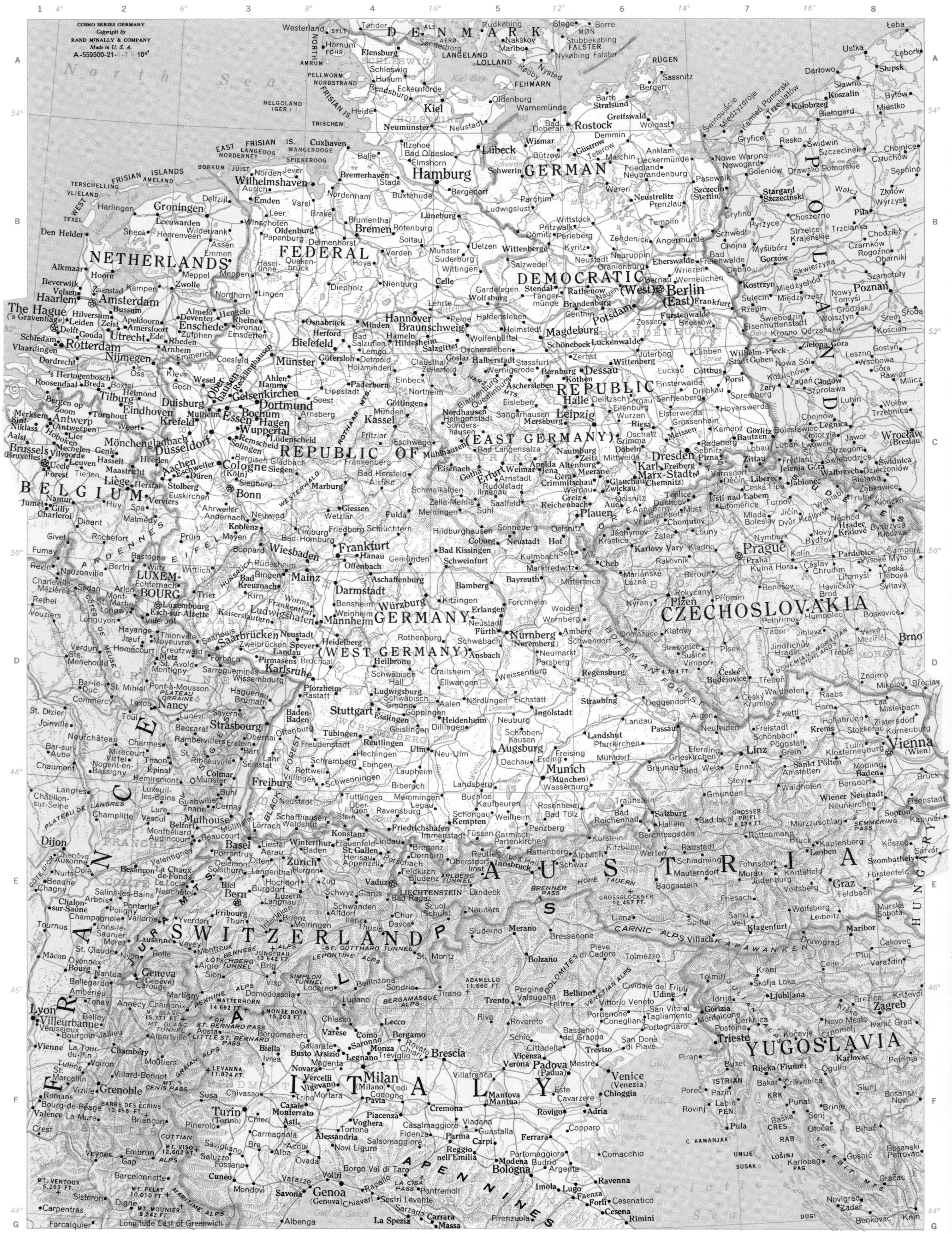

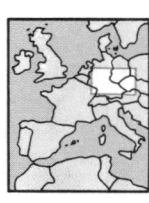

Lambert Conformal Conic Projection
SCALE 1:2,000,000  1 Inch = 32 Statute Miles

Statute Miles 5 0 5 10 20 30 40 50
Kilometers 5 0 5 10 20 30 40 50 60

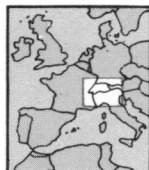

Statute Miles 5 0 5 10 20 30 40 50
Kilometers 5 0 5 10 20 30 40 50 60

Lambert Conformal Conic Projection
SCALE 1:2,000,000   1 Inch ≈ 32 Statute Miles

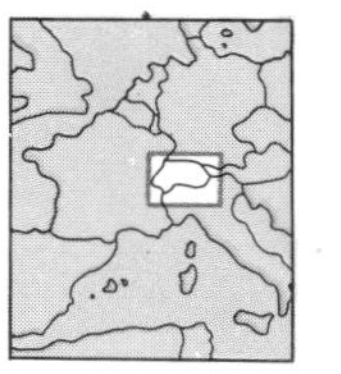

Lambert Conformal Conic Projection

SCALE 1 : 1,100,000   1 Inch = 17 Statute Miles

Statute Miles 5   0   5   10   20   30

Kilometers 5   0   5   10   20   30   40

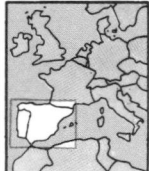

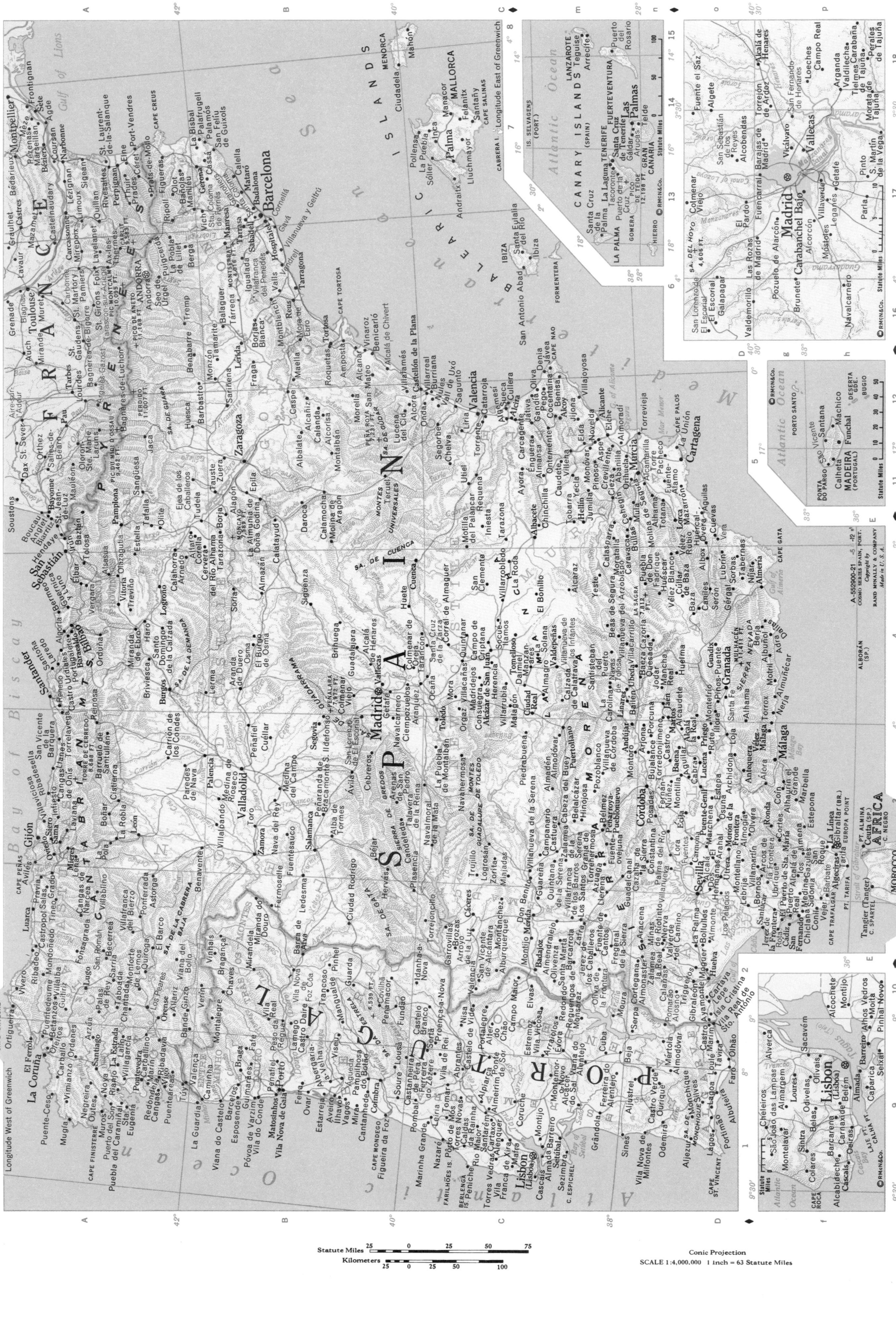

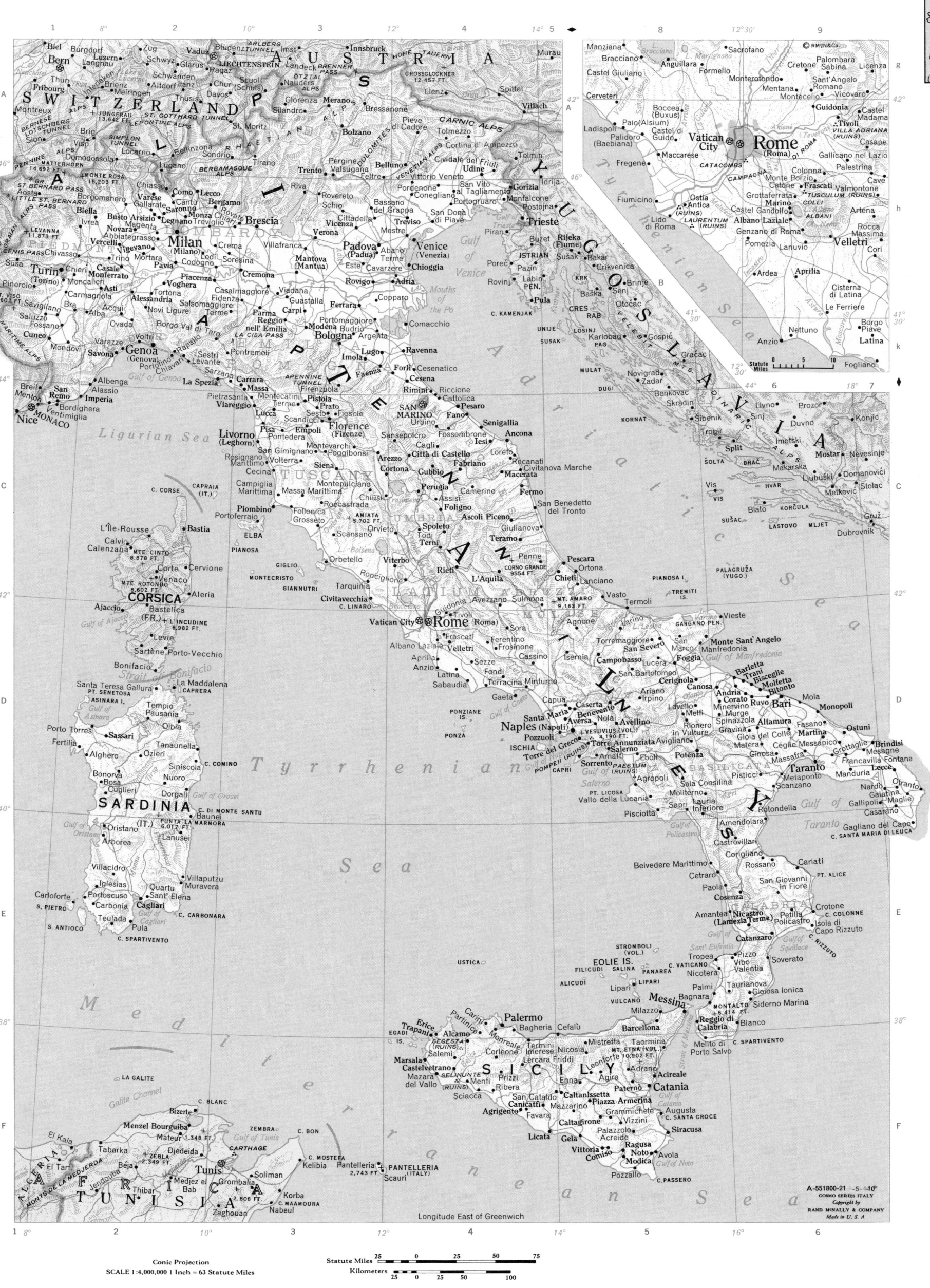

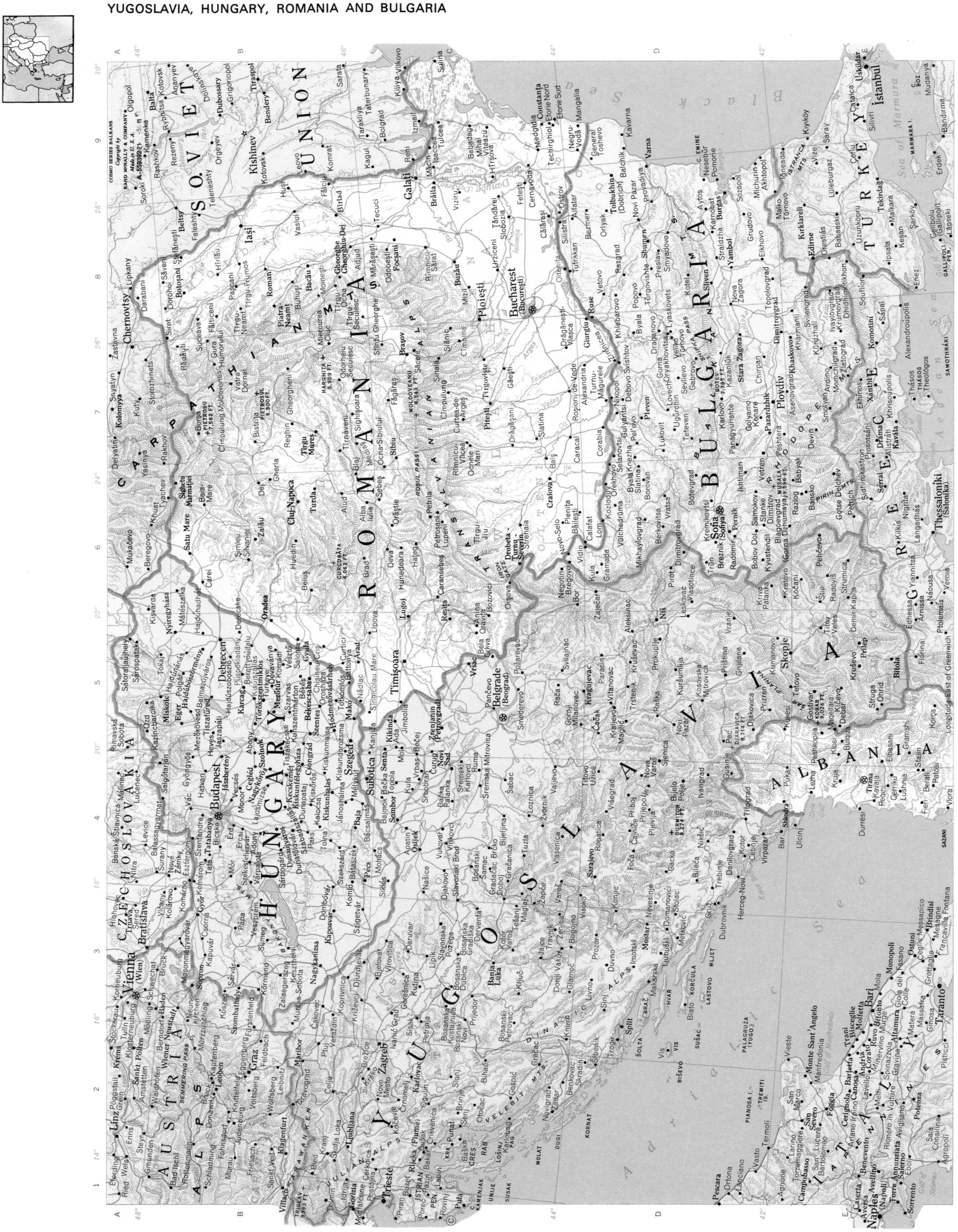

Statute Miles 25 0 25 50 75

Kilometers 25 0 25 50 75 100

Conic Projection

SCALE 1:4,000,000  1 Inch = 63 Statute Miles

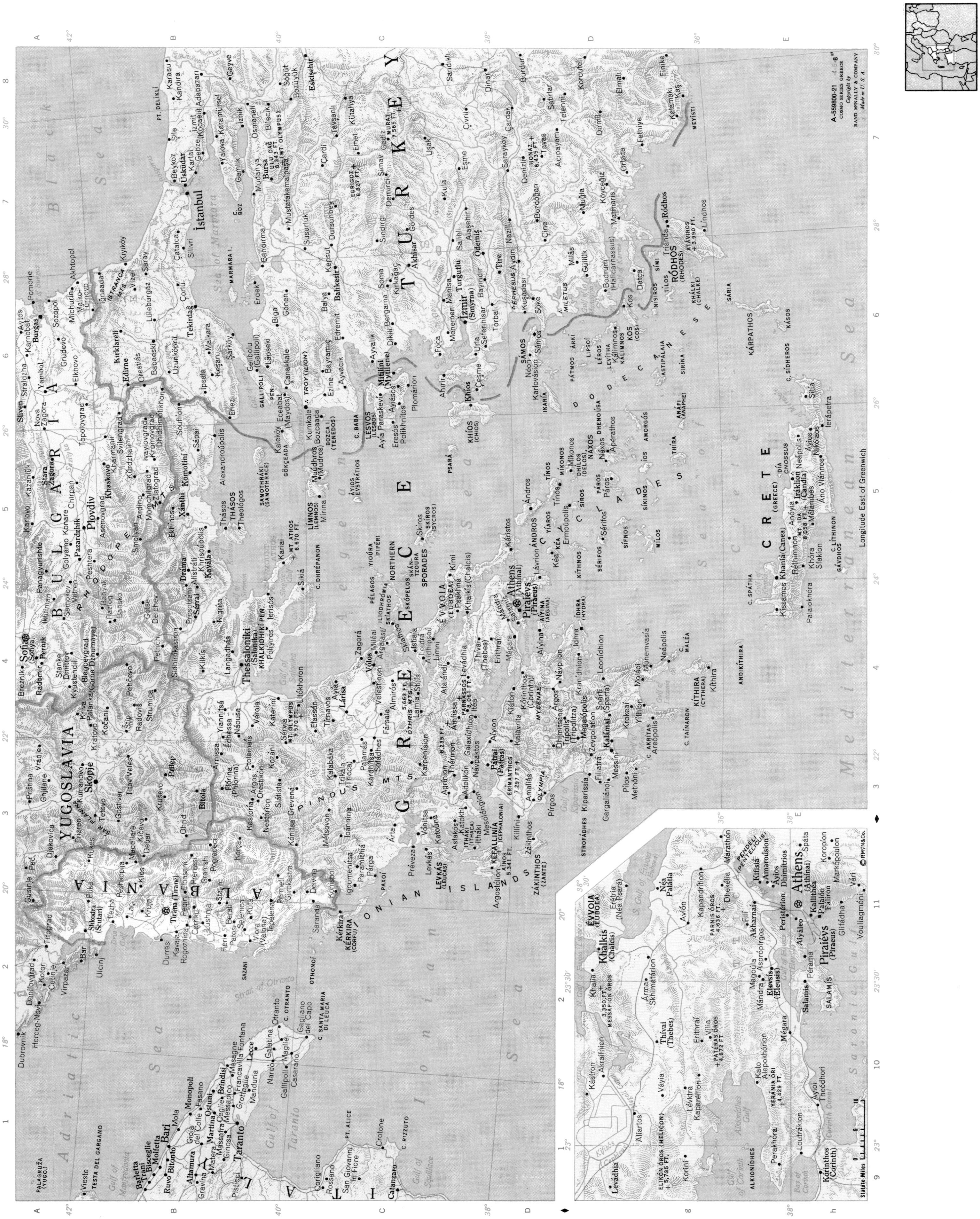

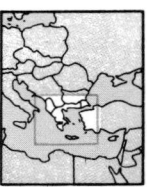

Conic Projection
SCALE 1:4,000,000  1 Inch = 63 Statute Miles

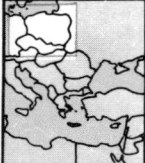

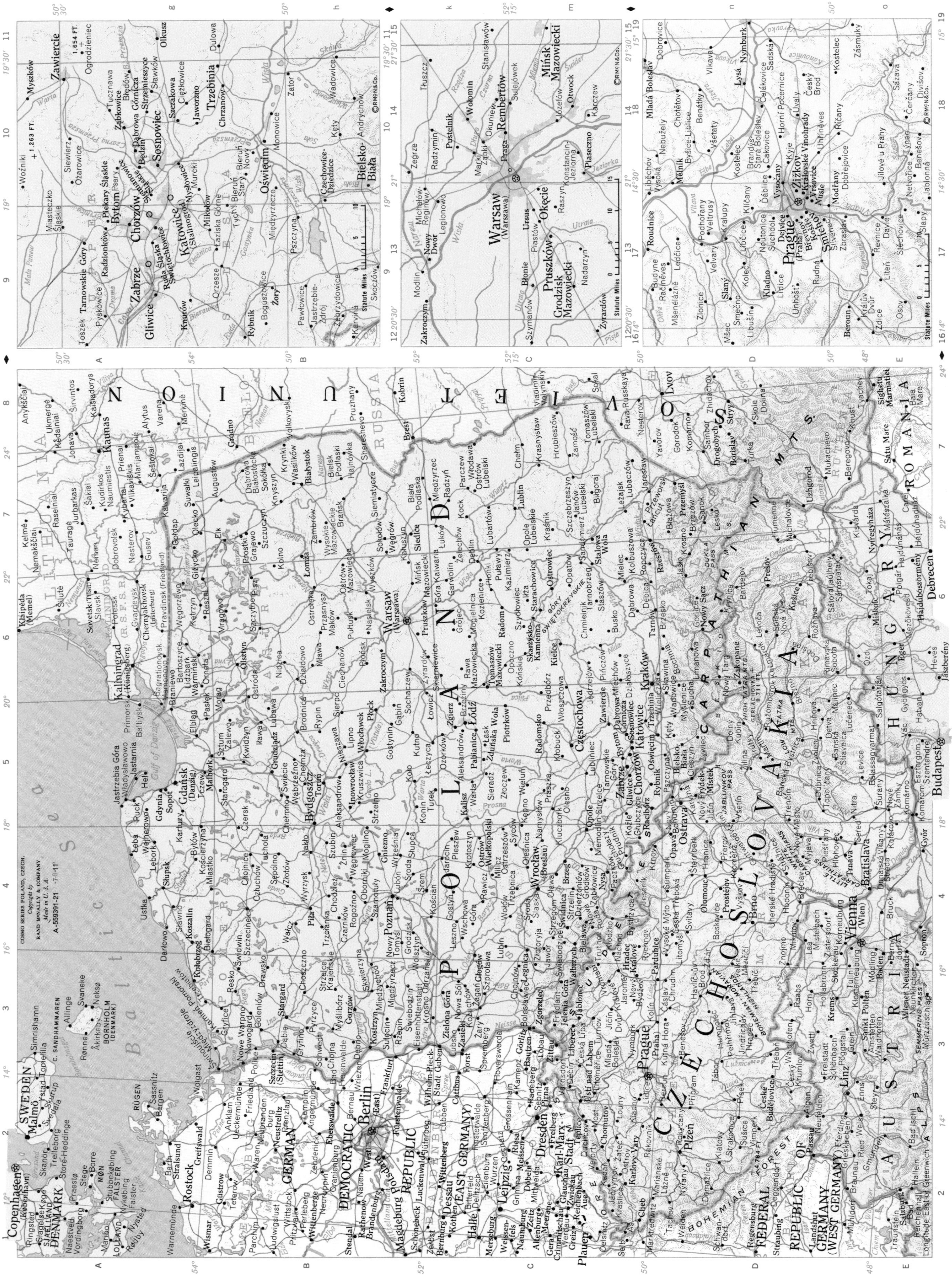

Statute Miles  25  0  25  50  75
Kilometers  25  0  25  50  100

Conic Projection
SCALE 1:4,000,000  1 Inch = 63 Statute Miles

COSMO SERIES POLAND, CZECH.
Copyright by
RAND McNALLY & COMPANY
Made in U.S.A.
A-559391-21

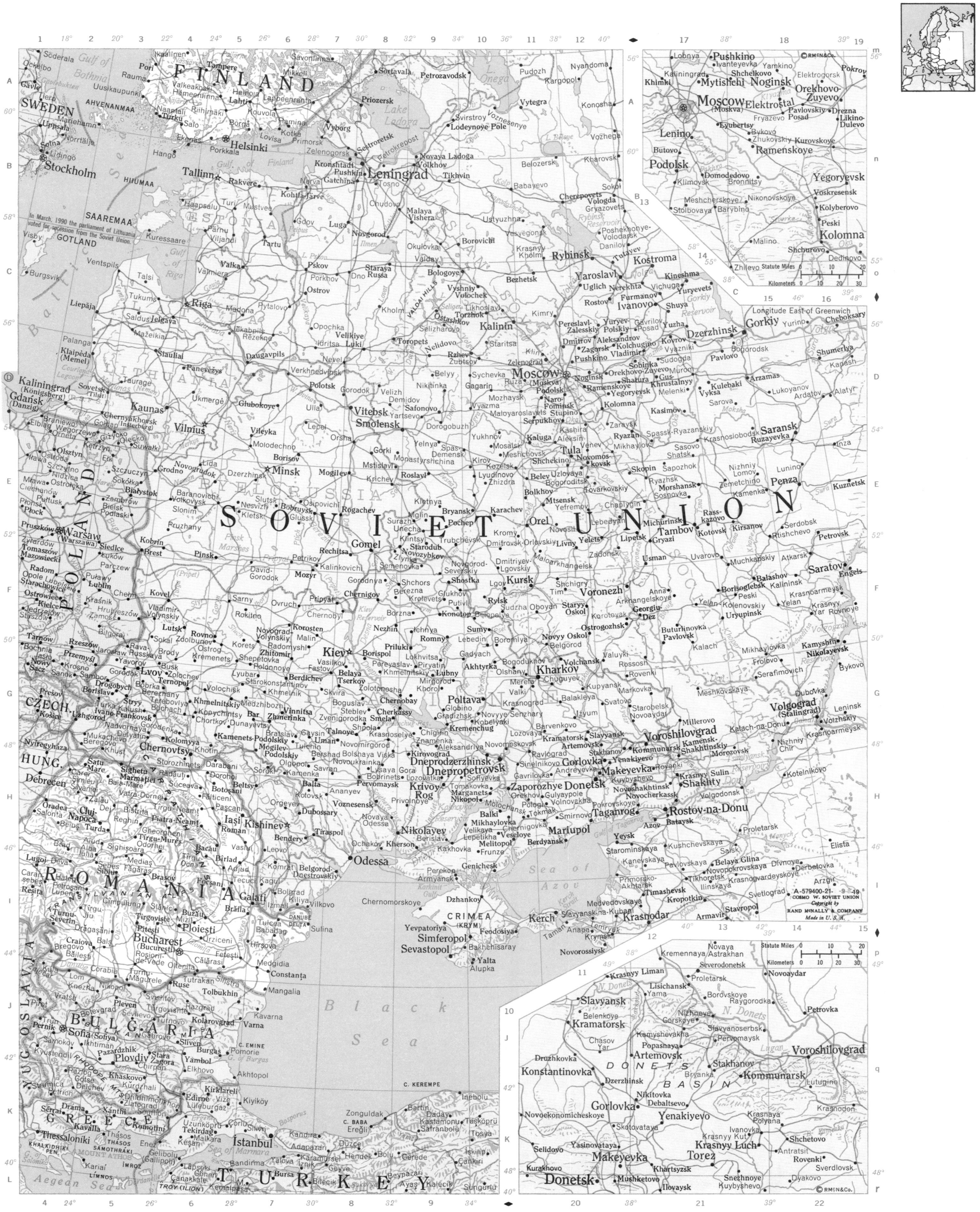

Statute Miles 50 0 50 100 150 200 250

Kilometers 50 0 50 100 150 200 250 300

Sinusoidal Projection

SCALE 1: 11,400,000    1 Inch = 180 Statute Miles

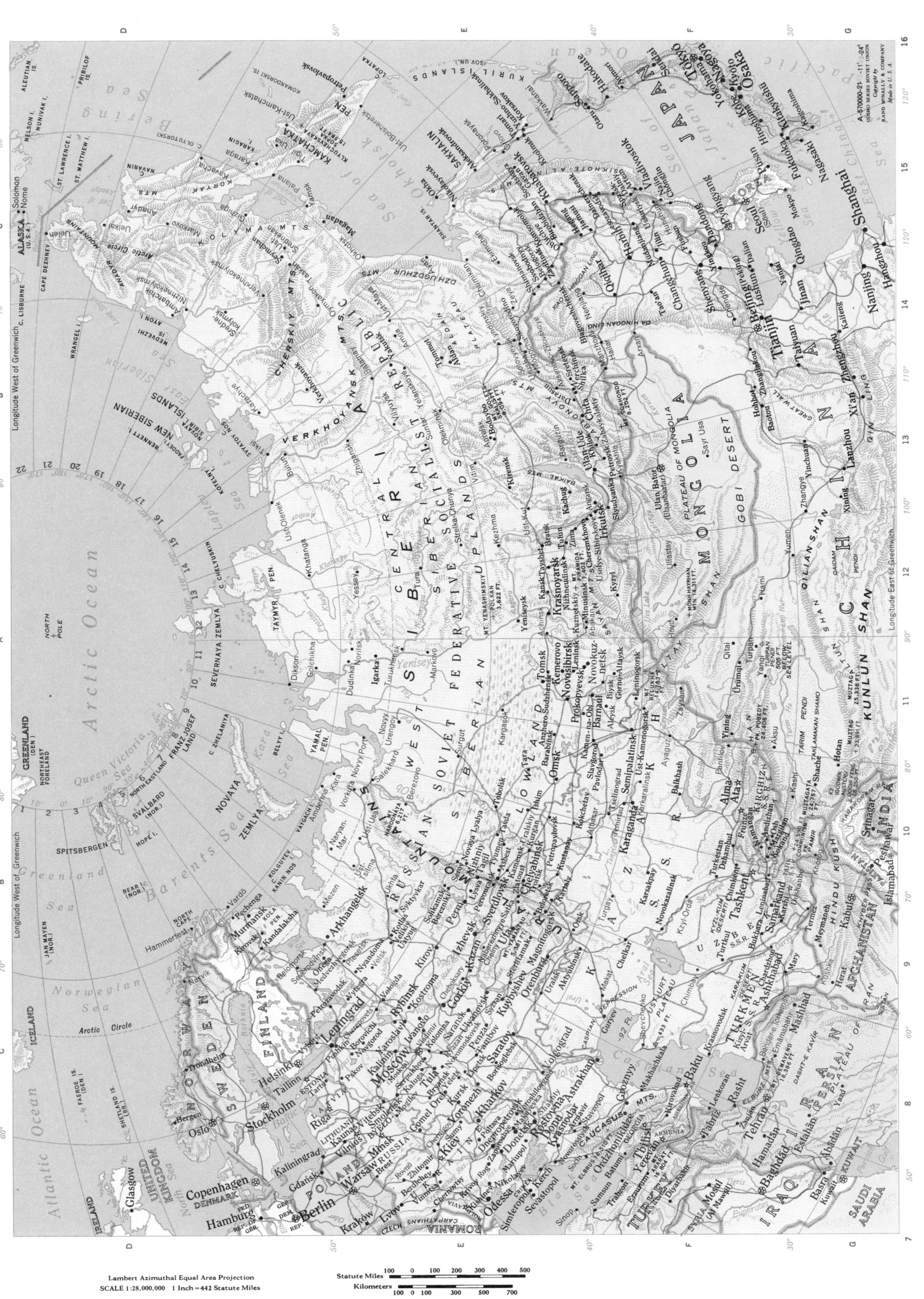

Lambert Azimuthal Equal Area Projection
SCALE 1:28,000,000   1 Inch = 442 Statute Miles

Statute Miles
100  0  100  200  300  400  500

Kilometers
100  0  100  300  500  700

A-570000-21 -111 -24°
RAND McNALLY & COMPANY
Copyright by
RAND McNALLY & COMPANY
Made in U.S.A.

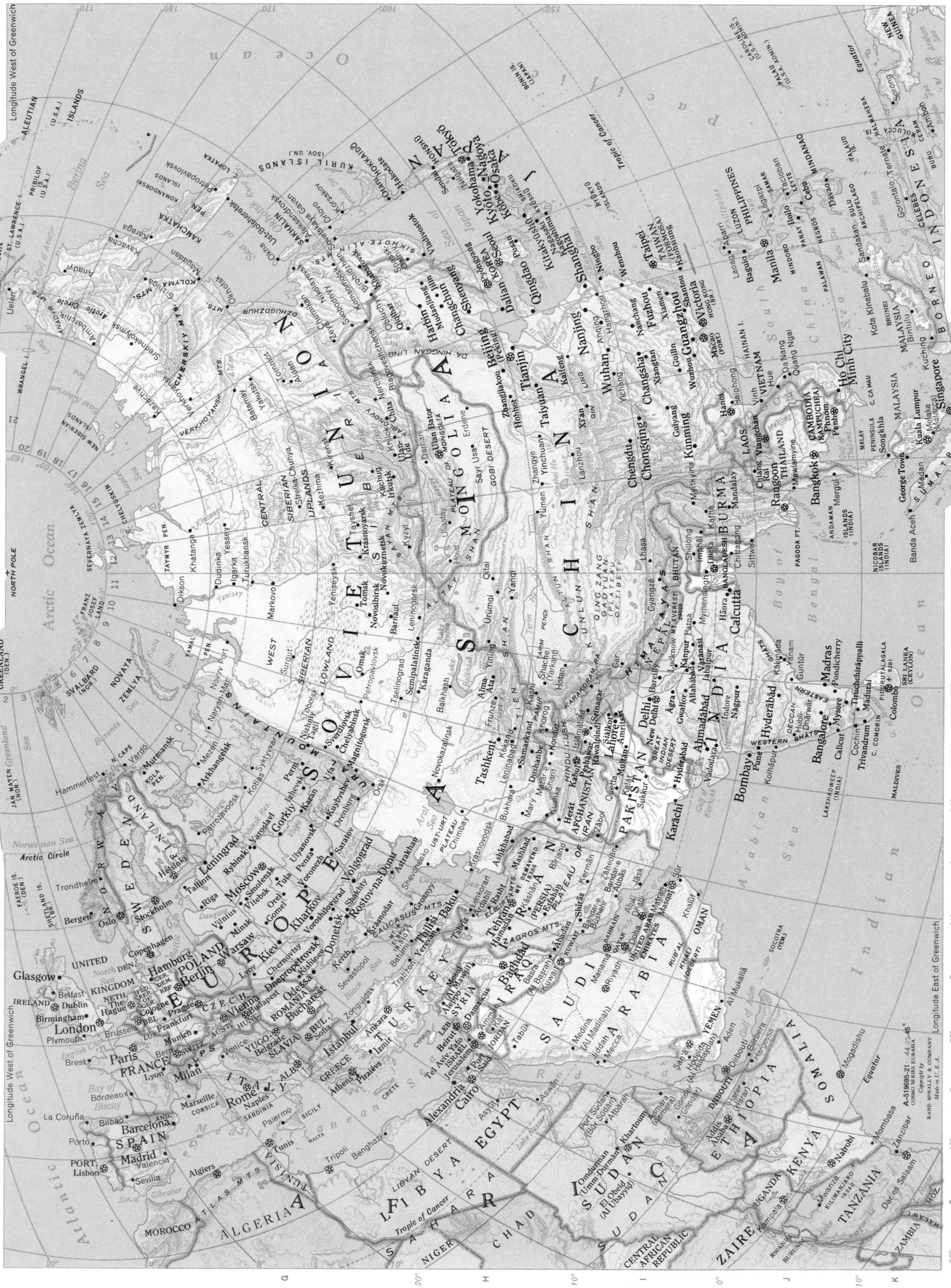

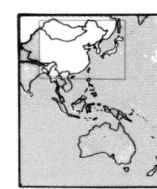

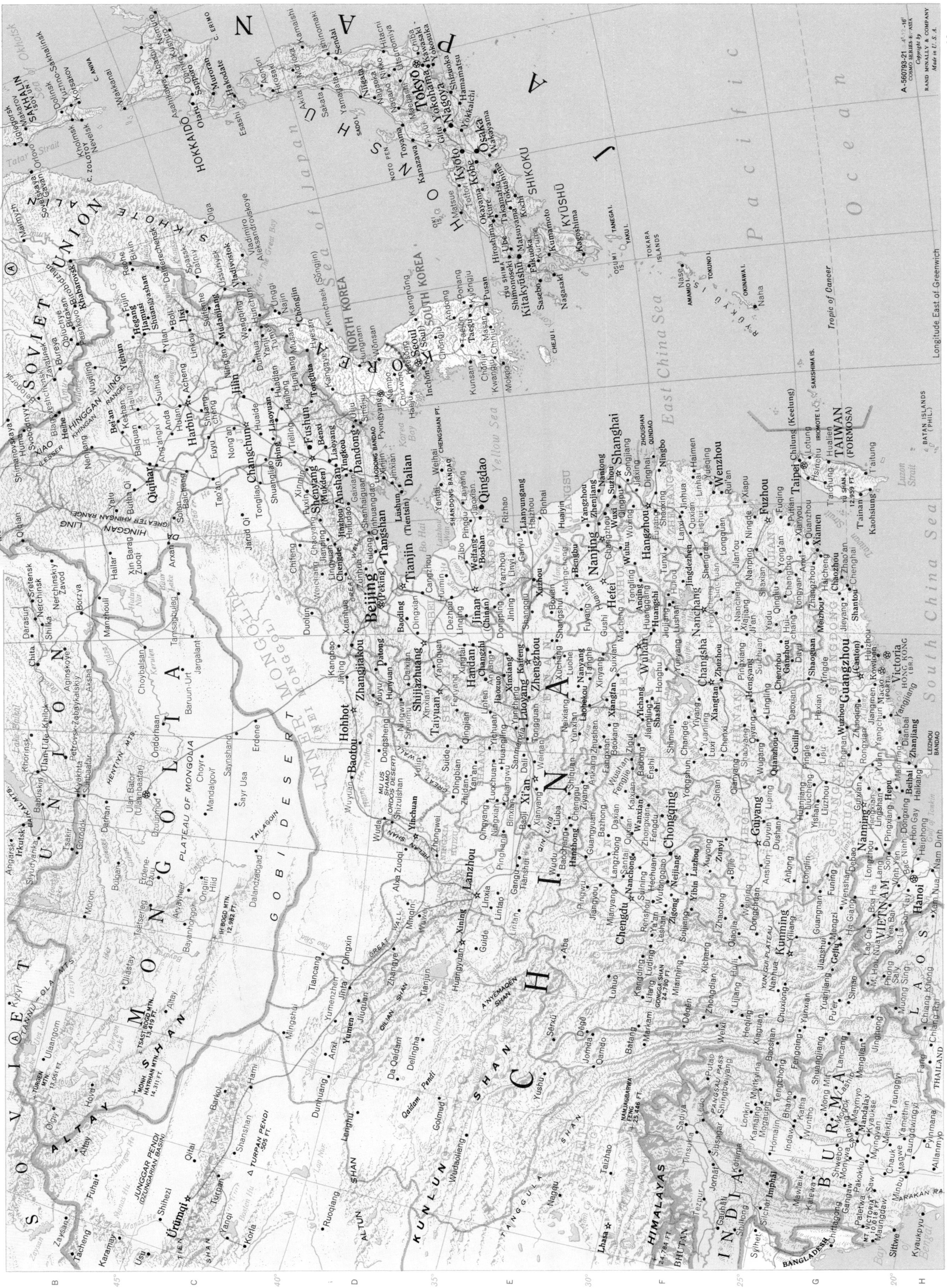

Polyconic Projection
SCALE 1:16,000,000 1 Inch = 252 Statute Miles

Statute Miles 100 0 100 200 300
Kilometers 100 0 100 200 300 400

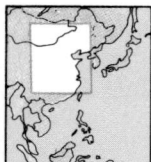

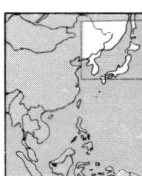

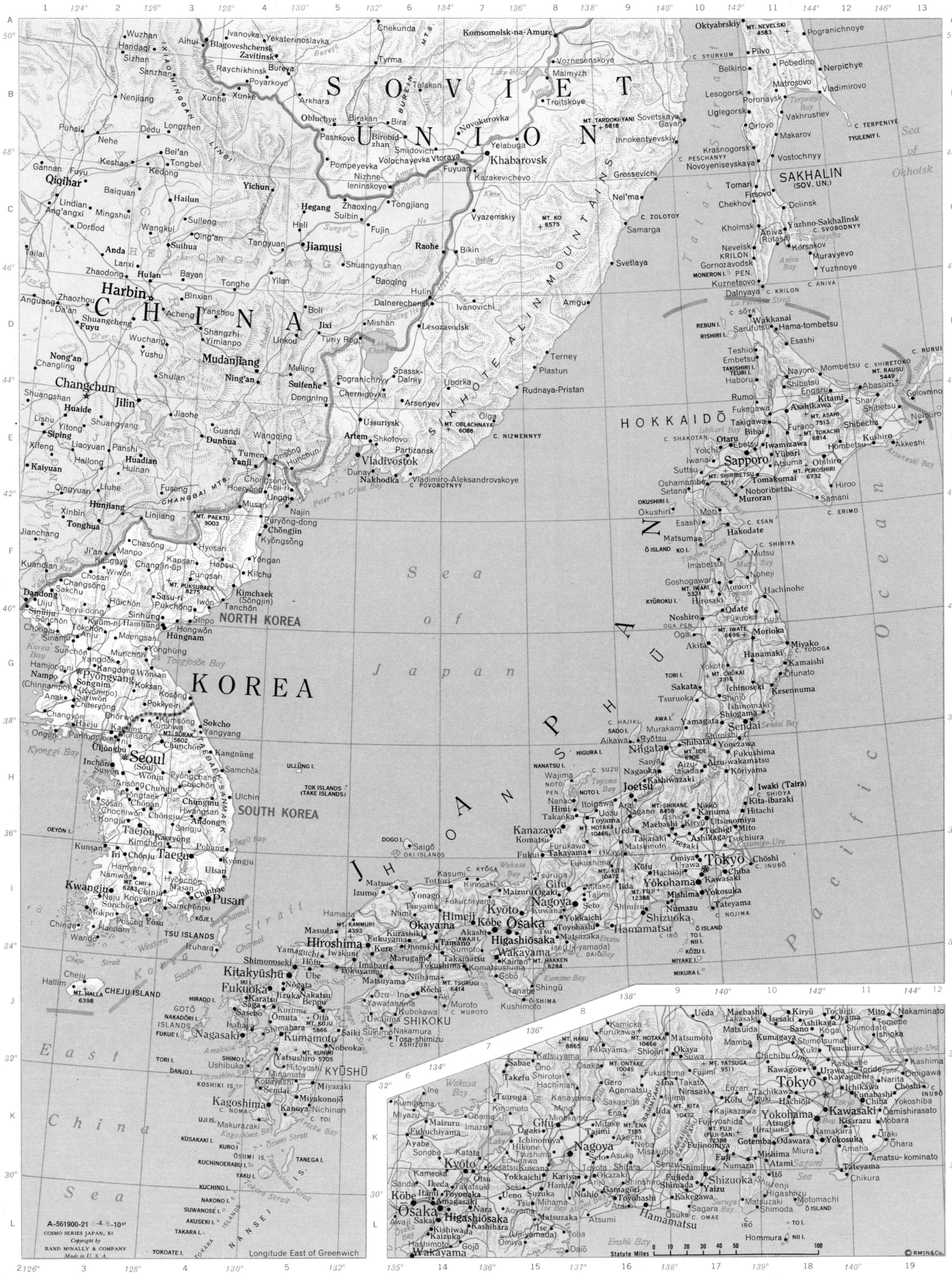

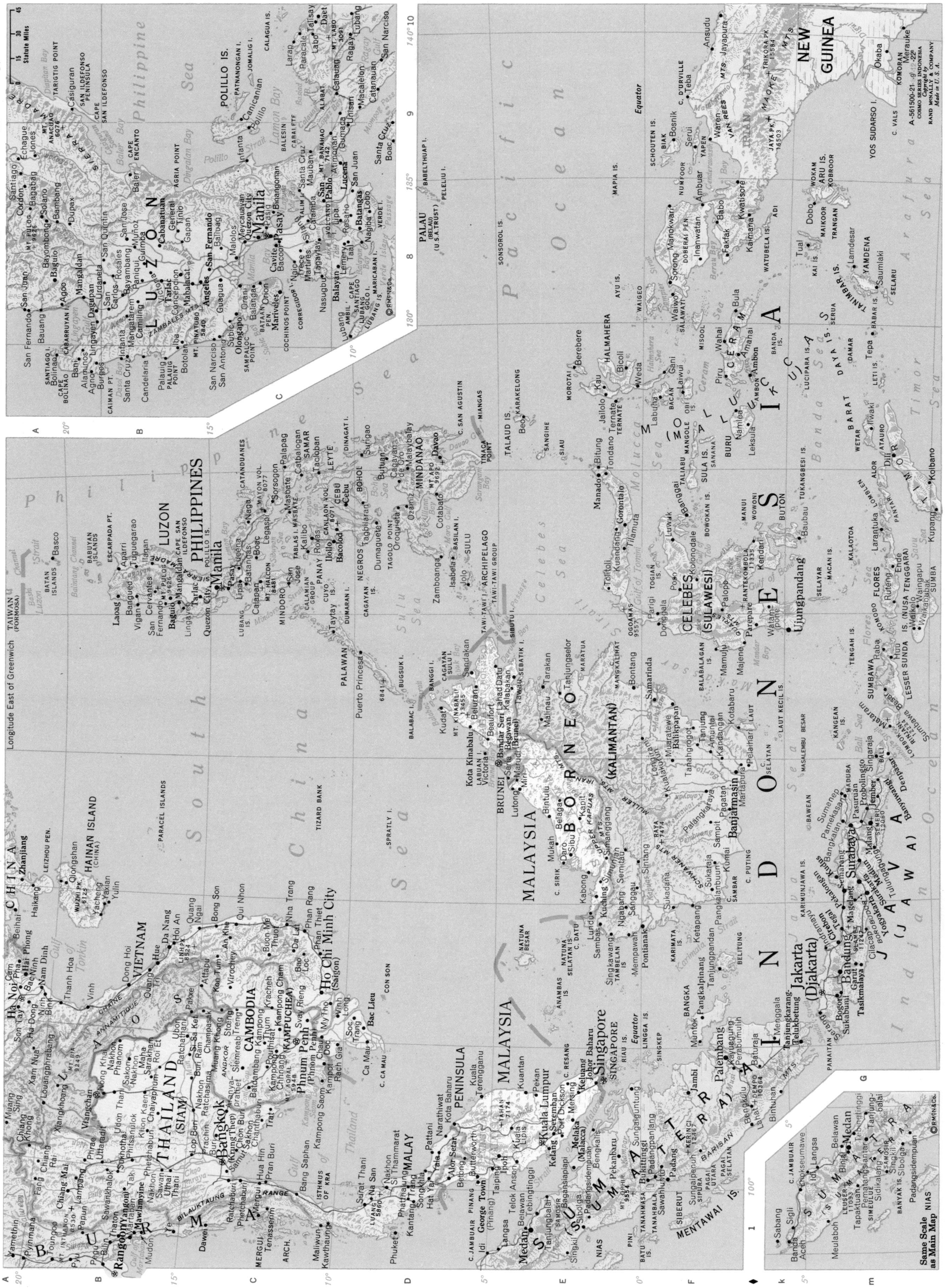

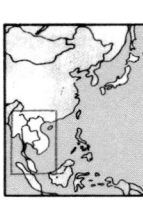

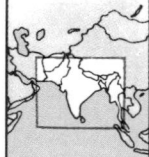

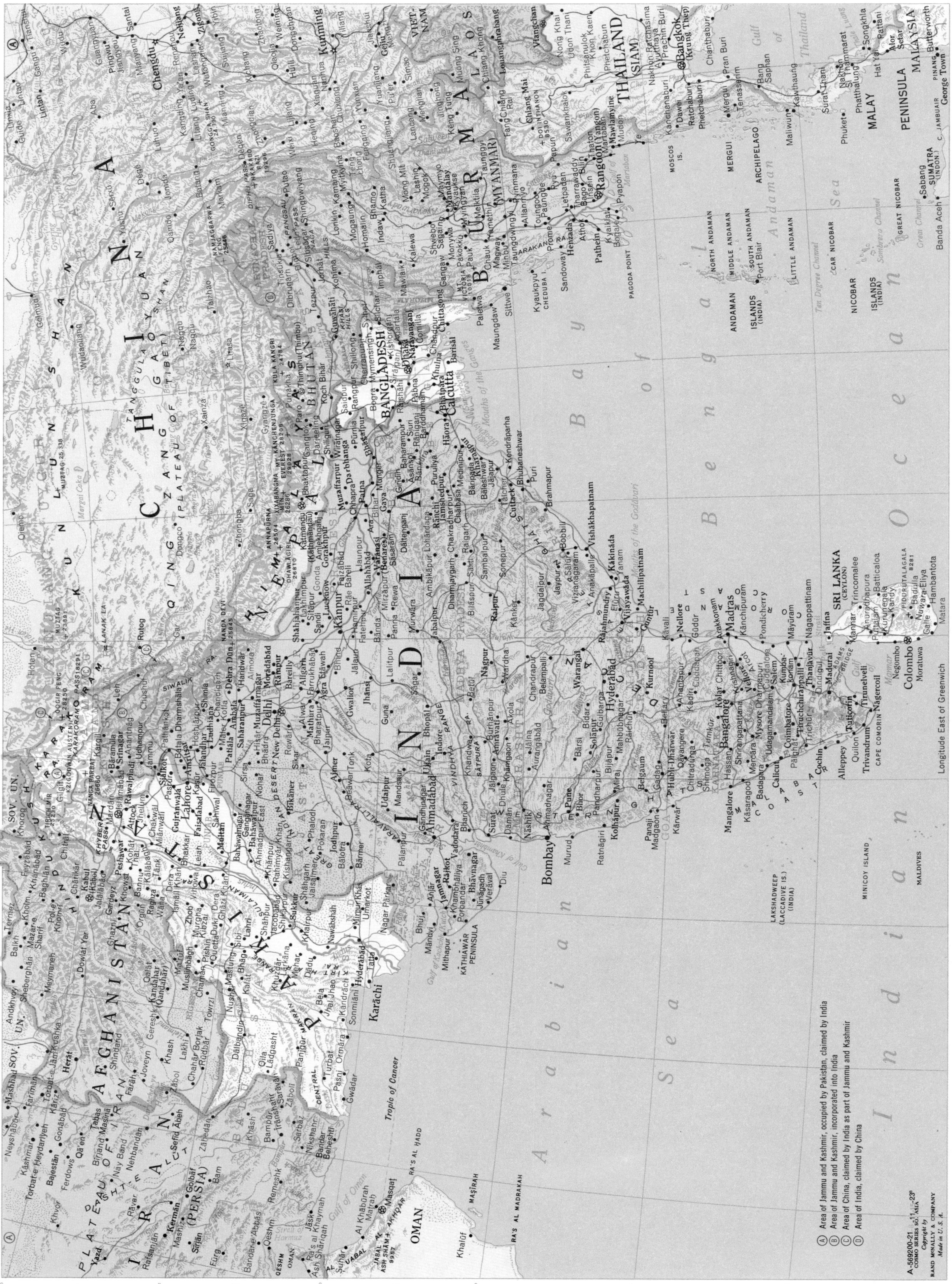

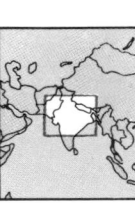

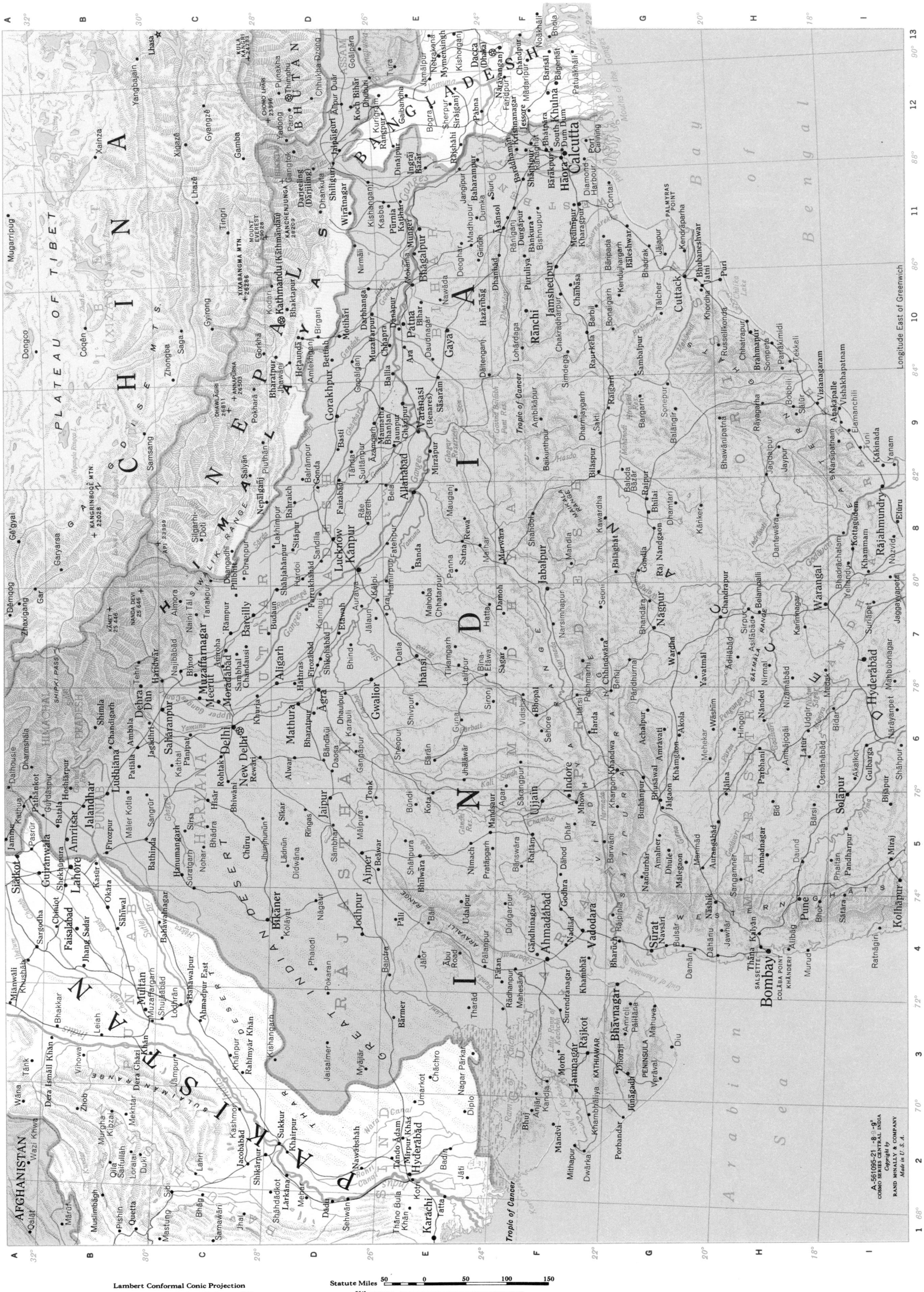


Lambert Conformal Conic Projection
SCALE 1 : 8,000,000 1 Inch = 126 Statute Miles

Statute Miles 50 0 50 100 150
Kilometers 50 0 50 100 200

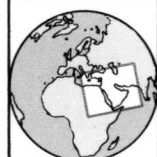

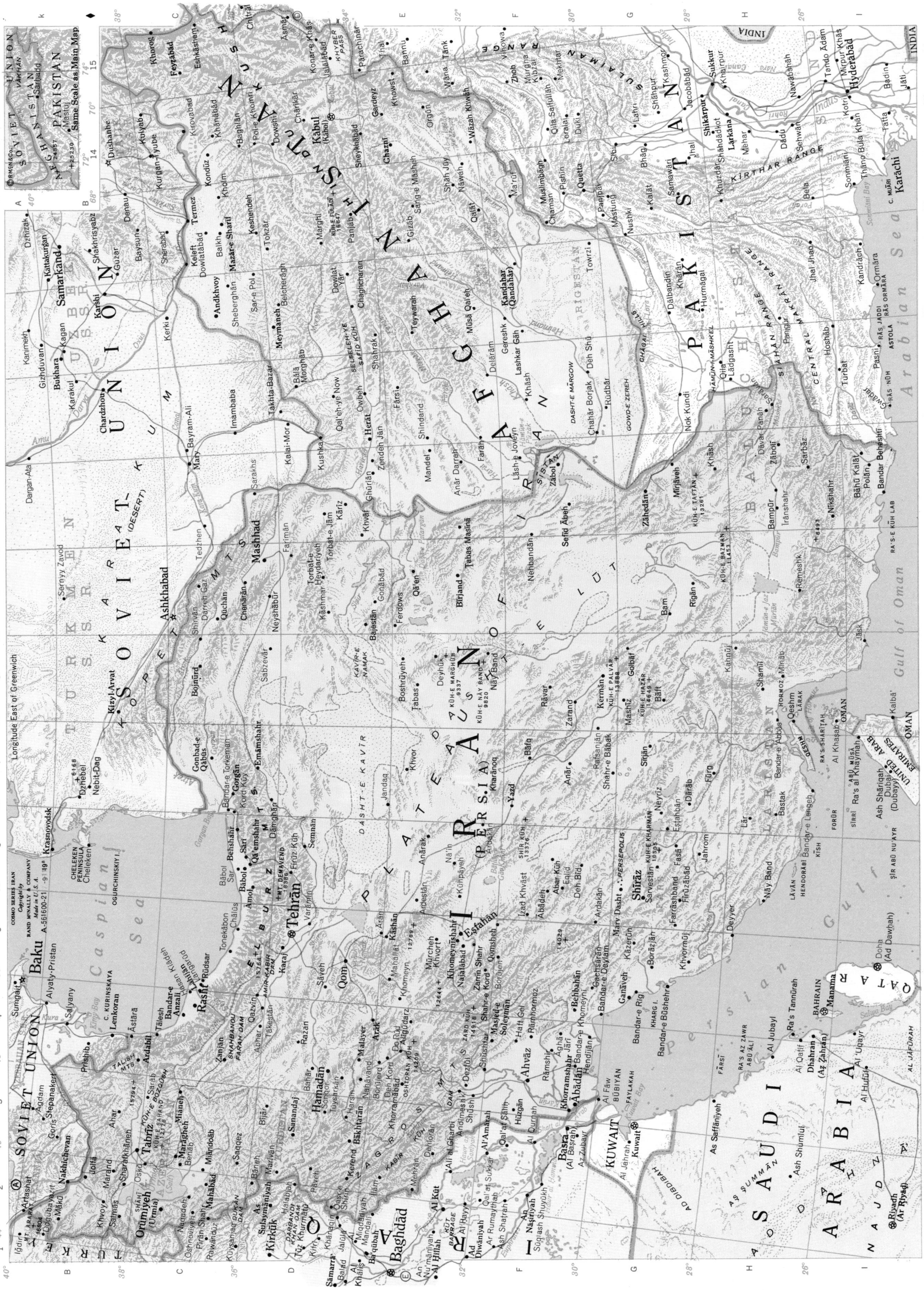

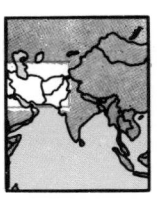

# IRAN AND AFGHANISTAN

SOVIET UNION

U Z B E K   S. S. R.

T U R K M E N   S. S. R.   (SOVIET)

A F G H A N I S T A N

P A K I S T A N

I R A N   (P E R S I A)

PLATEAU   OF   IRAN

DASHT-E KAVIR

DASHT-E LUT

SAUDI ARABIA

KUWAIT

QATAR

BAHRAIN

UNITED ARAB EMIRATES

OMAN

INDIA

TURKEY

Caspian Sea

Persian Gulf

Gulf of Oman

Arabian Sea

Longitude East of Greenwich

Lambert Conformal Conic Projection
SCALE 1 : 8,000,000   1 Inch = 126 Statute Miles

Statute Miles    50    0    50    100    150
Kilometers    50    0    50    100    200

COSMO SERIES IRAN
Copyrighted by
RAND McNALLY & COMPANY
MADE IN U.S.A.
A-561600-21 —9- 19!

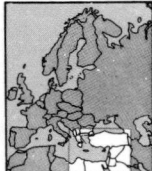

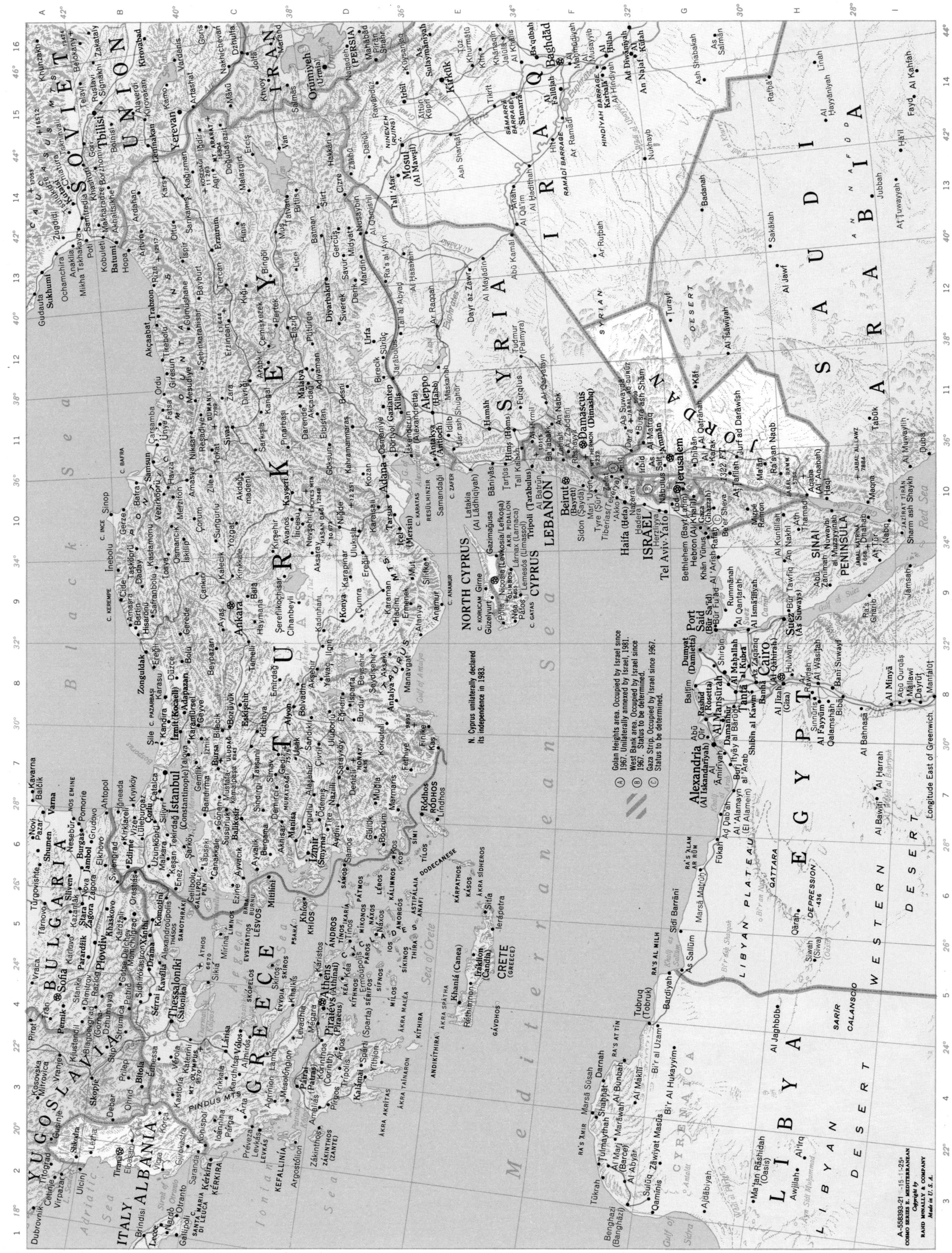

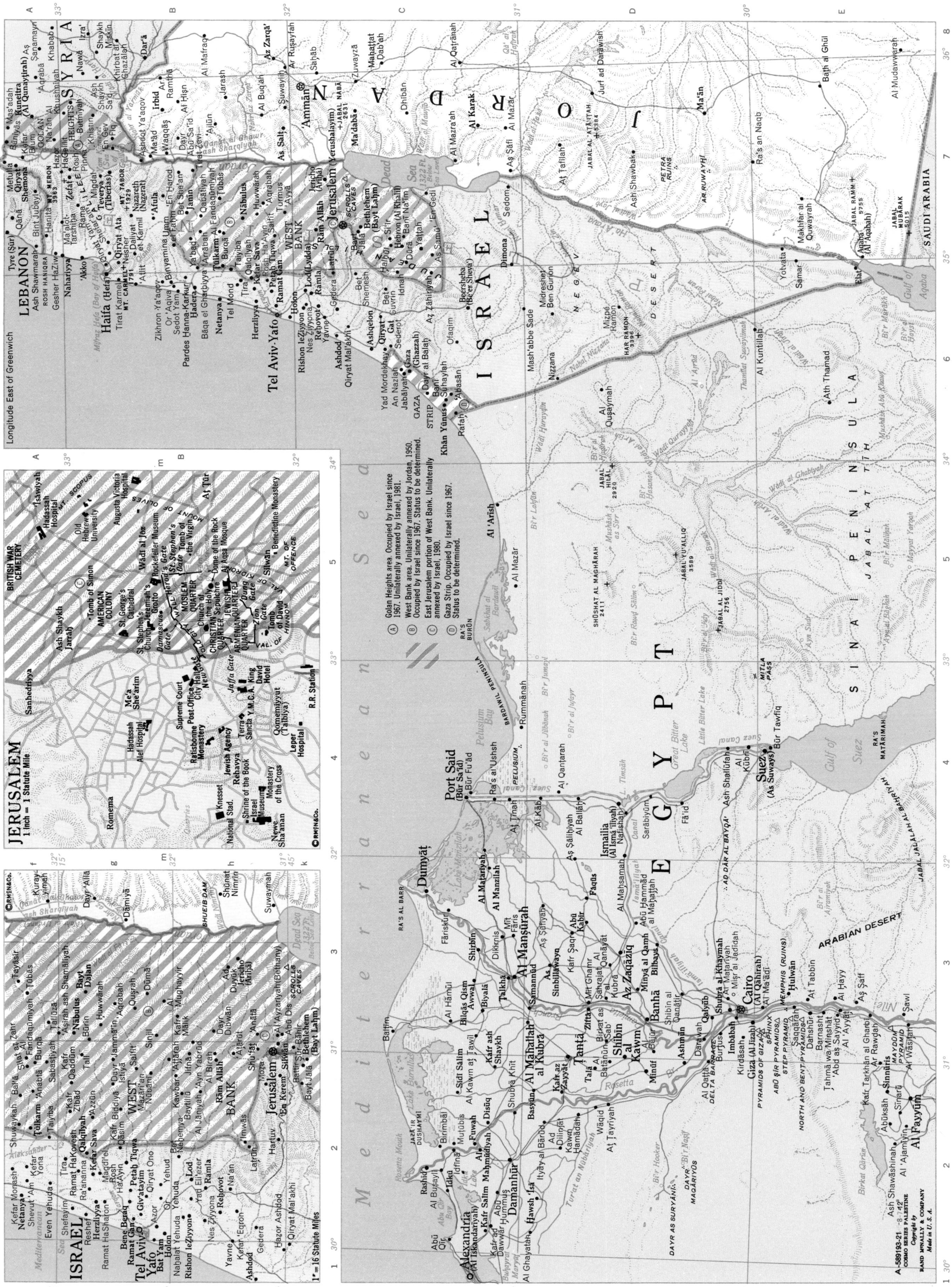

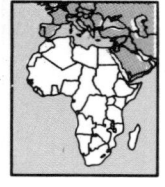

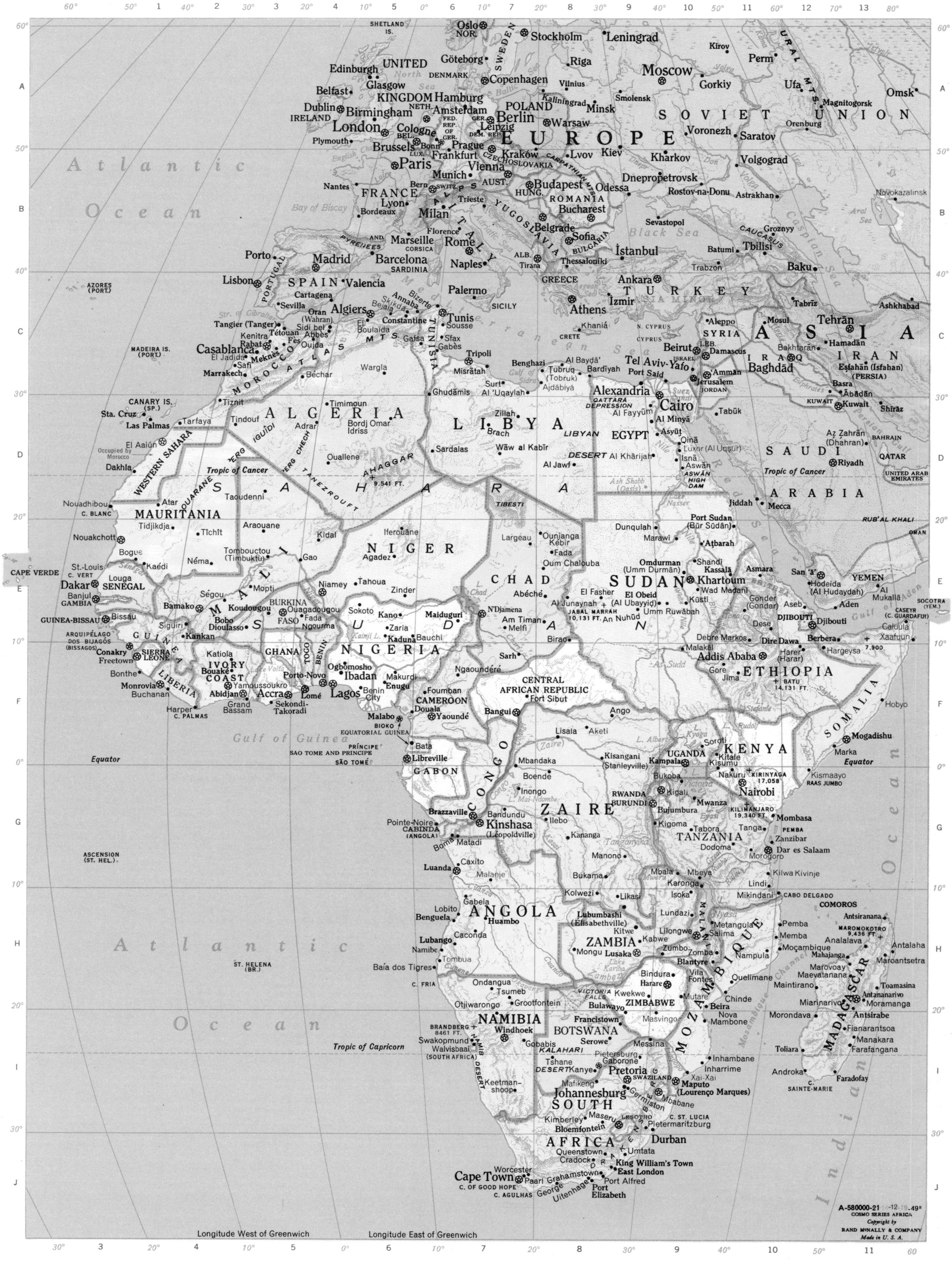

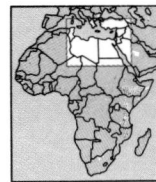

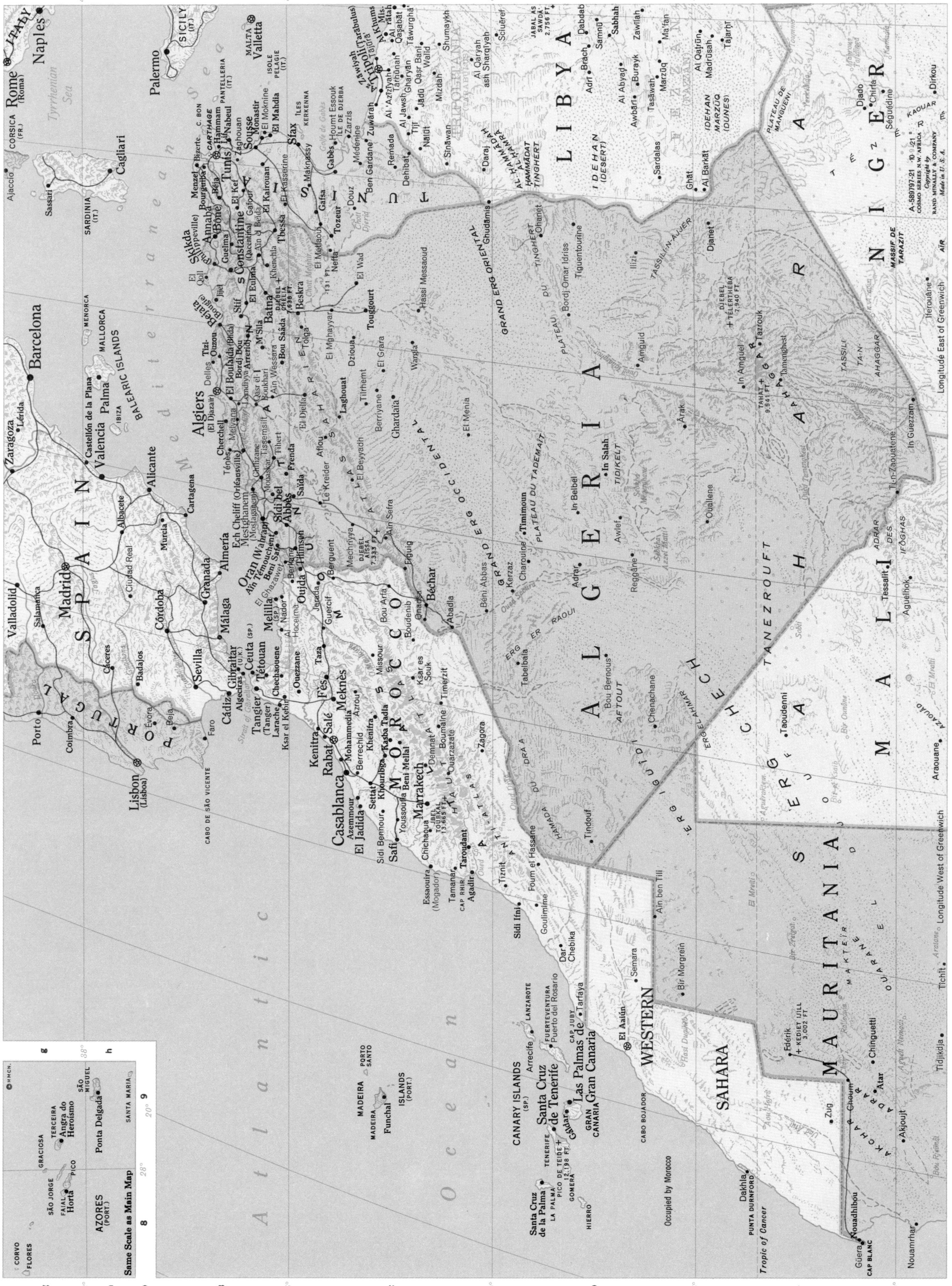

Statute Miles 50  25  0      50     100    150    200    250

50  0  50  100  150  200  250  300

Sinusoidal Projection
SCALE 1 : 11,400,000      1 Inch = 180 Statute Miles

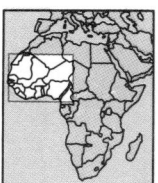

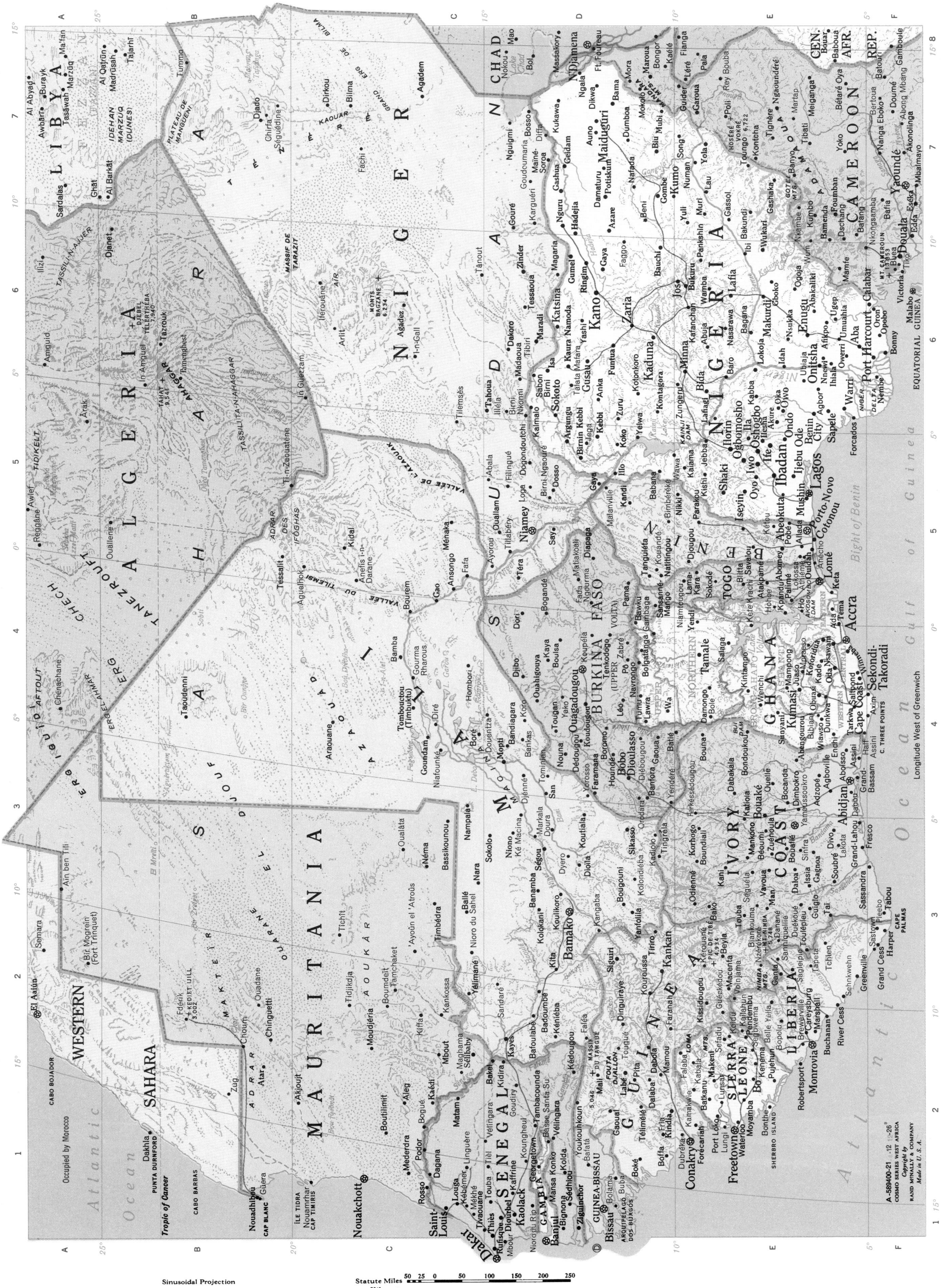

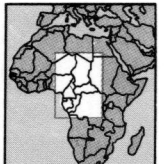

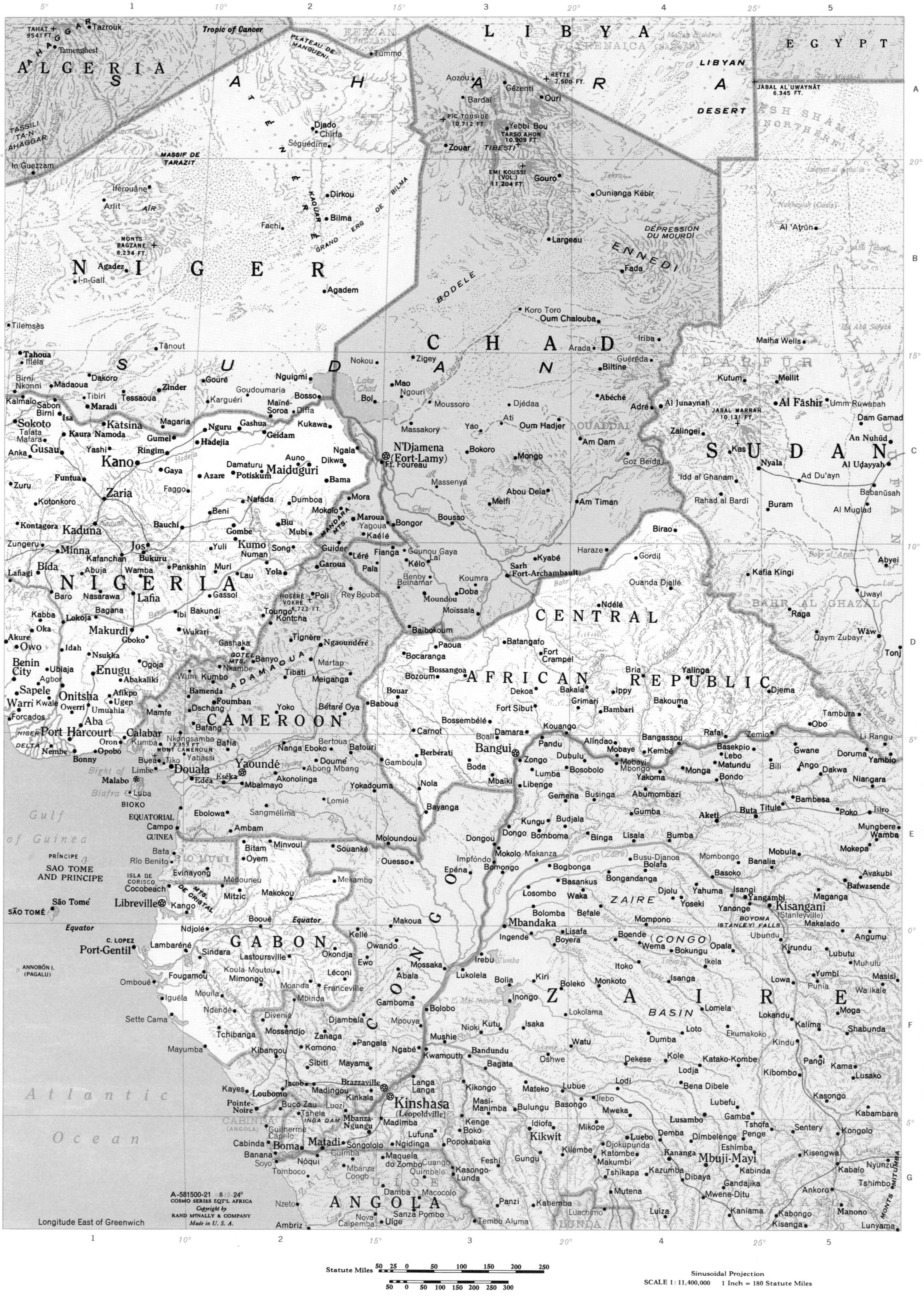

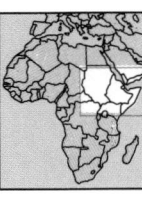

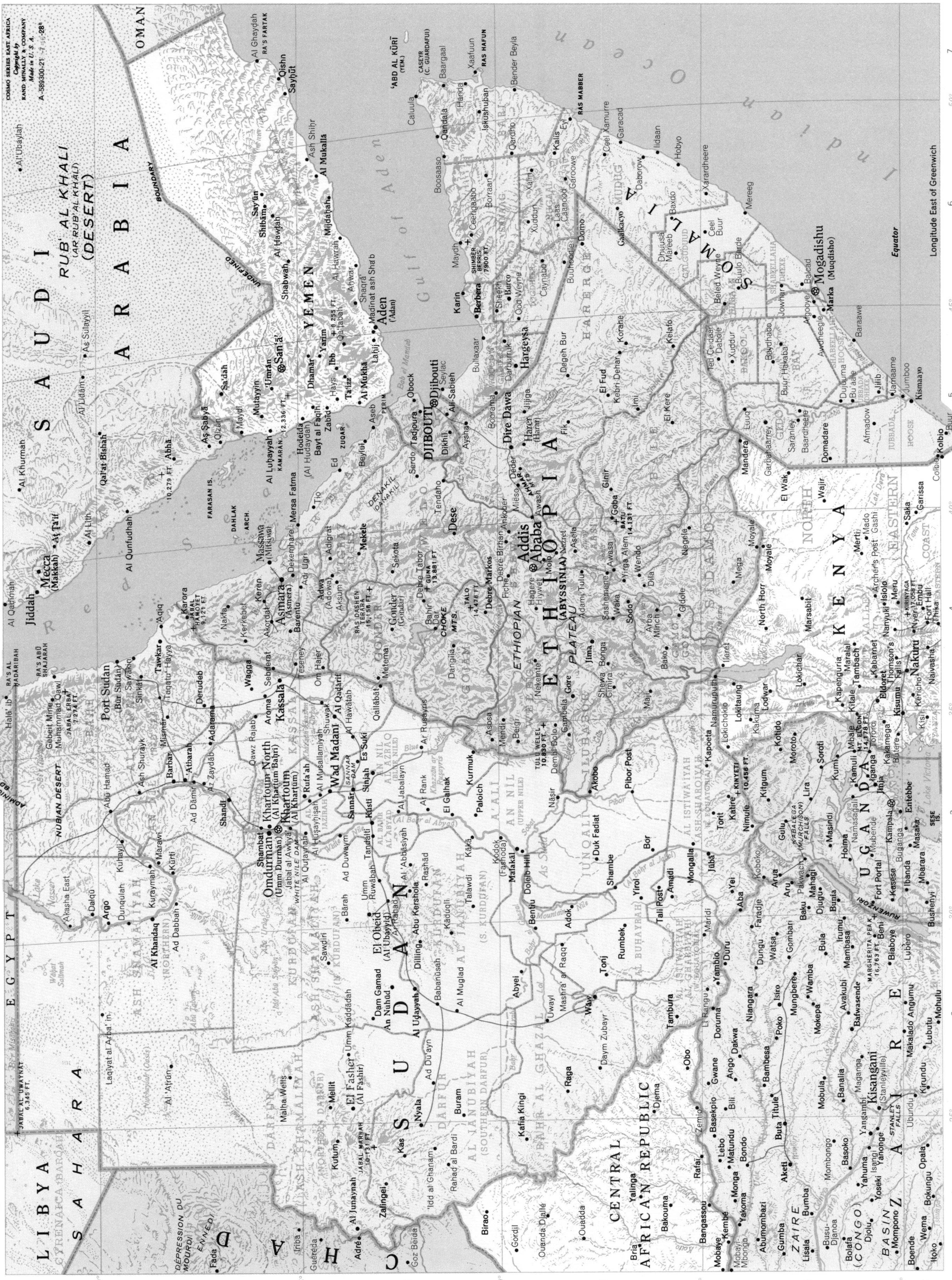


Sinusoidal Projection
SCALE 1 : 11,400,000   1 Inch = 180 Statute Miles

Statute Miles 50 25 0 50 100 150 200 250
Kilometers 50 0 50 100 150 200 250 300

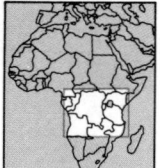

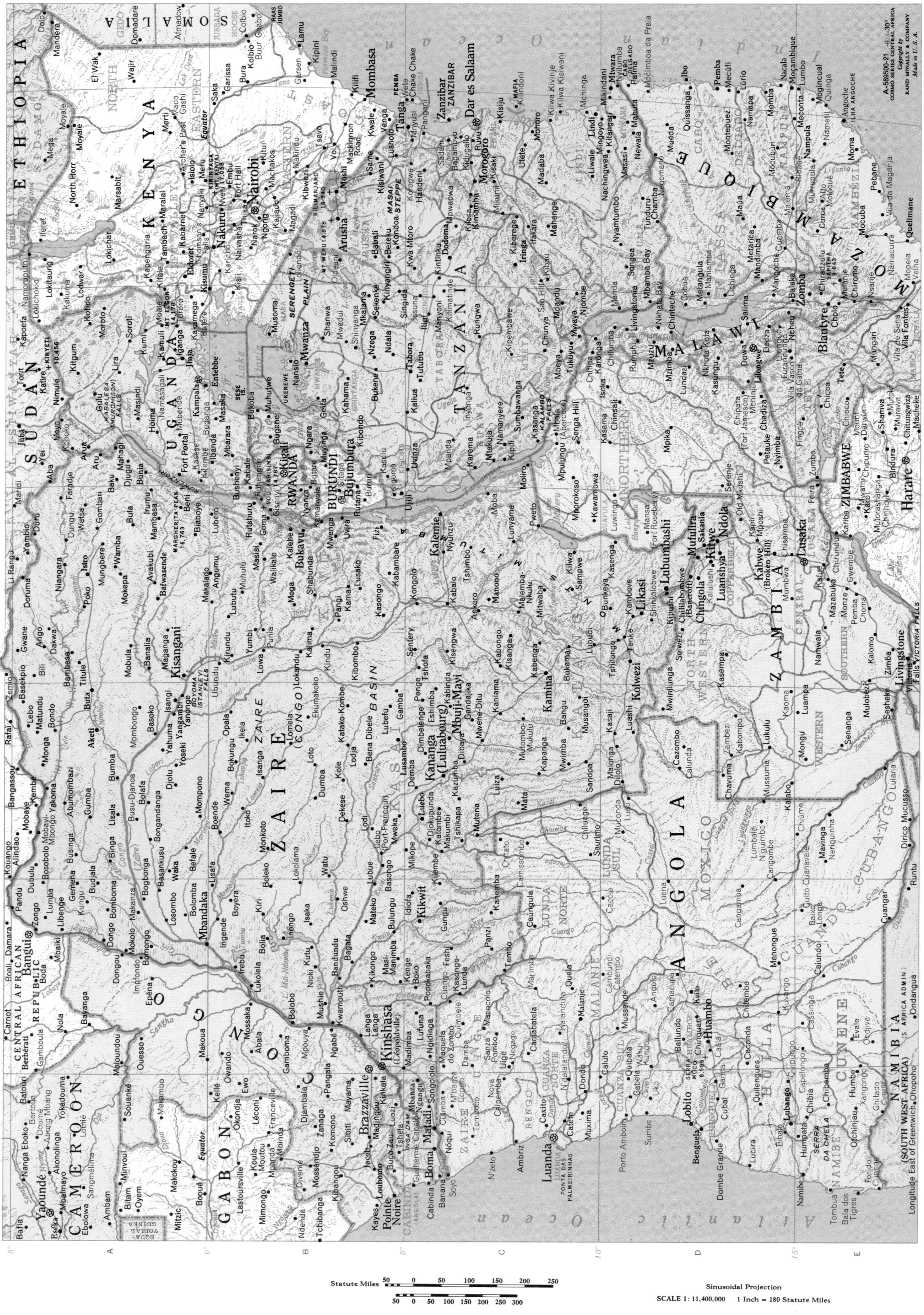

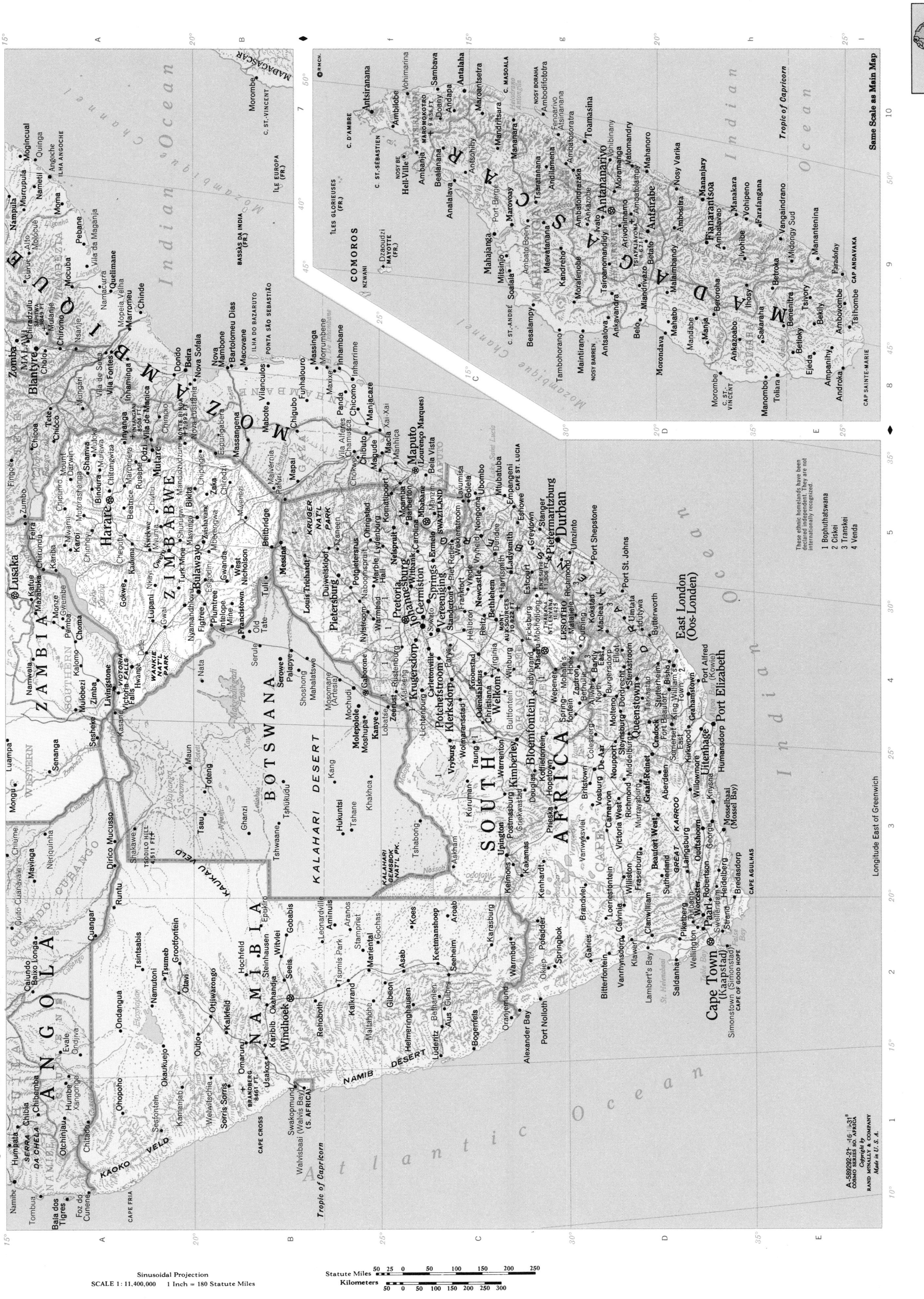

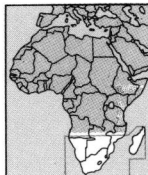

Same Scale as Main Map

These ethnic homelands have been declared independent. They are not internationally recognized.

1 Bophuthatswana
2 Ciskei
3 Transkei
4 Venda

A-589292-2t -16 I -31"
COSMO SERIES SO. AFRICA
Copyright by
RAND MCNALLY & COMPANY
Made in U.S.A.

Sinusoidal Projection
SCALE 1:11,400,000   1 Inch = 180 Statute Miles

Statute Miles   50 25 0   50   100   150   200   250
Kilometers   50 0 50 100 150 200 250 300

Longitude East of Greenwich

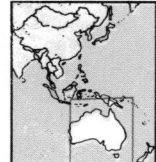

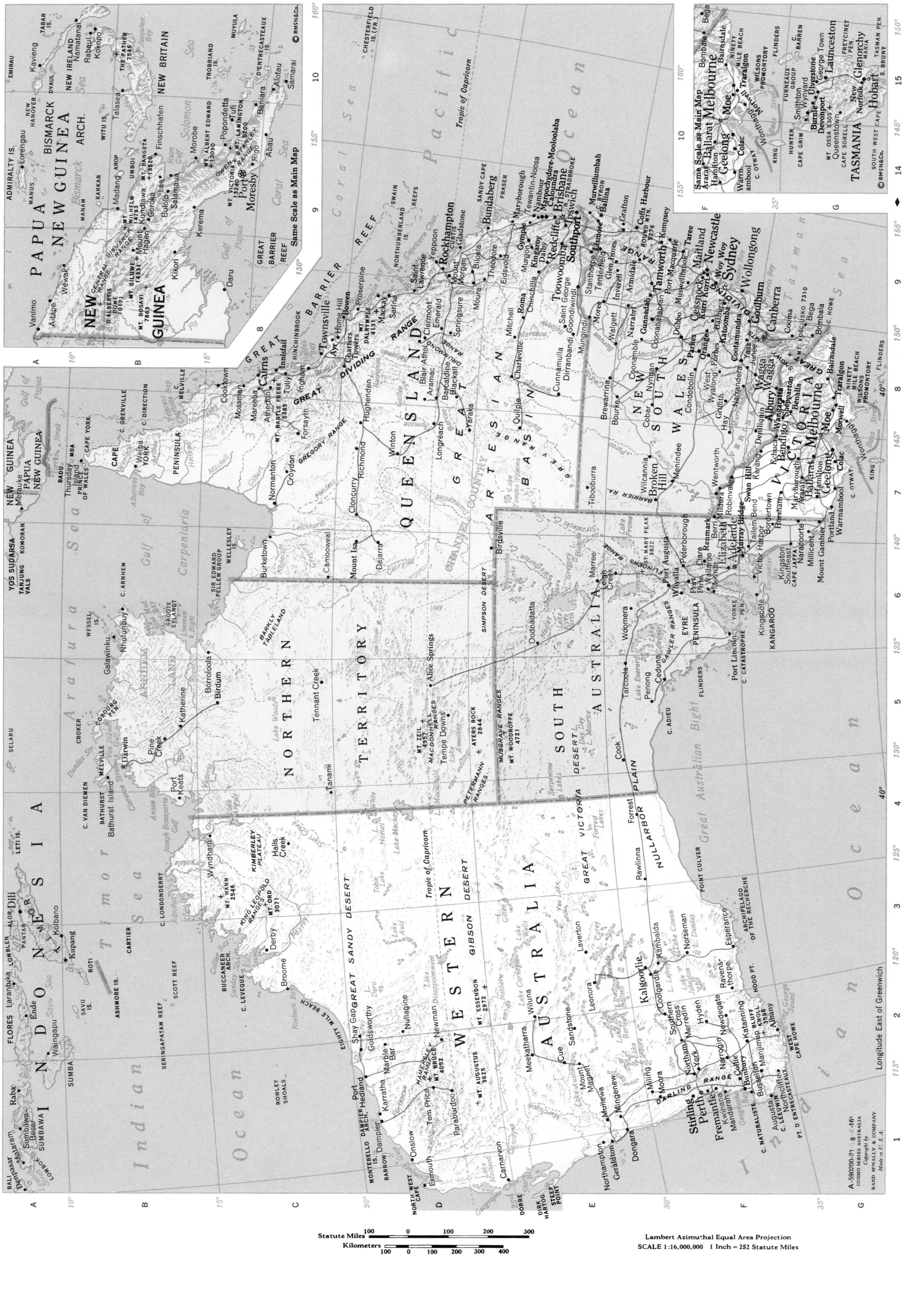

Statute Miles 100 0 100 200 300

Kilometers 100 0 100 200 300 400

Lambert Azimuthal Equal Area Projection

SCALE 1:16,000,000 1 Inch = 252 Statute Miles

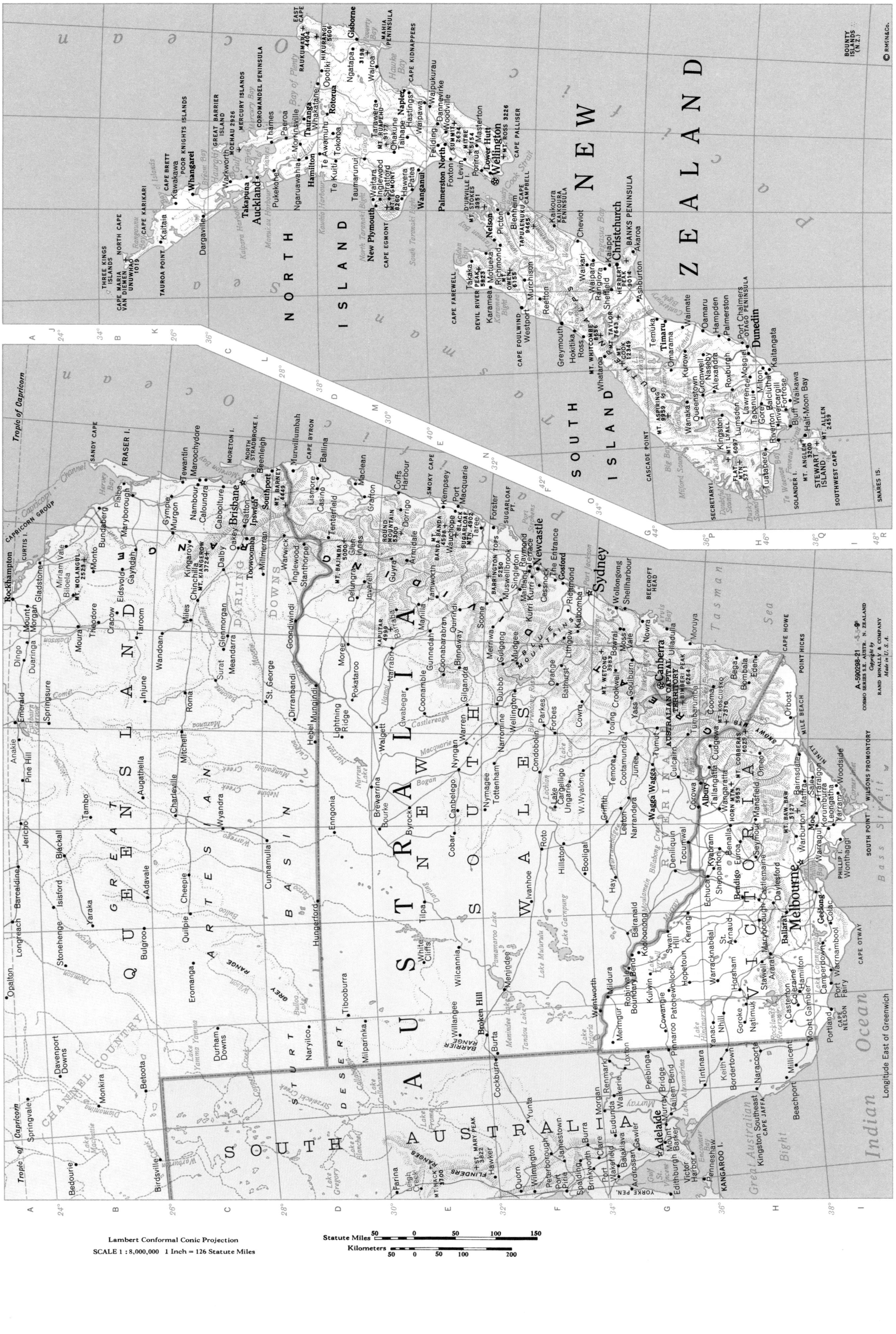

NORTH ISLAND

SOUTH ISLAND

NEW ZEALAND

QUEENSLAND

NEW SOUTH WALES

SOUTH AUSTRALIA

VICTORIA

Tasman Sea

Indian Ocean

Lambert Conformal Conic Projection
SCALE 1 : 8,000,000   1 Inch = 126 Statute Miles

Statute Miles
50   0   50   100   150

Kilometers
50   0   50   100   200

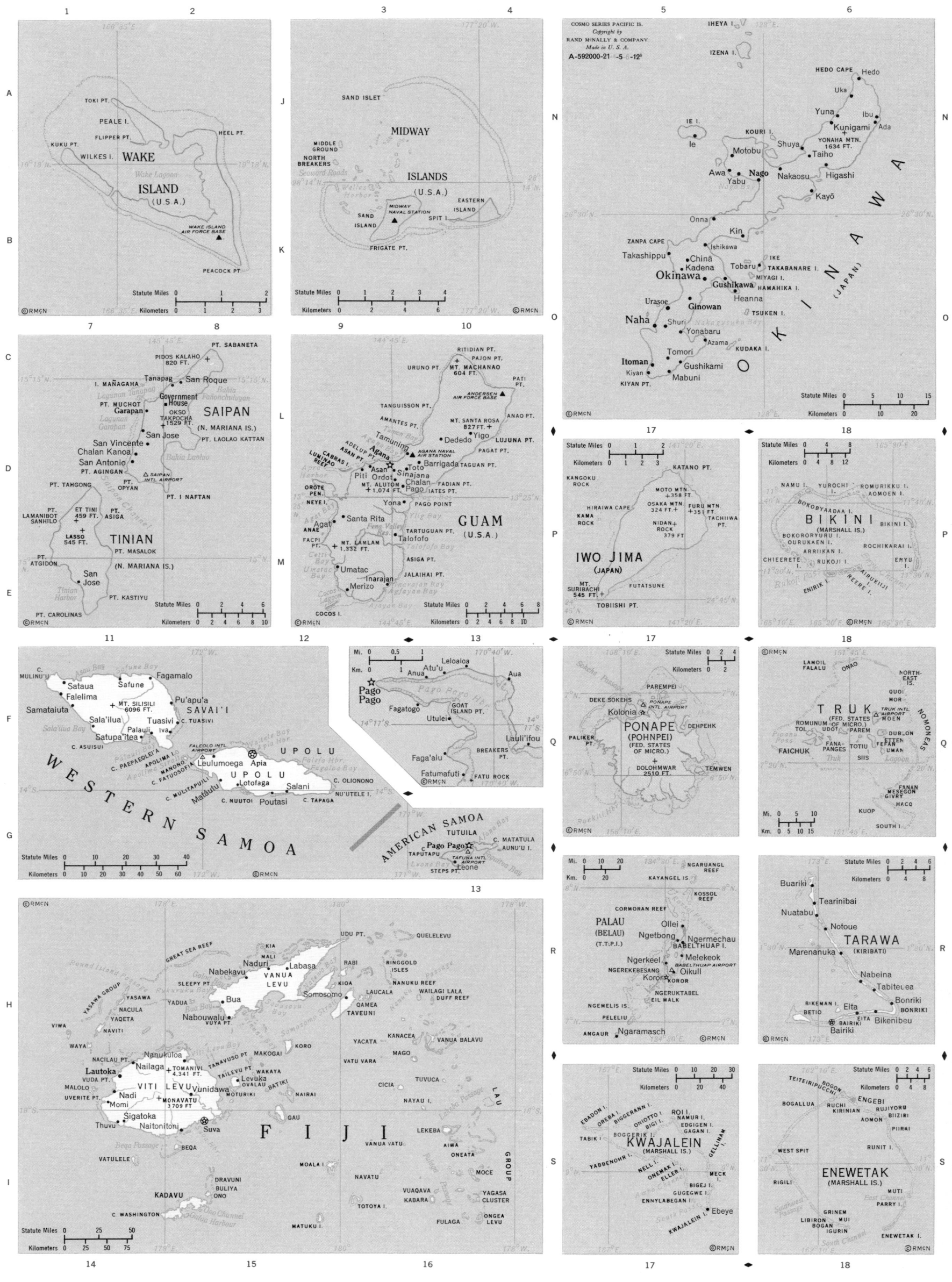

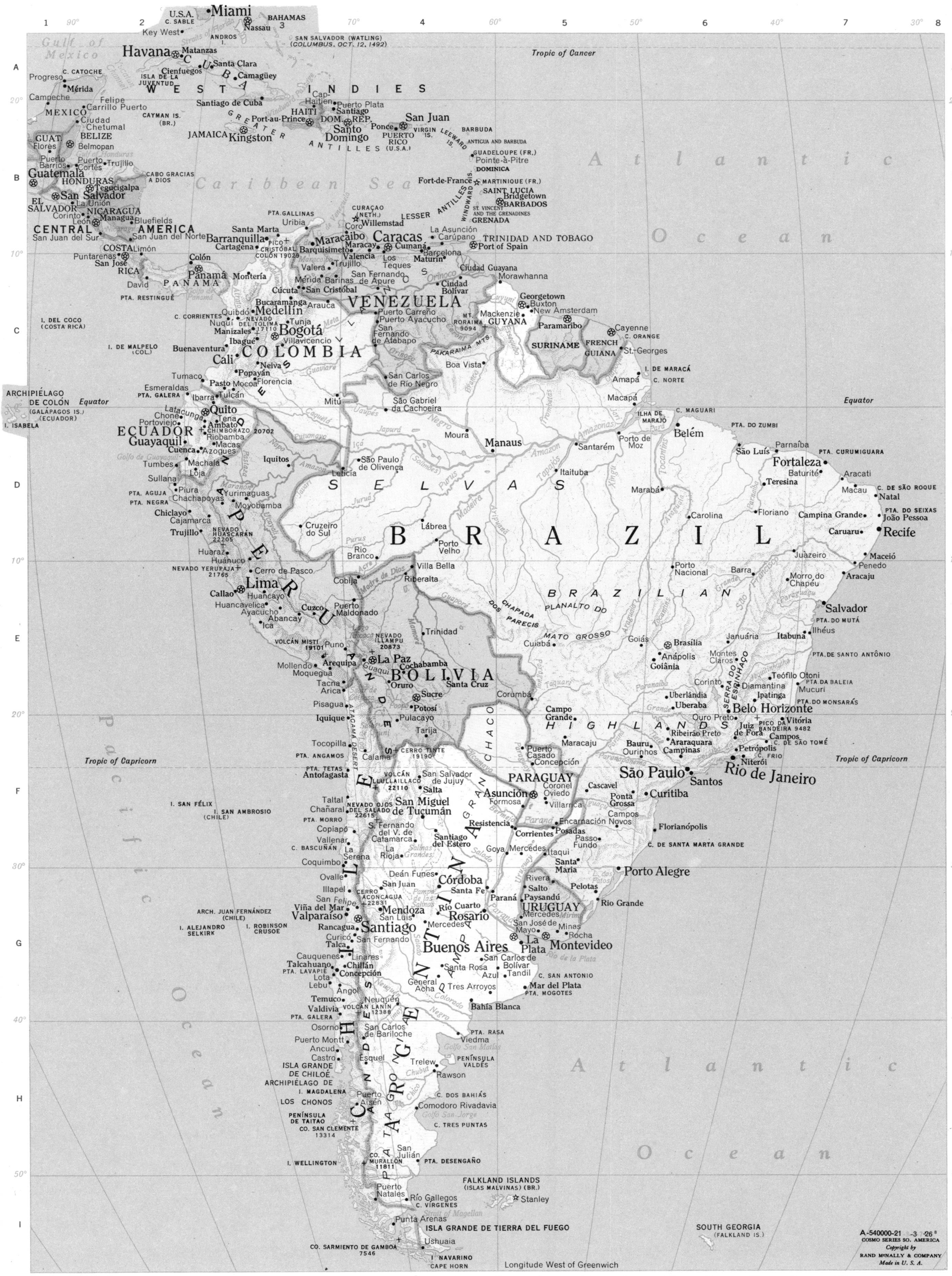

Miami · Key West · BAHAMAS · Nassau · ANDROS
Gulf of Mexico · C. SABLE · SAN SALVADOR (WATLING) (COLUMBUS, OCT. 12, 1492) · Tropic of Cancer
Havana · Matanzas · Santa Clara · Camagüey · Santiago de Cuba
WEST · INDIES
Progreso · C. CATOCHE · ISLA DE LA JUVENTUD · CAYMAN IS. (BR.) · JAMAICA · Kingston · HAITI · Port-au-Prince · DOM. REP. · Santo Domingo · Ponce · San Juan · PUERTO RICO (U.S.A.) · VIRGIN IS.
Campeche · Mérida · Felipe · Carrillo Puerto · Ciudad · Chetumal
MEXICO · GUAT. · Flores · BELIZE · Belmopan
Puerto Barrios · Puerto Cortés · Trujillo · CABO GRACIAS A DIOS
Guatemala · HONDURAS · Tegucigalpa
EL SALVADOR · San Salvador · La Unión · NICARAGUA · Managua · Bluefields
Corinto · León
CENTRAL · AMERICA
San Juan del Sur · COSTA RICA · Limón · Colón · PANAMÁ · Monteria · David
Puntarenas · San José · PTA. RESTINGUÉ
I. DEL COCO (COSTA RICA) · I. DE MALPELO (COL.)
ARCHIPIÉLAGO DE COLÓN (GALÁPAGOS IS.) (ECUADOR) · Equator
I. ISABELA

Caribbean Sea · LESSER · ANTILLES · GREATER · ANTILLES · WINDWARD IS. · LEEWARD IS.
ANTIGUA AND BARBUDA · GUADELOUPE (FR.) · Pointe-à-Pitre · DOMINICA · Fort-de-France · MARTINIQUE (FR.) · SAINT LUCIA · Bridgetown · BARBADOS · SAINT VINCENT AND THE GRENADINES · GRENADA
Santa Marta · Barranquilla · Uribia · PTA. GALLINAS · CURAÇAO (NETH.) · Willemstad · La Asunción · Carúpano · TRINIDAD AND TOBAGO · Port of Spain
Cartagena · Maracaibo · Maracay · Caracas · Cumaná · Barcelona · Maturín
Valera · Valencia · Los Teques
Medellín · Cúcuta · Barinas · San Fernando de Apure · Ciudad Guayana · Morawhanna
Bucaramanga · Arauca · Puerto Carreño · Ciudad Bolívar · Georgetown · Buxton · New Amsterdam
VENEZUELA · San Fernando de Atabapo · MT. RORAIMA 9094 · GUYANA · Paramaribo · Cayenne · C. ORANGE
Bogotá · Villavicencio · Puerto Ayacucho · SURINAME · FRENCH GUIANA · St.-Georges
COLOMBIA · Cali · Neiva · San Carlos de Río Negro · PAKARAIMA MTS. · Boa Vista · I. DE MARACÁ · C. NORTE
Buenaventura · Popayán · Florencia · São Gabriel da Cachoeira · Amapá · Macapá · ILHA DE MARAJÓ · C. MAGUARI · Equator
Tumaco · Pasto · Mocoa · Mitú
Esmeraldas · PTA. GALERA · Ibarra · Tulcán · Quito · Moura · Manaus · Santarém · Porto de Moz · Belém · PTA. DO ZUMBI · São Luís · Parnaíba · PTA. CURUMIGUARA
ECUADOR · Ambato · CHIMBORAZO 20702 · Riobamba · Macas
Guayaquil · Cuenca · Azogues · Iquitos · São Paulo de Olivença · Itaituba · Marabá · Carolina · Fortaleza · Baturité · Teresina · Aracati · C. DE SÃO ROQUE · Macau · Natal
Machala · Loja · Leticia · SELVAS · PTA. DO SEIXAS · João Pessoa
Sullana · Tumbes · PTA. AGUJA · PTA. NEGRA · Piura · Chachapoyas · Moyobamba · Floriano · Campina Grande · Caruaru · Recife
Chiclayo · Cajamarca · Yurimaguas · BRAZIL · Juazeiro · Maceió · Penedo
Trujillo · NEVADO HUASCARÁN 22205 · Huaraz · Cruzeiro do Sul · Lábrea · Porto Velho · Villa Bella · Porto Nacional · Barra · Morro do Chapéu · Aracaju
NEVADO YERUPAJÁ 21765 · Huánuco · Río Branco · Riberalta · Cobija · BRAZILIAN · Salvador · PTA. DO MUTÁ
Cerro de Pasco · Puerto Maldonado · CHAPADA DOS PARECIS · PLANALTO DO · Januária · Itabuna · Ilhéus
PERU · Huancayo · Cuzco · MATO GROSSO · Goiás · Brasília · Montes Claros · Teófilo Otoni · PTA. DE SANTO ANTÔNIO
Lima · Callao · Huancavelica · Ayacucho · Abancay · Trinidad · Cuiabá · Anápolis · Goiânia · Uberlândia · Ipatinga · Diamantina · PTA. DA BALEIA
Ica · VOLCÁN MISTI 19101 · NEVADO ILLAMPU 20873 · Uberaba · PICO DA BANDEIRA 9482 · PTA. DO MONSARÁS
Mollendo · Arequipa · La Paz · Cochabamba · Corumbá · Ouro Preto · Belo Horizonte · Vitória · PICO DE SÃO TOMÉ
Moquegua · Puno · Oruro · Santa Cruz · Campo Grande · HIGHLANDS · Juiz de Fora · Campos
Tacna · Sucre · Maracaju · Bauru · Ribeirão Preto · Araraquara · Petrópolis · C. FRIO
Arica · Pisagua · Potosí · Pulacayo · Tarija · Maracaju · Ourinhos · Campinas · Niterói · Tropic of Capricorn
Iquique · Tocopila · CHACO · Puerto Casado · Concepción · São Paulo · Rio de Janeiro
Calama · CERRO TINTE 19190 · Santos
PTA. ANGAMOS · PARAGUAY · Asunción · Curitiba
Antofagasta · PTA. TETAS · VOLCÁN LLULLAILLACO 22110 · San Salvador de Jujuy · Salta · Coronel Oviedo · Ponta Grossa · Florianópolis
Taltal · Chañaral · NEVADO OJOS DEL SALADO 22615 · San Miguel de Tucumán · Resistencia · Villarrica · Campos · Passo Fundo · C. DE SANTA MARTA GRANDE
PTA. MORRO · Copiapó · S. Fernando del V. de Catamarca · Corrientes · Posadas · Encarnación Novos
Vallenar · Santiago del Estero · Goya · Mercedes · Itaquí · Santa Maria · Porto Alegre
C. BASCUÑÁN · La Rioja · Paraná · Salto · Pelotas
La Serena · Coquimbo · Deán Funes · Rivera · Paysandú · Rio Grande
Ovalle · San Juan · Córdoba · Santa Fe · URUGUAY · Mercedes · Minas · Rocha
Illapel · CERRO ACONCAGUA 22831 · San Luis · Río Cuarto · Paraná · San José de Mayo
Viña del Mar · Mendoza · Rosario · La Plata · Montevideo
Valparaíso · Rancagua · Santiago · San Fernando · Buenos Aires · Mercedes · San Carlos de Bolívar · C. SAN ANTONIO
Curicó · Talca · Linares · Santa Rosa · Azul · Tandil
Cauquenes · Chillán · PTA. LAVAPIE · Lota · Lebu · General Acha · Tres Arroyos · Mar del Plata · PTA. MOGOTES
Talcahuano · Concepción · Angol · Neuquén · Bahía Blanca
Temuco · VOLCÁN LANÍN 12389 · Río Negro
Valdivia · PTA. GALERA · Osorno · San Carlos de Bariloche · PTA. RASA
Puerto Montt · Ancud · Viedma · PENÍNSULA VALDÉS
Castro · Esquel · Rawson · ARGENTINA
ISLA GRANDE DE CHILOÉ · ARCHIPIÉLAGO DE LOS CHONOS · Trelew · Chubut · GOLFO SAN JORGE
PENÍNSULA DE TAITAO · CO. SAN CLEMENTE 13314 · Comodoro Rivadavia · C. DOS BAHÍAS · C. TRES PUNTAS
CO. MURALLÓN 1811 · San Julián · PTA. DESENGAÑO
I. WELLINGTON · Puerto Natales · Río Gallegos · C. VÍRGENES · FALKLAND ISLANDS (ISLAS MALVINAS) (BR.) · Stanley
Punta Arenas · ISLA GRANDE DE TIERRA DEL FUEGO · SOUTH GEORGIA (FALKLAND IS.)
CO. SARMIENTO DE GAMBOA 7546 · Ushuaia · I. NAVARINO · CAPE HORN · Strait of Magellan · Longitude West of Greenwich

Gulf of Mexico · Caribbean Sea · Atlantic Ocean · Pacific Ocean
Tropic of Cancer · Equator · Tropic of Capricorn

Sinusoidal Projection
SCALE 1:29,465,000 · 1 Inch = 465 Statute Miles
Statute Miles · 100 · 0 · 100 · 300 · 500 · 700
Kilometers · 100 · 0 · 100 · 300 · 500 · 700 · 900 · 1100

A-540000-21 · -3 -26 ⁸
COSMO SERIES SO. AMERICA
Copyright by
RAND McNALLY & COMPANY
Made in U.S.A.

53

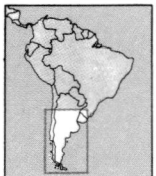

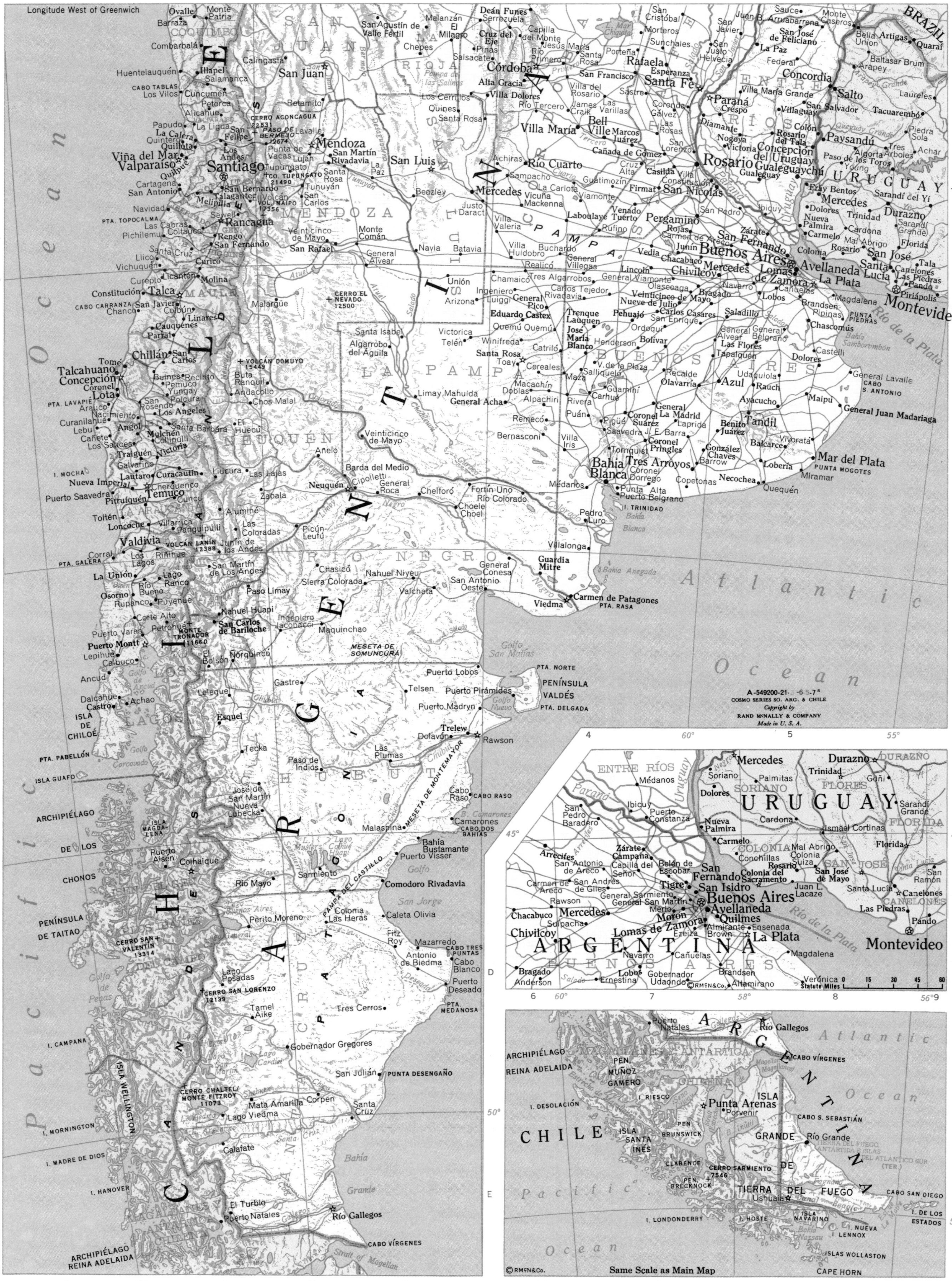


Statute Miles 50 0 50 100 150
Kilometers 50 0 50 100 150 200

Oblique Conic Conformal Projection
SCALE 1:8,000,000 1 Inch = 126 Statute Miles

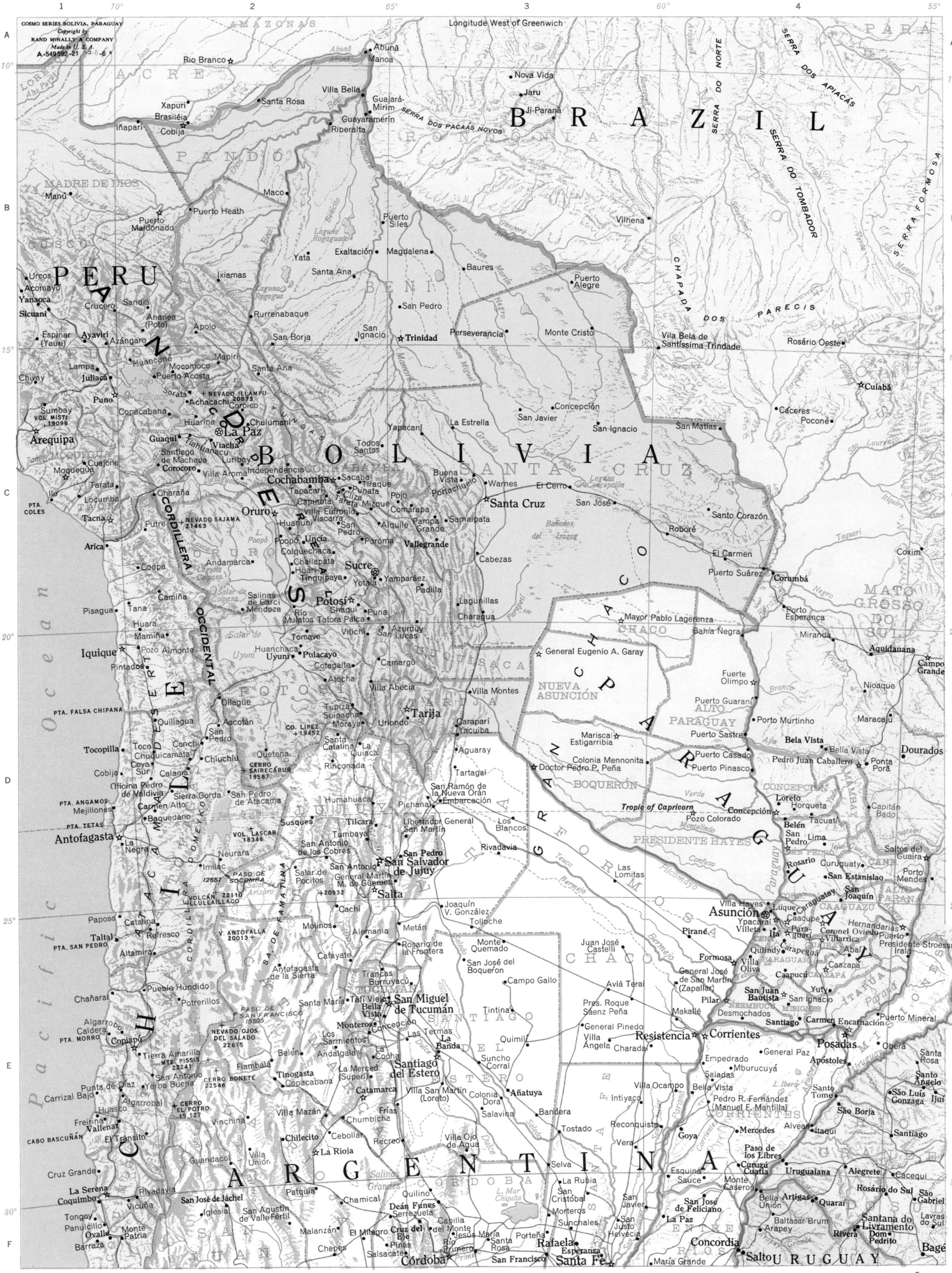

COSMO SERIES BOLIVIA, PARAGUAY
Copyright by
RAND McNALLY & COMPANY
Made in U.S.A.
A-549592-21

**PERU**

**BOLIVIA**

**BRAZIL**

**PARAGUAY**

**ARGENTINA**

**CHILE**

**URUGUAY**

MATO GROSSO DO SUL

Longitude West of Greenwich

Tropic of Capricorn

Pacific Ocean

Oblique Conic Conformal Projection
SCALE 1:8,000,000    1 Inch = 126 Statute Miles

Statute Miles
Kilometers

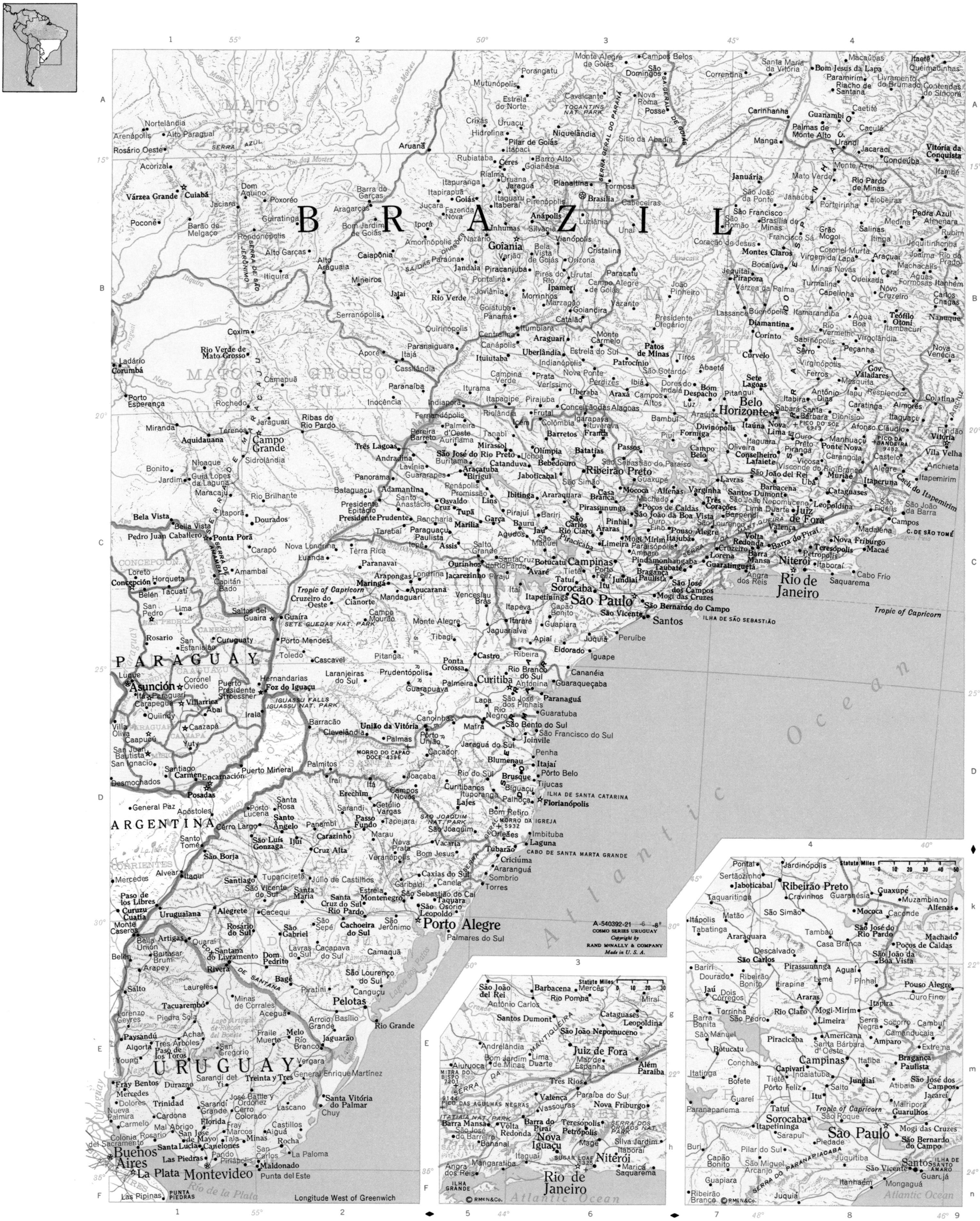

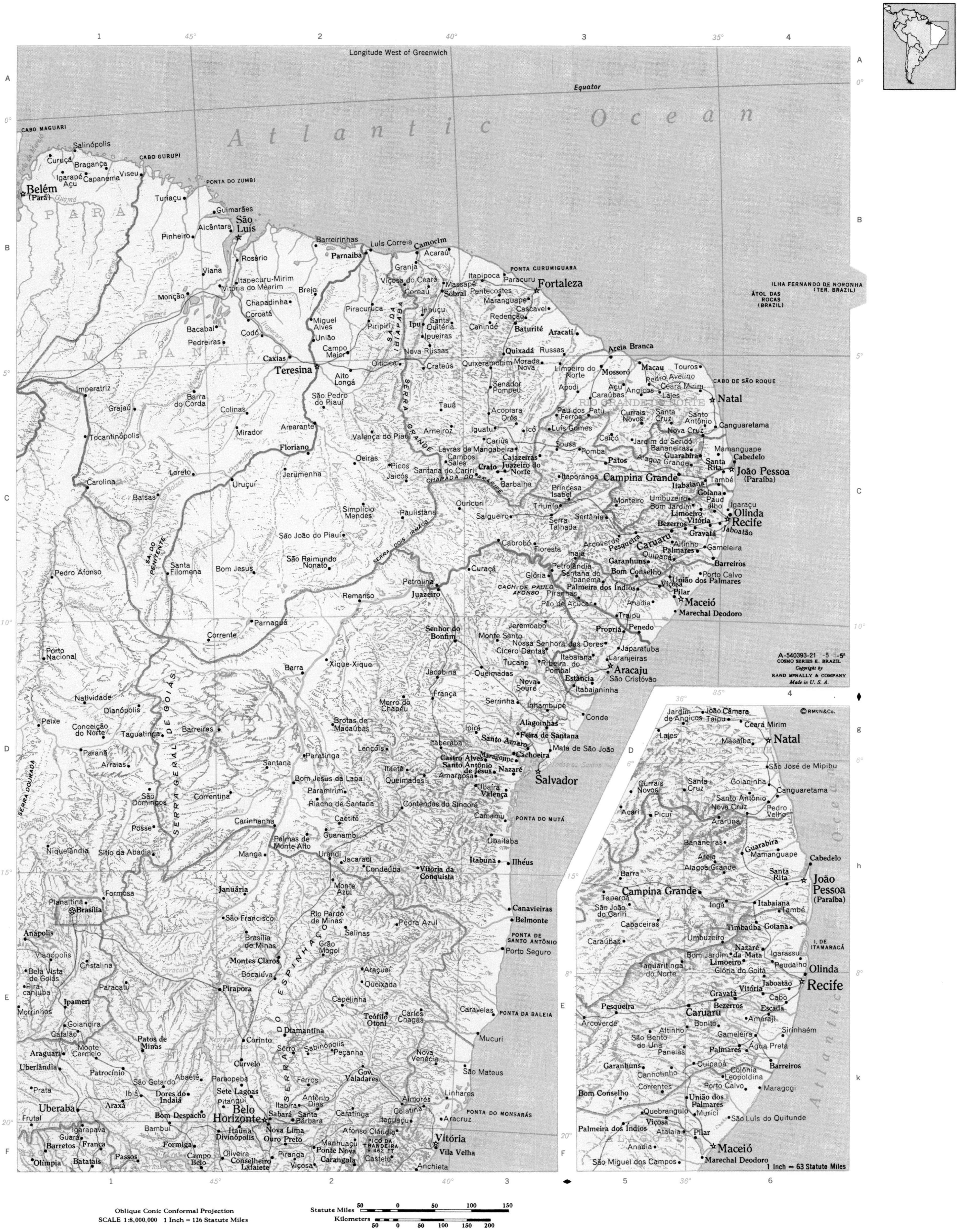

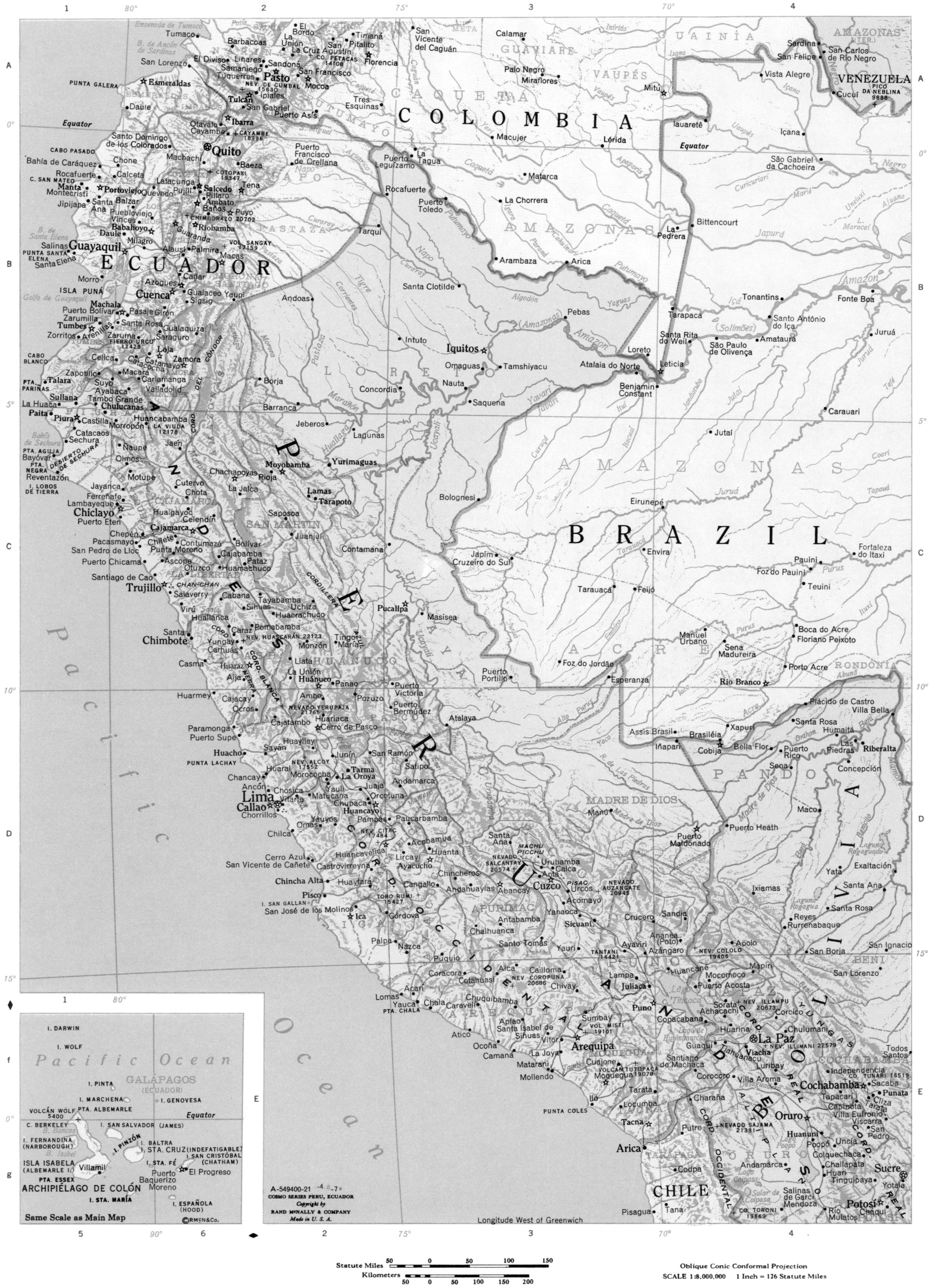

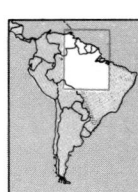

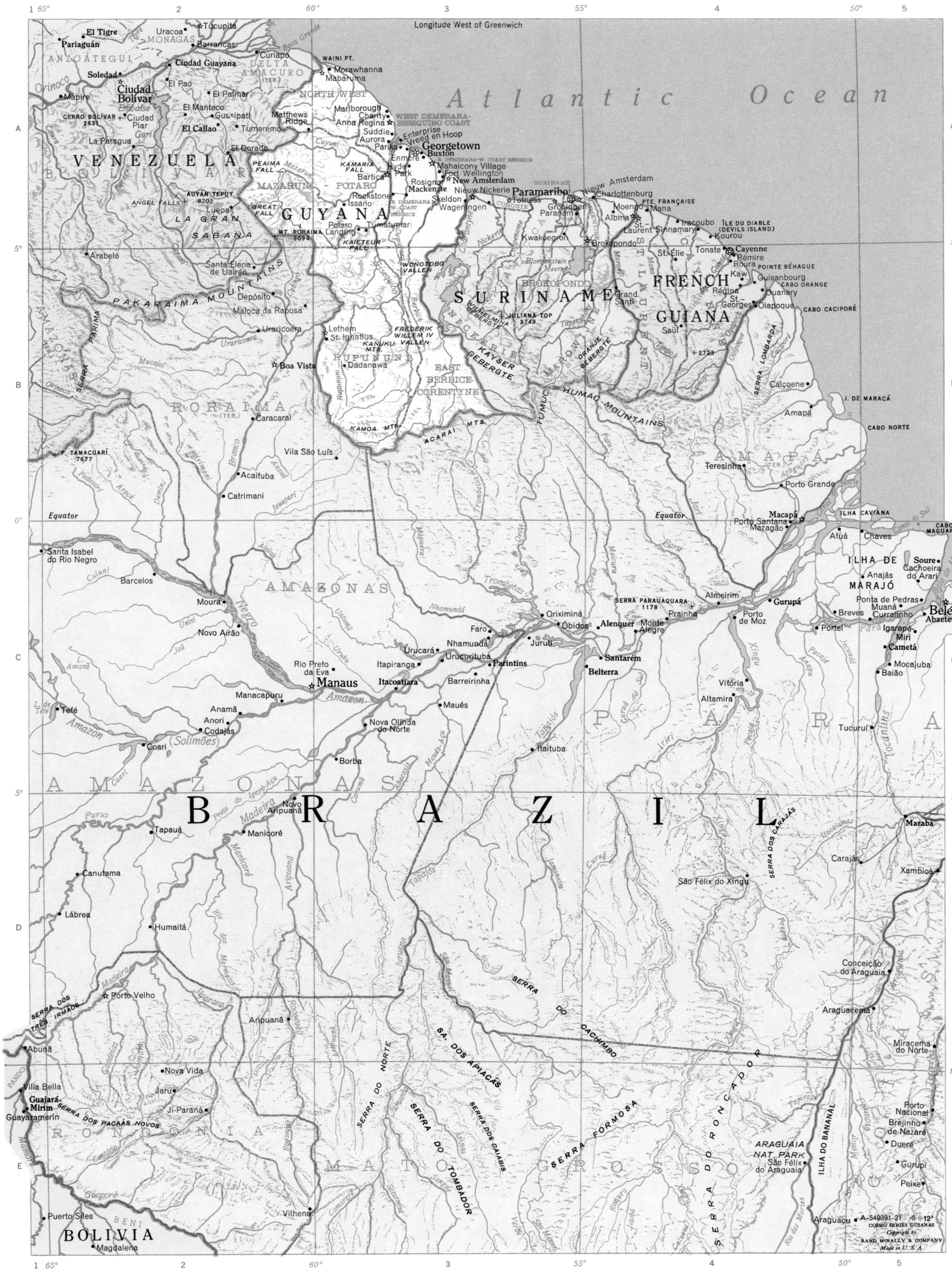


Oblique Conic Conformal Projection
SCALE 1:8,000,000 1 Inch = 126 Statute Miles

Statute Miles 50 0 50 100 150
Kilometers 50 0 50 100 150 200

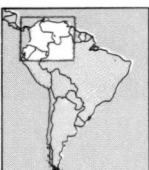

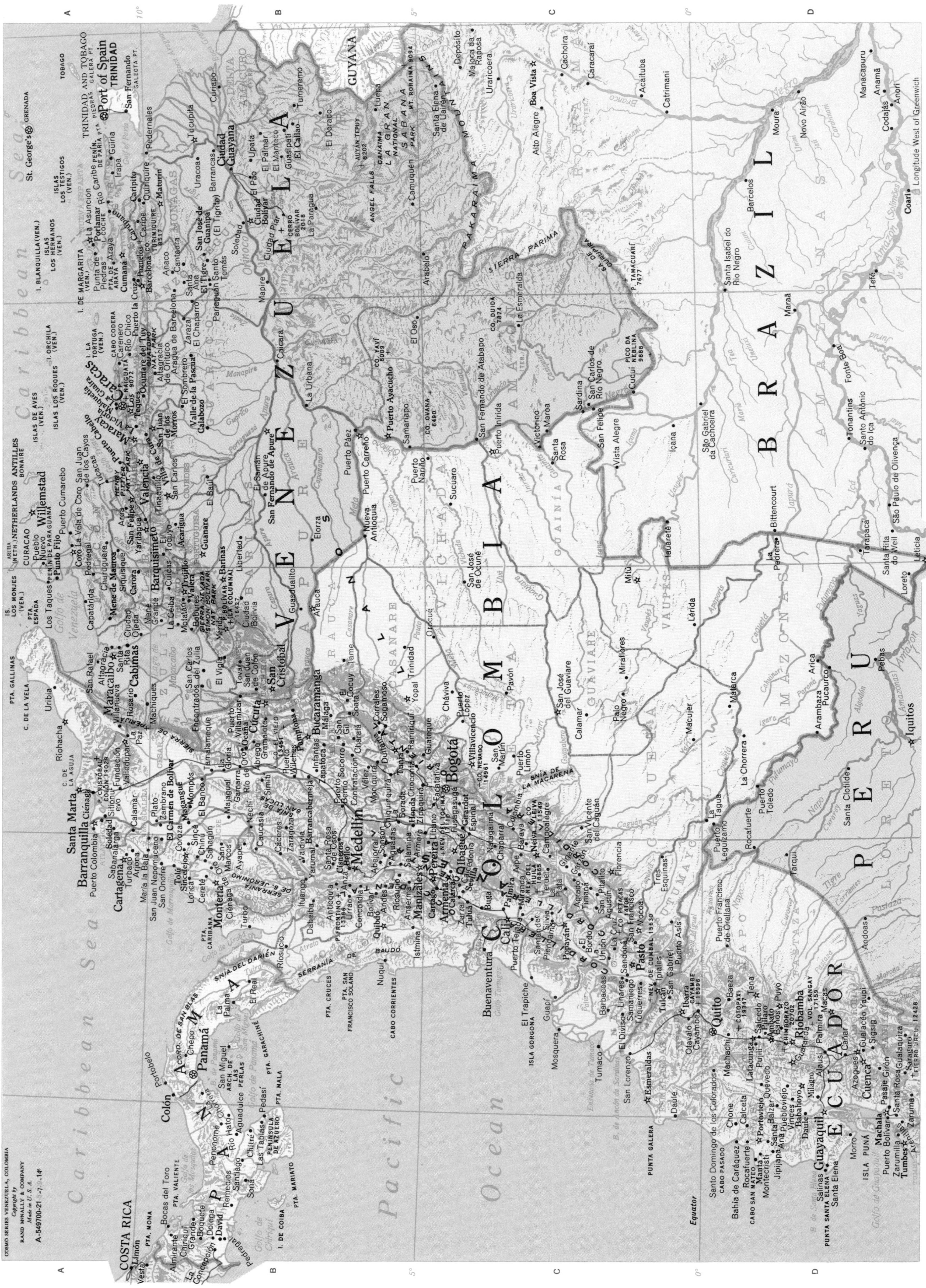

VENEZUELA
COLOMBIA
ECUADOR
PERU
BRAZIL
PANAMA
GUYANA
Caribbean Sea
Pacific Ocean
COSMO SERIES VENEZUELA, COLOMBIA
Copyright by RAND MCNALLY & COMPANY
Made in U.S.A.
Statute Miles 50 0 50 100 150
Kilometers 50 0 50 100 150 200
Oblique Conic Conformal Projection
SCALE 1:8,000,000 1 Inch = 126 Statute Miles

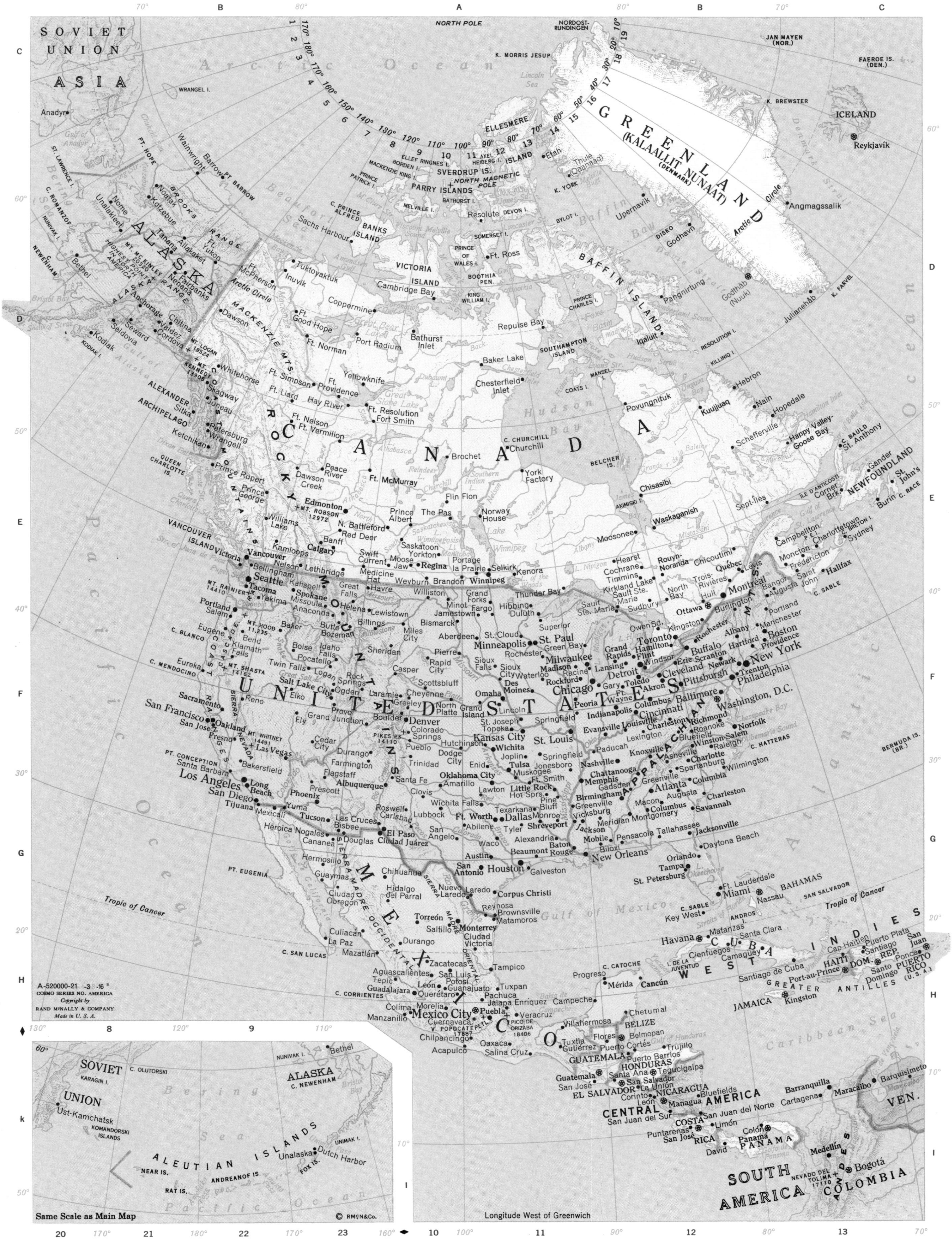

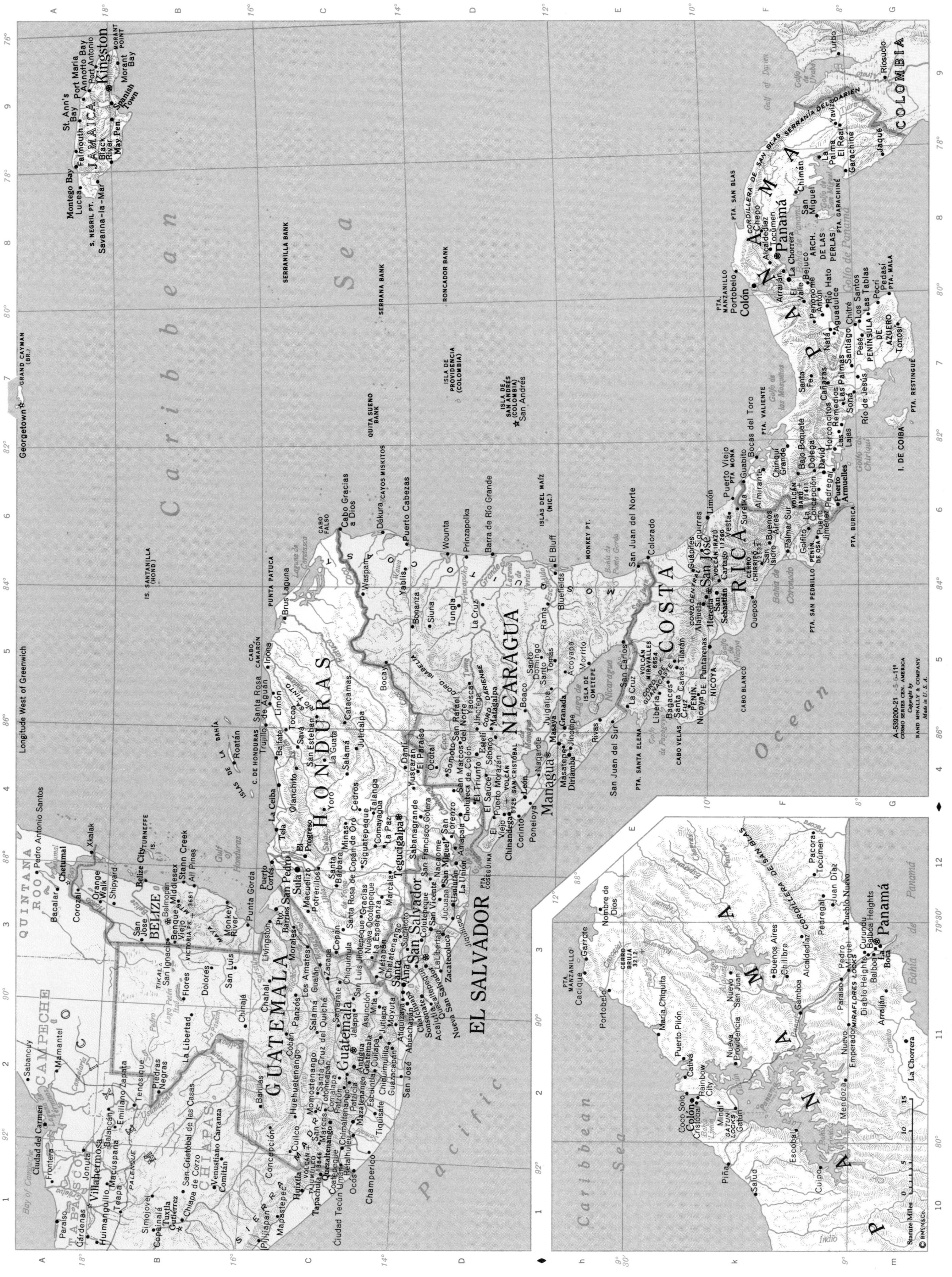

Oblique Conic Conformal Projection
SCALE 1:6,000,000  1 Inch = 95 Statute Miles

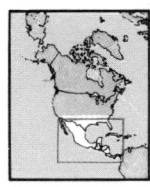

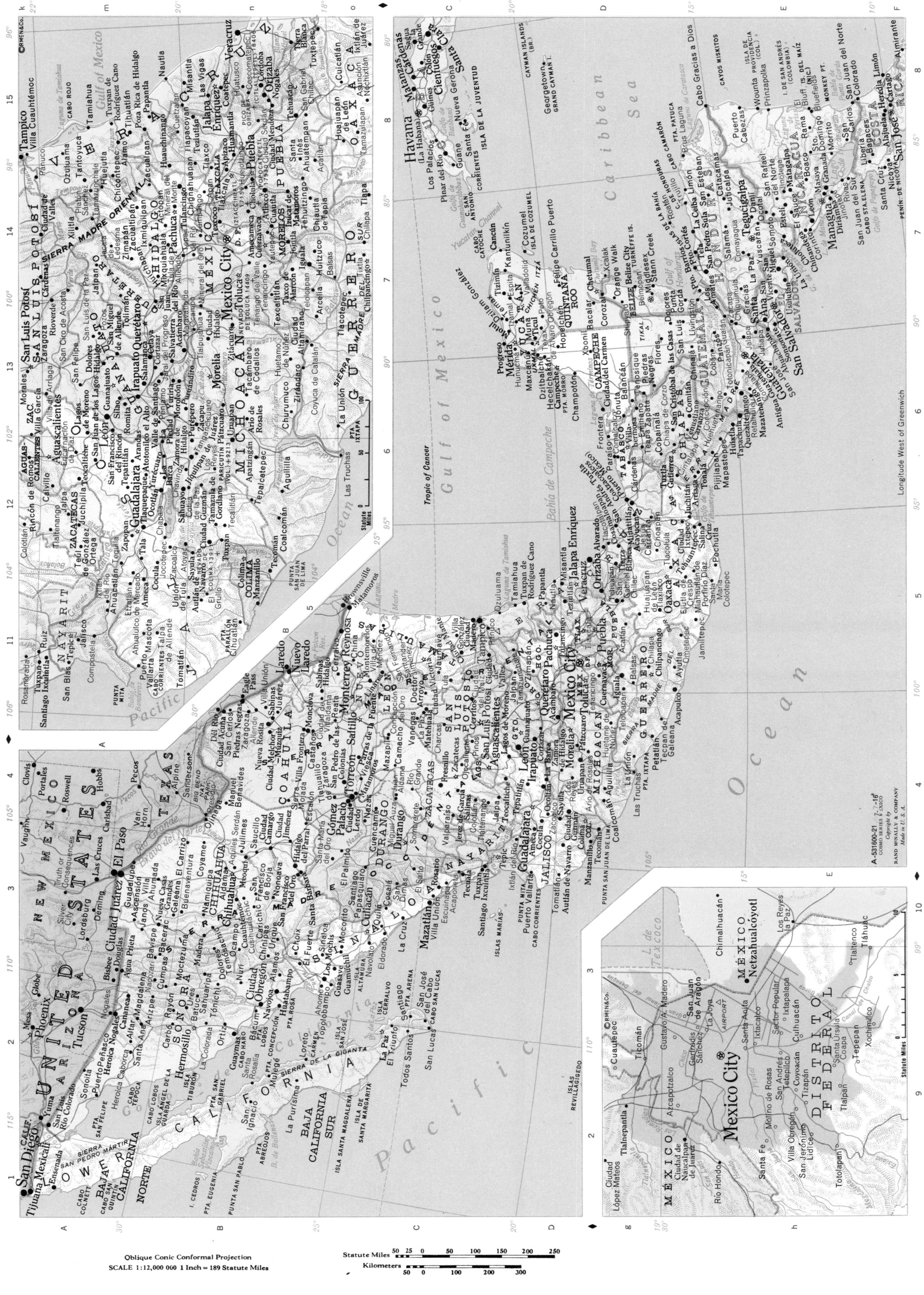
Gulf of Mexico
Caribbean Sea
Pacific Ocean
Bahía de Campeche
Tropic of Cancer
UNITED STATES
Mexico City
MÉXICO
DISTRITO FEDERAL
Longitude West of Greenwich
Oblique Conic Conformal Projection
SCALE 1:12,000 000 1 Inch = 189 Statute Miles
Statute Miles
Kilometers

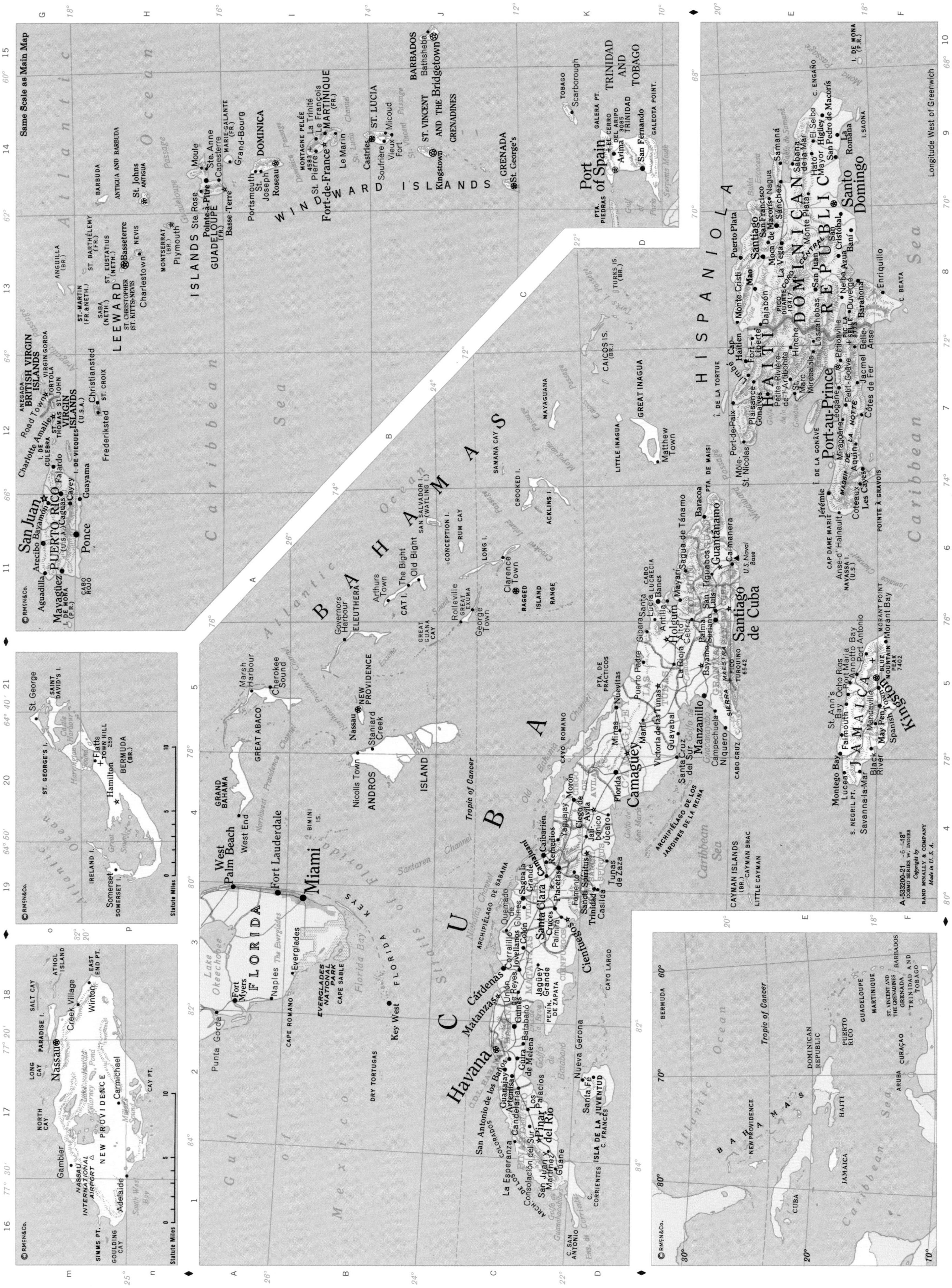

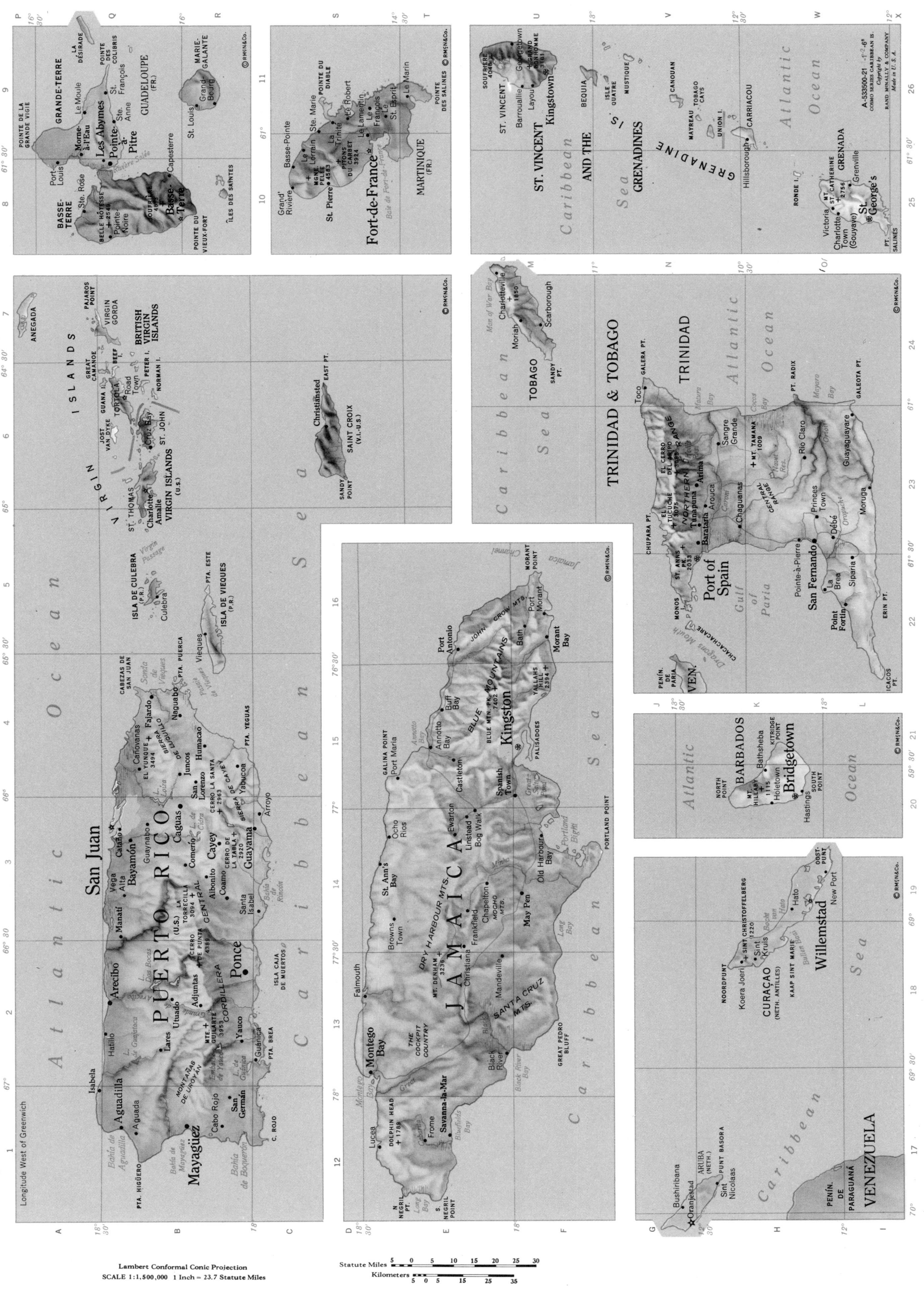

GUADELOUPE (FR.)

MARTINIQUE (FR.)

ST. VINCENT AND THE GRENADINES

GRENADA

VIRGIN ISLANDS

PUERTO RICO

San Juan

Mayagüez

Ponce

JAMAICA

Kingston

Montego Bay

TRINIDAD & TOBAGO

TRINIDAD

TOBAGO

Port of Spain

San Fernando

BARBADOS

Bridgetown

CURACAO (NETH. ANTILLES)

Willemstad

ARUBA (NETH.)

Oranjestad

VENEZUELA

Lambert Conformal Conic Projection
SCALE 1:1,500,000  1 Inch = 23.7 Statute Miles

Statute Miles

Kilometers

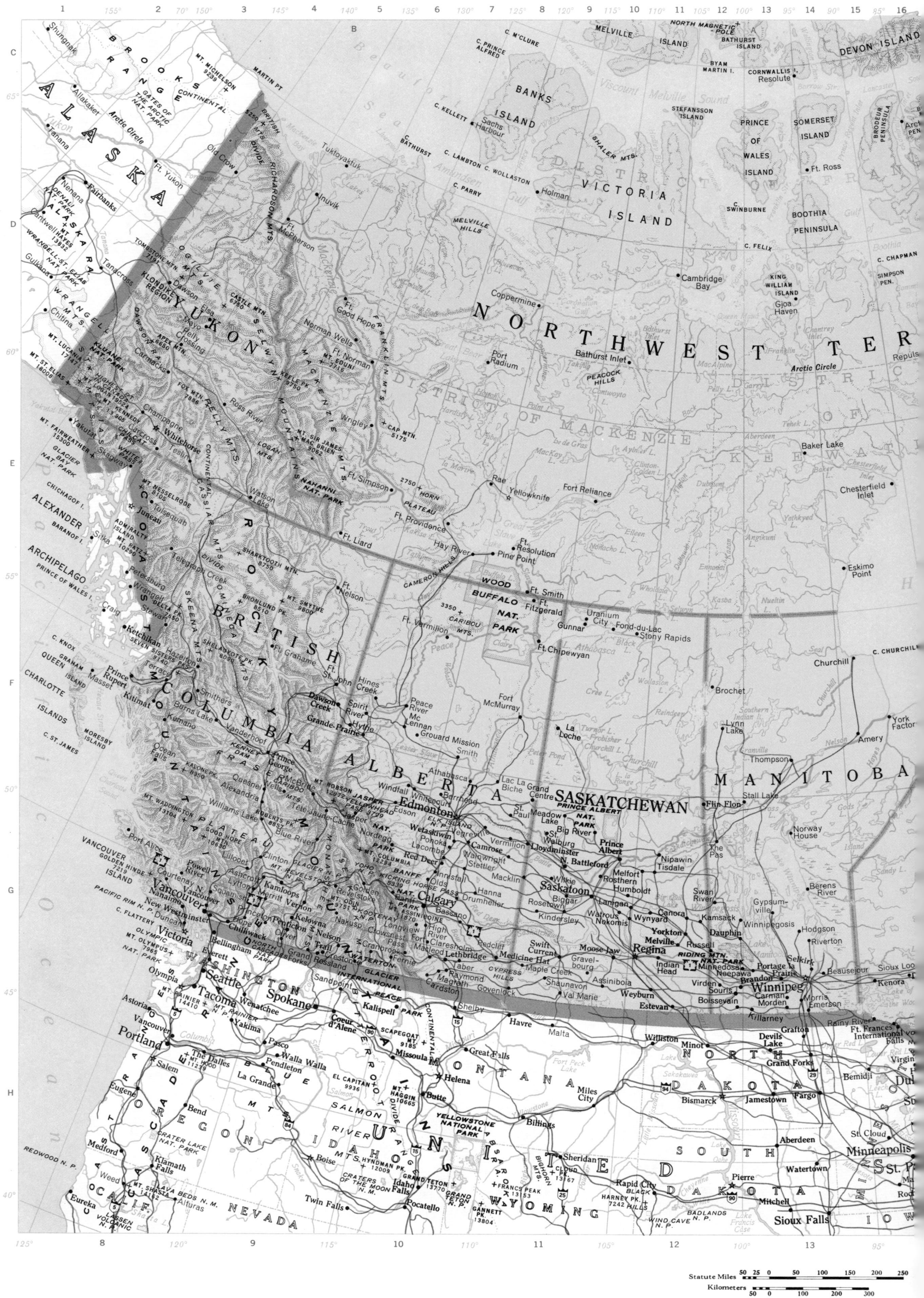

Lambert Conformal Conic Projection
SCALE 1:12,000,000  1 Inch = 189 Statute Miles

Longitude West of Greenwich

A-52020-72  -8 · 12°
COSMO SERIES CANADA
Copyright by
RAND McNALLY & COMPANY
Made in U.S.A.

Same Scale as Main Map  ©RM&N Co.

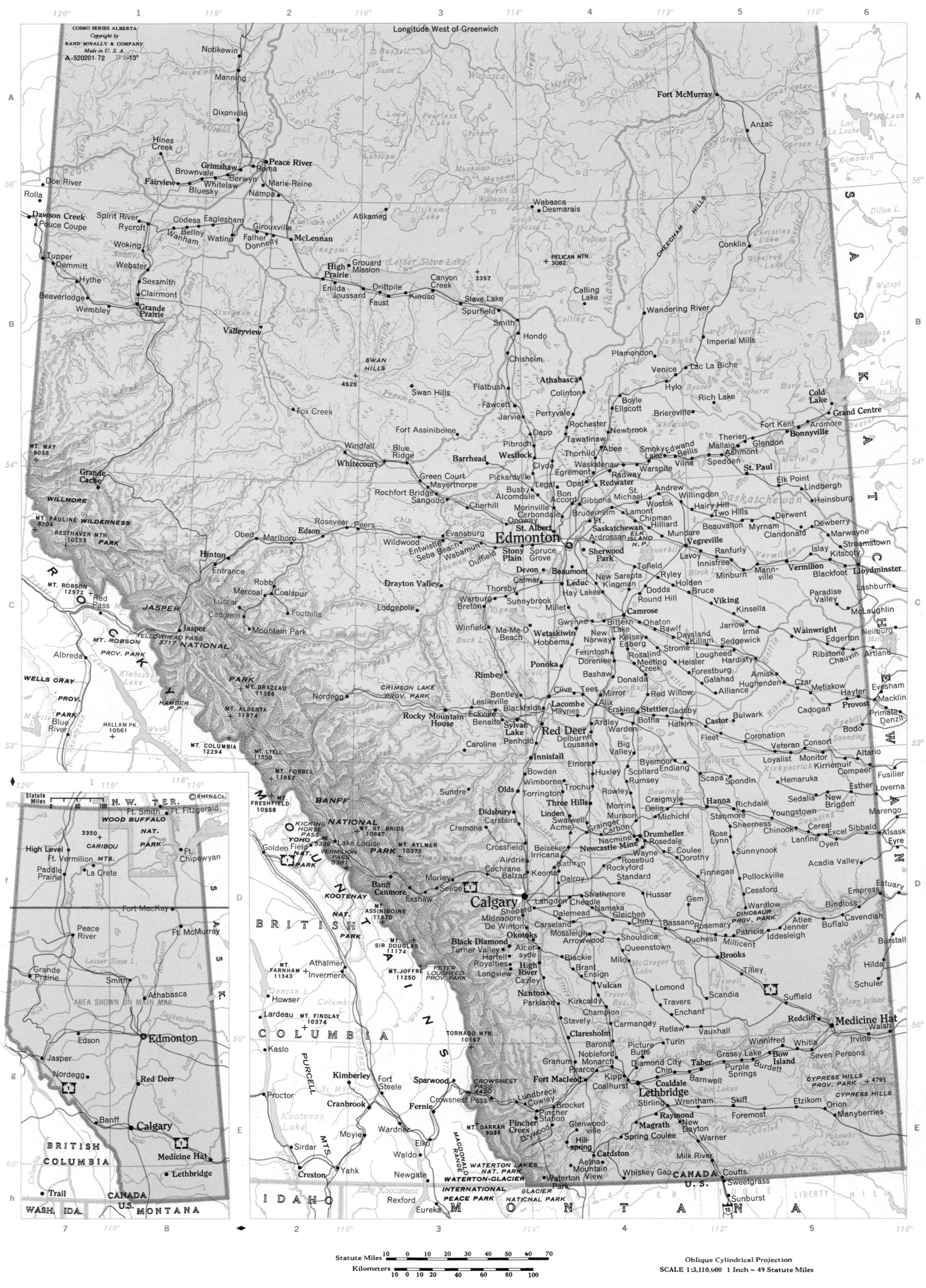

Oblique Cylindrical Projection
SCALE 1:4,255,000 1 Inch = 67 Statute Miles

Statute Miles 10 0 10 20 30 40 50 60 70 80 90 100
Kilometers 10 0 10 20 40 60 80 100 120 140

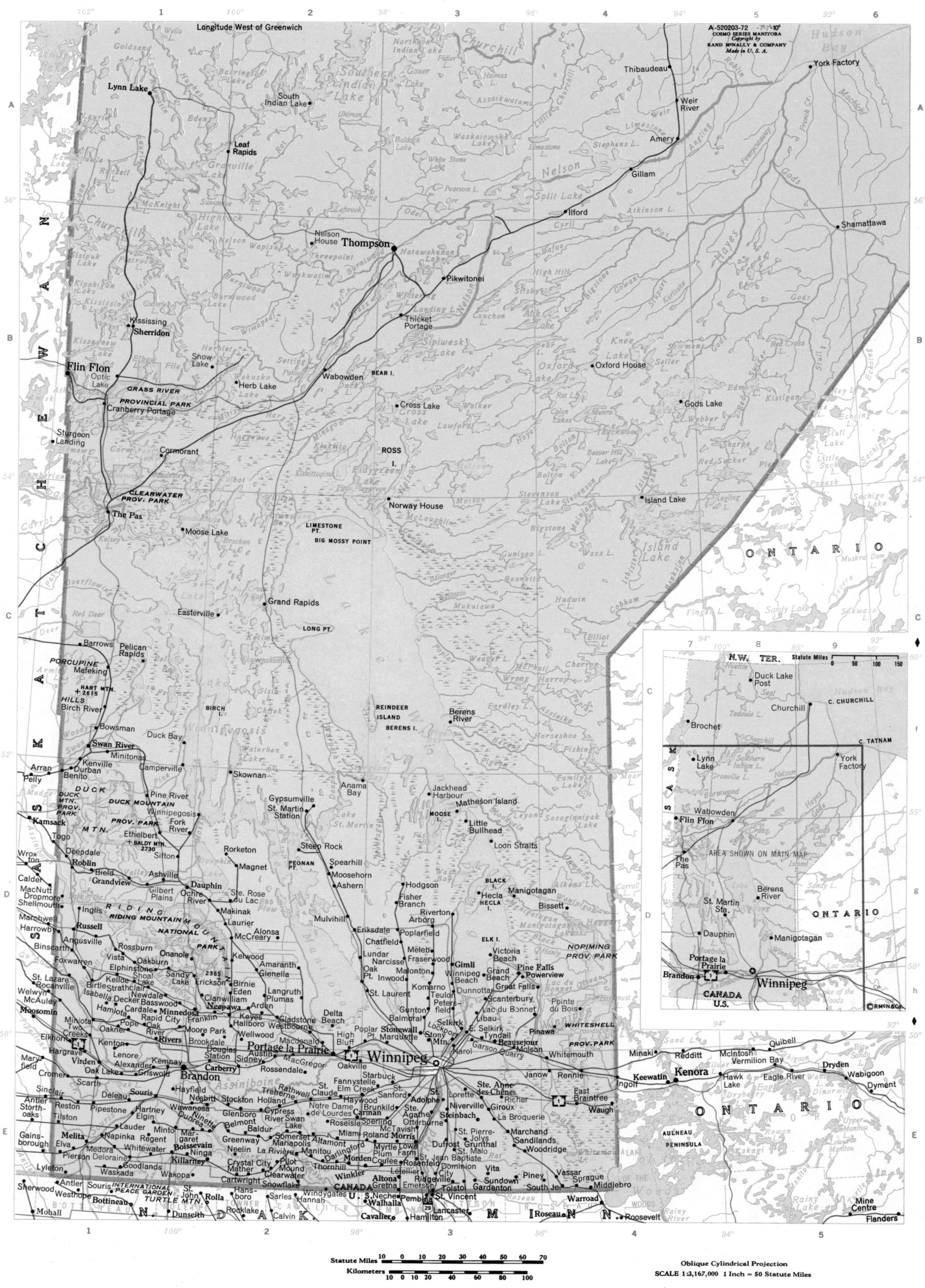

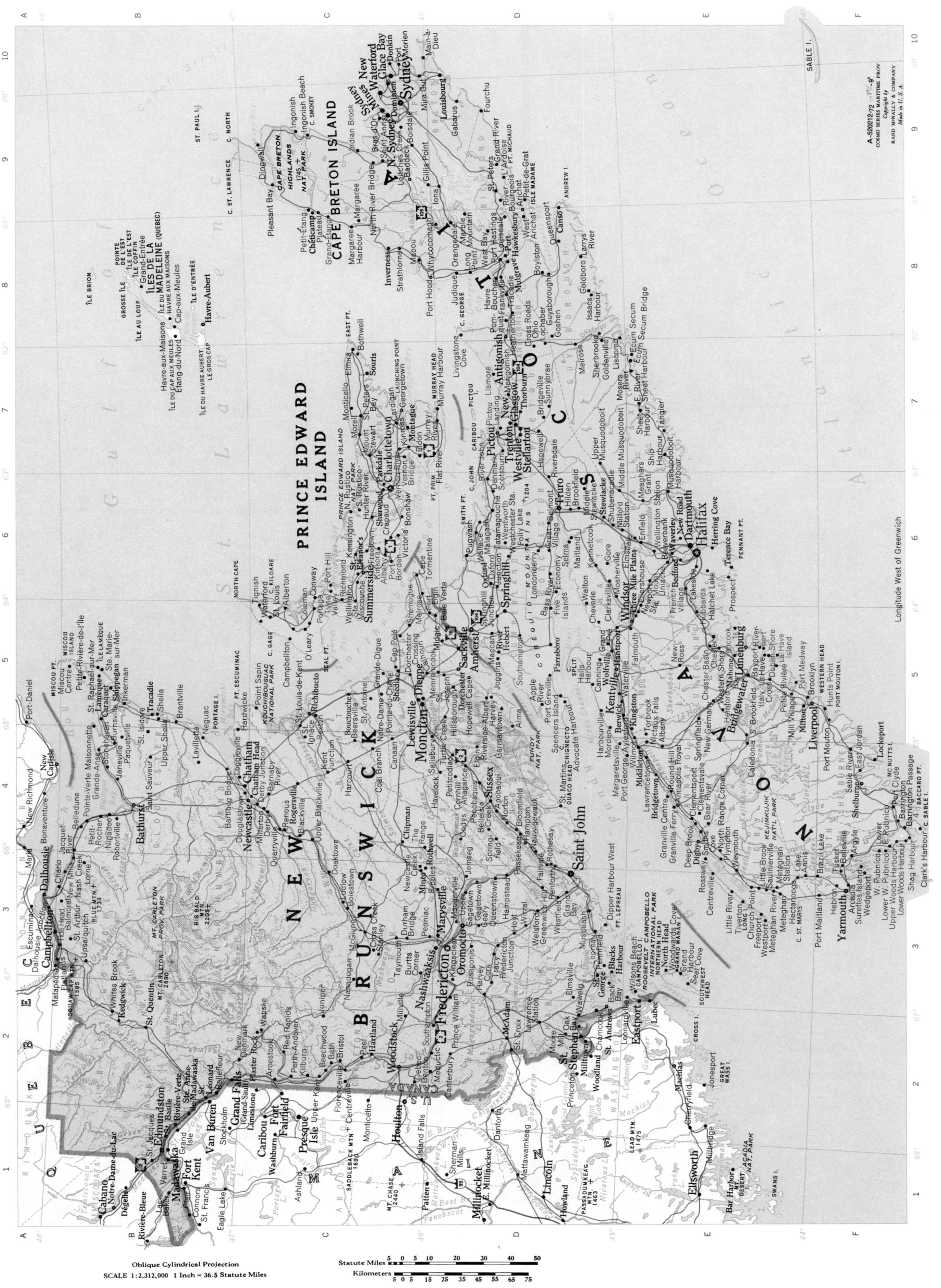

Oblique Cylindrical Projection
SCALE 1:2,312,000   1 Inch = 36.5 Statute Miles

Statute Miles
5  0  5  10     20     30     40     50

Kilometers
5  0  5    15    25    35    45    55    65    75

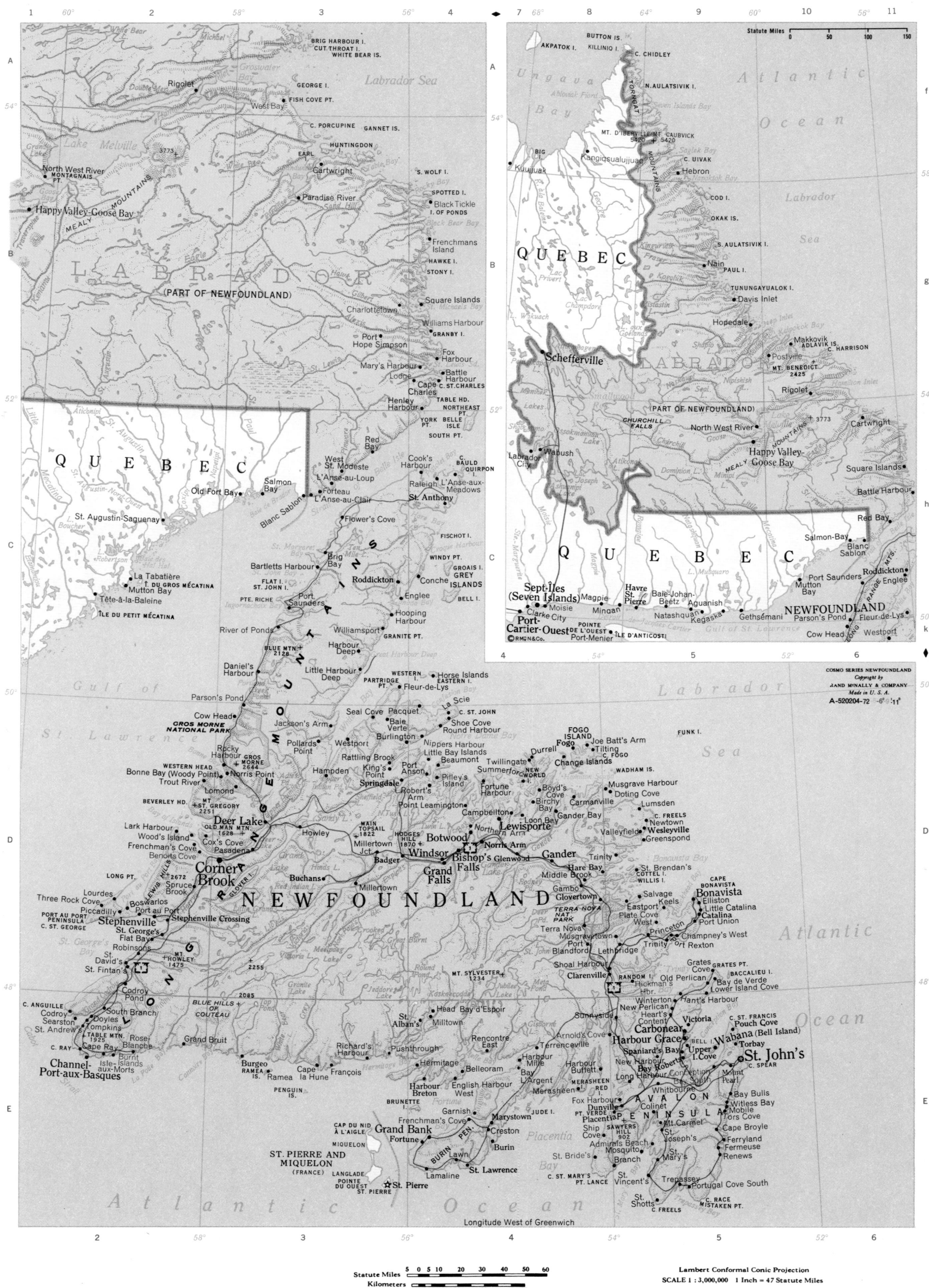

NEWFOUNDLAND

LABRADOR
(PART OF NEWFOUNDLAND)

QUEBEC

QUEBEC

ST. PIERRE AND MIQUELON
(FRANCE)

AVALON PENINSULA

St. John's

Corner Brook

Channel-Port-aux-Basques

Stephenville

Deer Lake

Gander

Grand Falls

Bonavista

Grand Bank

Statute Miles
0    50    100    150

Lambert Conformal Conic Projection
SCALE 1 : 3,000,000    1 Inch = 47 Statute Miles

Statute Miles
5 0 5 10    20    30    40    50    60
Kilometers
5 0 5 10 20 30 40 50 60 70 80

Longitude West of Greenwich

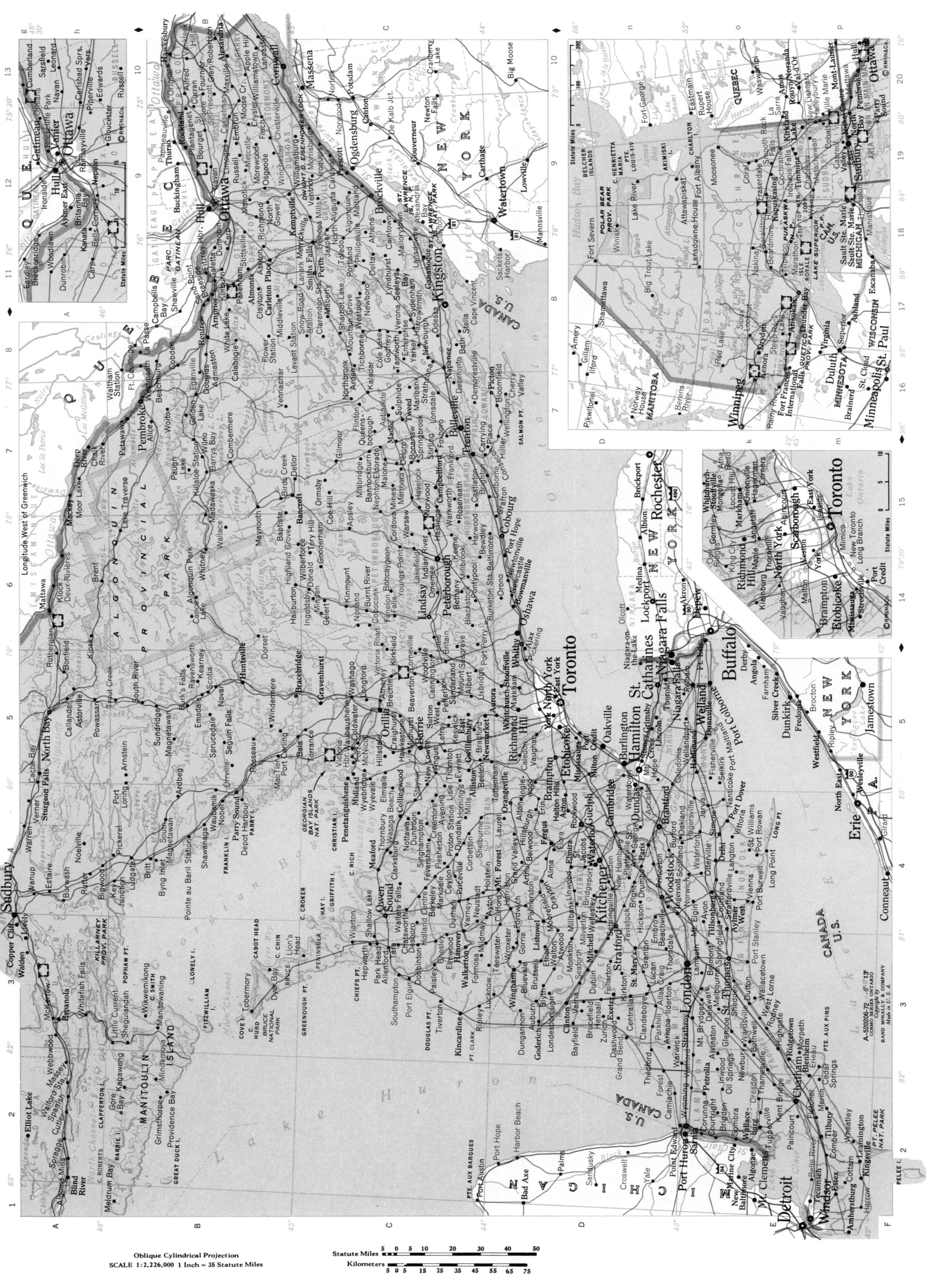

Oblique Cylindrical Projection
SCALE 1:2,226,000  1 Inch = 35 Statute Miles

Statute Miles
Kilometers

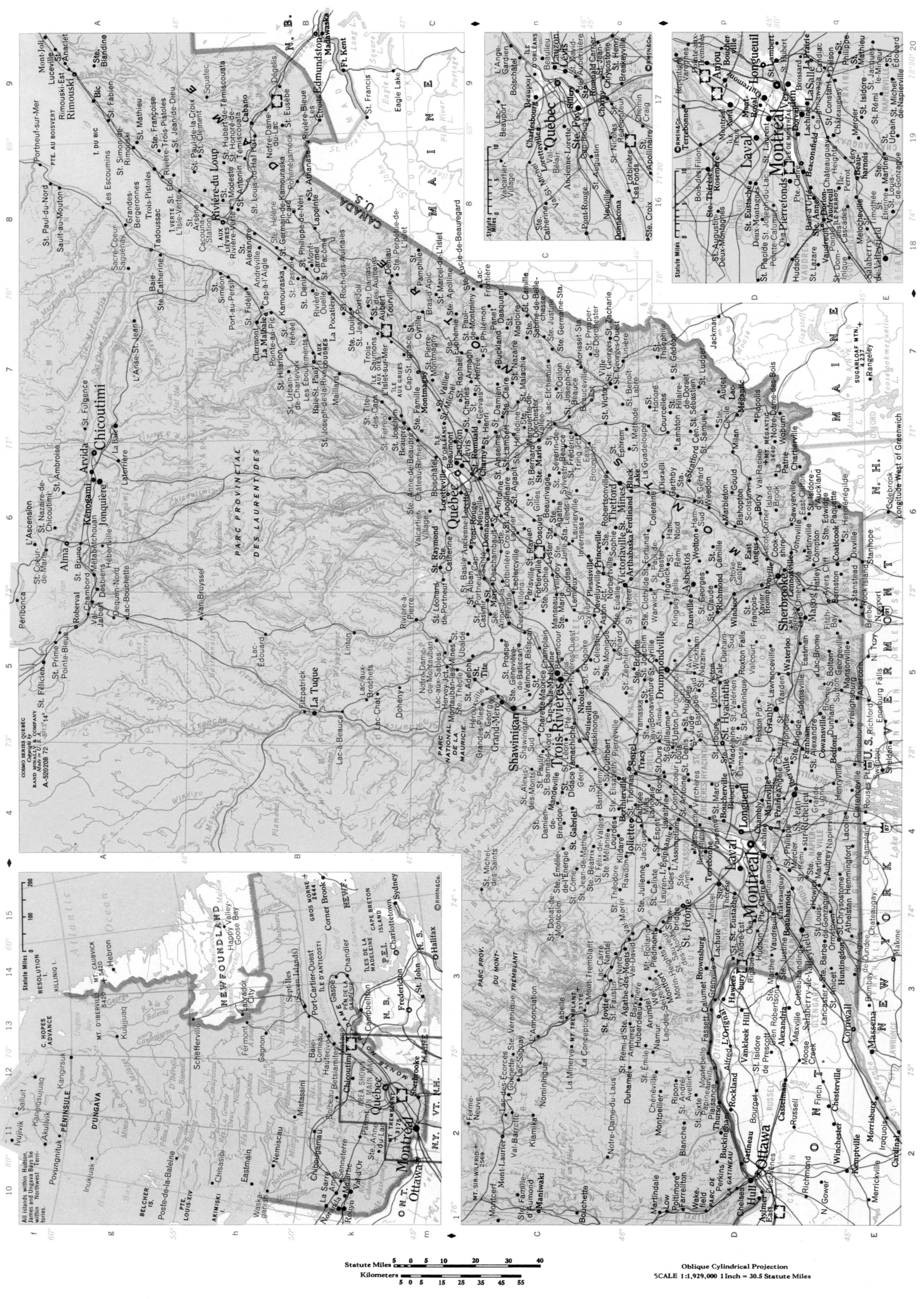

Statute Miles 5 0 5 10 20 30 40
Kilometers 5 0 5 15 25 35 45 55

Oblique Cylindrical Projection
SCALE 1:1,929,000 1 Inch = 30.5 Statute Miles

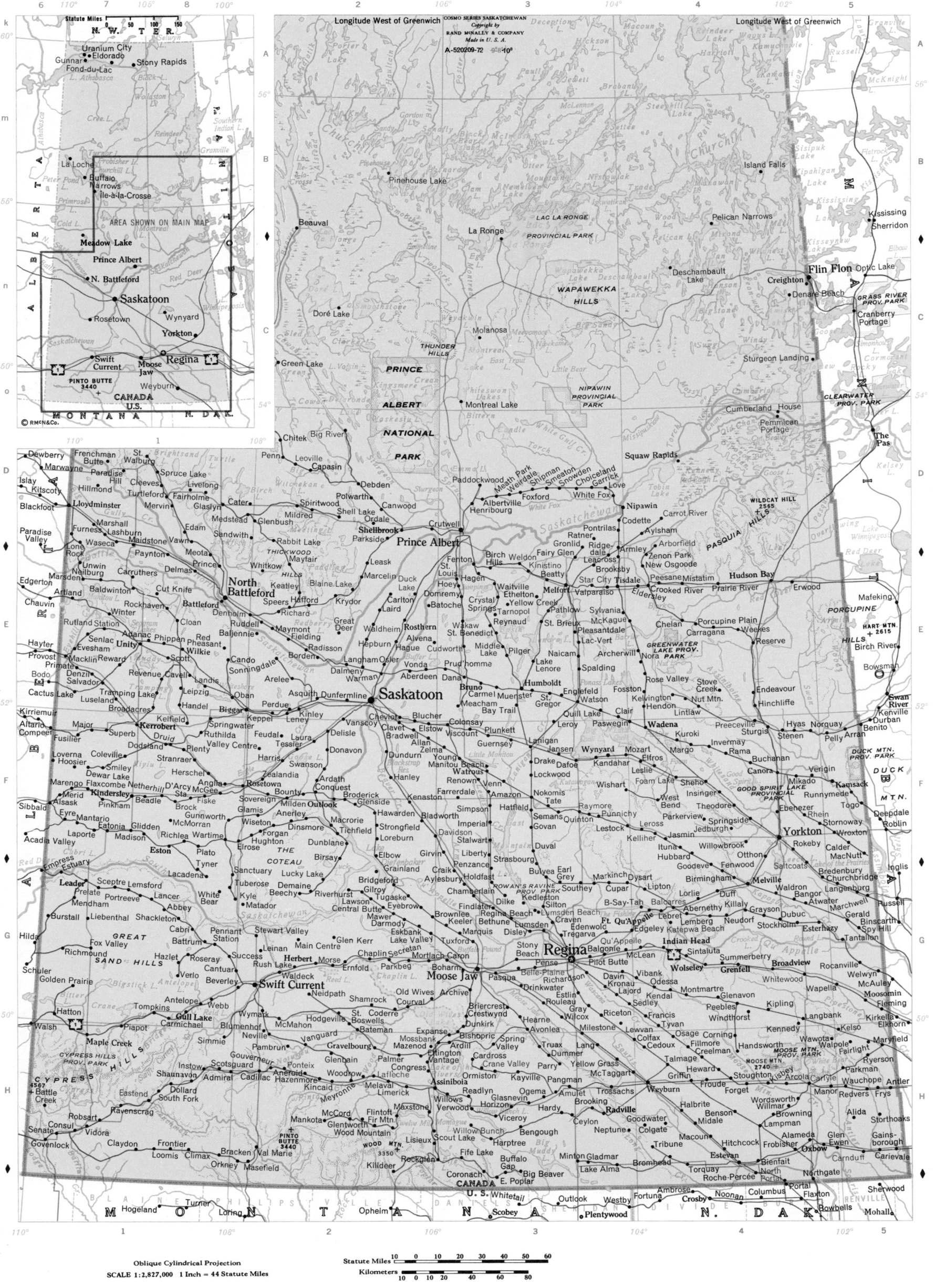

Oblique Cylindrical Projection
SCALE 1:2,827,000   1 Inch = 44 Statute Miles

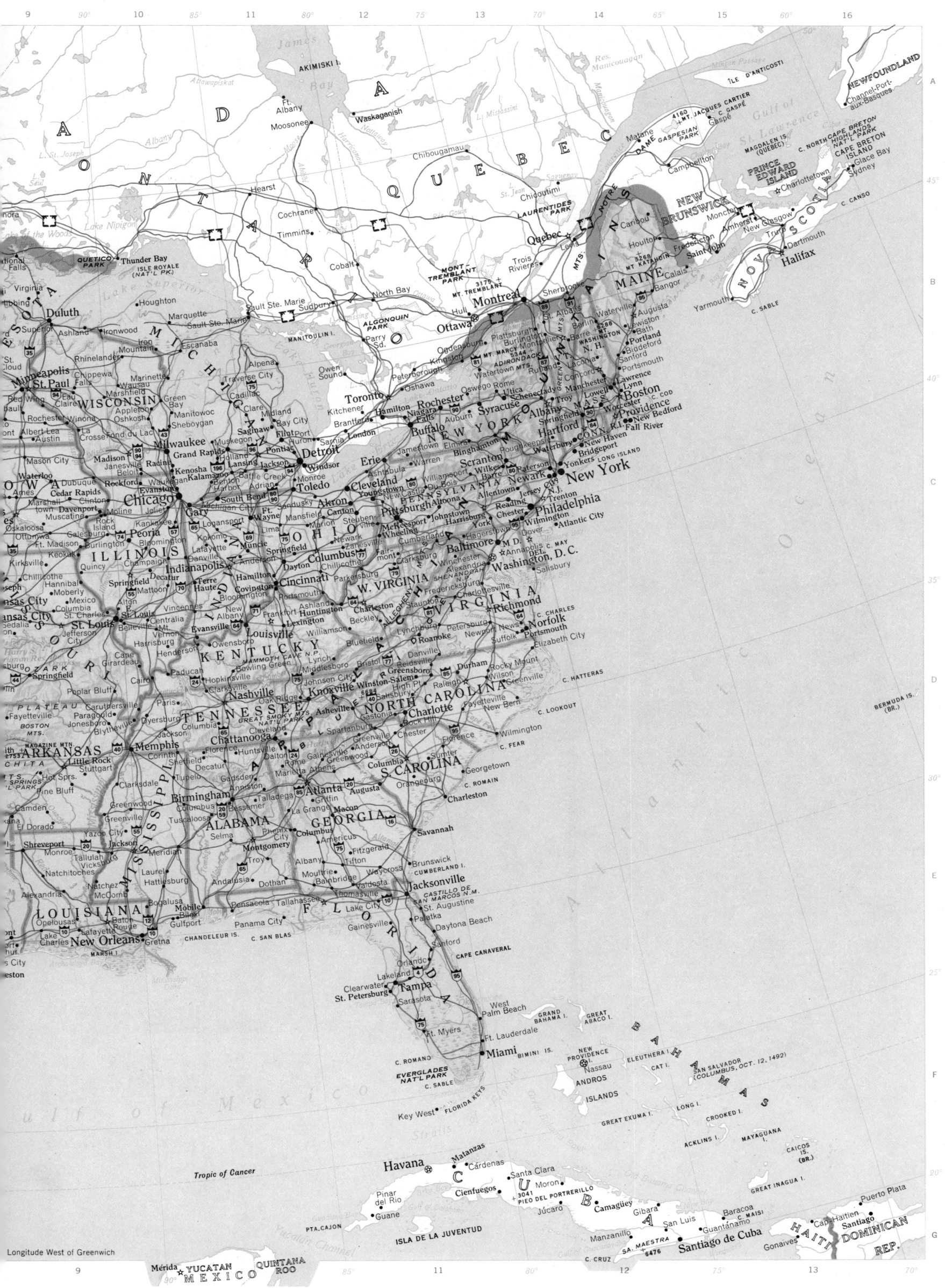

Lambert Conformal Conic Projection
SCALE 1:12,000,000   1 Inch = 189 Statute Miles

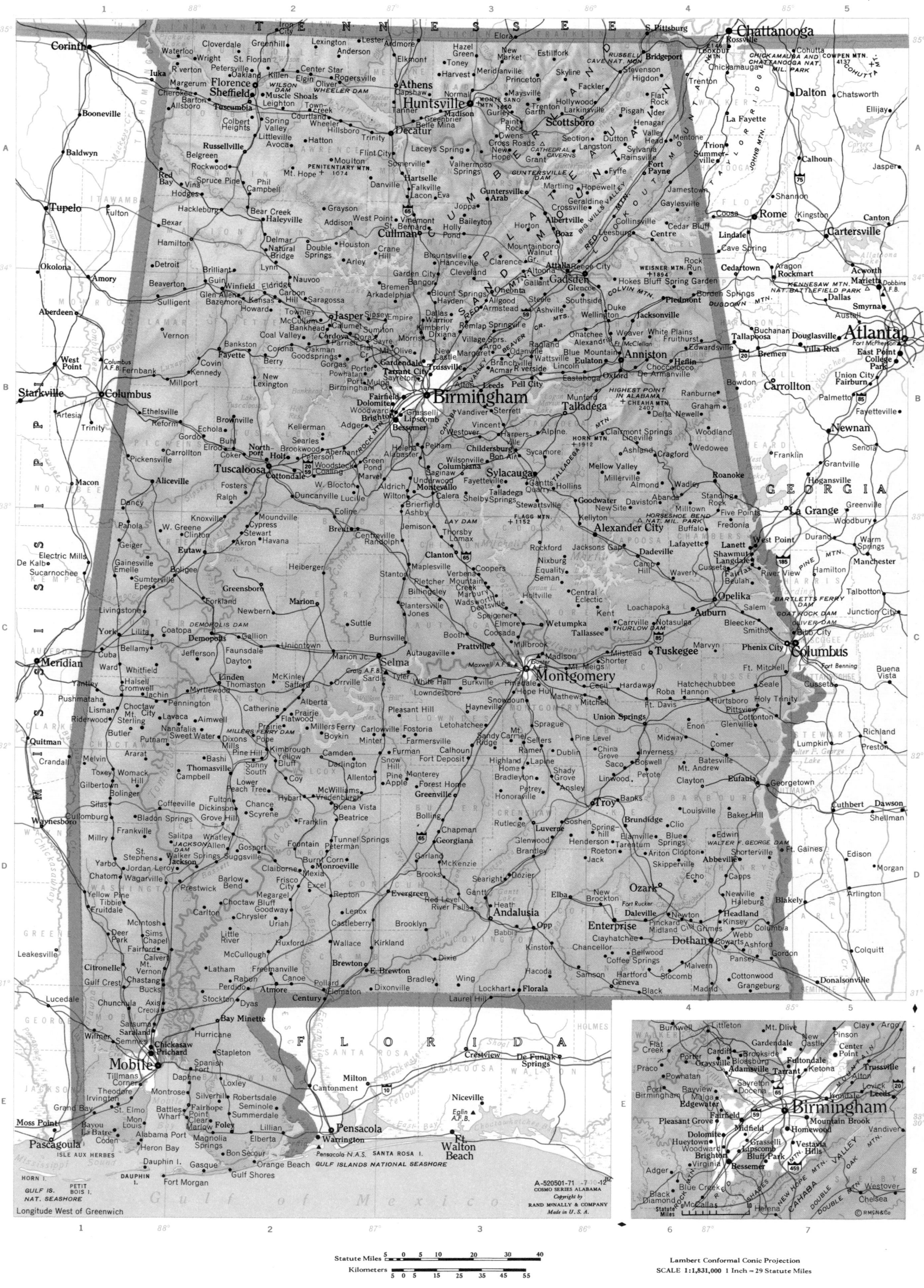

Statute Miles 5 0 5 10 20 30 40
Kilometers 5 0 5 15 25 35 45 55

A-520501-71  7 10 12
COSMO SERIES ALABAMA
Copyright by
RAND McNALLY & COMPANY
Made in U.S.A.

Lambert Conformal Conic Projection
SCALE 1:1,831,000  1 Inch = 29 Statute Miles

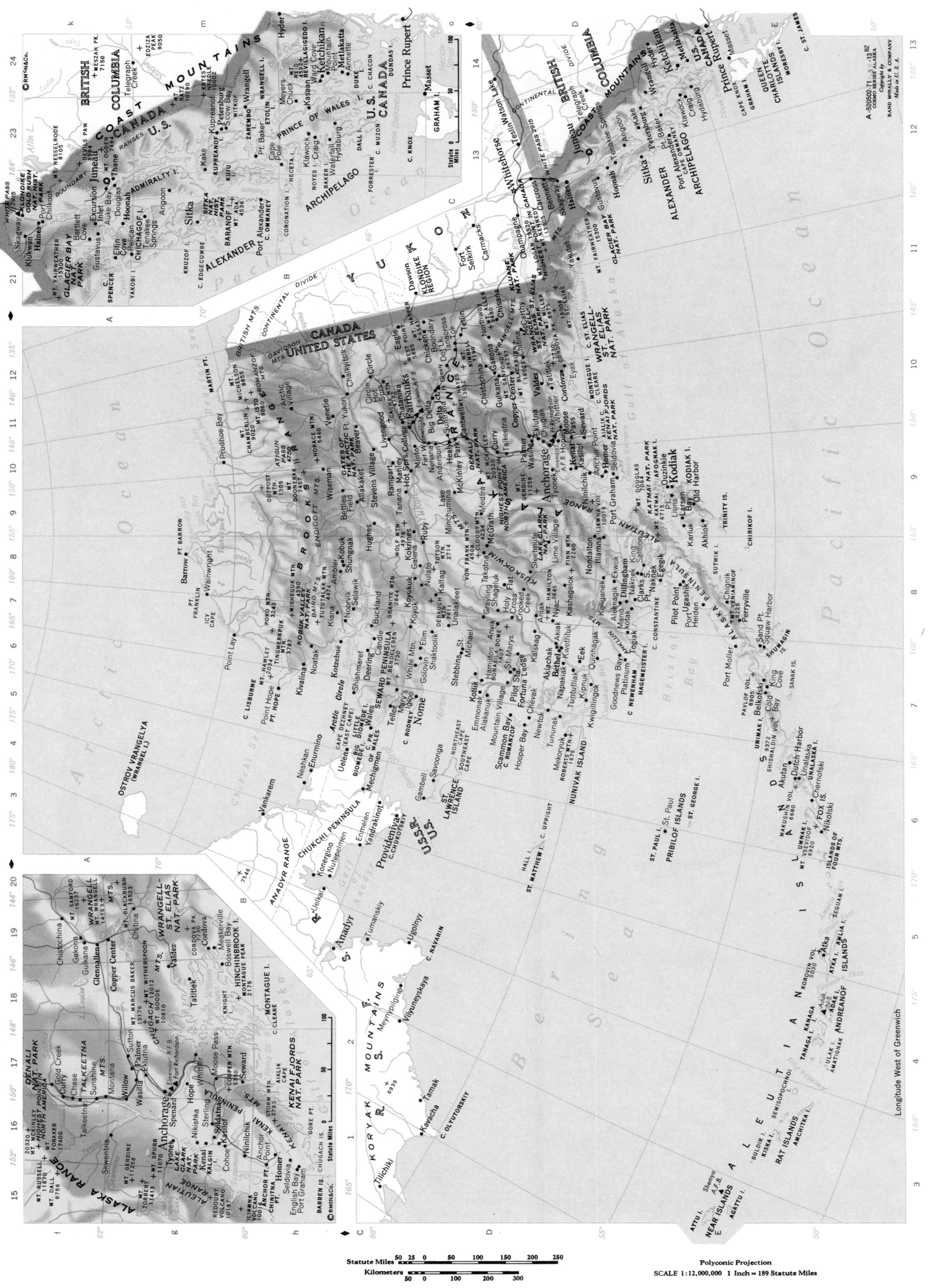

Statute Miles 50 25 0  50   100   150   200   250
Kilometers 50 0  100   200   300

Polyconic Projection
SCALE 1:12,000,000  1 Inch = 189 Statute Miles

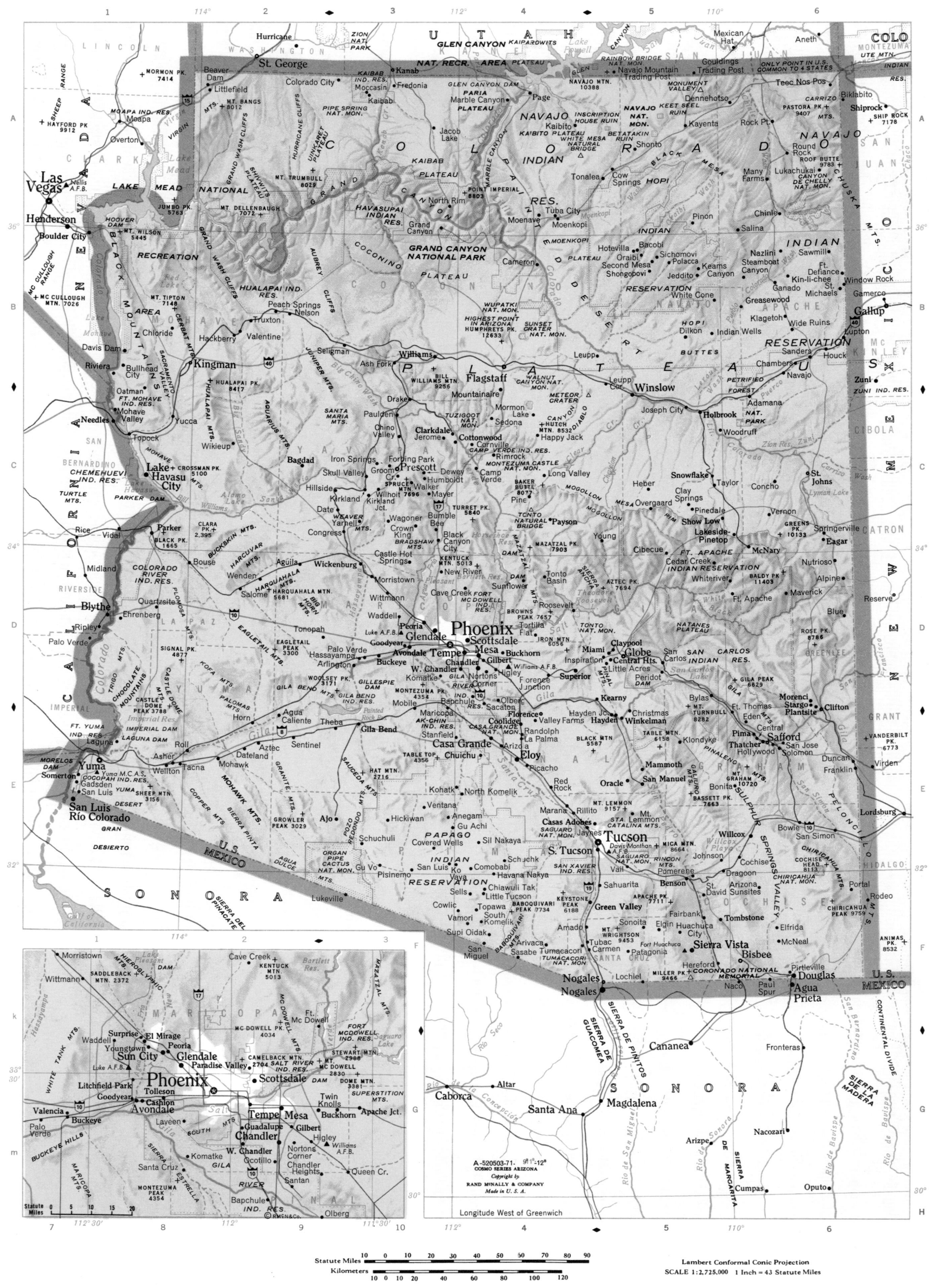

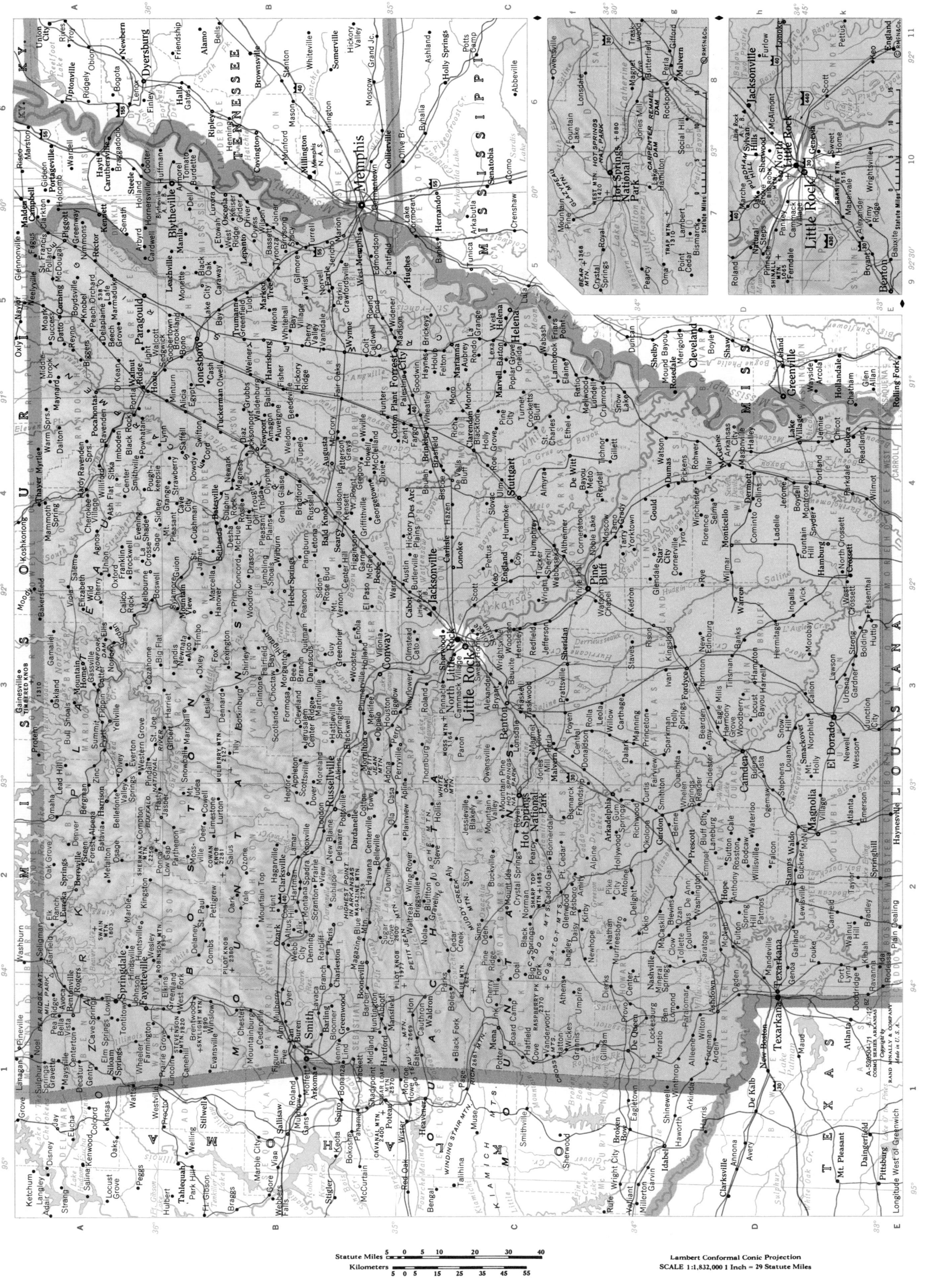

Statute Miles
Kilometers

Lambert Conformal Conic Projection
SCALE 1:1,832,000 1 Inch = 29 Statute Miles

Statute Miles  5  0  5  10    20    30    40    50
Kilometers  5 0 5  15  25  35  45  55  65  75

Lambert Conformal Conic Projection
SCALE 1:2,186,000    1 Inch = 34.5 Statute Miles

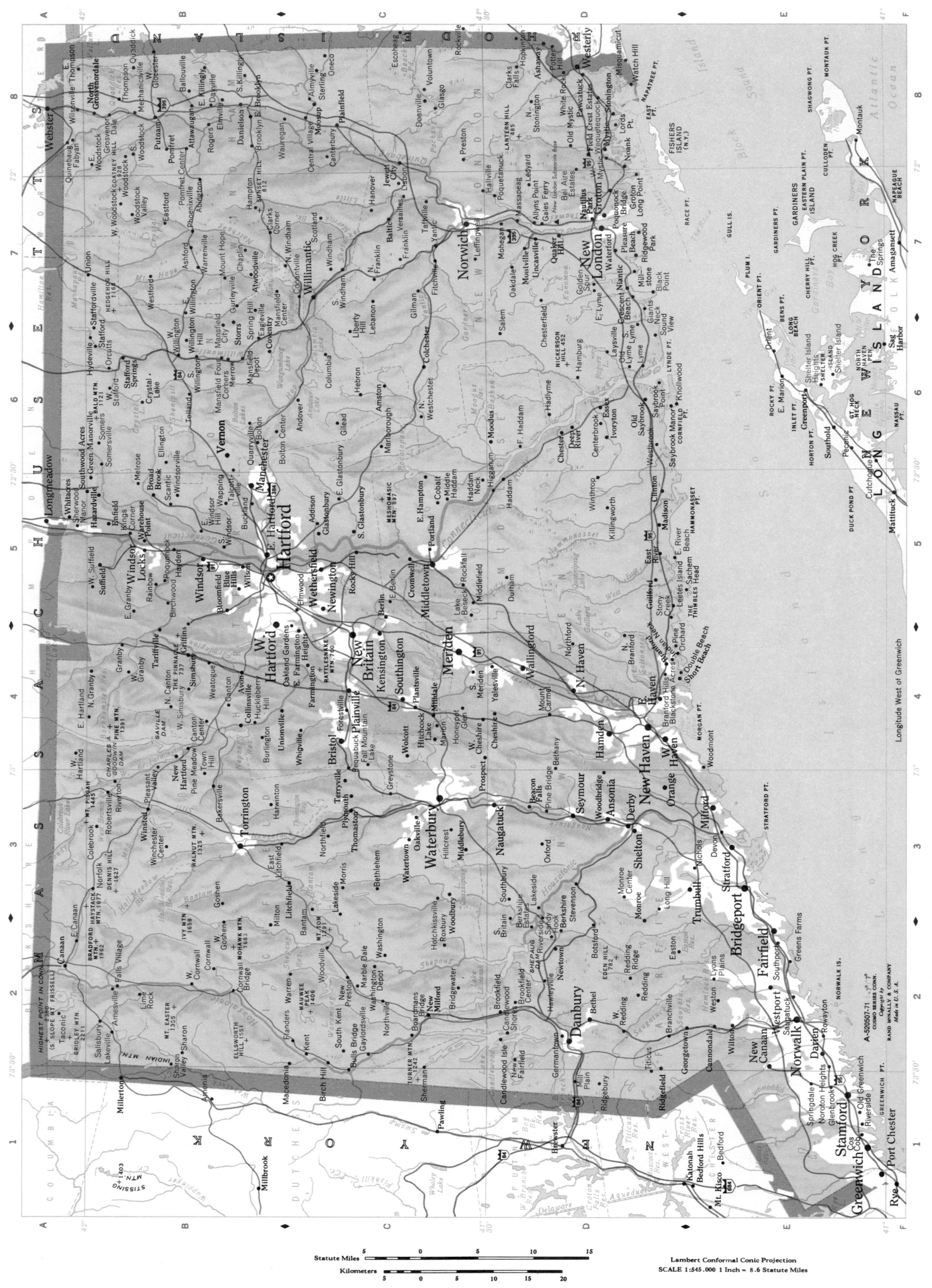

Statute Miles

Kilometers

Lambert Conformal Conic Projection
SCALE 1:545.000 1 Inch = 8.6 Statute Miles

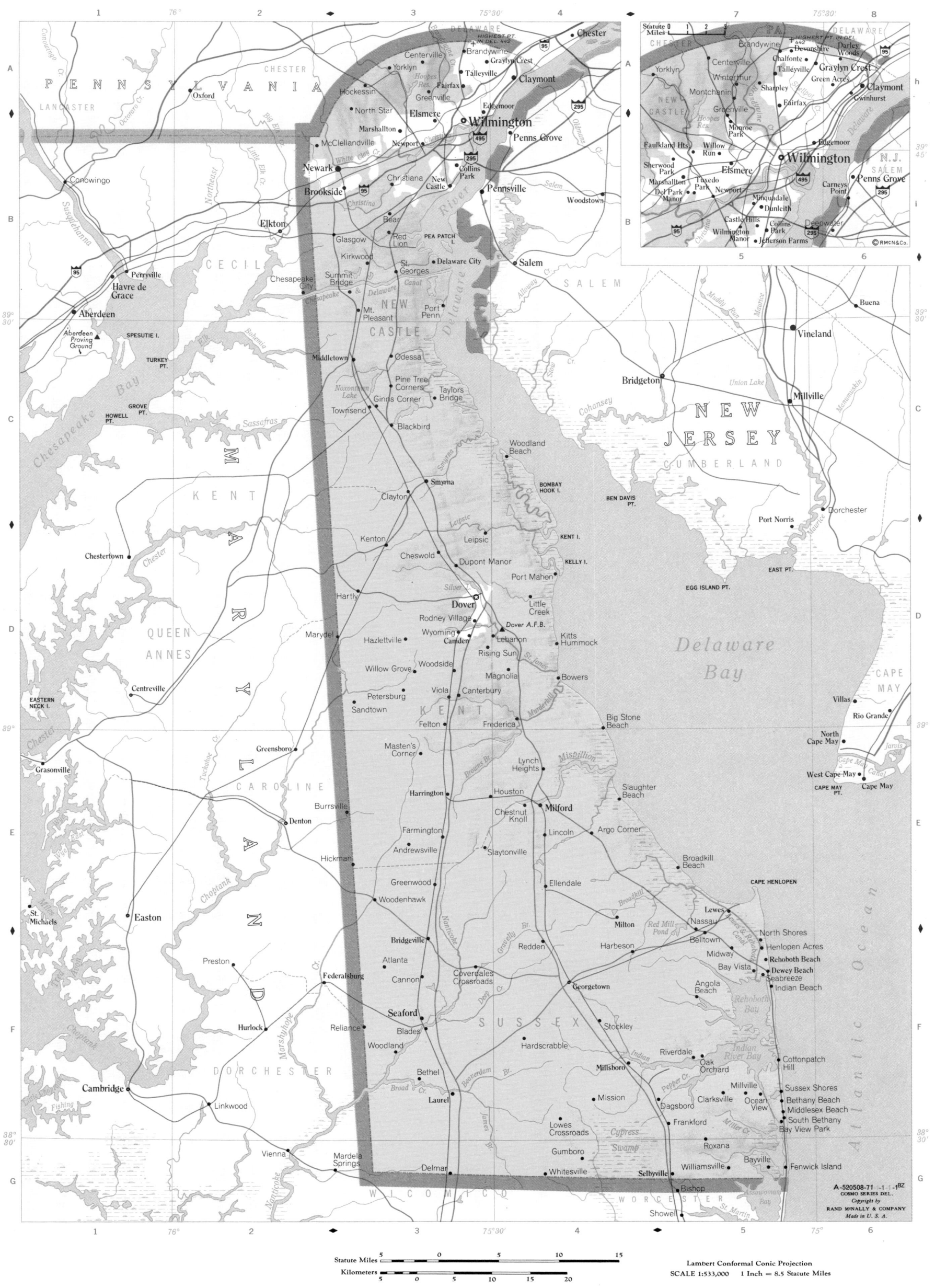

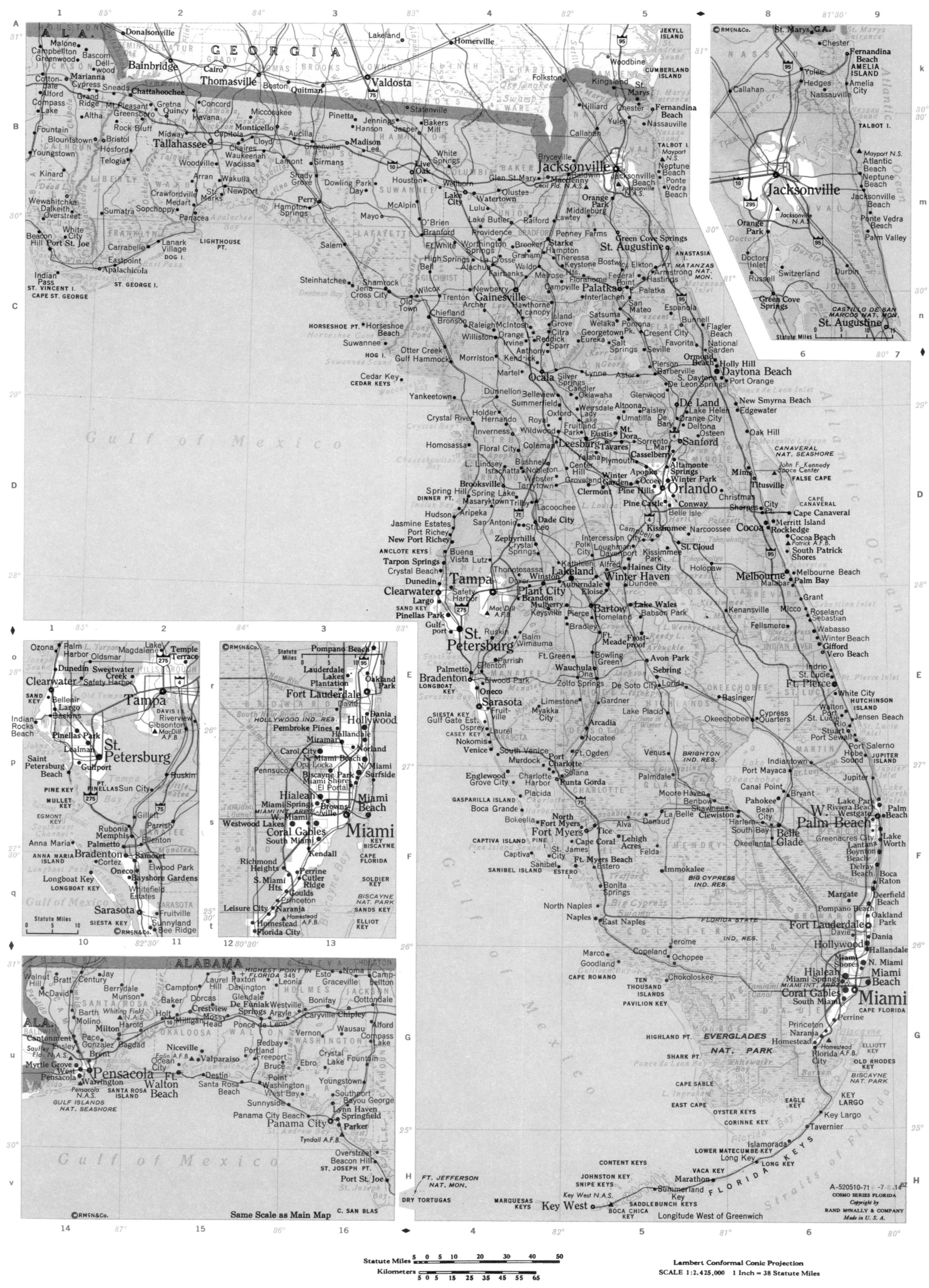

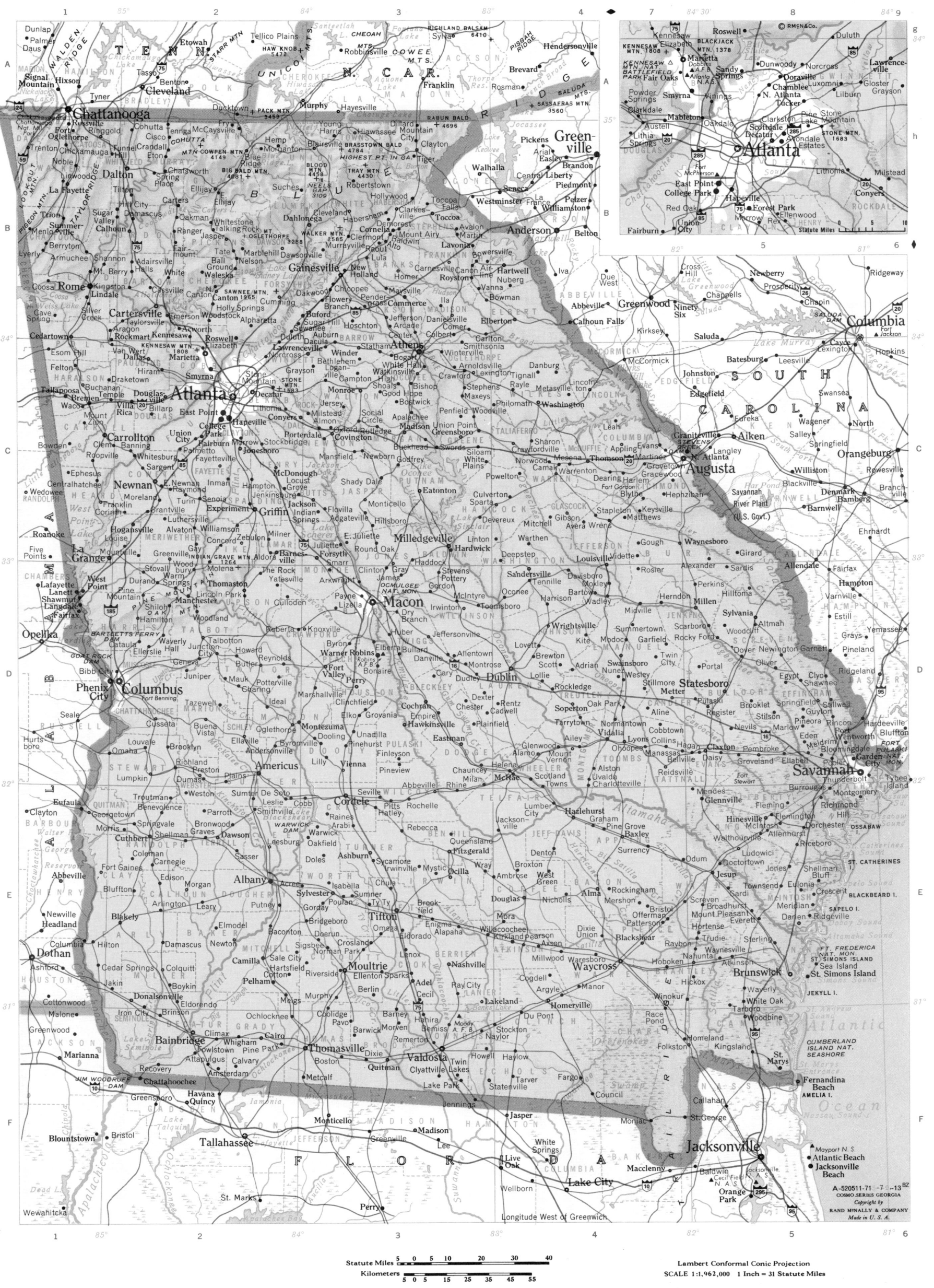

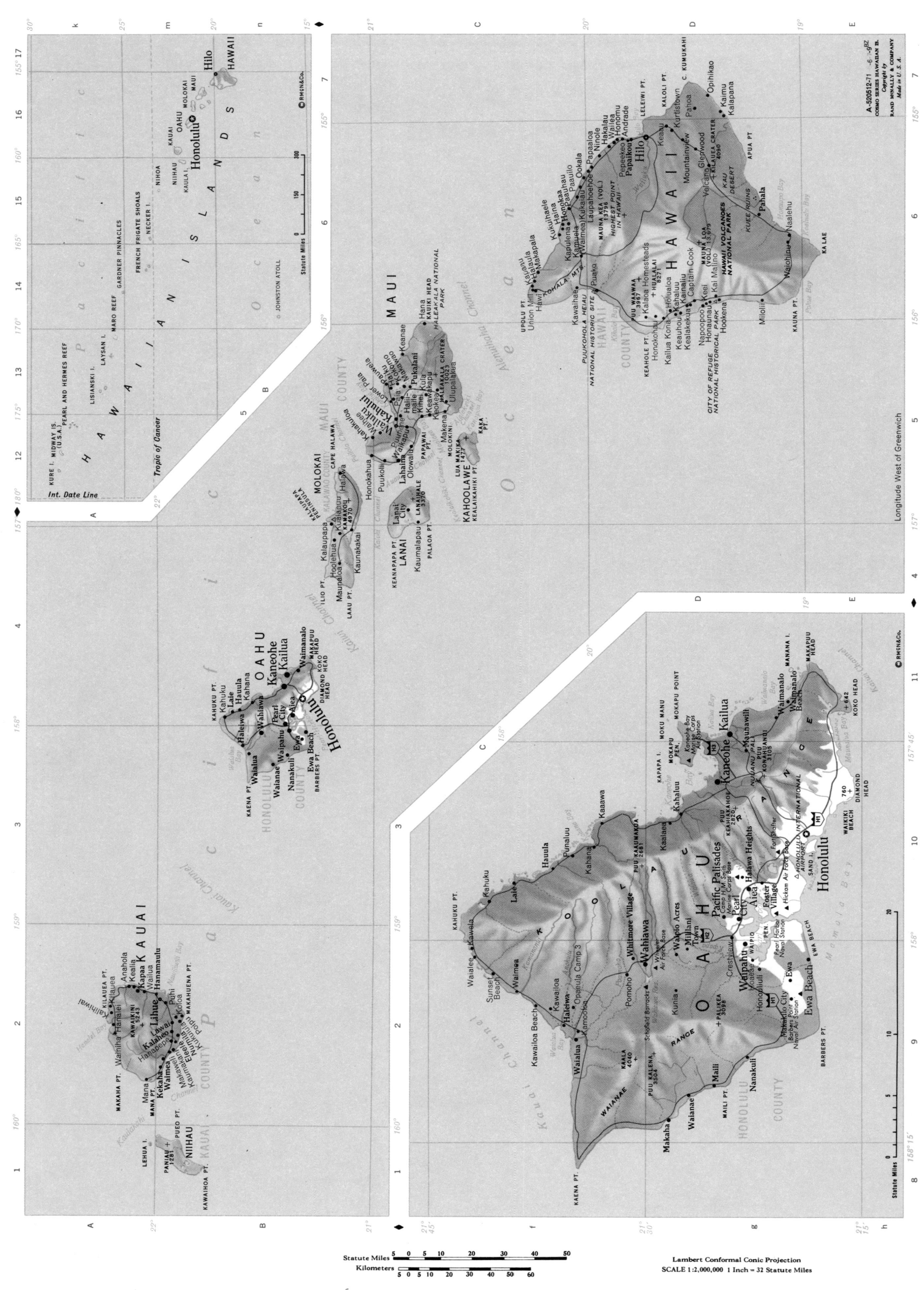

Lambert Conformal Conic Projection
SCALE 1:2,000,000  1 Inch = 32 Statute Miles

Statute Miles
Kilometers

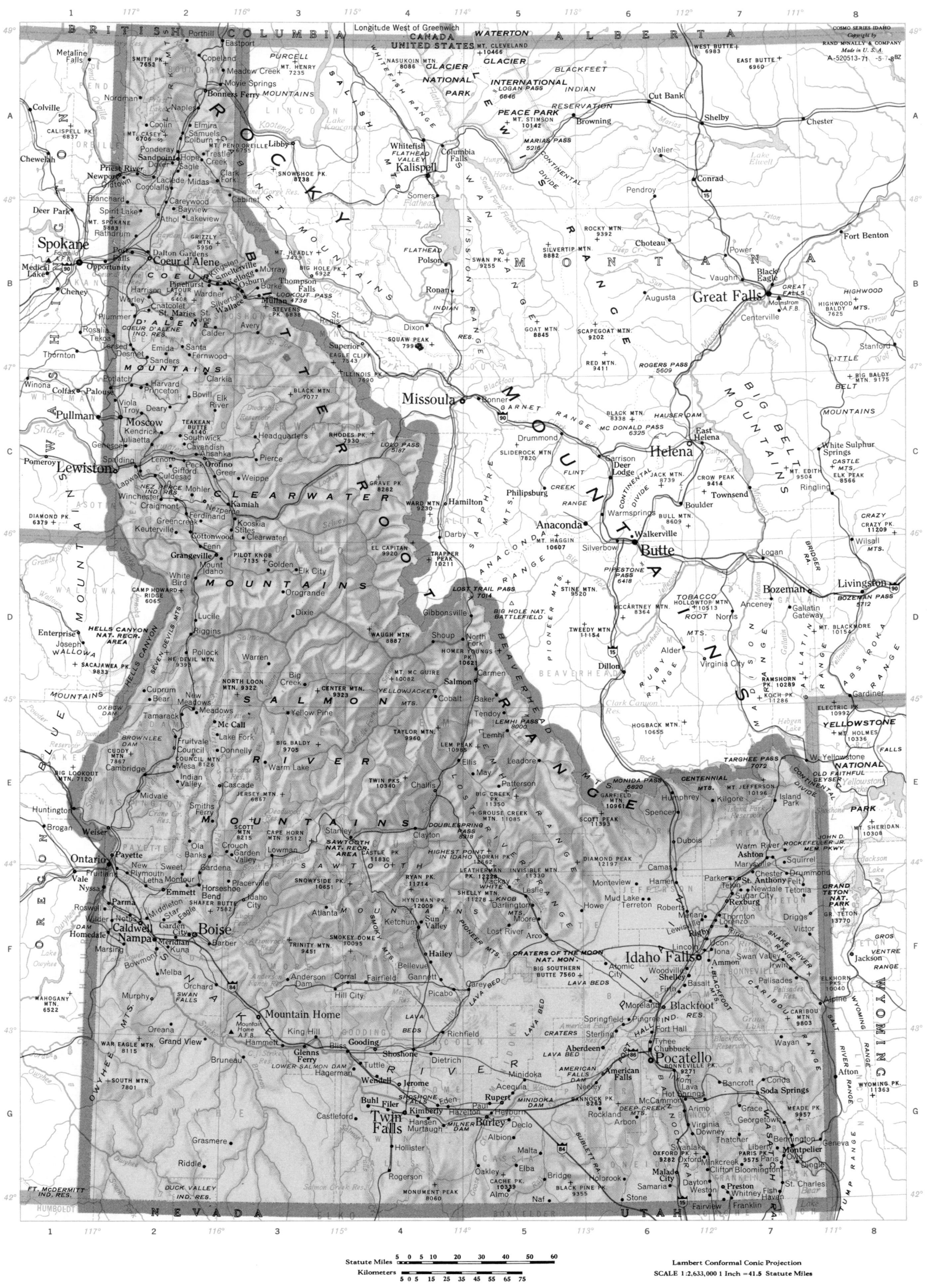

Statute Miles 5 0 5 10 20 30 40 50 60

Kilometers 5 0 5 15 25 35 45 65 75

Lambert Conformal Conic Projection
SCALE 1:2,633,000 1 Inch = 41.5 Statute Miles

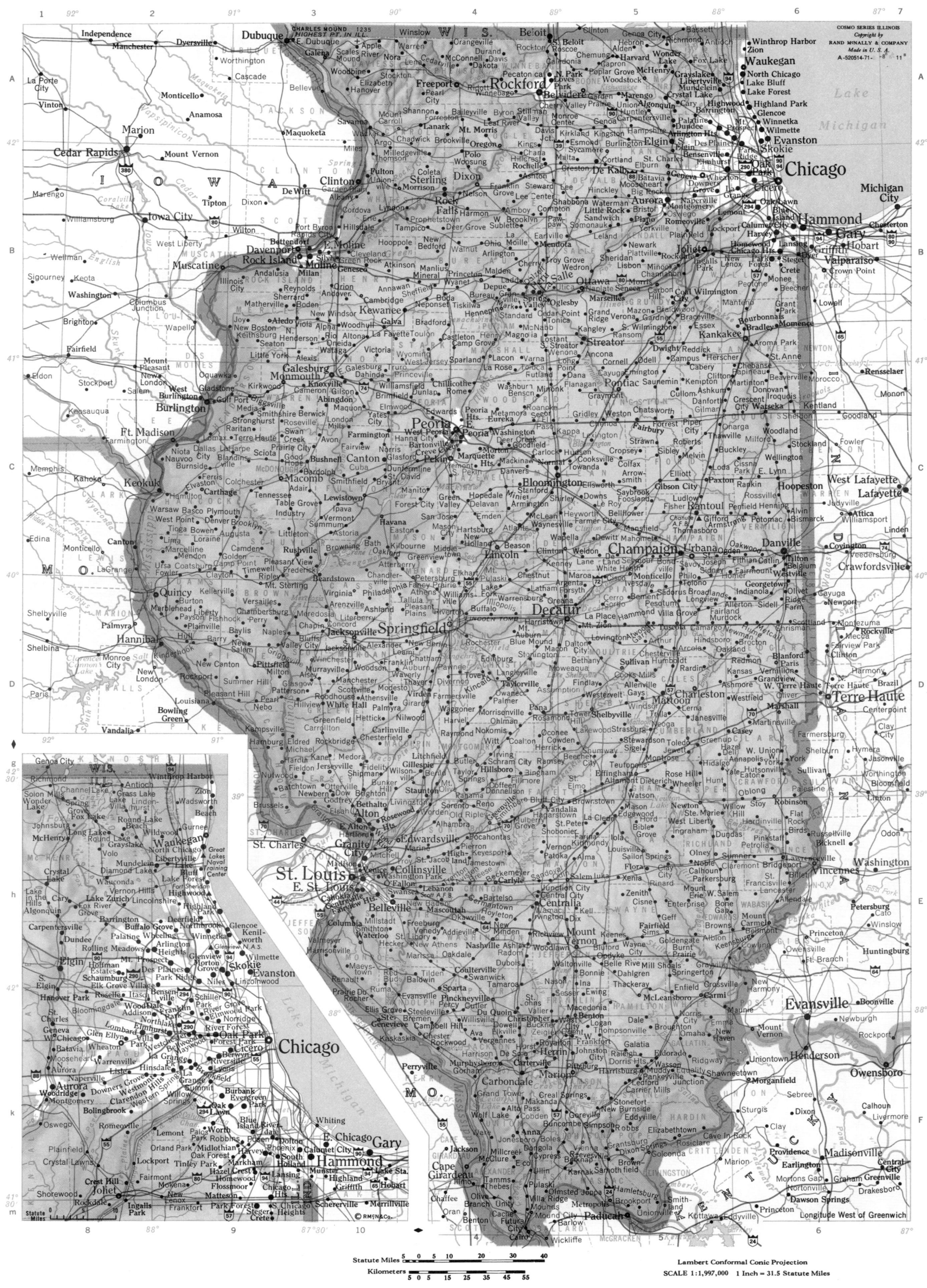

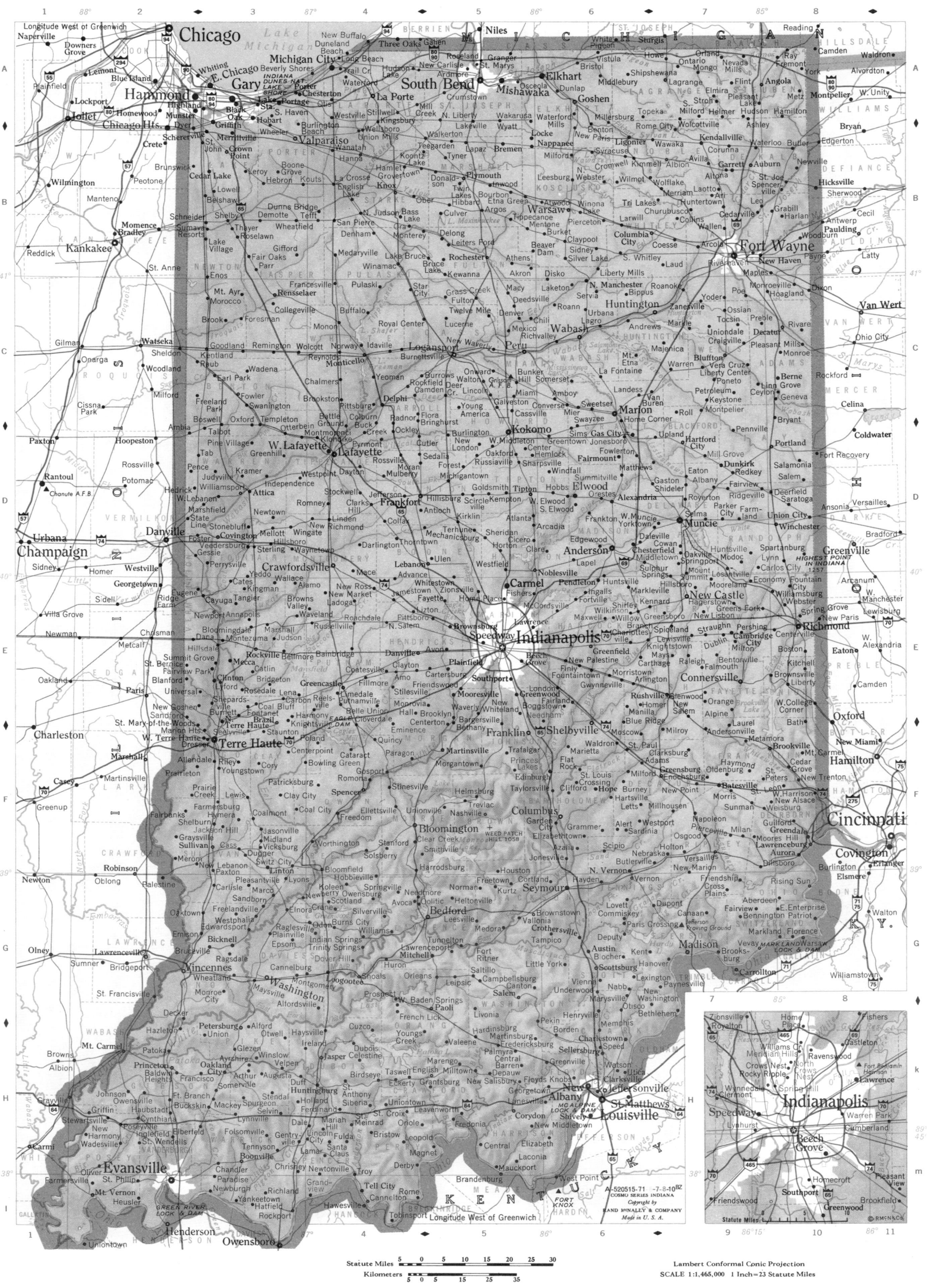

Statute Miles 5  0  5  10  15  20  25  30
Kilometers 5  0  5  15  25  35

Lambert Conformal Conic Projection
SCALE 1:1,465,000  1 Inch=23 Statute Miles

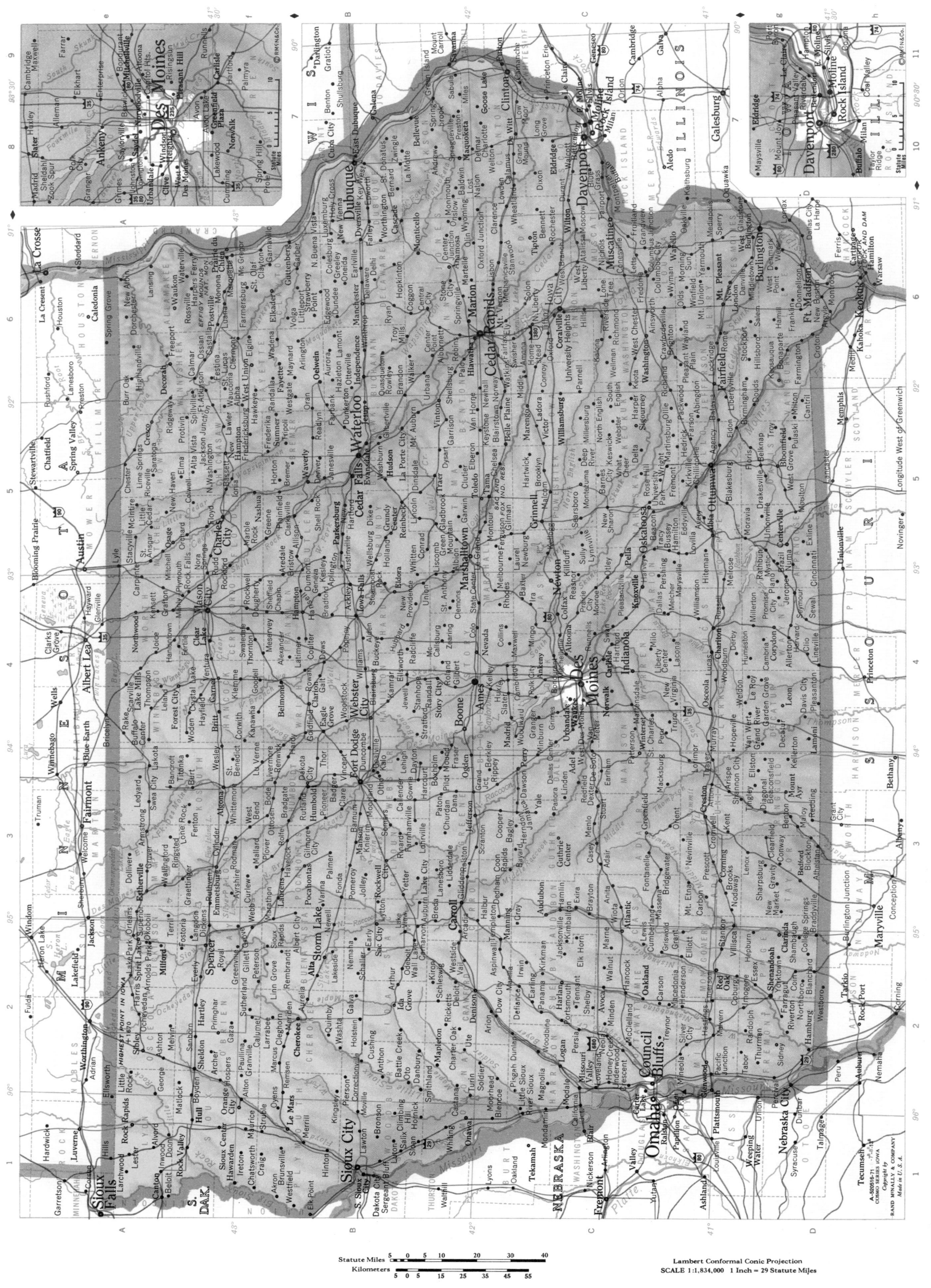

Statute Miles 5 0 5 10 20 30 40
Kilometers 5 0 5 15 25 35 45 55

Lambert Conformal Conic Projection
SCALE 1:1,834,000  1 Inch = 29 Statute Miles

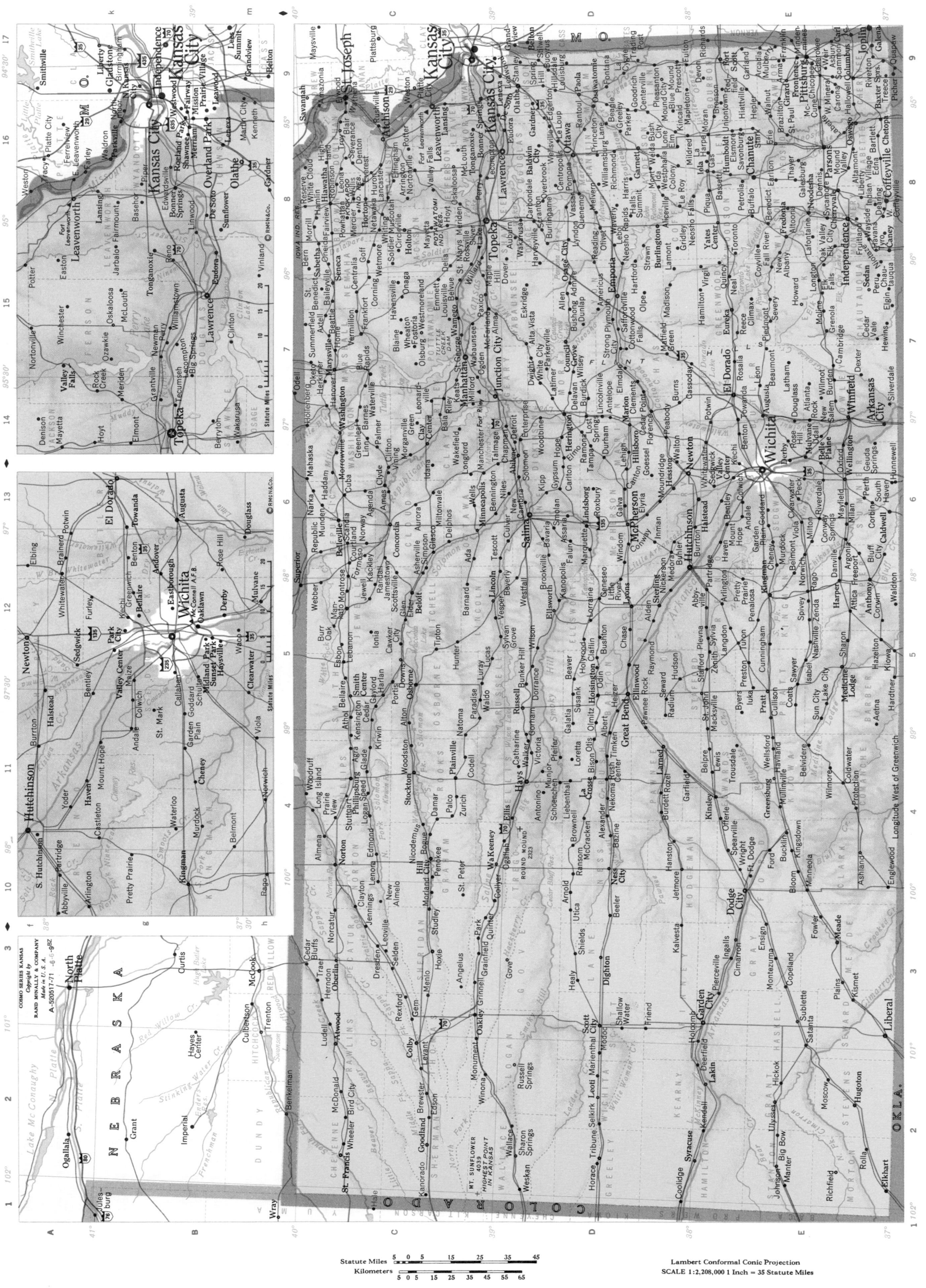

Statute Miles
Kilometers

Lambert Conformal Conic Projection
SCALE 1:2,208,000 1 Inch = 35 Statute Miles

COSMO SERIES KANSAS
Copyright by
RAND McNALLY & COMPANY
Made in U.S.A.
A-520517-271 -6-0-9BZ

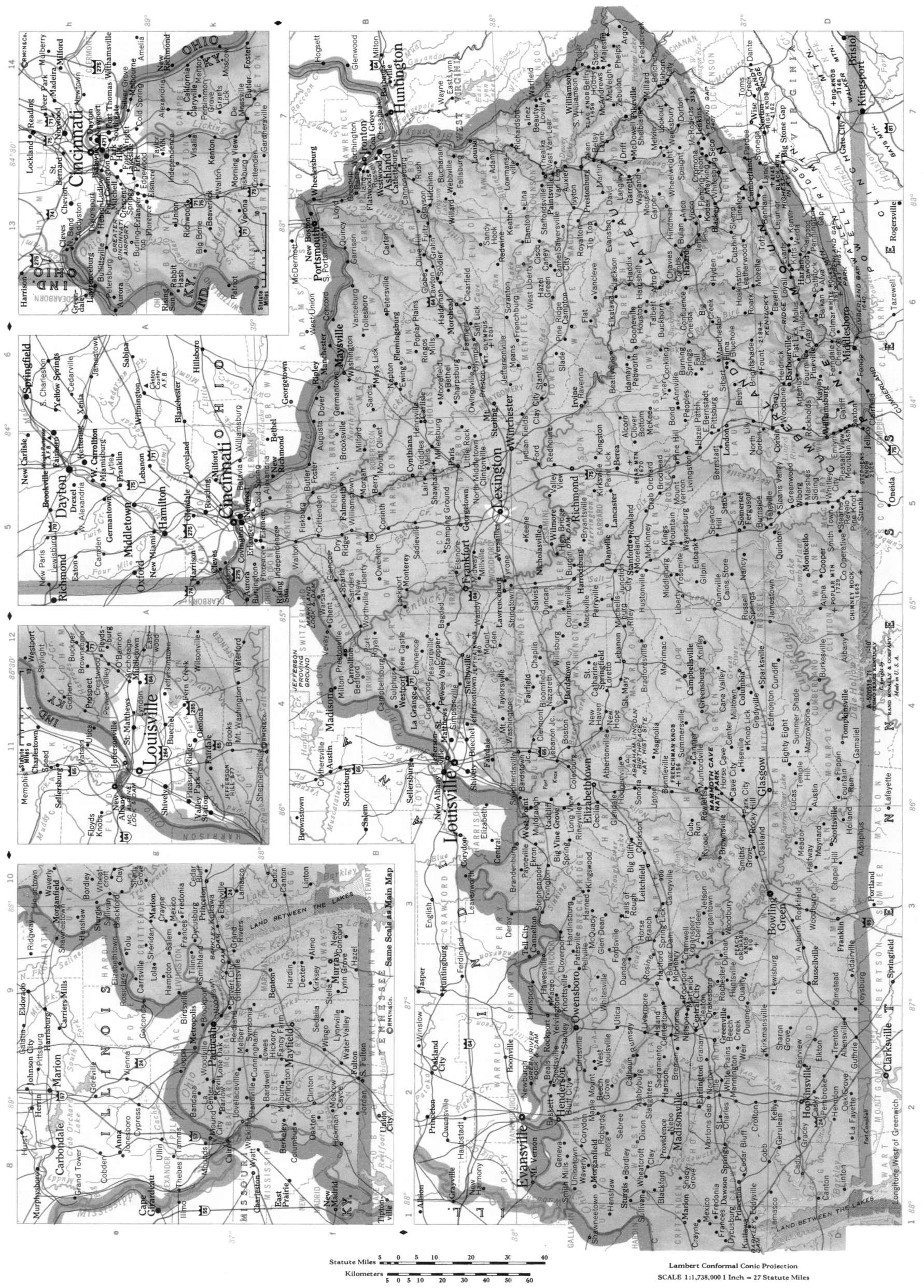

Statute Miles  5  0  5  10  20  30  40

Kilometers  5  0  5 10  20  30  40  50  60

Lambert Conformal Conic Projection
SCALE 1:1,738,000 1 Inch = 27 Statute Miles

Statute Miles 5  0  5  10      20      30    40

Kilometers  5 0 5  15  25  35  45  55

Lambert Conformal Conic Projection

SCALE 1:2,083,000  1 Inch = 33 Statute Miles

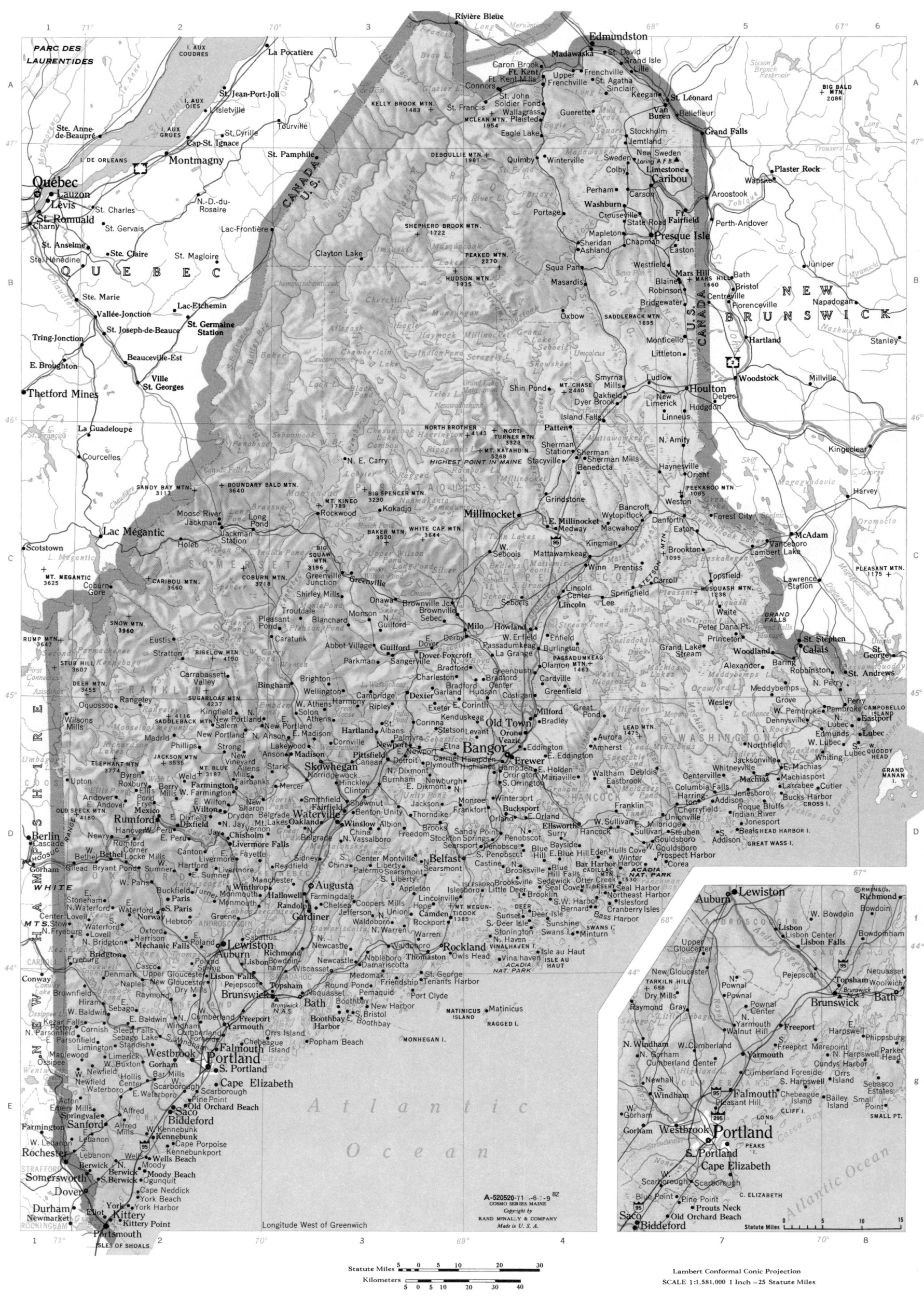

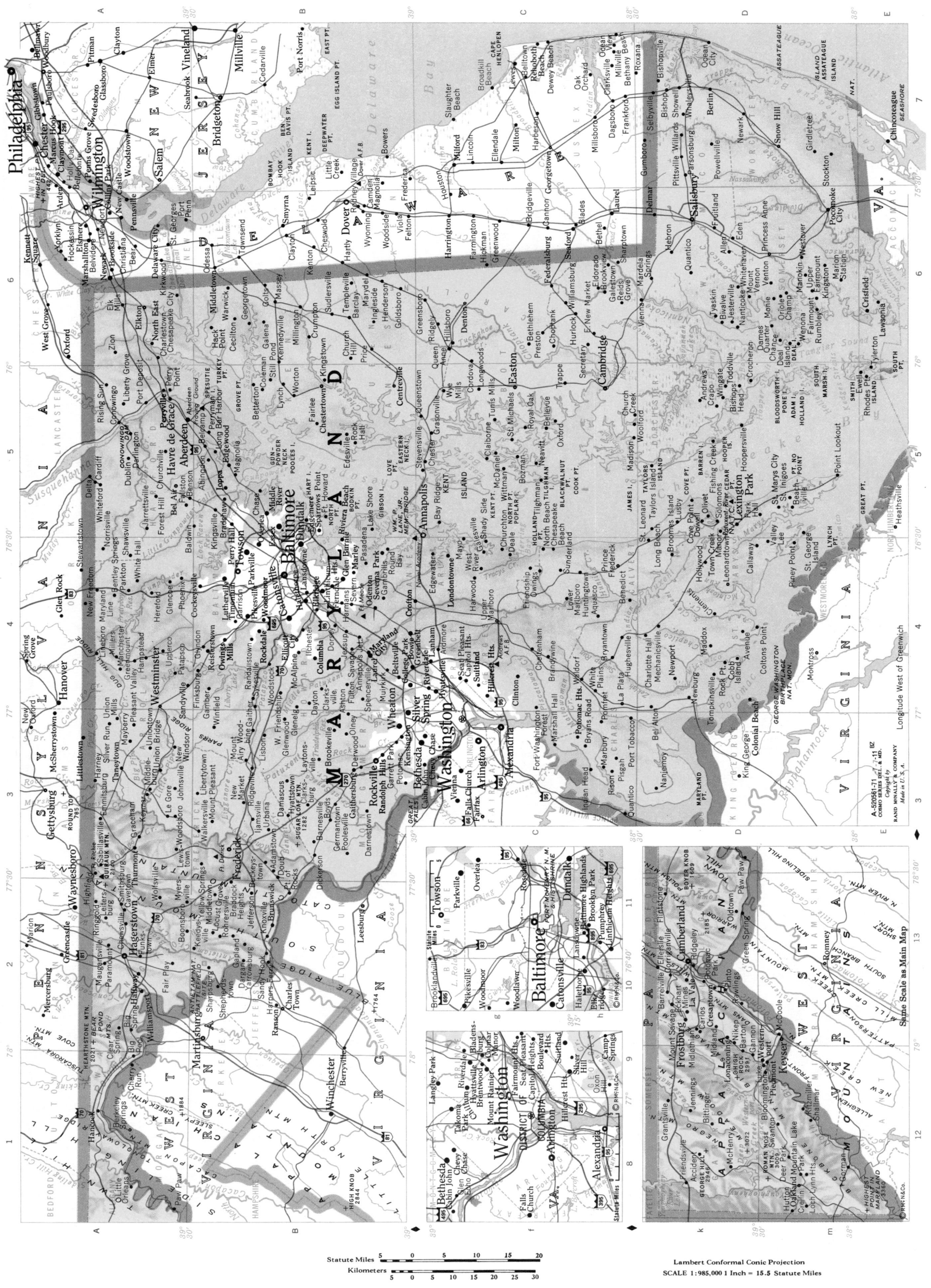

Statute Miles

Kilometers

Lambert Conformal Conic Projection
SCALE 1:985,000 1 Inch = 15.5 Statute Miles

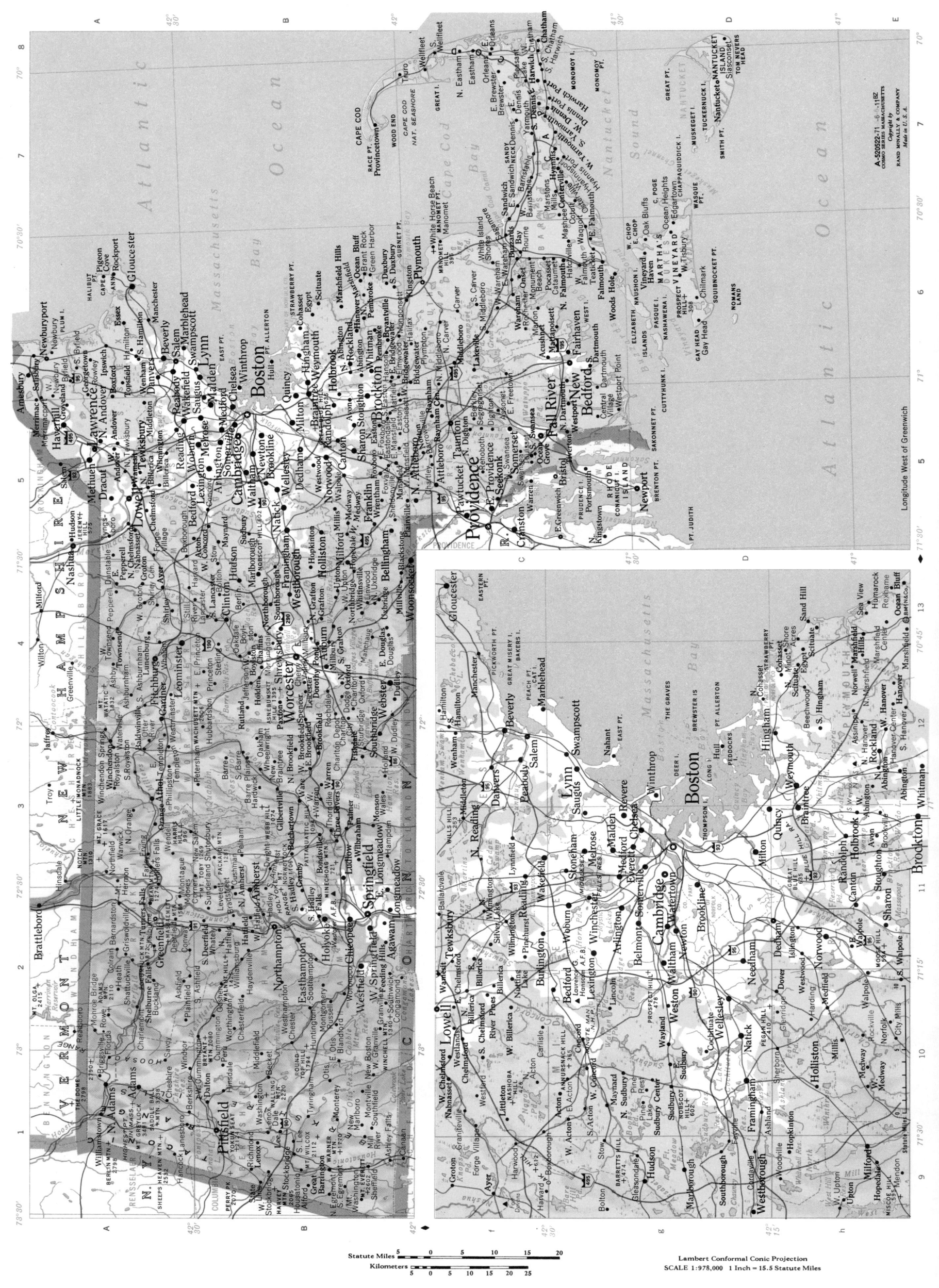

Statute Miles

Kilometers

Lambert Conformal Conic Projection
SCALE 1:978,000   1 Inch = 15.5 Statute Miles

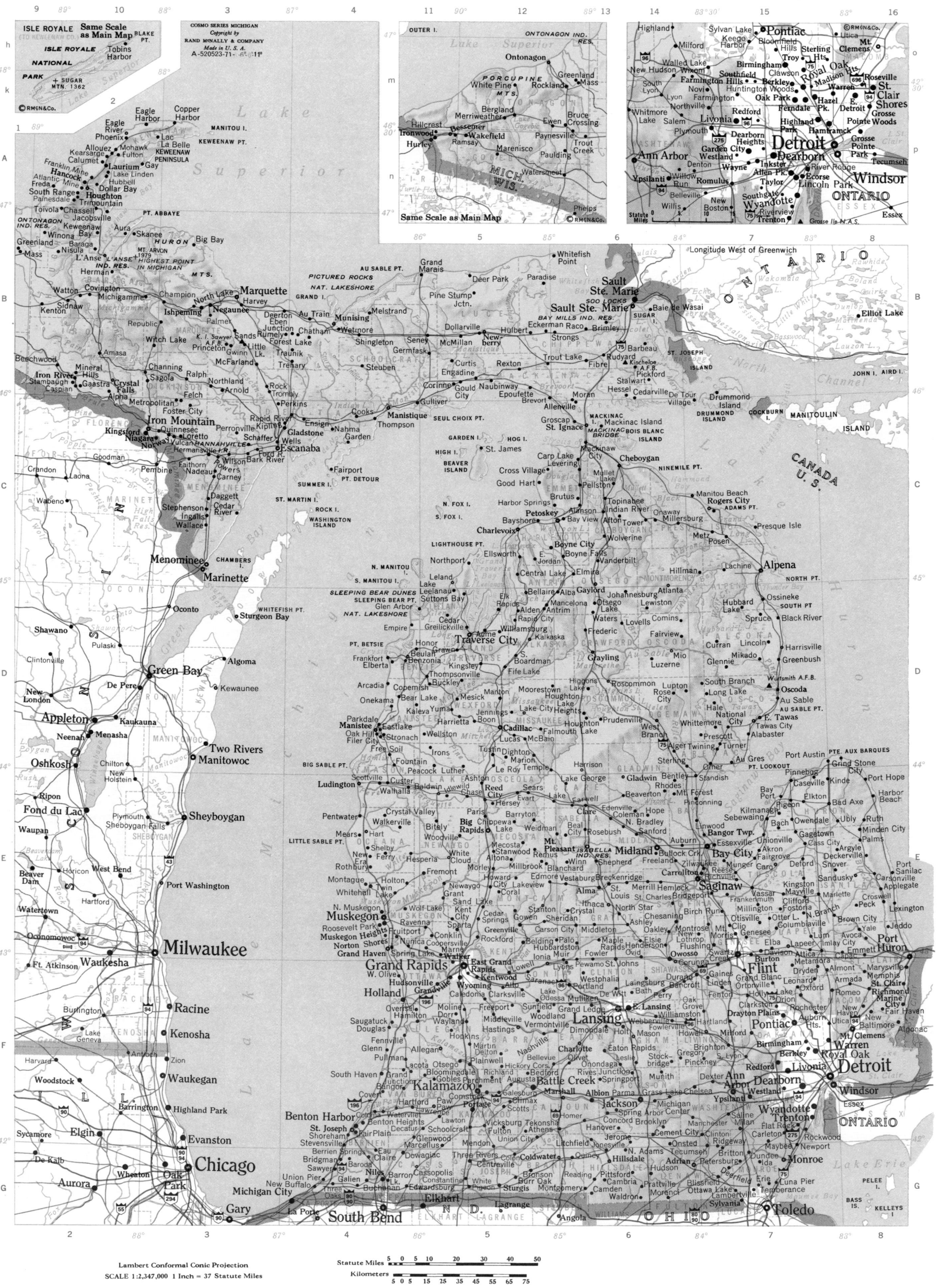

Isle Royale — Same Scale as Main Map

ISLE ROYALE NATIONAL PARK
+ SUGAR MTN. 1362
© R.M. & Co.

COSMO SERIES MICHIGAN
Copyright by
RAND McNALLY & COMPANY
Made in U.S.A.
A-520523-71-

Lambert Conformal Conic Projection
SCALE 1:2,347,000 1 Inch = 37 Statute Miles

Statute Miles 5 0 5 10 20 30 40 50
Kilometers 5 0 5 15 25 35 45 55 65 75

99

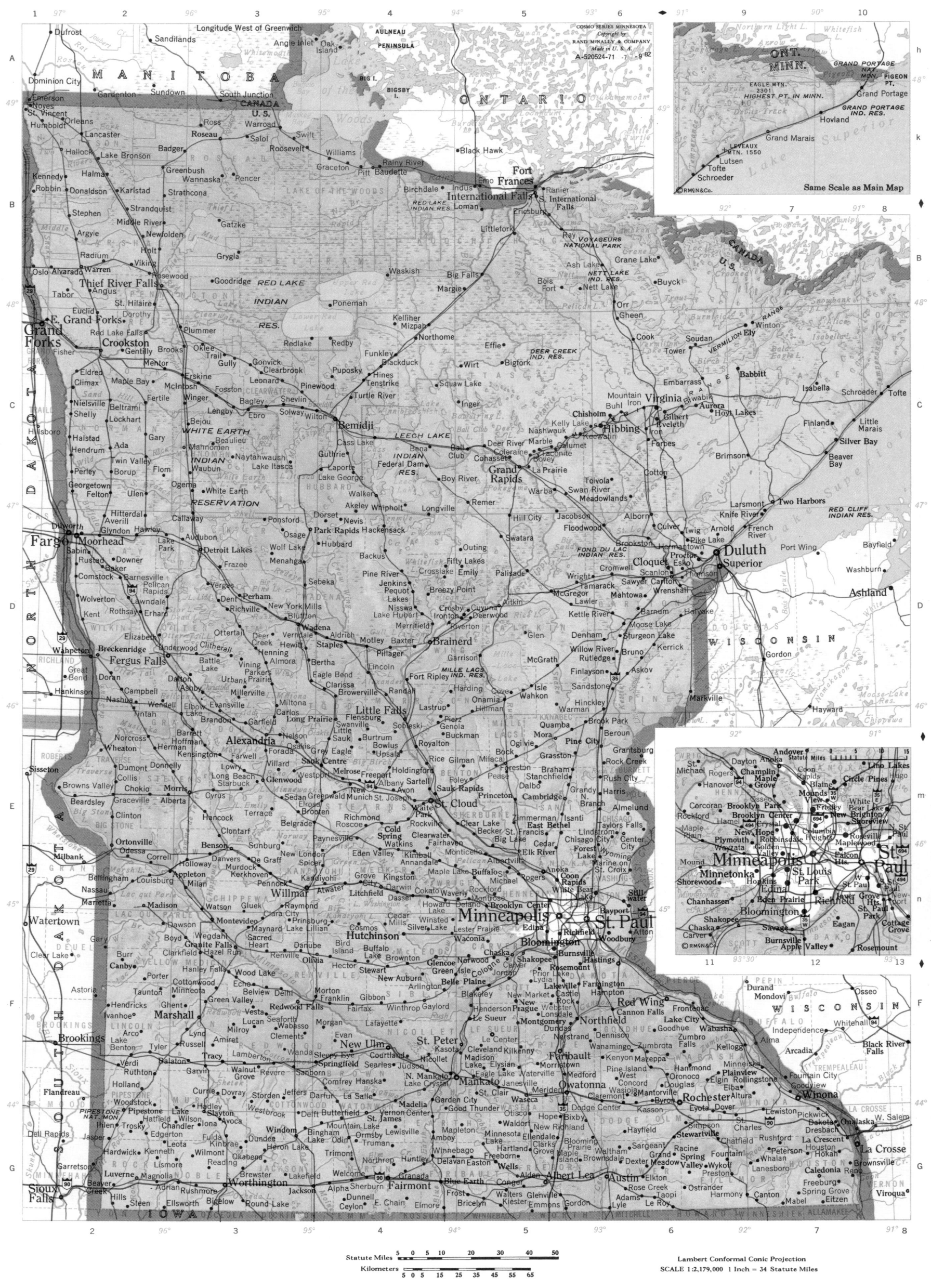

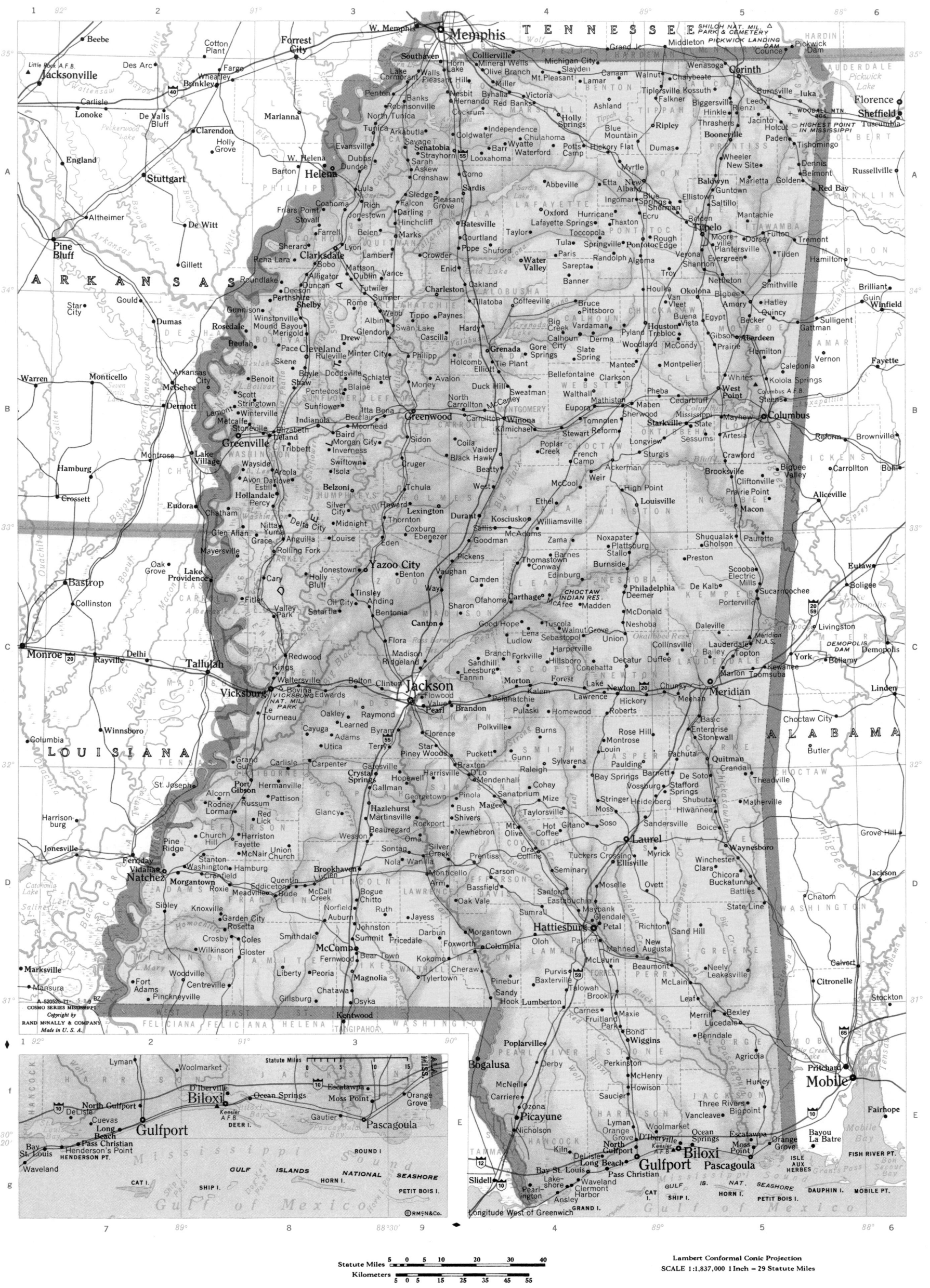

Lambert Conformal Conic Projection
SCALE 1:1,837,000  1 Inch = 29 Statute Miles

Statute Miles  5 0 5 10 20 30 40
Kilometers  5 0 5 15 25 35 45 55

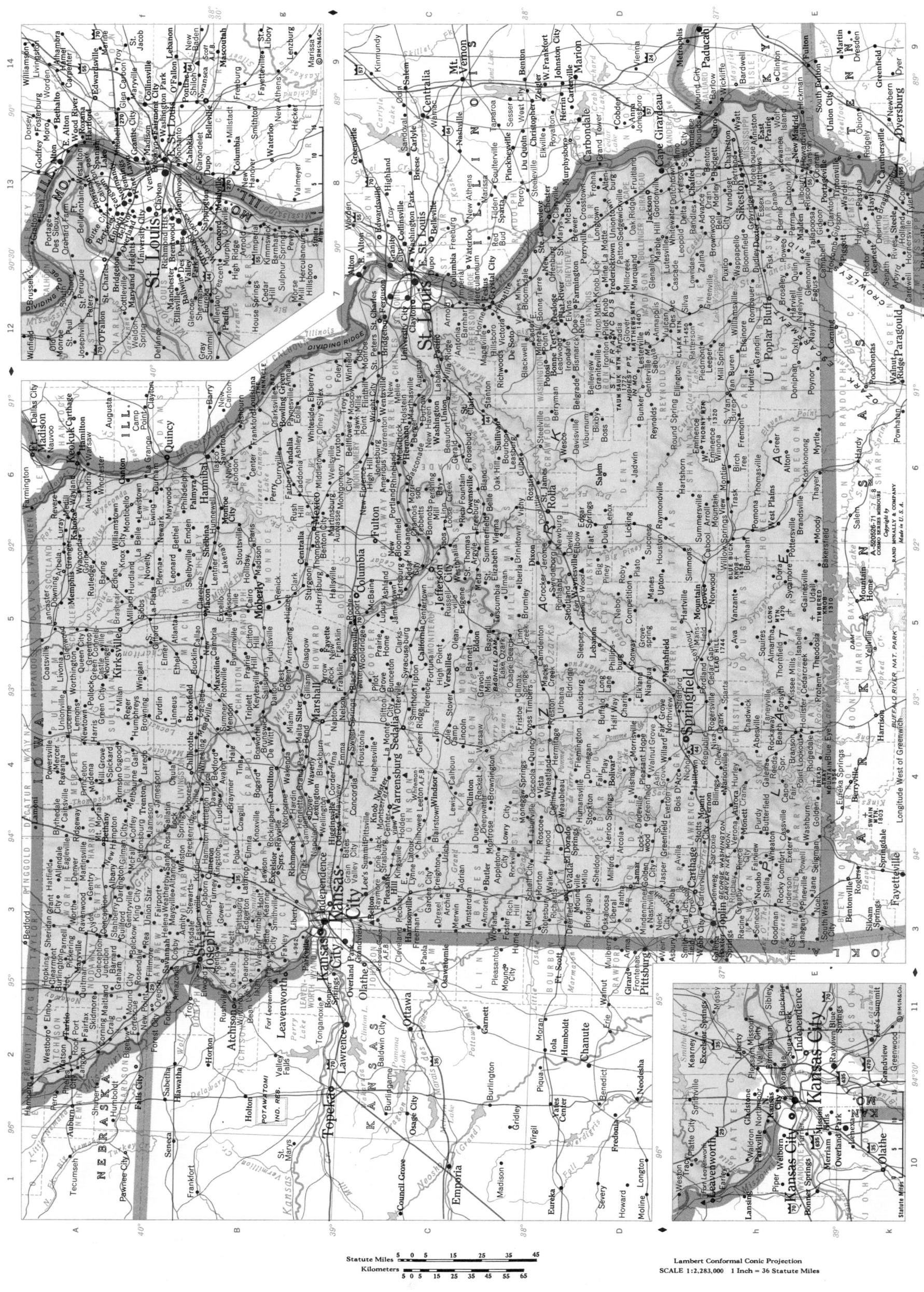

Statute Miles 5 0 5 15 25 35 45
Kilometers 5 0 5 15 25 35 45 55 65

Lambert Conformal Conic Projection
SCALE 1:2,283,000  1 Inch = 36 Statute Miles

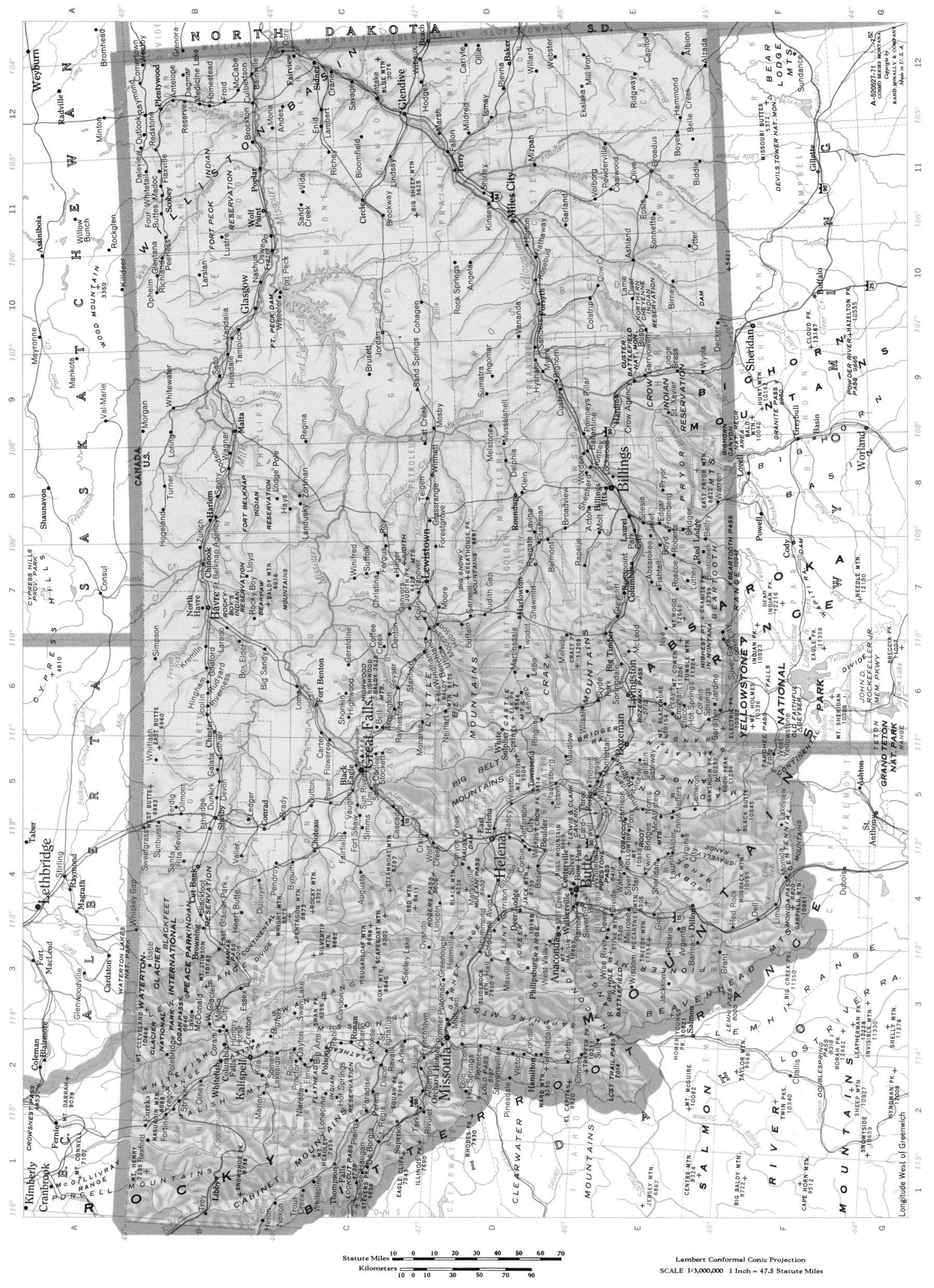

Statute Miles 10 0 10 20 30 40 50 60 70
Kilometers 10 0 10 30 50 70 90

Lambert Conformal Conic Projection
SCALE 1:3,000,000   1 Inch = 47.5 Statute Miles

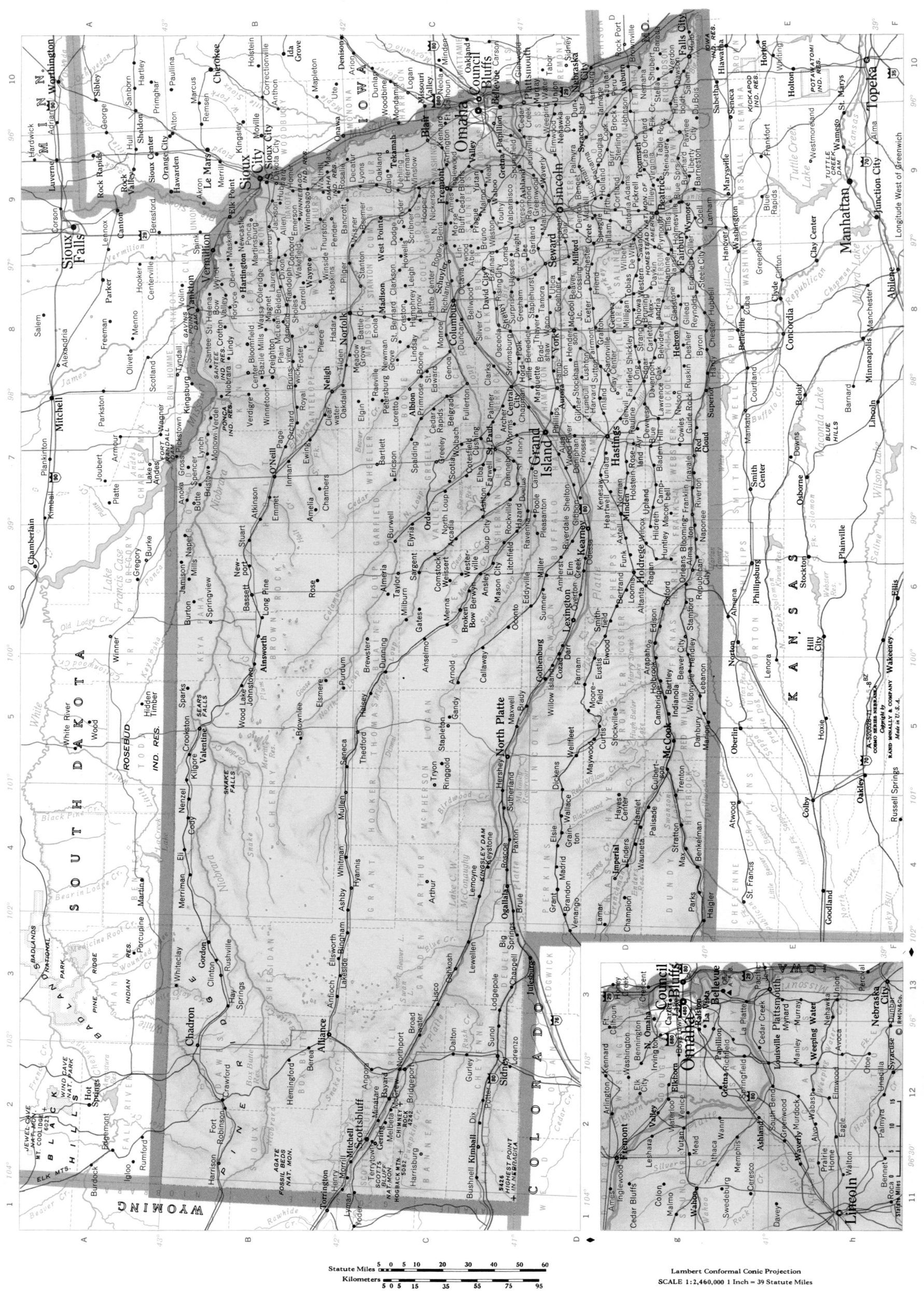

Statute Miles 5 0 5 10 20 30 40 50 60

Kilometers 5 0 5 15 35 55 75 95

Lambert Conformal Conic Projection
SCALE 1:2,460,000 1 Inch = 39 Statute Miles

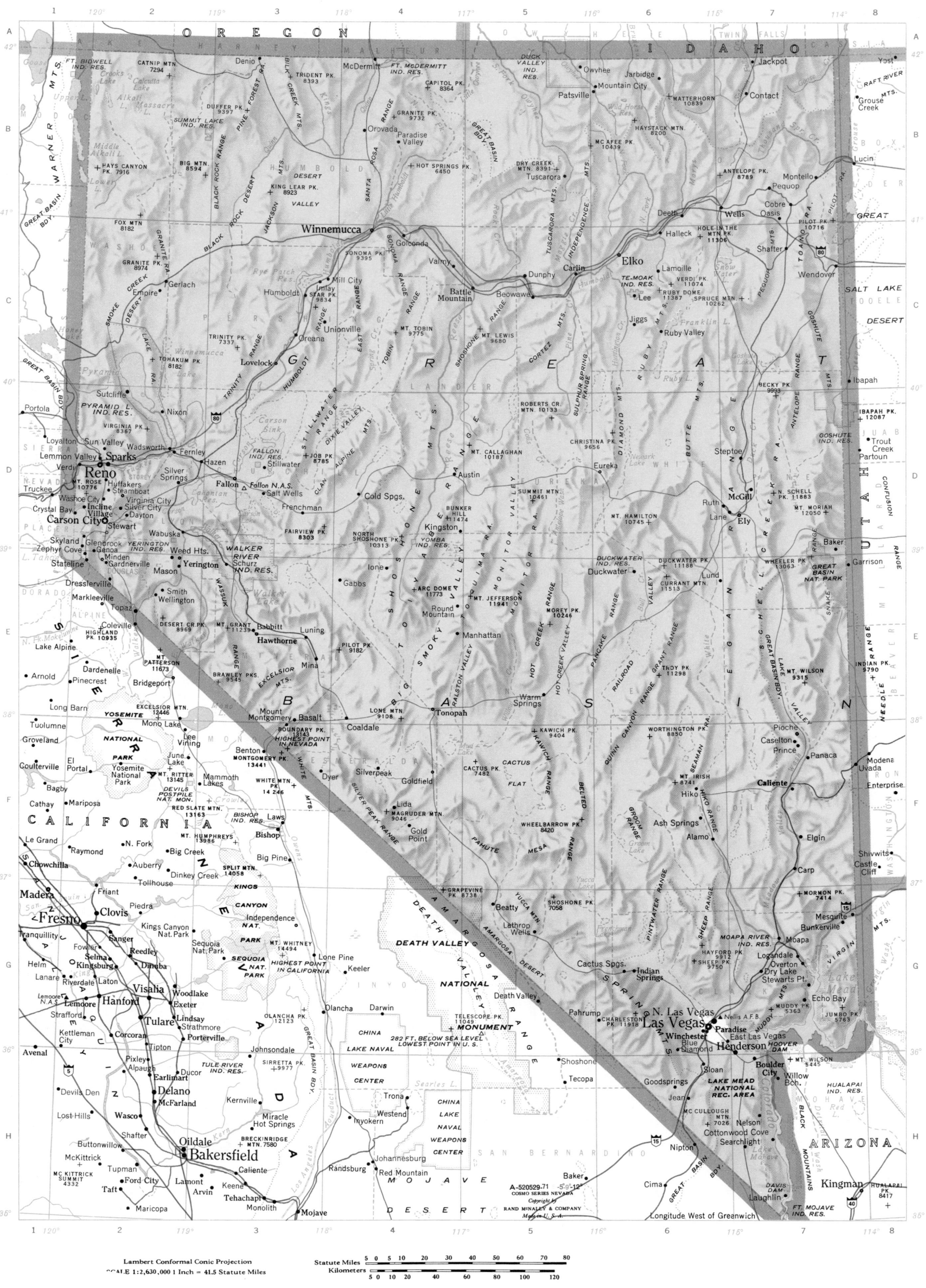

Lambert Conformal Conic Projection
SCALE 1:2,630,000 1 Inch = 41.5 Statute Miles

Statute Miles 5 0 5 10    20    30    40    50    60    70    80
Kilometers 5 0 10 20    40    60    80    100    120

A-520529-71 -5-9-12
COSMO SERIES NEVADA
Copyright by
RAND McNALLY & COMPANY
Made in U.S.A.

Longitude West of Greenwich

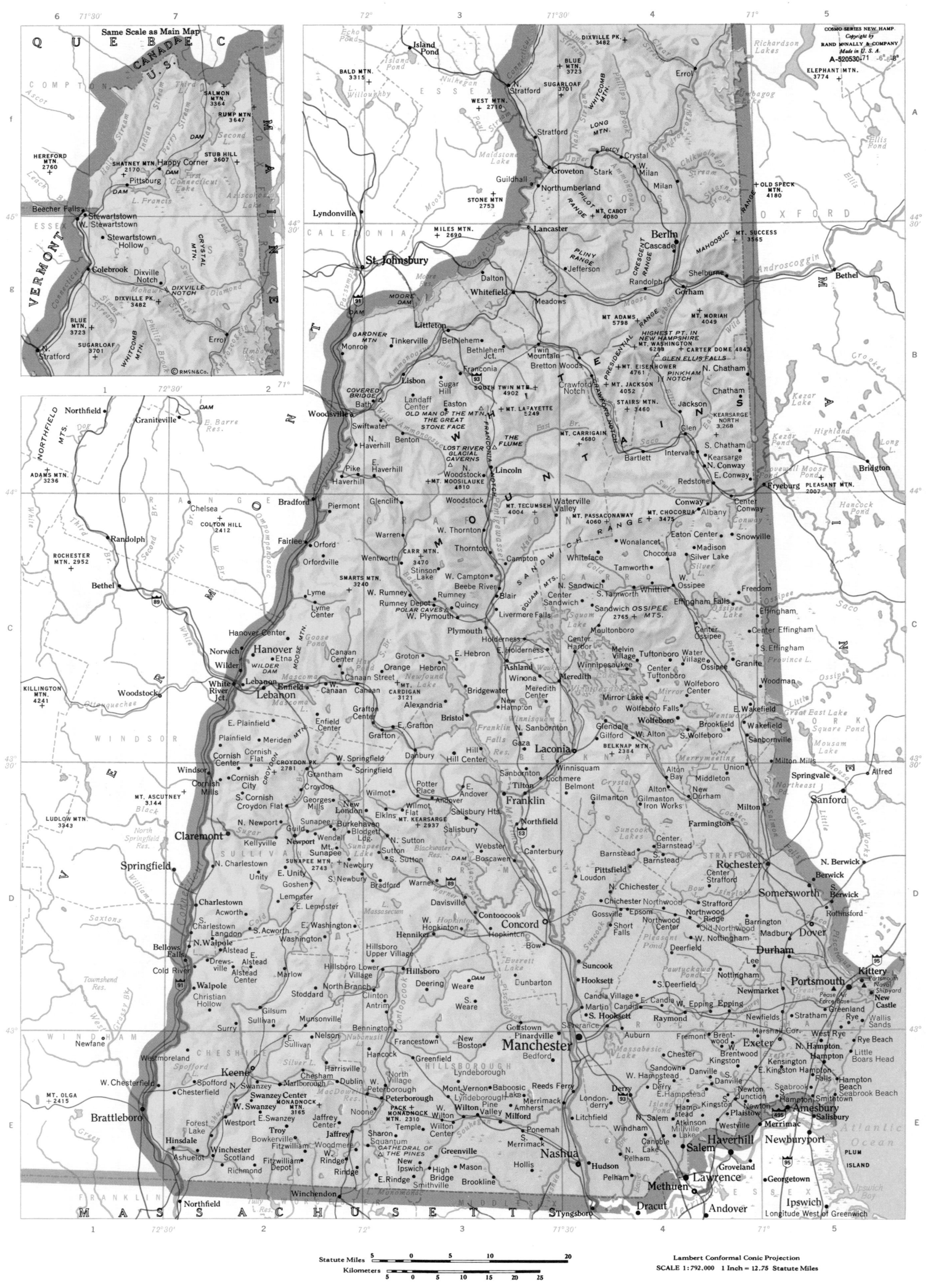

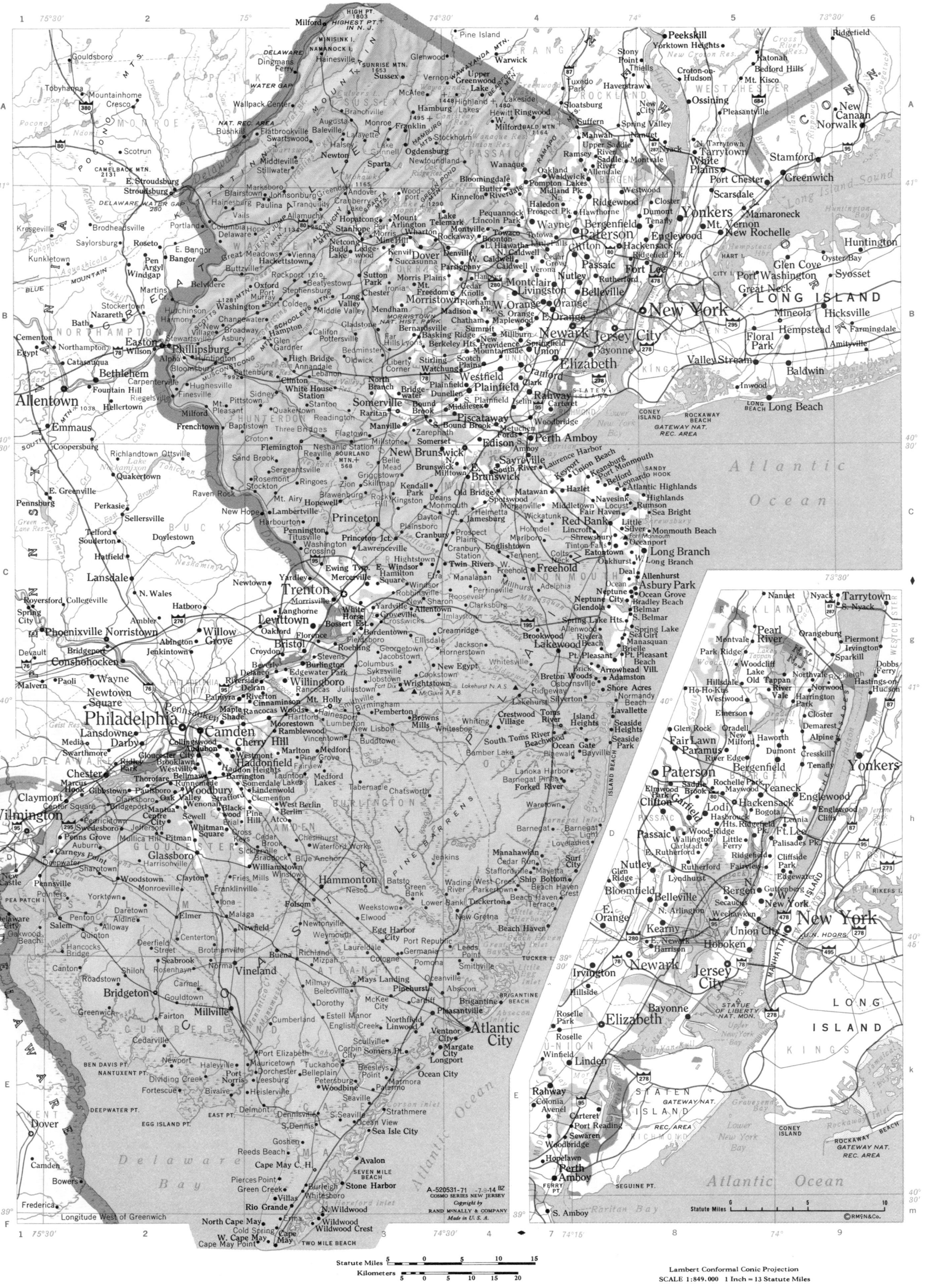

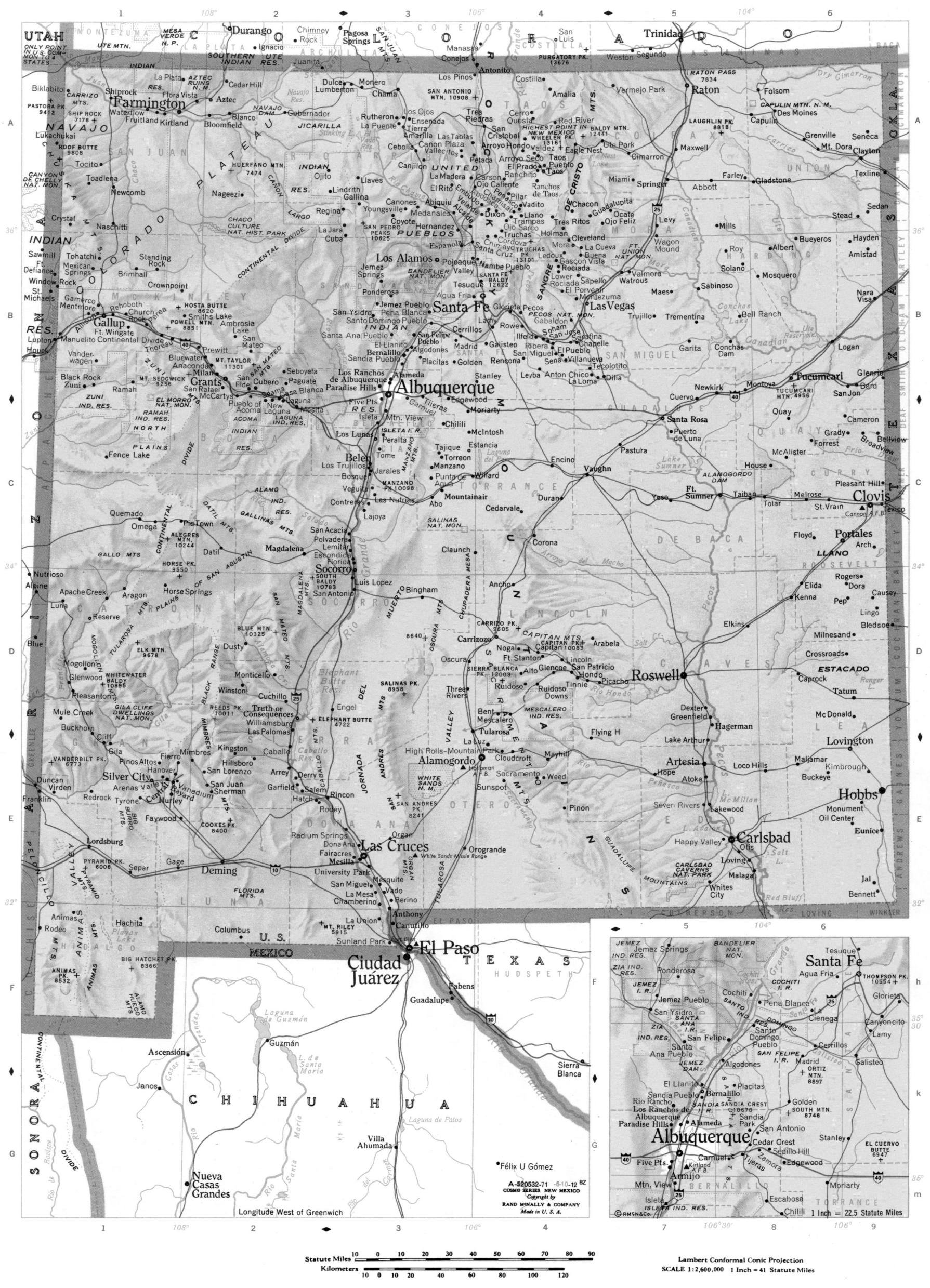

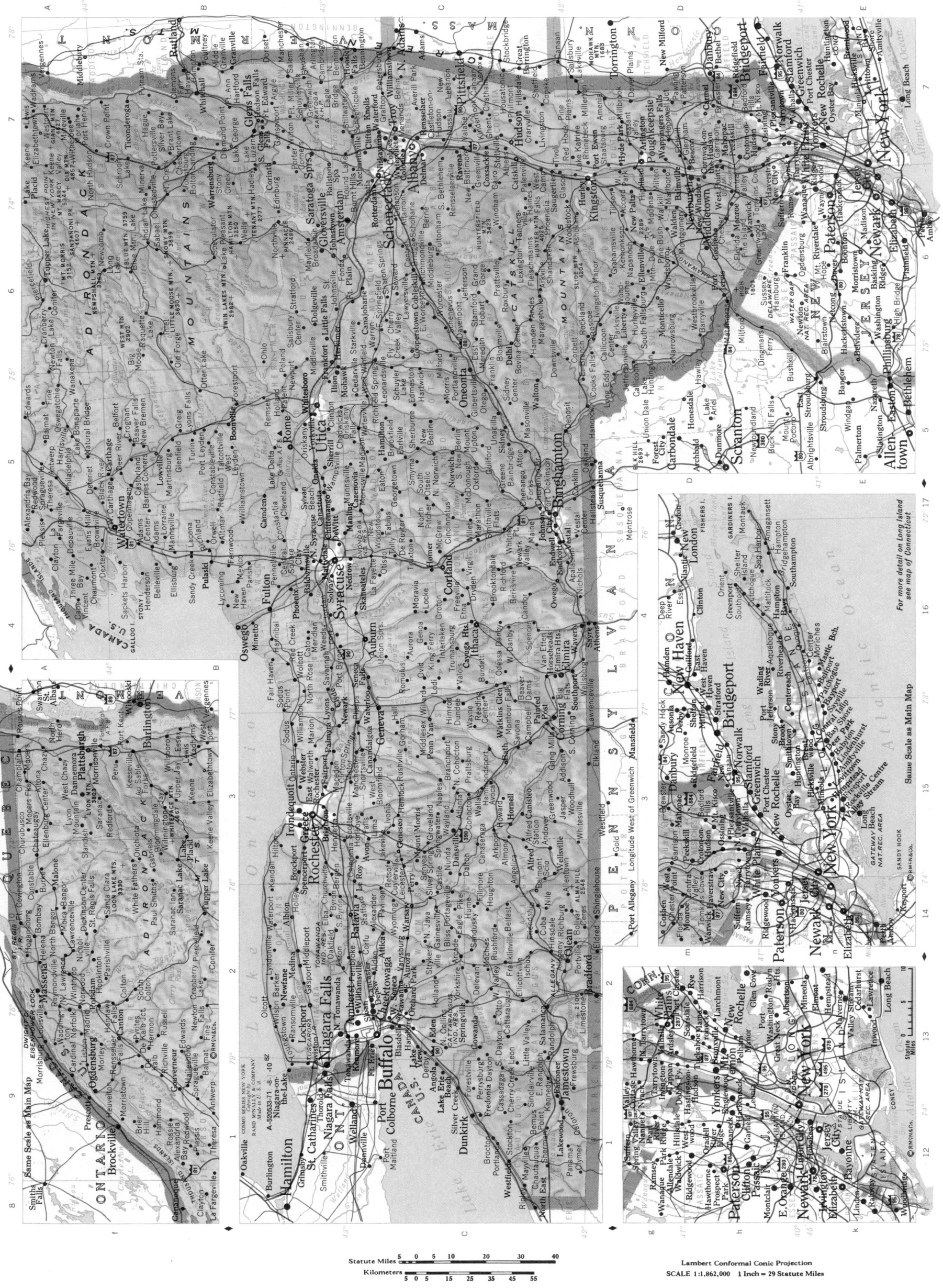

Statute Miles 5 0 5 10 20 30 40
Kilometers 5 0 5 15 25 35 45 55

Lambert Conformal Conic Projection
SCALE 1:1,862,000   1 Inch = 29 Statute Miles

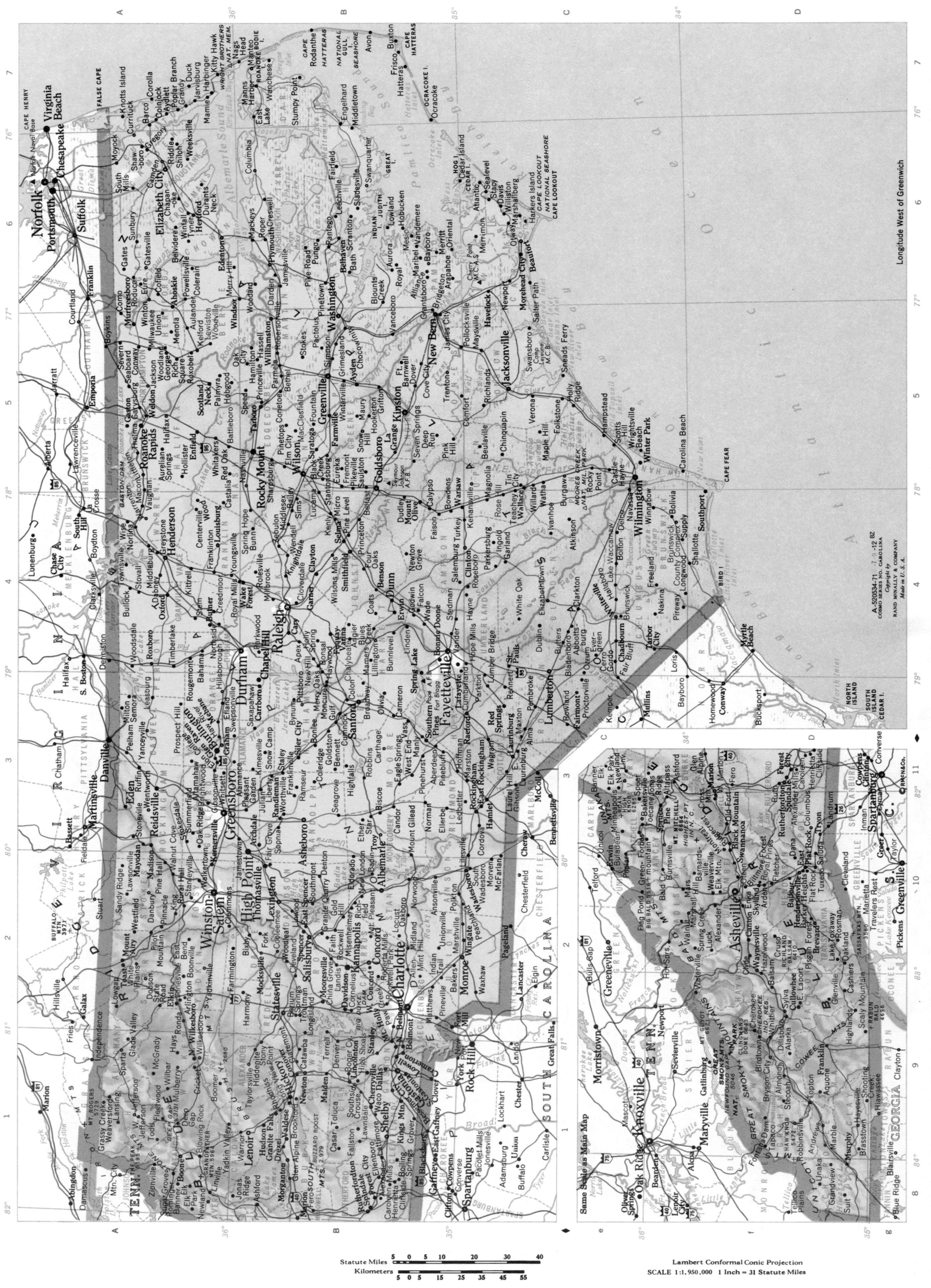

Statute Miles
Kilometers

Lambert Conformal Conic Projection
SCALE 1:1,950,000   1 Inch = 31 Statute Miles

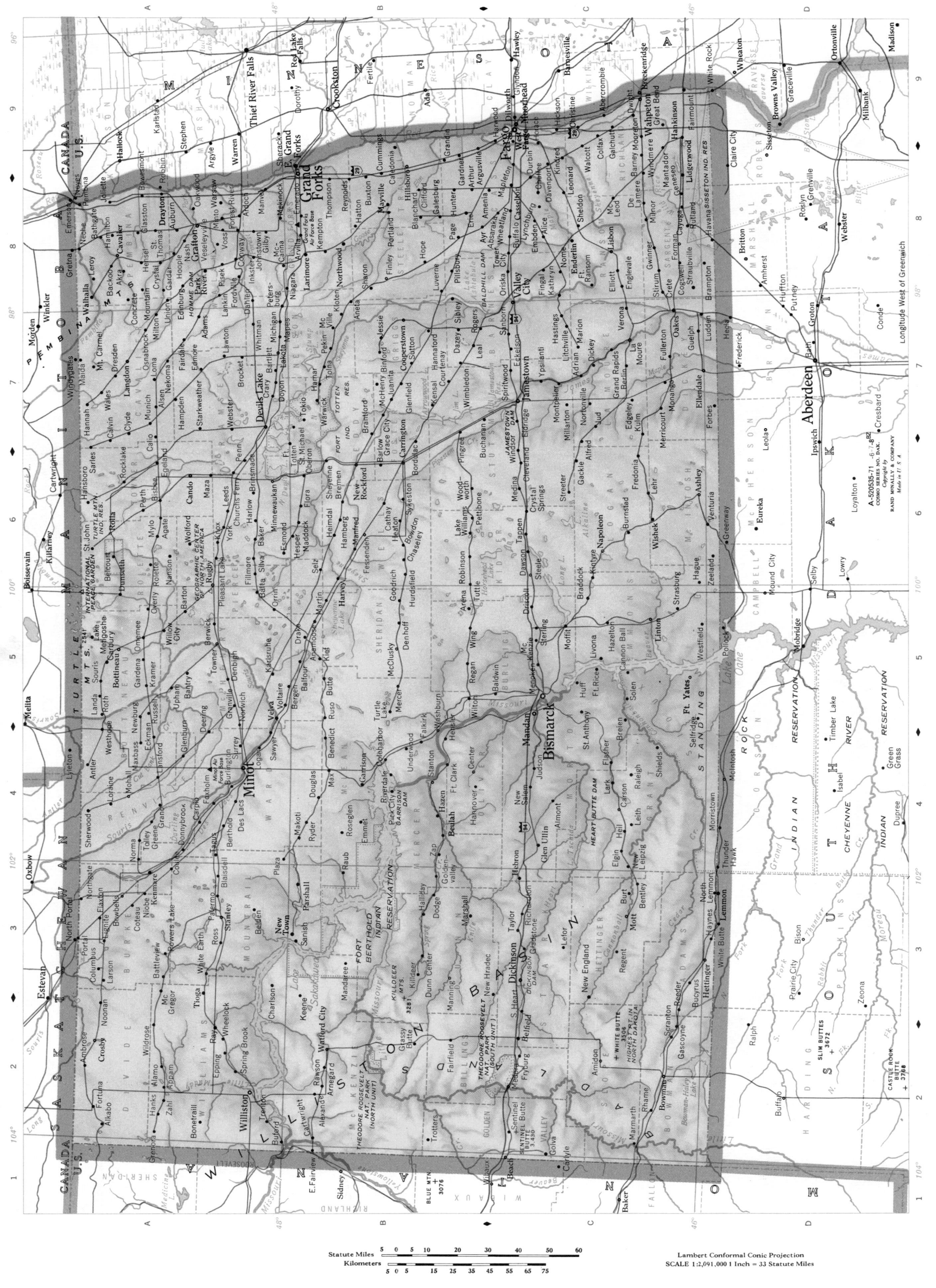

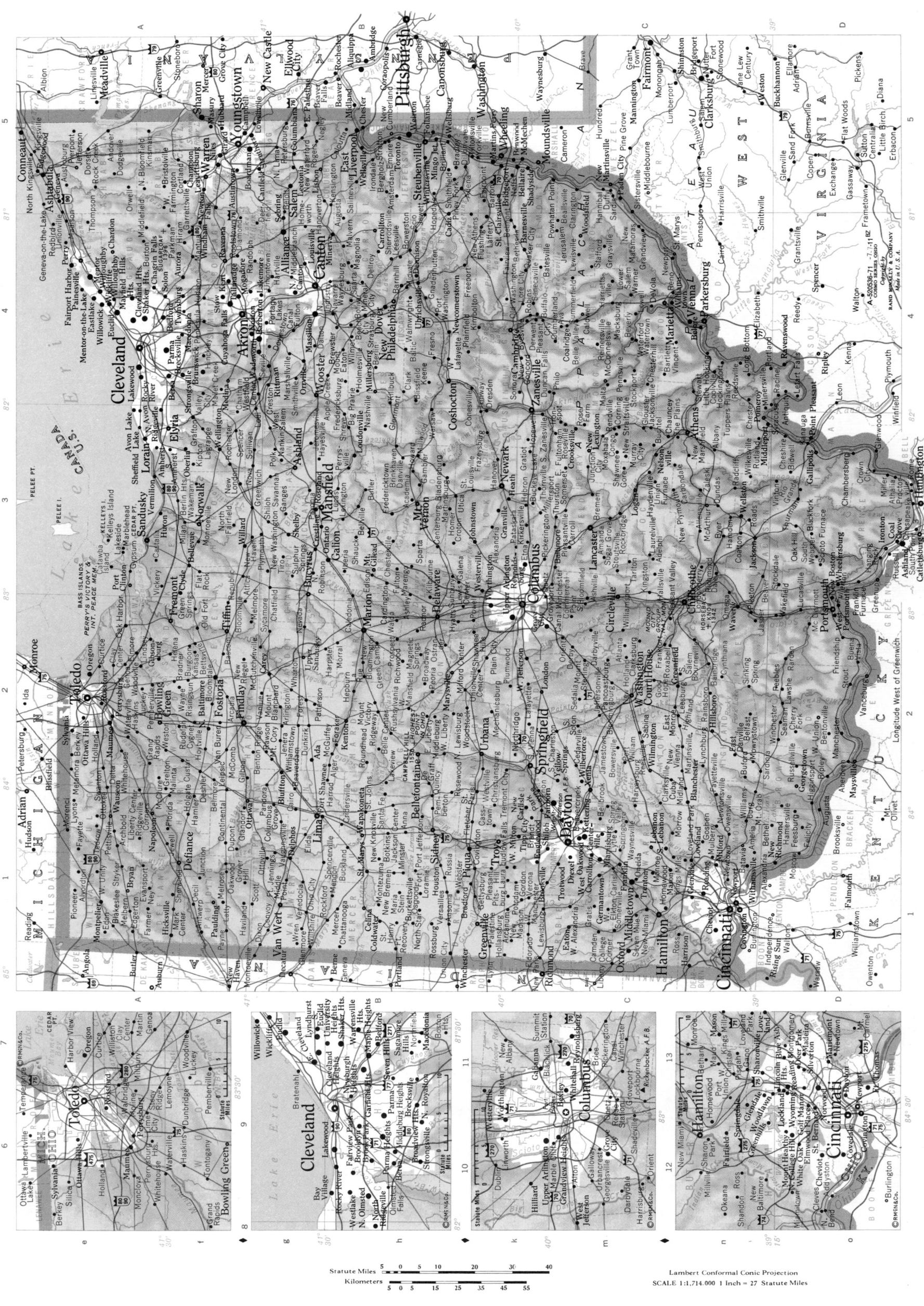

Statute Miles

Kilometers

Lambert Conformal Conic Projection
SCALE 1:1,714.000  1 Inch = 27 Statute Miles

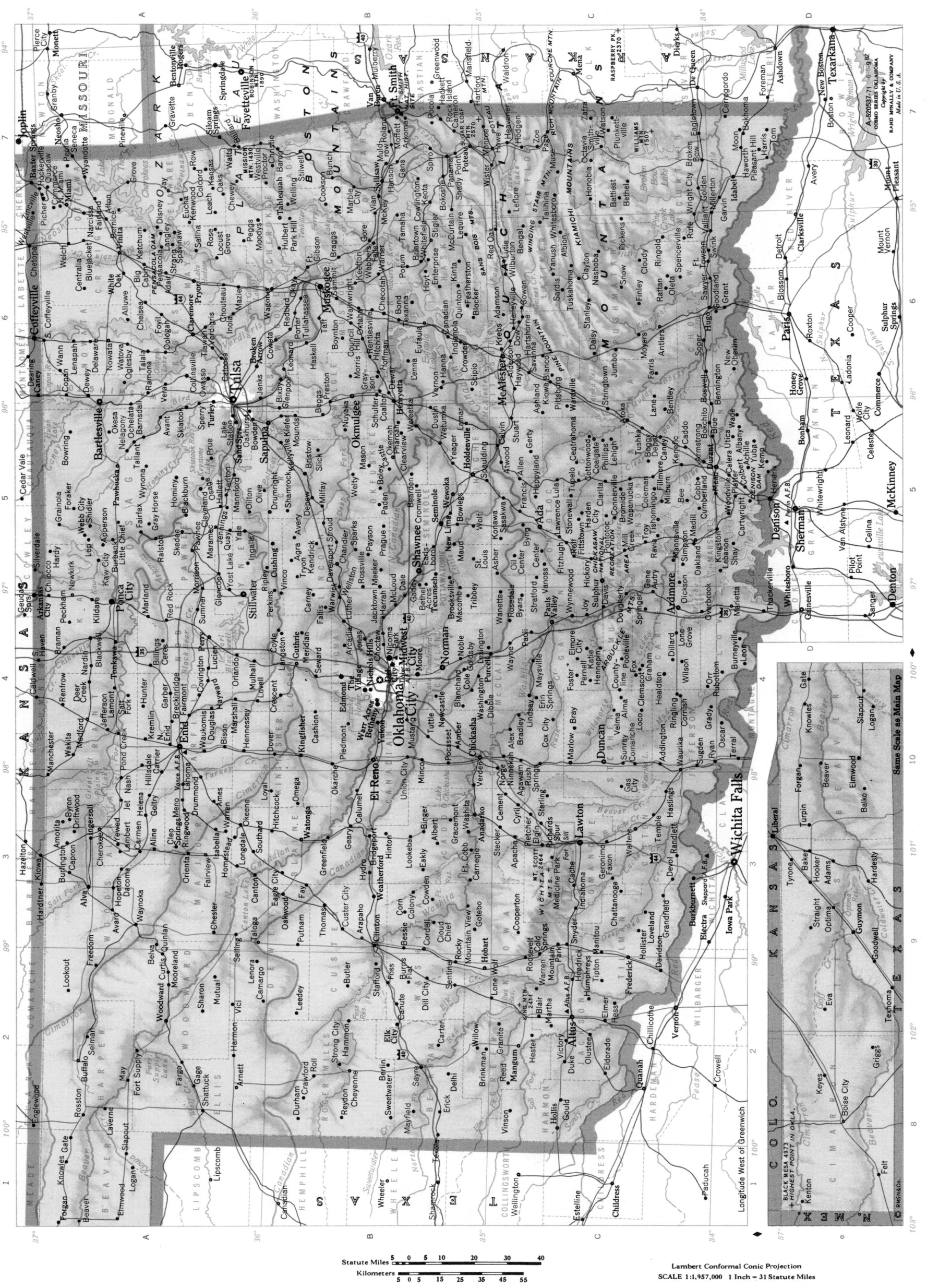

Statute Miles 5 0 5 10 20 30 40
Kilometers 5 0 5 15 25 35 45 55

Lambert Conformal Conic Projection
SCALE 1:1,957,000  1 Inch = 31 Statute Miles

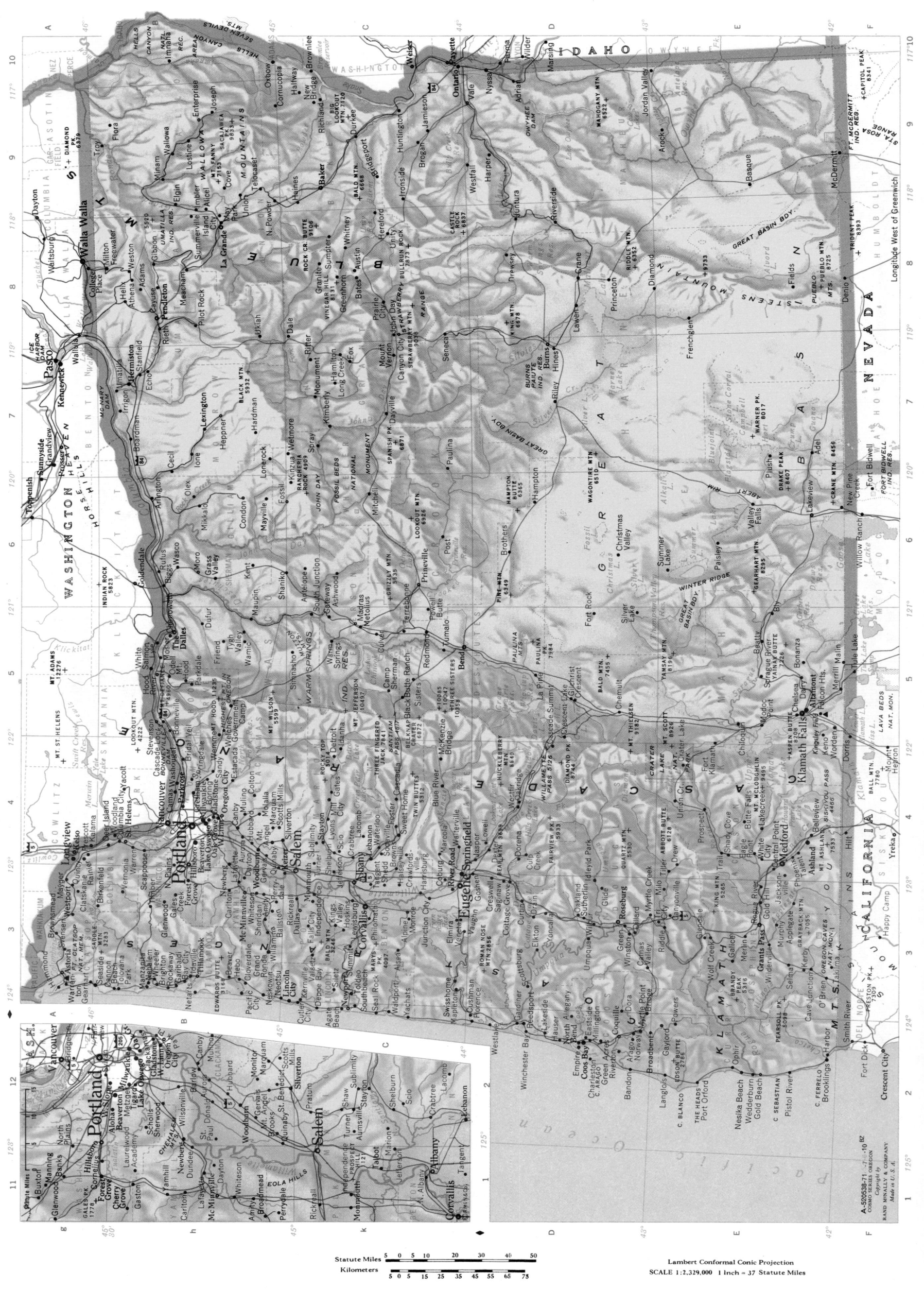

Lambert Conformal Conic Projection
SCALE 1:2,329,000  1 Inch = 37 Statute Miles

Statute Miles
Kilometers

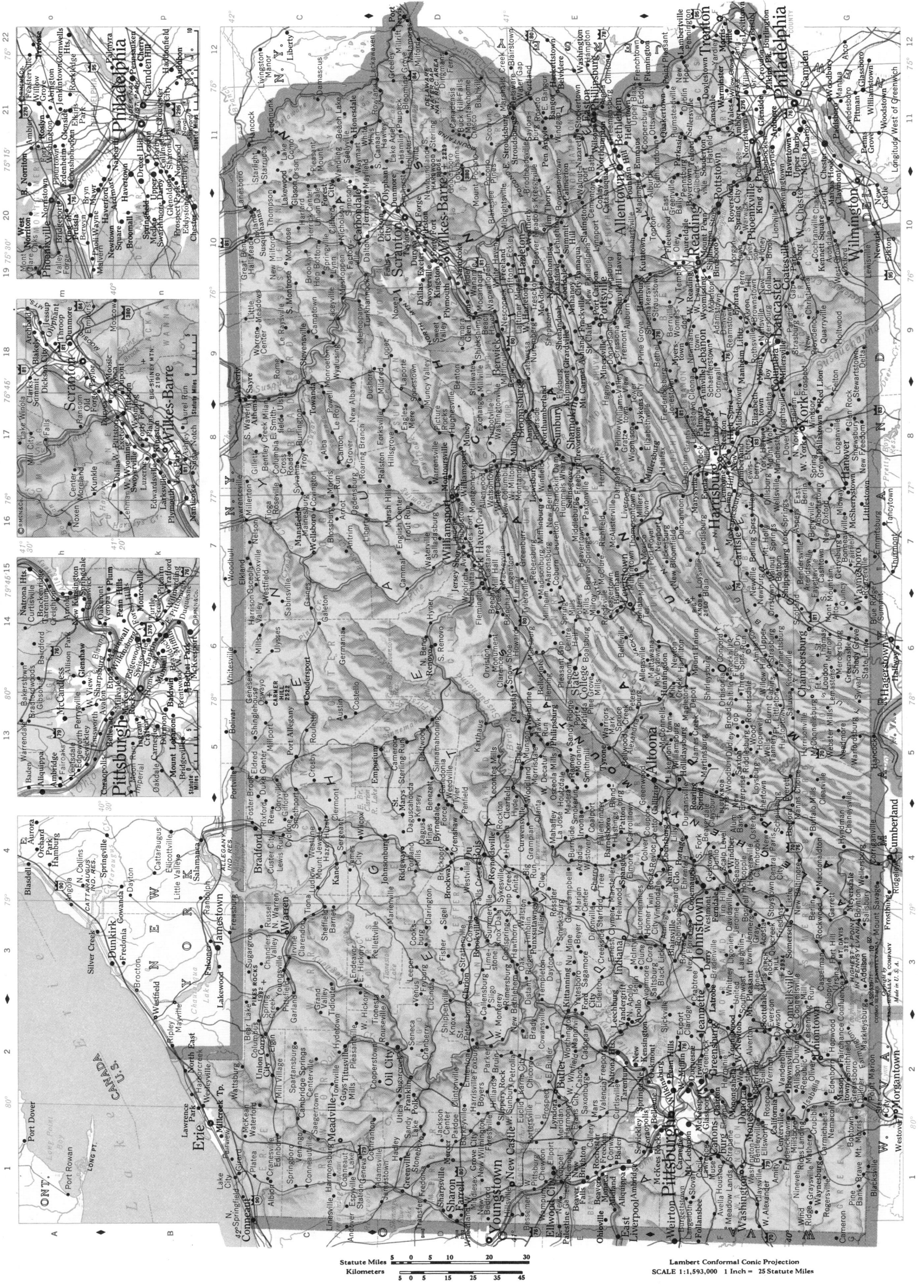

Statute Miles
Kilometers

Lambert Conformal Conic Projection
SCALE 1:1,593,000   1 Inch = 25 Statute Miles

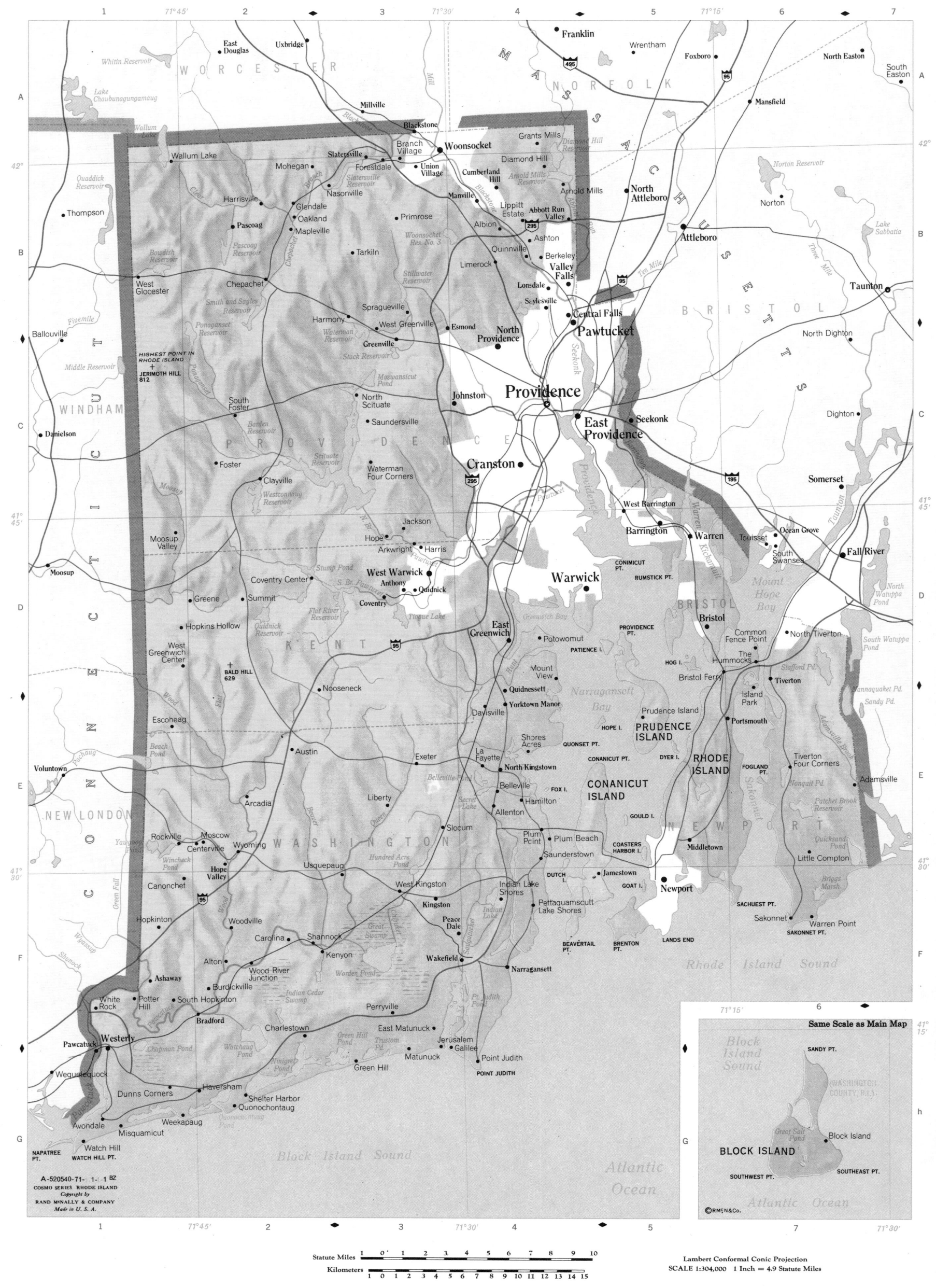

# RHODE ISLAND

Franklin
Wrentham
North Easton
South Easton
East Douglas
Uxbridge
Foxboro

Whitin Reservoir
WORCESTER
NORFOLK
Mansfield

Lake Chaubunagungamaug
Millville
Norton Reservoir

Wallum Lake
Wallum Lake
Blackstone
Grants Mills
North Attleboro
Norton

Slatersville
Branch Village
Woonsocket
Diamond Hill
Diamond Hill Reservoir

Mohegan
Forestdale
Union Village
Cumberland Hill
Arnold Mills Reservoir
Arnold Mills

Harrisville
Nasonville
Slatersville Reservoir
Manville
Attleboro

Thompson
Glendale
Oakland
Primrose
Albion
Lippitt Estate
Abbott Run Valley
North Attleboro

Pascoag
Mapleville
Woonsocket Res. No. 3
Ashton

Quaddick Reservoir
Tarkiln
Limerock
Quinnville
Berkeley

West Glocester
Stillwater Reservoir
Lonsdale
Valley Falls
Taunton

Chepachet
Harmony
Spragueville
Esmond
Saylesville
North Dighton

Balllouville
West Greenville
North Providence
Central Falls
Pawtucket

Fivemile
Greenville
Stock Reservoir
Pawtucket

Middle Reservoir
HIGHEST POINT IN RHODE ISLAND JERIMOTH HILL 812
Maswansicut Pond
Providence

Danielson
South Foster
North Scituate
Johnston
East Providence
Seekonk

Saundersville
Cranston
Somerset

Foster
Scituate Reservoir
Waterman Four Corners
West Barrington

Clayville
Westconnaug Reservoir
Jackson
Barrington
Warren
Ocean Grove

Moosup Valley
Hope
Arkwright
Harris
Touisset
South Swansea
Fall River

Moosup
West Warwick
Anthony
Quidnick
Warwick
CONIMICUT PT.
RUMSTICK PT.

Greene
Coventry Center
Coventry
Providence Pt.
Bristol
North Tiverton

Summit
Flat River Reservoir
Tiogue Lake
Patience I.
Common Fence Point
The Hummocks

Hopkins Hollow
Bald Hill 629
East Greenwich
Bristol Ferry
Tiverton

West Greenwich Center
Nooseneck
Potowomut
Quonset Pt.
Island Park

Escoheag
Mount View
Quidnessett
Hope I.
PRUDENCE ISLAND
Portsmouth

Voluntown
Austin
Yorktown Manor
Prudence Island
RHODE ISLAND

Arcadia
Daysville
Conanicut Pt.
Fogland Pt.
Tiverton Four Corners

Liberty
Exeter
La Fayette
Shores Acres
CONANICUT ISLAND
Adamsville

Rockville
Moscow
Belleville
North Kingstown
Fox I.
Gould I.

Centerville
Wyoming
Hamilton
Allenton
Dutch I.
Middletown
Little Compton

Hope Valley
Usquepaug
Slocum
Plum Point
Plum Beach
Saunderstown
Jamestown
Newport

Canonchet
West Kingston
Kingston
Indian Lake Shores
Goat I.
Sachuest Pt.

Hopkinton
Woodville
Peace Dale
Pettaquamscutt Lake Shores
Lands End
Sakonnet

Ashaway
Carolina
Shannock
Kenyon
Wakefield
Narragansett
Sakonnet Pt.
Warren Point

White Rock
Potter Hill
South Hopkinton
Alton
Wood River Junction
Burdickville
Perryville
Pt. Judith Pond

Bradford
Charlestown
East Matunuck
Jerusalem
Galilee
Point Judith

Westerly
Pawcatuck
Haversham
Matunuck
Green Hill
Point Judith

Weequapaug
Dunns Corners
Shelter Harbor
Quonochontaug

Avondale
Misquamicut
Weekapaug

Watch Hill
Watch Hill Pt.

Block Island Sound
Atlantic Ocean

BLOCK ISLAND
Sandy Pt.
Great Salt Pond
Block Island
Southwest Pt.
Southeast Pt.

Same Scale as Main Map

Statute Miles  1 0 1 2 3 4 5 6 7 8 9 10
Kilometers  1 0 1 2 3 4 5 6 7 8 9 10 11 12 13 14 15

Lambert Conformal Conic Projection
SCALE 1:304,000   1 Inch = 4.9 Statute Miles

A-520540-71- 1- 1 BZ
COSMO SERIES  RHODE ISLAND
Copyright by
RAND McNALLY & COMPANY
Made in U.S.A.

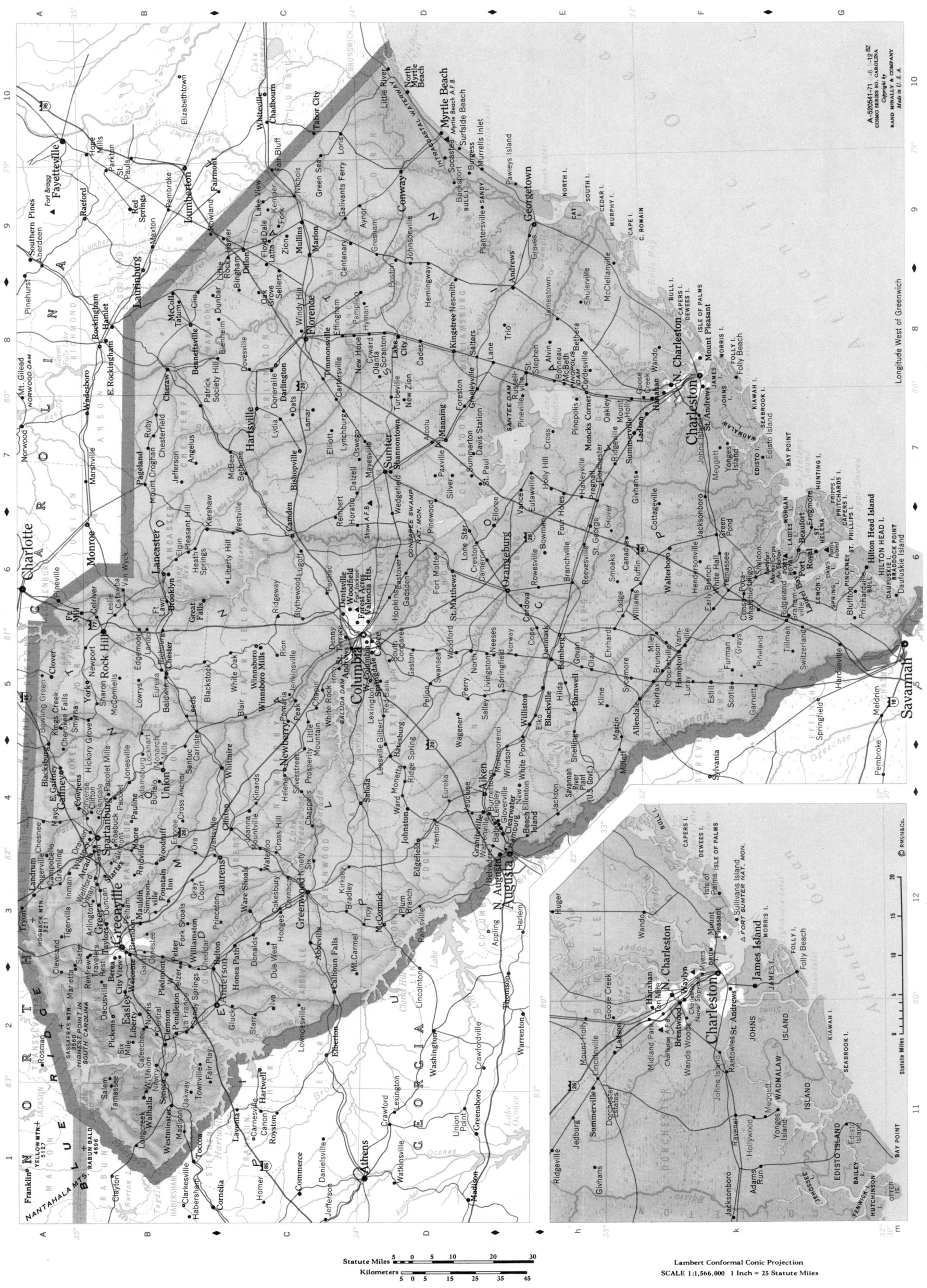

Statute Miles 5 0 5 10 20 30
Kilometers 5 0 5 15 25 35 45

Lambert Conformal Conic Projection
SCALE 1:1,566,000  1 Inch = 25 Statute Miles

A-500541-71  -6-,12 82
COSMO SERIES SO. CAROLINA
Copyright by
RAND McNALLY & COMPANY
Made in U.S.A.

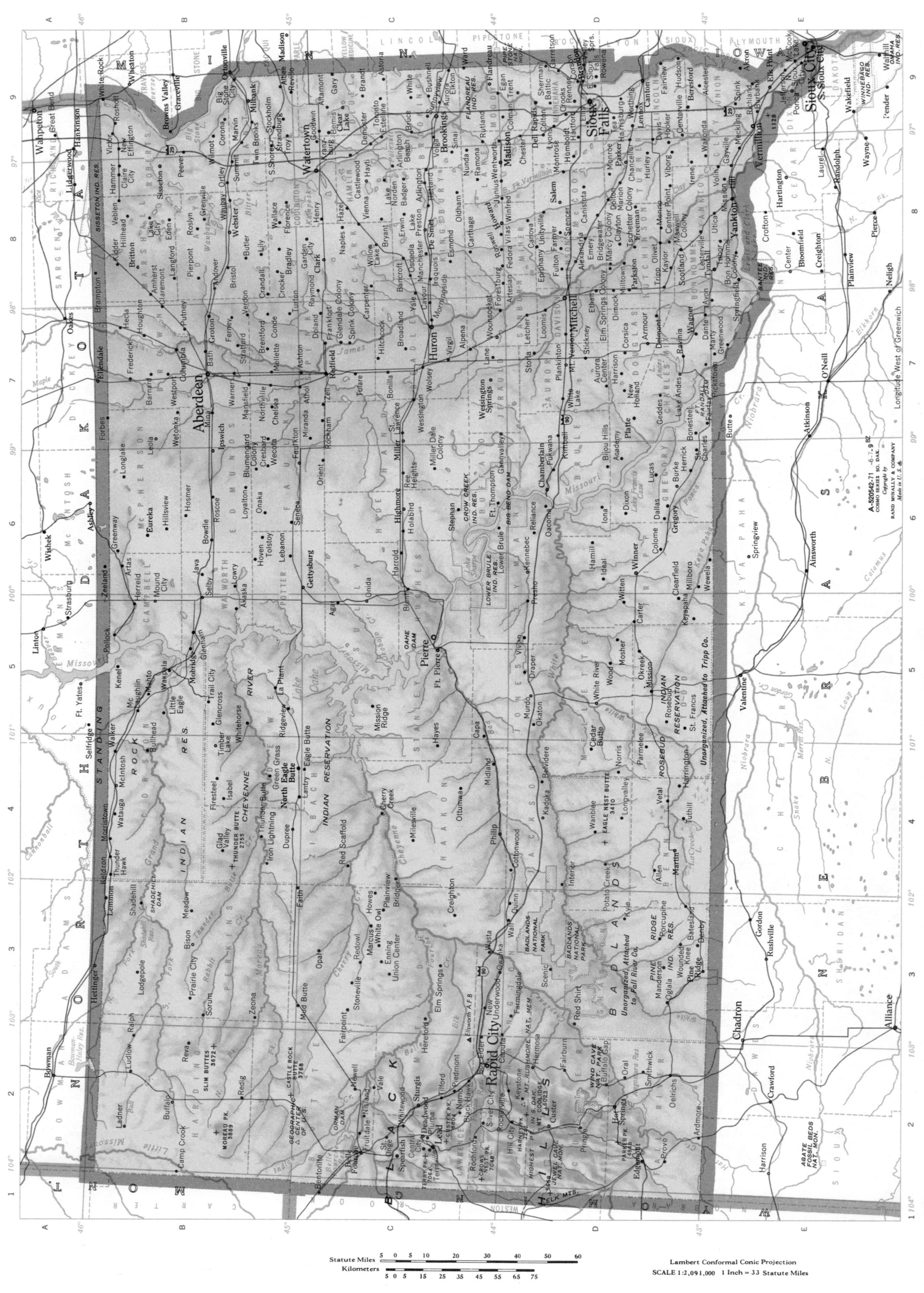

Statute Miles 5 0 5 10 20 30 40 50 60
Kilometers 5 0 5 15 25 35 45 55 65 75

Lambert Conformal Conic Projection
SCALE 1:2,091,000 1 Inch = 33 Statute Miles

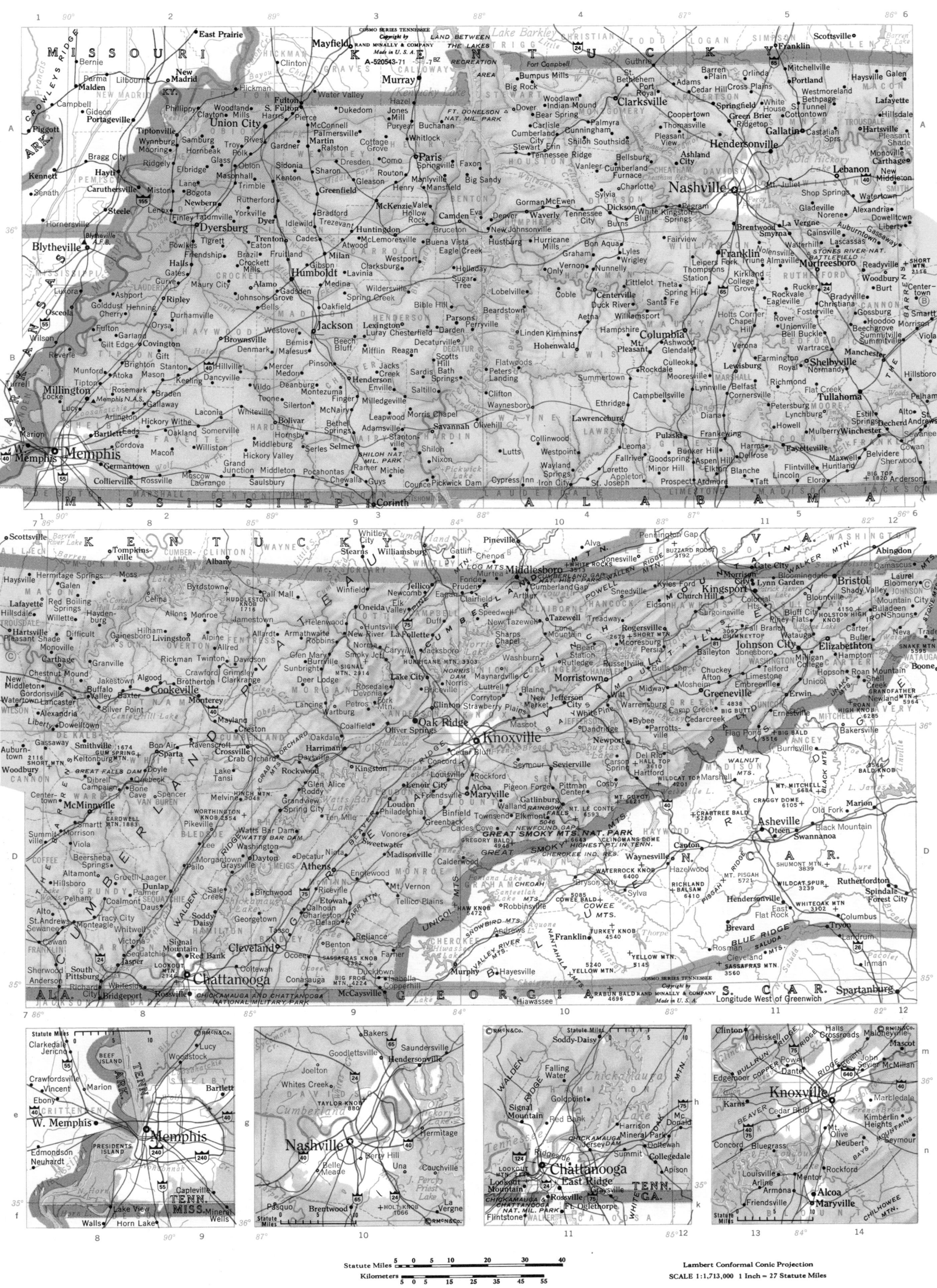

Statute Miles 5 0 5 10 20 30 40
Kilometers 5 0 5 15 25 35 45 55

Lambert Conformal Conic Projection
SCALE 1:1,713,000  1 Inch = 27 Statute Miles

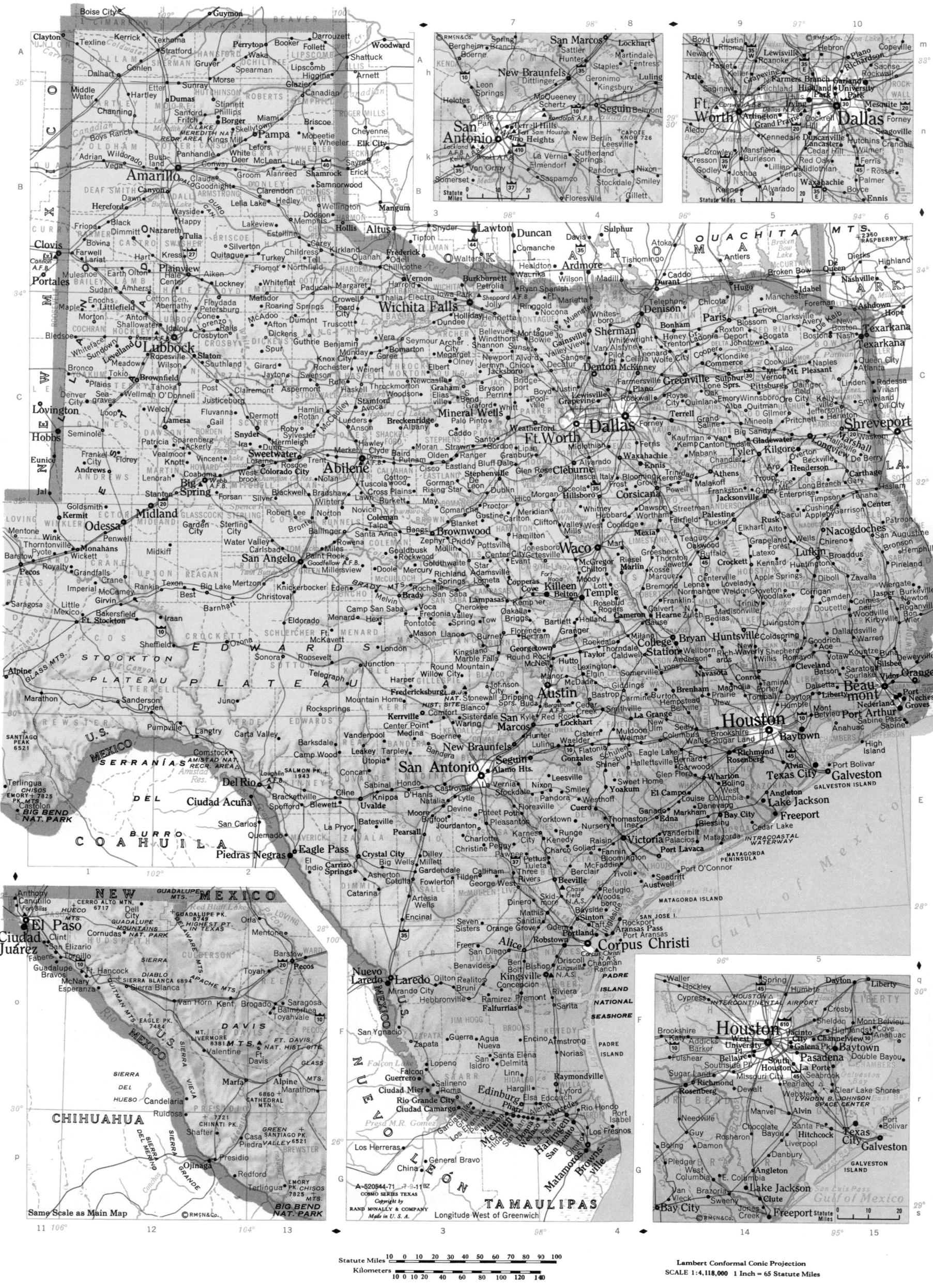

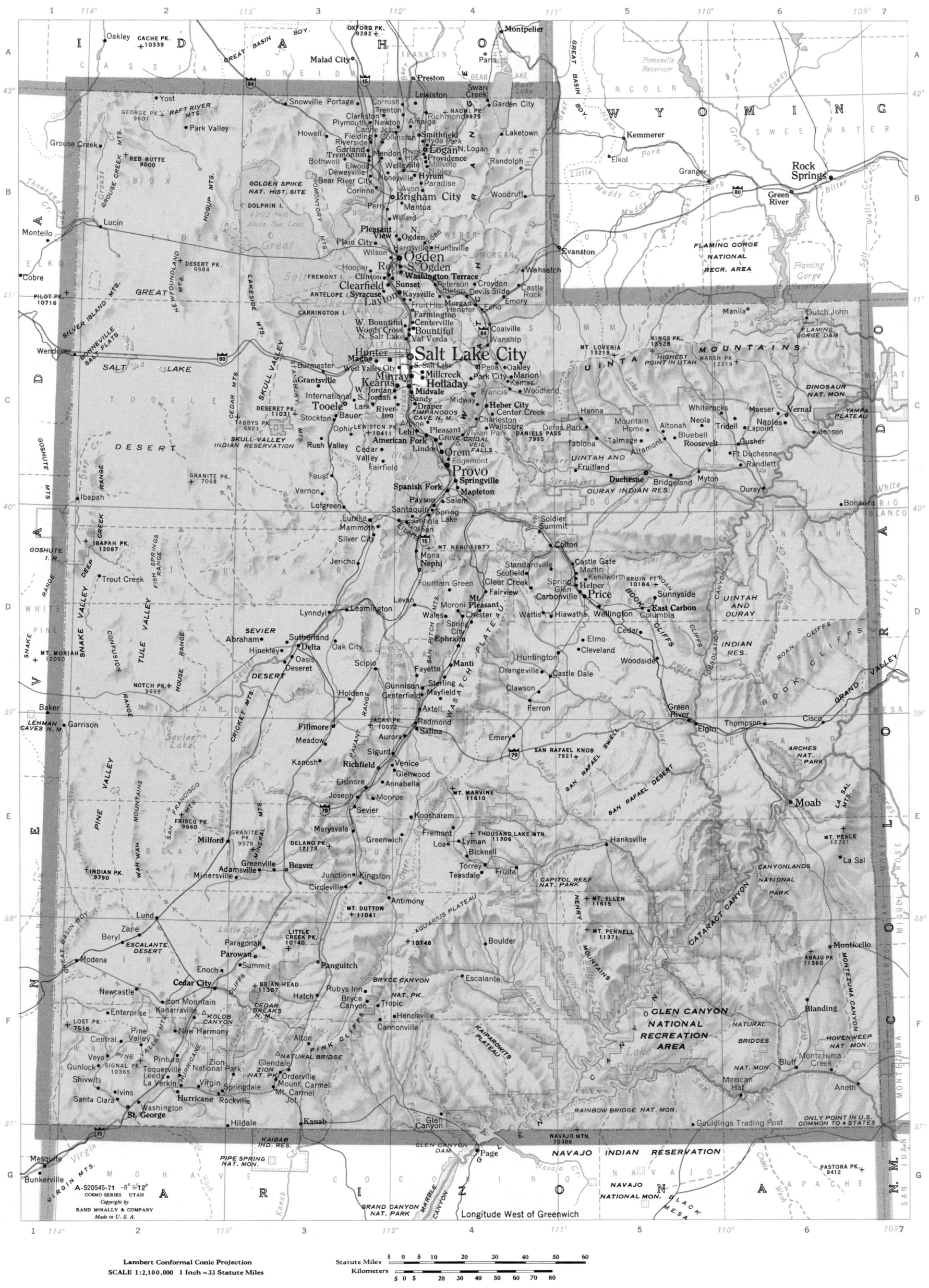

Longitude West of Greenwich

Lambert Conformal Conic Projection
SCALE 1:2,100,000  1 Inch =33 Statute Miles

Statute Miles
Kilometers

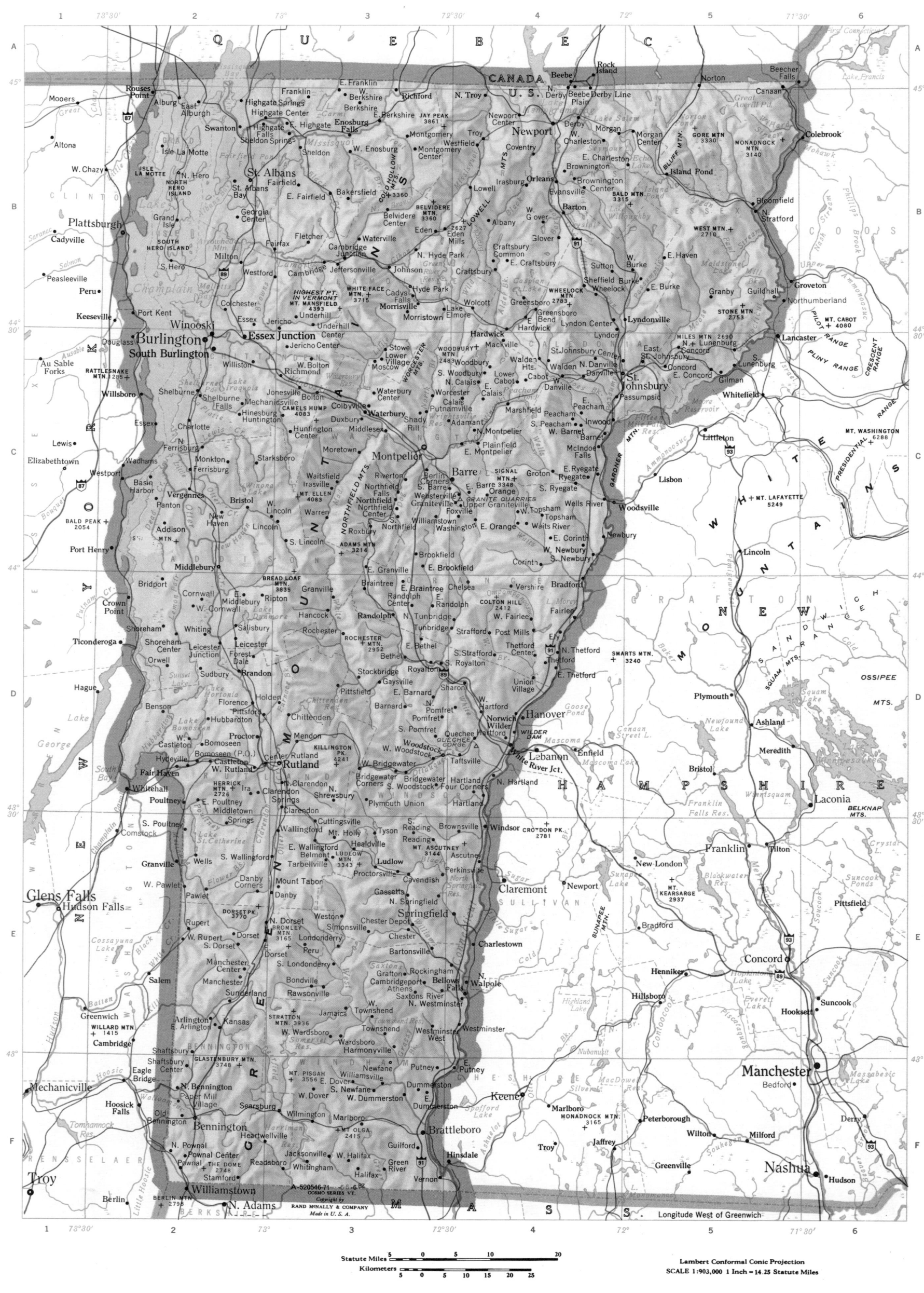

Statute Miles 5 0 5 20

Kilometers 5 0 5 10 15 20 25

Lambert Conformal Conic Projection
SCALE 1:903,000 1 Inch = 14.25 Statute Miles

A-520546-71 -6-5-6
COSMO SERIES VT.
Copyright by
RAND MCNALLY & COMPANY
Made in U.S.A.

Longitude West of Greenwich

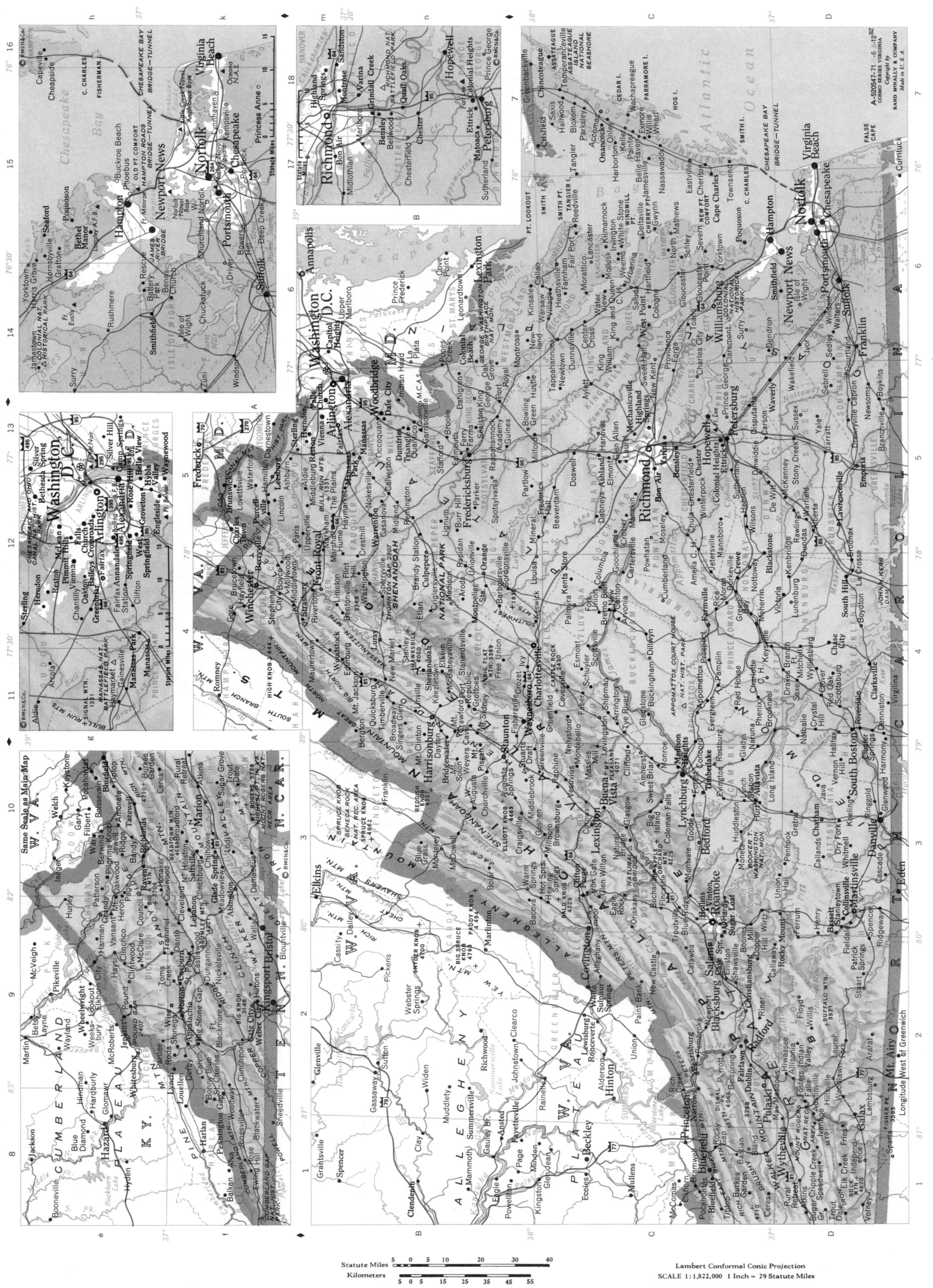

Statute Miles 5 0 5 10 20 30 40
Kilometers 5 0 5 15 25 35 45 55

Lambert Conformal Conic Projection
SCALE 1:1,822,000  1 Inch = 29 Statute Miles

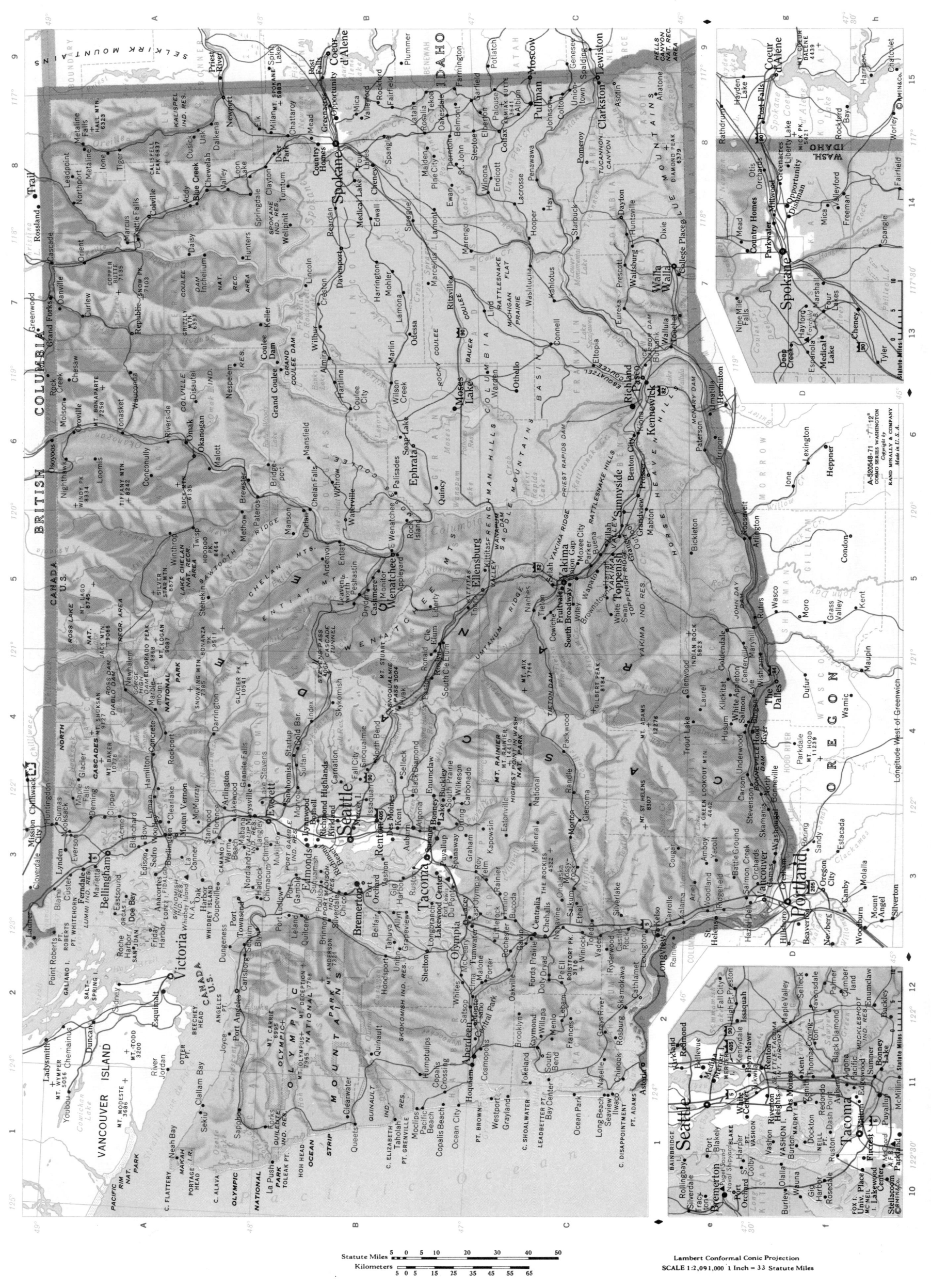

Statute Miles 5 0 5 10 20 30 40 50
Kilometers 5 0 5 15 25 35 45 55 65

Lambert Conformal Conic Projection
SCALE 1:2,091,000 1 Inch = 33 Statute Miles

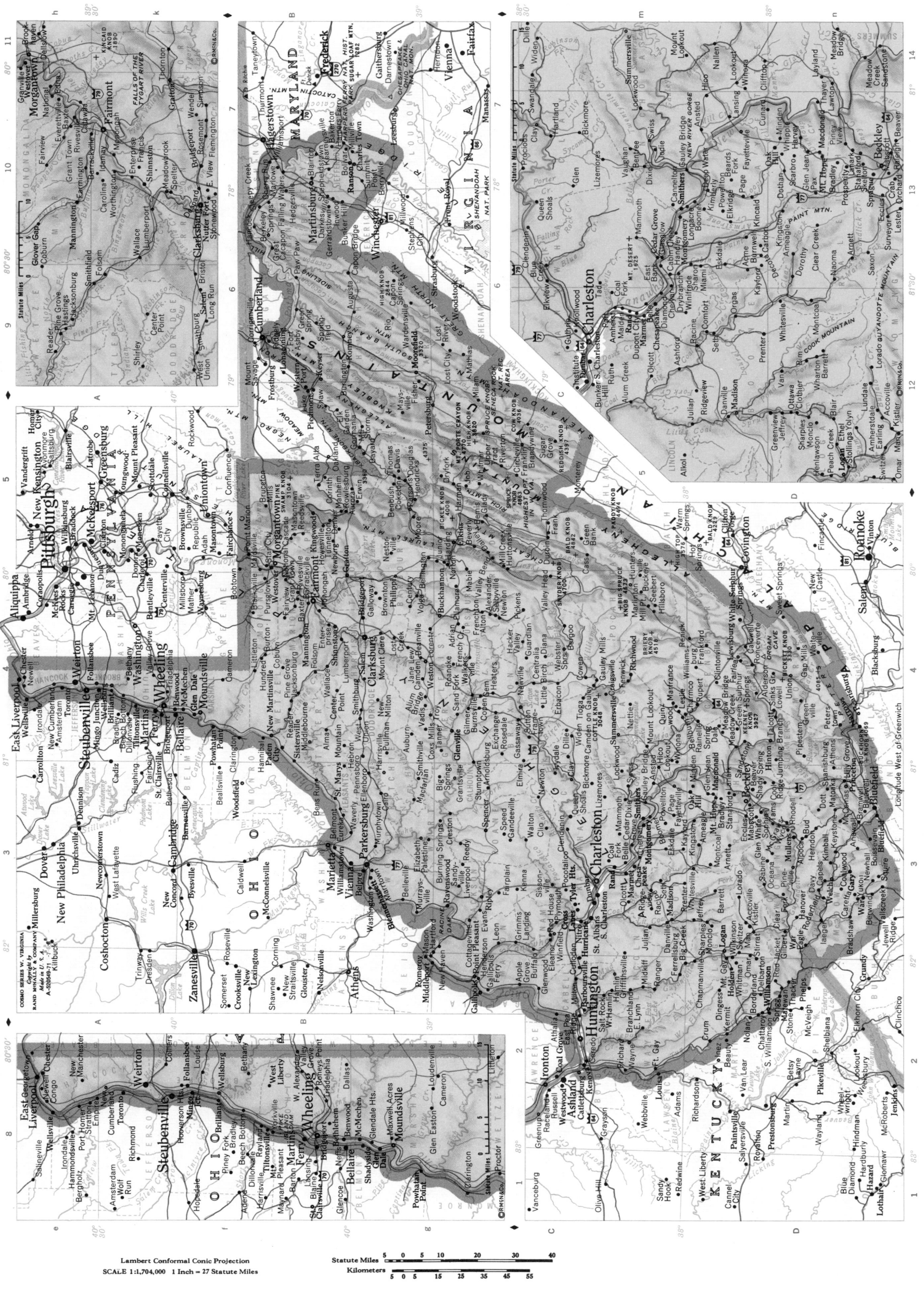

Lambert Conformal Conic Projection
SCALE 1:1,704,000   1 Inch = 27 Statute Miles

Statute Miles
Kilometers

Cosmo Series W. Virginia
Copyright by
RAND M?NALLY & COMPANY
Made in U.S.A.
A-020045-71

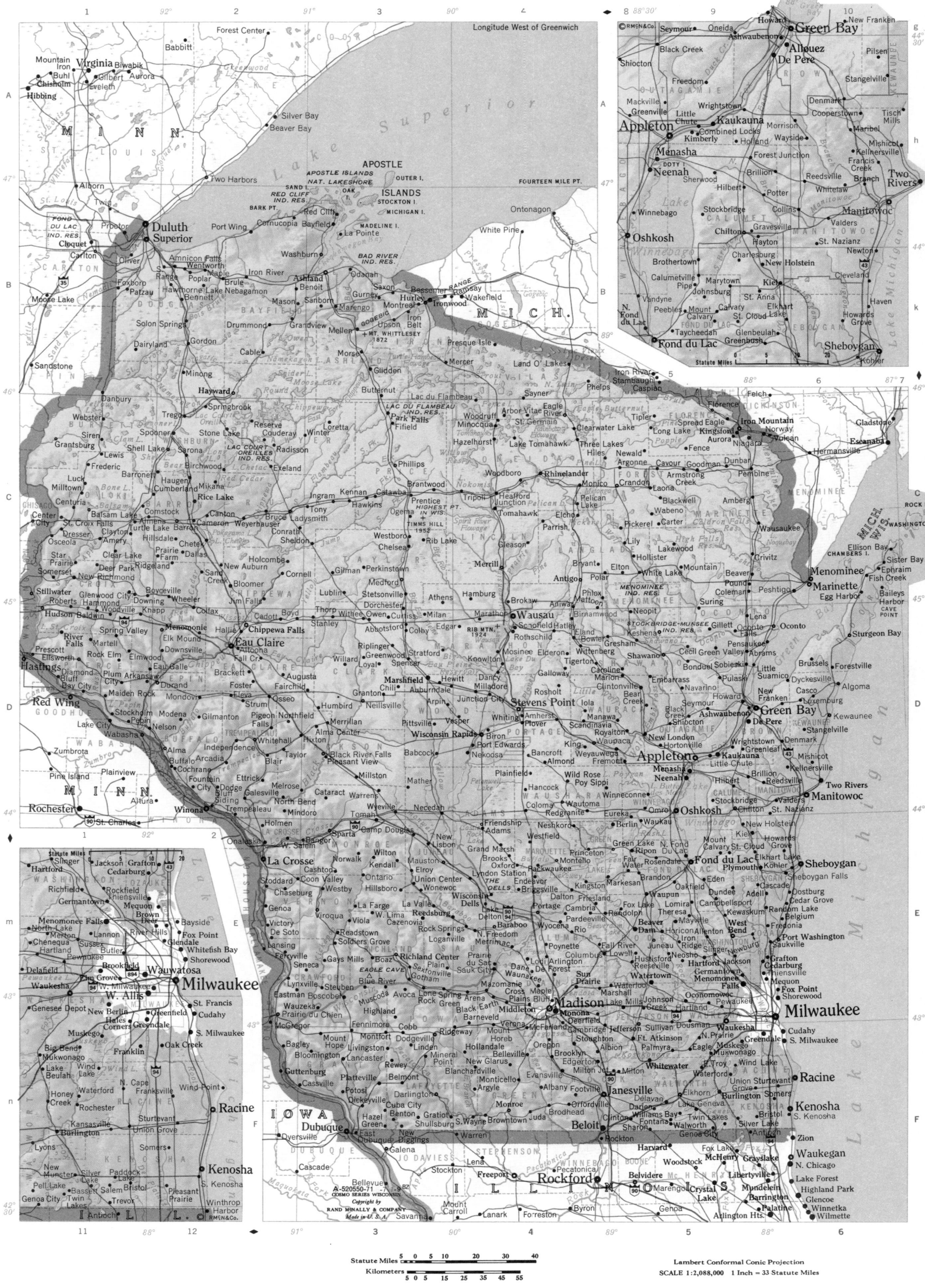

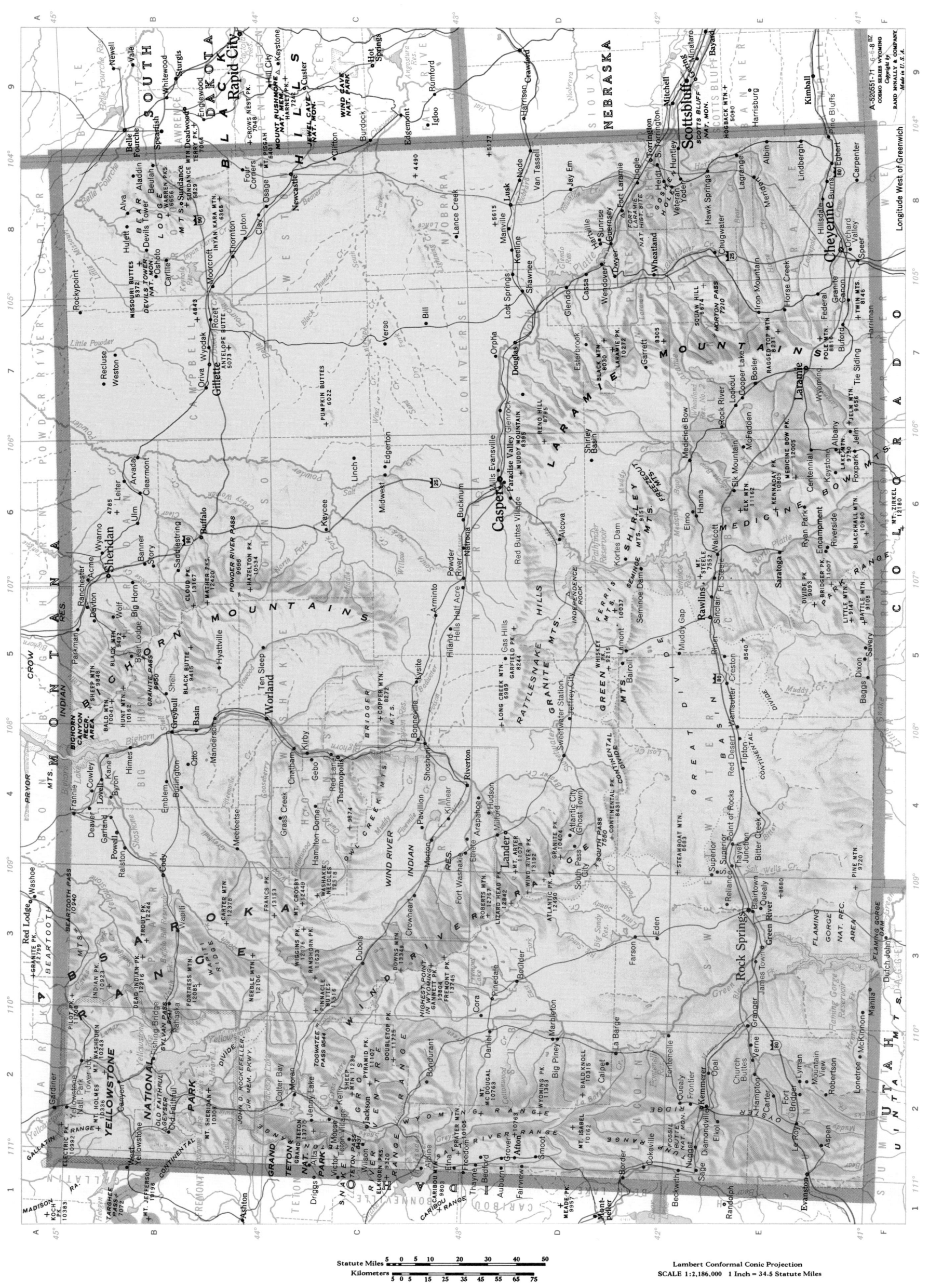

Statute Miles 5 0 5 10 20 30 40 50
Kilometers 5 0 5 15 25 35 45 55 65 75

Lambert Conformal Conic Projection
SCALE 1:2,186,000 1 Inch = 34.5 Statute Miles

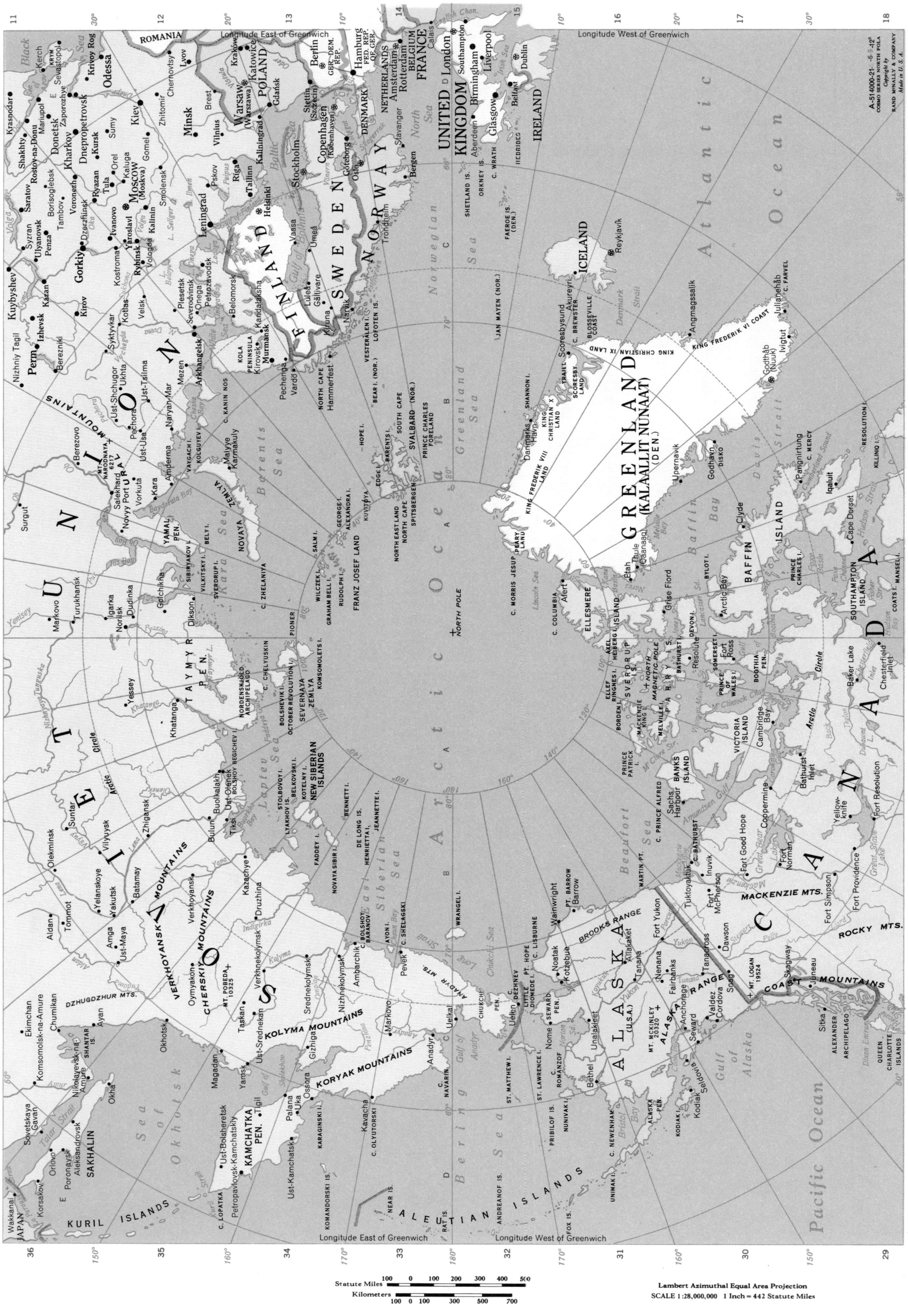

# INDEX TO WORLD REFERENCE MAPS

## INTRODUCTION TO THE INDEX

This universal index includes in a single alphabetical list approximately 78,000 names of features that appear on the reference maps. Each name is followed by the name of the country or continent in which it is located, a map-reference key and a page reference.

**Names** The names of cities appear in the index in regular type. The names of all other features appear in *italics*, followed by descriptive terms (hill, mtn., state) to indicate their nature.

Names that appear in shortened versions on the maps due to space limitations are spelled out in full in the index. The portions of these names omitted from the maps are enclosed in brackets — for example, Acapulco [de Juárez].

Abbreviations of names on the maps have been standardized as much as possible. Names that are abbreviated on the maps are generally spelled out in full in the index.

Country names and names of features that extend beyond the boundaries of one country are followed by the name of the continent in which each is located. Country designations follow the names of all other places in the index. The locations of places in the United States, Canada, and the United Kingdom are further defined by abbreviations that indicate the state, province, or political division in which each is located.

All abbreviations used in the index are defined in the List of Abbreviations below.

**Alphabetization** Names are alphabetized in the order of the letters of the English alphabet. Spanish *ll* and *ch*, for example, are not treated as distinct letters. Furthermore, diacritical marks are disregarded in alphabetization — German or Scandinavian *ä* or *ö* are treated as *a* or *o*.

The names of physical features may appear inverted, since they are always alphabetized under the proper, not the generic, part of the name, thus: 'Gibraltar, Strait of'. Otherwise every entry, whether consisting of one word or more, is alphabetized as a single continuous entity. 'Lakeland', for example, appears after 'La Crosse' and before 'La Salle'. Names beginning with articles (Le Havre, Den Helder, Al Manşūrah) are not inverted. Names beginning 'St.', 'Ste.' and 'Sainte' are alphabetized as though spelled 'Saint'.

In the case of identical names, towns are listed first, then political divisions, then physical features. Entries that are completely identical are listed alphabetically by country name.

**Map-Reference Keys and Page References** The map-reference keys and page references are found in the last two columns of each entry.

Each map-reference key consists of a letter and number. The letters appear along the sides of the maps. Lowercase letters indicate reference to inset maps. Numbers appear across the tops and bottoms of the maps.

Map reference keys for point features, such as cities and mountain peaks, indicate the locations of the symbols. For extensive areal features, such as countries or mountain ranges, locations are given for the approximate centers of the features. Those for linear features, such as canals and rivers, are given for the locations of the names.

Names of some important places or features that are omitted from the maps due to space limitations are included in the index. Each of these places is identified by an asterisk (*) preceding the map-reference key.

The page number generally refers to the main map for the country in which the feature is located. Page references to two-page maps always refer to the left-hand page.

## LIST OF ABBREVIATIONS

| | | | | | | | | | |
|---|---|---|---|---|---|---|---|---|---|
| Afg. | Afghanistan | De., U.S. | Delaware, U.S. | Ks., U.S. | Kansas, U.S. | Nmb. | Namibia | St. Luc. | St. Lucia |
| Afr. | Africa | Den. | Denmark | Kuw. | Kuwait | Nor. | Norway | *stm.* | stream (river, creek) |
| Ak., U.S. | Alaska, U.S. | *dep.* | dependency, colony | Ky., U.S. | Kentucky, U.S. | Norf. I. | Norfolk Island | S. Tom./P. | Sao Tome and |
| Al., U.S. | Alabama, U.S. | *depr.* | depression | *l.* | lake, pond | N.S. | Nova Scotia, Can. | | Principe |
| Alb. | Albania | *dept.* | department, district | La., U.S. | Louisiana, U.S. | Nv., U.S. | Nevada, U.S. | St. P./M. | St. Pierre and |
| Alg. | Algeria | *des.* | desert | Leb. | Lebanon | N.W. Ter. | Northwest | | Miquelon |
| Alta. | Alberta, Can. | Dji. | Djibouti | Leso. | Lesotho | | Territories, Can. | *strt.* | strait, channel, |
| Am. Sam. | American Samoa | Dom. | Dominica | Lib. | Liberia | N.Y., U.S. | New York, U.S. | | sound |
| *anch.* | anchorage | Dom. Rep. | Dominican Republic | Liech. | Liechtenstein | N.Z. | New Zealand | St. Vin. | St. Vincent and the |
| And. | Andorra | Ec. | Ecuador | Lux. | Luxembourg | Oc. | Oceania | | Grenadines |
| Ang. | Angola | Eg. | Egypt | Ma., U.S. | Massachusetts, | Oh., U.S. | Ohio, U.S. | Sud. | Sudan |
| Ant. | Antarctica | E. Ger. | German Democratic | | U.S. | Ok., U.S. | Oklahoma, U.S. | Sur. | Suriname |
| Antig. | Antigua and | | Republic | Madag. | Madagascar | Ont. | Ontario, Can. | *sw.* | swamp, marsh |
| | Barbuda | El Sal. | El Salvador | Malay. | Malaysia | Or., U.S. | Oregon, U.S. | Swaz. | Swaziland |
| Ar., U.S. | Arkansas, U.S. | Eng., U.K. | England, U.K. | Mald. | Maldives | Pa., U.S. | Pennsylvania, U.S. | Swe. | Sweden |
| Arg. | Argentina | Eq. Gui. | Equatorial Guinea | Man. | Manitoba, Can. | Pak. | Pakistan | Switz. | Switzerland |
| Aus. | Austria | *est.* | estuary | Marsh. Is. | Marshall Islands | Pan. | Panama | Tai. | Taiwan |
| Austl. | Australia | Eth. | Ethiopia | Mart. | Martinique | Pap. N. Gui. | Papua New Guinea | Tan. | Tanzania |
| Az., U.S. | Arizona, U.S. | Eur. | Europe | Maur. | Mauritania | Para. | Paraguay | T./C. Is. | Turks and Caicos |
| *b.* | bay, gulf, inlet, | Faer. Is. | Faeroe Islands | May. | Mayotte | P.E.I. | Prince Edward | | Islands |
| | lagoon | Falk. Is. | Falkland Islands | Md., U.S. | Maryland, U.S. | | Island, Can. | *ter.* | territory |
| Bah. | Bahamas | Fin. | Finland | Me., U.S. | Maine, U.S. | *pen.* | peninsula | Thai. | Thailand |
| Bahr. | Bahrain | Fl., U.S. | Florida, U.S. | Mex. | Mexico | Phil. | Philippines | Tn., U.S. | Tennessee, U.S. |
| Barb. | Barbados | *for.* | forest, moor | Mi., U.S. | Michigan, U.S. | Pit. | Pitcairn | Tok. | Tokelau |
| B.A.T. | British Antarctic | Fr. | France | Micron. | Federated States of | *pl.* | plain, flat | Trin. | Trinidad and |
| | Territory | Fr. Gu. | French Guiana | | Micronesia | *plat.* | plateau, highland | | Tobago |
| B.C. | British Columbia, | Fr. Poly. | French Polynesia | Mid. Is. | Midway Islands | Pol. | Poland | T.T.P.I. | Trust Territory of |
| | Can. | F.S.A.T. | French Southern | *mil.* | military installation | Port. | Portugal | | the Pacific Islands |
| Bdi. | Burundi | | and Antarctic | Mn., U.S. | Minnesota, U.S. | P.R. | Puerto Rico | Tun. | Tunisia |
| Bel. | Belgium | | Territory | Mo., U.S. | Missouri, U.S. | *prov.* | province, region | Tur. | Turkey |
| Ber. | Bermuda | Ga., U.S. | Georgia, U.S. | Mon. | Monaco | Que. | Quebec, Can. | Tx., U.S. | Texas, U.S. |
| Bhu. | Bhutan | Gam. | Gambia | Mong. | Mongolia | *reg.* | physical region | U.A.E. | United Arab |
| B.I.O.T. | British Indian Ocean | Gib. | Gibraltar | Monts. | Montserrat | *res.* | reservoir | | Emirates |
| | Territory | Grc. | Greece | Mor. | Morocco | Reu. | Reunion | Ug. | Uganda |
| Bngl. | Bangladesh | Gren. | Grenada | Moz. | Mozambique | *rf.* | reef, shoal | U.K. | United Kingdom |
| Bol. | Bolivia | Grnld. | Greenland | Mrts. | Mauritius | R.I., U.S. | Rhode Island, U.S. | Ur. | Uruguay |
| Boph. | Bophuthatswana | Guad. | Guadeloupe | Ms., U.S. | Mississippi, U.S. | Rom. | Romania | U.S. | United States |
| Bots. | Botswana | Guat. | Guatemala | Mt., U.S. | Montana, U.S. | Rw. | Rwanda | Ut., U.S. | Utah, U.S. |
| Braz. | Brazil | Gui. | Guinea | *mth.* | river mouth or | S.A. | South America | Va., U.S. | Virginia, U.S. |
| Bru. | Brunei | Gui.-B. | Guinea-Bissau | | channel | S. Afr. | South Africa | *val.* | valley, watercourse |
| Bul. | Bulgaria | Guy. | Guyana | *mtn.* | mountain | Sask. | Saskatchewan, | Vat. | Vatican City |
| Burkina | Burkina Faso | Hi., U.S. | Hawaii, U.S. | *mts.* | mountains | | Can. | Ven. | Venezuela |
| *c.* | cape, point | *hist.* | historic site, ruins | Mwi. | Malawi | Sau. Ar. | Saudi Arabia | V.I., Br. | Virgin Islands, |
| Ca., U.S. | California, U.S. | *hist. reg.* | historic region | N.A. | North America | S.C., U.S. | South Carolina, U.S. | | British |
| Cam. | Cameroon | H.K. | Hong Kong | N.B. | New Brunswick, | *sci.* | scientific station | Viet. | Vietnam |
| Camb. | Cambodia | Hond. | Honduras | | Can. | Scot., U.K. | Scotland, U.K. | V.I.U.S. | Virgin Islands (U.S.) |
| Can. | Canada | Hung. | Hungary | N.C., U.S. | North Carolina, U.S. | S.D., U.S. | South Dakota, U.S. | *vol.* | volcano |
| Cay. Is. | Cayman Islands | *i.* | island | N. Cal. | New Caledonia | Sen. | Senegal | Vt., U.S. | Vermont, U.S. |
| Cen. Afr. | Central African | Ia., U.S. | Iowa, U.S. | N. Cyp. | North Cyprus | Sey. | Seychelles | Wa., U.S. | Washington, U.S. |
| Rep. | Republic | I.C. | Ivory Coast | N.D., U.S. | North Dakota, U.S. | Sing. | Singapore | Wal./F. | Wallis and Futuna |
| Christ. I. | Christmas Island | Ice. | Iceland | Ne., U.S. | Nebraska, U.S. | S. Kor. | South Korea | W. Ger. | Federal Republic of |
| *clf.* | cliff, escarpment | *ice* | ice feature, glacier | Neth. | Netherlands | S.L. | Sierra Leone | | Germany |
| *co.* | county, parish | Id., U.S. | Idaho, U.S. | Neth. Ant. | Netherlands Antilles | S. Mar. | San Marino | Wi., U.S. | Wisconsin, U.S. |
| Co., U.S. | Colorado, U.S. | Il., U.S. | Illinois, U.S. | Newf. | Newfoundland, Can. | Sol. Is. | Solomon Islands | W. Sah. | Western Sahara |
| Col. | Colombia | In., U.S. | Indiana, U.S. | N.H., U.S. | New Hampshire, | Som. | Somalia | W. Sam. | Western Samoa |
| Com. | Comoros | Indon. | Indonesia | | U.S. | Sov. Un. | Soviet Union | *wtfl.* | waterfall |
| *cont.* | continent | I. of Man | Isle of Man | Nic. | Nicaragua | Sp. N. Afr. | Spanish North | W.V., U.S. | West Virginia, U.S. |
| C.R. | Costa Rica | Ire. | Ireland | Nig. | Nigeria | | Africa | Wy., U.S. | Wyoming, U.S. |
| *crat.* | crater | *is.* | islands | N. Ire., U.K. | Northern Ireland, | Sri L. | Sri Lanka | Yugo. | Yugoslavia |
| Ct., U.S. | Connecticut, U.S. | Isr. | Israel | | U.K. | *state* | state, republic, | Yukon | Yukon Territory, |
| *ctry.* | country | Isr. Occ. | Israeli Occupied | N.J., U.S. | New Jersey, U.S. | | canton | | Can. |
| C.V. | Cape Verde | | Territories | N. Kor. | North Korea | St. C.-N. | St. Christopher- | Zam. | Zambia |
| Cyp. | Cyprus | Jam. | Jamaica | N.M., U.S. | New Mexico, U.S. | | Nevis | Zimb. | Zimbabwe |
| Czech. | Czechoslovakia | Jord. | Jordan | N. Mar. Is. | Northern Mariana | St. Hel. | St. Helena | | |
| D.C., U.S. | District of Columbia, | Kir. | Kiribati | | Islands | | | | |
| | U.S. | | | | | | | | |

# INDEX

## A

| Name | Map Ref. | Page |
|---|---|---|
| Aachen, W. Ger. | C3 | 18 |
| Aalen, W. Ger. | D5 | 18 |
| A'alī an Nīl (Upper Nile), prov., Sud. | D3 | 47 |
| Aalsmeer, Neth. | B4 | 17 |
| Aalst (Alost), Bel. | B6 | 16 |
| Aalten, Neth. | C6 | 17 |
| Äänekoski, Fin. | F11 | 14 |
| Aarau, Switz. | E4 | 18 |
| Aare, stm., Switz. | E3 | 18 |
| Aargau, state, Switz. | B4 | 20 |
| Aaronsburg, Pa., U.S. | E7 | 115 |
| Aarschot, Bel. | D4 | 17 |
| Aba, China | E5 | 31 |
| Aba, Nig. | E6 | 45 |
| Aba, Zaire | A5 | 48 |
| Abacaxis, stm., Braz. | C3 | 59 |
| Abādān, Iran | B4 | 38 |
| Ābādeh, Iran | F6 | 39 |
| Abadla, Alg. | C4 | 44 |
| Abaeté, Braz. | B3 | 56 |
| Abaetetuba, Braz. | C5 | 59 |
| Abagnar Qi, China | C7 | 32 |
| Abag Qi, China | C6 | 32 |
| Abaí, Para. | E4 | 55 |
| Abajo Peak, mtn., Ut., U.S. | F6 | 121 |
| Abakaliki, Nig. | E6 | 45 |
| Abakan, Sov. Un. | D12 | 29 |
| Abala, Congo | B2 | 48 |
| Abala, Niger | D5 | 45 |
| Abancay, Peru | D3 | 58 |
| Abanda, Al., U.S. | B4 | 78 |
| Abanilla, Spain | C5 | 22 |
| Abano Terme, Italy | B3 | 23 |
| Abar Kūh, Iran | F6 | 39 |
| 'Abasān, Isr. Occ. | C6 | 41 |
| Abashiri, Japan | C13 | 31 |
| Abau, Pap. N. Gui. | m12 | 50 |
| Abaya, Lake, l., Eth. | D4 | 47 |
| Abbaye, Point, c., Mi., U.S. | B2 | 99 |
| Abbeville, Fr. | B4 | 16 |
| Abbeville, Al., U.S. | D4 | 78 |
| Abbeville, Ga., U.S. | E3 | 87 |
| Abbeville, La., U.S. | E3 | 95 |
| Abbeville, Ms., U.S. | A4 | 101 |
| Abbeville, S.C., U.S. | C3 | 117 |
| Abbeville, co., S.C., U.S. | C2 | 117 |
| Abbey, Sask. | G1 | 75 |
| Abbeydorney, Ire. | E2 | 11 |
| Abbeyfeale, Ire. | E2 | 11 |
| Abbey Head, c., Scot., U.K. | F5 | 13 |
| Abbeyleix, Ire. | E4 | 11 |
| Abbiategrasso, Italy | B2 | 23 |
| Abbotsford, B.C. | f13 | 69 |
| Abbotsford, Wi., U.S. | D3 | 126 |
| Abbott, Ar., U.S. | B1 | 81 |
| Abbott Butte, mtn., Or., U.S. | E4 | 114 |
| Abbott Run, stm., U.S. | B4 | 116 |
| Abbott Run Valley, R.I., U.S. | B4 | 116 |
| Abbottsburg, N.C., U.S. | C4 | 110 |
| Abbottstown, Pa., U.S. | G7 | 115 |
| Abbot Village, Me., U.S. | C3 | 96 |
| Abbyville, Ks., U.S. | E5 | 93 |
| 'Abd al Kūrī, i., Yemen | D5 | 38 |
| Abdulino, Sov. Un. | E19 | 8 |
| Abe, Lake, l., Afr. | C5 | 47 |
| Abéché, Chad | C4 | 46 |
| Abee, Alta. | B4 | 68 |
| Abejorral, Col. | B2 | 60 |
| Abengourou, I.C. | E4 | 45 |
| Åbenrå, Den. | C3 | 15 |
| Abeokuta, Nig. | E5 | 45 |
| Aberaeron, Wales, U.K. | B3 | 12 |
| Aberchirder, Scot., U.K. | C6 | 13 |
| Abercorn, Que. | D5 | 74 |
| Abercrombie, N.D., U.S. | C9 | 111 |
| Aberdare, Wales, U.K. | E5 | 10 |
| Aberdaron, Wales, U.K. | B3 | 12 |
| Aberdeen, Sask. | E2 | 75 |
| Aberdeen, S. Afr. | D3 | 49 |
| Aberdeen, Scot., U.K. | B5 | 10 |
| Aberdeen, Id., U.S. | G6 | 89 |
| Aberdeen, In., U.S. | G8 | 91 |
| Aberdeen, Ky., U.S. | C3 | 94 |
| Aberdeen, Md., U.S. | A5 | 97 |
| Aberdeen, Ms., U.S. | B5 | 101 |
| Aberdeen, N.C., U.S. | B3 | 110 |
| Aberdeen, Oh., U.S. | D2 | 112 |
| Aberdeen, S.D., U.S. | B7 | 118 |
| Aberdeen Lake, l., N.W. Ter. | D13 | 66 |
| Aberdeen Proving Ground, mil., Md., U.S. | A5 | 97 |
| Aberdeen Township, N.J., U.S. | *C4 | 107 |
| Aberdyfi, Wales, U.K. | B3 | 12 |
| Aberfeldy, Scot., U.K. | B5 | 10 |
| Aberfoyle, Scot., U.K. | D4 | 13 |
| Abergavenny, Wales, U.K. | E5 | 10 |
| Abernant, Al., U.S. | B2 | 78 |
| Abernathy, Tx., U.S. | C2 | 120 |
| Abernethy, Sask. | G4 | 75 |
| Abert, Lake, l., Or., U.S. | E6 | 114 |
| Abert Rim, clf., Or., U.S. | E6 | 114 |
| Aberystwyth, Wales, U.K. | D4 | 10 |
| Abesville, Mo., U.S. | E4 | 102 |
| Abhā, Sau. Ar. | D4 | 38 |
| Abhar, Iran | C4 | 39 |
| Abidjan, I.C. | E4 | 45 |
| Abie, Ne., U.S. | C9 | 104 |
| Abilene, Ks., U.S. | D6 | 93 |
| Abilene, Tx., U.S. | C3 | 120 |
| Abingdon, Eng., U.K. | C6 | 12 |
| Abingdon, Il., U.S. | C3 | 90 |
| Abingdon, Va., U.S. | C5 | 92 |
| Abington, Ct., U.S. | B7 | 84 |
| Abington, Ma., U.S. | B6 | 98 |
| Abington [Township], Pa., U.S. | o21 | 115 |
| Abiquiu, N.M., U.S. | A3 | 108 |
| Abisko, Swe. | C8 | 14 |
| Abita Springs, La., U.S. | D5 | 95 |
| Abitibi, stm., Ont. | o19 | 73 |
| Abitibi, Lake, l., Can. | G16 | 66 |
| Ablon, Fr. | h10 | 16 |
| Abloviak Fiord, Que. | f8 | 72 |
| Aboisso, I.C. | E4 | 45 |
| Abomey, Benin | E5 | 45 |
| Abong Mbang, Cam. | E2 | 46 |
| Abony, Hung. | B5 | 24 |
| Abou Deïa, Chad | C3 | 46 |
| Aboyne, Scot., U.K. | C6 | 13 |
| Abraham Lake, res., Alta. | C2 | 68 |
| Abraham Lincoln Birthplace National Historic Site, hist., Ky., U.S. | C4 | 94 |
| Abrams, Wi., U.S. | D5 | 126 |
| Abrantes, Port. | C1 | 22 |
| Ábrego, Col. | B3 | 60 |
| Abreojos, Punta, c., Mex. | B2 | 63 |
| Abruzzi, prov., Italy | C4 | 23 |
| Absaraka, N.D., U.S. | C8 | 111 |
| Absaroka Range, mts., U.S. | F7 | 127 |
| Absarokee, Mt., U.S. | E7 | 103 |
| Absecon, N.J., U.S. | E4 | 107 |
| Absecon Inlet, b., N.J., U.S. | E4 | 107 |
| Abū 'Alī, i., Sau. Ar. | H4 | 39 |
| Abū Dīs, Isr. Occ. | h12 | 41 |
| Abū Ḥadd, Bi'r, well, Eg. | E6 | 43 |
| Abū Ḥamad, Sud. | C3 | 47 |
| Abū Ḥammād al Maḥaṭṭah, Eg. | D3 | 41 |
| Abū Ḥummuṣ, Eg. | C2 | 41 |
| Abuja, Nig. | E6 | 45 |
| Abū Kabīr, Eg. | D3 | 41 |
| Abū Kamāl, Syria | B4 | 38 |
| Abū Kershola, Sud. | C3 | 47 |
| Abū Khawf, Mushāsh, well, Eg. | E6 | 41 |
| Abūksāh, Eg. | E2 | 41 |
| Abumombazi, Zaire | A3 | 48 |
| Abū Mūsā, i., U.A.E. | I7 | 39 |
| Abunā, Braz. | A2 | 55 |
| Abunã (Abuná), stm., S.A. | A2 | 55 |
| Abunã (Abuná), stm., S.A. | A2 | 55 |
| Abū Qīr, Eg. | C2 | 41 |
| Abū Qīr Bay, b., Eg. | C2 | 41 |
| Abū Qurqāṣ, Eg. | I8 | 40 |
| Abū Road, India | E4 | 37 |
| Abū Shajarah, Ra's, c., Sud. | A4 | 47 |
| Abū Simbel (Abū Sunbul), hist., Eg. | E6 | 43 |
| Abū Sufyān, 'Idd, well, Sud. | B2 | 47 |
| Abū Ṭabarī, well, Sud. | B2 | 47 |
| Abū 'Urūq, well, Sud. | B3 | 47 |
| Abū Zanīmah, Eg. | D6 | 43 |
| Åby (part of Norrköping), Swe. | u34 | 14 |
| Åbybro, Den. | A3 | 15 |
| Abyei, Sud. | D2 | 47 |
| Abyssinia see Ethiopia, ctry., Afr. | D4 | 47 |
| Academia, Oh., U.S. | B3 | 112 |
| Academy, S.D., U.S. | D6 | 118 |
| Acadia, co., La., U.S. | D3 | 95 |
| Acadia National Park, Me., U.S. | D4 | 96 |
| Acadia Valley, Alta. | D5 | 68 |
| Acaituba, Braz. | B2 | 59 |
| Acajutla, El Sal. | D3 | 62 |
| Acámbaro, Mex. | C4 | 63 |
| Acaponeta, Mex. | C3 | 63 |
| Acapulco [de Juárez], Mex. | D4 | 63 |
| Acarai Mountains, mts., S.A. | B3 | 59 |
| Acaraú, Braz. | B2 | 57 |
| Acaray, stm., Para. | E5 | 55 |
| Acari, Braz. | h5 | 57 |
| Acarí, Peru | E3 | 58 |
| Acarigua, Ven. | B4 | 60 |
| Acatlán [de Osorio], Mex. | D5 | 63 |
| Acayucan, Mex. | D6 | 63 |
| Accident, Md., U.S. | k12 | 97 |
| Accomac, Va., U.S. | C7 | 123 |
| Accomack, co., Va., U.S. | C7 | 123 |
| Accord, N.Y., U.S. | D6 | 109 |
| Accord Pond, l., Ma., U.S. | h12 | 98 |
| Accoville, W.V., U.S. | D3 | 125 |
| Accra, Ghana | E4 | 45 |
| Accrington, Eng., U.K. | A5 | 12 |
| Ace, Tx., U.S. | D5 | 120 |
| Aceguá, Ur. | E2 | 56 |
| Acequia, Id., U.S. | G5 | 89 |
| Achacachi, Bol. | C2 | 55 |
| Achalpur, India | G6 | 37 |
| Achao, Chile | C2 | 54 |
| Achar, Ur. | E1 | 56 |
| Acharacle, Scot., U.K. | D3 | 13 |
| Acheng, China | B10 | 31 |
| Achenkirch, Aus. | B7 | 20 |
| Achen Lake, l., Aus. | B7 | 20 |
| Achern, W. Ger. | E3 | 19 |
| Achicourt, Fr. | D2 | 17 |
| Achill Head, c., Ire. | D1 | 11 |
| Achill Island, i., Ire. | D1 | 10 |
| Achill Sound, Ire. | D2 | 10 |
| Achinsk, Sov. Un. | D12 | 29 |
| Achiras, Arg. | A4 | 54 |
| Achisay, Sov. Un. | E7 | 28 |
| Achtubinsk, Sov. Un. | D3 | 28 |
| Achuapam, Tur. | D7 | 25 |
| Acireale, Italy | F5 | 23 |
| Ackerly, Tx., U.S. | C2 | 120 |
| Ackerman, Ms., U.S. | B4 | 101 |
| Ackley, Ia., U.S. | B4 | 92 |
| Acklins Island, i., Bah. | C6 | 64 |
| Acmar, Al., U.S. | B3 | 78 |
| Acme, Alta. | D4 | 68 |
| Acme, La., U.S. | C3 | 95 |
| Acme, Mi., U.S. | D5 | 99 |
| Acme, Wa., U.S. | A3 | 124 |
| Acme, W.V., U.S. | m13 | 125 |
| Acme, Wy., U.S. | B6 | 127 |
| Acobamba, Peru | D3 | 58 |
| Acoma Indian Reservation, N.M., U.S. | C2 | 108 |
| Acomayo, Peru | D3 | 58 |
| Aconcagua, Cerro, mtn., Arg. | A3 | 54 |
| Acopiara, Braz. | C3 | 57 |
| Acorizal, Braz. | B1 | 56 |
| Acosta, Braz. | F3 | 115 |
| Acoyapa, Nic. | E5 | 62 |
| Acquarossa, Switz. | D3 | 20 |
| Acqui [Terme], Italy | B2 | 23 |
| Acre, state, Braz. | C3 | 58 |
| Acre, stm., S.A. | C4 | 58 |
| Acree, Ga., U.S. | E2 | 87 |
| Actinolite, Ont. | C7 | 73 |
| Acton, Ont. | D4 | 73 |
| Acton Vale, Que. | D5 | 74 |
| Actopan, Mex. | m14 | 63 |
| Açu, Braz. | C3 | 57 |
| Acushnet, Ma., U.S. | C6 | 98 |
| Acworth, Ga., U.S. | B2 | 87 |
| Acworth, N.H., U.S. | D2 | 106 |
| Ada, Ghana | E5 | 45 |
| Ada, Japan | N6 | 52 |
| Ada, Ks., U.S. | C6 | 93 |
| Ada, Mn., U.S. | C2 | 100 |
| Ada, Oh., U.S. | B2 | 112 |
| Ada, Ok., U.S. | C5 | 113 |
| Ada, Yugo. | C5 | 24 |
| Ada, co., Id., U.S. | F2 | 89 |
| Ada, Cape, c., Sov. Un. | G19 | 8 |
| Ada, Mount, mtn., Ak., U.S. | m22 | 79 |
| Adair, Il., U.S. | C3 | 90 |
| Adair, Ia., U.S. | C3 | 92 |
| Adair, Ok., U.S. | A6 | 113 |
| Adair, co., Ia., U.S. | C3 | 92 |
| Adair, co., Ky., U.S. | C4 | 94 |
| Adair, co., Mo., U.S. | A5 | 102 |
| Adair, co., Ok., U.S. | B7 | 113 |
| Adairsville, Ga., U.S. | B2 | 87 |
| Adairville, Ky., U.S. | D3 | 94 |
| Adak Island, i., Ak., U.S. | E4 | 79 |
| Adak Naval Station, mil., Ak., U.S. | E4 | 79 |
| Adamant, Vt., U.S. | C3 | 122 |
| Adamantina, Braz. | C2 | 56 |
| Adamaoua, mts., Afr. | D2 | 46 |
| Adam Island, i., Md., U.S. | D5 | 97 |
| Adami Tulu, Eth. | D4 | 47 |
| Adams, In., U.S. | F6 | 91 |
| Adams, Ky., U.S. | B7 | 94 |
| Adams, Ma., U.S. | A1 | 98 |
| Adams, Mn., U.S. | G6 | 100 |
| Adams, Ne., U.S. | D9 | 104 |
| Adams, N.Y., U.S. | B4 | 109 |
| Adams, N.D., U.S. | A7 | 111 |
| Adams, Ok., U.S. | e9 | 113 |
| Adams, Or., U.S. | B8 | 114 |
| Adams, Tn., U.S. | A4 | 119 |
| Adams, Wi., U.S. | E4 | 126 |
| Adams, co., Co., U.S. | B6 | 83 |
| Adams, co., Id., U.S. | E2 | 89 |
| Adams, co., Il., U.S. | C8 | 91 |
| Adams, co., In., U.S. | C3 | 92 |
| Adams, co., Ia., U.S. | C3 | 92 |
| Adams, co., Ms., U.S. | D2 | 101 |
| Adams, co., Ne., U.S. | D7 | 104 |
| Adams, co., N.D., U.S. | C3 | 111 |
| Adams, co., Oh., U.S. | D2 | 112 |
| Adams, co., Pa., U.S. | G7 | 115 |
| Adams, co., Wa., U.S. | B7 | 124 |
| Adams, co., Wi., U.S. | D4 | 126 |
| Adams, Mount, mtn., N.H., U.S. | B4 | 106 |
| Adams, Mount, mtn., Wa., U.S. | C4 | 124 |
| Adams, Mount, mtn., Vt., U.S. | C3 | 122 |
| Adams Bridge, rf., Asia | G6 | 36 |
| Adams Center, N.Y., U.S. | B5 | 109 |
| Adams City, Co., U.S. | *B6 | 83 |
| Adams Lake, l., B.C. | D8 | 69 |
| Adams Mountain, mtn., Ma., U.S. | A2 | 98 |
| Adamson, Ok., U.S. | C6 | 113 |
| Adams Point, c., Mi., U.S. | C7 | 99 |
| Adams Run, S.C., U.S. | k11 | 117 |
| Adamston, N.J., U.S. | C4 | 107 |
| Adamstown, Md., U.S. | B3 | 97 |
| Adamstown, Pa., U.S. | F9 | 115 |
| Adamsville, Que. | D5 | 74 |
| Adamsville, Al., U.S. | f7 | 78 |
| Adamsville, Pa., U.S. | D1 | 115 |
| Adamsville, R.I., U.S. | E6 | 116 |
| Adamsville, Tn., U.S. | B3 | 119 |
| Adamsville, Tx., U.S. | D3 | 120 |
| Adamsville, Ut., U.S. | E3 | 121 |
| Adamsville Brook, stm., R.I., U.S. | E6 | 116 |
| Adana, Tur. | D10 | 40 |
| Adanac, Sask. | E1 | 75 |
| Adapazarı, Tur. | B8 | 40 |
| Adarama, Sud. | B4 | 47 |
| Adare, Ire. | E3 | 11 |
| Adare, Cape, c., Ant. | B30 | 7 |
| Adavale, Austl. | B5 | 51 |
| Adaza, Italy | B2 | 23 |
| Aḏ Dab'ah, Eg. | C5 | 43 |
| Ad Dabbah, Sud. | B3 | 47 |
| Ad Dahnā', des., Sau. Ar. | C4 | 38 |
| Ad Dammām, Sau. Ar. | C5 | 38 |
| Ad Dibdibah, pl., Sau. Ar. | C3 | 38 |
| Ad Dilinjāt, Eg. | D2 | 41 |
| Addicks Barker, Tx., U.S. | r14 | 120 |
| Addieville, Il., U.S. | E4 | 90 |
| Ad Dilinjāt, Eg. | D2 | 41 |
| Addis, La., U.S. | D4 | 95 |
| Addis Ababa (Adīs Abeba), Eth. | D4 | 47 |
| Addison, Al., U.S. | A2 | 78 |
| Addison, Ct., U.S. | C5 | 84 |
| Addison, Il., U.S. | k8 | 90 |
| Addison, Me., U.S. | D5 | 96 |
| Addison, N.Y., U.S. | C3 | 109 |
| Addison, Tx., U.S. | *n10 | 120 |
| Addison, Vt., U.S. | C2 | 122 |
| Addison, co., Vt., U.S. | C2 | 122 |
| Addis Zemen, Eth. | C4 | 47 |
| Ad Dīwānīyah, Iraq | B4 | 38 |
| Ad Duwaym, Sud. | C3 | 47 |
| Ad Duwaym, Sud. | C3 | 47 |
| Addy, Wa., U.S. | A8 | 124 |
| Addyston, Oh., U.S. | o12 | 112 |
| Adel, Ga., U.S. | E3 | 87 |
| Adel, Ia., U.S. | C3 | 92 |
| Adel, Or., U.S. | E7 | 114 |
| Adelaide, Austl. | F6 | 50 |
| Adelaide, Bah. | m17 | 64 |
| Adelaide Island, i., Ant. | C6 | 7 |
| Adelanto, Ca., U.S. | E5 | 82 |
| Adelboden, Switz. | E4 | 20 |
| Adélie Coast, Ant. | C26 | 7 |
| Adell, Wi., U.S. | *B4 | 97 |
| Adelphi, Md., U.S. | *B4 | 97 |
| Adelphi, Oh., U.S. | C3 | 112 |
| Adelphia, N.J., U.S. | C4 | 107 |
| Aden ('Adan), Yemen | D4 | 38 |
| Aden, Gulf of, b. | D4 | 38 |
| Adena, Oh., U.S. | B5 | 112 |
| Adenau, W. Ger. | C1 | 19 |
| Adgateville, Ga., U.S. | C3 | 87 |
| Adi, i., Indon. | F8 | 34 |
| Adige, stm., Italy | B3 | 23 |
| Adigrat, Eth. | C4 | 47 |
| Ādilābād, India | H7 | 37 |
| Adin, Ca., U.S. | B3 | 82 |
| Adirondack Mountains, mts., N.Y., U.S. | A6 | 109 |
| Adi Ugri, Eth. | C4 | 47 |
| Adiyaman, Tur. | C12 | 40 |
| Adjud, Rom. | D4 | 24 |
| Adjuntas, P.R. | B2 | 65 |
| Adlavik Islands, is., Newf. | g10 | 72 |
| Adliswil, Switz. | B6 | 21 |
| Admaston, Ont. | B8 | 73 |
| Admiral, Sask. | H1 | 75 |
| Admirals Beach, Newf. | E5 | 72 |
| Admiralty Bay, b., Ak. U.S. | A9 | 79 |
| Admiralty Gulf, b., Austl. | B4 | 50 |
| Admiralty Inlet, b., N.W. Ter. | B15 | 66 |
| Admiralty Island, i., Ak., U.S. | m22 | 79 |
| Admiralty Islands, is., Pap. N. Gui. | h12 | 50 |
| Admiralty Mountains, mts., Ant. | B29 | 7 |
| Admire, Ks., U.S. | D7 | 93 |
| Adobe Acres, N.M., U.S. | B3 | 108 |
| Adobe Creek, stm., Co., U.S. | C7 | 83 |
| Adobe Creek Reservoir, res., Co., U.S. | C7 | 83 |
| Ado-Ekiti, Nig. | *E6 | 45 |
| Adok, Sud. | D3 | 47 |
| Adolphus, Ky., U.S. | D3 | 94 |
| Adona, Ar., U.S. | B3 | 81 |
| Ādoni, India | *E6 | 36 |
| Adony, Hung. | B4 | 24 |
| Adorf, E. Ger. | C7 | 19 |
| Adour, stm., Fr. | F3 | 16 |
| Adowa see Adwa, Eth. | C4 | 47 |
| Adra, Spain | D4 | 22 |
| Adrano, Italy | F5 | 23 |
| Adrar, Alg. | D4 | 44 |
| Adrar, reg., Maur. | B2 | 45 |
| Adré, Chad | C4 | 46 |
| Adrī, Libya | D2 | 43 |
| Adria, Italy | B4 | 23 |
| Adrian, Ga., U.S. | D4 | 87 |
| Adrian, Mi., U.S. | G6 | 99 |
| Adrian, Mn., U.S. | G3 | 100 |
| Adrian, Mo., U.S. | C3 | 102 |
| Adrian, N.D., U.S. | C7 | 111 |
| Adrian, Or., U.S. | D9 | 114 |
| Adrian, Tx., U.S. | B1 | 120 |
| Adrian, W.V., U.S. | C4 | 125 |
| Adriatic Sea, Eur. | G12 | 8 |
| Adrigole, Ire. | F2 | 11 |
| Advance, In., U.S. | D4 | 91 |
| Advance, Mo., U.S. | D8 | 102 |
| Advocate Harbour, N.S. | D5 | 71 |
| Adwa (Adowa), Eth. | C4 | 47 |
| Æbelø, i., Den. | C4 | 15 |
| Aegean Sea | C5 | 40 |
| Aegeri, Lake, l., Switz. | B4 | 20 |
| Ærø, i., Den. | D4 | 15 |
| Ærøskøbing, Den. | D4 | 15 |
| Aesch, Switz. | B4 | 21 |
| Aetna, Alta. | E4 | 68 |
| Aetna, Tn., U.S. | B4 | 119 |
| Afars and Issas see Djibouti, ctry., Afr. | C5 | 47 |
| Affolterm am Albis, Switz. | B5 | 21 |
| Affton, Mo., U.S. | *f13 | 102 |
| Afghanistan, ctry., Asia | B3 | 36 |
| Afgooye, Som. | E6 | 47 |
| 'Afif, Sau. Ar. | C4 | 38 |
| Afikpo, Nig. | E6 | 45 |
| Aflou, Alg. | C5 | 44 |
| Afmadow, Som. | E5 | 47 |
| Afognak Island, i., Ak., U.S. | D9 | 79 |
| Afono Bay, b., Am. Sam. | G13 | 52 |
| Afonso Cláudio, Braz. | C4 | 56 |
| Africa, cont. | F8 | 42 |
| Afton, De., U.S. | *A4 | 85 |
| Afton, Ia., U.S. | C3 | 92 |
| Afton, Mi., U.S. | C6 | 99 |
| Afton, Mn., U.S. | F6 | 100 |
| Afton, N.Y., U.S. | C5 | 109 |
| Afton, Ok., U.S. | A7 | 113 |
| Afton, Tn., U.S. | C11 | 119 |
| Afton, Tx., U.S. | C2 | 120 |
| Afton, Wy., U.S. | D2 | 127 |
| Aftout, reg., Alg. | D4 | 44 |
| Afuá, Braz. | C4 | 59 |
| 'Afula, Isr. | B7 | 41 |
| Afyon, Tur. | C7 | 40 |
| Agadem, Niger | C7 | 45 |
| Agadez, Niger | C6 | 45 |
| Agadir, Mor. | C3 | 44 |
| Agana, Guam | L9 | 52 |
| Agana Bay, b., Guam | L9 | 52 |
| Agana Heights, Guam | *L9 | 52 |
| Agana Naval Air Station, mil., Guam | L10 | 52 |
| Agar, India | F5 | 37 |
| Agar, S.D., U.S. | C5 | 118 |
| Agartala, India | D9 | 36 |
| Agassiz, B.C. | E7 | 69 |
| Agassiz, Cape, c., Ant. | C7 | 7 |
| Agat, Guam | M9 | 52 |
| Agatayn Hiid, Mong. | A3 | 32 |
| Agat Bay, b., Guam | M9 | 52 |
| Agate, N.D., U.S. | A3 | 111 |
| Agate Beach, Or., U.S. | C2 | 114 |
| Agate Fossil Beds National Monument, Ne., U.S. | B2 | 104 |
| Agattu Island, i., Ak., U.S. | E2 | 79 |
| Agawam, Ma., U.S. | B2 | 98 |
| Agawam, Ok., U.S. | C4 | 113 |
| Agbor, Nig. | E6 | 45 |
| Agboville, I.C. | E5 | 45 |
| Agdam, Sov. Un. | B3 | 39 |
| Agde, Fr. | F5 | 16 |
| Agen, Fr. | E4 | 16 |
| Agency, Ia., U.S. | D5 | 92 |
| Agency, Mo., U.S. | B3 | 102 |
| Agenda, Ks., U.S. | C6 | 93 |
| Ageo, Japan | *I9 | 33 |
| Ageri, Lake, l., Switz. | C5 | 15 |
| Agersø, i., Den. | C5 | 15 |
| Agfayan Bay, b., Guam | L9 | 52 |
| Aghā Jārī, Iran | F4 | 39 |
| Aghleam, Ire. | C1 | 11 |
| Agincourt (part of Scarborough), Ont. | k15 | 73 |
| Aginskoye, Sov. Un. | A7 | 31 |
| Agira, Italy | F5 | 23 |
| Agno, Phil. | n12 | 34 |
| Agno, stm., Phil. | o13 | 34 |
| Agnone, Italy | D5 | 23 |
| Agnos, Ar., U.S. | A4 | 81 |
| Agogna, stm., Italy | B2 | 23 |
| Agoo, Phil. | n13 | 34 |
| Agordo, Italy | C8 | 20 |
| Agoura Hills, Ca., U.S. | m11 | 82 |
| Āgra, India | C6 | 36 |
| Āgra, stm., India | F5 | 37 |
| Agra, Ok., U.S. | B5 | 113 |
| Agrado, Col. | F5 | 60 |
| Ağrı (Karaköse), Tur. | C14 | 40 |
| Agri, stm., Italy | D6 | 23 |
| Agri Point, c., Phil. | o13 | 34 |
| Agricola, Ms., U.S. | E5 | 101 |
| Agrigento, Italy | F4 | 23 |
| Agrínion, Grc. | C3 | 40 |
| Agripoli, Italy | D5 | 23 |
| Agryz, Sov. Un. | D19 | 8 |
| Aguada Boa, Braz. | B4 | 56 |
| Aguada, P.R. | B1 | 65 |
| Aguadas, Col. | B2 | 60 |
| Aguadilla, P.R. | G11 | 64 |
| Aguadilla, Bahía de, b., P.R. | B1 | 65 |
| Aguadulce, Pan. | F7 | 62 |
| Agua Dulce Mountains, mts., Az., U.S. | E2 | 80 |
| Agua Fria, N.M., U.S. | B3 | 108 |
| Agua Fria, stm., Az., U.S. | C3 | 80 |
| Aguaí, Braz. | m8 | 56 |
| Aguán, stm., Hond. | C4 | 62 |
| Aguanish, Que. | h9 | 72 |
| Agua Nueva, Tx., U.S. | F3 | 120 |
| Aguapey, stm., Arg. | E4 | 55 |
| Água Preta, Braz. | k6 | 57 |
| Agua Prieta, Mex. | A3 | 63 |
| Aguaray, Arg. | D3 | 55 |
| Aguarico, stm., S.A. | B2 | 58 |
| Aguascalientes, Mex. | C4 | 63 |
| Aguascalientes, state, Mex. | C4 | 63 |
| Aguas Formosas, Braz. | B4 | 56 |
| Agudos, Braz. | C3 | 56 |
| Águeda, Port. | B1 | 22 |
| Águeda, stm., Eur. | B2 | 22 |
| Aguelhok, Mali | C5 | 45 |
| Aguérakrtem, well, Mali | B3 | 45 |
| Aguila, Az., U.S. | D2 | 80 |
| Aguilar, Spain | D3 | 22 |
| Aguilar, Co., U.S. | D6 | 83 |
| Águilas, Spain | D5 | 22 |
| Aguililla, Mex. | D4 | 63 |
| Aguja, Cabo de la, c., Col. | A3 | 60 |
| Aguja, Punta, c., Peru | C1 | 58 |
| Agulhas, Cape, c., S. Afr. | D3 | 49 |
| Agulhas Negras, Pico das, mtn., Braz. | h5 | 56 |
| Agusan, stm., Phil. | D7 | 34 |
| Ahaggar, mts., Afr. | E6 | 44 |
| Ahaggar, Tassili ta-n-, plat., Alg. | E6 | 44 |
| Ahar, Iran | B3 | 39 |
| Ahiachak, Ak., U.S. | C7 | 79 |
| Ahascragh, Ire. | D3 | 11 |
| Ahaus, W. Ger. | A2 | 19 |
| Ahimiski Island, i., N.W. Ter. | F16 | 66 |
| Ahklun Mountains, mts., Ak., U.S. | D7 | 79 |
| Ahlen, W. Ger. | F2 | 15 |
| Ahlhorn, W. Ger. | F2 | 15 |
| Ahmadābād (Ahmedabad), India | D5 | 36 |
| Ahmadnagar, India | E5 | 36 |
| Ahmadpur East, Pak. | C5 | 36 |
| Ahmar, 'Erg el, des., Afr. | E4 | 44 |
| Ahmar Mountains, mts., Eth. | D5 | 47 |
| Ahmic Lake, l., Ont. | B5 | 73 |
| Ahome, Mex. | B3 | 63 |
| Ahon, Tarso, mtn., Chad | A3 | 46 |
| Ahoskie, N.C., U.S. | A6 | 110 |
| Ahousat, B.C. | E4 | 69 |
| Ahrensbök, W. Ger. | C4 | 15 |
| Ahrweiler, W. Ger. | C3 | 18 |
| Ahsahka, Id., U.S. | C2 | 89 |
| Ahtanum Creek, stm., Wa., U.S. | C5 | 124 |
| Ahuacatlán, Mex. | m11 | 63 |
| Ahuachapán, El Sal. | E7 | 63 |
| Ahualulco de Mercado, Mex. | m11 | 63 |
| Åhus, Swe. | C8 | 15 |
| Ahvāz (Nāsiri), Iran | B4 | 38 |
| Ahvenanmaa (Åland), is., Fin. | G9 | 14 |
| Ahwahnee, Ca., U.S. | D4 | 82 |
| Aḥwar, Yemen | C6 | 47 |
| Aialik, Cape, c., Ak., U.S. | D10 | 79 |
| Aibonito, P.R. | B3 | 65 |
| Aichach, W. Ger. | E6 | 19 |
| Aiea, Hi., U.S. | B4 | 88 |
| Aigen [in Mühlkreis], Aus. | D6 | 18 |
| Aigle, Switz. | E3 | 20 |
| Aigues-Mortes, Fr. | F6 | 16 |
| Aiguilles, Fr. | E2 | 20 |
| Aija, Peru | C2 | 58 |
| Aikawa, Japan | G9 | 33 |
| Aiken, S.C., U.S. | D4 | 117 |
| Aiken, Tx., U.S. | B2 | 120 |
| Aiken, co., S.C., U.S. | C4 | 117 |
| Aikens Lake, l., Man. | D4 | 70 |
| Ailey, Ga., U.S. | D4 | 87 |
| Ailsa Craig, Ont. | D3 | 73 |
| Aimorés, Braz. | B3 | 80 |
| Ain, dept., Fr. | E1 | 78 |
| Ain, stm., Fr. | E6 | 16 |
| Aïn el Beïda, Alg. | B6 | 44 |
| Aïn ben Tili, Maur. | A3 | 45 |
| Aïn Sefra, Alg. | C4 | 44 |
| Aïn Témouchent, Alg. | B5 | 44 |
| Aïn Wessara, Alg. | B5 | 44 |
| Aipe, Col. | F5 | 60 |
| Aiquile, Bol. | C2 | 55 |
| Aïr, mts., Niger | C6 | 45 |
| Airabu, i., Indon. | K7 | 35 |
| Airaines, Fr. | E1 | 17 |
| Airdrie, Alta. | D3 | 68 |
| Airdrie, Scot., U.K. | D6 | 41 |
| Aire, stm., Eng., U.K. | A6 | 12 |
| Aire-sur-l'Adour, Fr. | F3 | 16 |
| Aire [-sur-la-Lys], Fr. | B5 | 16 |
| Air Force Island, i., N.W. Ter. | C18 | 66 |
| Airline, Ne., U.S. | D9 | 104 |
| Air Park West, Ne., U.S. | D9 | 104 |
| Airukiiji Island, i., Marsh Is. | P18 | 52 |
| Aisch, stm., W. Ger. | D5 | 19 |
| Aisén del General Carlos Ibáñez del Campo, prov., Chile | D2 | 54 |
| Aishihik Lake, l., Yukon | D5 | 66 |
| Aisne, dept., Fr. | E3 | 17 |
| Aisne, stm., Fr. | C6 | 16 |
| Aitape, Pap. N. Gui. | h11 | 50 |
| Aitkin, Mn., U.S. | D5 | 100 |
| Aitkin, co., Mn., U.S. | D5 | 100 |
| Aiud, Rom. | C6 | 24 |
| Aiuaba, Braz. | C2 | 57 |
| Aiuruoca, stm., Braz. | g5 | 56 |
| Aiwa, i., Fiji | I16 | 52 |
| Aix, Mount, mtn., Wa., U.S. | C4 | 124 |
| Aix-en-Provence, Fr. | F6 | 16 |
| Aix-les-Bains, Fr. | E6 | 16 |
| Aíyáleo, Grc. | h11 | 25 |
| Aíyina (Aegina), i., Grc. | D4 | 25 |
| Aiyion, Grc. | C4 | 25 |
| Aizu-takada, Japan | H9 | 33 |
| Aizu-wakamatsu, Japan | H9 | 33 |
| Ajaccio, Fr. | D2 | 23 |
| Ajaccio, Gulf of, b., Fr. | D2 | 23 |
| Ajax, Ont. | D6 | 73 |
| Ajayan Bay, b., Guam | M9 | 52 |
| Ajdābiyā, Libya | C4 | 43 |
| Ajlūn, Jord. | B7 | 41 |
| Ajmer, India | C5 | 36 |
| Ajo, Az., U.S. | E3 | 80 |
| 'Ajramīyah, Bi'r al, well, Eg. | E3 | 41 |
| Akaishi-sammyaku, mts., Japan | n17 | 33 |
| Akaki Beseka, Eth. | *D4 | 47 |
| Akalkot, India | I6 | 37 |
| Akaroa, N.Z. | O14 | 51 |
| 'Akasha East, Sud. | A3 | 47 |
| Akashi, Japan | I7 | 33 |
| Akbulak, Sov. Un. | E20 | 8 |
| Akçaabat, Tur. | B12 | 40 |
| Akçadağ, Tur. | C11 | 40 |
| Ak-Chin Indian Reservation, Az., U.S. | E3 | 80 |
| Akdağmadeni, Tur. | C10 | 40 |
| Akechi, Japan | n16 | 33 |
| Akeley, Mn., U.S. | C4 | 100 |
| Aken, E. Ger. | B7 | 19 |
| Akers, La., U.S. | D5 | 95 |
| Aketi, Zaire | A3 | 48 |
| Akhaltsikhe, Sov. Un. | B14 | 40 |
| Akhelóös, stm., Grc. | g11 | 25 |
| Akhḍar, Al Jabal al, mts., Libya | C4 | 43 |
| Akhḍar, Al Jabal al, mts., Oman | C5 | 38 |
| Akhelóös, stm., Grc. | C3 | 25 |
| Akhiok, Ak., U.S. | D9 | 79 |
| Akhisar, Tur. | C6 | 40 |
| Akhmīm, Eg. | D7 | 43 |
| Akhtopol, Bul. | D8 | 24 |
| Akhtyrka, Sov. Un. | F10 | 27 |
| Aki, Japan | J6 | 33 |
| Akiachak, Ak., U.S. | C7 | 79 |
| Akiak, Ak., U.S. | C7 | 79 |
| Akimiski Island, i., N.W. Ter. | F16 | 66 |
| Akita, Japan | D13 | 31 |
| Akjoujt, Maur. | C2 | 45 |
| 'Akko, Isr. | F10 | 40 |
| Akobo, Sud. | D3 | 47 |
| Akobo, stm., Afr. | D3 | 47 |
| Akola, India | D6 | 36 |
| Akonolinga, Cam. | E2 | 46 |
| Akordat, Eth. | B4 | 47 |
| Akosombo Dam, Ghana | E5 | 45 |
| Akpatok Island, i., N.W. Ter. | D19 | 66 |
| Akra, N.D., U.S. | A8 | 111 |
| Akraífnion, Grc. | g10 | 25 |
| Akranes, Ice. | n21 | 14 |
| Akrítas, Ákra, c., Grc. | D3 | 40 |
| Akron, Al., U.S. | C2 | 78 |
| Akron, Co., U.S. | A7 | 83 |
| Akron, In., U.S. | B5 | 91 |
| Akron, Ia., U.S. | B1 | 92 |
| Akron, Mi., U.S. | E7 | 99 |
| Akron, N.Y., U.S. | B2 | 109 |
| Akron, Oh., U.S. | A4 | 112 |
| Akron, Pa., U.S. | F9 | 115 |
| Aksaray, Tur. | C10 | 40 |
| Akşehir, Tur. | C8 | 40 |
| Akşehir, Tur. | C8 | 40 |
| Akseki, Tur. | D8 | 40 |
| Aksenovo-Zilovskoye, Sov. Un. | D14 | 29 |
| Aksha, Sov. Un. | A7 | 31 |
| Akshimrau, Sov. Un. | E4 | 28 |
| Aksoran, Mount, mtn., Sov. Un. | F24 | 8 |
| Aksu, China | E11 | 29 |
| Aksum, Eth. | C4 | 47 |
| Aktogay, Sov. Un. | D9 | 28 |
| Aktumsyk, Sov. Un. | D8 | 29 |
| Aktyubinsk, Sov. Un. | D5 | 28 |
| Akure, Nig. | E6 | 45 |
| Akureyri, Ice. | n23 | 14 |
| Akuseki Island, i., Japan | L4 | 33 |
| Akutan, Ak., U.S. | E6 | 79 |
| Akyab see Sittwe, Burma | D9 | 36 |
| Alabama, state, U.S. | C3 | 78 |
| Alabama, stm., Al., U.S. | D2 | 78 |
| Alabama Port, Al., U.S. | E1 | 78 |
| Alabaster, Al., U.S. | B3 | 78 |
| Alabaster, Mi., U.S. | D7 | 99 |
| Alabat, i., Phil. | o14 | 34 |
| Al 'Abbāsīyah, Sud. | C3 | 47 |
| Al Abyaḍ, Libya | F3 | 40 |
| Al Abyār, Libya | C4 | 43 |
| Alachua, Fl., U.S. | C4 | 86 |
| Alachua, co., Fl., U.S. | C4 | 86 |
| Aladdin, Wy., U.S. | B8 | 127 |
| Alagoa Grande, Braz. | D3 | 57 |
| Alagoas, state, Braz. | D3 | 57 |
| Alagoinhas, Braz. | D3 | 57 |
| Alagón, Spain | B5 | 22 |
| Alagón, stm., Spain | B2 | 22 |
| Al 'Ajamīyīn, Eg. | D2 | 41 |
| Al 'Ajrūd, well, Eg. | D6 | 41 |
| Alajuela, Lago, res., Pan. | k11 | 62 |
| Alakol, Lake, l., Sov. Un. | D10 | 29 |
| Alalakeiki Channel, strt., Hi., U.S. | C5 | 88 |
| Al 'Alamayn, Eg. | B2 | 43 |
| Alalaú, stm., Braz. | C2 | 59 |
| Alamance, N.C., U.S. | B3 | 110 |
| Alamance, co., N.C., U.S. | A3 | 110 |
| 'Alam ar Rūm, Ra's, c., Egypt | G6 | 40 |
| Alameda, Sask. | H4 | 75 |
| Alameda, Ca., U.S. | h8 | 82 |
| Alameda, co., Ca., U.S. | D3 | 82 |
| Alameda Naval Air Station, mil., Ca., U.S. | h8 | 82 |
| Al 'Āmirīyah, Eg. | G7 | 40 |
| Alamikamba, Nic. | D5 | 62 |
| Alamo, Mex. | m15 | 63 |
| Alamo, Ca., U.S. | *D2 | 82 |
| Alamo, Ga., U.S. | D4 | 87 |
| Alamo, Nv., U.S. | F6 | 105 |
| Alamo, Tn., U.S. | B2 | 119 |
| Alamo, Tx., U.S. | F3 | 120 |
| Alamo, stm., Ca., U.S. | F6 | 82 |
| Alamogordo, N.M., U.S. | E4 | 108 |
| Alamogordo Dam, N.M., U.S. | C5 | 108 |
| Alamo Heights, Tx., U.S. | E3 | 120 |

# Index

| Name | Map Ref. | Page |
|---|---|---|
| Alamo Hueco Mountains, mts., N.M., U.S. | F1 | 108 |
| Alamo Indian Reservation, N.M., U.S. | C2 | 108 |
| Alamo Lake, res., Az., U.S. | C2 | 80 |
| Alamos, Mex. | B3 | 63 |
| Alamosa, Co., U.S. | D5 | 83 |
| Alamosa, co., Co., U.S. | D5 | 83 |
| Alamosa, stm., Co., U.S. | D4 | 83 |
| Alamosa Creek, stm., N.M., U.S. | D2 | 108 |
| Alamosa East, Co., U.S. | D5 | 83 |
| Åland see Ahvenanmaa, is., Fin. | G9 | 14 |
| Alanreed, Tx., U.S. | B2 | 120 |
| Alanson, Mi., U.S. | C6 | 99 |
| Alanya, Tur. | D9 | 40 |
| Alaotra, Lac, l., Madag. | g9 | 49 |
| Alapaha, Ga., U.S. | E3 | 87 |
| Alapaha, stm., U.S. | E3 | 87 |
| Alapayevsk, Sov. Un. | B6 | 28 |
| Al 'Aqabah, Jord. | C3 | 38 |
| Al Aqsa Mosque, Isr. Occ. | m14 | 41 |
| Al 'Arīsh, Eg. | C6 | 43 |
| Alasdair, Sgurr, mtn., Scot., U.K. | C2 | 13 |
| Alaşehir, Tur. | C7 | 40 |
| Alaska, state, U.S. | C9 | 79 |
| Alaska, Gulf of, b., Ak., U.S. | D10 | 79 |
| Alaska Peninsula, pen., Ak., U.S. | D8 | 79 |
| Alaska Range, mts., Ak., U.S. | C9 | 79 |
| Alassio, Italy | C2 | 23 |
| Alatna, stm., Ak., U.S. | B9 | 79 |
| Al 'Aţrūn, Sud. | B2 | 47 |
| Alatyr, Sov. Un. | D16 | 29 |
| Alausí, Ec. | B2 | 58 |
| Alava, Cape, c., Wa., U.S. | A1 | 124 |
| Alaverdi, Sov. Un. | B15 | 40 |
| Al 'Ayyāţ, Eg. | E3 | 41 |
| Al 'Ayzarīyah (Bethany), Isr. Occ. | h12 | 41 |
| Al 'Azīzīyah, Libya | C2 | 43 |
| Alb, stm., W. Ger. | A5 | 21 |
| Alba, Italy | B2 | 23 |
| Alba, Mi., U.S. | D6 | 99 |
| Alba, Mo., U.S. | D3 | 102 |
| Alba, Pa., U.S. | C8 | 115 |
| Alba, Tx., U.S. | E5 | 120 |
| Albacete, Spain | C5 | 22 |
| Al Badārī, Eg. | D6 | 43 |
| Alba de Tormes, Spain | B3 | 22 |
| Ålbæk, Den. | A4 | 15 |
| Ålbæk Bugt, b., Den. | A4 | 15 |
| Al Bahnasā, Eg. | H8 | 40 |
| Al Bahr al Abyaḑ, prov., Sud. | C3 | 47 |
| Al Baḥr al Aḥmar (Red Sea), prov., Sud. | B4 | 47 |
| Alba Iulia, Rom. | B6 | 24 |
| Al Bājūr, Eg. | D3 | 41 |
| Albalate [del Arzobispo], Spain | B5 | 22 |
| Al Ballaḩ, Eg. | D4 | 41 |
| Albanel, Lac, l., Que. | F18 | 66 |
| Albani, Colli, hills, Italy | h9 | 23 |
| Albania, ctry., Eur. | B2 | 40 |
| Albano, Lake, l., Italy | h9 | 23 |
| Albano Laziale, Italy | D4 | 23 |
| Albany, Austl. | F2 | 50 |
| Albany, N.S. | E4 | 71 |
| Albany, P.E.I. | C6 | 71 |
| Albany, Ca., U.S. | *h8 | 82 |
| Albany, Ga., U.S. | E2 | 87 |
| Albany, In., U.S. | D7 | 91 |
| Albany, Ky., U.S. | D4 | 94 |
| Albany, La., U.S. | g10 | 95 |
| Albany, Mn., U.S. | E4 | 100 |
| Albany, Mo., U.S. | A3 | 102 |
| Albany, N.H., U.S. | C4 | 106 |
| Albany, N.Y., U.S. | C7 | 109 |
| Albany, Oh., U.S. | C3 | 112 |
| Albany, Or., U.S. | C3 | 114 |
| Albany, Tx., U.S. | C3 | 120 |
| Albany, Vt., U.S. | B4 | 122 |
| Albany, Wy., U.S. | E6 | 127 |
| Albany, co., N.Y., U.S. | C6 | 109 |
| Albany, co., Wy., U.S. | E7 | 127 |
| Albany, stm., Ont. | o18 | 73 |
| Al Barkāt, Libya | E2 | 43 |
| Al Baţānūn, Eg. | D2 | 41 |
| Albatross Bay, b., Austl. | B7 | 50 |
| Al Bawīţī, Eg. | D5 | 43 |
| Al Bayḑā, Libya | C4 | 43 |
| Albee, S.D., U.S. | B9 | 118 |
| Albemarle, N.C., U.S. | B2 | 110 |
| Albemarle, Va., U.S. | C4 | 123 |
| Albemarle, Punta, c., Ec. | f5 | 58 |
| Albemarle Lake, l., Ms., U.S. | C2 | 101 |
| Albemarle Sound, strt., N.C., U.S. | A6 | 110 |
| Albenga, Italy | B2 | 23 |
| Alberche, stm., Spain | B3 | 22 |
| Ålberga (part of Eskilstuna), Swe. | u34 | 14 |
| Albergaria-a-Velha, Port. | B1 | 22 |
| Albersdorf, W. Ger. | D3 | 15 |
| Albert, Fr. | B5 | 16 |
| Albert, Ks., U.S. | D5 | 93 |
| Albert, N.M., U.S. | B6 | 108 |
| Albert, co., N.B. | D5 | 71 |
| Albert, Lake, l., Afr. | A5 | 48 |
| Alberta, Va., U.S. | D5 | 123 |
| Alberta, Mn., U.S. | E2 | 100 |
| Alberta, prov., Can. | C4 | 68 |
| Alberta, Mount, mtn., Alta. | C2 | 68 |
| Albert Canyon, B.C. | D9 | 69 |
| Albert City, Ia., U.S. | B3 | 92 |
| Albert Edward, Mount, mtn., Pap. N. Gui. | k12 | 50 |
| Albert Lea, Mn., U.S. | G5 | 100 |
| Albert Markham, Mount, mtn., Ant. | A28 | 7 |
| Albert Nile, stm., Ug. | A5 | 48 |
| Alberton, P.E.I. | C5 | 71 |
| Alberton, Mt., U.S. | C2 | 103 |
| Albertson, N.Y., U.S. | k13 | 109 |
| Albertville, Sask. | D3 | 75 |
| Albertville, Fr. | E7 | 16 |
| Albertville, Al., U.S. | A3 | 78 |
| Albertville, Mn., U.S. | E5 | 100 |
| Albeuve, Switz. | E3 | 21 |
| Albi, Fr. | F5 | 16 |
| Albia, Ia., U.S. | C5 | 92 |
| Albin, Wy., U.S. | E8 | 127 |
| Albina, Sur. | A4 | 59 |
| Albino, Italy | E8 | 21 |
| Albion, Ca., U.S. | C2 | 82 |
| Albion, Il., U.S. | G5 | 90 |
| Albion, Il., U.S. | E5 | 90 |
| Albion, In., U.S. | B7 | 91 |
| Albion, Ia., U.S. | B5 | 92 |
| Albion, Me., U.S. | D3 | 96 |
| Albion, Mi., U.S. | F6 | 99 |
| Albion, Ne., U.S. | C7 | 104 |
| Albion, N.Y., U.S. | B2 | 109 |
| Albion, Ok., U.S. | C6 | 113 |
| Albion, Pa., U.S. | C1 | 115 |
| Albion, R.I., U.S. | B4 | 116 |
| Albion, Wa., U.S. | C8 | 124 |
| Albion, Wi., U.S. | F4 | 126 |
| Al Bīrah, Isr. Occ. | h11 | 41 |
| Alborán, i., Spain | E4 | 22 |
| Ålborg, Den. | I3 | 14 |
| Ålborg Bugt, b., Den. | B4 | 15 |
| Alborn, Mn., U.S. | D6 | 100 |
| Albox, Spain | D4 | 22 |
| Albrightsville, Pa., U.S. | D10 | 115 |
| Al Bu'ayrāt, Libya | C3 | 43 |
| Albufeira, Port. | D1 | 22 |
| Al Buhayrah, prov., Sud. | D2 | 47 |
| Al Bunbah, Libya | F4 | 40 |
| Albuñol, Spain | D4 | 22 |
| Al Buq'ah, Jord. | B7 | 41 |
| Albuquerque, N.M., U.S. | B3 | 108 |
| Al Buraymi, Oman | C5 | 38 |
| Alburg, Vt., U.S. | B2 | 122 |
| Alburnett, Ia., U.S. | B6 | 92 |
| Alburquerque, Spain | C2 | 22 |
| Alburtis, Pa., U.S. | F10 | 115 |
| Albury, Austl. | G8 | 50 |
| Alca, Peru | E3 | 58 |
| Alcabideche, Port. | f9 | 22 |
| Alcácer do Sal, Port. | C1 | 22 |
| Alcalá [de Guadaira], Spain | D3 | 22 |
| Alcalá de Henares, Spain | B4 | 22 |
| Alcalá de los Gazules, Spain | D3 | 22 |
| Alcalá la Real, Spain | D4 | 22 |
| Alcalde, N.M., U.S. | A3 | 108 |
| Alcaldediáz, Pan. | F8 | 62 |
| Alcamo, Italy | F4 | 23 |
| Alcanadre, stm., Spain | B5 | 22 |
| Alcanar, Spain | B6 | 22 |
| Alcañiz, Spain | B5 | 22 |
| Alcântara, Braz. | B2 | 57 |
| Alcantarilla, Spain | D5 | 22 |
| Alcaraz, Spain | C4 | 22 |
| Alcaudete, Spain | D3 | 22 |
| Alcázar de San Juan, Spain | C4 | 22 |
| Alcester, S.D., U.S. | D9 | 118 |
| Alcira, Spain | C5 | 22 |
| Alco, La., U.S. | C2 | 95 |
| Alcoa, Tn., U.S. | D10 | 119 |
| Alcobendas, Spain | o17 | 22 |
| Alcochete, Port. | f10 | 22 |
| Alcolu, S.C., U.S. | D7 | 117 |
| Alcomdale, Alta. | C4 | 68 |
| Alcona, co., Mi., U.S. | D7 | 99 |
| Alcorisa, Spain | B5 | 22 |
| Alcorcón, Spain | p17 | 22 |
| Alcorn, Ms., U.S. | D2 | 101 |
| Alcorn, co., Ms., U.S. | A5 | 101 |
| Alcova, Wy., U.S. | D6 | 127 |
| Alcovy, stm., Ga., U.S. | C3 | 87 |
| Alcoy, Spain | C5 | 22 |
| Alcoy, Nevado, mtn., Peru | D2 | 58 |
| Alda, Ne., U.S. | D7 | 104 |
| Aldama, Mex. | B3 | 63 |
| Aldan, Sov. Un. | D15 | 29 |
| Aldan, stm., Sov. Un. | C16 | 29 |
| Aldan Plateau, plat., Sov. Un. | D15 | 29 |
| Al Dār al Bayḑā', hist., Eg. | D3 | 41 |
| Aldeburgh, Eng., U.K. | B9 | 12 |
| Alden, Il., U.S. | A5 | 90 |
| Alden, Ia., U.S. | B4 | 92 |
| Alden, Mi., U.S. | D5 | 99 |
| Alden, Mn., U.S. | G5 | 100 |
| Alden, N.Y., U.S. | C2 | 109 |
| Alden, Pa., U.S. | D9 | 115 |
| Alder, Mt., U.S. | E4 | 103 |
| Alder, Ben, mtn., Scot., U.K. | D4 | 13 |
| Alder Brook, stm., Vt., U.S. | B4 | 122 |
| Alderney, i., Guernsey | F5 | 10 |
| Aldershot, Eng., U.K. | E6 | 10 |
| Alderson, Ok., U.S. | C6 | 113 |
| Alderson, W.V., U.S. | D4 | 125 |
| Aldersyde, Alta. | D4 | 68 |
| Alderwood Manor, Wa., U.S. | *B3 | 124 |
| Aldie, Va., U.S. | B5 | 123 |
| Aldora, Ga., U.S. | C2 | 87 |
| Aldrich, Al., U.S. | B3 | 78 |
| Aldrich, Mn., U.S. | D4 | 100 |
| Aldrich, Mo., U.S. | D4 | 102 |
| Aledo, Il., U.S. | B3 | 90 |
| Aledo, Tx., U.S. | n9 | 120 |
| Alegre, Maur. | C2 | 45 |
| Alegre, Braz. | C4 | 56 |
| Alegre, stm., Braz. | D1 | 56 |
| Alegrete, Braz. | C5 | 54 |
| Alejandro Selkirk, Isla, i., Chile | G2 | 53 |
| Aleknagik, Ak., U.S. | D8 | 79 |
| Aleksandriya, Sov. Un. | G9 | 27 |
| Aleksandrov-Gay, Sov. Un. | C3 | 28 |
| Aleksandrovsk [-Sakhalinskiy], Sov. Un. | D17 | 29 |
| Aleksandrów [Kujawski], Pol. | B5 | 26 |
| Aleksandrów [Łódzki], Pol. | C5 | 26 |
| Aleksin, Sov. Un. | D11 | 27 |
| Aleksinac, Yugo. | D5 | 24 |
| Alemania, Arg. | E2 | 55 |
| Além Paraíba, Braz. | g6 | 56 |
| Alençon, Fr. | C4 | 16 |
| Alenquer, Braz. | C4 | 59 |
| Alenquer, Port. | C1 | 22 |
| Alentejo, hist. reg., Port. | C2 | 22 |
| Alenuihaha Channel, strt., Hi., U.S. | C5 | 88 |
| Aleppo (Halab), Syria | B3 | 38 |
| Alert, N.W. Ter. | k39 | 66 |
| Alert Bay, B.C. | D4 | 69 |
| Alès, Fr. | E6 | 16 |
| Alessandria, Italy | B2 | 23 |
| Alestrup, Den. | B3 | 15 |
| Ålesund, Nor. | F2 | 14 |
| Aleutian Islands, is., Ak., U.S. | E3 | 79 |
| Aleutian Range, mts., Ak., U.S. | D9 | 79 |
| Alexander, Man. | E1 | 70 |
| Alexander, Ga., U.S. | C5 | 87 |
| Alexander, Il., U.S. | D3 | 90 |
| Alexander, Ks., U.S. | D4 | 93 |
| Alexander, Me., U.S. | C5 | 96 |
| Alexander, N.Y., U.S. | C2 | 109 |
| Alexander, N.C., U.S. | f10 | 110 |
| Alexander, N.D., U.S. | B2 | 111 |
| Alexander, W.V., U.S. | C4 | 125 |
| Alexander, co., Il., U.S. | F4 | 90 |
| Alexander, co., N.C., U.S. | B1 | 110 |
| Alexander, stm., Isr. | f10 | 41 |
| Alexander, Lake, l., Mn., U.S. | D4 | 100 |
| Alexander Archipelago, is., Ak., U.S. | D12 | 79 |
| Alexander Bay, S. Afr. | C2 | 49 |
| Alexander City, Al., U.S. | C4 | 78 |
| Alexander Island, i., Ant. | B5 | 7 |
| Alexander Mills, N.C., U.S. | B1 | 110 |
| Alexandretta see İskenderun, Tur. | D11 | 40 |
| Alexandria, B.C. | C6 | 69 |
| Alexandria, Ont. | B10 | 73 |
| Alexandria (Al Iskandarīyah), Eg. | B2 | 38 |
| Alexandria, Rom. | D7 | 24 |
| Alexandria, Al., U.S. | B4 | 78 |
| Alexandria, In., U.S. | D6 | 91 |
| Alexandria, Ky., U.S. | B5 | 94 |
| Alexandria, La., U.S. | C3 | 95 |
| Alexandria, Mn., U.S. | E3 | 100 |
| Alexandria, Mo., U.S. | A6 | 102 |
| Alexandria, Ne., U.S. | D8 | 104 |
| Alexandria, N.H., U.S. | C3 | 106 |
| Alexandria, Oh., U.S. | B3 | 112 |
| Alexandria, Pa., U.S. | E5 | 115 |
| Alexandria, S.D., U.S. | D8 | 118 |
| Alexandria, Tn., U.S. | A5 | 119 |
| Alexandria, Va., U.S. | B5 | 123 |
| Alexandria Bay, N.Y., U.S. | A5 | 109 |
| Alexandrina, Lake, l., Austl. | G2 | 51 |
| Alexandroúpolis, Grc. | B5 | 25 |
| Alexis, Il., U.S. | B3 | 90 |
| Alexis, stm., Newf. | B3 | 72 |
| Alexis Creek, B.C. | C6 | 69 |
| Aley, stm., Sov. Un. | E25 | 8 |
| Aleysk, Sov. Un. | D11 | 29 |
| Alfalfa, co., Ok., U.S. | A3 | 113 |
| Al Fallūjah, Iraq | F14 | 40 |
| Al Fandaqūmīyah, Isr. Occ. | B7 | 41 |
| Alfaro, Spain | A5 | 22 |
| Al Fashn, Eg. | D6 | 43 |
| Alfatar, Bul. | D8 | 24 |
| Al Fāw, Iraq | G4 | 39 |
| Al Fayyūm, Eg. | C3 | 38 |
| Alfeld, W. Ger. | B4 | 19 |
| Alfenas, Braz. | C3 | 56 |
| Alfiós (Alpheus), stm., Grc. | D3 | 25 |
| Alfonsine, Italy | E8 | 20 |
| Alford, Eng., U.K. | A8 | 12 |
| Alford, Scot., U.K. | C6 | 13 |
| Alford, Fl., U.S. | B1 | 86 |
| Alford, In., U.S. | H3 | 91 |
| Alford, Ma., U.S. | B1 | 98 |
| Alfordsville, In., U.S. | G4 | 91 |
| Alfortville, Fr. | g10 | 16 |
| Alfred, Ont. | B10 | 73 |
| Alfred, Me., U.S. | E2 | 96 |
| Alfred, N.Y., U.S. | C3 | 109 |
| Alfred, N.D., U.S. | C6 | 111 |
| Alfred Station, N.Y., U.S. | C3 | 109 |
| Al Fujayrah, U.A.E. | C5 | 38 |
| Al Fuqahā', Libya | D3 | 43 |
| Algarrobal, Chile | E1 | 55 |
| Algarrobo, Chile | E1 | 55 |
| Algarrobo del Águila, Arg. | B3 | 54 |
| Algarve, hist. reg., Port. | D1 | 22 |
| Algeciras, Spain | D3 | 22 |
| Algemesí, Spain | C5 | 22 |
| Alger, Mi., U.S. | D6 | 99 |
| Alger, co., Mi., U.S. | B4 | 99 |
| Algeria, ctry., Afr. | D5 | 44 |
| Algete, Spain | o18 | 22 |
| Al Ghayatah, Eg. | D2 | 41 |
| Al Ghaydah, Yemen | B7 | 47 |
| Alghero, Italy | D2 | 23 |
| Al Ghurdaqah, Eg. | B5 | 44 |
| Algiers (El Djazaïr), Alg. | A5 | 44 |
| Algoa, Ar., U.S. | *B4 | 81 |
| Algoa Bay, b., S. Afr. | D4 | 49 |
| Algodón, stm., Peru | D3 | 58 |
| Algodones, N.M., U.S. | B3 | 108 |
| Algoma, Ms., U.S. | A4 | 101 |
| Algoma, Wi., U.S. | D6 | 126 |
| Algoma, dept., Ont. | A2 | 73 |
| Algoma Mills, Ont. | A2 | 73 |
| Algona, Ia., U.S. | A3 | 92 |
| Algona, Wa., U.S. | f11 | 124 |
| Algonac, Mi., U.S. | F8 | 99 |
| Algonquin, Il., U.S. | A5 | 90 |
| Algonquin Park, Ont. | B6 | 73 |
| Algonquin Provincial Park, Ont. | B6 | 73 |
| Algorta (Guecho), Spain | A4 | 22 |
| Algorta, Ur. | E1 | 56 |
| Algrange, Fr. | E6 | 17 |
| Al Hadd, Oman | C5 | 38 |
| Al Hadīthah, Iraq | A9 | 38 |
| Alhama [de Granada], Spain | D4 | 22 |
| Alhama [de Murcia], Spain | D5 | 22 |
| Alhambra, Ca., U.S. | m12 | 82 |
| Al Hamūl, Eg. | C3 | 41 |
| Al Harrah, Egypt | H7 | 40 |
| Al Hasakah, Syria | D13 | 40 |
| Alhaurín el Grande, Spain | D3 | 22 |
| Al Hawātah, Sud. | C3 | 47 |
| Al Hawţah, Yemen | D4 | 47 |
| Al Hayy, Iraq | E3 | 41 |
| Al Hayyānīyah, Sau. Ar. | H4 | 39 |
| Al Hillah (Hilla), Iraq | B4 | 38 |
| Al Hindīyah, Iraq | F15 | 40 |
| Al Hirmil, Leb. | E11 | 40 |
| Al Hişn, Jord. | B7 | 41 |
| Al Hoceïma, Mor. | B4 | 44 |
| Alhos Vedros, Port. | f9 | 22 |
| Al Hufūf (Hofuf), Sau. Ar. | C4 | 38 |
| Al Husaynīyah, Sud. | C3 | 47 |
| Al Huşn, Jord. | B7 | 41 |
| 'Alī al Gharbī, Iraq | G14 | 40 |
| Aliartos, Grc. | g10 | 25 |
| Alibag, India | H4 | 37 |
| Alicahue, Chile | A2 | 54 |
| Alicante, Spain | C5 | 22 |
| Alicante, Gulf of, b., Spain | C5 | 22 |
| Alice, N.D., U.S. | C8 | 111 |
| Alice, Tx., U.S. | F3 | 120 |
| Alice, Point, c., Italy | E6 | 23 |
| Alice Lake, l., Mn., U.S. | C7 | 100 |
| Alice Springs, Austl. | D5 | 50 |
| Aliceville, Al., U.S. | B1 | 78 |
| Aliceville, Ks., U.S. | D8 | 93 |
| Alick, i., Indon. | B4 | 81 |
| Alicudi, i., Italy | E5 | 23 |
| Alida, Sask. | H5 | 75 |
| Alīgarh, India | C6 | 36 |
| Alīgūdarz, Iran | E4 | 39 |
| Alindao, Cen. Afr. Rep. | E4 | 46 |
| Aline, Ga., U.S. | D4 | 87 |
| Aline, Ok., U.S. | A3 | 113 |
| Alingsås, Swe. | I5 | 14 |
| Aliquippa, Pa., U.S. | E1 | 115 |
| Al 'Irq, Libya | D4 | 43 |
| Ali-Sabieh, Dji. | C5 | 47 |
| Alistráti, Grc. | B4 | 25 |
| Aliwal North, S. Afr. | D4 | 49 |
| Alix, Alta. | C4 | 68 |
| Alix, Ar., U.S. | B2 | 81 |
| Al Jabalayn, Sud. | C3 | 47 |
| Al Jāfūrah, des., Sau. Ar. | I5 | 39 |
| Al Jaghbūb, Libya | D4 | 43 |
| Al Jahrah, Kuw. | G3 | 39 |
| Al Jānīyah, Isr. Occ. | h11 | 41 |
| Al Jawf, Libya | E4 | 43 |
| Al Jawf, Sau. Ar. | C3 | 38 |
| Al Jawsh, Libya | C2 | 43 |
| Al Jazīrah, prov., Sud. | C3 | 47 |
| Aljezur, Port. | D1 | 22 |
| Al Jubayl, Sau. Ar. | H4 | 39 |
| Al Junaynah, Sud. | C1 | 47 |
| Aljustrel, Port. | D1 | 22 |
| Al Kāb, Eg. | D4 | 41 |
| Al Kahfah, Sau. Ar. | I14 | 40 |
| Alkali Lake, l., Nv., U.S. | B2 | 105 |
| Al Karak, Jord. | G10 | 40 |
| Al Karnak, Eg. | D6 | 43 |
| Al Kawm aţ Ţawīl, Eg. | C3 | 41 |
| Al Khābūr, stm., Syria | B4 | 38 |
| Al Khābūrah, Oman | C5 | 38 |
| Al Khālis, Iraq | E15 | 40 |
| Al Khandaq, Sud. | B3 | 47 |
| Al Khārijah, Eg. | C3 | 38 |
| Al Khartūm, prov., Sud. | B3 | 47 |
| Al Khaşab, Oman | C5 | 38 |
| Al Khums, Libya | C2 | 43 |
| Al Khurmah, Sau. Ar. | C4 | 38 |
| Al Khushnīyah, Isr. Occ. | A7 | 41 |
| Alkionídhes, is., Grc. | g9 | 25 |
| Alkionídhes Gulf, b., Grc. | g10 | 25 |
| Alkmaar, Neth. | A6 | 16 |
| Alkol, W.V., U.S. | m12 | 125 |
| Al Kūbrī, Eg. | D4 | 41 |
| Al Kūfah, Iraq | G15 | 40 |
| Al Kuntillah, Eg. | E6 | 41 |
| Al Kūt, Iraq | B4 | 38 |
| Allagash, stm., Me., U.S. | B3 | 96 |
| Allagash Lake, l., Me., U.S. | B3 | 96 |
| Allahābād, India | C7 | 36 |
| Allakaket, Ak., U.S. | B9 | 79 |
| Allamakee, co., Ia., U.S. | A6 | 92 |
| Allamuchy Mountain, mtn., N.J., U.S. | B3 | 107 |
| Allanmyo, Burma | E10 | 36 |
| 'Allāqī, Wādī al, val., Eg. | E6 | 43 |
| Allardt, Tn., U.S. | C9 | 119 |
| Allatoona Lake, res., Ga., U.S. | B2 | 87 |
| Alleene, Ar., U.S. | D1 | 81 |
| Allegan, Mi., U.S. | F5 | 99 |
| Allegan, co., Mi., U.S. | F5 | 99 |
| Allegany, N.Y., U.S. | C2 | 109 |
| Allegany, Or., U.S. | D3 | 114 |
| Allegany, co., Md., U.S. | k13 | 97 |
| Allegany, co., N.Y., U.S. | C2 | 109 |
| Allegany Indian Reservation, N.Y., U.S. | C2 | 109 |
| Alleghany, Ca., U.S. | C3 | 82 |
| Alleghany, co., N.C., U.S. | A1 | 110 |
| Alleghany, co., Va., U.S. | C2 | 123 |
| Allegheny, co., Pa., U.S. | E2 | 115 |
| Allegheny, stm., Pa., U.S. | E2 | 115 |
| Allegheny Front, mtn., W.V., U.S. | B5 | 125 |
| Allegheny Mountain, mts., U.S. | B3 | 123 |
| Allegheny Plateau, plat., U.S. | B4 | 125 |
| Allegheny Reservoir, res., U.S. | B4 | 115 |
| Allemand, Ia., U.S. | e8 | 92 |
| Allemands, Bayou Des, stm., La., U.S. | k11 | 95 |
| Allemands, Lac Des, l., La., U.S. | E5 | 95 |
| Allen, Al., U.S. | D2 | 78 |
| Allen, Ks., U.S. | D7 | 93 |
| Allen, Ky., U.S. | C7 | 94 |
| Allen, Md., U.S. | D6 | 97 |
| Allen, Ne., U.S. | B9 | 104 |
| Allen, Ok., U.S. | C5 | 113 |
| Allen, Tx., U.S. | *C4 | 120 |
| Allen, co., In., U.S. | B7 | 91 |
| Allen, co., Ks., U.S. | E8 | 93 |
| Allen, co., Ky., U.S. | D4 | 94 |
| Allen, co., Oh., U.S. | B1 | 112 |
| Allen, Lough, l., Ire. | C2 | 10 |
| Allen, Mount, mtn., N.Z. | Q11 | 51 |
| Allen, Mount, mtn., Ak., U.S. | C11 | 79 |
| Allendale, Il., U.S. | E6 | 90 |
| Allendale, Mo., U.S. | A3 | 102 |
| Allendale, N.J., U.S. | A4 | 107 |
| Allendale, S.C., U.S. | E5 | 117 |
| Allendale, co., S.C., U.S. | F5 | 117 |
| Allende, Mex. | B4 | 63 |
| Allenford, Ont. | C3 | 73 |
| Allenhurst, Ga., U.S. | E5 | 87 |
| Allenhurst, N.J., U.S. | C5 | 107 |
| Allen Park, Mi., U.S. | p15 | 99 |
| Allens, Mts., Me., U.S. | C2 | 96 |
| Allenspark, Co., U.S. | A5 | 83 |
| Allenstein see Olsztyn, Pol. | B6 | 26 |
| Allensville, Ky., U.S. | D2 | 94 |
| Allensville, Oh., U.S. | D3 | 112 |
| Allenton, Mo., U.S. | f12 | 102 |
| Allenton, R.I., U.S. | E4 | 116 |
| Allenton, Wi., U.S. | E5 | 126 |
| Allentown, Ga., U.S. | D3 | 87 |
| Allentown, N.J., U.S. | C3 | 107 |
| Allentown, N.Y., U.S. | C2 | 109 |
| Allentown, Pa., U.S. | E11 | 115 |
| Allenville, Mi., U.S. | C6 | 99 |
| Allenwood, Pa., U.S. | D8 | 115 |
| Alleppey, India | G6 | 36 |
| Aller, stm., Eur. | B4 | 18 |
| Allerton, Il., U.S. | D6 | 90 |
| Allerton, Ia., U.S. | D4 | 92 |
| Allerton, Point, c., Ma., U.S. | B6 | 98 |
| Alliance, Alta. | C5 | 68 |
| Alliance, Ne., U.S. | B3 | 104 |
| Alliance, N.C., U.S. | B6 | 110 |
| Alliance, Oh., U.S. | B4 | 112 |
| Allier, stm., Fr. | D5 | 16 |
| Alligator, Ms., U.S. | A3 | 101 |
| Alligator, stm., N.C., U.S. | B6 | 110 |
| Alligator Lake, l., Me., U.S. | D4 | 96 |
| Allihies, Ire. | F1 | 11 |
| Allinge [-Sandvig], Den. | C8 | 15 |
| Allison, Co., U.S. | D3 | 83 |
| Allison, Ia., U.S. | B5 | 92 |
| Allison, N.M., U.S. | B1 | 108 |
| Allison, Pa., U.S. | G2 | 115 |
| Allisonia, Va., U.S. | D12 | 123 |
| Allison Park, Pa., U.S. | h14 | 115 |
| Alliston, Ont. | C5 | 73 |
| Al Līth, Sau. Ar. | C4 | 38 |
| Alloa, Scot., U.K. | B5 | 10 |
| Allons, Tn., U.S. | C8 | 119 |
| Allouez, Mi., U.S. | A2 | 99 |
| Allouez, Wi., U.S. | h9 | 126 |
| Alloway, N.J., U.S. | D2 | 107 |
| Alloway Creek, stm., N.J., U.S. | D2 | 107 |
| Allred, Tn., U.S. | C8 | 119 |
| Allsboro, Al., U.S. | A1 | 78 |
| Allschwil, Switz. | A4 | 21 |
| Allumette Lake, l., Can. | B7 | 73 |
| Alluwe, Ok., U.S. | A6 | 113 |
| Allyn, Wa., U.S. | B3 | 124 |
| Alma, N.B. | D5 | 71 |
| Alma, Ont. | D4 | 73 |
| Alma, Que. | A6 | 74 |
| Alma, Ar., U.S. | B1 | 81 |
| Alma, Co., U.S. | B4 | 83 |
| Alma, Ga., U.S. | E4 | 87 |
| Alma, Il., U.S. | E5 | 90 |
| Alma, Ks., U.S. | C7 | 93 |
| Alma, Mi., U.S. | E6 | 99 |
| Alma, Mo., U.S. | B4 | 102 |
| Alma, Ne., U.S. | D6 | 104 |
| Alma, N.C., U.S. | C3 | 110 |
| Alma, W.V., U.S. | B4 | 125 |
| Alma, Wi., U.S. | D1 | 126 |
| Alma-Ata, Sov. Un. | E10 | 29 |
| Alma Center, Wi., U.S. | D3 | 126 |
| Almada, Port. | C1 | 22 |
| Almadén, Spain | C3 | 22 |
| Al Mafraq, Jord. | F11 | 40 |
| Almagro, Spain | C4 | 22 |
| Al Mahallah al Kubrá, Eg. | D3 | 41 |
| Al Mahmūdīyah, Eg. | D2 | 41 |
| Al Mahmūdīyah, Iraq | F15 | 40 |
| Al Makīlī, Libya | F4 | 40 |
| Almanor, Lake, l., Ca., U.S. | B3 | 82 |
| Almansa, Spain | C5 | 22 |
| Al Manşūrah, Eg. | B3 | 38 |
| Al Manzilah, Eg. | C3 | 41 |
| Almanzora, stm., Spain | D4 | 22 |
| Al Marj, Libya | C4 | 43 |
| Al Maţarīyah, Eg. | D3 | 41 |
| Al Maţarīyah, Eg. | D2 | 41 |
| Al Mayādīn, Syria | B4 | 38 |
| Al Mazār, Jord. | C5 | 41 |
| Al Mazār, Jord. | G11 | 40 |
| Al Mazra'ah, Jord. | C4 | 41 |
| Almeirim, Braz. | C4 | 59 |
| Almeirim, Port. | C1 | 22 |
| Almelo, Neth. | A7 | 16 |
| Almena, Ks., U.S. | C4 | 93 |
| Almena, Wi., U.S. | C1 | 126 |
| Almendralejo, Spain | C2 | 22 |
| Almería, Spain | D4 | 22 |
| Almería, Gulf of, b., Spain | D4 | 22 |
| Älmhult, Swe. | H5 | 15 |
| Al Minyā, Eg. | C3 | 38 |
| Al Miqdādīyah, Iraq | E15 | 40 |
| Almira, Wa., U.S. | B7 | 124 |
| Almirante, Pan. | F6 | 62 |
| Almirante Brown, Arg. | g7 | 54 |
| Almirós, Grc. | g10 | 25 |
| Almo, Id., U.S. | G5 | 89 |
| Almo, Ky., U.S. | f9 | 94 |
| Almodóvar [del Campo], Spain | C3 | 22 |
| Almodóvar [del Río], Spain | D3 | 22 |
| Almogía, Spain | D3 | 22 |
| Almond, Wi., U.S. | D4 | 126 |
| Almond, stm., N.Y., U.S. | C3 | 109 |
| Almont, Co., U.S. | C4 | 83 |
| Almont, Mi., U.S. | F8 | 99 |
| Almont, N.D., U.S. | C4 | 111 |
| Almonte, Ont. | B8 | 73 |
| Almonte, stm., Spain | C3 | 22 |
| Almora, India | C7 | 36 |
| Almyville, Ct., U.S. | C8 | 84 |
| Alness, Scot., U.K. | C4 | 13 |
| Alnwick, Eng., U.K. | C6 | 10 |
| Aloha, Or., U.S. | h12 | 114 |
| Alondra, Ca., U.S. | *n12 | 82 |
| Alonsa, Man. | D2 | 70 |
| Alor, i., Indon. | G6 | 34 |
| Álora, Spain | D3 | 22 |
| Alor Setar, Malay. | D2 | 34 |
| Alosno, Spain | D2 | 22 |
| Alost see Aalst, Bel. | B6 | 16 |
| Alotau, Pap. N. Gui. | m13 | 50 |
| Alpachiri, Arg. | B4 | 54 |
| Alpaugh, Ca., U.S. | E4 | 82 |
| Alpbach, Aus. | E5 | 18 |
| Alpena, Ar., U.S. | A2 | 81 |
| Alpena, Mi., U.S. | C7 | 99 |
| Alpena, S.D., U.S. | C7 | 118 |
| Alpena, co., Mi., U.S. | D7 | 99 |
| Alpha, Ia., U.S. | A5 | 92 |
| Alpha, Ky., U.S. | C6 | 94 |
| Alpha, Mi., U.S. | B2 | 99 |
| Alpha, Mn., U.S. | G4 | 100 |
| Alpha, N.J., U.S. | B2 | 107 |
| Alpharetta, Ga., U.S. | B2 | 87 |
| Alphen aan den Rijn, Neth. | B4 | 17 |
| Alpheus see Alfiós, stm., Grc. | D3 | 25 |
| Alpiarça, Port. | C1 | 22 |
| Alpine, Al., U.S. | B3 | 78 |
| Alpine, Az., U.S. | D6 | 80 |
| Alpine, Ca., U.S. | *F5 | 82 |
| Alpine, In., U.S. | E7 | 91 |
| Alpine, N.J., U.S. | h9 | 107 |
| Alpine, Or., U.S. | C3 | 114 |
| Alpine, Tn., U.S. | C8 | 119 |
| Alpine, Tx., U.S. | D1 | 120 |
| Alpine, Ut., U.S. | C4 | 121 |
| Alpine, co., Ca., U.S. | C4 | 82 |
| Alpine Junction, Wy., U.S. | *C1 | 127 |
| Alps, mts., Eur. | E4 | 18 |
| Al Qadārif, Sud. | C3 | 47 |
| Al Qaḑīmah, Sau. Ar. | C3 | 38 |
| Al Qā'im, Iraq | E13 | 40 |
| Al Qāmishlī, Syria | B4 | 38 |
| Al Qanāṭir, Eg. | D4 | 41 |
| Al Qanţarah, Eg. | D4 | 41 |
| Al Qaryah ash Sharqīyah, Libya | C2 | 43 |
| Al Qaryatayn, Syria | E11 | 40 |
| Al Qaşabāt, Libya | C2 | 43 |
| Al Qaşr, Eg. | C2 | 38 |
| Al Qaţrānah, Jord. | G11 | 40 |
| Al Qaţrūn, Libya | E2 | 43 |
| Al Qaţţā, Eg. | D2 | 41 |
| Al Qunfudhah, Sau. Ar. | D4 | 38 |
| Al Qurnah, Iraq | F3 | 39 |
| Al Quşaymah, Eg. | D6 | 41 |
| Al Qusayr, Eg. | C3 | 38 |
| Al Quţaynah, Sud. | C3 | 47 |
| Als, i., Den. | D3 | 15 |
| Alsace, hist. reg., Fr. | C7 | 16 |
| Alsasua, Spain | A4 | 22 |
| Alsdorf, W. Ger. | D6 | 17 |
| Alsea, Or., U.S. | C3 | 114 |
| Alsek, stm., N.A. | D5 | 66 |
| Alsen, N.D., U.S. | A7 | 111 |
| Alsey, Il., U.S. | D3 | 90 |
| Alsfeld, W. Ger. | C4 | 18 |
| Alsike (part of Uppsala), Swe. | I35 | 14 |
| Alsip, Il., U.S. | *k9 | 90 |
| Alstead, N.H., U.S. | D2 | 106 |
| Alstead, Sask. | B2 | 75 |
| Alstead Center, N.H., U.S. | D2 | 106 |
| Alston, Eng., U.K. | F6 | 13 |
| Alston, Ga., U.S. | D4 | 87 |
| Alta, Ia., U.S. | B2 | 92 |
| Alta, Ut., U.S. | *C4 | 121 |
| Alta, Wy., U.S. | C1 | 127 |
| Altadena, Ca., U.S. | m12 | 82 |
| Alta Gracia, Arg. | A4 | 54 |
| Altagracia, Ven. | A3 | 60 |
| Altagracia de Orituco, Ven. | B4 | 60 |
| Altamaha, stm., Ga., U.S. | E4 | 87 |
| Altamaha Sound, strt., Ga., U.S. | E5 | 87 |
| Altamahaw, N.C., U.S. | A3 | 110 |
| Altamira, Braz. | C4 | 59 |
| Altamira, Chile | E2 | 55 |
| Altamirano, Arg. | g7 | 54 |
| Altamont, Man. | E2 | 70 |
| Altamont, Il., U.S. | D5 | 90 |
| Altamont, Ks., U.S. | E8 | 93 |
| Altamont, Mo., U.S. | B3 | 102 |
| Altamont, N.Y., U.S. | C6 | 109 |
| Altamont, Or., U.S. | E5 | 114 |
| Altamont, S.D., U.S. | C9 | 118 |
| Altamont, Tn., U.S. | D8 | 119 |
| Altamont, Ut., U.S. | C5 | 121 |
| Altamonte Springs, Fl., U.S. | D5 | 86 |
| Altamura, Italy | D6 | 23 |
| Altamura, Isla, i., Mex. | C3 | 63 |
| Altar, Mex. | A2 | 63 |
| Altario, Alta. | C5 | 68 |
| Alta Vista, Ia., U.S. | A5 | 92 |
| Alta Vista, Ks., U.S. | D7 | 93 |
| Altavista, Va., U.S. | C3 | 123 |
| Altay, China | B4 | 31 |
| Altay, Mong. | B6 | 31 |
| Altay Shan, mts., Asia | B4 | 31 |
| Altdorf, Switz. | E4 | 21 |
| Altdorf [bei Nürnberg], W. Ger. | D6 | 19 |
| Altefähr, E. Ger. | D7 | 15 |
| Altenberg, E. Ger. | C8 | 19 |
| Altenbruch, W. Ger. | E2 | 15 |
| Altenburg, E. Ger. | C7 | 19 |
| Altenburg, Mo., U.S. | D8 | 102 |
| Altenkirchen, W. Ger. | C2 | 19 |
| Altenkirchen, W. Ger. | E7 | 15 |
| Altenmarkt [an der Alz], W. Ger. | A8 | 20 |
| Altentreptow, E. Ger. | E7 | 15 |
| Alter do Chão, Port. | C2 | 22 |
| Altha, Fl., U.S. | B1 | 86 |
| Altheim, Aus. | A9 | 20 |
| Altinho, Braz. | C3 | 57 |
| Altkirch, Fr. | B5 | 20 |
| Altman, Wy., U.S. | D5 | 127 |
| Altmühl, stm., W. Ger. | D5 | 19 |
| Altnaharra, Scot., U.K. | B3 | 13 |
| Alto, Ga., U.S. | B3 | 87 |
| Alto, La., U.S. | B4 | 95 |
| Alto, Mi., U.S. | F5 | 99 |
| Alto, Tn., U.S. | D8 | 119 |
| Alto, Tx., U.S. | D5 | 120 |
| Alto Araguaia, Braz. | B2 | 56 |
| Alto Cedro, Cuba | D5 | 64 |

| Name | Map Ref. | Page |
|---|---|---|
| Alto Garças, Braz. | B2 | 56 |
| Alto Longá, Braz. | C2 | 57 |
| Alto Molócuè, Moz. | A6 | 49 |
| Altomünster, W. Ger. | A7 | 20 |
| Alton, Ont. | D4 | 73 |
| Alton, Eng., U.K. | C7 | 12 |
| Alton, Al., U.S. | B3 | 78 |
| Alton, Il., U.S. | E3 | 90 |
| Alton, Ia., U.S. | B2 | 92 |
| Alton, Ks., U.S. | C5 | 93 |
| Alton, La., U.S. | h12 | 95 |
| Alton, Mo., U.S. | E6 | 102 |
| Alton, N.H., U.S. | D4 | 106 |
| Alton, Oh., U.S. | m10 | 112 |
| Alton, R.I., U.S. | F2 | 116 |
| Alton, Ut., U.S. | F3 | 121 |
| Alton, W.V., U.S. | C4 | 125 |
| Altona, Man. | E3 | 70 |
| Altona (part of Hamburg), W. Ger. | E3 | 15 |
| Altona, Il., U.S. | B3 | 90 |
| Altona, N.Y., U.S. | f11 | 109 |
| Altonah, Ut., U.S. | C5 | 121 |
| Alton Bay, N.H., U.S. | D4 | 106 |
| Altoona, Al., U.S. | A3 | 78 |
| Altoona, Fl., U.S. | D5 | 86 |
| Altoona, Ia., U.S. | C4 | 92 |
| Altoona, Ks., U.S. | E8 | 93 |
| Altoona, Pa., U.S. | E5 | 115 |
| Altoona, Wi., U.S. | D2 | 126 |
| Alto Parguai, Braz. | A1 | 56 |
| Alto Paraguay, dept., Para. | D4 | 55 |
| Alto Paraná, dept., Para. | D5 | 55 |
| Alto Pass, Il., U.S. | F4 | 90 |
| Alto Purus, stm., Peru | D3 | 58 |
| Altötting, W. Ger. | A8 | 20 |
| Altrincham, Eng., U.K. | A5 | 12 |
| Altro, Ky., U.S. | C6 | 94 |
| Altstätten, Switz. | B5 | 20 |
| Āltūn Kūprī, Iraq | E15 | 40 |
| Altun Shan, mts., China | D2 | 31 |
| Altura, Mn., U.S. | F7 | 100 |
| Alturas, Ca., U.S. | B3 | 82 |
| Altus, Ar., U.S. | B2 | 81 |
| Altus, Ok., U.S. | C2 | 113 |
| Altus Air Force Base, mil., Ok., U.S. | C2 | 113 |
| Altus Reservoir, res., Ok., U.S. | C2 | 113 |
| Altusried, W. Ger. | A9 | 21 |
| Alt Zachun, E. Ger. | E5 | 15 |
| Al 'Ubaylah, Sau. Ar. | C5 | 38 |
| Al Uqayyah, Sud. | C2 | 47 |
| Alum Bank, Pa., U.S. | F4 | 115 |
| Alum Bridge, W.V., U.S. | B4 | 125 |
| Alum Creek, W.V., U.S. | m12 | 125 |
| Alum Creek, stm., Oh., U.S. | k11 | 112 |
| Aluminé, Arg. | B2 | 54 |
| Alum Rock, Ca., U.S. | *k9 | 82 |
| Alupka, Sov. Un. | I10 | 27 |
| Al 'Uqaylah, Libya | C3 | 43 |
| Al 'Uqayr, Sau. Ar. | I5 | 39 |
| Alutom, Mount, hill, Guam | L9 | 52 |
| Alva, Fl., U.S. | F5 | 86 |
| Alva, Ky., U.S. | D6 | 94 |
| Alva, Ok., U.S. | A3 | 113 |
| Alva, Wy., U.S. | B8 | 127 |
| Alvarado, Mex. | D5 | 63 |
| Alvarado, Mn., U.S. | B2 | 100 |
| Alvarado, Tx., U.S. | C4 | 120 |
| Alvaton, Ga., U.S. | C2 | 87 |
| Älvdalen, Swe. | G6 | 14 |
| Alvear, Arg. | E4 | 55 |
| Alvena, Sask. | E2 | 75 |
| Alverca, Port. | f9 | 22 |
| Alverton, Pa., U.S. | F2 | 115 |
| Alvesta, Swe. | B8 | 15 |
| Alvin, Il., U.S. | C6 | 90 |
| Alvin, S.C., U.S. | E8 | 117 |
| Alvin, Tx., U.S. | E5 | 120 |
| Alvinston, Ont. | E3 | 73 |
| Alvo, Ne., U.S. | h12 | 104 |
| Alvord, Ia., U.S. | A1 | 92 |
| Alvord, Tx., U.S. | C4 | 120 |
| Alvord Lake, l., Or., U.S. | E8 | 114 |
| Alvordton, Oh., U.S. | A1 | 112 |
| Älvsborg, co., Swe. | A6 | 15 |
| Älvsered, Swe. | A6 | 15 |
| Älvsjö (part of Stockholm), Swe. | t36 | 14 |
| Al Wajh, Sau. Ar. | C3 | 38 |
| Alwar, India | C6 | 36 |
| Al Wāsiṭah, Eg. | E3 | 41 |
| Alxa Zuoqi, China | D6 | 31 |
| Alyat, Sov. Un. | F3 | 28 |
| Alyth, Scot., U.K. | D5 | 13 |
| Alytus, Sov. Un. | A8 | 26 |
| Alz, stm., W. Ger. | D6 | 18 |
| Alzada, Mt., U.S. | E12 | 103 |
| Alzey, W. Ger. | D3 | 19 |
| Ama, La., U.S. | k11 | 95 |
| Amacuzac, stm., Mex. | n14 | 63 |
| Amadeus, Lake, l., Austl. | D5 | 50 |
| Amadi, Sud. | D3 | 47 |
| Amadjuak Lake, l., N.W. Ter. | C18 | 66 |
| Amado, Az., U.S. | F4 | 80 |
| Amador, co., Ca., U.S. | C3 | 82 |
| Amagansett, N.Y., U.S. | n16 | 109 |
| Amagasaki, Japan | o14 | 33 |
| Amager, i., Den. | C6 | 15 |
| Amagon, Ar., U.S. | B4 | 81 |
| Amaha, Japan | n18 | 33 |
| Amahai, Indon. | F7 | 34 |
| Amakusa Sea, Japan | J4 | 33 |
| Åmål, Swe. | H5 | 14 |
| Amalfi, Italy | D5 | 23 |
| Amalga, Ut., U.S. | B4 | 121 |
| Amalia, N.M., U.S. | A4 | 108 |
| Amaliás, Grc. | D3 | 40 |
| Amalner, India | G5 | 37 |
| Amambaí, Braz. | C1 | 56 |
| Amambaí, Serra de, mts., S.A. | C1 | 56 |
| Amambay, dept., Para. | D4 | 55 |
| Amamio Island, i., Japan | F10 | 31 |
| Amana, Ia., U.S. | C6 | 92 |
| Amana, Lago, l., Braz. | C2 | 59 |
| Amancio, Fr. | B1 | 21 |
| Amanda, Oh., U.S. | C3 | 112 |
| Amangeldy, Sov. Un. | C7 | 28 |
| Amantea, Italy | E6 | 23 |
| Amantes Point, c., Guam | L10 | 52 |
| Amapá, Braz. | B4 | 59 |
| Amapá, ter., Braz. | B4 | 59 |
| Amapala, Hond. | D4 | 62 |
| Amaraji, Braz. | k6 | 57 |
| Amaranth, Man. | D2 | 70 |
| Amargosa, Braz. | D3 | 57 |
| Amargosa, stm., U.S. | D5 | 82 |
| Amargosa Desert, des., U.S. | G5 | 105 |
| Amargosa Range, mts., U.S. | G5 | 105 |
| Amarillo, Tx., U.S. | B2 | 120 |
| Amaro, Mount, mtn., Italy | C5 | 23 |
| Amaroúsion, Grc. | g11 | 25 |
| Amasa, Mi., U.S. | B2 | 99 |
| Amasra, Tur. | B9 | 40 |
| Amasya, Tur. | B10 | 40 |
| Amataurá, Braz. | B4 | 58 |
| Amatignak Island, i., Ak., U.S. | E4 | 79 |
| Amatsu-kominato, Japan | n19 | 33 |
| Amazon, Sask. | F3 | 75 |
| Amazon (Solimões) (Amazonas), stm., S.A. | D5 | 53 |
| Amazonas, state, Braz. | C2 | 59 |
| Amazonas, dept., Col. | D3 | 60 |
| Amazonas, dept., Peru | C2 | 58 |
| Amazonas, ter., Ven. | C4 | 60 |
| Amazonia, Mo., U.S. | B3 | 102 |
| Ambājogāi, India | H6 | 37 |
| Ambala, India | B6 | 36 |
| Ambalavao, Madag. | h9 | 49 |
| Ambam, Cam. | E2 | 46 |
| Ambanja, Madag. | f9 | 49 |
| Ambarchik, Sov. Un. | C19 | 29 |
| Ambato, Ec. | B2 | 58 |
| Ambato Boeny, Madag. | g9 | 49 |
| Ambatolampy, Madag. | g9 | 49 |
| Ambatondrazaka, Madag. | g9 | 49 |
| Ambatosoratra, Madag. | g9 | 49 |
| Amber, Ok., U.S. | B4 | 113 |
| Amberg, W. Ger. | D5 | 18 |
| Amberg, Wi., U.S. | C6 | 126 |
| Ambérieu [-en-Bugey], Fr. | E6 | 16 |
| Amberson, Pa., U.S. | F6 | 115 |
| Ambert, Fr. | E5 | 16 |
| Ambia, In., U.S. | D2 | 91 |
| Ambikāpur, India | D7 | 36 |
| Ambil Island, i., Phil. | p13 | 34 |
| Ambilobe, Madag. | f9 | 49 |
| Amble-by-the-Sea, Eng., U.K. | E7 | 13 |
| Ambler, Ak., U.S. | B8 | 79 |
| Ambler, Pa., U.S. | F11 | 115 |
| Ambo, Peru | D2 | 58 |
| Ambo Channel, strt., Marsh Is. | S17 | 52 |
| Ambodifototra, Madag. | g9 | 49 |
| Amboina see Ambon, Indon. | F7 | 34 |
| Amboise, Fr. | D4 | 16 |
| Ambon, Indon. | F7 | 34 |
| Ambon, i., Indon. | F7 | 34 |
| Ambositra, Madag. | h9 | 49 |
| Ambovombe, Madag. | h9 | 49 |
| Amboy, Ca., U.S. | E6 | 82 |
| Amboy, Il., U.S. | B4 | 90 |
| Amboy, In., U.S. | C6 | 91 |
| Amboy, Mn., U.S. | G4 | 100 |
| Amboy, Wa., U.S. | D3 | 124 |
| Ambridge, Pa., U.S. | E1 | 115 |
| Ambriz, Ang. | C1 | 48 |
| Ambrose, Ga., U.S. | E3 | 87 |
| Ambrose, N.D., U.S. | A2 | 111 |
| Ambrosia Lake, N.M., U.S. | B2 | 108 |
| Ambuar, Indon. | F8 | 34 |
| Amchitka Island, i., Ak., U.S. | E3 | 79 |
| Amchitka Pass, strt., Ak., U.S. | C4 | 79 |
| Am Dam, Chad | C4 | 46 |
| Amden, Switz. | B7 | 21 |
| Amderma, Sov. Un. | C9 | 29 |
| Ameagle, W.V., U.S. | D3 | 125 |
| Ameca, Mex. | C4 | 63 |
| Ameca, stm., Mex. | m11 | 63 |
| Amecameca [de Juárez], Mex. | A6 | 63 |
| Ameland, i., Neth. | A6 | 16 |
| Amelia, La., U.S. | E4 | 95 |
| Amelia, Ne., U.S. | B7 | 104 |
| Amelia, Oh., U.S. | C1 | 112 |
| Amelia, co., Va., U.S. | C4 | 123 |
| Amelia City, Fl., U.S. | k9 | 86 |
| Amelia Court House, Va., U.S. | C5 | 123 |
| Amelia Island, i., Fl., U.S. | k9 | 86 |
| Amendlinghausen, Ger. | E4 | 15 |
| Amendolara, Italy | E6 | 23 |
| Amenia, N.Y., U.S. | D7 | 109 |
| Amenia, N.D., U.S. | B8 | 111 |
| Amercuao, Mount, mtn., Phil. | n13 | 34 |
| Amadarko, Ok., U.S. | B3 | 113 |
| Amadia, Braz. | C3 | 57 |
| Americana, Braz. | m8 | 56 |
| American Canyon, Ca., U.S. | *C2 | 82 |
| American Falls, Id., U.S. | G6 | 89 |
| American Falls Dam, Id., U.S. | G6 | 89 |
| American Falls Reservoir, res., Id., U.S. | F5 | 89 |
| American Fork, Ut., U.S. | C4 | 121 |
| American Highland, plat., Ant. | B20 | 7 |
| American Samoa, dep., Oc. | G11 | 6 |
| Americus, Ga., U.S. | D2 | 87 |
| Americus, Ks., U.S. | D7 | 93 |
| Americus, Mo., U.S. | C6 | 102 |
| Amersfoort, Neth. | A6 | 16 |
| Amery, Man. | A4 | 70 |
| Amery, Wi., U.S. | C1 | 126 |
| Amery Ice Shelf, ice, Ant. | C20 | 7 |
| Ames, Ia., U.S. | B4 | 92 |
| Ames, Ks., U.S. | C6 | 93 |
| Ames, Ne., U.S. | C9 | 104 |
| Ames, Ok., U.S. | A3 | 113 |
| Amesbury, Ma., U.S. | A6 | 98 |
| Amesville, Ct., U.S. | B2 | 84 |
| Amfissa, Grc. | C4 | 25 |
| Amga, Sov. Un. | C16 | 29 |
| Amgu, Sov. Un. | D8 | 33 |
| Amguid, Alg. | D6 | 44 |
| Amgun, stm., Sov. Un. | D16 | 29 |
| Amherst, N.S. | D5 | 71 |
| Amherst, Co., U.S. | A8 | 83 |
| Amherst, Me., U.S. | D4 | 96 |
| Amherst, Ma., U.S. | B2 | 98 |
| Amherst, Ne., U.S. | D6 | 104 |
| Amherst, N.H., U.S. | E3 | 106 |
| Amherst, N.Y., U.S. | C2 | 109 |
| Amherst, Oh., U.S. | A3 | 112 |
| Amherst, S.D., U.S. | B8 | 118 |
| Amherst, Tx., U.S. | B1 | 120 |
| Amherst, Va., U.S. | C3 | 123 |
| Amherst, Wi., U.S. | D4 | 126 |
| Amherst, co., Va., U.S. | C3 | 123 |
| Amherstburg, Ont. | E1 | 73 |
| Amherstdale, W.V., U.S. | n12 | 125 |
| Amidon, N.D., U.S. | C2 | 111 |
| Amiens, Fr. | C5 | 16 |
| Aminuis, Nmb. | B2 | 49 |
| 'Āmir, Ra's, c., Libya | C4 | 43 |
| Amirante Islands, is., Sey. | G24 | 1 |
| Amir Kabir Dam, Iran | C5 | 39 |
| Amisk, Alta. | C5 | 68 |
| Amisk Lake, l., Sask. | C4 | 75 |
| Amistad, N.M., U.S. | B6 | 108 |
| Amistad National Recreation Area, Tx., U.S. | E2 | 120 |
| Amistad Reservoir, res., N.A. | E2 | 120 |
| Amite, La., U.S. | D5 | 95 |
| Amite, co., Ms., U.S. | D3 | 101 |
| Amite, stm., La., U.S. | D5 | 95 |
| Amity, Ar., U.S. | C2 | 81 |
| Amity, Mo., U.S. | B3 | 102 |
| Amity, Or., U.S. | B3 | 114 |
| Amity, Pa., U.S. | F1 | 115 |
| Amityville, N.Y., U.S. | E7 | 109 |
| Amlekhganj, Nepal | C7 | 36 |
| Amlia Island, i., Ak., U.S. | E5 | 79 |
| Amlwch, Wales, U.K. | A3 | 12 |
| 'Ammān, Jord. | B3 | 38 |
| Ammanford, Wales, U.K. | C3 | 12 |
| Ammeloe, W. Ger. | A1 | 19 |
| Ammendorf, E. Ger. | B6 | 19 |
| Ammon, Id., U.S. | F7 | 89 |
| Ammonoosuc, stm., N.H., U.S. | B3 | 106 |
| Amo, In., U.S. | E4 | 91 |
| Amol, Iran | C6 | 39 |
| Amonate, Va., U.S. | e10 | 123 |
| Amoret, Mo., U.S. | C3 | 102 |
| Amorgós, i., Grc. | D5 | 40 |
| Amorinópolis, Braz. | B2 | 56 |
| Amorita, Ok., U.S. | A3 | 113 |
| Amory, Ms., U.S. | B5 | 101 |
| Amos, Que. | k11 | 74 |
| Amoy see Xiamen, China | G8 | 31 |
| Ampanihy, Madag. | h8 | 49 |
| Amparo, Braz. | C3 | 56 |
| Ampelókipoi, Grc. | *B4 | 25 |
| Amper, stm., W. Ger. | E6 | 19 |
| Ampezzo, Italy | C8 | 20 |
| Amposta, Spain | B6 | 22 |
| Amrāvati (Amraoti), India | D6 | 36 |
| Amreli, India | G3 | 37 |
| Amriswil, Switz. | A7 | 21 |
| Amritsar, India | B5 | 36 |
| Amroha, India | C7 | 37 |
| Amrum, i., W. Ger. | A4 | 18 |
| Amsteg, Switz. | C6 | 21 |
| Amstelveen, Neth. | *B4 | 17 |
| Amsterdam, Neth. | A6 | 16 |
| Amsterdam, Ga., U.S. | F2 | 87 |
| Amsterdam, Mo., U.S. | C3 | 102 |
| Amsterdam, Mt., U.S. | E5 | 103 |
| Amsterdam, N.Y., U.S. | C6 | 109 |
| Amsterdam, Oh., U.S. | B5 | 112 |
| Amsterdam, Île, i., F.S.A.T. | I2 | 2 |
| Amstetten, Aus. | D7 | 18 |
| Amston, Ct., U.S. | C6 | 84 |
| Am Timan, Chad | C4 | 46 |
| Amu Darya, stm., Asia | F9 | 29 |
| Amukta Pass, strt., Ak., U.S. | E5 | 79 |
| Amulet, Sask. | H3 | 75 |
| Amund Ringnes Island, i., N.W. Ter. | m32 | 66 |
| Amundsen Bay, b., Ant. | C17 | 7 |
| Amundsen Gulf, b., N.W. Ter. | B8 | 66 |
| Amundsen-Scott, sci., Ant. | A17 | 7 |
| Amundsen Sea, Ant. | B36 | 7 |
| Amuntai, Indon. | F5 | 34 |
| Amur (Heilong Jiang), stm., Asia | E16 | 29 |
| Amvrakía, Gulf of, b., Grc. | C3 | 25 |
| Amy, Ar., U.S. | D3 | 81 |
| Amzi, Oued ti-n-, val., Afr. | E5 | 44 |
| 'Anabar, stm., Sov. Un. | B14 | 29 |
| 'Anabtā, Isr. Occ. | f11 | 41 |
| Anaco, Ven. | B5 | 60 |
| Anacoco, La., U.S. | C2 | 95 |
| Anacoco, Bayou, stm., La., U.S. | D2 | 95 |
| Anaconda, Mt., U.S. | D4 | 103 |
| Anaconda, N.M., U.S. | B2 | 108 |
| Anaconda Range, mts., Mt., U.S. | E3 | 103 |
| Anacortes, Wa., U.S. | A3 | 124 |
| Anacostia, stm., U.S. | C4 | 97 |
| Anacostia, Northwest Branch, stm., Md., U.S. | B3 | 97 |
| Anacuao, Mount, mtn., Phil. | n13 | 34 |
| Anadia, Braz. | C3 | 57 |
| Anadyr, Sov. Un. | C20 | 29 |
| Anadyr, stm., Sov. Un. | C20 | 29 |
| Anadyr, Gulf of, b., Sov. Un. | C21 | 29 |
| Anadyr Mountains, mts., Sov. Un. | C20 | 14 |
| Anae, i., Guam | M9 | 52 |
| Anáfi (Anaphe), i., Grc. | D5 | 40 |
| Anagance, N.B. | D4 | 71 |
| 'Ānah, Iraq | E13 | 40 |
| Anaheim, Ca., U.S. | F5 | 82 |
| Anahim Lake, B.C. | C5 | 69 |
| Anahola, Hi., U.S. | A2 | 88 |
| Anahuac, Tx., U.S. | E5 | 120 |
| Anahulu, stm., Hi., U.S. | f9 | 88 |
| Anajás, Braz. | D8 | 59 |
| Anak, N. Kor. | G2 | 33 |
| Anakāpalle, India | E7 | 36 |
| Anakie, Austl. | A6 | 51 |
| Anaklia, Sov. Un. | A13 | 40 |
| Analalava, Madag. | f9 | 49 |
| Anamã, Braz. | C2 | 59 |
| Anama Bay, Man. | D2 | 70 |
| Ana María, Golfo de, b., Cuba | D4 | 64 |
| Anambas Islands, is., Indon. | E3 | 34 |
| Anamoose, N.D., U.S. | B5 | 111 |
| Anamosa, Ia., U.S. | B6 | 92 |
| Anamur, Tur. | D9 | 40 |
| Anamur, Cape, c., Tur. | D9 | 40 |
| Anandale, La., U.S. | *C3 | 95 |
| Ananea (Poto), Peru | D3 | 58 |
| Anantapur, India | F6 | 36 |
| Anantnāg, India | B6 | 36 |
| Ananyev, Sov. Un. | H8 | 27 |
| Anao Point, c., Guam | L10 | 52 |
| Anefis i-n-Darane, Mali | C5 | 45 |
| Anégada, Bahía, b., Arg. | C4 | 54 |
| Anégada Passage, strt., N.A. | G13 | 64 |
| Anegam, Az., U.S. | D3 | 80 |
| Añelo, Arg. | B3 | 54 |
| Aneroid, Sask. | H2 | 75 |
| Aneta, N.D., U.S. | B8 | 111 |
| Aneth, Ut., U.S. | F6 | 121 |
| Aneto, Pico de, mtn., Spain | A6 | 22 |
| Añatone, Wa., U.S. | C8 | 124 |
| Anár, Iran | F7 | 39 |
| Anār Darreh, Afg. | E10 | 39 |
| Anastasia Island, i., Fl., U.S. | C5 | 86 |
| 'Anātā, Isr. Occ. | h12 | 41 |
| Anatone, Wa., U.S. | C8 | 124 |
| Añatuya, Arg. | A3 | 54 |
| Anauá, stm., Braz. | B2 | 59 |
| Anawalt, W.V., U.S. | D3 | 125 |
| Ancash, dept., Peru | C2 | 58 |
| Ancaster, Ont. | D4 | 73 |
| Ancenis, Fr. | D3 | 16 |
| Ancha, Sierra, mts., Az., U.S. | D4 | 80 |
| Anchieta, Braz. | C4 | 56 |
| Anching see Anqing, China | E8 | 31 |
| Anchorage, Ak., U.S. | C10 | 79 |
| Anchorage, Ky., U.S. | g11 | 94 |
| Anchor Point, Ak., U.S. | D9 | 79 |
| Anchor Point, c., Hi., U.S. | h15 | 79 |
| Ancienne-Lorette, Que. | C6 | 74 |
| Ancla Keys, is., Fl., U.S. | C6 | 86 |
| Anco, Ky., U.S. | C6 | 94 |
| Ancón, Peru | D2 | 58 |
| Ancona, Italy | C4 | 23 |
| Ancona, Il., U.S. | B5 | 90 |
| Ancón de Sardinas, Bahía de, b., S.A. | C2 | 60 |
| Ancud, Chile | C2 | 54 |
| Ancud, Golfo de, b., Chile | C2 | 54 |
| Anda, China | B10 | 31 |
| Andacollo, Arg. | B2 | 54 |
| Andahuaylas, Peru | D3 | 58 |
| Andale, Ks., U.S. | E6 | 93 |
| Andalgalá, Arg. | E2 | 55 |
| Andalsnes, Nor. | F2 | 14 |
| Andalusia, Al., U.S. | D3 | 78 |
| Andalusia, Il., U.S. | B3 | 90 |
| Andalusia, hist. reg., Spain | D3 | 22 |
| Andaman and Nicobar Islands, ter., India | *F9 | 36 |
| Andaman Islands, is., India | F9 | 36 |
| Andaman Sea, Asia | F10 | 36 |
| Andamarca, Bol. | C2 | 55 |
| Andamarca, Peru | D3 | 58 |
| Andapa, Madag. | f9 | 49 |
| Andavaka, Cap, c., Madag. | i9 | 49 |
| Andebu, Nor. | p28 | 14 |
| Andeer, Switz. | C7 | 21 |
| Andenne, Bel. | D5 | 17 |
| Andernach, W. Ger. | C3 | 18 |
| Anderslöv, Swe. | C7 | 15 |
| Anderson, Arg. | g6 | 54 |
| Anderson, Al., U.S. | A2 | 78 |
| Anderson, Ak., U.S. | C10 | 79 |
| Anderson, Ca., U.S. | B2 | 82 |
| Anderson, In., U.S. | D6 | 91 |
| Anderson, Mo., U.S. | E3 | 102 |
| Anderson, S.C., U.S. | B2 | 117 |
| Anderson, Tn., U.S. | D8 | 119 |
| Anderson, Tx., U.S. | D4 | 120 |
| Anderson, co., Ks., U.S. | D8 | 93 |
| Anderson, co., Ky., U.S. | B4 | 94 |
| Anderson, co., S.C., U.S. | B2 | 117 |
| Anderson, co., Tn., U.S. | C9 | 119 |
| Anderson, co., Tx., U.S. | D5 | 120 |
| Anderson, stm., N.W. Ter. | C7 | 66 |
| Anderson, stm., In., U.S. | H4 | 91 |
| Anderson, Mount, mtn., Wa., U.S. | B2 | 124 |
| Anderson Ranch Reservoir, res., Id., U.S. | F3 | 89 |
| Andersonville, Ga., U.S. | D2 | 87 |
| Andersonville, Tn., U.S. | C9 | 119 |
| Andes, Col. | B2 | 60 |
| Andes, N.Y., U.S. | C6 | 109 |
| Andes, mts., S.A. | E4 | 53 |
| Andes, Lake, l., S.D., U.S. | D7 | 118 |
| Andes, stm., U.S. | D3 | 83 |
| Andfjorden, strt., Nor. | C7 | 14 |
| Andhra Pradesh, state, India | E6 | 36 |
| Andikíthira, i., Grc. | E4 | 40 |
| Andilamena, Madag. | g9 | 49 |
| Andimeshk, Iran | E4 | 39 |
| Andizhan, Sov. Un. | E10 | 29 |
| Andkhvoy, Afg. | A4 | 36 |
| Andoas, Peru | B2 | 58 |
| Andong, S. Kor. | A6 | 22 |
| Andorra, And. | A6 | 22 |
| Andorra, ctry., Eur. | A6 | 22 |
| Andover, Eng., U.K. | C6 | 12 |
| Andover, Ct., U.S. | C6 | 84 |
| Andover, Il., U.S. | B3 | 90 |
| Andover, Ks., U.S. | g12 | 93 |
| Andover, Me., U.S. | D2 | 96 |
| Andover, Mn., U.S. | m12 | 100 |
| Andover, N.H., U.S. | D3 | 106 |
| Andover, N.Y., U.S. | C3 | 109 |
| Andover, Oh., U.S. | A5 | 112 |
| Andover, S.D., U.S. | B8 | 118 |
| Andover Lake, res., Ct., U.S. | C6 | 84 |
| Andøya, i., Nor. | C6 | 14 |
| Andrade, Hi., U.S. | D6 | 88 |
| Andradina, Braz. | C2 | 56 |
| Andraitx, Spain | C7 | 22 |
| Andreanof Islands, is., Ak., U.S. | E4 | 79 |
| Andrelândia, Braz. | g5 | 56 |
| Andrew, Alta. | C4 | 68 |
| Andrew, Ia., U.S. | B7 | 92 |
| Andrew, co., Mo., U.S. | B3 | 102 |
| Andrew Island, i., N.S. | D9 | 71 |
| Andrews, In., U.S. | C6 | 91 |
| Andrews, N.C., U.S. | f9 | 110 |
| Andrews, S.C., U.S. | E8 | 117 |
| Andrews, Tx., U.S. | C1 | 120 |
| Andrews, co., Tx., U.S. | C1 | 120 |
| Andrews Air Force Base, mil., Md., U.S. | C4 | 97 |
| Andrewsville, De., U.S. | E3 | 85 |
| Andreyevka, Sov. Un. | G11 | 27 |
| Andria, Italy | D6 | 23 |
| Androka, Madag. | h8 | 49 |
| Andros, Grc. | D5 | 40 |
| Ándros, i., Grc. | D5 | 40 |
| Androscoggin, co., Me., U.S. | D2 | 96 |
| Androscoggin, stm., Me., U.S. | D2 | 96 |
| Androscoggin Lake, l., Me., U.S. | D2 | 96 |
| Andros, i., Bah. | B5 | 64 |
| Andrychów, Pol. | h10 | 24 |
| Andújar, Spain | D3 | 22 |
| Andulo, Ang. | D2 | 48 |
| Anécho, Togo | E5 | 45 |
| Anefis i-n-Darane, Mali | C5 | 45 |
| Anegada, Bahía, b., Arg. | C4 | 54 |
| Anegada Passage, strt., N.A. | G13 | 64 |
| Anegam, Az., U.S. | D3 | 80 |
| Añelo, Arg. | B3 | 54 |
| Aneroid, Sask. | H2 | 75 |
| Aneta, N.D., U.S. | B8 | 111 |
| Aneth, Ut., U.S. | h12 | 41 |
| Aneto, Pico de, mtn., Spain | A6 | 22 |
| Añatone, Wa., U.S. | C8 | 124 |
| Añatuya, Arg. | A3 | 54 |
| Anauá, stm., Braz. | B2 | 59 |
| Anawalt, W.V., U.S. | D3 | 125 |
| Angers, Fr. | D3 | 16 |
| Angicos, Braz. | C3 | 57 |
| Angie, La., U.S. | D6 | 95 |
| Ängsjön, l., Swe. | u33 | 14 |
| An Nuhūd, Sud. | C2 | 47 |
| Angier, N.C., U.S. | B4 | 110 |
| Angikuni Lake, l., N.W. Ter. | D13 | 66 |
| An Nu'māniyah, Iraq | E2 | 39 |
| Angle Inlet, Mn., U.S. | A3 | 100 |
| Angle Lake, Wa., U.S. | *B3 | 124 |
| Anglem, Mount, mtn., N.Z. | Q11 | 51 |
| Anglesey, i., Wales, U.K. | D4 | 10 |
| Anglet, Fr. | E3 | 16 |
| Angleton, Tx., U.S. | E5 | 120 |
| Anori, Braz. | C2 | 59 |
| Áno Viánnos, Grc. | E5 | 25 |
| Anóyia, Grc. | E5 | 25 |
| Anping, China | E6 | 32 |
| Anping, China | E8 | 31 |
| Angmagssalik, Grnld. | C17 | 61 |
| Ansbach, W. Ger. | D5 | 18 |
| Ango, Zaire | A4 | 48 |
| Anse d'Hainault, Haiti | E6 | 64 |
| Angoche, Moz. | A6 | 49 |
| Anselmo, Col. | B2 | 60 |
| Angoche, Ilha, i., Moz. | A6 | 49 |
| Anserma, Col. | B2 | 60 |
| Angol, Chile | B2 | 54 |
| Anshan, China | C9 | 31 |
| Angola, In., U.S. | A7 | 91 |
| Anshun, China | F6 | 31 |
| Angola, N.Y., U.S. | C1 | 109 |
| Ansley, Al., U.S. | D3 | 78 |
| Angola, ctry., Afr. | D2 | 48 |
| Ansley, Ms., U.S. | E4 | 101 |
| Angola Beach, De., U.S. | F5 | 85 |
| Ansley, Ne., U.S. | C6 | 104 |
| Angola Swamp, sw., N.C., U.S. | C5 | 110 |
| Anson, Me., U.S. | D3 | 96 |
| Angoon, Ak., U.S. | D13 | 79 |
| Anson, Tx., U.S. | C3 | 120 |
| Angora, Ne., U.S. | C2 | 104 |
| Anson, co., N.C., U.S. | B2 | 110 |
| Angora see Ankara, Tur. | C9 | 40 |
| Anson Bay, b., Austl. | B5 | 50 |
| Angostura Reservoir, res., S.D., U.S. | D2 | 118 |
| Ansonia, Ct., U.S. | D3 | 84 |
| Angoulême, Fr. | E4 | 16 |
| Ansonia, Oh., U.S. | B1 | 112 |
| Angra do Heroísmo, Port. | g9 | 44 |
| Ansonville, Ont. | G16 | 66 |
| Angra dos Reis, Braz. | C4 | 56 |
| Ansonville, N.C., U.S. | B2 | 110 |
| Angren, Sov. Un. | E7 | 28 |
| Anstruther, Scot., U.K. | D6 | 13 |
| Anguang, China | B10 | 32 |
| Ansudu, Indon. | F9 | 34 |
| Anguilla, Ms., U.S. | C3 | 101 |
| Anta, Peru | D3 | 58 |
| Anguilla, ctry., N.A. | G13 | 64 |
| Antabamba, Peru | D3 | 58 |
| Anguillara [Sabazia], Italy | g8 | 23 |
| Antakya (Antioch), Tur. | D11 | 40 |
| Anguille, Cape, c., Newf. | E2 | 72 |
| Antalaha, Madag. | f10 | 49 |
| Angumu, Zaire | B4 | 48 |
| Antalya, Tur. | D8 | 40 |
| Angus, Ont. | C5 | 73 |
| Antalya, Gulf of, b., Tur. | D8 | 40 |
| Angus, stm., N.W. Ter. | B2 | 100 |
| Antananarivo, Madag. | g9 | 49 |
| Angusville, Man. | D1 | 70 |
| Antananarivo, prov., Madag. | g9 | 49 |
| Anhua, China | J4 | 32 |
| Antarctica, cont. | A19 | 7 |
| Anhui, prov., China | E8 | 31 |
| Antarctic Peninsula, pen., Ant. | C6 | 7 |
| Anhwei see Anhui, prov., China | E8 | 31 |
| Antelope, Sask. | G1 | 75 |
| Aniak, Ak., U.S. | C8 | 79 |
| Antelope, Ks., U.S. | D7 | 93 |
| Aniche, Fr. | D3 | 17 |
| Antelope, Mt., U.S. | B12 | 103 |
| Aniene (Teverone), stm., Italy | h9 | 23 |
| Antelope, Or., U.S. | C6 | 114 |
| Animas, N.M., U.S. | F1 | 108 |
| Antelope, S.D., U.S. | *D5 | 118 |
| Animas, stm., U.S. | D3 | 83 |
| Antelope, co., Ne., U.S. | B7 | 104 |
| Animas Mountains, mts., N.M., U.S. | F1 | 108 |
| Antelope Butte, mtn., Wy., U.S. | B7 | 127 |
| Animas Peak, mtn., N.M., U.S. | F2 | 108 |
| Antelope Creek, stm., Wy., U.S. | C7 | 127 |
| Animas Valley, val., N.M., U.S. | F1 | 108 |
| Antelope Island, i., Ut., U.S. | B3 | 121 |
| Anina, Rom. | C5 | 24 |
| Antelope Lake, l., Sask. | G1 | 75 |
| Anita, Ia., U.S. | C3 | 92 |
| Antelope Mine, Zimb. | B4 | 49 |
| Anita, Pa., U.S. | D4 | 115 |
| Antelope Peak, mtn., Nv., U.S. | B7 | 105 |
| Aniva, Sov. Un. | C11 | 33 |
| Antelope Range, mts., Nv., U.S. | D7 | 105 |
| Aniva, Cape, c., Sov. Un. | C11 | 33 |
| Antelope Reservoir, res., Or., U.S. | E9 | 114 |
| Aniva Bay, b., Sov. Un. | C11 | 33 |
| Antelope Wash, val., Nv., U.S. | D5 | 105 |
| Aniwa, Wi., U.S. | C4 | 126 |
| Antequera, Spain | D3 | 22 |
| Anizy-le-Château, Fr. | C5 | 16 |
| Antero, Mount, mtn., Co., U.S. | C4 | 83 |
| Anjar, India | D5 | 36 |
| Antero Reservoir, res., Co., U.S. | C5 | 83 |
| Anjò, Japan | o16 | 33 |
| Antes Fort, Pa., U.S. | D7 | 115 |
| Anjou, Que. | p19 | 74 |
| Anthon, Ia., U.S. | B2 | 92 |
| Anjou, hist. reg., Fr. | D3 | 16 |
| Anthony, Fl., U.S. | C4 | 86 |
| Anju, N. Kor. | G2 | 33 |
| Anthony, Ks., U.S. | E5 | 93 |
| Anjum, Neth. | A6 | 17 |
| Anthony, N.M., U.S. | F3 | 108 |
| Anka, Nig. | B5 | 45 |
| Anthony, R.I., U.S. | D3 | 116 |
| Ankang, China | E6 | 31 |
| Anthony Creek, stm., W.V., U.S. | C4 | 92 |
| Ankara, Tur. | C9 | 40 |
| Anti-Atlas, mts., Mor. | C3 | 44 |
| Ankavandra, Madag. | g9 | 49 |
| Antibes, Fr. | F7 | 16 |
| Ankazoabo, Madag. | h8 | 49 |
| Anticosti, Île d', i., Que. | k14 | 74 |
| Ankazobe, Madag. | g9 | 49 |
| Antietam Creek, stm., Md., U.S. | B2 | 97 |
| Ankeny, Ia., U.S. | C4 | 92 |
| Antietam National Battlefield Site, hist., Md., U.S. | B2 | 97 |
| An Khe, Viet. | C3 | 34 |
| Antigo, Wi., U.S. | C4 | 126 |
| Anklam, E. Ger. | B6 | 18 |
| Antigonish, N.S. | D8 | 71 |
| Ankober, Eth. | D4 | 47 |
| Antigonish, co., N.S. | D7 | 71 |
| Ankoro, Zaire | C4 | 48 |
| Antigua, i., Antig. | H14 | 64 |
| Anlong, China | F6 | 31 |
| Antigua and Barbuda, ctry., N.A. | H14 | 64 |
| Anlu, China | I5 | 32 |
| Antigua Guatemala, Guat. | E6 | 63 |
| Ann, Cape, c., Ant. | C18 | 7 |
| Antilla, Cuba | D6 | 64 |
| Ann, Cape, c., Ma., U.S. | A6 | 98 |
| Antioch, Ca., U.S. | h9 | 82 |
| Anna, Sov. Un. | F13 | 27 |
| Antioch, Il., U.S. | A5 | 90 |
| Anna, Il., U.S. | F4 | 90 |
| Antioch, Tn., U.S. | D5 | 91 |
| Anna, Oh., U.S. | B1 | 112 |
| Antioch see Antakya, Tur. | D11 | 40 |
| Anna, Tx., U.S. | C4 | 120 |
| Antioquia, Col. | B2 | 60 |
| Annaba (Bône), Alg. | B6 | 44 |
| Antioquia, dept., Col. | B2 | 60 |
| Annabella, Ut., U.S. | E3 | 121 |
| Antipodes Islands, is., N.Z. | J8 | 2 |
| Annabella-Buchholz, E. Ger. | C6 | 18 |
| Antiquity, Oh., U.S. | D4 | 112 |
| An Nabk, Syria | B8 | 19 |
| Annada, Mo., U.S. | B7 | 102 |
| Antofagasta, Chile | A2 | 54 |
| An Nafūd, des., Sau. Ar. | C4 | 38 |
| Antofagasta, prov., Chile | D1 | 55 |
| An Najaf, Iraq | F11 | 40 |
| Antofagasta de la Sierra, Arg. | E2 | 55 |
| An Nakhl, Eg. | B6 | 41 |
| Antofalla, Volcán, v., Arg. | E2 | 55 |
| Annalee Heights, Va., U.S. | *B5 | 123 |
| Antón, Pan. | F7 | 62 |
| Annam, hist. reg., Viet. | E7 | 35 |
| Anton, Tx., U.S. | B1 | 120 |
| Annamitique, Chaîne, mts., Asia | B3 | 34 |
| Anton Chico, N.M., U.S. | C1 | 108 |
| Annan, Scot., U.K. | C5 | 10 |
| Antongila, Helodrano, b., Madag. | f10 | 49 |
| Annan, stm., Scot., U.K. | E5 | 13 |
| Antonia, Mo., U.S. | g13 | 102 |
| Annandale, Mn., U.S. | E4 | 100 |
| Antonino, Ks., U.S. | D4 | 93 |
| Annandale, N.J., U.S. | B3 | 107 |
| António de Biedma, Arg. | g6 | 54 |
| Annandale, Va., U.S. | B5 | 123 |
| Antônio Dias, Braz. | D5 | 83 |
| Anna Maria, Fl., U.S. | p10 | 86 |
| Antonito, Co., U.S. | D5 | 83 |
| Anna Maria Island, i., Fl., U.S. | q10 | 86 |
| Antony, Fr. | g10 | 16 |
| Annapolis, Il., U.S. | D6 | 90 |
| Antora Peak, mtn., Co., U.S. | C4 | 83 |
| Annapolis, Md., U.S. | C4 | 97 |
| Antrim, N. Ire., U.K. | q22 | 117 |
| Annapolis, co., N.S. | E4 | 71 |
| Antrim, Mi., U.S. | C5 | 99 |
| Annapolis, stm., N.S. | E4 | 71 |
| Antrim, N.H., U.S. | D3 | 106 |
| Annapolis Junction, Md., U.S. | B4 | 97 |
| Antrim, co., Mi., U.S. | C5 | 99 |
| Annapolis Royal, N.S. | E4 | 71 |
| Antsalova, Madag. | g9 | 49 |
| Annapurna, mtn., Nepal | C7 | 36 |
| Antsirabe, Madag. | g9 | 49 |
| Anna Regina, Guy. | A3 | 59 |
| Antsiranana, Madag. | f9 | 49 |
| Annawan, Il., U.S. | B4 | 90 |
| Antsiranana, prov., Madag. | f9 | 49 |
| Annecy, Fr. | E6 | 16 |
| Antsohihy, Madag. | f9 | 49 |
| Annecy, Lake, l., Fr. | E1 | 21 |
| Antwerp (Antwerpen), Bel. | B5 | 64 |
| Annecy-le-Vieux, Fr. | E1 | 21 |
| Antwerp, N.Y., U.S. | A5 | 109 |
| Annemasse, Fr. | E1 | 21 |
| Antwerp, Oh., U.S. | A1 | 112 |
| Annestown, Ire. | E4 | 11 |
| Antwerp, prov., Bel. | C4 | 17 |
| Annette, Ak., U.S. | n24 | 79 |
| An Nhon, Viet. | F8 | 35 |
| An Nīl, prov., Sud. | B3 | 47 |
| An Nīl al Azraq (Blue Nile), prov., Sud. | *B3 | 47 |
| Anniston, Al., U.S. | B4 | 78 |
| Annobón Island (Pagalu), i., Eq. Gui. | F1 | 46 |
| Annone, Lago di, l., Italy | E7 | 21 |
| Annonay, Fr. | E6 | 16 |
| Annotto Bay, Jam. | E5 | 64 |
| Annotto Bay, b., Jam. | E15 | 65 |

| Name | Map Ref. | Page |
|---|---|---|

Antwerpen see Antwerp, Bel. — B5 16
Anua, Am. Sam. — F13 52
An Uaimh (Navan), Ire. — D3 10
Anuradhapura, Sri L. — G7 36
Anvers Island, i., Ant. — C6 7
Anvik, Ak., U.S. — C7 79
Anxi, China — F8 31
Anxi, China — C4 31
Anyang, China — D7 31
Anyang, S. Kor. — *H3 33
A'nyêmaqên Shan, mts., China — D4 31
Anyi, China — G4 32
Anykščiai, Sov. Un. — A8 26
Anzá, Col. — B2 60
Anza, stm., Italy — E5 21
Anzac, Alta. — A5 68
Anzhero-Sudzhensk, Sov. Un. — D11 29
Anzin, Fr. — D3 17
Anzio, Italy — D4 23
Anzoátegui, state, Ven. — B5 60
Aoji-ri, N. Kor. — E5 33
Aomoen Island, i., Marsh Is. — P18 52
Aomon, i., Marsh Is. — S18 52
Aomori, Japan — C13 31
Aoral, Mount, mtn., Camb. — C2 34
Aosta, Italy — B1 23
Aou Hofrit, well, W. Sah. — E2 44
Aouk, Bahr, stm., Afr. — D3 46
Aoukâr, reg., Maur. — C2 45
Aoyama, Japan — o15 33
Aozou, Chad — A3 46
Apa, stm., S.A. — D4 55
Apache, Ok., U.S. — C3 113
Apache, co., Az., U.S. — B6 80
Apache Creek, N.M., U.S. — D1 108
Apache Junction, Az., U.S. — m9 80
Apache Peak, mtn., Az., U.S. — F5 80
Apalachee, Ga., U.S. — B3 87
Apalachee Bay, b., Fl., U.S. — B2 86
Apalachicola, Fl., U.S. — C1 86
Apalachicola, stm., Fl., U.S. — B1 86
Apalachicola Bay, b., Fl., U.S. — C2 86
Apalachin, N.Y., U.S. — C4 109
Apan, Mex. — n14 63
Apaporis, stm., S.A. — D3 60
Aparri, Phil. — B6 34
Apatin, Yugo. — C4 24
Apatity, Sov. Un. — D15 14
Apatzingán [de la Constitución], Mex. — n12 63
Apeldoorn, Neth. — A6 16
Apennines, mts., Italy — C4 23
Apennine Tunnel, Italy — B3 23
Apérathos, Grc. — D5 25
Apex, N.C., U.S. — B4 110
Apex Mountain, mtn., Yukon — D5 66
Api, mtn., Nepal — C8 37
Apia, W. Sam. — F12 52
Apiacás, Serra dos, plat., Braz. — E3 59
Apia Harbour, b., W. Sam. — F12 52
Apiaí, Braz. — C3 56
Apishapa, stm., Co., U.S. — D6 83
Apison, Tn., U.S. — h11 119
Apizaco, Mex. — n14 63
Aplao, Peru — E3 58
Aplin, Ar., U.S. — C3 81
Aplington, Ia., U.S. — B5 92
Apo, Mount, mtn., Phil. — D7 34
Apodi, Braz. — C3 57
Apohaqui, N.B. — D4 71
Apolda, E. Ger. — C5 18
Apoland Island, i., W. Sam. — F11 52
Apolima Strait, strt., W. Sam. — F11 52
Apollo, Pa., U.S. — E2 115
Apolo, Bol. — B2 55
Apopka, Fl., U.S. — D5 86
Apopka, Lake, l., Fl., U.S. — D5 86
Aporé, Braz. — B2 56
Aporé, stm., Braz. — B2 56
Apostle Islands, is., Wi., U.S. — A3 126
Apostle Islands National Lakeshore, Wi., U.S. — A3 126
Apóstoles, Arg. — E4 55
Appalachia, Va., U.S. — f9 123
Appalachian Mountains, mts., N.A. — C11 76
Appam, N.D., U.S. — A2 111
Appanoose, co., Ia., U.S. — D5 92
Appenzell, Switz. — E4 18
Appenzell-Ausser Rhoden, state, Switz. — B5 20
Appenzell-Inner Rhoden, state, Switz. — B5 20
Apperson, Ok., U.S. — A5 113
Appingedam, Neth. — A6 17
Apple, Wi., U.S. — C1 126
Appleby, Eng., U.K. — F6 13
Appleby, Tx., U.S. — D5 120
Apple Creek, Oh., U.S. — B4 112
Applecross, Scot., U.K. — C4 13
Applegate, Mi., U.S. — E8 99
Applegate, Or., U.S. — E3 114
Applegate, stm., Or., U.S. — E3 114
Apple Grove, W.V., U.S. — C2 125
Apple Hill, Ont. — B10 73
Apple Orchard Mountain, mtn., Va., U.S. — C3 123
Apple River, N.S. — D5 71
Apple River, Il., U.S. — A3 90
Apple Springs, Tx., U.S. — D5 120
Appleton, Me., U.S. — D3 96
Appleton, Mn., U.S. — E2 100
Appleton, Tn., U.S. — D5 119
Appleton, Wa., U.S. — D4 124
Appleton, Wi., U.S. — D5 126
Appleton City, Mo., U.S. — C3 102
Apple Valley, Ca., U.S. — E5 82
Apple Valley, Mn., U.S. — n12 100
Apple Valley, N.D., U.S. — *C5 111
Applewood, Co., U.S. — B5 83
Appleyard, Wa., U.S. — B5 124
Appling, Ga., U.S. — C4 87
Appling, co., Ga., U.S. — D4 87
Appomattox, Va., U.S. — C4 123
Appomattox, stm., Va., U.S. — C4 123
Appomattox Court House National Historical Park, Va., U.S. — C4 123
Apra Harbor, b., Guam — L9 52
Aprelsk, Sov. Un. — D14 52
Aprilia, Italy — D4 23
Apsheron Peninsula, pen., Sov. Un. — G19 8
Apsley, Ont. — C6 73
Apt, Fr. — F6 16
Aptos, Ca., U.S. — *D3 82
Apua Point, c., Hi., U.S. — D6 88
Apucarana, Braz. — C2 56
Apulia (Puglia), prov., Italy — D6 23
Apure, stm., Ven. — B4 60
Apurímac, dept., Peru — D3 58

Apurímac, stm., Peru — D3 58
Aqaba, Gulf of, b. — C3 38
'Aqaba, Sud. — B4 47
'Aqīq, Sud. — B4 47
'Aqrabā, Syria — A8 41
'Aqrabah, Isr. Occ. — B7 41
Aquarius Mountains, mts., Az., U.S. — C2 80
Aquarius Plateau, plat., Ut., U.S. — E4 121
Aquasco, Md., U.S. — C4 97
Aquebogue, N.Y., U.S. — n16 109
Aquidauana, Braz. — C1 56
Aquila see L'Aquila, Italy — C4 23
Aquileia, Italy — D9 20
Aquin, Haiti — E7 64
Aquone, N.C., U.S. — f9 110
Ara, India — C7 36
Arab, Al., U.S. — A3 78
'Arab, Bahr al, stm., Sud. — D2 47
'Arab, Khalīj al, b., Egypt — G7 40
Arab, Shatt al, stm., Iraq — B4 38
Arabelo, Ven. — C5 60
Arabi, Ga., U.S. — E3 87
Arabi, La., U.S. — k11 95
Arabian Desert, des., Eg. — C3 38
Arabian Sea — H9 30
Araçá, stm., Braz. — B2 59
Aracaju, Braz. — D3 57
Aracati, Braz. — B3 57
Araçatuba, Braz. — C2 56
Aracena, Spain — D2 22
Aracruz, Braz. — B4 56
Araçuaí, Braz. — B4 56
Arad, Rom. — B5 24
Arada, Chad — B4 46
Araçon, Fr. — C1 21
Arcos de la Frontera, Spain — D3 22
Arcot, India — F6 36
Aragarças, Braz. — B2 56
Arago, Or., U.S. — D2 114
Arago, Cape, c., Or., U.S. — D2 114
Aragón, Ga., U.S. — B1 87
Aragon, N.M., U.S. — D1 108
Aragón, hist. reg., Spain — B5 22
Aragón, stm., Spain — A5 22
Aragua, state, Ven. — A4 60
Araguacema, Braz. — D5 59
Araguaçu, Braz. — E5 59
Aragua de Barcelona, Ven. — B5 60
Araguaia, stm., Braz. — D6 53
Araguaia, Braço Menor, stm., Braz. — E5 59
Araguaia National Park, Braz. — E4 59
Araguao, Boca, mth., Ven. — B5 60
Araguari, Braz. — B3 56
Araguari, stm., Braz. — B4 59
Arai, Japan — H9 33
Arai, Japan — o16 33
Arāk, Alg. — D5 44
Arāk, Iran — B4 38
Arakan Range, mts., Burma — E9 36
Árakhthos, stm., Grc. — C3 25
Arakkonam, India — F6 36
Araks, stm., Asia — B3 39
Aral Sea, Sov. Un. — E9 29
Aralsk, Sov. Un. — D6 28
Aramac, Austl. — D8 50
Arambaza, Col. — D3 60
Ārān, Iran — D5 39
Aranda de Duero, Spain — B4 22
Arandas, Mex. — m12 63
Aran Island, i., Ire. — C2 10
Aran Islands, is., Ire. — D2 10
Aranjuez, Spain — B4 22
Aranos, Nmb. — B2 49
Aransas, co., Tx., U.S. — E4 120
Aransas Bay, b., Tx., U.S. — E4 120
Aransas Pass, Tx., U.S. — F4 120
Aranyaprathet, Thai. — C2 34
Araouane, Mali — C4 45
Arapaho, Ok., U.S. — B3 113
Arapahoe, Co., U.S. — C8 83
Arapahoe, Ne., U.S. — D6 104
Arapahoe, N.C., U.S. — B6 110
Arapahoe, Wy., U.S. — D4 127
Arapahoe, co., Co., U.S. — B6 83
Arapey, Ur. — E1 56
Arapey Grande, stm., Ur. — E1 56
Arapkir, Tur. — C12 40
Arapongas, Braz. — C2 56
Araranguá, Braz. — D3 56
Araraquara, Braz. — C3 56
Araras, Braz. — C3 56
Ararat, Austl. — G7 50
Ararat, Va., U.S. — D2 123
Ararat, Mount, mtn., Tur. — C15 40
Araripe, Chapada do, plat., Braz. — C3 57
Araruna, Braz. — h6 57
Arauca, Col. — B3 60
Arauca, dept., Col. — B3 60
Arauca, stm., S.A. — B3 60
Arauco, Chile — B2 54
Araújos, Braz. — B3 56
Arāvalli Range, mts., India — D5 36
Araxá, Braz. — B3 56
Araya, Ven. — A5 60
Araya, Punta de, c., Ven. — A5 60
Arba Minch, Eth. — D4 47
Arbela, Mo., U.S. — A5 102
Arboga, Swe. — t33 14
Arbois, Fr. — D6 16
Arboles, Co., U.S. — D3 83
Arbon, Switz. — C9 20
Arbon, Id., U.S. — G6 89
Arborea (Mussolinia), Italy — E2 23
Arborfield, Sask. — D4 75
Arborg, Man. — D3 70
Arbor Vitae, Wi., U.S. — C4 126
Arbroath, Scot., U.K. — E6 13
Arbuckle, Ca., U.S. — C2 82
Arbuckle, Lake, l., Fl., U.S. — E5 86
Arbuckle Mountains, mts., Ok., U.S. — C4 113
Arbuckles, Lake of the, res., Ok., U.S. — C5 113
Arbyrd, Mo., U.S. — E7 102
Arc, Bayou des, stm., Ar., U.S. — B4 81
Arcachon, Fr. — E3 16
Arcade, Ca., U.S. — c3 82
Arcade, N.Y., U.S. — C2 109
Arcadia, Ca., U.S. — m12 82
Arcadia, Fl., U.S. — E5 86
Arcadia, In., U.S. — D5 91
Arcadia, Ks., U.S. — E9 93
Arcadia, La., U.S. — B3 95
Arcadia, Mi., U.S. — D4 99
Arcadia, Ne., U.S. — C6 104
Arcadia, Ok., U.S. — B4 113
Arcadia, Pa., U.S. — E4 115

Arcadia, R.I., U.S. — E2 116
Arcadia, S.C., U.S. — B4 117
Arcadia, Wi., U.S. — D2 126
Arcanum, Oh., U.S. — C1 112
Arcata, Ca., U.S. — B1 82
Arc Dome, mtn., Nv., U.S. — E4 105
Arcelia, Mex. — n13 63
Arcey, Fr. — A2 21
Archambault, Lac, l., Que. — C3 74
Archbald, Pa., U.S. — m18 115
Archbold, Oh., U.S. — A1 112
Archdale, N.C., U.S. — B3 110
Archer, Fl., U.S. — C4 86
Archer, Ia., U.S. — A2 92
Archer, Ne., U.S. — C7 104
Archer, co., Tx., U.S. — C3 120
Archer City, Tx., U.S. — C3 120
Archerwill, Sask. — E4 75
Arches National Park, Ut., U.S. — E6 121
Archidona, Spain — D3 22
Archie, Mo., U.S. — C3 102
Archive, Sask. — G3 75
Arco, Id., U.S. — F5 89
Arco, Mn., U.S. — F2 100
Arcola, Sask. — H4 75
Arcola, Il., U.S. — D5 90
Arcola, In., U.S. — B7 91
Arcola, Ms., U.S. — B3 101
Arcola, Mo., U.S. — D4 102
Arcola, Va., U.S. — g11 123
Arcon, Fr. — C1 21
Arcos de la Frontera, Spain — D3 22
Arcot, India — F6 36
Arcoverde, Braz. — C3 57
Arcueil, Fr. — g10 16
Arctic Bay, N.W. Ter. — B16 66
Arctic Ocean — A1 128
Arctic Village, Ak., U.S. — B10 79
Arda, stm., Eur. — E7 24
Ardabīl (Ardebil), Iran — B4 38
Ardagh, Ire. — E2 11
Ardahan, Tur. — B14 40
Ardakān, Iran — B5 38
Ardakān, Iran — B5 38
Ardara, Ire. — C3 11
Ardath, Sask. — F2 75
Ardatov, Sov. Un. — D16 27
Ardbeg, Ont. — B4 73
Ardea, Italy — h9 23
Ardee, Ire. — E2 10
Ardebil see Ardabīl, Iran — B4 38
Arden, Man. — D2 70
Arden, Ont. — C8 73
Arden, Den. — B3 15
Arden, Ar., U.S. — D1 81
Arden, Ca., U.S. — *C2 82
Arden, N.C., U.S. — f10 110
Arden Hills, Mn., U.S. — *m12 100
Ardennes, dept., Fr. — E4 17
Ardennes, reg., Eur. — B6 16
Ardenno, Italy — C5 20
Ardenvoir, Wa., U.S. — B5 124
Arderin, mtn., Ire. — E6 39
Ardglass, N. Ire., U.K. — C6 11
Ardgroom, Ire. — F2 11
Ardila, stm., Eur. — C2 22
Ardill, Sask. — H3 75
Ardino, Bul. — E7 24
Ardley, Alta. — C4 68
Ardmore, Ire. — F4 11
Ardmore, Al., U.S. — A3 78
Ardmore, Md., U.S. — C4 97
Ardmore, Ok., U.S. — C4 113
Ardmore, Pa., U.S. — F11 115
Ardmore, S.D., U.S. — D2 118
Ardmore, Tn., U.S. — B5 119
Ardnamurchan, Point of, c., Scot., U.K. — D2 13
Arkport, N.Y., U.S. — C3 109
Arkville, N.Y., U.S. — C6 109
Ardoch, N.D., U.S. — A8 111
Ardpatrick Point, c., Scot., U.K. — E3 13
Ardres, Fr. — D1 17
Ardrossan, Austl. — G1 51
Ardrossan, Alta. — C4 68
Ardrossan, Scot., U.K. — E4 13
Ardsley, N.Y., U.S. — g13 109
Arecibo, P.R. — G11 64
Aredale, Ia., U.S. — B5 92
Areia, Braz. — h6 57
Areia Branca, Braz. — B3 57
Arelee, Sask. — E2 75
Arena, N.D., U.S. — B5 111
Arena, Point, c., Ca., U.S. — C2 82
Arena, Punta, c., Mex. — C3 63
Arenac, co., Mi., U.S. — D7 99
Arenápolis, Braz. — A1 56
Arenas de San Pedro, Spain — B3 22
Arenas Valley, N.M., U.S. — E1 108
Arendal, Nor. — H3 14
Arendonk, Bel. — C5 17
Arendsee, E. Ger. — F5 15
Arendtsville, Pa., U.S. — G7 115
Arenillas, Ec. — D3 90
Arenys de Mar, Spain — D7 22
Areópolis, Grc. — E5 25
Arequipa, Peru — E3 58
Arequipa, dept., Peru — E3 58
Arezzo, Italy — C3 23
Arga, stm., Spain — A5 22
Argalastí, Grc. — C5 25
Arganda, Spain — p18 22
Argelès-Gazost, Fr. — F3 16
Argen, stm., W. Ger. — A8 21
Argenta, Italy — E6 20
Argenta, Il., U.S. — D5 90
Argentan, Fr. — C4 16
Argentat, Fr. — E4 16
Argenteuil, co., Que. — D3 74
Argentina, II., U.S. — C2 90
Argentino, Lago, l., Arg. — G2 54
Argenton-sur-Creuse, Fr. — D4 16
Argeş, stm., Rom. — C7 24
Arghandāb, Afg. — E13 39
Arghandāb, Band-e, stm., Afg. — F13 39
Argo, Sud. — B4 47
Argo, Al., U.S. — A3 78
Argo, Ky., U.S. — C7 94
Argo Corner, De., U.S. — k7 108
Argolis, Gulf of, b., Grc. — D4 25
Argonne, Mt., U.S. — C6 103
Argonne, Wi., U.S. — C5 126
Argonne, reg., Fr. — C6 16

Argonne, Forêt d', for., Fr. — E4 17
Argonk, N.Y., U.S. — *g13 109
Argos, Grc. — D4 40
Argos, In., U.S. — B5 91
Argos Orestikón, Grc. — B3 25
Argostólion, Grc. — C3 40
Argroup, Asia — D14 29
Argungu, Nig. — D5 45
Argyle, Fl., U.S. — C5 86
Argyle, Il., U.S. — C6 90
Argyle, N.S. — F4 71
Argyle, Fl., U.S. — u15 86
Argyle, Ga., U.S. — E4 87
Argyle, Ia., U.S. — D6 92
Argyle, Mi., U.S. — E8 99
Argyle, Mn., U.S. — B2 100
Argyle, Mo., U.S. — C5 102
Argyle, N.Y., U.S. — B7 109
Argyle, Wi., U.S. — F4 126
Argyle, Lake, res., Austl. — C4 50
Århus, Den. — I4 14
Århus, co., Den. — B4 15
Århus Bugt, b., Den. — B4 15
Ari, In., U.S. — B7 91
Ariake Bay, b., Japan — K5 33
Ariano Irpino, Italy — D5 23
Ariano nel Polesine, Italy — E8 20
Ariari, stm., Col. — C3 60
Arica, Chile — C1 55
Arica, Col. — D3 60
Arichat, N.S. — D8 71
Ariège, stm., Fr. — F4 16
Ariel, Wa., U.S. — D3 124
Ariel, stm., Rom. — B6 24
Arikaree, stm., U.S. — B8 83
Arima, Trin. — K14 64
Arimo, Id., U.S. — G6 89
Arinos, stm., Braz. — B4 55
Ario de Rosales, Mex. — D4 63
Arion, Ia., U.S. — C2 92
Aripo, El Cerro del, mtn., Trin. — K14 64
Aripuanã, Braz. — D2 59
Aripuanã, stm., Braz. — D2 59
'Arīsh, Wādī al, val., Eg. — D6 41
Aristazabal Island, i., B.C. — C3 69
Arivaca, Az., U.S. — F4 80
Arivonimamo, Madag. — g9 49
Arizaro, Salar de, pl., Arg. — D2 55
Arizona, Arg. — B3 54
Arizona, state, U.S. — C4 80
Arizona Sunsites, Az., U.S. — F6 80
Arizpe, Mex. — A2 63
Arjay, Ky., U.S. — D6 94
Arjeplog, Swe. — D8 14
Arjona, Col. — A2 60
Arjona, Spain — D3 22
Arkabutla, Ms., U.S. — A3 101
Arkabutla Lake, res., Ms., U.S. — A4 101
Arkadak, Sov. Un. — D16 27
Arkadelphia, Al., U.S. — B3 78
Arkadelphia, Ar., U.S. — C2 81
Arkagala, Sov. Un. — D13 15
Arkalyk, Sov. Un. — D7 28
Arkansas, state, U.S. — C3 81
Arkansas, co., Ar., U.S. — C4 81
Arkansas, Salt Fork, stm., U.S. — A3 113
Arkansas City, Ar., U.S. — E3 81
Arkansas City, Ks., U.S. — E6 93
Arkansaw, Wi., U.S. — D1 126
Arkelstorp, Swe. — B8 15
Arkhangelsk, Sov. Un. — C7 29
Arkhangelskoye, Sov. Un. — F13 27
Arkhara, Sov. Un. — H5 33
Árki, Grc. — D6 25
Arkinda, Ar., U.S. — D1 81
Arklow, Ire. — D3 10
Arkoma, Ok., U.S. — B7 113
Arkona, Ont. — D2 73
Arkona, Kap (The Skaw), c., E. Ger. — D7 15
Arkport, N.Y., U.S. — C3 109
Arkville, N.Y., U.S. — C6 109
Arkwright, N.Y., U.S. — C1 109
Arkwright, Scot., U.K. — D3 13
Arlanc, Fr. — E5 16
Arlanza, stm., Spain — A4 22
Arlanzón, stm., Spain — A4 22
Arlberg Tunnel, Aus. — A5 18
Arles, Mt., U.S. — C12 103
Arlee, Fr. — F6 16
Arles, Ala., U.S. — A2 78
Arlesheim, Switz. — A7 20
Arlington, Az., U.S. — D3 80
Arlington, Ga., U.S. — E2 87
Arlington, Ia., U.S. — B6 92
Arlington, Ks., U.S. — E5 93
Arlington, Ky., U.S. — f9 94
Arlington, Ma., U.S. — B5 98
Arlington, Mn., U.S. — F4 100
Arlington, Ne., U.S. — C9 104
Arlington, N.Y., U.S. — D7 109
Arlington, Oh., U.S. — B2 112
Arlington, S.C., U.S. — B6 117
Arlington, S.D., U.S. — C8 118
Arlington, Tn., U.S. — B2 119
Arlington, Tx., U.S. — n9 120
Arlington, Vt., U.S. — E2 122
Arlington, Va., U.S. — g12 123
Arlington, co., Va., U.S. — g12 123
Arlington, Lake, res., Tx., U.S. — n9 120
Arlington Beach, S.D., U.S. — C8 118
Arlington Heights, Il., U.S. — A5 90
Arlit, Niger — C6 45
Arlon, Bel. — C6 17
Arly, stm., Fr. — E7 16
Armada, Mi., U.S. — F8 99
Armagh, Que. — C7 74
Armagh, N. Ire., U.K. — F3 115
Armagh, co., N. Ire., U.K. — C3 11
Armant, Eg. — C3 38
Armavir, Sov. Un. — H13 27
Armenia, state, Sov. Un. — E7 29
Armenière, Fr. — D2 17
Armeria, stm., Mex. — n12 63
Armidale, Austl. — F9 50
Arminto, Wy., U.S. — C5 127
Armit Lake, l., Can. — C1 70

Armley, Sask. — D3 75
Armonk, N.Y., U.S. — *g13 109
Armorel, Ar., U.S. — B6 81
Armour, S.D., U.S. — D7 118
Armour, B.C. — D8 69
Armstead, Al., U.S. — B3 78
Armstrong, B.C. — D8 69
Armstrong, Fl., U.S. — C5 86
Armstrong, Il., U.S. — C6 90
Armstrong, Ia., U.S. — A3 92
Armstrong, Mo., U.S. — B5 102
Armstrong, Tx., U.S. — F4 120
Armstrong, co., Pa., U.S. — E2 115
Armstrong, co., Tx., U.S. — B2 120
Armstrong Creek, Wi., U.S. — C5 126
Armstrong Creek, stm., W.V., U.S. — m13 125
Armstrong Station, Ont. — F15 66
Armuchee, Ga., U.S. — B1 87
Armyansk, Sov. Un. — H9 27
Arnaud, stm., Que. — E18 66
Arnaudville, La., U.S. — D4 95
Arneburg, E. Ger. — F5 15
Arnedo, Spain — A4 22
Arnegard, N.D., U.S. — B2 111
Arneiroz, Braz. — C2 57
Arnett, Ok., U.S. — A2 113
Arnett, W.V., U.S. — D3 125
Arney, stm., N. Ire., U.K. — C4 11
Arnhem, Neth. — B6 16
Arnhem, Cape, c., Austl. — B6 50
Arnhem Land, reg., Austl. — B5 50
Arnissa, Grc. — B3 25
Arno, stm., Italy — C3 23
Arnold, Ca., U.S. — C3 82
Arnold, Ks., U.S. — D3 93
Arnold, Md., U.S. — *B4 97
Arnold, Mi., U.S. — B3 99
Arnold, Mo., U.S. — C7 102
Arnold, Ne., U.S. — C5 104
Arnold, Pa., U.S. — h14 115
Arnold Mills, R.I., U.S. — B4 116
Arnolds, Scot., U.K. — C4 11
Arnold Mills Reservoir, res., R.I., U.S. — B4 116
Arnoldsburg, W.V., U.S. — C3 125
Arnold's Cove, Newf. — E4 72
Arnolds Park, Ia., U.S. — A2 92
Arnoldsville, Ga., U.S. — C3 87
Arnouville, Fr. — g10 16
Arnøy, i., Nor. — B9 14
Arnprior, Ont. — B8 73
Arnsberg, W. Ger. — C4 18
Arnstadt, E. Ger. — C5 18
Arnstein, Ont. — B5 73
Aroa, i., Den. — C3 15
Aroa, Ven. — A4 60
Aroab, Nmb. — C2 49
Arock, Or., U.S. — E9 114
Aroda, Va., U.S. — B4 123
Arolla, Switz. — D3 21
Arolsen, W. Ger. — B4 18
Aroma, Sud. — B4 47
Aroma Park, Il., U.S. — B6 90
Arona, Italy — E6 21
Aroostook, N.B. — C2 71
Aroostook, co., Me., U.S. — B4 96
Aroostook, stm., N.A. — B4 96
Arop, i., Pap. N. Gui. — k12 50
Aros, Nor. — p28 14
Arosa, Switz. — C5 20
Arosa, Trin. — N23 65
Arp, Tx., U.S. — C5 120
Arpajon, Fr. — F2 17
Arpin, Wi., U.S. — D3 126
Arques-la-Bataille, Fr. — E9 12
'Arrābah, Isr. Occ. — B7 41
Ar Rahad, Sud. — C3 47
Arraias, Braz. — D1 57
Arraiján, Pan. — F8 62
Arraiolos, Port. — C2 22
Ar Ramādī, Iraq — B4 38
Ar Ramthā, Jord. — B7 41
Arran, Sask. — F5 75
Arran, Island of, i., Scot., U.K. — C4 10
Arran, Island of, i., Scot., U.K. — E4 13
Ar Raqqah, Syria — B3 38
Arras, Fr. — E9 12
Ar Rawdah, Eg. — E3 41
Arrecifes, Arg. — g6 54
Arrecifes, stm., Arg. — g7 54
Arrey, N.M., U.S. — E2 108
Arriaga, Mex. — D6 63
Arriba, Co., U.S. — B7 83
Arriken Island, i., Marsh Is. — P18 52
Arrington, Ks., U.S. — C8 93
Arrington, Va., U.S. — C4 123
Arroio Grande, Braz. — E2 56
Arroll, Mo., U.S. — D6 102
Arrone, stm., Italy — h8 23
Arrow, Lough, l., Ire. — C4 11
Arrow Creek, stm., Mt., U.S. — C6 103
Arrowhead Mountain Lake, res., Vt., U.S. — B2 122
Arrowhead Village, N.J., U.S. — C4 107
Arrowrock Reservoir, res., Id., U.S. — F3 89
Arrowsmith, Il., U.S. — C5 90
Arrowwood, Alta. — D4 68
Arrowwood Lake, res., N.D., U.S. — B7 111
Arroyo, P.R. — G11 64
Arroyo de la Luz, Spain — C3 22
Arroyo Grande, Ca., U.S. — E3 82
Arroyo Hondo, N.M., U.S. — A4 108
Arroyo Seco, N.M., U.S. — A4 108
Ar Rumaythah, Iraq — B4 38
Ar Ruṣayfah, Jord. — B8 41
Ar Ruṣayriṣ, Sud. — g10 47
Ar Ruṭbah, Iraq — B4 38
Ar Ruwayṭī, hist., Jord. — D5 41
Ārs, Den. — B3 15
Arsenyevo, Sov. Un. — D3 27
Arsi, prov., Eth. — D4 47
Årstad, Swe. — H5 14
Árta, Grc. — *C3 40
Arta, dept., Grc. — *g13 25
Artas, S.D., U.S. — B6 118
Artem, Sov. Un. — E7 29
Artemisa, Cuba — C2 64
Artemovsk, Sov. Un. — G11 27
Artemovsk, Sov. Un. — E21 29
Artemovskiy, Sov. Un. — D6 94
Artena, Italy — h9 23
Arter, Mount, mtn., Wy., U.S. — D4 127
Artern, E. Ger. — B6 19

Artesia, Ca., U.S. — *n12 82
Artesia, Ms., U.S. — B5 101
Artesia, N.M., U.S. — E5 108
Artesian, S.D., U.S. — C8 118
Arth, Switz. — B4 20
Arthabaska, Que. — C6 74
Arthabaska, co., Que. — C5 74
Arthur, Ont. — D4 73
Arthur, Il., U.S. — D5 90
Arthur, In., U.S. — H3 91
Arthur, Ia., U.S. — B2 92
Arthur, Ne., U.S. — C4 104
Arthur, N.D., U.S. — B8 111
Arthur, Tn., U.S. — C10 119
Arthur, co., Ne., U.S. — C4 104
Arthur, Lake, l., La., U.S. — D3 95
Arthur, Lake, res., Pa., U.S. — E1 115
Arthur Kill, stm., N.J., U.S. — k8 107
Arthurs Town, Bah. — B4 64
Artibonite, stm., Haiti — E7 64
Artigas, Ur. — E1 56
Artland, Sask. — E1 75
Artois, hist. reg., Fr. — B9 16
Artois, Collines de l', hills, Fr. — D2 17
Artvin, Tur. — B13 40
Aru, Zaire — A5 48
Aru, Ug. — A5 48
Aruanã, Braz. — A2 56
Aruba, ctry., N.A. — H17 65
Arucas, Spain — m14 22
Aru Islands, is., Indon. — G8 34
Arun, stm., Eng., U.K. — D7 12
Arunachal Pradesh, state, India — C10 36
Arundel, Que. — D3 74
Arundel, Eng., U.K. — D7 12
Arundel Village, Md., U.S. — *h11 97
Arusha, Tan. — B6 48
Arusha, prov., Tan. — B6 48
Aruwimi, stm., Zaire — A4 48
Arvada, Co., U.S. — B5 83
Arvada, Wy., U.S. — B6 127
Arvagh, Ire. — D4 11
Arvayheer, Mong. — B5 31
Arve, stm., Eur. — D2 20
Arvida, Que. — A6 74
Arvidsjaur, Swe. — E8 14
Arvigo, Switz. — D7 21
Arvika, Swe. — H5 14
Arvilla, N.D., U.S. — B8 111
Arvin, Ca., U.S. — E4 82
Arvon, Mount, mtn., Mi., U.S. — *B2 99
Arvonia, Va., U.S. — C4 123
Arxan, China — B8 31
Arys, Sov. Un. — E7 28
Arzamas, Sov. Un. — D14 27
Arzgir, Sov. Un. — I15 27
Arzúa, Spain — A1 22
Aš, Czech. — C2 26
Asā, Nmb. — A4 15
Asab, Nmb. — C2 49
Asad, Lake, res., Syria — B12 40
Asahi, Mount, mtn., Japan — E11 33
Asahikawa, Japan — C13 31
Asan, Guam — L9 52
Asan Bay, b., S. Kor. — H3 33
Asan Point, c., Guam — L9 52
Āsānsol, India — D8 36
Asau, b., W. Sam. — F11 52
Asbach, W. Ger. — C2 19
Asbest, Sov. Un. — D9 29
Asbestos, Que. — D6 74
Asbury, Mo., U.S. — D3 102
Asbury Park, N.J., U.S. — C4 107
Ascensión, Mex. — A3 63
Ascension, co., La., U.S. — D5 95
Ascension, i., St. Hel. — G4 42
Aschaffenburg, W. Ger. — D4 18
Aschersleben, E. Ger. — C5 18
Ascoli Piceno, Italy — C4 23
Ascona, Switz. — D6 21
Ascope, Peru — C2 58
Ascotán, Chile — D2 55
Ascot-Corner, Que. — D6 74
Ascutney, Vt., U.S. — E4 122
Ascutney, Mount, mtn., Vt., U.S. — E4 122
Aseb, Eth. — C5 47
Asela, Eth. — D4 47
Asenovgrad, Bul. — E7 24
Asha, Sov. Un. — D8 29
Ashanti, prov., Ghana — E4 45
Ashaway, R.I., U.S. — F1 116
Ashbourne, Eng., U.K. — A6 12
Ashburn, Ga., U.S. — E3 87
Ashburn, Mo., U.S. — B6 102
Ashburnham, Ma., U.S. — A4 98
Ashburton, N.Z. — O13 51
Ashburton, stm., Austl. — D3 50
Ashby, Al., U.S. — B3 78
Ashby, Mn., U.S. — D3 100
Ashby, Ne., U.S. — C4 104
Ashbyburg, Ky., U.S. — C2 94
Ashcroft, B.C. — D7 69
Ashdod, Isr. — C6 41
Ashdot Ya'aqov, Isr. — C7 41
Ashdown, Ar., U.S. — D1 81
Ashe, co., N.C., U.S. — A1 110
Asheboro, N.C., U.S. — B3 110
Ashepoo, stm., S.C., U.S. — C5 117
Asher, Ok., U.S. — C4 113
Asherton, Tx., U.S. — E3 120
Asheville, N.C., U.S. — f10 110
Ashford, Ala., U.S. — D4 78
Ashford, W.V., U.S. — m12 125
Ash Fork, Az., U.S. — B3 80
Ash Grove, Mo., U.S. — D4 102
Ashikaga, Japan — H9 33
Ashio, Japan — H9 33
Ashizuri, Cape, c., Japan — J6 33
Ashkhabad, Sov. Un. — F8 29
Ash Lake, Mn., U.S. — B6 100
Ashland, Al., U.S. — B4 78
Ashland, Ca., U.S. — E4 90
Ashland, Il., U.S. — D4 90
Ashland, Ks., U.S. — E4 93
Ashland, Ky., U.S. — B7 94
Ashland, Me., U.S. — B4 96
Ashland, Ma., U.S. — g10 98
Ashland, Ms., U.S. — A4 101

# Index

| Name | Map Ref. | Page |
|---|---|---|
| Ashland, Mo., U.S. | C5 | 102 |
| Ashland, Mt., U.S. | E10 | 103 |
| Ashland, Ne., U.S. | C9 | 104 |
| Ashland, N.H., U.S. | C3 | 106 |
| Ashland, Oh., U.S. | B3 | 112 |
| Ashland, Ok., U.S. | C5 | 113 |
| Ashland, Or., U.S. | E4 | 114 |
| Ashland, Pa., U.S. | E9 | 115 |
| Ashland, Va., U.S. | C5 | 123 |
| Ashland, Wi., U.S. | B3 | 126 |
| Ashland, co., Oh., U.S. | B3 | 112 |
| Ashland, co., Wi., U.S. | B3 | 126 |
| Ashland, Mount, mtn., Or., U.S. | E4 | 114 |
| Ashland City, Tn., U.S. | A4 | 119 |
| Ashland Reservoir, res., Ma., U.S. | h10 | 98 |
| Ashley, Il., U.S. | E4 | 90 |
| Ashley, In., U.S. | A7 | 91 |
| Ashley, Mi., U.S. | E6 | 99 |
| Ashley, Mo., U.S. | B6 | 102 |
| Ashley, N.D., U.S. | C6 | 111 |
| Ashley, Oh., U.S. | B3 | 112 |
| Ashley, Pa., U.S. | n17 | 115 |
| Ashley, co., Ar., U.S. | D4 | 81 |
| Ashley, co., S.C., U.S. | F7 | 117 |
| Ashley Creek, stm., Ut., U.S. | C6 | 121 |
| Ashley Falls, Ma., U.S. | B1 | 98 |
| Ashmont, Alta. | B5 | 68 |
| Ashmore, Il., U.S. | D5 | 90 |
| Ashmore Islands, is., Austl. | B3 | 50 |
| Ashmūn, Eg. | D2 | 41 |
| Ashnola, stm., N.A. | A5 | 124 |
| Ashokan, N.Y., U.S. | D6 | 109 |
| Ashokan Reservoir, res., N.Y., U.S. | D6 | 109 |
| Ashport, Tn., U.S. | B2 | 119 |
| Ashqelon, Isr. | B3 | 38 |
| Ash Shabakah, Iraq | B4 | 38 |
| Ash Shabb, well, Eg. | E5 | 43 |
| Ash Shallāl, Eg. | E6 | 43 |
| Ash Shallūfah, Eg. | D4 | 41 |
| Ash Shamālīyah (Northern), prov., Sud. | B2 | 47 |
| Ash Shāriqah, U.A.E. | C5 | 38 |
| Ash Sharqāt, Iraq | B4 | 38 |
| Ash Shaṭrah, Iraq | F3 | 39 |
| Ash Shawāshinah, Eg. | E2 | 41 |
| Ash Shawbak, Jord. | D7 | 41 |
| Ash Shawmarah, Leb. | A7 | 41 |
| Ash Shaykh Jarrāh (part of Jerusalem), Isr. Occ. | m14 | 41 |
| Ash Shaykh Sa'd, Syria | B7 | 41 |
| Ash Shiḥr, Yemen | D4 | 38 |
| Ash Shumlul, Sau. Ar. | H3 | 39 |
| Ash Shurayk, Sud. | B3 | 47 |
| Ash Springs, Nv., U.S. | F6 | 105 |
| Ashtabula, Oh., U.S. | A5 | 112 |
| Ashtabula, co., Oh., U.S. | A5 | 112 |
| Ashtabula, Lake, res., N.D., U.S. | B8 | 111 |
| Ashton, Ont. | B8 | 73 |
| Ashton, Id., U.S. | E7 | 89 |
| Ashton, Il., U.S. | B4 | 90 |
| Ashton, Ia., U.S. | A2 | 92 |
| Ashton, Md., U.S. | B3 | 97 |
| Ashton, Mi., U.S. | E5 | 99 |
| Ashton, Ne., U.S. | C7 | 104 |
| Ashton, R.I., U.S. | B4 | 116 |
| Ashton, S.D., U.S. | C7 | 118 |
| Ashuanipi Lake, l., Newf. | h8 | 72 |
| Ashuelot, N.H., U.S. | E2 | 106 |
| Ashuelot, stm., N.H., U.S. | E2 | 106 |
| Ashville, Man. | D1 | 70 |
| Ashville, Al., U.S. | B3 | 78 |
| Ashville, Oh., U.S. | C3 | 112 |
| Ashwaubenon, Wi., U.S. | D5 | 126 |
| Ashwood, Or., U.S. | C6 | 114 |
| Ashwood, Tn., U.S. | B4 | 119 |
| Asia, cont. | E11 | 30 |
| Asiago, Italy | D7 | 20 |
| Asia Minor, reg., Tur. | C10 | 40 |
| Asifābād, India | H7 | 37 |
| Asiga, Puntan, c., N. Mar. Is. | D7 | 52 |
| Asiga Point, c., Guam | M10 | 52 |
| Asinara, Gulf of, b., Italy | D2 | 23 |
| Asinara Island, i., Italy | D2 | 23 |
| Asino, Sov. Un. | B11 | 28 |
| 'Asīr, reg., Sau. Ar. | D4 | 38 |
| 'Aṣīrah ash Shamālīyah, Isr. Occ. | g12 | 41 |
| Asker, Nor. | p28 | 14 |
| Askersund, Swe. | H6 | 14 |
| Askew, Ms., U.S. | A3 | 101 |
| Askham, S. Afr. | C3 | 49 |
| Askim, Nor. | p29 | 14 |
| Askim, Swe. | A5 | 15 |
| Askival, mtn., Scot., U.K. | D2 | 13 |
| Askö, l., Swe. | u35 | 14 |
| Askov, Mn., U.S. | D6 | 100 |
| Āsmār, Afg. | D15 | 39 |
| Asmara (Asmera), Eth. | B4 | 47 |
| Asnæs, Den. | C5 | 15 |
| Asnebumskit Hill, hill, Ma., U.S. | B4 | 98 |
| Åsnen, l., Swe. | B8 | 15 |
| Asnières [-sur-Seine], Fr. | C5 | 16 |
| Asopós, stm., Grc. | g11 | 25 |
| Asosa, Eth. | C3 | 47 |
| Asotin, Wa., U.S. | C8 | 124 |
| Asotin, co., Wa., U.S. | C8 | 124 |
| Asotin Creek, stm., Wa., U.S. | C8 | 124 |
| Aspe, Spain | C5 | 22 |
| Aspen, Co., U.S. | B4 | 83 |
| Aspen Butte, mtn., Or., U.S. | E4 | 114 |
| Aspen Hill, Md., U.S. | *B3 | 97 |
| Aspen Hill, Il., U.S. | B4 | 90 |
| Asperg, W. Ger. | E4 | 19 |
| Aspermont, Tx., U.S. | C2 | 120 |
| Aspers, Pa., U.S. | G7 | 115 |
| Aspinwall, Ia., U.S. | C2 | 92 |
| Aspinwall, Pa., U.S. | k14 | 115 |
| Aspiring, Mount, mtn., N.Z. | P12 | 51 |
| Aspres [-sur-Buëch], Fr. | E1 | 20 |
| Aspropirgos, Grc. | g11 | 25 |
| Aspy Bay, b., N.S. | C9 | 71 |
| Asquith, Sask. | E2 | 75 |
| Assabet, stm., Ma., U.S. | g9 | 98 |
| Aş Şabyā, Sau. Ar. | C4 | 38 |
| Aş Şaff, Eg. | E3 | 41 |
| Aş Şaffānīyah, Sau. Ar. | C4 | 38 |
| Assaikwatam, stm., Man. | A3 | 70 |
| Aş Şāfī, Jord. | C7 | 41 |
| Aş Şāliḩīyah, Eg. | D4 | 41 |
| As Sallūm, Eg. | B2 | 38 |
| As Salṭ, Jord. | F10 | 41 |
| Assam, state, India | C9 | 36 |
| As Samū', Isr. Occ. | C7 | 41 |
| Aş Şanamayn, Syria | A8 | 41 |
| Assaria, Ks., U.S. | D6 | 93 |
| Assateague Island, i., U.S. | D7 | 97 |
| Assateague Island National Seashore, U.S. | D7 | 97 |
| Assawoman Bay, b., Md., U.S. | D7 | 97 |
| Assawompset Pond, l., Ma., U.S. | C6 | 98 |
| Assen, Neth. | A7 | 16 |
| Assens, Den. | C3 | 15 |
| Assens, Den. | B4 | 15 |
| As Sinbillāwayn, Eg. | D3 | 41 |
| Assini, I.C. | E4 | 45 |
| Assiniboia, Sask. | H2 | 75 |
| Assiniboine, stm., Can. | E2 | 70 |
| Assiniboine, Mount, mtn., Can. | D3 | 68 |
| Assinika, stm., Man. | C4 | 70 |
| Assinippi, Ma., U.S. | h12 | 98 |
| Assis, Braz. | C2 | 56 |
| Assis Brasil, Braz. | D4 | 58 |
| Assisi, Italy | C4 | 23 |
| Asso, Italy | E7 | 21 |
| Assonet, Ma., U.S. | C5 | 98 |
| As Sudd, reg., Sud. | D3 | 47 |
| Aş Şufīyah, Eg. | D3 | 41 |
| As Sulaymānīyah, Iraq | B4 | 38 |
| As Sulaymānīyah, Sau. Ar. | C4 | 38 |
| As Sulayyil, Sau. Ar. | A6 | 47 |
| As Sulṭān, Libya | C3 | 43 |
| Aş Şummān, plat., Sau. Ar. | H3 | 39 |
| Assumption, Il., U.S. | D4 | 90 |
| Assumption, co., La., U.S. | E4 | 95 |
| As Suwaydā', Syria | F11 | 40 |
| Astakós, Grc. | C3 | 25 |
| Āstārā, Iran | B5 | 39 |
| Asten, Neth. | C5 | 17 |
| Asterābād see Gorgān, Iran | | |
| Asti, Italy | B2 | 23 |
| Astipálaia, i., Grc. | l11 | 25 |
| Astola, i., Pak. | D6 | 40 |
| Aston, Pa., U.S. | *p20 | 115 |
| Aston Jonction, Que. | C5 | 74 |
| Astor, Fl., U.S. | C5 | 86 |
| Astorga, Spain | A2 | 22 |
| Astoria, Il., U.S. | C3 | 90 |
| Astoria, Or., U.S. | A3 | 114 |
| Astoria, S.D., U.S. | C9 | 118 |
| Astorville, Ont. | A5 | 73 |
| Astrakhan, Sov. Un. | E7 | 29 |
| Astura, stm., Italy | h9 | 23 |
| Asturias, hist. reg., Spain | A2 | 22 |
| Asuisui, Cape, c., W. Sam. | F11 | 52 |
| Asuke, Japan | n16 | 33 |
| Asunción, Para. | E4 | 55 |
| Asunción Mita, Guat. | C3 | 62 |
| Asunción Nochixtlán, Mex. | o15 | 63 |
| Asunden, l., Swe. | A7 | 15 |
| Aswān, Eg. | C3 | 38 |
| Aswān High Dam, Eg. | C3 | 38 |
| Asyūṭ, Eg. | C3 | 38 |
| Atacama, prov., Chile | B3 | 55 |
| Atacama, Salar de, pl., Chile | D2 | 55 |
| Atacama Desert, des., Chile | D2 | 55 |
| 'Aṭā'iṭah, Jabal al, mtn., Jord. | D7 | 41 |
| Atakpamé, Togo | E5 | 45 |
| Atalaia, Braz. | k5 | 57 |
| Atalaia do Norte, Braz. | B3 | 58 |
| Atalándi, Grc. | C4 | 25 |
| Atalaya, Peru | D3 | 58 |
| Atalissa, Ia., U.S. | C6 | 92 |
| Atami, Japan | n18 | 33 |
| Atar, Maur. | B2 | 45 |
| 'Aṭārūt, Isr. Occ. | h11 | 41 |
| Atascadero, Ca., U.S. | E3 | 82 |
| Atascosa, co., Tx., U.S. | E3 | 120 |
| Atasu, Sov. Un. | D8 | 28 |
| Ataúro, i., Indon. | G7 | 34 |
| Atáviros, mtn., Grc. | D6 | 25 |
| 'Aṭbarah, Sud. | B3 | 47 |
| 'Aṭbarah, stm., Afr. | B4 | 47 |
| Atbasar, Sov. Un. | D9 | 28 |
| Atchafalaya, stm., La., U.S. | D4 | 95 |
| Atchafalaya Bay, b., La., U.S. | E4 | 95 |
| Atchison, Ks., U.S. | C8 | 93 |
| Atchison, co., Ks., U.S. | C8 | 93 |
| Atchison, co., Mo., U.S. | A2 | 102 |
| Atco, N.J., U.S. | D3 | 107 |
| Atgidon, Puntan, c., N. Mar. Is. | E7 | 52 |
| Ath, Bel. | D3 | 17 |
| Athabasca, Alta. | B4 | 68 |
| Athabasca, stm., Alta. | f8 | 68 |
| Athabasca, Lake, l., Can. | m7 | 75 |
| Athalia, Oh., U.S. | D3 | 112 |
| Athalmer, B.C. | D10 | 69 |
| Athapapuskow Lake, l., Man. | B1 | 70 |
| Atha Road (part of Pickering), Ont. | k15 | 73 |
| Athboy, Ire. | D5 | 11 |
| Athelstan, Que. | D3 | 74 |
| Athenry, Ire. | D3 | 11 |
| Athens, Ont. | C9 | 73 |
| Athens, Al., U.S. | A3 | 78 |
| Athens, Ar., U.S. | C2 | 81 |
| Athens, Ga., U.S. | C3 | 87 |
| Athens, Il., U.S. | D4 | 90 |
| Athens, La., U.S. | B2 | 95 |
| Athens, Me., U.S. | D3 | 96 |
| Athens, Mi., U.S. | F5 | 99 |
| Athens, N.Y., U.S. | C7 | 109 |
| Athens, Oh., U.S. | C3 | 112 |
| Athens, Pa., U.S. | C8 | 115 |
| Athens, Tn., U.S. | D9 | 119 |
| Athens, Tx., U.S. | C5 | 120 |
| Athens, Vt., U.S. | E3 | 122 |
| Athens, W.V., U.S. | D3 | 125 |
| Athens, co., Oh., U.S. | C3 | 112 |
| Athens (Athínai), Grc. | D4 | 40 |
| Athensville, Il., U.S. | D3 | 90 |
| Atherley, Ont. | C5 | 73 |
| Atherton, Austl. | C8 | 50 |
| Athertonville, Ky., U.S. | *C4 | 94 |
| Athi, stm., Kenya | B6 | 48 |
| Athiémé, Benin | E5 | 45 |
| Athleague, Ire. | D3 | 10 |
| Athlone, Ire. | D3 | 10 |
| Athok, Burma | E10 | 36 |
| Athol, Id., U.S. | B2 | 89 |
| Athol, Ks., U.S. | C5 | 93 |
| Athol, Ma., U.S. | A3 | 98 |
| Athol, S.D., U.S. | C7 | 118 |
| Athol Island, i., Bah. | m18 | 64 |
| Ath Thamad, Eg. | D6 | 43 |
| Athy, Ire. | D3 | 11 |
| Ati, Chad | F9 | 45 |
| Atibaia, Braz. | m8 | 56 |
| Atico, Peru | E3 | 58 |
| Atikameg, Alta. | B3 | 68 |
| Atikameg Lake, l., Man. | B4 | 70 |
| Atikokan, Ont. | o17 | 73 |
| Atikonak Lake, l., Newf. | h8 | 72 |
| Atimonan, Phil. | p13 | 34 |
| Atiquizaya, El Sal. | D3 | 62 |
| Atka, Ak., U.S. | E5 | 79 |
| Atka Island, i., Ak., U.S. | E5 | 79 |
| Atkarsk, Sov. Un. | F15 | 27 |
| Atkins, Ar., U.S. | B3 | 81 |
| Atkins, Va., U.S. | D1 | 123 |
| Atkinson, Ga., U.S. | E5 | 87 |
| Atkinson, Il., U.S. | B3 | 90 |
| Atkinson, Ne., U.S. | B7 | 104 |
| Atkinson, N.H., U.S. | E4 | 106 |
| Atkinson, N.C., U.S. | C4 | 110 |
| Atkinson, co., Ga., U.S. | E4 | 87 |
| Atkinson Lake, l., Man. | A4 | 70 |
| Atlanta, Ga., U.S. | C2 | 87 |
| Atlanta, Id., U.S. | F3 | 89 |
| Atlanta, Il., U.S. | C4 | 90 |
| Atlanta, In., U.S. | D5 | 91 |
| Atlanta, Ks., U.S. | E7 | 93 |
| Atlanta, La., U.S. | C3 | 95 |
| Atlanta, Mi., U.S. | C6 | 99 |
| Atlanta, Mo., U.S. | B5 | 102 |
| Atlanta, Ne., U.S. | D6 | 104 |
| Atlanta, N.Y., U.S. | C3 | 109 |
| Atlanta, Oh., U.S. | C2 | 112 |
| Atlanta, Tx., U.S. | C5 | 120 |
| Atlantic, Ia., U.S. | C2 | 92 |
| Atlantic, N.C., U.S. | C6 | 110 |
| Atlantic, co., N.J., U.S. | E3 | 107 |
| Atlantic Beach, Fl., U.S. | m9 | 86 |
| Atlantic City, N.J., U.S. | E4 | 107 |
| Atlantic City, Wy., U.S. | D4 | 127 |
| Atlantic Highlands, N.J., U.S. | C4 | 107 |
| Atlantic Mine, Mi., U.S. | A2 | 99 |
| Atlantic Ocean | G8 | 2 |
| Atlántico, dept., Col. | A2 | 60 |
| Atlas Mountains, mts., Afr. | C4 | 44 |
| Atlas Saharien, mts., Alg. | C5 | 44 |
| Atlee, Alta. | D5 | 68 |
| Atlin, B.C. | m16 | 69 |
| Atlin Lake, l., Can. | E6 | 66 |
| 'Atlit, Isr. | B6 | 41 |
| Atlixco, Mex. | n14 | 63 |
| Atmore, Al., U.S. | D2 | 78 |
| Atna Peak, mtn., B.C. | C3 | 69 |
| Atocha, Bol. | D2 | 55 |
| Atoka, N.M., U.S. | E5 | 108 |
| Atoka, Ok., U.S. | C5 | 113 |
| Atoka, Tn., U.S. | B2 | 119 |
| Atoka, co., Ok., U.S. | C5 | 113 |
| Atoka Reservoir, res., Ok., U.S. | C5 | 113 |
| Atomic City, Id., U.S. | F6 | 89 |
| Atotonilco el Alto, Mex. | m12 | 63 |
| Atoyac, Mex. | m12 | 63 |
| Atoyac, stm., Mex. | n14 | 63 |
| Atrak, stm., Asia | B5 | 38 |
| Átran, stm., Swe. | B6 | 15 |
| Atrato, stm., Col. | B2 | 60 |
| Atrek (Atrak), stm., Asia | C7 | 39 |
| Atsugi, Japan | n18 | 33 |
| Atsukeshi Bay, b., Japan | E12 | 33 |
| Atsuma, Japan | E10 | 33 |
| Atsumi, Japan | o16 | 33 |
| Atsumi Bay, b., Japan | o16 | 33 |
| At Tabbīn, Eg. | E3 | 41 |
| Aṭ Ṭafīlah, Jord. | G10 | 40 |
| Aṭ Ṭā'if, Sau. Ar. | C4 | 38 |
| Attalla, Al., U.S. | A3 | 78 |
| Attalla, co., Ms., U.S. | B4 | 101 |
| Aṭ Ṭallāb, Libya | E4 | 43 |
| At Tamīmī, Libya | C4 | 43 |
| Attapu, Laos | C3 | 34 |
| Attapulgus, Ga., U.S. | F2 | 87 |
| 'Aṭṭārah, Isr. Occ. | h11 | 41 |
| Attawapiskat, Ont. | n19 | 73 |
| Attawapiskat, stm., Ont. | n18 | 73 |
| Attawaugan, Ct., U.S. | B8 | 84 |
| Aṭ Ṭayrīyah, Eg. | D2 | 41 |
| Attean Pond, l., Me., U.S. | C2 | 96 |
| Atterberry, Il., U.S. | C4 | 90 |
| Attica, In., U.S. | D3 | 91 |
| Attica, Ks., U.S. | E5 | 93 |
| Attica, Mi., U.S. | E7 | 99 |
| Attica, N.Y., U.S. | C2 | 109 |
| Attica, Oh., U.S. | A3 | 112 |
| Attica, hist. reg., Grc. | g11 | 25 |
| Attigny, Fr. | E4 | 17 |
| Attikamagen Lake, l., Newf. | g8 | 72 |
| Aṭ Ṭīnah, Eg. | C4 | 41 |
| Attleboro, Ma., U.S. | C5 | 98 |
| Attleborough, Eng., U.K. | B9 | 12 |
| Attock, Pak. | B5 | 36 |
| Attu Island, i., Ak., U.S. | E2 | 79 |
| Aṭ Ṭūr, Eg. | D6 | 43 |
| Aṭ Ṭūr, Isr. Occ. | m14 | 41 |
| Aṭ Ṭuwayyah, Sau. Ar. | I13 | 40 |
| Attymon, Ire. | D3 | 11 |
| Atuel, stm., Arg. | B3 | 54 |
| Atui, Uad, val., Afr. | B2 | 45 |
| Atu'u, Am. Sam. | F13 | 52 |
| Åtvidaberg, Swe. | H6 | 14 |
| Atwater, Sask. | G4 | 75 |
| Atwater, Ca., U.S. | D3 | 82 |
| Atwater, Mn., U.S. | E4 | 100 |
| Atwater, Oh., U.S. | A4 | 112 |
| Atwood, Ont. | D3 | 73 |
| Atwood, Co., U.S. | A7 | 83 |
| Atwood, Il., U.S. | D5 | 90 |
| Atwood, Ks., U.S. | C2 | 93 |
| Atwood, Ok., U.S. | C5 | 113 |
| Atwood, Tn., U.S. | B3 | 119 |
| Atwood Lake, res., Oh., U.S. | B4 | 112 |
| Atwoodville, Ct., U.S. | B7 | 84 |
| Aua, Am. Sam. | F13 | 52 |
| Auau Channel, strt., Hi., U.S. | C5 | 88 |
| Aubagne, Fr. | F6 | 16 |
| Aube, dept., Fr. | F4 | 17 |
| Aube, stm., Fr. | E5 | 16 |
| Aubenas, Fr. | E6 | 16 |
| Auberry, Ca., U.S. | D4 | 82 |
| Aubervilliers, Fr. | g10 | 16 |
| Aubière, Fr. | E5 | 16 |
| Aubigny-sur-Nère, Fr. | D5 | 16 |
| Aubin, Fr. | E4 | 16 |
| Aubrey, Que. | D4 | 74 |
| Aubrey Cliffs, clf., Az., U.S. | B2 | 80 |
| Auburn, Ont. | D3 | 73 |
| Auburn, Al., U.S. | C4 | 78 |
| Auburn, Ca., U.S. | C3 | 82 |
| Auburn, Ga., U.S. | B3 | 87 |
| Auburn, Il., U.S. | D4 | 90 |
| Auburn, In., U.S. | B7 | 91 |
| Auburn, Ia., U.S. | B2 | 92 |
| Auburn, Ks., U.S. | D8 | 93 |
| Auburn, Ky., U.S. | D3 | 94 |
| Auburn, Me., U.S. | D2 | 96 |
| Auburn, Ma., U.S. | B4 | 98 |
| Auburn, Mi., U.S. | E6 | 99 |
| Auburn, Ne., U.S. | D10 | 104 |
| Auburn, N.H., U.S. | E4 | 106 |
| Auburn, N.Y., U.S. | C4 | 109 |
| Auburn, Pa., U.S. | E9 | 115 |
| Auburn, Wa., U.S. | B3 | 124 |
| Auburn, W.V., U.S. | B4 | 125 |
| Auburn, Wy., U.S. | D1 | 127 |
| Auburndale, Fl., U.S. | D5 | 86 |
| Auburndale, Wi., U.S. | D3 | 126 |
| Auburn Heights, Mi., U.S. | F7 | 99 |
| Auburntown, Tn., U.S. | B5 | 119 |
| Aubusson, Fr. | E5 | 16 |
| Auch, Fr. | F4 | 16 |
| Auchterarder, Scot., U.K. | D5 | 13 |
| Auckland, N.Z. | B3 | 51 |
| Auckland Islands, is., N.Z. | J8 | 2 |
| Audet, Que. | D7 | 74 |
| Audierne, Fr. | C1 | 16 |
| Audincourt, Fr. | D7 | 16 |
| Audrain, co., Mo., U.S | B6 | 102 |
| Audubon, Ia., U.S. | C3 | 92 |
| Audubon, Mn., U.S. | D3 | 100 |
| Audubon, N.J., U.S. | D2 | 107 |
| Audubon, Pa., U.S. | *F11 | 115 |
| Audubon, co., Ia., U.S. | C2 | 92 |
| Aue, E. Ger. | C6 | 18 |
| Auerbach, E. Ger. | C7 | 19 |
| Augathella, Austl. | B6 | 51 |
| Auggen, W. Ger. | A4 | 21 |
| Aughnacloy, N. Ire., U.K. | C5 | 11 |
| Aughrim, Ire. | E5 | 11 |
| Auglaize, co., Oh., U.S. | B1 | 112 |
| Auglaize, stm., Oh., U.S. | A1 | 112 |
| Au Gres, Mi., U.S. | D7 | 99 |
| Augsburg, W. Ger. | D5 | 18 |
| August, Ca., U.S. | *D3 | 82 |
| Augusta, Austl. | F2 | 50 |
| Augusta, Italy | F5 | 23 |
| Augusta, Ar., U.S. | B4 | 81 |
| Augusta, Ga., U.S. | C5 | 87 |
| Augusta, Il., U.S. | C3 | 90 |
| Augusta, Ks., U.S. | E7 | 93 |
| Augusta, Ky., U.S. | B6 | 94 |
| Augusta, Me., U.S. | D3 | 96 |
| Augusta, Mi., U.S. | F5 | 99 |
| Augusta, Mo., U.S. | C7 | 102 |
| Augusta, Mt., U.S. | C4 | 103 |
| Augusta, N.J., U.S. | A3 | 107 |
| Augusta, Oh., U.S. | B4 | 112 |
| Augusta, W.V., U.S. | B6 | 125 |
| Augusta, Wi., U.S. | D2 | 126 |
| Augusta, co., Va., U.S. | B3 | 123 |
| Augusta Springs, Va., U.S. | B3 | 123 |
| Augusta Victoria Hospital, Isr. Occ. | m14 | 41 |
| Augustenborg, Den. | D3 | 15 |
| Augustów, Pol. | B7 | 26 |
| Augustus, Mount, mtn., Austl. | D2 | 50 |
| Aulander, N.C., U.S. | A5 | 110 |
| Auld, Lake, l., Austl. | D3 | 50 |
| Aulendorf, W. Ger. | B5 | 20 |
| Aulnay-sous-Bois, Fr. | g11 | 16 |
| Aulne, stm., Fr. | C2 | 16 |
| Aulneau Peninsula, pen., Ont. | E4 | 70 |
| Aulnoye [-Aymeries], Fr. | D3 | 17 |
| Ault, Co., U.S. | A6 | 83 |
| Ault, Piz, mtn., Switz. | C7 | 21 |
| Aumale, Fr. | E9 | 12 |
| Aumsville, Or., U.S. | k12 | 114 |
| Auneuil, Fr. | E2 | 17 |
| Auno, Nig. | D7 | 45 |
| Aunu'u Island, i., Am. Sam. | G13 | 52 |
| Aur, i., Malay. | K6 | 35 |
| Auraiya, India | D7 | 37 |
| Aurangābād, India | E6 | 36 |
| Auray, Fr. | D2 | 16 |
| Aurelia, Ia., U.S. | B2 | 92 |
| Aurelian Springs, N.C., U.S. | A5 | 110 |
| Aurich, W. Ger. | B3 | 18 |
| Auriflama, Braz. | C2 | 56 |
| Aurillac, Fr. | C5 | 16 |
| Aurora, Guy. | A3 | 59 |
| Aurora, Ont. | C5 | 73 |
| Aurora, Co., U.S. | B6 | 83 |
| Aurora, Il., U.S. | B5 | 90 |
| Aurora, In., U.S. | F8 | 91 |
| Aurora, Ks., U.S. | C6 | 93 |
| Aurora, Me., U.S. | D4 | 96 |
| Aurora, Mn., U.S. | C6 | 100 |
| Aurora, Mo., U.S. | D4 | 102 |
| Aurora, Ne., U.S. | D8 | 104 |
| Aurora, N.Y., U.S. | C4 | 109 |
| Aurora, N.C., U.S. | B6 | 110 |
| Aurora, Oh., U.S. | A4 | 112 |
| Aurora, Or., U.S. | B4 | 114 |
| Aurora, S.D., U.S. | C9 | 118 |
| Aurora, Ut., U.S. | E4 | 121 |
| Aurora, W.V., U.S. | B5 | 125 |
| Aurora, Wi., U.S. | C5 | 126 |
| Aurora, co., S.D., U.S. | D7 | 118 |
| Aurora Center, S.D., U.S. | D7 | 118 |
| Aurskog, Nor. | *p29 | 14 |
| Aus, Nmb. | E3 | 49 |
| Au Sable, stm., Mi., U.S. | D6 | 99 |
| Ausable, stm., N.Y., U.S. | f11 | 109 |
| Au Sable, North Branch, stm., Mi., U.S. | D6 | 99 |
| Au Sable Forks, N.Y., U.S. | f11 | 109 |
| Au Sable Point, c., Mi., U.S. | B4 | 99 |
| Au Sable Point, c., Mi., U.S. | D7 | 99 |
| Auschwitz see Oświęcim, Pol. | | |
| Aussa, stm., Eth. | C9 | 47 |
| Austell, Ga., U.S. | h7 | 87 |
| Austerlitz see Slavkov, Czech. | | |
| Austin, Man. | D2 | 70 |
| Austin, In., U.S. | G6 | 91 |
| Austin, Ky., U.S. | D4 | 94 |
| Austin, Mn., U.S. | G6 | 100 |
| Austin, Nv., U.S. | D4 | 105 |
| Austin, Pa., U.S. | C5 | 115 |
| Austin, Tx., U.S. | D4 | 120 |
| Austin, co., Tx., U.S. | E4 | 120 |
| Austin, Lake, l., Austl. | E3 | 50 |
| Austinburg, Oh., U.S. | A5 | 112 |
| Austintown, Oh., U.S. | A5 | 112 |
| Austinville, Ia., U.S. | B5 | 92 |
| Australia, ctry., Oc. | | |
| Australian Capital Territory, ter., Austl. | G7 | 51 |
| Austria, ctry., Eur. | E7 | 18 |
| Austvågøy, i., Nor. | B10 | 14 |
| Austwell, Tx., U.S. | E4 | 120 |
| Autauga, co., Al., U.S. | C3 | 78 |
| Autaugaville, Al., U.S. | C3 | 78 |
| Authie, stm., Fr. | D2 | 17 |
| Autlán de Navarro, Mex. | H7 | 63 |
| Au Train, Mi., U.S. | B4 | 99 |
| Autun, Fr. | E6 | 16 |
| Auvergne, Ar., U.S. | B4 | 81 |
| Auvergne, hist. reg., Fr. | E5 | 16 |
| Auvergne Mountains, mts., Fr. | E5 | 16 |
| Auvers [-sur-Oise], Fr. | E2 | 17 |
| Auxerre, Fr. | D5 | 16 |
| Auxi-le-Château, Fr. | D2 | 17 |
| Auxier, Ky., U.S. | C7 | 94 |
| Auxonne, Fr. | D6 | 16 |
| Auxvasse, Mo., U.S. | B6 | 102 |
| Auyán Tepuy, mtn., Ven. | B5 | 60 |
| Auyuittuq National Park, N.W. Ter. | C19 | 66 |
| Auzangate, Nevado, mtn., Peru | D3 | 58 |
| Ava, Il., U.S. | F4 | 90 |
| Ava, Mo., U.S. | E5 | 102 |
| Ava, Oh., U.S. | C4 | 112 |
| Avakubi, Zaire | A4 | 48 |
| Avallon, Fr. | D5 | 16 |
| Avalon, Ca., U.S. | F4 | 82 |
| Avalon, Ga., U.S. | B3 | 87 |
| Avalon, Ms., U.S. | B3 | 101 |
| Avalon, Mo., U.S. | B4 | 102 |
| Avalon, N.J., U.S. | E3 | 107 |
| Avalon, Pa., U.S. | h13 | 115 |
| Avalon, Lake, res., N.M., U.S. | E5 | 108 |
| Avalon Peninsula, pen., Newf. | E5 | 72 |
| Avanos, Tur. | C10 | 40 |
| Avant, Ok., U.S. | A5 | 113 |
| Avaré, Braz. | B2 | 56 |
| Aveiro, Port. | E2 | 22 |
| Avella, Pa., U.S. | F1 | 115 |
| Avellaneda, Arg. | A5 | 54 |
| Avellino, Italy | D5 | 23 |
| Avenal, Ca., U.S. | E3 | 82 |
| Avenches, Switz. | C3 | 21 |
| Avenel, Md., U.S. | *B4 | 97 |
| Avenel, N.J., U.S. | k7 | 107 |
| Avening, Ont. | C5 | 73 |
| Aventura, Fl., U.S. | *G6 | 86 |
| Avenue, Md., U.S. | D4 | 97 |
| Avenwedde, W. Ger. | B3 | 19 |
| Avera, Ga., U.S. | C4 | 87 |
| Averill Park, N.Y., U.S. | C7 | 109 |
| Averøy, i., Nor. | E7 | 14 |
| Avery, Id., U.S. | B3 | 89 |
| Avery, Ok., U.S. | A5 | 113 |
| Avery, Tx., U.S. | C5 | 120 |
| Avery, co., N.C., U.S. | e11 | 110 |
| Avery Island, La., U.S. | E4 | 95 |
| Avesnes, Fr. | D3 | 17 |
| Avesta, Swe. | G7 | 14 |
| Avezzano, Italy | C4 | 23 |
| Aviá Terai, Arg. | E5 | 55 |
| Aviemore, Scot., U.K. | C5 | 13 |
| Avigliano, Italy | D5 | 23 |
| Avignon, Fr. | F6 | 16 |
| Ávila, Spain | B3 | 22 |
| Avila Beach, Ca., U.S. | E3 | 82 |
| Avilés, Spain | A3 | 22 |
| Avis, Pa., U.S. | D7 | 115 |
| Avisio, stm., Italy | C7 | 20 |
| Aviston, Il., U.S. | E4 | 90 |
| Avlón, Grc. | g11 | 25 |
| Avoca, Al., U.S. | A2 | 78 |
| Avoca, Ar., U.S. | A1 | 81 |
| Avoca, Ia., U.S. | C2 | 92 |
| Avoca, Mi., U.S. | E8 | 99 |
| Avoca, Ne., U.S. | h12 | 104 |
| Avoca, N.Y., U.S. | C3 | 109 |
| Avoca, Pa., U.S. | m18 | 115 |
| Avoca, Tx., U.S. | C3 | 120 |
| Avoca, Wi., U.S. | E3 | 126 |
| Avola, B.C. | D8 | 69 |
| Avola, Italy | F5 | 23 |
| Avon, Ont. | E4 | 73 |
| Avon, Ct., U.S. | B4 | 84 |
| Avon, Il., U.S. | C3 | 90 |
| Avon, Ma., U.S. | B5 | 98 |
| Avon, Mn., U.S. | E4 | 100 |
| Avon, N.Y., U.S. | C3 | 109 |
| Avon, N.C., U.S. | B7 | 110 |
| Avon, Oh., U.S. | A3 | 112 |
| Avon, S.D., U.S. | D7 | 118 |
| Avon, stm., Eng., U.K. | C5 | 12 |
| Avon, stm., Austl. | F2 | 50 |
| Avon, stm., Eng., U.K. | E6 | 12 |
| Avon, stm., Eng., U.K. | E6 | 12 |
| Avon, stm., Scot., U.K. | C5 | 13 |
| Avon by the Sea, N.J., U.S. | *C4 | 107 |
| Avondale, Az., U.S. | m8 | 80 |
| Avondale, Co., U.S. | C6 | 83 |
| Avondale, La., U.S. | *E5 | 95 |
| Avondale, Mo., U.S. | h10 | 102 |
| Avondale, Pa., U.S. | *C1 | 112 |
| Avondale, R.I., U.S. | G1 | 116 |
| Avondale Estates, Ga., U.S. | h8 | 87 |
| Avon Lake, Ia., U.S. | e8 | 92 |
| Avon Lake, Oh., U.S. | A3 | 112 |
| Avonlea, Sask. | G3 | 75 |
| Avonmore, Pa., U.S. | E3 | 115 |
| Avon Park, Fl., U.S. | E5 | 86 |
| Avoyelles, co., La., U.S. | C3 | 95 |
| Avranches, Fr. | D5 | 16 |
| Awa, Japan | o14 | 33 |
| Awaji, Japan | H8 | 33 |
| Awaji Island, i., Japan | I7 | 33 |
| Awash, Eth. | D5 | 47 |
| Awash, stm., Eth. | C8 | 47 |
| Awbārī, Libya | C8 | 43 |
| Awe, Loch, l., Scot., U.K. | D3 | 13 |
| Awjilah, Libya | C10 | 43 |
| Awka, Nig. | E6 | 45 |
| Awo Island, i., Japan | o14 | 33 |
| Axel, Neth. | D3 | 17 |
| Axel Heiberg Island, i., N.W. Ter. | m33 | 66 |
| Axial Basin, Co., U.S. | A2 | 83 |
| Axim, Ghana | F4 | 45 |
| Axis, Al., U.S. | E1 | 78 |
| Axiós (Vardar), stm., Eur. | B4 | 25 |
| Ax-les-Thermes, Fr. | A6 | 22 |
| Axson, Ga., U.S. | E4 | 87 |
| Axtell, Ks., U.S. | C7 | 93 |
| Axtell, Ne., U.S. | D6 | 104 |
| Axtell, Ut., U.S. | D4 | 121 |
| Aÿ, Fr. | C5 | 16 |
| Ay, stm., Sov. Un. | B5 | 28 |
| Ayabaca, Peru | B2 | 58 |
| Ayabe, Japan | n14 | 33 |
| Ayacucho, Arg. | B5 | 54 |
| Ayacucho, Peru | D3 | 58 |
| Ayacucho, dept., Peru | D3 | 58 |
| Ayamonte, Spain | D2 | 22 |
| Ayan, Sov. Un. | E11 | 29 |
| Ayapel, Col. | B2 | 60 |
| Ayaş, Tur. | B9 | 40 |
| Aydar, stm., Sov. Un. | G12 | 27 |
| Ayden, N.C., U.S. | B5 | 110 |
| Aydın, Tur. | D6 | 40 |
| Aydlett, N.C., U.S. | A7 | 110 |
| Ayer, Ma., U.S. | A4 | 98 |
| Ayers Cliff, Que. | D5 | 74 |
| Ayers Rock, mtn., Austl. | E5 | 50 |
| Ayeyarwady, stm., Burma | D10 | 36 |
| Ayia, Grc. | C6 | 25 |
| Ayía Paraskeví, Grc. | C6 | 25 |
| Áyioi Theódhoroi, Grc. | h10 | 25 |
| Ayiásos, Grc. | C6 | 25 |
| Áyios Dhimítrios, Grc. | g11 | 25 |
| Áyios Evstrátios, i., Grc. | C5 | 25 |
| Áyios Nikólaos, Grc. | B7 | 25 |
| Aylen Lake, l., Ont. | B7 | 73 |
| Aylesbury, Sask. | G3 | 75 |
| Aylesbury, Eng., U.K. | E6 | 10 |
| Aylesford, N.S. | D5 | 71 |
| Aylett, Va., U.S. | C5 | 123 |
| Aylmer, Mount, mtn., Alta. | D3 | 68 |
| Aylmer East, Que. | D2 | 74 |
| Aylmer Lake, l., N.W. Ter. | D11 | 66 |
| Aylmer West, Ont. | E4 | 73 |
| Aylsham, Sask. | D4 | 75 |
| Aynor, S.C., U.S. | D9 | 117 |
| 'Ayn Yabrūd, Isr. Occ. | h11 | 41 |
| Ayon Island, i., Sov. Un. | B9 | 29 |
| Ayora, Spain | C5 | 22 |
| Ayorou, Niger | D5 | 45 |
| 'Ayoûn el 'Atroûs, Maur. | C3 | 45 |
| 'Ayoûn, i., Austl. | C8 | 50 |
| Ayr, Ont. | D4 | 73 |
| Ayr, N.D., U.S. | B8 | 111 |
| Ayr, Scot., U.K. | C4 | 10 |
| Ayr, Ne., U.S. | D7 | 104 |
| Ayr, stm., Scot., U.K. | E4 | 13 |
| Ayre, Point of, c., I. of Man | F4 | 13 |
| Ayrshire, In., U.S. | H3 | 91 |
| Ayrshire, Ia., U.S. | A3 | 92 |
| Aysary, Sov. Un. | C8 | 28 |
| Aysha, Eth. | G7 | 14 |
| Ayton, Ont. | C4 | 73 |
| Aytré, Fr. | D3 | 16 |
| Ayu Islands, is., Indon. | E8 | 34 |
| Ayutla [de los Libres], Mex. | D5 | 63 |
| Ayvacık, Tur. | C6 | 40 |
| Ayvalık, Tur. | C6 | 40 |
| Āzamgarh, India | D9 | 36 |
| Azaouâd, reg., Mali | C4 | 45 |
| Azaouak, Vallée de l', val., Afr. | D5 | 45 |
| Azare, Nig. | D7 | 45 |
| Āžar Shahr, Iran | B4 | 38 |
| Azcapotzalco (part of Mexico City), Mex. | h9 | 63 |
| Azemmour, Mor. | C3 | 44 |
| Azerbaijan, hist. reg., Iran | B4 | 38 |
| Azerbaijan S.S.R., state, Sov. Un. | E7 | 29 |
| Aziscohos Lake, l., Me., U.S. | C1 | 96 |
| Azle, Tx., U.S. | n9 | 120 |
| Azogues, Ec. | B2 | 58 |
| Azov, Sea of, Sov. Un. | E6 | 29 |
| Azov, Sov. Un. | E6 | 29 |
| Azrou, Mor. | C3 | 44 |
| Aztec, Az., U.S. | E2 | 80 |
| Aztec, N.M., U.S. | A2 | 108 |
| Aztec Peak, mtn., Az., U.S. | D5 | 80 |
| Aztec Ruins National Monument, N.M., U.S. | A1 | 108 |
| Azua, Dom. Rep. | E8 | 64 |
| Azuaga, Spain | C3 | 22 |
| Azuay, prov., Ec. | B2 | 58 |
| Azuero, Península de, pen., Pan. | G7 | 62 |
| Azul, Arg. | B5 | 54 |
| Azul, Cordillera, mts., Peru | C3 | 58 |
| Azul, Serra, plat., Braz. | A2 | 56 |
| Azusa, Ca., U.S. | m13 | 82 |
| Az Zabdānī, Syria | F11 | 40 |
| Az Zāhirīyah, Isr. Occ. | C6 | 41 |
| Az Zahrān (Dhahran), Sau. Ar. | C4 | 38 |
| Az Zaqāzīq, Eg. | D3 | 41 |
| Az Zarqā', Jord. | B3 | 38 |
| Az Zāwiyah, Libya | B8 | 43 |
| Az Zaydāb, Sud. | B3 | 47 |
| 'Azzah, Ra's, c., Libya | C4 | 43 |
| Azzel Matti, Sebkha, pl., Alg. | D5 | 44 |
| Az Zubayr, Iraq | F3 | 39 |
| 'Azzūn, Isr. Occ. | g11 | 41 |

**B**

| Name | Map Ref. | Page |
|---|---|---|
| Baal, W. Ger. | C6 | 17 |
| Baalbek, Leb. | B3 | 38 |
| Baar, Switz. | B6 | 21 |
| Baardheere, Som. | C7 | 47 |
| Baarle-Hertog, Bel. | C3 | 16 |
| Baargaal, Som. | C7 | 47 |
| Baba Burnu, c., Tur. | C6 | 40 |
| Baba, i., Indon. | G7 | 34 |
| Babaeski, Tur. | B6 | 25 |
| Babahoyo, Ec. | B2 | 58 |
| Babana, Nig. | D5 | 45 |
| Babanūsah, Sud. | C7 | 47 |
| Babar Islands, is., Indon. | G7 | 34 |
| Babayevo, Sov. Un. | B11 | 27 |
| Bābil, Iraq | B3 | 38 |
| Babb, Mt., U.S. | B3 | 103 |
| Babbie, Al., U.S. | D3 | 78 |
| Babbitt, Mn., U.S. | C7 | 100 |
| Babbitt, Nv., U.S. | E3 | 105 |
| Babcock, Wi., U.S. | D3 | 126 |
| Babelthuap International Airport, Palau | R17 | 52 |
| Babenhausen, W. Ger. | A6 | 20 |
| Babi, i., Indon. | K2 | 34 |
| Babine, stm., B.C. | B4 | 69 |
| Babine Range, mts., B.C. | B4 | 69 |
| Babo, Indon. | F8 | 34 |

Name | Map Ref. | Page


Bābol, Iran B5 38
Bābol Sar, Iran C6 39
Baboosic Lake, N.H., U.S. E3 106
*Baboquivari Mountains, mts., Az., U.S.* F4 80
*Baboquivari Peak, mtn., Az., U.S.* F4 80
Baboua, Cen. Afr. Rep. D2 46
Babson Park, Fl., U.S. E5 86
Babuškin, Sov. Un. A6 31
*Babuyan Islands, is., Phil.* B6 34
Babyak, Bul. E6 24
Babylon, N.Y., U.S. n15 109
*Baca, co., Co., U.S.* D8 83
Bacabal, Braz. B2 57
*Bacajá, stm., Braz.* C4 59
Bacalar, Mex. D7 63
*Bacan, i., Indon.* F7 34
Bacău, Rom. B8 24
*Baccalieu Island, i., Newf.* D5 72
Bac Can, Viet. A6 35
Baccarat, Fr. C7 16
*Baccaro Point, c., N.S.* F4 71
Bacerac, Mex. A3 63
Bach, Mi., U.S. E7 99
Bacharach, W. Ger. C2 19
*Bach Long Vi, i., Viet.* B7 35
*Back, stm., N.W. Ter.* C12 66
*Back, stm., S.C., U.S.* h12 117
Bačka Palanka, Yugo. C4 24
Bačka Topola, Yugo. C4 24
Back Bay, N.B. D3 71
*Backbone Mountain, mtn., U.S.* m12 97
Backnang, W. Ger. E4 19
Backoo, N.D., U.S. A8 111
Backus, Mn., U.S. D4 100
Bac Lieu, Viet. D3 34
Bac Ninh, Viet. A3 34
Bacobi, Az., U.S. B5 80
Bacolod, Phil. C6 34
*Bacon, co., Ga., U.S.* E4 87
Baconton, Ga., U.S. E2 87
Bacoor, Phil. o13 34
Bacova, Va., U.S. B3 123
Bac Quang, Viet. A6 35
Bacqueville-en-Caux, Fr. E9 12
Bácsalmás, Hung. B4 24
Bácum, Mex. B2 63
*Bad, stm., S.D., U.S.* C5 118
*Bad, stm., Wi., U.S.* B3 126
Badagara, India F6 36
Bad Aibling, W. Ger. B7 20
Badajoz, Spain C2 22
Badalona, Spain B7 22
Badanah, Sau. Ar. B4 38
Bad Axe, Mi., U.S. E8 99
Bad Bergzabern, W. Ger. D2 19
Bad Berneck, W. Ger. C6 19
Bad Bramstedt, W. Ger. C4 18
Baddeck, N.S. C9 71
Bad Doberan, E. Ger. A5 18
Bad Düben, E. Ger. B7 19
Baden, Ont. D4 73
Baden, Switz. E4 18
Baden, Pa., U.S. E1 115
*Baden, hist. reg., W. Ger.* D4 18
Baden-Baden, W. Ger. D4 18
Baden [bei Wien], Aus. D8 18
*Baden-Württemberg, state, W. Ger.* D4 19
Bad Freienwalde, E. Ger. B7 18
Bad Friedrichshall, W. Ger. D4 19
Badgastein, Aus. E6 18
Badger, Newf. D3 72
Badger, Ia., U.S. B3 92
Badger, Mn., U.S. B2 100
Badger, S.D., U.S. C8 118
*Badger Creek, stm., Co., U.S.* B7 83
Bad Godesberg, W. Ger. C2 19
Bad Hersfeld, W. Ger. C4 18
Bad Homburg [vor der Höhe], W. Ger. C4 18
Bad Honnef, W. Ger. C2 19
Bad Hönningen, W. Ger. C2 19
Badia Polesine, Italy D7 20
Badīn, Pak. E2 37
Badin, N.C., U.S. B2 110
*Badin Lake, res., N.C., U.S.* B2 110
Bad Ischl, Aus. E6 18
Bad Kissingen, W. Ger. C5 18
Bad Kreuznach, W. Ger. D3 18
*Badlands, hills, S.D., U.S.* D3 118
*Badlands, reg., U.S.* C2 111
*Badlands National Park, S.D., U.S.* D3 118
Bad Langensalza, E. Ger. C5 18
Bad Lauterberg, W. Ger. B5 19
Bad Leonfelden, Aus. E9 19
Bad Liebenwerda, E. Ger. B8 19
Bad Lippspringe, W. Ger. B3 19
Bad Mergentheim, W. Ger. D4 19
Bad Münstereifel, W. Ger. C1 19
Bad Muskau, E. Ger. B9 19
Bad Nauheim, W. Ger. C3 19
Bad Neustadt [an der Saale], W. Ger. C5 19
Bad Oeynhausen, W. Ger. A3 19
Bad Oldesloe, W. Ger. B5 18
Badong, China E7 31
Bad Orb, W. Ger. C4 19
Badoumbé, Mali D2 45
Bad Pyrmont, W. Ger. B4 19
Bad Ragaz, Switz. E4 18
Bad Reichenhall, W. Ger. E6 18
*Bad River Indian Reservation, Wi., U.S.* B3 126
Bad Salzuflen, W. Ger. B4 18
Bad Salzungen, E. Ger. C5 19
Bad Schandau, E. Ger. C9 19
Bad Segeberg, W. Ger. E4 15
Bad Sülze, E. Ger. D6 15
Bad Tennstedt, E. Ger. B5 19
Bad Tölz, W. Ger. E5 18
*Badu, i., Austl.* A7 50
Badulla, Sri L. G7 36
*Badwater Creek, stm., Wy., U.S.* C5 127
Bad Wildungen, W. Ger. B4 19
Bad Windsheim, W. Ger. D5 19
Bad Wörishofen, W. Ger. B6 20
Bad Wurzach, W. Ger. B5 20
Baena, Spain D3 22
Baependi, Braz. C4 56
Baeza, Ec. B2 58
Baeza, Spain D4 22
Bafang, Cam. D2 46
Bafatá, Gui.-B. D2 45
*Baffin Bay, b., N.A.* B14 61
*Baffin Bay, b., Tx., U.S.* E4 120
*Baffin Island, i., N.W. Ter.* C18 66
Bafia, Cam. E2 46
Bafoulabé, Mali D2 45
Bafoussam, Cam. *D2 46
Bāfq, Iran B5 38
Bafra, Tur. B10 40
*Bafra, Cape, c., Tur.* B11 40
Bāft, Iran G8 39
Bafwasende, Zaire A4 48
Bagabag, Phil. n13 34
Bagaces, C.R. E7 63
Bagamoyo, Tan. C6 48
Bagana, Nig. E6 45
Bagansiapiapi, Indon. E2 34
Bagata, Zaire B2 48
Bagdad, Az., U.S. C2 80
Bagdad, Fl., U.S. u14 86
Bagdad, Ky., U.S. B4 94
Bagé, Braz. E2 56
Bagenkop, Den. D4 15
Bāgerhāt, Bngl. F12 37
Baggs, Wy., U.S. E5 127
*Bāghah, 'Ayn al, well, Eg.* E5 41
Baghdād, Iraq B4 38
Bagheria, Italy E4 23
Baghlān, Afg. A4 36
Bagley, Ia., U.S. C3 92
Bagley, Mn., U.S. C3 100
Bagley, Wi., U.S. F2 126
Bagnacavallo, Italy E7 20
Bagnara [Calabra], Italy E5 23
*Bagnell Dam, Mo., U.S.* C5 102
Bagnères-de-Bigorre, Fr. F4 16
Bagnères-de-Luchon, Fr. F4 16
Bagnolet, Fr. g10 16
Bagnols, Fr. E6 16
Bago, Burma E10 36
*Bågø, i., Den.* C3 15
*Bagoé, stm., Afr.* D3 45
Bagolino, Italy D6 20
*Bagot, co., Que.* D5 74
Bagrationovsk, Sov. Un. A6 26
Baguio, Phil. B6 34
*Bagzane, Monts, mts., Niger* C6 45
Bahama, N.C., U.S. A4 110
*Bahamas, ctry., N.A.* B5 64
Bahār, Iran D4 39
Baharampur, India D8 36
Bahāwalnagar, Pak. C5 36
Bahāwalpur, Pak. C5 36
*Bahia, state, Braz.* D2 57
*Bahía, Islas de la, is., Hond.* D7 63
Bahía Blanca, Arg. B4 54
Bahia Bustamante, Arg. D3 54
Bahía de Caráquez, Ec. B1 58
Bahia Negra, Para. D4 55
Bahir Dar, Eth. C4 47
Bahraich, India D8 37
*Bahrain, ctry., Asia* C5 38
*Baḥr al Ghazāl, prov., Sud.* D2 47
*Baḥr aş Şāfī, des., Asia* D4 38
*Baḥrīyah, Al Wāḥāt al, well, Eg.* D5 43
Bāhū Kalāt, Iran I10 39
Baía dos Tigres, Ang. E1 48
Baia-Mare, Rom. B6 24
Baião, Braz. C5 59
Baibokoum, Chad D3 46
Baicheng, China E4 33
Baie-Comeau, Que. k13 74
Baie de Wasai, Mi., U.S. B6 99
Baie-d'Urfé, Que. q19 74
Baie-Johan-Beetz, Que. h9 72
Baiersbronn, W. Ger. E3 19
Baie-Sainte-Catherine, Que. A8 74
Baie-Saint-Paul, Que. B7 74
Baie Verte, N.B. C5 71
Baie Verte, Newf. D3 72
Baihe, China H4 32
*Baikal, Lake, l., Sov. Un.* D13 29
*Baikal Mountains, mts., Sov. Un.* D13 29
Baikunthpur, India F9 37
Bailén, Spain C4 22
Băilești, Rom. C6 24
Bailey, Co., U.S. B5 83
Bailey, Ms., U.S. C5 101
Bailey, N.C., U.S. B4 110
*Bailey, co., Tx., U.S.* B1 120
*Bailey Brook, stm., Me., U.S.* B2 96
Bailey Island, Me., U.S. g8 96
*Bailey Island, i., S.C., U.S.* k11 117
Baileys Crossroads, Va., U.S. g12 123
Baileys Harbor, Wi., U.S. C6 126
Baileyton, Al., U.S. A3 78
Baileyton, Tn., U.S. C11 119
Baileyville, Il., U.S. A4 90
Baileyville, Ks., U.S. C7 93
Bailieborough, Ire. D5 11
Bailundo, Ang. D2 48
Bainbridge, Ga., U.S. F2 87
Bainbridge, In., U.S. E4 91
Bainbridge, N.Y., U.S. C5 109
Bainbridge, Oh., U.S. C2 112
*Bainbridge Island, i., Wa., U.S.* e10 124
Bain-de-Bretagne, Fr. D3 16
Bains, La., U.S. D4 95
Bainville, Mt., U.S. B12 103
Baiquan, China B10 31
Baird, Ms., U.S. B3 101
Baird, Tx., U.S. C3 120
Bairdford, Pa., U.S. h14 115
*Baird Inlet, b., Ak., U.S.* C7 79
*Baird Mountains, mts., Ak., U.S.* B7 79
Bairiki, Kir. R18 52
*Bairiki, i., Kir.* R18 52
Bairin Youqi, China C8 32
Bairin Zuoqi, China B8 32
Bairnsdale, Austl. G8 50
Bairoil, Wy., U.S. D5 127
*Baïse, stm., Fr.* F4 16
Baixo Longa, Ang. E2 48
Baja, Hung. B4 24
*Baja California Norte, state, Mex.* A1 63
*Baja California Sur, state, Mex.* B2 63
Bajestān, Iran D9 39
*Bajimba, Mount, mtn., Austl.* D8 51
Bajmok, Yugo. C4 24
Bajo Boquete, Pan. F6 62
Bajram-Ali, Sov. Un. C11 39
Bakala, Cen. Afr. Rep. D4 46
Bakar, Yugo. C2 24
Bakel, Sen. D2 45
Baker, Ca., U.S. E5 82
Baker, Fl., U.S. u15 86
Baker, La., U.S. D4 95
Baker, Mn., U.S. D6 100
Baker, Mt., U.S. D12 103
Baker, Nv., U.S. D7 105
Baker, N.D., U.S. A6 111
Baker, Ok., U.S. e9 113
Baker, Or., U.S. C9 114
*Baker, co., Fl., U.S.* B4 86
*Baker, co., Ga., U.S.* E2 87
*Baker, co., Or., U.S.* C9 114
*Baker, stm., N.H., U.S.* C3 106
*Baker, Mount, mtn., Wa., U.S.* A4 124
*Baker Butte, mtn., Az., U.S.* C4 80
Baker Hill, Al., U.S. D4 78
*Baker Island, i., Oc.* F11 6
*Baker Island, i., Ak., U.S.* n22 79
Baker Lake, N.W. Ter. D13 66
*Baker Lake, l., N.W. Ter.* D13 66
*Baker Lake, l., Me., U.S.* B3 96
*Baker Lake, res., Wa., U.S.* A4 124
*Baker Mountain, mtn., Me., U.S.* C3 96
Bakers, N.C., U.S. B2 110
*Bakers Bayou, stm., Ar., U.S.* k11 81
Bakersfield, Ca., U.S. E4 82
Bakersfield, Mo., U.S. E5 102
Bakersfield, Vt., U.S. B3 122
*Bakers Island, i., Ma., U.S.* f12 98
Bakers Mill, Fl., U.S. B4 86
Bakerstown, Pa., U.S. h14 115
Bakersville, Ct., U.S. B3 84
Bakersville, N.C., U.S. e10 110
Bakerton, W.V., U.S. B7 125
Bakewell, Eng., U.K. A6 12
Bakhchisaray, Sov. Un. I9 27
*Bakhmut, stm., Sov. Un.* q21 27
Bākhtarān (Kermānshāh), Iran B4 38
*Bakır, stm., Tur.* C6 25
Bako, Eth. D4 47
Bako, I.C. E3 45
*Bakony Mountains, mts., Hung.* B3 24
*Bakool, prov., Som.* E5 47
Bakouma, Cen. Afr. Rep. D4 46
*Bakoye, stm., Afr.* D3 45
Baku, Sov. Un. E7 29
Baku, Zaire A5 48
Bakundi, Nig. E7 45
Bakungan, Indon. K2 35
Bala, Ont. B5 73
Bal'a, Isr. Occ. f11 41
Balâ, Tur. C9 40
Bala, Wales, U.K. B4 12
Bala, Ks., U.S. C7 93
*Balabac Island, i., Phil.* D5 34
*Balabac Strait, strt., Asia* D5 34
*Balabalagun Islands, is., Indon.* F5 34
Balad, Iraq D2 39
Bālāghāt, India G8 37
Balaguer, Spain B6 22
Balaka, Mwi. D6 48
Balakhna, Sov. Un. D17 8
Balakhna, Sov. Un. D27 8
Balaklava, Austl. G2 51
Balakleya, Sov. Un. G11 27
Balakovo, Sov. Un. *D7 29
Balallan, Scot., U.K. B2 13
Bālā Morghāb, Afg. D11 39
Balancán [de Dominguez], Mex. D6 63
Balanga, Phil. o13 34
Balāngīr, India G9 37
Balashov, Sov. Un. F14 27
Balassagyarmat, Hung. A4 24
Balaṭ, Eg. D5 43
Balaton, Mn., U.S. F3 100
*Balaton, Lake, l., Hung.* B3 24
Balayan, Phil. p13 34
*Balayan Bay, b., Phil.* p13 34
*Balbi, mtn., Pap. N. Gui.* *G9 6
Balboa, Pan. m11 62
Balboa Heights, Pan. m11 62
Balbriggan, Ire. D5 11
Balcad, Som. E6 47
Balcarce, Arg. B5 54
Balcarres, Sask. G4 75
Balch, Ar., U.S. B4 81
Balchik, Bul. D9 24
Balch Springs, Tx., U.S. *n10 120
Balclutha, N.Z. Q12 51
Bald Creek, N.C., U.S. f10 110
*Bald Eagle Lake, l., Mn., U.S.* m12 100
*Bald Eagle Lake, l., Mn., U.S.* C7 100
*Baldegger Lake, l., Switz.* B5 21
*Bald Hill, hill, R.I., U.S.* D2 116
*Baldhill Dam, N.D., U.S.* B7 111
Bald Knob, Ar., U.S. B4 81
*Bald Knob, mtn., Va., U.S.* c3 123
*Bald Knob, mtn., W.V., U.S.* C5 125
*Bald Knoll, mtn., Wy., U.S.* D2 127
*Bald Mountain, mtn., Ct., U.S.* B6 84
*Bald Mountain, mtn., N.J., U.S.* A4 107
*Bald Mountain, mtn., Or., U.S.* D5 114
*Bald Mountain, mtn., Or., U.S.* C9 114
*Bald Mountain, mtn., Vt., U.S.* B5 122
*Bald Mountain, mtn., Wy., U.S.* B5 127
*Bald Mountains, mts., N.C., U.S.* f10 110
*Baldock Lake, l., Man.* A3 70
Baldur, Man. E2 70
Baldwin, Fl., U.S. B5 86
Baldwin, Ga., U.S. B3 87
Baldwin, Il., U.S. E4 90
Baldwin, Ia., U.S. B7 92
Baldwin, La., U.S. E4 95
Baldwin, Md., U.S. B5 97
Baldwin, Mi., U.S. E5 99
Baldwin, N.Y., U.S. *E7 109
Baldwin, N.D., U.S. B5 111
Baldwin, Pa., U.S. k13 115
Baldwin, S.C., U.S. B5 117
Baldwin, Wi., U.S. D1 126
*Baldwin, co., Al., U.S.* E2 78
*Baldwin, co., Ga., U.S.* C3 87
Baldwin City, Ks., U.S. D8 93
Baldwin Heights, In., U.S. H2 91
Baldwin Park, Ca., U.S. *E4 82
Baldwinsville, N.Y., U.S. B4 109
Baldwinton, Sask. E1 75
Baldwinville, Ma., U.S. A3 98
Baldwyn, Ms., U.S. A5 101
*Baldy Mountain, mtn., B.C.* D7 69
*Baldy Mountain, mtn., Man.* D1 70
*Baldy Mountain, mtn., Mt., U.S.* B7 103
*Baldy Mountain, mtn., N.M., U.S.* A4 108
*Baldy Peak, mtn., Az., U.S.* D6 80
*Bale, prov., Eth.* D5 47
*Balearic Islands, is., Spain* C7 22
*Baleia, Ponta da, c., Braz.* E3 57
*Baleine, Rivière à la, stm., Que.* g13 74
Baler, Phil. o13 34
*Baler Bay, b., Phil.* o13 34
*Baleshare, i., Scot., U.K.* C1 13
Bāleshwar, India D8 36
*Balesin, i., Phil.* o14 34
Baleville, N.J., U.S. A3 107
Balfate, Hond. C4 62
Balfour, N.C., U.S. f10 110
Balfour, N.D., U.S. B5 111
Balgonie, Sask. G3 75
Bāli, India E4 37
*Bali, i., Indon.* G5 34
Balıkesir, Tur. C6 40
Balikpapan, Indon. F5 34
Balingen, W. Ger. A4 20
*Balintang Channel, strt., Phil.* B6 34
*Bali Sea, Indon.* G5 34
Baliuag, Phil. o13 34
Balje, W. Ger. B4 18
Baljennie, Sask. E2 75
Balkan, Ky., U.S. D6 94
*Balkan Mountains, mts., Eur.* D7 24
Balkh, Afg. A4 36
Balkhash, Sov. Un. E10 29
*Balkhash, Lake, l., Sov. Un.* E10 29
Balki, Sov. Un. H10 27
Balko, Ok., U.S. e10 113
Ball, La., U.S. C3 95
Balla, Ire. D2 11
Ballachulish, Scot., U.K. D3 13
Ballagh, Ire. E4 11
Ballaghaderreen, Ire. D3 11
Ballantine, Mt., U.S. E8 103
Ballantrae, Scot., U.K. C4 10
Ballarat (Ballaarat), Austl. G7 50
Ballard, Ok., U.S. A7 113
*Ballard, co., Ky., U.S.* e8 94
*Ballard, Lake, l., Austl.* E3 50
Ballardvale, Ma., U.S. f11 98
Ballater, Scot., U.K. B5 10
Ball Club, Mn., U.S. C5 100
*Ball Club Lake, l., Mn., U.S.* C5 100
Ballé, Mali C3 45
*Ballenas, Bahía de, b., Mex.* B2 63
Ballenstedt, E. Ger. B6 19
*Balleny Islands, is., Ant.* C29 7
Ballerup [-Målov], Den. C6 15
Ball Ground, Ga., U.S. B2 87
Ballia, India E10 37
Ballina, Austl. E9 50
Ballina, Ire. C2 10
Ballina, Ire. E3 11
Ballinakill, Ire. E4 11
Ballinalack, Ire. D4 11
Ballinascarty, Ire. F3 11
Ballinasloe, Ire. D2 10
Ballindine, Ire. D3 11
Ballineen, Ire. F3 11
Ballingarry, Ire. E3 11
Ballingeary, Ire. F2 11
Ballinger, Tx., U.S. D3 120
Ballinluig, Scot., U.K. D5 13
Ballinrobe, Ire. D2 11
*Ballinskelligs Bay, b., Ire.* F1 11
Ballintra, Ire. C3 11
Ballitore, Ire. D5 11
*Ball Mountain Lake, res., Vt., U.S.* E3 122
Ballouville, Ct., U.S. B8 84
Ballston, Or., U.S. B3 114
Ballston Spa, N.Y., U.S. B7 109
Ballwin, Mo., U.S. f12 102
Bally, Pa., U.S. F10 115
Ballybofey, Ire. C4 11
Ballybunnion, Ire. E2 11
Ballycanew, Ire. E5 11
Ballycastle, Ire. C2 11
Ballycastle, N. Ire., U.K. C3 10
Ballyconneely, Ire. D1 11
Ballyconnell, Ire. C4 11
Ballycroy, Ire. C2 11
Ballyduff, Ire. E3 11
Ballyduff, Ire. E2 11
Ballyferriter, Ire. E1 11
Ballygar, Ire. D3 11
Ballygorman, Ire. B4 11
Ballyhaunis, Ire. D3 11
Ballyheige, Ire. E2 11
*Ballyhoura Mountains, mts., Ire.* E3 11
Ballyjamesduff, Ire. D4 11
Ballykelly, N. Ire., U.K. B4 11
Ballylongford, Ire. E2 11
Ballymahon, Ire. D4 11
Ballymena, N. Ire., U.K. C3 10
Ballymoe, Ire. D3 11
Ballymoney, N. Ire., U.K. B5 11
Ballymote, Ire. C3 11
Ballymurray, Ire. D3 11
Ballynahinch, N. Ire., U.K. C6 11
Ballyneety, Ire. E3 11
Ballynoe, Ire. E3 11
Ballysadare, Ire. C3 11
Ballyshannon, Ire. C2 10
*Ballyteige Bay, b., Ire.* E5 11
Ballyvaghan, Ire. D2 11
Ballyvourney, Ire. F2 11
Balm, Fl., U.S. E4 86
Balmat, N.Y., U.S. A5 109
Balmazújváros, Hung. B5 24
*Balmhorn, mtn., Switz.* B3 21
Balmoral, Man. D3 70
Balmoral, N.B. B3 71
*Balmoral Castle, hist., Scot., U.K.* C5 13
Balmorhea, Tx., U.S. o13 120
Balmville, N.Y., U.S. D6 109
Baloda Bāzār, India G9 37
*Balonne, stm., Austl.* E8 50
Bālotra, India C5 36
Balrāmpur, India D9 37
Balranald, Austl. G4 51
Balș, Rom. C7 24
Balsam, N.C., U.S. f9 110
Balsam Lake, Wi., U.S. C1 126
*Balsam Lake, l., Ont.* C6 73
*Balsam Lake, l., Wi., U.S.* C1 126
Balsas, Braz. C1 57
Balsas, Mex. D5 63
*Balsas, stm., Braz.* C1 57
*Balsas, stm., Mex.* D4 63
*Balsas, Rio das, stm., Braz.* D1 57
Balsthal, Switz. B4 21
Balta, Sov. Un. H7 27
Balta, N.D., U.S. A5 111
Baltasar Brum, Ur. E1 56
Baltic, Ct., U.S. C7 84
Baltic, Oh., U.S. B4 112
Baltic, S.D., U.S. D9 118
*Baltic Sea, Eur.* I8 14
Baltīm, Eg. C3 41
Baltimore, Ont. C6 73
Baltimore, Ire. F2 11
Baltimore, Md., U.S. B4 97
Baltimore, Oh., U.S. C3 112
*Baltimore, co., Md., U.S.* B4 97
Baltimore Highlands, Md., U.S. h11 97
Baltinglass, Ire. E5 11
Baltiysk, Sov. Un. A5 26
*Baltra, Isla, i., Ec.* g5 58
Baltrum, W. Ger. A7 17
*Baltrum, i., W. Ger.* A7 17
*Baluchistan, hist. reg., Asia* C3 36
Balya, Tur. C6 25
Balzac, Alta. D3 68
Balzar, Ec. B2 58
Balzers, Liech. B8 21
Bam, Iran C5 38
Bama, Nig. D7 45
Bamako, Mali D3 45
Bamba, Mali C4 45
Bambang, Phil. n13 34
Bambari, Cen. Afr. Rep. D4 46
Bamberg, W. Ger. D5 18
Bamberg, S.C., U.S. E5 117
*Bamberg, co., S.C., U.S.* E5 117
Bamber Lake, N.J., U.S. D4 107
Bambesa, Zaire A4 48
Bambuí, Braz. C3 56
Bamburgh, Eng., U.K. E7 13
*Bam Co, l., China* B9 36
Bamenda, Cam. D2 46
Bampūr, Iran H10 39
*Bampūr, stm., Iran* H9 39
*Ban, Carn, mtn., Scot., U.K.* C4 13
Banagher, Ire. D4 11
*Banahao, Mount, mtn., Phil.* o13 34
Banalia, Zaire A4 48
Banamba, Mali D3 45
Banana, Zaire C1 48
Bananal, Braz. h5 56
*Bananal, Ilha do, i., Braz.* E4 59
*Banana River, b., Fl., U.S.* D6 86
Bananeiras, Braz. C3 57
*Banās, stm., India* E4 37
*Banās, Ra's, c., Eg.* C3 38
*Banat, hist. reg., Eur.* C5 24
Banbridge, N. Ire., U.K. C3 10
Banbury, Eng., U.K. D6 10
Banchory, Scot., U.K. C6 13
*Bancos, Bahía, b., Ec.* g5 58
Bancroft, Ont. B7 73
Bancroft, Id., U.S. G7 89
Bancroft, Ia., U.S. A3 92
Bancroft, Me., U.S. C4 96
Bancroft, Mi., U.S. F6 99
Bancroft, Ne., U.S. B9 104
Bancroft, S.D., U.S. C8 118
Bancroft, Wi., U.S. D4 126
Bānda, India C7 36
Banda Aceh, Indon. k11 34
*Banda Banda, Mount, mtn., Austl.* E9 51
*Banda Islands, is., Indon.* F7 34
*Bandama, stm., I.C.* E3 45
Bandana, Ky., U.S. e9 94
Bandar see Machilīpatnam, India E7 36
Bandar Baharu, Malay. J4 35
Bandar Beheshtī, Iran I10 39
Bandar-e 'Abbās, Iran C5 38
Bandar-e Anzalī (Bandar-e Pahlavī), Iran B4 38
Bandar-e Būshehr, Iran G5 39
Bandar-e Deylam, Iran F5 39
Bandar-e Khomeynī (Bandar-e Shāhpūr), Iran F4 39
Bandar-e Lengeh, Iran H7 39
Bandar-e Māhshahr, Iran *F4 39
Bandar-e Pahlavī see Bandar-e Anzalī, Iran B4 38
Bandar-e Rīg, Iran G5 39
Bandar-e Shāh see Bandar-e Torkeman, Iran B5 38
Bandar-e Shāhpūr see Bandar-e Khomeynī, Iran F4 39
Bandar-e Torkeman (Bandar-e Shāh), Iran B5 38
Bandar Maharani see Muar, Malay. K5 35
Bandar Seri Begawan (Brunei), Bru. E5 34
*Banda Sea, Indon.* G7 34
Bande, Spain A2 22
*Banded Peak, mtn., Co., U.S.* D4 83
*Bandeira, Pico da, mtn., Braz.* C4 56
*Bandelier National Monument, N.M., U.S.* B3 108
Bandera, Arg. E3 55
Bandera, Tx., U.S. E3 120
*Bandera, co., Tx., U.S.* E3 120
*Banderas, Bahía de, b., Mex.* m11 63
Bandholm, Den. D5 15
Bandiagara, Mali D4 45
Bāndīkūi, India D6 37
Bandırma, Tur. B7 40
Bandon, Ire. F3 11
Bandon, Or., U.S. D2 114
*Bandon, stm., Ire.* F3 11
Bandundu, Zaire B2 48
Bandung, Indon. G3 34
Bandy, Va., U.S. e10 123
Bāneh, Iran D2 39
Banes, Cuba D6 64
Banff, Alta. D3 68
Banff, Scot., U.K. B5 10
*Banff National Park, Alta.* D2 68
Banfora, Burkina D4 45
Bangalore, India F6 36
Bangassou, Cen. Afr. Rep. E4 46
*Bangeta, Mount, mtn., Pap. N. Gui.* k12 50
Banggai, Indon. F6 34
*Banggi Island, i., Malay.* D5 34
*Banggong Co, l., China* B6 36
*Bangka, i., Indon.* F3 34
Bangkalan, Indon. G4 34
Bangkok (Krung Thep), Thai. C2 34
*Bangladesh, ctry., Asia* D6 36
Bangor, Sask. G4 75
Bangor, Ire. C2 11
Bangor, N. Ire., U.K. C4 10
Bangor, Wales, U.K. B3 12
Bangor, Al., U.S. B3 78
Bangor, Me., U.S. D4 96
Bangor, Mi., U.S. F4 99
Bangor, N.Y., U.S. f10 109
Bangor, Pa., U.S. E11 115
Bangor, Wi., U.S. E3 126
Bangor Township, Mi., U.S. E7 99
Bangs, Tx., U.S. D3 120
*Bangs, Mount, mtn., Az., U.S.* A2 80
Bang Saphan, Thai. C1 34
Bangu, Zaire C3 48
Bangued, Phil. B6 34
Bangui, Cen. Afr. Rep. E3 46
*Bangweulu, Lake, l., Zam.* C4 48
Banhā, Eg. B3 38
Ban Hat Yai see Hat Yai, Thai. D2 34
Baní, Dom. Rep. E8 64
Bani, Phil. n12 34
*Bani, stm., Mali* D3 45
Baniara, Pap. N. Gui. k12 50
Banī Na'īm, Isr. Occ. C7 41
*Banister, stm., Va., U.S.* D4 123
Banī Suhaylah, Isr. Occ. C6 41
Banī Suwayf, Eg. B3 38
Bāniyās, Isr. Occ. B3 38
Banja Luka, Yugo. C3 24
Banjarmasin, Indon. F4 34
Banjul, Gam. D1 45
Bankas, Mali D4 45
Bankeryd, Swe. A8 15
Bankfoot, Scot., U.K. D5 13
Bankhead, Al., U.S. A2 78
*Bankhead Lake, res., Al., U.S.* B2 78
Banks, Al., U.S. D4 78
Banks, Ar., U.S. D3 81
Banks, Id., U.S. E2 89
Banks, Ms., U.S. A3 101
Banks, Or., U.S. g11 114
*Banks, co., Ga., U.S.* B3 87
*Banksian, stm., Can.* C4 70
*Banks Island, i., B.C.* C2 69
*Banks Island, i., N.W. Ter.* B8 66
*Banks Lake, res., Ga., U.S.* E3 87
*Banks Lake, res., Wa., U.S.* B6 124
*Banks Peninsula, pen., N.Z.* O14 51
Bankston, Al., U.S. B2 78
Bankstown, Austl. *F9 50
Bānkura, India D8 36
*Bann, stm., N. Ire., U.K.* B5 11
Bannack, Mt., U.S. E4 103
Banner, Ms., U.S. A4 101
Banner, Wy., U.S. B6 127
*Banner, co., Ne., U.S.* C2 104
Banner Elk, N.C., U.S. A1 110
Banning, Ca., U.S. F5 82
Banning, Ga., U.S. C2 87
*Bannock, co., Id., U.S.* G6 89
Bannockburn, Ont. C7 73
*Bannock Peak, mtn., Id., U.S.* F6 89
*Bannock Range, mts., Id., U.S.* G6 89
Bannu, Pak. B5 36
Bañolas, Spain A7 22
Baños, Ec. B2 58
Bansha, Ire. E3 11
Banská Bystrica, Czech. D5 26
Banská Štiavnica, Czech. D5 26
Bansko, Bul. E6 24
Bānswāra, India F5 37
Bantam, Ct., U.S. C3 84
*Bantam, stm., Ct., U.S.* B3 84
*Bantam Lake, l., Ct., U.S.* C3 84
Banteer, Ire. E3 11
Bantry, Ire. E2 10
Bantry, N.D., U.S. A5 111
*Bantry Bay, b., Ire.* E2 10
*Banyak Islands, is., Indon.* m11 34
Banyo, Cam. D2 46
Banyuwangi, Indon. G4 34
*Banzare Coast, Ant.* C25 7
Baocheng, China E6 31
Baode, China E4 32
Baodi, China E7 32
Baoding, China D8 31
Bao Ha, Viet. A6 35
Baoji, China E6 31
Baokang, China E7 31
Bao Loc, Viet. C3 34
Baoqing, China C6 33
Baoshan, China F4 31
Baoting, China C8 35
Baotou, China C6 31
*Baoulé, stm., Afr.* D3 45
*Baoulé, stm., Mali* D3 45
Baoying, China H8 32
Bapaume, Fr. D2 17
Bapchule, Az., U.S. D4 80
Baptiste, Ont. B6 73
Baptistown, N.J., U.S. B2 107
Bāqa el Gharbiyya, Isr. B7 41
Ba'qūbah, Iraq B4 38
Baquedano, Chile D2 55
Bar, Fr. C6 16
Bar, Sov. Un. G6 27
Bar, Yugo. D4 24
Baraawe, Som. E5 47
Barabinsk, Sov. Un. D10 29
Baraboo, Wi., U.S. E4 126
*Baraboo, stm., Wi., U.S.* E3 126
Baracaldo, Spain A4 22
Baracoa, Cuba D6 64
Barada, Ne., U.S. D10 104
Baradero, Arg. f7 54
Baraga, Mi., U.S. B2 99
*Baraga, co., Mi., U.S.* B2 99
Bārah, Sud. C3 47
Barahona, Dom. Rep. E8 64
Barajas de Madrid, Spain p17 22
Bārākpur, India F12 37
Bāramūla, India B5 36
Bārān, India E6 37
Baranagar, India *D8 36
*Baranof Island, i., Ak., U.S.* m22 79
*Baranov, Cape, c., Sov. Un.* C34 128
Baranovichi, Sov. Un. E5 27
Barão de Melgaço, Braz. B1 56
Barataria, Trin. N23 65
Barataria, La., U.S. E5 95
*Barataria, Bayou, stm., La., U.S.* k11 95
*Barataria Bay, b., La., U.S.* E6 95
*Barat Daya Islands, is., Indon.* G7 34
Baraya, Col. C2 60
Barbacena, Braz. C4 56
Barbacoas, Col. C2 60
*Barbado, stm., Braz.* C3 55
*Barbados, ctry., N.A.* J15 64
Barbalha, Braz. C3 57
Barbar, Sud. B3 47
Barbastro, Spain A6 22
Barbate [de Franco], Spain D3 22
Barbeau, Mi., U.S. B6 99
*Barbeau Peak, mtn., N.W. Ter.* k37 66
Barber, Ar., U.S. B1 81
*Barber, co., Ks., U.S.* E5 93
*Barbers Point, c., Hi., U.S.* B3 88
*Barbers Point Naval Air Station, mil., Hi., U.S.* g9 88
Barberton, S. Afr. C5 49
Barberton, Oh., U.S. A4 112
Barberville, Fl., U.S. C5 86
Barbezieux, Fr. E3 16
Barbil, India F10 37
*Barbour, co., Al., U.S.* D4 78
*Barbour, co., W.V., U.S.* B4 125
Barboursville, Va., U.S. B4 123
Barboursville, W.V., U.S. C2 125
Barbourville, Ky., U.S. D6 94
*Barbuda, i., Antig.* H14 64
Barby, E. Ger. B6 19
Barca de Alva, Port. B2 22
Barcaldine, Austl. D8 50
Barcarena, Port. f9 22
Barcarrota, Spain C2 22
Barcellona [Pozzo di Gotto], Italy E5 23
Barcelona, Spain B7 22
Barcelona, Ven. A5 60
Barcelonnette, Fr. E7 16
Barcelos, Braz. C2 59
Barcelos, Port. B1 22
Barclay, Md., U.S. B6 97

| Name | Map Ref. | Page |
|---|---|---|
| Barco, N.C., U.S. | A7 | 110 |
| Barcoo, stm., Austl. | D7 | 50 |
| Barcroft, Lake, res., Va., U.S. | g12 | 123 |
| Bard, N.M., U.S. | B6 | 108 |
| Barda del Medio, Arg. | B3 | 54 |
| Bardaï, Chad | C3 | 46 |
| Bardawīl, Sabkhat al, sw., Eg. | C5 | 41 |
| Bardawil Peninsula, spit, Eg. | C4 | 41 |
| Barddhamān, India | D8 | 36 |
| Bardejov, Czech. | D6 | 26 |
| Barden Reservoir, res., R.I., U.S. | C2 | 116 |
| Bardi, Italy | E5 | 20 |
| Bardīyah, Libya | C5 | 43 |
| Bardolph, Il., U.S. | C3 | 90 |
| Bardonecchia, Italy | D2 | 20 |
| Bardsey Island, i., Wales, U.K. | B3 | 12 |
| Bardstown, Ky., U.S. | C4 | 94 |
| Bardstown Junction, Ky., U.S. | C4 | 94 |
| Bardswell Group, is., B.C. | C3 | 69 |
| Bardwell, Ky., U.S. | f9 | 94 |
| Bardwell Lake, res., Tx., U.S. | C4 | 120 |
| Bare Hill Pond, l., Ma., U.S. | g9 | 98 |
| Bareilly, India | C6 | 36 |
| Barenburg, W. Ger. | F2 | 15 |
| Barentin, Fr. | C4 | 16 |
| Barents, i., Nor. | B12 | 128 |
| Barents Sea, Eur. | B6 | 29 |
| Barentu, Eth. | B4 | 47 |
| Barfleur, Pointe de, c., Fr. | C3 | 16 |
| Bargarh, India | G9 | 37 |
| Bargersville, In., U.S. | E5 | 91 |
| Barguzin, Sov. Un. | D13 | 29 |
| Bar Harbor, Me., U.S. | D4 | 96 |
| Bari, Italy | D6 | 23 |
| Bari, prov., Som. | D6 | 47 |
| Barillas, Guat. | C2 | 62 |
| Barinas, Ven. | B3 | 60 |
| Barinas, state, Ven. | B4 | 60 |
| Baring, Me., U.S. | C5 | 96 |
| Baring, Mo., U.S. | A5 | 102 |
| Bāripada, India | D8 | 36 |
| Bariri, Braz. | C3 | 56 |
| Bārīs, Eg. | E6 | 43 |
| Barisāl, Bngl. | D9 | 36 |
| Barisan Mountains, mts., Indon. | F2 | 34 |
| Barito, stm., Indon. | F4 | 34 |
| Barium Springs, N.C., U.S. | B2 | 110 |
| Barker, N.Y., U.S. | B2 | 109 |
| Barker Heights, N.C., U.S. | f10 | 110 |
| Barkerville, B.C. | C7 | 69 |
| Barkeyville, Pa., U.S. | D2 | 115 |
| Barkhamsted Reservoir, res., Ct., U.S. | B3 | 84 |
| Bark Lake, l., Ont. | B7 | 73 |
| Barkley, Lake, res., U.S. | f10 | 94 |
| Barkley Dam, Ky., U.S. | e9 | 94 |
| Barkley Sound, strt., B.C. | E5 | 69 |
| Barkly East, S. Afr. | D4 | 49 |
| Barkly Tableland, plat., Austl. | C6 | 50 |
| Barkmere, Que. | C3 | 74 |
| Barkol, China | C3 | 31 |
| Bark Point, c., Wi., U.S. | B2 | 126 |
| Bark River, Mi., U.S. | C3 | 99 |
| Barksdale, Tx., U.S. | E2 | 120 |
| Barksdale Air Force Base, mil., La., U.S. | B2 | 95 |
| Bar Lake, l., Sask. | B2 | 75 |
| Bar-le-Duc, Fr. | C6 | 16 |
| Barlee, Lake, l., Austl. | E2 | 50 |
| Barletta, Italy | D6 | 23 |
| Barling, Ar., U.S. | B1 | 81 |
| Barlow, Ky., U.S. | e8 | 94 |
| Barlow, N.D., U.S. | B6 | 111 |
| Barlow, Or., U.S. | h12 | 114 |
| Bärmer, India | C5 | 36 |
| Bar Mills, Me., U.S. | E2 | 96 |
| Barmouth, Wales, U.K. | D4 | 10 |
| Barna, Ire. | D2 | 11 |
| Barnaby River, N.B. | C4 | 71 |
| Barnard, Ks., U.S. | C5 | 93 |
| Barnard, Mo., U.S. | A3 | 102 |
| Barnard, S.D., U.S. | B7 | 118 |
| Barnard, Vt., U.S. | D3 | 122 |
| Barnard Castle, Eng., U.K. | F7 | 13 |
| Barnardsville, N.C., U.S. | f10 | 110 |
| Barnasht, Eg. | E3 | 41 |
| Barnaul, Sov. Un. | D11 | 29 |
| Barnegat, N.J., U.S. | D4 | 107 |
| Barnegat, b., N.J., U.S. | D4 | 107 |
| Barnegat Inlet, b., N.J., U.S. | D4 | 107 |
| Barnegat Light, N.J., U.S. | D4 | 107 |
| Barnegat Pines, N.J., U.S. | D4 | 107 |
| Barne Inlet, b., Ant. | g40 | 7 |
| Barnes, Ks., U.S. | C7 | 93 |
| Barnes, Pa., U.S. | C3 | 115 |
| Barnes, co., N.D., U.S. | B7 | 111 |
| Barnes City, Ia., U.S. | C5 | 92 |
| Barnes Corners, N.Y., U.S. | B5 | 109 |
| Barnes Creek, stm., La., U.S. | D2 | 95 |
| Barnes Sound, strt., Fl., U.S. | G6 | 86 |
| Barneston, Ne., U.S. | D9 | 104 |
| Barnesville, Ga., U.S. | C2 | 87 |
| Barnesville, Md., U.S. | B3 | 97 |
| Barnesville, Mn., U.S. | D2 | 100 |
| Barnesville, Oh., U.S. | C4 | 112 |
| Barnet (part of London), Eng., U.K. | k12 | 10 |
| Barnet, Vt., U.S. | C4 | 122 |
| Barnett, Mo., U.S. | C5 | 102 |
| Barneveld, Neth. | B5 | 17 |
| Barneveld, Wi., U.S. | E4 | 126 |
| Barneville-Carteret, Fr. | F6 | 10 |
| Barney, Ga., U.S. | F3 | 87 |
| Barney, N.D., U.S. | C8 | 111 |
| Barney, Mount, mtn., Austl. | D9 | 51 |
| Barnhart, Mo., U.S. | C7 | 102 |
| Barnhart, Tx., U.S. | D2 | 120 |
| Barnhill, Oh., U.S. | B4 | 112 |
| Barnsdall, Ok., U.S. | A5 | 113 |
| Barnsley, Eng., U.K. | A6 | 12 |
| Barnstable, Ma., U.S. | C7 | 98 |
| Barnstable, co., Ma., U.S. | C7 | 98 |
| Barnstaple, Eng., U.K. | E4 | 10 |
| Barnstaple Bay, b., Eng., U.K. | C3 | 12 |
| Barnstead, N.H., U.S. | D4 | 106 |
| Barnston, Que. | D6 | 74 |
| Barnum, Ia., U.S. | B3 | 92 |
| Barnum, Mn., U.S. | D6 | 100 |
| Barnwell, Alta. | E4 | 68 |
| Barnwell, S.C., U.S. | E5 | 117 |
| Barnwell, co., S.C., U.S. | E5 | 117 |
| Baro, Nig. | E6 | 45 |
| Baro, stm., Afr. | D3 | 47 |
| Baroda, Mi., U.S. | G4 | 99 |
| Baroda see Vadodara, India | D5 | 36 |
| Baron, Ok., U.S. | B7 | 113 |
| Barons, Alta. | E4 | 68 |
| Barques, Pointe aux, c., Mi., U.S. | D8 | 99 |
| Barquisimeto, Ven. | A4 | 60 |
| Barr, Fr. | C7 | 16 |
| Barr, Co., U.S. | B6 | 83 |
| Barr, Ra's al, c., Eg. | C3 | 41 |
| Barra, Braz. | h5 | 57 |
| Barra, Braz. | D2 | 57 |
| Barra, i., Scot., U.K. | B3 | 10 |
| Barra, Sound of, strt., Scot., U.K. | C1 | 13 |
| Barraba, Austl. | E8 | 51 |
| Barra Bonita, Braz. | m7 | 56 |
| Barracão, Braz. | D2 | 56 |
| Barrackville, W.V., U.S. | B4 | 125 |
| Barra de Río Grande, Nic. | D6 | 62 |
| Barra do Corda, Braz. | C1 | 57 |
| Barra do Garças, Braz. | B2 | 56 |
| Barra do Piraí, Braz. | C4 | 56 |
| Barra Head, c., Scot., U.K. | B3 | 10 |
| Barra Mansa, Braz. | C4 | 56 |
| Barranca, Peru | B2 | 58 |
| Barranca, N.M., U.S. | *A3 | 108 |
| Barrancabermeja, Col. | B3 | 60 |
| Barrancas, Ven. | B5 | 60 |
| Barranco, Peru | *D2 | 58 |
| Barranquilla, Col. | A3 | 60 |
| Barraza, Chile | A2 | 54 |
| Barre, Ma., U.S. | B3 | 98 |
| Barre, Vt., U.S. | C4 | 122 |
| Barre, Lake, l., La., U.S. | E5 | 95 |
| Barre des Écrins, mtn., Fr. | E7 | 16 |
| Barre Falls Reservoir, res., Ma., U.S. | B4 | 98 |
| Barreirinha, Braz. | C3 | 59 |
| Barreirinhas, Braz. | B2 | 57 |
| Barreiro, Port. | C1 | 22 |
| Barreiros, Braz. | C3 | 57 |
| Barrelville, Md., U.S. | k13 | 97 |
| Barren, co., Ky., U.S. | D4 | 94 |
| Barren, stm., Ky., U.S. | C3 | 94 |
| Barren, Nosy, is., Madag. | g8 | 49 |
| Barren Island, i., Md., U.S. | D5 | 97 |
| Barren Islands, is., Ak., U.S. | h15 | 79 |
| Barren Plain, Tn., U.S. | A5 | 119 |
| Barren River Lake, res., Ky., U.S. | D3 | 94 |
| Barre Plains, Ma., U.S. | B3 | 98 |
| Barretos, Braz. | C3 | 56 |
| Barrett, Mn., U.S. | E3 | 100 |
| Barrett, W.V., U.S. | D3 | 125 |
| Barretts Hill, hill, Ma., U.S. | g9 | 98 |
| Barrhead, Alta. | B3 | 68 |
| Barrhead, Scot., U.K. | E4 | 13 |
| Barrhill, Scot., U.K. | E4 | 13 |
| Barrie, Ont. | C5 | 73 |
| Barrie Island, i., Ont. | B2 | 73 |
| Barrier Bay, b., Ant. | C21 | 7 |
| Barrière, Fr. | D7 | 69 |
| Barrier Lake, l., Sask. | E4 | 75 |
| Barrier Range, mts., Austl. | F7 | 50 |
| Barrigada, Guam | L10 | 52 |
| Barrington, N.S. | F4 | 71 |
| Barrington, Il., U.S. | A5 | 90 |
| Barrington, N.H., U.S. | D4 | 106 |
| Barrington, N.J., U.S. | D2 | 107 |
| Barrington, R.I., U.S. | D5 | 116 |
| Barrington Lake, l., Man. | A1 | 70 |
| Barrington Passage, N.S. | F4 | 71 |
| Barrington Tops, mtn., Austl. | F8 | 51 |
| Barrio Obrero Industrial, Peru | *D2 | 58 |
| Barro Alto, Braz. | B3 | 56 |
| Barron, Wi., U.S. | C2 | 126 |
| Barron, co., Wi., U.S. | C2 | 126 |
| Barronett, Wi., U.S. | C2 | 126 |
| Barron Lake, Mi., U.S. | G4 | 99 |
| Barrouallie, St. Vin. | U26 | 65 |
| Barrow, Arg. | B4 | 54 |
| Barrow, Ak., U.S. | A8 | 79 |
| Barrow, co., Ga., U.S. | B3 | 87 |
| Barrow, i., Austl. | D2 | 50 |
| Barrow, stm., Ire. | D3 | 10 |
| Barrow, Point, c., Ak., U.S. | A8 | 79 |
| Barrow-in-Furness, Eng., U.K. | C5 | 10 |
| Barrows, Man. | C1 | 70 |
| Barrow Strait, strt., N.W. Ter. | B14 | 66 |
| Barrowsville, Ma., U.S. | C5 | 98 |
| Barruelo de Santullán, Spain | A3 | 22 |
| Barry (Vale of Glamorgan), Wales, U.K. | C4 | 12 |
| Barry, Il., U.S. | D2 | 90 |
| Barry, co., Mi., U.S. | F5 | 99 |
| Barry, co., Mo., U.S. | E4 | 102 |
| Barrys Bay, Ont. | B7 | 73 |
| Barryton, Mi., U.S. | E5 | 99 |
| Barryville, N.Y., U.S. | D6 | 109 |
| Bārsi, India | E6 | 36 |
| Barsinghausen, W. Ger. | A4 | 19 |
| Barsø, i., Den. | C3 | 15 |
| Barstow, Ca., U.S. | E5 | 82 |
| Barstow, Tx., U.S. | D1 | 120 |
| Bar-sur-Aube, Fr. | C6 | 16 |
| Bartelso, Il., U.S. | E4 | 90 |
| Barth, E. Ger. | A6 | 19 |
| Barth, Fl., U.S. | u14 | 86 |
| Bartholomew, Bayou, stm., U.S. | D4 | 81 |
| Bartibog Bridge, N.B. | B4 | 71 |
| Bartica, Guy. | A3 | 59 |
| Bartin, Tur. | B9 | 40 |
| Bartle Frere, Mount, mtn., Austl. | C8 | 50 |
| Bartlesville, Ok., U.S. | A6 | 113 |
| Bartlett, Il., U.S. | *k8 | 90 |
| Bartlett, Ne., U.S. | C7 | 104 |
| Bartlett, N.H., U.S. | B4 | 106 |
| Bartlett, Tn., U.S. | B2 | 119 |
| Bartlett, Tx., U.S. | D4 | 120 |
| Bartlett Cove, Ak., U.S. | k22 | 79 |
| Bartlett Reservoir, res., Az., U.S. | D4 | 80 |
| Bartletts Ferry Dam, U.S. | C2 | 87 |
| Bartletts Harbour, Newf. | C3 | 72 |
| Bartolomeu Dias, Moz. | B6 | 49 |
| Barton, Ar., U.S. | A2 | 78 |
| Barton, Md., U.S. | k12 | 97 |
| Barton, N.D., U.S. | A5 | 111 |
| Barton, Oh., U.S. | B5 | 112 |
| Barton, co., Ks., U.S. | D5 | 93 |
| Barton, co., Mo., U.S. | D3 | 102 |
| Barton, Vt., U.S. | B4 | 122 |
| Bartonsville, Vt., U.S. | E3 | 122 |
| Barton-upon-Humber, Eng., U.K. | A7 | 12 |
| Bartonville, Il., U.S. | C4 | 90 |
| Bartoszyce, Pol. | A6 | 26 |
| Bartow, Fl., U.S. | E5 | 86 |
| Bartow, Ga., U.S. | C4 | 87 |
| Bartow, co., Ga., U.S. | B2 | 87 |
| Barú, Volcán, vol., Pan. | F6 | 62 |
| Barun Su, China | C4 | 32 |
| Barus, Indon. | K3 | 35 |
| Baruth, E. Ger. | A8 | 19 |
| Baruun-Urt, Mong. | B7 | 31 |
| Barvas, Scot., U.K. | A3 | 10 |
| Barvenkovo, Sov. Un. | G11 | 27 |
| Barview, Or., U.S. | *D2 | 114 |
| Barwāni, India | F5 | 37 |
| Barwick, Ga., U.S. | F3 | 87 |
| Barwon, stm., Austl. | E8 | 50 |
| Barybino, Sov. Un. | n17 | 27 |
| Barycz, stm., Pol. | C4 | 26 |
| Basalt, Co., U.S. | B3 | 83 |
| Basalt, Id., U.S. | F6 | 89 |
| Basalt, Nv., U.S. | E3 | 105 |
| Basankusu, Zaire | A2 | 48 |
| Basbulak, Sov. Un. | E6 | 28 |
| Basco, Phil. | A6 | 34 |
| Basco, Il., U.S. | C2 | 90 |
| Bascom, Fl., U.S. | B1 | 86 |
| Bascom, Oh., U.S. | A2 | 112 |
| Bascuñán, Cabo, c., Chile | E1 | 55 |
| Basehor, Ks., U.S. | k16 | 93 |
| Basekpio, Zaire | A3 | 48 |
| Basel, Switz. | B3 | 20 |
| Basel-Land, state, Switz. | B3 | 20 |
| Basel-Stadt, state, Switz. | B3 | 20 |
| Bashan Lake, l., Ct., U.S. | D6 | 84 |
| Bashaw, Alta. | C4 | 68 |
| Bashi, Al., U.S. | D2 | 78 |
| Bashi Channel, strt., Asia | A6 | 34 |
| Basiad Bay, b., Phil. | o14 | 34 |
| Basilan Island, i., Phil. | D6 | 34 |
| Basildon, Eng., U.K. | C8 | 12 |
| Basile, La., U.S. | D3 | 95 |
| Basilicata (Lucania), prov., Italy | D6 | 23 |
| Basílio, Braz. | E2 | 56 |
| Basin, Mt., U.S. | D4 | 103 |
| Basin, Wy., U.S. | B4 | 127 |
| Basinger, Fl., U.S. | E5 | 86 |
| Basingstoke, Eng., U.K. | E6 | 10 |
| Basin Harbor, Vt., U.S. | C2 | 122 |
| Basin Lake, l., Sask. | E2 | 75 |
| Baška, Yugo. | C2 | 24 |
| Baskahegan Lake, l., Me., U.S. | C5 | 96 |
| Baskatong, Réservoir, res., Que. | k11 | 74 |
| Baskett, Ky., U.S. | C2 | 94 |
| Baskin, Fl., U.S. | p10 | 86 |
| Baskin, La., U.S. | B4 | 95 |
| Basking Ridge, N.J., U.S. | B3 | 107 |
| Basoko, Zaire | A3 | 48 |
| Basora, Punt, c., Neth. Ant. | H17 | 65 |
| Basque Provinces, hist. reg., Spain | A4 | 22 |
| Basra (Al Başrah), Iraq | B4 | 38 |
| Bas-Rhin, dept., Fr. | F7 | 17 |
| Bassano, Alta. | D4 | 68 |
| Bassano del Grappa, Italy | B3 | 23 |
| Bassas da India, rf., Reu. | B6 | 49 |
| Basse Santa Su, Gam. | D2 | 45 |
| Basse-Pointe, Mart. | S10 | 65 |
| Basse-Terre, Guad. | I14 | 64 |
| Basseterre, St. C.-N. | H13 | 64 |
| Basse-Terre, i., Guad. | Q8 | 65 |
| Bassett, Ar., U.S. | B5 | 81 |
| Bassett, Ne., U.S. | B6 | 104 |
| Bassett, Ks., U.S. | E8 | 93 |
| Bassett, Va., U.S. | D3 | 123 |
| Bassett, Wi., U.S. | n11 | 126 |
| Bassett Creek, stm., Al., U.S. | D2 | 78 |
| Bassett Peak, mtn., Az., U.S. | E5 | 80 |
| Bassfield, Ms., U.S. | D4 | 101 |
| Bassikounou, Maur. | C3 | 45 |
| Bass Islands, is., Oh., U.S. | A3 | 112 |
| Bass Lake, In., U.S. | B4 | 91 |
| Bass River, N.S. | D6 | 71 |
| Bass Strait, strt., Austl. | n15 | 50 |
| Bassum, W. Ger. | F2 | 15 |
| Basswood, Man. | D1 | 70 |
| Basswood Lake, l., Mn., U.S. | B7 | 100 |
| Bästad, Swe. | B5 | 15 |
| Bastak, Iran | H7 | 39 |
| Bastelica, Fr. | D2 | 23 |
| Basti, India | D9 | 37 |
| Bastia, Fr. | C2 | 23 |
| Bastian, Va., U.S. | C1 | 123 |
| Bastogne, Bel. | B6 | 16 |
| Bastrop, La., U.S. | B4 | 95 |
| Bastrop, Tx., U.S. | D4 | 120 |
| Bastrop, co., Tx., U.S. | D4 | 120 |
| Basţūn, Eg. | D2 | 41 |
| Bastuträsk, Swe. | E9 | 14 |
| Baxdo, Som. | E7 | 47 |
| Baxian, China | E7 | 32 |
| Bata, Eq. Gui. | A1 | 46 |
| Bataan Peninsula, pen., Phil. | o13 | 34 |
| Batabanó, Cuba | C2 | 64 |
| Batabanó, Golfo de, b., Cuba | C2 | 64 |
| Bataguaçu, Braz. | C2 | 56 |
| Batala, India | B6 | 36 |
| Batamay, Sov. Un. | C15 | 29 |
| Batang, China | E4 | 31 |
| Batangafo, Cen. Afr. Rep. | D3 | 46 |
| Batangas, Phil. | C6 | 34 |
| Batan Islands, is., Phil. | A6 | 34 |
| Bataszék, Hung. | B4 | 24 |
| Batatais, Braz. | C6 | 56 |
| Batavia, Arg. | A3 | 54 |
| Batavia, Ar., U.S. | A2 | 81 |
| Batavia, Il., U.S. | B5 | 90 |
| Batavia, Ia., U.S. | D5 | 92 |
| Batavia, N.Y., U.S. | C2 | 109 |
| Batavia, Oh., U.S. | C1 | 112 |
| Bataysk, Sov. Un. | H12 | 27 |
| Batchelor, La., U.S. | D4 | 95 |
| Batchelor Bay, b., N.C., U.S. | B6 | 110 |
| Batchtown, Il., U.S. | D3 | 90 |
| Batdambang, Camb. | C2 | 34 |
| Bateman, Sask. | G2 | 75 |
| Bates, Ar., U.S. | C1 | 81 |
| Bates, co., Mo., U.S. | C3 | 102 |
| Batesburg, S.C., U.S. | D4 | 117 |
| Bates City, Mo., U.S. | C3 | 102 |
| Batesland, S.D., U.S. | D3 | 118 |
| Batesville, Ar., U.S. | B4 | 81 |
| Batesville, In., U.S. | F7 | 91 |
| Batesville, Ms., U.S. | A4 | 101 |
| Batesville, Oh., U.S. | K3 | 35 |
| Batesville, Tx., U.S. | E3 | 120 |
| Bath, E. Ger. | A8 | 19 |
| Bath, N.B. | C1 | 71 |
| Bath, Ont. | C8 | 73 |
| Bath, Jam. | F16 | 65 |
| Bath, Eng., U.K. | E5 | 10 |
| Bath, Il., U.S. | *C3 | 90 |
| Bath, Me., U.S. | E3 | 96 |
| Bath, Mi., U.S. | F6 | 99 |
| Bath, N.H., U.S. | B3 | 106 |
| Bath, N.Y., U.S. | C3 | 109 |
| Bath, N.C., U.S. | B6 | 110 |
| Bath, Pa., U.S. | E11 | 115 |
| Bath, S.C., U.S. | D4 | 117 |
| Bath, S.D., U.S. | B7 | 118 |
| Bath, co., Ky., U.S. | B6 | 94 |
| Bath, co., Va., U.S. | B3 | 123 |
| Baṭḥ al Ghūl, Jord. | E7 | 41 |
| Bathgate, Scot., U.K. | E5 | 13 |
| Bathgate, N.D., U.S. | A8 | 111 |
| Bathinda, India | B5 | 37 |
| Bathsheba, Barb. | J15 | 64 |
| Bath Springs, Tn., U.S. | B3 | 119 |
| Bathurst, Austl. | F8 | 50 |
| Bathurst, N.B. | B4 | 71 |
| Bathurst, Cape, c., Banjul, Gam. | D1 | 45 |
| Bathurst, i., Austl. | B5 | 50 |
| Bathurst, Cape, c., N.W. Ter. | B7 | 66 |
| Bathurst Inlet, N.W. Ter. | C11 | 66 |
| Bathurst Inlet, b., N.W. Ter. | C11 | 66 |
| Bathurst Island, i., Austl. | B5 | 50 |
| Bathurst Island, i., N.W. Ter. | m31 | 66 |
| Batié, Burkina | E4 | 45 |
| Batiki, i., Fiji | H15 | 52 |
| Batiscan, Que. | C5 | 74 |
| Batiscan, stm., Que. | B5 | 74 |
| Batkanu, S.L. | E2 | 45 |
| Batman, Tur. | D13 | 40 |
| Batna, Alg. | B6 | 44 |
| Batoche, Sask. | E2 | 75 |
| Baton Rouge, La., U.S. | D4 | 95 |
| Batouri, Cam. | A2 | 46 |
| Batson, Tx., U.S. | D5 | 120 |
| Batsto, N.J., U.S. | D3 | 107 |
| Batsto, stm., N.J., U.S. | D3 | 107 |
| Batten Kill, stm., U.S. | E2 | 122 |
| Battery Park, Va., U.S. | k14 | 123 |
| Batticaloa, Sri L. | G7 | 36 |
| Battiest, Ok., U.S. | C7 | 113 |
| Battle, stm., Can. | F11 | 66 |
| Battleboro, N.C., U.S. | A5 | 110 |
| Battle, stm., Sask. | H1 | 75 |
| Battle Creek, Ia., U.S. | B2 | 92 |
| Battle Creek, Mi., U.S. | F5 | 99 |
| Battle Creek, Ne., U.S. | C8 | 104 |
| Battle Creek, stm., N.A | B7 | 103 |
| Battle Ground, In., U.S. | C4 | 91 |
| Battle Ground, Wa., U.S. | D3 | 124 |
| Battle Harbour, Newf. | B4 | 72 |
| Battle Lake, Mn., U.S. | D3 | 100 |
| Battlement Mesa, mtn., Co., U.S. | B2 | 83 |
| Battle Mountain, Nv., U.S. | C5 | 105 |
| Battle Mountain, mtn., Wy., U.S. | E5 | 127 |
| Battles, Ms., U.S. | D5 | 101 |
| Battles Wharf, Al., U.S. | E2 | 78 |
| Battleview, N.D., U.S. | A3 | 111 |
| Battonya, Hung. | B5 | 24 |
| Battram, Sask. | G1 | 75 |
| Batu, mtn., Eth. | D4 | 47 |
| Batuc, Mex. | B2 | 63 |
| Batu Islands, is., Indon. | F1 | 34 |
| Batumi, Sov. Un. | E7 | 29 |
| Batu Pahat, Malay. | L5 | 35 |
| Baturaja, Indon. | F2 | 34 |
| Baturino, Sov. Un. | B11 | 28 |
| Baturité, Braz. | B3 | 57 |
| Bat Yam, Isr. | g9 | 41 |
| Baubau, Indon. | G6 | 34 |
| Bauchi, Nig. | D6 | 45 |
| Baudette, Mn., U.S. | B4 | 100 |
| Baudó, Serranía de, mts., Col. | B3 | 60 |
| Bauer, Ut., U.S. | C3 | 121 |
| Bauer Coulee, val., Wa., U.S. | B7 | 124 |
| Baugé, Fr. | D3 | 16 |
| Bauld, Cape, c., Newf. | C4 | 72 |
| Bauma, Switz. | B5 | 21 |
| Baume-les-Dames, Fr. | B2 | 20 |
| Baunei, Italy | D2 | 23 |
| Baures, Bol. | B5 | 55 |
| Baures, stm., Bol. | B3 | 55 |
| Baurtregaum, mtn., Ire. | E2 | 11 |
| Bauru, Braz. | C3 | 56 |
| Bautzen, E. Ger. | C7 | 18 |
| Bauxite, Ar., U.S. | C3 | 81 |
| Bavaria, Ks., U.S. | D6 | 93 |
| Bavaria, hist. reg., W. Ger. | D5 | 18 |
| Bavarian Alps, mts., Eur. | B7 | 20 |
| Bavay, Fr. | D5 | 17 |
| Båven, l., Swe. | t34 | 14 |
| Bavispe, Mex. | B2 | 63 |
| Baw Baw, Mount, mtn., Austl. | H6 | 51 |
| Bawcomville, La., U.S. | *B3 | 95 |
| Bawean, i., Indon. | G4 | 34 |
| Bawku, Ghana | E5 | 45 |
| Bawlf, Alta. | C4 | 68 |
| Baxley, Ga., U.S. | E4 | 87 |
| Baxter, Ia., U.S. | C4 | 92 |
| Baxter, Mn., U.S. | D4 | 100 |
| Baxter, Tn., U.S. | C8 | 119 |
| Baxter, W.V., U.S. | B4 | 125 |
| Baxter, co., Ar., U.S. | A3 | 81 |
| Baxter Springs, Ks., U.S. | E9 | 93 |
| Baxterville, Co., U.S. | D4 | 83 |
| Baxterville, Ms., U.S. | D4 | 101 |
| Bay, Ar., U.S. | B5 | 81 |
| Bay, prov., Som. | E6 | 47 |
| Bay, co., Fl., U.S. | u16 | 86 |
| Bay, co., Mi., U.S. | E6 | 99 |
| Bay, Laguna de, l., Phil. | o13 | 34 |
| Bay al Kabīr, Wādī, val., Libya | C2 | 43 |
| Bayambang, Phil. | o13 | 34 |
| Bayamo, Cuba | D5 | 64 |
| Bayamón, P.R. | G11 | 64 |
| Bayan, China | C3 | 32 |
| Bayanaul, Sov. Un. | C9 | 28 |
| Bayanga, Cen. Afr. Rep. | B3 | 46 |
| Bayan Obo, China | A1 | 32 |
| Bayard, Ia., U.S. | C3 | 92 |
| Bayard, Ne., U.S. | C2 | 104 |
| Bayard, N.M., U.S. | E1 | 108 |
| Bayberry, N.Y., U.S. | B4 | 109 |
| Bayboro, N.C., U.S. | B6 | 110 |
| Bay Bulls, Newf. | E5 | 72 |
| Bayburt, Tur. | B13 | 40 |
| Bay Center, Wa., U.S. | C2 | 124 |
| Bay City, Mi., U.S. | E7 | 99 |
| Bay City, Or., U.S. | B3 | 114 |
| Bay City, Tx., U.S. | E5 | 120 |
| Baydabo, Som. | E5 | 47 |
| Baydrag, stm., Mong. | B6 | 31 |
| Bayeux, Fr. | C7 | 16 |
| Bayfield, Ont. | D3 | 73 |
| Bayfield, Co., U.S. | D3 | 83 |
| Bayfield, Wi., U.S. | B3 | 126 |
| Bayfield, co., Wi., U.S. | B2 | 126 |
| Bay Head, N.J., U.S. | *C4 | 107 |
| Bayındır, Tur. | C6 | 25 |
| Baykonyr, Sov. Un. | D7 | 28 |
| Baylis, Il., U.S. | D3 | 90 |
| Baylor, co., Tx., U.S. | C3 | 120 |
| Baymak, Sov. Un. | C5 | 28 |
| Bay Mills Indian Reservation, Mi., U.S. | B6 | 99 |
| Bay Minette, Al., U.S. | E2 | 78 |
| Bayombong, Phil. | n13 | 34 |
| Bayonet Point, Fl., U.S. | *D4 | 86 |
| Bayonne, Fr. | F3 | 16 |
| Bayonne, N.J., U.S. | B4 | 107 |
| Bayou Bodcau Reservoir, res., La., U.S. | B3 | 95 |
| Bayou Cane, La., U.S. | *E5 | 95 |
| Bayou D'Arbonne Lake, res., La., U.S. | B3 | 95 |
| Bayou George, Fl., U.S. | u16 | 86 |
| Bayou Goula, La., U.S. | D4 | 95 |
| Bayou La Batre, Al., U.S. | E1 | 78 |
| Bay Pines, Fl., U.S. | *E4 | 86 |
| Bay Point, c., S.C., U.S. | G7 | 117 |
| Bayport, N.S. | E5 | 71 |
| Bay Port, Mi., U.S. | E7 | 99 |
| Bayport, Mn., U.S. | E6 | 100 |
| Bayport, N.Y., U.S. | n15 | 109 |
| Bayramıç, Tur. | C6 | 25 |
| Bay Ridge, Md., U.S. | C5 | 97 |
| Bayrischzell, W. Ger. | B7 | 20 |
| Bay Roberts, Newf. | E5 | 72 |
| Bay Saint Louis, Ms., U.S. | E4 | 101 |
| Bayshore, Mi., U.S. | C5 | 99 |
| Bay Shore, N.Y., U.S. | E7 | 109 |
| Bayshore Gardens, Fl., U.S. | q10 | 86 |
| Bayside, Tx., U.S. | E4 | 120 |
| Bayside, Wi., U.S. | m12 | 126 |
| Bays Mountains, mtn., Tn., U.S. | n14 | 119 |
| Bayson, Sov. Un. | E5 | 28 |
| Bayt al Faqīh, Yemen | C5 | 47 |
| Bayt Dajan, Isr. Occ. | g12 | 41 |
| Baytīllū, Isr. Occ. | h11 | 41 |
| Baytown, Tx., U.S. | E5 | 120 |
| Bay Trail, Sask. | E5 | 75 |
| Bayview, Al., U.S. | f7 | 78 |
| Bayview, Id., U.S. | B2 | 89 |
| Bay View, Mi., U.S. | C6 | 99 |
| Bay View Park, De., U.S. | F5 | 85 |
| Bay Village, Oh., U.S. | h9 | 112 |
| Bayville, N.J., U.S. | D4 | 107 |
| Bayville, N.Y., U.S. | *E7 | 109 |
| Bayzah, Bi'r, well, Eg. | D6 | 43 |
| Baza, Spain | D4 | 22 |
| Bazaruto, Ilha do, i., Moz. | B6 | 49 |
| Bazemore, Al., U.S. | B2 | 78 |
| Bazhong, China | E6 | 31 |
| Bazile Mills, Ne., U.S. | B8 | 104 |
| Bazine, Ks., U.S. | D4 | 93 |
| Bazmān, Küh-e, mtn., Iran | G10 | 39 |
| Baztán, Spain | A5 | 22 |
| Be, Nosy, i., Madag. | f9 | 49 |
| Beach, N.D., U.S. | C1 | 111 |
| Beachburg, Ont. | B8 | 73 |
| Beach City, Oh., U.S. | B4 | 112 |
| Beach Haven, N.J., U.S. | D4 | 107 |
| Beach Haven, Pa., U.S. | D9 | 115 |
| Beach Haven Crest, N.J., U.S. | D4 | 107 |
| Beach Haven Inlet, b., N.J., U.S. | D4 | 107 |
| Beach Haven Terrace, N.J., U.S. | D4 | 107 |
| Beach Lake, Pa., U.S. | C11 | 115 |
| Beach Pond, res., U.S. | C8 | 84 |
| Beachport, Austl. | H3 | 51 |
| Beachville, Ont. | D4 | 73 |
| Beachwood, N.J., U.S. | D4 | 107 |
| Beachwood, Oh., U.S. | *h10 | 112 |
| Beachy Head, c., Eng., U.K. | D8 | 12 |
| Beacon, N.Y., U.S. | D7 | 109 |
| Beacon Falls, Ct., U.S. | D3 | 84 |
| Beaconsfield, Que. | q19 | 74 |
| Beacon Square, Fl., U.S. | *D4 | 86 |
| Beadle, Sask. | F1 | 75 |
| Beadle, co., S.D., U.S. | C7 | 118 |
| Beagh, Slieve, hill, N. Ire., U.K. | C4 | 13 |
| Beagle, Canal, strt., S.A. | h12 | 54 |
| Bealanana, Madag. | f9 | 49 |
| Beal City, Mi., U.S. | E6 | 99 |
| Beale, Cape, c., B.C. | E5 | 69 |
| Beale Air Force Base, mil., Ca., U.S. | C3 | 82 |
| Beallsville, Oh., U.S. | C4 | 112 |
| Beals, Ky., U.S. | C2 | 94 |
| Beals, Me., U.S. | D5 | 96 |
| Bean Lake, Mo., U.S. | B3 | 102 |
| Bean Station, Tn., U.S. | C10 | 119 |
| Bear, De., U.S. | B3 | 85 |
| Bear, i., Nor. | B13 | 128 |
| Bear, stm., U.S. | B3 | 121 |
| Bearcreek, Mt., U.S. | E7 | 103 |
| Bear Creek, Al., U.S. | A2 | 78 |
| Bear Creek, Wi., U.S. | D5 | 126 |
| Bear Creek, stm., Al., U.S. | A1 | 78 |
| Bear Creek, stm., Or., U.S. | E4 | 114 |
| Bear Creek, stm., Wy., U.S. | E3 | 127 |
| Bear Creek, stm., N.D., U.S. | C1 | 111 |
| Bear Creek, stm., Ok., U.S. | D3 | 113 |
| Bear Creek, stm., Wy., U.S. | m13 | 127 |
| Bear Creek Mountains, mts., Al., U.S. | B3 | 78 |
| Bear Crossing, Ne., U.S. | D8 | 104 |
| Bear Mountain, mtn., Ky., U.S. | C5 | 94 |
| Bear Mountain, mtn., Ma., U.S. | A3 | 98 |
| Bear Mountain, mtn., Or., U.S. | D4 | 114 |
| Béarn, hist. reg., Fr. | F3 | 16 |
| Bearpaw Mountains, mts., Mt., U.S. | B7 | 103 |
| Bear Peninsula, pen., Ant. | B1 | 7 |
| Bear Pond Mountains, mts., Md., U.S. | A2 | 97 |
| Bear River, N.S. | E4 | 71 |
| Bear River City, Ut., U.S. | B3 | 121 |
| Bear Spring, Tn., U.S. | A4 | 119 |
| Bear Swamp, sw., Ma., U.S. | h11 | 98 |
| Beartooth Range, mts., U.S. | E7 | 103 |
| Bear Town, Ms., U.S. | D3 | 101 |
| Beartown Mountain, mtn., Va., U.S. | f10 | 123 |
| Beas de Segura, Spain | C4 | 22 |
| Beason, Il., U.S. | C4 | 90 |
| Beata, Cabo, c., Dom. Rep. | F8 | 64 |
| Beatrice, Al., U.S. | D2 | 78 |
| Beatrice, Ne., U.S. | D9 | 104 |
| Beatrice, Zimb. | A5 | 49 |
| Beattie, Ks., U.S. | C7 | 93 |
| Beatton, stm., B.C. | A7 | 69 |
| Beatty, Nv., U.S. | G5 | 105 |
| Beatty, Or., U.S. | E5 | 114 |
| Beattyville, Ky., U.S. | C6 | 94 |
| Beattyestown, N.J., U.S. | B3 | 107 |
| Beaucaire, Fr. | F6 | 16 |
| Beauce, co., Que. | C7 | 74 |
| Beauceville, Que. | C7 | 74 |
| Beauceville-Est, Que. | C7 | 74 |
| Beaucoup Creek, stm., La., U.S. | B3 | 95 |
| Beaucourt, Fr. | D7 | 16 |
| Beaufort, Fr. | E2 | 21 |
| Beaufort, Malay. | D5 | 34 |
| Beaufort, Mo., U.S. | C6 | 102 |
| Beaufort, N.C., U.S. | C6 | 110 |
| Beaufort, S.C., U.S. | G6 | 117 |
| Beaufort, co., N.C., U.S. | B5 | 110 |
| Beaufort, co., S.C., U.S. | G6 | 117 |
| Beaufort Island, i., Ant. | e38 | 7 |
| Beaufort Marine Corps Air Station, mil., S.C., U.S. | F6 | 117 |
| Beaufort Sea, N.A. | B7 | 61 |
| Beaufort West, S. Afr. | D3 | 49 |
| Beaugency, Fr. | D4 | 16 |
| Beauharnois, Que. | D4 | 74 |
| Beauharnois, co., Que. | D3 | 74 |
| Beau Lake, l., Me., U.S. | A3 | 96 |
| Beaulieu, Que. | n17 | 74 |
| Beaulieu, Mn., U.S. | C3 | 100 |
| Beauly, Scot., U.K. | C4 | 13 |
| Beauly, stm., Scot., U.K. | C4 | 13 |
| Beaumaris, Wales, U.K. | A3 | 12 |
| Beaumont, Bel. | D4 | 17 |
| Beaumont, Alta. | C4 | 68 |
| Beaumont, Newf. | D4 | 72 |
| Beaumont, Que. | C6 | 74 |
| Beaumont, Ca., U.S. | *F5 | 82 |
| Beaumont, Ks., U.S. | E7 | 93 |
| Beaumont, Ms., U.S. | D5 | 101 |
| Beaumont, Tx., U.S. | D5 | 120 |
| Beaumont [-sur-Oise], Fr. | E2 | 17 |
| Beaune, Fr. | D6 | 16 |
| Beauport, Que. | n17 | 74 |
| Beaupré, Que. | B7 | 74 |
| Beauraing, Bel. | D4 | 17 |
| Beauregard, Ms., U.S. | D3 | 101 |
| Beauregard, co., La., U.S. | D2 | 95 |
| Beaurivage, Que. | C6 | 74 |
| Beausejour, Man. | D3 | 70 |
| Beauty, Ky., U.S. | C7 | 94 |
| Beauvais, Fr. | C5 | 16 |
| Beauval, Sask. | B2 | 75 |
| Beauvallon, Alta. | C5 | 68 |
| Beaver, Ak., U.S. | B10 | 79 |
| Beaver, Ar., U.S. | *A2 | 81 |
| Beaver, Ks., U.S. | D5 | 93 |
| Beaver, Or., U.S. | B3 | 114 |
| Beaver, Ut., U.S. | E3 | 121 |
| Beaver, Wi., U.S. | D5 | 126 |
| Beaver, W.V., U.S. | C6 | 125 |
| Beaver, co., Ok., U.S. | e10 | 113 |
| Beaver, co., Pa., U.S. | E1 | 115 |
| Beaver, co., Ut., U.S. | E3 | 121 |
| Beaver, stm., Can. | B2 | 75 |
| Beaver, stm., N.Y., U.S. | B6 | 109 |
| Beaver, stm., Ut., U.S. | E2 | 121 |
| Beaver, stm., U.S. | e9 | 113 |
| Beaver Bay, Mn., U.S. | C7 | 100 |
| Beaver Brook, stm., U.S. | E4 | 106 |
| Beaver City, Ne., U.S. | D6 | 104 |
| Beaver Creek, Mn., U.S. | G2 | 100 |
| Beavercreek, Oh., U.S. | C1 | 112 |
| Beaver Creek, Sask. | F2 | 75 |
| Beaver Creek, stm., U.S. | E4 | 104 |
| Beaver Creek, stm., U.S. | C8 | 127 |
| Beaver Creek, stm., Ia., U.S. | e8 | 92 |
| Beaver Creek, stm., U.S. | C7 | 94 |
| Beaver Creek, stm., Md., U.S. | A2 | 97 |
| Beaver Creek, stm., N.D., U.S. | C1 | 111 |
| Beaver Creek, stm., Or., U.S. | E4 | 114 |
| Beaver Creek, stm., Ok., U.S. | C5 | 113 |
| Beaver Creek, stm., N.D., U.S. | m13 | 111 |
| Beaver Creek, stm., Wy., U.S. | m13 | 127 |
| Beaver Creek Mountains, mts., Al., U.S. | B3 | 78 |
| Beaverdale, Pa., U.S. | F4 | 115 |
| Beaver Dam, Az., U.S. | A2 | 80 |
| Beaver Dam, In., U.S. | B5 | 91 |
| Beaver Dam, Ky., U.S. | C3 | 94 |
| Beaver Dam, Oh., U.S. | B2 | 112 |
| Beaver Dam, Ut., U.S. | *B3 | 121 |
| Beaver Dam, Wi., U.S. | E5 | 126 |
| Beaverdam Branch, stm., De., U.S. | F3 | 85 |
| Beaverdam Lake, res., Wi. | E5 | 126 |
| Beaver Dams, N.Y., U.S. | C4 | 109 |
| Beaverdell, B.C. | E8 | 69 |
| Beaver Falls, N.Y., U.S. | B5 | 109 |
| Beaver Falls, Pa., U.S. | E1 | 115 |
| Beaverhead, co., Mt., U.S. | E3 | 103 |
| Beaverhead, stm., Mt., U.S. | E4 | 103 |

| Name | Map Ref. | Page |
|---|---|---|
| Beaverhead Mountains, mts., U.S. | D5 | 89 |
| Beaverhill Lake, l., Alta. | C4 | 68 |
| Beaver Hill Lake, l., Man. | B4 | 70 |
| Beaver Island, i., Mi., U.S. | C5 | 99 |
| Beaver Lake, l., Alta. | B5 | 68 |
| Beaver Lake, res., Ar., U.S. | A2 | 81 |
| Beaverlick, Ky., U.S. | k13 | 94 |
| Beaverlodge, Alta. | B1 | 68 |
| Beaver Meadows, Pa., U.S. | E10 | 115 |
| Beaver Point, Co., U.S. | A5 | 83 |
| Beaver Ridge, mtn., Tn., U.S. | D9 | 119 |
| Beaver Run Reservoir, res., Pa., U.S. | F2 | 115 |
| Beaver Springs, Pa., U.S. | E7 | 115 |
| Beavertail Point, c., R.I., U.S. | F4 | 116 |
| Beaverton, Ont. | C5 | 73 |
| Beaverton, Al., U.S. | B1 | 78 |
| Beaverton, Mi., U.S. | E6 | 99 |
| Beaverton, Or., U.S. | B4 | 114 |
| Beavertown, Pa., U.S. | E7 | 115 |
| Beaverville, Il., U.S. | C6 | 90 |
| Beāwar, India | C5 | 36 |
| Beazley, Arg. | A3 | 54 |
| Bebedouro, Braz. | C3 | 56 |
| Bebra, W. Ger. | C4 | 19 |
| Bécancour, Que. | C5 | 74 |
| Bécancour, stm., Que. | C6 | 74 |
| Beccles, Eng., U.K. | B9 | 12 |
| Bečej, Yugo. | C5 | 24 |
| Bécerreá, Spain | A2 | 22 |
| Béchar, Alg. | C4 | 44 |
| Becharof Lake, l., Ak., U.S. | D8 | 79 |
| Bechyně, Czech. | D9 | 19 |
| Beckemeyer, Il., U.S. | E4 | 90 |
| Becker, Mn., U.S. | E5 | 100 |
| Becker, Ms., U.S. | B5 | 101 |
| Becker, co., Mn., U.S. | D3 | 100 |
| Becket, Ma., U.S. | B1 | 98 |
| Beckhām, co., Ok., U.S. | B2 | 113 |
| Beckley, W.V., U.S. | D3 | 125 |
| Beckum, W. Ger. | B3 | 19 |
| Beckville, Tx., U.S. | C5 | 120 |
| Beckwith Creek, stm., La., U.S. | D2 | 95 |
| Becky Peak, mtn., Nv., U.S. | D7 | 105 |
| Bedale, Eng., U.K. | F7 | 13 |
| Bédarieux, Fr. | F5 | 16 |
| Bedburg, W. Ger. | C1 | 19 |
| Bederkesa, W. Ger. | E2 | 15 |
| Bedford, N.S. | E6 | 71 |
| Bedford, Que. | D5 | 74 |
| Bedford, Eng., U.K. | D6 | 10 |
| Bedford, In., U.S. | G5 | 91 |
| Bedford, Ia., U.S. | D3 | 92 |
| Bedford, Ky., U.S. | B4 | 94 |
| Bedford, Ma., U.S. | B5 | 98 |
| Bedford, Mi., U.S. | F5 | 99 |
| Bedford, Mo., U.S. | B4 | 102 |
| Bedford, N.H., U.S. | E3 | 106 |
| Bedford, Oh., U.S. | A4 | 112 |
| Bedford, Pa., U.S. | F4 | 115 |
| Bedford, Tx., U.S. | *n9 | 120 |
| Bedford, Va., U.S. | C3 | 123 |
| Bedford, Wy., U.S. | D2 | 127 |
| Bedford, co., Pa., U.S. | G4 | 115 |
| Bedford, co., Tn., U.S. | B5 | 119 |
| Bedford, co., Va., U.S. | C3 | 123 |
| Bedford Heights, Oh., U.S. | *h9 | 112 |
| Bedford Hills, N.Y., U.S. | D7 | 109 |
| Bedfordshire, co., Eng., U.K. | B7 | 12 |
| Bedias, Tx., U.S. | D5 | 120 |
| Bedlington, Eng., U.K. | C6 | 10 |
| Bedminster, N.J., U.S. | B3 | 107 |
| Bedourie, Austl. | B2 | 51 |
| Bedrock, Co., U.S. | C2 | 83 |
| Będzin, Pol. | g10 | 26 |
| Bee, Ne., U.S. | C8 | 104 |
| Bee, co., Tx., U.S. | E4 | 120 |
| Beebe, Que. | D5 | 74 |
| Beebe, Ar., U.S. | B4 | 81 |
| Beebe Plain, Vt., U.S. | A4 | 122 |
| Beebe River, N.H., U.S. | C3 | 106 |
| Bee Branch, Ar., U.S. | B3 | 81 |
| Beech Bluff, Tn., U.S. | B3 | 119 |
| Beech Bottom, W.V., U.S. | f8 | 125 |
| Beech Creek, Ky., U.S. | C2 | 94 |
| Beech Creek, Pa., U.S. | D6 | 115 |
| Beecher, Il., U.S. | B6 | 90 |
| Beecher, Mi., U.S. | E7 | 99 |
| Beecher City, Il., U.S. | D5 | 90 |
| Beechey Head, c., B.C. | h12 | 69 |
| Beech Fork, stm., Ky., U.S. | C4 | 94 |
| Beech Grove, Ar., U.S. | A5 | 81 |
| Beech Grove, In., U.S. | E5 | 91 |
| Beech Grove, Tn., U.S. | C2 | 94 |
| Beechgrove, Tn., U.S. | B5 | 119 |
| Beech Island, S.C., U.S. | E4 | 117 |
| Beechwood, N.B. | C2 | 71 |
| Beechwood, Ma., U.S. | h12 | 98 |
| Beechwood, Mi., U.S. | B2 | 99 |
| Beechy, Sask. | G2 | 75 |
| Beecroft Head, c., Austl. | G8 | 51 |
| Beedeville, Ar., U.S. | B4 | 81 |
| Beef Island, i., Tn., U.S. | e8 | 119 |
| Beef Island, i., V.I., Br. | B6 | 65 |
| Beek, Neth. | D5 | 17 |
| Beeler, Ks., U.S. | D3 | 93 |
| Beelitz, E. Ger. | A7 | 19 |
| Beemer, Ne., U.S. | C9 | 104 |
| Beenleigh, Austl. | C9 | 51 |
| Bee Ridge, Fl., U.S. | q11 | 86 |
| Beersheba (Be'er Sheva'), Isr. | B3 | 38 |
| Beersheba Springs, Tn., U.S. | D8 | 119 |
| Beersville, N.B. | C4 | 71 |
| Beeskow, E. Ger. | B7 | 18 |
| Beesleys Point, N.J., U.S. | E3 | 107 |
| Beethoven Peninsula, pen., Ant. | B5 | 7 |
| Beeton, Ont. | C5 | 73 |
| Beetzendorf, E. Ger. | F5 | 15 |
| Beeville, Tx., U.S. | E4 | 120 |
| Befale, Zaire | A3 | 48 |
| Beg, Lough, l., N. Ire. U.K. | C5 | 11 |
| Bega, Austl. | G8 | 50 |
| Beggs, Ok., U.S. | B5 | 113 |
| Begicheva, i., Sov. Un. | B3 | 128 |
| Béhague, Pointe, c., Fr. Gu. | B4 | 59 |
| Behāla (South Suburban), India | *D8 | 36 |
| Behbahān, Iran | F5 | 39 |
| Behm Canal, strt., Ak., U.S. | n24 | 79 |
| Behshahr, Iran | C6 | 39 |
| Bei'an, China | B10 | 31 |
| Beigi, Eth. | D3 | 47 |
| Beihai, China | G6 | 31 |
| Beijing (Peking), China | D8 | 31 |
| Beili, China | D8 | 31 |
| Beilngries, W. Ger. | D6 | 19 |
| Beinamar, Chad | D3 | 48 |
| Beipiao, China | *C9 | 31 |
| Beira, Moz. | A5 | 49 |
| Beira, hist. reg., Port. | B2 | 22 |
| Beirne, Ar., U.S. | D2 | 81 |
| Beirut (Bayrūt), Leb. | B3 | 38 |
| Beiseker, Alta. | D4 | 68 |
| Beitbridge, Zimb. | B5 | 49 |
| Beius, Rom. | B6 | 24 |
| Beja, Port. | C2 | 22 |
| Bejaïa (Bougie), Alg. | B6 | 44 |
| Béja, Tun. | B6 | 44 |
| Béjar, Spain | B3 | 22 |
| Bejou, Mn., U.S. | C3 | 100 |
| Bejuco, Pan. | F8 | 62 |
| Bekabad, Sov. Un. | G22 | 8 |
| Bekdash, Sov. Un. | E4 | 28 |
| Békés, Hung. | B5 | 24 |
| Békéscsaba, Hung. | B5 | 24 |
| Bekily, Madag. | h9 | 49 |
| Bela, India | E8 | 37 |
| Bela, Pak. | C4 | 36 |
| Bela Crkva, Yugo. | C5 | 24 |
| Belaga, Malay. | E4 | 34 |
| Bel Air, Md., U.S. | A5 | 97 |
| Bel Aire, Ks., U.S. | g12 | 93 |
| Bel Aire Estates, Ct., U.S. | D7 | 84 |
| Belalcázar, Spain | C3 | 22 |
| Bel Alton, Md., U.S. | D4 | 97 |
| Belampalli, India | E6 | 36 |
| Belas, Port. | f9 | 22 |
| Bela Vista, Braz. | C1 | 56 |
| Bela Vista, Moz. | C5 | 49 |
| Bela Vista de Goiás, Braz. | B3 | 56 |
| Belawan, Indon. | E1 | 34 |
| Belaya, stm., Sov. Un. | B4 | 28 |
| Belaya Glina, Sov. Un. | H13 | 27 |
| Belaya Tserkov, Sov. Un. | G8 | 27 |
| Belcamp, Md., U.S. | B5 | 97 |
| Belcher, La., U.S. | B2 | 95 |
| Belcher, Ky., U.S. | C7 | 94 |
| Belcherāgh, Afg. | D12 | 39 |
| Belcher Islands, is., N.W. Ter. | E17 | 66 |
| Belchertown, Ma., U.S. | B3 | 98 |
| Belcourt, N.D., U.S. | A6 | 111 |
| Belcoville, N.J., U.S. | E3 | 107 |
| Belden, Ms., U.S. | A5 | 101 |
| Belden, Ne., U.S. | B8 | 104 |
| Belden, N.D., U.S. | A3 | 111 |
| Belding, Mi., U.S. | E5 | 99 |
| Belecke, W. Ger. | B3 | 19 |
| Beled Weyne, Som. | E6 | 47 |
| Belém (Pará), Braz. | B1 | 57 |
| Belém, Port. | f9 | 22 |
| Belén, Arg. | E2 | 55 |
| Belén, Para. | D4 | 55 |
| Belén, Ms., U.S. | A3 | 101 |
| Belén, N.M., U.S. | C3 | 108 |
| Belén, Ur. | E1 | 56 |
| Belén de Escobar, Arg. | g7 | 54 |
| Belenkoye, Sov. Un. | q20 | 27 |
| Belev, Sov. Un. | E11 | 27 |
| Belfair, Wa., U.S. | B3 | 124 |
| Belfast, N. Ire., U.K. | C4 | 10 |
| Belfast, Me., U.S. | D3 | 96 |
| Belfast, N.Y., U.S. | C2 | 109 |
| Belfast, N.C., U.S. | B5 | 110 |
| Belfast, Oh., U.S. | C2 | 112 |
| Belfast, Tn., U.S. | B5 | 119 |
| Belfast Lough, b., N. Ire., U.K. | C6 | 11 |
| Belfield, N.D., U.S. | C2 | 111 |
| Belford, Eng., U.K. | E7 | 13 |
| Belford, N.J., U.S. | C4 | 107 |
| Belfort, Fr. | D7 | 16 |
| Belfort, N.Y., U.S. | B5 | 109 |
| Belfort, ter., Fr. | B2 | 20 |
| Belfry, Ky., U.S. | C7 | 94 |
| Belfry, Mt., U.S. | E8 | 103 |
| Belgaum, India | E5 | 36 |
| Belgica Mountains, mts., Ant. | B16 | 7 |
| Belgium, Il., U.S. | C6 | 90 |
| Belgium, Wi., U.S. | E6 | 126 |
| Belgium, ctry., Eur. | B6 | 16 |
| Belgorod, Sov. Un. | F11 | 27 |
| Belgorod-Dnestrovskiy, Sov. Un. | H8 | 27 |
| Belgrade, Mn., U.S. | E3 | 100 |
| Belgrade, Mo., U.S. | D7 | 102 |
| Belgrade, Mt., U.S. | E5 | 103 |
| Belgrade, Ne., U.S. | C7 | 104 |
| Belgrade (Beograd), Yugo. | C5 | 24 |
| Belgrade Lakes, Me., U.S. | D3 | 96 |
| Belgreen, Al., U.S. | A2 | 78 |
| Belhaven, N.C., U.S. | B6 | 110 |
| Belice, stm., Italy | F4 | 23 |
| Beli Lom, stm., Bul. | D8 | 24 |
| Belington, W.V., U.S. | B5 | 125 |
| Belitung, i., Indon. | F3 | 34 |
| Belize, ctry., N.A. | D7 | 63 |
| Belize, stm., Belize | B3 | 62 |
| Belize City, Belize | D7 | 63 |
| Belkino, Sov. Un. | B11 | 30 |
| Belknap, Il., U.S. | F5 | 90 |
| Belknap, co., N.H., U.S. | C3 | 106 |
| Belknap Crater, crat., Or., U.S. | C5 | 114 |
| Belknap Mountain, mtn., N.H., U.S. | C4 | 106 |
| Belkovskiy, stm., Sov. Un. | B1 | 128 |
| Bell, Ca., U.S. | *E4 | 82 |
| Bell, Fl., U.S. | C4 | 86 |
| Bell, co., Ky., U.S. | D6 | 94 |
| Bell, co., Tx., U.S. | D4 | 120 |
| Bella Bella, B.C. | C3 | 69 |
| Bellac, Fr. | D4 | 16 |
| Bella Coola, B.C. | C4 | 69 |
| Bella Coola, stm., B.C. | C4 | 69 |
| Bellagio, Italy | D5 | 20 |
| Bellaire, Fl., U.S. | *m8 | 86 |
| Bellaire, Ks., U.S. | D5 | 93 |
| Bellaire, Mi., U.S. | D5 | 99 |
| Bellaire, Oh., U.S. | B5 | 112 |
| Bellaire, Tx., U.S. | r14 | 120 |
| Bellamy, Al., U.S. | C1 | 78 |
| Bellano, Italy | D7 | 21 |
| Bellary, India | E4 | 36 |
| Bella Unión, Ur. | E1 | 56 |
| Bella Vista, Arg. | E2 | 55 |
| Bella Vista, Arg. | B4 | 54 |
| Bella Vista, Ar., U.S. | A1 | 81 |
| Belledune, N.B. | B4 | 71 |
| Belleek, N. Ire., U.K. | C3 | 11 |
| Bellefleur, N.B. | B2 | 71 |
| Bellefontaine, Ms., U.S. | B4 | 101 |
| Bellefontaine, Oh., U.S. | B2 | 112 |
| Bellefontaine Neighbors, Mo., U.S. | *f13 | 102 |
| Bellefonte, Ar., U.S. | A2 | 81 |
| Bellefonte, De., U.S. | *A3 | 85 |
| Bellefonte, Pa., U.S. | E6 | 115 |
| Belle Fourche, S.D., U.S. | C2 | 118 |
| Belle Fourche, stm., U.S. | C3 | 118 |
| Belle Fourche Reservoir, res., S.D., U.S. | C2 | 118 |
| Bellegarde, Fr. | F6 | 16 |
| Belle Glade, Fl., U.S. | F6 | 86 |
| Belle Haven, Va., U.S. | C7 | 123 |
| Belleherbe, Fr. | B2 | 21 |
| Belle Isle, Fl., U.S. | D5 | 86 |
| Belle Isle, i., Newf. | C4 | 72 |
| Belle Isle, Strait of, strt., Newf. | C4 | 72 |
| Belleisle Creek, N.B. | D4 | 71 |
| Belle Mead, N.J., U.S. | C3 | 107 |
| Belle Meade, Tn., U.S. | g10 | 119 |
| Belle Mina, Al., U.S. | A3 | 78 |
| Bellemoor, De., U.S. | *B3 | 85 |
| Belleoram, Newf. | E4 | 72 |
| Belleplain, N.J., U.S. | E3 | 107 |
| Belle Plaine, Sask. | G3 | 75 |
| Belle Plaine, Ia., U.S. | C5 | 92 |
| Belle Plaine, Ks., U.S. | E6 | 93 |
| Belle Plaine, Mn., U.S. | F5 | 100 |
| Belle Rive, Il., U.S. | E5 | 90 |
| Belle River, Ont. | E2 | 73 |
| Belle Rose, La., U.S. | D4 | 95 |
| Belleu, Fr. | E3 | 17 |
| Belle Union, In., U.S. | E4 | 91 |
| Belle Valley, Oh., U.S. | C4 | 112 |
| Belle Vernon, Pa., U.S. | F2 | 115 |
| Belleview, Fl., U.S. | C4 | 86 |
| Belleview, Mo., U.S. | D7 | 102 |
| Belle View, Va., U.S. | g12 | 123 |
| Belleville, N.S. | F4 | 71 |
| Belleville, Ont. | C7 | 73 |
| Belleville, Fr. | D6 | 16 |
| Belleville, Il., U.S. | E4 | 90 |
| Belleville, Ks., U.S. | C6 | 93 |
| Belleville, Mi., U.S. | p15 | 99 |
| Belleville, N.J., U.S. | B4 | 107 |
| Belleville, N.Y., U.S. | B4 | 109 |
| Belleville, Pa., U.S. | E6 | 115 |
| Belleville, R.I., U.S. | E4 | 116 |
| Belleville, W.V., U.S. | B3 | 125 |
| Belleville, Wi., U.S. | F4 | 126 |
| Bellevue, Alta. | E3 | 68 |
| Bellevue, Id., U.S. | F4 | 89 |
| Bellevue, Ia., U.S. | B7 | 92 |
| Bellevue, Ky., U.S. | h13 | 94 |
| Bellevue, Md., U.S. | C5 | 97 |
| Bellevue, Mi., U.S. | F5 | 99 |
| Bellevue, Ne., U.S. | C10 | 104 |
| Bellevue, Oh., U.S. | A3 | 112 |
| Bellevue, Pa., U.S. | F1 | 115 |
| Bellevue, Tx., U.S. | C3 | 120 |
| Bellevue, Wa., U.S. | e11 | 124 |
| Belley, Fr. | E6 | 16 |
| Belle Yella, Lib. | E3 | 45 |
| Bellflower, Ca., U.S. | n12 | 82 |
| Bellflower, Il., U.S. | C5 | 90 |
| Bellflower, Mo., U.S. | B6 | 102 |
| Bell Gardens, Ca., U.S. | *n12 | 82 |
| Bellingham, Eng., U.K. | C6 | 10 |
| Bellingham, Ma., U.S. | B5 | 98 |
| Bellingham, Mn., U.S. | E2 | 100 |
| Bellingham, Wa., U.S. | A3 | 124 |
| Bellingshausen Sea, Ant. | B3 | 7 |
| Bellinzona, Switz. | E4 | 18 |
| Bell-Irving, stm., B.C. | A3 | 69 |
| Bellis, Alta. | B4 | 68 |
| Bell Island, i., Newf. | E5 | 72 |
| Bell Island, i., Newf. | C4 | 72 |
| Bellmawr, N.J., U.S. | D2 | 107 |
| Bellmead, Tx., U.S. | *D4 | 120 |
| Bellmont, Il., U.S. | E6 | 90 |
| Bellmore, In., U.S. | E3 | 91 |
| Bellmore, N.Y., U.S. | *m15 | 109 |
| Bello, Col. | B2 | 60 |
| Bellows Falls, Vt., U.S. | E4 | 122 |
| Belloy, Alta. | B1 | 68 |
| Bellport, N.Y., U.S. | n16 | 109 |
| Bell Ranch, N.M., U.S. | B5 | 108 |
| Bells, Tn., U.S. | B2 | 119 |
| Bellsburg, Tn., U.S. | A4 | 119 |
| Bells Corners, Ont. | h12 | 73 |
| Bells Creek, stm., W.V., U.S. | m13 | 125 |
| Bellshill, Scot., U.K. | *E4 | 13 |
| Belltown, De., U.S. | F5 | 85 |
| Bellview, N.M., U.S. | C6 | 108 |
| Bell Ville, Arg. | A4 | 54 |
| Bellville, Ga., U.S. | D5 | 87 |
| Bellville, Oh., U.S. | B3 | 112 |
| Bellville, Tx., U.S. | E4 | 120 |
| Bellvue, Co., U.S. | A5 | 83 |
| Bellwood, Al., U.S. | D4 | 78 |
| Bellwood, Il., U.S. | k9 | 90 |
| Bellwood, Ne., U.S. | C8 | 104 |
| Bellwood, Pa., U.S. | E5 | 115 |
| Bellwood, Va., U.S. | n18 | 123 |
| Belly, stm., N.A. | E4 | 68 |
| Belmar, N.J., U.S. | C4 | 107 |
| Bélmez, Spain | C3 | 22 |
| Belmond, Ia., U.S. | B4 | 92 |
| Belmont, Man. | E2 | 70 |
| Belmont, N.S. | D6 | 71 |
| Belmont, Ca., U.S. | h8 | 82 |
| Belmont, Ms., U.S. | A5 | 101 |
| Belmont, N.H., U.S. | D4 | 106 |
| Belmont, N.Y., U.S. | C2 | 109 |
| Belmont, N.C., U.S. | B1 | 110 |
| Belmont, Oh., U.S. | B4 | 112 |
| Belmont, Tx., U.S. | E4 | 120 |
| Belmont, Vt., U.S. | E3 | 122 |
| Belmont, W.V., U.S. | B3 | 125 |
| Belmont, Wi., U.S. | F3 | 126 |
| Belmont, co., Oh., U.S. | C4 | 112 |
| Belmont Heights, Ut., U.S. | *C4 | 121 |
| Belmopan, Belize | D7 | 63 |
| Belmore, Oh., U.S. | A2 | 112 |
| Belmullet, Ire. | C1 | 11 |
| Bel-Nor, Mo., U.S. | f13 | 102 |
| Belo, Madag. | g8 | 49 |
| Belœil, Que. | D4 | 74 |
| Belogorsk, Sov. Un. | D15 | 29 |
| Belo Horizonte, Braz. | A6 | 56 |
| Beloit, Ia., U.S. | A1 | 92 |
| Beloit, Ks., U.S. | C5 | 93 |
| Beloit, Oh., U.S. | B5 | 112 |
| Beloit, Wi., U.S. | F4 | 126 |
| Beloit North, Wi., U.S. | F4 | 126 |
| Belokany, Sov. Un. | B16 | 40 |
| Belomorsk, Sov. Un. | C6 | 29 |
| Belopolye, Sov. Un. | F10 | 27 |
| Beloretsk, Sov. Un. | D8 | 29 |
| Belovo, Sov. Un. | E26 | 8 |
| Beloye, Lake, l., Sov. Un. | A11 | 27 |
| Belozersk, Sov. Un. | B11 | 27 |
| Belp, Switz. | C4 | 21 |
| Belpre, Ks., U.S. | E4 | 93 |
| Belpre, Oh., U.S. | C4 | 112 |
| Belshaw, In., U.S. | B3 | 91 |
| Belspring, Va., U.S. | C2 | 123 |
| Belt, Mt., U.S. | C6 | 103 |
| Belt Creek, stm., Mt., U.S. | C6 | 103 |
| Belted Range, mts., Nv., U.S. | F5 | 105 |
| Belterra, Braz. | C3 | 59 |
| Belton, Mo., U.S. | C3 | 102 |
| Belton, S.C., U.S. | B3 | 117 |
| Belton, Tx., U.S. | D4 | 120 |
| Belton Lake, res., Tx., U.S. | D4 | 120 |
| Beltra, Ire. | C3 | 11 |
| Beltrami, Mn., U.S. | C2 | 100 |
| Beltrami, co., Mn., U.S. | B3 | 100 |
| Beltsville, Md., U.S. | B4 | 97 |
| Beltsy, Sov. Un. | H6 | 27 |
| Belturbet, Ire. | C4 | 11 |
| Belukha, Mount, mtn., Sov. Un. | E11 | 29 |
| Belumut, mtn., Malay. | L5 | 35 |
| Beluran, Malay. | D5 | 34 |
| Belvedere, Ga., U.S. | *C2 | 87 |
| Belvedere Marittimo, Italy | E5 | 23 |
| Belvedere Park, Ga., U.S. | *h8 | 87 |
| Belvidere, De., U.S. | *B3 | 85 |
| Belvidere, Il., U.S. | A5 | 90 |
| Belvidere, Ks., U.S. | E4 | 93 |
| Belvidere, Ne., U.S. | D8 | 104 |
| Belvidere, N.J., U.S. | B2 | 107 |
| Belvidere, N.C., U.S. | A6 | 110 |
| Belvidere, S.D., U.S. | D4 | 118 |
| Belvidere, Tn., U.S. | B5 | 119 |
| Belvidere Center, Vt., U.S. | B3 | 122 |
| Belvidere Mountain, mtn., Vt., U.S. | B3 | 122 |
| Belview, Mn., U.S. | F3 | 100 |
| Belvue, Ks., U.S. | C7 | 93 |
| Belwood, Ont. | D4 | 73 |
| Belyando, stm., Austl. | D8 | 50 |
| Belyy, Sov. Un. | D9 | 27 |
| Belyy Bom, Sov. Un. | E26 | 8 |
| Belyy Island, i., Sov. Un. | B9 | 29 |
| Belyy Yar, Sov. Un. | B11 | 28 |
| Belzig, E. Ger. | A7 | 19 |
| Belzoni, Ms., U.S. | B3 | 101 |
| Bembézar, stm., Spain | C3 | 22 |
| Bement, Il., U.S. | D5 | 90 |
| Bemidji, Mn., U.S. | C3 | 100 |
| Bemidji, Lake, l., Mn., U.S. | C4 | 100 |
| Bemis, S.D., U.S. | C9 | 118 |
| Bemis, Tn., U.S. | B3 | 119 |
| Bemis, W.V., U.S. | C5 | 125 |
| Bemiss, Ga., U.S. | F3 | 87 |
| Bemus Point, N.Y., U.S. | C1 | 109 |
| Bena, Mn., U.S. | C4 | 100 |
| Benāb, Iran | C3 | 39 |
| Benabarre, Spain | A6 | 22 |
| Bena Dibele, Zaire | B4 | 48 |
| Benalla, Austl. | G8 | 50 |
| Benalto, Alta. | D3 | 68 |
| Benares see Vārānasi, India | C7 | 36 |
| Benátky [nad Jizerou], Czech. | n18 | 29 |
| Benavente, Spain | A3 | 22 |
| Benavides, Tx., U.S. | F3 | 120 |
| Benbane Head, c., N. Ire., U.K. | A5 | 11 |
| Benbaun, mtn., Ire. | D2 | 11 |
| Benbecula, i., Scot., U.K. | C1 | 13 |
| Ben Bolt, Tx., U.S. | F3 | 120 |
| Benbow, Fl., U.S. | F5 | 86 |
| Benbrook, Tx., U.S. | *n9 | 120 |
| Benbrook Lake, res., Tx., U.S. | n9 | 120 |
| Benbush, W.V., U.S. | B5 | 125 |
| Bend, Or., U.S. | C5 | 114 |
| Ben Davis Point, c., N.J., U.S. | E2 | 107 |
| Bendeleben, Mount, mtn., Ak., U.S. | B7 | 79 |
| Bender Beyla, Som. | F4 | 47 |
| Bendersville, Pa., U.S. | G7 | 115 |
| Bendery, Sov. Un. | H7 | 27 |
| Bendigo, Austl. | G7 | 50 |
| Bendorf, W. Ger. | C2 | 19 |
| Bene Beraq, Isr. | g10 | 41 |
| Benedict, Ks., U.S. | E8 | 93 |
| Benedict, Md., U.S. | C4 | 97 |
| Benedict, Ne., U.S. | C8 | 104 |
| Benedict, N.D., U.S. | B4 | 111 |
| Benedict, Mount, mtn., Newf. | g10 | 72 |
| Benenitra, Madag. | h9 | 49 |
| Beneraird, hill, Scot., U.K. | E4 | 13 |
| Beneŝov, Czech. | D3 | 19 |
| Bénestroff, Fr. | F6 | 17 |
| Benevento, Italy | D6 | 23 |
| Benevolence, Ga., U.S. | D2 | 87 |
| Benewah, co., Id., U.S. | B2 | 89 |
| Benezett, Pa., U.S. | D5 | 115 |
| Benfeld, Fr. | A3 | 20 |
| Bengal, hist. reg., Asia | D6 | 36 |
| Bengal, Bay of, b., Asia | F8 | 36 |
| Ben Gardane, Tun. | C7 | 44 |
| Bengbu, China | C4 | 31 |
| Benghazi (Banghāzī), Libya | C8 | 44 |
| Bengkalis, Indon. | E3 | 34 |
| Bengkalis, i., Indon. | L5 | 34 |
| Bengkulu, Indon. | F3 | 34 |
| Bengo, dept., Ang. | C1 | 48 |
| Bengough, Sask. | H3 | 75 |
| Benguela, Ang. | D1 | 49 |
| Benguela, dept., Ang. | D7 | 48 |
| Benham, Ky., U.S. | D7 | 94 |
| Ben Hill, co., Ga., U.S. | E3 | 87 |
| Beni, Nig. | A4 | 48 |
| Beni, dept., Bol. | B2 | 55 |
| Beni, stm., Bol. | B2 | 55 |
| Béni Abbès, Alg. | C4 | 44 |
| Benicarló, Spain | B6 | 22 |
| Benicia, Ca., U.S. | C2 | 82 |
| Benin, ctry., Afr. | G6 | 45 |
| Benin, Bight of, Afr. | H6 | 45 |
| Benin City, Nig. | G6 | 45 |
| Benisa, Spain | C6 | 22 |
| Beni Saf, Alg. | B4 | 44 |
| Benito, Man. | D1 | 70 |
| Benito Juárez, Arg. | B5 | 54 |
| Benjamin, Tx., U.S. | C3 | 120 |
| Benjamin Constant, Braz. | B3 | 58 |
| Benkelman, Ne., U.S. | D4 | 104 |
| Ben Lomond, Ar., U.S. | D1 | 81 |
| Ben Lomond, Ca., U.S. | *D2 | 82 |
| Benmore, Lake, res., N.Z. | P12 | 51 |
| Bennet, Ne., U.S. | D9 | 104 |
| Bennett, Co., U.S. | B6 | 83 |
| Bennett, Ia., U.S. | C7 | 92 |
| Bennett, N.C., U.S. | B3 | 110 |
| Bennett, Wi., U.S. | B2 | 126 |
| Bennett, co., S.D., U.S. | D4 | 118 |
| Bennett Creek, stm., Md., U.S. | B3 | 97 |
| Bennett Island, i., Sov. Un. | B18 | 29 |
| Bennett Lake, l., Man. | C3 | 70 |
| Bennettsville, S.C., U.S. | B8 | 117 |
| Bennington, Id., U.S. | G7 | 89 |
| Bennington, In., U.S. | G7 | 91 |
| Bennington, Ks., U.S. | C6 | 93 |
| Bennington, Ne., U.S. | g12 | 104 |
| Bennington, N.H., U.S. | D3 | 106 |
| Bennington, Ok., U.S. | C5 | 113 |
| Bennington, Vt., U.S. | F2 | 122 |
| Bennington, co., Vt., U.S. | E2 | 122 |
| Benns Church, Va., U.S. | k14 | 123 |
| Benoit, Wi., U.S. | B2 | 126 |
| Benoit, Ms., U.S. | B2 | 101 |
| Bénoué (Benue), stm., Afr. | E7 | 45 |
| Benoy, Chad | D3 | 46 |
| Benque Viejo, Belize | B3 | 62 |
| Bensalem, Pa., U.S. | *F12 | 115 |
| Bensbergün, Switz. | C8 | 21 |
| Bensberg, W. Ger. | C2 | 19 |
| Bensenville, Il., U.S. | B6 | 90 |
| Bensheim, W. Ger. | D4 | 18 |
| Benson, Sask. | H4 | 75 |
| Benson, Az., U.S. | F5 | 80 |
| Benson, Il., U.S. | C4 | 90 |
| Benson, La., U.S. | C2 | 95 |
| Benson, Md., U.S. | A5 | 97 |
| Benson, Mn., U.S. | E3 | 100 |
| Benson, N.C., U.S. | B4 | 110 |
| Benson, Vt., U.S. | D2 | 122 |
| Benson, co., N.D., U.S. | A6 | 111 |
| Bent, N.M., U.S. | D4 | 108 |
| Bent, co., Co., U.S. | D7 | 83 |
| Bentheim, W. Ger. | A2 | 19 |
| Bentinck, i., Burma | G2 | 35 |
| Bentiu, Sud. | D2 | 47 |
| Bentley, Alta. | C3 | 68 |
| Bentley, Ks., U.S. | E6 | 93 |
| Bentley, La., U.S. | C3 | 95 |
| Bentley, N.D., U.S. | C3 | 111 |
| Bentley, Ok., U.S. | C5 | 113 |
| Bentley Creek, Pa., U.S. | C8 | 115 |
| Bentleyville, Pa., U.S. | F1 | 115 |
| Benton, N.B. | D2 | 71 |
| Benton, Ar., U.S. | C3 | 81 |
| Benton, Ca., U.S. | D4 | 82 |
| Benton, Il., U.S. | E5 | 90 |
| Benton, Ia., U.S. | D3 | 92 |
| Benton, Ks., U.S. | E6 | 93 |
| Benton, Ky., U.S. | f9 | 94 |
| Benton, La., U.S. | B2 | 95 |
| Benton, Me., U.S. | D3 | 96 |
| Benton, Mo., U.S. | D8 | 102 |
| Benton, Pa., U.S. | D9 | 115 |
| Benton, Tn., U.S. | D9 | 119 |
| Benton, Wi., U.S. | F3 | 126 |
| Benton, co., Ar., U.S. | A1 | 81 |
| Benton, co., In., U.S. | C3 | 91 |
| Benton, co., Ia., U.S. | B5 | 92 |
| Benton, co., Mn., U.S. | E5 | 100 |
| Benton, co., Mo., U.S. | C4 | 102 |
| Benton, co., Ms., U.S. | A4 | 101 |
| Benton, co., Or., U.S. | C3 | 114 |
| Benton, co., Tn., U.S. | A3 | 119 |
| Benton, co., Wa., U.S. | C6 | 124 |
| Benton City, Wa., U.S. | C6 | 124 |
| Benton Harbor, Mi., U.S. | F4 | 99 |
| Benton Heights, Mi., U.S. | F4 | 99 |
| Bentonia, Ms., U.S. | C3 | 101 |
| Bentonville, Ar., U.S. | A1 | 81 |
| Bentonville, Oh., U.S. | D2 | 112 |
| Bentonville, Va., U.S. | B4 | 123 |
| Bentree, W.V., U.S. | m13 | 125 |
| Bent's Old Fort National Historic Site, hist., Co., U.S. | C7 | 83 |
| Benue (Bénoué), stm., Afr. | E6 | 45 |
| Benwee Head, c., Ire. | B2 | 11 |
| Benwood, W.V., U.S. | f8 | 125 |
| Benxi, China | C9 | 31 |
| Benzie, co., Mi., U.S. | D4 | 99 |
| Beo, Indon. | E7 | 34 |
| Beograd (Belgrade), Yugo. | C5 | 24 |
| Beowawe, Nv., U.S. | C5 | 105 |
| Beppu, Japan | J5 | 33 |
| Beqa, Fiji | I15 | 52 |
| Beqa Passage, strt., Fiji | U26 | 65 |
| Bequia, i., St. Vin. | U26 | 65 |
| Berach, stm., India | H6 | 36 |
| Berati, Alb. | E3 | 24 |
| Berau Bay, b., Indon. | F8 | 34 |
| Berbera, Som. | E4 | 47 |
| Berbérati, Cen. Afr. Rep. | E3 | 46 |
| Berbice, stm., Guy. | B7 | 59 |
| Berceto, Italy | E4 | 20 |
| Berchogur, Sov. Un. | D5 | 28 |
| Berchtesgaden, W. Ger. | E8 | 18 |
| Berck, Fr. | B4 | 16 |
| Berclair, Tx., U.S. | E4 | 120 |
| Berdichev, Sov. Un. | G6 | 27 |
| Berdyansk, Sov. Un. | H11 | 27 |
| Berea, Ky., U.S. | C5 | 94 |
| Berea, Ne., U.S. | B3 | 104 |
| Berea, Oh., U.S. | A4 | 112 |
| Berea, S.C., U.S. | *B3 | 117 |
| Beregovo, Sov. Un. | G4 | 27 |
| Bereku, Tan. | B6 | 48 |
| Berens, stm., Can. | C3 | 70 |
| Berens Island, i., Man. | C3 | 70 |
| Berens River, Man. | C3 | 70 |
| Beresford, S.D., U.S. | D9 | 118 |
| Berettyóújfalu, Hung. | B5 | 24 |
| Berezhany, Sov. Un. | G5 | 27 |
| Berezina, stm., Sov. Un. | E7 | 27 |
| Berezna, Sov. Un. | F8 | 27 |
| Berezniki, Sov. Un. | D8 | 29 |
| Berezovo, Sov. Un. | C9 | 29 |
| Berg, Nor. | q27 | 14 |
| Berga, Spain | A6 | 22 |
| Berga, Swe. | B8 | 15 |
| Bergama, Tur. | C6 | 25 |
| Bergamasque Alps, mts., Italy | A2 | 23 |
| Bergamo, Italy | B2 | 23 |
| Bergedorf, W. Ger. | B5 | 18 |
| Bergen, W. Ger. | F3 | 15 |
| Bergen, Nor. | G1 | 14 |
| Bergen, N.Y., U.S. | B3 | 109 |
| Bergen, N.D., U.S. | A5 | 111 |
| Bergen, co., N.J., U.S. | A4 | 107 |
| Bergen aan Zee, Neth. | B4 | 17 |
| Bergen [auf Rügen], E. Ger. | A6 | 18 |
| Bergenfield, N.J., U.S. | B4 | 107 |
| Bergen see Mons, Bel. | B5 | 16 |
| Bergen op Zoom, Neth. | B6 | 16 |
| Berger, Mo., U.S. | C6 | 102 |
| Bergerac, Fr. | E4 | 16 |
| Bergheim, Tx., U.S. | h7 | 120 |
| Bergisch Gladbach, W. Ger. | C3 | 18 |
| Bergkamen, W. Ger. | B2 | 19 |
| Bergland, Mi., U.S. | m12 | 99 |
| Bergman, Ar., U.S. | A2 | 81 |
| Bergoo, W.V., U.S. | C4 | 125 |
| Bergstrom Air Force Base, mil., Tx., U.S. | D4 | 120 |
| Berguent, Mor. | C4 | 44 |
| Bergün, Switz. | C8 | 21 |
| Bering Sea | D32 | 128 |
| Bering Strait, strt. | C6 | 79 |
| Berino, N.M., U.S. | E3 | 108 |
| Berislav, Sov. Un. | H9 | 27 |
| Berja, Spain | D4 | 22 |
| Berkane, Mor. | C4 | 44 |
| Berkeley, Ont. | C4 | 73 |
| Berkeley, Ca., U.S. | *D2 | 82 |
| Berkeley, Il., U.S. | *k9 | 90 |
| Berkeley, Ky., U.S. | f8 | 94 |
| Berkeley, Mo., U.S. | f13 | 102 |
| Berkeley, R.I., U.S. | B4 | 116 |
| Berkeley, co., S.C., U.S. | E8 | 117 |
| Berkeley, co., W.V., U.S. | B6 | 125 |
| Berkeley, Cabo, c., Ec. | f5 | 58 |
| Berkeley Heights, N.J., U.S. | B4 | 107 |
| Berkeley Springs, W.V., U.S. | B6 | 125 |
| Berkey, Oh., U.S. | A2 | 112 |
| Berkley, Ia., U.S. | C3 | 92 |
| Berkley, Ma., U.S. | C5 | 98 |
| Berkley, Mi., U.S. | F7 | 99 |
| Berkner Island, i., Ant. | B7 | 7 |
| Berkovitsa, Bul. | D6 | 24 |
| Berks, co., Pa., U.S. | F9 | 115 |
| Berkshire, Ma., U.S. | A1 | 98 |
| Berkshire, N.Y., U.S. | C4 | 109 |
| Berkshire, Vt., U.S. | B3 | 122 |
| Berkshire, co., Eng., U.K. | C6 | 12 |
| Berkshire, co., Ma., U.S. | B1 | 98 |
| Berkshire Estates, Ct., U.S. | D2 | 84 |
| Berkshire Hills, hills, Ma., U.S. | B1 | 98 |
| Berland, stm., Alta. | C1 | 68 |
| Berleburg, W. Ger. | B3 | 19 |
| Berlenga Islands, is., Port. | C1 | 22 |
| Berlin (East), E. Ger. | B6 | 18 |
| Berlin (West), W. Ger. | B6 | 18 |
| Berlin, Ct., U.S. | C5 | 84 |
| Berlin, Ga., U.S. | E3 | 87 |
| Berlin, Md., U.S. | D7 | 97 |
| Berlin, Ma., U.S. | B4 | 98 |
| Berlin, N.H., U.S. | B4 | 106 |
| Berlin, N.J., U.S. | D3 | 107 |
| Berlin, N.Y., U.S. | C7 | 109 |
| Berlin, Pa., U.S. | G4 | 115 |
| Berlin, Wi., U.S. | E5 | 126 |
| Berlin, Mount, mtn., Ant. | B35 | 7 |
| Berlin Corners, Vt., U.S. | C3 | 122 |
| Berlin Heights, Oh., U.S. | A3 | 112 |
| Berlin Lake, res., Oh., U.S. | A4 | 112 |
| Berlin Mountain, mtn., U.S. | A1 | 98 |
| Berlin [West], state, W. Ger. | F7 | 15 |
| Bermagui, Austl. | A3 | 54 |
| Bermejo, Spain | A4 | 55 |
| Bermejo, stm., S.A. | E4 | 55 |
| Bermeo, Spain | A4 | 22 |
| Bermuda, dep., N. A. | F14 | 61 |
| Bermuda, i., Ber. | p20 | 64 |
| Bern, Switz. | C4 | 18 |
| Bern, Ks., U.S. | C8 | 93 |
| Bern, state, Switz. | C3 | 20 |
| Bernalillo, N.M., U.S. | B3 | 108 |
| Bernalillo, co., N.M., U.S. | C3 | 108 |
| Bernam, stm., Malay. | K4 | 35 |
| Bernard, Me., U.S. | D4 | 96 |
| Bernard, Ia., U.S. | B7 | 92 |
| Bernardston, Ma., U.S. | A2 | 98 |
| Bernard Lake, l., Ont. | B5 | 73 |
| Bernasconi, Arg. | B4 | 54 |
| Bernau [bei Berlin], E. Ger. | B6 | 18 |
| Bernay, Fr. | C4 | 16 |
| Bernburg, E. Ger. | C5 | 18 |
| Berndorf, Aus. | E8 | 18 |
| Berne, In., U.S. | C8 | 91 |
| Berne, N.Y., U.S. | C6 | 109 |
| Berneray, i., Scot., U.K. | C3 | 13 |
| Bernese Alps, mts., Switz. | C3 | 18 |
| Bernice, Ok., U.S. | A7 | 113 |
| Bernina, Piz, mtn., Eur. | C5 | 18 |
| Bernina Pass, Switz. | C5 | 18 |
| Bernville, Pa., U.S. | F9 | 115 |
| Beroroha, Madag. | h9 | 49 |
| Beroun, Czech. | D3 | 26 |
| Berounka, stm., Czech. | E6 | 100 |
| Berre [-l'Étang], Fr. | F6 | 16 |
| Berri, Austl. | F7 | 50 |
| Berrien, co., Ga., U.S. | E3 | 87 |
| Berrien, co., Mi., U.S. | F4 | 99 |
| Berrien Springs, Mi., U.S. | G4 | 99 |
| Berry, Al., U.S. | B2 | 78 |
| Berry, Ky., U.S. | B5 | 94 |
| Berry, hist. reg., Fr. | C4 | 16 |
| Berry Creek, stm., Alta. | D5 | 68 |
| Berryessa, Lake, res., U.S. | C2 | 82 |
| Berry Hill, Tn., U.S. | g10 | 119 |
| Berryman, Mo., U.S. | D6 | 102 |
| Berryton, Ga., U.S. | B1 | 87 |
| Berryville, Fl., U.S. | u14 | 86 |

| Name | Map Ref. | Page |
|------|----------|------|
| Berryton, Ks., U.S. | m14 | 93 |
| Berryville, Ar., U.S. | A2 | 81 |
| Berryville, Va., U.S. | A5 | 123 |
| Bersenbrück, W. Ger. | B7 | 17 |
| Bershad, Sov. Un. | G7 | 27 |
| Bertha, Mn., U.S. | D3 | 100 |
| Berthier, co., Que. | C4 | 74 |
| Berthierville, Que. | C4 | 74 |
| Berthold, N.D., U.S. | A4 | 111 |
| Berthoud, Co., U.S. | A5 | 83 |
| Berthoud Pass, Co., U.S. | B5 | 83 |
| Bertie, co., N.C., U.S. | A5 | 110 |
| Bertoua, Cam. | E2 | 46 |
| Bertraghboy Bay, b., Ire. | D2 | 11 |
| Bertram, Tx., U.S. | D4 | 120 |
| Bertrand, Mi., U.S. | *G5 | 99 |
| Bertrand, Mo., U.S. | E8 | 102 |
| Bertrand, Ne., U.S. | D6 | 104 |
| Bertrandville, La., U.S. | E5 | 95 |
| Bertrix, Bel. | C6 | 16 |
| Berwick, N.S. | D5 | 71 |
| Berwick, Il., U.S. | C3 | 90 |
| Berwick, Ia., U.S. | e8 | 92 |
| Berwick, La., U.S. | E4 | 95 |
| Berwick, Me., U.S. | E2 | 96 |
| Berwick, N.D., U.S. | A5 | 111 |
| Berwick, Pa., U.S. | D9 | 115 |
| Berwick-upon-Tweed, Eng., U.K. | C6 | 10 |
| Berwind, W.V., U.S. | D3 | 125 |
| Berwyn, Alta. | A2 | 68 |
| Berwyn, Il., U.S. | k9 | 90 |
| Berwyn, Ne., U.S. | C6 | 104 |
| Berwyn, Pa., U.S. | o20 | 115 |
| Beryl, Ut., U.S. | F2 | 121 |
| Besalampy, Madag. | g8 | 49 |
| Besançon, Fr. | D7 | 16 |
| Besar Hantu, mtn., Malay. | K4 | 35 |
| Beskid Mountains, mts., Eur. | D5 | 26 |
| Beskra, Alg. | C6 | 44 |
| Besnard Lake, l., Sask. | B2 | 75 |
| Besni, Tur. | D11 | 40 |
| Bessèges, Fr. | E6 | 16 |
| Bessemer, Al., U.S. | B3 | 78 |
| Bessemer, Mi., U.S. | n11 | 99 |
| Bessemer, Pa., U.S. | E1 | 115 |
| Bessemer City, N.C., U.S. | B1 | 110 |
| Bessie, Ok., U.S. | B3 | 113 |
| Best, Tx., U.S. | D2 | 120 |
| Bestfield, De., U.S. | *B3 | 85 |
| Bestobe, Sov. Un. | C8 | 28 |
| Betafo, Madag. | g9 | 49 |
| Betanzos, Spain | A1 | 22 |
| Bétaré Oya, Cam. | D2 | 46 |
| Betatakin Ruin, hist., Az., U.S. | A5 | 80 |
| Bet Guvrin, Isr. | C6 | 41 |
| Bethalto, Il., U.S. | E3 | 90 |
| Bethanien, Nmb. | C2 | 49 |
| Bethany, Ont. | C6 | 73 |
| Bethany, Ct., U.S. | D4 | 84 |
| Bethany, Il., U.S. | D5 | 90 |
| Bethany, In., U.S. | F5 | 91 |
| Bethany, La., U.S. | B1 | 95 |
| Bethany, Mo., U.S. | A3 | 102 |
| Bethany, Oh., U.S. | n13 | 112 |
| Bethany, Ok., U.S. | B4 | 113 |
| Bethany, W.V., U.S. | A4 | 125 |
| Bethany see Al ʿAyzarīyah, Isr. Occ. | h12 | 41 |
| Bethany Beach, De., U.S. | F5 | 85 |
| Bethel, Ak., U.S. | C7 | 79 |
| Bethel, Ct., U.S. | D2 | 84 |
| Bethel, De., U.S. | F3 | 85 |
| Bethel, Ky., U.S. | B6 | 94 |
| Bethel, Me., U.S. | D2 | 96 |
| Bethel, Mo., U.S. | B5 | 102 |
| Bethel, N.C., U.S. | B5 | 110 |
| Bethel, Oh., U.S. | D1 | 112 |
| Bethel, Oh., U.S. | C7 | 113 |
| Bethel, Pa., U.S. | F9 | 115 |
| Bethel, Vt., U.S. | D3 | 122 |
| Bethel Acres, Ok., U.S. | #C2 | 113 |
| Bethel Park, Pa., U.S. | k14 | 115 |
| Bethel Springs, Tn., U.S. | B3 | 119 |
| Bethera, S.C., U.S. | E8 | 117 |
| Bethesda, Wales, U.K. | A3 | 12 |
| Bethesda, Ar., U.S. | B4 | 81 |
| Bethesda, Md., U.S. | C3 | 97 |
| Bethesda, Oh., U.S. | B4 | 112 |
| Bethlehem (Bayt Laḥm), Isr. Occ. | G10 | 40 |
| Bethlehem, S. Afr. | C4 | 49 |
| Bethlehem, Ct., U.S. | C3 | 84 |
| Bethlehem, Ga., U.S. | C3 | 87 |
| Bethlehem, In., U.S. | G7 | 91 |
| Bethlehem, Md., U.S. | C6 | 97 |
| Bethlehem, N.H., U.S. | B3 | 106 |
| Bethlehem, Pa., U.S. | E11 | 115 |
| Bethlehem, W.V., U.S. | f8 | 125 |
| Bethlehem Junction, N.H., U.S. | B3 | 106 |
| Bethpage, N.Y., U.S. | *E7 | 109 |
| Bethpage, Tn., U.S. | A5 | 119 |
| Bethulie, S. Afr. | D4 | 49 |
| Bethune, Sask. | G3 | 75 |
| Bethune, Co., U.S. | B8 | 83 |
| Bethune, S.C., U.S. | C7 | 117 |
| Betio, i., Kir. | R18 | 52 |
| Betioky, Madag. | h8 | 49 |
| Bet Neḥemya, Isr. | h10 | 41 |
| Betong, Thai. | D2 | 34 |
| Betoota, Austl. | B3 | 51 |
| Betpak-Dala, des., Sov. Un. | D7 | 28 |
| Betroka, Madag. | h9 | 49 |
| Bet Sh'ean, Isr. | B7 | 41 |
| Bet Shemesh, Isr. | C6 | 41 |
| Betsiamites, Que. | k13 | 74 |
| Betsiboka, stm., Madag. | g9 | 49 |
| Betsie, Point, c., Mi., U.S. | D4 | 99 |
| Betsy Layne, Ky., U.S. | C7 | 94 |
| Bette, mtn., Libya | E3 | 43 |
| Bettendorf, Ia., U.S. | C7 | 92 |
| Betterton, Md., U.S. | B5 | 97 |
| Bettiah, India | D10 | 37 |
| Bettles Field, Ak., U.S. | B9 | 79 |
| Bettsville, Oh., U.S. | A2 | 112 |
| Bettyhill, Scot., U.K. | A4 | 10 |
| Betūl, India | D6 | 36 |
| Betwa, stm., India | D6 | 36 |
| Betzdorf, W. Ger. | E7 | 19 |
| Beulah, Al., U.S. | C4 | 78 |
| Beulah, Co., U.S. | C6 | 83 |
| Beulah, Mi., U.S. | D4 | 99 |
| Beulah, Ms., U.S. | B3 | 101 |
| Beulah, N.D., U.S. | B4 | 111 |
| Beulah, Wy., U.S. | B8 | 127 |
| Beulah, Lake, l., Ms., U.S. | B3 | 101 |
| Beulaville, N.C., U.S. | C5 | 110 |
| Beuthen see Bytom, Pol. | C5 | 26 |
| B. Everett Jordan Lake, res., N.C., U.S. | B3 | 110 |
| Beverley, Sask. | G1 | 75 |
| Beverley, Eng., U.K. | D6 | 10 |
| Beverley Head, c., Newf. | D2 | 72 |
| Beverly, Ks., U.S. | C6 | 93 |
| Beverly, Ky., U.S. | D6 | 94 |
| Beverly, Ma., U.S. | A6 | 98 |
| Beverly, N.J., U.S. | C3 | 107 |
| Beverly, Oh., U.S. | C4 | 112 |
| Beverly, Tn., U.S. | m14 | 119 |
| Beverly, W.V., U.S. | C5 | 125 |
| Beverly Hills, Ca., U.S. | m12 | 82 |
| Beverly Hills, Mi., U.S. | *o15 | 99 |
| Beverly Shores, In., U.S. | A4 | 91 |
| Beverstedt, W. Ger. | A6 | 16 |
| Beverwijk, Neth. | A6 | 16 |
| Bewdley, Ont. | C6 | 73 |
| Bex, Switz. | D3 | 21 |
| Bexar, co., Tx., U.S. | E3 | 120 |
| Bexhill-on-Sea, Eng., U.K. | D8 | 12 |
| Bexley, Ms., U.S. | E5 | 101 |
| Bexley, Oh., U.S. | m11 | 112 |
| Beya, Sov. Un. | E27 | 8 |
| Beyer, Pa., U.S. | E3 | 115 |
| Beykoz, Tur. | B7 | 25 |
| Beyla, Gui. | E3 | 45 |
| Beylul, Eth. | C5 | 47 |
| Beypazarı, Tur. | B8 | 40 |
| Beyşehir, Tur. | D8 | 40 |
| Beyşehir, Lake, l., Tur. | D8 | 40 |
| Bezau, Aus. | B5 | 20 |
| Bezerros, Braz. | C3 | 57 |
| Bezhetsk, Sov. Un. | C11 | 27 |
| Béziers, Fr. | F5 | 16 |
| Bezmer, Bul. | D8 | 24 |
| Bezons, Fr. | g9 | 16 |
| Bhādra, India | C6 | 36 |
| Bhadrāchalam, India | I8 | 37 |
| Bhadrak, India | G11 | 37 |
| Bhāg, Pak. | C4 | 36 |
| Bhāgalpur, India | C8 | 36 |
| Bhakkar, Pak. | B5 | 36 |
| Bhaktapur, Nepal | C8 | 36 |
| Bhamo, Burma | D10 | 34 |
| Bhandāra, India | G7 | 37 |
| Bharatpur, India | C6 | 36 |
| Bharatpur, Nepal | D10 | 37 |
| Bharūch, India | D5 | 36 |
| Bhātpāra, India | D8 | 36 |
| Bhāvnagar, India | D5 | 36 |
| Bhawānipatna, India | H9 | 37 |
| Bheigeir, Beinn, hill, Scot., U.K. | E2 | 13 |
| Bhilai (Bhilainagar), India | *D7 | 36 |
| Bhilai, India | G8 | 37 |
| Bhīlwāra, India | E5 | 37 |
| Bhīma, stm., India | E6 | 36 |
| Bhind, India | C6 | 37 |
| Bhiwāni, India | C6 | 36 |
| Bhola, Bngl. | F13 | 37 |
| Bhopāl, India | D6 | 36 |
| Bhor, India | E5 | 36 |
| Bhubaneshwar, India | D8 | 36 |
| Bhuj, India | D4 | 36 |
| Bhumiphol (Yanhee) Dam, Thai. | D3 | 35 |
| Bhusāwal, India | G5 | 37 |
| Bhutan, ctry., Asia | C9 | 36 |
| Bia, mont., mtn., Laos | D4 | 34 |
| Biaboye, Zaire | A4 | 48 |
| Biafra, Bight of, Afr. | E1 | 46 |
| Biak, i., Indon. | F9 | 34 |
| Biała, stm., Pol. | h10 | 26 |
| Biała Podlaska, Pol. | B7 | 26 |
| Biała Przemsza, stm., Pol. | g11 | 26 |
| Białogard (Belgard), Pol. | A4 | 26 |
| Białystok, Pol. | B7 | 26 |
| Bian, Bidean nam, mtn., Scot., U.K. | E2 | 13 |
| Bianco, Italy | E6 | 23 |
| Biankouma, I.C. | E3 | 45 |
| Biarritz, Fr. | F3 | 16 |
| Biasca, Switz. | C4 | 20 |
| Bibā, Eg. | D6 | 43 |
| Bibai, Japan | E10 | 33 |
| Bibala, Ang. | D1 | 48 |
| Bibb, co., Al., U.S. | C2 | 78 |
| Bibb, co., Ga., U.S. | D3 | 87 |
| Bibb City, Ga., U.S. | D2 | 87 |
| Biberach, W. Ger. | D4 | 18 |
| Biberist, Switz. | B4 | 21 |
| Bibiani, Ghana | E4 | 45 |
| Bible Grove, Il., U.S. | E5 | 90 |
| Bible Hill, Tn., U.S. | B3 | 119 |
| Bic, Que. | A9 | 74 |
| Bic, Île du, i., Que. | A9 | 74 |
| Bicaz, Lac les, Rom. | B8 | 24 |
| Bicester, Eng., U.K. | C6 | 12 |
| Biche, Lac la, l., Alta. | B4 | 68 |
| Bichl, W. Ger. | B7 | 20 |
| Bickerton, Cape, c., Ant. | C26 | 7 |
| Bickett Knob, mtn., W.V., U.S. | D4 | 125 |
| Bickle Knob, mtn., W.V., U.S. | C5 | 125 |
| Bickleton, Wa., U.S. | D5 | 124 |
| Bickmore, W.V., U.S. | C3 | 125 |
| Bicknell, In., U.S. | G3 | 91 |
| Bicknell, Ut., U.S. | E4 | 121 |
| Bicoli, Indon. | F7 | 34 |
| Bicske, Hung. | H5 | 37 |
| Bīd, India | D5 | 36 |
| Bida, Nig. | E6 | 45 |
| Bīdar, India | E6 | 36 |
| Biddeford, Me., U.S. | E2 | 96 |
| Biddiyā, Isr. Occ. | g11 | 41 |
| Biddle, Mt., U.S. | E11 | 103 |
| Bideford, Eng., U.K. | E4 | 10 |
| Bidwell, Oh., U.S. | D3 | 112 |
| Bidwell, Mount, mtn., Ca., U.S. | B3 | 82 |
| Bié, dept., Ang. | D2 | 48 |
| Biebrza, stm., Pol. | B7 | 26 |
| Biedenkopf, W. Ger. | C3 | 19 |
| Bieber, Ca., U.S. | B3 | 82 |
| Biel, Switz. | C1 | 21 |
| Biel (Bienne), Lake, l., Switz. | B3 | 20 |
| Bield, Man. | D1 | 70 |
| Bielefeld, W. Ger. | C4 | 18 |
| Biella, Italy | B2 | 23 |
| Bielsko-Biała, Pol. | D5 | 26 |
| Bielsk Podlaski, Pol. | B7 | 26 |
| Bienfait, Sask. | H4 | 75 |
| Bien Hoa, Viet. | G7 | 35 |
| Bienville, co., La., U.S. | B2 | 95 |
| Bienville, Lac, l., Que. | g12 | 74 |
| Bierawka, stm., Pol. | g9 | 26 |
| Bière, Switz. | C1 | 21 |
| Bieruń Nowy, Pol. | g10 | 26 |
| Bieruń Stary, Pol. | g10 | 26 |
| Biese, stm., E. Ger. | F5 | 15 |
| Bietigheim, W. Ger. | F5 | 19 |
| Bièvre, stm., Fr. | g9 | 16 |
| Bièvres, Fr. | h9 | 16 |
| Biferno, stm., Italy | D5 | 23 |
| Big, stm., Mo., U.S. | B2 | 105 |
| Big, stm., Mo., U.S. | c7 | 102 |
| Biga, Tur. | B6 | 25 |
| Big A Mountain, mtn., Va., U.S. | e9 | 123 |
| Big Arm, Mt., U.S. | C2 | 103 |
| Big Bald, Mtn., U.S. | f10 | 119 |
| Big Bald, mtn., Ga., U.S. | B2 | 87 |
| Big Bald Mountain, mtn., N.B. | B3 | 71 |
| Big Baldy, mtn., Id., U.S. | E3 | 89 |
| Big Baldy Mountain, mtn., Mt., U.S. | D6 | 103 |
| Big Bay, Mi., U.S. | B3 | 99 |
| Big Bay, b., N.Z. | P11 | 51 |
| Big Bay De Noc, b., Mi., U.S. | C4 | 99 |
| Big Bayou, stm., Ar., U.S. | D4 | 81 |
| Big Bear, Ca., U.S. | *E5 | 82 |
| Big Bear City, Ca., U.S. | E5 | 82 |
| Big Beaver, Sask. | H3 | 75 |
| Big Belt Mountains, mts., Mt., U.S. | D5 | 103 |
| Big Bend, Ca., U.S. | B3 | 82 |
| Big Bend, La., U.S. | C4 | 95 |
| Big Bend, Wi., U.S. | n11 | 126 |
| Big Bend Dam, S.D., U.S. | C6 | 118 |
| Big Bend National Park, Tx., U.S. | E1 | 120 |
| Big Bend Reservoir, res., Alta. | C3 | 68 |
| Big Birch Lake, l., Mn., U.S. | E4 | 100 |
| Big Black, stm., Me., U.S. | B3 | 96 |
| Big Black, stm., Ms., U.S. | C3 | 101 |
| Big Blue, stm., In., U.S. | E6 | 91 |
| Big Bone, Ky., U.S. | k13 | 94 |
| Big Bow, Ks., U.S. | E2 | 93 |
| Big Burro Mountains, mts., N.M., U.S. | E1 | 108 |
| Big Butt, mtn., Tn., U.S. | C11 | 119 |
| Big Cabin, Ok., U.S. | A6 | 113 |
| Big Cabin Creek, stm., Ok., U.S. | A6 | 113 |
| Big Canyon, val., Tx., U.S. | D1 | 120 |
| Big Chino Wash, val., Az., U.S. | B3 | 80 |
| Big Clifty, Ky., U.S. | C3 | 94 |
| Big Coal, stm., W.V., U.S. | C3 | 125 |
| Big Corney Bayou, stm., U.S. | D3 | 81 |
| Big Costilla Peak, mtn., N.M., U.S. | A4 | 108 |
| Big Creek, B.C. | D6 | 69 |
| Big Creek, Ca., U.S. | D4 | 82 |
| Big Creek, Id., U.S. | D3 | 89 |
| Big Creek, Ky., U.S. | C6 | 94 |
| Big Creek, Ms., U.S. | B4 | 101 |
| Big Creek, W.V., U.S. | C2 | 125 |
| Big Creek, stm., B.C. | D6 | 69 |
| Big Creek, stm., Ar., U.S. | C5 | 81 |
| Big Creek, stm., In., U.S. | H2 | 91 |
| Big Creek, stm., In., U.S. | G7 | 91 |
| Big Creek, stm., Ks., U.S. | D4 | 93 |
| Big Creek, stm., La., U.S. | B4 | 95 |
| Big Creek, stm., Ms., U.S. | D5 | 101 |
| Big Creek, stm., Mo., U.S. | C3 | 102 |
| Big Creek, stm., Tn., U.S. | e8 | 119 |
| Big Creek Lake, res., Al., U.S. | E1 | 78 |
| Big Creek Peak, mtn., Id., U.S. | E5 | 89 |
| Big Cypress Indian Reservation, Fl., U.S. | F5 | 86 |
| Big Cypress Swamp, sw., Fl., U.S. | F5 | 86 |
| Big Darby Creek, stm., Oh., U.S. | C2 | 112 |
| Big Delta, Ak., U.S. | C10 | 79 |
| Big Dry Creek, stm., Mt., U.S. | C10 | 103 |
| Big Duke Dam, N.C., U.S. | B2 | 110 |
| Big Eau Pleine, stm., Wi., U.S. | D3 | 126 |
| Big Eau Pleine Reservoir, res., Wi., U.S. | D4 | 126 |
| Bigej Island, i., Marsh Is. | S17 | 52 |
| Big Elk Creek, stm., U.S. | A6 | 97 |
| Bigelow, Ar., U.S. | B3 | 81 |
| Bigelow, Mn., U.S. | G3 | 100 |
| Bigelow, Mo., U.S. | A2 | 102 |
| Bigelow, Mount, mtn., Me., U.S. | C3 | 96 |
| Bigstick, Lake, l., Sask. | G1 | 75 |
| Big Stone, co., Mn., U.S. | E2 | 100 |
| Bigstone, stm., Man. | B4 | 70 |
| Big Stone Beach, Ct., U.S. | D4 | 85 |
| Big Stone City, S.D., U.S. | B9 | 118 |
| Big Stone Gap, Va., U.S. | f9 | 123 |
| Big Stone Lake, l., U.S. | B4 | 123 |
| Bigstone Lake, l., Sask. | C4 | 75 |
| Bigstone Lake, l., Man. | E2 | 100 |
| Big Sunflower, stm., Ms., U.S. | B3 | 101 |
| Big Sur, Ca., U.S. | D3 | 82 |
| Big Thompson, stm., Co., U.S. | A5 | 83 |
| Big Timber, Mt., U.S. | E7 | 103 |
| Big Top, mtn., Tn., U.S. | B5 | 119 |
| Big Trout Lake, Ont. | n17 | 73 |
| Big Trout Lake, l., Ont. | n17 | 73 |
| Biguaçu, Braz. | D3 | 56 |
| Big Valley, Alta. | C4 | 68 |
| Big Walnut Creek, stm., Oh., U.S. | m11 | 112 |
| Big Wells, Tx., U.S. | E3 | 120 |
| Big Wills Creek, stm., Al., U.S. | A3 | 78 |
| Big Wills Valley, val., Al., U.S. | A3 | 78 |
| Bigwood, Ont. | A4 | 73 |
| Big Gull Lake, l., Ont. | C8 | 73 |
| Big Gully Creek, stm., Sask. | D1 | 75 |
| Big Hatchet Peak, mtn., N.M., U.S. | F1 | 108 |
| Big Hole, stm., Mt., U.S. | E4 | 103 |
| Big Hole National Battlefield, hist., Mt., U.S. | E3 | 103 |
| Bighorn, Mt., U.S. | D9 | 103 |
| Big Horn, Wy., U.S. | B5 | 127 |
| Big Horn, co., Mt., U.S. | E9 | 103 |
| Big Horn, co., Wy., U.S. | B4 | 127 |
| Bighorn Canyon National Recreation Area, U.S. | F8 | 103 |
| Bighorn Lake, res., U.S. | E8 | 103 |
| Bighorn Mountains, mts., Az., U.S. | D2 | 80 |
| Bigi Island, i., Marsh Is. | S17 | 52 |
| Big Island, Va., U.S. | C3 | 123 |
| Big Island, i., N.W. Ter. | D18 | 66 |
| Big Kandiyohi Lake, l., Mn., U.S. | F4 | 100 |
| Big Knob, mtn., Pa., U.S. | F6 | 115 |
| Big Lake, mtn., Va., U.S. | f9 | 123 |
| Big Lake, Mn., U.S. | E5 | 100 |
| Big Lake, Tx., U.S. | D2 | 120 |
| Big Lake, l., Me., U.S. | C5 | 96 |
| Big Lake, l., Mn., U.S. | E5 | 100 |
| Biglerville, Pa., U.S. | G7 | 115 |
| Big Lookout Mountain, mtn., Or., U.S. | C9 | 114 |
| Big Lost, stm., Id., U.S. | F5 | 89 |
| Big Moose, N.Y., U.S. | B6 | 109 |
| Big Mossy Point, c., Man. | C2 | 70 |
| Big Mountain, mtn., Nv., U.S. | B2 | 105 |
| Big Muddy, stm., Il., U.S. | F4 | 90 |
| Big Muddy Creek, stm., Mt., U.S. | B12 | 103 |
| Big Muddy Lake, l., Sask. | H3 | 75 |
| Big Nemaha, stm., Ne., U.S. | D10 | 104 |
| Bignona, Sen. | D1 | 45 |
| Big North Mountain, mts., Va., U.S. | B4 | 123 |
| Bigonville, Lux. | E5 | 17 |
| Big Otter, stm., Va., U.S. | C3 | 123 |
| Big Pine, Ca., U.S. | D4 | 82 |
| Big Pine Creek, stm., In., U.S. | D3 | 91 |
| Big Pine Lake, l., Mn., U.S. | D3 | 100 |
| Big Pine Mountain, mtn., Ca., U.S. | E4 | 82 |
| Big Piney, Mo., U.S. | D5 | 102 |
| Big Piney, Wy., U.S. | D2 | 127 |
| Big Piney, stm., Mo., U.S. | D5 | 102 |
| Big Piney Creek, stm., Ar., U.S. | B2 | 81 |
| Big Pipe Creek, stm., Md., U.S. | A3 | 97 |
| Bigpoint, Ms., U.S. | E5 | 101 |
| Big Pool, Md., U.S. | A1 | 97 |
| Big Prairie, Oh., U.S. | B3 | 112 |
| Big Quill Lake, l., Sask. | F3 | 75 |
| Big Raccoon Creek, stm., In., U.S. | E4 | 91 |
| Big Rapids, Mi., U.S. | E5 | 99 |
| Big Rib, stm., Wi., U.S. | C3 | 126 |
| Big River, Sask. | D2 | 75 |
| Big Rock, Il., U.S. | B5 | 90 |
| Big Rock, Tn., U.S. | A4 | 119 |
| Big Rock Mountain, mtn., Ar., U.S. | h10 | 81 |
| Big Run, Pa., U.S. | E4 | 115 |
| Big Sable Point, c., Mi., U.S. | D4 | 99 |
| Big Sandy, Mt., U.S. | B6 | 103 |
| Big Sandy, Tn., U.S. | A3 | 119 |
| Big Sandy, Tx., U.S. | C5 | 120 |
| Big Sandy, stm., U.S. | C2 | 125 |
| Big Sandy, stm., Az., U.S. | C2 | 80 |
| Big Sandy, stm., Tn., U.S. | A3 | 119 |
| Big Sandy, stm., Wy., U.S. | D3 | 127 |
| Big Sandy Creek, stm., Co., U.S. | C8 | 83 |
| Big Sandy Creek, stm., Mt., U.S. | B6 | 103 |
| Big Sandy Creek, stm., W.V., U.S. | C3 | 125 |
| Big Sandy Creek, stm., Wy., U.S. | D3 | 127 |
| Big Sandy Lake, l., Mn., U.S. | D5 | 100 |
| Big Sandy Reservoir, res., Wy., U.S. | D3 | 127 |
| Big Satilla Creek, stm., Ga., U.S. | E4 | 87 |
| Big Savage Mountain, mtr., U.S. | k12 | 97 |
| Big Sheep Mountain, mtn., Mt., U.S. | C11 | 103 |
| Big Shiney Mountain, mtn., Pa., U.S. | B6 | 41 |
| Big Sioux, stm., U.S. | E9 | 118 |
| Big Slough, stm., Ga., U.S. | F2 | 87 |
| Big Smoky Valley, val., Nv., U.S. | E4 | 105 |
| Big Snowy Mountains, mts., Mt., U.S. | D7 | 103 |
| Big Southern Butte, mtn., Id., U.S. | F5 | 89 |
| Big South Fork, stm., Ky., U.S. | k13 | 94 |
| Big Spencer Mountain, mtn., Me., U.S. | C3 | 96 |
| Big Spring, Ky., U.S. | C3 | 94 |
| Big Spring, Md., U.S. | A2 | 97 |
| Big Spring, Tx., U.S. | C2 | 120 |
| Big Springs, Ks., U.S. | k15 | 93 |
| Big Springs, Ne., U.S. | C3 | 104 |
| Big Springs, W.V., U.S. | C3 | 125 |
| Big Spruce Knob, mtn., W.V., U.S. | C4 | 125 |
| Big Squaw Mountain, mtn., Me., U.S. | C3 | 96 |
| Bigstick, Lake, l., Sask. | G1 | 75 |
| Big Stone, co., Mn., U.S. | E2 | 100 |
| Bigstone, stm., Man. | B4 | 70 |
| Big Stone Beach, Ct., U.S. | D4 | 85 |
| Big Stone City, S.D., U.S. | B9 | 118 |
| Big Stone Gap, Va., U.S. | f9 | 123 |
| Bigstone Lake, l., Sask. | C4 | 75 |
| Bigstone Lake, l., Man. | E2 | 100 |
| Big Sunflower, stm., Ms., U.S. | B3 | 101 |
| Big Sur, Ca., U.S. | D3 | 82 |
| Big Thompson, stm., Co., U.S. | A5 | 83 |
| Big Timber, Mt., U.S. | E7 | 103 |
| Big Top, mtn., Tn., U.S. | B5 | 119 |
| Big Trout Lake, Ont. | n17 | 73 |
| Big Trout Lake, l., Ont. | n17 | 73 |
| Biguaçu, Braz. | D3 | 56 |
| Big Valley, Alta. | C4 | 68 |
| Big Walnut Creek, stm., Oh., U.S. | m11 | 112 |
| Big Wells, Tx., U.S. | E3 | 120 |
| Big Wills Creek, stm., Al., U.S. | A3 | 78 |
| Big Wills Valley, val., Al., U.S. | A3 | 78 |
| Bigwood, Ont. | A4 | 73 |
| Bihać, Yugo. | C2 | 24 |
| Bihar, state, India | D8 | 36 |
| Bihār, India | D8 | 36 |
| Bīiziri, i., Marsh Is. | S18 | 52 |
| Bijagós, Arquipélago dos, is., Gui.-B. | D1 | 45 |
| Bīijapūr, India | E6 | 36 |
| Bijār, Iran | D3 | 39 |
| Bijeljina, Yugo. | C4 | 24 |
| Bijelo Polje, Yugo. | C4 | 24 |
| Bijie, China | F6 | 31 |
| Bijnor, India | C7 | 37 |
| Bijou Creek, stm., Co., U.S. | B6 | 83 |
| Bijou Hills, S.D., U.S. | D6 | 118 |
| Bīkāner, India | C5 | 36 |
| Bikeman Island, i., Kir. | R18 | 52 |
| Bikenibeu, Kir. | R18 | 52 |
| Bikin, Sov. Un. | B11 | 31 |
| Bikin, Sov. Un. | C7 | 33 |
| Bikini, atoll, Marsh Is. | F10 | 6 |
| Bikini Island, i., Marsh Is. | P18 | 52 |
| Bikita, Zimb. | B5 | 49 |
| Bilāspur, India | D7 | 36 |
| Bilauktaung Range, mts., Asia | C3 | 34 |
| Bilbao, Spain | A4 | 22 |
| Bilbays, Eg. | D2 | 43 |
| Bildudalur, Ice. | n21 | 14 |
| Bileća, Yugo. | D4 | 24 |
| Bilecik, Tur. | B7 | 40 |
| Bili, Zaire | A4 | 48 |
| Bili, Burma | E10 | 34 |
| Bilina, Czech. | C8 | 19 |
| Bilk Creek Mountains, mts., Nv., U.S. | B3 | 105 |
| Billabong, see Moonie, stm., Austl. | C7 | 51 |
| Billarp, Ga., U.S. | C2 | 87 |
| Billerica, Ma., U.S. | A5 | 98 |
| Billet, Il., U.S. | E6 | 90 |
| Billings, Mo., U.S. | D4 | 102 |
| Billings, Mt., U.S. | E8 | 103 |
| Billings, Ok., U.S. | A4 | 113 |
| Billings, co., N.D., U.S. | B2 | 111 |
| Billings Heights, Mt., U.S. | E8 | 103 |
| Billingsley, Al., U.S. | C3 | 78 |
| Bill Williams, stm., Az., U.S. | C1 | 80 |
| Bill Williams Mountain, mtn., Az., U.S. | B3 | 80 |
| Biloela, Austl. | D9 | 50 |
| Biloxi, Ms., U.S. | E5 | 101 |
| Biloxi, stm., Ms., U.S. | E4 | 101 |
| Biloxi Bay, b., Ms., U.S. | f8 | 101 |
| Bilqās Qism Awwal, Eg. | C3 | 43 |
| Biltine, Chad | C4 | 46 |
| Biltmore Forest, N.C., U.S. | f10 | 110 |
| Bilugyun, i., Burma | D2 | 35 |
| Bilzen, Bel. | D5 | 17 |
| Bimbéréké, Benin | D5 | 45 |
| Bimberi Peak, mtn., Austl. | G7 | 51 |
| Bimini Islands, is., Bah. | B4 | 64 |
| Bīna-Etāwa, India | E7 | 37 |
| Binangonan, Phil. | o13 | 34 |
| Bindloss, Alta. | D5 | 68 |
| Bindura, Zimb. | A5 | 49 |
| Binefar, Zaire | A3 | 48 |
| Binfield, Tn., U.S. | D9 | 119 |
| Binford, N.D., U.S. | B7 | 111 |
| Binga, Zaire | A3 | 48 |
| Binga, Monte, mtn., Afr. | A5 | 49 |
| Bingamon Creek, stm., W.V., U.S. | k10 | 125 |
| Bingen, W. Ger. | D3 | 18 |
| Bingen, W. Ger. | D4 | 124 |
| Binger, Ok., U.S. | B3 | 113 |
| Bingham, Il., U.S. | D4 | 90 |
| Bingham, Me., U.S. | C3 | 96 |
| Bingham, Ne., U.S. | B3 | 104 |
| Bingham, co., Id., U.S. | F6 | 89 |
| Bingham Lake, Mn., U.S. | G3 | 100 |
| Binghamton, N.Y., U.S. | C5 | 109 |
| Bingöl, Tur. | C13 | 40 |
| Binhai, China | E8 | 31 |
| Binjai, Indon. | m11 | 34 |
| Binnaway, Austl. | E7 | 51 |
| Binningen, Switz. | A4 | 21 |
| Binscarth, Man. | D1 | 70 |
| Bintan, i., Indon. | L6 | 35 |
| Bintuan, Indon. | F2 | 34 |
| Bintulu, Malay. | E4 | 34 |
| Binxian, China | D6 | 31 |
| Binxian, China | D3 | 33 |
| Binyamina, Isr. | B6 | 41 |
| Biobío, prov., Chile | B2 | 54 |
| Biobío, stm., Chile | B2 | 54 |
| Bioko, i., Eq. Gui. | E1 | 46 |
| Bippus, In., U.S. | C6 | 91 |
| Bira, Sov. Un. | B6 | 33 |
| Birakan, Sov. Un. | B11 | 31 |
| Bir al Uzam, Libya | G4 | 40 |
| Birao, Cen. Afr. Rep. | C4 | 46 |
| Birch, stm., W.V., U.S. | C4 | 125 |
| Birchdale, Mn., U.S. | B4 | 100 |
| Birch Hill, Ct., U.S. | C2 | 84 |
| Birch Hills, Sask. | E3 | 75 |
| Birch Island, B.C. | D8 | 69 |
| Birch Island, i., Man. | C2 | 70 |
| Birch Lake, l., Alta. | C5 | 68 |
| Birch Lake, l., Man. | D1 | 70 |
| Birch Lake, l., Mn., U.S. | C7 | 100 |
| Birch River, Man. | C1 | 70 |
| Birch Rock Hill, mtn., Pa., U.S. | F3 | 115 |
| Birch Run, Mi., U.S. | E7 | 99 |
| Birch Tree, Mo., U.S. | E6 | 102 |
| Birchwood, Ct., U.S. | C1 | 84 |
| Birchwood, Tn., U.S. | D9 | 119 |
| Birchwood, Wi., U.S. | C2 | 126 |
| Birchwood City, Md., U.S. | f9 | 97 |
| Birchwood Park, De., U.S. | *B3 | 85 |
| Birchy Bay, Newf. | D4 | 72 |
| Bird City, Ks., U.S. | C2 | 93 |
| Bird Creek, stm., Ok., U.S. | A6 | 113 |
| Bird Island, Mn., U.S. | F4 | 100 |
| Bird Island, i., N.C., U.S. | D4 | 110 |
| Birds, Il., U.S. | D6 | 90 |
| Birdsboro, Pa., U.S. | F10 | 115 |
| Birdseye, In., U.S. | H4 | 91 |
| Birdsong, Ar., U.S. | e9 | 94 |
| Birdsville, Austl. | E6 | 50 |
| Birdsville, Ky., U.S. | e9 | 94 |
| Birdtail Creek, stm., Man. | D1 | 70 |
| Birdtown, N.C., U.S. | f9 | 110 |
| Birdum, Austl. | C5 | 50 |
| Birdwood Creek, stm., Ne., U.S. | C4 | 104 |
| Birecik, Tur. | D11 | 40 |
| Bireun, Indon. | J2 | 35 |
| Bīrganj, Nepal | D10 | 37 |
| Birigui, Braz. | C2 | 56 |
| Birinci, Braz. | F5 | 57 |
| Birjand, Iran | B5 | 38 |
| Birkat as Sabʿ, Isr. Occ. | D3 | 41 |
| Birkenfeld, W. Ger. | D6 | 36 |
| Birkenfeld, W. Ger. | B3 | 114 |
| Birkenhead, Eng., U.K. | B5 | 12 |
| Bîrlad, Rom. | B8 | 24 |
| Bîrlad, stm., Rom. | B8 | 24 |
| Birmingham, Sask. | G4 | 75 |
| Birmingham, Eng., U.K. | B6 | 12 |
| Birmingham, Al., U.S. | B3 | 78 |
| Birmingham, Ia., U.S. | D6 | 92 |
| Birmingham, Mi., U.S. | F7 | 99 |
| Birmingham, Mo., U.S. | h11 | 102 |
| Birmingham, N.J., U.S. | D3 | 107 |
| Birney, Mt., U.S. | E10 | 103 |
| Birni Ngaouré, Niger | D5 | 45 |
| Birni Kebbi, Nig. | D5 | 45 |
| Birni Nkonni, Niger | D6 | 45 |
| Birobidzhan, Sov. Un. | E16 | 29 |
| Biron, Wi., U.S. | D4 | 126 |
| Birr, Ire. | D4 | 11 |
| Birs, stm., Switz. | B3 | 21 |
| Birsay, Sask. | F2 | 75 |
| Birsk, Sov. Un. | D20 | 8 |
| Birtle, Man. | D1 | 70 |
| Biruaca, Mong. | A6 | 32 |
| Bisalpur, Az., U.S. | F6 | 80 |
| Biscarrosse, Fr. | A6 | 111 |
| Biscay, Bay of, b., Eur. | G8 | 8 |
| Biscayne, Key, i., Fl., U.S. | s13 | 86 |
| Biscayne Bay, b., Fl., U.S. | G6 | 86 |
| Biscayne Gardens, Fl., U.S. | *s13 | 86 |
| Biscayne National Monument, Fl., U.S. | G6 | 86 |
| Biscayne Park, Fl., U.S. | s13 | 86 |
| Bisceglie, Italy | D6 | 23 |
| Bischheim, Fr. | F7 | 17 |
| Bischofshofen, Aus. | B9 | 20 |
| Bischofswerda, E. Ger. | B9 | 19 |
| Bischwiller, Fr. | F7 | 17 |
| Biscoe, Ar., U.S. | C4 | 81 |
| Biscoe, N.C., U.S. | B3 | 110 |
| Biscoe Islands, is., Ant. | C6 | 7 |
| Biševo, i., Yugo. | D3 | 24 |
| Bishārah, Maʿtan, well, Libya | E4 | 43 |
| Bishnupur, India | F11 | 37 |
| Bisho, Ciskei | D4 | 82 |
| Bishop, Ca., U.S. | D4 | 82 |
| Bishop, Ga., U.S. | C3 | 87 |
| Bishop, Md., U.S. | D7 | 97 |
| Bishop, Tx., U.S. | n12 | 125 |
| Bishop Auckland, Eng., U.K. | F7 | 13 |
| Bishopric, Sask. | H3 | 75 |
| Bishop's Castle, Eng., U.K. | B5 | 12 |
| Bishop's Falls, Newf. | D4 | 72 |
| Bishops Head, Md., U.S. | D5 | 97 |
| Bishops Mills, Ont. | C9 | 73 |
| Bishop's Stortford, Eng., U.K. | E7 | 10 |
| Bishopton, Que. | D6 | 74 |
| Bishopville, Md., U.S. | D7 | 97 |
| Bishopville, S.C., U.S. | C7 | 117 |
| Bismarck, Ar., U.S. | C2 | 81 |
| Bismarck, Il., U.S. | C6 | 90 |
| Bismarck, Mo., U.S. | D7 | 102 |
| Bismarck, N.D., U.S. | C5 | 111 |
| Bismarck, Cape, c., Grnld. | A16 | 128 |
| Bismarck Archipelago, is., Pap. N. Gui. | h12 | 50 |
| Bismarck Range, mts., Pap. N. Gui. | k11 | 50 |
| Bismarck Sea, Pap. N. Gui. | h12 | 50 |
| Bismark, E. Ger. | F5 | 15 |
| Bison, Ok., U.S. | A4 | 113 |
| Bison, S.D., U.S. | B3 | 118 |
| Bison Lake, l., Alta. | A2 | 68 |
| Bison Peak, mtn., Co., U.S. | B5 | 83 |
| Bissau, Gui.-B. | D1 | 45 |
| Bissett, Man. | D4 | 70 |
| Bistineau, Lake, res., La., U.S. | B2 | 95 |
| Bistriţa, Rom. | B7 | 24 |
| Bistriţa, stm., Rom. | B7 | 24 |
| Bitam, Gabon | A2 | 46 |
| Bitburg, W. Ger. | E6 | 17 |
| Bitche, Fr. | F7 | 17 |
| Bitely, Mi., U.S. | E5 | 99 |
| Bitlis, Tur. | C14 | 40 |
| Bitola, Yugo. | E5 | 24 |
| Bitonto, Italy | D6 | 23 |
| Bitter Creek, stm., Wy., U.S. | E4 | 127 |
| Bitterfeld, E. Ger. | B7 | 19 |
| Bitterfontein, S. Afr. | D2 | 49 |
| Bitter Lake, l., Sask. | G1 | 75 |
| Bitter Lake, l., S.D., U.S. | B8 | 118 |
| Bitter Lake, l., Sask. | C4 | 68 |
| Bitterroot, stm., Mt., U.S. | D2 | 103 |
| Bitterroot Range, mts., U.S. | B3 | 89 |
| Bittinger, Md., U.S. | k12 | 97 |
| Bituig, Indon. | E7 | 34 |
| Bityug, stm., Sov. Un. | F13 | 27 |
| Biu, Nig. | E8 | 45 |
| Bivalve, Md., U.S. | D6 | 97 |
| Bivalve, N.J., U.S. | E2 | 107 |
| Biwabik, Mn., U.S. | C6 | 100 |
| Biwa Lake, l., Japan | n15 | 33 |
| Bixby, Mn., U.S. | G5 | 100 |
| Bixby, Mo., U.S. | D7 | 102 |
| Bixby, Ok., U.S. | B6 | 113 |
| Bixby, N.C., U.S. | B2 | 110 |
| Biya, stm., Sov. Un. | *E26 | 8 |
| Biyalā, Eg. | C3 | 43 |
| Biyang, China | H5 | 32 |
| Biysk, Sov. Un. | D11 | 29 |
| Bizerte, Tun. | B6 | 44 |
| Bjelovar, Yugo. | C2 | 24 |
| Bjerringbro, Den. | B3 | 15 |
| Bjork Lake, l., Sask. | C4 | 75 |
| Black, stm., Az., U.S. | D5 | 80 |
| Black, stm., La., U.S. | B1 | 120 |
| Black, stm., Asia | C9 | 34 |
| Black, stm., Jam. | E13 | 65 |
| Black, stm., N.A. | D5 | 80 |
| Black, stm., N.Y., U.S. | B5 | 109 |
| Black, stm., S.C., U.S. | D8 | 117 |
| Black, stm., Vt., U.S. | B4 | 122 |
| Black, stm., Vt., U.S. | E4 | 122 |
| Black, stm., Wi., U.S. | D3 | 126 |
| Black, stm., Ms., U.S. | C4 | 101 |
| Black, stm., S.C., U.S. | C9 | 117 |
| Black Bayou, stm., La., U.S. | B2 | 95 |
| Black Bear Bay, b., Newf. | B4 | 72 |
| Black Bear Creek, stm., Ok., U.S. | A4 | 113 |
| Blackbeard Island, i., Ga., U.S. | E5 | 87 |
| Black Bear Island Lake, l., Sask. | B3 | 75 |
| Blackbird, De., U.S. | B3 | 85 |
| Blackburn, Eng., U.K. | D5 | 12 |
| Blackburn, Mo., U.S. | B4 | 102 |
| Blackburn, Mount, mtn., Ak., U.S. | C11 | 79 |
| Black Butte, mtn., Mt., U.S. | F5 | 103 |
| Black Butte, mtn., Wy., U.S. | *B5 | 127 |
| Black Butte Lake, res., Ca., U.S. | C2 | 82 |
| Black Butte Ranch, Or., U.S. | C5 | 114 |
| Black Canyon, val., Co., U.S. | C3 | 83 |
| Black Canyon City, Az., U.S. | C3 | 80 |
| Black Canyon of the Gunnison National Monument, Co., U.S. | C3 | 83 |
| Black Creek, B.C. | E5 | 69 |
| Black Creek, N.C., U.S. | *D5 | 110 |
| Black Creek, Wi., U.S. | D5 | 126 |
| Black Creek, stm., B.C. | E5 | 69 |
| Black Creek, stm., Ms., U.S. | D4 | 101 |
| Black Creek, stm., S.C., U.S. | B7 | 117 |
| Black Diamond, Alta. | D3 | 68 |
| Black Diamond, Wa., U.S. | B4 | 124 |
| Black Down Hills, hills, Eng., U.K. | E5 | 10 |
| Blackduck, Mn., U.S. | C4 | 100 |
| Black Eagle, Mt., U.S. | C5 | 103 |
| Black Earth, Wi., U.S. | E4 | 126 |
| Blackey, Ky., U.S. | C7 | 94 |
| Blackfalds, Alta. | C4 | 68 |

| Name | Map Ref. | Page |
|---|---|---|

Blackfeet Indian Reservation, Mt., U.S. — B4 103
Blackfoot, Alta. — C5 68
Blackfoot, Id., U.S. — F6 89
Blackfoot, Mt., U.S. — B4 103
Blackfoot, stm., Mt., U.S. — C3 103
Blackfoot Mountains, mts., Id., U.S. — F7 89
Blackfoot Reservoir, res., Id., U.S. — G7 89
Blackford, Ky., U.S. — C2 94
Blackford, co., In., U.S. — D7 91
Black Forest, Co., U.S. — C6 83
Black Forest, mts., W. Ger. — D4 18
Blackfork, Oh., U.S. — D3 112
Blackhall Mountain, mtn., Wy., U.S. — E6 127
Black Hawk, In., U.S. — B3 101
Black Hawk, S.D., U.S. — C2 118
Black Hawk, co., Ia., U.S. — B5 92
Blackhead Bay, b., Newf. — D5 72
Black Hills, mts., U.S. — C2 118
Blackie, Alta. — D4 68
Black Island, i., Ant. — f38 7
Black Island, i., Man. — D3 70
Black Jack, Mo., U.S. — *f13 102
Blackjack Mountain, mtn., Ga., U.S. — h7 87
Black Lake, Que. — C6 74
Black Lake, l., Sask. — m7 75
Black Lake, l., Mi., U.S. — C6 99
Black Lake, l., N.Y., U.S. — f9 109
Black Lake Bayou, stm., La., U.S. — B2 95
Blacklick, Oh., U.S. — m11 112
Black Lick, Pa., U.S. — F3 115
Blacklick Estates, Oh., U.S. — m11 112
Black Mesa, mtn., Az., U.S. — A5 80
Black Mesa, mtn., Ok., U.S. — e8 113
Black Mingo Creek, stm., S.C., U.S. — D9 117
Blackmore, Mount, mtn., Mt., U.S. — E6 103
Black Mountain, N.C., U.S. — f10 110
Black Mountain, mtn., U.S. — D7 94
Black Mountain, mtn., Az., U.S. — E4 80
Black Mountain, mtn., Co., U.S. — A5 83
Black Mountain, mtn., Id., U.S. — C3 89
Black Mountain, mtn., Mt., U.S. — D4 103
Black Mountain, mtn., Or., U.S. — B7 114
Black Mountain, mtn., Wy., U.S. — D7 127
Black Mountain, mtn., Wy., U.S. — B5 127
Black Mountains, mts., Wales, U.K. — C4 12
Black Mountains, mts., Az., U.S. — B1 80
Black Oak, Ar., U.S. — B5 81
Black Oak, In., U.S. — A3 91
Black Peak, mtn., Az., U.S. — C1 80
Black Pine Peak, mtn., Id., U.S. — G5 89
Black Point, Ct., U.S. — D7 84
Black Point Beach Club, Ct., U.S. — *D7 84
Black Pond, l., Me., U.S. — B3 96
Blackpool, Eng., U.K. — D5 10
Black Range, mts., N.M., U.S. — D2 108
Black River, Jam. — E5 64
Black River, Mi., U.S. — D7 99
Black River, N.Y., U.S. — A5 109
Black River Bay, b., Jam. — F13 65
Black River Falls, Wi., U.S. — D3 126
Black Rock, Ar., U.S. — A4 81
Black Rock, N.M., U.S. — B1 108
Black Rock Desert, des., Nv., U.S. — B3 105
Black Rock Range, mts., Nv., U.S. — B3 105
Blacksburg, S.C., U.S. — A4 117
Blacksburg, Va., U.S. — C2 123
Black Sea — G15 8
Blacks Fork, stm., U.S. — E3 127
Blacks Harbour, N.B. — D3 71
Blackshear, Ga., U.S. — E4 87
Blackshear, Lake, res., Ga., U.S. — E2 87
Blacksod Bay, b., Ire. — C1 10
Black Springs, Ar., U.S. — C2 81
Black Springs, Nv., U.S. — *D2 105
Black Squirrel Creek, stm., Co., U.S. — C6 83
Blackstock, Ont. — C6 73
Blackstock, S.C., U.S. — B5 117
Blackstone, Ma., U.S. — B4 98
Blackstone, Va., U.S. — C5 123
Blackstone, stm., Alta. — C2 68
Blackstone, stm., R.I., U.S. — B4 116
Blackstrap Reservoir, res., Sask. — F2 75
Black Sugarloaf Mountain, mtn., Austl. — E9 51
Blacksville, W.V., U.S. — B4 125
Black Thunder Creek, stm., Wy., U.S. — C8 127
Black Tickle, Newf. — D5 72
Blacktown, Austl. — *F9 50
Blackville, N.B. — C4 71
Blackville, S.C., U.S. — E5 117
Black Volta (Volta Noire), stm., Afr. — E4 45
Blackwalnut Point, c., Md., U.S. — C5 97
Black Warrior, stm., Al., U.S. — C2 78
Blackwater, Ire. — E5 11
Blackwater, Mo., U.S. — C5 102
Blackwater, Va., U.S. — f8 123
Blackwater, stm., Ire. — E5 11
Blackwater, stm., Fl., U.S. — u15 86
Blackwater, stm., Md., U.S. — D5 97
Blackwater, stm., N.H., U.S. — D3 106
Blackwater, stm., Va., U.S. — D6 123
Blackwater Reservoir, res., Scot., U.K. — D4 13
Blackwater Reservoir, res., N.H., U.S. — D3 106
Blackwell, Ar., U.S. — B3 81
Blackwell, Mo., U.S. — C7 102
Blackwell, Ok., U.S. — A4 113
Blackwell, Tx., U.S. — C2 120
Blackwell, Wi., U.S. — C5 126
Blackwood, N.J., U.S. — D2 107
Blackwood Creek, stm., Ne., U.S. — D7 104
Bladen, Ne., U.S. — D7 104
Bladen, co., N.C., U.S. — C4 110
Bladenboro, N.C., U.S. — C4 110
Bladensburg, Md., U.S. — B3 97
Bladensburg, Oh., U.S. — B3 112
Blades, De., U.S. — F3 85

Bladon Springs, Al., U.S. — D1 78
Bladworth, Sask. — F2 75
Blaeberry, stm., B.C. — D2 68
Blagnac, Fr. — F4 16
Blagodarnoye, Sov. Un. — D2 28
Blagoevgrad (Gorna Dzhumaya), Bul. — D6 24
Blagoveshchensk, Sov. Un. — D20 8
Blagoveshchensk, Sov. Un. — D15 29
Blain, Fr. — D3 16
Blain, Pa., U.S. — F7 115
Blaine, Ks., U.S. — C7 93
Blaine, Me., U.S. — B5 96
Blaine, Mn., U.S. — m12 100
Blaine, Ms., U.S. — B3 101
Blaine, Tn., U.S. — C10 119
Blaine, Wa., U.S. — A3 124
Blaine, co., Id., U.S. — F4 89
Blaine, co., Mt., U.S. — B7 103
Blaine, co., Ne., U.S. — C6 104
Blaine, co., Ok., U.S. — B3 113
Blaine Creek, stm., Ky., U.S. — B7 94
Blair, Ks., U.S. — C8 93
Blair, Ne., U.S. — C9 104
Blair, Ok., U.S. — C2 113
Blair, S.C., U.S. — C5 117
Blair, W.V., U.S. — n12 125
Blair, Wi., U.S. — D2 126
Blair, co., Pa., U.S. — E5 115
Blair Athol, Austl. — D8 50
Blair Athol, Scot., U.K. — D5 13
Blairgowrie, Scot., U.K. — B5 10
Blairsburg, Ia., U.S. — B4 92
Blairsden, Ca., U.S. — C3 82
Blairstown, Ia., U.S. — C5 92
Blairstown, Mo., U.S. — C4 102
Blairsville, Ga., U.S. — B3 87
Blairsville, Pa., U.S. — F3 115
Blairton, W.V., U.S. — B7 125
Blaisdell, N.D., U.S. — A3 111
Blaj, Rom. — B6 24
Blake Island, i., Wa., U.S. — e11 124
Blakely, Mn., U.S. — F5 100
Blakely, Ar., U.S. — C2 81
Blakely, Ga., U.S. — E2 87
Blakely, Pa., U.S. — m18 115
Blake Point, c., Mi., U.S. — h10 99
Blakesburg, Ia., U.S. — D5 92
Blakeslee, Oh., U.S. — A1 112
Blakeslee, Pa., U.S. — D10 115
Blâmont, Fr. — F6 17
Blanc, Cap, c., Afr. — B1 45
Blanc, Cap, c., Tun. — F2 23
Blanc, Mont, mtn., Eur. — E7 16
Blanca, Bahía, b., Arg. — B4 54
Blanca, Cordillera, mts., Peru — C2 58
Blanca, Sierra, mtn., Tx., U.S. — o12 120
Blanca, Peak, mtn., Co., U.S. — D5 83
Blanchard, Id., U.S. — A2 89
Blanchard, Ia., U.S. — D2 92
Blanchard, La., U.S. — B2 95
Blanchard, Me., U.S. — C3 96
Blanchard, Mi., U.S. — E5 99
Blanchard, N.D., U.S. — B8 111
Blanchard, Ok., U.S. — B4 113
Blanchard, Pa., U.S. — D6 115
Blanchard, Wa., U.S. — A3 124
Blanchard, stm., Oh., U.S. — A1 112
Blanchardville, Wi., U.S. — F4 126
Blanche, Que. — D2 74
Blanche, Tn., U.S. — B5 119
Blanche, Lake, l., Austl. — E6 50
Blanchester, Oh., U.S. — C2 112
Blanco, N.M., U.S. — A2 108
Blanco, Ok., U.S. — C6 113
Blanco, Tx., U.S. — D3 120
Blanco, co., Tx., U.S. — D3 120
Blanco, stm., Arg. — E2 55
Blanco, Cabo, c., C.R. — F5 62
Blanco, Cabo, c., Peru — B1 58
Blanco, Cape, c., Or., U.S. — E2 114
Blanc Sablon, Que. — C3 72
Bland, Mo., U.S. — C6 102
Bland, Va., U.S. — C1 123
Bland, co., Va., U.S. — C1 123
Blandburg, Pa., U.S. — E5 115
Blandford, Ma., U.S. — B2 98
Blandford Forum, Eng., U.K. — D5 12
Blanding, Ut., U.S. — F6 121
Blandinsville, Il., U.S. — C3 90
Blandville, Ky., U.S. — f9 94
Blanford, In., U.S. — E2 91
Blangkejeren, Indon. — K2 35
Blangy-sur-Bresle, Fr. — E9 12
Blankenberge, Bel. — C3 17
Blankenburg, E. Ger. — C5 18
Blankenfelde, E. Ger. — A8 19
Blankenheim, W. Ger. — C1 19
Blanket, Tx., U.S. — D3 120
Blanquilla, Isla, i., Ven. — A5 60
Blantyre, Mwi. — E6 48
Blarney, Ire. — F3 11
Blasdell, N.Y., U.S. — C2 109
Blatná, Czech. — D8 19
Blato, Yugo. — D3 24
Blaubeuren, W. Ger. — E4 19
Blauvelt, N.Y., U.S. — *g13 109
Blåvands Huk, c., Den. — C2 15
Blawenburg, N.J., U.S. — C3 107
Blawnox, Pa., U.S. — k14 115
Blaye, Fr. — E3 16
Błażowa, Pol. — D7 26
Bleckede, W. Ger. — B5 18
Bleckley, co., Ga., U.S. — D3 87
Błędów, Pol. — g10 26
Bledsoe, Tx., U.S. — C1 120
Bledsoe, co., Tn., U.S. — D8 119
Bleecker, N.Y., U.S. — B6 109
Bleicherode, E. Ger. — B5 19
Blekinge, co., Swe. — B8 15
Blencoe, Ia., U.S. — C1 92
Blende, Co., U.S. — C6 83
Blendecques, Fr. — D2 17
Blenheim, Ont. — E3 73
Blenheim, N.Z. — N14 51
Blenheim, S.C., U.S. — B8 117
Blennerhassett, W.V., U.S. — B3 125
Blessing, Tx., U.S. — E4 120
Blessington, Ire. — D5 11
Bletchley, Eng., U.K. — C7 12
Blevins, Ar., U.S. — D2 81
Blija, Neth. — A5 17
Blind, stm., La., U.S. — h10 95
Blind River, Ont. — A2 73
Bliss, Id., U.S. — G4 89
Bliss, N.Y., U.S. — C2 109
Blissfield, Mi., U.S. — G7 99
Blissfield, Oh., U.S. — B4 112
Blitar, Indon. — *G4 34
Blitta, Togo — E5 45

Blocher, In., U.S. — G6 91
Blocker, Ok., U.S. — B6 113
Block Island, R.I., U.S. — h7 116
Block Island, i., R.I., U.S. — h7 116
Block Island Sound, strt., U.S. — G2 116
Blockton, Ia., U.S. — D3 92
Blodgett, Mo., U.S. — D8 102
Blodgett Landing, N.H., U.S. — D3 106
Bloedel, B.C. — D5 69
Bloemfontein, S. Afr. — C4 49
Blois, Fr. — D4 16
Blokhus, Den. — A3 15
Blomberg, W. Ger. — B4 19
Blommesteinmeer, res., Sur. — B3 59
Blönduós, Ice. — n22 14
Błonie, Pol. — m13 26
Blood Mountain, mtn., Ga., U.S. — B3 87
Bloodsworth Island, i., Md., U.S. — D5 97
Bloodvein, stm., Can. — D3 70
Bloody Foreland, c., Ire. — B3 11
Bloom, Ks., U.S. — E4 93
Bloom, Slieve, mts., Ire. — D4 11
Bloomdale, Oh., U.S. — A2 112
Bloomer, Ar., U.S. — B1 81
Bloomer, Wi., U.S. — C2 126
Bloomfield, N.B. — D4 71
Bloomfield, Ont. — D7 73
Bloomfield, Ct., U.S. — B5 84
Bloomfield, In., U.S. — F4 91
Bloomfield, Ia., U.S. — D5 92
Bloomfield, Ky., U.S. — C4 94
Bloomfield, Mo., U.S. — E8 102
Bloomfield, Ne., U.S. — B8 104
Bloomfield, N.J., U.S. — h8 107
Bloomfield, N.M., U.S. — A2 108
Bloomfield, Vt., U.S. — B5 122
Bloomfield Hills, Mi., U.S. — o15 99
Bloomfield Township, Mi., U.S. — *F7 99
Bloomingburg, Oh., U.S. — C2 112
Bloomingdale, Ga., U.S. — D5 87
Bloomingdale, Il., U.S. — k8 90
Bloomingdale, In., U.S. — E3 91
Bloomingdale, Mi., U.S. — F5 99
Bloomingdale, N.J., U.S. — A4 107
Bloomingdale, N.Y., U.S. — f10 109
Bloomingdale, Tn., U.S. — C11 119
Blooming Grove, Pa., U.S. — D11 115
Blooming Grove, Tx., U.S. — C4 120
Blooming Prairie, Mn., U.S. — G5 100
Bloomington, Ca., U.S. — *m14 82
Bloomington, Id., U.S. — G7 89
Bloomington, Il., U.S. — C4 90
Bloomington, In., U.S. — F4 91
Bloomington, Md., U.S. — m12 97
Bloomington, Mn., U.S. — F5 100
Bloomington, Ne., U.S. — D6 104
Bloomington, Tx., U.S. — E4 120
Bloomington, Ut., U.S. — *F2 121
Bloomington, Wi., U.S. — F3 126
Bloomington, Lake, res., Il., U.S. — C5 90
Bloomsburg, Pa., U.S. — E9 115
Bloomsbury, N.J., U.S. — B2 107
Bloomsdale, Mo., U.S. — C7 102
Bloomville, N.Y., U.S. — C6 109
Bloomville, Oh., U.S. — A2 112
Blossburg, Al., U.S. — f7 78
Blossom, Tx., U.S. — C5 120
Blosseville Coast, Grnld. — C17 128
Blossom, Tx., U.S. — C5 114
Blount, co., Al., U.S. — B3 78
Blount, co., Tn., U.S. — D10 119
Blounts Creek, N.C., U.S. — B6 110
Blount Springs, Al., U.S. — A3 78
Blountstown, Fl., U.S. — B1 86
Blountsville, Al., U.S. — A3 78
Blountville, Tn., U.S. — C11 119
Blovice, Czech. — D8 19
Blowing Rock, N.C., U.S. — A1 110
Bloxom, Va., U.S. — C7 123
Blucher, Sask. — E2 75
Bludenz, Aus. — E4 18
Blue, Az., U.S. — D6 80
Blue, Ok., U.S. — C5 113
Blue, stm., Co., U.S. — B4 83
Blue, stm., In., U.S. — H5 91
Blue, stm., Mo., U.S. — k10 102
Blue, Bayou, stm., La., U.S. — E5 95
Blue, Mount, mtn., Me., U.S. — D2 96
Blue Anchor, N.J., U.S. — D3 107
Blue Ash, Oh., U.S. — o13 112
Bluebell, Ut., U.S. — C5 121
Blueberry, stm., B.C. — A7 69
Blue Buck Knob, hill, Mo., U.S. — E5 102
Blue Buck Point, c., La., U.S. — E5 95
Blue Creek, Al., U.S. — g6 78
Blue Creek, Wa., U.S. — A8 124
Blue Creek, stm., Ne., U.S. — C3 104
Blue Creek, stm., W.V., U.S. — m13 125
Blue Cypress Lake, l., Fl., U.S. — E6 86
Blue Diamond, Nv., U.S. — G6 105
Blue Earth, Mn., U.S. — G4 100
Blue Earth, co., Mn., U.S. — G4 100
Blue Earth, stm., Mn., U.S. — G4 100
Bluefield, Va., U.S. — C1 123
Bluefield, W.V., U.S. — D3 125
Bluefields, Nic. — E6 62
Bluefields Bay, b., Jam. — E12 65
Blue Glacier, ice., Ant. — e39 7
Blue Grass, Ia., U.S. — C7 92
Blue Grass, Va., U.S. — B3 123
Blue Hill, Me., U.S. — D4 96
Blue Hill, Ne., U.S. — D7 104
Blue Hill Falls, Me., U.S. — D4 96
Blue Hill Range, hills, Ma., U.S. — h11 98
Blue Hills of Couteau, hills, Newf. — E3 72
Bluehole, Ky., U.S. — C6 94
Bluejacket, Ok., U.S. — A6 113
Bluejoint Lake, l., Or., U.S. — E7 114
Blue Knob, mtn., Pa., U.S. — F4 115
Blue Lake, Ca., U.S. — B2 82
Blue Mesa Reservoir, res., Co., U.S. — C3 83
Blue Mound, Il., U.S. — D4 90
Blue Mound, Ks., U.S. — D8 93
Blue Mountain, Al., U.S. — B4 78
Blue Mountain, Co., U.S. — A2 83
Blue Mountain, Ms., U.S. — A4 101
Blue Mountain, mtn., N.B. — D3 71
Blue Mountain, mtn., Newf. — C3 72
Blue Mountain, mtn., Ar., U.S. — C1 81
Blue Mountain, mtn., N.H., U.S. — A4 106

Blue Mountain, mtn., N.M., U.S. — D2 108
Blue Mountain, mtn., N.Y., U.S. — B6 109
Blue Mountain, mtn., Pa., U.S. — F6 115
Blue Mountain, mtn., U.S. — B6 109
Blue Mountain Lake, N.Y., U.S. — B6 109
Blue Mountain Lake, res., Ar., U.S. — B2 81
Blue Mountain Peak, mtn., Jam. — E5 64
Blue Mountains, mts., Austl. — F8 51
Blue Mountains, mts., Jam. — E15 65
Blue Mountains, mts., U.S. — A4 76
Blue Mud Bay, b., Austl. — B6 50
Blue Nile, stm., Afr. — C3 47
Bluenose Lake, l., N.W. Ter. — C9 66
Blue Point, Me., U.S. — g7 96
Blue Rapids, Ks., U.S. — C7 93
Blue Ridge, Alta. — B3 68
Blue Ridge, Ga., U.S. — B2 87
Blue Ridge, In., U.S. — E6 91
Blue Ridge, Va., U.S. — C3 123
Blue Ridge, mtn., U.S. — C11 76
Blue Ridge Lake, res., Ga., U.S. — B2 87
Blue Ridge Summit, Pa., U.S. — G7 115
Blue River, B.C. — C8 69
Blue River, Or., U.S. — C4 114
Blue River, Wi., U.S. — E3 126
Bluesky, Alta. — A1 68
Blue Springs, Al., U.S. — D4 78
Blue Springs, Ms., U.S. — A5 101
Blue Springs, Mo., U.S. — h11 102
Blue Springs, Ne., U.S. — D9 104
Bluestone, stm., W.V., U.S. — D3 125
Bluestone Lake, res., U.S. — D4 125
Bluevale, Ont. — D3 73
Bluewater, N.M., U.S. — B2 108
Bluewell, W.V., U.S. — D3 125
Bluff, N.Z. — Q12 51
Bluff, Ut., U.S. — F6 121
Bluff City, Ar., U.S. — D2 81
Bluff City, Il., U.S. — E4 90
Bluff City, Ks., U.S. — E6 93
Bluff City, Ky., U.S. — C2 94
Bluff City, Tn., U.S. — C11 119
Bluff Creek, stm., Ks., U.S. — E4 93
Bluff Creek, stm., Ok., U.S. — A4 113
Bluff Dale, Tx., U.S. — C3 120
Bluffdale, Ut., U.S. — *C4 121
Bluff Knoll, mtn., Austl. — F2 50
Bluff Lake, res., Ms., U.S. — B5 101
Bluff Mountain, mtn., Vt., U.S. — B5 122
Bluff Park, Al., U.S. — g7 78
Bluffs, Il., U.S. — D3 90
Bluffton, Ga., U.S. — E2 87
Bluffton, In., U.S. — C7 91
Bluffton, Mn., U.S. — D3 100
Bluffton, Oh., U.S. — B2 112
Bluffton, S.C., U.S. — G6 117
Bluford, Il., U.S. — E5 90
Blumenau, Braz. — D3 56
Blumenfeld, W. Ger. — A6 21
Blumengard Colony, S.D., U.S. — B6 118
Blumenhof, Sask. — G2 75
Blumenthal (part of Bremen), W. Ger. — B4 18
Blunt, S.D., U.S. — C6 118
Bly, Or., U.S. — E5 114
Blying Sound, strt., Ak., U.S. — h17 79
Blyth, Ont. — D3 73
Blythe, Ca., U.S. — F6 82
Blythe, Ga., U.S. — C4 87
Blythedale, Mo., U.S. — A4 102
Blytheville, Ar., U.S. — B6 81
Blytheville Air Force Base, mil., Ar., U.S. — B6 81
Blythewood, S.C., U.S. — C6 117
Bo, S.L. — E2 45
Boac, Phil. — E6 34
Boaco, Nic. — E5 62
Bo'ai (Qinghua), China — G5 32
Boali, Cen. Afr. Rep. — B3 46
Boalsburg, Pa., U.S. — E6 115
Board Camp, Ar., U.S. — C1 81
Boardman, Oh., U.S. — A5 112
Boardman, Or., U.S. — B7 114
Boa Vista, Braz. — B2 59
Boaz, Al., U.S. — A3 78
Boaz, W.V., U.S. — B3 125
Bobbili, India — E7 37
Bobbio, Italy — E5 20
Bobcaygeon, Ont. — C6 73
Bobigny, Fr. — g10 16
Böblingen, W. Ger. — E4 19
Bobo, Ms., U.S. — A3 101
Bobo Dioulasso, Burkina — D4 45
Bobov Dol, Bul. — D6 24
Bóbr, stm., Pol. — C3 26
Bobrinets, Sov. Un. — G5 27
Bobruysk, Sov. Un. — D7 27
Bobtown, Pa., U.S. — G2 115
Bobures, Ven. — C3 60
Boca Chica Key, i., Fl., U.S. — H5 86
Boca Ciega Bay, b., Fl., U.S. — p10 86
Boca Grande, Fl., U.S. — F4 86
Bôca do Acre, Braz. — B4 56
Boca Raton, Fl., U.S. — F6 86
Bocaiúva, Braz. — D6 56
Bocanda, I.C. — E4 45
Bocaranga, Cen. Afr. Rep. — D2 46
Bocas del Toro, Pan. — F6 62
Bocay, Nic. — D5 62
Boccea (Buxus), Italy — h8 21
Bochnia, Pol. — B1 19
Bocholt, W. Ger. — B1 19
Bochov, Czech. — C7 19
Bochum, W. Ger. — B3 19
Bock, Mn., U.S. — E5 100
Bockhorn, W. Ger. — A8 18
Bockum-Hövel, W. Ger. — B2 19
Boda, Cen. Afr. Rep. — B3 46
Bodafors, Sov. Un. — D14 29
Bodcau Creek, stm., Ar., U.S. — D2 81
Boddam, Scot., U.K. — C7 13
Bode, Ia., U.S. — B3 92
Bode, reg., Chad — E9 46
Bodega Head, c., Ca., U.S. — C2 82
Bodélé, reg., Chad — E9 46
Boden, Swe. — C13 14
Boden, Il., U.S. — A4 90
Boderg, Lough, l., Ire. — C4 11
Bodie Island, i., N.C., U.S. — B7 110
Bodine, Mount, mtn., B.C. — B1 69
Bodkin Point, c., Md., U.S. — B5 97
Bodmin, Eng., U.K. — E4 10
Bodmin Moor, for., Eng., U.K. — E4 10

Bodo, Alta. — C5 68
Bodö, Nor. — D6 14
Bodrog, stm., Eur. — A5 24
Bodrum, Tur. — D6 40
Bodva, stm., Eur. — A5 24
Boelus, Ne., U.S. — C7 104
Boende, Zaire — B3 48
Boerne, Tx., U.S. — E3 120
Boesing, Al., U.S. — D3 78
Boeuf, stm., La., U.S. — C4 95
Boeuf, Bayou, stm., La., U.S. — D3 95
Boeuf, Lake, l., La., U.S. — k10 95
Bofete, Braz. — m7 56
Boffa, Gui. — D2 45
Bogale, Burma — E10 36
Bogalusa, La., U.S. — D6 95
Bogan, i., Marsh Is. — S18 52
Bogan, stm., Austl. — E6 51
Bogandé, Burkina — D4 45
Bogard, Mo., U.S. — B4 102
Bogart, Ga., U.S. — C3 87
Bogotnoye, Sov. Un. — B10 28
Bogata, Tx., U.S. — C5 120
Bogatynia, Pol. — *C4 26
Bogatynia, Pol. — C9 19
Bogen, W. Ger. — E7 19
Bogenfels, Nmb. — C2 49
Bogense, Den. — C4 15
Boger City, N.C., U.S. — B1 110
Boggeragh Mountains, mts., Ire. — E3 11
Boggerik Island, i., Marsh Is. — S17 52
Boggstown, In., U.S. — E6 91
Bogno, i., Marsh Is. — S18 52
Bogno, Switz. — D7 21
Bognor Regis, Eng., U.K. — D7 12
Bogo, Indon. — G3 34
Bogor (Buitenzorg), Indon. — G3 34
Bogoroditsk, Sov. Un. — E12 27
Bogorodsk, Sov. Un. — C14 27
Bogotá, Col. — C3 60
Bogota, N.J., U.S. — h8 107
Bogota, Tn., U.S. — A2 119
Bogotol, Sov. Un. — D26 8
Bogra, Bngl. — D8 36
Bogue, Ks., U.S. — C4 93
Bogué, Maur. — C2 45
Bogue Chitto, Ms., U.S. — D3 101
Bogue Chitto, stm., U.S. — D5 95
Bogue Inlet, b., N.C., U.S. — C5 110
Bogue Phalia, stm., Ms., U.S. — B3 101
Boguslav, Sov. Un. — G8 27
Bo Hai, b., China — D8 31
Bohain[-en-Vermandois], Fr. — C5 16
Boharm, Sask. — G3 75
Bohemia, N.Y., U.S. — *n15 109
Bohemia, hist. reg., Czech. — D6 18
Bohemian Forest, mts., Eur. — D6 18
Bohemian-Moravian Highlands, plat., Czech. — D3 26
Böhmte, W. Ger. — A3 19
Bohol, i., Phil. — D6 34
Bohol Sea, Phil. — D6 34
Boiestown, N.B. — C3 71
Boiling Springs, N.C., U.S. — B1 110
Boiling Springs, Pa., U.S. — F7 115
Bois, Lac des, l., N.W. Ter. — C7 66
Bois, Rio dos, stm., Braz. — B2 56
Bois Blanc Island, i., Mi., U.S. — C6 99
Boischâtel, Que. — C6 74
Bois-Colombes, Fr. — g10 16
Boisdale, N.S. — C9 71
Bois D'Arc, Mo., U.S. — D4 102
Bois de Sioux, stm., U.S. — E2 100
Boise, Id., U.S. — F2 89
Boise, co., Id., U.S. — F3 89
Boise City, Ok., U.S. — e8 113
Boise Fort, Mn., U.S. — B5 100
Boissevain, Man. — E1 70
Boissevain, Va., U.S. — e10 123
Boistfort Peak, mtn., Wa., U.S. — C2 124
Boizenburg, E. Ger. — B5 18
Bojador, Cabo, c., W. Sah. — B2 45
Bojnûrd, Iran — B5 38
Bokchito, Ok., U.S. — C5 113
Boké, Gui. — D2 45
Bokeelia, Fl., U.S. — F4 86
Bokhoma, Ok., U.S. — D7 113
Boko, Zaire — C2 48
Bokobyaadaa Island, i., Marsh Is. — P18 52
Bokoro, Chad — C3 46
Bokoryuru Island, i., Marsh Is. — P18 52
Bokoshe, Ok., U.S. — B7 113
Bokungu, Zaire — B3 48
Bol, Chad — C2 46
Bolafa, Zaire — A3 48
Bolama, Gui.-B. — D5 126
Bolaños, stm., Mex. — m12 63
Bolar, Va., U.S. — B3 123
Bolbec, Fr. — C4 16
Bolckow, Mo., U.S. — A3 102
Bole, Ghana — E4 45
Boles, Ar., U.S. — C1 81
Boles, N.M., U.S. — *E4 108
Bolesławiec, Pol. — C3 26
Boley, Ok., U.S. — B5 113
Bolgatanga, Ghana — D4 45
Bolgrad, Sov. Un. — I7 27
Boli, China — B11 31
Bolia, Zaire — B3 48
Boligee, Al., U.S. — C1 78
Bolinao, Phil. — n12 34
Bolinao, Cape, c., Phil. — n12 34
Boling, Tx., U.S. — E5 120
Bolingbrook, Il., U.S. — k8 90
Bolívar, Arg. — B4 54
Bolívar, Col. — B2 60
Bolívar, Peru — B2 58
Bolivar, Mo., U.S. — D4 102
Bolivar, N.Y., U.S. — C2 109
Bolivar, Oh., U.S. — B4 112
Bolivar, Tn., U.S. — B3 119
Bolívar, W.V., U.S. — B7 125
Bolivar, co., Ms., U.S. — B3 101
Bolívar, state, Ven. — C6 60
Bolívar, prov., Ec. — B5 58
Bolívar, dept., Col. — B2 60
Bolívar, Cerro, mtn., Ven. — C6 60
Bolívar, Lake, l., Ms., U.S. — B3 101

Bolívar, Pico, mtn., Ven. — B3 60
Bolivia, N.C., U.S. — C4 110
Bolivia, ctry., S.A. — C2 55
Bolkhov, Sov. Un. — E11 27
Bollebygd, Swe. — A6 15
Bollène, Fr. — E6 16
Bolligen, Switz. — C4 21
Bolling, Al., U.S. — D3 78
Bollinger, co., Mo., U.S. — D7 102
Bollnäs, Swe. — G7 14
Bollullos [par del Condado], Spain — D2 22
Bolmen, l., Swe. — B7 15
Bolnisi, Sov. Un. — B15 40
Bologna, Italy — B3 23
Bolognesi, Peru — C3 58
Bologoye, Sov. Un. — C10 27
Bolomba, Zaire — A2 48
Bolon, Lake, l., Sov. Un. — B8 33
Bolotnoye, Sov. Un. — B10 28
Bolovens, Plateau des, plat., Laos — E7 35
Bolsena, Lake, l., Italy — C3 23
Bolshaya Kamenka, stm., Sov. Un. — q22 27
Bolshevik, i., Sov. Un. — B4 128
Bolshevik, i., Sov. Un. — C3 28
Bolshoy Irgiz, stm., Sov. Un. — C3 28
Bolshoy Uzen, stm., Sov. Un. — D3 28
Bolshoy Yugan, stm., Sov. Un. — B8 28
Bolsward, Neth. — A5 17
Bolton, Eng., U.K. — D5 10
Bolton, Ct., U.S. — B6 84
Bolton, Ma., U.S. — B4 98
Bolton, Ms., U.S. — C3 101
Bolton, N.C., U.S. — C4 110
Bolton, Vt., U.S. — C3 122
Bolton, stm., Man. — B4 70
Bolton Center, Ct., U.S. — B6 84
Bolton Lake, l., Man. — B4 70
Bolton Lakes, l., Ct., U.S. — B6 84
Bolton Landing, N.Y., U.S. — B7 109
Bolu, Tur. — B8 40
Bolus Head, c., Ire. — F1 11
Bolvadin, Tur. — C8 40
Bolzano, Italy — A3 23
Boma, Zaire — C1 48
Bombala, Austl. — G8 50
Bombay, India — E5 36
Bombay Hook Island, i., De., U.S. — C4 85
Bomboma, Zaire — A2 48
Bom Conselho, Braz. — C5 57
Bom Despacho, Braz. — B3 56
Bom Jardim de Goiás, Braz. — B2 56
Bom Jardim de Minas, Braz. — g5 56
Bom Jesus, Braz. — D2 56
Bom Jesus da Lapa, Braz. — A4 56
Bomokandi, stm., Zaire — A4 48
Bomongo, Zaire — A2 48
Bomoseen, Vt., U.S. — D2 122
Bomoseen, Lake, l., Vt., U.S. — D2 122
Bom Retiro, Braz. — D3 56
Bomu, stm., Afr. — E4 46
Bon, Cap, c., Tun. — B7 44
Bon Accord, Alta. — C4 68
Bonaigarh, India — G10 37
Bon Air, Al., U.S. — B3 78
Bon Air, Va., U.S. — C5 123
Bonaire, i., Neth. Ant. — A4 60
Bonanza, Nic. — D5 62
Bonanza, Or., U.S. — B1 81
Bonanza, Ut., U.S. — C6 121
Bonanza City, Co., U.S. — C6 83
Bonanza Peak, mtn., Wa., U.S. — A5 124
Bonaparte, Ia., U.S. — D6 92
Bonaparte, Mount, mtn., Wa., U.S. — A7 124
Bonaparte Lake, l., B.C. — D7 69
Bon Aqua, Tn., U.S. — B4 119
Boñar, Spain — A3 22
Bonar Bridge, Scot., U.K. — C4 13
Bonarlaw, Ont. — C7 73
Bonasila Dome, mtn., Ak., U.S. — C7 79
Bonaventure, Fl., U.S. — *F6 86
Bonaventure, Newf. — D5 72
Bonavista, Newf. — D5 72
Bonavista Bay, b., Newf. — D5 72
Bond, Co., U.S. — B4 83
Bond, Ky., U.S. — C6 94
Bond, Ms., U.S. — E4 101
Bond, co., Il., U.S. — E4 90
Bondeno, Italy — E7 20
Bondo, Zaire — A3 48
Bondoukou, I.C. — E4 45
Bondsville, Ma., U.S. — B3 98
Bonduel, Wi., U.S. — D5 126
Bondurant, Ia., U.S. — C4 92
Bondurant, Wy., U.S. — C2 127
Bondville, Il., U.S. — C5 90
Bondville, Vt., U.S. — E3 122
Bondy, Fr. — g10 16
Bone Cave, Tn., U.S. — D8 119
Bone Gap, Il., U.S. — E6 90
Bone Lake, l., Wi., U.S. — C1 126
Bonesteel, S.D., U.S. — D7 118
Bonete, Cerro, mtn., Arg. — E2 55
Bonetraill, N.D., U.S. — A2 111
Bonfield, Ont. — A5 73
Bonfouca, La., U.S. — h12 95
Bonga, Eth. — D4 47
Bongandanga, Zaire — A3 48
Bongor, Chad — C3 46
Bong Son, Viet. — D9 35
Bonham, Tx., U.S. — C4 120
Bonhomme Colony, S.D., U.S. — D8 118
Bonifacio, Fr. — F8 23
Bonifacio, Strait of, strt., Eur. — D2 23
Bonifay, Fl., U.S. — u16 86
Bonin Islands, is., Japan — *F5 82
Bonita, La., U.S. — B4 95
Bonita Springs, Fl., U.S. — F5 86
Bonito, Braz. — C1 56
Bonlee, N.C., U.S. — B3 110
Bonn, W. Ger. — C2 19
Bonneau, S.C., U.S. — E8 117
Bonneauville, Pa., U.S. — G7 115

# Index

| Name | Map Ref. | Page |
|---|---|---|
| Bonne Bay (Woody Point), Newf. | D3 | 72 |
| Bonne Bay, b., Newf. | D3 | 72 |
| Bonne Idee, Bayou, stm., La., U.S. | B4 | 95 |
| Bonner, Mt., U.S. | D3 | 103 |
| Bonner, co., Id., U.S. | A2 | 89 |
| Bonnerdale, Ar., U.S. | C2 | 81 |
| Bonners Ferry, Id., U.S. | A2 | 89 |
| Bonner Springs, Ks., U.S. | C9 | 93 |
| Bonnerup Strand, Den. | B4 | 15 |
| Bonne-sur-Ménoge, Fr. | D1 | 21 |
| Bonnet, Lac du, l., Man. | D4 | 70 |
| Bonnétable, Fr. | C4 | 16 |
| Bonne Terre, Mo., U.S. | D7 | 102 |
| Bonneville, Fr. | C2 | 20 |
| Bonneville, Or., U.S. | B5 | 114 |
| Bonneville, co., Id., U.S. | F7 | 89 |
| Bonneville Dam, U.S. | B4 | 114 |
| Bonneville Peak, mtn. Id., U.S. | F6 | 89 |
| Bonneville Salt Flats, pl., Ut., U.S. | C2 | 121 |
| Bonnevoie-Sud, Lux. | *E6 | 17 |
| Bonney Lake, Wa., U.S. | B3 | 124 |
| Bonnie, Il., U.S. | E5 | 90 |
| Bonnie Doone, N.C., U.S. | B4 | 110 |
| Bonnieville, Ky., U.S. | C4 | 94 |
| Bonnots Mill, Mo., U.S. | C6 | 102 |
| Bonny, Nig. | F6 | 45 |
| Bonny Blue, Va., U.S. | f8 | 123 |
| Bonny Reservoir, res., Co., U.S. | B8 | 83 |
| Bono, Ar., U.S. | B5 | 81 |
| Bono, Oh., U.S. | *A2 | 112 |
| Bonorva, Italy | D2 | 23 |
| Bonriki, Kir. | R18 | 52 |
| Bonriki, i., Kir. | R18 | 52 |
| Bons, Fr. | D1 | 21 |
| Bonsal, N.C., U.S. | B4 | 110 |
| Bon Secour, Al., U.S. | E2 | 78 |
| Bonshaw, P.E.I. | C6 | 71 |
| Bontang, Indon. | E5 | 34 |
| Bonthe, S.L. | E2 | 45 |
| Bon Wier, Tx., U.S. | D6 | 120 |
| Book Cliffs, clf., U.S. | D6 | 121 |
| Booker, Tx., U.S. | A2 | 120 |
| Booker T. Washington National Monument, Va., U.S. | C3 | 123 |
| Booligal, Austl. | F5 | 51 |
| Boolyglass, Ire. | E4 | 11 |
| Boomer, N.C., U.S. | A1 | 110 |
| Boomer, W.V., U.S. | C3 | 125 |
| Boone, Co., U.S. | D5 | 99 |
| Boone, Ia., U.S. | C6 | 83 |
| Boone, Ne., U.S. | B4 | 92 |
| Boone, N.C., U.S. | C8 | 104 |
| Boone, co., Ar., U.S. | A1 | 110 |
| Boone, co., Il., U.S. | A2 | 81 |
| Boone, co., In., U.S. | A5 | 90 |
| Boone, co., Ia., U.S. | D4 | 91 |
| Boone, co., Ky., U.S. | B3 | 92 |
| Boone, co., Mo., U.S. | B5 | 94 |
| Boone, co., Ne., U.S. | B5 | 102 |
| Boone, co., W.V., U.S. | C7 | 104 |
| Boone, stm., Ia., U.S. | C3 | 125 |
| Boone Grove, In., U.S. | B4 | 92 |
| Boone Lake, res., Tn., U.S. | B3 | 91 |
| Boones Mill, Va., U.S. | C11 | 119 |
| Booneville, Ar., U.S. | C3 | 123 |
| Booneville, Ky., U.S. | B2 | 81 |
| Booneville, Ms., U.S. | C6 | 94 |
| Boonsboro, Md., U.S. | A5 | 101 |
| Boons Pond, l., Ma., U.S. | A2 | 97 |
| Boonton, N.J., U.S. | g10 | 98 |
| Boonville, Ca., U.S. | B4 | 107 |
| Boonville, In., U.S. | C2 | 82 |
| Boonville, Mo., U.S. | H3 | 91 |
| Boonville, N.Y., U.S. | C5 | 102 |
| Boonville, N.C., U.S. | B5 | 109 |
| Boorama, Som. | A2 | 110 |
| Boosaaso, Som. | C5 | 47 |
| Booth, Al., U.S. | C6 | 47 |
| Boothbay, Me., U.S. | C3 | 78 |
| Boothbay Harbor, Me., U.S. | E3 | 96 |
| Boothby, Cape of, c., Ant. | E3 | 96 |
| Boothia, Gulf of, b., N.W. Ter. | C18 | 7 |
| Boothia Peninsula, pen., N.W. Ter. | B14 | 66 |
| Booths Creek, stm., W.V., U.S. | B14 | 66 |
| Boothville, La., U.S. | h11 | 125 |
| Bootle, Eng., U.K. | E6 | 95 |
| Booué, Gabon | A4 | 12 |
| Bophuthatswana, ctry., Afr. | F2 | 46 |
| Bopolu, Lib. | C4 | 49 |
| Boppard, W. Ger. | E2 | 45 |
| Boquerón, dept., Para. | C3 | 18 |
| Boquerón, Bahía de, b., P.R. | D3 | 55 |
| Boquerón, P.R. | k11 | 65 |
| Bor, Sud. | B1 | 65 |
| Bor, Yugo. | D3 | 47 |
| Boraha, Nosy, i., Madag. | C6 | 24 |
| Borah Peak, mtn., Id., U.S. | g10 | 49 |
| Borås, Swe. | E5 | 89 |
| Borāzjān, Iran | I5 | 14 |
| Borba, Braz. | G5 | 39 |
| Borculo, Neth. | C3 | 59 |
| Bordeaux, Fr. | B6 | 17 |
| Bordelonville, La., U.S. | E3 | 16 |
| Borden, Sask. | C4 | 95 |
| Borden, co., Tx., U.S. | E2 | 75 |
| Borden Island, i., N.W. Ter. | C2 | 120 |
| Borden Peninsula, pen., N.W. Ter. | m29 | 66 |
| Borden Springs, Al., U.S. | B16 | 66 |
| Bordentown, N.J., U.S. | B4 | 78 |
| Borderland, W.V., U.S. | C3 | 107 |
| Borders, prov., Scot., U.K. | D2 | 125 |
| Bordertown, Austl. | F9 | 13 |
| Bordighera, Italy | G7 | 50 |
| Bordj Bou Arreridj, Alg. | C1 | 23 |
| Bordj Omar Idriss, Alg. | B5 | 44 |
| Bordley, co., Tx., U.S. | D6 | 44 |
| Bordulac, N.D., U.S. | C2 | 94 |
| Boré, Mali | B7 | 111 |
| Boren, I., Indon. | C4 | 45 |
| Borensberg, Swe. | u33 | 14 |
| Borgå, Fin. | u33 | 14 |
| Börger, W. Ger. | G11 | 14 |
| Borger, Neth. | B7 | 17 |
| Borger, Tx., U.S. | B6 | 17 |
| Borgholm, Swe. | B2 | 120 |
| Borghorst, W. Ger. | H11 | 14 |
| Borg Mountain, mtn., Ant. | A2 | 19 |
| Borgne, stm., Switz. | B12 | 7 |
| Borgne, Lake, b., La., U.S. | D3 | 21 |
| Borgomanero, Italy | D6 | 95 |
| Borgo Piave, Italy | B2 | 23 |
| Borgosesia, Italy | k9 | 23 |
| Borgo Val di Taro, Italy | E5 | 21 |
| Borgo Val Sugana, Italy | B2 | 23 |
| Boring, Or., U.S. | C7 | 20 |
| Borislav, Sov. Un. | B4 | 114 |
| Borisoglebsk, Sov. Un. | G4 | 27 |
| Borisov, Sov. Un. | D7 | 29 |
| Borispol, Sov. Un. | D7 | 27 |
| Borja, Peru | F8 | 27 |
| Borja, Spain | B2 | 58 |
| Borjas Blancas, Spain | B5 | 22 |
| Borken, W. Ger. | B6 | 22 |
| Borken, W. Ger. | B1 | 19 |
| Børkop, Den. | B4 | 19 |
| Borkou, hist. reg., Chad | C3 | 15 |
| Borkum, W. Ger. | B3 | 46 |
| Borkum, i., W. Ger. | A6 | 17 |
| Borlänge, Swe. | B3 | 18 |
| Bormes, Fr. | G6 | 14 |
| Bormida, stm., Italy | F7 | 16 |
| Bormio, Italy | E4 | 20 |
| Borna, E. Ger. | C6 | 20 |
| Borne, Neth. | B7 | 19 |
| Borneo (Kalimantan), i., Asia | B6 | 17 |
| Bornheim, W. Ger. | E4 | 34 |
| Bornholm, co., Den. | C1 | 19 |
| Bornholm, i., Den. | C8 | 15 |
| Bornholmsgat, strt., Eur. | J6 | 14 |
| Bornos, Spain | C8 | 15 |
| Borobudur, hist., Indon. | D3 | 22 |
| Boromlya, Sov. Un. | G4 | 34 |
| Boromo, Burkina | F10 | 27 |
| Boron, Ca., U.S. | D4 | 45 |
| Borovan, Bul. | E5 | 82 |
| Borovichi, Sov. Un. | D6 | 24 |
| Borovskoye, Sov. Un. | D6 | 29 |
| Borraan, Som. | q21 | 27 |
| Borrby, Swe. | C6 | 47 |
| Borre, Den. | C8 | 15 |
| Borrego Springs, Ca., U.S. | C8 | 15 |
| Borris, Ire. | F5 | 82 |
| Borrisokane, Ire. | E4 | 11 |
| Borrisoleigh, Ire. | E3 | 11 |
| Borroloola, Austl. | E4 | 11 |
| Borşa, Rom. | C6 | 50 |
| Bort-les-Orgues, Fr. | B7 | 24 |
| Borūjen, Iran | E5 | 16 |
| Borūjerd, Iran | F5 | 39 |
| Borup, Mn., U.S. | B4 | 38 |
| Borzhomi, Sov. Un. | C2 | 100 |
| Borzna, Sov. Un. | B14 | 40 |
| Borzonasca, Italy | F9 | 27 |
| Borzya, Sov. Un. | E5 | 20 |
| Bosa, Italy | A8 | 31 |
| Bosanska Dubica, Yugo. | D2 | 23 |
| Bosanska Gradiška, Yugo. | C3 | 24 |
| Bosanska Kostajnica, Yugo. | C3 | 24 |
| Bosanski Novi, Yugo. | C3 | 24 |
| Bosanski Petrovac, Yugo. | C3 | 24 |
| Bosanski Šamac, Yugo. | C4 | 24 |
| Bosavi, Mount, mtn., Pap. N. Gui. | k11 | 51 |
| Boscawen, N.H., U.S. | D3 | 106 |
| Boscobel, Wi., U.S. | E3 | 126 |
| Boshan, China | D8 | 31 |
| Boshrūyeh, Iran | E8 | 39 |
| Boskovice, Czech. | D4 | 26 |
| Bosler, Wy., U.S. | E7 | 127 |
| Bosna, stm., Yugo. | C3 | 24 |
| Bosnia, hist. reg., Yugo. | C3 | 24 |
| Bosnik, Indon. | F9 | 34 |
| Bosobolo, Zaire | A2 | 48 |
| Bosporus, strt. | B7 | 40 |
| Bosque, N.M., U.S. | C3 | 108 |
| Bosque, co., Tx., U.S. | D4 | 120 |
| Boss, Mo., U.S. | D6 | 102 |
| Bossangoa, Cen. Afr. Rep. | D3 | 46 |
| Bossembélé, Cen. Afr. Rep. | D3 | 46 |
| Bossert Estates, N.J., U.S. | C3 | 107 |
| Bossier, co., La., U.S. | B2 | 95 |
| Bossier City, La., U.S. | B2 | 95 |
| Bosso, Niger | D7 | 45 |
| Bosso, Dallol, val., Niger | D5 | 45 |
| Bosten Lake, l., China | C2 | 31 |
| Boston, Eng., U.K. | D6 | 10 |
| Boston, Ga., U.S. | F3 | 87 |
| Boston, In., U.S. | E8 | 91 |
| Boston, Ky., U.S. | C4 | 94 |
| Boston, Ma., U.S. | B5 | 98 |
| Boston Bar, B.C. | E7 | 69 |
| Boston Bay, b., Ma., U.S. | g12 | 98 |
| Boston Heights, Oh., U.S. | h9 | 112 |
| Boston Mountains, mts., Ar., U.S. | B2 | 81 |
| Bostonnais, stm., Que. | B5 | 74 |
| Bostwick, Fl., U.S. | C5 | 86 |
| Bostwick, Ga., U.S. | C3 | 87 |
| Boswarlos, Newf. | D2 | 72 |
| Boswell, B.C. | E9 | 69 |
| Boswell, In., U.S. | D4 | 91 |
| Boswell, Ok., U.S. | C6 | 113 |
| Boswell, Pa., U.S. | F3 | 115 |
| Bosworth, Mo., U.S. | B4 | 102 |
| Botany Bay, b., Austl. | *F9 | 50 |
| Boteti, stm., Bots. | B3 | 49 |
| Botetourt, co., Va., U.S. | C3 | 123 |
| Botev, mtn., Bul. | D7 | 24 |
| Botevgrad, Bul. | D6 | 24 |
| Botha, Alta. | C4 | 68 |
| Bothell, Wa., U.S. | B3 | 124 |
| Bothnia, Gulf of, b., Eur. | F9 | 14 |
| Bothwell, Ont. | E3 | 73 |
| Bothwell, P.E.I. | C7 | 71 |
| Botkins, Oh., U.S. | B1 | 112 |
| Botkyrka, Swe. | t35 | 14 |
| Botolan, Phil. | o13 | 34 |
| Botoşani, Rom. | B8 | 24 |
| Botsford, Ct., U.S. | D2 | 84 |
| Botswana, ctry., Afr. | B3 | 49 |
| Bottineau, N.D., U.S. | A5 | 111 |
| Bottineau, co., N.D., U.S. | A4 | 111 |
| Bottrop, W. Ger. | B1 | 19 |
| Botucatu, Braz. | C3 | 56 |
| Botwood, Newf. | D4 | 72 |
| Bouaflé, I.C. | E3 | 45 |
| Bouaké, I.C. | E3 | 45 |
| Bouar, Cen. Afr. Rep. | D3 | 46 |
| Bou Arfa, Mor. | C4 | 44 |
| Boucau, Fr. | F3 | 16 |
| Boucher, Lac, l., Que. | C2 | 72 |
| Boucherville, Que. | D4 | 74 |
| Bouchette, Que. | C2 | 74 |
| Bouctouche, N.B. | C5 | 71 |
| Boudenib, Mor. | C4 | 44 |
| Boú Djébéha, well, Mali | C4 | 45 |
| Boudreaux, Lake, l., La., U.S. | E5 | 95 |
| Boudry, Switz. | C2 | 21 |
| Bougainville, i., Pap. N. Gui. | G9 | 6 |
| Bougouni, Mali | D3 | 45 |
| Bouillon, Bel. | E5 | 17 |
| Boulder, Co., U.S. | A5 | 83 |
| Boulder, Mt., U.S. | D4 | 103 |
| Boulder, Ut., U.S. | F4 | 121 |
| Boulder, Wy., U.S. | D3 | 127 |
| Boulder, co., Co., U.S. | A5 | 83 |
| Boulder City, Nv., U.S. | H7 | 105 |
| Boulder Creek, Ca., U.S. | *D2 | 82 |
| Boulder Hill, Il., U.S. | *B5 | 90 |
| Boulevard, Ca., U.S. | F5 | 82 |
| Boulevard Heights, Md., U.S. | f9 | 97 |
| Boulevard Park, Wa., U.S. | *B3 | 124 |
| Bouligny, Fr. | E5 | 17 |
| Boulogne, La., U.S. | n10 | 120 |
| Boulogne-Billancourt, Fr. | C5 | 16 |
| Boulogne-sur-Mer, Fr. | B4 | 16 |
| Boulsa, Burkina | D4 | 45 |
| Boumalne, Mor. | C3 | 44 |
| Boumdeït, Maur. | C2 | 45 |
| Bouna, I.C. | E4 | 45 |
| Boundary, Ak., U.S. | C11 | 79 |
| Boundary, co., Id., U.S. | A2 | 89 |
| Boundary Bald Mountain, mtn., Me., U.S. | C2 | 96 |
| Boundary Bay, b., Wa., U.S. | A3 | 124 |
| Boundary Bend, Austl. | G4 | 51 |
| Boundary Peak, mtn., Nv., U.S. | F3 | 105 |
| Boundary Ranges, mts., N.A. | k22 | 79 |
| Bound Brook, N.J., U.S. | B3 | 107 |
| Boundiali, I.C. | E3 | 45 |
| Bountiful, Ut., U.S. | C4 | 121 |
| Bounty Islands, is., N.Z. | Q17 | 51 |
| Bourbeuse, stm., Mo., U.S. | C6 | 102 |
| Bourbon, In., U.S. | B5 | 91 |
| Bourbon, Mo., U.S. | C6 | 102 |
| Bourbon, co., Ks., U.S. | E9 | 93 |
| Bourbon, co., Ky., U.S. | B5 | 94 |
| Bourbonnais, Il., U.S. | B6 | 90 |
| Bourbonnais, hist. reg., Fr. | D5 | 16 |
| Bourbonne-les-Bains, Fr. | B1 | 20 |
| Bourem, Mali | C4 | 45 |
| Bourg, La., U.S. | E5 | 95 |
| Bourg-de-Péage, Fr. | E6 | 16 |
| Bourg [-en-Bresse], Fr. | D6 | 16 |
| Bourges, Fr. | D5 | 16 |
| Bourget, Ont. | B9 | 73 |
| Bourget, Lake, l., Fr. | E6 | 16 |
| Bourg-la-Reine, Fr. | g10 | 16 |
| Bourgoin [-Jallieu], Fr. | E6 | 16 |
| Bourg-Saint-Andéol, Fr. | E6 | 16 |
| Bourg-Saint-Maurice, Fr. | G3 | 115 |
| Bou Rjeïmat, well, Maur. | C2 | 45 |
| Bourke, Austl. | F8 | 50 |
| Bourne, Eng., U.K. | B7 | 12 |
| Bourne, Ma., U.S. | C6 | 98 |
| Bournemouth, Eng., U.K. | E6 | 10 |
| Bourneville, Oh., U.S. | C2 | 112 |
| Bou Saâda, Alg. | B5 | 44 |
| Bouse, Az., U.S. | D2 | 80 |
| Bousso, Chad | C3 | 46 |
| Boutilimit, Maur. | C2 | 45 |
| Boutte, La., U.S. | k11 | 95 |
| Bouvet, i., Ant. | D13 | 7 |
| Bovey, Mn., U.S. | C5 | 100 |
| Bovill, Id., U.S. | C2 | 89 |
| Bovina, Ms., U.S. | C3 | 101 |
| Bovina, Tx., U.S. | B1 | 120 |
| Bovina Center, N.Y., U.S. | C6 | 109 |
| Bow, N.H., U.S. | D3 | 106 |
| Bow, Wa., U.S. | A3 | 124 |
| Bow, stm., Alta. | D4 | 68 |
| Bowbells, N.D., U.S. | A3 | 111 |
| Bowden, Alta. | D4 | 68 |
| Bowden, Ok., U.S. | A5 | 113 |
| Bowdens, N.C., U.S. | B4 | 110 |
| Bowdish Reservoir, res., R.I., U.S. | B1 | 116 |
| Bowdle, S.D., U.S. | B6 | 118 |
| Bowdoin, Me., U.S. | f8 | 96 |
| Bowdoinham, Me., U.S. | D3 | 96 |
| Bowdon, Ga., U.S. | C1 | 87 |
| Bowdon, N.D., U.S. | B6 | 111 |
| Bowen, Austl. | C8 | 50 |
| Bowen, Il., U.S. | C2 | 90 |
| Bowers, De., U.S. | D4 | 85 |
| Bowersville, Ga., U.S. | B3 | 87 |
| Bowersville, Oh., U.S. | C2 | 112 |
| Bowesmont, N.D., U.S. | A8 | 111 |
| Bowie, Az., U.S. | E6 | 80 |
| Bowie, Co., U.S. | C3 | 83 |
| Bowie, Md., U.S. | B4 | 97 |
| Bowie, Tx., U.S. | C4 | 120 |
| Bowie, co., Tx., U.S. | C5 | 120 |
| Bowie Creek, stm., Ms., U.S. | D4 | 101 |
| Bowkerville, N.H., U.S. | E2 | 106 |
| Bowdon Point, c., S.C., U.S. | G6 | 117 |
| Bowlegs, Ok., U.S. | B5 | 113 |
| Bowler, Wi., U.S. | D5 | 126 |
| Bowling Green, Fl., U.S. | E4 | 86 |
| Bowling Green, In., U.S. | F3 | 91 |
| Bowling Green, Ky., U.S. | D3 | 94 |
| Bowling Green, Mo., U.S. | B6 | 102 |
| Bowling Green, Oh., U.S. | A2 | 112 |
| Bowling Green, S.C., U.S. | A5 | 117 |
| Bowling Green, Va., U.S. | B5 | 123 |
| Bowlus, Mn., U.S. | E4 | 100 |
| Bowman, Ga., U.S. | B3 | 87 |
| Bowman, N.D., U.S. | C2 | 111 |
| Bowman, S.C., U.S. | E6 | 117 |
| Bowman, co., N.D., U.S. | C2 | 111 |
| Bowman Creek, stm., Pa., U.S. | m16 | 115 |
| Bowman-Haley Lake, res., N.D., U.S. | C2 | 111 |
| Bowman Island, i., Ant. | C23 | 7 |
| Bowmanstown, Pa., U.S. | E10 | 115 |
| Bowmanville (part of Newcastle), Ont. | D6 | 73 |
| Bow Mar, Col., U.S. | *B5 | 83 |
| Bowmore, Scot., U.K. | E2 | 13 |
| Bowokan Islands, is., Indon. | F6 | 34 |
| Bowral, Austl. | G8 | 51 |
| Bowring, Ok., U.S. | B6 | 113 |
| Bowron, stm., B.C. | C7 | 69 |
| Bowron Lake Provincial Park, B.C. | C7 | 69 |
| Bowser Lake, l., B.C. | A3 | 69 |
| Bowsman, Man. | C1 | 70 |
| Bowstring Lake, l., Mn., U.S. | C5 | 100 |
| Bow Valley, Ne., U.S. | B8 | 104 |
| Boxborough, Ma., U.S. | A5 | 98 |
| Box Butte, co., Ne., U.S. | B2 | 104 |
| Box Butte Creek, stm., Ne., U.S. | B3 | 104 |
| Box Butte Reservoir, res., Ne., U.S. | B2 | 104 |
| Box Elder, Mt., U.S. | B6 | 103 |
| Box Elder, S.D., U.S. | C2 | 118 |
| Box Elder, co., Ut., U.S. | B2 | 121 |
| Box Elder Creek, stm., Co., U.S. | A6 | 83 |
| Boxelder Creek, stm., Mt., U.S. | E12 | 103 |
| Box Elder Creek, stm., Mt., U.S. | C8 | 103 |
| Boxford, Ma., U.S. | A6 | 98 |
| Boxholm, Ia., U.S. | B3 | 92 |
| Boxian, China | E8 | 31 |
| Boxmeer, Neth. | C5 | 17 |
| Boxtel, Neth. | B6 | 16 |
| Boyacá, dept., Col. | B3 | 60 |
| Boyang, China | J7 | 32 |
| Boyce, La., U.S. | C3 | 95 |
| Boyce, Va., U.S. | A4 | 123 |
| Boyceville, Wi., U.S. | C1 | 126 |
| Boyd, Mn., U.S. | F3 | 100 |
| Boyd, Mt., U.S. | E7 | 103 |
| Boyd, Tx., U.S. | C4 | 120 |
| Boyd, Wi., U.S. | D2 | 126 |
| Boyd, co., Ky., U.S. | B7 | 94 |
| Boyd, co., Ne., U.S. | B7 | 104 |
| Boyd Glacier, ice, Ant. | B34 | 7 |
| Boyd Lake, l., Me., U.S. | C4 | 96 |
| Boyds, Md., U.S. | B3 | 97 |
| Boyd's Cove, Newf. | D4 | 72 |
| Boydsville, Ar., U.S. | A5 | 81 |
| Boydton, Va., U.S. | D4 | 123 |
| Boyer, stm., Ia., U.S. | C2 | 92 |
| Boyero, Zaire | B2 | 48 |
| Boyer Knob, mtn., Md., U.S. | k13 | 97 |
| Boyero, Co., U.S. | C7 | 83 |
| Boyers, Pa., U.S. | D2 | 115 |
| Boyertown, Pa., U.S. | F10 | 115 |
| Boyes, Mt., U.S. | E11 | 103 |
| Boykin, Al., U.S. | C2 | 78 |
| Boykin, Ga., U.S. | E2 | 87 |
| Boykins, Va., U.S. | D5 | 123 |
| Boyle, Alta. | B4 | 68 |
| Boyle, Ire. | C2 | 10 |
| Boyle, Ms., U.S. | B3 | 101 |
| Boyle, co., Ky., U.S. | C5 | 94 |
| Boylston, N.S. | D8 | 71 |
| Boylston, Ma., U.S. | B4 | 98 |
| Boylston, La., U.S. | D3 | 95 |
| Boyne City, Mi., U.S. | C6 | 99 |
| Boyne Falls, Mi., U.S. | C6 | 99 |
| Boynton, Ok., U.S. | B6 | 113 |
| Boynton, Pa., U.S. | G3 | 115 |
| Boynton Beach, Fl., U.S. | F6 | 86 |
| Boyoma Falls (Stanley Falls), wtfl., Zaire | A4 | 48 |
| Boysen Reservoir, res., Wy., U.S. | C4 | 127 |
| Boys Ranch, Tx., U.S. | B1 | 120 |
| Boys Town, Ne., U.S. | g12 | 104 |
| Bozcaada, Tur. | B7 | 25 |
| Bozcaada (Tenedos), i., Tur. | C6 | 25 |
| Bozdoğan, Tur. | D7 | 25 |
| Bozeman, Mt., U.S. | E5 | 103 |
| Bozeman Pass, Mt., U.S. | E6 | 103 |
| Bozman, Md., U.S. | C5 | 97 |
| Bozoum, Cen. Afr. Rep. | D3 | 46 |
| Bozovici, Rom. | C5 | 24 |
| Bozüyük, Tur. | C8 | 40 |
| Bra, Italy | B1 | 23 |
| Brabant, prov., Bel. | D4 | 17 |
| Brabant, co., Bel. | C6 | 7 |
| Brabant Lake, l., Sask. | A4 | 75 |
| Brač, i., Yugo. | D3 | 24 |
| Bracadale, Loch, b., Scot., U.K. | C2 | 13 |
| Bracciano, Italy | g8 | 23 |
| Bracciano, Lake, l., Italy | C4 | 23 |
| Bracebridge, Ont. | B5 | 73 |
| Braceville, Il., U.S. | B5 | 90 |
| Brach, Libya | D2 | 43 |
| Bracken, Sask. | H1 | 75 |
| Bracken, co., Ky., U.S. | B5 | 94 |
| Bracken Lake, l., Man. | C2 | 70 |
| Brackenridge, Pa., U.S. | h15 | 115 |
| Brackett, Wi., U.S. | D2 | 126 |
| Brackettville, Tx., U.S. | E2 | 120 |
| Brackley, Eng., U.K. | B6 | 12 |
| Bracknell, Eng., U.K. | C7 | 12 |
| Brackwede, W. Ger. | B3 | 19 |
| Braden, Tx., U.S. | B2 | 120 |
| Bradano, stm., Italy | D6 | 23 |
| Bradenton, Fl., U.S. | E4 | 86 |
| Bradenton Beach, Fl., U.S. | F3 | 115 |
| Bradford, Ont. | C5 | 73 |
| Bradford, Eng., U.K. | D6 | 10 |
| Bradford, Ar., U.S. | B4 | 81 |
| Bradford, Il., U.S. | B4 | 90 |
| Bradford, N.H., U.S. | D3 | 106 |
| Bradford, Oh., U.S. | B1 | 112 |
| Bradford, Pa., U.S. | C4 | 115 |
| Bradford, R.I., U.S. | F2 | 116 |
| Bradford, Tn., U.S. | A3 | 119 |
| Bradford, Vt., U.S. | D4 | 122 |
| Bradford, co., Fl., U.S. | C4 | 86 |
| Bradford, co., Pa., U.S. | C8 | 115 |
| Bradford Mountain, mtn., Ct., U.S. | B2 | 84 |
| Bradfordsville, Ky., U.S. | C4 | 94 |
| Bradfordwoods, Pa., U.S. | h13 | 115 |
| Bradgate, Ia., U.S. | B3 | 92 |
| Bradley, Al., U.S. | D3 | 78 |
| Bradley, Ar., U.S. | D2 | 81 |
| Bradley, Fl., U.S. | E5 | 86 |
| Bradley, Il., U.S. | B6 | 90 |
| Bradley, Me., U.S. | D4 | 96 |
| Bradley, Ok., U.S. | C4 | 113 |
| Bradley, S.C., U.S. | C3 | 117 |
| Bradley, S.D., U.S. | B8 | 118 |
| Bradley, W.V., U.S. | D3 | 125 |
| Bradley, co., Ar., U.S. | D3 | 81 |
| Bradley, co., Tn., U.S. | D9 | 119 |
| Bradley Beach, N.J., U.S. | C4 | 107 |
| Bradner, Oh., U.S. | A2 | 112 |
| Brador, Baie de, b., Que. | B3 | 72 |
| Bradshaw, Ne., U.S. | D8 | 104 |
| Bradshaw, W.V., U.S. | D3 | 125 |
| Bradshaw Mountains, mts., Az., U.S. | C3 | 80 |
| Bradstreet, Ma., U.S. | B2 | 98 |
| Bradwell, Sask. | F2 | 75 |
| Brady, Mt., U.S. | B5 | 103 |
| Brady, Ne., U.S. | C5 | 104 |
| Brady, Tx., U.S. | D3 | 120 |
| Bradyville, Tn., U.S. | B5 | 119 |
| Braeside, Ont. | B8 | 73 |
| Braemar, Scot., U.K. | D5 | 13 |
| Braga, Port. | B1 | 22 |
| Bragado, Arg. | B4 | 54 |
| Bragança, Braz. | B1 | 57 |
| Bragança, Port. | B2 | 22 |
| Bragança Paulista, Braz. | C3 | 56 |
| Braggadocio, Mo., U.S. | E8 | 102 |
| Braggs, Ok., U.S. | B6 | 113 |
| Braham, Mn., U.S. | E5 | 100 |
| Brāhmani, stm., India | D7 | 36 |
| Brahmapur, India | E7 | 36 |
| Brahmaputra (Yarlung Zangbo Jiang), stm., Asia | C9 | 36 |
| Braidwood, Il., U.S. | B5 | 90 |
| Braila, Rom. | C8 | 24 |
| Brainard, Ne., U.S. | C9 | 104 |
| Braine-le-Comte, Bel. | D4 | 17 |
| Brainerd, Ks., U.S. | g12 | 93 |
| Brainerd, Mn., U.S. | D4 | 100 |
| Braintree, Eng., U.K. | C8 | 12 |
| Braintree, Ma., U.S. | B5 | 98 |
| Braintree, Vt., U.S. | D3 | 122 |
| Braithwaite, La., U.S. | k12 | 95 |
| Brake, W. Ger. | B4 | 18 |
| Brakel, W. Ger. | B4 | 19 |
| Brakpan, S. Afr. | *C4 | 49 |
| Bralorne, B.C. | D6 | 69 |
| Braman, Ok., U.S. | A4 | 113 |
| Bramming, Den. | C2 | 15 |
| Brampton, Ont. | D5 | 73 |
| Brampton, Eng., U.K. | F6 | 13 |
| Brampton, N.D., U.S. | B8 | 111 |
| Bramsche, W. Ger. | B7 | 17 |
| Bramwell, W.V., U.S. | D3 | 125 |
| Branch, Newf. | E5 | 72 |
| Branch, Ar., U.S. | B1 | 81 |
| Branch, La., U.S. | D3 | 95 |
| Branch, Wi., U.S. | h10 | 126 |
| Branch, co., Mi., U.S. | G5 | 99 |
| Branch, stm., R.I., U.S. | B3 | 116 |
| Branch, stm., Wi., U.S. | h10 | 126 |
| Branch Lake, l., Me., U.S. | D4 | 96 |
| Branchland, W.V., U.S. | C2 | 125 |
| Branchport, N.Y., U.S. | C3 | 109 |
| Branch Village, R.I., U.S. | B3 | 116 |
| Branchville, Al., U.S. | B3 | 78 |
| Branchville, Ct., U.S. | D2 | 84 |
| Branchville, S.C., U.S. | E6 | 117 |
| Branco, Cape, c., Tur. | B7 | 25 |
| Branco, stm., Braz. | D4 | 55 |
| Branco, stm., Braz. | B2 | 59 |
| Brande, Den. | C3 | 15 |
| Brandberg, mtn., Nmb. | B1 | 49 |
| Brandbu, Bul. | C6 | 24 |
| Brandenburg, E. Ger. | B6 | 18 |
| Brandenburg, Ky., U.S. | C3 | 94 |
| Brandenburg, hist. reg., E. Ger. | B6 | 18 |
| Brandon, Man. | E2 | 70 |
| Brandon, Co., U.S. | C8 | 83 |
| Brandon, Fl., U.S. | E4 | 86 |
| Brandon, Ms., U.S. | C4 | 101 |
| Brandon, Ne., U.S. | C4 | 104 |
| Brandon, S.C., U.S. | B3 | 117 |
| Brandon, S.D., U.S. | D9 | 118 |
| Brandon, Vt., U.S. | D2 | 122 |
| Brandon, Wi., U.S. | E5 | 126 |
| Brandon Head, c., Ire. | D1 | 10 |
| Brandon Mountain, mtn., Ire. | D1 | 10 |
| Brandsen, Arg. | B5 | 54 |
| Brandsville, Mo., U.S. | E6 | 102 |
| Brandt, Oh., U.S. | C1 | 112 |
| Brandt, S.D., U.S. | C9 | 118 |
| Brandvlei, S. Afr. | D3 | 49 |
| Brandy Peak, mtn., Or., U.S. | E3 | 114 |
| Brandys nad Labem, Czech. | C9 | 19 |
| Brandýs-Stará Boleslav, Czech. | n18 | 26 |
| Brandy Station, Va., U.S. | B5 | 123 |
| Brandywine, Md., U.S. | C4 | 97 |
| Brandywine Creek, stm., U.S. | A3 | 85 |
| Branford, Ct., U.S. | D4 | 84 |
| Branford, Fl., U.S. | C4 | 86 |
| Branford Hills, Ct., U.S. | D4 | 84 |
| Braniewo, Pol. | A5 | 26 |
| Brańsk, Pol. | B7 | 26 |
| Branson, Co., U.S. | D7 | 83 |
| Branson, Mo., U.S. | E4 | 102 |
| Brant, Alta. | D4 | 68 |
| Brant, co., Ont. | D4 | 73 |
| Brantford, Ont. | D4 | 73 |
| Brantford, N.D., U.S. | B7 | 111 |
| Brant Lake, N.Y., U.S. | B7 | 109 |
| Brantley, Al., U.S. | D3 | 78 |
| Brantley, co., Ga., U.S. | E4 | 87 |
| Brant Rock, Ma., U.S. | B6 | 98 |
| Brantville, N.B. | B5 | 71 |
| Brantwood, Wi., U.S. | C3 | 126 |
| Bras-d'Apic, Que. | C7 | 74 |
| Bras-d'Or, Que. | C9 | 71 |
| Bras d'Or Lake, l., N.S. | D9 | 71 |
| Brasfield, Ar., U.S. | C4 | 81 |
| Brashear, Mo., U.S. | A5 | 102 |
| Brasília, Braz. | B2 | 55 |
| Brasiléia, Braz. | B2 | 55 |
| Brasília de Minas, Braz. | B4 | 56 |
| Braşov (Orașul-Stalin), Rom. | C7 | 24 |
| Brasstown, N.C., U.S. | f9 | 110 |
| Brasstown Bald, mtn., Ga., U.S. | B3 | 87 |
| Brassua Lake, res., Me., U.S. | C2 | 96 |
| Bratenahl, Oh., U.S. | g9 | 112 |
| Bratsk, Sov. Un. | D13 | 29 |
| Bratsk Reservoir, res., Sov. Un. | D13 | 29 |
| Bratt, Fl., U.S. | u14 | 86 |
| Braunau [am Inn], Aus. | D6 | 18 |
| Braunfels, W. Ger. | C3 | 18 |
| Braunschweig, W. Ger. | B5 | 18 |
| Brâviken, b., Swe. | u34 | 14 |
| Brawley, Ca., U.S. | F6 | 82 |
| Brawley Peaks, mts., Nv., U.S. | E3 | 105 |
| Braxton, Ms., U.S. | C4 | 101 |
| Braxton, co., W.V., U.S. | C4 | 125 |
| Bray, Ire. | C5 | 11 |
| Bray, Ok., U.S. | C4 | 113 |
| Bray Head, c., Ire. | F1 | 11 |
| Braymer, Mo., U.S. | B3 | 102 |
| Brayton, Ia., U.S. | C2 | 92 |
| Brazeau, stm., Alta. | C2 | 68 |
| Brazeau, Mount, mtn., Alta. | C2 | 68 |
| Brazil, In., U.S. | E3 | 91 |
| Brazil, Ia., U.S. | D5 | 92 |
| Brazil, Tn., U.S. | B2 | 119 |
| Brazil, ctry., S.A. | D5 | 53 |
| Brazilian Highlands, plat., Braz. | E5 | 53 |
| Brazil Lake, N.S. | F4 | 71 |
| Braziltown, Ks., U.S. | E9 | 93 |
| Brazoria, Tx., U.S. | r14 | 120 |
| Brazoria, co., Tx., U.S. | E5 | 120 |
| Brazos, co., Tx., U.S. | D4 | 120 |
| Brazos, stm., Tx., U.S. | D4 | 120 |
| Brazzaville, Congo | B2 | 48 |
| Brčko, Yugo. | C4 | 24 |
| Brda, stm., Pol. | B4 | 26 |
| Brea, Ca., U.S. | n13 | 82 |
| Brea, Punta, c., P.R. | C2 | 65 |
| Bread Loaf Mountain, mtn., Vt., U.S. | D3 | 122 |
| Breakenridge, Mount, mtn., B.C. | E7 | 69 |
| Breakers Point, c., Am. Sam. | F13 | 52 |
| Breakeyville, Que. | o17 | 74 |
| Bream Bay, b., N.Z. | K15 | 51 |
| Breared, Swe. | B7 | 15 |
| Breathitt, co., Ky., U.S. | C6 | 94 |
| Breaux Bridge, La., U.S. | D4 | 95 |
| Brechin, Ont. | C5 | 73 |
| Brechin, Scot., U.K. | B5 | 10 |
| Breckenridge, Que. | h12 | 73 |
| Breckenridge, Co., U.S. | B4 | 83 |
| Breckenridge, Mi., U.S. | E6 | 99 |
| Breckenridge, Mn., U.S. | D2 | 100 |
| Breckenridge, Mo., U.S. | B4 | 102 |
| Breckenridge, Ok., U.S. | A4 | 113 |
| Breckenridge, Tx., U.S. | C3 | 120 |
| Breckenridge Hills, Mo., U.S. | *f13 | 102 |
| Breckinridge, co., Ky., U.S. | C3 | 94 |
| Brecknock, Península, pen., Chile | h11 | 54 |
| Brecksville, Oh., U.S. | A4 | 112 |
| Břeclav, Czech. | D4 | 26 |
| Brecon (Brecknock), Wales, U.K. | E5 | 10 |
| Brecon Beacons, mtn., Wales, U.K. | E5 | 10 |
| Breda, Neth. | B6 | 16 |
| Breda, Ia., U.S. | B3 | 92 |
| Bredasdorp, S. Afr. | D3 | 49 |
| Bredenbury, Sask. | G4 | 75 |
| Bredstedt, W. Ger. | D2 | 15 |
| Bredy, Sov. Un. | E21 | 8 |
| Bree, Bel. | C5 | 17 |
| Breese, Il., U.S. | E4 | 90 |
| Breezy Point, Mn., U.S. | D4 | 100 |
| Bregalnica, stm., Yugo. | E6 | 24 |
| Bregenz, Aus. | E4 | 18 |
| Bregenzerach, stm., Aus. | B8 | 21 |
| Bregovo, Bul. | C6 | 24 |
| Breidafjördur, b., Ice. | n21 | 14 |
| Breid Bay, b., Ant. | B15 | 7 |
| Breien, N.D., U.S. | C5 | 111 |
| Breil, Fr. | F7 | 16 |
| Breisach, W. Ger. | A3 | 20 |
| Brejinho de Nazaré, Braz. | B2 | 57 |
| Brejo, Braz. | B3 | 57 |
| Bremen, Al., U.S. | B2 | 78 |
| Bremen, Ga., U.S. | C1 | 87 |
| Bremen, Il., U.S. | F4 | 90 |
| Bremen, In., U.S. | B5 | 91 |
| Bremen, Ky., U.S. | C2 | 94 |
| Bremen, N.D., U.S. | B6 | 111 |
| Bremen, Oh., U.S. | C3 | 112 |
| Bremen, state, W. Ger. | E2 | 15 |
| Bremer, co., Ia., U.S. | B5 | 92 |
| Bremerhaven (Wesermünde), W. Ger. | B4 | 18 |
| Bremerton, Wa., U.S. | B3 | 124 |
| Bremervörde, W. Ger. | E3 | 15 |
| Bremond, Tx., U.S. | D4 | 120 |
| Breña, Peru | *D2 | 58 |
| Brenham, Tx., U.S. | D4 | 120 |
| Brenish, Scot., U.K. | B1 | 13 |
| Brenner Pass, Eur. | A3 | 23 |
| Brent, Ont. | A6 | 73 |
| Brent, Al., U.S. | C2 | 78 |
| Brent, Fl., U.S. | u14 | 86 |
| Brenta, stm., Italy | D7 | 20 |
| Brentford, S.D., U.S. | B7 | 118 |
| Brenton, W.V., U.S. | *D3 | 125 |
| Brenton Point, c., R.I., U.S. | F5 | 116 |
| Brentwood, Eng., U.K. | k13 | 10 |
| Brentwood, Ca., U.S. | h9 | 82 |
| Brentwood, Md., U.S. | f9 | 97 |
| Brentwood, Mo., U.S. | *f13 | 102 |
| Brentwood, N.H., U.S. | E4 | 106 |
| Brentwood, N.Y., U.S. | E7 | 109 |
| Brentwood, Oh., U.S. | *o12 | 112 |
| Brentwood, Pa., U.S. | k14 | 115 |
| Brentwood, S.C., U.S. | k11 | 117 |
| Brentwood, Tn., U.S. | A5 | 119 |
| Brescia, Italy | B3 | 23 |
| Breskens, Neth. | C3 | 17 |
| Breslau see Wrocław, Pol. | C4 | 26 |
| Bresle, stm., Fr. | C4 | 16 |
| Bressanone, Italy | A3 | 23 |
| Bressuire, Fr. | C3 | 16 |
| Brest, Fr. | C1 | 16 |
| Brest (Brest-Litovsk), Sov. Un. | D5 | 29 |
| Bretagne see Brittany, Fr. | E2 | 17 |
| Bretigny [-Notre-Dame], Fr. | C7 | 17 |
| Breton, Alta. | C3 | 68 |
| Breton, Pertuis, strt., Fr. | D3 | 16 |
| Breton Islands, is., La., U.S. | E6 | 95 |
| Breton Sound, strt., La., U.S. | E6 | 95 |
| Breton Woods, N.J., U.S. | C4 | 107 |
| Brett, Cape, c., N.Z. | K15 | 51 |
| Bretton Woods, N.H., U.S. | B4 | 106 |
| Breuil, Italy | | |
| Brevard, N.C., U.S. | f10 | 110 |
| Brevard, co., Fl., U.S. | D6 | 86 |
| Breves, Braz. | C4 | 59 |
| Brevik (part of Porsgrunn), Nor. | p27 | 14 |
| Břevnov (part of Prague), Czech. | n17 | 26 |
| Brevort Lake, l., Mi., U.S. | B5 | 99 |
| Brewarrina, Austl. | F5 | 50 |
| Brewer, Me., U.S. | D4 | 96 |
| Brewerville, Lib. | E2 | 45 |
| Brewster, Ks., U.S. | C2 | 93 |
| Brewster, Ma., U.S. | C7 | 98 |
| Brewster, Mn., U.S. | G3 | 100 |
| Brewster, Ne., U.S. | C6 | 104 |
| Brewster, N.Y., U.S. | D7 | 109 |
| Brewster, Oh., U.S. | B4 | 112 |
| Brewster, Wa., U.S. | A6 | 124 |
| Brewster, co., Tx., U.S. | E1 | 120 |
| Brewster, Kap, c., Grnld. | B18 | 61 |

**Name — Map Ref. — Page**

Brewster Islands, is., Ma., U.S. ... g12 98
Brewton, Al., U.S. ... D2 78
Brewton, Al., U.S. ... D4 87
Brezhnev see Naberezhnyye Chelny, Sov. Un. ... D8 29
Brežice, Yugo. ... C2 24
Březnice, Czech. ... D8 19
Breznik, Bul. ... D6 24
Brezno, Czech. ... D5 26
Bria, Cen. Afr. Rep. ... D4 46
Brian Boru Peak, mtn., B.C. ... B4 69
Briançon, Fr. ... E7 16
Brian Head, mtn., Ut., U.S. ... F3 121
Briarcliff, Pa., U.S. ... p20 115
Briarcliff Manor, N.Y., U.S. ... *D7 109
Briare, Fr. ... D5 16
Briartown, Ok., U.S. ... B6 113
Brice, Oh., U.S. ... m11 112
Bricelyn, Mn., U.S. ... G5 100
Briceville, Tn., U.S. ... C9 119
Brickeys, Ar., U.S. ... C5 81
Brick [Township], N.J., U.S. ... C4 107
Bridal Veil, Or., U.S. ... B4 114
Bridal Veil Falls, wtfl., Ut., U.S. ... C4 121
Bride, stm., Ire. ... E3 11
Bridesville, B.C. ... E8 69
Bridge, stm., B.C. ... D6 69
Bridgeboro, Ga., U.S. ... E3 87
Bridge City, La., U.S. ... *E5 95
Bridge City, Tx., U.S. ... *D6 120
Bridge Creek, stm., Sask. ... H1 75
Bridgeford, Sask. ... G2 75
Bridgehampton, N.Y., U.S. ... n16 109
Bridge Lake, B.C. ... D7 69
Bridgeland, Ut., U.S. ... C5 121
Bridgend, Wales, U.K. ... C4 12
Bridgeport (part of Kitchener), Ont. ... D4 73
Bridgeport, Al., U.S. ... A4 78
Bridgeport, Ca., U.S. ... C4 82
Bridgeport, Ct., U.S. ... E3 84
Bridgeport, Il., U.S. ... E6 90
Bridgeport, Mi., U.S. ... E7 99
Bridgeport, Ne., U.S. ... C2 104
Bridgeport, N.J., U.S. ... D2 107
Bridgeport, Oh., U.S. ... B5 112
Bridgeport, Ok., U.S. ... B3 113
Bridgeport, Or., U.S. ... C9 114
Bridgeport, Pa., U.S. ... o20 115
Bridgeport, Tx., U.S. ... C4 120
Bridgeport, Wa., U.S. ... B6 124
Bridgeport, W.V., U.S. ... B4 125
Bridger, Mt., U.S. ... E8 103
Bridger, S.D., U.S. ... C4 118
Bridger Mountains, mts., Wy., U.S. ... C5 127
Bridger Peak, mtn., Wy., U.S. ... E5 127
Bridger Range, mts., Mt., U.S. ... E6 103
Bridgeton, In., U.S. ... E3 91
Bridgeton, Mo., U.S. ... C7 102
Bridgeton, N.J., U.S. ... E2 107
Bridgeton, N.C., U.S. ... B5 110
Bridgetown, Barb. ... J15 64
Bridgetown, N.S. ... E4 71
Bridgetown, Oh., U.S. ... *o12 112
Bridgeview, Il., U.S. ... *k9 90
Bridgeville, N.S. ... D7 71
Bridgeville, Pa., U.S. ... F3 85
Bridgeville, Pa., U.S. ... k13 115
Bridgewater, N.S. ... E5 71
Bridgewater, Ct., U.S. ... C2 84
Bridgewater, Ia., U.S. ... C3 92
Bridgewater, Me., U.S. ... B5 96
Bridgewater, Ma., U.S. ... C6 98
Bridgewater, N.H., U.S. ... C3 106
Bridgewater, N.J., U.S. ... B3 107
Bridgewater, S.D., U.S. ... D8 118
Bridgewater, Vt., U.S. ... D3 122
Bridgewater, Va., U.S. ... B4 123
Bridgewater Corners, Vt., U.S. ... D3 122
Bridgman, Mi., U.S. ... G4 99
Bridgnorth, Eng., U.K. ... B5 12
Bridgton, Me., U.S. ... D2 96
Bridgwater, Eng., U.K. ... E5 10
Bridgwater Bay, b., Eng., U.K. ... C4 12
Bridlington, Eng., U.K. ... C6 10
Bridport, Eng., U.K. ... D5 12
Bridport, Vt., U.S. ... D2 122
Brielle, N.J., U.S. ... C4 107
Brienz, Switz. ... E4 18
Brienz, Lake, l., Switz. ... C3 20
Brier Creek, stm., Ga., U.S. ... C5 87
Briercrest, Sask. ... G3 75
Briereville, Alta. ... B5 68
Brierfield, Al., U.S. ... B3 78
Brier Hill, N.Y., U.S. ... f9 109
Briery Knob, mtn., W.V., U.S. ... C4 125
Briey, Fr. ... E5 17
Brig, Switz. ... E3 18
Brigantine, N.J., U.S. ... E4 107
Brigantine Beach, N.J., U.S. ... E4 107
Brig Bay, Newf. ... C3 72
Brigden, Ont. ... E2 73
Brigg, Eng., U.K. ... A7 12
Briggs, In., U.S. ... *C10 104
Briggs, Tx., U.S. ... D4 120
Briggsdale, Co., U.S. ... A6 83
Briggs Marsh, sw., R.I., U.S. ... F6 116
Briggsville, Ar., U.S. ... C2 81
Briggsville, Ma., U.S. ... A1 98
Briggsville, Wi., U.S. ... E4 126
Brigham City, Ut., U.S. ... B3 121
Brig Harbour Island, i., Newf. ... A3 72
Bright, Ont. ... D4 73
Brighton, Ont. ... C7 73
Brighton, Eng., U.K. ... E6 10
Brighton, Al., U.S. ... B3 78
Brighton, Co., U.S. ... B6 83
Brighton, Il., U.S. ... D3 90
Brighton, Ia., U.S. ... C6 92
Brighton, Me., U.S. ... C3 96
Brighton, Mi., U.S. ... F7 99
Brighton, N.Y., U.S. ... B3 109
Brighton, Or., U.S. ... B3 114
Brighton, Tn., U.S. ... B2 119
Brighton, Wi., U.S. ... *C4 126
Brighton Indian Reservation, Fl., U.S. ... E5 86
Brightsand Lake, l., Sask. ... D1 75
Brightshade, Ky., U.S. ... C6 94
Brignoles, Fr. ... F7 16
Brihuega, Spain ... B4 22
Brilhante, stm., Braz. ... C1 56
Brilliant, B.C. ... E9 69
Brilliant, Al., U.S. ... A2 78
Brilliant, Oh., U.S. ... B5 112
Brillion, Wi., U.S. ... D5 126
Brilon, W. Ger. ... B3 19
Brimfield, Il., U.S. ... C4 90
Brimfield, Ma., U.S. ... *B3 98
Brimhall, N.M., U.S. ... B1 108
Brimley, Mi., U.S. ... B6 99
Brimson, Mn., U.S. ... C7 100
Brimson, Mo., U.S. ... A4 102

Brindisi, Italy ... D6 23
Bringhurst, In., U.S. ... C5 91
Brinje, Yugo. ... C2 24
Brinkhaven, Oh., U.S. ... B3 112
Brinkley, Ar., U.S. ... C4 81
Brinkman, Ok., U.S. ... B2 113
Brinktown, Mo., U.S. ... C5 102
Brinkworth, Austl. ... F2 51
Brinnon, Wa., U.S. ... B3 124
Brinsmade, N.D., U.S. ... A6 111
Brinson, Ga., U.S. ... F2 87
Brion, Île, i., Que. ... B8 71
Brione (Verzasca), Switz. ... D6 21
Brioude, Fr. ... E5 16
Brisbane, Austl. ... E9 50
Briscoe, Tx., U.S. ... B2 120
Briscoe, co., Tx., U.S. ... B2 120
Brissago, Switz. ... D6 21
Bristol, N.B. ... C2 71
Bristol, Eng., U.K. ... E5 10
Bristol, Co., U.S. ... C8 83
Bristol, Ct., U.S. ... C4 84
Bristol, Fl., U.S. ... B2 86
Bristol, Ga., U.S. ... E4 87
Bristol, Il., U.S. ... B5 90
Bristol, Me., U.S. ... *E3 96
Bristol, N.H., U.S. ... C3 106
Bristol, R.I., U.S. ... D5 116
Bristol, S.D., U.S. ... B8 118
Bristol, Tn., U.S. ... C11 119
Bristol, Vt., U.S. ... C2 122
Bristol, Va., U.S. ... f9 123
Bristol, W.V., U.S. ... k9 125
Bristol, Wi., U.S. ... F5 126
Bristol, co., Ma., U.S. ... C5 98
Bristol, co., R.I., U.S. ... D5 116
Bristol Bay, b., Ak., U.S. ... D7 79
Bristol Channel, strt., U.K. ... E4 10
Bristol Ferry, R.I., U.S. ... D5 116
Bristol [Township], Pa., U.S. ... F12 115
Bristolville, Oh., U.S. ... A5 112
Bristow, In., U.S. ... H4 91
Bristow, Ia., U.S. ... B5 92
Bristow, Ne., U.S. ... B7 104
Bristow, Ok., U.S. ... B5 113
Britannia Bay (part of Ottawa), Ont. ... h12 73
Britannia Beach, B.C. ... E6 69
Britannia Range, mts., Ant. ... B28 7
British Antarctic Territory, dep., S.A. ... *C7 7
British Columbia, prov., Can. ... C6 69
British Indian Ocean Territory, dep., Afr. ... *G25 7
British Mountains, mts., N.A. ... B12 79
British Virgin Islands, dep., N.A. ... G12 64
Britstown, S. Afr. ... D3 49
Britt, Ont. ... B4 73
Britt, Ia., U.S. ... A4 92
Brittany, hist. reg., Fr. ... C2 16
Britton, Mi., U.S. ... G7 99
Britton, S.D., U.S. ... B8 118
Brive [-la-Gaillarde], Fr. ... E4 16
Briviesca, Spain ... A4 22
Brixham, Eng., U.K. ... D4 12
Brno, Czech. ... D4 26
Broa, Ensenada de la, b., Cuba ... C3 64
Broad, stm., Ga., U.S. ... B4 87
Broad, stm., S.C., U.S. ... C5 117
Broadacres, Sask. ... E1 75
Broadalbin, N.Y., U.S. ... B6 109
Broadback, stm., Que. ... F17 66
Broad Bay, b., Scot., U.K. ... B2 13
Broadbent, Or., U.S. ... E2 114
Broaddus, Tx., U.S. ... D5 120
Broadford, Scot., U.K. ... C3 13
Broadford, Va., U.S. ... f10 123
Broad Haven, b., Ire. ... C2 11
Broadhurst, Ga., U.S. ... E5 87
Broadkill, stm., De., U.S. ... E4 85
Broadkill Beach, De., U.S. ... E5 85
Broadlands, Il., U.S. ... D6 90
Broadlands, S.D., U.S. ... C7 118
Broadmeadows, Austl. ... *G7 50
Broadmoor, Co., U.S. ... C6 83
Broad Run, stm., Va., U.S. ... g11 123
Broad Sound, strt., Austl. ... D8 50
Broad Top, Pa., U.S. ... F5 115
Broadus, Mt., U.S. ... E11 103
Broadview, Sask. ... G4 75
Broadview, Il., U.S. ... *k9 90
Broadview, Mt., U.S. ... D8 103
Broadview, N.M., U.S. ... C6 108
Broadview Heights, Oh., U.S. ... h9 112
Broadview Park, Fl., U.S. ... F6 86
Broadwater, Ne., U.S. ... C3 104
Broadwater, co., Mt., U.S. ... D5 103
Broadway, N.C., U.S. ... B3 110
Broadway, Oh., U.S. ... B2 112
Broadway, Va., U.S. ... B4 123
Brochet, Man. ... f7 70
Brock, Sask. ... F1 75
Brock, Ne., U.S. ... D10 104
Brocken, mtn., E. Ger. ... B5 19
Brocket, Alta. ... E4 68
Brocket, N.D., U.S. ... A7 111
Brock Island, i., N.W. Ter. ... m29 66
Brockport, N.Y., U.S. ... B3 109
Brockport, Pa., U.S. ... D4 115
Brockton, Ma., U.S. ... B5 98
Brockton, Mt., U.S. ... B12 103
Brockton Reservoir, res., Ma., U.S. ... h11 98
Brockville, Ont. ... C9 73
Brockway, Mt., U.S. ... C11 103
Brockway, Pa., U.S. ... D4 115
Brockwell, Ar., U.S. ... A4 81
Brocton, Il., U.S. ... D6 90
Brocton, N.Y., U.S. ... C1 109
Broderick, Sask. ... F2 75
Brodeur Peninsula, pen., N.W. Ter. ... B15 66
Brodhead, Ky., U.S. ... C5 94
Brodhead, Wi., U.S. ... F4 126
Brodheadsville, Pa., U.S. ... E11 115
Brodick, Scot., U.K. ... E3 13
Brodnax, Va., U.S. ... D4 123
Brodnica, Pol. ... B5 26
Brody, Sov. Un. ... F5 27
Brogan, Or., U.S. ... C9 114
Brokaw, Wi., U.S. ... C4 126
Broke Inlet, b., Austl. ... F3 50
Broken Arrow, Ok., U.S. ... A6 113
Broken Bow, Ne., U.S. ... C6 104
Broken Bow, Ok., U.S. ... C7 113
Broken Bow Lake, res., Ok., U.S. ... C7 113
Broken Hill, Austl. ... F7 50

Brokopondo, Sur. ... A3 59
Brokopondo, dept., Sur. ... B3 59
Brome, Que. ... D5 74
Brome, W. Ger. ... F4 15
Brome, co., Que. ... D5 74
Brome, Lac, l., Que. ... D5 74
Bromhead, Sask. ... H4 75
Bromide, Ok., U.S. ... C5 113
Bromley (part of London), Eng., U.K. ... m13 10
Bromley Mountain, mtn., Vt., U.S. ... E3 122
Bromptonville, Que. ... D6 74
Bromsgrove, Eng., U.K. ... B5 12
Bromyard, Eng., U.K. ... B5 12
Bronaugh, Mo., U.S. ... D3 102
Bronco, Tx., U.S. ... C1 120
Brong-Ahafo, prov., Ghana ... E4 45
Bronlund Peak, mtn., B.C. ... E7 66
Brönnitsy, Sov. Un. ... n18 27
Brönnöysund, Nor. ... E5 14
Bronson, Fl., U.S. ... C4 86
Bronson, Ia., U.S. ... B1 92
Bronson, Ks., U.S. ... E8 93
Bronson, Mi., U.S. ... G5 99
Bronson, Tx., U.S. ... D6 120
Bronte, Tx., U.S. ... D2 120
Bronwood, Ga., U.S. ... E2 87
Bronx, co., N.Y., U.S. ... E7 109
Bronxville, N.Y., U.S. ... h13 109
Brook, In., U.S. ... C3 91
Brookdale, Man. ... D2 70
Brooke, Va., U.S. ... B5 123
Brooke, co., W.V., U.S. ... A4 125
Brooker, Fl., U.S. ... C4 86
Brookeville, Md., U.S. ... B3 97
Brookfield, N.S. ... D6 71
Brookfield, Ct., U.S. ... D2 84
Brookfield, Ga., U.S. ... E3 87
Brookfield, Il., U.S. ... k9 90
Brookfield, In., U.S. ... m11 91
Brookfield, Ma., U.S. ... B3 98
Brookfield, Mo., U.S. ... B4 102
Brookfield, N.H., U.S. ... C4 106
Brookfield, N.Y., U.S. ... C5 109
Brookfield, Vt., U.S. ... C3 122
Brookfield, Wi., U.S. ... m11 126
Brookfield Center, Ct., U.S. ... D2 84
Brookford, N.C., U.S. ... B1 110
Brookhaven, Ms., U.S. ... D3 101
Brookhaven, Pa., U.S. ... *p20 115
Brookhaven, W.V., U.S. ... h11 125
Brooking, Sask. ... H3 75
Brookings, Or., U.S. ... E2 114
Brookings, S.D., U.S. ... C9 118
Brookings, co., S.D., U.S. ... C9 118
Brookland, Ar., U.S. ... B5 81
Brooklandville, Md., U.S. ... g10 97
Brooklawn, N.J., U.S. ... D2 107
Brooklet, Ga., U.S. ... D5 87
Brooklin, Me., U.S. ... D4 96
Brooklin, Ont. ... D6 73
Brookline, Ma., U.S. ... B5 98
Brookline, N.H., U.S. ... E3 106
Brooklyn, N.S. ... E5 71
Brooklyn, Al., U.S. ... D3 78
Brooklyn, Ct., U.S. ... B8 84
Brooklyn, Ga., U.S. ... D2 87
Brooklyn, Il., U.S. ... C3 90
Brooklyn, In., U.S. ... E5 91
Brooklyn, Ia., U.S. ... C5 92
Brooklyn, Mi., U.S. ... F6 99
Brooklyn, Ms., U.S. ... D4 101
Brooklyn, Oh., U.S. ... h9 112
Brooklyn, Pa., U.S. ... C10 115
Brooklyn, S.C., U.S. ... B6 117
Brooklyn, Tn., U.S. ... B2 119
Brooklyn, Wi., U.S. ... F4 126
Brooklyn Center, Mn., U.S. ... E5 100
Brooklyn Park, Md., U.S. ... h11 97
Brooklyn Park, Mn., U.S. ... m12 100
Brookmere, B.C. ... E7 69
Brookneal, Va., U.S. ... C4 123
Brook Park, Mn., U.S. ... E5 100
Brook Park, Oh., U.S. ... h9 112
Brookport, Il., U.S. ... F5 90
Brookridge, Co., U.S. ... *B6 83
Brooks, Alta. ... D5 68
Brooks, Ia., U.S. ... D3 92
Brooks, Ky., U.S. ... g11 94
Brooks, Mn., U.S. ... C2 100
Brooks, Or., U.S. ... h12 114
Brooks, Wi., U.S. ... E4 126
Brooks, co., Ga., U.S. ... F3 87
Brooks, co., Tx., U.S. ... F3 120
Brooks Air Force Base, mil., Tx., U.S. ... k7 120
Brooksburg, In., U.S. ... G7 91
Brooksby, Sask. ... E3 75
Brookshire, Tx., U.S. ... E5 120
Brookside, Al., U.S. ... f7 78
Brookside, Co., U.S. ... C5 83
Brookside, De., U.S. ... B3 85
Brookston, In., U.S. ... C4 91
Brookston, Mn., U.S. ... C6 100
Brooksville, Fl., U.S. ... D4 86
Brooksville, Ky., U.S. ... B5 94
Brooksville, Me., U.S. ... D4 96
Brooksville, Ms., U.S. ... B5 101
Brookton, Me., U.S. ... C5 96
Brooktondale, N.Y., U.S. ... C4 109
Brookvale, Co., U.S. ... *B5 83
Brookview, Md., U.S. ... C6 97
Brookville, In., U.S. ... A4 91
Brookville, Ks., U.S. ... D6 93
Brookville, N.Y., U.S. ... *E7 109
Brookville, Oh., U.S. ... C1 112
Brookville, Pa., U.S. ... D3 115
Brookville Lake, res., In., U.S. ... E7 91
Brookwood, Al., U.S. ... B2 78
Brookwood, N.J., U.S. ... C4 107
Broom, Loch, b., Scot., U.K. ... B4 10
Broomall, Pa., U.S. ... p20 115
Broome, Austl. ... C3 50
Broome, co., N.Y., U.S. ... C5 109
Broomes Island, Md., U.S. ... C5 97
Broomfield, Co., U.S. ... B5 83
Brooten, Mn., U.S. ... E3 100
Brora, Scot., U.K. ... B5 13
Brora, stm., Scot., U.K. ... B5 13
Brösarp, Swe. ... C8 15
Broseley, Mo., U.S. ... E7 102
Brosna, stm., Ire. ... D4 11
Brossard, Que. ... q20 74
Brotas de Macaúbas, Braz. ... D2 57
Brothers, Or., U.S. ... D6 114
Brotherton, Tn., U.S. ... C8 119
Brothertown, Wi., U.S. ... k9 126

Brotmanville, N.J., U.S. ... D2 107
Brou, Fr. ... C4 16
Brough, Eng., U.K. ... F6 13
Brough Head, c., Scot., U.K. ... A5 13
Broughton, Il., U.S. ... F5 90
Broughton, co., Que. ... D5 74
Broussard, La., U.S. ... D4 95
Brovst, Den. ... A3 15
Broward, co., Fl., U.S. ... F6 86
Browardale, Fl., U.S. ... r13 86
Browerville, Mn., U.S. ... D4 100
Brown, co., Il., U.S. ... D3 90
Brown, co., In., U.S. ... F5 91
Brown, co., Ks., U.S. ... C8 93
Brown, co., Mn., U.S. ... F4 100
Brown, co., Ne., U.S. ... B6 104
Brown, co., Oh., U.S. ... D2 112
Brown, co., S.D., U.S. ... B7 118
Brown, co., Tx., U.S. ... D3 120
Brown, co., Wi., U.S. ... D6 126
Brown, Point, c., Wa., U.S. ... C1 124
Brown City, Mi., U.S. ... E8 99
Brown Deer, Wi., U.S. ... m12 126
Brownell, Ks., U.S. ... D4 93
Brownfield, Me., U.S. ... E2 96
Brownfield, Tx., U.S. ... C1 120
Brownfields, La., U.S. ... *D4 95
Browning, Il., U.S. ... C3 90
Browning, Mo., U.S. ... A4 102
Browning, Mt., U.S. ... B3 103
Browning Entrance, strt., B.C. ... C2 69
Brownington, Mo., U.S. ... C4 102
Brownington Center, Vt., U.S. ... B4 122
Brownlee, Sask. ... G2 75
Brownlee, Ne., U.S. ... B5 104
Brownlee Dam, U.S. ... E2 89
Brownlee Reservoir, res., U.S. ... C10 114
Browns, Il., U.S. ... E6 90
Browns, stm., Vt., U.S. ... B2 122
Brownsboro, Ky., U.S. ... g11 94
Browns Branch, stm., De., U.S. ... E3 85
Brownsburg, Que. ... D3 74
Brownsburg, In., U.S. ... E5 91
Brownsburg, Va., U.S. ... C3 123
Brownsdale, Mn., U.S. ... G6 100
Browns Inlet, b., N.C., U.S. ... C5 110
Browns Mills, N.J., U.S. ... C3 107
Browns Peak, mtn., Az., U.S. ... D4 80
Browns Town, Jam. ... E14 65
Brownstown, Il., U.S. ... E5 90
Brownstown, In., U.S. ... G5 91
Brownstown, Pa., U.S. ... F9 115
Brownstown Head, c., Ire. ... E4 11
Browns Valley, Mn., U.S. ... E2 100
Brownsville, Or., U.S. ... C4 114
Brownsville, Ky., U.S. ... C3 94
Brownsville, La., U.S. ... B3 95
Brownsville, Or., U.S. ... C4 114
Brownsville, Pa., U.S. ... F2 115
Brownsville, Tn., U.S. ... B2 119
Brownsville, Tx., U.S. ... G4 120
Brownsville, Vt., U.S. ... E4 122
Brownton, Mn., U.S. ... F4 100
Brownton, W.V., U.S. ... B4 125
Brownvale, Alta. ... A2 68
Brownville, Me., U.S. ... C3 96
Brownville, Ne., U.S. ... D10 104
Brownville, N.Y., U.S. ... A5 109
Brownville Junction, Me., U.S. ... C3 96
Brown Willy, hill, Eng., U.K. ... D3 12
Brownwood, Tx., U.S. ... D3 120
Brownwood, Lake, res., Tx., U.S. ... D3 120
Broxton, Ga., U.S. ... E4 87
Broye, stm., Switz. ... C2 21
Broyhill Park, Va., U.S. ... *B5 123
Brozas, Spain ... B5 22
Bruay [-en-Artois], Fr. ... B5 16
Bruce, Alta. ... C4 68
Bruce, Fl., U.S. ... u16 86
Bruce, Ms., U.S. ... B4 101
Bruce, Wi., U.S. ... C2 126
Bruce, co., Ont. ... C3 73
Bruce, Mount, mtn., Austl. ... D2 50
Bruce Crossing, Mi., U.S. ... m12 99
Brucefield, Ont. ... D3 73
Bruce Lake, In., U.S. ... B5 91
Bruce National Park, Ont. ... B3 73
Bruce Peninsula, pen., Ont. ... B3 73
Bruceton, Tn., U.S. ... A3 119
Bruceton Mills, W.V., U.S. ... B5 125
Brucetown, Va., U.S. ... A4 123
Bruceville, In., U.S. ... G2 91
Bruck, Aus. ... B8 20
Brück, E. Ger. ... A7 19
Bruck [an der Leitha], Aus. ... H16 21
Bruck [an der Mur], Aus. ... H15 21
Brückenau, W. Ger. ... C4 19
Bruderheim, Alta. ... C4 68
Bruff, Ire. ... D3 11
Bruges see Brugge, Bel. ... B5 16
Brugg, Switz. ... B5 21
Brugge (Bruges), Bel. ... B5 16
Brühl, W. Ger. ... B3 19
Bruin Point, mtn., Ut., U.S. ... D5 121
Bruja, Cerro, mtn., Pan. ... k11 62
Brule, Ne., U.S. ... C4 104
Brule, Wi., U.S. ... B2 126
Brule, co., S.D., U.S. ... D6 118
Brûlé Lake, l., Alta. ... C2 68
Brule Lake, l., Mn., U.S. ... k9 100
Brumath, Fr. ... C7 16
Brumley Mountain, mtn., Va., U.S. ... f9 123
Brundidge, Al., U.S. ... D4 78
Bruneau, Id., U.S. ... G3 89
Bruneau, stm., U.S. ... G3 89
Brunei, ctry., Asia ... E5 34
Brunei Bay, b., Asia ... D5 34
Brunete, Spain ... p16 21
Brunette Island, i., Newf. ... E4 72
Bruni, Tx., U.S. ... F3 120
Brunico, Italy ... C6 20
Bruning, Ne., U.S. ... D8 104
Brunkild, Man. ... E3 70
Brunnen, Switz. ... C6 21
Brunner, Lake, l., N.Z. ... O13 51
Bruno, Sask. ... E3 75
Bruno, Mn., U.S. ... D6 100

Bruno, Ne., U.S. ... C9 104
Brunsbüttel, W. Ger. ... E3 15
Brunson, S.C., U.S. ... F5 117
Brunsville, Ia., U.S. ... B1 92
Brunswick, Ga., U.S. ... E5 87
Brunswick, In., U.S. ... D2 91
Brunswick, Me., U.S. ... E3 96
Brunswick, Md., U.S. ... B2 97
Brunswick, Mo., U.S. ... B4 102
Brunswick, Ne., U.S. ... B8 104
Brunswick, N.C., U.S. ... C4 110
Brunswick, Oh., U.S. ... A4 112
Brunswick, co., N.C., U.S. ... C4 110
Brunswick, co., Va., U.S. ... D5 123
Brunswick, Peninsula, pen., Chile ... h11 54
Brunswick see Braunschweig, W. Ger. ... B5 18
Brunswick Naval Air Station, mil., Me., U.S. ... E3 96
Bruree, Ire. ... E3 11
Brusett, Mt., U.S. ... C10 103
Brush, Co., U.S. ... A7 83
Brushy Mountain, mtn., Va., U.S. ... C1 123
Brushy Mountains, mts., N.C., U.S. ... B1 110
Brus Laguna, Hond. ... D8 63
Brusly, La., U.S. ... D4 95
Brusque, Braz. ... D3 56
Brussels (Bruxelles), Bel. ... B6 16
Brussels, Ont. ... D3 73
Brussels, Il., U.S. ... D3 90
Brussels, Wi., U.S. ... D6 126
Brusson, Italy ... E4 21
Bruton, Eng., U.K. ... C5 12
Bruton, Zaire ... A2 20
Bruyères, Fr. ... A2 20
Budrio, Italy ... B3 23
Bryan, Oh., U.S. ... A1 112
Bryan, Tx., U.S. ... D4 120
Bryan, co., Ga., U.S. ... D5 87
Bryan, co., Ok., U.S. ... D5 113
Bryanka, Sov. Un. ... q21 27
Bryans Road, Md., U.S. ... C3 97
Bryant, Ar., U.S. ... C3 81
Bryant, Fl., U.S. ... F6 86
Bryant, Il., U.S. ... C3 90
Bryant, In., U.S. ... C8 91
Bryant, S.D., U.S. ... C8 118
Bryant, Wi., U.S. ... C4 126
Bryant Creek, stm., Mo., U.S. ... E5 102
Bryant Mountain, mtn., Ma., U.S. ... B2 98
Bryantown, Md., U.S. ... C4 97
Bryantsville, Ky., U.S. ... C5 94
Bryantville, Ma., U.S. ... B6 98
Bryce Canyon, Ut., U.S. ... F3 121
Bryce Canyon National Park, Ut., U.S. ... F3 121
Bryceland, La., U.S. ... B3 95
Bryceville, Fl., U.S. ... B5 86
Brynica, stm., Pol. ... g9 26
Bryn Mawr, Pa., U.S. ... G7 100
Bryn Mawr, Wa., U.S. ... e11 124
Bryson, Tx., U.S. ... C3 120
Bryson City, N.C., U.S. ... f9 110
Brzeg, Pol. ... C4 26
Brzesko, Pol. ... D6 26
Brzeziny, Pol. ... C5 26
Brzozów, Pol. ... D7 26
B-Say-Tah, Sask. ... G4 75
Bua, Fiji ... H15 52
Bu'aale, Som. ... E5 47
Bua Bay, b., Fiji ... H15 52
Buariki, Kir. ... R18 52
Buba, Gui.-B. ... D2 45
Bübiyān, i., Kuw. ... C4 38
Bucaramanga, Col. ... B3 60
Buccaneer Archipelago, is., Austl. ... C3 50
Buchach, Sov. Un. ... G5 27
Buchanan, Sask. ... F4 75
Buchanan, Lib. ... E2 45
Buchanan, Ga., U.S. ... C1 87
Buchanan, Mi., U.S. ... G4 99
Buchanan, N.D., U.S. ... B7 111
Buchanan, Tn., U.S. ... A3 119
Buchanan, Va., U.S. ... C3 123
Buchanan, co., Ia., U.S. ... B6 92
Buchanan, co., Mo., U.S. ... B3 102
Buchanan, co., Va., U.S. ... e9 123
Buchanan, Lake, l., Austl. ... D8 50
Buchanan, Lake, l., Tx., U.S. ... D3 120
Buchan Ness, c., Scot., U.K. ... C7 13
Buchans, Newf. ... D3 72
Bucharest (Bucureşti), Rom. ... C8 24
Buchen, W. Ger. ... B4 19
Buchholz, W. Ger. ... A9 15
Buchloe, W. Ger. ... B5 20
Buchs, Switz. ... B5 21
Buchtel, Oh., U.S. ... C4 112? 
Buckatunna, Ms., U.S. ... D5 101
Buck Creek, stm., Ga., U.S. ... D2 87
Buck Creek, stm., Ky., U.S. ... C5 94
Bückeburg, W. Ger. ... A4 19
Buckeye, Az., U.S. ... D3 80
Buckeye, Co., U.S. ... A5 83
Buckeye, W.V., U.S. ... C4 125
Buckeye Hills, Az., U.S. ... m7 80
Buckeye Lake, Oh., U.S. ... C3 112
Buckeystown, Md., U.S. ... B3 97
Buckfield, Me., U.S. ... D2 96
Buckhannon, W.V., U.S. ... C4 125
Buckhaven, Scot., U.K. ... B5 10
Buckhead, Ga., U.S. ... C3 87
Buck Hill Falls, Pa., U.S. ... D11 115
Buckhorn, Ky., U.S. ... C6 94
Buckhorn, Mn., U.S. ... k9 100
Buckhorn Knob, mtn., W.V., U.S. ... ...
Buckhorn Lake, res., Ky., U.S. ... C6 94
Buckie, Scot., U.K. ... D10 13
Buckingham, Que. ... D2 74
Buckingham, Eng., U.K. ... C6 12
Buckingham, co., Va., U.S. ... C4 123
Buckinghamshire, co., Eng., U.K. ... C7 12
Buck Lake, l., Alta. ... C3 68
Buckland, Que. ... C7 74
Buckland, Ma., U.S. ... A2 98
Buckland, Oh., U.S. ... B1 112
Buckley, Il., U.S. ... C5 90
Buckley, Mi., U.S. ... D5 99
Buckley, Wa., U.S. ... B3 124
Bucklin, Ks., U.S. ... E4 93
Bucklin, Mo., U.S. ... B5 102
Buckman, Mn., U.S. ... E4 100

Buck Mountain, mtn., Va., U.S. ... D1 123
Buck Mountain, mtn., Wa., U.S. ... A6 124
Bucknell Manor, Va., U.S. ... *B5 123
Buckner, Ar., U.S. ... D2 81
Buckner, Il., U.S. ... F4 90
Buckner, Ky., U.S. ... g12 94
Buckner, Mo., U.S. ... h11 102
Bucks, Al., U.S. ... D1 78
Bucks, co., Pa., U.S. ... F11 115
Bucks Harbor, Me., U.S. ... D5 96
Buckskin, In., U.S. ... H3 91
Buckskin Mountains, mts., Az., U.S. ... C2 80
Bucksport, Me., U.S. ... D4 96
Bucksport, S.C., U.S. ... D9 117
Buckville, Ar., U.S. ... C2 81
Bucoda, Wa., U.S. ... C3 124
Buco Zau, Ang. ... B1 48
Bucyrus, Ks., U.S. ... D9 93
Bucyrus, N.D., U.S. ... C3 111
Bucyrus, Oh., U.S. ... B3 112
Bud, W.V., U.S. ... D3 125
Buda, Il., U.S. ... B4 90
Buda, Tx., U.S. ... D4 120
Budapest, Hung. ... B4 24
Budaun, India ... C7 37
Budd Coast, Ant. ... C24 7
Budd Lake, l., N.J., U.S. ... B3 107
Buddon Ness, c., Scot., U.K. ... D6 13
Buddonovsk, Sov. Un. ... G17 8
Bude, Eng., U.K. ... E4 10
Bude, Ms., U.S. ... D3 101
Bude Bay, b., Eng., U.K. ... D3 12
Budrio, Italy ... B3 23
Budyně [nad Ohří], Czech. ... n17 26
Buea, Cam. ... E1 46
Buechel, Ky., U.S. ... B4 94
Buellton, Ca., U.S. ... E3 82
Buena, N.J., U.S. ... D3 107
Buena, Wa., U.S. ... C5 124
Buena Park, Ca., U.S. ... n12 82
Buenaventura, Col. ... C2 60
Buenaventura, Mex. ... B3 63
Buena Vista, Bol. ... B4 56
Buena Vista, Al., U.S. ... D2 78
Buena Vista, Co., U.S. ... C4 83
Buena Vista, Ga., U.S. ... D2 87
Buena Vista, Ms., U.S. ... B5 101
Buena Vista, N.M., U.S. ... A4 108
Buena Vista, Oh., U.S. ... D2 112
Buena Vista, Va., U.S. ... C3 123
Buena Vista, co., Ia., U.S. ... B2 92
Buena Vista, Lago (Lago General Carrera), l., S.A. ... D2 54
Buenópolis, Braz. ... B4 56
Buenos Aires, Arg. ... C2 54
Buenos Aires, C.R. ... F6 62
Buenos Aires, Pan. ... k11 62
Buenos Aires, prov., Arg. ... B4 54
Buenos Aires, Lago (Lago General Carrera), l., S.A. ... D2 54
Bueyeros, N.M., U.S. ... B6 108
Buffalo, Alta. ... D5 68
Buffalo, Il., U.S. ... C4 90
Buffalo, Ia., U.S. ... C7 92
Buffalo, Ks., U.S. ... E8 93
Buffalo, Mn., U.S. ... E5 100
Buffalo, Mo., U.S. ... D4 102
Buffalo, N.Y., U.S. ... C2 109
Buffalo, N.D., U.S. ... C8 111
Buffalo, Oh., U.S. ... C4 117? 
Buffalo, Ok., U.S. ... A2 113
Buffalo, S.C., U.S. ... B4 117
Buffalo, S.D., U.S. ... B2 118
Buffalo, Tx., U.S. ... D5 120
Buffalo, W.V., U.S. ... C3 125
Buffalo, Wy., U.S. ... B6 127
Buffalo, co., Ne., U.S. ... D6 104
Buffalo, co., S.D., U.S. ... C6 118
Buffalo, co., Wi., U.S. ... D2 126
Buffalo, stm., Ar., U.S. ... B3 81
Buffalo, stm., Mn., U.S. ... D2 100
Buffalo, stm., Tn., U.S. ... B4 119
Buffalo, stm., Wi., U.S. ... D2 126
Buffalo Bill Reservoir, res., Wy., U.S. ... B3 127
Buffalo Center, Ia., U.S. ... A4 92
Buffalo Creek, stm., U.S. ... f8 125
Buffalo Creek, stm., W.V., U.S. ... h10 125
Buffalo Creek, stm., W.V., U.S. ... n12 125
Buffalo Gap, Sask. ... H3 75
Buffalo Gap, S.D., U.S. ... D2 118
Buffalo Grove, Il., U.S. ... h9 90
Buffalo Lake, Alta. ... C4 68
Buffalo Lake, l., Mn., U.S. ... F4 100
Buffalo Lake, l., N.W. Ter. ... D9 66
Buffalo Lake, res., Wi., U.S. ... E4 126
Buffalo Mills, Pa., U.S. ... G4 115
Buffalo Mountain, mtn., Va., U.S. ... D2 123
Buffalo Narrows, Sask. ... m7 75
Buffalo Pound Lake, l., Sask. ... G3 75
Buffalo Valley, Tn., U.S. ... C8 119
Buffer Lake, l., Sask. ... E2 75
Buffumville Lake, res., Ma., U.S. ... B4 98
Buford, Co., U.S. ... B3 83
Buford, Ga., U.S. ... B2 87
Buford, Oh., U.S. ... C2 112
Buford, Wy., U.S. ... E7 127
Bug, stm., Eur. ... B6 26
Buga, Col. ... C2 60
Buganga, Ug. ... B5 48
Bugene, Tan. ... B5 48
Bugojno, Yugo. ... E12 21
Bugsuk Island, i., Phil. ... D5 34
Bugt, China ... C9 28
Buguruslan, Sov. Un. ... C4 28
Buhl, Fr. ... *D7 16
Bühl, W. Ger. ... B4 19
Buhl, Al., U.S. ... B2 78
Buhl, Id., U.S. ... G4 89
Buhl, Mn., U.S. ... C6 100
Buhler, Ks., U.S. ... D6 93
Bühlertal, W. Ger. ... E3 19
Buhuşi, Rom. ... B8 24
Bui Dam, Ghana ... E4 45
Buies Creek, N.C., U.S. ... B4 110

| Name | Map Ref. | Page |
|---|---|---|
| Builth Wells, Wales, U.K. | B4 | 12 |
| Buitenpost, Neth. | A6 | 17 |
| Bujalance, Spain | D3 | 22 |
| Bujumbura, Bdi. | B4 | 48 |
| Bukavu, Zaire | B4 | 48 |
| Bukama, Zaire | C4 | 48 |
| Bukavu, Zaire | B4 | 48 |
| Bukene, Tan. | B5 | 48 |
| Bukhara, Sov. Un. | F9 | 29 |
| Bukittinggi, Indon. | F2 | 34 |
| Bukoba, Tan. | B5 | 48 |
| Bukovina, hist. reg., Eur. | B7 | 24 |
| Bukuru, Nig. | E6 | 45 |
| Bula, Indon. | F8 | 34 |
| Bula, Zaire | A4 | 48 |
| Bülach, Switz. | A6 | 21 |
| Buladean, N.C., U.S. | e10 | 110 |
| Buladeen, Tn., U.S. | C11 | 119 |
| Bulan, Ky., U.S. | C6 | 94 |
| Bulan, Phil. | n12 | 34 |
| Bulawayo, Zimb. | B4 | 49 |
| Buldir Island, i., Ak., U.S. | E3 | 79 |
| Bulgan, Mong. | B5 | 31 |
| Bulgaria, ctry., Eur. | D7 | 24 |
| Bulgroo, Austl. | B4 | 51 |
| Buliya, i., Fiji | I15 | 52 |
| Bulkley, stm., B.C. | B4 | 69 |
| Bulkley Ranges, mts., B.C. | B4 | 69 |
| Bull, stm., B.C. | E3 | 68 |
| Bullange see Büllingen, Bel. | D6 | 17 |
| Bullaque, stm., Spain | C3 | 22 |
| Bullard, Ga., U.S. | D3 | 87 |
| Bullas, Spain | C5 | 22 |
| Bullaxaar, Som. | C5 | 47 |
| Bullay, W. Ger. | C2 | 19 |
| Bull Creek, stm., Nv., U.S. | E6 | 105 |
| Bull Creek, stm., S.D., U.S. | B2 | 118 |
| Bulle, Switz. | C3 | 20 |
| Bullen Baai, b., Neth. Ant. | H18 | 65 |
| Bullfrog Creek, stm., Ut., U.S. | F5 | 121 |
| Bullhead, S.D., U.S. | B4 | 118 |
| Bullhead City, Az., U.S. | B1 | 80 |
| Büllingen (Bullange), Bel. | D6 | 17 |
| Bull Island, i., S.C., U.S. | G6 | 117 |
| Bull Island, i., S.C., U.S. | F8 | 117 |
| Bull Island, i., S.C., U.S. | D9 | 117 |
| Bullitt, co., Ky., U.S. | C4 | 94 |
| Bullittsville, Ky., U.S. | h13 | 94 |
| Bull Mountain, mtn., Mt., U.S. | D4 | 103 |
| Bulloch, co., Ga., U.S. | D5 | 87 |
| Bullock, N.C., U.S. | A4 | 110 |
| Bullock, co., Al., U.S. | C4 | 78 |
| Bullock Creek, Mi., U.S. | E6 | 99 |
| Bulloo, stm., Austl. | E7 | 50 |
| Bulloo Lake, l., Austl. | D4 | 51 |
| Bull Run, stm., Va., U.S. | g11 | 123 |
| Bull Run, stm., Va., U.S., | | |
| Bullrun Ridge, mtn., Tn., U.S. | m13 | 119 |
| Bullrun Rock, mtn., Or., U.S. | C8 | 114 |
| Bulls Bay, b., S.C., U.S. | F8 | 117 |
| Bulls Bridge, Ct., U.S. | C1 | 84 |
| Bulls Gap, Tn., U.S. | C10 | 119 |
| Bull Shoals, Ar., U.S. | A3 | 81 |
| Bull Shoals Lake, res., U.S. | A3 | 81 |
| Bull Sluice Lake, res., Ga., U.S. | h8 | 87 |
| Bully Creek Reservoir, res., Or., U.S. | C9 | 114 |
| Bulnes, Chile | B2 | 54 |
| Bulolo, Pap. N. Gui. | k12 | 50 |
| Bulsār, India | G4 | 37 |
| Bultfontein, S. Afr. | C4 | 49 |
| Bulun, Sov. Un. | B15 | 29 |
| Bulungu, Zaire | B2 | 48 |
| Bulwark, Alta. | C5 | 68 |
| Bulyea, Sask. | G3 | 75 |
| Bumba, Zaire | A3 | 48 |
| Bumping, stm., Wa., U.S. | C4 | 124 |
| Bumpus Mills, Tn., U.S. | A4 | 119 |
| Buna, Tx., U.S. | D6 | 120 |
| Bunbury, Austl. | F2 | 50 |
| Bunceton, Mo., U.S. | C5 | 102 |
| Bunch, Ok., U.S. | B7 | 113 |
| Bunche Park, Fl., U.S. | *s13 | 86 |
| Buncombe, Il., U.S. | F5 | 90 |
| Buncombe, co., N.C., U.S. | f10 | 110 |
| Buncrana, Ire. | B4 | 11 |
| Bundaberg, Austl. | D9 | 50 |
| Bünde, W. Ger. | A3 | 19 |
| Bündi, India | E5 | 37 |
| Bundick Creek, stm., La., U.S. | D2 | 95 |
| Bundoran, Ire. | C3 | 11 |
| Bunessan, Scot., U.K. | D2 | 13 |
| Bungay, Eng., U.K. | B9 | 12 |
| Bunger Hills, hills, Ant. | C23 | 7 |
| Bungo Strait, strt., Japan | J6 | 33 |
| Bunia, Zaire | A5 | 48 |
| Bunker, Mo., U.S. | D6 | 102 |
| Bunker Hill, Il., U.S. | D4 | 90 |
| Bunker Hill, In., U.S. | C5 | 91 |
| Bunker Hill, Ks., U.S. | D5 | 93 |
| Bunker Hill, Or., U.S. | *D2 | 114 |
| Bunker Hill, Tn., U.S. | B5 | 119 |
| Bunker Hill, W.V., U.S. | B6 | 125 |
| Bunker Hill, W.V., U.S. | m12 | 125 |
| Bunker Hill, mtn., Nv., U.S. | D4 | 105 |
| Bunkerville, Nv., U.S. | G7 | 105 |
| Bunkeya, Zaire | D5 | 48 |
| Bunkie, La., U.S. | D3 | 95 |
| Bunn, N.C., U.S. | B4 | 110 |
| Bunnahowen, Ire. | C2 | 11 |
| Bunnell, Fl., U.S. | C5 | 86 |
| Bunnlevel, N.C., U.S. | B4 | 110 |
| Buolkalakh, Sov. Un. | B2 | 128 |
| Buon Me Thuot, Viet. | C3 | 34 |
| Buor-Khaya Bay, b., Sov. Un. | B1 | 128 |
| Bura, Kenya | B7 | 48 |
| Buram, Sud. | E6 | 48 |
| Buras, La., U.S. | E6 | 95 |
| Buraydah, Sau. Ar. | C4 | 38 |
| Burayk, Libya | D2 | 43 |
| Burbank, Ca., U.S. | E4 | 82 |
| Burbank, Il., U.S. | k9 | 90 |
| Burbank, Ok., U.S. | A5 | 113 |
| Burbank, S.D., U.S. | E9 | 118 |
| Burchard, Ne., U.S. | D9 | 104 |
| Burco, Som. | D6 | 47 |
| Burdekin, stm., Austl. | C8 | 50 |
| Burden, Ks., U.S. | E7 | 93 |
| Burdett, Alta. | E5 | 68 |
| Burdett, Ks., U.S. | D4 | 93 |
| Burdett, N.Y., U.S. | C4 | 109 |
| Burdette, Ar., U.S. | B6 | 81 |
| Burdick, Ks., U.S. | D7 | 93 |
| Burdickville, R.I., U.S. | F2 | 116 |
| Burdur, Tur. | D8 | 40 |
| Bureau, Il., U.S. | B4 | 90 |
| Bureau, co., Il., U.S. | B4 | 90 |
| Burein Mountains, mts., Sov. Un. | B6 | 33 |
| Büren, Sov. Un. | B6 | 33 |
| Büren [an der Aare], Switz. | B3 | 21 |
| Bureya, Sov. Un. | B10 | 31 |
| Bureya, Sov. Un. | A5 | 33 |
| Burford, Ont. | D4 | 73 |
| Bür Fu'ād, Eg. | C4 | 41 |
| Burg, E. Ger. | A6 | 19 |
| Burg, W. Ger. | D5 | 15 |
| Burgas, Bul. | D8 | 24 |
| Burgas, Gulf of, b., Bul. | D8 | 24 |
| Burgaw, N.C., U.S. | C5 | 110 |
| Burgdorf, W. Ger. | F3 | 15 |
| Burgdorf, Switz. | E3 | 18 |
| Burgeo, Newf. | E3 | 72 |
| Burgersdorp, S. Afr. | D4 | 49 |
| Burgess, S.C., U.S. | D9 | 117 |
| Burgess, co., U.K. | D7 | 12 |
| Burgettstown, Pa., U.S. | F1 | 115 |
| Burghausen, W. Ger. | A8 | 20 |
| Burghead, Scot., U.K. | C5 | 13 |
| Burgin, Ky., U.S. | C5 | 94 |
| Burglengenfeld, W. Ger. | D7 | 19 |
| Burgoon, Oh., U.S. | A2 | 112 |
| Burgos, Phil. | n12 | 34 |
| Burgos, Spain | A4 | 22 |
| Burgstädt, E. Ger. | C7 | 19 |
| Burgsteinfurt, W. Ger. | A2 | 19 |
| Burgsvik, Swe. | I8 | 14 |
| Burgundy, hist. reg., Fr. | D6 | 16 |
| Burhānpur, India | D6 | 36 |
| Burhi Gandak, stm., India | E10 | 37 |
| Buri, Braz. | m7 | 56 |
| Burica, Punta, c., N.A. | F6 | 62 |
| Burin, Newf. | E4 | 72 |
| Burin, Isr. Occ. | g12 | 41 |
| Burin Peninsula, pen., Newf. | E4 | 72 |
| Buritama, Braz. | C2 | 56 |
| Buri Ram, Thai. | C2 | 34 |
| Bûr Safâjah, Eg. | C3 | 38 |
| Bursey, Mount, mtn., Ant. | B35 | 7 |
| Burj al 'Arab, Eg. | G7 | 40 |
| Burkburnett, Tx., U.S. | B3 | 120 |
| Burke, Id., U.S. | B3 | 89 |
| Burke, N.Y., U.S. | f10 | 109 |
| Burke, S.D., U.S. | D6 | 118 |
| Burke, Vt., U.S. | B5 | 122 |
| Burke, Va., U.S. | *B5 | 123 |
| Burke, co., Ga., U.S. | C4 | 87 |
| Burke, co., N.C., U.S. | B1 | 110 |
| Burke, co., N.D., U.S. | A3 | 111 |
| Burke Channel, strt., B.C. | C4 | 69 |
| Burke City, Mo., U.S. | f13 | 102 |
| Burkehaven, N.H., U.S. | D2 | 106 |
| Burke Island, i., Ant. | B2 | 7 |
| Burkes Garden, Va., U.S. | C1 | 123 |
| Burkesville, Ky., U.S. | D4 | 94 |
| Burketon Station (part of Newcastle), Ont. | C6 | 73 |
| Burketown, Austl. | C6 | 50 |
| Burkett, Tx., U.S. | C3 | 120 |
| Burkettsville, Oh., U.S. | B1 | 112 |
| Burkeville, Tx., U.S. | D6 | 120 |
| Burkeville, Va., U.S. | C4 | 123 |
| Burkina Faso, ctry., Afr. | D4 | 45 |
| Burk's Falls, Ont. | B5 | 73 |
| Burkville, Al., U.S. | C3 | 78 |
| Burleigh, N.J., U.S. | E3 | 107 |
| Burleigh, co., N.D., U.S. | C5 | 111 |
| Burleson, Tx., U.S. | n9 | 120 |
| Burleson, co., Tx., U.S. | D4 | 120 |
| Burley, Id., U.S. | G5 | 89 |
| Burley, Wa., U.S. | f10 | 124 |
| Burlingame, Ca., U.S. | h8 | 82 |
| Burlingame, Ks., U.S. | D7 | 93 |
| Burlington, Newf. | D3 | 72 |
| Burlington, Ont. | D5 | 73 |
| Burlington, Co., U.S. | B8 | 83 |
| Burlington, Ct., U.S. | B4 | 84 |
| Burlington, Il., U.S. | A5 | 90 |
| Burlington, In., U.S. | C5 | 91 |
| Burlington, Ia., U.S. | D6 | 92 |
| Burlington, Ks., U.S. | D8 | 93 |
| Burlington, Ky., U.S. | A5 | 94 |
| Burlington, Me., U.S. | C4 | 96 |
| Burlington, Ma., U.S. | f11 | 98 |
| Burlington, N.C., U.S. | A3 | 110 |
| Burlington, N.D., U.S. | A4 | 111 |
| Burlington, N.J., U.S. | C3 | 107 |
| Burlington, Pa., U.S. | C8 | 115 |
| Burlington, Vt., U.S. | C2 | 122 |
| Burlington, Wi., U.S. | F5 | 126 |
| Burlington, Wy., U.S. | B4 | 127 |
| Burlington, co., N.J., U.S. | D3 | 107 |
| Burlington Beach, In., U.S. | B3 | 91 |
| Burlington Junction, Mo., U.S. | A2 | 102 |
| Burlyu-Tobe, Sov. Un. | D9 | 28 |
| Burma (Myanmar), ctry., Asia | D10 | 36 |
| Burnaby, B.C. | E6 | 69 |
| Burnaby Island, i., B.C. | C2 | 69 |
| Burnet, Tx., U.S. | D3 | 120 |
| Burnet, co., Tx., U.S. | D3 | 120 |
| Burnett, In., U.S. | E3 | 91 |
| Burnett, co., Wi., U.S. | C1 | 126 |
| Burnett, stm., Austl. | B8 | 51 |
| Burnettown, S.C., U.S. | D4 | 117 |
| Burnettsville, In., U.S. | C4 | 91 |
| Burney, Ca., U.S. | B3 | 82 |
| Burneyville, Ok., U.S. | D4 | 113 |
| Burnham, Me., U.S. | D3 | 96 |
| Burnham, Pa., U.S. | E6 | 115 |
| Burnham-on-Sea / Highbridge, Eng., U.K. | C5 | 12 |
| Burnie, Austl. | o15 | 50 |
| Burning Springs, Ky., U.S. | C6 | 94 |
| Burning Springs, W.V., U.S. | C3 | 125 |
| Burnley, Eng., U.K. | D5 | 10 |
| Burns, Co., U.S. | B4 | 83 |
| Burns, Ks., U.S. | D7 | 93 |
| Burns, Or., U.S. | D7 | 114 |
| Burns, Tn., U.S. | A4 | 119 |
| Burns, Wy., U.S. | E8 | 127 |
| Burns City, In., U.S. | G4 | 91 |
| Burns Flat, Ok., U.S. | B2 | 113 |
| Burnside, Ky., U.S. | D5 | 94 |
| Burnside, Pa., U.S. | E4 | 115 |
| Burns Paiute Indian Reservation, Or., U.S. | D7 | 114 |
| Burnstad, N.D. | C6 | 111 |
| Burnsville, Al., U.S. | C3 | 78 |
| Burnsville, Mn., U.S. | F5 | 100 |
| Burnsville, Ms., U.S. | A5 | 101 |
| Burnsville, N.C., U.S. | f10 | 110 |
| Burnsville, W.V., U.S. | C4 | 125 |
| Burnsville Lake, res., W.V., U.S. | C4 | 125 |
| Burnt, stm., Or., U.S. | C9 | 114 |
| Burnt Cabins, Pa., U.S. | F6 | 115 |
| Burnt Corn, Al., U.S. | D2 | 78 |
| Burnt Hills, N.Y., U.S. | C7 | 109 |
| Burntisland, Scot., U.K. | D5 | 13 |
| Burnt Islands, Newf. | E2 | 72 |
| Burnt Mills, Lake, l., Va., U.S. | k14 | 123 |
| Burnt Prairie, Il., U.S. | E5 | 90 |
| Burnt River, Ont. | C6 | 73 |
| Burntside Lake, l., Mn., U.S. | C6 | 100 |
| Burntwood, stm., Man. | B2 | 70 |
| Burntwood Lake, l., Man. | B1 | 70 |
| Burnwell, Al., U.S. | f6 | 78 |
| Burnwell, W.V., U.S. | m13 | 125 |
| Burqā, Isr. Occ. | b7 | 41 |
| Burr, Mn., U.S. | F2 | 100 |
| Burr, Ne., U.S. | D9 | 104 |
| Burra, Austl. | F2 | 51 |
| Burragorang, Lake, l., Austl. | G8 | 51 |
| Burray, i., Scot., U.K. | B6 | 13 |
| Burrendong Reservoir, res., Austl. | F7 | 51 |
| Burr Ferry, La., U.S. | C2 | 95 |
| Burr Hill, Va., U.S. | B5 | 123 |
| Burriana, Spain | C5 | 22 |
| Burr Oak, Ia., U.S. | A6 | 92 |
| Burr Oak, Ks., U.S. | C5 | 93 |
| Burr Oak, Mi., U.S. | G5 | 99 |
| Burr Oak Reservoir, res., Oh., U.S. | C3 | 112 |
| Burroughs, Ga., U.S. | E5 | 87 |
| Burrow Head, c., Scot., U.K. | F4 | 13 |
| Burrows, In., U.S. | C5 | 91 |
| Burr Ridge, Il., U.S. | *B6 | 89 |
| Burrton, Ks., U.S. | D6 | 93 |
| Burruyacú, Arg. | E3 | 55 |
| Burrville, Tn., U.S. | C9 | 119 |
| Burrwood, La., U.S. | F6 | 95 |
| Burry Port, Wales, U.K. | C3 | 12 |
| Bursa, Tur. | B7 | 40 |
| Bûr Safâjah, Eg. | C3 | 38 |
| Burstall, Sask. | G1 | 75 |
| Burt, Ia., U.S. | A3 | 92 |
| Burt, N.D., U.S. | C3 | 111 |
| Burt, co., Ne., U.S. | C9 | 104 |
| Burta, Austl. | F3 | 51 |
| Burt Lake, l., Mi., U.S. | C6 | 99 |
| Burton, B.C. | D9 | 69 |
| Burton, Il., U.S. | D2 | 90 |
| Burton, Mi., U.S. | E7 | 99 |
| Burton, Ne., U.S. | B6 | 104 |
| Burton, Oh., U.S. | A4 | 112 |
| Burton, Tx., U.S. | D4 | 120 |
| Burton, Wa., U.S. | f11 | 124 |
| Burton, W.V., U.S. | B4 | 125 |
| Burton, Lake, res., Ga., U.S. | B3 | 87 |
| Burtonport, Ire. | C3 | 11 |
| Burton upon Trent, Eng., U.K. | D6 | 10 |
| Burträsk, Swe. | E9 | 14 |
| Burtrum, Mn., U.S. | E4 | 100 |
| Burṭus, Eg. | C3 | 41 |
| Burtts Corner, N.B. | C3 | 71 |
| Buru, i., Indon. | F7 | 34 |
| Burūk, Wādī al, val., Eg. | D5 | 41 |
| Burullus, Lake, l., Eg. | C2 | 41 |
| Burūn, Ra's, c., Eg. | C5 | 41 |
| Bururi, Bdi. | B5 | 48 |
| Burwash, Ont. | A4 | 73 |
| Burwell, Ne., U.S. | C6 | 104 |
| Burwell, Que. | D6 | 74 |
| Bury, Eng., U.K. | A5 | 12 |
| Bury, Que. | D6 | 74 |
| Burynshik, Sov. Un. | D4 | 28 |
| Bury Saint Edmunds, Eng., U.K. | D7 | 10 |
| Busby, Alta. | C4 | 68 |
| Busby, Mt., U.S. | E10 | 103 |
| Büschfeld, W. Ger. | D1 | 19 |
| Bush, Ky., U.S. | C6 | 94 |
| Bush, La., U.S. | D6 | 95 |
| Bush City, Ks., U.S. | D8 | 93 |
| Bushenyi, Ug. | B5 | 48 |
| Bushimaie, stm., Zaire | C3 | 48 |
| Bushiribana, Aruba | G17 | 65 |
| Bushkill, Pa., U.S. | D11 | 115 |
| Bushland, Tx., U.S. | B1 | 120 |
| Bushmills, N. Ire., U.K. | B6 | 11 |
| Bushnell, Fl., U.S. | D4 | 86 |
| Bushnell, Il., U.S. | C3 | 90 |
| Bushnell, Ne., U.S. | C2 | 104 |
| Bushnell, S.D., U.S. | C9 | 118 |
| Bushong, Ks., U.S. | D7 | 93 |
| Bush River, b., Md., U.S. | B5 | 97 |
| Bushton, Ks., U.S. | D5 | 93 |
| Bushong, Mo. | A3 | 48 |
| Busk, Sov. Un. | G5 | 27 |
| Busko [Zdrój], Pol. | C6 | 26 |
| Bussang, Fr. | D8 | 16 |
| Busselton, Austl. | F2 | 50 |
| Busseto, Italy | E6 | 20 |
| Bussey, Ia., U.S. | C5 | 92 |
| Busto Arsizio, Italy | B2 | 23 |
| Busu-Djanoa, Zaire | A3 | 48 |
| Büsum, W. Ger. | D2 | 15 |
| Buta, Zaire | A3 | 48 |
| Buta Ranquil, Arg. | B3 | 54 |
| Butare, Rw. | B4 | 48 |
| Butedale, B.C. | C3 | 69 |
| Bute Inlet, b., B.C. | D5 | 69 |
| Butere, Kenya | A5 | 48 |
| Butha Qi, China | B9 | 31 |
| Butler, stm., Italy | D3 | 20 |
| Butler, Al., U.S. | C1 | 78 |
| Butler, Ga., U.S. | D2 | 87 |
| Butler, Il., U.S. | D4 | 90 |
| Butler, In., U.S. | B8 | 91 |
| Butler, Ky., U.S. | B5 | 94 |
| Butler, Mo., U.S. | C3 | 102 |
| Butler, N.J., U.S. | B4 | 107 |
| Butler, Oh., U.S. | B3 | 112 |
| Butler, Pa., U.S. | E2 | 115 |
| Butler, S.D., U.S. | C8 | 118 |
| Butler, Tn., U.S. | C11 | 119 |
| Butler, Wi., U.S. | m11 | 126 |
| Butler, co., Al., U.S. | D3 | 78 |
| Butler, co., Ia., U.S. | B5 | 92 |
| Butler, co., Ks., U.S. | E7 | 93 |
| Butler, co., Ky., U.S. | C3 | 94 |
| Butler, co., Mo., U.S. | E7 | 102 |
| Butler, co., Ne., U.S. | C8 | 104 |
| Butler, co., Oh., U.S. | C1 | 112 |
| Butler, co., Pa., U.S. | E2 | 115 |
| Butlers Bridge, Ire. | C4 | 11 |
| Butlerville, In., U.S. | F6 | 91 |
| Butmīyah, Isr. Occ. | B7 | 41 |
| Butner, N.C., U.S. | A4 | 110 |
| Butovo, Sov. Un. | n17 | 27 |
| Buttahatchee, stm., U.S. | B5 | 101 |
| Butte, Mt., U.S. | E4 | 103 |
| Butte, Ne., U.S. | B6 | 104 |
| Butte, N.D., U.S. | B5 | 111 |
| Butte, co., Ca., U.S. | C3 | 82 |
| Butte, co., Id., U.S. | F5 | 89 |
| Butte, co., S.D., U.S. | *C2 | 118 |
| Butte des Morts, Lake, l., Wi., U.S. | D5 | 126 |
| Butte Falls, Or., U.S. | E4 | 114 |
| Butte Mountains, mts., Nv., U.S. | D6 | 105 |
| Butterfield, Mn., U.S. | G4 | 100 |
| Butterfield, Mo., U.S. | E4 | 102 |
| Butternut, Wi., U.S. | B3 | 126 |
| Butternut Lake, l., Wi., U.S. | C5 | 126 |
| Butters, N.C., U.S. | C4 | 110 |
| Butterworth, Malay. | D2 | 34 |
| Butterworth, Transkei | D4 | 49 |
| Buttevant, Ire. | E3 | 11 |
| Button Islands, is., N.W. Ter. | f8 | 72 |
| Button Islands, is., N.W. Ter. | f8 | 72 |
| Buttonwillow, Ca., U.S. | E4 | 82 |
| Butuan, Phil. | D7 | 34 |
| Butung, i., Indon. | F7 | 34 |
| Buturlinovka, Sov. Un. | F13 | 27 |
| Butzbach, W. Ger. | C3 | 19 |
| Bützow, E. Ger. | B5 | 18 |
| Buuhoodle, Som. | D6 | 47 |
| Buulo Berde, Som. | E6 | 47 |
| Buur Gaabo, Som. | F5 | 47 |
| Buur Hakaba, Som. | E5 | 47 |
| Buxtehude, W. Ger. | B4 | 18 |
| Buxton, Guy. | A3 | 59 |
| Buxton, Eng., U.K. | A6 | 12 |
| Buxton, N.C., U.S. | B7 | 110 |
| Buxton, N.D., U.S. | B8 | 111 |
| Buxton, Or., U.S. | g11 | 114 |
| Buxton, Mount, mtn., B.C. | D3 | 69 |
| Buxton Center, Me., U.S. | *E2 | 96 |
| Buy, Sov. Un. | B2 | 28 |
| Buyck, Sov. Un. | B6 | 100 |
| Buynaksk, Sov. Un. | E3 | 28 |
| Büyükliman see Vakfıkebir, Tur. | B12 | 40 |
| Büyükmenderes, stm., Tur. | D7 | 40 |
| Buzachi Peninsula, pen., Sov. Un. | E4 | 28 |
| Buzancy, Fr. | C6 | 16 |
| Buzău, Rom. | C8 | 24 |
| Buzău, stm., Rom. | C8 | 24 |
| Buzaymah, Libya | E4 | 43 |
| Buzet, Yugo. | D7 | 23 |
| Buzuluk, Sov. Un. | C4 | 28 |
| Buzzard Roost, mtn., N.C., | B1 | 110 |
| Buzzards Bay, Ma., U.S. | C6 | 98 |
| Buzzards Bay, b., Ma., U.S. | C6 | 98 |
| Byala, Bul. | D7 | 24 |
| Byala Slatina, Bul. | D6 | 24 |
| Byam Martin Island, i., N.W. Ter. | m31 | 66 |
| Byars, Ok., U.S. | C4 | 113 |
| Bybee, Tn., U.S. | C10 | 119 |
| Bydgoszcz, Pol. | B5 | 26 |
| Byelorussia (White Russie), state, Sov. Un. | D5 | 29 |
| Byemoor, Alta. | D4 | 68 |
| Byer, Oh., U.S. | C3 | 112 |
| Byers, Co., U.S. | B6 | 83 |
| Byers, Ks., U.S. | E5 | 93 |
| Byers, Tx., U.S. | C4 | 120 |
| Byesville, Oh., U.S. | C4 | 112 |
| Byfield, Ma., U.S. | A6 | 98 |
| Byhalia, Ms., U.S. | A4 | 101 |
| Bykovo, Sov. Un. | n18 | 27 |
| Bykovo, Sov. Un. | G15 | 27 |
| Bylas, Az., U.S. | D5 | 80 |
| Bylot Island, i., N.W. Ter. | B17 | 66 |
| Byng, Ok., U.S. | C5 | 113 |
| Byng Inlet, Ont. | B4 | 73 |
| Bynum, Mt., U.S. | C4 | 103 |
| Bynum, N.C., U.S. | B3 | 110 |
| Bynumville, Mo., U.S. | B5 | 102 |
| Byram, Ms., U.S. | C3 | 101 |
| Byrd, sci., Ant. | A36 | 7 |
| Byrd Glacier, ice, Ant. | g40 | 7 |
| Byrdstown, Tn., U.S. | C8 | 119 |
| Byrnedale, Pa., U.S. | D5 | 115 |
| Byrock, Austl. | E6 | 51 |
| Byromville, Ga., U.S. | D3 | 87 |
| Byron, Ca., U.S. | h9 | 82 |
| Byron, Il., U.S. | A4 | 90 |
| Byron, Me., U.S. | D2 | 96 |
| Byron, Mn., U.S. | F6 | 100 |
| Byron, Ne., U.S. | D8 | 104 |
| Byron, N.Y., U.S. | B2 | 109 |
| Byron, Ga., U.S. | D3 | 87 |
| Byron, Cape, c., Austl. | E9 | 51 |
| Byron, Den. | A5 | 15 |
| Byron, Wy., U.S. | B4 | 127 |
| Byšice-Liblice, Czech. | n18 | 26 |
| Bystrzyca [Kłodzka], Pol. | C4 | 26 |
| Bytom (Beuthen), Pol. | C5 | 26 |
| Bytów, Pol. | A5 | 26 |
| Byzantium see İstanbul, Tur. | B7 | 40 |

**C**

| Ca, stm., Asia | C6 | 35 |
| Caacupé, Para. | E4 | 55 |
| Caaguazú, dept., Para. | E4 | 55 |
| Čačk, Yugo. | D5 | 24 |
| Caála, Ang. | D2 | 48 |
| Caamaño Sound, strt., B.C. | C3 | 69 |
| Caapucú, Para. | E4 | 55 |
| Caazapá, Para. | E4 | 55 |
| Caazapá, dept., Para. | E4 | 55 |
| Cabaceiras, Braz. | h5 | 57 |
| Cabalete, i., Phil. | o13 | 34 |
| Caballo, N.M., U.S. | E2 | 108 |
| Caballo Mountains, mts., N M., U.S. | E2 | 108 |
| Caballo Reservoir, res., N.M., U.S. | E2 | 108 |
| Cabana, Peru | C11 | 119 |
| Cabanatuan, Phil. | m11 | 126 |
| Cabano, Que. | B9 | 74 |
| Cabarita, stm., Jam. | E12 | 65 |
| Cabarrus, co., N.C., U.S. | B2 | 110 |
| Cabarruyan Island, i., Phil. | n12 | 34 |
| Cabbage Swamp, sw., Fl., U.S. | m9 | 86 |
| Cabedelo, Braz. | C4 | 57 |
| Cabell, co., W.V., U.S. | C2 | 125 |
| Cabery, Il., U.S. | C5 | 90 |
| Cabeza del Buey, Spain | C3 | 22 |
| Cabezas, Bol. | C3 | 55 |
| Cabimas, Ven. | A3 | 60 |
| Cabin Creek, W.V., U.S. | m13 | 125 |
| Cabin Creek, W.V., U.S. | m13 | 125 |
| Cabinda, Ang. | C1 | 48 |
| Cabinda, dept., Ang. | C1 | 48 |
| Cabinet Gorge Reservoir, res., U.S. | B1 | 103 |
| Cabinet Mountains, mts., Mt., U.S. | B1 | 103 |
| Cabin John, Md., U.S. | C3 | 97 |
| Cable, Wi., U.S. | B2 | 126 |
| Cabo, Braz. | k6 | 57 |
| Cabo Blanco, Arg. | D3 | 54 |
| Cabo Delgado, dept., Moz. | D6 | 48 |
| Cabo Frio, Braz. | C4 | 56 |
| Cabo Gracias a Dios, Nic. | D8 | 63 |
| Cabonga, Réservoir, res., Que. | k11 | 74 |
| Cabool, Mo., U.S. | D5 | 102 |
| Caboolture, Austl. | C9 | 51 |
| Cabora Bassa Lake, res., Moz. | A5 | 49 |
| Cabo Raso, Arg. | C3 | 54 |
| Cabo Rojo, P.R. | B1 | 65 |
| Cabot, Ar., U.S. | C3 | 81 |
| Cabot, Pa., U.S. | E2 | 115 |
| Cabot, Vt., U.S. | C4 | 122 |
| Cabot, Mount, mtn., N.H., U.S. | A4 | 106 |
| Cabot Head, c., Ont. | B3 | 73 |
| Cabot Strait, strt., Can. | G20 | 66 |
| Cabra, Spain | D3 | 22 |
| Cabras Island, i., Guam | L9 | 52 |
| Cabrera Baja, Sierra de la, mts., Spain | B5 | 22 |
| Cabrera Island, i., Spain | C7 | 22 |
| Cabri, Sask. | G1 | 75 |
| Cabriel, stm., Spain | C5 | 22 |
| Cabri Lake, l., Sask. | F1 | 75 |
| Cabrobó, Braz. | C3 | 57 |
| Caçador, Braz. | D2 | 56 |
| Caçapava do Sul, Braz. | E2 | 56 |
| Cacapon, stm., W.V., U.S. | B6 | 125 |
| Cacequi, Braz. | D2 | 56 |
| Cáceres, Braz. | D6 | 57 |
| Cáceres, Col. | B2 | 60 |
| Cáceres, Spain | C5 | 22 |
| Cáceres, dept., Peru | C2 | 58 |
| Cachan, Fr. | g10 | 16 |
| Cache, Ok., U.S. | C3 | 113 |
| Cache, co., Ut., U.S. | B4 | 121 |
| Cache, stm., Ar., U.S. | C4 | 81 |
| Cache, stm., Il., U.S. | F4 | 90 |
| Cache Bay, Ont. | A5 | 73 |
| Cache Creek, B.C. | D7 | 69 |
| Cache Creek, stm., Ca., U.S. | C2 | 82 |
| Cache Junction, Ut., U.S. | B3 | 121 |
| Cache la Poudre, stm., Co., U.S. | A5 | 83 |
| Cache la Poudre, North Fork, stm., Co., U.S. | A5 | 83 |
| Cache Mountain, mtn., Ak., U.S. | B10 | 79 |
| Cache Peak, mtn., Id., U.S. | G5 | 89 |
| Cachi, Arg. | E2 | 55 |
| Cachimbo, Serra do, mts., Braz. | D4 | 59 |
| Cachoeira, Braz. | D3 | 57 |
| Cachoeira do Arari, Braz. | C5 | 59 |
| Cachoeira do Sul, Braz. | D2 | 56 |
| Cachoeiro de Itapemirim, Braz. | C4 | 56 |
| Caçiporé, stm., Braz. | B4 | 59 |
| Caçiporé, Cabo, c., Braz. | B4 | 59 |
| Cacique, Pan. | h11 | 62 |
| Cacolo, Ang. | D2 | 48 |
| Caconda, Ang. | D2 | 48 |
| Caconde, Braz. | k8 | 56 |
| Cactus Flat, pl., Nv., U.S. | F5 | 105 |
| Cactus Lake, Sask. | E1 | 75 |
| Cactus Peak, mtn., Nv., U.S. | F5 | 105 |
| Cactus Springs, Nv., U.S. | G6 | 105 |
| Caculé, Braz. | A4 | 56 |
| Caddo, Ok., U.S. | C5 | 113 |
| Caddo, Tx., U.S. | C3 | 120 |
| Caddo, co., La., U.S. | B2 | 95 |
| Caddo, co., Ok., U.S. | B3 | 113 |
| Caddo, stm., Ar., U.S. | C2 | 81 |
| Caddo Gap, Ar., U.S. | C2 | 81 |
| Caddo Lake, res., U.S. | B2 | 95 |
| Caddo Mountains, mtn., Ar., U.S. | C2 | 81 |
| Cade, La., U.S. | D4 | 95 |
| Cader Idris, mtn., Wales, U.K. | D4 | 10 |
| Cades, Tn., U.S. | B3 | 119 |
| Cades Cove, Tn., U.S. | D10 | 119 |
| Cadet, Mo., U.S. | C7 | 102 |
| Cadillac, Sask. | H2 | 75 |
| Cadillac, Mi., U.S. | D5 | 99 |
| Cadillac Mountain, mtn., Me., U.S. | D4 | 96 |
| Cadiz, Ca., U.S. | E6 | 82 |
| Cadiz, Ky., U.S. | D2 | 94 |
| Cadiz, Oh., U.S. | B4 | 112 |
| Cádiz, Spain | D2 | 22 |
| Cadiz, Gulf of, b., Eur. | D2 | 22 |
| Cadogan, Alta. | C5 | 68 |
| Cadomin, Alta. | C2 | 68 |
| Cadott, Wi., U.S. | D2 | 126 |
| Cadotte, stm., Alta. | A2 | 68 |
| Cadron Creek, stm., Ar., U.S. | B3 | 81 |
| Cadwell, Ga., U.S. | D3 | 87 |
| Cadys Falls, Vt., U.S. | B3 | 122 |
| Caen, Fr. | D4 | 16 |
| Caernarfon, Wales, U.K. | D4 | 10 |
| Caernarfon Bay, b., Wales, U.K. | D4 | 10 |
| Caerphilly, Wales, U.K. | C4 | 12 |
| Caesar Creek Lake, res., Oh., U.S. | C2 | 112 |
| Caetité, Braz. | A4 | 56 |
| Cafayate, Arg. | E2 | 55 |
| Cagayan, stm., Phil. | B6 | 34 |
| Cagayan de Oro, Phil. | D7 | 34 |
| Cagayan Islands, is., Phil. | D6 | 34 |
| Cagayan Sulu Island, i., Phil. | D5 | 34 |
| Cagiallo, Switz. | D5 | 21 |
| Cagles Mill Lake, res., In., U.S. | F4 | 91 |
| Cagli, Italy | F7 | 21 |
| Cagliari, Italy | K4 | 23 |
| Cagliari, Gulf of, b., Italy | K4 | 23 |
| Cagnes-sur-Mer, Fr. | F7 | 16 |
| Caguán, stm., Col. | G5 | 60 |
| Caguas, P.R. | G11 | 64 |
| Cahaba, stm., Al., U.S. | C2 | 78 |
| Cahaba Heights, Al., U.S. | *B3 | 78 |
| Cahaba Valley, stm., Al., U.S. | B3 | 78 |
| Caher, Ire. | F2 | 11 |
| Caherdaniel, Ire. | F1 | 11 |
| Cahersiveen, Ire. | F1 | 11 |
| Cahokia, Il., U.S. | E3 | 90 |
| Cahone, Co., U.S. | D2 | 83 |
| Cahore Point, c., Ire. | E5 | 11 |
| Cahors, Fr. | D4 | 16 |
| Cahuinari, stm., Col. | D3 | 60 |
| Caiabis, Serra dos, plat., Braz. | E3 | 59 |
| Caiapônia, Braz. | B2 | 56 |
| Caibarién, Cuba | C4 | 64 |
| Cai Bau, i., Viet. | B7 | 35 |
| Caicara, Ven. | B4 | 60 |
| Caicedonia, Col. | C2 | 60 |
| Caicó, Braz. | C4 | 57 |
| Caicos Islands, is., T./C. Is. | D8 | 64 |
| Caicos Passage, strt., N.A. | C7 | 64 |
| Cailloma, Peru | E3 | 58 |
| Caillou Bay, b., La., U.S. | E5 | 95 |
| Caillou Lake, l., La., U.S. | E5 | 95 |
| Caimanera, Cuba | E6 | 64 |
| Caiman Point, c., Phil. | o12 | 34 |
| Caimito, stm., Pan. | m11 | 62 |
| Cains, stm., N.B. | C4 | 71 |
| Cains Store, Ky., U.S. | C5 | 94 |
| Cainsville, Mo., U.S. | A4 | 102 |
| Cainsville, Tn., U.S. | B5 | 119 |
| Caintown, Ont. | C9 | 73 |
| Cairnbrook, Pa., U.S. | F4 | 115 |
| Cairngorm Mountains, mts., Scot., U.K. | C5 | 13 |
| Cairns, Austl. | C8 | 50 |
| Cairnsmore of Carsphairn, mtn., Scot., U.K. | E4 | 13 |
| Cairn Table, mtn., Scot., U.K. | E5 | 13 |
| Cairo (Al Qāhirah), Eg. | B3 | 38 |
| Cairo, Ga., U.S. | F2 | 87 |
| Cairo, Il., U.S. | F4 | 90 |
| Cairo, Mo., U.S. | B5 | 102 |
| Cairo, Ne., U.S. | D7 | 104 |
| Cairo, N.Y., U.S. | C6 | 109 |
| Cairo, Oh., U.S. | B1 | 112 |
| Cairo, W.V., U.S. | B3 | 125 |
| Caiundo, Ang. | E2 | 48 |
| Cajabamba, Peru | C2 | 58 |
| Cajacay, Peru | D2 | 58 |
| Caja de Muertos, Isla, i., P.R. | C2 | 65 |
| Cajamarca, Peru | C2 | 58 |
| Cajamarca, dept., Peru | C2 | 58 |
| Cajatambo, Peru | D2 | 58 |
| Cajàzeiras, Braz. | C3 | 57 |
| Čajniče, Yugo. | D4 | 24 |
| Čakovec, Yugo. | B2 | 24 |
| Čakovice, Czech. | n18 | 26 |
| Calabar, Nig. | H5 | 45 |
| Calabasas, Ca., U.S. | m11 | 82 |
| Calabogie Lake, l., Ont. | B8 | 73 |
| Calabozo, Ven. | B4 | 60 |
| Calabria, prov., Italy | E6 | 23 |
| Calafat, Rom. | D6 | 24 |
| Calafate, Arg. | E2 | 54 |
| Calagua Islands, is., Phil. | o14 | 34 |
| Calahorra, Spain | A5 | 22 |
| Calais, Fr. | B4 | 16 |
| Calais, Me., U.S. | C5 | 96 |
| Calais, Vt., U.S. | C4 | 122 |
| Calamar, Col. | A3 | 60 |
| Calamar, Col. | C3 | 60 |
| Calamba, Phil. | o13 | 34 |
| Calamian Group, is., Phil. | C6 | 34 |
| Calamocha, Spain | B5 | 22 |
| Calamus, Ia., U.S. | C7 | 92 |
| Calamus, stm., Ne., U.S. | B6 | 104 |
| Calañas, Spain | D2 | 22 |
| Calanda, Spain | B5 | 22 |
| Calanscio, Sarīr, des., Afr. | H5 | 43 |
| Calanscio, Sarīr, des., Libya | D4 | 43 |
| Calapan, Phil. | C6 | 34 |
| Calàrasi, Rom. | C8 | 24 |
| Calarcá, Col. | C2 | 60 |
| Calasparra, Spain | C5 | 22 |
| Calatayud, Spain | B5 | 22 |
| Calau, E. Ger. | B8 | 19 |
| Calauag, Phil. | p14 | 34 |
| Calauag Bay, stm., Phil. | o14 | 34 |
| Calaveras, co., Ca., U.S. | C3 | 82 |
| Calavo Gardens, Ca., U.S. | *o16 | 82 |
| Calbe, E. Ger. | B6 | 19 |
| Calbuco, Chile | D2 | 54 |
| Calca, Peru | D3 | 58 |
| Calcasieu, co., La., U.S. | D2 | 95 |
| Calcasieu, stm., La., U.S. | D2 | 95 |
| Calcasieu Lake, l., La., U.S. | E2 | 95 |
| Calcasieu Pass, strt., La., U.S. | E2 | 95 |
| Calceta, Ec. | B1 | 60 |
| Calchaquí, Arg. | B4 | 55 |
| Calçoene, Braz. | B4 | 59 |
| Calcutta, Oh., U.S. | B5 | 112 |
| Calcutta, India | I13 | 37 |
| Calcutta Lake, l., Nv., U.S. | B2 | 105 |
| Caldaro, Italy | C6 | 20 |
| Caldas, dept., Col. | E5 | 60 |
| Caldas da Rainha, Port. | C1 | 22 |
| Calder, Sask. | F5 | 75 |
| Calder, stm., Eng., U.K. | A6 | 12 |
| Calder, Loch, l., Scot., U.K. | B5 | 13 |
| Caldera, Chile | E1 | 55 |
| Calderwood, Tn., U.S. | D10 | 119 |
| Caldron Falls Reservoir, res., Wi., U.S. | C5 | 126 |
| Caldwell, Ar., U.S. | B5 | 81 |
| Caldwell, Id., U.S. | F2 | 89 |
| Caldwell, Ks., U.S. | E6 | 93 |
| Caldwell, Oh., U.S. | C4 | 112 |
| Caldwell, Tx., U.S. | D4 | 120 |
| Caldwell, W.V., U.S. | D5 | 125 |
| Caldwell, co., Ky., U.S. | C2 | 94 |
| Caldwell, co., Mo., U.S. | B3 | 102 |
| Caldwell, co., N.C., U.S. | B1 | 110 |
| Caldwell, co., Tx., U.S. | E4 | 120 |
| Cale, Ar., U.S. | D2 | 81 |
| Caledon, Ont. | D5 | 73 |
| Caledon, N. Ire., U.K. | C5 | 11 |
| Caledonia, Ont. | D5 | 73 |
| Caledonia, Ms., U.S. | B5 | 101 |
| Caledonia, Mn., U.S. | G7 | 100 |
| Caledonia, N.Y., U.S. | C3 | 109 |
| Caledonia, Oh., U.S. | B3 | 112 |
| Caledonia, co., Vt., U.S. | C4 | 122 |
| Caledonian Canal, Scot., U.K. | D4 | 13 |

| Name | Map Ref. | Page |
|------|------|------|

Calhoun, Ky., U.S. — C2 94
Calhoun, La., U.S. — B3 95
Calhoun, Mo., U.S. — C4 102
Calhoun, Tn., U.S. — D9 119
Calhoun, co., Al., U.S. — B4 78
Calhoun, co., Ar., U.S. — D3 81
Calhoun, co., Fl., U.S. — B1 86
Calhoun, co., Ga., U.S. — E2 87
Calhoun, co., Il., U.S. — D3 90
Calhoun, co., Ia., U.S. — B3 92
Calhoun, co., Mi., U.S. — F5 99
Calhoun, co., Ms., U.S. — B4 101
Calhoun, co., S.C., U.S. — D6 117
Calhoun, co., Tx., U.S. — E4 120
Calhoun, co., W.V., U.S. — C3 125
Calhoun City, Ms., U.S. — B4 101
Calhoun Falls, S.C., U.S. — C3 117
Cali, Col. — C2 60
Calico Rock, Ar., U.S. — A3 81
Calicut (Kozhikode), India — F6 36
Caliente, Ca., U.S. — E4 82
Caliente, Nv., U.S. — F7 105
Califon, N.J., U.S. — B3 107
California, Ky., U.S. — k14 94
California, Md., U.S. — *D4 97
California, Mo., U.S. — C5 102
California, Pa., U.S. — F2 115
California, state, U.S. — D4 82
California, Golfo de, b., Mex. — B2 63
California Aqueduct, Ca., U.S. — E4 82
California Junction, Ia., U.S. — C1 92
California Oil Camp, Co., U.S. — A2 83
Calingasta, Arg. — A3 54
Calio, N.D., U.S. — A7 111
Calion, Ar., U.S. — D3 81
Calipatria, Ca., U.S. — F6 82
Calispell Peak, mtn., Wa., U.S. — A8 124
Calistoga, Ca., U.S. — C2 82
Callabonna, Austl. — D3 51
Callabonna, Lake, l., Austl. — D3 51
Callaghan, Mount, mtn., Nv., U.S. — D5 105
Callahan, Fl., U.S. — B5 86
Callahan, Ks., U.S. — g12 93
Callahan, co., Tx., U.S. — C3 120
Callan, Ire. — E4 11
Callander, Ont. — A5 73
Callander, Scot., U.K. — B4 10
Callands, Va., U.S. — D3 123
Callao, Peru — D2 58
Callao, Mo., U.S. — B5 102
Callao, Va., U.S. — C6 123
Callao, dept., Peru — *D2 58
Callaway, Fl., U.S. — u16 86
Callaway, Md., U.S. — D4 97
Callaway, Mn., U.S. — D3 100
Callaway, Ne., U.S. — C6 104
Callaway, Va., U.S. — C2 123
Callaway, co., Mo., U.S. — C6 102
Callender, Ia., U.S. — B3 92
Callensburg, Pa., U.S. — D2 115
Callery, Pa., U.S. — E1 115
Callicoon, N.Y., U.S. — D5 109
Callicoon Center, N.Y., U.S. — D6 109
Calliham, Tx., U.S. — E3 120
Calling Lake, Alta. — B4 68
Calling Lake, l., Alta. — B4 68
Calloway, co., Ky., U.S. — f9 94
Calmar, Alta. — C4 68
Calmar, Ia., U.S. — A6 92
Calne, Eng., U.K. — C5 12
Caloosahatchee, stm., Fl., U.S. — F5 86
Caloundra, Austl. — E9 50
Calpella, Ca., U.S. — C2 82
Calpet, Wy., U.S. — D2 127
Caltagirone, Italy — F5 23
Caltanissetta, Italy — F5 23
Caltra, Ire. — D3 11
Caluire [-et-Cuire], Fr. — E6 16
Calulo, Ang. — D1 48
Calumet, Que. — D3 74
Calumet, Al., U.S. — B2 78
Calumet, Ia., U.S. — B2 92
Calumet, Mi., U.S. — A2 99
Calumet, Mn., U.S. — C5 100
Calumet, Ok., U.S. — B3 113
Calumet, co., Wi., U.S. — D5 126
Calumet, Lake, l., Il., U.S. — k9 90
Calumet City, Il., U.S. — B6 90
Calumet Park, Il., U.S. — *k9 90
Calumet Sag Channel, Il., U.S. — k9 90
Calumetville, Wi., U.S. — k9 126
Calunda, Ang. — D3 48
Caluula, Som. — C7 47
Calvary, Ga., U.S. — F2 87
Calvary, Wi., U.S. — k9 126
Calvert, Al., U.S. — D1 78
Calvert, Tx., U.S. — D4 120
Calvert, co., Md., U.S. — C4 97
Calvert City, Ky., U.S. — e9 94
Calvert Island, i., B.C. — D3 69
Calverton, Md., U.S. — B4 97
Calverton, N.Y., U.S. — n16 109
Calverton, Va., U.S. — B5 123
Calverton Park, Mo., U.S. — f13 102
Calvi, Fr. — C2 23
Calvillo, Mex. — m12 63
Calvin, La., U.S. — C3 95
Calvin, N.D., U.S. — A7 111
Calvin, Ok., U.S. — C5 113
Calvinia, S. Afr. — D2 49
Calvörde, E. Ger. — A6 19
Calw, W. Ger. — D4 19
Calwa, Ca., U.S. — *D4 82
Calypso, N.C., U.S. — B4 110
Calzada de Calatrava, Spain — C4 22
Cam, stm., Eng., U.K. — D7 10
Camabatela, Ang. — C2 48
Camacho, Mex. — C4 63
Camacupa, Ang. — D2 48
Camaguán, Cuba — D5 64
Camagüey, prov., Cuba — D5 64
Camajuaní, Cuba — C4 64
Camak, Ga., U.S. — C4 87
Camamu, Braz. — D3 57
Camaná, Peru — E3 58
Camanche, Ia., U.S. — C7 92
Camanducaia, Braz. — m8 56
Camano Island, i., Wa., U.S. — A3 124
Camapuã, Braz. — B2 56
Camaquã, Braz. — E2 56
Camaquã, stm., Braz. — E2 56
Camararé, stm., Braz. — E3 59
Camargo, Bol. — D5 59
Camargo, Mex. — D5 90
Camargo, Ok., U.S. — A2 113
Camarillo, Ca., U.S. — *E4 82
Camarón, Cabo, c., Hond. — D7 63
Camarones, Arg. — C3 54
Camarones, Bahía, b., Arg. — C3 54
Camas, Wa., U.S. — D3 124
Camas, co., Id., U.S. — F4 89
Camas Valley, Or., U.S. — D3 114
Ca Mau, Viet. — D3 34
Ca Mau, Cape, c., Viet. — D2 34

Camberwell, Austl. — *G8 50
Cambodia, ctry., Asia — C3 34
Camborne [-Redruth], Eng., U.K. — E4 10
Cambrai, Fr. — B5 16
Cambria, Ca., U.S. — E3 82
Cambria, Ia., U.S. — D4 92
Cambria, Mi., U.S. — G6 99
Cambria, Wi., U.S. — E4 126
Cambrian Mountains, mts., Wales, U.K. — D5 10
Cambridge, Ont. — D4 73
Cambridge, Eng., U.K. — D7 10
Cambridge, Id., U.S. — E2 89
Cambridge, Il., U.S. — B3 90
Cambridge, Ia., U.S. — C4 92
Cambridge, Ks., U.S. — E7 93
Cambridge, Me., U.S. — C3 96
Cambridge, Md., U.S. — C5 97
Cambridge, Ma., U.S. — B5 98
Cambridge, Mn., U.S. — E5 100
Cambridge, N.Y., U.S. — B7 109
Cambridge, Oh., U.S. — B4 112
Cambridge, Vt., U.S. — B3 122
Cambridge, Wi., U.S. — E4 126
Cambridge Bay, N.W. Ter. — C12 66
Cambridge City, In., U.S. — E7 91
Cambridge Junction, Vt., U.S. — B3 122
Cambridgeport, Vt., U.S. — E3 122
Cambridge Reservoir, res., Ma., U.S. — g10 98
Cambridgeshire, co., Eng., U.K. — B7 12
Cambridge Springs, Pa., U.S. — C1 115
Cambuí, Braz. — m8 56
Cambundi-Catembo (Nova Gaia), Ang. — D2 48
Camden, Al., U.S. — D2 78
Camden, Ar., U.S. — D3 81
Camden, De., U.S. — D3 85
Camden, Il., U.S. — C3 90
Camden, In., U.S. — C4 91
Camden, Me., U.S. — D3 96
Camden, Mi., U.S. — G6 99
Camden, Mo., U.S. — C4 101
Camden, N.J., U.S. — B3 102
Camden, N.Y., U.S. — D2 107
Camden, N.C., U.S. — B5 109
Camden, Oh., U.S. — A6 110
Camden, S.C., U.S. — C1 112
Camden, Tn., U.S. — C6 117
Camden, Tx., U.S. — D5 120
Camden, W.V., U.S. — B4 125
Camden, co., Ga., U.S. — F5 87
Camden, co., Mo., U.S. — C5 102
Camden, co., N.J., U.S. — D3 107
Camden, co., N.C., U.S. — A6 110
Camden on Gauley, W.V., U.S. — C4 125
Camdenton, Mo., U.S. — D5 102
Camelback Mountain, mtn., Az., U.S. — k9 80
Camelot, Wa., U.S. — *B3 124
Camels Hump, mtn., Vt., U.S. — C3 122
Camerino, Italy — C4 23
Cameron, Az., U.S. — B4 80
Cameron, Il., U.S. — C3 90
Cameron, La., U.S. — E2 95
Cameron, Mo., U.S. — B3 102
Cameron, Mt., U.S. — E5 103
Cameron, N.C., U.S. — B3 110
Cameron, Ok., U.S. — B7 113
Cameron, Tx., U.S. — D5 115
Cameron, S.C., U.S. — D6 117
Cameron, Tx., U.S. — D4 120
Cameron, W.V., U.S. — B4 125
Cameron, Wi., U.S. — C2 126
Cameron, co., La., U.S. — E2 95
Cameron, co., Pa., U.S. — D5 115
Cameron, co., Tx., U.S. — F4 120
Cameron Hills, hills, Can. — E9 66
Cameron Island, i., N.W. Ter. — m31 66
Cameron Park, Ca., U.S. — *C3 82
Cameroon, ctry., Afr. — D2 46
Cameroun, Mont, mtn., Cam. — E1 46
Cametá, Braz. — B4 57
Camiling, Phil. — o13 34
Camilla, Ga., U.S. — E2 87
Camino, Ca., U.S. — C3 82
Camissombo (Verísimo Sarmento), Ang. — C3 48
Camlachie, Ont. — D2 73
Camp Verde, Az., U.S. — C4 80
Camp Verde Indian Reservation, Az., U.S. — C4 80
Campville, Fl., U.S. — C4 86
Camp Wood, Tx., U.S. — E2 120
Cam Ranh, Viet. — G8 35
Cam Ranh Bay, b., Viet. — G8 35
Camrose, Alta. — C4 68
Camuquén, Ven. — B5 60
Canaan, N.B. — C4 71
Canaan, Ct., U.S. — A2 84
Canaan, In., U.S. — G7 91
Canaan, Me., U.S. — D3 96
Canaan, Ms., U.S. — A4 101
Canaan, N.H., U.S. — C2 106
Canaan, N.Y., U.S. — C7 109
Canaan, Vt., U.S. — A5 122
Canaan, stm., N.B. — C4 71
Canaan Center, N.H., U.S. — C2 106
Canaan Street, N.H., U.S. — C2 106
Canada, Ky., U.S. — *C7 94
Canada Bay, b., Newf. — C3 72
Canada Falls Lake, res., Me., U.S. — C2 96
Canadensis, Pa., U.S. — D11 115
Canadian, Ok., U.S. — B6 113
Canadian, Tx., U.S. — B2 120
Canadian, co., Ok., U.S. — B3 113
Canadian, stm., U.S. — C7 76
Canadys, S.C., U.S. — E6 117
Canajoharie, N.Y., U.S. — C6 109
Canakkale, Tur. — B6 40
Canal Flats, B.C. — D10 69
Canal Fulton, Oh., U.S. — B4 112
Canalou, Mo., U.S. — E8 102
Canal Point, Fl., U.S. — F6 86
Canal Winchester, Oh., U.S. — C3 112
Canandaigua, N.Y., U.S. — C3 109
Canandaigua Lake, l., N.Y., U.S. — C3 109
Cananea, Mex. — A2 63
Cananéia, Braz. — D3 56
Canápolis, Braz. — B3 56
Cañar, Ec. — D2 58
Cañar, prov., Ec. — C3 22
Canary Islands, is., Spain — m14 22
Cañas, C.R. — E5 62
Canaseraga, N.Y., U.S. — C3 109
Canastota, N.Y., U.S. — B5 109
Canaveral, Cape, c., Fl., U.S. — D6 86
Canaveral National Seashore, Fl., U.S. — D6 86
Cañavieiras, Braz. — C9 57
Cañazas, Pan. — F7 62
Canazei, Italy — C6 21
Canberra, Austl. — G8 50
Canby, Ca., U.S. — B3 82
Canby, Mn., U.S. — F2 100
Canby, Or., U.S. — B4 114
Canche, stm., Fr. — B8 16
Cancún, Mex. — C7 63
Candeias, stm., Braz. — D2 59
Candela, Mex. — D4 90
Candelaria, Phil. — o12 34
Candelaria, Tx., U.S. — o12 120
Candelaria, stm., Mex. — A2 62
Candeleda, Spain — B3 22
Candia see Iráklion, Grc. — E5 40
Candia, N.H., U.S. — D4 106
Candia Village, N.H., U.S. — D4 106
Candiac, Que. — q19 74
Candle Lake, l., Sask. — D3 75
Candor, Fl., U.S. — C5 86
Candor, N.C., U.S. — B3 110
Candor, N.Y., U.S. — C4 109

Canton Lake, res., Ok., U.S. — A3 113
Cantonment, Fl., U.S. — u14 86
Cantril, Ia., U.S. — D5 92
Cantù, Italy — B2 23
Cantuar, Sask. — G1 75
Cantwell, Ak., U.S. — C10 79
Canuelas, Arg. — B5 54
Canumã, stm., Braz. — C3 59
Canutama, Braz. — D2 59
Canute, Ok., U.S. — B2 113
Canutillo, Tx., U.S. — o11 120
Canwood, Sask. — D2 75
Cany-Barville, Fr. — E8 12
Canyon, Tx., U.S. — B2 120
Canyon, co., Id., U.S. — F2 89
Canyon City, Or., U.S. — C8 114
Canyon Country, Ca., U.S. — *E4 82
Canyon Creek, Alta. — B3 68
Canyon Creek, Mt., U.S. — D4 103
Canyon de Chelly National Monument, Az., U.S. — A6 80
Canyon Ferry Lake, res., Mt., U.S. — D5 103
Canyon Lake, res., Tx., U.S. — E3 120
Canyonlands National Park, Ut., U.S. — E6 121
Canyonville, Or., U.S. — E3 114
Cao Bang, Viet. — A7 35
Caonao, stm., Cuba — D4 64
Caorle, Italy — D8 20
Capac, Mi., U.S. — F8 99
Capacho, Ven. — C4 60
Capanaparo, stm., S.A. — B4 60
Capanema, Braz. — B1 57
Capão Bonito, Braz. — C3 57
Capão Doce, Morro do, mtn., Braz. — D2 56
Caparica, Port. — f9 22
Caparo, stm., Ven. — B3 60
Capasin, Sask. — D2 75
Capatárida, Ven. — A3 60
Cap-aux-Meules, Que. — B8 71
Cap-aux-Meules, Île du, i., Que. — B8 71
Capbreton, Fr. — F3 16
Cap-Chat, Que. — G19 66
Cap-de-la-Madeleine, Que. — C5 74
Capdenac-Gare, Fr. — E5 16
Cape, prov., S. Afr. — D3 49
Cape Barren, i., Austl. — o15 50
Cape Breton, i., N.S. — C9 71
Cape Breton Highlands National Park, N.S. — C9 71
Cape Breton Island, i., N.S. — C9 71
Cape Broyle, Newf. — E5 72
Cape Canaveral, Fl., U.S. — D6 86
Cape Charles, Newf. — B4 72
Cape Charles, Va., U.S. — C6 123
Cape Coast, Ghana — E4 45
Cape Cod Bay, b., Ma., U.S. — C7 98
Cape Cod Canal, Ma., U.S. — C6 98
Cape Cod National Seashore, Ma., U.S. — C7 98
Cape Dorset, N.W. Ter. — D17 66
Cape Elizabeth, Me., U.S. — E2 96
Cape Fair, Mo., U.S. — E4 102
Cape Fear, stm., N.C., U.S. — C4 110
Cape Girardeau, Mo., U.S. — D8 102
Cape Girardeau, co., Mo., U.S. — D8 102
Cape Hatteras National Seashore, N.C., U.S. — B7 110
Cape Horn Mountain, mtn., Id., U.S. — E3 89
Cape la Hune, Newf. — E3 72
Capelinha, Braz. — D7 57
Capelongo, Ang. — E2 48
Cape Lookout National Seashore, N.C., U.S. — C6 110
Capels, W.V., U.S. — D3 125
Cape May, N.J., U.S. — F3 107
Cape May, co., N.J., U.S. — E3 107
Cape May Court House, N.J., U.S. — E3 107
Cape May Point, N.J., U.S. — F3 107
Cape Neddick, Me., U.S. — E2 96
Cape Pole, Ak., U.S. — n23 79
Cape Porpoise, Me., U.S. — E2 96
Cape Ray, Newf. — E2 72
Capers Island, i., S.C., U.S. — G6 117
Capers Island, i., S.C., U.S. — F8 117
Cape Sable Island, i., N.S. — F4 71
Capesterre, Guad. — H14 64
Cape Tormentine, N.B. — C6 71
Cape Town (Kaapstad), S. Afr. — D2 49
Cape Verde, ctry., Afr. — A2 45
Capeville, Va., U.S. — h16 123
Cape Vincent, N.Y., U.S. — A4 109
Cap-Haïtien, Haiti — E7 64
Capibaribe, stm., Braz. — k5 57
Capilla del Monte, Arg. — g7 54
Capilla del Señor, Arg. — g7 54
Capim, stm., Braz. — B1 57
Capinota, Bol. — G8 59
Capitachouane, stm., Que. — *F9 50
Capitan, N.M., U.S. — D4 108
Capitán Bado, Para. — D4 55
Capitan Mountains, mts., N.M., U.S. — D4 108
Capitán Sarmiento, Arg. — C5 54
Capitol, Mt., U.S. — E12 103
Capitol Heights, Md., U.S. — C4 97
Capitol Peak, mtn., Nv., U.S. — B4 105
Capitol Reef National Park, Ut., U.S. — E4 121
Capitol View, S.C., U.S. — *D6 117
Capivari, Braz. — m8 56
Capleville, Tn., U.S. — B2 119
Cap Mountain, mtn., N.W. Ter. — D8 66
Capon Bridge, W.V., U.S. — B6 125
Capon Springs, W.V., U.S. — B6 125
Capote Peak, mtn., Tx., U.S. — k8 120
Cap-Pelé, N.B. — C5 71
Cappoquin, Ire. — I4 11
Capraia, i., Italy — C2 23
Capraprock, Point, c., Italy — *E4 23
Caprara, Point, c., Italy — B2 23
Caprera, i., Italy — B2 23
Capri, i., Italy — D5 23
Capricorn, Cape, c., Austl. — D9 50
Capricorn Group, is., Austl. — A8 51
Caprock, N.M., U.S. — D6 108
Capron, Il., U.S. — A5 90

Capron, Ok., U.S. — A3 113
Capron, Va., U.S. — D5 123
Cap-Rouge, Que. — n17 74
Cap-Saint-Ignace, Que. — B7 74
Cap-Santé, Que. — C6 74
Capshaw, Al., U.S. — A3 78
Captain Cook, Hi., U.S. — D6 88
Captiva, Fl., U.S. — F4 86
Captiva Island, i., Fl., U.S. — F4 86
Capua, Italy — D5 23
Capulin, N.M., U.S. — A6 108
Capulin Mountain National Monument, N.M., U.S. — A6 108
Caputa, S.D., U.S. — D3 118
Caquetá, dept., Col. — C3 60
Caquetá (Japurá), stm., S.A. — D3 60
Carabaña, Spain — p18 22
Carabanchel Bajo, Spain — p17 22
Carabinani, Braz. — D5 60
Carabobo, state, Ven. — A4 60
Caracal, Rom. — C7 24
Caracaraí, Braz. — B2 59
Caracas, Ven. — A4 60
Caraguatay, Para. — E4 55
Caraí, Braz. — D5 59
Carajás, Braz. — D5 59
Carajás, Serra dos, mts., Braz. — D4 59
Caranga, Braz. — C4 56
Caransebeş, Rom. — C6 24
Carapari, Bol. — D3 55
Carapeguá, Para. — E4 55
Carapó, Braz. — C1 56
Caraquet, N.B. — B5 71
Caratasca, Laguna de, b., Hond. — D8 63
Caratinga, Braz. — B4 56
Carauari, Braz. — D2 59
Caraúbas, Braz. — h5 57
Caraúbas, Braz. — C5 57
Caravaca, Spain — C5 22
Caravelas, Braz. — E3 57
Caravelí, Peru — E3 58
Caraway, Ar., U.S. — B5 81
Caraz, Peru — C2 58
Carazinho, Braz. — D2 56
Carballino, Spain — A1 22
Carballo, Spain — A1 22
Carberry, Man. — E2 70
Carbet, Pitons du, mts., Mart. — S10 65
Carbó, Mex. — B2 63
Carbon, In., U.S. — E3 91
Carbon, Ia., U.S. — C3 92
Carbon, W.V., U.S. — m13 125
Carbon, co., Mt., U.S. — E7 103
Carbon, co., Pa., U.S. — E10 115
Carbon, co., Ut., U.S. — D5 121
Carbon, co., Wy., U.S. — E5 127
Carbonara, Cape, c., Italy — E3 23
Carbondale, Alta. — C4 68
Carbondale, Co., U.S. — B3 83
Carbondale, Il., U.S. — F4 90
Carbondale, Ks., U.S. — D8 93
Carbondale, Oh., U.S. — C3 112
Carbondale, Pa., U.S. — C10 115
Carbonear, Newf. — E5 72
Carbon Hill, Al., U.S. — B2 78
Carbon Hill, Il., U.S. — B5 90
Carbonia, Italy — E2 23
Carbonne, Fr. — F4 16
Carbonville, Ut., U.S. — D5 121
Carbury, N.D., U.S. — A5 111
Carcagente, Spain — C5 22
Carcans, Étang de b., Fr. — E3 16
Carcassonne, Fr. — F5 16
Carchi, prov., Ec. — A2 58
Carcross, Yukon — D6 66
Çardak, Tur. — D7 25
Cardale, Man. — D1 70
Cárdenas, Cuba — C3 64
Cárdenas, Mex. — m14 63
Cárdenas, Mex. — D6 63
Cardeña, Spain — C7 25
Cardiel, Lago, l., Arg. — D2 54
Cardiff, Wales, U.K. — E5 10
Cardiff, Al., U.S. — f7 78
Cardiff, Md., U.S. — A5 97
Cardiff, N.J., U.S. — E3 107
Cardigan, P.E.I. — C7 71
Cardigan, Wales, U.K. — D4 10
Cardigan, Mount, mtn., N.H., U.S. — C3 106
Cardigan Bay, b., P.E.I. — C7 71
Cardigan Bay, b., Wales, U.K. — D4 10
Cardinal, Ont. — C9 73
Cardinal Lake, l., Alta. — B2 68
Cardington, Oh., U.S. — B3 112
Cardona, Ur. — C4 54
Cardross, Sask. — H3 75
Cardston, Alta. — E4 68
Cardville, Me., U.S. — C4 96
Cardwell, Mo., U.S. — E7 102
Cardwell, Mt., U.S. — E5 103
Cardwell Mountain, mtn., Tn., U.S. — D8 119
Carega, mtn., Italy — D7 20
Carei, Rom. — B6 24
Carencro, La., U.S. — D3 95
Carentan, Fr. — C5 16
Carenero, Ven. — A4 60
Caretta, W.V., U.S. — D3 125
Carey, Oh., U.S. — B2 112
Careysburg, Lib. — G3 45
Careywood, Id., U.S. — A2 89
Carhaix, Fr. — D2 16
Carhué, Arg. — B4 54
Cariamanga, Ec. — D2 58
Cariati, Italy — E6 23
Caribana, Punta, c., Col. — B3 53
Caribbean Sea — E5 65
Cariboo Mountains, mts., B.C. — C7 69
Caribou, Me., U.S. — B5 96
Caribou, co., Id., U.S. — G7 89
Caribou Island, i., N.S. — D7 71
Caribou Lake, l., Me., U.S. — C3 96
Caribou Mountain, mtn., Id., U.S. — F7 89
Caribou Mountain, mtn., Me., U.S. — C2 96
Caribou Mountains, mts., Alta. — f7 68
Caribou Range, mts., Id., U.S. — F7 89
Carichíc, Mex. — C3 63
Carievale, Sask. — H5 75
Carignan, Fr. — C6 16
Carinhanha, Braz. — A4 56
Carini, Italy — F4 23
Carinish, Scot., U.K. — C1 13
Carinthia, hist. reg., Aus. — E6 18

| Name | Map Ref. | Page |
|---|---|---|
| Caripe, Ven. | A5 | 60 |
| Caripito, Ven. | A5 | 60 |
| Cariús, Braz. | C3 | 57 |
| Carl Blackwell, Lake, res., Ok., U.S. | A4 | 113 |
| Carle Place, N.Y., U.S. | *n15 | 109 |
| Carleton, Mi., U.S. | F7 | 99 |
| Carleton, Ne., U.S. | D8 | 104 |
| Carleton, co., N.B. | C2 | 71 |
| Carleton, Mount, mtn., N.B. | B3 | 71 |
| Carleton Place, Ont. | B8 | 73 |
| Carleton, S. Afr. | C4 | 49 |
| Carlile, Wy., U.S. | B8 | 127 |
| Carlin, Nv., U.S. | C5 | 105 |
| Carlingford, Ire. | C5 | 11 |
| Carlingford Lough, b., Eur. | C5 | 11 |
| Carlinville, Il., U.S. | D4 | 90 |
| Carlisle, Eng., U.K. | C5 | 10 |
| Carlisle, Ar., U.S. | C4 | 81 |
| Carlisle, In., U.S. | G3 | 91 |
| Carlisle, Ia., U.S. | C4 | 92 |
| Carlisle, Ky., U.S. | B5 | 94 |
| Carlisle, Ma., U.S. | f10 | 98 |
| Carlisle, Ms., U.S. | C3 | 101 |
| Carlisle, Oh., U.S. | C1 | 112 |
| Carlisle, Pa., U.S. | F7 | 115 |
| Carlisle, S.C., U.S. | B5 | 117 |
| Carlisle, Tn., U.S. | A4 | 119 |
| Carlisle, co., Ky., U.S. | f8 | 94 |
| Carlit, Pic, mtn., Fr. | F4 | 16 |
| Carl Junction, Mo., U.S. | D3 | 102 |
| Carlock, Il., U.S. | C4 | 90 |
| Carloforte, Italy | E2 | 23 |
| Carlos, Md., U.S. | k13 | 97 |
| Carlos, Mn., U.S. | E3 | 100 |
| Carlos Casares, Arg. | B4 | 54 |
| Carlos Chagas, Braz. | B4 | 56 |
| Carlos City, In., U.S. | D7 | 91 |
| Carlos Tejedor, Arg. | B4 | 54 |
| Carlotta, Ca., U.S. | B1 | 82 |
| Carlow, Ire. | D3 | 10 |
| Carlow, co., Ire. | E5 | 11 |
| Carloway, Scot., U.K. | B2 | 13 |
| Carlowville, Al., U.S. | C2 | 78 |
| Carlsbad, Ca., U.S. | F5 | 82 |
| Carlsbad, N.M., U.S. | E5 | 108 |
| Carlsbad, Tx., U.S. | D2 | 120 |
| Carlsbad Caverns National Park, N.M., U.S. | E5 | 108 |
| Carlsbad Springs, Ont. | h13 | 73 |
| Carlsborg, Wa., U.S. | A2 | 124 |
| Carlstadt, N.J., U.S. | h8 | 107 |
| Carlton, Sask. | E2 | 75 |
| Carlton, Eng., U.K. | B6 | 12 |
| Carlton, Al., U.S. | D2 | 78 |
| Carlton, Ga., U.S. | B3 | 87 |
| Carlton, Ks., U.S. | D6 | 93 |
| Carlton, Mn., U.S. | D6 | 100 |
| Carlton, Or., U.S. | B3 | 114 |
| Carlton, Tx., U.S. | D3 | 120 |
| Carlton, co., Mn., U.S. | D6 | 100 |
| Carluke, Scot., U.K. | E5 | 13 |
| Carlyle, Sask. | H4 | 75 |
| Carlyle, Il., U.S. | E4 | 90 |
| Carlyle, Mt., U.S. | D12 | 103 |
| Carlyle Lake, res., Il., U.S. | E4 | 90 |
| Carmacks, Yukon | D5 | 66 |
| Carmagnola, Italy | B1 | 23 |
| Carman, Man. | E2 | 70 |
| Carmangay, Alta. | D4 | 68 |
| Carmanville, Newf. | D4 | 72 |
| Carmarthen, Wales, U.K. | E4 | 10 |
| Carmarthen Bay, b., Wales, U.K. | E4 | 10 |
| Carmaux, Fr. | E5 | 16 |
| Carmel, Sask. | E3 | 75 |
| Carmel, Ca., U.S. | D3 | 82 |
| Carmel, In., U.S. | E5 | 91 |
| Carmel, La., U.S. | B2 | 95 |
| Carmel, Me., U.S. | D3 | 96 |
| Carmel, N.J., U.S. | E2 | 107 |
| Carmel, N.Y., U.S. | D7 | 109 |
| Carmel, Mount, mtn., Isr. | B7 | 41 |
| Carmel Head, c., Wales, U.K. | A3 | 12 |
| Carmelo, Ur. | E1 | 56 |
| Carmen, Az., U.S. | F4 | 80 |
| Carmen, Id., U.S. | D5 | 89 |
| Carmen, Ok., U.S. | A3 | 113 |
| Carmen, Isla i., Mex. | B2 | 63 |
| Carmen, Río del, stm., Chile | E1 | 55 |
| Carmen Alto, Chile | D2 | 55 |
| Carmen de Areco, Arg. | A5 | 54 |
| Carmen [del Paraná], Para. | E4 | 55 |
| Carmen de Patagones, Arg. | C4 | 54 |
| Carmer Hill, hill, Pa., U.S. | C6 | 115 |
| Carmi, Il., U.S. | E5 | 90 |
| Carmi, Lake, I., Vt., U.S. | B3 | 122 |
| Carmichael, Bah. | m17 | 64 |
| Carmichael, Sask. | G1 | 75 |
| Carmichael, Ca., U.S. | *C3 | 82 |
| Carmichaels, Pa., U.S. | G2 | 115 |
| Carmine, Tx., U.S. | D4 | 120 |
| Carmona, Port. | D3 | 22 |
| Carnarvon, Austl. | D1 | 50 |
| Carnarvon, S. Afr. | D3 | 49 |
| Carnarvon, Ia., U.S. | B2 | 92 |
| Carnation, Wa., U.S. | B4 | 124 |
| Carnaxide, Port. | f9 | 22 |
| Carndonagh, Ire. | B4 | 11 |
| Carndonagh, Ire. | H5 | 75 |
| Carnduff, Sask. | | |
| Carnegie, Ga., U.S. | E2 | 87 |
| Carnegie, Ok., U.S. | B3 | 113 |
| Carnegie, Pa., U.S. | F1 | 115 |
| Carnegie, Lake, I., Austl. | E3 | 50 |
| Carnes, Ms., U.S. | E4 | 101 |
| Carnesville, Ga., U.S. | B3 | 87 |
| Carnew, Ire. | E5 | 11 |
| Carney, Md., U.S. | *B4 | 97 |
| Carney, Mi., U.S. | C3 | 99 |
| Carney, Ok., U.S. | B4 | 113 |
| Carneys Point, N.J., U.S. | D2 | 107 |
| Carnforth, Eng., U.K. | F6 | 13 |
| Carnic Alps, mts., Eur. | A4 | 23 |
| Car Nicobar, i., India | G9 | 36 |
| Carnlough, N. Ire., U.K. | C6 | 11 |
| Carnot, Cen. Afr. Rep. | D3 | 46 |
| Carnot, Pa., U.S. | *F1 | 115 |
| Carnoustie, Scot., U.K. | D6 | 13 |
| Carnsore Point, c., Ire. | D3 | 10 |
| Carnuel, N.M., U.S. | B3 | 108 |
| Caro, Mi., U.S. | E7 | 99 |
| Carol City, Fl., U.S. | s13 | 86 |
| Caroleen, N.C., U.S. | B1 | 110 |
| Carolina, Braz. | C3 | 57 |
| Carolina, P.R. | *B4 | 65 |
| Carolina, S. Afr. | C5 | 49 |
| Carolina, R.I., U.S. | F2 | 116 |
| Carolina, W.V., U.S. | k10 | 125 |
| Carolina Beach, N.C., U.S. | C5 | 110 |
| Carolinas, Puntan, c., N. Mar. Is. | E7 | 52 |
| Caroline, Alta. | D3 | 68 |
| Caroline, Wi., U.S. | D5 | 126 |
| Caroline, co., Md., U.S. | C6 | 97 |
| Caroline, co., Va., U.S. | C5 | 123 |

| Caroline, atoll, Kir. | G13 | 6 |
| Caroline Islands, is., T.T.P.I. | F8 | 6 |
| Carol Stream, Il., U.S. | *k8 | 90 |
| Caron, Sask. | G3 | 75 |
| Carona, Ks., U.S. | E9 | 93 |
| Caroni, stm., Trin. | N23 | 65 |
| Caroní, stm., Ven. | B5 | 60 |
| Carora, Ven. | A3 | 60 |
| Carouge, Switz. | E13 | 18 |
| Carp, Ont. | B8 | 73 |
| Carpathian Mountains, mts., Eur. | F13 | 8 |
| Carpentaria, Gulf of, b., Austl. | B6 | 50 |
| Carpenter, Ia., U.S. | A4 | 92 |
| Carpenter, S.D., U.S. | C8 | 118 |
| Carpenter, Wy., U.S. | E8 | 127 |
| Carpenter Dam, Ar., U.S. | g7 | 81 |
| Carpentersville, Il., U.S. | A5 | 90 |
| Carpentersville, N.J., U.S. | B2 | 107 |
| Carpentras, Fr. | E6 | 16 |
| Carpi, Italy | B3 | 23 |
| Carpinteria, Ca., U.S. | E4 | 82 |
| Carpio, N.D., U.S. | A4 | 111 |
| Carp Lake, Mi., U.S. | C6 | 99 |
| Carp Lake, l., B.C. | B6 | 69 |
| Carr, Co., U.S. | A6 | 83 |
| Carrabassett Valley, Me., U.S. | C2 | 96 |
| Carrabelle, Fl., U.S. | C2 | 86 |
| Carradale, Scot., U.K. | E3 | 13 |
| Carraganga, Sask. | E4 | 75 |
| Carranza, Cabo, c., Chile | B2 | 54 |
| Carrantoohil, mtn., Ire. | D2 | 10 |
| Carrara, Italy | B3 | 23 |
| Carrauntoohil, mtn., Ire. | D2 | 10 |
| Carbbboro, N.C., U.S. | B3 | 110 |
| Carrboro, N.C., U.S. | B3 | 110 |
| Carrcroft Crest, De., U.S. | *A3 | 85 |
| Carriacou, i., Gren. | W26 | 65 |
| Carrickfergus, N. Ire., U.K. | C4 | 10 |
| Carrickmacross, Ire. | D5 | 11 |
| Carrick on Shannon, Ire. | D3 | 11 |
| Carrick on Suir, Ire. | D3 | 10 |
| Carrie, Mount, mtn., Wa., U.S. | B2 | 124 |
| Carrier, Que. | o17 | 74 |
| Carrier, Ok., U.S. | A3 | 113 |
| Carrier Mills, Il., U.S. | F5 | 90 |
| Carrigahorig, Ire. | D3 | 11 |
| Carrigaline, Ire. | F3 | 11 |
| Carrigan, Mount, mtn., N.H., U.S. | B4 | 106 |
| Carrigan Head, c., Ire. | C3 | 11 |
| Carrington, N.D., U.S. | B6 | 111 |
| Carrington, Pa., U.S., I., Ut., U.S. | C3 | 121 |
| Carrión, stm., Spain | A3 | 22 |
| Carrión de los Condes, Spain | A3 | 22 |
| Carrizal Bajo, Chile | E1 | 55 |
| Carrizo Creek, stm., U.S. | A1 | 108 |
| Carrizo Mountain, mtn., N.M., U.S. | D4 | 108 |
| Carrizo Mountains, mts., U.S. | A6 | 80 |
| Carrizo Springs, Tx., U.S. | E3 | 120 |
| Carrizo Wash, val., U.S. | C6 | 80 |
| Carrizozo, N.M., U.S. | D4 | 108 |
| Carroll, Ia., U.S. | B3 | 92 |
| Carroll, Ne., U.S. | B8 | 104 |
| Carroll, Oh., U.S. | C3 | 112 |
| Carroll, co., Ar., U.S. | A2 | 81 |
| Carroll, co., Ga., U.S. | C1 | 87 |
| Carroll, co., Il., U.S. | A4 | 90 |
| Carroll, co., In., U.S. | C4 | 91 |
| Carroll, co., Ia., U.S. | B3 | 92 |
| Carroll, co., Ky., U.S. | B4 | 94 |
| Carroll, co., Md., U.S. | A3 | 97 |
| Carroll, co., Ms., U.S. | B4 | 101 |
| Carroll, co., Mo., U.S. | B4 | 102 |
| Carroll, co., N.H., U.S. | C4 | 106 |
| Carroll, co., Oh., U.S. | B4 | 112 |
| Carroll, co., Tn., U.S. | B3 | 119 |
| Carroll, co., Va., U.S. | D2 | 123 |
| Carroll Lake, l., Can. | D4 | 70 |
| Carrolls, Wa., U.S. | C3 | 124 |
| Carrollton, Al., U.S. | B1 | 78 |
| Carrollton, Ga., U.S. | C1 | 87 |
| Carrollton, Il., U.S. | D3 | 90 |
| Carrollton, Ky., U.S. | B4 | 94 |
| Carrollton, Mi., U.S. | E7 | 99 |
| Carrollton, Ms., U.S. | B4 | 101 |
| Carrollton, Mo., U.S. | B4 | 102 |
| Carrollton, Oh., U.S. | B4 | 112 |
| Carrollton, Tx., U.S. | *n10 | 120 |
| Carrolltown, Pa., U.S. | E4 | 115 |
| Carrollwood, Fl., U.S. | *E4 | 86 |
| Carron, stm., Scot., U.K. | D4 | 13 |
| Carron, Loch, b., Scot., U.K. | B4 | 10 |
| Carrot River, Sask. | D4 | 75 |
| Carrot, stm., Can. | D4 | 75 |
| Carrowmore Lake, l., Ire. | C2 | 11 |
| Carrsville, Ky., U.S. | e9 | 94 |
| Carruthers, Sask. | E1 | 75 |
| Carrville, Al., U.S. | C4 | 78 |
| Carry Falls Reservoir, res., N.Y., U.S. | f10 | 109 |
| Carrying Place, Ont. | C7 | 73 |
| Carşamba, Tur. | B11 | 40 |
| Carseland, Alta. | D4 | 68 |
| Carson, Ca., U.S. | *E4 | 82 |
| Carson, Ia., U.S. | C2 | 92 |
| Carson, Me., U.S. | B4 | 96 |
| Carson, Ms., U.S. | D4 | 101 |
| Carson, N.M., U.S. | A4 | 108 |
| Carson, N.D., U.S. | C4 | 111 |
| Carson, Va., U.S. | C5 | 123 |
| Carson, Wa., U.S. | D4 | 124 |
| Carson, co., Tx., U.S. | B2 | 120 |
| Carson, stm., Nv., U.S. | D2 | 105 |
| Carson City, Mi., U.S. | E6 | 99 |
| Carson City, Nv., U.S. | D2 | 105 |
| Carson Lake, l., Nv., U.S. | D3 | 105 |
| Carson Sink, l., Nv., U.S. | D3 | 105 |
| Carson Spring, Tn., U.S. | D10 | 119 |
| Carsonville, Mi., U.S. | E8 | 99 |
| Carstairs, Alta. | D3 | 68 |
| Carswell Air Force Base, mil., Tx., U.S. | n9 | 120 |
| Cartagena, Chile | A2 | 54 |
| Cartagena, Col. | A2 | 60 |
| Cartagena, Spain | D5 | 22 |
| Cartago, Col. | C2 | 60 |
| Cartago, C.R. | F8 | 63 |
| Carta Valley, Tx., U.S. | E2 | 120 |
| Cartaxo, Port. | C1 | 22 |
| Cartaya, Spain | D2 | 22 |
| Carter, Ky., U.S. | B6 | 94 |
| Carter, Mt., U.S. | C6 | 103 |
| Carter, Ok., U.S. | B2 | 113 |
| Carter, S.D., U.S. | D5 | 118 |
| Carter, Tn., U.S. | C11 | 119 |
| Carter, Wi., U.S. | C5 | 126 |
| Carter, co., Ky., U.S. | B6 | 94 |
| Carter, co., Mo., U.S. | E7 | 102 |
| Carter, co., Mt., U.S. | E12 | 103 |

| Carter, co., Ok., U.S. | C4 | 113 |
| Carter, co., Tn., U.S. | C11 | 119 |
| Carter Dome, mtn., N.H., U.S. | B4 | 106 |
| Carteret, N.J., U.S. | B4 | 107 |
| Carteret, co., N.C., U.S. | C6 | 110 |
| Carter Lake, Ia., U.S. | C2 | 92 |
| Carter Mountain, mtn., Wy., U.S. | B3 | 127 |
| Cartersburg, In., U.S. | E5 | 91 |
| Carters Lake, res., Ga., U.S. | B2 | 87 |
| Cartersville, Ga., U.S. | B2 | 87 |
| Cartersville, S.C., U.S. | C7 | 117 |
| Cartersville, Va., U.S. | C4 | 123 |
| Carterville, Il., U.S. | F4 | 90 |
| Carterville, Mo., U.S. | D3 | 102 |
| Carthage, Ar., U.S. | C3 | 81 |
| Carthage, Il., U.S. | C2 | 90 |
| Carthage, In., U.S. | E6 | 91 |
| Carthage, Ms., U.S. | C4 | 101 |
| Carthage, Mo., U.S. | D3 | 102 |
| Carthage, N.Y., U.S. | B5 | 109 |
| Carthage, N.C., U.S. | B3 | 110 |
| Carthage, S.D., U.S. | C8 | 118 |
| Carthage, Tn., U.S. | C8 | 119 |
| Carthage, Tx., U.S. | C5 | 120 |
| Carthage, hist., Tun. | B7 | 44 |
| Cartier, i., Austl. | B3 | 50 |
| Cartier, i., Austl. | B3 | 50 |
| Cartwright, Man. | E2 | 70 |
| Cartwright, Newf. | B3 | 72 |
| Cartwright, N.D., U.S. | B2 | 111 |
| Cartwright, Ok., U.S. | D5 | 113 |
| Caruaru, Braz. | C3 | 57 |
| Carúpano, Ven. | A5 | 60 |
| Caruthers, Ca., U.S. | D4 | 82 |
| Caruthersville, Mo., U.S. | E8 | 102 |
| Carver, Ma., U.S. | C6 | 98 |
| Carver, Mn., U.S. | F5 | 100 |
| Carver, co., Mn., U.S. | F5 | 100 |
| Carver Ranch Estates, Fl., U.S. | *r13 | 86 |
| Carville, La., U.S. | h9 | 95 |
| Carvin, Fr. | D2 | 17 |
| Cary, Ga., U.S. | D3 | 87 |
| Cary, Il., U.S. | A5 | 90 |
| Cary, Ms., U.S. | C3 | 101 |
| Cary, N.C., U.S. | B4 | 110 |
| Caryville, Fl., U.S. | u16 | 86 |
| Caryville, Tn., U.S. | C9 | 119 |
| Casa, Ar., U.S. | B2 | 81 |
| Casablanca, Mor. | C3 | 44 |
| Casa Blanca, N.M., U.S. | B2 | 108 |
| Casa Branca, Braz. | C3 | 56 |
| Casa de Oro, Ca., U.S. | *F5 | 82 |
| Casa Grande, Az., U.S. | E4 | 80 |
| Casa Grande National Monument, Az., U.S. | E4 | 80 |
| Casale Monferrato, Italy | B2 | 23 |
| Casalmaggiore, Italy | B3 | 23 |
| Casanare, dept., Col. | B3 | 60 |
| Casanare, stm., Col. | B3 | 60 |
| Casape, Italy | h9 | 23 |
| Casa Piedra, Tx., U.S. | p12 | 120 |
| Casar, N.C., U.S. | B1 | 110 |
| Casarano, Italy | D7 | 23 |
| Casas Adobes, Az., U.S. | E5 | 80 |
| Cascade, B.C. | E8 | 69 |
| Cascade, Co., U.S. | C6 | 83 |
| Cascade, Id., U.S. | E2 | 89 |
| Cascade, Ia., U.S. | B6 | 92 |
| Cascade, Mo., U.S. | D7 | 102 |
| Cascade, Mt., U.S. | C5 | 103 |
| Cascade, Va., U.S. | D3 | 123 |
| Cascade, Wi., U.S. | E5 | 126 |
| Cascade, co., Mt., U.S. | C5 | 103 |
| Cascade Locks, Or., U.S. | B5 | 114 |
| Cascade Point, c., N.Z. | O12 | 51 |
| Cascade Range, mts., N.A. | B3 | 76 |
| Cascade Reservoir, res., Id., U.S. | E3 | 89 |
| Cascade Summit, Or., U.S. | D4 | 114 |
| Cascade Tunnel, Wa., U.S. | B4 | 124 |
| Cascade Vista, Wa., U.S. | *B3 | 124 |
| Cascadia, Or., U.S. | C4 | 114 |
| Cascais, Port. | C1 | 22 |
| Cascais Bay, b., Port. | f9 | 22 |
| Cascajal, stm., Pan. | h11 | 62 |
| Cascavel, Braz. | C2 | 56 |
| Cascavel, Braz. | B3 | 57 |
| Cascilla, Ms., U.S. | B3 | 101 |
| Casco, Me., U.S. | D2 | 96 |
| Casco, Wi., U.S. | D6 | 126 |
| Casco Bay, b., Me., U.S. | E3 | 96 |
| Caselton, Nv., U.S. | F7 | 105 |
| Caserta, Italy | D5 | 23 |
| Caseville, Mi., U.S. | E7 | 99 |
| Casey, Il., U.S. | D6 | 90 |
| Casey, Ia., U.S. | C3 | 92 |
| Casey, co., Ky., U.S. | C5 | 94 |
| Casey, sci., Ant. | C24 | 7 |
| Casey Bay, b., Ant. | C17 | 7 |
| Casey Key, i., Fl., U.S. | E4 | 86 |
| Caseyr (Cape Guardafui), c., Som. | C7 | 47 |
| Cash, Ar., U.S. | B5 | 81 |
| Cashel, Ire. | C3 | 10 |
| Cashel, Ire. | D2 | 11 |
| Cashiers, N.C., U.S. | f9 | 110 |
| Cashion, Az., U.S. | m8 | 80 |
| Cashion, Ok., U.S. | B4 | 113 |
| Cashmere, Wa., U.S. | B5 | 124 |
| Cashton, Wi., U.S. | E3 | 126 |
| Cashtown, Pa., U.S. | G7 | 115 |
| Casiguran Sound, strt., Phil. | n14 | 34 |
| Casilda, Cuba | D4 | 64 |
| Casino, Austl. | D9 | 51 |
| Casiquiare, stm., Ven. | C4 | 60 |
| Casky, Ky., U.S. | D2 | 94 |
| Casma, Peru | C2 | 58 |
| Casmalia, Ca., U.S. | E3 | 82 |
| Caspar, Ca., U.S. | C2 | 82 |
| Caspe, Spain | B5 | 22 |
| Casper, Wy., U.S. | D6 | 127 |
| Caspian, La., U.S. | B2 | 95 |
| Caspian, Mi., U.S. | B2 | 99 |
| Caspiana, La., U.S. | B2 | 95 |
| Caspian Depression, pl., Sov. Un. | E8 | 29 |
| Caspian Lake, l., Vt., U.S. | B4 | 122 |
| Caspian Sea | E8 | 29 |
| Cass, In., U.S. | F3 | 91 |
| Cass, W.V., U.S. | C5 | 125 |
| Cass, co., Ia., U.S. | C3 | 92 |
| Cass, co., In., U.S. | C5 | 91 |
| Cass, co., Mi., U.S. | G4 | 99 |
| Cass, co., Mn., U.S. | D4 | 100 |
| Cass, co., Mo., U.S. | C3 | 102 |
| Cass, co., Ne., U.S. | D9 | 104 |
| Cass, co., N.D., U.S. | C8 | 111 |

| Cass, co., Tx., U.S. | C5 | 120 |
| Cass, stm., Mi., U.S. | E7 | 99 |
| Cassà [de la Selva], Spain | B7 | 22 |
| Cassai (Kasai), stm., Afr | D3 | 48 |
| Cass City, Mi., U.S. | E7 | 99 |
| Cassel, Fr. | D2 | 17 |
| Casselberry, Fl., U.S. | D5 | 86 |
| Cassel see Kassel, W. Ger. | C4 | 18 |
| Casselman, Ont. | B9 | 73 |
| Casselman, Pa., U.S. | G3 | 115 |
| Casselman, stm., U.S. | k12 | 97 |
| Casselton, N.D., U.S. | C8 | 111 |
| Cassia, co., Id., U.S. | G5 | 89 |
| Cassiar, B.C. | m17 | 69 |
| Cassiar Mountains, mts. Can. | E6 | 66 |
| Cassidy, B.C. | f12 | 69 |
| Cassilândia, Braz. | B2 | 56 |
| Cassinga, Ang. | E2 | 48 |
| Cassino, Italy | D4 | 23 |
| Cass Lake, Mn., U.S. | C4 | 100 |
| Cass Lake, l., Mn., U.S. | C4 | 100 |
| Cassoday, Ks., U.S. | D7 | 93 |
| Cassopolis, Mi., U.S. | G4 | 99 |
| Casstown, Oh., U.S. | B1 | 112 |
| Cassville, Ga., U.S. | B2 | 87 |
| Cassville, In., U.S. | C5 | 91 |
| Cassville, Mo., U.S. | E4 | 102 |
| Cassville, Wi., U.S. | F3 | 126 |
| Castalia, Ia., U.S. | A6 | 92 |
| Castalia, N.C., U.S. | A4 | 110 |
| Castalia, Oh., U.S. | A3 | 112 |
| Castalian Springs, Tn., U.S. | A5 | 119 |
| Castana, Ia., U.S. | B2 | 92 |
| Castanea, Pa., U.S. | D7 | 115 |
| Castanheira de Pêra, Po't. | C1 | 22 |
| Castaños, Mex. | B4 | 63 |
| Castel di Guido, Italy | h8 | 23 |
| Castelfranco Emilia, Italy | E7 | 20 |
| Castelfranco Veneto, Italy | D7 | 20 |
| Castel Gandolfo, Italy | h9 | 23 |
| Castel Giuliano, Italy | g8 | 23 |
| Casteljaloux, Fr. | E4 | 16 |
| Castella, Ca., U.S. | B2 | 82 |
| Castellamonte, Italy | D3 | 20 |
| Castellammare, Italy | B5 | 54 |
| Castellón de la Plana, Spain | C5 | 22 |
| Castel Madama, Italy | h9 | 23 |
| Castelnaudary, Fr. | F4 | 16 |
| Castelo, Braz. | C4 | 56 |
| Castelo Branco, Port. | C2 | 22 |
| Castelo de Vide, Port. | C2 | 22 |
| Castel San Pietro dell'Emilia, Italy | E7 | 20 |
| Castelsarrasin, Fr. | E4 | 16 |
| Castelvetrano, Italy | F4 | 23 |
| Casterton, Austl. | H3 | 51 |
| Castile, N.Y., U.S. | C2 | 109 |
| Castile, hist. reg., Spain | B3 | 22 |
| Castilla, Pampa del, pl., Arg. | D3 | 54 |
| Castillo de San Marcos National Monument, Fl., U.S. | n9 | 86 |
| Castillos, Ur. | E2 | 56 |
| Castine, Me., U.S. | D4 | 96 |
| Castione [della Presolana], Italy | E9 | 21 |
| Castle, Ok., U.S. | B5 | 113 |
| Castle Air Force Base, mil., Ca., U.S. | D3 | 82 |
| Castlebar, Ire. | D2 | 10 |
| Castlebay, Scot., U.K. | D1 | 13 |
| Castlebellingham, Ire. | D5 | 11 |
| Castleberry, Al., U.S. | D2 | 78 |
| Castleblayney, Ire. | C5 | 11 |
| Castlecomer, Ire. | E4 | 11 |
| Castle Dale, Ut., U.S. | D4 | 121 |
| Castlederg, N. Ire., U.K. | C4 | 11 |
| Castle Dome Mountains, mts., Az., U.S. | D1 | 80 |
| Castle Dome Peak, mtn., Az., U.S. | D1 | 80 |
| Castle Douglas, Scot., U.K. | C4 | 11 |
| Castlefinn, Ire. | C4 | 11 |
| Castleford, Id., U.S. | G4 | 89 |
| Castlegar, B.C. | E9 | 69 |
| Castlegregory, Ire. | E1 | 11 |
| Castle Harbour, b., Ber. | o20 | 64 |
| Castle Hayne, N.C., U.S. | C5 | 110 |
| Castle Hills, De., U.S. | i7 | 85 |
| Castle Hot Springs, Az., U.S. | D3 | 80 |
| Castleisland, Ire. | D1 | 11 |
| Castlemaine, Austl. | H5 | 51 |
| Castlemaine, Ire. | D1 | 11 |
| Castlemartyr, Ire. | F3 | 11 |
| Castle Mountain, mtn., Yukon | D5 | 66 |
| Castle Mountains, mts., Mt., U.S. | D6 | 103 |
| Castle Park, Ca., U.S. | *o15 | 82 |
| Castle Peak, mtn., Co., U.S. | B4 | 83 |
| Castle Peak, mtn., Id., U.S. | E4 | 89 |
| Castle Point, Mo., U.S. | f13 | 102 |
| Castlepollard, Ire. | D4 | 11 |
| Castlerea, Ire. | D3 | 11 |
| Castlereagh, N. Ire., U.K. | *C6 | 11 |
| Castlereagh, stm., Austl. | E7 | 51 |
| Castle Rock, Co., U.S. | B6 | 83 |
| Castle Rock, Wa., U.S. | F5 | 100 |
| Castle Rock, mtn., Or., U.S. | C3 | 124 |
| Castle Rock, mtn., Or., U.S. | C5 | 114 |
| Castle Rock, mtn., U.S. | C4 | 123 |
| Castle Rock Butte, mtn., S.D., U.S. | B2 | 118 |
| Castle Rock Lake, res., Wi., U.S. | E4 | 126 |
| Castle Shannon, Pa., U.S. | *k13 | 115 |
| Castleton, Ont. | C7 | 73 |
| Castleton, Jam. | E15 | 65 |
| Castleton, Il., U.S. | C4 | 90 |
| Castleton, Ks., U.S. | g11 | 93 |
| Castleton on Hudson, N.Y., U.S. | C7 | 109 |
| Castleton, I. of Man | F4 | 13 |
| Castleton Geoghegan, Ire. | D4 | 11 |
| Castletown, Jam. | E3 | 11 |
| Castletownroche, Ire. | E3 | 11 |
| Castletownshend, N. Ire., U.K. | C6 | 11 |
| Castlewood, S.D., U.S. | C8 | 118 |
| Castlewood, Va., U.S. | f9 | 123 |
| Castor, Alta. | C5 | 68 |
| Castor, La., U.S. | B2 | 95 |
| Castor, stm., Mo., U.S. | D7 | 102 |
| Castor Creek, stm., La., U.S. | C3 | 95 |
| Castorland, N.Y., U.S. | B5 | 109 |
| Castres, Fr. | E5 | 16 |
| Castries [St. Luc.] | J14 | 64 |
| Castro, Chile | C2 | 54 |
| Castro, Braz. | B2 | 56 |
| Castro, co., Tx., U.S. | B1 | 120 |
| Castro Alves, Braz. | B4 | 57 |
| Castro Daire, Port. | C2 | 22 |
| Castro [del Río], Spain | D3 | 22 |
| Castro Marim, Port. | D2 | 22 |
| Castropol, Spain | A2 | 22 |
| Castrop-Rauxel, W. Ger. | *C3 | 18 |
| Castro Urdiales, Spain | A4 | 22 |

| Castro Valley, Ca., U.S. | h8 | 82 |
| Castro Verde, Port. | D1 | 22 |
| Castrovillari, Italy | E6 | 23 |
| Castroville, Ca., U.S. | D3 | 82 |
| Castroville, Tx., U.S. | E3 | 120 |
| Castrovirreyna, Peru | D2 | 58 |
| Castuera, Spain | C3 | 22 |
| Caswell, co., N.C., U.S. | A3 | 110 |
| Catacamas, Hond. | E7 | 63 |
| Cataguases, Braz. | C4 | 56 |
| Cataingan, Phil. | C4 | 34 |
| Catalão, Braz. | B3 | 56 |
| Çatalca, Tur. | B7 | 40 |
| Catalina, Newf. | D5 | 72 |
| Catalina, Chile | E2 | 55 |
| Catalina Foothills, Az., U.S. | *E5 | 80 |
| Catalonia, hist. reg., Spain | B6 | 22 |
| Catamarca, Arg. | E2 | 55 |
| Catamarca, prov., Arg. | E2 | 55 |
| Catamayo, Ec. | B2 | 58 |
| Catanauan, Phil. | p14 | 34 |
| Catanduanes, i., Phil. | C6 | 34 |
| Catanduva, Braz. | C3 | 56 |
| Catania, Italy | F5 | 23 |
| Catania, Gulf of, b., Italy | F5 | 23 |
| Catanzaro, Italy | E6 | 23 |
| Cataouatche, Lake, l., La., U.S. | k11 | 95 |
| Cataract, In., U.S. | F4 | 91 |
| Cataract, Wi., U.S. | D3 | 126 |
| Cataract Canyon, val., Ut., U.S. | F5 | 121 |
| Catarroja, Spain | C5 | 22 |
| Catasauqua, Pa., U.S. | E11 | 115 |
| Catastrophe, Cape, c., Austl. | F6 | 50 |
| Cataula, Ga., U.S. | D2 | 87 |
| Cataumet, Ma., U.S. | C6 | 98 |
| Catawba, N.C., U.S. | B1 | 110 |
| Catawba, S.C., U.S. | B6 | 117 |
| Catawba, Va., U.S. | C2 | 123 |
| Catawba, Wi., U.S. | C3 | 126 |
| Catawba, co., N.C., U.S. | B1 | 110 |
| Catawba, stm., S.C., U.S. | B6 | 117 |
| Catawba, South Fork, stm., N.C., U.S. | B1 | 110 |
| Catawba Island, Oh., U.S. | A3 | 112 |
| Catawissa, Pa., U.S. | E9 | 115 |
| Cat Ba, i., Viet. | B7 | 35 |
| Catbalogan, Phil. | C6 | 34 |
| Cat Creek, stm., Al., U.S. | C8 | 103 |
| Cateechee, S.C., U.S. | B2 | 117 |
| Cater, Sask. | D1 | 75 |
| Cates, In., U.S. | E3 | 91 |
| Catete, Ang. | C1 | 48 |
| Cathance, Lake, l., Me., U.S. | D5 | 96 |
| Catharine, Ks., U.S. | D4 | 93 |
| Cathay, N.D., U.S. | B6 | 111 |
| Cathedral Bluffs, clf., Co., U.S. | B2 | 83 |
| Cathedral Caverns, Al., U.S. | A3 | 78 |
| Cathedral City, Ca., U.S. | F5 | 82 |
| Cathedral Mountain, mtn., Tx., U.S. | o13 | 120 |
| Cathedral of the Pines, N.H., U.S. | E3 | 106 |
| Catherine, Al., U.S. | C2 | 78 |
| Catherine, Lake, res., Ar., U.S. | C3 | 81 |
| Cathlamet, Wa., U.S. | C2 | 124 |
| Cat Island, i., Bah. | B6 | 64 |
| Cat Island, i., Ms., U.S. | E4 | 101 |
| Cat Island, i., S.C., U.S. | E9 | 117 |
| Cativá, Pan. | k11 | 62 |
| Catlettsburg, Ky., U.S. | B7 | 94 |
| Catlin, Il., U.S. | C6 | 90 |
| Catlin, In., U.S. | E3 | 91 |
| Catnip Mountain, mtn., Nv., U.S. | B2 | 105 |
| Cato, N.Y., U.S. | B4 | 109 |
| Catoche, Cabo, c., Mex. | C7 | 63 |
| Catoctin Mountain, mtn., U.S. | B2 | 97 |
| Catonsville, Md., U.S. | B4 | 97 |
| Catoosa, co., Ga., U.S. | B1 | 87 |
| Catoosa, Ok., U.S. | A6 | 113 |
| Catrilo, Arg. | B3 | 54 |
| Catrimani, Braz. | B2 | 59 |
| Catrimani, stm., Braz. | B2 | 59 |
| Catron, Mo., U.S. | E7 | 102 |
| Catron, co., N.M., U.S. | D1 | 108 |
| Catskill, N.Y., U.S. | C7 | 109 |
| Catskill Mountains, mts., N.Y., U.S. | C6 | 109 |
| Catt, Mount, mtn., B.C. | C6 | 69 |
| Cattaraugus, N.Y., U.S. | C2 | 109 |
| Cattaraugus, co., N.Y., U.S. | C2 | 109 |
| Cattaraugus Creek, stm., N.Y., U.S. | C2 | 109 |
| Cattaraugus Indian Reservation, N.Y., U.S. | C2 | 109 |
| Cattolica, Italy | C4 | 23 |
| Catumbela, stm., Ang. | D1 | 48 |
| Catwick, Îles is., Viet. | G8 | 35 |
| Caubvick, Mount (Mont d'Iberville), mtn., Can. | f9 | 72 |
| Cauca, dept., Col. | B2 | 60 |
| Cauca, stm., Col. | B2 | 60 |
| Caucaia, Col. | B2 | 60 |
| Caucasus Mountains, mts., Sov. Un. | E7 | 29 |
| Cauchon Lake, l., Man. | B3 | 70 |
| Caucomgomoc Lake, l., Me., U.S. | B3 | 96 |
| Caudebec, Fr. | C7 | 16 |
| Caudete, Spain | C5 | 22 |
| Caudry, Fr. | B5 | 16 |
| Caughnawaga, Que. | D4 | 74 |
| Caulfield, Mo., U.S. | E5 | 102 |
| Caungula, Ang. | C2 | 48 |
| Caúngula, Ang. | C2 | 48 |
| Cauquenes, Chile | B2 | 54 |
| Caura, stm., Ven. | B5 | 60 |
| Causey, N.M., U.S. | C6 | 108 |
| Caussade, Fr. | E4 | 16 |
| Cauthron, Ar., U.S. | B1 | 81 |
| Caution, Cape, c., B.C. | D4 | 69 |
| Cauto, stm., Cuba | D5 | 64 |
| Cauvery, stm., India | F5 | 36 |
| Cávado, stm., Port. | C1 | 22 |
| Cavaillon, Fr. | F6 | 16 |
| Cavalcante, Braz. | B3 | 57 |
| Cavalier, N.D., U.S. | A8 | 111 |
| Cavalier, co., N.D., U.S. | A7 | 111 |
| Cavalla, stm., Afr. | H5 | 45 |
| Cavan, Ire. | C4 | 11 |
| Cavan, co., Ire. | C4 | 11 |
| Cavarzere, Italy | D7 | 20 |
| Cave, Italy | h9 | 23 |
| Cave City, Ar., U.S. | B4 | 81 |

| Cave City, Ky., U.S. | C4 | 94 |
| Cave Creek, Az., U.S. | D4 | 80 |
| Cave In Rock, Il., U.S. | F5 | 90 |
| Cave Junction, Or., U.S. | E3 | 114 |
| Cavell, Sask. | D5 | 75 |
| Cavendish, Alta. | C2 | 89 |
| Cavendish, Vt., U.S. | E3 | 122 |
| Cave Point, c., Wi., U.S. | D6 | 126 |
| Cave Run Lake, res., Ky., U.S. | B6 | 94 |
| Cave Spring, Braz. | B1 | 87 |
| Cave Spring, Va., U.S. | C2 | 123 |
| Cave Springs, Ar., U.S. | A1 | 81 |
| Cavetown, Md., U.S. | A2 | 97 |
| Caviana, Ilha i., Braz. | B4 | 59 |
| Cavite, Phil. | o13 | 34 |
| Cavour, S.D., U.S. | C7 | 118 |
| Cavour, Wi., U.S. | C5 | 126 |
| Cawdor, Scot., U.K. | C5 | 13 |
| Cawker City, Ks., U.S. | C5 | 93 |
| Cawood, Ky., U.S. | D6 | 94 |
| Cawston, B.C. | E8 | 69 |
| Caxias, Braz. | B3 | 57 |
| Caxias do Sul, Braz. | D2 | 56 |
| Caxito, Ang. | C1 | 48 |
| Cayambe, Ec. | A2 | 58 |
| Cayambe, vol., Ec. | A2 | 58 |
| Cayce, Ky., U.S. | f8 | 94 |
| Cayce, S.C., U.S. | D5 | 117 |
| Cayenne, Fr. Gu. | B4 | 59 |
| Cayenne, ter., Fr. Gu. | B4 | 59 |
| Cayeux-sur-Mer, Fr. | D9 | 17 |
| Cayey, P.R. | G11 | 64 |
| Cayey, Sierra de, mts., P.R. | B3 | 65 |
| Cayley, Alta. | D4 | 68 |
| Caylus, Fr. | E4 | 16 |
| Cayman Brac, i., Cay. Is. | E6 | 64 |
| Cayman Islands, dep., N.A. | D8 | 63 |
| Caynabo, Som. | D6 | 47 |
| Cay Point, c., Bah. | n17 | 64 |
| Cayuga, Ont. | E5 | 73 |
| Cayuga, In., U.S. | E3 | 91 |
| Cayuga, Ms., U.S. | C3 | 101 |
| Cayuga, N.D., U.S. | C8 | 111 |
| Cayuga, co., N.Y., U.S. | C4 | 109 |
| Cayuga Heights, N.Y., U.S. | C4 | 109 |
| Cayuga Lake, l., N.Y., U.S. | C4 | 109 |
| Cayuse, Or., U.S. | B8 | 114 |
| Cazalla de la Sierra, Spain | D3 | 22 |
| Cazaux, Étang de, b., Fr. | E3 | 16 |
| Cazenovia, N.Y., U.S. | C5 | 109 |
| Cazenovia, Wi., U.S. | E3 | 126 |
| Cazombo, Ang. | D3 | 48 |
| Cazorla, Spain | D4 | 22 |
| Cea, stm., Spain | A3 | 22 |
| Ceanannus Mór (Kells), Ire. | D5 | 11 |
| Ceará, state, Braz. | B3 | 57 |
| Ceará Mirim, Braz. | B3 | 57 |
| Ceará-Mirim, stm., Braz. | g6 | 57 |
| Cebolla, N.M., U.S. | A3 | 108 |
| Cebolla Creek, stm., Co., U.S. | C3 | 83 |
| Cebollar, Arg. | E2 | 55 |
| Cebollati, stm., Ur. | E2 | 56 |
| Cebreros, Spain | B3 | 22 |
| Cebu, Phil. | C6 | 34 |
| Cebu, i., Phil. | C6 | 34 |
| Cecil, Al., U.S. | C3 | 78 |
| Cecil, Ga., U.S. | E3 | 87 |
| Cecil, Oh., U.S. | A1 | 112 |
| Cecil, Pa., U.S. | F1 | 115 |
| Cecil, Wi., U.S. | D5 | 126 |
| Cecil, co., Md., U.S. | A6 | 97 |
| Cecil Field Naval Air Station, mil., Fl., U.S. | B5 | 86 |
| Cecilia, Ky., U.S. | C4 | 94 |
| Cecilton, Md., U.S. | B6 | 97 |
| Cecina, Italy | C3 | 23 |
| Cedar, Ks., U.S. | C5 | 93 |
| Cedar, Mi., U.S. | D5 | 99 |
| Cedar, Mn., U.S. | E5 | 100 |
| Cedar, co., Ia., U.S. | C6 | 92 |
| Cedar, co., Mo., U.S. | D4 | 102 |
| Cedar, co., Ne., U.S. | B8 | 104 |
| Cedar, stm., U.S. | A4 | 128 |
| Cedar, stm., Ia., U.S. | B5 | 92 |
| Cedar, stm., Ne., U.S. | B7 | 104 |
| Cedar, stm., Wa., U.S. | f11 | 124 |
| Cedar Bluff, Al., U.S. | A4 | 78 |
| Cedar Bluff, Va., U.S. | C2 | 94 |
| Cedarbluff, Ms., U.S. | B5 | 101 |
| Cedar Bluff, Tn., U.S. | D9 | 119 |
| Cedar Bluff Reservoir, res., Ks., U.S. | D4 | 93 |
| Cedar Bluffs, Ks., U.S. | C3 | 93 |
| Cedar Bluffs, Ne., U.S. | C9 | 104 |
| Cedar Breaks National Monument, Ut., U.S. | F3 | 121 |
| Cedarburg, Wi., U.S. | E6 | 126 |
| Cedarbutte, S.D., U.S. | D4 | 118 |
| Cedar City, Mo., U.S. | C6 | 102 |
| Cedar City, Ut., U.S. | F2 | 121 |
| Cedar Creek, Az., U.S. | D5 | 80 |
| Cedarcreek, Mo., U.S. | e7 | 112 |
| Cedar Creek, stm., Co., U.S. | A7 | 83 |
| Cedar Creek, stm., In., U.S. | B7 | 91 |
| Cedar Creek, stm., N.D., U.S. | D6 | 92 |
| Cedar Creek, stm., Mo., U.S. | C5 | 102 |
| Cedar Creek, stm., Oh., U.S. | e7 | 112 |
| Cedar Creek Lake, res., Tx., U.S. | C4 | 120 |
| Cedar Crest, N.M., U.S. | k8 | 108 |
| Cedaredge, Co., U.S. | C3 | 83 |
| Cedar Falls, Ia., U.S. | B5 | 92 |
| Cedar Gap, Mo., U.S. | F8 | 91 |
| Cedar Grove, N.J., U.S. | B4 | 107 |
| Cedar Grove, W.V., U.S. | C3 | 125 |
| Cedar Hill, Mo., U.S. | g12 | 102 |
| Cedar Hill, N.M., U.S. | A5 | 108 |
| Cedar Hills, Or., U.S. | *h12 | 114 |
| Cedarhurst, N.Y., U.S. | k13 | 109 |
| Cedar Island, N.C., U.S. | C6 | 110 |
| Cedar Island, i., S.C., U.S. | E9 | 117 |
| Cedar Island, i., Va., U.S. | C7 | 123 |
| Cedar Key, Fl., U.S. | C3 | 86 |
| Cedar Keys, is., Fl., U.S. | C3 | 86 |
| Cedar Knolls, N.J., U.S. | B4 | 107 |
| Cedar Lake, l., Ont. | A6 | 73 |
| Cedar Lake, l., Man. | C1 | 70 |
| Cedar Lake, res., Il., U.S. | F4 | 90 |
| Cedar Lake, Mn., U.S. | C3 | 100 |
| Cedar Mountain, mtn., Ca., U.S. | B3 | 82 |
| Cedar Mountains, mts., Ut., U.S. | C2 | 121 |
| Cedar Point, Il., U.S. | B4 | 90 |

| Name | Map Ref. | Page |
|---|---|---|
| Cedar Point, Ks., U.S. | D7 | 93 |
| Cedar Point, c., Md., U.S. | D5 | 97 |
| Cedar Point, c., Oh., U.S. | A3 | 112 |
| Cedar Point, c., Oh., U.S. | e7 | 112 |
| Cedar Rapids, Ia., U.S. | C6 | 92 |
| Cedar Rapids, Ne., U.S. | C7 | 104 |
| Cedar River, Mi., U.S. | C3 | 99 |
| Cedar Run, N.J., U.S. | D4 | 107 |
| Cedar Springs, Ont. | E2 | 73 |
| Cedar Springs, Ga., U.S. | E1 | 87 |
| Cedar Springs, Mi., U.S. | E5 | 99 |
| Cedar Swamp, sw., Ma., U.S. | f11 | 98 |
| Cedartown, Ga., U.S. | B1 | 87 |
| Cedarvale, B.C. | B3 | 69 |
| Cedarvale, N.M., U.S. | C4 | 108 |
| Cedar Vale, Ks., U.S. | E7 | 93 |
| Cedar Valley, Ut., U.S. | C3 | 121 |
| Cedarville, Ar., U.S. | B1 | 81 |
| Cedarville, Ca., U.S. | B3 | 82 |
| Cedarville, Il., U.S. | A4 | 90 |
| Cedarville, In., U.S. | B7 | 91 |
| Cedarville, Ma., U.S. | *C6 | 98 |
| Cedarville, N.J., U.S. | E2 | 107 |
| Cedarville, N.Y., U.S. | C5 | 109 |
| Cedarville, Oh., U.S. | C2 | 112 |
| Cedoux, Sask. | H4 | 75 |
| Cedros, Hond. | C4 | 62 |
| Cedros, Isla, i., Mex. | B1 | 63 |
| Ceduna, Austl. | F5 | 50 |
| Ceel Buur, Som. | E6 | 47 |
| Ceel Xamurre, Som. | D6 | 47 |
| Ceepeecee, B.C. | E4 | 69 |
| Ceerigaabo, Som. | C6 | 47 |
| Cefalù, Italy | E5 | 23 |
| Cega, stm., Spain | B4 | 22 |
| Cegléd, Hung. | B4 | 24 |
| Ceglie Messapico, Italy | D6 | 23 |
| Cehegín, Spain | C5 | 22 |
| Čelákovice, Czech. | n18 | 26 |
| Celaya, Mex. | m13 | 63 |
| Celebes (Sulawesi), i., Indon. | F6 | 34 |
| Celebes Sea, Asia | E6 | 34 |
| Celendín, Peru | C2 | 58 |
| Celestine, In., U.S. | H4 | 91 |
| Celica, Ec. | B2 | 58 |
| Celina, Oh., U.S. | B1 | 112 |
| Celina, Tn., U.S. | C8 | 119 |
| Celina, Tx., U.S. | C4 | 120 |
| Celje, Yugo. | B2 | 24 |
| Celle, W. Ger. | B5 | 18 |
| Cellina, stm., Italy | C8 | 20 |
| Celoron, N.Y., U.S. | C1 | 109 |
| Celriver, S.C., U.S. | B6 | 117 |
| Celtic Sea, Eur. | F5 | 11 |
| Cemaes Head, c., Wales, U.K. | B3 | 12 |
| Cement, Ok., U.S. | C3 | 113 |
| Cement City, Mi., U.S. | F6 | 99 |
| Cementon, Pa., U.S. | E10 | 115 |
| Çemişgezek, Tur. | C12 | 40 |
| Cenon, Fr. | E3 | 16 |
| Centenary, S.C., U.S. | C9 | 117 |
| Centennial, Wy., U.S. | E7 | 127 |
| Centennial Lake, res., Ont. | B7 | 73 |
| Centennial Mountains, mts., Id., U.S. | E7 | 89 |
| Center, Co., U.S. | D4 | 83 |
| Center, Ga., U.S. | B3 | 87 |
| Center, In., U.S. | D5 | 91 |
| Center, Ky., U.S. | C4 | 94 |
| Center, Mo., U.S. | B6 | 102 |
| Center, N.D., U.S. | B8 | 104 |
| Center, Ok., U.S. | C5 | 113 |
| Center, Tx., U.S. | D5 | 120 |
| Center Barnstead, N.H., U.S. | D4 | 106 |
| Centerbrook, Ct., U.S. | D6 | 84 |
| Centerburg, Oh., U.S. | B3 | 112 |
| Center City, Mn., U.S. | E6 | 100 |
| Center City, Tx., U.S. | D3 | 120 |
| Center Conway, N.H., U.S. | C4 | 106 |
| Center Cross, Va., U.S. | C6 | 123 |
| Centereach, N.Y., U.S. | n15 | 109 |
| Center Effingham, N.H., U.S. | C4 | 106 |
| Centerfield, Ut., U.S. | D4 | 121 |
| Center Harbor, N.H., U.S. | C4 | 106 |
| Center Hill, Ar., U.S. | B4 | 81 |
| Center Hill, Fl., U.S. | D5 | 86 |
| Center Hill Lake, res., Tn., U.S. | C8 | 119 |
| Center Junction, Ia., U.S. | B6 | 92 |
| Center Line, Mi., U.S. | *p15 | 99 |
| Center Lovell, Me., U.S. | D2 | 96 |
| Center Montville, Me., U.S. | D3 | 96 |
| Center Moreland, Pa., U.S. | m17 | 115 |
| Center Moriches, N.Y., U.S. | n16 | 109 |
| Center Mountain, mtn., Id., U.S. | D3 | 89 |
| Center Ossipee, N.H., U.S. | C4 | 106 |
| Center Point, Al., U.S. | f7 | 78 |
| Center Point, Ar., U.S. | C2 | 81 |
| Centerpoint, In., U.S. | F3 | 91 |
| Center Point, Ia., U.S. | B6 | 92 |
| Center Point, La., U.S. | C3 | 95 |
| Center Point, S.D., U.S. | D8 | 118 |
| Center Point, Tx., U.S. | E3 | 120 |
| Center Point, W.V., U.S. | B4 | 125 |
| Center Ridge, Ar., U.S. | B3 | 81 |
| Center Rutland, Vt., U.S. | D2 | 122 |
| Center Sandwich, N.H., U.S. | C4 | 106 |
| Center Square, N.J., U.S. | D2 | 107 |
| Center Star, Al., U.S. | A2 | 78 |
| Center Strafford, N.H., U.S. | D4 | 106 |
| Centerton, Ar., U.S. | A1 | 81 |
| Centerton, In., U.S. | E5 | 91 |
| Centerton, N.J., U.S. | D2 | 107 |
| Centertown, Ky., U.S. | C3 | 94 |
| Centertown, Mo., U.S. | C5 | 102 |
| Centertown, Tn., U.S. | D8 | 119 |
| Center Tuftonboro, N.H., U.S. | C4 | 106 |
| Centerview, Mo., U.S. | C4 | 102 |
| Centerville, De., U.S. | A3 | 85 |
| Centerville, Ga., U.S. | E8 | 91 |
| Centerville, Ia., U.S. | D5 | 92 |
| Centerville, Ks., U.S. | E8 | 93 |
| Centerville, La., U.S. | E4 | 95 |
| Centerville, Ma., U.S. | C7 | 98 |
| Centerville, Mo., U.S. | D7 | 102 |
| Centerville, Nv., U.S. | *E2 | 105 |
| Centerville, Oh., U.S. | C1 | 112 |
| Centerville, Pa., U.S. | F2 | 115 |
| Centerville, R.I., U.S. | E2 | 116 |
| Centerville, S.D., U.S. | D9 | 118 |
| Centerville, Tn., U.S. | B4 | 119 |
| Centerville, Tx., U.S. | D5 | 120 |
| Centerville, Ut., U.S. | C4 | 121 |
| Centerville, Wa., U.S. | D5 | 124 |
| Cento, Italy | E7 | 20 |
| Centrahoma, Ok., U.S. | C5 | 113 |
| Central, Al., U.S. | C3 | 78 |
| Central, Az., U.S. | E6 | 80 |
| Central, In., U.S. | H5 | 91 |
| Central, N.M., U.S. | E1 | 108 |
| Central, S.C., U.S. | B2 | 117 |
| Central, Ut., U.S. | F2 | 121 |
| Central, prov., Ghana | E4 | 45 |
| Central, prov., Kenya | B6 | 48 |
| Central, prov., Mwi. | D5 | 48 |
| Central, prov., Scot., U.K. | D4 | 13 |
| Central, prov., Zam. | E4 | 48 |
| Central, dept., Para. | E4 | 55 |
| Central, Cordillera, mts., Col. | C2 | 60 |
| Central, Cordillera, mts., C.R. | E5 | 62 |
| Central, Cordillera, mts., Dom. Rep. | E8 | 64 |
| Central, Cordillera, mts., P.R. | B2 | 65 |
| Central African Republic, ctry., Afr. | D4 | 46 |
| Central Barren, In., U.S. | H5 | 91 |
| Central Bridge, N.Y., U.S. | C6 | 109 |
| Central Butte, Sask. | G2 | 75 |
| Central City, Co., U.S. | B5 | 83 |
| Central City, Il., U.S. | E4 | 90 |
| Central City, Ia., U.S. | B6 | 92 |
| Central City, Ky., U.S. | C2 | 94 |
| Central City, Ne., U.S. | C7 | 104 |
| Central City, Pa., U.S. | F4 | 115 |
| Central City, S.D., U.S. | C2 | 118 |
| Central Falls, R.I., U.S. | B4 | 116 |
| Centralhatchee, Ga., U.S. | C1 | 87 |
| Central Heights, Az., U.S. | D5 | 80 |
| Centralia, Ont. | D3 | 73 |
| Centralia, Il., U.S. | E4 | 90 |
| Centralia, Ks., U.S. | C7 | 93 |
| Centralia, Mo., U.S. | B5 | 102 |
| Centralia, Ok., U.S. | A6 | 113 |
| Centralia, Wa., U.S. | C3 | 124 |
| Centralia, W.V., U.S. | C4 | 125 |
| Centralina, Braz. | B3 | 56 |
| Central Islip, N.Y., U.S. | n15 | 109 |
| Central Lake, Mi., U.S. | C5 | 99 |
| Central Makrān Range, mts., Pak. | C3 | 36 |
| Central Park, Wa., U.S. | C2 | 124 |
| Central Point, Or., U.S. | E4 | 114 |
| Central Range, mts., Pap. N. Gui. | h11 | 50 |
| Central Range, hills, Trin. | O23 | 65 |
| Central Siberian Uplands, plat., Sov. Un. | C13 | 29 |
| Central Square, N.Y., U.S. | B4 | 109 |
| Central Valley, Ca., U.S. | B2 | 82 |
| Central Valley, N.Y., U.S. | D6 | 109 |
| Central Village, Ct., U.S. | C8 | 84 |
| Central Village, Ma., U.S. | C5 | 98 |
| Centre, co., Pa., U.S. | E6 | 115 |
| Centre City, N.J., U.S. | D2 | 107 |
| Centre Hall, Pa., U.S. | E6 | 115 |
| Centre Peak, mtn., B.C. | B4 | 69 |
| Centreville, N.B. | C2 | 71 |
| Centreville, N.S. | E3 | 71 |
| Centreville, Al., U.S. | C2 | 78 |
| Centreville, Il., U.S. | E3 | 90 |
| Centreville, Md., U.S. | B5 | 97 |
| Centreville, Mi., U.S. | G5 | 99 |
| Centreville, Ms., U.S. | D2 | 101 |
| Centreville, Va., U.S. | *B5 | 123 |
| Centropolis, Ks., U.S. | D8 | 93 |
| Centuria, Wi., U.S. | C1 | 126 |
| Century, Fl., U.S. | u14 | 86 |
| Century, W.V., U.S. | B4 | 125 |
| Century Village, Fl., U.S. | *F6 | 86 |
| Cephalonia see Kefallinía, i., Grc. | C3 | 40 |
| Cephisus see Kifisós, stm., Grc. | g9 | 25 |
| Ceram, i., Indon. | F7 | 34 |
| Ceram Sea, Indon. | F7 | 34 |
| Cerbat Mountains, mts., Az., U.S. | B1 | 80 |
| Čerčany, Czech. | o18 | 26 |
| Cereal, Alta. | D5 | 68 |
| Cereales, Arg. | B4 | 54 |
| Ceredo, W.V., U.S. | C2 | 125 |
| Ceres, Braz. | B5 | 56 |
| Ceres, Italy | D3 | 20 |
| Ceres, Ca., U.S. | D3 | 82 |
| Ceres, N.Y., U.S. | C2 | 109 |
| Ceres, Ok., U.S. | A4 | 113 |
| Ceres, Va., U.S. | C1 | 123 |
| Ceres, Ne., U.S. | C9 | 117 |
| Céret, Fr. | F5 | 16 |
| Cereté, Col. | B2 | 60 |
| Cerignola, Italy | D5 | 23 |
| Cerknica, Yugo. | C2 | 24 |
| Cernavodă, Rom. | C9 | 24 |
| Cernay, Fr. | D7 | 16 |
| Cerralvo, Mex. | B5 | 63 |
| Cerralvo, Isla, i., Mex. | C3 | 63 |
| Cërriku, Alb. | B2 | 25 |
| Cerrillos, N.M., U.S. | B3 | 108 |
| Cerritos, Mex. | C4 | 63 |
| Cerritos, Ca., U.S. | *E4 | 82 |
| Cerro, N.M., U.S. | A4 | 108 |
| Cerro Alto Mountain, mtn., Tx., U.S. | o12 | 120 |
| Cerro Azul, Peru | E1 | 58 |
| Cerro Colorado, Ur. | E1 | 54 |
| Cerro de Pasco, Peru | D2 | 58 |
| Cerro Gordo, Il., U.S. | D5 | 90 |
| Cerro Gordo, N.C., U.S. | C4 | 110 |
| Cerro Gordo, co., Ia., U.S. | A4 | 92 |
| Cêrro Largo, Braz. | D2 | 56 |
| Cerulean, Ky., U.S. | D2 | 94 |
| Cervera del Río Alhama, Spain | A5 | 22 |
| Cerveteri, Italy | g8 | 23 |
| Cervignano del Friuli, Italy | D9 | 20 |
| Cervione, Fr. | C2 | 23 |
| Cesar, dept., Col. | B3 | 60 |
| Cesena, Italy | E6 | 20 |
| Cesenatico, Italy | E7 | 20 |
| Česká Kamenice, Czech. | C9 | 19 |
| Česká Lípa, Czech. | D4 | 26 |
| České Budějovice, Czech. | D3 | 26 |
| Český Brod, Czech. | n18 | 26 |
| Český Krumlov, Czech. | D3 | 26 |
| Çeşme, Tur. | C6 | 25 |
| Cessnock, Austl. | F9 | 50 |
| Cestos, stm., Lib. | E3 | 45 |
| Cetina, stm., Yugo. | C3 | 24 |
| Cetinje, Yugo. | D3 | 24 |
| Cetraro, Italy | E6 | 23 |
| Cetti Bay, b., Guam | M9 | 52 |
| Ceuta, Sp. N. Afr. | B3 | 44 |
| Cévennes, reg., Fr. | E5 | 16 |
| Cevio, Switz. | C4 | 20 |
| Ceyhan, Tur. | *D10 | 40 |
| Ceyhan, stm., Tur. | D11 | 40 |
| Ceylon, Ont. | C4 | 73 |
| Ceylon, Sask. | H3 | 75 |
| Ceylon, In., U.S. | C8 | 91 |
| Ceylon, Mn., U.S. | G4 | 100 |
| Ceylon see Sri Lanka, ctry., Asia | G7 | 36 |
| Chabařovice, Czech. | C8 | 19 |
| Chacabuco, Arg. | A4 | 54 |
| Chacachacare, i., Trin. | N22 | 65 |
| Chachapoyas, Peru | C2 | 58 |
| Chachoengsao, Thai. | F4 | 35 |
| Cháchro, Pak. | E3 | 37 |
| Chaco, prov., Arg. | E3 | 55 |
| Chaco, dept., Para. | D3 | 55 |
| Chaco, stm., N.M., U.S. | A1 | 108 |
| Chaco Culture National Historic Park, N.M., U.S. | A2 | 108 |
| Chacon, N.M., U.S. | A4 | 108 |
| Chacon, Cape, c., Ak., U.S. | n24 | 79 |
| Chacuaco Creek, stm., Co., U.S. | D7 | 83 |
| Chad, ctry., Afr. | B3 | 46 |
| Chad, Lake, l., Afr. | C2 | 46 |
| Chadbourn, N.C., U.S. | C4 | 110 |
| Chadds Ford, Pa., U.S. | G10 | 115 |
| Chadileuvu, stm., Arg. | B3 | 54 |
| Chadiza, Zam. | D5 | 48 |
| Chadron, Ne., U.S. | B3 | 104 |
| Chadwick, Il., U.S. | A4 | 90 |
| Chadwick, Mo., U.S. | E4 | 102 |
| Chadwicks, N.Y., U.S. | B5 | 109 |
| Chaeryŏng, N. Kor. | G2 | 33 |
| Chaffee, Mo., U.S. | D8 | 102 |
| Chaffee, N.D., U.S. | C8 | 111 |
| Chaffee, co., Co., U.S. | C4 | 83 |
| Chaffin, Ma., U.S. | B4 | 98 |
| Chaffois, Fr. | C1 | 21 |
| Chāgai Hills, mts., Asia | G11 | 39 |
| Chaghcharan, Afg. | D12 | 39 |
| Chagny, Fr. | D6 | 16 |
| Chagodoshcha, stm., Sov. Un. | B10 | 27 |
| Chagos Archipelago, is., B.I.O.T. | G25 | 2 |
| Chagres, stm., Pan. | k11 | 62 |
| Chagrin Falls, Oh., U.S. | A4 | 112 |
| Chaguanas, Trin. | N23 | 65 |
| Chagyl, Sov. Un. | E5 | 28 |
| Chahal, Guat. | C3 | 62 |
| Chahar Borjak, Afg. | B3 | 36 |
| Chāībāsa, India | D8 | 36 |
| Chai Nat, Thai. | E4 | 35 |
| Chaiyaphum, Thai. | B2 | 34 |
| Chakachamna Lake, l., Ak., U.S. | g15 | 79 |
| Chake Chake, Tan. | C6 | 48 |
| Chakradharpur, India | D8 | 36 |
| Chakwāl, Pak. | B5 | 36 |
| Chala, Peru | E3 | 58 |
| Chala, Punta, c., Peru | E3 | 58 |
| Chalan Kanoa, N. Mar. Is. | D7 | 52 |
| Chalan Pago, Guam | L10 | 52 |
| Chalatenango, El Sal. | C3 | 62 |
| Chalchuapa, El Sal. | D3 | 62 |
| Chalcis see Khalkís, Grc. | C4 | 40 |
| Chalco, Canal de, Mex. | h9 | 63 |
| Chalfant, De., U.S. | h7 | 85 |
| Chalfonte, De., U.S. | B5 | 97 |
| Chalhuanca, Peru | D3 | 58 |
| Chalk River, Ont. | A7 | 73 |
| Chalkyitsik, Ak., U.S. | B11 | 79 |
| Challans, Fr. | D3 | 16 |
| Challapata, Bol. | C2 | 55 |
| Challis, Id., U.S. | E4 | 89 |
| Chalmette, La., U.S. | E6 | 95 |
| Châlons-sur-Marne, Fr. | C6 | 16 |
| Chalon-sur-Saône, Fr. | D6 | 16 |
| Chaltel, Cerro see Fitzroy, Monte, mtn., S.A. | D2 | 54 |
| Chālūs, Iran | C5 | 39 |
| Chalybeate, Ms., U.S. | A5 | 101 |
| Chalybeate, N.C., U.S. | B4 | 110 |
| Cham, W. Ger. | D7 | 19 |
| Cham, Switz. | B5 | 21 |
| Cham, i., Viet. | E8 | 35 |
| Chama, stm., U.S. | D5 | 83 |
| Chama, N.M., U.S. | A3 | 108 |
| Chama, Rio, stm., N.M., U.S. | A3 | 108 |
| Chamaicó, Arg. | B4 | 54 |
| Chamalières, Fr. | E5 | 16 |
| Chaman, Pak. | B4 | 36 |
| Chamba, Tan. | D6 | 48 |
| Chamba, stm., India | C6 | 36 |
| Chamberino, N.M., U.S. | E3 | 108 |
| Chamberlain, Sask. | G3 | 75 |
| Chamberlain, S.D., U.S. | D6 | 118 |
| Chamberlain Lake, l., Me., | B3 | 96 |
| Chamberlin, Mount, mtn., Ak., U.S. | B10 | 79 |
| Chambers, Az., U.S. | B6 | 80 |
| Chambers, La., U.S. | D5 | 95 |
| Chambers, Ne., U.S. | B7 | 104 |
| Chambers, co., Al., U.S. | C4 | 78 |
| Chambers, co., Tx., U.S. | E5 | 120 |
| Chambersburg, Il., U.S. | D3 | 90 |
| Chambersburg, Oh., U.S. | D3 | 112 |
| Chambersburg, Pa., U.S. | G6 | 115 |
| Chambers Island, i., Wi., U.S. | C6 | 126 |
| Chambéry, Fr. | E6 | 16 |
| Chambeshi, stm., Zam. | D5 | 48 |
| Chamblee, Ga., U.S. | h8 | 87 |
| Chambly, Que. | D4 | 74 |
| Chambly, co., Que. | D4 | 74 |
| Chambord, Que. | A5 | 74 |
| Chamcook, N.B. | D2 | 71 |
| Chamical, Arg. | F2 | 55 |
| Chamisal, N.M., U.S. | A4 | 108 |
| Chamois, Mo., U.S. | C6 | 102 |
| Chamonix [-Mont-Blanc], Fr. | E7 | 16 |
| Champagne, Yukon | | |
| Champagne, hist. reg., Fr. | C5 | 16 |
| Champagney, Fr. | A2 | 21 |
| Champagnole, Fr. | D6 | 16 |
| Champaign, Il., U.S. | C5 | 90 |
| Champaign, co., Il., U.S. | C5 | 90 |
| Champaign, co., Oh., U.S. | B2 | 112 |
| Champasak, Laos | C3 | 34 |
| Champdoré, Lac, l., Que. | g8 | 72 |
| Champerico, Guat. | G4 | 62 |
| Champex, Switz. | C3 | 20 |
| Champigneulles, Fr. | D7 | 16 |
| Champigny-sur-Marne, Fr. | g11 | 16 |
| Champion, Alta. | D4 | 68 |
| Champion, Mi., U.S. | B3 | 99 |
| Champion, Ne., U.S. | D4 | 104 |
| Champion, N.Y., U.S. | A5 | 112 |
| Champlain Creek Reservoir, res., Tx., U.S. | C2 | 120 |
| Champions, Tx., U.S. | *E5 | 120 |
| Champlain, Que. | C5 | 74 |
| Champlain, N.Y., U.S. | f11 | 109 |
| Champlain, co., Que. | B4 | 74 |
| Champlain, Lake, l., N.A. | B2 | 122 |
| Champlin, Mn., U.S. | m12 | 100 |
| Champlitte [-et-le-Prélot], Fr. | D6 | 16 |
| Champney's West, Newf. | D5 | 72 |
| Champotón, Mex. | D6 | 63 |
| Chana, Il., U.S. | B4 | 90 |
| Chañaral, Chile | E1 | 55 |
| Chancay, Peru | D2 | 58 |
| Chance, Al., U.S. | D2 | 78 |
| Chance, Md., U.S. | D6 | 97 |
| Chancellor, Al., U.S. | D4 | 78 |
| Chancellor, S.D., U.S. | D8 | 118 |
| Chanchelulla Peak, mtn., Ca., U.S. | B2 | 82 |
| Chanco, Chile | B2 | 54 |
| Chandalar, stm., Ak., U.S. | B10 | 79 |
| Chandausi, India | C7 | 37 |
| Chandeleur Islands, is., La., U.S. | E7 | 95 |
| Chandeleur Sound, strt., La., U.S. | E6 | 95 |
| Chandīgarh, India | *B6 | 36 |
| Chandīgarh, ter., India | *B6 | 36 |
| Chandler, Que. | k14 | 74 |
| Chandler, Az., U.S. | D4 | 80 |
| Chandler, In., U.S. | H3 | 91 |
| Chandler, Mn., U.S. | G3 | 100 |
| Chandler, Ok., U.S. | B5 | 113 |
| Chandler, Tx., U.S. | C5 | 120 |
| Chandler Heights, Az., U.S. | m9 | 80 |
| Chandlers Valley, Pa., U.S. | C3 | 115 |
| Chandlerville, Il., U.S. | C3 | 90 |
| Chandos Lake, l., Ont. | C6 | 73 |
| Chāndpur, Bngl. | D9 | 36 |
| Chandrapur, India | E6 | 36 |
| Chaneysville, Pa., U.S. | G5 | 115 |
| Chang, i., Thai. | F5 | 35 |
| Changbai Mountains, mts., Asia | E3 | 33 |
| Changchou see Zhangzhou, China | G8 | 31 |
| Changchun, China | C10 | 31 |
| Change Islands, Newf. | D4 | 72 |
| Changewater, N.J., U.S. | B3 | 107 |
| Changhua, China | I8 | 31 |
| Chang Jiang see Yangtze, stm., China | E8 | 31 |
| Changjin-ho, N. Kor. | F3 | 33 |
| Changle, China | L8 | 32 |
| Changli, China | E8 | 32 |
| Changling, China | B10 | 32 |
| Changping, China | D7 | 32 |
| Changsha, China | F7 | 31 |
| Changsŏng, N. Kor. | F2 | 33 |
| Changting, China | F8 | 31 |
| Changwu, China | D6 | 31 |
| Changxing, China | I8 | 32 |
| Changyŏn, N. Kor. | G2 | 33 |
| Changzhi, China | D7 | 31 |
| Changzhou, China | E8 | 31 |
| Chanhassen, Mn., U.S. | n11 | 100 |
| Channahon, Il., U.S. | B5 | 90 |
| Channel Country, reg., Austl. | D5 | 50 |
| Channel Islands, is., Eur. | F5 | 10 |
| Channel Islands National Park, Ca., U.S. | F4 | 82 |
| Channel-Port-aux-Basques, Newf. | E2 | 72 |
| Channelview, Tx., U.S. | r14 | 120 |
| Channing, Mi., U.S. | B2 | 99 |
| Channing, Tx., U.S. | B1 | 120 |
| Chantada, Spain | A2 | 22 |
| Chanthaburi, Thai. | C2 | 34 |
| Chantilly, Fr. | C5 | 16 |
| Chantilly, Va., U.S. | g12 | 123 |
| Chantrey Inlet, b., N.W. Ter. | C13 | 66 |
| Chanute, Ks., U.S. | E8 | 93 |
| Chanute Air Force Base, mil., Il., U.S. | C5 | 90 |
| Chao'an, China | G8 | 31 |
| Chao Lake, l., China | I7 | 32 |
| Chao Phraya, stm., Thai. | C2 | 34 |
| Chaor He, stm., China | B9 | 31 |
| Chaoyang, China | C9 | 31 |
| Chaoyang, China | *G8 | 31 |
| Chapadinha, Braz. | B2 | 57 |
| Chapala, Mex. | m12 | 63 |
| Chapala, Lago de, l., Mex. | m12 | 63 |
| Chaparral, Col. | C2 | 60 |
| Chapayev, Sov. Un. | G8 | 28 |
| Chapayevsk, Sov. Un. | C7 | 28 |
| Chapel Hill, De., U.S. | *B3 | 85 |
| Chapel Hill, N.C., U.S. | B3 | 110 |
| Chapel Hill, Tn., U.S. | B5 | 119 |
| Chapel Square, Va., U.S. | *B5 | 123 |
| Chapelton, Jam. | E14 | 65 |
| Chapin, Il., U.S. | D3 | 90 |
| Chapin, Ia., U.S. | B4 | 92 |
| Chapin, S.C., U.S. | C5 | 117 |
| Chaplin, Ct., U.S. | B7 | 84 |
| Chaplin, Sask. | G2 | 75 |
| Chaplin, co., Que. | C6 | 74 |
| Chaplin Lake, l., Sask. | G2 | 75 |
| Chaplygin, Sov. Un. | E12 | 27 |
| Chapman, Al., U.S. | D3 | 78 |
| Chapman, Ks., U.S. | D7 | 93 |
| Chapman, Ne., U.S. | C7 | 104 |
| Chapman, Me., U.S. | B4 | 96 |
| Chapman, Mount, mtn., Tn., U.S. | D10 | 119 |
| Chapman, Cape, c., N.W. Ter. | C15 | 66 |
| Chapman Ranch, Tx., U.S. | F4 | 120 |
| Chappaqua, N.Y., U.S. | *D7 | 109 |
| Chappaquiddick Island, i., Ma., U.S. | D7 | 98 |
| Chappell, Ne., U.S. | C3 | 104 |
| Chappells, S.C., U.S. | C4 | 117 |
| Chaptico Creek, stm., Md., U.S. | D4 | 97 |
| Chaqui, Bol. | C2 | 55 |
| Chara, well, Maur. | B2 | 45 |
| Charadai, Arg. | B5 | 54 |
| Charagua, Bol. | C3 | 55 |
| Charalá, Col. | D6 | 60 |
| Charaña, Bol. | C2 | 55 |
| Charata, Arg. | B4 | 54 |
| Charcas, Mex. | C4 | 63 |
| Charco, Tx., U.S. | E4 | 120 |
| Charcot Island, i., Ant. | C5 | 7 |
| Chardara, Sov. Un. | E7 | 28 |
| Chardon, Oh., U.S. | A4 | 112 |
| Chardzhou, Sov. Un. | F9 | 29 |
| Charente, stm., Fr. | E3 | 16 |
| Charenton, La., U.S. | E4 | 95 |
| Charenton-le-Pont, Fr. | g10 | 16 |
| Charette, Que. | C5 | 74 |
| Chari, stm., Afr. | C3 | 46 |
| Chārīkār, Afg. | A4 | 36 |
| Charing, Ga., U.S. | D2 | 87 |
| Chariton, Ia., U.S. | C4 | 92 |
| Chariton, co., Mo., U.S. | B4 | 102 |
| Chariton, stm., U.S. | A5 | 102 |
| Charity, Guy. | A3 | 59 |
| Charity, Mo., U.S. | D4 | 102 |
| Charlemont, Ma., U.S. | A2 | 98 |
| Charleroi, Bel. | B6 | 16 |
| Charleroi, Pa., U.S. | F2 | 115 |
| Charles, co., Md., U.S. | C3 | 97 |
| Charles, stm., Ma., U.S. | B5 | 98 |
| Charles, Cape, c., Va., U.S. | C6 | 123 |
| Charles A. Goodwin Dam, Ct., U.S. | B3 | 84 |
| Charlesbourg, Que. | n17 | 74 |
| Charlesburg, Wi., U.S. | k9 | 126 |
| Charles City, Ia., U.S. | A5 | 92 |
| Charles City, Va., U.S. | C5 | 123 |
| Charles City, co., Va., U.S. | C5 | 123 |
| Charles Mill Lake, res., Oh., U.S. | B3 | 112 |
| Charles Mix, co., S.D., U.S. | D7 | 118 |
| Charles Mound, hill, Il., U.S. | A3 | 90 |
| Charleston, Ar., U.S. | B1 | 81 |
| Charleston, Il., U.S. | D5 | 90 |
| Charleston, Me., U.S. | C3 | 96 |
| Charleston, Ms., U.S. | A3 | 101 |
| Charleston, Mo., U.S. | E8 | 102 |
| Charleston, Or., U.S. | D2 | 114 |
| Charleston, S.C., U.S. | F8 | 117 |
| Charleston, Tn., U.S. | D9 | 119 |
| Charleston, Ut., U.S. | C4 | 121 |
| Charleston, W.V., U.S. | C3 | 125 |
| Charleston, co., S.C., U.S. | F8 | 117 |
| Charleston Air Force Base, mil., S.C., U.S. | k11 | 117 |
| Charleston Naval Shipyard, mil., S.C., U.S. | k12 | 117 |
| Charleston Park, Nv., U.S. | *G6 | 105 |
| Charleston Peak, mtn., Nv., U.S. | G6 | 105 |
| Charlestown, Ire. | D3 | 11 |
| Charlestown, St. C.-N. | H13 | 64 |
| Charlestown, In., U.S. | H6 | 91 |
| Charlestown, Md., U.S. | A6 | 97 |
| Charlestown, N.H., U.S. | D2 | 106 |
| Charlestown, R.I., U.S. | F2 | 116 |
| Charles Town, W.V., U.S. | B7 | 125 |
| Charleville, Austl. | E8 | 50 |
| Charleville-Mézières, Fr. | C6 | 16 |
| Charlevoix, Mi., U.S. | C5 | 99 |
| Charlevoix, co., Mi., U.S. | C5 | 99 |
| Charlevoix, Lake, l., Mi., U.S. | C5 | 99 |
| Charlevoix-Est, co., Que. | B7 | 74 |
| Charlevoix-Ouest, co., Que. | B7 | 74 |
| Charlie Lake, B.C. | A7 | 69 |
| Charlieu, Fr. | D6 | 16 |
| Charlo, Mt., U.S. | C2 | 103 |
| Charlo, N.B. | B3 | 71 |
| Charlotte, Ia., U.S. | C7 | 92 |
| Charlotte, Mi., U.S. | F6 | 99 |
| Charlotte, N.C., U.S. | B2 | 110 |
| Charlotte, Tn., U.S. | A4 | 119 |
| Charlotte, Tx., U.S. | E3 | 120 |
| Charlotte, Vt., U.S. | C2 | 122 |
| Charlotte, co., N.B. | D2 | 71 |
| Charlotte, co., Fl., U.S. | F5 | 86 |
| Charlotte, co., Va., U.S. | C4 | 123 |
| Charlotte Amalie, V.I.U.S. | G12 | 64 |
| Charlotte Court House, Va., U.S. | C4 | 123 |
| Charlotte Harbor, Fl., U.S. | F4 | 86 |
| Charlotte Harbor, b., Fl., U.S. | F4 | 86 |
| Charlotte Lake, l., B.C. | C5 | 69 |
| Charlottenburg, Sur. | A4 | 59 |
| Charlottesville, In., U.S. | E6 | 91 |
| Charlottesville, Va., U.S. | B4 | 123 |
| Charlottetown, Newf. | B3 | 72 |
| Charlottetown, P.E.I. | C6 | 71 |
| Charlotte Town (Gouyave), Gren. | W25 | 67 |
| Charlotteville, Trin. | M24 | 65 |
| Charlotteville, Ga., U.S. | D4 | 87 |
| Charlson, N.D., U.S. | A3 | 111 |
| Charlton, Ma., U.S. | B4 | 98 |
| Charlton, co., Ga., U.S. | F4 | 87 |
| Charlton City, Ma., U.S. | B4 | 98 |
| Charlton Depot, Ma., U.S. | B4 | 98 |
| Charlton Island, i., N.W. Ter. | n20 | 73 |
| Charly [-sur-Marne], Fr. | F3 | 17 |
| Charmco, W.V., U.S. | C4 | 125 |
| Charmes, Fr. | C7 | 16 |
| Charmey, Switz. | C3 | 21 |
| Charny, Que. | C6 | 74 |
| Charouine, Alg. | D4 | 44 |
| Charquemont, Fr. | B2 | 21 |
| Charron Lake, l., Man. | C4 | 70 |
| Charsk, Sov. Un. | D10 | 29 |
| Charters Towers, Austl. | D9 | 50 |
| Chartierville, Que. | D6 | 74 |
| Chartley, Ma., U.S. | C5 | 98 |
| Chartres, Fr. | C4 | 16 |
| Charysh, stm., Sov. Un. | C10 | 28 |
| Chascomús, Arg. | B5 | 54 |
| Chase, B.C. | D5 | 69 |
| Chase, Ks., U.S. | D5 | 93 |
| Chase, Mi., U.S. | E5 | 99 |
| Chase, co., Ks., U.S. | D7 | 93 |
| Chase, co., Ne., U.S. | D4 | 104 |
| Chase, Mount, mtn., Me., U.S. | B4 | 96 |
| Chaseburg, Wi., U.S. | E2 | 126 |
| Chase City, Va., U.S. | D4 | 123 |
| Chase Field Naval Air Station, mil., Tx., U.S. | E4 | 120 |
| Chaseley, N.D., U.S. | B6 | 111 |
| Chase River, B.C. | f12 | 69 |
| Chasico, Arg. | C3 | 54 |
| Chaska, Mn., U.S. | F5 | 100 |
| Chasov Yar, Sov. Un. | q20 | 27 |
| Chassahowitzka Bay, b., Fl., U.S. | D4 | 86 |
| Chassell, Mi., U.S. | A2 | 99 |
| Chasseral, mtn., Switz. | C2 | 21 |
| Chasseron, Mont, mtn., Switz. | C2 | 21 |
| Chataignier, La., U.S. | D3 | 95 |
| Chatanika, Ak., U.S. | B10 | 79 |
| Chatawa, Ms., U.S. | D3 | 101 |
| Chatcolet, Id., U.S. | B2 | 89 |
| Château-d'Oex, Switz. | D3 | 21 |
| Château-du-Loir, Fr. | C4 | 16 |
| Châteaugay, N.Y., U.S. | f10 | 109 |
| Château-Gontier, Fr. | D3 | 16 |
| Châteauguay, Que. | D4 | 74 |
| Châteauguay, co., Que. | D4 | 74 |
| Châteauguay Heights, Que. | q19 | 74 |
| Châteauneuf, Fr. | D5 | 16 |
| Château-Renault, Fr. | C4 | 16 |
| Château-Richer, Que. | C6 | 74 |
| Châteauroux, Fr. | D4 | 16 |
| Château-Salins, Fr. | F6 | 17 |
| Château-Thierry, Fr. | C5 | 16 |
| Châtel, Fr. | D2 | 21 |
| Châtellerault, Fr. | C4 | 16 |
| Chatfield, Ar., U.S. | B5 | 81 |
| Chatfield, Mn., U.S. | G6 | 100 |
| Chatfield, Oh., U.S. | B3 | 112 |
| Chatham, N.B. | B4 | 71 |
| Chatham, Ont. | E2 | 73 |
| Chatham, Eng., U.K. | D7 | 10 |
| Chatham, Il., U.S. | D4 | 90 |
| Chatham, La., U.S. | B3 | 95 |
| Chatham, Ma., U.S. | C8 | 98 |
| Chatham, Mi., U.S. | B4 | 99 |
| Chatham, N.J., U.S. | B4 | 107 |
| Chatham, N.Y., U.S. | C7 | 109 |
| Chatham, Oh., U.S. | A3 | 112 |
| Chatham, Va., U.S. | D3 | 123 |
| Chatham, co., Ga., U.S. | E5 | 87 |
| Chatham, co., N.C., U.S. | B3 | 110 |
| Chatham Head, N.B. | C4 | 71 |
| Chatham Islands, is., | I11 | 6 |
| Chatham Sound, strt., B.C. | B2 | 69 |
| Chatham Strait, strt., Ak., U.S. | m22 | 79 |
| Châtillon, Italy | D2 | 20 |
| Châtillon-sur-Seine, Fr. | D6 | 16 |
| Chatkal Range, mts., Sov. Un. | E8 | 28 |
| Chatom, Al., U.S. | D1 | 78 |
| Chatsworth, Ont. | C4 | 73 |
| Chatsworth, Ga., U.S. | B2 | 87 |
| Chatsworth, Il., U.S. | C5 | 90 |
| Chatsworth, N.J., U.S. | D3 | 107 |
| Chatsworth Reservoir, res., Ca., U.S. | m11 | 82 |
| Chattahoochee, Fl., U.S. | B2 | 86 |
| Chattahoochee, co., Ga., U.S. | D1 | 87 |
| Chattahoochee, stm., U.S. | E1 | 87 |
| Chattanooga, Oh., U.S. | B1 | 112 |
| Chattanooga, Tn., U.S. | D8 | 119 |
| Chattaroy, Wa., U.S. | B8 | 124 |
| Chattaroy, W.V., U.S. | D2 | 125 |
| Chatteris, Eng., U.K. | B1 | 12 |
| Chattooga, co., Ga., U.S. | B1 | 87 |
| Chattooga, stm., U.S. | B1 | 87 |
| Chatuge Lake, res., U.S. | g9 | 110 |
| Chaudière, stm., Que. | C7 | 74 |
| Chau Doc, Viet. | C3 | 34 |
| Chauk, Burma | D9 | 36 |
| Chaumont, Fr. | C6 | 16 |
| Chaumont, N.Y., U.S. | A4 | 109 |
| Chaun Bay, b., Sov. Un. | B34 | 128 |
| Chauncey, Ga., U.S. | D3 | 87 |
| Chauncey, Oh., U.S. | C3 | 112 |
| Chauncy Lake, l., Ma., U.S. | g9 | 98 |
| Chauny, Fr. | C5 | 16 |
| Chautauqua, Ks., U.S. | E7 | 93 |
| Chautauqua, co., Ks., U.S. | E7 | 93 |
| Chautauqua, co., N.Y., U.S. | C1 | 109 |
| Chautauqua Lake, l., N.Y., U.S. | C1 | 109 |
| Chauvigny, Fr. | D4 | 16 |
| Chauvin, Alta. | C5 | 68 |
| Chauvin, La., U.S. | E5 | 95 |
| Chavanga, Sov. Un. | D17 | 14 |
| Chaves, Braz. | C5 | 59 |
| Chaves, Port. | B3 | 22 |
| Chaves, co., N.M., U.S. | D5 | 108 |
| Chavies, Ky., U.S. | C6 | 94 |
| Chavinda, Mex. | m12 | 63 |
| Cháviva, Col. | C3 | 60 |
| Chavuma, Zam. | D3 | 48 |
| Chazelles, Fr. | D6 | 16 |
| Chazy, N.Y., U.S. | f11 | 109 |
| Cheadle, Alta. | D4 | 68 |
| Cheaha Mountain, mtn., Al., U.S. | B4 | 78 |
| Cheam (part of London), Eng., U.K. | | |
| Cheapside, Va., U.S. | h16 | 123 |
| Cheat, Shavers Fork, stm., W.V., U.S. | B5 | 125 |
| Cheatham, co., Tn., U.S. | A4 | 119 |
| Cheatham Reservoir, res., Tn., U.S. | A4 | 119 |
| Cheat Mountain, mtn., W.V., U.S. | C5 | 125 |
| Cheb, Czech. | C2 | 26 |
| Chebacco Lake, l., Ma., U.S. | f12 | 98 |
| Chebanse, Il., U.S. | C6 | 90 |
| Chebeague Island, Me., U.S. | E2 | 96 |
| Cheboksary, Sov. Un. | D7 | 28 |
| Cheboygan, Mi., U.S. | C6 | 99 |
| Cheboygan, co., Mi., U.S. | C6 | 99 |
| Chech, 'Erg des., Afr. | E4 | 44 |
| Chechaouèn, Mor. | B3 | 44 |
| Chechŏn, S. Kor. | F3 | 33 |
| Checotah, Ok., U.S. | B6 | 113 |
| Chedabucto Bay, b., N.S. | D8 | 71 |
| Cheddar, Eng., U.K. | C5 | 12 |
| Cheduba Island, i., Burma | E9 | 36 |
| Cheecham Hills, hills, Alta. | | |
| Cheektowaga, N.Y., U.S. | C2 | 109 |
| Cheepie, Austl. | C5 | 51 |
| Cheesman Lake, res., Co., U.S. | B5 | 83 |
| Chegutu, Zimb. | A5 | 49 |
| Chehalem Mountains, mts., Or., U.S. | h12 | 114 |
| Chehalis, Wa., U.S. | C2 | 124 |
| Chehalis, stm., Wa., U.S. | C2 | 124 |
| Cheju, S. Kor. | J3 | 33 |
| Cheju Island, i., S. Kor. | D10 | 31 |
| Cheju Strait, strt., S. Kor. | J3 | 33 |
| Chekhov, Sov. Un. | C10 | 31 |
| Chekiang see Zhejiang, prov., China | F9 | 31 |
| Chekunda, Sov. Un. | A6 | 33 |
| Chela, Serra da, mtn., Ang. | E1 | 48 |
| Chelan, Wa., U.S. | B5 | 124 |
| Chelan, co., Wa., U.S. | B4 | 124 |
| Chelan, Lake, l., Wa., U.S. | A5 | 124 |
| Chelan Falls, Wa., U.S. | B5 | 124 |
| Chelan Mountains, mts., Wa., U.S. | A5 | 124 |
| Cheleiros, Port. | f9 | 22 |
| Cheleken, Sov. Un. | B6 | 39 |

| Name | Map Ref. | Page |
|---|---|---|
| Cheleken Peninsula, pen., Sov. Un. | B6 | 39 |
| Chelforó, Arg. | B3 | 54 |
| Chélia, Djebel, mtn., Alg. | B6 | 44 |
| Chéliff, Oued, stm., Alg. | B5 | 44 |
| Chelkar, Sov. Un. | E8 | 29 |
| Chelles, Fr. | F2 | 17 |
| Chelm, Pol. | C7 | 26 |
| Chelmno, Pol. | B5 | 26 |
| Chelmsford, Eng., U.K. | E7 | 10 |
| Chelmsford, Ma., U.S. | A5 | 98 |
| Chelmza, Pol. | B5 | 26 |
| Chelsea, Que. | D2 | 74 |
| Chelsea (part of London), Eng., U.K. | m12 | 10 |
| Chelsea, Al., U.S. | g7 | 78 |
| Chelsea, Ia., U.S. | C5 | 92 |
| Chelsea, Ma., U.S. | D3 | 98 |
| Chelsea, Mi., U.S. | F6 | 99 |
| Chelsea, Ok., U.S. | A6 | 113 |
| Chelsea, S.D., U.S. | B7 | 118 |
| Chelsea, Vt., U.S. | D4 | 122 |
| Chelsea, Wi., U.S. | C3 | 126 |
| Chelsea Estates, De., U.S. | *B3 | 85 |
| Cheltenham, Eng., U.K. | E5 | 10 |
| Cheltenham, Md., U.S. | C4 | 97 |
| Cheltenham Township, Pa., U.S. | *o21 | 115 |
| Chelva, Spain | C5 | 22 |
| Chelyabinsk, Sov. Un. | D9 | 29 |
| Chelyan, W.V., U.S. | C3 | 125 |
| Chelyuskin, Cape, c., Sov. Un. | B13 | 29 |
| Chelyuskintsy Ice Tongue, ice, Ant. | C21 | 7 |
| Chemainus, B.C. | E6 | 69 |
| Chemal, Sov. Un. | E26 | 8 |
| Chemehuevi Indian Reservation, Ca., U.S. | E6 | 82 |
| Chemillé, Fr. | D3 | 16 |
| Chemin Craig, Que. | o17 | 74 |
| Chemnitz see Karl-Marx-Stadt, E. Ger. | C6 | 18 |
| Chemquasabamticook Lake (Ross Lake), l., Me., U.S. | B3 | 96 |
| Chemult, Or., U.S. | D5 | 114 |
| Chemung, Al., U.S. | A5 | 90 |
| Chemung, co., N.Y., U.S. | C4 | 109 |
| Chemung, stm., Pa., U.S. | C8 | 115 |
| Chemung Lake, l., Ont. | C6 | 73 |
| Chenāb, stm., Asia | B5 | 36 |
| Chenachane, Alg. | D4 | 44 |
| Chenango, co., N.Y., U.S. | C5 | 109 |
| Chenango, stm., N.Y., U.S. | C5 | 109 |
| Chenango Bridge, N.Y., U.S. | C5 | 109 |
| Chenango Forks, N.Y., U.S. | C5 | 109 |
| Chenārān, Iran | C9 | 39 |
| Chene, Bayou, stm., La., U.S. | k9 | 95 |
| Chenequa, Wi., U.S. | m11 | 126 |
| Chenes, River Aux, b., La., U.S. | k12 | 95 |
| Chénéville, Que. | D2 | 74 |
| Cheney, Ks., U.S. | E6 | 93 |
| Cheney, Wa., U.S. | B8 | 124 |
| Cheney Reservoir, res., Ks., U.S. | E6 | 93 |
| Cheneyville, La., U.S. | C3 | 95 |
| Chengchou see Zhengzhou, China | E7 | 31 |
| Chengde, China | C8 | 31 |
| Chengdu (Chengtu), China | E5 | 31 |
| Chenggu, China | E6 | 31 |
| Chenghai, China | G8 | 31 |
| Chengkou, China | I3 | 32 |
| Chengmai, China | C8 | 35 |
| Chengshan Point, c., China | D9 | 31 |
| Chengtu see Chengdu, China | E5 | 31 |
| Chenoa, Il., U.S. | C5 | 90 |
| Chenoa, Ky., U.S. | D6 | 94 |
| Chenôve, Fr. | D6 | 16 |
| Chenoweth, Or., U.S. | B5 | 114 |
| Chenxi, China | F7 | 31 |
| Chenzhou, China | F7 | 31 |
| Chepachet, R.I., U.S. | B2 | 116 |
| Chepachet, stm., R.I., U.S. | B2 | 116 |
| Chepén, Peru | C2 | 58 |
| Chepes, Arg. | A3 | 54 |
| Chepo, Pan. | F8 | 62 |
| Chepstow, Wales, U.K. | E5 | 10 |
| Cheptsa, stm., Sov. Un. | D19 | 8 |
| Chequamegon Bay, b., Wi., U.S. | B3 | 126 |
| Cher, stm., Fr. | D4 | 16 |
| Cheraw, Co., U.S. | C7 | 83 |
| Cheraw, S.C., U.S. | B8 | 117 |
| Cherbourg, Fr. | C3 | 16 |
| Cherchell, Alg. | B5 | 44 |
| Cherdyn, Sov. Un. | A5 | 28 |
| Cheremkhovo, Sov. Un. | D13 | 29 |
| Cherepanovo, Sov. Un. | C10 | 29 |
| Cherepovets, Sov. Un. | D6 | 29 |
| Cherhill, Alta. | C3 | 68 |
| Cheriton, Va., U.S. | C7 | 123 |
| Cherkassy, Sov. Un. | G9 | 27 |
| Cherkessk, Sov. Un. | G17 | 8 |
| Cherlakskiy, Sov. Un. | C8 | 28 |
| Chernigov, Sov. Un. | D6 | 33 |
| Chernigovka, Sov. Un. | H11 | 27 |
| Chernobay, Sov. Un. | G9 | 27 |
| Chernobyl, Sov. Un. | F8 | 27 |
| Chernogorsk, Sov. Un. | E27 | 8 |
| Chernomorskoye, Sov. Un. | I9 | 27 |
| Chernovtsy, Sov. Un. | E5 | 29 |
| Chernoye, Sov. Un. | r32 | 14 |
| Chernyakhovsk (Insterburg), Sov. Un. | D3 | 27 |
| Cherokee, Al., U.S. | A2 | 78 |
| Cherokee, Ia., U.S. | B2 | 92 |
| Cherokee, Ks., U.S. | E9 | 93 |
| Cherokee, N.C., U.S. | f9 | 110 |
| Cherokee, Ok., U.S. | A3 | 113 |
| Cherokee, Tx., U.S. | D3 | 120 |
| Cherokee, co., Al., U.S. | A4 | 78 |
| Cherokee, co., Ga., U.S. | B2 | 87 |
| Cherokee, co., Ia., U.S. | B2 | 92 |
| Cherokee, co., Ks., U.S. | E9 | 93 |
| Cherokee, co., N.C., U.S. | f8 | 110 |
| Cherokee, co., Ok., U.S. | B6 | 113 |
| Cherokee, co., S.C., U.S. | A4 | 117 |
| Cherokee, co., Tx., U.S. | D5 | 120 |
| Cherokee Falls, S.C., U.S. | A4 | 117 |
| Cherokee Indian Reservation, N.C., U.S. | f9 | 110 |
| Cherokee Lake, res., Tn., U.S. | C10 | 119 |
| Cherokees, Lake O' The res., Ok., U.S. | A7 | 113 |
| Cherokee Sound, Bah. | A5 | 64 |
| Cherokee Village, Ar., U.S. | *A4 | 81 |
| Cherquenco, Chile | B2 | 54 |
| Cherrapunji, India | C9 | 36 |
| Cherry, Il., U.S. | B4 | 90 |
| Cherry, Tn., U.S. | B2 | 119 |
| Cherry, co., Ne., U.S. | B4 | 104 |
| Cherry Creek, N.Y., U.S. | C1 | 109 |
| Cherry Creek, S.D., U.S. | C4 | 118 |
| Cherry Creek, stm., Co., U.S. | B6 | 83 |
| Cherry Creek, stm., S.D., U.S. | C3 | 118 |
| Cherryfield, Me., U.S. | D5 | 96 |
| Cherry Fork, Oh., U.S. | D2 | 112 |
| Cherry Grove, Or., U.S. | g11 | 114 |
| Cherry Hill, N.J., U.S. | D2 | 107 |
| Cherry Hills Village, Co., U.S. | *B6 | 83 |
| Cherryland, Ca., U.S. | *D2 | 82 |
| Cherry Point, c., Va., U.S. | C6 | 123 |
| Cherry Point Marine Corps Air Station, mil., N.C., U.S. | C6 | 110 |
| Cherry Run, W.V., U.S. | B6 | 125 |
| Cherry Tree, Pa., U.S. | E4 | 115 |
| Cherryvale, Ks., U.S. | E8 | 93 |
| Cherry Valley, Ont. | D7 | 73 |
| Cherry Valley, Ar., U.S. | B5 | 81 |
| Cherry Valley, Ca., U.S. | *F5 | 82 |
| Cherry Valley, Il., U.S. | A5 | 90 |
| Cherry Valley, Ma., U.S. | B4 | 98 |
| Cherry Valley, N.Y., U.S. | C6 | 109 |
| Cherryville, N.C., U.S. | B1 | 110 |
| Cherskiy Mountains, mts., Sov. Un. | C17 | 29 |
| Chesaning, Mi., U.S. | E6 | 99 |
| Chesapeake, Oh., U.S. | D3 | 112 |
| Chesapeake, Va., U.S. | D6 | 123 |
| Chesapeake, W.V., U.S. | C3 | 125 |
| Chesapeake and Delaware Canal, U.S. | B3 | 85 |
| Chesapeake Bay, b., U.S. | C12 | 76 |
| Chesapeake Bay Bridge-Tunnel, Va., U.S. | D7 | 123 |
| Chesapeake Beach, Md., U.S. | C4 | 97 |
| Chesapeake City, Md., U.S. | A6 | 97 |
| Chesaw, Wa., U.S. | A6 | 124 |
| Chesdin, Lake, res., Va., U.S. | C5 | 123 |
| Chesha Bay, b., Sov. Un. | B18 | 8 |
| Chesham, Eng., U.K. | k11 | 10 |
| Chesham, N.H., U.S. | E2 | 106 |
| Cheshire, Ct., U.S. | D4 | 84 |
| Cheshire, Ma., U.S. | A1 | 98 |
| Cheshire, Oh., U.S. | D3 | 112 |
| Cheshire, co., Eng., U.K. | A5 | 12 |
| Cheshire, co., N.H., U.S. | E2 | 106 |
| Cheshire Reservoir, res., Ma., U.S. | A1 | 98 |
| Cheshunt, Eng., U.K. | k12 | 10 |
| Chesilhurst, N.J., U.S. | D3 | 107 |
| Chesley, Ont. | C3 | 73 |
| Chesnee, S.C., U.S. | A4 | 117 |
| Chester, N.S. | E5 | 71 |
| Chester, Eng., U.K. | D5 | 10 |
| Chester, Ar., U.S. | B1 | 81 |
| Chester, Ca., U.S. | B3 | 82 |
| Chester, Ct., U.S. | D6 | 84 |
| Chester, Fl., U.S. | B5 | 86 |
| Chester, Ga., U.S. | D3 | 87 |
| Chester, Il., U.S. | F4 | 90 |
| Chester, Ia., U.S. | A5 | 92 |
| Chester, Md., U.S. | C5 | 97 |
| Chester, Ma., U.S. | B2 | 98 |
| Chester, Mt., U.S. | B6 | 103 |
| Chester, Ne., U.S. | D8 | 104 |
| Chester, N.H., U.S. | E4 | 106 |
| Chester, N.J., U.S. | B3 | 107 |
| Chester, N.Y., U.S. | D6 | 109 |
| Chester, Oh., U.S. | C4 | 112 |
| Chester, Pa., U.S. | G11 | 115 |
| Chester, S.C., U.S. | B5 | 117 |
| Chester, S.D., U.S. | D9 | 118 |
| Chester, Ut., U.S. | D4 | 121 |
| Chester, Vt., U.S. | E3 | 122 |
| Chester, Va., U.S. | C5 | 123 |
| Chester, W.V., U.S. | A4 | 125 |
| Chester, co., Pa., U.S. | G10 | 115 |
| Chester, co., S.C., U.S. | B5 | 117 |
| Chester, co., Tn., U.S. | B3 | 119 |
| Chester, stm., Md., U.S. | B5 | 97 |
| Chester Basin, N.S. | E5 | 71 |
| Chester Depot, Vt., U.S. | E3 | 122 |
| Chesterfield, Eng., U.K. | D6 | 10 |
| Chesterfield, In., U.S. | D6 | 91 |
| Chesterfield, Ma., U.S. | B2 | 98 |
| Chesterfield, N.H., U.S. | E2 | 106 |
| Chesterfield, S.C., U.S. | B7 | 117 |
| Chesterfield, Tn., U.S. | B3 | 119 |
| Chesterfield, co., S.C., U.S. | B7 | 117 |
| Chesterfield, co., Va., U.S. | C5 | 123 |
| Chesterfield, Îles, is., N. Cal. | H9 | 6 |
| Chesterfield Inlet, N.W. Ter. | D14 | 66 |
| Chesterfield Inlet, b., N.W. Ter. | D14 | 66 |
| Chesterhill, Oh., U.S. | C4 | 112 |
| Chesterton, In., U.S. | A3 | 91 |
| Chestertown, Md., U.S. | B5 | 97 |
| Chestertown, N.Y., U.S. | B7 | 109 |
| Chester Township, Pa., U.S. | *p20 | 115 |
| Chesterville, Ont. | B9 | 73 |
| Chesterville, Oh., U.S. | B3 | 112 |
| Chestnut, Il., U.S. | C4 | 90 |
| Chestnut, La., U.S. | B2 | 95 |
| Chestnut Hill Estates, De., U.S. | *B3 | 85 |
| Chestnut Knoll, De., U.S. | *B3 | 85 |
| Chestnut Mound, Tn., U.S. | C8 | 119 |
| Chestnut Ridge, N.Y., U.S. | *D6 | 109 |
| Chesuncook Lake, l., Me., U.S. | C3 | 96 |
| Cheswick, Pa., U.S. | h14 | 115 |
| Cheswold, De., U.S. | D3 | 85 |
| Chetac, Lake, l., Wi., U.S. | C2 | 126 |
| Chetco, stm., Or., U.S. | E2 | 114 |
| Chetek, Wi., U.S. | C2 | 126 |
| Chetek, Lake, l., Wi., U.S. | C2 | 126 |
| Chéticamp, N.S. | C8 | 71 |
| Chetopa, Ks., U.S. | E8 | 93 |
| Chetumal, Mex. | D7 | 63 |
| Chetumal Bay, b., N.A. | D7 | 63 |
| Chetwynd, B.C. | B7 | 69 |
| Chevak, Ak., U.S. | C6 | 79 |
| Chevelon Creek, stm., Az., U.S. | C5 | 80 |
| Cheverie, N.S. | E5 | 71 |
| Cheverly, Md., U.S. | *C4 | 97 |
| Cheviot, N.Z. | O14 | 51 |
| Cheviot, Oh., U.S. | C1 | 112 |
| Chevreuil, Bayou, stm., La., U.S. | k10 | 95 |
| Chevreuil, Point, c., La., U.S. | E4 | 95 |
| Chevy Chase, Md., U.S. | g13 | 97 |
| Chewack, stm., Wa., U.S. | A5 | 124 |
| Chewalla, Tn., U.S. | B3 | 119 |
| Chewelah, Wa., U.S. | A8 | 124 |
| Chewsville, Md., U.S. | A2 | 97 |
| Chewton, Pa., U.S. | E1 | 115 |
| Cheyenne, Ok., U.S. | B2 | 113 |
| Cheyenne, Wy., U.S. | E8 | 127 |
| Cheyenne, co., Co., U.S. | C8 | 83 |
| Cheyenne, co., Ks., U.S. | C2 | 93 |
| Cheyenne, co., Ne., U.S. | C2 | 104 |
| Cheyenne, stm., U.S. | C4 | 118 |
| Cheyenne, Dry Fork, stm., Wy., U.S. | C7 | 127 |
| Cheyenne River Indian Reservation, S.D., U.S. | B4 | 118 |
| Cheyenne Wells, Co., U.S. | C8 | 83 |
| Chhapra, India | C7 | 36 |
| Chhatarpur, India | E7 | 37 |
| Chhatrapur, India | H10 | 37 |
| Chhindwāra, India | F7 | 37 |
| Chhukha Dzong, Bhu. | D12 | 37 |
| Chi, stm., Thai. | E6 | 35 |
| Chiai, Tai. | *G9 | 31 |
| Chiang Kham, Thai. | C4 | 35 |
| Chiang Khong, Thai. | A2 | 34 |
| Chiang Mai, Thai. | B1 | 34 |
| Chiang Rai, Thai. | B1 | 34 |
| Chiapa de Corzo, Mex. | D6 | 63 |
| Chiapas, state, Mex. | D6 | 63 |
| Chiari, Italy | B2 | 23 |
| Chiasso, Switz. | E7 | 21 |
| Chiatura, Sov. Un. | A14 | 40 |
| Chiautla de Tapia, Mex. | n14 | 63 |
| Chiavari, Italy | B2 | 23 |
| Chiavenna, Italy | C5 | 20 |
| Chiawuli Tak, Az., U.S. | F4 | 80 |
| Chiba, Japan | D13 | 31 |
| Chibemba, Ang. | E1 | 48 |
| Chibia, Ang. | E1 | 48 |
| Chiblow Lake, l., Ont. | A1 | 73 |
| Chibougamau, Que. | k12 | 74 |
| Chibuto, Moz. | B5 | 49 |
| Chicago, Il., U.S. | B6 | 90 |
| Chicago Heights, Il., U.S. | B6 | 90 |
| Chicago Ridge, Il., U.S. | *k9 | 90 |
| Chicago Sanitary and Ship Canal, Il., U.S. | k8 | 90 |
| Chicamacomico, stm., Md., U.S. | D6 | 97 |
| Chicapa, stm., Afr. | C3 | 48 |
| Chichagof Island, i., Ak., U.S. | m22 | 79 |
| Chichaoua, Mor. | C3 | 44 |
| Chicheng, China | D6 | 32 |
| Chichén Itzá, hist., Mex. | C7 | 63 |
| Chichester, Eng., U.K. | E6 | 10 |
| Chichester, N.H., U.S. | D4 | 106 |
| Chichibu, Japan | n18 | 31 |
| Chickahominy, stm., Va., U.S. | C5 | 123 |
| Chickamauga, Ga., U.S. | B1 | 87 |
| Chickamauga and Chattanooga National Military Park, U.S. | k11 | 119 |
| Chickamauga Dam, res., Tn., U.S. | h11 | 119 |
| Chickamauga Lake, res., Tn., U.S. | D8 | 119 |
| Chickasaw, Al., U.S. | E1 | 78 |
| Chickasaw, co., Ia., U.S. | A5 | 92 |
| Chickasaw, co., Ms., U.S. | B5 | 101 |
| Chickasawhay, stm., Ms., U.S. | D5 | 101 |
| Chickasaw National Recreation Area, Ok., U.S. | C5 | 113 |
| Chickasha, Ok., U.S. | B4 | 113 |
| Chickasha, Lake, res., Ok., U.S. | B3 | 113 |
| Chicken, Ak., U.S. | C11 | 79 |
| Chickwolnepy Stream, stm., N.H., U.S. | A4 | 106 |
| Chiclana [de la Frontera], Spain | D2 | 22 |
| Chiclayo, Peru | C2 | 58 |
| Chico, Ca., U.S. | C3 | 82 |
| Chico, Tx., U.S. | C4 | 120 |
| Chico, Wa., U.S. | B3 | 124 |
| Chico, stm., Arg. | C3 | 54 |
| Chico, stm., Arg. | D3 | 54 |
| Chico, stm., Mex. | h9 | 63 |
| Chicoa, Moz. | A5 | 49 |
| Chico Creek, stm., Co., U.S. | C6 | 83 |
| Chico Hot Springs, Mt., U.S. | E6 | 103 |
| Chicomo, Moz. | B5 | 49 |
| Chico North, Ca., U.S. | *C3 | 82 |
| Chicontepec, Mex. | m14 | 63 |
| Chicopee, Ga., U.S. | B3 | 87 |
| Chicopee, Ks., U.S. | E9 | 93 |
| Chicopee, Ma., U.S. | B2 | 98 |
| Chicora, Ms., U.S. | D5 | 101 |
| Chicora, Pa., U.S. | E2 | 115 |
| Chicot, co., Ar., U.S. | D4 | 81 |
| Chicot, Lake, l., Ar., U.S. | D4 | 81 |
| Chicota, Tx., U.S. | C5 | 120 |
| Chicot Island, i., La., U.S. | E6 | 95 |
| Chicoutimi, Que. | A6 | 74 |
| Chicoutimi, co., Que. | A6 | 74 |
| Chicoutimi, stm., Que. | A6 | 74 |
| Chico West, Ca., U.S. | *C3 | 82 |
| Chidester, Ar., U.S. | D2 | 81 |
| Chidley, Cape, c., Can. | f8 | 72 |
| Chieerete Island, i., Marsh Is. | P18 | 52 |
| Chiefland, Fl., U.S. | C4 | 86 |
| Chiefs Point, c., Ont. | C3 | 73 |
| Chiem Lake, l., W. Ger. | E6 | 18 |
| Chien, Bayou de, stm., Ky., U.S. | f8 | 94 |
| Chieri, Italy | B1 | 23 |
| Chiers, stm., Eur. | E5 | 17 |
| Chiese, stm., Italy | C5 | 20 |
| Chieti, Italy | C5 | 23 |
| Chifeng, China | C8 | 31 |
| Chigasaki, Japan | *I9 | 33 |
| Chigirin, Sov. Un. | G9 | 27 |
| Chignahuapan, Mex. | n14 | 63 |
| Chignecto, Cape, c., N.S. | D5 | 71 |
| Chignecto Bay, b., Can. | D5 | 71 |
| Chignik, Ak., U.S. | D8 | 79 |
| Chigubo, Moz. | B5 | 49 |
| Chigwell, Eng., U.K. | k13 | 10 |
| Chihli, Gulf of see Bo Hai, b., China | D8 | 31 |
| Chihuahua, Mex. | B3 | 63 |
| Chihuahua, state, Mex. | B3 | 63 |
| Chii, Mount, mtn., S. Kor. | I3 | 33 |
| Chikaskia, stm., U.S. | A4 | 113 |
| Chikura, Japan | o18 | 31 |
| Chilapa [de Alvarez], Mex. | D5 | 63 |
| Chilca, Peru | D2 | 58 |
| Chilcotin, stm., B.C. | D6 | 69 |
| Childersburg, Al., U.S. | B3 | 78 |
| Childress, Tx., U.S. | B2 | 120 |
| Childress, co., Tx., U.S. | B2 | 120 |
| Chile, ctry., S.A. | G3 | 53 |
| Chilecito, Arg. | E2 | 55 |
| Chilete, Peru | C2 | 58 |
| Chilhowee, Mo., U.S. | C4 | 102 |
| Chilhowee Mountain, mtn., Tn., U.S. | n14 | 119 |
| Chilhowie, Va., U.S. | f10 | 123 |
| Chili, In., U.S. | C5 | 91 |
| Chili, N.M., U.S. | *A3 | 108 |
| Chili, Wi., U.S. | D3 | 126 |
| Chilibre, Peru | k11 | 62 |
| Chili Center, N.Y., U.S. | *B3 | 109 |
| Chilika Lake, l., India | H10 | 37 |
| Chililabombwe (Bancroft), Zam. | D4 | 48 |
| Chilili, N.M., U.S. | C3 | 108 |
| Chilkat Pass, B.C. | E5 | 66 |
| Chilko, stm., B.C. | D6 | 69 |
| Chilko Lake, l., B.C. | D5 | 69 |
| Chillán, Chile | B2 | 54 |
| Chilli, Sov. Un. | E7 | 28 |
| Chillicothe, Il., U.S. | C4 | 90 |
| Chillicothe, Ia., U.S. | C5 | 92 |
| Chillicothe, Mo., U.S. | B4 | 102 |
| Chillicothe, Oh., U.S. | C3 | 112 |
| Chillicothe, Tx., U.S. | B3 | 120 |
| Chilliwack, B.C. | E7 | 69 |
| Chilliwack, stm., N.A. | A4 | 124 |
| Chillum, Md., U.S. | f9 | 97 |
| Chilmark, Ma., U.S. | D6 | 98 |
| Chilocco, Ok., U.S. | A4 | 113 |
| Chiloé, Isla de, i., Chile | C2 | 54 |
| Chiloquin, Or., U.S. | E5 | 114 |
| Chilpancingo [de los Bravos], Mex. | D5 | 63 |
| Chilton, Tx., U.S. | D4 | 120 |
| Chilton, Wi., U.S. | D5 | 126 |
| Chilton, co., Al., U.S. | C3 | 78 |
| Chiluage, Ang. | C3 | 48 |
| Chilumba, Mwi. | D5 | 48 |
| Chilung (Keelung), Tai. | F9 | 31 |
| Chilwa, Lake, l., Afr. | E6 | 48 |
| Chimacum, Wa., U.S. | A3 | 124 |
| Chimalhuacán, Mex. | h10 | 63 |
| Chimaltenango, Guat. | C2 | 62 |
| Chimán, Pan. | F8 | 62 |
| Chimay, Bel. | D4 | 17 |
| Chimayo, N.M., U.S. | A4 | 108 |
| Chimbay, Sov. Un. | E8 | 29 |
| Chimborazo, prov., Ec. | B2 | 58 |
| Chimborazo, vol., Ec. | B2 | 58 |
| Chimbote, Peru | C2 | 58 |
| Chimkent, Sov. Un. | E9 | 29 |
| Chimney Rock, Co., U.S. | D3 | 83 |
| Chimney Rock, mtn., Ky., U.S. | D5 | 94 |
| Chimney Rock, mtn., Ne., U.S. | C2 | 104 |
| Chimneytop, mtn., Tn., U.S. | C11 | 119 |
| Chimoio, Moz. | A5 | 49 |
| Chin, Alta. | E4 | 68 |
| Chin, co., Ar., U.S. | B3 | 73 |
| Chinā, Japan | O5 | 52 |
| China, Mex. | B5 | 63 |
| China, Me., U.S. | D3 | 96 |
| China, ctry., Asia | E6 | 31 |
| China Grove, N.C., U.S. | B2 | 110 |
| China Lake, l., Me., U.S. | D3 | 96 |
| Chinaja, Guat. | D6 | 63 |
| Chinan see Jinan, China | D8 | 31 |
| Chinandega, Nic. | E7 | 63 |
| Chinati Peak, mtn., Tx., U.S. | p12 | 120 |
| Chincha Alta, Peru | D2 | 58 |
| Chincheros, Peru | D3 | 58 |
| Chinchilla, Austl. | E9 | 50 |
| Chinchilla [de Monte Aragón], Spain | C5 | 22 |
| Chincoteague, Va., U.S. | C7 | 123 |
| Chincoteague Bay, b., U.S. | D7 | 97 |
| Chinde, Moz. | A6 | 49 |
| Chindo, S. Kor. | I3 | 33 |
| Chindwinn, stm., Burme | C10 | 36 |
| Chingola, Zam. | D4 | 48 |
| Chinguar, Ang. | D2 | 48 |
| Chinguetti, Maur. | B2 | 44 |
| Chinhae, S. Kor. | I4 | 33 |
| Chinhoyi, Zimb. | A5 | 49 |
| Chiniot, Pak. | B4 | 37 |
| Chinipas, Mex. | B3 | 63 |
| Chinit, stm., Camb. | F6 | 35 |
| Chinitna Point, c., Ak., U.S. | h15 | 79 |
| Chinju, S. Kor. | D10 | 31 |
| Chinko, stm., Cen. Afr. Rep. | D4 | 46 |
| Chin Lakes, l., Alta. | E4 | 63 |
| Chinle, Az., U.S. | A6 | 80 |
| Chinle Wash, val., U.S. | A6 | 80 |
| Chinnampo see Nampo, N. Kor. | D10 | 31 |
| Chino, Ca., U.S. | F5 | 82 |
| Chinon, Fr. | D6 | 16 |
| Chinook, Alta. | D5 | 68 |
| Chinook, Mt., U.S. | B7 | 103 |
| Chinook, Wa., U.S. | C2 | 124 |
| Chinook, Lake, res., Or., U.S. | C5 | 114 |
| Chinook Cove, B.C. | D7 | 69 |
| Chino Valley, Az., U.S. | C3 | 80 |
| Chinquapin, N.C., U.S. | C5 | 110 |
| Chinsali, Zam. | D5 | 48 |
| Chinteche, Mwi. | D5 | 48 |
| Chinú, Col. | B2 | 58 |
| Chioco, Moz. | A5 | 49 |
| Chioggia, Italy | C4 | 20 |
| Chios see Khios, i., Grc | C5 | 40 |
| Chipata (Fort Jameson), Zam. | D5 | 48 |
| Chipewyan, stm., Alta. | A4 | 68 |
| Chipinge, Zimb. | B6 | 49 |
| Chipita Park, Co., U.S. | C5 | 83 |
| Chip Lake, l., Alta. | C3 | 68 |
| Chipley, Fl., U.S. | u16 | 86 |
| Chipman, Alta. | C4 | 68 |
| Chipman, N.B. | C4 | 71 |
| Chipola, stm., Fl., U.S. | B1 | 86 |
| Chippenham, Eng., U.K. | C5 | 12 |
| Chippewa, co., Mi., U.S. | B6 | 99 |
| Chippewa, co., Mn., U.S. | E3 | 100 |
| Chippewa, co., Wi., U.S. | D2 | 126 |
| Chippewa, stm., Mi., U.S. | E6 | 99 |
| Chippewa, stm., Mn., U.S. | E3 | 100 |
| Chippewa, stm., Wi., U.S. | D2 | 126 |
| Chippewa, East Branch, stm., Mn., U.S. | E3 | 100 |
| Chippewa, East Fork, stm., Wi., U.S. | C3 | 126 |
| Chippewa Falls, Wi., U.S. | D2 | 126 |
| Chippewa Lake, l., Wi., U.S. | C2 | 126 |
| Chippewa Lake, Mi., U.S. | E5 | 99 |
| Chipping Norton, Eng., U.K. | C5 | 12 |
| Chipuriro, Zimb. | A5 | 49 |
| Chiputneticook Lakes, l., N.A. | C5 | 96 |
| Chipuxet, stm., R.I., U.S. | F3 | 116 |
| Chiquibul, Guat. | E7 | 63 |
| Chiquimula, Guat. | C2 | 62 |
| Chiquinquirá, Col. | B3 | 58 |
| Chira, S.A. | B1 | 58 |
| Chiradzulu, Mwi. | E6 | 48 |
| Chirchik, Sov. Un. | E9 | 29 |
| Chiredzi, Zimb. | B5 | 49 |
| Chireno, Tx., U.S. | D5 | 120 |
| Chirfa, Niger | E8 | 44 |
| Chiricahua Mountains, mts., Az., U.S. | E6 | 80 |
| Chiricahua National Monument, Az., U.S. | F6 | 80 |
| Chiricahua Peak, mtn., Az., U.S. | F6 | 80 |
| Chirikof Island, i., Ak., U.S. | D8 | 79 |
| Chiriquí, Golfo de, b., Pan. | F6 | 62 |
| Chiriquí Grande, Pan. | F6 | 62 |
| Chiromo, Mwi. | E6 | 48 |
| Chirpan, Bul. | D7 | 24 |
| Chirripó, Cerro, mtn., C.R. | F6 | 62 |
| Chirundu, Zimb. | A4 | 49 |
| Chisago, co., Mn., U.S. | E6 | 100 |
| Chisago City, Mn., U.S. | E6 | 100 |
| Chisamba, Zam. | D4 | 48 |
| Chisana, Ak., U.S. | C11 | 79 |
| Chisasibi, Que. | h11 | 74 |
| Chisholm, Alta. | B3 | 68 |
| Chisholm, Mn., U.S. | C6 | 100 |
| Chisholm, Me., U.S. | D2 | 96 |
| Chişineu-Criş, Rom. | B5 | 24 |
| Chisos Mountains, mts., Tx., U.S. | E12 | 120 |
| Chistochina, Ak., U.S. | C11 | 79 |
| Chistopol, Sov. Un. | B24 | 28 |
| Chita, Sov. Un. | D14 | 29 |
| Chitado, Ang. | E1 | 48 |
| Chitek, Sask. | D2 | 75 |
| Chitek Lake, l., Man. | C2 | 70 |
| Chitina, Ak., U.S. | C11 | 79 |
| Chitina, stm., Ak., U.S. | g19 | 79 |
| Chitipa, Mwi. | C5 | 48 |
| Chitose, Japan | *E10 | 33 |
| Chitradurga, India | F6 | 36 |
| Chitrāl, Pak. | A5 | 36 |
| Chitré, Pan. | G7 | 62 |
| Chittagong, Bngl. | D9 | 36 |
| Chittaranjan, India | *I5 | 37 |
| Chittenango, N.Y., U.S. | B5 | 109 |
| Chittenden, Vt., U.S. | D3 | 122 |
| Chittenden, co., Vt., U.S. | C2 | 122 |
| Chittenden Reservoir, res., Vt., U.S. | D3 | 122 |
| Chittoor, India | F6 | 36 |
| Chitungwiza, Zimb. | A5 | 49 |
| Chiuchiu, Chile | D2 | 55 |
| Chiumbe, stm., Afr. | C3 | 48 |
| Chiúme, Ang. | E3 | 48 |
| Chiusi, Italy | C3 | 23 |
| Chivasso, Italy | B1 | 23 |
| Chivay, Peru | E3 | 58 |
| Chivhu, Zimb. | A5 | 49 |
| Chivilcoy, Arg. | A4 | 54 |
| Chixoy, stm., Guat. | C2 | 62 |
| Chizhapka, stm., Sov. Un. | B9 | 28 |
| Chloride, Az., U.S. | B1 | 80 |
| Chmielnik, Pol. | C6 | 26 |
| Choapa, stm., Chile | A2 | 54 |
| Choapan, Mex. | D5 | 63 |
| Chobe, stm., Afr. | A3 | 49 |
| Choccolocco, Al., U.S. | B4 | 78 |
| Choccolocco Creek, stm., Al., U.S. | B3 | 78 |
| Chochiwŏn, S. Kor. | H3 | 33 |
| Chocó, dept., Col. | B2 | 60 |
| Chocolate Mountains, mts., U.S. | F6 | 82 |
| Chocorua, N.H., U.S. | C4 | 106 |
| Chocorua, Mount, mtn., N.H., U.S. | C4 | 106 |
| Chocowinity, N.C., U.S. | B5 | 110 |
| Choctaw, Ar., U.S. | B3 | 81 |
| Choctaw, Ok., U.S. | B4 | 113 |
| Choctaw, co., Al., U.S. | C1 | 78 |
| Choctaw, co., Ms., U.S. | B4 | 101 |
| Choctaw, co., Ok., U.S. | C6 | 113 |
| Choctawhatchee, East Fork, stm., Al., U.S. | D4 | 78 |
| Choctawhatchee, West Fork, stm., Al., U.S. | D4 | 78 |
| Choctawhatchee Bay, b., Fl., U.S. | u15 | 86 |
| Choctaw Indian Reservation, Ms., U.S. | C4 | 101 |
| Chodzież, Pol. | B5 | 26 |
| Choele Choel, Arg. | B3 | 54 |
| Choiceland, Sask. | D3 | 75 |
| Choiseul, i., Sol. Is. | G9 | 6 |
| Choisy-le-Roi, Fr. | g10 | 16 |
| Chojna, Pol. | B3 | 26 |
| Chojnice, Pol. | B5 | 26 |
| Chojnów, Pol. | B4 | 26 |
| Chōkai, Mount, mtn., Japan | G10 | 33 |
| Choke Mountains, mts., Eth. | C4 | 47 |
| Chokio, Mn., U.S. | E2 | 100 |
| Chokoloskee, Fl., U.S. | G5 | 86 |
| Chokwé, Moz. | B5 | 49 |
| Cholame, Ca., U.S. | E3 | 82 |
| Cholet, Fr. | D6 | 16 |
| Cholo, Mwi. | E6 | 48 |
| Cholula [de Rivadabia], Mex. | n14 | 63 |
| Choluteca, Hond. | E7 | 63 |
| Choluteca, stm., Hond. | C5 | 62 |
| Choma, Zam. | E4 | 48 |
| Chomo Lhāri, mtn., Asia | D12 | 37 |
| Chomutov, Czech. | C3 | 26 |
| Chonan, S. Kor. | H3 | 33 |
| Chon Buri, Thai. | C2 | 34 |
| Chone, Ec. | E6 | 69 |
| Chong'an, China | K8 | 32 |
| Chongjin, N. Kor. | C10 | 31 |
| Chŏngju, N. Kor. | G2 | 33 |
| Chongju, S. Kor. | *I3 | 33 |
| Chongqing (Chungking), China | F6 | 31 |
| Chongren (Chengren), China | K6 | 32 |
| Chongsŏng, N. Kor. | D10 | 31 |
| Chŏnju, S. Kor. | D10 | 31 |
| Chonos, Archipiélago de los, is., Chile | C2 | 54 |
| Chopim, stm., Braz. | C5 | 56 |
| Choptank, Md., U.S. | C6 | 97 |
| Choptank, stm., Md., U.S. | C5 | 97 |
| Chorrillos, Peru | D2 | 58 |
| Chortkov, Sov. Un. | G5 | 27 |
| Chŏrwŏn, S. Kor. | D10 | 31 |
| Chorzów, Pol. | C5 | 26 |
| Chosan, N. Kor. | C10 | 31 |
| Chōshi, Japan | I10 | 33 |
| Chosica, Peru | D2 | 58 |
| Chos Malal, Arg. | B2 | 54 |
| Choszczno, Pol. | B3 | 26 |
| Chota, Peru | C2 | 58 |
| Choteau, Mt., U.S. | C4 | 103 |
| Chotětov, Czech. | n18 | 26 |
| Choudrant, La., U.S. | B3 | 95 |
| Choudrant, Bayou, stm., La., U.S. | B3 | 95 |
| Choum, Maur. | B2 | 45 |
| Choushan Islands see Zhoushan Islands is., China | E9 | 31 |
| Chouteau, Ok., U.S. | A6 | 113 |
| Chouteau, co., Mt., U.S. | C6 | 103 |
| Chowan, co., N.C., U.S. | A6 | 110 |
| Chowan, stm., N.C., U.S. | A6 | 110 |
| Chowchilla, Ca., U.S. | D3 | 82 |
| Choybalsan, Mong. | B7 | 31 |
| Choyr, Mong. | B6 | 31 |
| Chrisman, Il., U.S. | D6 | 90 |
| Chrisney, In., U.S. | H3 | 91 |
| Christchurch, N.Z. | O14 | 51 |
| Christchurch, Eng., U.K. | D6 | 12 |
| Christian, co., Il., U.S. | D4 | 90 |
| Christian, co., Ky., U.S. | D2 | 94 |
| Christian, co., Mo., U.S. | E4 | 102 |
| Christiana, Jam. | E14 | 65 |
| Christiana, S. Afr. | C4 | 49 |
| Christiana, De., U.S. | B3 | 85 |
| Christiana, Pa., U.S. | G9 | 115 |
| Christiana, Tn., U.S. | B5 | 119 |
| Christian Hollow, N.H., U.S. | D2 | 106 |
| Christian Island, i., Ont. | C4 | 73 |
| Christiansburg, Oh., U.S. | B1 | 112 |
| Christiansburg, Va., U.S. | C2 | 123 |
| Christiansfeld, Den. | G3 | 15 |
| Christian Sound, strt., Ak., U.S. | n22 | 79 |
| Christiansted, V.I.U.S. | H12 | 64 |
| Christina, stm., Alta. | A5 | 68 |
| Christina, stm., Alta. | A5 | 68 |
| Christina, Lake, l., Mn., U.S. | D3 | 100 |
| Christina Peak, mtn., Nv., U.S. | D6 | 105 |
| Christine, N.D., U.S. | C9 | 111 |
| Christine, Tx., U.S. | E3 | 120 |
| Christmas, Fl., U.S. | D5 | 86 |
| Christmas Island, dep., Oc. | G6 | 6 |
| Christmas Island see Kiritimati Island, i., Kir. | F12 | 6 |
| Christmas Lake, l., Or., U.S. | D6 | 114 |
| Christmas Valley, Or., U.S. | D6 | 114 |
| Christopher, Il., U.S. | F4 | 90 |
| Christoval, Tx., U.S. | D2 | 120 |
| Chromo, Co., U.S. | D4 | 83 |
| Chrudim, Czech. | D3 | 26 |
| Chrysler, Al., U.S. | D2 | 78 |
| Chrzanów, Pol. | g10 | 26 |
| Chu, stm., Sov. Un. | G23 | 8 |
| Chu Chua, B.C. | D7 | 69 |
| Chuckey, Tn., U.S. | C11 | 119 |
| Chudovo, Sov. Un. | B8 | 27 |
| Chugach Mountains, mts., Ak., U.S. | g18 | 79 |
| Chuguyev, Sov. Un. | G11 | 27 |
| Chugwater, Wy., U.S. | E8 | 127 |
| Chugwater Creek, stm., Wy., U.S. | E8 | 127 |
| Chuichu, Az., U.S. | E4 | 80 |
| Chuius Mountain, mtn., B.C. | B5 | 69 |
| Chukai (Kemaman), Malay. | J5 | 35 |
| Chukchi Sea | C32 | 128 |
| Chukotsk Peninsula, pen., Sov. Un. | C32 | 128 |
| Chula, Ga., U.S. | E3 | 87 |
| Chula, Mo., U.S. | B4 | 102 |
| Chula, Va., U.S. | C5 | 123 |
| Chula Vista, Ca., U.S. | F5 | 82 |
| Chulucanas, Peru | B1 | 58 |
| Chulumani, Bol. | G5 | 58 |
| Chulym, Sov. Un. | B10 | 29 |
| Chulym, stm., Sov. Un. | D11 | 29 |
| Chumbicha, Arg. | D16 | 29 |
| Chumikan, Sov. Un. | D16 | 29 |
| Chumphon, Thai. | G3 | 35 |
| Chumysh, stm., Sov. Un. | C10 | 28 |
| Chunchŏn, S. Kor. | H3 | 33 |
| Chunchula, Al., U.S. | E1 | 78 |
| Chungju, S. Kor. | H3 | 33 |
| Chungking see Chongqing, China | F6 | 31 |
| Chungmu, S. Kor. | H4 | 33 |
| Chunya, Tan. | H5 | 35 |
| Chuoi, i., Viet. | H6 | 35 |
| Chupaca, Peru | D2 | 58 |
| Chupadera Mesa, mtn., N.M., U.S. | D3 | 108 |
| Chupadero, Co., U.S. | *B4 | 108 |
| Chuquibamba, Peru | E3 | 58 |
| Chuquicamata, Chile | D2 | 55 |
| Chuquisaca, dept., Bol. | D3 | 55 |
| Chur, Switz. | E4 | 19 |
| Churchbridge, Sask. | G5 | 75 |
| Church Creek, Md., U.S. | C5 | 97 |
| Church Hill, Md., U.S. | B6 | 97 |
| Church Hill, Ms., U.S. | D2 | 101 |
| Church Hill, Tn., U.S. | C11 | 119 |
| Churchill, Man. | f9 | 70 |
| Churchill, Oh., U.S. | *A5 | 112 |
| Churchill, co., Nv., U.S. | D2 | 105 |
| Churchill, stm., Newf. | h9 | 72 |
| Churchill, stm., Can. | f9 | 70 |
| Churchill, Cape, c., Man. | f9 | 70 |
| Churchill, Mount, mtn., B.C. | E6 | 69 |
| Churchill Falls, wtfl., Newf. | h8 | 72 |
| Churchill Lake, l., Sask. | m7 | 75 |
| Churchill Mountain, mtn., B.C. | f14 | 69 |
| Church Point, N.S. | E3 | 71 |
| Church Point, La., U.S. | D3 | 95 |
| Church Rock, N.M., U.S. | B1 | 108 |
| Churchs Ferry, N.D., U.S. | A6 | 111 |
| Church Stretton, Eng., U.K. | C5 | 12 |
| Churchville, N.Y., U.S. | B3 | 109 |
| Churchville, Va., U.S. | B3 | 123 |
| Churdan, Ia., U.S. | B3 | 92 |
| Churia, India | C5 | 37 |
| Churu, India | D5 | 37 |
| Churubusco, In., U.S. | B7 | 91 |
| Churuguara, Ven. | A4 | 60 |
| Churumuco, Mex. | n13 | 63 |
| Chushul, India | C7 | 37 |
| Chuska Mountains, mts., Az., U.S. | A6 | 80 |
| Chusovoy, Sov. Un. | D20 | 8 |
| Chusovaya, stm., Sov. Un. | G23 | 8 |
| Chuxian, China | H8 | 32 |
| Chuxiong, China | F5 | 31 |
| Chuy, Ur. | E2 | 56 |
| Cianjur, Indon. | *G3 | 34 |
| Ciano d'Enza, Italy | E3 | 23 |
| Cianorte, Braz. | C2 | 57 |
| Cibecue, Az., U.S. | C5 | 80 |
| Cibola, co., N.M., U.S. | C1 | 108 |
| Cibolo, stm., Tx., U.S. | h7 | 120 |
| Cicero, Il., U.S. | B6 | 90 |
| Cicero, In., U.S. | D5 | 91 |
| Cicero Dantas, Braz. | F11 | 57 |
| Ciche, Sgurr na, mtn., Scot., U.K. | D20 | 8 |
| Cicia, i., Fiji | H16 | 52 |
| Cide, Tur. | B9 | 27 |

| Name | Map Ref. | Page |
|---|---|---|
| Cidra, Lago de, res., P.R. | B3 | 65 |
| Ciechanów, Pol. | B6 | 26 |
| Ciego de Avila, Cuba | D4 | 64 |
| Ciego de Avila, prov., Cuba | C4 | 64 |
| Ciempozuelos, Spain | B4 | 22 |
| Ciénaga, Col. | A3 | 60 |
| Ciénaga de Oro, Col. | B2 | 60 |
| Cienfuegos, Cuba | C3 | 64 |
| Cienfuegos, prov., Cuba | C3 | 64 |
| Cieszyn, Pol. | D5 | 26 |
| Cieżkowice, Pol. | g10 | 27 |
| Cigüela, stm., Spain | C4 | 22 |
| Cihanbeyli, Tur. | C9 | 40 |
| Cihuatlán, Mex. | n11 | 63 |
| Cilacap, Indon. | G3 | 34 |
| Cili, China | J4 | 32 |
| Cima, Ca., U.S. | E6 | 82 |
| Cimarron, Co., U.S. | C3 | 83 |
| Cimarron, Ks., U.S. | E3 | 93 |
| Cimarron, N.M., U.S. | A5 | 108 |
| Cimarron, co., Ok., U.S. | e8 | 113 |
| Cimarron, stm., U.S. | C8 | 76 |
| Cimarron, North Fork, stm., U.S. | E2 | 93 |
| Cimarron Hills, Co., U.S. | *C6 | 83 |
| Cîmpina, Rom. | C7 | 24 |
| Cîmpulung, Rom. | C7 | 24 |
| Cîmpulung Moldovenesc, Rom. | B7 | 24 |
| Cincinnati, Ia., U.S. | D5 | 92 |
| Cincinnati, Oh., U.S. | C1 | 112 |
| Cincinnatus, N.Y., U.S. | C5 | 109 |
| Cinconsine, Lac, l., Que. | B4 | 74 |
| Cine, Tur. | D7 | 25 |
| Cinnaminson, N.J., U.S. | D3 | 107 |
| Cintalapa [de Figueroa], Mex. | D6 | 63 |
| Cinto, Monte, mtn., Fr. | C2 | 23 |
| Cipolletti, Arg. | B3 | 54 |
| Circle, Ak., U.S. | B11 | 79 |
| Circle, Mt., U.S. | C11 | 103 |
| Circle Hot Springs, Ak., U.S. | B11 | 79 |
| Circle Pines, Mn., U.S. | m12 | 100 |
| Circleville, Ks., U.S. | C8 | 93 |
| Circleville, Oh., U.S. | C3 | 112 |
| Circleville, Ut., U.S. | E3 | 121 |
| Circleville, W.V., U.S. | C5 | 125 |
| Cirebon, Indon. | G3 | 34 |
| Cirencester, Eng., U.K. | E6 | 10 |
| Cirí, stm., Pan. | m10 | 62 |
| Cisco, Ga., U.S. | B2 | 87 |
| Cisco, Il., U.S. | C5 | 90 |
| Cisco, Ky., U.S. | C6 | 94 |
| Cisco, Tx., U.S. | C3 | 120 |
| Cisco, Ut., U.S. | E6 | 121 |
| Ciskei, ctry., Afr. | D4 | 49 |
| Cisne, Il., U.S. | E5 | 90 |
| Cisneros, Col. | B2 | 60 |
| Cisnes, stm., Chile | C2 | 54 |
| Cispus, stm., Wa., U.S. | C4 | 124 |
| Cissna Park, Il., U.S. | C6 | 90 |
| Cistern, Tx., U.S. | E4 | 120 |
| Cisterna di Latina, Italy | h9 | 23 |
| Cistierna, Spain | A3 | 22 |
| Citac, Nevado, mtn., Peru | D2 | 58 |
| Citra, Fl., U.S. | C4 | 86 |
| Citronelle, Al., U.S. | D1 | 78 |
| Citrus, Ca., U.S. | *E5 | 82 |
| Citrus, co., Fl., U.S. | D4 | 86 |
| Citrus Heights, Ca., U.S. | *C3 | 82 |
| Cittadella, Italy | B3 | 23 |
| Città di Castello, Italy | C4 | 23 |
| City Mills, Ma., U.S. | h10 | 98 |
| City of Commerce, Ca., U.S. | n12 | 82 |
| City of Refuge National Historical Park, Hi., U.S. | D5 | 88 |
| City Point, Fl., U.S. | D6 | 86 |
| City View, S.C., U.S. | B3 | 117 |
| Ciudad Acuña, Mex. | A4 | 63 |
| Ciudad Altamirano, Mex. | n13 | 63 |
| Ciudad Bolívar, Ven. | B5 | 60 |
| Ciudad Bolivia, Ven. | B3 | 60 |
| Ciudad Camargo, Mex. | B3 | 63 |
| Ciudad de la Habana, prov., Cuba | C2 | 64 |
| Ciudad del Carmen, Mex. | D6 | 63 |
| Ciudad del Maíz, Mex. | C5 | 63 |
| Ciudad de Naucalpan de Juárez, Mex. | h9 | 63 |
| Ciudad de Valles, Mex. | C5 | 63 |
| Ciudad de Villaldama, Mex. | B4 | 63 |
| Ciudadela, Spain | B7 | 22 |
| Ciudad Guayana, Ven. | B5 | 60 |
| Ciudad Guzmán, Mex. | D4 | 63 |
| Ciudad Hidalgo, Mex. | n13 | 63 |
| Ciudad Ixtepec, Mex. | D5 | 63 |
| Ciudad Jiménez, Mex. | B3 | 63 |
| Ciudad Juárez, Mex. | A3 | 63 |
| Ciudad Lerdo, Mex. | C5 | 63 |
| Ciudad López Mateos, Mex. | g9 | 63 |
| Ciudad Madero, Mex. | C5 | 63 |
| Ciudad Mante, Mex. | C5 | 63 |
| Ciudad Melchor Múzquiz, Mex. | B4 | 63 |
| Ciudad Mendoza, Mex. | n15 | 63 |
| Ciudad Obregón, Mex. | B3 | 63 |
| Ciudad Ojeda, Ven. | A3 | 60 |
| Ciudad Piar, Ven. | B5 | 60 |
| Ciudad Real, Spain | C4 | 22 |
| Ciudad Rodrigo, Spain | B2 | 22 |
| Ciudad Serdán, Mex. | n15 | 63 |
| Ciudad Tecún Umán, Guat. | C1 | 62 |
| Ciudad Victoria, Mex. | C5 | 63 |
| Cividale del Friuli, Italy | A4 | 23 |
| Civitanova Marche, Italy | C4 | 23 |
| Civitavecchia, Italy | C3 | 23 |
| Civray, Fr. | D4 | 16 |
| Çivril, Tur. | C7 | 40 |
| Cizre, Tur. | D14 | 40 |
| C.J. Strike Reservoir, res., Id., U.S. | G3 | 89 |
| Clackamas, Or., U.S. | h12 | 114 |
| Clackamas, co., Or., U.S. | B4 | 114 |
| Clacton-on-Sea, Eng., U.K. | C9 | 12 |
| Claflin, Ks., U.S. | D5 | 93 |
| Claiborne, Al., U.S. | D2 | 78 |
| Claiborne, La., U.S. | *B3 | 95 |
| Claiborne, Md., U.S. | C5 | 97 |
| Claiborne, co., Ms., U.S. | D3 | 101 |
| Claiborne, co., Ms., U.S. | C10 | 119 |
| Claiborne, Lake, res., La., U.S. | B3 | 95 |
| Clair, N.B. | B1 | 71 |
| Clair, Sask. | B3 | 75 |
| Claire, Lake, l., Alta. | f8 | 68 |
| Clair City, S.D., U.S. | B8 | 118 |
| Clair Engle Lake, res., Ca., U.S. | B2 | 82 |
| Clairfield, Tn., U.S. | C10 | 119 |
| Clairton, Pa., U.S. | F2 | 115 |
| Clallam, co., Wa., U.S. | A1 | 124 |
| Clallam Bay, Wa., U.S. | A1 | 124 |
| Clamart, Fr. | g10 | 16 |
| Clamecy, Fr. | D5 | 16 |
| Clam Lake, l., Sask. | B3 | 75 |
| Clam Lake, l., Wi., U.S. | C1 | 126 |
| Clan Alpine Mountains, mts., Nv., U.S. | D4 | 105 |
| Clancy, Mt., U.S. | D5 | 103 |
| Clandeboye, Ont. | D3 | 73 |
| Clandonald, Alta. | C5 | 68 |
| Clanton, Al., U.S. | C3 | 78 |
| Clanwilliam, Man. | D2 | 70 |
| Clanwilliam, S. Afr. | D2 | 49 |
| Clapperton Island, i., Ont. | A2 | 73 |
| Clara, Ire. | D4 | 11 |
| Clara, Ms., U.S. | D5 | 101 |
| Clara City, Mn., U.S. | F3 | 100 |
| Clara Peak, mtn., Az., U.S. | C2 | 80 |
| Clare, Austl. | F6 | 50 |
| Clare, Ia., U.S. | D6 | 91 |
| Clare, Mi., U.S. | E6 | 99 |
| Clare, co., Ire. | E3 | 11 |
| Clare, co., Mi., U.S. | E6 | 99 |
| Clarecastle (Clare), Ire. | E3 | 11 |
| Claregalway, Ire. | E3 | 11 |
| Clare Island, i., Ire. | D1 | 10 |
| Claremont, Ca., U.S. | m13 | 82 |
| Claremont, Il., U.S. | E6 | 90 |
| Claremont, Mn., U.S. | F6 | 100 |
| Claremont, N.H., U.S. | D2 | 106 |
| Claremont, N.C., U.S. | B1 | 110 |
| Claremont, S.D., U.S. | B7 | 118 |
| Claremont, Va., U.S. | C6 | 123 |
| Claremore, Ok., U.S. | A6 | 113 |
| Claremorris, Ire. | D2 | 10 |
| Clarence, Al., U.S. | A3 | 78 |
| Clarence, Ia., U.S. | C6 | 92 |
| Clarence, La., U.S. | C2 | 95 |
| Clarence, Mo., U.S. | B5 | 102 |
| Clarence, Pa., U.S. | D6 | 115 |
| Clarence, stm., N.Z. | O14 | 51 |
| Clarence, Isla, i., Chile | h11 | 54 |
| Clarence Cannon Lake, res., Mo., U.S. | B6 | 102 |
| Clarence Island, i., B.A.T. | C7 | 7 |
| Clarence Strait, strt., Austl. | B5 | 50 |
| Clarence Strait, strt., Ak., U.S. | n23 | 79 |
| Clarence Town, Bah. | C6 | 64 |
| Clarenceville, Que. | D4 | 74 |
| Clarendon, Ar., U.S. | C4 | 81 |
| Clarendon, Pa., U.S. | C3 | 115 |
| Clarendon, Tx., U.S. | B2 | 120 |
| Clarendon, Vt., U.S. | D3 | 122 |
| Clarendon, co., S.C., U.S. | D7 | 117 |
| Clarendon, co., Vt., U.S. | E2 | 122 |
| Clarendon Hills, Il., U.S. | k9 | 90 |
| Clarendon Springs, Vt., U.S. | D2 | 122 |
| Clarendon Station, Ont. | C8 | 73 |
| Clarenville, Newf. | D4 | 72 |
| Claresholm, Alta. | D4 | 68 |
| Claridge, Pa., U.S. | F2 | 115 |
| Clarie Coast, Ant. | C26 | 7 |
| Clarinda, Ia., U.S. | D2 | 92 |
| Clarington, Oh., U.S. | C5 | 112 |
| Clarington, Pa., U.S. | D3 | 115 |
| Clarion, Ia., U.S. | B4 | 92 |
| Clarion, Pa., U.S. | D3 | 115 |
| Clarion, co., Pa., U.S. | D3 | 115 |
| Clarion, stm., Pa., U.S. | D3 | 115 |
| Clarissa, Mn., U.S. | D4 | 100 |
| Clarita, Ok., U.S. | C5 | 113 |
| Clark, Co., U.S. | A4 | 83 |
| Clark, Mo., U.S. | B5 | 102 |
| Clark, N.J., U.S. | B4 | 107 |
| Clark, Oh., U.S. | B4 | 112 |
| Clark, S.D., U.S. | C8 | 118 |
| Clark, co., Ar., U.S. | C2 | 81 |
| Clark, co., Id., U.S. | E6 | 89 |
| Clark, co., Il., U.S. | D6 | 90 |
| Clark, co., In., U.S. | H6 | 91 |
| Clark, co., Ks., U.S. | E4 | 93 |
| Clark, co., Ky., U.S. | C5 | 94 |
| Clark, co., Mo., U.S. | A6 | 102 |
| Clark, co., Nv., U.S. | G6 | 105 |
| Clark, co., Oh., U.S. | C2 | 112 |
| Clark, co., S.D., U.S. | C8 | 118 |
| Clark, co., Wa., U.S. | D3 | 124 |
| Clark, co., Wi., U.S. | D3 | 126 |
| Clark, Lake, l., Ak., U.S. | C9 | 79 |
| Clark, Point, c., Ont. | C3 | 73 |
| Clark Colony, S.D., U.S. | *C8 | 118 |
| Clarkdale, Az., U.S. | C3 | 80 |
| Clarkdale, Ga., U.S. | h7 | 87 |
| Clarke, co., Al., U.S. | D2 | 78 |
| Clarke, co., Ga., U.S. | C3 | 87 |
| Clarke, co., Ia., U.S. | C4 | 92 |
| Clarke, co., Ms., U.S. | C5 | 101 |
| Clarke, co., Va., U.S. | A4 | 123 |
| Clarke City, Que. | h8 | 72 |
| Clarke Lake, l., Sask. | C2 | 75 |
| Clarkesville, Ga., U.S. | B3 | 87 |
| Clarkfield, Mn., U.S. | F3 | 100 |
| Clark Fork, Id., U.S. | A2 | 89 |
| Clark Fork, stm., U.S. | C1 | 103 |
| Clarkia, Id., U.S. | B2 | 89 |
| Clark Mountain, mtn., Mo., U.S. | D7 | 102 |
| Clarkrange, Tn., U.S. | C8 | 119 |
| Clarks, La., U.S. | B3 | 95 |
| Clarks, Ne., U.S. | C8 | 104 |
| Clarks, stm., Ky., U.S. | f9 | 94 |
| Clarks, West Fork, stm., Ky., U.S. | f9 | 94 |
| Clarksboro, N.J., U.S. | D2 | 107 |
| Clarksburg, Ont. | C4 | 73 |
| Clarksburg, In., U.S. | F7 | 91 |
| Clarksburg, Md., U.S. | B3 | 97 |
| Clarksburg, Mo., U.S. | C5 | 102 |
| Clarksburg, N.J., U.S. | C4 | 107 |
| Clarksburg, Oh., U.S. | C2 | 112 |
| Clarksburg, W.V., U.S. | B4 | 125 |
| Clarksdale, Ms., U.S. | A3 | 101 |
| Clarksdale, Mo., U.S. | B3 | 102 |
| Clark's Grove, Mn., U.S. | G5 | 100 |
| Clark's Harbour, N.S. | F4 | 71 |
| Clarks Hill, In., U.S. | D4 | 91 |
| Clarkson, Ky., U.S. | C3 | 94 |
| Clarks Point, Ak., U.S. | D7 | 79 |
| Clarks Summit, Pa., U.S. | m18 | 115 |
| Clarkston, Ga., U.S. | h8 | 87 |
| Clarkston, Mi., U.S. | F7 | 99 |
| Clarkston, Wa., U.S. | C8 | 124 |
| Clarksville, Ar., U.S. | B2 | 81 |
| Clarksville, De., U.S. | F5 | 85 |
| Clarksville, Ia., U.S. | B5 | 92 |
| Clarksville, Mi., U.S. | F5 | 99 |
| Clarksville, Mo., U.S. | B7 | 102 |
| Clarksville, Oh., U.S. | C2 | 112 |
| Clarksville, Tn., U.S. | A4 | 119 |
| Clarksville, Tx., U.S. | C5 | 120 |
| Clarksville, Va., U.S. | D4 | 123 |
| Clarkton, Mo., U.S. | E8 | 102 |
| Clarkton, N.C., U.S. | C4 | 110 |
| Claryville, Ky., U.S. | k14 | 94 |
| Claryville, Mo., U.S. | D8 | 102 |
| Clashmore, Ire. | E4 | 11 |
| Clatonia, Ne., U.S. | D9 | 104 |
| Clatskanie, Or., U.S. | A3 | 114 |
| Clatsop, co., Or., U.S. | A3 | 114 |
| Claude, Tx., U.S. | B2 | 120 |
| Claudy, N. Ire., U.K. | C4 | 11 |
| Claunch, N.M., U.S. | C3 | 108 |
| Clausthal-Zellerfeld, W. Ger. | C5 | 18 |
| Clavet, Sask. | F2 | 75 |
| Clawson, Mi., U.S. | o15 | 99 |
| Claxton, Ga., U.S. | D5 | 87 |
| Clay, Al., U.S. | f7 | 78 |
| Clay, Ky., U.S. | C2 | 94 |
| Clay, La., U.S. | B3 | 95 |
| Clay, N.Y., U.S. | B4 | 109 |
| Clay, W.V., U.S. | C3 | 125 |
| Clay, Wy., U.S. | B8 | 127 |
| Clay, co., Al., U.S. | B4 | 78 |
| Clay, co., Ar., U.S. | A5 | 81 |
| Clay, co., Fl., U.S. | B5 | 86 |
| Clay, co., Ga., U.S. | E2 | 87 |
| Clay, co., Il., U.S. | E5 | 90 |
| Clay, co., In., U.S. | F3 | 91 |
| Clay, co., Ia., U.S. | A2 | 92 |
| Clay, co., Ks., U.S. | C6 | 93 |
| Clay, co., Ky., U.S. | C6 | 94 |
| Clay, co., Mn., U.S. | D2 | 100 |
| Clay, co., Ms., U.S. | B5 | 101 |
| Clay, co., Mo., U.S. | B3 | 102 |
| Clay, co., Ne., U.S. | D7 | 104 |
| Clay, co., N.C., U.S. | f9 | 110 |
| Clay, co., S.D., U.S. | E8 | 118 |
| Clay, co., Tn., U.S. | C8 | 119 |
| Clay, co., Tx., U.S. | C3 | 120 |
| Clay, co., W.V., U.S. | C3 | 125 |
| Clay Center, Ks., U.S. | C6 | 93 |
| Clay Center, Ne., U.S. | D7 | 104 |
| Clay Center, Oh., U.S. | A2 | 112 |
| Clay City, Il., U.S. | E5 | 90 |
| Clay City, In., U.S. | F3 | 91 |
| Clay City, Ky., U.S. | C6 | 94 |
| Clay Creek, stm., S.D., U.S. | D8 | 118 |
| Clayhatchee, Al., U.S. | D4 | 78 |
| Claydon, Sask. | H1 | 75 |
| Clay Head, c., I. of Man | F4 | 13 |
| Claymont, De., U.S. | A4 | 85 |
| Claypool, Az., U.S. | D5 | 80 |
| Claypool, In., U.S. | B6 | 91 |
| Claysburg, Pa., U.S. | F5 | 115 |
| Clay Springs, Az., U.S. | C5 | 80 |
| Claysville, Pa., U.S. | F1 | 115 |
| Clayton, Al., U.S. | D4 | 78 |
| Clayton, De., U.S. | C3 | 85 |
| Clayton, Ga., U.S. | B3 | 87 |
| Clayton, Id., U.S. | E4 | 89 |
| Clayton, Il., U.S. | C3 | 90 |
| Clayton, In., U.S. | E4 | 91 |
| Clayton, Ks., U.S. | C3 | 93 |
| Clayton, La., U.S. | C4 | 95 |
| Clayton, Mo., U.S. | C7 | 102 |
| Clayton, N.J., U.S. | D2 | 107 |
| Clayton, N.M., U.S. | A6 | 108 |
| Clayton, N.Y., U.S. | A4 | 109 |
| Clayton, N.C., U.S. | B4 | 110 |
| Clayton, Ok., U.S. | C6 | 113 |
| Clayton, S.D., U.S. | D8 | 118 |
| Clayton, Tn., U.S. | A2 | 119 |
| Clayton, Wa., U.S. | B8 | 124 |
| Clayton, Wi., U.S. | C1 | 126 |
| Clayton, co., Ga., U.S. | C2 | 87 |
| Clayton, co., Ia., U.S. | B6 | 92 |
| Clayton Lake, Me., U.S. | B3 | 96 |
| Claytor Lake, res., Va., U.S. | C2 | 123 |
| Clayville, R.I., U.S. | C2 | 116 |
| Clear, stm., Alta. | A1 | 68 |
| Clear, stm., R.I., U.S. | B2 | 116 |
| Clear, Cape, c., Ire. | E2 | 10 |
| Clear, Lake, l., Ont. | B7 | 73 |
| Clear Boggy Creek, stm., Ok., U.S. | C5 | 113 |
| Clearbrook, Mn., U.S. | C3 | 100 |
| Clear Creek, In., U.S. | F4 | 91 |
| Clear Creek, Ut., U.S. | D4 | 121 |
| Clear Creek, W.V., U.S. | n13 | 125 |
| Clear Creek, co., Co., U.S. | B5 | 83 |
| Clear Creek, stm., Az., U.S. | C4 | 80 |
| Clear Creek, stm., Ne., U.S. | C6 | 104 |
| Clear Creek, stm., Tn., U.S. | C9 | 119 |
| Clear Creek, stm., Wy., U.S. | B6 | 127 |
| Clear Creek, c., Ak., U.S. | D10 | 79 |
| Clearfield, Pa., U.S. | D5 | 115 |
| Clearfield, Ky., U.S. | B6 | 94 |
| Clearfield, Ut., U.S. | B3 | 121 |
| Clearfield, co., Pa., U.S. | D5 | 115 |
| Clear Fork, stm., W.V., U.S. | D3 | 125 |
| Clear Fork, stm., W.V., U.S. | n13 | 125 |
| Clear Fork, West Fork, stm., Ky., U.S. | f9 | 94 |
| Clearlake, Ca., U.S. | C2 | 82 |
| Clear Lake, Ia., U.S. | A4 | 92 |
| Clear Lake, Mn., U.S. | E5 | 100 |
| Clear Lake, S.D., U.S. | C9 | 118 |
| Clearlake, Wa., U.S. | A3 | 124 |
| Clear Lake, l., Man. | D1 | 70 |
| Clear Lake, l., Ia., U.S. | A4 | 92 |
| Clear Lake, l., Ut., U.S. | D3 | 121 |
| Clear Lake, res., Ca., U.S. | B3 | 82 |
| Clear Lake City, Tx., U.S. | r14 | 120 |
| Clear Lake Reservoir, res., Ca., U.S. | B3 | 82 |
| Clearwater, stm., Alta. | D3 | 68 |
| Clearwater, stm., Can. | A5 | 68 |
| Clearwater, stm., B.C. | C7 | 69 |
| Clearwater, stm., Id., U.S. | C2 | 89 |
| Clearwater, stm., Mn., U.S. | C3 | 100 |
| Clearwater Lake, Wi., U.S. | C4 | 126 |
| Clearwater Lake, l., B.C. | C7 | 69 |
| Clearwater Lake, l., Man. | B1 | 70 |
| Clearwater Mountains, mts., Id., U.S. | C2 | 89 |
| Clearwater Provincial Park, Man. | C1 | 70 |
| Cleaton, Ky., U.S. | C2 | 94 |
| Cleator Moor, Eng., U.K. | F5 | 13 |
| Cleburne, Tx., U.S. | C4 | 120 |
| Cleburne, co., Al., U.S. | B4 | 78 |
| Cleburne, co., Ar., U.S. | B3 | 81 |
| Cle Elum, Wa., U.S. | B5 | 124 |
| Cle Elum, stm., Wa., U.S. | B4 | 124 |
| Cle Elum Lake, res., Wa., U.S. | B4 | 124 |
| Cleethorpes, Eng., U.K. | A7 | 12 |
| Cleeves, Sask. | D1 | 75 |
| Cleggan, Ire. | D1 | 11 |
| Cleghorn, Ia., U.S. | B2 | 92 |
| Cleland Heights, De., U.S. | *B3 | 85 |
| Clem, Ga., U.S. | C1 | 87 |
| Clementon, N.J., U.S. | D3 | 107 |
| Clements, Ks., U.S. | D7 | 93 |
| Clements, Md., U.S. | D4 | 97 |
| Clements, Mn., U.S. | F3 | 100 |
| Clementsport, N.S. | E4 | 71 |
| Clementsvale, N.S. | E4 | 71 |
| Clemmons, N.C., U.S. | A2 | 110 |
| Clemons, Ia., U.S. | B4 | 92 |
| Clemscot, Ok., U.S. | C4 | 113 |
| Clemson, S.C., U.S. | B2 | 117 |
| Clendenin, W.V., U.S. | C3 | 125 |
| Clendening Lake, res., Oh., U.S. | B4 | 112 |
| Cleona, Pa., U.S. | F9 | 115 |
| Cleo Springs, Ok., U.S. | A3 | 113 |
| Clermont, Austl. | D8 | 50 |
| Clermont, Que. | B7 | 74 |
| Clermont, Fr. | E2 | 17 |
| Clermont, Fl., U.S. | D5 | 86 |
| Clermont, Ga., U.S. | B3 | 87 |
| Clermont, Ia., U.S. | A6 | 92 |
| Clermont, Ky., U.S. | C4 | 94 |
| Clermont, co., Oh., U.S. | C1 | 112 |
| Clermont-Ferrand, Fr. | E5 | 16 |
| Clermont Harbor, Ms., U.S. | E4 | 101 |
| Clermont-l'Hérault, Fr. | F5 | 16 |
| Clerval, Fr. | B1 | 21 |
| Clervaux, Lux. | D6 | 17 |
| Clevedon, Eng., U.K. | C5 | 12 |
| Cleveland, Al., U.S. | A3 | 78 |
| Cleveland, Ar., U.S. | B3 | 81 |
| Cleveland, Ga., U.S. | B3 | 87 |
| Cleveland, Mn., U.S. | F5 | 100 |
| Cleveland, Ms., U.S. | B3 | 101 |
| Cleveland, Mo., U.S. | C3 | 102 |
| Cleveland, N.M., U.S. | A4 | 108 |
| Cleveland, N.Y., U.S. | B5 | 109 |
| Cleveland, N.C., U.S. | B2 | 110 |
| Cleveland, N.D., U.S. | C6 | 111 |
| Cleveland, Oh., U.S. | A4 | 112 |
| Cleveland, Ok., U.S. | A5 | 113 |
| Cleveland, S.C., U.S. | A2 | 117 |
| Cleveland, Tn., U.S. | D9 | 119 |
| Cleveland, Tx., U.S. | D5 | 120 |
| Cleveland, Ut., U.S. | D5 | 121 |
| Cleveland, Va., U.S. | f9 | 123 |
| Cleveland, Wi., U.S. | k10 | 126 |
| Cleveland, co., Ar., U.S. | D3 | 81 |
| Cleveland, co., N.C., U.S. | B1 | 110 |
| Cleveland, co., Ok., U.S. | B4 | 113 |
| Cleveland, Mount, mtn., Mt., U.S. | B3 | 103 |
| Cleveland Heights, Oh., U.S. | A4 | 112 |
| Cleveland Hills, hills, Eng., U.K. | F7 | 13 |
| Clevelândia, Braz. | D2 | 56 |
| Clever, Mo., U.S. | D4 | 102 |
| Cleves, Oh., U.S. | o12 | 112 |
| Cleves see Kleve, W. Ger. | C3 | 18 |
| Clew Bay, b., Ire. | D2 | 10 |
| Clewiston, Fl., U.S. | F6 | 86 |
| Clichy, Fr. | g10 | 16 |
| Clifden, Ire. | D1 | 10 |
| Cliff, N.M., U.S. | E1 | 108 |
| Cliff Island, l., Me., U.S. | g7 | 96 |
| Clifford, Ont. | D4 | 73 |
| Clifford, In., U.S. | F6 | 91 |
| Clifford, Mi., U.S. | E7 | 99 |
| Clifford, N.D., U.S. | B8 | 111 |
| Clifford, Pa., U.S. | C10 | 115 |
| Cliffside, N.C., U.S. | B1 | 110 |
| Cliffside Park, N.J., U.S. | h9 | 107 |
| Clifftop, W.V., U.S. | m14 | 125 |
| Clifton, Az., U.S. | D6 | 80 |
| Clifton, Co., U.S. | B2 | 83 |
| Clifton, Il., U.S. | C6 | 90 |
| Clifton, Ks., U.S. | C6 | 93 |
| Clifton, N.J., U.S. | B4 | 107 |
| Clifton, S.C., U.S. | A4 | 117 |
| Clifton, Tn., U.S. | B4 | 119 |
| Clifton, Tx., U.S. | D4 | 120 |
| Clifton, Va., U.S. | g12 | 123 |
| Clifton City, Mo., U.S. | C5 | 102 |
| Clifton Forge, Va., U.S. | C3 | 123 |
| Clifton Heights, Pa., U.S. | *p20 | 115 |
| Clifton Hill, Mo., U.S. | B5 | 102 |
| Clifton Knolls, N.Y., U.S. | C7 | 109 |
| Clifton Springs, N.Y., U.S. | C3 | 109 |
| Cliftonville, Ms., U.S. | B5 | 101 |
| Climax, Sask. | H1 | 75 |
| Climax, Ga., U.S. | F2 | 87 |
| Climax, Mi., U.S. | F5 | 99 |
| Climax, Mn., U.S. | C2 | 100 |
| Climax Springs, Mo., U.S. | C4 | 102 |
| Climbing Hill, Ia., U.S. | B1 | 92 |
| Clinch, co., Ga., U.S. | F4 | 87 |
| Clinch, stm., U.S. | C10 | 119 |
| Clinchburg, Va., U.S. | f10 | 123 |
| Clinchco, Va., U.S. | e9 | 123 |
| Clinchfield, Ga., U.S. | D3 | 87 |
| Clinch Mountain, mtn., U.S. | C10 | 119 |
| Clinchport, Va., U.S. | f9 | 123 |
| Clingmans Dome, mtn., U.S. | D10 | 119 |
| Clint, Tx., U.S. | o11 | 120 |
| Clinton, B.C. | D7 | 69 |
| Clinton, Ont. | D3 | 73 |
| Clinton, Ar., U.S. | B3 | 81 |
| Clinton, Ct., U.S. | D5 | 84 |
| Clinton, Ga., U.S. | D3 | 87 |
| Clinton, Il., U.S. | C5 | 90 |
| Clinton, In., U.S. | E3 | 91 |
| Clinton, Ia., U.S. | C7 | 92 |
| Clinton, Ks., U.S. | m15 | 93 |
| Clinton, Ky., U.S. | f9 | 94 |
| Clinton, La., U.S. | D4 | 95 |
| Clinton, Me., U.S. | D3 | 96 |
| Clinton, Md., U.S. | C4 | 97 |
| Clinton, Ma., U.S. | B4 | 98 |
| Clinton, Mi., U.S. | F7 | 99 |
| Clinton, Mn., U.S. | E2 | 100 |
| Clinton, Ms., U.S. | C3 | 101 |
| Clinton, Mo., U.S. | C4 | 102 |
| Clinton, Mt., U.S. | D3 | 103 |
| Clinton, Ne., U.S. | B3 | 104 |
| Clinton, N.J., U.S. | B3 | 107 |
| Clinton, N.Y., U.S. | B5 | 109 |
| Clinton, N.C., U.S. | C4 | 110 |
| Clinton, Ok., U.S. | B3 | 113 |
| Clinton, S.C., U.S. | C4 | 117 |
| Clinton, Tn., U.S. | C9 | 119 |
| Clinton, Ut., U.S. | B3 | 121 |
| Clinton, Wa., U.S. | B3 | 124 |
| Clinton, Wi., U.S. | F5 | 126 |
| Clinton, co., Il., U.S. | E4 | 90 |
| Clinton, co., In., U.S. | D4 | 91 |
| Clinton, co., Ia., U.S. | C7 | 92 |
| Clinton, co., Ky., U.S. | D4 | 94 |
| Clinton, co., Mi., U.S. | F6 | 99 |
| Clinton, co., Mo., U.S. | B3 | 102 |
| Clinton, co., N.Y., U.S. | f11 | 109 |
| Clinton, co., Oh., U.S. | C2 | 112 |
| Clinton, co., Pa., U.S. | D6 | 115 |
| Clinton, Lake, res., Il., U.S. | C5 | 90 |
| Clinton-Colden Lake, l., N.W. Ter. | D11 | 66 |
| Clinton Lake, res., Ks., U.S. | m15 | 93 |
| Clinton Reservoir, res., N.J., U.S. | A4 | 107 |
| Clinton Township, Mi., U.S. | *F8 | 99 |
| Clintonville, Pa., U.S. | D2 | 115 |
| Clintonville, W.V., U.S. | D4 | 125 |
| Clintonville, Wi., U.S. | D5 | 126 |
| Clintwood, Va., U.S. | e9 | 123 |
| Clio, Al., U.S. | D4 | 78 |
| Clio, Ca., U.S. | C3 | 82 |
| Clio, Mi., U.S. | E7 | 99 |
| Clio, S.C., U.S. | B8 | 117 |
| Clio, W.V., U.S. | C3 | 125 |
| Clipperton, atoll, Fr. Poly. | F15 | 6 |
| Clisham, mtn., Scot., U.K. | C2 | 13 |
| Clisson, Fr. | E5 | 16 |
| Clitheroe, Eng., U.K. | G6 | 13 |
| Clive, Alta. | C4 | 68 |
| Clive, Ia., U.S. | e8 | 92 |
| Cliza, Bol. | C5 | 59 |
| Cloan, Sask. | E1 | 75 |
| Cloe, Pa., U.S. | E3 | 115 |
| Cloghan, Ire. | C4 | 11 |
| Cloghan, Ire. | E1 | 11 |
| Cloghane, Ire. | E1 | 11 |
| Clogheen, Ire. | E4 | 11 |
| Clogher Head, c., Ire. | D5 | 11 |
| Clonakilty, Ire. | E2 | 10 |
| Clonakilty Bay, b., Ire. | E2 | 10 |
| Cloncurry, Austl. | D7 | 50 |
| Clones, Ire. | D3 | 11 |
| Clonmany, Ire. | A4 | 10 |
| Clonmel, Ire. | E3 | 10 |
| Clonmellon, Ire. | D3 | 10 |
| Clontarf, Mn., U.S. | E3 | 100 |
| Cloone, Ire. | D5 | 11 |
| Clo-oose, B.C. | E5 | 69 |
| Cloppenburg, W. Ger. | C4 | 18 |
| Clopton, Al., U.S. | D4 | 78 |
| Cloquet, Mn., U.S. | D6 | 100 |
| Cloquet, stm., Mn., U.S. | C6 | 100 |
| Closter, N.J., U.S. | B5 | 107 |
| Clothier, W.V., U.S. | n12 | 125 |
| Cloud, co., Ks., U.S. | C6 | 93 |
| Cloud Chief, Ok., U.S. | B3 | 113 |
| Cloudcroft, N.M., U.S. | E4 | 108 |
| Cloud Peak, mtn., Wy., U.S. | B5 | 127 |
| Cloudy, Ok., U.S. | C6 | 113 |
| Cloudy Bay, b., N.Z. | N15 | 51 |
| Cloudy Mountain, mtn., Ar., U.S. | C8 | 79 |
| Cloutierville, La., U.S. | C3 | 95 |
| Clover, S.C., U.S. | A5 | 117 |
| Clover, Va., U.S. | D4 | 123 |
| Clover Bottom, Ky., U.S. | C5 | 94 |
| Cloverdale, B.C. | f13 | 69 |
| Cloverdale, Ca., U.S. | C2 | 82 |
| Cloverdale, In., U.S. | E4 | 91 |
| Cloverdale, Or., U.S. | B3 | 114 |
| Cloverleaf, Tx., U.S. | *r14 | 120 |
| Cloverport, Ky., U.S. | C3 | 94 |
| Clovis, Ca., U.S. | D4 | 82 |
| Clovis, N.M., U.S. | C6 | 108 |
| Clow, Ar., U.S. | D2 | 81 |
| Cloyne, Ire. | F3 | 11 |
| Cluanie, Loch, l., Scot., U.K. | C3 | 13 |
| Cluj-Napoca, Rom. | B6 | 24 |
| Clune, Pa., U.S. | E3 | 115 |
| Cluny, Alta. | D4 | 68 |
| Cluny, Fr. | D6 | 21 |
| Cluses, Fr. | D2 | 21 |
| Clusone, Italy | D4 | 23 |
| Cluster Springs, Va., U.S. | D4 | 123 |
| Clute, Tx., U.S. | r14 | 120 |
| Clutha, stm., N.Z. | P12 | 51 |
| Clutier, Ia., U.S. | B5 | 92 |
| Clwyd, co., Wales, U.K. | A4 | 12 |
| Clyattville, Ga., U.S. | F3 | 87 |
| Clyde, Alta. | B4 | 68 |
| Clyde, N.W. Ter. | B19 | 66 |
| Clyde, Ks., U.S. | C6 | 93 |
| Clyde, Mo., U.S. | A3 | 102 |
| Clyde, N.C., U.S. | f10 | 110 |
| Clyde, N.Y., U.S. | B3 | 109 |
| Clyde, Oh., U.S. | A3 | 112 |
| Clyde, Tx., U.S. | C3 | 120 |
| Clyde, stm., Scot., U.K. | E4 | 13 |
| Clyde, Firth of, est., Scot., U.K. | C4 | 10 |
| Clydebank, Scot., U.K. | C4 | 10 |
| Clyde Park, Mt., U.S. | E6 | 103 |
| Clymer, N.Y., U.S. | C1 | 109 |
| Clymer, Pa., U.S. | E3 | 115 |
| Clyo, Ga., U.S. | D5 | 87 |
| Cnossus, hist., Grc. | E5 | 25 |
| Côa, stm., Port. | D4 | 22 |
| Coachella, Ca., U.S. | F5 | 82 |
| Coachella Canal, Ca., U.S. | F6 | 82 |
| Coachford, Ire. | F3 | 11 |
| Coahoma, Ms., U.S. | A3 | 101 |
| Coahoma, Tx., U.S. | C2 | 120 |
| Coahoma, co., Ms., U.S. | A3 | 101 |
| Coahuayana, stm., Mex. | n12 | 63 |
| Coahuila, state, Mex. | B4 | 63 |
| Coal, co., Ok., U.S. | C5 | 113 |
| Coal Bluff, In., U.S. | E3 | 91 |
| Coal Branch, N.B. | C4 | 71 |
| Coal City, Il., U.S. | B5 | 90 |
| Coal City, In., U.S. | F3 | 91 |
| Coalcomán [de Matamoros], Mex. | D4 | 63 |
| Coal Creek, Co., U.S. | C5 | 83 |
| Coal Creek, stm., In., U.S. | E3 | 91 |
| Coal Creek, stm., Ok., U.S. | B6 | 113 |
| Coaldale, Alta. | E4 | 68 |
| Coaldale, Co., U.S. | C5 | 83 |
| Coaldale, Nv., U.S. | E4 | 105 |
| Coaldale, Pa., U.S. | E10 | 115 |
| Coalfield, Tn., U.S. | C9 | 119 |
| Coal Fork, W.V., U.S. | C3 | 125 |
| Coal Fork, stm., W.V., U.S. | m13 | 125 |
| Coalgate, Ok., U.S. | C5 | 113 |
| Coalgood, Ky., U.S. | D6 | 94 |
| Coal Grove, Oh., U.S. | D3 | 112 |
| Coal Harbour, B.C. | D4 | 69 |
| Coal Hill, Ar., U.S. | B2 | 81 |
| Coalhurst, Alta. | E4 | 68 |
| Coaling, Al., U.S. | B2 | 78 |
| Coalinga, Ca., U.S. | D3 | 82 |
| Coalmont, B.C. | E7 | 69 |
| Coalmont, Co., U.S. | A4 | 83 |
| Coalmont, In., U.S. | F3 | 91 |
| Coalmont, Tn., U.S. | D8 | 119 |
| Coalport, Pa., U.S. | E5 | 115 |
| Coalridge, Oh., U.S. | C4 | 112 |
| Coalspur, Alta. | C2 | 68 |
| Coalton, Il., U.S. | D4 | 90 |
| Coalton, Oh., U.S. | C3 | 112 |
| Coalville, Eng., U.K. | B6 | 12 |
| Coalville, Ia., U.S. | B3 | 92 |
| Coalville, Ut., U.S. | C4 | 121 |
| Coalwood, W.V., U.S. | D3 | 125 |
| Coamo, P.R. | B3 | 65 |
| Coari, Braz. | C2 | 59 |
| Coari, stm., Braz. | C2 | 59 |
| Coast, prov., Kenya | B6 | 48 |
| Coast Mountains, mts., N.A. | E6 | 66 |
| Coast Ranges, mts., U.S. | B3 | 76 |
| Coatbridge, Scot., U.K. | C5 | 10 |
| Coatepec, Mex. | n15 | 63 |
| Coatepeque, Guat. | C2 | 62 |
| Coatesville, In., U.S. | E4 | 91 |
| Coatesville, Pa., U.S. | G10 | 115 |
| Coaticook, Que. | D6 | 74 |
| Coatney Hill, mtn., Ct., U.S. | B7 | 84 |
| Coatopa, Al., U.S. | C1 | 78 |
| Coats, Ks., U.S. | E5 | 93 |
| Coats, N.C., U.S. | B4 | 110 |
| Coatsburg, Il., U.S. | C2 | 90 |
| Coats Island, i., N.W. Ter. | D16 | 66 |
| Coats Land, reg., Ant. | B9 | 7 |
| Coatsville, Mo., U.S. | A5 | 102 |
| Coatzacoalcos (Puerto México), Mex. | D6 | 63 |
| Cobalt, Ont. | p19 | 73 |
| Cobalt, Ct., U.S. | C5 | 84 |
| Cobalt, Id., U.S. | D4 | 89 |
| Cobán, Guat. | D6 | 63 |
| Cobar, Austl. | F8 | 50 |
| Cobb, Ga., U.S. | E3 | 87 |
| Cobb, Ky., U.S. | D2 | 94 |
| Cobb, Ok., U.S. | C5 | 113 |
| Cobb, Wi., U.S. | F3 | 126 |
| Cobb, co., Ga., U.S. | C2 | 87 |
| Cobb, stm., Mn., U.S. | G5 | 100 |
| Cobberas, Mount, mtn., Austl. | H7 | 51 |
| Cobb Island, Md., U.S. | D4 | 97 |
| Cobble Hill, B.C. | g12 | 69 |
| Cobble Mountain Reservoir, res., Ma., U.S. | B2 | 98 |
| Cobbosseecontee Lake, l., Me., U.S. | D3 | 96 |
| Cobbtown, Ga., U.S. | D4 | 87 |
| Cobden, Ont. | B8 | 73 |
| Cobden, Il., U.S. | F4 | 90 |
| Cobequid Mountains, mts., N.S. | D5 | 71 |
| Cobh, Ire. | E2 | 10 |
| Cobham, Eng., U.K. | m12 | 10 |
| Cobham, stm., Can. | C4 | 70 |
| Cobija, Bol. | B2 | 55 |
| Cobija, Chile | D2 | 55 |
| Coble, Tn., U.S. | B4 | 119 |
| Coblence see Koblenz, W. Ger. | C3 | 18 |
| Cobleskill, N.Y., U.S. | C6 | 109 |
| Coboconk, Ont. | C6 | 73 |
| Cobourg, Ont. | D6 | 73 |
| Cobourg Peninsula, pen., Austl. | B5 | 50 |
| Cobre, Nv., U.S. | B7 | 105 |
| Cóbuè, Moz. | D6 | 44 |
| Cobun Creek, stm., W.V., U.S. | h11 | 125 |
| Coburg, Austl. | *G7 | 51 |
| Coburg, W. Ger. | C5 | 18 |
| Coburg, Ia., U.S. | D2 | 92 |
| Coburg, Or., U.S. | C3 | 114 |
| Coburg Island, i., N.W. Ter. | m36 | 67 |
| Coburn Gore, Me., U.S. | C2 | 96 |
| Coburn Mountain, mtn., Me., U.S. | C2 | 96 |
| Cocentaina, Spain | C5 | 22 |
| Cochabamba, Bol. | C2 | 55 |
| Cochabamba, dept., Bol. | C5 | 55 |
| Coche, Isla, i., Ven. | A5 | 60 |
| Cocheco, stm., N.H., U.S. | D5 | 106 |
| Cochem, W. Ger. | C2 | 19 |
| Cochesett, Ma., U.S. | B5 | 98 |
| Cochetopa Creek, stm., Co., U.S. | C4 | 83 |
| Cochetopa Hills, mts., Co., U.S. | C4 | 83 |
| Cochin, India | G3 | 37 |
| Cochin China, hist. reg., Viet. | H6 | 35 |
| Cochinos Point, c., Phil. | o13 | 34 |
| Cochise, Az., U.S. | E6 | 80 |
| Cochise, co., Az., U.S. | F5 | 80 |
| Cochise Head, mtn., Az., U.S. | E6 | 80 |
| Cochiti, N.M., U.S. | h8 | 108 |
| Cochiti Indian Reservation, N.M., U.S. | h8 | 108 |
| Cochiti Reservoir, res., N.M., U.S. | B3 | 108 |
| Cochituate, Ma., U.S. | g10 | 98 |
| Cochituate, Lake, l., Ma., U.S. | g10 | 98 |
| Cochran, Ga., U.S. | D3 | 87 |
| Cochran, co., Tx., U.S. | C1 | 120 |
| Cochrane, Alta. | D3 | 68 |
| Cochrane, Ont. | o19 | 73 |
| Cochrane, Wi., U.S. | D2 | 126 |
| Cochrane, dept., Ont. | o19 | 73 |
| Cochranton, Pa., U.S. | C1 | 115 |
| Cochranville, Pa., U.S. | G10 | 115 |

Cockburn, Austl. . . . . . . . F3 51
Cocke, co., Tn., U.S. . . . . . D10 119
Cockermouth, Eng., U.K. . . . F5 13
Cockeysville, Md., U.S. . . . . B4 97
Cockpit Country, reg., Jam. . E13 65
Cockrell Hill, Tx., U.S. . . . . n10 120
Cockrum, Ms., U.S. . . . . . . A4 101
Coco, stm., N.A. . . . . . . . E8 63
Coco, Isla del, i., C.R. . . . . C2 53
Cocoa, Fl., U.S. . . . . . . . . D6 86
Cocoa Beach, Fl., U.S. . . . . D6 86
Cocoa West, Fl., U.S. . . . . *D6 86
Cocobeach, Gabon . . . . . . E1 46
Cocolalla, Id., U.S. . . . . . . A2 89
Coconino, co., Az., U.S. . . . B3 80
Coconino Plateau, plat., Az.,
U.S. . . . . . . . . . . . . . B3 80
Coconut Creek, Fl., U.S. . . . *F6 86
Cocopah Indian Reservation,
Az., U.S. . . . . . . . . . . . E1 80
Cocos Bay, b., Trin. . . . . . . O23 65
Cocos Island, i., Guam . . . . M9 52
Cocos Islands (Keeling
Islands), is., Oc. . . . . . . G3 2
Cocos Lagoon, b., Guam . . . M9 52
Coco Solo, Pan. . . . . . . . . k11 62
Cocula, Mex. . . . . . . . . . . C4 63
Cod, Cape, c., Ma., U.S. . . . C7 98
Codajás, Braz. . . . . . . . . . C2 59
Codell, Ks., U.S. . . . . . . . . C4 93
Coden, Al., U.S. . . . . . . . . E1 78
Codera, Cabo, c., Ven. . . . . A4 60
Coderre, Sask. . . . . . . . . . G2 75
Codette, Sask. . . . . . . . . . D3 75
Codigoro, Italy . . . . . . . . . E8 20
Codington, co., S.D., U.S. . . C8 118
Cod Island, i., Newf. . . . . . g9 72
Codó, Braz. . . . . . . . . . . . B2 57
Codogno, Italy . . . . . . . . . B2 23
Codpa, Chile . . . . . . . . . . C2 55
Codroipo, Italy . . . . . . . . . D8 20
Codroy, Newf. . . . . . . . . . E2 72
Codroy Pond, Newf. . . . . . . D2 72
Cody, Ne., U.S. . . . . . . . . B4 104
Cody, Wy., U.S. . . . . . . . . B3 127
Codys, N.B. . . . . . . . . . . . D4 71
Coeburn, Va., U.S. . . . . . . f9 123
Coe Hill, Ont. . . . . . . . . . C7 73
Coesfeld, W. Ger. . . . . . . . C3 18
Coessе, In., U.S. . . . . . . . B7 91
Coeur d'Alene, Id., U.S. . . . B2 89
Coeur d'Alene, stm., Id., U.S. B2 89
Coeur d'Alene Indian
Reservation, Id., U.S. . . . B2 89
Coeur d'Alene Lake, res., Id.,
U.S. . . . . . . . . . . . . . B2 89
Coeur d'Alene Mountains,
mts., Id., U.S. . . . . . . . B2 89
Coevorden, Neth. . . . . . . . B6 17
Coffee, co., Al., U.S. . . . . . D3 78
Coffee, co., Ga., U.S. . . . . . E4 87
Coffee, co., Tn., U.S. . . . . . B5 119
Coffee Creek, Mt., U.S. . . . C6 103
Coffeen, Il., U.S. . . . . . . . . D4 90
Coffee Springs, Al., U.S. . . . D4 78
Coffeeville, Al., U.S. . . . . . D1 78
Coffeeville, Ms., U.S. . . . . . B4 101
Coffey, Mo., U.S. . . . . . . . A3 102
Coffey, co., Ks., U.S. . . . . . D8 93
Coffeyville, Ks., U.S. . . . . . E8 93
Coffin, Île, i., Que. . . . . . . B8 71
Coffs Harbour, Austl. . . . . . F9 50
Cofield, N.C., U.S. . . . . . . A6 110
Cogdell, Ga., U.S. . . . . . . . E4 87
Coggon, Ia., U.S. . . . . . . . B6 92
Coghinas, stm., Italy . . . . . D2 23
Cognac, Fr. . . . . . . . . . . . E3 16
Cogswell, N.D., U.S. . . . . . C8 111
Cohagen, Mt., U.S. . . . . . . C10 103
Cohansey, stm., N.J., U.S. . . E2 107
Cohasset, Ma., U.S. . . . . . . B6 98
Cohasset, Mn., U.S. . . . . . . C5 100
Cohocton, N.Y., U.S. . . . . . C3 109
Cohocton, stm., N.Y., U.S. . . C3 109
Cohoe, Ak., U.S. . . . . . . . . g16 79
Cohoes, N.Y., U.S. . . . . . . C7 109
Cohoon, Lake, res., Va., U.S. k14 123
Cohutta, Ga., U.S. . . . . . . . B2 87
Cohutta Mountain, mtn., Ga.,
U.S. . . . . . . . . . . . . . B2 87
Coiba, Isla de, i., Pan. . . . . G7 62
Coig, stm., Arg. . . . . . . . . E2 54
Coihaique, Chile . . . . . . . . D2 54
Coila, Ms., U.S. . . . . . . . . B4 101
Coils Creek, stm., Nv., U.S. . D5 105
Coimbatore, India . . . . . . . F6 36
Coimbra, Port. . . . . . . . . . B1 22
Coín, Spain . . . . . . . . . . . D3 22
Coin, Ia., U.S. . . . . . . . . . D2 92
Coinjock, N.C., U.S. . . . . . A7 110
Coipasa, Laguna, l., Bol. . . . C2 55
Coipasa, Salar de, pl., S.A. . C2 55
Coire, Loch, l., Scot., U.K. . . B4 13
Cojedes, state, Ven. . . . . . . B4 60
Cojutepeque, El Sal. . . . . . . D3 62
Cokato, Mn., U.S. . . . . . . . E4 100
Coke, co., Tx., U.S. . . . . . . D2 120
Coker, Al., U.S. . . . . . . . . B2 78
Cokesbury, S.C., U.S. . . . . . C3 117
Coketon, W.Va., U.S. . . . . . B5 125
Cokeville, Wy., U.S. . . . . . . D2 127
Colába Point, c., India . . . . H4 37
Colac, Austl. . . . . . . . . . . G7 50
Colares, Port. . . . . . . . . . . f9 22
Colatina, Braz. . . . . . . . . . B4 56
Colbeck, Cape, c., Ant. . . . . B33 7
Colbert, Ga., U.S. . . . . . . . B3 87
Colbert, Ok., U.S. . . . . . . . D5 113
Colbert, co., Al., U.S. . . . . . A2 78
Colbert Heights, Al., U.S. . . A2 78
Colbio, Som. . . . . . . . . . . F5 47
Colborne, Ont. . . . . . . . . . C7 73
Colbún, Chile . . . . . . . . . . B2 54
Colburn, Id., U.S. . . . . . . . A2 89
Colburn, In., U.S. . . . . . . . C4 91
Colby, Ks., U.S. . . . . . . . . C2 93
Colby, Me., U.S. . . . . . . . . B4 96
Colby, Wi., U.S. . . . . . . . . D3 126
Colbyville, Vt., U.S. . . . . . . C3 122
Colchester, Eng., U.K. . . . . E7 10
Colchester, Ct., U.S. . . . . . C6 84
Colchester, Il., U.S. . . . . . . C3 90
Colchester, Vt., U.S. . . . . . B2 122
Colchester, co., N.S. . . . . . D6 71
Colcord, Ok., U.S. . . . . . . . A7 113
Cold, N.H., U.S. . . . . . . . . C4 106
Cold, stm., N.H., U.S. . . . . . D2 106
Cold Bay, Ak., U.S. . . . . . . E7 79
Cold Fell, mtn., Eng., U.K. . . F6 13
Cold Hollow Mountains, mts.,
Vt., U.S. . . . . . . . . . . . B3 122
Colditz, E. Ger. . . . . . . . . . B7 19
Cold Lake, Alta. . . . . . . . . B5 68
Cold Lake, l., Can. . . . . . . . B5 68

Cold River, N.H., U.S. . . . . . D2 106
Cold Spring, Ky., U.S. . . . . . A5 94
Cold Spring, Mn., U.S. . . . . E4 100
Cold Spring, N.J., U.S. . . . . F3 107
Coldspring, Tx., U.S. . . . . . D5 120
Cold Spring Harbor, N.Y., U.S. *n15 109
Cold Springs, Nv., U.S. . . . . D4 105
Cold Stream Pond, l., Me.,
U.S. . . . . . . . . . . . . . . C4 96
Coldwater, Ont. . . . . . . . . C5 73
Coldwater, Ks., U.S. . . . . . . E4 93
Coldwater, Mi., U.S. . . . . . . G5 99
Coldwater, Ms., U.S. . . . . . A4 101
Coldwater, Oh., U.S. . . . . . B1 112
Coldwater, stm., Ms., U.S. . . A3 101
Coldwater Creek, stm., U.S. . e9 113
Cole, Ok., U.S. . . . . . . . . . B4 113
Cole, co., Mo., U.S. . . . . . . C5 102
Colebrook, Ct., U.S. . . . . . . B3 84
Colebrook, N.H., U.S. . . . . . g7 106
Colebrook River Lake, res.,
Ct., U.S. . . . . . . . . . . . A3 84
Cole Camp, Mo., U.S. . . . . . C4 102
Coleen, stm., Ak., U.S. . . . . B11 79
Coleharbor, N.D., U.S. . . . . B4 111
Cole Lake, Ont. . . . . . . . . C8 73
Coleman, P.E.I. . . . . . . . . . C5 71
Coleman, Fl., U.S. . . . . . . . D4 86
Coleman, Ga., U.S. . . . . . . E2 87
Coleman, Md., U.S. . . . . . . B5 97
Coleman, Mi., U.S. . . . . . . . E6 99
Coleman, Ok., U.S. . . . . . . C5 113
Coleman, Tx., U.S. . . . . . . . D3 120
Coleman, Wi., U.S. . . . . . . C5 126
Coleman, co., Tx., U.S. . . . . D3 120
Coleman Falls, Va., U.S. . . . C3 123
Colen Lakes, l., Man. . . . . . B4 70
Colerain, N.C., U.S. . . . . . . A6 110
Coleraine, Austl. . . . . . . . . H3 51
Coleraine, Que. . . . . . . . . . D6 74
Coleraine, N. Ire., U.K. . . . . C3 10
Coleraine, Mn., U.S. . . . . . . C5 100
Coleridge, Ne., U.S. . . . . . . B8 104
Coles, Ms., U.S. . . . . . . . . D2 101
Coles, co., Il., U.S. . . . . . . . D5 90
Coles, Punta, c., Peru . . . . . E3 58
Colesburg, S. Afr. . . . . . . . D4 49
Colesburg, Ia., U.S. . . . . . . B6 92
Colesburg, Ky., U.S. . . . . . . C4 94
Coleta, Il., U.S. . . . . . . . . . B4 90
Coleville, Sask. . . . . . . . . . F1 75
Colfax, Ca., U.S. . . . . . . . . C3 82
Colfax, Il., U.S. . . . . . . . . . C5 90
Colfax, In., U.S. . . . . . . . . . D4 91
Colfax, Ia., U.S. . . . . . . . . C4 92
Colfax, La., U.S. . . . . . . . . C3 95
Colfax, N.D., U.S. . . . . . . . C9 111
Colfax, Wa., U.S. . . . . . . . . C8 124
Colfax, Wi., U.S. . . . . . . . . D2 126
Colfax, co., Ne., U.S. . . . . . C8 104
Colfax, co., N.M., U.S. . . . . A5 108
Colgate, Sask. . . . . . . . . . H4 75
Colhué Huapi, Lago, l., Arg. . D3 54
Colibris, Pointe des, c., Guad. Q9 65
Colico, Italy . . . . . . . . . . . C3 20
Colijnsplaat, Neth. . . . . . . . C3 17
Colima, Mex. . . . . . . . . . . D4 63
Colima, state, Mex. . . . . . . D4 63
Colima, Nevado de, mtn.,
Mex. . . . . . . . . . . . . . . n12 63
Colinas, Braz. . . . . . . . . . . C2 57
Colinton, Newf. . . . . . . . . . E5 72
Colinton, Alta. . . . . . . . . . B4 68
Coll, i., Scot., U.K. . . . . . . . B3 10
Collbran, Co., U.S. . . . . . . . B3 83
College, Ak., U.S. . . . . . . . B10 79
College City, Ar., U.S. . . . . . *A5 81
College Corner, Oh., U.S. . . C1 112
Collegedale, Tn., U.S. . . . . . h11 119
College Grove, Tn., U.S. . . . B5 119
College Park, Ga., U.S. . . . . C2 87
College Park, Md., U.S. . . . . C4 97
College Place, Wa., U.S. . . . C7 124
College Springs, Ia., U.S. . . . D2 92
College Station, Ar., U.S. . . . C3 81
College Station, Tx., U.S. . . . D4 120
Collegeville, Ar., U.S. . . . . . *C3 81
Collegeville, In., U.S. . . . . . C3 91
Collegeville, Pa., U.S. . . . . . F11 115
College Ward, Ut., U.S. . . . . *B4 121
Colleton, co., S.C., U.S. . . . *F6 117
Colleyville, Tx., U.S. . . . . . . *n9 120
Collie, Austl. . . . . . . . . . . . F2 50
Collier, co., Fl., U.S. . . . . . . F5 86
Collier Bay, b., Austl. . . . . . C4 50
Collier City, Fl., U.S. . . . . . . *F6 86
Colliers, W.Va., U.S. . . . . . . f8 125
Collierville, Tn., U.S. . . . . . . B2 119
Collingdale, Pa., U.S. . . . . . p20 115
Collingswood, N.J., U.S. . . . D2 107
Collingsworth, co., Tx., U.S. . B2 120
Collingwood, Ont. . . . . . . . C4 73
Collins, Ar., U.S. . . . . . . . . D4 81
Collins, Ga., U.S. . . . . . . . . D4 87
Collins, In., U.S. . . . . . . . . . B7 91
Collins, Ia., U.S. . . . . . . . . C4 92
Collins, Ms., U.S. . . . . . . . . D4 101
Collins, Mo., U.S. . . . . . . . . C4 102
Collins, Wi., U.S. . . . . . . . . h10 126
Collins Park, De., U.S. . . . . . B3 85
Collinston, La., U.S. . . . . . . B4 95
Collinston, Ut., U.S. . . . . . . B3 121
Collinsville, Al., U.S. . . . . . . A4 78
Collinsville, Ct., U.S. . . . . . . B4 84
Collinsville, Il., U.S. . . . . . . E4 90
Collinsville, Ms., U.S. . . . . . C5 101
Collinsville, Ok., U.S. . . . . . A6 113
Collinsville, Va., U.S. . . . . . . D3 123
Collinwood, Tn., U.S. . . . . . B4 119
Collipulli, Chile . . . . . . . . . D2 54
Collis, Mn., U.S. . . . . . . . . E2 100
Collooney, Ire. . . . . . . . . . . C3 11
Collyer, Ks., U.S. . . . . . . . . C3 93
Colmar, Fr. . . . . . . . . . . . . C7 16
Colmar, Ky., U.S. . . . . . . . . D6 94
Colmar Manor, Md., U.S. . . . f9 97
Colmenar de Oreja, Spain . . B4 22
Colmenar Viejo, Spain . . . . B4 22
Colnett, Cabo, c., Mex. . . . . A1 63
Cologne (Köln), W. Ger. . . . C3 18
Cologne, Mn., U.S. . . . . . . . F5 100
Cologne, N.J., U.S. . . . . . . . D3 107
Coloma, Ca., U.S. . . . . . . . C3 82
Coloma, Mi., U.S. . . . . . . . F4 99
Colombes, Fr. . . . . . . . . . . g10 16
Colômbia, Braz. . . . . . . . . . C3 56

Colombia, Col. . . . . . . . . . . C3 60
Colombia, ctry., S.A. . . . . . . C3 60
Colombo, Sri L. . . . . . . . . . G6 36
Colome, S.D., U.S. . . . . . . . D6 118
Colón, Arg. . . . . . . . . . . . A5 54
Colón, Cuba . . . . . . . . . . . C3 64
Colón, Pan. . . . . . . . . . . . . F8 62
Colon, Mi., U.S. . . . . . . . . . G5 99
Colon, Ne., U.S. . . . . . . . . . g11 104
Colon, N.C., U.S. . . . . . . . . B3 110
Colón, Archipiélago de
(Galápagos Islands), is., Ec. g5 58
Colona, Co., U.S. . . . . . . . . C3 83
Colonia, Italy . . . . . . . . . . . k7 107
Colonia, dept., Ur. . . . . . . . g8 54
Colonia del Sacramento, Ur. . E1 56
Colonia Dora, Arg. . . . . . . . E3 55
Colonia Las Heras, Arg. . . . . D3 54
Colonial Beach, Va., U.S. . . . B6 123
Colônia Leopoldina, Braz. . . k6 57
Colonial Heights, Tn., U.S. . . C11 119
Colonial Heights, Va., U.S. . . C5 123
Colonial National Historical
Park, Va., U.S. . . . . . . . . C6 123
Colonial Park, Pa., U.S. . . . . *F8 115
Colonia Mennonita, Para. . . . D3 55
Colonia Suiza, Ur. . . . . . . . g8 54
Colonie, N.Y., U.S. . . . . . . . C7 109
Colonna, stm., Italy . . . . . . . h9 23
Colonne, Cape, c., Italy . . . . E6 23
Colonsay, Sask. . . . . . . . . . F3 75
Colonsay, i., Scot., U.K. . . . . B3 10
Colony, Ks., U.S. . . . . . . . . D8 93
Colony, Ok., U.S. . . . . . . . . B3 113
Colorado, C.R. . . . . . . . . . E8 63
Colorado, co., Tx., U.S. . . . . E4 120
Colorado, state, U.S. . . . . . . B5 83
Colorado, stm., Arg. . . . . . . B4 54
Colorado, stm., N.A. . . . . . . D5 76
Colorado, stm., U.S. . . . . . . D3 120
Colorado City, Az., U.S. . . . . A3 80
Colorado City, Co., U.S. . . . . D6 83
Colorado City, Tx., U.S. . . . . E3 120
Colorado City, Lake, res., Tx.,
U.S. . . . . . . . . . . . . . . C2 120
Colorado National Monument,
Co., U.S. . . . . . . . . . . . B2 83
Colorado Plateau, plat., U.S. . B4 80
Colorado River Aqueduct, Ca.,
U.S. . . . . . . . . . . . . . . F6 82
Colorado River Indian
Reservation, U.S. . . . . . . D1 80
Colorados, Archipiélago de
los, is., Cuba . . . . . . . . . C1 64
Colorado Springs, Co., U.S. . C6 83
Colotlán, Mex. . . . . . . . . . . C4 63
Colquechaca, Bol. . . . . . . . C2 55
Colquitt, Ga., U.S. . . . . . . . E2 87
Colquitt, co., Ga., U.S. . . . . . E3 87
Colrain, Ma., U.S. . . . . . . . . A2 98
Colstrip, Mt., U.S. . . . . . . . . E10 103
Colt, Ar., U.S. . . . . . . . . . . B5 81
Coltauco, Chile . . . . . . . . . A2 54
Colter Bay, Wy., U.S. . . . . . C2 127
Colton, Ca., U.S. . . . . . . . . *E5 82
Colton, N.Y., U.S. . . . . . . . . f10 109
Colton, Or., U.S. . . . . . . . . B4 114
Colton, S.D., U.S. . . . . . . . . D9 118
Colton, Wa., U.S. . . . . . . . . C8 124
Colton Hill, mtn., Vt., U.S. . . D4 122
Colton, Ca., U.S. . . . . . . . . *E5 82
Colts Neck, N.J., U.S. . . . . . C4 107
Columbia, Al., U.S. . . . . . . . D4 78
Columbia, Ct., U.S. . . . . . . . C6 84
Columbia, Il., U.S. . . . . . . . E3 90
Columbia, Ky., U.S. . . . . . . . C4 94
Columbia, La., U.S. . . . . . . . B3 95
Columbia, Md., U.S. . . . . . . B4 97
Columbia, Mo., U.S. . . . . . . C5 102
Columbia, Ms., U.S. . . . . . . D4 101
Columbia, N.C., U.S. . . . . . . B6 110
Columbia, Pa., U.S. . . . . . . . F9 115
Columbia, S.C., U.S. . . . . . . C5 117
Columbia, S.D., U.S. . . . . . . B7 118
Columbia, Tn., U.S. . . . . . . . B4 119
Columbia, Va., U.S. . . . . . . . C4 123
Columbia, co., Ar., U.S. . . . . D2 81
Columbia, co., Fl., U.S. . . . . B4 86
Columbia, co., Ga., U.S. . . . . C4 87
Columbia, co., N.Y., U.S. . . . C7 109
Columbia, co., Or., U.S. . . . . B3 114
Columbia, co., Pa., U.S. . . . . D9 115
Columbia, co., Wa., U.S. . . . . C7 124
Columbia, co., Wi., U.S. . . . . E4 126
Columbia, stm., N.A. . . . . . . A3 76
Columbia, Cape, c., N.W. Ter. k37 66
Columbia, Mount, mtn., Can. . C2 68
Columbia Basin, Wa., U.S. . . C6 124
Columbia City, In., U.S. . . . . B7 91
Columbia City, Or., U.S. . . . . B4 114
Columbia Cross Roads, Pa.,
U.S. . . . . . . . . . . . . . . C8 115
Columbia Falls, Me., U.S. . . . D5 96
Columbia Falls, Mt., U.S. . . . B2 103
Columbia Heights, Mn., U.S. . m12 100
Columbia Lake, B.C. . . . . . . D10 69
Columbia Lake, res., Ct., U.S. C6 84
Columbia Mountains, mts.,
B.C. . . . . . . . . . . . . . . C7 69
Columbiana, Al., U.S. . . . . . B3 78
Columbiana, Oh., U.S. . . . . . B5 112
Columbiana, co., Oh., U.S. . . B5 112
Columbiaville, Mi., U.S. . . . . E7 99
Columbine, Co., U.S. . . . . . . *B5 83
Columbus, Ar., U.S. . . . . . . . D2 81
Columbus, Ga., U.S. . . . . . . D1 87
Columbus, In., U.S. . . . . . . . F6 91
Columbus, Ks., U.S. . . . . . . E9 93
Columbus, Ky., U.S. . . . . . . . f8 94
Columbus, Ms., U.S. . . . . . . B5 101
Columbus, Mt., U.S. . . . . . . E7 103
Columbus, Ne., U.S. . . . . . . C8 104
Columbus, N.J., U.S. . . . . . . C3 107
Columbus, N.M., U.S. . . . . . F2 108
Columbus, N.C., U.S. . . . . . . f10 110
Columbus, N.D., U.S. . . . . . . A3 111
Columbus, Oh., U.S. . . . . . . C2 112
Columbus, Tx., U.S. . . . . . . . E4 120
Columbus, Wi., U.S. . . . . . . . E4 126
Columbus, co., N.C., U.S. . . . C4 110
Columbus Air Force Base,
mil., Ms., U.S. . . . . . . . . B5 101
Columbus City, Ia., U.S. . . . . C6 92
Columbus Grove, Oh., U.S. . . B1 112
Columbus Junction, Ia., U.S. . C6 92
Columbus Lake, res., Ms.,
U.S. . . . . . . . . . . . . . . B5 101
Colusa, Ca., U.S. . . . . . . . . C2 82
Colusa, co., Ca., U.S. . . . . . C2 82
Colver, Pa., U.S. . . . . . . . . E4 115
Colville, Wa., U.S. . . . . . . . . A8 124
Colville, stm., Ak., U.S. . . . . B9 79
Colville, stm., Wa., U.S. . . . . A8 124

Colville Indian Reservation,
Wa., U.S. . . . . . . . . . . . A6 124
Colville Lake, l., N.W. Ter. . . C7 66
Colvin Mountain, mtn., Al.,
U.S. . . . . . . . . . . . . . . B4 78
Colvos Passage, strt., Wa.,
U.S. . . . . . . . . . . . . . . f10 124
Colwell, Ia., U.S. . . . . . . . . A5 92
Colwich, Ks., U.S. . . . . . . . . E6 93
Colwood, B.C. . . . . . . . . . . h12 69
Colwyn Bay, Wales, U.K. . . . A4 12
Colyell Creek, stm., La., U.S. h10 95
Comabbio, Lago di, l., Italy . . E6 21
Comacchio, Italy . . . . . . . . E8 20
Comacchio, Valli di, b., Italy . E8 20
Comal, co., Tx., U.S. . . . . . . E3 120
Comalapa, Guat. . . . . . . . . E6 63
Comalcalco, Mex. . . . . . . . . D6 63
Coman, Mount, mtn., Ant. . . . B6 7
Comanche, Ok., U.S. . . . . . . C4 113
Comanche, Tx., U.S. . . . . . . D3 120
Comanche, co., Ks., U.S. . . . E4 93
Comanche, co., Ok., U.S. . . . C3 113
Comanche, co., Tx., U.S. . . . D3 120
Comarapa, Bol. . . . . . . . . . C3 55
Comayagua, Hond. . . . . . . . E7 63
Combahee, stm., S.C., U.S. . F6 117
Combeaufontaine, Fr. . . . . . . B1 20
Combee Settlement, Fl., U.S. . *D5 86
Comber, Ont. . . . . . . . . . . E2 73
Comber, N. Ire., U.K. . . . . . . C6 11
Combermere, Ont. . . . . . . . B7 73
Combined Locks, Wi., U.S. . . h9 126
Combs, Ar., U.S. . . . . . . . . B2 81
Combs, Ky., U.S. . . . . . . . . C6 94
Comer, Al., U.S. . . . . . . . . . C4 78
Comer, Ga., U.S. . . . . . . . . B3 87
Comerío, P.R. . . . . . . . . . . B3 65
Comet, stm., Austl. . . . . . . . B7 51
Comfort, N.C., U.S. . . . . . . . B5 110
Comfort, Tx., U.S. . . . . . . . . E3 120
Comfort, W.V., U.S. . . . . . . . m12 125
Comfrey, Mn., U.S. . . . . . . . F4 100
Comilla, Bngl. . . . . . . . . . . D9 36
Comines, Bel. . . . . . . . . . . D2 17
Comino, Cape, c., Italy . . . . D2 23
Comins, Mi., U.S. . . . . . . . . D6 99
Cominto, Ar., U.S. . . . . . . . . D4 81
Comiso, Italy . . . . . . . . . . . F5 23
Comitán [de Dominguez]
Mex. . . . . . . . . . . . . . . D6 63
Comite, stm., La., U.S. . . . . . D4 95
Commack, N.Y., U.S. . . . . . . *n15 109
Commentry, Fr. . . . . . . . . . D5 16
Commerce, Ga., U.S. . . . . . B3 87
Commerce, Mo., U.S. . . . . . D8 102
Commerce, Ok., U.S. . . . . . . A7 113
Commerce, Tx., U.S. . . . . . . C5 120
Commerce City, Co., U.S. . . . B6 83
Commercial Point, Oh., U.S. . C2 112
Commercy, Fr. . . . . . . . . . . C6 16
Commewijne, dept., Sur. . . . A4 59
Commiskey, In., U.S. . . . . . . G6 91
Commissaires, Lac des, l.,
Que. . . . . . . . . . . . . . . A5 74
Committee Bay, b., N.W. Ter. . C15 66
Common Fence Point, R.,
U.S. . . . . . . . . . . . . . . E6 116
Commonwealth Bay, b., Ant. . C27 7
Commonwealth Range, mts.,
Ant. . . . . . . . . . . . . . . . A30 7
Communism Peak, mtn., Sov.
Un. . . . . . . . . . . . . . . . F10 29
Como, Italy . . . . . . . . . . . . B2 23
Como, Co., U.S. . . . . . . . . . B5 83
Como, Ms., U.S. . . . . . . . . . A4 101
Como, N.C., U.S. . . . . . . . . A5 110
Como, Tn., U.S. . . . . . . . . . A3 119
Como, Lake, l., Italy . . . . . . B2 23
Comobabi, Az., U.S. . . . . . . E4 80
Comodoro Rivadavia, Arg. . . D3 54
Comorin, Cape, c., India . . . G6 36
Comoros, ctry., Afr. . . . . . . . H10 42
Comox, B.C. . . . . . . . . . . . E5 69
Compass Lake, Fl., U.S. . . . . B1 86
Compeer, Alta. . . . . . . . . . . D5 68
Competition, Mo., U.S. . . . . . D5 102
Compiègne, Fr. . . . . . . . . . . C5 16
Compostela, Mex. . . . . . . . . m11 63
Comptche, Ca., U.S. . . . . . . C2 82
Compton, Que. . . . . . . . . . D6 74
Compton, Ar., U.S. . . . . . . . A2 81
Compton, Il., U.S. . . . . . . . . B4 90
Compton, co., Que. . . . . . . . D6 74
Compton, stm., N.A. . . . . . . A3 76

Concarneau, Fr. . . . . . . . . . D2 16
Conceição das Alagoas, Braz. B3 78
Conceição do Araguaia, Braz. D5 59
Conceição do Norte, Braz. . . D1 57
Conceição do Uruguai, Arg. . A3 102
Concepción, Arg. . . . . . . . . E2 55
Concepción, Bol. . . . . . . . . B2 54
Concepción, Chile . . . . . . . . B2 54
Concepción, Guat. . . . . . . . E6 63
Concepción, Para. . . . . . . . D4 55
Concepción, Phil. . . . . . . . . o13 34
Concepción, Laguna, l., Bol. . C3 55
Concepción, Punta, c., Mex. . D4 63
Concepción del Oro, Mex. . . C4 63
Concepción del Uruguay, Arg. A3 102
Conception, Mo., U.S. . . . . . A3 102
Conception, Point, c., Ca.,
U.S. . . . . . . . . . . . . . . . E3 82
Conception Bay, b., Newf. . . E5 72
Conception Island, i., Bah. . . C6 64
Conception Junction, Mo.,
U.S. . . . . . . . . . . . . . . . A3 102
Conchas, Braz. . . . . . . . . . m7 56
Conchas Dam, N.M., U.S. . . B5 108
Conchas Lake, res., N.M.,
U.S. . . . . . . . . . . . . . . . B5 108
Conche, Newf. . . . . . . . . . . C4 72
Conchi, Chile . . . . . . . . . . . A3 55
Conchillas, Ur. . . . . . . . . . . g7 54
Concho, Az., U.S. . . . . . . . . C6 80
Concho, Ok., U.S. . . . . . . . . B4 113
Concho, co., Tx., U.S. . . . . . D3 120
Concho, stm., Tx., U.S. . . . . D2 120
Conchos, stm., Mex. . . . . . . B4 63
Conchos, stm., Mex. . . . . . . C4 63
Concord, Ca., U.S. . . . . . . . h8 82
Concord, Fl., U.S. . . . . . . . . B2 86
Concord, Ga., U.S. . . . . . . . C2 87
Concord, Il., U.S. . . . . . . . . D3 90
Concord, Ky., U.S. . . . . . . . B6 94
Concord, Ma., U.S. . . . . . . . B5 98
Concord, Mi., U.S. . . . . . . . F6 99
Concord, Mi., U.S. . . . . . . . g13 102
Concord, Ne., U.S. . . . . . . . B9 104
Concord, N.H., U.S. . . . . . . D3 106
Concord, N.C., U.S. . . . . . . B2 110
Concord, Pa., U.S. . . . . . . . F6 115
Concord, Tn., U.S. . . . . . . . D10 119
Concord, Vt., U.S. . . . . . . . C5 122
Concord, Va., U.S. . . . . . . . C4 123
Concord, stm., Ma., U.S. . . . A5 98
Concordia, Arg. . . . . . . . . . A5 54
Concordia, Col. . . . . . . . . . B2 60
Concordia, Peru . . . . . . . . . B3 58
Concordia, Ks., U.S. . . . . . . C6 93
Concordia, Mo., U.S. . . . . . . C4 102
Concordia, co., La., U.S. . . . C4 95
Concrete, N.D., U.S. . . . . . . A8 111
Concrete, Wa., U.S. . . . . . . A4 124
Conda, Id., U.S. . . . . . . . . . G7 89
Condamine, stm., Austl. . . . . E9 50
Condé, Braz. . . . . . . . . . . . D3 57
Condé-sur-l'Escaut, Fr. . . . . D3 17
Condé-sur-Marne, Fr. . . . . . D1 20
Condé-sur-Noireau, Fr. . . . . C3 16
Condeúba, Braz. . . . . . . . . A4 56
Condino, Italy . . . . . . . . . . D6 20
Condobolin, Austl. . . . . . . . F4 16
Condom, Fr. . . . . . . . . . . . C3 103
Condon, Mt., U.S. . . . . . . . . B6 114
Condon, Or., U.S. . . . . . . . . B2 58
Cóndor, Cordillera del, mts.,
S.A. . . . . . . . . . . . . . . . B2 58
Cone, Tx., U.S. . . . . . . . . . C2 120
Conecuh, co., Al., U.S. . . . . . D2 78
Conecuh, stm., U.S. . . . . . . D3 78
Conegliano [Veneto], Italy . . B4 23
Conehatta, Ms., U.S. . . . . . . C4 101
Conejos, co., Co., U.S. . . . . D4 83
Conejos, stm., Co., U.S. . . . D4 83
Conejos Peak, mtn., Co., U.S. D4 83
Conemaugh, Pa., U.S. . . . . . F4 115
Conemaugh River Lake, res.,
Pa., U.S. . . . . . . . . . . . . F3 115
Conestee, S.C., U.S. . . . . . . B3 117
Conesville, Ia., U.S. . . . . . . C6 92
Conetoe, N.C., U.S. . . . . . . B5 110
Coney Island (part of New
York), N.Y., U.S. . . . . . . . k13 109
Conflans-en-Jarnisy, Fr. . . . . C6 16
Conflans-Sainte-Honorine, Fr. g9 16
Confluence, Ky., U.S. . . . . . C6 94
Confluence, Pa., U.S. . . . . . G3 115
Confolens, Fr. . . . . . . . . . . D4 16
Confusion Bay, b., Newf. . . . D4 72
Confusion Range, mts., Ut.,
U.S. . . . . . . . . . . . . . . . D2 121
Confuso, stm., Para. . . . . . . D4 55
Cong, Ire. . . . . . . . . . . . . . D2 11
Congamond, Ma., U.S. . . . . B2 98
Congaree, stm., S.C., U.S. . . D6 117
Congaree Swamp National
Monument, S.C., U.S. . . . . D6 117
Conger, Mn., U.S. . . . . . . . . G5 100
Congers, N.Y., U.S. . . . . . . . *D7 109
Congleton, Eng., U.K. . . . . . A5 12
Congo, Oh., U.S. . . . . . . . . B2 112
Congo, W.V., U.S. . . . . . . . . e8 125
Congo, ctry., Afr. . . . . . . . . B2 48
Congo (Zaire), stm., Afr. . . . . B2 48
Congress, Sask. . . . . . . . . . C3 80
Congress, Az., U.S. . . . . . . . C3 80
Conifer, N.Y., U.S. . . . . . . . . A6 109
Conil [de la Frontera], Spain . D5 116
Conimicut Point, c., R.I., U.S. D5 116
Coniston Water, l., Eng., U.K. E4 83
Conklin, Alta. . . . . . . . . . . . B5 68
Conklin, N.Y., U.S. . . . . . . . C5 109
Conlen, Tx., U.S. . . . . . . . . A1 120
Conley, Ga., U.S. . . . . . . . . *C2 87
Conn, Lough, l., Ire. . . . . . . C2 10
Connacht (Connaught), hist.
reg., Ire. . . . . . . . . . . . . D2 11
Connaught see Connacht,
hist. reg., Ire. . . . . . . . . . D2 11
Conneaut, Oh., U.S. . . . . . . A5 112
Conneaut Creek, stm., Oh.,
U.S. . . . . . . . . . . . . . . . A5 112
Conneaut Lake, Pa., U.S. . . . C1 115
Conneaut Lake, l., Pa., U.S. . C1 115
Conneautville, Pa., U.S. . . . . C1 115
Connecticut, state, U.S. . . . . C5 84
Connecticut, stm., U.S. . . . . C5 84
Connell, Wa., U.S. . . . . . . . . C7 124
Connells Creek, stm., R.,
U.S. . . . . . . . . . . . . . . . F2 115
Connellsville, Pa., U.S. . . . . . F2 115
Connellys, Mo., U.S. . . . . . . E5 102
Conner, Mt., U.S. . . . . . . . . E2 103
Connerville, Ok., U.S. . . . . . C5 113
Connersville, In., U.S. . . . . . E7 91
Connors, N.B. . . . . . . . . . . B1 71
Conococheague Creek, stm.,
Md., U.S. . . . . . . . . . . . . A2 97
Conover, N.C., U.S. . . . . . . . B1 110
Conover, Wi., U.S. . . . . . . . . C4 126
Conowingo, Md., U.S. . . . . . A5 97
Conowingo Dam, Md., U.S. . A5 97
Conquest, Sask. . . . . . . . . . F2 75
Conrad, Ia., U.S. . . . . . . . . B5 92
Conrad, Mt., U.S. . . . . . . . . B5 103
Conrath, Wi., U.S. . . . . . . . . C2 126
Conroe, Tx., U.S. . . . . . . . . D5 120
Conroy, Ia., U.S. . . . . . . . . . C5 92
Consecon, Ont. . . . . . . . . . C7 73
Conselheiro Lafaiete, Braz. . . F7 57
Consett, Eng., U.K. . . . . . . . F7 13
Consolación del Sur, Cuba . . C2 64
Con Son, i., Viet. . . . . . . . . D5 34
Consort, Alta. . . . . . . . . . . . D5 68
Constable, N.Y., U.S. . . . . . . f10 109
Constableville, N.Y., U.S. . . . B5 109
Constance, Lake, l., Eur. . . . . A3 102
Constance, Lake, l., Eur. . . . . A3 102
Constance see Konstanz, W.
Ger. . . . . . . . . . . . . . . . E4 18
Constancia, Rom. . . . . . . . . C5 24
Constantina, Braz. . . . . . . . B5 109
Constantine, Mi., U.S. . . . . . G5 99
Constantine, Cape, c., Ak.,
U.S. . . . . . . . . . . . . . . . D8 79
Constantine (Qacentina), Alg. B6 44
Constantinople see İstanbul,
Tur. . . . . . . . . . . . . . . . B7 24
Constitución, Chile . . . . . . . B2 54
Constitución, Ur. . . . . . . . . C4 22

Consul, Sask. . . . . . . . . . . H1 75
Contact, Nv., U.S. . . . . . . . . B7 105
Contai, India . . . . . . . . . . . G11 37
Contamana, Peru . . . . . . . . C3 58
Contas, Rio de, stm., Braz. . . D3 57
Contendas do Sincorá, Braz. . A4 56
Content Keys, is., Fl., U.S. . . H5 86
Continental, Oh., U.S. . . . . . A1 112
Continental Divide, N.M., U.S. B1 108
Continental Peak, mtn., Wy.,
U.S. . . . . . . . . . . . . . . . D4 127
Continental Reservoir, res.,
Co., U.S. . . . . . . . . . . . . D3 83
Contoocook, N.H., U.S. . . . . D3 106
Contoocook, stm., N.H., U.S. D3 106
Contra Costa, co., Ca., U.S. . D3 82
Contracoeur, Que. . . . . . . . D4 74
Contratación, Col. . . . . . . . . B3 60
Contrecoeur, Que. . . . . . . . D4 74
Contrexéville, Fr. . . . . . . . . A1 20
Contreras, N.M., U.S. . . . . . C4 102
Contumazá, Peru . . . . . . . . C2 58
Contwoyto Lake, l., N.W. Ter. C10 66
Converse, In., U.S. . . . . . . . C6 91
Converse, La., U.S. . . . . . . . C2 95
Converse, S.C., U.S. . . . . . . B4 117
Converse, Tx., U.S. . . . . . . . *E3 120
Converse, co., Wy., U.S. . . . C7 127
Convoy, Oh., U.S. . . . . . . . . B1 112
Conway, P.E.I. . . . . . . . . . . C6 71
Conway, Ar., U.S. . . . . . . . . B3 81
Conway, Fl., U.S. . . . . . . . . D5 86
Conway, Ia., U.S. . . . . . . . . D3 92
Conway, Ks., U.S. . . . . . . . . D6 93
Conway, Ma., U.S. . . . . . . . A2 98
Conway, Mo., U.S. . . . . . . . D5 102
Conway, N.H., U.S. . . . . . . . C4 106
Conway, N.C., U.S. . . . . . . . A5 110
Conway, N.D., U.S. . . . . . . . A8 111
Conway, Pa., U.S. . . . . . . . . E1 115
Conway, S.C., U.S. . . . . . . . D9 117
Conway, co., Ar., U.S. . . . . . B3 81
Conway, Lake, l., Ar., U.S. . . B3 81
Conway Springs, Ks., U.S. . . E6 93
Conwy, Wales, U.K. . . . . . . A4 12
Conyers, Ga., U.S. . . . . . . . C2 87
Cook, Austl. . . . . . . . . . . . F5 50
Cook, Mn., U.S. . . . . . . . . . C6 100
Cook, Ne., U.S. . . . . . . . . . D9 104
Cook, co., Ga., U.S. . . . . . . E3 87
Cook, co., Il., U.S. . . . . . . . B6 90
Cook, co., Mn., U.S. . . . . . . k9 100
Cook, Cape, c., B.C. . . . . . . D4 69
Cook, Mount, mtn., N.Z. . . . . O13 51
Cooke, co., Tx., U.S. . . . . . . C4 120
Cooke City, Mt., U.S. . . . . . . E7 103
Cookes Peak, mtn., N.M.,
U.S. . . . . . . . . . . . . . . . E2 108
Cookeville, Tn., U.S. . . . . . . C8 119
Cook Ice Shelf, ice, Ant. . . . C28 7
Cooking Lake, l., Alta. . . . . . C4 68
Cook Inlet, b., Ak., U.S. . . . . D9 79
Cook Islands, ctry., Oc. . . . . G12 6
Cook Mountain, mtn., W.V.,
U.S. . . . . . . . . . . . . . . . n12 125
Cook Point, c., Md., U.S. . . . C5 97
Cooks, Mi., U.S. . . . . . . . . . B3 99
Cooksburg, Pa., U.S. . . . . . . D3 115
Cooks Falls, N.Y., U.S. . . . . . D6 109
Cookshire, Que. . . . . . . . . . D6 74
Cooks Mills, Il., U.S. . . . . . . D5 90
Cookson, Ok., U.S. . . . . . . . B7 113
Cookstown, N. Ire., U.K. . . . . C5 11
Cookstown, Austl. . . . . . . . . C8 50
Cook Strait, strt., N.Z. . . . . . N15 51
Cooktown, Austl. . . . . . . . . C8 50
Cookville, Tn., U.S. . . . . . . . C8 119
Coolah, Austl. . . . . . . . . . . F8 50
Coolamon, Austl. . . . . . . . . G8 50
Coolgardie, Austl. . . . . . . . . F3 50
Coolidge, Alta. . . . . . . . . . . E3 87
Coolidge, Ga., U.S. . . . . . . . D2 87
Coolidge, Ks., U.S. . . . . . . . D2 93
Coolidge, Tx., U.S. . . . . . . . D4 120
Coolidge, Mount, mtn., S.D.,
U.S. . . . . . . . . . . . . . . . *D2 118
Coolin, Id., U.S. . . . . . . . . . A2 89
Cool Ridge, W.V., U.S. . . . . D3 125
Coolspring, Pa., U.S. . . . . . . D3 115
Coolville, Oh., U.S. . . . . . . . C4 112
Cooma, Austl. . . . . . . . . . . G8 50
Coonabarabran, Austl. . . . . . F8 50
Coonamble, Austl. . . . . . . . F8 50
Coon Rapids, Ia., U.S. . . . . . C3 92
Coon Rapids, Mn., U.S. . . . . E5 100
Coon Valley, Wi., U.S. . . . . . E2 126
Cooper, Tx., U.S. . . . . . . . . C5 120
Cooper, co., Mo., U.S. . . . . . C5 102
Cooper, East Branch, stm.,
S.C., U.S. . . . . . . . . . . . E8 117
Cooper, West Branch, stm.,
S.C., U.S. . . . . . . . . . . . E8 117
Cooper City, Fl., U.S. . . . . . *F6 86
Cooper Creek, stm., Austl. . . E7 50
Cooper Mountain, mtn., Ak.,
U.S. . . . . . . . . . . . . . . . g17 79
Cooper Road, La., U.S. . . . . *B2 95
Coopersburg, Pa., U.S. . . . . F11 115
Coopers Mills, Me., U.S. . . . D3 96
Cooperstown, N.Y., U.S. . . . C6 109
Cooperstown, N.D., U.S. . . . B7 111
Cooperton, Ok., U.S. . . . . . . C2 113
Cooperville, Wi., U.S. . . . . . . h10 126
Coopersville, Mi., U.S. . . . . . E5 99
Coos, co., N.H., U.S. . . . . . . A4 106
Coos, co., Or., U.S. . . . . . . . D2 114
Coos, stm., Or., U.S. . . . . . . D2 114
Coosa, co., Al., U.S. . . . . . . C3 78
Coosa, stm., U.S. . . . . . . . . B1 87
Coosada, Al., U.S. . . . . . . . C3 78
Coosawattee, stm., Ga., U.S. *A5 94
Coosawhatchie, S.C., U.S. . . F6 117
Coosawhatchie, stm., S.C.,
U.S. . . . . . . . . . . . . . . . F5 117
Coos Bay, Or., U.S. . . . . . . . D2 114
Cootamundra, Austl. . . . . . . G8 50
Cootehill, Ire. . . . . . . . . . . . C5 11
Cooter, Mo., U.S. . . . . . . . . E8 102
Copacabana, Bol. . . . . . . . . C2 55
Copacabana, Arg. . . . . . . . . E2 55
Copainalá, Mex. . . . . . . . . . D6 63
Copake, N.Y., U.S. . . . . . . . C7 109
Copalis Beach, Wa., U.S. . . . B1 124
Copalis Crossing, Wa., U.S. . B1 124
Copán, Hond. . . . . . . . . . . C3 62

| Name | Map Ref. | Page |
|---|---|---|
| Copan, Ok., U.S. | A6 | 113 |
| *Copan Reservoir, res., Ok., U.S.* | A6 | 113 |
| Cope, Co., U.S. | B8 | 83 |
| Cope, S.C., U.S. | E5 | 117 |
| Copeland, Fl., U.S. | G5 | 86 |
| Copeland, Ks., U.S. | E3 | 93 |
| Copemish, Mi., U.S. | D5 | 99 |
| Copen, W.V., U.S. | C4 | 125 |
| Copenhagen (København), Den. | J5 | 14 |
| Copenhagen, N.Y., U.S. | B5 | 109 |
| Copetonas, Arg. | B4 | 54 |
| Copeville, Tx., U.S. | m10 | 120 |
| Copiague, N.Y., U.S. | *n15 | 109 |
| Copiah, co., Ms., U.S. | D3 | 101 |
| Copiapó, Chile | E1 | 55 |
| *Copiapó, stm., Chile* | E1 | 55 |
| *Copinsay, i., Scot., U.K.* | B6 | 13 |
| Coplay, Pa., U.S. | E10 | 115 |
| Copparo, Italy | B3 | 23 |
| *Coppename, stm., Sur.* | A3 | 59 |
| *Copper, stm., Ak., U.S.* | C11 | 79 |
| Copperas Cove, Tx., U.S. | D4 | 120 |
| *Copperbelt, prov., Zam.* | D4 | 48 |
| *Copper Butte, mtn., Wa., U.S.* | A7 | 124 |
| Copper Center, Ak., U.S. | C10 | 79 |
| Copper Cliff (part of Sudbury), Ont. | A3 | 73 |
| Copper Harbor, Mi., U.S. | A3 | 99 |
| Copperhill, Tn., U.S. | D9 | 119 |
| Copper Hill, Va., U.S. | C2 | 123 |
| Coppermine, N.W. Ter. | C9 | 66 |
| *Coppermine, stm., N.W. Ter.* | C10 | 66 |
| Copper Mountain, B.C. | E7 | 69 |
| *Copper Mountain, mtn., Wy., U.S.* | C5 | 127 |
| *Copper Mountains, mts., Az., U.S.* | E2 | 80 |
| *Copper Ridge, mtn., Tn., U.S.* | m13 | 119 |
| *Copper Ridge, mtn., Va., U.S.* | f9 | 123 |
| Copperton, Ut., U.S. | *C3 | 121 |
| Coppet, Switz. | D1 | 21 |
| *Copton Creek, stm., Alta.* | B1 | 68 |
| Coqên, China | B10 | 37 |
| *Coquet, stm., Eng., U.K.* | E7 | 13 |
| Coquille, Or., U.S. | D2 | 114 |
| Coquimbo, Chile | E1 | 55 |
| *Coquimbo, prov., Chile* | F1 | 55 |
| Cora, Wy., U.S. | D3 | 127 |
| Corabia, Rom. | D7 | 24 |
| Coração de Jesus, Braz. | B4 | 56 |
| Coracora, Peru | E3 | 58 |
| Coral, Ont. | o19 | 73 |
| Coral, Mi., U.S. | E5 | 99 |
| Coral, Pa., U.S. | F3 | 115 |
| Coral Gables, Fl., U.S. | G6 | 86 |
| Coral Hills, Md., U.S. | *C4 | 97 |
| *Coral Sea, Oc.* | G9 | 6 |
| Coral Springs, Fl., U.S. | *F6 | 86 |
| Coral Terrace, Fl., U.S. | *G6 | 86 |
| Coralville, Ia., U.S. | C6 | 92 |
| *Coralville Lake, res., Ia., U.S.* | C5 | 92 |
| Coral Way Village, Fl., U.S. | *G6 | 86 |
| Coram, Mt., U.S. | B2 | 103 |
| Coram, N.Y., U.S. | *n15 | 109 |
| *Corangamite, Lake, l., Austl.* | I4 | 51 |
| Coraopolis, Pa., U.S. | E1 | 115 |
| Corato, Italy | D6 | 23 |
| Corbeil [-Essonnes], Fr. | C5 | 16 |
| Corbeny, Fr. | E3 | 17 |
| Corbett, N.Y., U.S. | C5 | 109 |
| Corbetton, Ont. | C4 | 73 |
| Corbie, Fr. | C5 | 16 |
| Corbin, Ks., U.S. | E6 | 93 |
| Corbin, Ky., U.S. | D5 | 94 |
| Corbin, Mt., U.S. | D4 | 103 |
| Corbin City, N.J., U.S. | E3 | 107 |
| Corby, Eng., U.K. | B7 | 12 |
| Corcoran, Ca., U.S. | D4 | 82 |
| Corcoran, Mn., U.S. | m11 | 100 |
| *Corcovado, Golfo, b., Chile* | C2 | 54 |
| Cord, Ar., U.S. | B4 | 81 |
| Cordaville, Ma., U.S. | g9 | 98 |
| Cordele, Ga., U.S. | E3 | 87 |
| Cordell, Ok., U.S. | B3 | 113 |
| *Cordell Hull Lake, res., Tn., U.S.* | C8 | 119 |
| Corder, Mo., U.S. | B4 | 102 |
| Cordesville, S.C., U.S. | E8 | 117 |
| *Cordillera, dept., Para.* | A4 | 54 |
| Córdoba, Mex. | n15 | 63 |
| Córdoba, Spain | D3 | 22 |
| *Córdoba, prov., Arg.* | B3 | 54 |
| *Córdoba, dept., Col.* | B2 | 60 |
| Cordon, Phil. | n13 | 34 |
| Córdova, Peru | D2 | 58 |
| Cordova, Al., U.S. | B2 | 78 |
| Cordova, Ak., U.S. | C10 | 79 |
| Cordova, Il., U.S. | B3 | 90 |
| Cordova, Md., U.S. | C6 | 97 |
| Cordova, Ne., U.S. | *D8 | 104 |
| Cordova, N.M., U.S. | A4 | 108 |
| Cordova, N.C., U.S. | C3 | 110 |
| Cordova, S.C., U.S. | E6 | 117 |
| Cordova, Tn., U.S. | B2 | 119 |
| Cordova Mines, Ont. | C7 | 73 |
| *Cordova Peak, mtn., Ak., U.S.* | C10 | 79 |
| Corea, Me., U.S. | D5 | 96 |
| Coreaú, Braz. | B2 | 57 |
| Corella, Spain | A5 | 22 |
| Corfu, N.Y., U.S. | C2 | 109 |
| *Corfu see Kérkira, i., Grc.* | C2 | 40 |
| Cori, Italy | h9 | 23 |
| Corigliano, Italy | E6 | 23 |
| Corinna, Me., U.S. | D3 | 96 |
| Corinne, Ut., U.S. | B3 | 121 |
| Corinne, W.V., U.S. | *D3 | 125 |
| *Corinne Key, i., Fl., U.S.* | G6 | 86 |
| *Corinth see Kórinthos, Grc.* | D4 | 40 |
| Corinth, Me., U.S. | D4 | 96 |
| Corinth, Ms., U.S. | A5 | 101 |
| Corinth, N.Y., U.S. | B7 | 109 |
| Corinth, Vt., U.S. | C4 | 122 |
| Corinth, W.V., U.S. | B5 | 125 |
| *Corinth, Bay of, b., Grc.* | h9 | 25 |
| *Corinth, Gulf of, b., Grc.* | C4 | 25 |
| *Corinth Canal, Grc.* | h10 | 25 |
| Corinto, Braz. | B4 | 56 |
| Corinto, Nic. | E7 | 64 |
| *Corisco, Isla de, i., Eq. Gui.* | E1 | 46 |
| Cork, N.B. | D3 | 71 |
| Cork, Ire. | E2 | 10 |
| *Cork, co., Ire.* | F3 | 11 |
| *Cork Harbour, b., Ire.* | E2 | 10 |
| Corleone, Italy | F4 | 23 |
| Çorlu, Tur. | B6 | 40 |
| Cormeilles-en-Parisis, Fr. | g9 | 16 |
| *Cormoran Reef, rf., Palau* | R17 | 52 |
| Cormorant, Man. | B1 | 70 |
| *Cormorant Lake, l., Man.* | B1 | 70 |
| Corn, Ok., U.S. | B3 | 113 |
| Cornaca, S.C., U.S. | C3 | 117 |
| Cornelia, Ga., U.S. | B3 | 87 |
| Cornelius, N.C., U.S. | B2 | 110 |
| Cornelius, Or., U.S. | g11 | 114 |
| Cornell, Il., U.S. | C5 | 90 |
| Cornell, Wi., U.S. | C2 | 126 |
| Cornellà, Spain | B7 | 22 |
| Corner Brook, Newf. | D3 | 72 |
| *Corner Inlet, b., Austl.* | I6 | 51 |
| Cornerstone, Ar., U.S. | C4 | 81 |
| Cornersville, Tn., U.S. | B5 | 119 |
| Cornfield, Or., U.S. | D4 | 81 |
| *Cornfield Point, c., Ct., U.S.* | D6 | 84 |
| Cornie, Ky., U.S. | H5 | 91 |
| Cornimont, Fr. | B2 | 20 |
| Corning, Sask. | H4 | 75 |
| Corning, Ar., U.S. | A5 | 81 |
| Corning, Ca., U.S. | C2 | 82 |
| Corning, Ia., U.S. | D3 | 92 |
| Corning, Ks., U.S. | C7 | 93 |
| Corning, Mo., U.S. | A2 | 102 |
| Corning, N.Y., U.S. | C3 | 109 |
| Corning, Oh., U.S. | C3 | 112 |
| Cornish, Me., U.S. | E2 | 96 |
| Cornish, Ok., U.S. | C4 | 113 |
| Cornish, Ut., U.S. | B4 | 121 |
| Cornish Center, N.H., U.S. | D2 | 106 |
| Cornish Flat, N.H., U.S. | D2 | 106 |
| Cornish Mills, N.H., U.S. | D2 | 106 |
| Cornishville, Ky., U.S. | C5 | 94 |
| *Corno Grande, mtn., Italy* | C4 | 23 |
| Cornucopia, Wi., U.S. | B2 | 126 |
| Cornville, Az., U.S. | C4 | 80 |
| Cornville, Me., U.S. | D3 | 96 |
| Cornwall, Ont. | B10 | 73 |
| Cornwall, Ct., U.S. | B2 | 84 |
| Cornwall, Pa., U.S. | F9 | 115 |
| Cornwall, Vt., U.S. | D2 | 122 |
| *Cornwall, co., Eng., U.K.* | D3 | 12 |
| *Cornwall Bridge, Ct., U.S.* | B2 | 84 |
| *Cornwallis Island, i., N.W. Ter.* | m33 | 66 |
| *Cornwall Island, i., N.W. Ter.* | m32 | 66 |
| Cornwall-on-Hudson, N.Y., U.S. | D6 | 109 |
| Cornwells Heights, Pa., U.S. | o22 | 115 |
| Coro, Ven. | A4 | 60 |
| Coroatá, Braz. | B2 | 57 |
| Corocoro, Bol. | C5 | 55 |
| Corofin, N.C., U.S. | A7 | 110 |
| Coroico, Bol. | C5 | 55 |
| Coromandel, Braz. | B2 | 59 |
| *Coromandel Coast, India* | F7 | 36 |
| *Coromandel Peninsula, pen., N.Z.* | L15 | 51 |
| Corona, Al., U.S. | B2 | 78 |
| Corona, Ca., U.S. | F5 | 82 |
| Corona, N.M., U.S. | C4 | 108 |
| Corona, S.D., U.S. | B9 | 118 |
| Coronach, Sask. | H3 | 75 |
| Coronado, Ca., U.S. | F5 | 82 |
| *Coronado, Bahía de, b., C.R.* | F6 | 62 |
| *Coronado National Memorial, Az., U.S.* | F5 | 80 |
| Coronation, Alta. | C5 | 68 |
| *Coronation Gulf, b., N.W. Ter.* | C10 | 66 |
| *Coronation Island, i., B.A.T.* | C8 | 7 |
| *Coronation Island, i., Ak., U.S.* | n22 | 79 |
| Coronda, Arg. | A4 | 54 |
| Coronel, Chile | B2 | 54 |
| Coronel Dorrego, Arg. | B4 | 54 |
| Coronel Murta, Braz. | B4 | 56 |
| Coronel Oviedo, Para. | E4 | 55 |
| Coronel Pringles, Arg. | B4 | 54 |
| Coronel Suárez, Arg. | B4 | 54 |
| *Coronie, dept., Sur.* | A3 | 59 |
| *Coropuna, Nevado, mtn., Peru* | E3 | 58 |
| Corowa, Austl. | G6 | 51 |
| Corozal, Belize | D7 | 63 |
| Corozal, Col. | B2 | 60 |
| Corpataux, Switz. | C3 | 21 |
| Corpen, Arg. | D3 | 54 |
| Corps, Fr. | E1 | 20 |
| Corpus Christi, Tx., U.S. | F4 | 120 |
| *Corpus Christi Naval Air Station, mil., Tx., U.S.* | F4 | 120 |
| Corral, Chile | B2 | 54 |
| Corral, Id., U.S. | F4 | 89 |
| *Corral de Almaguer, Spain* | C4 | 22 |
| Corrales, Cuba | C3 | 64 |
| Corralillo, Cuba | C3 | 64 |
| Corraun, Ire. | D2 | 11 |
| Correctionville, Ia., U.S. | B2 | 92 |
| *Corregidor Island, i., Phil.* | o13 | 34 |
| Correll, Mn., U.S. | E2 | 100 |
| Corrente, Braz. | D1 | 57 |
| Correntina, Braz. | k5 | 57 |
| Correntes, Braz. | A4 | 56 |
| *Correntes, prov., Arg.* | A4 | 54 |
| *Correntes, stm., Arg.* | A4 | 54 |
| *Correntes, stm., S.A.* | B2 | 59 |
| *Correntes, Cabo, c., Col.* | B2 | 60 |
| *Correntes, Cabo, c., Cuba* | D1 | 64 |
| *Correntes, Cabo, c., Mex.* | G6 | 62 |
| *Correntes, Ensenada de, b., Cuba* | D1 | 64 |
| Corrigan, Tx., U.S. | D5 | 120 |
| Corrigan, Md., U.S. | k13 | 97 |
| Corrigin, Austl. | F3 | 50 |
| Corrofin, Ire. | E2 | 11 |
| Corry, Pa., U.S. | C2 | 115 |
| Corryton, Tn., U.S. | C10 | 119 |
| *Corse, Cap, c., Fr.* | C2 | 23 |
| Corsica, Pa., U.S. | D3 | 115 |
| Corsica, S.D., U.S. | D7 | 118 |
| *Corsica, i., Fr.* | C2 | 23 |
| Corsicana, Tx., U.S. | C4 | 120 |
| Corson, S.D., U.S. | D9 | 118 |
| *Corson, co., S.D., U.S.* | B4 | 118 |
| *Corson Inlet, b., N.J., U.S.* | E3 | 107 |
| Cortazar, Mex. | C4 | 63 |
| Corte, Fr. | C2 | 23 |
| *Corte Alto, Chile* | C2 | 54 |
| Corte Madera, Ca., U.S. | *h7 | 82 |
| Cortemilia, Italy | E4 | 20 |
| *Cortes [de la Frontera], Spain* | D3 | 22 |
| Cortez, Co., U.S. | D2 | 83 |
| Cortez, Fl., U.S. | q10 | 86 |
| *Cortez Mountains, mts., Nv., U.S.* | C5 | 105 |
| Cortina d'Ampezzo, Italy | A4 | 23 |
| Cortland, Il., U.S. | B5 | 90 |
| Cortland, In., U.S. | G6 | 91 |
| Cortland, Ne., U.S. | D9 | 104 |
| Cortland, N.Y., U.S. | C4 | 109 |
| Cortland, Oh., U.S. | A5 | 112 |
| *Cortland, co., N.Y., U.S.* | C4 | 109 |
| Cortona, Italy | C3 | 23 |
| Coruche, Port. | C1 | 22 |
| *Çoruh, stm., Asia* | B13 | 40 |
| Çorum, Tur. | B10 | 40 |
| Corumbá, Braz. | B1 | 56 |
| *Corumbá, stm., Braz.* | B3 | 56 |
| Corunna, Ont. | E2 | 73 |
| Corunna, In., U.S. | B7 | 91 |
| Corunna, Mi., U.S. | F6 | 99 |
| Corvallis, Mt., U.S. | D2 | 103 |
| Corvallis, Or., U.S. | C3 | 114 |
| Corwin, Ks., U.S. | E5 | 93 |
| Corwith, Ia., U.S. | B4 | 92 |
| Corydon, In., U.S. | H5 | 91 |
| Corydon, Ia., U.S. | D4 | 92 |
| Corydon, Ky., U.S. | C2 | 94 |
| *Coryell, co., Tx., U.S.* | D4 | 120 |
| Cos see Kos, i., Grc. | D6 | 40 |
| Cosalá, Mex. | C3 | 63 |
| Cosamaloapan [de Carpio], Mex. | D5 | 63 |
| Cosby, Mo., U.S. | A3 | 102 |
| Cosby, Tn., U.S. | D10 | 119 |
| Coscomatepec [de Bravo], Mex. | n15 | 63 |
| Coseguina, Punta, c., Nic. | D4 | 62 |
| Cosenza, Italy | E6 | 23 |
| Coshocton, Oh., U.S. | B4 | 112 |
| *Coshocton, co., Oh., U.S.* | B4 | 112 |
| Cosmopolis, Wa., U.S. | C2 | 124 |
| Cosmos, Mn., U.S. | F4 | 100 |
| Cosne, Fr. | D5 | 16 |
| *Cossato, stm., Ar., U.S.* | C1 | 81 |
| *Cossatot Mountains, mtn., Ar., U.S.* | C1 | 81 |
| Cossonay, Switz. | C2 | 20 |
| Costa Mesa, Ca., U.S. | n13 | 82 |
| *Costa Rica, ctry., N.A.* | F6 | 62 |
| Costelloe, Ire. | D2 | 11 |
| Costigan, Me., U.S. | C4 | 96 |
| Costilla, N.M., U.S. | A4 | 108 |
| *Costilla, co., Co., U.S.* | D5 | 83 |
| Coswig, E. Ger. | B8 | 18 |
| Coswig, E. Ger. | B7 | 19 |
| Cotabato, Phil. | D6 | 34 |
| Cotagaita, Bol. | D2 | 55 |
| Cotahuasi, Peru | E3 | 58 |
| *Côte d'Or, reg., Fr.* | D6 | 16 |
| *Côtes de Fer, Haiti* | E7 | 64 |
| Cotesfield, Ne., U.S. | C7 | 104 |
| *Cotija de la Paz, Mex.* | n12 | 63 |
| *Cotingo, stm., Braz.* | B2 | 59 |
| Cotonou, Benin | E5 | 45 |
| Cotopaxi, Co., U.S. | C5 | 83 |
| *Cotopaxi, prov., Ec.* | B2 | 58 |
| *Cotopaxi, vol., Ec.* | B2 | 58 |
| *Cotswold Hills, hills, Eng., U.K.* | J11 | 13 |
| Cottage Grove, Mn., U.S. | n13 | 100 |
| Cottage Grove, Or., U.S. | D3 | 114 |
| Cottage Grove, Tn., U.S. | A3 | 119 |
| *Cottage Grove Reservoir, res., Or., U.S.* | D3 | 114 |
| Cottageville, S.C., U.S. | F7 | 117 |
| Cottageville, W.V., U.S. | C3 | 125 |
| Cottam, Ont. | E2 | 73 |
| Cottbus, E. Ger. | C7 | 18 |
| *Cottel Island, i., Newf.* | D5 | 72 |
| Cotter, Ar., U.S. | A3 | 81 |
| *Cottian Alps, mts., Eur.* | E7 | 16 |
| Cottle, co., Tx., U.S. | B2 | 120 |
| *Cottle Knob, mtn., W.V., U.S.* | G3 | 51 |
| Cottleville, Mo., U.S. | f12 | 102 |
| Cotton, Ga., U.S. | E2 | 87 |
| Cotton, Mn., U.S. | C6 | 100 |
| *Cotton, co., Ok., U.S.* | C3 | 113 |
| Cotton Center, Tx., U.S. | B1 | 120 |
| Cottondale, Al., U.S. | B2 | 78 |
| Cottondale, Fl., U.S. | B1 | 86 |
| *Cottonpatch Hill, De., U.S.* | F5 | 85 |
| Cotton Plant, Ar., U.S. | B4 | 81 |
| Cottonport, La., U.S. | C3 | 95 |
| Cottonton, Al., U.S. | C4 | 78 |
| Cottontown, Tn., U.S. | A5 | 119 |
| Cotton Valley, La., U.S. | B2 | 95 |
| Cottonwood, Az., U.S. | C3 | 80 |
| Cottonwood, Ca., U.S. | B2 | 82 |
| Cottonwood, Id., U.S. | C2 | 89 |
| Cottonwood, Ia., U.S. | C3 | 92 |
| Cottonwood, Mn., U.S. | F3 | 100 |
| Cottonwood, S.D., U.S. | D4 | 118 |
| Cottonwood, Tx., U.S. | C3 | 120 |
| Cottonwood, Ut., U.S. | *C4 | 121 |
| *Cottonwood, co., Mn., U.S.* | G3 | 100 |
| *Cottonwood, stm., Ks., U.S.* | D7 | 93 |
| *Cottonwood, stm., Mn., U.S.* | F3 | 100 |
| Cottonwood Cove, Nv., U.S. | H7 | 105 |
| *Cottonwood Creek, stm., Wy., U.S.* | D2 | 127 |
| *Cottonwood Creek, stm., Wy., U.S.* | C4 | 127 |
| Cottonwood Falls, Ks., U.S. | D7 | 93 |
| Cottonwood Heights, Ut., U.S. | *C4 | 121 |
| *Cottonwood Wash, val., Ut., U.S.* | F6 | 121 |
| Cotuit, Ma., U.S. | C7 | 98 |
| Cotulla, Tx., U.S. | E3 | 120 |
| *Couchiching, Lake, l., Ont.* | C5 | 73 |
| Coudekerque-Branche, Fr. | B5 | 16 |
| Coudersport, Pa., U.S. | C5 | 115 |
| *Coudres, Île aux, i., Que.* | B7 | 74 |
| Couëron, Fr. | D3 | 16 |
| *Cougar Reservoir, res., Or., U.S.* | C4 | 114 |
| Coulee, N.D., U.S. | A3 | 111 |
| Coulee City, Wa., U.S. | B6 | 124 |
| *Coulee Creek, stm., Wa., U.S.* | g13 | 124 |
| Coulee Dam, Wa., U.S. | B7 | 124 |
| *Coulee Dam National Recreation Area, Wa., U.S.* | A7 | 124 |
| *Coulman Island, i., Ant.* | B29 | 7 |
| Coulommiers, Fr. | C5 | 16 |
| *Coulsdon (part of London), Eng., U.K.* | m12 | 10 |
| Coulter, Ia., U.S. | B4 | 92 |
| Coulterville, Il., U.S. | E4 | 90 |
| Coulterville, Ca., U.S. | D3 | 82 |
| Coulwood, Va., U.S. | f9 | 123 |
| Council, Id., U.S. | E2 | 89 |
| Council, Ga., U.S. | F4 | 87 |
| Council, N.C., U.S. | C4 | 110 |
| Council Bluffs, Ia., U.S. | C2 | 92 |
| *Council Grove Lake, res., Ks., U.S.* | D7 | 93 |
| Council Hill, Ok., U.S. | B6 | 113 |
| *Council Mountain, mtn., Id., U.S.* | E2 | 89 |
| Country Club Hills, Il., U.S. | *k9 | 90 |
| Country Homes, Wa., U.S. | B8 | 124 |
| Countryside, Il., U.S. | *k9 | 90 |
| Countyline, Ok., U.S. | C4 | 113 |
| *Coupar Angus, Scot., U.K.* | B5 | 10 |
| Coupeville, Wa., U.S. | A3 | 124 |
| Coupon, Pa., U.S. | E4 | 115 |
| Courantyne, stm., S.A. | A3 | 59 |
| Courbevoie, Fr. | g10 | 16 |
| Courcelles, Que. | D7 | 74 |
| Courland Lagoon, b., Sov. Un. | D2 | 20 |
| Courmayeur, Italy | D2 | 20 |
| Coursan, Fr. | F5 | 16 |
| Courtenay, B.C. | E5 | 69 |
| Courtenay, N.D., U.S. | B7 | 111 |
| *Courtmacsherry, Ire.* | F3 | 11 |
| *Courtrai see Kortrijk, Bel.* | B5 | 16 |
| Courtright, Ont. | E2 | 73 |
| Courval, Sask. | G2 | 75 |
| Coushatta, La., U.S. | B2 | 95 |
| Coutances, Fr. | C3 | 16 |
| Coutras, Fr. | E3 | 16 |
| Coutts, Alta. | E5 | 68 |
| Couvin, Bel. | D4 | 17 |
| Cove, Scot., U.K. | C3 | 13 |
| Cove, Ar., U.S. | C1 | 81 |
| Cove, Or., U.S. | B9 | 114 |
| Cove City, N.C., U.S. | B5 | 110 |
| *Cove Creek, stm., Ut., U.S.* | E3 | 121 |
| Covedale, Oh., U.S. | o12 | 112 |
| *Cove Island, i., Ont.* | B3 | 73 |
| Covelo, Ca., U.S. | C2 | 82 |
| Coventry, Eng., U.K. | D6 | 10 |
| Coventry, Ct., U.S. | B6 | 84 |
| Coventry, De., U.S. | *B3 | 85 |
| Coventry, R.I., U.S. | D3 | 116 |
| Coventry, Vt., U.S. | B4 | 122 |
| Cove Point, Md., U.S. | D5 | 97 |
| *Cove Point, c., Md., U.S.* | D5 | 97 |
| Coverdale Crossroads, De., U.S. | F3 | 85 |
| *Covered Wells, Az., U.S.* | E3 | 80 |
| Covert, Mi., U.S. | F4 | 99 |
| Covesville, Va., U.S. | C4 | 123 |
| Covilhã, Port. | E3 | 22 |
| Covina, Ca., U.S. | m13 | 82 |
| Covington, Ga., U.S. | C3 | 87 |
| Covington, In., U.S. | D3 | 91 |
| Covington, Ky., U.S. | A5 | 94 |
| Covington, La., U.S. | D5 | 95 |
| Covington, Mi., U.S. | B2 | 99 |
| Covington, Oh., U.S. | B1 | 112 |
| Covington, Ok., U.S. | A4 | 113 |
| Covington, Tn., U.S. | C7 | 115 |
| Covington, Tn., U.S. | B2 | 119 |
| Covington, Va., U.S. | C3 | 123 |
| *Covington, co., Al., U.S.* | D3 | 78 |
| *Covington, co., Ms., U.S.* | D4 | 101 |
| Cowal, Lake, l., Austl. | F6 | 51 |
| Cowan, In., U.S. | D7 | 91 |
| Cowan, Tn., U.S. | B5 | 119 |
| *Cowan, stm., Sask.* | C2 | 75 |
| *Cowan, Lake, l., Austl.* | F3 | 50 |
| Cowangie, Austl. | G3 | 51 |
| *Cowan Knob, mtn., Ar., U.S.* | B2 | 81 |
| *Cowan Lake, l., Sask.* | C2 | 75 |
| Cowansville, Que. | D5 | 74 |
| Cowansville, Pa., U.S. | E2 | 115 |
| Coward, S.C., U.S. | D8 | 117 |
| Cow Creek, stm., Ks., U.S. | D5 | 93 |
| *Cow Creek, stm., Wa., U.S.* | C7 | 124 |
| Cowden, Il., U.S. | D5 | 90 |
| Cowden, Ok., U.S. | B3 | 113 |
| Cowdenbeath, Scot., U.K. | D5 | 13 |
| Cowdrey, Co., U.S. | A4 | 83 |
| *Cowee Mountains, mts., N.C., U.S.* | f9 | 110 |
| Cowen, W.V., U.S. | C4 | 125 |
| *Cowen, Mount, mtn., Mt., U.S.* | E6 | 103 |
| Cowes, Eng., U.K. | E6 | 10 |
| Coweta, Ok., U.S. | B6 | 113 |
| Coweta, co., Ga., U.S. | C2 | 87 |
| Cowgill, Mo., U.S. | B4 | 102 |
| Cow Head, Newf. | D3 | 72 |
| Cowichan Bay, B.C. | g12 | 69 |
| *Cowichan Lake, l., B.C.* | E5 | 69 |
| Cow Knob, mtn., W.V., U.S. | C5 | 125 |
| *Cow Lakes, l., Or., U.S.* | D9 | 114 |
| Cowles, Ne., U.S. | D7 | 104 |
| Cowley, Alta. | E3 | 68 |
| Cowley, Wy., U.S. | B4 | 127 |
| *Cowley, co., Ks., U.S.* | E7 | 93 |
| Cowlic, Az., U.S. | F4 | 80 |
| Cowling, Il., U.S. | E6 | 90 |
| *Cowlitz, co., Wa., U.S.* | C3 | 124 |
| *Cowlitz, stm., Wa., U.S.* | C3 | 124 |
| Cowpasture, stm., Va., U.S. | B3 | 123 |
| *Cowpen Mountain, mtn., Ga., U.S.* | B2 | 87 |
| Cowpens, S.C., U.S. | A4 | 117 |
| Cowra, Austl. | F7 | 51 |
| *Cowskin Creek, stm., Ks., U.S.* | g11 | 93 |
| Cox, Tex., Newf. | B3 | 50 |
| Coxim, Braz. | B2 | 56 |
| Coxipó, stm., Can. | *C2 | 59 |
| Coxsackie, N.Y., U.S. | C7 | 109 |
| Cox's Cove, Newf. | D2 | 72 |
| Coxwold, Ms., U.S. | B3 | 101 |
| Coy, Al., U.S. | D2 | 78 |
| Coy, Ar., U.S. | C4 | 81 |
| *Coyanosa Draw, val., Tx., U.S.* | D1 | 120 |
| Coya Sur, Chile | D2 | 55 |
| Coyoacán (part of Mexico City), Mex. | h9 | 63 |
| Coyote, N.M., U.S. | A3 | 108 |
| *Coyote Basin, Ca., U.S.* | A2 | 83 |
| Coyuca de Catalán, Mex. | n13 | 63 |
| Coyville, Ks., U.S. | E8 | 93 |
| Cozad, Ne., U.S. | D6 | 104 |
| Cozahome, Ar., U.S. | A3 | 81 |
| Cozumel, Mex. | C7 | 63 |
| Cozumel, Isla de, i., Mex. | C7 | 63 |
| *Crab Creek, stm., Wa., U.S.* | B7 | 124 |
| *Crab Creek, stm., Wa., U.S.* | C5 | 124 |
| Crab Orchard, Ky., U.S. | C5 | 94 |
| Crab Orchard, Ne., U.S. | D9 | 104 |
| Crab Orchard, Tn., U.S. | D9 | 119 |
| Crab Orchard, W.V., U.S. | n13 | 125 |
| *Crab Orchard Lake, res., Il., U.S.* | F4 | 90 |
| *Crab Orchard Mountains, mts., Tn., U.S.* | D9 | 119 |
| Crabtree, Or., U.S. | C4 | 114 |
| Crabtree, Pa., U.S. | F3 | 115 |
| Crellin, Md., U.S. | m12 | 97 |
| *Crabtree Mills, Que.* | D4 | 74 |
| Cracking, stm., Sask. | D4 | 75 |
| Cracow, Austl. | B8 | 51 |
| Cradock, S. Afr. | D4 | 49 |
| Crafton, Pa., U.S. | k13 | 115 |
| Craftsbury, Vt., U.S. | B4 | 122 |
| Craftsbury Common, Vt., U.S. | B4 | 122 |
| Cragford, Al., U.S. | B4 | 78 |
| Craig, Ak., U.S. | D13 | 79 |
| Craig, Co., U.S. | A3 | 83 |
| Craig, Ia., U.S. | B1 | 92 |
| Craig, Mo., U.S. | A2 | 102 |
| Craig, Mt., U.S. | C5 | 103 |
| Craig, Ne., U.S. | C9 | 104 |
| *Craig, co., Ok., U.S.* | A6 | 113 |
| *Craig, co., Va., U.S.* | C2 | 123 |
| *Craig Air Force Base, mil., Al., U.S.* | C3 | 78 |
| *Craig Creek, stm., Va., U.S.* | C2 | 123 |
| Craigellachie, B.C. | D8 | 69 |
| *Craighead, co., Ar., U.S.* | B5 | 81 |
| Craighouse, Scot., U.K. | E3 | 13 |
| Craighurst, Ont. | C5 | 73 |
| Craigmont, Id., U.S. | C2 | 89 |
| Craigmyle, Alta. | D4 | 68 |
| Craigsville, Va., U.S. | B3 | 123 |
| Craigsville, W.V., U.S. | C4 | 125 |
| Craigville, In., U.S. | C7 | 91 |
| Craik, Sask. | F3 | 75 |
| Crail, Scot., U.K. | D6 | 13 |
| Crailsheim, W. Ger. | D5 | 18 |
| Craiova, Rom. | C6 | 24 |
| Cramerton, N.C., U.S. | B1 | 110 |
| Cranberry, Pa., U.S. | D2 | 115 |
| Cranberry Isles, Me., U.S. | D4 | 96 |
| *Cranberry Lake, N.Y., U.S.* | A6 | 109 |
| *Cranberry Lake, l., N.Y., U.S.* | A6 | 109 |
| Cranberry Portage, Man. | B1 | 70 |
| Cranbrook, B.C. | E10 | 69 |
| Cranbury, N.J., U.S. | C3 | 107 |
| Crandall, Ga., U.S. | B2 | 87 |
| Crandall, S.D., U.S. | B8 | 118 |
| Crandall, Tx., U.S. | n10 | 120 |
| Crandon, Wi., U.S. | C5 | 126 |
| Crane, Az., U.S. | E1 | 80 |
| Crane, In., U.S. | G4 | 91 |
| Crane, Mo., U.S. | E4 | 102 |
| Crane, Mt., U.S. | C12 | 103 |
| Crane, Or., U.S. | D8 | 114 |
| Crane, Tx., U.S. | D1 | 120 |
| *Crane, co., Tx., U.S.* | D1 | 120 |
| *Crane Creek, stm., Oh., U.S.* | e7 | 112 |
| *Crane Creek Reservoir, res., Id., U.S.* | E2 | 89 |
| Crane Lake, Mn., U.S. | B6 | 100 |
| *Crane Lake, l., Sask.* | G1 | 75 |
| *Crane Lake, l., Il., U.S.* | C3 | 90 |
| *Crane Lake, l., Mn., U.S.* | B6 | 100 |
| *Crane Mountain, mtn., Or., U.S.* | E6 | 114 |
| *Crane Prairie Reservoir, res., Or., U.S.* | D5 | 114 |
| Cranesville, Pa., U.S. | C1 | 115 |
| Crane Valley, Sask. | H3 | 75 |
| Cranfield, Al., U.S. | D2 | 101 |
| Cranford, N.J., U.S. | B4 | 107 |
| Cransac, Fr. | E5 | 16 |
| Cranston, R.I., U.S. | D4 | 116 |
| *Cranstown, Cape, c., Grnld.* | B20 | 128 |
| Crapaud, P.E.I. | C6 | 71 |
| Crapo, Md., U.S. | D5 | 97 |
| Crary, N.D., U.S. | A7 | 111 |
| *Crary Mountains, mts., Ant.* | B1 | 7 |
| Craryville, N.Y., U.S. | C7 | 109 |
| Crasna, stm., Eur. | B6 | 24 |
| Crater Lake, l., Or., U.S. | E4 | 114 |
| Crater Lake, l., St. Vin. | U26 | 65 |
| *Crater Lake National Park, Or., U.S.* | E4 | 114 |
| *Craters of the Moon National Monument, Id., U.S.* | F5 | 89 |
| Crateús, Braz. | C2 | 57 |
| Crato, Braz. | C3 | 57 |
| Craughwell, Ire. | D3 | 11 |
| Craven, Sask. | G3 | 75 |
| *Craven, co., N.C., U.S.* | B5 | 110 |
| Cravinhos, Braz. | k8 | 56 |
| Crawford, Ga., U.S. | C3 | 87 |
| Crawford, Ms., U.S. | B5 | 101 |
| Crawford, Ne., U.S. | B2 | 104 |
| Crawford, Tx., U.S. | D4 | 120 |
| Crawford, co., Ar., U.S. | B1 | 81 |
| Crawford, co., Ga., U.S. | D2 | 87 |
| Crawford, co., Il., U.S. | D6 | 90 |
| Crawford, co., In., U.S. | H4 | 91 |
| Crawford, co., Ia., U.S. | B2 | 92 |
| Crawford, co., Ks., U.S. | E9 | 93 |
| Crawford, co., Mi., U.S. | D6 | 99 |
| Crawford, co., Mo., U.S. | D6 | 102 |
| Crawford, co., Oh., U.S. | B3 | 112 |
| Crawford, co., Pa., U.S. | C1 | 115 |
| Crawford, co., Wi., U.S. | E3 | 126 |
| Crawford Bay, B.C. | E10 | 69 |
| *Crawford Lake, l., Me., U.S.* | C5 | 96 |
| Crawford Notch, N.H., U.S. | B4 | 106 |
| *Crawford Notch State Park, N.H., U.S.* | B4 | 106 |
| Crawfordsville, Ar., U.S. | B5 | 81 |
| Crawfordsville, In., U.S. | D4 | 91 |
| Crawfordsville, Or., U.S. | C4 | 114 |
| Crawfordville, Fl., U.S. | B2 | 86 |
| Crawfordville, Ga., U.S. | C4 | 87 |
| Crawley, Eng., U.K. | C7 | 12 |
| Crayne, Ky., U.S. | e9 | 94 |
| Crazy Mountains, mts., Mt., U.S. | D7 | 103 |
| Crazy Peak, mtn., Mt., U.S. | D6 | 103 |
| *Crazy Woman Creek, stm., Wy., U.S.* | B6 | 127 |
| Creal Springs, Il., U.S. | F5 | 90 |
| Creamridge, N.J., U.S. | C3 | 107 |
| *Crean Lake, l., Sask.* | D3 | 75 |
| Crediton, Eng., U.K. | D4 | 12 |
| Cree, stm., Sask. | E11 | 66 |
| Creede, Co., U.S. | D4 | 83 |
| Creedmoor, N.C., U.S. | A4 | 110 |
| *Creek, co., Ok., U.S.* | B5 | 113 |
| Creekside, Pa., U.S. | E3 | 115 |
| Creek Village, Bah. | m18 | 64 |
| *Cree Lake, l., Sask.* | m7 | 75 |
| Creelman, Sask. | H4 | 75 |
| Creemore, Ont. | C4 | 73 |
| Cregganbaun, Ire. | D2 | 11 |
| Creighton, Sask. | C5 | 75 |
| Creighton, Mo., U.S. | C3 | 102 |
| Creighton, Ne., U.S. | B8 | 104 |
| Creighton, Pa., U.S. | h14 | 115 |
| Creighton, S.D., U.S. | C3 | 118 |
| Creil, Fr. | C5 | 16 |
| Crellin, Md., U.S. | m12 | 97 |
| Crema, Italy | B2 | 23 |
| Cremona, Alta. | D3 | 68 |
| Cremona, Italy | B3 | 23 |
| Crenshaw, Ms., U.S. | A3 | 101 |
| Crenshaw, co., Al., U.S. | D3 | 78 |
| Creola, Al., U.S. | E1 | 78 |
| Creole, La., U.S. | E2 | 95 |
| Crépy-en-Valois, Fr. | E2 | 17 |
| Cres, i., Yugo. | C2 | 24 |
| Cresaptown, Md., U.S. | k13 | 97 |
| Cresbard, S.D., U.S. | B7 | 118 |
| Crescent, Ga., U.S. | E5 | 87 |
| Crescent, Ia., U.S. | C2 | 92 |
| Crescent, Ok., U.S. | A6 | 113 |
| Crescent, Or., U.S. | f12 | 102 |
| Crescent, co., Ok., U.S. | C2 | 123 |
| Crescent, Or., U.S. | B4 | 113 |
| Crescent, Or., U.S. | D5 | 114 |
| *Crescent, Lake, l., Wa., U.S.* | A2 | 124 |
| Crescent City, Ca., U.S. | B1 | 82 |
| Crescent City, Fl., U.S. | C5 | 86 |
| Crescent City, Il., U.S. | C6 | 90 |
| Crescent Lake, Or., U.S. | D5 | 114 |
| *Crescent Lake, l., Fl., U.S.* | C5 | 86 |
| *Crescent Lake, l., Or., U.S.* | D5 | 114 |
| Crescent Mills, Ca., U.S. | B3 | 82 |
| *Crescent Range, mtn., N.H., U.S.* | B4 | 106 |
| Crescent Springs, Ky., U.S. | h13 | 94 |
| Crescent Spur, B.C. | C7 | 69 |
| Cresco, Ia., U.S. | A5 | 92 |
| Cresco, Pa., U.S. | D11 | 115 |
| Crespo, Arg. | A4 | 54 |
| Cresskill, N.J., U.S. | h9 | 107 |
| Cresson, Pa., U.S. | F4 | 115 |
| Cresson, Tx., U.S. | n9 | 120 |
| Cressona, Pa., U.S. | E9 | 115 |
| Crest, Fr. | E6 | 16 |
| Cresta, Switz. | D8 | 21 |
| Crested Butte, Co., U.S. | C4 | 83 |
| Cresthaven, Fl., U.S. | *F6 | 86 |
| Crest Hill, Il., U.S. | k8 | 90 |
| Crestline, Ca., U.S. | *E5 | 82 |
| Crestline, Oh., U.S. | B3 | 112 |
| Creston, B.C. | E9 | 69 |
| Creston, Newf. | E4 | 72 |
| Creston, Il., U.S. | B5 | 90 |
| Creston, Ia., U.S. | C3 | 92 |
| Creston, Mt., U.S. | B2 | 103 |
| Creston, Ne., U.S. | C8 | 104 |
| Creston, Oh., U.S. | B4 | 112 |
| Creston, S.C., U.S. | D6 | 117 |
| Creston, Tn., U.S. | C8 | 119 |
| Creston, Wa., U.S. | B7 | 124 |
| Creston, W.V., U.S. | C3 | 125 |
| Creston, Wy., U.S. | E5 | 127 |
| Crestone, Co., U.S. | D5 | 83 |
| *Crestone Peak, mtn., Co., U.S.* | D5 | 83 |
| Crestview, Fl., U.S. | u15 | 86 |
| Crestview, Ky., U.S. | g10 | 88 |
| Crestwood, Il., U.S. | *k9 | 90 |
| Crestwood, Ky., U.S. | B4 | 94 |
| Crestwood, Mo., U.S. | *f13 | 102 |
| Crestwood Village, N.J., U.S. | D4 | 107 |
| Crestwynd, Sask. | G3 | 75 |
| Creswell, N.C., U.S. | B6 | 110 |
| Creswell, Or., U.S. | D3 | 114 |
| Crete, Il., U.S. | B6 | 90 |
| Crete, Ne., U.S. | D9 | 104 |
| Crete, i., Grc. | C8 | 111 |
| *Crete, Sea of, Grc.* | E5 | 40 |
| Créteil, Fr. | g10 | 16 |
| Cretone, Italy | g9 | 23 |
| *Creus, Cape, c., Spain* | A7 | 22 |
| Creuse, Fr. | C7 | 16 |
| Creutzwald, Fr. | C7 | 16 |
| *Crevasse Valley Glacier, ice, Ant.* | B34 | 7 |
| Creve Coeur, Il., U.S. | C4 | 90 |
| Creve Coeur, Mo., U.S. | *f13 | 102 |
| Crèvecœur-le-Grand, Fr. | E2 | 17 |
| Crevillente, Spain | C5 | 22 |
| Crewe, Eng., U.K. | D5 | 10 |
| Crewe, Va., U.S. | C4 | 123 |
| Crewkerne, Eng., U.K. | D5 | 12 |
| Criciúma, Braz. | D3 | 56 |
| Cricket, N.C., U.S. | A1 | 110 |
| *Cricket Mountains, mts., Ut., U.S.* | E3 | 121 |
| Cridersville, Oh., U.S. | B1 | 112 |
| Crieff, Scot., U.K. | B5 | 10 |
| *Criffell, mtn., Scot., U.K.* | F5 | 13 |
| Criglersville, Va., U.S. | B4 | 123 |
| Crikvenica, Yugo. | C2 | 24 |
| Crimea, pen., Sov. Un. | E6 | 29 |
| *Crimson Lake Provincial Park, Alta.* | C3 | 68 |
| Crinan, Scot., U.K. | D3 | 13 |
| Cripple Creek, Co., U.S. | C5 | 83 |
| Cripple Creek, Va., U.S. | D1 | 123 |
| *Crisana-Maramures, hist. reg., Rom.* | B6 | 24 |
| Crisfield, Md., U.S. | E6 | 97 |
| Crisp, co., Ga., U.S. | E3 | 87 |
| Criss Creek, B.C. | D7 | 69 |
| Crissolo, Italy | E2 | 20 |
| *Cristal, Monts de, mts., Gabon* | E2 | 46 |
| Cristalina, Braz. | B3 | 56 |
| Cristalândia, Braz. | k11 | 57 |
| Cristóbal, Pan. | k11 | 62 |
| *Cristóbal Colón, Pico, mtn., Col.* | A3 | 60 |
| Crisu Alb, stm., Eur. | B5 | 24 |
| Crittenden, Ky., U.S. | B5 | 94 |
| *Crittenden, co., Ar., U.S.* | B5 | 81 |
| *Crittenden, co., Ky., U.S.* | e9 | 94 |
| Crivitz, Wi., U.S. | C6 | 126 |
| Crixás, Braz. | A3 | 56 |
| Crna, stm., Yugo. | E5 | 24 |
| Crnomelj, Yugo. | C2 | 24 |
| *Croatia, hist. reg., Yugo.* | C2 | 24 |
| Croche, stm., Que. | A5 | 74 |
| Crocheron, Md., U.S. | D5 | 97 |
| Crocker, Mo., U.S. | D5 | 102 |
| Crocker, S.D., U.S. | B8 | 118 |
| Crockett, Ca., U.S. | g8 | 82 |
| Crockett, Tx., U.S. | D5 | 120 |
| *Crockett, co., Tn., U.S.* | B2 | 119 |
| *Crockett, co., Tx., U.S.* | D2 | 120 |
| Crockett Mills, Tn., U.S. | B2 | 119 |
| Crocketts Bluff, Ar., U.S. | C4 | 81 |
| Crocketville, S.C., U.S. | F5 | 117 |
| Crofton, Ky., U.S. | C2 | 94 |
| Crofton, Md., U.S. | B4 | 97 |
| Crofton, Ne., U.S. | B8 | 104 |
| Croghan, N.Y., U.S. | B5 | 109 |

| Name | Map Ref. | Page |
|---|---|---|
| Croghan Mountain, mtn., Ire. | E5 | 11 |
| Crohy Head, c., Ire. | C3 | 11 |
| Croix, Fr. | D3 | 17 |
| Croix, Lac la, l., Mn., U.S. | B6 | 100 |
| Croker, i., Austl. | B5 | 50 |
| Croker, Cape, c., Ont. | C4 | 73 |
| Cromarty, Scot., U.K. | B4 | 10 |
| Cromer, Man. | E1 | 70 |
| Cromer, Eng., U.K. | B9 | 12 |
| Cromona, Ky., U.S. | C7 | 94 |
| Cromwell, N.Z. | P12 | 51 |
| Cromwell, Al., U.S. | C1 | 78 |
| Cromwell, Ct., U.S. | C5 | 84 |
| Cromwell, In., U.S. | B6 | 91 |
| Cromwell, Ia., U.S. | C3 | 92 |
| Cromwell, Ky., U.S. | C3 | 94 |
| Cromwell, Mn., U.S. | D6 | 100 |
| Cromwell, Ok., U.S. | B5 | 113 |
| Crook, Eng., U.K. | F7 | 13 |
| Crook, Co., U.S. | A8 | 83 |
| Crook, co., Or., U.S. | C6 | 114 |
| Crook, co., Wy., U.S. | B8 | 127 |
| Crooked, stm., B.C. | B6 | 69 |
| Crooked, stm., U.S. | C6 | 114 |
| Crooked Creek, Ak., U.S. | C8 | 79 |
| Crooked Creek, stm., U.S. | E3 | 93 |
| Crooked Creek, stm., Ar., U.S. | A3 | 81 |
| Crooked Creek, stm., In., U.S. | k10 | 91 |
| Crooked Creek, stm., Pa., U.S. | C7 | 115 |
| Crooked Creek Lake, res., Pa., U.S. | E3 | 115 |
| Crooked Island, i., Bah. | C6 | 64 |
| Crooked Island Passage, strt., Bah. | C6 | 64 |
| Crooked Lake, l., Newf. | D3 | 72 |
| Crooked Lake, l., Sask. | G4 | 75 |
| Crooked Lake, l., Fl., U.S. | E5 | 86 |
| Crooked Lake, l., Mn., U.S. | B7 | 100 |
| Crooked River, Sask. | E4 | 75 |
| Crooks, S.D., U.S. | D9 | 118 |
| Crooks Lake, l., Nv., U.S. | B2 | 105 |
| Crookston, Mn., U.S. | C2 | 100 |
| Crookston, Ne., U.S. | B5 | 104 |
| Crookstown, Ire. | F3 | 11 |
| Crooksville, Oh., U.S. | C3 | 112 |
| Crookwell, Austl. | G7 | 51 |
| Croom, Ire. | E3 | 11 |
| Cropper, Ky., U.S. | B4 | 94 |
| Cropsey, Il., U.S. | C5 | 90 |
| Croque Harbour, b., Newf. | C4 | 72 |
| Crosby, Mn., U.S. | D5 | 100 |
| Crosby, Ms., U.S. | D2 | 101 |
| Crosby, N.D., U.S. | A2 | 111 |
| Crosby, Pa., U.S. | C5 | 115 |
| Crosby, Tx., U.S. | r14 | 120 |
| Crosby, co., Tx., U.S. | C2 | 120 |
| Crosby, Mount, mtn., Wy., U.S. | C3 | 127 |
| Crosbyton, Tx., U.S. | C2 | 120 |
| Crosland, Ga., U.S. | E3 | 87 |
| Cross, S.C., U.S. | E7 | 117 |
| Cross, co., Ar., U.S. | B5 | 81 |
| Cross, stm., Afr. | E6 | 45 |
| Cross, Cape, c., Nmb. | B1 | 49 |
| Cross Anchor, S.C., U.S. | B4 | 117 |
| Cross Bay, b., Man. | C2 | 70 |
| Crossbost, Scot., U.K. | B2 | 13 |
| Cross City, Fl., U.S. | C3 | 86 |
| Cross Creek, N.B. | C3 | 71 |
| Cross Creek, stm., W.V., U.S. | f8 | 125 |
| Crossett, Ar., U.S. | D4 | 81 |
| Cross Fell, mtn., Eng., U.K. | F6 | 13 |
| Crossfield, Alta. | D3 | 68 |
| Crosshaven, Ire. | F3 | 11 |
| Cross Hill, S.C., U.S. | C4 | 117 |
| Cross Island, i., Me., U.S. | D5 | 96 |
| Cross Keys, N.J., U.S. | D2 | 107 |
| Cross Lake, Man. | B3 | 70 |
| Crosslake, Mn., U.S. | D4 | 100 |
| Cross Lake, l., Man. | B3 | 70 |
| Cross Lake, l., Me., U.S. | A4 | 96 |
| Cross Lake, res., La., U.S. | B2 | 95 |
| Cross Lanes, W.V., U.S. | C3 | 125 |
| Crossman Peak, mtn., Az., U.S. | C1 | 80 |
| Cross Mill, N.C., U.S. | f10 | 110 |
| Crossmolina, Ire. | C2 | 11 |
| Cross Mountains, mtn., Ar., U.S. | C1 | 81 |
| Cross Plains, In., U.S. | G7 | 91 |
| Cross Plains, Tn., U.S. | A5 | 119 |
| Cross Plains, Tx., U.S. | C3 | 120 |
| Cross Plains, Wi., U.S. | E4 | 126 |
| Crossroads, N.M., U.S. | D6 | 108 |
| Cross Roads Ohio, Tn., U.S. | D7 | 71 |
| Cross Sound, strt., Ak., U.S. | k21 | 79 |
| Cross Timbers, Mo., U.S. | C4 | 102 |
| Crosstown, Mo., U.S. | D8 | 102 |
| Cross Village, Mi., U.S. | C5 | 99 |
| Crossville, Al., U.S. | A4 | 78 |
| Crossville, Il., U.S. | E5 | 90 |
| Crossville, Tn., U.S. | D8 | 119 |
| Crosswicks, N.J., U.S. | C3 | 107 |
| Croswell, Mi., U.S. | E8 | 99 |
| Crothersville, In., U.S. | G6 | 91 |
| Croton, Ia., U.S. | D6 | 92 |
| Croton, N.J., U.S. | B3 | 107 |
| Croton, Oh., U.S. | B3 | 112 |
| Crotone, Italy | E6 | 23 |
| Croton-on-Hudson, N.Y., U.S. | D7 | 109 |
| Crottendorf, E. Ger. | C7 | 19 |
| Crouch, Id., U.S. | E3 | 89 |
| Crouse, N.C., U.S. | B1 | 110 |
| Crouseville, Me., U.S. | A4 | 96 |
| Crow, stm., Mn., U.S. | F4 | 100 |
| Crow, North Fork, stm., Mn., U.S. | E4 | 100 |
| Crow Agency, Mt., U.S. | E9 | 103 |
| Crow Creek, stm., U.S. | A6 | 83 |
| Crow Creek Indian Reservation, S.D., U.S. | C6 | 118 |
| Crowder, Ms., U.S. | A3 | 101 |
| Crowder, Ok., U.S. | B6 | 113 |
| Crowduck Lake, l., Man. | D4 | 70 |
| Crowell, Tx., U.S. | C3 | 120 |
| Crowheart, Wy., U.S. | C3 | 127 |
| Crow Indian Reservation, Mt., U.S. | E9 | 103 |
| Crowley, Co., U.S. | C7 | 83 |
| Crowley, La., U.S. | D3 | 95 |
| Crowley, Tx., U.S. | n9 | 120 |
| Crowley, co., Co., U.S. | C7 | 83 |
| Crowley, Lake, res., Ca., U.S. | D4 | 82 |
| Crowleys Ridge, mtn., U.S. | B5 | 81 |
| Crown City, Oh., U.S. | D3 | 112 |
| Crown King, Az., U.S. | C3 | 80 |
| Crown Point, In., U.S. | B3 | 91 |
| Crown Point, La., U.S. | k11 | 95 |
| Crownpoint, N.M., U.S. | B1 | 108 |
| Crown Point, N.Y., U.S. | B7 | 109 |
| Crow Peak, mtn., Mt., U.S. | D5 | 103 |
| Crowsnest, B.C. | E10 | 69 |
| Crowsnest Pass, Alta. | E3 | 68 |
| Crowsnest Pass, Can. | E3 | 68 |
| Crows Nest Peak, mtn., S.D., U.S. | C2 | 118 |
| Crowville, La., U.S. | B4 | 95 |
| Crow Wing, co., Mn., U.S. | D4 | 100 |
| Crow Wing, stm., Mn., U.S. | D4 | 100 |
| Croydon, Austl. | C7 | 50 |
| Croydon (part of London), Eng., U.K. | E6 | 10 |
| Croydon, N.H., U.S. | D2 | 106 |
| Croydon, Pa., U.S. | F12 | 115 |
| Croydon, Ut., U.S. | B4 | 121 |
| Croydon Flat, N.H., U.S. | D2 | 106 |
| Croydon Peak, mtn., N.H., U.S. | D2 | 106 |
| Crozet, Va., U.S. | B4 | 123 |
| Crozet, Îles, is., F.S.A.T. | J24 | 2 |
| Crozier, Va., U.S. | C5 | 123 |
| Crozon, Fr. | C1 | 16 |
| Cruachan, Ben, mtn., Scot., U.K. | D3 | 13 |
| Cruagh Island, i., Ire. | D1 | 11 |
| Crucero, Peru | D3 | 58 |
| Cruces, Cuba | C3 | 64 |
| Cruces, Punta, c., Col. | B2 | 60 |
| Crucible, Pa., U.S. | G1 | 115 |
| Cruden Bay, Scot., U.K. | B6 | 10 |
| Cruger, Ms., U.S. | B3 | 101 |
| Crum, W.V., U.S. | D2 | 125 |
| Crumlin, N. Ire., U.K. | C5 | 11 |
| Crummock Water, l., Eng., U.K. | F5 | 13 |
| Crump Lake, l., Or., U.S. | E7 | 114 |
| Crumpton, Md., U.S. | B6 | 97 |
| Crumrod, Ar., U.S. | C5 | 81 |
| Crumstown, In., U.S. | A5 | 91 |
| Cruseilles, Fr. | C2 | 20 |
| Crusheen, Ire. | E3 | 11 |
| Cruso, N.C., U.S. | f10 | 110 |
| Crutwell, Sask. | D2 | 75 |
| Cruz, Cabo, c., Cuba | E5 | 64 |
| Cruz Alta, Arg. | A4 | 54 |
| Cruz Alta, Braz. | D2 | 56 |
| Cruz del Eje, Arg. | A4 | 54 |
| Cruzeiro, Braz. | C4 | 56 |
| Cruzeiro do Oeste, Braz. | C2 | 56 |
| Cruzeiro do Sul, Braz. | C3 | 58 |
| Cruz Grande, Chile | E1 | 53 |
| Crysler, Ont. | B9 | 73 |
| Crystal, Mi., U.S. | E6 | 99 |
| Crystal, Mn., U.S. | m12 | 100 |
| Crystal, N.D., U.S. | A8 | 111 |
| Crystal, stm., Co., U.S. | B3 | 83 |
| Crystal Bay, Nv., U.S. | D1 | 105 |
| Crystal Bay, b., Fl., U.S. | D4 | 86 |
| Crystal Beach, Fl., U.S. | D4 | 86 |
| Crystal City, Man. | E2 | 70 |
| Crystal City, Mo., U.S. | C7 | 102 |
| Crystal City, Tx., U.S. | E3 | 120 |
| Crystal Falls, Mi., U.S. | B2 | 99 |
| Crystal Hill, Va., U.S. | D4 | 123 |
| Crystal Lake, Ct., U.S. | B6 | 84 |
| Crystal Lake, Il., U.S. | A5 | 90 |
| Crystal Lake, Ia., U.S. | A4 | 92 |
| Crystal Lake, l., Ct., U.S. | B6 | 84 |
| Crystal Lake, l., Fl., U.S. | u16 | 86 |
| Crystal Lake, l., Il., U.S. | A5 | 90 |
| Crystal Lake, l., Mi., U.S. | D4 | 99 |
| Crystal Lake, l., N.H., U.S. | D4 | 106 |
| Crystal Lake, l., Vt., U.S. | B4 | 122 |
| Crystal Lawns, Il., U.S. | k8 | 90 |
| Crystal Manor, Il., U.S. | k8 | 90 |
| Crystal Mountain, mtn., N.H., U.S. | g7 | 106 |
| Crystal Pond, res., Ct., U.S. | B7 | 84 |
| Crystal River, Fl., U.S. | D4 | 86 |
| Crystal Springs, Sask. | E3 | 75 |
| Crystal Springs, Ar., U.S. | C2 | 81 |
| Crystal Springs, Fl., U.S. | D4 | 86 |
| Crystal Springs, Ms., U.S. | D3 | 101 |
| Crystal Springs, N.D., U.S. | C6 | 111 |
| Crystal Valley, Mi., U.S. | E4 | 99 |
| Csongrád, Hung. | B5 | 24 |
| Csorna, Hung. | B3 | 24 |
| Cuajone, Peru | E3 | 58 |
| Cuamba, Moz. | D6 | 48 |
| Cuando, stm., Afr. | H8 | 42 |
| Cuando Cubango, dept., Ang. | E2 | 48 |
| Cuangar, Ang. | E2 | 48 |
| Cuango, Ang. | C2 | 48 |
| Cuango (Kwango), stm., Afr. | C2 | 48 |
| Cuanza, Ang. | C2 | 48 |
| Cuanza-Norte, dept., Ang. | C1 | 48 |
| Cuanza-Sul, dept., Ang. | D1 | 48 |
| Cuarto, stm., Arg. | A4 | 54 |
| Cuauhtémoc, Mex. | B3 | 63 |
| Cuautepec (part of Mexico City), Mex. | g9 | 63 |
| Cuautla [Morelos], Mex. | n14 | 63 |
| Cuba, Port. | C2 | 22 |
| Cuba, Al., U.S. | C1 | 78 |
| Cuba, Il., U.S. | C3 | 90 |
| Cuba, Ks., U.S. | C6 | 93 |
| Cuba, Mo., U.S. | C6 | 102 |
| Cuba, N.M., U.S. | A3 | 108 |
| Cuba, N.Y., U.S. | C2 | 109 |
| Cuba, Oh., U.S. | C2 | 112 |
| Cuba, ctry., N.A. | C4 | 64 |
| Cuba City, Wi., U.S. | F3 | 126 |
| Cubal, Ang. | D1 | 48 |
| Cubero, N.M., U.S. | B2 | 108 |
| Cub Run, Ky., U.S. | C3 | 94 |
| Cucamonga, Ca., U.S. | *m13 | 82 |
| Cuchara, Co., U.S. | D5 | 83 |
| Cucharas, stm., Co., U.S. | D6 | 83 |
| Cuchillo, N.M., U.S. | D2 | 108 |
| Cuchivero, stm., Ven. | B4 | 60 |
| Cucuí, Braz. | C4 | 60 |
| Cúcuta, Col. | C5 | 60 |
| Cudahy, Ca., U.S. | *E4 | 82 |
| Cudahy, Wi., U.S. | F6 | 126 |
| Cuddalore, India | F6 | 36 |
| Cuddapah, India | F6 | 36 |
| Cudgewa, Austl. | H6 | 51 |
| Cudworth, Sask. | E3 | 75 |
| Cue, Austl. | E2 | 50 |
| Cuéllar, Spain | B3 | 22 |
| Cuenca, Ec. | B2 | 58 |
| Cuenca, Spain | B2 | 22 |
| Cuenca, Sierra de, mts., Spain | B4 | 22 |
| Cuencamé [de Ceniceros], Mex. | C4 | 63 |
| Cuernavaca, Mex. | D5 | 63 |
| Cuero, Tx., U.S. | E4 | 120 |
| Cuervo, N.M., U.S. | B5 | 108 |
| Cuetzalan, Mex. | m15 | 63 |
| Cuevas, Ms., U.S. | f7 | 101 |
| Cuevas [del Almanzora], Spain | D5 | 22 |
| Cuglieri, Italy | D2 | 23 |
| Cuiabá, Braz. | B1 | 56 |
| Cuiabá, stm., Braz. | B1 | 56 |
| Cuicas, Ven. | B3 | 60 |
| Cuicatlán, Mex. | o15 | 63 |
| Cuilapa, Guat. | C2 | 62 |
| Cuilcagh, mtn., Eur. | C4 | 11 |
| Cuilco, Guat. | C2 | 62 |
| Cuillin Hills, hills, Scot., U.K. | C2 | 13 |
| Cuimba, Ang. | C1 | 48 |
| Cuipo, Pan. | k10 | 62 |
| Cuito, stm., Ang. | E2 | 48 |
| Cuito-Cuanavale, Ang. | E2 | 48 |
| Cuitzeo, Lago de, l., Mex. | n13 | 63 |
| Ciuiuni, stm., Braz. | C2 | 59 |
| Cuivre, West Fork, stm., Mo., U.S. | B6 | 102 |
| Culberson, co., Tx., U.S. | o12 | 120 |
| Culbertson, Mt., U.S. | B12 | 103 |
| Culbertson, Ne., U.S. | D5 | 104 |
| Culcairn, Austl. | G6 | 51 |
| Culdaff Bay, b., Ire. | B4 | 11 |
| Culdesac, Id., U.S. | C2 | 89 |
| Culebra, P.R. | B5 | 65 |
| Culebra, Isla de, i., P.R. | G12 | 64 |
| Culebra Peak, mtn., Co., U.S. | D5 | 83 |
| Culgoa, stm., Austl. | E8 | 50 |
| Culhuacán (part of Mexico City), Mex. | h9 | 63 |
| Culiacán, Mex. | C3 | 63 |
| Cúllar de Baza, Spain | D4 | 22 |
| Cullen, Scot., U.K. | C6 | 13 |
| Cullen, La., U.S. | B2 | 95 |
| Culleoka, Tn., U.S. | B5 | 119 |
| Cullera, Spain | C5 | 22 |
| Cullison, Ks., U.S. | E5 | 93 |
| Cullman, Al., U.S. | A3 | 78 |
| Cullman, co., Al., U.S. | A3 | 78 |
| Culloden, Ga., U.S. | D2 | 87 |
| Culloden, W.V., U.S. | C2 | 125 |
| Cullom, Il., U.S. | C5 | 90 |
| Cullomburg, Al., U.S. | D1 | 78 |
| Cullowhee, N.C., U.S. | f9 | 110 |
| Culoz, Fr. | D1 | 20 |
| Culp Creek, Or., U.S. | D4 | 114 |
| Culpeper, Va., U.S. | B5 | 123 |
| Culpeper, co., Va., U.S. | B5 | 123 |
| Cultus Lake, B.C. | f14 | 69 |
| Culuene, stm., Braz. | A2 | 56 |
| Culver, In., U.S. | B5 | 91 |
| Culver, Ks., U.S. | D6 | 93 |
| Culver, Mn., U.S. | D6 | 100 |
| Culver, Or., U.S. | C5 | 114 |
| Culver, Point, c., Austl. | F3 | 50 |
| Culver City, Ca., U.S. | m12 | 82 |
| Culvers Lake, l., N.J., U.S. | A3 | 107 |
| Culverton, Ga., U.S. | C4 | 87 |
| Culzean Bay, b., Scot., U.K. | C8 | 21 |
| Cumaná, Ven. | A5 | 60 |
| Cumbal, Nevado de, mtn., Col. | C3 | 60 |
| Cumberland, B.C. | E5 | 69 |
| Cumberland, Ont. | g13 | 73 |
| Cumberland, Ia., U.S. | C3 | 92 |
| Cumberland, Ky., U.S. | D7 | 94 |
| Cumberland, Md., U.S. | k13 | 97 |
| Cumberland, N.J., U.S. | E2 | 107 |
| Cumberland, N.C., U.S. | B4 | 110 |
| Cumberland, Oh., U.S. | C4 | 112 |
| Cumberland, Va., U.S. | C4 | 123 |
| Cumberland, Wa., U.S. | f12 | 124 |
| Cumberland, Wi., U.S. | C1 | 126 |
| Cumberland, co., N.S. | D5 | 71 |
| Cumberland, co., Il., U.S. | D5 | 90 |
| Cumberland, co., Ky., U.S. | D4 | 94 |
| Cumberland, co., Me., U.S. | E2 | 96 |
| Cumberland, co., N.J., U.S. | E2 | 107 |
| Cumberland, co., N.C., U.S. | B4 | 110 |
| Cumberland, co., Pa., U.S. | F7 | 115 |
| Cumberland, co., Tn., U.S. | D8 | 119 |
| Cumberland, co., Va., U.S. | C4 | 123 |
| Cumberland, stm., U.S. | C11 | 76 |
| Cumberland, Lake, res., Ky., U.S. | D5 | 94 |
| Cumberland, South Fork, stm., U.S. | D5 | 94 |
| Cumberland Center, Me., U.S. | g7 | 96 |
| Cumberland City, Tn., U.S. | A4 | 119 |
| Cumberland Foreside, Me., U.S. | E2 | 96 |
| Cumberland Furnace, Tn., U.S. | A4 | 119 |
| Cumberland Gap, Tn., U.S. | C10 | 119 |
| Cumberland Gap, U.S. | D6 | 94 |
| Cumberland Gap National Historical Park, U.S. | D6 | 94 |
| Cumberland Hill, R.I., U.S. | B4 | 116 |
| Cumberland House, Sask. | D4 | 75 |
| Cumberland Island National Seashore, Ga., U.S. | F5 | 87 |
| Cumberland Lake, l., Sask. | C4 | 75 |
| Cumberland Mountain, mtn., Tn., U.S. | C9 | 119 |
| Cumberland Peninsula, pen., N.W. Ter. | C20 | 66 |
| Cumberland Plateau, plat., U.S. | D8 | 119 |
| Cumberland Sound, strt., N.W. Ter. | C19 | 66 |
| Cumbernauld, Scot., U.K. | *E5 | 13 |
| Cumbres Pass, Co., U.S. | D4 | 83 |
| Cumbria, co., Eng., U.K. | F6 | 13 |
| Cuming, co., Ne., U.S. | C9 | 104 |
| Cumming, Ga., U.S. | B2 | 87 |
| Cumming, Ia., U.S. | f8 | 92 |
| Cummings, Ks., U.S. | C8 | 93 |
| Cummings, N.D., U.S. | B8 | 111 |
| Cummington, Ma., U.S. | B2 | 98 |
| Cumnock [and Holmhead], Scot., U.K. | E4 | 13 |
| Cumnock, N.C., U.S. | B3 | 110 |
| Cumpas, Mex. | A3 | 63 |
| Cumra, Tur. | D7 | 25 |
| Cunard, W.V., U.S. | m13 | 125 |
| Cunco, Chile | B2 | 54 |
| Cuncumén, Chile | A2 | 54 |
| Cundiff, Ky., U.S. | D4 | 94 |
| Cundinamarca, dept., Col. | C3 | 60 |
| Cundiyo, N.M., U.S. | *B4 | 108 |
| Cundys Harbor, Me., U.S. | g8 | 96 |
| Cunene, dept., Ang. | E1 | 48 |
| Cunene, stm., Afr. | E1 | 48 |
| Cuneo, Italy | B1 | 23 |
| Cuney, Tx., U.S. | C5 | 120 |
| Cunnamulla, Austl. | E8 | 50 |
| Cunningham, Ks., U.S. | E5 | 93 |
| Cunningham, Ky., U.S. | f9 | 94 |
| Cunningham, Tn., U.S. | A4 | 119 |
| Cupar, Sask. | G3 | 75 |
| Cupar, Scot., U.K. | D5 | 13 |
| Cupertino, Ca., U.S. | *k8 | 82 |
| Cupica, Col. | B2 | 60 |
| Curaçá, Braz. | D3 | 57 |
| Curaçao, i., Neth. Ant. | H18 | 65 |
| Curacautín, Chile | B2 | 54 |
| Curacó, stm., Arg. | B3 | 54 |
| Curanilahue, Chile | B2 | 54 |
| Curaray, stm., S.A. | B3 | 58 |
| Curcubica, mtn., Rom. | B6 | 24 |
| Curdsville, Ky., U.S. | C2 | 94 |
| Curecanti National Recreation Area, Co., U.S. | C3 | 83 |
| Curepto, Chile | B2 | 54 |
| Curiapo, Ven. | B5 | 60 |
| Curicó, Chile | A2 | 54 |
| Curicuriari, stm., Braz. | D4 | 60 |
| Curimataú, stm., Braz. | h6 | 57 |
| Curitiba, Braz. | D3 | 56 |
| Curitibanos, Braz. | D2 | 56 |
| Curlew, Wa., U.S. | A7 | 124 |
| Curlew, Wa., U.S. | A7 | 124 |
| Curlew Creek, stm., Wa., U.S. | A7 | 124 |
| Curlew Lake, l., Wa., U.S. | A7 | 124 |
| Curon Venosta, Italy | C6 | 20 |
| Currais Novos, Braz. | C3 | 57 |
| Curralinho, Braz. | C5 | 59 |
| Curran, Ont. | B10 | 73 |
| Curran, Mi., U.S. | D7 | 99 |
| Currans, Ire. | E2 | 11 |
| Currant, Nv., U.S. | *D7 | 105 |
| Currant Creek, stm., Co., U.S. | C5 | 83 |
| Currant Mountain, mtn., Nv., U.S. | E6 | 105 |
| Current, stm., U.S. | A5 | 81 |
| Currie, Nv., U.S. | F3 | 100 |
| Curituck, N.C., U.S. | A6 | 110 |
| Currituck, co., N.C., U.S. | A6 | 110 |
| Curry, co., N.M., U.S. | C6 | 108 |
| Curry, co., Or., U.S. | E2 | 114 |
| Curryville, Mo., U.S. | B6 | 102 |
| Curtea-de-Argeș, Rom. | C7 | 24 |
| Curtice, Oh., U.S. | A2 | 112 |
| Curtici, Rom. | C5 | 24 |
| Curtin, Or., U.S. | D3 | 114 |
| Curtis, Ar., U.S. | D2 | 81 |
| Curtis, Ne., U.S. | D5 | 104 |
| Curtis, Wi., U.S. | D3 | 126 |
| Curtis, i., Austl. | D9 | 50 |
| Curtiss, Wi., U.S. | D3 | 126 |
| Curtisville, Pa., U.S. | E2 | 115 |
| Curuá, stm., Braz. | C4 | 59 |
| Curuá, stm., Braz. | C4 | 59 |
| Curuá do Sul, stm., Braz. | C4 | 59 |
| Curuçá, Braz. | B1 | 57 |
| Curuçá, stm., Braz. | C5 | 59 |
| Ćuprija, Yugo. | C5 | 24 |
| Curupira, Sierra de, mts., S.A. | E4 | 55 |
| Curuzú Cuatiá, Arg. | B5 | 54 |
| Curve, Tn., U.S. | B2 | 119 |
| Curvelo, Braz. | B4 | 56 |
| Curvér, mtn., Switz. | C8 | 21 |
| Curwensville, Pa., U.S. | E4 | 115 |
| Curwensville Lake, res., Pa., U.S. | E4 | 115 |
| Curwood, Mount, mtn., Mi., U.S. | B2 | 99 |
| Cushendall, N. Ire., U.K. | B5 | 11 |
| Cushing, Ia., U.S. | B2 | 92 |
| Cushing, Ne., U.S. | C7 | 104 |
| Cushing, Ok., U.S. | B5 | 113 |
| Cushing, Tx., U.S. | D5 | 120 |
| Cushman, Ar., U.S. | B4 | 81 |
| Cushman, Ma., U.S. | B2 | 98 |
| Cushman, Lake, res., Wa., U.S. | B2 | 124 |
| Cusick, Wa., U.S. | A8 | 124 |
| Cusihuiriáchic, Mex. | B3 | 63 |
| Cusseta, Al., U.S. | C4 | 78 |
| Cusset, Fr. | D5 | 16 |
| Cusseta, Ga., U.S. | D2 | 87 |
| Custar, Oh., U.S. | A2 | 112 |
| Custer, Mi., U.S. | E4 | 99 |
| Custer, Mt., U.S. | D9 | 103 |
| Custer, S.D., U.S. | D2 | 118 |
| Custer, Wa., U.S. | A3 | 124 |
| Custer, co., Co., U.S. | C5 | 83 |
| Custer, co., Id., U.S. | E4 | 89 |
| Custer, co., Mt., U.S. | D11 | 103 |
| Custer, co., Ne., U.S. | C6 | 104 |
| Custer, co., Ok., U.S. | B2 | 113 |
| Custer, co., S.D., U.S. | D2 | 118 |
| Custer Battlefield National Monument, Mt., U.S. | E9 | 103 |
| Custer City, Ok., U.S. | B3 | 113 |
| Custer City, Pa., U.S. | C5 | 115 |
| Custer Peak, mtn., S.D., U.S. | C2 | 118 |
| Cut Bank, Mt., U.S. | B4 | 103 |
| Cutbank, stm., Alta. | B1 | 68 |
| Cut Bank Creek, stm., N.D., U.S. | A4 | 111 |
| Cut Beaver Lake, l., Sask. | D4 | 75 |
| Cutchogue, N.Y., U.S. | m16 | 109 |
| Cutervo, Peru | C2 | 58 |
| Cuthbert, Ga., U.S. | E2 | 87 |
| Cut Knife, Sask. | E1 | 75 |
| Cutler, Ont. | A2 | 73 |
| Cutler, Fl., U.S. | *G6 | 86 |
| Cutler, In., U.S. | C5 | 91 |
| Cutler, Me., U.S. | D5 | 96 |
| Cutler Ridge, Fl., U.S. | s13 | 86 |
| Cutlerville, Mi., U.S. | *F5 | 99 |
| Cut Off, La., U.S. | E5 | 95 |
| Cutshin, Ky., U.S. | C6 | 94 |
| Cuttack, India | J11 | 37 |
| Cuttingsville, Vt., U.S. | E3 | 122 |
| Cuttyhunk Island, i., Ma., U.S. | D6 | 98 |
| Cutzamalá, stm., Mex. | n13 | 63 |
| Cuvo, stm., Ang. | D1 | 48 |
| Cuxhaven, W. Ger. | B8 | 19 |
| Cuyahoga, co., Oh., U.S. | A4 | 112 |
| Cuyahoga, stm., Oh., U.S. | A4 | 112 |
| Cuyahoga Falls, Oh., U.S. | A4 | 112 |
| Cuyama, stm., Ca., U.S. | E4 | 82 |
| Cuyamaca Peak, mtn., Ca., U.S. | F5 | 82 |
| Cuyamungue, N.M., U.S. | *B4 | 108 |
| Cuyo Islands, is., Phil. | C6 | 34 |
| Cuyuna, Mn., U.S. | D5 | 100 |
| Cuyuni, stm., S.A. | A3 | 59 |
| Cuzco, In., U.S. | H4 | 91 |
| Cuzco, dept., Peru | D4 | 58 |
| Cwmbran, Wales, U.K. | C5 | 12 |
| C.W. McConaughy, Lake, res., Ne., U.S. | C4 | 104 |
| Cybinka, Pol. | A9 | 19 |
| Cyclades, is., Grc. | D5 | 40 |
| Cyclone, Pa., U.S. | C4 | 115 |
| Cygnet, Oh., U.S. | A2 | 112 |
| Cylinder, Ia., U.S. | A3 | 92 |
| Cynthiana, In., U.S. | H2 | 91 |
| Cynthiana, Ky., U.S. | B5 | 94 |
| Cynthiana, Oh., U.S. | C2 | 112 |
| Cypress, Al., U.S. | C2 | 78 |
| Cypress, Ca., U.S. | *n12 | 82 |
| Cypress, Fl., U.S. | B5 | 86 |
| Cypress, Tx., U.S. | r14 | 120 |
| Cypress Bayou, stm., Tx., U.S. | B4 | 120 |
| Cypress Creek, stm., Tx., U.S. | r14 | 120 |
| Cypress Hills, hills, Can. | G10 | 66 |
| Cypress Hills Provincial Park, Alta. | E5 | 68 |
| Cypress Hills Provincial Park, Sask. | H1 | 75 |
| Cypress Inn, Tn., U.S. | B4 | 119 |
| Cypress Lake, Fl., U.S. | *F6 | 86 |
| Cypress Lake, l., Sask. | H1 | 75 |
| Cypress Lake, l., Fl., U.S. | D5 | 86 |
| Cypress Quarters, Fl., U.S. | E6 | 86 |
| Cypress River, Man. | E2 | 70 |
| Cypress Swamp, sw., Fl., U.S. | F4 | 85 |
| Cyprus, ctry., Asia | E9 | 40 |
| Cyprus, North, ctry., Asia | E9 | 40 |
| Cyrenaica (Barqah), hist. reg., Libya | D4 | 43 |
| Cyril, Ok., U.S. | C3 | 113 |
| Cyril, stm., Man. | B4 | 70 |
| Cyrus, Mn., U.S. | E3 | 100 |
| Cythera see Kíthira, i., Grc. | D4 | 40 |
| Czar, Alta. | C5 | 68 |
| Czarna, stm., Pol. | k14 | 26 |
| Czarna Przemsza, stm., Pol. | g10 | 26 |
| Czarnków, Pol. | B4 | 26 |
| Czechoslovakia, ctry., Eur. | D6 | 14 |
| Czechowice-Dziedzice, Pol. | h10 | 26 |
| Czersk, Pol. | B4 | 26 |
| Częstochowa, Pol. | C5 | 26 |
| Człuchów, Pol. | B4 | 26 |

**D**

| Name | Map Ref. | Page |
|---|---|---|
| Da'an, China | B11 | 32 |
| Daaquam, Que. | C7 | 74 |
| Dabakala, I.C. | E4 | 45 |
| Daba Mountains, mts., China | I4 | 32 |
| Dabdab, Libya | D2 | 43 |
| Dabeiba, Col. | B2 | 60 |
| Dabie (part of Szczecin), Pol. | B3 | 26 |
| Dabie Mountains, mts., China | I5 | 32 |
| Dáblice, Czech. | n18 | 21 |
| Dabneys, Va., U.S. | C5 | 123 |
| Dabola, Gui. | F3 | 45 |
| Daborow, Som. | C2 | 47 |
| Dabou, I.C. | E4 | 45 |
| Dąbrowa Białostocka, Pol. | B7 | 26 |
| Dąbrowa Górnicza, Pol. | C5 | 26 |
| Dąbrowa [Tarnowska], Pol. | C6 | 26 |
| Dacca see Dhaka, Bngl. | D9 | 36 |
| Dachau, W. Ger. | D11 | 19 |
| Dacoma, Ok., U.S. | A3 | 113 |
| Dacono, Co., U.S. | B6 | 83 |
| Dacula, Ga., U.S. | C3 | 87 |
| Dadanawa, Guy. | E13 | 59 |
| Daday, Tur. | B9 | 40 |
| Dade, co., Fl., U.S. | B1 | 87 |
| Dade, co., Ga., U.S. | B1 | 87 |
| Dade, co., Mo., U.S. | D4 | 102 |
| Dade City, Fl., U.S. | D4 | 86 |
| Dadeville, Al., U.S. | C4 | 78 |
| Dadeville, Mo., U.S. | D4 | 102 |
| Dādra and Nagar Haveli, ter., India | *D5 | 36 |
| Dādu, Pak. | G4 | 37 |
| Daet, Phil. | o14 | 34 |
| Dafoe, Sask. | F3 | 75 |
| Dafoe, stm., Man. | B4 | 70 |
| Dagana, Sen. | C1 | 45 |
| Dagenham (part of London), Eng., U.K. | k13 | 10 |
| Daggett, Ca., U.S. | E5 | 82 |
| Daggett, Mi., U.S. | C3 | 99 |
| Daggett, co., Ut., U.S. | C6 | 121 |
| Dagmar, Mt., U.S. | B12 | 103 |
| Dagsboro, De., U.S. | F5 | 85 |
| Dagu, China | E7 | 32 |
| Dagupan, Phil. | n13 | 34 |
| Daguscahonda, Pa., U.S. | D4 | 115 |
| Dagus Mines, Pa., U.S. | D4 | 115 |
| Da Hinggan Ling (Greater Khingan Range), mts., China | B9 | 31 |
| Dahlak Archipelago, is., Eth. | E3 | 47 |
| Dahlen, N.D., U.S. | A8 | 111 |
| Dahlgren, Il., U.S. | E5 | 90 |
| Dahlgren, Va., U.S. | B5 | 123 |
| Dahlonega, Ga., U.S. | B3 | 87 |
| Dahme, E. Ger. | B12 | 19 |
| Dahod, India | I5 | 36 |
| Dahomey see Benin, ctry., Afr. | E5 | 45 |
| Dahra, Libya | B3 | 43 |
| Dahshūr, Eg. | D14 | 41 |
| Dahūk, Iraq | D14 | 41 |
| Daicheng, China | E7 | 32 |
| Dailey, W.V., U.S. | C5 | 125 |
| Daimiel, Spain | C4 | 22 |
| Daingean, Ire. | D5 | 11 |
| Daingerfield, Tx., U.S. | C5 | 120 |
| Daiō, Japan | o15 | 33 |
| Daiō, Cape, c., Japan | I8 | 33 |
| Dairen see Dalian, China | D9 | 31 |
| Dairy, Or., U.S. | E5 | 114 |
| Dairyland, Wi., U.S. | B1 | 126 |
| Daisetta, Tx., U.S. | D5 | 120 |
| Daisy, Ar., U.S. | C2 | 81 |
| Daisy, Ga., U.S. | D5 | 87 |
| Daixian, China | D7 | 32 |
| Dajābon, Dom. Rep. | E8 | 64 |
| Dajarra, Austl. | D6 | 50 |
| Dakar, Sen. | D1 | 45 |
| Dākhilah, Al Wāḥāt ad, well, Eg. | E1 | 43 |
| Dakhla, W. Sah. | D1 | 45 |
| Dakoro, Niger | A6 | 45 |
| Dakota, Il., U.S. | A4 | 90 |
| Dakota, Mn., U.S. | G7 | 100 |
| Dakota, co., Mn., U.S. | F5 | 100 |
| Dakota, co., Ne., U.S. | B9 | 104 |
| Dakota City, Ia., U.S. | B3 | 92 |
| Dakota City, Ne., U.S. | B9 | 104 |
| Dākura, Nic. | C6 | 62 |
| Dakwaa, Zaire | A4 | 48 |
| Dalaas, Aus. | B9 | 21 |
| Dalālven, stm., Swe. | G6 | 14 |
| Dalaman, Tur. | D7 | 25 |
| Dalandzadgad, Mong. | C7 | 31 |
| Dalark, Ar., U.S. | C2 | 81 |
| Dalaro, Swe. | i36 | 14 |
| Da Lat, Viet. | C3 | 34 |
| Dalbandin, Pak. | F1 | 36 |
| Dalbeattie, Scot., U.K. | F5 | 13 |
| D'Albertis Dome, mtn., Pap. N. Gui. | k11 | 50 |
| Dalbo, Mn., U.S. | E5 | 100 |
| Dalby, Austl. | E9 | 50 |
| Dalby, Swe. | C7 | 15 |
| Dalcahue, Chile | B2 | 54 |
| Dale, In., U.S. | H4 | 91 |
| Dale, Or., U.S. | C8 | 114 |
| Dale, co., Al., U.S. | D4 | 78 |
| Dale City, Va., U.S. | B5 | 123 |
| Dale Hollow Lake, res., U.S. | C8 | 119 |
| Dalemead, Alta. | D4 | 68 |
| Daleville, Al., U.S. | D4 | 78 |
| Daleville, In., U.S. | D6 | 91 |
| Daleville, Ms., U.S. | C5 | 101 |
| Dalhart, Tx., U.S. | A1 | 120 |
| Dalhousie, N.B. | A3 | 71 |
| Dalhousie, India | A5 | 37 |
| Dalhousie Junction, N.B. | A3 | 71 |
| Dali, China | E6 | 31 |
| Dalian (Lüda), China | D9 | 31 |
| Dalías, Spain | D4 | 22 |
| Daliyat el Karmil, Isr. | B7 | 41 |
| Dalkeith, Scot., U.K. | E5 | 13 |
| Dalkeith, Fl., U.S. | B1 | 86 |
| Dalkena, Wa., U.S. | A8 | 124 |
| Dalkey, Ire. | D5 | 11 |
| Dall, Mount, mtn., Ak., U.S. | f15 | 79 |
| Dallam, co., Tx., U.S. | A1 | 120 |
| Dallardsville, Tx., U.S. | D5 | 120 |
| Dallas, Ga., U.S. | C2 | 87 |
| Dallas, Ia., U.S. | C4 | 92 |
| Dallas, N.C., U.S. | B1 | 110 |
| Dallas, Or., U.S. | C3 | 114 |
| Dallas, Pa., U.S. | D10 | 115 |
| Dallas, S.D., U.S. | D6 | 118 |
| Dallas, Tx., U.S. | C4 | 120 |
| Dallas, W.V., U.S. | f8 | 125 |
| Dallas, Wi., U.S. | C2 | 126 |
| Dallas, co., Al., U.S. | C2 | 78 |
| Dallas, co., Ar., U.S. | D3 | 81 |
| Dallas, co., Ia., U.S. | C3 | 92 |
| Dallas, co., Mo., U.S. | D4 | 102 |
| Dallas, co., Tx., U.S. | C4 | 120 |
| Dallas Center, Ia., U.S. | C4 | 92 |
| Dallas City, Il., U.S. | C2 | 90 |
| Dallas Naval Air Station, mil., Tx., U.S. | n9 | 120 |
| Dallastown, Pa., U.S. | G8 | 115 |
| Dall Island, i., Ak., U.S. | n23 | 79 |
| Dalmally, Scot., U.K. | D4 | 13 |
| Dalmatia, Pa., U.S. | E8 | 115 |
| Dalmatia, hist. reg., Yugo. | D3 | 24 |
| Dalmellington, Scot., U.K. | C4 | 10 |
| Dalnerechensk, Sov. Un. | E16 | 29 |
| Dalnyaya, Sov. Un. | D11 | 33 |
| Daloa, I.C. | E3 | 45 |
| Dalou Mountains, mts., China | K2 | 32 |
| Dalqū, Sud. | A3 | 47 |
| Dalroy, Alta. | D4 | 68 |
| Dalry, Scot., U.K. | E4 | 13 |
| Dalrymple, Mount, mtn., Austl. | D8 | 50 |
| Dāltenganj, India | D7 | 36 |
| Dalton, Ar., U.S. | A4 | 81 |
| Dalton, Ga., U.S. | B2 | 87 |
| Dalton, Ma., U.S. | B1 | 98 |
| Dalton, Mn., U.S. | D3 | 100 |
| Dalton, Mo., U.S. | B5 | 102 |
| Dalton, Ne., U.S. | C3 | 104 |
| Dalton, N.H., U.S. | B3 | 106 |
| Dalton, N.Y., U.S. | C3 | 109 |
| Dalton, Oh., U.S. | B4 | 112 |
| Dalton, Wi., U.S. | E4 | 126 |
| Dalton City, Il., U.S. | D5 | 90 |
| Dalton Gardens, Id., U.S. | B2 | 89 |
| Dalton Iceberg Tongue, ice, Ant. | C25 | 7 |
| Dalwhinnie, Scot., U.K. | D4 | 13 |
| Daly, stm., Austl. | B5 | 50 |
| Dalzell, Il., U.S. | B4 | 90 |
| Dalzell, S.C., U.S. | C7 | 117 |
| Damän, India | *D5 | 36 |
| Damān and Diu, ter., India | *D5 | 36 |
| Dāhānu, India | G4 | 37 |
| Dahinda, Il., U.S. | C3 | 90 |
| Damaqun Mountains, mts., | D7 | 32 |
| Damar, Ks., U.S. | C4 | 93 |
| Damar, i., Indon. | G7 | 34 |
| Damaraland, | D3 | 49 |
| Damariscotta, Me., U.S. | D3 | 96 |
| Damariscotta Lake, l., Me., | D3 | 96 |
| Damascus (Dimashq), Syria | B3 | 41 |
| Damascus, Ar., U.S. | B3 | 81 |
| Damascus, Ga., U.S. | E2 | 87 |
| Damascus, Md., U.S. | B3 | 97 |
| Damascus, Pa., U.S. | C11 | 115 |
| Damascus, Va., U.S. | f10 | 123 |
| Damascus Gate, hist., Isr. Occ. | m14 | 41 |
| Damaturu, Nig. | D7 | 45 |
| Damba, Ang. | C2 | 48 |
| Dame Marie, Cap, c., Haiti | E6 | 64 |
| Damdama, Sud. | C2 | 47 |
| Dam Gamad, Sud. | C2 | 47 |
| Dāmghān, Iran | B5 | 38 |
| Damietta Branch, stm., Eg. | B3 | 41 |
| Daming, China | D3 | 32 |
| Damme, W. Ger. | B8 | 19 |
| Dāmodar, stm., India | F10 | 37 |
| Damoh, India | I8 | 36 |
| Damon, Tx., U.S. | r14 | 120 |
| Damongo, Ghana | E4 | 45 |
| Dampier, Austl. | D2 | 50 |
| Dampier Archipelago, is., Austl. | D2 | 50 |
| Dampier Strait, strt., Indon. | F8 | 34 |
| Damvant, Switz. | B2 | 21 |
| Dan, stm., U.S. | D3 | 123 |
| Dana, In., U.S. | E3 | 91 |
| Dana, Ia., U.S. | B3 | 92 |
| Dana, Sask. | E3 | 75 |
| Dana Point, Ca., U.S. | *F5 | 82 |
| Dānāpur, India | H11 | 37 |
| Danané, I.C. | E3 | 45 |
| Da Nang, Viet. | B4 | 34 |
| Danbury, Ct., U.S. | D2 | 84 |
| Danbury, Ia., U.S. | B2 | 92 |
| Danbury, Ne., U.S. | D5 | 104 |
| Danbury, N.H., U.S. | D3 | 106 |
| Danbury, N.C., U.S. | A2 | 110 |
| Danbury, Tx., U.S. | r14 | 120 |
| Danbury, Wi., U.S. | B1 | 126 |
| Danby, N.Y., U.S. | C4 | 109 |
| Danby, Vt., U.S. | E3 | 122 |
| Danby Corners, Vt., U.S. | E2 | 122 |
| Dancy, Wi., U.S. | D3 | 126 |
| Dandeldhura, Nep. | E2 | 37 |
| Dande, stm., Ang. | C1 | 48 |
| Dandenong, Austl. | *G8 | 50 |
| Dandong, China | C9 | 31 |
| Dandridge, Tn., U.S. | C10 | 119 |

| Name | Map Ref. | Page |
|---|---|---|
| Dane, Wi., U.S. | E4 | 126 |
| Dane, co., Wi., U.S. | E4 | 126 |
| Danevang, Tx., U.S. | E4 | 120 |
| Danfeng, China | H4 | 32 |
| Danforth, Il., U.S. | C6 | 90 |
| Danforth, Me., U.S. | C5 | 96 |
| Danforth Hills, mts., Co., U.S. | A2 | 83 |
| Dangila, Eth. | C4 | 47 |
| Dangshan, China | G7 | 32 |
| Dangtu, China | I8 | 32 |
| Dangyang, China | I4 | 32 |
| Dania, Fl., U.S. | F6 | 86 |
| Daniel, Ut., U.S. | *C4 | 121 |
| Daniel, Wy., U.S. | D2 | 127 |
| Daniels, co., Mt., U.S. | B11 | 103 |
| Daniel's Harbour, Newf. | C3 | 72 |
| Danielson, Ct., U.S. | B8 | 84 |
| Daniels Pass, Ut., U.S. | C4 | 121 |
| Danielsville, Ga., U.S. | B3 | 87 |
| Danilov, Sov. Un. | B13 | 27 |
| Danilovgrad, Yugo. | D4 | 24 |
| Danli, Hond. | E7 | 63 |
| Danjo Island, i., Japan | J4 | 33 |
| Dannebrog, Ne., U.S. | C7 | 104 |
| Dannemarie, Fr. | A3 | 21 |
| Dannemora, N.Y., U.S. | f11 | 109 |
| Dannenberg, W. Ger. | E5 | 15 |
| Dannevirke, N.Z. | N16 | 51 |
| Dannike, Swe. | A7 | 15 |
| Dans Mountain, mtn., Md., U.S. | k13 | 97 |
| Dansville, N.Y., U.S. | C3 | 109 |
| Dante, S.D., U.S. | D7 | 118 |
| Dante, Tn., U.S. | m14 | 119 |
| Dante, Va., U.S. | f9 | 123 |
| Dantewāra, India | H8 | 37 |
| Danube, Mn., U.S. | F3 | 100 |
| Danube, stm., Eur. | G14 | 8 |
| Danube Delta, Eur. | I7 | 27 |
| Danubyu, Burma | D1 | 35 |
| Danvers, Il., U.S. | C4 | 90 |
| Danvers, Ma., U.S. | A6 | 98 |
| Danvers, Mn., U.S. | E3 | 100 |
| Danvers, Mt., U.S. | C7 | 103 |
| Danville, Que. | D5 | 74 |
| Danville, Al., U.S. | A2 | 78 |
| Danville, Ar., U.S. | B2 | 81 |
| Danville, Ca., U.S. | h9 | 82 |
| Danville, Ga., U.S. | D3 | 87 |
| Danville, Il., U.S. | C6 | 90 |
| Danville, In., U.S. | E4 | 91 |
| Danville, Ia., U.S. | D6 | 92 |
| Danville, Ks., U.S. | E6 | 93 |
| Danville, Ky., U.S. | C5 | 94 |
| Danville, La., U.S. | B3 | 95 |
| Danville, N.H., U.S. | E4 | 106 |
| Danville, Oh., U.S. | B3 | 112 |
| Danville, Pa., U.S. | E8 | 115 |
| Danville, Vt., U.S. | C4 | 122 |
| Danville, Va., U.S. | D3 | 123 |
| Danville, Wa., U.S. | A7 | 124 |
| Danville, W.V., U.S. | C3 | 125 |
| Danxian, China | C8 | 35 |
| Danzhai, China | K2 | 32 |
| Danzig, Gulf of b., Eur. | A5 | 26 |
| Danzig see Gdańsk, Pol. | A5 | 26 |
| Daosa, India | D6 | 37 |
| Dacxian, China | F7 | 31 |
| Daphne, Al., U.S. | E2 | 78 |
| Da Qaidam, China | D4 | 31 |
| Daqing (Anda), China | *B10 | 31 |
| Darʿā, Syria | F11 | 40 |
| Dārāb, Iran | G7 | 39 |
| Darabani, Rom. | A8 | 24 |
| Daraj, Libya | C2 | 43 |
| Darasun, Sov. Un. | D14 | 29 |
| Darawah, Eg. | D3 | 41 |
| Darbandi Khan Dam, Iraq | D2 | 39 |
| Darbhanga, India | C8 | 36 |
| D'Arbonne, Bayou, stm., La., U.S. | B3 | 95 |
| Darburruk, Som. | D5 | 47 |
| Darby, Mt., U.S. | D2 | 103 |
| Darby, Pa., U.S. | G11 | 115 |
| Darbydale, Oh., U.S. | m10 | 112 |
| Darby Township, Pa., U.S. | *G11 | 115 |
| Darbyville, Oh., U.S. | C2 | 112 |
| Dar Chebika, Mor. | D2 | 44 |
| D'Arcy Station, Sask. | F1 | 75 |
| Dardanelle, Ar., U.S. | B2 | 81 |
| Dardanelle, Ca., U.S. | C4 | 82 |
| Dardanelle Lake, res., Ar., U.S. | B2 | 81 |
| Dardanelles, strt. | B5 | 40 |
| Darden, N.C., U.S. | B6 | 110 |
| Darden, Tn., U.S. | B3 | 119 |
| Dardenne Creek, stm., Mo., U.S. | f12 | 102 |
| Dare, co., N.C., U.S. | B7 | 110 |
| Darende, Tur. | C11 | 40 |
| Dar es Salaam, Tan. | C6 | 48 |
| Daretown, N.J., U.S. | D2 | 107 |
| Darfo, Italy | D6 | 20 |
| Darfur, Mn., U.S. | F4 | 100 |
| Dārfūr al Janūbīyah (Southern Darfur), prov., Sud. | C1 | 47 |
| Dārfūr ash Shamālīyah (Northern Darfur), prov., Sud. | B2 | 47 |
| Dargan, Md., U.S. | G3 | 97 |
| Dargan-Ata, Sov. Un. | A11 | 39 |
| Dargaville, N.Z. | K14 | 51 |
| Darhan, Mong. | B6 | 31 |
| Darhan Muminggan Lianheqi, China | D4 | 32 |
| Darien, Ct., U.S. | E2 | 84 |
| Darien, Ga., U.S. | E5 | 87 |
| Darien, Il., U.S. | *k9 | 90 |
| Darien, Wi., U.S. | F5 | 126 |
| Darien, Gulf of, b. | F9 | 62 |
| Darien, Serranía del, mts. | F9 | 62 |
| Dariense, Cordillera, mts., Nic. | D5 | 62 |
| Darjeeling, India | C8 | 36 |
| Darke, co., Oh., U.S. | B1 | 112 |
| Darkesville, W.V., U.S. | B6 | 125 |
| Darley Woods, De., U.S. | h8 | 85 |
| Darling, Ms., U.S. | A3 | 101 |
| Darling, stm., Austl. | F7 | 50 |
| Darling, Lake, res., N.D., U.S. | A4 | 111 |
| Darling Downs, reg., Austl. | E9 | 50 |
| Darlingford, Man. | E2 | 70 |
| Darling Range, mts., Austl. | F2 | 50 |
| Darlington, Eng., U.K. | C6 | 10 |
| Darlington, Al., U.S. | D2 | 78 |
| Darlington, Fl., U.S. | v15 | 86 |
| Darlington, In., U.S. | D4 | 91 |
| Darlington, Mo., U.S. | A3 | 102 |
| Darlington, S.C., U.S. | C8 | 117 |
| Darlington, Wi., U.S. | F3 | 126 |
| Darlington, co., S.C., U.S. | C8 | 117 |
| Darłowo, Pol. | A4 | 26 |
| Darmody, Sask. | G2 | 75 |
| Darmstadt, W. Ger. | D4 | 18 |
| Darnah, Libya | C4 | 43 |
| Darnell, La., U.S. | B4 | 95 |
| Darnestown, Md., U.S. | B3 | 97 |
| Darney, Fr. | A2 | 20 |
| Darnley, Cape, c., Ant. | C19 | 7 |
| Daro, Malay. | E4 | 34 |
| Daroca, Spain | B5 | 22 |
| Darr, Ne., U.S. | D6 | 104 |
| Darrah, Mount, mtn., Can. | E3 | 68 |
| Darreh Gaz, Iran | C9 | 39 |
| Darrington, Wa., U.S. | A4 | 124 |
| Darrouzett, Tx., U.S. | A2 | 120 |
| Darrow, La., U.S. | h10 | 95 |
| Darsser Ort, c., E. Ger. | D6 | 15 |
| Dart, stm., Eng., U.K. | D4 | 12 |
| Dart, Cape, c., Ant. | E7 | 7 |
| Dartmoor, for., Eng., U.K. | E5 | 10 |
| Dartmouth, N.S. | E6 | 71 |
| Dartmouth, Eng., U.K. | E5 | 10 |
| Dartmouth Woods, De., U.S. | *A3 | 85 |
| Daruvar, Yugo. | C3 | 24 |
| Darvel Bay, b., Malay. | E5 | 34 |
| Darwin, Austl. | B5 | 50 |
| Darwin, Ca., U.S. | D5 | 82 |
| Darwin, Mn., U.S. | E4 | 100 |
| Darwin Glacier, ice, Ant. | f41 | 7 |
| Dasht, strt., Pak. | C3 | 36 |
| Dashwood, Ont. | D3 | 73 |
| Dasol Bay, b., Phil. | o12 | 34 |
| Dassel, Mn., U.S. | E4 | 100 |
| Dassel, Tur. | D6 | 25 |
| Datça, Tur. | D6 | 25 |
| Dateland, Az., U.S. | E2 | 80 |
| Datia, India | E7 | 37 |
| Datian, China | L7 | 32 |
| Datil, N.M., U.S. | C2 | 108 |
| Datong, China | C7 | 31 |
| Datto, Ar., U.S. | A5 | 81 |
| Datu, Cape, c., Asia | E3 | 34 |
| Datu, Cape, stm., E. Ger. | E7 | 15 |
| Daudnagar, India | E10 | 37 |
| Daufuskie Island, S.C., U.S. | G6 | 117 |
| Daufuskie Island, i., S.C., U.S. | G6 | 117 |
| Daugava (Western Dvina), stm., Sov. Un. | C5 | 27 |
| Daugavpils (Dvinsk), Sov. Un. | D6 | 27 |
| Daule, Ec. | A2 | 58 |
| Daule, Ec. | B2 | 58 |
| Daun, W. Ger. | C1 | 19 |
| Daung, i., Burma | H5 | 37 |
| Dauphin, Man. | D1 | 70 |
| Dauphin, Pa., U.S. | F8 | 115 |
| Dauphin, co., Pa., U.S. | F8 | 115 |
| Dauphin, stm., Man. | D2 | 70 |
| Dauphiné, hist. reg., Fr. | E6 | 16 |
| Dauphin Island, Al., U.S. | E1 | 78 |
| Dauphin Island, i., Al., U.S. | E1 | 78 |
| Dauphin Lake, l., Man. | D2 | 70 |
| Davao, Phil. | D7 | 34 |
| Davao Gulf, b., Phil. | D7 | 34 |
| Davenport, Ca., U.S. | D2 | 82 |
| Davenport, Fl., U.S. | D5 | 86 |
| Davenport, Ia., U.S. | C7 | 92 |
| Davenport, Ne., U.S. | D8 | 104 |
| Davenport, N.Y., U.S. | C6 | 109 |
| Davenport, N.D., U.S. | C8 | 111 |
| Davenport, Ok., U.S. | B5 | 113 |
| Davenport, Wa., U.S. | B7 | 124 |
| Davenport Downs, Austl. | B3 | 51 |
| Daventry, Eng., U.K. | B6 | 12 |
| Davey, Ne., U.S. | h11 | 104 |
| David, Pan. | F6 | 62 |
| David, Ky., U.S. | C7 | 94 |
| David City, Ne., U.S. | C8 | 104 |
| David-Gorodok, Sov. Un. | E6 | 27 |
| Davidson, Sask. | F3 | 75 |
| Davidson, N.C., U.S. | B2 | 110 |
| Davidson, Ok., U.S. | C2 | 113 |
| Davidson, Tn., U.S. | C8 | 119 |
| Davidson, co., N.C., U.S. | B2 | 110 |
| Davidson, co., Tn., U.S. | A5 | 119 |
| Davidson Mountains, mts., Ak., U.S. | B11 | 79 |
| Davidsville, Pa., U.S. | F4 | 115 |
| Davie, Fl., U.S. | F6 | 86 |
| Davie, co., N.C., U.S. | B2 | 110 |
| Davie, co., N.C., U.S. | G3 | 91 |
| Daviess, co., Ky., U.S. | C2 | 94 |
| Daviess, co., Mo., U.S. | B3 | 102 |
| Davin, Sask. | G3 | 75 |
| Davis, Ca., U.S. | C3 | 82 |
| Davis, Il., U.S. | A4 | 90 |
| Davis, N.C., U.S. | C6 | 110 |
| Davis, Ok., U.S. | C4 | 113 |
| Davis, W.V., U.S. | B5 | 125 |
| Davis, co., Ia., U.S. | D5 | 92 |
| Davis, co., Ut., U.S. | C3 | 121 |
| Davis, Mount, mtn., Pa., U.S. | G3 | 115 |
| Davisboro, Ga., U.S. | D4 | 87 |
| Davis Creek, stm., W.V., U.S. | m12 | 125 |
| Davis Dam, U.S. | H7 | 105 |
| Davis Inlet, Newf. | g9 | 72 |
| Davis Islands, is., Fl., U.S. | p11 | 86 |
| Davis Junction, Il., U.S. | A4 | 90 |
| Davis Lake, l., Or., U.S. | E5 | 114 |
| Davis-Monthan Air Force Base, mil., Az., U.S. | E5 | 80 |
| Davis Mountains, mts., Tx., U.S. | o12 | 120 |
| Daviston, Al., U.S. | B4 | 78 |
| Davisville, N.H., U.S. | D3 | 106 |
| Davisville, R.I., U.S. | E4 | 116 |
| Davle, Czech. | o17 | 26 |
| Davos, Switz. | E4 | 18 |
| Dawa, China | *C9 | 31 |
| Dawasir, Wādī ad, val., Sau. Ar. | C4 | 38 |
| Dawei, Burma | F10 | 36 |
| Daweloor, i., Indon. | B2 | 34 |
| Dawn, Mo., U.S. | B4 | 102 |
| Dawn, Tx., U.S. | B1 | 120 |
| Dawna Range, mts., Burma | D3 | 35 |
| Dawros Head, c., Ire. | C3 | 11 |

| Name | Map Ref. | Page |
|---|---|---|
| Daws Island, i., S.C., U.S. | G6 | 117 |
| Dawson, Yukon | D5 | 66 |
| Dawson, Ga., U.S. | E2 | 87 |
| Dawson, Ia., U.S. | C3 | 92 |
| Dawson, Mn., U.S. | F2 | 100 |
| Dawson, Ne., U.S. | D10 | 104 |
| Dawson, N.D., U.S. | C6 | 111 |
| Dawson, Pa., U.S. | F2 | 115 |
| Dawson, Tx., U.S. | D4 | 120 |
| Dawson, co., Ga., U.S. | B2 | 87 |
| Dawson, co., Mt., U.S. | C11 | 103 |
| Dawson, co., Ne., U.S. | D6 | 104 |
| Dawson, co., Ks., U.S. | C1 | 120 |
| Dawson, stm., Austl. | D8 | 50 |
| Dawson, Mount, mtn., B.C. | D9 | 69 |
| Dawson-Lambton Glacier, ice, Ant. | B10 | 7 |
| Dawson Range, mts., Yukon | D5 | 66 |
| Dawson Creek, B.C. | B7 | 69 |
| Dawson Springs, Ky., U.S. | C2 | 94 |
| Dawsonville, Ga., U.S. | B2 | 87 |
| Daxian, China | E6 | 31 |
| Daxin, China | B3 | 86 |
| Daykin, Ne., U.S. | D8 | 104 |
| Daylesford, Austl. | H5 | 51 |
| Daym Zubayr, Sud. | D2 | 47 |
| Dayr Abū Saʿīd, Jord. | B7 | 41 |
| Dayr al Balaḥ, Isr. Occ. | C6 | 41 |
| Dayr ʿAllā, Jord. | g13 | 41 |
| Dayr az Zawr, Syria | B4 | 38 |
| Dayr Dibwān, Isr. Occ. | h12 | 41 |
| Dayr Istiyā, Isr. Occ. | g11 | 41 |
| Dayrūṭ, Eg. | D6 | 43 |
| Daysland, Alta. | C4 | 68 |
| Daysville, Tn., U.S. | D9 | 119 |
| Dayton, Al., U.S. | C2 | 78 |
| Dayton, Id., U.S. | G7 | 89 |
| Dayton, In., U.S. | D4 | 91 |
| Dayton, Ia., U.S. | B3 | 92 |
| Dayton, Ky., U.S. | h14 | 94 |
| Dayton, Md., U.S. | B4 | 97 |
| Dayton, Mn., U.S. | m12 | 100 |
| Dayton, Mt., U.S. | C2 | 103 |
| Dayton, Nv., U.S. | D2 | 105 |
| Dayton, N.J., U.S. | C3 | 107 |
| Dayton, N.Y., U.S. | C2 | 109 |
| Dayton, Oh., U.S. | C1 | 112 |
| Dayton, Or., U.S. | B3 | 114 |
| Dayton, Pa., U.S. | E3 | 115 |
| Dayton, Tn., U.S. | D8 | 119 |
| Dayton, Tx., U.S. | D5 | 120 |
| Dayton, Va., U.S. | B4 | 123 |
| Dayton, Wa., U.S. | C8 | 124 |
| Dayton, Wy., U.S. | B5 | 127 |
| Daytona Beach, Fl., U.S. | C5 | 86 |
| Dayu, China | F7 | 31 |
| Dayville, Ct., U.S. | B8 | 84 |
| Dayville, Or., U.S. | C7 | 114 |
| Dazey, N.D., U.S. | B7 | 111 |
| De Aar, S. Afr. | D3 | 49 |
| Dead, North Branch, stm., Me., U.S. | C2 | 96 |
| Dead, South Branch, stm., Me., U.S. | C2 | 96 |
| Dead Creek, stm., Vt., U.S. | C2 | 122 |
| Dead Diamond, stm., N.H., U.S. | g7 | 106 |
| Dead Indian Peak, mtn., Wy., U.S. | B3 | 127 |
| Dead Lake, l., Mn., U.S. | D3 | 100 |
| Dead Lake, res., Fl., U.S. | B1 | 86 |
| Deadman Bay, b., Fl., U.S. | C3 | 86 |
| Deadman Creek, stm., Wa., U.S. | g14 | 124 |
| Dead Sea, l., Asia | B3 | 38 |
| Deadwood, S.D., U.S. | C2 | 118 |
| Deadwood Reservoir, res., Id., U.S. | E3 | 89 |
| Deaf Smith, co., Tx., U.S. | B1 | 120 |
| Deakin Bay, b., Ant. | C28 | 7 |
| Deal, Eng., U.K. | C9 | 12 |
| Deal, N.J., U.S. | C4 | 107 |
| Deale, Md., U.S. | C4 | 97 |
| Deal Island, Md., U.S. | D6 | 97 |
| Deal Island, i., Md., U.S. | D6 | 97 |
| Deam, B.C. | C4 | 69 |
| Deanburg, Tn., U.S. | B3 | 119 |
| Dean Channel, strt., B.C. | C4 | 69 |
| Deán Funes, Arg. | A4 | 54 |
| Deanville, W.V., U.S. | C3 | 107 |
| Dearborn, Mi., U.S. | F7 | 99 |
| Dearborn, Mo., U.S. | B3 | 102 |
| Dearborn, co., In., U.S. | F7 | 91 |
| Dearborn Heights, Mi., U.S. | p15 | 99 |
| Dearg, Beinn, mtn., Scot., U.K. | B4 | 10 |
| Dearing, Ga., U.S. | E8 | 93 |
| Dearing, Ks., U.S. | C2 | 89 |
| De Armanville, Al., U.S. | B4 | 78 |
| Deary, Id., U.S. | C2 | 89 |
| Dease Arm, b., N.W. Ter. | A4 | 111 |
| Dease Lake, B.C. | m16 | 69 |
| Dease Strait, strt., N.W. Ter. | C11 | 66 |
| Death Valley, val., Ca., U.S. | D5 | 82 |
| Death Valley Junction, Ca., U.S. | D5 | 82 |
| Death Valley National Monument, U.S. | D5 | 82 |
| Deatsville, Al., U.S. | C3 | 78 |
| Deauville, Fr. | C7 | 16 |
| Deba, Nig. | *D6 | 45 |
| De Baca, co., N.M., U.S. | C5 | 108 |
| Debao, China | G6 | 31 |
| Debar, Yugo. | E5 | 24 |
| Debary, Fl., U.S. | D5 | 86 |
| Debden, Sask. | D2 | 75 |
| Debec, N.B. | C2 | 71 |
| De Beque, Co., U.S. | B2 | 83 |
| De Berry, Tx., U.S. | C5 | 120 |
| Dębica, Pol. | C6 | 26 |
| Deblin, Pol. | B6 | 26 |
| Deblois, Me., U.S. | D4 | 96 |
| Debno, Pol. | B3 | 26 |
| Debo, Lac, l., Mali | C4 | 45 |
| De Borgia, Mt., U.S. | C1 | 103 |
| Deboullie Mountain, mtn., Me., U.S. | B4 | 96 |
| Debovo, Bul. | D7 | 24 |
| Debre Birhan, Eth. | D4 | 47 |
| Debrecen, Hung. | B5 | 24 |
| Debre Markos, Eth. | C4 | 47 |
| Debre Tabor, Eth. | C4 | 47 |
| Debre Zeyit, Eth. | *D4 | 47 |
| De Cade, Lake, l., La., U.S. | E5 | 95 |
| Decatur, Ar., U.S. | A1 | 81 |

| Name | Map Ref. | Page |
|---|---|---|
| Decatur, Ga., U.S. | C2 | 87 |
| Decatur, Il., U.S. | D5 | 90 |
| De Funiak Springs, Fl., U.S. | u15 | 86 |
| Dêgê, China | E4 | 31 |
| Degeberga, Swe. | C8 | 15 |
| Degeh Bur, Eth. | D5 | 47 |
| Degélis, Que. | B9 | 74 |
| Degerön, Swe. | u33 | 14 |
| Degersheim, Switz. | B7 | 21 |
| Deggendorf, W. Ger. | D6 | 18 |
| De Graff, Mn., U.S. | E3 | 100 |
| De Graff, Oh., U.S. | B2 | 112 |
| De Gray Lake, res., Ar., U.S. | C2 | 81 |
| Deh Bīd, Iran | B5 | 38 |
| Dehibat, Tun. | C7 | 44 |
| Dehiwala-Mount Lavinia, Sri L. | *G6 | 35 |
| Deh Kord, Iran | E4 | 39 |
| Dehlorān, Iran | E3 | 39 |
| Dehpehk, i., Micron. | Q17 | 52 |
| Dehra Dūn, India | B6 | 36 |
| Deh Shū, Afg. | F11 | 39 |
| Deinze, Bel. | D3 | 17 |
| Děčín, Czech. | C3 | 26 |
| Decize, Fr. | D5 | 16 |
| Decker, Man. | D1 | 70 |
| Decker, In., U.S. | G2 | 91 |
| Decker, Mt., U.S. | E10 | 103 |
| Decker Lake, B.C. | B5 | 69 |
| Deckers, Co., U.S. | B5 | 83 |
| Deckerville, Mi., U.S. | E8 | 99 |
| Declo, Id., U.S. | G5 | 89 |
| De Cocksdorp, Neth. | A4 | 17 |
| Decorah, Ia., U.S. | A6 | 92 |
| Decota, W.V., U.S. | m13 | 125 |
| Dededo, Guam | L10 | 52 |
| Dedemsvaart, Neth. | B6 | 17 |
| Deder, Eth. | D5 | 47 |
| Dedham, Ia., U.S. | C3 | 92 |
| Dedham, Ma., U.S. | B5 | 98 |
| Dedinovo, Sov. Un. | n19 | 27 |
| Dedougou, Burkina | D4 | 45 |
| Dedu, China | B3 | 33 |
| Dedza, Mwi. | D5 | 48 |
| Dee, stm., U.K. | D5 | 10 |
| Dee, stm., Scot., U.K. | B5 | 10 |
| Deedsville, In., U.S. | C5 | 91 |
| Deel, stm., Ire. | E3 | 11 |
| Deemer, Ms., U.S. | C4 | 101 |
| Deep, stm., N.C., U.S. | B3 | 110 |
| Deep Brook, N.S. | E4 | 71 |
| Deep Creek, stm., De., U.S. | F3 | 85 |
| Deep Creek, stm., Mt., U.S. | C4 | 103 |
| Deep Creek, stm., Ut., U.S. | B3 | 121 |
| Deep Creek, stm., Ut., U.S. | C2 | 121 |
| Deep Creek, stm., Va., U.S. | F3 | 121 |
| Deep Creek, stm., Wa., U.S. | g13 | 124 |
| Deep Creek Lake, res., Md., U.S. | K12 | 97 |
| Deep Creek Mountains, mts., Id., U.S. | G6 | 89 |
| Deep Creek Range, mts., Ut., U.S. | D2 | 121 |
| Deep Fork, stm., Ok., U.S. | B5 | 113 |
| Deep Gap, N.C., U.S. | A1 | 110 |
| Deep Inlet, b., Newf. | g10 | 72 |
| Deep Red Creek, stm., Ok., U.S. | C3 | 113 |
| Deep River, Ont. | A7 | 73 |
| Deep River, Ct., U.S. | D6 | 84 |
| Deep River, Ia., U.S. | C5 | 92 |
| Deep Run, N.C., U.S. | B5 | 110 |
| Deepstep, Ga., U.S. | C4 | 87 |
| Deepwater, Mo., U.S. | C4 | 102 |
| Deepwater, N.J., U.S. | D2 | 107 |
| Deep Water, W.V., U.S. | m13 | 125 |
| Deer, Ar., U.S. | B2 | 81 |
| Deer Creek, Il., U.S. | C4 | 90 |
| Deer Creek, Mn., U.S. | D3 | 100 |
| Deer Creek, Ok., U.S. | A4 | 113 |
| Deer Creek, stm., In., U.S. | C5 | 91 |
| Deer Creek, stm., Md., U.S. | A5 | 97 |
| Deer Creek, stm., Oh., U.S. | C2 | 112 |
| Deer Creek Indian Reservation, Mn., U.S. | C5 | 100 |
| Deerfield, Il., U.S. | h9 | 90 |
| Deerfield, Ks., U.S. | E2 | 93 |
| Deerfield, Ma., U.S. | A2 | 98 |
| Deerfield, Mi., U.S. | G7 | 99 |
| Deerfield, Mo., U.S. | D3 | 102 |
| Deerfield, N.H., U.S. | D4 | 106 |
| Deerfield, Oh., U.S. | A4 | 112 |
| Deerfield, Wi., U.S. | E4 | 126 |
| Deerfield, stm., U.S. | A2 | 98 |
| Deerfield Beach, Fl., U.S. | F6 | 86 |
| Deerfield Street, N.J., U.S. | D2 | 107 |
| Deer Grove, Il., U.S. | B4 | 90 |
| Deering, Ak., U.S. | B7 | 79 |
| Deering, N.H., U.S. | D3 | 106 |
| Deering, N.D., U.S. | A4 | 111 |
| Deer Island, Or., U.S. | B4 | 114 |
| Deer Island, i., Ms., U.S. | g12 | 98 |
| Deer Isle, Me., U.S. | D4 | 96 |
| Deer Isle, i., Me., U.S. | D4 | 96 |
| Deer Lake, Newf. | D3 | 72 |
| Deer Lake, l., Newf. | D3 | 72 |
| Deer Lodge, Mt., U.S. | D4 | 103 |
| Deer Lodge, Tn., U.S. | C9 | 119 |
| Deer Lodge, co., Mt., U.S. | E3 | 103 |
| Deer Mountain, mtn., Me., U.S. | C2 | 96 |
| Deer Park, Al., U.S. | D1 | 78 |
| Deer Park, Md., U.S. | m12 | 97 |
| Deer Park, N.Y., U.S. | n15 | 109 |
| Deer Park, Oh., U.S. | o13 | 112 |
| Deer Park, Tx., U.S. | *r14 | 120 |
| Deer Park, Wa., U.S. | B8 | 124 |
| Deer Pond, l., Newf. | D4 | 72 |
| Deer River, Mn., U.S. | C5 | 100 |
| Deer River, N.Y., U.S. | B5 | 109 |
| Deerton, Mi., U.S. | B3 | 99 |
| Deer Trail, Co., U.S. | B6 | 83 |
| Deerwood, Mn., U.S. | D5 | 100 |
| Deeson, Ms., U.S. | A3 | 101 |
| Deex Nugaaleed, stm., Som. | D6 | 47 |
| Defas Park, Ut., U.S. | C5 | 121 |
| Deferiet, N.Y., U.S. | A5 | 109 |
| Defiance, Ia., U.S. | C2 | 92 |
| Defiance, Mo., U.S. | f12 | 102 |
| Defiance, Oh., U.S. | A1 | 112 |
| Defiance, co., Oh., U.S. | A1 | 112 |
| Defiance, Mount, mtn., Or., U.S. | B5 | 114 |
| Deford, Mi., U.S. | E7 | 99 |

| Name | Map Ref. | Page |
|---|---|---|
| De Forest, Wi., U.S. | E4 | 126 |
| Delmita, Tx., U.S. | F3 | 120 |
| Delmont, N.J., U.S. | E3 | 107 |
| Delmont, S.D., U.S. | D7 | 118 |
| Del Norte, Co., U.S. | D4 | 83 |
| Del Norte, co., Ca., U.S. | B2 | 82 |
| Deloit, Ia., U.S. | B2 | 92 |
| Delong, In., U.S. | B5 | 91 |
| De Long Islands, is., Sov. Un. | B35 | 128 |
| Deloraine, Man. | E1 | 70 |
| Delorme, Lac, l., Que. | F18 | 66 |
| Deloro, Ont. | C7 | 73 |
| Delos see Dhílos, i., Grc. | D5 | 25 |
| Del Park Manor, De., U.S. | i7 | 85 |
| Delphi, In., U.S. | C4 | 91 |
| Delphia, Mt., U.S. | D8 | 103 |
| Delphos, Ks., U.S. | C6 | 93 |
| Delphos, Oh., U.S. | B1 | 112 |
| Delran, N.J., U.S. | C3 | 107 |
| Delray Beach, Fl., U.S. | F6 | 86 |
| Del Rio, Fl., U.S. | *D4 | 86 |
| Del Rio, Tn., U.S. | D10 | 119 |
| Del Rio, Tx., U.S. | E2 | 120 |
| Delson, Que. | q19 | 74 |
| Delta, Ont. | C8 | 73 |
| Delta, Al., U.S. | B4 | 78 |
| Delta, Co., U.S. | C2 | 83 |
| Delta, Ia., U.S. | C5 | 92 |
| Delta, La., U.S. | B5 | 95 |
| Delta, Mo., U.S. | D8 | 102 |
| Delta, Oh., U.S. | A1 | 112 |
| Delta, Pa., U.S. | G9 | 115 |
| Delta, Ut., U.S. | D3 | 121 |
| Delta, co., Co., U.S. | C2 | 83 |
| Delta, co., Mi., U.S. | C3 | 99 |
| Delta, co., Tx., U.S. | C5 | 120 |
| Delta, reg., Ms., U.S. | B3 | 101 |
| Delta Amacuro, ter., Ven. | B5 | 60 |
| Delta Barrage, Eg. | D3 | 41 |
| Delta Beach, Man. | D2 | 70 |
| Delta City, Ms., U.S. | B3 | 101 |
| Delta Junction, Ak., U.S. | C10 | 79 |
| Delta Peak, mtn., B.C. | A3 | 69 |
| Delta Reservoir, res., N.Y., U.S. | B5 | 109 |
| Deltaville, Va., U.S. | C6 | 123 |
| Delton, Mi., U.S. | F5 | 99 |
| Deltona, Fl., U.S. | D5 | 86 |
| Delungra, Austl. | D8 | 51 |
| Delvin, Ire. | D4 | 11 |
| Delvina, Alb. | C3 | 25 |
| Delyatin, Sov. Un. | G5 | 27 |
| Demaine, Sask. | G2 | 75 |
| Demanda, Sierra de la, mts., Spain | A4 | 22 |
| Demarest, N.J., U.S. | h9 | 107 |
| Demavend, Mount, mtn., Iran | B5 | 38 |
| Demba, Zaire | C3 | 48 |
| Dembi Dolo, Eth. | D3 | 47 |
| Demerara, stm., Guy. | A5 | 59 |
| Demidov, Sov. Un. | D8 | 27 |
| Deming, N.M., U.S. | E2 | 108 |
| Deming, Wa., U.S. | A3 | 124 |
| Demini, stm., Braz. | B2 | 59 |
| Demirci, Tur. | C7 | 40 |
| Demir Kapija, Yugo. | E6 | 24 |
| Demmin, E. Ger. | B6 | 18 |
| Demmitt, Alta. | B1 | 68 |
| Demnat, Mor. | C3 | 44 |
| Demopolis, Al., U.S. | C2 | 78 |
| Demopolis Dam, Al., U.S. | C2 | 78 |
| Demorest, Ga., U.S. | B3 | 87 |
| Demorestville, Ont. | C7 | 73 |
| De Mossville, Ky., U.S. | k14 | 94 |
| Demotte, In., U.S. | B3 | 91 |
| Dempo, mtn., Indon. | F2 | 34 |
| Dempster, S.D., U.S. | C9 | 118 |
| Dêmqog, China | B6 | 36 |
| Demyansk, Sov. Un. | C8 | 27 |
| Denain, Fr. | B5 | 16 |
| Denakil (Dankali), pl., Eth. | C5 | 47 |
| Denali National Park, Ak., U.S. | C9 | 79 |
| Denare Beach, Sask. | C4 | 75 |
| Denau, Sov. Un. | H22 | 8 |
| Denaud, Fl., U.S. | F5 | 86 |
| Denbigh, Wales, U.K. | A5 | 111 |
| Denbigh, N.D., U.S. | A5 | 111 |
| Den Burg, Neth. | A4 | 17 |
| Denby, D3 | 118 |
| Dendermonde, Bel. | D3 | 17 |
| Dendron, Va., U.S. | C6 | 123 |
| Denezhkin Kamen, Mount, mtn., Sov. Un. | A5 | 39 |
| Denham, W.V., U.S. | D2 | 125 |
| Denham, Mn., U.S. | D6 | 100 |
| Denham, Mount, mtn., Jam. | E13 | 65 |
| Denham Springs, La., U.S. | D5 | 95 |
| Den Helder, Neth. | A6 | 18 |
| Denholm, Sask. | E1 | 75 |
| Den Hoorn, Neth. | A4 | 17 |
| Denia, Spain | C6 | 22 |
| Deniau, Que. | B8 | 74 |
| Deniliquin, Austl. | G7 | 50 |
| Denio, Nv., U.S. | B3 | 105 |
| Denison, Ia., U.S. | B2 | 92 |
| Denison, Ks., U.S. | C8 | 93 |
| Denison, Tx., U.S. | C4 | 120 |
| Denison Dam, U.S. | D5 | 113 |
| Denizli, Tur. | D7 | 40 |
| Denman Glacier, ice, Ant. | C22 | 7 |
| Denmark, Ia., U.S. | D6 | 92 |
| Denmark, Me., U.S. | E2 | 96 |
| Denmark, S.C., U.S. | E5 | 117 |
| Denmark, Tn., U.S. | B3 | 119 |
| Denmark, Wi., U.S. | D6 | 126 |
| Denmark, ctry., Eur. | I3 | 13 |
| Denmark Strait, strt. | C17 | 128 |
| Dennard, Ar., U.S. | B3 | 81 |
| Dennehotso, Az., U.S. | A6 | 80 |
| Denning, Ar., U.S. | B2 | 81 |
| Dennis, Ma., U.S. | C7 | 98 |
| Dennis, Ms., U.S. | A5 | 101 |
| Dennis Hill, mtn., Ct., U.S. | B3 | 84 |
| Dennison, Il., U.S. | D6 | 90 |
| Dennison, Mn., U.S. | F6 | 100 |
| Dennison, Oh., U.S. | B4 | 112 |
| Dennis Port, Ma., U.S. | C7 | 98 |
| Dennisville, N.J., U.S. | E3 | 107 |
| Denny, Scot., U.K. | *D5 | 95 |
| Dennysville, Me., U.S. | D5 | 96 |
| Denny Terrace, S.C., U.S. | C5 | 117 |
| Den Oever, Neth. | B5 | 17 |
| Denpasar, Indon. | G5 | 34 |
| Dent, Mn., U.S. | D3 | 100 |
| Dent, co., Mo., U.S. | D6 | 102 |
| Denton, Ga., U.S. | E4 | 87 |
| Denton, Md., U.S. | C6 | 97 |
| Denton, Mt., U.S. | C7 | 103 |
| Denton, Ne., U.S. | D9 | 104 |
| Denton, N.C., U.S. | B2 | 110 |
| Denton, Tx., U.S. | C4 | 120 |

| Name | Map Ref. | Page |
|---|---|---|
| Denton, co., Tx., U.S. | C4 | 120 |
| D'Entrecasteaux, Point, c., Austl. | F2 | 50 |
| D'Entrecasteaux Islands, is., Pap. N. Gui. | k13 | 50 |
| Dents Du Midi, mts., Switz. | D2 | 21 |
| Dentsville, S.C., U.S. | C6 | 117 |
| Denver, Ar., U.S. | A2 | 81 |
| Denver, Co., U.S. | B6 | 83 |
| Denver, Il., U.S. | C2 | 90 |
| Denver, In., U.S. | C5 | 91 |
| Denver, Ia., U.S. | B5 | 92 |
| Denver, Mo., U.S. | A3 | 102 |
| Denver, N.C., U.S. | B1 | 110 |
| Denver, Pa., U.S. | F9 | 115 |
| Denver, Tn., U.S. | A4 | 119 |
| Denver, W.V., U.S. | B5 | 125 |
| Denver, co., Co., U.S. | B6 | 83 |
| Denver City, Tx., U.S. | C1 | 120 |
| Denville, N.J., U.S. | B4 | 107 |
| Denzil, Sask. | E1 | 75 |
| Deoghar, India | E11 | 37 |
| De Panne, Bel. | C2 | 17 |
| Departure Bay, B.C. | f12 | 69 |
| Depauville, N.Y., U.S. | A4 | 109 |
| Depauw, In., U.S. | H5 | 91 |
| De Pere, Wi., U.S. | D5 | 126 |
| Depew, N.Y., U.S. | C2 | 109 |
| Depew, Ok., U.S. | B5 | 113 |
| Depoe Bay, Or., U.S. | C2 | 114 |
| Depok, Indon. | *G3 | 34 |
| Deport, Tx., U.S. | C5 | 120 |
| Deposit, N.Y., U.S. | C5 | 109 |
| Depósito, Braz. | B2 | 59 |
| Depot Harbour, Ont. | B4 | 73 |
| Depue, Il., U.S. | B4 | 90 |
| Deputy, In., U.S. | G6 | 91 |
| De Queen, Ar., U.S. | C1 | 81 |
| De Queen Lake, res., Ar., U.S. | C1 | 81 |
| Dequen-Nord, Que. | A5 | 74 |
| De Quincy, La., U.S. | D2 | 95 |
| Dera, Lat., Asia | E5 | 47 |
| Dera Ghāzi Khān, Pak. | B5 | 36 |
| Dera Ismāil Khān, Pak. | B5 | 36 |
| Derbent, Sov. Un. | E3 | 28 |
| Derbetovka, Sov. Un. | I14 | 27 |
| Derby, Austl. | C3 | 50 |
| Derby, N.B. | C4 | 71 |
| Derby, Eng., U.K. | D6 | 10 |
| Derby, Ct., U.S. | D3 | 84 |
| Derby, In., U.S. | H4 | 91 |
| Derby, Ia., U.S. | D4 | 92 |
| Derby, Ks., U.S. | E6 | 93 |
| Derby, Me., U.S. | C4 | 96 |
| Derby, Ms., U.S. | E4 | 101 |
| Derby, N.Y., U.S. | C2 | 109 |
| Derby, Oh., U.S. | C2 | 112 |
| Derby, Va., U.S. | f9 | 123 |
| Derby Junction, N.B. | C4 | 71 |
| Derby Line, Vt., U.S. | A4 | 122 |
| Derbyshire, Eng., U.K. | A6 | 12 |
| Derecske, Hung. | B5 | 24 |
| Derg, Lough, l., Ire. | D2 | 10 |
| Der Grabow, b., E. Ger. | D6 | 15 |
| De Ridder, La., U.S. | D2 | 95 |
| Derik, Tur. | D13 | 40 |
| Derma, Ms., U.S. | B4 | 101 |
| Dermott, Ar., U.S. | D4 | 81 |
| Dernieres, Isles, is., La., U.S. | E5 | 95 |
| Derravaragh, Lough, l., Ire. | D3 | 10 |
| Derrieusseaux Creek, stm., Ar., U.S. | C3 | 81 |
| Derry, La., U.S. | C3 | 95 |
| Derry, N.H., U.S. | E4 | 106 |
| Derry, N.M., U.S. | E2 | 108 |
| Derry, Pa., U.S. | F3 | 115 |
| Derrybrien, Ire. | D3 | 11 |
| Derry see Londonderry, N. Ire., U.K. | C3 | 10 |
| Derudeb, Sud. | B4 | 47 |
| De Ruyter, N.Y., U.S. | C5 | 109 |
| Derventa, Yugo. | C3 | 24 |
| Derwent, Alta. | C5 | 68 |
| Derwent, Oh., U.S. | C4 | 112 |
| Derwent, stm., Eng., U.K. | F8 | 13 |
| Derwent, stm., Eng., U.K. | F6 | 13 |
| Derwent, stm., Eng., U.K. | F5 | 13 |
| Derwood, Md., U.S. | B3 | 97 |
| Derzhavinsk, Sov. Un. | C7 | 28 |
| Desaguadero, stm., Arg. | A3 | 54 |
| Desaguadero, stm., Bol. | C2 | 55 |
| Des Allemands, La., U.S. | E5 | 95 |
| Desamparados, C.R. | *F5 | 62 |
| Des Arc, Ar., U.S. | C4 | 81 |
| Des Arc, Mo., U.S. | D7 | 102 |
| Desbiens, Que. | A6 | 74 |
| Desboro, Ont. | C3 | 73 |
| Descalvado, Braz. | k8 | 56 |
| Descartes, Fr. | D4 | 16 |
| Deschaillons [-sur-Saint-Laurent], Que. | C5 | 74 |
| Deschambault, Que. | C6 | 74 |
| Deschambault Lake, Sask. | C4 | 75 |
| Deschambault Lake, l., Sask. | C4 | 75 |
| Deschênes, Que. | D2 | 74 |
| Deschutes, co., Or., U.S. | D5 | 114 |
| Deschutes, stm., Or., U.S. | B6 | 114 |
| Dese, Eth. | C4 | 47 |
| Deseado, stm., Arg. | D3 | 54 |
| Desengaño, Punta, c., Arg. | D3 | 54 |
| Desenzano del Garda, Italy | D6 | 20 |
| Deseret, Ut., U.S. | D3 | 121 |
| Deseret Peak, mtn., Ut., U.S. | C3 | 121 |
| Deseronto, Ont. | C7 | 73 |
| Desert, Mount, mtn., W.V., U.S. | m13 | 125 |
| Deserta Grande, i., Port. | h12 | 22 |
| Desert Center, Ca., U.S. | F6 | 82 |
| Desert Creek Peak, mtn., Nv., U.S. | E2 | 105 |
| Desert Hot Springs, Ca., U.S. | F5 | 82 |
| Desert Peak, mtn., Ut., U.S. | B2 | 121 |
| Desert Valley, val., Nv., U.S. | B3 | 105 |
| Desha, Ar., U.S. | B4 | 81 |
| Desha, co., Ar., U.S. | D4 | 81 |
| Deshler, Ne., U.S. | D8 | 104 |
| Deshler, Oh., U.S. | A2 | 112 |
| Desio, Italy | D5 | 20 |
| Des Lacs, N.D., U.S. | A4 | 111 |
| Des Lacs, stm., N.D., U.S. | A4 | 111 |
| Desloge, Mo., U.S. | D7 | 102 |
| Desmarais, Alta. | B4 | 68 |
| Desmet, Id., U.S. | B2 | 89 |
| De Smet, S.D., U.S. | C8 | 118 |
| Desmochados, Para. | E4 | 55 |
| Des Moines Ia., U.S. | C4 | 92 |
| Des Moines, N.M., U.S. | A6 | 108 |
| Des Moines, Wa., U.S. | B3 | 124 |
| Des Moines, co., Ia., U.S. | D6 | 92 |
| Des Moines, stm., U.S. | D5 | 92 |
| Des Moines, East Fork, stm., U.S. | A3 | 92 |
| Desna, stm., Sov. Un. | F8 | 27 |
| Desolación, Isla, i., Chile | h11 | 54 |
| Desolation Canyon, val., Ut., U.S. | D5 | 121 |
| De Soto, Ga., U.S. | E2 | 87 |
| De Soto, Il., U.S. | F4 | 90 |
| De Soto, Ia., U.S. | C3 | 92 |
| De Soto, Ks., U.S. | D9 | 93 |
| De Soto, Ms., U.S. | D5 | 101 |
| De Soto, Mo., U.S. | C7 | 102 |
| De Soto, Tx., U.S. | *n10 | 120 |
| De Soto, Wi., U.S. | E2 | 126 |
| De Soto, co., Fl., U.S. | E5 | 86 |
| De Soto, co., La., U.S. | B2 | 95 |
| De Soto, co., Ms., U.S. | A3 | 101 |
| De Soto City, Fl., U.S. | E5 | 86 |
| Despard, W.V., U.S. | k10 | 125 |
| Des Peres, Mo., U.S. | f13 | 102 |
| Des Plaines, Il., U.S. | A6 | 90 |
| Des Plaines, stm., U.S. | k8 | 90 |
| Dessau, E. Ger. | D5 | 18 |
| Destin, Fl., U.S. | u15 | 86 |
| Destrehan, La., U.S. | E5 | 95 |
| Desvres, Fr. | D1 | 17 |
| Dete, Zimb. | A4 | 49 |
| Detlor, Ont. | B7 | 73 |
| Detmold, W. Ger. | C4 | 18 |
| De Tour Village, Mi., U.S. | C7 | 99 |
| Detroit, Al., U.S. | A1 | 78 |
| Detroit, Ks., U.S. | D6 | 93 |
| Detroit, Me., U.S. | D3 | 96 |
| Detroit, Mi., U.S. | F7 | 99 |
| Detroit, Or., U.S. | C4 | 114 |
| Detroit, Tx., U.S. | C5 | 120 |
| Detroit, stm., N.A. | F7 | 99 |
| Detroit Lake, res., Or., U.S. | C4 | 114 |
| Detroit Lakes, Mn., U.S. | D3 | 100 |
| Detva, Czech. | D5 | 26 |
| Deuel, co., Ne., U.S. | C3 | 104 |
| Deuel, co., S.D., U.S. | C9 | 118 |
| Deurne (part of Antwerp), Bel. | B6 | 16 |
| Deux Frères, Les, is., Viet. | H7 | 35 |
| Deux-Montagnes, Que. | p19 | 74 |
| Deux-Montagnes, Que. | D3 | 74 |
| Deux-Montagnes, Lac des, l., Que. | q19 | 74 |
| Deux-Rivières, Ont. | A6 | 73 |
| Deva, Rom. | C6 | 24 |
| Dévaványa, Hung. | B5 | 24 |
| Deventer, Neth. | A7 | 16 |
| Devereux, Ga., U.S. | C3 | 87 |
| Deveron, stm., Scot., U.K. | C6 | 13 |
| DeView, Bayou, stm., Ar., U.S. | B4 | 81 |
| Devil River Peak, mtn., N.Z. | N14 | 51 |
| Devils Elbow, Mo., U.S. | D5 | 102 |
| Devils Island see Diable, Île du, i., Fr. Gu. | A4 | 59 |
| Devils Lake, N.D., U.S. | A7 | 111 |
| Devils Lake, l., N.D., U.S. | A6 | 111 |
| Devils Paw, mtn., Ak., U.S. | k23 | 79 |
| Devils Postpile National Monument, Ca., U.S. | D4 | 82 |
| Devils Slide, Ut., U.S. | B4 | 121 |
| Devils Tower, Wy., U.S. | B8 | 127 |
| Devils Tower National Monument, Wy., U.S. | B8 | 127 |
| Devil Track Lake, l., Mn., U.S. | k9 | 100 |
| Devin, Bul. | E7 | 24 |
| Devine, Tx., U.S. | E3 | 120 |
| Devizes, Eng., U.K. | C6 | 12 |
| Devol, Ok., U.S. | C3 | 113 |
| Devola, Oh., U.S. | C4 | 112 |
| Devolli, stm., Alb. | B3 | 25 |
| Devon, Alta. | C4 | 68 |
| Devon, Ks., U.S. | E9 | 93 |
| Devon, Mt., U.S. | B5 | 103 |
| Devon, Pa., U.S. | *o20 | 115 |
| Devon, co., Eng., U.K. | D4 | 12 |
| Devonia, Tn., U.S. | C9 | 119 |
| Devon Island, i., N.W. Ter. | m34 | 66 |
| Devonport, Austl. | o15 | 50 |
| Devonshire, De., U.S. | h7 | 85 |
| Dewalt, Tx., U.S. | r14 | 120 |
| Dewar, Ok., U.S. | B6 | 113 |
| Dewar Lake, Sask. | F1 | 75 |
| Dewberry, Alta. | C5 | 68 |
| Dewdney, B.C. | E6 | 69 |
| Deweese, Ne., U.S. | D7 | 104 |
| Dewees Inlet, b., S.C., U.S. | k12 | 117 |
| Dewees Island, i., S.C., U.S. | F8 | 117 |
| Dewey, Az., U.S. | C3 | 80 |
| Dewey, Mt., U.S. | E4 | 103 |
| Dewey, Ok., U.S. | A6 | 113 |
| Dewey, co., Ok., U.S. | B2 | 113 |
| Dewey, co., S.D., U.S. | B4 | 118 |
| Dewey Beach, De., U.S. | F5 | 85 |
| Dewey Lake, res., Ky., U.S. | C7 | 94 |
| Deweyville, Tx., U.S. | D6 | 120 |
| Deweyville, Ut., U.S. | B3 | 121 |
| De Winton, Alta. | D3 | 68 |
| De Witt, Ar., U.S. | C4 | 81 |
| Dewitt, Il., U.S. | C5 | 90 |
| De Witt, Ia., U.S. | C7 | 92 |
| De Witt, Mi., U.S. | F6 | 99 |
| DeWitt, Mo., U.S. | B4 | 102 |
| De Witt, Ne., U.S. | D9 | 104 |
| De Witt, N.Y., U.S. | B4 | 109 |
| DeWitt, Va., U.S. | C5 | 123 |
| De Witt, co., Il., U.S. | C5 | 90 |
| De Witt, co., Tx., U.S. | E4 | 120 |
| Dewsbury, Eng., U.K. | A6 | 12 |
| Dexing, China | J7 | 32 |
| Dexter, Ga., U.S. | D3 | 87 |
| Dexter, Id., U.S. | G6 | 89 |
| Dexter, Ks., U.S. | E7 | 93 |
| Dexter, Ky., U.S. | f9 | 94 |
| Dexter, Me., U.S. | C3 | 96 |
| Dexter, Mi., U.S. | F7 | 99 |
| Dexter, Mo., U.S. | E8 | 102 |
| Dexter, N.M., U.S. | D5 | 108 |
| Dexter, N.Y., U.S. | A4 | 109 |
| Dexter, Or., U.S. | D4 | 114 |
| Dey-Dey, Lake, l., Austl. | E5 | 50 |
| Deyyer, Iran | H6 | 39 |
| Dezhneva, Cape, c., Sov. Un. | C21 | 29 |
| Dezhou, China | D8 | 31 |
| Dhahab, Eg. | H10 | 40 |
| Dhahran see Aẓ Ẓahrān, Sau. | C4 | 38 |
| Dhaka (Dacca), Bngl. | D9 | 36 |
| Dhamār, Yemen | D4 | 38 |
| Dhamtari, India | G8 | 37 |
| Dhangadhī, Nepal | C8 | 37 |
| D'Hanis, Tx., U.S. | E3 | 120 |
| Dhār, India | F5 | 36 |
| Dharmapuri, India | F6 | 36 |
| Dharmjaygarh, India | D7 | 36 |
| Dharmshāla, India | B6 | 36 |
| Dhaulpur, India | D6 | 37 |
| Dhawlāgiri, mtn., Nepal | C7 | 36 |
| Dhekélia, Grc. | g11 | 25 |
| Dhenoúsa, i., Grc. | D5 | 25 |
| Dhībān, Jord. | G10 | 40 |
| Dhidhimótikhon, Grc. | B6 | 25 |
| Dhílos (Delos), i., Grc. | D5 | 25 |
| Dhimitsána, Grc. | D4 | 25 |
| Dhomhnuill, Sgurr, mtn., Scot., U.K. | D3 | 13 |
| Dhorāji, India | G3 | 37 |
| Dhrépanon, Cape, c., Grc. | C4 | 25 |
| Dhuburi, India | D12 | 37 |
| Dhule, India | D5 | 36 |
| Dhuusa Mareeb, Som. | D6 | 47 |
| Día, i., Grc. | E5 | 25 |
| Diable, Île du (Devils Island), i., Fr. Gu. | A4 | 59 |
| Diable, Pointe du, c., Mart. | S11 | 65 |
| Diablerets, mtn., Switz. | C3 | 20 |
| Diablo, Canyon, val., Az., U.S. | *C4 | 80 |
| Diablo, Mount, mtn., Ca., U.S. | h9 | 82 |
| Diablo Dam, Wa., U.S. | A4 | 124 |
| Diablo Heights, Pan. | m11 | 62 |
| Diablo Lake, res., Wa., U.S. | A4 | 124 |
| Diablo Range, mts., Ca., U.S. | D3 | 82 |
| Diagonal, Ia., U.S. | D3 | 92 |
| Diamante, Arg. | A4 | 54 |
| Diamantina, Braz. | B4 | 56 |
| Diamantina, stm., Austl. | D7 | 50 |
| Diamond, Oh., U.S. | A4 | 112 |
| Diamond, W.V., U.S. | m12 | 125 |
| Diamond Bar, Ca., U.S. | *n13 | 82 |
| Diamond Bluff, Wi., U.S. | D1 | 126 |
| Diamond City, Alta. | E4 | 68 |
| Diamond Harbour, India | F12 | 37 |
| Diamond Head, crat., Hi., U.S. | B4 | 88 |
| Diamond Hill, R.I., U.S. | B4 | 116 |
| Diamond Hill Reservoir, res., R.I., U.S. | A4 | 116 |
| Diamond Lake, Il., U.S. | h9 | 90 |
| Diamond Lake, l., Or., U.S. | D4 | 114 |
| Diamond Mountains, mts., Nv., U.S. | D6 | 105 |
| Diamond Peak, mtn., Co., U.S. | A2 | 83 |
| Diamond Peak, mtn., Id., U.S. | E5 | 89 |
| Diamond Peak, mtn., Or., U.S. | D4 | 114 |
| Diamond Peak, mtn., Wa., U.S. | C8 | 124 |
| Diamond Point, N.Y., U.S. | B7 | 109 |
| Diamond Springs, Ca., U.S. | C3 | 82 |
| Diamondville, Wy., U.S. | E2 | 127 |
| Diana, Tn., U.S. | B5 | 119 |
| Diana, W.V., U.S. | C4 | 125 |
| Dianalund, Den. | C5 | 15 |
| Dianbai, China | G7 | 31 |
| Dianjiang, China | I2 | 32 |
| Dianópolis, Braz. | D1 | 57 |
| Diapaga, Burkina | D5 | 45 |
| Diapitan Bay, b., Phil. | n14 | 34 |
| Dibaya, Zaire | C3 | 48 |
| Dibble Iceberg Tongue, ice, Ant. | C26 | 7 |
| D'Iberville, Ms., U.S. | E5 | 101 |
| D'Iberville, Lac, l., Que. | g12 | 74 |
| Diboll, Tx., U.S. | D5 | 120 |
| Dibrell, Tn., U.S. | D8 | 119 |
| Dibrugarh, India | C9 | 36 |
| Dickens, Ia., U.S. | A2 | 92 |
| Dickens, Ne., U.S. | D5 | 104 |
| Dickens, Tx., U.S. | C2 | 120 |
| Dickens, co., Tx., U.S. | C2 | 120 |
| Dickenson, co., Va., U.S. | e9 | 123 |
| Dickerson, Md., U.S. | B3 | 97 |
| Dickey, N.D., U.S. | C7 | 111 |
| Dickey, co., N.D., U.S. | C7 | 111 |
| Dickeyville, Wi., U.S. | F3 | 126 |
| Dickinson, Al., U.S. | D2 | 78 |
| Dickinson, N.D., U.S. | D4 | 111 |
| Dickinson, Tx., U.S. | *r14 | 120 |
| Dickinson, co., Ia., U.S. | A2 | 92 |
| Dickinson, co., Ks., U.S. | D6 | 93 |
| Dickinson, co., Mi., U.S. | B3 | 99 |
| Dickinson Center, N.Y., U.S. | f10 | 109 |
| Dickinson Dam, N.D., U.S. | C3 | 111 |
| Dickson, Tn., U.S. | A4 | 119 |
| Dickson, co., Tn., U.S. | A4 | 119 |
| Dickson City, Pa., U.S. | D10 | 115 |
| Dicle (Tigris), stm., Asia | D13 | 40 |
| Didcot, Eng., U.K. | C6 | 12 |
| Dīdwāna, India | D5 | 37 |
| Diébougou, Burkina | D4 | 45 |
| Dieburg, W. Ger. | D4 | 18 |
| Diefenbaker, Lake, res., Sask. | F2 | 75 |
| Diégo-Suarez see Antsiranana, Madag. | f9 | 49 |
| Diekirch, Lux. | E6 | 17 |
| Diemel, stm., W. Ger. | B3 | 19 |
| Dien Bien Phu, Viet. | B5 | 35 |
| Diepholz, W. Ger. | B4 | 18 |
| Dieppe, N.B. | C5 | 71 |
| Dieppe, Fr. | C4 | 16 |
| Dierks, Ar., U.S. | C1 | 81 |
| Di'er Songhua, stm., China | D2 | 33 |
| Diessen, W. Ger. | B7 | 20 |
| Diest, Bel. | D5 | 17 |
| Dieterich, Il., U.S. | D5 | 90 |
| Dietikon, Switz. | B5 | 21 |
| Dietrich, Id., U.S. | G4 | 89 |
| Dieuze, Fr. | F6 | 17 |
| Diever, Neth. | B6 | 17 |
| Diez, W. Ger. | C2 | 19 |
| Diffa, Niger | D7 | 45 |
| Differdange, Lux. | E5 | 17 |
| Difficult, Tn., U.S. | C8 | 119 |
| Digboi, India | C10 | 36 |
| Digby, N.S. | E4 | 71 |
| Digby, co., N.S. | E4 | 71 |
| Dighton, Ks., U.S. | D3 | 93 |
| Dighton, Ma., U.S. | C5 | 98 |
| Digne, Fr. | E7 | 16 |
| Digoin, Fr. | D6 | 16 |
| Digul, stm., Indon. | G10 | 34 |
| Dijon, Fr. | D6 | 16 |
| Dike, Tx., U.S. | C5 | 120 |
| Dikhil, Dji. | C6 | 47 |
| Dikili, Tur. | C6 | 25 |
| Diksmuide, Bel. | C2 | 17 |
| Dikwa, Nig. | D7 | 45 |
| Dili, Indon. | G7 | 34 |
| Dilã, Eth. | D4 | 47 |
| Dilke, Sask. | G3 | 75 |
| Dilkon, Az., U.S. | B5 | 80 |
| Dillard, Ga., U.S. | B3 | 87 |
| Dillard, Or., U.S. | D3 | 114 |
| Dill City, Ok., U.S. | B2 | 113 |
| Dille, W.V., U.S. | C4 | 125 |
| Dillenburg, W. Ger. | C3 | 19 |
| Diller, Ne., U.S. | D9 | 104 |
| Dilley, Tx., U.S. | E3 | 120 |
| Dilliner, Pa., U.S. | G2 | 115 |
| Dilling, Sud. | C2 | 47 |
| Dillingen, W. Ger. | D1 | 19 |
| Dillingen [an der Donau], W. Ger. | D5 | 18 |
| Dillingham, Ak., U.S. | D8 | 79 |
| Dillon, Co., U.S. | B4 | 83 |
| Dillon, Mt., U.S. | E4 | 103 |
| Dillon, S.C., U.S. | C9 | 117 |
| Dillon, co., S.C., U.S. | C9 | 117 |
| Dillon, stm., Can. | B5 | 68 |
| Dillon Lake, l., Sask. | B5 | 68 |
| Dillon Lake, res., Oh., U.S. | B3 | 112 |
| Dillon Reservoir, res., Co., U.S. | B4 | 83 |
| Dillonvale, Oh., U.S. | B5 | 112 |
| Dillsboro, In., U.S. | F7 | 91 |
| Dillsboro, N.C., U.S. | f9 | 110 |
| Dillsburg, Pa., U.S. | F7 | 115 |
| Dillwyn, Va., U.S. | C4 | 123 |
| Dilolo, Zaire | D3 | 48 |
| Dilworth, Mn., U.S. | D2 | 100 |
| Dimbelenge, Zaire | C3 | 48 |
| Dimbokro, I.C. | E4 | 45 |
| Dimboola, Austl. | G8 | 50 |
| Dîmboviţa, stm., Rom. | C7 | 24 |
| Dimitrovgrad, Bul. | D7 | 24 |
| Dimitrovgrad, Yugo. | C4 | 24 |
| Dimmit, co., Tx., U.S. | E3 | 120 |
| Dimmitt, Tx., U.S. | B1 | 120 |
| Dimock, S.D., U.S. | D8 | 118 |
| Dimona, Isr. | C7 | 41 |
| Dimondale, Mi., U.S. | F6 | 99 |
| Dinagat Island, i., Phil. | C7 | 34 |
| Dinājpur, Bngl. | E12 | 37 |
| Dinan, Fr. | C2 | 16 |
| Dinant, Bel. | B6 | 16 |
| Dinar, Tur. | C8 | 25 |
| Dinard, Fr. | C2 | 16 |
| Dinaric Alps, mts., Yugo. | C3 | 24 |
| Dindigul, India | F6 | 36 |
| Dinero, Tx., U.S. | E4 | 120 |
| Dingalan Bay, b., Phil. | o13 | 34 |
| Dingbian, China | D6 | 31 |
| Dingelstädt, E. Ger. | B5 | 19 |
| Dingess, W.V., U.S. | D2 | 125 |
| Dinghai, China | E9 | 31 |
| Dingle, Ire. | D1 | 10 |
| Dingle, Id., U.S. | G7 | 89 |
| Dingle Bay, b., Ire. | D1 | 10 |
| Dingmans Ferry, Pa., U.S. | D12 | 115 |
| Dingo, Austl. | A7 | 51 |
| Dingolfing, W. Ger. | E7 | 19 |
| Dinguiraye, Gui. | D2 | 45 |
| Dingwall, N.S. | C9 | 71 |
| Dingwall, Scot., U.K. | C4 | 14 |
| Dingxian, China | D8 | 31 |
| Dingxin, China | C4 | 31 |
| Dingxing, China | E6 | 32 |
| Dinh Lap, Viet. | B7 | 35 |
| Dinkelsbühl, W. Ger. | D5 | 19 |
| Dinkey Creek, Ca., U.S. | D4 | 82 |
| Dinklage, W. Ger. | F2 | 15 |
| Dinner Point, c., Fl., U.S. | g12 | 74 |
| Dinorwic Lake, l., Ont. | E5 | 70 |
| Dinosaur, Ca., U.S. | A1 | 83 |
| Dinosaur National Monument, U.S. | C6 | 121 |
| Dinosaur Provincial Park, Alta. | D5 | 68 |
| Dinsdale, Ia., U.S. | B5 | 92 |
| Dinslaken, W. Ger. | B1 | 19 |
| Dinsmore, Sask. | F2 | 75 |
| Dinuba, Ca., U.S. | D4 | 82 |
| Dinwiddie, Va., U.S. | C5 | 123 |
| Dinwiddie, co., Va., U.S. | C5 | 123 |
| Diöla, Mali | C4 | 45 |
| Dionísio, Braz. | B4 | 56 |
| Diourbel, Sen. | D1 | 45 |
| Diphu Pass, Asia | C10 | 36 |
| Diplo, Pak. | E1 | 36 |
| Dipper Harbour West, N.B. | D3 | 71 |
| Dippoldiswalde, E. Ger. | C6 | 18 |
| Diré, Mali | C4 | 45 |
| Direction, Cape, c., Austl. | B7 | 50 |
| Dire Dawa, Eth. | C5 | 47 |
| Diriamba, Nic. | H4 | 63 |
| Dirico, Ang. | E3 | 48 |
| Dirk Hartog, i., Austl. | E1 | 50 |
| Dirkou, Niger | C7 | 45 |
| Dirmil, Tur. | C8 | 25 |
| Dirranbandi, Austl. | E8 | 50 |
| Dirty Devil, stm., Ut., U.S. | E5 | 121 |
| Disappointment, Cape, c., Falk. Is. | D9 | 7 |
| Disappointment, Cape, c., Wa., U.S. | C1 | 124 |
| Disappointment, Lake, l., Austl. | D3 | 50 |
| Disappointment Creek, stm., Co., U.S. | C2 | 83 |
| Discovery, Mount, mtn., Ant. | f39 | 7 |
| Dishman, Wa., U.S. | g14 | 124 |
| Dishnā, Eg. | D6 | 40 |
| Disko, i., Grnld. | B6 | 91 |
| Disko, i., Grnld. | C15 | 61 |
| Disley, Sask. | G3 | 75 |
| Dismal, stm., Ne., U.S. | C5 | 104 |
| Dismal Peak, mtn., Va., U.S. | C2 | 123 |
| Disney, Ok., U.S. | A6 | 113 |
| Disputanta, Va., U.S. | C5 | 123 |
| Disraëli, Que. | D6 | 74 |
| Diss, Eng., U.K. | B9 | 12 |
| Distant, Pa., U.S. | E3 | 115 |
| District Heights-Forestville, Md., U.S. | *C4 | 97 |
| District of Columbia, dept., U.S. | f8 | 97 |
| Distrito Especial (Bogotá), dept., Col. | C5 | 60 |
| Distrito Federal (Federal District), state, Mex. | h9 | 63 |
| Distrito Federal, dept., Arg. | g7 | 54 |
| Distrito Federal, dept., Braz. | A4 | 56 |
| Distrito Federal, dept., Ven | A4 | 60 |
| Disūq, Eg. | C6 | 43 |
| Ditzum, W. Ger. | A7 | 17 |
| Diu, India | E4 | 36 |
| Divernie, Congo | B1 | 48 |
| Divernon, Il., U.S. | D4 | 90 |
| Dives-sur-Mer, Fr. | C3 | 16 |
| Divide, co., N.D., U.S. | A2 | 111 |
| Divide Peak, mtn., Wy., U.S. | E5 | 127 |
| Dividing Creek, N.J., U.S. | E2 | 107 |
| Dividing Creek, stm., Md., U.S. | D6 | 97 |
| Divinópolis, Braz. | C4 | 56 |
| Divion, Fr. | D2 | 17 |
| Divisões, Serra das, hills, Braz. | D1 | 57 |
| Dog, stm., Vt., U.S. | C3 | 122 |
| Dogai Coring, l., China | B8 | 36 |
| Divišov, Czech. | o18 | 26 |
| Divnoye, Sov. Un. | I14 | 27 |
| Dog Creek, B.C. | D6 | 69 |
| Divo, I.C. | E3 | 45 |
| Divriği, Tur. | C12 | 40 |
| Dix, Il., U.S. | E5 | 90 |
| Dix, Ne., U.S. | C2 | 104 |
| Dix, stm., Ky., U.S. | C5 | 94 |
| Dix Dam, Ky., U.S. | C5 | 94 |
| Dixence, stm., Switz. | D3 | 21 |
| Dixfield, Me., U.S. | D2 | 96 |
| Dix Hills, N.Y., U.S. | *n15 | 109 |
| Dixiana, Al., U.S. | B3 | 78 |
| Dixie, Ar., U.S. | B4 | 81 |
| Dixie, Ga., U.S. | F3 | 87 |
| Dixie, Id., U.S. | D3 | 89 |
| Dixie, Wa., U.S. | C7 | 124 |
| Dixie, W.V., U.S. | C3 | 125 |
| Dixie, co., Fl., U.S. | C3 | 86 |
| Dixie Valley, val., Nv., U.S. | D4 | 105 |
| Dixie Union, Ga., U.S. | E4 | 87 |
| Dix Mountain, mtn., N.Y., U.S. | A7 | 109 |
| Dixon, Ca., U.S. | C3 | 82 |
| Dixon, Il., U.S. | B4 | 90 |
| Dixon, Ky., U.S. | C2 | 94 |
| Dixon, Mo., U.S. | C5 | 102 |
| Dixon, Mt., U.S. | C2 | 103 |
| Dixon, Ne., U.S. | B9 | 104 |
| Dixon, N.M., U.S. | A4 | 108 |
| Dixon, Oh., U.S. | B1 | 112 |
| Dixon, S.D., U.S. | D6 | 118 |
| Dixon, Wy., U.S. | E5 | 127 |
| Dixon, co., Ne., U.S. | B9 | 104 |
| Dixon Entrance, strt., N.A. | B1 | 69 |
| Dixons Mills, Al., U.S. | C2 | 78 |
| Dixon Springs, Il., U.S. | F5 | 90 |
| Dixonville, Alta. | A2 | 68 |
| Dixonville, Pa., U.S. | E3 | 115 |
| Dixville, Que. | D6 | 74 |
| Dixville Notch, N.H., U.S. | g7 | 106 |
| Dixville Peak, mtn., N.H., U.S. | g7 | 106 |
| Diyarbakır, Tur. | D13 | 40 |
| Dizy-le-Gros, Fr. | E3 | 17 |
| Dizy-Magenta, Fr. | E3 | 17 |
| Dja, stm., Afr. | E3 | 45 |
| Djado, Niger | B7 | 45 |
| Djakarta see Jakarta, Indon. | G3 | 34 |
| Djakovica, Yugo. | D5 | 24 |
| Djakovo, Yugo. | C3 | 24 |
| Djambala, Congo | B1 | 48 |
| Djanet, Alg. | E6 | 44 |
| Djaravica, mtn., Yugo. | D5 | 24 |
| Djédaa, Chad | C3 | 46 |
| Djedeida, Tun. | F2 | 23 |
| Djema, Cen. Afr. Rep. | D4 | 46 |
| Djénné, Mali | D4 | 45 |
| Djerba, Île de, i., Tun. | C7 | 44 |
| Djerid, Chott, sw., Tun. | C6 | 44 |
| Djibo, Burkina | C4 | 45 |
| Djibouti, Dji. | C5 | 47 |
| Djibouti, ctry., Afr. | C5 | 47 |
| Djokupunda, Zaire | C3 | 48 |
| Djolu, Zaire | A3 | 48 |
| Djougou, Benin | D5 | 45 |
| Djugu, Zaire | A5 | 48 |
| Djursholm, Swe. | t36 | 14 |
| Długa, stm., Pol. | k14 | 26 |
| Dmitriyev-Lgovskiy, Sov. Un. | E10 | 27 |
| Dmitrov, Sov. Un. | C11 | 27 |
| Dmitrovsk-Orlovskiy, Sov. Un. | E10 | 27 |
| Dnepr, stm., Sov. Un. | D5 | 29 |
| Dneprodzerzhinsk, Sov. Un. | G10 | 27 |
| Dnepropetrovsk, Sov. Un. | E6 | 29 |
| Dnestr, stm., Sov. Un. | H7 | 27 |
| Dnieper see Dnepr, stm., Sov. Un. | D5 | 29 |
| Dno, Sov. Un. | D5 | 27 |
| Doaktown, N.B. | C3 | 71 |
| Doany, Madag. | f9 | 49 |
| Doba, Chad | D3 | 46 |
| Dobbinton, Ont. | C3 | 73 |
| Dobbs Ferry, N.Y., U.S. | g13 | 109 |
| Döbeln, E. Ger. | C6 | 18 |
| Doberai Peninsula, pen., Indon. | F8 | 34 |
| Doberlug-Kirchhain, E. Ger. | B8 | 18 |
| Doblas, Arg. | B4 | 54 |
| Dobo, Indon. | G9 | 34 |
| Doboj, Yugo. | C4 | 24 |
| Doboy Sound, b., Ga., U.S. | E5 | 87 |
| Dobřejovice, Czech. | o18 | 26 |
| Dobříš, Czech. | B4 | 26 |
| Dobrovice, Czech. | n18 | 26 |
| Dobrovskiy, Sov. Un. | A7 | 29 |
| Dobruja, Eur. | C9 | 24 |
| Dobšiná, Czech. | C3 | 26 |
| Dobson, N.C., U.S. | A2 | 110 |
| Doce, stm., Braz. | f7 | 78 |
| Docena, Al., U.S. | f7 | 78 |
| Dock Junction, Ga., U.S. | E5 | 87 |
| Dockton, Wa., U.S. | f11 | 124 |
| Doctor Arroyo, Mex. | F10 | 63 |
| Doctor Pedro P. Peña, Para. | C3 | 55 |
| Doctors Inlet, Fl., U.S. | m8 | 86 |
| Doctors Lake, l., Fl., U.S. | m8 | 86 |
| Doctortown, Ga., U.S. | E5 | 87 |
| Doddridge, Ar., U.S. | D2 | 81 |
| Doddridge, co., W.V., U.S. | B4 | 125 |
| Dodds, Alta. | C4 | 68 |
| Doddsville, Ms., U.S. | B3 | 101 |
| Dodecanese, is., Grc. | D6 | 40 |
| Dodge, Ma., U.S. | f11 | 98 |
| Dodge, Ne., U.S. | C9 | 104 |
| Dodge, Wi., U.S. | D2 | 126 |
| Dodge, co., Ga., U.S. | D3 | 87 |
| Dodge, co., Mn., U.S. | G6 | 100 |
| Dodge, co., Ne., U.S. | C9 | 104 |
| Dodge, co., Wi., U.S. | E5 | 126 |
| Dodge Center, Mn., U.S. | F6 | 100 |
| Dodge City, Ks., U.S. | E3 | 93 |
| Dodge Park, Md., U.S. | *C4 | 97 |
| Dodgeville, Wi., U.S. | F3 | 126 |
| Dodoma, Zaire | C6 | 48 |
| Dodoma, Tan. | C6 | 48 |
| Dodoma, prov., Tan. | C6 | 48 |
| Dodsland, Sask. | F1 | 75 |
| Dodson, Mt., U.S. | B8 | 103 |
| Dodson, Tx., U.S. | B2 | 120 |
| Dodson Peninsula, pen., Ant. | B6 | 7 |
| Doe River, B.C. | A7 | 69 |
| Doerun, Ga., U.S. | E3 | 87 |
| Doe Run, Mo., U.S. | D7 | 102 |
| Doetinchem, Neth. | C6 | 17 |
| Dog, stm., Vt., U.S. | C3 | 122 |
| Dogai Coring, l., China | B8 | 36 |
| Dog Creek, B.C. | D6 | 69 |
| Dog Island, i., Fl., U.S. | C2 | 86 |
| Dog Keys Pass, strt., Ms., U.S. | g8 | 101 |
| Dog Lake, l., Man. | D2 | 70 |
| Dog Lake, l., Ont. | H6 | 33 |
| Do Gonbadān, Iran | *F5 | 39 |
| Doğubayazıt, Tur. | C15 | 40 |
| Doha (Ad Dawḩah), Qatar | C5 | 38 |
| Doheny, Que. | B5 | 74 |
| Doiran, Lake, l., Eur. | E6 | 25 |
| Dois Córregos, Braz. | m7 | 56 |
| Dokkum, Neth. | A6 | 17 |
| Doksy, Czech. | C9 | 19 |
| Dol, Fr. | C3 | 16 |
| Doland, S.D., U.S. | C7 | 118 |
| Dolavón, Arg. | C3 | 54 |
| Dolbeau, Que. | k12 | 74 |
| Dôle, Fr. | D6 | 16 |
| Dolega, Pan. | F6 | 62 |
| Doleib Hill, Sud. | D3 | 47 |
| Doles, Ga., U.S. | E3 | 87 |
| Dolgellau, Wales, U.K. | B4 | 12 |
| Dolgeville, N.Y., U.S. | B6 | 109 |
| Dolinsk, Sov. Un. | B13 | 31 |
| Dolinskoye, Sov. Un. | B9 | 24 |
| Dollar Bay, Mi., U.S. | A2 | 99 |
| Dollard, Sask. | H1 | 75 |
| Dollart, b., Eur. | A7 | 17 |
| Dollarville, Mi., U.S. | B5 | 99 |
| Dolliver, Ia., U.S. | A3 | 92 |
| Dolný Kubín, Czech. | A3 | 92 |
| Dolomites, mts., Italy | A3 | 20 |
| Dolomwhar, mtn., Micron. | Q17 | 52 |
| Dolores, Arg. | B5 | 54 |
| Dolores, Guat. | D7 | 63 |
| Dolores, Mex. | B3 | 63 |
| Dolores, Co., U.S. | D2 | 83 |
| Dolores, Ur. | E1 | 56 |
| Dolores, co., Co., U.S. | D2 | 83 |
| Dolores Hidalgo, Mex. | m13 | 63 |
| Dolphin and Union Strait, strt., N.W. Ter. | C9 | 66 |
| Dolphin Head, mtn., Jam. | E12 | 65 |
| Dolphin Island, i., Ut., U.S. | B3 | 121 |
| Dolton, Il., U.S. | k9 | 90 |
| Dolton, S.D., U.S. | D8 | 118 |
| Dom, stm., Switz. | D4 | 21 |
| Dom Aquino, Braz. | B2 | 56 |
| Domat-Ems, Switz. | C7 | 21 |
| Domažlice, Czech. | D2 | 26 |
| Dombarovskiy, Sov. Un. | C5 | 28 |
| Dombås, Nor. | F3 | 14 |
| Dombasle[-sur-Meurthe], Fr. | F6 | 17 |
| Dombe Grande, Ang. | D1 | 48 |
| Dombóvár, Hung. | B4 | 24 |
| Domburg, Neth. | C3 | 17 |
| Dôme, Puy de, mtn., Fr. | E5 | 16 |
| Dome Mountain, mtn., Az., U.S. | k9 | 80 |
| Dome of the Rock, Isr. Occ. | m14 | 41 |
| Dome Peak, mtn., Co., U.S. | B3 | 83 |
| Domeyko, Cordillera, mts., Chile | D2 | 53 |
| Domfront, Fr. | C3 | 16 |
| Dominica, ctry., N.A. | i14 | 64 |
| Dominican Republic, ctry., N.A. | E8 | 64 |
| Dominica Passage, strt., N.A. | I14 | 64 |
| Dominion, N.S. | C9 | 71 |
| Dominion City, Man. | E3 | 70 |
| Dominion Lake, l., Newf. | h9 | 72 |
| Dömitz, E. Ger. | B5 | 18 |
| Dommel, stm., Eur. | C5 | 17 |
| Domo, Eth. | D6 | 47 |
| Domodedovo, Sov. Un. | n17 | 27 |
| Domodossola, Italy | A2 | 20 |
| Dom Pedrito, Braz. | E2 | 56 |
| Dompierre [-sur-Authie], Fr. | D1 | 17 |
| Domremy, Sask. | E3 | 75 |
| Domuyo, Volcán, vol., Arg. | H13 | 27 |
| Don, stm., Scot., U.K. | C6 | 13 |
| Don, stm., Eng., U.K. | C6 | 13 |
| Dona Ana, N.M., U.S. | E3 | 108 |
| Dona Ana, co., N.M., U.S. | C4 | 10 |
| Donaghadee, N. Ire., U.K. | C6 | 73 |
| Donald, Or., U.S. | h12 | 114 |
| Donalda, Alta. | C4 | 68 |
| Donaldson, S.C., U.S. | C3 | 117 |
| Donaldson, Mn., U.S. | B2 | 100 |
| Donaldsonville, La., U.S. | D4 | 95 |
| Donalsonville, Ga., U.S. | E1 | 87 |
| Donard, Ire. | D5 | 11 |
| Donard, Slieve, mtn., N. Ire., U.K. | C4 | 10 |
| Donaueschingen, W. Ger. | B4 | 20 |
| Donauwörth, W. Ger. | E5 | 19 |
| Donavon, Sask. | F2 | 75 |
| Don Benito, Spain | C3 | 22 |
| Doncaster, Eng., U.K. | A6 | 12 |
| Doncaster and Templestowe, Austl. | *G8 | 51 |
| Dondo, Ang. | C1 | 48 |
| Dondo, Moz. | A5 | 49 |
| Donegal, Ire. | C3 | 11 |
| Donegal, co., Ire. | C4 | 11 |
| Donegal Bay, b., Ire. | C3 | 11 |
| Donegal Point, c., Ire. | D2 | 11 |
| Donerail, S.C., U.S. | C8 | 117 |
| Donets Basin, Sov. Un. | q21 | 27 |
| Donetsk, Sov. Un. | E1 | 50 |
| Dongara, Austl. | E1 | 50 |
| Dongchuan, China | B7 | 35 |
| Dongfang, China | F5 | 34 |
| Dongguang, China | B7 | 35 |
| Dong Hoi, Viet. | D5 | 35 |
| Dongning, China | D5 | 31 |
| Dongola, Il., U.S. | F4 | 90 |
| Dongou, Congo | A2 | 48 |
| Dongping, China | D8 | 31 |
| Dongsheng, China | D6 | 31 |
| Dongtai, China | H9 | 32 |
| Dongting Hu, l., China | F7 | 31 |
| Dong Ujimqin Qi, China | B7 | 32 |
| Dongxiang, China | J7 | 32 |
| Dongxing, China | G6 | 31 |
| Dongzhi, China | I7 | 32 |
| Donington, Eng., U.K. | B7 | 13 |
| Doniphan, Mo., U.S. | E7 | 102 |
| Doniphan, Ne., U.S. | D7 | 104 |
| Doniphan, co., Ks., U.S. | C8 | 93 |
| Donji Vakuf, Yugo. | C3 | 24 |
| Donkey Creek, stm., Wy., U.S. | B7 | 127 |

| Name | Map Ref. | Page |
|---|---|---|
| Donkin, N.S. | C10 | 71 |
| Donley, co., Tx., U.S. | B2 | 120 |
| Donna, Tx., U.S. | F3 | 120 |
| Donnacona, Que. | C6 | 74 |
| Donnellson, Il., U.S. | D4 | 90 |
| Donnelly, Ia., U.S. | D6 | 92 |
| Donnelly, Alta. | B2 | 68 |
| Donnelly, Id., U.S. | E2 | 89 |
| Donnelly, Mn., U.S. | E2 | 100 |
| Donner, La., U.S. | E5 | 95 |
| Donner Pass, Ca., U.S. | C3 | 82 |
| Donnybrook, N.D., U.S. | A4 | 111 |
| Donora, Pa., U.S. | F2 | 115 |
| Donovan, Il., U.S. | C6 | 90 |
| Don Peninsula, pen., B.C. | C3 | 69 |
| Donzère, Fr. | E6 | 16 |
| Dooagh, Ire. | D1 | 11 |
| Doogort, Ire. | C1 | 11 |
| Doole, Tx., U.S. | D3 | 120 |
| Dooling, Ga., U.S. | D3 | 87 |
| Doolittle, Mo., U.S. | D6 | 102 |
| Dooly, co., Ga., U.S. | D3 | 87 |
| Doon, Ia., U.S. | A1 | 92 |
| Doon, Loch, l., Scot., U.K. | E4 | 13 |
| Doonbeg, Ire. | E2 | 11 |
| Doonerak, Mount, mtn., Ak., U.S. | B9 | 79 |
| Door, co., Wi., U.S. | D6 | 126 |
| Doornik see Tournai, Bel. | D3 | 17 |
| Dora, Al., U.S. | B2 | 78 |
| Dora, Mo., U.S. | E5 | 102 |
| Dora, N.M., U.S. | D6 | 108 |
| Dora, Lake, l., U.S. | D3 | 50 |
| Dora Baltea, stm., Italy | B1 | 23 |
| Doran, Mn., U.S. | D2 | 100 |
| Doraville, Ga., U.S. | h8 | 87 |
| Dorbod, China | A11 | 32 |
| Dorcas, Bayou, stm., U.S. | u15 | 86 |
| Dorcheat, Bayou, stm., U.S. | B2 | 95 |
| Dorchester, N.B. | D5 | 71 |
| Dorchester, Eng., U.K. | E5 | 10 |
| Dorchester, Ne., U.S. | D8 | 104 |
| Dorchester, N.J., U.S. | E3 | 107 |
| Dorchester, S.C., U.S. | E7 | 117 |
| Dorchester, Wi., U.S. | C3 | 126 |
| Dorchester, co., Que. | C7 | 74 |
| Dorchester, co., Md., U.S. | D5 | 97 |
| Dorchester, co., S.C., U.S. | E7 | 117 |
| Dorchester, Cape, c., N.W. Ter. | C17 | 66 |
| Dorchester Crossing, N.B. | C5 | 71 |
| Dorchester Estates, S.C., U.S. | k11 | 117 |
| Dorcyville, La., U.S. | h9 | 95 |
| Dordogne, stm., Fr. | E4 | 16 |
| Dordrecht, Neth. | B6 | 16 |
| Dordrecht, S. Afr. | D4 | 49 |
| Doré, stm., Sask. | C2 | 75 |
| Doré, Lake, l., Ont. | B7 | 73 |
| Doré Lake, Sask. | C2 | 75 |
| Doré Lake, l., Sask. | C2 | 75 |
| Dorena, Or., U.S. | D4 | 114 |
| Dorena Lake, res., Or., U.S. | D3 | 114 |
| Dorenlee, Alta. | C4 | 68 |
| Dores, Scot., U.K. | C4 | 13 |
| Dores do Indaiá, Braz. | B3 | 56 |
| Dorfen, W. Ger. | A8 | 20 |
| Dorgali, Italy | D2 | 23 |
| Dörgön Lake, l., Mong. | B3 | 31 |
| Dori, Burkina | D4 | 45 |
| Dorion-Vaudreuil, Que. | q18 | 74 |
| Dorking, Eng., U.K. | m12 | 10 |
| Dormagen, W. Ger. | *C3 | 18 |
| Dormans, Fr. | E3 | 17 |
| Dormont, Pa., U.S. | k13 | 115 |
| Dornbirn, Aus. | E4 | 18 |
| Dornie, Scot., U.K. | C3 | 13 |
| Dornoch, Scot., U.K. | C4 | 10 |
| Dornoch Firth, est., Scot., U.K. | B5 | 10 |
| Dorogobuzh, Sov. Un. | D9 | 27 |
| Dorohoi, Rom. | B8 | 24 |
| Dorothy, Alta. | D4 | 68 |
| Dorothy, Mn., U.S. | C2 | 100 |
| Dorothy, N.J., U.S. | E3 | 107 |
| Dorothy, W.V., U.S. | n13 | 125 |
| Dorothy Pond, Ma., U.S. | B4 | 98 |
| Dorr, Mi., U.S. | F5 | 99 |
| Dorrance, Ks., U.S. | D5 | 93 |
| Dorre, i., Austl. | E1 | 50 |
| Dorrigo, Austl. | E9 | 51 |
| Dorris, Ca., U.S. | B3 | 82 |
| Dorris Heights, Il., U.S. | F5 | 90 |
| Dorset, Ont. | B6 | 73 |
| Dorset, Mn., U.S. | D4 | 100 |
| Dorset, Oh., U.S. | A5 | 112 |
| Dorset, Vt., U.S. | E2 | 122 |
| Dorset, co., Eng., U.K. | D5 | 12 |
| Dorset Peak, mtn., Vt., U.S. | E2 | 122 |
| Dorsey, Md., U.S. | B4 | 97 |
| Dorsey, Ms., U.S. | A5 | 101 |
| Dorsten, W. Ger. | B1 | 19 |
| Dortmund, W. Ger. | B2 | 18 |
| Dortmund Ems Canal, W. Ger. | B7 | 17 |
| Dorton, Ky., U.S. | C7 | 94 |
| Dörtyol, Tur. | D11 | 40 |
| Do Rüd, Iran | E4 | 39 |
| Dorum, W. Ger. | E2 | 15 |
| Doruma, Zaire | A4 | 48 |
| Dorval, Que. | q19 | 74 |
| Dos Bahías, Cabo, c., Arg. | C3 | 54 |
| Dos Bocas, Lago, res., P.R. | B2 | 65 |
| Dos Hermanas, Spain | D3 | 22 |
| Dos Quebradas, Col. | *C2 | 60 |
| Dosquet, Que. | C6 | 74 |
| Dos Rios, Ca., U.S. | C2 | 82 |
| Dosse, stm., E. Ger. | E6 | 15 |
| Dosso, Niger | D5 | 45 |
| Dossor, Sov. Un. | D4 | 28 |
| Doswell, Va., U.S. | C5 | 123 |
| Dothan, Al., U.S. | D4 | 78 |
| Dothan, W.V., U.S. | n13 | 125 |
| Doting Cove, Newf. | D5 | 72 |
| Dot Lake, Ak., U.S. | C11 | 79 |
| Dott, W.V., U.S. | D3 | 125 |
| Doty, Wa., U.S. | C2 | 124 |
| Douai, Fr. | B5 | 16 |
| Douala, Cam. | E1 | 46 |
| Douarnenez, Fr. | D2 | 16 |
| Double Bayou, Tx., U.S. | r15 | 120 |
| Double Beach, Ct., U.S. | D4 | 84 |
| Double Mer, b., Newf. | A2 | 72 |
| Double Mountain, mtn., Al., U.S. | g7 | 78 |
| Double Oak Mountain, mtn., Al., U.S. | g7 | 78 |
| Doublespring Pass, Id., U.S. | E5 | 89 |
| Double Springs, Al., U.S. | A2 | 78 |
| Doubletop Peak, mtn., Wy., U.S. | C2 | 127 |
| Doubs, Md., U.S. | B3 | 97 |
| Doubs, dept., Fr. | B2 | 20 |
| Doubs, stm., Eur. | D7 | 16 |
| Doubtful Sound, strt., N.Z. | P11 | 51 |
| Doucette, Tx., U.S. | D5 | 120 |
| Douds, Ia., U.S. | D5 | 92 |
| Doué, Fr. | D3 | 16 |
| Douentza, Mali | D4 | 45 |
| Dougherty, Ia., U.S. | B4 | 92 |
| Dougherty, Ok., U.S. | C4 | 113 |
| Dougherty, co., Ga., U.S. | E2 | 87 |
| Douglas, Ont. | B8 | 73 |
| Douglas, I. of Man | C4 | 10 |
| Douglas, S. Afr. | C3 | 49 |
| Douglas, Scot., U.K. | E5 | 13 |
| Douglas, Az., U.S. | F6 | 80 |
| Douglas, Ga., U.S. | E4 | 87 |
| Douglas, Mi., U.S. | F4 | 99 |
| Douglas, Ne., U.S. | D9 | 104 |
| Douglas, N.D., U.S. | B4 | 111 |
| Douglas, Ok., U.S. | A4 | 113 |
| Douglas, W.V., U.S. | B5 | 125 |
| Douglas, Wy., U.S. | D7 | 127 |
| Douglas, co., Co., U.S. | B6 | 83 |
| Douglas, co., Ga., U.S. | C2 | 87 |
| Douglas, co., Il., U.S. | D5 | 90 |
| Douglas, co., Ks., U.S. | D8 | 93 |
| Douglas, co., Mn., U.S. | E3 | 100 |
| Douglas, co., Mo., U.S. | E5 | 102 |
| Douglas, co., Ne., U.S. | C9 | 104 |
| Douglas, co., Nv., U.S. | E2 | 105 |
| Douglas, co., Or., U.S. | D3 | 114 |
| Douglas, co., S.D., U.S. | D7 | 118 |
| Douglas, co., Wa., U.S. | B6 | 124 |
| Douglas, co., Wi., U.S. | B2 | 126 |
| Douglas, Mount, mtn., Ak., U.S. | D9 | 79 |
| Douglas Channel, strt., B.C. | C3 | 69 |
| Douglas Creek, stm., Co., U.S. | B2 | 83 |
| Douglas Lake, B.C. | D7 | 69 |
| Douglas Lake, l., Mi., U.S. | C6 | 99 |
| Douglas Lake, res., Tn., U.S. | D10 | 119 |
| Douglas Point, c., Ont. | C3 | 73 |
| Douglass, Ks., U.S. | E7 | 93 |
| Douglas Station, Man. | E2 | 70 |
| Douglastown, N.B. | B4 | 71 |
| Douglasville, Ga., U.S. | C2 | 87 |
| Doullens, Fr. | B5 | 16 |
| Doulus Head, c., Ire. | F1 | 11 |
| Doumé, Cam. | E2 | 46 |
| Dour, Bel. | D3 | 17 |
| Doura, Mali | D3 | 45 |
| Dourados, Braz. | m7 | 56 |
| Dourados, Braz. | C2 | 56 |
| Douro (Duero), stm., Eur. | B1 | 22 |
| Dousman, Wi., U.S. | E5 | 126 |
| Douz, Tun. | C6 | 44 |
| Dove Creek, Co., U.S. | D2 | 83 |
| Dover, Eng., U.K. | E7 | 10 |
| Dover, Ar., U.S. | B2 | 81 |
| Dover, De., U.S. | D3 | 85 |
| Dover, Fl., U.S. | D4 | 86 |
| Dover, Ga., U.S. | D5 | 87 |
| Dover, Id., U.S. | A2 | 89 |
| Dover, Ks., U.S. | D8 | 93 |
| Dover, Ky., U.S. | B6 | 94 |
| Dover, Ma., U.S. | h10 | 98 |
| Dover, Mn., U.S. | G6 | 100 |
| Dover, Mo., U.S. | B4 | 102 |
| Dover, N.H., U.S. | D5 | 106 |
| Dover, N.J., U.S. | B3 | 107 |
| Dover, N.C., U.S. | B5 | 110 |
| Dover, Oh., U.S. | B4 | 112 |
| Dover, Ok., U.S. | B4 | 113 |
| Dover, Pa., U.S. | F8 | 115 |
| Dover, Tn., U.S. | A4 | 119 |
| Dover, stm., Alta. | A4 | 68 |
| Dover, Strait of, strt., Eur. | B5 | 16 |
| Dover Air Force Base, mil., De., U.S. | D4 | 85 |
| Dover-Foxcroft, Me., U.S. | C3 | 96 |
| Dover Hill, In., U.S. | G4 | 91 |
| Dover Plains, N.Y., U.S. | D7 | 109 |
| Dovesville, S.C., U.S. | C8 | 117 |
| Dovray, Mn., U.S. | F3 | 100 |
| Dow, Il., U.S. | D3 | 90 |
| Dow, Ok., U.S. | C6 | 113 |
| Dowa, Mwi. | D5 | 48 |
| Dowagiac, Mi., U.S. | G4 | 99 |
| Dow City, Ia., U.S. | C2 | 92 |
| Dowell, Il., U.S. | F4 | 90 |
| Dowell, Md., U.S. | D5 | 97 |
| Dowelltown, Tn., U.S. | C8 | 119 |
| Dowlatābād, Afg. | C13 | 39 |
| Dowlat Yar, Afg. | B4 | 36 |
| Dowling Lake, l., Alta. | D4 | 68 |
| Dowling Park, Fl., U.S. | B3 | 86 |
| Downer, Mn., U.S. | D2 | 100 |
| Downers Grove, Il., U.S. | B5 | 90 |
| Downey, Ca., U.S. | n12 | 82 |
| Downey, Id., U.S. | G6 | 89 |
| Downham Market, Eng., U.K. | B8 | 12 |
| Downieville, Ca., U.S. | C3 | 82 |
| Downing, Mo., U.S. | A5 | 102 |
| Downing, Wi., U.S. | C1 | 126 |
| Downingtown, Pa., U.S. | F10 | 115 |
| Downpatrick, N. Ire., U.K. | C4 | 10 |
| Downpatrick Head, c., Ire. | C2 | 11 |
| Downs, Ks., U.S. | C5 | 93 |
| Downs Mountain, mtn., Wy., U.S. | C3 | 127 |
| Downsville, La., U.S. | B3 | 95 |
| Downsville, N.Y., U.S. | C6 | 109 |
| Downsville, Wi., U.S. | D2 | 126 |
| Downton, Mount, mtn., B.C. | C5 | 69 |
| Dows, Ia., U.S. | B4 | 92 |
| Dowshī, Afg. | D14 | 39 |
| Doyle, Ca., U.S. | B3 | 82 |
| Doyle, Tn., U.S. | D8 | 119 |
| Doyles, Newf. | E2 | 72 |
| Doylestown, Oh., U.S. | B4 | 112 |
| Doylestown, Pa., U.S. | F11 | 115 |
| Doyline, La., U.S. | B2 | 95 |
| Dozier, Al., U.S. | D3 | 78 |
| Dra'a, Hamada du, des., Alg. | C3 | 44 |
| Drâa, Oued, val., Afr. | D3 | 44 |
| Drabenderhöhe, W. Ger. | C2 | 18 |
| Drachten, Neth. | A6 | 17 |
| Drăgănești-Vlașca, Rom. | C7 | 24 |
| Draganovo, Bul. | D7 | 24 |
| Drăgășani, Rom. | C7 | 24 |
| Dragons Mouth, strt. | N22 | 65 |
| Dragoon, Az., U.S. | E5 | 80 |
| Dragør, Den. | C6 | 15 |
| Draguignan, Fr. | F7 | 16 |
| Dragovac, Yugo. | B2 | 24 |
| Drain, Or., U.S. | D3 | 114 |
| Drake, Sask. | F3 | 75 |
| Drake, Az., U.S. | C3 | 80 |
| Drake, Co., U.S. | A5 | 83 |
| Drake, N.D., U.S. | B5 | 111 |
| Drakensberg, mts., Afr. | D4 | 49 |
| Drake Passage, strt. | J16 | 2 |
| Drake Peak, mtn., Or., U.S. | E6 | 114 |
| Drakesboro, Ky., U.S. | C2 | 94 |
| Drakes Branch, Va., U.S. | D4 | 123 |
| Drakes Creek, stm., Ky., U.S. | D3 | 94 |
| Drakes Creek, West Fork, stm., Ky., U.S. | D3 | 94 |
| Drakesville, Ia., U.S. | D5 | 92 |
| Draketown, Ga., U.S. | C1 | 87 |
| Dráma, Grc. | B5 | 40 |
| Drama, stm., Pol. | g9 | 26 |
| Drammen, Nor. | H4 | 14 |
| Dramselva, stm., Nor. | p27 | 14 |
| Drancy, Fr. | g10 | 16 |
| Dranse, stm., Fr. | C2 | 20 |
| Draper, S.D., U.S. | D5 | 118 |
| Draper, Ut., U.S. | C4 | 121 |
| Draperstown, N. Ire., U.K. | C5 | 11 |
| Drasco, Ar., U.S. | B4 | 81 |
| Drava (Drau), stm., Eur. | C4 | 24 |
| Draveil, Fr. | F2 | 17 |
| Dravuni, i., Fiji | l15 | 52 |
| Drawsko [Pomorskie], Pol. | B3 | 26 |
| Drayton, Ont. | D4 | 73 |
| Drayton, N.D., U.S. | A8 | 111 |
| Drayton, S.C., U.S. | B4 | 117 |
| Drayton Plains, Mi., U.S. | F7 | 99 |
| Drayton Valley, Alta. | C3 | 68 |
| Dreamland Villa, Az., U.S. | *D4 | 80 |
| Drebkau, E. Ger. | C7 | 18 |
| Dreisdorf, W. Ger. | D3 | 15 |
| Drenthe, prov., Neth. | B6 | 17 |
| Dresbach, Mn., U.S. | G7 | 100 |
| Dresden, Ont. | E2 | 73 |
| Dresden, E. Ger. | C6 | 18 |
| Dresden, Ks., U.S. | C3 | 93 |
| Dresden, Oh., U.S. | B3 | 112 |
| Dresden, Tn., U.S. | A3 | 119 |
| Dresser, In., U.S. | F3 | 91 |
| Dresser, Wi., U.S. | C1 | 126 |
| Dresslerville, Nv., U.S. | E2 | 105 |
| Dreux, Fr. | C4 | 16 |
| Drew, Ms., U.S. | B3 | 101 |
| Drew, co., Ar., U.S. | D4 | 81 |
| Drewryville, Va., U.S. | D5 | 123 |
| Drewsey, Or., U.S. | D8 | 114 |
| Drews Reservoir, res., Or., U.S. | E6 | 114 |
| Drewsville, N.H., U.S. | D2 | 106 |
| Drexel, Mo., U.S. | C3 | 102 |
| Drexel, N.C., U.S. | B1 | 110 |
| Drexel, Oh., U.S. | C1 | 112 |
| Drexel Hill, Pa., U.S. | p20 | 115 |
| Drezna, Sov. Un. | n18 | 27 |
| Drift, Ky., U.S. | C7 | 94 |
| Drifton, Pa., U.S. | D10 | 115 |
| Driftpile, Alta. | B3 | 68 |
| Driftpile, stm., Alta. | B3 | 68 |
| Driftwood, Ok., U.S. | A3 | 113 |
| Driftwood, Pa., U.S. | D5 | 115 |
| Driftwood Creek, stm., Ne., U.S. | D4 | 104 |
| Driggs, Id., U.S. | F7 | 89 |
| Drimoleague, Ire. | F2 | 11 |
| Drina, stm., Yugo. | C4 | 24 |
| Drin Gulf, b., Alb. | B2 | 25 |
| Drini, stm., Alb. | A3 | 25 |
| Drinkwater, Sask. | G3 | 75 |
| Dripping Springs, Tx., U.S. | D3 | 120 |
| Driscoll, N.D., U.S. | C5 | 111 |
| Driscoll, Tx., U.S. | F4 | 120 |
| Driskill Mountain, hill, La., U.S. | B3 | 95 |
| Driver, Ar., U.S. | B5 | 81 |
| Dröbak, Nor. | H4 | 14 |
| Drobeta-Turnu-Severin, Rom. | C6 | 24 |
| Drogheda, Ire. | D3 | 10 |
| Drogobych, Sov. Un. | G4 | 27 |
| Droitwich, Eng., U.K. | B5 | 12 |
| Dromahair, Ire. | C3 | 11 |
| Drôme, stm., Fr. | E6 | 16 |
| Dromod, Ire. | C3 | 11 |
| Dromore, N. Ire., U.K. | C4 | 11 |
| Dromore West, Ire. | C3 | 11 |
| Dronero, Italy | E3 | 20 |
| Dronfield, Eng., U.K. | A6 | 12 |
| Dronninglund, Den. | A4 | 15 |
| Dropmore, Man. | D1 | 70 |
| Druid, Sask. | F1 | 75 |
| Druid Hills, Ga., U.S. | *C2 | 87 |
| Drulingen, Fr. | E2 | 19 |
| Drumbeg, Scot., U.K. | B3 | 13 |
| Drumbo, Ont. | D4 | 73 |
| Drumcliff, Ire. | B3 | 11 |
| Drumheller, Alta. | D4 | 68 |
| Drum Island, i., S.C., U.S. | k12 | 117 |
| Drumlish, Ire. | C4 | 11 |
| Drummond, Id., U.S. | F7 | 89 |
| Drummond, Mt., U.S. | D3 | 103 |
| Drummond, Ok., U.S. | A3 | 113 |
| Drummond, Wi., U.S. | B2 | 126 |
| Drummond, co., Que. | D5 | 74 |
| Drummond, Lake, l., Va., U.S. | D6 | 123 |
| Drummond Island, Mi., U.S. | C7 | 99 |
| Drummond Island, i., Mi., U.S. | C7 | 99 |
| Drummond Range, mts., Austl. | D8 | 51 |
| Drummondville, Que. | D5 | 74 |
| Drummondville-Sud, Que. | D5 | 74 |
| Drummore, Scot., U.K. | F4 | 13 |
| Drumquin, N. Ire., U.K. | *C4 | 11 |
| Drumright, Ok., U.S. | B5 | 113 |
| Drumshanbo, Ire. | C3 | 11 |
| Druzhina, Sov. Un. | C36 | 128 |
| Druzhkovka, Sov. Un. | q20 | 27 |
| Drweca, stm., Pol. | B5 | 26 |
| Dryad, Wa., U.S. | C2 | 124 |
| Dryberry Lake, l., Ont. | E5 | 70 |
| Dry Branch, Ga., U.S. | D3 | 87 |
| Dry Cimarron, stm., U.S. | A6 | 108 |
| Dry Creek, La., U.S. | D2 | 95 |
| Dry Creek, stm., Ks., U.S. | g12 | 93 |
| Dry Creek Mountain, mtn., Nv., U.S. | B5 | 105 |
| Dryden, Ont. | o16 | 73 |
| Dryden, Me., U.S. | D2 | 96 |
| Dryden, Mi., U.S. | F7 | 99 |
| Dryden, N.Y., U.S. | C4 | 109 |
| Dryden, Tx., U.S. | D1 | 120 |
| Dryden, Va., U.S. | f8 | 123 |
| Dryden, Wa., U.S. | B5 | 124 |
| Dryfork, W.V., U.S. | C5 | 125 |
| Dry Fork, stm., Mo., U.S. | D6 | 102 |
| Dry Fork, stm., W.V., U.S. | C5 | 125 |
| Dry Fork, stm., W.V., U.S. | m13 | 125 |
| Drygalski Island, i., Ant. | C22 | 7 |
| Dry Harbour Mountains, mts., Jam. | E14 | 65 |
| Drymen, Scot., U.K. | D4 | 13 |
| Dry Mills, Me., U.S. | E2 | 96 |
| Dry Prong, La., U.S. | C3 | 95 |
| Dry Ridge, Ky., U.S. | B5 | 94 |
| Dry Run, Pa., U.S. | F6 | 115 |
| Drysdale, stm., Austl. | B4 | 50 |
| Dry Tortugas, is., Fl., U.S. | H5 | 86 |
| Drywood, Alta. | E4 | 68 |
| Dschang, Cam. | D2 | 46 |
| Duaiheb, Hasi, well, W. Sah. | D6 | 34 |
| Duaringa, Austl. | A7 | 51 |
| Duarte, Ca., U.S. | *E5 | 82 |
| Duarte, Pico, mtn., Dom. Rep. | E8 | 64 |
| Duart Point, c., Scot., U.K. | C3 | 13 |
| Dubā, Sau. Ar. | C3 | 38 |
| Dubach, La., U.S. | B3 | 95 |
| Dubai (Dubayy), U.A.E. | C5 | 38 |
| Dubawnt, stm., N.W. Ter. | D12 | 66 |
| Dubawnt Lake, l., N.W. Ter. | D12 | 66 |
| Du Bay, Lake, res., Wi., U.S. | D4 | 126 |
| Dubbo, Austl. | F8 | 50 |
| Dübendorf, Switz. | B6 | 21 |
| Dublin (Baile Átha Cliath), Ire. | D3 | 10 |
| Dublin, Al., U.S. | C3 | 78 |
| Dublin, Ca., U.S. | *D3 | 82 |
| Dublin, Ga., U.S. | D4 | 87 |
| Dublin, In., U.S. | E7 | 91 |
| Dublin, Md., U.S. | A5 | 97 |
| Dublin, Ms., U.S. | A3 | 101 |
| Dublin, N.H., U.S. | E2 | 106 |
| Dublin, N.C., U.S. | C4 | 110 |
| Dublin, Oh., U.S. | k10 | 112 |
| Dublin, Pa., U.S. | F11 | 115 |
| Dublin, Tx., U.S. | C3 | 120 |
| Dublin, Va., U.S. | C2 | 123 |
| Dublin, co., Ire. | D3 | 11 |
| Dublin Bay, b., Ire. | D3 | 11 |
| Dublin Shore, N.S. | E5 | 71 |
| Dubna [nad Váhom], Czech. | D5 | 26 |
| Dubois, Id., U.S. | E6 | 89 |
| Dubois, In., U.S. | H4 | 91 |
| Du Bois, Pa., U.S. | D4 | 115 |
| Dubois, Wy., U.S. | C3 | 127 |
| Dubois, co., In., U.S. | H4 | 91 |
| Duboistown, Pa., U.S. | D7 | 115 |
| Dubossary, Sov. Un. | H7 | 27 |
| Dubossary Reservoir, res., Sov. Un. | B9 | 24 |
| Dubovka, Sov. Un. | D2 | 28 |
| Dubréka, Gui. | E2 | 45 |
| Dubrovka, Sov. Un. | s31 | 14 |
| Dubrovnik, Yugo. | D4 | 24 |
| Dubuc, Sask. | G4 | 75 |
| Dubulu, Zaire | A3 | 48 |
| Dubuque, Ia., U.S. | B7 | 92 |
| Dubuque, co., Ia., U.S. | B7 | 92 |
| Duchcov, Czech. | C4 | 26 |
| Duchesne, Ut., U.S. | C5 | 121 |
| Duchesne, co., Ut., U.S. | C5 | 121 |
| Duchesne, stm., Ut., U.S. | C5 | 121 |
| Duchess, Alta. | D5 | 68 |
| Ducie, atoll, Pit. | H14 | 6 |
| Duck, N.C., U.S. | A7 | 110 |
| Duck, stm., Tn., U.S. | B4 | 119 |
| Duck Bay, Man. | C1 | 70 |
| Duck Creek, stm., De., U.S. | C4 | 85 |
| Duck Creek, stm., Nv., U.S. | D7 | 105 |
| Duck Creek, stm., Oh., U.S. | C4 | 112 |
| Duck Creek, stm., Wi., U.S. | h9 | 126 |
| Duck Hill, Ms., U.S. | B4 | 101 |
| Duck Lake, Sask. | E2 | 75 |
| Duck Lake, l., Man. | B2 | 70 |
| Duck Lake, l., Me., U.S. | C4 | 96 |
| Duck Lake Post, Man. | f8 | 70 |
| Duck Mountain, hills, Man. | D1 | 70 |
| Duck Mountain Provincial Park, Man. | D1 | 70 |
| Duck Mountain Provincial Park, Man. | F5 | 75 |
| Duck River, Tn., U.S. | B4 | 119 |
| Duck Valley Indian Reservation, U.S. | B5 | 105 |
| Ducktown, Tn., U.S. | D9 | 119 |
| Duckwater, Nv., U.S. | E6 | 105 |
| Duckwater Indian Reservation, Nv., U.S. | E6 | 105 |
| Duckwater Peak, mtn., Nv., U.S. | E6 | 105 |
| Ducor, Ca., U.S. | E4 | 82 |
| Dudelange, Lux. | E6 | 17 |
| Duderstadt, W. Ger. | B5 | 19 |
| Dudinka, Sov. Un. | C11 | 29 |
| Dudley, Eng., U.K. | D5 | 10 |
| Dudley, Ga., U.S. | D3 | 87 |
| Dudley, Ma., U.S. | B4 | 98 |
| Dudley, Mo., U.S. | E7 | 102 |
| Dudley, N.C., U.S. | B4 | 110 |
| Dudley, Pa., U.S. | F5 | 115 |
| Dudweiler, W. Ger. | F2 | 19 |
| Duékoué, I.C. | E3 | 45 |
| Duenweg, Mo., U.S. | D3 | 102 |
| Dueré, Braz. | E5 | 59 |
| Duero (Douro), stm., Eur. | B1 | 22 |
| Due West, S.C., U.S. | C3 | 117 |
| Duff, In., U.S. | H3 | 91 |
| Duff, Tn., U.S. | C9 | 119 |
| Duffee, Ms., U.S. | C5 | 101 |
| Duffer Peak, mtn., Nv., U.S. | B3 | 105 |
| Duffield, Alta. | C3 | 68 |
| Duff Reef, rf., Fiji | H16 | 52 |
| Dufftown, Scot., U.K. | C5 | 13 |
| Duffy, Oh., U.S. | C5 | 112 |
| Dufur, Or., U.S. | B5 | 114 |
| Dugdemona, stm., La., U.S. | B3 | 95 |
| Dugger, In., U.S. | F3 | 91 |
| Dug Hill Ridge, mtn., Md., U.S. | A4 | 97 |
| Dugi, i., Yugo. | C2 | 24 |
| Dug Gate, hist., Isr. Occ. | m14 | 41 |
| Duich, Loch, b., Scot., U.K. | C3 | 13 |
| Duida, Cerro, mtn., Ven. | C4 | 60 |
| Duisburg, W. Ger. | B2 | 18 |
| Duitama, Col. | B5 | 60 |
| Duiwelskloof, S. Afr. | B5 | 49 |
| Dujuuma, Som. | E8 | 47 |
| Dūkān Dam, Iraq | C2 | 39 |
| Duke, Mo., U.S. | D5 | 102 |
| Duke, Ok., U.S. | C2 | 113 |
| Duke Center, Pa., U.S. | C3 | 115 |
| Dukedom, Tn., U.S. | A3 | 119 |
| Duke Island, i., Ak., U.S. | n24 | 79 |
| Dukes, co., Ma., U.S. | D6 | 98 |
| Duk Fadiat, Sud. | D3 | 47 |
| Duki, Pak. | D6 | 36 |
| Dukla Pass, Eur. | D6 | 26 |
| Dukou, China | *F5 | 31 |
| Dulac, La., U.S. | E5 | 95 |
| Dulce, N.M., U.S. | A2 | 108 |
| Dulce, stm., Arg. | C3 | 55 |
| Dülken, W. Ger. | B2 | 19 |
| Dulowa, Pol. | g11 | 26 |
| Duluth, Ga., U.S. | B2 | 87 |
| Duluth, Mn., U.S. | D6 | 100 |
| Dūma, Isr. Occ. | g12 | 41 |
| Dūmā, Syria | *F11 | 40 |
| Dumaguete, Phil. | D6 | 34 |
| Dumanli, mtn., Tur. | B11 | 40 |
| Dumaran Island, i., Phil. | C5 | 34 |
| Dumas, Ar., U.S. | D4 | 81 |
| Dumas, Ga., U.S. | D2 | 87 |
| Dumas, Ms., U.S. | A5 | 101 |
| Dumas, Tx., U.S. | B2 | 120 |
| Dumba, Zaire | B3 | 48 |
| Dumbarton, Scot., U.K. | E4 | 13 |
| Dumboa, Nig. | D7 | 45 |
| Dumfries, Va., U.S. | B5 | 123 |
| Dumfries, Scot., U.K. | E4 | 13 |
| Dumfries and Galloway, prov., Scot., U.K. | E4 | 13 |
| Dumka, India | E11 | 37 |
| Dummer, Sask. | H3 | 75 |
| Dümmer, l., W. Ger. | F2 | 15 |
| Dummerston, Vt., U.S. | F3 | 122 |
| Dumont, Ia., U.S. | B5 | 92 |
| Dumont, Mn., U.S. | E2 | 100 |
| Dumont, N.J., U.S. | B5 | 107 |
| Dumont, Ne., U.S. | C5 | 104 |
| Dumont, Tx., U.S. | C2 | 120 |
| Dumont d'Urville, sci., Ant. | C27 | 7 |
| Dumyat (Damietta), Eg. | B3 | 38 |
| Dunaff Head, c., Ire. | B4 | 11 |
| Dunafoldvár, Hung. | B4 | 24 |
| Dunaújváros, Hung. | B4 | 24 |
| Dunajec, stm., Eur. | D6 | 26 |
| Dunajská Streda, Czech. | D4 | 26 |
| Dunany Point, c., Ire. | D5 | 11 |
| Dunapataj, Hung. | B4 | 24 |
| Dunbar, Scot., U.K. | D5 | 13 |
| Dunbar, Ky., U.S. | C3 | 94 |
| Dunbar, Ne., U.S. | D9 | 104 |
| Dunbar, Pa., U.S. | G2 | 115 |
| Dunbar, S.C., U.S. | B8 | 117 |
| Dunbar, W.V., U.S. | C3 | 125 |
| Dunbarton, N.H., U.S. | D3 | 106 |
| Dunblane, Sask. | F2 | 75 |
| Dunblane, Scot., U.K. | D5 | 13 |
| Dunboyne, Ire. | D5 | 11 |
| Dunbridge, Oh., U.S. | f6 | 112 |
| Duncan, B.C. | E6 | 69 |
| Duncan, Az., U.S. | E6 | 80 |
| Duncan, Ky., U.S. | C5 | 94 |
| Duncan, Ms., U.S. | A3 | 101 |
| Duncan, Ne., U.S. | C8 | 104 |
| Duncan, Ok., U.S. | C4 | 113 |
| Duncan, S.C., U.S. | B3 | 117 |
| Duncan, stm., B.C. | D9 | 69 |
| Duncan Falls, Oh., U.S. | C4 | 112 |
| Duncan Lake, res., B.C. | D9 | 69 |
| Duncannon, Pa., U.S. | F7 | 115 |
| Duncansby Head, c., Scot., U.K. | A5 | 10 |
| Duncansville, Pa., U.S. | F5 | 115 |
| Duncanville, Al., U.S. | B2 | 78 |
| Duncanville, Tx., U.S. | n10 | 120 |
| Duncombe, Ia., U.S. | B4 | 92 |
| Duncormick, Ire. | E5 | 11 |
| Dundalk, Ont. | C4 | 73 |
| Dundalk, Ire. | C3 | 10 |
| Dundalk, Md., U.S. | B4 | 97 |
| Dundalk Bay, b., Ire. | D3 | 10 |
| Dundas, Ont. | D5 | 73 |
| Dundas, Il., U.S. | E5 | 90 |
| Dundas, Mn., U.S. | F5 | 100 |
| Dundas, Va., U.S. | D4 | 123 |
| Dundas, co., Ont. | B9 | 73 |
| Dundas, Lake, l., Austl. | F3 | 50 |
| Dundas Island, i., B.C. | B2 | 69 |
| Dundas Strait, strt., Austl. | B5 | 50 |
| Dundee, S. Afr. | C5 | 49 |
| Dundee, Scot., U.K. | C5 | 13 |
| Dundee, Fl., U.S. | D5 | 86 |
| Dundee, Il., U.S. | B6 | 92 |
| Dundee, Ky., U.S. | C3 | 94 |
| Dundee, Mi., U.S. | G7 | 99 |
| Dundee, Mn., U.S. | G3 | 100 |
| Dundee, N.Y., U.S. | C4 | 109 |
| Dundee, Oh., U.S. | h11 | 114 |
| Dundee, Or., U.S. | E5 | 11 |
| Dundrum, Ire. | D5 | 11 |
| Dundrum Bay, b., N. Ire., U.K. | C4 | 10 |
| Dundurn, Sask. | F2 | 75 |
| Dundy, co., Ne., U.S. | D4 | 104 |
| Dunedin, N.Z. | P13 | 51 |
| Dunedin, Fl., U.S. | D4 | 86 |
| Duneland Beach, In., U.S. | A4 | 91 |
| Dunellen, N.J., U.S. | B4 | 107 |
| Dunfanaghy, Ire. | B4 | 11 |
| Dunfermline, Scot., U.K. | C5 | 13 |
| Dunfermline, Il., U.S. | C3 | 90 |
| Dungannon, Ont. | C3 | 73 |
| Dungannon, N. Ire., U.K. | C5 | 11 |
| Dungannon, Va., U.S. | f9 | 123 |
| Dungarpur, India | F4 | 37 |
| Dungarvan, Ire. | E4 | 11 |
| Dungarvan Harbour, b., Ire. | E4 | 11 |
| Dungeness, Wa., U.S. | A2 | 124 |
| Dungeness, c., Eng., U.K. | D8 | 12 |
| Dung Gate, hist., Isr. Occ. | m14 | 41 |
| Dunglow, Ire. | B3 | 11 |
| Dungu, Zaire | A5 | 48 |
| Dungun, Malay. | J5 | 35 |
| Dunhua, China | C10 | 31 |
| Dunkard Creek, stm., U.S. | B4 | 125 |
| Dunkeld, Scot., U.K. | D5 | 13 |
| Dunkerque, Fr. | B5 | 16 |
| Dunkerton, Ia., U.S. | B5 | 92 |
| Dunkineely, Ire. | C3 | 11 |
| Dunkirk, In., U.S. | D7 | 91 |
| Dunkirk, N.Y., U.S. | C1 | 109 |
| Dunkirk, Oh., U.S. | B2 | 112 |
| Dunkirk, co., Mo., U.S. | E7 | 102 |
| Dunkwa, Ghana | E4 | 45 |
| Dún Laoghaire, Ire. | D3 | 10 |
| Dunlap, Ia., U.S. | C2 | 92 |
| Dunlap, Il., U.S. | C4 | 90 |
| Dunlap, In., U.S. | A6 | 91 |
| Dunlap, Ks., U.S. | D7 | 93 |
| Dunlap, Tn., U.S. | D8 | 119 |
| Dunlavin, Ire. | D5 | 11 |
| Dunleer, Ire. | D5 | 11 |
| Dunleith, De., U.S. | i7 | 85 |
| Dunlo, Pa., U.S. | F4 | 115 |
| Dunloup Creek, stm., W.V., U.S. | n13 | 125 |
| Dunmanway, Ire. | F2 | 11 |
| Dunmore, Ky., U.S. | C2 | 94 |
| Dunmore, Ire. | D3 | 11 |
| Dunmore, Pa., U.S. | D10 | 115 |
| Dunmore, Lake, l., Vt., U.S. | D2 | 122 |
| Dunmore East, Ire. | E5 | 11 |
| Dunn, N.C., U.S. | B4 | 110 |
| Dunn, co., N.D., U.S. | B3 | 111 |
| Dunn, co., Wi., U.S. | D2 | 126 |
| Dunnamanagh, N. Ire., U.K. | C4 | 11 |
| Dunn Center, N.D., U.S. | B3 | 111 |
| Dunnellon, Fl., U.S. | C4 | 86 |
| Dunnet Head, c., Scot., U.K. | B5 | 13 |
| Dunn Loring Woods, Va., U.S. | *B5 | 123 |
| Dunnottar, Man. | D3 | 70 |
| Dunns Bridge, In., U.S. | B4 | 91 |
| Dunns Corners, R.I., U.S. | G1 | 116 |
| Dunnsville, Va., U.S. | C6 | 123 |
| Dunnville, Ont. | E5 | 73 |
| Dunnville, Ky., U.S. | C5 | 94 |
| Dunoon, Scot., U.K. | C4 | 10 |
| Dunphy, Nv., U.S. | C5 | 105 |
| Dunqulah, Sud. | B3 | 47 |
| Dunrea, Man. | E2 | 70 |
| Dunrobin, Ont. | B8 | 73 |
| Duns, Scot., U.K. | E6 | 13 |
| Dunseith, N.D., U.S. | A5 | 111 |
| Dunsmuir, Ca., U.S. | B2 | 82 |
| Dunstable, Eng., U.K. | C7 | 12 |
| Dunstable, Ma., U.S. | A5 | 98 |
| Dun-sur-Auron, Fr. | D5 | 16 |
| Dun [-sur-Meuse], Fr. | E5 | 17 |
| Duntroon, Ont. | C4 | 73 |
| Dunvegan, Scot., U.K. | C2 | 13 |
| Dunvegan, Loch, b., Scot., U.K. | C2 | 13 |
| Dunvegan Head, c., Scot., U.K. | C2 | 13 |
| Dunville, Newf. | E5 | 72 |
| Dunwoody, Ga., U.S. | h8 | 87 |
| Duolun, China | C8 | 31 |
| Du Page, co., Il., U.S. | B5 | 90 |
| Du Page, stm., Il., U.S. | k8 | 90 |
| Dupax, Phil. | n13 | 34 |
| Duplessis, La., U.S. | h10 | 95 |
| Duplin, co., N.C., U.S. | C5 | 110 |
| Dupont, Ga., U.S. | F4 | 87 |
| Dupont, In., U.S. | G6 | 91 |
| Dupont, La., U.S. | *D4 | 95 |
| Dupont, Oh., U.S. | A1 | 112 |
| Dupont, Pa., U.S. | n18 | 115 |
| Du Pont, Wa., U.S. | B3 | 124 |
| Dupont, Bayou, stm., La., U.S. | k11 | 95 |
| Dupont City, W.V., U.S. | m12 | 125 |
| Dupont Manor, De., U.S. | D3 | 85 |
| Dupree, S.D., U.S. | B4 | 118 |
| Dupuyer, Mt., U.S. | B4 | 103 |
| Du Quoin, Il., U.S. | E4 | 90 |
| Dūrā, Isr. Occ. | C7 | 41 |
| Durance, stm., Fr. | F6 | 16 |
| Durand, Ga., U.S. | D2 | 87 |
| Durand, Il., U.S. | A4 | 90 |
| Durand, Mi., U.S. | F6 | 99 |
| Durand, Wi., U.S. | D2 | 126 |
| Durango (Victoria de Durango), Mex. | C4 | 63 |
| Durango, state, Mex. | C4 | 63 |
| Durango, Co., U.S. | D3 | 83 |
| Durant, Ia., U.S. | C7 | 92 |
| Durant, Ms., U.S. | B4 | 101 |
| Durant, Ok., U.S. | D5 | 113 |
| Durants Neck, N.C., U.S. | A6 | 110 |
| Duraton, stm., Spain | B4 | 22 |
| Durazno, Ur. | E1 | 56 |
| Durazno, dept., Ur. | f8 | 54 |
| Durban, S. Afr. | C5 | 49 |
| Durbin, N.D., U.S. | C8 | 111 |
| Durbin, W.V., U.S. | C5 | 125 |
| Durbin Creek, stm., Fl., U.S. | m8 | 86 |
| Düren, W. Ger. | C2 | 18 |
| Durg, India | *D7 | 37 |
| Durgāpur, India | F11 | 37 |
| Durham, Ont. | C4 | 73 |
| Durham, Eng., U.K. | C6 | 13 |
| Durham, Ca., U.S. | C3 | 82 |
| Durham, Ct., U.S. | D5 | 84 |
| Durham, Ks., U.S. | D6 | 93 |
| Durham, Mo., U.S. | B6 | 102 |
| Durham, N.H., U.S. | D5 | 106 |
| Durham, N.C., U.S. | B4 | 110 |
| Durham, Or., U.S. | *B2 | 113 |
| Durham (Regional Municipality), co., Ont. | C6 | 73 |
| Durham, co., Eng., U.K. | F7 | 13 |
| Durham, co., N.C., U.S. | A4 | 110 |
| Durham Bridge, N.B. | C3 | 71 |
| Durham Downs, Austl. | E7 | 51 |
| Durham-Sud, Que. | D5 | 74 |
| Durhamville, Tn., U.S. | B2 | 119 |
| Durkee, Or., U.S. | C9 | 114 |
| Durmersheim, W. Ger. | E3 | 19 |
| Durmitor, mtn., Yugo. | C4 | 24 |
| Durness, Scot., U.K. | B4 | 13 |
| Durness, Kyle of, b., Scot., U.K. | B4 | 13 |
| Dürnford, Punta, c., W. Sah. | E1 | 44 |
| Dürrboden, Switz. | C8 | 21 |
| Durrell, Newf. | D4 | 72 |
| Durrës, Alb. | B2 | 25 |
| Durrow, Ire. | E4 | 11 |
| Dursey Island, i., Ire. | F1 | 11 |
| Dursunbey, Tur. | B12 | 40 |
| Duru, Zaire | A4 | 48 |
| D'Urville, Cape, c., Indon. | F9 | 34 |
| D'Urville Island, i., N.Z. | N14 | 51 |
| Duryea, Pa., U.S. | D10 | 115 |
| Dushan, China | F6 | 31 |
| Dushanbe, Sov. Un. | F9 | 29 |
| Dushaymī, Jazā'ir, is., Eg. | C2 | 41 |
| Dushore, Pa., U.S. | C9 | 115 |
| Dusky Sound, strt., N.Z. | P11 | 51 |
| Düsseldorf, W. Ger. | C3 | 18 |
| Dustin, Ok., U.S. | B6 | 113 |
| Dusty, N.M., U.S. | D2 | 108 |
| Dutch Creek, stm., Ar., U.S. | C2 | 81 |
| Dutchess, co., N.Y., U.S. | D7 | 109 |
| Dutch Harbor, Ak., U.S. | E6 | 79 |
| Dutch Island, i., R.I., U.S. | F4 | 116 |

Dutch John, Ut., U.S. — C6 121
Dutchtown, Mo., U.S. — D8 102
Dutton, Ont. — E3 73
Dutton, Al., U.S. — A4 78
Dutton, Mt., U.S. — C5 103
Dutton, Mount, mtn., Ut., U.S. — E3 121
Dutzow, Mo., U.S. — C7 102
Duval, Sask. — F3 75
Duval, co., Fl., U.S. — B5 86
Duval, co., Tx., U.S. — F3 120
Duvergé, Dom. Rep. — E8 64
Duvno, Yugo. — D3 24
Duxbury, Ma., U.S. — B6 98
Duxbury, Vt., U.S. — C3 122
Duyun, China — F6 31
Düzce, Tur. — B8 40
Dvina Bay, b., Sov. Un. — C16 8
Dvůr Králové [nad Labem], Czech. — C3 26
Dwārka, India — F2 37
Dwight, Il., U.S. — B5 90
Dwight, Ks., U.S. — D7 93
Dwight, Ma., U.S. — B3 98
Dwight, Ne., U.S. — C8 104
Dwight, N.D., U.S. — C9 111
Dwight D. Eisenhower Lock, N.Y., U.S. — f9 109
Dworshak Reservoir, res., Id., U.S. — C3 89
Dwyer, Wy., U.S. — D8 127
Dyakovo, Sov. Un. — r22 17
Dyatkovo, Sov. Un. — E10 27
Dyaul, i., Pap. N. Gui. — h13 50a
Dyce, Scot., U.K. — C6 13
Dyckesville, Wi., U.S. — D6 126
Dycusburg, Ky., U.S. — e9 94
Dyer, In., U.S. — B1 91
Dyer, Nv., U.S. — F3 105
Dyer, Tn., U.S. — A3 119
Dyer, co., Tn., U.S. — A2 119
Dyer Bay, Ont. — B3 73
Dyer Bay, b., Ont. — B3 73
Dyer Brook, Me., U.S. — B4 96
Dyer Island, i., R.I., U.S. — E5 116
Dyero, Mali — D3 45
Dyersburg, Tn., U.S. — A2 119
Dyersville, Ia., U.S. — B6 92
Dyess, Ar., U.S. — B5 81
Dyess Air Force Base, mil., Tx., U.S. — C3 120
Dyfed, co., Wales, U.K. — C3 12
Dyje, stm., Eur. — D3 26
Dykh-Tau, Mount, mtn., Sov. Un. — *E7 29
Dyment, Ont. — E5 70
Dysart, Sask. — G3 75
Dysart, Ia., U.S. — B5 92
Dzalaâta, Mong. — B2 32
Dzamîn Üüd, Mong. — B4 32
Dzaoudzi, May. — f9 49
Dzaudzhikau see Ordzhonikidze, Sov. Un. — E7 29
Dzavhan, stm., Mong. — B3 31
Dzerzhinsk, Sov. Un. — q20 27
Dzerzhinsk, Sov. Un. — C14 27
Dzerzhinsk, Sov. Un. — E6 27
Dzhalal-Abad, Sov. Un. — E8 28
Dzhambul, Sov. Un. — E10 29
Dzhankoy, Sov. Un. — I10 27
Dzhebel, Sov. Un. — B7 39
Dzhetygara, Sov. Un. — C6 28
Dzhezkazgan, Sov. Un. — D7 28
Dzhizak, Sov. Un. — G22 8
Dzhugdzhur Mountains, mts., Sov. Un. — D16 29
Dzhungarian Alatau Mountains, mts., Asia — D9 28
Dzhusaly, Sov. Un. — D6 28
Działdowo, Pol. — B6 26
Działoszyce, Pol. — C6 26
Dzierżoniów, Pol. — C4 26
Dzilam González, Mex. — C7 63
Dzioua, Cam. — C6 44
Dzitbalché, Mex. — C15 40
Dzungarian Basin see Junggar Pendi, China — B2 31
Dzuunmod, Mong. — B6 31

**E**

Eads, Co., U.S. — C8 83
Eads, Tn., U.S. — B2 119
Eagan, Mn., U.S. — n12 100
Eagan, Tn., U.S. — C10 119
Eagar, Az., U.S. — C6 80
Eagle, Ak., U.S. — C11 79
Eagle, Co., U.S. — B4 83
Eagle, Id., U.S. — F2 89
Eagle, Ne., U.S. — h12 104
Eagle, N.Y., U.S. — C2 109
Eagle, Wi., U.S. — F5 126
Eagle, co., Co., U.S. — B4 83
Eagle, stm., Newf. — B2 72
Eagle Bend, Mn., U.S. — D3 100
Eagle Bridge, N.Y., U.S. — C7 109
Eagle Butte, S.D., U.S. — C4 118
Eagle Cave, Wi., U.S. — E3 126
Eagle City, Ok., U.S. — B3 113
Eagle Cliff, mtn., U.S. — B3 89
Eagle Creek, Tn., U.S. — B4 119
Eagle Creek, stm., Sask. — F2 75
Eagle Creek, stm., In., U.S. — D5 91
Eagle Creek, stm., Ky., U.S. — B5 94
Eagle Creek Reservoir, res., In., U.S. — E5 91
Eagle Dam, In., U.S. — E4 91
Eagle Grove, Ia., U.S. — B4 92
Eagle Harbor, Mi., U.S. — A2 99
Eagle Key, i., Fl., U.S. — G6 86
Eagle Lake, Me., U.S. — A4 96
Eagle Lake, Mn., U.S. — F5 100
Eagle Lake, Tx., U.S. — E4 120
Eagle Lake, Wi., U.S. — *F5 126
Eagle Lake, l., U.S. — C5 70
Eagle Lake, l., Ca., U.S. — B3 82
Eagle Lake, l., Me., U.S. — B3 96
Eagle Lake, l., Me., U.S. — A4 96
Eagle Lake, l., Wi., U.S. — C4 126
Eagle Mills, Ar., U.S. — D3 81
Eagle Mountain, mtn., Mn., U.S. — k9 100
Eagle Mountain Lake, res., Tx., U.S. — m9 120
Eagle Nest, N.M., U.S. — A4 108
Eagle Nest Butte, mtn., S.D., U.S. — D4 118
Eaglenest Lake, l., Can. — D4 70
Eagle Nest Lake, l., N.M., U.S. — A4 108
Eagle Pass, Tx., U.S. — E2 120
Eagle Peak, mtn., Ca., U.S. — B3 82
Eagle Peak, mtn., Tx., U.S. — o12 120

Eagle Point, Or., U.S. — E4 114
Eagle River, Ont. — E5 70
Eagle River, Mi., U.S. — A2 99
Eagle River, Wi., U.S. — C4 126
Eagle Rock, Va., U.S. — C3 123
Eaglesham, Alta. — B2 68
Eagles Mere, Pa., U.S. — D8 115
Eagle Springs, N.C., U.S. — B3 110
Eagletail Mountains, mts., Az., U.S. — D2 80
Eagletail Peak, mtn., Az., U.S. — D2 80
Eagleton Village, Tn., U.S. — *D10 119
Eagletown, Ok., U.S. — C7 113
Eagleville, Ca., U.S. — B3 82
Eagleville, Ct., U.S. — B6 84
Eagleville, Mo., U.S. — A4 102
Eagleville, Tn., U.S. — B5 119
Eakly, Ok., U.S. — B3 113
Earle, Ar., U.S. — B5 81
Eardley, Que. — g11 73
Eardley Lake, l., Man. — C3 70
Earl Grey, Sask. — G3 75
Earlham, Ia., U.S. — C3 92
Earlimart, Ca., U.S. — E4 82
Earling, Ia., U.S. — C2 92
Earling, W.V., U.S. — n12 125
Earlington, Ky., U.S. — C2 94
Earl Island, i., Newf. — B3 72
Earl Park, In., U.S. — C3 91
Earlsboro, Ok., U.S. — B5 113
Earlton, Ks., U.S. — E8 93
Earlville, Il., U.S. — B5 90
Earlville, Ia., U.S. — B6 92
Earlville, N.Y., U.S. — C5 109
Early, Ia., U.S. — B2 92
Early, co., Ga., U.S. — E2 87
Early Branch, S.C., U.S. — F6 117
Earn, stm., Scot., U.K. — D5 13
Earn, Loch, l., Scot., U.K. — D4 13
Earth, Tx., U.S. — B1 120
Easky, Ire. — C3 11
Easley, S.C., U.S. — B2 117
East, stm., Ont. — B5 73
East, stm., Ct., U.S. — D5 84
East, stm., N.Y., U.S. — k13 109
East, stm., Wi., U.S. — h9 126
Eastaboga, Al., U.S. — B3 78
Eastabuchie, Ms., U.S. — D4 101
East Acton, Ma., U.S. — g10 98
East Alburgh, Vt., U.S. — B2 122
East Alstead, N.H., U.S. — D2 106
East Alton, Il., U.S. — E3 90
East Andover, Me., U.S. — D2 96
East Andover, N.H., U.S. — D3 106
East Angus, Que. — D6 74
East Arlington, Vt., U.S. — E2 122
East Aurora, N.Y., U.S. — C2 109
East Baldwin, Me., U.S. — E2 96
East Bangor, Pa., U.S. — E11 115
East Bank, W.V., U.S. — m13 125
East Barnard, Vt., U.S. — D3 122
East Barre, Vt., U.S. — C4 122
East Baton Rouge, co., La., U.S. — D4 95
East Bay, b., Fl., U.S. — u16 86
East Bay, b., Tx., U.S. — R15 120
East Beckwith Mountain, mtn., Co., U.S. — C3 83
East Bend, N.C., U.S. — A2 110
East Berbice-Corentyne, dept., Guy. — B3 59
East Berlin, Ct., U.S. — C5 84
East Berlin, Pa., U.S. — G8 115
East Bernard, Tx., U.S. — E4 120
East Bernstadt, Ky., U.S. — C5 94
East Bethel, Mn., U.S. — E5 100
East Bethel, Vt., U.S. — D3 122
East Billerica, Ma., U.S. — f11 98
East Blue Hill, Me., U.S. — D4 96
East Bonne Terre, Mo., U.S. — D7 102
East Boothbay, Me., U.S. — E3 96
East Borough, Ks., U.S. — g12 93
East Brady, Pa., U.S. — E2 115
East Braintree, Man. — E4 70
East Braintree, Vt., U.S. — D3 122
East Branch, N.Y., U.S. — D5 109
East Branch Clarion River Lake, res., Pa., U.S. — C4 115
East Brewster, Ma., U.S. — C7 98
East Brewton, Al., U.S. — D2 78
East Bridgewater, Ma., U.S. — B6 98
East Brimfield Lake, res., Ma., U.S. — B3 98
Eastbrook, Me., U.S. — D4 96
East Brookfield, Ma., U.S. — B3 98
East Brookfield, Vt., U.S. — C3 122
East Brooklyn, Ct., U.S. — B8 84
East Broughton, Que. — C6 74
East Brunswick, N.J., U.S. — C4 107
East Burke, Vt., U.S. — B5 122
East Butler, Pa., U.S. — E2 115
East Butte, mtn., Mt., U.S. — B5 103
East Cache Creek, stm., Ok., U.S. — C3 113
East Calais, Vt., U.S. — C4 122
East Canaan, Ct., U.S. — A2 84
East Candia, N.H., U.S. — D4 106
East Cape, c., N.Z. — L17 51
East Cape, c., Fl., U.S. — G5 86
East Carbon, Ut., U.S. — D5 121
East Carroll, co., La., U.S. — B4 95
East Chain, Mn., U.S. — G3 100
East Charleston, Vt., U.S. — B5 122
East Chelmsford, Ma., U.S. — f10 98
Eastchester, N.Y., U.S. — *n15 109
East Chicago, Il., U.S. — B3 90
East Chicago Heights, Il., U.S. — *k9 90
East China Sea, Asia — F10 31
East Chop, c., Ma., U.S. — D6 98
East Cleveland, Oh., U.S. — g9 112
East-Clifton, Que. — D6 74
East Columbia, Tx., U.S. — r14 120
East Compton, Ca., U.S. — *F4 82
East Concord, Vt., U.S. — C5 122
East Conway, N.H., U.S. — B4 106
East Corinth, Me., U.S. — D3 96
East Corinth, Vt., U.S. — C4 122
East Cote Blanche Bay, b., La., U.S. — E4 95
East Coulee, Alta. — D4 68
East Danville, Oh., U.S. — C2 112
East Dennis, Ma., U.S. — C7 98
East Detroit, Mi., U.S. — p16 99
East Dixfield, Me., U.S. — D2 96
East Dixmont, Me., U.S. — D3 96
East Dorset, Vt., U.S. — E2 122

East Douglas, Ma., U.S. — B4 98
East Dover, Me., U.S. — C3 96
East Dover, Vt., U.S. — F3 122
East Dubuque, Il., U.S. — A3 90
East Dummerston, Vt., U.S. — F3 122
East Eddington, Me., U.S. — D4 96
East Ellijay, Ga., U.S. — B2 87
East End Point, c., Bah. — m18 64
East Enterprise, In., U.S. — G8 91
East Falmouth, Ma., U.S. — C6 98
Eastern, prov., Ghana — E5 45
Eastern, prov., Kenya — B6 48
Eastern, prov., Zam. — D5 48
Eastern Channel, strt., Japan — J4 33
Eastern Ghāts, mts., India — E7 36
Eastern Island, i., Newf. — C4 72
Eastern Island, i., Mid. Is. — K4 52
Eastern Neck Island, i., Md., U.S. — B5 97
Eastern Point, c., Ma., U.S. — f13 98
Easterville, Man. — C2 70
East Fairfield, Vt., U.S. — B3 122
East Fairview, N.D., U.S. — B1 111
East Falmouth, Ma., U.S. — C6 98
East Farmingdale, N.Y., U.S. — *E7 109
East Farmington Heights, Ct., U.S. — C4 84
East Feliciana, co., La., U.S. — D4 95
East Flanders, prov., Bel. — C3 17
East Flat Rock, N.C., U.S. — f10 110
East Flevoland, reg., Neth. — B5 17
Eastford, Ct., U.S. — B7 84
East Fork, stm., Wy., U.S. — D3 127
East Fork Lake, res., Oh., U.S. — C1 112
East Foxboro, Ma., U.S. — B5 98
East Franklin, Vt., U.S. — B3 122
East Freetown, Ma., U.S. — C6 98
East Frisian Islands, is., W. Ger. — B3 18
East Fultonham, Oh., U.S. — C3 112
East Gaffney, S.C., U.S. — A4 117
East Galesburg, Il., U.S. — C3 90
Eastgate, Wa., U.S. — *e11 124
East Glacier Park, Mt., U.S. — B3 103
East Glastonbury, Ct., U.S. — C5 84
East Glenville, N.Y., U.S. — *C7 109
East Grafton, N.H., U.S. — C3 106
East Granby, Ct., U.S. — B5 84
East Grand Forks, Mn., U.S. — C2 100
East Grand Rapids, Mi., U.S. — F5 99
East Granville, Vt., U.S. — C3 122
East Greenville, Pa., U.S. — F10 115
East Greenwich, R.I., U.S. — D4 116
East Grinstead, Eng., U.K. — C8 12
East Gwillimbury, Ont. — C5 73
East Haddam, Ct., U.S. — D6 84
East Half Hollow Hills, N.Y., U.S. — *n15 109
Eastham, Ma., U.S. — C8 98
East Hampden, Me., U.S. — *D4 96
East Hampstead, N.H., U.S. — E4 106
East Hampton, Ct., U.S. — C5 84
Easthampton, Ma., U.S. — B2 98
East Hampton, N.Y., U.S. — n16 109
East Hanover, N.J., U.S. — *B4 107
East Hardwick, Vt., U.S. — B4 122
East Harpswell, Me., U.S. — g8 96
East Hartford, Ct., U.S. — B5 84
East Haven, Ct., U.S. — D4 84
East Haven, Vt., U.S. — B5 122
East Haverhill, N.H., U.S. — B3 106
East Hebron, N.H., U.S. — C3 106
East Helena, Mt., U.S. — D5 103
East Hemet, Ca., U.S. — *F5 82
East Hickory, Pa., U.S. — C3 115
East Highgate, Vt., U.S. — B3 122
East Hills, N.Y., U.S. — *E7 109
East Holden, Me., U.S. — D4 96
East Holderness, N.H., U.S. — C3 106
East Islip, N.Y., U.S. — *n15 109
East Jordan, Mi., U.S. — C5 99
East Jordan, N.S. — F5 71
East Juliette, Ga., U.S. — C3 87
East Kelowna, B.C. — E8 69
East Kilbride, Scot., U.K. — E4 13
East Killingly, Ct., U.S. — B8 84
East Kingston, N.H., U.S. — E4 106
Eastlake, Mi., U.S. — D4 99
East Lake, N.C., U.S. — B7 110
Eastlake, Oh., U.S. — A4 112
East Lake Tohopekaliga, l., Fl., U.S. — D5 86
East La Mirada, Ca., U.S. — *F5 82
East Lansing, Mi., U.S. — F6 99
East Laport, N.C., U.S. — f9 110
East Las Vegas, Nv., U.S. — G6 105
East Laurinburg, N.C., U.S. — C3 110
East Lebanon, Me., U.S. — E2 96
Eastleigh, Eng., U.K. — D6 12
East Lempster, N.H., U.S. — D2 106
East Liberty, Oh., U.S. — B2 112
East Litchfield, Ct., U.S. — B3 84
East Livermore, Me., U.S. — D2 96
East Liverpool, Oh., U.S. — B5 112
East Longmeadow, Ma., U.S. — B2 98
East Los Angeles, Ca., U.S. — m12 82
East Lynn, Il., U.S. — C6 90
East Lynn, W.V., U.S. — C2 125
East Lynne, Mo., U.S. — C3 102
East Lynn Lake, res., W.V., U.S. — C2 125
East Machias, Me., U.S. — D5 96
East Madison, Me., U.S. — D3 96
Eastmain, stm., Que. — F18 66
Eastmain-Opinaca, Réservoir, res., Que. — h11 74
Eastman, Que. — D5 74
Eastman, Ga., U.S. — D3 87
Eastman, Wi., U.S. — E2 126

East Meredith, N.Y., U.S. — C6 109
East Middlebury, Vt., U.S. — D2 122
East Midvale, Ut., U.S. — *C4 121
East Millbury, Ma., U.S. — *B4 98
East Millinocket, Me., U.S. — C4 96
East Moline, Il., U.S. — B3 90
East Monroe, Oh., U.S. — C2 112
East Montpelier, Vt., U.S. — C4 122
East Naples, Fl., U.S. — F5 86
East Newark, N.J., U.S. — k8 107
East New Market, Md., U.S. — C6 97
East Newnan, Ga., U.S. — C2 87
East New Portland, Me., U.S. — D2 96
East Nishnabotna, stm., Ia., U.S. — C2 92
East Northport, N.Y., U.S. — *n15 109
East Norriton, Pa., U.S. — o20 115
East Olympia, Wa., U.S. — C3 124
Easton, Ct., U.S. — D2 84
Easton, Il., U.S. — C4 90
Easton, Ks., U.S. — k15 93
Easton, Me., U.S. — B5 96
Easton, Md., U.S. — C5 97
Easton, Ma., U.S. — B5 98
Easton, Mn., U.S. — G5 100
Easton, Mo., U.S. — B3 102
Easton, N.H., U.S. — B3 106
Easton, Pa., U.S. — E11 115
Easton, Wa., U.S. — B4 124
Eastondale, Ma., U.S. — B5 98
Easton Reservoir, res., Ct., U.S. — E2 84
East Orange, N.J., U.S. — B4 107
East Orange, Vt., U.S. — C4 122
East Orland, Me., U.S. — D4 96
East Orleans, Ma., U.S. — C8 98
East Otis, Ma., U.S. — B1 98
East Otto, N.Y., U.S. — C2 109
East Palatka, Fl., U.S. — C5 86
East Palestine, Oh., U.S. — B5 112
East Palo Alto, Ca., U.S. — *D2 82
East Parsonfield, Me., U.S. — E2 96
East Pass, strt., Fl., U.S. — C2 86
East Patchogue, N.Y., U.S. — *n16 109
East Peacham, Vt., U.S. — C4 122
East Pea Ridge, W.V., U.S. — C2 125
East Pepperell, Ma., U.S. — A4 98
East Peru, Me., U.S. — D2 96
East Petersburg, Pa., U.S. — F9 115
East Pittsburg, Pa., U.S. — k14 115
East Point, B.C. — B7 69
East Point, Ga., U.S. — C2 87
East Point, c., P.E.I. — C8 71
East Point, c., Ma., U.S. — B6 98
East Point, c., N.J., U.S. — E2 107
East Point, c., V.I.U.S. — C6 65
East Poland, Me., U.S. — D2 96
East Poplar, Sask. — H3 75
East Portal, Co., U.S. — B5 83
East Porterville, Ca., U.S. — *D5 82
East Poultney, Vt., U.S. — D2 122
East Prairie, Mo., U.S. — E8 102
East Princeton, Ma., U.S. — B4 98
East Prospect, Pa., U.S. — G8 115
East Pryor Mountain, mtn., Mt., U.S. — E8 103
East Quogue, N.Y., U.S. — n16 109
East Randolph, N.Y., U.S. — C2 109
East Randolph, Vt., U.S. — D3 122
East Range, mts., Nv., U.S. — C4 105
East Retford, Eng., U.K. — A7 12
East Ridge, Tn., U.S. — h11 119
East Rindge, N.H., U.S. — E3 106
East River, Ct., U.S. — D5 84
East River Mountain, mts., U.S. — C1 123
East River Sheet Harbour, N.S. — E7 71
East Rochester, N.Y., U.S. — B3 109
East Rockaway, N.Y., U.S. — *k13 109
East Rockingham, N.C., U.S. — C3 110
East Rutherford, N.J., U.S. — h8 107
East Ryegate, Vt., U.S. — C4 122
East Saint Johnsbury, Vt., U.S. — C5 122
East Saint Louis, Il., U.S. — E3 90
East Salt Creek, stm., Co., U.S. — B2 83
East Sandwich, Ma., U.S. — C7 98
East Sebago, Me., U.S. — E2 96
East Siberian Sea, Sov. Un. — B18 29
Eastside, Or., U.S. — D2 114
East Sioux Falls, S.D., U.S. — D9 118
East Smithfield, Pa., U.S. — C8 115
Eastsound, Wa., U.S. — A3 124
East Sparta, Oh., U.S. — B4 112
East Spencer, N.C., U.S. — B2 110
East Springfield, N.Y., U.S. — C6 109
East Stoneham, Ma., U.S. — D2 96
East Stroudsburg, Pa., U.S. — D11 115
East Sudbury, Ma., U.S. — g10 98
East Sullivan, Me., U.S. — D4 96
East Sullivan, N.H., U.S. — E2 106
East Sumner, Me., U.S. — D2 96
East Sussex, co., Eng., U.K. — D7 12
East Swanzey, N.H., U.S. — E2 106
East Tawas, Mi., U.S. — D7 99
East Templeton, Ma., U.S. — A4 98
East Thermopolis, Wy., U.S. — *C4 127
East Thetford, Vt., U.S. — D4 122
East Thompson, Ct., U.S. — A8 84
East Troy, Wi., U.S. — F5 126
East Tustin, Ca., U.S. — *n13 82
East Unity, N.H., U.S. — D2 106
East Vestal, N.Y., U.S. — C5 109
East View, W.V., U.S. — k10 125
Eastville, Va., U.S. — C7 123
East Wakefield, N.H., U.S. — C4 106
East Walker, stm., U.S. — E2 105
East Wallingford, Vt., U.S. — E3 122
East Walpole, Ma., U.S. — h11 98
East Wareham, Ma., U.S. — C6 98
East Washington, Pa., U.S. — F1 115
East Waterboro, Me., U.S. — E2 96
East Waterford, Me., U.S. — D2 96
East Wenatchee, Wa., U.S. — B5 124
East Wilton, Me., U.S. — D2 96
East Windsor, N.J., U.S. — C3 107
East Windsor Hill, Ct., U.S. — B5 84
Eastwood, Ky., U.S. — g12 94
Eastwood, Mi., U.S. — *F5 99
Eastwood Hills, Ut., U.S. — *C4 121
East Woodstock, Ct., U.S. — B8 84

East Worcester, N.Y., U.S. — C6 109
East York, Ont. — D5 73
Eaton, Co., U.S. — A6 83
Eaton, In., U.S. — D6 91
Eaton, N.Y., U.S. — C5 109
Eaton, Oh., U.S. — C1 112
Eaton, Tn., U.S. — B2 119
Eaton, co., Mi., U.S. — F6 99
Eaton Center, N.H., U.S. — C4 106
Eatonia, Sask. — F1 75
Eaton Rapids, Mi., U.S. — F6 99
Eatonton, Ga., U.S. — C3 87
Eatontown, N.J., U.S. — C4 107
Eatonville, Wa., U.S. — C3 124
Eau Claire, Mi., U.S. — G4 99
Eau Claire, Wi., U.S. — D2 126
Eau Claire, co., Wi., U.S. — D2 126
Eau Claire, stm., Wi., U.S. — *D2 126
Eau Claire, Lac à l', l., Que. — g11 74
Eau Galle, Wi., U.S. — D1 126
Ebadon Island, i., Marsh Is. — S17 52
Ebb and Flow Lake, l., Man. — D2 70
Ebbw Vale (Blaenau Gwent), Wales, U.K. — C4 12
Ebeleben, E. Ger. — B5 19
Ebeltoft, Den. — B4 15
Ebenezer, Sask. — F4 75
Ebenezer, Ms., U.S. — C3 101
Ebenezer, Oh., U.S. — A1 112
Ebensburg, Pa., U.S. — F4 115
Eberbach, W. Ger. — D3 19
Ebermannstadt, W. Ger. — D6 19
Ebersbach, E. Ger. — B9 19
Ebersbach, W. Ger. — D5 19
Eberswalde [-Finow], E. Ger. — B6 18
Ebetsu, Japan — E10 33
Ebeye, Marsh Is. — S17 52
Ebinger, W. Ger. — D4 18
Eboli, Italy — D5 23
Ebolowa, Cam. — E2 46
Ebro, Fl., U.S. — u16 86
Ebro, Mn., U.S. — C3 100
Ebro, stm., Spain — B6 22
Eccles, W.V., U.S. — n13 125
Eceabat, Tur. — B6 25
Echague, Phil. — n13 34
Echallens, Switz. — C2 21
Ech Cheliff (Orléansville), Alg. — B5 44
Echeconnee Creek, stm., Ga., U.S. — D3 87
Echigawa, Japan — n15 33
Echo, Al., U.S. — D4 78
Echo, La., U.S. — C3 95
Echo, Mn., U.S. — F3 100
Echo, Or., U.S. — B7 114
Echo, Ut., U.S. — C4 121
Echo Bay, Nv., U.S. — G7 105
Echoing, stm., Can. — B6 70
Echo Lake, l., Me., U.S. — D3 96
Echo Lake, l., Vt., U.S. — B5 122
Echols, co., Ga., U.S. — F4 87
Echt, Neth. — C5 17
Echt, Scot., U.K. — C6 13
Echternach, Lux. — C6 17
Echuca, Austl. — G7 50
Écija, Spain — D3 22
Eckelson, N.D., U.S. — C7 111
Eckerman, Mi., U.S. — B5 99
Eckernförde, W. Ger. — A4 18
Eckernförder Bucht, b., W. Ger. — D4 15
Eckerty, In., U.S. — H4 91
Eckhart Mines, Md., U.S. — k13 97
Eckley, Co., U.S. — A8 83
Eckley, Pa., U.S. — E10 115
Eckman, N.D., U.S. — A4 111
Eckman, W.V., U.S. — *D3 125
Eckville, Alta. — C3 68
Eclectic, Al., U.S. — C3 78
Eclipse Sound, strt., N.W. Ter. — B17 66
Econfina, stm., Fl., U.S. — B3 86
Economy, In., U.S. — E7 91
Economy, N.S. — D6 71
Economy, Pa., U.S. — E1 115
Écorces, Rivière aux, stm., Que. — A6 74
Ecorse, Mi., U.S. — p15 99
Ecru, Ms., U.S. — A4 101
Ector, co., Tx., U.S. — D1 120
Ecuador, ctry., S.A. — B2 58
Ecum Secum, N.S. — E7 71
Ecum Secum Bridge, N.S. — E7 71
Ed, Eth. — G5 47
Eda, Sask. — D1 75
Edam, Sask. — D1 75
Edam, Neth. — B5 17
Edberg, Alta. — C4 68
Edcouch, Tx., U.S. — F4 120
Eddiceton, Ms., U.S. — D3 101
Eddington, Me., U.S. — D4 96
Eddrachillis Bay, b., Scot., U.K. — B3 13
Eddy, co., N.M., U.S. — E5 108
Eddy, co., N.D., U.S. — B7 111
Eddystone, Pa., U.S. — p20 115
Eddystone Rocks, Eng., U.K. — E4 11
Eddyville, Il., U.S. — F5 90
Eddyville, Ia., U.S. — C5 92
Eddyville, Ky., U.S. — e9 94
Eddyville, Ne., U.S. — C6 104
Ede, Neth. — B5 17
Ede, Nig. — *E5 45
Edéa, Cam. — E2 46
Eden, Austl. — H7 51
Eden, Man. — D2 70
Eden, Az., U.S. — D6 80
Eden, Ga., U.S. — D5 87
Eden, Id., U.S. — G4 89
Eden, Md., U.S. — D6 97
Eden, N.Y., U.S. — C2 109
Eden, N.C., U.S. — A3 110
Eden, S.D., U.S. — B8 118
Eden, Tx., U.S. — D3 120
Eden, Vt., U.S. — B4 122
Eden, Wi., U.S. — E5 126
Eden, Wy., U.S. — D3 127
Eden, stm., Eng., U.K. — C5 12
Edenborn, Pa., U.S. — G2 115
Edenderry, Ire. — C4 11
Eden Hill, hill, Ct., U.S. — B2 84
Eden Mills, Vt., U.S. — B4 122
Eden Prairie, Mn., U.S. — n12 100
Eden Valley, Mn., U.S. — E4 100

Edenville, Mi., U.S. — E6 99
Eder, stm., W. Ger. — C4 18
Edesville, Md., U.S. — B5 97
Edgar, Ne., U.S. — D8 104
Edgar, Wi., U.S. — D4 126
Edgar, co., Il., U.S. — D6 90
Edgard, La., U.S. — D5 95
Edgar Springs, Mo., U.S. — D6 102
Edgartown, Ma., U.S. — D6 98
Edge, i., Nor. — B12 128
Edgecombe, co., N.C., U.S. — B5 110
Edgecumbe, Cape, c., Ak., U.S. — m21 79
Edgefield, S.C., U.S. — D4 117
Edgefield, co., S.C., U.S. — D4 117
Edgeley, Sask. — G4 75
Edgeley, N.D., U.S. — C7 111
Edgemere, Md., U.S. — B5 97
Edgemont, Ar., U.S. — *B3 81
Edgemont, Ca., U.S. — *F5 82
Edgemont, S.D., U.S. — D2 118
Edgemoor, De., U.S. — A3 85
Edgemoor, S.C., U.S. — B5 117
Edgerly, La., U.S. — D2 95
Edgerton, Alta. — C5 68
Edgerton, Ks., U.S. — D8 93
Edgerton, Mn., U.S. — G2 100
Edgerton, Mo., U.S. — B3 102
Edgerton, Oh., U.S. — A1 112
Edgerton, Wi., U.S. — F4 126
Edgerton, Wy., U.S. — C6 127
Edgewater, Al., U.S. — f7 78
Edgewater, Co., U.S. — *B5 83
Edgewater, Fl., U.S. — D6 86
Edgewater, Md., U.S. — C4 97
Edgewater, N.J., U.S. — h9 107
Edgewater Park, N.J., U.S. — C3 107
Edgewood, B.C. — E8 69
Edgewood, Il., U.S. — E5 90
Edgewood, In., U.S. — D6 91
Edgewood, Ia., U.S. — B6 92
Edgewood, Ky., U.S. — h13 94
Edgewood, Md., U.S. — B5 97
Edgewood, N.M., U.S. — B3 108
Edgewood, Oh., U.S. — A5 112
Edgewood, Pa., U.S. — k14 115
Edgewood, Tx., U.S. — C5 120
Edgeworth, Pa., U.S. — h13 115
Edgeworthstown see Mostrim, Ire. — D4 11
Edgigen Island, i., Marsh Is. — S17 52
Édhessa, Grc. — B4 40
Edina, Mo., U.S. — A5 102
Edina, Mn., U.S. — F5 100
Edinboro, Pa., U.S. — C1 115
Edinburg, Il., U.S. — D4 90
Edinburg, Ms., U.S. — C4 101
Edinburg, N.Y., U.S. — B6 109
Edinburg, N.D., U.S. — A8 111
Edinburg, Tx., U.S. — F3 120
Edinburg, Va., U.S. — B4 123
Edinburgh, Scot., U.K. — C5 10
Edinburgh, In., U.S. — F6 91
Edirne, Tur. — B6 40
Edison, Ne., U.S. — D6 104
Edison, N.J., U.S. — *C4 107
Edison, Oh., U.S. — B3 112
Edison, Wa., U.S. — A3 124
Edisto, stm., S.C., U.S. — E6 117
Edisto, North Fork, stm., S.C., U.S. — D5 117
Edisto, South Fork, stm., S.C., U.S. — E5 117
Edisto Island, S.C., U.S. — F7 117
Edisto Island, i., S.C., U.S. — F7 117
Edith, Mount, mtn., Mt., U.S. — D5 103
Edithburgh, Austl. — G1 51
Edmeston, N.Y., U.S. — C5 109
Edmond, Ok., U.S. — B4 113
Edmond, W.V., U.S. — n13 125
Edmonds, Wa., U.S. — B3 124
Edmondson, Ar., U.S. — B5 81
Edmondson Heights, Md., U.S. — g10 97
Edmonson, co., Ky., U.S. — C3 94
Edmonton, Alta. — C4 68
Edmonton, Ky., U.S. — D4 94
Edmore, N.D., U.S. — A7 111
Edmore, Mi., U.S. — E5 99
Edmund Lake, l., Man. — B4 70
Edmunds, co., S.D., U.S. — B6 118
Edmundston, N.B. — B1 71
Edna, Ks., U.S. — E8 93
Edna, Tx., U.S. — E4 120
Edna, W.V., U.S. — h10 125
Edolo, Italy — D3 21
Edon, Oh., U.S. — A1 112
Édouard, Lac, l., Que. — C6 74
Edremit, Tur. — C6 25
Edremit, Gulf of, b., Tur. — C6 25
Edson, Alta. — C2 68
Edson, Ks., U.S. — C2 93
Edson Butte, mtn., Or., U.S. — E2 114
Eduardo Castex, Arg. — C4 56
Eduni, Mount, mtn., N.W. Ter. — D7 66
Edwall, Wa., U.S. — B8 124
Edwand, Alta. — B4 68
Edward, Lake, l., Afr. — B5 48
Edward, Ont. — h13 73
Edwards, Co., U.S. — C4 83
Edwards, Il., U.S. — C4 90
Edwards, Ms., U.S. — C3 101
Edwards, N.Y., U.S. — A5 109
Edwards, co., Il., U.S. — E5 90
Edwards, co., Ks., U.S. — E4 93
Edwards, co., Tx., U.S. — E2 120
Edwards Air Force Base, mil., Ca., U.S. — E5 82
Edwardsburg, Mi., U.S. — G4 99
Edwards Butte, mtn., Or., U.S. — B3 114
Edwards Plateau, plat., Tx., U.S. — D2 120
Edwardsport, In., U.S. — G3 91
Edwardsville, Al., U.S. — B4 78
Edwardsville, Il., U.S. — E4 90
Edwardsville, Ks., U.S. — k16 93
Edwardsville, Pa., U.S. — n17 115
Edwin, Al., U.S. — D4 78
Edzell, Scot., U.K. — C6 13
Eek, Ak., U.S. — C7 79
Eeklo, Bel. — B2 17
Eel, stm., Ca., U.S. — B2 82
Eel, stm., In., U.S. — C5 91
Eel, stm., In., U.S. — F5 91
Eferding, Aus. — D7 18
Effie, Mn., U.S. — C5 100
Effigy Mounds National Monument, Ia., U.S. — A6 92

| Name | Map Ref. | Page |
|---|---|---|
| Effingham, Il., U.S. | D5 | 90 |
| Effingham, Ks., U.S. | C8 | 93 |
| Effingham, N.H., U.S. | C5 | 106 |
| Effingham, S.C., U.S. | C8 | 117 |
| Effingham, co., Ga., U.S. | D5 | 87 |
| Effingham, co., Il., U.S. | D5 | 90 |
| Effingham Falls, N.H., U.S. | C4 | 106 |
| Effon-Alaiye, Nig. | *E5 | 45 |
| Efland, N.C., U.S. | A3 | 110 |
| Eforie Nord, Rom. | C9 | 24 |
| Eforie Sud (Vasile Roaită), Rom. | C9 | 24 |
| Ega, stm., Spain | A4 | 22 |
| Egadi Islands, is., Italy | E4 | 23 |
| Egan, S.D., U.S. | D9 | 118 |
| Egan Range, mts., Nv., U.S. | E7 | 105 |
| Eganville, Ont. | B7 | 73 |
| Egbert, Wy., U.S. | E8 | 127 |
| Egedesminde, Grnld. | *C15 | 61 |
| Egegik, Ak., U.S. | D8 | 79 |
| Egeland, N.D., U.S. | A6 | 111 |
| Egeln, E. Ger. | B6 | 19 |
| Eger, Hung. | B5 | 24 |
| Egersund, Nor. | H2 | 14 |
| Egerton, Mount, mtn., Ant. | A28 | 7 |
| Eggebek, W. Ger. | D3 | 15 |
| Eggenfelden, W. Ger. | E7 | 19 |
| Egg Harbor, Wi., U.S. | C6 | 126 |
| Egg Harbor City, N.J., U.S. | D3 | 107 |
| Egg Island Point, c., N.J., U.S. | E2 | 107 |
| Egg Lake, l., Sask. | C3 | 75 |
| Egilsstadir, Ice. | n25 | 14 |
| Égletons, Fr. | E5 | 16 |
| Eglin Air Force Base, mil., Fl., U.S. | u15 | 86 |
| Eglinton Island, i., N.W. Ter. | m28 | 61 |
| Eglisau, Switz. | A6 | 21 |
| Egmond aan Zee, Neth. | B4 | 17 |
| Egmont, Cape, c., N.Z. | M14 | 51 |
| Egmont, Mount, mtn., N.Z. | M15 | 51 |
| Egmont Bay, b., P.E.I. | C5 | 71 |
| Egmont Channel, strt., Fl., U.S. | p10 | 86 |
| Egmont Key, i., Fl., U.S. | p10 | 86 |
| Egnar, Co., U.S. | D2 | 83 |
| Egremont, Alta. | B4 | 68 |
| Egremont, Eng., U.K. | G9 | 13 |
| Eğridir, Tur. | D8 | 40 |
| Eğridir, l., Tur. | C8 | 40 |
| Eğrigöz, mtn., Tur. | C7 | 25 |
| Egtved, Den. | C3 | 15 |
| Egypt, Ar., U.S. | B5 | 81 |
| Egypt, Ga., U.S. | D5 | 87 |
| Egypt, Ma., U.S. | B6 | 98 |
| Egypt, Ms., U.S. | B5 | 101 |
| Egypt, ctry., Afr. | C2 | 38 |
| Egypt, Lake of, res., Il., U.S. | F5 | 90 |
| Egypt Lake, Fl., U.S. | *D4 | 86 |
| Ehrenberg, Az., U.S. | D1 | 80 |
| Ehrenfeld, Pa., U.S. | F4 | 115 |
| Ehrhardt, S.C., U.S. | E5 | 117 |
| Éibar, Spain | A4 | 22 |
| Eibau, E. Ger. | C9 | 19 |
| Eibenstock, E. Ger. | C7 | 19 |
| Eichstätt, W. Ger. | D5 | 18 |
| Eider, stm., W. Ger. | A4 | 18 |
| Eidsberg, Nor. | H4 | 14 |
| Eidson, Tn., U.S. | C10 | 119 |
| Eidsvold, Austl. | E9 | 50 |
| Eidsvoll, Nor. | G4 | 14 |
| Eielson Air Force Base, mil., Ak., U.S. | C10 | 79 |
| Eifel, mts., W. Ger. | C3 | 18 |
| Eiger, mtn., Switz. | C5 | 21 |
| Eigg, i., Scot., U.K. | B3 | 10 |
| Eigg, Sound of, strt., Scot., U.K. | D2 | 13 |
| Eightmile Creek, stm., Ks., U.S. | h12 | 93 |
| Eights Coast, Ant. | B3 | 7 |
| Eighty Eight, Ky., U.S. | D4 | 94 |
| Eikeren, l., Nor. | p28 | 14 |
| Eildon, Lake, res., Austl. | H6 | 51 |
| Eileen Lake, l., N.W. Ter. | D11 | 66 |
| Eilenburg, E. Ger. | C6 | 18 |
| Eiler Rasmussen, Cape, c., Grnld. | A16 | 128 |
| Eil Malk, i., Palau | R17 | 52 |
| Einbeck, W. Ger. | C4 | 18 |
| Eindhoven, Neth. | B6 | 16 |
| Einsiedeln, Switz. | B4 | 20 |
| Eirunepé, Braz. | C4 | 58 |
| Eisenach, E. Ger. | C5 | 18 |
| Eisenberg, E. Ger. | C6 | 19 |
| Eisenhower, Mount, mtn., N.H., U.S. | B4 | 106 |
| Eisenhüttenstadt, E. Ger. | B7 | 18 |
| Eisenstadt, Aus. | E8 | 18 |
| Eiserfeld, W. Ger. | C2 | 19 |
| Eisfeld, E. Ger. | C5 | 19 |
| Eisleben, E. Ger. | C5 | 18 |
| Eita, Kir. | R18 | 52 |
| Eita, i., Kir. | R18 | 52 |
| Eitorf, W. Ger. | C2 | 19 |
| Eitzen, Mn., U.S. | G7 | 100 |
| Ejby, Den. | C3 | 15 |
| Ejea de los Caballeros, Spain | A5 | 22 |
| Ejeda, Madag. | h8 | 49 |
| Ejigbo, Nig. | *E5 | 45 |
| Ejstrup, Den. | C3 | 15 |
| Ejutla de Crespo, Mex. | D5 | 63 |
| Ekalaka, Mt., U.S. | E12 | 103 |
| Ekenäs, Fin. | G10 | 14 |
| Ekeren (part of Antwerp), Bel. | C4 | 17 |
| Ekeren, Sov. Un. | D16 | 29 |
| Ekimchan, Sov. Un. | G21 | 29 |
| Ekoln, l., Swe. | t35 | 14 |
| Ekron, Ky., U.S. | C3 | 94 |
| Eksjö, Swe. | I6 | 14 |
| Ekumakoko, Zaire | B3 | 48 |
| Ekwan, stm., Ont. | F15 | 66 |
| Ekwok, Ak., U.S. | D8 | 79 |
| El Aaiún, W. Sah. | D2 | 44 |
| Elaine, Ar., U.S. | C5 | 81 |
| Elamanchili, India | I9 | 37 |
| Elamton, Ky., U.S. | C6 | 94 |
| Elamville, Al., U.S. | D4 | 78 |
| Eland, Wi., U.S. | D4 | 126 |
| El Arahal, Spain | D3 | 22 |
| Elassón, Grc. | C4 | 25 |
| Elat, Isr. | E6 | 41 |
| Elazığ, Tur. | C12 | 40 |
| Elba, Al., U.S. | D3 | 78 |
| Elba, Mi., U.S. | G5 | 89 |
| Elba, Mi., U.S. | E7 | 99 |
| Elba, Ne., U.S. | F6 | 100 |
| Elba, Ne., U.S. | C7 | 104 |
| Elba, N.Y., U.S. | *B2 | 109 |
| Elba, i., Italy | C3 | 23 |
| El Banco, Col. | B3 | 60 |
| Elbasani, Alb. | B3 | 40 |
| El Baúl, Ven. | B4 | 60 |
| Elbe (Labe), stm., Eur. | B4 | 18 |
| Elberfeld, In., U.S. | H3 | 91 |
| Elberon, Ia., U.S. | B5 | 92 |
| Elbert, Co., U.S. | B6 | 83 |
| Elbert, Tx., U.S. | C3 | 120 |
| Elbert, co., Co., U.S. | B6 | 83 |
| Elbert, co., Ga., U.S. | B4 | 87 |
| Elbert, Mount, mtn., Co., U.S. | B4 | 83 |
| Elberta, Al., U.S. | E2 | 78 |
| Elberta, Ga., U.S. | D3 | 87 |
| Elberta, Mi., U.S. | D4 | 99 |
| Elberta, Ut., U.S. | D4 | 121 |
| Elberton, Ga., U.S. | B4 | 87 |
| Elbeuf, Fr. | C4 | 16 |
| El Beyyadh, Alg. | C5 | 44 |
| Elbigenalp, Aus. | B6 | 20 |
| Elbing, Ks., U.S. | f12 | 93 |
| Elbistan, Tur. | C11 | 40 |
| Elblag, Pol. | A5 | 26 |
| El Bluff, Nic. | E8 | 63 |
| El Bolsón, Arg. | C2 | 54 |
| El Bonillo, Spain | C4 | 22 |
| El Bordo, Col. | C2 | 60 |
| El Boulaïda (Blida), Alg. | B5 | 44 |
| Elbow, Sask. | F2 | 75 |
| Elbow, stm., Alta. | D3 | 68 |
| Elbow Lake, Mn., U.S. | E3 | 100 |
| Elbow Lake, l., Man. | B1 | 70 |
| Elbridge, Tn., U.S. | A2 | 119 |
| Elbrus, Mount, mtn., Sov. Un. | E7 | 29 |
| Elburg, Neth. | B5 | 17 |
| El Burgo de Osma, Spain | B4 | 22 |
| Elburn, Il., U.S. | B5 | 90 |
| Elburz Mountains, mts., Iran | B5 | 38 |
| El Cajon, Ca., U.S. | F5 | 82 |
| El Callao, Ven. | B5 | 60 |
| El Campo, Tx., U.S. | E4 | 120 |
| El Capitan, mtn., Mt., U.S. | D2 | 103 |
| El Capitan Reservoir, res., Ca., U.S. | o16 | 82 |
| El Carmen, Bol. | C4 | 55 |
| El Carmen de Bolívar, Col. | B2 | 60 |
| El Carrizo, Mex. | B3 | 63 |
| El Centro, Ca., U.S. | F6 | 82 |
| El Cerrito, Ca., U.S. | h8 | 82 |
| El Cerro, Bol. | C3 | 55 |
| El Chaparro, Ven. | B4 | 60 |
| Elche, Spain | C5 | 22 |
| Elcho, Wi., U.S. | C4 | 126 |
| Elco, Il., U.S. | F4 | 90 |
| El Cocuy, Col. | B3 | 60 |
| El Cuervo Butte, mtn., N.M., U.S. | k9 | 108 |
| Elda, Spain | C5 | 22 |
| Elde, stm., E. Ger. | B5 | 18 |
| Elderon, Wi., U.S. | D4 | 126 |
| Eldersley, Sask. | E4 | 75 |
| Elderton, Pa., U.S. | E3 | 115 |
| El Diviso, Col. | C2 | 60 |
| El Djelfa, Alg. | C5 | 44 |
| El Djouf, des., Afr. | B3 | 45 |
| Eldon, P.E.I. | C7 | 71 |
| Eldon, Ia., U.S. | D5 | 92 |
| Eldon, Mo., U.S. | C5 | 102 |
| Eldora, Ia., U.S. | B4 | 92 |
| Eldorado, Braz. | C3 | 56 |
| Eldorado, Ont. | C7 | 73 |
| Eldorado, Sask. | m7 | 75 |
| Eldorado, Mex. | C3 | 63 |
| El Dorado, Ar., U.S. | D3 | 81 |
| Eldorado, Ga., U.S. | E3 | 87 |
| Eldorado, Il., U.S. | F5 | 90 |
| El Dorado, Ks., U.S. | E7 | 93 |
| Eldorado, Md., U.S. | C6 | 97 |
| Eldorado, N.C., U.S. | B2 | 110 |
| El Dorado, Oh., U.S. | C1 | 112 |
| El Dorado, Ok., U.S. | C2 | 113 |
| Eldorado, Tx., U.S. | D2 | 120 |
| El Dorado, Ven. | B5 | 60 |
| El Dorado, co., Ca., U.S. | C3 | 82 |
| Eldorado Peak, mtn., Wa., U.S. | A4 | 124 |
| Eldorado Springs, Co., U.S. | B5 | 83 |
| El Dorado Springs, Mo., U.S. | D3 | 102 |
| Eldorendo, Ga., U.S. | E2 | 87 |
| Eldoret, Kenya | A6 | 48 |
| Eldred, Mn., U.S. | C2 | 100 |
| Eldred, Pa., U.S. | C5 | 115 |
| Eldridge, Al., U.S. | B2 | 78 |
| Eldridge, Ca., U.S. | C2 | 82 |
| Eldridge, Mo., U.S. | D5 | 102 |
| Eldridge, N.D., U.S. | C7 | 111 |
| Eleanor, W.V., U.S. | C3 | 125 |
| Electra, Tx., U.S. | B3 | 120 |
| Electra Lake, res., Co., U.S. | D3 | 83 |
| Electric Mills, Ms., U.S. | C5 | 101 |
| Electric Peak, mtn., Co., U.S. | C5 | 83 |
| Electric Peak, mtn., Mt., U.S. | E6 | 103 |
| Elektrogorsk, Sov. Un. | n18 | 27 |
| Elektrostal, Sov. Un. | n18 | 27 |
| El Encanto Heights, Ca., U.S. | *E4 | 82 |
| Elephant Butte, mtn., N.M., U.S. | D2 | 108 |
| Elephant Butte Reservoir, res., N.M., U.S. | D2 | 108 |
| Elephant Island, i., B.A.T. | C7 | 7 |
| Elephant Mountain, mtn., Me., U.S. | D2 | 96 |
| El Escorial, Spain | o16 | 22 |
| El Eulma, Alg. | B6 | 44 |
| Eleusis see Elevsís, Grc. | g11 | 25 |
| Eleuthera, i., Bah. | B5 | 56 |
| Eleva, Wi., U.S. | D2 | 126 |
| Eleven Mile Canyon Reservoir, res., Co., U.S. | C5 | 83 |
| Eleven Point, stm., U.S. | A4 | 81 |
| Elevsís (Eleusis), Grc. | g11 | 25 |
| Elevsís, Gulf of, b., Grc. | g11 | 25 |
| Elfin Cove, Ak., U.S. | k21 | 79 |
| Elfros, Sask. | F4 | 75 |
| Elfrida, Az., U.S. | F6 | 80 |
| El Fud, Eth. | D5 | 47 |
| El Fuerte, Mex. | B3 | 63 |
| El Galhak, Sud. | C3 | 47 |
| El Ghazawet, Alg. | B4 | 44 |
| Elgin, Man. | E1 | 70 |
| Elgin, N.B. | D4 | 71 |
| Elgin, Scot., U.K. | B5 | 10 |
| Elgin, Al., U.S. | A2 | 78 |
| Elgin, Az., U.S. | F5 | 80 |
| Elgin, Ia., U.S. | B6 | 92 |
| Elgin, Il., U.S. | A5 | 90 |
| Elgin, Mn., U.S. | F6 | 100 |
| Elgin, N.D., U.S. | C4 | 111 |
| Elgin, Ne., U.S. | C7 | 104 |
| Elgin, Or., U.S. | B9 | 114 |
| Elgin, S.C., U.S. | C6 | 117 |
| Elgin, Tn., U.S. | C9 | 119 |
| Elgin, Tx., U.S. | D4 | 120 |
| Elgin, Ut., U.S. | E5 | 121 |
| Elgin, co., Ont. | E3 | 73 |
| Elgol, Scot., U.K. | C2 | 13 |
| Elgon, Mount, mtn., Afr. | A5 | 48 |
| El Grara, Alg. | C5 | 44 |
| El Grullo, Mex. | n11 | 63 |
| El Hecú, Arg. | B2 | 54 |
| Eli, Ne., U.S. | B4 | 104 |
| Eliasville, Tx., U.S. | C3 | 120 |
| Elida, N.M., U.S. | D6 | 108 |
| Elida, Oh., U.S. | B1 | 112 |
| Elikón Óros (Helicon), mtn., Grc. | g9 | 25 |
| Elila, stm., Zaire | B4 | 48 |
| Elim, Ak., U.S. | C7 | 79 |
| El Indio, Tx., U.S. | E2 | 120 |
| Eliot, Me., U.S. | E2 | 96 |
| Élisabethville see Lubumbashi, Zaire | D4 | 48 |
| Elista, Sov. Un. | H15 | 27 |
| Elizabeth, Austl. | F6 | 50 |
| Elizabeth, Co., U.S. | B6 | 83 |
| Elizabeth, Ga., U.S. | C2 | 87 |
| Elizabeth, Il., U.S. | A3 | 90 |
| Elizabeth, In., U.S. | H6 | 91 |
| Elizabeth, La., U.S. | D3 | 95 |
| Elizabeth, Mn., U.S. | D2 | 100 |
| Elizabeth, Ms., U.S. | B3 | 101 |
| Elizabeth, N.J., U.S. | B4 | 107 |
| Elizabeth, W.V., U.S. | B3 | 125 |
| Elizabeth, Cape, c., Wa., U.S. | B1 | 124 |
| Elizabeth City, N.C., U.S. | A6 | 110 |
| Elizabeth Islands, is., Ma., U.S. | D6 | 98 |
| Elizabethton, Tn., U.S. | C11 | 119 |
| Elizabethtown, Il., U.S. | F5 | 90 |
| Elizabethtown, In., U.S. | F6 | 91 |
| Elizabethtown, Ky., U.S. | C4 | 94 |
| Elizabethtown, N.Y., U.S. | A7 | 109 |
| Elizabethtown, N.C., U.S. | C4 | 110 |
| Elizabethtown, Pa., U.S. | F8 | 115 |
| Elizabethville, Pa., U.S. | E8 | 115 |
| El Jadida, Mor. | C3 | 44 |
| El Jebel, Co., U.S. | B3 | 83 |
| Elk, Pol. | B7 | 26 |
| Elk, Ca., U.S. | C2 | 82 |
| Elk, Wa., U.S. | A8 | 124 |
| Elk, co., Ks., U.S. | E7 | 93 |
| Elk, co., Pa., U.S. | D4 | 115 |
| Elk, stm., B.C. | D10 | 69 |
| Elk, stm., U.S. | A2 | 78 |
| Elk, stm., Co., U.S. | A4 | 83 |
| Elk, stm., Ks., U.S. | E7 | 93 |
| Elk, stm., W.V., U.S. | C3 | 125 |
| Elk, stm., Wi., U.S. | C3 | 126 |
| Elk, stm., N.H., U.S. | B4 | 106 |
| El Kairouan, Tun. | B7 | 44 |
| El Kala, Alg. | F2 | 23 |
| El Kasserine, Tun. | B6 | 44 |
| Elkatawa, Ky., U.S. | C6 | 94 |
| Elk City, Id., U.S. | D3 | 89 |
| Elk City, Ks., U.S. | E8 | 93 |
| Elk City, Ne., U.S. | g12 | 104 |
| Elk City, Ok., U.S. | B2 | 113 |
| Elk Creek Lake, res., Ks., U.S. | E7 | 93 |
| Elk Creek, Ca., U.S. | C2 | 82 |
| Elk Creek, Ne., U.S. | D9 | 104 |
| Elk Creek, Va., U.S. | D1 | 123 |
| Elk Creek, stm., Ok., U.S. | B2 | 113 |
| Elk Creek, stm., S.D., U.S. | C3 | 118 |
| El Kef, Tun. | B6 | 44 |
| Elk Falls, Ks., U.S. | E7 | 93 |
| Elkford, B.C. | D10 | 69 |
| Elk Garden, W.V., U.S. | B5 | 125 |
| Elk Grove, Ca., U.S. | C3 | 82 |
| Elk Grove Village, Il., U.S. | h9 | 90 |
| Elkhart, Il., U.S. | C4 | 90 |
| Elkhart, In., U.S. | A6 | 91 |
| Elkhart, Ia., U.S. | e8 | 92 |
| Elkhart, Ks., U.S. | E2 | 93 |
| Elkhart, Tx., U.S. | D5 | 120 |
| Elkhart, co., In., U.S. | A6 | 91 |
| Elkhart, stm., In., U.S. | B6 | 91 |
| Elkhead Mountains, mts., Co., U.S. | A4 | 83 |
| Elk Horn, Ia., U.S. | C2 | 92 |
| Elkhorn, Man. | E1 | 70 |
| Elkhorn, Wi., U.S. | F5 | 126 |
| Elkhorn, W.V., U.S. | *D3 | 125 |
| Elkhorn, North Fork, stm., Ne., U.S. | B8 | 104 |
| Elkhorn, South Fork, stm., Ne., U.S. | B8 | 104 |
| Elkhorn City, Ky., U.S. | C7 | 94 |
| Elkhorn Peaks, mts., Id., U.S. | F7 | 89 |
| Elkhovo, Bul. | D8 | 24 |
| Elkin, N.C., U.S. | A2 | 110 |
| Elkins, Ar., U.S. | A1 | 81 |
| Elkins, N.H., U.S. | D3 | 106 |
| Elkins, W.V., U.S. | C5 | 125 |
| Elkins Park, Pa., U.S. | F11 | 115 |
| Elk Island, i., Man. | D3 | 70 |
| Elk Island National Park, Alta. | C4 | 68 |
| Elkland, Mo., U.S. | D4 | 102 |
| Elkland, Pa., U.S. | C7 | 115 |
| Elk Mills, Md., U.S. | A6 | 97 |
| Elkmont, Al., U.S. | A3 | 78 |
| Elkmont, Tn., U.S. | D10 | 119 |
| Elk Mound, Wi., U.S. | D2 | 126 |
| Elk Mountain, Wy., U.S. | E6 | 127 |
| Elk Mountain, mtn., N.M., U.S. | D1 | 108 |
| Elk Mountain, mtn., Wy., U.S. | E6 | 127 |
| Elk Mountains, mts., U.S. | D1 | 118 |
| Elk Mountains, mts., Co., U.S. | B3 | 83 |
| Elko, B.C. | E10 | 69 |
| Elko, Ga., U.S. | D3 | 87 |
| Elko, Nv., U.S. | C6 | 105 |
| Elko, S.C., U.S. | E5 | 117 |
| Elko, co., Nv., U.S. | B5 | 105 |
| Elk Park, N.C., U.S. | A1 | 110 |
| Elk Peak, mtn., Mt., U.S. | D5 | 103 |
| Elk Point, Alta. | C5 | 68 |
| Elk Point, S.D., U.S. | E9 | 118 |
| Elk Ranch, Ar., U.S. | A2 | 81 |
| Elk Rapids, Mi., U.S. | D5 | 99 |
| Elkridge, Md., U.S. | B4 | 97 |
| Elk River, Id., U.S. | C2 | 89 |
| Elk River, Mn., U.S. | E5 | 100 |
| Elk Springs, Co., U.S. | A2 | 83 |
| Elkton, Fl., U.S. | C5 | 86 |
| Elkton, Ky., U.S. | D2 | 94 |
| Elkton, Md., U.S. | A6 | 97 |
| Elkton, Mi., U.S. | E7 | 99 |
| Elkton, Or., U.S. | D3 | 114 |
| Elkton, S.D., U.S. | C9 | 118 |
| Elkton, Tn., U.S. | B5 | 119 |
| Elkton, Va., U.S. | B4 | 123 |
| Elk Valley, Tn., U.S. | C9 | 119 |
| Elkville, Il., U.S. | F4 | 90 |
| Ellabell, Ga., U.S. | D5 | 87 |
| Ellamore, W.V., U.S. | C4 | 125 |
| Ellaville, Ga., U.S. | D2 | 87 |
| Ellen, Mount, mtn., Ut., U.S. | E5 | 121 |
| Ellen, Mount, mtn., Vt., U.S. | C3 | 122 |
| Ellenboro, N.C., U.S. | B1 | 110 |
| Ellenboro, W.V., U.S. | B3 | 125 |
| Ellenburg Center, N.Y., U.S. | f11 | 109 |
| Ellendale, De., U.S. | E4 | 85 |
| Ellendale, Mn., U.S. | G5 | 100 |
| Ellendale, N.D., U.S. | C7 | 111 |
| Ellensburg, Wa., U.S. | C5 | 124 |
| Ellenton, Fl., U.S. | E4 | 86 |
| Ellenton, Ga., U.S. | E3 | 87 |
| Ellenville, N.Y., U.S. | D6 | 109 |
| Ellenwood, Ga., U.S. | h8 | 87 |
| Ellerbe, N.C., U.S. | B3 | 110 |
| Eller Island, i., Marsh Is. | S17 | 52 |
| Ellershouse, N.S. | E6 | 71 |
| Ellerslie, Ga., U.S. | D2 | 87 |
| Ellerslie, Md., U.S. | k13 | 97 |
| Ellesmere Island, i., N.W. Ter. | m35 | 66 |
| Ellesmere Port, Eng., U.K. | A5 | 12 |
| Ellettsville, In., U.S. | F4 | 91 |
| Ellice Islands see Tuvalu, ctry., Oc. | G10 | 6 |
| Ellichpur see Achalpur, India | G6 | 37 |
| Ellicottville, N.Y., U.S. | C2 | 109 |
| Ellijay, Ga., U.S. | B2 | 87 |
| Ellington, Ct., U.S. | B6 | 84 |
| Ellington, Mo., U.S. | D7 | 102 |
| Ellinwood, Ks., U.S. | D5 | 93 |
| Elliot, S. Afr. | H5 | 49 |
| Elliot Lake, Ont. | A2 | 73 |
| Elliott, Il., U.S. | C5 | 90 |
| Elliott, Ms., U.S. | B4 | 101 |
| Elliott, N.D., U.S. | C8 | 111 |
| Elliott, S.C., U.S. | C7 | 117 |
| Elliott, co., Ky., U.S. | B6 | 94 |
| Elliott Bay, b., Wa., U.S. | e11 | 124 |
| Elliott Key, i., Fl., U.S. | G6 | 86 |
| Elliott Knob, mtn., Va., U.S. | B3 | 123 |
| Ellis, Ks., U.S. | D4 | 93 |
| Ellis, S.D., U.S. | D9 | 118 |
| Ellis, co., Ks., U.S. | D4 | 93 |
| Ellis, co., Ok., U.S. | A2 | 113 |
| Ellis, co., Tx., U.S. | C4 | 120 |
| Ellis, stm., N.H., U.S. | B4 | 106 |
| Ellisburg, N.Y., U.S. | B4 | 109 |
| Ellisdale, N.J., U.S. | C3 | 107 |
| Ellison Bay, Wi., U.S. | C6 | 126 |
| Ellis Pond, l., Me., U.S. | D2 | 96 |
| Elliston, Mt., U.S. | D4 | 103 |
| Elliston, Newf. | D5 | 72 |
| Elliston, Va., U.S. | C2 | 123 |
| Ellistown, Ms., U.S. | A5 | 101 |
| Ellisville, Il., U.S. | C3 | 90 |
| Ellisville, Mo., U.S. | f12 | 102 |
| Ellon, Scot., U.K. | B5 | 10 |
| Ellore see Elūru, India | E7 | 36 |
| Elloree, S.C., U.S. | D6 | 117 |
| Ellport, Pa., U.S. | E1 | 115 |
| Ellrich, E. Ger. | B5 | 19 |
| Ells, stm., Alta. | A4 | 68 |
| Ellsinore, Mo., U.S. | E7 | 102 |
| Ellston, Ia., U.S. | D3 | 92 |
| Ellsworth, Il., U.S. | C5 | 90 |
| Ellsworth, Ks., U.S. | D5 | 93 |
| Ellsworth, Me., U.S. | D4 | 96 |
| Ellsworth, Mi., U.S. | C5 | 99 |
| Ellsworth, Mn., U.S. | G2 | 100 |
| Ellsworth, Pa., U.S. | F1 | 115 |
| Ellsworth, Wi., U.S. | D1 | 126 |
| Ellsworth, co., Ks., U.S. | D5 | 93 |
| Ellsworth Air Force Base, mil., S.D., U.S. | C2 | 118 |
| Ellsworth Hill, mtn., Ct., U.S. | B2 | 84 |
| Ellsworth Land, reg., Ant. | B4 | 7 |
| Ellsworth Mountains, mts., Ant. | B5 | 7 |
| Ellwangen, W. Ger. | D5 | 18 |
| Ellwood City, Pa., U.S. | E1 | 115 |
| Elm, stm., N.D., U.S. | B8 | 111 |
| Elma, Ia., U.S. | A5 | 92 |
| Elma, Wa., U.S. | C2 | 124 |
| El Mahdia, Tun. | B7 | 44 |
| Elmali, Tur. | D7 | 25 |
| El Manteco, Ven. | B5 | 60 |
| Elm City, N.C., U.S. | B5 | 110 |
| Elm Creek, Man. | E2 | 70 |
| Elm Creek, Ne., U.S. | D6 | 104 |
| Elm Creek, stm., Ks., U.S. | D7 | 93 |
| Elmdale, Ks., U.S. | D7 | 93 |
| Elmendorf, Tx., U.S. | k7 | 120 |
| Elmendorf Air Force Base, mil., Ak., U.S. | C10 | 79 |
| El Menia, Alg. | C5 | 44 |
| Elmer, Mo., U.S. | B5 | 102 |
| Elmer, N.J., U.S. | D2 | 107 |
| Elmer, Ok., U.S. | C2 | 113 |
| El Metlaoui, Tun. | C6 | 44 |
| El Mghayra, Alg. | C5 | 44 |
| Elm Grove, La., U.S. | B2 | 95 |
| Elmhurst, Il., U.S. | B6 | 90 |
| Elmhurst, Pa., U.S. | D10 | 115 |
| El Milagro, Arg. | A3 | 54 |
| Elmira, P.E.I. | C7 | 71 |
| Elmira, Mi., U.S. | C6 | 99 |
| Elmira, N.Y., U.S. | C4 | 109 |
| Elmira, Or., U.S. | C3 | 114 |
| Elmira, W.V., U.S. | C4 | 125 |
| Elmira Heights, N.Y., U.S. | C4 | 109 |
| Elmo, Mo., U.S. | A2 | 102 |
| Elmo, Ut., U.S. | D5 | 121 |
| Elmodel, Ga., U.S. | E2 | 87 |
| El Moknine, Tun. | B7 | 44 |
| Elmont, N.Y., U.S. | k13 | 109 |
| El Monte, Ca., U.S. | *E4 | 82 |
| Elmore, Al., U.S. | C3 | 78 |
| Elmore, Mn., U.S. | G4 | 100 |
| Elmore, Oh., U.S. | A2 | 112 |
| Elmore, co., Al., U.S. | C3 | 78 |
| Elmore, co., Id., U.S. | F3 | 89 |
| Elmore City, Ok., U.S. | C4 | 113 |
| El Morro National Monument, N.M., U.S. | B1 | 108 |
| El Mreïti, well, Maur. | B3 | 45 |
| Elmsdale, N.S. | E6 | 71 |
| Elmshorn, W. Ger. | B4 | 18 |
| Elm Springs, Ar., U.S. | A1 | 81 |
| Elm Springs, S.D., U.S. | C3 | 118 |
| Elm Springs Colony, S.D., U.S. | D8 | 118 |
| Elmsville, N.B. | D3 | 71 |
| Elmvale, Ont. | C5 | 73 |
| Elmwood, Ont. | C3 | 73 |
| Elmwood, Il., U.S. | C3 | 90 |
| Elmwood, Ma., U.S. | B6 | 98 |
| Elmwood, Ne., U.S. | D9 | 104 |
| Elmwood, Ok., U.S. | A1 | 113 |
| Elmwood, Wi., U.S. | D1 | 126 |
| Elmwood Park, Il., U.S. | k9 | 90 |
| Elmwood Park, N.J., U.S. | h8 | 107 |
| Elmwood Place, Oh., U.S. | o13 | 112 |
| Elna, Ky., U.S. | C7 | 94 |
| Elne, Fr. | F5 | 16 |
| El Nevado, Cerro, mtn., Arg. | B3 | 54 |
| Elnora, Alta. | D4 | 68 |
| Elnora, In., U.S. | G3 | 91 |
| Eloise, Fl., U.S. | E5 | 86 |
| Elon College, N.C., U.S. | A3 | 110 |
| Elora, Ont. | D4 | 73 |
| Elora, Tn., U.S. | B5 | 119 |
| El Oro, prov., Ec. | B2 | 58 |
| Elorza, Ven. | B4 | 60 |
| El Oso, Ven. | B4 | 60 |
| Eloy, Az., U.S. | E4 | 80 |
| El Palmar, Ven. | B5 | 60 |
| El Palmito, Mex. | B3 | 63 |
| El Pao, Ven. | B5 | 60 |
| El Paraíso, Hond. | D4 | 62 |
| Elphin, Ire. | D3 | 11 |
| Elphinstone, Man. | D1 | 70 |
| El Portal, Ca., U.S. | D4 | 82 |
| El Porvenir, N.M., U.S. | B4 | 108 |
| El Prado, N.M., U.S. | A4 | 108 |
| El Progreso, Ec. | g6 | 58 |
| El Progreso, Hond. | C4 | 62 |
| El Puerto de Santa María, Spain | D2 | 22 |
| El Qoll, Alg. | B6 | 44 |
| Elquí, stm., Chile | F1 | 55 |
| Elrama, Pa., U.S. | F2 | 115 |
| El Real, Pan. | F9 | 62 |
| El Reno, Ok., U.S. | B4 | 113 |
| El Rio, Ca., U.S. | D3 | 82 |
| El Rito, N.M., U.S. | A3 | 108 |
| Elrod, Al., U.S. | B2 | 78 |
| El Rosa, Mn., U.S. | E4 | 100 |
| Elrose, Sask. | F1 | 75 |
| Elroy, Wi., U.S. | E3 | 126 |
| Elsa, Yukon | D5 | 66 |
| Elsa, Tx., U.S. | F4 | 120 |
| Elsah, Il., U.S. | D3 | 90 |
| El Salto, Mex. | C3 | 63 |
| El Salvador, ctry., N.A. | E7 | 63 |
| El Samán de Apure, Ven. | B4 | 60 |
| El Sauce, Nic. | E7 | 62 |
| Elsberry, Mo., U.S. | B7 | 102 |
| El Segundo, Ca., U.S. | *n12 | 82 |
| El Seibo, Dom. Rep. | E9 | 64 |
| Elsie, Mi., U.S. | E6 | 99 |
| Elsie, Ne., U.S. | D4 | 104 |
| Elsinore see Helsingør, Den. | I5 | 14 |
| Elsinore, Mo., U.S. | D7 | 102 |
| Elsinore, Ut., U.S. | E3 | 121 |
| Elsmere, De., U.S. | B3 | 85 |
| Elsmere, Ky., U.S. | B5 | 94 |
| Elsmere, N.Y., U.S. | *n15 | 109 |
| El Sobrante, Ca., U.S. | h8 | 82 |
| El Sombrero, Ven. | B4 | 60 |
| Elsterwerda, E. Ger. | C6 | 18 |
| Elstow, Sask. | F2 | 75 |
| El Tarf, Alg. | F2 | 23 |
| El Tigre, Ven. | B5 | 60 |
| El Tocuyo, Ven. | B4 | 60 |
| Elton, La., U.S. | D3 | 95 |
| Elton, Wi., U.S. | C5 | 126 |
| Eltopia, Wa., U.S. | C7 | 124 |
| El Turbio, Arg. | F2 | 54 |
| Eltville, W. Ger. | C3 | 19 |
| Elūru (Ellore), India | C6 | 37 |
| Elva, Man. | E1 | 70 |
| Elvas, Port. | C3 | 22 |
| Elvaston, Il., U.S. | C2 | 90 |
| Elverson, Pa., U.S. | F10 | 115 |
| Elverum, Nor. | F4 | 14 |
| El Viejo, Nic. | E7 | 62 |
| El Vigía, Ven. | B4 | 60 |
| El Volcán, Chile | A2 | 54 |
| El Wad, Alg. | C6 | 44 |
| El Wak, Kenya | A7 | 48 |
| Elwell, Lake, res., Mt., U.S. | B5 | 103 |
| Elwha, stm., Wa., U.S. | A2 | 124 |
| Elwood, Il., U.S. | k8 | 90 |
| Elwood, In., U.S. | D6 | 91 |
| Elwood, Ks., U.S. | C9 | 93 |
| Elwood, Ne., U.S. | D6 | 104 |
| Elwood, N.J., U.S. | D3 | 107 |
| Elwood, N.Y., U.S. | *n15 | 109 |
| Elwood, Ut., U.S. | B3 | 121 |
| Ely, Eng., U.K. | D7 | 10 |
| Ely, Ia., U.S. | C6 | 92 |
| Ely, Mn., U.S. | C7 | 100 |
| Ely, Nv., U.S. | D7 | 105 |
| Ely, Vt., U.S. | D4 | 122 |
| Elyria, Ne., U.S. | C6 | 104 |
| Elyria, Oh., U.S. | A3 | 112 |
| Elysburg, Pa., U.S. | E8 | 115 |
| Elysian, Mn., U.S. | F5 | 100 |
| El Yunque, mtn., P.R. | A4 | 65 |
| Elzach, W. Ger. | B5 | 20 |
| Emämshahr (Shährūd), Iran | B5 | 38 |
| Emanuel, co., Ga., U.S. | D4 | 87 |
| Emba, Sov. Un. | D5 | 28 |
| Emba, stm., Sov. Un. | D5 | 28 |
| Embarcación, Arg. | D3 | 55 |
| Embarras, stm., Il., U.S. | E6 | 90 |
| Embarrass, Mn., U.S. | C6 | 100 |
| Embarrass, Wi., U.S. | D5 | 126 |
| Embarrass, stm., Wi., U.S. | D5 | 126 |
| Embden, N.D., U.S. | C8 | 111 |
| Embden Pond, l., Me., U.S. | D3 | 96 |
| Embetsu, Japan | D10 | 33 |
| Embira, stm., Braz. | C3 | 58 |
| Emblem, Wy., U.S. | B4 | 127 |
| Embreeville, Tn., U.S. | C11 | 119 |
| Embrun, Ont. | B9 | 73 |
| Embrun, Fr. | E7 | 16 |
| Embu, Kenya | B6 | 48 |
| Embudo, N.M., U.S. | A4 | 108 |
| Emden, W. Ger. | B4 | 18 |
| Emden, Il., U.S. | C4 | 90 |
| Emden, Mo., U.S. | B6 | 102 |
| Emelle, Al., U.S. | C1 | 78 |
| Emerald, Austl. | D8 | 50 |
| Emerado, N.D., U.S. | B8 | 111 |
| Emerald, i. | *D9 | 104 |
| Emerson, Man. | E3 | 70 |
| Emerson, Ar., U.S. | D2 | 81 |
| Emerson, Ga., U.S. | B2 | 87 |
| Emerson, Ia., U.S. | C2 | 92 |
| Emerson, Ne., U.S. | B9 | 104 |
| Emerson, N.J., U.S. | h8 | 107 |
| Emery, S.D., U.S. | D8 | 118 |
| Emery, Ut., U.S. | E5 | 121 |
| Emery, co., Ut., U.S. | E5 | 121 |
| Emery Mills, Me., U.S. | E2 | 96 |
| Emet, Tur. | C7 | 25 |
| Emida, Id., U.S. | B2 | 89 |
| Emigrant, Mt., U.S. | E6 | 103 |
| Emigrant Gap, Ca., U.S. | C3 | 82 |
| Emiliano Zapata, Mex. | D6 | 63 |
| Emilia-Romagna, prov., Italy | B3 | 23 |
| Emily, Mn., U.S. | D5 | 100 |
| Emily, Lake, l., Mn., U.S. | E3 | 100 |
| Eminence, In., U.S. | F4 | 91 |
| Eminence, Ky., U.S. | B4 | 94 |
| Eminence, Mo., U.S. | D6 | 102 |
| Emington, Il., U.S. | C5 | 90 |
| Emirdağ, Tur. | C8 | 40 |
| Emlenton, Pa., U.S. | D2 | 115 |
| Emlyn, Ky., U.S. | D5 | 94 |
| Emma, Mo., U.S. | C4 | 102 |
| Emma Lake, l., Sask. | D3 | 75 |
| Emmaus, Pa., U.S. | E11 | 115 |
| Emmeline Lake, l., Sask. | C2 | 75 |
| Emme, stm., Switz. | B4 | 21 |
| Emmen, Neth. | A7 | 16 |
| Emmen, Switz. | B5 | 21 |
| Emmendingen, W. Ger. | A3 | 20 |
| Emmerich, W. Ger. | C3 | 18 |
| Emmet, Ne., U.S. | B7 | 104 |
| Emmet, co., Ia., U.S. | A3 | 92 |
| Emmet, co., Mi., U.S. | C6 | 99 |
| Emmetsburg, Ia., U.S. | A3 | 92 |
| Emmett, Id., U.S. | F2 | 89 |
| Emmett, Ks., U.S. | C7 | 93 |
| Emmett, Mi., U.S. | E8 | 99 |
| Emmitsburg, Md., U.S. | A3 | 97 |
| Emmonak, Ak., U.S. | C7 | 79 |
| Emmons, co., N.D., U.S. | C5 | 111 |
| Emmons, Mount, mtn., Ut., U.S. | C5 | 121 |
| Emory, Tx., U.S. | C5 | 120 |
| Emory Peak, mtn., Tx., U.S. | E1 | 120 |
| Empedrado, Arg. | E4 | 55 |
| Empire, Al., U.S. | B2 | 78 |
| Empire, Co., U.S. | B5 | 83 |
| Empire, Ga., U.S. | D3 | 87 |
| Empire, La., U.S. | E6 | 95 |
| Empire, Mi., U.S. | D4 | 99 |
| Empire, Nv., U.S. | C2 | 105 |
| Empire, Oh., U.S. | B5 | 112 |
| Empoli, Italy | C3 | 23 |
| Emporia, Ks., U.S. | D7 | 93 |
| Emporia, Va., U.S. | D5 | 123 |
| Emporium, Pa., U.S. | D5 | 115 |
| Empress, Alta. | D5 | 68 |
| Emptinne, Bel. | D5 | 17 |
| Ems, stm., Eur. | B4 | 18 |
| Emsdetten, W. Ger. | C4 | 18 |
| Ems Jade Canal, W. Ger. | A7 | 17 |
| Emsworth, Pa., U.S. | h13 | 115 |
| Emyvale, Ire. | C5 | 11 |
| Ena, Japan | n16 | 33 |
| Enard Bay, b., Scot., U.K. | B3 | 13 |
| Encampment, Wy., U.S. | E6 | 127 |
| Encarnación de Díaz, Mex. | m12 | 63 |
| Enchant, Alta. | D4 | 68 |
| Encinal, Tx., U.S. | E3 | 120 |
| Encinitas, Ca., U.S. | F5 | 82 |
| Encino, N.M., U.S. | C4 | 108 |
| Encino, Tx., U.S. | F3 | 120 |
| Encontrados, Ven. | B3 | 60 |
| Encounter Bay, b., Austl. | G6 | 50 |
| Endako, B.C. | B5 | 69 |
| Endako, stm., B.C. | B5 | 69 |
| Ende, Indon. | G6 | 34 |
| Endeavor, Wi., U.S. | E4 | 126 |
| Endeavour, Sask. | E5 | 75 |
| Endelave, Den. | C4 | 15 |
| Endelave, i., Den. | C4 | 15 |
| Enderby, B.C. | D8 | 69 |
| Enderby Land, reg., Ant. | C18 | 7 |
| Enderlin, N.D., U.S. | C8 | 111 |
| Enders Reservoir, res., Ne., U.S. | D4 | 104 |
| Endiang, Alta. | D4 | 68 |
| Endicott, Ne., U.S. | D8 | 104 |
| Endicott, N.Y., U.S. | C4 | 109 |
| Endicott, Wa., U.S. | C8 | 124 |
| Endicott Mountains, mts., Ak., U.S. | B9 | 79 |
| Endwell, N.Y., U.S. | C4 | 109 |
| Ene, stm., Peru | D3 | 58 |
| Energetik, Sov. Un. | p29 | 14 |
| Enewetak, atoll, Marsh Is. | S18 | 52 |
| Enez, Tur. | B6 | 40 |
| Enfield, Austl. | *F6 | 50 |
| Enfield, N.S. | E6 | 71 |

| Name | Map Ref. | Page |
|---|---|---|
| Enfield (part of London), Eng., U.K. | k12 | 10 |
| Enfield, Ct., U.S. | B5 | 84 |
| Enfield, Il., U.S. | E5 | 90 |
| Enfield, Me., U.S. | C4 | 96 |
| Enfield, N.H., U.S. | C2 | 106 |
| Enfield, N.C., U.S. | A5 | 110 |
| Enfield Center, N.H., U.S. | C2 | 106 |
| Engadine, Mi., U.S. | B5 | 99 |
| Engaño, Cabo, c., Dom. Rep. | E9 | 64 |
| Engaru, Japan | D11 | 33 |
| Engebi, i., Marsh Is. | S18 | 52 |
| 'En Gedi, Isr. | C7 | 41 |
| Engelberg, Switz. | C4 | 21 |
| Engelhard, N.C., U.S. | B7 | 110 |
| Engels, Sov. Un. | F16 | 27 |
| Engen, W. Ger. | A6 | 21 |
| 'En Gev, Isr. | B7 | 41 |
| Enghien, Bel. | D4 | 17 |
| Enghien, Fr. | g10 | 16 |
| England, Ar., U.S. | C4 | 81 |
| England, ter., U.K. | D6 | 10 |
| England Air Force Base, mil., La., U.S. | C3 | 95 |
| Englee, Newf. | C3 | 72 |
| Englefeld, Sask. | E3 | 75 |
| Engleside, Va., U.S. | g12 | 123 |
| Englevale, N.D., U.S. | C8 | 111 |
| Englewood, Co., U.S. | B6 | 83 |
| Englewood, Fl., U.S. | F4 | 86 |
| Englewood, Ks., U.S. | E4 | 93 |
| Englewood, N.J., U.S. | B5 | 107 |
| Englewood, Oh., U.S. | C1 | 112 |
| Englewood, Tn., U.S. | D9 | 119 |
| Englewood Cliffs, N.J., U.S. | h9 | 107 |
| English, In., U.S. | H5 | 91 |
| English Bay, b., U.S. | h16 | 79 |
| English Center, Pa., U.S. | D7 | 115 |
| English Channel, strt., Eur. | F5 | 10 |
| English Coast, Ant. | B5 | 7 |
| English Creek, N.J., U.S. | E3 | 107 |
| English Harbour West, Newf. | E4 | 72 |
| English Lake, In., U.S. | B4 | 91 |
| Englishtown, N.J., U.S. | C4 | 107 |
| Enguera, Spain | C5 | 22 |
| 'En Harod, Isr. | B7 | 41 |
| Enid, Ms., U.S. | A4 | 101 |
| Enid, Mt., U.S. | C12 | 103 |
| Enid, Ok., U.S. | A4 | 113 |
| Enid Lake, res., Ms., U.S. | A4 | 101 |
| Enigma, Ga., U.S. | E3 | 87 |
| Enilda, Alta. | B2 | 68 |
| Enirik Island, i., Marsh Is. | P18 | 52 |
| eNjesuthi, mtn., S. Afr. | C4 | 49 |
| Enka, N.C., U.S. | f10 | 110 |
| 'En Kerem, Isr. | h11 | 41 |
| Enkhuizen, Neth. | B5 | 17 |
| Enköping, Swe. | H7 | 14 |
| Enmore, Guy. | A3 | 59 |
| Enna, Italy | F5 | 23 |
| Ennadai Lake, l., N.W. Ter. | D12 | 66 |
| Ennedi, plat., Chad | B4 | 46 |
| Ennell, Lough, l., Ire. | D4 | 11 |
| Enngonia, Austl. | D5 | 51 |
| Ennigerloh, W. Ger. | B3 | 19 |
| Enning, S.D., U.S. | C3 | 118 |
| Ennis, Ire. | D2 | 10 |
| Ennis, Mt., U.S. | E5 | 103 |
| Ennis, Tx., U.S. | C4 | 120 |
| Enniscorthy, Ire. | D3 | 10 |
| Enniskillen, N. Ire., U.K. | C3 | 10 |
| Ennistimon, Ire. | D2 | 10 |
| Enns, Aus. | D7 | 18 |
| Enns, stm., Aus. | D7 | 18 |
| Ennylabegan Island, i., Marsh Is. | S17 | 52 |
| Enoch, Ut., U.S. | F3 | 121 |
| Enochs, Tx., U.S. | C1 | 120 |
| Enola, Ar., U.S. | B3 | 81 |
| Enola, Ne., U.S. | C8 | 104 |
| Enola, Pa., U.S. | F8 | 115 |
| Enon, Cape, c., Japan | C13 | 31 |
| Enon, Oh., U.S. | C2 | 112 |
| Enoree, S.C., U.S. | B4 | 117 |
| Enoree, stm., S.C., U.S. | B3 | 117 |
| Enos, In., U.S. | B3 | 91 |
| Enosburg Falls, Vt., U.S. | B3 | 122 |
| Enriquillo, Dom. Rep. | E8 | 64 |
| Enriquillo, Lago, l., Dom. Rep. | E8 | 64 |
| Enschede, Neth. | A7 | 16 |
| Ensenada, Arg. | g8 | 54 |
| Ensenada, Mex. | A1 | 63 |
| Ensenada, N.M., U.S. | A3 | 108 |
| Enshi, China | E6 | 31 |
| Enshu Bay, b., Japan | I8 | 33 |
| Ensign, Alta. | D4 | 68 |
| Ensign, Ks., U.S. | E3 | 93 |
| Ensign, Mi., U.S. | C4 | 99 |
| Ensisheim, Fr. | B3 | 20 |
| Ensley, Fl., U.S. | u14 | 86 |
| Enterprise, Ont. | A5 | 109 |
| Entebbe, Ug. | A5 | 48 |
| Enterprise, Ont. | C8 | 73 |
| Enterprise, Guy. | A3 | 59 |
| Enterprise, Al., U.S. | D4 | 78 |
| Enterprise, Il., U.S. | E5 | 90 |
| Enterprise, Ia., U.S. | e8 | 92 |
| Enterprise, Ks., U.S. | D6 | 93 |
| Enterprise, La., U.S. | C4 | 95 |
| Enterprise, Ms., U.S. | C5 | 101 |
| Enterprise, Ok., U.S. | B6 | 113 |
| Enterprise, Or., U.S. | B9 | 114 |
| Enterprise, Ut., U.S. | F2 | 121 |
| Enterprise, W.V., U.S. | B4 | 125 |
| Entiat, Wa., U.S. | B5 | 124 |
| Entiat, stm., Wa., U.S. | B5 | 124 |
| Entiat Lake, l., Wa., U.S. | B5 | 124 |
| Entiat Mountains, mts., Wa., U.S. | B5 | 124 |
| Entrance, Alta. | C2 | 68 |
| Entraygues, Fr. | E5 | 16 |
| Entrée, Île d', Que. | B8 | 71 |
| Entre Minho e Douro, hist. reg., Port. | B1 | 22 |
| Entre Ríos, prov., Arg. | A5 | 54 |
| Entwistle, Alta. | C3 | 68 |
| Enugu, Nig. | E6 | 45 |
| Enumclaw, Wa., U.S. | B4 | 124 |
| Envermeu, Fr. | E9 | 12 |
| Envigado, Col. | *B2 | 60 |
| Enville, Tn., U.S. | B3 | 119 |
| Envira, Braz. | C3 | 58 |
| Enyu Channel, strt., Marsh Is. | P18 | 52 |
| Enyu Island, i., Marsh Is. | P18 | 52 |
| Enz, stm., W. Ger. | D4 | 18 |
| Enza, stm., Italy | E5 | 20 |
| Enzan, Japan | n17 | 33 |
| Eola, La., U.S. | D3 | 95 |
| Eola Hills, hills, Or., U.S. | h11 | 114 |
| Eolie, Ut., U.S. | B6 | 102 |
| Eoline, Al., U.S. | C2 | 78 |
| Eolie Islands, is., Italy | E5 | 23 |
| Epe, Neth. | B5 | 17 |
| Épéna, Congo | A2 | 48 |
| Épernay, Fr. | C5 | 16 |
| Epes, Al., U.S. | C1 | 78 |
| Ephesus, Ga., U.S. | C1 | 87 |
| Ephesus, hist., Tur. | D6 | 25 |
| Ephraim, Ut., U.S. | D4 | 121 |
| Ephraim, Wi., U.S. | C6 | 126 |
| Ephrata, Pa., U.S. | F9 | 115 |
| Ephrata, Wa., U.S. | B6 | 124 |
| Épila, Spain | B5 | 22 |
| Épinal, Fr. | C7 | 16 |
| Épinay [-sur-Seine], Fr. | g10 | 16 |
| Epiphany, S.D., U.S. | D8 | 118 |
| Epirus, hist. reg., Grc. | C3 | 25 |
| Epoufette, Mi., U.S. | B5 | 99 |
| Epping, Eng., U.K. | k13 | 10 |
| Epping, N.H., U.S. | D4 | 106 |
| Epping, N.D., U.S. | A2 | 111 |
| Eppingen, W. Ger. | D3 | 19 |
| Epps, La., U.S. | B4 | 95 |
| Epsom, In., U.S. | G3 | 91 |
| Epsom, N.H., U.S. | D4 | 106 |
| Epsom [and Ewell], Eng., U.K. | m12 | 10 |
| Epukiro, Nmb. | B2 | 49 |
| Epworth, Ia., U.S. | B7 | 92 |
| Eqlid, Iran | F6 | 39 |
| Equality, Al., U.S. | C3 | 78 |
| Equality, Il., U.S. | F5 | 90 |
| Equatorial Guinea, ctry., Afr. | E1 | 46 |
| Équeurdreville, Fr. | C3 | 16 |
| Equinunk, Pa., U.S. | C11 | 115 |
| Erath, La., U.S. | E3 | 95 |
| Erath, co., Tx., U.S. | C3 | 120 |
| Erba, Italy | E7 | 21 |
| Erba, Jabal, mtn., Sud. | A4 | 47 |
| Erbach, W. Ger. | D3 | 19 |
| Erbacon, W.V., U.S. | C4 | 125 |
| Erbendorf, W. Ger. | D7 | 19 |
| Erciş, Tur. | C14 | 40 |
| Erciyes Mountain, mtn., Tur. | C10 | 40 |
| Ercsi, Hung. | B4 | 24 |
| Érd, Hung. | B4 | 24 |
| Erdek, Tur. | B6 | 25 |
| Erdene, Mong. | C7 | 31 |
| Erdene-Dzuu, Mong. | B5 | 31 |
| Erdenetsagaan, Mong. | B6 | 32 |
| Erdenheim, Pa., U.S. | o21 | 115 |
| Erding, W. Ger. | D5 | 18 |
| Erdre, stm., Fr. | D5 | 16 |
| Erebus, Mount, mtn., Ant. | B29 | 7 |
| Erechim, Braz. | D2 | 56 |
| Ereğli, Tur. | D10 | 40 |
| Ereğli, Tur. | B8 | 40 |
| Erenhot, China | C4 | 32 |
| Eresós, Grc. | C7 | 25 |
| Erétria (Néa Psará), Grc. | g11 | 25 |
| Erfurt, E. Ger. | C5 | 18 |
| Ergene, stm., Tur. | B6 | 40 |
| Eriboll, Loch, b., Scot., U.K. | B4 | 13 |
| Erice, Italy | E4 | 23 |
| Ericht, Loch, l., Scot., U.K. | D4 | 13 |
| Erick, Ok., U.S. | B2 | 113 |
| Erickson, B.C. | E9 | 69 |
| Ericsburg, Mn., U.S. | B5 | 100 |
| Erickson, Man. | D2 | 70 |
| Ericson, Ne., U.S. | C7 | 104 |
| Erie, Co., U.S. | A5 | 83 |
| Erie, Il., U.S. | B3 | 90 |
| Erie, Ks., U.S. | E8 | 93 |
| Erie, Mi., U.S. | G7 | 99 |
| Erie, N.D., U.S. | B8 | 111 |
| Erie, Pa., U.S. | B1 | 115 |
| Erie, co., N.Y., U.S. | C2 | 109 |
| Erie, co., Oh., U.S. | A3 | 112 |
| Erie, co., Pa., U.S. | C1 | 115 |
| Erie, Lake, l., N.A. | B11 | 76 |
| Erieau, Ont. | E3 | 73 |
| Erie Canal, N.Y., U.S. | B5 | 109 |
| Eriksdale, Man. | D2 | 70 |
| Érimanthos, mtn., Grc. | D3 | 25 |
| Erimo, Cape, c., Japan | C13 | 31 |
| Erin, Ont. | D4 | 73 |
| Erin, Tn., U.S. | A4 | 119 |
| Erin Point, c., Trin. | O22 | 65 |
| Erin Springs, Ok., U.S. | C4 | 113 |
| Eriskay, i., Scot., U.K. | C1 | 13 |
| Erisort, Loch, b., Scot., U.K. | B2 | 13 |
| Erithraí, Grc. | C4 | 25 |
| Eritrea, prov., Eth. | B4 | 47 |
| Erkelenz, W. Ger. | C6 | 17 |
| Erken, l., Swe. | t36 | 14 |
| Erkner, W. Ger. | D5 | 18 |
| Erlangen, W. Ger. | D5 | 18 |
| Erlanger, Ky., U.S. | A5 | 94 |
| Erling, Lake, res., Ar., U.S. | D2 | 81 |
| Ermelo, Neth. | B5 | 17 |
| Ermelo, S. Afr. | C5 | 49 |
| Ermenek, Tur. | D9 | 40 |
| Ermont, Fr. | g10 | 16 |
| Ermoúpolis (Syros), Grc. | D5 | 40 |
| Erne, Upper Lough, l., Eur. | C3 | 10 |
| Ernée, Fr. | C3 | 16 |
| Ernest, Pa., U.S. | E3 | 115 |
| Ernestina, Arg. | g7 | 54 |
| Ernestville, Pa., U.S. | C11 | 119 |
| Ernfold, Sask. | G2 | 75 |
| Erode, India | *F6 | 36 |
| Eromanga, Austl. | C4 | 51 |
| Eros, La., U.S. | B3 | 95 |
| Errigal Mountain, mtn., Ire. | C2 | 10 |
| Erris Head, c., Ire. | C1 | 10 |
| Errol, N.H., U.S. | A4 | 106 |
| Errol Heights, Or., U.S. | *h12 | 114 |
| Erskine, Alta. | C4 | 68 |
| Erskine, Mn., U.S. | C3 | 100 |
| Erstein, Fr. | C7 | 16 |
| Erstfeld, Switz. | C4 | 20 |
| Erving, Ma., U.S. | A3 | 98 |
| Erwin, N.C., U.S. | B4 | 110 |
| Erwin, S.D., U.S. | C8 | 118 |
| Erwin, Tn., U.S. | C11 | 119 |
| Erwin, W.V., U.S. | B5 | 125 |
| Erwinville, La., U.S. | D4 | 95 |
| Erwood, Sask. | E4 | 75 |
| Erzincan, Tur. | C12 | 40 |
| Erzurum, Tur. | C13 | 40 |
| Esashi, Japan | C13 | 31 |
| Esashi, Japan | D11 | 33 |
| Esbjerg, Den. | J3 | 14 |
| Escabosa, N.M., U.S. | m8 | 108 |
| Escada, Braz. | k6 | 57 |
| Escalante, Ut., U.S. | F4 | 121 |
| Escalante, stm., Ut., U.S. | F4 | 121 |
| Escalante Creek, stm., Co., U.S. | C2 | 83 |
| Escalante Desert, des., Ut., U.S. | | |
| Escalón, Mex. | B4 | 63 |
| Escambia, co., Al., U.S. | D2 | 78 |
| Escambia, co., Fl., U.S. | u14 | 86 |
| Escambia, stm., Fl., U.S. | u14 | 86 |
| Escanaba, Mi., U.S. | C3 | 99 |
| Escanaba, stm., Mi., U.S. | B3 | 99 |
| Escarpada Point, c., Phil. | B6 | 34 |
| Escatawpa, Ms., U.S. | E5 | 101 |
| Escatawpa, stm., U.S. | D5 | 101 |
| Eschede, W. Ger. | F4 | 15 |
| Eschenbach, W. Ger. | D6 | 19 |
| Eschholzmatt, Switz. | C4 | 21 |
| Esch-sur-Alzette, Lux. | C7 | 16 |
| Eschwege, W. Ger. | C5 | 18 |
| Eschweiler, W. Ger. | C3 | 18 |
| Escobal, Pan. | k11 | 62 |
| Escocesa, Bahía, b., Dom. Rep. | E9 | 64 |
| Escoheag, R.I., U.S. | E1 | 116 |
| Escondida, N.M., U.S. | C3 | 108 |
| Escondido, Ca., U.S. | F5 | 82 |
| Escondido, stm., Nic. | D6 | 62 |
| Escouminac, Que. | A8 | 74 |
| Escouminac, Point, c., N.B. | B5 | 71 |
| Escuinapa [de Hidalgo], Mex. | C3 | 63 |
| Escuintla, Guat. | C2 | 62 |
| Escuminac, Que. | A3 | 71 |
| Eséka, Cam. | E2 | 46 |
| Esens, W. Ger. | A7 | 17 |
| Eşfahān (Isfahan), Iran | B5 | 38 |
| Esgueva, stm., Spain | A3 | 22 |
| Eshkāshem, Afg. | C15 | 39 |
| Eshowe, S. Afr. | C5 | 49 |
| Esigodini, Zimb. | B4 | 49 |
| Esk, stm., U.K. | E6 | 13 |
| Eskdale, W.V., U.S. | C3 | 125 |
| Eske, Lough, l., Ire. | C3 | 11 |
| Eskilstuna, Swe. | H7 | 14 |
| Eskimo Lakes, l., N.W. Ter. | C6 | 66 |
| Eskimo Point, N.W. Ter. | D14 | 66 |
| Eskişehir, Tur. | C8 | 40 |
| Esko, Mn., U.S. | D6 | 100 |
| Eskridge, Ks., U.S. | D7 | 93 |
| Eslāmābād, Iran | *D3 | 39 |
| Eslarn, W. Ger. | D7 | 19 |
| Eslava, stm., Mex. | h9 | 63 |
| Eslöv, Swe. | C7 | 15 |
| Eşme, Tur. | C7 | 25 |
| Esmeralda, co., Nv., U.S. | F4 | 105 |
| Esmeraldas, Ec. | A2 | 58 |
| Esmeraldas, prov., Ec. | A2 | 58 |
| Esmond, Il., U.S. | A5 | 90 |
| Esmond, N.D., U.S. | A6 | 111 |
| Esmond, R.I., U.S. | B4 | 116 |
| Esom Hill, Ga., U.S. | C1 | 87 |
| Espada, Point, c., Col. | A3 | 60 |
| Espanola, Ont. | A3 | 73 |
| Espanola, Fl., U.S. | C5 | 86 |
| Espanola, N.M., U.S. | B3 | 108 |
| Española, Isla (Hood), i., Ec. | g6 | 58 |
| Esparto, Ca., U.S. | C2 | 82 |
| Esperance, Austl. | F3 | 50 |
| Esperance, Wa., U.S. | *B3 | 124 |
| Esperanza, Arg. | A4 | 54 |
| Esperanza, Peru | o12 | 58 |
| Esperanza, Tx., U.S. | o12 | 120 |
| Esperanza, stm., Pan. | k12 | 62 |
| Espichel, Cape, c., Port. | C1 | 22 |
| Espinal, Col. | C3 | 60 |
| Espinhaço, Serra do, mts., Braz. | E6 | 53 |
| Espírito Santo, state, Braz. | E8 | 53 |
| Espíritu Santo, i., Vanuatu | H10 | 6 |
| Espita, Mex. | | |
| Espoo, Fin. | *G11 | 14 |
| Esposende, Port. | B1 | 22 |
| Espungabera, Moz. | B5 | 49 |
| Espy, Pa., U.S. | D9 | 115 |
| Espyville Station, Pa., U.S. | C1 | 115 |
| Esquatzel Coulee, val., Wa., U.S. | C6 | 124 |
| Esquel, Arg. | C2 | 54 |
| Esquimalt, B.C. | E6 | 69 |
| Esquina, Arg. | A4 | 54 |
| Essaouira (Mogador), Mor. | C3 | 44 |
| Essen, Bel. | C4 | 17 |
| Essen, W. Ger. | C3 | 18 |
| Essendon, Austl. | *G7 | 50 |
| Essendon, Mount, mtn., Austl. | D3 | 50 |
| Essequibo, stm., Guy. | B3 | 59 |
| Essex, Ont. | E2 | 73 |
| Essex, Ct., U.S. | D6 | 84 |
| Essex, Ia., U.S. | D2 | 92 |
| Essex, Md., U.S. | B5 | 97 |
| Essex, Ma., U.S. | A6 | 98 |
| Essex, Mo., U.S. | E8 | 102 |
| Essex, Mt., U.S. | B3 | 103 |
| Essex, N.Y., U.S. | f11 | 109 |
| Essex, Vt., U.S. | B2 | 122 |
| Essex, co., Eng., U.K. | C2 | 73 |
| Essex, co., Ma., U.S. | A6 | 98 |
| Essex, co., N.J., U.S. | B4 | 107 |
| Essex, co., N.Y., U.S. | B7 | 109 |
| Essex, co., Vt., U.S. | B5 | 122 |
| Essex, co., Va., U.S. | C6 | 123 |
| Essex Fells, N.J., U.S. | *B4 | 107 |
| Essex Junction, Vt., U.S. | C2 | 122 |
| Essexville, Mi., U.S. | E7 | 99 |
| Es Sider, Libya | B4 | 46 |
| Essling, W. Ger. | | |
| Essonne, dept., Fr. | F2 | 17 |
| Es Suki, Sud. | C3 | 47 |
| Est, Île de l', i., Que. | B8 | 71 |
| Est, Pointe de l', c., Que. | B8 | 71 |
| Estacada, Or., U.S. | B4 | 114 |
| Estacado, Llano, pl., U.S. | C7 | 120 |
| Estados, Isla de los, i., Arg. | h13 | 54 |
| Estahbān, Iran | G7 | 39 |
| Estaire, Ont. | A4 | 73 |
| Estância, Braz. | F11 | 57 |
| Estancia, N.M., U.S. | C3 | 108 |
| Estcourt, S. Afr. | C4 | 49 |
| Este, Italy | D5 | 21 |
| Este, Punta, c., P.R. | E7 | 64 |
| Estelí, Nic. | E7 | 62 |
| Estella, Spain | A4 | 22 |
| Estelline, S.D., U.S. | *C9 | 118 |
| Estelline, Tx., U.S. | B2 | 120 |
| Estell Manor, N.J., U.S. | E3 | 107 |
| Estepa, Spain | D3 | 22 |
| Estepona, Spain | D3 | 22 |
| Esterbrook, Wy., U.S. | D7 | 127 |
| Esterhazy, Sask. | G4 | 75 |
| Esternay, Fr. | F3 | 17 |
| Esternberg, Aus. | E8 | 19 |
| Estero Bay, b., Ca., U.S. | E3 | 82 |
| Estero Bay, b., Fl., U.S. | F5 | 86 |
| Estero Island, i., Fl., U.S. | F5 | 86 |
| Estes Park, Co., U.S. | A5 | 83 |
| Estevan, Sask. | H4 | 75 |
| Estevan Group, is., B.C. | C3 | 69 |
| Estevan Point, B.C. | E4 | 69 |
| Esther, Alta. | D5 | 68 |
| Estherville, Ia., U.S. | A3 | 92 |
| Estherwood, La., U.S. | D3 | 95 |
| Estill, S.C., U.S. | F5 | 117 |
| Estill, co., Ky., U.S. | C6 | 94 |
| Estillfork, Al., U.S. | A3 | 78 |
| Estill Springs, Tn., U.S. | B5 | 119 |
| Estlin, Sask. | G3 | 75 |
| Eston, Sask. | F1 | 75 |
| Estonia, state, Sov. Un. | D5 | 29 |
| Estrées-Saint-Denis, Fr. | E2 | 17 |
| Estrela, Braz. | D2 | 56 |
| Estrela, mtn., Port. | *B2 | 22 |
| Estrela, Serra da, mts., Port. | B2 | 22 |
| Estrela do Norte, Braz. | A3 | 56 |
| Estrela do Sul, Braz. | B3 | 56 |
| Estremadura, hist. reg., Port. | C1 | 22 |
| Estremadura, hist. reg., Spain | C2 | 22 |
| Estremoz, Port. | C2 | 22 |
| Estuary, Sask. | G1 | 75 |
| Esztergom, Hung. | B4 | 24 |
| Étain, Fr. | E5 | 17 |
| Étampes, Fr. | C5 | 16 |
| Étang-du-Nord, Que. | B8 | 71 |
| Étaples, Fr. | B4 | 16 |
| Etāwah, India | C6 | 37 |
| Eternity Range, mts., Ant. | C6 | 7 |
| Ethan, S.D., U.S. | D8 | 118 |
| Ethel, La., U.S. | D4 | 95 |
| Ethel, Ms., U.S. | B4 | 101 |
| Ethel, Mo., U.S. | B5 | 102 |
| Ethel, Wa., U.S. | C3 | 124 |
| Ethelbert, Man. | D1 | 70 |
| Ethelsville, Al., U.S. | B1 | 78 |
| Ethelton, Sask. | E3 | 75 |
| Ether, N.C., U.S. | B3 | 110 |
| Ethete, Wy., U.S. | C4 | 127 |
| Ethiopia, ctry., Afr. | D4 | 47 |
| Ethiopian Plateau, plat., Eth. | D4 | 47 |
| Ethridge, Mt., U.S. | B5 | 103 |
| Ethridge, Tn., U.S. | B4 | 119 |
| Etive, Loch, l., Scot., U.K. | D3 | 13 |
| Etna, Ca., U.S. | B2 | 82 |
| Etna, Me., U.S. | D3 | 96 |
| Etna, N.H., U.S. | C2 | 106 |
| Etna, N.Y., U.S. | C4 | 109 |
| Etna, Oh., U.S. | C3 | 112 |
| Etna, Pa., U.S. | k14 | 115 |
| Etna, Mount, mtn., Italy | F5 | 23 |
| Etna Green, In., U.S. | B5 | 91 |
| Etobicoke, Ont. | D5 | 73 |
| Etolin Island, i., Ak., U.S. | m23 | 79 |
| Etolin Strait, strt., Ak., U.S. | C6 | 79 |
| Etosha Pan, pl., Nmb. | A2 | 49 |
| Etowah, Tn., U.S. | D9 | 119 |
| Etowah, co., Al., U.S. | A3 | 78 |
| Etowah, stm., Ga., U.S. | B2 | 87 |
| Étreat, Fr. | C4 | 16 |
| Étroubles, Italy | E3 | 21 |
| Etta, Ms., U.S. | A4 | 101 |
| Ettelbruck, Lux. | B6 | 25 |
| Etten, i., Micron. | Q18 | 52 |
| Etterbeek, Bel. | *D4 | 17 |
| Ettington, Sask. | H2 | 75 |
| Ettlingen, W. Ger. | E3 | 19 |
| Ettrick, Wi., U.S. | D2 | 126 |
| Ettrick, Va., U.S. | C5 | 123 |
| Et Tini, hill, N. Mar. Is. | D7 | 52 |
| Etzatlán, Mex. | m11 | 63 |
| Etzikom, Alta. | E5 | 68 |
| Etzikom Coulee, stm., Alta. | E5 | 68 |
| Eu, Fr. | B4 | 16 |
| Euboea see Évvoia, i., Grc. | C4 | 40 |
| Eucha, Ok., U.S. | A7 | 113 |
| Euclid, Mn., U.S. | C2 | 100 |
| Euclid, Oh., U.S. | A4 | 112 |
| Eucumbene, Lake, l., Austl. | H7 | 51 |
| Eudora, Ar., U.S. | D4 | 81 |
| Eudora, Ks., U.S. | D8 | 93 |
| Eudora, Mo., U.S. | E4 | 102 |
| Eufaula, Al., U.S. | D4 | 78 |
| Eufaula, Ok., U.S. | B6 | 113 |
| Eufaula Lake, res., Ok., U.S. | B6 | 113 |
| Eugene, Mo., U.S. | C5 | 102 |
| Eugene, Or., U.S. | C3 | 114 |
| Eugenia, Punta, c., Mex. | B1 | 63 |
| Eulaton, Al., U.S. | B4 | 78 |
| Euless, Tx., U.S. | *n9 | 120 |
| Eulonia, Ga., U.S. | E5 | 87 |
| Eunice, La., U.S. | D3 | 95 |
| Eunice, N.M., U.S. | E6 | 108 |
| Eupen, Bel. | B7 | 16 |
| Euphrates, stm., Asia | B4 | 38 |
| Eupora, Ms., U.S. | B4 | 101 |
| Eure, dept., Fr. | C4 | 16 |
| Eure, stm., Fr. | C4 | 16 |
| Eureka, N.W. Ter. | m34 | 66 |
| Eureka, Ca., U.S. | B1 | 82 |
| Eureka, Ks., U.S. | E7 | 93 |
| Eureka, Mo., U.S. | f12 | 102 |
| Eureka, Mt., U.S. | B1 | 103 |
| Eureka, Nv., U.S. | D6 | 105 |
| Eureka, S.D., U.S. | B6 | 118 |
| Eureka, Ut., U.S. | D3 | 121 |
| Eureka, Wa., U.S. | C7 | 124 |
| Eureka, Wi., U.S. | D5 | 126 |
| Eureka, co., Nv., U.S. | C5 | 105 |
| Eureka Sound, strt., N.W. Ter. | m34 | 66 |
| Eureka Springs, Ar., U.S. | A2 | 81 |
| Euroa, Austl. | H5 | 51 |
| Europa Point, c., Gib. | D3 | 22 |
| Europe, cont. | E13 | 8 |
| Euskirchen, W. Ger. | C3 | 18 |
| Eustis, Fl., U.S. | D5 | 86 |
| Eustis, Me., U.S. | C2 | 96 |
| Eustis, Ne., U.S. | D5 | 104 |
| Eutaw, Al., U.S. | C2 | 78 |
| Eutawville, S.C., U.S. | E7 | 117 |
| Eutin, W. Ger. | D4 | 15 |
| Eutsuk Lake, l., B.C. | C4 | 69 |
| Eva, Al., U.S. | A3 | 78 |
| Eva, Tn., U.S. | A3 | 119 |
| Evale, Ang. | E2 | 48 |
| Evan, Mn., U.S. | F4 | 100 |
| Evangeline, La., U.S. | D3 | 95 |
| Evangeline, co., La., U.S. | D3 | 95 |
| Evans, Co., U.S. | A6 | 83 |
| Evans, La., U.S. | C2 | 95 |
| Evans, W.V., U.S. | C3 | 125 |
| Evans, co., Ga., U.S. | D5 | 87 |
| Evans, Mount, mtn., Co., U.S. | B5 | 83 |
| Evans City, Pa., U.S. | E1 | 115 |
| Evans Mills, N.Y., U.S. | A5 | 109 |
| Evansburg, Alta. | C3 | 68 |
| Evansdale, Ia., U.S. | B5 | 92 |
| Evansport, Oh., U.S. | A1 | 112 |
| Evans Strait, strt., N.W. Ter. | D16 | 66 |
| Evanston, Il., U.S. | A6 | 90 |
| Evanston, Ky., U.S. | C6 | 94 |
| Evanston, Wy., U.S. | E2 | 127 |
| Evansville, Ar., U.S. | B1 | 81 |
| Evansville, Il., U.S. | E4 | 90 |
| Evansville, In., U.S. | I2 | 91 |
| Evansville, Mn., U.S. | D3 | 100 |
| Evansville, Ms., U.S. | A3 | 101 |
| Evansville, Vt., U.S. | B4 | 122 |
| Evansville, Wi., U.S. | F4 | 126 |
| Evansville, Wy., U.S. | D6 | 127 |
| Evant, Tx., U.S. | D3 | 120 |
| Evanton, Scot., U.K. | C4 | 13 |
| Evart, Mi., U.S. | E5 | 99 |
| Evarts, Ky., U.S. | D6 | 94 |
| Eveleth, Mn., U.S. | C6 | 100 |
| Evelyn, La., U.S. | C2 | 95 |
| Evening Shade, Ar., U.S. | A4 | 81 |
| Even Yehuda, Isr. | f10 | 41 |
| Everard, Lake, l., Austl. | F5 | 50 |
| Everest, Mount, mtn., Asia | C8 | 36 |
| Everett, Ont. | C5 | 73 |
| Everett, Ga., U.S. | g11 | 98 |
| Everett, Ma., U.S. | g11 | 98 |
| Everett, Pa., U.S. | F5 | 115 |
| Everett, Wa., U.S. | B3 | 124 |
| Everett, Mount, mtn., Ma., U.S. | B1 | 98 |
| Everett Lake, res., N.H., U.S. | D3 | 106 |
| Everettville, W.V., U.S. | h10 | 125 |
| Evergem, Bel. | C3 | 17 |
| Everglades National Park, Fl., U.S. | G5 | 86 |
| Evergreen, Al., U.S. | D3 | 78 |
| Evergreen, Co., U.S. | B5 | 83 |
| Evergreen, N.C., U.S. | C4 | 110 |
| Evergreen, Ms., U.S. | A5 | 101 |
| Evergreen Park, Il., U.S. | k9 | 90 |
| Everly, Ia., U.S. | A2 | 92 |
| Everman, Tx., U.S. | *n9 | 120 |
| Everson, Pa., U.S. | F2 | 115 |
| Everson, Wa., U.S. | A3 | 124 |
| Everton, Ar., U.S. | A3 | 81 |
| Everton, Mo., U.S. | D4 | 102 |
| Evesham, Sask. | E1 | 75 |
| Evesham, Eng., U.K. | B6 | 12 |
| Évian-les-Bains, Fr. | C2 | 20 |
| Evinayong, Eq. Gui. | E2 | 46 |
| Evington, Va., U.S. | C3 | 123 |
| Evolène, Switz. | D3 | 21 |
| Évora, Port. | C2 | 22 |
| Évreux, Fr. | C4 | 16 |
| Evstratios, i., Grc. | C5 | 40 |
| Évvoia (Euboea), i., Grc. | C5 | 40 |
| Ewa, Hi., U.S. | B3 | 88 |
| Ewa Beach, Hi., U.S. | g9 | 88 |
| Ewan, Wa., U.S. | B8 | 124 |
| Ewarton, Jam. | E14 | 63 |
| Ewe, Loch, b., Scot., U.K. | C4 | 13 |
| Ewell, Mi., U.S. | m12 | 99 |
| Ewen, Mi., U.S. | B2 | 99 |
| Ewing, Il., U.S. | E5 | 90 |
| Ewing, Ky., U.S. | B6 | 94 |
| Ewing, Ne., U.S. | B7 | 104 |
| Ewing, Va., U.S. | E1 | 123 |
| Ewing Township, N.J., U.S. | C3 | 107 |
| Ewo, Congo | B2 | 48 |
| Exaltación, Bol. | D5 | 58 |
| Excel, Al., U.S. | D2 | 78 |
| Excello, Mo., U.S. | B5 | 102 |
| Excelsior Mountain, mtn., Ca., U.S. | C4 | 82 |
| Excelsior Mountains, mts., Nv., U.S. | E3 | 105 |
| Excelsior Springs, Mo., U.S. | B3 | 102 |
| Exchange, Pa., U.S. | D8 | 115 |
| Exchange, W.V., U.S. | C4 | 125 |
| Exe, stm., Eng., U.K. | D4 | 12 |
| Executive Committee Range, mts., Ant. | B36 | 7 |
| Exeland, Wi., U.S. | C2 | 126 |
| Exeter, Ont. | D3 | 73 |
| Exeter, Eng., U.K. | E5 | 10 |
| Exeter, Ca., U.S. | D4 | 82 |
| Exeter, Me., U.S. | D4 | 96 |
| Exeter, Mo., U.S. | E4 | 102 |
| Exeter, N.H., U.S. | E5 | 106 |
| Exeter, R.I., U.S. | E2 | 116 |
| Exira, Ia., U.S. | C3 | 92 |
| Exline, Ia., U.S. | D5 | 92 |
| Exmoor, for., Eng., U.K. | C7 | 123 |
| Exmore, Va., U.S. | C7 | 123 |
| Exmouth, Austl. | D1 | 50 |
| Exmouth, Eng., U.K. | E5 | 10 |
| Exmouth Gulf, b., Austl. | D1 | 50 |
| Expanse, Sask. | H3 | 75 |
| Experiment, Ga., U.S. | C2 | 87 |
| Exploits, stm., Newf. | D3 | 72 |
| Exploits, Bay of, b., Newf. | D4 | 72 |
| Export, Pa., U.S. | F2 | 115 |
| Exshaw, Alta. | D3 | 68 |
| Extension, B.C. | f12 | 69 |
| Extrema, Braz. | m8 | 56 |
| Exuma Sound, strt., Bah. | B5 | 64 |
| Eyasi, Lake, l., Tan. | B6 | 48 |
| Eyebrow, Sask. | G2 | 75 |
| Eyehill Creek, stm., Can. | C5 | 68 |
| Eyemouth, Scot., U.K. | C5 | 10 |
| Eye Peninsula, pen., Scot., U.K. | B2 | 13 |
| Eyl, Som. | D6 | 47 |
| Eylar Mountain, mtn., Ca., U.S. | D3 | 82 |
| Eynort, Loch, b., Scot., U.K. | C1 | 13 |
| Eyota, Mn., U.S. | G6 | 100 |
| Eyre, Sask. | F1 | 75 |
| Eyrecourt, Ire. | D3 | 11 |
| Eyre North, Lake, l., Austl. | E6 | 50 |
| Eyre Peninsula, pen., Austl. | F6 | 50 |
| Ezeiza, Arg. | g7 | 54 |
| Ezine, Tur. | C6 | 40 |

**F**

| Name | Map Ref. | Page |
|---|---|---|
| Fabens, Tx., U.S. | o11 | 120 |
| Faber, Va., U.S. | C4 | 123 |
| Faber Lake, l., N.W. Ter. | D9 | 66 |
| Fabius, N.Y., U.S. | C5 | 109 |
| Fabius, stm., Mo., U.S. | A6 | 102 |
| Fåborg, Den. | C4 | 15 |
| Fabriano, Italy | C4 | 23 |
| Fabyan, Ct., U.S. | A8 | 84 |
| Facatativá, Col. | C3 | 60 |
| Fachi, Niger | C7 | 45 |
| Fackler, Al., U.S. | A4 | 78 |
| Facpi Point, c., Guam | M9 | 52 |
| Factoryville, Pa., U.S. | C10 | 115 |
| Fada, Chad | B4 | 46 |
| Fada Ngourma, Burkina | D5 | 45 |
| Faddeya Gulf, b., Sov. Un. | B13 | 28 |
| Faddey Island, i., Sov. Un. | B17 | 29 |
| Fadian Point, c., Guam | L10 | 52 |
| Faenza, Italy | E5 | 20 |
| Faeroe Islands, ctry., Eur. | C7 | 8 |
| Fafa, Mali | C5 | 45 |
| Fafe, Port. | B1 | 22 |
| Fafen, stm., Eth. | D5 | 47 |
| Faga'alu, Am. Sam. | F13 | 52 |
| Fagaitua Bay, b., Am. Sam. | G13 | 52 |
| Fagaloa Bay, b., W. Sam. | F12 | 52 |
| Fagamalo, W. Sam. | F11 | 52 |
| Fágáras, Rom. | C7 | 24 |
| Fagatogo, Am. Sam. | F13 | 52 |
| Fagernes, Nor. | G3 | 14 |
| Fagersta, Swe. | G6 | 14 |
| Faggo, Nig. | D6 | 45 |
| Fagnano, Lago, l., S.A. | h12 | 54 |
| Faguibine, Lac, l., Mali | C4 | 45 |
| Fagus, Mo., U.S. | E7 | 102 |
| Fahan, Ire. | B4 | 11 |
| Faial, i., Port. | g8 | 44 |
| Faichuk, is., Micron. | Q18 | 52 |
| Fã'id, Eg. | D4 | 41 |
| Faido, Switz. | D6 | 21 |
| Fairacres, N.M., U.S. | A5 | 101 |
| Fairbairn Reservoir, res., Austl. | A7 | 51 |
| Fairbank, Az., U.S. | F5 | 80 |
| Fairbank, Ia., U.S. | B5 | 92 |
| Fairbanks, Ak., U.S. | C10 | 79 |
| Fairbanks, Fl., U.S. | C4 | 86 |
| Fairbanks, In., U.S. | F2 | 91 |
| Fairbanks, Me., U.S. | D2 | 96 |
| Fair Bluff, N.C., U.S. | C3 | 110 |
| Fairborn, Oh., U.S. | C1 | 112 |
| Fairburn, Ga., U.S. | C2 | 87 |
| Fairburn, S.D., U.S. | D2 | 118 |
| Fairbury, Il., U.S. | C5 | 90 |
| Fairbury, Ne., U.S. | D8 | 104 |
| Fairchance, Pa., U.S. | G2 | 115 |
| Fairchild, Wi., U.S. | D3 | 126 |
| Fairchild Air Force Base, mil., Wa., U.S. | g13 | 124 |
| Fairdale, Ky., U.S. | B4 | 94 |
| Fairdale, N.D., U.S. | A7 | 111 |
| Fairfax, Ca., U.S. | C2 | 82 |
| Fairfax, De., U.S. | A3 | 85 |
| Fairfax, Mn., U.S. | F4 | 100 |
| Fairfax, Mo., U.S. | A2 | 102 |
| Fairfax, Oh., U.S. | o13 | 112 |
| Fairfax, S.C., U.S. | F5 | 117 |
| Fairfax, S.D., U.S. | D7 | 118 |
| Fairfax, Vt., U.S. | B2 | 122 |
| Fairfax, Va., U.S. | B5 | 123 |
| Fairfax, co., Va., U.S. | B5 | 123 |
| Fairfax Station, Va., U.S. | g12 | 123 |
| Fairfield, Austl. | *F9 | 50 |
| Fairfield, Al., U.S. | B3 | 78 |
| Fairfield, Ca., U.S. | C2 | 82 |
| Fairfield, Ct., U.S. | E2 | 84 |
| Fairfield, Id., U.S. | F4 | 89 |
| Fairfield, Il., U.S. | E5 | 90 |
| Fairfield, Ia., U.S. | C6 | 92 |
| Fairfield, Me., U.S. | D3 | 96 |
| Fairfield, Mt., U.S. | C5 | 103 |
| Fairfield, Ne., U.S. | D7 | 104 |
| Fairfield, N.J., U.S. | *B4 | 107 |
| Fairfield, N.C., U.S. | B6 | 110 |
| Fairfield, Oh., U.S. | n12 | 112 |
| Fairfield, Pa., U.S. | G7 | 115 |
| Fairfield, Tx., U.S. | D4 | 120 |
| Fairfield, Ut., U.S. | C4 | 121 |
| Fairfield, Vt., U.S. | B3 | 122 |
| Fairfield, co., Ct., U.S. | D2 | 84 |
| Fairfield, co., Oh., U.S. | C3 | 112 |
| Fairfield, co., S.C., U.S. | C5 | 117 |
| Fairfield Bay, Ar., U.S. | B3 | 81 |
| Fairfield Pond, l., Vt., U.S. | B3 | 122 |
| Fairgrove, Mi., U.S. | E7 | 99 |
| Fair Grove, Mo., U.S. | D4 | 102 |
| Fair Grove, N.C., U.S. | B1 | 110 |
| Fairhaven, Ma., U.S. | C6 | 98 |
| Fair Haven, Mi., U.S. | F8 | 99 |
| Fair Haven, N.J., U.S. | C4 | 107 |
| Fair Haven, N.Y., U.S. | B4 | 109 |
| Fair Haven, Vt., U.S. | D2 | 122 |
| Fair Head, c., N. Ire., U.K. | B5 | 11 |
| Fairhope, Al., U.S. | E2 | 78 |
| Fairland, In., U.S. | E6 | 91 |
| Fairland, Ok., U.S. | A7 | 113 |
| Fair Lawn, N.J., U.S. | h8 | 107 |
| Fairlawn, Oh., U.S. | *A4 | 112 |
| Fairlawn, Va., U.S. | C2 | 123 |
| Fairlea, W.V., U.S. | D4 | 125 |
| Fairlee, Vt., U.S. | D3 | 122 |
| Fairlight, Sask. | H5 | 75 |
| Fairmont, Il., U.S. | C6 | 90 |
| Fairmont, Mn., U.S. | G4 | 100 |
| Fairmont, Ne., U.S. | D8 | 104 |

| Name | Map Ref. | Page |
|---|---|---|

Fairmont, N.C., U.S. — C3 110
Fairmont, Ok., U.S. — A4 113
Fairmont, S.C., U.S. — B3 117
Fairmont, W.V., U.S. — B4 125
Fairmount, Ga., U.S. — B2 87
Fairmount, Il., U.S. — C6 90
Fairmount, In., U.S. — D6 91
Fairmount, Ks., U.S. — k16 93
Fairmont, Md., U.S. — D6 97
Fairmont, N.Y., U.S. — *B4 109
Fairmont, N.D., U.S. — C9 111
Fairmount Heights, Md., U.S. — f9 97
Fair Oaks, Ar., U.S. — B4 81
Fair Oaks, Ca., U.S. — *C3 82
Fair Oaks, Ga., U.S. — h7 87
Fairoaks, Pa., U.S. — h13 115
Fair Plain, Mi., U.S. — F4 99
Fairplay, Co., U.S. — C3 125
Fair Play, Md., U.S. — A2 97
Fair Play, Mo., U.S. — D4 102
Fair Play, S.C., U.S. — B2 117
Fairpoint, Oh., U.S. — B5 112
Fairpoint, S.D., U.S. — C3 118
Fairport, Ia., U.S. — C7 92
Fairport, Mi., U.S. — C4 99
Fairport, Mo., U.S. — B3 102
Fairport, N.Y., U.S. — B3 109
Fair Port, Va., U.S. — C6 123
Fairton, N.J., U.S. — E2 107
Fairvale, N.B. — D4 71
Fairview, Alta. — A1 68
Fairview, Ar., U.S. — *D4 81
Fairview, Il., U.S. — C3 90
Fairview, In., U.S. — D7 91
Fairview, Ks., U.S. — C8 93
Fairview, Ky., U.S. — D2 94
Fairview, Mi., U.S. — D6 99
Fairview, Mo., U.S. — E3 102
Fairview, Mt., U.S. — C12 103
Fairview, N.J., U.S. — D3 107
Fairview, N.J., U.S. — h8 107
Fairview, N.M., U.S. — E4 108
Fairview, N.Y., U.S. — *D7 109
Fairview, Oh., U.S. — B4 112
Fairview, Ok., U.S. — A3 113
Fairview, Or., U.S. — *B4 114
Fairview, Pa., U.S. — B1 115
Fairview, S.D., U.S. — D9 118
Fairview, Tn., U.S. — B4 119
Fairview, Ut., U.S. — D4 121
Fairview, W.V., U.S. — B4 125
Fairview, Wy., U.S. — D2 127
Fairview Heights, Il., U.S. — E3 90
Fairview Park, In., U.S. — E3 91
Fairview Park, Oh., U.S. — g9 112
Fairview Peak, mtn., Nv., U.S. — D3 105
Fairview Peak, mtn., Or., U.S. — D4 114
Fairview Shores, Fl., U.S. — *D5 86
Fair Water, Wi., U.S. — E5 126
Fairway, Ks., U.S. — k16 93
Fairweather, Mount, mtn., N.A. — D12 79
Fairwood, Wa., U.S. — *B8 124
Fairwood, Wa., U.S. — *B3 124
Fairy Glen, Sask. — D3 75
Faisalabad (Lyallpur), Pak. — B5 36
Faison, N.C., U.S. — B4 110
Faith, N.C., U.S. — B2 110
Faith, S.D., U.S. — B3 118
Faithorn, Mi., U.S. — C3 99
Faizābād (Fyzabad), India — C9 36
Fajardo, P.R. — G12 64
Fakenham, Eng., U.K. — B8 12
Fakfak, Indon. — F8 34
Fakse, Den. — C6 15
Fakse Bugt, b., Den. — C6 15
Fakse Ladeplads, Den. — C6 15
Faku, China — C10 32
Fal, stm., Eng., U.K. — D3 12
Falaba, S.L. — E2 45
Falaise, Fr. — C3 16
Falalu, i., Micron. — Q18 52
Fălciu, Rom. — B9 24
Falcon, Ar., U.S. — D2 81
Falcon, Co., U.S. — C6 83
Falcon, Ms., U.S. — A3 101
Falcon, N.C., U.S. — B4 110
Falcón, state, Ven. — A4 60
Falconer, N.Y., U.S. — C1 109
Falcon Heights, Mn., U.S. — n12 100
Falcon Heights, Or., U.S. — E5 114
Falcon Lake, res., N.A. — F3 120
Faléa, Mali — D2 45
Falefa Harbour, b., W. Sam. — F12 52
Falelima, W. Sam. — F11 52
Falémé, stm., Afr. — D2 45
Faleolo International Airport, W. Sam. — F12 52
Faleshty, Sov. Un. — B8 24
Falfurrias, Tx., U.S. — F3 120
Falher, Alta. — B2 68
Falkenberg, E. Ger. — B8 19
Falkenberg, Swe. — B6 15
Falkenstein, E. Ger. — C7 19
Falkirk, Scot., U.K. — C5 10
Falkland, N.D., U.S. — B4 111
Falkland, i. — D8 69
Falkland Islands (Islas Malvinas), dep., S.A. — I5 53
Falkner, Ms., U.S. — A5 101
Falköping, Swe. — H5 14
Falkville, Al., U.S. — A3 78
Fall, W. Ger. — B7 20
Fall, stm., Ks., U.S. — E7 93
Fall Branch, Tn., U.S. — C11 119
Fallbrook, Ca., U.S. — F5 82
Fall City, Wa., U.S. — B4 124
Fall Creek, Wi., U.S. — D2 126
Fall Creek, stm., In., U.S. — k10 91
Fallentimber, Pa., U.S. — E4 115
Falling Creek, stm., Va., U.S. — n17 123
Falling Rock Creek, stm., W.V., U.S. — m13 125
Falling Water, Tn., U.S. — h11 119
Falling Waters, W.V., U.S. — B6 125
Fallis, Ok., U.S. — B4 113
Fall Mountain Lake, Ct., U.S. — C4 84
Fållnäs, Swe. — u35 14
Fallon, Il., U.S. — D11 103
Fallon, Nv., U.S. — D3 105
Fallon, co., Mt., U.S. — D12 103
Fallon Indian Reservation, Nv., U.S. — D3 105
Fallon Naval Air Station, mil., Nv., U.S. — D3 105
Fall River, Ks., U.S. — E7 93
Fall River, Ma., U.S. — C5 98
Fallriver, Wi., U.S. — E5 126
Fall River, co., S.D., U.S. — D2 118
Fall River Lake, res., Ks., U.S. — E7 93
Fall River Mills, Ca., U.S. — B3 82
Fall Rock, Ky., U.S. — C6 94
Falls, Pa., U.S. — D10 115

Falls, co., Tx., U.S. — D4 120
Fallsburg, Ky., U.S. — B7 94
Falls Church, Va., U.S. — g12 123
Falls City, Ne., U.S. — D10 104
Falls City, Or., U.S. — C3 114
Falls Creek, Pa., U.S. — D4 115
Falls of Rough, Ky., U.S. — C3 94
Fallston, Md., U.S. — A5 97
Fallston, N.C., U.S. — B1 110
Falls Township, Pa., U.S. — *F12 115
Falls Village, Ct., U.S. — B2 84
Falmouth, N.S. — E5 71
Falmouth, Jam. — E5 64
Falmouth, Eng., U.K. — E4 10
Falmouth, In., U.S. — E7 91
Falmouth, Ky., U.S. — B5 94
Falmouth, Me., U.S. — E2 96
Falmouth, Ma., U.S. — C6 98
Falmouth, Mi., U.S. — D5 99
Falmouth, Va., U.S. — B5 123
Falmouth Bay, b., Eng., U.K. — D2 12
Falsa Chipana, Punta, c., Chile — D1 56
False Bay, b., S. Afr. — H3 49
False Cape, c., Fl., U.S. — D6 86
False Cape, c., Va., U.S. — D7 123
Falso, Cabo, c., Hond. — C6 62
Falster, i., Den. — D5 15
Falsterbo, Swe. — C6 15
Fălticeni, Rom. — B8 24
Falun, Swe. — G6 14
Falun, Ks., U.S. — D6 93
Famagusta see Gazimağusa, N. Cyp. — E9 40
Famatina, Sierra de, mts., Arg. — E2 55
Family Lake, l., Man. — D4 70
Fana, i., Micron. — Q18 52
Fanapanges, i., Micron. — Q18 52
Fancy Farm, Ky., U.S. — f9 94
Fancy Prairie, Il., U.S. — D4 90
Fang, Thai. — B1 34
Fangcheng, China — H5 32
Fangxian, China — E7 31
Fannettsburg, Pa., U.S. — F6 115
Fannin, Tx., U.S. — E4 120
Fannin, co., Ga., U.S. — B2 87
Fannin, co., Tx., U.S. — C4 120
Fanning Island see Tabuaeran Island, atoll, Kir. — F12 6
Fanny, Mount, mtn., Or., U.S. — B9 114
Fanny Bay, B.C. — E5 69
Fannystelle, Man. — E3 70
Fano, Italy — C4 23
Fanø, i., Den. — C2 15
Fanø Bugt, b., Den. — C2 15
Fañonchuluyan, Bahia, b., N. Mar. Is. — D8 52
Fan Si Pan, mtn., Viet. — A5 35
Faradje, Zaire — A4 48
Faradofay, Madag. — h9 49
Farafangana, Madag. — h9 49
Farāfirah, Al Wāḥat al, well, Eg. — C2 38
Farāh, Afg. — B3 36
Farah, stm., Afg. — B3 36
Farallón, Punta, c., Mex. — n11 63
Faramana, Burkina — D4 45
Faranah, Gui. — D2 45
Farasan Islands, is., Sau. Ar. — D4 38
Farber, Mo., U.S. — B6 102
Fareham, Eng., U.K. — D6 12
Farewell, Cape, c., N.Z. — N14 51
Fargo, Ga., U.S. — F4 87
Fargo, N.D., U.S. — C9 111
Fargo, Ok., U.S. — A2 113
Far Hills, N.J., U.S. — B3 107
Farībah, Wādī al, val., Isr. Occ. — g12 41
Fārghah, Wādī al, val., Libya — G3 40
Farīmān, Iran — D9 39
Farina, Austl. — E2 51
Farina, Il., U.S. — E5 90
Farisita, Co., U.S. — D5 83
Färiskūr, Eg. — C3 41
Farley, Ia., U.S. — B6 92
Farley, Ma., U.S. — A3 98
Farley, Mo., U.S. — B3 102
Farley, N.M., U.S. — A5 108
Farlington, Ks., U.S. — E9 93
Farm, stm., Ky., U.S. — B6 94
Farmer, Oh., U.S. — A1 112
Farmer, S.D., U.S. — D8 118
Farmer City, Il., U.S. — C5 90
Farmersburg, In., U.S. — F3 91
Farmersburg, Ia., U.S. — B6 92
Farmersville, Ca., U.S. — *D4 82
Farmersville, Il., U.S. — D4 90
Farmersville, Tx., U.S. — C4 120
Farmerville, La., U.S. — B3 95
Farmingdale, Me., U.S. — D3 96
Farmingdale, N.J., U.S. — *C4 107
Farmingdale, N.Y., U.S. — *n15 109
Farmington, Ar., U.S. — A1 81
Farmington, Ct., U.S. — C4 84
Farmington, De., U.S. — E3 85
Farmington, Il., U.S. — C3 90
Farmington, Ia., U.S. — D6 92
Farmington, Me., U.S. — D2 96
Farmington, Mi., U.S. — p15 99
Farmington, Mn., U.S. — F5 100
Farmington, Mo., U.S. — D7 102
Farmington, N.H., U.S. — D4 106
Farmington, N.M., U.S. — A1 108
Farmington, N.C., U.S. — A2 110
Farmington, Pa., U.S. — G2 115
Farmington, Tn., U.S. — B5 119
Farmington, Ut., U.S. — C4 121
Farmington, Wa., U.S. — B8 124
Farmington, W.V., U.S. — h10 125
Farmington, stm., Ct., U.S. — B4 84
Farmington, West Branch, stm., U.S. — B4 84
Farmington Hills, Mi., U.S. — *o15 99
Farmingville, N.Y., U.S. — *n15 109
Farmland, In., U.S. — D7 91
Farmville, N.C., U.S. — B5 110
Farmville, Va., U.S. — C4 123
Farnborough, Eng., U.K. — C7 12
Farne Islands, is., Eng., U.K. — C6 10
Farner, Tn., U.S. — D9 119
Farnham, Que. — D5 74
Farnham, Va., U.S. — C6 123
Farnham, Mount, mtn., B.C. — D9 69
Farnhamville, Ia., U.S. — B3 92
Färnigen, Switz. — C6 21
Faro, Port. — D2 22
Faro, Port. — D2 22
Farragut, Ia., U.S. — D2 92

Farragut, Tn., U.S. — *D9 119
Farrar, Ia., U.S. — e9 92
Farrar, stm., Scot., U.K. — C4 13
Farrāshband, Iran — G6 39
Farrell, Ms., U.S. — A3 101
Farrell, Pa., U.S. — D1 115
Farrellton, Que. — D2 74
Farrerdale, Sask. — F3 75
Farris, Ok., U.S. — C6 113
Farrukhābād, India — C6 36
Fars, hist. reg., Iran — C5 38
Fársala (Pharsalus), Grc. — C4 25
Farsī, Afg. — E11 39
Farsø, Den. — B3 15
Farson, Ia., U.S. — C5 92
Farson, Wy., U.S. — D3 127
Farsund, Nor. — H2 14
Fartak, Ra's, c., Yemen — D5 38
Fårup, Den. — B3 15
Farvel, Kap, c., Grnld. — D16 61
Farwell, Mi., U.S. — E6 99
Farwell, Ne., U.S. — C7 104
Farwell, Tx., U.S. — B1 120
Fasā, Iran — G6 39
Fashoda see Kodok, Sudan — D3 47
Fassett, Que. — D3 74
Fastov, Sov. Un. — F7 27
Fatehpur, India — C7 36
Fatsa, Tur. — B11 40
Fatumafuti, Am. Sam. — F13 52
Fatuosofia, Cape, c., W. Sam. — F11 52
Fatu Rock, rock, Am. Sam. — F13 52
Faucett, Mo., U.S. — B3 102
Faulenfürst, W. Ger. — A5 21
Faulk, co., S.D., U.S. — B6 118
Faulkland Heights, De., U.S. — i7 85
Faulkner, co., Ar., U.S. — B3 81
Faulkton, S.D., U.S. — B6 118
Faunsdale, Al., U.S. — C2 78
Fauquembergues, Fr. — D10 12
Fauquier, B.C. — E8 69
Fauquier, co., Va., U.S. — B5 123
Faust, Alta. — B3 68
Favara, Italy — F4 23
Faverges, Fr. — D2 20
Faverney, Fr. — A1 21
Faversham, Eng., U.K. — C8 12
Favorita, Fl., U.S. — C5 86
Fawcett, Alta. — B3 68
Fawcett Lake, l., Alta. — B4 68
Fawnie Nose, mtn., B.C. — C5 69
Fawnie Range, mts., B.C. — C5 69
Faxälven, stm., Swe. — F6 14
Faxon, Ok., U.S. — C3 113
Faxon, Tn., U.S. — A3 119
Fay, Ok., U.S. — B3 113
Fayd, Sau. Ar. — I14 40
Fayette, Al., U.S. — B2 78
Fayette, Ia., U.S. — B6 92
Fayette, Me., U.S. — D2 96
Fayette, Ms., U.S. — D2 101
Fayette, Oh., U.S. — A1 112
Fayette, Ut., U.S. — D4 121
Fayette, co., Al., U.S. — B3 78
Fayette, co., Ga., U.S. — C2 87
Fayette, co., Il., U.S. — D5 90
Fayette, co., In., U.S. — E7 91
Fayette, co., Ia., U.S. — B6 92
Fayette, co., Ky., U.S. — B5 94
Fayette, co., Oh., U.S. — C2 112
Fayette, co., Pa., U.S. — G2 115
Fayette, co., Tn., U.S. — B2 119
Fayette, co., Tx., U.S. — E4 120
Fayette, co., W.V., U.S. — C3 125
Fayetteville, Ar., U.S. — A1 81
Fayetteville, Ga., U.S. — C2 87
Fayetteville, N.C., U.S. — B4 110
Fayetteville, Oh., U.S. — C2 112
Fayetteville, Pa., U.S. — G6 115
Fayetteville, Tn., U.S. — B5 119
Fayetteville, W.V., U.S. — C3 125
Faylakah, i., Kuw. — G4 39
Fays-Billot, Fr. — B1 20
Fayville, Ma., U.S. — g9 98
Faywood, N.M., U.S. — E1 108
Fazenda Nova, Braz. — B2 56
Féderik, Maur. — B2 45
Fear, Cape, c., N.C., U.S. — C5 110
Feasterville, Pa., U.S. — o21 115
Feather, Middle Fork, stm., Ca., U.S. — C3 82
Feather, Mount, mtn., Ant. — e40 7
Feather Falls, Ca., U.S. — C3 82
Featherston, Ok., U.S. — B6 113
Fécamp, Fr. — C4 16
Federal, Arg. — A5 54
Federal, Mn., U.S. — C5 100
Federal Heights, Co., U.S. — *B6 83
Federal Point, Fl., U.S. — C5 86
Federalsburg, Md., U.S. — C6 97
Federal Way, Wa., U.S. — *f11 124
Fedora, S.D., U.S. — C8 118
Feeds Creek, Ky., U.S. — C7 94
Feeding Hills, Ma., U.S. — B2 98
Feesburg, Oh., U.S. — D2 112
Fefan, i., Micron. — Q18 52
Fehmarn, i., W. Ger. — A5 18
Fehmarn Strait, strt., Eur. — D5 15
Feia, Lagoa, b., Braz. — C4 56
Feijó, Braz. — E3 56
Feilding, N.Z. — N15 51
Feira, Port. — B1 22
Feira (Luangwa), Zam. — E5 48
Feira de Santana, Braz. — D3 57
Fejø, i., Den. — D5 15
Felanitx, Spain — C3 22
Felch, Mi., U.S. — C3 99
Felda, Fl., U.S. — F5 86
Feldbach, Aus. — E7 18
Feldberg, mtn., W. Ger. — B4 20
Feldkirch, Aus. — E4 18
Felicity, Oh., U.S. — D1 112
Felipe Carrillo Puerto, Mex. — D7 63
Felix, Cape, c., N.W. Ter. — C13 66
Felixstowe, Eng., U.K. — C9 12
Felixville, La., U.S. — D5 95
Fellbach, W. Ger. — E4 19
Fellingsbro, Swe. — t33 14
Fellowship, N.J., U.S. — *D3 107
Fellsmere, Fl., U.S. — E6 86
Fellsenthal, Ar., U.S. — D3 81
Felt, Id., U.S. — F7 89
Felt, Ok., U.S. — e8 113
Felton, Ca., U.S. — D2 82

Felton, De., U.S. — D3 85
Felton, Ga., U.S. — C1 87
Felton, Mn., U.S. — C2 100
Felton, Pa., U.S. — G8 115
Feltre, Italy — A3 23
Femø, i., Den. — D5 15
Femunden, l., Nor. — F4 14
Fena Valley Reservoir, res., Guam — M9 52
Fence, Wi., U.S. — C5 126
Fence, stm., Mi., U.S. — B2 99
Fence Lake, N.M., U.S. — C1 108
Fence Lake, l., Wi., U.S. — C4 126
Fenelon Falls, Ont. — C6 73
Fengcheng, China — F8 31
Fengcheng, China — D11 32
Fengdu, China — E6 31
Fengjie, China — E6 31
Fengning, China — D7 32
Fenging, China — G4 31
Fengxian, China — H2 32
Fengxiang, China — G2 32
Fengzhen, China — D5 32
Fenimore Pass, strt., Ak., U.S. — E4 79
Fenn, Id., U.S. — D2 89
Fennimore, Wi., U.S. — F3 126
Fennville, Mi., U.S. — F4 99
Fenoarivo Atsinanana, Madag. — g9 49
Fenton, Sask. — D3 75
Fenton, Ia., U.S. — A3 92
Fenton, La., U.S. — D3 95
Fenton, Mi., U.S. — F7 99
Fentress, Tx., U.S. — h8 120
Fentress, co., Tn., U.S. — C9 119
Fenwick, W.V., U.S. — C4 125
Fenwick Island, De., U.S. — G5 85
Fenwick Island, i., S.C., U.S. — k11 117
Fenwood, Sask. — G4 75
Fenyang, China — D7 31
Feodosiya, Sov. Un. — I10 27
Fer, Point au, c., La., U.S. — E4 95
Ferbane, Ire. — D4 11
Ferdig, Mt., U.S. — B5 103
Ferdinand, Id., U.S. — C2 89
Ferdinand, In., U.S. — H4 91
Ferdinandshof, E. Ger. — B7 15
Ferdows, Iran — B5 38
Père-Champenoise, Fr. — F3 17
Ferentino, Italy — D4 23
Fergana, Sov. Un. — E8 28
Fergana Mountains, mts., Sov. Un. — E8 28
Fergus, Ont. — D4 73
Fergus, Mt., U.S. — C7 103
Fergus, co., Mt., U.S. — C7 103
Fergus Falls, Mn., U.S. — D2 100
Ferguson, B.C. — D9 69
Ferguson, Ia., U.S. — C5 92
Ferguson, Ky., U.S. — C5 94
Ferguson, Mo., U.S. — C7 102
Ferkéssédougou, I.C. — E3 45
Ferme-Neuve, Que. — C2 74
Fermeuse, Newf. — E5 72
Fermo, Italy — C4 23
Fermont, Que. — h13 74
Fermoselle, Spain — B2 22
Fermoy, Ire. — D2 10
Fernández, Isla (Narborough), i., Ec. — g5 58
Fernandina Beach, Fl., U.S. — B5 86
Fernando de Noronha, Ilha, i., Braz. — B4 57
Fernandópolis, Braz. — C2 56
Fernando Póo see Bioko, i., Eq. Gui. — E1 46
Fernán-Núñez, Spain — D3 22
Fernbank, Al., U.S. — B1 78
Fern Creek, Ky., U.S. — g11 94
Fern Creek, stm., Ky., U.S. — g11 94
Ferndale, Ar., U.S. — h9 81
Ferndale, Ca., U.S. — B1 82
Ferndale, Md., U.S. — B4 97
Ferndale, Mi., U.S. — P15 99
Ferndale, Pa., U.S. — F4 115
Ferndale, Wa., U.S. — A3 124
Ferney, S.D., U.S. — B7 118
Fernie, B.C. — E10 69
Fernley, Nv., U.S. — D2 105
Fern Park, Fl., U.S. — *D5 86
Fern Ridge Lake, res., Or., U.S. — C3 114
Ferns, Ire. — E5 11
Fernwood, Id., U.S. — B2 89
Fernwood, Ms., U.S. — D3 101
Fernwood, N.Y., U.S. — B4 109
Ferrara, Italy — B3 23
Ferreira do Alentejo, Port. — C1 22
Ferreira do Zêzere, Port. — C1 22
Ferrelsburg, W.V., U.S. — C2 125
Ferrelo, Cape, c., Or., U.S. — E2 114
Ferreñafe, Peru — C2 58
Ferriday, La., U.S. — C4 95
Ferriere, Italy — B2 23
Ferris, Il., U.S. — C2 90
Ferris, Tx., U.S. — C4 120
Ferrisburg, Vt., U.S. — C2 122
Ferris Mountains, mts., Wy., U.S. — D5 127
Ferron, Ut., U.S. — D4 121
Ferros, Braz. — E7 57
Ferrum, Va., U.S. — D2 123
Ferry, Mi., U.S. — E4 99
Ferry, co., Wa., U.S. — A7 124
Ferry Farms, Va., U.S. — B5 123
Ferryland, Newf. — E5 72
Ferry Point, c., N.J., U.S. — k7 107
Ferryville, Wi., U.S. — E2 126
Fertile, Ia., U.S. — A4 92
Fertile, Mn., U.S. — C2 100
Fertília, Italy — D2 23
Firmat, Arg. — A4 54
Firminy, Fr. — D3 20
Fès, Mor. — B4 44
Feshi, Zaire — C3 48
Fessenden, N.D., U.S. — B6 111
Festina, Ia., U.S. — A6 92
Festus, Mo., U.S. — C7 102
Fetești, Rom. — C8 24
Fethard, Ire. — D4 11
Fethiye, Tur. — D7 40
Fetisovo, Sov. Un. — I7 28
Fettercairn, Scot., U.K. — E10 13
Feucht, W. Ger. — D6 19
Feuchtwangen, W. Ger. — D5 19
Feudal, Sask. — F2 75
Feuilles, Rivière aux, stm., Que. — g12 74
Feurs, Fr. — E6 16
Feversham, Ont. — C4 73
Feyẕābād, Afg. — A5 36
Fezzan (Fazzān), hist. reg., Libya — D2 43
Ffestiniog, Wales, U.K. — D5 10

Fhada, Beinn, mtn., Scot., U.K. — B4 10
Fiambalá, Arg. — E2 55
Fianarantsoa, Madag. — h9 49
Fianarantsoa, prov., Madag. — h9 49
Fianga, Chad — D3 46
Fibre, Mi., U.S. — B6 99
Ficarolo, Italy — E7 20
Fiche, Eth. — D4 47
Fichtelgebirge, mts., W. Ger. — C6 19
Ficksburg, S. Afr. — C4 49
Fidalgo Island, i., Wa., U.S. — A3 124
Fidelity, Il., U.S. — D3 90
Fidenza, Italy — B3 23
Fidler Lake, l., Man. — A3 70
Field, B.C. — D9 69
Fieldale, Va., U.S. — D3 123
Field Crest Estates, Ct., U.S. — D8 84
Fielding, Sask. — E2 75
Fielding, Ut., U.S. — B3 121
Fieldon, Il., U.S. — D3 90
Fields, La., U.S. — D2 95
Fields, Or., U.S. — E8 114
Fields, Lake, l., Ak., U.S. — k10 95
Fields, Lake, stm., Fl., U.S. — B3 86
Fieldsboro, N.J., U.S. — C3 107
Fier, Alb. — B2 25
Fierro Urco, mtn., Ec. — B2 58
Fiesch, Switz. — D5 21
Fiesole, Italy — C3 23
Fife, prov., Scot., U.K. — C5 13
Fife Lake, Mi., U.S. — D5 99
Fife Lake, Sask. — H3 75
Fife Lake, l., Sask. — H3 75
Fife Ness, c., Scot., U.K. — B5 10
Fifield, Wi., U.S. — C3 126
Fifteenmile Creek, stm., Wy., U.S. — B4 127
Fifteen Mile Falls Reservoir, res., U.S. — C5 122
Fifty Lakes, Mn., U.S. — D4 100
Figeac, Fr. — E5 16
Fig Garden, Ca., U.S. — *D4 82
Figtree, Zimb. — B4 49
Figueira da Foz, Port. — B1 22
Figueras, Spain — A7 22
Figuig, Mor. — C4 44
Fiji, ctry., Oc. — H10 6
Fik, Eth. — D5 47
Fik, Eth. — D5 47
Filchner Ice Shelf, ice, Ant. — B8 7
File Lake, l., Man. — B1 70
Filer, Id., U.S. — G4 89
Filer City, Mi., U.S. — D4 99
Filey, Eng., U.K. — F8 13
Filiatrá, Grc. — D3 25
Filicudi, i., Italy — E5 23
Filingué, Niger — D5 45
Filisur, Switz. — C8 21
Filley, Ne., U.S. — D9 104
Fillmore, Sask. — H4 75
Fillmore, Ca., U.S. — E4 82
Fillmore, Il., U.S. — D5 90
Fillmore, In., U.S. — E4 91
Fillmore, Mo., U.S. — A2 102
Fillmore, N.Y., U.S. — C2 109
Fillmore, N.D., U.S. — A6 111
Fillmore, Ok., U.S. — C5 113
Fillmore, Ut., U.S. — E3 121
Fillmore, co., Mn., U.S. — G6 100
Fillmore, co., Ne., U.S. — D8 104
Fimi, stm., Zaire — B3 48
Finale Emilia, Italy — E7 20
Fincastle, Va., U.S. — C3 123
Finch, Ont. — B9 73
Findhorn, Scot., U.K. — C5 13
Findhorn, stm., Scot., U.K. — C5 13
Findlater, Sask. — G3 75
Findlay, Il., U.S. — D5 90
Findlay, Oh., U.S. — A2 112
Findlay, Mount, mtn., B.C. — D9 69
Fine, N.Y., U.S. — A5 109
Finesville, N.J., U.S. — B2 107
Fingal, N.D., U.S. — C8 111
Finger, Tn., U.S. — B3 119
Finger Lake, l., Ont. — C5 70
Fingerville, S.C., U.S. — A3 117
Fingoè, Moz. — A5 49
Finike, Tur. — D7 40
Finisterre, Cape, c., Spain — A1 22
Finksburg, Md., U.S. — B4 97
Finland, Mn., U.S. — C7 100
Finland, ctry., Eur. — E12 14
Finland, Gulf of, b., Eur. — H12 14
Finlay, stm., B.C. — m17 69
Finlayson, Mn., U.S. — D6 100
Finley, N.D., U.S. — B8 111
Finley, Ok., U.S. — C6 113
Finley, Tn., U.S. — A2 119
Finleyson, Ga., U.S. — D3 87
Finly, In., U.S. — E6 91
Finmoore, B.C. — C6 69
Finnegan, Alta. — D5 68
Finney, co., Ks., U.S. — D3 93
Finn Mountain, hill, Ak., U.S. — C7 79
Finnsnes, Nor. — G10 14
Finschhafen, Pap. N. Gui. — k12 50
Finspång, Swe. — u33 14
Finsteraarhorn, mtn., Switz. — C5 21
Finsterwalde, E. Ger. — C6 19
Fintona, N. Ire., U.K. — C4 11
Fintown, Ire. — C3 11
Fionn Loch, l., Scot., U.K. — C3 13
Fiorenzuola, Italy — B2 23
Fiq, Isr. Occ. — F10 40
Fir, Wa., U.S. — *D4 124
Fircrest, Wa., U.S. — f10 124
Firebaugh, Ca., U.S. — D3 82
Firenzuola, Italy — A5 23
Firesteel, S.D., U.S. — B4 118
Firestone, Co., U.S. — A6 83
Firmat, Arg. — A4 54
Firozabad, India — H8 36
Firozpur, India — E5 36
Firūzābād, Iran — G6 39
Firūz Kūh, Iran — C5 39
Firth, Id., U.S. — F6 89
Firth, Ne., U.S. — D9 104
Firth, stm., N.A. — C5 66
Fischbach, W. Ger. — D6 19
Fischot Island, i., Newf. — C4 72
Fish, stm., Nmb. — D3 48
Fish, stm., Me., U.S. — A4 96
Fish, stm., Mn., U.S. — E2 100
Fish Cove Point, c., Newf. — A3 72
Fish Creek, Wi., U.S. — C6 126
Fish Creek, stm., W.V., U.S. — g8 125
Fisheating Creek, stm., Fl., U.S. — F5 86

Fisher, Ar., U.S. — B5 81
Fisher, La., U.S. — C2 95
Fisher, Mn., U.S. — C2 100
Fisher, Pa., U.S. — D3 115
Fisher, W.V., U.S. — B5 125
Fisher, co., Tx., U.S. — C2 120
Fisher, stm., Man. — D3 70
Fisher Bay, b., Man. — D3 70
Fisher Branch, Man. — D3 70
Fisher Glacier, ice, Ant. — B19 7
Fisher Lake, l., Man. — E4 71
Fishermans Island, i., Va., U.S. — h15 123
Fishers, In., U.S. — E5 91
Fishers Island, i., N.Y., U.S. — m16 109
Fishers Peak, mtn., Co., U.S. — D6 83
Fisher Strait, strt., N.W. Ter. — D16 66
Fishersville, Va., U.S. — B4 123
Fishertown, Pa., U.S. — F4 115
Fisherville, Ont. — E5 73
Fishguard [and Goodwick], Wales, U.K. — E4 10
Fish Haven, Id., U.S. — G7 89
Fishhook, Il., U.S. — D3 90
Fishing Bay, b., Md., U.S. — D5 97
Fishing Creek, Md., U.S. — D5 97
Fishing Creek, stm., N.C., U.S. — A5 110
Fishing Creek, stm., S.C., U.S. — B5 117
Fishing Creek, stm., W.V., U.S. — B4 125
Fishing Creek, North Fork, stm., W.V., U.S. — h9 125
Fishing Creek, South Fork, stm., W.V., U.S. — h9 125
Fishing Creek Reservoir, res., S.C., U.S. — B6 117
Fishing Lake, l., Man. — C4 70
Fishing Lake, l., Sask. — F4 75
Fishkill, N.Y., U.S. — D7 109
Fish Lake, l., Ut., U.S. — E4 121
Fish River Lake, l., Me., U.S. — B4 96
Fish Springs Range, mts., Ut., U.S. — D2 121
Fishtail, Mt., U.S. — E7 103
Fishtail Point, c., Ant. — f39 7
Fishtrap Lake, res., Ky., U.S. — C7 94
Fishville, La., U.S. — C3 95
Fisk, Mo., U.S. — E7 102
Fiskburg, Ky., U.S. — B5 94
Fiskdale, Ma., U.S. — B3 98
Fiske, Sask. — F1 75
Fismes, Fr. — E3 17
Fitch-Bay, Que. — D5 74
Fitchburg, Ma., U.S. — A4 98
Fitchburg, Wi., U.S. — *F4 126
Fitchville, Ct., U.S. — C7 84
Fithian, Il., U.S. — C6 90
Fitler, Ms., U.S. — C2 101
Fittstown, Ok., U.S. — C5 113
Fitzgerald, Ga., U.S. — E3 87
Fitzhugh, Ok., U.S. — C5 113
Fitz Hugh Sound, strt., B.C. — C4 69
Fitzpatrick, Que. — B5 74
Fitz Roy, Arg. — D3 54
Fitzroy, stm., Austl. — C3 50
Fitzroy, stm., Austl. — D9 50
Fitzroy, Monte (Cerro Chaltel), mtn., S.A. — D2 54
Fitzroy Harbour, Ont. — B8 73
Fitzwilliam Depot, N.H., U.S. — E2 106
Fitzwilliam Island, i., Ont. — B3 73
Fiume see Rijeka, Yugo. — C2 24
Fiumicino, Italy — h8 23
Five Island Lake, l., Ia., U.S. — A3 92
Five Islands, N.S. — D5 71
Fivemile Creek, stm., Wy., U.S. — C4 127
Fivemiletown, N. Ire., U.K. — C4 11
Five Points, Al., U.S. — B4 78
Five Points, N.M., U.S. — B3 108
Fizi, Zaire — B5 48
Fjärås Kyrkby, Swe. — A6 15
Fjärdhundra, Swe. — t34 14
Fjerritslev, Den. — A3 15
Flagg Mountain, hill, Al., U.S. — C3 78
Flag Knob, mtn., Ky., U.S. — C7 94
Flagler, Co., U.S. — B7 83
Flagler, co., Fl., U.S. — C5 86
Flagler Beach, Fl., U.S. — C5 86
Flag Pond, Tn., U.S. — C11 119
Flagstaff, Az., U.S. — B4 80
Flagstaff Lake, l., Or., U.S. — E7 114
Flagtown, N.J., U.S. — B3 107
Flamand, Lac, l., Que. — B4 74
Flambeau, stm., Wi., U.S. — C3 126
Flambeau, South Fork, stm., Wi., U.S. — C3 126
Flamborough Head, c., Eng., U.K. — C6 10
Flaming Gorge Dam, Ut., U.S. — C6 121
Flaming Gorge National Recreation Area, U.S. — E3 127
Flaming Gorge Reservoir, res., U.S. — E3 127
Flanagan, Il., U.S. — C5 90
Flanders, Ont. — E5 70
Flanders, Ct., U.S. — C7 84
Flanders, N.J., U.S. — *B3 107
Flanders, hist. reg., Eur. — B5 16
Flandreau, S.D., U.S. — C9 118
Flandreau Indian Reservation, S.D., U.S. — C9 118
Flannan Islands, is., Scot., U.K. — A3 10
Flåren, l., Swe. — H10 14
Flasher, N.D., U.S. — C4 111
Flat, Ak., U.S. — C8 79
Flat, Ky., U.S. — C6 94
Flat, Mo., U.S. — D6 102
Flat, stm., Mi., U.S. — E5 99
Flat, stm., N.C., U.S. — A4 110
Flat, stm., R.I., U.S. — E2 116
Flat Bay, Newf. — D2 72
Flat Brook, stm., N.J., U.S. — A3 107
Flatbush, Alta. — B3 68
Flat Creek, Al., U.S. — B3 78
Flat Creek, Tn., U.S. — B5 119
Flathead, co., Mt., U.S. — B2 103
Flathead, stm., N.A. — E10 69
Flathead, North Fork, stm., N.A. — B2 103
Flathead, South Fork, stm., Mt., U.S. — C3 103
Flathead Indian Reservation, Mt., U.S. — C2 103
Flathead Lake, l., Mt., U.S. — C2 103
Flathead Valley, val., Mt., U.S. — C2 103
Flat Island, i., Newf. — D4 72
Flat Lake, l., Alta. — B4 68
Flat Lake, l., La., U.S. — k9 95
Flatlands, N.B. — B3 71
Flat Lick, Ky., U.S. — D6 94
Flat Mountain, mtn., N.Z. — P11 51

| Name | Map Ref. | Page |
|---|---|---|
| Flatonia, Tx., U.S. | E4 | 120 |
| Flat River, P.E.I. | C7 | 71 |
| Flat River, Mo., U.S. | D7 | 102 |
| *Flat River Reservoir, res., R.I., U.S.* | D3 | 116 |
| Flat Rock, Al., U.S. | A4 | 78 |
| Flat Rock, Il., U.S. | E6 | 90 |
| Flat Rock, In., U.S. | F6 | 91 |
| Flat Rock, Mi., U.S. | F7 | 99 |
| Flat Rock, N.C., U.S. | f10 | 110 |
| Flat Rock, Oh., U.S. | A3 | 112 |
| *Flatrock, stm., In., U.S.* | F6 | 91 |
| *Flatrock Lake, l., Man.* | B1 | 70 |
| Flats, In., U.S. | D5 | 92 |
| *Flattery, Cape, c., Wa., U.S.* | A1 | 124 |
| Flatts, Ber. | p20 | 64 |
| Flatwood, Al., U.S. | C2 | 78 |
| Flatwoods, Ky., U.S. | B7 | 94 |
| Flatwoods, La., U.S. | C3 | 95 |
| Flatwoods, Tn., U.S. | B4 | 119 |
| Flatwoods, W.V., U.S. | *C4 | 125 |
| Flawil, Switz. | B5 | 20 |
| Flaxcombe, Sask. | F1 | 75 |
| Flaxton, N.D., U.S. | A3 | 111 |
| Flaxville, Mt., U.S. | B11 | 103 |
| Fleet, Alta. | C5 | 68 |
| Fleet, Eng., U.K. | C7 | 12 |
| Fleetwood, Eng., U.K. | G5 | 13 |
| Fleetwood, N.C., U.S. | A1 | 110 |
| Fleetwood, Pa., U.S. | F10 | 115 |
| Fleischmanns, N.Y., U.S. | C6 | 109 |
| Flekkefjord, Nor. | H2 | 14 |
| Fleming, Sask. | G5 | 75 |
| Fleming, Co., U.S. | A8 | 83 |
| Fleming, Ga., U.S. | E5 | 87 |
| Fleming, co., Ky., U.S. | B6 | 94 |
| Fleming-Neon, Ky., U.S. | C7 | 94 |
| Flemingsburg, Ky., U.S. | B6 | 94 |
| Flemington, Ga., U.S. | E5 | 87 |
| Flemington, Mo., U.S. | D4 | 102 |
| Flemington, N.J., U.S. | B3 | 107 |
| Flemington, Pa., U.S. | D7 | 115 |
| Flemington, W.V., U.S. | k10 | 125 |
| Flen, Swe. | t34 | 14 |
| Flensburg, W. Ger. | A4 | 18 |
| Flensburg, Mn., U.S. | E4 | 100 |
| *Flensburg Fjord, b., Eur.* | D3 | 15 |
| Flers, Fr. | C3 | 16 |
| Flesherton, Ont. | C4 | 73 |
| Fletcher, N.C., U.S. | f10 | 110 |
| Fletcher, Oh., U.S. | B1 | 112 |
| Fletcher, Ok., U.S. | C3 | 113 |
| Fletcher, Vt., U.S. | B3 | 122 |
| *Fletcher Islands, is., Ant.* | B3 | 7 |
| Fleur-de-Lys, Newf. | C3 | 72 |
| Fleurier, Switz. | C2 | 20 |
| Flieden, W. Ger. | C4 | 19 |
| Flims, Switz. | C7 | 21 |
| *Flinders, stm., Austl.* | C7 | 50 |
| *Flinders Island, i., Austl.* | F5 | 50 |
| *Flinders Range, mts., Austl.* | F6 | 50 |
| Flin Flon, Man. | B1 | 70 |
| Flint, Wales, U.K. | A4 | 12 |
| Flint, In., U.S. | A7 | 91 |
| Flint, Mi., U.S. | E7 | 99 |
| *Flint, stm., Ga., U.S.* | E2 | 87 |
| Flint City, Al., U.S. | A3 | 78 |
| *Flint Creek, stm., Al., U.S.* | A3 | 78 |
| *Flint Creek Range, mts., Mt., U.S.* | D3 | 103 |
| Flinthill, Mo., U.S. | C7 | 102 |
| Flint Hill, Va., U.S. | B4 | 123 |
| *Flint Hills, hills, Ks., U.S.* | D7 | 93 |
| *Flint Island, i., Kir.* | G12 | 6 |
| Flintoft, Sask. | H2 | 75 |
| Flinton, Ont. | C7 | 73 |
| *Flint Run, stm., W.V., U.S.* | k9 | 125 |
| Flintstone, Md., U.S. | k13 | 97 |
| Flintville, Tn., U.S. | B5 | 119 |
| *Flipper Point, c., Wake I.* | A2 | 52 |
| Flippin, Ar., U.S. | A3 | 81 |
| Flippin, Ky., U.S. | D4 | 94 |
| Flixecourt, Fr. | D2 | 17 |
| Flöha, E. Ger. | C8 | 19 |
| Flom, Mn., U.S. | C2 | 100 |
| Flomaton, Al., U.S. | D2 | 78 |
| Flomot, Tx., U.S. | B2 | 120 |
| *Flood Range, mts., Ant.* | B35 | 7 |
| Floodwood, Mn., U.S. | D6 | 100 |
| Flora, Il., U.S. | E5 | 90 |
| Flora, In., U.S. | C4 | 91 |
| Flora, Ms., U.S. | C3 | 101 |
| Flora, N.D., U.S. | B6 | 111 |
| Florahome, Fl., U.S. | C5 | 86 |
| Florala, Al., U.S. | D3 | 78 |
| Floral City, Fl., U.S. | D4 | 86 |
| Floral Park, N.Y., U.S. | *k13 | 109 |
| Flora Vista, N.M., U.S. | A1 | 108 |
| Florence (Firenze), Italy | C3 | 23 |
| Florence, Al., U.S. | A2 | 78 |
| Florence, Az., U.S. | D4 | 80 |
| Florence, Ca., U.S. | *n12 | 82 |
| Florence, Co., U.S. | C5 | 83 |
| Florence, In., U.S. | G8 | 91 |
| Florence, Ks., U.S. | D7 | 93 |
| Florence, Ky., U.S. | A5 | 94 |
| Florence, Ms., U.S. | C3 | 101 |
| Florence, Mo., U.S. | C5 | 102 |
| Florence, Mt., U.S. | D2 | 103 |
| Florence, N.J., U.S. | C3 | 107 |
| Florence, Or., U.S. | D2 | 114 |
| Florence, S.C., U.S. | C8 | 117 |
| Florence, S.D., U.S. | B8 | 118 |
| Florence, Tx., U.S. | D4 | 120 |
| Florence, Vt., U.S. | D2 | 122 |
| Florence, Wa., U.S. | A3 | 124 |
| Florence, Wi., U.S. | C5 | 126 |
| *Florence, co., S.C., U.S.* | C8 | 117 |
| *Florence, co., Wi., U.S.* | C5 | 126 |
| Florence Junction, Az., U.S. | D4 | 80 |
| Florenceville, N.B. | C2 | 71 |
| Florencia, Col. | C2 | 59 |
| Florenville, Bel. | E5 | 17 |
| Flores, Guat. | D7 | 63 |
| *Flores, dept., Ur.* | f8 | 54 |
| *Flores, i., Indon.* | G6 | 34 |
| *Flores, i., Port.* | g8 | 44 |
| *Flores Island, i., B.C.* | E4 | 69 |
| *Flores Sea, Indon.* | G5 | 34 |
| Floresta, Braz. | E3 | 57 |
| Floresville, Tx., U.S. | E3 | 120 |
| Florham Park, N.J., U.S. | B4 | 107 |
| Floriano, Braz. | C2 | 57 |
| Florianópolis, Braz. | D3 | 56 |
| Floriano Peixoto, Braz. | C4 | 58 |
| Florida, Cuba | D5 | 64 |
| Florida, Ma., U.S. | A1 | 98 |
| Florida, N.M., U.S. | C3 | 108 |
| Florida, N.Y., U.S. | D6 | 109 |
| Florida, Ur. | A1 | 112 |
| *Florida, dept., Ur.* | f8 | 54 |
| *Florida, state, U.S.* | E5 | 86 |
| *Florida, Cape, c., Fl., U.S.* | G6 | 86 |
| *Florida, Straits of, strt., N.A.* | F11 | 76 |
| *Florida Bay, b., Fl., U.S.* | H6 | 86 |
| Floridablanca, Col. | *B3 | 60 |
| Florida City, Fl., U.S. | G6 | 86 |
| *Florida Keys, is., Fl., U.S.* | H6 | 86 |
| *Florida Mountains, mts., N.M., U.S.* | E2 | 108 |
| *Florida State Indian Reservation, Fl., U.S.* | F5 | 86 |
| Florien, La., U.S. | C2 | 95 |
| Florin, Ca., U.S. | *C3 | 82 |
| Florina (Phlorina), Grc. | B3 | 25 |
| Floris, Ia., U.S. | D5 | 92 |
| Florissant, Co., U.S. | C5 | 83 |
| Florissant, Mo., U.S. | f13 | 102 |
| *Florissant Fossil Beds National Monument, Co., U.S.* | C5 | 83 |
| Flossmoor, Il., U.S. | k9 | 90 |
| Flournoy, Ca., U.S. | C2 | 82 |
| Flourtown, Pa., U.S. | o21 | 115 |
| Flovilla, Ga., U.S. | C3 | 87 |
| *Flower Brook, stm., Vt., U.S.* | E2 | 122 |
| Floweree, Mt., U.S. | C5 | 103 |
| Flower Hill, N.Y., U.S. | *E7 | 109 |
| Flower's Cove, Newf. | C3 | 72 |
| Flower Station, Ont. | B8 | 73 |
| Flowery Branch, Ga., U.S. | B3 | 87 |
| Flowood, Ms., U.S. | C3 | 101 |
| Floyd, Ia., U.S. | A5 | 92 |
| Floyd, N.M., U.S. | C6 | 108 |
| Floyd, Va., U.S. | D2 | 123 |
| *Floyd, co., Ga., U.S.* | B1 | 87 |
| *Floyd, co., In., U.S.* | H6 | 91 |
| *Floyd, co., Ia., U.S.* | A5 | 92 |
| *Floyd, co., Ky., U.S.* | C7 | 94 |
| *Floyd, co., Tx., U.S.* | B2 | 120 |
| *Floyd, stm., Ia., U.S.* | B1 | 92 |
| Floydada, Tx., U.S. | C2 | 120 |
| Floyd Dale, S.C., U.S. | C9 | 117 |
| Floydsburg, Ky., U.S. | g12 | 94 |
| *Floyds Fork, stm., Ky., U.S.* | B4 | 94 |
| Floyds Knobs, In., U.S. | H6 | 91 |
| *Fluchthorn, mtn., Eur.* | C9 | 21 |
| *Fluessen, l., Neth.* | B5 | 17 |
| *Flumendosa, stm., Italy* | E2 | 23 |
| Flumet, Switz. | B7 | 21 |
| Flushing, Mi., U.S. | E7 | 99 |
| Flushing, Oh., U.S. | B4 | 112 |
| Fluvanna, Tx., U.S. | C2 | 120 |
| *Fluvanna, co., Va., U.S.* | C4 | 123 |
| *Fly, stm.* | k11 | 50 |
| Fly Creek, N.Y., U.S. | C6 | 109 |
| Flyinge, Swe. | C7 | 15 |
| Flying H, N.M., U.S. | D4 | 108 |
| Foam Lake, Sask. | F4 | 75 |
| *Foam Lake, l., Sask.* | F4 | 75 |
| *Foard, co., Tx., U.S.* | B3 | 120 |
| Foça, Tur. | C6 | 25 |
| Foča, Yugo. | D4 | 24 |
| Focşani, Rom. | C8 | 24 |
| Foggia, Italy | D5 | 23 |
| *Fogland Point, c., R.I., U.S.* | E6 | 116 |
| Fogliano, Italy | k9 | 23 |
| Fogo, Newf. | D4 | 72 |
| *Fogo, Cape, c., Newf.* | D5 | 72 |
| *Fogo Island, i., Newf.* | D4 | 72 |
| Fohnsdorf, Aus. | E7 | 18 |
| *Föhr, i., W. Ger.* | A4 | 18 |
| Foix, Fr. | F4 | 16 |
| Folcroft, Pa., U.S. | *p20 | 115 |
| Foley, Al., U.S. | E2 | 78 |
| Foley, Mn., U.S. | E5 | 100 |
| Foley, Mo., U.S. | B7 | 102 |
| *Foley Island, i., N.W. Ter.* | C17 | 66 |
| Folkestone, Eng., U.K. | E7 | 10 |
| Folkston, Ga., U.S. | F4 | 87 |
| Folkston, N.C., U.S. | C5 | 110 |
| Folkstone, N.C., U.S. | C5 | 110 |
| Follansbee, W.V., U.S. | A4 | 125 |
| Follett, Tx., U.S. | A2 | 120 |
| Follonica, Italy | C3 | 23 |
| Folly Beach, S.C., U.S. | F8 | 117 |
| *Folly Island, i., S.C., U.S.* | F8 | 117 |
| Folly Mountain, Tn., U.S. | C9 | 119 |
| Folly River, Man. | D1 | 70 |
| Folsom, Ca., U.S. | C3 | 82 |
| Folsom, La., U.S. | D5 | 95 |
| Folsom, N.J., U.S. | D3 | 107 |
| Folsom, N.M., U.S. | A6 | 108 |
| Folsom, W.V., U.S. | B4 | 125 |
| Folsomville, In., U.S. | H3 | 91 |
| Fomento, Cuba | C4 | 64 |
| Fonda, Ia., U.S. | B3 | 92 |
| Fonda, N.Y., U.S. | C6 | 109 |
| Fond du Lac, Sask. | m7 | 75 |
| Fond du Lac, Wi., U.S. | E5 | 126 |
| *Fond du Lac, co., Wi., U.S.* | E5 | 126 |
| *Fond du Lac Indian Reservation, Mn., U.S.* | D6 | 100 |
| Fonde, Ky., U.S. | D6 | 94 |
| Fondi, Italy | D4 | 23 |
| Fonsagrada, Spain | A2 | 22 |
| *Fonseca, Golfo de, b., N.A.* | E7 | 63 |
| Fontainebleau, Fr. | C5 | 16 |
| Fontana, Ca., U.S. | m14 | 82 |
| Fontana, Ks., U.S. | D9 | 93 |
| Fontana, Wi., U.S. | F5 | 126 |
| Fontana Dam, N.C., U.S. | f9 | 110 |
| *Fontana Lake, res., N.C., U.S.* | f9 | 110 |
| Fontanelle, Ia., U.S. | C3 | 92 |
| Fontanet, In., U.S. | E3 | 91 |
| Fonte Boa, Braz. | D4 | 60 |
| Fontenay-le-Comte, Fr. | D3 | 16 |
| Fontenay [-sous-Bois], Fr. | g10 | 16 |
| Fontenelle, Wy., U.S. | E2 | 127 |
| *Fontenelle Reservoir, res., Wy., U.S.* | D2 | 127 |
| Foosland, Il., U.S. | C5 | 90 |
| Foothill Farms, Ca., U.S. | *C3 | 82 |
| Foothills, Alta. | C2 | 68 |
| Footville, Wi., U.S. | F4 | 126 |
| Foping, China | H2 | 32 |
| Forada, Mn., U.S. | E3 | 100 |
| Foraker, Ok., U.S. | A5 | 113 |
| *Foraker, Mount, mtn., Ak., U.S.* | f16 | 79 |
| Forbach, Fr. | C7 | 16 |
| Forbes, Austl. | F8 | 50 |
| Forbes, Mn., U.S. | C6 | 100 |
| Forbes, Mo., U.S. | B2 | 102 |
| Forbes, N.D., U.S. | D7 | 111 |
| *Forbes, Lac, l., Que.* | *B3 | 74 |
| Forcados, Nig. | E6 | 45 |
| Forcalquier, Fr. | F6 | 16 |
| Forchheim, W. Ger. | D5 | 18 |
| Ford, Scot., U.K. | D3 | 13 |
| Ford, Ky., U.S. | C5 | 94 |
| Ford, Ks., U.S. | E4 | 93 |
| *Ford, co., Il., U.S.* | C5 | 90 |
| *Ford, co., Ks., U.S.* | E4 | 93 |
| *Ford, stm., Mi., U.S.* | C3 | 99 |
| Ford City, Ca., U.S. | E4 | 82 |
| Ford City, Pa., U.S. | E2 | 115 |
| Fordland, Mo., U.S. | D5 | 102 |
| Fordoche, La., U.S. | D4 | 95 |
| Ford River, Mi., U.S. | C3 | 99 |
| Fords, N.J., U.S. | B4 | 107 |
| Fords Prairie, Wa., U.S. | C2 | 124 |
| Fordsville, Ky., U.S. | C3 | 94 |
| Fordville, N.D., U.S. | A8 | 111 |
| Fordwich, Ont. | D3 | 73 |
| Fordyce, Ar., U.S. | D3 | 81 |
| Fordyce, Ne., U.S. | B8 | 104 |
| Forécariah, Gui. | E2 | 45 |
| Foreman, Ar., U.S. | D1 | 81 |
| Foremost, Alta. | E5 | 68 |
| Foresman, In., U.S. | C3 | 91 |
| Forest, Bel. | B6 | 16 |
| Forest, Ont. | D2 | 73 |
| Forest, In., U.S. | D5 | 91 |
| Forest, Ms., U.S. | C4 | 101 |
| Forest, Oh., U.S. | B2 | 112 |
| Forest, Tx., U.S. | D5 | 120 |
| Forest, Va., U.S. | C3 | 123 |
| *Forest, co., Pa., U.S.* | C3 | 115 |
| *Forest, co., Wi., U.S.* | C5 | 126 |
| *Forest, stm., N.D., U.S.* | A8 | 111 |
| Forest Acres, S.C., U.S. | C6 | 117 |
| Forestburg, Alta. | C4 | 68 |
| Forestburg, S.D., U.S. | C7 | 118 |
| Forest City, Ia., U.S. | A4 | 92 |
| Forest City, Me., U.S. | C5 | 96 |
| Forest City, Mo., U.S. | B2 | 102 |
| Forest City, N.C., U.S. | B1 | 110 |
| Forest City, Pa., U.S. | C11 | 115 |
| Forestdale, R.I., U.S. | B3 | 116 |
| Forest Dale, Vt., U.S. | D2 | 122 |
| Forest Glen, La., U.S. | h12 | 95 |
| Forest Green, Mo., U.S. | B5 | 102 |
| Forestgrove, Mt., U.S. | D7 | 103 |
| Forest Grove, Or., U.S. | B3 | 114 |
| Forest Hill, La., U.S. | C3 | 95 |
| Forest Hill, Md., U.S. | A5 | 97 |
| Forest Hill, Tx., U.S. | *n9 | 120 |
| Forest Hills, Pa., U.S. | k14 | 115 |
| Forest Home, Al., U.S. | D3 | 78 |
| Forest Junction, Wi., U.S. | h9 | 126 |
| Forest Knolls, Ca., U.S. | g7 | 82 |
| Forest Lake, Mi., U.S. | B4 | 99 |
| Forest Lake, Mn., U.S. | E6 | 100 |
| Forest Lake, N.H., U.S. | E2 | 106 |
| Forest Park, Ga., U.S. | h8 | 87 |
| Forest Park, Il., U.S. | k9 | 90 |
| Forest Park, La., U.S. | B3 | 95 |
| Forest Park, Oh., U.S. | n12 | 112 |
| Forestport, N.Y., U.S. | B5 | 109 |
| *Forest River, N.D., U.S.* | A8 | 111 |
| Forestville, Md., U.S. | *C4 | 97 |
| Forestville, N.Y., U.S. | C1 | 109 |
| Forestville, Pa., U.S. | D1 | 115 |
| Forestville, Wi., U.S. | D6 | 126 |
| Forfar, Scot., U.K. | E10 | 13 |
| Forgan, Sask. | F2 | 75 |
| Forgan, Ok., U.S. | A1 | 113 |
| Forges-les-Eaux, Fr. | C4 | 16 |
| Forge Village, Ma., U.S. | A5 | 98 |
| *Forillon, Parc National de, Que.* | k14 | 74 |
| Fork, N.C., U.S. | B2 | 110 |
| Fork, S.C., U.S. | C9 | 117 |
| *Fork Creek, stm., W.V., U.S.* | m12 | 125 |
| *Forked Deer, stm., Tn., U.S.* | B2 | 119 |
| *Forked Deer, Middle Fork, stm., Tn., U.S.* | D3 | 119 |
| *Forked Deer, North Fork, stm., Tn., U.S.* | B3 | 119 |
| *Forked Deer, South Fork, stm., Tn., U.S.* | B2 | 119 |
| Forked Island, La., U.S. | E3 | 95 |
| Forked River, N.J., U.S. | D4 | 107 |
| Forkland, Al., U.S. | C2 | 78 |
| Fork Mountain, Tn., U.S. | C9 | 119 |
| Fork River, Man. | D1 | 70 |
| Forks, Wa., U.S. | B1 | 124 |
| Fork Shoals, S.C., U.S. | B3 | 117 |
| Forksville, Pa., U.S. | D8 | 115 |
| Fork Union, Va., U.S. | C4 | 123 |
| Forkville, Ms., U.S. | C4 | 101 |
| Forlì, Italy | B4 | 23 |
| Forman, N.D., U.S. | C8 | 111 |
| Formazza, Italy | C4 | 20 |
| Formby, Eng., U.K. | A4 | 12 |
| *Formentera, i., Spain* | C6 | 22 |
| Formia, Italy | C6 | 23 |
| Formiga, Braz. | C3 | 56 |
| Formosa, Arg. | E4 | 55 |
| Formosa, Braz. | B3 | 56 |
| Formosa, Ont. | C3 | 73 |
| *Formosa, prov., Arg.* | D5 | 55 |
| *Formosa, Serra, plat., Braz.* | E4 | 59 |
| *Formosa Bay, b., Kenya* | B7 | 48 |
| *Formosa see Taiwan, ctry., Asia* | G9 | 31 |
| Formoso, Ks., U.S. | C6 | 93 |
| *Formoso, stm., Braz.* | A4 | 56 |
| Fornovo di Taro, Italy | E6 | 20 |
| Forres, Scot., U.K. | D9 | 13 |
| Forrest, Austl. | F4 | 50 |
| Forrest, Il., U.S. | C5 | 90 |
| *Forrest, co., Ms., U.S.* | D4 | 101 |
| Forrest City, Ar., U.S. | B5 | 81 |
| *Forrester Island, i., Ak., U.S.* | n23 | 79 |
| *Forrest Lakes, l., Austl.* | E4 | 50 |
| Forreston, Il., U.S. | A4 | 90 |
| Forsayth, Austl. | C7 | 50 |
| Förslövsholm, Swe. | B6 | 15 |
| Forst [Lausitz], E. Ger. | C7 | 18 |
| Forsyth, Ga., U.S. | C3 | 87 |
| Forsyth, Il., U.S. | D5 | 90 |
| Forsyth, Mo., U.S. | E4 | 102 |
| Forsyth, Mt., U.S. | D10 | 103 |
| *Forsyth, co., Ga., U.S.* | B2 | 87 |
| *Forsyth, co., N.C., U.S.* | A2 | 110 |
| Fort Adams, Ms., U.S. | D2 | 101 |
| Fort Albany, Ont. | n19 | 73 |
| Fortaleza, Braz. | B3 | 57 |
| Fortaleza de Ituxi, Braz. | C4 | 58 |
| Fort Apache, Az., U.S. | D6 | 80 |
| *Fort Apache Indian Reservation, Az., U.S.* | D5 | 80 |
| *Fort-Archambault see Sarh, Chad* | D3 | 46 |
| Fort Ashby, W.V., U.S. | B6 | 125 |
| Fort Assiniboine, Alta. | B3 | 68 |
| Fort Atkinson, Ia., U.S. | A6 | 92 |
| Fort Atkinson, Wi., U.S. | F5 | 126 |
| Fort Augustus, Scot., U.K. | C4 | 13 |
| Fort Barnwell, N.C., U.S. | B5 | 110 |
| Fort Beaufort, S. Afr. | D4 | 49 |
| Fort Belknap Agency, Mt., U.S. | B8 | 103 |
| *Fort Belknap Indian Reservation, Mt., U.S.* | B8 | 103 |
| Fort Belvoir, mil., Va., U.S. | g12 | 123 |
| *Fort Bend, co., Tx., U.S.* | E5 | 120 |
| Fort Benjamin Harrison, mil., In., U.S. | k10 | 91 |
| Fort Benning, mil., Ga., U.S. | D1 | 87 |
| Fort Benton, Mt., U.S. | C6 | 103 |
| *Fort Berthold Indian Reservation, N.D., U.S.* | B3 | 111 |
| Fort Bidwell, Ca., U.S. | B3 | 82 |
| *Fort Bidwell Indian Reservation, Ca., U.S.* | B3 | 82 |
| Fort Blackmore, Va., U.S. | f9 | 123 |
| Fort Bliss, mil., Tx., U.S. | o11 | 120 |
| Fort Bragg, Ca., U.S. | C2 | 82 |
| Fort Bragg, mil., N.C., U.S. | B3 | 110 |
| Fort Branch, In., U.S. | H2 | 91 |
| Fort Bridger, Wy., U.S. | E2 | 127 |
| Fort Calhoun, Ne., U.S. | C9 | 104 |
| Fort Campbell, mil., Ky., U.S. | A4 | 119 |
| Fort Carson, mil., Co., U.S. | C6 | 83 |
| Fort Chipewyan, Alta. | f8 | 68 |
| Fort Clark, N.D., U.S. | B4 | 111 |
| *Fort Clatsop National Memorial, hist., Or., U.S.* | A3 | 114 |
| Fort Cobb, Ok., U.S. | B3 | 113 |
| *Fort Cobb Reservoir, res., Ok., U.S.* | B3 | 113 |
| Fort Collins, Co., U.S. | A5 | 83 |
| Fort Coulonge, Que. | B8 | 73 |
| Fort Covington, N.Y., U.S. | f10 | 109 |
| Fort Crampel, Cen. Afr. Rep. | C4 | 78 |
| Fort Davis, Al., U.S. | C4 | 78 |
| *Fort Davis National Historic Site, hist., Tx., U.S.* | o13 | 120 |
| Fort Defiance, Az., U.S. | B6 | 80 |
| Fort-de-France, Mart. | I14 | 64 |
| *Fort-de-France, Baie de, b., Mart.* | S10 | 65 |
| Fort Deposit, Al., U.S. | D3 | 78 |
| Fort Detrick, mil., Md., U.S. | B3 | 97 |
| Fort Devens, mil., Ma., U.S. | f9 | 98 |
| Fort Dix, mil., N.J., U.S. | C3 | 107 |
| Fort Dodge, Ia., U.S. | B3 | 92 |
| Fort Dodge, Ks., U.S. | D4 | 93 |
| *Fort Donelson National Military Park, Tn., U.S.* | A4 | 119 |
| Fort Duchesne, Ut., U.S. | C6 | 121 |
| Forteau, Newf. | C3 | 72 |
| Fort Edward, N.Y., U.S. | B7 | 109 |
| Fort Erie, Ont. | E6 | 73 |
| Fortescue, Mo., U.S. | A2 | 102 |
| Fortescue, N.J., U.S. | E2 | 107 |
| *Fortescue, stm., Austl.* | D2 | 50 |
| Fort Eustis, mil., Va., U.S. | h14 | 123 |
| Fort Fairfield, Me., U.S. | B5 | 96 |
| Fort Fitzgerald, Alta. | f8 | 68 |
| Fort Foureau, Cam. | C3 | 46 |
| Fort-Foureau, Chad | C3 | 46 |
| Fort Frances, Ont. | o16 | 73 |
| Fort Fraser, B.C. | B5 | 69 |
| Fort Gaines, Ga., U.S. | E1 | 87 |
| Fort Garland, Co., U.S. | D5 | 83 |
| Fort Gay, W.V., U.S. | C2 | 125 |
| Fort Gibson, Ok., U.S. | B6 | 113 |
| *Fort Gibson Lake, res., Ok., U.S.* | A6 | 113 |
| Fort Good Hope, N.W. Ter. | C7 | 66 |
| Fort Gordon, mil., Ga., U.S. | C4 | 87 |
| Fort Graham, B.C. | f8 | 68 |
| Fort Greely, mil., Ak., U.S. | C10 | 79 |
| Fort Green, Fl., U.S. | E5 | 86 |
| *Forth, stm., Scot., U.K.* | D4 | 13 |
| *Forth, Firth of, est., Scot., U.K.* | B5 | 10 |
| Fort Hall, Kenya | B6 | 48 |
| Fort Hall, Id., U.S. | F6 | 89 |
| *Fort Hall Indian Reservation, Id., U.S.* | F6 | 89 |
| Fort Hancock, Tx., U.S. | o12 | 120 |
| Fort Hill, Pa., U.S. | G3 | 115 |
| Fort Hood, mil., Tx., U.S. | D4 | 120 |
| Fort Howard, Md., U.S. | B5 | 97 |
| Fort Huachuca, mil., Az., U.S. | F5 | 80 |
| Fortierville, Que. | C5 | 74 |
| Fortine, Mt., U.S. | B2 | 103 |
| Fortín Uno, Arg. | B3 | 54 |
| Fort Jackson, mil., S.C., U.S. | C6 | 117 |
| *Fort Jefferson National Monument, Fl., U.S.* | H4 | 86 |
| Fort Jennings, Oh., U.S. | B1 | 112 |
| Fort Jones, Ca., U.S. | B2 | 82 |
| Fort Kent, Alta. | B5 | 68 |
| Fort Kent, Me., U.S. | A4 | 96 |
| Fort Kent Mills, Me., U.S. | A4 | 96 |
| Fort Klamath, Or., U.S. | E5 | 114 |
| Fort Knox, mil., Ky., U.S. | B4 | 94 |
| *Fort-Lamy see N'Djamena, Chad* | C3 | 46 |
| Fort Langley, B.C. | f13 | 69 |
| Fort Laramie, Wy., U.S. | D8 | 127 |
| *Fort Laramie National Historic Site, hist., Wy., U.S.* | D8 | 127 |
| Fort Lauderdale, Fl., U.S. | F6 | 86 |
| Fort Lawn, S.C., U.S. | B6 | 117 |
| Fort Leavenworth, mil., Ks., U.S. | C9 | 93 |
| Fort Lee, mil., Va., U.S. | C5 | 123 |
| Fort Leonard Wood, mil., Mo., U.S. | D5 | 102 |
| Fort Lewis, mil., Wa., U.S. | B3 | 124 |
| Fort Liard, N.W. Ter. | D8 | 66 |
| Fort Littleton, Pa., U.S. | F5 | 115 |
| Fort Loramie, Oh., U.S. | B1 | 112 |
| Fort Loudon, Pa., U.S. | G6 | 115 |
| *Fort Loudoun Lake, res., Tn., U.S.* | D9 | 119 |
| Fort Lupton, Co., U.S. | A6 | 83 |
| Fort MacArthur, mil., Ca., U.S. | n12 | 82 |
| Fort MacKay, Alta. | f8 | 68 |
| Fort Macleod, Alta. | E4 | 68 |
| Fort Madison, Ia., U.S. | D6 | 92 |
| *Fort Matanzas National Monument, Fl., U.S.* | C5 | 86 |
| Fort McClellan, mil., Al., U.S. | B4 | 78 |
| *Fort McDermitt Indian Reservation, Az., U.S.* | B4 | 105 |
| *Fort McDowell Indian Reservation, Az., U.S.* | D4 | 80 |
| *Fort McHenry National Monument And Historic Shrine, Md., U.S.* | g11 | 97 |
| Fort McKavett, Tx., U.S. | D2 | 120 |
| Fort McKinley, Oh., U.S. | *C1 | 112 |
| Fort McMurray, Alta. | A5 | 68 |
| Fort McPherson, N.W. Ter. | C6 | 66 |
| Fort Meade, Fl., U.S. | E5 | 86 |
| Fort Meade, mil., Md., U.S. | B4 | 97 |
| *Fort Meadow Reservoir, res., Ma., U.S.* | g9 | 98 |
| Fort Mill, S.C., U.S. | A6 | 117 |
| Fort Miller, N.Y., U.S. | B7 | 109 |
| Fort Mitchell, Al., U.S. | C4 | 78 |
| Fort Mitchell, Ky., U.S. | h13 | 94 |
| Fort Mitchell, Va., U.S. | D4 | 123 |
| *Fort Mojave Indian Reservation, U.S.* | C1 | 80 |
| Fort Monmouth, mil., N.J., U.S. | C4 | 107 |
| Fort Monroe, mil., Va., U.S. | h15 | 123 |
| Fort Morgan, Al., U.S. | E1 | 78 |
| Fort Morgan, Co., U.S. | A7 | 83 |
| Fort Motte, S.C., U.S. | D6 | 117 |
| Fort Myer, mil., Va., U.S. | g12 | 123 |
| Fort Myers, Fl., U.S. | F5 | 86 |
| Fort Myers Beach, Fl., U.S. | F5 | 86 |
| Fort Necessity, La., U.S. | B4 | 95 |
| Fort Nelson, B.C. | m18 | 69 |
| Fort Norman, N.W. Ter. | D7 | 66 |
| Fort Ogden, Fl., U.S. | E5 | 86 |
| Fort Oglethorpe, Ga., U.S. | B1 | 87 |
| Fort Ord, mil., Ca., U.S. | D3 | 82 |
| Fort Payne, Al., U.S. | A4 | 78 |
| Fort Peck, Mt., U.S. | B10 | 103 |
| Fort Peck Dam, Mt., U.S. | B10 | 103 |
| *Fort Peck Indian Reservation, Mt., U.S.* | B11 | 103 |
| *Fort Peck Lake, res., Mt., U.S.* | C9 | 103 |
| Fort Pierce, Fl., U.S. | E6 | 86 |
| *Fort Pierce Inlet, b., Fl., U.S.* | E6 | 86 |
| Fort Pierre, S.D., U.S. | C5 | 118 |
| Fort Plain, N.Y., U.S. | C6 | 109 |
| Fort Polk, mil., La., U.S. | C2 | 95 |
| Fort Portal, Ug. | A5 | 48 |
| Fort Providence, N.W. Ter. | D9 | 66 |
| Fort Qu'Appelle, Sask. | G4 | 75 |
| Fort Randall Dam, S.D., U.S. | D7 | 118 |
| Fort Ransom, N.D., U.S. | C8 | 111 |
| Fort Recovery, Oh., U.S. | B1 | 112 |
| Fort Reliance, N.W. Ter. | D11 | 66 |
| Fort Resolution, N.W. Ter. | D10 | 66 |
| Fort Rice, N.D., U.S. | C5 | 111 |
| Fort Richardson, mil., Ak., U.S. | C10 | 79 |
| Fort Riley, mil., Ks., U.S. | C7 | 93 |
| Fort Ripley, Mn., U.S. | D4 | 100 |
| Fort Ritchie, mil., Md., U.S. | A3 | 97 |
| Fort Ritner, In., U.S. | G5 | 91 |
| Fort Robinson, Ne., U.S. | B2 | 104 |
| Fort Rock, Or., U.S. | D5 | 114 |
| Fortrose, N.Z. | Q12 | 51 |
| Fortrose, Scot., U.K. | C4 | 13 |
| Fort Ross, N.W. Ter. | B14 | 66 |
| Fort Rucker, mil., Al., U.S. | D4 | 78 |
| Fort Saint James, B.C. | B5 | 69 |
| Fort Saint John, B.C. | A7 | 69 |
| Fort Sam Houston, mil., Tx., U.S. | k7 | 120 |
| Fort Saskatchewan, Alta. | C4 | 68 |
| Fort Scott, Ks., U.S. | E9 | 93 |
| Fort Severn, Ont. | n18 | 73 |
| Fort Shafter, mil., Hi., U.S. | g10 | 88 |
| Fort Shaw, Mt., U.S. | C5 | 103 |
| Fort Shawnee, Oh., U.S. | B1 | 112 |
| Fort Sheridan, mil., Il., U.S. | h9 | 90 |
| Fort-Shevchenko, Sov. Un. | E4 | 28 |
| Fort Sibut, Cen. Afr. Rep. | D3 | 46 |
| Fort Sill, mil., Ok., U.S. | C3 | 113 |
| Fort Simpson, N.W. Ter. | D8 | 66 |
| Fort Smith, Ar., U.S. | B1 | 81 |
| Fort Smith, N.W. Ter. | D10 | 66 |
| Fort Stanton, N.M., U.S. | D4 | 108 |
| Fort Steele, B.C. | E10 | 69 |
| Fort Steele, Wy., U.S. | E6 | 127 |
| Fort Stewart, mil., Ga., U.S. | D5 | 87 |
| Fort Stockton, Tx., U.S. | D1 | 120 |
| *Fort Sumter National Monument, S.C., U.S.* | k12 | 117 |
| Fort Supply, Ok., U.S. | A2 | 113 |
| *Fort Supply Lake, res., Ok., U.S.* | A2 | 113 |
| Fort Thomas, Az., U.S. | D6 | 80 |
| Fort Thomas, Ky., U.S. | h14 | 94 |
| Fort Thompson, S.D., U.S. | C6 | 118 |
| Fort Totten, N.D., U.S. | B7 | 111 |
| *Fort Totten Indian Reservation, N.D., U.S.* | B7 | 111 |
| Fort Towson, Ok., U.S. | C6 | 113 |
| Fortuna, Ca., U.S. | B1 | 82 |
| Fortuna, Mo., U.S. | C5 | 102 |
| Fortuna, N.D., U.S. | A2 | 111 |
| Fortuna Ledge (Marshall), Ak., U.S. | C7 | 79 |
| Fortune, Newf. | E4 | 72 |
| *Fortune Bay, b., Newf.* | E4 | 72 |
| Fortune Harbour, Newf. | D4 | 72 |
| *Fort Union National Monument, N.M., U.S.* | B5 | 108 |
| Fort Valley, Ga., U.S. | D3 | 87 |
| Fort Vermilion, Alta. | f7 | 68 |
| Fort Walton Beach, Fl., U.S. | u15 | 86 |
| Fort Washakie, Wy., U.S. | C4 | 127 |
| Fort Washington, Pa., U.S. | o21 | 115 |
| *Fort Washington Forest, Md., U.S.* | | |
| Fort Wayne, In., U.S. | B7 | 91 |
| Fort Wellington, Guy. | C4 | 59 |
| Fort White, Fl., U.S. | C4 | 86 |
| Fort William, Scot., U.K. | C3 | 13 |
| Fort Wingate, N.M., U.S. | B1 | 108 |
| Fort Worth, Tx., U.S. | C4 | 120 |
| Fort Wright, Ky., U.S. | h13 | 94 |
| Forty Fort, Pa., U.S. | D10 | 115 |
| Fort Yukon, Ak., U.S. | B10 | 79 |
| Fort Yates, N.D., U.S. | C5 | 111 |
| *Foss Reservoir, res., Ok., U.S.* | B2 | 113 |
| Fosston, Sask. | E4 | 75 |
| Fosston, Mn., U.S. | C3 | 100 |
| Foster, In., U.S. | D3 | 91 |
| Foster, Ky., U.S. | B5 | 94 |
| Foster, Mo., U.S. | C3 | 102 |
| Foster, Ne., U.S. | B8 | 104 |
| Foster, Ok., U.S. | C4 | 113 |
| Foster, Or., U.S. | C4 | 114 |
| Foster, R.I., U.S. | C2 | 116 |
| Foster, Wi., U.S. | D2 | 126 |
| *Foster, co., N.D., U.S.* | B6 | 111 |
| *Foster, stm., Sask.* | A3 | 75 |
| Foster Brook, Pa., U.S. | C4 | 115 |
| Foster City, Ca., U.S. | *h8 | 82 |
| Foster City, Mi., U.S. | C3 | 99 |
| Fosters, Al., U.S. | B2 | 78 |
| Fosters Falls, Va., U.S. | D2 | 123 |
| *Fosters Pond, l., Ma., U.S.* | f11 | 98 |
| Foster Village, Hi., U.S. | g10 | 88 |
| Fosterville, Tn., U.S. | B5 | 119 |
| Fostoria, Al., U.S. | C3 | 78 |
| Fostoria, Ia., U.S. | A2 | 92 |
| Fostoria, Ks., U.S. | C7 | 93 |
| Fostoria, Mi., U.S. | E7 | 99 |
| Fostoria, Oh., U.S. | A2 | 112 |
| Fougamou, Gabon | F2 | 46 |
| Fougères, Fr. | C3 | 16 |
| *Foula, i., Scot., U.K.* | g9 | 10 |
| Foulke, Ar., U.S. | D2 | 81 |
| *Foulness Island, i., Eng., U.K.* | C8 | 12 |
| *Foulwind, Cape, c., N.Z.* | N13 | 51 |
| Foumban, Cam. | D2 | 46 |
| Foum el Hassane, Mor. | D3 | 44 |
| Fount, Ky., U.S. | C6 | 94 |
| Fountain, Al., U.S. | D2 | 78 |
| Fountain, Co., U.S. | C6 | 83 |
| Fountain, Fl., U.S. | B1 | 86 |
| Fountain, Mi., U.S. | D4 | 99 |
| Fountain, Mn., U.S. | G6 | 100 |
| Fountain, N.C., U.S. | B5 | 110 |
| *Fountain, co., In., U.S.* | D3 | 91 |
| Fountain City, In., U.S. | E8 | 91 |
| Fountain City, Wi., U.S. | D2 | 126 |
| *Fountain Creek, stm., Co., U.S.* | C6 | 83 |
| Fountain Green, Ut., U.S. | D4 | 121 |
| Fountain Hill, Ar., U.S. | D4 | 81 |
| Fountain Hill, Pa., U.S. | E11 | 115 |
| Fountain Inn, S.C., U.S. | B3 | 117 |
| Fountain Lake, Ar., U.S. | f8 | 81 |
| *Fountain Peak, mtn., Ca., U.S.* | E6 | 82 |
| Fountain Place, La., U.S. | D4 | 95 |
| Fountain Run, Ky., U.S. | D4 | 94 |
| Fountaintown, In., U.S. | E6 | 91 |
| Fountain Valley, Ca., U.S. | *n13 | 82 |
| Four Buttes, Mt., U.S. | B11 | 103 |
| Fourchambault, Fr. | D5 | 16 |
| Fourche, Ar., U.S. | *C3 | 81 |
| *Fourche Creek, stm., Ar., U.S.* | k10 | 81 |
| *Fourche LaFave, stm., Ar., U.S.* | C2 | 81 |
| *Fourche Maline, stm., Ok., U.S.* | C6 | 113 |
| *Fourche Mountain, mtn., Ar., U.S.* | C2 | 81 |
| Fourchu, N.S. | D9 | 71 |
| Four Corners, Ca., U.S. | E5 | 82 |
| Four Corners, Or., U.S. | *C4 | 114 |
| Four Corners, Wy., U.S. | B8 | 127 |
| Four Lakes, Wa., U.S. | B8 | 124 |
| Fourmies, Fr. | B6 | 16 |
| Fourmile, Ky., U.S. | D6 | 94 |
| *Fourmile Creek, stm., Ia., U.S.* | e8 | 92 |
| *Four Mountains, Islands of, is., Ak., U.S.* | E6 | 79 |
| Fournier, Ont. | B10 | 73 |
| Four Oaks, N.C., U.S. | B4 | 110 |
| *Fouta Djallon, reg., Gui.* | E2 | 45 |
| *Foveaux Strait, strt., N.Z.* | Q11 | 51 |
| Fowey, Eng., U.K. | D3 | 12 |
| Fowler, Ca., U.S. | D4 | 82 |
| Fowler, Co., U.S. | C6 | 83 |
| Fowler, Il., U.S. | C2 | 90 |
| Fowler, In., U.S. | C3 | 91 |
| Fowler, Ks., U.S. | E3 | 93 |
| Fowler, Mi., U.S. | E6 | 99 |
| Fowlerton, In., U.S. | D6 | 91 |
| Fowlerville, Mi., U.S. | F6 | 99 |
| Fowlkes, Tn., U.S. | B2 | 119 |
| Fowlstown, Ga., U.S. | F2 | 87 |
| Fox, Ar., U.S. | B3 | 81 |
| Fox, Ok., U.S. | C4 | 113 |
| *Fox, stm., Man.* | B4 | 70 |
| *Fox, stm., Il., U.S.* | B5 | 90 |
| *Fox, stm., Wi., U.S.* | D5 | 126 |
| Foxboro, Ont. | C7 | 73 |
| Foxboro, Ma., U.S. | B5 | 98 |
| Foxboro, Wi., U.S. | B1 | 126 |
| Fox Chapel, Pa., U.S. | *h14 | 115 |
| Fox Creek, Alta. | B2 | 68 |
| Foxdale, I. of Man | F4 | 13 |
| *Foxe Basin, b., N.W. Ter.* | C17 | 66 |
| *Foxe Channel, strt., N.W. Ter.* | D16 | 66 |
| *Foxe Peninsula, pen., N.W. Ter.* | C17 | 66 |
| Foxford, Ire. | D3 | 11 |
| Fox Harbour, Newf. | B5 | 108 |
| Fox Harbour, Newf. | B4 | 72 |
| Foxholm, N.D., U.S. | A4 | 111 |
| Fortville, In., U.S. | E6 | 91 |
| *Fox Island, i., R.I., U.S.* | E4 | 116 |
| *Fox Island, i., Wa., U.S.* | f10 | 124 |
| *Fox Islands, is., Ak., U.S.* | E6 | 79 |
| Fox Lake, Il., U.S. | A5 | 90 |
| Fox Lake, Wi., U.S. | E5 | 126 |
| *Fox Lake, l., Il., U.S.* | h8 | 90 |
| *Fox Mountain, mtn., Yukon* | D6 | 66 |
| *Fox Mountain, mtn., Nv., U.S.* | B2 | 105 |
| Foxpark, Wy., U.S. | E6 | 127 |
| Fox Point, Wi., U.S. | *E6 | 126 |
| Fox River Grove, Il., U.S. | h8 | 90 |
| Foxton, N.Z. | N15 | 51 |
| Foxvale, Ma., U.S. | B5 | 98 |
| Fox Valley, Sask. | G1 | 75 |
| Foxville, Md., U.S. | A3 | 97 |
| Foxwarren, Man. | D1 | 70 |
| Foxworth, Ms., U.S. | D4 | 101 |
| Foyil, Ok., U.S. | A6 | 113 |
| *Foyle, stm., Eur.* | D2 | 11 |
| *Foyle, Lough, b., Eur.* | D2 | 11 |
| Foynes, Ire. | D2 | 11 |
| Foz do Cunene, Ang. | E1 | 48 |
| Foz do Iguaçu, Braz. | C6 | 56 |
| Foz do Jordão, Braz. | C4 | 58 |
| Foz do Pauini, Braz. | C4 | 58 |
| Fraga, Spain | B6 | 22 |
| Fraile Muerto, Ur. | C5 | 54 |
| Frametown, W.V., U.S. | C4 | 125 |
| Framingham, Ma., U.S. | B5 | 98 |

Name   Map Ref.   Page

Framnes Mountains, mts., Ant. C19 7
Franca, Braz. C3 56
França, Braz. D2 57
Française, Pointe, c., Fr. Gu. A4 59
Francavilla Fontana, Italy D6 23
France, ctry., Eur. D5 16
Frances, Ky., U.S. e9 94
Francés, Cabo, c., Cuba D2 64
Francestown, N.H., U.S. E3 106
Franceville, In., U.S. C4 91
Franceville, Gabon F2 46
Franche-Comté, hist. reg., Fr. D6 16
Francis, Sask. G4 75
Francis, Ok., U.S. C5 113
Francis, Ut., U.S. C4 121
Francis, W.V., U.S. k10 125
Francis, Lake, l., N.H., U.S. f7 106
Francis Case, Lake, res., S.D., U.S. D6 118
Francisco, In., U.S. H3 91
Francisco Sá, Braz. B4 56
Francis Creek, Wi., U.S. h10 126
Francistown, Bots. B4 49
François, Newf. E3 72
François Lake, l., B.C. C5 69
Franconia, N.H., U.S. E3 106
Franconia, Va., U.S. *B5 123
Franconia Notch, N.H., U.S. B3 106
Franconville, Fr. g9 16
Francs Peak, mtn., Wy., U.S. C3 127
Franeker, Neth. A5 17
Frank, W.V., U.S. C5 125
Frankel City, Tx., U.S. C1 120
Frankenberg, Ger. C8 19
Frankenberg [-Eder], W. Ger. C4 18
Frankenmuth, Mi., U.S. E7 99
Frankenthal, W. Ger. D4 18
Frankewing, Tn., U.S. B5 119
Frankfield, Jam. E14 65
Frankford, Ont. C7 73
Frankford, De., U.S. F5 85
Frankford, Mo., U.S. B6 102
Frankford, W.V., U.S. D4 125
Frankford see Kilcormac, Ire. D4 11
Frankfort, S. Afr. C4 49
Frankfort, Il., U.S. m9 90
Frankfort, In., U.S. D4 91
Frankfort, Ks., U.S. C7 93
Frankfort, Ky., U.S. B5 94
Frankfort, Me., U.S. D4 96
Frankfort, Mi., U.S. D4 99
Frankfort, N.Y., U.S. B5 109
Frankfort, Oh., U.S. C2 112
Frankfort, S.D., U.S. C7 118
Frankfurt [am Main], W. Ger. C4 18
Frankfurt [an der Oder], E. Ger. B7 18
Fränkische Saale, stm., W. Ger. C5 19
Frank Lake, l., Alta. D4 68
Franklin, Man. D2 70
Franklin, Al., U.S. D2 78
Franklin, Ar., U.S. E6 80
Franklin, Ar., U.S. A4 81
Franklin, Ct., U.S. C7 84
Franklin, Ga., U.S. C1 87
Franklin, Id., U.S. G7 89
Franklin, Il., U.S. D3 90
Franklin, In., U.S. F5 91
Franklin, Ia., U.S. D6 92
Franklin, Ks., U.S. E9 93
Franklin, Ky., U.S. D3 94
Franklin, La., U.S. E4 95
Franklin, Me., U.S. D4 96
Franklin, Ma., U.S. B5 98
Franklin, Mn., U.S. F4 100
Franklin, Mo., U.S. B5 102
Franklin, Ne., U.S. D7 104
Franklin, N.H., U.S. D3 106
Franklin, N.J., U.S. A3 107
Franklin, N.Y., U.S. C5 109
Franklin, N.C., U.S. f9 110
Franklin, Oh., U.S. C1 112
Franklin, Pa., U.S. D2 115
Franklin, Tn., U.S. B5 119
Franklin, Tx., U.S. D4 120
Franklin, Va., U.S. D6 123
Franklin, W.V., U.S. C5 125
Franklin, Wi., U.S. n11 126
Franklin, dept., N.W. Ter. B15 66
Franklin, co., Al., U.S. A2 78
Franklin, co., Ar., U.S. B2 81
Franklin, co., Fl., U.S. C2 86
Franklin, co., Ga., U.S. B3 87
Franklin, co., Id., U.S. G7 89
Franklin, co., Il., U.S. E4 90
Franklin, co., In., U.S. F7 91
Franklin, co., Ia., U.S. B4 92
Franklin, co., Ks., U.S. D8 93
Franklin, co., Ky., U.S. B5 94
Franklin, co., La., U.S. B4 95
Franklin, co., Me., U.S. C2 96
Franklin, co., Ma., U.S. A2 98
Franklin, co., Ms., U.S. D3 101
Franklin, co., Mo., U.S. C6 102
Franklin, co., Ne., U.S. D7 104
Franklin, co., N.Y., U.S. f10 109
Franklin, co., N.C., U.S. A4 110
Franklin, co., Oh., U.S. B2 112
Franklin, co., Pa., U.S. G6 115
Franklin, co., Tn., U.S. B5 119
Franklin, co., Tx., U.S. C5 120
Franklin, co., Vt., U.S. B2 122
Franklin, co., Va., U.S. D3 123
Franklin, co., Wa., U.S. C6 124
Franklin, Point, c., Ak., U.S. A8 79
Franklin D. Roosevelt Lake, res., Wa., U.S. B7 124
Franklin Falls Reservoir, res., N.H., U.S. C3 106
Franklin Grove, Il., U.S. B4 90
Franklin Island, i., Ont. B4 73
Franklin Lake, l., N.W. Ter. C13 66
Franklin Lake, l., Nv., U.S. C6 105
Franklin Lakes, N.J., U.S. *B4 107
Franklin Mine, Mi., U.S. A2 99
Franklin Mountains, mts., N.W. Ter. C8 66
Franklin Park, Il., U.S. k9 90
Franklin Park, Pa., U.S. h13 115
Franklin Square, N.Y., U.S. *F7 109
Franklin Strait, strt., N.W. Ter. B13 66
Franklinton, La., U.S. D5 95
Franklinton, N.C., U.S. A4 110
Franklinville, N.J., U.S. D2 107
Franklinville, N.Y., U.S. C2 109
Frankston, Austl. *G8 50
Frankston, Tx., U.S. C5 120
Franksville, Wi., U.S. n12 126
Franktown, In., U.S. D6 91
Franktown, Co., U.S. B6 83
Frankville, Que. D8 71
Frankville, Al., U.S. D1 78
Frannie, Wy., U.S. B4 127

Franz Josef Land, is., Sov. Un. B8 29
Frascati, Italy D4 23
Fraser, Co., U.S. B5 83
Fraser, Ia., U.S. B4 92
Fraser, Mi., U.S. *o16 99
Fraser, i., Austl. E9 50
Fraser, stm., B.C. E7 69
Fraser, stm., Newf. g9 72
Fraser, Mount, mtn., Can. C8 69
Fraserburg, S. Afr. D3 49
Fraserburgh, Scot., U.K. B6 10
Fraserdale, Ont. o19 73
Fraser Lake, B.C. B5 69
Fraser Lake, l., B.C. B5 69
Fraser Plateau, plat., B.C. D6 69
Fraserwood, Man. D3 70
Frauenfeld, Switz. E4 18
Fray Bentos, Ur. E1 56
Fray Marcos, Ur. E1 56
Frazee, Mn., U.S. D3 100
Frazer, Mt., U.S. B10 103
Frazeysburg, Oh., U.S. B3 112
Frazier Park, Ca., U.S. E4 82
Freda, Mi., U.S. A2 99
Frederic, Mi., U.S. D6 99
Frederic, Wi., U.S. C1 126
Frederica, De., U.S. D4 85
Fredericia, Den. J3 14
Frederick, Co., U.S. A6 83
Frederick, Il., U.S. C3 90
Frederick, Md., U.S. B3 97
Frederick, Ok., U.S. C2 113
Frederick, S.D., U.S. B7 118
Frederick, co., Md., U.S. B3 97
Frederick, co., Va., U.S. A4 123
Frederick Hall, Va., U.S. C5 123
Fredericksburg, In., U.S. H5 91
Fredericksburg, Ia., U.S. B5 92
Fredericksburg, Oh., U.S. B4 112
Fredericksburg, Pa., U.S. F9 115
Fredericksburg, Tx., U.S. D3 120
Fredericksburg, Va., U.S. B5 123
Frederick Sound, strt., Ak., U.S. m23 79
Fredericktown, Mo., U.S. D7 102
Fredericktown, Oh., U.S. B3 112
Fredericktown, Pa., U.S. F1 115
Fredericton, N.B. D3 71
Fredericton Junction, N.B. D3 71
Frederika, Ia., U.S. B5 92
Frederiksberg, Den. *J5 14
Frederiksborg, co., Den. C6 15
Frederikshavn, Den. I4 14
Frederikssund, Den. C6 15
Frederik Willem IV Vallen, wtfl., Sur. B3 59
Frederiksted, V.I.U.S. H12 64
Frederiksvaerk, Den. C6 15
Fredonia, Az., U.S. A3 80
Fredonia, Ia., U.S. C6 92
Fredonia, Ks., U.S. E8 93
Fredonia, Ky., U.S. C1 94
Fredonia, N.Y., U.S. C1 109
Fredonia, N.D., U.S. C6 111
Fredonia, Pa., U.S. D1 115
Fredonia, Tx., U.S. D3 120
Fredonia, Wi., U.S. E6 126
Fredrikstad, Nor. H4 14
Freeborn, Mn., U.S. G5 100
Freeborn, co., Mn., U.S. G5 100
Freeburg, Il., U.S. E4 90
Freeburg, Mo., U.S. C6 102
Freedom, Ca., U.S. *D3 82
Freedom, In., U.S. F4 91
Freedom, Me., U.S. D3 96
Freedom, N.H., U.S. C4 106
Freedom, Ok., U.S. A2 113
Freedom, Pa., U.S. E1 115
Freedom, Wi., U.S. h9 126
Freedom, Wy., U.S. C2 127
Freehold, N.J., U.S. C4 107
Freeland, Mi., U.S. E6 99
Freeland, Pa., U.S. E10 115
Freeland, N.C., U.S. C4 110
Freeland Park, In., U.S. C3 91
Freelandville, In., U.S. G3 91
Freel Peak, mtn., Ca., U.S. C4 82
Freels, Cape, c., Newf. E5 72
Freels, Cape, c., Newf. D5 72
Freeman, Mo., U.S. C3 102
Freeman, S.D., U.S. D8 118
Freeman, Wa., U.S. g14 124
Freeman, stm., Alta. B3 68
Freeman, Lake, l., In., U.S. C4 91
Freemansburg, Pa., U.S. E11 115
Freemason Islands, is., La., U.S. E7 95
Freemount, Ire. E3 11
Freeport, Bah. *A4 64
Freeport, Fl., U.S. u15 86
Freeport, Il., U.S. A4 90
Freeport, Ks., U.S. E6 93
Freeport, Me., U.S. E2 96
Freeport, Mn., U.S. E4 100
Freeport, N.Y., U.S. n15 109
Freeport, Oh., U.S. B4 112
Freeport, Pa., U.S. E2 115
Freeport, Tx., U.S. E5 120
Freer, Tx., U.S. F3 120
Free Soil, Mi., U.S. D4 99
Freestone, co., Tx., U.S. D4 120
Freetown, P.E.I. C6 71
Freetown, S.L. G2 42
Freetown, In., U.S. G5 91
Free Union, Va., U.S. B4 123
Freeville, N.Y., U.S. C4 109
Fregenal de la Sierra, Spain C2 22
Fregene, Italy h8 23
Freiberg, E. Ger. C8 18
Freiberger Mulde, stm., Eur. B8 19
Freiburg [im Breisgau], W. Ger. D3 18
Freienbach, Switz. B6 21
Freirina, Chile E1 55
Freising, W. Ger. D5 18
Freistadt, Aus. D7 18
Freital, E. Ger. B8 19
Fréjus, Fr. F7 16
Fréjus Tunnel, Eur. D2 20
Frelighsburg, Que. D5 74
Fremantle, Austl. F2 50
Fremont, Ca., U.S. D2 82

Fremont, In., U.S. A8 91
Fremont, Ia., U.S. C5 92
Fremont, Mi., U.S. E5 99
Fremont, Mo., U.S. E6 102
Fremont, Ne., U.S. C9 104
Fremont, N.H., U.S. E4 106
Fremont, N.C., U.S. B5 110
Fremont, Oh., U.S. A2 112
Fremont, Ut., U.S. E4 121
Fremont, Wi., U.S. D5 126
Fremont, co., Co., U.S. C5 83
Fremont, co., Id., U.S. E7 89
Fremont, co., Ia., U.S. D2 92
Fremont, co., Wy., U.S. C4 127
Fremont, stm., Ut., U.S. E4 121
Fremont Island, i., Ut., U.S. B3 121
Fremont Lake, l., Wy., U.S. D3 127
Fremont Peak, mtn., Wy., U.S. D3 127
French Broad, stm., U.S. D10 119
Frenchburg, Ky., U.S. C6 94
French Camp, Ms., U.S. B4 101
French Creek, W.V., U.S. C4 125
French Creek, stm., Man. A5 70
French Creek, stm., Pa., U.S. C2 115
French Frigate Shoals, rf., Hi., U.S. m14 88
Frenchglen, Or., U.S. E8 114
French Guiana, dep., S.A. B4 59
French Gulch, Ca., U.S. B2 82
French Island, Wi., U.S. *E2 126
French Lick, In., U.S. G4 91
Frenchman, Nv., U.S. D5 105
Frenchman, stm., N.A. A8 103
Frenchman Bay, b., Me., U.S. D4 96
Frenchman Butte, Sask. D1 75
Frenchman Creek, stm., U.S. D4 104
Frenchman Hills, hills, Wa., U.S. C6 124
Frenchman Knob, mtn., Ky., U.S. C4 94
Frenchman Lake, l., Nv., U.S. G6 105
Frenchman's Cove, Newf. D2 72
Frenchman's Cove, Newf. E4 72
Frenchmans Island, Newf. D3 72
Frenchpark, Ire. H3 11
French Polynesia, dep., Oc. H13 6
French River, Mn., U.S. D7 100
French Settlement, La., U.S. D5 95
French Southern and Antarctic Territories, dep., Afr. *J1 2
Frenchton, W.V., U.S. C4 125
Frenchtown, Mt., U.S. C2 103
Frenchtown, N.J., U.S. B2 107
French Village, N.S. E6 71
Frenchville, Me., U.S. A4 96
Frenda, Alg. B5 44
Fresco, I.C. E3 42
Fresco, stm., Braz. C3 56
Freshfield, Mount, mtn., Can. D2 68
Freshford, Ire. E4 11
Freshwater, Eng., U.K. D6 12
Fresnillo [de González Echeverría], Mex. C4 63
Fresno, Ca., U.S. D4 82
Fresno, Oh., U.S. B4 112
Fresno, co., Ca., U.S. D4 82
Fresno Reservoir, res., Mt., U.S. B6 103
Freudenstadt, W. Ger. D4 18
Frévent, Fr. B5 16
Frewsburg, N.Y., U.S. C1 109
Freyburg, E. Ger. B6 19
Freycinet Peninsula, pen., Austl. o15 50
Freyenstein, E. Ger. E6 15
Freyming-Merlebach, Fr. E6 17
Freyung, W. Ger. E8 19
Fria, Gui. D2 42
Fria, Cape, c., Nmb. A1 49
Friant, Ca., U.S. D4 82
Friars Point, Ms., U.S. A3 101
Fribourg, Switz. E3 18
Fribourg, state, Switz. C3 20
Friday Harbor, Wa., U.S. A2 124
Fridtjof Nansen, Mount, mtn., Ant. A32 7
Friedberg, W. Ger. C4 18
Friedens, Pa., U.S. F3 115
Friedland, E. Ger. B6 18
Friedrichroda, E. Ger. C5 19
Friedrichshafen, W. Ger. E5 18
Friedrichskoog, W. Ger. D2 15
Friedrichsthal, W. Ger. D2 19
Friedrichsthal, W. Ger. D2 19
Friend, Ks., U.S. D3 93
Friend, Ne., U.S. D8 104
Friendship, Ar., U.S. C3 81
Friendship, In., U.S. G7 91
Friendship, Me., U.S. E3 96
Friendship, N.Y., U.S. C2 109
Friendship, Tn., U.S. B2 119
Friendship, Wi., U.S. E4 126
Friendsville, Md., U.S. k12 97
Friendsville, Tn., U.S. D9 119
Friendswood, In., U.S. E5 91
Friendswood, Tx., U.S. *r14 120
Frierson, La., U.S. B2 95
Fries, Va., U.S. D1 123
Friesach, Aus. E7 18
Friesland, prov., Neth. A5 17
Friesland, Wi., U.S. E4 126
Friesoythe, W. Ger. A7 17
Frigate Point, c., Mid. Is. k3 52
Frio, co., Tx., U.S. E3 120
Frio, stm., Tx., U.S. E3 120
Frio Draw, val., U.S. B1 120
Frisco, Co., U.S. B4 83
Frisco, N.C., U.S. B7 110
Frisco City, Al., U.S. D2 78
Frisco Peak, mtn., Ut., U.S. E2 121
Frissell, Mount, mtn., U.S. A2 84
Fristoe, Mo., U.S. C4 102
Fritch, Tx., U.S. B2 120
Fritsla, Swe. A6 15
Fritzlar, W. Ger. C4 18
Friuli-Venezia Giulia, prov., Italy C8 20
Frobisher, Sask. H4 75
Frobisher Bay, b., N.W. Ter. D19 66
Frobisher Lake, l., Sask. m7 75
Frog Lake, l., Alta. C5 68
Frogmore, La., U.S. C4 95
Frogmore, S.C., U.S. G6 117
Frohna, Mo., U.S. D8 102
Froid, Mt., U.S. B12 103

Frolovo, Sov. Un. G14 27
Fromberg, Mt., U.S. E8 103
Frome, Jam. E12 65
Frome, Eng., U.K. C5 12
Frome, Bay of, b., Can. D4 71
Frome, stm., Eng., U.K. D5 12
Frome, Lake, l., Austl. F6 50
Fromentine, Fr. F5 16
Frontenac, Ks., U.S. E9 93
Frontenac, Mn., U.S. F6 100
Frontenac, co., Ont. C8 73
Frontenac, co., Que. D7 74
Frontera, Mex. D6 63
Frontier, Wy., U.S. E2 127
Frontier, co., Ne., U.S. D5 104
Frontignan, Fr. F5 16
Frontino, Páramo, mtn., Col. B2 60
Front Range, mts., Co., U.S. A5 83
Front Royal, Va., U.S. B4 123
Frosinone, Italy D4 23
Frost, Mn., U.S. G5 100
Frost, Tx., U.S. C4 120
Frostburg, Md., U.S. k13 97
Frostproof, Fl., U.S. E5 86
Frouard, Fr. F6 17
Froude, Sask. H4 75
Frøya, i., Nor. F3 14
Fruges, Fr. D2 17
Fruita, Co., U.S. B2 83
Fruita, Ut., U.S. E4 121
Fruitdale, Al., U.S. D1 78
Fruitdale, S.D., U.S. C2 118
Fruit Heights, Ut., U.S. B4 121
Fruithurst, Al., U.S. B4 78
Fruitland, Ia., U.S. C6 92
Fruitland, Id., U.S. F2 89
Fruitland, Md., U.S. D6 97
Fruitland, Mo., U.S. D8 102
Fruitland, N.M., U.S. A1 108
Fruitland, Tn., U.S. B3 119
Fruitland, Ut., U.S. C5 121
Fruitland Park, Fl., U.S. D5 86
Fruitland Park, Ms., U.S. E4 101
Fruitport, Mi., U.S. E4 99
Fruitvale, B.C. E9 69
Fruitvale, Co., U.S. B2 83
Fruitvale, Tn., U.S. B2 119
Fruitvale, Wa., U.S. C5 124
Fruitville, Fl., U.S. E4 86
Frunze, Sov. Un. H10 27
Frunze, Sov. Un. E10 29
Frutal, Braz. C3 56
Frutigen, Switz. C4 21
Fry, Ga., U.S. B2 87
Fryazevo, Sov. Un. n18 27
Fryburg, Pa., U.S. D2 115
Frye, Me., U.S. D2 96
Fryeburg, La., U.S. B2 95
Fryeburg, Me., U.S. D2 96
Frys, Sask. H5 75
Fu'an, China K8 32
Fuchou see Fuzhou, China F8 31
Fuchū, Japan *I9 33
Fuding, China K9 32
Fuencarral, Spain p17 22
Fuente-Álamo [de Murcia], Spain D5 22
Fuente de Cantos, Spain C2 22
Fuente el Saz, Spain o17 22
Fuente Obejuna, Spain C3 22
Fuentesaúco, Spain C2 22
Fuentes [de Andalucía], Spain D3 22
Fuerte, stm., Mex. B3 63
Fuerte Olimpo, Para. D4 55
Fuerteventura, i., Spain m14 22
Fuglbjerg, Den. C5 15
Fugou, China G6 32
Fuhai, China B2 31
Fuji, Mount, vol., Japan I9 33
Fujian, prov., China F8 31
Fujieda, Japan o17 33
Fujimi, Japan n17 33
Fujin, China B11 31
Fujinomiya, Japan *I9 33
Fujisawa, Japan n17 33
Fuji-yoshida, Japan I9 33
Fukagawa, Japan E10 33
Fūkah, Egypt G6 40
Fukien see Fujian, prov., China F8 31
Fukuchiyama, Japan I7 33
Fukue Island, i., Japan J4 33
Fukui, Japan D12 31
Fukuoka, Japan E11 31
Fukuoka, Japan F10 33
Fukushima, Japan I8 33
Fukuyama, Japan I6 33
Fulaga, i., Fiji I16 52
Fulaga Passage, strt., Fiji I16 52
Fulda, W. Ger. C4 18
Fulda, Mn., U.S. G3 100
Fulda, stm., W. Ger. B4 19
Fuling, China J2 32
Fullerton, Ca., U.S. n13 82
Fullerton, Ne., U.S. C8 104
Fullerton, N.D., U.S. C7 111
Fulshear, Tx., U.S. r14 120
Fulton, Al., U.S. D2 78
Fulton, Ar., U.S. D2 81
Fulton, Il., U.S. B3 90
Fulton, In., U.S. C5 91
Fulton, Ks., U.S. D9 93
Fulton, Ky., U.S. f9 94
Fulton, Md., U.S. B4 97
Fulton, Mi., U.S. F5 99
Fulton, Ms., U.S. A5 101
Fulton, Mo., U.S. C6 102
Fulton, N.Y., U.S. B4 109
Fulton, Oh., U.S. B3 112
Fulton, S.D., U.S. D8 118
Fulton, Tx., U.S. E4 120
Fulton, co., Ar., U.S. A4 81
Fulton, co., Ga., U.S. C2 87
Fulton, co., Il., U.S. C3 90
Fulton, co., In., U.S. C5 91
Fulton, co., Ky., U.S. f9 94
Fulton, co., N.Y., U.S. B6 109
Fulton, co., Oh., U.S. A1 112
Fulton, co., Pa., U.S. G6 115
Fultondale, Al., U.S. f7 78
Fultonham, N.Y., U.S. C6 109
Fultz, Ky., U.S. B6 94
Fumay, Fr. C6 16
Funabashi, Japan n19 33
Funafuti, Tuvalu G10 6
Funchal, Port. h12 22

Fundación, Col. A3 60
Fundão, Braz. B4 56
Fundão, Port. B2 22
Fundy, Bay of, b., Can. D4 71
Fundy National Park, N.B. D4 71
Funhalouro, Moz. E7 49
Funing, China G6 31
Funing, China J6 32
Funing Bay, b., China K9 32
Funk, Ne., U.S. D6 104
Funkley, Mn., U.S. C4 100
Funkstown, Md., U.S. A2 97
Funtua, Nig. D6 45
Fuqing, China F8 31
Fuquay-Varina, N.C., U.S. B4 110
Fur, i., Den. B3 15
Furancungo, Moz. D5 48
Furano, Japan E11 33
Fürg, Iran C5 38
Furka Pass, Switz. C5 21
Furley, Ks., U.S. g12 93
Furman, Al., U.S. C3 78
Furman, S.C., U.S. F5 117
Furmanov, Sov. Un. C13 27
Furmanovka, Sov. Un. E8 28
Furnace Brook, stm., Vt., U.S. D3 122
Furnas, co., Ne., U.S. D6 104
Furnas, Represa de, res., Braz. C3 56
Furneaux Group, is., Austl. o15 50
Furness, Sask. D1 75
Furqlus, Syria E11 40
Fürstenau, W. Ger. B7 17
Fürstenfeld, Aus. E8 18
Fürstenfeldbruck, W. Ger. D5 18
Fürstenwalde [Spree], E. Ger. A7 18
Fürth, W. Ger. D5 18
Furth im Wald, W. Ger. D7 19
Furukawa, Japan H8 33
Furu Mountain, hill, Japan P17 52
Fusagasugá, Col. C3 60
Fushan, China C9 31
Fushun, China C11 31
Fusilier, Sask. F1 75
Fusong, China E3 33
Füssen, W. Ger. E5 18
Fusui, China C10 32
Futatsune, rock, Japan P17 52
Future City, Il., U.S. F4 90
Fuwah, Egypt Y2 41
Fuxian, China F3 32
Fuxian Hu, l., China B7 34
Fuxin, China C11 31
Fuyang, China E8 31
Fuyang, China G6 31
Fuyu, China B8 31
Fuyu, China B11 31
Fuyuan, China B3 31
Fuyun, China B3 31
Fuzhou (Fuchou), China F8 31
Fuzhou, China K7 32
Fyffe, Al., U.S. A4 78
Fyn, i., Den. C4 15
Fyn, i., Den. J4 14
Fyne, Loch, b., Scot., U.K. B4 10

G

Gaalkacyo, Som. D6 47
Gaastra, Mi., U.S. B2 99
Gabaldon, N.M., U.S. B4 108
Gabarus, N.S. D9 71
Gabela, Ang. D1 48
Gabès, Tun. C7 44
Gabès, Golfe de, b., Tun. C7 44
Gabin, Pol. B5 26
Gabon, ctry., Afr. F2 46
Gaborone, Bots. B4 49
Gabriel, Mount, hill, Ire. F2 11
Gabriels, N.Y., U.S. f10 109
Gabriola, B.C. f12 69
Gabrovo, Bul. D7 24
Gachsārān, Iran F5 39
Gacko, Yugo. E6 36
Gadag, India E3 37
Gadmen, Switz. C5 21
Gadsby, Alta. C4 68
Gadsden, Al., U.S. A3 78
Gadsden, Az., U.S. E1 80
Gadsden, S.C., U.S. D6 117
Gadsden, Tn., U.S. B3 119
Gadsden, co., Fl., U.S. B2 86
Gadyach, Sov. Un. F10 27
Gaeşti, Rom. C7 24
Gaeta, Italy D4 23
Gaeta, Gulf of, b., Italy D4 23
Gafour, Tun. B6 44
Gafsa, Tun. C6 44
Gagan Island, i., Marsh Is. S17 52
Gagarin, Sov. Un. D10 27
Gage, Ok., U.S. A2 113
Gage, co., Ne., U.S. D9 104
Gage, Cape, c., P.E.I. C7 71
Gagetown, N.B. D3 71
Gagetown, Mi., U.S. E7 99
Gaggenau, W. Ger. E7 19
Gagliano del Capo, Italy E7 23
Gagnoa, I.C. E4 42
Gagnon, Que. h13 74
Gagny, Fr. g11 16
Gahanna, Oh., U.S. k11 112
Gaibandha, Bngl. E12 37
Gail, Tx., U.S. C2 120
Gail, stm., Aus. C9 20
Gaillac, Fr. E4 16
Gaillard, Lake, l., Ct., U.S. D4 84
Gaines, Mi., U.S. F7 99
Gaines, co., Tx., U.S. C1 120
Gainesboro, Tn., U.S. C8 119
Gainesborough, Sask. H5 75
Gainesborough, Eng., U.K. H12 13
Gainesville, Fl., U.S. C4 86
Gainesville, Ga., U.S. B3 87
Gainesville, Mo., U.S. E5 102
Gainesville, Tx., U.S. C4 120

Galapagar, Spain o16 22
Galápagos, Ec. g5 58
Galapagos Islands see Colón, Archipiélago de, is., Ec. g5 58
Galashiels, Scot., U.K. C5 10
Galata, Mt., U.S. B5 103
Galați (Galacz), Rom. C9 24
Galatia, Il., U.S. F5 90
Galatia, Ks., U.S. D5 93
Galatina, Italy D7 23
Galátsion, Grc. *C4 25
Galawinku, Austl. B6 50
Galax, Va., U.S. D2 123
Galaxidhion, Grc. C4 25
Galchutt, N.D., U.S. C9 111
Gáldar, Spain m14 22
Galeana, Mex. A3 63
Galena, Ak., U.S. C8 79
Galena, Il., U.S. A3 90
Galena, Ks., U.S. E9 93
Galena, Md., U.S. B6 97
Galena, Mo., U.S. E4 102
Galena, Oh., U.S. B3 112
Galena Park, Tx., U.S. r14 120
Galeota Point, c., Trin. K14 64
Galera, Punta, c., Chile B2 54
Galera, Punta, c., Ec. A1 58
Galera Point, c., Trin. K14 64
Galesburg, Il., U.S. C3 90
Galesburg, Ks., U.S. E8 93
Galesburg, Mi., U.S. F5 99
Galesburg, N.D., U.S. B8 111
Galesville, Md., U.S. C4 97
Galesville, Wi., U.S. D2 126
Galeton, Co., U.S. A6 83
Galeton, Pa., U.S. C6 115
Galetta, Ont. B8 73
Galeville, N.Y., U.S. *B4 109
Galgaduud, prov., Som. D6 47
Galiano Island, i., B.C. f12 69
Galich, Sov. Un. C13 27
Galicia, hist. reg., Eur. D6 26
Galicia, hist. reg., Spain B2 22
Galien, Mi., U.S. G4 99
Galilee, Lake, l., Austl. D8 50
Galilee, hist. reg., Isr. B7 41
Galilee, Sea of see Kinneret, Yam, l., Isr. B7 41
Galina Point, c., Jam. E15 65
Galion, Oh., U.S. B3 112
Galisteo Creek, stm., N.M., U.S. k8 108
Galite Channel, strt., Tun. F2 23
Galiuro Mountains, mts., Az., U.S. E5 80
Galivants Ferry, S.C., U.S. C9 117
Gallan Head, c., Scot., U.K. B1 13
Gallant, Al., U.S. B3 78
Gallarate, Italy B2 23
Gallatin, Mo., U.S. B4 102
Gallatin, Tn., U.S. A5 119
Gallatin, co., Il., U.S. F5 90
Gallatin, co., Ky., U.S. B5 94
Gallatin, co., Mt., U.S. E5 103
Gallatin, stm., Mt., U.S. E5 103
Gallatin Gateway, Mt., U.S. E5 103
Gallatin Range, mts., Mt., U.S. E5 103
Gallaway, Tn., U.S. B2 119
Galle, Sri L. I6 37
Gállego, stm., Spain A5 22
Gallegos, stm., Arg. G2 54
Galley Head, c., Ire. F3 11
Gallia, co., Oh., U.S. D3 112
Galliano, La., U.S. E5 95
Gallicano nel Lazio, Italy h9 23
Gallinas, Punta, c., Col. A3 60
Gallinas Mountains, mts., N.M., U.S. C2 108
Gallipoli, Italy D7 23
Gallipoli see Gelibolu, Tur. B6 40
Gallipoli Peninsula, pen., Tur. B6 40
Gallipolis, Oh., U.S. D3 112
Gallipolis Ferry, W.V., U.S. C2 125
Gallitzin, Pa., U.S. F4 115
Gallneukirchen, Aus. D9 14
Gallo, stm., Spain B5 22
Gallo Mountains, mts., N.M., U.S. C1 108
Galloo Island, i., N.Y., U.S. A4 109
Galloway, Oh., U.S. m10 112
Galloway, W.V., U.S. D4 125
Galloway, Mull of, c., Scot., U.K. F4 13
Gällstad, Swe. A7 15
Gallup, N.M., U.S. B1 108
Galoa Bay, b., Fiji H15 52
Galoa Harbour, b., Fiji I15 52
Galt, Ont. D4 73
Galt, Ca., U.S. C3 82
Galt, Ia., U.S. B4 92
Galt, Mo., U.S. A4 102
Galten, Den. t34 14
Galtür, Aus. B3 11
Galtymore Mountain, mtn., Ire. E3 11
Galva, Il., U.S. B3 90
Galva, Ia., U.S. B2 92
Galva, Ks., U.S. D6 93
Gálvez, Arg. C4 54
Galveston, In., U.S. C5 91
Galveston, Tx., U.S. E5 120
Galveston, co., Tx., U.S. E5 120
Galveston Bay, b., Tx., U.S. E5 120
Galveston Island, i., Tx., U.S. E5 120
Galway, co., Ire. H3 11
Galway, Ire. D2 10
Galway Bay, b., Ire. E9 12
Gamaches, Fr. E9 12
Gamagōri, Japan A3 81
Gamaliel, Ar., U.S. A3 81
Gamaliel, Ky., U.S. D4 94
Gamarra, Col. B3 60
Gamba, China C12 37
Gamba, Zaire D3 48
Gambaga, Ghana D4 45
Gambela, Eth. E12 47
Gamber, Md., U.S. B3 97
Gambia, ctry., Afr. D2 42
Gambia, stm., Afr. D2 42
Gambia, Bah. m17 64
Gambier, B3 112
Gamboa, Pan. k11 62
Gamboma, Congo B2 48

Gamboula, Cen. Afr. Rep. — E3 46
Gambrills, Md., U.S. — B4 97
Gameleira, Braz. — C3 57
Gamerco, N.M., U.S. — B1 108
Gammertingen, W. Ger. — A5 20
Gammon, stm., Can. — D4 70
Gamo Gofa, prov., Eth. — D4 47
Gamph, Slieve, mts., Ire. — C3 11
Ganado, Az., U.S. — B6 80
Ganado, Tx., U.S. — E4 120
Gananoque, Ont. — C8 73
Gancheng, China — C8 35
Ganda, Ang. — D1 48
Gandajika, Zaire — C3 48
Gandak, stm., Asia — D10 37
Gandeeville, W.V., U.S. — C3 125
Gander, Newf. — D4 72
Gander, stm., Newf. — D4 72
Gander Bay, Newf. — D4 72
Gander Lake, l., Newf. — D4 72
Gāndhīnagar, India — D5 36
Gandhi Reservoir, res., India — E5 37
Gandia, Spain — C5 22
Gandy, Ne., U.S. — C5 104
Gangānagar, India — C5 36
Gangāpur, India — D6 37
Gangaw, Burma — D9 36
Gangdise Mountains, mts., China — B9 37
Ganges, B.C. — g12 69
Ganges, Fr. — F5 16
Ganges, Oh., U.S. — B3 112
Ganges, stm., Asia — D8 36
Ganges, Mouths of the, mth., Asia — D8 36
Gang Mills, N.Y., U.S. — C3 109
Gangtok, India — C8 36
Gangu, China — E6 31
Gani, Indon. — F7 34
Gan Jiang, stm., China — K6 32
Gannan, China — C1 33
Gannat, Fr. — D5 16
Gannet Islands, is., Newf. — B3 72
Gannett Peak, mtn., Wy., U.S. — C3 127
Gannon, Md., U.S. — k12 97
Gannvalley, S.D., U.S. — C7 118
Gano, Oh., U.S. — n13 112
Gans, Ok., U.S. — B7 113
Gansevoort, N.Y., U.S. — B7 109
Gansu, prov., China — D5 31
Ganta, Lib. — E3 45
Gantt, Al., U.S. — D3 78
Gantt, S.C., U.S. — B3 117
Gantt Lake, res., Al., U.S. — D3 78
Gantts Quarry, Al., U.S. — B3 78
Ganyu, China — E8 31
Ganzhou, China — F7 31
Gao, Mali — C5 45
Gao'an, China — J6 32
Gaoil, Sliabh, mtn., Scot., U.K. — E3 13
Gaoua, Burkina — D4 45
Gaoual, Gui. — D2 45
Gaoyou, China — H8 32
Gaoyou Lake, l., China — H8 32
Gap, Fr. — E7 16
Gap, Pa., U.S. — G9 115
Gapan, Phil. — o13 34
Gapland, Md., U.S. — B2 97
Gap Mills, W.V., U.S. — D4 125
Gar, China — B7 36
Gara, Lough, l., Ire. — D2 10
Garacad, Som. — D6 47
Garachiné, Pan. — F8 62
Garachiné, Punta, c., Pan. — F8 62
Garanhuns, Braz. — C3 57
Garapan, N. Mar. Is. — D7 52
Garapan, Lagunan, b., N. Mar. Is. — D7 52
Garau, Canal la, Mex. — h9 63
Garbaharrey, Som. — E5 47
Garber, Ia., U.S. — B6 92
Garber, Ok., U.S. — A4 113
Garberville, Ca., U.S. — B2 82
Garbsen, W. Ger. — *B4 18
Garça, Braz. — C3 56
Garching [an der Alz], W. Ger. — A8 20
Garcia, Co., U.S. — D5 83
Garciasville, Tx., U.S. — F3 120
Gard, stm., Fr. — E6 16
Garda, Lake, l., Italy — B3 23
Gardanne, Fr. — F6 16
Gardar, N.D., U.S. — A8 111
Gardelegen, E. Ger. — B5 18
Garden, Mi., U.S. — C4 99
Garden, co., Ne., U.S. — C3 104
Gardena, Ca., U.S. — n12 82
Gardena, N.D., U.S. — A5 111
Garden City, Al., U.S. — A3 78
Garden City, Co., U.S. — *A6 83
Garden City, Ga., U.S. — D5 87
Garden City, Id., U.S. — F2 89
Garden City, Ks., U.S. — E3 93
Garden City, La., U.S. — E4 95
Garden City, Mi., U.S. — p15 99
Garden City, Mn., U.S. — F4 100
Garden City, Mo., U.S. — C3 102
Garden City, N.Y., U.S. — *E7 109
Garden City, S.D., U.S. — C8 118
Garden City, Tx., U.S. — D2 120
Garden City, Ut., U.S. — B4 121
Garden City Park, N.Y., U.S. — *n15 109
Gardendale, Al., U.S. — B3 78
Gardendale, Tx., U.S. — D1 120
Garden Grove, Ca., U.S. — n13 82
Garden Grove, Ia., U.S. — D4 92
Garden Home, Or., U.S. — *B4 114
Garden Island, i., Mi., U.S. — C5 99
Garden of Gethsemane, Isr. Occ. — m14 41
Garden Plain, Il., U.S. — B3 90
Garden Prairie, Il., U.S. — A5 90
Garden Reach, India — *D8 36
Gardenton, Man. — E3 70
Garden Valley, Id., U.S. — E3 89
Gardez, Afg. — B4 36
Gardi, Ga., U.S. — E5 87
Gardiner, Me., U.S. — D3 96
Gardiner, Mt., U.S. — E6 103
Gardiner, Or., U.S. — D2 114
Gardiners Island, i., N.Y., U.S. — m16 109
Gardner, Ar., U.S. — D3 81
Gardner, Co., U.S. — D5 83
Gardner, Fl., U.S. — E5 86
Gardner, Il., U.S. — B5 90
Gardner, Ks., U.S. — D9 93
Gardner, Ma., U.S. — A4 98
Gardner, N.D., U.S. — B9 111
Gardner, Tn., U.S. — A3 119
Gardner Canal, strt., B.C. — C3 69
Gardner Lake, l., Ct., U.S. — C6 84
Gardner Lake, l., Me., U.S. — D5 96

Gardner Mountain, mtn., N.H., U.S. — B3 106
Gardner Pinnacles, Hi., U.S. — k14 88
Gardnersville, Ky., U.S. — k14 94
Gardnerville, Nv., U.S. — E2 105
Gardone Riviera, Italy — D6 20
Gardone Val Trompia, Italy — D6 20
Garešnica, Yugo. — C3 24
Garfield, Ar., U.S. — A2 81
Garfield, Co., U.S. — C4 83
Garfield, Ga., U.S. — D4 87
Garfield, Ks., U.S. — D4 93
Garfield, Mn., U.S. — E3 100
Garfield, N.J., U.S. — h8 107
Garfield, N.M., U.S. — E2 108
Garfield, Wa., U.S. — B8 124
Garfield, co., Co., U.S. — B2 83
Garfield, co., Mt., U.S. — C9 103
Garfield, co., Ne., U.S. — C6 104
Garfield, co., Ok., U.S. — A4 113
Garfield, co., Ut., U.S. — F4 121
Garfield, co., Wa., U.S. — C8 124
Garfield Heights, Oh., U.S. — h9 112
Garfield Mountain, mtn., Mt., U.S. — F4 103
Garfield Park, De., U.S. — *B3 85
Garfield Peak, mtn., Wy., U.S. — D5 127
Gargaliánoi, Grc. — D3 25
Gargano, Italy — D2 56
Gargano Peninsula, pen., Italy — D6 20
Garibaldi, Braz. — B3 114
Garibaldi, Or., U.S. — B3 114
Garibaldi, Mount, mtn., B.C. — E6 69
Garibaldi Provincial Park, B.C. — D6 69
Garies, S. Afr. — D2 49
Garissa, Kenya — B6 48
Garita, N.M., U.S. — D3 78
Garland, Ar., U.S. — D2 81
Garland, Ks., U.S. — E9 93
Garland, Me., U.S. — D3 96
Garland, Ne., U.S. — D9 104
Garland, N.C., U.S. — C4 110
Garland, Pa., U.S. — C3 115
Garland, Tn., U.S. — B2 119
Garland, Tx., U.S. — n10 120
Garland, Ut., U.S. — B3 121
Garland, Wy., U.S. — B4 127
Garland, co., Ar., U.S. — C2 81
Garm, Sov. Un. — H23 8
Garmisch-Partenkirchen, W. Ger. — E5 18
Garmouth, Scot., U.K. — C5 13
Garnavillo, Ia., U.S. — B6 92
Garneill, Mt., U.S. — D7 103
Garner, Ar., U.S. — B4 81
Garner, Ia., U.S. — A4 92
Garner, Ky., U.S. — C7 94
Garner, N.C., U.S. — B4 110
Garnet Range, mts., Mt., U.S. — D3 103
Garnett, S.C., U.S. — F5 117
Garnett, Ks., U.S. — D8 93
Garnish, Newf. — E4 72
Garnpung, Lake, l., Austl. — F4 51
Garonne, stm., Eur. — E3 16
Garoowe, Som. — D6 47
Garou, Lac, l., Mali — C4 45
Garoua, Cam. — D2 46
Garrard, co., Ky., U.S. — C5 94
Garrilovka, Sov. Un. — G11 27
Garrett, Il., U.S. — D5 90
Garrett, In., U.S. — B7 91
Garrett, Ky., U.S. — C7 94
Garrett, Pa., U.S. — G3 115
Garrett, Wy., U.S. — D7 127
Garrett, co., Md., U.S. — k12 97
Garrett Park, Md., U.S. — *B3 97
Garrettsville, Oh., U.S. — A4 112
Garrick, Sask. — D3 75
Garrison, Ia., U.S. — B5 92
Garrison, Ky., U.S. — B6 94
Garrison, Md., U.S. — B4 97
Garrison, Mn., U.S. — D5 100
Garrison, Mt., U.S. — D4 103
Garrison, N.Y., U.S. — D7 109
Garrison, N.D., U.S. — B4 111
Garrison, Tx., U.S. — D5 120
Garrison, Ut., U.S. — E1 121
Garrison Dam, N.D., U.S. — B4 111
Garristown, Ire. — D5 11
Garron Point, c., N. Ire., U.K. — B6 11
Garrote, Pan. — h11 62
Garrovillas, Spain — C2 22
Garry, stm., Scot., U.K. — D5 13
Garry Lake, l., N.W. Ter. — C13 66
Garryowen, Mt., U.S. — E9 103
Garsen, Kenya — B7 48
Garson Lake, l., Can. — A5 68
Garson Quarry, Man. — D7 70
Garstang, Eng., U.K. — G6 13
Garth, Al., U.S. — A3 78
Garthby Station (Beaulac), Que. — D6 74
Gartz, E. Ger. — E8 15
Garut, Indon. — G3 34
Garvagh, N. Ire., U.K. — C5 11
Garvin, Ok., U.S. — C7 113
Garvin, co., Ok., U.S. — C4 113
Garwa, Scot., U.K. — C4 13
Garwolin, Pol. — C6 26
Garwood, N.J., U.S. — *B4 107
Garwood, Tx., U.S. — E4 120
Gary, In., U.S. — A3 91
Gary, Mn., U.S. — C2 100
Gary, S.D., U.S. — C9 118
Gary, Tx., U.S. — D5 120
Gary, W.V., U.S. — D3 125
Garyarsa, China — B8 37
Garysburg, N.C., U.S. — A5 110
Garyville, La., U.S. — D5 95
Garza, co., Tx., U.S. — C2 120
Garza García, Mex. — *B4 63
Garza-Little Elm Reservoir, res., Tx., U.S. — C4 120
Garzón, Col. — C2 60
Gas, Ks., U.S. — E8 93
Gascogne, hist. reg., Fr. — E3 16
Gasconade, Mo., U.S. — C6 102
Gasconade, co., Mo., U.S. — C6 102
Gasconade, stm., Mo., U.S. — C6 102
Gasconade, Osage Fork, stm., Mo., U.S. — D5 102
Gascoyne, N.D., U.S. — C2 111
Gascoyne, stm., Austl. — E2 50
Gashaka, Nig. — E7 45
Gasherbrum, mtn., Asia — *A6 36
Gas Hills, Wy., U.S. — D5 127
Gashua, Nig. — D7 45
Gasparilla Island, i., Fl., U.S. — F4 86
Gaspé, Que. — k14 74
Gaspé, Cap, c., Que. — G20 66

Gaspésie, Péninsule de la, pen., Que. — k13 74
Gasport, N.Y., U.S. — B2 109
Gasque, Al., U.S. — E2 78
Gassaway, Tn., U.S. — D8 119
Gassaway, W.V., U.S. — C4 125
Gassetts, Vt., U.S. — E3 122
Gassol, Nig. — E7 45
Gassville, Ar., U.S. — A3 81
Gaston, In., U.S. — D7 91
Gaston, N.C., U.S. — A5 110
Gaston, Or., U.S. — h11 114
Gaston, S.C., U.S. — D5 117
Gaston, co., N.C., U.S. — B1 110
Gaston, Lake, res., U.S. — A5 110
Gaston Dam, N.C., U.S. — A5 110
Gastonia, N.C., U.S. — B1 110
Gastre, Arg. — C3 54
Gata, Cape, c., Spain — D4 22
Gata, Sierra de, mts., Spain — B2 22
Gatas, Cape, c., Cyp. — E9 40
Gatchina, Sov. Un. — B8 27
Gate, Ok., U.S. — e9 113
Gate City, Va., U.S. — f9 123
Gatehouse of Fleet, Scot., U.K. — F4 13
Gates, Ne., U.S. — C6 104
Gates, N.Y., U.S. — B3 109
Gates, N.C., U.S. — A6 110
Gates, Or., U.S. — C4 114
Gates, Tn., U.S. — B2 119
Gates, co., N.C., U.S. — A6 110
Gates, Lake, res., N.Y., U.S. — C2 109
Gatesville, Ms., U.S. — C3 101
Gatesville, N.C., U.S. — A6 110
Gatesville, Tx., U.S. — D4 120
Gateway, Ar., U.S. — *A2 81
Gateway, Co., U.S. — C2 83
Gateway, Or., U.S. — C5 114
Gatineau, Que. — D2 74
Gatineau, stm., Que. — C2 74
Gatineau, Parc de la, Que. — D2 74
Gatliff, Ky., U.S. — D5 94
Gatlinburg, Tn., U.S. — D10 119
Gato, Co., U.S. — D3 83
Gattman, Ms., U.S. — B5 101
Gatton, Austl. — C9 51
Gatún, Pan. — k11 62
Gatún, Lago, res., Pan. — k11 62
Gatún Locks, Pan. — k11 62
Gau, i., Fiji — I15 52
Gauer Lake, l., Man. — A3 70
Gauhati, India — C8 36
Gauja, stm., Sov. Un. — C5 27
Gaula, stm., Nor. — F4 14
Gauley, stm., W.V., U.S. — C3 125
Gauley Bridge, W.V., U.S. — C3 125
Gauley Mills, W.V., U.S. — C4 125
Gautier, Ms., U.S. — f8 101
Gavá, Spain — B7 22
Gávdhos, i., Grc. — E5 40
Gavins Point Dam, U.S. — E8 104
Gāv Khūnī, Bāṭlāq-e, sw., Iran — E6 39
Gävle, Swe. — G7 14
Gävlebukten, b., Swe. — G7 14
Gavrilovka, Sov. Un. — G11 27
Gavrilov Posad, Sov. Un. — C13 27
Gawler, Austl. — G2 51
Gawler Ranges, mts., Austl. — F6 50
Gay, Ga., U.S. — C2 87
Gay, Mi., U.S. — A2 99
Gaya, India — D7 36
Gaya, Niger — D5 45
Gaya, Nig. — D6 45
Gay Head, Ma., U.S. — D6 98
Gay Head, c., Ma., U.S. — D6 98
Gaylesville, Al., U.S. — A4 78
Gaylord, Ks., U.S. — C5 93
Gaylord, Mi., U.S. — C6 99
Gaylord, Mn., U.S. — F4 100
Gaylord, Or., U.S. — E2 114
Gaylordsville, Ct., U.S. — C2 84
Gayndah, Austl. — B8 51
Gays, Il., U.S. — D5 90
Gays Mills, Wi., U.S. — E3 126
Gaysville, Vt., U.S. — D3 122
Gaza (Ghazzah), Isr. Occ. — B3 38
Gaza, Ia., U.S. — A2 92
Gaza, dept., Moz. — B5 49
Gaza Strip, ter., Isr. Occ. — D3 40
Gaziantep, Tur. — D11 40
Gazimağusa, N. Cyp. — E9 40
Gboko, Nig. — E6 45
Gdańsk (Danzig), Pol. — A5 26
Gdov, Sov. Un. — B6 27
Gdynia, Pol. — A5 26
Gearhart, Or., U.S. — A3 114
Gearhart Mountain, mtn., Or., U.S. — E6 114
Geary, N.B. — D3 71
Geary, Ok., U.S. — B3 113
Geary, co., Ks., U.S. — D7 93
Geauga, co., Oh., U.S. — A4 112
Gebeit Mine, Sud. — A4 47
Gebze, Tur. — B7 25
Ged, La., U.S. — D2 95
Geddes, S.D., U.S. — D7 118
Gedern, W. Ger. — C6 18
Gedinne, Bel. — E4 17
Gediz, Tur. — C7 40
Gediz, stm., Tur. — C6 40
Gedo, prov., Som. — E5 47
Gedser, Den. — D5 15
Geel, Bel. — C4 17
Geelong, Austl. — G7 50
Geetbets, Bel. — D5 17
Geeveston, Austl. — G5 50
Geidam, Nig. — D7 45
Geiger, Al., U.S. — C1 78
Geisenfeld, W. Ger. — C2 60
Geislingen, W. Ger. — D4 18
Geistown, Pa., U.S. — F4 115
Geita, Tan. — B5 48
Gejiu, China — G5 31
Gela, Italy — F5 23
Gelderland, prov., Neth. — B5 17
Geldermalsen, Neth. — C5 17
Geldern, W. Ger. — B6 18
Geldrop, Neth. — C5 17
Geleen, Neth. — D5 17
Gelert, Ont. — C6 73
Gelibolu (Gallipoli), Tur. — B6 40
Gelligaer, Wales, U.K. — C4 12
Gellinam Island, i., Marsh Is. — S17 52

Gelnhausen, W. Ger. — C4 19
Gelsenkirchen, W. Ger. — C3 18
Gelting, W. Ger. — D3 15
Gem, Alta. — D4 68
Gem, Id., U.S. — *B3 89
Gem, Ks., U.S. — C3 93
Gem, W.V., U.S. — C4 125
Gem, co., Id., U.S. — E2 89
Gemas, Malay. — K5 35
Gembloux, Bel. — D4 17
Gemena, Zaire — A2 48
Gemert, Neth. — C5 17
Gemlik, Tur. — B8 15
Gemlik, Tur. — B7 40
Gemona del Friuli, Italy — C9 20
Gemünden, W. Ger. — C4 18
Gem Village, Co., U.S. — D3 83
Genale (Jubba), stm., Afr. — D5 47
Genarp, Swe. — C7 15
Gene Autry, Ok., U.S. — C4 113
General Acha, Arg. — B4 54
General Alvear, Arg. — B5 54
General Alvear, Arg. — A3 54
General Belgrano, Arg. — B5 54
General Carrera, Lago (Lago Buenos Aires), l., S.A. — D2 54
General Conesa, Arg. — C4 54
General Enrique Martínez, Ur. — E2 56
General Eugenio A. Garay, Para. — D3 55
General José de San Martín, Arg. — E4 55
General La Madrid, Arg. — B4 54
General Lavalle, Arg. — B5 54
General Martín Miguel de Güemes, Arg. — D2 55
General Paz, Arg. — E4 55
General Pico, Arg. — B4 54
General Pinedo, Arg. — B3 55
General Roca, Arg. — B3 54
General San Martín, Arg. — g7 54
General Sarmiento, Arg. — g7 54
General Tinio, Phil. — o13 34
General Toshevo, Bul. — D9 24
General Viamonte, Arg. — B4 54
General Villegas, Arg. — B4 54
Genesee, Mi., U.S. — E7 99
Genesee, co., Mi., U.S. — E7 99
Genesee, co., N.Y., U.S. — B2 109
Genesee, stm., N.Y., U.S. — C2 109
Genesee Depot, Wi., U.S. — n11 126
Geneseo, Il., U.S. — B3 90
Geneseo, Ks., U.S. — D5 93
Geneseo, N.Y., U.S. — C3 109
Geneva (Genève), Switz. — E3 18
Geneva, Al., U.S. — D4 78
Geneva, Ga., U.S. — D2 87
Geneva, Il., U.S. — B5 90
Geneva, Ia., U.S. — B4 92
Geneva, Ky., U.S. — C2 94
Geneva, Ne., U.S. — D8 104
Geneva, N.Y., U.S. — C4 109
Geneva, Oh., U.S. — A5 112
Geneva, Pa., U.S. — C1 115
Geneva, co., Al., U.S. — D4 78
Geneva, Lake, l., Eur. — E3 18
Geneva, Lake, l., Wi., U.S. — F5 126
Geneva-on-the-Lake, Oh., U.S. — A5 112
Genève, state, Switz. — C2 20
Genichesk, Sov. Un. — H10 27
Genil, stm., Spain — D3 22
Génissiat, Fr. — C1 20
Genk, Bel. — B6 16
Gennep, Neth. — C5 17
Gennevilliers, Fr. — g10 16
Genoa (Genova), Italy — B2 23
Genoa, Ar., U.S. — D1 81
Genoa, Co., U.S. — B7 83
Genoa, Il., U.S. — A5 90
Genoa, Ne., U.S. — C8 104
Genoa, Nv., U.S. — D2 105
Genoa, Oh., U.S. — A2 112
Genoa, Wi., U.S. — E2 126
Genoa City, Wi., U.S. — F5 126
Genoa, Gulf of, b., Italy — B2 23
Genola, Ut., U.S. — D4 121
Genolier, Switz. — D1 21
Genovesa, Isla, i., Ec. — f6 58
Gent (Ghent), Bel. — B3 16
Genthin, E. Ger. — B6 18
Gentilly, Fr. — g10 16
Gentilly, Mn., U.S. — *C6 100
Gentofte, Den. — *C6 15
Gentry, Ar., U.S. — A1 81
Gentry, Mo., U.S. — A3 102
Gentry, co., Mo., U.S. — A3 102
Gentryville, In., U.S. — H3 91
Genzano di Roma, Italy — h9 23
Geographe Bay, b., Austl. — F2 50
Geographe Channel, strt., Austl. — D1 50
Geographical Society Island, i., Grnld. — B16 128
Geokchay, Sov. Un. — G18 19
George, S. Afr. — D3 49
George, Ia., U.S. — A2 92
George, N.C., U.S. — A5 110
George, co., Ms., U.S. — E5 101
George, i., Sov. Un. — B10 128
George, stm., Que. — g13 74
George, Cape, c., N.S. — D8 71
George, Lake, l., Austl. — G7 50
George, Lake, l., Fl., U.S. — C5 86
George, Lake, l., Mi., U.S. — E3 71
George, Lake, l., N.Y., U.S. — B7 109
George Air Force Base, mil., Ca., U.S. — E5 82
George B. Stevenson Reservoir, res., Pa., U.S. — D6 115
George Hill, mtn., Ma., U.S. — k12 97
George Island, i., Newf. — A3 72
George Peak, mtn., Ut., U.S. — E6 121
Georges Mills, N.H., U.S. — D2 106
George Town, Austl. — o15 50
George Town, Bah. — C7 64
George Town, P.E.I. — C7 71
Georgetown, Gam. — C2 45
Georgetown, Guy. — B7 58
George Town (Pinang), Malay. — D2 34
Georgetown, St. Vin. — U26 65
Georgetown, Ca., U.S. — C3 82
Georgetown, Co., U.S. — B5 83

Georgetown, Ct., U.S. — D2 84
Georgetown, De., U.S. — F4 85
Georgetown, Fl., U.S. — C5 86
Georgetown, Ga., U.S. — E1 87
Georgetown, Id., U.S. — G7 89
Georgetown, Il., U.S. — D6 90
Georgetown, In., U.S. — H6 91
Georgetown, Ky., U.S. — B5 94
Georgetown, La., U.S. — C3 95
Georgetown, Ma., U.S. — A6 98
Georgetown, Mn., U.S. — C2 100
Georgetown, Ms., U.S. — D3 101
Georgetown, N.J., U.S. — C3 107
Georgetown, N.Y., U.S. — C5 109
Georgetown, Oh., U.S. — D2 112
Georgetown, S.C., U.S. — E9 117
Georgetown, Tx., U.S. — D4 120
Georgetown, co., S.C., U.S. — E9 117
George V Coast, Ant. — C28 7
Georgeville, Que. — D5 74
George VI Sound, strt., Ant. — B6 7
Georgia, state, Sov. Un. — D3 8
Georgia, state, U.S. — E5 69
Georgia, Strait of, strt., N.A. — E5 69
Georgia Center, Vt., U.S. — B2 122
Georgiana, Al., U.S. — D3 78
Georgian Bay, b., Ont. — B3 73
Georgina, stm., Austl. — D6 50
Georgiu-Dez, Sov. Un. — F12 27
Georgiyevsk, Sov. Un. — G17 8
Gera, E. Ger. — C6 18
Geraardsbergen, Bel. — D3 17
Geral, Serra, clf., Braz. — D2 56
Gerald, Sask. — G5 75
Gerald, Mo., U.S. — C6 102
Geral de Goiás, Serra, clf., Braz. — D1 57
Geraldine, Al., U.S. — A4 78
Geraldine, Mt., U.S. — C6 103
Geral do Paraná, Serra, mts., Braz. — A3 56
Geraldton, Austl. — E1 50
Geraldton, Ont. — o18 73
Gérardmer, Fr. — A2 20
Gerber, Ca., U.S. — B2 82
Gerber Reservoir, res., Or., U.S. — E5 114
Gerbstedt, E. Ger. — B6 19
Gerciş, Tur. — D13 40
Gerdau, stm., W. Ger. — F4 15
Gerdine, Mount, mtn., Ak., U.S. — C9 79
Gerede, Tur. — B9 40
Gereshk, Afg. — B3 36
Gérgal, Spain — D4 22
Gérin, Que. — C4 74
Gering, Ne., U.S. — C2 104
Gerlach, Nv., U.S. — C2 105
Gerlachovka, mtn., Czech. — D6 26
German Democratic Republic (East Germany), ctry., Eur. — B6 18
Germania, N.J., U.S. — D3 107
Germania, Pa., U.S. — C6 115
Germansen Lake, l., B.C. — B5 69
Germantown, N.B. — D5 71
Germantown, Il., U.S. — E4 90
Germantown, Md., U.S. — B3 97
Germantown, Oh., U.S. — C1 112
Germantown, Tn., U.S. — B2 119
Germantown, Wi., U.S. — E5 126
Germany, Federal Republic of (West Germany), ctry., Eur. — C4 18
Germersheim, W. Ger. — D3 18
Germfask, Mi., U.S. — B5 99
Germiston, S. Afr. — B5 49
Gernrode, E. Ger. — B6 19
Gernsheim, W. Ger. — D3 18
Gero, Japan — n16 33
Gerolzhofen, W. Ger. — C5 18
Gerona, Spain — B7 22
Geronimo, Ok., U.S. — C3 113
Gerrardstown, W.V., U.S. — B6 125
Gersfeld, W. Ger. — C4 18
Gersthofen, W. Ger. — C5 18
Gertrudis Sánchez (part of Mexico City), Mex. — h9 63
Gerty, Ok., U.S. — C5 113
Gervais, Or., U.S. — B4 114
Gerze, Tur. — B10 40
Geseke, W. Ger. — B3 19
Gesher HaZiw, Isr. — A7 41
Gessie, In., U.S. — D2 91
Getafe, Spain — B4 22
Gethsémani, Que. — h9 72
Gettysburg, Oh., U.S. — B1 112
Gettysburg, Pa., U.S. — G7 115
Gettysburg, S.D., U.S. — C6 118
Getz Ice Shelf, ice, Ant. — B36 7
Geuda Springs, Ks., U.S. — E6 93
Gevelsberg, W. Ger. — B2 19
Gex, Fr. — C1 20
Geyser, Mt., U.S. — C6 103
Geyserville, Ca., U.S. — C2 82
Geyve, Tur. — B8 40
Gēzenti, Chad — E3 46
Ghabīyah, Wādī al, val., Eg. — B8 41
Ghaggar, stm., India — C6 36
Ghāghara, stm., India — G10 37
Ghaghar Reservoir, res., India — E4 37
Ghana, ctry., Afr. — E4 45
Ghanzi, Bots. — C5 44
Ghardaïa, Alg. — C4 44
Gharyān, Libya — D2 43
Ghāt, Libya — C8 43
Ghawr ash Sharqīyah, Qanāt al, Jord. — B7 41
Ghazāl, Bahr al, stm., Sud. — B7 41
Ghazal, Bahr el, stm., Chad — C3 46
Ghāziābād, India — *C6 37
Ghāzīpur, India — C6 37
Ghaznī, Afg. — C6 36
Gheen, Mn., U.S. — C6 100
Gheens, La., U.S. — E5 95
Ghent, Ky., U.S. — B4 94
Ghent, Mn., U.S. — F3 100
Ghent, N.Y., U.S. — C7 109
Ghent see Gent, Bel. — B5 16
Gheorghe Gheorghiu-Dej, Rom. — B8 24
Gheorgheni, Rom. — B7 24
Gherla, Rom. — B6 24
Ghilizane, Alg. — B5 44

Ghlò, Beinn a', mtn., Scot., U.K. — D5 13
Ghudāmis, Libya — C1 43
Ghūrīān, Afg. — D10 39
Giannutri, i., Italy — C3 23
Giant Mountain, mtn., N.Y., U.S. — A7 109
Giants Neck, Ct., U.S. — D7 84
Giaveno, Italy — D3 20
Gibara, Cuba — D5 64
Gibbon, Mn., U.S. — F4 100
Gibbon, Ne., U.S. — D7 104
Gibbons, Alta. — C4 68
Gibbonsville, Id., U.S. — D5 89
Gibbs, Mo., U.S. — A5 102
Gibbstown, N.J., U.S. — D2 107
Gibeon, Nmb. — C2 49
Gibraléon, Spain — D3 22
Gibraltar, dep., Eur. — D3 22
Gibraltar, Strait of, strt. — D2 22
Gibraltar Point, c., Eng., U.K. — A8 12
Gibsland, La., U.S. — B2 95
Gibson, Ga., U.S. — C4 87
Gibson, La., U.S. — E5 95
Gibson, Ms., U.S. — B5 101
Gibson, Mo., U.S. — E7 102
Gibson, N.C., U.S. — C3 110
Gibson, Pa., U.S. — C10 115
Gibson, Tn., U.S. — B3 119
Gibson, co., In., U.S. — H2 91
Gibson, co., Tn., U.S. — A3 119
Gibsonburg, Oh., U.S. — A2 112
Gibson City, Il., U.S. — C5 90
Gibson Desert, des., Austl. — *D5 86
Gibsonia, Fl., U.S. — h14 115
Gibson Island, i., Md., U.S. — B5 97
Gibsons, B.C. — E6 69
Gibsonton, Fl., U.S. — p11 86
Gibsonville, N.C., U.S. — A3 110
Giddings, Tx., U.S. — D4 120
Gideon, Mo., U.S. — E8 102
Gidole, Eth. — C6 47
Gien, Fr. — D5 16
Giessen, W. Ger. — C4 18
Gifford, Ar., U.S. — g8 81
Gifford, Fl., U.S. — E6 86
Gifford, Id., U.S. — C2 89
Gifford, Il., U.S. — C5 90
Gifford, In., U.S. — B3 91
Gifford, Pa., U.S. — C4 115
Giffre, stm., Fr. — D21 21
Gifhorn, W. Ger. — F4 15
Gift, Tn., U.S. — B2 119
Gifu, Japan — D12 31
Giganta, Sierra de la, mts., Mex. — B2 63
Gigante, Col. — C2 60
Gigha Island, i., Scot., U.K. — E3 13
Giglio, i., Italy — C3 23
Gihon, stm., Vt., U.S. — B3 122
Gijón, Spain — A3 22
Gila, N.M., U.S. — E1 108
Gila, stm., U.S. — D5 80
Gila, stm., Az., U.S. — D5 76
Gila Bend, Az., U.S. — E3 80
Gila Bend Indian Reservation, Az., U.S. — D3 80
Gila Bend Mountains, mts., Az., U.S. — D2 80
Gila Cliff Dwellings National Monument, N.M., U.S. — D1 108
Gila Mountains, mts., Az., U.S. — D6 80
Gila Peak, mtn., Az., U.S. — D6 80
Gila River Indian Reservation, Az., U.S. — D4 80
Gilbert, Ar., U.S. — B3 81
Gilbert, Az., U.S. — *D4 80
Gilbert, Ia., U.S. — B4 92
Gilbert, La., U.S. — B4 95
Gilbert, Mn., U.S. — C6 100
Gilbert, Or., U.S. — *B4 114
Gilbert, S.C., U.S. — D5 117
Gilbert, W.V., U.S. — D3 125
Gilbert, stm., Austl. — C8 51
Gilbert, stm., Newf. — B3 72
Gilbert Islands see Kiribati, ctry., Oc. — G11 6
Gilbert Islands, is., Kir. — G10 6
Gilbert, Al., U.S. — D1 78
Gilbert Peak, mtn., Wa., U.S. — C4 124
Gilbert Plains, Man. — D1 70
Gilbertsville, Ky., U.S. — f9 94
Gilbertsville, N.Y., U.S. — C5 109
Gilbertsville, Pa., U.S. — F10 115
Gilbertville, Ia., U.S. — B5 92
Gilbertville, Ma., U.S. — B3 98
Gilboa, Oh., U.S. — A2 112
Gilby, N.D., U.S. — A8 111
Gilchrist, Or., U.S. — D5 114
Gilchrist, co., Fl., U.S. — C4 86
Gilcrest, Co., U.S. — A6 83
Gildford, Mt., U.S. — B6 103
Gilead, Ct., U.S. — C6 84
Gilead, Me., U.S. — D2 96
Gilead, Ne., U.S. — D8 104
Gilead, Oh., U.S. — B3 112
Giles, co., Tn., U.S. — B4 119
Giles, co., Va., U.S. — C2 123
Gilford, N. Ire., U.K. — C5 11
Gilford, N.H., U.S. — C4 106
Gilford, i., B.C. — D4 69
Gilford Park, N.J., U.S. — *D4 107
Gilgandra, Austl. — E7 51
Gilgit, Pak. — C6 36
Gil Island, i., B.C. — C3 69
Gill, Co., U.S. — A6 83
Gill, Lough, l., Ire. — C3 11
Gillam, Man. — A4 70
Gillespie, Il., U.S. — D4 90
Gillespie, co., Tx., U.S. — D3 120
Gillespie Dam, Az., U.S. — D3 80
Gillett, Ar., U.S. — C4 81
Gillett, Pa., U.S. — C8 115
Gillett, Wi., U.S. — D5 126
Gillett Grove, Ia., U.S. — A2 92
Gillette, Wy., U.S. — B7 127
Gilliam, La., U.S. — B2 95
Gilliam, Mo., U.S. — B4 102
Gilliam, co., Or., U.S. — B6 114
Gillingham, Eng., U.K. — C8 12
Gillis, La., U.S. — D2 95
Gillsville, Ga., U.S. — B3 87
Gilman, Ia., U.S. — C5 92
Gilman, Il., U.S. — C5 90
Gilman, Vt., U.S. — C5 122
Gilman, Wi., U.S. — C3 126
Gilman City, Mo., U.S. — A4 102
Gilman, Mn., U.S. — E5 100

| Name | Map Ref. | Page |
|---|---|---|
| Gilman, Vt., U.S. | C5 | 122 |
| Gilman, Wi., U.S. | C3 | 126 |
| Gilman City, Mo., U.S. | A4 | 102 |
| Gilmanton, N.H., U.S. | D4 | 106 |
| Gilmanton, Wi., U.S. | D2 | 126 |
| Gilmanton Iron Works, N.H., U.S. | D4 | 106 |
| Gilmer, Tx., U.S. | C5 | 120 |
| Gilmer, W.V., U.S. | C4 | 125 |
| Gilmer, co., Ga., U.S. | B2 | 87 |
| Gilmer, co., W.V., U.S. | C4 | 125 |
| Gilmore, Ar., U.S. | B5 | 81 |
| Gilmore City, Ia., U.S. | B3 | 92 |
| Gilmour, Ont. | C7 | 73 |
| Gilo, stm., Eth. | D3 | 47 |
| Gilpin, Ky., U.S. | C5 | 94 |
| Gilpin, co., Co., U.S. | B5 | 83 |
| Gilroy, Sask. | G2 | 75 |
| Gilroy, Ca., U.S. | D3 | 82 |
| Gilson, Il., U.S. | C3 | 90 |
| Gilsum, N.H., U.S. | D2 | 106 |
| Gilt Edge, Tn., U.S. | B2 | 119 |
| Giltner, Ne., U.S. | D7 | 104 |
| Giluwe, Mount, mtn., Pap. N. Gui. | k11 | 50 |
| Gimli, Man. | D3 | 70 |
| Ginir, Eth. | D5 | 47 |
| Ginns Corner, De., U.S. | C3 | 85 |
| Ginosa, Italy | D6 | 23 |
| Ginowan, Japan | O5 | 52 |
| Ginzo [de Limia], Spain | A2 | 22 |
| Gioia del Colle, Italy | D6 | 23 |
| Gioiosa Ionica, Italy | E6 | 23 |
| Girard, Ga., U.S. | C5 | 87 |
| Girard, Il., U.S. | D4 | 90 |
| Girard, Ks., U.S. | E9 | 93 |
| Girard, La., U.S. | B4 | 95 |
| Girard, Oh., U.S. | A5 | 112 |
| Girard, Pa., U.S. | B1 | 115 |
| Girard, Tx., U.S. | C2 | 120 |
| Girardot, Col. | C3 | 60 |
| Girardville, Pa., U.S. | E9 | 115 |
| Girdletree, Md., U.S. | D7 | 97 |
| Giresun, Tur. | B12 | 40 |
| Giri, stm., Zaire | A2 | 48 |
| Girīdīh, India | D8 | 36 |
| Girna, stm., India | G5 | 37 |
| Girne, N. Cyp. | E9 | 40 |
| Giromagny, Fr. | D7 | 16 |
| Girón, Ec. | B2 | 58 |
| Gironde, est., Fr. | E3 | 16 |
| Giroux, Man. | E3 | 70 |
| Girouxville, Alta. | B2 | 68 |
| Girvan, Scot., U.K. | C4 | 10 |
| Girvin, Sask. | F3 | 75 |
| Girvin, Tx., U.S. | D1 | 120 |
| Gisborne, N.Z. | M17 | 51 |
| Gisborne Lake, l., Newf. | E4 | 72 |
| Giscome, B.C. | B6 | 69 |
| Gisenyi, Rw. | B4 | 48 |
| Gisors, Fr. | C4 | 16 |
| Gislaved, Swe. | A7 | 15 |
| Gitega, Bdi. | B4 | 48 |
| Giulianova, Italy | C4 | 23 |
| Giurgiu, Rom. | D7 | 24 |
| Giv'atayim, Isr. | g10 | 41 |
| Give, Den. | C3 | 15 |
| Givet, Fr. | B6 | 16 |
| Givhans, S.C., U.S. | E7 | 117 |
| Givors, Fr. | E6 | 16 |
| Givry, l., Micron. | Q18 | 52 |
| Giza (Al Jīzah), Eg. | B3 | 38 |
| Giza, Pyramids of, hist., Egypt | E3 | 41 |
| Gīzāb, Afg. | E13 | 39 |
| Gizhiga, Sov. Un. | C19 | 31 |
| Gizycko, Pol. | A6 | 26 |
| Gjirokastra, Alb. | B3 | 40 |
| Gjoa Haven, N.W. Ter. | C13 | 66 |
| Gjøvik, Nor. | G4 | 14 |
| Glace Bay, N.S. | C10 | 71 |
| Glacier, B.C. | D9 | 69 |
| Glacier, Wa., U.S. | A4 | 124 |
| Glacier, co., Mt., U.S. | B3 | 103 |
| Glacier Bay, b., Ak., U.S. | k21 | 79 |
| Glacier Bay National Park, Ak., U.S. | D12 | 79 |
| Glacier National Park, B.C. | D9 | 69 |
| Glacier National Park, Mt., U.S. | B2 | 103 |
| Glacier Peak, mtn., Wa., U.S. | A4 | 124 |
| Gladbeck, W. Ger. | B1 | 19 |
| Gladbrook, Ia., U.S. | B5 | 92 |
| Glade, Ks., U.S. | C4 | 93 |
| Glade Creek, stm., W.V., U.S. | C6 | 124 |
| Glade Creek, stm., W.V., U.S. | n14 | 125 |
| Glade Creek, stm., W.V., U.S. | n13 | 125 |
| Glade Park, Co., U.S. | B2 | 83 |
| Glades, co., Fl., U.S. | F5 | 86 |
| Glade Spring, Va., U.S. | f10 | 123 |
| Glade Valley, N.C., U.S. | A1 | 110 |
| Gladeview, Fl., U.S. | *G6 | 86 |
| Gladeville, Tn., U.S. | A5 | 119 |
| Gladewater, Tx., U.S. | C5 | 120 |
| Gladmar, Sask. | H3 | 75 |
| Gladstone, Austl. | D9 | 50 |
| Gladstone, Man. | D2 | 70 |
| Gladstone, Il., U.S. | C3 | 90 |
| Gladstone, Mi., U.S. | C3 | 99 |
| Gladstone, Mo., U.S. | h10 | 102 |
| Gladstone, Ne., U.S. | D8 | 104 |
| Gladstone, N.J., U.S. | B3 | 107 |
| Gladstone, N.M., U.S. | A6 | 108 |
| Gladstone, N.D., U.S. | C3 | 111 |
| Gladstone, Or., U.S. | B4 | 114 |
| Gladstone, Va., U.S. | C4 | 123 |
| Glad Valley, S.D., U.S. | B4 | 118 |
| Gladwin, Mi., U.S. | E6 | 99 |
| Gladwin, co., Mi., U.S. | D6 | 99 |
| Glady, W.V., U.S. | C5 | 125 |
| Gladys, Va., U.S. | C3 | 123 |
| Glåma, stm., Nor. | G5 | 14 |
| Glamis, Sask. | F2 | 75 |
| Glamoč, Yugo. | C3 | 24 |
| Glan, l., Swe. | u33 | 14 |
| Glan, sm., W. Ger. | D2 | 19 |
| Gland, Switz. | D1 | 21 |
| Glandorf, Oh., U.S. | A1 | 112 |
| Glanshammar (part of Örebro), Swe. | t33 | 14 |
| Glärnisch, mts., Switz. | C4 | 20 |
| Glarus, Switz. | C4 | 20 |
| Glarus, state, Switz. | B5 | 21 |
| Glarus Alps, mts., Switz. | C8 | 21 |
| Glasco, Ks., U.S. | C6 | 93 |
| Glasco, N.Y., U.S. | C7 | 109 |
| Glascock, co., Ga., U.S. | C4 | 87 |
| Glasford, Il., U.S. | C4 | 90 |
| Glasgo, Ct., U.S. | C8 | 84 |
| Glasgow, Scot., U.K. | C4 | 10 |
| Glasgow, Ky., U.S. | D3 | 90 |
| Glasgow, Mo., U.S. | B5 | 102 |
| Glasgow, Va., U.S. | C3 | 123 |
| Glasgow, W.V., U.S. | m13 | 125 |
| Glasgow Village, Mo., U.S. | *f13 | 102 |
| Glaslyn, Sask. | D1 | 75 |
| Glasnevin, Sask. | H3 | 75 |
| Glass, Tn., U.S. | A2 | 119 |
| Glassboro, N.J., U.S. | D2 | 107 |
| Glasscock, co., Tx., U.S. | D2 | 120 |
| Glass Mountains, mts., Tx., U.S. | D1 | 120 |
| Glassmanor, Md., U.S. | *C4 | 97 |
| Glassport, Pa., U.S. | F2 | 115 |
| Glasston, N.D., U.S. | A8 | 111 |
| Glastenbury Mountain, mtn., Vt., U.S. | F2 | 122 |
| Glastonbury, Eng., U.K. | C5 | 12 |
| Glastonbury, Ct., U.S. | C5 | 84 |
| Glauchau, E. Ger. | C6 | 18 |
| Glazier, Tx., U.S. | A2 | 120 |
| Glazier Lake, l., Me., U.S. | A3 | 96 |
| Glazov, Sov. Un. | B4 | 28 |
| Glazypeau Mountain, mtn., Ar., U.S. | f7 | 81 |
| Gleason, Tn., U.S. | A3 | 119 |
| Gleason, Wi., U.S. | C4 | 126 |
| Gleasondale, Ma., U.S. | g9 | 98 |
| Gleichen, Alta. | D4 | 68 |
| Gleiwitz see Gliwice, Pol. | C5 | 26 |
| Glen, Mn., U.S. | D5 | 100 |
| Glen, Mt., U.S. | E4 | 103 |
| Glen, N.H., U.S. | B4 | 106 |
| Glen, W.V., U.S. | m13 | 125 |
| Glenade, Ire. | C3 | 11 |
| Glen Alice, Tn., U.S. | D9 | 119 |
| Glen Allan, Ms., U.S. | B2 | 101 |
| Glen Allen, Al., U.S. | B2 | 78 |
| Glen Allen, Mo., U.S. | D7 | 102 |
| Glen Allen, Va., U.S. | C5 | 123 |
| Glenalpine, Ire. | B1 | 110 |
| Glenamaddy, Ire. | D3 | 11 |
| Glenamoy, Ire. | C2 | 11 |
| Glénan, Îles de, is., Fr. | D1 | 16 |
| Glenavon, Sask. | G4 | 75 |
| Glenavon, N. Ire., U.K. | C6 | 11 |
| Glen Avon, Ca., U.S. | m14 | 82 |
| Glenbain, Sask. | H2 | 75 |
| Glenbarr, Scot., U.K. | E3 | 13 |
| Glenbeigh, Ire. | E2 | 11 |
| Glenbeulah, Wi., U.S. | k9 | 126 |
| Glenbrook, Man. | D1 | 70 |
| Glenbrook, Nv., U.S. | D2 | 105 |
| Glenburn, Man. | D2 | 70 |
| Glenburn, N.D., U.S. | A4 | 111 |
| Glen Burnie, Md., U.S. | B4 | 97 |
| Glen Burnie Park, Md., U.S. | *B4 | 97 |
| Glenbush, Sask. | D2 | 75 |
| Glen Campbell, Pa., U.S. | E4 | 115 |
| Glen Canyon, Ut., U.S. | F4 | 121 |
| Glen Canyon Dam, Az., U.S. | A4 | 80 |
| Glen Canyon National Recreation Area, U.S. | F5 | 121 |
| Glencar, Ire. | E2 | 11 |
| Glen Carbon, Il., U.S. | *E4 | 90 |
| Glencliff, N.H., U.S. | C3 | 106 |
| Glencoe, Ont. | E3 | 73 |
| Glencoe, Al., U.S. | B4 | 78 |
| Glencoe, Il., U.S. | A6 | 90 |
| Glencoe, Ky., U.S. | B5 | 94 |
| Glencoe, Md., U.S. | A4 | 97 |
| Glencoe, Mn., U.S. | F4 | 100 |
| Glencoe, Mo., U.S. | f12 | 102 |
| Glencoe, N.M., U.S. | D4 | 108 |
| Glencoe, Ok., U.S. | A5 | 113 |
| Glen Cove, N.Y., U.S. | h13 | 109 |
| Glencross, S.D., U.S. | B5 | 118 |
| Glendale, Az., U.S. | D3 | 80 |
| Glendale, Ca., U.S. | m12 | 82 |
| Glendale, Co., U.S. | *B6 | 83 |
| Glendale, Fl., U.S. | v15 | 86 |
| Glendale, Ms., U.S. | C4 | 94 |
| Glendale, Ms., U.S. | *B1 | 98 |
| Glendale, Mo., U.S. | *f13 | 102 |
| Glendale, N.H., U.S. | E3 | 106 |
| Glendale, Oh., U.S. | C1 | 112 |
| Glendale, Or., U.S. | E3 | 114 |
| Glendale, R.I., U.S. | B2 | 116 |
| Glendale, S.C., U.S. | B4 | 117 |
| Glendale, Ut., U.S. | B5 | 119 |
| Glen Dale, W.V., U.S. | B4 | 125 |
| Glendale Colony, S.D., U.S. | C7 | 118 |
| Glendale Heights, Il., U.S. | *k8 | 90 |
| Glendale Heights, W.V., U.S. | g8 | 125 |
| Glen Dean, Ky., U.S. | C3 | 94 |
| Glendevey, Co., U.S. | A5 | 83 |
| Glendive, Mt., U.S. | C12 | 103 |
| Glendo, Wy., U.S. | D7 | 127 |
| Glendola, N.J., U.S. | C4 | 107 |
| Glendon, Alta. | B5 | 68 |
| Glendora, Ca., U.S. | m13 | 82 |
| Glendora, Ms., U.S. | B3 | 101 |
| Glendora, N.J., U.S. | *D2 | 107 |
| Glendowan, Ire. | C4 | 11 |
| Glen Easton, W.V., U.S. | g8 | 125 |
| Glen Echo, Md., U.S. | f8 | 97 |
| Glen Elder, Ks., U.S. | C5 | 93 |
| Glenelg, Scot., U.K. | C3 | 13 |
| Glenelg, Md., U.S. | B4 | 97 |
| Glenella, Man. | D2 | 70 |
| Glen Ellis Falls, wtfl., N.H., U.S. | B4 | 106 |
| Glen Ellyn, Il., U.S. | k8 | 90 |
| Glen Ewen, Sask. | H4 | 75 |
| Glenfarne, Ire. | C4 | 11 |
| Glenferrie, W.V., U.S. | *C3 | 125 |
| Glenfield, N.Y., U.S. | B5 | 109 |
| Glenfield, N.D., U.S. | B7 | 111 |
| Glenfinnan, Scot., U.K. | D3 | 13 |
| Glen Flora, Tx., U.S. | E4 | 120 |
| Glengad Head, c., Ire. | B4 | 11 |
| Glengarriff, Ire. | F2 | 11 |
| Glengarry, co., Ont. | B10 | 73 |
| Glenham, N.Y., U.S. | D7 | 109 |
| Glenham, S.D., U.S. | B5 | 118 |
| Glen Haven, Co., U.S. | A5 | 83 |
| Glen Head, N.Y., U.S. | *h13 | 109 |
| Glen Innes, Austl. | E9 | 50 |
| Glen Jean, W.V., U.S. | D3 | 125 |
| Glen Kerr, Sask. | G2 | 75 |
| Glen Lake, l., Mi., U.S. | D5 | 99 |
| Glenluce, Scot., U.K. | D4 | 13 |
| Glenlyon, Scot., U.K. | D4 | 13 |
| Glenmont, Oh., U.S. | B3 | 112 |
| Glenmora, La., U.S. | D3 | 95 |
| Glenmore, Oh., U.S. | B1 | 112 |
| Glenmorgan, Austl. | E8 | 50 |
| Glenn, Mi., U.S. | F4 | 99 |
| Glenn, co., Ca., U.S. | C2 | 82 |
| Glennallen, Ak., U.S. | f19 | 79 |
| Glenn Dale, Md., U.S. | *C4 | 97 |
| Glennie, Mi., U.S. | D7 | 99 |
| Glennonville, Mo., U.S. | E7 | 102 |
| Glenns Ferry, Id., U.S. | G3 | 89 |
| Glennville, Ga., U.S. | E5 | 87 |
| Glenolden, Pa., U.S. | p20 | 115 |
| Glenoma, Wa., U.S. | C3 | 124 |
| Glenorchy, Austl. | o15 | 50 |
| Glenpool, Ok., U.S. | B5 | 113 |
| Glen Raven, N.C., U.S. | A3 | 110 |
| Glenridge, Man. | h10 | 98 |
| Glen Ridge, N.J., U.S. | h8 | 107 |
| Glenrio, W.V., U.S. | B6 | 108 |
| Glen Robertson, Ont. | B10 | 73 |
| Glen Rock, N.J., U.S. | h8 | 107 |
| Glen Rock, Pa., U.S. | G8 | 115 |
| Glenrock, Wy., U.S. | D7 | 127 |
| Glen Rose, Tx., U.S. | C4 | 120 |
| Glenrothes, Scot., U.K. | D5 | 13 |
| Glen Saint Mary, Fl., U.S. | B4 | 86 |
| Glens Falls, N.Y., U.S. | B7 | 109 |
| Glenshaw, Pa., U.S. | h14 | 115 |
| Glenside, Sask. | F2 | 75 |
| Glenside, Pa., U.S. | *o21 | 115 |
| Glentana, Mt., U.S. | B10 | 103 |
| Glenties, Ire. | C3 | 11 |
| Glentworth, Sask. | H2 | 75 |
| Glen Ullin, N.D., U.S. | C4 | 111 |
| Glenview, Il., U.S. | h9 | 90 |
| Glenview Naval Air Station, mil., Il., U.S. | h9 | 90 |
| Glenvil, Ne., U.S. | D7 | 104 |
| Glenville, Ire. | E3 | 11 |
| Glenville, Mn., U.S. | G5 | 100 |
| Glenville, N.C., U.S. | f9 | 110 |
| Glenville, W.V., U.S. | C4 | 125 |
| Glen White, W.V., U.S. | D3 | 125 |
| Glen Wilton, Va., U.S. | C3 | 123 |
| Glin, Ire. | E2 | 11 |
| Glina, stm., Scot., U.K. | D6 | 23 |
| Glittertinden, mtn., Nor. | G3 | 14 |
| Gliwice (Gleiwitz), Pol. | C5 | 26 |
| Globe, Az., U.S. | D5 | 80 |
| Globe, Ky., U.S. | B6 | 94 |
| Globino, Sov. Un. | G9 | 27 |
| Głogów, Pol. | C4 | 26 |
| Glorenza, Italy | A3 | 23 |
| Glória, Braz. | C3 | 57 |
| Glória de Goitá, Braz. | k6 | 57 |
| Glorieta, N.M., U.S. | B4 | 108 |
| Glorieuses, Îles es, i., Reu. | f9 | 49 |
| Glossop, Eng., U.K. | A6 | 12 |
| Glossopteris, Mount, mtn., Ant. | A1 | 7 |
| Gloster, Ga., U.S. | h8 | 87 |
| Gloster, La., U.S. | B2 | 95 |
| Gloster, Ms., U.S. | D2 | 101 |
| Glostrup, Den. | C6 | 15 |
| Gloucester, Ont. | m12 | 73 |
| Gloucester, Eng., U.K. | E5 | 10 |
| Gloucester, Ma., U.S. | A6 | 98 |
| Gloucester, co., N.B. | B4 | 71 |
| Gloucester, co., N.J., U.S. | D2 | 107 |
| Gloucester, co., Va., U.S. | C6 | 123 |
| Gloucester City, N.J., U.S. | D2 | 107 |
| Gloucester Point, Va., U.S. | C6 | 123 |
| Gloucestershire, co., Eng., U.K. | C7 | 12 |
| Glouster, Oh., U.S. | C3 | 112 |
| Glover, Mo., U.S. | D7 | 102 |
| Glover, Vt., U.S. | B4 | 122 |
| Glover Gap, W.V., U.S. | h10 | 125 |
| Glover Island, l., Newf. | D3 | 72 |
| Gloversville, N.Y., U.S. | B6 | 109 |
| Glovertown, Newf. | D4 | 72 |
| Gloverville, S.C., U.S. | E4 | 117 |
| Głubczyce, Pol. | C4 | 26 |
| Glubokoye, Sov. Un. | D6 | 27 |
| Głuchołazy, Pol. | C4 | 26 |
| Gluck, S.C., U.S. | B2 | 117 |
| Glücksburg, W. Ger. | E3 | 15 |
| Glückstadt, W. Ger. | E3 | 15 |
| Gluek, Mn., U.S. | F3 | 100 |
| Glukhov, Sov. Un. | F9 | 27 |
| Glussk, Sov. Un. | E6 | 27 |
| Glyndon, Md., U.S. | B4 | 97 |
| Glyndon, Mn., U.S. | D2 | 100 |
| Glyngøre, Den. | B2 | 15 |
| Glynn, co., Ga., U.S. | E5 | 87 |
| Gmunden, Aus. | D6 | 18 |
| Gnadenhutten, Oh., U.S. | B4 | 112 |
| Gnesta, Swe. | t35 | 14 |
| Gniezno, Pol. | B4 | 26 |
| Gnjilane, Yugo. | D5 | 24 |
| Gnoien, E. Ger. | B5 | 18 |
| Goa, state, India | E5 | 36 |
| Goālpāra, India | D13 | 37 |
| Goat Fell, mtn., Scot., U.K. | E3 | 13 |
| Goat Island, i., R.I., U.S. | F5 | 116 |
| Goat Island Point, c., Am. Sam. | f13 | 52 |
| Goat Mountain, mtn., Mt., U.S. | C3 | 103 |
| Goat Rock Dam, U.S. | C4 | 78 |
| Goba, Eth. | D5 | 47 |
| Gobabis, Nmb. | B3 | 49 |
| Gobernador, N.M., U.S. | A2 | 108 |
| Gobernador Gregores, Arg. | D2 | 54 |
| Gobernador Udaondo, Arg. | g7 | 54 |
| Gobi Desert, des., Asia | C7 | 33 |
| Gobles, Mi., U.S. | F5 | 99 |
| Goboō, Japan | J7 | 33 |
| Gochas, Nmb. | B2 | 49 |
| Godāvari, stm., India | E6 | 36 |
| Godāvari, Mouths of the, mth., India | E7 | 36 |
| Goddard, Ks., U.S. | E6 | 93 |
| Goderich, Ont. | D3 | 73 |
| Godfrey, Ga., U.S. | C3 | 87 |
| Godfrey, Il., U.S. | E3 | 90 |
| Godhavn, Grnld. | C15 | 61 |
| Godhra, India | F4 | 37 |
| Godley, Tx., U.S. | n9 | 120 |
| Gods, stm., Man. | A5 | 70 |
| Gods Lake, Man. | B4 | 70 |
| Gods Lake, l., Man. | B4 | 70 |
| Godthåb (Nuuk), Grnld. | C15 | 61 |
| Godwin, N.C., U.S. | B4 | 110 |
| Godwin Austen, see K2, mtn., Asia | A6 | 36 |
| Goehner, Ne., U.S. | D8 | 104 |
| Goes, Neth. | C3 | 17 |
| Goessel, Ks., U.S. | D6 | 93 |
| Goff, Ks., U.S. | C8 | 93 |
| Goff Creek, stm., Ok., U.S. | e9 | 113 |
| Goffstown, N.H., U.S. | D3 | 106 |
| Gogebic, co., Mi., U.S. | n12 | 99 |
| Gogebic, Lake, l., Mi., U.S. | m12 | 99 |
| Gogebic Range, hills, U.S. | B3 | 126 |
| Goglio, Italy | D5 | 21 |
| Godfield, Il., U.S. | A3 | 19 |
| Göhren, E. Ger. | D7 | 15 |
| Goiana, Braz. | C4 | 57 |
| Goiandira, Braz. | B3 | 56 |
| Goianésia, Braz. | B3 | 56 |
| Goiânia, Braz. | B3 | 56 |
| Goianinha, Braz. | h6 | 57 |
| Goiás, Braz. | B2 | 56 |
| Goiás, state, Braz. | B3 | 56 |
| Goiatuba, Braz. | D4 | 13 |
| Goil, Loch, b., Scot., U.K. | D6 | 23 |
| Goito, Italy | A4 | 47 |
| Gojam, prov., Eth. | C4 | 47 |
| Gojō, Japan | o14 | 33 |
| Gojōb, Japan | B2 | 56 |
| Gökçeada, i., Tur. | B5 | 25 |
| Göksun, Tur. | C11 | 40 |
| Gokwe, Zimb. | A4 | 49 |
| Gol, Nor. | G3 | 14 |
| Gola Island, i., Ire. | B3 | 11 |
| Golam Head, c., Ire. | D2 | 11 |
| Golan Heights, ter., Syria | A7 | 41 |
| Golbāf, Iran | C5 | 38 |
| Golchikha, Sov. Un. | B11 | 29 |
| Golconda, Il., U.S. | F5 | 90 |
| Golconda, Nv., U.S. | C4 | 105 |
| Goldach, Switz. | B7 | 21 |
| Gotdap, Pol. | A7 | 26 |
| Goldbach, W. Ger. | C4 | 19 |
| Gold Bar, Wa., U.S. | B4 | 124 |
| Goldberg, E. Ger. | E6 | 15 |
| Goldboro, N.S. | D8 | 71 |
| Gold Coast see Southport, Austl. | E9 | 50 |
| Gold Creek, Ak., U.S. | f17 | 79 |
| Goldcreek, Mt., U.S. | D4 | 103 |
| Golddust, Tn., U.S. | B2 | 119 |
| Golden, B.C. | D9 | 69 |
| Golden, Ire. | E4 | 11 |
| Golden, Co., U.S. | B5 | 83 |
| Golden, Il., U.S. | C2 | 90 |
| Golden, Ms., U.S. | A5 | 101 |
| Golden, Ok., U.S. | E4 | 102 |
| Golden, S.D., U.S. | B3 | 108 |
| Golden, Ok., U.S. | C7 | 113 |
| Golden Bay, b., N.Z. | N14 | 51 |
| Golden Beach, Fl., U.S. | *G6 | 86 |
| Golden City, Mo., U.S. | D3 | 102 |
| Goldenvalley, N.D., U.S. | D5 | 124 |
| Golden Ears Provincial Park, B.C. | E6 | 69 |
| Goldengate, Il., U.S. | E5 | 90 |
| Golden Gate Bridge, Ca., U.S. | h7 | 82 |
| Golden Gate National Recreation Area, Ca., U.S. | h7 | 82 |
| Golden Glades, Fl., U.S. | *G6 | 86 |
| Golden Hinde, B.C. | E5 | 69 |
| Golden Lake, Ont. | B7 | 73 |
| Golden Lake, l., Ont. | B7 | 73 |
| Golden Meadow, La., U.S. | E5 | 95 |
| Golden Prairie, Sask. | G1 | 75 |
| Golden Spike National Historic Site, hist., Ut., U.S. | B3 | 121 |
| Golden Spur, Ct., U.S. | D7 | 84 |
| Golden Valley, Mn., U.S. | n12 | 100 |
| Goldenvalley, N.D., U.S. | B3 | 111 |
| Golden Valley, co., Mt., U.S. | D7 | 103 |
| Golden Valley, co., N.D., U.S. | B2 | 111 |
| Goldenville, N.S. | D7 | 71 |
| Goldfield, Ia., U.S. | B4 | 92 |
| Goldfield, Nv., U.S. | F4 | 105 |
| Gold Hill, N.C., U.S. | B2 | 110 |
| Gold Hill, Or., U.S. | E3 | 114 |
| Goldonna, La., U.S. | B3 | 95 |
| Goldsand Lake, l., Man. | A1 | 70 |
| Goldsboro, Md., U.S. | B6 | 97 |
| Goldsboro, N.C., U.S. | B5 | 110 |
| Goldsby, Ok., U.S. | B4 | 113 |
| Goldschmidt, Cape, c., Ant. | g40 | 7 |
| Goldsmith, In., U.S. | D6 | 91 |
| Goldsmith, Tx., U.S. | D1 | 120 |
| Goldston, N.C., U.S. | B3 | 110 |
| Goldsworthy, Austl. | D3 | 50 |
| Goldthwaite, Tx., U.S. | D3 | 120 |
| Goleen, Ire. | F2 | 11 |
| Golela, S. Afr. | C5 | 49 |
| Goleniów, Pol. | B3 | 26 |
| Goleta, Ca., U.S. | E4 | 82 |
| Golets-Skalistyy, Mount, mtn., Sov. Un. | D14 | 29 |
| Golfito, C.R. | F6 | 62 |
| Golf Manor, Oh., U.S. | o13 | 112 |
| Goliad, Tx., U.S. | E4 | 120 |
| Goliad, co., Tx., U.S. | E4 | 120 |
| Golling [an der Salzach], Aus. | B9 | 20 |
| Golmud, China | D3 | 31 |
| Golo, stm., Fr. | G2 | 16 |
| Golo Island, i., Phil. | p13 | 34 |
| Golovin, Ak., U.S. | C7 | 79 |
| Golpāyegān, Iran | C4 | 38 |
| Golspie, Scot., U.K. | A3 | 13 |
| Goltry, Ok., U.S. | A3 | 113 |
| Golts, Md., U.S. | B6 | 97 |
| Golva, N.D., U.S. | C2 | 111 |
| Golyamo Konare, Bul. | D7 | 24 |
| Goma, Zaire | B4 | 48 |
| Gomati, stm., India | A4 | 48 |
| Gombari, Zaire | A5 | 48 |
| Gombe, Nig. | D6 | 45 |
| Gomel, Sov. Un. | E8 | 27 |
| Gomera, i., Spain | m13 | 22 |
| Gómez Palacio, Mex. | C7 | 63 |
| Gommern, E. Ger. | A6 | 19 |
| Gonābād, Iran | B6 | 39 |
| Gonaïves, Haiti | E7 | 64 |
| Gonâve, Golfe de la, b., Haiti | E7 | 64 |
| Gonâve, Île de la, i., Haiti | E7 | 64 |
| Gonbad-e Qābūs, Iran | E7 | 39 |
| Gonda, India | C7 | 36 |
| Gonder (Gondar), Eth. | C4 | 47 |
| Gondia, India | A5 | 48 |
| Gondrecourt-le-Château, Fr. | F5 | 17 |
| Gönen, Tur. | G8 | 37 |
| Gonesse, Fr. | g10 | 16 |
| Gongga Shan, mtn., China | F5 | 31 |
| Gongola, stm., Nig. | D7 | 45 |
| Goñi, Ur. | f8 | 54 |
| Gonvick, Mn., U.S. | C3 | 100 |
| Gonzales, Ca., U.S. | D3 | 82 |
| Gonzales, La., U.S. | D5 | 95 |
| Gonzales, Tx., U.S. | E4 | 120 |
| Gonzales, co., Tx., U.S. | E4 | 120 |
| González, Fl., U.S. | u14 | 86 |
| González Chaves, Arg. | B4 | 54 |
| Goochland, Va., U.S. | C5 | 123 |
| Goochland, co., Va., U.S. | C5 | 123 |
| Goode, Va., U.S. | C3 | 123 |
| Goode, Mount, mtn., Ak., U.S. | g18 | 79 |
| Goodell, Ia., U.S. | B4 | 92 |
| Gooderham, Ont. | C6 | 73 |
| Goodeve, Sask. | F4 | 75 |
| Goodfellow Air Force Base, mil., Tx., U.S. | D2 | 120 |
| Goodfield, Il., U.S. | C4 | 90 |
| Good Hart, Mi., U.S. | C5 | 99 |
| Good Hope, Ga., U.S. | C3 | 87 |
| Good Hope, Il., U.S. | C3 | 90 |
| Good Hope, Ms., U.S. | C4 | 101 |
| Good Hope, Oh., U.S. | C2 | 112 |
| Good Hope, Cape of, c., S. Afr. | D2 | 49 |
| Good Hope Mountain, mtn., B.C. | D5 | 69 |
| Goodhue, Mn., U.S. | F6 | 100 |
| Goodhue, co., Mn., U.S. | F6 | 100 |
| Gooding, Id., U.S. | G4 | 89 |
| Gooding, co., Id., U.S. | G4 | 89 |
| Goodland, Fl., U.S. | G5 | 86 |
| Goodland, In., U.S. | C3 | 91 |
| Goodland, Ks., U.S. | C2 | 93 |
| Goodland, Ok., U.S. | D6 | 113 |
| Goodlands, Man. | E1 | 70 |
| Goodlettsville, Tn., U.S. | g10 | 119 |
| Goodman, Ms., U.S. | C4 | 101 |
| Goodman, Mo., U.S. | E3 | 102 |
| Goodman, Wi., U.S. | C5 | 126 |
| Goodnews Bay, Ak., U.S. | D7 | 79 |
| Goodnight, Tx., U.S. | B2 | 120 |
| Good Pine, La., U.S. | C3 | 95 |
| Goodrich, Ks., U.S. | A6 | 83 |
| Goodrich, N.D., U.S. | B5 | 111 |
| Goodrich, Tx., U.S. | D5 | 120 |
| Goodridge, Mn., U.S. | B3 | 100 |
| Good Spirit Lake, l., Sask. | F4 | 75 |
| Good Spirit Lake Provincial Park, Sask. | F4 | 75 |
| Goodsprings, Tn., U.S. | B4 | 119 |
| Goodsprings, Al., U.S. | B2 | 78 |
| Goodsprings, Nv., U.S. | H6 | 105 |
| Good Thunder, Mn., U.S. | F4 | 100 |
| Goodview, Mn., U.S. | F7 | 100 |
| Goodwater, Sask. | H4 | 75 |
| Goodwater, Al., U.S. | B3 | 78 |
| Goodway, Al., U.S. | D2 | 78 |
| Goodwell, Ok., U.S. | e9 | 113 |
| Goodwin, Ar., U.S. | C4 | 81 |
| Goodwin, S.D., U.S. | C9 | 118 |
| Goodyear, Az., U.S. | D3 | 80 |
| Goole, Eng., U.K. | H12 | 12 |
| Goondiwindi, Austl. | E9 | 50 |
| Goor, Neth. | B6 | 17 |
| Goose, stm., Newf. | h9 | 72 |
| Goose, stm., N.D., U.S. | B8 | 111 |
| Goose Bay, b., Newf. | B1 | 72 |
| Goose Bay see Happy Valley-Goose Bay, Newf. | B1 | 72 |
| Gooseberry Creek, stm., Wy., U.S. | B4 | 127 |
| Goose Creek, S.C., U.S. | F7 | 117 |
| Goose Creek, stm., U.S. | G5 | 89 |
| Goose Creek, stm., Va., U.S. | C3 | 123 |
| Goose Creek Reservoir, res., S.C., U.S. | k11 | 117 |
| Goose Island, i., B.C. | D3 | 69 |
| Goose Lake, l., Man. | B1 | 70 |
| Goose Lake, l., U.S. | F2 | 75 |
| Goose Lake, l., Sask. | F2 | 75 |
| Goose Pond, l., N.H., U.S. | C2 | 106 |
| Gopālganj, India | D10 | 37 |
| Gopło Lake, l., Pol. | B4 | 26 |
| Góra, Pol. | C4 | 26 |
| Góra Kalwaria, Pol. | C6 | 26 |
| Gorakhpur, India | C7 | 36 |
| Gorday, Ga., U.S. | E3 | 87 |
| Gördes, Tur. | D6 | 40 |
| Gordil, Cen. Afr. Rep. | B2 | 46 |
| Gordo, Al., U.S. | B2 | 78 |
| Gordon, Al., U.S. | D3 | 78 |
| Gordon, Ga., U.S. | D3 | 87 |
| Gordon, Ne., U.S. | B3 | 104 |
| Gordon, Tx., U.S. | C3 | 120 |
| Gordon, Wi., U.S. | B2 | 126 |
| Gordon, co., Ga., U.S. | B2 | 87 |
| Gordon Creek, stm., Ne., U.S. | B5 | 104 |
| Gordon Horne Peak, mtn., B.C. | D8 | 69 |
| Gordon Lake, l., Alta. | A5 | 68 |
| Gordon Lake, l., Sask. | B1 | 75 |
| Gordon's Corner, N.J., U.S. | *C4 | 107 |
| Gordonsville, Tn., U.S. | C8 | 119 |
| Gordonsville, Va., U.S. | B4 | 123 |
| Gordonville, Mo., U.S. | D8 | 102 |
| Gore, N.S. | D6 | 71 |
| Gore, N.Z. | Q12 | 51 |
| Gore, Ok., U.S. | B6 | 113 |
| Gore, Ok., U.S. | B6 | 113 |
| Gore Bay, Ont. | B2 | 73 |
| Gore Mountain, mtn., Vt., U.S. | B5 | 122 |
| Gore Point, c., Ak., U.S. | h16 | 79 |
| Gore Range, mts., Co., U.S. | B4 | 83 |
| Gore Springs, Ms., U.S. | B4 | 101 |
| Goreville, Il., U.S. | F5 | 90 |
| Gorey, Ire. | E5 | 11 |
| Gorgān (Astarābād), Iran | B5 | 38 |
| Gorgān, stm., Iran | B5 | 38 |
| Gorgan Bay, b., Iran | C6 | 39 |
| Gorgas, Al., U.S. | B2 | 78 |
| Gorge High Dam, Wa., U.S. | A4 | 124 |
| Gorgona, Isla, i., Col. | C2 | 60 |
| Gorgona, i., Italy | C4 | 23 |
| Gorham, Ks., U.S. | D4 | 93 |
| Gorham, Me., U.S. | E2 | 96 |
| Gorham, N.H., U.S. | B4 | 106 |
| Gorham, N.Y., U.S. | C3 | 109 |
| Gori, Sov. Un. | E2 | 28 |
| Gorinchem, Neth. | C5 | 17 |
| Goris, Sov. Un. | B3 | 39 |
| Gorizia, Italy | B4 | 23 |
| Gorkhā, Nepal | C10 | 37 |
| Gorki, Sov. Un. | D8 | 27 |
| Gorkiy, Sov. Un. | D7 | 29 |
| Gorkiy Reservoir, res., Sov. Un. | D7 | 29 |
| Gørlev, Den. | C5 | 15 |
| Gorlice, Pol. | D6 | 26 |
| Görlitz, E. Ger. | C7 | 18 |
| Gorlovka, Sov. Un. | G12 | 27 |
| Gorman, Md., U.S. | m12 | 97 |
| Gorman, Tn., U.S. | A4 | 119 |
| Gorman, Tx., U.S. | C3 | 120 |
| Gormania, W.V., U.S. | B5 | 125 |
| Gormley (part of Whitchurch-Stouffville), Ont. | k15 | 73 |
| Gorna Oryakhovitsa, Bul. | D7 | 24 |
| Gornji Milanovac, Yugo. | C5 | 24 |
| Gorno-Altaysk, Sov. Un. | D11 | 29 |
| Gornozavodsk, Sov. Un. | C10 | 33 |
| Gorodenka, Sov. Un. | G5 | 27 |
| Gorodets, Sov. Un. | D17 | 8 |
| Gorodnya, Sov. Un. | F8 | 27 |
| Gorodok, Mong. | A5 | 31 |
| Gorodok, Sov. Un. | G4 | 27 |
| Gorodok, Sov. Un. | D8 | 27 |
| Goroka, Pap. N. Gui. | k12 | 50 |
| Gorontalo, Indon. | E6 | 34 |
| Gorrie, Ont. | D3 | 73 |
| Gorskoye, Sov. Un. | q21 | 19 |
| Gort, Ire. | D3 | 11 |
| Gortahork, Ire. | B3 | 11 |
| Gorum, La., U.S. | C3 | 95 |
| Gorumna, i., Ire. | D2 | 11 |
| Goryn, stm., Sov. Un. | F6 | 27 |
| Gorzów [Wielkopolski], Pol. | B3 | 26 |
| Gosford, Austl. | F8 | 51 |
| Goshen, Austl. | D8 | 71 |
| Goshen, Al., U.S. | D3 | 78 |
| Goshen, Ct., U.S. | B3 | 84 |
| Goshen, In., U.S. | A6 | 91 |
| Goshen, Ky., U.S. | g11 | 94 |
| Goshen, Ma., U.S. | B2 | 98 |
| Goshen, N.H., U.S. | D2 | 106 |
| Goshen, N.J., U.S. | E3 | 107 |
| Goshen, N.Y., U.S. | D6 | 109 |
| Goshen, Oh., U.S. | C1 | 112 |
| Goshen, Or., U.S. | D3 | 114 |
| Goshen, Ut., U.S. | D4 | 121 |
| Goshen, Va., U.S. | C3 | 123 |
| Goshen, co., Wy., U.S. | D8 | 127 |
| Goshen Hole, Wy., U.S. | D8 | 127 |
| Goshogawara, Japan | F10 | 33 |
| Goshute Indian Reservation, U.S. | D7 | 105 |
| Goshute Lake, l., Nv., U.S. | C7 | 105 |
| Goshute Mountains, mts., Nv., U.S. | C7 | 105 |
| Goslar, W. Ger. | C5 | 18 |
| Gosnell, Ar., U.S. | *B6 | 81 |
| Gosnells, Austl. | *F2 | 50 |
| Gosper, co., Ne., U.S. | D6 | 104 |
| Gospić, Yugo. | C2 | 24 |
| Gosport, Eng., U.K. | D6 | 12 |
| Gosport, In., U.S. | D2 | 78 |
| Gosport, Al., U.S. | F4 | 91 |
| Gossau, Switz. | B7 | 21 |
| Gossburg, N.H., U.S. | B5 | 119 |
| Gossville, N.H., U.S. | D4 | 106 |
| Gostivar, Yugo. | C5 | 24 |
| Gostyń, Pol. | B5 | 26 |
| Gostynin, Pol. | g9 | 26 |
| Gotebo, Ok., U.S. | B3 | 113 |
| Göteborg (Gothenburg), Swe. | I4 | 14 |
| Göteborg och Bohus, co., Swe. | A5 | 15 |
| Gotemba, Japan | n18 | 33 |
| Gotel Mountains, mts., Afr. | D2 | 46 |
| Gotha, E. Ger. | C5 | 18 |
| Gotham, Wi., U.S. | E3 | 126 |
| Gothenburg, Ne., U.S. | D5 | 104 |
| Gotland, i., Swe. | I8 | 14 |
| Gotō Islands, is., Japan | J4 | 33 |
| Gotse Delchev (Nevrokop), Bul. | E6 | 24 |
| Göttingen, W. Ger. | C4 | 18 |
| Gottwaldov (Zlín), Czech. | B4 | 26 |
| Götzis, Aus. | B8 | 21 |
| Goubangzi, China | B9 | 32 |
| Gouda, Neth. | B4 | 17 |
| Goudeau, Sen. | D2 | 45 |
| Goudiry, Sen. | D2 | 45 |
| Goudoumaria, Niger | D7 | 45 |
| Goudswaard, Neth. | C4 | 17 |
| Gough, Ga., U.S. | C4 | 87 |
| Gough Island, i., St. Hel. | I9 | 5 |
| Gough Lake, l., Alta. | C4 | 68 |
| Gouin, Réservoir, res., Que. | k12 | 74 |
| Goulburn, Austl. | F8 | 51 |
| Goulburn, Que. | D6 | 74 |
| Gould, Ar., U.S. | D4 | 81 |
| Gould, Ok., U.S. | C2 | 113 |
| Gould City, Mi., U.S. | B5 | 99 |
| Goulding, Fl., U.S. | u14 | 86 |
| Goulding Cay, i., Bah. | m16 | 64 |
| Gouldings Trading Post, Ut., U.S. | F5 | 121 |
| Gould Island, i., R.I., U.S. | E5 | 116 |
| Goulds, Fl., U.S. | s13 | 86 |
| Gouldsboro, Me., U.S. | D4 | 96 |
| Gouldsboro, Pa., U.S. | D11 | 115 |
| Goulmime, Mor. | D2 | 44 |
| Goum, Mali | E4 | 45 |
| Gounamitz, stm., N.B. | B2 | 71 |
| Goundam, Mali | C4 | 45 |
| Gounou Gaya, Chad | D3 | 46 |
| Gourdon, Fr. | E4 | 16 |
| Gouré, Niger | D7 | 45 |
| Gourma Rharous, Mali | C4 | 45 |
| Gournay-en-Bray, Fr. | C4 | 16 |
| Gouro, Chad | C3 | 46 |
| Gouverneur, Sask. | H2 | 75 |
| Gouverneur, N.Y., U.S. | f9 | 109 |
| Govan, Sask. | F3 | 75 |
| Govan, S.C., U.S. | E5 | 117 |
| Gove, Ks., U.S. | D3 | 93 |
| Gove, co., Ks., U.S. | D3 | 93 |
| Govenlock, Sask. | H1 | 75 |
| Governador Valadares, Braz. | B4 | 56 |
| Government Camp, Or., U.S. | B5 | 114 |
| Governors Harbour, Bah. | B5 | 64 |

161

| Name | Ref. | Page |
|---|---|---|
| Govind Ballabh Pant Reservoir, res., India | F9 | 37 |
| Govind Reservoir, res., India | B6 | 37 |
| Gowan, stm., Man. | B4 | 70 |
| Gowanda, N.Y., U.S. | C2 | 109 |
| Gowen, Mi., U.S. | C5 | 99 |
| Gowen, Ok., U.S. | C6 | 113 |
| Gower, Mo., U.S. | B3 | 102 |
| Gowna, Lough, l., Ire. | D3 | 10 |
| Gowrie, Ia., U.S. | B3 | 92 |
| Goya, Arg. | E4 | 55 |
| Goz Beïda, Chad | C4 | 46 |
| Graaff-Reinet, S. Afr. | D3 | 49 |
| Grabill, In., U.S. | B8 | 91 |
| Grabow, E. Ger. | E5 | 15 |
| Gračac, Yugo. | C2 | 24 |
| Gračanica, Yugo. | C4 | 24 |
| Grace, Id., U.S. | G7 | 89 |
| Grace, Ms., U.S. | C3 | 101 |
| Grace, Mount, mtn., Ma., U.S. | A3 | 98 |
| Grace City, N.D., U.S. | B7 | 111 |
| Graceham, Md., U.S. | A3 | 97 |
| Gracemont, Ok., U.S. | B3 | 113 |
| Graceton, Mn., U.S. | B4 | 100 |
| Graceville, Fl., U.S. | u16 | 86 |
| Graceville, Mn., U.S. | E2 | 100 |
| Gracewood, Ga., U.S. | C4 | 87 |
| Gracey, Ky., U.S. | D2 | 94 |
| Gracias, Hond. | E7 | 63 |
| Graciosa, i., Port. | g9 | 44 |
| Gradačac, Yugo. | C4 | 24 |
| Gradizhsk, Sov. Un. | G9 | 27 |
| Grado, Italy | D9 | 20 |
| Grado, Spain | A2 | 22 |
| Grady, Ar., U.S. | C4 | 81 |
| Grady, N.M., U.S. | C6 | 108 |
| Grady, Ok., U.S. | C4 | 113 |
| Grady, co., Ga., U.S. | F2 | 87 |
| Grady, co., Ok., U.S. | C4 | 113 |
| Gradyville, Ky., U.S. | C4 | 94 |
| Graettinger, Ia., U.S. | A3 | 92 |
| Grafenau, W. Ger. | E8 | 19 |
| Graford, Tx., U.S. | C3 | 120 |
| Grafton, Austl. | E9 | 50 |
| Grafton, Ont. | D6 | 73 |
| Grafton, Il., U.S. | E3 | 90 |
| Grafton, Ia., U.S. | A4 | 92 |
| Grafton, Ma., U.S. | B4 | 98 |
| Grafton, Ne., U.S. | D8 | 104 |
| Grafton, N.H., U.S. | C3 | 106 |
| Grafton, N.Y., U.S. | C7 | 109 |
| Grafton, N.D., U.S. | A8 | 111 |
| Grafton, Oh., U.S. | A3 | 112 |
| Grafton, Vt., U.S. | E3 | 122 |
| Grafton, Va., U.S. | h15 | 123 |
| Grafton, W.V., U.S. | B4 | 125 |
| Grafton, Wi., U.S. | E6 | 126 |
| Grafton, co., N.H., U.S. | C3 | 106 |
| Grafton Center, N.H., U.S. | C3 | 106 |
| Graham, N.C., U.S. | B4 | 78 |
| Graham, Ca., U.S. | *n12 | 82 |
| Graham, Fl., U.S. | C4 | 86 |
| Graham, Ky., U.S. | C2 | 94 |
| Graham, Mo., U.S. | A2 | 102 |
| Graham, N.C., U.S. | A3 | 110 |
| Graham, Ok., U.S. | C4 | 113 |
| Graham, Tn., U.S. | B4 | 119 |
| Graham, Tx., U.S. | C3 | 120 |
| Graham, Wa., U.S. | B3 | 124 |
| Graham, co., Az., U.S. | E5 | 80 |
| Graham, co., Ks., U.S. | C4 | 93 |
| Graham, co., N.C., U.S. | f9 | 110 |
| Graham, stm., B.C. | A6 | 69 |
| Graham, Lake, res., Tx., U.S. | C3 | 120 |
| Graham, Mount, mtn., Az., U.S. | E6 | 80 |
| Graham Bell, i., Sov. Un. | A7 | 128 |
| Graham Creek, stm., In., U.S. | G6 | 91 |
| Graham Island, i., B.C. | C1 | 69 |
| Graham Island, i., N.W. Ter. | m33 | 66 |
| Graham Lake, l., Alta. | A3 | 68 |
| Graham Lake, l., Me., U.S. | D4 | 96 |
| Graham Land, reg., Ant. | C6 | 7 |
| Grahamstown, S. Afr. | D4 | 49 |
| Grahamsville, N.Y., U.S. | D6 | 109 |
| Grahamville, S.C., U.S. | G6 | 117 |
| Grahn, Ky., U.S. | B6 | 94 |
| Graian Alps, mts., Eur. | E7 | 16 |
| Grainfield, Ks., U.S. | C3 | 93 |
| Grainger, Alta. | D4 | 68 |
| Grainger, co., Tn., U.S. | C10 | 119 |
| Grainland, Sask. | F2 | 75 |
| Grainola, Ok., U.S. | A5 | 113 |
| Grainton, Ne., U.S. | D4 | 104 |
| Grain Valley, Mo., U.S. | B3 | 102 |
| Grajaú, Braz. | C1 | 57 |
| Grajaú, stm., Braz. | B1 | 57 |
| Grajewo, Pol. | B7 | 26 |
| Gram, Den. | C3 | 15 |
| Gramada, Bul. | D6 | 24 |
| Gramalote, Col. | B3 | 60 |
| Gramastetten, Aus. | E9 | 19 |
| Grambling, La., U.S. | B3 | 95 |
| Gramercy, La., U.S. | h10 | 95 |
| Gramling, S.C., U.S. | A3 | 117 |
| Grammer, In., U.S. | F6 | 91 |
| Grammichele, Italy | F5 | 23 |
| Grampian, Pa., U.S. | E4 | 115 |
| Grampian, prov., Scot., U.K. | C6 | 13 |
| Grampian Mountains, mts., Scot., U.K. | B4 | 10 |
| Gramshi, Alb. | B3 | 25 |
| Gramzow, E. Ger. | E8 | 15 |
| Gran, Mount, mtn., Ant. | B29 | 7 |
| Granada, Nic. | E7 | 63 |
| Granada, Spain | D4 | 22 |
| Granada, Co., U.S. | C8 | 83 |
| Granada, Mn., U.S. | G4 | 100 |
| Granard, Ire. | D4 | 11 |
| Granbury, Tx., U.S. | C4 | 120 |
| Granby, Que. | D5 | 74 |
| Granby, Co., U.S. | A5 | 83 |
| Granby, Ct., U.S. | B4 | 84 |
| Granby, Ma., U.S. | B2 | 98 |
| Granby, Mo., U.S. | E3 | 102 |
| Granby, Vt., U.S. | B5 | 122 |
| Granby, Lake, res., Co., U.S. | A5 | 83 |
| Granby, Lake, l., Newf. | B4 | 72 |
| Gran Canal del Desagüe, Mex. | g9 | 63 |
| Gran Canaria, i., Spain | n14 | 22 |
| Gran Chaco, pl., S.A. | D3 | 55 |
| Grand, co., Co., U.S. | A4 | 83 |
| Grand, co., Ut., U.S. | E6 | 121 |
| Grand, stm., Ont. | D3 | 73 |
| Grand, stm., Mi., U.S. | E5 | 99 |
| Grand, stm., Mo., U.S. | A3 | 102 |
| Grand, stm., Oh., U.S. | A4 | 112 |
| Grand, stm., S.D., U.S. | B4 | 118 |
| Grand, North Fork, stm., U.S. | B2 | 118 |
| Grand, South Fork, stm., S.D., U.S. | B3 | 118 |
| Grand Bahama, i., Bah. | A4 | 64 |
| Grand Bank, Newf. | E4 | 72 |
| Grand-Bassam, I.C. | E4 | 45 |
| Grand Bay, N.B. | D3 | 71 |
| Grand Bay, Al., U.S. | E1 | 78 |
| Grand Bayou, stm., La., U.S. | k10 | 95 |
| Grand Bayou, stm., La., U.S. | h9 | 95 |
| Grand Bend, Ont. | D3 | 73 |
| Grand Blanc, Mi., U.S. | F7 | 99 |
| Grand Bonhomme, mtn., St. Vin. | U26 | 65 |
| Grand-Bourg, Guad. | I14 | 64 |
| Grand Bruit, Newf. | E2 | 72 |
| Grand Caillou, La., U.S. | E5 | 95 |
| Grand Canal (Da Yunhe), China | E8 | 31 |
| Grand Canal, Ire. | D4 | 11 |
| Grand Cane, La., U.S. | B2 | 95 |
| Grand Canyon, Az., U.S. | A3 | 80 |
| Grand Canyon, val., Az., U.S. | A3 | 80 |
| Grand Canyon National Park, Az., U.S. | B3 | 80 |
| Grand Cayman, i., Cay. Is. | D8 | 63 |
| Grand Centre, Alta. | B5 | 68 |
| Grand Cess, Lib. | F3 | 45 |
| Grand Chenier, La., U.S. | E3 | 95 |
| Grand Combin, mtn., Switz. | D3 | 20 |
| Grand Coteau, La., U.S. | D3 | 95 |
| Grand Coulee, Wa., U.S. | B6 | 124 |
| Grand Coulee Dam, Wa., U.S. | B6 | 124 |
| Grande, stm., Arg. | B3 | 54 |
| Grande, stm., Arg. | D2 | 55 |
| Grande, stm., Bol. | C3 | 55 |
| Grande, stm., Braz. | B2 | 56 |
| Grande, stm., Braz. | D2 | 57 |
| Grande, Bahía, b., Arg. | E3 | 54 |
| Grande, Boca, mth., Ven. | B5 | 60 |
| Grande, Ilha, i., Braz. | h5 | 56 |
| Grande, Rio, stm., N.A. | E7 | 76 |
| Grande, Serra, mts., Braz. | C2 | 57 |
| Grande-Anse, N.B. | B4 | 71 |
| Grande Cache, Alta. | C1 | 68 |
| Grande Ecore, La., U.S. | C2 | 95 |
| Grande de Arecibo, stm., P.R. | B2 | 65 |
| Grande [de Matagalpa], stm., Nic. | E8 | 63 |
| Grande de Santiago, stm., Mex. | C3 | 63 |
| Grande de Tarija, stm., S.A. | D3 | 55 |
| Grande-Digue, N.B. | C5 | 71 |
| Grande-Ligne, Que. | D4 | 74 |
| Grande-Entrée, Que. | B8 | 71 |
| Grande Prairie, Alta. | B1 | 68 |
| Grand Erg de Bilma, des., Niger | C7 | 45 |
| Grand Erg Occidental, des., Alg. | C5 | 44 |
| Grand Erg Oriental, des., Alg. | C6 | 44 |
| Grande rivière de la Baleine, stm., Que. | g11 | 74 |
| Grande Ronde, stm., U.S. | C8 | 124 |
| Grandes, Salinas, pl., Arg. | F2 | 55 |
| Grandes-Bergeronnes, Que. | A8 | 74 |
| Grandes-Piles, Que. | C5 | 74 |
| Grande-Étang, N.S. | C8 | 71 |
| Grande-Terre, i., Guad. | Q9 | 65 |
| Grande Vigie, Pointe de la, c., Guad. | P9 | 65 |
| Grand Falls (Grand-Sault), N.B. | B2 | 71 |
| Grand Falls, Newf. | D4 | 72 |
| Grandfalls, Tx., U.S. | D1 | 120 |
| Grand Falls, wtfl., Me., U.S. | C5 | 96 |
| Grand Falls Lake, l., N.A. | C5 | 96 |
| Grandfather Mountain, mtn., N.C., U.S. | A1 | 110 |
| Grandfield, Ok., U.S. | C3 | 113 |
| Grand Forks, B.C. | E8 | 69 |
| Grand Forks, N.D., U.S. | B8 | 111 |
| Grand Forks, co., N.D., U.S. | B8 | 111 |
| Grand Forks Air Force Base, mil., N.D., U.S. | B8 | 111 |
| Grand Glaise, Ar., U.S. | B4 | 81 |
| Grand Gorge, N.Y., U.S. | C6 | 109 |
| Grand Gulf, Ms., U.S. | C2 | 101 |
| Grand Harbour, N.B. | E3 | 71 |
| Grand Haven, Mi., U.S. | E4 | 99 |
| Grand Hogback, mtn., Co., U.S. | B3 | 83 |
| Grandin, Mo., U.S. | E7 | 102 |
| Grandin, N.D., U.S. | B9 | 111 |
| Grand Island, Ne., U.S. | D7 | 104 |
| Grand Island, i., La., U.S. | D6 | 95 |
| Grand Island, i., Mi., U.S. | B4 | 99 |
| Grand Isle, La., U.S. | E6 | 95 |
| Grand Isle, Me., U.S. | A4 | 96 |
| Grand Isle, Vt., U.S. | B2 | 122 |
| Grand Isle, co., Vt., U.S. | B2 | 122 |
| Grand Junction, Co., U.S. | B2 | 83 |
| Grand Junction, Ia., U.S. | B3 | 92 |
| Grand Junction, Mi., U.S. | F4 | 99 |
| Grand Junction, Tn., U.S. | B2 | 119 |
| Grand lac Bostonnais, l., Que. | B5 | 74 |
| Grand-Lahou, I.C. | E3 | 45 |
| Grand Lake, Co., U.S. | A5 | 83 |
| Grand Lake, La., U.S. | D2 | 95 |
| Grand Lake, l., Newf. | D3 | 72 |
| Grand Lake, l., Newf. | B1 | 72 |
| Grand Lake, l., Newf. | D3 | 72 |
| Grand Lake, l., N.A. | C5 | 96 |
| Grand Lake, l., La., U.S. | E6 | 95 |
| Grand Lake, l., La., U.S. | E3 | 95 |
| Grand Lake, l., Mi., U.S. | C7 | 99 |
| Grand Lake, l., Oh., U.S. | B1 | 112 |
| Grand Lake Matagamon, l., Me., U.S. | B4 | 96 |
| Grand Lake Seboeis, l., Me., U.S. | B4 | 96 |
| Grand Lake Stream, Me., U.S. | C5 | 96 |
| Grand Ledge, Mi., U.S. | F6 | 99 |
| Grand Lieu, Lac de, l., Fr. | D3 | 16 |
| Grand Manan Channel, strt., N.A. | D6 | 96 |
| Grand Manan Island, i., N.B. | E3 | 71 |
| Grand Marais, Mi., U.S. | B5 | 99 |
| Grand Marais, Mn., U.S. | k9 | 100 |
| Grand Marsh, Wi., U.S. | E4 | 126 |
| Grand Meadow, Mn., U.S. | G6 | 100 |
| Grand-Mère, Que. | C5 | 74 |
| Grand Mesa, mtn., Co., U.S. | C2 | 83 |
| Grand Mound, Ia., U.S. | C7 | 92 |
| Grand Pass, Mo., U.S. | B4 | 102 |
| Grand Portage Indian Reservation, Mn., U.S. | k10 | 100 |
| Grand Portage National Monument, Mn., U.S. | h10 | 100 |
| Grand Prairie, Tx., U.S. | n10 | 120 |
| Grand Pré, N.S. | D5 | 71 |
| Grand Rapids, Man. | U26 | 66 |
| Grand Rapids, Mi., U.S. | F5 | 99 |
| Grand Rapids, Mn., U.S. | C5 | 100 |
| Grand Rapids, N.D., U.S. | C7 | 111 |
| Grand Ridge, Fl., U.S. | B1 | 86 |
| Grand Ridge, Il., U.S. | B5 | 90 |
| Grand River, N.S. | D9 | 71 |
| Grand River, Ia., U.S. | D4 | 92 |
| Grand Rivers, Ky., U.S. | f9 | 94 |
| Grand' Rivière, Mart. | S10 | 65 |
| Grand Ronde, Or., U.S. | B3 | 114 |
| Grand Saline, Tx., U.S. | C5 | 120 |
| Grand Santi, Fr. Gu. | B4 | 59 |
| Grandson, Switz. | C2 | 21 |
| Grand Terrace, Ca., U.S. | *E5 | 82 |
| Grand Terre Islands, is., La., U.S. | E6 | 95 |
| Grand Teton, mtn., Wy., U.S. | C2 | 127 |
| Grand Teton National Park, Wy., U.S. | C2 | 127 |
| Grand Tower, Il., U.S. | F4 | 90 |
| Grand Traverse, co., Mi., U.S. | D5 | 99 |
| Grand Traverse Bay, b., Mi., U.S. | C5 | 99 |
| Grand Traverse Bay, East Arm, b., Mi., U.S. | D5 | 99 |
| Grand Traverse Bay, West Arm, b., Mi., U.S. | D5 | 99 |
| Grand Valley, Ont. | D4 | 73 |
| Grand Valley, Pa., U.S. | C2 | 115 |
| Grand Valley, val., U.S. | B2 | 83 |
| Grand View, Id., U.S. | G2 | 89 |
| Grandview, Il., U.S. | D6 | 90 |
| Grandview, In., U.S. | I4 | 91 |
| Grandview, Ia., U.S. | C6 | 92 |
| Grandview, Mo., U.S. | C3 | 102 |
| Grandview, Oh., U.S. | C4 | 112 |
| Grandview, Tn., U.S. | D9 | 119 |
| Grandview, Wa., U.S. | C6 | 124 |
| Grand View, Wi., U.S. | B3 | 126 |
| Grandview Heights, Oh., U.S. | m10 | 112 |
| Grandville, Mi., U.S. | F5 | 99 |
| Grandvilliers, Fr. | E1 | 17 |
| Grand Wash Cliffs, clf., Az., U.S. | B2 | 80 |
| Grandy, Mn., U.S. | E5 | 100 |
| Grandy, N.C., U.S. | A7 | 110 |
| Grängärde (part of Ludvika), Swe. | G6 | 14 |
| Grangemouth, Scot., U.K. | D5 | 13 |
| Grange-over-Sands, Eng., U.K. | F6 | 13 |
| Granger, In., U.S. | A5 | 91 |
| Granger, Ia., U.S. | C4 | 92 |
| Granger, Mo., U.S. | A6 | 102 |
| Granger, Tx., U.S. | D4 | 120 |
| Granger, Wa., U.S. | C5 | 124 |
| Granges [-sur-Vologne], Fr. | A2 | 17 |
| Grangeville, Id., U.S. | D2 | 89 |
| Grangeville, La., U.S. | D5 | 95 |
| Granisle, B.C. | B4 | 69 |
| Granite, Co., U.S. | B4 | 83 |
| Granite, Ok., U.S. | C2 | 113 |
| Granite, Or., U.S. | C8 | 114 |
| Granite, Ut., U.S. | *C4 | 121 |
| Granite, co., Mt., U.S. | D3 | 103 |
| Granite Canon, Wy., U.S. | E7 | 127 |
| Granite City, Il., U.S. | E3 | 90 |
| Granite Falls, Mn., U.S. | F3 | 100 |
| Granite Falls, N.C., U.S. | B1 | 110 |
| Granite Falls, Wa., U.S. | A4 | 124 |
| Granite Harbor, b., Ant. | e39 | 7 |
| Granite Lake, res., Newf. | D3 | 72 |
| Granite Mountain, mtn., Ak., U.S. | B7 | 79 |
| Granite Mountain, mtn., Ar., U.S. | k10 | 81 |
| Granite Mountains, mts., Az., U.S. | E2 | 80 |
| Granite Mountains, mts., Wy., U.S. | D5 | 127 |
| Granite Park, Ut., U.S. | *C4 | 121 |
| Granite Pass, Wy., U.S. | B5 | 127 |
| Granite Peak, mtn., Mt., U.S. | E7 | 103 |
| Granite Peak, mtn., Nv., U.S. | C2 | 105 |
| Granite Peak, mtn., Nv., U.S. | B4 | 105 |
| Granite Peak, mtn., Ut., U.S. | E3 | 121 |
| Granite Peak, mtn., Ut., U.S. | C2 | 121 |
| Granite Peak, mtn., Wy., U.S. | C2 | 127 |
| Granite Point, c., Newf. | C3 | 72 |
| Granite Quarry, N.C., U.S. | B2 | 110 |
| Granite Range, mts., Nv., U.S. | C2 | 105 |
| Graniteville, Ma., U.S. | f10 | 98 |
| Graniteville, Mo., U.S. | D7 | 102 |
| Graniteville, S.C., U.S. | D4 | 117 |
| Graniteville, Vt., U.S. | C4 | 122 |
| Granja, Braz. | B2 | 57 |
| Granja de Torrehermosa, Spain | C3 | 22 |
| Granma, prov., Cuba | D5 | 64 |
| Grannis, Ar., U.S. | C1 | 81 |
| Grano, N.D., U.S. | A4 | 111 |
| Granollers, Spain | B7 | 22 |
| Gran Paradiso, mtn., Italy | D3 | 20 |
| Gransee, E. Ger. | E7 | 15 |
| Grant, Al., U.S. | A3 | 78 |
| Grant, Co., U.S. | B5 | 83 |
| Grant, Fl., U.S. | E6 | 86 |
| Grant, Ia., U.S. | C2 | 92 |
| Grant, Mi., U.S. | E5 | 99 |
| Grant, Mt., U.S. | E3 | 103 |
| Grant, Ne., U.S. | D4 | 104 |
| Grant, Ok., U.S. | D6 | 113 |
| Grant, Or., U.S. | C7 | 114 |
| Grant, co., Ar., U.S. | C3 | 81 |
| Grant, co., In., U.S. | D6 | 91 |
| Grant, co., Ks., U.S. | E2 | 93 |
| Grant, co., Ky., U.S. | B5 | 94 |
| Grant, co., La., U.S. | C3 | 95 |
| Grant, co., Mn., U.S. | E2 | 100 |
| Grant, co., Ne., U.S. | C4 | 104 |
| Grant, co., N.M., U.S. | E1 | 108 |
| Grant, co., N.D., U.S. | C4 | 111 |
| Grant, co., Ok., U.S. | A4 | 113 |
| Grant, co., Or., U.S. | C7 | 114 |
| Grant, co., S.D., U.S. | B8 | 118 |
| Grant, co., Wa., U.S. | B6 | 124 |
| Grant, co., W.V., U.S. | B5 | 125 |
| Grant, co., Wi., U.S. | F2 | 126 |
| Grant, Mount, mtn., Nv., U.S. | E3 | 105 |
| Grant City, Mo., U.S. | A3 | 102 |
| Grantham, Eng., U.K. | D6 | 10 |
| Grantham, N.H., U.S. | D2 | 106 |
| Granton, Ont. | D3 | 73 |
| Grantown-on-Spey, Scot., U.K. | C5 | 13 |
| Grant Range, mts., Nv., U.S. | E6 | 105 |
| Grants, N.M., U.S. | B2 | 108 |
| Grantsboro, N.C., U.S. | B6 | 110 |
| Grantsburg, Il., U.S. | F5 | 90 |
| Grantsburg, Wi., U.S. | C1 | 126 |
| Grantsdale, Mt., U.S. | D2 | 103 |
| Grants Lick, Ky., U.S. | k14 | 94 |
| Grants Pass, Or., U.S. | E3 | 114 |
| Grantsville, Md., U.S. | k12 | 97 |
| Grantsville, Ut., U.S. | C3 | 121 |
| Grantsville, W.V., U.S. | C3 | 125 |
| Grant Town, W.V., U.S. | B4 | 125 |
| Grantville, Ga., U.S. | C2 | 87 |
| Grantville, Ks., U.S. | k14 | 93 |
| Grantville, Pa., U.S. | F8 | 115 |
| Granum, Alta. | E4 | 68 |
| Granville, Fr. | C3 | 16 |
| Granville, Il., U.S. | B4 | 90 |
| Granville, Ia., U.S. | B2 | 92 |
| Granville, Ma., U.S. | B2 | 98 |
| Granville, N.Y., U.S. | B7 | 109 |
| Granville, N.D., U.S. | A5 | 111 |
| Granville, Oh., U.S. | B3 | 112 |
| Granville, Tn., U.S. | C8 | 119 |
| Granville, Vt., U.S. | D3 | 122 |
| Granville, co., N.C., U.S. | A4 | 110 |
| Granville Centre, N.S. | E4 | 71 |
| Granville Ferry, N.S. | E4 | 71 |
| Grão Mogol, Braz. | B4 | 56 |
| Grapeland, Tx., U.S. | D5 | 120 |
| Grapeview, Wa., U.S. | B3 | 124 |
| Grapevine, Tx., U.S. | C4 | 120 |
| Grapevine Lake, res., Tx., U.S. | n9 | 120 |
| Grapevine Peak, mtn., Nv., U.S. | G4 | 105 |
| Gras, Lac de, l., N.W. Ter. | D10 | 66 |
| Grasonville, Md., U.S. | C5 | 97 |
| Grass, stm., Man. | B2 | 70 |
| Grass, stm., N.Y., U.S. | f9 | 109 |
| Grass Creek, In., U.S. | C5 | 91 |
| Grasse, Fr. | F7 | 16 |
| Grasselli, Al., U.S. | B3 | 78 |
| Grassflat, Pa., U.S. | D5 | 115 |
| Grassington, Eng., U.K. | F7 | 13 |
| Grass Lake, Il., U.S. | h8 | 90 |
| Grass Lake, Mi., U.S. | F6 | 99 |
| Grass Lake, l., Il., U.S. | h8 | 90 |
| Grassrange, Mt., U.S. | C8 | 103 |
| Grass River Provincial Park, Man. | B1 | 70 |
| Grasston, Mn., U.S. | E5 | 100 |
| Grass Valley, Ca., U.S. | C3 | 82 |
| Grass Valley, Or., U.S. | B6 | 114 |
| Grassy Brook, stm., Vt., U.S. | E3 | 122 |
| Grassy Butte, N.D., U.S. | B2 | 111 |
| Grassy Creek, N.C., U.S. | A1 | 110 |
| Grassy Lake, Alta. | E5 | 68 |
| Grassy Lake, l., La., U.S. | k9 | 95 |
| Gråsten, Den. | D3 | 15 |
| Grates Cove, Newf. | D5 | 72 |
| Grates Point, c., Newf. | D5 | 72 |
| Gratiot, Oh., U.S. | C3 | 112 |
| Gratiot, Wi., U.S. | F3 | 126 |
| Gratiot, co., Mi., U.S. | E6 | 99 |
| Gratis, Oh., U.S. | C1 | 112 |
| Gratz, Pa., U.S. | E8 | 115 |
| Graubünden, state, Switz. | C5 | 20 |
| Graulhet, Fr. | F4 | 16 |
| Gravatá, Braz. | C3 | 57 |
| Grave Creek, stm., W.V., U.S. | g8 | 125 |
| Gravedona, Italy | D7 | 21 |
| Gravelbourg, Sask. | H2 | 75 |
| Gravelines, Fr. | D2 | 17 |
| Gravelly, Ar., U.S. | C2 | 81 |
| Gravelly Branch, stm., De., U.S. | F4 | 85 |
| Gravelly Range, mts., Mt., U.S. | E4 | 103 |
| Gravenhurst, Ont. | C5 | 73 |
| Grave Peak, mtn., Id., U.S. | C4 | 89 |
| Graves, Ga., U.S. | E2 | 87 |
| Graves, co., Ky., U.S. | f9 | 94 |
| Gravesend, Eng., U.K. | E7 | 10 |
| Gravesville, Wi., U.S. | h9 | 126 |
| Gravette, Ar., U.S. | A1 | 81 |
| Gravina [in Puglia], Italy | D6 | 23 |
| Gravity, Ia., U.S. | D3 | 92 |
| Gravois, Pointe à, c., Haiti | E7 | 64 |
| Gravois Mills, Mo., U.S. | C5 | 102 |
| Grawn, Mi., U.S. | D5 | 99 |
| Gray, Fr. | D6 | 16 |
| Gray, Ga., U.S. | C3 | 87 |
| Gray, Ky., U.S. | D5 | 94 |
| Gray, La., U.S. | k10 | 95 |
| Gray, Me., U.S. | g7 | 96 |
| Gray, Pa., U.S. | F3 | 115 |
| Gray, Sask. | G4 | 75 |
| Gray, co., Ks., U.S. | E3 | 93 |
| Gray, co., Tx., U.S. | B2 | 120 |
| Grayback Mountain, mtn., Or., U.S. | E3 | 114 |
| Gray Court, S.C., U.S. | B3 | 117 |
| Gray Gables, Ma., U.S. | *C6 | 98 |
| Gray Horse, Ok., U.S. | A5 | 113 |
| Grayland, Wa., U.S. | C1 | 124 |
| Grayling, Ak., U.S. | C7 | 79 |
| Grayling, Mi., U.S. | D6 | 99 |
| Graylyn Crest, De., U.S. | A3 | 85 |
| Graymont, Il., U.S. | C5 | 90 |
| Grays, Eng., U.K. | m13 | 10 |
| Grays, Ar., U.S. | B4 | 81 |
| Grays Harbor, co., Wa., U.S. | B2 | 124 |
| Grays Harbor, b., Wa., U.S. | C1 | 124 |
| Grayslake, Il., U.S. | A5 | 90 |
| Grays Lake, sw., Id., U.S. | F7 | 89 |
| Grayson, Sask. | G4 | 75 |
| Grayson, Ky., U.S. | B6 | 94 |
| Grayson, La., U.S. | B3 | 95 |
| Grayson, co., Ky., U.S. | C3 | 94 |
| Grayson, co., Tx., U.S. | C4 | 120 |
| Grayson, co., Va., U.S. | D1 | 123 |
| Grayson Lake, res., Ky., U.S. | B7 | 94 |
| Grays River, Wa., U.S. | C2 | 124 |
| Gray Summit, Mo., U.S. | g12 | 102 |
| Grayville, Al., U.S. | f7 | 78 |
| Grayville, Il., U.S. | E5 | 90 |
| Graz, Aus. | E7 | 18 |
| Greasewood, Az., U.S. | B6 | 80 |
| Great, stm., Jam. | E13 | 65 |
| Great Abaco, i., Bah. | A7 | 64 |
| Great Alföld, pl., Hung. | B5 | 24 |
| Great Artesian Basin, Austl. | D8 | 50 |
| Great Australian Bight, Austl. | F4 | 50 |
| Great Averill Pond, l., Vt., U.S. | B5 | 122 |
| Great Barrier Island, i., N.Z. | L15 | 51 |
| Great Barrier Reef, rf., Austl. | C9 | 50 |
| Great Barrington, Ma., U.S. | B1 | 98 |
| Great Basin, U.S. | C4 | 76 |
| Great Basin National Park, Nv., U.S. | E7 | 105 |
| Great Bay, b., N.H., U.S. | D5 | 106 |
| Great Bay, b., N.J., U.S. | D4 | 107 |
| Great Bear Lake, l., N.W. Ter. | C8 | 66 |
| Great Bend, Ks., U.S. | D5 | 93 |
| Great Bend, N.D., U.S. | C9 | 111 |
| Great Bend, Pa., U.S. | C10 | 115 |
| Great Bitter Lake, l., Eg. | D4 | 41 |
| Great Blasket Island, i., Ire. | E1 | 11 |
| Great Blue Hill, hill, Ma., U.S. | B5 | 98 |
| Great Burnt Lake, l., Newf. | D3 | 72 |
| Great Cacapon, W.V., U.S. | B6 | 125 |
| Great Camanoe, i., V.I., Br. | B6 | 65 |
| Great Captain Island, i., Ct., U.S. | F1 | 84 |
| Great Channel, strt., Asia | G9 | 36 |
| Great Deer, Sask. | E2 | 75 |
| Great Dismal Swamp, sw., U.S. | D6 | 123 |
| Great Divide Basin, Wy., U.S. | E4 | 127 |
| Great Dividing Range, mts., Austl. | F9 | 50 |
| Great Driffield, Eng., U.K. | F8 | 13 |
| Great Duck Island, i., Ont. | B2 | 73 |
| Great East Lake, l., U.S. | C5 | 106 |
| Great Egg Harbor, stm., N.J., U.S. | D3 | 107 |
| Greater Antilles, is., N.A. | H13 | 61 |
| Greater Cincinnati Airport, Ky., U.S. | h13 | 94 |
| Greater Khingan Range see Da Hinggan Ling, mts., China | B9 | 31 |
| Greater London, co., Eng., U.K. | C7 | 12 |
| Greater Manchester, co., Eng., U.K. | *A5 | 12 |
| Great Exuma, i., Bah. | C6 | 64 |
| Great Fall, wtfl., Guy. | A2 | 59 |
| Great Falls, Man. | D3 | 70 |
| Great Falls, Mt., U.S. | C5 | 103 |
| Great Falls, S.C., U.S. | B6 | 117 |
| Great Falls, wtfl., Md., U.S. | B3 | 97 |
| Great Falls Dam, Tn., U.S. | D6 | 119 |
| Great Guana Cay, i., Bah. | B5 | 64 |
| Great Harbour Deep, b., Newf. | C3 | 72 |
| Greathouse Peak, mtn., Mt., U.S. | D7 | 103 |
| Great Inagua, i., Bah. | D7 | 64 |
| Great Indian Desert (Thar Desert), des., Asia | C5 | 36 |
| Great Island, spit, Ma., U.S. | C7 | 98 |
| Great Island, i., N.C., U.S. | B6 | 110 |
| Great Karroo, plat., S. Afr. | D3 | 49 |
| Great Lake, l., Austl. | o15 | 50 |
| Great Lakes Naval Training Center, mil., Il., U.S. | h9 | 90 |
| Great Malvern, Eng., U.K. | B5 | 12 |
| Great Miami, stm., U.S. | C1 | 112 |
| Great Misery Island, i., Ma., U.S. | f12 | 98 |
| Great Moose Lake, l., Me., U.S. | D3 | 96 |
| Great Neck, N.Y., U.S. | h13 | 109 |
| Great Neck Estates, N.Y., U.S. | *E7 | 109 |
| Great Nicobar, i., India | G9 | 36 |
| Great North Mountain, mtn., U.S. | C6 | 125 |
| Great Ouse, stm., Eng., U.K. | D7 | 10 |
| Great Pee Dee, stm., U.S. | D9 | 117 |
| Great Point, c., Ma., U.S. | D7 | 98 |
| Great Pond, Me., U.S. | D4 | 96 |
| Great Pond, l., Ma., U.S. | D3 | 96 |
| Great Pond, l., Ma., U.S. | h12 | 98 |
| Great Pond, l., Ma., U.S. | h11 | 98 |
| Great Quittacas Pond, l., Ma., U.S. | C6 | 98 |
| Great Ruaha, stm., Tan. | C6 | 48 |
| Great Sacandaga Lake, l., N.Y., U.S. | C6 | 109 |
| Great Saint Bernard Pass, Eur. | B1 | 23 |
| Great Salt Lake, l., Ut., U.S. | B3 | 121 |
| Great Salt Lake Desert, des., Ut., U.S. | C2 | 121 |
| Great Salt Plains Lake, res., Ok., U.S. | A3 | 113 |
| Great Salt Pond, b., R.I., U.S. | h7 | 116 |
| Great Salt Pond, l., Jam. | F15 | 65 |
| Great Sand Dunes National Monument, Co., U.S. | D5 | 83 |
| Great Sand Hills, hills, Sask. | G1 | 75 |
| Great Sandy Desert, des., Austl. | D3 | 50 |
| Great Sea Reef, rf., Fiji | H15 | 52 |
| Great Seneca Creek, stm., Md., U.S. | B3 | 97 |
| Great Skellig Island, i., Ire. | F1 | 11 |
| Great Slave Lake, l., N.W. Ter. | D10 | 66 |
| Great Smoky Mountains, mts., U.S. | B8 | 119 |
| Great Smoky Mountains National Park, U.S. | B8 | 119 |
| Great Sound, strt., Ber. | p19 | 64 |
| Great Swamp, sw., R.I., U.S. | F3 | 116 |
| Great Tenasserim, stm., Burma | F3 | 35 |
| Great Torrington, Eng., U.K. | B2 | 12 |
| Great Valley, val., U.S. | C2 | 123 |
| Great Victoria Desert, des., Austl. | E4 | 50 |
| Great Village, N.S. | D6 | 71 |
| Great Wall, hist., China | C8 | 31 |
| Great Wass Island, i., Me., U.S. | D5 | 96 |
| Great Yarmouth, Eng., U.K. | D7 | 10 |
| Great Zab, stm., Asia | D14 | 40 |
| Gredos, Sierra de, mts., Spain | B3 | 22 |
| Greece, N.Y., U.S. | B3 | 109 |
| Greece, ctry., Eur. | F2 | 25 |
| Greeley, Co., U.S. | A6 | 83 |
| Greeley, Ks., U.S. | D8 | 93 |
| Greeley, Ne., U.S. | C7 | 104 |
| Greeley, Pa., U.S. | D12 | 115 |
| Greeley, co., Ks., U.S. | D2 | 93 |
| Greeley, co., Ne., U.S. | C7 | 104 |
| Greely Fiord, N.W. Ter. | k35 | 66 |
| Green, Or., U.S. | D3 | 114 |
| Green, co., Ky., U.S. | C4 | 94 |
| Green, co., Wi., U.S. | F4 | 126 |
| Green, stm., N.B. | B1 | 71 |
| Green, stm., U.S. | C6 | 76 |
| Green, stm., Il., U.S. | B4 | 90 |
| Green, stm., Ky., U.S. | C2 | 94 |
| Green, stm., Wa., U.S. | C4 | 124 |
| Green Acres, U.S. | *E4 | 82 |
| Green Acres, De., U.S. | h8 | 85 |
| Greenacres, Wa., U.S. | B8 | 124 |
| Greenacres City, Fl., U.S. | F6 | 86 |
| Greenback, Tn., U.S. | D9 | 119 |
| Greenbackville, Va., U.S. | C7 | 123 |
| Green Bank, N.J., U.S. | D3 | 107 |
| Green Bank, W.V., U.S. | C5 | 125 |
| Green Bay, Va., U.S. | C4 | 123 |
| Green Bay, Wi., U.S. | D6 | 126 |
| Green Bay, b., U.S. | D3 | 99 |
| Greenbelt, Md., U.S. | C4 | 97 |
| Greenbrier, Al., U.S. | A3 | 78 |
| Greenbrier, Ar., U.S. | B3 | 81 |
| Green Brier, Tn., U.S. | A5 | 119 |
| Greenbrier, co., W.V., U.S. | D4 | 125 |
| Greenbrier, stm., W.V., U.S. | D4 | 125 |
| Green Brook, N.J., U.S. | *B4 | 107 |
| Greenburr, Pa., U.S. | D7 | 115 |
| Greenbush, Me., U.S. | C4 | 96 |
| Greenbush, Mn., U.S. | B2 | 100 |
| Greenbush, Wi., U.S. | k9 | 126 |
| Green Camp, Oh., U.S. | B2 | 112 |
| Greencastle, In., U.S. | A5 | 91 |
| Greencastle, Mo., U.S. | A5 | 102 |
| Greencastle, Pa., U.S. | G6 | 115 |
| Green City, Mo., U.S. | A5 | 102 |
| Green Cove Springs, Fl., U.S. | C5 | 86 |
| Greencreek, Id., U.S. | C2 | 89 |
| Green Creek, N.J., U.S. | E3 | 107 |
| Greendale, In., U.S. | F8 | 91 |
| Greendale, Ut., U.S. | *C6 | 121 |
| Greendale, Wi., U.S. | F6 | 126 |
| Greendell, N.J., U.S. | B3 | 107 |
| Greene, Me., U.S. | D2 | 96 |
| Greene, N.Y., U.S. | C5 | 109 |
| Greene, N.D., U.S. | A4 | 111 |
| Greene, co., Al., U.S. | C1 | 78 |
| Greene, co., Ar., U.S. | A5 | 81 |
| Greene, co., Ga., U.S. | C3 | 87 |
| Greene, co., Il., U.S. | D3 | 90 |
| Greene, co., In., U.S. | F4 | 91 |
| Greene, co., Ia., U.S. | B3 | 92 |
| Greene, co., Mo., U.S. | D4 | 102 |
| Greene, co., N.Y., U.S. | C6 | 109 |
| Greene, co., N.C., U.S. | B5 | 110 |
| Greene, co., Oh., U.S. | C2 | 112 |
| Greene, co., Pa., U.S. | G1 | 115 |
| Greene, co., Tn., U.S. | C11 | 119 |
| Greene, co., Va., U.S. | B4 | 123 |
| Greeneville, Tn., U.S. | C11 | 119 |
| Green Fall, stm., U.S. | F1 | 116 |
| Greenfield, Ca., U.S. | D3 | 82 |
| Greenfield, Il., U.S. | D3 | 90 |
| Greenfield, In., U.S. | E6 | 91 |
| Greenfield, Ia., U.S. | C3 | 92 |
| Greenfield, Me., U.S. | C4 | 96 |
| Greenfield, Ma., U.S. | A2 | 98 |
| Greenfield, Mo., U.S. | D4 | 102 |
| Greenfield, N.H., U.S. | E3 | 106 |
| Greenfield, N.M., U.S. | D5 | 108 |
| Greenfield, Oh., U.S. | C2 | 112 |
| Greenfield, Ok., U.S. | B3 | 113 |
| Greenfield, Tn., U.S. | A3 | 119 |
| Greenfield, Va., U.S. | C4 | 123 |
| Greenfield, Wi., U.S. | n11 | 126 |
| Greenfield Plaza, Ia., U.S. | e8 | 92 |
| Green Forest, Ar., U.S. | A2 | 81 |
| Green Grass, S.D., U.S. | B4 | 118 |
| Green Harbor, Ma., U.S. | B6 | 98 |
| Greenhill, Al., U.S. | A2 | 78 |
| Greenhill, In., U.S. | D3 | 91 |
| Green Hill, R.I., U.S. | G3 | 116 |
| Green Hill Pond, l., R.I., U.S. | G3 | 116 |
| Greenhills, Oh., U.S. | n12 | 112 |
| Greenhorn, Or., U.S. | C8 | 114 |
| Greenhorn Creek, stm., Co., U.S. | D6 | 83 |
| Green Island, Ia., U.S. | B7 | 92 |
| Green Island, N.Y., U.S. | *C7 | 109 |
| Green Isle, Mn., U.S. | F4 | 100 |
| Green Lake, Sask. | C2 | 75 |
| Green Lake, Ut., U.S. | *C6 | 121 |
| Green Lake, Wi., U.S. | E5 | 126 |
| Green Lake, co., Wi., U.S. | E4 | 126 |
| Green Lake, l., B.C. | D7 | 69 |
| Green Lake, l., Sask. | C2 | 75 |
| Green Lake, l., Me., U.S. | D4 | 96 |
| Green Lake, l., Wi., U.S. | E5 | 126 |
| Greenland, Ar., U.S. | B1 | 81 |
| Greenland, Mi., U.S. | B1 | 99 |
| Greenland (Kalaallit Nunaat), ctry., N.A. | B16 | 61 |
| Greenland Sea | B15 | 128 |
| Greenlawn, N.Y., U.S. | *h13 | 109 |
| Greenleaf, Id., U.S. | F2 | 89 |
| Greenleaf, Ks., U.S. | C7 | 93 |
| Greenleaf, Wi., U.S. | D5 | 126 |
| Greenlee, co., Az., U.S. | D6 | 80 |
| Green Lookout Mountain, mtn., Wa., U.S. | C4 | 124 |
| Green Lowther, mtn., Scot., U.K. | E5 | 13 |
| Green Manorville, Ct., U.S. | B5 | 84 |
| Greenmount, Md., U.S. | A4 | 97 |
| Greenmountain, Ia., U.S. | B5 | 92 |
| Green Mountain Falls, Co., U.S. | *C6 | 83 |
| Green Mountain Reservoir, res., Co., U.S. | B4 | 83 |
| Green Mountains, mts., Vt., U.S. | F2 | 122 |
| Green Mountains, mts., Wy., U.S. | D5 | 127 |
| Greenock, Scot., U.K. | C4 | 10 |
| Greenore Point, c., Ire. | E5 | 11 |
| Greenough Point, c., Ont. | C3 | 73 |
| Green Peter Lake, res., Or., U.S. | C4 | 114 |
| Green Pond, Al., U.S. | B2 | 78 |
| Green Pond, S.C., U.S. | F6 | 117 |
| Green Pond Mountain, mtn., N.J., U.S. | A4 | 107 |
| Greenport, N.Y., U.S. | m16 | 109 |
| Green Ridge, Mo., U.S. | C4 | 102 |
| Green River, Ut., U.S. | E5 | 121 |
| Green River, Wy., U.S. | E3 | 127 |
| Green River Lake, res., Ky., U.S. | C4 | 94 |
| Green River Lock and Dam, Ky., U.S. | I2 | 91 |
| Green River Reservoir, res., Vt., U.S. | B3 | 122 |
| Green Rock, Il., U.S. | B3 | 90 |
| Greensboro, Al., U.S. | C2 | 78 |
| Greensboro, Fl., U.S. | B2 | 86 |
| Greensboro, Ga., U.S. | C3 | 87 |
| Greensboro, Md., U.S. | C6 | 97 |

| Name | Map Ref. | Page |
|---|---|---|
| Greensboro, N.C., U.S. | A3 | 110 |
| Greensboro, Pa., U.S. | G2 | 115 |
| Greensboro, Vt., U.S. | B4 | 122 |
| Greensboro Bend, Vt., U.S. | B4 | 122 |
| Greensburg, In., U.S. | F7 | 91 |
| Greensburg, Ks., U.S. | E4 | 93 |
| Greensburg, Ky., U.S. | C4 | 94 |
| Greensburg, La., U.S. | D5 | 95 |
| Greensburg, Pa., U.S. | F2 | 115 |
| Green Sea, N.C., U.S. | C10 | 117 |
| Greens Fork, In., U.S. | E7 | 91 |
| Greens Peak, mtn., Az., U.S. | C6 | 80 |
| Greenspond, Newf. | D5 | 72 |
| Green Spring, W.V., U.S. | B6 | 125 |
| Green Springs, Oh., U.S. | A2 | 112 |
| Greenstone Point, c., Scot., U.K. | C3 | 13 |
| Green Sulphur Springs, W.V., U.S. | D4 | 125 |
| Greensville, co., Va., U.S. | D5 | 123 |
| Green Swamp, sw., N.C., U.S. | C4 | 110 |
| Greentop, Mo., U.S. | A5 | 102 |
| Greentown, In., U.S. | D6 | 91 |
| Green Tree, Pa., U.S. | *k13 | 115 |
| Greenup, Il., U.S. | D5 | 90 |
| Greenup, Ky., U.S. | B7 | 94 |
| Greenup, co., Ky., U.S. | B7 | 94 |
| Green Valley, Az., U.S. | F5 | 80 |
| Green Valley, Il., U.S. | C4 | 90 |
| Green Valley, Mn., U.S. | F3 | 100 |
| Green Valley, Wi., U.S. | D5 | 126 |
| Green Valley, val., Tx., U.S. | p13 | 120 |
| Greenview, Il., U.S. | C4 | 90 |
| Greenview, W.V., U.S. | n12 | 125 |
| Greenville, Lib. | E3 | 45 |
| Greenville, Al., U.S. | D3 | 78 |
| Greenville, Ca., U.S. | B3 | 82 |
| Greenville, De., U.S. | A3 | 85 |
| Greenville, Fl., U.S. | B3 | 86 |
| Greenville, Ga., U.S. | C2 | 87 |
| Greenville, Il., U.S. | E4 | 90 |
| Greenville, In., U.S. | H6 | 91 |
| Greenville, Ia., U.S. | A2 | 92 |
| Greenville, Ky., U.S. | C2 | 94 |
| Greenville, Me., U.S. | C3 | 96 |
| Greenville, Mi., U.S. | E5 | 99 |
| Greenville, Ms., U.S. | B2 | 101 |
| Greenville, Mo., U.S. | D7 | 102 |
| Greenville, N.H., U.S. | E3 | 106 |
| Greenville, N.Y., U.S. | *n15 | 109 |
| Greenville, N.C., U.S. | B5 | 110 |
| Greenville, Oh., U.S. | B1 | 112 |
| Greenville, Pa., U.S. | D1 | 115 |
| Greenville, R.I., U.S. | C3 | 116 |
| Greenville, S.C., U.S. | B3 | 117 |
| Greenville, Tx., U.S. | C4 | 120 |
| Greenville, Ut., U.S. | E3 | 121 |
| Greenville, Va., U.S. | B3 | 123 |
| Greenville, W.V., U.S. | D4 | 125 |
| Greenville, co., S.C., U.S. | B3 | 117 |
| Greenville Creek, stm., Oh., U.S. | B1 | 112 |
| Greenville Junction, Me., U.S. | C3 | 96 |
| Greenwald, Mn., U.S. | E4 | 100 |
| Greenwater Lake Provincial Park, Sask. | E4 | 75 |
| Greenway, Man. | E2 | 70 |
| Greenway, Ar., U.S. | A5 | 81 |
| Greenwell Springs, La., U.S. | D5 | 95 |
| Greenwich (part of London), Eng., U.K. | m13 | 10 |
| Greenwich, Ct., U.S. | E1 | 84 |
| Greenwich, Ks., U.S. | g12 | 93 |
| Greenwich, N.J., U.S. | E2 | 107 |
| Greenwich, N.Y., U.S. | B7 | 109 |
| Greenwich, Oh., U.S. | A3 | 112 |
| Greenwich, Ut., U.S. | E4 | 121 |
| Greenwich, Va., U.S. | *B5 | 123 |
| Greenwich Bay, b., R.I., U.S. | D4 | 116 |
| Greenwich Hill, N.B. | D3 | 71 |
| Greenwich Point, c., Ct., U.S. | E1 | 84 |
| Greenwood, B.C. | E8 | 69 |
| Greenwood, Ar., U.S. | B1 | 81 |
| Greenwood, De., U.S. | E3 | 85 |
| Greenwood, Fl., U.S. | B1 | 86 |
| Greenwood, In., U.S. | E5 | 91 |
| Greenwood, Ky., U.S. | D5 | 94 |
| Greenwood, La., U.S. | B2 | 95 |
| Greenwood, Ms., U.S. | B3 | 101 |
| Greenwood, Mo., U.S. | k11 | 102 |
| Greenwood, Ne., U.S. | D9 | 104 |
| Greenwood, N.Y., U.S. | C3 | 109 |
| Greenwood, S.C., U.S. | C3 | 117 |
| Greenwood, S.D., U.S. | E7 | 118 |
| Greenwood, Wi., U.S. | D3 | 126 |
| Greenwood, co., Ks., U.S. | E7 | 93 |
| Greenwood, co., S.C., U.S. | C3 | 117 |
| Greenwood, Lake, res., In., U.S. | G4 | 91 |
| Greenwood, Lake, res., S.C., U.S. | C4 | 117 |
| Greenwood Lake, N.Y., U.S. | D6 | 109 |
| Greenwood Lake, l., N.J., U.S. | A4 | 107 |
| Greenwood Lake, l., Mn., U.S. | C6 | 100 |
| Greenwood Village, co., U.S. | *B6 | 83 |
| Greer, Id., U.S. | C2 | 89 |
| Greer, Mo., U.S. | E6 | 102 |
| Greer, S.C., U.S. | B3 | 117 |
| Greer, co., Ok., U.S. | C2 | 113 |
| Greers Ferry Lake, res., Ar., U.S. | B3 | 81 |
| Greeson, Lake, res., Ar., U.S. | C2 | 81 |
| Gregg, co., Tx., U.S. | C5 | 120 |
| Gregoire Lake, l., Alta. | A5 | 68 |
| Gregory, Mi., U.S. | F6 | 99 |
| Gregory, S.D., U.S. | D6 | 118 |
| Gregory, co., S.D., U.S. | D6 | 118 |
| Gregory, stm., Austl. | C6 | 50 |
| Gregory Bald, mtn., Tn., U.S. | D10 | 119 |
| Gregory Range, mts., Austl. | C7 | 50 |
| Greifswald, E. Ger. | A6 | 18 |
| Greifswalder Bodden, b., E. Ger. | D7 | 15 |
| Greig, N.Y., U.S. | B5 | 109 |
| Greilickville, Mi., U.S. | D5 | 99 |
| Grein, Aus. | D7 | 18 |
| Greiz, E. Ger. | C6 | 18 |
| Grelton, Oh., U.S. | A1 | 112 |
| Gremyachinsk, Sov. Un. | D20 | 8 |
| Grená, Den. | B4 | 15 |
| Grenada, Ms., U.S. | B4 | 101 |
| Grenada, co., Ms., U.S. | B4 | 101 |
| Grenada, ctry., N.A. | J14 | 64 |
| Grenada Lake, res., Ms., U.S. | B4 | 101 |
| Grenade, Fr. | I8 | 17 |
| Grenadine Islands, is., N.A. | V26 | 65 |
| Grenagh, Ire. | E3 | 11 |
| Grenay, Fr. | D2 | 17 |
| Grenchen, Switz. | B3 | 20 |
| Grenen (The Skaw), spit, Den. | A4 | 15 |
| Grenfell, Sask. | G4 | 75 |
| Grenoble, Fr. | E6 | 16 |
| Grenola, Ks., U.S. | E7 | 93 |
| Grenora, N.D., U.S. | A2 | 111 |
| Grenville, Que. | D3 | 74 |
| Grenville, Gren. | W25 | 65 |
| Grenville, N.M., U.S. | A6 | 108 |
| Grenville, S.D., U.S. | B8 | 118 |
| Grenville, co., Ont. | C9 | 73 |
| Grenville, Cape, c., Austl. | B7 | 50 |
| Grenville, Point, c., Wa., U.S. | B1 | 124 |
| Grenville Channel, strt., B.C. | C3 | 69 |
| Gresham, Or., U.S. | B4 | 114 |
| Gresham, S.C., U.S. | D9 | 117 |
| Gresham, Wi., U.S. | D5 | 126 |
| Gresham Park, Ga., U.S. | *h8 | 87 |
| Gretna, Man. | E3 | 70 |
| Gretna, Scot., U.K. | F5 | 13 |
| Gretna, Fl., U.S. | B2 | 86 |
| Gretna, La., U.S. | E5 | 95 |
| Gretna, Ne., U.S. | C9 | 104 |
| Gretna, Va., U.S. | D3 | 123 |
| Greven, W. Ger. | A2 | 19 |
| Grevená, Grc. | B3 | 25 |
| Grevenbroich, W. Ger. | B1 | 19 |
| Grevesmühlen, E. Ger. | E5 | 15 |
| Grey, co., Ont. | C4 | 73 |
| Grey, stm., Newf. | E3 | 72 |
| Grey, stm., N.Z. | O13 | 51 |
| Greybull, Wy., U.S. | B4 | 127 |
| Greybull, stm., Wy., U.S. | B4 | 127 |
| Grey Eagle, Mn., U.S. | E4 | 100 |
| Grey Islands, is., Newf. | C4 | 72 |
| Greylock, Mount, mtn., Ma., U.S. | A1 | 98 |
| Greymouth, N.Z. | O13 | 51 |
| Grey Range, mts., Austl. | E7 | 50 |
| Greys, stm., Wy., U.S. | C2 | 127 |
| Greystone, Ct., U.S. | C3 | 84 |
| Greystone, N.C., U.S. | A4 | 110 |
| Greytown, S. Afr. | C5 | 49 |
| Gribbell Island, i., B.C. | C3 | 69 |
| Gridley, Ca., U.S. | C3 | 82 |
| Gridley, Il., U.S. | C5 | 90 |
| Gridley, Ks., U.S. | D8 | 93 |
| Gridley Mountain, mtn., Ct., U.S. | A2 | 84 |
| Griekwastad, S. Afr. | C3 | 49 |
| Grieskirchen, Aus. | D6 | 18 |
| Griffin, Sask. | H4 | 75 |
| Griffin, Ga., U.S. | C2 | 87 |
| Griffin, In., U.S. | H2 | 91 |
| Griffiss Air Force Base, mil., N.Y., U.S. | B5 | 109 |
| Griffith, Austl. | F8 | 50 |
| Griffith, In., U.S. | A3 | 91 |
| Griffith Island, i., Ont. | C4 | 73 |
| Griffithsville, W.V., U.S. | C3 | 125 |
| Griffithville, Ar., U.S. | B4 | 81 |
| Grifton, N.C., U.S. | B5 | 110 |
| Griggs, Ok., U.S. | e8 | 113 |
| Griggs, co., N.D., U.S. | B7 | 111 |
| Griggsville, Il., U.S. | D3 | 90 |
| Grigoriopol, Sov. Un. | B9 | 24 |
| Grijalva, stm., Mex. | D6 | 63 |
| Grim, Cape, c., Austl. | o14 | 50 |
| Grimari, Cen. Afr. Rep. | D4 | 46 |
| Grimes, Al., U.S. | D4 | 78 |
| Grimes, Ia., U.S. | C4 | 92 |
| Grimes, co., Tx., U.S. | D4 | 120 |
| Grimesland, N.C., U.S. | B5 | 110 |
| Grimma, E. Ger. | C6 | 18 |
| Grimmen, E. Ger. | D7 | 15 |
| Grimmialp, Switz. | C4 | 21 |
| Grimms Landing, W.V., U.S. | C3 | 125 |
| Grimsby, Ont. | D5 | 73 |
| Grimsby, Eng., U.K. | D6 | 10 |
| Grímsey, i., Ice. | m23 | 14 |
| Grimshaw, Alta. | A2 | 68 |
| Grimsley, Tn., U.S. | C9 | 119 |
| Grimstad, Nor. | H3 | 14 |
| Grimsthorpe, Ont. | B7 | 73 |
| Grindall Creek, Va., U.S. | n18 | 123 |
| Grindelwald, Switz. | C5 | 21 |
| Grindsted, Den. | C2 | 15 |
| Grindstone, Me., U.S. | C4 | 96 |
| Grind Stone City, Mi., U.S. | D8 | 99 |
| Grinem, i., Marsh Is. | S18 | 52 |
| Grinnell, Ia., U.S. | C5 | 92 |
| Grinnell Peninsula, pen., N.W. Ter. | m32 | 66 |
| Grise Fiord, N.W. Ter. | m35 | 66 |
| Gris-Nez, Cap, c., Fr. | D9 | 12 |
| Griswold, Man. | E1 | 70 |
| Griswold, Ia., U.S. | C2 | 92 |
| Griswoldville, Ma., U.S. | A2 | 98 |
| Grizzly Mountain, mtn., Id., U.S. | B2 | 89 |
| Grizzly Mountain, mtn., Or., U.S. | C6 | 114 |
| Grizzly Mountain, mtn., Wa., U.S. | A7 | 124 |
| Grodków, Pol. | C4 | 26 |
| Grodno, Sov. Un. | E4 | 27 |
| Grodzisk Mazowiecki, Pol. | m13 | 26 |
| Grodzisk (Wielkopolski), Pol. | B4 | 26 |
| Groenlo, Neth. | B6 | 17 |
| Groesbeck, Oh., U.S. | *o12 | 120 |
| Groesbeck, Tx., U.S. | D4 | 120 |
| Groix, Île de, i., Fr. | D2 | 16 |
| Grójec, Pol. | C6 | 26 |
| Grombalia, Tun. | F3 | 23 |
| Gronau, W. Ger. | B3 | 18 |
| Gronau, W. Ger. | A7 | 16 |
| Groningen, Sur. | A3 | 59 |
| Groningen, prov., Neth. | A6 | 17 |
| Grönlid, Sask. | D3 | 75 |
| Groom, Tx., U.S. | B2 | 120 |
| Groom Lake, l., Nv., U.S. | F6 | 105 |
| Groom Range, mts., Nv., U.S. | F6 | 105 |
| Groote Eylandt, i., Austl. | B6 | 50 |
| Grootfontein, Nmb. | A2 | 49 |
| Grootvloer, pl., S. Afr. | C3 | 49 |
| Groscap, Mi., U.S. | C6 | 99 |
| Grosio, Italy | D9 | 21 |
| Groslay, Fr. | g10 | 16 |
| Gros-Mécatina, Île du, i., Que. | D2 | 16 |
| Gros Morne, mtn., Newf. | D3 | 72 |
| Gros Morne National Park, Newf. | D3 | 72 |
| Gross, Ne., U.S. | B7 | 104 |
| Grossbreitenbach, E. Ger. | C6 | 19 |
| Grosse Ile, Mi., U.S. | *F7 | 99 |
| Grosse Île, i., Que. | B8 | 71 |
| Grosse Isle Naval Air Station, mil., Mi., U.S. | p15 | 99 |
| Grosse Laaber, stm., W. Ger. | E7 | 19 |
| Grossenhain, E. Ger. | C6 | 18 |
| Grosse Pointe, Mi., U.S. | p16 | 99 |
| Grosse Pointe Farms, Mi., U.S. | *F8 | 99 |
| Grosse Pointe Park, Mi., U.S. | p16 | 99 |
| Grosse Pointe Woods, Mi., U.S. | p16 | 99 |
| Grosser Arber, mtn., W. Ger. | D8 | 19 |
| Grosse Röder, stm., E. Ger. | B8 | 19 |
| Grösser Plön, l., W. Ger. | D4 | 15 |
| Grosser Priel, mtn., Aus. | E7 | 18 |
| Grosse Tete, La., U.S. | D4 | 95 |
| Grosseto, Italy | C3 | 23 |
| Gross-Gerau, W. Ger. | D3 | 19 |
| Grossglockner, mtn., Aus. | E6 | 18 |
| Grossmont, Ca., U.S. | o16 | 82 |
| Grossostheim, W. Ger. | D4 | 19 |
| Grossräschen, E. Ger. | B9 | 19 |
| Grossröhrsdorf, E. Ger. | B9 | 19 |
| Grosvenor Dale, Ct., U.S. | B8 | 84 |
| Gros Ventre, stm., Wy., U.S. | C2 | 127 |
| Gros Ventre Range, mts., Wy., U.S. | C2 | 127 |
| Groswater Bay, b., Newf. | A3 | 72 |
| Groton, Ct., U.S. | D7 | 84 |
| Groton, Ma., U.S. | A4 | 98 |
| Groton, N.H., U.S. | C3 | 106 |
| Groton, N.Y., U.S. | C4 | 109 |
| Groton, S.D., U.S. | B7 | 118 |
| Groton, Vt., U.S. | C4 | 122 |
| Groton Long Point, Ct., U.S. | D7 | 84 |
| Grottaferrata, Italy | h9 | 23 |
| Grottaglie, Italy | D6 | 23 |
| Grottoes, Va., U.S. | B4 | 123 |
| Grouard Mission, Alta. | B2 | 68 |
| Grouse Creek, Ut., U.S. | B2 | 121 |
| Grouse Creek, stm., Ks., U.S. | E7 | 93 |
| Grouse Creek, stm., Ut., U.S. | B2 | 121 |
| Grouse Creek Mountain, mtn., Id., U.S. | E5 | 89 |
| Grouse Creek Mountains, mts., Ut., U.S. | B2 | 121 |
| Grovania, Ga., U.S. | D3 | 87 |
| Grove, Me., U.S. | C5 | 96 |
| Grove, Ok., U.S. | A7 | 113 |
| Grove City, Fl., U.S. | F4 | 86 |
| Grove City, Mn., U.S. | E4 | 100 |
| Grove City, Oh., U.S. | C2 | 112 |
| Grove City, Pa., U.S. | D1 | 115 |
| Grove Hill, Al., U.S. | D2 | 78 |
| Groveland, Ca., U.S. | D3 | 82 |
| Groveland, Fl., U.S. | D5 | 86 |
| Groveland, Ga., U.S. | D5 | 87 |
| Groveland, Ma., U.S. | A5 | 98 |
| Groveland, N.Y., U.S. | C3 | 109 |
| Grove Mountains, mts., Ant. | B21 | 7 |
| Grove Point, c., Md., U.S. | B5 | 97 |
| Groveport, Oh., U.S. | C3 | 112 |
| Grover, Co., U.S. | A6 | 83 |
| Grover, N.C., U.S. | B1 | 110 |
| Grover, Pa., U.S. | C8 | 115 |
| Grover, S.C., U.S. | E6 | 117 |
| Grover, Wy., U.S. | D2 | 127 |
| Grover City, Ca., U.S. | E3 | 82 |
| Grover Hill, Oh., U.S. | A1 | 112 |
| Grovertown, In., U.S. | B4 | 91 |
| Groves, Tx., U.S. | E6 | 120 |
| Grovespring, Mo., U.S. | D5 | 102 |
| Groveton, N.H., U.S. | A3 | 106 |
| Groveton, Tx., U.S. | D5 | 120 |
| Groveton, Va., U.S. | g12 | 123 |
| Groveton Gardens, Va., U.S. | *B5 | 123 |
| Grovetown, Ga., U.S. | C4 | 87 |
| Groveville, N.J., U.S. | C3 | 107 |
| Growler Peak, mtn., Az., U.S. | E2 | 80 |
| Groznyy, Sov. Un. | E7 | 29 |
| Grubbs, Ar., U.S. | B4 | 81 |
| Grudovo, Bul. | D8 | 24 |
| Grudziadz, Pol. | B5 | 26 |
| Grues, Île aux, i., Que. | B7 | 74 |
| Gruetli-Laager, Tn., U.S. | D8 | 119 |
| Gruinard Bay, b., Scot., U.K. | C3 | 13 |
| Grulla, Tx., U.S. | F3 | 120 |
| Grünberg, W. Ger. | C3 | 19 |
| Grundy, Va., U.S. | e9 | 123 |
| Grundy, co., Il., U.S. | B5 | 90 |
| Grundy, co., Ia., U.S. | B5 | 92 |
| Grundy, co., Mo., U.S. | A4 | 102 |
| Grundy, co., Tn., U.S. | D8 | 119 |
| Grundy Center, Ia., U.S. | B5 | 92 |
| Grünstadt, W. Ger. | D3 | 19 |
| Grunthal, Man. | E3 | 70 |
| Grüsch, Switz. | C8 | 21 |
| Gruver, Ia., U.S. | A3 | 92 |
| Gruver, Tx., U.S. | A2 | 120 |
| Gruyères, Switz. | C3 | 21 |
| Gruž (part of Dubrovnik), Yugo. | D4 | 24 |
| Gryazi, Sov. Un. | E13 | 27 |
| Gryazovets, Sov. Un. | B13 | 27 |
| Gryfice, Pol. | B3 | 26 |
| Gryfino, Pol. | B2 | 26 |
| Grygla, Mn., U.S. | B3 | 100 |
| Gstaad, Switz. | C3 | 20 |
| Guabito, Pan. | F6 | 62 |
| Guacanayabo, Golfo de, b., Cuba | D5 | 64 |
| Gu Achi, Az., U.S. | E3 | 80 |
| Guadalajara, Mex. | C4 | 63 |
| Guadalcanal, Spain | C3 | 22 |
| Guadalcanal, i., Sol.Is. | G9 | 6 |
| Guadalentin, stm., Spain | D5 | 22 |
| Guadalhorce, stm., Spain | D3 | 22 |
| Guadalmena, stm., Spain | C4 | 22 |
| Guadalope, stm., Spain | B6 | 22 |
| Guadalquivir, stm., Spain | D2 | 22 |
| Guadalupe [Bravos], Mex. | *B4 | 63 |
| Guadalupe Mountains, mts., U.S. | E5 | 108 |
| Guadalupe Mountains National Park, Tx., U.S. | o12 | 120 |
| Guadalupe Peak, mtn., Tx., U.S. | o12 | 120 |
| Guadalupe, N.M., U.S. | A4 | 108 |
| Guadarrama, stm., Spain | *p17 | 22 |
| Guadarrama, Sierra de, mts., Spain | B4 | 22 |
| Guadeloupe, dept., N.A. | H14 | 64 |
| Guadeloupe Passage, strt., N.A. | H14 | 64 |
| Guadiana, stm., Eur. | D2 | 22 |
| Guadiana Menor, stm., Spain | D4 | 22 |
| Guadiela, stm., Spain | B4 | 22 |
| Guadilla, Bahía de, b., P.R. | B1 | 65 |
| Guadix, Spain | D4 | 22 |
| Guafo, Isla, i., Chile | C2 | 54 |
| Guagua, Phil. | o13 | 34 |
| Guainía, dept., Col. | C4 | 60 |
| Guainía, stm., S.A. | C4 | 60 |
| Guaíra, Braz. | C2 | 56 |
| Guajará Mirim, Braz. | E1 | 59 |
| Guajataca, Lago de, res., P.R. | B2 | 65 |
| Guajira, dept., Col. | A3 | 60 |
| Gualaceo, Ec. | B2 | 58 |
| Gualala, Ca., U.S. | C2 | 82 |
| Gualán, Guat. | D7 | 63 |
| Gualaquiza, Ec. | B2 | 58 |
| Gualeguay, Arg. | A5 | 54 |
| Gualeguaychú, Arg. | A5 | 54 |
| Guam, dept., Oc. | F8 | 6 |
| Guamá, stm., Braz. | B1 | 57 |
| Guamini, Arg. | B4 | 54 |
| Guamúchil, Mex. | B3 | 63 |
| Guanacaste, Cordillera de, mts., C.R. | E5 | 62 |
| Guanahacabibes, Golfo de, b., Cuba | C1 | 64 |
| Guana Island, i., V.I., Br. | B6 | 65 |
| Guanajay, Cuba | C2 | 64 |
| Guanajuato, Mex. | C4 | 63 |
| Guanajuato, state, Mex. | C4 | 63 |
| Guanambi, Braz. | A4 | 56 |
| Guanare, Ven. | B4 | 60 |
| Guandacol, Arg. | E2 | 55 |
| Guandi, China | E4 | 33 |
| Guane, Cuba | C1 | 64 |
| Guang'an, China | I2 | 32 |
| Guangchang, China | K7 | 32 |
| Guangde, China | I8 | 32 |
| Guangdong, prov., China | G7 | 31 |
| Guangnan, China | G6 | 31 |
| Guangxi Zhuangzu, prov., China | G6 | 31 |
| Guangyuan, China | E6 | 31 |
| Guangzhou (Canton), China | G7 | 31 |
| Guánica, P.R. | C2 | 65 |
| Guánica, Laguna de, l., P.R. | B2 | 65 |
| Guano Lake, l., Or., U.S. | E7 | 114 |
| Guantánamo, Cuba | D6 | 64 |
| Guantánamo, prov., Cuba | D6 | 64 |
| Guanxian, China | F6 | 32 |
| Guanyun, China | G8 | 32 |
| Guapi, Col. | C2 | 60 |
| Guapiara, Braz. | C3 | 56 |
| Guápiles, C.R. | E6 | 62 |
| Guaporé (Iténez), stm., S.A. | C2 | 55 |
| Guaqui, Bol. | C2 | 55 |
| Guará, Braz. | F1 | 57 |
| Guarabira, Braz. | C3 | 57 |
| Guaranda, Ec. | B2 | 58 |
| Guaranésia, Braz. | k8 | 56 |
| Guarapuava, Braz. | D2 | 56 |
| Guaraqueçaba, Braz. | D2 | 56 |
| Guararapes, Braz. | C2 | 56 |
| Guaratinguetá, Braz. | C2 | 56 |
| Guaratuba, Braz. | D3 | 56 |
| Guarda, Port. | B2 | 22 |
| Guardafui, Cape see Caseyr, c., Som. | C7 | 47 |
| Guardia Mitre, Arg. | C4 | 54 |
| Guardian, W.V., U.S. | C4 | 125 |
| Guareí, Braz. | m7 | 56 |
| Guareña, Spain | C2 | 22 |
| Guárico, state, Ven. | B4 | 60 |
| Guárico, stm., Ven. | B4 | 60 |
| Guarujá, Braz. | n8 | 56 |
| Guarulhos, Braz. | m8 | 56 |
| Guasave, Mex. | B3 | 63 |
| Guasdualito, Ven. | B3 | 60 |
| Guasipati, Ven. | B5 | 60 |
| Guastalla, Italy | D5 | 23 |
| Guatemala, Guat. | E6 | 63 |
| Guatemala, ctry., N.A. | D6 | 63 |
| Guateque, Col. | C3 | 60 |
| Guatimozín, Arg. | A4 | 54 |
| Guatopo National Park, Ven. | A4 | 60 |
| Guaviare, dept., Col. | C3 | 60 |
| Guaviare, stm., Col. | C3 | 60 |
| Guaxupé, Braz. | C3 | 56 |
| Guayabal, Cuba | D5 | 64 |
| Guayaguayare, Trin. | O23 | 65 |
| Guayama, P.R. | C3 | 65 |
| Guayaquil, Ec. | B1 | 58 |
| Guayaquil, Golfo de, b., S.A. | B1 | 58 |
| Guayaramerín, Bol. | C2 | 55 |
| Guayas, prov., Ec. | B1 | 58 |
| Guaymas, Mex. | B2 | 63 |
| Guaynabo, P.R. | C3 | 65 |
| Guazacapán, Guat. | E6 | 63 |
| Gubakha, Sov. Un. | B5 | 28 |
| Gubbio, Italy | C4 | 23 |
| Gubin, Pol. | B9 | 19 |
| Gucheng, China | H4 | 32 |
| Gúdar, Sierra de, mts., Spain | B5 | 22 |
| Gudauta, Sov. Un. | A13 | 40 |
| Gudenå, stm., Den. | C3 | 15 |
| Gudermes, Sov. Un. | E7 | 29 |
| Gudhjem, Den. | C8 | 15 |
| Güdür, India | F6 | 36 |
| Guebwiller, Fr. | D7 | 16 |
| Guéckédou, Gui. | E2 | 45 |
| Guelma, Alg. | B6 | 44 |
| Guelph, Ont. | D4 | 73 |
| Guelph, N.D., U.S. | C7 | 111 |
| Guénette, Que. | C2 | 74 |
| Güera, W. Sah. | E1 | 44 |
| Guercif, Mor. | B4 | 44 |
| Guéréda, Chad | C4 | 46 |
| Guéret, Fr. | C4 | 16 |
| Guerette, Me., U.S. | A4 | 96 |
| Guernica y Luno, Spain | A4 | 22 |
| Guernsey, Sask. | F3 | 75 |
| Guernsey, Wy., U.S. | D8 | 127 |
| Guernsey, co., Oh., U.S. | B4 | 112 |
| Guernsey, dep., Eur. | F5 | 10 |
| Guernsey, i., Guernsey | F5 | 10 |
| Guerrero, state, Mex. | D4 | 63 |
| Guest Peninsula, pen., Ant. | B34 | 7 |
| Gueugnon, Fr. | D6 | 16 |
| Gueydan, La., U.S. | D3 | 95 |
| Guffey, Co., U.S. | C5 | 83 |
| Gugegwe Island, i., Marsh Is. | S17 | 52 |
| Guia Lopes da Laguna, Braz. | D1 | 56 |
| Guibes, Nmb. | C3 | 49 |
| Guichi, China | I7 | 32 |
| Guide, China | D8 | 31 |
| Guider, Cam. | D2 | 46 |
| Guide Rock, Ne., U.S. | D7 | 104 |
| Guidong, China | K5 | 32 |
| Guidonia [Montecelio], Italy | h9 | 23 |
| Guiglo, I.C. | E3 | 45 |
| Guildford, Eng., U.K. | E6 | 10 |
| Guildhall, Vt., U.S. | B5 | 122 |
| Guilford, Ct., U.S. | D5 | 84 |
| Guilford, In., U.S. | F8 | 91 |
| Guilford, Me., U.S. | C3 | 96 |
| Guilford, Mo., U.S. | A3 | 102 |
| Guilford, N.Y., U.S. | C5 | 109 |
| Guilford, Vt., U.S. | F3 | 122 |
| Guilford, co., N.C., U.S. | A3 | 110 |
| Guilherme Capelo, Ang. | C1 | 48 |
| Guilin, China | F7 | 31 |
| Guillaume-Delisle, Lac, l., Que. | E17 | 66 |
| Guillestre, Fr. | D12 | 16 |
| Guimaraes, Braz. | B2 | 57 |
| Guimarães, Port. | B1 | 22 |
| Guimba, Phil. | o13 | 34 |
| Guin, Al., U.S. | B2 | 78 |
| Guinea, Va., U.S. | B5 | 123 |
| Guinea, ctry., Afr. | D2 | 45 |
| Guinea, Gulf of, b., Afr. | F6 | 6 |
| Guinea-Bissau, ctry., Afr. | D1 | 45 |
| Güines, Cuba | C2 | 64 |
| Guînes, Fr. | D11 | 12 |
| Guingamp, Fr. | C2 | 16 |
| Guion, Ar., U.S. | B4 | 81 |
| Güira de Melena, Cuba | C2 | 64 |
| Guiratinga, Braz. | B2 | 56 |
| Güiria, Ven. | A5 | 60 |
| Guisanbourg, Fr. Gu. | B4 | 59 |
| Guisborough, Eng., U.K. | F7 | 13 |
| Guise, Fr. | C5 | 16 |
| Guist Creek, stm., Ky., U.S. | B4 | 94 |
| Guitiriz, Spain | A2 | 22 |
| Guixi, China | J7 | 32 |
| Guixian, China | G6 | 31 |
| Guiyang, China | F6 | 31 |
| Guizhou, prov., China | F6 | 31 |
| Gujan, Fr. | E4 | 33 |
| Gujarat, state, India | D5 | 36 |
| Gujrānwāla, Pak. | B5 | 36 |
| Gujrāt, Pak. | *B5 | 36 |
| Gulbarga, India | D6 | 36 |
| Gulbene, Sov. Un. | B13 | 39 |
| Gülchö, Sov. Un. | D13 | 27 |
| Gulf, co., Fl., U.S. | C1 | 86 |
| Gulf Breeze, Fl., U.S. | *u14 | 86 |
| Gulf Gate Estates, Fl., U.S. | E4 | 86 |
| Gulf Hammock, Fl., U.S. | C4 | 86 |
| Gulf Islands National Seashore, U.S. | E5 | 101 |
| Gulfport, Fl., U.S. | E4 | 86 |
| Gulf Port, Il., U.S. | C2 | 90 |
| Gulfport, Ms., U.S. | E4 | 101 |
| Gulf Shores, Al., U.S. | E2 | 78 |
| Gulgong, Austl. | F7 | 51 |
| Gulkana, Ak., U.S. | C10 | 79 |
| Gullion, Slieve, mtn., N. Ire., U.K. | C5 | 11 |
| Gull Island, i., N.C., U.S. | B7 | 110 |
| Gullivan Bay, b., Fl., U.S. | G5 | 86 |
| Gulliver, Mi., U.S. | B5 | 99 |
| Gull Lake, Sask. | G1 | 75 |
| Gull Lake, l., Alta. | C4 | 68 |
| Gull Lake, l., Mn., U.S. | D4 | 100 |
| Güllük, Tur. | D6 | 40 |
| Gully, Mn., U.S. | C3 | 100 |
| Gulu, Ug. | A5 | 48 |
| Gulyantsi, Bul. | D6 | 24 |
| Gulyaypole, Sov. Un. | H11 | 27 |
| Gumaca, Phil. | p14 | 34 |
| Gumba, Zaire | A3 | 48 |
| Gumboro, De., U.S. | G4 | 85 |
| Gumefens, Switz. | C3 | 21 |
| Gumel, Nig. | D6 | 45 |
| Gummersbach, W. Ger. | B2 | 19 |
| Gum Spring Mountain, mtn., Tn., U.S. | D8 | 119 |
| Gum Swamp Creek, stm., Ga., U.S. | C2 | 81 |
| Gümüşhane, Tur. | B12 | 40 |
| Guna, India | D6 | 36 |
| Guna, Eth. | C4 | 47 |
| Gundelfingen, W. Ger. | E5 | 19 |
| Gungu, Zaire | C2 | 48 |
| Gunisao, stm., Man. | C3 | 70 |
| Gunisao Lake, l., Man. | C3 | 70 |
| Gunlock, Ut., U.S. | F2 | 121 |
| Gunn, Alta. | C3 | 68 |
| Gunnar, Sask. | m7 | 75 |
| Gunnbjørn Fjeld, mtn., Grnld. | *C17 | 128 |
| Gunnedah, Austl. | F9 | 51 |
| Gunnison, Co., U.S. | C3 | 83 |
| Gunnison, Ms., U.S. | B3 | 101 |
| Gunnison, Ut., U.S. | D4 | 121 |
| Gunnison, co., Co., U.S. | C3 | 83 |
| Gunnison, stm., Co., U.S. | C2 | 83 |
| Gunnison, Mount, mtn., Co., U.S. | C3 | 83 |
| Gunworth, Sask. | F1 | 75 |
| Gunpowder Creek, stm., Ky., U.S. | k13 | 94 |
| Gunpowder Neck, c., Md., U.S. | B5 | 97 |
| Gunpowder River, b., Md., U.S. | B5 | 97 |
| Gunter Air Force Base, mil., Al., U.S. | C3 | 78 |
| Guntersville, Al., U.S. | A3 | 78 |
| Guntersville Dam, Al., U.S. | A3 | 78 |
| Guntersville Lake, res., Al., U.S. | A3 | 78 |
| Gunton, Man. | D3 | 70 |
| Guntown, Ms., U.S. | A5 | 101 |
| Guntūr, India | E6 | 36 |
| Gunungsitoli, Indon. | L2 | 35 |
| Günz, stm., W. Ger. | E5 | 19 |
| Günzburg, W. Ger. | E5 | 19 |
| Gunzenhausen, W. Ger. | D5 | 19 |
| Guoyang, China | H7 | 32 |
| Gura Humorului, Rom. | B8 | 24 |
| Gurdāspur, India | A5 | 37 |
| Gurdon, Ar., U.S. | D2 | 81 |
| Gurguéia, stm., Braz. | C2 | 57 |
| Guri, Embalse, res., Ven. | B5 | 60 |
| Gurjevsk, Sov. Un. | *E26 | 8 |
| Gurk, stm., Aus. | A3 | 78? |
| Gurley, Al., U.S. | A3 | 78 |
| Gurley, Ne., U.S. | C2 | 104 |
| Gurnee, Il., U.S. | h9 | 90 |
| Gurnet Point, c., Ma., U.S. | B6 | 98 |
| Gurney, Wi., U.S. | B3 | 126 |
| Gurué, Moz. | A6 | 49 |
| Gurupá, Braz. | C3 | 59 |
| Gurupi, Braz. | B1 | 57 |
| Gurupi, stm., Braz. | B1 | 57 |
| Gurupi, Cabo, c., Braz. | B1 | 57 |
| Guryev, Sov. Un. | H7 | 29 |
| Gusau, Nig. | D6 | 45 |
| Gusev, Sov. Un. | *E26 | 8 |
| Gusher, Ut., U.S. | C6 | 121 |
| Gushi, China | H5 | 32 |
| Gushikami, Japan | O5 | 52 |
| Gushikawa, Japan | O5 | 52 |
| Gusinje, Yugo. | D4 | 24 |
| Gus-Khrustalnyy, Sov. Un. | D13 | 27 |
| Gustavo A. Madero (part of Mexico City), Mex. | h9 | 63 |
| Gustavus, Ak., U.S. | D12 | 79 |
| Güsten, E. Ger. | B6 | 19 |
| Gustine, Ca., U.S. | D3 | 82 |
| Gustine, Tx., U.S. | D3 | 120 |
| Güstrow, E. Ger. | B6 | 18 |
| Gutau, Aus. | E9 | 19 |
| Gütersloh, W. Ger. | B3 | 19 |
| Guthrie, Ky., U.S. | D2 | 94 |
| Guthrie, Mn., U.S. | C4 | 100 |
| Guthrie, Ok., U.S. | B4 | 113 |
| Guthrie, Tx., U.S. | C2 | 120 |
| Guthrie, W.V., U.S. | m12 | 125 |
| Guthrie, co., Ia., U.S. | C3 | 92 |
| Guthrie Center, Ia., U.S. | C3 | 92 |
| Guthrie Lake, l., Man. | B1 | 70 |
| Guttenberg, Ia., U.S. | B6 | 92 |
| Guttenberg, N.J., U.S. | h8 | 107 |
| Gu Vo, Az., U.S. | E3 | 80 |
| Guwāhāti, India | C9 | 36 |
| Guy, Ar., U.S. | B3 | 81 |
| Guy, Tx., U.S. | r14 | 120 |
| Guyana, ctry., S.A. | A3 | 59 |
| Guyandotte, stm., W.V., U.S. | C2 | 125 |
| Guyandotte Mountain, mtn., W.V., U.S. | n12 | 125 |
| Guyang, China | D4 | 32 |
| Guyenne, hist. reg., Fr. | E4 | 16 |
| Guymon, Ok., U.S. | e9 | 113 |
| Guyot, Mount, mtn., U.S. | D10 | 119 |
| Guyra, Austl. | E8 | 51 |
| Guys, Tn., U.S. | B3 | 119 |
| Guysborough, N.S. | D8 | 71 |
| Guysborough, co., N.S. | D7 | 71 |
| Guys Mills, Pa., U.S. | C2 | 115 |
| Guyton, Ga., U.S. | D5 | 87 |
| Guyuan, China | G2 | 32 |
| Guyuan, China | D6 | 32 |
| Guzar, Sov. Un. | B13 | 39 |
| Güzelyurt, N. Cyp. | C8 | 40 |
| Guzhen, China | H7 | 32 |
| Gvardeysk, Sov. Un. | *E26 | 8 |
| Gwabegar, Austl. | E7 | 51 |
| Gwādar, Pak. | B4 | 36 |
| Gwai, Zimb. | A4 | 49 |
| Gwalior, India | C6 | 36 |
| Gwanda, Zimb. | B4 | 49 |
| Gwane, Zaire | A4 | 48 |
| Gwda, stm., Pol. | B3 | 26 |
| Gweebarra Bay, b., Ire. | C3 | 11 |
| Gweesalia, Ire. | C2 | 11 |
| Gwembe, Zam. | A4 | 49 |
| Gwent, co., Wales, U.K. | C5 | 12 |
| Gweru, Zimb. | A4 | 49 |
| Gwinhurst, De., U.S. | h8 | 85 |
| Gwinn, Mi., U.S. | B3 | 99 |
| Gwinner, N.D., U.S. | C8 | 111 |
| Gwinnett, co., Ga., U.S. | C2 | 87 |
| Gwydir Bay, b., Ak., U.S. | A10 | 79 |
| Gwynedd, co., Wales, U.K. | A3 | 12 |
| Gwynn, Va., U.S. | C6 | 123 |
| Gwynne, Alta. | C4 | 68 |
| Gwynneville, In., U.S. | E6 | 91 |
| Gwynns Falls, stm., Md., U.S. | g10 | 97 |
| Gyangzê, China | C8 | 36 |
| Gyaring Co, l., China | E4 | 31 |
| Gyaring Hu, l., China | E4 | 31 |
| Gyirong, China | C10 | 37 |
| Gympie, Austl. | E9 | 50 |
| Gyöngyös, Hung. | B3 | 24 |
| Györ (Raab), Hung. | B3 | 24 |
| Gypsera, Switz. | C3 | 21 |
| Gypsum, Co., U.S. | B4 | 83 |
| Gypsum, Ks., U.S. | D6 | 93 |
| Gypsum, Oh., U.S. | A3 | 112 |
| Gypsumville, Man. | D2 | 70 |
| Gyula, Hung. | B5 | 24 |

## H

| Name | Map Ref. | Page |
|---|---|---|
| Haag [in Oberbayern], W. Ger. | A8 | 19 |
| Haakon, co., S.D., U.S. | C4 | 118 |
| Haaksbergen, Neth. | B6 | 17 |
| Haamstede, Neth. | C3 | 17 |
| Haapamäki, Fin. | F11 | 14 |
| Haapsalu, Sov. Un. | B4 | 27 |
| Ha Arava (Wādī al Jayb), val., Asia | D7 | 41 |
| Haarlem, Neth. | A6 | 16 |
| Haarlemmermeer, Neth. | A6 | 16 |
| Hab, stm., Pak. | I13 | 39 |
| Habarmehl Peak, mtn., Ant. | B13 | 7 |
| Habersham, Ga., U.S. | B3 | 87 |
| Habersham, co., Ga., U.S. | B3 | 87 |
| Haboro, Japan | D10 | 52 |
| Hachiman, Japan | n15 | 52 |
| Hachinohe, Japan | F10 | 53 |
| Hachiōji, Japan | I9 | 52 |
| Hachita, N.M., U.S. | F1 | 108 |
| Hacienda Heights, Ca., U.S. | *n13 | 82 |
| Hack, Mount, mtn., Austl. | E2 | 51 |
| Hackberry, Az., U.S. | B2 | 80 |
| Hackberry, La., U.S. | E2 | 95 |
| Hackberry Creek, stm., Ks., U.S. | D3 | 93 |
| Hackensack, Mn., U.S. | D4 | 100 |
| Hackensack, N.J., U.S. | h8 | 107 |
| Hackensack, stm., N.J., U.S. | h8 | 107 |
| Hacker Valley, W.V., U.S. | C4 | 125 |
| Hackett, Ar., U.S. | B1 | 81 |
| Hackettstown, N.J., U.S. | B3 | 107 |
| Hackleburg, Al., U.S. | A2 | 78 |
| Hackney (part of London), Eng., U.K. | k12 | 10 |
| Hack Point, Md., U.S. | B6 | 97 |
| Hacoda, Al., U.S. | D3 | 78 |
| Hacq, i., Micron. | Q18 | 52 |
| Ḥaḍāribah, Ra's al, c., Sud. | A4 | 47 |
| Hadassah Alef Hospital, Isr. | m14 | 41 |
| Ḥadd, Ra's al, c., Oman | C6 | 35 |
| Haddam, Ks., U.S. | C6 | 93 |
| Haddam, Ct., U.S. | D5 | 84 |
| Haddington, Scot., U.K. | C6 | 13 |
| Haddix, Ky., U.S. | C6 | 94 |
| Haddock, Ga., U.S. | C3 | 87 |
| Haddon Heights, N.J., U.S. | D2 | 107 |
| Haddonfield, N.J., U.S. | D2 | 107 |
| Hadejia, Nig. | D7 | 45 |
| Hadejia, stm., Nig. | D7 | 45 |
| Hadera, Isr. | F10 | 40 |
| Haderslev, Den. | C2 | 15 |
| Hadim, Tur. | D9 | 40 |
| Ḥadīthah, Bi'r al, well, Eg. | D6 | 41 |
| Hadleigh, Eng., U.K. | E3 | 11 |
| Hadley, Mn., U.S. | F3 | 100 |
| Hadley, N.Y., U.S. | B7 | 109 |
| Hadley, Pa., U.S. | D1 | 115 |

| Name | Map Ref. | Page |
|---|---|---|
| Hadley Bay, b., N.W. Ter. | B11 | 66 |
| Hadley Lake, l., Me., U.S. | D5 | 96 |
| Hadlock, Wa., U.S. | A3 | 124 |
| Hadlyme, Ct., U.S. | D6 | 84 |
| Ha Dong, Viet. | A3 | 34 |
| Hadramawt, reg., Yemen | D4 | 38 |
| Hadsten, Den. | B4 | 15 |
| Hadsund, Den. | B4 | 15 |
| Haeju, N. Kor. | C10 | 31 |
| Haenam, S. Kor. | I3 | 33 |
| Haerhpin see Harbin, China | B10 | 31 |
| Hafford, Sask. | E2 | 75 |
| Ḩafīra, Qā'al, pl., Jord. | C8 | 41 |
| Hafnarfjördur, Ice. | n22 | 14 |
| Haft Gel, Iran | F4 | 39 |
| Hafun, Ras, c., Som. | C7 | 47 |
| Hagan, La., U.S. | D5 | 87 |
| Hagari, stm., India | F6 | 36 |
| Hagarstown, Il., U.S. | E4 | 90 |
| Hagarville, Ar., U.S. | B2 | 81 |
| Hagemeister Island, i., Ak., U.S. | D7 | 79 |
| Hagen, Sask. | E3 | 75 |
| Hagen, W. Ger. | C3 | 18 |
| Hagenow, E. Ger. | E5 | 15 |
| Hagensborg, B.C. | C4 | 69 |
| Hagere Hiywet, Eth. | D4 | 47 |
| Hagerman, Id., U.S. | G4 | 89 |
| Hagerman, N.M., U.S. | D5 | 108 |
| Hagerman Corners, Ont. | k15 | 73 |
| Hagerstown, In., U.S. | E7 | 91 |
| Hagerstown, Md., U.S. | A2 | 97 |
| Hagersville, Ont. | E4 | 73 |
| Haggart Lake, l., Ont. | D4 | 70 |
| Haggin, Mount, mtn., Mt., U.S. | D3 | 103 |
| Ha Giang, Viet. | A6 | 34 |
| Hags Head, c., Ire. | E2 | 11 |
| Hague, Sask. | E2 | 75 |
| Hague, N.Y., U.S. | B7 | 109 |
| Hague, N.D., U.S. | C6 | 111 |
| Hague, Cap de la, c., Fr. | C3 | 16 |
| Haguenau, Fr. | C7 | 16 |
| Hagues Peak, mtn., Co., U.S. | A5 | 83 |
| Ha! Ha!, Baie des, b., Que. | C2 | 72 |
| Ha! Ha!, Lac, l., Que. | A7 | 74 |
| Hahira, Ga., U.S. | F3 | 87 |
| Hahnville, La., U.S. | E5 | 95 |
| Haicheng, China | G8 | 31 |
| Haicheng, China | D10 | 32 |
| Haichow Bay see Haizhou Bay, b., China | G8 | 32 |
| Hai Duong, Viet. | B7 | 35 |
| Haifa (Hefa), Isr. | C3 | 38 |
| Haifa, Bay of see Hefa, Mifraz, b., Isr. | B6 | 41 |
| Haigerloch, W. Ger. | A4 | 20 |
| Haigler, Ne., U.S. | D4 | 104 |
| Haikang, China | G6 | 31 |
| Haikou, China | B4 | 34 |
| Haiku, Hi., U.S. | C5 | 88 |
| Ḩā'il, Sau. Ar. | C4 | 38 |
| Hailar, China | B8 | 31 |
| Haile, La., U.S. | B3 | 95 |
| Hailesboro, N.Y., U.S. | f9 | 109 |
| Hailey, Id., U.S. | F4 | 89 |
| Haileybury, Ont. | p20 | 73 |
| Haileyville, Ok., U.S. | C6 | 113 |
| Hailong, China | C10 | 31 |
| Hailun, China | B10 | 31 |
| Haimen, China | F9 | 31 |
| Haimen, China | I9 | 32 |
| Hainan Island, i., China | B3 | 34 |
| Hainaut, prov., Bel. | D3 | 17 |
| Haines, Ak., U.S. | D12 | 79 |
| Haines, Or., U.S. | C9 | 114 |
| Hainesburg, N.J., U.S. | B2 | 107 |
| Haines City, Fl., U.S. | D5 | 86 |
| Haines Falls, N.Y., U.S. | C6 | 109 |
| Hainesport, N.J., U.S. | D3 | 107 |
| Hainesville, N.J., U.S. | A3 | 107 |
| Hainichen, E. Ger. | C8 | 19 |
| Haining, China | I9 | 32 |
| Hai Phong, Viet. | A3 | 34 |
| Hairy Hill, Alta. | C5 | 68 |
| Haiti, ctry., N.A. | E7 | 64 |
| Haiyang, China | F9 | 32 |
| Haiyuan, China | F1 | 32 |
| Haizhou, China | E8 | 31 |
| Haizhou Bay, b., China | G8 | 32 |
| Hajdúböszörmény, Hung. | B5 | 24 |
| Hajdúhadház, Hung. | B5 | 24 |
| Hajdúnánás, Hung. | B5 | 24 |
| Hajdúszoboszló, Hung. | B5 | 24 |
| Hajiki, Cape, c., Japan | G9 | 33 |
| Hajnowka, Pol. | B7 | 26 |
| Hakalau, Hi., U.S. | D6 | 88 |
| Hakkâri, Tur. | D14 | 40 |
| Hakken, Mount, mtn., Japan | I7 | 33 |
| Hakodate, Japan | C13 | 31 |
| Hākra Branch, stm., Pak. | C4 | 37 |
| Haku, China | m15 | 33 |
| Ḩalabjah, Iraq | D2 | 39 |
| Ḩalā'ib, Eg. | E7 | 43 |
| Halaula, Hi., U.S. | C6 | 88 |
| Halawa, Cape, c., Hi., U.S. | B5 | 88 |
| Halawa Heights, Hi., U.S. | g10 | 88 |
| Halberstadt, E. Ger. | C5 | 18 |
| Halbrite, Sask. | H4 | 75 |
| Halbur, Ia., U.S. | C3 | 92 |
| Halcon, Mount, mtn., Phil. | C6 | 34 |
| Haldeman, Ky., U.S. | B6 | 94 |
| Halden, Nor. | H4 | 14 |
| Haldensleben, E. Ger. | B5 | 18 |
| Haldimand, Ont. | E5 | 73 |
| Haldimand, co., Ont. | E5 | 73 |
| Hale, Co., U.S. | B8 | 83 |
| Hale, Mi., U.S. | D7 | 99 |
| Hale, Mo., U.S. | B4 | 102 |
| Hale, co., Al., U.S. | C2 | 78 |
| Hale, co., Tx., U.S. | B2 | 120 |
| Haleakala Crater, crat., Hi., U.S. | C5 | 88 |
| Haleakala National Park, Hi., U.S. | C6 | 88 |
| Hale Center, Tx., U.S. | B2 | 120 |
| Haledon, N.J., U.S. | *B4 | 107 |
| Haleiwa, Hi., U.S. | B3 | 88 |
| Hales Corners, Wi., U.S. | n11 | 126 |
| Halesowen, Eng., U.K. | B5 | 12 |
| Halesworth, Eng., U.K. | B9 | 12 |
| Halethorpe, Md., U.S. | B4 | 97 |
| Haleyville, Al., U.S. | A2 | 78 |
| Haleyville, N.J., U.S. | E2 | 107 |
| Half Assini, Ghana | G4 | 45 |
| Half Hollow Hills, N.Y., U.S. | *h13 | 109 |
| Half-Moon Bay, N.Z. | Q12 | 51 |
| Half Moon Bay, Ca., U.S. | k8 | 82 |
| Halfway, Ky., U.S. | D3 | 94 |
| Halfway, Md., U.S. | A2 | 97 |
| Halfway, Mo., U.S. | D4 | 102 |
| Half Way, Mo., U.S. | D4 | 102 |
| Halfway, Or., U.S. | C9 | 114 |
| Halfway, stm., B.C. | A6 | 69 |
| Halfway Nunatak, mtn., Ant. | f40 | 7 |
| Ḩalḩūl, Isr. Occ. | C7 | 41 |
| Haliburton, Ont. | B6 | 73 |
| Haliburton, co., Ont. | B6 | 73 |
| Halibut Point, c., Ma., U.S. | A6 | 98 |
| Halifax, N.S. | E6 | 71 |
| Halifax, Eng., U.K. | D6 | 10 |
| Halifax, Ma., U.S. | C6 | 98 |
| Halifax, N.C., U.S. | A5 | 110 |
| Halifax, Pa., U.S. | F8 | 115 |
| Halifax, Vt., U.S. | F3 | 122 |
| Halifax, Va., U.S. | D4 | 123 |
| Halifax, co., N.S. | E6 | 71 |
| Halifax, co., N.C., U.S. | A5 | 110 |
| Halifax, co., Va., U.S. | D4 | 123 |
| Halifax Bay, b., Austl. | C8 | 50 |
| Haliimaile, Hi., U.S. | C5 | 88 |
| Halkirk, Alta. | C4 | 68 |
| Hall, Mt., U.S. | D3 | 103 |
| Hall, N.Y., U.S. | C3 | 109 |
| Hall, co., Ga., U.S. | B3 | 87 |
| Hall, co., Ne., U.S. | D7 | 104 |
| Hall, co., Tx., U.S. | B2 | 120 |
| Halladale, stm., Scot., U.K. | B5 | 13 |
| Hallam, Ne., U.S. | D9 | 104 |
| Hallam Peak, mtn., B.C. | C8 | 69 |
| Halland, co., Swe. | B6 | 15 |
| Hallandale, Fl., U.S. | G6 | 86 |
| Hallands Väderö, i., Swe. | B6 | 15 |
| Hallberg, Man. | k39 | 66 |
| Halle, Bel. | D4 | 17 |
| Halle, W. Ger. | A3 | 19 |
| Halleck, Nv., U.S. | C6 | 105 |
| Hallein, Aus. | E6 | 18 |
| Halle-Neustadt, E. Ger. | *C6 | 18 |
| Hällestad, Swe. | u33 | 14 |
| Hallett, Ok., U.S. | A5 | 113 |
| Hallettsville, Tx., U.S. | E4 | 120 |
| Halley, Ar., U.S. | D4 | 81 |
| Halley Bay, sci., Ant. | B10 | 7 |
| Halliday, N.D., U.S. | B3 | 111 |
| Hallie, Wi., U.S. | D2 | 126 |
| Hallim, S. Kor. | J3 | 33 |
| Hall Island, i., Ak., U.S. | C5 | 79 |
| Hall Meadow Brook, stm., Ct., U.S. | B3 | 84 |
| Hall Meadow Brook Reservoir, res., Ct., U.S. | B3 | 84 |
| Hall Mountain, mtn., Wa., U.S. | A8 | 124 |
| Hallock, Mn., U.S. | B2 | 100 |
| Hallowell, Ks., U.S. | E9 | 93 |
| Hallowell, Me., U.S. | D3 | 96 |
| Hall Peninsula, pen., N.W. Ter. | D19 | 66 |
| Halls, Ga., U.S. | B2 | 87 |
| Halls, Tn., U.S. | B2 | 119 |
| Halls, Tn., U.S. | *C10 | 119 |
| Hallsberg, Swe. | t33 | 14 |
| Hallsboro, N.C., U.S. | C4 | 110 |
| Halls Creek, austl. | C4 | 50 |
| Halls Creek, stm., Ut., U.S. | F5 | 121 |
| Halls Crossroads, Tn., U.S. | m14 | 119 |
| Halls Harbour, N.S. | D5 | 71 |
| Halls Stream, stm., N.H., U.S. | f7 | 106 |
| Halls Summit, Ks., U.S. | D8 | 93 |
| Hallstead, Pa., U.S. | C10 | 115 |
| Hall Summit, La., U.S. | B2 | 95 |
| Hallsville, Mo., U.S. | B5 | 102 |
| Hallsville, Oh., U.S. | C3 | 112 |
| Hallsville, Tx., U.S. | C5 | 120 |
| Hall Top, mtn., Tn., U.S. | D10 | 119 |
| Hallville, Ct., U.S. | D7 | 84 |
| Hallwil Lake, l., Switz. | B4 | 20 |
| Hallwood, Va., U.S. | C7 | 123 |
| Halma, Mn., U.S. | B2 | 100 |
| Halmahera, i., Indon. | E7 | 34 |
| Halmahera Sea, Indon. | F7 | 34 |
| Halmstad, Swe. | I5 | 14 |
| Hals, Den. | B4 | 15 |
| Halsell, Al., U.S. | C1 | 78 |
| Halsey, Ne., U.S. | C5 | 104 |
| Halsey, N.J., U.S. | A3 | 107 |
| Halsey, Or., U.S. | C3 | 114 |
| Hälsö, i., Swe. | A5 | 15 |
| Halstad, Mn., U.S. | C2 | 100 |
| Halstead, Eng., U.K. | C8 | 12 |
| Halstead, Ks., U.S. | E6 | 93 |
| Haltern, W. Ger. | B2 | 19 |
| Haltia, mtn., Eur. | A9 | 14 |
| Haltom City, Tx., U.S. | *n9 | 120 |
| Halton, co., Ont. | D5 | 73 |
| Halton Hills, Ont. | D5 | 73 |
| Haltwhistle, Eng., U.K. | F6 | 13 |
| Ham, Fr. | E3 | 17 |
| Hamada, Japan | I6 | 33 |
| Hamadān, Iran | B4 | 38 |
| Hamāh, Syria | B3 | 38 |
| Hamahika Island, i., Japan | O5 | 52 |
| Hamamatsu, Japan | E12 | 31 |
| Hamar, Nor. | G4 | 14 |
| Hama-tombetsu, Japan | D11 | 33 |
| Hambantota, Sri L. | G7 | 36 |
| Hamberg, N.D., U.S. | B6 | 111 |
| Hamber Provincial Park, B.C. | C8 | 69 |
| Hamblen, co., Tn., U.S. | C10 | 119 |
| Hamburg, W. Ger. | B5 | 18 |
| Hamburg, Ar., U.S. | D4 | 81 |
| Hamburg, Ia., U.S. | D6 | 84 |
| Hamburg, Ia., U.S. | D2 | 92 |
| Hamburg, Ms., U.S. | D2 | 101 |
| Hamburg, N.Y., U.S. | A3 | 109 |
| Hamburg, N.Y., U.S. | C2 | 109 |
| Hamburg, Wi., U.S. | C4 | 126 |
| Hamburg, state, W. Ger. | E4 | 15 |
| Hamburg Mountains, mts., N.J., U.S. | A3 | 107 |
| Ḩamd, Wādī al, val., Sau. Ar. | C3 | 38 |
| Hamden, Ct., U.S. | D4 | 84 |
| Hamden, N.Y., U.S. | C6 | 109 |
| Hamden, Oh., U.S. | C3 | 112 |
| Hämeenlinna, Fin. | G11 | 14 |
| Hamel, Mn., U.S. | m11 | 100 |
| Hameln, W. Ger. | B4 | 18 |
| Hamer, Id., U.S. | F6 | 89 |
| Hamer, S.C., U.S. | C9 | 117 |
| Hamersley Range, mts., Austl. | D2 | 50 |
| Hamersville, Oh., U.S. | D2 | 112 |
| Hamhŭng, N. Kor. | G3 | 33 |
| Hami, China | C3 | 31 |
| Hamill, S.D., U.S. | D6 | 118 |
| Hamilton, Austl. | G8 | 51 |
| Hamilton, Ber. | p20 | 64 |
| Hamilton, Ont. | D5 | 73 |
| Hamilton, N.Z. | L15 | 51 |
| Hamilton, Scot., U.K. | C4 | 10 |
| Hamilton, Al., U.S. | A2 | 78 |
| Hamilton, Ak., U.S. | C7 | 79 |
| Hamilton, Co., U.S. | A3 | 83 |
| Hamilton, Ga., U.S. | D2 | 87 |
| Hamilton, Il., U.S. | C2 | 90 |
| Hamilton, In., U.S. | A8 | 91 |
| Hamilton, Ia., U.S. | C5 | 92 |
| Hamilton, Ks., U.S. | E7 | 93 |
| Hamilton, Ma., U.S. | A6 | 98 |
| Hamilton, Mi., U.S. | F4 | 99 |
| Hamilton, Ms., U.S. | B5 | 101 |
| Hamilton, Mo., U.S. | B3 | 102 |
| Hamilton, Mt., U.S. | D2 | 103 |
| Hamilton, N.Y., U.S. | C5 | 109 |
| Hamilton, N.C., U.S. | B5 | 110 |
| Hamilton, N.D., U.S. | A8 | 111 |
| Hamilton, Oh., U.S. | C1 | 112 |
| Hamilton, Or., U.S. | C7 | 114 |
| Hamilton, R.I., U.S. | E4 | 116 |
| Hamilton, Tx., U.S. | D3 | 120 |
| Hamilton, Va., U.S. | A5 | 123 |
| Hamilton, Wa., U.S. | A4 | 124 |
| Hamilton, co., Fl., U.S. | B3 | 86 |
| Hamilton, co., Il., U.S. | E5 | 90 |
| Hamilton, co., In., U.S. | D5 | 91 |
| Hamilton, co., Ia., U.S. | B4 | 92 |
| Hamilton, co., Ks., U.S. | E2 | 93 |
| Hamilton, co., Ne., U.S. | D7 | 104 |
| Hamilton, co., N.Y., U.S. | B6 | 109 |
| Hamilton, co., Oh., U.S. | C1 | 112 |
| Hamilton, co., Tn., U.S. | D8 | 119 |
| Hamilton, co., Tx., U.S. | D3 | 120 |
| Hamilton, Lake, res., Ar., U.S. | C2 | 81 |
| Hamilton, Mount, mtn., Ak., U.S. | C8 | 79 |
| Hamilton, Mount, mtn., Ca., U.S. | k9 | 82 |
| Hamilton, Mount, mtn., Nv., U.S. | D6 | 105 |
| Hamilton City, Ca., U.S. | C2 | 82 |
| Hamilton Dome, Wy., U.S. | C4 | 127 |
| Hamilton Inlet, b., Newf. | A2 | 72 |
| Hamilton Mountain, mtn., N.Y., U.S. | B6 | 109 |
| Hamilton Reservoir, res., Ma., U.S. | B3 | 98 |
| Hamilton Sound, strt., Newf. | D4 | 72 |
| Hamilton Square, N.J., U.S. | C3 | 107 |
| Hamina, Fin. | G12 | 14 |
| Hamīrpur, India | C7 | 36 |
| Hamjong-ni, N. Kor. | G2 | 33 |
| Ham Lake, Mn., U.S. | *m12 | 100 |
| Hamler, Oh., U.S. | A1 | 112 |
| Hamlet, In., U.S. | B4 | 91 |
| Hamlet, Ne., U.S. | D4 | 104 |
| Hamlet, N.C., U.S. | C3 | 110 |
| Hamlet, Mount, mtn., Ak., U.S. | B6 | 79 |
| Hamletsburg, Il., U.S. | F5 | 90 |
| Hamlin, Ks., U.S. | C8 | 93 |
| Hamlin, Pa., U.S. | D11 | 115 |
| Hamlin, Tx., U.S. | C2 | 120 |
| Hamlin, W.V., U.S. | C2 | 125 |
| Hamlin, co., S.D., U.S. | C8 | 118 |
| Hamlin, Lake, l., Mi., U.S. | D4 | 99 |
| Hammam Lif, Tun. | B7 | 44 |
| Hammām, Ḩawr al, l., Iraq | F3 | 39 |
| Hammamet, Tun. | B7 | 44 |
| Hammarby, Swe. | t35 | 14 |
| Hammarsjön, l., Swe. | C8 | 15 |
| Hamme, Bel. | C4 | 17 |
| Hammel, Den. | B3 | 15 |
| Hammelburg, W. Ger. | C4 | 19 |
| Hammerfest, Nor. | B10 | 14 |
| Hamm [in Westfalen], W. Ger. | C3 | 18 |
| Hammonasset, stm., Ct., U.S. | D5 | 84 |
| Hammonasset Point, c., Ct., U.S. | E5 | 84 |
| Hammond, Il., U.S. | D5 | 90 |
| Hammond, In., U.S. | A2 | 91 |
| Hammond, La., U.S. | D5 | 95 |
| Hammond, Mn., U.S. | F6 | 100 |
| Hammond, Mt., U.S. | E12 | 103 |
| Hammond, N.Y., U.S. | f9 | 109 |
| Hammond, Or., U.S. | A3 | 114 |
| Hammond, Wi., U.S. | D1 | 126 |
| Hammond Bay, b., Mi., U.S. | C6 | 99 |
| Hammondsport, N.Y., U.S. | C3 | 109 |
| Hammonton, N.J., U.S. | D3 | 107 |
| Hamneda, Swe. | B7 | 15 |
| Ham-Nord, Que. | D6 | 74 |
| Hamoyet, Jabal, mtn., Afr. | B4 | 47 |
| Hampden, Newf. | D3 | 72 |
| Hampden, N.Z. | P13 | 51 |
| Hampden, Me., U.S. | D4 | 96 |
| Hampden, co., Ma., U.S. | B2 | 98 |
| Hampden Highlands, Me., U.S. | D4 | 96 |
| Hampshire, Il., U.S. | A5 | 90 |
| Hampshire, co., Eng., U.K. | C6 | 12 |
| Hampshire, co., Ma., U.S. | B2 | 98 |
| Hampshire, co., W.V., U.S. | B6 | 125 |
| Hampstead (part of London), Eng., U.K. | k12 | 12 |
| Hampstead, Md., U.S. | A4 | 97 |
| Hampstead, N.C., U.S. | C5 | 110 |
| Hampstead, N.H., U.S. | E4 | 106 |
| Hampton, N.B. | D4 | 71 |
| Hampton, Ar., U.S. | D3 | 81 |
| Hampton, Ct., U.S. | B7 | 84 |
| Hampton, Fl., U.S. | C4 | 86 |
| Hampton, Ia., U.S. | B4 | 92 |
| Hampton, Ky., U.S. | e9 | 94 |
| Hampton, Ne., U.S. | D8 | 104 |
| Hampton, N.H., U.S. | E5 | 106 |
| Hampton, N.J., U.S. | B3 | 107 |
| Hampton, S.C., U.S. | F5 | 117 |
| Hampton, Tn., U.S. | C11 | 119 |
| Hampton, Va., U.S. | C6 | 123 |
| Hampton, co., S.C., U.S. | F5 | 117 |
| Hampton Bays, N.Y., U.S. | n16 | 109 |
| Hampton Beach, N.H., U.S. | E5 | 106 |
| Hampton Butte, mtn., Or., U.S. | D6 | 114 |
| Hampton Falls, N.H., U.S. | E5 | 106 |
| Hampton Roads, anch., Va., U.S. | k15 | 123 |
| Hampton Roads Bridge-Tunnel, Va., U.S. | k15 | 123 |
| Ḩamrā, Al Ḩammādah al, pl., Libya | B2 | 42 |
| Hams Fork, stm., Wy., U.S. | E2 | 127 |
| Ham-sud, Que. | D6 | 74 |
| Ham-Tan, Viet. | G7 | 35 |
| Hamtramck, Mi., U.S. | p15 | 99 |
| Hamyang, S. Kor. | I3 | 33 |
| Han, stm., Asia | H4 | 33 |
| Hana, Hi., U.S. | C6 | 88 |
| Hanahan, S.C., U.S. | F7 | 117 |
| Hanalei, Hi., U.S. | A2 | 88 |
| Hanalei Bay, b., Hi., U.S. | A2 | 88 |
| Hanamaki, Japan | G10 | 33 |
| Hanamaulu, Hi., U.S. | B2 | 88 |
| Hanapepe, Hi., U.S. | B2 | 88 |
| Hanau, W. Ger. | C4 | 18 |
| Hanceville, B.C. | D6 | 69 |
| Hanceville, Al., U.S. | A3 | 78 |
| Hancheng, China | G4 | 32 |
| Hancock, Ia., U.S. | C2 | 92 |
| Hancock, Me., U.S. | D4 | 96 |
| Hancock, Md., U.S. | A1 | 97 |
| Hancock, Mi., U.S. | A2 | 99 |
| Hancock, Mn., U.S. | E3 | 100 |
| Hancock, N.H., U.S. | E3 | 106 |
| Hancock, N.Y., U.S. | D5 | 109 |
| Hancock, Vt., U.S. | D3 | 122 |
| Hancock, W.V., U.S. | B6 | 125 |
| Hancock, Wi., U.S. | D4 | 126 |
| Hancock, co., Ga., U.S. | C3 | 87 |
| Hancock, co., Il., U.S. | C2 | 90 |
| Hancock, co., In., U.S. | E6 | 91 |
| Hancock, co., Ia., U.S. | A4 | 92 |
| Hancock, co., Ky., U.S. | C3 | 94 |
| Hancock, co., Me., U.S. | D4 | 96 |
| Hancock, co., Ms., U.S. | E4 | 101 |
| Hancock, co., Oh., U.S. | A2 | 112 |
| Hancock, co., Tn., U.S. | C10 | 119 |
| Hancock, co., W.V., U.S. | A4 | 125 |
| Hancock Pond, l., Me., U.S. | E2 | 96 |
| Hancocks Bridge, N.J., U.S. | D2 | 107 |
| Hand, co., S.D., U.S. | C6 | 118 |
| Handa, Japan | o15 | 33 |
| Handa, Som. | C7 | 47 |
| Handa, i., Scot., U.K. | B3 | 13 |
| Handan, China | D7 | 31 |
| Handaqi, China | A3 | 33 |
| Handel, Sask. | E1 | 75 |
| Handeni, Tan. | C6 | 48 |
| Handley, W.V., U.S. | m13 | 125 |
| Hando, China | A7 | 41 |
| Handsworth, Sask. | H4 | 75 |
| Hanford, Ca., U.S. | D4 | 82 |
| Hangchou see Hangzhou, China | E9 | 31 |
| Hangchow Bay see Hangzhou Bay, b., China | I9 | 32 |
| Hangelsberg, E. Ger. | F7 | 15 |
| Hanging Rock, Oh., U.S. | D3 | 112 |
| Hangingstone, stm., Alta | A5 | 68 |
| Hangman Creek, stm., Wa., U.S. | B8 | 124 |
| Hangö, Fin. | H10 | 14 |
| Hangu, China | *D8 | 31 |
| Hangzhou (Hangchou), China | E9 | 31 |
| Hangzhou Bay, b., China | I9 | 32 |
| HaNiqra, Rosh, c., Asia | A7 | 41 |
| Hanita, Isr. | A7 | 41 |
| Hankinson, N.D., U.S. | C9 | 111 |
| Hanks, N.D., U.S. | A2 | 111 |
| Hanksville, Ut., U.S. | E5 | 121 |
| Hanley, Sask. | F2 | 75 |
| Hanley Falls, Mn., U.S. | F3 | 100 |
| Hanlontown, Ia., U.S. | A4 | 92 |
| Hann, Mount, mtn., Austl. | C4 | 50 |
| Hanna, Alta. | D5 | 68 |
| Hanna, In., U.S. | B4 | 91 |
| Hanna, Ok., U.S. | B6 | 113 |
| Hanna, Ut., U.S. | C5 | 121 |
| Hanna, Wy., U.S. | E6 | 127 |
| Hanna City, Il., U.S. | C4 | 90 |
| Hannaford, N.D., U.S. | B7 | 111 |
| Hannah, N.D., U.S. | A7 | 111 |
| Hannahville Indian Reservation, Mi., U.S. | C3 | 99 |
| Hannawa Falls, N.Y., U.S. | f10 | 109 |
| Hannibal, Mo., U.S. | B6 | 102 |
| Hannibal, N.Y., U.S. | B4 | 109 |
| Hannibal, Oh., U.S. | C5 | 112 |
| Hannover, W. Ger. | B4 | 18 |
| Hanöbukten, b., Swe. | J6 | 14 |
| Hanoi (Ha Noi), Viet. | A3 | 34 |
| Hanover, Ont. | C3 | 73 |
| Hanover, Il., U.S. | B3 | 81 |
| Hanover, In., U.S. | A3 | 90 |
| Hanover, Ks., U.S. | G7 | 91 |
| Hanover, Ma., U.S. | C7 | 93 |
| Hanover, Mn., U.S. | B6 | 98 |
| Hanover, N.H., U.S. | F6 | 100 |
| Hanover, Pa., U.S. | G8 | 115 |
| Hanover, Va., U.S. | C5 | 123 |
| Hanover, co., Va., U.S. | C5 | 123 |
| Hanover, hist. reg., W. Ger. | B4 | 18 |
| Hanover, Isla, i., Chile | E2 | 54 |
| Hanover Center, Ma., U.S. | h12 | 98 |
| Hanover Center, N.H., U.S. | C2 | 106 |
| Hanover Park, Il., U.S. | k8 | 90 |
| Hanoverton, Oh., U.S. | B5 | 112 |
| Hanover Township, N.J., U.S. | B4 | 107 |
| Hansard, B.C. | B7 | 69 |
| Hansboro, N.D., U.S. | A6 | 111 |
| Hansell, Ia., U.S. | B4 | 92 |
| Hansen, Id., U.S. | G4 | 89 |
| Hansford, co., Tx., U.S. | A2 | 120 |
| Han Shui, stm., China | E7 | 31 |
| Hanson, Ky., U.S. | C2 | 94 |
| Hanson, Ma., U.S. | *B6 | 98 |
| Hanson, Ok., U.S. | B7 | 113 |
| Hanson, co., S.D., U.S. | D8 | 118 |
| Hanson, Lake, l., Sask. | D1 | 75 |
| Hansted (Hanstholm), Den. | A2 | 15 |
| Hants, co., N.S. | D6 | 71 |
| Hant's Harbour, Newf. | D5 | 72 |
| Hantsport, N.S. | D5 | 71 |
| Hanumangarh, India | C5 | 37 |
| Hanyin, China | H3 | 32 |
| Hanzhong, China | E8 | 31 |
| Hāora, India | D8 | 36 |
| Haparanda, Swe. | E10 | 14 |
| Hapeville, Ga., U.S. | C2 | 87 |
| Happy, Tx., U.S. | B2 | 120 |
| Happy Camp, Ca., U.S. | B2 | 82 |
| Happy Corner, N.H., U.S. | f7 | 106 |
| Happy Jack, Az., U.S. | C4 | 80 |
| Happyland, Sask. | G1 | 75 |
| Happy Valley, N.M., U.S. | E5 | 108 |
| Happy Valley-Goose Bay, Newf. | B1 | 72 |
| Hapsu, N. Kor. | F4 | 33 |
| Ḩaql, Sau. Ar. | C3 | 38 |
| Ḩaraḍ, Sau. Ar. | C4 | 38 |
| Hārādbāck, Swe. | B8 | 15 |
| Harahan, La., U.S. | k11 | 95 |
| Haralson, co., Ga., U.S. | C1 | 87 |
| Harare, Zimb. | A5 | 49 |
| Ḩarash, Bi'r al, well, Libya | D5 | 86 |
| Haraze, Chad | D4 | 46 |
| Harbeson, De., U.S. | F4 | 85 |
| Harbin (Haerhpin), China | B10 | 31 |
| Harbinger, N.C., U.S. | A7 | 110 |
| Harboør, Den. | B2 | 15 |
| Harbor, Or., U.S. | E2 | 114 |
| Harbor Beach, Mi., U.S. | E8 | 99 |
| Harborcreek, Pa., U.S. | B2 | 115 |
| Harbor Springs, Mi., U.S. | C6 | 99 |
| Harborton, Va., U.S. | C7 | 123 |
| Harbor View, Oh., U.S. | e7 | 112 |
| Harbour Breton, Newf. | E4 | 72 |
| Harbour Buffett, Newf. | E4 | 72 |
| Harbour Deep, Newf. | C3 | 72 |
| Harbour Grace, Newf. | E5 | 72 |
| Harbour Mille, Newf. | E4 | 72 |
| Harbourton, N.J., U.S. | C3 | 107 |
| Harbourville, N.S. | D5 | 71 |
| Harburg (part of Hamburg), W. Ger. | B5 | 18 |
| Hårby, Den. | C4 | 15 |
| Harcourt, N.B. | B4 | 71 |
| Harcourt, Ia., U.S. | B3 | 92 |
| Harcuvar Mountains, mts., Az., U.S. | D2 | 80 |
| Harda, India | I7 | 36 |
| Hardangerfjorden, Nor. | H1 | 14 |
| Hardangerjøkulen, ice, Nor. | G2 | 14 |
| Hardangervidda, plat., Nor. | G2 | 14 |
| Hardaway, Al., U.S. | C4 | 78 |
| Hardeeville, S.C., U.S. | G5 | 117 |
| Harden City, Ok., U.S. | C5 | 113 |
| Hardeman, co., Tn., U.S. | B2 | 119 |
| Hardeman, co., Tx., U.S. | B3 | 120 |
| Hardenberg, Neth. | B6 | 17 |
| Harderwijk, Neth. | B5 | 17 |
| Hardesty, Ok., U.S. | e9 | 113 |
| Hardin, Il., U.S. | D3 | 90 |
| Hardin, Ky., U.S. | f9 | 94 |
| Hardin, Mo., U.S. | B4 | 102 |
| Hardin, Mt., U.S. | E9 | 103 |
| Hardin, co., Il., U.S. | F5 | 90 |
| Hardin, co., Ia., U.S. | B4 | 92 |
| Hardin, co., Ky., U.S. | C4 | 94 |
| Hardin, co., Oh., U.S. | B2 | 112 |
| Hardin, co., Tn., U.S. | B3 | 119 |
| Hardin, co., Tx., U.S. | D5 | 120 |
| Harding, Mn., U.S. | D4 | 100 |
| Harding, W.V., U.S. | C5 | 125 |
| Harding, co., N.M., U.S. | B5 | 108 |
| Harding, co., S.D., U.S. | B2 | 118 |
| Harding, Lake, res., U.S. | C4 | 78 |
| Harding Lake, l., Man. | B3 | 70 |
| HaNiqra, Rosh, c., Asia | A7 | 41 |
| Hardinsburg, In., U.S. | H5 | 91 |
| Hardinsburg, Ky., U.S. | C3 | 94 |
| Hardinville, Il., U.S. | E6 | 90 |
| Hardisty, Alta. | C5 | 68 |
| Hardisty Lake, l., N.W. Ter. | D9 | 66 |
| Hardman, Or., U.S. | B7 | 114 |
| Hardoi, India | D8 | 37 |
| Hardshell, Ky., U.S. | C6 | 94 |
| Hardtner, Ks., U.S. | E5 | 93 |
| Hardwick, Ga., U.S. | C3 | 87 |
| Hardwick, Mn., U.S. | G2 | 100 |
| Hardwick, Vt., U.S. | B4 | 122 |
| Hardwick, Vt., U.S. | B5 | 71 |
| Hardwood Ridge, mtn., Pa., U.S. | D11 | 115 |
| Hardy, Sask. | H3 | 75 |
| Hardy, Ar., U.S. | A4 | 81 |
| Hardy, Ms., U.S. | B3 | 101 |
| Hardy, Ne., U.S. | D8 | 104 |
| Hardy, Ok., U.S. | A5 | 113 |
| Hardy, co., W.V., U.S. | B5 | 125 |
| Hardy Lake, res., In., U.S. | G6 | 91 |
| Hare Bay, Newf. | C4 | 72 |
| Hare Bay, b., Newf. | C4 | 72 |
| Haren, Neth. | B6 | 17 |
| Harer (Harar), Eth. | D5 | 47 |
| Harerge, prov., Eth. | C6 | 47 |
| Harfleur, Fr. | C4 | 16 |
| Harford, Pa., U.S. | C10 | 115 |
| Harford, co., Md., U.S. | A5 | 97 |
| Hargeysa, Som. | B8 | 48 |
| Harghita, mtn., Rom. | B7 | 24 |
| Hargill, Tx., U.S. | F3 | 120 |
| Hargrave, Man. | E1 | 70 |
| Hargrave, stm., Man. | B2 | 70 |
| Hargrave Lake, l., Man. | B2 | 70 |
| Hari, stm., China | F2 | 34 |
| Haridwār, India | C6 | 36 |
| Harlan, Ia., U.S. | C2 | 92 |
| Harlan, Ky., U.S. | D6 | 94 |
| Harlan, co., Ky., U.S. | D6 | 94 |
| Harlan, co., Ne., U.S. | D6 | 104 |
| Harlan County Lake, res., Ne., U.S. | E6 | 104 |
| Harlech, Wales, U.K. | I8 | 13 |
| Harlem, Ga., U.S. | C4 | 87 |
| Harlem, Mt., U.S. | B8 | 103 |
| Harleton, Tx., U.S. | C5 | 120 |
| Harleysville, Pa., U.S. | F11 | 115 |
| Harlingen, Neth. | B5 | 17 |
| Harlingen, Tx., U.S. | F4 | 120 |
| Harlow, Eng., U.K. | k13 | 11 |
| Harlow, N.D., U.S. | A6 | 111 |
| Harlowton, Mt., U.S. | D7 | 103 |
| Harmans, Md., U.S. | B4 | 97 |
| Harmarville, Pa., U.S. | h14 | 115 |
| Harmon, Ok., U.S. | B7 | 113 |
| Harmon, co., Ok., U.S. | C2 | 113 |
| Harmon Creek, stm., W.V., U.S. | f8 | 125 |
| Harmony, Ca., U.S. | E3 | 82 |
| Harmony, In., U.S. | E3 | 91 |
| Harmony, Mn., U.S. | G6 | 100 |
| Harmony, Pa., U.S. | E1 | 115 |
| Harmony, R.I., U.S. | B3 | 116 |
| Harmony, Va., U.S. | D4 | 123 |
| Harmony, Wi., U.S. | F5 | 126 |
| Harmony Grove, Ar., U.S. | A4 | 81 |
| Harmony Hills, De., U.S. | *B3 | 85 |
| Harmonyvale, Vt., U.S. | C3 | 122 |
| Harmony, Tn., U.S. | B5 | 119 |
| Harned, Ky., U.S. | C3 | 94 |
| Harnett, co., N.C., U.S. | B4 | 110 |
| Harney, Md., U.S. | A3 | 97 |
| Harney, co., Or., U.S. | D7 | 114 |
| Harney, Lake, l., Fl., U.S. | D5 | 86 |
| Harney Lake, l., Or., U.S. | D7 | 114 |
| Harney Peak, mtn., S.D., U.S. | D2 | 118 |
| Härnösand, Swe. | F8 | 14 |
| Haro, Spain | A4 | 22 |
| Haro, Cabo, c., Mex. | B2 | 63 |
| Harold, Fl., U.S. | u15 | 86 |
| Harold Pond, l., Bah. | m17 | 64 |
| Haro Strait, strt., Wa., U.S. | A2 | 124 |
| Harper, Lib. | F3 | 45 |
| Harper, Ia., U.S. | C5 | 92 |
| Harper, Ks., U.S. | E5 | 93 |
| Harper, Or., U.S. | D9 | 114 |
| Harper, Tx., U.S. | D3 | 120 |
| Harper, Wa., U.S. | e10 | 124 |
| Harper, co., Ks., U.S. | E5 | 93 |
| Harper, co., Ok., U.S. | A2 | 113 |
| Harper, Mount, mtn., Ak., U.S. | C11 | 79 |
| Harpers Ferry, Ia., U.S. | A6 | 92 |
| Harpers Ferry, W.V., U.S. | B7 | 125 |
| Harpers Ferry National Historical Park, W.V., U.S. | B7 | 125 |
| Harpersville, Al., U.S. | B3 | 78 |
| Harperville, Ms., U.S. | C4 | 101 |
| Harper Woods, Mi., U.S. | *p16 | 99 |
| Harpeth, stm., Tn., U.S. | A5 | 119 |
| Harpster, Oh., U.S. | B2 | 112 |
| Harpswell Center, Me., U.S. | *E3 | 96 |
| Harptree, Sask. | H3 | 75 |
| Harquahala Mountain, mtn., Az., U.S. | D2 | 80 |
| Harquahala Mountains, mts., Az., U.S. | D2 | 80 |
| Harrah, Ok., U.S. | B4 | 113 |
| Harrah, Wa., U.S. | C5 | 124 |
| Harray, Loch of, l., Scot., U.K. | A5 | 13 |
| Harrell, Ar., U.S. | D3 | 81 |
| Harricana, stm., Can. | F17 | 66 |
| Harriet, Ar., U.S. | B3 | 81 |
| Harriet, Mi., U.S. | D5 | 99 |
| Harriettsville, Oh., U.S. | C4 | 112 |
| Harriman, Tn., U.S. | D9 | 119 |
| Harriman, Wy., U.S. | E7 | 127 |
| Harriman Reservoir, res., Vt., U.S. | F3 | 122 |
| Harrington, De., U.S. | E8 | 85 |
| Harrington, Wa., U.S. | B7 | 124 |
| Harrington Park, N.J., U.S. | h9 | 107 |
| Harrington Pond, l., Me., U.S. | B4 | 96 |
| Harrington Sound, strt., Ber. | o20 | 64 |
| Harriott Lake, l., Sask. | A4 | 75 |
| Harris, Sask. | F2 | 75 |
| Harris, Scot., U.K. | B3 | 10 |
| Harris, Ia., U.S. | A2 | 92 |
| Harris, Mn., U.S. | E6 | 100 |
| Harris, Mo., U.S. | A4 | 102 |
| Harris, Ok., U.S. | D7 | 113 |
| Harris, R.I., U.S. | D3 | 116 |
| Harris, co., Ga., U.S. | D2 | 87 |
| Harris, co., Tx., U.S. | E5 | 120 |
| Harris, Lake, l., Fl., U.S. | D5 | 86 |
| Harris, Sound of, strt., Scot., U.K. | C1 | 13 |
| Harrisburg, Ar., U.S. | B5 | 81 |
| Harrisburg, Il., U.S. | F5 | 90 |
| Harrisburg, Ne., U.S. | C2 | 104 |
| Harrisburg, Oh., U.S. | m10 | 112 |
| Harrisburg, Or., U.S. | C3 | 114 |
| Harrisburg, Pa., U.S. | F8 | 115 |
| Harrisburg, S.D., U.S. | D9 | 118 |
| Harris Grove, Ia., U.S. | h15 | 123 |
| Harris Hill, N.Y., U.S. | *C2 | 109 |
| Harris Hill, hill, Ma., U.S. | A3 | 98 |
| Harrismith, S. Afr. | C4 | 49 |
| Harrison, Ar., U.S. | A2 | 81 |
| Harrison, Id., U.S. | B2 | 89 |
| Harrison, Mi., U.S. | D6 | 99 |
| Harrison, N.J., U.S. | k8 | 107 |
| Harrison, N.Y., U.S. | h13 | 109 |
| Harrison, Oh., U.S. | C1 | 112 |
| Harrison, S.D., U.S. | D7 | 118 |
| Harrison, Tn., U.S. | h11 | 119 |
| Harrison, co., In., U.S. | H5 | 91 |
| Harrison, co., Ia., U.S. | C2 | 92 |
| Harrison, co., Ky., U.S. | B5 | 94 |
| Harrison, co., Ms., U.S. | E4 | 101 |
| Harrison, co., Mo., U.S. | A3 | 102 |
| Harrison, co., Oh., U.S. | B4 | 112 |
| Harrison, co., Tx., U.S. | C5 | 120 |
| Harrison, co., W.V., U.S. | B4 | 125 |
| Harrison Bay, b., Ak., U.S. | A9 | 79 |
| Harrisonburg, La., U.S. | C4 | 95 |
| Harrisonburg, Va., U.S. | B4 | 123 |
| Harrison Hot Springs, B.C. | f14 | 69 |
| Harrison Lake, l., B.C. | E7 | 69 |
| Harrison Township, Mi., U.S. | *F8 | 99 |
| Harrison Valley, Pa., U.S. | C6 | 115 |
| Harrisonville, Il., U.S. | E3 | 90 |
| Harrisonville, Mo., U.S. | C3 | 102 |
| Harrisonville, Pa., U.S. | G6 | 115 |
| Harriston, Ont. | D4 | 73 |
| Harriston, Ms., U.S. | D2 | 101 |
| Harristown, Il., U.S. | D4 | 90 |
| Harrisville, Mi., U.S. | D7 | 99 |
| Harrisville, Ms., U.S. | D3 | 101 |
| Harrisville, N.H., U.S. | E3 | 106 |
| Harrisville, N.Y., U.S. | A5 | 109 |
| Harrisville, R.I., U.S. | B2 | 116 |
| Harrisville, W.V., U.S. | B3 | 125 |
| Harrod, Oh., U.S. | B2 | 112 |
| Harrodsburg, In., U.S. | F4 | 91 |
| Harrodsburg, Ky., U.S. | C5 | 94 |
| Harrods Creek, stm., Ky., U.S. | g11 | 94 |
| Harrogate, Eng., U.K. | C6 | 10 |
| Harrold, S.D., U.S. | C6 | 118 |
| Harrow, Ont. | E2 | 73 |
| Harrowby, Man. | D1 | 70 |
| Harrowsmith, Ont. | C8 | 73 |
| Harrys, stm., Newf. | D2 | 72 |
| Harry S. Truman Reservoir, res., Mo., U.S. | C4 | 102 |
| Harry Strunk Lake, res., Ne., U.S. | D5 | 104 |
| Harsīn, Iran | B4 | 38 |
| Harstad, Nor. | C7 | 14 |
| Hart, Mi., U.S. | E4 | 99 |
| Hart, Tx., U.S. | B1 | 120 |
| Hart, co., Ga., U.S. | B4 | 87 |

| Name | Map Ref. | Page |
|---|---|---|
| Hart, co., Ky., U.S. | C4 | 94 |
| Hart, Lake, l., Fl., U.S. | D5 | 86 |
| Hartell, Alta. | D3 | 68 |
| Hartfield, Va., U.S. | C6 | 123 |
| Hartford, Al., U.S. | D4 | 78 |
| Hartford, Ar., U.S. | B1 | 81 |
| Hartford, Ct., U.S. | B5 | 84 |
| Hartford, Il., U.S. | E3 | 90 |
| Hartford, In., U.S. | *G8 | 91 |
| Hartford, Ia., U.S. | C4 | 92 |
| Hartford, Ks., U.S. | D8 | 93 |
| Hartford, Ky., U.S. | C3 | 94 |
| Hartford, Me., U.S. | D2 | 96 |
| Hartford, Mi., U.S. | F4 | 99 |
| Hartford, N.J., U.S. | D3 | 107 |
| Hartford, N.Y., U.S. | B7 | 109 |
| Hartford, S.D., U.S. | D9 | 118 |
| Hartford, Tn., U.S. | D10 | 119 |
| Hartford, Vt., U.S. | D4 | 122 |
| Hartford, W.V., U.S. | C3 | 125 |
| Hartford, Wi., U.S. | E5 | 126 |
| Hartford, co., Ct., U.S. | B4 | 84 |
| Hartford City, In., U.S. | D7 | 91 |
| Hartha, E. Ger. | B7 | 19 |
| Hartington, Ne., U.S. | B8 | 104 |
| Hart Island, i., Md., U.S. | B5 | 97 |
| Hart Lake, l., Or., U.S. | E7 | 114 |
| Hartland, N.B. | C2 | 71 |
| Hartland, Me., U.S. | D3 | 96 |
| Hartland, Mi., U.S. | F7 | 99 |
| Hartland, Mn., U.S. | G5 | 100 |
| Hartland, Vt., U.S. | D4 | 122 |
| Hartland, W.V., U.S. | m13 | 125 |
| Hartland, Wi., U.S. | E5 | 126 |
| Hartland Four Corners, Vt., U.S. | D4 | 122 |
| Hartland Point, c., Eng., U.K. | E4 | 12 |
| Hartlepool, Eng., U.K. | C6 | 10 |
| Hartley, Ia., U.S. | A2 | 92 |
| Hartley, Tx., U.S. | B1 | 120 |
| Hartley, co., Tx., U.S. | B1 | 120 |
| Hartline, Wa., U.S. | B6 | 124 |
| Hartly, De., U.S. | D3 | 85 |
| Hartman, Ar., U.S. | B2 | 81 |
| Hartman, Co., U.S. | C8 | 83 |
| Hart Mountain, mtn., Man. | C1 | 70 |
| Hartney, Man. | E1 | 70 |
| Hartsburg, Il., U.S. | C4 | 90 |
| Hartsburg, Mo., U.S. | C5 | 102 |
| Hartsdale, N.Y., U.S. | *n15 | 109 |
| Hartsel, Co., U.S. | B5 | 83 |
| Hartselle, Al., U.S. | A3 | 78 |
| Hartsfield, Ga., U.S. | E3 | 87 |
| Hartshorn, Mo., U.S. | D6 | 102 |
| Hartshorne, Ok., U.S. | C6 | 113 |
| Hartsville, In., U.S. | F6 | 91 |
| Hartsville, S.C., U.S. | C7 | 117 |
| Hartsville, Tn., U.S. | A5 | 119 |
| Hartuv, Isr. | h11 | 41 |
| Hartville, Mo., U.S. | D5 | 102 |
| Hartville, Oh., U.S. | B4 | 112 |
| Hartville, Wy., U.S. | D8 | 127 |
| Hartwell, Ga., U.S. | B4 | 87 |
| Hartwell Lake, res., U.S. | B1 | 117 |
| Hartwick, Ia., U.S. | C5 | 92 |
| Hartwick, N.Y., U.S. | C5 | 109 |
| Har Us Lake, l., Mong. | B3 | 31 |
| Hārūt, stm., Afg. | E10 | 39 |
| Harvard, Id., U.S. | C2 | 89 |
| Harvard, Il., U.S. | A5 | 90 |
| Harvard, Ia., U.S. | D4 | 92 |
| Harvard, Ma., U.S. | B4 | 98 |
| Harvard, Ne., U.S. | D7 | 104 |
| Harvard, Mount, mtn., Co., U.S. | C4 | 83 |
| Harvel, Il., U.S. | D4 | 90 |
| Harvest, Al., U.S. | A3 | 78 |
| Harvey, N.B. | D3 | 71 |
| Harvey, N.B. | D5 | 71 |
| Harvey, Il., U.S. | B6 | 90 |
| Harvey, Ia., U.S. | C5 | 92 |
| Harvey, La., U.S. | E5 | 95 |
| Harvey, Mi., U.S. | B3 | 99 |
| Harvey, N.D., U.S. | B6 | 111 |
| Harvey, W.V., U.S. | n13 | 125 |
| Harvey, co., Ks., U.S. | D6 | 93 |
| Harvey, Lake, res., Pa., U.S. | m16 | 115 |
| Harvey Mountain, mtn., U.S. | B1 | 98 |
| Harveysburg, Oh., U.S. | C1 | 112 |
| Harveys Creek, stm., Pa., U.S. | n16 | 115 |
| Harveyville, Ks., U.S. | D8 | 93 |
| Harviell, Mo., U.S. | E7 | 102 |
| Harwich, Eng., U.K. | E7 | 10 |
| Harwich, Ma., U.S. | C7 | 98 |
| Harwich Port, Ma., U.S. | C7 | 98 |
| Harwinton, Ct., U.S. | B3 | 84 |
| Harwood, Ont. | C6 | 73 |
| Harwood, Md., U.S. | C4 | 97 |
| Harwood, Mo., U.S. | f9 | 98 |
| Harwood, Mo., U.S. | D3 | 102 |
| Harwood, N.D., U.S. | C9 | 111 |
| Harwood Heights, Il., U.S. | *k9 | 90 |
| Haryāna, state, India | C6 | 36 |
| Harzgerode, E. Ger. | B6 | 19 |
| Harz Mountains, mts., Eur. | C5 | 18 |
| Hasā, Wādī al, val., Jord. | D7 | 41 |
| Hasanah, Bi'r, well, Eg. | D5 | 41 |
| Hasan Dağı, mtn., Tur. | C10 | 40 |
| Ḥasan Kīādeh, Iran | C4 | 39 |
| Hasbrouck Heights, N.J., U.S. | h8 | 107 |
| Hasdo, stm., India | F9 | 37 |
| Hase, stm., W. Ger. | B3 | 18 |
| Haselünne, W. Ger. | B3 | 18 |
| Hashimoto, Japan | o14 | 33 |
| Haskell, Ar., U.S. | C3 | 81 |
| Haskell, Ok., U.S. | B6 | 113 |
| Haskell, Tx., U.S. | C3 | 120 |
| Haskell, co., Ks., U.S. | E3 | 93 |
| Haskell, co., Ok., U.S. | B6 | 113 |
| Haskell, co., Tx., U.S. | C3 | 120 |
| Haskins, Oh., U.S. | A2 | 112 |
| Haslach, Aus. | E9 | 19 |
| Hasle, Den. | C8 | 15 |
| Haslemere, Eng., U.K. | C7 | 12 |
| Haslet, Tx., U.S. | n9 | 120 |
| Haslett, Mi., U.S. | *F6 | 99 |
| Haslev, Den. | C6 | 15 |
| Hassan, India | F6 | 36 |
| Hassayampa, stm., Az., U.S. | D3 | 80 |
| Hassell, N.C., U.S. | B5 | 110 |
| Hasselt, Bel. | B6 | 16 |
| Hassfurt, W. Ger. | C5 | 19 |
| Hassi Messaoud, Alg. | C6 | 44 |
| Hassleben, E. Ger. | E7 | 15 |
| Hässleholm, Swe. | I5 | 14 |
| Hassloch, W. Ger. | F8 | 19 |
| Hastings, Barb. | K20 | 65 |
| Hastings, Ont. | C7 | 73 |
| Hastings, N.Z. | M16 | 51 |
| Hastings, Eng., U.K. | E7 | 10 |
| Hastings, Fl., U.S. | C5 | 86 |
| Hastings, Ia., U.S. | C2 | 92 |
| Hastings, Mi., U.S. | F5 | 99 |
| Hastings, Mn., U.S. | F6 | 100 |

| Hastings, Ne., U.S. | D7 | 104 |
| Hastings, N.D., U.S. | C7 | 111 |
| Hastings, Ok., U.S. | C3 | 113 |
| Hastings, Pa., U.S. | E4 | 115 |
| Hastings, W.V., U.S. | h9 | 125 |
| Hastings-on-Hudson, N.Y., U.S. | h13 | 109 |
| Hasvik, Nor. | | |
| Hästveda, Swe. | B7 | 15 |
| Hasty, Ar., U.S. | A2 | 81 |
| Hasty, Co., U.S. | C8 | 83 |
| Haswell, Co., U.S. | C7 | 83 |
| Hatboro, Pa., U.S. | *F11 | 115 |
| Hatch, N.M., U.S. | E2 | 108 |
| Hatch, Ut., U.S. | F3 | 121 |
| Hatch Lake, Ont. | | |
| Hatchechubbee, Al., U.S. | C4 | 78 |
| Hatchet Creek, stm., Al., U.S. | B3 | 78 |
| Hatchet Lake, N.S. | E6 | 71 |
| Hatchie, stm., Tn., U.S. | B2 | 119 |
| Hatchineha, Lake, l., Fl., U.S. | D5 | 86 |
| Hatchville, Ma., U.S. | C6 | 98 |
| Hateg, Rom. | C6 | 24 |
| Hatfield, Sask. | F3 | 75 |
| Hatfield, Ar., U.S. | C1 | 81 |
| Hatfield, In., U.S. | I3 | 91 |
| Hatfield, Ma., U.S. | B2 | 98 |
| Hatfield, Mo., U.S. | A3 | 102 |
| Hatfield, Pa., U.S. | F11 | 115 |
| Hathaway, Mt., U.S. | D10 | 103 |
| Hāthras, India | D7 | 37 |
| Hatillo, P.R. | B2 | 65 |
| Ha Tien, Viet. | G6 | 35 |
| Ha Tinh, Viet. | C6 | 35 |
| Hatteras, N.C., U.S. | B7 | 110 |
| Hatteras, Cape, c., N.C., U.S. | B7 | 110 |
| Hatteras Inlet, b., N.C., U.S. | B7 | 110 |
| Hattfjelldal, Nor. | E6 | 14 |
| Hattiesburg, Ms., U.S. | D4 | 101 |
| Hattieville, Ar., U.S. | B3 | 81 |
| Hatton, Sask. | G1 | 75 |
| Hatton, Al., U.S. | A2 | 78 |
| Hatton, Ar., U.S. | C1 | 81 |
| Hatton, N.D., U.S. | B8 | 111 |
| Hatvan, Hung. | B4 | 24 |
| Hat Yai (Ban Hat Yai), Thai. | D2 | 34 |
| Hatzic, B.C. | f13 | 69 |
| Haubourdin, Fr. | D3 | 17 |
| Haubstadt, In., U.S. | H2 | 91 |
| Haugan, Mt., U.S. | C1 | 103 |
| Haugen, Wi., U.S. | C2 | 126 |
| Haugesund, Nor. | H1 | 14 |
| Haughton, La., U.S. | B2 | 95 |
| Hauppauge, N.Y., U.S. | *n15 | 109 |
| Hauraki Gulf, b., N.Z. | L15 | 51 |
| Hausach, W. Ger. | A4 | 20 |
| Hauser, Or., U.S. | D2 | 114 |
| Hauser Dam, Mt., U.S. | D5 | 103 |
| Haus Stock, mtn., Switz. | C7 | 21 |
| Haut, Isle au, i., Me., U.S. | D4 | 96 |
| Haut Atlas, mts., Mor. | C3 | 44 |
| Haute-Marne, dept., Fr. | A1 | 20 |
| Hauterive (part of Baie-Comeau), Que. | k13 | 74 |
| Hautes-Alpes, dept., Fr. | E2 | 20 |
| Haute-Saône, dept., Fr. | B2 | 20 |
| Haute-Savoie, dept., Fr. | C2 | 20 |
| Hautes Fagnes, mts., Eur. | D6 | 17 |
| Hautmont, Fr. | B5 | 16 |
| Haut-Rhin, dept., Fr. | B3 | 20 |
| Hauula, Hi., U.S. | B4 | 88 |
| Hauzenberg, W. Ger. | E8 | 19 |
| Havana (La Habana), Cuba | C2 | 64 |
| Havana, Al., U.S. | C2 | 78 |
| Havana, Fl., U.S. | B2 | 86 |
| Havana, Il., U.S. | C3 | 90 |
| Havana, Ks., U.S. | E8 | 93 |
| Havana, N.D., U.S. | D8 | 111 |
| Havana Nakya, Az., U.S. | E4 | 80 |
| Havana, Lake, res., U.S. | C1 | 80 |
| Havasupai Indian Reservation, Az., U.S. | A3 | 80 |
| Havel, stm., Eur. | F6 | 15 |
| Havelberg, E. Ger. | F6 | 15 |
| Havelock, N.B. | D4 | 71 |
| Havelock, Ont. | C7 | 73 |
| Havelock, Ia., U.S. | B3 | 92 |
| Havelock, N.C., U.S. | C6 | 110 |
| Haven, Ks., U.S. | E6 | 93 |
| Haven, Wi., U.S. | k10 | 126 |
| Haverford [Township], Pa., U.S. | o20 | 115 |
| Haverfordwest, Wales, U.K. | C3 | 12 |
| Haverhill, Eng., U.K. | B8 | 12 |
| Haverhill, N.H., U.S. | A5 | 98 |
| Haverhill, Ma., U.S. | B2 | 106 |
| Haversham, R.I., U.S. | G2 | 116 |
| Haverstraw, N.Y., U.S. | D7 | 109 |
| Havertown, Pa., U.S. | G11 | 115 |
| Haviland, Ks., U.S. | E4 | 93 |
| Haviland, Oh., U.S. | A1 | 112 |
| Havířov, Czech. | *D5 | 26 |
| Havlíčkův Brod, Czech. | C3 | 120 |
| Havoc Point, Boucher, N.S. | D8 | 71 |
| Havre de Grace, Md., U.S. | A5 | 97 |
| Havre North, Mt., U.S. | B7 | 103 |
| Havre Saint Pierre, Que. | h9 | 72 |
| Havza, Tur. | B10 | 40 |
| Haw, stm., N.C., U.S. | B3 | 110 |
| Hawaii, co., Hi., U.S. | D6 | 88 |
| Hawaii, state, U.S. | C5 | 88 |
| Hawaii, i., Hi., U.S. | D6 | 88 |
| Hawaiian Gardens, Ca., U.S. | *n12 | 82 |
| Hawaiian Islands, is., Hi., U.S. | m14 | 88 |
| Hawaii Volcanoes National Park, Hi., U.S. | D6 | 88 |
| Hawarden, Sask. | F2 | 75 |
| Hawarden, Ia., U.S. | A1 | 92 |
| Hawea, Lake, l., N.Z. | P12 | 51 |
| Hawera, N.Z. | M15 | 51 |
| Hawes, Eng., U.K. | F6 | 13 |
| Hawesville, Ky., U.S. | C3 | 94 |

| Hawi, Hi., U.S. | C6 | 88 |
| Hawick, Scot., U.K. | C5 | 10 |
| Hawke Bay, b., N.Z. | M16 | 51 |
| Hawke, stm., Newf. | B3 | 72 |
| Hawke Island, i., Newf. | B4 | 72 |
| Hawker, Austl. | E2 | 51 |
| Hawkesbury, Ont. | C7 | 73 |
| Hawkesbury, Ont. | B10 | 73 |
| Hawkesbury Island, i., B.C. | C3 | 69 |
| Hawkestone, Ont. | C5 | 73 |
| Hawkeye, Ia., U.S. | B6 | 92 |
| Hawkins, Wi., U.S. | C3 | 126 |
| Hawkins, co., Tn., U.S. | C11 | 119 |
| Hawkinsville, Ga., U.S. | D3 | 87 |
| Hawk Lake, Ont. | E5 | 70 |
| Hawk Point, Mo., U.S. | C6 | 102 |
| Haw Knob, mtn., U.S. | D9 | 119 |
| Hawk Run, Pa., U.S. | E5 | 115 |
| Hawk Springs, Wy., U.S. | E8 | 127 |
| Hawley, Mn., U.S. | D2 | 100 |
| Hawley, Pa., U.S. | D11 | 115 |
| Hawley, Tx., U.S. | C3 | 120 |
| Hawleyville, Ct., U.S. | D2 | 84 |
| Haworth, N.J., U.S. | h9 | 107 |
| Haworth, Ok., U.S. | D7 | 113 |
| Haw River, N.C., U.S. | A3 | 110 |
| Ḥawsh ʿĪsā, Eg. | D2 | 41 |
| Hawthorne, Ca., U.S. | n12 | 82 |
| Hawthorne, Fl., U.S. | C4 | 86 |
| Hawthorne, Nv., U.S. | E3 | 105 |
| Hawthorne, N.J., U.S. | B4 | 107 |
| Hawthorne, N.Y., U.S. | g13 | 109 |
| Hawthorne, Wi., U.S. | B2 | 126 |
| Haxtun, Co., U.S. | A8 | 83 |
| Hay, Austl. | F7 | 50 |
| Hay, Wa., U.S. | C8 | 124 |
| Hay, stm., Austl. | D6 | 50 |
| Hay, stm., Can. | E9 | 66 |
| Hayange, Fr. | C7 | 16 |
| Haybes, Fr. | D4 | 17 |
| Hayden, Al., U.S. | B3 | 78 |
| Hayden, Az., U.S. | E5 | 80 |
| Hayden, Co., U.S. | A3 | 83 |
| Hayden, Ct., U.S. | B5 | 84 |
| Hayden, Id., U.S. | *B2 | 89 |
| Hayden, In., U.S. | G6 | 91 |
| Haydenburg, Tn., U.S. | C8 | 119 |
| Hayden Lake, l., Id., U.S. | B2 | 89 |
| Haydenville, Ma., U.S. | B2 | 98 |
| Haydenville, Oh., U.S. | C3 | 112 |
| Hayes, La., U.S. | D3 | 95 |
| Hayes, S.D., U.S. | C4 | 118 |
| Hayes, co., Ne., U.S. | D4 | 104 |
| Hayes, stm., Man. | B5 | 70 |
| Hayes, Mount, mtn., Ak., U.S. | C10 | 79 |
| Hayes Center, Ne., U.S. | D4 | 104 |
| Hayesville, N.C., U.S. | f9 | 110 |
| Hayesville, Oh., U.S. | B3 | 112 |
| Hayesville, Or., U.S. | *C4 | 114 |
| Hayfield, Man. | E1 | 70 |
| Hayfield, Ia., U.S. | A4 | 92 |
| Hayfield, Mn., U.S. | G6 | 100 |
| Hayfield, Va., U.S. | *B5 | 123 |
| Hayfield, Va., U.S. | A4 | 123 |
| Hayford Peak, mtn., Nv., U.S. | G6 | 105 |
| Hay Island, i., Ont. | C4 | 73 |
| Hay Lakes, Alta. | C4 | 68 |
| Haylow, Ga., U.S. | F4 | 87 |
| Hayman, Tur. | C9 | 40 |
| Haymarket, Va., U.S. | B5 | 123 |
| Haymock Lake, l., Me., U.S. | B3 | 96 |
| Haymond, In., U.S. | F7 | 91 |
| Haynes, Alta. | C4 | 68 |
| Haynes, Ar., U.S. | C5 | 81 |
| Haynes, N.D., U.S. | D3 | 111 |
| Haynesville, La., U.S. | B2 | 95 |
| Haynesville, Me., U.S. | C5 | 96 |
| Hayneville, Al., U.S. | C3 | 78 |
| Hay-on-Wye, Wales, U.K. | B4 | 12 |
| Hay River, N.W. Ter. | D9 | 66 |
| Hays, Ks., U.S. | D4 | 93 |
| Hays, Mt., U.S. | C8 | 103 |
| Hays, N.C., U.S. | A1 | 110 |
| Hays, Yemen | C5 | 47 |
| Hays, co., Tx., U.S. | D3 | 120 |
| Hays Canyon Peak, mtn., Nv., U.S. | B2 | 105 |
| Haysi, Va., U.S. | e9 | 123 |
| Ḥayṣī, Bi'r al, well, Eg. | E6 | 41 |
| Hay Springs, Ne., U.S. | B3 | 104 |
| Haystack Mountain, mtn., Ct., U.S. | B3 | 84 |
| Haystack Mountain, mtn., Nv., U.S. | B6 | 105 |
| Haysville, In., U.S. | H4 | 91 |
| Haysville, Ks., U.S. | g12 | 93 |
| Haysville, Tn., U.S. | A5 | 119 |
| Hayter, Alta. | C5 | 68 |
| Hayti, Mo., U.S. | E8 | 102 |
| Hayti, S.D., U.S. | C8 | 118 |
| Hayti Heights, Mo., U.S. | E8 | 102 |
| Hayward, Ca., U.S. | h8 | 82 |
| Hayward, Ok., U.S. | A4 | 113 |
| Hayward Addition, S.D., U.S. | *D8 | 118 |
| Haywards Heath, Eng., U.K. | C7 | 12 |
| Haywood, Man. | E2 | 70 |
| Haywood, N.C., U.S. | B3 | 110 |
| Haywood, co., N.C., U.S. | f10 | 110 |
| Haywood, co., Tn., U.S. | B2 | 119 |
| Hazār, Kūh-e, mtn., Iran | G8 | 39 |
| Hazard, Ky., U.S. | C6 | 94 |
| Hazard, Ne., U.S. | C6 | 104 |
| Hazardville, Ct., U.S. | B5 | 84 |
| Hazebrouck, Fr. | B5 | 16 |
| Hazel, Ky., U.S. | f9 | 94 |
| Hazel, S.D., U.S. | C8 | 118 |
| Hazel Crest, Il., U.S. | k9 | 90 |
| Hazel Dell, Il., U.S. | D5 | 90 |
| Hazel Dell, Wa., U.S. | D3 | 124 |
| Hazel Green, Al., U.S. | A3 | 78 |
| Hazel Green, Ky., U.S. | C6 | 94 |
| Hazel Green, Wi., U.S. | F3 | 126 |
| Hazelhurst, Wi., U.S. | C4 | 126 |
| Hazel Park, Mi., U.S. | p15 | 99 |
| Hazel Patch, Ky., U.S. | C5 | 94 |
| Hazel Run, Mn., U.S. | F3 | 100 |
| Hazelton, B.C. | B4 | 69 |
| Hazelton, Id., U.S. | G5 | 89 |
| Hazelton, Ks., U.S. | E5 | 93 |
| Hazelton, N.D., U.S. | C5 | 111 |
| Hazelton Peak, mtn., Wy., U.S. | B5 | 127 |
| Hazelwood, Mo., U.S. | *f13 | 102 |
| Hazelwood, N.C., U.S. | f9 | 110 |
| Hazen, Ar., U.S. | C4 | 81 |
| Hazen, Nv., U.S. | D2 | 105 |

| Hazen, N.D., U.S. | B4 | 111 |
| Hazen Bay, b., Ak., U.S. | C6 | 79 |
| Hazenmore, Sask. | H2 | 75 |
| Hazen Strait, strt., N.W. Ter. | m29 | 66 |
| Hazlehurst, Ga., U.S. | E4 | 87 |
| Hazlehurst, Ms., U.S. | D3 | 101 |
| Hazlet, Sask. | G1 | 75 |
| Hazlet, N.J., U.S. | C4 | 107 |
| Hazleton, Ia., U.S. | B6 | 92 |
| Hazleton, In., U.S. | H2 | 91 |
| Hazleton, Pa., U.S. | E10 | 115 |
| Hazlett, Lake, l., Austl. | D4 | 50 |
| Hazlettville, De., U.S. | D3 | 85 |
| Ḥazōr Ashdod, Isr. | h9 | 41 |
| Ḥazor HaGelilit, Isr. | B7 | 41 |
| Head Bay d'Espoir (part of Milltown-Head Bay d'Espoir, Newf. | E4 | 72 |
| Head Harbor Island, i., Me., U.S. | D5 | 96 |
| Headland, Al., U.S. | D4 | 78 |
| Headley, Mount, mtn., Mt., U.S. | C1 | 103 |
| Head of Island, La., U.S. | h10 | 95 |
| Headquarters, Id., U.S. | C3 | 89 |
| Headrick, Ok., U.S. | C2 | 113 |
| Heafford Junction, Wi., U.S. | C4 | 126 |
| Healdsburg, Ca., U.S. | C2 | 82 |
| Healdton, Ok., U.S. | C4 | 113 |
| Healdville, Vt., U.S. | E3 | 122 |
| Healing Springs, Va., U.S. | C3 | 123 |
| Healy, Ak., U.S. | C10 | 79 |
| Healy, Ks., U.S. | D3 | 93 |
| Heanna, Japan | O5 | 52 |
| Heard, co., Ga., U.S. | C1 | 87 |
| Heard Island, i., Austl. | J1 | 2 |
| Hearne, Sask. | G3 | 75 |
| Hearne, Tx., U.S. | D4 | 120 |
| Hearst, Ont. | o19 | 73 |
| Hearst Island, i., Ant. | C6 | 7 |
| Heart, stm., Alta. | B2 | 68 |
| Heart, stm., N.D., U.S. | C3 | 111 |
| Heart Butte, Mt., U.S. | B4 | 103 |
| Heart Butte Dam, N.D., U.S. | C4 | 111 |
| Hearthstone Mountain, mtn., Md., U.S. | A2 | 97 |
| Heart Lake, l., Alta. | B5 | 68 |
| Heart Lake, l., Wy., U.S. | B2 | 127 |
| Heart's Content, Newf. | E5 | 72 |
| Heartwell, Ne., U.S. | D7 | 104 |
| Heaters, W.V., U.S. | C4 | 125 |
| Heath, Al., U.S. | D3 | 78 |
| Heath, Ma., U.S. | A2 | 98 |
| Heath, Oh., U.S. | B3 | 112 |
| Heath, co., Ne., U.S. | D8 | 71 |
| Heathrow, N.S. | | |
| Healdsburg, S.C., U.S. | B6 | 117 |
| Heathsville, Va., U.S. | C6 | 123 |
| Heaton, N.D., U.S. | B6 | 111 |
| Heaundā, Nepal | D10 | 37 |
| Heavener, Ok., U.S. | C7 | 113 |
| Hebbronville, Tx., U.S. | F3 | 120 |
| Hebei, prov., China | D8 | 31 |
| Hebel, Austl. | D6 | 51 |
| Heber, Az., U.S. | C5 | 80 |
| Heber City, Ut., U.S. | C4 | 121 |
| Heber Springs, Ar., U.S. | B3 | 81 |
| Hebert, La., U.S. | B4 | 95 |
| Hebertville, Que. | A6 | 74 |
| Hebgen Lake, res., Mt., U.S. | F5 | 103 |
| Hebi, China | *D7 | 31 |
| Hebo, Or., U.S. | B3 | 114 |
| Hebrides, Sea of the, Scot., U.K. | B3 | 10 |
| Hebron, Newf. | f9 | 72 |
| Hebron, N.S. | F3 | 71 |
| Hebron (Al Khalīl), Isr. Occ. | G10 | 40 |
| Hebron, Ct., U.S. | C6 | 84 |
| Hebron, Il., U.S. | A5 | 90 |
| Hebron, In., U.S. | B3 | 91 |
| Hebron, Ky., U.S. | h13 | 94 |
| Hebron, Md., U.S. | D2 | 96 |
| Hebron, Ne., U.S. | D8 | 104 |
| Hebron, N.H., U.S. | C3 | 106 |
| Hebron, N.D., U.S. | C3 | 111 |
| Hebron, Oh., U.S. | C3 | 112 |
| Hebron, Tx., U.S. | m10 | 120 |
| Hebron, W.V., U.S. | B3 | 125 |
| Heby, Swe. | t34 | 14 |
| Hecate Strait, strt., B.C. | C2 | 69 |
| Hecelchakán, Mex. | C6 | 63 |
| Heceta Island, i., Ak., U.S. | n23 | 79 |
| Hechingen, W. Ger. | D4 | 21 |
| Hechtel, Bel. | C5 | 17 |
| Hechuan, China | E8 | 31 |
| Hecker, Il., U.S. | E4 | 90 |
| Hecklingen, E. Ger. | B6 | 19 |
| Hecla, Man. | D3 | 70 |
| Hecla, S.D., U.S. | B7 | 118 |
| Hecla, i., Man. | D3 | 70 |
| Hectanooga, N.S. | E3 | 71 |
| Hector, Ar., U.S. | B3 | 81 |
| Hector, Mn., U.S. | F4 | 100 |
| Hede, Swe. | F5 | 14 |
| Hedemora, Swe. | G6 | 14 |
| Hedensted, Den. | C3 | 15 |
| He Devil, Mt., Id., U.S. | D2 | 89 |
| Hedgehog Hill, hill, Ct., U.S. | k8 | 86 |
| Hedges, Fl., U.S. | E7 | 69 |
| Hedgesville, W.V., U.S. | B6 | 125 |
| Hedley, B.C. | | |
| Hedley, Tx., U.S. | B2 | 120 |
| Hedo, Japan | N6 | 52 |
| Hedo Cape, c., Japan | N6 | 52 |
| Hedon, Eng., U.K. | A7 | 12 |
| Hedrick, In., U.S. | G5 | 91 |
| Hedrick, Ia., U.S. | C5 | 92 |
| Heeia, Hi., U.S. | *B4 | 88 |
| Heek, W. Ger. | A2 | 19 |
| Heel Point, c., Wake I. | E8 | 2 |
| Heeney, Co., U.S. | B4 | 83 |
| Heerde, Neth. | C6 | 16 |
| Heerenveen, Neth. | A6 | 16 |
| Heerlen, Neth. | D5 | 16 |
| Heessen, W. Ger. | B2 | 19 |
| Ḥefa, Mifraẕ (Bay of Haifa), b., Isr. | B6 | 41 |
| Hefei, China | E6 | 31 |
| Heflin, Al., U.S. | B4 | 78 |
| Hefner, Lake, res., Ok., U.S. | B4 | 113 |
| Hegang, China | B11 | 31 |
| Hegins, Pa., U.S. | E9 | 115 |
| Heide, W. Ger. | m29 | 66 |
| Heidelberg, Austl. | *G8 | 50 |
| Heidelberg, W. Ger. | D4 | 49 |
| Heidelberg, S. Afr. | D3 | 49 |
| Heidelberg, Ms., U.S. | D5 | 101 |
| Hazelton, N.D., U.S. | C5 | 111 |
| Heiden, Switz. | B8 | 21 |
| Heidenau, E. Ger. | D5 | 18 |
| Heidenheim, W. Ger. | C5 | 19 |
| Heidrick, Ky., U.S. | D6 | 94 |
| Heihe (Aihui), China | A10 | 31 |
| Heil, N.D., U.S. | C4 | 111 |

| Heilbron, S. Afr. | C4 | 49 |
| Heilbronn, W. Ger. | D4 | 18 |
| Heiligenblut, Aus. | B8 | 20 |
| Heiligenhafen, W. Ger. | D4 | 15 |
| Heiligenstadt, E. Ger. | C5 | 18 |
| Heilongjiang, prov., China | B10 | 31 |
| Heilong Jiang (Amur), stm., Asia | B10 | 31 |
| Heilungkiang see Heilongjiang, prov., China | B10 | 31 |
| Heilwood, Pa., U.S. | E4 | 115 |
| Heimbach, W. Ger. | D6 | 17 |
| Heimdal, N.D., U.S. | B6 | 111 |
| Heimenkirch, W. Ger. | A8 | 21 |
| Heinola, Fin. | G12 | 14 |
| Heinsberg, W. Ger. | C6 | 17 |
| Heinsburg, Alta. | C5 | 68 |
| Heiskell, Tn., U.S. | m13 | 119 |
| Heisler, Alta. | C4 | 68 |
| Heislerville, N.J., U.S. | E3 | 107 |
| Heizer, Ks., U.S. | D5 | 93 |
| Hejaz, reg., Sau. Ar. | C3 | 38 |
| Hejian, China | E7 | 32 |
| Hekla, Mount, vol., Ice. | n23 | 14 |
| Hekou, China | A5 | 35 |
| Hel, Pol. | A5 | 26 |
| Helagsfjället, mtn., Swe. | F5 | 14 |
| Helan Shan, mts., China | D6 | 31 |
| Helbra, E. Ger. | B6 | 19 |
| Helena, Al., U.S. | B3 | 78 |
| Helena, Ar., U.S. | C5 | 81 |
| Helena, Ga., U.S. | D4 | 87 |
| Helena, Mo., U.S. | B3 | 102 |
| Helena, Mt., U.S. | D4 | 103 |
| Helena, N.Y., U.S. | f10 | 109 |
| Helena, Oh., U.S. | A2 | 112 |
| Helena, Ok., U.S. | A3 | 113 |
| Helena, S.C., U.S. | C4 | 117 |
| Helendale, Ca., U.S. | E5 | 82 |
| Helenwood, Tn., U.S. | C9 | 119 |
| Helga å, stm., Swe. | B8 | 15 |
| Helgasjön, l., Swe. | B8 | 15 |
| Helgeröd, Nor. | p28 | 14 |
| Helgoland, i., W. Ger. | A3 | 18 |
| Helgoland Bay, b., W. Ger. | A3 | 18 |
| Heli, China | C5 | 33 |
| Helicon see Elikón Óros, mtn., Grc. | g9 | 25 |
| Helix, Or., U.S. | B8 | 114 |
| Hellam, Pa., U.S. | G8 | 115 |
| Hellenthal, W. Ger. | D6 | 17 |
| Hellertown, Pa., U.S. | E11 | 115 |
| Hellín, Spain | C5 | 22 |
| Hells Canyon, val., U.S. | B10 | 114 |
| Hells Canyon National Recreation Area, U.S. | B10 | 114 |
| Hell-Ville, Madag. | f9 | 49 |
| Helm, Ca., U.S. | D3 | 82 |
| Helmand, stm., Asia | B3 | 36 |
| Helmbrechts, W. Ger. | C6 | 19 |
| Helmer, Id., U.S. | *C2 | 89 |
| Helmer, In., U.S. | A7 | 91 |
| Helmeringhausen, Nmb. | C2 | 49 |
| Helmetta, N.J., U.S. | C4 | 107 |
| Helmond, Neth. | B6 | 16 |
| Helmsburg, In., U.S. | F5 | 91 |
| Helmsdale, Scot., U.K. | A5 | 10 |
| Helmsdale, stm., Scot., U.K. | B5 | 13 |
| Helmsley, Eng., U.K. | F7 | 13 |
| Helmstedt, W. Ger. | B5 | 18 |
| Helmville, Mt., U.S. | D4 | 103 |
| Helnæs, i., Den. | C3 | 15 |
| Helotes, Tx., U.S. | h7 | 120 |
| Helper, Ut., U.S. | D5 | 121 |
| Helsingborg, Swe. | I5 | 14 |
| Helsingör, Den. | I5 | 14 |
| Helsinki, Fin. | G11 | 14 |
| Helston, Eng., U.K. | D2 | 12 |
| Heltonville, In., U.S. | G5 | 91 |
| Helvecia, Arg. | A4 | 54 |
| Helvellyn, mtn., Eng., U.K. | F6 | 13 |
| Helvetia, Pa., U.S. | D4 | 115 |
| Helvick Head, c., Ire. | E4 | 11 |
| Ḥemar, Naḥal, val., Isr. | C7 | 41 |
| Hemaruka, Alta. | D5 | 68 |
| Hematite, Mo., U.S. | C7 | 102 |
| Hemau, W. Ger. | D6 | 19 |
| Hemel Hempstead, Eng., U.K. | k12 | 10 |
| Hemet, Ca., U.S. | F5 | 82 |
| Hemford, N.S. | E5 | 71 |
| Hemingford, Ne., U.S. | B2 | 104 |
| Hemingway, S.C., U.S. | D9 | 117 |
| Hemlock, Mi., U.S. | E6 | 99 |
| Hemlock, N.Y., U.S. | C3 | 109 |
| Hemlock Reservoir, res., Ct., U.S. | E2 | 84 |
| Hemmesta, Swe. | t36 | 14 |
| Hemmingford, Que. | D4 | 74 |
| Hemnesberget, Nor. | E6 | 14 |
| Hemphill, Tx., U.S. | D6 | 120 |
| Hemphill, co., Tx., U.S. | B2 | 120 |
| Hemple, Mo., U.S. | B3 | 102 |
| Hempstead, N.Y., U.S. | n15 | 109 |
| Hempstead, Tx., U.S. | D4 | 120 |
| Hempstead, co., Ar., U.S. | D2 | 81 |
| Hemsedal, Al., U.S. | A4 | 78 |
| Henan, prov., China | E4 | 31 |
| Henares, stm., Spain | B4 | 22 |
| Hendaye, Fr. | F6 | 17 |
| Henderson, Arg. | B4 | 54 |
| Henderson, Co., U.S. | D5 | 83 |
| Henderson, Ky., U.S. | C2 | 94 |
| Henderson, La., U.S. | D4 | 95 |
| Henderson, Md., U.S. | B6 | 97 |
| Henderson, Mn., U.S. | F5 | 100 |
| Henderson, Ne., U.S. | D8 | 104 |
| Henderson, N.C., U.S. | A4 | 110 |
| Henderson, Tn., U.S. | B3 | 119 |
| Henderson, Tx., U.S. | C5 | 120 |
| Henderson, co., Il., U.S. | C3 | 90 |
| Henderson, co., Ky., U.S. | C2 | 94 |
| Henderson, co., N.C., U.S. | f10 | 110 |
| Henderson, co., Tn., U.S. | B3 | 119 |
| Henderson, co., Tx., U.S. | C5 | 120 |
| Henderson's Point, Ms., U.S. | g7 | 101 |
| Hendersonville, N.C., U.S. | f10 | 110 |
| Hendersonville, Tn., U.S. | A5 | 119 |
| Hendijān, Iran | F4 | 39 |
| Hendley, Ne., U.S. | D6 | 104 |
| Hendon, Sask. | E4 | 75 |
| Hendon (part of London), Eng., U.K. | k12 | 10 |
| Hendorābī, i., Iran | H6 | 39 |
| Hendricks, Mn., U.S. | F2 | 100 |
| Hendricks, W.V., U.S. | B5 | 125 |
| Hendricks, co., In., U.S. | E4 | 91 |

| Hendrik Verwoerd Dam, res., S. Afr. | D4 | 49 |
| Hendrix, Ok., U.S. | D5 | 113 |
| Hendrum, Mn., U.S. | C2 | 100 |
| Hendry, co., Fl., U.S. | F5 | 86 |
| Henefer, Ut., U.S. | C4 | 121 |
| Hengelo, Neth. | A7 | 16 |
| Hengshan, China | F3 | 32 |
| Hengshan, China | K5 | 32 |
| Hengxian, China | G6 | 31 |
| Hengyang, China | F7 | 31 |
| Hénin-Beaumont, Fr. | D2 | 17 |
| Henlawson, W.V., U.S. | n12 | 125 |
| Henley Harbour, Newf. | B4 | 72 |
| Henley-on-Thames, Eng., U.K. | C7 | 12 |
| Henlopen, Cape, c., De., U.S. | E5 | 85 |
| Henlopen Acres, De., U.S. | F5 | 85 |
| Hennebont, Fr. | D2 | 16 |
| Hennef, W. Ger. | C2 | 19 |
| Hennepin, Il., U.S. | B4 | 90 |
| Hennepin, Ok., U.S. | C4 | 113 |
| Hennepin, co., Mn., U.S. | E5 | 100 |
| Hennessey, Ok., U.S. | A4 | 113 |
| Henniker, N.H., U.S. | D3 | 106 |
| Henning, Il., U.S. | C6 | 90 |
| Henning, Mn., U.S. | D3 | 100 |
| Henning, Tn., U.S. | B2 | 119 |
| Henribourg, Sask. | D2 | 75 |
| Henrico, co., Va., U.S. | C5 | 123 |
| Henrietta, Mo., U.S. | B4 | 102 |
| Henrietta, N.Y., U.S. | B3 | 109 |
| Henrietta, N.C., U.S. | B1 | 110 |
| Henrietta, Tx., U.S. | C3 | 120 |
| Henrietta Island, i., Sov. Un. | B35 | 128 |
| Henrietta Maria, Cape, c., Ont. | n19 | 73 |
| Henrieville, Ut., U.S. | F4 | 121 |
| Henry, Ne., U.S. | C1 | 104 |
| Henry, S.D., U.S. | C8 | 118 |
| Henry, Ne., U.S. | A3 | 119 |
| Henry, Va., U.S. | D3 | 123 |
| Henry, co., Al., U.S. | D4 | 78 |
| Henry, co., Ga., U.S. | C2 | 87 |
| Henry, co., Il., U.S. | B3 | 90 |
| Henry, co., In., U.S. | E7 | 91 |
| Henry, co., Ia., U.S. | C6 | 92 |
| Henry, co., Ky., U.S. | B4 | 94 |
| Henry, co., Mo., U.S. | C4 | 102 |
| Henry, co., Oh., U.S. | A1 | 112 |
| Henry, co., Tn., U.S. | A3 | 119 |
| Henry, co., Va., U.S. | D3 | 123 |
| Henry, Mount, mtn., Mt., U.S. | B1 | 103 |
| Henryetta, Ok., U.S. | B6 | 113 |
| Henry Kater, Cape, c., N.W. Ter. | C19 | 66 |
| Henry Mountains, mts., Ut., U.S. | E5 | 121 |
| Henry Pittier National Park, Ven. | A4 | 58 |
| Henrys Fork, stm., U.S. | E2 | 127 |
| Henryville, Que. | D4 | 74 |
| Henryville, In., U.S. | G6 | 91 |
| Hensall, Ont. | D3 | 73 |
| Hensel, N.D., U.S. | A8 | 111 |
| Henshaw, Ky., U.S. | e9 | 94 |
| Hensler, N.D., U.S. | B4 | 111 |
| Hensley, Ar., U.S. | C3 | 81 |
| Henson Creek, stm., Md., U.S. | f9 | 97 |
| Hentiyn Mountains, mts., Mong. | B6 | 31 |
| Henzada, Burma | E10 | 36 |
| Hepburn, Sask. | E2 | 75 |
| Hepburn, Ia., U.S. | D2 | 92 |
| Hepburn, Oh., U.S. | B2 | 112 |
| Hephzibah, Ga., U.S. | C4 | 87 |
| Hepler, Ks., U.S. | E9 | 93 |
| Heppenheim, W. Ger. | D3 | 19 |
| Heppner, Or., U.S. | B7 | 114 |
| Hepworth, Ont. | C3 | 73 |
| Hepu, China | G6 | 31 |
| Heqing, China | F5 | 31 |
| Herāt, Afg. | B3 | 36 |
| Herbert, Sask. | G2 | 75 |
| Herbertingen, W. Ger. | A5 | 20 |
| Herbert Peak, mtn., N.Z. | O14 | 51 |
| Herbes, Isle aux, i., Al., U.S. | E1 | 78 |
| Herblay, Fr. | B7 | 70 |
| Herblet Lake, l., Man. | B7 | 70 |
| Herborn, W. Ger. | C4 | 19 |
| Herceg-Novi, Yugo. | D4 | 24 |
| Hercegovina, hist. reg., Yugo. | C3 | 24 |
| Herculaneum, Mo., U.S. | C7 | 102 |
| Hercules, Ca., U.S. | *g8 | 82 |
| Herdecke, W. Ger. | E8 | 63 |
| Heredia, C.R. | | |
| Hereford, Eng., U.K. | D5 | 10 |
| Hereford, Az., U.S. | F5 | 80 |
| Hereford, Co., U.S. | A6 | 83 |
| Hereford, Or., U.S. | C8 | 114 |
| Hereford, S.D., U.S. | D3 | 118 |
| Hereford, Tx., U.S. | B1 | 120 |
| Hereford and Worcester, co., Eng. and U.K. | B5 | 12 |
| Hereford Inlet, b., N.J., U.S. | E3 | 107 |
| Hérémence, Switz. | D3 | 21 |
| Herencia, Spain | C4 | 22 |
| Herentals, Bel. | B4 | 16 |
| Herfølge, Den. | B8 | 15 |
| Herford, W. Ger. | B4 | 18 |
| Héricourt, Fr. | B2 | 21 |
| Hérimoncourt, Fr. | B2 | 21 |
| Herington, Ks., U.S. | D7 | 93 |
| Herisau, Switz. | E4 | 18 |
| Heritage Range, mts., Ant. | A9 | 7 |
| Heritage Village, Ct., U.S. | *D3 | 84 |
| Herkimer, N.Y., U.S. | B6 | 109 |
| Herkimer, co., N.Y., U.S. | B5 | 109 |
| Herman, Mn., U.S. | E2 | 100 |
| Herman, Ne., U.S. | C9 | 104 |
| Herman, Pa., U.S. | C2 | 102 |
| Hermano Peak, mtn., Co., U.S. | D2 | 83 |
| Hermansville, Mi., U.S. | C3 | 99 |
| Herman, co., Il., U.S. | D6 | 100 |
| Hermanville, Ms., U.S. | D3 | 101 |
| Hermeskeil, W. Ger. | F2 | 19 |
| Herminie, Pa., U.S. | F2 | 115 |
| Hermiston, Or., U.S. | B7 | 114 |
| Hermitage, Newf. | E4 | 72 |
| Hermitage, Pa., U.S. | D4 | 95 |
| Hermitage, Pa., U.S. | *D1 | 115 |
| Hermitage Bay, b., Newf. | E3 | 72 |
| Hermitage Springs, U.S. | C8 | 119 |
| Hermleigh, Tx., U.S. | C2 | 120 |
| Hermon, N.Y., U.S. | f9 | 109 |
| Hermon, Mount, mtn., Asia | *D4 | 96 |
| Hermon, Mount, mtn., Asia | F11 | 40 |
| Hermosa, S.D., U.S. | D2 | 118 |

**Name** — Map Ref. — Page

Hermosa Beach, Ca., U.S. — *n12 82
Hermosillo, Mex. — B2 63
Hernåd, stm., Eur. — A5 24
Hernandarias, Para. — E5 55
Hernandez, N.M., U.S. — A3 108
Hernando, Fl., U.S. — D4 86
Hernando, Ms., U.S. — A4 101
Hernando, co., Fl., U.S. — D4 86
Herndon, Ga., U.S. — D4 87
Herndon, Ia., U.S. — C3 92
Herndon, Ks., U.S. — C3 93
Herndon, Ky., U.S. — D2 94
Herndon, Pa., U.S. — E8 115
Herndon, Va., U.S. — B5 123
Herndon, W.V., U.S. — D3 125
Herne, W. Ger. — B2 19
Herning, Den. — I3 14
Herod's Gate, hist., Isr. Occ. — m14 41
Heroica Caborca, Mex. — A2 63
Heroica Nogales, Mex. — A2 63
Heron, Mt., U.S. — B1 103
Heron Bay, Al., U.S. — E1 78
Heron Lake, Mn., U.S. — G3 100
Hérouxville, Que. — C5 74
Herreid, S.D., U.S. — B5 118
Herrenberg, W. Ger. — E3 19
Herrick, Il., U.S. — D5 90
Herrick, S.D., U.S. — D6 118
Herrick Center, Pa., U.S. — C11 115
Herrick Creek, stm., B.C. — B7 69
Herrick Mountain, mtn., Vt., U.S. — D2 122
Herriman, Ut., U.S. — *C3 121
Herrin, Il., U.S. — F4 90
Herring Bay, b., Md., U.S. — C4 97
Herring Cove, N.S. — E6 71
Herring Run, stm., Md., U.S. — g11 97
Herrington Lake, res., Ky., U.S. — C5 94
Hersbruck, W. Ger. — D6 19
Herschel, Sask. — F1 75
Herscher, Il., U.S. — B5 90
Hersey, Mi., U.S. — E5 99
Hershey, Ne., U.S. — C5 104
Hershey, Pa., U.S. — F8 115
Herstal, Bel. — B6 16
Herten, W. Ger. — *C3 19
Hertford, Eng., U.K. — E6 10
Hertford, N.C., U.S. — A6 110
Hertford, co., N.C., U.S. — A5 110
Hertfordshire, co., Eng., U.K. — C7 12
Hervás, Spain — B3 22
Hervey Bay, b., Austl. — D9 50
Hervey-Jonction, Que. — C5 74
Herxheim, W. Ger. — D3 19
Herzberg, E. Ger. — F7 15
Herzberg, E. Ger. — B8 19
Herzberg [am Harz], W. Ger. — B5 19
Herzliyya, Isr. — F10 40
Herzogenaurach, W. Ger. — D5 19
Herzogenbuchsee, Switz. — B4 21
Hesdin, Fr. — D2 17
Hesel, W. Ger. — A7 17
Hesper, N.D., U.S. — B6 111
Hesperia, Ca., U.S. — E5 82
Hesperia, Mi., U.S. — E4 99
Hesperus, Co., U.S. — D2 83
Hesperus Mountain, mtn., Co., U.S. — D2 83
Hess, Ok., U.S. — C2 113
Hesse, hist. reg., W. Ger. — C4 18
Hessel, Mi., U.S. — B6 99
Hesselager, Den. — C4 15
Hesselø, i., Den. — B5 15
Hessen, state, W. Ger. — C3 19
Hessmer, La., U.S. — C3 95
Hesston, Ks., U.S. — D6 93
Hetland, S.D., U.S. — C8 118
Hettick, Il., U.S. — D3 90
Hettinger, N.D., U.S. — D3 111
Hettinger, co., N.D., U.S. — C3 111
Hettstedt, E. Ger. — B6 19
Heusler, In., U.S. — I2 91
Heuvelton, N.Y., U.S. — f9 109
Heves, Hung. — B5 24
Heward, Sask. — H4 75
Hewins, Ks., U.S. — E7 93
Hewitt, Mn., U.S. — D3 100
Hewitt, N.J., U.S. — A4 107
Hewitt, Tx., U.S. — *D4 120
Hewitt, Wi., U.S. — D3 126
Hewlett, N.Y., U.S. — *n14 109
Hexham, Eng., U.K. — F6 13
Hexian, China — G7 31
Hexigten Qi, China — C7 32
Hext, Tx., U.S. — D3 120
Heyang, China — G4 32
Heyburn, Id., U.S. — G5 89
Heyworth, Il., U.S. — C5 90
Heze (Caozhou), China — *D8 31
Heze, China — G6 32
Hialeah, Fl., U.S. — G6 86
Hiattville, Ks., U.S. — E9 93
Hiawassee, Ga., U.S. — B3 87
Hiawatha, Ia., U.S. — B6 92
Hiawatha, Ks., U.S. — C8 93
Hiawatha, Ut., U.S. — D5 121
Hiawatha Camp, Co., U.S. — A2 83
Hibbard, In., U.S. — B5 91
Hibbing, Mn., U.S. — C6 100
Hickam Air Force Base, mil., Hi., U.S. — g10 88
Hickiwan, Az., U.S. — E3 80
Hickman, De., U.S. — E3 85
Hickman, Ky., U.S. — f8 94
Hickman, Ne., U.S. — D9 104
Hickman, co., Ky., U.S. — f8 94
Hickman, co., Tn., U.S. — B4 119
Hickman's Harbour, Newf. — D5 72
Hickok, Ks., U.S. — E2 93
Hickory, Ky., U.S. — f9 94
Hickory, Ms., U.S. — C4 101
Hickory, N.C., U.S. — B1 110
Hickory, Ok., U.S. — C5 113
Hickory, co., Mo., U.S. — D4 102
Hickory Corners, Mi., U.S. — F5 99
Hickory Flat, Ms., U.S. — A4 101
Hickory Grove, S.C., U.S. — B5 117
Hickory Hills, Il., U.S. — *k9 90
Hickory Plains, Ar., U.S. — C4 81
Hickory Ridge, Ar., U.S. — B5 81
Hickory Valley, Tn., U.S. — B2 119
Hickory Withe, Tn., U.S. — B2 119
Hickox, Ga., U.S. — E5 87
Hicks, La., U.S. — C2 95
Hickson, Ont. — D4 73
Hickson Lake, l., Sask. — A3 75
Hicksville, N.Y., U.S. — E7 109
Hicksville, Oh., U.S. — A1 112
Hico, Tx., U.S. — D3 120
Hico, W.V., U.S. — C3 125
Hida, Japan — n16 33
Hidalgo, Il., U.S. — D5 90
Hidalgo, Tx., U.S. — F3 120

Hidalgo, state, Mex. — C5 63
Hidalgo, co., N.M., U.S. — F1 108
Hidalgo, co., Tx., U.S. — F3 120
Hidalgo del Parral, Mex. — B3 63
Hiddenite, N.C., U.S. — B1 110
Hiddensee, i., E. Ger. — D7 15
Hideaway Park, Co., U.S. — B5 83
Hidrolina, Braz. — A3 56
Hieroglyphic Mountains, mts., Az., U.S. — k8 80
Hierro, i., Spain — n13 22
Higashi, Japan — N6 52
Higashiizu, Japan — o18 33
Higashiōsaka, Japan — I7 33
Higbee, Mo., U.S. — B5 102
Higden, Ar., U.S. — B3 81
Higganum, Ct., U.S. — D5 84
Higgins, Tx., U.S. — A2 120
Higgins Lake, Mi., U.S. — D6 99
Higgins Lake, l., Mi., U.S. — D6 99
Higgins Millpond, res., Md., U.S. — C6 97
Higginson, Ar., U.S. — B4 81
Higginsport, Oh., U.S. — D2 112
Higginsville, Mo., U.S. — B4 102
High Bluff, Man. — D2 70
High Bridge, Ky., U.S. — C5 94
High Bridge, N.H., U.S. — E3 106
High Bridge, N.J., U.S. — B3 107
Highfalls, N.C., U.S. — B3 110
High Falls Reservoir, res., Wi., U.S. — C5 126
Highfield, Md., U.S. — A3 97
Highgate, Ont. — E3 73
Highgate Falls, Vt., U.S. — B2 122
High Hill, Mo., U.S. — C6 102
High Hill, stm., Can. — A5 68
High Hill Lake, l., Man. — B4 70
High Island, Tx., U.S. — E5 120
High Island, i., Mi., U.S. — C5 99
High Knob, mtn., U.S. — A4 123
High Knob, mtn., W.V., U.S. — C5 125
Highland, Ca., U.S. — *E5 82
Highland, Il., U.S. — E4 90
Highland, In., U.S. — A3 91
Highland, Ks., U.S. — C8 93
Highland, Mi., U.S. — o14 99
Highland, N.Y., U.S. — D7 109
Highland, Oh., U.S. — C2 112
Highland, Wi., U.S. — E3 126
Highland, prov., Scot., U.K. — B4 13
Highland, co., Oh., U.S. — C2 112
Highland, co., Va., U.S. — B3 123
Highland Falls, N.Y., U.S. — *D6 109
Highland Grove, Ont. — B6 73
Highland Heights, Oh., U.S. — *g10 112
Highland Home, Al., U.S. — D3 78
Highland Lake, l., Me., U.S. — g7 96
Highland Lakes, N.J., U.S. — A4 107
Highland Park, Il., U.S. — A6 90
Highland Park, Mi., U.S. — p15 99
Highland Park, N.J., U.S. — *C4 107
Highland Park, Tx., U.S. — n10 120
Highland Peak, mtn., Ca., U.S. — C3 82
Highland Point, c., Fl., U.S. — G5 86
Highlands, N.J., U.S. — C5 107
Highlands, N.C., U.S. — f9 110
Highlands Heights, De., U.S. — r14 120
Highlands, co., Fl., U.S. — E5 86
Highlands Springs, Va., U.S. — C5 123
Highlandville, Ia., U.S. — A6 92
High Level, Alta. — F7 68
Highmore, S.D., U.S. — C6 118
High Point, Ms., U.S. — B4 101
High Point, N.C., U.S. — B2 110
High Point, Wa., U.S. — e12 124
High Prairie, Alta. — B2 68
High Ridge, Mo., U.S. — g12 102
High River, Alta. — D4 68
High Rock, mtn., Md., U.S. — k12 97
High Rock Lake, l., N.C. — B1 70
High Rolls Mountain Park, N.M., U.S. — E4 108
High Shoals, Ga., U.S. — C3 87
High Shoals, N.C., U.S. — B1 110
High Spire, Pa., U.S. — F8 115
High Springs, Fl., U.S. — C4 86
High Tatra Mountains, mts., Eur. — D5 26
High Top, mtn., W.V., U.S. — C5 125
High Wycombe, Eng., U.K. — E6 10
Higley, Az., U.S. — D4 80
Higüero, Punta, c., P.R. — B1 65
Higura Island, i., Japan — H8 33
Hiiraan, Som. — E6 47
Hiiumaa, i., Sov. Un. — B4 27
Hiko, Nv., U.S. — F6 105
Hikone, Japan — n15 33
Hiko Range, mts., Nv., U.S. — F6 105
Hikurangi, mtn., N.Z. — L17 51
Hīlāl, Jabal, mts., Eg. — D5 41
Hiland, Wy., U.S. — C5 127
Hilbert, Wi., U.S. — D5 126
Hilda, Alta. — D5 68
Hilda, S.C., U.S. — E5 117
Hildale, Ut., U.S. — F3 121
Hildburghausen, E. Ger. — C5 18
Hilden, N.C., U.S. — D6 71
Hildesheim, W. Ger. — B4 18
Hildreth, Ne., U.S. — D6 104
Hiles, Wi., U.S. — C5 126
Hilham, Tn., U.S. — C8 119
Hill, co., Mt., U.S. — B6 103
Hill, co., Tx., U.S. — D4 120
Hilla see Al Ḥillah, Iraq — B4 38
Hillaby, Mount, mtn., Barb. — K20 65
Hillared, Swe. — A7 15
Hill City, Id., U.S. — F3 89
Hill City, Ks., U.S. — C4 93
Hill City, Mn., U.S. — D5 100
Hill City, S.D., U.S. — D2 118
Hillcrest, Il., U.S. — B4 90
Hillcrest, N.Y., U.S. — *n15 109
Hillcrest Center, Ca., U.S. — *E4 82
Hillcrest Heights, Md., U.S. — C4 97
Hillegom, Neth. — B4 17

Hillerage, Ne., U.S. — *C2 104
Hillerød, Den. — C6 15
Hillesheim, W. Ger. — C1 19
Hillhead, S.D., U.S. — B8 118
Hilliard, Alta. — C4 68
Hilliard, Fl., U.S. — B5 86
Hilliard, Oh., U.S. — k10 112
Hilliards, Pa., U.S. — D2 115
Hillier, Ont. — D7 73
Hillisburg, In., U.S. — D5 91
Hill Lake, l., Ar., U.S. — h10 81
Hillman, Mi., U.S. — C7 99
Hillman, Mn., U.S. — D5 100
Hillmond, Sask. — D1 75
Hillrose, Co., U.S. — A7 83
Hills, Ia., U.S. — C6 92
Hills, Mn., U.S. — G2 100
Hillsboro, Al., U.S. — A2 78
Hillsboro, Ga., U.S. — C3 87
Hillsboro, Il., U.S. — D4 90
Hillsboro, In., U.S. — D3 91
Hillsboro, Ia., U.S. — D6 92
Hillsboro, Ks., U.S. — D6 93
Hillsboro, Md., U.S. — C6 97
Hillsboro, Ms., U.S. — C4 101
Hillsboro, Mo., U.S. — C7 102
Hillsboro, N.H., U.S. — D3 106
Hillsboro, N.M., U.S. — E2 108
Hillsboro, N.D., U.S. — B8 111
Hillsboro, Oh., U.S. — C2 112
Hillsboro, Or., U.S. — B4 114
Hillsboro, Tn., U.S. — D8 119
Hillsboro, Tx., U.S. — C4 120
Hillsboro, W.V., U.S. — C4 125
Hillsboro, Wi., U.S. — E3 126
Hillsboro Canal, Fl., U.S. — F6 86
Hillsborough, N.B. — D5 71
Hillsborough, Gren. — W25 65
Hillsborough, St. Vin. — W26 65
Hillsborough, Ca., U.S. — *h8 82
Hillsborough, N.C., U.S. — A3 110
Hillsborough, co., Fl., U.S. — E4 86
Hillsborough, co., N.H., U.S. — E3 106
Hillsborough Bay, b., P.E.I. — C6 71
Hillsborough Lower Village, N.H., U.S. — D3 106
Hillsborough Upper Village, N.H., U.S. — D3 106
Hillsburgh, Ont. — D4 73
Hills Creek Lake, res., Or., U.S. — D4 114
Hillsdale, Ont. — C5 73
Hillsdale, Il., U.S. — B3 90
Hillsdale, In., U.S. — E3 91
Hillsdale, Ks., U.S. — D9 93
Hillsdale, Mi., U.S. — G6 99
Hillsdale, N.J., U.S. — g8 107
Hillsdale, N.Y., U.S. — C7 109
Hillsdale, Ok., U.S. — A4 113
Hillsdale, Tn., U.S. — A5 119
Hillsdale, Wi., U.S. — C2 126
Hillsdale, Wy., U.S. — E8 127
Hillsdale, co., Mi., U.S. — G6 99
Hillsgrove, Pa., U.S. — D8 115
Hillside, Az., U.S. — C3 80
Hillside, Co., U.S. — C5 83
Hillside, Il., U.S. — *k9 90
Hillside, N.J., U.S. — k8 107
Hillside Heights, De., U.S. — *B3 85
Hillspring, Alta. — E4 68
Hillston, Austl. — F5 51
Hillsview, S.D., U.S. — B6 118
Hillsville, Pa., U.S. — D1 115
Hillsville, Va., U.S. — D2 123
Hilltonia, Ga., U.S. — D5 87
Hilltown, N. Ire., U.K. — C5 11
Hillview, Il., U.S. — D3 90
Hillview, Ky., U.S. — *g11 94
Hilo, Hi., U.S. — D6 88
Hilo Bay, b., Hi., U.S. — D6 88
Hilpoltstein, W. Ger. — D6 19
Hilton, Ga., U.S. — E1 87
Hilton, N.Y., U.S. — B3 109
Hilton Head Island, S.C., U.S. — G6 117
Hilton Head Island, i., S.C., U.S. — G6 117
Hiltons, Va., U.S. — f9 123
Hilversum, Neth. — A6 16
Hima, Ky., U.S. — C6 94
Himachal Pradesh, state, India — D6 36
Himalayas, mts., Asia — C8 36
Himeji, Japan — I7 33
Himi, Japan — H8 33
Himrod, N.Y., U.S. — C4 109
Hinche, Haiti — E7 64
Hinchinbrook, i., Austl. — C8 50
Hinchinbrook Island, i., Ak., U.S. — g18 79
Hinckley, Eng., U.K. — B6 12
Hinckley, Il., U.S. — B5 90
Hinckley, Me., U.S. — D3 96
Hinckley, Mn., U.S. — D6 100
Hinckley, Oh., U.S. — A4 112
Hinckley, Ut., U.S. — D3 121
Hinckley Reservoir, res., N.Y., U.S. — B5 109
Hindaun, India — H6 37
Hindīyah Barrage, Iraq — F15 40
Hindman, Ky., U.S. — C7 94
Hindmarsh, Lake, l., Austl. — G3 51
Hinds, co., Ms., U.S. — C3 101
Hindsboro, Il., U.S. — D5 90
Hinds Lake, l., Newf. — D3 72
Hindu Kush, mts., Asia — A5 36
Hines, Mn., U.S. — C4 100
Hines, Or., U.S. — D7 114
Hinesburg, Vt., U.S. — C2 122
Hines Creek, Alta. — A1 68
Hineston, La., U.S. — C3 95
Hinesville, Ga., U.S. — E5 87
Hingham, Ma., U.S. — B6 98
Hingham, Mt., U.S. — B6 103
Hingham Bay, b., Ma., U.S. — g12 98
Hingoli, India — H6 37
Hinis, Tur. — C13 40
Hinnøy, i., Nor. — B6 15
Hinojosa [del Duque], Spain — C3 22
Hinsdale, Il., U.S. — k9 90
Hinsdale, Ma., U.S. — B1 98
Hinsdale, N.H., U.S. — E2 106
Hinsdale, N.Y., U.S. — C2 109
Hinsdale, co., Co., U.S. — D3 83
Hinterrhein, Switz. — C7 21
Hinterrhein, stm., Switz. — C7 21
Hinton, Alta. — C2 68

Hinton, Ia., U.S. — B1 92
Hinton, Ok., U.S. — B3 113
Hinton, W.V., U.S. — D4 125
Hirado Island, i., Japan — J4 33
Hiraiwa Cape, c., Japan — P17 52
Hirakata, Japan — *I7 33
Hirakūd Reservoir, res., India — G9 37
Hiram, Ga., U.S. — C2 87
Hiram, Me., U.S. — E2 96
Hiram, Oh., U.S. — A4 112
Hiratsuka, Japan — n17 33
Hirlău, Rom. — B8 24
Hiroo, Japan — E11 33
Hirosaki, Japan — C13 31
Hiroshima, Japan — E11 31
Hirschberg see Jelenia Góra, Pol. — C3 26
Hirson, Fr. — C6 16
Hîrșova, Rom. — C8 24
Hirtshals, Den. — A3 15
Hisar, India — C6 36
Hisarönü, Tur. — B9 40
Hispaniola, i., N.A. — E8 64
Ḥīt, Iraq — F14 40
Hitachi, Japan — D13 31
Hitchcock, Ok., U.S. — B3 113
Hitchcock, S.D., U.S. — C7 118
Hitchcock, Tx., U.S. — r14 120
Hitchcock, co., Ne., U.S — D4 104
Hitchcock Lake, Ct., U.S. — C4 84
Hitchin, Eng., U.K. — C7 12
Hitchins, Ky., U.S. — B7 94
Hitchita, Ok., U.S. — B6 113
Hiteman, Ia., U.S. — C5 92
Hitoyoshi, Japan — J5 33
Hitra, i., Nor. — F3 14
Hitterdal, Mn., U.S. — D2 100
Hittisau, Aus. — B8 21
Hitzacker, W. Ger. — E5 15
Hiwannee, Ms., U.S. — D5 101
Hiwassee, Va., U.S. — G3 75
Hiwassee, stm., Tn., U.S. — D9 119
Hiwassee Lake, res., N.C., U.S. — f8 110
Hixon, B.C. — C6 69
Hixton, Wi., U.S. — D2 126
Hjälmaren, l., Swe. — H7 14
Hjälmseryd, Swe. — A8 15
Hjo, Swe. — H6 14
Hjørring, Den. — I3 14
Hkakabo Razi, mtn., Burma — C10 36
Hlohovec, Czech. — D4 26
Ho, Ghana — E5 45
Hoa Binh, Viet. — B6 35
Hoaeae, Hi., U.S. — g9 88
Hoagland, In., U.S. — C8 91
Hoback, stm., Wy., U.S. — C2 127
Hobart, Austl. — o15 50
Hobart, In., U.S. — A3 91
Hobart, N.Y., U.S. — C6 109
Hobart, Ok., U.S. — B2 113
Hobbema, Alta. — C4 68
Hobbieville, In., U.S. — G4 91
Hobbs, In., U.S. — D6 91
Hobbs, N.M., U.S. — E6 108
Hobe Sound, Fl., U.S. — E6 86
Hobgood, N.C., U.S. — A5 110
Hoboken (part of Antwerp), Bel. — B6 16
Hoboken, Ga., U.S. — E4 87
Hoboken, N.J., U.S. — k8 107
Hobro, Den. — B3 15
Hobson, Mt., U.S. — D7 103
Hobson Lake, l., B.C. — C7 69
Hobucken, N.C., U.S. — B6 110
Hobyo, Som. — D6 47
Hochdorf, Switz. — E4 21
Hochfeld, Nmb. — B2 49
Hochfelden, Fr. — F7 17
Ho Chi Minh City (Saigon), Viet. — C3 34
Höchst (part of Frankfurt am Main), W. Ger. — C3 19
Höchstadt [an der Aisch], W. Ger. — D5 19
Hockenheim, W. Ger. — D3 19
Hockerville, Ok., U.S. — A7 113
Hockessin, De., U.S. — A3 85
Hocking, co., Oh., U.S. — C3 112
Hocking, stm., Oh., U.S. — C3 112
Hockingport, Oh., U.S. — C4 112
Hockley, Tx., U.S. — q14 120
Hockley, co., Tx., U.S. — C1 120
Hodeida (Al Ḥudaydah), Yemen — k13 10
Hodgdon, Me., U.S. — B5 96
Hodge, La., U.S. — B3 95
Hodgeman, co., Ks., U.S. — D4 93
Hodgen, Ok., U.S. — C7 113
Hodgenville, Ky., U.S. — C4 94
Hodges, S.C., U.S. — C3 117
Hodges Village Reservoir, res., Ma., U.S. — B4 98
Hodgeville, Sask. — G2 75
Hodgson, Man. — D3 70
Hódmezővásárhely, Hung. — B5 24
Hodonín, Czech. — D4 26
Hoehne, Co., U.S. — D6 83
Hoek van Holland (part of Rotterdam), Neth. — C4 17
Hoensbroek, Neth. — D5 17
Hōeryŏng, N. Kor. — E4 33
Hoey, Sask. — E3 75
Hof, W. Ger. — C5 18
Hof, Nor. — p28 14
Hoffman, Mn., U.S. — E3 100
Hoffman, N.C., U.S. — B3 110
Hoffman, Ok., U.S. — B6 113
Hoffman Estates, Il., U.S. — h8 90
Hofgeismar, W. Ger. — B4 18
Höfn, Ice. — n25 14
Hofors, Swe. — n23 14
Hofsjökull, ice, Ice. — n23 14
Höfu, Japan — I5 33
Hōgānäs, Swe. — B6 15
Hogansville, Ga., U.S. — C2 87
Hogback Mountain, mtn., Mt., U.S. — F4 103
Hogback Mountain, mtn., Ne., U.S. — C2 104
Hogback Mountain, mtn., N.C., U.S. — f9 110
Hogeland, Mt., U.S. — B8 103
Hog Island, i., Mi., U.S. — C5 99
Hog Island, i., N.C., U.S. — B6 110
Hog Island, i., R.I., U.S. — D5 116
Hog Island, i., Va., U.S. — C7 123
Hogup Mountains, mts., Ut., U.S. — B2 121

Hoh, stm., Wa., U.S. — B1 124
Hohen Solms, La., U.S. — h9 95
Hohenwald, Tn., U.S. — B4 119
Hohe Tauern, mts., Aus. — E6 18
Hoh Head, c., Wa., U.S. — B1 124
Hohhot, China — C7 31
Hohoe, Ghana — E5 45
Ho-Ho-Kus, N.J., U.S. — h8 107
Hohwachter Bucht, b., W. Ger. — D4 15
Hoi An, Viet. — B3 34
Hoima, Ug. — A5 48
Hoisington, Ks., U.S. — D5 93
Hoi Xuan, Viet. — B6 35
Højer, Den. — D2 15
Hokah, Mn., U.S. — G7 100
Hoke, co., N.C., U.S. — B3 110
Hokes Bluff, Al., U.S. — B4 78
Hokitika, N.Z. — O13 51
Hokkaidō, i., Japan — C13 31
Holabird, S.D., U.S. — C6 118
Holbæk, Den. — C5 15
Holbeach, Eng., U.K. — B8 12
Holbrook, Az., U.S. — C5 80
Holbrook, Id., U.S. — G6 89
Holbrook, Ma., U.S. — B5 98
Holbrook, Ne., U.S. — D5 104
Holbrook, N.Y., U.S. — *n15 109
Holcomb, Ks., U.S. — E3 93
Holcomb, Mo., U.S. — E7 102
Holcomb, N.Y., U.S. — C3 109
Holcombe, Wi., U.S. — C2 126
Holden, Alta. — C4 68
Holden, La., U.S. — g10 95
Holden, Ma., U.S. — B4 98
Holden, Mo., U.S. — C4 102
Holden, Ut., U.S. — D3 121
Holden, W.V., U.S. — D2 125
Holden Heights, Fl., U.S. — D5 86
Holdenville, Ok., U.S. — B5 113
Holder, Fl., U.S. — D4 86
Holderness, N.H., U.S. — C3 106
Holdfast, Sask. — G3 75
Holdingford, Mn., U.S. — E4 100
Holdrege, Ne., U.S. — D6 104
Hole in the Mountain Peak, mtn., Nv., U.S. — C6 105
Holetown, Barb. — K20 65
Holgate, Oh., U.S. — A1 112
Holguín, Cuba — D5 64
Holguín, prov., Cuba — D6 64
Holiday, Fl., U.S. — *D4 86
Holiday City at Berkeley, N.J., U.S. — *D4 107
Hollabrunn, Aus. — D8 18
Holladay, Tn., U.S. — B3 119
Holladay, Ut., U.S. — C4 121
Holland, Man. — E2 70
Holland, Ar., U.S. — B3 81
Holland, Ia., U.S. — B5 92
Holland, Ky., U.S. — D3 94
Holland, Ma., U.S. — B3 98
Holland, Mn., U.S. — F2 100
Holland, Ne., U.S. — D9 104
Holland, N.Y., U.S. — C2 109
Holland, Oh., U.S. — A2 112
Holland, Pa., U.S. — *F12 115
Holland, Tx., U.S. — D4 120
Holland, Wi., U.S. — h9 126
Holland Centre, Ont. — C4 73
Holland Island, i., Md., U.S. — D5 97
Holland Patent, N.Y., U.S. — B5 109
Holland Point, c., Md., U.S. — C4 97
Holland Straits, strt., Md., U.S. — D5 97
Holland see Netherlands, ctry., Eur. — A6 16
Hollandale, Ms., U.S. — B3 101
Hollandale, Wi., U.S. — F4 126
Hollenberg, Ks., U.S. — C6 93
Holley, N.Y., U.S. — B2 109
Hollick-Kenyon Plateau, plat., Ant. — B2 7
Holliday, Mo., U.S. — B5 102
Holliday, Tx., U.S. — C3 120
Hollidaysburg, Pa., U.S. — F5 115
Hollins, Al., U.S. — B3 78
Hollins, Va., U.S. — C3 123
Hollis, N.H., U.S. — E3 106
Hollis, Ok., U.S. — C2 113
Hollis Center, Me., U.S. — E2 96
Hollis Reservoir, res., Trin. — N23 65
Hollister, Ca., U.S. — D3 82
Hollister, Id., U.S. — G4 89
Hollister, Mo., U.S. — E4 102
Hollister, N.C., U.S. — A5 110
Hollister, Ok., U.S. — C3 113
Hollister, Wi., U.S. — C5 126
Hollisterville, Pa., U.S. — D11 115
Holliston, Ma., U.S. — B5 98
Holloman Air Force Base, mil., N.M., U.S. — E3 108
Holloway, In., U.S. — G4 91
Holloway Terrace, De., U.S. — *B3 85
Hollow Rock, Tn., U.S. — A3 119
Hollollow Mountain, mtn., Mt., U.S. — F4 103
Hollsopple, Pa., U.S. — F4 115
Hollum, Neth. — A5 17
Holly, Co., U.S. — C8 83
Holly, Mi., U.S. — F7 99
Holly Beach, La., U.S. — E2 95
Holly Bluff, Ms., U.S. — C3 101
Holly Grove, Ar., U.S. — C4 81
Holly Hill, Fl., U.S. — C5 86
Holly Hill, S.C., U.S. — E7 117
Holly Pond, Al., U.S. — A3 78
Holly Ridge, N.C., U.S. — C5 110
Holly Shelter Swamp, sw., N.C., U.S. — C5 110
Holly Springs, Ar., U.S. — D3 81
Holly Springs, Ms., U.S. — A4 101
Holly Springs, N.C., U.S. — B3 110
Hollywood, Al., U.S. — A4 78
Hollywood, Az., U.S. — C2 80
Hollywood (part of Los Angeles), Ca., U.S. — m12 82
Hollywood, Fl., U.S. — F6 86
Hollywood, S.C., U.S. — k11 117
Hollywood Indian Reservation, Fl., U.S. — r13 86
Holman, Ar., U.S. — B3 81
Holman, N.W. Ter. — B5 66
Holmdel, N.J., U.S. — C4 107
Holmen, Wi., U.S. — E2 126
Holmes, co., Fl., U.S. — u16 86

Holmes, co., Ms., U.S. — B3 101
Holmes, co., Oh., U.S. — B4 112
Holmes, Mount, mtn., Wy., U.S. — B2 127
Holmes Lake, l., Man. — A3 70
Holmestrand, Nor. — p28 14
Holmesville, Ne., U.S. — D9 104
Holmesville, Oh., U.S. — B4 112
Holmsbu, Nor. — p28 14
Holmsund, Swe. — F9 14
Holon, Isr. — B6 41
Holopaw, Fl., U.S. — D5 86
Holroyd, Austl. — *F9 50
Holroyd, stm., Austl. — B7 50
Holstebro, Den. — I3 14
Holsted, Den. — C2 15
Holstein, Ont. — C4 73
Holstein, Ia., U.S. — B2 92
Holstein, Mo., U.S. — C6 102
Holstein, Ne., U.S. — D7 104
Holsteinsborg, Grnld. — *C15 61
Holston, stm., Tn., U.S. — C11 119
Holston, Middle Fork, stm., Va., U.S. — f10 123
Holston High Knob, mtn., Tn., U.S. — C11 119
Holsworthy, Eng., U.K. — D3 12
Holt, Al., U.S. — B2 78
Holt, Fl., U.S. — u15 86
Holt, Mi., U.S. — F6 99
Holt, Mn., U.S. — B2 100
Holt, Mo., U.S. — B3 102
Holt, co., Mo., U.S. — A2 102
Holt, co., Ne., U.S. — B7 104
Holt Creek, stm., Ne., U.S. — B7 104
Holt Knob, mtn., Tn., U.S. — g10 119
Holton, In., U.S. — G7 91
Holton, Ks., U.S. — C8 93
Holton, Mi., U.S. — E4 99
Holt Reservoir, res., Al., U.S. — B2 78
Holts Corner, Tn., U.S. — B5 119
Holtville, Al., U.S. — C3 78
Holtville, Ca., U.S. — F6 82
Holtwood, Pa., U.S. — G9 115
Holualoa, Hi., U.S. — D6 88
Holy Cross, Ak., U.S. — C8 79
Holy Cross, Mountain of the, mtn., Co., U.S. — B4 83
Holyhead, Wales, U.K. — D4 12
Holy Island, i., Eng., U.K. — C6 10
Holy Island, i., Wales, U.K. — D4 12
Holyoke, Co., U.S. — A8 83
Holyoke, Ma., U.S. — B2 98
Holyoke, Mn., U.S. — D6 100
Holyoke Range, hills, Ma., U.S. — B2 98
Holyrood, Ks., U.S. — D5 93
Holy Sepulchre, The Church of the, Isr. Occ. — m14 41
Holy Trinity, Al., U.S. — C4 78
Holzgau, Aus. — B9 21
Holzkirchen, W. Ger. — B7 20
Holzminden, W. Ger. — B4 18
Homalin, Burma — D9 36
Homathko, stm., B.C. — D5 69
Homberg, W. Ger. — B4 19
Homberg, W. Ger. — B1 19
Hombori, Mali — C4 45
Hombourg-Haut, Fr. — E6 17
Homburg, W. Ger. — D2 19
Homburg see Bad Homburg, W. Ger. — C4 19
Home, Ks., U.S. — C7 93
Home Corner, In., U.S. — C6 91
Homécourt, Fr. — C6 16
Homecroft, In., U.S. — m10 91
Homedale, Id., U.S. — F2 89
Home Gardens, Ca., U.S. — *n13 82
Home Hill, Austl. — C8 50
Homelake, Co., U.S. — D4 83
Homeland, Fl., U.S. — E5 86
Homeland, Ga., U.S. — F4 87
Homeland Park, S.C., U.S. — *B2 117
Home Place, In., U.S. — E5 91
Homer, Ak., U.S. — D9 79
Homer, Ga., U.S. — B3 87
Homer, Il., U.S. — C6 90
Homer, In., U.S. — B5 91
Homer, La., U.S. — B2 95
Homer, Mi., U.S. — F6 99
Homer, N.Y., U.S. — C4 109
Homer City, Pa., U.S. — E3 115
Homer Youngs Peak, mtn., Mt., U.S. — E3 103
Homestead, Fl., U.S. — G6 86
Homestead, Mt., U.S. — B12 103
Homestead, Ok., U.S. — A3 113
Homestead Air Force Base, mil., Fl., U.S. — G6 86
Homestead National Monument of America, Ne., U.S. — D9 104
Hometown, Il., U.S. — *k9 90
Homewood, Al., U.S. — g7 78
Homewood, Il., U.S. — B6 90
Homewood, Ms., U.S. — C4 101
Homeworth, Oh., U.S. — B5 112
Hominy, Ok., U.S. — A5 113
Hominy Creek, stm., Ok., U.S. — A5 113
Homme Dam, N.D., U.S. — A8 111
Hommura, Japan — o18 33
Homochitto, stm., Ms., U.S. — D2 101
Homosassa, Fl., U.S. — D4 86
Homs (Ḥimṣ), Syria — B3 38
Hon, Ar., U.S. — B1 81
Honan see Henan, prov., China — E7 31
Honaunau, Hi., U.S. — D6 88
Honaz, mtn., Tur. — B7 40
Honda, Col. — B5 60
Hondo, Alta. — B3 68
Hondo, N.M., U.S. — D4 108
Hondo, Tx., U.S. — E3 120
Hondo, stm., Mex. — h9 63
Hondo, Rio, stm., N.M., U.S. — D4 108
Honduras, ctry., N.A. — D7 63
Honduras, Cabo de, c., Hond. — D7 63
Honduras, Gulf of, b., N.A. — D7 63
Honea Path, S.C., U.S. — C3 117
Hönefoss, Nor. — G4 14
Honeoye Falls, N.Y., U.S. — C3 109
Honesdale, Pa., U.S. — C11 115

| Name | Map Ref. | Page |
|---|---|---|
| Honey Brook, Pa., U.S. | F10 | 115 |
| Honey Creek, Ia., U.S. | C2 | 92 |
| Honey Creek, Wi., U.S. | n11 | 126 |
| Honey Grove, Tx., U.S. | C5 | 120 |
| Honey Lake, l., Ca., U.S. | B3 | 82 |
| Honeymoon Bay, B.C. | E5 | 69 |
| Honeypot Glen, Ct., U.S. | C4 | 84 |
| Honeyville, Ut., U.S. | B3 | 121 |
| Honfleur, Fr. | C4 | 16 |
| Høng, Den. | C5 | 15 |
| Hon Gai, Viet. | B7 | 35 |
| Hong'an, China | I6 | 32 |
| Honga River, b., Md., U.S. | D5 | 97 |
| Honghu, China | F7 | 31 |
| Hong Kong, dep., Asia | G7 | 31 |
| Hongshui He, stm., China | G6 | 31 |
| Hongwŏn, N. Kor. | G3 | 33 |
| Hongze Hu, l., China | E8 | 31 |
| Honiara, Sol.Is. | G9 | 6 |
| Honichin Hural, Mong. | C3 | 32 |
| Honiton, Eng., U.K. | D4 | 12 |
| Hönö, i., Swe. | A5 | 15 |
| Honobia, Ok., U.S. | C7 | 113 |
| Honokaa, Hi., U.S. | C6 | 88 |
| Honokahua, Hi., U.S. | B5 | 88 |
| Honokohau, Hi., U.S. | D6 | 88 |
| Honolulu, Hi., U.S. | B4 | 88 |
| Honolulu, Hi., U.S. | D6 | 88 |
| Honolulu International Airport, Hi., U.S. | g10 | 88 |
| Honomu, Hi., U.S. | D6 | 88 |
| Honor, Mi., U.S. | D4 | 99 |
| Honoraville, Al., U.S. | D3 | 78 |
| Honouliuli, Hi., U.S. | g9 | 88 |
| Hon Quan, Viet. | G7 | 35 |
| Honshū, i., Japan | D12 | 31 |
| Honuapo Bay, b., Hi., U.S. | D6 | 88 |
| Hood, co., Tx., U.S. | C4 | 120 |
| Hood, Mount, mtn., Or., U.S. | B5 | 114 |
| Hood Canal, b., Wa., U.S. | B2 | 124 |
| Hoodoo, Tn., U.S. | B5 | 119 |
| Hoodoo Peak, mtn., Wa., U.S. | A5 | 124 |
| Hood Point, c., Austl. | F2 | 50 |
| Hood River, Or., U.S. | B5 | 114 |
| Hood River, co., Or., U.S. | B5 | 114 |
| Hoodsport, Wa., U.S. | B2 | 124 |
| Hoogeveen, Neth. | B6 | 17 |
| Hoogezand, Neth. | A6 | 17 |
| Hookena, Hi., U.S. | D6 | 88 |
| Hooker, Ok., U.S. | e9 | 113 |
| Hooker, S.D., U.S. | D8 | 118 |
| Hooker, co., Ne., U.S. | C4 | 104 |
| Hooker, Bi'r, well, Eg. | D2 | 41 |
| Hooker, Mount, mtn., Can. | C8 | 69 |
| Hookerton, N.C., U.S. | B5 | 110 |
| Hook Head, c., Ire. | E5 | 11 |
| Hooksett, N.H., U.S. | D4 | 106 |
| Hoolehua, Hi., U.S. | B4 | 88 |
| Hoonah, Ak., U.S. | D12 | 79 |
| Hoopa Valley Indian Reservation, Ca., U.S. | B2 | 82 |
| Hooper, Co., U.S. | D5 | 83 |
| Hooper, Ne., U.S. | C9 | 104 |
| Hooper, Ut., U.S. | B3 | 121 |
| Hooper, Wa., U.S. | C7 | 124 |
| Hooper Bay, Ak., U.S. | C6 | 79 |
| Hooper Creek, stm., Ne., U.S. | h12 | 104 |
| Hooper Islands, is., U.S. | D5 | 97 |
| Hooper Strait, strt., Md., U.S. | D5 | 97 |
| Hoopersville, Md., U.S. | D5 | 97 |
| Hoopes Reservoir, res., De., U.S. | A3 | 85 |
| Hoopeston, Il., U.S. | C6 | 90 |
| Hooping Harbour, Newf. | C3 | 72 |
| Hoople, N.D., U.S. | A8 | 111 |
| Hooppole, Il., U.S. | B4 | 90 |
| Hoorn, Neth. | A6 | 16 |
| Hoosac Range, mts., U.S. | A1 | 98 |
| Hoosic, stm., U.S. | C7 | 109 |
| Hoosick Falls, N.Y., U.S. | C7 | 109 |
| Hoosier, Sask. | F1 | 75 |
| Hoosuc Range, mts., U.S. | C6 | 124 |
| Hoover, Al., U.S. | *g7 | 78 |
| Hoover Dam, U.S. | G7 | 105 |
| Hoover Reservoir, res., Oh., U.S. | B3 | 112 |
| Hooverson Heights, W.V., U.S. | f8 | 125 |
| Hooversville, Pa., U.S. | F4 | 115 |
| Hopa, Tur. | B13 | 40 |
| Hopatcong, N.J., U.S. | B3 | 107 |
| Hopatcong, Lake, l., N.J., U.S. | A3 | 107 |
| Hop Bottom, Pa., U.S. | C10 | 115 |
| Hope, B.C. | E7 | 69 |
| Hope, Ak., U.S. | C10 | 79 |
| Hope, Ar., U.S. | D2 | 81 |
| Hope, Id., U.S. | A2 | 89 |
| Hope, In., U.S. | F6 | 91 |
| Hope, Ks., U.S. | D6 | 93 |
| Hope, Me., U.S. | D3 | 96 |
| Hope, Mn., U.S. | E6 | 99 |
| Hope, N.M., U.S. | E5 | 108 |
| Hope, N.D., U.S. | B8 | 111 |
| Hope, R.I., U.S. | D3 | 116 |
| Hope, i., Nor. | B12 | 128 |
| Hope, Ben, mtn., Scot., U.K. | A4 | 10 |
| Hope, Loch, l., Scot., U.K. | B4 | 10 |
| Hope, Point, c., Ak., U.S. | B6 | 79 |
| Hopedale, Newf. | g9 | 72 |
| Hopedale, Il., U.S. | C4 | 90 |
| Hopedale, La., U.S. | E6 | 95 |
| Hopedale, Ma., U.S. | B4 | 98 |
| Hopedale, Oh., U.S. | B5 | 112 |
| Hopeh see Hebei, prov., China | D8 | 31 |
| Hope Hull, Al., U.S. | C3 | 78 |
| Hope Island, i., B.C. | D4 | 69 |
| Hope Island, i., R.I., U.S. | E5 | 116 |
| Hopelchén, Mex. | D7 | 63 |
| Hope Mills, N.C., U.S. | B4 | 110 |
| Hopes Advance, Cap, c., Que. | f13 | 74 |
| Hopeton, Ok., U.S. | A3 | 113 |
| Hopetoun, Austl. | G4 | 51 |
| Hopetown, S. Afr. | G4 | 49 |
| Hope Valley, R.I., U.S. | E2 | 116 |
| Hopeville, Ia., U.S. | C3 | 92 |
| Hopewell, N.S. | D7 | 71 |
| Hopewell, N.J., U.S. | C3 | 107 |
| Hopewell, Oh., U.S. | B3 | 112 |
| Hopewell, Pa., U.S. | F5 | 115 |
| Hopewell, Va., U.S. | C5 | 123 |
| Hopewell Cape, N.B. | D5 | 71 |
| Hopewell Junction, N.Y., U.S. | D7 | 109 |
| Hopi Buttes, mtn., Az., U.S. | B5 | 80 |
| Hopi Indian Reservation, Az., U.S. | A5 | 80 |
| Hopkins, Mn., U.S. | n12 | 100 |
| Hopkins, Mo., U.S. | A3 | 102 |
| Hopkins, co., Ky., U.S. | D6 | 117 |
| Hopkins, co., Ky., U.S. | C2 | 94 |
| Hopkins, co., Tx., U.S. | C5 | 120 |
| Hopkinsville, Ky., U.S. | D2 | 94 |
| Hopkinton, Ia., U.S. | B6 | 92 |
| Hopkinton, Ma., U.S. | B4 | 98 |
| Hopkinton, N.H., U.S. | D3 | 106 |
| Hopkinton, N.Y., U.S. | f10 | 109 |
| Hopkinton, R.I., U.S. | F1 | 116 |
| Hopkinton Lake, res., N.H., U.S. | D3 | 106 |
| Hopland, Ca., U.S. | C2 | 82 |
| Hopwood, Pa., U.S. | G2 | 115 |
| Hopson, Tn., U.S. | C11 | 119 |
| Hoquiam, Wa., U.S. | C2 | 124 |
| Horace, Ks., U.S. | D2 | 93 |
| Horace, N.D., U.S. | C9 | 111 |
| Horace Mountain, mtn., Ak., U.S. | B10 | 79 |
| Horatio, Ar., U.S. | D1 | 81 |
| Horatio, S.C., U.S. | C6 | 117 |
| Horažďovice, Czech. | D8 | 19 |
| Horb, W. Ger. | E3 | 19 |
| Hørby, Den. | A4 | 15 |
| Hörby, Swe. | C7 | 15 |
| Horconcitos, Pan. | F6 | 62 |
| Hord, Il., U.S. | E5 | 90 |
| Horden, Switz. | E4 | 18 |
| Horicon, Wi., U.S. | E5 | 126 |
| Horine, Mo., U.S. | C7 | 102 |
| Hörle, Swe. | D6 | 99 |
| Horlick Mountains, mts., Ant. | A36 | 7 |
| Hormoz, i., Iran | H8 | 39 |
| Hormuz, Strait of, strt., Asia | C5 | 38 |
| Horn, Aus. | G15 | 18 |
| Horn, Cape, c., Chile | k12 | 54 |
| Horn, i., Ice. | m21 | 14 |
| Hornavan, l., Swe. | D7 | 14 |
| Hornbeak, Tn., U.S. | A2 | 119 |
| Hornbeck, La., U.S. | C2 | 95 |
| Hornburg, W. Ger. | A5 | 19 |
| Horncastle, Eng., U.K. | A7 | 12 |
| Hornell, N.Y., U.S. | C3 | 109 |
| Hornerstown, N.J., U.S. | C3 | 107 |
| Hornersville, Mo., U.S. | E7 | 102 |
| Horn Head, c., Ire. | B4 | 11 |
| Hornick, Ia., U.S. | B1 | 92 |
| Horning's Mills, Ont. | C4 | 73 |
| Horní Počernice, Czech. | n18 | 26 |
| Horn Island, i., Ms., U.S. | E5 | 101 |
| Horn Island Pass, strt., Ms., U.S. | g8 | 101 |
| Horn Lake, Ms., U.S. | A3 | 101 |
| Horn Mountain, mtn., Al., U.S. | B3 | 78 |
| Horn Plateau, plat., N.W. Ter. | D9 | 66 |
| Horn Pond, l., Ma., U.S. | g11 | 98 |
| Hornsby, Tn., U.S. | B3 | 119 |
| Hornsby, Eng., U.K. | D6 | 10 |
| Hornsea, Eng., U.K. | D6 | 10 |
| Hornslet, Den. | B4 | 15 |
| Hořovice, Czech. | D8 | 19 |
| Horqin Youyi Qianqi, China | A10 | 32 |
| Horqin Youyi Zhongqi, China | B9 | 32 |
| Horqueta, Para. | D4 | 55 |
| Horred, Swe. | A6 | 15 |
| Horry, co., S.C., U.S. | D10 | 117 |
| Horse, stm., Alta. | A5 | 68 |
| Horse Branch, Ky., U.S. | C3 | 94 |
| Horse Cave, Ky., U.S. | C4 | 94 |
| Horse Creek, Wy., U.S. | E7 | 127 |
| Horse Creek, stm., U.S. | E8 | 127 |
| Horse Creek, stm., Co., U.S. | C7 | 83 |
| Horse Creek, stm., Wy., U.S. | D4 | 102 |
| Horse Creek Reservoir, res., Co., U.S. | C7 | 83 |
| Horsefly, B.C. | C7 | 69 |
| Horsefly Lake, l., B.C. | C7 | 69 |
| Horsehead Lake, l., N.D., U.S. | B6 | 111 |
| Horseheads, N.Y., U.S. | C4 | 109 |
| Horse Heaven Hills, hills, Wa., U.S. | C6 | 124 |
| Horse Islands, Newf. | C4 | 72 |
| Horse Mountain, mtn., N.M., U.S. | D1 | 108 |
| Horsens, Den. | J3 | 14 |
| Horseshoe Beach, Fl., U.S. | C3 | 86 |
| Horseshoe Bend, Id., U.S. | F2 | 89 |
| Horseshoe Bend National Military Park, Al., U.S. | C4 | 78 |
| Horseshoe Cove, b., Fl., U.S. | C3 | 86 |
| Horseshoe Lake, l., Man. | C4 | 70 |
| Horseshoe Point, c., Fl., U.S. | C3 | 86 |
| Horseshoe Reservoir, res., Az., U.S. | C4 | 80 |
| Horse Springs, N.M., U.S. | D1 | 108 |
| Horsham, Austl. | G7 | 50 |
| Horsham, Eng., U.K. | J12 | 12 |
| Horsham, Pa., U.S. | *F11 | 115 |
| Horšovský Týn, Czech. | D7 | 19 |
| Horta, Port. | g8 | 44 |
| Horten, Nor. | H4 | 14 |
| Hortense, Ga., U.S. | E5 | 87 |
| Horton, Al., U.S. | A3 | 78 |
| Horton, In., U.S. | D5 | 91 |
| Horton, Ks., U.S. | C8 | 93 |
| Horton, Mo., U.S. | D3 | 102 |
| Horton, stm., N.W. Ter. | C8 | 66 |
| Horton Lake, l., Vt., U.S. | D2 | 122 |
| Hortonia, Lake, l., Vt., U.S. | D2 | 122 |
| Hortonville, Wi., U.S. | D5 | 126 |
| Hörvik, Swe. | C5 | 15 |
| Hørve, Den. | B8 | 18 |
| Hörwe, Switz. | B5 | 21 |
| Hoschton, Ga., U.S. | B3 | 87 |
| Hosford, Fl., U.S. | B2 | 86 |
| Hoshāb, Pak. | H11 | 39 |
| Hoshiārpur, India | B6 | 36 |
| Hoskins, Newf. | B8 | 104 |
| Hoskins, Or., U.S. | C3 | 114 |
| Hoskinston, Ky., U.S. | C6 | 94 |
| Hosmer, B.C. | E10 | 69 |
| Hosmer, S.D., U.S. | B6 | 118 |
| Hospers, Ia., U.S. | A2 | 92 |
| Hospet, India | E3 | 11 |
| Hospitalet, Spain | B7 | 22 |
| Hosta Butte, mtn., N.M., U.S. | B1 | 108 |
| Hoste, Isla, i., Chile | k12 | 54 |
| Hot, Thai. | C3 | 35 |
| Hotaka, Mount, mtn., Japan | H8 | 33 |
| Hotan, China | A6 | 36 |
| Hotan He, stm., China | A7 | 36 |
| Hotchkiss, Co., U.S. | C3 | 83 |
| Hotchkissville, Ct., U.S. | C3 | 84 |
| Hot Coffee, Ms., U.S. | D4 | 101 |
| Hot Creek Range, mts., Nv., U.S. | E5 | 105 |
| Hot Creek Valley, val., Nv., U.S. | E5 | 105 |
| Hotevilla, Az., U.S. | B5 | 80 |
| Hoting, Swe. | E7 | 14 |
| Hot Spring, co., Ar., U.S. | C2 | 81 |
| Hot Springs, Mt., U.S. | C2 | 103 |
| Hot Springs see Truth or Consequences, N.M., U.S. | D2 | 108 |
| Hot Springs, N.C., U.S. | f10 | 110 |
| Hot Springs, S.D., U.S. | D2 | 118 |
| Hot Springs, Va., U.S. | C3 | 123 |
| Hot Springs, co., Wy., U.S. | C4 | 127 |
| Hot Springs National Park, Ar., U.S. | C2 | 81 |
| Hot Springs National Park, Ar., U.S. | C2 | 81 |
| Hot Springs Peak, mtn., Ca., U.S. | B3 | 82 |
| Hot Springs Peak, mtn., Nv., U.S. | B4 | 105 |
| Hot Sulphur Springs, Co., U.S. | A4 | 83 |
| Hottah Lake, l., N.W. Ter. | C9 | 66 |
| Hotte, Massif de la, mts., Haiti | E7 | 64 |
| Houck, Az., U.S. | B6 | 80 |
| Houffalize, Bel. | D5 | 17 |
| Houghton, Mi., U.S. | A2 | 99 |
| Houghton, N.Y., U.S. | C2 | 109 |
| Houghton, S.D., U.S. | B7 | 118 |
| Houghton, co., Mi., U.S. | B2 | 99 |
| Houghton Lake, Mi., U.S. | D6 | 99 |
| Houghton Lake, l., Mi., U.S. | D6 | 99 |
| Houghton Lake Heights, Mi., U.S. | D6 | 99 |
| Houilles, Fr. | g9 | 16 |
| Houlka, La., U.S. | A4 | 101 |
| Houlton, Me., U.S. | B5 | 96 |
| Houltonville, La., U.S. | h11 | 95 |
| Houma, La., U.S. | E5 | 95 |
| Houmt Essouk, Tun. | C7 | 44 |
| Houndé, Burkina | D4 | 45 |
| Hourn, Loch, b., Scot., U.K. | C3 | 13 |
| Housatonic, Ma., U.S. | B1 | 98 |
| Housatonic, stm., U.S. | D3 | 84 |
| House, N.M., U.S. | C6 | 108 |
| House, stm., Alta. | B4 | 68 |
| House Range, mts., Ut., U.S. | D2 | 121 |
| House Springs, Mo., U.S. | g12 | 102 |
| Houston, B.C. | B4 | 69 |
| Houston, Al., U.S. | A2 | 78 |
| Houston, Ar., U.S. | B3 | 81 |
| Houston, De., U.S. | E3 | 85 |
| Houston, In., U.S. | F5 | 91 |
| Houston, Mn., U.S. | G7 | 100 |
| Houston, Mo., U.S. | D6 | 102 |
| Houston, Ms., U.S. | B4 | 101 |
| Houston, Oh., U.S. | B1 | 112 |
| Houston, Pa., U.S. | F1 | 115 |
| Houston, Tx., U.S. | E5 | 120 |
| Houston, co., Al., U.S. | D4 | 78 |
| Houston, co., Ga., U.S. | D3 | 87 |
| Houston, co., Mn., U.S. | G7 | 100 |
| Houston, co., Tn., U.S. | A4 | 119 |
| Houston, co., Tx., U.S. | D5 | 120 |
| Houston, stm., La., U.S. | D2 | 95 |
| Houston, Lake, res., Tx., U.S. | r14 | 120 |
| Houstonia, Mo., U.S. | C4 | 102 |
| Houston Intercontinental Airport, Tx., U.S. | r14 | 120 |
| Houtzdale, Pa., U.S. | E5 | 115 |
| Hov, Mong. | B3 | 31 |
| Hovd, stm., Mong. | B3 | 31 |
| Hove, Eng., U.K. | E6 | 10 |
| Hövelhof, W. Ger. | B3 | 19 |
| Hoven, S.D., U.S. | B6 | 118 |
| Hovenweep National Monument, Ut., U.S. | F6 | 121 |
| Hövsgöl Lake, l., Mong. | A5 | 31 |
| Howar, Wādī, val., Afr. | B2 | 47 |
| Howard, Co., U.S. | B2 | 78 |
| Howard, Ga., U.S. | D2 | 87 |
| Howard, Ks., U.S. | E7 | 93 |
| Howard, Pa., U.S. | E7 | 115 |
| Howard, S.D., U.S. | D8 | 118 |
| Howard, Wi., U.S. | D5 | 126 |
| Howard, co., Ar., U.S. | C2 | 81 |
| Howard, co., In., U.S. | C5 | 91 |
| Howard, co., Ia., U.S. | A5 | 92 |
| Howard, co., Md., U.S. | B4 | 97 |
| Howard, co., Mo., U.S. | B5 | 102 |
| Howard, co., Ne., U.S. | C7 | 104 |
| Howard, co., Tx., U.S. | C2 | 120 |
| Howard City, Mi., U.S. | E5 | 99 |
| Howard Hanson Reservoir, res., Wa., U.S. | B4 | 124 |
| Howard Lake, Mn., U.S. | E4 | 100 |
| Howard Prairie Lake, res., Or., U.S. | E4 | 114 |
| Howards Grove-Millersville, Wi., U.S. | E6 | 126 |
| Howardville, Mo., U.S. | E8 | 102 |
| Howe, Id., U.S. | F6 | 89 |
| Howe, In., U.S. | A7 | 91 |
| Howe, Ok., U.S. | C7 | 113 |
| Howe, Cape, c., Austl. | G9 | 50 |
| Howell, Mi., U.S. | F7 | 99 |
| Howell, Ut., U.S. | B3 | 121 |
| Howell, co., Mo., U.S. | E6 | 102 |
| Howells, Ne., U.S. | C8 | 104 |
| Howes, S.D., U.S. | C3 | 118 |
| Howe Sound, strt., B.C. | E6 | 69 |
| Howesville, W.V., U.S. | B5 | 125 |
| Howick, Austl. | D4 | 74 |
| Howison, Ms., U.S. | E4 | 101 |
| Howland, Me., U.S. | C4 | 96 |
| Howland, Oh., U.S. | *A5 | 112 |
| Howland Island, i., Oc. | F11 | 6 |
| Howley, Newf. | D3 | 72 |
| Howley, Mount, mtn., Newf. | D2 | 72 |
| Howser, B.C. | D9 | 69 |
| Howson Peak, mtn., B.C. | B3 | 69 |
| Howth (part of Dublin), Ire. | D5 | 11 |
| Hoxie, Ar., U.S. | A5 | 81 |
| Hoxie, Ks., U.S. | C3 | 93 |
| Höxter, W. Ger. | B3 | 19 |
| Hoy, i., Scot., U.K. | A5 | 10 |
| Hoya, W. Ger. | A4 | 19 |
| Hoyerswerda, E. Ger. | C7 | 18 |
| Hoyland, Eng., U.K. | D6 | 10 |
| Hoyleton, Il., U.S. | E4 | 90 |
| Hoyo, Sierra del, mts., Spain | o17 | 22 |
| Hoyt, Co., U.S. | A6 | 83 |
| Hoyt, Ks., U.S. | C8 | 93 |
| Hoyt, Ok., U.S. | B6 | 113 |
| Hoyt Lakes, Mn., U.S. | C6 | 100 |
| Hradec Králové, Czech. | C3 | 19 |
| Hranice, Czech. | D5 | 26 |
| Hronov, Czech. | D5 | 26 |
| Hříňová, Czech. | D5 | 26 |
| Hrubieszów, Pol. | C7 | 26 |
| Hsinchu, Tai. | G9 | 31 |
| Hsipaw, Burma | A2 | 35 |
| Huacho, Peru | D2 | 58 |
| Huachuca City, Az., U.S. | F5 | 80 |
| Huacrachuco, Peru | C2 | 58 |
| Huade, China | D5 | 32 |
| Huadian, China | C10 | 31 |
| Huai'an (Huaicheng), China | H8 | 32 |
| Huaibei, China | *E8 | 31 |
| Huaide, China | C9 | 31 |
| Huailai, China | D6 | 32 |
| Huainan, China | E8 | 31 |
| Huaiyang, China | H6 | 32 |
| Huaiyin, China | E8 | 31 |
| Huaiyin, China | H7 | 32 |
| Huajuapan de León, Mex. | D5 | 63 |
| Hualapai Indian Reservation, Az., U.S. | B2 | 80 |
| Hualapai Mountains, mts., Az., U.S. | B2 | 80 |
| Hualapai Peak, mtn., Az., U.S. | B2 | 80 |
| Hualgayoc, Peru | C2 | 58 |
| Hualien, Tai. | G9 | 31 |
| Huallaga, stm., Peru | C2 | 58 |
| Huallanca, Peru | C2 | 58 |
| Huamachuco, Peru | C2 | 58 |
| Huamantla, Mex. | n15 | 63 |
| Huambo, Ang. | D2 | 48 |
| Huambo, dept., Ang. | D2 | 48 |
| Huancabamba, Peru | C2 | 58 |
| Huancané, Peru | E4 | 58 |
| Huancavelica, Peru | D2 | 58 |
| Huancavelica, dept., Peru | D2 | 58 |
| Huancayo, Peru | D2 | 58 |
| Huanchaca, Bol. | D2 | 55 |
| Huangchuan, China | H6 | 32 |
| Huanggang, China | E8 | 31 |
| Huang He (Yellow), stm., China | D8 | 31 |
| Huangling, China | D6 | 31 |
| Huangmei, China | I6 | 32 |
| Huangpang, China | K2 | 32 |
| Huangshi, China | E8 | 31 |
| Huangxian, China | F9 | 32 |
| Huangyan, China | D5 | 31 |
| Huanjiang, China | G6 | 31 |
| Huanta, Peru | D3 | 58 |
| Huánuco, Peru | C2 | 58 |
| Huánuco, dept., Peru | C2 | 58 |
| Huanuni, Bol. | C2 | 55 |
| Huara, Chile | D2 | 55 |
| Huaral, Peru | D2 | 58 |
| Huaraz, Peru | C2 | 58 |
| Huari, Bol. | C2 | 55 |
| Huariaca, Peru | D2 | 58 |
| Huarina, Bol. | C2 | 55 |
| Huarmey, Peru | D2 | 58 |
| Huascarán, Nevado, mtn., Peru | C2 | 58 |
| Huasco, Chile | E1 | 55 |
| Huasco, stm., Chile | E1 | 55 |
| Huatabampo, Mex. | B3 | 63 |
| Huatusco [de Chicuellar], Mex. | H11 | 63 |
| Huauchinango, Mex. | m14 | 63 |
| Huaxian, China | G6 | 32 |
| Huayllay, Peru | D2 | 58 |
| Huaytará, Peru | D2 | 58 |
| Huayuan, China | J3 | 32 |
| Hubbard, Sask. | F4 | 75 |
| Hubbard, Ia., U.S. | B4 | 92 |
| Hubbard, Mn., U.S. | D4 | 100 |
| Hubbard, Ne., U.S. | B9 | 104 |
| Hubbard, Oh., U.S. | A5 | 112 |
| Hubbard, Or., U.S. | B4 | 114 |
| Hubbard, Tx., U.S. | D4 | 120 |
| Hubbard, co., Mn., U.S. | C4 | 100 |
| Hubbard Creek Lake, res., Tx., U.S. | C3 | 120 |
| Hubbard Lake, Mi., U.S. | D7 | 99 |
| Hubbard Lake, l., Mi., U.S. | D7 | 99 |
| Hubbards, N.S. | E5 | 71 |
| Hubbardston, Ma., U.S. | B3 | 98 |
| Hubbardton, Vt., U.S. | D2 | 122 |
| Hubbardton, stm., Vt., U.S. | D2 | 122 |
| Hubbell, Mi., U.S. | A2 | 99 |
| Hubbell, Ne., U.S. | D8 | 104 |
| Hubei, prov., China | E7 | 31 |
| Huben, Aus. | D3 | 87 |
| Huber, Ga., U.S. | D3 | 87 |
| Huber Heights, Oh., U.S. | *C1 | 112 |
| Huber Ridge, Oh., U.S. | *B3 | 112 |
| Huber South, Oh., U.S. | *C1 | 112 |
| Hubli-Dhārwār, India | E3 | 36 |
| Huckleberry Hill, Ct., U.S. | B4 | 84 |
| Huckleberry Mountain, mtn., Or., U.S. | D4 | 114 |
| Huddersfield, Eng., U.K. | *H7 | 10 |
| Huddinge, Swe. | B11 | 100 |
| Huddleston, Va., U.S. | C3 | 123 |
| Huddleston Knob, mtn., Tn., U.S. | D8 | 119 |
| Huddy, Ky., U.S. | C7 | 94 |
| Hude, W. Ger. | B8 | 19 |
| Hudgin Creek, stm., Ar., U.S. | D3 | 81 |
| Hudiksvall, Swe. | F7 | 14 |
| Hudson, Que. | D3 | 74 |
| Hudson, Co., U.S. | A5 | 83 |
| Hudson, Fl., U.S. | D4 | 86 |
| Hudson, Il., U.S. | C5 | 90 |
| Hudson, In., U.S. | A7 | 91 |
| Hudson, Ia., U.S. | B5 | 92 |
| Hudson, Ks., U.S. | D5 | 93 |
| Hudson, Me., U.S. | D4 | 96 |
| Hudson, Ma., U.S. | B4 | 98 |
| Hudson, Mi., U.S. | G6 | 99 |
| Hudson, N.H., U.S. | E4 | 106 |
| Hudson, N.Y., U.S. | C7 | 109 |
| Hudson, N.C., U.S. | B1 | 110 |
| Hudson, Oh., U.S. | A4 | 112 |
| Hudson, S.D., U.S. | D9 | 118 |
| Hudson, Wi., U.S. | D1 | 126 |
| Hudson, Wy., U.S. | D4 | 127 |
| Hudson, co., N.J., U.S. | B4 | 107 |
| Hudson, stm., U.S. | E7 | 109 |
| Hudson, Lake, res., Ok., U.S. | A6 | 113 |
| Hudson Bay, Sask. | E4 | 75 |
| Hudson Bay, b., Can. | D15 | 66 |
| Hudson Falls, N.Y., U.S. | B7 | 109 |
| Hudson Hope, B.C. | A6 | 69 |
| Hudson Lake, In., U.S. | A4 | 91 |
| Hudson Mountain, mtn., Me., U.S. | C3 | 96 |
| Hudson Mountains, mts., Ant. | B3 | 7 |
| Hudson Strait, strt., Can. | D18 | 66 |
| Hudsonville, Mi., U.S. | F5 | 99 |
| Hudspeth, co., Tx., U.S. | o12 | 120 |
| Hudwin Lake, l., Man. | C4 | 70 |
| Hue, Viet. | B4 | 35 |
| Huedin, Rom. | B6 | 24 |
| Huehuetenango, Guat. | n14 | 63 |
| Huehuetla, Mex. | — | — |
| Huejotzingo, Mex. | n14 | 63 |
| Huejutla [de Reyes], Mex. | m14 | 63 |
| Huelma, Spain | D4 | 22 |
| Huelva, Spain | D2 | 22 |
| Huentelauquén, Chile | A2 | 54 |
| Huércal-Overa, Spain | D5 | 22 |
| Huerfano, co., Co., U.S. | D5 | 83 |
| Huerfano, stm., Co., U.S. | D6 | 83 |
| Huerfano Mountain, mtn., N.M., U.S. | A2 | 108 |
| Huerva, stm., Spain | B5 | 22 |
| Huesca, Spain | A5 | 22 |
| Huéscar, Spain | D4 | 22 |
| Huetamo de Núñez, Mex. | D4 | 63 |
| Huete, Spain | B4 | 22 |
| Huetter, Id., U.S. | *B2 | 89 |
| Hueytown, Al., U.S. | g6 | 78 |
| Huff, N.D., U.S. | C5 | 111 |
| Huffakers, Nv., U.S. | D2 | 105 |
| Huger, S.C., U.S. | h12 | 117 |
| Huggins, Mount, mtn., Ant. | B29 | 7 |
| Hugh Butler Lake, res., Ne., U.S. | D5 | 104 |
| Hughenden, Austl. | D7 | 50 |
| Hughenden, Alta. | C5 | 68 |
| Hughes, Ak., U.S. | B9 | 79 |
| Hughes, Ar., U.S. | C5 | 81 |
| Hughes, co., Ok., U.S. | B5 | 113 |
| Hughes, co., S.D., U.S. | C5 | 118 |
| Hughes, stm., Man. | A1 | 70 |
| Hughes, North Fork, stm., W.V., U.S. | B3 | 125 |
| Hughes, South Fork, stm., W.V., U.S. | B3 | 125 |
| Hughesville, Mo., U.S. | C4 | 102 |
| Hughesville, Md., U.S. | C4 | 97 |
| Hughesville, Pa., U.S. | D8 | 115 |
| Hughton, Sask. | F2 | 75 |
| Hugli, stm., India | D8 | 36 |
| Hugo, Co., U.S. | B7 | 83 |
| Hugo, Mn., U.S. | m13 | 100 |
| Hugo, Ok., U.S. | C6 | 113 |
| Hugo Lake, res., Ok., U.S. | C6 | 113 |
| Hugoton, Ks., U.S. | E2 | 93 |
| Huguley, Al., U.S. | *C4 | 78 |
| Huichang, China | F8 | 31 |
| Huichapan, Mex. | m14 | 63 |
| Hŭichŏn, N. Kor. | F3 | 33 |
| Huíla, dept., Ang. | D2 | 48 |
| Huila, dept., Col. | C2 | 60 |
| Huila, Nevado del, mtn., Col. | C2 | 60 |
| Huili, China | F5 | 31 |
| Huimanguillo, Mex. | B1 | 62 |
| Huinan, China | E3 | 33 |
| Huitzuco [de los Figueroa], Mex. | n14 | 63 |
| Huixtla, Mex. | D6 | 63 |
| Huizen, Neth. | B5 | 17 |
| Huizhou, China | G7 | 31 |
| Hukou, China | F8 | 31 |
| Hukuntsi, Bots. | B3 | 49 |
| Hulah Lake, res., Ok., U.S. | A5 | 113 |
| Hulan, China | B10 | 31 |
| Hulbert, Mi., U.S. | B5 | 99 |
| Hulbert, Ok., U.S. | B6 | 113 |
| Hulen, Ky., U.S. | D6 | 94 |
| Hulett, Wy., U.S. | B8 | 127 |
| Hulin, China | C6 | 33 |
| Hull, Que. | D2 | 74 |
| Hull, Il., U.S. | D4 | 100 |
| Hull, Ia., U.S. | A1 | 92 |
| Hull, Ma., U.S. | B6 | 98 |
| Hull, Or., U.S. | D2 | 74 |
| Hull, co., Que. | D2 | 74 |
| Hull Glacier, ice, Ant. | B35 | 7 |
| Hull see Kingston upon Hull, Eng., U.K. | D6 | 10 |
| Hulls Cove, Me., U.S. | D4 | 96 |
| Hulst, Neth. | D4 | 17 |
| Huludao, China | C9 | 31 |
| Hulun Nur, l., China | B9 | 31 |
| Hŭlwān, Eg. | E3 | 41 |
| Huma, China | A10 | 31 |
| Humacao, P.R. | B4 | 65 |
| Humahuaca, Arg. | D2 | 55 |
| Humaitá, Braz. | D2 | 59 |
| Humansdorp, S. Afr. | H4 | 49 |
| Humansville, Mo., U.S. | D4 | 102 |
| Humarock, Ma., U.S. | h13 | 98 |
| Humbe, Ang. | E1 | 49 |
| Humber, stm., Eng., U.K. | D6 | 10 |
| Humberside, co., Eng., U.K. | G8 | 13 |
| Humbird, Wi., U.S. | D3 | 126 |
| Humble, Tx., U.S. | E5 | 120 |
| Humboldt, Az., U.S. | C3 | 80 |
| Humboldt, Ia., U.S. | B3 | 92 |
| Humboldt, Ks., U.S. | E8 | 93 |
| Humboldt, Mn., U.S. | B1 | 100 |
| Humboldt, Ne., U.S. | D10 | 104 |
| Humboldt, S.D., U.S. | D8 | 118 |
| Humboldt, Tn., U.S. | B3 | 119 |
| Humboldt, co., Ca., U.S. | B2 | 82 |
| Humboldt, co., Ia., U.S. | B3 | 92 |
| Humboldt, co., Nv., U.S. | B3 | 105 |
| Humboldt, stm., Nv., U.S. | C3 | 105 |
| Humboldt, North Fork, stm., Nv., U.S. | B6 | 105 |
| Humboldt Mountains, mts., Ant. | B14 | 7 |
| Humboldt Range, mts., Nv., U.S. | C3 | 105 |
| Hume, Mo., U.S. | C3 | 102 |
| Hume, Va., U.S. | B5 | 123 |
| Hume, Lake, res., Austl. | G6 | 51 |
| Humenné, Czech. | D6 | 19 |
| Humeston, Ia., U.S. | D4 | 92 |
| Hummels Wharf, Pa., U.S. | E8 | 115 |
| Humpata, Ang. | D1 | 48 |
| Humphrey, Ar., U.S. | C4 | 81 |
| Humphrey, Ne., U.S. | C8 | 104 |
| Humphreys, co., Ms., U.S. | B3 | 101 |
| Humphreys, co., Tn., U.S. | A4 | 119 |
| Humphreys, Mount, mtn., Ca., U.S. | D4 | 82 |
| Humphreys Peak, mtn., Az., U.S. | B4 | 80 |
| Humpolec, Czech. | D3 | 19 |
| Humptulips, Wa., U.S. | B2 | 124 |
| Hūn, Libya | D3 | 43 |
| Hun, stm., China | B9 | 32 |
| Hunan, prov., China | F7 | 31 |
| Hunchun, China | C11 | 31 |
| Hundested, Den. | C5 | 15 |
| Hundred, W.V., U.S. | B4 | 125 |
| Hundred Acre Pond, l., R.I., U.S. | E3 | 116 |
| Hunedoara, Rom. | D5 | 24 |
| Hünfeld, W. Ger. | C4 | 19 |
| Hungary, ctry., Eur. | B4 | 24 |
| Hungerford, Austl. | D5 | 51 |
| Hüngnam, N. Kor. | D10 | 31 |
| Hungry Hill, mtn., Ire. | F2 | 11 |
| Hungry Horse, Mt., U.S. | B2 | 103 |
| Hungry Horse Reservoir, res., Mt., U.S. | B3 | 103 |
| Huningue, Fr. | B3 | 20 |
| Hunish, Rubha, c., Scot., U.K. | C10 | 31 |
| Hunjiang, China | C10 | 31 |
| Hunn, l., Swe. | u33 | 14 |
| Hunnewell, Ks., U.S. | E6 | 93 |
| Hunnewell, Mo., U.S. | B6 | 102 |
| Hunt, China | B9 | 32 |
| Hunt, Ar., U.S. | B2 | 81 |
| Hunt, Il., U.S. | D5 | 90 |
| Hunt, co., Tx., U.S. | C4 | 120 |
| Hunt, stm., R.I., U.S. | D4 | 116 |
| Hunte, stm., W. Ger. | F2 | 15 |
| Hunter, Ar., U.S. | B4 | 81 |
| Hunter, Ks., U.S. | C5 | 93 |
| Hunter, N.D., U.S. | B8 | 111 |
| Hunter, i., Austl. | A4 | 113 |
| Hunter, i., Austl. | o14 | 50 |
| Hunter, Cape, c., N.W. Ter. | B18 | 66 |
| Hunter Island, i., B.C. | D3 | 69 |
| Hunterdon, co., N.J., U.S. | B3 | 107 |
| Hunter Mountain, mtn., N.Y., U.S. | C6 | 109 |
| Hunter River, P.E.I. | C6 | 71 |
| Hunters, Wa., U.S. | A7 | 124 |
| Huntersfield Mountain, mtn., N.Y., U.S. | C6 | 109 |
| Huntersville, W.V., U.S. | C4 | 125 |
| Huntertown, In., U.S. | B7 | 91 |
| Huntingburg, In., U.S. | H4 | 91 |
| Hunting Creek, stm., Md., U.S. | C4 | 97 |
| Huntingdon, Que. | D3 | 74 |
| Huntingdon, Eng., U.K. | B7 | 12 |
| Huntingdon, Pa., U.S. | F6 | 115 |
| Huntingdon, Tn., U.S. | A3 | 119 |
| Huntingdon, co., Pa., U.S. | F5 | 115 |
| Huntingdon, co., Que. | D3 | 74 |
| Huntington, Ar., U.S. | B1 | 81 |
| Huntington, In., U.S. | C7 | 91 |
| Huntington, Ma., U.S. | B2 | 98 |
| Huntington, N.Y., U.S. | E7 | 109 |
| Huntington, Or., U.S. | C9 | 114 |
| Huntington, Tx., U.S. | D5 | 120 |
| Huntington, Ut., U.S. | D5 | 121 |
| Huntington, Vt., U.S. | C3 | 122 |
| Huntington, Va., U.S. | *B5 | 123 |
| Huntington, W.V., U.S. | C2 | 125 |
| Huntington, co., In., U.S. | C6 | 91 |
| Huntington Bay, N.Y., U.S. | *E7 | 109 |
| Huntington Beach, Ca., U.S. | F4 | 82 |
| Huntington Center, Vt., U.S. | C3 | 122 |
| Huntington Creek, stm., Nv., U.S. | C6 | 105 |
| Huntington Lake, res., In., U.S. | C7 | 91 |
| Huntington Park, Ca., U.S. | *E4 | 82 |
| Huntington Station, N.Y., U.S. | *E7 | 109 |
| Huntington Woods, Mi., U.S. | p15 | 99 |
| Huntland, Tn., U.S. | B5 | 119 |
| Huntley, Il., U.S. | A5 | 90 |
| Huntley, Mn., U.S. | G4 | 100 |
| Huntley, Mt., U.S. | E8 | 103 |
| Huntley, Ne., U.S. | D6 | 104 |
| Huntley, Wy., U.S. | E8 | 127 |
| Huntly, Scot., U.K. | B5 | 10 |
| Hunt Mountain, mtn., Wy., U.S. | B5 | 127 |
| Hunts Point, N.S. | F5 | 71 |
| Huntsville, Ont. | B5 | 73 |
| Huntsville, Al., U.S. | A3 | 78 |
| Huntsville, Ar., U.S. | A2 | 81 |
| Huntsville, Mo., U.S. | B5 | 102 |
| Huntsville, Oh., U.S. | B2 | 112 |
| Huntsville, Tn., U.S. | C9 | 119 |
| Huntsville, Tx., U.S. | D5 | 120 |
| Huntsville, Ut., U.S. | B4 | 121 |
| Hunucmá, Mex. | C7 | 63 |
| Hunyuan, China | C7 | 32 |
| Huon Gulf, b., Pap. N. Gui. | k12 | 50 |
| Huoshan, China | I7 | 32 |
| Huoxian, China | F4 | 32 |
| Hupeh see Hubei, prov., China | E7 | 31 |
| Ḩurayḍīn, Wādī, val., Eg. | D6 | 41 |
| Hurd, Cape, c., Ont. | B3 | 73 |
| Hurdland, Mo., U.S. | A5 | 102 |
| Hurdsfield, N.D., U.S. | B6 | 111 |
| Hure Qi, China | C10 | 32 |
| Hurley, Mo., U.S. | E4 | 102 |
| Hurley, N.M., U.S. | E1 | 108 |
| Hurley, N.Y., U.S. | D6 | 109 |
| Hurley, S.D., U.S. | D8 | 118 |
| Hurley, Va., U.S. | e9 | 123 |
| Hurley, Wi., U.S. | B3 | 126 |
| Hurleyville, N.Y., U.S. | D6 | 109 |
| Hurliness, Scot., U.K. | C5 | 13 |
| Hurlock, Md., U.S. | C6 | 97 |
| Hurmägai, Pak. | G12 | 39 |
| Huron, Ca., U.S. | G4 | 82 |
| Huron, Ks., U.S. | C8 | 93 |
| Huron, Oh., U.S. | A3 | 112 |
| Huron, S.D., U.S. | C7 | 118 |
| Huron, co., Mi., U.S. | E8 | 99 |
| Huron, co., Oh., U.S. | A3 | 112 |
| Huron, Lake, l., N.A. | B11 | 76 |
| Huron, stm., Mi., U.S. | p14 | 99 |
| Huron, Lake, l., N.A. | B11 | 76 |
| Huron Mountains, hills, Mi., U.S. | B3 | 99 |
| Hurricane, Ut., U.S. | F2 | 121 |
| Hurricane, W.V., U.S. | C2 | 125 |
| Hurricane, Ms., U.S. | A4 | 101 |
| Hurricane Cliffs, clf., U.S. | A2 | 80 |
| Hurricane Creek, stm., Ar. | C3 | 81 |
| Hurricane Creek, stm., Ga. | D4 | 87 |
| Hurricane Mills, Tn., U.S. | B4 | 119 |
| Hurricane Mountain, mtn., Tn., U.S. | C9 | 119 |
| Hurst, Il., U.S. | F4 | 90 |
| Hurst, Tx., U.S. | *n9 | 120 |
| Hurstville, Austl. | *F9 | 50 |
| Hürth, W. Ger. | C1 | 19 |
| Hurtsboro, Al., U.S. | C4 | 78 |
| Hurup, Den. | B9 | 24 |
| Huşi, Rom. | B9 | 24 |

| Name | Map Ref. | Page |
|---|---|---|

Huskvarna (part of Jönköping), Swe. ... I6 14
Huson, Mt., U.S. ... C2 103
Hussar, Alta. ... D4 68
Husser, La., U.S. ... D5 95
Hustburg, Tn., U.S. ... B4 119
Hustisford, Wi., U.S. ... E5 126
Hustle, Va., U.S. ... B5 123
Hustontown, Pa., U.S. ... F5 115
Hustonville, Ky., U.S. ... C5 94
Husum, W. Ger. ... A4 18
Husum, Wa., U.S. ... D4 124
Hutchins, Tx., U.S. ... n10 120
Hutchinson, Ks., U.S. ... D6 93
Hutchinson, Mn., U.S. ... F4 100
Hutchinson, N.J., U.S. ... B2 107
Hutchinson, co., S.D., U.S. ... D8 118
Hutchinson, co., Tx., U.S. ... B2 120
Hutchinson Island, i., Fl., U.S. ... E6 86
Hutchinson Island, i., S.C., U.S. ... k11 117
Hutch Mountain, mtn., Az., U.S. ... C4 80
Hutsonville, Il., U.S. ... D6 90
Hüttental, W. Ger. ... C3 19
Huttig, Ar., U.S. ... D3 81
Hutto, Tx., U.S. ... D4 120
Hutton, Md., U.S. ... m12 97
Huttonsville, W.V., U.S. ... C5 125
Huttwil, Switz. ... B4 21
Hutuo He, stm., China ... E5 32
Huu, Indon. ... G5 34
Huwwärah, Isr. Occ. ... g12 41
Huwwärah, Isr. Occ. ... B7 41
Huxford, Al., U.S. ... D2 78
Huxley, Alta. ... D4 68
Huxley, Ia., U.S. ... C4 92
Huy, Bel. ... B6 16
Hüzgän, Iran ... F4 39
Huzhou, China ... *E9 31
Hvalpsund, Den. ... B3 15
Hvannadalshnúkur, mtn., Ice. ... n24 14
Hvar, i., Yugo. ... D3 24
Hvidbjerg, Den. ... B2 15
Hvide Sande, Den. ... C2 15
Hvidovre, Den. ... *C6 15
Hvitstein, Nor. ... p28 14
Hvittingfoss (part of Kongsberg), Nor. ... p28 14
Hwange, Zimb. ... A4 49
Hwang Ho see Huang He, stm., China ... D8 31
Hyak, Wa., U.S. ... B4 124
Hyampom, Ca., U.S. ... B2 82
Hyannis, Ma., U.S. ... C7 98
Hyannis, Ne., U.S. ... C4 104
Hyannis Port, Ma., U.S. ... C7 98
Hyargas Lake, l., Mong. ... B3 31
Hyas, Sask. ... F4 75
Hyatts, Oh., U.S. ... B2 112
Hyattstown, Md., U.S. ... B3 97
Hyattsville, Md., U.S. ... C4 97
Hyattville, Wy., U.S. ... B5 127
Hybart, Al., U.S. ... D2 78
Hybla Valley, Va., U.S. ... g12 123
Hyco, stm., Va., U.S. ... D3 123
Hyco Lake, res., N.C., U.S. ... A3 110
Hydaburg, Ak., U.S. ... D13 79
Hyde, Pa., U.S. ... D5 115
Hyde, co., N.C., U.S. ... B6 110
Hyde, co., S.D., U.S. ... C6 118
Hyden, Austl. ... F2 50
Hyden, Ky., U.S. ... C6 94
Hyde Park, Guy. ... A3 59
Hyde Park, N.Y., U.S. ... D7 109
Hyde Park, Ut., U.S. ... B4 121
Hyde Park, Vt., U.S. ... B3 122
Hyder, Ak., U.S. ... D13 79
Hyderābād, India ... E6 36
Hyderābād, Pak. ... C4 36
Hydetown, Pa., U.S. ... C2 115
Hydeville, Ct., U.S. ... B6 84
Hydeville, Vt., U.S. ... D2 122
Hydra (Ídhra), i., Grc. ... D4 25
Hydraulic, B.C. ... C7 69
Hydro, Ok., U.S. ... B3 113
Hyères, Fr. ... F7 16
Hyères, Îles d', is., Fr. ... F7 16
Hyesan, N. Kor. ... C10 31
Hygiene, Co., U.S. ... A5 83
Hylo, Alta. ... B4 68
Hyman, S.C., U.S. ... D8 117
Hymera, In., U.S. ... F3 91
Hyndman, Pa., U.S. ... G4 115
Hyndman Peak, mtn., Id., U.S. ... F4 89
Hyner, Pa., U.S. ... D6 115
Hyŏpchŏn, S. Kor. ... I4 33
Hyrum, Ut., U.S. ... B4 121
Hyrynsalmi, Fin. ... E13 14
Hysham, Mt., U.S. ... D9 103
Hythe, Alta. ... B1 68
Hythe, Eng., U.K. ... C9 12
Hyvinkää, Fin. ... *G11 14

**I**

Iaco (Yaco), stm., S.A. ... D4 58
Iaeger, W.V., U.S. ... D3 125
Ialomiţa, stm., Rom. ... C8 24
Iamonia, Lake, l., Fl., U.S. ... B2 86
Iantha, Mo., U.S. ... D3 102
Iapu, Braz. ... B4 56
Iaşi, Rom. ... B8 24
Iatan, Mo., U.S. ... B3 102
Iates Point, c., Guam ... L10 52
Iatt, Lake, res., La., U.S. ... C3 95
Iauaretê, Braz. ... C4 60
Iba, Phil. ... o12 34
Ibadan, Nig. ... E5 45
Ibagué, Col. ... C2 60
Ibanda, Ug. ... B5 48
Ibapah, Ut., U.S. ... C2 121
Ibapah Peak, mtn., Ut., U.S. ... D2 121
Ibar, stm., Yugo. ... D5 24
Ibaraki, Japan ... *I7 33
Ibarra, Ec. ... A2 58
Ibb, Yemen ... C5 47
Ibbenbüren, W. Ger. ... A2 19
Iberá, Laguna, l., Arg. ... E4 55
Iberia, Mo., U.S. ... C5 102
Iberia, co., La., U.S. ... B3 112
Iberia, co., La., U.S. ... E4 95
Iberville, Que. ... D4 74
Iberville, La., U.S. ... D4 95
Iberville, co., La., U.S. ... D4 95
Iberville, Mont d' (Mount Caubvick), mtn., Can. ... g14 74
Ibi, Nig. ... E6 45
Ibi, stm., Japan ... n15 33
Ibiá, Braz. ... B5 56
Ibiapaba, Serra da, mts., Braz. ... B2 57
Ibicuí, stm., Braz. ... D1 56
Ibicuy, Arg. ... A5 54

Ibirapuitã, stm., Braz. ... E1 56
Ibitinga, Braz. ... C3 56
Ibiza (Iviza), Spain ... C6 22
Ibiza (Isana), i., Spain ... C6 22
Ibiza, i., Spain ... C6 22
Ibo, Moz. ... D7 48
Ibo, Japan ... N6 52
Ibrī, Oman ... C5 38
Ibu, Japan ... N6 52
Ibug, W. Ger. ... A3 19
Ica, Peru ... D2 58
Ica, dept., Peru ... D2 58
Içá (Putumayo), stm., S.A. ... D4 60
Icana, Braz. ... A4 58
Içana (Isana), stm., S.A. ... C4 60
Içana (Isana) stm. ... C4 60
Içel (Mersin), Tur. ... D10 40
Iceland, ctry., Eur. ... n23 14
Ice Harbor Dam, Wa., U.S. ... C7 124
Ice Mountain, mtn., B.C. ... B7 69
Ichikawa, Japan ... n18 33
Ichinomiya, Japan ... n15 33
Ichinoseki, Japan ... G10 33
Ichnya, Sov. Un. ... F9 27
Ickesburg, Pa., U.S. ... F7 115
Icó, Braz. ... C3 57
Icy Cape, c., Ak., U.S. ... A7 79
Icy Strait, strt., Ak., U.S. ... k22 79
Ida, La., U.S. ... A2 95
Ida, co., Ia., U.S. ... B2 92
Ida, Lake, l., Mn., U.S. ... D3 100
Ida, Mount, mtn., Grc. ... E5 25
Idabel, Ok., U.S. ... D7 113
Ida Grove, Ia., U.S. ... B2 92
Idah, Nig. ... E6 45
Idaho, co., Id., U.S. ... D3 89
Idaho, state, U.S. ... E3 89
Idaho City, Id., U.S. ... F3 89
Idaho Falls, Id., U.S. ... F6 89
Idaho Springs, Co., U.S. ... B5 83
Idalia, Co., U.S. ... B8 83
Idalou, Tx., U.S. ... C2 120
Idamay, W.V., U.S. ... k10 125
Idana, Ks., U.S. ... C6 93
Idanha, Or., U.S. ... C4 114
Idanha-a-Nova, Port. ... C2 22
Idar-Oberstein, W. Ger. ... D2 19
Idaville, In., U.S. ... C4 91
Idaville, Or., U.S. ... B3 114
'Idd al Ghanam, Sud. ... C1 47
Iddesleigh, Alta. ... D5 68
Ideal, Ga., U.S. ... D2 87
Ideal, S.D., U.S. ... D6 118
Idehan, des., Libya ... D2 43
Ider, Al., U.S. ... A4 78
Ider, stm., Mong. ... B4 31
Idfina, Eg. ... C2 41
Idfū, Eg. ... C3 38
Ídhra, Grc. ... D4 25
Ídhra (Hydra), i., Grc. ... D4 25
Idi, Indon. ... D1 34
Idiofa, Zaire ... C2 48
Idkū, Eg. ... C2 41
Idkū Lake, l., Eg. ... C2 41
Idlewild, Mi., U.S. ... E5 99
Idlewild, Tn., U.S. ... A3 119
Idleyld Park, Or., U.S. ... D3 114
Idlib, Syria ... E11 40
Idmenau, E. Ger. ... C5 18
Idna, Isr. Occ. ... C6 41
Idrigill Point, c., Scot., U.K. ... C2 13
Idrija, Yugo. ... B2 24
Idritsa, Sov. Un. ... C7 27
Idro, Lake, l., Italy ... D6 20
Idutywa, Transkei ... D4 49
Ie Island, i., Japan ... N5 52
Ie Island, i., Japan ... N5 52
Ieper (Ypres), Bel. ... B5 16
Ierápetra, Grc. ... E5 40
Ierisós, Grc. ... B4 25
Iesi (Jesi), Italy ... C4 23
Ifakara, Tan. ... C6 48
Ife, Nig. ... E5 45
Iferouâne, Niger ... C6 45
Ifôghas, Adrar des, mts., Afr. ... C5 45
Ifon-Oshogbo, Nig. ... *E5 45
Iganga, Ug. ... A5 48
Igaraçu, Braz. ... C4 57
Igara Paraná, stm., Col. ... D3 60
Igarapava, Braz. ... C3 56
Igarapé Açu, Braz. ... B1 57
Igarapé-Miri, Braz. ... C5 59
Igarka, Sov. Un. ... C11 29
Igbo-Ora, Nig. ... *E5 45
Igdır, Tur. ... C15 40
Igharghar, Oued, val., Afr. ... E6 44
Igharghar, Oued, val., Alg. ... D6 44
Iglesia, Arg. ... F2 55
Iglesias, Italy ... E2 23
Ignacio, Col., U.S. ... D3 83
Ignacio, Tur. ... B6 40
Igny, Fr. ... h9 16
Igoumenitsa, Grc. ... C3 25
Igra, Sov. Un. ... B4 28
Igreja, Morro da, mtn., Braz. ... D3 56
Iguaçu, stm., S.A. ... D2 56
Iguala, Mex. ... D5 63
Igualada, Spain ... B6 22
Iguassu Falls, wtfl., S.A. ... D1 56
Iguatemi, stm., Braz. ... C2 56
Iguatu, Braz. ... C3 57
Iguéla, Gabon ... F1 46
Iguidi, 'Erg, dunes, Afr. ... D3 44
Igurin, i., Marsh Is. ... S18 52
Ih Bogd Mountain, mtn., Mong. ... C5 31
Iheya Island, i., Japan ... N5 52
Ihiala, Nig. ... *E6 45
Ihlen, Mn., U.S. ... G2 100
Ihosy, Madag. ... h9 49
Iida, Japan ... I8 33
Iide, Mount, mtn., Japan ... H9 33
Iijoki, stm., Fin. ... n16 33
Iisalmi, Fin. ... F12 14
Iizuka, Japan ... J3 33
Ijamsville, Md., U.S. ... B3 97
Ijebu Igbo, Nig. ... *E5 45
Ijebu Ode, Nig. ... E5 45
Ijill, Kediet, mtn., Maur. ... B4 17
Inajá, Braz. ... C3 57
IJssel, stm., Neth. ... B6 17
IJsselmeer (Zuider Zee), l., Neth. ... A6 16
Ijuí, Braz. ... D2 56
Ijuí, stm., Braz. ... D2 56
Ikare, Nig. ... *E6 45
Ikaría, i., Grc. ... D6 40
Ikast, Den. ... B3 15
Ike, i., Japan ... O6 52
Ikeda, Japan ... o14 33

Ikela, Zaire ... B3 48
Ikerre, Nig. ... *E6 45
Ikhtiman, Bul. ... D6 24
Iki Island, i., Japan ... J4 33
Ikire, Nig. ... *E5 45
Ikirun, Nig. ... *E5 45
Ikole, Nig. ... *E6 45
Ikorodu, Nig. ... *E5 45
Ikot Ekpene, Nig. ... *E6 45
Ila, Nig. ... E5 45
Ila, Ga., U.S. ... B3 87
Ilagan, Phil. ... B6 34
Īlām, Iran ... E3 39
Ilanz, Switz. ... E4 18
Ilasco, Mo., U.S. ... B6 102
Ilawa, Pol. ... B5 26
Ilawe-Ekiti, Nig. ... *E6 45
Ilchester, Md., U.S. ... B4 97
Ilderton, Ont. ... D3 73
Île-à-la-Crosse, Sask. ... m7 75
Île-à-la-Crosse, Lac, l., Sask. ... B2 75
Ilebo (Port-Francqui), Zaire ... B3 48
Île-de-France, hist. reg., Fr. ... C5 16
Ilek, stm., Sov. Un. ... E20 8
Île-Perrot, Que. ... q19 74
Îles, Lac des, l., Sask. ... B6 68
Ilesha, Nig. ... E5 45
Ilfeld, N.M., U.S. ... B4 108
Ilford, Man. ... A4 70
Ilfracombe, Eng., U.K. ... E4 10
Ilgin, Tur. ... C8 40
Ilhavo, Port. ... B1 22
Ilhéus, Braz. ... D3 57
Ili, stm., Asia ... E10 29
Iliamna, l., Ak., U.S. ... D8 79
Iliamna Lake, l., Ak., U.S. ... D8 79
Iliamna Volcano, vol., Ak., U.S. ... C9 79
Iliff, Co., U.S. ... A7 83
Iliki, Lake, l., Grc. ... g10 25
Ilinskaya, Sov. Un. ... I13 27
Iliodhrómia, i., Grc. ... C4 25
Ilion, N.Y., U.S. ... B5 109
Ilioúpolis, Grc. ... *D4 25
Ilkeston, Eng., U.K. ... B6 12
Ilkley, Eng., U.K. ... G7 13
Illampu, Nevado, mtn., Bol. ... C2 55
Illana Bay, b., Phil. ... D6 34
Illapel, Chile ... A2 54
Ille, Fr. ... F5 16
Illéla, Niger ... D6 45
Iller, stm., W. Ger. ... D5 18
Illfurth, Fr. ... A3 21
Illiers, Fr. ... C4 16
Illinois, state, U.S. ... C4 90
Illinois, stm., U.S. ... A7 113
Illinois, stm., Il., U.S. ... B5 90
Illinois, stm., Or., U.S. ... E3 114
Illinois City, Il., U.S. ... B3 90
Illinois Peak, mtn., Id., U.S. ... B3 89
Iliopolis, Il., U.S. ... D4 90
Illizi, Alg. ... D6 44
Illkirch-Graffenstaden, Fr. ... F7 17
Illmo, Mo., U.S. ... D8 102
Illnau [-Effretikon], Switz. ... B6 21
Illo, Nig. ... *D5 45
Illora, Spain ... D4 22
Ilmajoki, Fin. ... F5 116
Ilmenau, E. Ger. ... C5 18
Ilmenau, stm., W. Ger. ... B5 18
Ilo, Peru ... E3 58
Ilobu, Nig. ... *E5 45
Iloilo, Phil. ... C6 34
Ilorin, Nig. ... E5 45
Ilovaysk, Sov. Un. ... r21 27
Ilovlya, Sov. Un. ... D2 28
Ilsenburg, E. Ger. ... B5 19
Ilubabor, prov., Eth. ... D3 47
Ilwaco, Wa., U.S. ... C1 124
Ilwaki, Indon. ... G7 34
Iłża, Pol. ... C6 26
Imabari, Japan ... I6 33
Imabetsu, Japan ... F10 33
Imambaba, Sov. Un. ... C11 39
Iman, Sov. Un. ... B11 31
Imandra, Lake, l., Sov. Un. ... C6 14
Imari, Japan ... B3 33
Imatra, Fin. ... *G13 14
Imazu, Japan ... n14 33
Imbābah (part of Giza), Eg. ... D3 41
Imbabura, prov., Ec. ... A2 58
Imbituba, Braz. ... D3 56
Imbler, Or., U.S. ... B9 114
Imboden, Ar., U.S. ... A4 81
Ime, Beinn, mtn., Scot., U.K. ... B3 10
Imgyt Marsh, sw., Sov. Un. ... B8 28
Imi, Eth. ... D5 47
Imilac, Chile ... D2 55
Imlay, Nv., U.S. ... C3 105
Imlay City, Mi., U.S. ... E7 99
Imlaystown, N.J., U.S. ... C3 107
Immeln, l., Swe. ... B8 15
Immenstadt, W. Ger. ... E5 18
Immokalee, Fl., U.S. ... F5 86
Imnaha, Or., U.S. ... B10 114
Imnaha, stm., Or., U.S. ... B10 114
Imogene, Ia., U.S. ... D2 92
Imola, Italy ... B3 23
Imotski, Yugo. ... D3 24
Imperatriz, Braz. ... C1 57
Imperia, Italy ... C2 23
Imperial, Sask. ... F3 75
Imperial, Ca., U.S. ... F6 82
Imperial, Mo., U.S. ... g13 102
Imperial, Ne., U.S. ... D4 104
Imperial, Pa., U.S. ... k13 115
Imperial, Tx., U.S. ... D1 120
Imperial, co., Ca., U.S. ... F6 82
Imperial Beach, Ca., U.S. ... o15 82
Imperial Dam, U.S. ... E1 80
Imperial Mills, Alta. ... B5 68
Imperial Reservoir, res., U.S. ... E1 80
Imperial Valley, val., Ca., U.S. ... F6 82
Impfondo, Congo ... A2 48
Imphāl, India ... D9 36
Imst, Aus. ... E5 18
'Imwâs, Isr. Occ. ... h11 41
Ina, Japan ... n16 33
Ina, stm., Pol. ... B3 26
I Naftan, Puntan, c., N. Mar. Is. ... D8 52
Inajá, Braz. ... C3 57
I-n-Aleï, well, Mali ... C4 45
Inanwatan, Indon. ... F8 34
Iñapari, Peru ... D5 58
Inarajan, Guam ... M9 52
Inarajan Bay, b., Guam ... M10 52
Inari, Fin. ... C12 14
Inari, l., Fin. ... C12 14
Inavale, Ne., U.S. ... D7 104
Inawashiro, l., Japan ... H10 33
In Azaoua, well, Niger ... B6 45

In Belbel, Alg. ... D5 44
Inca, Spain ... C7 22
Incastro, stm., Italy ... h9 23
Ince, Cape, c., Tur. ... A10 40
Íncesu, Tur. ... C10 40
Inchard, Loch, b., Scot. U.K. ... B3 13
Inchelium, Wa., U.S. ... A7 124
Inchŏn, S. Kor. ... D10 31
Incline Village, Nv., U.S. ... D2 105
Indaiatuba, Braz. ... m8 56
Indaw, Burma ... D10 36
Independence, Ca., U.S. ... D4 82
Independence, Ia., U.S. ... B6 92
Independence, Ks., U.S. ... E8 93
Independence, Ky., U.S. ... B5 94
Independence, La., U.S. ... D5 95
Independence, Mo., U.S. ... B3 102
Independence, Oh., U.S. ... *h9 112
Independence, Or., U.S. ... C3 114
Independence, Va., U.S. ... D1 123
Independence, Wi., U.S. ... D2 126
Independence, co., Ar., U.S. ... B4 81
Independence, co., N.Y., U.S. ... B5 109
Independence Mountains, mts., Nv., U.S. ... C5 105
Independence National Historical Park, Pa., U.S. ... p21 115
Independence Rock, mtn., Wy., U.S. ... D5 127
Independencia, Bol. ... C2 55
Inderborskiy, Sov. Un. ... D4 28
Index, Wa., U.S. ... B4 124
India, ctry., Asia ... D6 36
Indiahoma, Ok., U.S. ... C3 113
Indian, stm., Ont. ... B7 73
Indian, stm., De., U.S. ... F4 85
Indian, stm., Mi., U.S. ... B4 99
Indian, stm., N.Y., U.S. ... A5 109
Indiana, Pa., U.S. ... E3 115
Indiana, co., Pa., U.S. ... E3 115
Indiana, state, U.S. ... E5 91
Indiana Dunes National Lakeshore, In., U.S. ... A3 91
Indian Agency, Co., U.S. ... D3 83
Indianapolis, In., U.S. ... E5 91
Indian Bay, b., Fl., U.S. ... D4 86
Indian Beach, De., U.S. ... F5 85
Indian Brook, U.S. ... C9 71
Indian Cedar Swamp, sw., R.I., U.S. ... F2 116
Indian Cove, Ct., U.S. ... *D4 84
Indian Creek, stm., In., U.S. ... H5 91
Indian Creek, stm., Md., U.S. ... C4 97
Indian Creek, stm., Oh., U.S. ... C1 112
Indian Creek, stm., S.D., U.S. ... B2 118
Indian Creek, stm., Tn., U.S. ... B3 119
Indian Creek, stm., W.V., U.S. ... k9 125
Indian Creek, stm., W.V., U.S. ... D4 125
Indian Grave Mountain, hill, Ga., U.S. ... C2 87
Indian Harbour Beach, Fl., U.S. ... *D6 86
Indian Head, Sask. ... G4 75
Indian Head, Md., U.S. ... C3 97
Indian Heights, In., U.S. ... *D5 91
Indian Hills, Co., U.S. ... *B5 83
Indian Island, i., N.C., U.S. ... B6 110
Indian Lake, N.Y., U.S. ... B6 109
Indian Lake, l., Mi., U.S. ... C4 99
Indian Lake, l., N.Y., U.S. ... B6 109
Indian Lake, l., Oh., U.S. ... B2 112
Indian Lake, l., R.I., U.S. ... F4 116
Indian Lake Shores, R.I., U.S. ... F4 116
Indian Mound, Tn., U.S. ... A4 119
Indian Mound Beach, Ma., U.S. ... C6 98
Indian Mountain, mtn., Ct., U.S. ... B2 84
Indian Neck, Ct., U.S. ... D4 84
Indian Ocean ... G2 2
Indianola, Il., U.S. ... D6 90
Indianola, Ia., U.S. ... C4 92
Indianola, Ms., U.S. ... B3 101
Indianola, Ne., U.S. ... D5 104
Indianola, Ok., U.S. ... B6 113
Indiánopolis, Braz. ... B5 56
Indian Peak, mtn., Ut., U.S. ... E2 121
Indian Peak, mtn., Wy., U.S. ... B3 127
Indian Pond, l., Me., U.S. ... C3 96
Indian Pond, l., Me., U.S. ... D3 96
Indian Pond, l., Me., U.S. ... D3 96
Indian Prairie Canal, Fl., U.S. ... E5 86
Indian Ridge Estates, Az., U.S. ... E5 80
Indian River, Ont. ... C6 73
Indian River, Mi., U.S. ... D5 99
Indian River, co., Fl., U.S. ... E6 86
Indian River, b., Fl., U.S. ... F5 85
Indian River Bay, b., De., U.S. ... F5 85
Indian Rock, mtn., Wa., U.S. ... D5 124
Indian Rocks Beach, Fl., U.S. ... p10 86
Indian Springs, Ga., U.S. ... C3 87
Indian Springs, Nv., U.S. ... G5 105
Indiantown, Fl., U.S. ... E6 86
Indian Trail, N.C., U.S. ... B2 110
Indian Valley, Id., U.S. ... E2 89
Indian Valley, Va., U.S. ... C2 123
Indian Village, Ks., U.S. ... E8 93
Indian Village, La., U.S. ... D4 95
Indian Wells, Az., U.S. ... B5 80
Indiaporã, Braz. ... B4 56
Indio, Ca., U.S. ... F5 82
Indigirka, stm., Sov. Un. ... C17 29
Indio, stm., Pan. ... k10 62
Indochina, reg., Asia ... D4 34
Indonesia, ctry., Asia ... F5 34
Indore, India ... B4 36
Indragiri, stm., Indon. ... F2 34
Indramayu, Indon. ... G3 34
Indrāvati, stm., India ... E7 36
Indrio, Fl., U.S. ... E6 86
Indus, Mn., U.S. ... B5 100
Indus, stm., Asia ... C4 36
Industry, Il., U.S. ... C3 90
Ine, Japan ... n14 33
Inebolu, Tur. ... B9 40
Ineğol, Tur. ... *B7 40
Inez, Ky., U.S. ... C7 94
Inez, Tx., U.S. ... E4 120
Infanta, Phil. ... o13 34
Infanta, Phil. ... o12 34
Infantas, Col. ... B5 60
Inferrillo, Presa del, res., Mex. ... h6 57
Infiesto, Spain ... A3 22
Inga Dam, Zaire ... C1 48
In-Gall, Niger ... C6 45
Ingalls, Ar., U.S. ... D3 81

Ingalls, In., U.S. ... E6 91
Ingalls, Ks., U.S. ... E3 93
Ingalls, Mi., U.S. ... C3 99
Ingalls, Ok., U.S. ... A5 113
Ingalls Park, Il., U.S. ... B5 90
Ingelheim, W. Ger. ... D3 19
Ingende, Zaire ... B2 48
Ingeniero Jacobacci, Arg. ... C3 54
Ingeniero Luiggi, Arg. ... B4 54
Ingenika, stm., B.C. ... A5 69
Inger, Mn., U.S. ... C5 100
Ingersheim, Fr. ... A3 20
Ingersoll, Ont. ... D4 73
Ingersoll, Ok., U.S. ... A3 113
Ingham, Austl. ... C8 50
Ingham, co., Mi., U.S. ... F6 99
Ingleside, Md., U.S. ... B6 97
Ingleside, Tx., U.S. ... F4 120
Inglewood, Austl. ... D8 51
Inglewood, Ont. ... D4 73
Inglewood, N.Z. ... M15 51
Inglewood, Ca., U.S. ... n12 82
Inglewood, Ne., U.S. ... C9 104
Inglewood, Tx., U.S. ... *B3 124
Inglis, Man. ... D1 70
Ingoda, stm., Sov. Un. ... B7 31
Ingold, N.C., U.S. ... C4 110
Ingoldsby, Ont. ... C6 73
Ingolf, Ont. ... E4 70
Ingolstadt, W. Ger. ... D6 18
Ingomar, Ms., U.S. ... A4 101
Ingomar, Mt., U.S. ... D9 103
Ingonish, N.S. ... C9 71
Ingonish Beach, N.S. ... C9 71
Ingornachoix Bay, b., Newf. ... C3 72
Ingraham, Il., U.S. ... E5 90
Ingraham, Lake, l., Fl., U.S. ... G5 86
India ... E12 37
Ingram, Pa., U.S. ... k13 115
Ingram, Wi., U.S. ... C3 126
Ingrid Christensen Coast, Ant. ... C20 7
In Guezzam, Alg. ... F6 44
Ingul, stm., Sov. Un. ... I11 27
Ingulets, stm., Sov. Un. ... H9 27
Inhambane, Moz. ... B6 49
Inhambane, dept., Moz. ... B5 49
Inhambane, Baía de, b., Moz. ... B6 49
Inhambupe, Braz. ... D3 57
Inhaminga, Moz. ... A5 49
Inharrime, Moz. ... B6 49
Inhuçu, Braz. ... B2 57
Inhumas, Braz. ... B3 56
Iniesta, Spain ... C4 22
Inírida, stm., Col. ... C4 60
Inisa, Nig. ... *E5 45
Inishark, i., Ire. ... D11 11
Inishbofin, i., Ire. ... D11 11
Inishcrone, Ire. ... C2 11
Inisheer, i., Ire. ... D2 11
Inishkea Islands, is., Ire. ... C1 11
Inishmaan, i., Ire. ... D2 11
Inishmore, i., Ire. ... D2 11
Inishmurray, i., Ire. ... C2 11
Inishowen Head, c., Ire. ... B5 11
Inishtooskert, i., Ire. ... E1 11
Inishtrahull, rock, Ire. ... C3 10
Inishturk, i., Ire. ... D1 10
Inishvickillane, i., Ire. ... E1 11
Inistioge, Ire. ... I6 11
Injune, Austl. ... B7 51
Inkerman, N.B. ... B5 71
Inkom, Id., U.S. ... G6 89
Inkster, Mi., U.S. ... p15 99
Inkster, N.D., U.S. ... A8 111
Inland, Ne., U.S. ... D7 104
Inle, Lake, l., Burma ... D10 36
Inlet, N.Y., U.S. ... B6 109
Inman, Ga., U.S. ... C2 87
Inman, Ks., U.S. ... D6 93
Inman, Ne., U.S. ... B7 104
Inman, S.C., U.S. ... A3 117
Inn, stm., Eur. ... D6 18
Inner Hebrides, is., Scot., U.K. ... B3 10
Innerleithen, Scot., U.K. ... D7 10
Inner Mongolia (Nei Mongol), prov., China ... C7 31
Inner Sound, strt., Scot., U.K. ... B4 10
Innisfail, Austl. ... C8 50
Innisfail, Alta. ... C4 68
Innisfree, Alta. ... C5 68
Inniswold, La., U.S. ... *D4 95
Innokenteyevskiy, Sov. Un. ... E5 31
Innsbruck, Aus. ... E5 18
Inny, stm., Ire. ... C4 11
Ino, Japan ... J6 33
Inocência, Braz. ... B2 56
Inola, Ok., U.S. ... A6 113
Inongo, Zaire ... B3 48
Inowrocław, Pol. ... B5 26
Ins, Switz. ... B3 21
In Salah, Alg. ... D5 44
Insch, Scot., U.K. ... C6 13
Inscription House Ruin, hist., Az., U.S. ... A5 80
Insein, Burma ... E10 36
Insinger, Sask. ... F4 75
Inspiration, Az., U.S. ... D5 80
Institute, W.V., U.S. ... m12 125
Instow, Sask. ... H1 75
Inta, Sov. Un. ... B21 8
Intercession City, Fl., U.S. ... D5 86
Intercourse, Pa., U.S. ... F9 115
Interior, S.D., U.S. ... D4 118
Interlaken, Switz. ... E3 18
Interlaken, Ma., U.S. ... *B1 98
Interlaken, N.Y., U.S. ... C4 109
International Falls, Mn., U.S. ... B5 100
International Peace Garden, N.A. ... A5 111
Intersection Mountain, mtn., Can. ... C8 69
Intervale, N.H., U.S. ... B4 106
Inthanon, Mount, mtn., Thai. ... B1 34
Intiyaco, Arg. ... B3 55
Intracoastal City, La., U.S. ... E3 95
Intracoastal Waterway, U.S. ... E4 95
Introbio, Italy ... B2 23
Intuto, Peru ... B3 58
Inubō-zaki, c., Japan ... H10 33
Inútil, Bahía, b., Chile ... h12 54
Inuvik, N.W. Ter. ... C6 66
Inveraray, Scot., U.K. ... B4 10
Inverbervie, Scot., U.K. ... C5 13
Invercargill, N.Z. ... Q12 51
Inverell, Austl. ... D8 51
Invergarry, Scot., U.K. ... C4 13
Invergordon, Scot., U.K. ... C4 13
Inver Grove Heights, Mn., U.S. ... n12 100
Invermay, Sask. ... F4 75
Invermere, B.C. ... D9 69
Inverness, N.S. ... C8 71
Inverness, Que. ... C6 74

Inverness, Scot., U.K. ... B4 10
Inverness, Al., U.S. ... C4 78
Inverness, Ca., U.S. ... C2 82
Inverness, Fl., U.S. ... D4 86
Inverness, Il., U.S. ... *A5 90
Inverness, Ms., U.S. ... B3 101
Inverness, Mt., U.S. ... B6 103
Inverurie, Scot., U.K. ... C6 13
Invisible Mountain, mtn., Id., U.S. ... F5 89
Inwood, Man. ... D3 70
Inwood, Ont. ... E3 73
Inwood, Fl., U.S. ... *D5 86
Inwood, In., U.S. ... B5 91
Inwood, Ia., U.S. ... A1 92
Inwood, N.Y., U.S. ... k13 109
Inwood, Vt., U.S. ... C4 122
Inwood, W.V., U.S. ... B6 125
Inyanga, Zimb. ... A5 49
Inyangani, mtn., Zimb. ... A5 49
Inyan Kara Creek, stm., Wy., U.S. ... B8 127
Inyan Kara Mountain, mtn., Wy., U.S. ... B8 127
Inyo, co., Ca., U.S. ... D5 82
Inyo, Mount, mtn., Ca., U.S. ... D5 82
Inyokern, Ca., U.S. ... E5 82
Inyo Mountains, mts., Ca., U.S. ... D4 82
Inyonga, Tan. ... C5 48
Inza, Sov. Un. ... E16 27
Inzana Lake, l., B.C. ... B5 69
Ioánnina, Grc. ... C3 25
Iokanga, Sov. Un. ... D18 14
Iola, Ks., U.S. ... E8 93
Iola, Wi., U.S. ... D4 126
Iona, N.S. ... C8 71
Iona, Id., U.S. ... F7 89
Iona, Mn., U.S. ... G3 100
Iona, N.J., U.S. ... D2 107
Iona, S.D., U.S. ... D6 118
Iona, i., Scot., U.K. ... D2 13
Ione, Ca., U.S. ... C3 82
Ione, Nv., U.S. ... E4 105
Ione, Or., U.S. ... B7 114
Ionia, Ia., U.S. ... A5 92
Ionia, Ks., U.S. ... C5 93
Ionia, Mi., U.S. ... F5 99
Ionia, Mo., U.S. ... C4 102
Ionia, co., Mi., U.S. ... F5 99
Ionian Islands, is., Grc. ... C3 25
Ionian Sea, Eur. ... H12 8
Íos, i., Grc. ... D5 40
Iosco, co., Mi., U.S. ... D7 99
Iosegun, stm., Alta. ... B2 68
Iota, La., U.S. ... D3 95
Iowa, co., Ia., U.S. ... C5 92
Iowa, co., Wi., U.S. ... E3 126
Iowa, state, U.S. ... C4 92
Iowa, West Branch, stm., Ia., U.S. ... B4 92
Iowa City, Ia., U.S. ... C6 92
Iowa Falls, Ia., U.S. ... B4 92
Iowa Indian Reservation, U.S. ... C8 93
Iowa Lake, l., U.S. ... A3 92
Iowa Park, Tx., U.S. ... C3 120
Ipameri, Braz. ... B5 56
Ipava, Il., U.S. ... C3 90
Ipel (Ipoly), stm., Eur. ... D5 26
Iphigenia Bay, b., Ak., U.S. ... n22 79
Ipiales, Col. ... C2 60
Ipirá, Braz. ... D3 57
Ipoh, Malay. ... L6 34
Ipoly (Ipel'), stm., Eur. ... E5 26
Iporá, Braz. ... B4 56
Ippy, Cen. Afr. Rep. ... B6 25
İpsala, Tur. ... I10 40
Ipswich, Austl. ... E9 50
Ipswich, Eng., U.K. ... D7 10
Ipswich, Ma., U.S. ... A6 98
Ipswich, S.D., U.S. ... B6 118
Ipswich, stm., Ma., U.S. ... A5 98
Ipu, Braz. ... B2 57
Ipueiras, Braz. ... B3 57
Iqaluit, N.W. Ter. ... D19 66
Iquique, Chile ... D1 55
Iquitos, Peru ... B3 58
Ira, Ia., U.S. ... C4 92
Ira, Tx., U.S. ... C2 120
Iraan, Tx., U.S. ... D2 120
Iracoubo, Fr. Gu. ... A4 59
Irai, Braz. ... B5 56
Iráklion (Candia), Grc. ... E5 40
Irala, Para. ... B6 56
Iran, ctry., Asia ... B5 38
Iran, Plateau of, plat., Asia ... B5 38
Iran, Plateau of, plat., Asia ... H10 39
Tränshahr, Iran ... H10 39
Irapa, Ven. ... A5 60
Irapuato, Mex. ... C4 63
Iraq, ctry., Asia ... B4 38
Irasburg, Vt., U.S. ... B4 122
Irasville, Vt., U.S. ... C3 122
Irazú, Volcán, vol., C.R. ... F6 62
Irbid, Jord. ... B3 38
Irbil, Iraq ... B4 38
Irbit, Sov. Un. ... D21 8
Irebu, Zaire ... B3 48
Iredell, co., N.C., U.S. ... B2 110
Ireland, ctry., Eur. ... H3 9
Ireland, In., U.S. ... H4 91
Ireland Island, i., Ber. ... p19 57
Irene, S.D., U.S. ... D8 118
Irene, Tx., U.S. ... C4 120
Ireton, Ia., U.S. ... B1 92
Irgiz, Sov. Un. ... D8 28
Irgiz, stm., Sov. Un. ... I3 8
Iri, S. Kor. ... I3 33
Irian Jaya, prov., Indon. ... F9 34
Iriba, Chad ... B4 46
Iringa, Tan. ... C6 48
Iringa, prov., Tan. ... C6 48
Iriomote Island, i., Japan ... G9 31
Irion, co., Tx., U.S. ... D2 120
Iriona, Hond. ... C5 62
Iriri, stm., Braz. ... C5 59
Irish, Mount, mtn., Nv., U.S. ... F6 105
Irish Sea, Eur. ... H10 9
Irkutsk, Sov. Un. ... D13 29
Irma, Alta. ... C5 68
Irmo, S.C., U.S. ... C5 117
Irō, Cape, c., Japan ... I9 33
Iron, Mn., U.S. ... C6 100
Iron, co., Mi., U.S. ... B2 99
Iron, co., Mo., U.S. ... D7 102
Iron, co., Ut., U.S. ... F2 121
Iron, co., Wi., U.S. ... B3 126

| Name | Map Ref. | Page |
|---|---|---|
| Iron Belt, Wi., U.S. | B3 | 126 |
| Iron City, Ga., U.S. | E2 | 87 |
| Iron City, Tn., U.S. | B4 | 119 |
| Irondale, Al., U.S. | f7 | 78 |
| Irondale, Mo., U.S. | D7 | 102 |
| Irondale, Oh., U.S. | B5 | 112 |
| Irondequoit, N.Y., U.S. | B3 | 109 |
| Iron Gate, Va., U.S. | C3 | 123 |
| Iron Gate, val., Eur. | C6 | 24 |
| Iron Gate Reservoir, res., Eur. | C5 | 24 |
| Iron Gate Reservoir, res., Ca., U.S. | B2 | 82 |
| Ironia, N.J., U.S. | B3 | 107 |
| Iron Lightning, S.D., U.S. | B4 | 118 |
| Iron Mountain, Mi., U.S. | C2 | 99 |
| Iron Mountain, Mo., U.S. | D7 | 102 |
| Iron Mountain, Wy., U.S. | E7 | 127 |
| Iron Mountain, mtn., Az., U.S. | D4 | 80 |
| Iron Mountains, mts., U.S. | D1 | 123 |
| Iron Ridge, Wi., U.S. | E5 | 126 |
| Iron River, Mi., U.S. | B2 | 99 |
| Iron River, Wi., U.S. | B2 | 126 |
| Irons, Mi., U.S. | D5 | 99 |
| Ironside, Que. | h12 | 73 |
| Ironside, Or., U.S. | C9 | 114 |
| Ironspot, Oh., U.S. | C3 | 112 |
| Iron Springs, Az., U.S. | C3 | 80 |
| Ironton, Mn., U.S. | D5 | 100 |
| Ironton, Mo., U.S. | D7 | 102 |
| Ironton, Oh., U.S. | D3 | 112 |
| Ironwood, Mi., U.S. | n11 | 99 |
| Iroquois, Ont. | C9 | 73 |
| Iroquois, Il., U.S. | C6 | 90 |
| Iroquois, S.D., U.S. | C8 | 118 |
| Iroquois, co., Il., U.S. | C6 | 90 |
| Iroquois, stm., U.S. | C6 | 90 |
| Iroquois, Lake, l., Vt., U.S. | B2 | 122 |
| Iroquois Falls, Ont. | o19 | 73 |
| Irrawaddy see Ayeyarwady, stm., Burma | D10 | 36 |
| Irricana, Alta. | D4 | 68 |
| Irrigon, Or., U.S. | B7 | 114 |
| Irt, stm., Eng., U.K. | F5 | 13 |
| Irthing, stm., Eng., U.K. | F6 | 13 |
| Irtysh, Sov. Un. | C8 | 28 |
| Irtysh, stm., Sov. Un. | D9 | 29 |
| Irumu, Zaire | A4 | 48 |
| Irún, Spain | A5 | 22 |
| Irvine, Alta. | E5 | 68 |
| Irvine, Scot., U.K. | C4 | 10 |
| Irvine, Ca., U.S. | n13 | 82 |
| Irvine, Fl., U.S. | C4 | 86 |
| Irvine, Ky., U.S. | C6 | 94 |
| Irvine, Pa., U.S. | C3 | 115 |
| Irvine, stm., Scot., U.K. | E4 | 13 |
| Irvines Landing, B.C. | E5 | 69 |
| Irving, Il., U.S. | D4 | 90 |
| Irving, Tx., U.S. | n10 | 120 |
| Irvington, Al., U.S. | E1 | 78 |
| Irvington, Il., U.S. | E4 | 90 |
| Irvington, Ky., U.S. | C3 | 94 |
| Irvington, Ne., U.S. | g12 | 104 |
| Irvington, N.J., U.S. | k8 | 107 |
| Irvington, N.Y., U.S. | g13 | 109 |
| Irvington, Va., U.S. | C6 | 123 |
| Irvona, Pa., U.S. | E4 | 115 |
| Irwin, Id., U.S. | F7 | 89 |
| Irwin, Ia., U.S. | C2 | 92 |
| Irwin, Pa., U.S. | F2 | 115 |
| Irwin, co., Ga., U.S. | E3 | 87 |
| Irwinton, Ga., U.S. | D3 | 87 |
| Irwinville, Ga., U.S. | E3 | 87 |
| Isa, Nig. | D6 | 45 |
| Isaac Lake, l., B.C. | C7 | 69 |
| Isaacs Harbour, N.S. | D8 | 71 |
| Isabel, Ks., U.S. | E5 | 93 |
| Isabel, S.D., U.S. | B4 | 118 |
| Isabel, Bahía, b., Ec. | g5 | 58 |
| Isabel, Mount, mtn., Wy., U.S. | D2 | 127 |
| Isabela, Phil. | D6 | 34 |
| Isabela, P.R. | A1 | 65 |
| Isabela, Isla (Albemarle Island), i., Ec. | g5 | 58 |
| Isabela, Cordillera, mts., Nic. | D5 | 62 |
| Isabella, Braz. | D1 | 70 |
| Isabella, Ga., U.S. | E3 | 87 |
| Isabella, Mn., U.S. | C7 | 100 |
| Isabella, Ok., U.S. | A3 | 113 |
| Isabella, Tn., U.S. | D9 | 119 |
| Isabella, co., Mi., U.S. | E6 | 99 |
| Isabella Indian Reservation, Mi., U.S. | E6 | 99 |
| Isabella Lake, l., Mn., U.S. | C7 | 100 |
| Isaccea, Rom. | C9 | 24 |
| Isachsen, N.W. Ter. | m31 | 66 |
| Ísafjarðardjúp, Ice. | m21 | 14 |
| Ísafjörður, Ice. | m21 | 14 |
| Isahaya, Japan | J5 | 33 |
| Isaka, Zaire | B2 | 48 |
| Isana (Içana), stm., S.A. | C4 | 60 |
| Isanga, Zaire | B3 | 48 |
| Isangi, Zaire | A3 | 48 |
| Isanti, Mn., U.S. | E5 | 100 |
| Isanti, co., Mn., U.S. | E5 | 100 |
| Isar, stm., Eur. | D6 | 18 |
| Isarco, stm., Italy | A3 | 23 |
| 'Īsāwīyah, Isr. Occ. | m14 | 41 |
| 'Īsāwīyah, Sau. Ar. | G12 | 40 |
| Isbergues, Fr. | D2 | 17 |
| Isbister, stm., Man. | C4 | 70 |
| Ischgl, Aus. | B9 | 21 |
| Ischia, i., Italy | D4 | 23 |
| Ischua, N.Y., U.S. | C2 | 109 |
| Ise, stm., W. Ger. | F4 | 15 |
| Ise (Uji-yamada), Japan | I8 | 33 |
| Ise Bay, b., Japan | o15 | 33 |
| Isefjord, b., Den. | C5 | 15 |
| Isel, stm., Aus. | E6 | 18 |
| Iselin, N.J., U.S. | B4 | 107 |
| Iselin, Pa., U.S. | E3 | 115 |
| Isen, stm., W. Ger. | A8 | 20 |
| Isenthal, Switz. | C6 | 21 |
| Iseo, Lake, l., Italy | B3 | 23 |
| Isère, dept., Fr. | D1 | 20 |
| Isère, stm., Fr. | E6 | 16 |
| Iserlohn, W. Ger. | B2 | 19 |
| Isernia, Italy | D5 | 23 |
| Isesaki, Japan | H9 | 33 |
| Iseyin, Nig. | E5 | 45 |
| Isfahan see Eşfahān, Iran | B5 | 38 |
| Ishikari Bay, b., Japan | E10 | 33 |
| Ishikawa, Japan | O5 | 52 |
| Ishim, Sov. Un. | D9 | 29 |
| Ishim, stm., Sov. Un. | C5 | 28 |
| Ishimbay, Sov. Un. | C5 | 28 |
| Ishinomaki, Japan | D13 | 33 |
| Ishioka, Japan | m19 | 33 |
| Ishpeming, Mi., U.S. | B3 | 99 |
| Isigny-sur-Mer, Fr. | C3 | 16 |
| Isil-Kul, Sov. Un. | C8 | 28 |
| Isinglass, stm., N.H., U.S. | D4 | 106 |
| Isiolo, Kenya | A6 | 48 |
| Isiro, Zaire | A4 | 48 |
| Isisford, Austl. | B5 | 51 |
| İskenderun (Alexandretta), Tur. | D11 | 40 |
| İskilip, Tur. | B10 | 40 |
| İskitim, Sov. Un. | E25 | 37 |
| İskūr, stm., Bul. | D6 | 24 |
| Iskushuban, Som. | C7 | 47 |
| Isla Cristina, Spain | D2 | 22 |
| Islāmābād, Pak. | B5 | 36 |
| Islamorada, Fl., U.S. | H6 | 86 |
| Island, Ky., U.S. | C2 | 94 |
| Island, co., Wa., U.S. | A3 | 124 |
| Island Beach, N.J., U.S. | D4 | 107 |
| Island-Brook, Que. | D6 | 74 |
| Island City, Or., U.S. | B8 | 114 |
| Island Creek, Ma., U.S. | *B6 | 98 |
| Island Falls, Sask. | B4 | 75 |
| Island Falls, Me., U.S. | B4 | 96 |
| Island Grove, Fl., U.S. | C4 | 86 |
| Island Heights, N.J., U.S. | D4 | 107 |
| Island Lake, Man. | C4 | 70 |
| Island Lake, l., Man. | C4 | 70 |
| Island Lake, stm., Man. | B4 | 70 |
| Island Park, Id., U.S. | E7 | 89 |
| Island Park, N.Y., U.S. | *E7 | 109 |
| Island Park Reservoir, res., Id., U.S. | E7 | 89 |
| Island Pond, Vt., U.S. | B5 | 122 |
| Island Pond, l., N.H., U.S. | E4 | 106 |
| Islands, Bay of, b., Newf. | D2 | 72 |
| Islands, Bay of, b., N.Z. | K15 | 51 |
| Isla Vista, Ca., U.S. | E4 | 82 |
| Islay, Alta. | C5 | 68 |
| Islay, i., Scot., U.K. | C3 | 10 |
| Islay, Sound of, strt., Scot., U.K. | E3 | 13 |
| Isle, Mn., U.S. | D5 | 100 |
| Isle, stm., Fr. | E4 | 16 |
| Isle au Haut, Me., U.S. | D4 | 96 |
| Isle-aux-Morts, Newf. | E2 | 72 |
| Isle La Motte, Vt., U.S. | B2 | 122 |
| Isle of Man, ctry., Eur. | C4 | 10 |
| Isle of Palms, S.C., U.S. | k12 | 117 |
| Isle of Wight, Va., U.S. | D6 | 123 |
| Isle of Wight, co., Eng., U.K. | D6 | 10 |
| Isle of Wight, co., Va., U.S. | D6 | 123 |
| Isle of Wight Bay, b., Md., U.S. | D7 | 97 |
| Isle Pierre, B.C. | C6 | 69 |
| Isle Royale National Park, Mi., U.S. | h9 | 99 |
| Islesboro, Me., U.S. | D4 | 96 |
| Islesboro Island, i., Me., U.S. | D4 | 96 |
| Islesford, Me., U.S. | D4 | 96 |
| Isleta, N.M., U.S. | C3 | 108 |
| Isleta Indian Reservation, N.M., U.S. | C3 | 108 |
| Isleton, Ca., U.S. | C3 | 82 |
| Islington, Ma., U.S. | h11 | 98 |
| Islip, N.Y., U.S. | *n15 | 109 |
| Islip Terrace, N.Y., U.S. | *n15 | 109 |
| Ismael Cortinas, Ur. | f5 | 54 |
| Ismailia, Eg. | B3 | 38 |
| Ismā'īlīyah Canal, Eg. | D3 | 41 |
| Ismay, Mt., U.S. | D12 | 103 |
| Isna, Eg. | C3 | 38 |
| Isny, W. Ger. | A9 | 21 |
| Isoka, Zam. | D5 | 48 |
| Isola, Ms., U.S. | B3 | 101 |
| Isola della Scala, Italy | D7 | 20 |
| Isola di Capo Rizzuto, Italy | E6 | 23 |
| Isonzo, stm., Eur. | A4 | 23 |
| Isparta, Tur. | D8 | 40 |
| İspir, Tur. | B13 | 40 |
| Israel, ctry., Asia | B3 | 38 |
| Israel, stm., N.H., U.S. | B3 | 106 |
| Israeli Occupied Areas, dep., Asia | B7 | 41 |
| Issano, Guy. | A3 | 59 |
| Issaquah, Wa., U.S. | B3 | 124 |
| Issaquena, co., Ms., U.S. | C2 | 101 |
| Issia, I.C. | E3 | 45 |
| Issoire, Fr. | E5 | 16 |
| Issoudun, Fr. | D4 | 16 |
| Issuna, Tan. | C5 | 48 |
| Issy, Fr. | g10 | 16 |
| Issyk-Kul, Lake, l., Sov. Un. | E10 | 29 |
| Istachatta, Fl., U.S. | D4 | 86 |
| Īstādeh-ye Moqor, Āb-e, l., Afg. | B4 | 36 |
| İstanbul (Constantinople) (Byzantium), Tur. | B7 | 40 |
| Istiaía, Grc. | C4 | 25 |
| Istmina, Col. | B2 | 60 |
| Isto, Mount, mtn., Ak., U.S. | B11 | 79 |
| Istokpoga, Lake, l., Fl., U.S. | E5 | 86 |
| Istra, stm., Braz. | C3 | 59 |
| Istranca Mountains, mts., Tur. | B7 | 25 |
| Istres, Fr. | F6 | 16 |
| Istrian Peninsula, pen., Yugo. | C1 | 24 |
| Itá, Braz. | D1 | 70 |
| Itá, Para. | E4 | 55 |
| Itabaiana, Braz. | C3 | 57 |
| Itabaiana, Braz. | D3 | 57 |
| Itabaianinha, Braz. | D3 | 57 |
| Itabapoana, stm., Braz. | C2 | 57 |
| Itaberaba, Braz. | D2 | 57 |
| Itaberaí, Braz. | A3 | 57 |
| Itabira, Braz. | B4 | 56 |
| Itaboraí, Braz. | D3 | 57 |
| Itabuna, Braz. | D3 | 57 |
| Itacaiunas, stm., Braz. | C3 | 59 |
| Itacoatiara, Braz. | C3 | 59 |
| Itacuaí, stm., Braz. | D2 | 57 |
| Itaeté, Braz. | D2 | 57 |
| Itaguaçu, Braz. | h6 | 56 |
| Itaguara, Braz. | B3 | 56 |
| Itaguaru, Braz. | B3 | 56 |
| Itaguí, Col. | *B2 | 60 |
| Itaí, Braz. | B3 | 56 |
| Itaituba, Braz. | C3 | 59 |
| Itajá, Braz. | D2 | 57 |
| Itajubá, Braz. | B4 | 56 |
| Italy, Tx., U.S. | C4 | 120 |
| Italy, ctry., Eur. | C4 | 23 |
| Italy Cross, N.S. | E5 | 71 |
| Itamaracá, Ilha de, i., Braz. | h6 | 57 |
| Itamarandiba, Braz. | B4 | 56 |
| Itambacuri, Braz. | B4 | 56 |
| Itambé, Braz. | D3 | 57 |
| Itami, Japan | o14 | 33 |
| Itanhaém, Braz. | n16 | 56 |
| Itapaci, Braz. | A3 | 56 |
| Itapecuru, stm., Braz. | B2 | 57 |
| Itapecuru-Mirim, Braz. | C2 | 57 |
| Itapemirim, Braz. | C4 | 56 |
| Itaperuna, Braz. | C4 | 56 |
| Itapetinga, Braz. | C3 | 57 |
| Itapetininga, Braz. | B3 | 56 |
| Itapetininga, stm., Braz. | m7 | 56 |
| Itapeva, Braz. | B3 | 56 |
| Itapicuru, stm., Braz. | B4 | 56 |
| Itapipoca, Braz. | B3 | 57 |
| Itapira, Braz. | m8 | 56 |
| Itapiranga, Braz. | C3 | 59 |
| Itapirapuã, Braz. | B2 | 56 |
| Itápolis, Braz. | k7 | 56 |
| Itaporã, Braz. | C2 | 56 |
| Itaporanga, Braz. | C3 | 57 |
| Itapúa, dept., Para. | E4 | 55 |
| Itapuranga, Braz. | B2 | 56 |
| Itaqui, Braz. | D1 | 56 |
| Itararé, Braz. | C3 | 56 |
| Itararé, stm., Braz. | C3 | 56 |
| Itārsi, India | F6 | 37 |
| Itasca, Il., U.S. | k8 | 90 |
| Itasca, Tx., U.S. | C4 | 120 |
| Itasca, co., Mn., U.S. | C5 | 100 |
| Itasca, Lake, l., Mn., U.S. | C3 | 100 |
| Itatiaia National Park, Braz. | h5 | 56 |
| Itatiba, Braz. | m8 | 56 |
| Itatinga, Braz. | m7 | 56 |
| Itaúna, Braz. | C4 | 56 |
| Itéa, Grc. | C4 | 25 |
| Iténez (Guaporé), stm., S.A. | B3 | 55 |
| Itenhém, Braz. | B4 | 56 |
| Ithaca, Mi., U.S. | E6 | 99 |
| Ithaca, Ne., U.S. | g11 | 104 |
| Ithaca, N.Y., U.S. | C4 | 109 |
| Ithaca see Itháki, i., Grc. | C3 | 25 |
| Itháki, Grc. | C3 | 25 |
| Itháki (Ithaca), i., Grc. | C3 | 25 |
| Itigi, Tan. | C5 | 48 |
| Itimbiri, stm., Zaire | A3 | 48 |
| Itinga, Braz. | B4 | 56 |
| Itiquira, Braz. | B2 | 56 |
| Itiquira, stm., Braz. | *B1 | 56 |
| Itiquira, stm., Braz. | B1 | 56 |
| Itirapina, Braz. | m8 | 56 |
| Itō, Japan | o18 | 33 |
| Itoigawa, Japan | H8 | 33 |
| Itoko, Zaire | B3 | 48 |
| Itoman, Japan | O5 | 52 |
| Itta Bena, Ms., U.S. | B3 | 101 |
| Itu, Braz. | C3 | 56 |
| Itu, stm., Braz. | D2 | 60 |
| Ituí, stm., Braz. | B3 | 58 |
| Ituiutaba, Braz. | B3 | 56 |
| Itumbiara, Braz. | B3 | 56 |
| Ituna, Sask. | F4 | 75 |
| Ituporanga, Braz. | D3 | 56 |
| Iturama, Braz. | B3 | 56 |
| Ituverava, Braz. | C3 | 56 |
| Ituxi, stm., Braz. | C4 | 58 |
| Ityaí al Bārūd, Eg. | D2 | 41 |
| Itzehoe, W. Ger. | B4 | 18 |
| Iuka, Il., U.S. | E5 | 90 |
| Iuka, Ks., U.S. | E5 | 93 |
| Iuka, Ms., U.S. | A5 | 101 |
| Iva, S.C., U.S. | C2 | 117 |
| Iva, W. Sam. | F11 | 52 |
| Ivaí, stm., Braz. | C2 | 56 |
| Ivalo, Fin. | C12 | 14 |
| Ivan, Ar., U.S. | D3 | 81 |
| Ivangrad, Yugo. | D4 | 24 |
| Ivanhoe, Austl. | F5 | 51 |
| Ivanhoe, Mn., U.S. | F2 | 100 |
| Ivanhoe, N.C., U.S. | C4 | 110 |
| Ivanhoe, Va., U.S. | D2 | 123 |
| Ivanić Grad, Yugo. | C3 | 24 |
| Ivano-Frankovsk, Sov. Un. | G5 | 27 |
| Ivanovichi, Sov. Un. | D7 | 33 |
| Ivanovka, Sov. Un. | q21 | 27 |
| Ivanovo, Sov. Un. | D7 | 29 |
| Ivanteyevka, Sov. Un. | n17 | 27 |
| Ivato, Madag. | g9 | 49 |
| Ivaylovgrad, Bul. | B6 | 28 |
| Ivdel, Sov. Un. | A6 | 28 |
| Ivesdale, Il., U.S. | D5 | 90 |
| Ives Estates, Fl., U.S. | *G6 | 86 |
| Ivigtut, Grnld. | C19 | 128 |
| Ivinheima, stm., Braz. | C2 | 56 |
| Ivins, Ut., U.S. | F2 | 121 |
| Ivohibe, Madag. | h9 | 49 |
| Ivor, Va., U.S. | D6 | 123 |
| Ivory Coast, ctry., Afr. | E3 | 45 |
| Ivoryton, Ct., U.S. | D6 | 84 |
| Ivösjön, l., Swe. | B10 | 15 |
| Ivrea, Italy | B1 | 23 |
| Ivrey-Nord, Que. | C3 | 74 |
| Ivry-sur-Seine, Fr. | g10 | 16 |
| Ivujivik, Que. | f11 | 74 |
| Ivy, Va., U.S. | B4 | 123 |
| Ivydale, W.V., U.S. | C3 | 125 |
| Ivy Mountain, mtn., Ct., U.S. | C7 | 84 |
| Iwaki (Taira), Japan | H10 | 33 |
| Iwaki, Mount, mtn., Japan | F10 | 33 |
| Iwakuni, Japan | I6 | 33 |
| Iwamizawa, Japan | E10 | 33 |
| Iwanai, Japan | E10 | 33 |
| Iwate, Mount, mtn., Japan | G10 | 33 |
| Iwo, Nig. | E5 | 45 |
| Iwo Jima, i., Japan | E8 | 6 |
| Iwŏn, N. Kor. | F4 | 33 |
| Ixelles (Elsene), Bel. | *D4 | 17 |
| Ixiamas, Bol. | B2 | 57 |
| Ixmiquilpan, Mex. | m14 | 63 |
| Ixtacalco (part of Mexico City), Mex. | h9 | 63 |
| Ixtapa, Punta, c., Mex. | D4 | 63 |
| Ixtapalapa (part of Mexico City), Mex. | h9 | 63 |
| Ixtlán de Juárez, Mex. | o15 | 63 |
| Ixtlán del Río, Mex. | C4 | 63 |
| Izabal, Lago de, l., Guat. | F3 | 63 |
| Izad Khvāst, Iran | F6 | 39 |
| Izamal, Mex. | C7 | 63 |
| Izard, co., Ar., U.S. | A4 | 81 |
| Izberbash, Sov. Un. | B1 | 38 |
| Izegem, Bel. | D3 | 17 |
| Izena Island, i., Japan | N5 | 52 |
| Izhevsk (Ustinov), Sov. Un. | D8 | 29 |
| Izhma, stm., Sov. Un. | C19 | 8 |
| Izmail, Sov. Un. | I7 | 27 |
| İzmir (Smyrna), Tur. | C4 | 25 |
| İzmir, Gulf of, b., Tur. | C6 | 25 |
| İzmit (Kocaeli) (Nicomedia), Tur. | B7 | 40 |
| İznik Lake, l., Tur. | B7 | 25 |
| Izozog, Bañados de, sw., Bol. | C3 | 55 |
| Izra', Syria | B8 | 41 |
| Iztaccíhuatl, vol., Mex. | n14 | 63 |
| Izúcar de Matamoros, Mex. | n14 | 63 |
| Izuhara, Japan | I4 | 33 |
| Izu Islands, is., Japan | D8 | 6 |
| Izumo, Japan | I6 | 33 |
| Izyum, Sov. Un. | G11 | 27 |

## J

| Name | Map Ref. | Page |
|---|---|---|
| Jabal al Awliyā', Sud. | B3 | 47 |
| Jabalón, stm., Spain | C4 | 22 |
| Jabalpur, India | D6 | 36 |
| Jabālyah, Isr. Occ. | C6 | 41 |
| Jablonec [nad Nisou], Czech. | C3 | 26 |
| Jablonná, Czech. | o17 | 26 |
| Jablunkov Pass, Czech. | D5 | 26 |
| Jaboatão, Braz. | C4 | 57 |
| Jaboticabal, Braz. | C3 | 56 |
| Jabrīn, l., Iran | C5 | 38 |
| Jaca, Spain | A5 | 22 |
| Jacala de Ledesma, Mex. | m14 | 63 |
| Jacaraci, Braz. | A4 | 56 |
| Jacaré, stm., Braz. | D2 | 57 |
| Jacareí, Braz. | m9 | 56 |
| Jacarezinho, Braz. | C2 | 56 |
| Jachin, Al., U.S. | C1 | 78 |
| Jáchymov, Czech. | B1 | 26 |
| Jacinto, Braz. | A5 | 56 |
| Jacinto City, Tx., U.S. | r14 | 120 |
| Jack, Al., U.S. | D3 | 78 |
| Jack, co., Tx., U.S. | C3 | 120 |
| Jackfish Lake, l., Sask. | D1 | 75 |
| Jackhead Harbour, Man. | D3 | 70 |
| Jackman, Me., U.S. | C2 | 96 |
| Jackman Station, Me., U.S. | C2 | 96 |
| Jack Mountain, mtn., Mt., U.S. | D4 | 103 |
| Jack Mountain, mtn., Va., U.S. | B3 | 123 |
| Jack Mountain, mtn., Wa., U.S. | A5 | 124 |
| Jackpot, Nv., U.S. | B7 | 105 |
| Jacksboro, Tn., U.S. | C9 | 119 |
| Jacksboro, Tx., U.S. | C3 | 120 |
| Jacks Creek, Tn., U.S. | B3 | 119 |
| Jacks Mountain, mtn., Pa., U.S. | E6 | 115 |
| Jackson, Al., U.S. | D2 | 78 |
| Jackson, Ca., U.S. | C3 | 82 |
| Jackson, Ga., U.S. | C3 | 87 |
| Jackson, Ky., U.S. | C6 | 94 |
| Jackson, Me., U.S. | D3 | 96 |
| Jackson, Mi., U.S. | F6 | 99 |
| Jackson, Mn., U.S. | G4 | 100 |
| Jackson, Mo., U.S. | D8 | 102 |
| Jackson, Ms., U.S. | C3 | 101 |
| Jackson, N.H., U.S. | B4 | 106 |
| Jackson, N.J., U.S. | C4 | 107 |
| Jackson, N.C., U.S. | A5 | 110 |
| Jackson, Oh., U.S. | C3 | 112 |
| Jackson, S.C., U.S. | E4 | 117 |
| Jackson, Tn., U.S. | B3 | 119 |
| Jackson, Wi., U.S. | E5 | 126 |
| Jackson, Wy., U.S. | C2 | 127 |
| Jackson, co., Al., U.S. | A3 | 78 |
| Jackson, co., Ar., U.S. | B4 | 81 |
| Jackson, co., Co., U.S. | A4 | 83 |
| Jackson, co., Fl., U.S. | B1 | 86 |
| Jackson, co., Ga., U.S. | B3 | 87 |
| Jackson, co., Il., U.S. | F4 | 90 |
| Jackson, co., In., U.S. | G5 | 91 |
| Jackson, co., Ia., U.S. | B7 | 92 |
| Jackson, co., Ks., U.S. | C8 | 93 |
| Jackson, co., Ky., U.S. | C5 | 94 |
| Jackson, co., La., U.S. | B3 | 95 |
| Jackson, co., Mi., U.S. | F6 | 99 |
| Jackson, co., Mn., U.S. | G3 | 100 |
| Jackson, co., Ms., U.S. | E5 | 101 |
| Jackson, co., Mo., U.S. | B3 | 102 |
| Jackson, co., N.C., U.S. | f9 | 110 |
| Jackson, co., Oh., U.S. | C3 | 112 |
| Jackson, co., Ok., U.S. | C2 | 113 |
| Jackson, co., Or., U.S. | E4 | 114 |
| Jackson, co., S.D., U.S. | D4 | 118 |
| Jackson, co., Tn., U.S. | C8 | 119 |
| Jackson, co., Tx., U.S. | E4 | 120 |
| Jackson, co., W.V., U.S. | C3 | 125 |
| Jackson, co., Wi., U.S. | D3 | 126 |
| Jackson, stm., Va., U.S. | C3 | 123 |
| Jackson, Lake, l., Fl., U.S. | B2 | 86 |
| Jackson, Lake, l., Fl., U.S. | E5 | 86 |
| Jackson, Mount, mtn., Ant. | B6 | 7 |
| Jackson, Port, b., Austl. | F8 | 51 |
| Jacksonboro, S.C., U.S. | F7 | 117 |
| Jacksonburg, W.V., U.S. | B4 | 125 |
| Jackson Center, Oh., U.S. | B1 | 112 |
| Jackson Center, Pa., U.S. | D1 | 115 |
| Jackson Dam, N.D., U.S. | C7 | 111 |
| Jackson Hill, In., U.S. | F3 | 91 |
| Jackson Junction, Ia., U.S. | A5 | 92 |
| Jackson Lake, res., Ga., U.S. | C3 | 87 |
| Jackson Lake, res., Wy., U.S. | C2 | 127 |
| Jackson Mountain, mtn., Me., U.S. | C2 | 96 |
| Jackson Mountains, mts., Nv., U.S. | B3 | 105 |
| Jacksonport, Ar., U.S. | B4 | 81 |
| Jackson's Gap, Al., U.S. | C4 | 78 |
| Jackson Town, Wy., U.S. | C2 | 127 |
| Jacksonville, Al., U.S. | B4 | 78 |
| Jacksonville, Ar., U.S. | C3 | 81 |
| Jacksonville, Fl., U.S. | B5 | 86 |
| Jacksonville, Ga., U.S. | E4 | 87 |
| Jacksonville, Il., U.S. | D3 | 90 |
| Jacksonville, Me., U.S. | D5 | 96 |
| Jacksonville, Mo., U.S. | B5 | 102 |
| Jacksonville, N.C., U.S. | C5 | 110 |
| Jacksonville, Or., U.S. | E4 | 114 |
| Jacksonville, Tx., U.S. | D5 | 120 |
| Jacksonville, Vt., U.S. | F3 | 122 |
| Jacksonville Beach, Fl., U.S. | B5 | 86 |
| Jacksonville Naval Air Station, mil., Fl., U.S. | B5 | 86 |
| Jacks Peak, mtn., Ut., U.S. | E3 | 121 |
| Jacktown, Ok., U.S. | B4 | 113 |
| Jacmel, Haiti | E7 | 64 |
| Jacob, Congo | B1 | 48 |
| Jacobina, Braz. | D3 | 57 |
| Jacob Lake, Az., U.S. | A3 | 80 |
| Jacobson, Mn., U.S. | C5 | 100 |
| Jacobstown, N.J., U.S. | C3 | 107 |
| Jacques-Cartier, stm., Que. | B6 | 74 |
| Jacques-Cartier, Détroit de, strt., Que. | h8 | 72 |
| Jacques-Cartier, Mont, mtn., Que. | G19 | 66 |
| Jacquet River, N.B. | B4 | 71 |
| Jacquinot Bay, b., Pap. N. Gui. | k13 | 50 |
| Jacuí, stm., Braz. | C6 | 56 |
| Jacuípe, stm., Braz. | D3 | 57 |
| Jacundá, stm., Braz. | C4 | 59 |
| Jadabpur, India | *D8 | 36 |
| Jaddi, Rās, c., Pak. | I11 | 39 |
| Jade, W. Ger. | B4 | 17 |
| Jade Bay, b., W. Ger. | B4 | 18 |
| Jādū, Libya | C2 | 43 |
| Jadwin, Mo., U.S. | D6 | 102 |
| Jægerspris, Den. | C5 | 15 |
| Jaén, Peru | C2 | 58 |
| Jaén, Spain | D4 | 22 |
| Jaffa, Cape, c., Austl. | G3 | 51 |
| Jaffa, Sea of, Asia | C12 | 31 |
| Jaffa Gate, hist., Isr. Occ. | m14 | 41 |
| Jaffna, Sri L. | G7 | 36 |
| Jaffrey, N.H., U.S. | E2 | 106 |
| Jaffrey Center, N.H., U.S. | E2 | 106 |
| Jagādhri, India | B6 | 37 |
| Jagdalpur, India | C6 | 36 |
| Jaggayyapeta, India | I8 | 37 |
| Jagin, stm., Iran | H9 | 39 |
| Jagst, stm., W. Ger. | D4 | 19 |
| Jaguarão, Braz. | E2 | 56 |
| Jaguarari, Braz. | C3 | 56 |
| Jaguariaíva, Braz. | C3 | 56 |
| Jagüey Grande, Cuba | C3 | 64 |
| Jahrom, Iran | C5 | 38 |
| Jaicós, Braz. | C2 | 57 |
| Jailolo, Indon. | E7 | 34 |
| Jaipur, India | C6 | 36 |
| Jājapur, India | D8 | 36 |
| Jajce, Yugo. | C3 | 24 |
| Jakarta (Djakarta), Indon. | G3 | 34 |
| Jakin, Ga., U.S. | E2 | 87 |
| Jakobstad, Fin. | F10 | 14 |
| Jal, N.M., U.S. | E6 | 108 |
| Jalaihai Point, c., Guam | M10 | 52 |
| Jalālābād, Afg. | B5 | 36 |
| Jalālah al Baḥrīyah, Jabal, plat., Eg. | E4 | 41 |
| Jalandhar, India | B6 | 36 |
| Jalapa, Guat. | E6 | 63 |
| Jalapa, Mex. | C6 | 36 |
| Jalapa Enríquez, Mex. | D5 | 63 |
| Jālgaon, India | D6 | 36 |
| Jālor, India | E4 | 37 |
| Jalpa, Mex. | C5 | 63 |
| Jalpan, Mex. | C5 | 63 |
| Jālū, Wāḥat, well, Libya | D4 | 43 |
| Jalūlā, Iraq | D2 | 39 |
| Jamaame, Som. | E5 | 47 |
| Jamaica, Ia., U.S. | C3 | 92 |
| Jamaica, Vt., U.S. | E3 | 122 |
| Jamaica, ctry., N.A. | E9 | 64 |
| Jamaica Bay, b., N.Y., U.S. | k13 | 109 |
| Jamaica Channel, strt., N.A. | D4 | 64 |
| Jamālpur, Bngl. | E12 | 37 |
| Jamanxim, stm., Braz. | D3 | 59 |
| Jamari, stm., Braz. | D2 | 59 |
| Jambi, Indon. | F2 | 34 |
| Jambuair, Cape, c., Indon. | D1 | 34 |
| James, stm., Alta. | D3 | 68 |
| James, stm., Mo., U.S. | E4 | 102 |
| James, stm., Va., U.S. | C5 | 123 |
| James, Lake, l., In., U.S. | A7 | 91 |
| James, Lake, l., N.C., U.S. | B1 | 110 |
| James Bay, b., Can. | F16 | 66 |
| James Branch, stm., De., U.S. | F3 | 85 |
| James City, N.C., U.S. | B5 | 110 |
| James City, Pa., U.S. | C4 | 115 |
| James City, co., Va., U.S. | C5 | 123 |
| James Craik, Arg. | A4 | 54 |
| James Creek, Pa., U.S. | F5 | 115 |
| James Island, B.C. | g12 | 69 |
| James Island, i., Md., U.S. | C5 | 97 |
| James Island, i., S.C., U.S. | F8 | 117 |
| Jameson, Mo., U.S. | A4 | 102 |
| Jamesport, Mo., U.S. | B4 | 102 |
| James River Bridge, Va., U.S. | k15 | 123 |
| James Ross Island, i., Ant. | C7 | 7 |
| James Ross Strait, strt., N.W. Ter. | C13 | 66 |
| Jamestown, Austl. | F3 | 51 |
| Jamestown, Ire. | D3 | 11 |
| Jamestown, Ca., U.S. | D3 | 82 |
| Jamestown, In., U.S. | E4 | 91 |
| Jamestown, Ky., U.S. | D4 | 94 |
| Jamestown, Mo., U.S. | C5 | 102 |
| Jamestown, N.Y., U.S. | C1 | 109 |
| Jamestown, N.C., U.S. | B3 | 110 |
| Jamestown, N.D., U.S. | C7 | 111 |
| Jamestown, Oh., U.S. | C2 | 112 |
| Jamestown, Pa., U.S. | D1 | 115 |
| Jamestown, R.I., U.S. | E5 | 116 |
| Jamestown, Tn., U.S. | C9 | 119 |
| Jamestown Dam, N.D., U.S. | C7 | 111 |
| Jamestown Reservoir, res., N.D., U.S. | C7 | 111 |
| Jamesville, N.C., U.S. | B6 | 110 |
| Jamesville, N.Y., U.S. | C4 | 109 |
| Jamiltepec, Mex. | D5 | 63 |
| Jamison, Pa., U.S. | F11 | 115 |
| Jammā'īn, Isr. Occ. | g11 | 41 |
| Jammerbugten, b., Den. | A3 | 15 |
| Jammu, India | C6 | 36 |
| Jammu and Kashmir, dep., Asia | A6 | 36 |
| Jāmnagar (Navanagar), India | D5 | 36 |
| Jāmpur, India | E4 | 37 |
| Jāmshedpur, India | D8 | 36 |
| Jāmul, Ca., U.S. | F5 | 82 |
| Jan, stm., Bngl. | E12 | 37 |
| Janaúba, Braz. | B4 | 56 |
| Jandaia, Braz. | B3 | 56 |
| Jandaq, Iran | B6 | 38 |
| Jandiatuba, stm., Braz. | A4 | 58 |
| Jándula, stm., Spain | C4 | 22 |
| Jane Lew, W.V., U.S. | B4 | 125 |
| Janesville, Ca., U.S. | B3 | 82 |
| Janesville, Il., U.S. | D5 | 90 |
| Janesville, Ia., U.S. | B5 | 92 |
| Janesville, Mn., U.S. | F5 | 100 |
| Janesville, Wi., U.S. | F4 | 126 |
| Jangīpur, India | B2 | 36 |
| Janīn, Isr. Occ. | B7 | 41 |
| Jan Lake, l., Sask. | C4 | 75 |
| Jan Mayen, i., Nor. | B15 | 128 |
| Janos, Mex. | A3 | 63 |
| Jánoshalma, Hung. | B4 | 24 |
| Janow, Man. | E4 | 70 |
| Janów, Pol. | C7 | 26 |
| Janów Lubelski, Pol. | C7 | 26 |
| Jansen, Sask. | F3 | 75 |
| Jansen, Co., U.S. | D6 | 83 |
| Jansen, Ne., U.S. | D8 | 104 |
| Januária, Braz. | B4 | 56 |
| Japan, ctry., Asia | D12 | 31 |
| Japan, Sea of, Asia | C12 | 31 |
| Japaratuba, Braz. | D3 | 57 |
| Japim, Braz. | C3 | 58 |
| Japurá (Caquetá), stm., S.A. | D4 | 60 |
| Jaqué, Pan. | B8 | 62 |
| Jarābulus, Syria | D12 | 40 |
| Jaraguá, Braz. | B3 | 56 |
| Jaraguari, Braz. | B2 | 56 |
| Jaraguá do Sul, Braz. | D3 | 56 |
| Jaral del Progreso, Mex. | m13 | 63 |
| Jarales, N.M., U.S. | C3 | 108 |
| Jarama, stm., Spain | B4 | 22 |
| Jaramānah, Syria | *F11 | 40 |
| Jarash, Jord. | B7 | 41 |
| Jarbalo, Ks., U.S. | k15 | 93 |
| Jarbidge, Nv., U.S. | B6 | 105 |
| Jardim, Braz. | C1 | 56 |
| Jardim de Angicos, Braz. | g6 | 57 |
| Jardim do Seridó, Braz. | C3 | 57 |
| Jardín, Mt., U.S. | E6 | 103 |
| Jardines de la Reina, Archipiélago de los, is., Cuba | D4 | 64 |
| Jardinópolis, Braz. | k8 | 56 |
| Järfälla, Swe. | *H7 | 14 |
| Jargalang, China | C10 | 32 |
| Jargalant, Mong. | B7 | 31 |
| Jari, stm., Braz. | B4 | 59 |
| Järlåsa (part of Uppsala), Swe. | t35 | 14 |
| Järna (part of Södertälje), Swe. | t35 | 14 |
| Jarnac, Fr. | E5 | 16 |
| Jarny, Fr. | E5 | 17 |
| Jarocin, Pol. | C4 | 26 |
| Jaromĕř, Czech. | C3 | 26 |
| Jarosław, Pol. | C7 | 26 |
| Jaroso, Co., U.S. | D5 | 83 |
| Jarratt, Va., U.S. | D5 | 123 |
| Jarrettsville, Md., U.S. | A5 | 97 |
| Jarrow, Alta. | C5 | 68 |
| Jaru, Braz. | B3 | 55 |
| Jarud Qi, China | C9 | 31 |
| Jarvie, Alta. | B4 | 68 |
| Jarvis, Ont. | E5 | 73 |
| Jarvis, i., Oc. | G12 | 6 |
| Jarvisburg, N.C., U.S. | A7 | 110 |
| Jasień, Pol. | B10 | 19 |
| Jāsk, Iran | I8 | 39 |
| Jasło, Pol. | D6 | 26 |
| Jasmine Estates, Fl., U.S. | D4 | 86 |
| Jason Peninsula, pen., Ant. | C6 | 7 |
| Jasonville, In., U.S. | F3 | 91 |
| Jasper, Alta. | C1 | 68 |
| Jasper, Ont. | C9 | 73 |
| Jasper, Al., U.S. | B2 | 78 |
| Jasper, Ar., U.S. | B2 | 81 |
| Jasper, Fl., U.S. | B4 | 86 |
| Jasper, Ga., U.S. | B2 | 87 |
| Jasper, In., U.S. | H4 | 91 |
| Jasper, Mn., U.S. | G2 | 100 |
| Jasper, Mo., U.S. | D3 | 102 |
| Jasper, N.Y., U.S. | C3 | 109 |
| Jasper, Oh., U.S. | C2 | 112 |
| Jasper, Or., U.S. | C4 | 114 |
| Jasper, Tn., U.S. | D8 | 119 |
| Jasper, Tx., U.S. | D6 | 120 |
| Jasper, co., Ga., U.S. | C3 | 87 |
| Jasper, co., Il., U.S. | D5 | 90 |
| Jasper, co., In., U.S. | B3 | 91 |
| Jasper, co., Ia., U.S. | C4 | 92 |
| Jasper, co., Ms., U.S. | D4 | 101 |
| Jasper, co., Mo., U.S. | D3 | 102 |
| Jasper, co., S.C., U.S. | G5 | 117 |
| Jasper, co., Tx., U.S. | D6 | 120 |
| Jasper Lake, l., Alta. | C1 | 68 |
| Jasper National Park, Alta. | C1 | 68 |
| Jastarnia, Pol. | A5 | 26 |
| Jastrzebie Góra, Pol. | A5 | 26 |
| Jastrzebie-Zdrój, Pol. | h9 | 26 |
| Jászapáti, Hung. | B5 | 24 |
| Jászberény, Hung. | B4 | 24 |
| Jataí, Braz. | B2 | 56 |
| Jāti, Pak. | B2 | 36 |
| Jatibonico, Cuba | D4 | 64 |
| Játiva, Spain | C5 | 22 |
| Jatni, India | G10 | 37 |
| Jatobá, stm., Braz. | E4 | 59 |
| Jaú, Braz. | A3 | 56 |
| Jauaperi, stm., Braz. | C2 | 59 |
| Jaunpur, India | C7 | 36 |
| Java (Jawa), i., Indon. | G13 | 34 |
| Java, S.D., U.S. | B6 | 118 |
| Java, Va., U.S. | D3 | 123 |
| Javari see Yavarí, stm., S.A. | B3 | 58 |
| Java Sea, Asia | G4 | 34 |
| Jávea, Spain | C6 | 22 |
| Jawhār, India | H4 | 37 |
| Jawor, Pol. | C3 | 26 |
| Jaworzno, Pol. | g10 | 26 |
| Jay, Fl., U.S. | u14 | 86 |
| Jay, Me., U.S. | D2 | 96 |
| Jay, Ok., U.S. | A7 | 113 |
| Jay, co., In., U.S. | D7 | 91 |
| Jaya Peak, mtn., Indon. | F9 | 34 |
| Jayapura, Indon. | F10 | 34 |
| Jay Em, Wy., U.S. | D8 | 127 |
| Jay Peak, mtn., Vt., U.S. | B3 | 122 |
| Jaypur, India | C7 | 36 |
| Jayton, Tx., U.S. | C2 | 120 |
| Jaz Mūrīān, Hāmūn-e, l., Iran | H9 | 39 |
| J. B. Thomas, Lake, res., Tx., U.S. | C2 | 120 |
| Jean, Nv., U.S. | H6 | 105 |
| Jeanerette, La., U.S. | E4 | 95 |
| Jean Lafitte National Historical Park, La., U.S. | k12 | 95 |
| Jeannette, Pa., U.S. | F2 | 115 |
| Jeannette Island, i., Sov. Un. | B35 | 128 |
| Jebba, Nig. | E5 | 45 |
| Jeberos, Peru | C2 | 58 |
| Jedburgh, Sask. | F4 | 75 |
| Jedburgh, Scot., U.K. | F9 | 13 |
| Jeddito, Az., U.S. | B6 | 80 |
| Jeddo, Mi., U.S. | E8 | 99 |
| Jeddore Lake, res., Newf. | D3 | 72 |
| Jędrzejów, Pol. | C5 | 26 |
| Jeetze, stm., Eur. | B2 | 19 |
| Jeff, Ky., U.S. | C6 | 94 |
| Jeff Davis, co., Ga., U.S. | E4 | 87 |
| Jeff Davis, co., Tx., U.S. | o12 | 120 |
| Jeffers, Mn., U.S. | F3 | 100 |

| Name | Map Ref. | Page |
|---|---|---|

Jeffers, Mt., U.S. — E5 103
Jefferson, Al., U.S. — C2 78
Jefferson, Ar., U.S. — C3 81
Jefferson, Co., U.S. — B5 83
Jefferson, Ga., U.S. — B3 87
Jefferson, In., U.S. — D4 91
Jefferson, Ia., U.S. — B3 92
Jefferson, La., U.S. — k11 95
Jefferson, Me., U.S. — D3 96
Jefferson, Md., U.S. — B2 97
Jefferson, Ma., U.S. — B4 98
Jefferson, N.H., U.S. — B4 106
Jefferson, N.J., U.S. — D2 107
Jefferson, N.Y., U.S. — C6 109
Jefferson, N.C., U.S. — A1 110
Jefferson, Oh., U.S. — A5 112
Jefferson, Ok., U.S. — A4 113
Jefferson, Or., U.S. — C3 114
Jefferson, Pa., U.S. — *F2 115
Jefferson, S.C., U.S. — B7 117
Jefferson, S.D., U.S. — E9 118
Jefferson, Tx., U.S. — C5 120
Jefferson, Wi., U.S. — E5 126
Jefferson, co., Al., U.S. — B3 78
Jefferson, co., Ar., U.S. — C3 81
Jefferson, co., Co., U.S. — B5 83
Jefferson, co., Fl., U.S. — B3 86
Jefferson, co., Ga., U.S. — C4 87
Jefferson, co., Id., U.S. — F6 89
Jefferson, co., Il., U.S. — E5 90
Jefferson, co., In., U.S. — G6 91
Jefferson, co., Ia., U.S. — C5 92
Jefferson, co., Ks., U.S. — C8 93
Jefferson, co., Ky., U.S. — B4 94
Jefferson, co., La., U.S. — E5 95
Jefferson, co., Ms., U.S. — D2 101
Jefferson, co., Mo., U.S. — C7 102
Jefferson, co., Mt., U.S. — D4 103
Jefferson, co., Ne., U.S. — D8 104
Jefferson, co., N.Y., U.S. — A5 109
Jefferson, co., Oh., U.S. — B5 112
Jefferson, co., Ok., U.S. — C4 113
Jefferson, co., Or., U.S. — C5 114
Jefferson, co., Pa., U.S. — D3 115
Jefferson, co., Tn., U.S. — C10 119
Jefferson, co., Tx., U.S. — E5 120
Jefferson, co., Wa., U.S. — B1 124
Jefferson, co., W.V., U.S. — B7 125
Jefferson, co., Wi., U.S. — E5 126
Jefferson, stm., Mt., U.S. — E5 103
Jefferson, Mount, mtn., Id., U.S. — E7 89
Jefferson, Mount, mtn., Nv., U.S. — E5 105
Jefferson, Mount, mtn., Or., U.S. — C5 114
Jefferson City, Mo., U.S. — C5 102
Jefferson City, Mt., U.S. — D5 103
Jefferson City, Tn., U.S. — C10 119
Jefferson Davis, co., La., U.S. — D3 95
Jefferson Davis, co., Ms., U.S. — D4 101
Jefferson Farms, De., U.S. — i7 85
Jefferson Hill, hill, Ky., U.S. — g11 94
Jefferson Manor, Va., U.S. — *B5 123
Jefferson Proving Ground, mil., In., U.S. — G7 91
Jeffersontown, Ky., U.S. — B4 94
Jefferson Valley, N.Y., U.S. — *D7 109
Jefferson Village, Va., U.S. — *B5 123
Jeffersonville, Ga., U.S. — D3 87
Jeffersonville, In., U.S. — H6 91
Jeffersonville, Ky., U.S. — C6 94
Jeffersonville, N.Y., U.S. — D6 109
Jeffersonville, Oh., U.S. — C2 112
Jeffersonville, Vt., U.S. — B3 122
Jeffrey, W.V., U.S. — D3 125
Jeffrey City, Wy., U.S. — D5 127
Jeffries Creek, stm., S.C., U.S. — C7 117
Jega, Nig. — D5 45
Jehossee Island, i., S.C., U.S. — k11 117
Jejui-Guazú, stm., Para. — D4 55
Jēkabpils, Sov. Un. — C4 18
Jekyll Island, i., Ga., U.S. — E5 87
Jelenia Góra (Hirschberg), Pol. — C3 26
Jelgava (Yelgava), Sov. Un. — C4 27
Jellico, Tn., U.S. — C9 119
Jelling, Den. — C3 15
Jelm, Wy., U.S. — E6 127
Jelm Mountain, mtn., Wy., U.S. — E7 127
Jelöya, i., Nor. — p28 14
Jemaja, i., Indon. — K6 35
Jember, Indon. — G4 34
Jemez, stm., N.M., U.S. — k7 108
Jemez Dam, N.M., U.S. — k7 108
Jemez Indian Reservation, N.M., U.S. — h7 108
Jemez Pueblo, N.M., U.S. — B3 108
Jemez Springs, N.M., U.S. — B3 108
Jemison, Al., U.S. — C3 78
Jemseg, N.B. — D3 71
Jemtland, Me., U.S. — A4 96
Jena, E. Ger. — C5 18
Jena, Fl., U.S. — C3 86
Jena, La., U.S. — C3 95
Jenaz, Switz. — C8 21
Jenbach, Aus. — B7 20
Jendouba, Tun. — F2 23
Jenera, Oh., U.S. — B2 112
Jenison, Mi., U.S. — *F5 99
Jenkins, Ky., U.S. — C7 94
Jenkins, Mn., U.S. — D4 100
Jenkins, N.J., U.S. — D3 107
Jenkins, co., Ga., U.S. — D5 87
Jenkinsburg, Ga., U.S. — C2 87
Jenkinsville, S.C., U.S. — C5 117
Jenkintown, Pa., U.S. — o21 115
Jenks, Ok., U.S. — A6 113
Jenner, Alta. — D5 68
Jenners, Pa., U.S. — F3 115
Jennie, Ar., U.S. — D4 81
Jennings, Fl., U.S. — B3 86
Jennings, Ks., U.S. — C3 93
Jennings, La., U.S. — D3 95
Jennings, Md., U.S. — k12 97
Jennings, Mi., U.S. — D5 99
Jennings, Mo., U.S. — f13 102
Jennings, Ok., U.S. — A5 113
Jennings, co., In., U.S. — G6 91
Jennings Lodge, Or., U.S. — *B4 114
Jenny Jump Mountain, mtn., N.J., U.S. — B3 107
Jenny Lind, Ar., U.S. — B1 81
Jensen, Ut., U.S. — C6 121
Jensen Beach, Fl., U.S. — E6 86
Jeptha Knob, hill, Ky., U.S. — B4 94
Jequié, Braz. — B4 56
Jequitaí, Braz. — D6 57
Jequitinhonha, Braz. — D6 57
Jequitinhonha, stm., Braz. — E2 57
Jerada, Mor. — C4 44
Jerauld, co., S.D., U.S. — C7 118
Jérémie, Haiti — E6 65
Jeremoabo, Braz. — D3 57
Jerez de García Salinas, Mex. — C4 63

Jerez de la Frontera, Spain — D2 22
Jerez de los Caballeros, Spain — C2 22
Jericho, Austl. — A6 51
Jericho (Arīhā), Isr. Occ. — C7 41
Jericho, Ar., U.S. — B5 81
Jericho, N.Y., U.S. — *E7 109
Jericho, Vt., U.S. — B3 122
Jericho Center, Vt., U.S. — C3 122
Jerico Springs, Mo., U.S. — D4 102
Jerimoth Hill, hill, R.I., U.S. — C1 116
Jermyn, Pa., U.S. — C10 115
Jermyn, Tx., U.S. — C3 120
Jerome, Az., U.S. — C3 80
Jerome, Fl., U.S. — F5 86
Jerome, Id., U.S. — G4 89
Jerome, Ia., U.S. — D4 92
Jerome, Mi., U.S. — F6 99
Jerome, Mo., U.S. — D6 102
Jerome, Pa., U.S. — F4 115
Jerome, co., Id., U.S. — G4 89
Jeromesville, Oh., U.S. — B3 112
Jersey, dep., Eur. — F5 10
Jersey City, N.J., U.S. — B4 107
Jersey Mountain, mtn., Id., U.S. — E3 89
Jersey Shore, Pa., U.S. — D7 115
Jerseyville, Il., U.S. — D3 90
Jerumenha, Braz. — B3 56
Jerusalem (Yerushalayim), Isr. — B3 38
Jerusalem, Oh., U.S. — C4 112
Jervis Bay, b., Austl. — G9 50
Jervis Inlet, b., B.C. — D6 69
Jesenice, Czech. — C4 26
Jessamine, co., Ky., U.S. — C5 94
Jessen, E. Ger. — B7 19
Jessie, N.D., U.S. — B7 111
Jessieville, Ar., U.S. — C2 81
Jessnitz, E. Ger. — B7 19
Jessore, Bngl. — F12 37
Jessup, Md., U.S. — B4 97
Jessup, Pa., U.S. — m18 115
Jesterville, Md., U.S. — D6 97
Jesup, Ga., U.S. — E5 87
Jesup, Ia., U.S. — B5 92
Jesup, Lake, l., Fl., U.S. — D5 86
Jésus, Île, i., Que. — p19 74
Jesús Carranza, Mex. — D5 63
Jesús María, Arg. — A4 54
Jesús María, Peru — *D2 58
Jet, Ok., U.S. — A3 113
Jetersville, Va., U.S. — C4 123
Jetmore, Ks., U.S. — D4 93
Jet Peak, mtn., Nv., U.S. — D3 105
Jetson, Ky., U.S. — C3 94
Jette, Bel. — D4 17
Jeumont, Fr. — D4 17
Jever, W. Ger. — B3 18
Jewell, Ia., U.S. — B4 92
Jewell, Ks., U.S. — C5 93
Jewell, Oh., U.S. — A1 112
Jewell, co., Ks., U.S. — C5 93
Jewell Ridge, Va., U.S. — e10 123
Jewett, Il., U.S. — D5 90
Jewett, Oh., U.S. — B4 112
Jewett, Tx., U.S. — D4 120
Jewett City, Ct., U.S. — C8 84
Jewett Lake, l., Sask. — A3 75
Jeziorka, stm., Pol. — m14 26
Jezioraka, stm., Pol. — m14 26
Jhal, Pak. — C1 37
Jhālāwār, India — E6 37
Jhal Jhao, Pak. — C4 36
Jhang Sadar, Pak. — B4 37
Jhānsi, India — C6 36
Jhawāni, Nepal — D10 37
Jhelum, Pak. — B5 36
Jhelum, stm., Asia — B5 36
Jhunjhunūn, India — C5 37
Jialing Jiang, stm., China — C8 114
Jiamusi, China — B11 31
Ji'an, China — F7 31
Ji'an, China — D12 31
Jianchang, China — D11 32
Jiande, China — J8 32
Jiangling, China — E7 31
Jiangmen, China — G7 31
Jiangsu, prov., China — E9 31
Jiangxi, prov., China — F8 31
Jiangyou (Chengjiang), China — I9 32
Jianli, China — J5 32
Jian'ou, China — F8 31
Jianping, China — C8 31
Jianshi, China — I3 32
Jianshui, China — G5 31
Jianyang, China — G5 31
Jiaohe, China — E3 33
Jiaozhou Bay, b., China — F9 32
Jiaozuo, China — D7 31
Jiashan, China — H8 32
Jiaxian, China — E4 32
Jiaxing, China — E9 31
Jiayu, China — I5 32
Jieyang, China — G8 31
Jifnā, Isr. Occ. — h11 41
Jigger, La., U.S. — B4 95
Jiggs, Nv., U.S. — C6 105
Jihlava, Czech. — D3 26
Jihočeský, prov., Czech. — D9 19
Jijel, Alg. — B6 44
Jijiga, Eth. — D5 47
Jilbānah, Bi'r al, well, Eg. — D4 41
Jilib, Som. — E5 47
Jilin, China — C10 31
Jilin, prov., China — C10 31
Jiloca, stm., Spain — B5 22
Jílové u Prahy, Czech. — o18 26
Jima, Eth. — D4 47
Jimbolia, Rom. — C5 24
Jimena [de los Frontera], Spain — D3 22
Jim Falls, Wi., U.S. — C2 126
Jim Hogg, co., Tx., U.S. — F3 120
Jim Lake, res., N.D., U.S. — B7 111
Jimo, China — F9 32
Jim Thorpe, Pa., U.S. — E10 115
Jim Wells, co., Tx., U.S. — F3 120

Jināh, Eg. — D6 43
Jincheng, China — G5 32
Jindřichův Hradec, Czech. — D3 26
Jingbian, China — F3 32
Jingchuan, China — G2 32
Jingde, China — I8 32
Jingdezhen, China — F8 31
Jing He, stm., China — G3 32
Jinghong, China — G5 31
Jingmen, China — I5 32
Jingning, China — G1 32
Jingshan, China — I5 32
Jingxi, China — D9 32
Jingxian, China — K3 32
Jingxian, China — I8 32
Jingxing, China — A10 32
Jingziguan, China — H4 32
Jinhua, China — F8 31
Jining, China — D8 31
Jining, China — C7 31
Jinja, Ug. — A5 48
Jinniu, China — I6 32
Jinotega, Nic. — E7 63
Jinotepe, Nic. — E7 63
Jinsha Jiang, stm., China — F4 31
Jinshi, China — J4 32
Jinxi, China — C4 31
Jinxi, China — *C9 31
Jinxian, China — D9 31
Jinyun, China — J9 32
Jinzhou, China — C9 31
Jinta, China — E4 31
Jīrjā, Eg. — C3 38
Jirkov, Czech. — C8 19
Jisr ash Shughūr, Syria — E11 40
Jiu, stm., Rom. — C6 24
Jiujiang, China — F8 31
Jiuquan, China — D4 31
Jiurongcheng, China — F7 32
Jixi, China — B11 31
Jixian, China — G6 32
Jizera, stm., Czech. — C9 19
Joaçaba, Braz. — D2 56
Joaíma, Braz. — B4 56
João Belo see Xai-Xai, Moz. — C5 49
João Câmara, Braz. — g6 57
João Pessoa (Paraíba), Braz. — C4 57
João Pinheiro, Braz. — B3 56
Joaquín V. González, Arg. — E3 55
Job, W.V., U.S. — C5 125
Job Peak, mtn., Nv., U.S. — D3 105
Jobstown, N.J., U.S. — C3 107
Jocassee, Lake, res., U.S. — B1 117
Jocotepec, Mex. — m12 63
Jódar, Spain — D4 22
Jo Daviess, co., Il., U.S. — A3 90
Jodhpur, India — C5 36
Jodie, W.V., U.S. — m13 125
Jodoigne, Bel. — D4 17
Joe Batt's Arm [-Barr'd Islands-Shoal Bay], Newf. — D4 72
Joensuu, Fin. — F13 14
Joes, Co., U.S. — B8 83
Joes Brook, stm., Vt., U.S. — C4 122
Joes Creek, stm., W.V., U.S. — m12 125
Joetsu, Japan — H9 33
Jœuf, Fr. — C6 16
Joffre, Mount, mtn., Can. — D3 68
Joggins, N.S. — D5 71
Jogjakarta see Yogyakarta, Indon. — G4 34
Johannesburg, S. Afr. — C4 49
Johannesburg, Ca., U.S. — E5 82
Johannesburg, Mi., U.S. — D6 99
John, Cape, c., N.S. — D6 71
John Crow Mountains, mts., Jam. — E16 65
John Day, Or., U.S. — C8 114
John Day, stm., Or., U.S. — B6 114
John Day, North Fork, stm., Or., U.S. — C7 114
John Day, South Fork, stm., Or., U.S. — C7 114
John Day Fossil Beds National Monument, Or., U.S. — C6 114
John F. Kennedy Space Center, sci., Fl., U.S. — D6 86
John H. Kerr Dam, Va., U.S. — D4 123
John H. Kerr Reservoir, res., U.S. — D4 123
John Martin Reservoir, res., Co., U.S. — C7 83
John Muir National Historical Site, hist., Ca., U.S. — h8 82
John o'Groats, Scot., U.K. — B5 13
John Redmond Reservoir, res., Ks., U.S. — D8 93
Johnsburg, Il., U.S. — h8 90
Johnsburg, N.Y., U.S. — B7 109
Johnsburg, Wi., U.S. — k9 126
John Sevier, Tn., U.S. — m14 119
Johns Island, S.C., U.S. — F7 117
Johns Island, i., S.C., U.S. — F7 117
Johnson, Ar., U.S. — A1 81
Johnson, In., U.S. — H2 91
Johnson, Ks., U.S. — E2 93
Johnson, Ne., U.S. — D10 104
Johnson, Vt., U.S. — B3 122
Johnson, Wa., U.S. — C8 124
Johnson, co., Ar., U.S. — B2 81
Johnson, co., Ga., U.S. — D4 87
Johnson, co., Il., U.S. — F5 90
Johnson, co., In., U.S. — F5 91
Johnson, co., Ia., U.S. — C6 92
Johnson, co., Ks., U.S. — D9 93
Johnson, co., Ky., U.S. — C7 94
Johnson, co., Mo., U.S. — C4 102
Johnson, co., Ne., U.S. — D9 104
Johnson, co., Tn., U.S. — C12 119
Johnson, co., Tx., U.S. — C4 120
Johnson, co., Wy., U.S. — B6 127
Johnsonburg, Pa., U.S. — D4 115
Johnson City, N.Y., U.S. — C5 109
Johnson City, Tn., U.S. — C11 119
Johnson City, Tx., U.S. — D3 120
Johnson Creek, Wi., U.S. — E5 126
Johnsonville, S.C., U.S. — D9 117
Johnston, Ia., U.S. — e8 92
Johnston, R.I., U.S. — C4 116
Johnston, S.C., U.S. — D4 117
Johnston, co., N.C., U.S. — B4 110
Johnston, co., Ok., U.S. — C5 113
Johnston City, Il., U.S. — F5 90

Johnstone, Scot., U.K. — *E4 13
Johnstone Strait, strt., B.C. — D4 69
Johnston Key, i., Fl., U.S. — H5 86
Johnston's Point, c., Scot., U.K. — E3 13
Johnstown, Co., U.S. — A6 83
Johnstown, Ne., U.S. — B5 104
Johnstown, N.Y., U.S. — B6 109
Johnstown, N.D., U.S. — A8 111
Johnstown, Oh., U.S. — B3 112
Johnstown, Pa., U.S. — F4 115
Johnsville, Md., U.S. — A3 97
Johnville, Que. — D6 74
John W. Flannagan Reservoir, res., Va., U.S. — e9 123
Johor, state, Malay. — K5 35
Johor Baharu, Malay. — E2 34
Joice, Ia., U.S. — A4 92
Joigny, Fr. — D5 16
Joinville, Braz. — D3 56
Joinville, Fr. — C6 16
Joinville Island, i., Ant. — C7 7
Jojutla, Mex. — n14 63
Jokkmokk, Swe. — D8 14
Jolfā, Iran — B2 39
Joliet, Il., U.S. — B5 90
Joliet, Mt., U.S. — E8 103
Joliette, Que. — C4 74
Joliette, co., Que. — C3 74
Jolley, Ia., U.S. — B3 92
Jolo, Phil. — D6 34
Jolo, Phil. — o14 34
Jomda, China — E4 31
Jonava, Sov. Un. — A8 26
Jones, Al., U.S. — C3 78
Jones, Ga., U.S. — E5 87
Jones, La., U.S. — B4 95
Jones, Ok., U.S. — B4 113
Jones, co., Ga., U.S. — C3 87
Jones, co., Ia., U.S. — B6 92
Jones, co., Ms., U.S. — D4 101
Jones, co., N.C., U.S. — B5 110
Jones, co., S.D., U.S. — D5 118
Jones, co., Tx., U.S. — C3 120
Jonesboro, Ar., U.S. — B5 81
Jonesboro, Ga., U.S. — C2 87
Jonesboro, Il., U.S. — F4 90
Jonesboro, In., U.S. — D6 91
Jonesboro, La., U.S. — B3 95
Jonesboro, Me., U.S. — D5 96
Jonesboro, Tn., U.S. — C11 119
Jonesboro, Tx., U.S. — D4 120
Jonesburg, Mo., U.S. — C6 102
Jones Creek, Tx., U.S. — s14 120
Jones Mill, Ar., U.S. — C3 81
Jones Mill, Tn., U.S. — A3 119
Jones Mills, Pa., U.S. — F3 115
Jones Mountains, mts., Ant. — B3 7
Jonesport, Me., U.S. — D5 96
Jones Sound, strt., N.W. Ter. — m34 66
Jonestown, Ms., U.S. — A3 101
Jonestown, Pa., U.S. — F9 115
Jonesville, In., U.S. — F6 91
Jonesville, La., U.S. — C4 95
Jonesville, Mi., U.S. — G6 99
Jonesville, N.C., U.S. — A2 110
Jonesville, S.C., U.S. — B4 117
Jonesville, Vt., U.S. — C3 122
Jonesville, Va., U.S. — f8 123
Jönköping, Swe. — I6 14
Jönköping, co., Swe. — A8 15
Jonquière, Que. — A6 74
Jonuta, Mex. — D6 63
Jonzac, Fr. — E3 16
Joplin, Mo., U.S. — D3 102
Joplin, Mt., U.S. — B6 103
Joppa, Al., U.S. — A3 78
Joppa, Il., U.S. — F5 90
Joppa, Md., U.S. — B5 97
Jordan, Al., U.S. — D1 78
Jordan, Mn., U.S. — F5 100
Jordan, Mt., U.S. — C10 103
Jordan, N.Y., U.S. — B4 109
Jordan, ctry., Asia — B3 38
Jordan, stm., Asia — B7 41
Jordan, stm., Ut., U.S. — C4 121
Jordan Creek, stm., U.S. — E9 114
Jordan Lake, l., N.C., U.S. — E4 71
Jordan Lake, res., Al., U.S. — C3 78
Jordan Valley, Or., U.S. — D9 114
Jordânia, Braz. — D1 56
Jorhāt, India — C9 36
Jörn, Swe. — E9 14
Jornado del Muerto, des., N.M., U.S. — D3 108
Jos, Nig. — E6 45
José Battle y Ordóñez, Ur. — E1 56
José de San Martín, Arg. — C2 54
José María Blanco, Arg. — B4 54
Joseph, Or., U.S. — B9 114
Joseph, Ut., U.S. — E3 121
Joseph, Lac, l., Newf. — h8 72
Joseph, Lake, l., Ont. — B5 73
Joseph Bonaparte Gulf, b., Austl. — B4 50
Joseph City, Az., U.S. — C5 80
Josephine, co., Or., U.S. — E3 114
Josephville, Mo., U.S. — f12 102
Joshua, Tx., U.S. — n9 120
Joshua Tree, Ca., U.S. — E5 82
Joshua Tree National Monument, Ca., U.S. — F6 82
Josselin, Fr. — D2 16
Jostedalsbreen, ice, Nor. — G2 14
Jost Van Dyke, i., V.I. Br. — E11 65
Jotunheimen, mts., Nor. — G3 14
Joussard, Alta. — B3 68
Jouy-en-Josas, Fr. — g9 16
Jovellanos, Cuba — B3 64
Joviânia, Braz. — B4 56
Jowhar, Som. — E6 47
Joy, Il., U.S. — B3 90
Joy, Ok., U.S. — C4 113
Joyce, La., U.S. — C3 95
Joyce, Wa., U.S. — A2 124
Jozefów, Pol. — m14 26
Juab, co., Ut., U.S. — D3 121
Juaja, Peru — C2 58
Juan Aldama, Mex. — C4 63
Juan B. Arruabarrena, Arg. — A5 54
Juan de Fuca, Strait of, strt., N.A. — A1 124

Juan Díaz (part of Panamá), Pan. — k12 62
Juan E. Barra, Arg. — B4 54
Juan Fernández, Archipiélago, is., Chile — G2 53
Juanita, N.D., U.S. — B7 111
Juanita, Wa., U.S. — *B3 124
Juan José Castelli, Arg. — E3 55
Juan L. Lacaze, Ur. — g8 54
Juárez, Mex. — B4 63
Juaso, Ghana — E4 45
Juazeiro, Braz. — C2 57
Juazeiro do Norte, Braz. — C3 57
Jūbā, Sud. — E5 47
Jubba (Genale), stm., Afr. — E5 47
Jubbada Dhexe, prov., Som. — E5 47
Jubbada Hoose, prov., Som. — E5 47
Jubbulpore, Sau. Ar. — I13 40
Jubilee Lake, l., Newf. — D4 72
Juby, Cap, c., Mor. — D2 44
Júcar, stm., Spain — C5 22
Juçara, Braz. — B2 56
Júcaro, Cuba — D4 64
Juchipila, Mex. — m12 63
Juchipila, stm., Mex. — m12 63
Juchitán [de Zaragoza], Mex. — D5 63
Jucuapa, El Sal. — D3 62
Juda, Wi., U.S. — F4 126
Judean Hills, hills, Asia — C7 41
Jude Island, i., Newf. — E4 72
Judenburg, Aus. — E7 18
Judique, N.S. — D8 71
Judith, stm., Mt., U.S. — C7 103
Judith, Point, c., R.I., U.S. — G4 85
Judith Basin, co., Mt., U.S. — C6 103
Judith Gap, Mt., U.S. — D7 103
Judith Island, i., N.C., U.S. — B6 110
Judith Mountains, mts., Mt., U.S. — C7 103
Judith Peak, mtn., Mt., U.S. — C7 103
Judson, In., U.S. — E3 91
Judson, Mn., U.S. — F4 100
Judson, N.D., U.S. — C4 111
Judsonia, Ar., U.S. — B4 81
Judyville, In., U.S. — D3 91
Juelsminde, Den. — C4 15
Jufary, Bi'r al, well, Eg. — D4 41
Juigalpa, Nic. — D5 62
Juist, i., W. Ger. — B3 18
Juiz de Fora, Braz. — D6 57
Jujuy, prov., Arg. — D2 55
Jukkasjärvi (part of Kiruna), Swe. — D9 14
Julesburg, Co., U.S. — A8 83
Juliaca, Peru — E3 58
Juliaetta, Id., U.S. — C2 89
Julian, Ca., U.S. — F5 82
Julian, N.C., U.S. — B3 110
Julian, W.V., U.S. — C3 125
Julian Alps, mts., Eur. — C2 24
Juliana Top, mtn., Sur. — B3 59
Julianehåb, Grnld. — C16 61
Jülich, W. Ger. — D6 17
Juliette, Ga., U.S. — C3 87
Julimes, Mex. — B3 63
Júlio de Castilhos, Braz. — D2 56
Julita, Swe. — t34 14
Juliustown, N.J., U.S. — C3 107
Julu, China — F5 32
Jumayl, Bi'r, well, Eg. — D5 41
Jumboo, Som. — F5 47
Jumbo Peak, mtn., Nv., U.S. — G7 105
Jumet (part of Charleroi), Bel. — C5 22
Jumilla, Spain — C5 22
Jump, stm., Wi., U.S. — C3 126
Jump, North Fork, stm., Wi., U.S. — C3 126
Jump, South Fork, stm., Wi., U.S. — C3 126
Jumping Branch, W.V., U.S. — D4 125
Jumping Lake, l., Sask. — B3 75
Jūnāgadh, India — D5 36
Juncos, P.R. — F5 90
Junction, Il., U.S. — F5 90
Junction, Tx., U.S. — D3 120
Junction, Ut., U.S. — E3 121
Junction City, Ar., U.S. — D3 81
Junction City, Il., U.S. — E5 90
Junction City, Ks., U.S. — C7 93
Junction City, Ky., U.S. — C5 94
Junction City, Oh., U.S. — C3 112
Junction City, Or., U.S. — C3 114
Junction City, Wi., U.S. — D4 126
Jundiaí, Braz. — D2 56
Juneau, Ak., U.S. — D13 79
Juneau, Wi., U.S. — E5 126
Juneau, co., Wi., U.S. — E3 126
Junee, Austl. — F8 50
June in Winter, Lake, l., Fl., U.S. — E5 86
June Lake, Ca., U.S. — D4 82
Jungfrau, mtn., Switz. — B3 21
Junggar Pendi (Dzungarian Basin), China — B5 73
Junglinster, Lux. — E6 17
Juniata, Ne., U.S. — D7 104
Juniata, Pa., U.S. — F7 115
Juniata, co., Pa., U.S. — F7 115
Juniata, Raystown Branch, stm., Pa., U.S. — F6 115
Juniata Terrace, Pa., U.S. — E6 115
Junín, Peru — A4 54
Junín, Peru — C2 58
Junín, Lago, l., Peru — C2 58
Junín de los Andes, Arg. — C2 54
Junior, W.V., U.S. — C5 125
Juniper, N.B. — C2 71
Juniper Mountains, mts., Az., U.S. — B2 80
Junipero Serra Peak, mtn., Ca., U.S. — D3 82

Jurbarkas, Sov. Un. — A7 27
Jurf ad Darāwīsh, Jord. — G10 40
Juruá, Braz. — B4 58
Juruá, stm., Braz. — B4 58
Juruena, stm., Braz. — D3 59
Juruti, Braz. — C3 59
Juskatla, B.C. — C1 69
Jussey, Fr. — B1 20
Justice, Il., U.S. — *k9 90
Justiceburg, Tx., U.S. — C2 120
Justin, Tx., U.S. — C4 120
Justo Daract, Arg. — A3 54
Jutaí, Braz. — B4 58
Jutaí, stm., Braz. — B4 58
Jüterbog, E. Ger. — C6 18
Jutiapa, Guat. — E7 63
Juticalpa, Hond. — E7 63
Jutland, pen., Den. — I3 14
Juventud, Isla de la (Isle of Pines), i., Cuba — D2 64
Juxian, China — G8 32
Juyongguan Pass, China — D7 32
Južna Morava, stm., Yugo. — C5 24
Jyderup, Den. — C5 15
Jyväskylä, Fin. — F11 14

## K

K2 (Godwin Austen), mtn., Asia — A6 36
Kaawaa, Hi., U.S. — f10 88
Kaala, mtn., Hi., U.S. — f9 88
Kaalualu Bay, b., Hi., U.S. — E6 88
Kaaumakua, Puu, mtn., Hi., U.S. — f10 88
Kabala, S.L. — E2 45
Kabale, Ug. — B4 48
Kabalega Falls (Murchison Falls), wtfl., Ug. — A5 48
Kabalo, Zaire — C4 48
Kabambare, Zaire — B4 48
Kabara, i., Fiji — I16 52
Kabarnet, Kenya — A6 48
Kabba, Nig. — E6 45
Kabenga, Zaire — C4 48
Kabetogama Lake, l., Mn., U.S. — B5 100
Kabinda, Zaire — C3 48
Kabīr Kūh, mts., Iran — E3 39
Kabompo, Zam. — D3 48
Kabompo, stm., Zam. — D3 48
Kabong, Malay. — E4 34
Kabongo, Zaire — C4 48
Kabul (Kābol), Afg. — D14 39
Kabwe (Broken Hill), Zam. — D4 48
Kachchh, Gulf of (Kutch), b., India — D4 36
Kachess Lake, res., Wa., U.S. — B4 124
Kachug, Sov. Un. — D13 29
Kackley, Ks., U.S. — C6 93
Kadaň, Czech. — C2 26
Kadan, i., Burma — F3 35
Kadavu, i., Fiji — I15 52
Kadavu Passage, strt., Fiji — I15 52
Kade, Ghana — E4 45
Kadena, Japan — O5 52
Kadet Channel, strt., Eur. — A6 18
Kading, stm., Laos — C9 40
Kadınhanı, Tur. — C9 40
Kadiolo, Mali — D3 45
Kadiri, India — F6 36
Kadirli, Tur. — *D11 40
Kadoka, S.D., U.S. — D4 118
Kadoma, Zimb. — A4 49
Kaduna, Nig. — D6 45
Kaduna, stm., Nig. — D6 45
Kāduqlī, Sud. — C2 47
Kaédi, Maur. — C2 45
Kaélé, Cam. — C2 46
Kaena Point, c., Hi., U.S. — B3 88
Kaeryong, S. Kor. — H4 33
Kaesŏng, N. Kor. — D10 31
Kāf, Sau. Ar. — D1 41
Kafanchan, Nig. — D6 45
Kaffrine, Sen. — D1 45
Kafia Kingi, Sud. — D1 47
Kafr ad Dawwār, Eg. — D1 41
Kafr ash Shaykh, Eg. — D2 41
Kafr az Zayyāt, Eg. — D2 41
Kafr Mālik, Isr. Occ. — h12 41
Kafr Qaddūm, Isr. Occ. — g11 41
Kafr Qāsim, Isr. — g10 41
Kafr Saīm, Eg. — D2 41
Kafr Saqr, Eg. — D2 41
Kafr Ṭarkhān al Gharbī, Eg. — D2 41
Kafr Yabād, Isr. Occ. — g10 41
Kafue, Zam. — E4 48
Kafue, stm., Zam. — E4 48
Kagan, Sov. Un. — B12 39
Kagawong, Ont. — B2 73
Kagera, stm., Afr. — B5 48
Kağızman, Tur. — B14 40
Kagoshima, Japan — E11 31
Kagoshima Bay, b., Japan — K5 33
Kagul, Sov. Un. — I7 27
Kahakuloa, Hi., U.S. — B5 88
Kahalu'u, Hi., U.S. — g10 88
Kahama, Tan. — B5 48
Kahana, Hi., U.S. — B4 88
Kahana Bay, b., Hi., U.S. — f10 88
Kahayan, stm., Indon. — F4 34
Kahemba, Zaire — C2 48
Kahla, E. Ger. — C5 18
Kahlotus, Wa., U.S. — C7 124
Kahnūj, Iran — A6 102
Kahoka, Mo., U.S. — A6 102
Kahoolawe, i., Hi., U.S. — C5 88
Kahramanmaraş, Tur. — D11 40
Kahuku, Hi., U.S. — B4 88
Kahuku Point, c., Hi., U.S. — B4 88
Kahului, Hi., U.S. — C5 88
Kahului Bay, b., Hi., U.S. — C5 88
Kaiama, Nig. — O14 51
Kaiapoi, N.Z. — O14 51
Kaibab Indian Reservation, Az., U.S. — A3 80
Kaibab Plateau, plat., Az., U.S. — A3 80
Kaibito, Az., U.S. — A4 80
Kaibito Plateau, plat., Az., U.S. — A4 80
Kaieteur Fall, wtfl., Guy. — A3 59
Kaifeng, China — J8 32
Kaihua, China — J8 32
Kai Islands, is., Indon. — G8 34
Kaikoura, N.Z. — O14 51
Kaikoura Peninsula, pen., N.Z. — E2 64
Kailas Range see Gangdise Mountains, China — B9 37
Kailu, China — C10 31
Kailua, Hi., U.S. — B4 88
Kailua, Hi., U.S. — g11 88
Kailua Bay, b., Hi., U.S. — g11 88

| Name | Map Ref. | Page |
|---|---|---|
| Kailua Kona, Hi., U.S. | D6 | 88 |
| Kai Malino, Hi., U.S. | D6 | 88 |
| Kaimana, Indon. | F8 | 34 |
| Kaimu, Hi., U.S. | D7 | 88 |
| Kainaliu, Hi., U.S. | D6 | 88 |
| Kainan, Japan | I7 | 33 |
| Kainji Dam, Nig. | E5 | 45 |
| Kainji Lake, res., Nig. | D5 | 45 |
| Kaipara Harbour, b., N.Z. | L15 | 51 |
| Kaiparowits Plateau, plat., Ut., U.S. | F4 | 121 |
| Kaipokok Bay, b., Newf. | g10 | 72 |
| Kaiserslautern, W. Ger. | D3 | 18 |
| Kaiserstuhl, Switz. | A5 | 21 |
| Kaišiadorys, Sov. Un. | A8 | 26 |
| Kaitaia, N.Z. | K14 | 51 |
| Kaitangata, N.Z. | Q12 | 51 |
| Kaithal, India | C6 | 37 |
| Kaiwi Channel, strt., Hi., U.S. | B4 | 88 |
| Kaixian, China | E6 | 31 |
| Kaiyuan, China | C11 | 32 |
| Kaizuka, Japan | o14 | 33 |
| Kajaani, Fin. | E12 | 14 |
| Kajakī, Band-e, res., Afg. | E12 | 39 |
| Kajiado, Kenya | B6 | 48 |
| Kajikazawa, Japan | n17 | 33 |
| Kākā, Sud. | C3 | 47 |
| Kakagi Lake, l., Ont. | E5 | 70 |
| Kakamas, S. Afr. | C3 | 49 |
| Kakamega, Kenya | A5 | 48 |
| Kaka Point, c., Hi., U.S. | C5 | 88 |
| Kake, Ak., U.S. | D13 | 79 |
| Kakegawa, Japan | o17 | 33 |
| Kakhovka, Sov. Un. | H9 | 27 |
| Kakhovka Reservoir, res., Sov. Un. | E6 | 29 |
| Kākināda (Cocanada), India | E7 | 36 |
| Kakisa Lake, l., N.W. Ter. | D9 | 66 |
| Kakogawa, Japan | *I7 | 33 |
| Kakuma, Kenya | A5 | 48 |
| Kakwa, stm., Can. | B1 | 68 |
| Kālābagh, Pak. | B5 | 36 |
| Kalabáka, Grc. | C3 | 25 |
| Kalabakan, Malay. | E5 | 34 |
| Kalābishah, Eg. | E6 | 43 |
| Kalabo, Zam. | D3 | 48 |
| Kalach, Sov. Un. | F13 | 27 |
| Kalach-na-Donu, Sov. Un. | G14 | 27 |
| Kaladar, Ont. | C7 | 73 |
| Ka Lae, c., Hi., U.S. | E6 | 88 |
| Kalahari Desert, des., Afr. | B3 | 49 |
| Kalahari Gemsbok National Park, S. Afr. | C3 | 49 |
| Kalaheo, Hi., U.S. | B2 | 88 |
| Kalaho, Pidos, hill, N. Mar. Is. | C8 | 52 |
| Kalai-Mor, Sov. Un. | D11 | 39 |
| Kalama, Wa., U.S. | C3 | 124 |
| Kalámai, Grc. | D4 | 40 |
| Kalamariá, Grc. | *B4 | 25 |
| Kalamazoo, Mi., U.S. | f5 | 99 |
| Kalamazoo, co., Mi., U.S. | F5 | 99 |
| Kalamazoo, stm., Mi., U.S. | F5 | 99 |
| Kalambo Falls, wtfl., Afr. | C5 | 48 |
| Kalandula, Ang. | C2 | 48 |
| Kalaoa Homesteads, Hi., U.S. | D6 | 88 |
| Kalaotoa, i., Indon. | G6 | 34 |
| Kalapana, Hi., U.S. | D7 | 88 |
| Kalasin, Thai. | D5 | 35 |
| Kalāt, Pak. | C4 | 36 |
| Kalaupapa, Hi., U.S. | C5 | 88 |
| Kalaupapa Peninsula, pen., Hi., U.S. | B5 | 88 |
| Kalávrita, Grc. | C4 | 25 |
| Kalawao, co., Hi., U.S. | B5 | 88 |
| Kalb, Ra's al, c., Yemen | D4 | 38 |
| Kalbā', U.A.E. | C5 | 38 |
| Kalecik, Tur. | B9 | 40 |
| Kaleden, B.C. | E8 | 69 |
| Kalegauk, i., Burma | E2 | 35 |
| Kalehe, Zaire | B4 | 48 |
| Kaleköy, Tur. | B5 | 25 |
| Kalemie (Albertville), Zaire | C4 | 48 |
| Kalena, Puu, mtn., Hi., U.S. | g9 | 88 |
| Kaleva, Mi., U.S. | D4 | 99 |
| Kalevala, Sov. Un. | E14 | 14 |
| Kalewa, Burma | D9 | 36 |
| Kalgalaksha, Sov. Un. | E16 | 14 |
| Kalgin Island, i., Ak., U.S. | g16 | 79 |
| Kalgoorlie, Austl. | F3 | 50 |
| Kalibo, Phil. | C6 | 34 |
| Kalihiwai, Hi., U.S. | A2 | 88 |
| Kalima, Zaire | B4 | 48 |
| Kálimnos, Grc. | D6 | 25 |
| Kálimnos, i., Grc. | D6 | 40 |
| Kalinin, Sov. Un. | D6 | 29 |
| Kaliningrad (Königsberg), Sov. Un. | n17 | 27 |
| Kalininsk, Sov. Un. | F15 | 27 |
| Kalinkovichi, Sov. Un. | E7 | 27 |
| Kalis, Som. | D6 | 47 |
| Kāli Sindh, stm., India | E6 | 37 |
| Kalispel Indian Reservation, Wa., U.S. | A8 | 124 |
| Kalispell, Mt., U.S. | B2 | 103 |
| Kalisz, Pol. | C5 | 26 |
| Kaliua, Tan. | C5 | 48 |
| Kalixälven, stm., Swe. | D10 | 14 |
| Kalkaska, Mi., U.S. | D5 | 99 |
| Kalkaska, co., Mi., U.S. | D5 | 99 |
| Kalkfeld, Nmb. | B2 | 49 |
| Kalkrand, Nmb. | B2 | 49 |
| Kallithéa, Grc. | h11 | 25 |
| Kallsjön, l., Swe. | F5 | 14 |
| Kalmalo, Nig. | D6 | 45 |
| Kalmar, Swe. | H11 | 14 |
| Kalmarsund, strt., Swe. | I7 | 14 |
| Kalmykovo, Sov. Un. | D4 | 28 |
| Kalo, Ia., U.S. | B3 | 92 |
| Kalocsa, Hung. | B4 | 24 |
| Kalohi Channel, strt., Hi., U.S. | C5 | 88 |
| Kaloli Point, c., Hi., U.S. | D7 | 88 |
| Kalomo, Zam. | E4 | 48 |
| Kalona, Ia., U.S. | C6 | 92 |
| Kalone Peak, mtn., B.C. | C4 | 69 |
| Kālpi, India | D7 | 37 |
| Kalskag, Ak., U.S. | C7 | 79 |
| Kaltag, Ak., U.S. | C8 | 79 |
| Kaluga, Sov. Un. | D6 | 29 |
| Kalulushi, Zam. | D4 | 48 |
| Kalundborg, Den. | C5 | 15 |
| Kalush, Sov. Un. | G5 | 27 |
| Kałuszyn, Pol. | B6 | 26 |
| Kalvarija, Sov. Un. | A7 | 26 |
| Kalvehave, Den. | D6 | 15 |
| Kalvesta, Ks., U.S. | D3 | 93 |
| Kalvsjön, l., Swe. | A7 | 15 |
| Kalyān, India | H4 | 37 |
| Kama, Zaire | B5 | 48 |
| Kama, stm., Sov. Un. | D8 | 29 |
| Kamaing, Burma | C10 | 36 |
| Kamaishi, Japan | D13 | 31 |
| Kamakou, mtn., Hi., U.S. | B5 | 88 |
| Kamakura, Japan | n18 | 33 |
| Kamakwie, S.L. | E2 | 45 |
| Kamananui Stream, stm., Hi., U.S. | f9 | 88 |
| Kamaniskeg Lake, l., Ont. | B7 | 73 |
| Kamanjab, Nmb. | A1 | 49 |
| Kamanyola, Zaire | B4 | 48 |
| Kamarān, i., Yemen | D4 | 38 |
| Kama Reservoir, res., Sov. Un. | D8 | 29 |
| Kāmārhāti, India | *D8 | 36 |
| Kamaria Fall, wtfl., Guy. | A3 | 59 |
| Kama Rock, i., Japan | P17 | 52 |
| Kamatsi Lake, l., Sask. | A4 | 75 |
| Kambalda, Austl. | F3 | 50 |
| Kambove, Zaire | D4 | 48 |
| Kamchatka Peninsula, pen., Sov. Un. | D18 | 29 |
| Kamenets-Podolskiy, Sov. Un. | G6 | 27 |
| Kamenjak, Cape, c., Yugo. | C1 | 24 |
| Kamenka, Sov. Un. | G7 | 27 |
| Kamenka, Sov. Un. | C2 | 28 |
| Kamen-na-Obi, Sov. Un. | D11 | 29 |
| Kamensk-Shakhtinskiy, Sov. Un. | G13 | 27 |
| Kamensk-Uralskiy, Sov. Un. | D9 | 29 |
| Kamenz, E. Ger. | C7 | 18 |
| Kameoka, Japan | o14 | 33 |
| Kamiah, Id., U.S. | C2 | 103 |
| Kamiak Butte, mtn., Wa., U.S. | C8 | 124 |
| Kamień Pomorski, Pol. | B3 | 26 |
| Kamina, Zaire | C4 | 48 |
| Kamioka, Japan | m16 | 33 |
| Kamloops, B.C. | D7 | 69 |
| Kammuri, Mount, mtn., Japan | I6 | 33 |
| Kamo, Sov. Un. | B15 | 40 |
| Kamoa Mountains, mts., Guy. | B3 | 59 |
| Kamooloa, Hi., U.S. | f9 | 88 |
| Kamouraska, Que. | B8 | 74 |
| Kamouraska, co., Que. | B8 | 74 |
| Kampala, Ug. | A5 | 48 |
| Kampar, Malay. | J4 | 35 |
| Kampar, stm., Indon. | E2 | 34 |
| Kampen, Neth. | A6 | 16 |
| Kampeska, Lake, l., S.D., U.S. | C8 | 118 |
| Kamphaeng Phet, Thai. | D3 | 35 |
| Kampong Cham, Camb. | C3 | 34 |
| Kampong Chhnang, Camb. | C2 | 34 |
| Kampong Khleang, Camb. | F6 | 35 |
| Kampong Saom, Camb. | C2 | 34 |
| Kampong Saom Bay, b., Camb. | C2 | 34 |
| Kampong Spoe, Camb. | G6 | 35 |
| Kampong Thum, Camb. | C2 | 34 |
| Kampot, Camb. | C2 | 34 |
| Kampsville, Il., U.S. | D3 | 90 |
| Kampuchea see Cambodia, ctry., Asia | F6 | 34 |
| Kamrar, Ia., U.S. | B4 | 92 |
| Kamsack, Sask. | F5 | 75 |
| Kamuchawie Lake, l., Can. | A4 | 75 |
| Kamuela (Waimea), Hi., U.S. | C6 | 88 |
| Kamuli, Ug. | A5 | 48 |
| Kamyshevakha, Sov. Un. | q21 | 27 |
| Kamyshin, Sov. Un. | F15 | 27 |
| Kamyshlov, Sov. Un. | B6 | 28 |
| Kanab, Ut., U.S. | F3 | 121 |
| Kanab Creek, stm., U.S. | A3 | 80 |
| Kanabec, co., Mn., U.S. | E5 | 100 |
| Kanacea, i., Fiji | H16 | 52 |
| Kanaga Island, i., Ak., U.S. | E4 | 79 |
| Kanairiktok, stm., Newf. | g9 | 72 |
| Kananaskis, stm., Alta. | D3 | 68 |
| Kananga (Luluabourg), Zaire | C3 | 48 |
| Kanapou Bay, b., Hi., U.S. | C5 | 88 |
| Kanarraville, Ut., U.S. | F2 | 121 |
| Kanash, Sov. Un. | D16 | 27 |
| Kanata, Ont. | B9 | 73 |
| Kanauga, Oh., U.S. | D3 | 112 |
| Kanawha, Ia., U.S. | B4 | 92 |
| Kanawha, co., W.V., U.S. | C3 | 125 |
| Kanawha, stm., W.V., U.S. | C3 | 125 |
| Kanayama, Japan | m16 | 33 |
| Kanazawa, Japan | D12 | 31 |
| Kanbe, Burma | *E10 | 36 |
| Kanchanaburi, Thai. | E3 | 35 |
| Kanchenjunga, mtn., Asia | C6 | 36 |
| Kānchipuram (Conjeeveram), India | F7 | 36 |
| Kānchrāpāra, India | *D8 | 36 |
| Kandahar (Qandahār), Afg. | B4 | 36 |
| Kandahar, Sask. | F3 | 75 |
| Kandalaksha, Sov. Un. | C6 | 29 |
| Kandalaksha Bay, b., Sov. Un. | B15 | 8 |
| Kandangan, Indon. | F5 | 34 |
| Kandel, W. Ger. | D3 | 19 |
| Kandern, W. Ger. | A4 | 21 |
| Kandersteg, Switz. | C3 | 20 |
| Kandi, Benin | D5 | 45 |
| Kandira, Tur. | B8 | 40 |
| Kandiyohi, Mn., U.S. | E4 | 100 |
| Kandiyohi, co., Mn., U.S. | E3 | 100 |
| Kandla, India | F3 | 37 |
| Kandrāch, Pak. | C4 | 36 |
| Kandreho, Madag. | g9 | 49 |
| Kandy, Sri L. | G7 | 36 |
| Kane, Il., U.S. | D3 | 90 |
| Kane, Pa., U.S. | C4 | 115 |
| Kane, co., Il., U.S. | B5 | 90 |
| Kane, co., Ut., U.S. | F3 | 121 |
| Kane Basin, strt., N.A. | m38 | 66 |
| Kaneohe, Hi., U.S. | B4 | 88 |
| Kaneohe, Hi., U.S. | g10 | 88 |
| Kaneohe Bay Marine Corps Air Station, mil., Hi., U.S. | g10 | 88 |
| Kanevskaya, Sov. Un. | H12 | 27 |
| Kang, Bots. | B3 | 49 |
| Kangaba, Mali | D3 | 45 |
| Kangal, Tur. | C11 | 40 |
| Kangar, Malay. | I4 | 35 |
| Kangaroo, i., Austl. | G6 | 50 |
| Kangbao, China | C7 | 31 |
| Kangding, China | E5 | 31 |
| Kangean Islands, is., Indon. | G5 | 34 |
| Kanggye, N. Kor. | C10 | 31 |
| Kangiqsualujjuaq, Que. | f8 | 72 |
| Kangiqsujuaq, Que. | f12 | 74 |
| Kangley, Il., U.S. | B5 | 90 |
| Kangnŭng, S. Kor. | D10 | 31 |
| Kango, Gabon | E2 | 46 |
| Kangrinboqê Mountain, mtn., China | B8 | 37 |
| Kani, Burma | A1 | 37 |
| Kani, I.C. | E3 | 45 |
| Kaniama, Zaire | C3 | 48 |
| Kanimekh, Sov. Un. | A12 | 39 |
| Kanin Nos, Cape, c., Sov. Un. | C7 | 29 |
| Kaniža, Yugo. | A5 | 24 |
| Kankakee, Il., U.S. | B6 | 90 |
| Kankakee, co., Il., U.S. | B6 | 90 |
| Kankakee, stm., U.S. | B5 | 90 |
| Kankan, Gui. | D3 | 45 |
| Känker, India | D7 | 36 |
| Kankossa, Maur. | C2 | 45 |
| Kannapolis, N.C., U.S. | B2 | 110 |
| Kannauj, India | D7 | 37 |
| Kano, Nig. | D6 | 45 |
| Kanopolis, Ks., U.S. | D5 | 93 |
| Kanopolis Lake, res., Ks., U.S. | D5 | 93 |
| Kanorado, Ks., U.S. | C1 | 93 |
| Kanosh, Ut., U.S. | E3 | 121 |
| Kanoya, Japan | K5 | 33 |
| Kānpur, India | C7 | 36 |
| Kansas, Al., U.S. | B2 | 78 |
| Kansas, Il., U.S. | D6 | 90 |
| Kansas, Oh., U.S. | A2 | 112 |
| Kansas, Ok., U.S. | A7 | 113 |
| Kansas, state, U.S. | D5 | 93 |
| Kansas, stm., Ks., U.S. | C7 | 93 |
| Kansas City, Ks., U.S. | C9 | 93 |
| Kansas City, Mo., U.S. | B3 | 102 |
| Kansasville, Wi., U.S. | n11 | 126 |
| Kansk, Sov. Un. | D12 | 29 |
| Kansu see Gansu, prov., China | D5 | 31 |
| Kantang, Thai. | D1 | 34 |
| Kanton Island, i., Kir. | G11 | 6 |
| Kantunilkin, Mex. | C7 | 63 |
| Kanturk, Ire. | I4 | 12 |
| Kanuku Mountains, mts., Guy. | B3 | 59 |
| Kanuma, Japan | H9 | 33 |
| Kanye, Bots. | B4 | 49 |
| Kaohsiung, Tai. | G9 | 31 |
| Kaoko Veld, plat., Nmb. | A1 | 49 |
| Kaolack, Sen. | D1 | 45 |
| Kaoma, Zam. | D3 | 48 |
| Kaouar, reg., Niger | C7 | 45 |
| Kapaa, Hi., U.S. | A2 | 88 |
| Kapaau, Hi., U.S. | C6 | 88 |
| Kapal, Sov. Un. | F24 | 8 |
| Kapandrítion, Grc. | g11 | 25 |
| Kapanga, Zaire | C3 | 48 |
| Kapapa Island, i., Hi., U.S. | g10 | 88 |
| Kaparéllion, Grc. | g10 | 25 |
| Kapchagay, Sov. Un. | E9 | 28 |
| Kapchagay Reservoir, res., Sov. Un. | E9 | 28 |
| Kapenguria, Kenya | A6 | 48 |
| Kapfenberg, Aus. | E7 | 18 |
| Kapiri Mposhi, Zam. | D4 | 48 |
| Kapit, Malay. | E4 | 34 |
| Kaplan, La., U.S. | D3 | 95 |
| Kaplice, Czech. | E9 | 19 |
| Kapoeta, Sud. | E3 | 47 |
| Kaposvár Creek, stm., Sask. | G4 | 75 |
| Kapowsin, Wa., U.S. | C3 | 124 |
| Kappa, Il., U.S. | C4 | 90 |
| Kapuas, stm., Indon. | E4 | 34 |
| Kapulena, Hi., U.S. | C6 | 88 |
| Kapuskasing, Ont. | o19 | 73 |
| Kapustin Yar, Sov. Un. | D3 | 28 |
| Kaputar, mtn., Austl. | E8 | 51 |
| Kapuvár, Hung. | B3 | 24 |
| Kara, Sov. Un. | C9 | 29 |
| Karabash, Sov. Un. | D21 | 8 |
| Kara-Bogaz-Gol, Sov. Un. | E4 | 28 |
| Kara-Bogaz-Gol Gulf, b., Sov. Un. | E4 | 28 |
| Karabük, Tur. | *B9 | 40 |
| Karachev, Sov. Un. | E10 | 27 |
| Karāchi, Pak. | D4 | 36 |
| Karāchi Cantonment, Pak. | *D4 | 36 |
| Karaga, Sov. Un. | D19 | 29 |
| Karaganda, Sov. Un. | E10 | 29 |
| Karagin Island, i., Sov. Un. | D19 | 29 |
| Karaisalı, Tur. | D10 | 40 |
| Karaj, Iran | D5 | 39 |
| Karakas, Sov. Un. | D10 | 29 |
| Karakelong, i., Indon. | E7 | 34 |
| Karakoram Pass, Asia | A6 | 36 |
| Karakoram Range, mts., Asia | A6 | 36 |
| Karaköse see Ağrı, Tur. | C14 | 40 |
| Kara-Kum, des., Sov. Un. | B5 | 38 |
| Kara-Kum Canal, Sov. Un. | H21 | 8 |
| Karaman, Tur. | D9 | 40 |
| Karamay, China | B1 | 31 |
| Karambu, Indon. | F5 | 34 |
| Karamea Bight, N.Z. | N13 | 51 |
| Karamürsel, Tur. | B7 | 40 |
| Karapınar, Tur. | D9 | 40 |
| Karasburg, Nmb. | C2 | 49 |
| Kara Sea, Sov. Un. | B9 | 29 |
| Karasu, Tur. | B8 | 40 |
| Karasu, stm., Sov. Un. | C9 | 28 |
| Karasuk, Sov. Un. | D9 | 29 |
| Karatal, stm., Sov. Un. | D10 | 29 |
| Karatau, China | E7 | 28 |
| Karatau Range, mts., Sov. Un. | E7 | 28 |
| Karatobe, Sov. Un. | D5 | 28 |
| Karatsu, Japan | J4 | 33 |
| Karauli, India | D6 | 37 |
| Karaulkeldy, Sov. Un. | D5 | 28 |
| Karawanken, mts., Eur. | E7 | 18 |
| Karbalā', Iraq | B3 | 38 |
| Karcag, Hung. | B4 | 24 |
| Karczew, Pol. | m14 | 26 |
| Kardhítsa, Grc. | C3 | 40 |
| Karema, Tan. | C5 | 48 |
| Karesuando (part of Kiruna), Swe. | C10 | 14 |
| Kargasok, Sov. Un. | D11 | 29 |
| Kargat, Sov. Un. | D25 | 8 |
| Kargil, India | B6 | 36 |
| Kargopol, Sov. Un. | C6 | 29 |
| Kariai, Grc. | B5 | 25 |
| Kariba, Zimb. | A4 | 49 |
| Kariba, Lake, res., Afr. | A4 | 49 |
| Karibib, Nmb. | B2 | 49 |
| Karimata Islands, is., Indon. | E3 | 34 |
| Karimata Strait, strt., Indon. | F3 | 34 |
| Karimganj, India | H7 | 37 |
| Karimunjawa Islands, is., Indon. | F4 | 34 |
| Karin, Som. | C6 | 47 |
| Karisimbi, Volcán, vol., Afr. | C5 | 48 |
| Káristos, Grc. | C5 | 25 |
| Karkaralinsk, Sov. Un. | E10 | 29 |
| Karkar Island, i., Pap. N. Gui. | m15 | 50a |
| Karkinit Gulf, b., Sov. Un. | I9 | 27 |
| Karl-Marx-Stadt (Chemnitz), E. Ger. | C6 | 18 |
| Karloske, stm., Man. | B4 | 70 |
| Karlovac, Yugo. | A10 | 24 |
| Karlovo, Bul. | D7 | 24 |
| Karlovy Vary, Czech. | C6 | 18 |
| Karlshamn, Swe. | I6 | 14 |
| Karlskoga, Swe. | H6 | 14 |
| Karlskrona, Swe. | I6 | 14 |
| Karlsruhe, W. Ger. | D4 | 18 |
| Karlsruhe, N.D., U.S. | A5 | 111 |
| Karlstad, Swe. | H5 | 14 |
| Karlstad, Mn., U.S. | B2 | 100 |
| Karlstadt, W. Ger. | D4 | 19 |
| Karluk, Ak., U.S. | D9 | 79 |
| Karnak, Il., U.S. | F5 | 90 |
| Karnāl, India | *C6 | 36 |
| Karnālī, stm., Nepal | C8 | 37 |
| Karnataka, state, India | F6 | 36 |
| Karnes, co., Tx., U.S. | E4 | 120 |
| Karnes City, Tx., U.S. | E4 | 120 |
| Karnobat, Bul. | D8 | 24 |
| Karns, Tn., U.S. | n13 | 119 |
| Karns City, Pa., U.S. | E2 | 115 |
| Kärnten, state, Aus. | C9 | 20 |
| Karoi, Zimb. | A4 | 49 |
| Karonga, Mwi. | C5 | 48 |
| Karora, Sud. | B4 | 47 |
| Karow, E. Ger. | B6 | 18 |
| Kárpathos, i., Grc. | E6 | 40 |
| Karpenísion, Grc. | C3 | 25 |
| Karratha, Austl. | D2 | 50 |
| Kars, Tur. | B14 | 40 |
| Karsakpay, Sov. Un. | E9 | 29 |
| Karsha, Sov. Un. | D4 | 28 |
| Karshi, Sov. Un. | F9 | 29 |
| Karstädt, E. Ger. | B6 | 18 |
| Kartal, Tur. | B6 | 25 |
| Kartaly, Sov. Un. | D9 | 29 |
| Karthaus, Pa., U.S. | D5 | 115 |
| Kartuzy, Pol. | A5 | 26 |
| Kārūn, stm., Iran | F4 | 39 |
| Karup, Den. | B3 | 15 |
| Karup Å, stm., Den. | B3 | 15 |
| Karval, Co., U.S. | C7 | 83 |
| Karvia, Fin. | F10 | 14 |
| Karviná, Czech. | D5 | 26 |
| Kārwār, India | F5 | 36 |
| Kås, Den. | A3 | 15 |
| Kas, Sud. | C1 | 47 |
| Kaş, Tur. | D7 | 40 |
| Kasaan, Ak., U.S. | n23 | 79 |
| Kasai (Cassai), stm., Afr. | B2 | 48 |
| Kasaji, Zaire | D3 | 48 |
| Kasama, Zam. | D5 | 48 |
| Kasane, Bots. | A4 | 49 |
| Kasanga, Tan. | C5 | 48 |
| Kāsaragod, India | F3 | 36 |
| Kasba, India | E11 | 37 |
| Kasba Lake, l., N.W. Ter. | D12 | 66 |
| Kasba Tadla, Mor. | C3 | 44 |
| Kasempa, Zam. | D4 | 48 |
| Kasenga, Zaire | D4 | 48 |
| Kasese, Ug. | A5 | 48 |
| Kāshān, Iran | B5 | 38 |
| Kashi, China | F10 | 29 |
| Kashihara, Japan | o14 | 33 |
| Kashima, Japan | n19 | 33 |
| Kashira, Sov. Un. | D12 | 27 |
| Kashiwa, stm., Japan | n18 | 33 |
| Kashiwazaki, Japan | H9 | 33 |
| Kāshmar (Turshīz), Iran | C2 | 37 |
| Kashmor, Pak. | C2 | 37 |
| Kasilof, Ak., U.S. | C9 | 79 |
| Kasimov, Sov. Un. | D13 | 27 |
| Kaskaskia, Il., U.S. | D5 | 90 |
| Kaskaskia, stm., Il., U.S. | D5 | 90 |
| Kaskö, Fin. | F9 | 14 |
| Kaslo, B.C. | E9 | 69 |
| Kasongo, Zaire | B4 | 48 |
| Kasongo-Lunda, Zaire | C2 | 48 |
| Kásos, i., Grc. | E6 | 40 |
| Kasota, Mn., U.S. | F5 | 100 |
| Kassalā, Sud. | B4 | 47 |
| Kassalā, prov., Sud. | B4 | 47 |
| Kassel (Cassel), W. Ger. | C4 | 18 |
| Kasson, Mn., U.S. | F6 | 100 |
| Kastamonu, Tur. | B9 | 40 |
| Kastoría, Grc. | C3 | 40 |
| Kástron, Grc. | g10 | 25 |
| Kasukabe, Japan | n18 | 33 |
| Kasulu, Tan. | B5 | 48 |
| Kasumi, Japan | I7 | 33 |
| Kasumiga-ura, l., Japan | H10 | 33 |
| Kasungu, Mwi. | D5 | 48 |
| Katako-Kombe, Zaire | B3 | 48 |
| Katanga, hist. reg., Zaire | C3 | 48 |
| Katanning, Austl. | F2 | 50 |
| Katano, Japan | P17 | 52 |
| Katata, Japan | n14 | 33 |
| Katepwa Beach, Sask. | G3 | 75 |
| Kateríni, Grc. | B4 | 40 |
| Kates Needle, mtn., Ak., U.S. | m24 | 79 |
| Katha, Burma | D10 | 36 |
| Katherine, Austl. | B5 | 50 |
| Kāthiāwār Peninsula, pen., India | I4 | 37 |
| Kathleen, Fl., U.S. | D4 | 86 |
| Kathmandu (Kāthmāndāū), Nepal | C8 | 36 |
| Kathryn, Alta. | D4 | 68 |
| Kathryn, N.D., U.S. | C8 | 111 |
| Kathua, India | A5 | 37 |
| Katie, Ok., U.S. | C4 | 113 |
| Katihar, India | E11 | 37 |
| Katikati, N.Z. | B5 | 51 |
| Katire, Sud. | E3 | 47 |
| Katlehong, S. Afr. | *C4 | 49 |
| Katmai, Mount, mtn., Ak., U.S. | D9 | 79 |
| Katmai National Park, Ak., U.S. | D9 | 79 |
| Kato Alepokhórion, Grc. | g10 | 25 |
| Katokhí, Grc. | C3 | 25 |
| Katombe, Zaire | B3 | 48 |
| Katoomba, Austl. | F9 | 50 |
| Katowice (Stalinogród), Pol. | C5 | 26 |
| Kätrine, Jabal, mtn., Eg. | D4 | 43 |
| Katrine, Loch, l., Scot., U.K. | D4 | 43 |
| Katrineholm, Swe. | H7 | 14 |
| Katsina, Nig. | C6 | 45 |
| Katsina Ala, stm., Afr. | H7 | 45 |
| Katsuta, Japan | *H10 | 33 |
| Katsuyama, Japan | m15 | 33 |
| Kattakurgan, Sov. Un. | H22 | 8 |
| Kattegat, strt., Eur. | E26 | 8 |
| Katun, stm., Sov. Un. | E26 | 8 |
| Katwijk aan Zee, Neth. | A4 | 16 |
| Katy, Tx., U.S. | r14 | 120 |
| Kau, Indon. | E7 | 34 |
| Kauai, co., Hi., U.S. | B1 | 88 |
| Kauai, i., Hi., U.S. | A2 | 88 |
| Kauai Channel, strt., Hi., U.S. | A2 | 88 |
| Kau Desert, des., Hi., U.S. | D6 | 88 |
| Kaufbeuren, W. Ger. | E5 | 18 |
| Kaufman, Tx., U.S. | C4 | 120 |
| Kaufman, co., Tx., U.S. | C4 | 120 |
| Kauhajoki, Fin. | F10 | 14 |
| Kauhava, Fin. | F10 | 14 |
| Kauiki Head, c., Hi., U.S. | C6 | 88 |
| Kaukauna, Wi., U.S. | D5 | 126 |
| Kaukau Veld, plat., Afr. | B3 | 49 |
| Kaula Island, i., Hi., U.S. | m15 | 88 |
| Kaulakahi Channel, strt., Hi., U.S. | A2 | 88 |
| Kauliranta, Fin. | D10 | 14 |
| Kaumakani, Hi., U.S. | B2 | 88 |
| Kaumalapau, Hi., U.S. | C5 | 88 |
| Kaunakakai, Hi., U.S. | B5 | 88 |
| Kauna Point, c., Hi., U.S. | D6 | 88 |
| Kaunas, Sov. Un. | D5 | 29 |
| Kaura Namoda, Nig. | D6 | 45 |
| Kautokeino, Nor. | C10 | 14 |
| Kavacha, Sov. Un. | C19 | 29 |
| Kavaja, Alb. | B2 | 25 |
| Kavála, Grc. | B5 | 40 |
| Kavála, Gulf of, b., Grc. | B5 | 40 |
| Kāvali, India | F6 | 36 |
| Kavarna, Bul. | D9 | 24 |
| Kavieng, Pap. N. Gui. | h13 | 50 |
| Kävlinge, Swe. | C7 | 15 |
| Kaw, Fr. Gu. | B4 | 59 |
| Kawagama Lake, l., Ont. | B6 | 73 |
| Kawagoe, Japan | n18 | 33 |
| Kawaguchi, Japan | n18 | 33 |
| Kawaihae, Hi., U.S. | C6 | 88 |
| Kawaihoa Point, c., Hi., U.S. | B1 | 88 |
| Kawaikini, mtn., Hi., U.S. | A2 | 88 |
| Kawailoa, Hi., U.S. | f9 | 88 |
| Kawailoa Beach, Hi., U.S. | f9 | 88 |
| Kawakawa, N.Z. | K15 | 51 |
| Kawambwa, Zam. | C4 | 48 |
| Kawardha, India | F8 | 37 |
| Kawasaki, Japan | D12 | 31 |
| Kawbar, Isr. Occ. | h11 | 41 |
| Kaweah Lake, l., Ca., U.S. | A5 | 113 |
| Kawela, Hi., U.S. | f9 | 88 |
| Kawhia Harbour, b., N.Z. | M15 | 51 |
| Kawich Peak, mtn., Nv., U.S. | F5 | 105 |
| Kawich Range, mts., Nv., U.S. | F5 | 105 |
| Kawkareik, Burma | B3 | 35 |
| Kaw Lake, res., Ok., U.S. | A5 | 113 |
| Kawm Imbū, Eg. | D2 | 41 |
| Kawm Ūmbū, Eg. | C3 | 38 |
| Kawthaung, Burma | F10 | 36 |
| Kay, co., Ok., U.S. | A4 | 113 |
| Kaya, Burkina | D5 | 45 |
| Kayan, stm., Indon. | E5 | 34 |
| Kayangel Islands, is., Palau | R17 | 52 |
| Kaycee, Wy., U.S. | C6 | 127 |
| Kayenta, Az., U.S. | A5 | 80 |
| Kayes, Congo | B1 | 48 |
| Kayes, Mali | D2 | 45 |
| Kayford, W.V., U.S. | C3 | 125 |
| Kayjay, Ky., U.S. | D6 | 94 |
| Kaylor, S.D., U.S. | D8 | 118 |
| Kayō, Japan | N6 | 52 |
| Kayser Gebergte, mts., Sur. | B3 | 59 |
| Kayseri, Tur. | C10 | 40 |
| Kaysville, Ut., U.S. | B4 | 121 |
| Kayuagung, Indon. | F2 | 34 |
| Kayville, Sask. | H3 | 75 |
| Kazachye, Sov. Un. | B16 | 29 |
| Kazakevichevo, Sov. Un. | B7 | 33 |
| Kazakh Hills, hills, Sov. Un. | D7 | 28 |
| Kazakh S.S.R., state, Sov. Un. | E9 | 29 |
| Kazalinsk, Sov. Un. | D6 | 28 |
| Kazan, Sov. Un. | D7 | 29 |
| Kazan, stm., N.W. Ter. | D12 | 66 |
| Kazanlŭk, Bul. | D7 | 24 |
| Kazbek, mtn., Sov. Un. | A4 | 38 |
| Kazhim, Sov. Un. | A4 | 28 |
| Kazi-Magomed, Sov. Un. | A8 | 38 |
| Kazimierz [Dolny], Pol. | C7 | 26 |
| Kazincbarcika, Hung. | A4 | 24 |
| Kazym, stm., Sov. Un. | C22 | 8 |
| Kdyně, Czech. | D8 | 19 |
| Kéa, i., Grc. | D8 | 25 |
| Kéa, i., Grc. | g10 | 25 |
| Keaau, Hi., U.S. | D6 | 88 |
| Keady, N. Ir., U.K. | G6 | 11 |
| Keahiakahoe, Puu, mtn., Hi., U.S. | g10 | 88 |
| Keahole Point, c., Hi., U.S. | D5 | 88 |
| Kealaikahiki Channel, strt., Hi., U.S. | C5 | 88 |
| Kealaikahiki Point, c., Hi., U.S. | C5 | 88 |
| Kealakekua, Hi., U.S. | D6 | 88 |
| Kealia, Hi., U.S. | A2 | 88 |
| Keams Canyon, Az., U.S. | B5 | 80 |
| Keanae, Hi., U.S. | C5 | 88 |
| Keanapapa Point, c., Hi., U.S. | C4 | 88 |
| Kearney, Mo., U.S. | B3 | 102 |
| Kearney, Ne., U.S. | D7 | 104 |
| Kearney, Ont. | B5 | 73 |
| Kearney, co., Ne., U.S. | D7 | 104 |
| Kearneysville, W.V., U.S. | B7 | 125 |
| Kearns, Ut., U.S. | C4 | 121 |
| Kearny, Az., U.S. | D5 | 80 |
| Kearny, N.J., U.S. | h8 | 107 |
| Kearny, co., Ks., U.S. | E3 | 93 |
| Kearsarge, N.H., U.S. | B4 | 106 |
| Kearsarge, Mount, mtn., N.H., U.S. | D3 | 106 |
| Kearsarge North, mtn., N.H., U.S. | B4 | 106 |
| Keatchie, La., U.S. | B2 | 95 |
| Keating, Or., U.S. | C9 | 114 |
| Keaton, Ky., U.S. | C7 | 94 |
| Keauhou, Hi., U.S. | D6 | 88 |
| Keats, Ks., U.S. | C7 | 93 |
| Keban Reservoir, res., Tur. | C12 | 40 |
| Kebbi, Nig. | C6 | 45 |
| Kébémer, Sen. | C1 | 45 |
| Kebnekaise, mtn., Swe. | C10 | 14 |
| Kebock Head, c., Scot., U.K. | B2 | 11 |
| Kebri Dehar, Eth. | C8 | 47 |
| Kecskemét, Hung. | B4 | 24 |
| Kédainiai, Sov. Un. | A8 | 26 |
| Keddie, Ca., U.S. | B3 | 82 |
| Kedges Straits, strt., Md., U.S. | D5 | 97 |
| Kedgwick, N.B. | B2 | 71 |
| Kedgwick, Can. | B2 | 71 |
| Kedleston, Sask. | G3 | 75 |
| Kedong, China | D12 | 29 |
| Kédougou, Sen. | D2 | 45 |
| Kedzierzyn-Koźle, Pol. | *C5 | 26 |
| Keedysville, Md., U.S. | B2 | 97 |
| Keefers, B.C. | D7 | 69 |
| Keefton, Ok., U.S. | B6 | 113 |
| Keego Harbor, Mi., U.S. | o15 | 99 |
| Keei, Hi., U.S. | D6 | 88 |
| Keele Peak, mtn., Yukon | D6 | 66 |
| Keeler, Sask. | G3 | 75 |
| Keeler, Ca., U.S. | D5 | 82 |
| Keeline, Wy., U.S. | D8 | 127 |
| Keeling, Tn., U.S. | B2 | 119 |
| Keeling, Va., U.S. | D3 | 123 |
| Keels, Newf. | D5 | 72 |
| Keelung see Chilung, Tai. | F9 | 31 |
| Keene, Ont. | C6 | 73 |
| Keene, Ca., U.S. | E4 | 82 |
| Keene, Ky., U.S. | C5 | 94 |
| Keene, N.H., U.S. | E2 | 106 |
| Keene, N.Y., U.S. | A7 | 109 |
| Keene, N.D., U.S. | B3 | 111 |
| Keene, Oh., U.S. | B4 | 112 |
| Keenes, Il., U.S. | E5 | 90 |
| Keene Valley, N.Y., U.S. | f11 | 109 |
| Keeney Knob, mtn., W.V., U.S. | D4 | 125 |
| Keensburg, Il., U.S. | E6 | 90 |
| Keeseville, N.Y., U.S. | f11 | 109 |
| Keesler Air Force Base, mil., Ms., U.S. | E5 | 101 |
| Keetmanshoop, Nmb. | C2 | 49 |
| Keet Seel Ruin, hist., Az., U.S. | A5 | 80 |
| Keewatin, Mn., U.S. | C5 | 100 |
| Keewatin, dept., N.W. Ter. | D13 | 66 |
| Keewatin, stm., Man. | A1 | 70 |
| Keezletown, Va., U.S. | B4 | 123 |
| Kefa, prov., Eth. | D4 | 47 |
| Kefallinía (Cephalonia), i., Grc. | C3 | 40 |
| Kefar Blum, Isr. | A7 | 41 |
| Kefar 'Eqron, Isr. | h10 | 41 |
| Kefar Monash, Isr. | f10 | 41 |
| Kefar Sava, Isr. | B6 | 41 |
| Kefar Yona, Isr. | f10 | 41 |
| Keffi, Nig. | *E6 | 45 |
| Keflavík, Ice. | o21 | 14 |
| Ke Ga, Cape, c., Viet. | F8 | 35 |
| Kegaska, Que. | h9 | 72 |
| Kegonsa, Lake, l., Wi., U.S. | F4 | 126 |
| Kehl, W. Ger. | E2 | 19 |
| Keho Lake, l., Alta. | E4 | 68 |
| Kehsi Mansam, Burma | B3 | 35 |
| Keighley, Eng., U.K. | H11 | 10 |
| Keilor, Austl. | *G7 | 50 |
| Keimoes, S. Afr. | C3 | 49 |
| Keiser, Ar., U.S. | B5 | 81 |
| Keitele, l., Fin. | F11 | 14 |
| Keith, Austl. | H3 | 51 |
| Keith, Scot., U.K. | B5 | 10 |
| Keith, co., Ne., U.S. | C4 | 104 |
| Keithley Creek, B.C. | C7 | 69 |
| Keithsburg, Il., U.S. | B3 | 90 |
| Keithville, La., U.S. | B2 | 95 |
| Keitum, W. Ger. | D2 | 15 |
| Kejimkujik Lake, l., N.S. | E4 | 71 |
| Kejimkujik National Park, N.S. | E4 | 71 |
| Kekaha, Hi., U.S. | B2 | 88 |
| Kékes, mtn., Hung. | *B5 | 24 |
| Kelafo, Eth. | D5 | 47 |
| Kelang, China | E3 | 34 |
| Kelang, Malay. | E2 | 34 |
| Kelantan, state, Malay. | J4 | 35 |
| Kelantan, stm., Malay. | J5 | 35 |
| Keldron, S.D., U.S. | B4 | 118 |
| Kelfield, Sask. | F1 | 75 |
| Kelford, N.C., U.S. | A5 | 110 |
| Kelheim, W. Ger. | E6 | 19 |
| Kelibia, Tun. | F3 | 23 |
| Kelkit, stm., Tur. | B11 | 40 |
| Kell, Il., U.S. | E5 | 90 |
| Kellé, Congo | B2 | 48 |
| Kellerhusen, W. Ger. | D5 | 15 |
| Keller, Tx., U.S. | n9 | 120 |
| Keller, Va., U.S. | C7 | 123 |
| Kellerman, Al., U.S. | B2 | 78 |
| Kellerton, Ia., U.S. | D3 | 92 |
| Kellett, Cape, c., N.W. Ter. | B7 | 66 |
| Kellettville, Pa., U.S. | C3 | 115 |
| Kelleys Island, Oh., U.S. | A3 | 112 |
| Kelleys Island, i., Oh., U.S. | A3 | 112 |
| Kelliher, Sask. | F4 | 75 |
| Kelliher, Mn., U.S. | C4 | 100 |
| Kellmünz, W. Ger. | A6 | 20 |
| Kellnersville, Wi., U.S. | D6 | 126 |
| Kelloe, Man. | D1 | 70 |
| Kellogg, Id., U.S. | B3 | 103 |
| Kellogg, Ia., U.S. | C5 | 92 |
| Kellogg, Mn., U.S. | F7 | 100 |
| Kelloselkä, Fin. | C13 | 14 |
| Kells see Ceanannus Mór, Ire. | H6 | 12 |
| Kelly, Ky., U.S. | D2 | 94 |
| Kelly, La., U.S. | C3 | 95 |
| Kelly Air Force Base, mil., Tx., U.S. | k7 | 120 |
| Kelly Brook Mountain, mtn., Me., U.S. | A3 | 96 |
| Kelly Island, i., De., U.S. | D4 | 85 |
| Kelly Lake, B.C. | D7 | 69 |
| Kelly Lake, Mn., U.S. | C5 | 100 |
| Kellyton, Al., U.S. | B3 | 78 |
| Kellyville, Tx., U.S. | C5 | 120 |
| Kélo, Chad | F3 | 46 |
| Kelowna, B.C. | E8 | 69 |
| Kelsey, Alta. | C4 | 68 |
| Kelsey, Man. | C1 | 70 |
| Kelseyville, Ca., U.S. | C2 | 82 |
| Kelso, Sask. | H5 | 75 |
| Kelso, Scot., U.K. | C6 | 10 |
| Kelso, Wa., U.S. | C3 | 124 |
| Keltie, Mount, mtn., Ant. | f40 | 7 |
| Keltonburg, Tn., U.S. | B2 | 119 |
| Keluang, Malay. | E2 | 34 |
| Kelvington, Sask. | F4 | 75 |
| Kelwood, Man. | D2 | 70 |
| Kê Macina, Mali | D4 | 45 |
| Kemano, B.C. | C3 | 69 |
| Kembé, Cen. Afr. Rep. | G9 | 47 |
| Kemerovo, Sov. Un. | D11 | 29 |
| Kemi, Fin. | D11 | 14 |
| Kemijärvi, Fin. | C12 | 14 |
| Kemijoki, stm., Fin. | D11 | 14 |
| Kemmer, well, Libya | | |
| Kemmerer, Wy., U.S. | E2 | 127 |
| Kemnath, W. Ger. | D6 | 19 |
| Kemnay, Man. | D1 | 70 |
| Kemp, Tx., U.S. | C4 | 120 |
| Kemp, Lake, res., Tx., U.S. | C3 | 120 |

| Name | Map Ref. | Page |
|---|---|---|

Kemp Coast, Ant. — C18 7
Kempen, W. Ger. — C6 17
Kemper, S.C., U.S. — C9 117
Kemper, co., Ms., U.S. — C5 101
Kempner, Tx., U.S. — D4 120
Kemp Peninsula, pen., Ant. — B6 7
Kempsey, Austl. — F9 50
Kempshall Mountain, mtn., N.Y., U.S. — A6 109
Kempten [in Allgäu], W. Ger. — E5 18
Kempton, Il., U.S. — C5 90
Kempton, In., U.S. — D5 91
Kempton, N.D., U.S. — B8 111
Kemptville, Ont. — B9 73
Kenai, Ak., U.S. — C9 79
Kenai Fjords National Park, Ak., U.S. — D10 79
Kenai Mountains, mts., Ak., U.S. — h16 79
Kenai Peninsula, pen., Ak., U.S. — h16 79
Kenamu, stm., Newf. — B1 72
Kenansville, Fl., U.S. — E6 86
Kenansville, N.C., U.S. — C5 110
Kenaston, Sask. — F2 75
Kenbridge, Va., U.S. — D4 123
Ken Caryl, Co., U.S. — *B5 83
Kendal, Sask. — G4 75
Kendal, Eng., U.K. — C5 10
Kendall, Fl., U.S. — s13 86
Kendall, Ks., U.S. — E2 93
Kendall, N.Y., U.S. — B2 109
Kendall, Wi., U.S. — E3 126
Kendall, co., Il., U.S. — B5 90
Kendall, co., Tx., U.S. — E3 120
Kendall Green, Fl., U.S. — *F6 86
Kendall Park, N.J., U.S. — C3 107
Kendallville, In., U.S. — B7 91
Kendari, Indon. — F6 34
Kendrāparha, India — D8 36
Kendrick, Id., U.S. — C2 89
Kendrick, Ok., U.S. — B5 113
Kendujhargarh, India — G10 37
Kenduskeag, Me., U.S. — D4 96
Kenedy, Tx., U.S. — E4 120
Kenedy, co., Tx., U.S. — F4 120
Kenefic, Ok., U.S. — C5 113
Kenel, S.D., U.S. — B5 118
Kenema, S.L. — E2 45
Kenesaw, Ne., U.S. — D7 104
Kenge, Zaire — B2 48
Kēng Tung, Burma — D10 36
Kenhardt, S. Afr. — C3 49
Kéniéba, Mali — D2 45
Kenilworth, Il., U.S. — h9 90
Kenilworth, N.J., U.S. — *B4 107
Kenilworth, Ut., U.S. — D5 121
Kenilworth, Eng., U.K. — C6 12
Kenitra, Mor. — C3 44
Kenly, N.C., U.S. — B4 110
Kenmare, Ire. — E2 10
Kenmare, N.D., U.S. — A3 111
Kenmare, stm., Ire. — E1 10
Kenmore, N.Y., U.S. — C2 109
Kenmore, Wa., U.S. — *B3 124
Kenna, N.M., U.S. — D6 108
Kenna, W.V., U.S. — C3 125
Kennaday Peak, mtn., Wy., U.S. — E6 127
Kennan, Wi., U.S. — C3 126
Kennard, In., U.S. — E6 91
Kennard, Ne., U.S. — C9 104
Kennard, Tx., U.S. — D5 120
Kennebago Lake, l., Me., U.S. — C2 96
Kennebec, S.D., U.S. — D5 118
Kennebec, co., Me., U.S. — D3 96
Kennebec, stm., Me., U.S. — D3 96
Kennebunk, Me., U.S. — E2 96
Kennebunkport, Me., U.S. — E2 96
Kennedale, Tx., U.S. — n9 120
Kennedy, Sask. — G4 75
Kennedy, Al., U.S. — B2 78
Kennedy, Mn., U.S. — B2 100
Kennedy, N.Y., U.S. — C1 109
Kennedy, Mount, mtn., Yukon — D5 66
Kennedy Channel, strt., N.A. — k38 66
Kennedy Entrance, strt., Ak., U.S. — D9 79
Kennedy Heights, La., U.S. — *E5 95
Kennedy Lake, l., Sask. — D4 75
Kennedy Township, Pa., U.S. — *F1 115
Kennedyville, Md., U.S. — B6 97
Kenner, La., U.S. — E5 95
Kennesaw, Ga., U.S. — B2 87
Kennesaw Mountain, mtn., Ga., U.S. — C2 87
Kennesaw Mountain National Battlefield Park, Ga., U.S. — h7 87
Kennet, stm., Eng., U.K. — C6 12
Kennetcook, N.S. — D6 71
Kenneth, Mn., U.S. — m16 93
Kenneth, Mo., U.S. — G2 100
Kennett, Mo., U.S. — E7 102
Kennett Square, Pa., U.S. — G10 115
Kennewick, Wa., U.S. — C6 124
Kenney, Il., U.S. — C4 90
Kenney Dam, B.C. — C5 69
Kennisis Lake, l., Ont. — B6 73
Kennydale, Wa., U.S. — e11 124
Keno, Or., U.S. — E5 114
Kénogami, Que. — A6 74
Kénogami, Lac, l., Que. — A6 74
Kenora, Ont. — o16 73
Kenora, dept., Ont. — o17 73
Kenosha, Wi., U.S. — F6 126
Kenosha, co., Wi., U.S. — F5 126
Kenova, W.V., U.S. — C2 125
Ken Rock, Il., U.S. — *A4 90
Kensal, N.D., U.S. — B7 111
Kensett, Ar., U.S. — B4 81
Kensett, Ia., U.S. — A4 92
Kensico Reservoir, res., N.Y., U.S. — g13 109
Kensington, P.E.I. — C6 71
Kensington (part of London), Eng., U.K. — k12 10
Kensington, Ca., U.S. — *h8 82
Kensington, Ct., U.S. — C4 84
Kensington, Ks., U.S. — C4 93
Kensington, Md., U.S. — B3 97
Kensington, Mn., U.S. — E3 100
Kensington, N.H., U.S. — E5 106
Kensington, Oh., U.S. — B5 112
Kent, Al., U.S. — C4 78
Kent, Ct., U.S. — C2 84
Kent, In., U.S. — G6 91
Kent, Ia., U.S. — D3 92
Kent, Mn., U.S. — D2 100
Kent, Oh., U.S. — A4 112
Kent, Or., U.S. — C5 114
Kent, Tx., U.S. — B3 120
Kent, Wa., U.S. — B3 124
Kent, co., N.B. — C4 71
Kent, co., Eng., U.K. — C8 12
Kent, co., De., U.S. — D3 85

Kent, co., Md., U.S. — B5 97
Kent, co., Mi., U.S. — E5 99
Kent, co., R.I., U.S. — D2 116
Kent, co., Tx., U.S. — C2 120
Kent Bridge, Ont. — E2 73
Kent City, Mi., U.S. — E5 99
Kent Island, i., De., U.S. — D4 85
Kent Island, i., Md., U.S. — C5 97
Kent Junction, N.B. — C4 71
Kenton, Man. — E1 70
Kenton, De., U.S. — D3 85
Kenton, Ky., U.S. — k14 94
Kenton, Mi., U.S. — B2 99
Kenton, Oh., U.S. — B2 112
Kenton, Ok., U.S. — e8 113
Kenton, Tn., U.S. — A2 119
Kenton, co., Ky., U.S. — B5 94
Kent Point, c., Md., U.S. — C5 97
Kents Store, Va., U.S. — C4 123
Kentucky, state, U.S. — C4 94
Kentucky, stm., Ky., U.S. — B5 94
Kentucky, Middle Fork, stm., Ky., U.S. — C6 94
Kentucky, North Fork, stm., Ky., U.S. — C6 94
Kentucky, South Fork, stm., Ky., U.S. — C6 94
Kentucky Dam, Ky., U.S. — e9 94
Kentucky Lake, res., U.S. — C10 76
Kentucky Ridge, mtn., Ky., U.S. — D6 94
Kentville, N.S. — D5 71
Kentwood, La., U.S. — D5 95
Kentwood, Mi., U.S. — F5 99
Kenvil, N.J., U.S. — B3 107
Kenvir, Ky., U.S. — D6 94
Kenwood, Oh., U.S. — *A4 112
Kenwood, Ca., U.S. — A7 113
Kenya, ctry., Afr. — A6 48
Kenya, Mount see Kirinyaga, mtn., Kenya — B6 48
Kenyon, Mn., U.S. — F6 100
Kenyon, R.I., U.S. — F2 116
Keo, Ar., U.S. — C3 81
Keokea, Hi., U.S. — C5 88
Keokuk, Ia., U.S. — D6 92
Keokuk, co., Ia., U.S. — C5 92
Keokuk Lock and Dam, U.S. — D6 92
Keoma, Alta. — D4 68
Keosauqua, Ia., U.S. — D6 92
Keota, Co., U.S. — A6 83
Keota, Ia., U.S. — C6 92
Keota, Ok., U.S. — B7 113
Keowee, Lake, res., S.C., U.S. — B2 117
Kepno, Pol. — C5 26
Keppel, Sask. — E2 75
Kepsut, Tur. — B5 25
Kerala, state, India — F6 36
Kerang, Austl. — G7 50
Keratsínion, Grc. — *D4 25
Kerby, Or., U.S. — E3 114
Kerch, Sov. Un. — E6 27
Kerchemya, Sov. Un. — C19 8
Kerema, Pap. N. Gui. — k12 50a
Keremeos, B.C. — E8 69
Keren, Eth. — B4 47
Kerend, Iran — D3 39
Kerens, Tx., U.S. — C4 120
Kerguélen, Îles, is., F.S.A.T. — J1 2
Kerhonkson, N.Y., U.S. — D6 109
Kericho, Kenya — B6 48
Kerinci, mtn., Indon. — F2 34
Kerkebet, Eth. — B4 47
Kerkenna, Îles, is., Tun. — C7 44
Kerkhoven, Mn., U.S. — E3 100
Kérki, Sov. Un. — C2 40
Kérkira (Corfu), i., Grc. — C2 40
Kérkira, Grc. — C2 40
Kerkrade, Neth. — B7 16
Kermadec Islands, is., N.Z. — I11 6
Kermān, Iran — I8 39
Kermānshāh see Bakhtarān, Iran — B4 38
Kerme, Gulf of, b., Tur. — D6 25
Kermit, Tx., U.S. — D1 120
Kermit, W.V., U.S. — D2 125
Kermode, Mount, mtn., B.C. — C2 69
Kern, co., Ca., U.S. — E4 82
Kern, stm., Ca., U.S. — E4 82
Kernersville, N.C., U.S. — A2 110
Kernville, Ca., U.S. — E4 82
Kernville, Or., U.S. — C3 114
Kérouané, Gui. — E3 45
Kerpen, W. Ger. — C1 19
Kerr, co., Tx., U.S. — D3 120
Kerr, Lake, l., Fl., U.S. — C5 86
Kerrick, Mn., U.S. — D6 100
Kerrick, Tx., U.S. — A1 120
Kerrobert, Sask. — F1 75
Kerrville, Tx., U.S. — D3 120
Kerry, co., Ire. — E2 11
Kerry Head, c., Ire. — E1 11
Kersey, Co., U.S. — A6 83
Kersey, Pa., U.S. — D4 115
Kershaw, S.C., U.S. — B6 117
Kershaw, co., S.C., U.S. — C6 117
Kersley, B.C. — C6 69
Kerteminde, Den. — C4 15
Kerulen, stm., Asia — B7 31
Kerzaz, Alg. — D4 44
Kerzers, Switz. — C3 21
Keşan, Tur. — B6 40
Keshena, Wi., U.S. — D5 126
Keshendeh, Afg. — C13 39
Kestenga, Sov. Un. — E14 14
Keswick, Ont. — C5 73
Keswick, Eng., U.K. — F5 13
Keswick, Va., U.S. — B4 123
Keszthely, Hung. — D16 18
Ket, stm., Sov. Un. — B10 28
Keta, Ghana — E6 45
Ketapang, Indon. — F3 34
Ketchikan, Ak., U.S. — D13 79
Ketchum, Id., U.S. — F4 89
Ketchum, Ok., U.S. — A6 113
Kete Krachi, Ghana — E4 45
Ketmen Range, mts., Asia — E10 28
Ketona, Al., U.S. — f7 78
Kétou, Benin — E5 45
Kętrzyn, Pol. — A6 26
Kettering, Eng., U.K. — I12 13
Kettering, Md., U.S. — *C4 97
Kettering, Oh., U.S. — C1 112
Kettle, stm., N.A. — E8 69
Kettle, stm., Mn., U.S. — D6 100

Kettle Creek, stm., Pa., U.S. — D6 115
Kettle Creek Lake, res., Pa., U.S. — D6 115
Kettle Falls, Wa., U.S. — A7 124
Kettleman City, Ca., U.S. — E4 82
Kettle River, Mn., U.S. — D6 100
Kettwig, W. Ger. — B1 19
Kęty, Pol. — D5 26
Ketzin, E. Ger. — A7 19
Keuka Lake, l., N.Y., U.S. — C3 109
Keuterville, Id., U.S. — C2 89
Kevil, Ky., U.S. — e9 94
Kevin, Mt., U.S. — B5 103
Kewanee, Il., U.S. — B4 90
Kewanee, Ms., U.S. — C5 101
Kewanee, Mo., U.S. — E8 102
Kewanna, In., U.S. — B5 91
Kewaskum, Wi., U.S. — E5 126
Kewaunee, Wi., U.S. — D6 126
Kewaunee, co., Wi., U.S. — D6 126
Keweenaw, co., Mi., U.S. — A2 99
Keweenaw Bay, Mi., U.S. — B2 99
Keweenaw Bay, b., Mi., U.S. — B2 99
Keweenaw Peninsula, pen., Mi., U.S. — A3 99
Keweenaw Point, c., Mi., U.S. — A3 99
Key, Lough, l., Ire. — C3 11
Keyapaha, S.D., U.S. — D5 118
Keya Paha, co., Ne., U.S. — B6 104
Keya Paha, stm., Ne., U.S. — A5 104
Key Biscayne, Fl., U.S. — *G6 86
Keyes, Man. — D2 70
Keyes, Ok., U.S. — e8 113
Keyesport, Il., U.S. — E4 90
Keyhole Reservoir, res., Wy., U.S. — B8 127
Key Junction, Ont. — B4 73
Key Largo, Fl., U.S. — G6 86
Keymar, Md., U.S. — A3 97
Keynsham, Eng., U.K. — C5 12
Keyport, N.J., U.S. — C4 107
Keysburg, Ky., U.S. — D2 94
Keyser, W.V., U.S. — B6 125
Keystone, In., U.S. — C7 91
Keystone, Ia., U.S. — C5 92
Keystone, Ne., U.S. — C4 104
Keystone, S.D., U.S. — D2 118
Keystone, W.V., U.S. — D3 125
Keystone, Wy., U.S. — E6 127
Keystone Heights, Fl., U.S. — C4 86
Keystone Lake, res., Ok., U.S. — A5 113
Keystone Peak, mtn., Az., U.S. — F4 80
Keysville, Ga., U.S. — C4 87
Keysville, Va., U.S. — C4 123
Keytesville, Mo., U.S. — B5 102
Key West, Fl., U.S. — H5 86
Key West, Ia., U.S. — B7 92
Key West Naval Air Station, mil., Fl., U.S. — H5 86
Kezar Falls, Me., U.S. — E2 96
Kezar Lake, l., Me., U.S. — D2 96
Kezhma, Sov. Un. — D13 29
Khabab, Syria — A8 41
Khabarovsk, Sov. Un. — E16 29
Khabis see Shahdād, Iran — F8 39
Khachmas, Sov. Un. — A9 40
Khaïdhárion, Grc. — *C4 25
Khairpur, Pak. — C4 36
Khakhea, Bots. — B3 49
Khalándrion, Grc. — *C4 25
Khalia, Grc. — g11 25
Khálki (Chalke), i., Grc. — D6 25
Khalkís, Grc. — C4 40
Khalkidhikí Penninsula, pen., Grc. — B4 25
Khalūf, Oman — C5 38
Khambhāliya, India — D4 36
Khambhāt, India — F4 37
Khambhāt, Gulf of, b., India — B5 36
Khāmgaon, India — D6 36
Khāmgaon, India — G6 37
Khammam, India — I8 37
Khānābād, Afg. — A4 36
Khānaqīn, Iraq — B4 38
Khānderi, i., India — H4 37
Khandwa, India — D6 36
Khaniá (Canea), Grc. — E5 40
Khanka, Lake see Xingkai Hu, l., Asia — B11 31
Khānpur, Pak. — C4 36
Khanty-Mansiysk, Sov. Un. — A7 28
Kharagpur, India — D8 36
Kharaḡah, Pak. — G12 39
Khārg Island, i., Iran — C4 38
Khargon, India — G5 37
Khārijah, Al Wāḥāt al, well, Eg. — C3 38
Kharkov, Sov. Un. — G9 29
Kharmān, Kūh-e, mtn., Iran — G6 39
Kharmanli, Bul. — E7 24
Kharovsk, Sov. Un. — B13 27
Khartoum (Al Kharṭūm), Sud. — B3 47
Khartoum North (Al Kharṭūm Baḥrī), Sud. — B3 47
Khasavyurt, Sov. Un. — q21 27
Khashm al Qirbah, Khazzān, res., Sud. — C4 47
Khashuri, Sov. Un. — B14 40
Khāsi Hills, hills, India — C9 36
Khaskovo, Bul. — E7 24
Khatanga, Sov. Un. — B13 29
Khatanga, stm., Sov. Un. — B13 29
Khemisset, Mor. — *C3 44
Khemmarat, Thai. — D6 35
Khenchla, Alg. — B6 44
Khenifra, Mor. — B3 44
Kherson, Sov. Un. — H9 27
Kheta, stm., Sov. Un. — B12 29
Khieo Peak, mtn., Thai. — E4 35
Khíos (Chios), i., Grc. — C6 40
Khirbat al Ghazālah, Syria — B8 41
Khisfin, Isr. Occ. — C6 41
Khlebarovo (Tsar Kaloyan), Bul. — E8 24
Khmelnik, Sov. Un. — n17 27
Khmelnitskiy, Sov. Un. — G6 27
Khoai, i., Viet. — H5 35
Kholm, Afg. — B4 36
Kholm, Sov. Un. — D1 27
Kholmsk, Sov. Un. — E17 29
Khomeyn, Iran — E5 39

Khomeynīshahr, Iran — E5 39
Khon Kaen, Thai. — B2 34
Khoper, stm., Sov. Un. — F14 27
Khor, strm., Sov. Un. — B12 31
Khóra Sfakíon, Grc. — E5 25
Khordha, India — G10 37
Khorinsk, Sov. Un. — A6 31
Khorog, Sov. Un. — F10 29
Khorol, Sov. Un. — G9 27
Khorramābād, Iran — E4 39
Khorramshahr, Iran — B4 38
Khotin, Sov. Un. — G6 27
Khouribga, Mor. — C3 44
Khowst, Afg. — B4 36
Khram Yai, i., Thai. — F4 35
Khulna, Bngl. — D8 36
Khunjarāb, Sov. Un. — A16 40
Khurja, India — C6 37
Khurr, Wādī al, val., Asia — G14 40
Khushāb, Pak. — A4 37
Khust, Sov. Un. — G4 27
Khuzdār, Pak. — C4 36
Khvāf, Iran — B6 38
Khvor, Iran — E7 39
Khvormūj, Iran — G5 39
Khvoy, Iran — B4 38
Khwae Noi, stm., Thai. — E3 35
Khyber Pass, Asia — B5 36
Kia, i., Fiji — H15 52
Kiamichi, stm., Ok., U.S. — C6 113
Kiamika, Que. — C2 74
Kiamika, stm., Que. — C2 74
Kiana, Ak., U.S. — B7 79
Kiangarow, Mount, mtn., Austl. — C8 51
Kiangsi see Jiangxi, prov., China — F8 31
Kiangsu see Jiangsu, prov., China — E9 31
Kiáton, Grc. — C4 25
Kiawah Island, i., S.C., U.S. — F7 117
Kibangou, Congo — B1 48
Kibaya, Tan. — C6 48
Kiberege, Tan. — C6 48
Kibombo, Zaire — B4 48
Kibondo, Tan. — B5 48
Kibwezi, Kenya — B6 48
Kičevo, Yugo. — E5 24
Kickamuit, stm., R.I., U.S. — D5 116
Kickapoo, stm., Wi., U.S. — E3 126
Kickapoo, Lake, res., Tx., U.S. — C3 120
Kickapoo Creek, stm., Il., U.S. — C4 90
Kickapoo Indian Reservation, Ks., U.S. — C8 93
Kicking Horse Pass, Can. — D2 68
Kidal, Mali — C5 45
Kidder, Mo., U.S. — B3 102
Kidder, S.D., U.S. — B8 118
Kidder, co., N.D., U.S. — C6 111
Kidderminster, Eng., U.K. — D5 10
Kidira, Sen. — D2 45
Kidnappers, Cape, c., N.Z. — M16 51
Kidron, Valley of, val., Isr. Occ. — m14 41
Kidsgrove, Eng., U.K. — A5 12
Kidugallo, Tan. — C6 48
Kidwelly, Wales, U.K. — C3 12
Kief, N.D., U.S. — B5 111
Kiel, Ok., U.S. — B5 113
Kiel, W. Ger. — A5 18
Kiel, Wi., U.S. — E5 126
Kiel Bay, b., W. Ger. — A5 18
Kiel Canal, W. Ger. — A4 18
Kielce, Pol. — C6 26
Kienester, Switz. — C4 21
Kiester, Mn., U.S. — G5 100
Kiev Reservoir, res., Sov. Un. — F8 27
Kiffa, Maur. — C2 45
Kifisiá, Grc. — g11 25
Kifisós (Cephissus), stm., Grc. — g9 25
Kifisós, stm., Grc. — g11 25
Kifrī, Iraq — E15 40
Kigali, Rw. — B5 48
Kiği, Tur. — C13 40
Kigoma, Tan. — B4 48
Kigoma, prov., Tan. — B5 48
Kihei, Hi., U.S. — C5 88
Kiholo Bay, b., Hi., U.S. — D5 88
Kii Strait, strt., Japan — J7 33
Kikinda, Yugo. — C5 24
Kikongo, Zaire — B2 48
Kikori, Pap. N. Gui. — k11 50a
Kikori, stm., Pap. N. Gui. — k11 50a
Kikwit, Zaire — C3 48
Kila, Mt., U.S. — B2 103
Kilauea, Hi., U.S. — A2 88
Kilauea Crater, crat., Hi., U.S. — D6 88
Kilauea Point, c., Hi., U.S. — A2 88
Kilbaha, Ire. — E2 11
Kilbeggan, Ire. — D4 11
Kilbirnie, Scot., U.K. — C4 13
Kilbourne, Il., U.S. — C4 90
Kilbourne, La., U.S. — B4 95
Kilbourne, Oh., U.S. — B3 112
Kilbrannan Sound, strt., Scot., U.K. — E3 13
Kilburn, N.B. — C2 71
Kilcar, Ire. — C3 11
Kilchreest, Ire. — D3 11
Kilchu, N. Kor. — F4 33
Kilcock, Ire. — D5 11
Kilcolgan, Ire. — D3 11
Kilconnell, Ire. — D3 11
Kilcormac (Frankford), Ire. — D4 11
Kilcullen, Ire. — D5 11
Kildare (Saint-Ambroise-ce-Kildare), Que. — C4 74
Kildare, Ire. — D5 11
Kildare, co., Ire. — D5 11
Kildare, Cape, c., P.E.I. — C6 71
Kildorrery, Ire. — E3 11
Kilembe, Zaire — C2 48
Kilfenora, Ire. — D3 11
Kilfinnane, Ire. — E3 11
Kilgarvan, Ire. — F2 11
Kilgore, Ne., U.S. — B5 104
Kilgore, Tx., U.S. — C5 120
Kilifi, Kenya — B6 48
Kilimanjaro, prov., Tan. — B6 48
Kilimanjaro, mtn., Tan. — B6 48
Kilindoni, Tan. — C6 48
Kilis, Tur. — D11 40
Kiliya, Sov. Un. — I7 27
Kilkee, Ire. — D2 11
Kilkeel, N. Ire., U.K. — C5 11
Kilkenny, Ire. — D3 10

Kilkenny, Mn., U.S. — F5 100
Kilkenny, co., Ire. — E4 11
Kilkerrin, Ire. — D3 11
Kilkieran, Ire. — D2 11
Kilkieran Bay, b., Ire. — D2 11
Kilkís, Grc. — B4 25
Killadysert, Ire. — E2 11
Killala, Ire. — C2 10
Killala Bay, b., Ire. — C2 11
Killaloe, Ire. — E3 11
Killaloe Station, Ont. — B7 73
Killaly, Sask. — G4 75
Killam, Alta. — C5 68
Killarney, Man. — E2 70
Killarney, Ire. — D2 10
Killarney Provincial Park, Ont. — A3 73
Killashandra, Ire. — C4 11
Killavally, Ire. — D2 11
Killbuck, Oh., U.S. — B4 112
Killdeer, Sask. — H2 75
Killdeer, N.D., U.S. — B3 111
Killdeer Mountains, mts., N.D., U.S. — B3 111
Killduff, Ia., U.S. — C5 92
Killearn, Fl., U.S. — *B2 86
Killeen, Tx., U.S. — D4 120
Killen, Al., U.S. — A2 78
Killenaule, Ire. — E4 11
Killeter, N. Ire., U.K. — C4 11
Killian, La., U.S. — h10 95
Killiecrankie, Pass of, Scot., U.K. — D5 13
Killik, stm., Ak., U.S. — B9 79
Killilan, Scot., U.K. — B4 10
Killimor, Ire. — D3 11
Killin, Scot., U.K. — D4 13
Killington Peak, mtn., Vt., U.S. — D3 122
Killingworth, Ct., U.S. — D5 84
Killíni, Grc. — D3 25
Killiniq Island, i., Can. — f8 72
Killona, La., U.S. — h11 95
Killorglin, Ire. — D2 11
Killucan, Ire. — D4 11
Killybegs, Ire. — C3 11
Killyleagh, N. Ire., U.K. — C6 11
Kilmacthomas, Ire. — E4 11
Kilmaine, Ire. — D2 11
Kilmallock, Ire. — E3 11
Kilmanagh, Mi., U.S. — E7 99
Kilmarnock, Scot., U.K. — C4 10
Kilmarnock, Va., U.S. — C6 123
Kilmelford, Scot., U.K. — D3 13
Kilmez, Sov. Un. — B4 28
Kilmichael, Ms., U.S. — B4 101
Kiln, Ms., U.S. — E4 101
Kilosa, Tan. — C6 48
Kilrea, N. Ire., U.K. — C5 11
Kilrush, Ire. — D2 11
Kilsyth, Scot., U.K. — E4 13
Kilteen, Ire. — D3 11
Kiltimagh, Ire. — D3 11
Kiltoom, Ire. — D3 11
Kilwa, Zaire — C4 48
Kilwa Kisiwani, Tan. — C6 48
Kilwa Kivinje, Tan. — C6 48
Kim, Co., U.S. — D7 83
Kimamba, Tan. — C6 48
Kimball, Mn., U.S. — E4 100
Kimball, Ne., U.S. — C2 104
Kimball, S.D., U.S. — D7 118
Kimball, W.V., U.S. — D3 125
Kimball, co., Ne., U.S. — C2 104
Kimball, Mount, mtn., Ak., U.S. — C11 79
Kimballton, Ia., U.S. — C2 92
Kimberley, B.C. — E9 69
Kimberley, S. Afr. — C3 49
Kimberley Plateau, plat., Austl. — C4 50
Kimberlin Heights, Tn., U.S. — n14 119
Kimberly, Al., U.S. — B3 78
Kimberly, Id., U.S. — G4 89
Kimberly, Or., U.S. — C7 114
Kimberly, W.V., U.S. — m13 125
Kimberly, Wi., U.S. — h9 126
Kimble, co., Tx., U.S. — D3 120
Kimbolton, Oh., U.S. — B4 112
Kimbrough, Al., U.S. — C2 78
Kimbrough, Ar., U.S. — D3 81
Kimchaek (Sŏngjin), N. Kor. — C10 31
Kimch'ŏn, S. Kor. — H4 33
Kimesville, N.C., U.S. — B3 110
Kimmell, In., U.S. — B6 91
Kimmins, Tn., U.S. — B4 119
Kimmswick, Mo., U.S. — g13 102
Kimmowin, stm., Sask. — A6 68
Kimry, Sov. Un. — C11 27
Kin, Japan — O5 52
Kinabalu, Mount, mtn., Malay. — A5 34
Kinard, Fl., U.S. — B1 86
Kinards, S.C., U.S. — C4 117
Kinbasket Lake, res., B.C. — D7 69
Kinbrace, Scot., U.K. — B5 13
Kinbrae, Mn., U.S. — G3 100
Kinburn, Ont. — B9 73
Kincaid, Sask. — H2 75
Kincaid, Il., U.S. — D4 90
Kincaid, Ks., U.S. — D8 93
Kincaid, W.V., U.S. — m13 125
Kincaid, Lake, res., Il., U.S. — D4 90
Kincaid Knob, mtn., W.V., U.S. — k11 125
Kincardine, Ont. — C3 73
Kinchafoonee Creek, stm., Ga., U.S. — E2 87
Kincheloe Air Force Base, mil., Mi., U.S. — B6 99
Kinde, La., U.S. — D3 95
Kinder, La., U.S. — D3 95
Kinderhook, N.Y., U.S. — C7 109
Kinder Scout, mtn., Eng., U.K. — A5 —
Kindersley, Sask. — F1 75
Kindia, Gui. — D2 45
Kindred, N.D., U.S. — C9 111
Kineo, Mount, mtn., Me., U.S. — C3 96
Kineshma, Sov. Un. — C14 27
King, N.C., U.S. — A2 110
King, Wi., U.S. — D4 126
King, co., Tx., U.S. — C2 120
King, co., Wa., U.S. — B4 124
King, i., Austl. — G7 50
King and Queen Court House, Va., U.S. — C6 123
Kingaroy, Austl. — E9 50
King Christian IX Land, reg., Grnld. — C18 128
King Christian X Land, reg., Grnld. — B17 128
King City, Ont. — k14 73

King City, Ca., U.S. — D3 82
King City, Mo., U.S. — A3 102
King Cove, Ak., U.S. — E7 79
King David Hotel, Isr. — m14 41
King Ferry, N.Y., U.S. — C4 109
Kingfield, Me., U.S. — D2 96
Kingfisher, Ok., U.S. — B4 113
Kingfisher, co., Ok., U.S. — B3 113
King Frederik VI Coast, Grnld. — C19 128
King Frederik VIII Land, reg., Grnld. — B17 128
King George, Va., U.S. — B5 123
King George, co., Va., U.S. — B5 123
King George, Mount, mtn., B.C. — D10 69
King George Island, i., B.A.T. — C7 7
King George Sound, strt., Austl. — G2 50
King Hill, Id., U.S. — F3 89
King Island, i., B.C. — C4 69
King Lake, Mn., U.S. — *C9 104
King Lear Peak, mtn., Nv., U.S. — B3 105
King Leopold Ranges, mts., Austl. — C4 50
Kingman, Alta. — C4 68
Kingman, Az., U.S. — B1 80
Kingman, In., U.S. — E3 91
Kingman, Ks., U.S. — E5 93
Kingman, Me., U.S. — C4 96
Kingman, co., Ks., U.S. — E5 93
King Mountain, mtn., Ok., U.S. — C2 113
King Mountain, mtn., Or., U.S. — D8 114
King of Prussia, Pa., U.S. — F11 115
King Peak, mtn., Ca., U.S. — B1 82
Kings, Il., U.S. — A4 90
Kings, Ms., U.S. — C3 101
Kings, co., N.B. — D4 71
Kings, co., N.S. — E5 71
Kings, co., P.E.I. — C7 71
Kings, co., Ca., U.S. — D3 82
Kings, co., N.Y., U.S. — E7 109
Kings, stm., Ire. — E4 11
Kings, stm., Ca., U.S. — D4 82
Kings, stm., Nv., U.S. — B3 105
Kings Salmon, Ak., U.S. — D8 79
Kingsbridge, Eng., U.K. — D4 12
Kingsburg, Ca., U.S. — D4 82
Kingsbury, In., U.S. — A4 91
Kingsbury, Tx., U.S. — h8 120
Kingsbury, co., S.D., U.S. — C8 118
Kings Canyon National Park, Ca., U.S. — D4 82
Kingsclear, N.B. — D3 71
Kingscote, Austl. — G6 50
Kings Creek, S.C., U.S. — A5 117
Kingsdown, Ks., U.S. — E4 93
Kingsey-Falls, Que. — D5 74
Kingsford, Mi., U.S. — C2 99
Kingsgate, B.C. — E9 69
Kingsgate, Wa., U.S. — *B3 124
Kings Grant, N.C., U.S. — *C5 110
Kingsland, Ar., U.S. — D3 81
Kingsland, Ga., U.S. — F5 87
Kingsland, Tx., U.S. — D3 120
Kingsley, Ia., U.S. — B2 92
Kingsley, Mi., U.S. — D5 99
Kingsley Dam, Ne., U.S. — C4 104
King's Lynn, Eng., U.K. — D7 10
Kingsmere Lake, l., Sask. — C2 75
Kings Mills, Oh., U.S. — C1 112
Kings Mountain, Ky., U.S. — C5 94
Kings Mountain, N.C., U.S. — B1 110
Kings Park, N.Y., U.S. — *E7 109
Kings Park West, Va., U.S. — *B5 123
Kings Peak, mtn., Ut., U.S. — C5 121
King's Point, Newf. — D3 72
Kings Point, Fl., U.S. — *F6 86
Kings Point, N.Y., U.S. — *E7 109
Kingsport, Tn., U.S. — C11 119
Kingston, N.S. — E5 71
Kingston, Ont. — C8 73
Kingston, Jam. — F5 64
Kingston, N.Z. — P12 51
Kingston, Ga., U.S. — B2 87
Kingston, Id., U.S. — B3 89
Kingston, Il., U.S. — A5 90
Kingston, Ma., U.S. — C6 98
Kingston, Mi., U.S. — E7 99
Kingston, Mo., U.S. — B3 102
Kingston, N.H., U.S. — E4 106
Kingston, N.Y., U.S. — D6 109
Kingston, Oh., U.S. — C3 112
Kingston, Ok., U.S. — D5 113
Kingston, Pa., U.S. — D10 115
Kingston, R.I., U.S. — F3 116
Kingston, Tn., U.S. — D9 119
Kingston, Ut., U.S. — E3 121
Kingston, W.V., U.S. — n13 125
Kingston, Wi., U.S. — E4 126
Kingston Springs, Tn., U.S. — A4 119
Kingston upon Hull, Eng., U.K. — D6 10
Kingston upon Thames (part of London), Eng., U.K. — m12 10
Kingstown, St. Vin. — J14 64
Kingstree, S.C., U.S. — D8 117
Kingsville, Ont. — E1 73
Kingsville, Md., U.S. — B5 97
Kingsville, Mo., U.S. — C3 102
Kingsville, Tx., U.S. — F4 120
Kingsville Naval Air Station, mil., Tx., U.S. — F4 120
Kingswood, Ky., U.S. — C6 94
Kington, Eng., U.K. — B4 12
Kingurutik Lake, l., Newf. — g9 72
King William, Va., U.S. — C5 123
King William, co., Va., U.S. — C5 123
King William Island, i., N.W. Ter. — C13 66
King William's Town, S. Afr. — C4 49
Kingwood, Tx., U.S. — *E5 120
Kingwood, W.V., U.S. — B5 125
Kinistino, Sask. — E3 75
Kinkaid Lake, l., Il., U.S. — F4 90
Kinkala, Congo — B1 48
Kinkora, P.E.I. — C6 71
Kinley, Sask. — E2 75
Kin-Li-Chee, Az., U.S. — B6 80

| Name | Map Ref. | Page |
|---|---|---|
| Kinloch, Mo., U.S. | f13 | 102 |
| Kinlochewe, Scot., U.K. | C3 | 13 |
| Kinloch Hourn, Scot., U.K. | C3 | 13 |
| Kinmount, Ont. | C6 | 73 |
| Kinmundy, Il., U.S. | E5 | 90 |
| Kinnairds Head, c., Scot., U.K. | B6 | 13 |
| Kinnear, Wy., U.S. | C4 | 127 |
| Kinnelon, N.J., U.S. | B4 | 107 |
| Kinneret, Yam (Sea of Galilee), l., Isr. | B7 | 41 |
| Kinney, co., Tx., U.S. | E2 | 120 |
| Kinomoto, Japan | n15 | 33 |
| Kinosaki, Japan | I7 | 33 |
| Kinrooi, Bel. | C5 | 17 |
| Kinross, P.E.I. | C7 | 71 |
| Kinross, Scot., U.K. | C5 | 13 |
| Kinsale, Ire. | E2 | 10 |
| Kinsale, Va., U.S. | C6 | 123 |
| Kinsella, Alta. | C5 | 68 |
| Kinsey, Al., U.S. | D4 | 78 |
| Kinsey, Mt., U.S. | D11 | 103 |
| Kinshasa (Léopoldville), Zaire | B2 | 48 |
| Kinsley, Ks., U.S. | E4 | 93 |
| Kinsman, Oh., U.S. | A5 | 112 |
| Kinston, Al., U.S. | D3 | 78 |
| Kinston, N.C., U.S. | B5 | 110 |
| Kinta, Ok., U.S. | B6 | 113 |
| Kintampo, Ghana | E4 | 45 |
| Kintinku, Tan. | C6 | 48 |
| Kintore, Scot., U.K. | C6 | 13 |
| Kintyre, N.D., U.S. | C6 | 111 |
| Kintyre, Mull of, c., Scot. U.K. | E3 | 13 |
| Kinuso, Alta. | B3 | 68 |
| Kinvarra, Ire. | D3 | 11 |
| Kinyangiri, Tan. | B5 | 48 |
| Kinyeti, mtn., Sud. | E3 | 47 |
| Kinzig, stm., W. Ger. | C4 | 19 |
| Kinzig, stm., W. Ger. | E2 | 19 |
| Kinzua, Or., U.S. | C6 | 114 |
| Kioa, i., Fiji | H15 | 52 |
| Kiona, Wa., U.S. | C6 | 124 |
| Kioshkokwi Lake, l., Ont. | A6 | 73 |
| Kiosk, Ont. | A6 | 73 |
| Kiowa, Co., U.S. | B6 | 83 |
| Kiowa, Ks., U.S. | E5 | 93 |
| Kiowa, Ok., U.S. | C6 | 113 |
| Kiowa, co., Co., U.S. | C8 | 83 |
| Kiowa, co., Ks., U.S. | E4 | 93 |
| Kiowa, co., Ok., U.S. | C2 | 113 |
| Kiowa Creek, stm., Co., U.S. | B6 | 83 |
| Kiowa Creek, stm., Ok., U.S. | A1 | 113 |
| Kipahigan Lake, l., Can. | B5 | 75 |
| Kipahulu, Hi., U.S. | *C5 | 88 |
| Kipapa Stream, stm., Hi., U.S. | g9 | 88 |
| Kiparissia, Grc. | D3 | 25 |
| Kiparissia, Gulf of, b., Grc. | D3 | 25 |
| Kipembawe, Tan. | C5 | 48 |
| Kipili, Tan. | C5 | 48 |
| Kipini, Kenya | B7 | 48 |
| Kipling, Sask. | G4 | 75 |
| Kipling, Mi., U.S. | C3 | 99 |
| Kipnuk, Ak., U.S. | C7 | 79 |
| Kipp, Alta. | E4 | 68 |
| Kipp, Ks., U.S. | D6 | 93 |
| Kipton, Oh., U.S. | A3 | 112 |
| Kipushi, Zaire | D4 | 48 |
| Kirby, Ar., U.S. | C2 | 81 |
| Kirby, Tx., U.S. | *E3 | 120 |
| Kirby, Wy., U.S. | C4 | 127 |
| Kirbyville, Tx., U.S. | D6 | 120 |
| Kirchberg, Switz. | *B7 | 21 |
| Kirchdorf, E. Ger. | E5 | 15 |
| Kirchhain, W. Ger. | E5 | 15 |
| Kirchheimbolanden, W. Ger. | D2 | 19 |
| Kirchheim [unter Teck], W. Ger. | E4 | 19 |
| Kirchhundem, W. Ger. | B3 | 19 |
| Kirdāsah, Eg. | D3 | 41 |
| Kirensk, Sov. Un. | D13 | 29 |
| Kirghiz S.S.R., state, Sov. Un. | E10 | 29 |
| Kirgiz Range, mts., Sov. Un. | E8 | 28 |
| Kiri, Zaire | C3 | 48 |
| Kiribati, ctry., Oc. | G11 | 6 |
| Kırıkhan, Tur. | *D11 | 40 |
| Kırıkkale, Tur. | C9 | 40 |
| Kitridge Point, c., Barb. | K21 | 65 |
| Kirin see Jilin, prov., China | C10 | 31 |
| Kirinian, i., Marsh Is. | S18 | 52 |
| Kirinyaga (Mount Kenya), mtn., Kenya | B6 | 48 |
| Kiritimati Island (Christmas Island), i., Kir. | F12 | 6 |
| Kirk, Co., U.S. | B8 | 83 |
| Kirkby Lonsdale, Eng., U.K. | F6 | 13 |
| Kirkby Stephen, Eng., U.K. | F6 | 13 |
| Kirkcaldy, Alta. | D4 | 68 |
| Kirkcaldy, Scot., U.K. | B5 | 10 |
| Kirkcolm, Scot., U.K. | F3 | 13 |
| Kirkcudbright, Scot., U.K. | D5 | 13 |
| Kirkcudbright Bay, b., Scot., U.K. | F4 | 13 |
| Kirkenes, Nor. | C13 | 14 |
| Kirkersville, Oh., U.S. | C3 | 112 |
| Kirkfield, Ont. | C5 | 73 |
| Kirkintilloch, Scot., U.K. | E4 | 13 |
| Kirkland, Al., U.S. | D2 | 78 |
| Kirkland, Az., U.S. | C3 | 80 |
| Kirkland, Ga., U.S. | E4 | 87 |
| Kirkland, Il., U.S. | A5 | 90 |
| Kirkland, Tn., U.S. | B5 | 119 |
| Kirkland, Tx., U.S. | B2 | 120 |
| Kirkland, Wa., U.S. | B3 | 124 |
| Kirkland Lake, Ont. | o19 | 73 |
| Kirklareli, Tur. | B6 | 40 |
| Kirklin, In., U.S. | D5 | 91 |
| Kirkman, Ia., U.S. | C2 | 92 |
| Kirkmansville, Ky., U.S. | D2 | 94 |
| Kirkoswald, Eng., U.K. | F6 | 13 |
| Kirkpatrick, Mount, mtn., Ant. | A29 | 7 |
| Kirkpatrick Lake, l., Alta. | D5 | 68 |
| Kirksey, Ky., U.S. | f9 | 94 |
| Kirksey, S.C., U.S. | C3 | 117 |
| Kirksville, Ky., U.S. | C5 | 94 |
| Kirksville, Mo., U.S. | A5 | 102 |
| Kirkton, Ont. | D3 | 73 |
| Kirkton of Glenisla, Scot., U.K. | D5 | 13 |
| Kirkūk, Iraq | B4 | 38 |
| Kirkville, In., U.S. | C5 | 91 |
| Kirkwall, Scot., U.K. | A5 | 10 |
| Kirkwood, S. Afr. | D4 | 49 |
| Kirkwood, De., U.S. | B3 | 85 |
| Kirkwood, Il., U.S. | C3 | 90 |
| Kirkwood, Mo., U.S. | f13 | 102 |
| Kirn, W. Ger. | D3 | 19 |
| Kiron, Ia., U.S. | B2 | 92 |
| Kirov, Sov. Un. | E7 | 29 |
| Kirovabad, Sov. Un. | B15 | 40 |
| Kirov Bay, b., Sov. Un. | B4 | 39 |
| Kirovograd, Sov. Un. | G9 | 27 |
| Kirovsk, Sov. Un. | C6 | 29 |
| Kirriemuir, Alta. | D5 | 68 |
| Kirriemuir, Scot., U.K. | D5 | 13 |
| Kirsanov, Sov. Un. | E14 | 27 |
| Kırşehir, Tur. | C10 | 40 |
| Kirthar Range, mts., Pak. | C4 | 36 |
| Kirtland, N.M., U.S. | A1 | 108 |
| Kirtland, Oh., U.S. | *C1 | 112 |
| Kirtland Air Force Base, mil., N.M., U.S. | k7 | 108 |
| Kiruna, Swe. | D9 | 14 |
| Kirundu, Zaire | B4 | 48 |
| Kirwin, Ks., U.S. | C4 | 93 |
| Kirwin Reservoir, res., Ks., U.S. | C4 | 93 |
| Kiryū, Japan | H9 | 33 |
| Kisaki, Tan. | C6 | 48 |
| Kisanga, Zaire | C4 | 48 |
| Kisangani (Stanleyville), Zaire | A4 | 48 |
| Kisarazu, Japan | n18 | 33 |
| Kisatchie, La., U.S. | C2 | 95 |
| Kisbey, Sask. | H4 | 75 |
| Kisengwa, Zaire | C4 | 48 |
| Kiselevsk, Sov. Un. | C11 | 28 |
| Kishanganj, India | D11 | 37 |
| Kishangarh, India | C5 | 36 |
| Kishinev, Sov. Un. | E6 | 29 |
| Kishiwada, Japan | o14 | 33 |
| Kishorganj, Bngl. | D9 | 36 |
| Kishwaukee, stm., Il., U.S. | A5 | 90 |
| Kisii, Kenya | B5 | 48 |
| Kisiju, Tan. | C6 | 48 |
| Kiska Island, i., Ak., U.S. | E3 | 79 |
| Kiskatinaw, stm., B.C. | B7 | 69 |
| Kiskittogisu Lake, l., Man. | B2 | 70 |
| Kiskitto Lake, l., Man. | B2 | 70 |
| Kisköros, Hung. | B4 | 24 |
| Kiskundorozsma (part of Szeged), Hung. | B5 | 24 |
| Kiskunfélegyháza, Hung. | B4 | 24 |
| Kiskunhalas, Hung. | B4 | 24 |
| Kiskunmajsa, Hung. | B4 | 24 |
| Kislovodsk, Sov. Un. | E2 | 28 |
| Kismet, Ks., U.S. | E3 | 93 |
| Kiso-sammyaku, mts., Japan | n16 | 33 |
| Kissamos, Grc. | E4 | 25 |
| Kissee Mills, Mo., U.S. | E4 | 102 |
| Kissenew Lake, l., Can. | B1 | 70 |
| Kissidougou, Gui. | E2 | 45 |
| Kissimmee, Fl., U.S. | D5 | 86 |
| Kissimmee, stm., Fl., U.S. | E5 | 86 |
| Kissimmee, Lake, l., Fl., U.S. | E5 | 86 |
| Kissimmee Park, Fl., U.S. | D5 | 86 |
| Kississing, Man. | B1 | 70 |
| Kississing, stm., Man. | B1 | 70 |
| Kississing, Lake, l., Man. | B1 | 70 |
| Kisslegg, W. Ger. | A8 | 21 |
| Kistefjellet, mtn., Nor. | C8 | 14 |
| Kistigan Lake, l., Man. | B5 | 70 |
| Kistler, W.V., U.S. | D3 | 125 |
| Kistrand, Nor. | B11 | 14 |
| Kisújszállás, Hung. | B5 | 24 |
| Kisumu, Kenya | A5 | 48 |
| Kisvárda, Hung. | A6 | 24 |
| Kita, Mali | D3 | 45 |
| Kita, Mount, mtn., Japan | I9 | 33 |
| Kita-ibaraki, Japan | H10 | 33 |
| Kita-iwo, i., Japan | E8 | 6 |
| Kitakyūshū, Japan | E11 | 31 |
| Kitale, Kenya | A5 | 48 |
| Kitami, Japan | E11 | 33 |
| Kitangari, Tan. | D6 | 48 |
| Kit Carson, Co., U.S. | C8 | 83 |
| Kit Carson, co., Co., U.S. | B8 | 83 |
| Kitchell, In., U.S. | E8 | 91 |
| Kitchener, Ont. | D4 | 73 |
| Kite, Ga., U.S. | D4 | 87 |
| Kitgum, Ug. | A5 | 48 |
| Kithira, Grc. | D4 | 25 |
| Kithira (Cythera), i., Grc. | D4 | 25 |
| Kithnos, i., Grc. | D5 | 40 |
| Kitimat, B.C. | C3 | 69 |
| Kitsap, co., Wa., U.S. | B3 | 124 |
| Kitscoty, Alta. | C5 | 68 |
| Kittanning, Pa., U.S. | E2 | 115 |
| Kittatinny Mountain, mtn., U.S. | B2 | 107 |
| Kittery, Me., U.S. | E2 | 96 |
| Kittery Point, Me., U.S. | E2 | 96 |
| Kittilä, Fin. | D11 | 14 |
| Kittitas, Wa., U.S. | C5 | 124 |
| Kittitas, co., Wa., U.S. | B4 | 124 |
| Kittitas Valley, val., Wa., U.S. | B5 | 124 |
| Kittrell, N.C., U.S. | A4 | 110 |
| Kitts, Ky., U.S. | D6 | 94 |
| Kitts Hummock, De., U.S. | D4 | 85 |
| Kittson, co., Mn., U.S. | B2 | 100 |
| Kitty Hawk, N.C., U.S. | A7 | 110 |
| Kitty Hawk Bay, b., N.C., U.S. | A7 | 110 |
| Kitui, Kenya | B6 | 48 |
| Kitwanga, B.C. | B3 | 69 |
| Kitwe, Zam. | D4 | 48 |
| Kitzbühel, Aus. | E6 | 18 |
| Kitzingen, W. Ger. | D5 | 19 |
| Kitzmiller, Md., U.S. | m12 | 97 |
| Kivalina, Ak., U.S. | B7 | 79 |
| Kivu, Lac, l., Afr. | B4 | 48 |
| Kivu, hist. reg., Zaire | B4 | 48 |
| Kiya, stm., B.C. | D26 | 8 |
| Kiyan, Japan | O5 | 32 |
| Kiyan Point, c., Japan | O5 | 32 |
| Kiyiu Lake, l., Sask. | F1 | 75 |
| Kiyköy, Tur. | B7 | 40 |
| Kizel, Sov. Un. | B10 | 40 |
| Kizil, stm., Tur. | E3 | 28 |
| Kizlyar, Sov. Un. | F8 | 28 |
| Kizil-Arvat, Sov. Un. | C10 | 14 |
| Kjaekan, Nor. | C5 | 15 |
| Kjellerup, Den. | B12 | 14 |
| Kjelvik, Nor. | C3 | 26 |
| Kladno, Czech. | E7 | 18 |
| Klagenfurt, Aus. | B6 | 80 |
| Klagetoh, Az., U.S. | B1 | 27 |
| Klaipėda (Memel), Sov. Un. | E5 | 114 |
| Klamath, co., Or., U.S. | B2 | 82 |
| Klamath, stm., U.S. | E5 | 114 |
| Klamath Falls, Or., U.S. | B2 | 82 |
| Klamath Glen, Ca., U.S. | E2 | 114 |
| Klamath Mountains, mts., U.S. | | |
| Klanxbüll, W. Ger. | | |
| Klarälven, stm., Eur. | | |
| Klatovy, Czech. | k7 | 49 |
| Klawer, S. Afr. | D2 | 49 |
| Klawock, Ak., U.S. | D13 | 79 |
| Kleberg, co., Tx., U.S. | F4 | 120 |
| Kleena Kleene, B.C. | D5 | 69 |
| Klein, Tx., U.S. | *D5 | 120 |
| Klein, stm., B.C. | k14 | 69 |
| Klemme, Ia., U.S. | A4 | 92 |
| Klerksdorp, S. Afr. | C4 | 49 |
| Kletnya, Sov. Un. | E9 | 27 |
| Kletsk, Sov. Un. | E6 | 27 |
| Kleve (Cleves), W. Ger. | C3 | 18 |
| Klibreck, Ben, mtn., Scot., U.K. | B4 | 13 |
| Kličany, Czech. | n17 | 26 |
| Klickitat, Wa., U.S. | D4 | 124 |
| Klickitat, co., Wa., U.S. | D4 | 124 |
| Klickitat, stm., Wa., U.S. | C4 | 124 |
| Klimovsk, Sov. Un. | n17 | 27 |
| Klin, Sov. Un. | C11 | 27 |
| Klinaklini, stm., B.C. | D5 | 69 |
| Kline, S.C., U.S. | E5 | 117 |
| Klingenthal, E. Ger. | C7 | 19 |
| Klínovec, mtn., Czech. | C7 | 19 |
| Klintsy, Sov. Un. | E9 | 27 |
| Klippan, Swe. | B7 | 15 |
| Klitmøller, Den. | A2 | 15 |
| Ključ, Yugo. | C3 | 24 |
| Kłobuck, Pol. | C5 | 26 |
| Kloch Lake, l., B.C. | B5 | 69 |
| Klock, Ont. | A6 | 73 |
| Kłodnica, stm., Pol. | g9 | 26 |
| Kłodzko, Pol. | C4 | 26 |
| Klondike, In., U.S. | D4 | 91 |
| Klondike, Tx., U.S. | C5 | 120 |
| Klondike Gold Rush National Historical Park, Ak., U.S. | k22 | 79 |
| Klondike Region, hist. reg., Yukon | D5 | 66 |
| Klondyke, Az., U.S. | E5 | 80 |
| Klos, Alb. | B3 | 25 |
| Klostermansfeld, E. Ger. | B6 | 19 |
| Klosterneuburg, Aus. | D8 | 18 |
| Klosters [-Serneus], Switz. | C8 | 21 |
| Kloten, Switz. | B6 | 21 |
| Kloten, N.D., U.S. | B7 | 111 |
| Klötze, E. Ger. | F5 | 15 |
| Klotzsche, E. Ger. | B8 | 19 |
| Klotzville, La., U.S. | h9 | 95 |
| Kluane Lake, l., Yukon | D5 | 66 |
| Kluane National Park, Yukon | D5 | 66 |
| Kluczbork, Pol. | C5 | 26 |
| Klukwan, Ak., U.S. | k22 | 79 |
| Klutina Lake, l., Ak., U.S. | g19 | 79 |
| Klütz, E. Ger. | E5 | 15 |
| Klyazma, stm., Sov. Un. | C13 | 27 |
| Klyuchevskaya Sopka, vol., Sov. Un. | D18 | 29 |
| Knapp, Wi., U.S. | D1 | 126 |
| Knapp Creek, stm., W.V., U.S. | C5 | 125 |
| Knaresborough, Eng., U.K. | F7 | 13 |
| Knee Lake, l., Man. | B4 | 70 |
| Knee Lake, l., Sask. | B2 | 75 |
| Knesebeck, W. Ger. | F4 | 15 |
| Kneža, Bul. | D7 | 24 |
| Knickerbocker, Tx., U.S. | D2 | 120 |
| Knierim, Ia., U.S. | B3 | 92 |
| Knife, stm., N.D., U.S. | B3 | 111 |
| Knife River, Mn., U.S. | D7 | 100 |
| Knifley, Ky., U.S. | C4 | 94 |
| Knightdale, N.C., U.S. | B4 | 110 |
| Knight Inlet, b., B.C. | D5 | 69 |
| Knight Island, i., Ak., U.S. | g18 | 79 |
| Knighton, Wales, U.K. | B4 | 12 |
| Knights Landing, Ca., U.S. | C3 | 82 |
| Knights Town, Ire. | F1 | 11 |
| Knightstown, In., U.S. | E6 | 91 |
| Knightsville, In., U.S. | E3 | 91 |
| Knightville Reservoir, res., Ma., U.S. | B2 | 98 |
| Knin, Yugo. | C3 | 24 |
| Knippa, Tx., U.S. | E3 | 120 |
| Knislinge, Swe. | B8 | 15 |
| Knittelfeld, Aus. | E7 | 18 |
| Knob Creek, stm., Ky., U.S. | g11 | 94 |
| Knobel, Ar., U.S. | A5 | 81 |
| Knob Lick, Ky., U.S. | C4 | 94 |
| Knob Lick, Mo., U.S. | D7 | 102 |
| Knobly Mountain, mtn., W.V., U.S. | B5 | 125 |
| Knob Noster, Mo., U.S. | C4 | 102 |
| Knobsville, Pa., U.S. | F6 | 115 |
| Knockadoon Head, c., Ire. | F4 | 11 |
| Knockalongy, mtn., Ire. | B3 | 11 |
| Knockanefune, hill, Ire. | E2 | 11 |
| Knockboy, mtn., Ire. | F2 | 11 |
| Knocklong, Ire. | E3 | 11 |
| Knockmealdown Mountains, mts., Ire. | D2 | 10 |
| Knokke [-Heist], Bel. | C3 | 17 |
| Knollwood, Ct., U.S. | D6 | 84 |
| Knollwood, W.V., U.S. | m12 | 125 |
| Knops Pond, l., Ma., U.S. | f9 | 98 |
| Knott, Tx., U.S. | C2 | 120 |
| Knott, co., Ky., U.S. | C6 | 94 |
| Knotts Island, N.C., U.S. | A7 | 110 |
| Knottsville, Ky., U.S. | C3 | 94 |
| Knowles, Ok., U.S. | A1 | 113 |
| Knowlton, Wi., U.S. | D4 | 126 |
| Knox, Austl. | *G8 | 50 |
| Knox, In., U.S. | B4 | 91 |
| Knox, N.D., U.S. | A6 | 111 |
| Knox, co., Il., U.S. | B3 | 90 |
| Knox, co., In., U.S. | G3 | 91 |
| Knox, co., Ky., U.S. | D6 | 94 |
| Knox, co., Me., U.S. | D3 | 96 |
| Knox, co., Mo., U.S. | A5 | 102 |
| Knox, co., Ne., U.S. | B8 | 104 |
| Knox, co., Oh., U.S. | B3 | 112 |
| Knox, co., Tn., U.S. | C10 | 119 |
| Knox, co., Tx., U.S. | C3 | 120 |
| Knox, Cape, c., B.C. | B1 | 69 |
| Knox City, Mo., U.S. | A5 | 102 |
| Knox City, Tx., U.S. | C3 | 120 |
| Knox Coast, Ant. | C23 | 7 |
| Knox Dale, Pa., U.S. | D3 | 115 |
| Knoxville, Al., U.S. | C2 | 78 |
| Knoxville, Ga., U.S. | D3 | 87 |
| Knoxville, Ia., U.S. | C4 | 92 |
| Knoxville, Il., U.S. | C3 | 90 |
| Knoxville, Md., U.S. | B2 | 97 |
| Knoxville, Pa., U.S. | C7 | 115 |
| Knoxville, Tn., U.S. | D10 | 119 |
| Knysna, S. Afr. | D3 | 49 |
| Knyszyn, Pol. | B7 | 26 |
| Ko, Mount, mtn., Sov. Un. | C8 | 33 |
| Kobayashi, Japan | K5 | 33 |
| Kōbe, Japan | E11 | 31 |
| Kobelyaki, Sov. Un. | G10 | 27 |
| København, co., Den. | C6 | 15 |
| Koblenz (Coblence), W. Ger. | C3 | 18 |
| Koboko, Ug. | A5 | 48 |
| Kobon, stm., B.C. | r32 | 14 |
| Kobrin, Sov. Un. | E5 | 29 |
| Kobroor, i., Indon. | G8 | 52 |
| Kobuk, Ak., U.S. | B8 | 79 |
| Kobuk, stm., Ak., U.S. | B8 | 79 |
| Kobuk Valley National Park, Ak., U.S. | B8 | 79 |
| Kobuleti, Sov. Un. | B13 | 40 |
| Kocába, stm., Czech. | o17 | 26 |
| Kocaeli see İzmit, Tur. | B7 | 40 |
| Kočani, Yugo. | E6 | 24 |
| Kočevje, Yugo. | C2 | 24 |
| Koch Bihār, India | C8 | 36 |
| Kochel, W. Ger. | B7 | 20 |
| Kochel Lake, l., W. Ger. | B7 | 20 |
| Kocher, stm., W. Ger. | D4 | 19 |
| Kōchi, Japan | E11 | 31 |
| Koch Peak, mtn., Mt., U.S. | E5 | 103 |
| Kodak, Pol. | C7 | 26 |
| Kodari, Nepal | D10 | 37 |
| Kodiak, Ak., U.S. | D9 | 79 |
| Kodiak Island, i., Ak., U.S. | D9 | 79 |
| Kodok (Fashoda), Sud. | D3 | 47 |
| Koera Joeri, Neth. Ant. | H18 | 65 |
| Kofa Mountains, mts., Az., U.S. | D2 | 80 |
| Koffiefontein, S. Afr. | C3 | 49 |
| Koforidua, Ghana | E4 | 45 |
| Kōfu, Japan | I9 | 33 |
| Koga, Japan | m18 | 33 |
| Kogaluk, stm., Newf. | g9 | 72 |
| Køge, Den. | C6 | 15 |
| Køge Bugt, b., Den. | C6 | 15 |
| Kohala Mountains, mts., Hi., U.S. | C6 | 88 |
| Kohāt, Pak. | B5 | 36 |
| Kohatk, Az., U.S. | E3 | 80 |
| Kohīma, India | C9 | 36 |
| Kohler, Wi., U.S. | E6 | 126 |
| Kohtla-Järve, Sov. Un. | B6 | 27 |
| Koidu, S.L. | E2 | 45 |
| Kōinge, Swe. | A6 | 15 |
| Ko Island, i., Japan | F9 | 33 |
| Kōje Island, i., S. Kor. | I4 | 33 |
| Kokanee Glacier Provincial Park, B.C. | E9 | 69 |
| Kokchetav, Sov. Un. | D9 | 29 |
| Kokkola, Fin. | F10 | 14 |
| Koko, Nig. | D5 | 45 |
| Koko Head, c., Hi., U.S. | B4 | 88 |
| Kokolik, stm., Ak., U.S. | B7 | 79 |
| Kokomo, Hi., U.S. | C5 | 88 |
| Kokomo, In., U.S. | D5 | 91 |
| Kokomo, Ms., U.S. | D3 | 101 |
| Koko Nor see Qinghai Hu, l., China | A4 | 31 |
| Kokopo, Pap. N. Gui. | h13 | 50 |
| Kokosing, stm., Oh., U.S. | B3 | 112 |
| Kokrines, Ak., U.S. | C9 | 79 |
| Koksan, N. Kor. | G3 | 33 |
| Koksilah, B.C. | g12 | 69 |
| Koksoak, stm., Que. | E19 | 66 |
| Kokstad, S. Afr. | D4 | 49 |
| Kola, Sov. Un. | C15 | 14 |
| Ko Lanta, i., Thai. | I3 | 35 |
| Kola Peninsula, pen., Sov. Un. | C6 | 29 |
| Kolār, India | E5 | 36 |
| Kolār Gold Fields, India | *F6 | 36 |
| Kolari, Fin. | D10 | 14 |
| Kolárovo, Czech. | E4 | 26 |
| Kolasin, Yugo. | D4 | 24 |
| Kolbäck, Swe. | t34 | 14 |
| Kolbano, Indon. | G6 | 34 |
| Kolbio, Kenya | B7 | 48 |
| Kolbuszowa, Pol. | C6 | 26 |
| Kolchugino, Sov. Un. | C12 | 27 |
| Kolczewo, Pol. | E8 | 15 |
| Kolda, Sen. | D2 | 45 |
| Koldewey, i., Grnld. | B16 | 128 |
| Kole, Zaire | C3 | 48 |
| Kolec, Czech. | n17 | 26 |
| Koleczkowo, Pol. | g9 | 26 |
| Koleen, In., U.S. | G4 | 91 |
| Kolezhma, Sov. Un. | E16 | 14 |
| Kolguyev Island, i., Sov. Un. | C7 | 29 |
| Kolhāpur, India | E5 | 36 |
| Koliganek, Ak., U.S. | D8 | 79 |
| Kolimbine, stm., Afr. | C2 | 45 |
| Kolín, Czech. | C3 | 26 |
| Kölleda, E. Ger. | B6 | 19 |
| Kolno, Pol. | B6 | 26 |
| Koloa, Hi., U.S. | B2 | 88 |
| Kolob Canyon, val., Ut., U.S. | F2 | 121 |
| Kołobrzeg, Pol. | A3 | 26 |
| Kolokani, Mali | D3 | 45 |
| Kolola Springs, Ms., U.S. | B5 | 101 |
| Kolomna, Sov. Un. | D6 | 29 |
| Kolomyya, Sov. Un. | E5 | 29 |
| Kolondiéba, Mali | D3 | 45 |
| Kolonia, Micron. | Q17 | 52 |
| Kolonodale, Indon. | F6 | 34 |
| Kolp, stm., Sov. Un. | B10 | 27 |
| Kolpashevo, Sov. Un. | B10 | 28 |
| Kolpino, Sov. Un. | s31 | 14 |
| Kolwezi, Zaire | D4 | 48 |
| Kolyberovo, Sov. Un. | n18 | 27 |
| Kolyma, stm., Sov. Un. | C18 | 29 |
| Kolyma Mountains, mts., Sov. Un. | C18 | 29 |
| Komádi, Hung. | B5 | 24 |
| Komandorski Islands, is., Sov. Un. | D19 | 29 |
| Komarno, Man. | D3 | 70 |
| Komárno, Czech. | E5 | 26 |
| Komarno Marsh, sw., Sov. Un. | B10 | 28 |
| Komárom, Hung. | H17 | 24 |
| Komatipoort, S. Afr. | C5 | 49 |
| Komatke, Az., U.S. | m8 | 80 |
| Komatsu, Japan | H8 | 33 |
| Komatsushima, Japan | I9 | 33 |
| Komló, Hung. | B4 | 24 |
| Komodo, i., Indon. | G5 | 34 |
| Komono, Congo | B1 | 48 |
| Komoran, i., Indon. | G10 | 34 |
| Komotiní, Grc. | B5 | 40 |
| Komsomolets, i., Sov. Un. | A4 | 128 |
| Komsomolsk [-na-Amure], Sov. Un. | D16 | 29 |
| Konahuanui, Puu, mtn., Hi., U.S. | g10 | 88 |
| Konar, stm., Asia | B7 | 36 |
| Konar-e Khāş, Afg. | D15 | 29 |
| Konawa, Ok., U.S. | C5 | 113 |
| Kondinskoye, Sov. Un. | B7 | 28 |
| Kondoa, Tan. | B6 | 48 |
| Kondopoga, Sov. Un. | F16 | 14 |
| Kondūz, Afg. | C5 | 36 |
| Konečnaya, Sov. Un. | C9 | 29 |
| Kong, i., Camb. | I5 | 35 |
| Kong, stm., Asia | C3 | 35 |
| Kongeå, stm., Den. | C2 | 15 |
| Kongju, S. Kor. | H3 | 33 |
| Kongolo, Zaire | C4 | 48 |
| Kongsberg, Nor. | H3 | 14 |
| Kongsmark, Den. | C2 | 15 |
| Kongsvinger, Nor. | G5 | 14 |
| Königsberg see Kaliningrad, Sov. Un. | D5 | 29 |
| Königsbrück, E. Ger. | B8 | 19 |
| Königslutter, W. Ger. | A5 | 19 |
| Königstein, E. Ger. | C9 | 19 |
| Königs Wusterhausen, E. Ger. | A8 | 19 |
| Konin, Pol. | B5 | 26 |
| Konispoli, Alb. | C3 | 40 |
| Konjic, Yugo. | D4 | 24 |
| Konkouré, stm., Gui. | D2 | 45 |
| Könnern, E. Ger. | B6 | 19 |
| Konolfingen, Switz. | C4 | 21 |
| Konomoc, Lake, res., Ct., U.S. | D7 | 84 |
| Konotop, Sov. Un. | F9 | 27 |
| Końskie, Pol. | C6 | 26 |
| Konstancin-Jeziorna, Pol. | m14 | 26 |
| Konstantinovka, Sov. Un. | q20 | 27 |
| Konstanz (Constance), W. Ger. | E4 | 18 |
| Kontagora, Nig. | D6 | 45 |
| Kontcha, Cam. | D2 | 46 |
| Kontich, Bel. | C4 | 17 |
| Kontiomäki, Fin. | E13 | 14 |
| Kon Tum, Viet. | C3 | 34 |
| Konya, Tur. | D9 | 40 |
| Konyang, S. Kor. | I3 | 33 |
| Konzhakovskiy Kamen, mtn., Sov. Un. | B1 | 103 |
| Koocanusa, Lake, res., N.A. | B1 | 103 |
| Koochiching, co., Mn., U.S. | B4 | 100 |
| Koolau Range, mts., Hi., U.S. | f10 | 88 |
| Koondrook, Austl. | G4 | 51 |
| Koontz Lake, In., U.S. | B5 | 91 |
| Koosharem, Ut., U.S. | E4 | 121 |
| Ko Vaya, Az., U.S. | E4 | 80 |
| Kootenai, Id., U.S. | A2 | 89 |
| Kootenai, co., Id., U.S. | B2 | 89 |
| Kootenay, stm., N.A. | E10 | 69 |
| Kootenay National Park, B.C. | D9 | 69 |
| Kópasker, Ice. | m24 | 14 |
| Kopervik, Nor. | H1 | 14 |
| Kopet Mountains, mts., Asia | B8 | 39 |
| Köping, Swe. | H6 | 14 |
| Köppány, stm., Hung. | B4 | 24 |
| Koppel, Pa., U.S. | E1 | 115 |
| Koprivnica, Yugo. | B3 | 24 |
| Kopychintsy, Sov. Un. | G6 | 27 |
| Korab, mtn., Eur. | E5 | 24 |
| Korahe, Eth. | D5 | 47 |
| Korarou, Lac, l., Mali | C4 | 45 |
| Korba, India | F3 | 37 |
| Korbach, W. Ger. | B3 | 19 |
| Korbu, mtn., Malay. | J4 | 35 |
| Korça, Alb. | B3 | 40 |
| Korčula, i., Yugo. | D3 | 24 |
| Kord Kūy, Iran | C7 | 39 |
| Korea, North, ctry., Asia | D10 | 31 |
| Korea, South, ctry., Asia | D10 | 31 |
| Korea Bay, b., Asia | D9 | 31 |
| Korea Strait, strt., Asia | E10 | 31 |
| Korets, Sov. Un. | F6 | 27 |
| Korhogo, I.C. | E3 | 45 |
| Kori Creek, stm., India | F2 | 37 |
| Koridhallós, Grc. | *D4 | 25 |
| Korini, Grc. | q9 | 25 |
| Kōriyama, Japan | H10 | 33 |
| Korkino, Sov. Un. | E21 | 8 |
| Korkuteli, Tur. | D8 | 40 |
| Korla, China | C2 | 31 |
| Körmend, Hung. | B3 | 24 |
| Kornat, i., Yugo. | D8 | 18 |
| Korneuburg, Aus. | D8 | 18 |
| Kornwestheim, W. Ger. | E4 | 19 |
| Koro, Mali | B4 | 45 |
| Koro, i., Fiji | H15 | 52 |
| Korogwe, Tan. | B6 | 48 |
| Koronis, Lake, l., Mn., U.S. | E4 | 100 |
| Koropión, Grc. | h11 | 25 |
| Koror, Palau | R17 | 52 |
| Koror, i., Palau | R17 | 52 |
| Korosten, Sov. Un. | F7 | 27 |
| Koro Toro, Chad | D3 | 46 |
| Korotoyak, Sov. Un. | F12 | 27 |
| Korovin Volcano, vol., Ak., U.S. | E5 | 79 |
| Korsakov, Sov. Un. | E17 | 29 |
| Korsør, Den. | C6 | 15 |
| Kortrijk (Courtrai), Bel. | B5 | 17 |
| Korucam, Cape, c., N. Cyp. | A7 | 38 |
| Korumburra, Austl. | I5 | 51 |
| Koryak Mountains, mts., Sov. Un. | C19 | 29 |
| Kos (Cos), i., Grc. | D6 | 40 |
| Kos, i., Grc. | D6 | 40 |
| Koschagyl, Sov. Un. | q20 | 27 |
| Kościan, Pol. | B4 | 26 |
| Kościerzyna, Pol. | A4 | 26 |
| Kosciusko, Ms., U.S. | B4 | 101 |
| Kosciusko, co., In., U.S. | B6 | 91 |
| Kosciusko, Mount, mtn., Austl. | G8 | 50 |
| Kösdağı, mtn., Tur. | *C14 | 40 |
| Koshigaya, Japan | *I9 | 33 |
| Koshiki Islands, is., Japan | K4 | 33 |
| Koshkonong, Lake, l., Wi., U.S. | F5 | 126 |
| Košice, Czech. | D6 | 26 |
| Košíře (part of Prague), Czech. | n17 | 26 |
| Koskaecodde Lake, l., Newf. | C18 | 72 |
| Koslan, Sov. Un. | B4 | 28 |
| Kosovo, N. Kor. | H8 | 33 |
| Kosovska Mitrovica, Yugo. | D5 | 24 |
| Kosrae, i., Micron. | Q21 | 52 |
| Kosse, Tx., U.S. | D4 | 120 |
| Kössol Passage, strt., Palau | R17 | 52 |
| Kossol Reef, rf., Palau | R17 | 52 |
| Kossuth, co., Ia., U.S. | A3 | 92 |
| Kostelec, Czech. | o18 | 26 |
| Kostroma, Sov. Un. | D7 | 29 |
| Kostrzyn, Pol. | B2 | 26 |
| Koszalin (Köslin), Pol. | A4 | 26 |
| Kőszeg, Hung. | B3 | 24 |
| Kota, India | H5 | 36 |
| Kota Baharu, Malay. | J7 | 35 |
| Kotabaru, Indon. | F5 | 34 |
| Kota Kinabalu, Malay. | D6 | 34 |
| Kotatengah, Indon. | L4 | 35 |
| Kotel, Bul. | H8 | 24 |
| Kotelnich, Sov. Un. | C3 | 33 |
| Kotelnikovo, Sov. Un. | H14 | 27 |
| Kotelny Island, i., Sov. Un. | B16 | 29 |
| Köthen, E. Ger. | C5 | 18 |
| Kotido, Ug. | A5 | 48 |
| Kotka, Fin. | G12 | 14 |
| Kotlas, Sov. Un. | C7 | 29 |
| Kotlik, Ak., U.S. | C7 | 79 |
| Kotonkoro, Nig. | D6 | 45 |
| Kotor, Yugo. | D4 | 24 |
| Kotor Bay, b., Yugo. | D4 | 24 |
| Kotor Varoš, Yugo. | C3 | 24 |
| Kotovsk, Sov. Un. | B9 | 24 |
| Kotovsk, Sov. Un. | E13 | 27 |
| Kotovsk, Sov. Un. | H7 | 27 |
| Kotri, Pak. | E2 | 37 |
| Kottagūdem, India | I8 | 37 |
| Kotte, Sri L. | *G6 | 36 |
| Kotto, stm., Cen. Afr. Rep. | D4 | 46 |
| Kotzebue, Ak., U.S. | B7 | 79 |
| Kotzebue Sound, strt., Ak., U.S. | B7 | 79 |
| Kötzting, W. Ger. | F9 | 19 |
| Kouandé, Benin | D5 | 45 |
| Kouango, Cen. Afr. Rep. | D3 | 46 |
| Kouchibouguacis, stm., N.B. | C4 | 71 |
| Kouchibouguac National Park, N.B. | C5 | 71 |
| Koudougou, Burkina | D4 | 45 |
| Koula-Moutou, Gabon | F2 | 46 |
| Koulikoro, Mali | D3 | 45 |
| Koumra, Chad | D3 | 46 |
| Koungheul, Sen. | D2 | 45 |
| Kounradskiy, Sov. Un. | D9 | 28 |
| Kountze, Tx., U.S. | D5 | 120 |
| Koupéla, Burkina | D4 | 45 |
| Kouri Island, i., Japan | A4 | 59 |
| Kourou, Fr. Gu. | D3 | 45 |
| Koussi, Emi, mtn., Chad | D3 | 46 |
| Koutiala, Mali | D3 | 45 |
| Kouts, In., U.S. | B3 | 91 |
| Kouvola, Fin. | G12 | 14 |
| Kovel, Sov. Un. | F5 | 27 |
| Kovrov, Sov. Un. | G7 | 31 |
| Köwloon, H.K. | D7 | 25 |
| Köyceğiz, Tur. | D7 | 25 |
| Koyuk, Ak., U.S. | C8 | 79 |
| Koyukuk, Ak., U.S. | C8 | 79 |
| Koyukuk, stm., Ak., U.S. | B8 | 79 |
| Kozan, Tur. | D10 | 40 |
| Kozáni, Grc. | B3 | 25 |
| Kozelsk, Sov. Un. | D10 | 27 |
| Koziegłowy, Pol. | C5 | 26 |
| Kozienice, Pol. | C6 | 26 |
| Koźle, Pol. | C5 | 26 |
| Kozlovsky, Bul. | D6 | 24 |
| Kozuchów, Pol. | B3 | 26 |
| Közu Island, i., Japan | I9 | 33 |
| Kpandu, Ghana | E5 | 45 |
| Kra, Isthmus of, Asia | H3 | 35 |
| Krabi, Thai. | I3 | 35 |
| Kracheh, Camb. | C3 | 35 |
| Kraemer, La., U.S. | k10 | 95 |
| Kragerø, Nor. | H3 | 14 |
| Kragujevac, Yugo. | C5 | 24 |
| Kraków, Pol. | C6 | 26 |
| Krakower, l., E. Ger. | E6 | 15 |
| Kraljevo, Yugo. | D5 | 24 |
| Královské Vinohrady (part of Prague), Czech. | n17 | 26 |
| Kralupy [nad Vltavou], Czech. | n17 | 26 |
| Kráľov Dvůr, Czech. | o17 | 26 |
| Kramatorsk, Sov. Un. | G11 | 27 |
| Kramer, In., U.S. | *F2 | 91 |
| Kramer, N.D., U.S. | A5 | 111 |
| Kranidhion, Grc. | q9 | 25 |
| Kranj, Yugo. | B2 | 24 |
| Kranzburg, S.D., U.S. | C9 | 118 |
| Kraslice, Czech. | C2 | 26 |
| Krasnaya Polyana, Sov. Un. | q27 | 27 |
| Kraśnik, Pol. | C7 | 26 |
| Krasnoarmeysk, Sov. Un. | B3 | 24 |
| Krasnoarmeysk, Sov. Un. | D8 | 18 |
| Krasnodar, Sov. Un. | q22 | 27 |
| Krasnodon, Sov. Un. | H12 | 27 |
| Krasnogorsk, Sov. Un. | G10 | 27 |
| Krasnogvardeyskoye, Sov. Un. | H13 | 27 |
| Krasnokamsk, Sov. Un. | D9 | 28 |
| Krasnoselkup, Sov. Un. | B25 | 8 |
| Krasnoselye, Sov. Un. | G9 | 27 |
| Krasnoslobodsk, Sov. Un. | D14 | 27 |
| Krasnoturinsk, Sov. Un. | B2 | 28 |
| Krasnoufimsk, Sov. Un. | B5 | 28 |
| Krasnouralsk, Sov. Un. | D21 | 8 |
| Krasnovishersk, Sov. Un. | A5 | 28 |
| Krasnoyarsk, Sov. Un. | D12 | 29 |
| Krasnoye Selo, Sov. Un. | s31 | 14 |
| Krasnozavodsk, Sov. Un. | C7 | 28 |
| Krasnoznamenskiy, Sov. Un. | C7 | 28 |
| Krasnystaw, Pol. | C7 | 26 |
| Krasny Kholm, Sov. Un. | B11 | 27 |
| Krasny Kut, Sov. Un. | q21 | 27 |
| Krasny Liman, Sov. Un. | q22 | 27 |
| Krasny Luch, Sov. Un. | H13 | 27 |
| Krasny Sulin, Sov. Un. | H13 | 27 |
| Krasny Yar, Sov. Un. | F15 | 27 |
| Kratovo, Yugo. | F6 | 24 |
| Kraul Mountains, mts., Ant. | B11 | 7 |
| Krawang, Indon. | *G3 | 34 |
| Krebs, Ok., U.S. | C6 | 113 |
| Krefeld, W. Ger. | C3 | 18 |
| Kremenchug Reservoir, res., Sov. Un. | G9 | 27 |
| Kremenets, Sov. Un. | F5 | 27 |
| Kremennaya, Sov. Un. | q25 | 27 |
| Kremikovtsi, Bul. | p21 | 27 |
| Kremlin, Mt., U.S. | B6 | 103 |
| Kremlin, Ok., U.S. | A4 | 113 |
| Kremmling, Co., U.S. | A4 | 83 |
| Krems [am der Donau], Aus. | D7 | 18 |
| Kremsmünster, Aus. | E10 | 15 |
| Kress, Tx., U.S. | B2 | 120 |
| Kreuzlingen, Switz. | B6 | 20 |
| Kreuztal, W. Ger. | B3 | 19 |
| Kriens, Switz. | C4 | 21 |
| Krilon, Cape, c., Sov. Un. | D11 | 33 |
| Krishna, stm., India | E6 | 36 |
| Krishnagiri, India | F6 | 36 |
| Krishnanagar, India | F12 | 37 |
| Kristiansand, Nor. | H2 | 14 |
| Kristianstad, co., Swe. | B8 | 15 |
| Kristiansund, Nor. | I6 | 14 |
| Kristinehamn, Swe. | B6 | 15 |
| Kristinestad, Fin. | F9 | 14 |
| Kriva Palanka, Yugo. | F6 | 24 |
| Krivoy Rog, Sov. Un. | E7 | 29 |
| Krk, i., Yugo. | C2 | 24 |
| Krka, stm., Yugo. | D3 | 24 |

| Name | Map Ref. | Page |
|---|---|---|
| Krnov, Czech. | C4 | 26 |
| Krokeai, Grc. | D4 | 25 |
| Krokstadelva, Nor. | p28 | 14 |
| Krolevets, Sov. Un. | F9 | 27 |
| Kroměříž, Czech. | D4 | 26 |
| Kromy, Sov. Un. | E10 | 27 |
| Kronach, W. Ger. | C6 | 19 |
| Kronau, Sask. | G3 | 75 |
| Kronoberg, co., Swe. | B8 | 15 |
| Kronshtadt, Sov. Un. | B7 | 27 |
| Kroonstad, S. Afr. | C4 | 49 |
| Kröpelin, E. Ger. | D5 | 15 |
| Kropotkin, Sov. Un. | I13 | 27 |
| Krosno, Pol. | D6 | 26 |
| Krosno Odrzańskie, Pol. | B3 | 26 |
| Krotoszyn, Pol. | C4 | 26 |
| Krotz Springs, La., U.S. | D4 | 95 |
| Krško, Yugo. | C2 | 24 |
| Kruger National Park, S. Afr. | B5 | 49 |
| Krugersdorp, S. Afr. | C4 | 49 |
| Kruja, Alb. | B2 | 25 |
| Krumbach, W. Ger. | A6 | 20 |
| Krumovgrad, Bul. | E7 | 24 |
| Kruševac, Yugo. | D5 | 24 |
| Kruševo, Yugo. | E5 | 24 |
| Kruszwica, Pol. | B5 | 26 |
| Kruzof Island, i., Ak., U.S. | m21 | 79 |
| Krydor, Sask. | E2 | 75 |
| Krymsk, Sov. Un. | I11 | 27 |
| Krynica, Pol. | D6 | 26 |
| Krynki, Pol. | B7 | 26 |
| Ksar el Kebir, Mor. | B3 | 44 |
| Ksar es Souk, Mor. | C4 | 44 |
| Kuala Kangsar, Malay. | J4 | 35 |
| Kualakurun, Indon. | F4 | 34 |
| Kuala Lipis, Malay. | E2 | 34 |
| Kuala Lumpur, Malay. | E2 | 34 |
| Kualapuu, Hi., U.S. | B4 | 88 |
| Kuala Terengganu, Malay. | D2 | 34 |
| Kuandang, Indon. | E6 | 34 |
| Kuandian, China | D11 | 32 |
| Kuantan, Malay. | E2 | 34 |
| Kuba, Sov. Un. | I13 | 27 |
| Kuban, stm., Sov. Un. | I13 | 27 |
| Kubitzer Bodden, b., E. Ger. | D7 | 15 |
| Kubokawa, Japan | J6 | 33 |
| Kuching, Malay. | E4 | 34 |
| Kuchinoerabu Island, i., Japan | K5 | 33 |
| Kuchino Island, i., Japan | L4 | 33 |
| Kuçovë see Stalin, Alb. | B2 | 25 |
| Küçükmenderes, stm., Tur. | C6 | 25 |
| Kudaka Island, i., Japan | O5 | 52 |
| Kudat, Malay. | D5 | 34 |
| Kudirkos Naumiestis, Sov. Un. | A7 | 26 |
| Kudus, Indon. | G4 | 34 |
| Kudymkar, Sov. Un. | B4 | 28 |
| Kuee Ruins, hist., Hi., U.S. | D6 | 88 |
| Kufstein, Aus. | E6 | 18 |
| Kuhaylī, Sud. | B3 | 47 |
| Kuhësi, Alb. | A3 | 25 |
| Kūh Lab, Ra's-e, c., Iran | I10 | 39 |
| Kūhpāyeh, Iran | E6 | 39 |
| Kuito, Ang. | D2 | 48 |
| Kiui Island, i., Ak., U.S. | m23 | 79 |
| Kuji, Japan | F10 | 33 |
| Kujū, Mount, mtn., Japan | J5 | 33 |
| Kukaiau, Hi., U.S. | C6 | 88 |
| Kukawa, Nig. | D7 | 45 |
| Kuki, Japan | m18 | 33 |
| Kukuihaele, Hi., U.S. | C6 | 88 |
| Kukuiula, Hi., U.S. | B2 | 88 |
| Kuku Point, c., Wake I. | A1 | 52 |
| Kula, Bul. | D6 | 24 |
| Kula, Tur. | C7 | 25 |
| Kula, Hi., U.S. | C5 | 88 |
| Kula, Yugo. | C4 | 24 |
| Kula Kangri, mtn., Bhu. | C9 | 36 |
| Kulebaki, Sov. Un. | D14 | 27 |
| Kulim, Malay. | J4 | 35 |
| Kulltorp, Swe. | A7 | 15 |
| Kulm, N.D., U.S. | C7 | 111 |
| Kulmbach, W. Ger. | C5 | 18 |
| Kulpmont, Pa., U.S. | E9 | 115 |
| Kulunda, Sov. Un. | C9 | 28 |
| Kulunda, Lake, l., Sov. Un. | C9 | 28 |
| Kulwin, Austl. | G4 | 51 |
| Kulyab, Sov. Un. | H22 | 8 |
| Küm, stm., S. Kor. | H3 | 33 |
| Kuma, stm., Sov. Un. | F18 | 8 |
| Kumagaya, Japan | m18 | 33 |
| Kumai, Indon. | F4 | 34 |
| Kumamoto, Japan | E11 | 31 |
| Kumano Bay, b., Japan | J8 | 33 |
| Kumanovo, Yugo. | D5 | 24 |
| Kumasi, Ghana | E4 | 45 |
| Kumba, Cam. | E1 | 46 |
| Kumba-konam, India | F6 | 36 |
| Kumbo, Cam. | D2 | 46 |
| Kümhwa, S. Kor. | G3 | 33 |
| Kumi, Ug. | A5 | 48 |
| Kumihama, Japan | n14 | 33 |
| Kumla, Swe. | H6 | 14 |
| Kummerower Lake, l., E. Ger. | E6 | 15 |
| Kumo, Nig. | E7 | 45 |
| Kumukahi, Cape, c., Hi., U.S. | D7 | 88 |
| Kuna, Id., U.S. | F2 | 89 |
| Kundar, stm., Asia | B2 | 37 |
| Kundiawa, Pap. N. Gui. | k11 | 50 |
| Kuneitra (Al Qunaytirah), Isr. Occ. | A7 | 41 |
| Kunggyü Lake, l., China | B9 | 37 |
| Kunghit Island, i., B.C. | C2 | 69 |
| Kungrad, Sov. Un. | E5 | 28 |
| Kungsbacka, Swe. | H5 | 14 |
| Kungsör, Swe. | t34 | 14 |
| Kungu, Zaire | A2 | 48 |
| Kungur, Sov. Un. | B5 | 28 |
| Kunia, Hi., U.S. | g9 | 88 |
| Kunigami, Japan | N6 | 52 |
| Kunimi, Mount, mtn., Japan | J5 | 33 |
| Kunkle, Pa., U.S. | m17 | 115 |
| Kunlun Shan, mts., China | F11 | 30 |
| Kunming, China | F5 | 31 |
| Kunsan, S. Kor. | D10 | 31 |
| Kunszentmárton, Hung. | B5 | 24 |
| Künzelsau, W. Ger. | D13 | 14 |
| Kuolayarvi, Sov. Un. | D13 | 14 |
| Kuop, atoll, Micron. | Q18 | 52 |
| Kuopio, Fin. | F12 | 14 |
| Kupa, stm., Yugo. | C2 | 24 |
| Kupang, Indon. | G6 | 34 |
| Kupino, Sov. Un. | C9 | 28 |
| Kupreanof, Ak., U.S. | m23 | 79 |
| Kupreanof Island, i., Ak., U.S. | m23 | 79 |
| Kupyansk, Sov. Un. | G11 | 27 |
| Kur, stm., Sov. Un. | B7 | 33 |
| Kura, stm., Asia | E3 | 28 |
| Kurakhovo, Sov. Un. | r20 | 27 |
| Kurashiki, Japan | I6 | 33 |
| Kuray, Sov. Un. | E26 | 8 |
| Kuraymah, Sud. | B3 | 47 |
| Kurayyimah, Jord. | f13 | 41 |
| Kurdistan, hist. reg., Asia | B4 | 38 |
| Kurdufān al Janūbīyah (Southern Kurdufan), prov., Sud. | C2 | 47 |
| Kurdufān ash Shamālīyah (Northern Kurdufan), prov., Sud. | C2 | 47 |
| Kürdzhali, Bul. | E7 | 24 |
| Kure, Japan | E11 | 31 |
| Kure Island, i., Hi., U.S. | k12 | 88 |
| Kuressaare, Sov. Un. | B4 | 27 |
| Kureyka, stm., Sov. Un. | C12 | 29 |
| Kurgaldzhinskiy, Sov. Un. | C8 | 28 |
| Kurgan, Sov. Un. | D9 | 29 |
| Kurganinsk, Sov. Un. | G17 | 8 |
| Kurgan-Tyube, Sov. Un. | H22 | 8 |
| Kuria Muria Islands (Khūryān Mūryān), is., Oman | D5 | 38 |
| Kurīgrām, Bngl. | E12 | 37 |
| Kuril Islands, is., Sov. Un. | E17 | 29 |
| Kuril Strait, strt., Sov. Un. | D18 | 29 |
| Kurmuk, Sud. | C3 | 47 |
| Kurnool, India | E6 | 36 |
| Kuro Island, i., Japan | K4 | 33 |
| Kuroki, Sask. | F4 | 75 |
| Kurovskoye, Sov. Un. | n18 | 27 |
| Kurri Kurri, Austl. | F9 | 50 |
| Kursk, Sov. Un. | D6 | 29 |
| Kuršumlija, Yugo. | D5 | 24 |
| Kurthwood, La., U.S. | C2 | 95 |
| Kürtī, Sud. | B3 | 47 |
| Kurtistown, Hi., U.S. | D6 | 88 |
| Kurtz, In., U.S. | G5 | 91 |
| Kuruman, S. Afr. | C3 | 49 |
| Kurume, Japan | E11 | 31 |
| Kurunegala, Sri L. | G7 | 36 |
| Kuşadası, Tur. | D6 | 25 |
| Kusakaki Island, i., Japan | K4 | 33 |
| Kusatsu, Japan | n14 | 33 |
| Kusel, W. Ger. | D2 | 19 |
| Kushchevskaya, Sov. Un. | H12 | 27 |
| Kushimoto, Japan | J7 | 33 |
| Kushiro, Japan | C13 | 31 |
| Kushmurun, Sov. Un. | C6 | 28 |
| Kushmurun, Lake, l., Sov. Un. | C6 | 28 |
| Kuskokwim, stm., Ak., U.S. | C8 | 79 |
| Kuskokwim Bay, b., Ak., U.S. | D7 | 79 |
| Kuskokwim Mountains, mts., Ak., U.S. | C8 | 79 |
| Kuş Lake, l., Tur. | B6 | 25 |
| Küsnacht [am Rigi], Switz. | B5 | 21 |
| Küssnacht, Switz. | B6 | 21 |
| Küssnacht [am Rigi], Switz. | B5 | 21 |
| Kustanay, Sov. Un. | D9 | 29 |
| Küsten Canal, W. Ger. | B7 | 17 |
| Küstī, Sud. | C3 | 47 |
| Kuta, Alb. | B2 | 25 |
| Kutacane, Indon. | K2 | 35 |
| Kütahya, Tur. | C7 | 40 |
| Kutaisi, Sov. Un. | G17 | 8 |
| Kutawagan Lake, l., Sask. | F3 | 75 |
| Kūt Barrage, Iraq | E2 | 39 |
| Kutch, Gulf of see Kachchh, Gulf of, b., India | D4 | 36 |
| Kutch, Rann of, pl., Asia | D4 | 36 |
| Kutina, Yugo. | C3 | 24 |
| Kutná Hora, Czech. | D3 | 26 |
| Kutno, Pol. | B5 | 26 |
| Kuttawa, Ky., U.S. | e9 | 94 |
| Kutum, Zaire | B2 | 48 |
| Kutum, Sud. | C1 | 47 |
| Kuturaja see Banda Aceh, Indon. | k11 | 34 |
| Kuty, Sov. Un. | A7 | 24 |
| Kutztown, Pa., U.S. | E10 | 115 |
| Kuujjuaq, Que. | g13 | 74 |
| Kuūm-ni, N. Kor. | G2 | 33 |
| Kuusamo, Fin. | E13 | 14 |
| Kuvandyk, Sov. Un. | E20 | 8 |
| Kuvango (Capelongo), Ang. | D2 | 48 |
| Kuwait (Al Kuwayt), Kuw. | C4 | 38 |
| Kuwait, ctry., Asia | C4 | 38 |
| Kuwait Bay, b., Kuw. | G4 | 39 |
| Kuwana, Japan | I8 | 33 |
| Kuybyshev, Sov. Un. | B9 | 28 |
| Kuybyshev, Sov. Un. | D8 | 29 |
| Kuybyshevo, Sov. Un. | H12 | 27 |
| Kuybyshev Reservoir, res., Sov. Un. | D7 | 29 |
| Küysanjaq, Iraq | D15 | 40 |
| Kuyto, l., Sov. Un. | E14 | 14 |
| Kuznetsk, Sov. Un. | E16 | 27 |
| Kuznetsk Basin, Sov. Un. | D25 | 8 |
| Kuznetsovo, Sov. Un. | C10 | 33 |
| Kuzomen, Sov. Un. | D17 | 14 |
| Kvarner, b., Yugo. | C2 | 24 |
| Kvismare Kanal, Swe. | t33 | 14 |
| Kvitøya, i., Nor. | A11 | 128 |
| Kwajalein, atoll, Marsh Is. | F10 | 6 |
| Kwajalein Island, i., Marsh Is. | S17 | 52 |
| Kwakoegron, Sur. | A3 | 59 |
| Kwale, Kenya | C7 | 48 |
| Kwa Mashu, S. Afr. | *C5 | 49 |
| Kwamouth, Zaire | B2 | 48 |
| Kwa Mtoro, Tan. | C6 | 48 |
| Kwatisore, Indon. | F9 | 34 |
| Kwekwe, Zimb. | A4 | 49 |
| Kwenge, stm., Afr. | C2 | 48 |
| Kwethluk, Ak., U.S. | C7 | 79 |
| Kwidzyn, Pol. | B5 | 26 |
| Kwigillingok, Ak., U.S. | D7 | 79 |
| Kwilu, stm., Afr. | B2 | 48 |
| Kwinana, Austl. | F2 | 50 |
| Kyabé, Chad | D3* | 46 |
| Kyabram, Austl. | H5 | 51 |
| Kyaikto, Burma | E10 | 36 |
| Kyakhta, Sov. Un. | D13 | 29 |
| Kyaukpadaung, Burma | B1 | 35 |
| Kyaukpyu, Burma | E9 | 36 |
| Kyaukse, Burma | D10 | 36 |
| Kybartai, Sov. Un. | A7 | 26 |
| Kyje, Czech. | n18 | 26 |
| Kyle, Sask. | G1 | 75 |
| Kyle, S.D., U.S. | D3 | 118 |
| Kyle, Tx., U.S. | E4 | 120 |
| Kyles Ford, Tn., U.S. | C10 | 119 |
| Kylestrome, Scot., U.K. | C8 | 13 |
| Kyllburg, W. Ger. | D6 | 17 |
| Kyll, stm., W. Ger. | E6 | 17 |
| Kyōga, Cape, c., Japan | I7 | 33 |
| Kyōga, Lake, l., Ug. | A5 | 48 |
| Kyōmipo see Songnim, N. Kor. | G2 | 33 |
| Kyonggi Bay, b., Asia | H2 | 33 |
| Kyŏngju, S. Kor. | D10 | 31 |
| Kyŏngsŏng, N. Kor. | F4 | 33 |
| Kyōto, Japan | D12 | 31 |
| Kyritz, E. Ger. | B6 | 18 |
| Kyrkjebö, Nor. | G1 | 14 |
| Kyrock, Ky., U.S. | C3 | 94 |
| Kyshtovka, Sov. Un. | D24 | 8 |
| Kyshtym, Sov. Un. | B6 | 28 |
| Kyūquot, B.C. | D4 | 69 |
| Kyuquot Island, i., B.C. | E4 | 69 |
| Kyuquot Sound, strt., B.C. | E4 | 69 |
| Kyūroku Island, i., Japan | F9 | 33 |
| Kyūshū, i., Japan | E11 | 31 |
| Kyustendil, Bul. | D6 | 24 |
| Kyzyl, Sov. Un. | D12 | 29 |
| Kyzyl-Kiya, Sov. Un. | E8 | 28 |
| Kyzyl-Kum, des., Sov. Un. | E9 | 29 |
| Kyzyltas Mountains, mts., Sov. Un. | D9 | 28 |
| Kzyl-Orda, Sov. Un. | E9 | 29 |

### L

| Laa [an der Thaya], Aus. | D8 | 18 |
|---|---|---|
| Laage, E. Ger. | E6 | 15 |
| La Almunia de Doña Godina, Spain | B5 | 22 |
| La Araucanía, prov., Chile | B2 | 54 |
| Laas Caanood, Som. | D6 | 47 |
| La Asunción, Ven. | A5 | 60 |
| Laau Point, c., Hi., U.S. | B4 | 88 |
| Labadie, Mo., U.S. | C7 | 102 |
| Labadieville, La., U.S. | E5 | 95 |
| La Banda, Arg. | E3 | 55 |
| La Barca, Mex. | C4 | 63 |
| La Barge, Wy., U.S. | D2 | 127 |
| La Barge Creek, stm., Wy., U.S. | D2 | 127 |
| Labasa, Fiji | H15 | 52 |
| La Baule-Escoublac, Fr. | D2 | 16 |
| Labé, Gui. | D2 | 45 |
| Labe (Elbe), stm., Eur. | C7 | 18 |
| Labelle, Que. | C3 | 74 |
| La Belle, Fl., U.S. | F5 | 86 |
| La Belle, Mo., U.S. | A6 | 102 |
| Labelle, co., Que. | C2 | 74 |
| La Belle-Île, i., Fr. | D2 | 16 |
| Laberge, Lake, l., Yukon | D5 | 66 |
| Labette, Ks., U.S. | E8 | 93 |
| Labette, co., Ks., U.S. | E8 | 93 |
| Labette Creek, stm., Ks., U.S. | E8 | 93 |
| Labin, Yugo. | C2 | 24 |
| La Bisbal, Spain | B7 | 22 |
| Labo, Phil. | o14 | 34 |
| Labo, Mount, mtn., Phil. | p14 | 34 |
| La Boca, Pan. | m11 | 62 |
| Laboe, W. Ger. | D4 | 15 |
| La Bolt, S.D., U.S. | *B9 | 118 |
| Labouheyre, Fr. | E3 | 16 |
| Laboulaye, Arg. | A4 | 54 |
| Labrador, reg., Newf. | g9 | 72 |
| Labrador City, Newf. | h8 | 72 |
| Labrador Sea N.A. | g10 | 72 |
| Lábrea, Braz. | D2 | 59 |
| La Broquerie, Man. | E3 | 70 |
| Labuan Island, i., Malay. | D5 | 34 |
| Labuha, Indon. | F7 | 34 |
| Labuhanbilik, Indon. | K4 | 35 |
| Labuk Bay, b., Malay. | D5 | 34 |
| Lac-à-Beauce, Que. | B5 | 74 |
| Lacadena, Sask. | G1 | 75 |
| La Calera, Chile | A2 | 54 |
| Lacamp, La., U.S. | C3 | 95 |
| La Canada Flintridge, Ca., U.S. | m12 | 82 |
| La Capelle [-en-Thiérache], Fr. | B3 | 17 |
| La Carlota, Arg. | A4 | 54 |
| La Carolina, Spain | C4 | 22 |
| Lac-aux-Brochets, Que. | B5 | 74 |
| Lac-aux-Sables, Que. | C5 | 74 |
| Lac-Baker, N.B. | B1 | 71 |
| Lac-Beauport, Que. | n17 | 74 |
| Lac-Bouchette, Que. | A5 | 74 |
| Lac-Brome, Que. | D5 | 74 |
| Laccadive, Minicoy and Amīndīvi Islands see Lakshadweep, ter., India | *F5 | 36 |
| Laccadive Islands see Lakshadweep, is., India | *F5 | 36 |
| Lac-Carré, Que. | C3 | 74 |
| Lac-Chat, Que. | A5 | 74 |
| Lac Courte Oreilles Indian Reservation, Wi., U.S. | C2 | 126 |
| Lac-des-Écorces, Que. | C2 | 74 |
| Lac-des-Seize-Îles, Que. | D3 | 74 |
| Lac du Bonnet, Man. | D3 | 70 |
| Lac du Flambeau, Wi., U.S. | C4 | 126 |
| Lac du Flambeau Indian Reservation, Wi., U.S. | C3 | 126 |
| Lac-Édouard, Que. | B5 | 74 |
| La Ceiba, Hond. | D7 | 63 |
| La Ceiba, Ven. | B3 | 60 |
| La Center, Ky., U.S. | e9 | 94 |
| Lac-Etchemin, Que. | C7 | 74 |
| Laceyville, Pa., U.S. | C9 | 115 |
| Lac-Frontière, Que. | C7 | 74 |
| Lachachi, Punta c., Peru | D2 | 58 |
| Lachen, Switz. | B6 | 21 |
| Lachine, Que. | D4 | 74 |
| Lachine, Mi., U.S. | C7 | 99 |
| Lachlan, stm., Austl. | F8 | 50 |
| La Chorrera, Col. | D3 | 60 |
| La Chorrera, Pan. | F8 | 62 |
| Lachute, Que. | D3 | 74 |
| La Cienega, N.M., U.S. | h8 | 108 |
| La Ciotat, Fr. | F6 | 16 |
| La Cisa Pass, Italy | E5 | 23 |
| Lackawanna, N.Y., U.S. | C2 | 109 |
| Lackawanna, co., Pa., U.S. | D10 | 115 |
| Lackawaxen, Pa., U.S. | D12 | 115 |
| Lackland Air Force Base, mil., Tx., U.S. | k7 | 120 |
| Lac La Belle, Mi., U.S. | A2 | 99 |
| Lac la Biche, Alta. | B5 | 68 |
| Lac la Hache, B.C. | D7 | 69 |
| Lac la Ronge Provincial Park, Sask. | B3 | 75 |
| Laclede, Id., U.S. | A2 | 89 |
| La Clede, Il., U.S. | E5 | 90 |
| Laclede, Mo., U.S. | B4 | 102 |
| Laclede, co., Mo., U.S. | D5 | 102 |
| Lagny, Fr. | g9 | 16 |
| Lac-Mégantic, Que. | D7 | 74 |
| La Cocha, Arg. | E2 | 55 |
| La Colorada, Mex. | B2 | 63 |
| Lacomb, Or., U.S. | C4 | 114 |
| Lacombe, Alta. | C4 | 68 |
| Lacombe, La., U.S. | D6 | 95 |
| Lacombe Bayou, stm., La., U.S. | | | |
| La Goulette, Tun. | *B7 | 44 |
| Lago Viedma, Arg. | D2 | 54 |
| Lacon, Il., U.S. | B4 | 90 |
| Lacona, Ia., U.S. | C4 | 92 |
| Lacona, N.Y., U.S. | B4 | 109 |
| La Conception, Que. | C3 | 74 |
| La Concepción, Pan. | F6 | 62 |
| Laconia, In., U.S. | H5 | 91 |
| Laconia, N.H., U.S. | C4 | 106 |
| Laconia, Gulf of, b., Grc. | D4 | 25 |
| La Conner, Wa., U.S. | A3 | 124 |
| Lacoochee, Fl., U.S. | D4 | 86 |
| La Coruña, Spain | A1 | 22 |
| La Courneuve, Fr. | g10 | 16 |
| Lacq, Fr. | F3 | 16 |
| Lac qui Parle, co., Mn., U.S. | F2 | 100 |
| Lac qui Parle, stm., Mn., U.S. | F2 | 100 |
| Lac qui Parle, West Branch, stm., Mn., U.S. | F2 | 100 |
| La Creek Lake, l., S.D., U.S. | D4 | 118 |
| La Crescent, Mn., U.S. | G7 | 100 |
| La Crescenta, Ca., U.S. | *m12 | 82 |
| La Crete, Alta. | f7 | 68 |
| La Crosse, Fl., U.S. | C4 | 86 |
| La Crosse, Ar., U.S. | A4 | 81 |
| La Crosse, In., U.S. | B4 | 91 |
| La Crosse, Ks., U.S. | D4 | 93 |
| La Crosse, Va., U.S. | D4 | 123 |
| La Crosse, Wi., U.S. | C8 | 124 |
| La Crosse, co., Wi., U.S. | E2 | 126 |
| La Crosse, stm., Wi., U.S. | E2 | 126 |
| La Cruz, Col. | C2 | 60 |
| La Cruz, C.R. | E5 | 62 |
| La Cruz, Mex. | C3 | 63 |
| La Cruz [de Río Grande], Nic. | D5 | 62 |
| Lac-Saguay, Que. | C2 | 74 |
| Labelle, Que. | C3 | 74 |
| Lac-Saint-Jean-Est, co., Que. | A6 | 74 |
| Lac-Saint-Jean-Ouest, co., Que. | | | |
| Lac-Vert, Sask. | E3 | 75 |
| La Cygne, Ks., U.S. | D9 | 93 |
| Ladário, Braz. | B1 | 56 |
| Ladd, Il., U.S. | B4 | 90 |
| Ladder Creek, stm., Ks., U.S. | D2 | 93 |
| Laddonia, Mo., U.S. | B6 | 102 |
| Ladelle, Ar., U.S. | D4 | 81 |
| Ladera Heights, Ca., U.S. | *m12 | 82 |
| Ladies Island, i., S.C., U.S. | G6 | 117 |
| Ladispoli, Italy | h8 | 23 |
| Ladner, S.D., U.S. | B2 | 118 |
| Lādnūn, India | D5 | 37 |
| Ladoga, In., U.S. | E4 | 91 |
| Ladonia, Tx., U.S. | C5 | 120 |
| Ladora, Ia., U.S. | C5 | 92 |
| La Dorada, Col. | B3 | 60 |
| Ladson, S.C., U.S. | F7 | 117 |
| Ladue, Mo., U.S. | *C7 | 102 |
| Ladue, Mo., U.S. | f13 | 102 |
| Ladybank, Scot., U.K. | E5 | 13 |
| Ladybrand, S. Afr. | C4 | 49 |
| Lady Lake, Fl., U.S. | D5 | 86 |
| Lady Laurier, Mount, mtn., B.C. | A6 | 69 |
| Ladysmith, B.C. | E6 | 69 |
| Ladysmith, S. Afr. | C4 | 49 |
| Ladysmith, Wi., U.S. | C2 | 126 |
| Lae, Pap. N. Gui. | k12 | 50 |
| Laichow Bay see Laizhou Wan, b., China | D8 | 31 |
| La Esmeralda, Ven. | C4 | 60 |
| Læsø, i., Den. | A4 | 15 |
| La Esperanza, Cuba | C2 | 64 |
| La Esperanza, Hond. | C3 | 62 |
| La Estrada, Spain | A1 | 22 |
| La Estrella, Bol. | C3 | 57 |
| La Farge, Wi., U.S. | E3 | 126 |
| LaFargeville, N.Y., U.S. | A5 | 109 |
| Lafayette, Al., U.S. | C4 | 78 |
| Lafayette, Ca., U.S. | *h8 | 82 |
| Lafayette, Ga., U.S. | B1 | 87 |
| La Fayette, Il., U.S. | B4 | 90 |
| La Fayette, Ky., U.S. | D2 | 94 |
| Lafayette, Mn., U.S. | F4 | 100 |
| Lafayette, N.J., U.S. | A3 | 107 |
| La Fayette, N.Y., U.S. | C4 | 109 |
| Lafayette, N.C., U.S. | B4 | 110 |
| Lafayette, Oh., U.S. | B2 | 112 |
| Lafayette, R.I., U.S. | E4 | 116 |
| Lafayette, Tn., U.S. | A5 | 119 |
| Lafayette, co., Ar., U.S. | D2 | 81 |
| Lafayette, co., Fl., U.S. | C3 | 86 |
| Lafayette, co., La., U.S. | D3 | 95 |
| Lafayette, co., Ms., U.S. | A4 | 101 |
| Lafayette, co., Mo., U.S. | B4 | 102 |
| Lafayette, co., Wi., U.S. | F3 | 126 |
| Lafayette, Mount, mtn., N.H., U.S. | B3 | 106 |
| Lafayette Southwest, La., U.S. | *D3 | 95 |
| Lafe, Ar., U.S. | A5 | 81 |
| La Fère, Fr. | B5 | 16 |
| La Feria, Tx., U.S. | F4 | 120 |
| La Ferté-Bernard, Fr. | C4 | 16 |
| La Ferté-Macé, Fr. | D6 | 16 |
| La Ferté-sous-Jouarre, Fr. | C5 | 16 |
| Lafferty, Oh., U.S. | B4 | 112 |
| Lafia, Nig. | E6 | 45 |
| Lafiagi, Nig. | E6 | 45 |
| Lafitte, La., U.S. | k11 | 95 |
| Laflèche, Sask. | H2 | 75 |
| La Flèche, Fr. | D6 | 16 |
| La Follette, Tn., U.S. | C9 | 119 |
| La Fontaine, In., U.S. | C6 | 91 |
| Lafontaine, Ks., U.S. | E8 | 93 |
| Lafourche, co., La., U.S. | E5 | 95 |
| Lafourche, Bayou, stm., La., U.S. | E5 | 95 |
| La France, S.C., U.S. | B2 | 117 |
| La Galeria, stm., Italy | h8 | 23 |
| La Galite, i., Tun. | A7 | 44 |
| Lagan, stm., Swe. | I5 | 14 |
| Lagan, Sov. Un. | G3 | 14 |
| Lågen, stm., Nor. | G3 | 14 |
| Laghouat, Alg. | B6 | 44 |
| La Gloria, Col. | B3 | 60 |
| Lagny, Fr. | g9 | 16 |
| Lago, Mount, mtn., Wa., U.S. | A5 | 124 |
| Lagoa, La., U.S. | *E4 | 95 |
| Lagonda, La., U.S. | D4 | 94 |
| Lago Posadas, Arg. | D2 | 54 |
| Lagos, Nig. | E5 | 45 |
| Lagos, Port. | D1 | 22 |
| Lagos de Moreno, Mex. | C4 | 63 |
| Lago Vidal, Arg. | D2 | 54 |
| La Grand'Combe, Fr. | E6 | 16 |
| La Grande, Or., U.S. | B8 | 114 |
| La Grande, stm., Que. | h11 | 74 |
| La Grande Deux, Réservoir, res., Que. | h11 | 74 |
| La Grande Quatre, Réservoir, res., Que. | F18 | 66 |
| Lagrange, Fl., U.S. | *D6 | 86 |
| La Grange, Ga., U.S. | C1 | 87 |
| La Grange, Il., U.S. | B6 | 90 |
| Lagrange, In., U.S. | A7 | 91 |
| La Grange, Ky., U.S. | B4 | 94 |
| La Grange, Mo., U.S. | A6 | 102 |
| La Grange, N.C., U.S. | B5 | 110 |
| Lagrange, Oh., U.S. | A3 | 112 |
| La Grange, Tn., U.S. | B2 | 119 |
| La Grange, Tx., U.S. | E4 | 120 |
| Lagrange, Wy., U.S. | E8 | 127 |
| Lagrange, co., In., U.S. | A7 | 91 |
| La Grange Highlands, Il., U.S. | *k9 | 90 |
| La Grange Park, Il., U.S. | k9 | 90 |
| La Gran Sabana, pl., Ven. | B5 | 60 |
| Lagro, In., U.S. | C6 | 91 |
| La Grue Bayou, stm., Ar., U.S. | C4 | 81 |
| La Guadeloupe (Saint-Évariste), Que. | D7 | 74 |
| La Guaira, Ven. | A4 | 60 |
| La Guardia, Spain | B1 | 22 |
| La Guata, Hond. | C4 | 62 |
| Laguna, Braz. | D3 | 56 |
| Laguna, N.M., U.S. | B2 | 108 |
| Laguna Beach, Ca., U.S. | F5 | 82 |
| Laguna Dam, U.S. | E1 | 80 |
| Laguna Hills, Ca., U.S. | *n13 | 82 |
| Laguna Indian Reservation, N.M., U.S. | C2 | 108 |
| Laguna Niguel, Ca., U.S. | *F5 | 82 |
| Lagunas, Peru | C2 | 58 |
| Lagunillas, Bol. | C3 | 55 |
| La Habana, prov., Cuba | C2 | 64 |
| La Habra, Ca., U.S. | n13 | 82 |
| Lahad Datu, Malay. | E5 | 34 |
| Lahaina, Hi., U.S. | C5 | 88 |
| La Harpe, Il., U.S. | C3 | 90 |
| La Harpe, Ks., U.S. | E8 | 93 |
| Lahat, Indon. | F2 | 34 |
| La Have, N.S. | E5 | 71 |
| La Have, stm., N.S. | E5 | 71 |
| La Have Island, N.S. | E5 | 71 |
| Lahāfān, Bi'r, well, Eg. | D5 | 41 |
| Lādnūn, India | D5 | 37 |
| Lahij, Yemen | C5 | 47 |
| Lāhījān, Iran | C5 | 39 |
| Lahn, stm., W. Ger. | C5 | 18 |
| Laholm, Swe. | B7 | 15 |
| Laholmsbukten, b., Swe. | B6 | 15 |
| Lahoma, Ok., U.S. | A3 | 113 |
| Lahontan Reservoir, res., Nv., U.S. | D2 | 105 |
| Lahore, Pak. | E5 | 36 |
| Lahore Cantonment, Pak. | *B5 | 36 |
| Lahr, W. Ger. | D3 | 18 |
| Lahri, Pak. | C4 | 36 |
| Lahti, Fin. | G11 | 14 |
| La Huaca, Peru | B1 | 58 |
| La'i, Chad | D3 | 46 |
| Lai Chau, Viet. | A5 | 35 |
| Laichow Bay see Laizhou Wan, b., China | D8 | 31 |
| Laide, Scot., U.K. | C4 | 13 |
| Laidon, Loch, l., Scot., U.K. | D4 | 13 |
| Laie, Hi., U.S. | A4 | 88 |
| Laifeng, China | J3 | 32 |
| La Jalca, Peru | C2 | 58 |
| La Jara, N.M., U.S. | A3 | 108 |
| Laje Point, c., Port. | f9 | 22 |
| Lajes, Braz. | D3 | 56 |
| Lajes, Braz. | C3 | 57 |
| La Jolla, Point, c., Ca., U.S. | o15 | 82 |
| Lajord, Sask. | G3 | 75 |
| La Jose, Pa., U.S. | E4 | 115 |
| Lajosmizse, Hung. | B4 | 24 |
| La Joya (part of Mexico City), Mex. | h9 | 63 |
| La Joya, Peru | D2 | 58 |
| Lajoya, N.M., U.S. | C3 | 108 |
| La Junta, Col., U.S. | D7 | 83 |
| Lake, Ms., U.S. | C4 | 101 |
| Lake, co., Ca., U.S. | C2 | 82 |
| Lake, co., Co., U.S. | B4 | 83 |
| Lake, co., Fl., U.S. | D5 | 86 |
| Lake, co., Il., U.S. | A6 | 90 |
| Lake, co., In., U.S. | B3 | 91 |
| Lake, co., Mi., U.S. | E5 | 99 |
| Lake, co., Mn., U.S. | C7 | 100 |
| Lake, co., Mt., U.S. | C2 | 103 |
| Lake, co., Oh., U.S. | A4 | 112 |
| Lake, co., Or., U.S. | E6 | 114 |
| Lake, co., S.D., U.S. | D8 | 118 |
| Lake, co., Tn., U.S. | A2 | 119 |
| Lake Alfred, Fl., U.S. | D5 | 86 |
| Lake Alma, Sask. | H3 | 75 |
| Lake Andes, S.D., U.S. | D7 | 118 |
| Lake Annis, N.S. | E4 | 71 |
| Lake Ariel, Pa., U.S. | D11 | 115 |
| Lake Arrowhead, Ca., U.S. | *E5 | 82 |
| Lake Arthur, La., U.S. | D3 | 95 |
| Lake Arthur, N.M., U.S. | E5 | 108 |
| Lake Barcroft, Va., U.S. | *g12 | 123 |
| Lake Benton, Mn., U.S. | F2 | 100 |
| Lake Beseck, Ct., U.S. | C5 | 84 |
| Lake Bluff, Il., U.S. | A6 | 90 |
| Lake Bonaparte, N.Y., U.S. | A5 | 109 |
| Lake Bronson, Mn., U.S. | B2 | 100 |
| Lake Bruce, In., U.S. | B4 | 91 |
| Lake Butler, Fl., U.S. | C4 | 86 |
| Lake Cargelligo, Austl. | F6 | 51 |
| Lake Carmel, N.Y., U.S. | *D7 | 109 |
| Lake Carroll, Il., U.S. | *A4 | 90 |
| Lake Charles, La., U.S. | D2 | 95 |
| Lake Chelan National Recreation Area, Wa., U.S. | A5 | 124 |
| Lake City, Ar., U.S. | B5 | 81 |
| Lake City, Co., U.S. | D3 | 83 |
| Lake City, Co., U.S. | C3 | 83 |
| Lake City, Fl., U.S. | B4 | 86 |
| Lake City, Ia., U.S. | B3 | 92 |
| Lake City, Ks., U.S. | E5 | 93 |
| Lake City, Mi., U.S. | D5 | 99 |
| Lake City, Mn., U.S. | F6 | 100 |
| Lake City, Pa., U.S. | B1 | 115 |
| Lake City, S.C., U.S. | D8 | 117 |
| Lake City, S.D., U.S. | C9 | 119 |
| Lake Clark National Park, Ak., U.S. | C9 | 79 |
| Lake Como, Pa., U.S. | C11 | 115 |
| Lake Cormorant, Ms., U.S. | A3 | 101 |
| Lake Cowichan, B.C. | g11 | 69 |
| Lakecreek, Or., U.S. | E4 | 114 |
| Lake Creek, stm., Wa., U.S. | B7 | 124 |
| Lake Crystal, Mn., U.S. | F4 | 100 |
| Lake Delta, N.Y., U.S. | B5 | 109 |
| Lake Delton, Wi., U.S. | E4 | 126 |
| Lake District, reg., Eng., U.K. | C5 | 10 |
| Lake Elmo, Mn., U.S. | *n13 | 100 |
| Lake Elmore, Vt., U.S. | B3 | 122 |
| Lake Elsinore, Ca., U.S. | F5 | 82 |
| Lake Erie Beach, N.Y., U.S. | C1 | 109 |
| Lakefield, Ont. | C6 | 73 |
| Lakefield, Mn., U.S. | G3 | 100 |
| Lake Forest, Fl., U.S. | *s13 | 86 |
| Lake Forest, Il., U.S. | A6 | 90 |
| Lake Fork, Id., U.S. | E2 | 89 |
| Lake Fork, Il., U.S. | D4 | 90 |
| Lake Fork, stm., Co., U.S. | C3 | 83 |
| Lake Fork, stm., Ut., U.S. | C5 | 121 |
| Lake Geneva, Wi., U.S. | F5 | 126 |
| Lake George, Co., U.S. | C5 | 83 |
| Lake George, Mi., U.S. | E6 | 99 |
| Lake George, Mn., U.S. | C4 | 100 |
| Lake George, N.Y., U.S. | B7 | 109 |
| Lake Grinnell, N.J., U.S. | A3 | 107 |
| Lake Grove, N.Y., U.S. | *E7 | 109 |
| Lake Hamilton, Ar., U.S. | g7 | 81 |
| Lake Harbour, N.W. Ter. | D19 | 66 |
| Lake Havasu City, Az., U.S. | C1 | 80 |
| Lake Helen, Fl., U.S. | D5 | 86 |
| Lake Hiawatha, N.J., U.S. | B4 | 107 |
| Lake Hubert, Mn., U.S. | D4 | 100 |
| Lake Hughes, Ca., U.S. | E4 | 82 |
| Lake Huntington, N.Y., U.S. | D5 | 109 |
| Lakehurst, N.J., U.S. | C4 | 107 |
| Lakehurst Naval Air Station, mil., N.J., U.S. | C4 | 107 |
| Lake in the Hills, Il., U.S. | h8 | 90 |
| Lake Itasca, Mn., U.S. | C3 | 100 |
| Lake Jackson, Tx., U.S. | E5 | 120 |
| Lake Katrine, N.Y., U.S. | D7 | 109 |
| Lakeland, Fl., U.S. | D5 | 86 |
| Lakeland, Ga., U.S. | E3 | 87 |
| Lakeland Highlands, Fl., U.S. | *E5 | 86 |
| Lake Leelanau, Mi., U.S. | D5 | 99 |
| Lake Lenore, Sask. | E3 | 75 |
| Lake Lillian, Mn., U.S. | F4 | 100 |
| Lake Linden, Mi., U.S. | A2 | 99 |
| Lake Lindsey, Fl., U.S. | D4 | 86 |
| Lake Lorraine, Fl., U.S. | *u15 | 86 |
| Lake Louise, Alta. | D2 | 68 |
| Lake Luzerne, N.Y., U.S. | B7 | 109 |
| Lake Magdalene, Fl., U.S. | o11 | 86 |
| Lake Mary, Fl., U.S. | D5 | 86 |
| Lake Mcdonald, Mt., U.S. | B3 | 103 |
| Lake Mead National Recreation Area, U.S. | H7 | 105 |
| Lake Meredith National Recreation Area, Tx., U.S. | B2 | 120 |
| Lake Metigoshe, N.D., U.S. | A5 | 111 |
| Lake Mills, Ia., U.S. | A4 | 92 |
| Lake Mills, Wi., U.S. | E5 | 126 |
| Lake Minchumina, Ak., U.S. | C9 | 79 |
| Lakemont, Pa., U.S. | F5 | 115 |
| Lakemore, Oh., U.S. | A4 | 112 |
| Lake Mountain, mtn., Wy., U.S. | E6 | 127 |
| Lakenan, Mo., U.S. | B5 | 102 |
| Lake Nebagamon, Wi., U.S. | B2 | 126 |
| Lake Norden, S.D., U.S. | C8 | 118 |
| Lake Odessa, Mi., U.S. | F5 | 99 |
| Lake Of The Woods, co., Mn., U.S. | B4 | 100 |
| Lake Orion, Mi., U.S. | F7 | 99 |
| Lake Oswego, Or., U.S. | B4 | 114 |
| Lake Ozark, Mo., U.S. | C5 | 102 |
| Lake Park, Fl., U.S. | F6 | 86 |
| Lake Park, Ga., U.S. | F3 | 87 |
| Lake Park, Ia., U.S. | A2 | 92 |
| Lake Park, Mn., U.S. | D2 | 100 |
| Lake Placid, Fl., U.S. | E5 | 86 |
| Lake Placid, N.Y., U.S. | A7 | 109 |
| Lake Pleasant, N.Y., U.S. | B6 | 109 |
| Lake Pontchartrain Causeway, La., U.S. | h11 | 95 |
| Lakeport, Ca., U.S. | C2 | 82 |
| Lakeport, S.D., U.S. | C8 | 118 |
| Lake Preston, S.D., U.S. | C8 | 118 |
| Lake Providence, La., U.S. | B4 | 95 |
| Lake Range, mts., Nv., U.S. | C2 | 105 |
| Lakeridge, Nv., U.S. | *E2 | 105 |
| Lake Ridge, Va., U.S. | B5 | 123 |
| Lake River, Ont. | n19 | 73 |
| Lake Ronkonkoma, N.Y., U.S. | *n15 | 109 |
| Lakeshore, Md., U.S. | B5 | 97 |
| Lake Shore, Mn., U.S. | D4 | 100 |
| Lake Shore, Ut., U.S. | *C4 | 121 |
| Lakeside, N.S. | E6 | 71 |
| Lakeside, Az., U.S. | C6 | 80 |
| Lakeside, Ca., U.S. | *F5 | 82 |
| Lakeside, Ct., U.S. | C3 | 84 |
| Lakeside, Mt., U.S. | B2 | 103 |
| Lakeside, Oh., U.S. | *A3 | 112 |
| Lakeside, Or., U.S. | D2 | 114 |
| Lakeside, Va., U.S. | *C5 | 123 |
| Lakeside Mountains, mts., Ut., U.S. | B3 | 121 |
| Lakeside Park, Ky., U.S. | h13 | 94 |
| Lakeside-Pinetop, Az., U.S. | C6 | 80 |
| Lake Station, In., U.S. | A3 | 91 |
| Lake Stevens, Wa., U.S. | A3 | 124 |
| Lake Superior Provincial Park, Ont. | p18 | 73 |
| Lake Swamp, stm., S.C., U.S. | D8 | 117 |
| Lake Tansi, Tn., U.S. | D8 | 119 |
| Lake Telemark, N.J., U.S. | A4 | 107 |
| Lake Tomahawk, Wi., U.S. | C4 | 126 |
| Laketon, In., U.S. | C6 | 91 |
| Laketown, Ut., U.S. | B4 | 121 |
| Lake Toxaway, N.C., U.S. | f10 | 110 |
| Lake Traverse, Ont. | A6 | 73 |
| Lake Valley, val., Nv., U.S. | E7 | 105 |
| Lakeview, Ga., U.S. | *B1 | 87 |

**Name — Map Ref. — Page**

Lakeview, Id., U.S. — B2 89
Lake View, Ia., U.S. — B2 92
Lakeview, Mi., U.S. — E5 99
Lakeview, Mt., U.S. — F5 103
Lakeview, N.Y., U.S. — *E7 109
Lake View, N.Y., U.S. — C2 109
Lakeview, Oh., U.S. — B2 112
Lakeview, Or., U.S. — E6 114
Lake View, S.C., U.S. — C9 117
Lakeview, Tx., U.S. — B2 120
Lake Villa, Il., U.S. — h8 90
Lake Village, Ar., U.S. — D4 81
Lake Village, In., U.S. — B3 91
Lakeville, Ct., U.S. — B2 84
Lakeville, In., U.S. — A5 91
Lakeville, Ma., U.S. — C6 98
Lakeville, Mn., U.S. — F5 100
Lakeville, N.Y., U.S. — C3 109
Lake Waccamaw, N.C., U.S. — C4 110
Lake Wales, Fl., U.S. — E5 86
Lake Williams, N.D., U.S. — B6 111
Lake Wilson, Mn., U.S. — G3 100
Lake Winola, Pa., U.S. — m17 115
Lake Wissota, Wi., U.S. — *D2 126
Lakewood, Ca., U.S. — n12 82
Lakewood, Co., U.S. — B5 83
Lakewood, Il., U.S. — D5 90
Lakewood, In., U.S. — f8 92
Lakewood, Me., U.S. — D3 96
Lakewood, N.J., U.S. — C4 107
Lakewood, N.M., U.S. — E5 108
Lakewood, N.Y., U.S. — C1 109
Lakewood, Oh., U.S. — A4 112
Lakewood, Pa., U.S. — C10 115
Lakewood, Wa., U.S. — A3 124
Lakewood, Wi., U.S. — C5 126
Lakewood Center, Wa., U.S. — B3 124
Lake Worth, Fl., U.S. — F6 86
Lake Worth Inlet, b., Fl., U.S. — F7 86
Lake Zurich, Il., U.S. — h8 90
Lakhī, Afg. — B3 36
Lakhīmpur, India — C7 36
Lakhta (part of Leningrad), Sov. Un. — r31 14
Lakin, Ks., U.S. — E2 93
Lakota, I.C. — E3 45
Lakota, Ia., U.S. — A3 92
Lakota, N.D., U.S. — A7 111
Laksefjorden, Nor. — B12 14
Lakshadweep (Laccadive, Minicoy and Amīndīvi Islands), ter., India — *F5 36
Lakshadweep (Laccadive Islands), is., India — F5 36
La Laguna, Spain — m13 22
La Libertad, El Sal. — D3 62
La Libertad, Guat. — B2 62
La Libertad, dept., Peru — C2 58
La Ligua, Chile — A2 54
Lalín, Spain — A1 22
La Línea, Spain — D3 22
La Loche, Sask. — m7 75
La Loche, Lac, l., Sask. — A6 68
La Loma, N.M., U.S. — B4 108
La Louvière, Bel. — D4 17
La Luz, N.M., U.S. — D4 108
La Macarena, Serranía de, mts., Col. — C3 60
La Machine, Fr. — D5 16
La Maddalena, Italy — D2 23
La Madera, N.M., U.S. — A3 108
Lama-Kara, Togo — E5 45
La Malbaie, Que. — B7 74
Lamaline, Newf. — E4 72
La Mancha, reg., Spain — C4 22
Lamanibot Sanhilo, Puntan, c., N. Mar. Is. — D7 52
Lamar, Ar., U.S. — B2 81
Lamar, Co., U.S. — C8 83
Lamar, In., U.S. — H4 91
Lamar, Ms., U.S. — A4 101
Lamar, Mo., U.S. — D3 102
Lamar, Ne., U.S. — D4 104
Lamar, Ok., U.S. — B5 113
Lamar, Pa., U.S. — D7 115
Lamar, S.C., U.S. — C7 117
Lamar, co., Al., U.S. — B1 78
Lamar, co., Ga., U.S. — C2 87
Lamar, co., Ms., U.S. — D4 101
Lamar, co., Tx., U.S. — C5 120
Lamar, stm., Wy., U.S. — B2 127
Lamarche, Fr. — A1 20
La Marmora, Punta, mtn., Italy — D2 23
La Marque, Tx., U.S. — *r15 120
Lamas, Peru — C2 58
Lamasco, Ky., U.S. — f10 94
La Mauricie, Parc National de, Que. — C5 74
Lamb, co., Tx., U.S. — B1 120
Lamballe, Fr. — C2 16
Lambaréné, Gabon — F2 46
Lambayeque, Peru — C2 58
Lambayeque, dept., Peru — C2 58
Lambay Island, i., Ire. — D5 11
Lambert, Ms., U.S. — A3 101
Lambert, Mt., U.S. — C12 103
Lambert, Ok., U.S. — A3 113
Lambert Glacier, ice, Ant. — B19 7
Lambert Lake, Me., U.S. — C5 96
Lamberton, Mn., U.S. — F3 100
Lambert's Bay, S. Afr. — D2 49
Lambertville, Mi., U.S. — G7 99
Lambertville, N.J., U.S. — C3 107
Lambeth, Ont. — E3 73
Lambeth (part of London), Eng., U.K. — m12 10
Lambourn, Eng., U.K. — C6 12
Lambrecht (Pfalz), W. Ger. — D3 19
Lambro, stm., Italy — D5 20
Lambrook, Ar., U.S. — C5 81
Lambsburg, Va., U.S. — D2 123
Lamb's Head, c., Ire. — F1 11
Lambton, Que. — D6 74
Lambton, co., Ont. — E2 73
Lambton, Cape, c., N.W. Ter. — B8 66
Lamdesar, Indon. — G8 34
Lame Deer, Mt., U.S. — E10 103
Lamego, Port. — D3 22
Lamèque, N.B. — B5 71
Lamèque, Île, i., N.B. — B5 71
La Merced (Superí), Arg. — E2 55
La Mesa, Ca., U.S. — F5 82
La Mesa, N.M., U.S. — E3 108
Lamesa, Tx., U.S. — C2 120
Lamía, Grc. — C4 40
La Minerve, Que. — C3 74
Lamington, Mount, mtn., Pap. N. Gui. — k12 50
La Mirada, Ca., U.S. — *E4 82
Lamlam, Mount, mtn., Guam — M9 52
Lamlash, Scot., U.K. — E3 13
Lammermuir Hills, hills, Scot., U.K. — E6 13
Lammhult, Swe. — A8 15
Lamoil, i., Micron. — Q18 52

La Moille, Il., U.S. — B4 90
Lamoille, Nv., U.S. — C6 105
Lamoille, co., Vt., U.S. — B3 122
Lamoille, stm., Vt., U.S. — B3 122
Lamoille, North Branch, stm., Vt., U.S. — B3 122
La Moine, stm., Il., U.S. — C3 90
Lamon Bay, b., Phil. — C6 34
La Monte, Mo., U.S. — C4 102
La Motte, Ia., U.S. — B7 92
La Motte, Isle, i., Vt., U.S. — B2 122
La Moure, N.D., U.S. — C7 111
La Moure, co., N.D., U.S. — C7 111
Lampa, Peru — E3 58
Lampang, Thai. — B1 34
Lampasas, Tx., U.S. — D3 120
Lampasas, co., Tx., U.S. — D3 120
Lampertheim, W. Ger. — D3 19
Lampeter, Wales, U.K. — B3 12
Lamphun, Thai. — C3 35
Lampman, Sask. — H4 75
Lamprey, stm., N.H., U.S. — D4 106
Lamu, Kenya — B7 48
La Mure, Fr. — E6 16
Lamy, N.M., U.S. — B4 108
Lanai, i., Hi., U.S. — C4 88
Lanai City, Hi., U.S. — C5 88
Lanaihale, mtn., Hi., U.S. — C5 88
Lanak La, Asia — B7 36
Lanao, Lake, l., Phil. — D6 34
Lanare, Ca., U.S. — D4 82
Lanark, Ont. — C8 73
Lanark, Scot., U.K. — E5 13
Lanark, Il., U.S. — A4 90
Lanark, W.V., U.S. — D3 125
Lanark, co., Ont. — B8 73
Lanark Village, Fl., U.S. — C2 86
Lanbi, i., Burma — G3 35
Lancang, China — G3 35
Lancashire, De., U.S. — *A4 85
Lancashire, co., Eng., U.K. — C5 10
Lancaster, Ont. — B10 73
Lancaster, Eng., U.K. — C5 10
Lancaster, Ca., U.S. — E4 82
Lancaster, Ky., U.S. — C5 94
Lancaster, Ks., U.S. — C8 93
Lancaster, Ma., U.S. — B4 98
Lancaster, Mn., U.S. — B2 100
Lancaster, Mo., U.S. — A5 102
Lancaster, N.H., U.S. — B3 106
Lancaster, N.Y., U.S. — C2 109
Lancaster, Oh., U.S. — C3 112
Lancaster, Pa., U.S. — F9 115
Lancaster, S.C., U.S. — B6 117
Lancaster, Tn., U.S. — C8 119
Lancaster, Tx., U.S. — n10 120
Lancaster, Va., U.S. — C6 123
Lancaster, Wi., U.S. — F3 126
Lancaster, co., Ne., U.S. — D9 104
Lancaster, co., Pa., U.S. — G9 115
Lancaster, co., S.C., U.S. — B6 117
Lancaster, co., Va., U.S. — C6 123
Lancaster Sound, strt., N.W. Ter. — B15 66
Lancaster Village, De., U.S. — *A3 85
Lance, Point, c., Newf. — E4 72
Lance Creek, Wy., U.S. — C8 127
Lance Creek, stm., Wy., U.S. — C8 127
Lancer, Sask. — G1 75
Lanchou see Lanzhou, China — D5 31
Lanciano, Italy — C5 23
Lancing, Tn., U.S. — C9 119
Lancut, Pol. — C7 26
Lancy, Switz. — D1 21
Landa, N.D., U.S. — A5 111
Landaff Center, N.H., U.S. — B3 106
Landau [an der Isar], W. Ger. — D6 18
Landau [in der Pfalz], W. Ger. — D4 18
Land Between the Lakes, U.S. — f9 94
Landeck, Aus. — E5 18
Landen, Bel. — D5 17
Lander, Wy., U.S. — D4 127
Lander, co., Nv., U.S. — C4 105
Landerneau, Fr. — C1 16
Landess, In., U.S. — C6 91
Landing Lake, l., Man. — B3 70
Landis, Sask. — E1 75
Landis, N.C., U.S. — B2 110
Landisburg, Pa., U.S. — F7 115
Landivisiau, Fr. — C1 16
Land O' Lakes, Wi., U.S. — B4 126
Landover, Md., U.S. — *C4 97
Landrum, S.C., U.S. — A3 117
Landsberg, W. Ger. — D5 18
Land's End, c., Eng., U.K. — E4 10
Landshut, W. Ger. — D6 18
Landskrona, Swe. — J5 14
Landsman Creek, stm., Co., U.S. — B8 83
Landsort, Swe. — u35 14
Landusky, Mt., U.S. — C8 103
Lane, Il., U.S. — D5 90
Lane, Ks., U.S. — D8 93
Lane, Nv., U.S. — D7 105
Lane, Ok., U.S. — C6 113
Lane, S.C., U.S. — D8 117
Lane, Tn., U.S. — A2 119
Lane, co., Ks., U.S. — D3 93
Lane, co., Or., U.S. — C4 114
Laneburg, Ar., U.S. — D2 81
Lanesboro, Ia., U.S. — B3 92
Lanesboro, Ma., U.S. — A1 98
Lanesboro, Mn., U.S. — G7 100
Lanesville, In., U.S. — H6 91
Lanett, Al., U.S. — C4 78
Lanfine, Alta. — D5 68
Langå, Den. — C3 15
Langadhás, Grc. — B4 25
Langa Langa, Zaire — B2 48
Langanes, c., Ice. — m25 14
Langarūd, Iran — C5 39
Långås, Swe. — H6 15
Langbank, Sask. — G4 75
Lang Bay, B.C. — E5 69

Langdale, Al., U.S. — C4 78
Langdon, Alta. — D4 68
Langdon, Ia., U.S. — A2 92
Langdon, Ks., U.S. — E5 93
Langdon, Mo., U.S. — A2 102
Langdon, N.H., U.S. — D2 106
Langdon, N.D., U.S. — A7 111
Langeac, Fr. — E5 16
Langeland, i., Den. — D4 15
Langelandsbaelt, strt., Den. — D4 15
Langeloth, Pa., U.S. — F1 115
Langen, W. Ger. — D3 19
Langenau, W. Ger. — E5 19
Langenburg, Sask. — G5 75
Langenfeld, W. Ger. — C4 19
Langenthal, Switz. — E3 18
Langenzenn, W. Ger. — D5 19
Langeoog, W. Ger. — A7 17
Langeoog, i., W. Ger. — B3 18
Langesund, Nor. — H3 14
Langford, B.C. — h12 69
Langford, S.D., U.S. — B8 118
Långhalsen, l., Swe. — u34 14
Langham, Sask. — E2 75
Langham, Swe. — A7 15
Langholm, Scot., U.K. — E5 13
Langhorne, Pa., U.S. — F12 115
Langjökull, ice, Ice. — n22 14
Langkawi, i., Malay. — I3 35
Langley, B.C. — f13 69
Langley, Ar., U.S. — C2 81
Langley, Ky., U.S. — C7 94
Langley, Ok., U.S. — A6 113
Langley, S.C., U.S. — E4 117
Langley, Wa., U.S. — A3 124
Langley Air Force Base, mil., Va., U.S. — h15 123
Langley Park, Md., U.S. — f9 97
Langleyville, Il., U.S. — D4 90
Langlois, Or., U.S. — E2 114
Langnau [in Emmental], Switz. — E3 18
Langogne, Fr. — E5 16
Langon, Fr. — E3 16
Langøya, i., Nor. — C6 14
Langres, Fr. — D6 16
Langres, Plateau de, plat., Fr. — D6 16
Langruth, Man. — D2 70
Langsa, Indon. — E1 34
Lang Son, Viet. — B7 35
Langstaff, Ont. — k15 73
Langston, Al., U.S. — A3 78
Langston, Ok., U.S. — B4 113
Langton, Ont. — E4 73
Langtry, Tx., U.S. — E2 120
Languedoc, hist. reg., Fr. — F5 16
L'Anguille, stm., Ar., U.S. — B5 81
Langzhong, China — E6 31
Lanham, Md., U.S. — C4 97
Lanier, co., Ga., U.S. — E3 87
Lanigan, Sask. — F3 75
Lanigan Creek, stm., Sask. — F3 75
Lankin, N.D., U.S. — A8 111
Lanklaar, Bel. — C5 17
Lannion, Fr. — C2 16
Lannon, Wi., U.S. — m11 126
Lanoka Harbor, N.J., U.S. — D4 107
Lanoraie, Que. — D4 74
Lansdale, Pa., U.S. — F11 115
Lansdowne, Ont. — C8 73
Lansdowne, Md., U.S. — *B4 97
Lansdowne, Pa., U.S. — *p20 115
Lansdowne House, Ont. — n18 73
Lansford, N.D., U.S. — A4 111
Lansford, Pa., U.S. — E10 115
Lansing, Il., U.S. — B6 90
Lansing, Ia., U.S. — A6 92
Lansing, Ks., U.S. — C9 93
Lansing, Mi., U.S. — F6 99
Lansing, N.C., U.S. — A1 110
Lansing, W.V., U.S. — m13 125
Lanslebourg, Fr. — D2 20
Lantana, Fl., U.S. — F6 86
Lantry, S.D., U.S. — B4 118
Lanusei, Italy — E2 23
Lanuvio, Italy — h9 23
Lanxi, China — F8 31
Lanxi, China — A12 32
Lanzada, Italy — D8 21
Lanzarote, i., Spain — m15 22
Lanzhou (Lanchou), China — D5 31
Laoag, Phil. — B6 34
Lao Cai, Viet. — A6 35
Laohekou, China — E7 31
Laoighis see Laois, co., Ire. — D4 11
Laolao, Bahia, b., N. Mar. Is. — D8 52
Laolao Kattan, Puntan, c., N. Mar. Is. — D8 52
Laon, Fr. — C5 16
Laona, Wi., U.S. — C5 126
La Oroya, Peru — D2 58
Laos, ctry., Asia — B2 35
Laotto, In., U.S. — B7 91
Lapa, Braz. — B7 56
La Palma, Pan. — F8 64
La Palma, Az., U.S. — E4 80
La Palma, Ca., U.S. — n12 82
La Palma [del Condado], Spain — D2 22
La Paloma, Ur. — C6 56
La Pampa, prov., Arg. — D3 54
La Paragua, Ven. — B5 60
La Pasión, stm., Guat. — B2 62
La Passe, Ont. — B8 73
La Patrie, Que. — D6 74
La Paz, Arg. — A5 54
La Paz, Bol. — C2 55
La Paz, Col. — C2 60
La Paz, Hond. — A3 63
La Paz, Mex. — E7 63
La Paz, Mex. — C2 63
Lapaz, In., U.S. — B5 91
La Paz, dept., Bol. — C2 55
La Paz, co., Az., U.S. — D2 80
La Paz, Bahía de, b., Mex. — D4 63
La Pedrera, Col. — D4 60
Lapeer, Mi., U.S. — E7 99
Lapeer, co., Mi., U.S. — E7 99

Lapel, In., U.S. — D6 91
La Perouse Strait, strt., Asia — D10 33
La Piedad [Cavadas], Mex. — m12 63
Lapine, Al., U.S. — D3 78
La Pine, Or., U.S. — D5 114
La Place, Il., U.S. — D5 90
La Place, La., U.S. — h11 95
Lapland, reg., Eur. — C11 14
La Plant, S.D., U.S. — B5 118
La Plata, Arg. — A5 54
La Plata, Col. — C2 60
La Plata, Md., U.S. — C4 97
La Plata, Mo., U.S. — A5 102
La Plata, N.M., U.S. — A1 108
La Plata, co., Co., U.S. — D3 83
La Plata Mountains, mts., Co., U.S. — D3 83
La Plata Peak, mtn., Co., U.S. — B4 83
La Platte, Ne., U.S. — g13 104
La Platte, stm., Vt., U.S. — C2 122
La Pobla de Lillet, Spain — A6 22
La Pocatière, Que. — B7 74
La Poile Bay, b., Newf. — E2 72
Lapoint, Ut., U.S. — C6 121
La Pointe, Wi., U.S. — B3 126
Lapola [de Gordón], Spain — A3 22
La Porte, Co., U.S. — A5 83
La Porte, In., U.S. — A4 91
La Porte, Mn., U.S. — C4 100
La Porte, Pa., U.S. — D9 115
La Porte, Tx., U.S. — r14 120
La Porte City, Ia., U.S. — B5 92
Läppe, Swe. — t33 14
Lappeenranta, Fin. — G13 14
La Prairie, Que. — D4 74
La Prairie, Mn., U.S. — C5 100
Laprairie, co., Que. — D4 74
Laprida, Arg. — B4 54
La Pryor, Tx., U.S. — E3 120
Lâpseki, Tur. — B6 40
Laptev Sea, Sov. Un. — B15 29
La Puebla, Spain — C7 22
La Puebla de Montalbán, Spain — C3 22
La Puente, Ca., U.S. — *m13 82
La Puente, N.M., U.S. — A3 108
La Puerta, Mex. — B2 63
La Push, Wa., U.S. — B1 124
Laqīyat al Arba'īn, Sud. — B2 47
La Quiaca, Arg. — D2 55
L'Aquila (Aguila), Italy — C4 23
Lār, Iran — C5 38
Lara, state, Ven. — A3 60
Larache, Mor. — B3 44
Laramie, Wy., U.S. — E7 127
Laramie, co., Wy., U.S. — E8 127
Laramie Mountains, mts., Wy., U.S. — D7 127
Laramie Peak, mtn., Wy., U.S. — D7 127
Laranjeiras, Braz. — D3 57
Laranjeiras do Sul, Braz. — D2 56
Larap, Phil. — o14 34
Larche Pass, Eur. — E2 20
Larchmont, N.Y., U.S. — h13 109
Larchmont North, N.Y., U.S. — *h13 109
Larchwood, Ia., U.S. — A1 92
Lardeau, stm., B.C. — D9 69
L'Ardoise, N.S. — D9 71
Laredo, Spain — A4 22
Laredo, Mo., U.S. — A4 102
Laredo, Tx., U.S. — F3 120
Laredo Sound, strt., B.C. — C3 69
La Réole, Fr. — E4 16
Lares, P.R. — B2 65
Largeau, Chad — B4 46
Largentière, Fr. — E6 16
Largo, Fl., U.S. — E4 86
Largo, Cañon, val., N.M., U.S. — A2 108
Largo, Cayo, i., Cuba — D3 64
Largo, Key, i., Fl., U.S. — G6 86
Largs, Scot., U.K. — E4 13
Lariat, Tx., U.S. — B1 120
La Ricamarie, Fr. — E6 16
Larimer, co., Co., U.S. — A5 83
Larimore, N.D., U.S. — B8 111
Larino, Italy — D5 23
La Rioja, Arg. — B2 54
La Rioja, Cuba — D5 64
La Rioja, prov., Arg. — B2 54
Lárisa, Grc. — C4 40
Laristan, hist. reg., Iran — C5 38
La Riviera, Ca., U.S. — *C3 82
La Rivière, Man. — E2 70
Lark, N.D., U.S. — C4 111
Lark, Ut., U.S. — C3 121
Lärkäna, Pak. — C3 36
Lark Harbour, Newf. — D2 72
Larkinsville, Al., U.S. — A3 78
Larkspur, Ca., U.S. — h7 82
Larkspur, Co., U.S. — B6 83
Larned, Ks., U.S. — D4 93
La Robla, Spain — A3 22
La Rochelle, Fr. — D3 16

La Roche-sur-Foron, Fr. — C7 20
La Roche-sur-Yon, Fr. — D3 16
La Roda, Spain — C4 22
La Romana, Dom. Rep. — E9 64
La Ronge, Sask. — B3 75
Larose, La., U.S. — E5 95
Larrys River, N.S. — D8 71
Larslan, Mt., U.S. — B10 103
Larsmont, Mn., U.S. — D7 100
Larson, N.D., U.S. — A3 111
Larto, La., U.S. — C4 95
La Rubia, Arg. — F3 55
La Rue, Oh., U.S. — B2 112
Larue, co., Ky., U.S. — C4 94
Laruns, Fr. — F3 16
Larvik, Nor. — H3 14
Larwill, In., U.S. — B6 91
Laryak, Sov. Un. — C25 8
La Sagra, mtn., Spain — D4 22
LaSalle, Que. — q19 74
La Salle, Col. — D4 60
La Salle, Ont. — E2 73
La Salle, Il., U.S. — B4 90
La Salle, Mn., U.S. — F4 100
La Salle, co., Il., U.S. — B4 90
La Salle, co., La., U.S. — C3 95

La Salle, co., Tx., U.S. — E3 120
La Sal Mountains, mts., Ut., U.S. — E6 121
Las Animas, Co., U.S. — C7 83
Las Animas, co., Co., U.S. — D6 83
La Santa, Cerro, mtn., P.R. — B3 65
La Sarre, Que. — k11 74
Lasberg, Aus. — C10 18
Las Cabras, Chile — A2 54
Lascahobas, Haiti — E8 64
Lascano, Ur. — E2 56
Lascar, Volcán, vol., Chile — D2 55
Lascassas, Tn., U.S. — B5 119
L'Ascension, Que. — A6 74
La Scie, Newf. — D4 72
Las Coloradas, Arg. — B2 54
Las Cruces, N.M., U.S. — E3 108
La Serena, Chile — E1 55
La Seyne [-sur-Mer], Fr. — F6 16
Las Flores, Arg. — B5 54
Lashburn, Sask. — D1 75
Lashio, Burma — D10 36
Las Lajas, Arg. — B2 54
Las Lajas, Pan. — F7 62
Las Lomitas, Arg. — D3 55
Las Marismas, sw., Spain — D2 22
La Solana, Spain — C4 22
Las Palmas, Pan. — F7 62
Las Palmas [de Gran Canaria], Spain — m14 22
Las Piedras, Ur. — E1 56
Las Piedras, Río de, stm., Peru — D3 58
Las Plumas, Arg. — C3 54
Las Rosas, Arg. — F3 55
Las Rozas de Madrid, Spain — p17 22
Lassance, Braz. — A6 56
Lassen, co., Ca., U.S. — B3 82
Lassen Peak, vol., Ca., U.S. — B3 82
Lassen Volcanic National Park, Ca., U.S. — B3 82
Lasso, hill, N. Mar. Is. — D7 52
L'Assomption, Que. — D4 74
L'Assomption, co., Que. — D4 74
Las Tablas, Pan. — G7 62
Las Tablas, N.M., U.S. — A3 108
Last Chance, Co., U.S. — B7 83
Las Termas, Arg. — E3 55
Last Mountain Lake, l., Sask. — F3 75
Lastoursville, Gabon — F2 46
Lastovo, i., Yugo. — D3 24
Lastrup, W. Ger. — B7 17
Lastrup, Mn., U.S. — D4 100
Las Tunas, prov., Cuba — D6 64
Las Varillas, Arg. — A4 54
Las Vegas, Nv., U.S. — G6 105
Las Vegas, N.M., U.S. — B4 108
Las Vigas, Mex. — n15 63
La Tabatière, Que. — C2 72
Latacunga, Ec. — H3 60
Latady Island, i., Ant. — B5 7
La Tagua, Col. — D3 60
Latah, Wa., U.S. — B8 124
Latah, co., Id., U.S. — C2 89
Latakia (Al Lādhiqīyah), Syria — B3 38
Laterrière, Que. — A6 74
La Teste-de-Buch, Fr. — E3 16
Latexo, Tx., U.S. — D5 120
Latham, Il., U.S. — D4 90
Latham, Ks., U.S. — E7 93
Latham, N.Y., U.S. — *n15 109
Lathrop, Mo., U.S. — B3 102
Lathrop Wells, Nv., U.S. — G5 105
Latimer, Ia., U.S. — B4 92
Latimer, Ks., U.S. — D7 93
Latimer, co., Ok., U.S. — C6 113
Latina, Italy — D4 23
Latium (Lazio), prov., Italy — C4 23
Latoritsa (Latorica), stm., Sov. Un. — D7 26
La Torrecilla, mtn., P.R. — B4 65
La Tortuga, Isla, i., Ven. — A4 60
Latour, Mo., U.S. — C3 102
La Tour-du-Pin, Fr. — E6 16
Latour Peak, mtn., Id., U.S. — B2 89
La Tremblade, Fr. — E3 16
La Trinité, Mart. — I14 64
Latrobe, Pa., U.S. — F3 115
Latrún, Isr. Occ. — C4 41
Latta, S.C., U.S. — C9 117
Lattimer Mines, Pa., U.S. — E10 115
Lattimore, N.C., U.S. — B1 110
Latty, Oh., U.S. — A1 112
La Tuque, Que. — B5 74
Latvia, state, Sov. Un. — D5 29
Lau, Nig. — G8 46
Lauca, stm., Bol. — G5 58
Laucala, i., Fiji — H16 52
Lauchhammer, E. Ger. — B8 19
Laud, In., U.S. — B7 91
Lauda, W. Ger. — E5 19
Lauderdale, Ms., U.S. — C5 101
Lauderdale, co., Al., U.S. — A2 78
Lauderdale, co., Ms., U.S. — C5 101
Lauderdale, co., Tn., U.S. — B2 119
Lauderdale Lakes, Fl., U.S. — *r13 86
Lauderhill, Fl., U.S. — *r13 86
Lauenburg, E. Ger. — B6 19
Lauf [an der Pegnitz], W. Ger. — D6 19
Laufen, Switz. — D5 21
Laufen, W. Ger. — E9 18
Laughery Creek, stm., In., U.S. — F7 91
Laughlin, Nv., U.S. — H7 105
Laughlin Air Force Base, mil., Tx., U.S. — E2 120
Laughlin Peak, mtn., N.M., U.S. — A5 108
Lau Group, is., Fiji — I16 52
Lau'ili'ifou, Am. Sam. — F13 52
Launceston, Austl. — o15 50
Launceston, Eng., U.K. — E4 10
Launching Point, c., P.E.I. — C7 71
La Unión, Chile — C2 54
La Unión, El Sal. — D3 62
La Unión, Mex. — H9 63
La Unión, Peru — B2 58
La Unión, Spain — E7 22
La Unión, N.M., U.S. — F3 108
Laupahoehoe, Hi., U.S. — C6 88
Laupheim, W. Ger. — D5 18
Laura, Oh., U.S. — B1 112
Laura, Braz. — B3 57
La Urbana, Ven. — B4 60

Laurbjerg, Den. — B3 15
Laurel, Ont. — C4 73
Laurel, De., U.S. — F3 85
Laurel, Fl., U.S. — E4 86
Laurel, In., U.S. — F7 91
Laurel, Md., U.S. — B4 97
Laurel, Ms., U.S. — D4 101
Laurel, Mt., U.S. — E8 103
Laurel, Ne., U.S. — B8 104
Laurel, Va., U.S. — C5 123
Laurel, co., Ky., U.S. — C5 94
Laurel, stm., Ky., U.S. — D5 94
Laurel Bay, S.C., U.S. — G6 117
Laurel Bloomery, Tn., U.S. — C12 119
Laurel Creek, stm., W.V., U.S. — n14 125
Laurel Creek, stm., W.V., U.S. — m12 125
Laureldale, N.J., U.S. — D3 107
Laureldale, Pa., U.S. — F10 115
Laureles, Ur. — E1 56
Laurel Fork, Va., U.S. — D2 123
Laurel Fork, stm., W.V., U.S. — C5 125
Laurel Hill, Fl., U.S. — u15 86
Laurel Hill, N.C., U.S. — C3 110
Laurel Mountain, mtn., W.V., U.S. — B5 125
Laurel River Lake, res., Ky., U.S. — D5 94
Laurelton, Pa., U.S. — E7 115
Laurelville, Oh., U.S. — C3 112
Laurelwood Academy, Or., U.S. — h11 114
Laurence G. Hanscom Air Force Base, mil., Ma., U.S. — g10 98
Laurence Harbor, N.J., U.S. — C4 107
Laurencekirk, Scot., U.K. — D6 13
Laurens, Ia., U.S. — B3 92
Laurens, S.C., U.S. — C3 117
Laurens, co., Ga., U.S. — D4 87
Laurens, co., S.C., U.S. — C3 117
Laurentides, Que. — D4 74
Laurentides, Parc Provincial des, Que. — B6 74
Laurentum, hist., Italy — h8 23
Lauria Inferiore, Italy — D5 23
Laurie, stm., Man. — A1 70
Laurie Island, i., B.A.T. — C8 7
Laurie Lake, l., Can. — A1 70
Laurier, Man. — D2 70
Laurier, Que. — C6 74
Laurierville, Que. — C6 74
Laurin, Mt., U.S. — E4 103
Laurinburg, N.C., U.S. — C3 110
Lauritzen Bay, b., Ant. — C28 7
Laurium, Mi., U.S. — A2 99
Laurium see Lávrion, Grc. — D5 25
Lausanne, Switz. — E3 18
Lauscha, E. Ger. — C6 19
Laut, i., Indon. — F5 34
Laut, i., Indon. — J8 35
Lautaro, Chile — B2 54
Lauterbach, W. Ger. — C4 19
Lauterbrunnen, Switz. — C4 21
Lauterecken, W. Ger. — D2 19
Laut Kecil Islands, is., Indon. — F5 34
Lautoka, Fiji — H14 52
Lauzon, Que. — C6 74
Lava Beds National Monument, Ca., U.S. — B3 82
Lavaca, Ar., U.S. — C1 81
Lavaca, co., Tx., U.S. — E4 120
Lavaca, stm., Tx., U.S. — E4 120
La Vale, Md., U.S. — k13 97
La Valle, Wi., U.S. — E3 126
Lavallette, N.J., U.S. — D4 107
La Valley, Co., U.S. — D5 83
Lavaltrie, Que. — D4 74
Lāvān, i., Iran — H6 39
Lavant Station, Ont. — B8 73
Lavapié, Punta, c., Chile — B2 54
Lavaur, Fr. — E4 16
Lavaveix-les-Mines, Fr. — D5 16
Laveen, Az., U.S. — m8 80
La Vega, Dom. Rep. — E8 64
La Vela de Coro, Ven. — A4 60
Lavelanet, Fr. — F4 16
Lavello, Italy — D5 23
L'Avenir, Que. — D5 74
La Vergne, Tn., U.S. — A5 119
La Verkin, Ut., U.S. — F2 121
La Verne, Ok., U.S. — A2 113
La Vernia, Tx., U.S. — E3 120
Laverton, Austl. — E4 50
La Veta, Co., U.S. — D5 83
Laviana, Spain — A3 22
Lavina, Mt., U.S. — D8 103
Lavínia, Braz. — F3 57
La Vista, Ga., U.S. — h8 87
La Vista, Ne., U.S. — g12 104
La Viuda, mtn., Peru — C2 58
Lavonia, Ga., U.S. — B3 87
Lavon Lake, res., Tx., U.S. — m10 120
Lavoy, Alta. — C5 68
Lavras, Braz. — F6 57
Lavras da Mangabeira, Braz. — E11 54
Lavras do Sul, Braz. — E2 57
Lávrion (Laurium), Grc. — D5 25
Lavumisa, Swaz. — D5 49
Lawai, Hi., U.S. — B2 88
Lawers, Ben, mtn., Scot., U.K. — D8 13
Lawford Lake, l., Man. — B3 70
Lawit, mtn., Malay. — J5 35
Lawler, Ia., U.S. — A5 92
Lawler, Mn., U.S. — D5 100
Lawn, Newf. — E4 72
Lawn, Tx., U.S. — C3 120
Lawndale, N.C., U.S. — B1 110
Lawndale, Ca., U.S. — *E4 82
Lawra, Ghana — F5 45
Lawrence, N.Z. — P12 51
Lawrence, In., U.S. — E5 91
Lawrence, Ks., U.S. — D8 93
Lawrence, Ma., U.S. — A5 98
Lawrence, Mi., U.S. — F4 99
Lawrence, Ms., U.S. — C4 101
Lawrence, N.Y., U.S. — k13 109
Lawrence, Pa., U.S. — F1 115
Lawrence, co., Al., U.S. — A2 78
Lawrence, co., Ar., U.S. — A4 81

Lawrence, co., Il., U.S. — E6 90
Lawrence, co., In., U.S. — G4 91
Lawrence, co., Ky., U.S. — B7 94
Lawrence, co., Ms., U.S. — D3 101
Lawrence, co., Mo., U.S. — D4 102
Lawrence, co., Oh., U.S. — D3 112
Lawrence, co., Pa., U.S. — E1 115
Lawrence, co., S.D., U.S. — E2 32
Lawrence, co., Tn., U.S. — B4 119
Lawrenceburg, In., U.S. — F8 91
Lawrenceburg, Ky., U.S. — B5 94
Lawrenceburg, Tn., U.S. — B4 119
Lawrence Park, Pa., U.S. — B1 115
Lawrenceport, In., U.S. — G5 91
Lawrence Station, N.B. — D2 71
Lawrencetown, N.S. — E4 71
Lawrenceville, Que. — D5 74
Lawrenceville, Ga., U.S. — C3 87
Lawrenceville, Il., U.S. — E6 90
Lawrenceville, N.J., U.S. — C3 107
Lawrenceville, N.Y., U.S. — f10 109
Lawrenceville, Pa., U.S. — C7 115
Lawrenceville, Va., U.S. — D5 123
Lawshe, Oh., U.S. — D2 112
Lawson, Sask. — G2 75
Lawson, Ar., U.S. — D3 81
Lawson, Mo., U.S. — B3 102
Lawsonia, Md., U.S. — E6 97
Lawsonville, N.C., U.S. — A2 110
Lawtell, La., U.S. — D3 95
Lawtey, Fl., U.S. — B4 86
Lawton, Ia., U.S. — B1 92
Lawton, Ky., U.S. — B6 94
Lawton, Mi., U.S. — F5 99
Lawton, N.D., U.S. — A7 111
Lawton, Ok., U.S. — C3 113
Lawyersville, N.Y., U.S. — C6 109
Lawz, Jabal al, mtn., Sau. Ar. — H10 40
Lax Kw'alaams, B.C. — B2 69
Laxou, Fr. — C7 16
Lay, Point, c., Viet. — D7 35
Lay Dam, Al., U.S. — C3 78
Lay Lake, res., Al., U.S. — B3 78
Layland, W.V., U.S. — n14 125
Layou, St. Vin. — U26 65
Laysan Island, i., Hi., U.S. — k13 88
Laysville, Ct., U.S. — D6 84
Layton, Ut., U.S. — B4 121
Laytonsville, Md., U.S. — B3 97
Laytonville, Ca., U.S. — C2 82
Lazdijai, Sov. Un. — A7 26
Lazear, Co., U.S. — C3 83
Łaziska Górne, Pol. — g9 26
Lea, co., N.M., U.S. — D6 108
Lea, stm., Eng., U.K. — k12 10
Leach, co., Tx., U.S. — A7 113
Leachville, Ar., U.S. — B5 81
Leacross, Sask. — D3 75
Lead, S.D., U.S. — C2 118
Leadbetter Point, c., Wa., U.S. — C1 124
Leader, Sask. — G1 75
Lead Hill, Ar., U.S. — A3 81
Lead Hill, hill, Mo., U.S. — D5 102
Lead Mountain, mtn., Me., U.S. — D4 96
Lead Mountain Ponds, l., Me., U.S. — D4 96
Leadore, Id., U.S. — E5 89
Leadville, Co., U.S. — B4 83
Leadwood, Mo., U.S. — D7 102
Leaf, Ms., U.S. — D5 101
Leaf, stm., Ms., U.S. — D5 101
Leaf Lake, l., Sask. — E4 75
Leaf Rapids, Man. — A1 70
Leaf River, Il., U.S. — A4 90
League City, Tx., U.S. — *r14 120
Leah, Ga., U.S. — C4 87
Leake, co., Ms., U.S. — C4 101
Leakesville, Ms., U.S. — D5 101
Leakey, Tx., U.S. — E3 120
Leal, N.D., U.S. — B7 111
Lealman, Fl., U.S. — p10 86
Leamington, Ont. — E2 73
Leamington, Ut., U.S. — D3 121
Leamington see Royal Leamington Spa, U.K. — D6 10
Leane, Lough, l., Ire. — E2 11
Leapwood, Tn., U.S. — B3 119
Learned, Ms., U.S. — C3 101
Leary, Ga., U.S. — E2 87
Leasburg, Mo., U.S. — C6 102
Leasburg, N.C., U.S. — A3 110
Leaside (part of East York), Ont. — m15 73
Leask, Sask. — E2 75
Leatherhead, Eng., U.K. — m12 10
Leatherman Peak, mtn., Id., U.S. — E5 89
Leatherwood, Ky., U.S. — C6 94
L'Eau Frais Creek, stm., Ar., U.S. — C3 81
Leavenworth, In., U.S. — H5 91
Leavenworth, Ks., U.S. — C9 93
Leavenworth, Wa., U.S. — B5 124
Leavenworth, co., Ks., U.S. — C8 93
Leavittsburg, Oh., U.S. — A5 112
Leawood, Ks., U.S. — D9 93
Łeba, Pol. — A4 26
Lebam, Wa., U.S. — C2 124
Lebanon, Ct., U.S. — C7 84
Lebanon, De., U.S. — D4 85
Lebanon, Il., U.S. — E4 90
Lebanon, In., U.S. — D5 91
Lebanon, Ks., U.S. — C5 93
Lebanon, Ky., U.S. — C4 94
Lebanon, Mo., U.S. — D5 102
Lebanon, Ne., U.S. — D5 104
Lebanon, N.H., U.S. — C2 106
Lebanon, N.J., U.S. — B3 107
Lebanon, Oh., U.S. — C1 112
Lebanon, Ok., U.S. — D5 113
Lebanon, Or., U.S. — C4 114
Lebanon, Pa., U.S. — F9 115
Lebanon, S.D., U.S. — B6 118
Lebanon, Tn., U.S. — A5 119
Lebanon, Va., U.S. — f9 123
Lebanon, co., Pa., U.S. — F8 115
Lebanon, ctry., Asia — B3 38
Lebanon Junction, Ky., U.S. — C4 94
Le Bardo, Tun. — *B7 42
Lebeau, La., U.S. — D4 95
Lebec, Ca., U.S. — E4 82
Lebedin, Sov. Un. — F10 27
Lebedyan, Sov. Un. — E12 27
Le Biot, Fr. — D2 21
Le Blanc, Fr. — D7 16
Le Blanc-Mesnil, Fr. — g10 16
Lebo, Ks., U.S. — D8 93
Lebo, Zaire — A3 48
Lębork, Pol. — A4 26
Le Bourg-d'Oisans, Fr. — D2 20
Le Bourget, Fr. — g10 16
Le Bouscat, Fr. — E3 16
Le Brassus, Switz. — C1 21
Lebret, Sask. — G4 75

Lebrija, Spain — D2 22
Lebu, Chile — B2 54
Lebyazhye, Sov. Un. — B7 28
Le Cateau, Fr. — B5 16
Lecce, Italy — D7 23
Lecco, Italy — B2 23
Lecco, Lake, l., Italy — E7 21
Le Center, Mn., U.S. — F5 100
Lech, stm., Eur. — D5 18
Le Chambon-Feugerolles, Fr. — E6 16
Le-Château, Fr. — E3 16
Lechbruck, W. Ger. — B6 20
Le Chesnay, Fr. — g9 16
Le Chesne, Fr. — E4 17
Leck, W. Ger. — D2 15
Le Claire, Ia., U.S. — C7 92
Leclercville, Que. — C6 74
Le Creusot, Fr. — D6 16
Le Croisic, Fr. — D9 12
Le Crotoy, Fr. — B3 16
Lectoure, Fr. — F9 16
Łęczyca, Pol. — B5 26
Ledbetter, N.C., U.S. — B3 110
Ledbury, Eng., U.K. — B5 12
Ledčice, Czech. — n17 26
Ledeberg (part of Gent), Bel. — C3 17
Ledesma, Spain — B2 22
Ledford, Il., U.S. — F5 90
Ledger, Mt., U.S. — B5 103
Ledgewood, N.J., U.S. — B3 107
Ledo, India — C10 36
Ledoux, N.M., U.S. — B4 108
Leduc, Alta. — C4 68
Ledyard, Ct., U.S. — D7 84
Ledyard, Ia., U.S. — A3 92
Lee, Fl., U.S. — B3 86
Lee, Il., U.S. — B5 90
Lee, Me., U.S. — C4 96
Lee, Ma., U.S. — B1 98
Lee, Nv., U.S. — C6 105
Lee, N.H., U.S. — D4 106
Lee, Tn., U.S. — D8 119
Lee, co., Al., U.S. — C4 78
Lee, co., Ar., U.S. — C5 81
Lee, co., Fl., U.S. — F5 86
Lee, co., Ga., U.S. — E2 87
Lee, co., Il., U.S. — B4 90
Lee, co., Ia., U.S. — D6 92
Lee, co., Ky., U.S. — C6 94
Lee, co., N.C., U.S. — B3 110
Lee, co., S.C., U.S. — C7 117
Lee, co., Tx., U.S. — D4 120
Lee, co., Va., U.S. — f8 123
Lee, Lake, l., Ms., U.S. — B3 101
Lee Center, Il., U.S. — B4 90
Leechburg, Pa., U.S. — E2 115
Leech Lake, l., Sask. — F4 75
Leech Lake, l., Mn., U.S. — C4 100
Leech Lake Indian Reservation, Mn., U.S. — C4 100
Leechville, N.C., U.S. — B6 110
Leedey, Ok., U.S. — B2 113
Leedom Estates, De., U.S. — *B3 85
Leeds, Eng., U.K. — D6 10
Leeds, Al., U.S. — B3 78
Leeds, N.D., U.S. — A6 111
Leeds, S.C., U.S. — B5 117
Leeds, Ut., U.S. — F2 121
Leeds [and Grenville], co., Ont. — C8 73
Leeds Point, N.J., U.S. — E4 107
Leeds-Village, Que. — C6 74
Leek, Eng., U.K. — A5 12
Leelanau, co., Mi., U.S. — D5 99
Leelanau, Lake, l., Mi., U.S. — C5 99
Leenaun, Ire. — D2 11
Lee Park, Pa., U.S. — n17 115
Leeper, Mo., U.S. — D7 102
Leeper, Pa., U.S. — D2 115
Leer, W. Ger. — B3 18
Leesburg, Al., U.S. — A4 78
Leesburg, Fl., U.S. — D5 86
Leesburg, Ga., U.S. — E2 87
Leesburg, In., U.S. — B6 91
Leesburg, N.J., U.S. — E3 107
Leesburg, Oh., U.S. — C2 112
Leesburg, Va., U.S. — A5 123
Lees Summit, Mo., U.S. — C3 102
Leesville, Ct., U.S. — *C6 84
Leesville, In., U.S. — G5 91
Leesville, La., U.S. — C2 95
Leesville, Oh., U.S. — B4 112
Leesville, S.C., U.S. — D4 117
Leesville, Tx., U.S. — E4 120
Leesville Lake, res., Va., U.S. — C3 123
Leetes Island, Ct., U.S. — D5 84
Leeton, Austl. — G4 51
Leeton, Mo., U.S. — C4 102
Leetonia, Oh., U.S. — B5 112
Leetsdale, Pa., U.S. — h13 115
Leeuwarden, Neth. — A6 16
Leeuwin, Cape, c., Austl. — F2 50
Leeville, La., U.S. — E5 95
Lee Vining, Ca., U.S. — D4 82
Leeward Islands, is., N.A. — H13 64
Le Ferriere, Italy — h9 23
Leffingwell, Ct., U.S. — C7 84
Leflore, Ok., U.S. — C7 113
Leflore, co., Ms., U.S. — B3 101
Lefor, N.D., U.S. — C3 111
Lefors, Tx., U.S. — B2 120
Le François, Mart. — I14 64
Lefroy, Ont. — C5 73
Lefroy, Lake, l., Austl. — F3 50
Leftrook Lake, l., Man. — A2 70
Legal, Alta. — C4 68
Leganés, Spain — p17 22
Legaspi, Phil. — C6 34
Legau, W. Ger. — E5 18
Leggett, Ca., U.S. — C2 82
Leghorn see Livorno, Italy — C3 23
Legionowo, Pol. — k13 26
Legnago, Italy — D7 20
Legnano, Italy — B2 23
Legnica (Liegnitz), Pol. — C4 26
Le Gore, Md., U.S. — A3 97
Le Grand, Ca., U.S. — D3 82
Le Grand, Ia., U.S. — B5 92
Le Grand-Quevilly, Fr. — C4 16
Le Gros Cap, c., Que. — B7 74
Leh, India — B6 36
Le Havre, Fr. — C4 16
Lehi, Ut., U.S. — C4 121

Lehigh, Ia., U.S. — B3 92
Lehigh, Ks., U.S. — D6 93
Lehigh, Ok., U.S. — C5 113
Lehigh, co., Pa., U.S. — E10 115
Lehigh, stm., Pa., U.S. — E10 115
Lehigh Acres, Fl., U.S. — F5 86
Lehighton, Pa., U.S. — E10 115
Lehinch, Ire. — E2 11
Lehman, Pa., U.S. — n16 115
Lehr, N.D., U.S. — C6 111
Lehrte, W. Ger. — B4 18
Lehua Island, i., Hi., U.S. — A1 88
Leiah, Pak. — B5 36
Leibnitz, Aus. — E7 18
Leicester, Eng., U.K. — D6 10
Leicester, Ma., U.S. — B4 98
Leicester, N.Y., U.S. — C3 109
Leicester, Vt., U.S. — D2 122
Leicester Junction, Vt., U.S. — D2 122
Leicestershire, co., Eng., U.K. — B6 12
Leichhardt, Austl. — *F9 51
Leichhardt, stm., Austl. — C7 50
Leiden, Neth. — A6 16
Leigh, Ne., U.S. — C8 104
Leigh Creek, Austl. — F6 50
Leighlinbridge, Ire. — E5 11
Leighton, Al., U.S. — A2 78
Leinan, Sask. — G2 75
Leinster, hist. reg., Ire. — D4 11
Leinster, Mount, mtn., Ire. — E5 11
Leipalingis, Sov. Un. — A7 26
Leipers Fork, Tn., U.S. — B5 119
Leipsic, De., U.S. — D3 85
Leipsic, In., U.S. — G5 91
Leipsic, Oh., U.S. — A2 112
Leipsic, stm., De., U.S. — C3 85
Leipzig, Sask. — E1 75
Leipzig, E. Ger. — C6 18
Leiria, Port. — C1 22
Leisnig, E. Ger. — B7 19
Leiston, Eng., U.K. — B9 12
Leisure City, Fl., U.S. — s13 86
Leitchfield, Ky., U.S. — C3 94
Leiter, Wy., U.S. — B6 127
Leitersburg, Md., U.S. — A2 97
Leiters Ford, In., U.S. — B5 91
Leith, N.D., U.S. — C4 111
Leitha, stm., Eur. — B3 24
Leitrim, co., Ire. — C3 11
Leixlip, Ire. — D5 11
Leiva, Cerro, mtn., Col. — C3 60
Leizhou Bandao, pen., China — G7 31
Leizhou Bay, b., China — B9 35
Lejunior, Ky., U.S. — D6 94
Lek, stm., Neth. — A5 16
Leka, i., Nor. — E4 14
Lekeba, i., Fiji — I16 52
Lekoa, S. Afr. — *C4 49
Le Kreider, Alg. — C5 44
Leksand, Swe. — G6 14
Leksula, Indon. — F7 34
Lela, Tx., U.S. — B2 120
Le Lamentin, Mart. — S10 65
Leland, Il., U.S. — B5 90
Leland, Ia., U.S. — A4 92
Leland, Mi., U.S. — C5 99
Leland, Ms., U.S. — B3 101
Leland, Wa., U.S. — B3 124
Leleiwi Point, c., Hi., U.S. — D7 88
Leleque, Arg. — B2 54
Leleloaloa, Am. Sam. — F13 52
Le Locle, Switz. — B3 18
Le Lorrain, Mart. — S10 65
Leloup, Ks., U.S. — D8 93
Lelystad, Neth. — B5 17
Le Maire, Estrecho de, strt., Arg. — h12 54
Le Mans, Fr. — C4 16
Le Marin, Mart. — I14 64
Le Mars, Ia., U.S. — B1 92
Lemasters, Pa., U.S. — G6 115
Lembach, Fr. — F7 17
Lemberg, Sask. — G4 75
Lemdiyya, Alg. — B5 44
Leme, Braz. — m8 56
Lemelerveld, Neth. — B6 17
Lemery, Phil. — p13 34
Lemesós (Limassol), Cyp. — E9 40
Lemgo, W. Ger. — B4 18
Lemhi, co., Id., U.S. — E4 89
Lemhi, stm., Id., U.S. — E5 89
Lemhi Pass, Id., U.S. — E5 89
Lemhi Range, mts., Id., U.S. — E5 89
Lemieux, Que. — C5 74
Lemitar, N.M., U.S. — C3 108
Lemmer, Neth. — B5 17
Lemmon, S.D., U.S. — B3 118
Lemmon, Mount, mtn., Az., U.S. — E5 80
Lemmon Valley, Nv., U.S. — D2 105
Lemnos see Límnos, i., Grc. — F5 91
Lemon, Lake, l., In., U.S. — F5 91
Lemon Fair, stm., Vt., U.S. — C2 122
Lemon Grove, Ca., U.S. — o15 82
Lemon Island, i., S.C., U.S. — G6 117
Lemons, Mo., U.S. — A4 102
Lemont, Il., U.S. — B5 90
Lemont, Pa., U.S. — E6 115
Lemonweir, stm., Wi., U.S. — D3 126
Lemoore, Ca., U.S. — D4 82
Lemoore Naval Air Station, mil., Ca., U.S. — D4 82
Lemoore Station, Ca., U.S. — *D4 82
Le Moyen, La., U.S. — D3 95
Lemoyne, Ne., U.S. — C4 104
Lemoyne, Oh., U.S. — f7 112
Lempa, stm., N.A. — D3 62
Lem Peak, mtn., Id., U.S. — E5 89
Lempster, N.H., U.S. — D2 106
Lemsford, Sask. — G1 75
Lemvig, Den. — C2 15
Lena, Spain — A3 22
Lena, Il., U.S. — A4 90
Lena, La., U.S. — C3 95
Lena, Ms., U.S. — C4 101
Lena, Wi., U.S. — D5 126
Lena, stm., Sov. Un. — C15 29
Lenapah, Ok., U.S. — A6 113
Lenawee, co., Mi., U.S. — G6 99
Lençóis, Braz. — B7 57
Lend, Aus. — B9 20
Lendinara, Italy — D7 20
Lenexa, Ks., U.S. — D9 93
Leney, Sask. — E2 75
Lengby, Mn., U.S. — C3 100
Lengede, W. Ger. — B4 18
Lengerich, W. Ger. — A2 18
Lenghu, China — D3 31

Lengshuijiang, China — *F7 31
Lenhartsville, Pa., U.S. — E10 115
Leninabad, Sov. Un. — E9 29
Leninakan, Sov. Un. — E2 28
Leningrad, Sov. Un. — C6 29
Leningradskaya, sci., Ant. — C28 7
Leninogorsk, Sov. Un. — D11 29
Lenino, Sov. Un. — n17 27
Leninsk, Sov. Un. — G15 27
Leninsk-Kuznetskiy, Sov. Un. — D11 29
Leninskoye, Sov. Un. — C7 28
Lenkoran, Sov. Un. — F7 29
Lenna, Ok., U.S. — B6 113
Lenne, stm., W. Ger. — B2 19
Lennox, Ca., U.S. — *n12 82
Lennox, S.D., U.S. — D9 118
Lennox and Addington, co., Ont. — C7 73
Lennoxville, Que. — D6 74
Leno, Italy — D6 20
Lenoir, N.C., U.S. — B1 110
Lenoir, co., N.C., U.S. — B5 110
Lenoir City, Tn., U.S. — D9 119
Lenora, Ks., U.S. — C4 93
Lenorah, Tx., U.S. — C2 120
Lenore, Man. — E1 70
Lenore, Id., U.S. — C2 89
Lenore Lake, l., Sask. — E3 75
Lenore Lake, l., Wa., U.S. — B6 124
Lenox, Al., U.S. — D2 78
Lenox, Ga., U.S. — E3 87
Lenox, Ia., U.S. — D3 92
Lenox, Ma., U.S. — B1 98
Lenox, Mo., U.S. — D6 102
Lenox, Tn., U.S. — A2 119
Lenox Dale, Ma., U.S. — B1 98
Lens, Fr. — B5 16
Lentner, Mo., U.S. — B5 102
Lenzburg, Switz. — B5 21
Lenzen, E. Ger. — E5 15
Lenzerheide, Switz. — C8 21
Léo, Burkina — D4 45
Leo, In., U.S. — B7 91
Leola, Ar., U.S. — C3 81
Leola, S.D., U.S. — B7 118
Leoma, Tn., U.S. — B4 119
Leominster, Eng., U.K. — B5 12
Leominster, Ma., U.S. — A4 98
Leon, Nic. — E7 63
León, Spain — A3 22
Leon, Ia., U.S. — D4 92
Leon, Ks., U.S. — E7 93
Leon, N.Y., U.S. — C1 109
Leon, Ok., U.S. — D4 113
Leon, W.V., U.S. — C3 125
Leon, co., Fl., U.S. — B2 86
Leon, co., Tx., U.S. — D4 120
León, hist. reg., Spain — B3 22
Leona, Tx., U.S. — D5 120
Leonard, Mi., U.S. — h13 73
Leonard, Mo., U.S. — B5 102
Leonard, N.D., U.S. — C8 111
Leonard, Ok., U.S. — B6 113
Leonard, Tx., U.S. — C4 120
Leonardo, N.J., U.S. — C4 107
Leonardtown, Md., U.S. — D4 97
Leonardsville, N.Y., U.S. — C5 109
Leonardville, Ks., U.S. — C7 93
Leonberg, W. Ger. — C5 19
León [de los Aldamas], Mex. — G9 62
Leone, Am. Sam. — G13 52
Leone Bay, b., Am. Sam. — G13 52
Leonforte, Italy — L9 23
Leongatha, Austl. — I5 51
Leonia, N.J., U.S. — h9 107
Leonídhion, Grc. — C4 40
Leonora, Austl. — E3 50
Leon Valley, Tx., U.S. — *E3 120
Leopold, In., U.S. — H4 91
Leopold, Mo., U.S. — D8 102
Leopold and Astrid Coast, Ant. — C21 7
Leopoldina, Braz. — C4 56
Léopoldsburg, Bel. — C5 17
Léopoldville see Kinshasa, Zaire — B2 48
Leoti, Ks., U.S. — D2 93
Leoville, Sask. — D2 75
Leoville, Ks., U.S. — C3 93
Leovo, Sov. Un. — H7 27
Lepanto, Ar., U.S. — B5 81
Lepe, Spain — D2 22
Le Petit-Quevilly, Fr. — C4 16
Lephué, Chile — C2 54
Leping, China — J7 32
Le Plessis-Belleville, Fr. — G11 16
Le Plessis-Robinson, Fr. — G10 16
Le Pont, Switz. — C1 21
Lepontine Alps, mts., Eur. — C2 23
Le Portel, Fr. — B3 16
Lepreau, N.B. — D3 71
Lepreau, Point, c., N.B. — D3 71
Lepsinsk, Sov. Un. — F25 8
Lepsy, Sov. Un. — H9 28
Le Puy [-en-Velay], Fr. — E5 16
Lequire, Ok., U.S. — B6 113
Le Raincy, Fr. — g11 16
Le Raysville, Pa., U.S. — C9 115
Lercara Friddi, Italy — F4 23
Léré, Chad — D2 46
Lérida, Col. — C3 60
Lérida, Spain — B6 22
Lerma, stm., Mex. — m13 63
Lermoos, Aus. — D5 18
Lerna, Il., U.S. — D5 90
Le Robert, Mart. — S11 65
Léros, i., Grc. — D6 41
Leross, Sask. — F3 75
Leroux Wash, val., Az., U.S. — B5 80
Leroy, Sask. — F3 75
Le Roy, Il., U.S. — C5 90
Le Roy, Ks., U.S. — D8 93
Le Roy, Mi., U.S. — D5 99
Le Roy, Mn., U.S. — G6 100

Le Roy, N.Y., U.S. — C3 109
Leroy, N.D., U.S. — A8 111
Le Roy, Pa., U.S. — C8 115
Lerum, Swe. — A6 15
Le Russey, Fr. — B2 21
Lerwick, Scot., U.K. — g10 10
Léry, Que. — q19 74
Léry, Lake, l., La., U.S. — k12 95
Les Abymes, Guad. — Q8 65
Le Saint-Esprit, Mart. — S11 65
Lesbos see Lésvos, i., Grc. — C5 40
Les Cayes, Haiti — E7 64
Les Diablerets, Switz. — C3 20
Les Éboulements, Que. — B7 74
Les Echelles, Fr. — D1 20
Le Sentier, Switz. — C1 21
Le Sépey, Switz. — D3 21
Les Escoumins, Que. — A8 74
Les Étroits, Que. — B9 74
Les Fonds, Que. — o16 74
Leshan, China — F5 31
Leshara, Ne., U.S. — g12 104
Les Haudères, Switz. — C3 20
Lesina, Lake, b., Italy — D5 23
Lesko, Pol. — D7 26
Leskovac, Yugo. — D5 24
Leslie, Sask. — F4 75
Leslie, Ar., U.S. — B3 81
Leslie, Ga., U.S. — E2 87
Leslie, Id., U.S. — F5 89
Leslie, Mi., U.S. — F6 99
Leslie, S.C., U.S. — B6 117
Leslie, W.V., U.S. — C4 125
Leslie, co., Ky., U.S. — C6 94
Leslieville, Alta. — C3 68
Les Lilas, Fr. — g10 16
Lesneven, Fr. — C1 16
Lesnoy, Sov. Un. — B4 28
Lesogorsk, Sov. Un. — B11 33
Lesosavodsk, Sov. Un. — E3 16
Lesotho, ctry., Afr. — C4 49
Les Ponts-de-Cé, Fr. — D3 16
Les Rousses, Fr. — D1 21
Les Sables-d'Olonne, Fr. — D4 16
Lesser Antilles, is. — H14 53
Lesser Khing Range see Xiao Hinggan Ling), mts., China — B10 31
Lesser Slave Lake, l., Alta. — B3 68
Lesser Sunda Islands (Nusa Tenggara), is., Indon. — G5 34
Lessines, Bel. — D3 17
Lester, Al., U.S. — A1 92
Lester, W.V., U.S. — n13 125
Lester Prairie, Mn., U.S. — F4 100
Lesterville, Mo., U.S. — D7 102
Lesterville, S.D., U.S. — D8 118
Lestock, Sask. — F3 75
Le Sueur, Mn., U.S. — F5 100
Le Sueur, co., Mn., U.S. — F5 100
Les Verrières, Switz. — C1 21
Lésvos (Lesbos), i., Grc. — C4 26
Leszno, Pol. — C4 26
Letart Falls, Oh., U.S. — C4 112
Letcher, S.D., U.S. — D7 118
Letcher, co., Ky., U.S. — C7 94
Le Teil, Fr. — E6 16
Letellier, Man. — E3 70
Letha, Id., U.S. — F2 89
Lethbridge, Alta. — E4 68
Lethbridge, Newf. — D5 72
Lethem, Guy. — B3 59
Le Thillot, Fr. — B2 20
Letiahau, stm., Bots. — D4 49
Leticia, Col. — D4 60
Leti Islands, is., Indon. — G7 34
Leto, Fl., U.S. — *E4 86
Letohatchee, Al., U.S. — B4 81
Letona, Ar., U.S. — D9 17
Le Touquet-Paris-Plage, Fr. — D1 16
Le Tourneau, Ms., U.S. — C3 101
Letpadan, Burma — E10 36
Le Tréport, Fr. — B4 16
Letsok-Aw, i., Burma — G3 35
Letterkenny, Ire. — D2 11
Letterfrack, Ire. — D2 11
Lettermullan, Ire. — D2 11
Letts, In., U.S. — F6 91
Lettsworth, La., U.S. — D4 95
Leucas see Levkás, i., Grc. — C3 40
Leuctra see Lévktra, Grc. — g10 25
Leuk, Switz. — D4 21
Leukerbad, Switz. — D4 21
Leulumoega, W. Sam. — F12 52
Leupp, Az., U.S. — B5 80
Leupp Corner, Az., U.S. — B5 80
Leuser, mtn., Indon. — k11 34
Leushinskiy Tuman, Lake, l., Sov. Un. — I2 28
Leutkirch, W. Ger. — E5 18
Leuven (Louvain), Bel. — B6 16
Leuze, Bel. — D3 17
Levádhia, Grc. — C4 40
Levallois-Perret, Fr. — g10 16
Levan, Ut., U.S. — D4 121
Levanger, Nor. — E4 14
Levant, Ks., U.S. — C2 93
Levant, Me., U.S. — D4 96
Levanna, mtn., Eur. — k9 100
Levelland, Tx., U.S. — C1 120
Leven, Scot., U.K. — B5 10
Leveque, Cape, c., Austl. — C3 50
Leverett, Ma., U.S. — B2 98
Leverett Glacier, ice, Ant. — A32 7
Levering, Mi., U.S. — C6 99
Leverkusen, W. Ger. — B1 19
Levice, Czech. — D5 26
Levick, Mount, mtn., Ant. — B29 7
Levie, Fr. — C1 21
Le Vigan, Fr. — E5 16
Levin, N.Z. — N15 51
Lévis, Que. — C6 74
Lévis, co., Que. — C6 74
Levisa Fork, stm., U.S. — C7 94
Levítha, i., Grc. — D6 41
Levittown, N.Y., U.S. — E7 109
Levittown, Pa., U.S. — F12 115
Levkás, Grc. — C3 40
Levkás (Leucas), i., Grc. — C3 40
Levočа, Czech. — D5 26
Levuka, Fiji — H15 52
Levy, co., Fl., U.S. — C4 86
Levy Lake, l., Fl., U.S. — C4 86
Lewvan, Sask. — G3 75
Lewellen, Ne., U.S. — C3 104
Lewes, Eng., U.K. — E7 10
Lewes, De., U.S. — E5 85
Lewes and Rehoboth Canal, De., U.S. — F5 85
Lewis, In., U.S. — F3 91

Lewis, Ia., U.S. — C2 92
Lewis, Ks., U.S. — E4 93
Lewis, Mo., U.S. — C4 102
Lewis, N.Y., U.S. — A7 109
Lewis, Wi., U.S. — C1 126
Lewis, co., Id., U.S. — C2 89
Lewis, co., Ky., U.S. — B6 94
Lewis, co., Mo., U.S. — A6 102
Lewis, co., N.Y., U.S. — B5 109
Lewis, co., Tn., U.S. — B4 119
Lewis, co., Wa., U.S. — C4 124
Lewis, co., W.V., U.S. — C4 125
Lewis, stm., Wa., U.S. — C4 124
Lewis, Butt of, c., Scot., U.K. — A3 10
Lewis, Isle of, i., Scot., U.K. — A3 10
Lewis, Mount, mtn., Nv., U.S. — C5 105
Lewis and Clark, co., Mt., U.S. — C4 103
Lewis and Clark Cavern, Mt., U.S. — D5 103
Lewis and Clark Lake, res., U.S. — E8 118
Lewisberry, Pa., U.S. — F8 115
Lewisburg, Ky., U.S. — D3 94
Lewisburg, La., U.S. — D3 95
Lewisburg, Oh., U.S. — C1 112
Lewisburg, Pa., U.S. — E8 115
Lewisburg, Tn., U.S. — B5 119
Lewisburg, W.V., U.S. — D4 125
Lewis Center, Oh., U.S. — B2 112
Lewis Creek, stm., Sask. — F3 75
Lewis Creek, stm., Vt., U.S. — C2 122
Lewis Hills, hills, Newf. — D2 72
Lewis Lake, l., Wy., U.S. — B2 127
Lewisport, Ky., U.S. — C3 94
Lewisporte, Newf. — D4 72
Lewis Range, mts., N.A. — A5 76
Lewis Run, Pa., U.S. — C4 115
Lewis Smith Lake, res., Al., U.S. — B2 78
Lewiston, Id., U.S. — C1 89
Lewiston, Me., U.S. — D2 96
Lewiston, Mn., U.S. — G7 100
Lewiston, N.Y., U.S. — B1 109
Lewiston, Ut., U.S. — B4 121
Lewiston Peak, mtn., Ut., U.S. — C3 121
Lewiston Woodville, N.C., U.S. — A5 110
Lewistown, Il., U.S. — C3 90
Lewistown, Md., U.S. — A3 97
Lewistown, Mo., U.S. — A6 102
Lewistown, Mt., U.S. — C7 103
Lewistown, Pa., U.S. — E6 115
Lewisville, N.B. — C5 71
Lewisville, Ar., U.S. — D2 81
Lewisville, Id., U.S. — F6 89
Lewisville, In., U.S. — E7 91
Lewisville, Mn., U.S. — G4 100
Lewisville, Oh., U.S. — C4 112
Lewisville, Tx., U.S. — C4 120
Lewisville Lake, res., Tx., U.S. — C4 120
Lexa, Ar., U.S. — C5 81
Lexington, Al., U.S. — A2 78
Lexington, Ga., U.S. — C3 87
Lexington, Il., U.S. — C5 90
Lexington, In., U.S. — G6 91
Lexington, Ky., U.S. — B5 94
Lexington, Ma., U.S. — B5 98
Lexington, Mi., U.S. — E8 99
Lexington, Mn., U.S. — m12 100
Lexington, Mo., U.S. — B4 102
Lexington, Ne., U.S. — D6 104
Lexington, N.Y., U.S. — C6 109
Lexington, N.C., U.S. — B2 110
Lexington, Oh., U.S. — B3 112
Lexington, Ok., U.S. — B4 113
Lexington, Or., U.S. — B7 114
Lexington, S.C., U.S. — D5 117
Lexington, Tn., U.S. — B3 119
Lexington, Tx., U.S. — D4 120
Lexington, Va., U.S. — C3 123
Lexington, co., S.C., U.S. — D5 117
Lexington Park, Md., U.S. — D4 108
Leyburn, Eng., U.K. — B4 108
Leyte, i., Phil. — C6 34
Leyte Gulf, b., Phil. — C6 34
Lezajsk, Pol. — B2 40
Lézignan, Fr. — F5 16
Lgov, Sov. Un. — F10 27
Lhasa, China — F3 31
Lhazê, China — C11 31
Lhokseumawe, Indon. — k11 34
Lhoksukon, Indon. — J2 35
Liancheng, China — I2 32
Liangping, China — D5 32
Lianhua, China — K5 32
Lianjiang, China — B9 35
Lianyungang, China — E8 31
Liaocheng, China — F6 32
Liaodong Bay, b., China — E9 31
Liao He, stm., China — C9 31
Liaoning, prov., China — C9 31
Liaotung Bay see Liaodong Bay, b., China — E9 31
Liaotung Peninsula, pen., China — D9 31
Liaoyang, China — D9 31
Liaoyuan, China — C10 31
Liard, stm., Can. — E7 66
Liart, Fr. — E4 17
Liathach, mtn., Scot., U.K. — C3 13
Líbano, Col. — C2 60
Libau, Man. — D3 70
Libby, Mt., U.S. — B1 103
Libčice [nad Vltavou], Czech. — n17 26
Libčchov, Czech. — n17 26
Libenge, Zaire — A2 48
Liberal, Ks., U.S. — E3 93
Liberal, Mo., U.S. — D3 102
Liberec, Czech. — E7 63
Liberia, C.R. — E4 63
Liberia, ctry., Afr. — G4 45
Libertad General Bernardo O'Higgins, prov., Chile — A2 54
Libertador General San Martín, Arg. — D3 55
Liberty, Sask. — G3 75
Liberty, Id., U.S. — G7 89
Liberty, Il., U.S. — D2 90
Liberty, In., U.S. — E8 91
Liberty, Ky., U.S. — C5 94
Liberty, Me., U.S. — D3 96
Liberty, Ms., U.S. — D3 101
Liberty, Mo., U.S. — B3 102
Liberty, Ne., U.S. — D9 104
Liberty, N.Y., U.S. — D6 109

| Name | Map Ref. | Page |
|---|---|---|

Liberty, N.C., U.S. — B3 110
Liberty, Pa., U.S. — C7 115
Liberty, S.C., U.S. — B2 117
Liberty, Tn., U.S. — C8 119
Liberty, Tx., U.S. — D5 120
Liberty, Wa., U.S. — B5 124
Liberty, co., Fl., U.S. — B2 86
Liberty, co., Ga., U.S. — E5 87
Liberty, co., Mt., U.S. — B5 103
Liberty, co., Tx., U.S. — D5 120
Liberty Acres, Ca., U.S. — *n12 82
Liberty Center, In., U.S. — C7 91
Liberty Center, Ia., U.S. — C4 92
Liberty Center, Oh., U.S. — A1 112
Liberty Corner, N.J., U.S. — B3 107
Liberty Grove, Md., U.S. — A5 97
Liberty Hill, Ct., U.S. — C6 84
Liberty Hill, S.C., U.S. — C6 117
Liberty Lake, Wa., U.S. — g14 124
Liberty Lake, res., Md., U.S. — B4 97
Liberty Mills, In., U.S. — B6 91
Libertytown, Md., U.S. — B3 97
Libertyville, Il., U.S. — A6 90
Libertyville, Ia., U.S. — D5 92
Libiron, i., Marsh Is. — S18 52
Liblar, W. Ger. — C1 19
Libourne, Fr. — E3 16
Libramont, Bel. — E5 17
Libreville, Gabon — E1 46
Libuse, La., U.S. — C3 95
Libušín, Czech. — n17 26
Libya, ctry., Afr. — D3 43
Libyan Desert, des., Afr. — D4 43
Libyan Plateau, plat., Afr. — C4 43
Licantén, Chile — B2 54
Licata, Italy — F4 23
Lice, Tur. — C13 40
Licenza, Italy — g9 23
Lichfield, Eng., U.K. — B6 12
Lichinga, Moz. — D6 48
Lichtenburg, S. Afr. — C4 49
Lichtenfels, W. Ger. — C6 19
Lichtenstein, E. Ger. — C7 19
Lick Creek, stm., Tn., U.S. — C11 119
Licking, Mo., U.S. — D6 102
Licking, co., Oh., U.S. — B3 112
Licking, stm., Ky., U.S. — B6 94
Licking, North Fork, stm., Ky., U.S. — B5 94
Licking, South Fork, stm., Ky., U.S. — B5 94
Licosa, Point, c., Italy — D5 23
Licungó, stm., Moz. — A6 49
Lida, Sov. Un. — E5 27
Lida, Lake, l., Mn., U.S. — D3 100
Liddel Water, stm., U.K. — E6 13
Lidderdale, Ia., U.S. — B3 92
Lidgerwood, N.D., U.S. — C8 111
Lidhult, Swe. — B7 15
Lidice, Czech. — C3 26
Lidingö, Swe. — H8 14
Lidköping, Swe. — H5 14
Lido di Roma, Italy — h8 23
Lidzbark Warmiński, Pol. — A6 26
Liebenthal, Sask. — G1 75
Liebenthal, Ks., U.S. — D4 93
Lieberose, E. Ger. — B9 19
Liechtenstein, ctry., Eur. — E4 18
Liège (Luik), Bel. — B6 16
Liège, prov., Bel. — D5 17
Liege, stm., Alta. — A4 68
Liegnitz see Legnica, Pol. — C4 26
Lieksa, Fin. — F14 14
Lienen, W. Ger. — A2 19
Lienz, Aus. — E6 18
Liepāja, Sov. Un. — C3 27
Lier (Lierre), Bel. — B6 16
Lierneux, Bel. — D5 17
Lierre see Lier, Bel. — B6 16
Liestal, Switz. — E3 18
Liévin, Fr. — D2 17
Lièvre, Rivière du, stm., Que. — D2 74
Lièvres, Île aux, i., Que. — B8 74
Liffey, stm., Ire. — D3 10
Lifford, Ire. — C3 10
Liftwood, De., U.S. — *A3 85
Light, Ar., U.S. — A5 81
Lighthouse Inlet, b., S.C., U.S. — k12 117
Lighthouse Point, Fl., U.S. — *F6 86
Lighthouse Point, c., Fl., U.S. — C2 86
Lighthouse Point, c., La., U.S. — E3 95
Lighthouse Point, c., Mi., U.S. — C5 99
Lightning Creek, stm., Wy., U.S. — C8 127
Lightning Ridge, Austl. — D6 51
Lignite, N.D., U.S. — A3 111
Lignum, Va., U.S. — B5 123
Ligny-en-Barrois, Fr. — F5 17
Ligonha, stm., Moz. — E6 48
Ligonier, In., U.S. — B6 91
Ligonier, Pa., U.S. — F3 115
Ligovo (part of Leningrad), Sov. Un. — s31 14
Liguria, prov., Italy — E4 20
Liguria, prov., Italy — B2 23
Ligurian Apennines, mts., Italy — E4 20
Ligurian Sea, Eur. — C2 23
Lihue, Hi., U.S. — B2 88
Lijiang, China — F5 31
Lijin, China — F8 32
Likasi, Zaire — C7 48
Likely, B.C. — D7 69
Likely, Ca., U.S. — B3 82
Likhoslavl, Sov. Un. — C10 27
Likino-Dulevo, Sov. Un. — n18 27
Lilbourn, Mo., U.S. — E8 102
Lilburn, Ga., U.S. — h8 87
L'Île-Rousse, Fr. — C2 23
Lilesville, N.C., U.S. — C3 110
Liling, China — K5 32
Lille, Fr. — B5 16
Lille, Me., U.S. — A4 96
Lille Bælt, strt., Den. — C3 15
Lillehammer, Nor. — G4 14
Lillers, Fr. — D2 17
Lillesand, Nor. — H3 14
Lilleström, Nor. — H4 14
Lillian, Al., U.S. — E2 78
Lillian, Tx., U.S. — n9 120
Lillie, La., U.S. — B3 95
Lillington, N.C., U.S. — B4 110
Lillinonah, Lake, l., Ct., U.S. — C2 84
Lilloet, B.C. — D7 69
Lilloet, Ca., U.S. — D6 69
Lilloet Lake, l., B.C. — D6 69
Lilloet Range, mts., B.C. — E7 69
Lilly, Ga., U.S. — D3 87
Lilly, Pa., U.S. — F4 115
Lilly Fork, stm., W.V., U.S. — m13 125
Lilly Grove, W.V., U.S. — D3 125
Lilongwe, Mwi. — D5 48
Lily, Ky., U.S. — h8 87
Lily, S.D., U.S. — B8 118
Lily, Wi., U.S. — C5 126
Lim, stm., Yugo. — D4 24

Lima, Para. — D4 55
Lima, Peru — D2 58
Lima, Il., U.S. — C2 90
Lima, Mt., U.S. — F4 103
Lima, N.Y., U.S. — C3 109
Lima, Oh., U.S. — B1 112
Lima, dept., Peru — D2 58
Lima Duarte, Braz. — C4 56
Lima Reservoir, res., Mt., U.S. — F4 103
Limanowa, Pol. — D6 26
Limassol see Lemesós, Cyp. — E9 40
Limavady, N. Ire., U.K. — B5 11
Limay, stm., Arg. — B3 54
Limay Mahuida, Arg. — B3 54
Limbach [-Oberfrohna], E. Ger. — C7 19
Limbe, Cam. — E1 46
Limbé, Haiti — E7 64
Limburg, W. Ger. — C4 18
Limburg, prov., Bel. — D5 17
Limburg, prov., Neth. — D5 17
Lime City, Oh., U.S. — e6 112
Limedale, In., U.S. — E4 91
Limeil-Brévannes, Fr. — h10 16
Limeira, Braz. — C3 56
Limerick, Sask. — H2 75
Limerick, Ire. — D2 10
Limerick, Me., U.S. — E2 96
Limerick, co., Ire. — E3 11
Lime Rock, Ct., U.S. — B2 84
Limerock, R.I., U.S. — B4 116
Limeshain, W. Ger. — ? ?
Lime Springs, Ia., U.S. — A5 92
Limestone, Ar., U.S. — B2 81
Limestone, Fl., U.S. — E5 86
Limestone, Me., U.S. — B5 96
Limestone, Pa., U.S. — D3 115
Limestone, Tn., U.S. — C11 119
Limestone, co., Al., U.S. — A2 78
Limestone, co., Tx., U.S. — D4 120
Limestone, co., Man. — A4 70
Limestone Bay, b., Man. — C2 70
Limestone Lake, l., Man. — A4 70
Limestone Point, pen., Man. — C2 70
Lime Village, Ak., U.S. — C8 79
Limfjorden, strt., Den. — B3 15
Limington, Me., U.S. — E2 96
Limmen Bight, Austl. — B6 50
Limni, Grc. — C4 25
Límnos (Lemnos), i., Grc. — C5 40
Limoeiro, Braz. — C3 57
Limoeiro do Norte, Braz. — C3 57
Limoges, Ont. — B9 73
Limoges, Fr. — E4 16
Limón, C.R. — E8 63
Limón, Hond. — D7 63
Limon, Co., U.S. — B7 83
Limón, Bahía, b., Pan. — k11 62
Limón, co., C.R. — ? ?
Limousin, hist. reg., Fr. — E4 16
Limousin Plateau, plat., Fr. — E4 16
Limoux, Fr. — F5 16
Limpopo, stm., Afr. — B5 49
Linah, Sau. Ar. — H14 40
Linard, mtn., Switz. — C9 21
Linares, Chile — B2 54
Linares, Col. — C2 60
Linares, Mex. — C5 63
Linares, Spain — C4 22
Linaro, Cape, c., Italy — C3 23
Lince, Peru — *D2 58
Linch, Wy., U.S. — C6 127
Linchuan, China — F8 31
Lincoln, Arg. — A4 54
Lincoln, Ont. — D5 73
Lincoln, Eng., U.K. — D6 10
Lincoln, Al., U.S. — B3 78
Lincoln, Ar., U.S. — B1 81
Lincoln, Ca., U.S. — C3 82
Lincoln, De., U.S. — E4 85
Lincoln, Id., U.S. — F7 89
Lincoln, Il., U.S. — C4 90
Lincoln, Ks., U.S. — C5 93
Lincoln, Me., U.S. — C4 96
Lincoln, Mi., U.S. — D7 99
Lincoln, Mo., U.S. — C4 102
Lincoln, Ne., U.S. — D9 104
Lincoln, N.M., U.S. — D4 108
Lincoln, Tn., U.S. — B5 119
Lincoln, Vt., U.S. — C3 122
Lincoln, Va., U.S. — A5 123
Lincoln, co., Ar., U.S. — D4 81
Lincoln, co., Co., U.S. — C7 83
Lincoln, co., Ga., U.S. — C4 87
Lincoln, co., Id., U.S. — G4 89
Lincoln, co., Ks., U.S. — C5 93
Lincoln, co., Ky., U.S. — C5 94
Lincoln, co., La., U.S. — B3 95
Lincoln, co., Me., U.S. — D3 96
Lincoln, co., Mn., U.S. — F2 100
Lincoln, co., Mo., U.S. — B7 102
Lincoln, co., Mt., U.S. — B1 103
Lincoln, co., Ne., U.S. — D5 104
Lincoln, co., Nv., U.S. — F6 105
Lincoln, co., N.M., U.S. — D4 108
Lincoln, co., N.C., U.S. — B1 110
Lincoln, co., Ok., U.S. — B5 113
Lincoln, co., Or., U.S. — C3 114
Lincoln, co., S.D., U.S. — D9 118
Lincoln, co., Tn., U.S. — B5 119
Lincoln, co., Wa., U.S. — B7 124
Lincoln, co., Wi., U.S. — C4 126
Lincoln, co., Wy., U.S. — D2 127
Lincoln, Mount, mtn., Co., U.S. — B4 83
Lincoln Acres, Ca., U.S. — o15 82
Lincoln Center, Me., U.S. — C4 96
Lincoln City, In., U.S. — H4 91
Lincoln City, Or., U.S. — C3 114
Lincoln Heights, Oh., U.S. — o13 112
Lincoln Park, Co., U.S. — C5 83
Lincoln Park, Ga., U.S. — D2 87
Lincoln Park, Mi., U.S. — p15 99
Lincoln Park, Nv., U.S. — *D2 105
Lincoln Park, N.J., U.S. — B4 107
Lincolnshire, co., Eng., U.K. — A7 12
Lincoln Tomb State Memorial, hist., Il., U.S. — D4 90
Lincolnton, Ga., U.S. — C4 87
Lincolnton, N.C., U.S. — B1 110
Lincoln Village, Ca., U.S. — *g10 82
Lincoln Village, Oh., U.S. — *m10 112
Lincolnville, Ks., U.S. — D7 93
Lincolnville, Me., U.S. — D3 96

Lincolnville, S.C., U.S. — h11 117
Lincolnwood, Il., U.S. — h9 90
Lincroft, N.J., U.S. — C4 107
L'Incudine, mtn., Fr. — D2 23
Lind, Wa., U.S. — C7 124
Linda, Ca., U.S. — *C3 82
Lindale, Ga., U.S. — B1 87
Lindale, Tx., U.S. — C5 120
Lindau, W. Ger. — E4 18
Lindbergh, Alta. — C5 68
Linden, Alta. — D4 68
Linden, Al., U.S. — C2 78
Linden, In., U.S. — D4 91
Linden, Mi., U.S. — F7 99
Linden, N.J., U.S. — k8 107
Linden, N.C., U.S. — B4 110
Linden, Pa., U.S. — D7 115
Linden, Tn., U.S. — B4 119
Linden, Tx., U.S. — C5 120
Linden, Wi., U.S. — F3 126
Lindenhurst, Il., U.S. — h8 90
Lindenhurst, N.Y., U.S. — n15 109
Lindenwold, N.J., U.S. — D3 107
Linderöd, Swe. — C7 15
Lindesberg, Swe. — H6 14
Lindgren Acres, Fl., U.S. — *G6 86
Líndhos, Grc. — D7 40
Lindi, Tan. — C6 48
Lindi, prov., Tan. — C6 48
Lindi, stm., Zaire — A4 48
Lindian, China — A11 32
Lindlar, W. Ger. — B2 19
Lindome, Swe. — A6 15
Lindon, Co., U.S. — B7 83
Lindon, Ut., U.S. — C4 121
Lindow, E. Ger. — F6 15
Lindrith, N.M., U.S. — A2 108
Lindsay, Ont. — C6 73
Lindsay, Ca., U.S. — D4 82
Lindsay, Mt., U.S. — C11 103
Lindsay, Ne., U.S. — C8 104
Lindsay, Ok., U.S. — C4 113
Lindsborg, Ks., U.S. — D6 93
Lindstrom, Mn., U.S. — E6 100
Lindy, Ne., U.S. — B8 104
Lineboro, Md., U.S. — A4 97
Linefork, Ky., U.S. — C7 94
Linesville, Pa., U.S. — C1 115
Lineville, Al., U.S. — B4 78
Lineville, Ia., U.S. — D4 92
Linfen, China — D7 31
Linganore Creek, stm., Md., U.S. — B3 97
Lingao, China — B8 35
Lingayen, Phil. — B6 34
Lingayen Gulf, b., Phil. — n13 34
Lingen, W. Ger. — B3 18
Lingga Islands, is., Indon. — F2 34
Lingle, Wy., U.S. — D8 127
Linglestown, Pa., U.S. — F8 115
Lingling, China — F7 31
Lingo, N.M., U.S. — D6 108
Linguère, Sen. — C1 45
Lingshan, China — G6 31
Lingwu, China — E2 32
Lingyuan, China — C8 31
Linhai, China — F9 31
Linhares, Braz. — E2 57
Linhe, China — D2 32
Linh Peak, mtn., Viet. — B3 34
Linière, Que. — C7 74
Linjiang, China — F3 33
Linköping, Swe. — H6 14
Linkou, China — B11 31
Linlithgow, Scot., U.K. — E5 13
Linn, Ks., U.S. — C6 93
Linn, Mo., U.S. — C6 102
Linn, Tx., U.S. — F3 120
Linn, co., Ia., U.S. — B6 92
Linn, co., Ks., U.S. — D9 93
Linn, co., Mo., U.S. — B4 102
Linn, co., Or., U.S. — C4 114
Linn Creek, Mo., U.S. — C5 102
Linneus, Me., U.S. — B5 96
Linneus, Mo., U.S. — B4 102
Linn Grove, In., U.S. — C7 91
Linn Grove, Ia., U.S. — B2 92
Linnhe, Loch, b., Scot., U.K. — B6 13
Lino Lakes, Mn., U.S. — m12 100
Linqing, China — D8 31
Linru, China — G5 32
Lins, Braz. — E14 65
Linstead, Jam. — E14 65
Lintan, China — E5 31
Lintao, China — D5 31
Linth, stm., Switz. — B5 20
Linthal, Switz. — C7 21
Linthicum Heights, Md., U.S. — B4 97
Lintlaw, Sask. — E4 75
Linton, Que. — C3 87
Linton, In., U.S. — F3 91
Linton, Ky., U.S. — D2 94
Linton, N.C., U.S. — C5 111
Linville, N.C., U.S. — A1 110
Linville, Va., U.S. — B4 123
Linwood, Ont. — D4 73
Linwood, Ks., U.S. — m15 93
Linwood, Mi., U.S. — E7 99
Linwood, N.J., U.S. — E3 107
Linwood, N.C., U.S. — B2 110
Linworth, Oh., U.S. — k10 112
Linxi, China — C8 32
Linxia, China — D5 31
Linyi, China — D8 31
Linz, Aus. — D7 18
Lions, La., U.S. — h10 95
Lions, Gulf of, b., Fr. — F6 16
Lion's Head, Ont. — C3 73
Lipa, Phil. — C7 34
Lipari, i., Italy — E5 23
Lipari, Italy — E5 23
Lipetsk, Sov. Un. — D6 29
Lipez, Cerro, mtn., Bol. — D2 55
Lipik, Yugo. — C11 24
Liping, China — F6 31
Lipkany, Sov. Un. — A8 24
Lipno, Pol. — B5 26
Lipno Reservoir, res., Czech. — B5 24
Lipova, Rom. — B5 24
Lippe, stm., W. Ger. — C3 18
Lippstadt, W. Ger. — B3 18
Lippitt Estate, R.I., U.S. — B4 116
Lipscomb, Al., U.S. — B3 78
Lipscomb, co., Tx., U.S. — A2 120
Lipsói, i., Grc. — D6 25
Lipton, Sask. — G4 75

Lipu, China — G7 31
Lira, Ug. — A5 48
Li Rangu, Sud. — E2 47
Lircay, Peru — D3 58
Liri, stm., Italy — D4 23
Liria, Spain — C5 22
Liro, stm., Italy — D7 21
Lisafa, Zaire — B2 48
Lisala, Zaire — A3 48
Lisbon (Lisboa), Port. — C1 22
Lisbon, Ct., U.S. — C7 84
Lisbon, Il., U.S. — B5 90
Lisbon, Ia., U.S. — C6 92
Lisbon, Me., U.S. — B3 95
Lisbon, N.H., U.S. — B3 106
Lisbon, N.Y., U.S. — f9 109
Lisbon, N.D., U.S. — C8 111
Lisbon, Oh., U.S. — B5 112
Lisbon Center, Me., U.S. — f7 96
Lisbon Falls, Me., U.S. — E2 96
Lisburn, N. Ire., U.K. — C3 10
Lisburne, Cape, c., Ak., U.S. — B5 79
Liscannor Bay, b., Ire. — E2 11
Liscarney, Ire. — D2 11
Lisco, Ne., U.S. — C3 104
Liscomb, Ia., U.S. — B5 92
Liscomb, N.S. — D7 71
Lisdoonvarna, Ire. — D2 11
Lishi, China — F4 32
Lishu, China — F8 31
Lishui, China — F9 31
Lisianski Island, i., Hi., U.S. — k13 88
Lisičansk, Sov. Un. — H2 75
Lisieux, Sask. — q21 27
Lisieux, Fr. — C4 16
Liskeard, Eng., U.K. — D3 12
Lisle, Ont. — C5 73
L'Isle, Switz. — C1 21
L'Isle [-sur-le-Doubs], Fr. — k8 90
L'Islet, co., Que. — B2 20
L'Islet-sur-Mer, Que. — B7 74
L'Isle-Verte, Que. — A8 74
Lisman, Al., U.S. — C1 78
Lismore, Austl. — E9 50
Lismore, N.S. — D7 71
Lismore, Ire. — E4 11
Lismore, Mn., U.S. — G3 100
Lismore Island, i., Scot., U.K. — D3 13
Lisnaskea, N. Ire., U.K. — C4 11
Listafjorden, b., Nor. — H2 14
Lister, B.C. — E9 69
Lister, Pa., U.S. — F3 115
Listie, Pa., U.S. — F3 115
Listowel, Ont. — D4 73
Listowel, Ire. — D2 10
Litang, China — F5 31
Litava, stm., Czech. — o16 26
Litchfield, Ct., U.S. — C3 84
Litchfield, Il., U.S. — D4 90
Litchfield, Mi., U.S. — F6 99
Litchfield, Mn., U.S. — E4 100
Litchfield, Ne., U.S. — C6 104
Litchfield, N.H., U.S. — E4 106
Litchfield, co., Ct., U.S. — B2 84
Litchfield Park, Az., U.S. — m8 80
Litchville, N.D., U.S. — C7 111
Liteň, Czech. — o17 26
Literberry, Il., U.S. — D3 90
Lithgow, Austl. — F8 51
Lithia Springs, Ga., U.S. — h7 87
Líthinon, Cape, c., Grc. — E5 25
Lithonia, Ga., U.S. — C2 87
Lithuania, state, Sov. Un. — D5 29
Lititz, Pa., U.S. — F9 115
Litókhoron, Grc. — B4 25
Litoměřice, Czech. — C3 26
Litomyšl, Czech. — D4 26
Litslena, Swe. — t35 14
Littau, Switz. — B5 21
Little, stm., U.S. — D7 113
Little, stm., Al., U.S. — A4 78
Little, stm., Ct., U.S. — C7 84
Little, stm., Ga., U.S. — E3 87
Little, stm., Ga., U.S. — E3 87
Little, stm., Ky., U.S. — D2 94
Little, stm., La., U.S. — B3 95
Little, stm., N.C., U.S. — B3 110
Little, stm., Ok., U.S. — B5 113
Little, stm., S.C., U.S. — C2 117
Little, stm., S.C., U.S. — B5 117
Little, stm., Tn., U.S. — n14 119
Little, stm., Tn., U.S. — D3 122
Little Acres, Az., U.S. — D5 80
Little Alfold, pl., Hung. — H3 27
Little America, Wy., U.S. — *E3 127
Little Andaman, i., India — F9 36
Little Arkansas, stm., Ks., U.S. — D6 93
Little Bay Islands, Newf. — D3 72
Little Bear Lake, l., Sask. — C3 75
Little Beaver Creek, stm., Ks., U.S. — C2 93
Little Belt Mountains, mts., Mt., U.S. — D6 103
Little Bighorn, stm., U.S. — E9 103
Little Birch, W.V., U.S. — C4 125
Little Bitter Lake, l., Eg. — D4 41
Little Black, stm., Me., U.S. — A3 96
Little Blue, stm., In., U.S. — H5 91
Little Blue, stm., U.S. — C6 104
Little Boars Head, N.H., U.S. — E5 106
Little Bow, stm., Alta. — D4 68
Little Britain, Ont. — C6 73
Little Brook, N.S. — E3 71
Little Bullhead, Man. — D3 70
Little Cacapon, stm., W.V., U.S. — B6 125
Little Cadotte, stm., Alta. — A2 68
Little Canada, Mn., U.S. — *m12 100
Little Carpathians, mts., Czech. — ? ?
Little Catalina, Newf. — D5 72
Little Cayman, i., Cay. Is. — E5 64
Little Cedar, stm., Ia., U.S. — A5 92
Little Chief, Ok., U.S. — A5 113
Little Choptank River, b., Md., U.S. — C5 97
Little Churchill, stm., Man. — A4 70
Little Chute, Wi., U.S. — D5 126
Little Coal, stm., W.V., U.S. — C3 125
Little Colorado, stm., Az., U.S. — B4 80
Little Compton, R.I., U.S. — E6 116
Little Creek, De., U.S. — D4 85
Little Creek Naval Amphibious Base, mil., Va., U.S. — k15 123
Little Creek Peak, mtn., Ut., U.S. — F3 121
Little Current, Ont. — B3 73
Little Deer Isle, Me., U.S. — D4 96

Little Diomede Island, i., Ak., U.S. — B6 79
Little Dry Creek, stm., Mt., U.S. — C10 103
Little Eagle, S.D., U.S. — B5 118
Little Egg Harbor, b., N.J., U.S. — D4 107
Little Egg Inlet, b., N.J., U.S. — D4 107
Little Falls, Mn., U.S. — E4 100
Little Falls, N.J., U.S. — B4 107
Little Falls, N.Y., U.S. — B6 109
Little Ferry, N.J., U.S. — h8 107
Little Fishing Creek, stm., W.V., U.S. — h9 125
Littlefork, Mn., U.S. — B5 100
Little Fork, stm., Mn., U.S. — B5 100
Little Frog Mountain, mtn., Tn., U.S. — D9 119
Little Goose Creek, stm., Wy., U.S. — B6 127
Little Grand Lake, l., Newf. — D3 72
Little Gunpowder Falls, stm., Md., U.S. — A4 97
Little Harbour Deep, Newf. — C3 72
Little Hocking, Oh., U.S. — C4 112
Little Humboldt, stm., Nv., U.S. — B4 105
Little Humboldt, North Fork, stm., Nv., U.S. — B4 105
Little Humboldt, South Fork, stm., Nv., U.S. — B4 105
Little Inagua, i., Bah. — D7 64
Little Kanawha, stm., W.V., U.S. — C4 125
Little Kanawha, West Fork, stm., W.V., U.S. — B3 125
Little Lake, Mi., U.S. — B3 99
Little Lake, l., La., U.S. — E5 95
Littlelot, Tn., U.S. — B4 119
Little Lynches, stm., S.C., U.S. — C7 117
Little Manatee, stm., Fl., U.S. — p11 86
Little Manitou Lake, l., Sask. — F3 75
Little Marais, Mn., U.S. — C7 100
Little Mazarn Creek, stm., Ar., U.S. — g7 81
Little Meadows, Pa., U.S. — C9 115
Little Mecatina, stm., Can. — h9 72
Little Mexico, Tx., U.S. — D1 120
Little Miami, stm., Oh., U.S. — C1 112
Little Miami, East Fork, stm., Oh., U.S. — C1 112
Little Miami, Todd Fork, stm., Oh., U.S. — C1 112
Little Missouri, stm., U.S. — A7 76
Little Moose Mountain, mtn., N.Y., U.S. — B6 109
Little Mountain, S.C., U.S. — C5 117
Little Mountain, mtn., Wy., U.S. — E3 127
Little Muddy, stm., Il., U.S. — E4 90
Little Muddy, stm., N.D., U.S. — A2 111
Little Orleans, Md., U.S. — A1 97
Little Osage, stm., Ks., U.S. — E9 93
Little Otter Creek, stm., Vt., U.S. — C2 122
Little Owyhee, stm., U.S. — B5 105
Little Pee Dee, stm., S.C. — C9 117
Little Pigeon Creek, stm., In., U.S. — I3 91
Little Pipe Creek, stm., Md., U.S. — A3 97
Little Playgreen Lake, l., Man. — B3 70
Littleport, Ia., U.S. — B6 92
Little Powder, stm., U.S. — F11 103
Little Quill Lake, l., Sask. — F3 75
Little Rann of Kachchh, pl., India — I5 36
Little Red, stm., Ar., U.S. — B4 81
Little Red, Middle Fork, stm., Ar., U.S. — B3 81
Little River, N.B. — E3 71
Little River, Al., U.S. — D2 78
Little River, Ks., U.S. — D6 93
Little River, S.C., U.S. — D10 117
Little River, co., Ar., U.S. — D1 81
Little River Inlet, b., S.C., U.S. — D10 117
Little Rock, Ar., U.S. — C3 81
Little Rock, Il., U.S. — B5 90
Little Rock, Ia., U.S. — A2 92
Little Rock, S.C., U.S. — B8 117
Littlerock, Wa., U.S. — C2 124
Little Rock Air Force Base, mil., Ar., U.S. — C3 81
Little Sable Point, c., Mi., U.S. — E4 99
Little Sachigo Lake, l., Ont. — A6 73
Little Saint Bernard Pass, Eur. — E7 16
Little Salt Lake, l., Ut., U.S. — F3 121
Little Sand Creek, stm., Mn., U.S. — B6 100
Little Sandy, stm., Ky., U.S. — B6 94
Little Sandy Creek, stm., Wy., U.S. — D3 127
Little Sauk, Mn., U.S. — E4 100
Little Sebago Lake, l., Me., U.S. — g7 96
Little Silver, N.J., U.S. — C4 107
Little Sioux, Ia., U.S. — C1 92
Little Sioux, stm., U.S. — B2 92
Little Sioux, West Fork, stm., Ia., U.S. — B2 92
Little Smoky, stm., Alta. — B2 68
Little Snake, stm., U.S. — A2 83
Little Southwest Miramichi, stm., N.B. — C3 71
Little Spokane, stm., Wa., U.S. — B8 124
Littlestown, Pa., U.S. — G7 115
Little Suamico, Wi., U.S. — D6 126
Little Tallapoosa, stm., U.S. — B4 78
Little Tenmile Creek, stm., W.V., U.S. — k10 125
Little Tennessee, stm., U.S. — D9 119
Littleton, Al., U.S. — f7 78
Littleton, Co., U.S. — B6 83
Littleton, Il., U.S. — C3 90
Littleton, Me., U.S. — B5 96
Littleton, N.H., U.S. — B3 106
Littleton, N.C., U.S. — A5 110
Littleton, W.V., U.S. — B4 125
Little Tucson, Az., U.S. — F3 80
Little Valley, Ca., U.S. — B3 82
Little Valley, N.Y., U.S. — C2 109
Littleville, Al., U.S. — A2 78
Little Wabash, stm., Il., U.S. — E5 90
Little Walnut, stm., Ks., U.S. — g13 93
Little West Fork, stm., Tn., U.S. — A4 119

Little White, stm., S.D., U.S. — D5 118
Little Wolf, stm., Wi., U.S. — D4 126
Little Wood, stm., Id., U.S. — F4 89
Little York, Il., U.S. — B3 90
Little York, In., U.S. — G6 91
Little Zab, stm., Asia — E15 40
Littoria see Latina, Italy — D4 23
Litvínov, Czech. — C8 19
Liuba, China — E6 31
Liucheng, China — G6 31
Liucura, Chile — B2 54
Liuhe, China — C11 32
Liupan Mountains, mts., China — F1 32
Liuyang, China — J5 32
Liuzhou, China — G6 31
Livelong, Sask. — D1 75
Lively, Ont. — A3 73
Livengood, Ak., U.S. — B10 79
Livenza, stm., Italy — D8 23
Live Oak, Ca., U.S. — C3 82
Live Oak, Ca., U.S. — *D3 82
Live Oak, Fl., U.S. — B3 86
Live Oak, Tx., U.S. — *E3 120
Live Oak, co., Tx., U.S. — E3 120
Live Oak Manor, La., U.S. — *E5 95
Livermore, Ca., U.S. — h9 82
Livermore, Co., U.S. — A5 83
Livermore, Ia., U.S. — B3 92
Livermore, Ky., U.S. — C2 94
Livermore, Mount, mtn., Tx., U.S. — o12 120
Livermore Falls, Me., U.S. — D2 96
Liverpool, Austl. — *F9 50
Liverpool, N.S. — E5 71
Liverpool, Eng., U.K. — D5 10
Liverpool, Pa., U.S. — F7 115
Liverpool, Tx., U.S. — r14 120
Liverpool Bay, b., N.W. Ter. — B7 66
Livigno, Italy — C9 21
Livingston, Guat. — D7 63
Livingston, Ca., U.S. — D3 82
Livingston, Il., U.S. — E4 90
Livingston, La., U.S. — C5 94
Livingston, Mt., U.S. — E6 103
Livingston, N.J., U.S. — B4 107
Livingston, S.C., U.S. — D5 117
Livingston, Tn., U.S. — C8 119
Livingston, Tx., U.S. — D5 120
Livingston, Wi., U.S. — F3 126
Livingston, co., Il., U.S. — C5 90
Livingston, co., Ky., U.S. — e9 94
Livingston, co., La., U.S. — D5 95
Livingston, co., Mi., U.S. — F7 99
Livingston, co., Mo., U.S. — B4 102
Livingston, co., N.Y., U.S. — C3 109
Livingston, Lake, res., Tx., U.S. — D5 120
Livingstone, Zam. — E4 48
Livingstone Cove, N.S. — D8 71
Livingstonia, Mwi. — C5 48
Livingston Island, i., B.A.T. — C6 7
Livingston Manor, N.Y., U.S. — D6 109
Livno, Yugo. — C2 24
Livny, Sov. Un. — E11 27
Livona, N.D., U.S. — C5 111
Livonia, In., U.S. — G5 91
Livonia, La., U.S. — D4 95
Livonia, Mi., U.S. — F7 99
Livonia, Mo., U.S. — A5 102
Livonia, N.Y., U.S. — C3 109
Livorno (Leghorn), Italy — C3 23
Livramento do Brumado, Braz. — A4 56
Livry-Gargan, Fr. — g11 16
Liwale, Tan. — C6 48
Lixian, China — J4 32
Liyang, China — I8 32
Lizard Creek, stm., Ia., U.S. — B3 92
Lizard Head Pass, Co., U.S. — D3 83
Lizard Head Peak, mtn., Wy., U.S. — D3 127
Lizard Point, c., Eng., U.K. — F4 10
Lizella, Ga., U.S. — D3 87
Lizemores, W.V., U.S. — C3 125
Lizton, In., U.S. — E4 91
Ljubljana, Yugo. — B9 24
Ljubuški, Yugo. — D2 24
Ljungby, Swe. — I5 14
Ljusdal, Swe. — G7 14
Ljusterö, Swe. — t36 14
Llandeilo, Wales, U.K. — C4 12
Llandovery, Wales, U.K. — C4 12
Llandrindod Wells, Wales, U.K. — D5 10
Llandudno, Wales, U.K. — D5 10
Llanelli, Wales, U.K. — D4 10
Llanes, Spain — B3 22
Llanfyllin, Wales, U.K. — B4 12
Llangefni, Wales, U.K. — A3 12
Llangollen, Wales, U.K. — B4 12
Llanidloes, Wales, U.K. — C4 12
Llangynog, Wales, U.K. — B4 12
Llanidloes Estates, De., U.S. — *B3 85
Llanidloes, Wales, U.K. — C4 12
Llano, N.M., U.S. — A4 108
Llano, Tx., U.S. — D3 120
Llano, co., Tx., U.S. — D3 120
Llano, stm., Tx., U.S. — D3 120
Llanos, pl., S.A. — A4 60
Llanquihue, Lago, l., Chile — C2 54
Llanrwst, Wales, U.K. — A4 12
Llata, Peru — C2 58
Llaves, N.M., U.S. — A3 108
Llera, Mex. — C5 63
Llerena, Spain — C2 22
Lleyn Peninsula, pen., Wales, U.K. — D4 10
Llico, Chile — B1 54
Llobregat, stm., Spain — B6 22
Lloyd, Fl., U.S. — B2 86
Lloyd, Ky., U.S. — B7 94
Lloyd, Mt., U.S. — B7 103
Lloyd Harbor, N.Y., U.S. — *E7 109
Lloydminster, Alta. — C5 68
Lloydminster (Alta. and Sask.) — D1 75
Lloyds, stm., Newf. — D3 72
Lluchmayor, Spain — C7 22
Llullaillaco, Volcán, vol., S.A. — D2 55
Lo, stm., Viet. — B5 35
Loa, Ut., U.S. — E4 121
Loa, stm., Chile — D2 55
Loachapoka, Al., U.S. — C4 78
Loami, Il., U.S. — D4 90
Loange, stm., Afr. — C4 48
Lobatse, Bots. — C4 49
Löbau, E. Ger. — C7 18
Lobaye, stm., Cen. Afr. Rep. — E1 46
Lobelville, Tn., U.S. — B4 119
Loberia, Arg. — B5 54
Lobito, Ang. — D1 48

177

| Name | Map Ref. | Page |
|---|---|---|

Lobnya, Sov. Un. — m17 27
Lobo, Phil. — p13 34
Lobos, Arg. — B5 54
Lobos, Cabo, c., Mex. — B2 63
Lobos, Punta, c., Mex. — B2 63
Lobos de Tierra, Isla, i., Peru — C1 58
Lobster Lake, l., Me., U.S. — C3 96
Loburg, E. Ger. — A7 19
Locarno, Switz. — E4 18
Lochaber, N.S. — D7 71
Lochaline, Scot., U.K. — D3 13
Lochcarron, Scot., U.K. — C3 13
Lochdonhead, Scot., U.K. — D3 13
Lochearnhead, Scot., U.K. — D4 13
Lochem, Neth. — B6 17
Loches, Fr. — D4 16
Lochgilphead, Scot., U.K. — D3 13
Lochinver, Scot., U.K. — B3 13
Loch Lomond, Va., U.S. — B5 123
Loch Lynn Heights, Md., U.S. — m12 97
Lochmaben, Scot., U.K. — E5 13
Lochmere, N.H., U.S. — D3 106
Lochnagar, mtn., Scot., U.K. — D5 13
Lochranza, Scot., U.K. — E3 13
Loch Raven Reservoir, res., Md., U.S. — B4 97
Lochsa, stm., Id., U.S. — C3 89
Lochy, Loch, l., Scot., U.K. — D4 13
Lockbourne, Oh., U.S. — m11 112
Locke, N.Y., U.S. — B5 91
Locke, N.Y., U.S. — C4 109
Locke, Tn., U.S. — B1 119
Locke Mills, Me., U.S. — D2 96
Lockeport, N.S. — F4 71
Lockerbie, Scot., U.K. — E5 13
Lockesburg, Ar., U.S. — D1 81
Lockhart, Al., U.S. — D3 78
Lockhart, Fl., U.S. — *D5 86
Lockhart, Mn., U.S. — C2 100
Lockhart, S.C., U.S. — B5 117
Lockhart, Tx., U.S. — E4 120
Lock Haven, Pa., U.S. — D7 115
Lockland, Oh., U.S. — o13 112
Lockney, Tx., U.S. — B2 120
Lockport, Man. — D3 70
Lockport, Il., U.S. — B5 90
Lockport, Ky., U.S. — B5 94
Lockport, La., U.S. — E5 95
Lockport, N.Y., U.S. — B2 109
Lockridge, Ia., U.S. — C6 92
Lock Springs, Mo., U.S. — B4 102
Lockwood, Sask. — F3 75
Lockwood, Mo., U.S. — D4 102
Lockwood, Mt., U.S. — E8 103
Lockwood, Ca., U.S. — D3 125
Loc Ninh, Viet. — G7 35
Loco, Ok., U.S. — C4 113
Loco Hills, N.M., U.S. — E6 108
Locumba, Peru — E3 58
Locust, N.J., U.S. — C4 107
Locust, N.C., U.S. — B2 110
Locust Bayou, Ar., U.S. — D3 81
Locust Creek, stm., Mo., U.S. — B4 102
Locust Fork, stm., Al., U.S. — B3 78
Locust Grove, Ga., U.S. — C2 87
Locust Grove, Md., U.S. — B2 97
Locust Grove, N.Y., U.S. — *C7 109
Locust Grove, Ok., U.S. — A6 113
Locust Hill (part of Markham), Ont. — k15 73
Lod, Isr. — G10 40
Loda, Il., U.S. — C5 90
Loděnice, stm., Czech. — n17 26
Löderup, Swe. — C8 15
Lodève, Fr. — F5 16
Lodeynoye Pole, Sov. Un. — A9 27
Lodge, Newf. — B4 72
Lodge, S.C., U.S. — E6 117
Lodge Creek, stm., N.A. — B7 103
Lodge Grass, Mt., U.S. — E9 103
Lodgepole, Alta. — C3 68
Lodge Pole, Mt., U.S. — B8 103
Lodgepole, Ne., U.S. — C2 104
Lodgepole, S.D., U.S. — B5 118
Lodgepole Creek, stm., U.S. — C3 104
Lodi, Italy — B2 23
Lodi, Ca., U.S. — C3 82
Lodi, N.J., U.S. — h8 107
Lodi, N.Y., U.S. — C4 109
Lodi, Oh., U.S. — A3 112
Lodi, Wi., U.S. — E4 126
Lodi, Zaire — B3 48
Lodja, Zaire — B3 48
Lodore, Canyon of, val., Co., U.S. — A2 83
Lods, Fr. — B2 20
Lodwar, Kenya — A6 48
Łódź, Pol. — C5 26
Loeches, Spain — p18 22
Loei, Thai. — D4 35
Loelli, l., Sud. — D3 47
Loeriesfontein, S. Afr. — D2 49
Lofer, Aus. — B8 20
Lofoten, i., Nor. — C5 14
Loftus, Eng., U.K. — F8 13
Loga, Niger — D5 45
Logan, Il., U.S. — F5 90
Logan, Ia., U.S. — C2 92
Logan, Ks., U.S. — C4 93
Logan, Mt., U.S. — E5 103
Logan, N.M., U.S. — B6 108
Logan, N.D., U.S. — A4 111
Logan, Oh., U.S. — C3 112
Logan, Ok., U.S. — A1 113
Logan, Ut., U.S. — B4 121
Logan, co., Ar., U.S. — B2 81
Logan, co., Co., U.S. — A7 83
Logan, co., Il., U.S. — C4 90
Logan, co., Ks., U.S. — D2 93
Logan, co., Ky., U.S. — D3 94
Logan, co., Ne., U.S. — C5 104
Logan, co., N.D., U.S. — C6 111
Logan, co., Oh., U.S. — B2 112
Logan, co., Ok., U.S. — B4 113
Logan, co., W.V., U.S. — D3 125
Logan, Mount, mtn., Yukon — D4 66
Logan, Mount, mtn., Wa., U.S. — A5 124
Logan Creek, stm., Ne., U.S. — B9 104
Logandale, Nv., U.S. — G7 105
Logan Lake, B.C. — D7 69
Logan Martin Lake, res., Al., U.S. — B3 78
Logan Mountains, mts., Yukon — D7 66
Logan Pass, Mt., U.S. — B2 103
Logansport, In., U.S. — C5 91
Logansport, La., U.S. — C2 95
Loganton, Pa., U.S. — D7 115
Loganville, Ga., U.S. — C3 87
Loganville, Pa., U.S. — G8 115
Loganville, Wi., U.S. — E3 126
Loge, stm., Ang. — C1 48
Loggieville, N.B. — B4 71
Log Lane Village, Co., U.S. — A7 83

Logone, stm., Afr. — C3 46
Logroño, Spain — A4 22
Logrosán, Spain — C3 22
Løgstør, Den. — B3 15
Løgumkloster, Den. — C2 15
Lohals, Den. — C4 15
Lohärdaga, India — D7 36
Lohr, W. Ger. — D4 19
Lohrville, Ia., U.S. — B3 92
Loi, mtn., Laos — B5 35
Loikaw, Burma — C2 35
Loir, stm., Fr. — D4 16
Loire, stm., Fr. — D3 16
Loíza, Lago, res., P.R. — B3 65
Loja, Ec. — B2 58
Loja, prov., Ec. — B2 58
Loja, Spain — D3 22
Lokandu, Zaire — B4 48
Lokan Reservoir, res., Fin. — C13 14
Lokeren, Bel. — C3 17
Lokichar, Kenya — A6 48
Lokichokio, Kenya — A5 48
Lokitaung, Kenya — A6 48
Løkken, Den. — A3 15
Lokoja, Nig. — E6 45
Lokolama, Zaire — B2 48
Lokossa, Benin — E5 45
Lol, stm., Sud. — D2 47
Lola, Ky., U.S. — e9 94
Lola, Mount, mtn., Ca., U.S. — C3 82
Loliondo, Tan. — B6 48
Lolland, i., Den. — C3 15
Lollar, W. Ger. — C3 19
Lollie, Ga., U.S. — D4 87
Lolo, Mt., U.S. — D2 103
Lolo Hot Springs, Mt., U.S. — D2 103
Lolo Pass, U.S. — C4 89
Lom, Bul. — D6 24
Loma, Co., U.S. — B2 83
Loma, Mt., U.S. — C6 103
Loma, Ne., U.S. — C9 104
Loma, N.D., U.S. — A7 111
Loma Linda, Ca., U.S. — *E5 82
Lomami, stm., Zaire — B3 48
Loma Mountains, mts., S.L. — E2 45
Loman, Mn., U.S. — B5 100
Lomas, Peru — E3 58
Lomas de Zamora, Arg. — C3 78
Lomax, Il., U.S. — C2 90
Lomax, Il., U.S. — k8 90
Lombarda, Serra, plat., Braz. — B4 59
Lombardy (Lombardia), prov., Italy — B2 23
Lomblen, i., Indon. — G6 34
Lombok, i., Indon. — G5 34
Lombok Strait, strt., Indon. — G5 34
Lomé, Togo — E5 45
Lomela, Zaire — B3 48
Lomela, stm., Zaire — B3 48
Lometa, Tx., U.S. — D3 120
Lomié, Cam. — E2 46
Lomira, Wi., U.S. — E5 126
Lomita, Ca., U.S. — *E4 82
Lommel, Bel. — C5 17
Lomond, Alta. — D4 68
Lomond, Newf. — D3 72
Lomond, Loch, l., Scot., U.K. — B4 10
Lomonosov, Sov. Un. — s30 14
Lomonosovka, Sov. Un. — C7 28
Lompoc, Ca., U.S. — E3 82
Lom Sak, Thai. — D4 35
Łomża, Pol. — B7 26
Lonaconing, Md., U.S. — k13 97
Loncoche, Chile — B2 54
Londesborough, Ont. — D3 73
London, Ont. — E3 73
London, Eng., U.K. — E6 10
London, Ar., U.S. — B2 81
London, In., U.S. — E6 91
London, Ky., U.S. — C5 94
London, Oh., U.S. — C2 112
London, Tx., U.S. — D3 120
London (Heathrow) Airport, Eng., U.K. — m12 10
Londonderry, N.S. — D6 71
Londonderry (Derry), N. Ire., U.K. — C3 10
Londonderry, N.H., U.S. — E4 106
Londonderry, Oh., U.S. — C3 112
Londonderry, Vt., U.S. — E3 122
Londonderry, Cape, c., Austl. — B4 50
Londonderry, Isla, i., Chile — k11 54
London Mills, Il., U.S. — C3 90
Londontowne, Md., U.S. — C4 97
Londrina, Braz. — C2 56
Lone Elm, Ks., U.S. — D8 93
Lone Grove, Ok., U.S. — C4 113
Lone Jack, Mo., U.S. — C3 102
Lonely Island, i., Ont. — B3 73
Lone Mountain, Tn., U.S. — C10 119
Lone Mountain, mtn., Nv., U.S. — E4 105
Lone Oak, Ky., U.S. — e9 94
Lone Oak, Tx., U.S. — C5 120
Lone Pine, Ca., U.S. — D4 82
Lone Rock, Sask. — D1 75
Lone Rock, Or., U.S. — B7 114
Lone Star, S.C., U.S. — D6 117
Lone Tree, Ia., U.S. — C6 92
Lonetree, Wy., U.S. — E2 127
Lone Tree Creek, stm., Co., U.S. — A6 83
Lone Wolf, Ok., U.S. — C2 113
Long, co., Ga., U.S. — E5 87
Longa, stm., Ang. — D1 48
Longá, stm., Braz. — B2 57
Longarone, Italy — C6 20
Long Bar Harbor, Md., U.S. — B5 97
Long Bay, b., Jam. — E12 65
Long Bay, b., Jam. — F14 65
Long Beach, Ca., U.S. — F4 82
Long Beach, In., U.S. — A4 91
Long Beach, Md., U.S. — C4 97
Long Beach, Mn., U.S. — E3 100
Long Beach, Ms., U.S. — g7 101
Long Beach, N.Y., U.S. — E7 109
Long Beach, Wa., U.S. — C1 124
Long Beach Naval Shipyard, mil., Ca., U.S. — n12 82
Longboat Key, Fl., U.S. — q10 86
Longboat Key, i., Fl., U.S. — E4 86
Longboat Pass, strt., Fl., U.S. — q10 86
Long Bottom, Oh., U.S. — C4 112
Long Branch (part of Etobicoke), Ont. — m14 73
Long Branch, N.J., U.S. — C5 107
Long Branch, Tx., U.S. — C5 120

Longbranch, Wa., U.S. — B3 124
Long Cay, i., Bah. — m17 64
Long Creek, Or., U.S. — C7 114
Longcreek, S.C., U.S. — B1 117
Long Creek, stm., N.A. — H3 75
Long Creek Mountain, mtn., Wy., U.S. — D5 127
Longdale, Ok., U.S. — A3 113
Long Eaton, Eng., U.K. — B6 12
Long Eddy, N.Y., U.S. — D5 109
Longford, Ont. — C5 73
Longford, Ire. — D3 10
Longford, Ks., U.S. — C6 93
Longford, co., Ire. — D4 11
Long Grove, Ia., U.S. — C7 92
Long Harbour [-Mount Arlington Heights], Newf. — E5 72
Longiram, Indon. — F5 34
Longisland, N.C., U.S. — B2 110
Long Island, Va., U.S. — C3 123
Long Island, i., Bah. — C6 64
Long Island, i., N.S. — E3 71
Long Island, i., Me., U.S. — g7 96
Long Island, i., Me., U.S. — g12 98
Long Island, i., N.Y., U.S. — E7 109
Long Island Sound, strt., U.S. — E7 109
Long Key, Fl., U.S. — H6 86
Long Key, i., Fl., U.S. — H6 86
Longkou, China — F9 32
Longlac, Ont. — G15 66
Long Lake, Mi., U.S. — D7 99
Long Lake, N.Y., U.S. — B6 109
Longlake, S.D., U.S. — B6 118
Long Lake, Wi., U.S. — C5 126
Long Lake, l., N.B. — B3 71
Long Lake, l., Me., U.S. — A4 96
Long Lake, l., Me., U.S. — D2 96
Long Lake, l., Mi., U.S. — D5 99
Long Lake, l., N.Y., U.S. — C7 99
Long Lake, l., N.Y., U.S. — D4 100
Long Lake, l., N.D., U.S. — C6 111
Long Lake, l., Wa., U.S. — f10 124
Long Lake, l., Wi., U.S. — C2 126
Long Lake Colony, S.D., U.S. — *B7 118
Long Lane, Mo., U.S. — D5 102
Longleaf, La., U.S. — C3 95
Longlin, China — G6 31
Longmeadow, Ma., U.S. — B2 98
Longmont, Co., U.S. — A5 83
Long Mountain, mtn., Mo., U.S. — E5 102
Long Mountain, mtn., N.H., U.S. — A4 106
Long Pine, Ne., U.S. — B6 104
Long Point, Ont. — E4 73
Long Point, c., Man. — C2 70
Long Point, c., Newf. — D2 72
Long Point, pen., Ont. — E4 73
Long Pond, l., Me., U.S. — C3 96
Long Pond, l., Me., U.S. — C2 96
Long Pond, l., Ma., U.S. — C6 98
Long Pond, l., Ma., U.S. — C6 98
Long Pond, res., Fl., U.S. — C4 86
Long Prairie, Mn., U.S. — E4 100
Long Range Mountains, mts., Newf. — D3 72
Longreach, Austl. — D7 50
Longridge, Eng., U.K. — G6 13
Long Run, W.V., U.S. — k9 125
Longstreet, La., U.S. — ... —
Longton, Ks., U.S. — E7 93
Longtown, Mo., U.S. — D8 102
Longueau, Fr. — E2 17
Longueuil, Que. — D4 74
Longuyon, Fr. — C6 16
Longvale, Ca., U.S. — C2 82
Long Valley, Az., U.S. — C4 80
Long Valley, N.J., U.S. — B3 107
Longvalley, S.D., U.S. — D4 118
Longview, Alta. — D3 68
Longview, Il., U.S. — D5 90
Long View, Ky., U.S. — C4 94
Longview, Ms., U.S. — B5 101
Long View, N.C., U.S. — B1 110
Longview, Tx., U.S. — C5 120
Longview, Wa., U.S. — C3 124
Longville, La., U.S. — D2 95
Longville, Mn., U.S. — C4 100
Longwood, Fl., U.S. — *D5 86
Longwood, N.C., U.S. — C4 110
Longwoods, Md., U.S. — C5 97
Longwy, Fr. — C6 16
Longxian, China — E8 31
Long Xuyen, Viet. — G6 35
Longyan, China — F8 31
Longyao, China — F6 32
Longzhen, China — B12 32
Longzhou, China — G6 31
Lonkin, Burma — C10 36
Lonoke, Ar., U.S. — C4 81
Lonoke, co., Ar., U.S. — C4 81
Lonerock, Or., U.S. — B7 114
Lonsdale, Ont. — C7 73
Lonsdale, Ar., U.S. — C3 81
Lonsdale, Mn., U.S. — F5 100
Lonsdale, R.I., U.S. — B4 116
Lons-le-Saunier, Fr. — D6 16
Lontzen, Bel. — D5 17
Looe, Eng., U.K. — D3 12
Lookeba, Ok., U.S. — B3 113
Lookout, Ca., U.S. — B3 82
Lookout, Ky., U.S. — C7 94
Lookout, Cape, c., N.C., U.S. — C7 110
Lookout, Cape, c., Mi., U.S. — d7 99
Lookout Mountain, Tn., U.S. — h11 119
Lookout Mountain, mtn., Or., U.S. — C6 114
Lookout Pass, U.S. — B3 89
Lookout Point Lake, res., Or., U.S. — D4 114
Loomis, Sask. — H1 75
Loomis, Ne., U.S. — D6 104
Loomis, S.D., U.S. — D7 118
Loomis, Wa., U.S. — A6 124
Loon, stm., Alta. — A3 68
Loon, stm., Man. — A1 70
Loon Bay, Newf. — D4 72
Loon Lake, Wa., U.S. — A8 124
Loon Lake, l., Can. — B1 70
Loon Lake, l., Me., U.S. — B3 96

Loon Lake Mountains, mtn., N.Y., U.S. — f10 109
Loon Straits, Man. — D3 70
Loop, Tx., U.S. — C1 120
Loop Creek, stm., W.V., U.S. — m13 125
Loop Head, c., Ire. — D1 10
Loose, Fr. — D3 17
Loosahatchie, stm., Tn., U.S. — B2 119
Loose Creek, Mo., U.S. — C6 102
Loosokonia, Ms., U.S. — A4 101
Lop Buri, Thai. — C2 34
Lopeno, Tx., U.S. — F3 120
Lopez, Pa., U.S. — D9 115
Lopez, Cap, c., Gabon — F1 46
Lopez Bay, b., Phil. — p14 34
Lopez Island, i., Wa., U.S. — A3 124
Lop Nur, l., China — D3 31
Lophavet, b., Nor. — B9 14
Lopori, stm., Zaire — A3 48
Lora, Hāmūn-i-, l., Asia — G12 39
Lora [del Río], Spain — D3 22
Lorado, W.V., U.S. — D3 125
Lorain, Oh., U.S. — A3 112
Lorain, co., Oh., U.S. — A3 112
Loraine, Il., U.S. — C2 90
Loraine, N.D., U.S. — A4 111
Loraine, Tx., U.S. — C2 120
Loralai, Pak. — B2 37
Loramie, Lake, res., Oh., U.S. — B1 112
Loranger, La., U.S. — D5 95
Lorca, Spain — D5 22
Lord Howe Island, i., Austl. — I9 6
Lordsburg, N.M., U.S. — E1 108
Lords Point, Ct., U.S. — D8 84
Loreauville, La., U.S. — D4 95
Lore City, Oh., U.S. — C4 112
Lorena, Braz. — C3 56
Lorengau, Pap. N. Gui. — h12 50
Lorentz, W.V., U.S. — B4 125
Lorenzo, Id., U.S. — F7 89
Lorenzo, Ne., U.S. — C2 104
Lorenzo, Tx., U.S. — C2 120
Lorenzo Geyres, Ur. — E1 56
Loreto, Braz. — C1 57
Loreto, Col. — D3 60
Loreto, Italy — C4 23
Loreto, Mex. — B2 63
Loreto, Para. — D4 57
Loreto, dept., Peru — B3 58
Loretta, Wi., U.S. — C3 126
Lorette, Man. — E3 70
Lorette, Que. — C6 74
Loretteville, Que. — C6 74
Loretto, Ky., U.S. — C4 94
Loretto, Mn., U.S. — m11 100
Loretto, Ne., U.S. — C7 104
Loretto, Pa., U.S. — F4 115
Loretto, Tn., U.S. — B4 119
Lorica, Col. — B2 60
Lorida, Fl., U.S. — E5 86
Lorient, Fr. — D2 16
L'Orignal, Ont. — B10 73
Lorimor, Ia., U.S. — C3 92
Loring, Mt., U.S. — B9 103
Loring Air Force Base, mil., Me., U.S. — B5 96
Loris, S.C., U.S. — C10 117
Lorlie, Sask. — G4 75
Lorman, Ms., U.S. — D2 101
Lorn, Firth of, est., Scot., U.K. — B4 10
Lorne, N.B. — B3 71
Lorneville, Ont. — C5 73
Lorquin, Fr. — F6 17
Lörrach, W. Ger. — E3 18
Lorraine, Ks., U.S. — D5 93
Lorraine, N.Y., U.S. — B5 109
Lorraine, hist. reg., Fr. — C6 16
Lorraine Plateau, plat., Fr. — C7 16
Lorsch, W. Ger. — D3 19
Lorton, Va., U.S. — *B5 123
Lorup, W. Ger. — B7 17
Los Alamitos, Ca., U.S. — *F5 82
Los Alamos, Ca., U.S. — E3 82
Los Alamos, N.M., U.S. — B3 108
Los Alamos, co., N.M., U.S. — B3 108
Los Altos, Ca., U.S. — k8 82
Los Altos Hills, Ca., U.S. — *k8 82
Los Amates, Guat. — D7 63
Los Angeles, Chile — B2 54
Los Angeles, Ca., U.S. — E4 82
Los Angeles, co., Ca., U.S. — E4 82
Los Angeles Aqueduct, Ca., U.S. — E4 82
Los Banos, Ca., U.S. — D3 82
Los Blancos, Arg. — A3 54
Los Cerrillos, Arg. — A3 54
Los Ebanos, Tx., U.S. — F3 120
Los Fresnos, Tx., U.S. — F4 120
Los Gatos, Ca., U.S. — D2 82
Los Hermanos, Islas, is., Ven. — A5 60
Los Lagos, Chile — B2 54
Los Lagos, prov., Chile — B2 54
Los Lunas, N.M., U.S. — B3 108
Los Mochis, Mex. — B3 63
Los Molinos, Ca., U.S. — B2 82
Los Monjes, Islas, is., Ven. — A3 60
Los Nietos, Ca., U.S. — *n12 82
Los Ojos, N.M., U.S. — A3 108
Los Padillas, N.M., U.S. — *B3 108
Los Palacios, Cuba — C6 64
Los Palacios [y Villafranca], Spain — D3 22
Los Peares, Spain — B2 22
Los Pinos, N.M., U.S. — A3 108
Los Pinos, stm., Co., U.S. — D3 83
Los Ranchos de Albuquerque, N.M., U.S. — B3 108
Los Remedios, stm., Mex. — D6 63
Los Reyes [de Salgado] Mex. — D4 63
Los Reyes la Paz, Mex. — h10 63
Los Ríos, prov., Ec. — B2 58
Los Roques, Islas, is., Ven. — A4 60
Los Santos, Pan. — G7 62
Los Santos [de Maimona], Spain — C2 22
Los Sarmientos, Arg. — A2 54
Los Sauces, Chile — B2 54
Lossiemouth, Scot., U.K. — C1 10
Lössnitz, E. Ger. — C7 19
Lost, stm., Wa., U.S. — A5 124
Lost, stm., W.V., U.S. — B6 125
Lost City, W.V., U.S. — B6 125
Lost Creek, stm., Ar., U.S. — C3 81
Lost Creek, stm., Wy., U.S. — D4 127

Los Teques, Ven. — A4 60
Los Testigos, Islas, is., Ven. — A5 60
Lost Hills, Ca., U.S. — E4 82
Lostine, Or., U.S. — B9 114
Lost Nation, Ia., U.S. — C7 92
Lost Peak, mtn., Ut., U.S. — F2 121
Lost Ranger Peak, mtn., Co., U.S. — C4 123
Lost River, Id., U.S. — F5 89
Lost River, W.V., U.S. — C6 125
Lost River Glacial Caverns, N.H., U.S. — B3 106
Lost River Range, mts., Id., U.S. — E5 89
Lost Springs, Ks., U.S. — D7 93
Lost Springs, Wy., U.S. — D8 127
Lost Trail Pass, U.S. — D5 89
Los Vigiles, N.M., U.S. — *B4 108
Los Vilos, Chile — A2 54
Lot, stm., Fr. — E4 16
Lota, Chile — B2 54
Lotawana, Lake, res., Mo., U.S. — k11 102
Lotbinière, Que. — C6 74
Lotbinière, co., Que. — C6 74
Lothair, Mt., U.S. — B5 103
Lothian, prov., Scot., U.K. — F2 89
Loto, Zaire — B3 48
Lotofaga, W. Sam. — F12 52
Lötschberg Tunnel, Switz. — E3 18
Lott, Tx., U.S. — D4 120
Lotung, Tai. — G9 31
Louang Namtha, Laos — B2 34
Louangphrabang, Laos — B2 34
Louann, Ar., U.S. — D3 81
Loubomo, Congo — B1 48
Loudéac, Fr. — D3 16
Loudon, N.H., U.S. — D4 106
Loudon, Tn., U.S. — D9 119
Loudon, co., Tn., U.S. — D9 119
Loudonville, N.Y., U.S. — *C7 109
Loudonville, Oh., U.S. — B3 112
Loudoun, co., Va., U.S. — A5 123
Loudun, Fr. — D4 16
Louga, Sen. — C1 45
Loughborough, Eng., U.K. — C6 13
Lougheed, Alta. — C5 68
Lougheed Island, i., N.W. Ter. — m31 66
Loughman, Fl., U.S. — D5 86
Loughrea, Ire. — C3 11
Loughros More Bay, b., Ire. — C3 11
Louin, Ms., U.S. — C4 101
Louisa, Ky., U.S. — B7 94
Louisa, Va., U.S. — B4 123
Louisa, co., Ia., U.S. — C6 92
Louisa, co., Va., U.S. — B5 123
Louisa, Lake, l., Fl., U.S. — D5 86
Louisburg, Ks., U.S. — D9 93
Louisburg, Mn., U.S. — E2 100
Louisburg, Mo., U.S. — D4 102
Louisburg, N.C., U.S. — A4 110
Louisburgh, Ire. — D2 11
Louisdale, N.S. — D8 71
Louise, Ms., U.S. — C3 101
Louise, Tx., U.S. — E4 120
Louise, Lake, l., Ak., U.S. — f18 79
Louise Island, i., B.C. — C2 69
Louiseville, Que. — C5 74
Louisiade Archipelago, is., Pap. N. Gui. — G9 6
Louisiana, Mo., U.S. — B6 102
Louisiana, state, U.S. — C3 95
Louisiana Point, c., La., U.S. — E2 95
Louis Trichardt, S. Afr. — B4 49
Louisville, Al., U.S. — D4 78
Louisville, Co., U.S. — B5 83
Louisville, Ga., U.S. — C4 87
Louisville, Il., U.S. — E5 90
Louisville, Ks., U.S. — C7 93
Louisville, Ky., U.S. — B4 94
Louisville, Ms., U.S. — B4 101
Louisville, Ne., U.S. — D9 104
Louisville, N.Y., U.S. — f9 109
Louisville, Oh., U.S. — B4 112
Louisville, Tn., U.S. — D9 119
Louis-XIV, Pointe, c., Que. — h11 74
Loukhi, Sov. Un. — D15 14
Loulé, Port. — D1 22
Louny, Czech. — C3 26
Loup, co., Ne., U.S. — C6 104
Loup, stm., Ne., U.S. — C7 104
Loup, Île au, i., Que. — B8 71
Loup, Rivière du, stm., Que. — D7 91
Loup, Rivière du, stm., Que. — D5 74
Loup City, Ne., U.S. — C7 104
Lourdes, Newf. — D2 72
Lourdes, Ok., U.S. — B3 113
Lourdes, Fr. — F3 16
Lourenço Marques see Maputo, Moz. — C5 49
Loures, Port. — B1 22
Lousã, Port. — B2 22
Lousana, Alta. — C4 68
Louth, Ire. — C5 11
Louth, Eng., U.K. — D5 11
Louth, co., Ire. — C5 11
Loutrá Aidhipsoú, Grc. — g9 25
Loutrákion, Grc. — h9 25
Loutre, Bayou de, stm., La., U.S. — B3 95
Louvain see Leuven, Bel. — D4 17
Louvale, Ga., U.S. — D2 87
Louviers, Co., U.S. — B6 83
Louviers, Fr. — C4 16
Lovat, stm., Sov. Un. — D9 27
Love, co., Ok., U.S. — D4 113
Love, Sask. — D3 75
Lovech, Bul. — g9 24
Lovelaceville, Ky., U.S. — f9 94
Loveladies, N.J., U.S. — D4 107
Lovelady, Tx., U.S. — D5 120
Loveland, Co., U.S. — A5 83
Loveland, Ia., U.S. — C2 92
Loveland, Oh., U.S. — C1 112
Loveland Park, Oh., U.S. — n13 112
Loveland Pass, Co., U.S. — B5 83
Lovell, Me., U.S. — D2 96
Lovell, Ok., U.S. — A4 113
Lovell, Wy., U.S. — B4 127
Lovells, Mi., U.S. — D6 99
Lovelock, Nv., U.S. — C3 105
Lovely, Ky., U.S. — C7 94
Lovenia, Mount, mtn., Ut., U.S. — C5 121
Love Point, Md., U.S. — B5 97
Loverna, Sask. — F1 75
Loves Park, Il., U.S. — A4 90
Lovett, Ga., U.S. — D4 87
Lovett, In., U.S. — G6 91

Lovettsville, Va., U.S. — A5 123
Lovewell Pond, l., Me., U.S. — f7 78
Lovick, Al., U.S. — f7 78
Lovilia, Ia., U.S. — C5 92
Loving, N.M., U.S. — E5 108
Loving, co., Tx., U.S. — D1 120
Lovington, Il., U.S. — D5 90
Lovington, Ia., U.S. — A3 92
Lovington, N.M., U.S. — E6 108
Lovosice, Czech. — C9 19
Low, Que. — D2 74
Lowa, Zaire — B4 48
Lowa, stm., Zaire — B4 48
Lowden, Ia., U.S. — C7 92
Lowe Farm, Man. — E3 70
Lowell, Ar., U.S. — A1 81
Lowell, In., U.S. — B3 91
Lowell, Ma., U.S. — A5 98
Lowell, Mi., U.S. — F5 99
Lowell, N.C., U.S. — B1 110
Lowell, Oh., U.S. — C4 112
Lowell, Or., U.S. — D4 114
Lowell, Vt., U.S. — B4 122
Lowell, W.V., U.S. — C3 125
Lowell, Wi., U.S. — E5 126
Lowell, Lake, res., Id., U.S. — F2 89
Lowell Mountains, mts., Vt., U.S. — B4 122
Lowellville, Oh., U.S. — A5 112
Lower Arrow Lake, res., B.C. — E8 69
Lower Bank, N.J., U.S. — D3 107
Lower Brule, S.D., U.S. — C6 118
Lower Brule Indian Reservation, S.D., U.S. — C6 118
Lower Burrell, Pa., U.S. — *h15 115
Lower Cabot, Vt., U.S. — C4 122
Lower California, pen., Mex. — B2 63
Lower East Pubnico, N.S. — F4 71
Lower Hutt, N.Z. — N15 51
Lower Island Cove, Newf. — D5 72
Lower Klamath Lake, l., Ca., U.S. — B3 82
Lower Loch Erne, l., N. Ire., U.K. — C3 10
Lower Manitou Lake, l., Ont. — E5 70
Lower Marlboro, Md., U.S. — C4 97
Lower Matecumbe Key, i., Fl., U.S. — H6 86
Lower Merion Township, Pa., U.S. — *F11 115
Lower Monumental Lake, res., Wa., U.S. — C7 124
Lower Moreland Township, Pa., U.S. — *F11 115
Lower New York Bay, b., N.J., U.S. — B4 107
Lower Otay Reservoir, res., Ca., U.S. — o16 82
Lower Paia, Hi., U.S. — C5 88
Lower Peach Tree, Al., U.S. — D2 78
Lower Red Lake, l., Mn., U.S. — C3 100
Lower Rice Lake, l., Mn., U.S. — C3 100
Lower Salem, Oh., U.S. — C4 112
Lower Salmon Dam, Id., U.S. — G4 89
Lower Southampton Township, Pa., U.S. — *G11 115
Lower Village, Vt., U.S. — C3 122
Lower West Pubnico, N.S. — F4 71
Lower Wilson Pond, l., Me., U.S. — C3 96
Lower Woods Harbour, N.S. — F4 71
Lowes, Ky., U.S. — f9 94
Lowestoft, Eng., U.K. — D7 10
Lowgap, N.C., U.S. — A2 110
Łowicz, Pol. — B5 26
Lowland, N.C., U.S. — B6 110
Lowman, Id., U.S. — E3 89
Lowmansville, Ky., U.S. — C7 94
Low Moor, Va., U.S. — C3 123
Lowndes, co., Al., U.S. — C3 78
Lowndes, co., Ga., U.S. — F3 87
Lowndes, co., Ms., U.S. — B5 101
Lowndesboro, Al., U.S. — C3 78
Lowndesville, S.C., U.S. — C2 117
Lowry, Mn., U.S. — E3 100
Lowry, S.D., U.S. — B6 118
Lowry Air Force Base, mil., Co., U.S. — B6 83
Lowry City, Mo., U.S. — C4 102
Lowrys, S.C., U.S. — B5 117
Low Tatra Mountains, mts., Czech. — D5 26
Lowville, N.Y., U.S. — B5 109
Loxley, Al., U.S. — E2 78
Loxton, Austl. — G3 51
Loyal, Ok., U.S. — B3 113
Loyal, Wi., U.S. — D3 126
Loyalist, Alta. — D5 68
Loyall, Ky., U.S. — D6 94
Loyalsock Creek, stm., Pa., U.S. — D8 115
Loyalton, Ca., U.S. — C3 82
Loyalton, S.D., U.S. — B6 118
Loyalty Islands, is., N. Cal. — H10 6
Loysburg, Pa., U.S. — F5 115
Loysville, Pa., U.S. — F7 115
Loznica, Yugo. — C4 24
Lozova, Sov. Un. — G11 27
Lozovaya, Sov. Un. — G11 27
Lozoya, Canal of, Spain — o17 22
Lualaba, stm., Zaire — B4 48
Luama, stm., Zaire — B4 48
Lua Makika, crat., Hi., U.S. — C5 88
Lu'an, China — I7 32
Luana, Ia., U.S. — A6 92
Luanda, Ang. — C1 48
Luanda, Braz. — C2 56
Luang, mtn., Thai. — D1 34
Luang Chiang Dao, mtn., Thai. — C3 35
Luangwa, stm., Afr. — C8 48
Luan He, stm., China — C8 31
Luanshya, Zam. — D6 48
Luanxian, China — C8 31
Luapula, prov., Zam. — A2 49
Luarca, Spain — A2 22
Luashi, Zaire — D3 48
Luau, Ang. — D3 48
Luba, Eq. Gui. — H7 45
Lubaczów, Pol. — E7 26
Lubang, Phil. — p13 34
Lubang, i., Phil. — p14 34
Lubang Islands, is., Phil. — C6 34
Lubango, Ang. — D1 48
Lubartów, Pol. — D7 26
Lubawa, Pol. — B5 26
Lübbecke, W. Ger. — A3 19
Lübben, E. Ger. — C6 18

| Name | Map Ref. | Page |
|---|---|---|

Lübbenau, E. Ger. — B8 19
Lubbock, Tx., U.S. — C2 120
Lubbock, co., Tx., U.S. — C2 120
Lubec, Me., U.S. — D6 96
Lübeck, W. Ger. — B5 18
Lübeck Bay, b., Eur. — A5 18
Lubefu, Zaire — B3 48
Lubero, Zaire — B4 48
Lubicon Lake, l., Alta. — A3 68
Lubilash, stm., Zaire — C3 48
Lubin, Pol. — C4 26
Lublin, Pol. — C7 26
Lublin, Wi., U.S. — C3 126
Lubliniec, Pol. — C5 26
Lubny, Sov. Un. — F9 27
Luboń, Pol. — B4 26
Lubsko, Pol. — C3 26
Lübtheen, E. Ger. — E5 15
Lubudi, Zaire — C4 48
Lubudi, stm., Zaire — C3 48
Lubue, Zaire — B2 48
Lubumbashi (Elisabethville), Zaire — D4 48
Lubutu, Zaire — B4 48
Lucama, N.C., U.S. — B4 110
Lucan, Ont. — D3 73
Lucan, Ire. — D5 11
Lucan, Mn., U.S. — F3 100
Lucania, Mount, mtn., Yukon — D4 66
Lucas, Ia., U.S. — C4 92
Lucas, Ks., U.S. — C5 93
Lucas, Ky., U.S. — D3 94
Lucas, Mi., U.S. — D5 99
Lucas, Oh., U.S. — B3 112
Lucas, S.D., U.S. — D6 118
Lucas, co., Ia., U.S. — C4 92
Lucas, co., Oh., U.S. — A2 112
Lucasville, Oh., U.S. — D3 112
Lucca, Italy — C3 23
Lucé, Fr. — C4 16
Luce, co., Mi., U.S. — B5 99
Luce Bay, b., Scot., U.K. — C4 10
Lucedale, Ms., U.S. — E5 101
Lucena, Phil. — C6 34
Lucena, Spain — D3 22
Lucena del Cid, Spain — B5 22
Lučenec, Czech. — D5 26
Lucera, Italy — D5 23
Lucerne, Ca., U.S. — C2 82
Lucerne, Co., U.S. — A6 83
Lucerne, In., U.S. — C5 91
Lucerne, Mo., U.S. — A4 102
Lucerne, Lake of, l., Switz. — E4 18
Lucernemines, Pa., U.S. — E3 115
Lucerne Valley, Ca., U.S. — E5 82
Luceville, Que. — A9 74
Luchow see Luzhou, China — F6 31
Lüchow, W. Ger. — F5 15
Luchuan, China — A9 35
Lucien, Ms., U.S. — D3 101
Lucien, Ok., U.S. — A4 113
Lucile, Id., U.S. — D2 89
Lucille, Al., U.S. — B2 78
Lucinda, Pa., U.S. — D2 115
Lucipara Islands, is., Indon. — G7 34
Lucira, Ang. — D1 48
Luck, Wi., U.S. — C1 126
Luckau, E. Ger. — C6 18
Luckenwalde, E. Ger. — B6 18
Luckey, Oh., U.S. — A2 112
Luck Lake, l., Sask. — G2 75
Lucknow, Ont. — D3 73
Lucknow, India — C7 36
Lucky Lake, Sask. — G2 75
Lucky MacCamp, Wy., U.S. — *D5 127
Lucky Peak Lake, res., Id., U.S. — F3 89
Luçon, Fr. — D3 16
Lucrecia, Cabo, c., Cuba — D6 64
Lucy, La., U.S. — h10 95
Lucy, Tn., U.S. — B2 119
Lüda see Dalian, China — D9 31
Luda Kamchiya, stm., Bul. — D8 24
Ludden, N.D., U.S. — C7 111
Ludell, Ks., U.S. — C3 93
Lüdenscheid, W. Ger. — C3 18
Lüderitz, Nmb. — C2 49
Ludgate, Ont. — B4 73
Ludhiāna, India — B6 36
Luding, China — F5 31
Lüdinghausen, W. Ger. — B2 19
Ludington, Mi., U.S. — E4 99
Ludlow, N.B. — C3 71
Ludlow, Eng., U.K. — D5 10
Ludlow, Il., U.S. — C5 90
Ludlow, Ky., U.S. — h13 94
Ludlow, Me., U.S. — B4 96
Ludlow, Ma., U.S. — B3 98
Ludlow, Ms., U.S. — C4 101
Ludlow, Mo., U.S. — B4 102
Ludlow, Pa., U.S. — C4 115
Ludlow, S.D., U.S. — B2 118
Ludlow, Vt., U.S. — E3 122
Ludlow Falls, Oh., U.S. — B1 112
Ludlow Mountain, mtn., Vt., U.S. — E3 122
Ludowici, Ga., U.S. — E5 87
Ludvika, Swe. — G6 14
Ludwigsburg, W. Ger. — D4 18
Ludwigshafen [am Rhein], W. Ger. — D4 18
Ludwigslust, E. Ger. — B5 18
Luebo, Zaire — C3 48
Lueders, Tx., U.S. — C3 120
Luena, Ang. — D2 48
Luepa, Ven. — B5 60
Lüeyang, China — H2 32
Lufkin, Tx., U.S. — D5 120
Lufuna, Zaire — C2 48
Luga, Sov. Un. — B7 27
Luga, stm., Sov. Un. — B7 27
Lugagnano Val d'Arda, Italy — E5 20
Lugan, stm., Sov. Un. — q22 27
Luganchik, stm., Sov. Un. — q22 27
Lugano, Switz. — E4 18
Lugano, Lake, l., Eur. — E7 21
Lugau, E. Ger. — C7 19
Lugenda, stm., Moz. — D6 48
Lugnaquillia Mountian, mtn., Ire. — D3 11
Lugo, Italy — B3 23
Lugo, Spain — A2 22
Lugoff, S.C., U.S. — C6 117
Lugoj, Rom. — C5 24
Lugovoy, Sov. Un. — E8 28
Luhuo, China — E5 31
Luiana, Ang. — E3 48
Luidhorn, Neth. — A6 17
Luik see Liège, Bel. — B6 16
Luing, l., Scot., U.K. — D3 13
Luís Correia, Braz. — B2 57
Luís Gomes, Braz. — C3 57
Luis Lopez, N.M., U.S. — D3 108
Luiza, Zaire — C3 48

Lujuna Point, c., Guam — L10 52
Lukachukai, Az., U.S. — A6 80
Luke, Md., U.S. — m12 97
Luke Air Force Base, mil., Az., U.S. — D3 80
Lukenie, stm., Zaire — B2 48
Lukeville, Az., U.S. — F3 80
Lukolela, Zaire — B2 48
Lukovit, Bul. — D7 24
Łuków, Pol. — C7 26
Lukoyanov, Sov. Un. — D15 27
Lukuga, stm., Zaire — C4 48
Lukulu, Zam. — D3 48
Lula, Ga., U.S. — B3 87
Lula, Ms., U.S. — A3 101
Lula, Ok., U.S. — C5 113
Luleå, Swe. — E10 14
Luleälven, stm., Swe. — D9 14
Lüleburgaz, Tur. — B6 40
Luling, La., U.S. — k11 95
Luling, Tx., U.S. — E4 120
Lulong, China — D8 31
Lulu, Fl., U.S. — B4 86
Lulua, stm., Zaire — C3 48
Luluabourg see Kananga, Zaire — C3 48
Lum, Mi., U.S. — E7 99
Lumba, Zaire — A2 48
Lumbala N'guimbo, Ang. — D3 48
Lumber, stm., U.S. — C9 117
Lumber Bridge, N.C., U.S. — C3 110
Lumber City, Ga., U.S. — E4 87
Lumberport, W.V., U.S. — B4 125
Lumberton, Ms., U.S. — D4 101
Lumberton, N.J., U.S. — D3 107
Lumberton, N.M., U.S. — A3 108
Lumberton, N.C., U.S. — C3 110
Lumbo, Moz. — E7 48
Lumby, B.C. — D8 69
Luminao Reef, rf., Guam — L9 52
Lummi Indian Reservation, Wa., U.S. — A3 124
Lumpkin, Ga., U.S. — D2 87
Lumpkin, co., Ga., U.S. — B2 87
Lumsden, Newf. — D5 72
Lumsden, Sask. — G3 75
Lumsden, N.Z. — P12 51
Lumsden, Scot., U.K. — C6 13
Lumsden Beach, Sask. — G3 75
Luna, N.M., U.S. — D1 108
Luna, co., N.M., U.S. — E2 108
Luna Pier, Mi., U.S. — G7 99
Lund, B.C. — D5 69
Lund, Swe. — J5 14
Lund, Nv., U.S. — E6 105
Lundale, W.V., U.S. — n12 125
Lunda Norte, dept., Ang. — C2 48
Lunda Sul, dept., Ang. — D3 48
Lundar, Man. — D2 70
Lundazi, Zam. — D5 48
Lundbreck, Alta. — E3 68
Lundby, Den. — C5 15
Lundby, Swe. — t34 14
Lunderskov, Den. — C3 15
Lundu, Malay. — E3 34
Lundy, i., Eng., U.K. — E4 10
Lune, stm., Eng., U.K. — F6 13
Lüneburg, W. Ger. — B5 18
Lunel, Fr. — F6 16
Lünen, W. Ger. — B2 19
Lunenburg, N.S. — E5 71
Lunenburg, Ma., U.S. — A4 98
Lunenburg, Vt., U.S. — C5 122
Lunenburg, Va., U.S. — D4 123
Lunenburg, co., N.S. — E5 71
Lunenburg, co., Va., U.S. — D4 123
Lunéville, Fr. — C7 16
Lungi, S.L. — E2 45
Lungué-Bungo, stm., Afr. — D3 48
Lüni, stm., India — C5 36
Luning, Nv., U.S. — E3 105
Lunino, Sov. Un. — E15 27
Lunsar, S.L. — E2 45
Lunyama, Zaire — C4 48
Luochuan, China — D1 31
Luoding, China — A9 35
Luohe, China — E7 31
Luoning, China — G4 32
Luoshan, China — H6 32
Luoyang, China — E7 31
Luozi, Zaire — B1 48
Lupani, Zimb. — A4 49
Lupeni, Rom. — C6 24
Lupton, Az., U.S. — B6 80
Lupton, Mi., U.S. — D6 99
Lupus, Mo., U.S. — C5 102
Luque, Para. — B4 56
Luquillo, Sierra de, mts., P.R. — B4 65
Lūrah, stm., Afg. — B4 36
Luray, Ks., U.S. — C5 93
Luray, Mo., U.S. — A6 102
Luray, S.C., U.S. — F5 117
Luray, Tn., U.S. — B3 119
Luray, Va., U.S. — B4 123
Lure, Fr. — D7 16
Lure, Lake, res., N.C., U.S. — f10 110
Lurgan, N. Ire., U.K. — C3 10
Luribay, Bol. — C2 55
Lúrio, Moz. — D7 48
Lúrio, stm., Moz. — D6 48
Lurton, Ar., U.S. — B2 81
Lusaka, Zam. — E4 48
Lusaka, prov., Zam. — E4 48
Lusako, Zaire — B4 48
Lusambo, Zaire — B3 48
Lusby, Md., U.S. — D5 97
Luscar, Alta. — C2 68
Luseland, Sask. — E1 75
Lushan, China — H5 32
Lushan, China — F8 34
Lushnja, Alb. — D1 24
Lushoto, Tan. — B6 48
Lushton, Ne., U.S. — D8 104
Lushun, China — D9 31
Lusignan, Fr. — D4 16
Lusk, Wy., U.S. — D8 127
Lusk, stm., U.S. — B11 103
Lutcher, La., U.S. — D5 95
Lutesville, Mo., U.S. — D8 102
Luther, Mi., U.S. — D5 99
Luther, Mt., U.S. — E7 103
Luther, Ok., U.S. — B4 113
Luthersville, Ga., U.S. — C2 87
Lutherville-Timonium, Md., U.S. — B4 97
Lutie, Ok., U.S. — C6 113
Lutong, Malay. — D4 34
Lütjenburg, W. Ger. — A5 18
Luton, Eng., U.K. — E6 10
Luton, Ia., U.S. — B1 92
Lutong, Malay. — E4 34
Lutsen, Mn., U.S. — k9 100
Lutsk, Sov. Un. — F5 27
Luttrell, Tn., U.S. — C10 119
Lutts, Tn., U.S. — B4 119

Lutugino, Sov. Un. — q22 27
Lutz, Fl., U.S. — D4 86
Lützow-Holm Bay, b., Ant. — C16 7
Luuq, Som. — E5 47
Luverne, Al., U.S. — D3 78
Lu Verne, Ia., U.S. — B3 92
Luverne, Mn., U.S. — G2 100
Luverne, N.D., U.S. — B8 111
Luvua, stm., Zaire — C4 48
Luwingu, Zam. — D4 48
Luwuk, Indon. — F6 34
Luxapallila Creek, stm., U.S. — B1 101
Luxembourg, Lux. — C7 16
Luxembourg, prov., Bel. — C7 16
Luxembourg, ctry., Eur. — C7 16
Luxemburg, Ia., U.S. — B6 92
Luxemburg, Wi., U.S. — D6 126
Luxeuil-les-Bains, Fr. — D7 16
Luxi, China — F7 31
Luxomni, Ga., U.S. — h8 87
Luxor (Al Uqsur), Eg. — C3 38
Luxor, hist., Egypt — D6 43
Luxora, Ar., U.S. — B6 81
Luz, Braz. — B3 56
Luza, Sov. Un. — A3 28
Luza, stm., Sov. Un. — A3 28
Lyall, Mount, mtn., N.Z. — P11 51
Lyallpur see Faisalabad, Pak. — B5 36
Lyaskovets, Bul. — D7 24
Lybster, Scot., U.K. — B5 13
Lychen, E. Ger. — E7 15
Lycksele, Swe. — E8 14
Lycoming, N.Y., U.S. — B4 109
Lycoming, co., Pa., U.S. — D7 115
Lycoming Creek, stm., Pa., U.S. — D7 115
Lydenburg, S. Afr. — C5 49
Lydia, Mn., U.S. — F5 100
Lydia, S.C., U.S. — C7 117
Lyell, Mount, mtn., Can. — D2 68
Lyell Island, i., B.C. — C2 69
Lyerly, Ga., U.S. — B1 87
Lyford, In., U.S. — E3 91
Lyford, Tx., U.S. — F4 120
Lygnern, l., Swe. — A6 15
Lyle, Mn., U.S. — G6 100
Lyle, Wa., U.S. — D4 124
Lyles, Tn., U.S. — B4 119
Lyleton, Man. — E1 70
Lyman, Ne., U.S. — C1 104
Lyman, S.C., U.S. — B3 117
Lyman, Ut., U.S. — E4 121
Lyman, Wa., U.S. — A3 124
Lyman, Wy., U.S. — E2 127
Lyman, co., S.D., U.S. — D6 118
Lyman Lake, res., Az., U.S. — C6 80
Lyme, Ct., U.S. — D6 84
Lyme, N.H., U.S. — C2 106
Lyme Bay, b., Eng., U.K. — D5 12
Lyme Center, N.H., U.S. — C2 106
Lymington, Eng., U.K. — D6 12
Łyna, stm., Eur. — B6 26
Lynbrook, N.Y., U.S. — *E7 109
Lynch, Ky., U.S. — D7 94
Lynch, Ne., U.S. — B7 104
Lynchburg, N.D., U.S. — C8 111
Lynchburg, Oh., U.S. — C2 112
Lynchburg, S.C., U.S. — C7 117
Lynchburg, Tn., U.S. — B5 119
Lynchburg, Va., U.S. — C3 123
Lynches, stm., S.C., U.S. — D8 117
Lynch Heights, De., U.S. — *E4 85
Lynch Station, Va., U.S. — C3 123
Lyncourt, N.Y., U.S. — *B4 109
Lynd, Mn., U.S. — F3 100
Lyndeborough, N.H., U.S. — E3 106
Lynden, Wa., U.S. — A3 124
Lynde Point, c., Ct., U.S. — D6 84
Lyndhurst, Ont. — C8 73
Lyndhurst, N.J., U.S. — h8 107
Lyndhurst, Oh., U.S. — g10 112
Lyndon, Il., U.S. — B4 90
Lyndon, Ks., U.S. — D8 93
Lyndon, Ky., U.S. — g11 94
Lyndon, Vt., U.S. — B4 122
Lyndon B. Johnson National Historical Site, hist., Tx., U.S. — D3 120
Lyndon B. Johnson Space Center, sci., Tx., U.S. — r14 120
Lyndon Center, Vt., U.S. — B4 122
Lyndon Station, Wi., U.S. — E4 126
Lyndonville, N.Y., U.S. — B2 109
Lyndonville, Vt., U.S. — B4 122
Lyndora, Pa., U.S. — E2 115
Lyngby [-Tårbæk], Den. — C6 15
Lynn, Al., U.S. — A2 78
Lynn, In., U.S. — D8 91
Lynn, Ma., U.S. — B6 98
Lynn, Pa., U.S. — C10 115
Lynn, co., Tx., U.S. — C2 120
Lynn, Lake, res., W.V., U.S. — B5 125
Lynn Canal, b., Ak., U.S. — k22 79
Lynndyl, Ut., U.S. — D3 121
Lynne, Fl., U.S. — C5 86
Lynne Acres, Md., U.S. — B4 97
Lynnfield, Ma., U.S. — f11 98
Lynn Garden, Tn., U.S. — C11 119
Lynn Grove, Ky., U.S. — f9 94
Lynn Haven, Fl., U.S. — u16 86
Lynnhaven Roads, b., Va., U.S. — k15 123
Lynn Lake, Man. — A1 70
Lynnport, Pa., U.S. — E10 115
Lynnville, Ia., U.S. — C5 92
Lynnville, In., U.S. — H3 91
Lynnville, Ky., U.S. — f9 94
Lynnville, Tn., U.S. — B4 119
Lynnwood, Wa., U.S. — B3 124
Lynton, Eng., U.K. — E4 12
Lynwood, Ca., U.S. — n12 82
Lynxville, Wi., U.S. — E2 126
Lyø, i., Den. — C4 15
Lyoffans, Fr. — A2 21
Lyon, Fr. — E6 16
Lyon, co., Ia., U.S. — A1 92
Lyon, co., Ks., U.S. — D7 93
Lyon, co., Ky., U.S. — C1 94

Lyon, co., Mn., U.S. — F3 100
Lyon, co., Nv., U.S. — D2 105
Lyon, stm., Scot., U.K. — D4 13
Lyon Creek, stm., Ks., U.S. — D7 93
Lyon Mountain, N.Y., U.S. — f11 109
Lyon Mountain, mtn., N.Y., U.S. — f11 109
Lyonnais, hist. reg., Fr. — E6 16
Lyons, Co., U.S. — A5 83
Lyons, Ga., U.S. — D4 87
Lyons, Il., U.S. — k9 90
Lyons, In., U.S. — G3 91
Lyons, Ks., U.S. — D5 93
Lyons, Mi., U.S. — F6 99
Lyons, Ne., U.S. — C9 104
Lyons, N.Y., U.S. — B3 109
Lyons, Oh., U.S. — A1 112
Lyons, Or., U.S. — C4 114
Lyons, S.D., U.S. — D9 118
Lyons, Tx., U.S. — D4 120
Lyons, Wi., U.S. — n11 126
Lyons Falls, N.Y., U.S. — B5 109
Lyons Plains, Ct., U.S. — E2 84
Lyracrumpane, Ire. — E2 11
Lys, stm., Eur. — D3 17
Lysá [nad Labem], Czech. — n18 26
Lysaya Gora, Sov. Un. — G8 27
Lysekil, Swe. — H4 14
Lysite, Wy., U.S. — C5 127
Lyss, Switz. — B3 21
Lysva, Sov. Un. — D8 29
Lytham Saint Anne's, Eng., U.K. — A5 12
Lytle, Tx., U.S. — E3 120
Lytton, B.C. — D7 69
Lytton, Ia., U.S. — B3 92
Lyuban, Sov. Un. — G6 27
Lyubertsy, Sov. Un. — n17 27
Lyudinovo, Sov. Un. — E10 27

## M

Ma, stm., Asia — A2 34
Ma'ād, Jord. — B7 41
Maalaea, Hi., U.S. — *C5 88
Maalaea Bay, b., Hi., U.S. — *C5 88
Ma'alot-Tarshiha, Isr. — B7 41
Maam Cross, Ire. — D2 11
Maamoura, Cap, c., Tun. — F3 23
Ma'ān, Jord. — G10 40
Ma'anshan, China — *E8 31
Ma'arrat an Nu'mān, Syria — *E11 40
Maas, Ire. — C11 11
Maas (Meuse), stm., Eur. — B5 17
Maaseik, Bel. — C5 17
Maasin, Phil. — C7 34
Maastricht, Neth. — B6 16
Mabalacat, Phil. — o13 34
Mabana, Wa., U.S. — A3 124
Mabank, Tx., U.S. — C4 120
Mabaruma, Guy. — A3 59
Mabber, Ras, c., Som. — D7 47
Mabel, Mn., U.S. — G7 100
Mabelvale, Ar., U.S. — k10 81
Maben, Ms., U.S. — B4 101
Maberly, Ont. — C8 73
Mabie, W.V., U.S. — C5 125
Mableton, Ga., U.S. — h7 87
Mablethorpe, Eng., U.K. — A8 12
Mabote, Moz. — B5 49
Mabou, N.S. — C8 71
Mabrous Tafidinga, well, Niger — D7 43
Mabscott, W.V., U.S. — D3 125
Mabton, Wa., U.S. — C5 124
Mabuni, Japan — o5 52
Macachin, Arg. — D4 56
Macaé, Braz. — C4 56
Macaíba, Braz. — g6 57
Macalelon, Phil. — p14 34
Macalister, B.C. — C6 69
MacAlpine Lake, l., N.W. Ter. — C12 66
Macan Islands, is., Indon. — G6 34
Macao, dep., Asia — M2 31
Macapá, Braz. — C8 59
Macará, Braz. — B2 58
Macas, Ec. — C3 57
Macau, Braz. — C3 57
Macaúbas, Braz. — D6 21
Maccagno [Superiore], Italy — D6 21
Maccan, N.S. — D5 71
Maccarese, Italy — h8 23
MacClenny, Fl., U.S. — B4 86
Macclesfield, Eng., U.K. — D5 10
MacClesfield, N.C., U.S. — B5 110
Macculloch, Cape, c., N.W. Ter. — B18 66
MacDill Air Force Base, mil., Fl., U.S. — E4 86
Macdonald, Man. — D2 70
Macdonald, W.V., U.S. — n13 125
Macdonald, Lake, l., Austl. — D4 50
Macdonald Range, mts., B.C. — E10 69
MacDonaldton, Pa., U.S. — G4 115
Macdonnell Ranges, mts., Austl. — D5 50
MacDowell Reservoir, res., N.H., U.S. — E2 106
Macduff, Scot., U.K. — C6 13
Macdui, Ben, mtn., Scot., U.K. — D5 13
Maceió, Braz. — C3 57
Macenta, Gui. — G4 44
Maceo, Ky., U.S. — C3 94
Macerata, Italy — C4 23
Maces Bay, b., N.B. — D3 71
Macgillycuddy's Reeks, mts., Ire. — E2 11
MacGregor, Man. — E2 70
Machachi, Ec. — B2 58
Machacalis, Braz. — B2 58
Machachi, Ec. — B2 58
Machado, Braz. — B2 58
Machakos, Kenya — B6 48
Machala, Ec. — B2 58
Machanao, Mount, hill, Guam — L10 52
Machattie, Lake, l., Austl. — D7 50
Macheng, China — *E8 31
Machesney Park, Il., U.S. — *A4 90
Machias, N.Y., U.S. — C2 109
Machias, stm., Me., U.S. — B4 96
Machias, Ct., U.S. — B4 96
Machias Bay, b., Me., U.S. — D5 96
Machias Lakes, l., Me., U.S. — C5 96
Machiasport, Me., U.S. — D5 96
Machichi, stm., Man. — A6 70

Machico, Port. — h12 22
Machida, Japan — *19 33
Machilīpatnam, India — E7 36
Machiques, Ven. — A3 60
Macho, Arroyo del, val., N.M., U.S. — C4 108
Machrihanish, Scot., U.K. — E8 13
Machu Picchu, hist., Peru — D3 58
Machynlleth, Wales, U.K. — B4 12
Macia, Moz. — C5 49
Măcin, Rom. — G9 24
Macina, reg., Mali — D4 45
Mack, Co., U.S. — B2 83
Mackay, Austl. — D8 50
Mackay, Id., U.S. — F5 89
MacKay, Lake, l., Austl. — D4 50
MacKay Lake, l., N.W. Ter. — D10 66
MacKenzie, B.C. — B6 69
Mackenzie, Guy. — A4 59
Mackenzie, dept., N.W. Ter. — D11 66
Mackenzie, stm., N.W. Ter. — C6 66
Mackenzie Bay, b., Ant. — C20 7
Mackenzie Bay, b., Can. — C6 66
Mackenzie King Island, i., N.W. Ter. — m29 66
Mackenzie Mountains, mts., Can. — D7 66
Mackey, Ont. — A7 73
Mackey, In., U.S. — H3 91
Mackeys, N.C., U.S. — B6 110
Mackeyville, Pa., U.S. — D7 115
Mackinac, co., Mi., U.S. — B5 99
Mackinac, Straits of, strt., Mi., U.S. — C6 99
Mackinac Bridge, Mi., U.S. — C6 99
Mackinac Island, Mi., U.S. — C6 99
Mackinac Island, i., Mi., U.S. — C6 99
Mackinaw, Il., U.S. — C4 90
Mackinaw, stm., Il., U.S. — C4 90
Mackinaw City, Mi., U.S. — C6 99
Macklin, Sask. — E1 75
Macksburg, Oh., U.S. — C4 112
Macks Creek, Mo., U.S. — D5 102
Mackville, Ky., U.S. — C4 94
Mackville, Wi., U.S. — h9 126
Maclean, Austl. — D9 51
Maclean Strait, strt., N.W. Ter. — m31 66
Maclear, S. Afr. — D4 49
Macleod, Lake, l., Austl. — D1 50
MacNutt, Sask. — F5 75
Maco, Bol. — B2 55
Macocolo, Ang. — C2 48
Macomb, Il., U.S. — C3 90
Macomb, Ok., U.S. — B4 113
Macomb, co., Mi., U.S. — F8 99
Mâcon, Fr. — D6 16
Macon, Ga., U.S. — D3 87
Macon, Il., U.S. — D5 90
Macon, Ms., U.S. — B5 101
Macon, Mo., U.S. — B5 102
Macon, Ne., U.S. — D7 104
Macon, N.C., U.S. — A4 110
Macon, Tn., U.S. — B2 119
Macon, co., Al., U.S. — C4 78
Macon, co., Ga., U.S. — D2 87
Macon, co., Il., U.S. — D5 90
Macon, co., Mo., U.S. — B5 102
Macon, co., N.C., U.S. — f9 110
Macon, Bayou, stm., U.S. — B4 95
Macoun, Sask. — H4 75
Macoun Lake, l., Sask. — A4 75
Macoupin, co., Il., U.S. — D3 90
Macoupin Creek, stm., Il., U.S. — D3 90
Macovane, Moz. — B6 49
Macquarie, stm., Austl. — F8 50
Macquarie Island, i., Austl. — J7 2
Macroom, Ire. — E3 11
Macrorie, Sask. — F2 75
MacTier, Ont. — B5 73
Macuelizo, Hond. — C3 63
Macujer, Col. — C3 60
Macungie, Pa., U.S. — E10 115
Macwahoc, Me., U.S. — C4 96
Macy, In., U.S. — C5 91
Macy, Ne., U.S. — B9 104
Mad, stm., Ct., U.S. — B3 84
Mad, stm., N.H., U.S. — C3 106
Mad, stm., Oh., U.S. — C2 112
Mad, stm., Vt., U.S. — C3 122
Ma'dabā, Jord. — C7 41
Madaba, Jord. — D7 43
Madagascar, ctry., Afr. — g9 49
Madalena, Braz. — D9 57
Madame, Isle, i., N.S. — D9 71
Madang, Pap. N. Gui. — k12 50
Madaoua, Niger — D6 45
Mādārīpur, Bngl. — F13 37
Madawaska, Me., U.S. — A4 96
Madawaska, co., N.B. — B1 71
Madawaska, stm., Ont. — B7 73
Madawaska Lake, l., Me., U.S. — A4 96
Madaya, Burma — C2 35
Madbury, N.H., U.S. — D5 106
Madden, Ms., U.S. — C4 101
Maddock, N.D., U.S. — B6 111
Maddox, Md., U.S. — D4 97
Madeira, Oh., U.S. — o13 112
Madeira, i., Port. — h11 22
Madeira, stm., S.A. — D2 59
Madeira Islands, is., Port. — C1 44
Madeleine, Îles de la, i., Que. — B8 71
Madelia, Mn., U.S. — F4 100
Madeline, Ca., U.S. — B3 82
Madeline Island, i., Wi., U.S. — B3 126
Madera, Mex. — B3 63
Madera, Ca., U.S. — D4 82
Madera, Pa., U.S. — E5 115
Madera, co., Ca., U.S. — D4 82
Madgaon, India — E5 36
Madge Lake, l., Sask. — F5 75
Madhupur, India — E11 37
Madhya Pradesh, state, India — D6 36
Madill, Ok., U.S. — C5 113
Madimba, Zaire — B2 48
Madīnat ash Sha'b, Yemen — F4 38
Madingou, Congo — B1 48
Madison, Sask. — F1 75
Madison, Ca., U.S. — C3 82
Madison, Ct., U.S. — D5 84
Madison, Fl., U.S. — B3 86
Madison, Ga., U.S. — C3 87
Madison, In., U.S. — G7 91
Madison, Ks., U.S. — D7 93

Madison, Me., U.S. — D3 96
Madison, Md., U.S. — C5 97
Madison, Mn., U.S. — E2 100
Madison, Ms., U.S. — C3 101
Madison, Mo., U.S. — B5 102
Madison, Ne., U.S. — C8 104
Madison, N.H., U.S. — C4 106
Madison, N.J., U.S. — B4 107
Madison, N.Y., U.S. — C5 109
Madison, N.C., U.S. — A3 110
Madison, Oh., U.S. — A4 112
Madison, S.C., U.S. — B1 117
Madison, S.D., U.S. — C8 118
Madison, Va., U.S. — B4 123
Madison, W.V., U.S. — C3 125
Madison, Wi., U.S. — E4 126
Madison, co., Al., U.S. — A3 78
Madison, co., Ar., U.S. — B2 81
Madison, co., Fl., U.S. — B3 86
Madison, co., Ga., U.S. — B3 87
Madison, co., Id., U.S. — F7 89
Madison, co., Il., U.S. — E4 90
Madison, co., In., U.S. — D6 91
Madison, co., Ia., U.S. — C3 92
Madison, co., Ky., U.S. — C5 94
Madison, co., La., U.S. — B4 95
Madison, co., Ms., U.S. — C4 101
Madison, co., Mo., U.S. — D7 102
Madison, co., Mt., U.S. — E5 103
Madison, co., Ne., U.S. — C8 104
Madison, co., N.Y., U.S. — C5 109
Madison, co., N.C., U.S. — f10 110
Madison, co., Oh., U.S. — C2 112
Madison, co., Tn., U.S. — B3 119
Madison, co., Tx., U.S. — D5 120
Madison, co., Va., U.S. — B4 123
Madison, stm., Mt., U.S. — E5 103
Madisonburg, Pa., U.S. — E7 115
Madison Heights, Mi., U.S. — o15 99
Madison Heights, Va., U.S. — C3 123
Madison Lake, Mn., U.S. — F5 100
Madison Range, mts., Mt., U.S. — E5 103
Madisonville, Ky., U.S. — C2 94
Madisonville, La., U.S. — D5 95
Madisonville, Tn., U.S. — D9 119
Madisonville, Tx., U.S. — D5 120
Madiun, Indon. — G4 34
Madoc, Ont. — C7 73
Madoc, Mt., U.S. — B11 103
Mado Gashi, Kenya — A6 48
Madon, stm., Fr. — A2 21
Madona, Sov. Un. — C6 27
Madonna di Campiglio, Italy — C6 20
Madrakah, Ra's al, c., Oman — D5 38
Madras, India — F7 36
Madras see Tamil Nadu, state, India — G6 36
Madras, Or., U.S. — C5 114
Madre, Laguna, b., Mex. — C5 63
Madre, Laguna, b., Tx., U.S. — F4 120
Madre, Sierra, mts., N.A. — D6 63
Madre, Sierra, mts., Phil. — B6 34
Madre de Dios, dept., Peru — D3 58
Madre de Dios, Isla, i., Chile — E1 54
Madre del Sur, Sierra, mts., Mex. — D4 63
Madre Occidental, Sierra, mts., Mex. — B3 63
Madre Oriental, Sierra, mts., Mex. — C5 63
Madrid, Spain — B4 22
Madrid, Al., U.S. — D4 78
Madrid, Ia., U.S. — C4 92
Madrid, Me., U.S. — D2 96
Madrid, Ne., U.S. — D4 104
Madrid, N.Y., U.S. — f9 109
Madridejos, Spain — C4 22
Madrūsah, Libya — E2 43
Madura, i., Indon. — G4 34
Madurai, India — G6 36
Maebashi, Japan — D12 33
Mae Hong Son, Thai. — D3 35
Maella, Spain — B6 22
Maengsan, N. Kor. — G3 33
Maesteg, Wales, U.K. — C6 12
Maestra, Sierra, mts., Cuba — D5 64
Maevatanana, Madag. — g9 49
Maewo, i., Van. — E3 90
Ma'fan, Libya — D2 43
Mafeking see Mafikeng, S. Afr. — C4 49
Maffra, Austl. — H6 51
Mafia, i., Tan. — C6 48
Mafikeng, S. Afr. — C4 49
Mafra, Braz. — D5 56
Mafra, Port. — C1 22
Magadan, Sov. Un. — D18 29
Magadi, Kenya — B6 48
Magaguadavic Lake, l., N.B. — D2 71
Magallanes y Antártica Chilena, prov., Chile — h11 54
Maganey, Ire. — E5 11
Maganga, Zaire — A4 48
Magangué, Col. — B3 60
Magaria, Niger — F7 45
Magat, stm., Phil. — n13 34
Magazine Mountain, mtn., Ar., U.S. — B2 81
Magdalena, Arg. — B5 54
Magdalena, Bol. — B2 55
Magdalena, N.M., U.S. — C2 108
Magdalena, dept., Col. — A3 60
Magdalena, Mex. — h9 63
Magdalena, Isla, i., Chile — E1 54
Magdalena [de Kino], Mex. — h9 63
Magdalena del Mar, Peru — *D2 58
Magdalena Mountains, mts., N.M., U.S. — D2 108
Magdi'el, Isr. — g10 41
Magé, Braz. — h6 56
Magee, Ms., U.S. — D4 101
Magellan, Strait of (Estrecho de Magallanes), strt., S.A. — h11 54
Magenta, Italy — B2 23
Maggia, Switz. — E3 21
Maggie Creek, stm., Nv., U.S. — C5 105
Maggiore, Lake, l., Eur. — A2 23
Maghāghah, Eg. — D6 43
Maghera, N. Ire., U.K. — C3 10
Magherafelt, N. Ire., U.K. — C3 10
Maghull, Eng., U.K. — B5 12
Magic Reservoir, res., Id., U.S. — F4 89
Magilligan Point, c., N. Ire., U.K. — B5 11
Maglaj, Yugo. — C4 24

| Name | Map Ref. | Page |
|---|---|---|

Maglić, Yugo. . . . . . . . . D5 24
Maglie, Italy . . . . . . . . . D7 23
Magna, Ut., U.S. . . . . . . C3 121
Magness, Ar., U.S. . . . . . B4 81
Magnet, Man. . . . . . . . . D2 70
Magnet, In., U.S. . . . . . . H5 91
Magnet, Ne., U.S. . . . . . . B8 104
Magnetawan, Ont. . . . . . . B5 73
Magnetawan, stm., Ont. . . . B4 73
Magnet Cove, Ar., U.S. . . . C3 81
Magnetic Springs, Oh., U.S. . B2 112
Magnitogorsk, Sov. Un. . . . D8 29
Magnolia, De., U.S. . . . . . D2 81
Magnolia, De., U.S. . . . . . D4 85
Magnolia, Il., U.S. . . . . . . B4 90
Magnolia, Ia., U.S. . . . . . . C2 92
Magnolia, Ky., U.S. . . . . . C4 94
Magnolia, Md., U.S. . . . . . B5 97
Magnolia, Mn., U.S. . . . . . G2 100
Magnolia, Ms., U.S. . . . . . D3 101
Magnolia, N.J., U.S. . . . . . *D2 107
Magnolia, N.C., U.S. . . . . . C4 110
Magnolia, Oh., U.S. . . . . . B4 112
Magnolia, Tx., U.S. . . . . . . C5 120
Magnolia Springs, Al., U.S. . . E2 78
Mago, i., Fiji . . . . . . . . . H16 52
Magoffin, co., Ky., U.S. . . . C6 94
Magog, Que. . . . . . . . . . D5 74
Magothy River, b., Md., U.S. . B4 97
Magoúla, Grc. . . . . . . . . g11 25
Magpie, Que. . . . . . . . . . h8 72
Magpie, stm., Que. . . . . . . h8 72
Magrath, Alta. . . . . . . . . E4 68
Magruder Mountain, mtn., Nv., U.S. . . . . . . . . . . . . . F4 105
Maguari, Cabo, c., Braz. . . . B1 57
Magude, Moz. . . . . . . . . B5 49
Magway, Burma . . . . . . . D9 36
Mahābād, Iran . . . . . . . . B4 38
Mahabo, Madag. . . . . . . . h8 49
Mahaffey, Pa., U.S. . . . . . E4 115
Mahagi, Zaire . . . . . . . . A5 48
Mahaicony Village, Guy. . . . A3 59
Mahajanga, Madag. . . . . . g9 49
Mahajanga, prov., Madag. . . g9 49
Mahakam, stm., Indon. . . . . F5 34
Mahalatswe, Bots. . . . . . . B4 49
Mahallāt, Iran . . . . . . . . E5 39
Mahānadi, stm., India . . . . D7 36
Mahanoro, Madag. . . . . . . g9 49
Mahanoy City, Pa., U.S. . . . E9 115
Mahārāshtra, state, India . . . D6 36
Mahaska, Ks., U.S. . . . . . . C6 93
Mahaska, co., Ia., U.S. . . . . C5 92
Maḩaṭṭat Ḑab'ah, Jord. . . . . C8 41
Mahbūbnagar, India . . . . . E6 36
Mahenge, Tan. . . . . . . . . C7 48
Mahesāna, India . . . . . . . F4 37
Mahi, stm., India . . . . . . . I6 37
Mahia Peninsula, pen., N.Z. . M16 51
Mahned, Ms., U.S. . . . . . . D4 101
Mahnomen, Mn., U.S. . . . . C3 100
Mahnomen, co., Mn., U.S. . . C3 100
Mahoba, India . . . . . . . . E7 37
Mahogany Mountain, mtn., Or., U.S. . . . . . . . . . . . D9 114
Mahomet, Il., U.S. . . . . . . C5 90
Mahón, Spain . . . . . . . . C8 22
Mahone Bay, N.S. . . . . . . E5 71
Mahoning, co., Oh., U.S. . . . A5 112
Mahoning, stm., U.S. . . . . . A5 112
Mahoosuc Range, mts., N.H., U.S. . . . . . . . . . . . . . B4 106
Mahopac, N.Y., U.S. . . . . . D7 109
Mahto, S.D., U.S. . . . . . . B5 118
Mahtowa, Mn., U.S. . . . . . D6 100
Mahuta, Tan. . . . . . . . . . D8 48
Mahuva, India . . . . . . . . G3 37
Mahwah, N.J., U.S. . . . . . . A4 107
Maĭche, Fr. . . . . . . . . . . B2 20
Maicurú, stm., Braz. . . . . . C4 59
Maida, N.D., U.S. . . . . . . . A7 111
Maiden, N.C., U.S. . . . . . . B1 110
Maidenhead, Eng., U.K. . . . C7 12
Maiden Rock, Wi., U.S. . . . . D1 126
Maidens, rock, N. Ire., U.K. . . C6 11
Maidstone, Sask. . . . . . . . D1 75
Maidstone, Eng., U.K. . . . . E7 10
Maidstone Lake, l., Vt., U.S. . B5 122
Maidsville, W.V., U.S. . . . . B5 125
Maiduguri, Nig. . . . . . . . . D7 45
Maihar, India . . . . . . . . . E8 37
Maikala Range, mts., India . . F8 37
Maiko, stm., Zaire . . . . . . B4 48
Maikoor, i., Indon. . . . . . . G8 34
Maili, Hi., U.S. . . . . . . . . g9 88
Maili Point, c., Hi., U.S. . . . g9 88
Maillard, Que. . . . . . . . . B7 74
Mailley-et-Chazelot, Fr. . . . A1 21
Main, stm., W. Ger. . . . . . . D4 18
Main, stm., N. Ire., U.K. . . . C5 11
Main-à-Dieu, N.S. . . . . . . . C10 71
Mainburg, W. Ger. . . . . . . E6 19
Main Centre, Sask. . . . . . . G2 75
Main Channel, strt., Ont. . . . B3 73
Mai-Ndombe, Lac, l., Zaire . . B2 48
Maine, i., U.S. . . . . . . . . C4 109
Maine, hist. reg., Fr. . . . . . C4 16
Maine, state, U.S. . . . . . . . C3 96
Mainesburg, Pa., U.S. . . . . C7 115
Maïné-Soroa, Niger . . . . . . D7 45
Mainland, i., Scot., U.K. . . . g10 10
Mainland, i., Scot., U.K. . . . A5 10
Mainland, stm., Man. . . . . . C4 70
Main Pass, strt., La., U.S. . . E6 95
Maintirano, Madag. . . . . . . g8 49
Main Topsail, mtn., Newf. . . . D3 72
Mainz (Mayence), W. Ger. . . D4 18
Maipo, Volcán, vol., S.A. . . . C3 56
Maipú, Arg. . . . . . . . . . . B5 54
Maiquetía, Ven. . . . . . . . . A4 60
Maira, stm., Italy . . . . . . . E3 20
Mairiporã, Braz. . . . . . . . m8 56
Maisí, Punta de, c., Cuba . . . D6 64
Maisons-Laffitte, Fr. . . . . . g9 16
Maitland, Austl. . . . . . . . . F9 51
Maitland, N.S. . . . . . . . . . D6 71
Maitland, Ont. . . . . . . . . . C9 73
Maitland, Fl., U.S. . . . . . . . *D5 86
Maitland, Mo., U.S. . . . . . . A2 102
Maíz, Islas del, is., Nic. . . . . E8 63
Maize, Ks., U.S. . . . . . . . . g12 93
Maizières-lès-Vic, Fr. . . . . . E1 19
Maizuru, Japan . . . . . . . . I7 33
Majagual, Col. . . . . . . . . B3 60
Majene, Indon. . . . . . . . . F5 34
Majenica, In., U.S. . . . . . . C7 91
Majestic, Ky., U.S. . . . . . . C7 94
Maji, Eth. . . . . . . . . . . . D4 47
Major, Sask. . . . . . . . . . . F1 75
Major, co., Ok., U.S. . . . . . A3 113
Majuro, atoll, Marsh Is. . . . . F10 6
Makaha, Hi., U.S. . . . . . . . g9 88

Makaha Point, c., Hi., U.S. . . A2 88
Makah Indian Reservation, Wa., U.S. . . . . . . . . . . A1 124
Makahuena Point, c., Hi., U.S. B2 88
Makakilo City, Hi., U.S. . . . . g9 88
Makalado, Zaire . . . . . . . A4 48
Makallé, Arg. . . . . . . . . . E4 55
Makālu, mtn., Asia . . . . . . *C8 37
Makanda, Il., U.S. . . . . . . . F4 90
Makanza, Zaire . . . . . . . . A2 48
Makapala, Hi., U.S. . . . . . . C6 88
Makapuu Head, c., Hi., U.S. . B4 88
Makarov, Sov. Un. . . . . . . B13 31
Makarska, Yugo. . . . . . . . D3 24
Makasar see Ujungpandang, Indon. . . . . . . . . . . . . G5 34
Makassar Strait, strt., Indon. . F5 34
Makat, Sov. Un. . . . . . . . . E8 29
Makawao, Hi., U.S. . . . . . . C5 88
Makaweli, Hi., U.S. . . . . . . B2 88
Makeni, S.L. . . . . . . . . . . E2 45
Makeyevka, Sov. Un. . . . . . E6 29
Makgadikgadi Pans, pl., Bots. . B4 49
Makhachkala, Sov. Un. . . . . E7 29
Makharadze, Sov. Un. . . . . B14 40
Makhfar al Quwayrah, Jord. . E7 41
Makinak, Man. . . . . . . . . D2 70
Makindu, Kenya . . . . . . . . B6 48
Makinsk, Sov. Un. . . . . . . C8 28
Makkinga, Neth. . . . . . . . . C6 16
Makkovik, Newf. . . . . . . . g10 72
Makkum, Neth. . . . . . . . . A5 17
Makó, Hung. . . . . . . . . . . B5 24
Makogai, i., Fiji . . . . . . . . H15 52
Makokou, Gabon . . . . . . . E2 46
Makoko, Isla de, i., Col. . . . . C2 53
Makoti, N.D., U.S. . . . . . . . A4 111
Makoua, Congo . . . . . . . . A2 48
Maków [Mazowiecki], Pol. . . B6 26
Maków [Mazowiecki], Pol. . . B2 45
Makteïr, reg., Maur. . . . . . B2 45
Mākū, Iran . . . . . . . . . . . B2 39
Mākū, Iran . . . . . . . . . . . C3 48
Makumbi, Zaire . . . . . . . . C3 48
Makurazaki, Japan . . . . . . K5 33
Makurdi, Nig. . . . . . . . . . E6 45
Makushin Volcano, vol., Ak., U.S. . . . . . . . . . . . . . E6 79
Mala, Punta, c., Pan. . . . . . G8 62
Malabar, Fl., U.S. . . . . . . . D6 86
Malabar Coast, India . . . . . F6 36
Malabo, Eq. Gui. . . . . . . . E1 46
Malabrigo, Phil. . . . . . . . . E1 56
Malabuñgan, Phil. . . . . . . . o19 115
Malacca see Melaka, Malay. . E2 34
Malacca, Strait of, strt., Asia . E2 34
Malad City, Id., U.S. . . . . . . G6 89
Malade, stm., Italy . . . . . . h8 23
Málaga, Col. . . . . . . . . . . B3 60
Málaga, Spain . . . . . . . . . D3 22
Malaga, N.J., U.S. . . . . . . . D2 107
Málaga, N.M., U.S. . . . . . . E5 108
Málaga, Bay, b., Spain . . . . D3 22
Malagarasi, stm., Tan. . . . . D6 71
Malagón, Spain . . . . . . . . C4 22
Malaimbandy, Madag. . . . . h9 49
Malaita, i., Sol.Is. . . . . . . . G9 6
Malakāl, Sud. . . . . . . . . . D3 47
Malakoff, Fr. . . . . . . . . . . g10 16
Malakoff, Tx., U.S. . . . . . . C4 120
Malalbergo, Italy . . . . . . . E7 20
Malambo, Col. . . . . . . . . . *A3 60
Malamyzh, Sov. Un. . . . . . . B12 31
Malang, Indon. . . . . . . . . G4 34
Malang see Malanje, Ang. . . C2 48
Malanje, Ang. . . . . . . . . . C2 48
Malanje, dept., Ang. . . . . . C2 48
Malanville, Benin . . . . . . . D5 45
Malanzán, Arg. . . . . . . . . A3 54
Mala Panew, stm., Pol. . . . . f9 26
Mälaren, l., Swe. . . . . . . . B3 54
Malartic, Que. . . . . . . . . . k11 74
Malaspina, Arg. . . . . . . . . C3 54
Malaspina Glacier, ice, Ak., U.S. . . . . . . . . . . . . . D11 79
Malatya, Tur. . . . . . . . . . . C12 40
Malatya, ctry., Afr. . . . . . . . D5 48
Malaya Vishera, Sov. Un. . . . B9 27
Malaybalay, Phil. . . . . . . . D7 34
Malāyer, Iran . . . . . . . . . . D4 39
Malay Peninsula, pen., Asia . D2 34
Malaysia, ctry., Asia . . . . . . E4 34
Malazgirt, Tur. . . . . . . . . . C14 40
Malbaie, stm., Que. . . . . . . B7 74
Mal Bay, b., Ire. . . . . . . . . D2 10
Malbork, Pol. . . . . . . . . . . A5 26
Malchin, E. Ger. . . . . . . . . B6 18
Malchow, E. Ger. . . . . . . . B6 18
Malcolm, Ne., U.S. . . . . . . D9 104
Malcolm, Il., U.S. . . . . . . . C5 92
Malden, Ma., U.S. . . . . . . . B5 98
Malden, Mo., U.S. . . . . . . . E8 102
Malden, Wa., U.S. . . . . . . . B8 124
Malden, W.V., U.S. . . . . . . m12 125
Malden Island, i., Kir. . . . . . G12 6
Maldives, ctry., Asia . . . . . . G5 36
Maldon, Eng., U.K. . . . . . . C8 12
Maldonado, Ur. . . . . . . . . E2 56
Malè, Italy . . . . . . . . . . . C6 20
Maléa, Ákra, c., Grc. . . . . . D4 40
Mālegaon, India . . . . . . . . G5 37
Malema, Moz. . . . . . . . . . D6 48
Malemba-Nkulu, Zaire . . . . C4 48
Mäler Kotla, India . . . . . . . B6 36
Malesus, Tn., U.S. . . . . . . . B3 119
Malha Wells, Sud. . . . . . . . B3 47
Malheur, co., Or., U.S. . . . . D9 114
Malheur, stm., Or., U.S. . . . . D8 114
Malheur Lake, l., Or., U.S. . . D8 114
Mali, Gui. . . . . . . . . . . . . D2 45
Mali, ctry., Afr. . . . . . . . . . C4 45
Mali, i., Burma . . . . . . . . . F3 35
Mali, i., Fiji . . . . . . . . . . . H15 52
Malibu, Ca., U.S. . . . . . . . m11 82
Maligne Lake, l., Alta. . . . . . D2 68
Mālihah, Bi'r, well, Eg. . . . . E5 41
Mālihah, Wādī al, val., Sud. . E5 41
Malin, Ire. . . . . . . . . . . . B4 11
Malin, Sov. Un. . . . . . . . . F7 27
Malin, Or., U.S. . . . . . . . . E5 114
Malin Beg, Ire. . . . . . . . . . C3 11
Malindi, Kenya . . . . . . . . . B7 48
Malines see Mechelen, Bel. . B6 16
Malinvac, Czech. . . . . . . . D5 26
Malinvav, Sov. Un. . . . . . . D8 40
Malinta, Oh., U.S. . . . . . . . A1 112
Maliwun, Burma . . . . . . . . F10 36
Maljamar, N.M., U.S. . . . . . E6 108
Malko Türnovo, Bul. . . . . . B4 40
Mallaig, Scot., U.K. . . . . . . B5 10
Mallaig, Alta. . . . . . . . . . B5 68
Mallaranny, Ire. . . . . . . . . D2 11
Mallard, Ia., U.S. . . . . . . . B3 92

Mallawī, Eg. . . . . . . . . . . C3 38
Mallersdorf, W. Ger. . . . . . E7 19
Malles Venosta, Italy . . . . . C6 20
Mallet Creek, Oh., U.S. . . . . A4 112
Mallorca, i., Spain . . . . . . . C7 22
Mallorytown, Ont. . . . . . . . C9 73
Mallow, Ire. . . . . . . . . . . D2 10
Malm, Nor. . . . . . . . . . . . f11 102
Malmbäck, Swe. . . . . . . . . A8 15
Malmberget, Swe. . . . . . . . D9 14
Malmédy, Bel. . . . . . . . . . B7 16
Malmköping, Swe. . . . . . . . t34 14
Malmö, Swe. . . . . . . . . . . J5 14
Malmo, Ne., U.S. . . . . . . . C9 104
Malmöhus, co., Swe. . . . . . C7 15
Malmstrom Air Force Base, mil., Mt., U.S. . . . . . . . . C5 103
Maloarkhangelsk, Sov. Un. . . E11 27
Maloggia (Maloja), Switz. . . D8 21
Maloja (Maloggia), Switz. . . D8 21
Maloja Pass, Switz. . . . . . . C5 20
Malolo, i., Fiji . . . . . . . . . H14 52
Malolos, Phil. . . . . . . . . . o13 34
Malone, Ont. . . . . . . . . . . C7 73
Malone, Fl., U.S. . . . . . . . . B1 86
Malone, N.Y., U.S. . . . . . . . f10 109
Malone, Wa., U.S. . . . . . . . C2 124
Maloney Reservoir, res., Ne., U.S. . . . . . . . . . . . . . C5 104
Malonga, Zaire . . . . . . . . . D3 48
Malonno, Italy . . . . . . . . . D9 21
Malonton, Man. . . . . . . . . D3 70
Malott, Wa., U.S. . . . . . . . A6 124
Malmö, Swe. . . . . . . . . . . D3 92
Maloyaroslavets, Sov. Un. . . D11 27
Malozemel'skaya Tundra, Sov. Un. . . . . . . . . . . . . . . D6 28
Malpaso, Phil. . . . . . . . . . o13 34
Malpelo, Isla de, i., Col. . . . . C2 53
Malpeque Bay, b., P.E.I. . . . C6 71
Malpura, India . . . . . . . . . D5 37
Malsch, W. Ger. . . . . . . . . E3 19
Malta, Id., U.S. . . . . . . . . . G5 89
Malta, Il., U.S. . . . . . . . . . B5 90
Malta, Mt., U.S. . . . . . . . . B9 103
Malta, Oh., U.S. . . . . . . . . C4 112
Malta, ctry., Eur. . . . . . . . . H11 8
Malta Bend, Mo., U.S. . . . . B4 102
Maltahöhe, Nmb. . . . . . . . D2 49
Malton (part of Mississauga), Ont. . . . . . . . . . . . . . . m14 73
Malton, Eng., U.K. . . . . . . . C6 10
Malung, Swe. . . . . . . . . . . C4 25
Malvern, Ar., U.S. . . . . . . . C3 81
Malvern, Ia., U.S. . . . . . . . D2 92
Malvern, Oh., U.S. . . . . . . B4 112
Malvern, N.Y., U.S. . . . . . . k13 109
Malvérnia, Moz. . . . . . . . . B5 49
Malyye Karmakuly, Sov. Un. . B9 28
Malyy Uzen, stm., Sov. Un. . . D8 28
Mamala Bay, b., Hi., U.S. . . . g10 88
Mamanguape, Braz. . . . . . A4 56
Mamantel, Mex. . . . . . . . . A2 62
Mamaroneck, N.Y., U.S. . . . h13 109
Mamba, Japan . . . . . . . . . m17 33
Mambasa, Zaire . . . . . . . . A4 48
Mamberamo, stm., Indon. . . F9 34
Mambo, i., Indon. . . . . . . . C4 34
Mamelodi, S.A. . . . . . . . . *C4 49
Mamers, Fr. . . . . . . . . . . C4 16
Mamers, N.C., U.S. . . . . . . B4 110
Mamfe, Cam. . . . . . . . . . . D1 46
Mamie, N.C., U.S. . . . . . . . A7 110
Mamiña, Chile . . . . . . . . . D2 55
Mamju, Indon. . . . . . . . . . F5 34
Mammern, Switz. . . . . . . . A6 21
Mammoth, Az., U.S. . . . . . . E5 80
Mammoth, Ut., U.S. . . . . . . D3 121
Mammoth, W.V., U.S. . . . . . C3 125
Mammoth Cave National Park, Ky., U.S. . . . . . . . . . . . C4 94
Mammoth Lakes, Ca., U.S. . . D4 82
Mammoth Spring, Ar., U.S. . . A4 81
Mamonovo, Sov. Un. . . . . . A5 26
Mamoré, stm., S.A. . . . . . . B2 55
Mamou, Gui. . . . . . . . . . . D2 45
Mamou, La., U.S. . . . . . . . D3 95
Mampong, Ghana . . . . . . . E4 45
Mamry Lake, l., Pol. . . . . . . A6 26
Mamuju, Indon. . . . . . . . . F5 34
Man, I.C. . . . . . . . . . . . . E3 45
Man, W.V., U.S. . . . . . . . . D3 125
Man, Isle of, i., I. of Man . . . C4 10
Mana, Fr. Gu. . . . . . . . . . A4 59
Mana, stm., Fr. Gu. . . . . . . A4 59
Mana, stm., Fr. Gu. . . . . . . B4 59
Manabí, prov., Ec. . . . . . . . B1 58
Manacacias, stm., Col. . . . . C3 60
Manacapuru, Braz. . . . . . . C2 59
Manacor, Spain . . . . . . . . C7 22
Manado, Indon. . . . . . . . . E6 34
Mañagaha, Isleta i., N. Mar. . D7 52
Managua, Nic. . . . . . . . . . E7 63
Managua, Lago de, l., Nic. . . D4 62
Manahawkin, N.J., U.S. . . . . D4 107
Manakara, Madag. . . . . . . h9 49
Manakin, Va., U.S. . . . . . . . C5 123
Manalapan, N.J., U.S. . . . . C3 107
Manam, i., Pap. N. Gui. . . . . h12 50
Manama, Bahr. . . . . . . . . . C5 38
Manana Island, i., Hi., U.S. . . g11 88
Manannara, stm., Madag. . . g9 49
Mananara, Madag. . . . . . . g9 49
Mananara, stm., Madag. . . . h9 49
Mananjary, Madag. . . . . . . h9 49
Manantenina, Madag. . . . . h9 49
Manantico Creek, stm., N.J., U.S. . . . . . . . . . . . . . E3 107
Manapire, stm., Ven. . . . . . B4 60
Manas, stm., Asia . . . . . . . B2 37
Mana Point, c., Hi., U.S. . . . A2 88
Manas He, stm., China . . . . B2 31
Manas Hu, l., China . . . . . . B2 31
Manassa, Co., U.S. . . . . . . D5 83
Manasquan, N.J., U.S. . . . . C4 107
Manasquan, stm., N.J., U.S. . C4 107
Manassas, Ga., U.S. . . . . . D4 87
Manassas, Va., U.S. . . . . . . B5 123
Manassas National Battlefield Park, Va., U.S. . . . . . . . . g11 123
Manassas Park, Va., U.S. . . . B5 123
Manati, P.R. . . . . . . . . . . B3 65
Manatee, co., Fl., U.S. . . . . E4 86
Manatee, stm., Fl., U.S. . . . E4 86
Manaus, Braz. . . . . . . . . . C2 59
Manavgat, Tur. . . . . . . . . . D8 40
Manawa, Wi., U.S. . . . . . . . D5 126
Manawan Lake, l., Sask. . . . B4 75
Mancelona, Mi., U.S. . . . . . D5 99
Manchac, Bayou, stm., La., U.S. . . . . . . . . . . . . . h10 95
Mancha Real, Spain . . . . . . D4 22
Manchaug, Ma., U.S. . . . . . B4 98
Manchester, Eng., U.K. . . . . D5 10
Manchester, Ct., U.S. . . . . . B5 84
Manchester, Ga., U.S. . . . . D2 87
Manchester, Il., U.S. . . . . . D3 90

Manchester, Ia., U.S. . . . . . B6 92
Manchester, Ks., U.S. . . . . . C6 93
Manchester, Ky., U.S. . . . . . C6 94
Manchester, Me., U.S. . . . . D3 96
Manchester, Md., U.S. . . . . A4 97
Manchester, Ma., U.S. . . . . A6 98
Manchester, Mi., U.S. . . . . . F6 99
Manchester, Mo., U.S. . . . . f12 102
Manchester, N.H., U.S. . . . . E4 106
Manchester, N.Y., U.S. . . . . C3 109
Manchester, Oh., U.S. . . . . D2 112
Manchester, Ok., U.S. . . . . . A3 113
Manchester, Pa., U.S. . . . . F8 115
Manchester, S.D., U.S. . . . . C8 118
Manchester, Tn., U.S. . . . . . B5 119
Manchester, Tx., U.S. . . . . . C5 120
Manchester, Vt., U.S. . . . . . E2 122
Manchester Center, Vt., U.S. . E2 122
Manchuria, hist. reg., China . B10 31
Mancos, Co., U.S. . . . . . . . D2 83
Mancos, stm., U.S. . . . . . . D2 83
Mand, stm., Iran . . . . . . . . G6 39
Manda, Tan. . . . . . . . . . . D5 48
Mandabe, Madag. . . . . . . . h8 49
Mandaguari, Braz. . . . . . . . C2 56
Mandal, Nor. . . . . . . . . . . H2 14
Mandalay, Burma . . . . . . . D10 36
Mandalgovi, Mong. . . . . . . B6 31
Mandalī, Iraq . . . . . . . . . . E2 39
Mandalya, Gulf of, b., Tur. . . D6 25
Mandan, N.D., U.S. . . . . . . C5 111
Mandara Mountains, mts. Afr. F2 46
Mandaree, N.D., U.S. . . . . . B3 111
Mandeb, Bab el, strt. . . . . . D4 38
Mandel, Afg. . . . . . . . . . . E10 39
Mandera, Kenya . . . . . . . . A7 48
Manderfeld, Bel. . . . . . . . . B7 16
Manderson, S.D., U.S. . . . . D3 118
Manderson, Wy., U.S. . . . . B5 127
Mandeure, Fr. . . . . . . . . . B2 21
Mandeville, Que. . . . . . . . C4 74
Mandeville, Jam. . . . . . . . E6 64
Mandeville, Ar., U.S. . . . . . D2 81
Mandeville, La., U.S. . . . . . D5 95
Mandidzudzure, Zimb. . . . . A5 49
Mandimba, Moz. . . . . . . . . D6 48
Mandla, India . . . . . . . . . . F8 37
Mandø, i., Den. . . . . . . . . C2 15
Mándra, Grc. . . . . . . . . . . C4 25
Mandritsara, Madag. . . . . . g9 49
Mandsaur, India . . . . . . . . E6 36
Mandurah, Austl. . . . . . . . F2 50
Manduria, Italy . . . . . . . . . D6 23
Mandvi, India . . . . . . . . . . D4 36
Mandvi (Cutch Māndvi), India D5 102
Manes, Mo., U.S. . . . . . . . D5 102
Manfalūṭ, Eg. . . . . . . . . . . C3 38
Manfred, N.D., U.S. . . . . . . B6 111
Manfredonia, Italy . . . . . . . D5 23
Manfredonia, Gulf of, b., Italy . D6 23
Manga, Braz. . . . . . . . . . . D6 23
Mangaldan, Phil. . . . . . . . . A6 34
Mangalia, Rom. . . . . . . . . D9 24
Mangalore, India . . . . . . . . F5 36
Mangatarem, Phil. . . . . . . . o13 34
Mangaldan, Phil. . . . . . . . A6 34
Mangerton Mountain, mtn., Ire. . . . . . . . . . . . . . . F2 11
Mangham, La., U.S. . . . . . . B4 95
Mangkalihat, Cape, c., Indon. E5 34
Mangoche, Mwi. . . . . . . . . D6 48
Mangoky, stm., Madag. . . . . h8 49
Mangonia, i., Indon. . . . . . . F7 34
Mangualde, Port. . . . . . . . B2 22
Mangueni, Plateau de, plat., Niger . . . . . . . . . . . . . B7 45
Mangum, Ok., U.S. . . . . . . C2 113
Manhasset, N.Y., U.S. . . . . . *h13 109
Manhattan, Ks., U.S. . . . . . C7 93
Manhattan, Mt., U.S. . . . . . E5 103
Manhattan, Nv., U.S. . . . . . E4 105
Manhattan Beach, Ca., U.S. . n12 82
Manhattan Island, i., N.Y., U.S. . . . . . . . . . . . . . h13 109
Manheim, Pa., U.S. . . . . . . F9 115
Manheim, W.V., U.S. . . . . . B5 125
Manhiça, Moz. . . . . . . . . . C5 49
Manhuaçu, Braz. . . . . . . . C4 56
Maniago, Italy . . . . . . . . . C8 20
Maniamba, Moz. . . . . . . . . D6 48
Manica, dept., Moz. . . . . . . A5 49
Manicoré, Braz. . . . . . . . . D2 59
Manicouagan, stm., Que. . . . G19 66
Manicouagan, Réservoir, res., Que. . . . . . . . . . . . . . h13 74
Manifest, La., U.S. . . . . . . . C3 95
Manigotagan, Man. . . . . . . D3 70
Manigotagan Lake, l., Man. . . D4 70
Manila, Phil. . . . . . . . . . . . C6 34
Manila, Ar., U.S. . . . . . . . . B5 81
Manila, Ut., U.S. . . . . . . . . C6 121
Manila Bay, b., Phil. . . . . . . o13 34
Manila, Austl. . . . . . . . . . . E8 51
Manila, In., U.S. . . . . . . . . E6 91
Manilla, Ia., U.S. . . . . . . . . C2 92
Manipur, state, India . . . . . D9 36
Manisa, Tur. . . . . . . . . . . C6 40
Manistee, Mi., U.S. . . . . . . D4 99
Manistee, co., Mi., U.S. . . . . D4 99
Manistee, stm., Mi., U.S. . . . D5 99
Manistique, Mi., U.S. . . . . . C4 99
Manistique Lake, l., Mi., U.S. . B5 99
Manitoba, prov., Can. . . . . . C3 70
Manitoba, Lake, l., Man. . . . D2 70
Manitou, Man. . . . . . . . . . E2 70
Manitou, Ok., U.S. . . . . . . . C3 113
Manitou, Lake, l., Ont. . . . . E5 70
Manitou Beach, Sask. . . . . . F3 75
Manitou Beach, Mi., U.S. . . . G6 99
Manitou Island, i., Mi., U.S. . A3 99
Manitou Lake, l., Ont. . . . . . E1 75
Manitou Lake, l., Sask. . . . . E1 75
Manitoulin Island, i., Ont. . . B2 73
Manitou Springs, Co., U.S. . . C6 83
Manitowaning, Ont. . . . . . . B3 73
Manitowic, Wi., U.S. . . . . . D6 126
Manitowoc, co., Wi., U.S. . . . D6 126
Manitowoc, stm., Wi., U.S. . . h10 126
Manitowoc, North Branch, stm., Wi., U.S. . . . . . . . . h9 126
Manitowoc, South Branch, stm., Wi., U.S. . . . . . . . . k9 126
Maniwaki, Que. . . . . . . . . . C2 74
Manizales, Col. . . . . . . . . . B2 60
Manja, Madag. . . . . . . . . . h8 49
Manjacaze, Moz. . . . . . . . . B5 49
Manjimup, Austl. . . . . . . . . F2 50
Mānjra, stm., India . . . . . . . E6 36
Mankato, Ks., U.S. . . . . . . . C5 93

Mankato, Mn., U.S. . . . . . . F5 100
Mankono, I.C. . . . . . . . . . . E3 45
Mankota, Sask. . . . . . . . . . H2 75
Manley, Ne., U.S. . . . . . . . h12 104
Manley Hot Springs, Ak., U.S. B9 79
Manlius, Il., U.S. . . . . . . . . B4 90
Manlius, N.Y., U.S. . . . . . . . C5 109
Manlléu, Spain . . . . . . . . . A7 22
Manly, Ia., U.S. . . . . . . . . . A4 92
Manlyville, Tn., U.S. . . . . . . A3 119
Manmād, India . . . . . . . . . G5 37
Mann, Sri L. . . . . . . . . . . . G6 36
Mannar, Gulf of, b., Asia . . . G6 36
Mannboro, Va., U.S. . . . . . . C5 123
Mannford, Ok., U.S. . . . . . . A5 113
Mannheim, W. Ger. . . . . . . D4 18
Manning, Alta. . . . . . . . . . A2 68
Manning, Ar., U.S. . . . . . . . C3 81
Manning, Ia., U.S. . . . . . . . C2 92
Manning, N.D., U.S. . . . . . . B3 111
Manning, Or., U.S. . . . . . . . g11 114
Manning, S.C., U.S. . . . . . . D7 117
Manning Provincial Park, B.C. E7 69
Mannington, Ky., U.S. . . . . . C2 94
Mannington, W.V., U.S. . . . . B4 125
Manns Choice, Pa., U.S. . . . G4 115
Manns Creek, stm., W.V., U.S. . . . . . . . . . . . . . n14 125
Manns Harbor, N.C., U.S. . . B7 110
Mannsville, N.Y., U.S. . . . . . B4 109
Mannsville, Ok., U.S. . . . . . C5 113
Mannu, stm., Italy . . . . . . . E2 23
Manoa, Bol. . . . . . . . . . . . A2 55
Man of War Bay, b., Trin. . . . M24 65
Manokin, Md., U.S. . . . . . . D6 97
Manokin, stm., Md., U.S. . . . D6 97
Manokotak, Ak., U.S. . . . . . D8 79
Manokwari, Indon. . . . . . . . F8 34
Manombo, Madag. . . . . . . . h8 49
Manomet, Ma., U.S. . . . . . . C6 98
Manomet Hill, hill, Ma., U.S. . C6 98
Manomet Point, c., Ma., U.S. C6 98
Manono, Zaire . . . . . . . . . C4 48
Manono, i., W. Sam. . . . . . . F11 52
Manor, Sask. . . . . . . . . . . H4 75
Manor, Ga., U.S. . . . . . . . . E4 87
Manor, Tx., U.S. . . . . . . . . D4 120
Manorhamilton, Ire. . . . . . . C3 11
Manorhaven, N.Y., U.S. . . . . *h13 109
Manorville, Pa., U.S. . . . . . E2 115
Manosque, Fr. . . . . . . . . . F6 16
Manotick, Ont. . . . . . . . . . B9 73
Manouane, Lac, l., Que. . . . . h12 74
Manpo, N. Kor. . . . . . . . . . F3 33
Manresa, Spain . . . . . . . . B6 22
Mansa (Fort Rosebery), Zam. . D4 48
Mansa Konko, Gam. . . . . . . D1 45
Månsarp, Swe. . . . . . . . . . A8 15
Manseau, Que. . . . . . . . . . C5 74
Mansel Island, i., N.W. Ter. . . D17 66
Mansfield, Austl. . . . . . . . . H6 51
Mansfield, Eng., U.K. . . . . . D6 10
Mansfield, Ar., U.S. . . . . . . B1 81
Mansfield, Ga., U.S. . . . . . . C3 87
Mansfield, Il., U.S. . . . . . . . C5 90
Mansfield, La., U.S. . . . . . . B2 95
Mansfield, Ma., U.S. . . . . . . B5 98
Mansfield, Mo., U.S. . . . . . . D5 102
Mansfield, Oh., U.S. . . . . . . B3 112
Mansfield, Pa., U.S. . . . . . . C7 115
Mansfield, S.D., U.S. . . . . . B7 118
Mansfield, Tn., U.S. . . . . . . A3 119
Mansfield, Tx., U.S. . . . . . . n9 120
Mansfield, Wa., U.S. . . . . . . B6 124
Mansfield, Mount, mtn., Vt., U.S. . . . . . . . . . . . . . B3 122
Mansfield Center, Ct., U.S. . . B7 84
Mansfield Depot, Ct., U.S. . . B6 84
Mansfield Four Corners, Ct., U.S. . . . . . . . . . . . . . B6 84
Mansfield Hollow Lake, res., Ct., U.S. . . . . . . . . . . . B7 84
Manso, stm., Braz. . . . . . . . B2 56
Manson, Ia., U.S. . . . . . . . . B3 92
Manson, Wa., U.S. . . . . . . . B5 124
Manson Creek, B.C. . . . . . . B5 69
Mansonville, Que. . . . . . . . D5 74
Manta, Ec. . . . . . . . . . . . . B1 58
Mantachie, Ms., U.S. . . . . . A5 101
Mantador, N.D., U.S. . . . . . C9 111
Mantantao, Sask. . . . . . . . F1 75
Mantaro, stm., Peru . . . . . . D3 58
Manteca, Ca., U.S. . . . . . . . D3 82
Mantee, Ms., U.S. . . . . . . . B4 101
Manteno, Il., U.S. . . . . . . . B6 90
Manteo, N.C., U.S. . . . . . . . B7 110
Mantes [-la-Jolie], Fr. . . . . . C4 16
Manti, Ut., U.S. . . . . . . . . . D4 121
Mantiqueira, Serra da, mts., Braz. . . . . . . . . . . . . . C4 56
Manton, Mi., U.S. . . . . . . . D5 99
Mantorville, Mn., U.S. . . . . . F6 100
Mantova (Mantua), Italy . . . B3 23
Mantua, Oh., U.S. . . . . . . . A4 112
Mantua, Ut., U.S. . . . . . . . . B4 121
Mantua Hills, Va., U.S. . . . . *B5 123
Manú, Peru . . . . . . . . . . . D3 58
Manuel Benavides, Mex. . . . B4 62
Manuel Urbano, Braz. . . . . . C4 58
Manui, i., Indon. . . . . . . . . F6 34
Manukau Harbour, b., N.Z. . . L15 51
Manulla, stm., Ire. . . . . . . . D2 11
Manumuskin, stm., N.J., U.S. E3 107
Manus, i., Pap. N. Gui. . . . . h12 50
Manvel, N.D., U.S. . . . . . . . A8 111
Manvel, Tx., U.S. . . . . . . . . r14 120
Manville, R.I., U.S. . . . . . . . B4 116
Manville, Wy., U.S. . . . . . . . D8 127
Many, La., U.S. . . . . . . . . . C2 95
Manyara, Lake, l., Tan. . . . . B6 48
Manyberries, Alta. . . . . . . . E5 68
Manych, stm., Sov. Un. . . . . H13 27
Manych Lake, l., Sov. Un. . . . H14 27
Many Farms, Az., U.S. . . . . A6 80
Manyoni, Tan. . . . . . . . . . C6 48
Manzanares, Spain . . . . . . C4 22
Manzanares, stm., Spain . . . o17 22
Manzanares Canal, Spain . . . p17 22
Manzanillo, Cuba . . . . . . . D5 64
Manzanillo, Mex. . . . . . . . . D4 63
Manzanillo, Punta, c., Pan. . . F8 62
Manzanita, Or., U.S. . . . . . . B3 114
Manzano, N.M., U.S. . . . . . C3 108
Manzanola, Co., U.S. . . . . . C7 83
Manzano Mountains, mts., N.M., U.S. . . . . . . . . . . C3 108

Manzano Peak, mtn., N.M., U.S. . . . . . . . . . . . . . C3 108
Manzhouli, China . . . . . . . . C8 31
Manziana, Italy . . . . . . . . . g8 23
Manzilah, Lake, l., Eg. . . . . . C3 41
Manzini, Swaz. . . . . . . . . . B5 49
Mao, Chad . . . . . . . . . . . . C3 46
Mao, Dom. Rep. . . . . . . . . E8 64
Maoke Mountains, mts., Indon. . . . . . . . . . . . . . F9 34
Maoming, China . . . . . . . . G7 31
Mapai, Moz. . . . . . . . . . . B5 49
Mapam Yumco, l., China . . . B7 36
Mapastepec, Mex. . . . . . . . D6 63
Mapaville, Mo., U.S. . . . . . . C7 102
Mapes, N.D., U.S. . . . . . . . A7 111
Mapia Islands, is., Indon. . . . E8 34
Mapire, Ven. . . . . . . . . . . B5 60
Mapiri, Bol. . . . . . . . . . . . C2 55
Maple (part of Vaughan), Ont. C1 120
Maple, Tx., U.S. . . . . . . . . . C1 120
Maple, Wi., U.S. . . . . . . . . D7 117
Maple, stm., U.S. . . . . . . . . A7 118
Maple, stm., Ia., U.S. . . . . . C2 92
Maple, stm., N.D., U.S. . . . . C8 111
Maple Bay, Mn., U.S. . . . . . G4 115
Maple Bluff, Wi., U.S. . . . . . E4 126
Maple Creek, Sask. . . . . . . H1 75
Maple Creek, stm., Ne., U.S. . C9 104
Maple Falls, Wa., U.S. . . . . . A3 124
Maple Grove, Mn., U.S. . . . . m12 100
Maple Heights, Oh., U.S. . . . h9 112
Maple Hill, Ks., U.S. . . . . . . C7 93
Maple Hill, N.C., U.S. . . . . . C5 110
Maple Island, Mn., U.S. . . . . G5 100
Maple Lake, Mn., U.S. . . . . E5 100
Maple Mount, Ky., U.S. . . . . C2 94
Maple Plain, Mn., U.S. . . . . m11 100
Maple Rapids, Mi., U.S. . . . . E6 99
Maple Ridge, B.C. . . . . . . . E6 69
Maples, In., U.S. . . . . . . . . B8 91
Maple Shade, N.J., U.S. . . . D2 107
Maplesville, Al., U.S. . . . . . C3 78
Mapleton, Ia., U.S. . . . . . . . B2 92
Mapleton, Ks., U.S. . . . . . . D9 93
Mapleton, Me., U.S. . . . . . . B4 96
Mapleton, Mn., U.S. . . . . . . G5 100
Mapleton, N.D., U.S. . . . . . . C8 111
Mapleton, Or., U.S. . . . . . . C3 114
Mapleton, Ut., U.S. . . . . . . C4 121
Mapleton Depot, Pa., U.S. . . F6 115
Maple Valley, Wa., U.S. . . . . f11 124
Maplewood, Me., U.S. . . . . . E2 96
Maplewood, Mn., U.S. . . . . n12 100
Maplewood, Mo., U.S. . . . . f13 102
Maplewood, N.J., U.S. . . . . B4 107
Mapuera, stm., Braz. . . . . . C3 59
Maputo (Lourenço Marques), Moz. . . . . . . . . . . . . . C5 49
Maputo, dept., Moz. . . . . . . C5 49
Maquela do Zombo, Ang. . . . C2 48
Maquinchao, Arg. . . . . . . . C3 54
Maquoketa, Ia., U.S. . . . . . . B7 92
Maquoketa, stm., Ia., U.S. . . B6 92
Maquoketa, North Fork, stm., Ia., U.S. . . . . . . . . . . . B7 92
Maquon, Il., U.S. . . . . . . . . C3 90
Mar, Serra do, clf., Braz. . . . D3 56
Mara, prov., Tan. . . . . . . . . B5 48
Marã, Braz. . . . . . . . . . . . D4 60
Marabá, Braz. . . . . . . . . . E9 59
Maracá, Ilha de, i., Braz. . . . A3 60
Maracaibo, Ven. . . . . . . . . A3 60
Maracaibo, Lago de, l., Ven. . C1 56
Maracaju, Braz. . . . . . . . . . C2 56
Maracaju, Serra de, hills, S.A. . . . . . . . . . . . . . . C2 56
Maracay, Ven. . . . . . . . . . A4 60
Marādah, Libya . . . . . . . . . D3 43
Maradi, Niger . . . . . . . . . . D6 45
Marāgheh, Iran . . . . . . . . . B2 38
Maragogi, Braz. . . . . . . . . k6 57
Maragojipe, Braz. . . . . . . . D5 57
Marais des Cygnes, stm., U.S. D6 93
Marajó, Baía de, b., Braz. . . C5 59
Marajó, Ilha de, i., Braz. . . . C5 59
Maralal, Kenya . . . . . . . . . A6 48
Maramec, Ok., U.S. . . . . . . A5 113
Marana, Az., U.S. . . . . . . . E4 80
Marand, Iran . . . . . . . . . . B4 38
Maranguape, Braz. . . . . . . B1 57
Maranhão, state, Braz. . . . . D9 59
Marano, Laguna di, b., Italy . C8 20
Maranoa, stm., Austl. . . . . . E8 51
Marañón, stm., Peru . . . . . . B2 54
Marans, Fr. . . . . . . . . . . . . D3 16
Marãşeşti, Rom. . . . . . . . . C18 24
Marathon, Ont. . . . . . . . . . o18 73
Marathon, Grc. . . . . . . . . . g11 25
Marathon, Fl., U.S. . . . . . . . H5 86
Marathon, Ia., U.S. . . . . . . . B3 92
Marathon, N.Y., U.S. . . . . . . C4 109
Marathon, Tx., U.S. . . . . . . D1 120
Marathon, Wi., U.S. . . . . . . D4 126
Marathon, co., Wi., U.S. . . . . D4 126
Maratua, i., Indon. . . . . . . . E5 34
Marau, Braz. . . . . . . . . . . D2 57
Maravato de Ocampo, Mex. . n13 63
Marãwah, Libya . . . . . . . . . B3 47
Marawī, Sud. . . . . . . . . . . B3 47
Marbach [am Neckar], W. Ger. D5 19
Marbella, Spain . . . . . . . . . D3 22
Marble, Ar., U.S. . . . . . . . . A2 81
Marble, Co., U.S. . . . . . . . . B3 83
Marble, Mn., U.S. . . . . . . . C5 100
Marble, N.C., U.S. . . . . . . . f9 110
Marble Canyon, Az., U.S. . . A4 80
Marble Canyon, val., Az., U.S. A4 80
Marble City, Ok., U.S. . . . . . B7 113
Marble Cliff, Oh., U.S. . . . . . m10 112
Marble Dale, Ct., U.S. . . . . . C2 84
Marbledale, Ct., U.S. . . . . . C2 84
Marble Falls, Ar., U.S. . . . . . n14 119
Marble Falls, Tx., U.S. . . . . . D3 120
Marble Hall, S. Afr. . . . . . . D4 49
Marblehead, Ma., U.S. . . . . B6 98
Marblehead, Oh., U.S. . . . . A3 112
Marble Hill, Mo., U.S. . . . . . D8 102
Marblemount, Wa., U.S. . . . A4 124
Marble Mountain, N.S. . . . . D8 71
Marble Rock, Ia., U.S. . . . . . B5 92
Marbleton, Que. . . . . . . . . D6 74
Marbleton, Wy., U.S. . . . . . D2 127
Marburg, W. Ger. . . . . . . . . C4 18
Marbury, Al., U.S. . . . . . . . C3 78
Marbury, Md., U.S. . . . . . . C3 97
Marcala, Hond. . . . . . . . . . D6 20
Marcaria, Italy . . . . . . . . . B3 23
Marcelin, Sask. . . . . . . . . . E2 75
Marceline, Mo., U.S. . . . . . . B5 102

| Name | Map Ref. | Page |
|---|---|---|
| Marcella, Ar., U.S. | B4 | 81 |
| Marcelline, Il., U.S. | C2 | 90 |
| Marcellus, Mi., U.S. | F5 | 99 |
| March, Eng., U.K. | B8 | 12 |
| March Air Force Base, mil., Ca., U.S. | F5 | 82 |
| Marchand, Man. | E3 | 70 |
| Marche, hist. reg., Fr. | D4 | 16 |
| Marche-en-Famenne, Bel. | D5 | 17 |
| Marchena, Spain | D3 | 22 |
| Marchena, Isla, i., Ec. | f5 | 58 |
| Marches (Marche), prov., Italy | C4 | 23 |
| Mar Chiquita, Laguna, l., Arg. | A4 | 54 |
| Marchwell, Sask. | G5 | 75 |
| Marco, Fl., U.S. | G5 | 86 |
| Marco, In., U.S. | G3 | 91 |
| Marcola, Or., U.S. | C4 | 114 |
| Marcos Juárez, Arg. | A4 | 54 |
| Marcus, Ia., U.S. | B2 | 92 |
| Marcus, S.D., U.S. | C3 | 118 |
| Marcus, Wa., U.S. | A7 | 124 |
| Marcus Baker, Mount, mtn., Ak., U.S. | g18 | 79 |
| Marcus Hook, Pa., U.S. | G11 | 115 |
| Marcy, Mount, mtn., N.Y., U.S. | A7 | 109 |
| Marcy Colony, S.D., U.S. | D8 | 118 |
| Mardān, Pak. | B5 | 36 |
| Mar de Espanha, Braz. | g6 | 56 |
| Mardela Springs, Md., U.S. | D6 | 97 |
| Mar del Plata, Arg. | B5 | 54 |
| Mardin, Tur. | D13 | 40 |
| Marechal Deodoro, Braz. | C3 | 57 |
| Maree, Loch, l., Scot., U.K. | C3 | 13 |
| Mareeba, Austl. | C8 | 50 |
| Marenanuka, Kir. | R18 | 52 |
| Marengo, Sask. | F1 | 75 |
| Marengo, Il., U.S. | A5 | 90 |
| Marengo, In., U.S. | H5 | 91 |
| Marengo, Ia., U.S. | C5 | 92 |
| Marengo, Oh., U.S. | B3 | 112 |
| Marengo, Wa., U.S. | B7 | 124 |
| Marengo, Wi., U.S. | B3 | 126 |
| Marengo, co., Al., U.S. | C2 | 78 |
| Marenisco, Mi., U.S. | n12 | 99 |
| Marennes, Fr. | E3 | 16 |
| Maretz, Fr. | D3 | 17 |
| Mareuil-sur-Ourcq, Fr. | E3 | 17 |
| Marfa, Tx., U.S. | o12 | 120 |
| Marfrance, W.V., U.S. | C4 | 125 |
| Margai Co, l., China | A8 | 36 |
| Marganets, Sov. Un. | H10 | 27 |
| Margaree, N.S. | C8 | 71 |
| Margaree Harbour, N.S. | C8 | 71 |
| Margaret, Man. | E2 | 70 |
| Margaret, Al., U.S. | B3 | 78 |
| Margaret, Tx., U.S. | B3 | 120 |
| Margaretsville, N.S. | D4 | 71 |
| Margaretville, N.Y., U.S. | C6 | 109 |
| Margarita, Isla de, i., Ven. | A5 | 60 |
| Margate, Eng., U.K. | E7 | 10 |
| Margate, Fl., U.S. | F6 | 86 |
| Margate, Md., U.S. | *B4 | 97 |
| Margate City, N.J., U.S. | E3 | 107 |
| Margerum, Al., U.S. | A1 | 78 |
| Margherita Peak, mtn., Afr. | A4 | 48 |
| Marghī, Afg. | D13 | 39 |
| Marghūb, Kūh-e, mtn., Iran | E8 | 39 |
| Margie, Mn., U.S. | B5 | 100 |
| Margilan, Sov. Un. | E10 | 29 |
| Margny-lès-Compiègne, Fr. | E2 | 17 |
| Margo, Sask. | F4 | 75 |
| Mārgow, Dasht-e, des., Afg. | F11 | 39 |
| Margrethe, Lake, l., Mi., U.S. | D6 | 99 |
| Marguerite Bay, b., Ant. | C6 | 7 |
| Maria, Que. | A3 | 71 |
| Maria, i., Austl. | o15 | 50 |
| María Chiquita, Pan. | k11 | 62 |
| Mariager, Den. | B3 | 15 |
| Mariager Fjord, Den. | B4 | 15 |
| Mariah Hill, In., U.S. | H4 | 91 |
| María la Baja, Col. | A2 | 60 |
| Marian, Lake, l., Fl., U.S. | E5 | 86 |
| Mariana Islands, is., Oc. | E8 | 6 |
| Marianna, Ar., U.S. | C5 | 81 |
| Marianna, Fl., U.S. | B1 | 86 |
| Mariánské Lázně, Czech. | D2 | 26 |
| Mariapolis, Man. | E2 | 70 |
| Marias, stm., Mt., U.S. | B4 | 103 |
| Marías, Islas, is., Mex. | C3 | 63 |
| Marias Pass, Mt., U.S. | B3 | 103 |
| Maria Stein, Oh., U.S. | B1 | 112 |
| Maria van Diemen, Cape, c., N.Z. | K14 | 51 |
| Mariaville, Me., U.S. | D4 | 96 |
| Maribel, N.C., U.S. | B6 | 110 |
| Maribel, Wi., U.S. | h10 | 126 |
| Maribo, Den. | D5 | 15 |
| Maribor, Yugo. | B2 | 24 |
| Maricá, Braz. | h6 | 56 |
| Maricaban Island, i., Phil. | p13 | 34 |
| Maricopa, Az., U.S. | E3 | 80 |
| Maricopa, Ca., U.S. | E4 | 82 |
| Maricopa, co., Az., U.S. | D3 | 80 |
| Maricopa Mountains, mts., Az., U.S. | m7 | 80 |
| Marīdī, Sud. | F2 | 47 |
| Marié, Sud. | D4 | 60 |
| Marie Byrd Land, reg., Ant. | B1 | 7 |
| Mariedamm, Swe. | u33 | 14 |
| Mariefred, Swe. | t35 | 14 |
| Marie-Galante, i., Guad. | I14 | 64 |
| Mariehamn, Fin. | G8 | 14 |
| Marie Lake, l., Alta. | B5 | 68 |
| Mariembourg, Bel. | D4 | 17 |
| Mariemont, Oh., U.S. | o13 | 112 |
| Marienberg, E. Ger. | C8 | 19 |
| Mariental, Nmb. | B2 | 49 |
| Marienthal, Ks., U.S. | D2 | 93 |
| Marienville, Pa., U.S. | D3 | 115 |
| Marie-Reine, Alta. | A2 | 68 |
| Maries, co., Mo., U.S. | C6 | 102 |
| Mariestad, Swe. | H5 | 14 |
| Marietta, Ga., U.S. | C2 | 87 |
| Marietta, Il., U.S. | C3 | 90 |
| Marietta, Ms., U.S. | A5 | 101 |
| Marietta, Oh., U.S. | C4 | 112 |
| Marietta, Ok., U.S. | D4 | 113 |
| Marietta, S.C., U.S. | A2 | 117 |
| Marietta, Wa., U.S. | A3 | 124 |
| Marieville, Que. | D4 | 74 |
| Mariinsk, Sov. Un. | B11 | 28 |
| Marijampolė, Sov. Un. | A7 | 26 |
| Mari Lake, l., Sask. | B5 | 75 |
| Marília, Braz. | F5 | 57 |
| Marimba, Ang. | C2 | 48 |
| Marín, Spain | A1 | 22 |
| Marin, co., Ca., U.S. | C2 | 82 |
| Marina, Ca., U.S. | *D3 | 82 |
| Marina del Rey, Ca., U.S. | *n12 | 82 |
| Marina di Ravenna, Italy | E8 | 20 |
| Marine, Il., U.S. | E4 | 90 |
| Marine City, Mi., U.S. | F8 | 99 |
| Marine On St. Croix, Mn., U.S. | E6 | 100 |
| Marinette, Wi., U.S. | C6 | 126 |
| Marinette, co., Wi., U.S. | C5 | 126 |
| Maringá, Braz. | C2 | 56 |
| Maringa, stm., Zaire | A3 | 48 |
| Maringouin, La., U.S. | D4 | 95 |
| Marinha Grande, Port. | C1 | 22 |
| Marino, Italy | h9 | 23 |
| Marion, Austl. | *G6 | 50 |
| Marion, Al., U.S. | C2 | 78 |
| Marion, Ar., U.S. | B5 | 81 |
| Marion, Ct., U.S. | C4 | 84 |
| Marion, Il., U.S. | F5 | 90 |
| Marion, In., U.S. | C6 | 91 |
| Marion, Ia., U.S. | B6 | 92 |
| Marion, Ks., U.S. | D6 | 93 |
| Marion, Ky., U.S. | e9 | 94 |
| Marion, La., U.S. | B3 | 95 |
| Marion, Ma., U.S. | C6 | 98 |
| Marion, Mi., U.S. | D5 | 99 |
| Marion, Ms., U.S. | C5 | 101 |
| Marion, Mt., U.S. | B2 | 103 |
| Marion, Ne., U.S. | D5 | 104 |
| Marion, N.Y., U.S. | B3 | 109 |
| Marion, N.C., U.S. | B1 | 110 |
| Marion, N.D., U.S. | C7 | 111 |
| Marion, Oh., U.S. | B2 | 112 |
| Marion, Or., U.S. | k12 | 114 |
| Marion, Pa., U.S. | G6 | 115 |
| Marion, S.C., U.S. | C9 | 117 |
| Marion, S.D., U.S. | D8 | 118 |
| Marion, Ut., U.S. | C4 | 121 |
| Marion, Va., U.S. | f10 | 123 |
| Marion, Wi., U.S. | D5 | 126 |
| Marion, co., Al., U.S. | A2 | 78 |
| Marion, co., Ar., U.S. | A3 | 81 |
| Marion, co., Fl., U.S. | C4 | 86 |
| Marion, co., Ga., U.S. | D2 | 87 |
| Marion, co., Il., U.S. | E4 | 90 |
| Marion, co., In., U.S. | E5 | 91 |
| Marion, co., Ia., U.S. | C4 | 92 |
| Marion, co., Ks., U.S. | D6 | 93 |
| Marion, co., Ky., U.S. | C4 | 94 |
| Marion, co., Ms., U.S. | D4 | 101 |
| Marion, co., Mo., U.S. | B6 | 102 |
| Marion, co., Oh., U.S. | B2 | 112 |
| Marion, co., Or., U.S. | C4 | 114 |
| Marion, co., S.C., U.S. | C9 | 117 |
| Marion, co., Tn., U.S. | D8 | 119 |
| Marion, co., Tx., U.S. | C5 | 120 |
| Marion, co., W.V., U.S. | B4 | 125 |
| Marion, Lake, res., S.C., U.S. | E7 | 117 |
| Marion Center, Pa., U.S. | E3 | 115 |
| Marion Heights, In., U.S. | F3 | 91 |
| Marion Junction, Al., U.S. | C2 | 78 |
| Marion Station, Md., U.S. | D6 | 97 |
| Marionville, Mo., U.S. | D4 | 102 |
| Mariposa, Ca., U.S. | D4 | 82 |
| Mariposa, co., Ca., U.S. | D3 | 82 |
| Mariscal Estigarribia, Para. | D3 | 55 |
| Marissa, Il., U.S. | E4 | 90 |
| Maritime Alps, mts., Eur. | E7 | 16 |
| Maritsa (Évros) (Meriç), stm., Eur. | A5 | 25 |
| Mariupol, Sov. Un. | E6 | 29 |
| Marīvān, Iran | D3 | 39 |
| Mariveles, Phil. | o13 | 34 |
| Marj, II., U.S. | B4 | 90 |
| Marka, Som. | E5 | 47 |
| Marka Kul, l., Sov. Un. | B2 | 31 |
| Markala, Mali | D3 | 45 |
| Markam, China | F4 | 31 |
| Markaryd, Swe. | I5 | 14 |
| Mark Center, Oh., U.S. | A1 | 112 |
| Markdale, Ont. | C4 | 73 |
| Markesan, Wi., U.S. | E5 | 126 |
| Market Drayton, Eng., U.K. | B5 | 12 |
| Market Harborough, Eng., U.K. | B7 | 12 |
| Markethill, N. Ire., U.K. | C5 | 11 |
| Market Rasen, Eng., U.K. | A7 | 12 |
| Market Weighton, Eng., U.K. | G8 | 13 |
| Markham, Ont. | D5 | 73 |
| Markham, Il., U.S. | k9 | 90 |
| Markham, Tx., U.S. | E4 | 120 |
| Markham, Va., U.S. | B5 | 123 |
| Markham, Mount, mtn., Ant. | A29 | 7 |
| Marki, Pol. | k14 | 26 |
| Markinch, Sask. | G3 | 75 |
| Markkleeberg, E. Ger. | B7 | 19 |
| Markland, Il., U.S. | G8 | 91 |
| Markland Lock and Dam, U.S. | B5 | 94 |
| Markle, In., U.S. | C7 | 91 |
| Markleeville, Ca., U.S. | C4 | 82 |
| Markleville, In., U.S. | E6 | 91 |
| Markleysburg, Pa., U.S. | G3 | 115 |
| Markneukirchen, E. Ger. | C7 | 19 |
| Markópoulon, Grc. | h11 | 25 |
| Markovka, Sov. Un. | G12 | 27 |
| Markovo, Sov. Un. | C11 | 29 |
| Markovo, Sov. Un. | C20 | 29 |
| Markranstädt, E. Ger. | B7 | 19 |
| Marks, Ms., U.S. | A3 | 101 |
| Marksboro, N.J., U.S. | B3 | 107 |
| Marksville, La., U.S. | C3 | 95 |
| Marktheidenfeld, W. Ger. | D4 | 19 |
| Marktredwitz, W. Ger. | C6 | 18 |
| Marl, W. Ger. | *C3 | 18 |
| Marland, Ok., U.S. | A4 | 113 |
| Marlbank, Ont. | C7 | 73 |
| Marlboro, Alta. | C2 | 68 |
| Marlboro, Ma., U.S. | C4 | 107 |
| Marlboro, N.J., U.S. | C4 | 107 |
| Marlboro, N.Y., U.S. | D6 | 109 |
| Marlboro, Vt., U.S. | F3 | 122 |
| Marlboro, co., S.C., U.S. | n17 | 123 |
| Marlboro, co., S.C., U.S. | B8 | 117 |
| Marlborough, Guy. | A3 | 59 |
| Marlborough, Eng., U.K. | C6 | 12 |
| Marlborough, Ct., U.S. | C6 | 84 |
| Marlborough, Ma., U.S. | B4 | 98 |
| Marlborough, N.H., U.S. | E2 | 106 |
| Marle, Fr. | E3 | 17 |
| Marlene Village, Or., U.S. | *B4 | 114 |
| Marlette, Mi., U.S. | E7 | 99 |
| Marley, Md., U.S. | *B4 | 97 |
| Marlin, Tx., U.S. | D4 | 120 |
| Marlin, Wa., U.S. | B7 | 124 |
| Marlinton, W.V., U.S. | C4 | 125 |
| Marlow, Eng., U.K. | D6 | 15 |
| Marlow, Al., U.S. | E2 | 78 |
| Marlow, Ok., U.S. | D5 | 87 |
| Marlow, N.H., U.S. | D2 | 106 |
| Marlowe, W.V., U.S. | A3 | 113 |
| Marlowe, W.V., U.S. | B7 | 125 |
| Marlow Heights, Md., U.S. | *C4 | 97 |
| Marlton, N.J., U.S. | D3 | 107 |
| Marly-le-Roi, Fr. | g9 | 16 |
| Marmande, Ar., U.S. | A5 | 81 |
| Marmande, Fr. | E4 | 16 |
| Marmara, Sea of | B7 | 40 |
| Marmara Island, i., Tur. | B6 | 25 |
| Marmaris, Tur. | D7 | 40 |
| Marmarth, N.D., U.S. | C2 | 111 |
| Marmelos, Rio dos, stm., Braz. | D2 | 59 |
| Marmet, W.V., U.S. | C3 | 125 |
| Marmolada, mtn., Italy | C7 | 20 |
| Marmora, Ont. | C7 | 73 |
| Marmora, N.J., U.S. | E3 | 107 |
| Marmore, stm., italy | E4 | 21 |
| Marnay, Fr. | B1 | 20 |
| Marnaz, Fr. | D2 | 21 |
| Marne, W. Ger. | E3 | 15 |
| Marne, Ia., U.S. | C2 | 92 |
| Marne, Mi., U.S. | E5 | 99 |
| Marne, dept., Fr. | F4 | 17 |
| Marne, stm., Fr. | C5 | 16 |
| Marne au Rhin, Canal de la, Fr. | F4 | 17 |
| Maroa, Il., U.S. | C5 | 90 |
| Maroa, Ven. | C4 | 60 |
| Maroantsetra, Madag. | g9 | 49 |
| Maromokotro, mtn., Madag. | f9 | 49 |
| Marondera, Zimb. | A5 | 49 |
| Marone, Italy | E9 | 21 |
| Maroni, stm., S.A. | B4 | 59 |
| Maroochydore-Mooloolaba, Austl. | E9 | 50 |
| Maro Reef, rf., Hi., U.S. | k13 | 88 |
| Maroua, Cam. | C2 | 46 |
| Marovoay, Madag. | g9 | 49 |
| Marowijne, dept., Sur. | B4 | 59 |
| Marquam, Or., U.S. | B4 | 114 |
| Marquard, Mo., U.S. | D7 | 102 |
| Marquesas Islands, is., Fr. Poly. | G13 | 6 |
| Marquesas Keys, is., Fl., U.S. | H4 | 86 |
| Marquette, Man. | D3 | 70 |
| Marquette, Ia., U.S. | A6 | 92 |
| Marquette, Ks., U.S. | D6 | 93 |
| Marquette, Mi., U.S. | B3 | 99 |
| Marquette, Ne., U.S. | D8 | 104 |
| Marquette, co., Mi., U.S. | B3 | 99 |
| Marquette, co., Wi., U.S. | E4 | 126 |
| Marquette Heights, Il., U.S. | C4 | 90 |
| Marquez, Tx., U.S. | D4 | 120 |
| Marquis, Sask. | G3 | 75 |
| Marquise, Fr. | D9 | 12 |
| Marrakech, Mor. | C3 | 44 |
| Marree, Austl. | E6 | 50 |
| Marrero, La., U.S. | E5 | 95 |
| Marrickville, Austl. | *F9 | 50 |
| Marriott, Ut., U.S. | *B3 | 121 |
| Marromeu, Moz. | A6 | 49 |
| Marrowbone, Ky., U.S. | D4 | 94 |
| Marrtown, W.V., U.S. | B3 | 125 |
| Mars, Rivière à, stm., Que. | A7 | 74 |
| Marsabit, Kenya | A6 | 48 |
| Marsā Burayqah, Libya | C3 | 43 |
| Marsala, Italy | F4 | 23 |
| Marsā Maṭrūḥ, Eg. | B2 | 38 |
| Marsā Sūsah, Libya | C4 | 43 |
| Marsden, Sask. | E1 | 75 |
| Marseille, Fr. | F5 | 16 |
| Marseille, Fr. | F6 | 16 |
| Marseilles, Il., U.S. | B5 | 90 |
| Marshall, Sask. | D1 | 75 |
| Marshall, Lib. | E2 | 45 |
| Marshall, Ar., U.S. | B3 | 81 |
| Marshall, Il., U.S. | D6 | 90 |
| Marshall, In., U.S. | E3 | 91 |
| Marshall, Mi., U.S. | F6 | 99 |
| Marshall, Mn., U.S. | F3 | 100 |
| Marshall, Mo., U.S. | B4 | 102 |
| Marshall, N.C., U.S. | f10 | 110 |
| Marshall, N.D., U.S. | B3 | 111 |
| Marshall, Ok., U.S. | A4 | 113 |
| Marshall, Tx., U.S. | C5 | 120 |
| Marshall, Va., U.S. | B5 | 123 |
| Marshall, Wa., U.S. | g13 | 124 |
| Marshall, co., Al., U.S. | A3 | 78 |
| Marshall, co., Il., U.S. | B4 | 90 |
| Marshall, co., In., U.S. | B5 | 91 |
| Marshall, co., Ia., U.S. | C4 | 92 |
| Marshall, co., Ks., U.S. | C7 | 93 |
| Marshall, co., Ky., U.S. | f9 | 94 |
| Marshall, co., Mn., U.S. | B2 | 100 |
| Marshall, co., Ms., U.S. | A4 | 101 |
| Marshall, co., Ok., U.S. | C5 | 113 |
| Marshall, co., S.D., U.S. | B8 | 118 |
| Marshall, co., Tn., U.S. | B5 | 119 |
| Marshall, co., W.V., U.S. | B4 | 125 |
| Marshallberg, N.C., U.S. | C6 | 110 |
| Marshall Corner, N.H., U.S. | E4 | 106 |
| Marshall Islands, ctry., T.T.P.I. | F10 | 6 |
| Marshalls Creek, Pa., U.S. | D11 | 115 |
| Marshalltown, Ia., U.S. | B5 | 92 |
| Marshallville, Ga., U.S. | D3 | 87 |
| Marshallville, Oh., U.S. | B4 | 112 |
| Marshes Siding, Ky., U.S. | D5 | 94 |
| Marshfield, In., U.S. | D3 | 91 |
| Marshfield, Mo., U.S. | D5 | 102 |
| Marshfield, Vt., U.S. | C4 | 122 |
| Marshfield, Wi., U.S. | D3 | 126 |
| Marsh Fork, stm., W.V., U.S. | n13 | 125 |
| Marsh Harbour, Bah. | A5 | 64 |
| Marsh Hill, Pa., U.S. | D8 | 115 |
| Mars Hill, Me., U.S. | B5 | 96 |
| Mars Hill, N.C., U.S. | f10 | 110 |
| Mars Island, i., La., U.S. | E4 | 95 |
| Marsh Lake, res., Mn., U.S. | E2 | 100 |
| Marsh Peak, mtn., Ut., U.S. | C6 | 121 |
| Marshyhope Creek, stm., Md., U.S. | C6 | 97 |
| Marsing, Id., U.S. | F2 | 89 |
| Marstal, Den. | D4 | 15 |
| Marsteller, Pa., U.S. | E4 | 115 |
| Marston, Mo., U.S. | E8 | 102 |
| Marston, N.C., U.S. | C3 | 110 |
| Marstons Mills, Ma., U.S. | C7 | 98 |
| Mart, Tx., U.S. | D4 | 120 |
| Martaban, Burma | E10 | 36 |
| Martaban, Gulf of, b., Burma | E10 | 36 |
| Martap, Cam. | C2 | 46 |
| Martapura, Indon. | F4 | 34 |
| Martel, Oh., U.S. | B2 | 112 |
| Martelange, Bel. | E5 | 17 |
| Martell, Ne., U.S. | D9 | 104 |
| Martell, Wi., U.S. | D1 | 126 |
| Martensdale, Ia., U.S. | C4 | 92 |
| Martha, Ok., U.S. | C2 | 113 |
| Marthasville, Mo., U.S. | C6 | 102 |
| Martha's Vineyard, i., Ma., U.S. | D6 | 98 |
| Martí, Cuba | D5 | 64 |
| Martignano, Lake, l., Italy | g8 | 23 |
| Martigny[-Ville], Switz. | E3 | 18 |
| Martigues, Fr. | F6 | 16 |
| Martin, Czech. | D5 | 26 |
| Martin, Ga., U.S. | B3 | 87 |
| Martin, Ky., U.S. | C7 | 94 |
| Martin, La., U.S. | B2 | 95 |
| Martin, Mi., U.S. | F5 | 99 |
| Martin, N.D., U.S. | B5 | 111 |
| Martin, Oh., U.S. | e7 | 112 |
| Martin, S.C., U.S. | E5 | 117 |
| Martin, S.D., U.S. | D4 | 118 |
| Martin, Tn., U.S. | A3 | 119 |
| Martin, Ut., U.S. | D5 | 121 |
| Martin, co., Fl., U.S. | E6 | 86 |
| Martin, co., In., U.S. | G4 | 91 |
| Martin, co., Ky., U.S. | C7 | 94 |
| Martin, co., Mn., U.S. | G4 | 100 |
| Martin, co., N.C., U.S. | B5 | 110 |
| Martin, co., Tx., U.S. | C2 | 120 |
| Martin City, Mt., U.S. | B3 | 103 |
| Martindale, Que. | D2 | 74 |
| Martindale, Tx., U.S. | h8 | 120 |
| Martinez, Ca., U.S. | C2 | 82 |
| Martinez, Ga., U.S. | C4 | 87 |
| Martinique, dep., N.A. | I14 | 64 |
| Martin Lake, res., Al., U.S. | C4 | 78 |
| Martin Peninsula, pen., Ant. | B1 | 7 |
| Martin Point, c., Ak., U.S. | A11 | 79 |
| Martinsburg, In., U.S. | H5 | 91 |
| Martinsburg, Mo., U.S. | C5 | 92 |
| Martinsburg, Ne., U.S. | B9 | 104 |
| Martinsburg, N.Y., U.S. | B5 | 109 |
| Martinsburg, Oh., U.S. | B3 | 112 |
| Martinsburg, Pa., U.S. | F5 | 115 |
| Martinsburg, W.V., U.S. | B7 | 125 |
| Martinsdale, Mt., U.S. | D6 | 103 |
| Martins Ferry, Oh., U.S. | B5 | 112 |
| Martins Pond, l., Ma., U.S. | f11 | 98 |
| Martinsville, Il., U.S. | D6 | 90 |
| Martinsville, In., U.S. | F5 | 91 |
| Martinsville, Mo., U.S. | A3 | 102 |
| Martinsville, Va., U.S. | D3 | 123 |
| Martinton, Il., U.S. | C6 | 90 |
| Martinville, Que. | D6 | 74 |
| Martos, Spain | D4 | 22 |
| Martre, Lac la, l., N.W. Ter. | D9 | 66 |
| Martwick, Ky., U.S. | C2 | 94 |
| Marty, S.D., U.S. | E7 | 118 |
| Marudi, Malay. | E4 | 34 |
| Ma'rūf, Afg. | B4 | 36 |
| Marugame, Japan | I6 | 33 |
| Marum, Neth. | A6 | 17 |
| Marumsconi Creek, stm., Md., U.S. | D6 | 97 |
| Marvell, Ar., U.S. | C5 | 81 |
| Marvelo, Chad | G6 | 39 |
| Marvejols, Fr. | E5 | 16 |
| Marvel, Al., U.S. | B2 | 78 |
| Marvel, Co., U.S. | D2 | 83 |
| Marvell, Ar., U.S. | C5 | 81 |
| Marvin, S.D., U.S. | B9 | 118 |
| Marvine, Mount, mtn., Ut., U.S. | E4 | 121 |
| Marvyn, Al., U.S. | C4 | 78 |
| Marwayne, Alta. | C5 | 68 |
| Mary, Sov. Un. | F9 | 29 |
| Mary, Lake, l., Mn., U.S. | E3 | 100 |
| Mary, Lake, l., Ms., U.S. | D2 | 101 |
| Maryborough, Austl. | E9 | 50 |
| Maryborough, Austl. | G7 | 50 |
| Marydel, De., U.S. | D3 | 85 |
| Marydel, Md., U.S. | B6 | 97 |
| Maryfield, Sask. | H5 | 75 |
| Maryland, state, U.S. | B4 | 97 |
| Maryland City, Md., U.S. | B4 | 97 |
| Maryland Heights, Mo., U.S. | f13 | 102 |
| Maryland Line, Md., U.S. | A4 | 97 |
| Maryland Point, c., Md., U.S. | D3 | 97 |
| Maryport, Eng., U.K. | D5 | 10 |
| Marys, stm., Nv., U.S. | B6 | 105 |
| Mary's Harbour, Newf. | B4 | 72 |
| Mary's Peak, mtn., Or., U.S. | C3 | 114 |
| Marystown, Newf. | E4 | 72 |
| Marysvale, Ut., U.S. | E3 | 121 |
| Marysville, N.B. | C3 | 71 |
| Marysville, Ca., U.S. | C3 | 82 |
| Marysville, Id., U.S. | E7 | 89 |
| Marysville, Ks., U.S. | C7 | 93 |
| Marysville, Mi., U.S. | F8 | 99 |
| Marysville, Oh., U.S. | B2 | 112 |
| Marysville, Pa., U.S. | F8 | 115 |
| Marysville, Wa., U.S. | A3 | 124 |
| Marytown, Wi., U.S. | k9 | 126 |
| Maryūt, Buhayrat, l., Eg. | C1 | 41 |
| Maryville, Mo., U.S. | A3 | 102 |
| Maryville, Tn., U.S. | D10 | 119 |
| Marzagão, Braz. | B3 | 56 |
| Marzūg, Libya | D2 | 43 |
| Marzūg, Idehan, dunes, Libya | E2 | 43 |
| Mas'adah, Isr. Occ. | A7 | 41 |
| Masai Steppe, pl., Tan. | B6 | 48 |
| Masaka, Ug. | B6 | 48 |
| Masalembu Besar, i., Indon. | G4 | 34 |
| Masalok, Puntan, c., N. Mar. Is. | D7 | 52 |
| Masan, S. Kor. | D10 | 31 |
| Masardis, Me., U.S. | B4 | 96 |
| Masaryktown, Fl., U.S. | D4 | 86 |
| Masasi, Tan. | D6 | 48 |
| Masatepe, Nic. | H4 | 62 |
| Masaya, Nic. | H4 | 62 |
| Masbate, i., Phil. | C6 | 34 |
| Masbate, i., Phil. | C6 | 34 |
| Mascarene Islands, is., Afr. | H24 | 2 |
| Mascoma, stm., N.H., U.S. | C2 | 106 |
| Mascoma, Lake, l., N.H., U.S. | C3 | 106 |
| Mascot, Tn., U.S. | C10 | 119 |
| Mascotte, Fl., U.S. | D5 | 86 |
| Mascoutah, Il., U.S. | E4 | 90 |
| Mascuspana, Mex. | D6 | 63 |
| Masefield, Sask. | H2 | 75 |
| Maseru, Leso. | C4 | 49 |
| Mash'abbe Sade, Isr. | D4 | 41 |
| Masham, Eng., U.K. | F7 | 13 |
| Mashapaug Pond, l., Ct., U.S. | A7 | 84 |
| Mashhad, Iran | D6 | 39 |
| Mashīz, Iran | E6 | 39 |
| Mashkel, Hāmūn-i-, reg., Pak. | G11 | 39 |
| MashkeL Island, Man. | B7 | 70 |
| Mashra, Asia | H11 | 39 |
| Mashra'ar Raqq, Sud. | C7 | 47 |
| Masi-Manimba, Zaire | B2 | 48 |
| Masindi, Ug. | A5 | 48 |
| Maşīrah, i., Oman | C6 | 38 |
| Masisea, Peru | C3 | 58 |
| Masisi, Zaire | B4 | 48 |
| Masjed-e Soleymān, Iran | B4 | 38 |
| Maskanah, Syria | D12 | 40 |
| Maskell, Ne., U.S. | B9 | 104 |
| Maskinongé, Que. | C4 | 74 |
| Maskinongé, co., Que. | C4 | 74 |
| Masnières, Fr. | D3 | 17 |
| Masoala, Cap, c., Madag. | g10 | 49 |
| Mason, Il., U.S. | E5 | 90 |
| Mason, Mi., U.S. | F6 | 99 |
| Mason, Nv., U.S. | E2 | 105 |
| Mason, N.H., U.S. | E3 | 106 |
| Mason, Oh., U.S. | C1 | 112 |
| Mason, Ok., U.S. | B5 | 113 |
| Mason, Tn., U.S. | B2 | 119 |
| Mason, Tx., U.S. | D3 | 120 |
| Mason, W.V., U.S. | B2 | 125 |
| Mason, co., Il., U.S. | C4 | 90 |
| Mason, co., Ky., U.S. | B6 | 94 |
| Mason, co., Mi., U.S. | D4 | 99 |
| Mason, co., Tx., U.S. | D3 | 120 |
| Mason, co., Wa., U.S. | B2 | 124 |
| Mason, co., W.V., U.S. | C2 | 125 |
| Mason City, Il., U.S. | C4 | 90 |
| Mason City, Ia., U.S. | A4 | 92 |
| Mason City, Ne., U.S. | C6 | 104 |
| Masonnville, Pa., U.S. | A2 | 119 |
| Masontown, Pa., U.S. | G2 | 115 |
| Masontown, W.V., U.S. | B5 | 125 |
| Masonville, Ar., U.S. | D4 | 81 |
| Masonville, Co., U.S. | A5 | 83 |
| Masonville, N.Y., U.S. | C5 | 109 |
| Masqaṭ, Oman | C6 | 38 |
| Massa, Italy | B3 | 23 |
| Massac, co., Il., U.S. | F5 | 90 |
| Massachusetts, state, U.S. | B4 | 98 |
| Massachusetts Bay, b., Ma., U.S. | B6 | 98 |
| Massacre Lake, l., Nv., U.S. | B2 | 105 |
| Massaemett Mountain, mtn., Ma., U.S. | A2 | 98 |
| Massafra, Italy | D6 | 23 |
| Massakory, Chad | C3 | 46 |
| Massa Marittima, Italy | C3 | 23 |
| Massangena, Moz. | B5 | 49 |
| Massanutten Mountain, mts., Va., U.S. | B4 | 123 |
| Massapê, Braz. | B2 | 57 |
| Massapequa, N.Y., U.S. | *E7 | 109 |
| Massapequa Park, N.Y., U.S. | *E7 | 109 |
| Massapoag Lake, l., Ma., U.S. | h11 | 98 |
| Massasecum, Lake, l., N.H., U.S. | D3 | 106 |
| Massawa (Mitsiwa), Eth. | D7 | 39 |
| Massena, Ia., U.S. | C3 | 92 |
| Massena, N.Y., U.S. | f10 | 109 |
| Massenya, Chad | C3 | 46 |
| Masset, B.C. | C1 | 69 |
| Masset Inlet, b., B.C. | C1 | 69 |
| Massey, Ont. | A2 | 73 |
| Massey, Md., U.S. | B6 | 97 |
| Massies Mill, Va., U.S. | C3 | 123 |
| Massillon, Oh., U.S. | B4 | 112 |
| Massinga, Moz. | B6 | 49 |
| Massive, Mount, mtn., Co., U.S. | B4 | 83 |
| Masson Island, i., Ant. | C22 | 7 |
| Masten's Corner, De., U.S. | E3 | 85 |
| Mastergeehy, Ire. | F1 | 11 |
| Masterton, N.Z. | N15 | 51 |
| Mastic, N.Y., U.S. | *n16 | 109 |
| Mastic Beach, N.Y., U.S. | n16 | 109 |
| Mastigouche, Réserve, Que. | C4 | 74 |
| Mastung, Pak. | C4 | 36 |
| Mastūrah, Sau. Ar. | C2 | 38 |
| Masuda, Japan | I5 | 33 |
| Masuria, reg., Pol. | A5 | 26 |
| Masury, Oh., U.S. | A5 | 112 |
| Masvingo (Nyanda), Zimb. | B5 | 49 |
| Mata, Zaire | B2 | 48 |
| Mata Amarilla, Arg. | C3 | 53 |
| Matachewan, Ont. | p19 | 73 |
| Mata de São João, Braz. | B3 | 57 |
| Matadi, Zaire | C1 | 48 |
| Matador, Sask. | G2 | 75 |
| Matador, Tx., U.S. | B2 | 120 |
| Matagalpa, Nic. | H4 | 62 |
| Matagorda, Tx., U.S. | E5 | 120 |
| Matagorda, co., Tx., U.S. | E4 | 120 |
| Matagorda Bay, b., Tx., U.S. | E4 | 120 |
| Matagorda Peninsula, pen., Tx., U.S. | E5 | 120 |
| Matak, i., Indon. | K7 | 35 |
| Matam, Sen. | C2 | 45 |
| Matamoros, Pa., U.S. | D12 | 115 |
| Matamoros, Mex. | B5 | 63 |
| Matamoros [de la Laguna], Mex. | C4 | 63 |
| Matane, Que. | k13 | 74 |
| Matanuska, stm., Ak., U.S. | g18 | 79 |
| Matanzas, Cuba | C3 | 64 |
| Matanzas, prov., Cuba | C3 | 64 |
| Matanzas Inlet, b., Fl., U.S. | C5 | 86 |
| Matão, Braz. | F4 | 57 |
| Matápedia, Que. | B3 | 71 |
| Matara, Sri L. | I7 | 36 |
| Mataram, Indon. | G5 | 34 |
| Matarani, Peru | D3 | 58 |
| Mataró, Spain | B7 | 22 |
| Matatiele, S. Afr. | C4 | 49 |
| Matatula, Cape, c., Am. Sam. | G13 | 52 |
| Matāutu, W. Sam. | F12 | 52 |
| Matawan, N.J., U.S. | C4 | 107 |
| Matehuala, Mex. | C4 | 63 |
| Mateko, Zaire | B2 | 48 |
| Matera, Italy | D6 | 23 |
| Mátészalka, Hung. | B5 | 24 |
| Mateur, Tun. | F2 | 23 |
| Matfield Green, Ks., U.S. | E7 | 93 |
| Matha, Fr. | E3 | 16 |
| Mather, Man. | E2 | 70 |
| Mather, Pa., U.S. | G2 | 115 |
| Mather, Wi., U.S. | D3 | 126 |
| Mather Air Force Base, mil., Ca., U.S. | C3 | 82 |
| Mather Peaks, mts., Wy., U.S. | B5 | 127 |
| Matherville, Il., U.S. | B3 | 90 |
| Matheson Island, Man. | D3 | 70 |
| Mathews, In., U.S. | D7 | 91 |
| Mathews, Mo., U.S. | B8 | 102 |
| Mathews, N.C., U.S. | B2 | 110 |
| Mathews, Va., U.S. | C6 | 123 |
| Mathews, co., Va., U.S. | C6 | 123 |
| Mathews, Lake, l., Ca., U.S. | n14 | 82 |
| Mathias, W.V., U.S. | B5 | 125 |
| Mathis, Tx., U.S. | E4 | 120 |
| Mathiston, Ms., U.S. | B4 | 101 |
| Mathura (Muttra), India | C6 | 36 |
| Mati, stm., Alb. | B2 | 25 |
| Matiakoali, Burkina | D5 | 45 |
| Matinenda Lake, l., Ont. | A2 | 73 |
| Matinicus, Me., U.S. | E4 | 96 |
| Matinicus Island, i., Me., U.S. | E3 | 96 |
| Matlock, Eng., U.K. | A6 | 12 |
| Matlock, In., U.S. | A2 | 92 |
| Matoaca, Va., U.S. | n18 | 123 |
| Matoaka, W.V., U.S. | D3 | 125 |
| Mato Grosso, state, Braz. | B4 | 55 |
| Mato Grosso, Planalto do, plat., Braz. | E5 | 53 |
| Mato Grosso do Sul, state, Braz. | B2 | 56 |
| Mato Verde, Braz. | B4 | 56 |
| Maṭraḥ, Oman | C5 | 38 |
| Matrosovo, Sov. Un. | B11 | 33 |
| Matsqui, B.C. | f13 | 69 |
| Matsudo, Japan | *I9 | 33 |
| Matsue, Japan | D11 | 31 |
| Matsuida, Japan | m17 | 33 |
| Matsumae, Japan | F10 | 33 |
| Matsumoto, Japan | H9 | 33 |
| Matsuyama, Japan | E11 | 31 |
| Matsuzaka, Japan | I8 | 33 |
| Matsuzaki, Japan | o17 | 33 |
| Mattamiscontis Lake, l., Me., U.S. | C4 | 96 |
| Mattamuskeet, Lake, l., N.C., U.S. | B6 | 110 |
| Mattapoisett, Ma., U.S. | C6 | 98 |
| Mattaponi, stm., Va., U.S. | C5 | 123 |
| Mattawa, Ont. | A6 | 73 |
| Mattawamkeag, Me., U.S. | C4 | 96 |
| Mattawamkeag, stm., Me., U.S. | C4 | 96 |
| Mattawamkeag, East Branch, stm., Me., U.S. | C4 | 96 |
| Mattawamkeag, West Branch, stm., Me., U.S. | C4 | 96 |
| Mattawana, Pa., U.S. | F6 | 115 |
| Mattawoman Creek, stm., Md., U.S. | C3 | 97 |
| Matterhorn, mtn., Eur. | B1 | 23 |
| Matterhorn, mtn., Nv., U.S. | B6 | 105 |
| Matterson Inlet, b., Ant. | g40 | 7 |
| Matter Vispa, stm., Switz. | C4 | 18 |
| Matteson, Il., U.S. | k9 | 90 |
| Matthews, In., U.S. | D7 | 91 |
| Matthews, Mo., U.S. | E8 | 102 |
| Matthews, N.C., U.S. | B2 | 110 |
| Matthews Mountain, mtn., Mo., U.S. | D6 | 102 |
| Matthews Ridge, Guy. | A2 | 59 |
| Matthew Town, Bah. | D7 | 64 |
| Mattituck, N.Y., U.S. | n16 | 109 |
| Mattoon, Il., U.S. | D5 | 90 |
| Mattoon, Wi., U.S. | C4 | 126 |
| Mattoon, Lake, res., Il., U.S. | D5 | 90 |
| Mattson, Ms., U.S. | A3 | 101 |
| Mattydale, N.Y., U.S. | B4 | 109 |
| Matucana, Peru | C3 | 58 |
| Matuku Island, i., Fiji | I15 | 52 |
| Matundu, Zaire | A3 | 48 |
| Matunuck, R.I., U.S. | G3 | 116 |
| Matura Bay, b., Trin. | N23 | 65 |
| Maturín, Ven. | B6 | 60 |
| Máa, Moz. | o17 | 49 |
| Mauban, Phil. | o13 | 34 |
| Maubeuge, Fr. | E4 | 17 |
| Ma-Ubin, Burma | D1 | 35 |
| Mauchline, Scot., U.K. | H5 | 91 |
| Mauckport, In., U.S. | H5 | 91 |
| Maud, Scot., U.K. | B11 | 13 |
| Maud, Tx., U.S. | C5 | 120 |
| Maudlow, Mt., U.S. | D5 | 103 |
| Maués, Braz. | C3 | 59 |
| Maués-Açu, stm., Braz. | C3 | 59 |
| Mauganj, India | E8 | 37 |
| Maugansville, Md., U.S. | A2 | 97 |
| Maugerville, N.B. | D3 | 71 |
| Maughold Head, c., I. of Man | F4 | 13 |
| Maui, co., Hi., U.S. | B5 | 88 |
| Maui, i., Hi., U.S. | C6 | 88 |
| Mauk, Ga., U.S. | D2 | 87 |
| Mauldin, S.C., U.S. | B3 | 117 |
| Maule, prov., Chile | B2 | 54 |
| Mauléon [-Licharre], Fr. | F3 | 16 |
| Maumakeogh, hill, Ire. | C2 | 11 |
| Maumee, Oh., U.S. | A2 | 112 |
| Maumee, stm., U.S. | A1 | 112 |
| Maumee Bay, b., U.S. | G7 | 99 |
| Maumelle, Lake, res., Ar., U.S. | C3 | 81 |
| Maun, Bots. | A3 | 49 |
| Mauna Kea, vol., Hi., U.S. | D6 | 88 |
| Maunaloa, Hi., U.S. | B4 | 88 |
| Mauna Loa, vol., Hi., U.S. | D6 | 88 |
| Maunabo, P.R. | n15 | 64 |
| Maunalua Bay, b., Hi., U.S. | g10 | 88 |
| Maunath Bhanjan, India | E9 | 37 |
| Maunawili, Hi., U.S. | g10 | 88 |
| Maungdaw, Burma | D9 | 36 |
| Maunie, Il., U.S. | E5 | 90 |
| Maunoir, Lac, l., N.W. Ter. | C8 | 66 |
| Maupin, Or., U.S. | B5 | 114 |
| Maupotiha, Hi., U.S. | h10 | 95 |
| Maurepas, Lake, l., La., U.S. | D5 | 95 |
| Maurertown, Va., U.S. | B4 | 123 |
| Maurice, La., U.S. | D3 | 95 |
| Maurice, stm., N.J., U.S. | E2 | 107 |
| Maurice, Lake, l., Austl. | E5 | 50 |
| Maurice, stm., N.J., U.S. | E3 | 107 |
| Mauricetown, N.J., U.S. | E3 | 107 |
| Mauritania, ctry., Afr. | E3 | 44 |
| Mauritius, ctry., Afr. | H24 | 2 |
| Maury, N.C., U.S. | B5 | 110 |
| Maury, co., Tn., U.S. | B5 | 119 |
| Maury City, Tn., U.S. | B2 | 119 |
| Maury Island, pen., Wa., U.S. | f11 | 124 |
| Mauston, Wi., U.S. | E3 | 126 |
| Mauterndorf, Aus. | E6 | 18 |
| Mauwee Peak, mtn., Ct., U.S. | E2 | 120 |
| Maverick, Tx., U.S. | E2 | 120 |
| Mavinga, Ang. | G1 | 115 |
| Mawdesley Lake, l., Man. | B1 | 70 |
| Mawer, Sask. | G2 | 75 |
| Mawjib, Wādī al, val., Jord. | C7 | 41 |
| Mawlaik, Burma | E10 | 36 |
| Mawlamyine, Burma | E10 | 36 |
| Mawson, sci., Ant. | C19 | 7 |
| Mawson Coast, Ant. | C19 | 7 |
| Mawson Escarpment, clf., Ant. | B19 | 7 |
| Mawson Glacier, ice, Ant. | e40 | 7 |
| Mawson Peninsula, pen., Ant. | C28 | 7 |
| Max, Ne., U.S. | D4 | 104 |
| Max, N.D., U.S. | B4 | 111 |
| Maxbass, N.D., U.S. | A4 | 111 |
| Maxcanú, Mex. | C6 | 63 |
| Maxeys, Ga., U.S. | C3 | 87 |

| Name | Map Ref. | Page |
|---|---|---|
| Maxie, La., U.S. | D3 | 95 |
| Maxinkuckee, Lake, l., In., U.S. | B5 | 91 |
| Maxixe, Moz. | B6 | 49 |
| Max Meadows, Va., U.S. | D2 | 123 |
| Maxstone, Sask. | H2 | 75 |
| Maxton, N.C., U.S. | C3 | 110 |
| Maxville, Ont. | B10 | 73 |
| Maxville, Mt., U.S. | D3 | 103 |
| Maxwell, Ca., U.S. | C2 | 82 |
| Maxwell, In., U.S. | E6 | 91 |
| Maxwell, Ia., U.S. | C4 | 92 |
| Maxwell, Ne., U.S. | C5 | 104 |
| Maxwell, N.M., U.S. | A5 | 108 |
| Maxwell, Tn., U.S. | B5 | 119 |
| Maxwell Acres, W.V., U.S. | g8 | 125 |
| Maxwell Air Force Base, mil., Al., U.S. | C3 | 78 |
| Maxwell Colony, S.D., U.S. | D8 | 118 |
| May, Il., U.S. | E5 | 89 |
| May, Ok., U.S. | A2 | 113 |
| May, Tx., U.S. | C3 | 120 |
| May, Isle of, i., Scot., U.K. | D6 | 13 |
| May, Mount, mtn., Alta. | B1 | 68 |
| Maya, Mesa de, mtn., Co., U.S. | D7 | 83 |
| Mayaguana, i., Bah. | C7 | 64 |
| Mayaguana Passage, strt., Bah. | C7 | 64 |
| Mayagüez, P.R. | G11 | 64 |
| Mayagüez, Bahía de, b., P.R. | B1 | 65 |
| Mayama, Congo | B1 | 48 |
| Maya Mountains, mts., N.A. | B3 | 62 |
| Mayarí, Cuba | D6 | 64 |
| Mayaro Bay, b., Trin. | O24 | 65 |
| Maybank, Ms., U.S. | D4 | 101 |
| Maybee, Mi., U.S. | F7 | 99 |
| Maybell, Co., U.S. | A2 | 83 |
| Mayberry, Md., U.S. | A3 | 97 |
| Maybeury, W.V., U.S. | *D3 | 125 |
| Maybole, Scot., U.K. | C4 | 10 |
| Maydh, Som. | C6 | 47 |
| Maydī, Yemen | D4 | 38 |
| Maydūm Pyramid, hist., Egypt | E3 | 41 |
| Mayen, W. Ger. | C3 | 18 |
| Mayence see Mainz, W. Ger. | D4 | 18 |
| Mayenne, Fr. | C3 | 16 |
| Mayenne, stm., Fr. | D3 | 16 |
| Mayer, Az., U.S. | C3 | 80 |
| Mayersville, Ms., U.S. | C2 | 101 |
| Mayerthorpe, Alta. | C3 | 68 |
| Mayes, co., Ok., U.S. | A6 | 113 |
| Mayesville, S.C., U.S. | D7 | 117 |
| Mayetta, Ks., U.S. | C8 | 93 |
| Mayetta, N.J., U.S. | D4 | 107 |
| Mayfair, Sask. | E2 | 75 |
| Mayfield, Ky., U.S. | f9 | 94 |
| Mayfield, N.Y., U.S. | B4 | 109 |
| Mayfield, Oh., U.S. | B12 | 113 |
| Mayfield, Pa., U.S. | C10 | 115 |
| Mayfield, Ut., U.S. | D4 | 121 |
| Mayfield Heights, Oh., U.S. | A4 | 112 |
| Mayfield Lake, res., Wa., U.S. | C3 | 124 |
| Mayflower, Ar., U.S. | C3 | 81 |
| Mayflower Village, Ca., U.S. | *E4 | 82 |
| Mayhew, Ms., U.S. | B5 | 101 |
| Mayhill, N.M., U.S. | E4 | 108 |
| Maykain, Sov. Un. | C9 | 28 |
| Mayking, Ky., U.S. | C7 | 94 |
| Maykop, Sov. Un. | G17 | 8 |
| Mayland, Tn., U.S. | C8 | 119 |
| Maymont, Sask. | E2 | 75 |
| Maymyo, Burma | D10 | 36 |
| Maynard, Ar., U.S. | A5 | 81 |
| Maynard, Ia., U.S. | B6 | 92 |
| Maynard, Ky., U.S. | D3 | 94 |
| Maynard, Ma., U.S. | B5 | 98 |
| Maynard, Mn., U.S. | F3 | 100 |
| Maynardville, Tn., U.S. | C10 | 119 |
| Mayne, Or., U.S. | B7 | 73 |
| Mayne Island, i., B.C. | g12 | 69 |
| Maynooth, Ont. | B7 | 73 |
| Maynooth, Ire. | D5 | 11 |
| Mayo, Yukon | D5 | 66 |
| Mayo, Fl., U.S. | B3 | 86 |
| Mayo, Md., U.S. | C4 | 97 |
| Mayo, S.C., U.S. | A4 | 117 |
| Mayo, co., Ire. | D2 | 11 |
| Mayo, stm., Arg. | D2 | 54 |
| Mayodan, N.C., U.S. | A3 | 110 |
| Mayo Lake, l., Yukon | D6 | 66 |
| Mayon Volcano, vol., Phil. | C6 | 34 |
| Mayor Pablo Lagerenza, Para. | C3 | 55 |
| Mayotte, dep., Afr. | f9 | 49 |
| May Park, Or., U.S. | B8 | 114 |
| May Pen, Jam. | E6 | 64 |
| Mayport Naval Station, mil., Fl., U.S. | B5 | 86 |
| Mayreau, i., St. Vin. | V26 | 65 |
| Mayrhofen, Aus. | B7 | 20 |
| Mays, In., U.S. | E7 | 91 |
| Mays Landing, N.J., U.S. | E3 | 107 |
| Mays Lick, Ky., U.S. | B6 | 94 |
| Maysville, Ar., U.S. | A1 | 81 |
| Maysville, Ga., U.S. | B3 | 87 |
| Maysville, In., U.S. | G3 | 91 |
| Maysville, Ia., U.S. | g10 | 92 |
| Maysville, Ky., U.S. | B6 | 94 |
| Maysville, Mo., U.S. | B3 | 102 |
| Maysville, N.C., U.S. | C5 | 110 |
| Maysville, Ok., U.S. | C4 | 113 |
| Maysville, W.V., U.S. | B5 | 125 |
| Mayumba, Gabon | F2 | 46 |
| Mayview, Mo., U.S. | B4 | 102 |
| Mayville, Mi., U.S. | E7 | 99 |
| Mayville, N.Y., U.S. | C1 | 109 |
| Mayville, N.D., U.S. | B8 | 111 |
| Mayville, Wi., U.S. | E5 | 126 |
| Maywood, Ca., U.S. | *n12 | 82 |
| Maywood, Il., U.S. | k9 | 90 |
| Maywood, Mo., U.S. | B6 | 102 |
| Maywood, Ne., U.S. | D5 | 104 |
| Maywood, N.J., U.S. | h8 | 107 |
| Maywood Park, Or., U.S. | B4 | 114 |
| Maza, Arg. | D4 | 54 |
| Maza, N.D., U.S. | A6 | 111 |
| Mazabuka, Zam. | E4 | 48 |
| Mazagão, Braz. | C4 | 59 |
| Mazamet, Fr. | F5 | 16 |
| Mazapil, Mex. | C4 | 63 |
| Mazara del Vallo, Italy | F4 | 23 |
| Mazār-e Sharīf, Afg. | A4 | 36 |
| Mazārī an Nūbānī, Isr. Occ. | g11 | 41 |
| Mazarn Creek, stm., Ar., U.S. | g7 | 81 |
| Mazarredo, Arg. | D3 | 54 |
| Mazarrón, Spain | D5 | 22 |
| Mazaruni, stm., Guy. | A2 | 59 |
| Mazaruni-Potaro, dept., Guy. | A3 | 59 |
| Mazatenango, Guat. | E6 | 63 |
| Mazatlán, Mex. | C3 | 63 |
| Mazatzal Mountains, mts., Az., U.S. | C4 | 80 |
| Mazatzal Peak, mtn., Az., U.S. | C4 | 80 |
| Mažeikiai, Sov. Un. | C4 | 27 |
| Mazenod, Sask. | H2 | 75 |
| Mazeppa, Mn., U.S. | F6 | 100 |
| Mazie, Ok., U.S. | A6 | 113 |
| Mazomanie, Wi., U.S. | E4 | 126 |
| Mazon, Il., U.S. | B5 | 90 |
| Mazzarino, Italy | F5 | 23 |
| Mbabane, Swaz. | C5 | 49 |
| Mbaiki, Cen. Afr. Rep. | E3 | 46 |
| Mbala (Abercorn), Zam. | C5 | 48 |
| Mbale, Ug. | A5 | 48 |
| Mbalmayo, Cam. | E2 | 46 |
| Mbamba Bay, Tan. | D5 | 48 |
| M'banza Congo, Ang. | C1 | 48 |
| Mbandaka, Zaire | A2 | 48 |
| Mbanza-Ngungu, Zaire | C1 | 48 |
| Mbari, stm., Cen. Afr. Rep. | D4 | 46 |
| Mbarara, Ug. | B5 | 48 |
| Mberengwa, Zimb. | B4 | 49 |
| Mbeya, Tan. | C5 | 48 |
| Mbeya, prov., Tan. | C5 | 48 |
| Mbinda, Congo | B1 | 48 |
| Mbour, Sen. | D1 | 45 |
| Mbout, Maur. | C2 | 45 |
| Mbuji-Mayi, Zaire | C3 | 48 |
| Mburucuyá, Arg. | E4 | 55 |
| McAdam, N.B. | D2 | 71 |
| McAdams, Ms., U.S. | B4 | 101 |
| McAdoo, Pa., U.S. | E9 | 115 |
| McAdoo, Tx., U.S. | C2 | 120 |
| McAfee, Ms., U.S. | C4 | 101 |
| McAfee Peak, mtn., Nv., U.S. | B6 | 105 |
| McAlester, Ok., U.S. | C6 | 113 |
| McAlester, Lake, res., Ok., U.S. | B6 | 113 |
| McAlister, N.M., U.S. | C6 | 108 |
| McAlisterville, Pa., U.S. | E7 | 115 |
| McAllen, Tx., U.S. | F3 | 120 |
| McAllister, Mt., U.S. | E5 | 103 |
| McAlmont, Ar., U.S. | h10 | 81 |
| McAlpin, Fl., U.S. | B4 | 86 |
| McAlpine, Md., U.S. | B4 | 97 |
| McAlpine Lock and Dam, U.S. | H6 | 91 |
| McAndrews, Ky., U.S. | C7 | 94 |
| McArthur, Oh., U.S. | C3 | 112 |
| McAuley, Man. | D1 | 70 |
| McBain, Mi., U.S. | D5 | 99 |
| McBaine, Mo., U.S. | C5 | 102 |
| McBee, S.C., U.S. | C7 | 117 |
| McBride, B.C. | C7 | 69 |
| Mcbride, Mo., U.S. | D8 | 102 |
| McCabe, Mt., U.S. | B12 | 103 |
| McCall, Id., U.S. | E2 | 89 |
| McCalla, Al., U.S. | g6 | 78 |
| McCall Creek, Ms., U.S. | D3 | 101 |
| McCallsburg, Ia., U.S. | B4 | 92 |
| McCamey, Tx., U.S. | D1 | 120 |
| McCammon, Id., U.S. | G6 | 89 |
| McCandless, Pa., U.S. | h13 | 115 |
| McCanna, N.D., U.S. | A8 | 111 |
| McCarley, Ms., U.S. | B4 | 101 |
| McCarthy, Ak., U.S. | C11 | 79 |
| McCartney Mountain, mtn., Mt., U.S. | E4 | 103 |
| McCartys, N.M., U.S. | B2 | 108 |
| McCaskill, Ar., U.S. | D2 | 81 |
| McCauley Island, i., B.C. | C2 | 69 |
| McCaulley, Tx., U.S. | C2 | 120 |
| McCaysville, Ga., U.S. | B2 | 87 |
| McChord Air Force Base, mil., Wa., U.S. | f11 | 124 |
| McClain, co., Ok., U.S. | C4 | 113 |
| McClave, Co., U.S. | C8 | 83 |
| McCleary, Wa., U.S. | B2 | 124 |
| McClellan Air Force Base, mil., Ca., U.S. | C3 | 82 |
| McClelland, Ar., U.S. | B4 | 81 |
| McClelland, Ia., U.S. | C2 | 92 |
| McClellandville, De., U.S. | B2 | 85 |
| McClellanville, S.C., U.S. | E9 | 117 |
| McCleod, Mt., U.S. | E6 | 103 |
| McClintock, Mount, mtn., Ant. | A28 | 7 |
| McCloud, Ca., U.S. | B2 | 82 |
| McClure, Il., U.S. | F4 | 90 |
| McClure, Oh., U.S. | A2 | 112 |
| McClure, Pa., U.S. | E7 | 115 |
| McClure, Va., U.S. | e9 | 123 |
| McClusky, N.D., U.S. | B5 | 111 |
| McColl, S.C., U.S. | B8 | 117 |
| McComas, W.V., U.S. | D3 | 125 |
| McComb, Ms., U.S. | D3 | 101 |
| McComb, Oh., U.S. | A2 | 112 |
| McCondy, Ms., U.S. | B5 | 101 |
| McCone, co., Mt., U.S. | C11 | 103 |
| McConnell, Il., U.S. | A4 | 90 |
| McConnell, Tn., U.S. | A3 | 119 |
| McConnell Air Force Base, mil., Ks., U.S. | g12 | 93 |
| McConnells, S.C., U.S. | B5 | 117 |
| McConnellsburg, Pa., U.S. | G6 | 115 |
| McConnelstown, Pa., U.S. | F5 | 115 |
| McConnelsville, Oh., U.S. | C4 | 112 |
| McCook, Ne., U.S. | D5 | 104 |
| McCook, co., S.D., U.S. | D8 | 118 |
| McCook Lake, S.D., U.S. | E9 | 118 |
| McCool, Ms., U.S. | B4 | 101 |
| McCoole, Md., U.S. | m13 | 97 |
| McCool Junction, Ne., U.S. | D8 | 104 |
| McCord, Sask. | H2 | 75 |
| McCordsville, In., U.S. | E6 | 91 |
| McCormick, S.C., U.S. | D3 | 117 |
| McCormick, co., S.C., U.S. | D3 | 117 |
| McCoy, Co., U.S. | B4 | 83 |
| McCracken, Ks., U.S. | D4 | 93 |
| McCracken, co., Ky., U.S. | e9 | 94 |
| McCreary, Man. | D2 | 70 |
| McCreary, co., Ky., U.S. | D5 | 94 |
| McCrory, Ar., U.S. | B4 | 81 |
| McCulloch, co., Tx., U.S. | D3 | 120 |
| McCullough, Al., U.S. | D2 | 78 |
| McCullough Mountain, mtn., Nv., U.S. | H6 | 105 |
| McCune, Ks., U.S. | E8 | 93 |
| McCurtain, Ok., U.S. | B7 | 113 |
| McCurtain, co., Ok., U.S. | C7 | 113 |
| McCutchenville, Oh., U.S. | A2 | 112 |
| McDade, Tx., U.S. | D4 | 120 |
| McDaniel, Md., U.S. | C5 | 97 |
| McDavid, Fl., U.S. | u14 | 86 |
| McDermitt, Nv., U.S. | B4 | 105 |
| McDermott, Oh., U.S. | D2 | 112 |
| McDonald, Ks., U.S. | C2 | 93 |
| McDonald, N.M., U.S. | D6 | 108 |
| McDonald, Pa., U.S. | F1 | 115 |
| McDonald, Tn., U.S. | h12 | 119 |
| McDonald, co., Mo., U.S. | E3 | 102 |
| McDonald Creek, stm., Mt., U.S. | C8 | 103 |
| McDonald Islands, is., Austl. | J1 | 2 |
| McDonough, Ga., U.S. | C2 | 87 |
| McDonough, N.Y., U.S. | C5 | 109 |
| McDonough, co., Il., U.S. | C3 | 90 |
| McDougal, Ar., U.S. | A5 | 81 |
| McDougall, Mount, mtn., Wy., U.S. | D2 | 127 |
| McDowell, Ky., U.S. | C7 | 94 |
| McDowell, Va., U.S. | B3 | 123 |
| McDowell, co., N.C., U.S. | f10 | 110 |
| McDowell, co., W.V., U.S. | D3 | 125 |
| McDowell Mountains, mts., Az., U.S. | k9 | 80 |
| McDowell Peak, mtn., Az., U.S. | k9 | 80 |
| McDuffie, co., Ga., U.S. | C4 | 87 |
| McElhattan, Pa., U.S. | D7 | 115 |
| McElroy Creek, stm., W.V., U.S. | k9 | 125 |
| McEwen, Tn., U.S. | A4 | 119 |
| McFadden, Wy., U.S. | E6 | 127 |
| McFaddin, Tx., U.S. | E4 | 120 |
| McFall, Mo., U.S. | A3 | 102 |
| McFarlan, N.C., U.S. | C3 | 110 |
| McFarland, Ca., U.S. | E4 | 82 |
| McFarland, Ks., U.S. | C7 | 93 |
| McFarland, Mi., U.S. | B3 | 99 |
| McFarland, Wi., U.S. | E4 | 126 |
| McGaheysville, Va., U.S. | B4 | 123 |
| McGee, Sask. | F1 | 75 |
| McGehee, Ar., U.S. | D4 | 81 |
| McGill, Nv., U.S. | D7 | 105 |
| McGivney, N.B. | C3 | 71 |
| McGrady, N.C., U.S. | A1 | 110 |
| McGrath, Ak., U.S. | C8 | 79 |
| McGrath, Mn., U.S. | D5 | 100 |
| McGraw, N.Y., U.S. | C4 | 109 |
| McGraws, W.V., U.S. | D3 | 125 |
| McGregor, Ia., U.S. | A6 | 92 |
| McGregor, Mn., U.S. | D5 | 100 |
| McGregor, N.D., U.S. | A3 | 111 |
| McGregor, Tx., U.S. | D4 | 120 |
| McGregor, stm., B.C. | B7 | 69 |
| McGregor Lake, l., Alta. | D4 | 68 |
| McGuffey, Oh., U.S. | B2 | 112 |
| McGuire, Mount, mtn., Id., U.S. | D4 | 89 |
| McGuire Air Force Base, mil., N.J., U.S. | C3 | 107 |
| McHenry, Il., U.S. | A5 | 90 |
| McHenry, Ky., U.S. | C3 | 94 |
| McHenry, Md., U.S. | k12 | 97 |
| McHenry, N.D., U.S. | B7 | 111 |
| McHenry, co., Il., U.S. | A5 | 90 |
| McHenry, co., N.D., U.S. | A5 | 111 |
| McHenry, stm., N.D., U.S. | B7 | 111 |
| McHinga, Tan. | C6 | 48 |
| Mchinji, Mwi. | D5 | 48 |
| McHue, Ar., U.S. | B4 | 81 |
| McIndoe Falls, Vt., U.S. | C4 | 122 |
| McIntire, Ia., U.S. | A5 | 92 |
| McIntosh, Ont. | E5 | 70 |
| McIntosh, Al., U.S. | D1 | 78 |
| McIntosh, Fl., U.S. | C4 | 86 |
| McIntosh, Mn., U.S. | C3 | 100 |
| McIntosh, N.M., U.S. | C3 | 108 |
| McIntosh, S.D., U.S. | B4 | 118 |
| McIntosh, co., Ga., U.S. | E5 | 87 |
| McIntosh, co., N.D., U.S. | C6 | 111 |
| McIntosh, co., Ok., U.S. | B6 | 113 |
| McIntosh Lake, l., Sask. | n7 | 75 |
| McIntosh Run, stm., Md., U.S. | D4 | 97 |
| McIntyre, Ga., U.S. | D3 | 87 |
| McIntyre, Pa., U.S. | E3 | 115 |
| McKague, Sask. | E4 | 75 |
| McKean, co., Pa., U.S. | C4 | 115 |
| McKee, Ky., U.S. | C6 | 94 |
| McKee City, N.J., U.S. | E3 | 107 |
| McKeesport, Pa., U.S. | F2 | 115 |
| McKees Rocks, Pa., U.S. | F1 | 115 |
| McKenney, Va., U.S. | D5 | 123 |
| McKenzie, Al., U.S. | D3 | 78 |
| McKenzie, N.D., U.S. | C5 | 111 |
| McKenzie, Tn., U.S. | A3 | 119 |
| McKenzie, co., N.D., U.S. | B2 | 111 |
| McKenzie, stm., Or., U.S. | C4 | 114 |
| McKenzie Bridge, Or., U.S. | C4 | 114 |
| McKerrow, Ont. | A3 | 73 |
| McKinley, Mn., U.S. | C6 | 100 |
| McKinley, Mount, mtn., Ak., U.S. | C9 | 79 |
| McKinley Park, Ak., U.S. | C10 | 79 |
| McKinleyville, Ca., U.S. | B1 | 82 |
| McKinney, Ky., U.S. | C5 | 94 |
| McKinney, Tx., U.S. | C4 | 120 |
| McKinney, Lake, l., Ks., U.S. | E2 | 93 |
| McKinnon, Wy., U.S. | E3 | 127 |
| McKittrick, Ca., U.S. | E4 | 82 |
| McKittrick, Mo., U.S. | C6 | 102 |
| McKittrick Summit, mtn., Ca., U.S. | E4 | 82 |
| McKnight Lake, l., Man. | A1 | 70 |
| McLain, Ms., U.S. | D5 | 101 |
| McLaughlin, S.D., U.S. | B5 | 118 |
| McLaughlin, stm., Man. | C3 | 70 |
| McLaurin, Ms., U.S. | D4 | 101 |
| McLean, Sask. | G3 | 75 |
| McLean, Il., U.S. | C4 | 90 |
| McLean, Tx., U.S. | B2 | 120 |
| McLean, Va., U.S. | g12 | 123 |
| McLean, co., Il., U.S. | C4 | 90 |
| McLean, co., Ky., U.S. | C2 | 94 |
| McLean, co., N.D., U.S. | B4 | 111 |
| McLean Lake, l., Sask. | A6 | 68 |
| McLean Mountain, mtn., Me., U.S. | A4 | 96 |
| McLeansboro, Il., U.S. | E5 | 90 |
| McLemoresville, Tn., U.S. | B3 | 119 |
| McLennan, Alta. | B2 | 68 |
| McLennan, co., Tx., U.S. | D4 | 120 |
| McLeod, N.D., U.S. | C8 | 111 |
| McLeod, co., Mn., U.S. | F4 | 100 |
| McLeod, stm., Alta. | C2 | 68 |
| McLeod Lake, B.C. | B6 | 69 |
| McLeod Lake, l., B.C. | B6 | 69 |
| M'Clintock Channel, strt., N.W. Ter. | B12 | 66 |
| McLoughlin, Mount, mtn., Or., U.S. | E4 | 114 |
| McLouth, Ks., U.S. | C8 | 93 |
| McMahon, Sask. | G2 | 75 |
| McMechen, W.V., U.S. | B4 | 125 |
| M'Clure Strait, strt., N.W. Ter. | B9 | 66 |
| McMillan, Lake, res., N.M., U.S. | E5 | 108 |
| McMillin, Wa., U.S. | f11 | 124 |
| McMinn, co., Tn., U.S. | D9 | 119 |
| McMinnville, Or., U.S. | B3 | 114 |
| McMinnville, Tn., U.S. | D8 | 119 |
| McMorran, Sask. | F1 | 75 |
| McMullen, co., Tx., U.S. | E3 | 120 |
| McMurdo, sci., Ant. | B29 | 7 |
| McMurdo Sound, strt., Ant. | B29 | 7 |
| McNab, Ar., U.S. | D2 | 81 |
| McNabb, Il., U.S. | B4 | 90 |
| McNair, Ms., U.S. | D2 | 101 |
| McNairy, Tn., U.S. | B3 | 119 |
| McNairy, co., Tn., U.S. | B3 | 119 |
| McNary, Az., U.S. | C6 | 80 |
| McNary, La., U.S. | D3 | 95 |
| McNary Dam, U.S. | B7 | 114 |
| McNaughton Lake, res., B.C. | C8 | 69 |
| McNeal, Az., U.S. | F6 | 80 |
| McNeil, Ar., U.S. | D2 | 81 |
| McNeil, Tx., U.S. | D4 | 120 |
| McNeil Island, i., Wa., U.S. | f10 | 124 |
| McNeill, Ms., U.S. | E4 | 101 |
| McNulty, Or., U.S. | *B4 | 114 |
| McNutts Island, i., N.S. | F4 | 71 |
| McPhail, stm., Man. | C3 | 70 |
| McPherson, Ks., U.S. | D6 | 93 |
| McPherson, co., Ks., U.S. | D6 | 93 |
| McPherson, co., Ne., U.S. | C4 | 104 |
| McPherson, co., S.D., U.S. | B6 | 118 |
| McQuady, Ky., U.S. | C3 | 94 |
| McQueeney, Tx., U.S. | h7 | 120 |
| McRae, Ar., U.S. | B4 | 81 |
| McRae, Ga., U.S. | D4 | 87 |
| McRoberts, Ky., U.S. | C7 | 94 |
| McSherrystown, Pa., U.S. | G7 | 115 |
| McTaggart, Sask. | H3 | 75 |
| McTavish, Man. | E3 | 70 |
| McVeigh, Ky., U.S. | C7 | 94 |
| McVeytown, Pa., U.S. | F6 | 115 |
| McVille, N.D., U.S. | B7 | 111 |
| McWilliams, Al., U.S. | D2 | 78 |
| Mdandu, Tan. | C5 | 48 |
| Mdantsane, Ciskei | *D4 | 49 |
| Me, i., Viet. | C6 | 35 |
| Meacham, Sask. | E3 | 75 |
| Meacham, Or., U.S. | B8 | 114 |
| Mead, Co., U.S. | A6 | 83 |
| Mead, Ne., U.S. | C9 | 104 |
| Mead, Ok., U.S. | D5 | 113 |
| Mead, Lake, res., U.S. | A1 | 80 |
| Meade, Ks., U.S. | E3 | 93 |
| Meade, co., Ks., U.S. | E3 | 93 |
| Meade, co., Ky., U.S. | C3 | 94 |
| Meade, co., S.D., U.S. | C3 | 118 |
| Meade, stm., Ak., U.S. | B9 | 79 |
| Meaden Peak, mtn., Co., U.S. | A3 | 83 |
| Meade Peak, mtn., Id., U.S. | G7 | 89 |
| Meador, Ky., U.S. | D3 | 94 |
| Meadow, S.D., U.S. | B3 | 118 |
| Meadow, Tx., U.S. | C1 | 120 |
| Meadow, Ut., U.S. | E3 | 121 |
| Meadow, stm., W.V., U.S. | C4 | 125 |
| Meadow Bridge, W.V., U.S. | D4 | 125 |
| Meadowbrook, Fl., U.S. | *D5 | 86 |
| Meadowbrook, W.V., U.S. | k10 | 125 |
| Meadow Creek, W.V., U.S. | D4 | 125 |
| Meadow Creek, stm., W.V., U.S. | n14 | 125 |
| Meadow Grove, Ne., U.S. | B8 | 104 |
| Meadow Lake, Sask. | n7 | 75 |
| Meadowlands, Mn., U.S. | C6 | 100 |
| Meadow Lands, Pa., U.S. | F1 | 115 |
| Meadow Mountain, mtn., U.S. | k12 | 97 |
| Meadowood, De., U.S. | *B3 | 85 |
| Meadows, Id., U.S. | E2 | 89 |
| Meadows, N.H., U.S. | B4 | 106 |
| Meadow Valley Wash, val., Nv., U.S. | F7 | 105 |
| Meadowview, Va., U.S. | f10 | 123 |
| Meadville, Mo., U.S. | B4 | 102 |
| Meadville, Ms., U.S. | D3 | 101 |
| Meadville, Pa., U.S. | C1 | 115 |
| Meaford, Ont. | C4 | 73 |
| Meagher, co., Mt., U.S. | D6 | 103 |
| Meaghers Grant, N.S. | E6 | 71 |
| Mealy Mountains, mts., Newf. | h9 | 72 |
| Meandarra, Austl. | C7 | 51 |
| Meander Creek Reservoir, res., Oh., U.S. | A5 | 112 |
| Means, Ky., U.S. | C6 | 94 |
| Mearim, stm., Braz. | C1 | 57 |
| Mears, Mi., U.S. | E4 | 99 |
| Me'a She'arim (part of Jerusalem), Isr. | m14 | 41 |
| Meath, co., Ire. | D5 | 11 |
| Meath Park, Sask. | D3 | 75 |
| Meaux, Fr. | C5 | 16 |
| Mebane, N.C., U.S. | A3 | 110 |
| Mecca (Makkah), Sau. Ar. | C3 | 38 |
| Mecca, Ca., U.S. | F5 | 82 |
| Mecca, In., U.S. | E3 | 91 |
| Mechanic Falls, Me., U.S. | D2 | 96 |
| Mechanicsburg, Il., U.S. | D5 | 90 |
| Mechanicsburg, Oh., U.S. | B2 | 112 |
| Mechanicsburg, Pa., U.S. | F7 | 115 |
| Mechanicsville, Ct., U.S. | B8 | 84 |
| Mechanicsville, Ia., U.S. | C6 | 92 |
| Mechanicsville, Md., U.S. | D4 | 97 |
| Mechanicsville, Va., U.S. | C5 | 123 |
| Mechanicville, N.Y., U.S. | C7 | 109 |
| Mechant, Lake, l., La., U.S. | E4 | 95 |
| Mechelen (Malines), Bel. | B6 | 16 |
| Mechriyya, Alg. | C4 | 44 |
| Meck Island, i., Marsh Is. | S17 | 2 |
| Mecklenburg, co., N.C., U.S. | B2 | 110 |
| Mecklenburg, co., Va., U.S. | D4 | 123 |
| Mecklenburg, hist. reg., E. Ger. | B5 | 18 |
| Mecklenburg Bay, b., Eur. | D5 | 15 |
| Meckling, S.D., U.S. | E8 | 118 |
| Meconta, Moz. | D7 | 48 |
| Mecosta, Mi., U.S. | E5 | 99 |
| Mecosta, co., Mi., U.S. | E5 | 99 |
| Mecúfi, Moz. | D8 | 48 |
| Medak, India | H7 | 37 |
| Medan, Indon. | E1 | 34 |
| Medanales, N.M., U.S. | A3 | 108 |
| Médanos, Arg. | D4 | 54 |
| Medanos, Punta, c., Arg. | D5 | 54 |
| Medart, Fl., U.S. | B2 | 86 |
| Meddybemps, Me., U.S. | C5 | 96 |
| Meddybumps Lake, l., Me., U.S. | C5 | 96 |
| Medellín, Col. | B2 | 60 |
| Medemblik, Neth. | C5 | 16 |
| Medfield, Ma., U.S. | h10 | 98 |
| Medford, Ma., U.S. | B5 | 98 |
| Medford, Mn., U.S. | F5 | 100 |
| Medford, N.J., U.S. | *D3 | 107 |
| Medford, N.Y., U.S. | *n15 | 109 |
| Medford, Ok., U.S. | A4 | 113 |
| Medford, Or., U.S. | E4 | 114 |
| Medford, Wi., U.S. | C3 | 126 |
| Medford Lakes, N.J., U.S. | D3 | 107 |
| Medfra, Ak., U.S. | C9 | 79 |
| Medgidia, Rom. | C9 | 24 |
| Media, Il., U.S. | C3 | 90 |
| Media, Pa., U.S. | G11 | 115 |
| Mediapolis, Ia., U.S. | C6 | 92 |
| Medical Lake, Wa., U.S. | B8 | 124 |
| Medicina, Italy | E7 | 20 |
| Medicine Bow, Wy., U.S. | E6 | 127 |
| Medicine Bow Mountains, mts., U.S. | E6 | 127 |
| Medicine Bow Peak, mtn., Wy., U.S. | E6 | 127 |
| Medicine Creek, stm., Mo., U.S. | B4 | 102 |
| Medicine Creek, stm., Ne., U.S. | D5 | 104 |
| Medicine Hat, Alta. | D5 | 68 |
| Medicine Lodge, Ks., U.S. | E5 | 93 |
| Medicine Lodge, stm., U.S. | E4 | 93 |
| Medicine Park, Ok., U.S. | C3 | 113 |
| Medill, Mo., U.S. | A6 | 102 |
| Medina (Al Madīnah), Sau. Ar. | C3 | 38 |
| Medina, N.Y., U.S. | B2 | 109 |
| Medina, N.D., U.S. | C6 | 111 |
| Medina, Oh., U.S. | A4 | 112 |
| Medina, Tn., U.S. | B3 | 119 |
| Medina, Tx., U.S. | E3 | 120 |
| Medina, Wa., U.S. | e11 | 124 |
| Medina, co., Oh., U.S. | A4 | 112 |
| Medina, co., Tx., U.S. | k7 | 120 |
| Medina, stm., Tx., U.S. | E3 | 120 |
| Medina del Campo, Spain | B3 | 22 |
| Medina de Rioseco, Spain | B3 | 22 |
| Medina-Sidonia, Spain | D3 | 22 |
| Medinīpur, India | D8 | 36 |
| Mediterranean Sea | H12 | 8 |
| Medjerda, stm., Tun. | F2 | 23 |
| Medjerda, Monts de la, mts., Afr. | F2 | 23 |
| Medjez el Bab, Tun. | F2 | 23 |
| Mednogorsk, Sov. Un. | C5 | 28 |
| Medomak, Me., U.S. | *D3 | 96 |
| Medon, Tn., U.S. | B3 | 119 |
| Medora, Man. | E1 | 70 |
| Medora, Il., U.S. | D3 | 90 |
| Medora, In., U.S. | G5 | 91 |
| Medora, Ks., U.S. | D6 | 93 |
| Medora, N.D., U.S. | C2 | 111 |
| Médouneu, Gabon | E2 | 46 |
| Medstead, Sask. | D1 | 75 |
| Meductic, N.B. | D2 | 71 |
| Medveditsa, stm., Sov. Un. | F15 | 27 |
| Medvedovskaya, Sov. Un. | I12 | 27 |
| Medvezhi Islands, is., Sov. Un. | B19 | 29 |
| Medvezhyegorsk, Sov. Un. | C6 | 28 |
| Medway, Me., U.S. | C4 | 96 |
| Medway, Ma., U.S. | B5 | 98 |
| Medway, stm., N.S. | E5 | 71 |
| Medzhibozh, Sov. Un. | G6 | 27 |
| Meekatharra, Austl. | E3 | 50 |
| Meeker, Co., U.S. | A3 | 83 |
| Meeker, Ok., U.S. | B5 | 113 |
| Meeker, co., Mn., U.S. | E4 | 100 |
| Meelpaeg Lake, res., Newf. | D3 | 72 |
| Meerane, E. Ger. | C6 | 18 |
| Meerbusch, W. Ger. | *C3 | 18 |
| Meerle, Bel. | C4 | 17 |
| Meersburg, W. Ger. | A7 | 21 |
| Meerut, India | *C6 | 36 |
| Meeteetse, Wy., U.S. | C3 | 127 |
| Meeting Creek, Alta. | C4 | 68 |
| Meeting Lake, l., Sask. | D2 | 75 |
| Meeyamoot Lake, l., Sask. | C3 | 75 |
| Mega, Eth. | E4 | 47 |
| Megali Canal, Grc. | g10 | 25 |
| Megalópolis, Grc. | C4 | 25 |
| Mégantic, Que. | C6 | 74 |
| Mégantic, Lac, l., Que. | C6 | 74 |
| Mégantic, Mont, mtn., Que. | D6 | 74 |
| Mégara, Grc. | C4 | 25 |
| Megargel, Al., U.S. | D2 | 78 |
| Megargel, Tx., U.S. | C3 | 120 |
| Megève, Fr. | E2 | 21 |
| Meggett, S.C., U.S. | F7 | 117 |
| Meghalaya, state, India | C9 | 36 |
| Meguntacook, Mount, mtn., Me., U.S. | D3 | 96 |
| Mehar, Pak. | G3 | 37 |
| Mehekar, India | B4 | 37 |
| Meherrin, Va., U.S. | A4 | 110 |
| Mehlville, Mo., U.S. | f13 | 102 |
| Mehoopany, Pa., U.S. | C9 | 115 |
| Mehrān, Iran | *C5 | 38 |
| Mehun-sur-Yèvre, Fr. | D5 | 16 |
| Meia Ponte, stm., Braz. | D4 | 57 |
| Meiganga, Cam. | D2 | 46 |
| Meighen Island, i., N.W. Ter. | K32 | 66 |
| Meigs, Ga., U.S. | E2 | 87 |
| Meigs, co., Oh., U.S. | C3 | 112 |
| Meigs, co., Tn., U.S. | D9 | 119 |
| Meiktila, Burma | D10 | 36 |
| Meiners Oaks, Ca., U.S. | *E4 | 82 |
| Meiningen, E. Ger. | C5 | 18 |
| Meiringen, Switz. | E4 | 18 |
| Meissen, E. Ger. | C7 | 18 |
| Meitan, China | F8 | 31 |
| Mejillones, Chile | A2 | 54 |
| Mékambo, Gabon | D2 | 46 |
| Mékhé, Sen. | C1 | 45 |
| Mekhtar, Pak. | E3 | 37 |
| Meknès, Mor. | B3 | 44 |
| Mekong, stm., Asia | H13 | 30 |
| Mekoryuk, Ak., U.S. | C6 | 79 |
| Melaka (Malacca), Malay. | E2 | 34 |
| Melaka, state, Malay. | M7 | 33 |
| Mélambes, Grc. | E5 | 25 |
| Melba, Id., U.S. | F2 | 89 |
| Melber, Ky., U.S. | f9 | 94 |
| Melbern, Oh., U.S. | A1 | 112 |
| Melbeta, Ne., U.S. | C2 | 104 |
| Melbourne, Austl. | G8 | 50 |
| Melbourne, Ont. | E3 | 73 |
| Melbourne, Fl., U.S. | D6 | 86 |
| Melbourne, Ia., U.S. | C4 | 92 |
| Melbourne, Ky., U.S. | h14 | 94 |
| Melbourne, Mo., U.S. | A4 | 102 |
| Melbourne Beach, Fl., U.S. | D6 | 86 |
| Melcher, Ia., U.S. | C4 | 92 |
| Melder, La., U.S. | C3 | 95 |
| Meldorf, W. Ger. | D3 | 15 |
| Meldrum Bay, Ont. | B1 | 73 |
| Meleb, Man. | D3 | 70 |
| Melekeok, Palau | R17 | 52 |
| Melekess, Sov. Un. | E18 | 8 |
| Melenki, Sov. Un. | D13 | 27 |
| Mélèzes, Rivière aux, stm., Que. | g12 | 74 |
| Melfi, Chad | C3 | 46 |
| Melfi, Italy | D5 | 23 |
| Melfort, Sask. | E3 | 75 |
| Melghir, Chott, l., Alg. | C6 | 44 |
| Melilla, Sp. N. Afr. | B4 | 44 |
| Melipilla, Chile | A2 | 54 |
| Mélisey, Fr. | A2 | 21 |
| Melita, Man. | E1 | 70 |
| Melito di Porto Salvo, Italy | F5 | 23 |
| Melitopol, Sov. Un. | H10 | 27 |
| Melle, Fr. | D3 | 16 |
| Melle, W. Ger. | A3 | 19 |
| Mellen, Wi., U.S. | B3 | 126 |
| Mellette, S.D., U.S. | B7 | 118 |
| Mellette, co., S.D., U.S. | D5 | 118 |
| Mellit, Sud. | C2 | 47 |
| Mellor Glacier, ice, Ant. | B19 | 7 |
| Mellott, In., U.S. | D3 | 91 |
| Mellow Valley, Al., U.S. | B4 | 78 |
| Mellrichstadt, W. Ger. | C5 | 19 |
| Mellum, i., W. Ger. | E2 | 15 |
| Mellwood, Ar., U.S. | C5 | 81 |
| Melmore, Oh., U.S. | A2 | 112 |
| Mělník, Czech. | n18 | 19 |
| Melo, Ur. | E2 | 56 |
| Melocheville, Que. | q19 | 74 |
| Melrose, N.B. | C6 | 71 |
| Melrose, N.S. | D7 | 71 |
| Melrose, Ct., U.S. | B5 | 84 |
| Melrose, Fl., U.S. | C4 | 86 |
| Melrose, Ia., U.S. | D4 | 92 |
| Melrose, La., U.S. | C3 | 95 |
| Melrose, Ma., U.S. | B5 | 98 |
| Melrose, Mn., U.S. | E4 | 100 |
| Melrose, N.M., U.S. | C6 | 108 |
| Melrose, Oh., U.S. | A1 | 112 |
| Melrose Park, Fl., U.S. | r13 | 86 |
| Melrose Park, Il., U.S. | *k9 | 90 |
| Mels, Switz. | B7 | 21 |
| Melstone, Mt., U.S. | D9 | 103 |
| Melstrand, Mi., U.S. | B4 | 99 |
| Melsungen, W. Ger. | B5 | 19 |
| Melton Hill Lake, res., Tn., U.S. | D9 | 119 |
| Melton Mowbray, Eng., U.K. | B7 | 13 |
| Melun, Fr. | C5 | 16 |
| Melvaig, Scot., U.K. | C3 | 13 |
| Melvern, Ks., U.S. | D8 | 93 |
| Melvern Lake, res., Ks., U.S. | D8 | 93 |
| Melville, Austl. | *F2 | 50 |
| Melville, Sask. | G4 | 75 |
| Melville, La., U.S. | D4 | 95 |
| Melville, Mt., U.S. | D7 | 103 |
| Melville, N.Y., U.S. | *n15 | 109 |
| Melville, i., Austl. | B5 | 50 |
| Melville, Cape, c., Austl. | B7 | 50 |
| Melville, Lake, l., Newf. | B14 | 72 |
| Melville Bugt, b., Grnld. | B14 | 61 |
| Melville Hills, hills, N.W. Ter. | C8 | 66 |
| Melville Island, i., N.W. Ter. | m30 | 66 |
| Melville Peninsula, pen., N.W. Ter. | C16 | 66 |
| Melvin, Al., U.S. | D1 | 78 |
| Melvin, Il., U.S. | C5 | 90 |
| Melvin, Ia., U.S. | A2 | 92 |
| Melvin, Ky., U.S. | C7 | 94 |
| Melvin, Tx., U.S. | D3 | 120 |
| Melvin, Lough, l., Eur. | C3 | 11 |
| Melvindale, Mi., U.S. | *p7 | 99 |
| Melvine, Tn., U.S. | C8 | 119 |
| Melvin Village, N.H., U.S. | C4 | 106 |
| Melyana, Alg. | B5 | 44 |
| Mélykút, Hung. | B4 | 24 |
| Memba, Moz. | D8 | 48 |
| Memboro, Indon. | G6 | 34 |
| Memmingen, W. Ger. | E5 | 19 |
| Mempawah, Indon. | E3 | 34 |
| Memphis, Fl., U.S. | p10 | 86 |
| Memphis, Mi., U.S. | F8 | 99 |
| Memphis, Mo., U.S. | A5 | 102 |
| Memphis, Tn., U.S. | B2 | 119 |
| Memphis, Tx., U.S. | B2 | 120 |
| Memphis, hist., Egypt | C6 | 38 |
| Memphis Naval Air Station, mil., Tn., U.S. | B2 | 119 |
| Memphremagog, Lake, l., N.A. | D5 | 74 |
| Memramcook, N.B. | C5 | 71 |
| Mena, Ar., U.S. | C1 | 81 |
| Ménaka, Mali | B5 | 45 |
| Menahga, Mn., U.S. | D3 | 100 |
| Menan, Id., U.S. | F7 | 89 |
| Menands, N.Y., U.S. | *C7 | 109 |
| Menard, Tx., U.S. | D3 | 120 |
| Menard, co., Il., U.S. | C4 | 90 |
| Menard, co., Tx., U.S. | D3 | 120 |
| Menasha, Wi., U.S. | D5 | 126 |
| Mendawai, stm., Indon. | F4 | 34 |
| Mende, Fr. | E5 | 16 |
| Menden, W. Ger. | B2 | 19 |
| Mendenhall, Ms., U.S. | D4 | 101 |
| Mendes, Braz. | E7 | 59 |
| Mendham, N.J., U.S. | B3 | 107 |
| Mendi, Eth. | C4 | 47 |
| Mendip Hills, hills, Eng., U.K. | C5 | 13 |
| Mendocino, co., Ca., U.S. | C2 | 82 |
| Mendocino, Cape, c., Ca., U.S. | C1 | 82 |
| Mendon, Ma., U.S. | h9 | 98 |
| Mendon, Mi., U.S. | F5 | 99 |
| Mendon, Mo., U.S. | B4 | 102 |
| Mendon, Oh., U.S. | B1 | 112 |
| Mendon, Ut., U.S. | B4 | 121 |
| Mendota, Ca., U.S. | D3 | 82 |
| Mendota, Il., U.S. | B4 | 90 |
| Mendota, Lake, l., Wi., U.S. | E4 | 126 |
| Mendota Heights, Mn., U.S. | *m13 | 100 |
| Mendoza, Arg. | A3 | 54 |
| Mendoza, Pan. | k11 | 62 |
| Mendoza, prov., Arg. | A3 | 54 |
| Mene de Mauroa, Ven. | A3 | 60 |
| Mene Grande, Ven. | C6 | 25 |
| Menemen, Tur. | C6 | 25 |
| Menen, Bel. | D13 | 27 |
| Menfi, Italy | F4 | 23 |
| Mengcheng, China | E8 | 31 |
| Menggala, Indon. | F3 | 34 |

| Name | Map Ref. | Page |
|---|---|---|
| Menghai, China | B4 | 35 |
| Menglian, China | G4 | 31 |
| Mengzi, China | G5 | 31 |
| Menifee, Ar., U.S. | B3 | 81 |
| Menifee, co., Ky., U.S. | C6 | 94 |
| Menihek Lakes, l., Newf. | g8 | 72 |
| Menindee, Austl. | F7 | 50 |
| Menindee Lake, l., Austl. | F4 | 51 |
| Menlo, Ga., U.S. | B1 | 87 |
| Menlo, Ia., U.S. | C3 | 92 |
| Menlo, Ks., U.S. | C3 | 93 |
| Menlo, Wa., U.S. | C2 | 124 |
| Menlo Park, Ca., U.S. | k8 | 82 |
| Menno, S.D., U.S. | D8 | 118 |
| Meno, Ok., U.S. | A3 | 113 |
| Menoken, N.D., U.S. | C5 | 111 |
| Menominee, Mi., U.S. | C3 | 99 |
| Menominee, co., Mi., U.S. | C3 | 99 |
| Menominee, co., Wi., U.S. | C5 | 126 |
| Menominee, stm., U.S. | C6 | 126 |
| Menominee Indian Reservation, Wi., U.S. | C5 | 126 |
| Menomonee, stm., Wi., U.S. | m11 | 126 |
| Menomonee Falls, Wi., U.S. | E5 | 126 |
| Menomonie, Wi., U.S. | D2 | 126 |
| Menongue, Ang. | D2 | 48 |
| Menor, Mar, b., Spain | D5 | 22 |
| Menorca, i., Spain | C8 | 22 |
| Mentakab, Malay. | K5 | 35 |
| Mentana, Italy | g9 | 23 |
| Mentawai Islands, is., Indon. | F1 | 34 |
| Mentmore, N.M., U.S. | B1 | 108 |
| Menton, Fr. | F7 | 16 |
| Mentone, Al., U.S. | A4 | 78 |
| Mentone, In., U.S. | B5 | 91 |
| Mentone, Tx., U.S. | D1 | 120 |
| Mentor, Ky., U.S. | k14 | 94 |
| Mentor, Mn., U.S. | C2 | 100 |
| Mentor, Oh., U.S. | A4 | 112 |
| Mentor, Tn., U.S. | n13 | 119 |
| Mentor-on-the-Lake, Oh., U.S. | A4 | 112 |
| Menzel Bourguiba, Tun. | B6 | 44 |
| Menzies, Mount, mtn., Ant. | B19 | 7 |
| Menziken, Switz. | B5 | 21 |
| Meoqui, Mex. | B3 | 63 |
| Meota, Sask. | D1 | 75 |
| Meppel, Neth. | A7 | 16 |
| Meppen, W. Ger. | B3 | 18 |
| Meqerghane, Sebkha, pl., Alg. | D5 | 44 |
| Mequon, Wi., U.S. | E6 | 126 |
| Merabolo, Gulf of, b., Grc. | E5 | 25 |
| Meramec, stm., Mo., U.S. | C7 | 102 |
| Merano, Italy | A3 | 23 |
| Merasheen, Newf. | E4 | 72 |
| Merasheen Island, i., Newf. | E4 | 72 |
| Merate, Italy | E7 | 21 |
| Merauke, Indon. | G10 | 34 |
| Meraux, La., U.S. | k12 | 95 |
| Mercāra, India | F6 | 36 |
| Merced, Ca., U.S. | D3 | 82 |
| Merced, co., Ca., U.S. | D3 | 82 |
| Merced, stm., Ca., U.S. | D3 | 82 |
| Mercedes, Arg. | A3 | 54 |
| Mercedes, Arg. | A5 | 54 |
| Mercedes, Arg. | E4 | 55 |
| Mercedes, Tx., U.S. | F4 | 120 |
| Mercedes, Ur. | E1 | 56 |
| Mercer, Me., U.S. | D3 | 96 |
| Mercer, Mo., U.S. | A4 | 102 |
| Mercer, N.D., U.S. | B5 | 111 |
| Mercer, Oh., U.S. | B1 | 112 |
| Mercer, Pa., U.S. | D1 | 115 |
| Mercer, Tn., U.S. | B2 | 119 |
| Mercer, Wi., U.S. | B3 | 126 |
| Mercer, co., Il., U.S. | B3 | 90 |
| Mercer, co., Ky., U.S. | C5 | 94 |
| Mercer, co., Mo., U.S. | A4 | 102 |
| Mercer, co., N.J., U.S. | C3 | 107 |
| Mercer, co., N.D., U.S. | B4 | 111 |
| Mercer, co., Oh., U.S. | B1 | 112 |
| Mercer, co., Pa., U.S. | D1 | 115 |
| Mercer, co., W.V., U.S. | D3 | 125 |
| Mercer Island, Wa., U.S. | B3 | 124 |
| Mercer Island, i., Wa., U.S. | e11 | 124 |
| Mercersburg, Pa., U.S. | G6 | 115 |
| Mercerville, N.J., U.S. | C3 | 107 |
| Mercês, Braz. | g6 | 56 |
| Merchantville, N.J., U.S. | *D2 | 107 |
| Mercier, Que. | D4 | 74 |
| Mercier, Ks., U.S. | C8 | 93 |
| Mercoal, Alta. | C2 | 68 |
| Mercury Bay, b., N.Z. | L15 | 51 |
| Mercury Islands, is., N.Z. | L15 | 51 |
| Mercy, Cape, c., N.W. Ter. | D20 | 66 |
| Meredith, N.H., U.S. | C3 | 106 |
| Meredith, Lake, l., Co., U.S. | C7 | 83 |
| Meredith, Lake, res., Tx., U.S. | B2 | 120 |
| Meredith Center, N.H., U.S. | C3 | 106 |
| Meredosia, Il., U.S. | D3 | 90 |
| Meredosia Lake, l., Il., U.S. | D3 | 90 |
| Mereeg, Som. | G4 | 47 |
| Merefa, Sov. Un. | G11 | 27 |
| Merepoint, Me., U.S. | g7 | 96 |
| Mergui, Burma | F10 | 36 |
| Mergui Archipelago, is., Burma | F10 | 36 |
| Meriç (Maritsa) (Evros), stm., Eur. | B6 | 25 |
| Merid, Sask. | F1 | 75 |
| Mérida, Mex. | C7 | 63 |
| Mérida, Spain | C2 | 22 |
| Mérida, Ven. | B3 | 60 |
| Mérida, state, Ven. | B3 | 60 |
| Meriden, Ct., U.S. | C4 | 84 |
| Meriden, Ia., U.S. | B2 | 92 |
| Meriden, Ks., U.S. | C8 | 93 |
| Meriden, Mn., U.S. | F5 | 100 |
| Meriden, N.H., U.S. | C2 | 106 |
| Meriden, Wy., U.S. | E8 | 127 |
| Meridian, Ga., U.S. | E5 | 87 |
| Meridian, Id., U.S. | F2 | 89 |
| Meridian, Ms., U.S. | C5 | 101 |
| Meridian, N.Y., U.S. | B4 | 109 |
| Meridian, Pa., U.S. | E2 | 115 |
| Meridian, Tx., U.S. | C4 | 120 |
| Meridian Hills, In., U.S. | k10 | 91 |
| Meridian Naval Air Station, mil., Ms., U.S. | C5 | 101 |
| Meridianville, Al., U.S. | A3 | 78 |
| Mérignac, Fr. | E3 | 16 |
| Merigold, Ms., U.S. | B3 | 101 |
| Merikarvia, Fin. | G9 | 14 |
| Merino, Austl. | G3 | 51 |
| Merino, Co., U.S. | A7 | 83 |
| Meriwether, co., Ga., U.S. | C2 | 87 |
| Merizo, Guam | M9 | 52 |
| Merkel, Tx., U.S. | C2 | 120 |
| Merkinė, Sov. Un. | A8 | 26 |
| Merksem (part of Antwerp), Bel. | B6 | 16 |
| Merksplas, Bel. | C4 | 17 |
| Merkys, stm., Sov. Un. | D5 | 27 |
| Merlin, Ont. | E2 | 73 |
| Merlin, Or., U.S. | E3 | 114 |
| Merlo, Arg. | g7 | 54 |
| Mermentau, La., U.S. | D3 | 95 |
| Mermentau, stm., La., U.S. | E3 | 95 |
| Mern, Den. | C6 | 15 |
| Merna, Ne., U.S. | C6 | 104 |
| Merom, In., U.S. | F2 | 91 |
| Meron, Mount, mtn., Isr. | A7 | 41 |
| Merredin, Austl. | F2 | 50 |
| Merriam, N.S. | E3 | 71 |
| Merriam, Ks., U.S. | k16 | 93 |
| Merrick, N.Y., U.S. | *n15 | 109 |
| Merrick, co., Ne., U.S. | C7 | 104 |
| Merrick, stm., Scot., U.K. | E4 | 13 |
| Merrick Brook, stm., Ct., U.S. | C7 | 84 |
| Merrickville, Ont. | C9 | 73 |
| Merricourt, N.D., U.S. | C7 | 111 |
| Merrifield, Mn., U.S. | D4 | 100 |
| Merrifield, Va., U.S. | *B5 | 123 |
| Merrill, Ia., U.S. | B1 | 92 |
| Merrill, Mi., U.S. | E6 | 99 |
| Merrill, Ms., U.S. | E5 | 101 |
| Merrill, Or., U.S. | E5 | 114 |
| Merrill, Wi., U.S. | C4 | 126 |
| Merrillan, Wi., U.S. | D3 | 126 |
| Merrillville, In., U.S. | B3 | 91 |
| Merrimac, Ky., U.S. | C4 | 94 |
| Merrimac, Ma., U.S. | A5 | 98 |
| Merrimac, Wi., U.S. | E4 | 126 |
| Merrimack, N.H., U.S. | E4 | 106 |
| Merrimack, co., N.H., U.S. | D3 | 106 |
| Merrimack, stm., U.S. | A5 | 98 |
| Merriman, Ne., U.S. | B4 | 104 |
| Merrimon, N.C., U.S. | C6 | 110 |
| Merritt, B.C. | D7 | 69 |
| Merritt, In., U.S. | A8 | 91 |
| Merritt Island, Fl., U.S. | D6 | 86 |
| Merritt Reservoir, res., Ne., U.S. | B5 | 104 |
| Merriwa, Austl. | F8 | 51 |
| Merriweather, Mi., U.S. | m12 | 99 |
| Mer Rouge, La., U.S. | B4 | 95 |
| Merrow, Ct., U.S. | B6 | 84 |
| Merry Hill, N.C., U.S. | A6 | 110 |
| Merrymeeting Lake, l., N.H., U.S. | D4 | 106 |
| Merry Oaks, N.C., U.S. | B3 | 110 |
| Merryville, La., U.S. | D2 | 95 |
| Mersa Fatma, Eth. | B5 | 47 |
| Mersey, stm., Eng., U.K. | D5 | 10 |
| Merseyside, co., Eng., U.K. | A4 | 12 |
| Mershon, Ga., U.S. | E4 | 87 |
| Mersing, Malay. | E2 | 34 |
| Merti, Kenya | A6 | 48 |
| Mértola, Port. | D3 | 22 |
| Merton, Wi., U.S. | m11 | 126 |
| Mertz Glacier, ice, Ant. | C27 | 7 |
| Mertzon, Tx., U.S. | D2 | 120 |
| Méru, Fr. | C5 | 16 |
| Meru, Kenya | A6 | 48 |
| Meru, Mount, mtn., Tan. | B6 | 48 |
| Mervelier, Switz. | B4 | 21 |
| Merville, Fr. | D2 | 17 |
| Mervin, Sask. | D1 | 75 |
| Merwin Lake, res., Wa., U.S. | C3 | 124 |
| Merwin [-sur-Seine], Fr. | F3 | 17 |
| Merzifon, Tur. | B10 | 40 |
| Merzig, W. Ger. | E6 | 17 |
| Mesa, Az., U.S. | D4 | 80 |
| Mesa, Co., U.S. | B2 | 83 |
| Mesa, Id., U.S. | E2 | 89 |
| Mesa, co., Co., U.S. | C2 | 83 |
| Mesabi Range, hills, Mn., U.S. | C6 | 100 |
| Mesa Mountain, mtn., Co., U.S. | D4 | 83 |
| Mesa Verde National Park, Co., U.S. | D2 | 83 |
| Mescalero, N.M., U.S. | D4 | 108 |
| Mescalero Indian Reservation, N.M., U.S. | D4 | 108 |
| Meschede, W. Ger. | B3 | 19 |
| Mesegon, i., Micron. | Q18 | 52 |
| Meservey, Ia., U.S. | B4 | 92 |
| Meshcherskoye, Sov. Un. | n17 | 27 |
| Meshchovsk, Sov. Un. | D10 | 27 |
| Meshkovskaya, Sov. Un. | G13 | 27 |
| Meshomasic Mountain, mtn., Ct., U.S. | C5 | 84 |
| Meshoppen, Pa., U.S. | C9 | 115 |
| Mesic, N.C., U.S. | B6 | 110 |
| Mesick, Mi., U.S. | D5 | 99 |
| Mesilinka, stm., B.C. | A5 | 69 |
| Mesilla, N.M., U.S. | E3 | 108 |
| Mesita, Co., U.S. | D5 | 83 |
| Mesita, N.M., U.S. | C2 | 108 |
| Mesocco, Switz. | C5 | 20 |
| Mesólongion, Grc. | C3 | 40 |
| Mesquita, Braz. | B4 | 56 |
| Mesquite, Nv., U.S. | G7 | 105 |
| Mesquite, N.M., U.S. | E3 | 108 |
| Mesquite, Tx., U.S. | n10 | 120 |
| Messalonskee Lake, l., Me., U.S. | D3 | 96 |
| Messápion Óros, mtn., Grc. | g10 | 25 |
| Messen, Switz. | B3 | 21 |
| Messina, Italy | E5 | 23 |
| Messina, S. Afr. | B5 | 49 |
| Messina, Strait of, strt., Italy | E5 | 23 |
| Messíni, Grc. | D3 | 25 |
| Messíni, Gulf of, b., Grc. | D4 | 25 |
| Messkirch, W. Ger. | B5 | 20 |
| Mesta (Néstos), stm., Eur. | B4 | 25 |
| Mestghanem (Mostaganem), Alg. | B5 | 44 |
| Mestre, Italy | B4 | 23 |
| Mesudiye, Tur. | B11 | 40 |
| Meta, Mo., U.S. | C5 | 102 |
| Meta, dept., Col. | C3 | 60 |
| Meta, stm., S.A. | B4 | 60 |
| Métabetchouane, stm., Que. | A5 | 74 |
| Meta Incognita Peninsula, pen., N.W. Ter. | D19 | 66 |
| Metairie, La., U.S. | k11 | 95 |
| Metaline Falls, Wa., U.S. | A8 | 124 |
| Metamora, Il., U.S. | C4 | 90 |
| Metamora, In., U.S. | F7 | 91 |
| Metamora, Mi., U.S. | F7 | 99 |
| Metamora, Oh., U.S. | A2 | 112 |
| Metán, Arg. | E3 | 55 |
| Metapán, El Sal. | C3 | 62 |
| Metaponto, Italy | D6 | 23 |
| Metarica, Moz. | D6 | 48 |
| Meta Pond, l., Newf. | D4 | 72 |
| Métascouac, Lac, l., Que. | B6 | 74 |
| Metasville, Ga., U.S. | C4 | 87 |
| Metcalf, Ga., U.S. | F3 | 87 |
| Metcalf, Il., U.S. | D6 | 90 |
| Metcalfe, Ont. | B9 | 73 |
| Metcalfe, Ms., U.S. | B2 | 101 |
| Metcalfe, co., Ky., U.S. | C4 | 94 |
| Metchosin, B.C. | h12 | 69 |
| Metedeconk, North Branch, stm., N.J., U.S. | C4 | 107 |
| Metedeconk, South Branch, stm., N.J., U.S. | C3 | 107 |
| Meteghan, N.S. | E3 | 71 |
| Meteghan River, N.S. | E3 | 71 |
| Meteghan Station, N.S. | E3 | 71 |
| Metema, Eth. | C4 | 47 |
| Meteor Crater, crat., Az., U.S. | C4 | 80 |
| Methóni, Grc. | D3 | 25 |
| Methow, Wa., U.S. | A5 | 124 |
| Methow, stm., Wa., U.S. | A5 | 124 |
| Methuen, Ma., U.S. | A5 | 98 |
| Metiskow, Alta. | C5 | 68 |
| Metković, Yugo. | D3 | 24 |
| Metlakatla, Ak., U.S. | D13 | 79 |
| Meto, Bayou, stm., Ar., U.S. | C4 | 81 |
| Metolius, Or., U.S. | C5 | 114 |
| Metonga, Lake, l., Wi., U.S. | C5 | 126 |
| Metropolis, Il., U.S. | F5 | 90 |
| Metropolitana, prov., Chile | A2 | 54 |
| Métsovon, Grc. | C3 | 25 |
| Mettawee, stm., U.S. | E2 | 122 |
| Metten, W. Ger. | E7 | 19 |
| Metter, Ga., U.S. | D4 | 87 |
| Mettet, Bel. | D4 | 17 |
| Mettingen, W. Ger. | A2 | 19 |
| Mettmann, W. Ger. | B1 | 19 |
| Metuchen, N.J., U.S. | B4 | 107 |
| Metula, Isr. | A7 | 41 |
| Metz, Fr. | C7 | 16 |
| Metz, In., U.S. | A8 | 91 |
| Metz, Mo., U.S. | C3 | 102 |
| Metzeral, Fr. | B3 | 20 |
| Metzger, Or., U.S. | h12 | 114 |
| Meudon, Fr. | g9 | 16 |
| Meulaboh, Indon. | m11 | 34 |
| Meung, Fr. | D4 | 16 |
| Meureudu, Indon. | J2 | 35 |
| Meurthe, stm., Fr. | D7 | 17 |
| Meurthe-et-Moselle, dept., Fr. | F6 | 17 |
| Meuse, dept., Fr. | E5 | 17 |
| Meuse (Maas), stm., Eur. | C6 | 16 |
| Meuse, Côtes de, mts., Fr. | C6 | 16 |
| Meuselwitz, E. Ger. | B7 | 19 |
| Mexia, Al., U.S. | D2 | 78 |
| Mexia, Tx., U.S. | D4 | 120 |
| Mexia, Lake, res., Tx., U.S. | D4 | 120 |
| Mexicali, Mex. | A1 | 63 |
| Mexican Hat, Ut., U.S. | F6 | 121 |
| Mexican Springs, N.M., U.S. | B1 | 108 |
| Mexico, In., U.S. | C5 | 91 |
| Mexico, Ky., U.S. | e9 | 94 |
| Mexico, Me., U.S. | D2 | 96 |
| Mexico, Mo., U.S. | B6 | 102 |
| Mexico, N.Y., U.S. | B4 | 109 |
| Mexico, Pa., U.S. | E7 | 115 |
| México, ctry., N.A. | D5 | 63 |
| Mexico, Gulf of, b., N.A. | G11 | 61 |
| Mexico City, Mex. | D5 | 63 |
| Meycauayan, Phil. | o13 | 34 |
| Meydân-e Gel, pl., Iran | G7 | 39 |
| Meydanī, Ra's-e, c., Iran | C5 | 38 |
| Meyers Chuck, Ak., U.S. | n23 | 79 |
| Meyersdale, Pa., U.S. | G3 | 115 |
| Meyísti, i., Grc. | D7 | 25 |
| Meymaneh, Afg. | A4 | 36 |
| Meyrin, Switz. | D1 | 21 |
| Meyronne, Sask. | H2 | 75 |
| Mèze, Fr. | F5 | 16 |
| Mezen, Sov. Un. | C7 | 29 |
| Mezen, stm., Sov. Un. | C7 | 29 |
| Mézenc, Mont, mtn., Fr. | E6 | 16 |
| Mézières, Fr. | C6 | 16 |
| Mezőkövesd, Hung. | B5 | 24 |
| Mezőtúr, Hung. | B5 | 24 |
| Mezzana, Italy | C6 | 20 |
| Mezzolombardo, Italy | C7 | 20 |
| Mga, Sov. Un. | s32 | 14 |
| Mga, stm., Sov. Un. | s32 | 14 |
| Mglin, Sov. Un. | E9 | 27 |
| Mhôr, Beinn, mtn., Scot., U.K. | C1 | 13 |
| Mhôr, Loch, l., Scot., U.K. | C4 | 13 |
| Mhow, India | F5 | 37 |
| Miahuatlán de Porfirio Díaz, Mex. | D5 | 63 |
| Miajadas, Spain | C3 | 22 |
| Miami, Man. | E2 | 70 |
| Miami, Az., U.S. | D5 | 80 |
| Miami, Fl., U.S. | G6 | 86 |
| Miami, In., U.S. | C5 | 91 |
| Miami, Mo., U.S. | B4 | 102 |
| Miami, N.M., U.S. | A5 | 108 |
| Miami, Ok., U.S. | A7 | 113 |
| Miami, Tx., U.S. | B2 | 120 |
| Miami, W.V., U.S. | m13 | 125 |
| Miami, co., In., U.S. | C5 | 91 |
| Miami, co., Ks., U.S. | D9 | 93 |
| Miami, co., Oh., U.S. | B1 | 112 |
| Miami Beach, Fl., U.S. | G6 | 86 |
| Miami Canal, Fl., U.S. | F6 | 86 |
| Miami International Airport, Fl., U.S. | *G6 | 86 |
| Miami Lakes, Fl., U.S. | *G6 | 86 |
| Miamisburg, Oh., U.S. | C1 | 112 |
| Miami Shores, Fl., U.S. | G6 | 86 |
| Miami Springs, Fl., U.S. | G6 | 86 |
| Miamitown, Oh., U.S. | o12 | 112 |
| Miāndoāb, Iran | C3 | 39 |
| Miandrivazo, Madag. | g9 | 49 |
| Miāneh, Iran | D7 | 34 |
| Miangas Island, i., Indon. | D7 | 34 |
| Mianning, China | F5 | 31 |
| Mianus Reservoir, res., U.S. | E1 | 84 |
| Miānwāli, Pak. | B5 | 36 |
| Mianyang, China | E1 | 32 |
| Mianyang, China | I5 | 32 |
| Miarinarivo, Madag. | g9 | 49 |
| Miass, Sov. Un. | C6 | 28 |
| Miass, stm., Sov. Un. | B6 | 28 |
| Miasteczko Śląskie, Pol. | f9 | 26 |
| Miastko, Pol. | A4 | 26 |
| Mica, Wa., U.S. | B8 | 124 |
| Mica Creek, B.C. | C9 | 69 |
| Mica Mountain, mtn., Az., U.S. | E5 | 80 |
| Micanopy, Fl., U.S. | C4 | 86 |
| Micco, Fl., U.S. | E6 | 86 |
| Miccosukee, Fl., U.S. | B2 | 86 |
| Miccosukee, Lake, res., Fl., U.S. | B2 | 86 |
| Michael, Il., U.S. | D3 | 90 |
| Michael, Lake, l., Newf. | A2 | 72 |
| Michalovce, Czech. | D6 | 24 |
| Michałów-Reginów, Pol. | k13 | 26 |
| Michaud, Point, c., N.S. | D9 | 71 |
| Michelson, Mount, mtn., Ak., U.S. | B11 | 79 |
| Michendorf, E. Ger. | A8 | 19 |
| Michichi, Alta. | D4 | 68 |
| Michie, Tn., U.S. | B3 | 119 |
| Michigamme, Mi., U.S. | B2 | 99 |
| Michigamme, Lake, l., Mi., U.S. | B2 | 99 |
| Michigamme Reservoir, res., Mi., U.S. | B2 | 99 |
| Michigan, N.D., U.S. | A7 | 111 |
| Michigan, state, U.S. | E6 | 99 |
| Michigan, stm., Co., U.S. | A4 | 83 |
| Michigan, Lake, l., U.S. | B10 | 76 |
| Michigan Center, Mi., U.S. | F6 | 99 |
| Michigan City, In., U.S. | A4 | 91 |
| Michigan City, Ms., U.S. | A4 | 101 |
| Michigan Island, i., Wi., U.S. | B3 | 126 |
| Michigan Prairie, reg., Wa., U.S. | C7 | 124 |
| Michigantown, In., U.S. | D5 | 91 |
| Michoacán, state, Mex. | D4 | 63 |
| Michurin (Tsarevo), Bul. | D8 | 24 |
| Michurinsk, Sov. Un. | E13 | 27 |
| Micoud, St. Luc. | J14 | 64 |
| Micro, N.C., U.S. | B4 | 110 |
| Micronesia, Federated States of, ter., T.T.P.I. | F9 | 6 |
| Midai, i., Indon. | K7 | 35 |
| Midale, Sask. | H4 | 75 |
| Midas, Id., U.S. | A2 | 89 |
| Middelburg, Neth. | B5 | 16 |
| Middelburg, S. Afr. | D4 | 49 |
| Middelfart, Den. | C3 | 15 |
| Middelharnis, Neth. | C4 | 17 |
| Middelkerke, Bel. | C2 | 17 |
| Middle, Ia., U.S. | C6 | 92 |
| Middle, stm., B.C. | B5 | 69 |
| Middle, stm., Ia., U.S. | C3 | 92 |
| Middle, stm., Mn., U.S. | B2 | 100 |
| Middle Andaman, i., India | F9 | 36 |
| Middleboro, Ma., U.S. | C6 | 98 |
| Middlebourne, W.V., U.S. | B4 | 125 |
| Middlebranch, Oh., U.S. | B4 | 112 |
| Middlebro, Man. | E4 | 70 |
| Middlebrook, Va., U.S. | B3 | 123 |
| Middleburg, Fl., U.S. | B5 | 86 |
| Middleburg, Ky., U.S. | C5 | 94 |
| Middleburg, Md., U.S. | A3 | 97 |
| Middleburg, N.C., U.S. | A4 | 110 |
| Middleburg, Pa., U.S. | E7 | 115 |
| Middleburg, Va., U.S. | B5 | 123 |
| Middleburgh, N.Y., U.S. | C6 | 109 |
| Middleburg Heights, Oh., U.S. | h9 | 112 |
| Middlebury, Ct., U.S. | C3 | 84 |
| Middlebury, In., U.S. | A6 | 91 |
| Middlebury, Vt., U.S. | C2 | 122 |
| Middlefield, Ct., U.S. | C5 | 84 |
| Middlefield, Ma., U.S. | B1 | 98 |
| Middlefield, Oh., U.S. | A4 | 112 |
| Middle Granville, N.Y., U.S. | B7 | 109 |
| Middle Ground, rf., Mid. Is. | J3 | 52 |
| Middle Island, Ct., U.S. | C5 | 84 |
| Middle Island, N.Y., U.S. | *n16 | 109 |
| Middle Island Creek, stm., W.V., U.S. | B3 | 125 |
| Middle Loup, stm., Ne., U.S. | C5 | 104 |
| Middle Musquodoboit, N.S. | D6 | 71 |
| Middle Nodaway, stm., Ia., U.S. | C3 | 92 |
| Middle Park, val., Co., U.S. | A4 | 83 |
| Middle Patuxent, stm., Md., U.S. | B4 | 97 |
| Middle Point, Oh., U.S. | B1 | 112 |
| Middleport, N.Y., U.S. | B2 | 109 |
| Middleport, Oh., U.S. | C3 | 112 |
| Middle Raccoon, stm., Ia., U.S. | C3 | 92 |
| Middle River, Md., U.S. | B5 | 97 |
| Middle River, Mn., U.S. | B2 | 100 |
| Middlesboro, Ky., U.S. | D6 | 94 |
| Middlesbrough (Teesside), Eng., U.K. | C6 | 10 |
| Middlesex, Belize | B2 | 62 |
| Middlesex, N.J., U.S. | B4 | 107 |
| Middlesex, N.Y., U.S. | C3 | 109 |
| Middlesex, N.C., U.S. | B4 | 110 |
| Middlesex, Vt., U.S. | C3 | 122 |
| Middlesex, co., Ct., U.S. | D5 | 84 |
| Middlesex, co., Ma., U.S. | A5 | 98 |
| Middlesex, co., N.J., U.S. | C3 | 107 |
| Middlesex, co., Ont. | D3 | 73 |
| Middlesex, co., Va., U.S. | C6 | 123 |
| Middlesex Fells Reservation, Ma., U.S. | g11 | 98 |
| Middle Stewiacke, N.S. | D6 | 71 |
| Middleton, N.S. | E4 | 71 |
| Middleton, Id., U.S. | F2 | 89 |
| Middleton, Ma., U.S. | A5 | 98 |
| Middleton, Mi., U.S. | E6 | 99 |
| Middleton, Tn., U.S. | B3 | 119 |
| Middleton, Wi., U.S. | E4 | 126 |
| Middletown, Ca., U.S. | C2 | 82 |
| Middletown, Ct., U.S. | C5 | 84 |
| Middletown, De., U.S. | C3 | 85 |
| Middletown, Il., U.S. | C4 | 90 |
| Middletown, In., U.S. | D6 | 91 |
| Middletown, Ia., U.S. | D6 | 92 |
| Middletown, Ky., U.S. | g11 | 94 |
| Middletown, Md., U.S. | B2 | 97 |
| Middletown, N.J., U.S. | C4 | 107 |
| Middletown, N.Y., U.S. | D6 | 109 |
| Middletown, Oh., U.S. | C1 | 112 |
| Middletown, Pa., U.S. | F8 | 115 |
| Middletown, R.I., U.S. | E5 | 116 |
| Middletown, Va., U.S. | A4 | 123 |
| Middletown Springs, Vt., U.S. | E2 | 122 |
| Middletown Township, Pa., U.S. | *G11 | 115 |
| Middle Valley, N.J., U.S. | B3 | 107 |
| Middleville, Mi., U.S. | F5 | 99 |
| Middleville, N.J., U.S. | A3 | 107 |
| Middleville, N.Y., U.S. | B6 | 109 |
| Midelt, Mor. | B4 | 44 |
| Midfield, Al., U.S. | g7 | 78 |
| Midgic, N.B. | D5 | 71 |
| Mid Glamorgan, co., Wales, U.K. | C4 | 12 |
| Midi d'Ossau, Pic du, mtn., Fr. | F3 | 16 |
| Midkiff, Tx., U.S. | D2 | 120 |
| Midkiff, W.V., U.S. | C2 | 125 |
| Midland, Ont. | C5 | 73 |
| Midland, Ar., U.S. | B1 | 81 |
| Midland, La., U.S. | D3 | 95 |
| Midland, Md., U.S. | k13 | 97 |
| Midland, Mi., U.S. | E6 | 99 |
| Midland, N.C., U.S. | B2 | 110 |
| Midland, Oh., U.S. | C2 | 112 |
| Midland, Pa., U.S. | E1 | 115 |
| Midland, S.D., U.S. | C4 | 118 |
| Midland, Tx., U.S. | D1 | 120 |
| Midland, co., Mi., U.S. | E6 | 99 |
| Midland, co., Tx., U.S. | D1 | 120 |
| Midland Basin, Co., U.S. | A2 | 83 |
| Midland City, Al., U.S. | D4 | 78 |
| Midland Park, Ks., U.S. | g12 | 93 |
| Midland Park, N.J., U.S. | B4 | 107 |
| Midland Park, S.C., U.S. | k11 | 117 |
| Midleton, Ire. | E2 | 10 |
| Midlothian, Il., U.S. | k9 | 90 |
| Midlothian, Md., U.S. | k13 | 97 |
| Midlothian, Tx., U.S. | C4 | 120 |
| Midlothian, Va., U.S. | m17 | 123 |
| Midnapore, Alta. | D3 | 68 |
| Midnight, Ms., U.S. | B3 | 101 |
| Midongy Sud, Madag. | h9 | 49 |
| Midpines, Ca., U.S. | D4 | 82 |
| Midreshet Ben Gurion, Isr. | D6 | 41 |
| Midvale, Id., U.S. | E2 | 89 |
| Midvale, Oh., U.S. | B4 | 112 |
| Midvale, Ut., U.S. | C4 | 121 |
| Midville, Ga., U.S. | D4 | 87 |
| Midway, B.C. | E8 | 69 |
| Midway, Al., U.S. | C4 | 78 |
| Midway, De., U.S. | F5 | 85 |
| Midway, Ga., U.S. | E5 | 87 |
| Midway, Ky., U.S. | B5 | 94 |
| Midway, Or., U.S. | *B4 | 114 |
| Midway, Pa., U.S. | G7 | 115 |
| Midway, Tn., U.S. | C11 | 119 |
| Midway, Ut., U.S. | C4 | 121 |
| Midway Islands, dep., Oc. | E11 | 6 |
| Midway Naval Station, mil., Mid. Is. | K3 | 52 |
| Midway Range, mts., B.C. | C6 | 69 |
| Midwest, Wy., U.S. | C6 | 127 |
| Midwest City, Ok., U.S. | B4 | 113 |
| Midyat, Tur. | D13 | 40 |
| Miechów, Pol. | C3 | 26 |
| Miedzychód, Pol. | B3 | 26 |
| Międzyrzec [Podlaski], Pol. | C7 | 26 |
| Międzyrzecz, Pol. | B3 | 26 |
| Międzyzdroje, Pol. | B3 | 26 |
| Mielec, Pol. | C7 | 26 |
| Mien, l., Swe. | B8 | 15 |
| Mienia, stm., Pol. | m14 | 26 |
| Mier, In., U.S. | C6 | 91 |
| Miercurea Ciuc, Rom. | C8 | 24 |
| Mieres, Spain | A3 | 22 |
| Miesbach, W. Ger. | D5 | 20 |
| Mieso, Eth. | D5 | 47 |
| Mifflin, Pa., U.S. | E7 | 115 |
| Mifflin, Tn., U.S. | B3 | 119 |
| Mifflin, co., Pa., U.S. | E6 | 115 |
| Mifflinburg, Pa., U.S. | E7 | 115 |
| Mifflintown, Pa., U.S. | E7 | 115 |
| Mifflinville, Pa., U.S. | D9 | 115 |
| Migdal, Isr. | B7 | 41 |
| Migennes, Fr. | D5 | 16 |
| Migliarino, Italy | E7 | 20 |
| Miguel Alemán, Presa, res., Mex. | D5 | 63 |
| Miguel Alves, Braz. | B2 | 57 |
| Miguel Auza, Mex. | C4 | 63 |
| Mihai Viteazu, Rom. | C9 | 24 |
| Mihama, Japan | o15 | 33 |
| Mijares, stm., Spain | B5 | 22 |
| Mijdahah, Yemen | C3 | 92 |
| Mikado, Sask. | F4 | 75 |
| Mikado, Mi., U.S. | D7 | 99 |
| Mikana, Wi., U.S. | C2 | 126 |
| Mikha Tskhakaya, Sov. Un. | A14 | 40 |
| Mikhaylov, Sov. Un. | D12 | 27 |
| Mikhaylovgrad, Bul. | D6 | 24 |
| Mikhaylovka, Sov. Un. | G14 | 27 |
| Mikhaylovka, Sov. Un. | H10 | 27 |
| Mikhaylovskiy, Sov. Un. | C9 | 28 |
| Mikindani, Tan. | D7 | 48 |
| Mikkalo, Or., U.S. | B6 | 114 |
| Mikkeli, Fin. | G12 | 14 |
| Mikołów, Pol. | g9 | 26 |
| Míkonos, Grc. | D5 | 25 |
| Míkonos, i., Grc. | D5 | 25 |
| Mikope, Zaire | C5 | 48 |
| Mikulov, Czech. | E6 | 24 |
| Mikumi, Tan. | C6 | 48 |
| Mikura Island, i., Japan | E5 | 33 |
| Milaca, Mn., U.S. | E5 | 100 |
| Milagro, Ec. | B2 | 58 |
| Milam, W.V., U.S. | C5 | 125 |
| Milam, co., Tx., U.S. | D4 | 120 |
| Milan, Que. | D6 | 74 |
| Milan (Milano), Italy | D3 | 23 |
| Milan, Ga., U.S. | D3 | 87 |
| Milan, Il., U.S. | B3 | 90 |
| Milan, In., U.S. | F7 | 91 |
| Milan, Mi., U.S. | F7 | 99 |
| Milan, Mo., U.S. | A4 | 102 |
| Milan, N.H., U.S. | B4 | 106 |
| Milan, N.M., U.S. | B2 | 108 |
| Milan, Oh., U.S. | A3 | 112 |
| Milan, Tn., U.S. | B3 | 119 |
| Milan, Wa., U.S. | B8 | 124 |
| Milano, Tx., U.S. | D4 | 120 |
| Milâs, Tur. | D7 | 25 |
| Milazzo, Italy | E5 | 23 |
| Milbank, S.D., U.S. | B9 | 118 |
| Milbanke Sound, strt., B.C. | C3 | 69 |
| Milbridge, Me., U.S. | D5 | 96 |
| Milburn, Ok., U.S. | C5 | 113 |
| Milden, Sask. | F2 | 75 |
| Mildenhall, Eng., U.K. | B8 | 12 |
| Mildmay, Ont. | C3 | 73 |
| Mildred, Sask. | D2 | 75 |
| Mildred, Mt., U.S. | D12 | 103 |
| Mildura, Austl. | F7 | 50 |
| Mile, stm., Que. | p19 | 74 |
| Miles, Austl. | E9 | 51 |
| Miles, Ia., U.S. | B7 | 92 |
| Miles, Tx., U.S. | D2 | 120 |
| Miles City, Mt., U.S. | D11 | 103 |
| Miles Mountain, mtn., Vt., U.S. | A6 | 122 |
| Milestone, Sask. | G3 | 75 |
| Miletus, hist., Tur. | D7 | 25 |
| Miley, S.C., U.S. | F5 | 117 |
| Milfay, Ok., U.S. | B5 | 113 |
| Milford, Ca., U.S. | B3 | 82 |
| Milford, Ct., U.S. | E3 | 84 |
| Milford, De., U.S. | E4 | 85 |
| Milford, Il., U.S. | C6 | 90 |
| Milford, In., U.S. | B6 | 91 |
| Milford, Ia., U.S. | A2 | 92 |
| Milford, Ks., U.S. | C7 | 93 |
| Milford, Ky., U.S. | B5 | 94 |
| Milford, Me., U.S. | D4 | 96 |
| Milford, Ma., U.S. | B4 | 98 |
| Milford, Mi., U.S. | F7 | 99 |
| Milford, Mo., U.S. | D3 | 102 |
| Milford, Ne., U.S. | D8 | 104 |
| Milford, N.H., U.S. | E3 | 106 |
| Milford, N.J., U.S. | B2 | 107 |
| Milford, N.Y., U.S. | C6 | 109 |
| Milford, Oh., U.S. | C1 | 112 |
| Milford, Pa., U.S. | D12 | 115 |
| Milford, Ut., U.S. | E2 | 121 |
| Milford, Va., U.S. | B5 | 123 |
| Milford Center, Oh., U.S. | B2 | 112 |
| Milford Haven, Wales, U.K. | E4 | 10 |
| Milford Lake, res., Ks., U.S. | C6 | 93 |
| Milford Sound, strt., N.Z. | P11 | 51 |
| Milford Station, N.S. | D6 | 71 |
| Milh, Ra's al, c., Libya | F5 | 40 |
| Milicz, Pol. | C4 | 26 |
| Mililani Town, Hi., U.S. | g9 | 88 |
| Miling, Austl. | F2 | 50 |
| Milk, stm., N.A. | B8 | 103 |
| Milk Creek, stm., Co., U.S. | A3 | 83 |
| Milk River, Alta. | E4 | 68 |
| Milk River Ridge Reservoir, res., Alta. | E4 | 68 |
| Mill, stm., Ma., U.S. | h9 | 98 |
| Milladore, Wi., U.S. | D4 | 126 |
| Millard, Ky., U.S. | C7 | 94 |
| Millard, Mo., U.S. | A5 | 102 |
| Millard, co., Ut., U.S. | D2 | 121 |
| Millarton, N.D., U.S. | C7 | 111 |
| Millau, Fr. | E5 | 16 |
| Millbank, Ont. | D4 | 73 |
| Millboro, S.D., U.S. | D6 | 118 |
| Millboro, Va., U.S. | C3 | 123 |
| Millbrae, Ca., U.S. | h8 | 82 |
| Millbridge, Ont. | C7 | 73 |
| Millbrook, Ont. | C6 | 73 |
| Millbrook, Al., U.S. | C3 | 78 |
| Millbrook, Mi., U.S. | E5 | 99 |
| Millbrook, N.Y., U.S. | D7 | 109 |
| Mill Brook, stm., Vt., U.S. | B5 | 122 |
| Millburn, N.J., U.S. | B4 | 107 |
| Millbury, Ma., U.S. | B4 | 98 |
| Millbury, Oh., U.S. | e7 | 112 |
| Mill City, Nv., U.S. | C3 | 105 |
| Mill City, Or., U.S. | C4 | 114 |
| Mill City, Pa., U.S. | m17 | 115 |
| Mill Creek, In., U.S. | A4 | 91 |
| Mill Creek, Ok., U.S. | C5 | 113 |
| Mill Creek, Pa., U.S. | F6 | 115 |
| Mill Creek, Ut., U.S. | C4 | 121 |
| Mill Creek, W.V., U.S. | C5 | 125 |
| Mill Creek, stm., In., U.S. | F4 | 91 |
| Mill Creek, stm., Ks., U.S. | C7 | 93 |
| Mill Creek, stm., Ks., U.S. | C6 | 93 |
| Mill Creek, stm., N.J., U.S. | n15 | 63 |
| Mill Creek, stm., Oh., U.S. | B2 | 112 |
| Mill Creek, stm., W.V., U.S. | B2 | 125 |
| Mill Creek, stm., In., U.S. | F5 | 85 |
| Mill Dale Colony, S.D., U.S. | G13 | 27 |
| Miller Peak, mtn., Az., U.S. | F5 | 80 |
| Miller Place, N.Y., U.S. | *n16 | 109 |
| Miller Run, stm., Vt., U.S. | B4 | 122 |
| Millers, stm., Ma., U.S. | A3 | 98 |
| Millersburg, In., U.S. | A6 | 91 |
| Millersburg, Ky., U.S. | B5 | 94 |
| Millersburg, Mi., U.S. | C6 | 99 |
| Millersburg, Oh., U.S. | B4 | 112 |
| Millersburg, Pa., U.S. | E8 | 115 |
| Millers Falls, Ma., U.S. | A3 | 98 |
| Millers Ferry, Al., U.S. | C2 | 78 |
| Millers Ferry Dam, Al., U.S. | C2 | 78 |
| Millerstown, Pa., U.S. | E7 | 115 |
| Millersview, Tx., U.S. | D3 | 120 |
| Millersville, Oh., U.S. | *n12 | 112 |
| Millersville, Pa., U.S. | F9 | 115 |
| Millerton, N.B. | B4 | 71 |
| Millerton, Ia., U.S. | D4 | 92 |
| Millerton, N.Y., U.S. | D7 | 109 |
| Millerton, Ok., U.S. | D6 | 113 |
| Millerton Lake, res., Ca., U.S. | D4 | 82 |
| Mill Grove, In., U.S. | D7 | 91 |
| Millgrove, Mo., U.S. | A4 | 102 |
| Mill Hall, Pa., U.S. | D7 | 115 |
| Millhousen, In., U.S. | F7 | 91 |
| Millhurst, N.J., U.S. | C4 | 107 |
| Millican, Alta. | D3 | 68 |
| Milligan, Fl., U.S. | u15 | 86 |
| Milligan, Ne., U.S. | D8 | 104 |
| Milligan College, Tn., U.S. | C11 | 119 |
| Milliken, Co., U.S. | A6 | 83 |
| Millington, Md., U.S. | B6 | 97 |
| Millington, Mi., U.S. | E7 | 99 |
| Millington, Tn., U.S. | B2 | 119 |
| Millinocket, Me., U.S. | C4 | 96 |
| Millinocket Lake, l., Me., U.S. | B4 | 96 |
| Millinocket Lake, l., Me., U.S. | C4 | 96 |

| Name | Map Ref. | Page |
|---|---|---|

Mill Iron, Mt., U.S. ........ E12 103
Millis, Ma., U.S. .......... B5 98
Mill Island, i., Ant. ....... C23 7
Millmerran, Austl. ........ C8 51
Millom, Eng., U.K. ....... F5 13
Mill Point, W.V., U.S. ..... C4 125
Millport, Scot., U.K. ...... E4 13
Millport, Al., U.S. ........ B1 78
Millport, Pa., U.S. ........ C5 115
Millrift, Pa., U.S. ........ D12 115
Mill River, Ma., U.S. ...... B1 98
Mill Run, Pa., U.S. ....... G3 115
Millry, Al., U.S. .......... D1 78
Mills, Ne., U.S. .......... B6 104
Mills, N.M., U.S. ......... A5 108
Mills, Pa., U.S. .......... C6 115
Mills, Wy., U.S. .......... D6 127
Mills, co., Ia., U.S. ....... C2 92
Mills, co., Tx., U.S. ....... D3 120
Millsboro, De., U.S. ....... F4 85
Millsboro, Pa., U.S. ....... G1 115
Mill Shoals, Il., U.S. ...... E5 90
Mills Lake, l., N.W. Ter. ... D9 66
Mill Spring, Mo., U.S. ..... D7 102
Millstadt, Il., U.S. ....... E3 90
Millston, Wi., U.S. ....... D3 126
Millstone, N.J., U.S. ...... B3 107
Millstone, stm., N.J., U.S. .. C4 107
Millstreet, Ire. .......... E2 11
Milltown, Al., U.S. ....... C4 78
Milltown, In., U.S. ....... H5 91
Milltown, Ky., U.S. ....... C4 94
Milltown, Mt., U.S. ....... D3 103
Milltown, N.J., U.S. ...... C4 107
Milltown, S.D., U.S. ...... D8 118
Milltown, Wi., U.S. ....... C1 126
Milltown [-Head of Bay d'Espoir], Newf. ...... E4 72
Milltown Malbay, Ire. ..... E2 11
Millvale, Pa., U.S. ....... k14 115
Mill Valley, Ca., U.S. ..... D2 82
Mill Village, N.S. ........ E5 71
Mill Village, Pa., U.S. ..... C2 115
Millville, N.B. ........... C2 71
Millville, De., U.S. ....... F5 85
Millville, Ky., U.S. ....... B5 94
Millville, Ma., U.S. ...... B4 98
Millville, N.J., U.S. ...... E2 107
Millville, Oh., U.S. ....... n12 112
Millville, Pa., U.S. ....... D9 115
Millville, Ut., U.S. ....... B4 121
Millville, W.V., U.S. ...... B7 125
Millville Lake, N.H., U.S. .. E4 106
Millwood, Ga., U.S. ...... E4 87
Millwood, Oh., U.S. ...... B3 112
Millwood, Va., U.S. ...... A4 123
Millwood, Wa., U.S. ...... g14 124
Millwood Lake, res., Ar., U.S. D1 81
Milmay, N.J., U.S. ....... E3 107
Milner, B.C. ............ f13 69
Milner, Co., U.S. ........ A3 83
Milner, Ga., U.S. ........ C2 87
Milner Dam, Id., U.S. ..... G5 89
Milner Ridge, Man. ....... D3 70
Milnesand, N.M., U.S. ..... D6 108
Milnor, N.D., U.S. ....... C8 111
Milo, Alta. ............. D4 68
Milo, Ia., U.S. .......... C4 92
Milo, Me., U.S. .......... C4 96
Milo, Or., U.S. .......... E3 114
Miloli'i, Hi., U.S. ........ D6 88
Mílos, i., Grc. .......... D5 40
Milparinka, Austl. ........ D3 51
Milpitas, Ca., U.S. ....... *k9 82
Milroy, In., U.S. ......... F7 91
Milroy, Mn., U.S. ........ F3 100
Milroy, Pa., U.S. ......... E6 115
Milstead, Al., U.S. ....... C4 78
Milstead, Ga., U.S. ....... C3 87
Miltenberg, W. Ger. ...... D4 19
Milton, N.S. ............ E5 71
Milton, Ont. ............ D5 73
Milton, N.Z. ............ Q12 51
Milton, Ct., U.S. ........ B2 84
Milton, De., U.S. ........ F4 85
Milton, Fl., U.S. ........ u14 86
Milton, Il., U.S. ........ D3 90
Milton, In., U.S. ........ E7 91
Milton, Ia., U.S. ........ D5 92
Milton, Ks., U.S. ........ E6 93
Milton, Ky., U.S. ........ B4 94
Milton, La., U.S. ........ D3 95
Milton, Ma., U.S. ........ B5 98
Milton, N.H., U.S. ....... D5 106
Milton, N.Y., U.S. ....... D7 109
Milton, N.C., U.S. ....... A3 110
Milton, N.D., U.S. ....... A7 111
Milton, Pa., U.S. ........ D8 115
Milton, Vt., U.S. ........ B2 122
Milton, Wa., U.S. ........ f11 124
Milton, W.V., U.S. ....... C2 125
Milton, Wi., U.S. ........ F5 126
Milton, Lake, l., Oh., U.S. .. A4 112
Miltona, Mn., U.S. ....... D3 100
Miltona, Lake, l., Mn., U.S. .. D3 100
Milton-Freewater, Or., U.S. .. B8 114
Milton Keynes, Eng., U.K. .. B7 12
Milton Mills, N.H., U.S. .... C5 106
Milton Reservoir, res., Co., U.S. .............. A6 83
Miltonvale, Ks., U.S. ..... C6 93
Milverton, Ont. ......... D4 73
Milwaukee, N.C., U.S. .... A5 110
Milwaukee, Wi., U.S. ..... E6 126
Milwaukee, co., Wi., U.S. .. E6 126
Milwaukee, stm., Wi., U.S. .. m12 126
Milwaukie, Or., U.S. ..... B4 114
Mimbres, N.M., U.S. ..... E2 108
Mimbres Mountains, mts., N.M., U.S. ......... E2 108
Mimico (part of Etobicoke), Ont. ............ m15 73
Mimizan, Fr. ........... E3 16
Mimoň, Czech. ......... C9 19
Mimongo, Gabon ........ E2 46
Mimosa Park, La., U.S. ... *E5 95
Mims, Fl., U.S. ......... D6 86
Mina, Nv., U.S. ......... E3 105
Mina, S.D., U.S. ........ B7 118
Minā' al Aḥmadī, Kuw. .... C4 38
Mīnāb, Iran ............ H8 39
Minago, stm., Man. ...... B2 70
Minaki, Ont. ........... o16 73
Minamata, Japan ........ J5 33
Minami-iwo, i., Japan ..... E8 6
Minami-Tori Island, i., Japan . E9 6
Minas, Cuba ........... D6 64
Minas, Ur. ............. E1 56
Minas Basin, b., N.S. ..... D5 71
Minas Channel, strt., N.S. .. D5 71
Minas de Corrales, Ur. .... E1 56
Minas de Ríotinto, Spain ... D2 22
Minas Gerais, state, Braz. .. B4 56

Minas Novas, Braz. ....... B4 56
Minatare, Ne., U.S. ....... C2 104
Minatitlán, Mex. ......... D6 63
Minbu, Burma .......... D9 36
Minbya, Burma .......... D9 36
Minburn, Alta. .......... C5 68
Minburn, Ia., U.S. ....... C3 92
Minco, Ok., U.S. ......... B4 113
Mindanao, i., Phil. ....... D6 34
Mindel, stm., W. Ger. ..... A6 20
Mindelheim, W. Ger. ...... A6 20
Mindemoya, Ont. ........ B2 73
Minden, Ont. ........... C6 73
Minden, W. Ger. ......... B4 18
Minden, La., U.S. ........ B2 95
Minden, Ne., U.S. ....... D7 104
Minden, Nv., U.S. ....... E2 105
Minden, W.V., U.S. ...... D3 125
Minden City, Mi., U.S. .... E8 99
Mindi, Pan. ............ k11 62
Mindoro, Wi., U.S. ....... D2 126
Mindoro, i., Phil. ........ C6 34
Mindoro Strait, strt., Phil. .. C6 34
Mine Centre, Ont. ....... E5 70
Minehead, Eng., U.K. ..... E5 10
Mine Head, c., Ire. ....... F4 11
Mine Hill, N.J., U.S. ...... B3 107
Mineiros, Braz. ......... B2 56
Mineola, Ia., U.S. ....... C2 92
Mineola, N.Y., U.S. ...... E7 109
Mineola, Tx., U.S. ....... C5 120
Miner, Mo., U.S. ........ E8 102
Miner, co., S.D., U.S. ..... D8 118
Mineral, Ca., U.S. ....... B3 82
Mineral, Il., U.S. ........ B4 90
Mineral, Va., U.S. ....... B5 123
Mineral, Wa., U.S. ....... C3 124
Mineral, co., Co., U.S. .... D4 83
Mineral, co., Mt., U.S. .... C1 103
Mineral, co., Nv., U.S. .... E3 105
Mineral, co., W.V., U.S. ... B6 125
Mineral City, Oh., U.S. .... B4 112
Mineral del Monte, Mex. ... m14 63
Mineral del Oro, Mex. ..... n13 63
Mineral Hills, Mi., U.S. .... B2 99
Mineral Mountains, mts., Ut., U.S. ............ E3 121
Mineral Park, Tn., U.S. .... h11 119
Mineral Point, Mo., U.S. ... D7 102
Mineral Point, Wi., U.S. ... F3 126
Mineral Springs, Ar., U.S. .. D2 81
Mineral Wells, Ms., U.S. ... A4 101
Mineral Wells, Tx., U.S. ... C3 120
Minersville, Oh., U.S. ..... C4 112
Minersville, Pa., U.S. ..... E9 115
Minersville, Ut., U.S. ..... E3 121
Minerva, N.Y., U.S. ...... B7 109
Minerva, Oh., U.S. ....... B4 112
Minervino Murge, Italy .... D6 23
Minetto, N.Y., U.S. ...... B4 109
Mineville, N.Y., U.S. ..... A7 109
Mingan, Que. ........... h8 72
Mingenew, Austl. ........ E2 50
Mingo, Ia., U.S. ........ C4 92
Mingo, co., W.V., U.S. .... D2 125
Mingo Junction, Oh., U.S. .. B5 112
Mingoyo, Tan. .......... D6 48
Mingshui, China ......... C4 31
Mingshui, China ......... C2 33
Mingue (Miño), stm., Eur. .. B1 22
Miñho, stm., Jam. ....... E14 65
Minho (Miño), stm., India .. G5 36
Minicoy Island, i., India ... G5 36
Minidoka, Id., U.S. ...... G5 89
Minidoka, co., Id., U.S. ... G5 89
Minidoka Dam, Id., U.S. ... G5 89
Minier, Il., U.S. ......... C4 90
Miniota, Man. .......... D1 70
Minipi Lake, l., Newf. ..... h9 72
Minisink Island, i., N.J., U.S. . A3 107
Minitonas, Man. ......... C1 70
Minna, Nig. ............ E6 45
Minna Bluff, pen., Ant. .... B29 7
Minneapolis, Ks., U.S. .... C6 93
Minneapolis, Mn., U.S. ... F5 100
Minneapolis, N.C., U.S. ... e11 110
Minnedosa, Man. ........ D2 70
Minnedosa, stm., Man. .... D1 70
Minnehaha, co., S.D., U.S. .. D9 118
Minneiska, Mn., U.S. ..... F7 100
Minneola, Ks., U.S. ...... E3 93
Minneola, Mn., U.S. ...... F3 100
Minneota, Mn., U.S. ...... F2 100
Minnesota, state, U.S. .... E4 100
Minnesota, stm., Mn., U.S. . F2 100
Minnesota Lake, Mn., U.S. . G5 100
Minnetonka, Mn., U.S. .... n12 100
Minnetonka, Lake, l., Mn., U.S. .............. n11 100
Minnewanka, Lake, l., Alta. .. D3 68
Minnewaska, Lake, l., Mn., U.S. ......... n15 100
Minnewaukan, N.D., U.S. .. A6 111
Minong, Wi., U.S. ....... C2 126
Miño (Minho), stm., Eur. ... A1 22
Minokamo, Japan ........ n15 33
Minong, Wi., U.S. ....... B2 126
Minonk, Il., U.S. ........ C4 90
Minooka, Il., U.S. ....... B5 90
Minor Hill, Tn., U.S. ..... B4 119
Minot, Ma., U.S. ........ h12 98
Minot, N.D., U.S. ....... A4 111
Minot Air Force Base, mil., N.D., U.S. ......... A4 111
Minqin, China .......... D5 31
Minquadale, De., U.S. .... i7 85
Minsen, W. Ger. ........ A7 17
Minsk, Sov. Un. ......... D5 29
Mińsk Mazowiecki, Pol. ... B6 26
Minster, Oh., U.S. ....... B1 112
Minter City, Ms., U.S. .... B3 101
Mint Hill, N.C., U.S. ..... B2 110
Minto, Man. ............ E1 70
Minto, N.B. ............ C3 71
Minto, Ak., U.S. ........ C10 79
Minto, N.D., U.S. ....... A8 111
Minto, Sask. ........... H3 75
Minto, Lac, l., Que. ...... g11 74
Minton, Sask. .......... H3 75
Minturn, Ar., U.S. ....... B4 81
Minturn, Co., U.S. ....... B4 83
Minturn, Me., U.S. ....... D4 96
Minturno, Italy ......... D4 23
Minūf, Eg. ............. D2 41
Minvoul, Gabon ........ E2 46

Minyā al Qamḥ, Eg. ...... D3 41
Minya Konka see Gongga Mountain, mtn., China ... F5 31
Mio, Mi., U.S. .......... D6 99
Miquelon, i., St. P./M. .... E3 72
Mira, Port. ............ B1 22
Mira, La., U.S. ......... B2 95
Mira, stm., Port. ........ D1 22
Mira, stm., S.A. ........ A2 58
Mira, Que. ............ D4 71
Miracema do Norte, Braz. .. D5 59
Miracle Hot Springs, Ca., U.S. E4 82
Mirador, Braz. .......... C2 57
Miraflores, Col. ......... C3 60
Miraflores, Peru ........ *D2 58
Miraflores Locks, Pan. .... m11 62
Miragoâne, Haiti ........ E7 64
Miraí, Braz. ........... g6 56
Miraj, India ........... D3 36
Mira Loma, Ca., U.S. .... *m13 82
Miramar, Arg. ......... B5 54
Miramar, Fl., U.S. ....... s13 86
Miramar Naval Air Station, mil., Ca., U.S. ....... F5 82
Miramichi Bay, b., N.B. .... B5 71
Miranda, Braz. ......... C1 56
Miranda, Col. .......... C2 60
Miranda, S.D., U.S. ...... C7 118
Miranda, state, Ven. ..... A4 60
Miranda, stm., Braz. ..... C1 56
Miranda de Ebro, Spain ... A4 22
Miranda do Douro, Port. ... B2 22
Mirande, Fr. ........... F4 16
Mirandela, Port. ........ B2 22
Mirando City, Tx., U.S. .... F3 120
Mirandola, Italy ........ E7 23
Mirassol, Braz. ......... C3 56
Miravalles, Volcán, vol., C.R. . E5 62
Mirbāṭ, Oman .......... D5 38
Mirebalais, Haiti ........ E7 64
Mirecourt, Fr. .......... C7 16
Mirgorod, Sov. Un. ...... G9 27
Miri, Malay. ........... E4 34
Miriam Vale, Austl. ...... B8 51
Mirim, Lagoa, b., S.A. .... E2 56
Mirina, Grc. ........... C6 40
Mirond Lake, l., Sask. ..... B4 75
Mirow, E. Ger. ......... E6 15
Mīrpur, Bngl. .......... *D9 36
Mīrpur Khās, Pak. ....... C4 36
Mirror, Alta. .......... C4 68
Mirror Lake, N.H., U.S. ... C4 106
Mirror Lake, l., N.H., U.S. .. C4 106
Mīrzāpur, India ......... H10 36
Misāhah, Bi'r, well, Eg. ... E5 43
Misakubo, Japan ........ n16 33
Misantla, Mex. ......... H5 63
Miscou Centre, N.B. ..... B5 71
Miscou Island, i., N.B. .... B5 71
Miscou Point, c., N.B. .... A5 71
Misenheimer, N.C., U.S. .. B2 110
Mishan, China ......... D6 33
Mishawaka, In., U.S. ..... A5 91
Misheguk Mountain, mtn., Ak., U.S. ......... B7 79
Mishicot, Wi., U.S. ...... D6 126
Mishima, Japan ........ I9 33
Misiones, prov., Arg. ..... E5 55
Misiones, dept., Para. .... E4 55
Miskitos, Cayos, is., Nic. .. E8 63
Miskolc, Hung. ........ A5 24
Misool, i., Indon. ....... F7 34
Misr al Jadīdah (Heliopolis) (part of Cairo), Eg. ..... D3 41
Misrātah, Libya ......... C3 43
Missaukee, co., Mi., U.S. .. D5 99
Missaukee, Lake, l., Mi., U.S. D5 99
Missinaibi, stm., Ont. ..... G16 66
Mission, Ks., U.S. ...... m16 93
Mission, S.D., U.S. ...... D5 118
Mission, Tx., U.S. ....... F3 120
Mission City, B.C. ....... E6 69
Mission Hill, S.D., U.S. ... E8 118
Mission Hills, Ks., U.S. ... *k16 93
Mission Mountain, mtn., Ok., U.S. ............ A7 113
Mission Range, mts., Mt., U.S. C3 103
Mission Ridge, S.D., U.S. .. C5 118
Mission Viejo, Ca., U.S. ... n13 82
Missinopuskiow, stm., Sask. . D4 75
Missisa Lake, l., Ont. ..... G16 66
Missisicoi, Que. ......... B3 122
Missisquoi, l., Que. ...... D4 74
Missisquoi, stm., Vt., U.S. .. B3 122
Missisquoi Bay, b., Vt., U.S. . A2 122
Mississauga, Ont. ....... D5 73
Mississinewa, stm., In., U.S. . D7 91
Mississinewa Lake, res., In., U.S. ........... C6 91
Mississippi, co., Ar., U.S. .. B5 81
Mississippi, co., Mo., U.S. .. E8 102
Mississippi, state, U.S. .... C4 101
Mississippi, stm., U.S. ..... D9 76
Mississippi Delta, La., U.S. .. E6 95
Mississippi Lake, l., Ont. ... B8 73
Mississippi Sound, strt., U.S. . E5 101
Mississippi State, Ms., U.S. .. B5 101
Missoula, Mt., U.S. ...... D2 103
Missoula, co., Mt., U.S. ... D2 103
Missouri, state, U.S. ..... C5 102
Missouri, stm., U.S. ...... B8 76
Missouri Buttes, mtn., Wy., U.S. .............. B8 127
Missouri City, Mo., U.S. ... h11 102
Missouri City, Tx., U.S. ... r14 120
Missouri Valley, Ia., U.S. ... C2 92
Mistaken Point, c., Newf. ... E5 72
Mistassini, Que. ........ h12 74
Mistassini, Lac, l., Que. .... h12 74
Mistastin Lake, l., Newf. ... g9 72
Mistatim, Sask. ........ F4 75
Misti, Volcán, vol., Peru ... E3 58
Miston, Tn., U.S. ....... A2 119
Mistretta, Italy ......... F5 23
Mita, Punta, c., Mex. ..... C3 63
Mitake, Japan ......... *I9 33
Mitake, Japan .......... I8 33
Mitcham, Austl. ........ *F6 50
Mitchell, Austl. ........ E8 50
Mitchell, Ont. ......... D3 73
Mitchell, Ga., U.S. ...... C4 87
Mitchell, In., U.S. ...... G5 91
Mitchell, Ia., U.S. ...... A5 92
Mitchell, La., U.S. ...... *D2 95

Mitchell, Ne., U.S. ...... C2 104
Mitchell, Or., U.S. ...... C6 114
Mitchell, S.D., U.S. ..... D7 118
Mitchell, co., Ga., U.S. ... E2 87
Mitchell, co., Ia., U.S. .... A5 92
Mitchell, co., Ks., U.S. .... C5 93
Mitchell, co., N.C., U.S. ... e10 110
Mitchell, co., Tx., U.S. .... C2 120
Mitchell, Lake, l., Mi., U.S. .. D5 99
Mitchell, Lake, res., Al., U.S. . C3 78
Mitchell, Mount, mtn., N.C., U.S. .............. f10 110
Mitchell Island, i., La., U.S. .. E6 95
Mitchellsburg, Ky., U.S. .... C5 94
Mitchell, co., U.S. ....... C4 92
Mitchellville, Ia., U.S. .... C4 92
Mitchellville, Tn., U.S. .... A5 119
Mitchelstown, Ire. ....... D2 10
Mitford, Ok., U.S. ....... B7 113
Mīt Fāris, Eg. .......... C3 41
Mīt Ghamr, Eg. ........ D3 41
Mithapur, India ........ D4 36
Mitilíni, Grc. .......... C6 40
Mitishto, stm., Man. ...... B2 70
Mitkof Island, i., Ak., U.S. .. m23 79
Mitla Pass, Eg. ......... E4 41
Mito, Japan ........... H10 33
Mitra do Bispo, mtn., Braz. . h5 56
Mitre, mtn., N.Z. ....... N15 51
Mitry-Mory, Fr. ........ E2 17
Mitsinjo, Madag. ....... g9 49
Mittelland Canal, Eur. .... B5 18
Mittenwald, W. Ger. ..... B7 20
Mittersill, Aus. ......... B8 20
Mitterteich, W. Ger. ..... D6 18
Mittie, La., U.S. ........ D3 95
Mittlerer Isar Kanal, W. Ger. . A7 20
Mittweida, E. Ger. ....... C6 18
Mitú, Col. ............ C3 60
Mitumba, Monts, mts., Zaire . C4 48
Mitzic, Gabon ......... E2 46
Mixquiahuala, Mex. ..... m14 63
Mixteco, stm., Mex. ...... o14 63
Miyagi Island, i., Japan ... O5 52
Miyake-shima, i., Japan ... I9 33
Miyako, Japan ......... G10 33
Miyakonojō, Japan ...... K5 33
Miyazaki, Japan ........ K5 33
Miyazu, Japan ......... n14 33
Mizdah, Libya ......... C2 43
Mize, Ms., U.S. ........ D4 101
Mizen Head, c., Ire. ..... F2 11
Mizil, Rom. ........... C8 24
Mizoram, state, India .... D9 36
Mizpah, Mn., U.S. ...... C4 100
Mizpah, N.J., U.S. ...... E3 107
Mizpah Creek, stm., Mt., U.S. E11 103
Mizpé Ramon, Isr. ...... G10 40
Mizque, Bol. .......... C2 55
Mjölby, Swe. .......... H6 14
Mjøsa, l., Nor. ......... G4 14
Mkalama, Tan. ......... B5 48
Mladá Boleslav, Czech. ... C3 26
Mława, Pol. ........... B6 26
Mljet, i., Yugo. ........ D3 24
Mnichovo Hradiště, Czech. .. C9 19
Mnyusi, Tan. .......... C6 48
Mo, Nor. ............. D6 14
Moa, i., Austl. ......... B7 50
Moa, i., Indon. ........ G7 34
Moab, Ut., U.S. ........ E6 121
Moala Island, i., Fiji ..... I15 52
Moamba, Moz. ........ C5 49
Moanda, Gabon ....... F2 46
Moapa, Nv., U.S. ....... G7 105
Moapa River Indian Reservation, U.S. ...... G7 105
Moark, Ar., U.S. ....... A5 81
Moar Lake, l., Can. ...... D4 70
Moate, Ire. ........... D4 11
Moba, Zaire .......... C4 48
Mobara, Japan ........ n19 33
Mobaye, Cen. Afr. Rep. .. E4 46
Mobayi-Mbongo, Zaire ... A3 48
Mobeetie, Tx., U.S. ..... B2 120
Moberly, Mo., U.S. ..... B5 102
Moberly Lake, B.C. ...... B7 69
Mobile, Newf. ......... E5 72
Mobile, Al., U.S. ....... E1 78
Mobile, Az., U.S. ....... D3 80
Mobile, co., Al., U.S. .... E1 78
Mobile, stm., Al., U.S. ... E1 78
Mobile Bay, b., Al., U.S. .. E1 78
Mobridge, S.D., U.S. .... B5 118
Mobutu, Zaire ......... A4 48
Moca, Dom. Rep. ...... E8 64
Mocajuba, Braz. ....... D7 48
Moçambique, Moz. ..... D7 48
Moçâmedes see Namibe, Ang. .............. A1 48
Mocanaqua, Pa., U.S. ... D9 115
Moccasin, Az., U.S. ..... A3 80
Moccasin, Mt., U.S. ..... C7 103
Moce, i., Fiji .......... I16 52
Mocha, Isla, i., Chile ..... B2 54
Moc Hoa, Viet. ........ l8 35
Mocho Mountains, mts., Jam. E14 65
Mochudi, Bots. ........ B4 49
Mocimboa da Praia, Moz. .. D7 48
Möckeln, l., Swe. ....... H8 15
Mocksville, N.C., U.S. ... B2 110
Moclips, Wa., U.S. ...... B1 124
Moco, Serra, mtn., Ang. .. D2 48
Mococa, Braz. ......... C3 56
Mocomoco, Bol. ....... C2 55
Mocorito, Mex. ........ B3 63
Moctezuma, Mex. ...... B3 63
Moctezuma, stm., Mex. ... m14 63
Mocuba, Moz. ......... A6 49
Mocúbri, Moz. ......... D6 48
Modane, Fr. .......... D7 16
Model, Co., U.S. ....... D6 83
Model Reservoir, res., Co., U.S. .............. D6 83
Modena, Italy ......... B3 23
Modena, Mo., U.S. ..... A4 102
Modena, N.Y., U.S. ..... D6 109
Modena, Wi., U.S. ...... D2 126
Modesto, Ca., U.S. ..... D3 82
Modesto, Il., U.S. ...... D4 90
Modica, Italy ......... F5 23
Modlin, Pol. .......... k13 26
Modoc, In., U.S. ...... D7 91
Modoc, co., Ca., U.S. ... B3 82
Modoc Point, Or., U.S. .. E5 114
Modřany, Czech. ....... o17 26
Moe, Austl. ........... G8 50
Moehau, mtn., N.Z. ..... L15 51

Moen, i., Micron. ....... Q18 52
Moenave, Az., U.S. ...... A4 80
Moengo, Sur. .......... A4 59
Moenkopi, Az., U.S. ..... A4 80
Moenkopi Plateau, plat., Az., U.S. .............. B4 80
Moenkopi Wash, val., Az., U.S. .............. A5 80
Moerbeke, Bel. ........ C3 17
Moers, W. Ger. ......... B1 19
Moesa, stm., Switz. ...... D7 21
Moeskroen see Mouscron, Bel. .............. B5 16
Moffat, Scot., U.K. ...... E5 13
Moffat, Co., U.S. ....... C5 83
Moffat, co., Co., U.S. .... A2 83
Moffat Tunnel, Co., U.S. .. B5 83
Moffett, Ok., U.S. ...... B7 113
Moffett Field Naval Air Station, mil., Ca., U.S. .... k8 82
Moffit, N.D., U.S. ...... C5 111
Moga, Zaire .......... C4 48
Mogadishu (Muqdisho), Som. E6 47
Mogadore, Oh., U.S. .... A4 112
Mogaung, Burma ...... C10 36
Mogi das Cruzes, Braz. ... C3 56
Mogielnica, Pol. ....... C6 26
Mogilev, Sov. Un. ...... D6 29
Mogilev-Podolskiy, Sov. Un. . G6 27
Mogilno, Pol. ......... B5 26
Mogi-Mirim, Braz. ...... C3 56
Mogocha, Sov. Un. ..... D14 29
Mogochin, Sov. Un. ..... B10 28
Mogollon, N.M., U.S. ... D1 108
Mogollon Mesa, mtn., Az., U.S. .............. C4 80
Mogollon Mountains, mts., N.M., U.S. ........ D1 108
Mogollon Rim, clf., Az., U.S. . C4 80
Mogote, Co., U.S. ...... D4 83
Mogotes, Punta, c., Arg. .. B5 54
Moguer, Spain ........ D2 22
Mohács, Hung. ........ C4 24
Mohale's Hoek, Leso. .... D4 49
Mohall, N.D., U.S. ...... A4 111
Mohammedia, Mor. ..... C3 44
Mohave, co., Az., U.S. ... B1 80
Mohave, Lake, res., U.S. .. H7 105
Mohave Mountains, mts., Az., U.S. .......... C1 80
Mohave Valley, Az., U.S. .. C1 80
Mohawk, Mi., U.S. ..... A2 99
Mohawk, N.Y., U.S. .... C5 109
Mohawk, stm., N.Y., U.S. . g7 106
Mohawk, stm., N.Y., U.S. . C6 109
Mohawk, Lake, l., N.J., U.S. . A3 107
Mohawk Mountain, mtn., Ct., U.S. ............ B2 84
Mohawk Mountains, mts., Az., U.S. .......... D8 69
Mohe, China .......... A9 31
Mohegan, Ct., U.S. ..... D7 84
Mohegan, R.I., U.S. ..... B2 116
Mohican, stm., Oh., U.S. .. B3 112
Mohican, Black Fork, stm., Oh., U.S. .......... B3 112
Mohican, Clear Fork, stm., Oh., U.S. .......... B3 112
Mohill, Ire. ........... C4 11
Mohler, Wa., U.S. ...... B8 124
Mohnton, Pa., U.S. ..... F10 115
Mohoro, Tan. ......... C7 48
Moiese, Mt., U.S. ...... C2 103
Moineşti, Rom. ........ B8 24
Moinkum Desert, des., Sov. Un. .............. D8 28
Mointy, Sov. Un. ....... D8 28
Moira, N.Y., U.S. ...... f10 109
Moisie, Que. .......... h8 72
Moisie, stm., Que. ...... h8 72
Moissac, Fr. .......... E4 16
Moïssala, Chad ........ F10 22
Moita, Port. .......... f10 22
Mojave, Ca., U.S. ...... E4 82
Mojave, stm., Ca., U.S. .. E5 82
Mojave Desert, des., Ca., U.S. E5 82
Moji-Guaçu, stm., Braz. .. k8 56
Mojo, Eth. ........... D4 47
Mojokerto, Indon. ...... *G4 34
Mokāma, India ........ E10 37
Mokane, Mo., U.S. ..... C6 102
Mokapu, Hi., U.S. ...... *B4 88
Mokapu Peninsula, pen., Hi., U.S. .............. g10 88
Mokapu Point, c., Hi., U.S. . g11 88
Mokelumne, stm., Ca., U.S. . C3 82
Mokelumne Hill, Ca., U.S. .. C3 82
Mokena, Il., U.S. ....... k9 90
Mokepa, Zaire ........ A4 49
Mokhotlong, Leso. ..... n8 56
Mokochu, mtn., Thai. .... E3 35
Mokokio, Cam. ........ D3 47
Mokolo, Cam. ........ A2 48
Mokp'o, S. Kor. ....... E10 31
Moksha, stm., Sov. Un. .. D14 27
Mol, Bel. ............ C5 17
Mola, Yugo. .......... D3 24
Mola [di Bari], Italy ..... D6 23
Molalla, Or., U.S. ...... B4 114
Molangul, Mount, mtn., Austl. B8 51
Molasses Pond, l., Me., U.S. . D4 96
Molat, i., Yugo. ........ C2 24
Mold, Wales, U.K. ...... A4 12
Moldau see Vltava, stm., Czech. ............. B3 31
Moldava, state, Sov. Un. .. E5 29
Moldavia, hist. reg., Rom. .. B8 24
Molde, Nor. .......... F2 14
Moldova, stm., Rom. .... C8 24
Moldoveanu, mtn., Rom. .. C7 24
Molega Lake, l., N.S. .... E5 71
Molena, Ga., U.S. ...... C2 87
Molepolole, Bots. ...... B4 49
Molenbeek-Saint Jean, Bel. . *D4 17
Môle-Saint-Nicolas, Haiti .. D6 64
Molfetta, Italy ........ D6 23
Molina, Chile ......... B2 54
Molina, Col. .......... B2 60
Molina de Aragón, Spain .. B5 22
Molina de Segura, Spain .. C5 22
Moline, Il., U.S. ....... B3 90
Moline, Ks., U.S. ...... E7 93
Moline, Oh., U.S. ...... e6 112
Molinella, Italy ....... E6 23
Molino, Fl., U.S. ...... u14 86
Molino de Rosas (part of Mexico City), Mex. .... h9 63
Molinos, Arg. ......... B2 54

Molise, prov., Italy ...... D5 23
Moliterno, Italy ........ D5 23
Möll, stm., Aus. ........ C9 20
Mölle, Swe. ........... B6 15
Mollendo, Peru ........ E3 58
Mollusk, Va., U.S. ...... C6 123
Mölndal, Swe. ......... I4 14
Molochansk, Sov. Un. .... H10 27
Molodechno, Sov. Un. ... D6 27
Molokai, i., Hi., U.S. .... B5 88
Molokini, i., Hi., U.S. .... C5 88
Molopo, stm., Afr. ...... C3 49
Moloundou, Cam. ...... E3 46
Molsheim, Fr. ......... F7 17
Molson, Man. .......... D3 70
Molson, Wa., U.S. ...... A6 124
Molson, stm., Man. ..... C3 70
Molson Lake, l., Man. .... B3 70
Molt, Mt., U.S. ........ E8 103
Molteno, S. Afr. ....... D4 49
Moluccas (Maluku), is., Indon. F7 34
Molucca Sea, Indon. ..... F7 34
Molus, Ky., U.S. ....... D6 94
Moma, Moz. .......... A6 49
Mombasa, Kenya ...... B6 48
Mombetsu, Japan ...... D11 33
Mombongo, Zaire ...... A3 48
Momboyo, stm., Zaire ... B2 48
Momchilgrad, Bul. ...... E7 24
Momence, Il., U.S. ..... B6 90
Momi, Fiji ............ H14 52
Momostenango, Guat. ... C2 62
Mompog Pass, strt., Phil. .. p14 34
Mompono, Zaire ....... A3 48
Mompós, Col. ......... B3 60
Møn, i., Den. .......... C6 15
Mona, Ut., U.S. ....... D4 121
Mona, Isla de, i., P.R. .... G11 64
Mona, Punta, c., C.R. .... F6 62
Monaca, Pa., U.S. ...... E1 115
Monaco, ctry., Eur. ..... F7 16
Monadhliath Mountains, mts., Scot., U.K. .......... C4 13
Monadnock, Mount, mtn., N.H., U.S. .......... E2 106
Monadnock Mountain, mtn., Vt., U.S. .......... B5 122
Monagas, state, Ven. .... C5 60
Monaghan, Ire. ........ C5 11
Monaghan, co., Ire. ..... C5 11
Monahans, Tx., U.S. .... D1 120
Monamolin, Ire. ....... E5 11
Monango, N.D., U.S. .... C7 111
Mona Passage, strt., N.A. .. E10 64
Monarch, Alta. ........ E4 68
Monarch, Mt., U.S. ..... C6 103
Monarch Mills, S.C., U.S. .. B4 117
Monarch Mountain, mtn., B.C. D5 69
Monarch Pass, Co., U.S. .. C4 83
Monashee Mountains, mts., B.C. .............. D8 69
Monastir, Tun. ........ B7 44
Monastyrshchina, Sov. Un. . D8 27
Monavatu, mtn., Fiji ..... H14 52
Moncalieri, Italy ....... B1 23
Monção, Braz. ........ B1 57
Monção, Port. ........ B1 22
Moncey, Fr. .......... B1 21
Monchegorsk, Sov. Un. ... D15 14
Mönchengladbach, W. Ger. . C3 18
Monchique, Port. ...... D1 22
Monchique, Serra de, mts., Port. ............. D1 22
Moncks Corner, S.C., U.S. . E7 117
Monclo, W.V., U.S. ..... D3 125
Monclova, Mex. ....... B4 63
Monclova, Oh., U.S. .... e6 112
Moncton, N.B. ........ C5 71
Moncure, N.C., U.S. .... B3 110
Mondamin, Ia., U.S. .... C1 92
Mondego, stm., Port. .... B1 22
Mondego, Cabo, c., Port. .. B1 22
Mond Lake, l., Aus. ..... B8 20
Mondoñedo, Spain ..... A2 22
Mondorf-les-Bains, Lux. .. E6 17
Mondovi, Wi., U.S. ..... D2 126
Mondovì, Italy ........ B1 23
Monee, Il., U.S. ....... B6 90
Monegaw Springs, Mo., U.S. C4 102
Monemvasía, Grc. ...... N16 40
Moneron Island, i., Sov. Un. . C10 33
Monessen, Pa., U.S. .... F2 115
Moneta, Va., U.S. ...... C3 123
Monett, Mo., U.S. ..... E4 102
Monetta, S.C., U.S. .... D4 117
Monette, Ar., U.S. ..... B5 81
Money, Ms., U.S. ...... B3 101
Moneymore, N. Ire., U.K. .. C5 11
Monfalcone, Italy ...... B4 23
Monforte de Lemos, Spain . A2 22
Monfort Heights, Oh., U.S. . o12 112
Monga, Zaire ......... A4 48
Mongaguá, Braz. ...... n8 56
Mongala, stm., Zaire .... A3 48
Mongalla, Sud. ....... D3 47
Möng Hsat, Burma ..... B3 35
Möng Mit, Burma ...... D10 36
Mongo, Chad ......... C3 46
Mongo, stm., Afr. ...... A7 91
Mongolia (part of Markham), Ont. .............. k15 73
Mongolia, ctry., Asia .... B5 31
Mongolia, Plateau of, plat., Mong. ............ B6 31
Möng Pan, Burma ...... B3 35
Mongu, Burma ........ E3 35
Möng Yai, Burma ...... A3 35
Monhegan Island, i., Me., U.S. E3 96
Mönh Hayrhan Mountain, mtn., Mong. ......... B3 31
Moniac, Ga., U.S. ...... F4 87
Moniaive, Scot., U.K. .... E5 13
Monico, Wi., U.S. ...... C4 126
Monida Pass, U.S. ...... D6 97
Monie, Md., U.S. ...... D6 97
Moninabad see Ambājogāi, India ............. H6 37
Moniquirá, Col. ....... B3 60
Moniteau, co., Mo., U.S. .. C5 102
Monitor, Alta. ........ D5 68
Monitor, Or., U.S. ...... h12 114
Monitor, Wa., U.S. ..... B5 124
Monitor Range, mts., Nv., U.S. E5 105
Monitor Valley, val., Nv., U.S. E5 105
Moniveea, Ire. ........ D3 11
Monkey Point, c., Nic. ... E8 63
Monkey River, Belize .... B3 62
Monkira, Austl. ....... D3 51
Monkoto, Zaire ....... B3 48
Monkton, Ont. ........ D3 73
Monkton, Vt., U.S. ..... C2 122
Mon Louis, Al., U.S. .... E1 78
Monmouth, Wales, U.K. .. C5 12
Monmouth, Il., U.S. .... C3 90
Monmouth, Ia., U.S. .... B7 92
Monmouth, Me., U.S. ... D2 96

Name — Map Ref. — Page

Monmouth, Or., U.S. C3 114
*Monmouth, co., N.J., U.S.* C4 107
Monmouth Beach, N.J., U.S. C5 107
Monmouth Junction, N.J., U.S. C3 107
*Monmouth Mountain, mtn., B.C.* D6 69
Monnickendam, Neth. B5 17
*Monnow, stm., U.K.* C5 12
*Mono, co., Ca., U.S.* D4 82
*Monocacy, stm., Md., U.S.* B3 97
*Mono Lake, l., Ca., U.S.* D4 82
*Monomonac, Lake, l., U.S.* E3 106
*Monomoy Island, i., Ma., U.S.* C7 98
*Monomoy Point, c., Ma., U.S.* C7 98
Monon, In., U.S. C4 91
Monona, Ia., U.S. A6 92
Monona, Wi., U.S. E4 126
*Monona, co., Ia., U.S.* B1 92
*Monona, Lake, l., Wi., U.S.* E4 126
Monongah, W.V., U.S. B4 125
Monongahela, Pa., U.S. F2 115
*Monongahela, stm., U.S.* G2 115
*Monongalia, co., W.V., U.S.* B4 125
Monopoli, Italy D6 23
Monor, Hung. B4 24
*Monos Island, i., Trin.* N22 65
Monóvar, Spain C5 22
Monoville, Tn., U.S. C8 119
Monowi, Ne., U.S. B7 104
Monowice, Pol. g10 26
Monponsett, Ma., U.S. B6 98
Monreale, Italy E4 23
Monroe, Ar., U.S. C4 81
Monroe, Ct., U.S. D3 84
Monroe, Ga., U.S. C3 87
Monroe, In., U.S. C8 91
Monroe, Ia., U.S. C4 92
Monroe, La., U.S. B3 95
Monroe, Me., U.S. D3 96
Monroe, Mi., U.S. G7 99
Monroe, Ne., U.S. C8 104
Monroe, N.H., U.S. B2 106
Monroe, N.J., U.S. A3 107
Monroe, N.Y., U.S. D6 109
Monroe, N.C., U.S. C2 110
Monroe, Oh., U.S. C1 112
Monroe, Ok., U.S. C7 113
Monroe, Or., U.S. C3 114
Monroe, S.D., U.S. D8 118
Monroe, Tn., U.S. C8 119
Monroe, Ut., U.S. E3 121
Monroe, Va., U.S. C3 123
Monroe, Wa., U.S. B4 124
Monroe, Wi., U.S. F4 126
*Monroe, co., Al., U.S.* D2 78
*Monroe, co., Ar., U.S.* C4 81
*Monroe, co., Fl., U.S.* G5 86
*Monroe, co., Ga., U.S.* D3 87
*Monroe, co., Il., U.S.* E3 90
*Monroe, co., In., U.S.* F4 91
*Monroe, co., Ia., U.S.* D5 92
*Monroe, co., Ky., U.S.* D4 94
*Monroe, co., Mi., U.S.* G7 99
*Monroe, co., Ms., U.S.* B5 101
*Monroe, co., Mo., U.S.* B5 102
*Monroe, co., N.Y., U.S.* B3 109
*Monroe, co., Oh., U.S.* C4 112
*Monroe, co., Pa., U.S.* D11 115
*Monroe, co., Tn., U.S.* D9 119
*Monroe, co., W.V., U.S.* D4 125
*Monroe, co., Wi., U.S.* E3 126
Monroe Bridge, Ma., U.S. A2 98
Monroe Center, Ct., U.S. D3 84
Monroe Center, Il., U.S. A5 90
Monroe City, In., U.S. G3 91
Monroe City, Mo., U.S. B6 102
*Monroe Lake, res., In., U.S.* F5 91
Monroe Park, De., U.S. h7 85
Monroeton, Pa., U.S. C9 115
Monroeville, Al., U.S. D2 78
Monroeville, In., U.S. C8 91
Monroeville, N.J., U.S. D2 107
Monroeville, Oh., U.S. A3 112
Monroeville, Pa., U.S. k14 115
Monrovia, Lib. E2 45
Monrovia, Ca., U.S. m13 82
Monrovia, In., U.S. E5 91
Mons (Bergen), Bel. B5 16
*Monsarás, Ponta do, c., Braz.* E3 57
Monschau, W. Ger. D6 17
Monselice, Italy D7 20
Monsey, N.Y., U.S. *m14 109
*Møns Klint, clf., Den.* D6 15
Monson, Me., U.S. C3 96
Monson, Ma., U.S. B3 98
Montabaur, W. Ger. C2 19
*Montagnais Point, c., Newf.* B1 72
Montagnana, Italy D7 20
Montague, P.E.I. C7 71
Montague, Ca., U.S. B2 82
Montague, Ma., U.S. A2 98
Montague, Mi., U.S. E4 99
Montague, Tx., U.S. C4 120
*Montague, co., Tx., U.S.* C4 120
*Montague Island, i., Ak., U.S.* D10 79
*Montague Lake, l., Sask.* H3 75
*Montague Peak, mtn., Ak., U.S.* g18 79
*Montague Strait, strt., Ak., U.S.* h18 79
Montalbán, Spain B5 22
Montalegre, Port. B2 22
Mont Alto, Pa., U.S. G6 115
*Montalto, mtn., Italy* E5 23
Montana, Ak., U.S. g17 79
*Montana, state, U.S.* D7 103
Montana-Vermala, Switz. D3 21
Montánchez, Spain C2 22
Montandon, Pa., U.S. E8 115
Montargis, Fr. D5 16
Montataire, Fr. E2 17
Montauban, Fr. E4 16
Montauban-les-Mines, Que. C5 74
Montauk, N.Y., U.S. m17 109
Montbard, Fr. D6 16
Montbéliard, Fr. D7 16
Mont Belvieu, Tx., U.S. E5 120
Montblanch, Spain B6 22
*Mont Blanc Tunnel, Eur.* E7 16
Montbozon, Fr. B1 21
Montbrison, Fr. E6 16
*Montcalm, co., Que.* C3 74
*Montcalm, co., Mi., U.S.* E5 99
*Montcalm, Pic de, mtn., Fr.* F4 16
Mont-Carmel, Que. B8 74
Montceau-les-Mines, Fr. D6 16
*Mont Cenis Pass, Fr.* E7 16
Montcerf, Que. C1 74
Montchanin, Fr. D6 16
Montchanin, De., U.S. h7 85
Montclair, Ca., U.S. m13 82
Montclair, N.J., U.S. B4 107
Mont Clare, Pa., U.S. o19 115
Montcoal, W.V., U.S. D3 125
Montcornet, Fr. E3 17
Mont-de-Marsan, Fr. F3 16
Montdidier, Fr. C5 16
Monteagle, Tn., U.S. D8 119
Monte Alegre, Braz. C2 56
Monte Alegre, Braz. C4 59
Monte Alegre de Goiás, Braz. A3 56
Monte Azul, Braz. B4 56
Montebello, Que. D3 74
Montebello, Ca., U.S. m12 82
Montebello, Va., U.S. C3 123
*Montebello Islands, is., Austl.* D2 50
Montebelluna, Italy D8 20
Monte Carmelo, Braz. B3 56
Monte Caseros, Arg. A5 54
Montecatini Terme, Italy C3 23
Montecchio, Italy g9 23
Montecito, Ca., U.S. *E4 82
Monte Comán, Arg. A3 54
Monte Cristi, Dom. Rep. E8 64
Montecristi, Ec. B1 58
Monte Cristo, Bol. B3 55
*Montecristo, i., Italy* C3 23
Montefrío, Spain D3 22
Montego Bay, Jam. E5 64
*Montego Bay, b., Jam.* E13 65
Montegut, La., U.S. E5 95
Monteiro, Braz. C3 57
*Monteith, Mount, mtn., B.C.* B6 69
Montelavar, Port. f9 22
Montélimar, Fr. E6 16
*Montelindo, stm., Para.* D4 55
Montellano, Spain D3 22
Montello, Nv., U.S. B7 105
Montello, Wi., U.S. E4 126
*Montemayor, Meseta de, plat., Arg.* C3 54
Montemorelos, Mex. B5 63
Montemor-o-Novo, Port. C1 22
Montenegro, Braz. D2 56
*Montenegro, hist. reg., Yugo.* D4 24
Monte Patria, Chile A2 54
Monte Plata, Dom. Rep. E9 64
Monte Porzio Catone, Italy h9 23
Montepuez, Moz. D6 48
Montepulciano, Italy C3 23
Monte Quemado, Arg. E3 55
Montereau [-faut-Yonne], Fr. C5 16
Monterey, Al., U.S. D3 78
Monterey, Ca., U.S. D3 82
Monterey, In., U.S. B4 91
Monterey, Ky., U.S. B5 94
Monterey, La., U.S. C4 95
Monterey, Ma., U.S. B1 98
Monterey, Tn., U.S. C8 119
Monterey, Va., U.S. B3 123
*Monterey, co., Ca., U.S.* D3 82
*Monterey Bay, b., Ca., U.S.* D2 82
Monterey Park, Ca., U.S. m12 82
Montería, Col. B2 60
Monteros, Arg. E2 55
Monterotondo, Italy g9 23
Monterrey, Mex. B4 63
Montesano, Wa., U.S. C2 124
*Monte Sano Mountain, mtn., Al., U.S.* A3 78
Monte Sant'Angelo, Italy D5 23
Monte Santo, Braz. D3 57
*Monte Santu, Capo di, c., Italy* D2 23
Montes Claros, Braz. B4 56
Montevallo, Al., U.S. B3 78
Montevarchi, Italy C3 23
Montevideo, Mn., U.S. F3 100
Montevideo, Ur. E1 56
Monteview, Id., U.S. F6 89
Monte Vista, Co., U.S. D4 83
Montezuma, Ga., U.S. D2 87
Montezuma, In., U.S. E3 91
Montezuma, Ia., U.S. C5 92
Montezuma, Ks., U.S. E3 93
Montezuma, N.M., U.S. B4 108
Montezuma, Oh., U.S. B1 112
Montezuma, Tn., U.S. B3 119
*Montezuma, co., Co., U.S.* D2 83
*Montezuma Canyon, val., Ut., U.S.* F6 121
*Montezuma Castle National Monument, Az., U.S.* C4 80
Montezuma Creek, Ut., U.S. F6 121
*Montezuma Peak, mtn., Az., U.S.* D3 80
Montfaucon, Switz. B3 21
Montfort, Que. D3 74
Montfort, Wi., U.S. F3 126
Montfort-sur-Meu, Fr. C3 16
Montgomery, Wales, U.K. B4 12
Montgomery, Al., U.S. C3 78
Montgomery, Ga., U.S. E5 87
Montgomery, Il., U.S. B5 90
Montgomery, In., U.S. G3 91
Montgomery, La., U.S. C3 95
Montgomery, Ma., U.S. B2 98
Montgomery, Mi., U.S. G6 99
Montgomery, Mn., U.S. F5 100
Montgomery, N.Y., U.S. D6 109
Montgomery, Oh., U.S. o13 112
Montgomery, Pa., U.S. D8 115
Montgomery, Vt., U.S. B3 122
Montgomery, W.V., U.S. C3 125
*Montgomery, co., Al., U.S.* C3 78
*Montgomery, co., Ar., U.S.* C2 81
*Montgomery, co., Ga., U.S.* D4 87
*Montgomery, co., Il., U.S.* D4 90
*Montgomery, co., In., U.S.* D4 91
*Montgomery, co., Ia., U.S.* C2 92
*Montgomery, co., Ks., U.S.* E8 93
*Montgomery, co., Ky., U.S.* B6 94
*Montgomery, co., Md., U.S.* B3 97
*Montgomery, co., Ms., U.S.* B4 101
*Montgomery, co., Mo., U.S.* C6 102
*Montgomery, co., N.Y., U.S.* C6 109
*Montgomery, co., N.C., U.S.* B3 110
*Montgomery, co., Oh., U.S.* C1 112
*Montgomery, co., Pa., U.S.* F11 115
*Montgomery, co., Tn., U.S.* A4 119
*Montgomery, co., Tx., U.S.* D5 120
*Montgomery, co., Va., U.S.* C2 123
Montgomery Center, Vt., U.S. B3 122
Montgomery City, Mo., U.S. C6 102
Montgomery Creek, Ca., U.S. B3 82
Montgomery see Sāhīwāl, Pak. B5 36
Montgomery Village, Md., U.S. *B3 97
Monthermé, Fr. E4 17
Monthey, Switz. C2 21
Monticello, P.E.I. C7 71
Monticello, Ar., U.S. D4 81
Monticello, Fl., U.S. B3 86
Monticello, Ga., U.S. C3 87
Monticello, Il., U.S. C5 90
Monticello, In., U.S. C4 91
Monticello, Ia., U.S. B6 92
Monticello, Ky., U.S. D5 94
Monticello, Me., U.S. B5 96
Monticello, Mn., U.S. E5 100
Monticello, Ms., U.S. D3 101
Monticello, Mo., U.S. A6 102
Monticello, N.M., U.S. D2 108
Monticello, N.Y., U.S. D6 109
Monticello, Ut., U.S. F6 121
Monticello, Wi., U.S. F4 126
Mont Ida, Ks., U.S. D8 93
Montier, Mo., U.S. D6 102
Montier-en-Der, Fr. F4 17
Montiers-sur-Saulx, Fr. F5 17
Montignac, Fr. E4 16
Montigny [-lés-Metz], Fr. C7 16
Montijo, Port. C1 22
Montijo, Spain C2 22
Montilla, Spain D3 22
Monti Verdi, Ut., U.S. *B4 121
Montivilliers, Fr. C4 16
Mont-Joli, Que. A9 74
Mont-Laurier, Que. C2 74
Montluçon, Fr. D5 16
Montmagny, Que. C7 74
*Montmagny, co., Que.* C7 74
Montmartre, Sask. G4 75
Montmédy, Fr. E5 17
Montmélian, Fr. D2 20
Montmirail, Fr. F3 17
Montmorenci, In., U.S. D3 91
Montmorenci, S.C., U.S. D4 117
Montmorency, Fr. g10 16
*Montmorency, co., Mi., U.S.* C6 99
*Montmorency, stm., Que.* B6 74
*Montmorency Number One, co., Que.* B6 74
*Montmorency Number Two, co., Que.* C7 74
Montmorillon, Fr. D4 16
Montney, B.C. A7 69
Monto, Austl. B8 51
*Montone, stm., Italy* B3 23
Montoro, Spain C3 22
Montour, Ia., U.S. C5 92
*Montour, co., Pa., U.S.* D8 115
Montour Falls, N.Y., U.S. C4 109
Montoursville, Pa., U.S. D8 115
Montoya, N.M., U.S. B5 108
Montpelier, Id., U.S. G7 89
Montpelier, In., U.S. C7 91
Montpelier, Ia., U.S. C7 92
Montpelier, La., U.S. D5 95
Montpelier, Ms., U.S. B5 101
Montpelier, N.D., U.S. C7 111
Montpelier, Oh., U.S. A1 112
Montpelier, Vt., U.S. C3 122
Montpelier Station, Va., U.S. B4 123
Montpellier, Que. D2 74
Montpellier, Fr. F5 16
Montréal, Que. D4 74
Montreal, Wi., U.S. B3 126
*Montreal, stm., Sask.* C3 75
*Montréal, Île de, i., Que.* q19 74
Montreal Lake, Sask. C3 75
*Montreal Lake, l., Sask.* C3 75
Montréal-Nord, Que. p19 74
Montreat, N.C., U.S. f10 110
Montreuil, Fr. C5 16
Montreuil [-sous-Bois], Fr. C5 16
Montreuil-sur-Mer, Fr. B4 16
Montreux, Switz. E3 18
Montricher, Switz. C1 21
Mont-Rolland, Que. D3 74
Montrose, B.C. E9 69
Montrose, Scot., U.K. E6 13
Montrose, Al., U.S. E2 78
Montrose, Ar., U.S. D4 81
Montrose, Co., U.S. C3 83
Montrose, Ga., U.S. D3 87
Montrose, Il., U.S. D5 90
Montrose, Ia., U.S. D6 92
Montrose, Ks., U.S. C5 93
Montrose, Mi., U.S. E7 99
Montrose, Ms., U.S. C4 101
Montrose, Mo., U.S. C4 102
Montrose, Pa., U.S. C10 115
Montrose, S.D., U.S. D8 118
Montrose, Va., U.S. m18 123
*Montrose, co., Co., U.S.* C2 83
Montross, Va., U.S. B6 123
Montrouge, Fr. g10 16
Mont-Royal, Que. p19 74
Mont-Saint-Martin, Fr. C6 16
Mont-Saint-Michel, Fr. C3 16
Montserrat, Mo., U.S. C4 102
*Montserrat, dep., N.A.* H13 64
*Montserrat, mtn., Spain* B6 22
*Mont-Tremblant, Parc Provincial du, Que.* C3 74
Montvale, N.J., U.S. A4 107
Montvale, Va., U.S. C3 123
Mont Vernon, N.H., U.S. E3 106
Montville, Ct., U.S. D7 84
Montville, Ma., U.S. B1 98
Montville, N.J., U.S. B4 107
Montz, La., U.S. h11 95
Montzen, Bel. D5 17
Monument, Co., U.S. B6 83
Monument, Ks., U.S. C2 93
Monument, N.M., U.S. E6 108
Monument, Or., U.S. C7 114
Monument, Pa., U.S. D6 115
Monument Beach, Ma., U.S. C6 98
Monument Heights, Va., U.S. *C5 123
*Monument Peak, mtn., Co., U.S.* B3 83
*Monument Peak, mtn., Id., U.S.* G4 89
Monument Valley, Ut., U.S. *F5 121
*Monument Valley, val., Az., U.S.* A5 80
Monywa, Burma D10 36
Monza, Italy B2 23
Monze, Zam. E4 48
Monzón, Peru C2 58
Monzón, Spain B6 22
Moodus, Ct., U.S. D6 84
*Moodus Reservoir, res., Ct., U.S.* C6 84
Moody, Me., U.S. E2 96
Moody, Mo., U.S. E6 102
Moody, Tx., U.S. D4 120
*Moody, co., S.D., U.S.* C9 118
*Moody Air Force Base, mil., Ga., U.S.* F3 87
Moody Beach, Me., U.S. E2 96
Moodys, Ok., U.S. A7 113
Mooers Forks, N.Y., U.S. f11 109
Moon, Ok., U.S. D7 113
Moonachie, N.J., U.S. *B4 107
*Moonie, stm., Austl.* C7 51
*Moon Lake, l., Ms., U.S.* A3 101
Moon Run, Pa., U.S. k13 115
Moonta, Austl. F6 50
Moora, Austl. F2 50
Moorabbin, Austl. *G8 50
Moorcroft, Wy., U.S. B8 127
Moore, Id., U.S. F5 89
Moore, Mt., U.S. D7 103
Moore, Ok., U.S. B4 113
Moore, S.C., U.S. B4 117
Moore, Tx., U.S. E3 120
Moore, W.V., U.S. B5 125
*Moore, co., N.C., U.S.* B3 110
*Moore, co., Tn., U.S.* B5 119
*Moore, co., Tx., U.S.* B2 120
*Moore, Lake, l., Austl.* E2 50
*Moore Dam, U.S.* B3 106
Moorefield, Ont. D4 73
Moorefield, Ky., U.S. B6 94
Moorefield, Ne., U.S. D5 104
Moorefield, W.V., U.S. B6 125
Moore Haven, Fl., U.S. F5 86
Mooreland, In., U.S. E7 91
Mooreland, Ok., U.S. A2 113
Moore Mill, N.B. D2 71
Moore Park, Man. D2 70
*Moore Reservoir, res., U.S.* B3 106
Mooresburg, Tn., U.S. C10 119
Moores Corner, Ma., U.S. A3 98
*Moores Creek National Military Park, N.C., U.S.* C4 110
Moores Hill, In., U.S. F7 91
Moorestown, Mi., U.S. D5 99
Moorestown, N.J., U.S. D3 107
Mooresville, In., U.S. E5 91
Mooresville, Mo., U.S. B4 102
Mooresville, N.C., U.S. B2 110
Mooresville, Tn., U.S. B5 119
Mooreton, N.D., U.S. C9 111
Mooreville, Ms., U.S. A5 101
Moorhead, Ia., U.S. C2 92
Moorhead, Mn., U.S. D2 100
Moorhead, Ms., U.S. B3 101
Mooring, Tn., U.S. A2 119
Mooringsport, La., U.S. B2 95
Moor Lake, Ont. A7 73
Moorland, Ia., U.S. B3 92
Moorman, Ky., U.S. C2 94
Moorpark, Ca., U.S. *E4 82
Moosburg, W. Ger. E6 19
Moose, Wy., U.S. C2 127
*Moose, stm., N.H., U.S.* B4 106
*Moose, stm., N.Y., U.S.* B5 109
*Moose, stm., Vt., U.S.* B5 122
Moose Creek, Ont. B10 73
Moose Factory, Ont. F16 66
*Moosehead Lake, l., Me., U.S.* C3 96
Mooseheart, Il., U.S. B5 90
Moose Heights, B.C. C6 69
*Moose Hill, hill, Ma., U.S.* h11 98
Moosehorn, Man. D2 70
*Moose Island, i., Man.* D3 70
Moose Jaw, Sask. G3 75
*Moose Jaw, stm., Sask.* G3 75
Moose Lake, Man. C1 70
Moose Lake, Mn., U.S. D6 100
*Moose Lake, l., B.C.* C8 68
*Moose Lake, l., Wi., U.S.* B2 126
*Mooseleuk Stream, stm., Me., U.S.* B4 96
*Mooselookmeguntic Lake, l., Me., U.S.* D2 96
*Moose Mountain, mtn., Sask.* H4 75
*Moose Mountain, mtn., N.H., U.S.* C2 106
*Moose Mountain Creek, stm., Sask.* H4 75
*Moose Mountain Provincial Park, Sask.* H4 75
Moose Pass, Ak., U.S. C10 79
Moose River, Me., U.S. C2 96
Moosic, Pa., U.S. m18 115
*Moosilauke, Mount, mtn., N.H., U.S.* B3 106
Moosomin, Sask. G5 75
Moosonee, Ont. o19 73
Moosup, Ct., U.S. C8 84
*Moosup, stm., U.S.* C1 116
Moosup Valley, R.I., U.S. D1 116
*Mopang Lake, l., Me., U.S.* D5 96
Mopeia Velha, Moz. A6 49
Mopti, Mali D4 45
Moquegua, Peru E3 58
*Moquegua, dept., Peru* E3 58
Mór, Hung. B4 24
*Mor, i., Micron.* Q18 52
*Mòr, Glen, val., Scot., U.K.* D4 13
*Mòr, Sgùrr, mtn., Scot., U.K.* C3 13
Mora, Cam. C2 46
Mora, Spain C4 22
Mora, Swe. G6 14
Mora, Ga., U.S. E4 87
Mora, Mn., U.S. E5 100
Mora, N.M., U.S. B4 108
*Mora, co., N.M., U.S.* A5 108
*Mora, stm., N.M., U.S.* B5 108
*Morača, stm., Yugo.* D4 24
Morādābād, India C6 36
Morada Nova, Braz. C3 57
Mora de Ebro, Spain B6 22
Morafenobe, Madag. g8 49
Morąg, Pol. B5 26
Moraga, Ca., U.S. *D2 82
Moraine, Oh., U.S. *C1 112
Morales, Guat. C3 62
Morales, Mex. k13 63
Moramanga, Madag. g9 49
Moran, In., U.S. D4 91
Moran, Ks., U.S. E8 93
Moran, Mi., U.S. B6 99
Moran, Tx., U.S. C3 120
Moran, Wy., U.S. C2 127
Morann, Pa., U.S. E5 115
Morant Bay, Jam. F5 64
*Morant Point, c., Jam.* F5 64
*Morar, Loch, l., Scot., U.K.* D3 13
*Morat, Lake, l., Switz.* C3 20
Morata de Tajuña, Spain p18 22
Moratalla, Spain C5 22
Morattico, Va., U.S. C6 123
Moratuwa, Sri L. G6 36
*Morava, stm., Eur.* D4 26
Moravia, Ia., U.S. D5 92
Moravia, N.Y., U.S. C4 109
*Moravia, hist. reg., Czech.* D4 26
Morawhanna, Guy. A3 59
Moraya, Bol. D2 55
*Moray Firth, est., Scot., U.K.* B5 10
Morbach, W. Ger. D2 19
Morbegno, Italy D8 21
Morbi, India F3 37
Morden, Man. E2 70
Morden, N.S. D5 71
*More, Ben, mtn., Scot., U.K.* D4 13
*More, Ben, mtn., Scot., U.K.* D3 13
*More Assynt, Ben, mtn., Scot., U.K.* A4 10
*Moreau, stm., S.D., U.S.* B3 118
*Moreau, North Fork, stm., S.D., U.S.* B2 118
*Moreau, South Fork, stm., S.D., U.S.* B2 118
*Moreau Peak, mtn., S.D., U.S.* B2 118
Moreauville, La., U.S. C4 95
Morecambe, Eng., U.K. F6 13
*Morecambe Bay, b., Eng., U.K.* D5 10
Moree, Austl. E8 50
Morehead, Ky., U.S. B6 94
Morehead City, N.C., U.S. C6 110
Morehouse, Mo., U.S. E8 102
*Morehouse, co., La., U.S.* B4 95
Mörel, Switz. D5 21
Moreland, Ar., U.S. B3 81
Moreland, Ga., U.S. C2 87
Moreland, Id., U.S. F6 89
Moreland, Ky., U.S. C5 94
Morelia, Mex. D4 63
Morell, P.E.I. C7 71
Morella, Spain B5 22
*Morelos, state, Mex.* D5 63
*Morena, Sierra, mts., Spain* C3 22
Morenci, Az., U.S. D6 80
Morenci, Mi., U.S. G6 99
Moreno Valley, Ca., U.S. *F5 82
*Moresby Island, i., B.C.* C2 69
*Moreton Bay, b., Austl.* C9 51
Moreton-in-Marsh, Eng., U.K. C6 12
*Moreton Island, i., Austl.* C9 51
Moretown, Vt., U.S. C3 122
Moreuil, Fr. E2 17
Morewood, Ont. B9 73
*Morey, Lake, l., Vt., U.S.* D4 122
*Morey Peak, mtn., Nv., U.S.* E5 105
Morez, Fr. D7 16
Morgan, Austl. G2 51
Morgan, Ga., U.S. E2 87
Morgan, Ky., U.S. B5 94
Morgan, Mn., U.S. F4 100
Morgan, Tx., U.S. C4 120
Morgan, Ut., U.S. B4 121
Morgan, Vt., U.S. B4 122
*Morgan, co., Al., U.S.* A3 78
*Morgan, co., Co., U.S.* A7 83
*Morgan, co., Ga., U.S.* C3 87
*Morgan, co., Il., U.S.* D3 90
*Morgan, co., In., U.S.* F5 91
*Morgan, co., Ky., U.S.* C6 94
*Morgan, co., Mo., U.S.* C5 102
*Morgan, co., Oh., U.S.* C4 112
*Morgan, co., Tn., U.S.* C9 119
*Morgan, co., Ut., U.S.* B4 121
*Morgan, co., W.V., U.S.* B6 125
Morgan Center, Vt., U.S. B5 122
Morgan City, La., U.S. E4 95
Morgan City, Ms., U.S. B3 101
Morganfield, Ky., U.S. C2 94
Morgan Hill, Ca., U.S. D3 82
*Morgan Island, i., S.C., U.S.* G6 117
*Morgan Point, c., Ct., U.S.* E4 84
Morganton, Ar., U.S. B3 81
Morganton, Ga., U.S. B2 87
Morganton, N.C., U.S. B1 110
Morgantown, In., U.S. F5 91
Morgantown, Ky., U.S. C3 94
Morgantown, Ms., U.S. D4 101
Morgantown, Ms., U.S. D2 101
Morgantown, Pa., U.S. F10 115
Morgantown, Tn., U.S. D8 119
Morgantown, W.V., U.S. B5 125
Morganville, Ks., U.S. C6 93
Morganville, N.J., U.S. C4 107
Morganza, La., U.S. D4 95
Morges, Switz. C2 20
Morgex, Italy D3 20
*Morghāb, stm., Asia* A3 36
Morhange, Fr. F6 17
Mori, Japan E10 34
Moriah, Trin. M24 65
Moriah, N.Y., U.S. A7 109
*Moriah, Mount, mtn., Nv., U.S.* D7 105
*Moriah, Mount, mtn., N.H., U.S.* B4 106
Moriarty, N.M., U.S. C3 108
*Morice, stm., B.C.* B4 69
*Morice Lake, l., B.C.* B4 69
Moriguchi, Japan *I7 33
Morin-Heights, Que. D3 74
Morinville, Alta. C4 68
Morioka, Japan D13 31
Morisset-Station, Que. C7 74
Morjärv, Swe. D10 14
*Morkill, stm., B.C.* C7 69
Morlaix, Fr. C2 16
Morland, Ks., U.S. C3 93
Morley, Alta. D3 68
Morley, Mi., U.S. E5 99
Morley, Mo., U.S. D8 102
Morley, N.Y., U.S. f9 109
Mormon Lake, Az., U.S. C4 80
*Mormon Peak, mtn., Nv., U.S.* G7 105
Morne-à-l'Eau, Guad. Q9 65
Morningdale, Ma., U.S. B4 98
Morningside, S.D., U.S. C7 118
Morning Sun, Ia., U.S. C6 92
*Mornington, Isla, i., Chile* D1 54
Morning View, Ky., U.S. k14 94
Moro, Ar., U.S. C5 81
Moro, Or., U.S. B6 114
Morobay, Ar., U.S. D3 81
Morobe, Pap. N. Gui. k12 50
Morocco, In., U.S. C3 91
*Morocco, ctry., Afr.* C3 44
Morococha, Peru D2 58
*Moro Creek, stm., Ar., U.S.* D3 81
Morogoro, Tan. C6 48
*Morogoro, prov., Tan.* C6 48
*Moro Gulf, b., Phil.* D6 34
Moroleón, Mex. m13 63
Morombe, Madag. h8 49
Morón, Arg. g7 54
Morón, Cuba C4 64
Mörön, Mong. B5 31
*Morona, stm., Peru* B2 58
*Morona-Santiago, prov., Ec.* B2 58
Morondava, Madag. h8 49
Morón de la Frontera, Spain D3 22
Moroni, Ut., U.S. D4 121
*Morotai, i., Indon.* E7 34
Moroto, Ug. A5 48
Morozovsk, Sov. Un. G13 27
Morpeth, Ont. E3 73
Morpeth, Eng., U.K. E7 13
Morrill, Ks., U.S. C8 93
Morrill, Ne., U.S. C2 104
*Morrill, co., Ne., U.S.* C2 104
Morrilton, Ar., U.S. B3 81
Morrin, Alta. D4 68
Morrinhos, Braz. B3 56
Morrinsville, N.Z. L15 51
Morris, Man. E3 70
Morris, Al., U.S. B3 78
Morris, Ct., U.S. C3 84
Morris, Ga., U.S. E2 87
Morris, Il., U.S. B5 90
Morris, In., U.S. F7 91
Morris, Mn., U.S. E3 100
Morris, N.Y., U.S. C5 109
Morris, Ok., U.S. B6 113
*Morris, co., Ks., U.S.* D7 93
*Morris, co., N.J., U.S.* B3 107
*Morris, co., Tx., U.S.* C5 120
*Morris, Mount, mtn., N.Y., U.S.* A6 109
Morrisburg, Ont. C9 73
Morris Chapel, Tn., U.S. B3 119
Morrisdale, Pa., U.S. E5 115
*Morris Island, i., S.C., U.S.* F8 117
*Morris Jesup, Kap, c., Grnld.* A17 61
Morrison, Co., U.S. B5 83
Morrison, Il., U.S. B4 90
Morrison, Mo., U.S. C6 102
Morrison, Ok., U.S. A4 113
Morrison, Tn., U.S. D8 119
Morrison, Wi., U.S. h10 126
*Morrison, co., Mn., U.S.* D4 100
Morrison City, Tn., U.S. C11 119
Morrisonville, Il., U.S. D4 90
Morrisonville, N.Y., U.S. f11 109
Morris Plains, N.J., U.S. B4 107
Morris Run, Pa., U.S. C7 115
Morriston, Fl., U.S. C4 86
Morristown, Az., U.S. D3 80
Morristown, In., U.S. E6 91
Morristown, Mn., U.S. F5 100
Morristown, N.J., U.S. B4 107
Morristown, N.Y., U.S. f9 109
Morristown, S.D., U.S. B4 118
Morristown, Tn., U.S. C10 119
Morristown, Vt., U.S. B3 122
*Morristown National Historical Park, N.J., U.S.* B3 107
Morrisville, Mo., U.S. D4 102
Morrisville, N.Y., U.S. C5 109
Morrisville, Pa., U.S. F12 115
Morrisville, Vt., U.S. B3 122
Morrito, Nic. E7 63
Morro, Ec. B1 58
*Morro, Punta, c., Chile* E1 55
*Morro, Punta, c., Mex.* D6 63
Morro Bay, Ca., U.S. E3 82
Morro do Chapéu, Braz. D2 57
Morropón, Peru C2 58
*Morrosquillo, Golfo de, b., Col.* B2 60
Morrow, Ga., U.S. C2 87
Morrow, La., U.S. D3 95
Morrow, Oh., U.S. C1 112
*Morrow, co., Oh., U.S.* B3 112
*Morrow, co., Or., U.S.* B7 114
Morrowville, Ks., U.S. C6 93
Morrumbene, Moz. B6 49
*Mors, i., Den.* B2 15
Morse, Sask. G2 75
Morse, La., U.S. D3 95
Morse, Tx., U.S. A2 120
Morse, Wi., U.S. B3 126
Morse Bluff, Ne., U.S. C9 104
Morse Mill, Mo., U.S. g12 102
*Morse Reservoir, res., In., U.S.* D5 91
*Morses Creek, stm., N.J., U.S.* k8 107
Morshansk, Sov. Un. E13 27
Mortagne, Fr. C4 16
Mortara, Italy B2 23
Morteau, Fr. D7 16
Morteros, Arg. A4 54
*Mortes, Rio das, stm., Braz.* E4 59
Mortlach, Sask. G2 75
Morton, Il., U.S. C4 90
Morton, Mn., U.S. F4 100
Morton, Ms., U.S. C4 101
Morton, Tx., U.S. C1 120
Morton, Wa., U.S. C3 124
*Morton, co., Ks., U.S.* E2 93
*Morton, co., N.D., U.S.* C4 111
Morton Grove, Il., U.S. h9 90
*Morton Pass, Wy., U.S.* E7 127
Mortons Gap, Ky., U.S. C2 94
Moruga, Trin. O23 65
Moruya, Austl. G8 51
*Morvan Mountains, mts., Fr.* D6 16
Morven, Ga., U.S. F3 87
Morven, N.C., U.S. C2 110
*Morven, mtn., Scot., U.K.* B5 13
Morwell, Austl. G8 50
Moryakovskiy Zaton, Sov. Un. B10 28
Morye, Sov. Un. r32 14
Mosalsk, Sov. Un. D10 27
Mosbach, W. Ger. D4 19
Mosby, Mo., U.S. h11 102
Mosby, Mt., U.S. D9 103
Mosca, Co., U.S. D5 83
*Moscarello, Italy* k9 23
*Moscos Islands, is., Burma* F10 36
Moscow (Moskva), Sov. Un. D6 29
Moscow, Ar., U.S. C4 81
Moscow, Id., U.S. C2 89
Moscow, In., U.S. F6 91
Moscow, Ia., U.S. C6 92
Moscow, Ks., U.S. E2 93
Moscow, Ky., U.S. f8 94
Moscow, Oh., U.S. D1 112
Moscow, Pa., U.S. m18 115
Moscow, R.I., U.S. E2 116
Moscow, Tn., U.S. B2 119
Moscow, Vt., U.S. C3 122
Moscow Mills, Mo., U.S. C7 102
*Mosel (Moselle), stm., Eur.* D3 18
Moselle, Va., U.S. C5 123
Moselle, Ms., U.S. D4 101
*Moselle, dept., Fr.* E6 17
*Moselle (Mosel), stm., Eur.* C7 16
Mosers River, N.S. E7 71
*Moses Coulee, val., Wa., U.S.* B6 124
Moses Lake, Wa., U.S. B6 124
*Moses Lake, l., Wa., U.S.* B6 124
Mosgiel, N.Z. P13 51
Mosheim, Tn., U.S. C11 119
Mosher, S.D., U.S. D5 118
Mosherville, N.S. D6 71
Moshi, Tan. B6 48
Moshupa, Bots. B4 49
Mosier, Or., U.S. B5 114
Mosinee, Wi., U.S. D4 126
Mosjöen, Nor. E5 14
*Moskva, stm., Sov. Un.* n18 27
*Mosley Creek, stm., B.C.* D5 69
Mosomane (Artesia), Bots. B4 49
Mosonmagyaróvár, Hung. B3 24
Mosquera, Col. C2 60
Mosquero, N.M., U.S. B6 108
Mosquito, Newf. E5 72
*Mosquito Coast, N.A.* D6 62
*Mosquito Creek, stm., Ia., U.S.* C2 92
*Mosquito Creek Lake, res., Oh., U.S.* A5 112
*Mosquito Lagoon, b., Fl., U.S.* D6 86
*Mosquitos, Golfo de los, b., Pan.* F7 62
Moss, Nor. H4 14

| Name | Map Ref. | Page |
|---|---|---|
| Moss, Ms., U.S. | D4 | 101 |
| Moss, Tn., U.S. | C8 | 119 |
| Mossaka, Congo | B2 | 48 |
| Mossbank, Sask. | H3 | 75 |
| Moss Bluff, La., U.S. | D2 | 95 |
| Mosselbaai (Mossel Bay), S. Afr. | D3 | 49 |
| Mossendjo, Congo | B1 | 48 |
| Mossleigh, Alta. | D4 | 68 |
| Mossman, Austl. | C8 | 50 |
| Moss Mountain, mtn., Ar., U.S. | C3 | 81 |
| Mossoró, Braz. | C3 | 57 |
| Moss Point, Ms., U.S. | E5 | 101 |
| Moss Vale, Austl. | G8 | 51 |
| Mossville, Ar., U.S. | B2 | 81 |
| Mossy, stm., Man. | D2 | 70 |
| Mossy, stm., Sask. | C4 | 75 |
| Mossy Head, Fl., U.S. | u15 | 86 |
| Mossyrock, Wa., U.S. | C3 | 124 |
| Most, Czech. | C2 | 26 |
| Mostar, Yugo. | D3 | 24 |
| Mostefa, Cap, c., Tun. | F3 | 23 |
| Móstoles, Spain | p17 | 22 |
| Mostrim (Edgeworthstown), Ire. | D4 | 11 |
| Mosul (Al Mawṣil), Iraq | B4 | 38 |
| Moswansicut Pond, l., R.I., U.S. | C3 | 116 |
| Motagua, stm., N.A. | E6 | 63 |
| Motala, Swe. | H6 | 14 |
| Motatán, Ven. | B3 | 60 |
| Motherwell, Scot., U.K. | C5 | 10 |
| Motīhāri, India | D10 | 37 |
| Motilla del Palancar, Spain | C5 | 22 |
| Motley, Mn., U.S. | D4 | 100 |
| Motley, co., Tx., U.S. | B2 | 120 |
| Motobu, Japan | N5 | 52 |
| Motomachi, Japan | o18 | 33 |
| Moto Mountain, hill, Japan | P17 | 52 |
| Motril, Spain | D4 | 22 |
| Motru, stm., Rom. | C6 | 24 |
| Mott, N.D., U.S. | C3 | 111 |
| Motta di Livenza, Italy | D8 | 20 |
| Motueka, N.Z. | N14 | 51 |
| Motul [de Felipe Carrillo Puerto], Mex. | C7 | 63 |
| Motupe, Peru | C2 | 58 |
| Moturiki, i., Fiji | H15 | 52 |
| Mou, Den. | B4 | 15 |
| Mouaskar, Alg. | B5 | 44 |
| Moúdhros (Mudros), Grc. | C5 | 25 |
| Moudjéria, Maur. | C2 | 45 |
| Moudon, Switz. | C2 | 20 |
| Mouila, Gabon | F2 | 46 |
| Moulamein Billabong Creek, stm., Austl. | G5 | 51 |
| Mould Bay, N.W. Ter. | m28 | 66 |
| Moule, Guad. | H14 | 64 |
| Moulins, Fr. | D5 | 16 |
| Moulouya, Oued, stm., Mor. | C4 | 44 |
| Moulton, Al., U.S. | A2 | 78 |
| Moulton, Ia., U.S. | D5 | 92 |
| Moultonboro, N.H., U.S. | C4 | 106 |
| Moultrie, Ga., U.S. | E3 | 87 |
| Moultrie, co., Il., U.S. | D5 | 90 |
| Moultrie, Lake, res., S.C., U.S. | E7 | 117 |
| Mound, La., U.S. | B4 | 95 |
| Mound, Mn., U.S. | n11 | 100 |
| Mound Bayou, Ms., U.S. | B3 | 101 |
| Mound City, Il., U.S. | F4 | 90 |
| Mound City, Ks., U.S. | D9 | 93 |
| Mound City, Mo., U.S. | A2 | 102 |
| Mound City, S.D., U.S. | B5 | 118 |
| Mound City Group National Monument, Oh., U.S. | C2 | 112 |
| Moundou, Chad | D3 | 46 |
| Moundridge, Ks., U.S. | D6 | 93 |
| Mounds, Il., U.S. | F4 | 90 |
| Mounds, Ok., U.S. | B5 | 113 |
| Mounds View, Mn., U.S. | m12 | 100 |
| Moundsville, W.V., U.S. | B4 | 125 |
| Mound Valley, Ks., U.S. | E8 | 93 |
| Moundville, Al., U.S. | C2 | 78 |
| Moundville, Mo., U.S. | D3 | 102 |
| Mounier, Mont, mtn., Fr. | E7 | 16 |
| Mountain, N.D., U.S. | A8 | 111 |
| Mountain, W.V., U.S. | B4 | 125 |
| Mountain, Wi., U.S. | C5 | 126 |
| Mountainair, N.M., U.S. | C3 | 108 |
| Mountainaire, Az., U.S. | B4 | 80 |
| Mountain Ash, Ky., U.S. | D5 | 94 |
| Mountainboro, Al., U.S. | A3 | 78 |
| Mountain Brook, Al., U.S. | g7 | 78 |
| Mountainburg, Ar., U.S. | B1 | 81 |
| Mountain City, Ga., U.S. | B3 | 87 |
| Mountain City, Nv., U.S. | B6 | 105 |
| Mountain City, Tn., U.S. | C12 | 119 |
| Mountain Dale, Pa., U.S. | D6 | 109 |
| Mountain Fork, stm., U.S. | C7 | 113 |
| Mountain Grove, Ont. | C8 | 73 |
| Mountain Grove, Mo., U.S. | D5 | 102 |
| Mountain Home, Ar., U.S. | A3 | 81 |
| Mountain Home, Id., U.S. | F3 | 89 |
| Mountainhome, Pa., U.S. | D11 | 115 |
| Mountain Home, Tx., U.S. | D3 | 120 |
| Mountain Home, Ut., U.S. | C5 | 121 |
| Mountain Home Air Force Base, mil., Id., U.S. | F3 | 89 |
| Mountain Iron, Mn., U.S. | C6 | 100 |
| Mountain Lake, l., Sask. | B3 | 75 |
| Mountain Lake Park, Md., U.S. | m12 | 97 |
| Mountain Nile (Al Baḥr al Jabal), stm., Sud. | D3 | 47 |
| Mountain Park, Alta. | C2 | 68 |
| Mountain Park, Fl., U.S. | *C2 | 87 |
| Mountain Park, Ok., U.S. | C3 | 113 |
| Mountain Pine, Ar., U.S. | C2 | 81 |
| Mountain Point, Ak., U.S. | n24 | 79 |
| Mountainside, N.J., U.S. | B4 | 107 |
| Mountain Springs, Nv., U.S. | *G6 | 105 |
| Mountain Valley, Ar., U.S. | C3 | 81 |
| Mountain View, Alta. | E4 | 68 |
| Mountain View, Ar., U.S. | B3 | 81 |
| Mountain View, Ca., U.S. | k8 | 82 |
| Mountain View, Ca., U.S. | *B5 | 83 |
| Mountain View, Co., U.S. | *A5 | 83 |
| Mountainview, Hi., U.S. | D6 | 88 |
| Mountain View, Mo., U.S. | D6 | 102 |
| Mountain View, N.M., U.S. | B3 | 113 |
| Mountain View, Ok., U.S. | B3 | 113 |
| Mountain View, Wy., U.S. | *D6 | 127 |
| Mountain Village, Ak., U.S. | C7 | 79 |
| Mount Airy, Md., U.S. | B3 | 97 |
| Mount Airy, N.C., U.S. | A2 | 110 |
| Mount Albert, Ont. | C5 | 73 |
| Mount Angel, Or., U.S. | B4 | 114 |
| Mount Arlington, N.J., U.S. | B3 | 107 |
| Mount Assiniboine Provincial Park, B.C. | D10 | 69 |
| Mount Athos, ter., Grc. | B5 | 25 |
| Mount Auburn, Il., U.S. | D4 | 90 |
| Mount Auburn, Ia., U.S. | B5 | 92 |
| Mount Ayr, In., U.S. | C3 | 91 |
| Mount Ayr, Ia., U.S. | D3 | 92 |
| Mount Barker, Austl. | G2 | 51 |
| Mount Bellew Bridge, Ire. | D3 | 11 |
| Mount Berry, Ga., U.S. | B1 | 87 |
| Mount Blanchard, Oh., U.S. | B2 | 112 |
| Mount Brydges, Ont. | E3 | 73 |
| Mount Carleton Provincial Park, N.B. | B3 | 71 |
| Mount Carmel, Il., U.S. | E6 | 90 |
| Mount Carmel, Il., U.S. | F8 | 91 |
| Mount Carmel, N.D., U.S. | A7 | 111 |
| Mount Carmel, Oh., U.S. | o13 | 112 |
| Mount Carmel, Pa., U.S. | E9 | 115 |
| Mount Carmel, S.C., U.S. | C2 | 117 |
| Mount Carmel, Ut., U.S. | F3 | 121 |
| Mount Carmel Junction, Ut., U.S. | F3 | 121 |
| Mount Carmel [-Mitchell's Brook-Saint Catherine's], Newf. | E5 | 72 |
| Mount Carroll, Il., U.S. | A4 | 90 |
| Mount Clare, W.V., U.S. | B4 | 125 |
| Mount Clemens, Mi., U.S. | F8 | 99 |
| Mount Clinton, Va., U.S. | B4 | 123 |
| Mount Cory, Oh., U.S. | B2 | 112 |
| Mount Crawford, Va., U.S. | B4 | 123 |
| Mount Croghan, S.C., U.S. | B7 | 117 |
| Mount Darwin, Zimb. | A5 | 49 |
| Mount Desert, Me., U.S. | *D4 | 96 |
| Mount Desert Island, i., Me., U.S. | D4 | 96 |
| Mount Dora, Fl., U.S. | D5 | 86 |
| Mount Dora, N.M., U.S. | A6 | 108 |
| Mount Eaton, Oh., U.S. | B4 | 112 |
| Mount Eden, Ky., U.S. | B4 | 94 |
| Mount Elgin, Ont. | E4 | 73 |
| Mount Emmons, Ut., U.S. | *C5 | 121 |
| Mount Ephraim, N.J., U.S. | *D2 | 107 |
| Mount Erie, Il., U.S. | E5 | 90 |
| Mount Etna, In., U.S. | C6 | 91 |
| Mount Etna, Ia., U.S. | C3 | 92 |
| Mount Forest, Ont. | D4 | 73 |
| Mount Forest, Mi., U.S. | E6 | 99 |
| Mount Freedom, N.J., U.S. | B3 | 107 |
| Mount Gambier, Austl. | G7 | 50 |
| Mount Gay, W.V., U.S. | D2 | 125 |
| Mount Gilead, N.C., U.S. | B3 | 110 |
| Mount Gilead, Oh., U.S. | B3 | 112 |
| Mount Hagen, Pap. N. Gui. | k11 | 50 |
| Mount Healthy, Oh., U.S. | o12 | 112 |
| Mount Hebron, Ca., U.S. | B2 | 82 |
| Mount Hermon, La., U.S. | D5 | 95 |
| Mount Hermon, Ma., U.S. | A3 | 98 |
| Mount Heron, Va., U.S. | e9 | 123 |
| Mount Holly, Ar., U.S. | D3 | 81 |
| Mount Holly, N.J., U.S. | C3 | 107 |
| Mount Holly, N.C., U.S. | B1 | 110 |
| Mount Holly, S.C., U.S. | E7 | 117 |
| Mount Holly, Vt., U.S. | E3 | 122 |
| Mount Holly Springs, Pa., U.S. | F7 | 115 |
| Mount Hood, Or., U.S. | B5 | 114 |
| Mount Hope, Ont. | D5 | 73 |
| Mount Hope, Al., U.S. | A2 | 78 |
| Mount Hope, Ks., U.S. | E6 | 93 |
| Mount Hope, W.V., U.S. | D3 | 125 |
| Mount Hope, Wi., U.S. | F3 | 126 |
| Mount Hope, stm., Ct., U.S. | B7 | 84 |
| Mount Hope Bay, b., U.S. | D6 | 116 |
| Mount Horeb, Wi., U.S. | E4 | 126 |
| Mount Ida, Ar., U.S. | C2 | 81 |
| Mount Idaho, Id., U.S. | D2 | 89 |
| Mount Isa, Austl. | D6 | 50 |
| Mount Jackson, Va., U.S. | B4 | 123 |
| Mount Jewett, Pa., U.S. | C4 | 115 |
| Mount Joy, Ia., U.S. | h10 | 92 |
| Mount Joy, Pa., U.S. | F9 | 115 |
| Mount Judea, Ar., U.S. | B2 | 81 |
| Mount Juliet, Tn., U.S. | A5 | 119 |
| Mount Kisco, N.Y., U.S. | D7 | 109 |
| Mountlake Terrace, Wa., U.S. | *B3 | 124 |
| Mount Lebanon, Pa., U.S. | F1 | 115 |
| Mount Lemmon, Az., U.S. | E5 | 80 |
| Mount Lookout, W.V., U.S. | C4 | 125 |
| Mount Magnet, Austl. | E3 | 50 |
| Mount Meigs, Al., U.S. | C3 | 78 |
| Mountmellick, Ire. | D4 | 11 |
| Mount Montgomery, Nv., U.S. | F3 | 105 |
| Mount Morgan, Austl. | D9 | 50 |
| Mount Moriah, Mo., U.S. | A4 | 102 |
| Mount Morris, Il., U.S. | A4 | 90 |
| Mount Morris, Mi., U.S. | E7 | 99 |
| Mount Morris, N.Y., U.S. | C3 | 109 |
| Mount Morris, Pa., U.S. | G1 | 115 |
| Mount of Olives, hill, Isr. Occ. | m14 | 41 |
| Mount Olive, Al., U.S. | B3 | 78 |
| Mount Olive, Il., U.S. | D4 | 90 |
| Mount Olive, Ms., U.S. | D4 | 101 |
| Mount Olive, N.C., U.S. | B4 | 110 |
| Mount Olive, Tn., U.S. | n14 | 119 |
| Mount Olivet, Ky., U.S. | B5 | 94 |
| Mount Olympus, Ut., U.S. | *C4 | 121 |
| Mount Orab, Oh., U.S. | C2 | 112 |
| Mount Pearl, Newf. | E5 | 72 |
| Mount Penn, Pa., U.S. | F10 | 115 |
| Mount Pleasant, Ar., U.S. | B4 | 81 |
| Mount Pleasant, Fl., U.S. | B2 | 86 |
| Mount Pleasant, Ia., U.S. | C6 | 92 |
| Mount Pleasant, Md., U.S. | B3 | 97 |
| Mount Pleasant, Mi., U.S. | E6 | 99 |
| Mount Pleasant, Ms., U.S. | A4 | 101 |
| Mount Pleasant, N.C., U.S. | B2 | 110 |
| Mount Pleasant, Pa., U.S. | F2 | 115 |
| Mount Pleasant, S.C., U.S. | F8 | 117 |
| Mount Pleasant, Tn., U.S. | B4 | 119 |
| Mount Pleasant, Tx., U.S. | C5 | 120 |
| Mount Pleasant, Ut., U.S. | D4 | 121 |
| Mount Pocono, Pa., U.S. | D11 | 115 |
| Mount Prospect, Il., U.S. | A6 | 90 |
| Mount Pulaski, Il., U.S. | C4 | 90 |
| Mountrail, co., N.D., U.S. | A3 | 111 |
| Mount Rainier National Park, Wa., U.S. | C4 | 124 |
| Mount Revelstoke National Park, B.C. | D8 | 69 |
| Mount Robson Provincial Park, B.C. | C8 | 69 |
| Mount Rogers National Recreation Area, Va., U.S. | D1 | 123 |
| Mount Rushmore National Memorial, hist., S.D., U.S. | D2 | 118 |
| Mount Savage, Md., U.S. | k13 | 97 |
| Mount's Bay, b., Eng., U.K. | D2 | 12 |
| Mount Shasta, Ca., U.S. | B2 | 82 |
| Mount Sidney, Va., U.S. | B4 | 123 |
| Mount Sinai, N.Y., U.S. | *n15 | 109 |
| Mount Solon, Va., U.S. | B3 | 123 |
| Mount Sterling, Il., U.S. | D3 | 90 |
| Mount Sterling, Ky., U.S. | B6 | 94 |
| Mount Sterling, Oh., U.S. | C2 | 112 |
| Mount Stewart, P.E.I. | C7 | 71 |
| Mount Storm, W.V., U.S. | B5 | 125 |
| Mount Summit, In., U.S. | D7 | 91 |
| Mount Sunapee, N.H., U.S. | D2 | 106 |
| Mount Tabor, Vt., U.S. | E3 | 122 |
| Mount Uniacke, N.S. | E6 | 71 |
| Mount Union, Ia., U.S. | C6 | 92 |
| Mount Union, Pa., U.S. | F6 | 115 |
| Mount Upton, N.Y., U.S. | C5 | 109 |
| Mount Vernon, Al., U.S. | D1 | 78 |
| Mount Vernon, Ga., U.S. | D4 | 87 |
| Mount Vernon, Il., U.S. | E5 | 90 |
| Mount Vernon, In., U.S. | I2 | 91 |
| Mount Vernon, Ia., U.S. | C6 | 92 |
| Mount Vernon, Ky., U.S. | C5 | 94 |
| Mount Vernon, Me., U.S. | D3 | 96 |
| Mount Vernon, Md., U.S. | D6 | 97 |
| Mount Vernon, Mo., U.S. | D4 | 102 |
| Mount Vernon, N.Y., U.S. | h13 | 109 |
| Mount Vernon, Oh., U.S. | B3 | 112 |
| Mount Vernon, Or., U.S. | C7 | 114 |
| Mount Vernon, S.D., U.S. | D7 | 118 |
| Mount Vernon, Tn., U.S. | D9 | 119 |
| Mount Vernon, Wa., U.S. | A3 | 124 |
| Mount Victory, Oh., U.S. | B2 | 112 |
| Mount View, R.I., U.S. | D4 | 116 |
| Mount Washington, Ky., U.S. | B4 | 94 |
| Mount Washington, Ma., U.S. | B1 | 98 |
| Mount Wolf, Pa., U.S. | F8 | 115 |
| Mount Zion, Ga., U.S. | C1 | 87 |
| Mount Zion, Il., U.S. | D5 | 90 |
| Moura, Austl. | D8 | 50 |
| Moura, Braz. | C2 | 59 |
| Moura, Port. | C2 | 22 |
| Mourdi, Dépression du, depr., Chad | B4 | 46 |
| Mourmelon-le-Grand, Fr. | E4 | 17 |
| Mourne Mountains, mts., N. Ire. (U.K.) | C10 | 10 |
| Mouscron (Moeskroen), Bel. | B5 | 16 |
| Mousie, Ky., U.S. | C7 | 94 |
| Moussoro, Chad | C3 | 46 |
| Mouthe, Fr. | C1 | 21 |
| Moutier, Switz. | B3 | 21 |
| Moûtiers[-Tarentaise], Fr. | E7 | 16 |
| Mouy, Fr. | F2 | 17 |
| Moville, Ire. | B4 | 11 |
| Moville, Ia., U.S. | B1 | 92 |
| Moweaqua, Il., U.S. | D4 | 90 |
| Mower, co., Mn., U.S. | G6 | 100 |
| Mowrystown, Oh., U.S. | C2 | 112 |
| Moxahala, Oh., U.S. | C3 | 112 |
| Moxee City, Wa., U.S. | C5 | 124 |
| Moxico, dept., Ang. | D3 | 48 |
| Moxie Pond, l., Me., U.S. | C3 | 96 |
| Moxley, Ga., U.S. | D4 | 87 |
| Moy, stm., Ire. | C2 | 11 |
| Moy, Cnoc, hill, Scot., U.K. | E3 | 13 |
| Moyale, Eth. | E4 | 47 |
| Moyale, Kenya | A6 | 48 |
| Moyamba, S.L. | E2 | 45 |
| Moycullen, Ire. | D2 | 11 |
| Moyers, Ok., U.S. | C6 | 113 |
| Moyeuvre[-Grande], Fr. | C7 | 16 |
| Moyie, B.C. | E10 | 69 |
| Moyie Springs, Id., U.S. | A2 | 89 |
| Moyo, Ug. | A5 | 48 |
| Moyobamba, Peru | C2 | 58 |
| Moyock, N.C., U.S. | A6 | 110 |
| Moyu, Guat. | C2 | 64 |
| Moža, Isr. | h11 | 41 |
| Mozambique, ctry., Afr. | H9 | 42 |
| Mozambique Channel, strt., Afr. | H10 | 42 |
| Mozart, Sask. | F3 | 75 |
| Mozdok, Sov. Un. | E2 | 28 |
| Mozelle, Ky., U.S. | D6 | 94 |
| Mozhaysk, Sov. Un. | F5 | 28 |
| Mozhga, Sov. Un. | D19 | 8 |
| Mozyr, Sov. Un. | E7 | 27 |
| Mpanda, Tan. | C5 | 48 |
| Mpika, Zam. | D5 | 48 |
| Mporokoso, Zam. | C5 | 48 |
| Mpouya, Congo | B2 | 48 |
| Mpraeso, Ghana | E4 | 45 |
| Mpulungu, Zam. | C5 | 48 |
| Mpwapwa, Tan. | C6 | 48 |
| Mragowo, Pol. | B5 | 26 |
| Mšec, Czech. | n16 | 26 |
| Mšeno, Czech. | n17 | 26 |
| Mšené-lázně, Czech. | n17 | 26 |
| M'Sila, Alg. | B5 | 44 |
| Msta, stm., Sov. Un. | B9 | 27 |
| Mstislavl', Sov. Un. | D8 | 27 |
| Mtakuja, Tan. | C5 | 48 |
| Mtsensk, Sov. Un. | E11 | 27 |
| Mtubatuba, S. Afr. | C5 | 49 |
| Mtwara, Tan. | D7 | 48 |
| Mtwara, prov., Tan. | D6 | 48 |
| Mu, stm., Burma | A1 | 35 |
| Muaná, Braz. | C5 | 57 |
| Muang Khammouan, Laos | D6 | 35 |
| Muang Khong, Laos | C3 | 34 |
| Muang Khongxedon, Laos | E6 | 35 |
| Muang Lan, Laos | C6 | 35 |
| Muang Ou Nua, Laos | A4 | 35 |
| Muang Ou Tai, Laos | A4 | 35 |
| Muang Pakxan, Laos | C5 | 35 |
| Muang Sing, Laos | A2 | 34 |
| Muang Souy, Laos | C5 | 35 |
| Muang Xaignabouri, Laos | C4 | 35 |
| Muang Xepon, Laos | D7 | 35 |
| Muar (Bandar Maharani), Malay. | *E2 | 34 |
| Muar, Malay. | K5 | 35 |
| Muaratewe, Indon. | F5 | 34 |
| Mubārī, Cape, c., Pak. | I13 | 39 |
| Mubārak, Jabal, mtn., Asia | E7 | 41 |
| Mubende, Ug. | A5 | 48 |
| Mubi, Nig. | D7 | 45 |
| Mucajaí, stm., Braz. | B2 | 59 |
| Mücheln, E. Ger. | B6 | 19 |
| Muchkapskiy, Sov. Un. | F14 | 27 |
| Muchot, Puntan, c., N. Mar. Is. | D7 | 52 |
| Much Wenlock (Wenlock), Eng., U.K. | B5 | 12 |
| Muck, i., Scot., U.K. | B3 | 10 |
| Muckalee Creek, stm., Ga., U.S. | D2 | 87 |
| Muckleshoot Indian Reservation, Wa., U.S. | f11 | 124 |
| Muconda, Ang. | D3 | 48 |
| Mucuri, Braz. | E3 | 57 |
| Mucuri, stm., Braz. | E3 | 57 |
| Mucusso, Ang. | E3 | 48 |
| Mud, stm., Ky., U.S. | C3 | 94 |
| Mud, stm., Mn., U.S. | B3 | 100 |
| Mud, stm., Malay. | I4 | 35 |
| Mudanjiang, China | C10 | 31 |
| Mudanya, Tur. | B7 | 25 |
| Mud Butte, S.D., U.S. | C3 | 118 |
| Mud Creek, stm., Al., U.S. | g6 | 78 |
| Mud Creek, stm., Co., U.S. | D8 | 83 |
| Mud Creek, stm., Ia., U.S. | e9 | 92 |
| Mud Creek, stm., Ne., U.S. | C6 | 104 |
| Mud Creek, stm., Ok., U.S. | C4 | 113 |
| Muddy, Il., U.S. | F5 | 90 |
| Muddy Boggy Creek, stm., Ok., U.S. | C6 | 113 |
| Muddy Creek, stm., Co., U.S. | A4 | 83 |
| Muddy Creek, stm., Ks., U.S. | k14 | 93 |
| Muddy Creek, stm., Ut., U.S. | E4 | 121 |
| Muddy Creek, stm., Wy., U.S. | C4 | 127 |
| Muddy Creek, stm., Wy., U.S. | D6 | 127 |
| Muddy Creek, stm., Wy., U.S. | E5 | 127 |
| Muddy Creek, stm., Wy., U.S. | E2 | 127 |
| Muddy Creek Mountain, mtn., Ar., U.S. | C2 | 81 |
| Muddy Lake, l., Sask. | E1 | 75 |
| Muddy Mountain, mtn., Wy., U.S. | D6 | 127 |
| Muddy Mountains, mts., Nv., U.S. | G7 | 105 |
| Muddy Peak, mtn., Nv., U.S. | G7 | 105 |
| Müden, W. Ger. | F4 | 15 |
| Mudgee, Austl. | F7 | 51 |
| Mudjatik, stm., Sask. | A2 | 75 |
| Mud Lake, Id., U.S. | F6 | 89 |
| Mud Lake, l., Me., U.S. | A4 | 96 |
| Mud Lake, l., Nv., U.S. | F4 | 105 |
| Mud Lick Creek, stm., Ky., U.S. | k13 | 94 |
| Mudon, Burma | E10 | 36 |
| Mudros see Moúdhros, Grc. | C5 | 25 |
| Mudug, prov., Som. | D6 | 47 |
| Mudug, stm., Som. | D6 | 48 |
| Mueda, Moz. | D6 | 48 |
| Mueller, stm., Sask. | E3 | 75 |
| Muenster, Tx., U.S. | C4 | 120 |
| Muff, Ire. | B4 | 11 |
| Mufulira, Zam. | D4 | 48 |
| Mugarripiga, China | A11 | 37 |
| Mugía, Spain | A1 | 22 |
| Muğla, Tur. | D7 | 40 |
| Mugodzhary Mountains, hills, Sov. Un. | D5 | 28 |
| Muhammad Qawl, Sud. | A4 | 47 |
| Mühlacker, W. Ger. | E3 | 19 |
| Mühldorf, W. Ger. | D6 | 18 |
| Muhlenberg, co., Ky., U.S. | C2 | 94 |
| Mühlhausen [in Thüringen], E. Ger. | C5 | 18 |
| Mühlig-Hofmann Mountains, mts., Ant. | B13 | 7 |
| Muhulu, Zaire | B4 | 48 |
| Muhutwe, Tan. | B5 | 48 |
| Mui, i., Marsh Is. | S18 | 52 |
| Muine Bheag, Ire. | E5 | 11 |
| Muir, Mi., U.S. | E6 | 99 |
| Muir, Scot., U.K. | E4 | 13 |
| Muirkirk, Md., U.S. | B4 | 97 |
| Muir Woods National Monument, Ca., U.S. | h7 | 82 |
| Mukachevo, Sov. Un. | G4 | 27 |
| Mukah, Malay. | E4 | 34 |
| Mukdahan, Thai. | D6 | 35 |
| Mukden see Shenyang, China | C9 | 31 |
| Mukilteo, Wa., U.S. | B3 | 124 |
| Mukutawa, stm., Man. | C3 | 70 |
| Mukwonago, Wi., U.S. | F5 | 126 |
| Mula, Spain | C5 | 22 |
| Mulanje, Mwi. | E6 | 48 |
| Mulberry, Ar., U.S. | B1 | 81 |
| Mulberry, Fl., U.S. | E4 | 86 |
| Mulberry, In., U.S. | D4 | 91 |
| Mulberry, Ks., U.S. | E9 | 93 |
| Mulberry, N.C., U.S. | A1 | 110 |
| Mulberry, Oh., U.S. | C1 | 112 |
| Mulberry, stm., Ar., U.S. | B1 | 81 |
| Mulberry Fork, stm., Al., U.S. | B3 | 78 |
| Mulberry Grove, Il., U.S. | E4 | 90 |
| Mulberry Mountain, mtn., Ar., U.S. | B1 | 81 |
| Mulchén, Chile | B2 | 54 |
| Mulde, stm., E. Ger. | C6 | 18 |
| Muldoon, Tx., U.S. | E4 | 120 |
| Muldraugh, Ky., U.S. | C4 | 94 |
| Muldrow, Ok., U.S. | B7 | 113 |
| Mule Creek, N.M., U.S. | D1 | 108 |
| Mulegé, Mex. | D2 | 63 |
| Muleshoe, Tx., U.S. | B1 | 120 |
| Mulga, Al., U.S. | B3 | 78 |
| Mulhacén, mtn., Spain | D4 | 22 |
| Mulhall, Ok., U.S. | A4 | 113 |
| Mülheim [an der Ruhr], W. Ger. | C3 | 18 |
| Mulhouse, Fr. | D7 | 16 |
| Muling, China | C13 | 31 |
| Muling He, stm., China | C7 | 33 |
| Mulinu'u, Cape, c., W. Sam. | F11 | 52 |
| Mulitapu'ili, Cape, c., W. Sam. | F12 | 52 |
| Mull, Island of, i., Scot., U.K. | B4 | 10 |
| Mull, Sound of, strt., Scot., U.K. | B3 | 10 |
| Mullaghcleevaun, mtn., Ire. | D5 | 11 |
| Mullan, Id., U.S. | B3 | 89 |
| Mullan Pass, Mt., U.S. | D4 | 103 |
| Mullen, Ne., U.S. | B4 | 104 |
| Mullens, W.V., U.S. | D3 | 125 |
| Muller Mountains, mts., Indon. | E4 | 34 |
| Mullet Key, i., Fl., U.S. | p10 | 86 |
| Mullet Lake, Mi., U.S. | C6 | 99 |
| Mullet Peninsula, pen., Ire. | C1 | 11 |
| Mullett Lake, l., Mi., U.S. | C6 | 99 |
| Mullewa, Austl. | E3 | 50 |
| Mullica, stm., N.J., U.S. | D3 | 107 |
| Mullica Hill, N.J., U.S. | D2 | 107 |
| Mulliken, Mi., U.S. | F6 | 99 |
| Mullin, Tx., U.S. | D3 | 120 |
| Mullinavat, Ire. | E4 | 11 |
| Mullingar, Ire. | D4 | 11 |
| Mullins, S.C., U.S. | C9 | 117 |
| Müllrose, E. Ger. | A9 | 19 |
| Mulobezi, Zam. | E4 | 48 |
| Mulroy Bay, b., Ire. | B4 | 11 |
| Mulshi Lake, res., India | n5 | 37 |
| Multan, Pak. | B5 | 36 |
| Multnomah, co., Or., U.S. | B4 | 114 |
| Mulukuru, Lake, l., Austl. | F4 | 51 |
| Mulvane, Ks., U.S. | E6 | 93 |
| Mulvihill, Man. | D2 | 70 |
| Mummy Range, mts., Co., U.S. | A5 | 83 |
| Mun, stm., Thai. | B2 | 34 |
| Muna, Mex. | C7 | 63 |
| Münchberg, W. Ger. | C6 | 19 |
| Münchenstein, Switz. | A4 | 21 |
| Munchön, N. Kor. | G3 | 33 |
| Muncie, In., U.S. | D7 | 91 |
| Muncy, Pa., U.S. | D8 | 115 |
| Mundare, Alta. | C4 | 68 |
| Munday, Tx., U.S. | C3 | 120 |
| Mundelein, Il., U.S. | A5 | 90 |
| Münden, W. Ger. | C4 | 18 |
| Munden, Ks., U.S. | C6 | 93 |
| Munford, Al., U.S. | B4 | 78 |
| Munford, Tn., U.S. | B2 | 119 |
| Munfordville, Ky., U.S. | C4 | 94 |
| Munger, India | C8 | 36 |
| Munger, Mi., U.S. | E7 | 99 |
| Mungindi, Austl. | E8 | 50 |
| Munhall, Pa., U.S. | k14 | 115 |
| Munich (München), W. Ger. | D5 | 18 |
| Munich, N.D., U.S. | A7 | 111 |
| Munising, Mi., U.S. | B4 | 99 |
| Munith, Mi., U.S. | F6 | 99 |
| Munjor, Ks., U.S. | D4 | 93 |
| Munnsville, N.Y., U.S. | C5 | 109 |
| Muñoz, Phil. | o13 | 34 |
| Muñoz Gamero, Península, pen., Chile | h11 | 54 |
| Munro Lake, l., Man. | B4 | 70 |
| Munsan-ni, S. Kor. | H3 | 33 |
| Münsingen, W. Ger. | E4 | 19 |
| Münsingen, Switz. | C4 | 21 |
| Munson, Alta. | D4 | 68 |
| Munson, Fl., U.S. | u15 | 86 |
| Munson, Pa., U.S. | E5 | 115 |
| Munsonville, N.H., U.S. | D2 | 106 |
| Munster, Fr. | D7 | 16 |
| Münster, W. Ger. | B5 | 18 |
| Munster, In., U.S. | A2 | 91 |
| Munster, hist. reg., Ire. | E3 | 11 |
| Münster [in Westfalen], W. Ger. | C3 | 18 |
| Munsungan Lake, l., Me., U.S. | B4 | 96 |
| Muntenia, hist. reg., Rom. | C7 | 24 |
| Muntok, Indon. | F3 | 34 |
| Munuscong Lake, l., Mi., U.S. | B6 | 99 |
| Muonio, Fin. | D10 | 14 |
| Muonio, stm., Eur. | D10 | 14 |
| Muotathal, Switz. | C6 | 21 |
| Mur (Mura), stm., Eur. | B2 | 24 |
| Mura (Mur), stm., Eur. | B2 | 24 |
| Murakami, Japan | G9 | 33 |
| Murākh, Bi'r, well, Eg. | E6 | 41 |
| Murano, Italy | D8 | 20 |
| Murash', Sov. Un. | B3 | 28 |
| Murat, Fr. | E5 | 16 |
| Murat, Tur. | C7 | 25 |
| Murat, stm., Tur. | C13 | 40 |
| Murau, Aus. | E7 | 18 |
| Muravera, Italy | E2 | 23 |
| Murayyevo, Sov. Un. | C11 | 33 |
| Murchison, N.Z. | N14 | 51 |
| Murchison, stm., Austl. | E2 | 50 |
| Murchison Falls see Kabalega Falls, wtfl., Ug. | A5 | 48 |
| Murcia, Spain | C5 | 22 |
| Murcia, hist. reg., Spain | C5 | 22 |
| Murcki, Pol. | g10 | 26 |
| Murderkill, stm., De., U.S. | D4 | 85 |
| Murdo, S.D., U.S. | D5 | 118 |
| Murdock, Fl., U.S. | E4 | 86 |
| Murdock, Il., U.S. | D5 | 90 |
| Murdock, Ks., U.S. | E6 | 93 |
| Murdock, Ne., U.S. | h12 | 104 |
| Mureş, stm., Eur. | C6 | 24 |
| Muret, Fr. | F4 | 16 |
| Murewa, Zimb. | A5 | 49 |
| Murfreesboro, Ar., U.S. | C2 | 81 |
| Murfreesboro, N.C., U.S. | A5 | 110 |
| Murfreesboro, Tn., U.S. | B5 | 119 |
| Murgha Kibzai, Pak. | B4 | 36 |
| Murgon, Austl. | E9 | 50 |
| Muri, Nig. | E7 | 45 |
| Muriaé, Braz. | C4 | 56 |
| Muri [-bei Bern], Switz. | C4 | 21 |
| Murici, Braz. | k6 | 57 |
| Muriege, Ang. | B2 | 54 |
| Muriel Lake, l., Alta. | B5 | 68 |
| Müritz Lake, l., E. Ger. | B6 | 18 |
| Murmansk, Sov. Un. | C6 | 29 |
| Murnau, W. Ger. | B7 | 20 |
| Murom, Sov. Un. | D13 | 27 |
| Muroran, Japan | C13 | 31 |
| Muros, Spain | A1 | 22 |
| Muroto, Japan | J7 | 33 |
| Muroto, Cape, c., Japan | J7 | 33 |
| Murphy, Id., U.S. | E3 | 87 |
| Murphy, Mo., U.S. | g13 | 102 |
| Murphy, N.C., U.S. | f8 | 110 |
| Murphy, Or., U.S. | E3 | 114 |
| Murphy Island, i., S.C., U.S. | E8 | 117 |
| Murphys, Ca., U.S. | C3 | 82 |
| Murphysboro, Il., U.S. | F4 | 90 |
| Murphysville, W.V., U.S. | B3 | 125 |
| Murr, Bi'r, well, Eg. | E6 | 43 |
| Murray, Ia., U.S. | C4 | 92 |
| Murray, Ky., U.S. | f9 | 94 |
| Murray, Ne., U.S. | D10 | 104 |
| Murray, Ut., U.S. | C4 | 121 |
| Murray, co., Ga., U.S. | B2 | 87 |
| Murray, co., Mn., U.S. | F3 | 100 |
| Murray, co., Ok., U.S. | C4 | 113 |
| Murray, stm., B.C. | B7 | 69 |
| Murray, stm., Austl. | F7 | 50 |
| Murray, Lake, l., Pap. N. Gui. | k15 | 50 |
| Murray, Lake, res., S.C., U.S. | C4 | 117 |
| Murray, Lake, res., Ok., U.S. | C4 | 113 |
| Murray Bridge, Austl. | G6 | 50 |
| Murray Harbour, P.E.I. | C7 | 71 |
| Murray Head, c., P.E.I. | C7 | 71 |
| Murray Lake, l., Alta. | E5 | 68 |
| Murray River, P.E.I. | C7 | 71 |
| Murraysburg, S. Afr. | D3 | 49 |
| Murrayville, B.C. | f13 | 69 |
| Murrayville, Il., U.S. | D3 | 90 |
| Murrells Inlet, S.C., U.S. | D10 | 117 |
| Murrells Inlet, b., S.C., U.S. | D10 | 117 |
| Mürren, Switz. | C4 | 21 |
| Murrhardt, W. Ger. | E4 | 19 |
| Murrieta, Ca., U.S. | F5 | 82 |
| Murrumbidgee, stm., Austl. | F8 | 50 |
| Murrupula, Moz. | A6 | 49 |
| Murrysville, Pa., U.S. | *k15 | 115 |
| Mursala, i., Indon. | K3 | 35 |
| Murska Sobota, Yugo. | B3 | 24 |
| Murtagud, Id., U.S. | G4 | 89 |
| Murten, Switz. | C3 | 21 |
| Murud, India | E5 | 36 |
| Murwāra, India | D7 | 36 |
| Murwillumbah, Austl. | E9 | 50 |
| Mürz, stm., Aus. | E7 | 18 |
| Mürzzuschlag, Aus. | E7 | 18 |
| Muş, Tur. | C13 | 40 |
| Musaid, Libya | C4 | 43 |
| Musala, mtn., Bul. | D6 | 24 |
| Musan, N. Kor. | C10 | 31 |
| Musangoi, Zaire | C3 | 48 |
| Müsá Qal'eh, Afg. | E12 | 39 |
| Musashino, Japan | *I9 | 33 |
| Muscatatuck, Vernon Fork, stm., In., U.S. | G6 | 91 |
| Muscat see Masqaṭ, Oman | C5 | 38 |
| Muscatine, Ia., U.S. | C6 | 92 |
| Muscatine, co., Ia., U.S. | C6 | 92 |
| Muscle Shoals, Al., U.S. | A2 | 78 |
| Musclow, Mount, mtn., B.C. | C4 | 69 |
| Muscoda, Wi., U.S. | E3 | 126 |
| Muscogee, co., Ga., U.S. | D2 | 87 |
| Musconetcong, stm., N.J., U.S. | B4 | 107 |
| Musconetcong Mountain, mtn., N.J., U.S. | B2 | 107 |
| Muscooten Bay, l., Il., U.S. | C3 | 90 |
| Muscotah, Ks., U.S. | C8 | 93 |
| Muscoy, Ca., U.S. | *E5 | 82 |
| Muse, Ok., U.S. | C7 | 113 |
| Muse, Pa., U.S. | F1 | 115 |
| Musgrave Harbour, Newf. | D5 | 72 |
| Musgrave Ranges, mts., Austl. | E5 | 50 |
| Musgravetown, Newf. | D5 | 72 |
| Mushie, Zaire | B2 | 48 |
| Mushin, Nig. | E5 | 45 |
| Mushketovo, Sov. Un. | r20 | 27 |
| Musi, stm., Indon. | F2 | 34 |
| Muskeg Bay, b., Mn., U.S. | B3 | 100 |
| Muskeget Channel, strt., Ma., U.S. | D7 | 98 |
| Muskeget Island, i., Ma., U.S. | D7 | 98 |
| Muskego, Wi., U.S. | F5 | 126 |
| Muskego Lake, l., Wi., U.S. | n11 | 126 |
| Muskegon, Mi., U.S. | E4 | 99 |
| Muskegon, co., Mi., U.S. | E4 | 99 |
| Muskegon, stm., Mi., U.S. | E4 | 99 |
| Muskegon Heights, Mi., U.S. | E4 | 99 |
| Muskegon Lake, l., Mi., U.S. | E4 | 99 |
| Muskingum, co., Oh., U.S. | B4 | 112 |
| Muskingum, stm., Oh., U.S. | C4 | 112 |
| Muskö, Swe. | u36 | 14 |
| Muskoge, Ok., U.S. | B6 | 113 |
| Muskogee, Ok., U.S. | B6 | 113 |
| Muskogee, co., Ok., U.S. | B6 | 113 |
| Muskoka, co., Ont. | B5 | 73 |
| Muskoka, Lake, l., Ont. | C5 | 73 |
| Muskrat Dam Lake, res., Ont. | A3 | 68 |
| Muskwa, stm., Alta. | A3 | 68 |
| Muskwa Lake, l., Alta. | B4 | 68 |
| Muslimbāgh, Pak. | B4 | 36 |
| Musoma, Tan. | B5 | 48 |
| Musquacook Lakes, l., Me., U.S. | B3 | 96 |
| Musquaro, Lac, l., Que. | h14 | 74 |
| Musquash, N.B. | D3 | 71 |
| Musquash Mountain, mtn., Me., U.S. | C5 | 96 |
| Musquodoboit Harbour, N.S. | E6 | 71 |
| Musselburgh, Scot., U.K. | C5 | 10 |
| Musselshell, Mt., U.S. | D9 | 103 |
| Musselshell, co., Mt., U.S. | D8 | 103 |
| Musselshell, stm., Mt., U.S. | D9 | 103 |
| Mussende, Ang. | C3 | 48 |
| Mussidan, Fr. | E4 | 16 |
| Mussolinia see Arborea, Italy | E2 | 23 |
| Mussuma, Ang. | D3 | 48 |
| Mustafakemalpaşa, Tur. | B7 | 40 |
| Mustang, Ok., U.S. | B4 | 113 |
| Musters, Lago, l., Arg. | B3 | 55 |
| Mustinka, stm., Mn., U.S. | E2 | 100 |
| Mustique, i., St. Vin. | V26 | 65 |
| Mustvee, Sov. Un. | B6 | 27 |
| Muswellbrook, Austl. | F9 | 50 |
| Müt, Eg. | D5 | 43 |
| Mut, Tur. | E7 | 40 |
| Mutá, Ponta do, c., Braz. | D3 | 57 |
| Mutare, Zimb. | A5 | 49 |
| Mutayyin, Yemen | B5 | 47 |
| Mutena, Zaire | A5 | 48 |
| Muti, i., Marsh Is. | S18 | 52 |
| Mutoko, Zimb. | A5 | 49 |
| Mutombo-Mukulu, Zaire | C3 | 48 |
| Mutorashanga, Zimb. | A5 | 49 |
| Mutsu, Japan | F10 | 33 |
| Mutsu Bay, b., Japan | F10 | 33 |
| Mutton Bay, Que. | C2 | 72 |
| Mutton Mountains, mts., Or., U.S. | C5 | 114 |
| Mutual, Ok., U.S. | A2 | 113 |
| Muṭūbis, Eg. | C2 | 41 |
| Mutunópolis, Braz. | A5 | 56 |
| Mutzig, Fr. | F7 | 17 |
| Mu Us Shamo (Ordos Desert), des., China | D6 | 31 |
| Muxima, Ang. | C1 | 48 |
| Muyinga, Bdi. | B5 | 48 |
| Muyombe, Zam. | D5 | 48 |
| Muyula, i., Pap. N. Gui. | k13 | 50 |
| Muzaffargarh, Pak. | B4 | 36 |
| Muzaffarnagar, India | C6 | 36 |
| Muzaffarpur, India | C8 | 36 |
| Muzambinho, Braz. | k8 | 56 |
| Muzhi, Sov. Un. | B21 | 8 |
| Muzon, Cape, c., Ak., U.S. | n23 | 79 |
| Muztag, mtn., China | A8 | 36 |
| Muztagata, mtn., China | A7 | 36 |
| Muztag, mtn., China | F10 | 29 |
| Mvuma, Zimb. | A5 | 49 |
| Mvurwi, Zimb. | A5 | 49 |
| Mwadui, Tan. | B5 | 48 |
| Mwami, Zimb. | A4 | 49 |
| Mwanza, Tan. | B5 | 48 |
| Mwanza, prov., Tan. | B5 | 48 |
| Mwaya, Tan. | D5 | 48 |
| Mweelrea, mtn., Ire. | D2 | 11 |
| Mwene-Ditu, Zaire | C3 | 48 |
| Mwenezi, Zimb. | B5 | 49 |
| Mwenga, Zaire | B4 | 48 |
| Mweru, Lake, l., Afr. | C5 | 48 |
| Mwimba, Zaire | C3 | 48 |
| Mwinilunga, Zam. | D4 | 48 |
| Myājlār, India | D3 | 37 |
| Myakka, stm., Fl., U.S. | E4 | 86 |
| Myakka City, Fl., U.S. | E4 | 86 |
| Myanaung, Burma | D1 | 35 |
| Myaungmya, Burma | D1 | 35 |
| Mycenae, hist., Grc. | C10 | 25 |
| Myers Corner, N.Y., U.S. | *D7 | 109 |
| Myerstown, Pa., U.S. | F9 | 115 |
| Myersville, Md., U.S. | A2 | 97 |

| Name | Map Ref. | Page |
|---|---|---|

| Name | Ref. | Page |
|---|---|---|
| Myingyan, Burma | D10 | 36 |
| Myitkyinā, Burma | C10 | 36 |
| Myitnge, stm., Burma | B2 | 35 |
| Myjava, Czech. | D4 | 26 |
| Mylo, N.D., U.S. | A6 | 111 |
| Mymensingh, Bngl. | D9 | 36 |
| Mynaral, Sov. Un. | D8 | 28 |
| Mynard, Ne., U.S. | h13 | 104 |
| Myrick, Ms., U.S. | D5 | 101 |
| Myrnam, Alta. | C5 | 68 |
| Myrtle, Man. | E3 | 70 |
| Myrtle, Ms., U.S. | A4 | 101 |
| Myrtle, Mo., U.S. | E6 | 102 |
| Myrtle Beach, S.C., U.S. | D10 | 117 |
| Myrtle Beach Air Force Base, mil., S.C., U.S. | D10 | 117 |
| Myrtle Creek, Or., U.S. | D3 | 114 |
| Myrtle Grove, Fl., U.S. | u14 | 86 |
| Myrtle Grove, La., U.S. | k12 | 95 |
| Myrtle Point, Or., U.S. | D2 | 114 |
| Myrtlewood, Al., U.S. | C2 | 78 |
| Mysen, Nor. | p29 | 14 |
| Myślenice, Pol. | D5 | 26 |
| Myślibórz, Pol. | B3 | 26 |
| Mysłowice, Pol. | g10 | 26 |
| Mysore, India | F6 | 36 |
| Mysore see Karnataka, state, India | F6 | 36 |
| Mystic, Ct., U.S. | D8 | 84 |
| Mystic, Ga., U.S. | E3 | 87 |
| Mystic, Ia., U.S. | D5 | 92 |
| Mystic Lakes, l., Ma., U.S. | g11 | 98 |
| Myszków, Pol. | f10 | 26 |
| My Tho, Viet. | C3 | 34 |
| Mytilene see Mitilini, Grc. | C6 | 40 |
| Mytishchi, Sov. Un. | n17 | 27 |
| Myton, Ut., U.S. | C5 | 121 |
| Mže, stm., Czech. | D8 | 19 |
| Mzimba, Mwi. | D5 | 48 |
| Mzuzu, Mwi. | D5 | 48 |

**N**

| Name | Ref. | Page |
|---|---|---|
| Naab, stm., W. Ger. | D7 | 19 |
| Naalehu, Hi., U.S. | D6 | 88 |
| Naamans Garden, De., U.S. | *A3 | 85 |
| Na'an, Isr. | h10 | 41 |
| Naantali, Fin. | G10 | 14 |
| Naas, Ire. | D3 | 10 |
| Nabā, Jabal (Mount Nebo), mtn., Jord. | C7 | 41 |
| Nabadwīp, India | *D8 | 36 |
| Nabb, In., U.S. | G6 | 91 |
| Nabberu, Lake, l., Austl. | E3 | 50 |
| Nabburg, W. Ger. | D7 | 19 |
| Nabeina, Kir. | R18 | 52 |
| Nabekavu, Fiji | H15 | 52 |
| Naberezhnyye Chelny (Brezhnev), Sov. Un. | D8 | 29 |
| Nabeul, Tun. | B7 | 44 |
| Nabi Shuayb, Mount, mtn., Yemen | *D4 | 38 |
| Nabnasset, Ma., U.S. | A5 | 98 |
| Naboomspruit, S. Afr. | B4 | 49 |
| Nabouwalu, Fiji | H15 | 52 |
| Nabq, Eg. | H10 | 40 |
| Nāblus, Isr. Occ. | B3 | 38 |
| Nacala, Moz. | D7 | 48 |
| Nacaome, Hond. | D4 | 62 |
| Naches, Wa., U.S. | C5 | 124 |
| Naches, stm., Wa., U.S. | C5 | 124 |
| Nachingwea, Tan. | D6 | 48 |
| Náchod, Czech. | C4 | 26 |
| Nacilau Point, c., Fiji | H14 | 52 |
| Nacimiento, Chile | B2 | 54 |
| Nacimiento Reservoir, res., Ca., U.S. | E3 | 82 |
| Nacka, Swe. | *H8 | 14 |
| Nacmine, Alta. | D4 | 68 |
| Naco, Az., U.S. | F6 | 80 |
| Nacogdoches, Tx., U.S. | D5 | 120 |
| Nacogdoches, co., Tx., U.S. | D5 | 120 |
| Nacozari [de Garcia], Mex. | A3 | 63 |
| Nacula, i., Fiji | H14 | 52 |
| Nadarzyn, Pol. | m13 | 26 |
| Nadeau, Mi., U.S. | C3 | 99 |
| Naden Harbour, b., B.C. | B1 | 69 |
| Nadi, Fiji | H14 | 52 |
| Nadiād, India | F4 | 37 |
| Nădlac, Rom. | B5 | 24 |
| Nador, Mor. | B4 | 44 |
| Naduri, Fiji | H15 | 52 |
| Nadvornaya, Sov. Un. | G5 | 27 |
| Nadym, stm., Sov. Un. | B23 | 8 |
| Næstved, Den. | J4 | 14 |
| Nafada, Nig. | D7 | 45 |
| Nafishah, Eg. | D4 | 41 |
| Naga, Phil. | C6 | 34 |
| Naga Hills, mts., Asia | C10 | 36 |
| Nāgāland, state, India | *C9 | 36 |
| Nagano, Japan | D12 | 31 |
| Nagaoka, Japan | D12 | 31 |
| Nāgappattinam, India | F6 | 36 |
| Nagarote, Nic. | D4 | 62 |
| Nagar Pārkar, Pak. | D5 | 36 |
| Nagasaki, Japan | E10 | 31 |
| Nāgaur, India | D4 | 37 |
| Nageezi, N.M., U.S. | A2 | 108 |
| Nāgercoil, India | G6 | 36 |
| Nagiba, Phil. | p13 | 34 |
| Nagles Mountains, mts., Ire. | E3 | 11 |
| Nago, Japan | N5 | 52 |
| Nago Bay, b., Japan | N5 | 52 |
| Nagog Pond, l., Ma., U.S. | f10 | 98 |
| Nagold, W. Ger. | E3 | 19 |
| Nagoya, Japan | D12 | 31 |
| Nāgpur, India | D6 | 36 |
| Nagqu, China | E3 | 31 |
| Nags Head, N.C., U.S. | B7 | 110 |
| Nagua, Dom. Rep. | E9 | 64 |
| Naguabo, P.R. | B4 | 65 |
| Nagykanizsa, Hung. | B3 | 24 |
| Nagykőrös, Hung. | B4 | 24 |
| Naha, Japan | F10 | 31 |
| Nahalat Yehuda, Isr. | h10 | 41 |
| Nahanni National Park, N.W. Ter. | D7 | 66 |
| Nahant, Ma., U.S. | g12 | 98 |
| Nahariyya, Isr. | B7 | 41 |
| Nahāvand, Iran | D4 | 39 |
| Nahe, stm., W. Ger. | D3 | 18 |
| Nahma, Mi., U.S. | C4 | 99 |
| Nahmakanta Lake, l., Me., U.S. | C3 | 96 |
| Nahuel Huapi, Arg. | C2 | 54 |
| Nahuel Huapi, Lago, l., Arg. | C2 | 54 |
| Nahunta, Ga., U.S. | E5 | 87 |
| Naic, Phil. | o13 | 34 |
| Naicam, Sask. | E3 | 75 |
| Naiguatá, Pico, mtn., Ven. | *A4 | 60 |
| Naihāti, India | *D8 | 36 |
| Naila, W. Ger. | C6 | 19 |
| Nailaga, Fiji | H14 | 52 |

| Name | Ref. | Page |
|---|---|---|
| Nain, Newf. | g9 | 72 |
| Nā'īn, Iran | E6 | 39 |
| Naini Tāl, India | C7 | 37 |
| Nairai, i., Fiji | H15 | 52 |
| Nairn, Scot., U.K. | B5 | 10 |
| Nairn, stm., Scot., U.K. | C4 | 13 |
| Nairobi, Kenya | B6 | 48 |
| Naitonitoni, Fiji | I15 | 52 |
| Naivasha, Kenya | B6 | 48 |
| Najafābād, Iran | E5 | 39 |
| Naj Ḥammādī, Eg. | D6 | 43 |
| Najibābād, India | C7 | 37 |
| Najin, N. Kor. | C11 | 31 |
| Najran, well, Sau. Ar. | D4 | 38 |
| Naju, S. Kor. | I3 | 33 |
| Nakadōri Island, i., Japan | J4 | 33 |
| Nakagusuku Bay, b., Japan | O5 | 52 |
| Nakaminato, Japan | m19 | 33 |
| Nakamura, Japan | J6 | 33 |
| Nakaoso, Japan | N6 | 52 |
| Nakatsu, Japan | J5 | 33 |
| Nakfa, Eth. | B4 | 47 |
| Nakhichevan, Sov. Un. | F3 | 28 |
| Nakhodka, Sov. Un. | E6 | 33 |
| Nakhon Chai Si, stm., Thai. | E4 | 35 |
| Nakhon Pathom, Thai. | F3 | 35 |
| Nakhon Phanom, Thai. | B2 | 34 |
| Nakhon Ratchasima, Thai. | C2 | 34 |
| Nakhon Sawan, Thai. | B1 | 34 |
| Nakhon Si Thammarat, Thai. | C2 | 34 |
| Nakina, Ont. | o18 | 73 |
| Nakina, stm., B.C. | C4 | 110 |
| Nakło [nad Notecią], Pol. | B4 | 26 |
| Naknek, Ak., U.S. | D8 | 79 |
| Naknek Lake, l., Ak., U.S. | D8 | 79 |
| Nakodar, India | L3 | 33 |
| Nakonde, Zam. | C6 | 48 |
| Nakskov, Den. | J4 | 14 |
| Nakuru, Kenya | B6 | 48 |
| Nakusp, B.C. | D9 | 69 |
| Nalchik, Sov. Un. | E2 | 28 |
| Nallen, W.V., U.S. | m14 | 125 |
| Nalón, stm., Spain | A2 | 22 |
| Nālūt, Libya | C2 | 43 |
| Nam, stm., Asia | B3 | 35 |
| Nam, stm., S. Kor. | I4 | 33 |
| Namacurra, Moz. | A6 | 49 |
| Namak, Daryācheh-ye, l., Iran | E6 | 39 |
| Namak, Kavīr-e, des., Iran | D8 | 39 |
| Namaka, Alta. | D4 | 68 |
| Namakan Lake, l., N.A. | B6 | 100 |
| Namangan, Sov. Un. | E10 | 29 |
| Namanock Island, i., N.J., U.S. | A3 | 107 |
| Namanyere, Tan. | C5 | 48 |
| Namapa, Moz. | D6 | 48 |
| Namasagali, Ug. | A5 | 48 |
| Namatanai, Pap. N. Gui. | h13 | 50 |
| Nambe Pueblo, N.M., U.S. | B4 | 108 |
| Nambour, Austl. | E9 | 50 |
| Nam Co, l., China | E3 | 31 |
| Nam Dinh, Viet. | A3 | 34 |
| Namdō, i., Swe. | t36 | 14 |
| Namekagon, stm., Wi., U.S. | B2 | 126 |
| Namekagon Lake, l., Wi., U.S. | B2 | 126 |
| Namen see Namur, Bel. | B6 | 16 |
| Nametil, Moz. | A6 | 49 |
| Namib Desert, des., Afr. | B1 | 49 |
| Namibe (Moçâmedes), Ang. | E1 | 48 |
| Namibe, dept., Ang. | E1 | 48 |
| Namibia (South West Africa), ctry., Afr. | B2 | 49 |
| Namiquipa, Mex. | B3 | 63 |
| Namjagbarwa Feng, mtn., China | F4 | 31 |
| Namlea, Indon. | F7 | 34 |
| Nam Ngum Reservoir, res., Laos | C5 | 35 |
| Namoi, stm., Austl. | F8 | 50 |
| Namoruputh, Kenya | A6 | 48 |
| Nampa, Alta. | A2 | 68 |
| Nampa, Id., U.S. | F2 | 89 |
| Nampala, Mali | C3 | 45 |
| Nampo (Chinnampo), N. Kor. | D10 | 31 |
| Nampula, Moz. | A6 | 49 |
| Nampula, dept., Moz. | D6 | 48 |
| Namsen, stm., Nor. | E4 | 14 |
| Namsos, Nor. | E4 | 14 |
| Namu, B.C. | D4 | 69 |
| Namu Island, i., Marsh Is. | P18 | 52 |
| Namur (Namen), Bel. | B6 | 16 |
| Namur, Que. | D3 | 74 |
| Namur, prov., Bel. | D3 | 16 |
| Namur, i., Marsh Is. | S17 | 52 |
| Namutoni, Nmb. | A2 | 49 |
| Namwala, Zam. | E4 | 48 |
| Namwon, S. Kor. | I3 | 33 |
| Namysłów, Pol. | C4 | 26 |
| Nan, Thai. | C4 | 35 |
| Nana, stm., Cen. Afr. Rep. | D3 | 46 |
| Nanafalia, Al., U.S. | C2 | 78 |
| Nanaimo, B.C. | E5 | 69 |
| Nanakuli, Hi., U.S. | B3 | 88 |
| Nanao, Japan | H8 | 33 |
| Nanatsu Island, i., Japan | H8 | 33 |
| Nance, co., Ne., U.S. | C7 | 104 |
| Nanchang, China | F8 | 31 |
| Nanchong, China | F8 | 31 |
| Nanchong, China | E6 | 31 |
| Nanchuan, China | J2 | 32 |
| Nancy, Fr. | C7 | 16 |
| Nancy, Ky., U.S. | C5 | 94 |
| Nancy Creek, stm., Ga., U.S. | h8 | 87 |
| Nanda Devi, mtn., India | B7 | 36 |
| Nānded, India | H6 | 37 |
| Nandurbār, India | G5 | 37 |
| Nanfeng, China | K7 | 32 |
| Nanga Eboko, Cam. | F2 | 46 |
| Nānga Parbat, mtn., Pak. | A5 | 36 |
| Nangis, Fr. | F21 | 16 |
| Nangong, China | F6 | 32 |
| Nang Rong, China | E6 | 31 |
| Nanhua, China | F5 | 31 |
| Nanjemoy, Md., U.S. | D3 | 97 |
| Nanjiang, China | D1 | 34 |
| Nanjing (Nanking), China | E8 | 31 |
| Nankin, Oh., U.S. | B3 | 112 |
| Nanking see Nanjing, China | E8 | 31 |
| Nanning, China | G6 | 31 |
| Nanoose Bay, B.C. | f11 | 69 |
| Nanowin, stm., Man. | E1 | 70 |
| Nanping, China | F8 | 31 |
| Nansio, Tan. | B5 | 48 |
| Nanson, N.D., U.S. | A6 | 111 |
| Nantel, Que. | C3 | 74 |
| Nanterre, Fr. | g9 | 16 |
| Nantes, Fr. | D3 | 16 |
| Nanteuil-le-Haudouin, Fr. | E2 | 17 |
| Nantian, China | J9 | 32 |

| Name | Ref. | Page |
|---|---|---|
| Nanticoke, Ont. | E4 | 73 |
| Nanticoke, Md., U.S. | D6 | 97 |
| Nanticoke, Pa., U.S. | D10 | 115 |
| Nanticoke, stm., U.S. | D6 | 97 |
| Nanton, Alta. | D4 | 68 |
| Nantong, China | E9 | 31 |
| Nantua, Fr. | D6 | 16 |
| Nantucket, Ma., U.S. | D7 | 98 |
| Nantucket, co., Ma., U.S. | D7 | 98 |
| Nantucket Island, i., Ma., U.S. | D7 | 98 |
| Nantucket Sound, strt., Ma., U.S. | C7 | 98 |
| Nantuxent Point, c., N.J., U.S. | E2 | 107 |
| Nantwich, Eng., U.K. | A5 | 12 |
| Nanty Glo, Pa., U.S. | F4 | 115 |
| Nanuet, N.Y., U.S. | g12 | 109 |
| Nanukuloa, Fiji | H15 | 52 |
| Nanuku Passage, strt., Fiji | H16 | 52 |
| Nanuku Reef, rf., Fiji | H16 | 52 |
| Nanuque, Braz. | B4 | 56 |
| Nanyang, China | E7 | 31 |
| Nanyuki, Kenya | A6 | 48 |
| Nanzhang, China | I4 | 32 |
| Nao, Cape, c., Spain | C6 | 22 |
| Naoli He, stm., China | C6 | 33 |
| Naoma, W.V., U.S. | n13 | 125 |
| Naomi Peak, mtn., Ut., U.S. | B4 | 121 |
| Náousa, Grc. | B4 | 25 |
| Napa, Ca., U.S. | C2 | 82 |
| Napa, co., Ca., U.S. | C2 | 82 |
| Napadogan, N.B. | C3 | 71 |
| Napakiak, Ak., U.S. | C7 | 79 |
| Napaktok Bay, b., Newf. | f9 | 72 |
| Napanee, Ont. | C8 | 73 |
| Napanoch, N.Y., U.S. | D6 | 109 |
| Napatree Point, c., R.I., U.S. | G1 | 116 |
| Napavine, Wa., U.S. | C3 | 124 |
| Nape, Laos | C6 | 35 |
| Naper, Ne., U.S. | B6 | 104 |
| Naperville, Il., U.S. | B5 | 90 |
| Napetipi, stm., Can. | C2 | 72 |
| Napf, mtn., Switz. | C4 | 21 |
| Napier, N.Z. | M16 | 51 |
| Napier Mountains, mts., Ant. | C18 | 7 |
| Napierville, Que. | D4 | 74 |
| Napierville, co., Que. | D4 | 74 |
| Napinka, Man. | E1 | 70 |
| Naplate, Il., U.S. | B5 | 90 |
| Naples (Napoli), Italy | D5 | 23 |
| Naples, Fl., U.S. | F5 | 86 |
| Naples, Id., U.S. | A2 | 89 |
| Naples, Il., U.S. | D3 | 90 |
| Naples, Me., U.S. | E2 | 96 |
| Naples, N.Y., U.S. | C3 | 109 |
| Naples, S.D., U.S. | C8 | 118 |
| Naples, Tx., U.S. | C5 | 120 |
| Naples, Ut., U.S. | C6 | 121 |
| Naples, Gulf of, b., Italy | D5 | 23 |
| Naples Park, Fl., U.S. | *F5 | 86 |
| Napo, prov., Ec. | B2 | 58 |
| Napo, stm., S.A. | B3 | 58 |
| Napoleon, In., U.S. | F7 | 91 |
| Napoleon, Mo., U.S. | B3 | 102 |
| Napoleon, N.D., U.S. | C6 | 111 |
| Napoleon, Oh., U.S. | A1 | 112 |
| Napoleonville, La., U.S. | E4 | 95 |
| Naponee, Ne., U.S. | D6 | 104 |
| Nappanee, In., U.S. | B5 | 91 |
| Napton, Mo., U.S. | B4 | 102 |
| Naqadeh, Iran | C2 | 39 |
| Nara, Japan | o14 | 33 |
| Nara, Mali | C3 | 45 |
| Nāra Canal, Pak. | D2 | 37 |
| Naracoorte, Austl. | G7 | 50 |
| Naramata, B.C. | E8 | 69 |
| Na'rān, Isr. Occ. | A7 | 41 |
| Naranja, Fl., U.S. | G6 | 86 |
| Narathiwat, Thai. | D2 | 34 |
| Nara Visa, N.M., U.S. | B6 | 108 |
| Nārāyanganj, Bngl. | D9 | 36 |
| Nārāyanpet, India | I6 | 37 |
| Narberth, Wales, U.K. | C3 | 12 |
| Narberth, Pa., U.S. | p20 | 115 |
| Narbonne, Fr. | F5 | 16 |
| Narcissa, Ok., U.S. | A7 | 113 |
| Narcisse, Man. | D3 | 70 |
| Narcoossee, Fl., U.S. | D5 | 86 |
| Nardin, Ok., U.S. | A4 | 113 |
| Nardò, Italy | D7 | 23 |
| Nares Strait, strt., N.A. | m37 | 66 |
| Narew, stm., Eur. | B6 | 26 |
| Nārī, Jabal an, hills, Libya | E4 | 43 |
| Nariño, dept., Col. | C2 | 60 |
| Narita, Japan | n19 | 33 |
| Narka, Ks., U.S. | C6 | 93 |
| Narmada, stm., India | D6 | 36 |
| Narodnaya, Mount, mtn., Sov. Un. | C9 | 29 |
| Naro-Fominsk, Sov. Un. | D11 | 27 |
| Narok, Kenya | B6 | 48 |
| Narol, Man. | D3 | 70 |
| Narrabri, Austl. | F8 | 50 |
| Narragansett, R.I., U.S. | F4 | 116 |
| Narragansett Bay, b., R.I., U.S. | E5 | 116 |
| Narraguagus, stm., Me., U.S. | D5 | 96 |
| Narran, stm., Austl. | D6 | 51 |
| Narran Lake, l., Austl. | D6 | 51 |
| Narraway, stm., Can. | F2 | 50 |
| Narrogin, Austl. | F2 | 50 |
| Narromine, Austl. | I9 | 51 |
| Narrows, Va., U.S. | C2 | 123 |
| Narrowsburg, N.Y., U.S. | D5 | 109 |
| Narsimhapur, India | F7 | 37 |
| Narsipatnam, India | I9 | 37 |
| Naruna, Va., U.S. | C3 | 123 |
| Narva, Sov. Un. | B9 | 27 |
| Narvik, Nor. | C7 | 14 |
| Naryan-Mar, Sov. Un. | B8 | 28 |
| Naryilco, Austl. | D3 | 51 |
| Narym, Sov. Un. | D25 | 8 |
| Naryn, stm., Sov. Un. | E9 | 28 |
| Naryn, Sov. Un. | E10 | 28 |
| Narynkol, Sov. Un. | E10 | 28 |
| Na San, Viet. | D1 | 34 |
| Nasarawa, Nig. | F6 | 45 |
| Nase, Japan | F10 | 31 |
| Naseby, N.Z. | P13 | 51 |
| Naselle, Wa., U.S. | C2 | 124 |
| Nash, Ok., U.S. | A3 | 113 |
| Nash, Tx., U.S. | C5 | 120 |
| Nash, co., N.C., U.S. | A4 | 110 |
| Nashawena Island, i., Ma., U.S. | D6 | 98 |
| Nash Creek, N.B. | B3 | 71 |
| Nāshik, India | E5 | 36 |
| Nashoba, Ok., U.S. | C6 | 113 |
| Nashoba Hill, hill, Ma., U.S. | f10 | 98 |
| Nash Stream, stm., N.H., U.S. | A4 | 106 |
| Nashua, Ia., U.S. | B5 | 92 |
| Nashua, Mn., U.S. | E2 | 100 |
| Nashua, Mt., U.S. | B10 | 103 |

| Name | Ref. | Page |
|---|---|---|
| Nashua, N.H., U.S. | E4 | 106 |
| Nashua, stm., U.S. | E3 | 106 |
| Nashville, Ar., U.S. | D2 | 81 |
| Nashville, Ga., U.S. | E3 | 87 |
| Nashville, Il., U.S. | E4 | 90 |
| Nashville, In., U.S. | F5 | 91 |
| Nashville, Ks., U.S. | E5 | 93 |
| Nashville, Mi., U.S. | F5 | 99 |
| Nashville, Mo., U.S. | D3 | 102 |
| Nashville, N.C., U.S. | B5 | 110 |
| Nashville, Oh., U.S. | B3 | 112 |
| Nashville, Tn., U.S. | A5 | 119 |
| Nashwaak, stm., N.B. | C3 | 71 |
| Nashwauk, Mn., U.S. | C5 | 100 |
| Našice, Yugo. | C4 | 24 |
| Nasielsk, Pol. | B6 | 26 |
| Nāṣir, Bi'r, well, Eg. | D2 | 41 |
| Nāsijärvi, l., Fin. | G10 | 14 |
| Nāsiri see Ahvāz, Iran | B4 | 38 |
| Naskaupi, stm., Newf. | g9 | 72 |
| Nason, Il., U.S. | E5 | 90 |
| Nasonville, R.I., U.S. | B3 | 116 |
| Nass, stm., B.C. | E7 | 66 |
| Nassau, Bah. | B5 | 64 |
| Nassau, De., U.S. | E5 | 85 |
| Nassau, Mn., U.S. | E2 | 100 |
| Nassau, N.Y., U.S. | C7 | 109 |
| Nassau, co., Fl., U.S. | B5 | 86 |
| Nassau, co., N.Y., U.S. | E7 | 109 |
| Nassau, stm., Fl., U.S. | k8 | 86 |
| Nassau, Bahía, b., Chile | k12 | 54 |
| Nassau International Airport, Bah. | m17 | 64 |
| Nassau Shores, N.Y., U.S. | *n15 | 109 |
| Nassau Sound, strt., Fl., U.S. | B5 | 86 |
| Nassauville, Fl., U.S. | B5 | 86 |
| Nassawadox, Va., U.S. | C7 | 123 |
| Nassawango Creek, stm., Md., U.S. | D7 | 97 |
| Nasser, Lake, res., Afr. | E6 | 43 |
| Nässjö, Swe. | I6 | 14 |
| Nasugbu, Phil. | o13 | 34 |
| Nasukoin Mountain, mtn., Mt., U.S. | B2 | 103 |
| Nata, Bots. | B4 | 49 |
| Natá, Pan. | F7 | 62 |
| Natagaima, Col. | C2 | 60 |
| Natal, Braz. | C7 | 57 |
| Natal, prov., S. Afr. | C5 | 49 |
| Natalbany, La., U.S. | D5 | 95 |
| Natalia, Tx., U.S. | E3 | 120 |
| Natanes Plateau, plat., Az., U.S. | D5 | 80 |
| Natashquan, Que. | h9 | 72 |
| Natashquan, stm., Can. | h9 | 72 |
| Natawatman Lake, l., Man. | B3 | 70 |
| Natchaug, stm., Ct., U.S. | B7 | 84 |
| Natchez, Ms., U.S. | D2 | 101 |
| Natchitoches, La., U.S. | C2 | 95 |
| Natchitoches, co., La., U.S. | C2 | 95 |
| Natewa Bay, b., Fiji | H15 | 52 |
| Nathalie, Va., U.S. | D4 | 123 |
| Nathrop, Co., U.S. | C4 | 83 |
| Natick, Ma., U.S. | B5 | 98 |
| Natimuk, Austl. | H3 | 51 |
| Nation, stm., B.C. | B6 | 69 |
| National City, Ca., U.S. | F5 | 82 |
| National City, Il., U.S. | E3 | 90 |
| National Gardens, Fl., U.S. | C5 | 86 |
| National Park, N.J., U.S. | *D2 | 107 |
| Natitingou, Benin | D5 | 45 |
| Natividade, Braz. | D1 | 57 |
| Natoma, Ks., U.S. | C4 | 93 |
| Natron, Lake, l., Afr. | B6 | 48 |
| Natrona, Wy., U.S. | C6 | 127 |
| Natrona Heights, Pa., U.S. | E2 | 115 |
| Nāttarö, i., Swe. | u36 | 14 |
| Nattaung, mtn., Burma | C2 | 35 |
| Natuna, is., Indon. | E3 | 34 |
| Natuna Besar, i., Indon. | E3 | 34 |
| Natural Bridge, Al., U.S. | A2 | 78 |
| Natural Bridge, N.Y., U.S. | A5 | 109 |
| Natural Bridge, Va., U.S. | C3 | 123 |
| Natural Bridge, Ut., U.S. | F3 | 121 |
| Natural Bridges National Monument, Ut., U.S. | F6 | 121 |
| Naturaliste, Cape, c., Austl. | F1 | 50 |
| Natural Steps, Ar., U.S. | h10 | 81 |
| Naturita, Co., U.S. | C2 | 83 |
| Naubinway, Mi., U.S. | C5 | 99 |
| Nauders, Aus. | E5 | 18 |
| Nauen, E. Ger. | C9 | 29 |
| Naugatuck, Ct., U.S. | D3 | 84 |
| Naugatuck, stm., Ct., U.S. | D3 | 84 |
| Naumburg, W. Ger. | B4 | 19 |
| Naumburg [an der Saale], E. Ger. | C5 | 18 |
| Naunhof, E. Ger. | B7 | 19 |
| Naupactus see Návpaktos, Grc. | C3 | 25 |
| Ñaupe, Peru | C2 | 58 |
| Nauru, ctry., Oc. | G10 | 6 |
| Naushon Island, i., Ma., U.S. | D6 | 98 |
| Nauta, Peru | B3 | 58 |
| Nautilus Park, Ct., U.S. | D7 | 84 |
| Nautla, Mex. | C5 | 63 |
| Nauvoo, Al., U.S. | B2 | 78 |
| Nauvoo, Il., U.S. | C2 | 90 |
| Nauwigewauk, N.B. | D4 | 71 |
| Nava del Rey, Spain | A3 | 22 |
| Navahermosa, Spain | B3 | 22 |
| Navajo, Az., U.S. | B5 | 80 |
| Navajo, co., Az., U.S. | B5 | 80 |
| Navajo Dam, N.M., U.S. | A2 | 108 |
| Navajo Indian Reservation, U.S. | A4 | 80 |
| Navajo Mountain, mtn., Ut., U.S. | F5 | 121 |
| Navajo National Monument, Az., U.S. | A5 | 80 |
| Navalcarnero, Spain | B3 | 22 |
| Navalmoral de la Mata, Spain | B3 | 22 |
| Navan, Ont. | B9 | 73 |
| Navan see An Uaimh, Ire. | C3 | 11 |
| Navarin, Cape, c., Sov. Un. | C20 | 29 |
| Navarino, Isla, i., Chile | k12 | 54 |
| Navarra, hist. reg., Spain | A5 | 22 |
| Navarre, co., Fl., U.S. | u15 | 86 |
| Navarre, Oh., U.S. | B4 | 112 |
| Navarro, co., Tx., U.S. | D4 | 120 |
| Navas de Tolosa, Spain | C4 | 22 |
| Navasota, Tx., U.S. | D4 | 120 |
| Navassa, N.C., U.S. | C4 | 110 |
| Navassa Island, i., N.A. | E6 | 64 |

| Name | Ref. | Page |
|---|---|---|
| Naver, stm., Scot., U.K. | B4 | 13 |
| Naver, Loch, l., Scot., U.K. | B4 | 13 |
| Navesink, N.J., U.S. | C4 | 107 |
| Navet Reservoir, res., Trin. | O23 | 65 |
| Navia, Arg. | A3 | 54 |
| Navia, i., Spain | A2 | 22 |
| Navidad, Chile | A2 | 54 |
| Naviti, i., Fiji | H14 | 52 |
| Navojoa, Mex. | B3 | 63 |
| Navolato, Mex. | C3 | 63 |
| Návpaktos (Naupactus), Grc. | C3 | 25 |
| Návplion, Grc. | D4 | 25 |
| Navrongo, Ghana | D4 | 45 |
| Navsāri, India | G4 | 37 |
| Nawá, Syria | B8 | 41 |
| Nawābshāh, Pak. | C4 | 36 |
| Nawāda, India | E10 | 37 |
| Nāwah, Afg. | E13 | 39 |
| Nawiliwili Bay, b., Hi., U.S. | B2 | 88 |
| Náxos, Grc. | D5 | 40 |
| Náxos, i., Grc. | D5 | 40 |
| Nay, Fr. | F3 | 16 |
| Nayarit, state, Mex. | C3 | 63 |
| Nayau Island, i., Fiji | H16 | 52 |
| Nāy Band, Iran | C5 | 38 |
| Nāy Band, Iran | E8 | 39 |
| Nāy Band, Kūh-e, mtn., Iran | E8 | 39 |
| Nāy Band, Ra's-e, c., Iran | H6 | 39 |
| Naylor, Ga., U.S. | F3 | 87 |
| Naylor, Mo., U.S. | E7 | 102 |
| Nayoro, Japan | D11 | 33 |
| Nazaré, Braz. | D3 | 57 |
| Nazaré, Port. | C1 | 22 |
| Nazaré da Mata, Braz. | h6 | 57 |
| Nazareth (Nazerat), Isr. | B3 | 38 |
| Nazareth, Ky., U.S. | C4 | 94 |
| Nazareth, Pa., U.S. | E11 | 115 |
| Nazareth, Tx., U.S. | B1 | 120 |
| Nazário, Braz. | B3 | 56 |
| Nazas, Mex. | B4 | 63 |
| Nazas, stm., Mex. | B4 | 63 |
| Nazca, Peru | D3 | 58 |
| Nazilli, Tur. | D7 | 40 |
| Nazimovo, Sov. Un. | D27 | 8 |
| Naziya, Sov. Un. | s32 | 14 |
| Nazko, stm., B.C. | C6 | 69 |
| Nazlini, Az., U.S. | B6 | 80 |
| Nazret, Eth. | D4 | 47 |
| Nazyvayevsk, Sov. Un. | D8 | 28 |
| Ncheu, Mwi. | D5 | 48 |
| Ndalatando, Ang. | C1 | 48 |
| Ndélé, Cen. Afr. Rep. | D4 | 46 |
| Ndendé, Gabon | F2 | 46 |
| N'Djamena (Fort-Lamy), Chad | C3 | 46 |
| Ndjolé, Gabon | F2 | 46 |
| Ndola, Zam. | D5 | 48 |
| Neagh, Lough, l., N. Ire., U.K. | C3 | 10 |
| Neah Bay, Wa., U.S. | A1 | 124 |
| Neale, stm., Austl. | E6 | 50 |
| Neales, stm., Austl. | E6 | 50 |
| Néa Iónia, Grc. | *C4 | 25 |
| Néa Liósia, Grc. | *C4 | 25 |
| Néa Páfos, Cyp. | g11 | 25 |
| Néa Palátia, Grc. | g11 | 25 |
| Neápolis, Grc. | D4 | 25 |
| Neápolis, Grc. | E6 | 25 |
| Néa Psará see Erétria, Grc. | g11 | 25 |
| Near Islands, is., Ak., U.S. | E2 | 79 |
| Néa Smírni, Grc. | *D4 | 25 |
| Neath, Wales, U.K. | C4 | 12 |
| Neavitt, Md., U.S. | C5 | 97 |
| Nebel, stm., E. Ger. | n16 | 15 |
| Nebine Creek, stm., Austl. | E6 | 51 |
| Nebit-Dag, Sov. Un. | B7 | 39 |
| Neblina, Pico da, mtn., S.A. | C4 | 60 |
| Nebo, Il., U.S. | D3 | 90 |
| Nebo, Ky., U.S. | C2 | 94 |
| Nebo, Mo., U.S. | D5 | 102 |
| Nebo, Mount, mtn., Ut., U.S. | D4 | 121 |
| Nebo, Mount see Nabā, Jabal, mtn., Jord. | C7 | 41 |
| Nebraska, state, U.S. | C6 | 104 |
| Nebraska City, Ne., U.S. | D10 | 104 |
| Nebuzely, Czech. | n18 | 26 |
| Necedah, Wi., U.S. | D3 | 126 |
| Nechako, stm., B.C. | C5 | 69 |
| Nechako Range, mts., B.C. | C5 | 69 |
| Neche, N.D., U.S. | A8 | 111 |
| Neches, stm., Tx., U.S. | D5 | 120 |
| Nechí, Col. | B3 | 60 |
| Nechí, stm., Col. | B3 | 60 |
| Nechranice Reservoir, res., Czech. | C2 | 19 |
| Neckar, stm., W. Ger. | D4 | 19 |
| Neckarsulm, W. Ger. | D5 | 19 |
| Necker Island, i., Hi., U.S. | m15 | 88 |
| Necochea, Arg. | B5 | 54 |
| Necoclí, Col. | B2 | 60 |
| Neder Rijn, stm., Neth. | C5 | 17 |
| Nedrow, N.Y., U.S. | C4 | 109 |
| Needham, Ma., U.S. | g11 | 98 |
| Needham, In., U.S. | F6 | 91 |
| Needham Market, Eng., U.K. | B7 | 13 |
| Needle Mountain, mtn., Wy., U.S. | B3 | 127 |
| Needles, Ca., U.S. | E6 | 82 |
| Needmore, In., U.S. | G4 | 91 |
| Needville, Tx., U.S. | r14 | 120 |
| Neelin, Man. | E2 | 70 |
| Neels Gap, Ga., U.S. | B3 | 87 |
| Neely, Ms., U.S. | D5 | 101 |
| Neelyton, Pa., U.S. | G6 | 115 |
| Neelyville, Mo., U.S. | E7 | 102 |
| Neenah, Wi., U.S. | D5 | 126 |
| Neepawa, Man. | D2 | 70 |
| Neerpelt, Bel. | C5 | 17 |
| Neeses, S.C., U.S. | D5 | 117 |
| Neffs, Oh., U.S. | B5 | 112 |
| Neffs, Pa., U.S. | E11 | 115 |
| Nefta, Tun. | C6 | 44 |
| Neftegorsk, Sov. Un. | G16 | 29 |
| Nefyn, Wales, U.K. | A3 | 12 |
| Negaunee, Mi., U.S. | B3 | 99 |
| Negele, Eth. | D4 | 47 |
| Negeri Sembilan, state, Malay. | K5 | 35 |
| Neger Desert, des., Isr. | D4 | 41 |
| Negley, Oh., U.S. | B5 | 112 |
| Negomane, Moz. | C6 | 48 |
| Negombo, Sri L. | G6 | 36 |
| Negreira, Spain | A2 | 22 |
| Negreet, La., U.S. | C2 | 95 |
| Negrești, Rom. | A3 | 101 |
| Negro, stm., Arg. | C4 | 54 |
| Negro, Punta, c., Peru | C1 | 58 |
| Negro, stm., Bol. | B3 | 55 |
| Negro, rf., Fiji | I16 | 52 |
| Negro, stm., Braz. | D2 | 56 |

| Name | Ref. | Page |
|---|---|---|
| Negro, stm., Braz. | B1 | 56 |
| Negro, stm., S.A. | D4 | 53 |
| Negro, stm., S.A. | E1 | 56 |
| Negro Mountain, mtn., Md., U.S. | k12 | 97 |
| Negros, i., Phil. | D6 | 34 |
| Negru-Vodă, Rom. | D9 | 24 |
| Neguac, N.B. | B4 | 71 |
| Nehalem, Or., U.S. | B3 | 114 |
| Nehalem, stm., Or., U.S. | B3 | 114 |
| Nehawka, Ne., U.S. | D10 | 104 |
| Nehbandān, Iran | F10 | 39 |
| Nehe, China | B2 | 33 |
| Neheim-Hüsten, W. Ger. | B3 | 19 |
| Neiba, Dom. Rep. | E8 | 64 |
| Neidpath, Sask. | G2 | 75 |
| Neiden, Nor. | C13 | 14 |
| Neihart, Mt., U.S. | D6 | 103 |
| Neihuang, China | G6 | 32 |
| Neijiang, China | F6 | 31 |
| Neilburg, Sask. | E1 | 75 |
| Neill Point, c., Wa., U.S. | f11 | 124 |
| Neillsville, Wi., U.S. | D3 | 126 |
| Nei Monggol see Inner Mongolia, prov., China | C7 | 31 |
| Neisse, stm., Eur. | C7 | 18 |
| Neiva, Col. | C2 | 60 |
| Neixiang, China | E7 | 31 |
| Nejd, reg., Sau. Ar. | C4 | 38 |
| Nejdek, Czech. | C7 | 19 |
| Nekemte, Eth. | D4 | 47 |
| Nekoma, Ks., U.S. | D4 | 93 |
| Nekoma, N.D., U.S. | A7 | 111 |
| Nekoosa, Wi., U.S. | D4 | 126 |
| Neksø, Den. | C8 | 15 |
| Nelidovo, Sov. Un. | C9 | 27 |
| Neligh, Ne., U.S. | B7 | 104 |
| Nellis Air Force Base, mil., Nv., U.S. | G6 | 105 |
| Nell Island, i., Marsh Is. | S17 | 52 |
| Nellore, India | F7 | 36 |
| Nellysford, Va., U.S. | C4 | 123 |
| Nelson, B.C. | E9 | 69 |
| Nelson, N.Z. | N14 | 51 |
| Nelson, Az., U.S. | B2 | 80 |
| Nelson, Ga., U.S. | B2 | 87 |
| Nelson, Il., U.S. | B4 | 90 |
| Nelson, Ky., U.S. | C4 | 94 |
| Nelson, Mn., U.S. | E3 | 100 |
| Nelson, Mo., U.S. | B4 | 102 |
| Nelson, Ne., U.S. | D7 | 104 |
| Nelson, Nv., U.S. | H7 | 105 |
| Nelson, N.H., U.S. | E2 | 106 |
| Nelson, Pa., U.S. | C7 | 115 |
| Nelson, Wi., U.S. | D1 | 126 |
| Nelson, co., Ky., U.S. | C4 | 94 |
| Nelson, co., N.D., U.S. | B7 | 111 |
| Nelson, co., Va., U.S. | C4 | 123 |
| Nelson, stm., Man. | A4 | 70 |
| Nelson, Cape, c., Austl. | I3 | 51 |
| Nelson Forks, B.C. | m18 | 69 |
| Nelson House, Man. | B2 | 70 |
| Nelson Lake, l., Man. | B2 | 70 |
| Nelsonville, Oh., U.S. | C3 | 112 |
| Nelspruit, S. Afr. | C5 | 49 |
| Néma, Maur. | C3 | 45 |
| Nemacolin, Pa., U.S. | G2 | 115 |
| Nemadji, stm., U.S. | B1 | 126 |
| Nemaha, Ia., U.S. | B2 | 92 |
| Nemaha, Ne., U.S. | D10 | 104 |
| Nemaha, co., Ks., U.S. | C7 | 93 |
| Nemaha, co., Ne., U.S. | D10 | 104 |
| Nemakščiai, Sov. Un. | A7 | 26 |
| Neman, Sov. Un. | A7 | 26 |
| Neman (Nemunas), stm., Sov. Un. | E5 | 27 |
| Nembe, Nig. | F6 | 45 |
| Nemegos, Ont. | B3 | 55 |
| Nemei, Lake, l., Italy | h9 | 23 |
| Nemiscau, Que. | h11 | 74 |
| Nemours, Fr. | C5 | 16 |
| Nemunas (Neman), stm., Sov. Un. | D4 | 27 |
| Nemuro, Japan | C14 | 31 |
| Nemuro Strait, strt., Asia | D12 | 33 |
| Nenagh, Ire. | D2 | 10 |
| Nenana, Ak., U.S. | C10 | 79 |
| Nendeln, Liech. | B8 | 21 |
| Nene, stm., Eng., U.K. | B10 | 12 |
| Nenjiang, China | B10 | 31 |
| Nen Jiang, stm., China | B9 | 31 |
| Nenzel, Ne., U.S. | B4 | 104 |
| Nenzing, Aus. | B8 | 21 |
| Neodesha, Ks., U.S. | E8 | 93 |
| Neoga, Il., U.S. | D5 | 90 |
| Neola, Ia., U.S. | C2 | 92 |
| Neola, Ut., U.S. | C5 | 121 |
| Néon Karlovásion, Grc. | D6 | 25 |
| Neopit, Wi., U.S. | D5 | 126 |
| Neosho, Mo., U.S. | E3 | 102 |
| Neosho, Wi., U.S. | E5 | 126 |
| Neosho, co., Ks., U.S. | E8 | 93 |
| Neosho, stm., U.S. | A6 | 113 |
| Neosho Falls, Ks., U.S. | D8 | 93 |
| Neosho Rapids, Ks., U.S. | D8 | 93 |
| Neotsu, Or., U.S. | B3 | 114 |
| Nepal, ctry., Asia | C7 | 36 |
| Nepālganj, Nepal | C8 | 36 |
| Nepaug Reservoir, res., Ct., U.S. | B3 | 84 |
| Nepean, Ont. | B9 | 73 |
| Nepewassi Lake, l., Ont. | A4 | 73 |
| Nephi, Ut., U.S. | D4 | 121 |
| Nepisiguit, stm., N.B. | B3 | 71 |
| Nepisiguit Bay, b., N.B. | B4 | 71 |
| Nepomuk, Czech. | D8 | 19 |
| Neponset, Il., U.S. | B4 | 90 |
| Neponset, stm., Ma., U.S. | h11 | 98 |
| Neptune, Sask. | H3 | 75 |
| Neptune, N.J., U.S. | C4 | 107 |
| Neptune Beach, Fl., U.S. | B5 | 86 |
| Neptune City, N.J., U.S. | C4 | 107 |
| Nera, stm., Italy | C4 | 23 |
| Nerchinsk, Sov. Un. | D14 | 29 |
| Nerekhta, Sov. Un. | A8 | 31 |
| Neriquinha, Ang. | E3 | 48 |
| Nerja, Spain | D4 | 22 |
| Nerópolis, Braz. | B12 | 33 |
| Nerstrand, Mn., U.S. | F5 | 100 |
| Nes, Neth. | B5 | 17 |
| Nesbit, Ms., U.S. | A3 | 101 |
| Nesbitt, Man. | E2 | 70 |
| Nescopeck, Pa., U.S. | E2 | 70 |
| Nesconset, N.Y., U.S. | *n15 | 109 |

| Name | Map Ref. | Page |
|---|---|---|
| Nescopeck, Pa., U.S. | D9 | 115 |
| Nesebŭr, Bul. | D8 | 24 |
| Neshanic, stm., N.J., U.S. | C3 | 107 |
| Neshanic Station, N.J., U.S. | B3 | 107 |
| Nesher, Isr. | B7 | 41 |
| Neshkoro, Wi., U.S. | E4 | 126 |
| Neshoba, Ms., U.S. | C4 | 101 |
| Neshoba, co., Ms., U.S. | C4 | 101 |
| Nesika Beach, Or., U.S. | E2 | 114 |
| Neskaupstadur, Ice. | n26 | 14 |
| Neskowin, Or., U.S. | B3 | 114 |
| Nesle, Fr. | E2 | 17 |
| Nesmith, S.C., U.S. | D8 | 117 |
| Nesodden, Nor. | p28 | 14 |
| Nesowadnehunk, l., Me., U.S. | B3 | 96 |
| Nespelem, Wa., U.S. | A7 | 124 |
| Nesquehoning, Pa., U.S. | E10 | 115 |
| Ness, co., Ks., U.S. | D4 | 93 |
| Ness, Loch, l., Scot., U.K. | C4 | 13 |
| Ness City, Ks., U.S. | D4 | 93 |
| Nesselrode, Mount, mtn., N.A. | E6 | 66 |
| Nesselwang, W. Ger. | B6 | 20 |
| Nesslau, Switz. | B5 | 20 |
| Nessmersiel, W. Ger. | A7 | 17 |
| Nesterov, Sov. Un. | C7 | 26 |
| Nesterov, Sov. Un. | A7 | 26 |
| Nestórion, Grc. | B3 | 25 |
| Nestorville, W.V., U.S. | B5 | 125 |
| Néstos (Mesta), stm., Eur. | B5 | 25 |
| Nesvizh, Sov. Un. | E6 | 27 |
| Nes Ziyyona, Isr. | C6 | 41 |
| Netanya, Isr. | B6 | 41 |
| Netarts, Or., U.S. | B3 | 114 |
| Netawaka, Ks., U.S. | C8 | 93 |
| Netcong, N.J., U.S. | B3 | 107 |
| Netherhill, Sask. | F1 | 75 |
| Netherlands, ctry., Eur. | A6 | 16 |
| Netherlands Antilles, ctry., N.A. | A4 | 60 |
| Nether Providence Township, Pa., U.S. | *G11 | 115 |
| Nethy Bridge, Scot., U.K. | C5 | 13 |
| Netolice, Czech. | D9 | 19 |
| Netrakona, Bngl. | E13 | 37 |
| Nettie, W.V., U.S. | C4 | 125 |
| Nettilling Lake, l., N.W. Ter. | C18 | 66 |
| Nett Lake, Mn., U.S. | B5 | 100 |
| Nett Lake, l., Mn., U.S. | B5 | 100 |
| Nett Lake Indian Reservation, Mn., U.S. | B6 | 100 |
| Nettleton, Ms., U.S. | A5 | 101 |
| Nettleton, Mo., U.S. | B4 | 102 |
| Nettuno, Italy | k9 | 23 |
| Netvořice, Czech. | o18 | 26 |
| Netzahualcóyotl, Mex. | h9 | 63 |
| Neubeckum, W. Ger. | B3 | 19 |
| Neubrandenburg, E. Ger. | B6 | 18 |
| Neuburg [an der Donau], W. Ger. | D5 | 18 |
| Neuchâtel, Switz. | E3 | 18 |
| Neuchâtel, state, Switz. | C2 | 20 |
| Neuchâtel, Lake, l., Switz. | E3 | 18 |
| Neudorf, Sask. | G4 | 75 |
| Neuenegg, Switz. | C3 | 21 |
| Neuenkirchen, W. Ger. | E3 | 15 |
| Neuenrade, W. Ger. | B2 | 19 |
| Neuerburg, W. Ger. | E6 | 17 |
| Neufchâteau, Bel. | E5 | 17 |
| Neufchâteau, Fr. | C6 | 16 |
| Neufchâtel-en-Bray, Fr. | C4 | 16 |
| Neufchâtel-sur-Aisne, Fr. | E4 | 17 |
| Neufelden, Aus. | D6 | 18 |
| Neugersdorf, E. Ger. | C9 | 19 |
| Neuharlingersiel, W. Ger. | A7 | 17 |
| Neuhaus, E. Ger. | E4 | 15 |
| Neuhaus, E. Ger. | C6 | 19 |
| Neuilly [-sur-Seine], Fr. | g11 | 16 |
| Neu-Isenburg, W. Ger. | C3 | 19 |
| Neukirchen am Grossvenediger, Aus. | B8 | 20 |
| Neumarkt, W. Ger. | D5 | 18 |
| Neumarkt-Sankt Veit, W. Ger. | A8 | 20 |
| Neumünster, W. Ger. | A4 | 18 |
| Neunburg vorm Wald, W. Ger. | D7 | 19 |
| Neunkirch, Switz. | A6 | 21 |
| Neunkirchen, Aus. | E8 | 18 |
| Neunkirchen, W. Ger. | D2 | 19 |
| Neuquén, Arg. | B3 | 54 |
| Neuquén, prov., Arg. | B3 | 54 |
| Neuquén, stm., Arg. | B3 | 54 |
| Neurara, Chile | D2 | 55 |
| Neuruppin, E. Ger. | B6 | 18 |
| Neuse, stm., N.C., U.S. | B6 | 110 |
| Neusiedler Lake, l., Eur. | E8 | 18 |
| Neuss, W. Ger. | C5 | 19 |
| Neustadt, Ont. | C4 | 73 |
| Neustadt, W. Ger. | B9 | 19 |
| Neustadt, E. Ger. | C6 | 19 |
| Neustadt, W. Ger. | E4 | 18 |
| Neustadt, W. Ger. | C4 | 19 |
| Neustadt am Rübenberge, W. Ger. | F3 | 15 |
| Neustadt [an der Aisch], W. Ger. | D5 | 18 |
| Neustadt [an der Dosse], E. Ger. | B6 | 18 |
| Neustadt an der Waldnaab, W. Ger. | D7 | 19 |
| Neustadt [an der Weinstrasse], W. Ger. | D4 | 18 |
| Neustadt [bei Coburg], W. Ger. | C5 | 18 |
| Neustadt-Glewe, E. Ger. | E5 | 15 |
| Neustadt [in Holstein], W. Ger. | A5 | 18 |
| Neustrelitz, E. Ger. | B6 | 18 |
| Neu-Ulm, W. Ger. | D5 | 18 |
| Neuville, Que. | C6 | 74 |
| Neuville-lès-Dieppe, Fr. | E9 | 12 |
| Neuwerk, i., W. Ger. | E2 | 15 |
| Neuwied, W. Ger. | C6 | 19 |
| Neva, Tn., U.S. | C12 | 119 |
| Neva, stm., Sov. Un. | s31 | 14 |
| Nevada, Ia., U.S. | B4 | 92 |
| Nevada, Mo., U.S. | D3 | 102 |
| Nevada, Oh., U.S. | B2 | 112 |
| Nevada, co., Ar., U.S. | D2 | 81 |
| Nevada, co., Ca., U.S. | C3 | 82 |
| Nevada, state, U.S. | D4 | 105 |
| Nevada, Sierra, mts., Spain | D4 | 22 |
| Nevada, Sierra, mts., U.S. | D4 | 82 |
| Nevada City, Ca., U.S. | C3 | 82 |
| Nevado, Cerro, mtn., Col. | C7 | 27 |
| Nevel, Sov. Un. | C7 | 27 |
| Nevelsk, Sov. Un. | B13 | 31 |
| Nevelski, Mount, mtn., Sov. Un. | A11 | 33 |
| Nevers, Fr. | D5 | 16 |
| Neversink, stm., N.Y., U.S. | D6 | 109 |
| Nevesinje, Yugo. | D4 | 24 |
| Neville, Sask. | H2 | 75 |
| Neville, Fr. | E8 | 12 |
| Nevils, Ga., U.S. | D5 | 87 |
| Nevinnomyssk, Sov. Un. | G17 | 8 |
| Nevinville, Ia., U.S. | C3 | 92 |
| Nevis, Mn., U.S. | D4 | 100 |
| Nevis, i., St. C.-N. | H13 | 64 |
| Nevis, Ben, mtn., Scot., U.K. | B4 | 10 |
| Nevis, Loch, b., Scot., U.K. | C3 | 13 |
| Nevşehir, Tur. | C10 | 40 |
| New, stm., U.S. | C3 | 125 |
| New, stm., N.C., U.S. | C5 | 110 |
| Newala, Tan. | D6 | 48 |
| New Albany, In., U.S. | H6 | 91 |
| New Albany, Ks., U.S. | E8 | 93 |
| New Albany, Ms., U.S. | A4 | 101 |
| New Albany, Oh., U.S. | k11 | 112 |
| New Albin, Ia., U.S. | A6 | 92 |
| Newald, Wi., U.S. | C5 | 126 |
| New Almelo, Ks., U.S. | C3 | 93 |
| New Alsace, In., U.S. | F8 | 91 |
| New Amsterdam, Guy. | A3 | 59 |
| Newark, Ar., U.S. | B4 | 81 |
| Newark, Ca., U.S. | h8 | 82 |
| Newark, De., U.S. | B3 | 85 |
| Newark, Il., U.S. | B5 | 90 |
| Newark, Md., U.S. | D7 | 97 |
| Newark, Mo., U.S. | B6 | 102 |
| Newark, N.J., U.S. | B4 | 107 |
| Newark, N.Y., U.S. | B3 | 109 |
| Newark, Oh., U.S. | B3 | 112 |
| Newark, Tx., U.S. | m9 | 120 |
| Newark Bay, b., N.J., U.S. | k8 | 107 |
| Newark Lake, l., Nv., U.S. | D6 | 105 |
| Newark Valley, N.Y., U.S. | C4 | 109 |
| New Athens, Il., U.S. | E4 | 90 |
| New Athens, Oh., U.S. | B4 | 112 |
| New Auburn, Mn., U.S. | F4 | 100 |
| New Auburn, Wi., U.S. | C2 | 126 |
| New Augusta, Ms., U.S. | D4 | 101 |
| New Baden, Il., U.S. | E4 | 90 |
| New Baltimore, Mi., U.S. | F8 | 99 |
| New Baltimore, N.Y., U.S. | C7 | 109 |
| New Baltimore, Oh., U.S. | n12 | 112 |
| New Baltimore, Pa., U.S. | G4 | 115 |
| New Bedford, Il., U.S. | B4 | 90 |
| New Bedford, Ma., U.S. | C6 | 98 |
| New Bedford, Pa., U.S. | D1 | 115 |
| New Berlin, Il., U.S. | D4 | 90 |
| New Berlin, N.Y., U.S. | C5 | 109 |
| New Berlin, Pa., U.S. | E7 | 115 |
| New Berlin, Tx., U.S. | k7 | 120 |
| New Berlin, Wi., U.S. | n11 | 126 |
| New Bern, N.C., U.S. | B5 | 110 |
| Newberg, Or., U.S. | B4 | 114 |
| Newberry, Fl., U.S. | C4 | 86 |
| Newberry, Mi., U.S. | B5 | 99 |
| Newberry, S.C., U.S. | C4 | 117 |
| Newberry, co., S.C., U.S. | C4 | 117 |
| Newberry Springs, Ca., U.S. | E5 | 82 |
| New Bethlehem, Pa., U.S. | D3 | 115 |
| New Blaine, Ar., U.S. | B2 | 81 |
| New Bloomfield, Mo., U.S. | C5 | 102 |
| New Bloomfield, Pa., U.S. | F7 | 115 |
| New Bloomington, Oh., U.S. | B2 | 112 |
| New Boston, Il., U.S. | B3 | 90 |
| New Boston, Mi., U.S. | p15 | 99 |
| New Boston, N.H., U.S. | E3 | 106 |
| New Boston, Oh., U.S. | D3 | 112 |
| New Boston, Tx., U.S. | C5 | 120 |
| New Braintree, Ma., U.S. | B3 | 98 |
| New Braunfels, Tx., U.S. | E3 | 120 |
| New Bremen, N.Y., U.S. | B5 | 109 |
| New Bremen, Oh., U.S. | B1 | 112 |
| New Bridge, Or., U.S. | C9 | 114 |
| New Brigden, Alta. | D5 | 68 |
| New Brighton, Mn., U.S. | m12 | 100 |
| New Brighton, Pa., U.S. | E1 | 115 |
| New Britain, Ct., U.S. | C4 | 84 |
| New Britain, i., Pap. N. Gui. | k13 | 50 |
| New Brockton, Al., U.S. | D4 | 78 |
| Newbrook, Alta. | B4 | 68 |
| New Brunswick, N.J., U.S. | C4 | 107 |
| New Brunswick, prov., Can. | C3 | 71 |
| New Buffalo, Mi., U.S. | G4 | 99 |
| Newburg, Ky., U.S. | g11 | 94 |
| Newburg, Mo., U.S. | D5 | 102 |
| Newburg, N.D., U.S. | A5 | 111 |
| Newburg, Pa., U.S. | F6 | 115 |
| Newburg, Wi., U.S. | E5 | 126 |
| Newburgh, Ont. | C8 | 73 |
| Newburgh, Scot., U.K. | C7 | 13 |
| Newburgh, In., U.S. | I3 | 91 |
| Newburgh, Me., U.S. | D4 | 96 |
| Newburgh, N.Y., U.S. | D6 | 109 |
| Newburgh Heights, Oh., U.S. | h9 | 112 |
| New Burnside, Il., U.S. | F5 | 90 |
| Newbury, Ont. | E3 | 73 |
| Newbury, Eng., U.K. | E6 | 10 |
| Newbury, Ma., U.S. | A6 | 98 |
| Newbury, N.H., U.S. | D2 | 106 |
| Newbury, Vt., U.S. | C4 | 122 |
| Newburyport, Ma., U.S. | A6 | 98 |
| New Caledonia, dep., Oc. | H10 | 6 |
| New Cambria, Ks., U.S. | D6 | 93 |
| New Cambria, Mo., U.S. | B5 | 102 |
| New Canaan, Ct., U.S. | E2 | 84 |
| New Canton, Il., U.S. | D2 | 90 |
| New Canton, Va., U.S. | C4 | 123 |
| New Carlisle, Que. | A4 | 71 |
| New Carlisle, Oh., U.S. | C2 | 112 |
| New Carlisle, In., U.S. | A4 | 91 |
| New Carrollton, Md., U.S. | *C4 | 97 |
| New Cassel, N.Y., U.S. | *n15 | 109 |
| New Castle, hist. reg., Spain | | |
| New Castle, Austl. | F8 | 51 |
| Newcastle, N.B. | C4 | 71 |
| Newcastle, Ont. | D6 | 73 |
| Newcastle, Ire. | E4 | 11 |
| Newcastle, S. Afr. | C4 | 49 |
| Newcastle, N. Ire., U.K. | C6 | 11 |
| Newcastle, Al., U.S. | B3 | 78 |
| Newcastle, Ca., U.S. | C3 | 82 |
| Newcastle, Co., U.S. | B3 | 83 |
| Newcastle, De., U.S. | B3 | 85 |
| Newcastle, In., U.S. | E7 | 91 |
| Newcastle, Ky., U.S. | B4 | 94 |
| Newcastle, Me., U.S. | D3 | 96 |
| Newcastle, Ne., U.S. | B9 | 104 |
| Newcastle, Ok., U.S. | B4 | 113 |
| Newcastle, Pa., U.S. | D1 | 115 |
| Newcastle, Tx., U.S. | C3 | 120 |
| New Castle, Ut., U.S. | F2 | 121 |
| Newcastle, Va., U.S. | C2 | 123 |
| Newcastle, Wy., U.S. | C8 | 127 |
| New Castle, co., De., U.S. | B3 | 85 |
| Newcastle Creek, N.B. | C3 | 71 |
| Newcastle Emlyn, Wales, U.K. | B3 | 12 |
| Newcastle Mine, Alta. | D4 | 68 |
| Newcastle-under-Lyme, Eng., U.K. | A5 | 12 |
| Newcastle upon Tyne, Eng., U.K. | C6 | 10 |
| Newcastle West, Ire. | E2 | 11 |
| Newcestown, Ire. | F3 | 11 |
| New City, N.Y., U.S. | D6 | 109 |
| New Columbia, Pa., U.S. | D8 | 115 |
| Newcomb, N.M., U.S. | A1 | 108 |
| Newcomb, N.Y., U.S. | B6 | 109 |
| Newcomerstown, Oh., U.S. | B4 | 112 |
| New Concord, Ky., U.S. | f9 | 94 |
| New Concord, Oh., U.S. | C4 | 112 |
| New Cumberland, Pa., U.S. | F8 | 115 |
| New Cumberland, W.V., U.S. | A4 | 125 |
| New Cumnock, Scot., U.K. | C4 | 10 |
| Newdale, Man. | D1 | 70 |
| Newdale, Id., U.S. | F7 | 89 |
| New Dayton, Alta. | E4 | 68 |
| Newdegate, Austl. | F2 | 50 |
| New Delhi, India | C6 | 36 |
| New Denver, B.C. | D9 | 69 |
| New Diggings, Wi., U.S. | F3 | 126 |
| New Durham, N.H., U.S. | D4 | 106 |
| New Edinburg, Ar., U.S. | D3 | 81 |
| New Effington, S.D., U.S. | B9 | 118 |
| New Egypt, N.J., U.S. | C3 | 107 |
| Newell, Al., U.S. | B4 | 78 |
| Newell, Ar., U.S. | D3 | 81 |
| Newell, Ia., U.S. | B2 | 92 |
| Newell, S.D., U.S. | C2 | 118 |
| Newell, W.V., U.S. | A4 | 125 |
| Newell, Lake, l., Alta. | D5 | 68 |
| New Ellenton, S.C., U.S. | E4 | 117 |
| Newellton, La., U.S. | B4 | 95 |
| New England, N.D., U.S. | C3 | 111 |
| Newenham, Cape, c., Ak., U.S. | D7 | 79 |
| New Enterprise, Pa., U.S. | F5 | 115 |
| New Era, Mi., U.S. | E4 | 99 |
| Newe Sha'anan, Isr. | m14 | 41 |
| New Fairfield, Ct., U.S. | D2 | 84 |
| Newfane, N.Y., U.S. | B2 | 109 |
| Newfane, Vt., U.S. | F3 | 122 |
| Newfield, Me., U.S. | E2 | 96 |
| Newfield, N.J., U.S. | D2 | 107 |
| Newfields, N.H., U.S. | D5 | 106 |
| New Florence, Mo., U.S. | C6 | 102 |
| New Florence, Pa., U.S. | F3 | 115 |
| Newfolden, Mn., U.S. | B2 | 100 |
| New Forest, for., Eng., U.K. | D6 | 12 |
| Newfound Gap, U.S. | I9 | 110 |
| Newfound Lake, l., N.H., U.S. | C3 | 106 |
| Newfoundland, Pa., U.S. | D11 | 115 |
| Newfoundland, prov., Can. | D4 | 72 |
| Newfoundland, i., Newf. | D3 | 72 |
| Newfoundland Mountains, mts., Ut., U.S. | B2 | 121 |
| New Franken, Wi., U.S. | D6 | 126 |
| New Franklin, Mo., U.S. | B5 | 102 |
| New Freedom, Pa., U.S. | G8 | 115 |
| New Galilee, Pa., U.S. | E1 | 115 |
| New Galloway, Scot., U.K. | C4 | 10 |
| Newgate, B.C. | E10 | 69 |
| New Gate, hist., Isr. | m14 | 41 |
| New Germany, N.S. | E5 | 71 |
| New Glarus, Wi., U.S. | F4 | 126 |
| New Glasgow, N.S. | D7 | 71 |
| New Gloucester, Me., U.S. | E2 | 96 |
| New Gretna, N.J., U.S. | D4 | 107 |
| New Guinea, i. | G8 | 6 |
| Newhalem, Wa., U.S. | A4 | 124 |
| Newhall, Ca., U.S. | E4 | 82 |
| Newhall, Ia., U.S. | C6 | 92 |
| Newhall, Me., U.S. | g7 | 96 |
| Newhall, W.V., U.S. | D3 | 125 |
| New Hamburg, Ont. | D4 | 73 |
| New Hampshire, state, U.S. | C3 | 106 |
| New Hampton, Ia., U.S. | A5 | 92 |
| New Hampton, Mo., U.S. | A3 | 102 |
| New Hampton, N.H., U.S. | C3 | 106 |
| New Hanover, co., N.C., U.S. | C5 | 110 |
| New Hanover, i., Pap. N. Gui. | h12 | 50 |
| New Harbor, Me., U.S. | E3 | 96 |
| New Harbour, Newf. | E5 | 72 |
| New Harmony, In., U.S. | H2 | 91 |
| New Harmony, Ut., U.S. | F2 | 121 |
| New Hartford, Ct., U.S. | B4 | 84 |
| New Hartford, Ia., U.S. | B5 | 92 |
| New Haven, Ct., U.S. | D4 | 84 |
| New Haven, Il., U.S. | F5 | 90 |
| New Haven, In., U.S. | B7 | 91 |
| New Haven, Ky., U.S. | C4 | 94 |
| New Haven, Mi., U.S. | F8 | 99 |
| New Haven, Mo., U.S. | C6 | 102 |
| New Haven, N.Y., U.S. | B4 | 109 |
| New Haven, Oh., U.S. | A3 | 112 |
| New Haven, Vt., U.S. | C2 | 122 |
| New Haven, W.V., U.S. | C3 | 125 |
| New Haven, co., Ct., U.S. | D4 | 84 |
| New Haven, stm., Vt., U.S. | C2 | 122 |
| New Haven Harbor, b., Ct., U.S. | E4 | 84 |
| New Hazelton, B.C. | B4 | 69 |
| New Hebrides see Vanuatu, ctry., Oc. | H10 | 6 |
| Newhebron, Ms., U.S. | D4 | 101 |
| New Hill, N.C., U.S. | B4 | 110 |
| New Holland, Ga., U.S. | B3 | 87 |
| New Holland, Il., U.S. | C4 | 90 |
| New Holland, Oh., U.S. | C2 | 112 |
| New Holland, Pa., U.S. | F9 | 115 |
| New Holstein, Wi., U.S. | E5 | 126 |
| Newhope, Ar., U.S. | C2 | 81 |
| New Hope, Al., U.S. | A3 | 78 |
| New Hope, Ga., U.S. | C2 | 87 |
| New Hope, Ky., U.S. | C4 | 94 |
| New Hope, Mn., U.S. | m12 | 100 |
| New Hope, N.C., U.S. | *B4 | 110 |
| New Hope, Pa., U.S. | F12 | 115 |
| New Hope Mountain, mtn., Al., U.S. | g7 | 78 |
| New Hradec, N.D., U.S. | B3 | 111 |
| New Hudson, Mi., U.S. | o14 | 99 |
| New Hyde Park, N.Y., U.S. | *E7 | 109 |
| New Iberia, La., U.S. | D4 | 95 |
| Newington, Ct., U.S. | C5 | 84 |
| Newington, Ga., U.S. | D5 | 87 |
| Newington, Va., U.S. | *B5 | 123 |
| New Inlet, b., N.C., U.S. | D5 | 110 |
| New Ipswich, N.H., U.S. | E3 | 106 |
| New Ireland, i., Pap. N. Gui. | h13 | 50 |
| New Jersey, state, U.S. | C4 | 107 |
| New Johnsonville, Tn., U.S. | A4 | 119 |
| New Kensington, Pa., U.S. | E2 | 115 |
| New Kent, Va., U.S. | C5 | 123 |
| New Kent, co., Va., U.S. | C5 | 123 |
| Newkirk, N.M., U.S. | B5 | 108 |
| Newkirk, Ok., U.S. | A4 | 113 |
| New Knoxville, Oh., U.S. | B1 | 112 |
| New Kowloon, H.K. | *G7 | 31 |
| New Lake, l., N.C., U.S. | B6 | 110 |
| Newland, N.C., U.S. | A1 | 110 |
| New Lebanon, In., U.S. | F3 | 91 |
| New Lebanon, N.Y., U.S. | C7 | 109 |
| New Leipzig, N.D., U.S. | C4 | 111 |
| New Lenox, Il., U.S. | B6 | 90 |
| New Lexington, Oh., U.S. | C3 | 112 |
| New Liberty, Ky., U.S. | B5 | 94 |
| New Lima, Ok., U.S. | B5 | 113 |
| New Limerick, Me., U.S. | B5 | 96 |
| New Lisbon, In., U.S. | E7 | 91 |
| New Lisbon, N.J., U.S. | D3 | 107 |
| New Lisbon, Wi., U.S. | E3 | 126 |
| New Liskeard, Ont. | p20 | 73 |
| Newllano, La., U.S. | C2 | 95 |
| Newlon, W.V., U.S. | C4 | 125 |
| New London, Ct., U.S. | D7 | 84 |
| New London, Ia., U.S. | D6 | 92 |
| New London, Mn., U.S. | E4 | 100 |
| New London, Mo., U.S. | B6 | 102 |
| New London, N.H., U.S. | D3 | 106 |
| New London, N.C., U.S. | B2 | 110 |
| New London, Oh., U.S. | A3 | 112 |
| New London, Wi., U.S. | D5 | 126 |
| New London, co., Ct., U.S. | C7 | 84 |
| New London Submarine Base, mil., Ct., U.S. | D7 | 84 |
| New Lothrop, Mi., U.S. | E7 | 99 |
| New Lowell, Ont. | C5 | 73 |
| New Madison, Oh., U.S. | C1 | 112 |
| New Madrid, Mo., U.S. | E8 | 102 |
| New Madrid, co., Mo., U.S. | E8 | 102 |
| Newman, Austl. | D3 | 50 |
| Newman, Ca., U.S. | D3 | 82 |
| Newman, Il., U.S. | D6 | 90 |
| Newman, Ks., U.S. | k15 | 93 |
| New Manchester, W.V., U.S. | e8 | 125 |
| Newman Lake, l., Wa., U.S. | B8 | 124 |
| Newman Lake, Wa., U.S. | B8 | 124 |
| Newmanstown, Pa., U.S. | F9 | 115 |
| New Marion, In., U.S. | F7 | 91 |
| Newmarket, Ont. | C5 | 73 |
| Newmarket, Ire. | E2 | 11 |
| New Market, Al., U.S. | A3 | 78 |
| New Market, In., U.S. | E4 | 91 |
| New Market, Md., U.S. | B3 | 97 |
| New Market, Mn., U.S. | F5 | 100 |
| New Market, Tn., U.S. | C10 | 119 |
| New Market, Va., U.S. | B4 | 123 |
| Newmarket on Fergus, Ire. | E3 | 11 |
| New Marlboro, Ma., U.S. | B1 | 98 |
| New Marshfield, Oh., U.S. | C3 | 112 |
| New Martinsville, W.V., U.S. | B4 | 125 |
| New Matamoras, Oh., U.S. | C4 | 112 |
| New Meadows, Id., U.S. | D2 | 89 |
| New Melle, Mo., U.S. | C7 | 102 |
| New Mexico, state, U.S. | C3 | 108 |
| New Miami, Oh., U.S. | C1 | 112 |
| New Middletown, In., U.S. | H5 | 91 |
| New Milford, Ct., U.S. | C2 | 84 |
| New Milford, N.J., U.S. | h8 | 107 |
| New Milford, Pa., U.S. | C10 | 115 |
| New Mills, N.B. | B3 | 71 |
| New Milton, W.V., U.S. | B4 | 125 |
| New Munich, Mn., U.S. | E4 | 100 |
| New Munster, Wi., U.S. | n11 | 126 |
| New Norfolk, Austl. | o15 | 50 |
| New Norway, Alta. | C4 | 68 |
| New Offenburg, Mo., U.S. | D7 | 102 |
| New Orleans, La., U.S. | E5 | 95 |
| New Orleans Naval Air Station, mil., La., U.S. | k11 | 95 |
| New Osgoode, Sask. | E7 | 75 |
| New Oxford, Pa., U.S. | G7 | 115 |
| New Palestine, In., U.S. | E6 | 91 |
| New Paltz, N.Y., U.S. | D6 | 109 |
| New Paris, In., U.S. | B6 | 91 |
| New Paris, Oh., U.S. | C1 | 112 |
| New Paris, Pa., U.S. | F4 | 115 |
| New Perlican, Newf. | E5 | 72 |
| New Philadelphia, Oh., U.S. | B4 | 112 |
| New Philadelphia, Pa., U.S. | E9 | 115 |
| New Pine Creek, Or., U.S. | E6 | 114 |
| New Plymouth, N.Z. | M15 | 51 |
| New Plymouth, Id., U.S. | F2 | 89 |
| New Plymouth, Oh., U.S. | C3 | 112 |
| New Point, In., U.S. | F6 | 91 |
| New Point, Mo., U.S. | A2 | 102 |
| New Point Comfort, c., Va., U.S. | C6 | 123 |
| Newport, Ire. | D2 | 11 |
| Newport, Eng., U.K. | E6 | 10 |
| Newport, Wales, U.K. | E5 | 10 |
| New Port, Neth. Ant. | H19 | 65 |
| Newport, Eng., U.K. | E6 | 10 |
| Newport, Ar., U.S. | B4 | 81 |
| Newport, De., U.S. | B3 | 85 |
| Newport, In., U.S. | E3 | 91 |
| Newport, Ky., U.S. | A5 | 94 |
| Newport, Me., U.S. | D3 | 96 |
| Newport, Mi., U.S. | G8 | 99 |
| Newport, Mn., U.S. | n13 | 100 |
| Newport, Ne., U.S. | B6 | 104 |
| Newport, N.H., U.S. | D2 | 106 |
| Newport, N.C., U.S. | C6 | 110 |
| Newport, Oh., U.S. | C4 | 112 |
| Newport, Or., U.S. | C2 | 114 |
| Newport, Pa., U.S. | F7 | 115 |
| Newport, R.I., U.S. | E6 | 116 |
| Newport, Tn., U.S. | D10 | 119 |
| Newport, Tx., U.S. | C3 | 120 |
| Newport, Vt., U.S. | B4 | 122 |
| Newport, Va., U.S. | C2 | 123 |
| Newport, Wa., U.S. | A8 | 124 |
| Newport, co., R.I., U.S. | E5 | 116 |
| Newport Beach, Ca., U.S. | *n13 | 82 |
| Newport Hills, Wa., U.S. | *e11 | 124 |
| Newport News, Va., U.S. | D6 | 123 |
| New Port Richey, Fl., U.S. | D4 | 86 |
| Newport Station, N.S. | E5 | 71 |
| New Prague, Mn., U.S. | F5 | 100 |
| New Preston, Ct., U.S. | C2 | 84 |
| New Providence, Ia., U.S. | B4 | 92 |
| New Providence, N.J., U.S. | B4 | 107 |
| New Providence, i., Bah. | B5 | 64 |
| Newquay, Eng., U.K. | E4 | 10 |
| New Quay, Wales, U.K. | B3 | 12 |
| New Raymer, Co., U.S. | A7 | 83 |
| New Richland, Mn., U.S. | G5 | 100 |
| New Richmond, Que. | A4 | 71 |
| New Richmond, In., U.S. | D4 | 91 |
| New Richmond, Oh., U.S. | D1 | 112 |
| New Richmond, Wi., U.S. | C1 | 126 |
| New Riegel, Oh., U.S. | A2 | 112 |
| New River, Az., U.S. | D3 | 80 |
| New River, Tn., U.S. | C9 | 119 |
| New River Gorge, val., W.V., U.S. | m13 | 125 |
| New River Inlet, b., N.C., U.S. | C5 | 110 |
| New River Station, N.C., U.S. | *C5 | 110 |
| New Road, N.S. | E6 | 71 |
| New Roads, La., U.S. | D4 | 95 |
| New Rochelle, N.Y., U.S. | E7 | 109 |
| New Rockford, N.D., U.S. | B6 | 111 |
| New Ross, N.S. | E5 | 71 |
| New Ross, Ire. | E4 | 11 |
| New Ross, In., U.S. | E4 | 91 |
| Newry, N. Ire., U.K. | C3 | 10 |
| Newry, Me., U.S. | D2 | 96 |
| Newry, S.C., U.S. | B2 | 117 |
| New Salem, Il., U.S. | D3 | 90 |
| New Salem, In., U.S. | E7 | 91 |
| New Salem, Ks., U.S. | E7 | 93 |
| New Salem, Ma., U.S. | A3 | 98 |
| New Salem, N.D., U.S. | C4 | 111 |
| New Sarepta, Alta. | C4 | 68 |
| New Sarpy, La., U.S. | k11 | 95 |
| New Sharon, Ia., U.S. | C5 | 92 |
| New Sharon, Me., U.S. | D2 | 96 |
| New Siberian Islands, is., Sov. Un. | B18 | 29 |
| New Site, Al., U.S. | B4 | 78 |
| New Site, Ms., U.S. | A5 | 101 |
| New Smyrna Beach, Fl., U.S. | C6 | 86 |
| Newsoms, Va., U.S. | D5 | 123 |
| New South Wales, state, Austl. | F8 | 50 |
| New Straitsville, Oh., U.S. | C3 | 112 |
| New Sweden, Me., U.S. | B4 | 96 |
| New Tazwell, Tn., U.S. | C10 | 119 |
| Newtok, Ak., U.S. | C7 | 79 |
| Newton, Al., U.S. | D4 | 78 |
| Newton, Ga., U.S. | E2 | 87 |
| Newton, Il., U.S. | D5 | 90 |
| Newton, Ia., U.S. | C4 | 92 |
| Newton, Ks., U.S. | D6 | 93 |
| Newton, Ma., U.S. | B5 | 98 |
| Newton, Ms., U.S. | C4 | 101 |
| Newton, N.H., U.S. | E4 | 106 |
| Newton, N.J., U.S. | A3 | 107 |
| Newton, N.C., U.S. | B1 | 110 |
| Newton, Tx., U.S. | D6 | 120 |
| Newton, Ut., U.S. | B4 | 121 |
| Newton, W.V., U.S. | C3 | 125 |
| Newton, co., Ar., U.S. | B2 | 81 |
| Newton, co., Ga., U.S. | C3 | 87 |
| Newton, co., In., U.S. | B3 | 91 |
| Newton, co., Ms., U.S. | C4 | 101 |
| Newton, co., Mo., U.S. | E3 | 102 |
| Newton, co., Tx., U.S. | D6 | 120 |
| Newton Abbot, Eng., U.K. | F5 | 13 |
| Newton Aycliffe, Eng., U.K. | F7 | 13 |
| Newton Falls, N.Y., U.S. | A6 | 109 |
| Newton Falls, Oh., U.S. | A5 | 112 |
| Newton Grove, N.C., U.S. | B4 | 110 |
| New Town, N.D., U.S. | B3 | 111 |
| New Toronto (part of Etobicoke), Ont. | m14 | 73 |
| Newtown, Newf. | D5 | 72 |
| Newtown, Wales, U.K. | D5 | 10 |
| Newtown, Ct., U.S. | D2 | 84 |
| Newtown, Mo., U.S. | A4 | 102 |
| Newtown, Oh., U.S. | C1 | 112 |
| Newtown, Va., U.S. | C5 | 123 |
| Newtownabbey, N. Ire., U.K. | C6 | 11 |
| Newtownards, N. Ire., U.K. | C6 | 11 |
| Newtown Crommelin, N. Ire., U.K. | C5 | 11 |
| Newtownhamilton, N. Ire., U.K. | C5 | 11 |
| Newtown Mount Kennedy, Ire. | E4 | 11 |
| Newtown Square, Pa., U.S. | p20 | 115 |
| Newtownstewart, N. Ire., U.K. | C4 | 11 |
| New Trenton, In., U.S. | F7 | 91 |
| New Ulm, Mn., U.S. | F4 | 100 |
| New Ulm, Tx., U.S. | E4 | 120 |
| New Underwood, S.D., U.S. | C3 | 118 |
| New Vienna, Ia., U.S. | B6 | 92 |
| New Vienna, Oh., U.S. | C2 | 112 |
| New Village, N.J., U.S. | B2 | 107 |
| New Virginia, Ia., U.S. | C4 | 92 |
| New Washington, In., U.S. | G6 | 91 |
| New Washington, Oh., U.S. | B3 | 112 |
| New Washoe City, Nv., U.S. | *D2 | 105 |
| New Waterford, N.S. | C9 | 71 |
| New Waterford, Oh., U.S. | B5 | 112 |
| New Waverly, In., U.S. | C5 | 91 |
| New Waverly, Tx., U.S. | D5 | 120 |
| New Westminster, B.C. | E6 | 69 |
| New Whiteland, In., U.S. | E5 | 91 |
| New Wilmington, Pa., U.S. | D1 | 115 |
| New Windsor, Il., U.S. | B3 | 90 |
| New Windsor, Md., U.S. | A3 | 97 |
| New Windsor, N.Y., U.S. | D6 | 109 |
| New Woodstock, N.Y., U.S. | C5 | 109 |
| New World Island, i., Newf. | D4 | 72 |
| New York, co., N.Y., U.S. | k13 | 109 |
| New York, state, U.S. | C5 | 109 |
| New York Mills, Mn., U.S. | D3 | 100 |
| New Zealand, ctry., Oc. | N14 | 51 |
| New Zion, S.C., U.S. | D7 | 117 |
| Neya, Oh., U.S. | A1 | 112 |
| Neya, Sov. Un. | B2 | 8 |
| Ney Lake, l., Can. | B5 | 70 |
| Neyrīz, Iran | C5 | 38 |
| Neyshābūr, Iran | B5 | 38 |
| Nezhin, Sov. Un. | F8 | 27 |
| Nezperce, Id., U.S. | *C2 | 89 |
| Nez Perce, co., Id., U.S. | C2 | 89 |
| Nez Perce Indian Reservation, Id., U.S. | C2 | 89 |
| Nezpique, Bayou, stm., La., U.S. | D3 | 95 |
| Ngabang, Indon. | E3 | 34 |
| Ngabé, Congo | B2 | 48 |
| Ngala, Nig. | D7 | 45 |
| Ngami, Lake, l., Bots. | B3 | 49 |
| Ngangla Ringco, l., China | B7 | 36 |
| Ngangzê Lake, l., China | B11 | 37 |
| Ngaoundéré, Cam. | D2 | 46 |
| Ngara, Tan. | B5 | 48 |
| Ngaramasch, Palau | R17 | 52 |
| Ngaruangl Reef, rf., Palau | R17 | 52 |
| Ngaruawahia, N.Z. | L15 | 51 |
| Ngatapa, N.Z. | M16 | 51 |
| Ngemelis Islands, is., Palau | R17 | 52 |
| Ngerekebesang, i., Palau | R17 | 52 |
| Ngerkeel, Palau | R17 | 52 |
| Ngermechau, Palau | R17 | 52 |
| Ngeruktabel, i., Palau | R17 | 52 |
| Ngetbong, Palau | R17 | 52 |
| Ngidinga, Zaire | C2 | 48 |
| Ngong, Kenya | B6 | 48 |
| Ngoring Hu, l., China | D4 | 31 |
| Ngounié, stm., Gabon | F2 | 46 |
| Ngouri, Chad | C3 | 46 |
| Nguigmi, Niger | D7 | 45 |
| Nguru, Nig. | D7 | 45 |
| Nhamundá, Braz. | C3 | 59 |
| Nhamundá, stm., Braz. | C3 | 59 |
| Nha Trang, Viet. | C3 | 34 |
| Nhill, Austl. | H3 | 51 |
| Nhulunbuy, Austl. | B6 | 50 |
| Niafounké, Mali | B5 | 44 |
| Niagara, N.D., U.S. | B8 | 111 |
| Niagara, Wi., U.S. | C6 | 126 |
| Niagara, co., Ont. | D5 | 73 |
| Niagara, co., N.Y., U.S. | B2 | 109 |
| Niagara, stm., N.A. | B1 | 109 |
| Niagara Falls, Ont. | D5 | 73 |
| Niagara Falls, N.Y., U.S. | B1 | 109 |
| Niagara-on-the-Lake, Ont. | D5 | 73 |
| Niagara Town, N.Y., U.S. | *B2 | 109 |
| Niamey, Niger | D5 | 45 |
| Niamtougou, Togo | E5 | 45 |
| Niangara, Zaire | A4 | 48 |
| Niangua, Mo., U.S. | D5 | 102 |
| Niangua, stm., Mo., U.S. | C5 | 102 |
| Niantic, Ct., U.S. | D7 | 84 |
| Niarada, Mt., U.S. | C2 | 103 |
| Nias, i., Indon. | E1 | 34 |
| Niassa, dept., Moz. | D6 | 48 |
| Nibe, Den. | B3 | 15 |
| Nibley, Ut., U.S. | B4 | 121 |
| Nicaragua, ctry., N.A. | E7 | 63 |
| Nicaragua, Lago de, l., Nic. | E7 | 63 |
| Nicastro (Lamezia Terme), Italy | E6 | 23 |
| Nicatous Lake, l., Me., U.S. | C4 | 96 |
| Nice, Fr. | E7 | 16 |
| Niceville, Fl., U.S. | u15 | 86 |
| Nichinan, Japan | K5 | 33 |
| Nicholas, co., Ky., U.S. | B6 | 94 |
| Nicholas, co., W.V., U.S. | C4 | 125 |
| Nicholas Channel, strt., N.A. | C5 | 94 |
| Nicholasville, Ky., U.S. | C5 | 94 |
| Nichols, Ia., U.S. | C6 | 92 |
| Nichols, N.Y., U.S. | C4 | 109 |
| Nichols, S.C., U.S. | C9 | 117 |
| Nichols Hills, Ok., U.S. | B4 | 113 |
| Nicholson, Ms., U.S. | C10 | 115 |
| Nicholville, N.Y., U.S. | f10 | 109 |
| Nickajack Lake, l., Tn., U.S. | D8 | 119 |
| Nickel Centre, Ont. | p19 | 73 |
| Nickelsville, Va., U.S. | f9 | 123 |
| Nickerie, dept., Sur. | B3 | 59 |
| Nickerie, stm., Sur. | D5 | 93 |
| Nickerson, Ks., U.S. | D5 | 93 |
| Nickerson, Ne., U.S. | C9 | 104 |
| Nickerson Hill, hill, Ct., U.S. | B4 | 84 |
| Nicobar Islands, is., India | J3 | 29 |
| Nicodemus, Ks., U.S. | C4 | 93 |
| Nicola, B.C. | D7 | 69 |
| Nicola, stm., B.C. | D7 | 69 |
| Nicolet, Que. | C5 | 74 |
| Nicolet, stm., Que. | C5 | 74 |
| Nicolet, Lake, l., Mi., U.S. | B6 | 99 |
| Nicollet, Mn., U.S. | F4 | 100 |
| Nicollet, co., Mn., U.S. | F4 | 100 |
| Nicolls Town, Bah. | B5 | 64 |
| Nicoma Park, Ok., U.S. | B4 | 113 |
| Nicosia (Levkosía / Lefkoşa), Cyp. | E9 | 40 |
| Nicosia [Sicilia], Italy | L9 | 23 |
| Nicotera, Italy | E7 | 23 |
| Nicoya, C.R. | E7 | 63 |
| Nicoya, Golfo de, b., C.R. | F5 | 62 |
| Nicoya, Península de, pen., C.R. | E7 | 63 |
| Nictaux Falls, N.S. | E4 | 71 |
| Nida, stm., Pol. | C6 | 26 |
| Nid à l'Aigle, Cap du, St. P./M. | E3 | 72 |
| Nidan Rock, hill, Japan | P17 | 33 |
| Nidd, stm., Eng., U.K. | F7 | 13 |
| Nidda, W. Ger. | C4 | 19 |
| Nidda, stm., W. Ger. | C4 | 19 |
| Nidwalden, state, Switz. | C4 | 21 |
| Nidzica, Pol. | B6 | 26 |
| Niebüll, W. Ger. | D2 | 15 |
| Niederbronn-les-Bains, Fr. | F7 | 17 |
| Niedermarsberg, W. Ger. | B3 | 19 |
| Niedersachsen, state, W. Ger. | C2 | 100 |
| Nielsville, Mn., U.S. | C2 | 100 |
| Niemodlin, Pol. | C4 | 18 |
| Nienburg, W. Ger. | B4 | 18 |
| Niers, stm., Eur. | C6 | 17 |
| Nierstein, W. Ger. | D3 | 19 |
| Niesky, E. Ger. | B9 | 18 |
| Nieszawa, Pol. | C5 | 26 |
| Nietleben, E. Ger. | B6 | 18 |
| Nieu Amsterdam, Sur. | A3 | 59 |
| Nieuw Amsterdam, Neth. | *B5 | 17 |
| Nieuweroord, Neth. | B5 | 17 |
| Nieuw Nickerie, Sur. | A3 | 59 |
| Nigadoo, N.B. | B4 | 71 |
| Niğde, Tur. | D10 | 40 |
| Niger, ctry., Afr. | E6 | 45 |
| Niger, stm., Afr. | E6 | 45 |
| Niger, stm., Afr. | E6 | 45 |
| Niger Delta, Nig. | F6 | 45 |
| Nigeria, ctry., Afr. | E6 | 45 |
| Nigg, Scot., U.K. | C5 | 13 |

Name — Map Ref. — Page

Nighthawk, Wa., U.S. A6 124
Nigríta, Grc. B4 25
*Nihing, stm., Asia* H11 39
*Nihoa, i., Hi., U.S.* m15 88
Niigata, Japan D12 31
Niihama, Japan J6 33
*Niihau, i., Hi., U.S.* B1 88
*Nii Island, i., Japan* I9 33
Niimi, Japan I6 33
Nijar, Spain D4 22
Nijkerk, Neth. B5 17
Nijmegen, Neth. B6 16
Nikaia, Grc. *D4 25
Nikep, Md., U.S. k13 97
Nikishka, Ak., U.S. g16 79
Nikitinka, Sov. Un. D9 27
Nikitovka, Sov. Un. q21 27
Nikki, Benin E5 45
Nikkō, Japan D12 31
Nikolayev, Sov. Un. E6 29
Nikolayevsk, Sov. Un. F15 27
Nikolayevsk [-na-Amure], Sov. Un. D17 29
Nikolsk, Sov. Un. B3 28
Nikolski, Ak., U.S. E6 79
Nikonovskoye, Sov. Un. n18 27
Nikopol, Bul. D7 24
Nikopol, Sov. Un. H10 27
Niksar, Tur. B11 40
Nikshahr, Iran H10 39
Nikšić, Yugo. D4 24
Niland, Ca., U.S. F6 82
Nile, N.Y., U.S. C2 109
*Nile, stm., Afr.* C4 41
Niles, Il., U.S. h9 90
Niles, Ks., U.S. D6 93
Niles, Mi., U.S. G4 99
Niles, Oh., U.S. A5 112
Nilvange, Fr. E6 17
Nilwood, Il., U.S. D4 90
Nīmach, India E5 37
*Nimba, Mont, mtn., Afr.* E3 45
*Nimba Mountains, mts., Afr.* E3 45
Nîmes, Fr. F6 16
Nimmons, Ar., U.S. A5 81
*Nimpkish, stm., B.C.* D4 69
*Nimrīn, Wādī, val., Jord.* h13 41
*Nimrod Glacier, ice, Ant.* A29 7
*Nimrod Lake, res., Ar., U.S.* C2 81
Nimule, Sud. E3 47
*Ninemile Creek, stm., Ks., U.S.* k15 93
*Nine Mile Creek, stm., Ut., U.S.* D5 121
Nine Mile Falls, Wa., U.S. g13 124
*Ninemile Point, c., Mi., U.S.* C6 99
Ninette, Man. E2 70
*Ninety Mile Beach, Austl.* G8 50
Ninety Six, S.C., U.S. C3 117
Nineveh, Pa., U.S. G1 115
*Nineveh, hist., Iraq* B4 38
Ninga, Man. E2 70
Ning'an, China C10 31
Ningbo, China F9 31
Ningde, China F8 31
Ningdu, China K6 32
Ninghai, China J9 32
Ninghua, China K7 32
Ningjin, China F6 32
Ningming, China A7 35
Ningqiang, China H2 32
*Ningsia Hui see Ningxia Huizu, prov., China* D6 31
Ningwu, China D7 31
*Ningxia Huizu, prov., China* D6 31
Ningxian, China D6 31
Ninh Binh, Viet. A3 34
*Ninigret Pond, l., R.I., U.S.* G2 116
Ninilchik, Ak., U.S. C9 79
Ninnekah, Ok., U.S. C4 113
*Ninnescah, stm., Ks., U.S.* E6 93
*Ninnescah, North Fork, stm., Ks., U.S.* E5 93
*Ninnescah, South Fork, stm., Ks., U.S.* E5 93
*Ninnis Glacier, ice, Ant.* C27 7
Ninole, Hi., U.S. D6 88
Ninove, Bel. B6 16
Nioaque, Braz. C1 56
Niobe, N.D., U.S. A3 111
Niobrara, Ne., U.S. B7 104
*Niobrara, co., Wy., U.S.* C8 127
*Niobrara, stm., U.S.* B7 104
Nioki, Zaire B2 48
Niono, Mali D3 45
Nioro du Rip, Sen. D1 45
Nioro du Sahel, Mali C3 45
Niort, Fr. D3 16
Niota, Il., U.S. C2 90
Niota, Tn., U.S. D9 119
Niotaze, Ks., U.S. E7 93
Nipawin, Sask. D4 75
*Nipawin Provincial Park, Sask.* C3 75
*Nipekamew Lake, l., Sask.* C3 75
*Nipew Lake, l., Sask.* B3 75
Nipigon, Ont. o17 73
*Nipigon, Lake, l., Ont.* o17 73
*Nipishish Lake, l., Newf.* g9 72
*Nipissing, dept., Ont.* A6 73
*Nipissing, Lake, l., Ont.* A5 73
Nipomo, Ca., U.S. E3 82
Nippers Harbour, Newf. D4 72
*Nipple Mountain, mtn., Co., U.S.* D2 83
Nipton, Ca., U.S. E6 82
Niquelândia, Braz. A3 56
Niquero, Cuba D5 64
Nirasaki, Japan n17 33
Nirmal, India H7 37
Nirmāli, India D11 37
Niš, Yugo. D5 24
Nisa, Port. C2 22
*Nišava, stm., Eur.* D6 24
Nishinomiya, Japan *I7 33
Nishio, Japan o16 33
*Nísiros, i., Grc.* D6 25
Niskayuna, N.Y., U.S. C7 109
Nisland, S.D., U.S. C2 118
*Nisqually, stm., Wa., U.S.* C3 124
*Nissan, stm., Swe.* B7 15
*Nissum Bredning, b., Den.* B2 15
*Nissum Fjord, Den.* B2 15
Nisswa, Mn., U.S. D4 100
*Nistowiak Lake, l., Sask.* B3 75
Nisula, Mi., U.S. B2 99
Niterói, Braz. C4 56
*Nith, stm., Scot., U.K.* E5 13
Nitra, Czech. D5 26
*Nitra, stm., Czech.* D5 26
Nitro, W.V., U.S. C3 125
Nitta Yuma, Ms., U.S. B3 101
Nittenau, W. Ger. D7 19
*Niue, ctry., Oc.* H11 6
Nivelles, Bel. B6 16
*Nivernais, hist. reg., Fr.* D5 16
*Nivernais, Côtes du, hills, Fr.* D5 16
Niverville, Man. E3 70
Nivskiy, Sov. Un. D15 14
Niwot, Co., U.S. A5 83
Nixa, Mo., U.S. D4 102
Nixburg, Al., U.S. C3 78
Nixon, Nv., U.S. D2 105
Nixon, Tn., U.S. B3 119
Nixon, Tx., U.S. E4 120
Nizāmābād, India H7 37
*Nizām Sāgar, res., India* H7 37
*Nīzgān, stm., Afg.* E11 39
Nizhmozero, Sov. Un. E18 14
Nizhnekamsk, Sov. Un. *D8 29
Nizhnekolymsk, Sov. Un. C19 29
Nizhne-Leninskoye, Sov. Un. C6 33
Nizhneudinsk, Sov. Un. D12 29
Nizhneye, Sov. Un. q21 27
Nizhniy Chir, Sov. Un. G14 27
Nizhniy Lomov, Sov. Un. E14 27
Nizhniy Pyandzh, Sov. Un. H22 8
Nizhniy Tagil, Sov. Un. D9 29
*Nizhnyaya Tunguska, stm., Sov. Un.* C12 29
Nizhnyaya Tura, Sov. Un. D8 29
Nizip, Tur. *D11 40
*Nizmennyy, Cape, c., Sov. Un.* E7 33
Nizza Monferrato, Italy E4 20
Nizzana, Isr. D6 41
*Nizzana, Nahal, val., Isr.* D6 41
Njombe, Tan. C5 48
Njurunda, Swe. F7 14
Nkambe, Cam. D2 46
Nkayi, Zimb. A4 49
Nkhata Bay, Mwi. D5 48
Nkhota Kota, Mwi. D5 48
Nkongsamba, Cam. E1 46
Nnewi, Nig. E6 45
Noākhāli, Bngl. F13 37
Noank, Ct., U.S. D8 84
Noasca, Italy D3 20
Noatak, Ak., U.S. B7 79
*Noatak, stm., Ak., U.S.* B7 79
Nobel, Ont. B4 73
Nobeoka, Japan J5 33
Noble, Ga., U.S. B1 87
Noble, Il., U.S. E5 90
Noble, La., U.S. C2 95
Noble, Ok., U.S. B4 113
*Noble, co., In., U.S.* B7 91
*Noble, co., Oh., U.S.* C4 112
*Noble, co., Ok., U.S.* A4 113
Nobleboro, Me., U.S. D3 96
Nobleford, Alta. E4 68
*Nobles, co., Mn., U.S.* G3 100
Noblesville, In., U.S. D6 91
Nobleton, Fl., U.S. D4 86
Noboribetsu, Japan E10 33
*Nobscot Hill, hill, Ma., U.S.* B5 98
Nocatee, Fl., U.S. E5 86
Nocona, Tx., U.S. C4 120
Nodaway, Ia., U.S. D3 92
*Nodaway, co., Mo., U.S.* A3 102
*Nodaway, stm., U.S.* A2 102
Node, Wy., U.S. D8 127
Noel, Mo., U.S. E3 102
*Noel Paul's Brook, stm., Newf.* D3 72
Noelville, Ont. A4 73
Nogal, N.M., U.S. D4 108
Nogales, Mex. n15 63
Nogales, Az., U.S. F5 80
Nogara, Italy D7 20
Nōgata, Japan J5 33
Nogent-en-Bassigny, Fr. C6 16
Nogent-le-Rotrou, Fr. C4 16
Nogent [-sur-Marne], Fr. g10 16
Nogent-sur-Seine, Fr. C5 16
Noginsk, Sov. Un. D12 27
*Nogoa, stm., Austl.* B6 51
Nogoyá, Arg. A5 54
Nohar, India C5 36
Noheji, Japan F10 33
*Noirmoutier, Île de, i., Fr.* D2 16
Noisy-le-Sec, Fr. g10 16
*Nojima, Cape, c., Japan* I9 33
Nokesville, Va., U.S. B5 123
Nok Kundi, Pak. G11 39
Nokomis, Sask. F3 75
Nokomis, Fl., U.S. E4 86
Nokomis, Il., U.S. D4 90
*Nokomis, Lake, res., Wi., U.S.* C4 126
Nokou, Chad C2 46
Nola, Cen. Afr. Rep. E3 46
Nola, Italy D5 23
Nola, Ms., U.S. D3 101
Nolan, Tx., U.S. C2 120
Nolan, W.V., U.S. D2 125
*Nolan, co., Tx., U.S.* C2 120
Nolensville, Tn., U.S. B5 119
*Nolichucky, stm., Tn., U.S.* C10 119
*Nolin, stm., Ky., U.S.* C3 94
*Nolin Lake, res., Ky., U.S.* C3 94
Nolinsk, Sov. Un. B3 28
Noma, Fl., U.S. u16 86
*Noma, Cape, c., Japan* K5 33
*Nomans Land, i., Ma., U.S.* D6 98
Nombre de Dios, Pan. h12 62
Nome, Ak., U.S. C6 79
Nome, N.D., U.S. C8 111
Noményn, Fr. F6 17
Nomgon, Mong. C1 32
Nominingue, Que. C2 74
*Nomoneas, is., Micron.* Q18 52
*Nonacho Lake, l., N.W. Ter.* D11 66
Nondalton, Ak., U.S. C8 79
*Nonesuch, stm., Me., U.S.* g7 96
Nong'an, China C10 31
Nong Khai, Thai. B2 34
Nongoma, S. Afr. C5 49
Nonoava, Mex. B3 63
*Nonquit Pond, l., R.I., U.S.* E6 116
Nooksack, Wa., U.S. A3 124
*Nooksack, North Fork, stm., Wa., U.S.* A4 124
*Nooksack, South Fork, stm., Wa., U.S.* A3 124
Noonan, N.D., U.S. A2 111
Noone, N.H., U.S. E3 106
*Noordpunt, c., Neth. Ant.* H18 65
Noordwijk-Binnen, Neth. B4 17
Noorvik, Ak., U.S. B7 79
*Nootka Island, i., B.C.* E4 69
*Nootka Sound, strt., B.C.* E4 69
*Nopiming Provincial Park, Man.* D4 70
*No Point, Point, c., Md., U.S.* D5 97
*Noquebay, Lake, l., Wi., U.S.* C6 126
Nóqui, Ang. C1 48
Nora, Sask. E4 75
Nora, Swe. H6 14
Nora, Il., U.S. A4 90
Noranda, Que. k11 74
Nora Springs, Ia., U.S. A5 92
Norbertville, Que. C6 74
Norborne, Mo., U.S. B4 102
Norcatur, Ks., U.S. C3 93
Norco, Ca., U.S. *n13 82
Norco, La., U.S. D5 95
Norcross, Ga., U.S. C2 87
Norcross, Mn., U.S. E2 100
*Nord, dept., Fr.* D2 17
*Nord, Canal du, Fr.* D3 17
Nordborg, Den. C3 15
Nordby, Den. C2 15
Nordby, Den. C4 15
Nordegg, Alta. C2 68
*Nordegg, stm., Alta.* C3 68
Norden, W. Ger. B3 18
Nordenham, W. Ger. B4 18
*Nordenskjöld Archipelago, is., Sov. Un.* B4 128
*Nordenskjöld Ice Tongue, ice, Ant.* e39 7
Norderney, W. Ger. A7 17
*Norderney, i., W. Ger.* B3 18
Norderstedt, W. Ger. *B5 18
*Nordfjord, Nor.* G1 14
Nordhausen, E. Ger. C5 18
Nordhorn, W. Ger. B3 18
*Nordjylland, co., Den.* B3 15
Nordland, Wa., U.S. A3 124
Nördlingen, W. Ger. D5 18
Nordmaling, Swe. F8 14
Nordman, Id., U.S. A2 89
*Nordostrundingen, c., Grnld.* A19 61
Nordreisa, Nor. C9 14
*Nordrhein-Westfalen, state, W. Ger.* B2 19
*Nordstrand, i., W. Ger.* A4 18
*Nore, stm., Ire.* D3 10
Norene, Tn., U.S. A5 119
Norfolk, Ct., U.S. B3 84
Norfolk, Ma., U.S. h10 98
Norfolk, Ne., U.S. B8 104
Norfolk, N.Y., U.S. f9 109
Norfolk, Va., U.S. D6 123
*Norfolk, co., Ont.* E4 73
*Norfolk, co., Eng., U.K.* B8 12
*Norfolk, co., Ma., U.S.* B5 98
*Norfolk Island, dep., Oc.* H10 6
*Norfolk Naval Base, mil., Va., U.S.* k15 123
*Norfolk Naval Shipyard, mil., Va., U.S.* k15 123
Norfork, Ar., U.S. A3 81
*Norfork Dam, Ar., U.S.* A3 81
*Norfork Lake, res., U.S.* A3 81
Norge, Ok., U.S. C4 113
Norias, Tx., U.S. F4 120
Norilsk, Sov. Un. C11 29
Norland, Ont. C6 73
Norland, Fl., U.S. s13 86
Norlina, N.C., U.S. A4 110
Norma, N.J., U.S. E2 107
Norma, N.D., U.S. A4 111
Norma, Tn., U.S. C9 119
Normal, Al., U.S. A3 78
Normal, Il., U.S. C5 90
Norman, Ar., U.S. C2 81
Norman, In., U.S. G5 91
Norman, Ne., U.S. D7 104
Norman, N.C., U.S. B3 110
Norman, Ok., U.S. B4 113
*Norman, co., Mn., U.S.* C2 100
*Norman, Lake, res., N.C., U.S.* B2 110
*Normanby, stm., Austl.* B7 50
Normandy, Mo., U.S. f13 102
Normandy, Tn., U.S. B5 119
*Normandy, hist. reg., Fr.* C3 16
*Normandy, Hills of, hills, Fr.* C3 16
Normandy Beach, N.J., U.S. C4 107
Normangee, Tx., U.S. D4 120
*Norman Island, i., V.I., Br.* B6 65
Norman Park, Ga., U.S. E3 87
Normanton, Austl. C7 50
Normantown, Ga., U.S. D4 87
Norman Wells, N.W. Ter. C7 66
Norphlet, Ar., U.S. D3 81
Norquay, Sask. F4 75
Ñorquincó, Arg. C2 54
Norrahammar, Swe. A8 15
Nørre Åby, Den. C3 15
Nørre Alslev, Den. D5 15
Nørresundby (part of Ålborg), Den. A3 15
Norridge, Il., U.S. k9 90
Norridgewock, Me., U.S. D3 96
Norris, Il., U.S. C3 90
Norris, Mt., U.S. E5 103
Norris, S.C., U.S. B2 117
Norris, S.D., U.S. D4 118
Norris, Tn., U.S. C9 119
Norris Arm, Newf. D4 72
Norris City, Il., U.S. F5 90
*Norris Dam, Tn., U.S.* C9 119
*Norris Lake, res., Tn., U.S.* C10 119
Norris Point, Newf. D3 72
Norristown, Pa., U.S. F11 115
Norrisville, Md., U.S. A4 97
Norrköping, Swe. H7 14
Norrtälje, Swe. H8 14
Norseman, Austl. F3 50
*Norte, Cabo, c., Braz.* B5 59
*Norte, Canal do, strt., Braz.* B4 59
*Norte, Punta, c., Arg.* C4 54
*Norte, Serra do, plat., Braz.* E3 59
*Norte de Santander, dept., Col.* B3 60
Nortelândia, Braz. A1 56
North, S.C., U.S. D5 117
North, Va., U.S. C6 123
*North, stm., Newf.* B3 72
*North, stm., Al., U.S.* B2 78
*North, stm., Ia., U.S.* f8 92
*North, stm., Ma., U.S.* h12 98
*North, stm., W.V., U.S.* B6 125
*North, Cape, c., N.S.* B9 71
North Abington, Ma., U.S. B6 98
North Acton, Ma., U.S. f10 98
North Adams, Ma., U.S. A1 98
North Adams, Mi., U.S. G6 99
North Albany, Or., U.S. k11 114
Northallerton, Eng., U.K. F7 13
Northam, Austl. F2 50
*North America, cont.* E11 61
North Amherst, Ma., U.S. B2 98
North Amity, Me., U.S. C5 96
North Amityville, N.Y., U.S. *n15 109
Northampton, Austl. E1 50
Northampton, Eng., U.K. D6 10
Northampton, Ma., U.S. B2 98
Northampton, Pa., U.S. E11 115
*Northampton, co., N.C., U.S.* A5 110
*Northampton, co., Pa., U.S.* E11 115
*Northampton, co., Va., U.S.* C7 123
*Northamptonshire, co., Eng., U.K.* B7 12
*North Andaman, i., India* F9 36
*North and Bent Pyramids, hist., Egypt* E3 41
North Andover, Ma., U.S. A5 98
North Andrews Gardens, Fl., U.S. r13 86
*North Anna, stm., Va., U.S.* B5 123
North Anson, Me., U.S. D3 96
North Apollo, Pa., U.S. E2 115
*North Arapaho Peak, mtn., Co., U.S.* A5 83
North Arlington, N.J., U.S. h8 107
North Atlanta, Ga., U.S. h8 87
North Attleboro, Ma., U.S. C5 98
North Auburn, Ca., U.S. *C3 82
North Augusta, Ont. C9 73
North Augusta, S.C., U.S. D4 117
*North Aulatsivik Island, i., Newf.* f9 72
North Aurora, Il., U.S. k8 90
North Avondale, Co., U.S. C6 83
North Babylon, N.Y., U.S. *n15 109
North Baltimore, Oh., U.S. A2 112
North Bangor, N.Y., U.S. f10 109
North Battleford, Sask. E1 75
North Bay, Ont. A5 73
North Bay Shore, N.Y., U.S. *n15 109
North Beach, Md., U.S. C4 97
North Belgrade, Me., U.S. D3 96
North Bellmore, N.Y., U.S. *n15 109
North Bellport, N.Y., U.S. *n16 109
North Belmont, N.C., U.S. B1 110
North Bend, B.C. E7 69
North Bend, Ne., U.S. C9 104
North Bend, Oh., U.S. o12 112
North Bend, Or., U.S. D2 114
North Bend, Pa., U.S. D6 115
North Bend, Wa., U.S. B4 124
North Bend, Wi., U.S. D2 126
North Bennington, Vt., U.S. F2 122
North Bergen, N.J., U.S. h8 107
North Berwick, Scot., U.K. D6 13
North Berwick, Me., U.S. E2 96
North Billerica, Ma., U.S. A5 98
North Bloomfield, Oh., U.S. A5 112
North Bonneville, Wa., U.S. D4 124
Northboro, Ia., U.S. D2 92
Northborough, Ma., U.S. B4 98
*North Brabant (Noord-Brabant), prov., Neth.* C4 17
North Braddock, Pa., U.S. *k14 115
North Bradford, Me., U.S. C4 96
North Bradley, Mi., U.S. E6 99
North Branch, Mi., U.S. E7 99
North Branch, Mn., U.S. E6 100
North Branch, N.H., U.S. D3 106
North Branch, N.J., U.S. B3 107
North Branford, Ct., U.S. D4 84
*North Breakers, rf., Mid. Is.* J3 52
Northbridge, Ma., U.S. B4 98
North Bridgton, Me., U.S. D2 96
Northbrook, Ont. C7 73
Northbrook, Il., U.S. h9 90
Northbrook, Oh., U.S. *n12 112
North Brookfield, Ma., U.S. B3 98
*North Brother, mtn., Me., U.S.* C4 96
North Brunswick, N.J., U.S. C4 107
North Buena Vista, Ia., U.S. B7 92
North Calais, Vt., U.S. C4 122
North Caldwell, N.J., U.S. B4 107
*North Canadian, stm., Ok., U.S.* A5 113
North Canton, Ct., U.S. B4 84
North Canton, Ga., U.S. B2 87
North Canton, Oh., U.S. B4 112
North Cape, Wi., U.S. n11 126
*North Cape, c., P.E.I.* B6 71
*North Cape, c., N.Z.* K14 51
*North Cape, c., Nor.* B11 14
North Cape May, N.J., U.S. F3 107
*North Carolina, state, U.S.* B3 110
North Carrollton, Ms., U.S. B4 101
North Carver, Ma., U.S. C6 98
*North Cascades National Park, Wa., U.S.* A4 124
*North Cay, i., Bah.* m17 64
*North Channel, strt., Ont.* A2 73
*North Channel, strt., U.K.* C3 10
North Charleston, S.C., U.S. F8 117
North Charlestown, N.H., U.S. D2 106
North Chatham, N.H., U.S. B4 106
North Chicago, Il., U.S. A6 90
North Chichester, N.H., U.S. D4 106
North City, Wa., U.S. *B3 124
North Clarendon, Vt., U.S. D3 122
Northcliffe, Austl. F2 50
North Cohasset, Ma., U.S. g12 98
North Cohocton, N.Y., U.S. C3 109
North College Hill, Oh., U.S. o12 112
North Collins, N.Y., U.S. C2 109
North Concord, Vt., U.S. C5 122
North Conway, N.H., U.S. B4 106
North Corbin, Ky., U.S. D5 94
Northcote, Austl. *G8 50
North Creek, N.Y., U.S. B7 109
North Crossett, Ar., U.S. D4 81
North Crows Nest, In., U.S. k10 91
*North Dakota, state, U.S.* B5 111
North Danville, Vt., U.S. C4 122
North Dartmouth, Ma., U.S. C6 98
North Decatur, Ga., U.S. *h8 87
North Derby, Vt., U.S. A4 122
North Dighton, Ma., U.S. C5 98
North Dixmont, Me., U.S. D3 96
*North Downs, plat., Eng., U.K.* E7 10
North Druid Hills, Ga., U.S. h8 87
North Eagle Butte, S.D., U.S. B4 118
North East, Md., U.S. A6 97
North East, Pa., U.S. B2 115
*Northeast, stm., Md., U.S.* A6 97
*Northeast Cape, c., Ak., U.S.* C6 79
*Northeast Cape Fear, stm., N.C., U.S.* C5 110
North East Carry, Me., U.S. C3 96
*North Eastern, prov., Kenya* A6 48
North Eastham, Ma., U.S. C8 98
Northeast Harbor, Me., U.S. D4 96
Northeast Henrietta, N.Y., U.S. B3 109
*Northeast Islands, is., Micron.* q18 52
*North East Land, i., Nor.* A13 128
North Easton, Ma., U.S. B5 98
*Northeast Point, c., Newf.* C3 72
*Northeast Polder, reg., Neth.* B5 17
*Northeast Pond, l., N.H., U.S.* D5 106
*Northeast Providence Channel, strt., Bah.* B5 64
*North Edisto, stm., S.C., U.S.* k11 117
North Egremont, Ma., U.S. B1 98
Northeim, W. Ger. C4 18
North English, Ia., U.S. C5 92
*North English, stm., Ia., U.S.* C5 92
North Enid, Ok., U.S. A4 113
*Northern, prov., Ghana* E4 45
*Northern, prov., Mwi.* D5 48
*Northern, prov., Zam.* D5 48
Northern Arm, Newf. D4 72
*Northern Cheyenne Indian Reservation, Mt., U.S.* E10 103
*Northern Donets, stm., Sov. Un.* G13 27
*Northern Dvina, stm., Sov. Un.* C7 29
*Northern Head, c., N.B.* E3 71
*Northern Indian Lake, l., Man.* A3 70
*Northern Ireland, ter., U.K.* C3 10
*Northern Mariana Islands, ter., T.T.P.I.* E8 6
*Northern Range, mts., Trin.* N23 65
*Northern Sporades, is., Grc.* C5 25
*Northern Territory, ter., Austl.* C5 50
*North Esk, stm., Scot., U.K.* D6 13
North Fairfield, Oh., U.S. A3 112
North Fair Oaks, Ca., U.S. *k8 82
North Falmouth, Ma., U.S. C6 98
North Ferrisburg, Vt., U.S. C2 122
Northfield, B.C. f12 69
Northfield, Ct., U.S. C3 84
Northfield, Il., U.S. *h9 90
Northfield, Me., U.S. D5 96
Northfield, Ma., U.S. A3 98
Northfield, Mn., U.S. F5 100
Northfield, N.H., U.S. D3 106
Northfield, N.J., U.S. E3 107
Northfield, Oh., U.S. h9 112
Northfield, Tx., U.S. B2 120
Northfield, Vt., U.S. C3 122
Northfield, Wi., U.S. D2 126
Northfield Center, Vt., U.S. C3 122
Northfield Falls, Vt., U.S. C3 122
*Northfield Mountains, mts., Vt., U.S.* C3 122
North Fond du Lac, Wi., U.S. E5 126
Northford, Ct., U.S. D4 84
*North Foreland, c., Eng., U.K.* E7 10
North Fork, Ca., U.S. D4 82
North Fork, Id., U.S. D5 89
*North Fork Reservoir, res., Or., U.S.* B4 114
North Fort Myers, Fl., U.S. F5 86
*North Fox Island, i., Mi., U.S.* C5 99
North Franklin, Ct., U.S. C7 84
North Freedom, Wi., U.S. E4 126
*North Frisian Islands, is., Eur.* A4 18
North Fryeburg, Me., U.S. D2 96
North Galiano, B.C. f12 69
Northgate, Sask. H4 75
Northgate, N.D., U.S. A3 111
Northglenn, Co., U.S. B6 83
North Gorham, Me., U.S. g7 96
North Gower, Ont. B9 73
North Grafton, Ma., U.S. B4 98
North Granby, Ct., U.S. B4 84
North Great River, N.Y., U.S. *n18 109
North Grosvenordale, Ct., U.S. B8 84
*North Gulf of Évvoia, b., Grc.* C4 25
North Gulfport, Ms., U.S. E4 101
*North Halawa Stream, stm., Hi., U.S.* g10 88
North Haledon, N.J., U.S. B4 107
North Hampton, N.H., U.S. E5 106
North Hanover, Ma., U.S. h12 98
North Harpswell, Me., U.S. g8 96
North Hartland, Vt., U.S. D4 122
*North Hartland Reservoir, res., Vt., U.S.* D4 122
North Hatfield, Ma., U.S. B2 98
North Hatley, Que. D6 74
North Haven, Ct., U.S. D4 84
North Haven, Me., U.S. D4 96
North Haverhill, N.H., U.S. B2 106
North Head, N.B. E3 71
North Henderson, Il., U.S. B3 90
North Hero, Vt., U.S. B2 122
*North Hero Island, i., Vt., U.S.* B2 122
North Highlands, Ca., U.S. *C3 82
North Hill, Wa., U.S. *B3 124
*North Holland (Noord-Holland), prov., Neth.* B4 17
North Holston, Va., U.S. f10 123
*North Horn Lake, l., Tn., U.S.* e8 119
North Horr, Kenya A6 48
North Houston, Tx., U.S. *E5 120
North Hudson, N.Y., U.S. B7 109
North Hudson, Wi., U.S. *C1 126
North Hyde Park, Vt., U.S. B3 122
North Industry, Oh., U.S. B4 112
*North Inlet, b., S.C., U.S.* E9 117
*North Island, i., N.Z.* M15 51
*North Island, i., S.C., U.S.* E9 117
*North Island Naval Air Station, mil., Ca., U.S.* o15 82
*North Islands, is., La., U.S.* E7 95
North Java, N.Y., U.S. C2 109
North Jay, Me., U.S. D2 96
North Judson, In., U.S. B4 91
North Kansas City, Mo., U.S. h10 102
North Kingstown, R.I., U.S. E4 116
North Kingsville, Oh., U.S. A5 112
North Komelik, Az., U.S. E4 80
North La Junta, Co., U.S. C7 83
Northlake, Il., U.S. k9 90
North Lake, Mi., U.S. B3 99
North Lake, Wi., U.S. m11 126
Northland, Mi., U.S. B3 99
*North Laramie, stm., Wy., U.S.* D7 127
North Las Vegas, Nv., U.S. G6 105
North Lauderdale, Fl., U.S. *r13 86
*North La Veta Pass, Co., U.S.* D5 83
North Lawrence, N.Y., U.S. f10 109
North Lemmon, N.D., U.S. D3 111
North Lewisburg, Oh., U.S. B2 112
North Liberty, In., U.S. A5 91
North Liberty, Ia., U.S. C6 92
North Lima, Oh., U.S. B5 112
North Lindenhurst, N.Y., U.S. *n15 109
North Little Rock, Ar., U.S. C3 81
North Logan, Ut., U.S. B4 121
North Long Beach, Ms., U.S. *E4 101
*North Loon Mountain, mtn., Id., U.S.* D3 89
North Loup, Ne., U.S. C7 104
*North Loup, stm., Ne., U.S.* B5 104
North Lubec, Me., U.S. D5 96
North Madison, Oh., U.S. *A4 112
*North Magnetic Pole, N.W. Ter.* m31 66
*North Mamm Peak, mtn., Co., U.S.* B3 83
North Manchester, In., U.S. C6 91
*North Manitou Island, i., Mi., U.S.* C4 99
North Mankato, Mn., U.S. F4 100
North Marshfield, Ma., U.S. h12 98
North Massapequa, N.Y., U.S. *E7 109
North Merrick, N.Y., U.S. *n15 109
North Merrydale, La., U.S. D4 95
North Miami, Fl., U.S. G6 86
North Miami, Ok., U.S. A7 113
North Miami Beach, Fl., U.S. s13 86
North Middleboro, Ma., U.S. C6 98
North Middletown, Ky., U.S. B5 94
North Monmouth, Me., U.S. D2 96
North Montpelier, Vt., U.S. C4 122
Northmoor, Mo., U.S. h10 102
*North Moose Lake, l., Man.* B1 70
*North Mountain, mtn., Pa., U.S.* D9 115
North Muskegon, Mi., U.S. E4 99
North Myrtle Beach, S.C., U.S. D10 117
North Naples, Fl., U.S. F5 86
*North Negril Point, c., Jam.* E12 65
North Newcastle, Me., U.S. D3 96
North New Hyde Park, N.Y., U.S. *E7 109
North Newport, N.H., U.S. D2 106
North New Portland, Me., U.S. D2 96
*North New River Canal, Fl., U.S.* F6 86
North Norwich, N.Y., U.S. C5 109
North Ogden, Ut., U.S. B4 121
North Olmsted, Oh., U.S. h9 112
North Omaha, Ne., U.S. g13 104
Northome, Mn., U.S. C4 100
North Orange, Ma., U.S. A3 98
North Oxford, Ma., U.S. B4 98
*North Palisade, mtn., Ca., U.S.* D4 82
North Palm Beach, Fl., U.S. *F6 86
North Park, Il., U.S. A4 90
*North Park, val., Co., U.S.* A4 83
North Parsonfield, Me., U.S. E2 96
*North Pass, strt., La., U.S.* E7 95
North Patchogue, N.Y., U.S. *n15 109
North Pembroke, Ma., U.S. B6 98
North Pitcher, N.Y., U.S. C5 109
North Plainfield, N.J., U.S. B4 107
North Plains, Or., U.S. B4 114
*North Plains, pl., N.M., U.S.* C1 108
North Platte, Ne., U.S. C5 104
*North Platte, stm., U.S.* B7 76
*North Point, c., Barb.* K20 65
*North Point, c., Md., U.S.* B5 97
*North Point, c., Md., U.S.* C5 97
*North Point, c., Mi., U.S.* C7 99
*North Pole* A1 128
North Pomfret, Vt., U.S. D4 122
*North Pond, l., Me., U.S.* D3 96
*North Pond, l., Ma., U.S.* h9 98
Northport, Al., U.S. B2 78
North Port, Fl., U.S. *D4 86
Northport, Mi., U.S. C5 99
Northport, Ne., U.S. C2 104
Northport, N.Y., U.S. *n15 109
Northport, Wa., U.S. A8 124
North Portal, Sask. H4 75
North Powder, Or., U.S. B9 114
North Pownal, Me., U.S. g7 96
North Pownal, Vt., U.S. F2 122
North Prairie, Wi., U.S. F5 126
North Providence, R.I., U.S. C4 116
*North Raccoon, stm., Ia., U.S.* C3 92
North Range Corner, N.S. E4 71
North Reading, Ma., U.S. f11 98
North Richland Hills, Tx., U.S. n9 120
Northridge, Oh., U.S. C2 112
Northridge, Oh., U.S. *C1 112
North Ridgeville, Oh., U.S. A3 112
*North Rim, Az., U.S.* A3 80
North River Bridge, N.S. C9 71
North Riverside, Il., U.S. *k9 90
North Robinson, Oh., U.S. B3 112
*North Ronaldsay, i., Scot., U.K.* A5 10
Northrop, Mn., U.S. G4 100
North Rose, N.Y., U.S. B4 109
North Royalton, Oh., U.S. h9 112
North Rustico, P.E.I. C6 71
North Salem, In., U.S. E4 91
North Salem, N.H., U.S. E4 106
North Salt Lake, Ut., U.S. C4 121
North Sanbornton, N.H., U.S. C3 106
North Sandwich, N.H., U.S. C4 106
*North Santee, stm., S.C., U.S.* E9 117
*North Saskatchewan, stm., Can.* F10 66
*North Schell Peak, mtn., Nv., U.S.* D7 105
North Scituate, Ma., U.S. h12 98
North Scituate, R.I., U.S. C3 116
*North Sea, Eur.* D9 8
*Norths Highland, plat., Ant.* C25 7
North Shores, De., U.S. F5 85
*North Shoshone Peak, mtn., Nv., U.S.* D4 105
North Shrewsbury, Vt., U.S. D3 122
Northside, N.C., U.S. A4 110
North Sioux City, S.D., U.S. E9 118
*North Skunk, stm., Ia., U.S.* C5 92
*North Sound, strt., Ire.* D2 11
*North Sound, strt., Scot., U.K.* A6 13
*North Spicer Island, i., N.W. Ter.* C17 66
North Springfield, Or., U.S. *C3 114
North Springfield, Pa., U.S. B1 115
North Springfield, Vt., U.S. E3 122
North Springfield, Va., U.S. *B5 123
*North Springfield Reservoir, res., Vt., U.S.* E4 122
North Star, De., U.S. A3 85
North Star, Mi., U.S. E6 99
North Star, Oh., U.S. B1 112
North Stonington, Ct., U.S. D8 84
North St. Paul, Mn., U.S. m13 100
*North Stradbroke, i., Austl.* E9 50
North Stratford, N.H., U.S. A3 106
North Sudbury, Ma., U.S. g10 98
North Sutton, N.H., U.S. D3 106
North Swansea, Ma., U.S. C5 98
North Swanzey, N.H., U.S. E2 106
North Sydney, Austl. *F9 50
North Sydney, N.S. C9 71
North Syracuse, N.Y., U.S. B4 109
*North Taranaki Bight, N.Z.* M15 51
North Tarrytown, N.Y., U.S. D7 109
*North Tea Lake, l., Ont.* B5 73
North Terre Haute, In., U.S. E3 91
North Tewksbury, Ma., U.S. A5 98
North Thetford, Vt., U.S. D4 122
*North Thompson, stm., B.C.* D8 69
North Tolsta, Scot., U.K. B2 13
North Tonawanda, N.Y., U.S. B2 109
North Trenholm, S.C., U.S. *C6 117
North Troy, Vt., U.S. B4 122
North Truro, Ma., U.S. *B7 98
North Tunbridge, Vt., U.S. D4 122
North Tunica, Ms., U.S. A3 101
*North Turner Mountain, mtn., Me., U.S.* C4 96
*North Twin Lake, l., Newf.* D4 72
*North Twin Lake, l., Wi., U.S.* B4 126
*North Tyne, stm., Eng., U.K.* E6 13
*North Uist, i., Scot., U.K.* B3 10
Northumberland, N.H., U.S. A3 106
Northumberland, Pa., U.S. E8 115
*Northumberland, co., N.B.* B3 71
*Northumberland, co., Ont.* C6 73
*Northumberland, co., Eng., U.K.* E6 13

| Name | Map Ref. | Page |
|---|---|---|
| Northumberland, co., Pa., U.S. | D8 | 115 |
| Northumberland, co., Va., U.S. | C6 | 123 |
| Northumberland Isles, is., Austl. | D9 | 50 |
| Northumberland Strait, strt., Can. | C6 | 71 |
| North Umpqua, stm., Or., U.S. | D3 | 114 |
| North Uxbridge, Ma., U.S. | B4 | 98 |
| Northvale, N.J., U.S. | g9 | 107 |
| North Valley Stream, N.Y., U.S. | *n15 | 109 |
| North Vancouver, B.C. | *E6 | 69 |
| North Vassalboro, Me., U.S. | D3 | 96 |
| North Vernon, In., U.S. | F6 | 91 |
| North Versailles, Pa., U.S. | *k14 | 115 |
| Northview, Mi., U.S. | *E5 | 99 |
| Northview, Mo., U.S. | D4 | 102 |
| Northview, Oh., U.S. | *C1 | 112 |
| North Village, N.H., U.S. | E3 | 106 |
| Northville, Ct., U.S. | C2 | 84 |
| Northville, Mi., U.S. | p15 | 99 |
| Northville, N.Y., U.S. | B6 | 109 |
| Northville, S.D., U.S. | B7 | 118 |
| North Wabasca Lake, l., Alta. | A4 | 68 |
| North Waldoboro, Me., U.S. | D3 | 96 |
| North Wales, Pa., U.S. | F11 | 115 |
| North Walpole, N.H., U.S. | D2 | 106 |
| North Walsham, Eng., U.K. | D7 | 10 |
| North Wantagh, N.Y., U.S. | *n15 | 109 |
| North Warren, Pa., U.S. | C3 | 115 |
| North Waterford, Me., U.S. | D2 | 96 |
| Northway, Ak., U.S. | C11 | 79 |
| North Webster, In., U.S. | B6 | 91 |
| North West, dept., Guy. | A3 | 59 |
| North West Cape, c., Austl. | D1 | 50 |
| North Westchester, Ct., U.S. | C6 | 84 |
| North-Western, prov., Zam. | D4 | 48 |
| North West Highlands, plat., Scot., U.K. | B4 | 10 |
| North Westminster, Vt., U.S. | E4 | 122 |
| Northwest Miramichi, stm., N.B. | B3 | 71 |
| Northwest Polder, reg., Neth. | B5 | 17 |
| Northwest Providence Channel, strt., Bah. | A4 | 64 |
| North West River, Newf. | B1 | 72 |
| Northwest Territories, prov., Can. | C13 | 66 |
| Northwest Upsalquitch, stm., N.B. | B2 | 71 |
| Northwich, Eng., U.K. | A5 | 12 |
| North Wildwood, N.J., U.S. | E3 | 107 |
| North Wilkesboro, N.C., U.S. | A1 | 110 |
| North Wilmington, Ma., U.S. | f11 | 98 |
| North Windham, Ct., U.S. | C7 | 84 |
| North Windham, Me., U.S. | E2 | 96 |
| Northwood, Ia., U.S. | A4 | 92 |
| Northwood, N.H., U.S. | D4 | 106 |
| Northwood, N.D., U.S. | B8 | 111 |
| Northwood, Oh., U.S. | *c7 | 112 |
| Northwood Center, N.H., U.S. | D4 | 106 |
| Northwood Ridge, N.H., U.S. | D4 | 106 |
| Northwoods, Mo., U.S. | *t13 | 102 |
| North Woodstock, N.H., U.S. | B3 | 106 |
| North Yarmouth, Me., U.S. | g7 | 96 |
| North York, Ont. | D5 | 73 |
| North York, Pa., U.S. | G8 | 115 |
| North York Moors, hills, Eng., U.K. | C6 | 10 |
| North Yorkshire, co., Eng., U.K. | F7 | 13 |
| North Zulch, Tx., U.S. | D4 | 120 |
| Norton, N.B. | D4 | 71 |
| Norton, Eng., U.K. | F8 | 13 |
| Norton, Ks., U.S. | C4 | 93 |
| Norton, Ma., U.S. | C5 | 98 |
| Norton, Oh., U.S. | A4 | 112 |
| Norton, Tx., U.S. | D2 | 120 |
| Norton, Va., U.S. | f9 | 123 |
| Norton, W.V., U.S. | C5 | 125 |
| Norton, co., Ks., U.S. | C4 | 93 |
| Norton Air Force Base, mil., Ca., U.S. | E5 | 82 |
| Norton Bay, b., Ak., U.S. | C7 | 79 |
| Norton Creek, stm., Al., U.S. | B1 | 78 |
| Norton Pond, l., Vt., U.S. | B5 | 122 |
| Norton Reservoir, res., Ks., U.S. | C3 | 93 |
| Nortons Corner, Az., U.S. | D4 | 80 |
| Norton Shores, Mi., U.S. | E4 | 99 |
| Norton Sound, strt., Ak., U.S. | C6 | 79 |
| Nortonville, Ks., U.S. | C8 | 93 |
| Nortonville, Ky., U.S. | C2 | 94 |
| Nortonville, N.D., U.S. | C7 | 111 |
| Nortorf, W. Ger. | D3 | 15 |
| Norvegia, Cape, c., Ant. | B11 | 7 |
| Norwalk, Ca., U.S. | n12 | 82 |
| Norwalk, Ct., U.S. | E2 | 84 |
| Norwalk, Ia., U.S. | C4 | 92 |
| Norwalk, Oh., U.S. | A3 | 112 |
| Norwalk, Wi., U.S. | E3 | 126 |
| Norwalk, stm., Ct., U.S. | E2 | 84 |
| Norwalk Islands, is., Ct., U.S. | E2 | 84 |
| Norway, In., U.S. | C4 | 91 |
| Norway, Ia., U.S. | C6 | 92 |
| Norway, Ks., U.S. | C6 | 93 |
| Norway, Me., U.S. | D2 | 96 |
| Norway, Mi., U.S. | C3 | 99 |
| Norway, Or., U.S. | D2 | 114 |
| Norway, S.C., U.S. | E5 | 117 |
| Norway, ctry., Eur. | F4 | 14 |
| Norway House, Man. | C3 | 70 |
| Norway Lake, l., Mn., U.S. | E3 | 100 |
| Norwegian Bay, b., N.W. Ter. | m33 | 66 |
| Norwegian Sea, Eur. | C14 | 128 |
| Norwell, Ma., U.S. | h12 | 98 |
| Norwich, Ct., U.S. | C7 | 84 |
| Norwich, Eng., U.K. | D7 | 10 |
| Norwich, Ks., U.S. | E6 | 93 |
| Norwich, N.Y., U.S. | C5 | 109 |
| Norwich, N.D., U.S. | A5 | 111 |
| Norwood, Ont. | C7 | 73 |
| Norwood, Co., U.S. | C2 | 83 |
| Norwood, Ga., U.S. | C4 | 87 |
| Norwood, La., U.S. | D4 | 95 |
| Norwood, Ma., U.S. | B5 | 98 |
| Norwood, Mn., U.S. | F5 | 100 |
| Norwood, Mo., U.S. | D5 | 102 |
| Norwood, N.J., U.S. | h9 | 107 |
| Norwood, N.Y., U.S. | f10 | 109 |
| Norwood, N.C., U.S. | B2 | 110 |
| Norwood, Oh., U.S. | o13 | 112 |
| Norwood, Pa., U.S. | p20 | 115 |
| Norwoodville, Ia., U.S. | e8 | 92 |
| Norwottock, Mount, mtn., Ma., U.S. | B3 | 98 |
| Nosbonsing, Lake, l., Ont. | A5 | 73 |
| Noshiro, Japan | F9 | 33 |
| Nösjön, l., Swe. | A6 | 15 |
| Nossa Senhora das Dores, Braz. | D3 | 57 |
| Nossen, E. Ger. | B8 | 19 |
| Noss Head, c., Scot., U.K. | B5 | 11 |
| Nossob, stm., Afr. | C3 | 49 |
| Nosy Varika, Madag. | h9 | 49 |
| Notasulga, Al., U.S. | C4 | 78 |
| Notch Hill, B.C. | D8 | 69 |
| Notch Mountain, mtn., Ma., U.S. | A3 | 98 |
| Notch Peak, mtn., Ut., U.S. | D2 | 121 |
| Noteć, stm., Pol. | B3 | 26 |
| Notikewin, Alta. | A2 | 68 |
| Notikewin, stm., Alta. | A1 | 68 |
| Noto, Italy | F5 | 23 |
| Noto, Gulf of, b., Italy | F5 | 23 |
| Noto Island, i., Japan | F9 | 33 |
| Noto Peninsula, pen., Japan | D12 | 31 |
| Notoue, Kir. | R18 | 52 |
| Notre-Dame, N.B. | C5 | 71 |
| Notre Dame, Monts, mts., Que. | k13 | 74 |
| Notre Dame Bay, b., Newf. | D4 | 72 |
| Notre Dame de Lourdes, Man. | E2 | 70 |
| Notre-Dame-de-Montauban, Que. | C5 | 74 |
| Notre-Dame-des-Bois, Que. | D6 | 74 |
| Notre-Dame-du-Lac, Que. | B9 | 74 |
| Notre-Dame-du-Laus, Que. | C2 | 74 |
| Nottawa, Ont. | C4 | 73 |
| Nottawasaga Bay, b., Ont. | C4 | 73 |
| Nottaway, stm., Que. | h11 | 74 |
| Nottely Lake, res., Ga., U.S. | B2 | 87 |
| Nottingham, Eng., U.K. | D6 | 10 |
| Nottingham, N.H., U.S. | D4 | 106 |
| Nottingham Island, i., N.W. Ter. | D17 | 66 |
| Nottinghamshire, co., Eng., U.K. | A7 | 12 |
| Nottoway, Va., U.S. | C4 | 123 |
| Nottoway, co., Va., U.S. | C4 | 123 |
| Nottoway, stm., Va., U.S. | D5 | 123 |
| Nottoway, stm., Va., U.S. | C4 | 123 |
| Notukeu Creek, stm., Sask. | H2 | 75 |
| Notus, Id., U.S. | F2 | 89 |
| Nouadhibou, Maur. | B1 | 45 |
| Nouakchott, Maur. | C1 | 45 |
| Nouamrhar, Maur. | C1 | 45 |
| Nouméa, N. Cal. | H10 | 6 |
| Nouna, Burkina | D4 | 45 |
| Noupoort, S. Afr. | D3 | 49 |
| Noutonice, Czech. | n17 | 26 |
| Nouvelle-France, Cap de c., Que. | D18 | 66 |
| Nouzonville, Fr. | C6 | 16 |
| Nova, Oh., U.S. | A3 | 112 |
| Nova Caipemba, Ang. | C1 | 48 |
| Nova Cruz, Braz. | C3 | 57 |
| Nova Friburgo, Braz. | C4 | 56 |
| Nova Iguaçu, Braz. | h6 | 56 |
| Nova Lima, Braz. | C4 | 56 |
| Nova Londrina, Braz. | C2 | 56 |
| Nova Lusitânia, Moz. | A5 | 49 |
| Nova Mambone, Moz. | B6 | 49 |
| Nova Olinda do Norte, Braz. | C3 | 59 |
| Nova Ponte, Braz. | B3 | 56 |
| Nova Prata, Braz. | D2 | 56 |
| Novar, Ont. | B5 | 73 |
| Novara, Italy | B2 | 23 |
| Nova Roma, Braz. | A3 | 56 |
| Nova Russas, Braz. | B2 | 57 |
| Nova Scotia, prov., Can. | D6 | 71 |
| Nova Sofala, Moz. | B5 | 49 |
| Nova Soure, Braz. | D3 | 57 |
| Novate Mezzola, Italy | D7 | 21 |
| Novato, Ca., U.S. | C2 | 82 |
| Nova Varoš, Yugo. | D4 | 24 |
| Nova Venécia, Braz. | B4 | 56 |
| Nova Vida, Braz. | B3 | 55 |
| Nova Zagora, Bul. | D8 | 24 |
| Novelda, Spain | C5 | 22 |
| Novelty, Mo., U.S. | A5 | 102 |
| Nové Město [nad Váhom], Czech. | D4 | 26 |
| Nové Strašecí, Czech. | C8 | 19 |
| Nové Zámky, Czech. | E5 | 26 |
| Novgorod, Sov. Un. | D6 | 29 |
| Novgorod-Severskiy, Sov. Un. | E9 | 27 |
| Novi, Mi., U.S. | p15 | 99 |
| Novice, Tx., U.S. | D3 | 120 |
| Novigrad, Yugo. | C2 | 24 |
| Novi Ligure, Italy | B2 | 23 |
| Novinger, Mo., U.S. | A5 | 102 |
| Novi Pazar, Bul. | D8 | 24 |
| Novi Pazar, Yugo. | D5 | 24 |
| Novi Sad, Yugo. | C4 | 24 |
| Novoaltaysk, Sov. Un. | E25 | 8 |
| Novoanninskiy, Sov. Un. | A8 | 19 |
| Novo Aripuanã, Braz. | D2 | 59 |
| Novoaydar, Sov. Un. | G12 | 27 |
| Novocherkassk, Sov. Un. | H13 | 27 |
| Nôvo Cruzeiro, Braz. | B4 | 56 |
| Novoekonomicheskoye, Sov. Un. | q20 | 27 |
| Novograd-Volynskiy, Sov. Un. | F6 | 27 |
| Novogrudok, Sov. Un. | E5 | 27 |
| Novokazalinsk, Sov. Un. | E9 | 29 |
| Novokurovka, Sov. Un. | B7 | 33 |
| Novokuybyshevsk, Sov. Un. | *D7 | 29 |
| Novokuznetsk, Sov. Un. | D11 | 29 |
| Novo Mesto, Yugo. | C2 | 24 |
| Novomirgorod, Sov. Un. | G8 | 27 |
| Novomoskovsk, Sov. Un. | G10 | 27 |
| Novomoskovsk, Sov. Un. | D6 | 29 |
| Novopokrovskaya, Sov. Un. | I13 | 27 |
| Novorossiysk, Sov. Un. | E6 | 29 |
| Novo-Selo, Bul. | B5 | 24 |
| Novoshakhtinsk, Sov. Un. | H12 | 27 |
| Novosibirsk, Sov. Un. | D11 | 29 |
| Novosibirsk Reservoir, res., Sov. Un. | C10 | 28 |
| Novosil, Sov. Un. | E11 | 27 |
| Novotroitsk, Sov. Un. | C5 | 28 |
| Novoukrainka, Sov. Un. | G8 | 27 |
| Novovoronezh, Sov. Un. | C3 | 28 |
| Novozybkov, Sov. Un. | H9 | 27 |
| Nový Bohumin, Czech. | D5 | 26 |
| Nový Bydžov, Czech. | C3 | 26 |
| Nový Jičín, Czech. | D5 | 26 |
| Novyye Senzhary, Sov. Un. | G10 | 27 |
| Novyy Oskol, Sov. Un. | F11 | 27 |
| Novyy Port, Sov. Un. | C10 | 29 |
| Novyy Urengoy, Sov. Un. | C10 | 29 |
| Novyy Uzen, Sov. Un. | G19 | 18 |
| Novyy Vasyugan, Sov. Un. | B9 | 28 |
| Nowagród, Pol. | B10 | 19 |
| Nowa Ruda, Pol. | C4 | 26 |
| Nowa Sól, Pol. | C3 | 26 |
| Nowata, Ok., U.S. | A6 | 113 |
| Nowata, co., Ok., U.S. | A6 | 113 |
| Nowe Warpno, Pol. | B3 | 26 |
| Nowogard, Pol. | B3 | 26 |
| Nowood, stm., Wy., U.S. | B5 | 127 |
| Nowra-Bomaderry, Austl. | G8 | 51 |
| Nowshāk, mtn., Asia | k17 | 39 |
| Nowy Dwór [Mazowiecki], Pol. | k13 | 26 |
| Nowy Sącz, Pol. | D6 | 26 |
| Nowy Targ, Pol. | D6 | 26 |
| Nowy Tomyśl, Pol. | B4 | 26 |
| Noxapater, Ms., U.S. | C4 | 101 |
| Noxen, Pa., U.S. | D9 | 115 |
| Noxon, Mt., U.S. | C1 | 103 |
| Noxon Reservoir, res., Mt., U.S. | C1 | 103 |
| Noxontown Lake, res., De., U.S. | C3 | 85 |
| Noxubee, co., Ms., U.S. | B5 | 101 |
| Noxubee, stm., U.S. | B5 | 101 |
| Noya, Spain | A1 | 22 |
| Noyes, Mn., U.S. | B1 | 100 |
| Noyes Island, i., Ak., U.S. | n22 | 79 |
| Noyon, Fr. | C5 | 16 |
| Nozeroy, Fr. | C1 | 21 |
| Nsanje, Mwi. | E6 | 48 |
| Nsawam, Ghana | E4 | 45 |
| Nsukka, Nig. | E6 | 45 |
| Ntem, stm., Afr. | E2 | 46 |
| Nuatabu, Kir. | R18 | 52 |
| Nubanusit Lake, l., N.H., U.S. | E2 | 106 |
| Nūbāriyah, Tur'at an, Eg. | D2 | 41 |
| Nubian Desert, des., Sud. | A3 | 47 |
| Nuckolls, co., Ne., U.S. | D7 | 104 |
| Nucla, Co., U.S. | C2 | 83 |
| Nueces, co., Tx., U.S. | F4 | 120 |
| Nueces, stm., Tx., U.S. | E3 | 120 |
| Nueltin Lake, l., Can. | D13 | 66 |
| Nueva Antioquia, Col. | B4 | 58 |
| Nueva Asunción, dept., Para. | D3 | 55 |
| Nueva Casas Grandes, Mex. | B5 | 63 |
| Nueva Esparta, state, Ven. | A5 | 60 |
| Nueva Gerona, Cuba | D2 | 64 |
| Nueva Imperial, Chile | B2 | 54 |
| Nueva Lubecka, Arg. | C2 | 54 |
| Nueva Ocotepeque, Hond. | C3 | 62 |
| Nueva Palmira, Ur. | E1 | 56 |
| Nueva Providencia, Pan. | k11 | 62 |
| Nueva Rosita, Mex. | B4 | 63 |
| Nueva San Salvador, El Sal. | D3 | 62 |
| Nueve de Julio, Arg. | B3 | 119 |
| Nuevitas, Cuba | D5 | 64 |
| Nuevo, Golfo, b., Arg. | C4 | 54 |
| Nuevo Emperador, Pan. | m11 | 62 |
| Nuevo Laredo, Mex. | B5 | 63 |
| Nuevo León, state, Mex. | B5 | 63 |
| Nuevo San Juan, Pan. | k11 | 62 |
| Nugaal, prov., Som. | D6 | 47 |
| Nūh, Rās, c., Pak. | I11 | 39 |
| Nuits, Fr. | D6 | 16 |
| Nukhayb, Iraq | G14 | 40 |
| Nukhaylah, well, Sud. | B2 | 47 |
| Nuku'alofa, Tonga | H11 | 6 |
| Nukus, Sov. Un. | E5 | 28 |
| Nulato, Ak., U.S. | C8 | 79 |
| Nules, Spain | C5 | 22 |
| Nulhegan, stm., Vt., U.S. | B5 | 122 |
| Nullagine, Austl. | D3 | 50 |
| Nullarbor Plain, pl., Austl. | F4 | 50 |
| Numa, Ia., U.S. | D5 | 92 |
| Numan, Nig. | E7 | 45 |
| Numazu, Japan | I9 | 33 |
| Numfoor, i., Indon. | F8 | 34 |
| Numila, Hi., U.S. | B2 | 88 |
| Nu Mine, Pa., U.S. | E3 | 115 |
| Nunawading, Austl. | *G8 | 50 |
| Nunda, N.Y., U.S. | C3 | 109 |
| Nunda, S.D., U.S. | C8 | 118 |
| Nuneaton, Eng., U.K. | B6 | 12 |
| Nunez, Ga., U.S. | D4 | 87 |
| Nunica, Mi., U.S. | E4 | 99 |
| Nunivak Island, i., Ak., U.S. | D6 | 79 |
| Nunn, Co., U.S. | A6 | 83 |
| Nunnelly, Tn., U.S. | B4 | 119 |
| Nuoro, Italy | D2 | 23 |
| Nuquí, Col. | B2 | 60 |
| Nura, stm., Sov. Un. | E23 | 8 |
| Nuremberg, Pa., U.S. | E9 | 115 |
| Nuremberg see Nürnberg, W. Ger. | D5 | 18 |
| Nuri, Mex. | B3 | 63 |
| Nurmes, Fin. | F13 | 14 |
| Nürnberg (Nuremberg), W. Ger. | D5 | 18 |
| Nursery, Tx., U.S. | E4 | 120 |
| Nürtingen, W. Ger. | E4 | 19 |
| Nus, Italy | E3 | 21 |
| Nusaybin, Tur. | D13 | 40 |
| Nushki, Pak. | C4 | 36 |
| Nusle (part of Prague), Czech. | n17 | 26 |
| Nuthe, stm., E. Ger. | A8 | 19 |
| Nut Lake, l., Sask. | E4 | 75 |
| Nutley, N.J., U.S. | B4 | 107 |
| Nut Mountain, Sask. | E4 | 75 |
| Nutrioso, Az., U.S. | D6 | 80 |
| Nutter Fort, W.V., U.S. | k10 | 125 |
| Nutting Lake, Ma., U.S. | f10 | 98 |
| Nutwood, Il., U.S. | D3 | 90 |
| Nuuanu Pali, Hi., U.S. | g10 | 88 |
| Nuutoi, Cape, c., W. Sam. | G12 | 52 |
| Nuwara-Eliya, Sri L. | H10 | 40 |
| Nuwaybi' al Muzayyinah, Eg. | H10 | 40 |
| Nyac, Ak., U.S. | C8 | 79 |
| Nyack, N.Y., U.S. | D7 | 109 |
| Nyala, Sud. | C1 | 47 |
| Nyamandhlovu, Zimb. | A4 | 49 |
| Nyamtumbo, Tan. | C7 | 48 |
| Nyandoma, Sov. Un. | C7 | 29 |
| Nyanza, Rw. | B5 | 48 |
| Nyanza, prov., Kenya | B5 | 48 |
| Nyasa, Lake, l., Afr. | C6 | 48 |
| Nyborg, Den. | C4 | 15 |
| Nybro, Swe. | I11 | 14 |
| Nyda, Sov. Un. | B23 | 8 |
| Nye, Mt., U.S. | E7 | 103 |
| Nye, co., Nv., U.S. | E5 | 105 |
| Nyeri, Kenya | B6 | 48 |
| Nyilumba, Tan. | D7 | 48 |
| Nyíregyháza, Hung. | B5 | 24 |
| Nyírbátor, Hung. | H8 | 24 |
| Nykøbing Falster, Den. | D5 | 15 |
| Nykøbing Sjælland, Den. | k13 | 26 |
| Nyköping, Swe. | H7 | 14 |
| Nylstroom, S. Afr. | B4 | 49 |
| Nymagee, Austl. | F6 | 51 |
| Nymburk, Czech. | C3 | 26 |
| Nymindegab, Den. | C2 | 15 |
| Nynäshamn, Swe. | H8 | 14 |
| Nyngan, Austl. | F8 | 50 |
| Nyon, Switz. | E3 | 18 |
| Nyong, stm., Cam. | E2 | 46 |
| Nýřany, Czech. | D2 | 26 |
| Nýrsko, Czech. | D8 | 19 |
| Nysa, Pol. | C4 | 26 |
| Nyssa, Or., U.S. | D9 | 114 |
| Nysted, Den. | D5 | 15 |
| Nyunzu, Zaire | C4 | 48 |
| Nzega, Tan. | B5 | 48 |
| Nzérékoré, Gui. | E3 | 45 |
| N'zeto, Ang. | C1 | 48 |
| Nzwani, i., Com. | f8 | 49 |

## O

| Name | Map Ref. | Page |
|---|---|---|
| Oacoma, S.D., U.S. | D6 | 118 |
| Oahe, Lake, res., U.S. | A7 | 76 |
| Oahe Dam, S.D., U.S. | C5 | 118 |
| Oahu, i., Hi., U.S. | B4 | 88 |
| Oak, Ne., U.S. | D8 | 104 |
| Oakalla, Tx., U.S. | D4 | 120 |
| Oak Bay, B.C. | h12 | 69 |
| Oak Bay, N.B. | D2 | 71 |
| Oak Bluffs, Ma., U.S. | D6 | 98 |
| Oakboro, N.C., U.S. | B2 | 110 |
| Oak Brook, Il., U.S. | *k9 | 90 |
| Oakburn, Man. | D1 | 70 |
| Oak City, N.C., U.S. | B5 | 110 |
| Oak City, Ut., U.S. | D3 | 121 |
| Oak Creek, Co., U.S. | A4 | 83 |
| Oak Creek, Wi., U.S. | n12 | 126 |
| Oakdale, Ca., U.S. | D3 | 82 |
| Oakdale, Ct., U.S. | D7 | 84 |
| Oakdale, Ga., U.S. | h8 | 87 |
| Oakdale, Il., U.S. | E4 | 90 |
| Oakdale, La., U.S. | D3 | 95 |
| Oakdale, Mn., U.S. | *n13 | 100 |
| Oakdale, Ne., U.S. | B8 | 104 |
| Oakdale, N.Y., U.S. | *n15 | 109 |
| Oakdale, Pa., U.S. | k13 | 115 |
| Oakdale, Tn., U.S. | D9 | 119 |
| Oakdale Manor, Ct., U.S. | *D2 | 84 |
| Oakdale, Oh., U.S. | A3 | 112 |
| Oakengates, Eng., U.K. | B5 | 12 |
| Oakes, N.D., U.S. | C7 | 111 |
| Oakesdale, Wa., U.S. | B8 | 124 |
| Oakey, Austl. | C8 | 51 |
| Oakfield, Ga., U.S. | E3 | 87 |
| Oakfield, Me., U.S. | B4 | 96 |
| Oakfield, N.Y., U.S. | B2 | 109 |
| Oakfield, Wi., U.S. | E5 | 126 |
| Oakford, Il., U.S. | C4 | 90 |
| Oakford, In., U.S. | D5 | 91 |
| Oak Forest, Il., U.S. | k9 | 90 |
| Oak Grove, Ar., U.S. | A2 | 81 |
| Oak Grove, Ky., U.S. | D2 | 94 |
| Oak Grove, La., U.S. | B4 | 95 |
| Oak Grove, Mi., U.S. | F7 | 99 |
| Oak Grove, Or., U.S. | B4 | 114 |
| Oak Grove, S.C., U.S. | C8 | 117 |
| Oak Grove, S.C., U.S. | *D5 | 117 |
| Oakham, Eng., U.K. | B7 | 12 |
| Oakham, Ma., U.S. | B3 | 98 |
| Oak Harbor, Oh., U.S. | A2 | 112 |
| Oak Harbor, Wa., U.S. | A3 | 124 |
| Oak Hill, De., U.S. | *B3 | 85 |
| Oak Hill, Fl., U.S. | D6 | 86 |
| Oakhill, Ks., U.S. | *C6 | 93 |
| Oak Hill, Mi., U.S. | D4 | 99 |
| Oak Hill, Oh., U.S. | D3 | 112 |
| Oak Hill, W.V., U.S. | D3 | 125 |
| Oak Hill, mtn., Ma., U.S. | f9 | 98 |
| Oakhurst, N.J., U.S. | C4 | 107 |
| Oakhurst, Ok., U.S. | A5 | 113 |
| Oak Island, i., Wi., U.S. | B2 | 126 |
| Oak Lake, Man. | E1 | 70 |
| Oak Lake, l., Man. | D4 | 73 |
| Oakland, Ont. | D4 | 73 |
| Oakland, Al., U.S. | A3 | 81 |
| Oakland, Ca., U.S. | D2 | 82 |
| Oakland, Fl., U.S. | D5 | 86 |
| Oakland, Il., U.S. | D5 | 90 |
| Oakland, Ia., U.S. | C2 | 92 |
| Oakland, Ky., U.S. | D3 | 96 |
| Oakland, Md., U.S. | m12 | 97 |
| Oakland, Ne., U.S. | C9 | 104 |
| Oakland, N.J., U.S. | A4 | 107 |
| Oakland, Ok., U.S. | C5 | 113 |
| Oakland, Or., U.S. | D3 | 114 |
| Oakland, R.I., U.S. | B2 | 116 |
| Oakland, Tn., U.S. | B2 | 119 |
| Oakland, co., Mi., U.S. | F7 | 99 |
| Oakland City, In., U.S. | H3 | 91 |
| Oakland Gardens, Ct., U.S. | C4 | 84 |
| Oakland Park, Fl., U.S. | r13 | 86 |
| Oak Lane Manor, De., U.S. | *A3 | 85 |
| Oak Lawn, Il., U.S. | B6 | 90 |
| Oaklawn, Ks., U.S. | g12 | 93 |
| Oakleigh, Austl. | *G8 | 50 |
| Oakley, Id., U.S. | G5 | 89 |
| Oakley, Ks., U.S. | C3 | 93 |
| Oakley, Mi., U.S. | E6 | 99 |
| Oakley, Ms., U.S. | C3 | 101 |
| Oakley, S.C., U.S. | C5 | 117 |
| Oakley, Ut., U.S. | C4 | 121 |
| Oaklyn, N.J., U.S. | *D2 | 107 |
| Oakman, Al., U.S. | B2 | 78 |
| Oakman, Ga., U.S. | B2 | 87 |
| Oakmont, Pa., U.S. | E2 | 115 |
| Oak Mountain, mtn., Ga., U.S. | B1 | 87 |
| Oak Mountain, mtn., N.Y., U.S. | h11 | 119 |
| Oakner, Man. | D1 | 70 |
| Oak Orchard, De., U.S. | F5 | 85 |
| Oak Park, Ca., U.S. | *E5 | 82 |
| Oak Park, Ga., U.S. | D4 | 87 |
| Oak Park, Il., U.S. | B6 | 90 |
| Oak Park, Mi., U.S. | p15 | 99 |
| Oak Point, Man. | D2 | 70 |
| Oak Ridge, Fl., U.S. | *D5 | 86 |
| Oak Ridge, La., U.S. | B4 | 95 |
| Oak Ridge, Mo., U.S. | D8 | 102 |
| Oak Ridge, N.C., U.S. | A3 | 110 |
| Oakridge, Or., U.S. | D4 | 114 |
| Oak Ridge, Tn., U.S. | C9 | 119 |
| Oak Ridge Reservoir, res., N.J., U.S. | A3 | 107 |
| Oak Ridges (part of Richmond Hill), Ont. | k15 | 73 |
| Oak River, Man. | D1 | 70 |
| Oaks, Ok., U.S. | A7 | 113 |
| Oaks, Pa., U.S. | o20 | 115 |
| Oakton, Ky., U.S. | f8 | 94 |
| Oakton, Va., U.S. | g12 | 123 |
| Oaktown, In., U.S. | G3 | 91 |
| Oak Vale, Ms., U.S. | D4 | 101 |
| Oakvale, W.V., U.S. | *D4 | 125 |
| Oak Valley, N.J., U.S. | D2 | 107 |
| Oakville, Man. | E2 | 70 |
| Oakville, Ont. | C5 | 73 |
| Oakville, Ct., U.S. | C3 | 84 |
| Oakville, Ia., U.S. | D7 | 91 |
| Oakville, Mo., U.S. | g13 | 102 |
| Oakville, Wa., U.S. | C2 | 124 |
| Oakway, S.C., U.S. | B1 | 117 |
| Oakwood, Ga., U.S. | B3 | 87 |
| Oakwood, Il., U.S. | C6 | 90 |
| Oakwood, N.D., U.S. | A8 | 111 |
| Oakwood, Oh., U.S. | A1 | 112 |
| Oakwood, Ok., U.S. | B3 | 113 |
| Oakwood, Tx., U.S. | D5 | 120 |
| Oakwood, Va., U.S. | e9 | 123 |
| Oakwood Beach, N.J., U.S. | m9 | 80 |
| Oamaru, N.Z. | P13 | 51 |
| Ōamishirasato, Japan | n19 | 33 |
| Oark, Ar., U.S. | B2 | 81 |
| Oasis, Ut., U.S. | D3 | 121 |
| Oatman, Az., U.S. | C1 | 80 |
| Oats, S.C., U.S. | C7 | 117 |
| Oaxaca, state, Mex. | D5 | 63 |
| Oaxaca [de Juárez], Mex. | D5 | 63 |
| Ob, stm., Sov. Un. | C9 | 29 |
| Oba, Ont. | G16 | 66 |
| Obama, Japan | n14 | 33 |
| Oban, Sask. | E1 | 75 |
| Oban, Scot., U.K. | B4 | 10 |
| O'Bannon, Ky., U.S. | g11 | 94 |
| Ob Bay, b., Sov. Un. | C10 | 29 |
| Obed, Alta. | C2 | 68 |
| Obed, stm., Tn., U.S. | C9 | 119 |
| Ober, In., U.S. | B4 | 91 |
| Oberá, Arg. | B4 | 55 |
| Oberammergau, W. Ger. | B7 | 20 |
| Oberdrauburg, Aus. | C8 | 20 |
| Oberhausen, W. Ger. | C6 | 18 |
| Oberkirch, W. Ger. | E3 | 19 |
| Oberlin, Ks., U.S. | C3 | 93 |
| Oberlin, La., U.S. | D3 | 95 |
| Oberlin, Oh., U.S. | A3 | 112 |
| Obernai, Fr. | C7 | 16 |
| Obernburg [am Main], W. Ger. | E4 | 19 |
| Oberon, N.D., U.S. | B6 | 111 |
| Oberösterreich, state, Aus. | E9 | 19 |
| Oberstaufen, W. Ger. | B6 | 20 |
| Oberstdorf, W. Ger. | B6 | 20 |
| Obert, Ne., U.S. | B8 | 104 |
| Oberursel, W. Ger. | C4 | 19 |
| Oberwald, Switz. | C4 | 21 |
| Obetz, Oh., U.S. | C3 | 112 |
| Óbidos, Braz. | C3 | 59 |
| Obihiro, Japan | C13 | 31 |
| Obi Islands, is., Indon. | F7 | 34 |
| Obion, Tn., U.S. | A2 | 119 |
| Obion, co., Tn., U.S. | A2 | 119 |
| Obion, stm., Tn., U.S. | A2 | 119 |
| Obion, Middle Fork, stm., Tn., U.S. | A3 | 119 |
| Obion, Rutherford Fork, stm., Tn., U.S. | A3 | 119 |
| Obion, South Fork, stm., Tn., U.S. | A3 | 119 |
| Obion Creek, stm., Ky., U.S. | f9 | 94 |
| Oblachnaya, Mount, mtn., Sov. Un. | E7 | 33 |
| Oblong, Il., U.S. | D6 | 90 |
| Obluchye, Sov. Un. | E16 | 29 |
| Obo, Cen. Afr. Rep. | D5 | 46 |
| Obock, Dji. | C5 | 47 |
| Oborniki, Pol. | B4 | 26 |
| Oboyan', Sov. Un. | F11 | 27 |
| O'Brien, Fl., U.S. | B4 | 86 |
| O'Brien, Or., U.S. | E3 | 114 |
| O'Brien, co., Ia., U.S. | A2 | 92 |
| Observation Peak, mtn., Ca., U.S. | B4 | 82 |
| Obuasi, Ghana | E4 | 45 |
| Obwalden, state, Switz. | C4 | 20 |
| Ocala, Fl., U.S. | C4 | 86 |
| Ocampo, Mex. | B3 | 63 |
| Ocaña, Col. | B3 | 60 |
| Ocaña, Spain | C4 | 22 |
| Ocate, N.M., U.S. | A5 | 108 |
| Occidental, Cordillera, mts., Col. | C2 | 60 |
| Occidental, Cordillera, mts., Peru | D3 | 58 |
| Occidental, Cordillera, mts., S.A. | C2 | 55 |
| Occoquan, Va., U.S. | B5 | 123 |
| Ocean, co., N.J., U.S. | D4 | 107 |
| Oceana, W.V., U.S. | D3 | 125 |
| Oceana, co., Mi., U.S. | E4 | 99 |
| Oceana Naval Air Station, mil., Va., U.S. | k15 | 123 |
| Ocean Bluff, Ma., U.S. | B6 | 98 |
| Ocean City, Fl., U.S. | E3 | 97 |
| Ocean City, Md., U.S. | D7 | 97 |
| Ocean City, N.J., U.S. | E3 | 107 |
| Ocean City, Wa., U.S. | B1 | 124 |
| Ocean Falls, B.C. | D4 | 69 |
| Ocean Gate, N.J., U.S. | D4 | 107 |
| Ocean Grove, Ma., U.S. | C5 | 98 |
| Ocean Grove, N.J., U.S. | C4 | 107 |
| Ocean Heights, N.J., U.S. | D6 | 97 |
| Ocean Park, Wa., U.S. | C1 | 124 |
| Ocean Port, N.J., U.S. | C4 | 107 |
| Oceanside, Ca., U.S. | F5 | 82 |
| Oceanside, N.Y., U.S. | *E7 | 109 |
| Ocean Springs, Ms., U.S. | E5 | 101 |
| Ocean [Township], N.J., U.S. | C4 | 107 |
| Ocean View, De., U.S. | F5 | 85 |
| Ocean View, N.J., U.S. | E3 | 107 |
| Oceanville, N.J., U.S. | E4 | 107 |
| Ochakov, Sov. Un. | H8 | 27 |
| Ocheda Lake, l., Mn., U.S. | G3 | 100 |
| Ocheyedan, Ia., U.S. | A2 | 92 |
| Ocheyedan, stm., Ia., U.S. | A2 | 92 |
| Ochil Hills, hills, Scot., U.K. | D5 | 13 |
| Ochiltree, co., Tx., U.S. | A2 | 120 |
| Ochlockonee, Ga., U.S. | F2 | 87 |
| Ochlockonee, stm., Fl., U.S. | C2 | 86 |
| Ochoco, Lake, res., Or., U.S. | C6 | 114 |
| Ochopee, Fl., U.S. | G5 | 86 |
| Ochre River, Man. | D2 | 70 |
| Ochsenfurt, W. Ger. | D5 | 18 |
| Ochtrup, W. Ger. | A3 | 19 |
| Ocilla, Ga., U.S. | E3 | 87 |
| Ockelbo, Swe. | A5 | 14 |
| Ocklawaha, stm., Fl., U.S. | C5 | 86 |
| Ocmulgee, stm., Ga., U.S. | D3 | 87 |
| Ocmulgee National Monument, Ga., U.S. | D3 | 87 |
| Ocna Sibiului, Rom. | C8 | 24 |
| Ocnele Mari, Rom. | C7 | 24 |
| Ocoee, Fl., U.S. | D5 | 86 |
| Ocoee, Tn., U.S. | D9 | 119 |
| Ocoee, Lake, res., Tn., U.S. | D9 | 119 |
| Ocoltán, Mex. | C4 | 63 |
| Ocoña, Peru | E3 | 58 |
| Oconee, Ga., U.S. | D4 | 87 |
| Oconee, Il., U.S. | D4 | 90 |
| Oconee, co., Ga., U.S. | C3 | 87 |
| Oconee, co., S.C., U.S. | B1 | 117 |
| Oconee, stm., Ga., U.S. | C3 | 87 |
| Oconee, Lake, res., Ga., U.S. | C3 | 87 |
| Oconomowoc, Wi., U.S. | E5 | 126 |
| Oconto, Ne., U.S. | C6 | 104 |
| Oconto, Wi., U.S. | D6 | 126 |
| Oconto, co., Wi., U.S. | D5 | 126 |
| Oconto, stm., Wi., U.S. | C5 | 126 |
| Oconto Falls, Wi., U.S. | D5 | 126 |
| Ocós, Guat. | L1 | 62 |
| Ocotal, Nic. | E7 | 63 |
| Ocotillo, Az., U.S. | m9 | 80 |
| Ocros, Peru | D2 | 58 |
| Octavia, Ne., U.S. | C8 | 104 |
| Octavia, Ok., U.S. | C7 | 113 |
| Octeville, Fr. | C3 | 16 |
| October Revolution Island, i., Sov. Un. | B4 | 128 |
| Octoraro Creek, stm., U.S. | A5 | 97 |
| Ocumare del Tuy, Ven. | A4 | 60 |
| Oda, Ghana | E4 | 45 |
| Odanah, Wi., U.S. | B3 | 126 |
| Ōdate, Japan | F10 | 33 |
| Odawara, Japan | n18 | 33 |
| Odd, W.V., U.S. | *D3 | 125 |
| Odda, Nor. | G2 | 14 |
| Odder, Den. | C4 | 15 |
| Odebolt, Ia., U.S. | B2 | 92 |
| Odei, stm., Man. | A3 | 70 |
| Odell, Il., U.S. | B5 | 90 |
| Odell, Ne., U.S. | D9 | 104 |
| Odell, Or., U.S. | B5 | 114 |
| Odell, Tx., U.S. | B3 | 120 |
| Odell Lake, l., Or., U.S. | E5 | 114 |
| Odem, Tx., U.S. | F4 | 120 |
| Odemira, Port. | D1 | 22 |
| Ödemiş, Tur. | C7 | 40 |
| Odensala, Swe. | t35 | 14 |
| Odensbacken (part of Örebro), Swe. | t33 | 14 |
| Odense, Den. | J4 | 14 |
| Odense Å, stm., Den. | C4 | 15 |
| Odenton, Md., U.S. | B4 | 97 |
| Odenville, Al., U.S. | B3 | 78 |
| Odenwald, mts., W. Ger. | D3 | 19 |
| Oder (Odra), stm., Eur. | B3 | 26 |
| Oder Spree Canal, E. Ger. | A9 | 19 |
| Odessa, Ont. | C8 | 73 |
| Odessa, Sask. | G4 | 75 |
| Odessa, Sov. Un. | E6 | 29 |
| Odessa, De., U.S. | C3 | 85 |
| Odessa, Fl., U.S. | *D4 | 86 |
| Odessa, Mn., U.S. | E2 | 100 |
| Odessa, Mo., U.S. | C4 | 102 |
| Odessa, N.Y., U.S. | C4 | 109 |
| Odessa, Tx., U.S. | D1 | 120 |
| Odessa, Wa., U.S. | B7 | 124 |
| Odiel, stm., Spain | D2 | 22 |
| Odienné, I.C. | E4 | 45 |
| Odin, Il., U.S. | E4 | 90 |
| Odin, Mn., U.S. | G4 | 100 |
| Odin, Mount, mtn., B.C. | D8 | 69 |
| Odivelas, Port. | f9 | 22 |
| Odobești, Rom. | C8 | 24 |
| Odon, In., U.S. | G4 | 91 |
| O'Donnell, Tx., U.S. | C2 | 120 |
| Odorheiu Secuiesc, Rom. | B7 | 24 |
| Odra (Oder), stm., Eur. | B3 | 26 |
| Odum, Ga., U.S. | E4 | 87 |
| Odzi, Zimb. | A5 | 49 |
| Oebisfelde, E. Ger. | A5 | 19 |
| Oeiras, Braz. | B3 | 57 |
| Oeiras, Port. | f9 | 22 |
| Oelde, W. Ger. | B4 | 19 |
| Oelrichs, S.D., U.S. | D2 | 118 |
| Oelsnitz [im Erzgebirge], E. Ger. | C6 | 18 |
| Oelsnitz [im Vogtland], E. Ger. | C7 | 19 |
| Oelwein, Ia., U.S. | B6 | 92 |
| Oensingen, Switz. | B4 | 21 |
| Oettingen [in Bayern], W. Ger. | E5 | 19 |
| Ofahoma, Ms., U.S. | C4 | 101 |
| O'Fallon, Il., U.S. | E4 | 90 |
| O'Fallon, Mo., U.S. | f12 | 102 |
| O'Fallon Creek, stm., Mt., U.S. | D12 | 103 |
| Ofanto, stm., Italy | D5 | 23 |
| Ofaqim, Isr. | D4 | 41 |
| Offa, Nig. | *E5 | 45 |
| Offaly, co., Ire. | D4 | 11 |
| Offenbach [am Main], W. Ger. | D3 | 18 |
| Offenburg, W. Ger. | D3 | 18 |
| Offence, Mount of, hist., Isr. Occ. | m14 | 93 |
| Offerle, Ks., U.S. | E4 | 93 |
| Offerman, Ga., U.S. | E4 | 87 |
| Offutt Air Force Base, mil., Ne., U.S. | g3 | 104 |
| Oficina Pedro de Valdivia, Chile | D2 | 55 |
| Oftringen, Switz. | B4 | 21 |
| Ōfunato, Japan | G9 | 33 |
| Ogaki, Japan | I8 | 33 |
| Ogallah, Ks., U.S. | C3 | 93 |
| Ogallala, Ne., U.S. | C5 | 104 |
| Oga Peninsula, pen., Japan | G10 | 33 |
| Ogbomosho, Nig. | D1 | 46 |
| Ogden, Ia., U.S. | B3 | 92 |
| Ogden, Ks., U.S. | C7 | 93 |
| Ogden, Ut., U.S. | B4 | 121 |
| Ogden, Mount, mtn., Ak., U.S. | k23 | 79 |
| Ogdensburg, N.J., U.S. | A3 | 107 |
| Ogdensburg, N.Y., U.S. | f9 | 109 |
| Ogdensburg, Pa., U.S. | C8 | 115 |
| Ogeechee, stm., Ga., U.S. | D5 | 87 |
| Ogema, Sask. | H3 | 75 |
| Ogema, Mn., U.S. | C3 | 100 |
| Ogema, Wi., U.S. | C3 | 126 |
| Ogemaw, co., Mi., U.S. | D6 | 99 |
| Ogilvie Mountains, mts., Yukon | D5 | 66 |
| Oglala, S.D., U.S. | D3 | 118 |
| Oglala, co., Il., U.S. | A4 | 90 |
| Oglesby, Il., U.S. | B4 | 90 |
| Oglesby, Ok., U.S. | A6 | 113 |

| Name | Map Ref. | Page |
|---|---|---|

Oglethorpe, Ga., U.S. . . . . . . D2 87
Oglethorpe, co., Ga., U.S. . . . C3 87
Oglethorpe, Mount, mtn., Ga.,
U.S. . . . . . . . . . . . . . . . B2 87
Oglio, stm., Italy . . . . . . . . . B3 23
Ognon, stm., Fr. . . . . . . . . . B1 20
Ogoamas, mtn., Indon. . . . . . E6 34
Ogoja, Nig. . . . . . . . . . . . . E6 45
Ogoki, stm., Ont. . . . . . . . . o18 73
Ogooué, stm., Afr. . . . . . . . F2 46
Ogosta, stm., Bul. . . . . . . . D6 24
Ogrodzieniec, Pol. . . . . . . . g11 26
Ogulin, Yugo. . . . . . . . . . . C2 24
Ogunquit, Me., U.S. . . . . . . E2 96
Ogurchinskiy Island, i., Sov.
Un. . . . . . . . . . . . . . . . . B6 39
Ohakune, N.Z. . . . . . . . . . M15 51
Ohanet, Alg. . . . . . . . . . . . D6 44
O'Hanly, stm., Man. . . . . . . D4 70
Ōhara, Japan . . . . . . . . . . n19 33
Ohatchee, Al., U.S. . . . . . . B3 78
Ohaton, Alta. . . . . . . . . . . C4 68
O'Higgins, Lago (Lago San
Martín), l., S.A. . . . . . . . D2 54
Ohio, Co., U.S. . . . . . . . . . C4 83
Ohio, Il., U.S. . . . . . . . . . . B4 90
Ohio, N.Y., U.S. . . . . . . . . B6 109
Ohio, co., In., U.S. . . . . . . . G7 91
Ohio, co., Ky., U.S. . . . . . . C3 94
Ohio, co., W.V., U.S. . . . . . A4 125
Ohio, state, U.S. . . . . . . . . B3 112
Ohio, stm., U.S. . . . . . . . . C11 76
Ohio Brush Creek, stm., Oh.,
U.S. . . . . . . . . . . . . . . . D2 112
Ohio City, Oh., U.S. . . . . . . B1 112
Ohio Peak, mtn., Co., U.S. . . C3 83
Ohiopyle, Pa., U.S. . . . . . . G3 115
Ohioville, Pa., U.S. . . . . . . E1 115
Ohiowa, Ne., U.S. . . . . . . . D8 104
Ohlman, Il., U.S. . . . . . . . . D4 90
Ohoopee, stm., Ga., U.S. . . . D4 87
Ohoopee, stm., Ga., U.S. . . . D4 87
Ohopoho, Nmb. . . . . . . . . . A1 49
Ohrdruf, E. Ger. . . . . . . . . C5 19
Ohfe, stm., Eur. . . . . . . . . . C2 19
Ohrid, Yugo. . . . . . . . . . . . E5 24
Ohrid, Lake, l., Eur. . . . . . . E5 24
Ohrigstad, S. Afr. . . . . . . . B5 49
Öhringen, W. Ger. . . . . . . . D4 19
Oiapoque, Braz. . . . . . . . . . B4 59
Oiapoque (Oyapock), stm.,
S.A. . . . . . . . . . . . . . . . B4 59
Oies, Île aux, i., Que. . . . . . B7 74
Oikull, Palau . . . . . . . . . . . R17 52
Oil Center, N.M., U.S. . . . . . E6 108
Oil City, La., U.S. . . . . . . . B2 95
Oil City, Ms., U.S. . . . . . . . C3 101
Oil City, Pa., U.S. . . . . . . . D2 115
Oil Creek, stm., Pa., U.S. . . . C2 115
Oildale, Ca., U.S. . . . . . . . E4 82
Oilmont, Mt., U.S. . . . . . . . B5 103
Oil Springs, Ont. . . . . . . . . E2 73
Oilton, Ok., U.S. . . . . . . . . A5 113
Oilton, Tx., U.S. . . . . . . . . F3 120
Oil Trough, Ar., U.S. . . . . . B4 81
Oir, Beinn an, mtn., Scot.,
U.K. . . . . . . . . . . . . . . . E3 13
Oise, dept., Fr. . . . . . . . . . E2 17
Oise, stm., Eur. . . . . . . . . . C5 16
Oiseau, stm., Can. . . . . . . . D4 70
Oisemont, Fr. . . . . . . . . . . E9 12
Ō Island, i., Japan . . . . . . . F9 33
Ō Island, i., Japan . . . . . . . I9 33
Oita, Japan . . . . . . . . . . . . J5 33
Oiticica, Braz. . . . . . . . . . . C2 57
Ojai, Ca., U.S. . . . . . . . . . . E4 82
Ojinaga, Mex. . . . . . . . . . . C4 63
Ojocaliente, Mex. . . . . . . . . C4 63
Ojo Caliente, N.M., U.S. . . . A3 108
Ojo Feliz, N.M., U.S. . . . . . A4 108
Ojo Sarco, N.M., U.S. . . . . . A4 108
Ojos del Salado, Nevado,
mtn., S.A. . . . . . . . . . . . E2 55
Oka, Que. . . . . . . . . . . . . . D3 74
Oka, Nig. . . . . . . . . . . . . . E6 45
Oka, stm., Sov. Un. . . . . . . C14 27
Okaba, Indon. . . . . . . . . . . G9 34
Okabena, Mn., U.S. . . . . . . G3 100
Okahandja, Nmb. . . . . . . . . B2 49
Okak Islands, is., Newf. . . . . g9 72
Okaloosa, co., Fl., U.S. . . . . u15 86
Okamanpeedan Lake, l., U.S. A3 92
Okanagan Centre, B.C. . . . . D8 69
Okanagan Falls, B.C. . . . . . E8 69
Okanagan Lake, l., B.C. . . . . D8 69
Okanagan Landing, B.C. . . . . D8 69
Okanagan Range, mts., N.A. . E7 69
Okanogan, Wa., U.S. . . . . . A6 124
Okanogan, co., Wa., U.S. . . . A5 124
Okanogan, stm., N.A. . . . . . A6 124
Okapilco Creek, stm., Ga.,
U.S. . . . . . . . . . . . . . . . E3 87
Okāra, Pak. . . . . . . . . . . . . E5 36
Okarche, Ok., U.S. . . . . . . . B4 113
Okatibbee Reservoir, res., Ms.,
U.S. . . . . . . . . . . . . . . . C5 101
Okatoma Creek, stm., Ms.,
U.S. . . . . . . . . . . . . . . . D4 101
Okaton, S.D., U.S. . . . . . . . D5 118
Okauchee, Wi., U.S. . . . . . . *E5 126
Okauchee Lake, Wi., U.S. . . . E5 126
Okaukuejo, Nmb. . . . . . . . . A2 49
Okavango, stm., Afr. . . . . . . H7 42
Okavango Swamps, sw.,
Bots. . . . . . . . . . . . . . . . A3 49
Okawville, Il., U.S. . . . . . . . E4 90
Okay, Ok., U.S. . . . . . . . . . B6 113
Okaya, Japan . . . . . . . . . . . H8 33
Okayama, Japan . . . . . . . . . E11 31
Okazaki, Japan . . . . . . . . . . o16 33
O'Kean, Ar., U.S. . . . . . . . A5 81
Okeana, Oh., U.S. . . . . . . . n12 112
Okęcie (part of Warsaw), Pol. . m13 26
Okecko, P.E.I. . . . . . . . . . . C5 71
Okeechobee, Fl., U.S. . . . . . E6 86
Okeechobee, co., Fl., U.S. . . . E6 86
Okeechobee, Lake, l., Fl., U.S. F6 86
Okeene, Ok., U.S. . . . . . . . A3 113
Okefenokee Swamp, sw., U.S. F4 87
Okehampton, Eng., U.K. . . . . K9 11
Okemah, Ok., U.S. . . . . . . . B5 113
Okemos, Mi., U.S. . . . . . . . *F6 99
Oker, stm., W. Ger. . . . . . . . F4 15
Okesa, Ok., U.S. . . . . . . . . A5 113
Oketo, Ks., U.S. . . . . . . . . . C7 93
Okfuskee, co., Ok., U.S. . . . . B5 113
Okha, Sov. Un. . . . . . . . . . D17 29
Okhotsk, Sea of, Asia . . . . . D17 29
Okiep, S. Afr. . . . . . . . . . . C2 49
Oki Islands, is., Japan . . . . . D11 31
Okinawa Island, i., Japan . . . F10 31
Oklahoma, co., Ok., U.S. . . . B4 113
Oklahoma, state, U.S. . . . . . B4 113
Oklahoma City, Ok., U.S. . . . B4 113
Oklawaha, Fl., U.S. . . . . . . . C5 86

Oklawaha, stm., Fl., U.S. . . . C5 86
Oklawaha, Lake, res., Fl., U.S. C5 86
Oklee, Mn., U.S. . . . . . . . . C3 100
Okmulgee, Ok., U.S. . . . . . . B6 113
Okmulgee, co., Ok., U.S. . . . B5 113
Okoboji, Ia., U.S. . . . . . . . . A2 92
Okobojo Creek, stm., S.D.,
U.S. . . . . . . . . . . . . . . . C5 118
Okolona, Ar., U.S. . . . . . . . D2 81
Okolona, Ky., U.S. . . . . . . . g11 94
Okolona, Ms., U.S. . . . . . . . B5 101
Okondja, Gabon . . . . . . . . . F2 46
Okotoks, Alta. . . . . . . . . . . D4 68
Okreek, S.D., U.S. . . . . . . . D5 118
Oktaha, Ok., U.S. . . . . . . . . B6 113
Oktyabrsk, Sov. Un. . . . . . . D5 28
Oktyabrskiy, Sov. Un. . . . . . C4 28
Okulovka, Sov. Un. . . . . . . . B9 27
Okuniew, Pol. . . . . . . . . . . k14 26
Okushiri, Japan . . . . . . . . . E9 33
Okushiri Island, i., Japan . . . E9 33
Ola, Ar., U.S. . . . . . . . . . . B2 81
Olalla, Wa., U.S. . . . . . . . . f10 124
Olamon, Me., U.S. . . . . . . . C4 96
Olancha, Ca., U.S. . . . . . . . D5 82
Olancha Peak, mtn., Ca., U.S. D4 82
Olanchito, Hond. . . . . . . . . C4 62
Öland, i., Swe. . . . . . . . . . . I7 14
Olanta, S.C., U.S. . . . . . . . D8 117
Olar, S.C., U.S. . . . . . . . . . E5 117
Olascoaga, Arg. . . . . . . . . . B4 54
Olathe, Co., U.S. . . . . . . . . C3 83
Olathe, Ks., U.S. . . . . . . . . D9 93
Olavarría, Arg. . . . . . . . . . B4 54
Olberg, Az., U.S. . . . . . . . . D4 80
Olbernhau, E. Ger. . . . . . . . C8 19
Olbia, Italy . . . . . . . . . . . . D2 23
Olcott, N.Y., U.S. . . . . . . . B2 109
Olcott, W.V., U.S. . . . . . . . C3 125
Old Bahama Channel, strt.,
N.A. . . . . . . . . . . . . . . . C4 64
Old Bennington, Vt., U.S. . . . F2 122
Old Bethpage, N.Y., U.S. . . . *n15 109
Old Bight, Bah. . . . . . . . . . B6 64
Old Bridge, N.J., U.S. . . . . . C4 107
Old Castile, hist. reg., Spain . B4 22
Oldcastle, Ire. . . . . . . . . . . D4 11
Old Crow, Yukon . . . . . . . . C5 66
Oldeani, Tan. . . . . . . . . . . . B6 48
Olden, Tx., U.S. . . . . . . . . . C3 120
Oldenburg, W. Ger. . . . . . . . B4 18
Oldenburg, In., U.S. . . . . . . F7 91
Oldenburg [in Holstein], W.
Ger. . . . . . . . . . . . . . . . A5 18
Oldenzaal, Neth. . . . . . . . . B6 17
Old Faithful Geyser, Wy., U.S. B2 127
Old Forge, N.Y., U.S. . . . . . B6 109
Old Forge, Pa., U.S. . . . . . . D10 115
Old Fort, N.C., U.S. . . . . . . f10 110
Old Fort, Oh., U.S. . . . . . . . A2 112
Old Fort Bay, Que. . . . . . . . C3 72
Oldham, Eng., U.K. . . . . . . . D5 10
Oldham, S.D., U.S. . . . . . . . C8 118
Oldham, co., Ky., U.S. . . . . . B4 94
Oldham, co., Tx., U.S. . . . . . B1 120
Old Harbor, Ak., U.S. . . . . . D9 79
Old Harbour Bay, Jam. . . . . F14 65
Old Head of Kinsale, c., Ire. . E2 10
Old Hickory Lake, res., Tn.,
U.S. . . . . . . . . . . . . . . . A5 119
Old Lyme, Ct., U.S. . . . . . . D6 84
Oldman, stm., Alta. . . . . . . . E4 68
Old Man Mountain, mtn.,
Newf. . . . . . . . . . . . . . . D3 72
Old Man of the Mountain,
N.H., U.S. . . . . . . . . . . . B3 106
Oldmans Creek, stm., N.J.,
U.S. . . . . . . . . . . . . . . . D2 107
Oldmeldrum, Scot., U.K. . . . . C6 13
Old Mkushi, Zam. . . . . . . . . D4 48
Old Monroe, Mo., U.S. . . . . . C7 102
Old Mystic, Ct., U.S. . . . . . . D8 84
Old Northwood, N.H., U.S. . . D4 106
Old Orchard Beach, Me., U.S. E2 96
Old Perlican, Newf. . . . . . . . D5 72
Old Point Comfort, c., Va.,
U.S. . . . . . . . . . . . . . . . h15 123
Old Rhodes Key, i., Fl., U.S. . G6 86
Old Ripley, Il., U.S. . . . . . . . E4 90
Old River Lake, l., Ar., U.S. . k10 81
Olds, Alta. . . . . . . . . . . . . . D3 68
Olds, Ia., U.S. . . . . . . . . . . C6 92
Old Saybrook, Ct., U.S. . . . . D6 84
Oldsmar, Fl., U.S. . . . . . . . . o10 86
Old Speck Mountain, mtn.,
U.S. . . . . . . . . . . . . . . . D2 96
Old Tampa Bay, b., Fl., U.S. . p10 86
Old Tappan, N.J., U.S. . . . . . g9 107
Old Tate, Bots. . . . . . . . . . . B4 49
Old Topsail Inlet, b., N.C.,
U.S. . . . . . . . . . . . . . . . C5 110
Old Town, Fl., U.S. . . . . . . . C4 86
Old Town, Me., U.S. . . . . . . A1 89
Old Town, Md., U.S. . . . . . . k13 97
Old Village, N.Y., U.S. . . . . . *E7 109
Old Washington, Oh., U.S. . . B4 112
Oldwick, N.J., U.S. . . . . . . . B3 107
Old Wives, Sask. . . . . . . . . G2 75
Old Wives Lake, l., Sask. . . . G2 75
Olean, N.Y., U.S. . . . . . . . . C2 109
O'Leary, P.E.I. . . . . . . . . . . C5 71
Oleiros, Spain . . . . . . . . . . A1 22
Olecko, Pol. . . . . . . . . . . . A7 26
Olekma, stm., Sov. Un. . . . . C15 29
Olekminsk, Sov. Un. . . . . . . C14 29
Olenek, stm., Sov. Un. . . . . . C14 29
Olentangy, stm., Oh., U.S. . . B3 112
Oleśnica (Oels), Pol. . . . . . . C4 26
Olesno, Pol. . . . . . . . . . . . C5 113
Oleta, Ok., U.S. . . . . . . . . . C6 113
Oley, Pa., U.S. . . . . . . . . . . F10 115
Olga, Sov. Un. . . . . . . . . . . C12 31
Olga, Mount, mtn., V., U.S. . F3 122
Ōlgiy, Mong. . . . . . . . . . . . B2 31
Olgopol, Sov. Un. . . . . . . . . G7 27
Olhão, Port. . . . . . . . . . . . . D2 22
Olifants, stm., Afr. . . . . . . . B5 49
Ólimbos, mtn., Cyp. . . . . . . E9 40
Olímpia, Braz. . . . . . . . . . . C3 56
Olin, Ia., U.S. . . . . . . . . . . B6 92
Olinda, Braz. . . . . . . . . . . . C4 57
Olionorio, Cape, c., W. Sam. . F12 52

Olite, Spain . . . . . . . . . . . . A5 22
Oliva, Spain . . . . . . . . . . . . C5 22
Oliva de la Frontera, Spain . . C2 22
Olivais, Port. . . . . . . . . . . . f9 22
Olive, Mt., U.S. . . . . . . . . . E11 103
Olive, Ok., U.S. . . . . . . . . . A5 113
Olive Branch, Il., U.S. . . . . . F4 90
Olive Branch, Ms., U.S. . . . . A4 101
Olive Hill, Ky., U.S. . . . . . . B6 94
Olivehill, Tn., U.S. . . . . . . . B3 119
Olivehurst, Ca., U.S. . . . . . . C3 82
Oliveira, Braz. . . . . . . . . . . C4 56
Olivenza, Spain . . . . . . . . . C2 22
Oliver, B.C. . . . . . . . . . . . . E8 69
Oliver, Al., U.S. . . . . . . . . . A2 78
Oliver, Ga., U.S. . . . . . . . . D5 87
Oliver, Il., U.S. . . . . . . . . . D6 90
Oliver, Pa., U.S. . . . . . . . . . G2 115
Oliver, Wi., U.S. . . . . . . . . . B1 126
Oliver, co., N.D., U.S. . . . . . B4 111
Oliver Dam, U.S. . . . . . . . . C5 78
Oliver Springs, Tn., U.S. . . . C9 119
Olivet, Il., U.S. . . . . . . . . . D6 90
Olivet, Ks., U.S. . . . . . . . . . D8 93
Olivet, Md., U.S. . . . . . . . . D5 97
Olivet, Mi., U.S. . . . . . . . . . F6 99
Olivette, Mo., U.S. . . . . . . . *f13 102
Olivia, Mn., U.S. . . . . . . . . . F4 100
Olivia, N.C., U.S. . . . . . . . . B3 110
Olivone, Switz. . . . . . . . . . . C4 20
Öljaren, l., Swe. . . . . . . . . . t34 14
Olkusz, Pol. . . . . . . . . . . . . g11 26
Olla, La., U.S. . . . . . . . . . . C3 95
Ollagüe, Chile . . . . . . . . . . D2 55
Ollei, Palau . . . . . . . . . . . . R17 52
Olmito, Tx., U.S. . . . . . . . . F4 120
Olmitz, Ks., U.S. . . . . . . . . D5 93
Olmos, Peru . . . . . . . . . . . C2 58
Olmos Park, Tx., U.S. . . . . . k7 120
Olmstead, Ky., U.S. . . . . . . D2 94
Olmstead, Ut., U.S. . . . . . . . *C4 121
Olmsted, Il., U.S. . . . . . . . . F5 90
Olmsted, co., Mn., U.S. . . . . G6 100
Olmsted Falls, Oh., U.S. . . . . h9 112
Olmstedville, N.Y., U.S. . . . . B7 109
Olney, Il., U.S. . . . . . . . . . . E5 90
Olney, Md., U.S. . . . . . . . . . B3 97
Olney, Mo., U.S. . . . . . . . . . B6 102
Olney, Mt., U.S. . . . . . . . . . B2 103
Olney, Tx., U.S. . . . . . . . . . C3 120
Olney Springs, Co., U.S. . . . C7 83
Oloh, Ms., U.S. . . . . . . . . . D4 101
Olomouc, Czech. . . . . . . . . D4 26
Olongapo, Phil. . . . . . . . . . o13 34
Oloron, Gave d', stm., Fr. . . . F3 16
Oloron-Sainte-Marie, Fr. . . . F3 16
Olot, Spain . . . . . . . . . . . . A7 22
Olpe, W. Ger. . . . . . . . . . . . B2 19
Olpe, Ks., U.S. . . . . . . . . . . D7 93
Olsburg, Ks., U.S. . . . . . . . . C7 93
Olshany, Sov. Un. . . . . . . . . F10 27
Olst, stm., Rom. . . . . . . . . . C7 24
Olsztyn (Allenstein), Pol. . . . B6 26
Olteniţa, Rom. . . . . . . . . . . E9 24
Oltenia, hist. reg., Rom. . . . . C6 24
Olteţ, stm., Rom. . . . . . . . . C6 24
Olton, Tx., U.S. . . . . . . . . . B1 120
Olupona, Nig. . . . . . . . . . . *E5 45
Olustee, Fl., U.S. . . . . . . . . B4 86
Olustee, Ok., U.S. . . . . . . . . C2 113
Olvenstedt, E. Ger. . . . . . . . A6 19
Olvera, Spain . . . . . . . . . . . D3 22
Olvey, Ar., U.S. . . . . . . . . . A3 81
Olympia, Ky., U.S. . . . . . . . B6 94
Olympia, Wa., U.S. . . . . . . . B3 124
Olympia, hist., Grc. . . . . . . . D3 25
Olympia Heights, Fl., U.S. . . *s13 86
Olympic Mountains, mts., Wa.,
U.S. . . . . . . . . . . . . . . . B2 124
Olympic National Park, Wa.,
U.S. . . . . . . . . . . . . . . . B2 124
Olympus, Mount, mtn., Grc. . B4 40
Olympus, Mount, mtn., Ky.,
U.S. . . . . . . . . . . . . . . . B6 94
Olympus, Mount, mtn., Wa.,
U.S. . . . . . . . . . . . . . . . B2 124
Olyphant, Ar., U.S. . . . . . . . B4 81
Olyphant, Pa., U.S. . . . . . . . D10 115
Olyutorski, Cape, c., Sov. Un. D20 29
Om, stm., Sov. Un. . . . . . . . B9 28
Oma, Ar., U.S. . . . . . . . . . . g7 81
Oma, Ms., U.S. . . . . . . . . . D3 101
Omae, Cape, c., Japan . . . . o17 33
Omagh, N. Ire., U.K. . . . . . . C3 10
Omaguas, Peru . . . . . . . . . B3 58
Omaha, Ar., U.S. . . . . . . . . A2 81
Omaha, Ga., U.S. . . . . . . . . D1 87
Omaha, Il., U.S. . . . . . . . . . F5 90
Omaha, Ne., U.S. . . . . . . . . C10 104
Omaha Indian Reservation,
Ne., U.S. . . . . . . . . . . . . B9 104
Omak, Wa., U.S. . . . . . . . . . A6 124
Omak Lake, l., Wa., U.S. . . . A6 124
Oman, ctry., Asia . . . . . . . . C5 38
Oman, Gulf of, b., Asia . . . . C6 38
Omar, W.V., U.S. . . . . . . . . D3 125
Omaramara, Braz. . . . . . . . . P12 51
Omaruru, Nmb. . . . . . . . . . B2 49
Omas, Peru . . . . . . . . . . . . D2 58
Omboué, Gabon . . . . . . . . . F1 46
Ombrone, stm., Italy . . . . . . C3 23
Omdurman (Umm Durmān),
Sud. . . . . . . . . . . . . . . . B3 47
Omega, Ga., U.S. . . . . . . . . E3 87
Omega, N.M., U.S. . . . . . . . C1 108
Omega, Ok., U.S. . . . . . . . . B3 113
Omegna, Italy . . . . . . . . . . E5 21
Omemee, Ont. . . . . . . . . . . C6 73
Omemee, N.D., U.S. . . . . . . A5 111
Omeo, Austl. . . . . . . . . . . . H6 51
Omer, Mi., U.S. . . . . . . . . . D7 99
Ometepe, Isla de, i., Nic. . . . E5 62
Ometepec, Mex. . . . . . . . . . D5 63
Om Hajer, Eth. . . . . . . . . . . C4 47
Ōmihachiman, Japan . . . . . . n19 33
Omineca, stm., B.C. . . . . . . B5 69
Omineca Mountains, mts.,
B.C. . . . . . . . . . . . . . . . A4 69
Ōmiya, Japan . . . . . . . . . . . I9 33
Ōmiya, Japan . . . . . . . . . . . o15 33
Ommanney, Cape, c., Ak., U.S. D12 79
Ommen, Neth. . . . . . . . . . . B6 17
Omo, stm., Eth. . . . . . . . . . C5 47
Omo, stm., Eth. . . . . . . . . . D4 47
Omolon, stm., Sov. Un. . . . . C18 29

Ompompanoosuc, stm., Vt.,
U.S. . . . . . . . . . . . . . . . D4 122
Ompompanoosuc, West
Branch, stm., Vt., U.S. . . . . D4 122
Omro, Wi., U.S. . . . . . . . . . D5 126
Omsk, Sov. Un. . . . . . . . . . D10 29
Ōmuta, Japan . . . . . . . . . . J5 33
Ona, Fl., U.S. . . . . . . . . . . . E5 86
Onaga, Ks., U.S. . . . . . . . . . C7 93
Onaka, S.D., U.S. . . . . . . . . B6 118
Onalaska, Wa., U.S. . . . . . . C3 124
Onalaska, Wi., U.S. . . . . . . . E2 126
Onamia, Mn., U.S. . . . . . . . D5 100
Onancock, Va., U.S. . . . . . . C7 123
Onano, Micron. . . . . . . . . . . D2 70
Onao, Il., Micron. . . . . . . . . Q18 52
Onarga, Il., U.S. . . . . . . . . . C6 90
Onawa, Ia., U.S. . . . . . . . . . B1 92
Onawa, Me., U.S. . . . . . . . . C3 96
Onawa, Lake, l., Me., U.S. . . *C2 89
Onaway, Id., U.S. . . . . . . . . C2 89
Onaway, Mi., U.S. . . . . . . . . C6 99
Onchiota, N.Y., U.S. . . . . . . f10 109
Onda, Spain . . . . . . . . . . . . C5 22
Ondangua, Nmb. . . . . . . . . A2 49
Ondjiva (Ngiva), Ang. . . . . . E2 48
Ondo, Nig. . . . . . . . . . . . . . E5 45
Öndörhaan, Mong. . . . . . . . B7 31
Oneata, i., Fiji . . . . . . . . . . I16 52
Oneco, Ct., U.S. . . . . . . . . . C8 84
Oneco, Fl., U.S. . . . . . . . . . E4 86
Onega, Sov. Un. . . . . . . . . . C6 29
Onega, stm., Sov. Un. . . . . . C16 8
Onega, Lake, l., Sov. Un. . . . C6 29
One Hundred Fifty Mile
House, B.C. . . . . . . . . . . C7 69
One Hundred Mile House,
B.C. . . . . . . . . . . . . . . . D7 69
Oneida, Ar., U.S. . . . . . . . . C5 81
Oneida, Il., U.S. . . . . . . . . . B3 90
Oneida, In., U.S. . . . . . . . . . A7 91
Oneida, Ks., U.S. . . . . . . . . C8 93
Oneida, Ky., U.S. . . . . . . . . C6 94
Oneida, N.Y., U.S. . . . . . . . B5 109
Oneida, Tn., U.S. . . . . . . . . C9 119
Oneida, co., Id., U.S. . . . . . . G6 89
Oneida, co., N.Y., U.S. . . . . . B5 109
Oneida, co., Wi., U.S. . . . . . C4 126
Oneida Lake, l., N.Y., U.S. . . B5 109
O'Neill, Ne., U.S. . . . . . . . . B7 104
Onekama, Mi., U.S. . . . . . . . D4 99
Onemak Island, i., Marsh Is. . S17 52
Oneonta, Al., U.S. . . . . . . . B3 78
Oneonta, N.Y., U.S. . . . . . . C5 109
Ong, Ne., U.S. . . . . . . . . . . D8 104
Ongea Levu, i., Fiji . . . . . . . I16 52
Ongjin, Hid, Mong. . . . . . . . B5 31
Ongiyn, stm., Mong. . . . . . . B5 31
Ongjin, N. Kor. . . . . . . . . . . H2 33
Onida, S.D., U.S. . . . . . . . . C5 118
Onilahy, stm., Madag. . . . . . h8 49
Oniotto Island, i., Marsh Is. . S17 52
Onitsha, Nig. . . . . . . . . . . . E6 45
Onley, Va., U.S. . . . . . . . . . C7 123
Only, Tn., U.S. . . . . . . . . . . B4 119
Onna, Japan . . . . . . . . . . . O5 52
Ono, Japan . . . . . . . . . . . . n15 33
Ono, i., Fiji . . . . . . . . . . . . . I15 52
Ono Channel, strt., Fiji . . . . . I15 52
Onomichi, Japan . . . . . . . . . I6 33
Onondaga, Mi., U.S. . . . . . . F6 99
Onondaga, co., N.Y., U.S. . . . C4 109
Onondaga Indian Reservation,
N.Y., U.S. . . . . . . . . . . . C4 109
Onota Lake, l., Ma., U.S. . . . B1 98
Onoway, Alta. . . . . . . . . . . C3 68
Onset, Ma., U.S. . . . . . . . . C6 98
Onslow, Austl. . . . . . . . . . . D2 50
Onslow, In., U.S. . . . . . . . . B6 92
Onslow, co., N.C., U.S. . . . . C5 110
Onsong, N. Kor. . . . . . . . . . E4 33
Onsted, Mi., U.S. . . . . . . . . F6 99
Ontake, Mount, mtn., Japan . n16 33
Ontario, Ca., U.S. . . . . . . . . E5 82
Ontario, In., U.S. . . . . . . . . A7 91
Ontario, N.Y., U.S. . . . . . . . B3 109
Ontario, Oh., U.S. . . . . . . . . B3 112
Ontario, Or., U.S. . . . . . . . . C10 114
Ontario, Wi., U.S. . . . . . . . . E3 126
Ontario, co., N.Y., U.S. . . . . C3 109
Ontario, prov., Can. . . . . . . C6 73
Ontario, Lake, l., N.A. . . . . . B12 76
Onteniente, Spain . . . . . . . . C5 22
Ontonagon, Mi., U.S. . . . . . . m12 99
Ontonagon, co., Mi., U.S. . . . m12 99
Ontonagon Indian Reservation,
Mi., U.S. . . . . . . . . . . . . C5 99
Onward, In., U.S. . . . . . . . . C5 91
Oodnadatta, Austl. . . . . . . . E6 50
Ood Weyne, Som. . . . . . . . . D6 47
Ookala, Hi., U.S. . . . . . . . . C6 88
Oolitic, In., U.S. . . . . . . . . . G4 91
Oologah, Ok., U.S. . . . . . . . A6 113
Oologah Lake, res., Ok., U.S. A6 113
Ooltgensplaat, Neth. . . . . . . D4 17
Oostburg, Neth. . . . . . . . . . C3 17
Oostburg, Wi., U.S. . . . . . . . E6 126
Oostende (Ostende), Bel. . . . A5 16
Oosterend, Neth. . . . . . . . . A5 17
Oosterend, Neth. . . . . . . . . A5 17
Oosterhout, Neth. . . . . . . . . C4 17
Oosterschelde, b., Neth. . . . . A5 16
Oostmahorn, Neth. . . . . . . . A6 17
Oostpunt, c., Neth. Ant. . . . . H19 65
Oost-Vlieland, Neth. . . . . . . A5 17
Oostvoorne, Neth. . . . . . . . C4 17
Ootsa Lake, B.C. . . . . . . . . C4 69
Ootsa Lake, l., B.C. . . . . . . . C4 69
Opal, Alta. . . . . . . . . . . . . . C4 68
Opal, S.D., U.S. . . . . . . . . . C3 118
Opal, Wy., U.S. . . . . . . . . . E2 127
Opala, Zaire . . . . . . . . . . . . B4 48
Opalton, Austl. . . . . . . . . . . A4 51
Opan, stm., Sov. Un. . . . . . . B2 102
Opava, Czech. . . . . . . . . . . D4 26
Opdyke, Il., U.S. . . . . . . . . . E5 90
Opelika, Al., U.S. . . . . . . . . C4 78
Opelousas, La., U.S. . . . . . . D3 95
Opeongo, stm., Ont. . . . . . . B6 73
Opeongo Lake, l., Ont. . . . . . B6 73
Opequon Creek, stm., W.V.,
U.S. . . . . . . . . . . . . . . . B6 125
Opfikon, Switz. . . . . . . . . . . B6 21
Ophem, M.I., U.S. . . . . . . . . B10 103
Ophir, Or., U.S. . . . . . . . . . E2 114
Ophir, Ut., U.S. . . . . . . . . . C3 121

Ophir, Mount, mtn., Indon. . . E1 34
Opihikao, Hi., U.S. . . . . . . . D7 88
Opiscotéo, Lac, l., Que. . . . . F19 66
Opobo, Nig. . . . . . . . . . . . . F6 45
Opochka, Sov. Un. . . . . . . . C7 27
Opoczno, Pol. . . . . . . . . . . C6 26
Opole, Pol. . . . . . . . . . . . . C4 8
Opole Lubelskie, Pol. . . . . . C7 26
Oporto see Porto, Port. . . . . B1 22
Oppdal, Nor. . . . . . . . . . . . F3 14
Oppelo, Ar., U.S. . . . . . . . . B3 81
Opportunity, Wa., U.S. . . . . . B8 124
Optic Lake, Man. . . . . . . . . B1 70
Optima, Ok., U.S. . . . . . . . . e9 113
Optima Reservoir, res., Ok.,
U.S. . . . . . . . . . . . . . . . e9 113
Opyan, Puntan, c., N. Mar. Is. D7 52
Oquawka, Il., U.S. . . . . . . . . C3 90
Oquossoc, Me., U.S. . . . . . . D2 96
Ora, Italy . . . . . . . . . . . . . . C7 20
Ora, In., U.S. . . . . . . . . . . . B4 91
Ora, Ms., U.S. . . . . . . . . . . D4 101
Oracle, Az., U.S. . . . . . . . . . E5 80
Oradea, Rom. . . . . . . . . . . . C5 24
Oradell, N.J., U.S. . . . . . . . . h8 107
Oradell Reservoir, res., N.J.,
U.S. . . . . . . . . . . . . . . . h9 107
Orahovica, Sov. Un. . . . . . . F37 85
Oraibi, Az., U.S. . . . . . . . . . B5 80
Oraibi Wash, val., Az., U.S. . B5 80
Oral, S.D., U.S. . . . . . . . . . D2 118
Oran (Wahran), Alg. . . . . . . B5 42
Oran, Ia., U.S. . . . . . . . . . . B5 92
Oran, Mo., U.S. . . . . . . . . . D8 102
Orange, Austl. . . . . . . . . . . F8 50
Orange, Fr. . . . . . . . . . . . . E6 16
Orange, Ca., U.S. . . . . . . . . n13 82
Orange, Ct., U.S. . . . . . . . . D3 84
Orange, In., U.S. . . . . . . . . . E7 91
Orange, Ma., U.S. . . . . . . . . A3 98
Orange, N.H., U.S. . . . . . . . C3 106
Orange, N.J., U.S. . . . . . . . . B4 107
Orange, Tx., U.S. . . . . . . . . D6 120
Orange, Va., U.S. . . . . . . . . B4 123
Orange, co., Ca., U.S. . . . . . F5 82
Orange, co., Fl., U.S. . . . . . . D5 86
Orange, co., In., U.S. . . . . . . G5 91
Orange, co., N.Y., U.S. . . . . D6 109
Orange, co., N.C., U.S. . . . . A3 110
Orange, co., Tx., U.S. . . . . . D6 120
Orange, co., Vt., U.S. . . . . . D4 122
Orange, Cabo, c., Braz. . . . . B4 59
Orangeburg, S.C., U.S. . . . . E6 117
Orangeburg, co., S.C., U.S. . . E6 117
Orange City, Fl., U.S. . . . . . . D5 86
Orange City, Ia., U.S. . . . . . . A1 92
Orangedale, N.S. . . . . . . . . D8 71
Orange Free State, prov., S.
Afr. . . . . . . . . . . . . . . . . C4 49
Orange Grove, Ms., U.S. . . . E5 101
Orange Grove, Tx., U.S. . . . . F4 120
Orange Lake, Fl., U.S. . . . . . C4 86
Orange Lake, l., Fl., U.S. . . . C4 86
Orangevale, Ca., U.S. . . . . . *C3 82
Orangeville, Ont. . . . . . . . . D4 73
Orangeville, Il., U.S. . . . . . . A4 90
Orangeville, Ut., U.S. . . . . . . D4 121
Orange Walk, Belize . . . . . . D7 63
Orani, Phil. . . . . . . . . . . . . o13 34
Oranienbaum, E. Ger. . . . . . B7 19
Oranienburg, E. Ger. . . . . . . B6 18
Oranje Gebergte, mts., Sur. . B4 59
Oranjemund, Nmb. . . . . . . . C2 49
Oranjestad, Aruba . . . . . . . . G17 65
Oranmore, Ire. . . . . . . . . . . D3 11
Or 'Aqiva, Isr. . . . . . . . . . . B6 41
Orăştie, Rom. . . . . . . . . . . . C6 24
Oravita, Rom. . . . . . . . . . . . C5 24
Orba, stm., Italy . . . . . . . . . B6 21
Orbe, Switz. . . . . . . . . . . . . C2 21
Orbetello, Italy . . . . . . . . . . A3 23
Orbey, Fr. . . . . . . . . . . . . . D7 16
Orbigo, stm., Spain . . . . . . . A3 22
Orbisonia, Pa., U.S. . . . . . . F6 115
Orbost, Austl. . . . . . . . . . . . H7 51
Örby, Swe. . . . . . . . . . . . . . A6 15
Orcas Island, i., Wa., U.S. . . A3 124
Orchard, Id., U.S. . . . . . . . . F2 89
Orchard, Ne., U.S. . . . . . . . B7 104
Orchard City, Co., U.S. . . . . C3 83
Orchard Farm, Mo., U.S. . . . f13 102
Orchard Homes, Mt., U.S. . . D2 103
Orchard Mesa, Co., U.S. . . . *B2 83
Orchard Park, N.Y., U.S. . . . C2 109
Orchards, Wa., U.S. . . . . . . D3 124
Orchard Valley, Wy., U.S. . . . E8 127
Orchies, Fr. . . . . . . . . . . . . D3 16
Orchila, Isla, i., Ven. . . . . . . A4 60
Orcotuna, Peru . . . . . . . . . D2 58
Orcutt, Ca., U.S. . . . . . . . . . E3 82
Orcutts, Ct., U.S. . . . . . . . . B2 84
Ord, Ne., U.S. . . . . . . . . . . C7 104
Ord, Mount, mtn., Austl. . . . C4 50
Ordale, Sask. . . . . . . . . . . . E2 75
Orderville, Ut., U.S. . . . . . . . F3 121
Ording, W. Ger. . . . . . . . . . D2 15
Ordu, Tur. . . . . . . . . . . . . . B11 40
Orduña, Spain . . . . . . . . . . A4 22
Ordway, Co., U.S. . . . . . . . . C7 83
Ordzhonikidze (Dzaudzhikau),
Sov. Un. . . . . . . . . . . . . C7 29
Oreana, Il., U.S. . . . . . . . . . D5 90
Oreana, Nv., U.S. . . . . . . . . C2 105
Oreba Island, i., Marsh Is. . . S17 52
Örebro, Swe. . . . . . . . . . . . H6 14
Ore City, Tx., U.S. . . . . . . . C5 120
Orós, Braz. . . . . . . . . . . . . C3 57
Orosei, Gulf of, b., Italy . . . . C3 23
Oroshaza, Hung. . . . . . . . . . C5 24
Orote Peninsula, pen., Guam . L9 52
Orovada, Nv., U.S. . . . . . . . B4 105
Oroville, Ca., U.S. . . . . . . . . C3 82
Oroville, Wa., U.S. . . . . . . . A6 124
Oroville, Lake, res., Ca., U.S. C3 82
Orpington (part of London),
Eng., U.K. . . . . . . . . . . . m13 11
Orr, Mn., U.S. . . . . . . . . . . B6 100
Orrick, Mo., U.S. . . . . . . . . B3 102
Orrin, N.D., U.S. . . . . . . . . A5 111

Orekhovo, Bul. . . . . . . . . . . D6 24
Orekhovo-Zuyevo, Sov. Un. . D12 27
Orel, Sov. Un. . . . . . . . . . . . D6 29
Orem, Ut., U.S. . . . . . . . . . . C4 121
Ore Mountains, mts., Eur. . . . C6 18
Orenburg, Sov. Un. . . . . . . . D8 29
Orense, Spain . . . . . . . . . . . A2 22
Orestes, In., U.S. . . . . . . . . D6 91
Orestiás, Grc. . . . . . . . . . . . B8 40
Øresund (The Sound), strt.,
Eur. . . . . . . . . . . . . . . . . J5 14
Oreti, stm., N.Z. . . . . . . . . . P12 51
Oretta, La., U.S. . . . . . . . . . D2 95
Orford, N.H., U.S. . . . . . . . . C2 106
Orford, Mont, mtn., Que. . . . D5 74
Orford Ness, c., Eng., U.K. . . B9 12
Orfordville, Wi., U.S. . . . . . . F4 126
Organ, N.M., U.S. . . . . . . . . D3 108
Organ Cave, W.V., U.S. . . . . D4 125
Organ Mountains, mts., N.M.,
U.S. . . . . . . . . . . . . . . . E3 108
Organ Pipe Cactus National
Monument, Az., U.S. . . . . E3 80
Orgas, W.V., U.S. . . . . . . . . m12 125
Orgaz, Spain . . . . . . . . . . . C4 22
Orgelet, Fr. . . . . . . . . . . . . C1 20
Orgeyev, Sov. Un. . . . . . . . . H7 27
Orgūn, Afg. . . . . . . . . . . . . B4 36
Orhon, stm., Mong. . . . . . . . B5 31
Orick, Ca., U.S. . . . . . . . . . B1 82
Orient, Il., U.S. . . . . . . . . . . F5 90
Orient, Ia., U.S. . . . . . . . . . C3 92
Orient, Me., U.S. . . . . . . . . C5 96
Orient, N.Y., U.S. . . . . . . . . m16 109
Orient, Oh., U.S. . . . . . . . . . C2 112
Orient, S.D., U.S. . . . . . . . . C6 118
Orient, Wa., U.S. . . . . . . . . A7 124
Orienta, Ok., U.S. . . . . . . . . A3 113
Oriental, N.C., U.S. . . . . . . . B6 110
Oriental, Cordillera, mts., Col. C3 60
Orihuela, Spain . . . . . . . . . . C5 22
Orillia, Ont. . . . . . . . . . . . . C5 73
Orinda, Ca., U.S. . . . . . . . . *h8 82
Orinoco, stm., S.A. . . . . . . . B5 60
Oriole, Md., U.S. . . . . . . . . . D6 97
Orion, Alta. . . . . . . . . . . . . E5 68
Orion, Phil. . . . . . . . . . . . . o13 34
Orion, Il., U.S. . . . . . . . . . . B3 90
Oriska, N.D., U.S. . . . . . . . . C8 111
Oriskany, N.Y., U.S. . . . . . . B5 109
Oriskany Falls, N.Y., U.S. . . . C5 109
Orissa, state, India . . . . . . . E7 36
Oristano, Italy . . . . . . . . . . D2 23
Oristano, Gulf of, b., Italy . . . E2 23
Orivesi, l., Fin. . . . . . . . . . . F13 14
Oriximiná, Braz. . . . . . . . . . C3 59
Orizaba, Mex. . . . . . . . . . . . D5 63
Orizaba, Pico de (Citlaltépetl),
vol., Mex. . . . . . . . . . . . . n15 63
Orizona, Braz. . . . . . . . . . . B3 56
Orkanger, Nor. . . . . . . . . . . F3 14
Örkelljunga, Swe. . . . . . . . . B7 15
Orkla, stm., Nor. . . . . . . . . . F4 14
Orkney, Sask. . . . . . . . . . . H2 75
Orkney, prov., Sask., U.S. . . A5 13
Orkney Islands, is., Scot., U.K. A5 10
Orla, Tx., U.S. . . . . . . . . . . o13 120
Orland, Ca., U.S. . . . . . . . . C2 82
Orland, In., U.S. . . . . . . . . . A7 91
Orland, Me., U.S. . . . . . . . . D4 96
Orlando, Fl., U.S. . . . . . . . . D5 86
Orlando, Ok., U.S. . . . . . . . A4 113
Orland Park, Il., U.S. . . . . . . k9 90
Orleães, Braz. . . . . . . . . . . D3 56
Orléanais, hist. reg., Fr. . . . . o13 34
Orléanais, hist. reg., Fr. . . . . h12 73
Orleans, Fr. . . . . . . . . . . . . D4 16
Orleans, Ca., U.S. . . . . . . . . B2 82
Orleans, In., U.S. . . . . . . . . G5 91
Orleans, Ma., U.S. . . . . . . . C7 98
Orleans, Ne., U.S. . . . . . . . . D6 104
Orleans, Vt., U.S. . . . . . . . . B4 122
Orleans, co., La., U.S. . . . . . E6 95
Orleans, co., N.Y., U.S. . . . . B2 109
Orleans, co., Vt., U.S. . . . . . B4 122
Orléans, Île d', i., Que. . . . . C6 74
Orlik Reservoir, res., Czech. . D9 19
Orlinda, Tn., U.S. . . . . . . . . A5 119
Orlová, Czech. . . . . . . . . . . *D5 26
Orlovista, Fl., U.S. . . . . . . . . *D5 86
Orlovo, Sov. Un. . . . . . . . . . E8 29
Orly, Fr. . . . . . . . . . . . . . . . h10 16
Orlyak, Bul. . . . . . . . . . . . . D8 24
Orman Dam, S.D., U.S. . . . . C2 118
Ormāra, Pak. . . . . . . . . . . . C5 36
Ormāra, Rās, c., Pak. . . . . . . I12 39
Ormiston, Sask. . . . . . . . . . H3 75
Ormond Beach, Fl., U.S. . . . . C5 86
Ormond By The Sea, Fl., U.S. *C5 86
Ormsby, Ont. . . . . . . . . . . . C7 73
Ormsby, co., Nv., U.S. . . . . . G4 100
Ormskirk, Eng., U.K. . . . . . . D5 12
Ormstown, Que. . . . . . . . . . D3 74
Ornans, Fr. . . . . . . . . . . . . B2 20
Orne, stm., Fr. . . . . . . . . . . D5 16
Orneta, Pol. . . . . . . . . . . . . A6 26
Örnö, Swe. . . . . . . . . . . . . . t36 14
Örnö, i., Swe. . . . . . . . . . . . t36 14
Örnsköldsvik, Swe. . . . . . . . F8 14
Orø, i., Den. . . . . . . . . . . . . I5 15
Orocué, Col. . . . . . . . . . . . . C3 60
Orodara, Burkina . . . . . . . . . D4 45
Orofino, Id., U.S. . . . . . . . . C2 89
Oro Grande, Ca., U.S. . . . . . E5 82
Orogrande, N.M., U.S. . . . . . E3 108
Orohena, mtn., Fr. Poly. . . . . *H13 6
Oromocto, N.B. . . . . . . . . . D3 71
Oromocto Lake, l., N.B. . . . . D2 71
Oron, Nig. . . . . . . . . . . . . . F6 45
Oron-la-Ville, Switz. . . . . . . C2 21
Orono, Ont. . . . . . . . . . . . . D6 73
Orono, Me., U.S. . . . . . . . . D4 96
Oronoco, Mn., U.S. . . . . . . . *n11 100
Oronoco, Mn., U.S. . . . . . . . F6 100
Oronsay, i., Scot., U.K. . . . . O23 13
Oropuche, stm., Trin. . . . . . . D7 60
Oroquieta, Phil. . . . . . . . . . D6 34

| Name | Map Ref. | Page |
|---|---|---|
| Orrington, Me., U.S. | D4 | 96 |
| Orr Lake, l., Man. | A3 | 70 |
| Orrs Island, Me., U.S. | E3 | 96 |
| Orrstown, Pa., U.S. | F6 | 115 |
| Orrum, N.C., U.S. | C4 | 110 |
| Orrville, Ont. | B5 | 73 |
| Orrville, Al., U.S. | C2 | 78 |
| Orrville, Oh., U.S. | B4 | 112 |
| Orsa, Swe. | G6 | 14 |
| Orsay, Fr. | F2 | 17 |
| Orsha, Sov. Un. | D8 | 27 |
| Orsières, Switz. | C3 | 20 |
| Orsk, Sov. Un. | D8 | 29 |
| Orson, Pa., U.S. | C11 | 115 |
| Orşova, Rom. | C6 | 24 |
| Ørsted, Den. | B4 | 15 |
| Örsundsbro, Swe. | t35 | 14 |
| Orta, Lake, l., Italy | D4 | 20 |
| Ortaca, Tur. | D7 | 25 |
| Orta [San Giulio], Italy | E5 | 21 |
| Ortegal, Cape, c., Spain | A2 | 22 |
| Orthez, Fr. | F3 | 16 |
| Ortigueira, Spain | A2 | 22 |
| Orting, Wa., U.S. | B3 | 124 |
| Ortisei, Italy | C7 | 20 |
| Ortiz, Mex. | B2 | 63 |
| Ortiz, Co., U.S. | D4 | 83 |
| Ortiz Mountain, mtn., N.M., U.S. | k8 | 108 |
| Ortley, S.D., U.S. | B8 | 118 |
| Ortoire, stm., Trin. | O23 | 65 |
| Ortona, Italy | C5 | 23 |
| Ortonville, Mi., U.S. | F7 | 99 |
| Ortonville, Mn., U.S. | E2 | 100 |
| Orümïyeh (Urmia), Iran | B4 | 38 |
| Oruro, Bol. | C2 | 55 |
| Oruro, dept., Bol. | C2 | 55 |
| Orvieto, Italy | C4 | 23 |
| Orviston, Pa., U.S. | D6 | 115 |
| Orwell, N.Y., U.S. | B4 | 109 |
| Orwell, Oh., U.S. | A5 | 112 |
| Orwell, Vt., U.S. | D2 | 122 |
| Orwigsburg, Pa., U.S. | E9 | 115 |
| Or Yehuda, Isr. | g10 | 41 |
| Orysa, Tn., U.S. | B2 | 119 |
| Orzesze, Pol. | g9 | 26 |
| Osa, Peninsula de, pen., C.R. | F6 | 62 |
| Osage, Sask. | H4 | 75 |
| Osage, Ia., U.S. | A5 | 92 |
| Osage, Mn., U.S. | D3 | 100 |
| Osage, Ok., U.S. | A5 | 113 |
| Osage, Wy., U.S. | C8 | 127 |
| Osage, co., Ks., U.S. | D8 | 93 |
| Osage, co., Mo., U.S. | C6 | 102 |
| Osage, co., Ok., U.S. | A5 | 113 |
| Osage, stm., Mo., U.S. | C3 | 102 |
| Osage Beach, Mo., U.S. | C5 | 102 |
| Osage City, Ks., U.S. | D8 | 93 |
| Osage Creek, stm., Ar., U.S. | A2 | 81 |
| Ōsaka, Japan | E12 | 31 |
| Osaka, Japan | n16 | 33 |
| Ōsaka Bay, b., Japan | o14 | 33 |
| Osaka Mountain, hill, Japan | P17 | 52 |
| Osakis, Mn., U.S. | E3 | 100 |
| Osakis, Lake, l., Mn., U.S. | E3 | 100 |
| Osawatomie, Ks., U.S. | D9 | 93 |
| Osborn, Mo., U.S. | B3 | 102 |
| Osborne, Ks., U.S. | C5 | 93 |
| Osborne, co., Ks., U.S. | C5 | 93 |
| Osbornsville, N.J., U.S. | C4 | 107 |
| Osburn, Id., U.S. | B3 | 89 |
| Osby, Swe. | B8 | 15 |
| Oscar, La., U.S. | D4 | 95 |
| Oscar, Ok., U.S. | D4 | 113 |
| Osceola, Ar., U.S. | B6 | 81 |
| Osceola, In., U.S. | A5 | 91 |
| Osceola, Mo., U.S. | C4 | 102 |
| Osceola, Ne., U.S. | C8 | 104 |
| Osceola, Pa., U.S. | C7 | 115 |
| Osceola, S.D., U.S. | C8 | 118 |
| Osceola, Tx., U.S. | C4 | 120 |
| Osceola, Wi., U.S. | C1 | 126 |
| Osceola, co., Fl., U.S. | E5 | 86 |
| Osceola, co., Ia., U.S. | A2 | 92 |
| Osceola, co., Mi., U.S. | E5 | 99 |
| Osceola Mills, Pa., U.S. | E5 | 115 |
| Oschatz, E. Ger. | C6 | 18 |
| Oschersleben, E. Ger. | B5 | 18 |
| Oscoda, Mi., U.S. | D7 | 99 |
| Oscoda, co., Mi., U.S. | D6 | 99 |
| Oscura Mountains, mts., N.M., U.S. | D3 | 108 |
| Osek, Czech. | C8 | 19 |
| Oselki, Sov. Un. | r31 | 14 |
| Osgood, In., U.S. | F7 | 91 |
| Osgood, Mo., U.S. | A4 | 102 |
| Osgood, Oh., U.S. | B1 | 112 |
| Osgoode, Ont. | B9 | 73 |
| Osh, Sov. Un. | E10 | 29 |
| Oshamambe, Japan | E10 | 31 |
| Oshawa, Ont. | D6 | 73 |
| Ōshima, i., Japan | J7 | 33 |
| Oshkosh, Ne., U.S. | C3 | 104 |
| Oshkosh, Wi., U.S. | D5 | 126 |
| Oshnovïyeh, Iran | C2 | 39 |
| Oshogbo, Nig. | E5 | 45 |
| Oshoto, Wy., U.S. | B8 | 127 |
| Oshtorān Kūh, mtn., Iran | E4 | 39 |
| Oshwe, Zaire | B2 | 48 |
| Osijek, Yugo. | C4 | 24 |
| Osilinka, stm., B.C. | A5 | 69 |
| Osinniki, Sov. Un. | E26 | 8 |
| Osipovichi, Sov. Un. | E7 | 27 |
| Oskaloosa, Ia., U.S. | C5 | 92 |
| Oskaloosa, Ks., U.S. | C8 | 93 |
| Oskaloosa, Mo., U.S. | D3 | 102 |
| Oskarshamn, Swe. | I7 | 14 |
| Oskol, Sov. Un. | G11 | 27 |
| Oskū, Iran | C2 | 39 |
| Osler, Sask. | E2 | 75 |
| Oslo, Nor. | H4 | 14 |
| Oslo, Mn., U.S. | B1 | 100 |
| Oslofjorden, Nor. | H4 | 14 |
| Osma, Spain | B4 | 22 |
| Osmānābād, India | H6 | 37 |
| Osmancik, Tur. | B10 | 40 |
| Osmaneli, Tur. | J14 | 25 |
| Osmaniye, Tur. | D11 | 40 |
| Osmond, Ne., U.S. | B8 | 104 |
| Osnabrock, N.D., U.S. | A7 | 111 |
| Osnabrück, W. Ger. | B4 | 18 |
| Osório, Braz. | D2 | 56 |
| Osorno, Chile | D2 | 56 |
| Osov, Czech. | o17 | 26 |
| Osoyoos, B.C. | E8 | 69 |
| Osoyoos Lake, l., Wa., U.S. | A6 | 124 |
| Ospika, stm., B.C. | A6 | 69 |
| Osprey, stm., B.C. | E4 | 86 |
| Oss, Neth. | B6 | 16 |
| Ossa, Mount, mtn., Austl. | o15 | 50 |
| Ossabaw Island, i., Ga., U.S. | E5 | 87 |
| Ossabaw Sound, strt., Ga., U.S. | E6 | 87 |
| Osseo, Mn., U.S. | m12 | 100 |
| Osseo, Wi., U.S. | D2 | 126 |
| Ossian, In., U.S. | C7 | 91 |
| Ossian, Ia., U.S. | A6 | 92 |
| Ossineke, Mi., U.S. | D7 | 99 |
| Ossining, N.Y., U.S. | D7 | 109 |
| Ossipee, N.H., U.S. | C4 | 106 |
| Ossipee, stm., U.S. | C5 | 106 |
| Ossipee Lake, l., N.H., U.S. | C4 | 106 |
| Ossipee Mountains, mts., N.H., U.S. | C4 | 106 |
| Ossokmanuan Lake, l., Newf. | h8 | 72 |
| Ossora, Sov. Un. | D34 | 128 |
| Östanå, Swe. | t36 | 14 |
| Osteen, Fl., U.S. | D5 | 86 |
| Ostende see Oostende, Bel. | B5 | 16 |
| Osterburg, E. Ger. | F5 | 15 |
| Osterburg, Pa., U.S. | F4 | 115 |
| Osterode, W. Ger. | B5 | 19 |
| Östersund, Swe. | F6 | 14 |
| Osterville, Ma., U.S. | C7 | 98 |
| Osterwieck, E. Ger. | B5 | 19 |
| Ostia Antica, Italy | h8 | 23 |
| Ostiglia, Italy | D7 | 20 |
| Ostrach, W. Ger. | B5 | 20 |
| Ostrander, Mn., U.S. | G6 | 100 |
| Ostrander, Oh., U.S. | B2 | 112 |
| Ostrava, Czech. | D5 | 26 |
| Ostróda, Pol. | B5 | 26 |
| Ostrog, Sov. Un. | F6 | 27 |
| Ostrogozhsk, Sov. Un. | F12 | 27 |
| Ostrołęka, Pol. | B6 | 26 |
| Ostrov, Czech. | C2 | 26 |
| Ostrov, Rom. | C8 | 24 |
| Ostrov, Sov. Un. | C7 | 27 |
| Ostrowiec 95Świętokrzyski], Pol. | C6 | 26 |
| Ostrów Lubelski, Pol. | C7 | 26 |
| Ostrów Mazowiecka, Pol. | B6 | 26 |
| Ostrów Wielkopolski, Pol. | C4 | 26 |
| Ostrzeszów, Pol. | C4 | 26 |
| Ostseebad Graal-Müritz, E. Ger. | D6 | 15 |
| Ostseebad Rerik, E. Ger. | D5 | 15 |
| Ostuni, Italy | D6 | 23 |
| Ōsuka, Japan | o16 | 33 |
| Osŭm, stm., Bul. | D7 | 24 |
| Osumi, stm., Alb. | B3 | 25 |
| Ōsumi Islands, is., Japan | E11 | 31 |
| Ōsumi Strait, strt., Japan | K5 | 33 |
| Osuna, Spain | D3 | 22 |
| Osvaldo Cruz, Braz. | C2 | 56 |
| Oswayo, Pa., U.S. | C5 | 115 |
| Oswegatchie, Ct., U.S. | *D7 | 84 |
| Oswegatchie, N.Y., U.S. | A5 | 109 |
| Oswegatchie, stm., N.Y., U.S. | f9 | 109 |
| Oswego, Il., U.S. | B5 | 90 |
| Oswego, Ks., U.S. | E8 | 93 |
| Oswego, Mt., U.S. | B11 | 103 |
| Oswego, N.Y., U.S. | B4 | 109 |
| Oswego, S.C., U.S. | C7 | 117 |
| Oswego, co., N.Y., U.S. | B4 | 109 |
| Oswego, stm., N.J., U.S. | D4 | 107 |
| Oswego, stm., N.Y., U.S. | B4 | 109 |
| Oświęcim (Auschwitz), Pol. | C5 | 26 |
| Osyka, Ms., U.S. | D3 | 101 |
| Ōta, Japan | *H9 | 33 |
| Otago Peninsula, pen., N.Z. | P13 | 51 |
| Ōtaki, Japan | n19 | 33 |
| Otar, Sov. Un. | E9 | 28 |
| Otaru, Japan | C13 | 31 |
| Otava, stm., Czech. | D8 | 19 |
| Otavalo, Ec. | A2 | 58 |
| Otavi, Nmb. | A2 | 49 |
| Otay, Ca., U.S. | *o15 | 82 |
| Otchinjau, Ang. | E1 | 48 |
| Oteen, N.C., U.S. | f10 | 110 |
| Otego, N.Y., U.S. | C5 | 109 |
| Otero, co., Co., U.S. | D7 | 83 |
| Otero, co., N.M., U.S. | E3 | 108 |
| Othello, Wa., U.S. | C6 | 124 |
| Otho, Ia., U.S. | B3 | 92 |
| Othonoí, i., Grc. | C2 | 25 |
| Oti, stm., Afr. | E5 | 45 |
| Otis, Co., U.S. | A8 | 83 |
| Otis, In., U.S. | A4 | 91 |
| Otis, Ks., U.S. | D4 | 93 |
| Otis, Ma., U.S. | B1 | 98 |
| Otisco, In., U.S. | G6 | 91 |
| Otisco, Mn., U.S. | G5 | 100 |
| Otisco, N.Y., U.S. | C4 | 109 |
| Otis Orchards, Wa., U.S. | g14 | 124 |
| Otis Reservoir, res., Ma., U.S. | B1 | 98 |
| Otisville, Mi., U.S. | E7 | 99 |
| Otjiwarongo, Nmb. | B2 | 49 |
| Otley, Ia., U.S. | C4 | 92 |
| Oto, Ia., U.S. | B2 | 92 |
| Otočac, Yugo. | C2 | 24 |
| Otoe, Ne., U.S. | D9 | 104 |
| Otoe, co., Ne., U.S. | D9 | 104 |
| Otra, stm., Nor. | H2 | 14 |
| Otradnoye, Sov. Un. | s31 | 14 |
| Otranto, Italy | D7 | 23 |
| Otranto, Strait of, strt., Eur. | B2 | 40 |
| Otsego, Mi., U.S. | F5 | 99 |
| Otsego, co., Mi., U.S. | C6 | 99 |
| Otsego, co., N.Y., U.S. | C5 | 109 |
| Otsego Lake, l., Mi., U.S. | D6 | 99 |
| Otsego Lake, l., N.Y., U.S. | C6 | 109 |
| Ōtsu, Japan | o14 | 33 |
| Ōtsuki, Japan | n17 | 33 |
| Ottawa, Ont. | B9 | 73 |
| Ottawa, Il., U.S. | B5 | 90 |
| Ottawa, Ks., U.S. | D8 | 93 |
| Ottawa, Oh., U.S. | B1 | 112 |
| Ottawa, W.V., U.S. | n12 | 125 |
| Ottawa, co., Ks., U.S. | C6 | 93 |
| Ottawa, co., Mi., U.S. | F4 | 99 |
| Ottawa, co., Oh., U.S. | A7 | 113 |
| Ottawa, co., Ok., U.S. | A7 | 113 |
| Ottawa, stm., Can. | G17 | 66 |
| Ottawa, stm., Oh., U.S. | e6 | 112 |
| Ottawa-Carleton, co., Ont. | B9 | 73 |
| Ottawa Hills, Mi., U.S. | e6 | 112 |
| Ottawa Islands, is., N.W. Ter. | E16 | 66 |
| Ottawa Lake, Mi., U.S. | G7 | 99 |
| Otter, Mt., U.S. | E10 | 103 |
| Otter, stm., Alta. | A2 | 68 |
| Otter, stm., Eng., U.K. | D4 | 12 |
| Otterbein, In., U.S. | D3 | 91 |
| Otterberg, W. Ger. | D2 | 19 |
| Otter Brook, stm., N.H., U.S. | E2 | 106 |
| Otter Brook Lake, res., N.H., U.S. | E2 | 106 |
| Otter Creek, Fl., U.S. | C4 | 86 |
| Otter Creek, Me., U.S. | D4 | 96 |
| Otter Creek, stm., Vt., U.S. | C2 | 122 |
| Otter Creek Reservoir, res., Ut., U.S. | E4 | 121 |
| Otter Islands, is., S.C., U.S. | m11 | 117 |
| Otter Lake, Mi., U.S. | E7 | 99 |
| Otter Lake, N.Y., U.S. | B5 | 109 |
| Otter Lake, l., Sask. | B3 | 75 |
| Otterndorf, W. Ger. | E2 | 15 |
| Otter River, stm., U.S. | A3 | 98 |
| Ottersberg, W. Ger. | E3 | 15 |
| Ottersleben, E. Ger. | A6 | 19 |
| Otter Tail, co., Mn., U.S. | D3 | 100 |
| Otter Tail, stm., Mn., U.S. | D2 | 100 |
| Otter Tail Lake, l., Mn., U.S. | D3 | 100 |
| Otterup, Den. | C4 | 15 |
| Otterville, Ont. | E4 | 73 |
| Otterville, Il., U.S. | D3 | 90 |
| Otterville, Ia., U.S. | B6 | 92 |
| Otterville, Mo., U.S. | C4 | 102 |
| Otthon, Sask. | F4 | 75 |
| Ottignies, Bel. | D4 | 17 |
| Otto, Ky., U.S. | B4 | 127 |
| Ottokee, Oh., U.S. | A1 | 112 |
| Ottone, Italy | E5 | 20 |
| Ottosen, Ia., U.S. | B3 | 92 |
| Ottoville, Oh., U.S. | B1 | 112 |
| Ottsville, Pa., U.S. | F11 | 115 |
| Ottumwa, Ia., U.S. | C5 | 92 |
| Ottumwa, S.D., U.S. | C4 | 118 |
| Otuzco, Peru | B2 | 58 |
| Otway, N.C., U.S. | C6 | 110 |
| Otway, Cape, c., Austl. | G7 | 50 |
| Otway, Seno, b., Chile | h11 | 54 |
| Otwell, In., U.S. | H3 | 91 |
| Otwell, In., U.S. | H3 | 91 |
| Otwock, Pol. | m14 | 26 |
| Ötztal Alps, mts., Eur. | C6 | 20 |
| Ötztaler Ach, stm., Aus. | B6 | 20 |
| Ou, stm., Laos | B5 | 35 |
| Ouachita, co., Ar., U.S. | D3 | 81 |
| Ouachita, co., La., U.S. | B3 | 95 |
| Ouachita, stm., U.S. | D9 | 76 |
| Ouachita, Lake, res., Ar., U.S. | C2 | 81 |
| Ouachita Mountains, mts., U.S. | D9 | 76 |
| Ouadane, Maur. | B2 | 45 |
| Ouaddaï, hist. reg., Chad | C4 | 46 |
| Ouagadougou, Burkina | D4 | 45 |
| Ouahigouya, Burkina | D4 | 45 |
| Ouaka, stm., Cen. Afr. Rep. | D4 | 46 |
| Oualâta, Maur. | C3 | 45 |
| Oualam, Niger | D5 | 45 |
| Oualleme, Alg. | D5 | 45 |
| Ouanary, Fr. Gu. | B4 | 59 |
| Ouanda Djallé, Cen. Afr. Rep. | D4 | 46 |
| Ouarane, reg., Maur. | C3 | 45 |
| Ouarzazate, Mor. | A2 | 44 |
| Oubangui (Ubangi), stm., Afr. | A2 | 48 |
| Ouddorp, Neth. | C3 | 17 |
| Oudenaarde, Bel. | D3 | 17 |
| Oude-Pekela, Neth. | A7 | 17 |
| Oudtshoorn, S. Afr. | D3 | 49 |
| Oued Zem, Mor. | *C3 | 44 |
| Ouellé, I.C. | E4 | 45 |
| Ouelle, stm., Que. | B8 | 74 |
| Ouémé, stm., Benin | E5 | 45 |
| Ouesso, Congo | A2 | 48 |
| Ouest, Pointe de l', Que. | k8 | 72 |
| Ouest, Pointe du, St. P./M. | E3 | 72 |
| Ouezzane, Mor. | A3 | 44 |
| Oughter, Lough, l., Ire. | D3 | 10 |
| Oughterard, Ire. | D2 | 11 |
| Ouham, stm., Afr. | D3 | 46 |
| Ouidah, Benin | E5 | 45 |
| Oujda, Mor. | A4 | 44 |
| Oulins, Fr. | E6 | 16 |
| Oulu, Fin. | E11 | 14 |
| Oulujärvi, l., Fin. | E12 | 14 |
| Oum Chalouba, Chad | B4 | 46 |
| Oum Hadjer, Chad | C3 | 46 |
| Ounâne, stm., Mali | B4 | 45 |
| Ounasjoki, stm., Fin. | D11 | 14 |
| Ounianga Kébir, Chad | B4 | 46 |
| Ouray, Co., U.S. | C3 | 83 |
| Ouray, Ut., U.S. | C6 | 121 |
| Ouray, co., Co., U.S. | C3 | 83 |
| Ouray, Mount, mtn., Co., U.S. | C5 | 83 |
| Ouri, Chad | A3 | 46 |
| Ouricuri, Braz. | C5 | 56 |
| Ourinhos, Braz. | C3 | 56 |
| Ourique, Port. | D1 | 22 |
| Ouro Fino, Braz. | C5 | 56 |
| Ouro Prêto, Braz. | C5 | 56 |
| Ourthe, stm., Bel. | D5 | 17 |
| Ouse, stm., Eng., U.K. | D6 | 10 |
| Outagamie, co., Wi., U.S. | D5 | 126 |
| Outardes Quatre, Réservoir, res., Que. | h13 | 74 |
| Outer Hebrides, is., Scot., U.K. | B3 | 10 |
| Outer Island, i., Wi., U.S. | A3 | 126 |
| Outer Santa Barbara Passage, strt., Ca., U.S. | F4 | 82 |
| Outes, Spain | A1 | 22 |
| Outing, Mn., U.S. | D5 | 100 |
| Outjo, Nmb. | B2 | 49 |
| Outlook, Sask. | F2 | 75 |
| Outlook, Mt., U.S. | B12 | 103 |
| Outlook, Wa., U.S. | C5 | 124 |
| Outpost Mountain, mtn., Ak., U.S. | B9 | 79 |
| Outreau, Fr. | B4 | 16 |
| Outremont, Que. | p19 | 74 |
| Ouville-la-Rivière, Fr. | E8 | 12 |
| Ouzinkie, Ak., U.S. | D9 | 79 |
| Ovada, Italy | B2 | 23 |
| Oval, Pa., U.S. | D7 | 115 |
| Ovalau, i., Fiji | H15 | 52 |
| Ovalle, Chile | A2 | 54 |
| Ovana, Cerro, mtn., Ven. | C4 | 60 |
| Ovando, Mt., U.S. | C3 | 103 |
| Ovar, Port. | B1 | 22 |
| Overath, W. Ger. | C2 | 19 |
| Overbrook, Ks., U.S. | D8 | 93 |
| Overbrook, Ok., U.S. | C4 | 113 |
| Overflowing, stm., Can. | C5 | 80 |
| Overgaard, Az., U.S. | C5 | 80 |
| Overijse, Bel. | D4 | 17 |
| Overijssel, prov., Neth. | B6 | 17 |
| Overisel, Mi., U.S. | F4 | 99 |
| Overland, Mo., U.S. | f13 | 102 |
| Overland Park, Ks., U.S. | m16 | 93 |
| Overlea, Md., U.S. | B5 | 97 |
| Overlook, Oh., U.S. | *C1 | 112 |
| Overly, N.D., U.S. | A5 | 111 |
| Overstreet, Fl., U.S. | B1 | 86 |
| Overton, Nv., U.S. | G7 | 105 |
| Overton, Tx., U.S. | C5 | 120 |
| Overton, co., Tn., U.S. | C8 | 119 |
| Overtorneå, Swe. | D10 | 14 |
| Ovett, Ms., U.S. | D4 | 101 |
| Ovid, Co., U.S. | A8 | 83 |
| Ovid, Id., U.S. | G7 | 89 |
| Ovid, Mi., U.S. | E6 | 99 |
| Ovid, N.Y., U.S. | C4 | 109 |
| Oviedo, Spain | A3 | 22 |
| Ovruch, Sov. Un. | F7 | 27 |
| Owando, Congo | B2 | 48 |
| Owaneco, Il., U.S. | D4 | 90 |
| Owanka, S.D., U.S. | C3 | 118 |
| Owasco Lake, l., N.Y., U.S. | C4 | 109 |
| Owasso, Ok., U.S. | A6 | 113 |
| Owatonna, Mn., U.S. | F5 | 100 |
| Owbeh, Afg. | D11 | 39 |
| Owego, N.Y., U.S. | C4 | 109 |
| Owen, Wi., U.S. | D3 | 126 |
| Owen, co., In., U.S. | F4 | 91 |
| Owen, co., Ky., U.S. | B5 | 94 |
| Owen, Lake, l., Wi., U.S. | B2 | 126 |
| Owen, Mount, mtn., N.Z. | N14 | 51 |
| Owen, Mount, mtn., Co., U.S. | C3 | 83 |
| Owendale, Mi., U.S. | E7 | 99 |
| Owens, stm., Ca., U.S. | D4 | 82 |
| Owensboro, Ky., U.S. | C2 | 94 |
| Owensburg, In., U.S. | G4 | 91 |
| Owens Creek, stm., Md., U.S. | A3 | 97 |
| Owens Cross Roads, Al., U.S. | A3 | 78 |
| Owens Lake, l., Ca., U.S. | D5 | 82 |
| Owen Sound, Ont. | C4 | 73 |
| Owen Sound, b., Ont. | C4 | 73 |
| Owen Stanley Range, mts., Pap. N. Gui. | k12 | 50 |
| Owensville, Ar., U.S. | C3 | 81 |
| Owensville, In., U.S. | H2 | 91 |
| Owensville, Mo., U.S. | C6 | 102 |
| Owensville, Oh., U.S. | C1 | 112 |
| Owenton, Ky., U.S. | B5 | 94 |
| Owerri, Nig. | E6 | 45 |
| Owey Island, i., Ire. | B3 | 11 |
| Owings, Md., U.S. | C4 | 97 |
| Owings Mills, Md., U.S. | B4 | 97 |
| Owingsville, Ky., U.S. | B6 | 94 |
| Owl Creek, stm., Wy., U.S. | C4 | 127 |
| Owl Creek Mountains, mts., Wy., U.S. | C4 | 127 |
| Owls Head, Me., U.S. | D3 | 96 |
| Owo, Nig. | E6 | 45 |
| Owosso, Mi., U.S. | E6 | 99 |
| Owsley, co., Ky., U.S. | C6 | 94 |
| Owyhee, Nv., U.S. | B5 | 105 |
| Owyhee, co., Id., U.S. | G2 | 89 |
| Owyhee, stm., U.S. | E9 | 114 |
| Owyhee, Lake, res., Or., U.S. | D9 | 114 |
| Owyhee, North Fork, stm., U.S. | E9 | 114 |
| Owyhee, South Fork, stm., U.S. | G2 | 89 |
| Owyhee Dam, Or., U.S. | D9 | 114 |
| Owyhee Mountains, mts., U.S. | G2 | 89 |
| Oxbow, Sask. | H4 | 75 |
| Oxbow, Me., U.S. | B4 | 96 |
| Oxbow, Or., U.S. | B10 | 114 |
| Oxbow Dam, U.S. | E2 | 89 |
| Oxelösund, Swe. | u35 | 14 |
| Oxford, N.S. | D6 | 71 |
| Oxford, Eng., U.K. | E6 | 10 |
| Oxford, Al., U.S. | B4 | 78 |
| Oxford, Ct., U.S. | D3 | 84 |
| Oxford, Fl., U.S. | D4 | 86 |
| Oxford, Ga., U.S. | C3 | 87 |
| Oxford, Id., U.S. | G6 | 89 |
| Oxford, In., U.S. | C3 | 91 |
| Oxford, Ks., U.S. | E6 | 93 |
| Oxford, La., U.S. | C2 | 95 |
| Oxford, Ma., U.S. | B4 | 98 |
| Oxford, Md., U.S. | C5 | 97 |
| Oxford, Ms., U.S. | A4 | 101 |
| Oxford, Ne., U.S. | D6 | 104 |
| Oxford, N.J., U.S. | B3 | 107 |
| Oxford, N.Y., U.S. | C5 | 109 |
| Oxford, N.C., U.S. | A4 | 110 |
| Oxford, Oh., U.S. | C1 | 112 |
| Oxford, Pa., U.S. | G10 | 115 |
| Oxford, co., Me., U.S. | D2 | 96 |
| Oxford, co., Ont. | D4 | 73 |
| Oxford House, Man. | B4 | 70 |
| Oxford Junction, N.S. | D6 | 71 |
| Oxford Junction, Ia., U.S. | C7 | 92 |
| Oxford Lake, l., Man. | B4 | 70 |
| Oxford Peak, mtn., Id., U.S. | G6 | 89 |
| Oxfordshire, co., Eng., U.K. | C5 | 12 |
| Oxly, Mo., U.S. | E7 | 102 |
| Oxnard, Ca., U.S. | E4 | 82 |
| Oxon Hill, Md., U.S. | f9 | 97 |
| Oyace, Italy | E3 | 21 |
| Oyama, B.C. | D8 | 69 |
| Oyama, Japan | m18 | 33 |
| Oyapock (Oiapoque), stm., S.A. | C4 | 57 |
| Oyat, stm., Sov. Un. | A10 | 27 |
| Oyem, Gabon | A2 | 48 |
| Oyen, Alta. | D5 | 68 |
| Oyens, Ia., U.S. | B1 | 92 |
| Oyeren, l., Nor. | p29 | 14 |
| Oykel, stm., Scot., U.K. | C4 | 13 |
| Oykel Bridge, Scot., U.K. | C4 | 13 |
| Oymyakon, Sov. Un. | C17 | 29 |
| Oyo, Nig. | E5 | 45 |
| Oyonnax, Fr. | F7 | 16 |
| Oyster Bay, N.Y., U.S. | E7 | 109 |
| Oyster Keys, is., Fl., U.S. | G6 | 86 |
| Oyster Ridge, mtn., Wy., U.S. | E2 | 127 |
| Ozamiz, Phil. | D7 | 34 |
| Ozan, Ar., U.S. | D2 | 81 |
| Ozark, Al., U.S. | D4 | 78 |
| Ozark, Ar., U.S. | B2 | 81 |
| Ozark, Mo., U.S. | D4 | 102 |
| Ozark, co., Mo., U.S. | E5 | 102 |
| Ozark Escarpment, clf., U.S. | B4 | 81 |
| Ozark Plateau, plat., U.S. | C9 | 76 |
| Ozark Reservoir, res., Ar., U.S. | B1 | 81 |
| Ozarks, Lake of the, res., Mo., U.S. | C5 | 102 |
| Ożarowice, Pol. | g10 | 26 |
| Ozaukee, co., Wi., U.S. | E6 | 126 |
| Ozawkie, Ks., U.S. | k15 | 93 |
| Ōzd, Hung. | A5 | 24 |
| Ozernyy, Sov. Un. | C6 | 28 |
| Ozette Lake, l., Wa., U.S. | A1 | 124 |
| Ozieri, Italy | D2 | 23 |
| Ozona, Fl., U.S. | o10 | 86 |
| Ozona, Tx., U.S. | D2 | 120 |
| Ozone, Ar., U.S. | B2 | 81 |
| Ozorków, Pol. | C5 | 26 |
| Ōzu, Japan | J6 | 33 |
| Ozuluama, Mex. | C5 | 63 |
| **P** | | |
| Paar, stm., W. Ger. | E6 | 19 |
| Paarl, S. Afr. | D2 | 49 |
| Paauhau, Hi., U.S. | C6 | 88 |
| Paauilo, Hi., U.S. | C6 | 88 |
| Pabbay, i., Scot., U.K. | C1 | 13 |
| Pabellón, Punta, c., Chile | C2 | 54 |
| Pabianice, Pol. | C5 | 26 |
| Pablo, Mt., U.S. | C2 | 103 |
| Pābna, Bngl. | D8 | 36 |
| Pacaás Novos, Serra dos, mts., Braz. | C4 | 59 |
| Pacajá, stm., Braz. | C4 | 59 |
| Pacasmayo, Peru | C2 | 58 |
| Pace, Fl., U.S. | u14 | 86 |
| Pace, Ms., U.S. | B3 | 101 |
| Pachaug Pond, l., Ct., U.S. | C8 | 84 |
| Pachmarhi, India | F7 | 37 |
| Pachuca [de Soto], Mex. | C5 | 63 |
| Pachuta, Ms., U.S. | C5 | 101 |
| Pacific, B.C. | B3 | 69 |
| Pacific, Mo., U.S. | C7 | 102 |
| Pacific, Wa., U.S. | f11 | 124 |
| Pacific, co., Wa., U.S. | C2 | 124 |
| Pacifica, Ca., U.S. | h8 | 82 |
| Pacific Beach, Wa., U.S. | B1 | 124 |
| Pacific City, Or., U.S. | C3 | 114 |
| Pacific Creek, stm., Wy., U.S. | D3 | 127 |
| Pacific Grove, Ca., U.S. | D3 | 82 |
| Pacific Islands, Trust Territory of the, dep., Oc. | F9 | 6 |
| Pacific Junction, Ia., U.S. | C2 | 92 |
| Pacific Ocean | E11 | 6 |
| Pacific Palisades, Hi., U.S. | g10 | 88 |
| Pacific Ranges, mts., B.C. | D4 | 69 |
| Pacific Rim National Park, B.C. | E5 | 69 |
| Packard Mountain, hill, Ma., U.S. | B3 | 98 |
| Pack Monadnock Mountain, mtn., N.H., U.S. | E3 | 106 |
| Packwaukee, Wi., U.S. | E4 | 126 |
| Packwood, Ia., U.S. | C5 | 92 |
| Packwood, Wa., U.S. | C4 | 124 |
| Pacolet, S.C., U.S. | B4 | 117 |
| Pacolet, stm., S.C., U.S. | A4 | 117 |
| Pacolet Mills, S.C., U.S. | B4 | 117 |
| Pacora, Pan. | k12 | 62 |
| Pacora, stm., Pan. | k12 | 62 |
| Pacov, Czech. | D9 | 19 |
| Pacquet, Newf. | D4 | 72 |
| Pactola Reservoir, res., S.D., U.S. | C2 | 118 |
| Pactolus, N.C., U.S. | B5 | 110 |
| Paczków, Pol. | C4 | 26 |
| Padang, Indon. | F2 | 34 |
| Padang, i., Indon. | L5 | 35 |
| Padang Endau, Malay. | K5 | 35 |
| Padangpanjang, Indon. | F2 | 34 |
| Padangsidempuan, Indon. | E1 | 34 |
| Padauiri, stm., Braz. | B3 | 59 |
| Paddle Prairie, Alta. | f7 | 68 |
| Paddling Lake, l., Sask. | E2 | 75 |
| Paddock Lake, Wi., U.S. | n11 | 126 |
| Paddockwood, Sask. | D3 | 75 |
| Paddy Knob, mtn., U.S. | C5 | 125 |
| Paden, Ms., U.S. | A5 | 101 |
| Paden, Ok., U.S. | B5 | 113 |
| Paderborn, W. Ger. | C4 | 18 |
| Padilla, Bol. | C3 | 55 |
| Padova (Padua), Italy | B3 | 23 |
| Padre Island, i., Tx., U.S. | F4 | 120 |
| Padre Island National Seashore, Tx., U.S. | F4 | 120 |
| Padroni, Co., U.S. | A7 | 83 |
| Padstow, Eng., U.K. | D3 | 12 |
| Paducah, Ky., U.S. | e9 | 94 |
| Paducah, Tx., U.S. | B2 | 120 |
| Paektu, Mount, mtn., Asia | F4 | 33 |
| Paepaeolei'a, Cape, c., W. Sam. | F11 | 52 |
| Paeroa, N.Z. | L15 | 51 |
| Paestum, hist., Italy | D5 | 23 |
| Pafúri, Moz. | B5 | 49 |
| Pag, i., Yugo. | C2 | 24 |
| Pagai Selatan, i., Indon. | F2 | 34 |
| Pagai Utara, i., Indon. | F2 | 34 |
| Pagasitikós Kólpos (Gulf of Vólos), g., Grc. | C4 | 40 |
| Pagatan, Indon. | F5 | 34 |
| Pagato, stm., Sask. | A4 | 75 |
| Pagat Point, c., Guam | L10 | 52 |
| Page, Az., U.S. | A4 | 80 |
| Page, Ne., U.S. | B7 | 104 |
| Page, N.D., U.S. | B8 | 111 |
| Page, Ok., U.S. | C7 | 113 |
| Page, W.V., U.S. | D3 | 125 |
| Page, co., Ia., U.S. | D2 | 92 |
| Page, co., Va., U.S. | B4 | 123 |
| Pageland, S.C., U.S. | B7 | 117 |
| Page Manor, Oh., U.S. | *C1 | 112 |
| Paglia, stm., Italy | C5 | 23 |
| Pagny [-sur-Moselle], Fr. | F5 | 17 |
| Pago Bay, b., Guam | M10 | 52 |
| Pago Pago, Am. Sam. | G13 | 52 |
| Pago Pago Harbor, b., Am. Sam. | F13 | 52 |
| Pago Point, c., Guam | M10 | 52 |
| Pagosa Springs, Co., U.S. | D3 | 83 |
| Paguate, N.M., U.S. | B2 | 108 |
| Pahala, Hi., U.S. | D6 | 88 |
| Pahang, state, Malay. | K5 | 35 |
| Pahang, stm., Malay. | E2 | 34 |
| Pahaska, Wy., U.S. | B3 | 127 |
| Pahoa, Hi., U.S. | D7 | 88 |
| Pahokee, Fl., U.S. | F6 | 86 |
| Pahrump, Nv., U.S. | G6 | 105 |
| Pahute Mesa, mtn., Nv., U.S. | F5 | 105 |
| Paia, Hi., U.S. | C5 | 88 |
| Paignton, Eng., U.K. | D4 | 12 |
| Päijänne, l., Fin. | G11 | 14 |
| Pailo, Tn., U.S. | D8 | 119 |
| Pailolo Channel, strt., Hi., U.S. | B5 | 88 |
| Paincourt, Ont. | E2 | 73 |
| Paincourtville, La., U.S. | k9 | 95 |
| Painesdale, Mi., U.S. | B2 | 99 |
| Painesville, Oh., U.S. | A4 | 112 |
| Paint, stm., Mi., U.S. | B2 | 99 |
| Paint Bank, Va., U.S. | C2 | 123 |
| Paint Creek, stm., Oh., U.S. | C2 | 112 |
| Paint Creek, North Fork, stm., Oh., U.S. | m13 | 112 |
| Paint Creek Lake, res., Oh., U.S. | C2 | 112 |
| Painted Desert, des., Az., U.S. | B4 | 80 |
| Painted Post, N.Y., U.S. | C3 | 109 |
| Painted Rock Reservoir, res., Az., U.S. | D3 | 80 |
| Painter, Va., U.S. | C7 | 123 |
| Paint Lake, l., Man. | B3 | 70 |
| Paint Lick, Ky., U.S. | C5 | 94 |
| Paint Mountain, mtn., W.V., U.S. | n13 | 125 |
| Paint Rock, Al., U.S. | A3 | 78 |
| Paint Rock, Tx., U.S. | D3 | 120 |
| Paintsville, Ky., U.S. | C7 | 94 |
| Paisley, Ont. | C3 | 73 |
| Paisley, Scot., U.K. | C4 | 10 |
| Paisley, Fl., U.S. | D5 | 86 |
| Paisley, Or., U.S. | E6 | 114 |
| Paita, Peru | C1 | 58 |
| Pajala, Swe. | D10 | 14 |
| Pajarito, N.M., U.S. | *B3 | 108 |
| Pajaros Point, c., V.I. Br. | A7 | 65 |
| Pajon Point, c., Guam | L10 | 52 |
| Pakhra, stm., Sov. Un. | n17 | 27 |
| Pakistan, ctry., Asia | C4 | 36 |
| Pakokku, Burma | D9 | 36 |
| Pakowki Lake, l., Alta. | E5 | 68 |
| Pakra, stm., Yugo. | C3 | 24 |
| Paks, Hung. | B4 | 24 |
| Pakwa Lake, l., Man. | B2 | 70 |
| Pakxe, Laos | B3 | 34 |
| Pala, Chad | D2 | 46 |
| Palacios, Tx., U.S. | E4 | 120 |
| Palafrugell, Spain | B7 | 22 |
| Palagruža, is., Yugo. | D3 | 24 |
| Palaiokhóra, Grc. | E4 | 25 |
| Palaión Fáliron, Grc. | h11 | 25 |
| Palamós, Grc. | A4 | 25 |
| Palamós, Spain | B7 | 22 |
| Palana, Sov. Un. | D18 | 29 |
| Palanga, Sov. Un. | D3 | 27 |
| Palangkaraya, Indon. | F4 | 34 |
| Pālanpur, India | D5 | 36 |
| Palaoa Point, c., Hi., U.S. | C4 | 88 |
| Palapag, Phil. | C7 | 34 |
| Palapye, Bots. | B4 | 49 |
| Palas de Rey, Spain | A2 | 22 |
| Palatine, Il., U.S. | A5 | 90 |
| Palatka, Fl., U.S. | C5 | 86 |
| Palau (Belau), ter., T.T.P.I. | F8 | 6 |
| Palaug, Phil. | o12 | 34 |
| Palaui Point, c., Phil. | o12 | 34 |
| Palauli (Vailoa), b., W. Sam. | F11 | 52 |
| Palauli Bay, b., W. Sam. | F11 | 52 |
| Palawan, i., Phil. | C5 | 34 |
| Palazzolo Acreide, Italy | *E4 | 23 |
| Palco, Ks., U.S. | C4 | 93 |
| Palembang, Indon. | F2 | 34 |
| Palena, stm., S.A. | C2 | 54 |
| Palencia, Spain | A3 | 22 |
| Palenque, hist., Mex. | B2 | 62 |
| Palermo, Italy | C6 | 109 |
| Palermo, Italy | D3 | 96 |
| Palermo, N.J., U.S. | E3 | 107 |
| Palermo, N.D., U.S. | A3 | 111 |
| Palestine, Ct., U.S. | *D2 | 84 |
| Palestine, Il., U.S. | D6 | 90 |
| Palestine, Oh., U.S. | B1 | 112 |
| Palestine, Tx., U.S. | D5 | 120 |
| Palestine, W.V., U.S. | B3 | 125 |
| Palestine, hist. reg., Asia | G10 | 40 |
| Palestine, Lake, res., Tx., U.S. | C5 | 120 |
| Palestrina, Italy | h9 | 23 |
| Paletwa, Burma | D9 | 36 |
| Palghāt, India | F6 | 36 |
| Palhoça, Braz. | D3 | 56 |
| Pāli, India | E4 | 37 |
| Palidoro (Baebiana), Italy | h8 | 23 |
| Palikea, mtn., Hi., U.S. | g9 | 88 |
| Paliker Point, c., Micron. | Q17 | 52 |
| Palimé, Togo | E5 | 45 |
| Palisade, Co., U.S. | B2 | 83 |
| Palisade, Mn., U.S. | D5 | 100 |
| Palisade, Ne., U.S. | D4 | 104 |
| Palisades, Wa., U.S. | B6 | 124 |
| Palisades Park, N.J., U.S. | h8 | 107 |
| Palisades Reservoir, res., U.S. | F7 | 89 |
| Palisades, spit, Jam. | F15 | 65 |
| Paliseul, Bel. | E5 | 17 |
| Pālitāna, India | G3 | 37 |
| Palk Strait, strt., Asia | E3 | 11 |
| Pallaskenry, Ire. | E3 | 11 |
| Palling, B.C. | C4 | 69 |
| Palliser, Cape, c., N.Z. | N15 | 51 |
| Pall Mall, Tn., U.S. | C9 | 119 |
| Palma, Moz. | D7 | 48 |
| Palma, i., Spain | D1 | 57 |
| Palma [de Mallorca], Spain | C7 | 22 |
| Palmares, Braz. | C3 | 57 |
| Palmar Sur, C.R. | F6 | 62 |
| Palmas, Braz. | D2 | 56 |
| Palmas, Cape, c., Lib. | F3 | 45 |
| Palmas de Monte Alto, Braz. | A4 | 56 |
| Palma Sola, Fl., U.S. | *E4 | 86 |
| Palma Soriano, Cuba | D5 | 64 |
| Palm Bay, Fl., U.S. | D6 | 86 |
| Palm Beach, Fl., U.S. | F6 | 86 |
| Palm Beach, co., Fl., U.S. | F6 | 86 |
| Palm Beach Gardens, Fl., U.S. | F6 | 86 |
| Palm Desert, Ca., U.S. | *F5 | 82 |
| Palm Harbor, Fl., U.S. | o10 | 86 |
| Palmdale, Fl., U.S. | F5 | 86 |
| Palmdale, Ca., U.S. | E4 | 82 |
| Palmeira, Braz. | B6 | 57 |
| Palmeira d'Oeste, Braz. | C2 | 56 |
| Palmeira dos Índios, Braz. | C3 | 57 |
| Palmeirais, Braz. | C1 | 57 |
| Palmeirinhas, Ponta das, c., Ang. | C1 | 48 |
| Palmer, Sask. | H2 | 75 |
| Palmer, Ak., U.S. | C10 | 79 |
| Palmer, Il., U.S. | D4 | 90 |
| Palmer, Ma., U.S. | B3 | 98 |
| Palmer, Mi., U.S. | B3 | 99 |
| Palmer, Ne., U.S. | C7 | 104 |
| Palmer, Tn., U.S. | D8 | 119 |
| Palmer, Tx., U.S. | n10 | 120 |
| Palmer, Wa., U.S. | f12 | 124 |
| Palmeras do Sul, Braz. | E2 | 56 |
| Palmer Lake, Co., U.S. | B6 | 83 |
| Palmer Land, reg., Ant. | B7 | 7 |
| Palmer Park, Md., U.S. | *C4 | 97 |
| Palmerston, Ont. | D4 | 73 |
| Palmerston, N.Z. | P13 | 51 |
| Palmerston North, N.Z. | N15 | 51 |
| Palmersville, Tn., U.S. | A3 | 119 |
| Palmerton, Pa., U.S. | E10 | 115 |
| Palmetto, Ga., U.S. | C2 | 87 |
| Palmetto, Fl., U.S. | E4 | 86 |
| Palmetto Estates, Fl., U.S. | *G6 | 86 |

| Name | Map Ref. | Page |
|---|---|---|

Palmi, Italy — E5 23
Palmira, Col. — C2 60
Palmira, Cuba — C3 64
Palmira, Ec. — B2 58
Palmitas, Ur. — f8 54
Palmitos, Braz. — D2 56
Palms, Mi., U.S. — E8 99
Palms, Isle of, i., S.C., U.S. — F8 117
Palm Springs, Ca., U.S. — F5 82
Palm Springs, Fl., U.S. — F6 86
Palm Valley, Fl., U.S. — m9 86
Palmyra, Il., U.S. — D4 90
Palmyra, In., U.S. — H5 91
Palmyra, i., U.S. — f9 92
Palmyra, Me., U.S. — D3 96
Palmyra, Mo., U.S. — B6 102
Palmyra, Ne., U.S. — D9 104
Palmyra, N.J., U.S. — C2 107
Palmyra, N.Y., U.S. — B3 109
Palmyra, N.C., U.S. — A5 110
Palmyra, Pa., U.S. — F8 115
Palmyra, Tn., U.S. — A4 119
Palmyra, Va., U.S. — C4 123
Palmyra, Wi., U.S. — F5 126
Palmyra, atoll, Oc. — F12 6
Palmyras Point, c., India — G11 37
Palo (Alsium), Italy — h8 23
Palo, Ia., U.S. — B6 92
Palo, Mi., U.S. — E6 99
Palo Alto, Ca., U.S. — D2 82
Palo Alto, co., Ia., U.S. — A3 92
Palo Duro Canyon, val., Tx., U.S. — B2 120
Paloich, Sud. — C3 47
Palomar Mountain, mtn., Ca., U.S. — F5 82
Palomas Mountains, mts., Az., U.S. — D2 80
Palombara Sabina, Italy — g9 23
Palo Negro, Col. — C3 60
Palo Pinto, Tx., U.S. — C3 120
Palo Pinto, co., Tx., U.S. — C3 120
Palopo, Indon. — F6 34
Palos, Cape, c., Spain — D5 22
Palos Heights, Il., U.S. — *k9 90
Palos Hills, Il., U.S. — *k9 90
Palos Park, Il., U.S. — k9 90
Palos Verdes Estates, Ca., U.S. — n12 82
Palourde, Lake, l., La., U.S. — k9 95
Palouse, Wa., U.S. — C8 124
Palouse, stm., Wa., U.S. — C7 124
Palo Verde, Az., U.S. — D3 80
Palo Verde, Ca., U.S. — F6 82
Palpa, Peru — D3 58
Pålsboda, Swe. — t33 14
Palu, Indon. — *F5 34
Palvär, Küh-e, mtn., Iran — F8 39
Pama, Burkina — D5 45
Pamamaroo Lake, l., Austl. — F4 51
Pambrun, Sask. — H2 75
Pamekasan, Indon. — G4 34
Pamiers, Fr. — F4 16
Pamir, mts., Asia — F10 29
Pamlico, co., N.C., U.S. — B6 110
Pamlico, stm., N.C., U.S. — B6 110
Pamlico Sound, strt., N.C., U.S. — B6 110
Pampa, Tx., U.S. — B2 120
Pampa, reg., Ar. — G4 53
Pampa Grande, Bol. — C3 55
Pampanga, stm., Phil. — o13 34
Pampas, Peru — D3 58
Pampilhosa do Botão, Port. — B1 22
Pamplico, S.C., U.S. — D8 117
Pamplin, Va., U.S. — C4 123
Pamplona, Col. — B3 60
Pamplona, Spain — A5 22
Pamunkey, stm., Va., U.S. — C5 123
Pana, Il., U.S. — D4 90
Panaca, Nv., U.S. — F7 105
Panacea, Fl., U.S. — B2 86
Panache, Lake, l., Ont. — A3 73
Panagyurishte, Bul. — D7 24
Panaitan, i., Indon. — G3 34
Panaji, India — E5 36
Panamá, Braz. — B3 56
Panamá, Pan. — F8 62
Panama, Il., U.S. — D4 90
Panama, Ne., U.S. — D9 104
Panama, N.Y., U.S. — C1 109
Panama, Ok., U.S. — B7 113
Panama, ctry., N.A. — F8 62
Panamá, Bahia de, b., Pan. — F8 62
Panamá, Golfo de, b., Pan. — F8 62
Panama Canal, Pan. — k11 62
Panama City, Fl., U.S. — u16 86
Panama City Beach, Fl., U.S. — u16 86
Panambi, Braz. — D2 56
Panamint Range, mts., Ca., U.S. — D5 82
Panao, Peru — C2 58
Panarea, i., Italy — E5 23
Panaro, stm., Italy — B3 23
Panay, i., Phil. — C6 34
Pancake Range, mts., Nv., U.S. — E6 105
Pančevo, Yugo. — C5 24
Panch'iao (T'aipeihsien), Tai. — *F9 31
Pancoastburg, Oh., U.S. — C2 112
Panda, Moz. — B5 49
Pandharpur, India — E6 36
Pāndhurna, India — G7 37
Pando, Ur. — E1 56
Pando, dept., Bol. — B2 55
Pandora, Oh., U.S. — B2 112
Pandora, C.R. — E4 120
Pandu, Zaire — A2 48
Panelas, Braz. — k5 57
Panet, Que. — C7 74
Panevežys, Sov. Un. — D5 27
Panfilov, Sov. Un. — E10 29
Pangala, Congo — B1 48
Pangani, Tan. — C6 48
Pangburn, Ar., U.S. — B4 81
Pangi, Zaire — B4 48
Pangkalanbuun, Indon. — F4 34
Pangkalpinang, Indon. — F3 34
Pangman, Sask. — H3 75
Pangnirtung, N.W. Ter. — C19 66
Pangsau Pass, Asia — C10 36
Panguipulli, Chile — B2 54
Panguitch, Ut., U.S. — F3 121
Panhandle, Tx., U.S. — B2 120
Paniau, mtn., Hi., U.S. — B1 88
Panié, Mont, mtn., N. Cal. — *H10 6
Pānihāti, India — *D8 36
Panīpat, India — C6 37
Paniqui, Phil. — o13 34
Panj, stm., Asia — k17 39
Panjāb, Afg. — D13 39
Panjgūr, Pak. — C3 36
Panjim see Panaji, India — E5 36
Panjpāi, Pak. — G13 39

Pankey, Ar., U.S. — h10 81
Pankeyville, Il., U.S. — F5 90
Pankshin, Nig. — E6 45
Panmunjŏm, N. Kor. — H3 33
Panna, India — D7 36
Panola, Al., U.S. — C1 78
Panola, co., Ms., U.S. — A3 101
Panola, co., Tx., U.S. — C5 120
Panora, Ia., U.S. — C3 92
Panorama, Braz. — C2 56
Panshan, China — D9 32
Panshi, China — C11 32
Pantai, i., Indon. — G6 34
Pantego, N.C., U.S. — B6 110
Pantelleria, Italy — F3 23
Pantelleria, i., Italy — F4 23
Panthersville, Ga., U.S. — *h8 87
Pantin, Fr. — g10 16
Panton, Vt., U.S. — C2 122
Pánuco, Mex. — C5 63
Panulcillo, Chile — F1 55
Panzi, Zaire — C2 48
Panzós, Guat. — D7 63
Paola, Italy — E6 23
Paola, Ks., U.S. — D9 93
Paoli, Co., U.S. — A8 83
Paoli, In., U.S. — G5 91
Paoli, Ok., U.S. — C4 113
Paoli, Pa., U.S. — o20 115
Paonia, Co., U.S. — C3 83
Paoua, Cen. Afr. Rep. — D3 46
Paoy Pet, Camb. — F5 35
Pápa, Hung. — B3 24
Papaaloa, Hi., U.S. — D6 88
Papagayo, Golfo de, b., C.R. — E7 63
Papago Indian Reservation, Az., U.S. — E3 80
Papaikou, Hi., U.S. — D6 88
Papantla [de Olarte], Mex. — C5 63
Papawai Point, c., Hi., U.S. — C5 88
Papeete, Fr. Poly. — H13 6
Papenburg, W. Ger. — B3 18
Paper Mill Village, Vt., U.S. — F2 122
Papillion, Ne., U.S. — C9 104
Papineau, In., U.S. — C6 90
Papineau, co., Que. — D2 74
Papineau, Lake, l., Ont. — B7 73
Papineauville, Que. — D2 74
Papoose, Chile — E1 55
Papua, Gulf of, b., Pap. N. Gui. — k11 6
Papua New Guinea, ctry., Oc. — G8 6
Papudo, Chile — A2 54
Papun, Burma — E10 36
Paquette, Que. — D6 74
Pará, state, Braz. — C4 59
Pará, dept., Sur. — A3 59
Paraburdoo, Austl. — D2 50
Paracale, Phil. — o14 34
Paracatu, Braz. — B3 56
Paracatu, Braz. — B3 56
Paracel Islands, is., Asia — B4 34
Paracho, Co., U.S. — B2 83
Paraćin, Yugo. — D5 24
Paracuru, Braz. — C5 59
Paradis, La., U.S. — k11 95
Paradise, Ca., U.S. — C3 82
Paradise, Ks., U.S. — C5 93
Paradise, Mi., U.S. — B5 99
Paradise, Mt., U.S. — C2 103
Paradise, Nv., U.S. — G6 105
Paradise, Pa., U.S. — G9 115
Paradise, Ut., U.S. — B4 121
Paradise, stm., Newf. — D3 72
Paradise Hill, Sask. — D1 75
Paradise Hills, N.M., U.S. — B3 108
Paradise Island, i., Bah. — m18 64
Paradise River, Newf. — B3 72
Paradise Valley, Alta. — C5 68
Paradise Valley, Az., U.S. — k9 80
Paradise Valley, Nv., U.S. — B4 105
Paradise Valley, Wy., U.S. — D6 127
Paradox, Co., U.S. — C2 83
Paragon, In., U.S. — F4 91
Paragonah, Ut., U.S. — F3 121
Paragould, Ar., U.S. — A5 81
Paragua, stm., Ven. — B5 60
Paraguaçu, stm., Braz. — D3 57
Paraguaçu Paulista, Braz. — C2 56
Paraguaçu (Paraguay), stm., S.A. — C4 55
Paraguaná, Península de, pen., Ven. — A4 60
Paraguari, Para. — A4 54
Paraguari, dept., Para. — E4 55
Paraguay, ctry., S.A. — D4 55
Paraguay (Paraguai), stm., S.A. — D4 55
Paraíba, state, Braz. — C3 57
Paraíba, stm., Braz. — h6 57
Paraíba do Sul, Braz. — h6 56
Paraíba do Sul, stm., Braz. — g6 57
Paraíso, Braz. — C3 56
Paraíso, Pan. — k11 62
Paraisópolis, Braz. — C3 56
Parakou, Benin — E5 45
Paralomar, Ar., U.S. — D1 81
Paramirim, Braz. — A4 56
Paramithía, Grc. — C3 25
Paramonga, Peru — C2 58
Paramount, Ca., U.S. — *n12 82
Paramount, Md., U.S. — A2 97
Paramus, N.J., U.S. — h8 107
Paraná, Arg. — A4 54
Paraná, Braz. — D1 57
Paraná, state, Braz. — C2 56
Paraná, stm., Braz. — D1 57
Paraná, stm., S.A. — G5 53
Paranaíba, Braz. — B2 56
Paranaíba, Braz. — B2 56
Paranaíba, stm., Braz. — B2 56
Paranaguá, Braz. — C2 56
Paranaiguara, Braz. — A3 59
Paranapanema, Braz. — m7 56
Paranapanema, stm., Braz. — C2 56
Paranapiacaba, Serra do, mts., Braz. — m8 56
Paranaví, Braz. — C2 56
Paraopeba, Braz. — E2 57
Parapetí, stm., Bol. — C3 55
Paratinga, Braz. — D2 57
Paraúna, Braz. — C4 59
Parauapebas, Serra, hill, Braz. — B2 56
Paray-le-Monial, Fr. — D6 16
Pārbati, stm., India — E6 37
Parbhani, India — H6 37

Parchim, E. Ger. — B5 18
Parchment, Mi., U.S. — F5 99
Parczew, Pol. — C7 26
Pardee, Va., U.S. — e9 123
Pardeeville, Wi., U.S. — E4 126
Pardes Hanna-Karkur, Isr. — B6 41
Pardo, stm., Braz. — C2 56
Pardo, stm., Braz. — C3 56
Pardo, stm., Braz. — E2 57
Pardo, Pa., U.S. — D1 115
Pardubice, Czech. — C3 26
Parecis, Chapada dos, mts., Braz. — B4 55
Paredes de Nava, Spain — A3 22
Parem, i., Micron. — Q18 52
Parempei, i., Micron. — Q17 52
Parent, Que. — k12 74
Parepare, Indon. — F5 34
Párga, Grc. — C3 40
Pargas, Ponta do, c., Port. — h11 22
Pargolovo, Sov. Un. — r31 14
Paria, stm., U.S. — A4 80
Paria, Gulf of, b. — A5 60
Paria, Península de, pen., Ven. — A5 60
Pariaguán, Ven. — B5 60
Paria Plateau, plat., Az., U.S. — A4 80
Paricutín, vol., Mex. — n12 63
Parigi, Indon. — F6 34
Parika, Guy. — A3 59
Parima, Serra, mts., S.A. — C2 59
Parima, Sierra (Serra Parima), mts., S.A. — C5 60
Pariñas, Punta, c., Peru — B1 58
Parintins, Braz. — C3 59
Paris, Ont. — D4 73
Paris, Fr. — C5 16
Paris, Ar., U.S. — B2 81
Paris, Id., U.S. — G7 89
Paris, Il., U.S. — D6 90
Paris, Ky., U.S. — B5 94
Paris, Me., U.S. — D2 96
Paris, Mi., U.S. — E5 99
Paris, Ms., U.S. — A4 101
Paris, Mo., U.S. — B5 102
Paris, Tn., U.S. — A3 119
Paris, Tx., U.S. — C5 120
Paris, Va., U.S. — A5 123
Paris Crossing, In., U.S. — G6 91
Parish, N.Y., U.S. — B4 109
Parishville, N.Y., U.S. — f10 109
Paris Peak, mtn., Id., U.S. — G7 89
Parisville, Que. — C5 74
Park, Ks., U.S. — C3 93
Park, co., Co., U.S. — B5 83
Park, co., Mt., U.S. — E6 103
Park, co., Wy., U.S. — B3 127
Park, stm., N.D., U.S. — A8 111
Parkbeg, Sask. — G2 75
Park City, Ks., U.S. — g12 93
Park City, Ky., U.S. — C3 94
Park City, Mt., U.S. — E8 103
Park City, Ut., U.S. — C4 121
Parkdale, P.E.I. — C6 71
Parkdale, Ar., U.S. — D4 81
Parkdale, Mi., U.S. — D4 99
Parkdale, Or., U.S. — B5 114
Parke, co., In., U.S. — E3 91
Parker, Az., U.S. — C1 80
Parker, Co., U.S. — B6 83
Parker, Fl., U.S. — u16 86
Parker, Id., U.S. — F7 89
Parker, Ks., U.S. — D9 93
Parker, Pa., U.S. — D2 115
Parker, S.D., U.S. — D8 118
Parker, Wa., U.S. — C5 124
Parker, co., Tx., U.S. — C4 120
Parker City, In., U.S. — D7 91
Parker Dam, Ca., U.S. — E6 82
Parker Dam, Ca., U.S. — C1 80
Parker Peak, mtn., S.D., U.S. — D2 118
Parkersburg, Ia., U.S. — B5 92
Parkersburg, Il., U.S. — E5 90
Parkersburg, W.V., U.S. — B3 125
Parkers Prairie, Mn., U.S. — D3 100
Parkertown, N.J., U.S. — D4 107
Parkerville, Ks., U.S. — D7 93
Parkes, Austl. — F8 50
Parkesburg, Pa., U.S. — G10 115
Park Falls, Wi., U.S. — C3 126
Park Forest, Il., U.S. — *B6 90
Park Forest South, Il., U.S. — *B6 90
Park Hall, Md., U.S. — D5 97
Park Head, Ont. — C3 73
Parkhill, Ont. — D3 73
Park Hill, Ok., U.S. — B7 113
Park Hills, Ky., U.S. — h13 94
Parkin, Ar., U.S. — B5 81
Parkland, Alta. — D4 68
Parkland, Wa., U.S. — f11 124
Park Layne, Oh., U.S. — C1 112
Parkman, Me., U.S. — C3 96
Parkman, Wy., U.S. — B5 127
Park Place, Or., U.S. — h12 114
Park Plateau, plat., Co., U.S. — D6 83
Park Range, mts., Co., U.S. — A4 83
Park Rapids, Mn., U.S. — D3 100
Park Ridge, Il., U.S. — B6 90
Park Ridge, N.J., U.S. — g8 107
Park River, N.D., U.S. — A8 111
Parkrose, Or., U.S. — B4 114
Parks, Az., U.S. — B3 80
Parks, La., U.S. — D4 95
Parks, Ne., U.S. — D4 104
Parksley, Va., U.S. — C7 123
Parkston, S.D., U.S. — D8 118
Parksville, B.C. — E5 69
Parksville, N.Y., U.S. — D6 109
Parksville, S.C., U.S. — D3 117
Park Valley, Ut., U.S. — B3 121
Parkton, Md., U.S. — A4 97
Parkton, N.C., U.S. — C3 110
Parkville, Md., U.S. — B4 97
Parkville, Mo., U.S. — B3 102
Parkwater, Wa., U.S. — g14 124
Parkway, Ca., U.S. — *C3 82
Parkwood, N.C., U.S. — A4 110
Parla, Spain — p17 22
Parląkimedi, India — H10 37
Parle, Lac qui, l., Mn., U.S. — E3 100
Parlier, Ca., U.S. — D4 82
Parma, Co., U.S. — C4 83
Parma, Id., U.S. — F2 89
Parma, Italy — B3 23
Parma, Mi., U.S. — F6 99
Parma, Mo., U.S. — E8 102
Parma, Oh., U.S. — A4 112
Parma, stm., Italy — E6 20
Parma Heights, Oh., U.S. — h9 112

Parmele, N.C., U.S. — B5 110
Parmelee, S.D., U.S. — D4 118
Parmer, co., Tx., U.S. — B1 120
Parnaguá, Braz. — D2 57
Parnaíba, Braz. — B2 57
Parnaíba, stm., Braz. — B2 57
Parnassós, mtn., Grc. — C4 25
Parnell, Ia., U.S. — C6 92
Parnell, Mo., U.S. — A3 102
Párnis Óros, mts., Grc. — g11 25
Pärnu, Sov. Un. — B5 27
Paro, Bhu. — C8 36
Paron, Ar., U.S. — C3 81
Paroo, stm., Austl. — F7 50
Páros, Grc. — D5 25
Páros, i., Grc. — D5 40
Parowan, Ut., U.S. — F3 121
Par Pond, res., S.C., U.S. — D5 117
Parr, In., U.S. — B3 91
Parral, Chile — *B2 54
Parramatta, Austl. — *F9 50
Parramore Island, i., Va., U.S. — C7 123
Parras de la Fuente, Mex. — B4 63
Parrett, stm., Eng., U.K. — C5 12
Parrish, Al., U.S. — B2 78
Parrish, Fl., U.S. — E4 86
Parrish, Wi., U.S. — C4 126
Parrott, Ga., U.S. — E2 87
Parrott, Va., U.S. — C2 123
Parrottsville, Tn., U.S. — C10 119
Parrsboro, N.S. — D5 71
Parrs Ridge, mtn., Md., U.S. — B3 97
Parry, Sask. — H3 75
Parry, Cape, c., N.W. Ter. — B8 66
Parry, Mount, mtn., B.C. — C3 69
Parry Island, i., Ont. — B4 73
Parry Island, i., Marsh Is. — S18 52
Parry Islands, is., N.W. Ter. — m29 66
Parry Sound, Ont. — B4 73
Parry Sound, dept., Ont. — B4 73
Parsberg, W. Ger. — D5 18
Parseta, stm., Pol. — A3 26
Parshall, Co., U.S. — A4 83
Parshall, N.D., U.S. — B3 111
Parsippany, N.J., U.S. — B4 107
Parsnip, stm., B.C. — B6 69
Parsons, Ks., U.S. — E8 93
Parsons, Tn., U.S. — B3 119
Parsons, W.V., U.S. — B5 125
Parsonsburg, Md., U.S. — D7 97
Parson's Pond, Newf. — C3 72
Partenen, Aus. — C6 20
Parthenay, Fr. — F6 16
Parthenon, Ar., U.S. — B3 81
Partinico, Italy — E4 23
Partridge, Ks., U.S. — E5 93
Partridge Point, c., Newf. — C3 72
Partry, Ire. — D2 11
Parys, S. Afr. — C4 49
Pasadena, Newf. — D3 72
Pasadena, Ca., U.S. — E4 82
Pasadena, Md., U.S. — B4 97
Pasadena, Tx., U.S. — r14 120
Pasado, Cabo, c., Ec. — B1 58
Pasaje, Ec. — B2 58
Pa Sak, stm., Thai. — D4 35
Pascagoula, Ms., U.S. — E5 101
Pascagoula Bay, b., Ms., U.S. — f8 101
Pascani, Rom. — B8 24
Pasco, Wa., U.S. — C6 124
Pasco, dept., Peru — D2 58
Pasco, co., Fl., U.S. — D4 86
Pascoag, R.I., U.S. — B2 116
Pascoag Reservoir, res., R.I., U.S. — B2 116
Pascola, Mo., U.S. — E8 102
Pascua, Isla de (Easter Island), i., Chile — H15 6
Pas-de-Calais, dept., Fr. — B7 16
Pasewalk, E. Ger. — B7 18
Pashkovo, Sov. Un. — B11 31
Pasig, Phil. — o13 34
Pasłęk, Pol. — A5 26
Pasni, Pak. — C3 36
Paso de Indios, Arg. — C3 54
Paso de los Libres, Arg. — E4 55
Paso de los Toros, Ur. — E1 56
Paso Limay, Arg. — C2 54
Paso Robles, Ca., U.S. — E3 82
Pasqua, stm., Italy — E6 20
Pasque Island, i., Ma., U.S. — D6 98
Pasquia, stm., Sask. — D4 75
Pasquia Hills, hills, Sask. — D4 75
Pasquotank, co., N.C., U.S. — A6 110
Pasrūr, Pak. — B5 36
Passaconaway, Mount, mtn., N.H., U.S. — C4 106
Passadumkeag, Me., U.S. — C4 96
Passadumkeag Mountain, mtn., Me., U.S. — C4 96
Passage East, Ire. — I5 11
Passage West, Ire. — F3 11
Passaic, N.J., U.S. — B4 107
Passaic, co., N.J., U.S. — A4 107
Passaic, stm., N.J., U.S. — h8 107
Passamaquoddy Bay, b., Me., U.S. — C6 96
Passau, W. Ger. — D6 18
Passero, Cape, c., Italy — F5 23
Passo Fundo, Braz. — D2 56
Passos, Braz. — C3 56
Passumpsic, Vt., U.S. — C4 122
Passumpsic, stm., Vt., U.S. — C4 122
Passy, Fr. — E2 21
Pastaza, prov., Ec. — B2 58
Pastaza, stm., S.A. — B2 58
Pasto, Col. — C2 60
Pastura, N.M., U.S. — C5 108
Pasuruan, Indon. — G4 34
Paswegin, Sask. — F3 75
Patagonia, Az., U.S. — F5 80
Patagonia, reg., Arg. — D3 54
Pātan, India — F4 37
Patan see Lalitpur, Nepal — C11 36
Patani, Indon. — E8 34
Patapedia, stm., Can. — A4 71
Patapsco, Md., U.S. — B4 97
Patapsco, stm., Md., U.S. — B4 97
Patapsco, North Branch, stm., Md., U.S. — A4 97
Patargan, Daqq-e, sw., Asia — E10 39
Pataskala, Oh., U.S. — C3 112
Patchewollock, Austl. — G4 51
Patchogue, N.Y., U.S. — n15 109

Pat Cleburne, Lake, res., Tx., U.S. — C4 120
Patea, N.Z. — M15 51
Pateley Bridge, Eng., U.K. — F7 13
Paterno, Italy — F5 23
Pateros, Wa., U.S. — A6 124
Paterson, N.J., U.S. — B4 107
Paterson, Wa., U.S. — D6 124
Pathánkot, India — B6 36
Pathein, Burma — E9 36
Pathfinder Reservoir, res., Wy., U.S. — D6 127
Pathfork, Ky., U.S. — D6 94
Pathlow, Sask. — E3 75
Patía, stm., Col. — C2 60
Patiāla, India — B6 36
Patience Island, i., R.I., U.S. — D5 116
Patman, Lake, res., Tx., U.S. — C5 120
Patmos, Ar., U.S. — D2 81
Pátmos, i., Grc. — D1 40
Patna, India — C8 36
Patnanongan Island, i., Phil. — o14 34
Patoka, Il., U.S. — E4 90
Patoka, In., U.S. — H2 91
Patoka, stm., In., U.S. — H2 91
Patoka Lake, res., In., U.S. — H4 91
Paton, Ia., U.S. — B3 92
Patos, Braz. — C3 57
Patos, Lagoa dos, b., Braz. — E2 56
Patos de Minas, Braz. — B3 56
Patosi, Alb. — B2 25
Patquía, Arg. — F2 55
Pátrai (Patras), Grc. — C3 40
Pátrai, Gulf of see Patraïkós Kólpos, b., Grc. — C3 40
Patraïkós Kólpos (Gulf of Pátrai), b., Grc. — C3 40
Patras see Pátrai, Grc.
Patricia, Alta. — D5 68
Patricia, Tx., U.S. — C1 120
Patrick, co., Va., U.S. — D2 123
Patrick, S.C., U.S. — C8 117
Patrick Air Force Base, mil., Fl., U.S. — D6 86
Patricksburg, In., U.S. — F4 91
Patrick Springs, Va., U.S. — D2 123
Patriot, In., U.S. — G8 91
Patrocínio, Braz. — B3 56
Patsaliga Creek, stm., Al., U.S. — D3 78
Patsville, Nv., U.S. — B6 105
Pattani, Thai. — I4 35
Pattani, stm., Thai. — I4 35
Pattaquattic Hill, hill, Ma., U.S. — A4 113
Patten, Me., U.S. — C4 96
Patterson, Ar., U.S. — B4 81
Patterson, Ca., U.S. — D3 82
Patterson, Ga., U.S. — E4 87
Patterson, Id., U.S. — E5 89
Patterson, Il., U.S. — D3 90
Patterson, La., U.S. — E4 95
Patterson, Mo., U.S. — D7 102
Patterson, N.Y., U.S. — D7 109
Patterson, Oh., U.S. — B2 112
Patterson Creek, stm., W.V., U.S. — B5 125

Pattison, Ms., U.S. — D3 101
Patton, Mo., U.S. — D7 102
Patton, Pa., U.S. — E4 115
Pattonsburg, Mo., U.S. — B3 102
Pattullo, Mount, mtn., B.C. — A3 69
Patu, Braz. — C3 57
Patuākhāli, Bngl. — F13 37
Patuca, stm., Hond. — D8 63
Patuca, Punta, c., Hond. — D8 63
Patuxent, stm., Md., U.S. — C4 97
Patuxent River Naval Air Test Center, mil., Md., U.S. — D5 97
Patzau, Wi., U.S. — B1 126
Pátzcuaro, Mex. — D4 63
Pátzcuaro, Lago de, l., Mex. — n13 63
Patzicía, Guat. — C2 62
Patzún, Guat. — G10 63
Pau, Fr. — F3 16
Pau, Gave de, stm., Fr. — F3 16
Paucarbamba, Peru — D3 58
Paudalho, Braz. — k6 57
Pau dos Ferros, Braz. — C3 57
Paugh Lake, Ont. — B7 73
Pauillac, Fr. — F3 16
Pauini, Braz. — C3 58
Pauk, Burma — D9 36
Paul, Id., U.S. — G5 89
Paulaya, stm., Hond. — C5 62
Paulden, Az., U.S. — C3 80
Paulding, Mi., U.S. — n12 99
Paulding, Oh., U.S. — A1 112
Paulding, co., Ga., U.S. — C2 87
Paulding, co., Oh., U.S. — A1 112
Paulding Bay, b., Ant. — C25 7
Paulette, Ms., U.S. — B5 101
Paulina, La., U.S. — h10 95
Paulina, Or., U.S. — C6 114
Paulina Mountains, mts., Or., U.S. — D5 114
Paulina Peak, mtn., Or., U.S. — E5 114
Pauline, S.C., U.S. — B4 117
Paulins Kill, stm., N.J., U.S. — A3 107
Paul Island, i., Newf. — g9 72
Paulista, Braz. — j6 57
Paull, stm., Sask. — B3 75
Paullina, Ia., U.S. — A2 92
Paul Smiths, N.Y., U.S. — f10 109
Paulo Afonso, Cachoeira de, wtfl., Braz. — C3 57
Pauls Valley, Ok., U.S. — C4 113
Paungde, Burma — E10 36
Pauto, stm., Col. — C3 60
Pauwela, Hi., U.S. — C5 88
Pavant Range, mts., Ut., U.S. — D3 121
Pavia, Italy — B3 23
Pavilion, Wy., U.S. — C4 127
Pavilion, N.Y., U.S. — C2 109
Pavlodar, Sov. Un. — D10 29
Pavlof Volcano, vol., Ak., U.S. — D7 79
Pavlograd, Sov. Un. — G10 27
Pavlovo, Sov. Un. — s31 14
Pavlovsk, Sov. Un. — F13 27
Pavlovskaya, Sov. Un. — H13 27
Pavlovskiy Posad, Sov. Un. — n18 27
Pavo, Ga., U.S. — F3 87
Pavón, Col. — C3 60
Pawcatuck, Ct., U.S. — D8 84
Pawcatuck, stm., R.I., U.S. — G1 116
Paw Creek, N.C., U.S. — B2 110
Pawhuska, Ok., U.S. — A5 113
Pawlet, Vt., U.S. — E2 122
Pawleys Island, S.C., U.S. — E9 117
Pawling, N.Y., U.S. — D7 109
Pawłowice, Pol. — h9 26
Pawn, stm., Burma — C2 35
Pawnee, Il., U.S. — D4 90
Pawnee, Ok., U.S. — A5 113
Pawnee, Tx., U.S. — E4 120
Pawnee, co., Ks., U.S. — D4 93
Pawnee, co., Ne., U.S. — D9 104
Pawnee, co., Ok., U.S. — A5 113
Pawnee City, Ne., U.S. — D9 104
Pawnee Creek, stm., Co., U.S. — A7 83
Pawnee Rock, Ks., U.S. — D5 93
Pawpaw, Il., U.S. — B5 90
Paw Paw, Mi., U.S. — F5 99
Paw Paw, W.V., U.S. — B6 125
Pawpaw Creek, stm., W.V., U.S. — h10 125
Pawtuckaway Pond, l., N.H., U.S. — D4 106
Pawtucket, R.I., U.S. — C4 116
Pawtuxet, stm., R.I., U.S. — C4 116
Pawtuxet, North Branch, stm., R.I., U.S. — D3 116
Pawtuxet, South Branch, stm., R.I., U.S. — D3 116
Pax, W.V., U.S. — n13 125
Paxico, Ks., U.S. — C7 93
Paxoí, i., Grc. — C3 25
Paxton, Fl., U.S. — u15 86
Paxton, Il., U.S. — C5 90
Paxton, In., U.S. — F3 91
Paxton, Ma., U.S. — B4 98
Paxton, Ne., U.S. — C4 104
Paxtonville, Pa., U.S. — E7 115
Paxville, S.C., U.S. — D7 117
Payakumbuh, Indon. — *F2 34
Payerne, Switz. — C2 21
Payette, Id., U.S. — E2 89
Payette, co., Id., U.S. — E2 89
Payette, North Fork, stm., Id., U.S. — E2 89
Payette, South Fork, stm., Id., U.S. — E3 89
Payette Lake, res., Id., U.S. — E3 89
Payne, Ga., U.S. — D3 87
Payne, Oh., U.S. — A1 112
Payne, co., Ok., U.S. — A4 113
Payne, Lac, l., Que. — g12 74
Paynes, Ms., U.S. — B3 101
Paynes Creek, Ca., U.S. — B3 82
Paynesville, Mn., U.S. — E4 100
Paynesville, Mo., U.S. — B7 102
Payneville, Ky., U.S. — C3 94
Paynton, Sask. — D1 75
Payson, Az., U.S. — C4 80
Payson, Il., U.S. — D2 90
Payson, Ut., U.S. — C4 121
Pazardžhik, Bul. — D7 24
Pazin, Yugo. — C1 24
Pea, stm., Al., U.S. — D3 78
Peabody, Ks., U.S. — D6 93
Peabody, Ma., U.S. — A6 98
Peabody, stm., N.H., U.S. — B4 106
Peace, stm., Can. — E5 66
Peace, stm., Fl., U.S. — E5 86
Peace Dale, R.I., U.S. — F3 116
Peace River, Alta. — A2 68
Peach, co., Ga., U.S. — D3 87
Peacham, Vt., U.S. — C4 122
Peacham Pond, res., Vt., U.S. — C4 122
Peach Creek, W.V., U.S. — D3 125
Peachland, B.C. — E8 69
Peachland, N.C., U.S. — C2 110
Peach Orchard, Ar., U.S. — A5 81
Peach Orchard, Ga., U.S. — *C4 87
Peach Point, c., Ma., U.S. — f12 98
Peach Springs, Az., U.S. — B2 80
Peachtree City, Ga., U.S. — *C2 87
Peacock, Mi., U.S. — D5 99
Peacock Hills, hills, N.W. Ter. — C10 66
Peacock Point, c., Wake I. — B2 52
Peacock Sound, strt., Ant. — B2 7
Peaima Fall, wtfl., Guy. — A5 59
Peaked Mountain, mtn., Me., U.S. — B4 96
Peaks Island, i., Me., U.S. — g7 96
Peale, Mount, mtn., Ut., U.S. — E6 121
Peale Island, i., Wake I. — A2 52
Pea Patch Island, i., De., U.S. — B3 85
Pearce, Alta. — E4 68
Pearcy, Ar., U.S. — A1 81
Pea Ridge, Ar., U.S. — A1 81
Pea Ridge National Military Park, Ar., U.S. — A1 81
Pearisburg, Va., U.S. — C2 123
Pearl, Il., U.S. — D3 90
Pearl, Ms., U.S. — C3 101
Pearl, stm., U.S. — D3 101
Pearland, Tx., U.S. — r14 120
Pearl and Hermes Reef, rf., Hi., U.S. — k12 88
Pearl City, Hi., U.S. — B4 88
Pearl City, Il., U.S. — A4 90
Pearl Harbor, b., Hi., U.S. — B3 88
Pearl Harbor Naval Station, mil., Hi., U.S. — g10 88
Pearlington, Ms., U.S. — E4 101
Pearl River, La., U.S. — D6 95
Pearl River, N.Y., U.S. — g12 109
Pearl River, co., Ms., U.S. — E4 101
Pearsall, Tx., U.S. — E3 120
Pearsoll Peak, mtn., Or., U.S. — E3 114
Pearson, Ga., U.S. — E4 87
Pearson Lake, l., Man. — A3 70
Peary Channel, strt., N.W. Ter. — m30 66
Peary Land, reg., Grnld. — A18 129
Pease, Mn., U.S. — E5 100
Pease, stm., Tx., U.S. — B2 120
Pease Air Force Base, mil., N.H., U.S. — D5 106
Pebane, Moz. — A6 49
Pebas, Peru — D3 58
Pebworth, Ky., U.S. — C6 94
Peć, Yugo. — D4 24
Peçanha, Braz. — B4 56
Pecatonica, Il., U.S. — A4 90

| Name | Map Ref. | Page |
|---|---|---|
| Pecatonica, stm., U.S. | A4 | 90 |
| Pecatonica, East Branch, stm., Wi., U.S. | F4 | 126 |
| Pechenga, Sov. Un. | C6 | 29 |
| Pechora, Sov. Un. | B20 | 8 |
| Pechora, stm., Sov. Un. | C8 | 29 |
| Pechora Bay, b., Sov. Un. | B19 | 8 |
| Peck, Id., U.S. | C2 | 89 |
| Peck, Ks., U.S. | E6 | 93 |
| Peck, Mi., U.S. | E8 | 99 |
| Peckerwood Lake, res., Ar., U.S. | C4 | 81 |
| Peckham, Ok., U.S. | A4 | 113 |
| Pecos, N.M., U.S. | B4 | 108 |
| Pecos, Tx., U.S. | D1 | 120 |
| Pecos, co., Tx., U.S. | D1 | 120 |
| Pecos, stm., U.S. | D7 | 76 |
| Pecos National Monument, N.M., U.S. | B4 | 108 |
| Pécs, Hung. | B4 | 24 |
| Peculiar, Mo., U.S. | C3 | 102 |
| Pedasí, Pan. | G7 | 62 |
| Peddocks Island, i., Ma., U.S. | g12 | 98 |
| Pedernales, Ven. | B5 | 60 |
| Pedra Azul, Braz. | B4 | 56 |
| Pedregal (part of Panamá), Pan. | k12 | 62 |
| Pedregal, Pan. | F6 | 62 |
| Pedregal, Pan. | A3 | 60 |
| Pedreiras, Braz. | B2 | 57 |
| Pedricktown, N.J., U.S. | D2 | 107 |
| Pedro Afonso, Braz. | C1 | 57 |
| Pedro Antonio Santos, Mex. | A3 | 62 |
| Pedro Avelino, Braz. | C3 | 57 |
| Pedro Juan Caballero, Para. | D4 | 55 |
| Pedro Luro, Arg. | B4 | 54 |
| Pedro Miguel, Pan. | k11 | 62 |
| Pedro R. Fernández (Manuel F. Mantilla), Arg. | E4 | 55 |
| Pedro Velho, Braz. | h6 | 57 |
| Peebinga, Austl. | G3 | 51 |
| Peebles, Sask. | G4 | 75 |
| Peebles, Scot., U.K. | C5 | 10 |
| Peebles, Oh., U.S. | D2 | 112 |
| Peebles, Wi., U.S. | k9 | 126 |
| Peekaboo Mountain, hill, Me., U.S. | C5 | 96 |
| Peekskill, N.Y., U.S. | D7 | 109 |
| Peel, N.B. | C2 | 71 |
| Peel, I. of Man | F4 | 13 |
| Peel, co., Ont. | D5 | 73 |
| Peel, stm., Can. | C5 | 66 |
| Peel Fell, mtn., U.K. | E6 | 13 |
| Pe Ell, Wa., U.S. | C2 | 124 |
| Peel Sound, strt., N.W. Ter. | B13 | 66 |
| Peene, stm., E. Ger. | B6 | 18 |
| Peer, Bel. | B6 | 18 |
| Peerless, Mt., U.S. | B11 | 103 |
| Peerless Lake, l., Alta. | A3 | 68 |
| Peers, Alta. | C3 | 68 |
| Peesane, Sask. | E4 | 75 |
| Peetz, Co., U.S. | A7 | 83 |
| Peever, S.D., U.S. | B9 | 118 |
| Pefferlaw, Ont. | C5 | 73 |
| Pegan Hill, hill, Ma., U.S. | g10 | 98 |
| Pegasus Bay, b., N.Z. | O14 | 51 |
| Pegau, E. Ger. | B7 | 19 |
| Peggs, Ok., U.S. | A6 | 113 |
| Peggy, Tx., U.S. | E3 | 120 |
| Pegnitz, W. Ger. | D6 | 19 |
| Pegnitz, stm., W. Ger. | D5 | 18 |
| Pego, Spain | C5 | 22 |
| Pegram, Tn., U.S. | A4 | 119 |
| Pegu Yoma, mts., Burma | C1 | 35 |
| Pehčevo, Yugo. | E6 | 24 |
| Pehuajó, Arg. | B4 | 54 |
| Peine, W. Ger. | B5 | 18 |
| Peiping see Beijing, China | D8 | 31 |
| Peipus, Lake, l., Sov. Un. | C6 | 29 |
| Peixe, Braz. | D1 | 57 |
| Peixian, China | G7 | 32 |
| Pejepscot, Me., U.S. | E3 | 96 |
| Pekalongan, Indon. | G3 | 34 |
| Pekan, Malay. | E2 | 34 |
| Pekanbaru, Indon. | E2 | 34 |
| Pekin, Il., U.S. | C4 | 90 |
| Pekin, In., U.S. | G5 | 91 |
| Pekin, N.D., U.S. | B7 | 111 |
| Peking see Beijing, China | D8 | 31 |
| Pelabuhan Kelang, Malay. | K4 | 35 |
| Pelagos, i., Grc. | C5 | 25 |
| Pelahatchie, Ms., U.S. | C4 | 101 |
| Pelaihari, Indon. | F4 | 34 |
| Pelat, Mont, mtn., Mart. | E7 | 16 |
| Pelee, Montagne, mtn., Mart. | I14 | 64 |
| Pelee Island, i., Ont. | F2 | 73 |
| Peleliu, i., Palau | R17 | 52 |
| Pelham, Al., U.S. | B3 | 78 |
| Pelham, Ga., U.S. | E2 | 87 |
| Pelham, Ma., U.S. | B3 | 98 |
| Pelham, N.H., U.S. | E4 | 106 |
| Pelham, N.Y., U.S. | *h13 | 109 |
| Pelham, N.C., U.S. | A3 | 110 |
| Pelham, S.C., U.S. | B3 | 117 |
| Pelham, Tn., U.S. | D8 | 119 |
| Pelham Manor, N.Y., U.S. | h13 | 109 |
| Pelhřimov, Czech. | D3 | 26 |
| Pelican, Ak., U.S. | m21 | 79 |
| Pelican, La., U.S. | C2 | 95 |
| Pelican Bay, b., Man. | C1 | 70 |
| Pelican Lake, Wi., U.S. | C4 | 126 |
| Pelican Lake, l., Alta. | B4 | 68 |
| Pelican Lake, l., Man. | C1 | 70 |
| Pelican Lake, l., Sask. | B4 | 75 |
| Pelican Lake, l., Mn., U.S. | D4 | 100 |
| Pelican Lake, l., Mn., U.S. | E5 | 100 |
| Pelican Lake, l., Mn., U.S. | B6 | 100 |
| Pelican Lake, l., Mn., U.S. | D3 | 100 |
| Pelican Lake, l., Wi., U.S. | C4 | 126 |
| Pelican Mountain, mtn., Alta. | B4 | 68 |
| Pelican Narrows, Sask. | B4 | 75 |
| Pelican Rapids, Man. | C1 | 70 |
| Pelican Rapids, Mn., U.S. | D2 | 100 |
| Péligre, Lac de, res., Haiti | E8 | 64 |
| Pelion, S.C., U.S. | D5 | 117 |
| Pella, Ia., U.S. | C5 | 92 |
| Pell City, Al., U.S. | B3 | 78 |
| Pellice, stm., Italy | E2 | 23 |
| Pell Lake, Wi., U.S. | n11 | 126 |
| Pellston, Mi., U.S. | C6 | 99 |
| Pellville, Ky., U.S. | C3 | 94 |
| Pellworm, i., W. Ger. | A4 | 18 |
| Pelly, Sask. | F5 | 75 |
| Pelly, stm., Yukon | D6 | 66 |
| Pelly Crossing, Yukon | D5 | 66 |
| Pelly Lake, l., N.W. Ter. | C12 | 66 |
| Pelly Mountains, mts., Yukon | D6 | 66 |
| Peloncillo Mountains, mts., U.S. | E1 | 108 |
| Peloponnesos, hist. reg., Grc. | D4 | 25 |
| Pelotas, Braz. | E2 | 56 |
| Pelotas, stm., Braz. | D2 | 56 |
| Pel'ovo, Bul. | D7 | 24 |
| Pelton, Lake, l., La., U.S. | E5 | 95 |
| Pelusium, hist., Eg. | C4 | 41 |
| Pelusium Bay, b., Eg. | C4 | 41 |
| Pelzer, S.C., U.S. | B3 | 117 |
| Pemadumcook Lake, l., Me., U.S. | C3 | 96 |
| Pemalang, Indon. | *G3 | 34 |
| Pemanggil, i., Malay. | K6 | 35 |
| Pemaquid, Me., U.S. | E3 | 96 |
| Pematangsiantar, Indon. | m11 | 34 |
| Pemba, Moz. | D7 | 48 |
| Pemba, Zam. | E4 | 48 |
| Pemba, prov., Tan. | C6 | 48 |
| Pemba, i., Tan. | C6 | 48 |
| Pemberton, B.C. | D6 | 69 |
| Pemberton, N.J., U.S. | D3 | 107 |
| Pemberton, Oh., U.S. | B1 | 112 |
| Pemberville, Oh., U.S. | A2 | 112 |
| Pembina, N.D., U.S. | A8 | 111 |
| Pembina, co., N.D., U.S. | A8 | 111 |
| Pembina, stm., Alta. | C3 | 68 |
| Pembina, stm., N.A. | E2 | 70 |
| Pembina Mountains, mts., N.A. | A7 | 111 |
| Pembine, Wi., U.S. | C6 | 126 |
| Pembroke, Ont. | B7 | 73 |
| Pembroke, Wales, U.K. | E4 | 10 |
| Pembroke, Ga., U.S. | D5 | 87 |
| Pembroke, Ky., U.S. | D2 | 94 |
| Pembroke, Me., U.S. | D5 | 96 |
| Pembroke, N.H., U.S. | D4 | 106 |
| Pembroke, N.Y., U.S. | B2 | 109 |
| Pembroke, N.C., U.S. | C3 | 110 |
| Pembroke, Va., U.S. | C2 | 123 |
| Pembroke Park, Fl., U.S. | *G6 | 86 |
| Pembroke Pines, Fl., U.S. | r13 | 86 |
| Pembuang, stm., Indon. | F4 | 34 |
| Pemigewasset, stm., N.H., U.S. | C3 | 106 |
| Pemigewasset, East Branch, stm., N.H., U.S. | B3 | 106 |
| Pemiscot, co., Mo., U.S. | E8 | 102 |
| Pemmican Portage, Sask. | D4 | 75 |
| Pemuco, Chile | B2 | 54 |
| Pena Blanca, N.M., U.S. | B3 | 108 |
| Penafiel, Port. | B1 | 22 |
| Peñafiel, Spain | B4 | 22 |
| Peñalara, mtn., Spain | B4 | 22 |
| Penalosa, Ks., U.S. | E5 | 93 |
| Penamacor, Port. | B2 | 22 |
| Penápolis, Braz. | C2 | 56 |
| Peñaranda de Bracamonte, Spain | B3 | 22 |
| Pen Argyl, Pa., U.S. | E11 | 115 |
| Peñarroya-Pueblonuevo, Spain | C3 | 22 |
| Peñas, Cape, c., Spain | A3 | 22 |
| Peñas, Golfo de, b., Chile | D2 | 54 |
| Penasco, N.M., U.S. | A4 | 108 |
| Peñasco, Rio, stm., N.M., U.S. | E4 | 108 |
| Penbrook, Pa., U.S. | F8 | 115 |
| Pence, In., U.S. | D2 | 91 |
| Pencer, Mn., U.S. | B3 | 100 |
| Penck Trough, val., Ant. | B12 | 7 |
| Pendéli (Pentelicus), mtn., Grc. | g11 | 25 |
| Pendembu, S.L. | E2 | 45 |
| Pender, Ne., U.S. | B9 | 104 |
| Pender, co., N.C., U.S. | C4 | 110 |
| Pendergrass, Ga., U.S. | B3 | 87 |
| Pender Island, B.C. | g12 | 69 |
| Pendleton, In., U.S. | E6 | 91 |
| Pendleton, Or., U.S. | B8 | 114 |
| Pendleton, S.C., U.S. | B2 | 117 |
| Pendleton, co., Ky., U.S. | B5 | 94 |
| Pendleton, co., W.V., U.S. | C5 | 125 |
| Pendleyville, Ga., U.S. | h8 | 87 |
| Pend Oreille, co., Wa., U.S. | A8 | 124 |
| Pend Oreille, stm., Wa., U.S. | A8 | 124 |
| Pend Oreille, Lake, l., Id., U.S. | A2 | 89 |
| Pend Oreille, Mount, mtn., Id., U.S. | A2 | 89 |
| Pendroy, Mt., U.S. | B4 | 103 |
| Penedo, Braz. | D3 | 57 |
| Penetanguishene, Ont. | C5 | 73 |
| Penfield, Il., U.S. | C6 | 90 |
| Penfield, Il., U.S. | C5 | 90 |
| Penfield, N.Y., U.S. | *B3 | 109 |
| Penfield, Pa., U.S. | D4 | 115 |
| Pen'ga, China | I2 | 32 |
| Penganga, stm., India | H6 | 37 |
| Penge, Zaire | C5 | 48 |
| Pengibu, i., Indon. | L7 | 35 |
| Penghu, China | F9 | 32 |
| Pengshui, China | J3 | 32 |
| Penguin Islands, is., Newf. | E3 | 72 |
| Penha, Braz. | D3 | 56 |
| Penhold, Alta. | C4 | 68 |
| Penhook, Va., U.S. | D3 | 123 |
| Peniche, Port. | C1 | 22 |
| Penicuik, Scot., U.K. | E5 | 13 |
| Peninsula, Oh., U.S. | A4 | 112 |
| Peninsular Malaysia, hist. reg., Malay. | E2 | 34 |
| Penitas, Tx., U.S. | F3 | 120 |
| Penitente, Serra do, hills, Braz. | C1 | 57 |
| Penitentiary Mountain, hill, Al., U.S. | A2 | 78 |
| Pénjamo, Mex. | m13 | 63 |
| Penn, Sask. | D2 | 75 |
| Penn, N.D., U.S. | A6 | 111 |
| Penn Acres, De., U.S. | *B3 | 85 |
| Pennant Point, c., N.S. | E6 | 71 |
| Pennant Station, Sask. | G2 | 75 |
| Pennask Mountain, mtn., B.C. | E7 | 69 |
| Penne, Italy | C4 | 23 |
| Pennell, Mount, mtn., Ut., U.S. | F5 | 121 |
| Pennellville, N.Y., U.S. | B4 | 109 |
| Penner, stm., India | F6 | 36 |
| Penneshaw, Austl. | G1 | 51 |
| Penney Farms, Fl., U.S. | C5 | 86 |
| Penn Hills, Pa., U.S. | k14 | 115 |
| Penniac, N.B. | C3 | 71 |
| Pennine Alps, mts., Eur. | C5 | 10 |
| Pennines, mts., Eng., U.K. | E3 | 18 |
| Pennington, N.J., U.S. | C3 | 107 |
| Pennington, co., Mn., U.S. | B2 | 100 |
| Pennington, co., S.D., U.S. | D2 | 118 |
| Pennington Gap, Va., U.S. | f8 | 123 |
| Pennock, Mn., U.S. | E3 | 100 |
| Pennsauken, N.J., U.S. | D2 | 107 |
| Pennsboro, W.V., U.S. | B4 | 125 |
| Penns Grove, N.J., U.S. | D2 | 107 |
| Pennsuco, Fl., U.S. | s13 | 86 |
| Pennsville, N.J., U.S. | D1 | 107 |
| Pennsylvania, state, U.S. | E7 | 115 |
| Penn Valley, Pa., U.S. | o20 | 115 |
| Pennville, In., U.S. | D7 | 91 |
| Penny, B.C. | C7 | 69 |
| Penn Yan, N.Y., U.S. | C3 | 109 |
| Pennycutaway, stm., Man. | A5 | 70 |
| Penobscot, Me., U.S. | D4 | 96 |
| Penobscot, co., Me., U.S. | C4 | 96 |
| Penobscot, stm., Me., U.S. | C4 | 96 |
| Penobscot, East Branch, stm., Me., U.S. | C4 | 96 |
| Penobscot, North Branch, stm., Me., U.S. | B2 | 96 |
| Penobscot, West Branch, stm., Me., U.S. | C3 | 96 |
| Penobscot Bay, b., Me., U.S. | D3 | 96 |
| Penobscot Lake, l., Me., U.S. | C2 | 96 |
| Penobsquis, N.B. | D4 | 71 |
| Penokee, Ks., U.S. | C4 | 93 |
| Penong, Austl. | F5 | 50 |
| Penonomé, Pan. | F7 | 62 |
| Penrhyn, Cape, c., N.W. Ter. | C16 | 66 |
| Penrith, Austl. | *F9 | 50 |
| Penrith, Eng., U.K. | F6 | 13 |
| Pensacola, Fl., U.S. | u14 | 86 |
| Pensacola, Ok., U.S. | A6 | 113 |
| Pensacola Bay, b., Fl., U.S. | u14 | 86 |
| Pensacola Dam, Ok., U.S. | A6 | 113 |
| Pensacola Mountains, mts., Ant. | A6 | 7 |
| Pensacola Naval Air Station, mil., Fl., U.S. | u14 | 86 |
| Pensaukee, Wi., U.S. | D6 | 126 |
| Pense, Sask. | G3 | 75 |
| Pentecostes, Braz. | B3 | 57 |
| Pentelicus see Pendéli, mtn., Grc. | g11 | 25 |
| Penticton, B.C. | E8 | 69 |
| Pentland Firth, strt., Scot., U.K. | A5 | 10 |
| Pentland Hills, hills, Scot., U.K. | E5 | 13 |
| Penton, N.J., U.S. | D2 | 107 |
| Pentwater, Mi., U.S. | E4 | 99 |
| Penwell, Tx., U.S. | D1 | 120 |
| Penza, Sov. Un. | D7 | 29 |
| Penzance, Sask. | F3 | 75 |
| Penzance, Eng., U.K. | E4 | 10 |
| Penzberg, W. Ger. | E5 | 18 |
| Penzhina, stm., Sov. Un. | C19 | 29 |
| Penzlin, E. Ger. | B7 | 19 |
| Peoa, Ut., U.S. | C4 | 121 |
| Peonan Point, c., Man. | D2 | 70 |
| Peoples, Ky., U.S. | C5 | 94 |
| Peoria, Az., U.S. | D3 | 80 |
| Peoria, Il., U.S. | C4 | 90 |
| Peoria, Oh., U.S. | B2 | 112 |
| Peoria, co., Il., U.S. | C4 | 90 |
| Peoria Heights, Il., U.S. | C4 | 90 |
| Peotone, Il., U.S. | B6 | 90 |
| Pep, N.M., U.S. | D6 | 108 |
| Pepacton Reservoir, res., N.Y., U.S. | C6 | 109 |
| Pepeekeo, Hi., U.S. | D6 | 88 |
| Pepin, Wi., U.S. | D1 | 126 |
| Pepin, co., Wi., U.S. | D1 | 126 |
| Pepin, Lake, l., U.S. | D1 | 126 |
| Pepper Creek, stm., De., U.S. | A4 | 98 |
| Pepperell, Ma., U.S. | A4 | 98 |
| Pepper Pike, Oh., U.S. | *h10 | 112 |
| Peqini, Alb. | B2 | 25 |
| Pequabuck, Ct., U.S. | C4 | 84 |
| Pequannock, N.J., U.S. | B4 | 107 |
| Pequeni, stm., Pan. | k12 | 62 |
| Pequest, stm., N.J., U.S. | B3 | 107 |
| Pequop Mountains, mts., Nv., U.S. | C7 | 105 |
| Pequot Lakes, Mn., U.S. | D4 | 100 |
| Perabumulih, Indon. | F2 | 34 |
| Perak, state, Malay. | J4 | 35 |
| Perak, stm., Malay. | J4 | 35 |
| Perakhóra, Grc. | g9 | 25 |
| Perales, stm., Spain | p16 | 22 |
| Perales de Tajuña, Spain | p18 | 22 |
| Peralta, N.M., U.S. | C3 | 108 |
| Pérama, Grc. | h11 | 25 |
| Percival, Ia., U.S. | D2 | 92 |
| Percy, Il., U.S. | E4 | 90 |
| Percy, N.H., U.S. | A4 | 106 |
| Perdido, stm., U.S. | D2 | 78 |
| Perdido, mtn., Spain | A6 | 22 |
| Perdido, Al., U.S. | E2 | 78 |
| Perdido Bay, b., Al., U.S. | E2 | 78 |
| Perdizes, Braz. | B5 | 56 |
| Perdu, Lake, l., La., U.S. | B5 | 95 |
| Perdue, Sask. | E2 | 75 |
| Perea, N.M., U.S. | B1 | 108 |
| Pereira, Col. | C2 | 60 |
| Pereira Barreto, Braz. | C2 | 56 |
| Perekop, Sov. Un. | H9 | 27 |
| Pere Marquette, stm., Mi., U.S. | E4 | 99 |
| Peremennyy, Cape, c., Ant. | C23 | 7 |
| Perené, stm., Peru | D3 | 58 |
| Pereslavl-Zalesskiy, Sov. Un. | C12 | 27 |
| Pereyaslav-Khmelnitskiy, Sov. Un. | G4 | 27 |
| Pergamino, Arg. | A4 | 54 |
| Pergine Valsugana, Italy | A3 | 23 |
| Perham, Me., U.S. | B4 | 96 |
| Perham, Mn., U.S. | D3 | 100 |
| Péribonca, Que. | A5 | 74 |
| Peridot, Az., U.S. | D5 | 80 |
| Périgueux, Fr. | E4 | 16 |
| Perijá, Sierra de, mts., S.A. | B3 | 60 |
| Perim, i., Yemen | D4 | 38 |
| Peristérion, Grc. | g11 | 25 |
| Perito Moreno, Arg. | D2 | 54 |
| Perkasie, Pa., U.S. | F11 | 115 |
| Perkins, Que. | D2 | 74 |
| Perkins, Ga., U.S. | D4 | 87 |
| Perkins, Ok., U.S. | B5 | 113 |
| Perkins, co., Ne., U.S. | D4 | 104 |
| Perkins, co., S.D., U.S. | B3 | 118 |
| Perkinston, Ms., U.S. | E4 | 101 |
| Perkinsville, Vt., U.S. | E3 | 122 |
| Perla, Ar., U.S. | C3 | 81 |
| Perlas, Archipiélago de las, is., Pan. | F8 | 62 |
| Perlas, Laguna de, b., Nic. | E8 | 63 |
| Perleberg, E. Ger. | B6 | 19 |
| Perley, Mn., U.S. | C2 | 100 |
| Perlis, state, Malay. | I4 | 35 |
| Perl-Mack, Co., U.S. | *B6 | 83 |
| Perm, Sov. Un. | D8 | 29 |
| Përmeti, Alb. | C3 | 25 |
| Pernambuco, state, Braz. | B3 | 57 |
| Pernell, Ok., U.S. | C4 | 113 |
| Pernik, Bul. | D6 | 24 |
| Péronne, Fr. | C5 | 16 |
| Perote, Mex. | h10 | 63 |
| Perpignan, Fr. | F5 | 16 |
| Perquimans, co., N.C., U.S. | A6 | 110 |
| Perrin, Tx., U.S. | C3 | 120 |
| Perrine, Fl., U.S. | G6 | 86 |
| Perrineville, N.J., U.S. | C4 | 107 |
| Perris, Ca., U.S. | F5 | 82 |
| Perro, Laguna del, l., N.M., U.S. | C4 | 108 |
| Perronville, Mi., U.S. | C3 | 99 |
| Perros-Guirec, Fr. | C2 | 16 |
| Perrot, Île, i., Que. | q19 | 74 |
| Perry, Ar., U.S. | B3 | 81 |
| Perry, Fl., U.S. | B3 | 86 |
| Perry, Ga., U.S. | D3 | 87 |
| Perry, Il., U.S. | D3 | 90 |
| Perry, Ia., U.S. | C3 | 92 |
| Perry, Ks., U.S. | C8 | 93 |
| Perry, La., U.S. | E3 | 95 |
| Perry, Me., U.S. | D5 | 96 |
| Perry, Mi., U.S. | F6 | 99 |
| Perry, Mo., U.S. | B6 | 102 |
| Perry, N.Y., U.S. | C2 | 109 |
| Perry, Oh., U.S. | A4 | 112 |
| Perry, Ok., U.S. | A4 | 113 |
| Perry, S.C., U.S. | D4 | 117 |
| Perry, Ut., U.S. | B3 | 121 |
| Perry, co., Ar., U.S. | C3 | 81 |
| Perry, co., Il., U.S. | E4 | 90 |
| Perry, co., In., U.S. | H4 | 91 |
| Perry, co., Ky., U.S. | C6 | 94 |
| Perry, co., Ms., U.S. | D4 | 101 |
| Perry, co., Mo., U.S. | D8 | 102 |
| Perry, co., Oh., U.S. | C3 | 112 |
| Perry, co., Pa., U.S. | F7 | 115 |
| Perry, co., Tn., U.S. | B4 | 119 |
| Perrydale, Or., U.S. | k11 | 114 |
| Perry Hall, Md., U.S. | B5 | 97 |
| Perry Heights, Oh., U.S. | *B4 | 112 |
| Perry Lake, res., Ks., U.S. | C8 | 93 |
| Perryman, Md., U.S. | B5 | 97 |
| Perry Peak, mtn., Ma., U.S. | B1 | 98 |
| Perry Point, Md., U.S. | A5 | 97 |
| Perrysburg, N.Y., U.S. | C1 | 109 |
| Perrysburg, Oh., U.S. | A2 | 112 |
| Perrysburg Heights, Oh., U.S. | e6 | 112 |
| Perry Stream, stm., N.H., U.S. | f7 | 106 |
| Perry's Victory and International Peace Memorial, hist., Oh., U.S. | A2 | 112 |
| Perrysville, Oh., U.S. | B3 | 112 |
| Perrysville, Pa., U.S. | h13 | 115 |
| Perryton, Tx., U.S. | A2 | 120 |
| Perryville, Ak., U.S. | D8 | 79 |
| Perryville, Ar., U.S. | B3 | 81 |
| Perryville, Ky., U.S. | C5 | 94 |
| Perryville, Md., U.S. | A5 | 97 |
| Perryville, Mo., U.S. | D8 | 102 |
| Perryville, R.I., U.S. | F3 | 116 |
| Persan, Fr. | E2 | 17 |
| Persepolis, hist., Iran | C5 | 38 |
| Perseverancia, Bol. | B3 | 55 |
| Persia, Ia., U.S. | C2 | 92 |
| Persia, Tn., U.S. | C10 | 119 |
| Persian Gulf, b., Asia | C5 | 38 |
| Persimmon Grove, Ky., U.S. | k14 | 94 |
| Person, co., N.C., U.S. | A3 | 110 |
| Perstorp, Swe. | B7 | 15 |
| Pertek, Tur. | C12 | 40 |
| Perth, Austl. | F2 | 50 |
| Perth, Ont. | C8 | 73 |
| Perth, Scot., U.K. | B5 | 10 |
| Perth, Ks., U.S. | E6 | 93 |
| Perth, N.D., U.S. | A6 | 111 |
| Perth, co., Ont. | D3 | 73 |
| Perth Amboy, N.J., U.S. | B4 | 107 |
| Perth-Andover, N.B. | D10 | 71 |
| Perthshire, Ms., U.S. | B3 | 101 |
| Pertuis, Fr. | F6 | 16 |
| Peru, Il., U.S. | B4 | 90 |
| Peru, In., U.S. | C5 | 91 |
| Peru, Ia., U.S. | C4 | 92 |
| Peru, Me., U.S. | D2 | 96 |
| Peru, Ne., U.S. | D10 | 104 |
| Peru, N.Y., U.S. | f11 | 109 |
| Peru, Vt., U.S. | E3 | 122 |
| Peru, ctry., S.A. | C4 | 58 |
| Perugia, Italy | C4 | 23 |
| Peruíbe, Braz. | G5 | 56 |
| Peruque, Mo., U.S. | f12 | 102 |
| Péruwelz, Bel. | E3 | 16 |
| Pervomaysk, Sov. Un. | G8 | 27 |
| Pervomaysk, Sov. Un. | C12 | 27 |
| Pervoural'sk, Sov. Un. | D9 | 29 |
| Pesaro, Italy | C4 | 23 |
| Pescadero, Ca., U.S. | D2 | 82 |
| Pescara, Italy | C4 | 23 |
| Pescara, stm., Italy | C4 | 23 |
| Peschanyy, Cape, c., Sov. Un. | B10 | 33 |
| Pescia, Italy | A3 | 23 |
| Peshastin, Wa., U.S. | B5 | 124 |
| Peshāwar, Pak. | B3 | 36 |
| Peshkopija, Alb. | B3 | 25 |
| Peshtera, Bul. | D6 | 24 |
| Peshtigo, Wi., U.S. | C6 | 126 |
| Peshtigo, stm., Wi., U.S. | C5 | 126 |
| Peski, Sov. Un. | F14 | 27 |
| Peski, Sov. Un. | n18 | 27 |
| Peso da Régua, Port. | D5 | 90 |
| Pesotum, Il., U.S. | D5 | 90 |
| Pesqueira, Braz. | E3 | 16 |
| Pessac, Fr. | E3 | 16 |
| Petaca, N.M., U.S. | A3 | 108 |
| Petacas, Cerro, mtn., Col. | C2 | 60 |
| Petah Tiqwa, Isr. | D4 | 41 |
| Petal, Ms., U.S. | D4 | 101 |
| Petaling Jaya, Malay. | K4 | 35 |
| Petaluma, Ca., U.S. | C2 | 82 |
| Petatlán, Mex. | D4 | 63 |
| Petauke, Zam. | D5 | 48 |
| Petawawa, Ont. | B7 | 73 |
| Petawawa, stm., Ont. | A6 | 73 |
| Petén Itzá, Lago, l., Guat. | B3 | 62 |
| Petenwell Lake, res., Wi., U.S. | F6 | 126 |
| Peterborough, Austl. | F6 | 50 |
| Peterborough, Ont. | C6 | 73 |
| Peterborough, Eng., U.K. | C3 | 10 |
| Peterborough, N.H., U.S. | E3 | 106 |
| Peterborough, co., Ont. | C6 | 73 |
| Peter Dana Point, Me., U.S. | C5 | 96 |
| Peterhead, Scot., U.K. | C6 | 10 |
| Peter I Island, i., Ant. | B6 | 7 |
| Peter Island, i., V.I. Br. | B6 | 7 |
| Peterlee, Eng., U.K. | F7 | 13 |
| Peter Lougheed Provincial Park, Alta. | D3 | 68 |
| Peterman, Al., U.S. | D2 | 78 |
| Petermann Ranges, mts., Austl. | E4 | 50 |
| Peter Pond Lake, l., Sask. | m7 | 75 |
| Petersburg, Ak., U.S. | D13 | 79 |
| Petersburg, De., U.S. | D3 | 85 |
| Petersburg, Il., U.S. | C4 | 90 |
| Petersburg, In., U.S. | H3 | 91 |
| Petersburg, Ky., U.S. | h13 | 94 |
| Petersburg, Mi., U.S. | G7 | 99 |
| Petersburg, Ne., U.S. | C7 | 104 |
| Petersburg, N.J., U.S. | E3 | 107 |
| Petersburg, N.Y., U.S. | C7 | 109 |
| Petersburg, N.D., U.S. | A8 | 111 |
| Petersburg, Oh., U.S. | B5 | 112 |
| Petersburg, Pa., U.S. | E5 | 115 |
| Petersburg, Tn., U.S. | B5 | 119 |
| Petersburg, Tx., U.S. | C2 | 120 |
| Petersburg, Va., U.S. | C5 | 123 |
| Petersburg, W.V., U.S. | B5 | 125 |
| Peters Creek, stm., W.V., U.S. | m14 | 125 |
| Petersdorf, W. Ger. | D15 | 18 |
| Petersfield, Man. | D3 | 70 |
| Petersham, Ma., U.S. | B3 | 98 |
| Peters Landing, Tn., U.S. | B4 | 119 |
| Peters Mountain, mtn., U.S. | A4 | 125 |
| Peterson, Al., U.S. | B2 | 78 |
| Peterson, Ia., U.S. | B2 | 92 |
| Peterson, Mn., U.S. | G7 | 100 |
| Peterson Field, mil., Co., U.S. | C6 | 83 |
| Peterstown, W.V., U.S. | D3 | 125 |
| Petersville, Al., U.S. | A2 | 78 |
| Petersville, Ky., U.S. | B6 | 94 |
| Peter the Great Bay, b., Sov. Un. | C11 | 31 |
| Petilia Policastro, Italy | E6 | 23 |
| Pétionville, Haiti | E7 | 64 |
| Petit Bois Island, i., Ms., U.S. | E5 | 101 |
| Petitcodiac, N.B. | D4 | 71 |
| Petitcodiac, stm., N.B. | C5 | 71 |
| Petit-de-Grat, N.S. | D9 | 71 |
| Petite Amite, stm., La., U.S. | h10 | 95 |
| Petite Rivière, N.B. | E5 | 71 |
| Petite-Rivière-de-l'Artibonite, Haiti | E7 | 64 |
| Petite-Rivière-de-l'Île, N.B. | C7 | 71 |
| Petit-Étang, N.S. | C9 | 71 |
| Petit-Goâve, Haiti | E7 | 64 |
| Petit Jean, stm., Ar., U.S. | B2 | 81 |
| Petit Jean Mountain, mtn., Ar., U.S. | C2 | 81 |
| Petit Lac Des Allemands, l., La., U.S. | k11 | 95 |
| Petit Lake, l., La., U.S. | k12 | 95 |
| Petit-Mécatina, Île du, i., Que. | C2 | 72 |
| Petit-Rocher, N.B. | B4 | 71 |
| Petitsikapau Lake, l., Newf. | g8 | 72 |
| Peto, Mex. | C7 | 63 |
| Petorca, Chile | A2 | 54 |
| Petoskey, Mi., U.S. | C6 | 99 |
| Petra, hist., Jord. | D7 | 41 |
| Petras, Mount, mtn., Ant. | B36 | 7 |
| Petrey, Al., U.S. | D3 | 78 |
| Petrich, Bul. | E6 | 24 |
| Petrified Forest National Park, Az., U.S. | B6 | 80 |
| Petrikov, Sov. Un. | E7 | 27 |
| Petrila, Rom. | C6 | 24 |
| Petrinja, Yugo. | A3 | 23 |
| Petrodvorets, Sov. Un. | s30 | 14 |
| Petrokrepost, Sov. Un. | B8 | 27 |
| Petrolândia, Braz. | C3 | 57 |
| Petroleum, Ky., U.S. | C3 | 94 |
| Petroleum, co., Mt., U.S. | C8 | 103 |
| Petrolia, Ont. | E2 | 73 |
| Petrolia, Ca., U.S. | B1 | 82 |
| Petrolia, Ks., U.S. | E8 | 93 |
| Petrolia, Pa., U.S. | D2 | 115 |
| Petrolia, Tx., U.S. | B3 | 120 |
| Petrolina, Braz. | C2 | 57 |
| Petropavlovsk, Sov. Un. | D9 | 29 |
| Petropavlovsk [-Kamchatskiy], Sov. Un. | D18 | 29 |
| Petrópolis, Braz. | C4 | 56 |
| Petros, Tn., U.S. | C9 | 119 |
| Petroşani, Rom. | C6 | 24 |
| Petrovgrad see Zrenjanin, Yugo. | C5 | 24 |
| Petrovsk, Sov. Un. | E15 | 27 |
| Petrovsk-Zabaykalskiy, Sov. Un. | D13 | 29 |
| Petrozavodsk, Sov. Un. | C6 | 29 |
| Pettaquamscutt Lake Shores, R.I., U.S. | F4 | 116 |
| Pettibone, N.D., U.S. | B6 | 111 |
| Pettigo, Ire. | E4 | 11 |
| Pettigrew, Ar., U.S. | B2 | 81 |
| Pettingell Peak, mtn., Co., U.S. | B5 | 83 |
| Pettis, co., Mo., U.S. | C4 | 102 |
| Pettisville, Oh., U.S. | A1 | 112 |
| Pettus, Tx., U.S. | E4 | 120 |
| Petukhovo, Sov. Un. | B7 | 28 |
| Pevek, Sov. Un. | C33 | 128 |
| Pevely, Mo., U.S. | g13 | 102 |
| Pewamo, Mi., U.S. | F6 | 99 |
| Pewaukee, Wi., U.S. | E5 | 126 |
| Pewaukee Lake, l., Wi., U.S. | m11 | 126 |
| Pewee Valley, Ky., U.S. | B4 | 94 |
| Peyton, Co., U.S. | C6 | 83 |
| Pézenas, Fr. | F5 | 16 |
| Phetchabun, Thai. | B2 | 34 |
| Phetchabun Range, mts., Thai. | E4 | 35 |
| Phetchaburi, Thai. | C1 | 34 |
| Phichit, Thai. | D4 | 35 |
| Philadelphia, Il., U.S. | D3 | 90 |
| Philadelphia, Ms., U.S. | C4 | 101 |
| Philadelphia, Mo., U.S. | B6 | 102 |
| Philadelphia, N.Y., U.S. | A5 | 109 |
| Philadelphia, Pa., U.S. | G11 | 115 |
| Philadelphia, co., Pa., U.S. | G12 | 115 |
| Philadelphia Naval Shipyard, mil., Pa., U.S. | P21 | 115 |
| Phil Campbell, Al., U.S. | A2 | 78 |
| Philip, S.D., U.S. | C4 | 118 |
| Philipp, Ms., U.S. | B3 | 101 |
| Philippeville see Skikda, Alg. | B6 | 44 |
| Philippeville, Bel. | D4 | 17 |
| Philippi, W.V., U.S. | B4 | 125 |
| Philippi Glacier, ice, Ant. | C21 | 7 |
| Philippines, ctry., Asia | C6 | 34 |
| Philippine Sea | E7 | 6 |
| Philipsburg, Que. | D4 | 74 |
| Philipsburg, Mt., U.S. | D3 | 103 |
| Philipsburg, Pa., U.S. | E5 | 115 |
| Philipsville, Ont. | C8 | 73 |
| Philleo Lake, l., Wa., U.S. | h14 | 124 |
| Phillip Island, i., Austl. | I5 | 51 |
| Phillippy, Tn., U.S. | A2 | 119 |
| Phillips, Me., U.S. | D2 | 96 |
| Phillips, Ne., U.S. | D7 | 104 |
| Phillips, Ok., U.S. | C5 | 113 |
| Phillips, Tx., U.S. | B2 | 120 |
| Phillips, Wi., U.S. | C3 | 126 |
| Phillips, co., Ar., U.S. | C5 | 81 |
| Phillips, co., Co., U.S. | A8 | 83 |
| Phillips, co., Ks., U.S. | C4 | 93 |
| Phillips, co., Mt., U.S. | B8 | 103 |
| Phillips Brook, stm., N.H., U.S. | A4 | 106 |
| Phillipsburg, Ks., U.S. | C4 | 93 |
| Phillipsburg, Mo., U.S. | D5 | 102 |
| Phillipsburg, N.J., U.S. | B2 | 107 |
| Phillipston, Ma., U.S. | A3 | 98 |
| Philmont, N.Y., U.S. | C7 | 109 |
| Philo, Il., U.S. | C5 | 90 |
| Philo, Oh., U.S. | C4 | 112 |
| Philomath, Ga., U.S. | C4 | 87 |
| Philomath, Or., U.S. | C3 | 114 |
| Philpott Reservoir, res., Va., U.S. | D2 | 123 |
| Phippen, Sask. | E1 | 75 |
| Phippsburg, Co., U.S. | A4 | 83 |
| Phippsburg, Me., U.S. | g8 | 96 |
| Phitsanulok, Thai. | B2 | 34 |
| Phlorina see Flórina, Grc. | B3 | 25 |
| Phnom Penh (Phnom Penh), Camb. | C2 | 34 |
| Phoenix, N.Y., U.S. | C6 | 109 |
| Phoenix, Az., U.S. | D3 | 80 |
| Phoenix, Il., U.S. | k9 | 90 |
| Phoenix, Md., U.S. | A4 | 97 |
| Phoenix, N.Y., U.S. | B4 | 109 |
| Phoenix, Or., U.S. | E4 | 114 |
| Phoenix Islands, is., Kir. | B1 | 6 |
| Phoenixville, Pa., U.S. | F10 | 115 |
| Phongsali, Laos | D5 | 35 |
| Phrae, Thai. | B2 | 34 |
| Phra Nakhon Si Ayutthaya, Thai. | E4 | 35 |
| Phuket, Thai. | D1 | 34 |
| Phuket, Thai. | I3 | 35 |
| Phumi Samraong, Camb. | E5 | 35 |
| Phu Quoc, Viet. | G5 | 35 |
| Phu Quoc, i., Viet. | G6 | 35 |
| Phutthaisong, Thai. | B3 | 35 |
| Piaanu Pass, strt., Micron. | Q18 | 52 |
| Piacenza, Italy | A3 | 23 |
| Pianguan, China | E4 | 32 |
| Pianosa, Italy | C3 | 23 |
| Pianosa Island, i., Italy | C5 | 23 |
| Piatra-Neamţ, Rom. | B8 | 24 |
| Piatt, co., Il., U.S. | D5 | 90 |
| Piauí, state, Braz. | C2 | 57 |
| Piauí, stm., Braz. | C2 | 57 |
| Piave, stm., Italy | A4 | 23 |
| Piazza Armerina, Italy | F5 | 23 |
| Pibor, stm., Afr. | D3 | 43 |
| Pibor Post, Sud. | F4 | 116 |
| Pibroch, Alta. | B4 | 68 |
| Picacho, Id., U.S. | F4 | 89 |
| Picacho, Az., U.S. | E4 | 80 |
| Picacho, N.M., U.S. | D4 | 108 |
| Picard, Que. | B8 | 74 |
| Picard, hist. reg., Fr. | C5 | 16 |
| Picayune, Ms., U.S. | E4 | 101 |
| Piccadilly, Newf. | D2 | 72 |
| Piceance Creek, stm., Co., U.S. | B2 | 83 |
| Pichanal, Arg. | A3 | 55 |
| Picher, Ok., U.S. | A7 | 113 |
| Pichilemu, Chile | A2 | 54 |
| Pichincha, prov., Ec. | B2 | 58 |
| Pickardville, Alta. | C4 | 68 |
| Pickaway, co., Oh., U.S. | C2 | 112 |
| Pickens, Ms., U.S. | C3 | 101 |
| Pickens, Ok., U.S. | C6 | 113 |
| Pickens, S.C., U.S. | B2 | 117 |
| Pickens, W.V., U.S. | C4 | 125 |
| Pickens, co., Al., U.S. | B1 | 78 |
| Pickens, co., Ga., U.S. | B2 | 87 |
| Pickens, co., S.C., U.S. | B2 | 117 |
| Pickensville, Al., U.S. | B1 | 78 |
| Pickerel, Ont. | D5 | 73 |
| Pickerel, stm., Ont. | A4 | 73 |
| Pickerel Lake, l., Wi., U.S. | C5 | 126 |
| Pickering, Ont. | D5 | 73 |
| Pickering, Eng., U.K. | F8 | 13 |
| Pickering, Mo., U.S. | A3 | 102 |
| Pickerington, Oh., U.S. | C3 | 112 |
| Pickett, co., Tn., U.S. | C8 | 119 |
| Pickford, Mi., U.S. | B6 | 99 |
| Pickstown, S.D., U.S. | D7 | 118 |
| Pickton, Tx., U.S. | C5 | 120 |
| Pickwick, Mn., U.S. | G7 | 100 |
| Pickwick Dam, Tn., U.S. | B3 | 119 |
| Pickwick Lake, res., U.S. | A6 | 101 |
| Pickworth Point, c., Ma., U.S. | f12 | 98 |
| Pico, i., Port. | g8 | 44 |
| Pico, Ponta do, mtn., Port. | *g8 | 44 |
| Pico Rivera, Ca., U.S. | n12 | 82 |
| Picos, Braz. | C2 | 57 |
| Picton, Ont. | D7 | 73 |
| Picton, N.Z. | N14 | 51 |
| Pictou, N.S. | D7 | 71 |

| Name | Map Ref. | Page |
|---|---|---|
| Pictou, co., N.S. | D7 | 71 |
| Pictou Island, i., N.S. | D7 | 71 |
| Pictou Landing, N.S. | D7 | 71 |
| Picture Butte, Alta. | E4 | 68 |
| Pictured Rocks National Lakeshore, Mi., U.S. | B4 | 99 |
| Picture Rocks, Pa., U.S. | D8 | 115 |
| Picuí, Braz. | h5 | 57 |
| Picún Leufú, Arg. | B3 | 54 |
| Pidálion, Akrotírion, c., Cyp. | E10 | 40 |
| Pidurutalagala, mtn., Sri L. | G7 | 36 |
| Piedade, Braz. | m8 | 56 |
| Piedal, stm., Mex. | h9 | 63 |
| Piedmont, Que. | D3 | 74 |
| Piedmont, Al., U.S. | B4 | 78 |
| Piedmont, Ca., U.S. | h8 | 82 |
| Piedmont, Ks., U.S. | E7 | 93 |
| Piedmont, Mo., U.S. | D7 | 102 |
| Piedmont, Ok., U.S. | B4 | 113 |
| Piedmont, S.C., U.S. | B3 | 117 |
| Piedmont, S.D., U.S. | C2 | 118 |
| Piedmont, W.V., U.S. | B5 | 125 |
| Piedmont (Piemonte), prov., Italy | B1 | 23 |
| Piedmont Lake, res., Oh., U.S. | B4 | 112 |
| Piedra, Ca., U.S. | D4 | 82 |
| Piedra, stm., Co., U.S. | D3 | 83 |
| Piedrabuena, Spain | C3 | 22 |
| Piedras, stm., Pan. | k12 | 62 |
| Piedras, stm., Pan. | k11 | 62 |
| Piedras, Punta, c., Arg. | B5 | 54 |
| Piedras, Punta, c., Ven. | A5 | 60 |
| Piedras Blancas, Point, c., Ca., U.S. | E3 | 82 |
| Piedras Negras, Guat. | D6 | 63 |
| Piedras Negras, Mex. | B4 | 63 |
| Piedra Sola, Ur. | E1 | 56 |
| Piekary Śląskie, Pol. | g9 | 26 |
| Pieksämäki, Fin. | F12 | 14 |
| Pielinen, l., Fin. | F13 | 14 |
| Piemonte, prov., Italy | D3 | 20 |
| Piendamó, Col. | C2 | 60 |
| Pierce, Co., U.S. | A6 | 83 |
| Pierce, Fl., U.S. | E5 | 86 |
| Pierce, Id., U.S. | C3 | 89 |
| Pierce, Ne., U.S. | B8 | 104 |
| Pierce, Tn., U.S. | A3 | 119 |
| Pierce, co., Ga., U.S. | E4 | 87 |
| Pierce, co., Ne., U.S. | B8 | 104 |
| Pierce, co., N.D., U.S. | A5 | 111 |
| Pierce, co., Wa., U.S. | C3 | 124 |
| Pierce, co., Wi., U.S. | D1 | 126 |
| Pierce, Lake, l., Fl., U.S. | E5 | 86 |
| Pierce City, Mo., U.S. | E3 | 102 |
| Piercefield, N.Y., U.S. | A6 | 109 |
| Pierce Lake, l., Can. | B5 | 70 |
| Pierce Pond, l., Me., U.S. | C2 | 96 |
| Pierces Point, N.J., U.S. | E3 | 107 |
| Pierceton, In., U.S. | B6 | 91 |
| Pierceville, In., U.S. | F7 | 91 |
| Pierceville, Ks., U.S. | E3 | 93 |
| Piercy, Ca., U.S. | C2 | 82 |
| Piermont, N.H., U.S. | C2 | 106 |
| Pierowall, Scot., U.K. | A6 | 13 |
| Pierpont, N.Y., U.S. | A5 | 112 |
| Pierpont, S.D., U.S. | B8 | 118 |
| Pierre, S.D., U.S. | C5 | 118 |
| Pierre, Bayou, stm., Ms., U.S. | D3 | 101 |
| Pierrefitte, Fr. | g10 | 16 |
| Pierrefitte-sur-Aire, Fr. | F5 | 17 |
| Pierrefonds, Que. | q19 | 74 |
| Pierre Part, La., U.S. | k9 | 95 |
| Pierreville, Que. | C5 | 74 |
| Pierron, Il., U.S. | E4 | 90 |
| Pierson, Man. | E1 | 70 |
| Pierson, Fl., U.S. | C5 | 86 |
| Pierson, Ia., U.S. | B2 | 92 |
| Pierz, Mn., U.S. | E4 | 100 |
| Piešťany, Czech. | D4 | 26 |
| Pietermaritzburg, S. Afr. | C5 | 49 |
| Pietersburg, S. Afr. | B4 | 49 |
| Pie Town, N.M., U.S. | C1 | 108 |
| Pietrasanta, Italy | C3 | 23 |
| Piet Retief, S. Afr. | C5 | 49 |
| Pietrosu, mtn., Rom. | B7 | 24 |
| Pietrosul, mtn., Rom. | B7 | 24 |
| Pieve di Cadore, Italy | A4 | 23 |
| Pigeon, Mi., U.S. | E7 | 99 |
| Pigeon, stm., Man. | C3 | 70 |
| Pigeon, stm., l., U.S. | f9 | 110 |
| Pigeon, stm., In., U.S. | A6 | 91 |
| Pigeon, stm., Mn., U.S. | h10 | 100 |
| Pigeon, stm., Wi., U.S. | k10 | 126 |
| Pigeon Bay, b., Man. | C3 | 70 |
| Pigeon Cove, Ma., U.S. | A6 | 98 |
| Pigeon Creek, stm., Al., U.S. | D3 | 78 |
| Pigeon Creek, stm., In., U.S. | H3 | 91 |
| Pigeon Falls, Wi., U.S. | D2 | 126 |
| Pigeon Forge, Tn., U.S. | D10 | 119 |
| Pigeon Lake, l., Alta. | C3 | 68 |
| Pigeon Mountain, mtn., U.S. | B1 | 87 |
| Pigeon Point, c., Mn., U.S. | h10 | 100 |
| Pigg, stm., Va., U.S. | D3 | 123 |
| Piggott, Ar., U.S. | A5 | 81 |
| Pigüé, Arg. | B4 | 54 |
| Piirai, i., Marsh Is. | S18 | 52 |
| Pijijiapan, Mex. | D6 | 63 |
| Pike, N.H., U.S. | B2 | 106 |
| Pike, N.Y., U.S. | C2 | 109 |
| Pike, co., Al., U.S. | D4 | 78 |
| Pike, co., Ar., U.S. | C2 | 81 |
| Pike, co., Ga., U.S. | C2 | 87 |
| Pike, co., Il., U.S. | D2 | 90 |
| Pike, co., In., U.S. | H3 | 91 |
| Pike, co., Ky., U.S. | C7 | 94 |
| Pike, co., Ms., U.S. | D3 | 101 |
| Pike, co., Mo., U.S. | B6 | 102 |
| Pike, co., Oh., U.S. | C2 | 112 |
| Pike, co., Pa., U.S. | D11 | 115 |
| Pike, stm., Wi., U.S. | C6 | 126 |
| Pike City, Ar., U.S. | C2 | 81 |
| Pike Island Dam, U.S. | f8 | 125 |
| Pike Lake, Mn., U.S. | D6 | 100 |
| Pike Road, N.C., U.S. | B6 | 110 |
| Pikes Peak, mtn., Co., U.S. | C5 | 83 |
| Pikes Rocks, mtn., Pa., U.S. | C3 | 115 |
| Pikesville, Md., U.S. | B4 | 97 |
| Piketberg, S. Afr. | D2 | 49 |
| Piketon, Oh., U.S. | C2 | 112 |
| Pikeville, Ky., U.S. | C7 | 94 |
| Pikeville, N.C., U.S. | B5 | 110 |
| Pikeville, Tn., U.S. | D8 | 119 |
| Pikou, China | E10 | 32 |
| Pikwitonei, Man. | B3 | 70 |
| Piła, Pol. | B4 | 26 |
| Pilar, Braz. | C3 | 57 |
| Pilar, Para. | E4 | 55 |
| Pilar do Goiás, Braz. | A3 | 56 |
| Pilar do Sul, Braz. | m8 | 56 |
| Pilatus, mtn., Switz. | C4 | 20 |
| Pilcomayo, stm., S.A. | D4 | 55 |
| Pilger, Sask. | E3 | 75 |
| Pilger, Ne., U.S. | B8 | 104 |
| Pilgrims Knob, Va., U.S. | e10 | 123 |
| Pilgrim, Ky., U.S. | C7 | 94 |
| Pīlībhīt, India | C7 | 37 |
| Pilica, stm., Pol. | C5 | 26 |
| Pillager, Mn., U.S. | D4 | 100 |
| Pillar Point, c., Ca., U.S. | k7 | 82 |
| Pilley's Island, Newf. | D4 | 72 |
| Pillow, Pa., U.S. | E6 | 115 |
| Pillsbury, N.D., U.S. | B8 | 111 |
| Pílos, Grc. | D3 | 25 |
| Pilot Butte, Sask. | G3 | 75 |
| Pilot Grove, Mo., U.S. | C5 | 102 |
| Pilot Knob, Mo., U.S. | D7 | 102 |
| Pilot Knob, mtn., Ar., U.S. | B2 | 81 |
| Pilot Knob, mtn., Ar., U.S. | C1 | 81 |
| Pilot Knob, mtn., Id., U.S. | D3 | 89 |
| Pilot Mound, Man. | E2 | 70 |
| Pilot Mound, Ia., U.S. | B3 | 92 |
| Pilot Mountain, N.C., U.S. | A2 | 110 |
| Pilot Peak, mtn., Nv., U.S. | B7 | 105 |
| Pilot Peak, mtn., Nv., U.S. | E4 | 105 |
| Pilot Peak, mtn., Wy., U.S. | B3 | 127 |
| Pilot Point, Ak., U.S. | D8 | 79 |
| Pilot Point, Tx., U.S. | C4 | 120 |
| Pilot Range, mts., Nv., U.S. | B7 | 105 |
| Pilot Range, mts., N.H., U.S. | A4 | 106 |
| Pilot Rock, Or., U.S. | B8 | 114 |
| Pilot Station, Ak., U.S. | C7 | 79 |
| Pilottown, La., U.S. | E6 | 95 |
| Pilsen, Wi., U.S. | h10 | 126 |
| Pilvo, Sov. Un. | A11 | 33 |
| Pima, Az., U.S. | E6 | 80 |
| Pima, co., Az., U.S. | E3 | 80 |
| Pimmit Hills, Va., U.S. | g12 | 123 |
| Pimpri-Chinchwad, India | *E5 | 36 |
| Piña, Pan. | k10 | 62 |
| Pinal, co., Az., U.S. | E4 | 80 |
| Pinaleno Mountains, mts., Az., U.S. | E5 | 80 |
| Pinal Mountains, mts., Az., U.S. | D5 | 80 |
| Pinang see George Town, Malay. | D2 | 34 |
| Pinang, state, Malay. | J4 | 35 |
| Pinang, i., Malay. | D2 | 34 |
| Pınarbaşı, Tur. | C11 | 40 |
| Pinar del Río, Cuba | C2 | 64 |
| Pinar del Río, prov., Cuba | C2 | 64 |
| Pinardville, N.H., U.S. | E3 | 106 |
| Pinás, Ec. | A3 | 54 |
| Pinawa, Man. | D4 | 70 |
| Pincher Creek, Alta. | E4 | 68 |
| Pincher Station, Alta. | E4 | 68 |
| Pinckard, Al., U.S. | D4 | 78 |
| Pinckney, Mi., U.S. | F7 | 99 |
| Pinckney Island, i., S.C., U.S. | G6 | 117 |
| Pinckneyville, Il., U.S. | E4 | 90 |
| Pinconning, Mi., U.S. | E7 | 99 |
| Pińczów, Pol. | C6 | 26 |
| Pindall, Ar., U.S. | A3 | 81 |
| Pindamonhangaba, Braz. | C3 | 56 |
| Pindaré, stm., Braz. | B1 | 57 |
| Pindiga, Nig. | *E7 | 45 |
| Pindus Mountains, mts., Grc. | D3 | 40 |
| Pine, Az., U.S. | C4 | 80 |
| Pine, Co., U.S. | B5 | 83 |
| Pine, co., Mn., U.S. | D6 | 100 |
| Pine, La., U.S. | D5 | 95 |
| Pine, stm., B.C. | B6 | 69 |
| Pine, stm., Man. | D1 | 70 |
| Pine, stm., Mi., U.S. | D7 | 99 |
| Pine, stm., Mi., U.S. | D5 | 99 |
| Pine, stm., N.H., U.S. | C4 | 106 |
| Pine, stm., Wi., U.S. | C5 | 126 |
| Pine, stm., Wi., U.S. | C4 | 126 |
| Pine Apple, Al., U.S. | D3 | 78 |
| Pine Bank, Pa., U.S. | G1 | 115 |
| Pine Barrens, reg., N.J., U.S. | D3 | 107 |
| Pine Bluff, Ar., U.S. | C3 | 81 |
| Pinebluff, N.C., U.S. | B3 | 110 |
| Pine Bluffs, Wy., U.S. | E8 | 127 |
| Pine Bridge, Ct., U.S. | D3 | 84 |
| Pinebur, Ms., U.S. | D4 | 101 |
| Pine Bush, N.Y., U.S. | D6 | 109 |
| Pine Castle, Fl., U.S. | D5 | 86 |
| Pine City, Ca., U.S. | C4 | 81 |
| Pine City, Mn., U.S. | E6 | 100 |
| Pine City, Wa., U.S. | B8 | 124 |
| Pine Creek, Austl. | B5 | 50 |
| Pine Creek, stm., Alta. | B4 | 68 |
| Pine Creek, stm., Nv., U.S. | C5 | 105 |
| Pine Creek, stm., Pa., U.S. | C6 | 115 |
| Pine Creek Lake, res., Ok. | C6 | 113 |
| Pinecrest, Ca., U.S. | C4 | 82 |
| Pinedale, Az., U.S. | C5 | 80 |
| Pinedale, Wy., U.S. | D3 | 127 |
| Pine Falls, Man. | D3 | 70 |
| Pine Forest Range, mts., Nv., U.S. | B3 | 105 |
| Pine Grove, Ca., U.S. | C3 | 82 |
| Pine Grove, La., U.S. | D5 | 95 |
| Pine Grove, N.J., U.S. | D3 | 107 |
| Pine Grove, Pa., U.S. | E9 | 115 |
| Pine Grove, W.V., U.S. | B4 | 125 |
| Pine Grove Mills, Pa., U.S. | E6 | 115 |
| Pine Hill, Austl. | A6 | 51 |
| Pine Hill, Al., U.S. | D2 | 78 |
| Pine Hill, Ky., U.S. | C5 | 94 |
| Pine Hill, N.J., U.S. | D3 | 107 |
| Pine Hills, Fl., U.S. | D5 | 86 |
| Pinehouse Lake, Sask. | B2 | 75 |
| Pinehouse Lake, l., Sask. | B2 | 75 |
| Pinehurst, Ga., U.S. | D3 | 87 |
| Pinehurst, Id., U.S. | B2 | 89 |
| Pinehurst, Ma., U.S. | f11 | 98 |
| Pinehurst, N.J., U.S. | E3 | 107 |
| Pinehurst, N.C., U.S. | B3 | 110 |
| Pinehurst Lake, l., Alta. | B5 | 68 |
| Pine Island, Mn., U.S. | F6 | 100 |
| Pine Island, N.Y., U.S. | D6 | 109 |
| Pine Island, i., Fl., U.S. | F4 | 86 |
| Pine Island Sound, strt., Fl., U.S. | F4 | 86 |
| Pine Key, i., Fl., U.S. | p10 | 86 |
| Pine Knot, Ky., U.S. | D5 | 94 |
| Pine Lake, Ga., U.S. | h8 | 87 |
| Pine Lake, Ma., U.S. | g10 | 98 |
| Pine Lake, l., In., U.S. | A4 | 91 |
| Pine Lake, l., Wi., U.S. | C5 | 126 |
| Pineland, S.C., U.S. | F5 | 117 |
| Pine Lawn, Mo., U.S. | f13 | 102 |
| Pine Level, Al., U.S. | C3 | 78 |
| Pine Level, N.C., U.S. | B4 | 110 |
| Pinellas, co., Fl., U.S. | D4 | 86 |
| Pinellas Park, Fl., U.S. | p10 | 86 |
| Pine Meadow, Ct., U.S. | B4 | 84 |
| Pine Mountain, Ga., U.S. | D2 | 87 |
| Pine Mountain, mtn., U.S. | D6 | 94 |
| Pine Mountain, mtn., Ct., U.S. | B4 | 84 |
| Pine Mountain, mtn., Ga., U.S. | D2 | 87 |
| Pine Mountain, mtn., Or., U.S. | D6 | 114 |
| Pine Mountain, mtn., Tn., U.S. | C9 | 119 |
| Pine Mountain, mtn., Wy., U.S. | E3 | 127 |
| Pine Mountain, hills, Ok., U.S. | C6 | 113 |
| Pine Orchard, Ct., U.S. | D4 | 84 |
| Pine Park, Ga., U.S. | F2 | 87 |
| Pine Plains, N.Y., U.S. | D7 | 109 |
| Pine Point, N.W. Ter. | D10 | 66 |
| Pine Prairie, La., U.S. | D3 | 95 |
| Piner Bay, b., Ant. | C27 | 7 |
| Pine Rest, Ma., U.S. | g10 | 98 |
| Pine Ridge, Ar., U.S. | C2 | 81 |
| Pine Ridge, Ky., U.S. | C6 | 94 |
| Pine Ridge, Ms., U.S. | D2 | 101 |
| Pine Ridge, S.D., U.S. | D3 | 118 |
| Pine Ridge, mtn., U.S. | B2 | 104 |
| Pine Ridge Indian Reservation, S.D., U.S. | D3 | 118 |
| Pine River, Man. | D1 | 70 |
| Pine River, Mn., U.S. | D4 | 100 |
| Pinerolo, Italy | B1 | 23 |
| Pines, Isle of see Juventud, Isla de la, i., Cuba | D2 | 64 |
| Pines, Lake o' the, res., Tx., U.S. | C5 | 120 |
| Pinesdale, Mt., U.S. | D2 | 103 |
| Pine Stump Junction, Mi., U.S. | B5 | 99 |
| Pine Swamp Knob, mtn., W.V., U.S. | B5 | 125 |
| Pinetops, N.C., U.S. | B5 | 110 |
| Pinetown, N.C., U.S. | B6 | 110 |
| Pine Tree Corners, De., U.S. | C3 | 85 |
| Pinetta, Fl., U.S. | B3 | 86 |
| Pine Valley, Ca., U.S. | F5 | 82 |
| Pine Valley, N.H., U.S. | E3 | 106 |
| Pine Valley, Ut., U.S. | F2 | 121 |
| Pine Valley, val., Ut., U.S. | E2 | 121 |
| Pine Valley Mountains, mts., Ut., U.S. | F2 | 121 |
| Pineview, Ga., U.S. | D3 | 87 |
| Pine Village, In., U.S. | D3 | 91 |
| Pineville, Ky., U.S. | D6 | 94 |
| Pineville, La., U.S. | C3 | 95 |
| Pineville, Mo., U.S. | E3 | 102 |
| Pineville, N.C., U.S. | B2 | 110 |
| Pineville, S.C., U.S. | E7 | 117 |
| Pineville, W.V., U.S. | D3 | 125 |
| Pinewald, N.J., U.S. | D4 | 107 |
| Pinewood, Fl., U.S. | s13 | 86 |
| Pinewood, Mn., U.S. | C3 | 100 |
| Pinewood, S.C., U.S. | D7 | 117 |
| Pinewood Park, Fl., U.S. | *G6 | 86 |
| Piney, Man. | E4 | 70 |
| Piney Creek, stm., W.V., U.S. | n13 | 125 |
| Piney Flats, Tn., U.S. | C11 | 119 |
| Piney Fork, Oh., U.S. | B5 | 112 |
| Piney Point, Md., U.S. | D4 | 97 |
| Piney View, W.V., U.S. | n13 | 125 |
| Piney Woods, Ms., U.S. | C3 | 101 |
| Ping, stm., Thai. | B1 | 34 |
| Pingding, China | F5 | 32 |
| Pingdingshan, China | H5 | 32 |
| Pingdu, China | D8 | 31 |
| Pingjiang, China | J5 | 32 |
| Pingle, China | G7 | 31 |
| Pingliang, China | D6 | 31 |
| Pingluo, China | E2 | 32 |
| Pingnan, China | G7 | 31 |
| Pingquan, China | D8 | 32 |
| Pingree, Id., U.S. | F6 | 89 |
| Pingree, N.D., U.S. | B7 | 111 |
| Pingwu, China | E5 | 31 |
| Pingxiang, China | F7 | 31 |
| Pingxiang, China | G6 | 31 |
| Pinhal, Braz. | C3 | 56 |
| Pinhal Novo, Port. | f10 | 22 |
| Pinheiro, Braz. | B1 | 57 |
| Pinhel, Port. | B2 | 22 |
| Pini, i., Indon. | E1 | 34 |
| Piniós (Peneus), stm., Grc. | C4 | 40 |
| Pink Cliffs, clf., Ut., U.S. | F3 | 121 |
| Pinkham, Sask. | F1 | 75 |
| Pinkham Notch, N.H., U.S. | B4 | 106 |
| Pink Hill, N.C., U.S. | B5 | 110 |
| Pinkstaff, Il., U.S. | E6 | 90 |
| Pinnacle, N.C., U.S. | A2 | 110 |
| Pinnacle, mtn., N.Y., U.S. | B6 | 109 |
| Pinnacle Buttes, mtn., Wy., U.S. | C3 | 127 |
| Pinnacles National Monument, Ca., U.S. | D3 | 82 |
| Pinnaroo, Austl. | G3 | 51 |
| Pinneberg, W. Ger. | E3 | 15 |
| Pinnebog, Mi., U.S. | E7 | 99 |
| Pinola, Ms., U.S. | D4 | 101 |
| Pinole, Ca., U.S. | h8 | 82 |
| Pinon, Az., U.S. | A5 | 80 |
| Piñon, N.M., U.S. | E4 | 108 |
| Pinopolis Dam, S.C., U.S. | E8 | 117 |
| Pinos, Mex. | C4 | 63 |
| Pinos, Mount, mtn., Ca., U.S. | E4 | 82 |
| Pinos, Point, c., Ca., U.S. | D3 | 82 |
| Pinos Altos, N.M., U.S. | E1 | 108 |
| Pinoso, Spain | C5 | 22 |
| Pinos-Puente, Spain | D4 | 22 |
| Pinrang, Oh., U.S. | C1 | 112 |
| Pins, Pointe aux, c., Ont. | E3 | 73 |
| Pins, Sov. Un. | E6 | 27 |
| Pinsk Marshes, sw., Sov. Un. | I7 | 8 |
| Pinson, Tn., U.S. | B3 | 119 |
| Pinta, Isla, i., Ec. | f5 | 58 |
| Pinta, Sierra, mts., Az., U.S. | E2 | 80 |
| Pintados, Chile | D2 | 55 |
| Pinto, Spain | p17 | 22 |
| Pinto, Md., U.S. | k13 | 97 |
| Pinto Butte, mtn., Sask. | H2 | 75 |
| Pinto Creek, stm., Sask. | H2 | 75 |
| Pintura, Ut., U.S. | F2 | 121 |
| Pintwater Range, mts., Nv., U.S. | G6 | 105 |
| Pinware, stm., Newf. | C3 | 72 |
| Pinzolo, Italy | C6 | 20 |
| Pinzón, Isla, i., Ec. | g5 | 58 |
| Pioche, Nv., U.S. | F7 | 105 |
| Piombino, Italy | C3 | 23 |
| Pioneer, La., U.S. | B4 | 95 |
| Pioneer, Oh., U.S. | A1 | 112 |
| Pioneer Mine, B.C. | D6 | 69 |
| Pioneer Mountains, mts., Id., U.S. | F5 | 89 |
| Pioneer Mountains, mts., Mt., U.S. | E3 | 103 |
| Pioner, i., Sov. Un. | B6 | 28 |
| Pionki, Pol. | C6 | 26 |
| Piopolis, Que. | D7 | 74 |
| Piotrków [Trybunalski], Pol. | C5 | 26 |
| Piove di Sacco, Italy | D8 | 20 |
| Pipe, Wi., U.S. | k9 | 126 |
| Pipe Creek, stm., In., U.S. | D6 | 91 |
| Piper, Ks., U.S. | k16 | 93 |
| Piper City, Il., U.S. | C5 | 90 |
| Pipéri, i., Grc. | C5 | 25 |
| Piperville, Ont. | h12 | 73 |
| Pipe Spring National Monument, Az., U.S. | A3 | 80 |
| Pipestem, W.V., U.S. | D4 | 125 |
| Pipestem Creek, stm., N.D., U.S. | B6 | 111 |
| Pipestone, Man. | E1 | 70 |
| Pipestone, Mn., U.S. | G2 | 100 |
| Pipestone, co., Mn., U.S. | F2 | 100 |
| Pipestone Creek, stm., Can. | E1 | 70 |
| Pipestone National Monument, Mn., U.S. | G2 | 100 |
| Pipestone Pass, Mt., U.S. | E4 | 103 |
| Pipmuacan, Réservoir, res., Que. | k12 | 74 |
| Piqua, Ks., U.S. | E8 | 93 |
| Piqua, Oh., U.S. | B1 | 112 |
| Piquiri, stm., Braz. | C2 | 56 |
| Piracanjuba, Braz. | B3 | 56 |
| Piracicaba, Braz. | C3 | 56 |
| Piracicaba, stm., Braz. | m8 | 56 |
| Piracuruca, Braz. | B2 | 57 |
| Piraeus see Piraiévs, Grc. | D4 | 40 |
| Piraiévs (Piraeus), Grc. | D4 | 40 |
| Piraju, Braz. | C3 | 56 |
| Pirajuba, Braz. | B3 | 56 |
| Pirajuí, Braz. | C3 | 56 |
| Piramida, Mount, mtn., Sov. Un. | D12 | 29 |
| Piran, Yugo. | C1 | 24 |
| Pirané, Arg. | A5 | 55 |
| Piranga, Braz. | C4 | 56 |
| Piranhas, Braz. | C3 | 57 |
| Pīrān Shahr, Iran | C2 | 39 |
| Pirapora, Braz. | C3 | 56 |
| Pirassununga, Braz. | C3 | 56 |
| Piratini, Braz. | D2 | 57 |
| Pirenópolis, Braz. | B3 | 56 |
| Pires do Rio, Braz. | B3 | 56 |
| Pírgos, Grc. | D3 | 40 |
| Piriápolis, Ur. | E1 | 56 |
| Piripiri, Braz. | B3 | 57 |
| Pirmasens, W. Ger. | D3 | 18 |
| Pirna, E. Ger. | C6 | 18 |
| Pirot, Yugo. | D6 | 24 |
| Pirovskoye, Sov. Un. | F6 | 28 |
| Pirtleville, Az., U.S. | F6 | 80 |
| Piru, Indon. | F8 | 34 |
| Piru, Ca., U.S. | E4 | 82 |
| Piryatin, Sov. Un. | F9 | 27 |
| Pisa, Italy | C3 | 23 |
| Pisagua, Chile | C1 | 55 |
| Pisac, hist., Peru | D3 | 58 |
| Piscataqua, stm., N.H., U.S. | D5 | 106 |
| Piscataquis, co., Me., U.S. | C3 | 96 |
| Piscataquis, stm., Me., U.S. | C3 | 96 |
| Piscataquog, stm., N.H., U.S. | E3 | 106 |
| Piscataway, N.J., U.S. | B4 | 107 |
| Piscataway Creek, stm., Md., U.S. | C4 | 97 |
| Pisciotta, Italy | D5 | 23 |
| Pisco, Peru | D2 | 58 |
| Piseco Lake, l., N.Y., U.S. | B6 | 109 |
| Písek, Czech. | D3 | 26 |
| Písek, N.D., U.S. | A8 | 111 |
| Pisgah, Al., U.S. | A4 | 78 |
| Pisgah, Ia., U.S. | C2 | 92 |
| Pisgah, Md., U.S. | C3 | 97 |
| Pisgah, Oh., U.S. | n13 | 112 |
| Pisgah, Mount, mtn., Ct., U.S. | B3 | 84 |
| Pisgah, Mount, mtn., Vt., U.S. | F3 | 122 |
| Pisgah, Mount, mtn., Wy., U.S. | B8 | 127 |
| Pisgah Forest, N.C., U.S. | f10 | 110 |
| Pishan, China | B4 | 36 |
| Pishin, Pak. | E2 | 38 |
| Pishin Lora, stm., Asia | E2 | 38 |
| Pisinemo, Az., U.S. | E3 | 80 |
| Pismo Beach, Ca., U.S. | E3 | 82 |
| Pisogne, Italy | D6 | 20 |
| Pissis, Monte, mtn., Arg. | B2 | 55 |
| Pisticci, Italy | D6 | 23 |
| Pistoia, Italy | C3 | 23 |
| Pistolet Bay, b., Newf. | C3 | 72 |
| Pistol River, Or., U.S. | E2 | 114 |
| Pisuerga, stm., Spain | C4 | 22 |
| Pisz, Pol. | B6 | 26 |
| Pit, stm., Ca., U.S. | B3 | 82 |
| Pita, Gui. | D2 | 45 |
| Pital, Cerro el, mtn., N.A. | *C3 | 62 |
| Pitalito, Col. | C2 | 60 |
| Pitanga, Braz. | B2 | 56 |
| Pitangui, Braz. | B4 | 56 |
| Pitcairn, dep., Oc. | H14 | 6 |
| Pitcairn, Pa., U.S. | k14 | 115 |
| Pitcher, N.Y., U.S. | C4 | 109 |
| Piteå, Swe. | E9 | 14 |
| Piteälven, stm., Swe. | C7 | 14 |
| Piteşti, Rom. | C7 | 24 |
| Pithiviers, Fr. | C5 | 16 |
| Piti, Guam | L9 | 52 |
| Pitkin, Co., U.S. | C4 | 83 |
| Pitkin, La., U.S. | D3 | 95 |
| Pitkin, co., Co., U.S. | B4 | 83 |
| Pitlochry, Scot., U.K. | B5 | 10 |
| Pitman, N.J., U.S. | D2 | 107 |
| Pitrufquén, Chile | B2 | 54 |
| Pittsburg, Oh., U.S. | C1 | 112 |
| Pitt, Mn., U.S. | B4 | 100 |
| Pitt, co., N.C., U.S. | B5 | 110 |
| Pitt Island, i., B.C. | C3 | 69 |
| Pittman Center, Tn., U.S. | D10 | 119 |
| Pitts, Ga., U.S. | E3 | 87 |
| Pittsboro, In., U.S. | E5 | 91 |
| Pittsboro, Ms., U.S. | B4 | 101 |
| Pittsboro, N.C., U.S. | B3 | 110 |
| Pittsburg, Ca., U.S. | h9 | 82 |
| Pittsburg, Il., U.S. | F5 | 90 |
| Pittsburg, Ks., U.S. | E9 | 93 |
| Pittsburg, Ky., U.S. | C5 | 94 |
| Pittsburg, Ok., U.S. | C6 | 113 |
| Pittsburg, Tx., U.S. | C5 | 120 |
| Pittsburg, co., Ok., U.S. | C6 | 113 |
| Pittsburgh, Pa., U.S. | F1 | 115 |
| Pittsfield, Il., U.S. | D3 | 90 |
| Pittsfield, Ma., U.S. | B1 | 98 |
| Pittsfield, N.H., U.S. | D4 | 106 |
| Pittsfield, Vt., U.S. | D3 | 122 |
| Pittsford, Mi., U.S. | G6 | 99 |
| Pittsford, Vt., U.S. | D2 | 122 |
| Pittston, Pa., U.S. | D10 | 115 |
| Pittstown, N.J., U.S. | B3 | 107 |
| Pittsview, Al., U.S. | C4 | 78 |
| Pittsville, Md., U.S. | D7 | 97 |
| Pittsville, Wi., U.S. | D3 | 126 |
| Piove di Sacco, Italy | D8 | 20 |
| Pipe, Wi., U.S. | k9 | 126 |
| Piúí, Braz. | C3 | 56 |
| Piura, Peru | C1 | 58 |
| Piura, dept., Peru | C1 | 58 |
| Piuthãn, Nepal | C9 | 37 |
| Piva, stm., Yugo. | A4 | 24 |
| Pixley, Ca., U.S. | E4 | 82 |
| Pizzo, Italy | E6 | 23 |
| P. K. le Roux Dam, res., S. Afr. | D3 | 49 |
| Placentia, Newf. | E5 | 72 |
| Placentia, Ca., U.S. | *n13 | 82 |
| Placentia Bay, b., Newf. | E4 | 72 |
| Placer, co., Ca., U.S. | C3 | 82 |
| Placerville, Ca., U.S. | C3 | 82 |
| Placerville, Co., U.S. | C2 | 83 |
| Placerville, Id., U.S. | F2 | 89 |
| Placetas, Cuba | C4 | 64 |
| Placid, Lake, l., Fl., U.S. | E5 | 86 |
| Placid, Lake, l., N.Y., U.S. | f11 | 109 |
| Placida, Fl., U.S. | F4 | 86 |
| Plácido de Castro, Braz. | D4 | 58 |
| Placitas, N.M., U.S. | B3 | 108 |
| Plaffeien, Switz. | C3 | 21 |
| Plain, Wi., U.S. | E3 | 126 |
| Plain City, Oh., U.S. | B2 | 112 |
| Plain City, Ut., U.S. | B3 | 121 |
| Plain Dealing, La., U.S. | B2 | 95 |
| Plainfield, Ct., U.S. | C8 | 84 |
| Plainfield, Il., U.S. | B5 | 90 |
| Plainfield, In., U.S. | E5 | 91 |
| Plainfield, Ia., U.S. | B5 | 92 |
| Plainfield, Ma., U.S. | A2 | 98 |
| Plainfield, N.H., U.S. | D2 | 106 |
| Plainfield, N.J., U.S. | B4 | 107 |
| Plainfield, Oh., U.S. | B4 | 112 |
| Plainfield, Vt., U.S. | C4 | 122 |
| Plainfield, Wi., U.S. | D4 | 126 |
| Plainfield Heights, Mi., U.S. | E5 | 99 |
| Plains, Ga., U.S. | D2 | 87 |
| Plains, Ks., U.S. | E3 | 93 |
| Plains, Mt., U.S. | C2 | 103 |
| Plains, Pa., U.S. | n17 | 115 |
| Plains, Tx., U.S. | C1 | 120 |
| Plainsboro, N.J., U.S. | C3 | 107 |
| Plainview, Ar., U.S. | C2 | 81 |
| Plainview, Mn., U.S. | F6 | 100 |
| Plainview, Ne., U.S. | B8 | 104 |
| Plainview, N.Y., U.S. | *E7 | 109 |
| Plainview, Tx., U.S. | B2 | 120 |
| Plainville, Ct., U.S. | C4 | 84 |
| Plainville, Ga., U.S. | B1 | 87 |
| Plainville, Il., U.S. | D2 | 90 |
| Plainville, Ks., U.S. | C4 | 93 |
| Plainville, Ma., U.S. | B5 | 98 |
| Plainwell, Mi., U.S. | F5 | 99 |
| Plaisance, Que. | D2 | 74 |
| Plaisance, Haiti | E7 | 64 |
| Plaisance, Baie de, b., Que. | B8 | 71 |
| Plaisance-du-Gers, Fr. | F4 | 16 |
| Plaisted, Me., U.S. | A4 | 96 |
| Plaistow, N.H., U.S. | E4 | 106 |
| Plamondon, Alta. | B4 | 68 |
| Planá, Czech. | D7 | 19 |
| Planaltina, Braz. | B3 | 56 |
| Plane, stm., E. Ger. | A7 | 19 |
| Plankinton, S.D., U.S. | D7 | 118 |
| Plano, Il., U.S. | B5 | 90 |
| Plano, Tx., U.S. | C4 | 120 |
| Plantagenet, Ont. | B9 | 73 |
| Plantation, Fl., U.S. | r13 | 86 |
| Plantersville, Al., U.S. | C3 | 78 |
| Plantersville, Ms., U.S. | A5 | 101 |
| Plantersville, S.C., U.S. | D9 | 117 |
| Plantsite, Az., U.S. | D6 | 80 |
| Plantsville, Ct., U.S. | C4 | 84 |
| Plaquemine, La., U.S. | D4 | 95 |
| Plaquemines, co., La., U.S. | E6 | 95 |
| Plasencia, Spain | B2 | 22 |
| Plast, Sov. Un. | E2 | 8 |
| Plaster Rock, N.B. | C2 | 71 |
| Plastun, Sov. Un. | D8 | 33 |
| Plasy, Czech. | D7 | 19 |
| Plata, Isla, i., Ec. | A1 | 54 |
| Plata, Río de la, est., S.A. | B5 | 54 |
| Platea, Pa., U.S. | C1 | 115 |
| Plateau, N.S. | C8 | 71 |
| Plateau City, Co., U.S. | B3 | 83 |
| Plateau Creek, stm., Co., U.S. | B3 | 83 |
| Plate Cove West, Newf. | D5 | 72 |
| Platina, Ca., U.S. | B2 | 82 |
| Platinum, Ak., U.S. | D7 | 79 |
| Platner, Co., U.S. | A7 | 83 |
| Plato, Col. | B5 | 60 |
| Plato, Mo., U.S. | D5 | 102 |
| Platón Sánchez, Mex. | m14 | 63 |
| Platte, S.D., U.S. | D7 | 118 |
| Platte, co., Mo., U.S. | B3 | 102 |
| Platte, co., Ne., U.S. | C8 | 104 |
| Platte, co., Wy., U.S. | D7 | 127 |
| Platte, stm., U.S. | E4 | 100 |
| Platte, stm., Mn., U.S. | E4 | 100 |
| Platte Center, Ne., U.S. | C8 | 104 |
| Platte City, Mo., U.S. | B3 | 102 |
| Plattekill, N.Y., U.S. | k9 | 109 |
| Platteville, Co., U.S. | A6 | 83 |
| Platteville, Wi., U.S. | F3 | 126 |
| Plattling, W. Ger. | D7 | 19 |
| Plattsburg, Mo., U.S. | B3 | 102 |
| Plattsburgh, N.Y., U.S. | f11 | 109 |
| Plattsburgh Air Force Base, mil., N.Y., U.S. | f11 | 109 |
| Plattsmouth, Ne., U.S. | D10 | 104 |
| Plattville, Ont. | D4 | 73 |
| Plau, E. Ger. | B5 | 18 |
| Plaucheville, La., U.S. | C4 | 95 |
| Plauen, E. Ger. | C6 | 18 |
| Plauer, l., E. Ger. | E6 | 15 |
| Play Cu, Viet. | F7 | 35 |
| Playgreen Lake, l., Man. | C2 | 70 |
| Plaza, N.D., U.S. | A4 | 111 |
| Pleasant, stm., Me., U.S. | D4 | 96 |
| Pleasant, Lake, res., Az., U.S. | D3 | 80 |
| Pleasant, Mount, mtn., Va., U.S. | C3 | 123 |
| Pleasant Bay, Que. | f9 | 71 |
| Pleasant City, Oh., U.S. | C4 | 112 |
| Pleasantdale, Sask. | E3 | 75 |
| Pleasant Dale, Ne., U.S. | D9 | 104 |
| Pleasant Gap, Pa., U.S. | E6 | 115 |
| Pleasant Garden, N.C., U.S. | B3 | 110 |
| Pleasant Grove, Al., U.S. | g7 | 78 |
| Pleasant Grove, Ms., U.S. | A3 | 101 |
| Pleasant Grove, Ut., U.S. | C4 | 121 |
| Pleasant Hill, Al., U.S. | C3 | 78 |
| Pleasant Hill, Ca., U.S. | h8 | 82 |
| Pleasant Hill, Il., U.S. | D3 | 90 |
| Pleasant Hill, Ia., U.S. | e8 | 92 |
| Pleasant Hill, La., U.S. | C2 | 95 |
| Pleasant Hill, Me., U.S. | g7 | 96 |
| Pleasant Hill, Mo., U.S. | C3 | 102 |
| Pleasant Hill, Oh., U.S. | B1 | 112 |
| Pleasant Hill, Ok., U.S. | D7 | 113 |
| Pleasant Hill, S.C., U.S. | B6 | 117 |
| Pleasant Hills, Pa., U.S. | *k14 | 115 |
| Pleasant Hope, Mo., U.S. | D4 | 102 |
| Pleasant Lake, In., U.S. | A7 | 91 |
| Pleasant Lake, Ma., U.S. | C7 | 98 |
| Pleasant Lake, l., Me., U.S. | C5 | 96 |
| Pleasant Lake, l., N.H., U.S. | D4 | 106 |
| Pleasant Mount, Pa., U.S. | C11 | 115 |
| Pleasanton, Ca., U.S. | h9 | 82 |
| Pleasanton, Ia., U.S. | D4 | 92 |
| Pleasanton, Ks., U.S. | D9 | 93 |
| Pleasanton, Ne., U.S. | D6 | 104 |
| Pleasanton, Tx., U.S. | E3 | 120 |
| Pleasant Plain, Ia., U.S. | C6 | 92 |
| Pleasant Plains, Ar., U.S. | B4 | 81 |
| Pleasant Plains, Il., U.S. | D4 | 90 |
| Pleasant Pond, Me., U.S. | C3 | 96 |
| Pleasant Pond, l., Me., U.S. | C3 | 96 |
| Pleasant Prairie, Wi., U.S. | n12 | 126 |
| Pleasants, co., W.V., U.S. | B3 | 125 |
| Pleasant Shade, Tn., U.S. | C8 | 119 |
| Pleasant Valley, Ct., U.S. | B4 | 84 |
| Pleasant Valley, Ia., U.S. | g11 | 92 |
| Pleasant Valley, Md., U.S. | A3 | 97 |
| Pleasant Valley, Mo., U.S. | h11 | 102 |
| Pleasant Valley, Nv., U.S. | *D2 | 105 |
| Pleasant Valley, N.Y., U.S. | D7 | 109 |
| Pleasant Valley, Oh., U.S. | C2 | 112 |
| Pleasant View, Co., U.S. | *B5 | 83 |
| Pleasant View, Il., U.S. | C3 | 90 |
| Pleasant View, In., U.S. | m11 | 91 |
| Pleasant View, Ky., U.S. | D5 | 94 |
| Pleasant View, Tn., U.S. | A4 | 119 |
| Pleasant View, Ut., U.S. | B3 | 121 |
| Pleasant View, Wi., U.S. | D3 | 126 |
| Pleasantville, In., U.S. | G3 | 91 |
| Pleasantville, Ia., U.S. | C4 | 92 |
| Pleasantville, N.J., U.S. | E3 | 107 |
| Pleasantville, N.Y., U.S. | D7 | 109 |
| Pleasantville, Oh., U.S. | C3 | 112 |
| Pleasure Beach, Ct., U.S. | D7 | 84 |
| Pleasure Ridge Park, Ky., U.S. | g11 | 94 |
| Pleasureville, Ky., U.S. | B4 | 94 |
| Pledger, Tx., U.S. | r14 | 120 |
| Pléhédel, Fr. | F3 | 45 |
| Pleneta, Rom. | C6 | 24 |
| Plenty, Sask. | F1 | 75 |
| Plenty, Bay of, b., N.Z. | L16 | 51 |
| Plentywood, Mt., U.S. | B12 | 103 |
| Plérin, Fr. | C2 | 16 |
| Plesetsk, Sov. Un. | C7 | 29 |
| Plessis, N.Y., U.S. | A5 | 109 |
| Plessisville, Que. | C6 | 74 |
| Pleszew, Pol. | C4 | 26 |
| Plétipi, Lac, l., Que. | h12 | 74 |
| Plettenberg, W. Ger. | D7 | 24 |
| Pleven, Bul. | E5 | 93 |
| Plevna, Mo., U.S. | B5 | 102 |
| Plevna, Mt., U.S. | D12 | 103 |
| Pliny Range, mts., N.H., U.S. | B4 | 106 |
| Pljevlja, Yugo. | D4 | 24 |
| Plochingen, W. Ger. | B5 | 26 |
| Płock, Pol. | D2 | 16 |
| Ploërmel, Fr. | C8 | 24 |
| Ploieşti, Rom. | C6 | 25 |
| Plomárion, Grc. | E5 | 15 |
| Plomb du Cantal, mtn., Fr. | B2 | 20 |
| Plombières-les-Bains, Fr. | | |
| Plomosa Mountains, mts., Az., U.S. | D1 | 80 |
| Plön, W. Ger. | D4 | 15 |
| Plonge, Lac la, l., Sask. | B2 | 75 |
| Plonsk, Pol. | B6 | 26 |
| Plougastel, Fr. | C1 | 16 |
| Plovdiv, Bul. | D7 | 24 |
| Plover, Ia., U.S. | B3 | 92 |
| Plover, Wi., U.S. | D4 | 126 |
| Plover, stm., Wi., U.S. | D4 | 126 |
| Plum, Pa., U.S. | k14 | 115 |
| Pluma, S.D., U.S. | C2 | 118 |
| Plumas, Man. | D2 | 70 |
| Plumas, co., Ca., U.S. | B3 | 82 |
| Plum Bayou, stm., Ar., U.S. | k10 | 81 |
| Plum Branch, S.C., U.S. | D3 | 117 |
| Plumbridge, N. Ire., U.K. | C4 | 11 |
| Plumerville, Ar., U.S. | B3 | 81 |
| Plum Island, i., Ma., U.S. | A6 | 98 |
| Plummer, Id., U.S. | B2 | 89 |
| Plummer, Mn., U.S. | C2 | 100 |
| Plum Point, R.I., U.S. | E4 | 116 |
| Plumsteadville, Pa., U.S. | F11 | 115 |
| Plumtree, Zimb. | B4 | 49 |
| Plumwood, Oh., U.S. | B2 | 112 |
| Plunkett, Sask. | F3 | 75 |
| Plunkettville, Ok., U.S. | C7 | 113 |
| Plush, Or., U.S. | E7 | 114 |
| Plymouth, Monts. | H13 | 64 |
| Plymouth, Eng., U.K. | C3 | 84 |
| Plymouth, Ct., U.S. | C4 | 84 |
| Plymouth, Fl., U.S. | D5 | 86 |
| Plymouth, Il., U.S. | C3 | 90 |
| Plymouth, In., U.S. | B5 | 91 |
| Plymouth, Ia., U.S. | A4 | 92 |
| Plymouth, Ma., U.S. | C6 | 98 |
| Plymouth, Mi., U.S. | p15 | 99 |
| Plymouth, Mn., U.S. | m12 | 100 |
| Plymouth, Ne., U.S. | D9 | 104 |
| Plymouth, N.H., U.S. | C3 | 106 |
| Plymouth, N.C., U.S. | B6 | 110 |
| Plymouth, Oh., U.S. | B3 | 112 |
| Plymouth, Pa., U.S. | D10 | 115 |
| Plymouth, Wi., U.S. | E6 | 126 |
| Plymouth, co., Ia., U.S. | B1 | 92 |
| Plymouth, co., Ma., U.S. | C6 | 98 |
| Plymouth Bay, b., Ma., U.S. | C6 | 98 |
| Plymouth Township, Pa., U.S. | *F11 | 115 |
| Plympton, N.S. | E4 | 71 |
| Plympton, Ma., U.S. | C6 | 98 |
| Plzeň, Czech. | D2 | 26 |
| Pô, Burkina | D4 | 45 |

| Name | Map Ref. | Page |
|---|---|---|
| Po, stm., Italy | B3 | 23 |
| Po, stm., Va., U.S. | B5 | 123 |
| Po, Mouths of the, mth., Italy | B4 | 23 |
| Poamoho Stream, stm., Hi., U.S. | f9 | 88 |
| Pobé, Benin | E5 | 45 |
| Pobeda, Mount, mtn., Sov. Un. | C36 | 128 |
| Pobedino, Sov. Un. | B11 | 33 |
| Pobedy, Peak, mtn., Asia | E11 | 29 |
| Poca, W.V., U.S. | *C3 | 125 |
| Pocahontas, Ar., U.S. | A5 | 81 |
| Pocahontas, Il., U.S. | E4 | 90 |
| Pocahontas, Il., U.S. | B3 | 92 |
| Pocahontas, Tn., U.S. | B3 | 119 |
| Pocahontas, Va., U.S. | e10 | 123 |
| Pocahontas, co., Ia., U.S. | B3 | 92 |
| Pocahontas, co., W.V., U.S. | C4 | 125 |
| Pocasset, Ma., U.S. | C6 | 98 |
| Pocasset, Ok., U.S. | B4 | 113 |
| Pocatalico, W.V., U.S. | C3 | 125 |
| Pocatalico, stm., W.V., U.S. | C3 | 125 |
| Pocatello, Id., U.S. | G6 | 89 |
| Pochep, Sov. Un. | E9 | 27 |
| Pochutla, Mex. | D5 | 63 |
| Pocola, Ok., U.S. | B7 | 113 |
| Pocomoke, stm., Md., U.S. | D7 | 97 |
| Pocomoke City, Md., U.S. | D6 | 97 |
| Pocomoke Sound, strt., Md., U.S. | E6 | 97 |
| Poconé, Braz. | B1 | 56 |
| Pocono Mountains, hills, Pa., U.S. | E11 | 115 |
| Pocono Pines, Pa., U.S. | D11 | 115 |
| Poços de Caldas, Braz. | C3 | 56 |
| Pocotopaug Lake, res., Ct., U.S. | C6 | 84 |
| Pocrí, Pan. | G7 | 62 |
| Pocumtuck Mountain, mtn., Ma., U.S. | A2 | 98 |
| Podbořany, Czech. | C8 | 19 |
| Podgornoye, Sov. Un. | D25 | 8 |
| Podhořany, Czech. | n17 | 26 |
| Podkamennaya Tunguska, Sov. Un. | C27 | 8 |
| Podkamennaya Tunguska, stm., Sov. Un. | C12 | 29 |
| Podolsk, Sov. Un. | D11 | 27 |
| Podor, Sen. | C2 | 45 |
| Podporozhye, Sov. Un. | G16 | 19 |
| Poe, In., U.S. | C7 | 91 |
| Poel, i., E. Ger. | E5 | 15 |
| Pofadder, S. Afr. | C2 | 49 |
| Poge, Cape, c., Ma., U.S. | D7 | 98 |
| Poggibonsi, Italy | C3 | 23 |
| Pöggstall, Aus. | D7 | 18 |
| Pogradeci, Alb. | B3 | 25 |
| Pogranichnoye, Sov. Un. | A11 | 33 |
| Pogranichnyy, Sov. Un. | D5 | 33 |
| Pohang, S. Kor. | D10 | 31 |
| Pohénégamook, Que. | B8 | 74 |
| Pohnpei, i., Micron. | F9 | 6 |
| Pohue Bay, b., Hi., U.S. | E6 | 88 |
| Poinsett, Cape, c., Ant. | C24 | 7 |
| Poinsett, Lake, l., Fl., U.S. | D6 | 86 |
| Poinsett, Lake, l., S.D., U.S. | C8 | 118 |
| Point Arena, Ca., U.S. | C2 | 82 |
| Point Baker, Ak., U.S. | D13 | 79 |
| Point Blue, La., U.S. | D3 | 95 |
| Point Cedar, Ar., U.S. | C2 | 81 |
| Point Clear, Al., U.S. | E2 | 78 |
| Pointe a la Hache, La., U.S. | E6 | 95 |
| Pointe-à-Pierre, Trin. | O23 | 65 |
| Pointe-à-Pitre, Guad. | H14 | 64 |
| Pointe au Baril Station, Ont. | B4 | 73 |
| Pointe-au-Pic, Que. | B7 | 74 |
| Pointe-aux-Trembles (part of Montréal), Que. | p20 | 74 |
| Pointe-Bleue, Que. | A5 | 74 |
| Pointe-Calumet, Que. | p19 | 74 |
| Pointe-Claire, Que. | D4 | 74 |
| Pointe Coupee, co., La., U.S. | D4 | 95 |
| Pointe-des-Cascades, Que. | q19 | 74 |
| Pointe-du-Bois, Man. | D4 | 70 |
| Pointe-du-Chêne, N.B. | C5 | 71 |
| Pointe-du-Lac, Que. | C5 | 74 |
| Point Edward, Ont. | D2 | 73 |
| Pointe-Noire, Congo | B1 | 48 |
| Pointe-Noire, Guad. | Q8 | 65 |
| Pointers, N.J., U.S. | D2 | 107 |
| Pointe-Verte, N.B. | B4 | 71 |
| Point Fortin, Trin. | O22 | 65 |
| Point Hope, Ak., U.S. | B6 | 79 |
| Point Imperial, mtn., Az., U.S. | A4 | 80 |
| Point Independence, Ma., U.S. | *C6 | 98 |
| Point Judith, R.I., U.S. | G4 | 116 |
| Point Judith Pond, l., R.I., U.S. | F4 | 116 |
| Point Lake, l., N.W. Ter. | C10 | 66 |
| Point Leamington, Newf. | D4 | 72 |
| Point Lookout, Md., U.S. | D5 | 97 |
| Point Marion, Pa., U.S. | G2 | 115 |
| Point Mugu Naval Air Station, mil., Ca., U.S. | E4 | 82 |
| Point of Rocks, Md., U.S. | B3 | 97 |
| Point of Rocks, Wy., U.S. | E4 | 127 |
| Point Pelee National Park, Ont. | F2 | 73 |
| Point Pleasant, N.J., U.S. | C4 | 107 |
| Point Pleasant, W.V., U.S. | C2 | 125 |
| Point Pleasant Beach, N.J., U.S. | C4 | 107 |
| Point Reyes National Seashore, Ca., U.S. | C2 | 82 |
| Point Roberts, Wa., U.S. | A2 | 124 |
| Point Sapin, N.B. | C5 | 71 |
| Point Washington, Fl., U.S. | u15 | 86 |
| Poipu, Hi., U.S. | B2 | 88 |
| Poirino, Italy | E3 | 20 |
| Poison Creek, stm., Wy., U.S. | C5 | 127 |
| Poisson Blanc, Lac du, res., Que. | C2 | 74 |
| Poissy, Fr. | C5 | 16 |
| Poitiers, Fr. | D4 | 16 |
| Poitou, hist. reg., Fr. | D3 | 16 |
| Poix, Fr. | E1 | 17 |
| Pojo, Bol. | C3 | 55 |
| Pojoaque Valley, N.M., U.S. | B3 | 108 |
| Pokaran, India | D4 | 36 |
| Pokataroo, Austl. | D7 | 51 |
| Pokegama Lake, l., Mn., U.S. | C5 | 100 |
| Pokegama Lake, l., Wi., U.S. | C2 | 126 |
| Pokhara, Nepal | C9 | 36 |
| Pokkve-ri, N. Kor. | G3 | 33 |
| Poko, Zaire | A4 | 48 |
| Poko Mountain, mtn., Ak., U.S. | B7 | 79 |
| Pokrov, Sov. Un. | n19 | 27 |
| Pokrovskoye, Sov. Un. | H12 | 27 |
| Polacca, Az., U.S. | B5 | 80 |
| Polän, Iran | C6 | 38 |
| Poland, In., U.S. | F4 | 91 |
| Poland, Me., U.S. | *D2 | 96 |
| Poland, N.Y., U.S. | B5 | 109 |
| Poland, ctry., Eur. | C5 | 26 |
| Poland Spring, Me., U.S. | D2 | 96 |
| Polar, Wi., U.S. | C5 | 126 |
| Polar Bear Provincial Park, Ont. | n18 | 73 |
| Polaris, Mt., U.S. | E3 | 103 |
| Polar Record Glacier, ice, Ant. | C20 | 7 |
| Polar Times Glacier, ice, Ant. | C20 | 7 |
| Polathane see Akçaabat, Tur. | B12 | 40 |
| Polatlı, Tur. | *C9 | 40 |
| Polbain, Scot., U.K. | B3 | 13 |
| Polch, W. Ger. | C2 | 19 |
| Polcura, Chile | B2 | 54 |
| Polebridge, Mt., U.S. | B2 | 103 |
| Polecat Creek, stm., Ok., U.S. | B5 | 113 |
| Polesella, Italy | E7 | 20 |
| Polevskoy, Sov. Un. | D21 | 8 |
| Polgár, Hung. | B5 | 24 |
| Poli, Cam. | D2 | 46 |
| Policastro, Gulf of, b., Italy | E5 | 23 |
| Police, Pol. | B3 | 26 |
| Polikhnitos, Grc. | C6 | 25 |
| Polillo, Phil. | o13 | 34 |
| Polillo Islands, is., Phil. | B6 | 34 |
| Polillo Strait, strt., Phil. | o13 | 34 |
| Pólis, Cyp. | E9 | 40 |
| Políyiros, Grc. | B4 | 25 |
| Polk, Ne., U.S. | C8 | 104 |
| Polk, Oh., U.S. | B3 | 112 |
| Polk, Pa., U.S. | D2 | 115 |
| Polk City, Fl., U.S. | D5 | 86 |
| Polk City, Ia., U.S. | C4 | 92 |
| Polk, co., Ar., U.S. | C1 | 81 |
| Polk, co., Fl., U.S. | E5 | 86 |
| Polk, co., Ga., U.S. | C1 | 87 |
| Polk, co., Ia., U.S. | C4 | 92 |
| Polk, co., Mn., U.S. | C2 | 100 |
| Polk, co., Mo., U.S. | D4 | 102 |
| Polk, co., Ne., U.S. | C8 | 104 |
| Polk, co., N.C., U.S. | f10 | 110 |
| Polk, co., Or., U.S. | C3 | 114 |
| Polk, co., Tn., U.S. | D9 | 119 |
| Polk, co., Tx., U.S. | D5 | 120 |
| Polk, co., Wi., U.S. | C1 | 126 |
| Polkton, N.C., U.S. | B2 | 110 |
| Polkville, Ms., U.S. | C4 | 101 |
| Pollard, Al., U.S. | D2 | 78 |
| Pollard, Ar., U.S. | A5 | 81 |
| Pollards Point, Newf. | D3 | 72 |
| Pollensa, Spain | C7 | 22 |
| Pollock, Id., U.S. | D2 | 89 |
| Pollock, La., U.S. | C3 | 95 |
| Pollock, Mo., U.S. | A4 | 102 |
| Pollock, S.D., U.S. | B5 | 118 |
| Pollocksville, N.C., U.S. | B5 | 110 |
| Pollockville, Alta. | D5 | 68 |
| Polo, Il., U.S. | B4 | 90 |
| Polo, Mo., U.S. | B3 | 102 |
| Polochic, stm., Guat. | C5 | 63 |
| Pologi, Sov. Un. | H11 | 27 |
| Polonnoye, Sov. Un. | F6 | 27 |
| Polotsk, Sov. Un. | D7 | 27 |
| Polson, Mt., U.S. | C2 | 103 |
| Poltava, Sov. Un. | E6 | 29 |
| Poltimore, Que. | D2 | 74 |
| Polunochnoye, Sov. Un. | A6 | 28 |
| Polvadera, N.M., U.S. | C3 | 108 |
| Polwarth, Sask. | D2 | 75 |
| Polyarnyy, Sov. Un. | C15 | 14 |
| Pomabamba, Peru | C2 | 58 |
| Pomarão, Port. | D2 | 22 |
| Pomba, stm., Braz. | g6 | 56 |
| Pombal, Braz. | C3 | 57 |
| Pombal, Port. | C1 | 22 |
| Pomerania, hist. reg., Pol. | B4 | 26 |
| Pomeranian Bay, b., Eur. | D8 | 15 |
| Pomerene, Az., U.S. | E5 | 80 |
| Pomeroy, N. Ire., U.K. | C5 | 11 |
| Pomeroy, Ia., U.S. | B3 | 92 |
| Pomeroy, Oh., U.S. | C3 | 112 |
| Pomeroy, Wa., U.S. | C8 | 124 |
| Pomezia, Italy | h9 | 23 |
| Pomfret, Ct., U.S. | B8 | 84 |
| Pomfret, Md., U.S. | C3 | 97 |
| Pomfret, Vt., U.S. | D3 | 122 |
| Pomfret Center, Ct., U.S. | B8 | 84 |
| Pomme de Terre, stm., Mn., U.S. | E3 | 100 |
| Pomme de Terre, stm., Mo., U.S. | D4 | 102 |
| Pomme de Terre Lake, res., Mo., U.S. | D4 | 102 |
| Pomoho, Hi., U.S. | f9 | 88 |
| Pomona, Ca., U.S. | E5 | 82 |
| Pomona, Ks., U.S. | D8 | 93 |
| Pomona, N.J., U.S. | E3 | 107 |
| Pomona, N.Y., U.S. | E6 | 109 |
| Pomona Park, Fl., U.S. | C5 | 86 |
| Pompano Beach, Fl., U.S. | F6 | 86 |
| Pompano Beach Highlands, Fl., U.S. | *F6 | 86 |
| Pompeii, hist., Italy | D5 | 23 |
| Pompeys Pillar, Mt., U.S. | E9 | 103 |
| Pompton Lakes, N.J., U.S. | A4 | 107 |
| Pomquet, N.S. | D8 | 71 |
| Ponaganset, stm., R.I., U.S. | C2 | 116 |
| Ponaganset Reservoir, res., R.I., U.S. | B2 | 116 |
| Ponape International Airport, Micron. | Q17 | 52 |
| Ponask Lake, l., Ont. | B5 | 70 |
| Ponass Lakes, l., Sask. | E3 | 75 |
| Ponca, Ar., U.S. | A2 | 81 |
| Ponca, Ne., U.S. | B9 | 104 |
| Ponca City, Ok., U.S. | A4 | 113 |
| Ponca Creek, stm., U.S. | A6 | 104 |
| Ponca Indian Reservation, Ne., U.S. | B7 | 104 |
| Ponce, P.R. | H11 | 64 |
| Ponce de Leon, Fl., U.S. | u16 | 86 |
| Ponce de Leon Bay, b., Fl., U.S. | G5 | 86 |
| Ponce de Leon Inlet, b., Fl., U.S. | C6 | 86 |
| Poncha Pass, Co., U.S. | C4 | 83 |
| Poncha Springs, Co., U.S. | C4 | 83 |
| Ponchatoula, La., U.S. | D5 | 95 |
| Pond, stm., Ky., U.S. | C2 | 94 |
| Pond, West Fork, stm., Ky., U.S. | C2 | 94 |
| Pond Creek, Ok., U.S. | A3 | 113 |
| Pond Creek, stm., Co., U.S. | C7 | 83 |
| Pond Creek, stm., Ky., U.S. | g11 | 94 |
| Pondera, co., Mt., U.S. | B4 | 103 |
| Ponderay, Id., U.S. | A2 | 89 |
| Ponderosa, N.M., U.S. | B3 | 108 |
| Pond Fork, stm., W.V., U.S. | D3 | 125 |
| Pond Fork, West Fork, stm., W.V., U.S. | n12 | 125 |
| Pondicherry, India | F6 | 36 |
| Pondicherry, ter., India | *F6 | 36 |
| Pond Inlet, N.W. Ter. | B17 | 66 |
| Ponds, Island of, i., Newf. | B4 | 72 |
| Pone Island, i., Md., U.S. | D5 | 97 |
| Poneloya, Nic. | D4 | 62 |
| Ponemah, Mn., U.S. | B4 | 100 |
| Poneto, In., U.S. | C7 | 91 |
| Ponferrada, Spain | A2 | 22 |
| Pongoma, Sov. Un. | E16 | 14 |
| Ponhook Lake, l., N.S. | E5 | 71 |
| Ponkapog Pond, l., Ma., U.S. | h11 | 98 |
| Ponoka, Alta. | C4 | 68 |
| Ponoy, Sov. Un. | D19 | 14 |
| Ponoy, stm., Sov. Un. | B16 | 8 |
| Pons, Fr. | E3 | 16 |
| Ponsford, Mn., U.S. | D3 | 100 |
| Ponta Delgada, Port. | h9 | 44 |
| Ponta de Pedras, Braz. | C5 | 59 |
| Ponta Grossa, Braz. | D2 | 56 |
| Pontal, Braz. | k7 | 56 |
| Pontalina, Braz. | B3 | 56 |
| Ponta Porã, Braz. | C1 | 56 |
| Pontarlier, Fr. | D7 | 16 |
| Pontchartrain, Lake, l., La., U.S. | D5 | 95 |
| Pont-de-Roide, Fr. | B2 | 20 |
| Pontedera, Italy | C3 | 23 |
| Ponte di Legno, Italy | C6 | 20 |
| Ponte de Sor, Port. | C2 | 22 |
| Pontefract, Eng., U.K. | A6 | 12 |
| Ponteix, Sask. | H2 | 75 |
| Ponte Nova, Braz. | C4 | 56 |
| Pontevedra, Spain | A1 | 22 |
| Ponte Vedra Beach, Fl., U.S. | B5 | 86 |
| Pontfaverger-Moronvilliers, Fr. | E4 | 17 |
| Pontiac, Il., U.S. | C5 | 90 |
| Pontiac, Mi., U.S. | F7 | 99 |
| Pontiac, S.C., U.S. | C6 | 117 |
| Pontianak, Indon. | F3 | 34 |
| Pontic Mountains, mts., Tur. | B11 | 40 |
| Pontivy, Fr. | C2 | 16 |
| Pont-l'Abbé, Fr. | D1 | 16 |
| Pontoise, Fr. | C5 | 16 |
| Pontoosuc Lake, l., Ma., U.S. | A1 | 98 |
| Pontotoc, Ms., U.S. | A4 | 101 |
| Pontotoc, Tx., U.S. | D3 | 120 |
| Pontotoc, co., Ms., U.S. | A4 | 101 |
| Pontotoc, co., Ok., U.S. | C5 | 113 |
| Pontremoli, Italy | B2 | 23 |
| Pontresina, Switz. | C5 | 20 |
| Pontrilas, Sask. | D3 | 75 |
| Pont-Rouge, Que. | C6 | 74 |
| Pont-Sainte-Maxence, Fr. | E2 | 17 |
| Pontypool, Wales, U.K. | C4 | 12 |
| Pontypool, Ont. | C6 | 73 |
| Pontypridd (Taff-Ely), Wales, U.K. | C4 | 12 |
| Pony, Mt., U.S. | E5 | 103 |
| Ponziane Islands, is., Italy | D4 | 23 |
| Poole, Eng., U.K. | E5 | 10 |
| Poole, Ky., U.S. | C2 | 94 |
| Poole, Ne., U.S. | D7 | 104 |
| Pooler, Ga., U.S. | D5 | 87 |
| Pooles Island, i., Md., U.S. | B5 | 97 |
| Poolesville, Md., U.S. | B3 | 97 |
| Pooleville, Ok., U.S. | C4 | 113 |
| Poolewe, Scot., U.K. | C3 | 13 |
| Pooley Island, i., B.C. | C3 | 69 |
| Poolowanna Lake, l., Austl. | E6 | 50 |
| Poolville, Tx., U.S. | C4 | 120 |
| Poona see Pune, India | E5 | 36 |
| Poopó, Bol. | C2 | 55 |
| Poopó, Lago, l., Bol. | C2 | 55 |
| Poor Knights Islands, is., N.Z. | K15 | 51 |
| Pootatuck Park, Ct., U.S. | *D2 | 84 |
| Popasnaya, Sov. Un. | q21 | 27 |
| Popayán, Col. | C2 | 60 |
| Pope, Man. | D1 | 70 |
| Pope, Ms., U.S. | A4 | 101 |
| Pope, co., Ar., U.S. | B2 | 81 |
| Pope, co., Il., U.S. | F5 | 90 |
| Pope, co., Mn., U.S. | E3 | 100 |
| Pope Air Force Base, mil., N.C., U.S. | B3 | 110 |
| Popejoy, Ia., U.S. | B4 | 92 |
| Poperinge, Bel. | D2 | 17 |
| Popham Beach, Me., U.S. | E3 | 96 |
| Popham Point, c., Ont. | B3 | 73 |
| Poplar, Mt., U.S. | B11 | 103 |
| Poplar, N.C., U.S. | e10 | 110 |
| Poplar, Wi., U.S. | B2 | 126 |
| Poplar, stm., Can. | C3 | 70 |
| Poplar, stm., N.A. | B11 | 103 |
| Poplar, stm., U.S. | C2 | 100 |
| Poplar, West Fork, stm., U.S. | B11 | 103 |
| Poplar Bluff, Mo., U.S. | E7 | 102 |
| Poplar Branch, N.C., U.S. | A7 | 110 |
| Poplar Creek, Ms., U.S. | B4 | 101 |
| Poplarfield, Man. | D3 | 70 |
| Poplar Grove, Ar., U.S. | C5 | 81 |
| Poplar Grove, Il., U.S. | A5 | 90 |
| Poplar Island, i., Md., U.S. | C5 | 97 |
| Poplar Mountain, mtn., Ky., U.S. | D5 | 94 |
| Poplar Plains, Ky., U.S. | B6 | 94 |
| Poplar Point, Man. | D3 | 70 |
| Popocatépetl, Volcán, vol., Mex. | n14 | 63 |
| Popokabaka, Zaire | C2 | 48 |
| Popondetta, Pap. N. Gui. | k12 | 50 |
| Popovo, Bul. | D8 | 24 |
| Poppel, Bel. | C5 | 17 |
| Popple, stm., Wi., U.S. | C5 | 126 |
| Poprad, Czech. | *D6 | 26 |
| Poquetanuck, Ct., U.S. | D7 | 84 |
| Poquonock, Ct., U.S. | B5 | 84 |
| Poquonock Bridge, Ct., U.S. | D7 | 84 |
| Poquoson, Va., U.S. | C6 | 123 |
| Porangatu, Braz. | A3 | 56 |
| Porbandar, India | D4 | 36 |
| Porcher Island, i., B.C. | C2 | 69 |
| Porcuna, Spain | D3 | 22 |
| Porcupine, S.D., U.S. | D3 | 118 |
| Porcupine, stm., N.A. | B11 | 79 |
| Porcupine, Cape, c., Newf. | B3 | 72 |
| Porcupine Hills, hills, Can. | E5 | 75 |
| Porcupine Mountains, mts., Mi., U.S. | m12 | 99 |
| Porcupine Plain, Sask. | E4 | 75 |
| Pordenone, Italy | C6 | 20 |
| Poreč, Yugo. | C1 | 24 |
| Pori, Fin. | G9 | 14 |
| Porirua, N.Z. | N15 | 51 |
| Porjus, Swe. | D8 | 14 |
| Porkhov, Sov. Un. | C7 | 27 |
| Porkkala, Fin. | G11 | 14 |
| Porlamar, Ven. | A5 | 60 |
| Porlezza, Italy | D7 | 21 |
| Pornic, Fr. | D2 | 16 |
| Poroma, Bol. | C2 | 55 |
| Poronaysk, Sov. Un. | E17 | 29 |
| Poroshiri, Mount, mtn., Japan | E11 | 33 |
| Porpoise Bay, b., Ant. | C25 | 7 |
| Porrentruy, Switz. | E3 | 18 |
| Porsangen, Nor. | B12 | 14 |
| Porsgrunn, Nor. | p27 | 14 |
| Portachuelo, Bol. | C3 | 55 |
| Portacloy, Ire. | C2 | 11 |
| Portadown, N. Ire., U.K. | C6 | 11 |
| Portaferry, N. Ire., U.K. | C6 | 11 |
| Portage, P.E.I. | C5 | 71 |
| Portage, In., U.S. | A3 | 91 |
| Portage, Me., U.S. | B4 | 96 |
| Portage, Mi., U.S. | F5 | 99 |
| Portage, Pa., U.S. | F4 | 115 |
| Portage, Ut., U.S. | B3 | 121 |
| Portage, Wi., U.S. | E4 | 126 |
| Portage, co., Oh., U.S. | A4 | 112 |
| Portage, co., Wi., U.S. | D4 | 126 |
| Portage, North Branch, stm., Oh., U.S. | f7 | 112 |
| Portage Bay, b., Man. | D2 | 70 |
| Portage Des Sioux, Mo., U.S. | f13 | 102 |
| Portage Head, c., Wa., U.S. | A1 | 124 |
| Portage Lake, l., N.B. | B3 | 96 |
| Portage Lake, l., Me., U.S. | B4 | 96 |
| Portage Lakes, Oh., U.S. | B4 | 112 |
| Portage la Prairie, Man. | E2 | 70 |
| Portageville, Mo., U.S. | E8 | 102 |
| Portageville, N.Y., U.S. | C2 | 109 |
| Portal, Az., U.S. | F6 | 80 |
| Portal, Ga., U.S. | D5 | 87 |
| Portal, N.D., U.S. | A3 | 111 |
| Portalegre, Port. | C2 | 22 |
| Portales, N.M., U.S. | C6 | 108 |
| Port Alexander, Ak., U.S. | D13 | 79 |
| Port-Alfred, Que. | A7 | 74 |
| Port Alfred (Kowie), S. Afr. | D4 | 49 |
| Port Alice, B.C. | D4 | 69 |
| Port Allegany, Pa., U.S. | C5 | 115 |
| Port Allen, La., U.S. | D4 | 95 |
| Port Amherst, W.V., U.S. | m12 | 125 |
| Port Angeles, Wa., U.S. | A2 | 124 |
| Port Anson, Newf. | D4 | 72 |
| Port Antonio, Jam. | E5 | 64 |
| Port Aransas, Tx., U.S. | F4 | 120 |
| Portarlington, Ire. | D3 | 10 |
| Port Arthur see Lüshun, China | D9 | 31 |
| Port Arthur, Tx., U.S. | E6 | 120 |
| Port Askaig, Scot., U.K. | C3 | 11 |
| Port Augusta, Austl. | F6 | 50 |
| Port au Port Bay, b., Newf. | D2 | 72 |
| Port au Port [West-Aghatuna-Felix Cove], Newf. | D2 | 72 |
| Port au Port Peninsula, pen., Newf. | D2 | 72 |
| Port-au-Prince, Haiti | E7 | 64 |
| Port Austin, Mi., U.S. | D7 | 99 |
| Port Barre, La., U.S. | D4 | 95 |
| Port-Bergé, Madag. | g9 | 49 |
| Port Birmingham, Al., U.S. | B2 | 78 |
| Port Blair, India | F9 | 36 |
| Port Blakely, Wa., U.S. | e10 | 124 |
| Port Blandford, Newf. | D4 | 72 |
| Port Bolivar, Tx., U.S. | E5 | 120 |
| Port Borden, P.E.I. | C6 | 71 |
| Port Burwell, Ont. | E4 | 73 |
| Port Byron, Il., U.S. | B3 | 90 |
| Port Byron, N.Y., U.S. | B4 | 109 |
| Port Canning, India | F12 | 37 |
| Port Carbon, Pa., U.S. | E9 | 115 |
| Port Carling, Ont. | B5 | 73 |
| Port-Cartier-Ouest, Que. | k13 | 74 |
| Port Chalmers, N.Z. | P13 | 51 |
| Port Charlotte, Fl., U.S. | F4 | 86 |
| Port Chester, N.Y., U.S. | E7 | 109 |
| Port Clements, B.C. | C1 | 69 |
| Port Clinton, Oh., U.S. | A3 | 112 |
| Port Clyde, Me., U.S. | E3 | 96 |
| Port Clyde, N.S. | F4 | 71 |
| Port Colborne, Ont. | E5 | 73 |
| Port Colden, N.J., U.S. | B3 | 107 |
| Port Coquitlam, B.C. | E6 | 69 |
| Port Credit, Ont. | D5 | 73 |
| Port-Daniel, Que. | A5 | 71 |
| Port-de-Bouc, Fr. | F6 | 16 |
| Port-de-Paix, Haiti | E7 | 64 |
| Port Deposit, Md., U.S. | A5 | 97 |
| Port Dickinson, N.Y., U.S. | C5 | 109 |
| Port Dickson, Malay. | E2 | 34 |
| Port Dover, Ont. | E4 | 73 |
| Port Eads, La., U.S. | E6 | 95 |
| Porte Crayon, Mount, mtn., W.V., U.S. | C5 | 125 |
| Port Edward, B.C. | B2 | 69 |
| Port Edwards, Wi., U.S. | D4 | 126 |
| Porteirinha, Braz. | B4 | 56 |
| Portel, Braz. | C5 | 59 |
| Port Elgin, N.B. | C5 | 71 |
| Port Elgin, Ont. | C3 | 73 |
| Port Elizabeth, S. Afr. | D4 | 49 |
| Port Elizabeth, N.J., U.S. | E3 | 107 |
| Port Ellen, Scot., U.K. | E2 | 11 |
| Porteña, Arg. | B5 | 54 |
| Porter, Me., U.S. | E2 | 96 |
| Porter, Ok., U.S. | B6 | 113 |
| Porter, Tx., U.S. | D5 | 120 |
| Porter, Wa., U.S. | C2 | 124 |
| Porter, co., In., U.S. | B3 | 91 |
| Porter Corners, N.Y., U.S. | B7 | 109 |
| Porter Creek, stm., W.V., U.S. | m13 | 125 |
| Porterdale, Ga., U.S. | C3 | 87 |
| Port Erin, I. of Man | F4 | 13 |
| Porter Lake, l., Sask. | A2 | 75 |
| Portersville, Ca., U.S. | D4 | 82 |
| Porterville, Ca., U.S. | D4 | 82 |
| Porterville, Ms., U.S. | C5 | 101 |
| Port Essington, B.C. | B3 | 69 |
| Port Ewen, N.Y., U.S. | D7 | 109 |
| Port Fairy, Austl. | I4 | 51 |
| Port Gamble, Wa., U.S. | B3 | 124 |
| Port Gamble Indian Reservation, Wa., U.S. | B3 | 124 |
| Port-Gentil, Gabon | F1 | 46 |
| Port Gibson, Ms., U.S. | D3 | 101 |
| Port Glasgow, Scot., U.K. | E4 | 13 |
| Port Graham, Ak., U.S. | D9 | 79 |
| Port Greville, N.S. | D5 | 71 |
| Port Harcourt, Nig. | F6 | 45 |
| Port Hardy, B.C. | D4 | 69 |
| Port Hastings, N.S. | D8 | 71 |
| Port Hawkesbury, N.S. | D8 | 71 |
| Porthcawl, Wales, U.K. | C4 | 12 |
| Port Hedland, Austl. | D2 | 50 |
| Port Heiden, Ak., U.S. | D8 | 79 |
| Port Henry, N.Y., U.S. | A7 | 109 |
| Port Hill, P.E.I. | C6 | 71 |
| Port Hood, N.S. | C8 | 71 |
| Port Hope, Ont. | D6 | 73 |
| Port Hope, Mi., U.S. | E8 | 99 |
| Port Hope Simpson, Newf. | B3 | 72 |
| Port Hueneme, Ca., U.S. | E4 | 82 |
| Port Huron, Mi., U.S. | F8 | 99 |
| Portia, Ar., U.S. | A4 | 81 |
| Portimão, Port. | D1 | 22 |
| Portis, Ks., U.S. | C5 | 93 |
| Port Isabel, Tx., U.S. | F4 | 120 |
| Port Jefferson, N.Y., U.S. | n15 | 109 |
| Port Jefferson, Oh., U.S. | B1 | 112 |
| Port Jefferson Station, N.Y., U.S. | *n15 | 109 |
| Port Jervis, N.Y., U.S. | D6 | 109 |
| Port Keats, Austl. | B4 | 50 |
| Port Kent, N.Y., U.S. | f11 | 109 |
| Portland, Austl. | G7 | 50 |
| Portland, Ont. | C8 | 73 |
| Portland, Ar., U.S. | D4 | 81 |
| Portland, Co., U.S. | C5 | 83 |
| Portland, Ct., U.S. | C5 | 84 |
| Portland, Fl., U.S. | u15 | 86 |
| Portland, In., U.S. | D8 | 91 |
| Portland, Me., U.S. | E2 | 96 |
| Portland, Mi., U.S. | F6 | 99 |
| Portland, Mo., U.S. | C6 | 102 |
| Portland, N.D., U.S. | B8 | 111 |
| Portland, Or., U.S. | B4 | 114 |
| Portland, Pa., U.S. | E11 | 115 |
| Portland, Tn., U.S. | A5 | 119 |
| Portland, Tx., U.S. | F4 | 120 |
| Portland, Bill of, c., Eng., U.K. | E5 | 10 |
| Portland Bight, Jam. | F14 | 65 |
| Portland Canal, b., N.A. | B2 | 69 |
| Portland Creek Pond, l., Newf. | C3 | 72 |
| Portland Inlet, b., B.C. | B2 | 69 |
| Portland Mills, Pa., U.S. | D4 | 115 |
| Portland Point, c., Jam. | F14 | 65 |
| Portlandville, N.Y., U.S. | C6 | 109 |
| Port Laoise, Ire. | D3 | 10 |
| Port Lavaca, Tx., U.S. | E4 | 120 |
| Port Leyden, N.Y., U.S. | B5 | 109 |
| Port Lincoln, Austl. | F6 | 50 |
| Port Lions, Ak., U.S. | D9 | 79 |
| Port Loko, S.L. | G2 | 45 |
| Port-Louis, Fr. | D2 | 16 |
| Port-Louis, Guad. | Q8 | 65 |
| Port Louis, Mrts. | H24 | 2 |
| Port Ludlow, Wa., U.S. | B3 | 124 |
| Port Macquarie, Austl. | F9 | 50 |
| Port Madison Indian Reservation, Wa., U.S. | B3 | 124 |
| Portmagee, Ire. | F1 | 11 |
| Portmahomack, Scot., U.K. | C5 | 13 |
| Port Maitland, N.S. | F3 | 71 |
| Port Maitland (part of Dunnville), Ont. | E5 | 73 |
| Port Maria, Jam. | E5 | 64 |
| Port Matilda, Pa., U.S. | E5 | 115 |
| Port Mayaca, Fl., U.S. | F6 | 86 |
| Port McNeil, B.C. | D4 | 69 |
| Port McNicoll, Ont. | C5 | 73 |
| Port Medway, N.S. | E5 | 71 |
| Port Mellon, B.C. | E6 | 69 |
| Port-Menier, Que. | k8 | 72 |
| Port Moller, Ak., U.S. | D7 | 79 |
| Port Monmouth, N.J., U.S. | C4 | 107 |
| Port Morant, Jam. | F16 | 65 |
| Port Moresby, Pap. N. Gui. | k12 | 50 |
| Port Morien, N.S. | C10 | 71 |
| Port Morris, N.J., U.S. | B3 | 107 |
| Port Mouton, N.S. | F5 | 71 |
| Port Mouton Island, i., N.S. | F5 | 71 |
| Port Murray, N.J., U.S. | B3 | 107 |
| Portnahaven, Scot., U.K. | E2 | 11 |
| Port Neches, Tx., U.S. | E6 | 120 |
| Portneuf, co., Que. | C5 | 74 |
| Portneuf-sur-Mer, Que. | A8 | 74 |
| Port Nolloth, S. Afr. | C2 | 49 |
| Port Norris, N.J., U.S. | E3 | 107 |
| Porto (Oporto), Port. | B1 | 22 |
| Porto Acre, Braz. | E2 | 56 |
| Porto Alegre, Braz. | E2 | 56 |
| Porto Alexandre see Tombua, Ang. | E1 | 48 |
| Porto Amboim, Ang. | D2 | 48 |
| Porto Belo, Braz. | D3 | 56 |
| Portobelo, Pan. | F8 | 62 |
| Porto Calvo, Braz. | C5 | 59 |
| Port O'Connor, Tx., U.S. | E4 | 120 |
| Pôrto de Mós, Port. | C1 | 22 |
| Porto de Moz, Braz. | C4 | 59 |
| Porto Esperança, Braz. | B1 | 56 |
| Porto Feliz, Braz. | C3 | 56 |
| Portoferraio, Italy | C3 | 23 |
| Portofino, Italy | C3 | 23 |
| Port of Ness, Scot., U.K. | B2 | 13 |
| Porto Garibaldi, Italy | B6 | 20 |
| Porto Grande, Braz. | C4 | 59 |
| Portogruaro, Italy | B4 | 20 |
| Portola, Ca., U.S. | C3 | 82 |
| Porto Lucena, Braz. | D1 | 56 |
| Portomaggiore, Italy | B5 | 20 |
| Porto Mendes, Braz. | C2 | 56 |
| Porto Murtinho, Braz. | C1 | 56 |
| Porto Nacional, Braz. | D1 | 57 |
| Porto-Novo, Benin | E5 | 45 |
| Port Orange, Fl., U.S. | C6 | 86 |
| Port Orchard, Wa., U.S. | B3 | 124 |
| Port Orford, Or., U.S. | E2 | 114 |
| Porto Santana, Braz. | C4 | 59 |
| Porto Santo, i., Port. | g12 | 44 |
| Portoscuso, Italy | E2 | 23 |
| Porto Seguro, Braz. | E3 | 57 |
| Porto Torres, Italy | D2 | 23 |
| Porto União, Braz. | D2 | 56 |
| Porto-Vecchio, Fr. | G2 | 16 |
| Porto Velho, Braz. | D2 | 59 |
| Portoviejo, Ec. | B1 | 58 |
| Port Penn, De., U.S. | B3 | 85 |
| Port Perry, Ont. | C6 | 73 |
| Port Phillip Bay, b., Austl. | G7 | 50 |
| Port Pirie, Austl. | F6 | 50 |
| Port Radium, N.W. Ter. | C9 | 66 |
| Port Reading, N.J., U.S. | k8 | 107 |
| Portree, Scot., U.K. | C2 | 13 |
| Port Renfrew, B.C. | E5 | 69 |
| Port Republic, N.J., U.S. | E3 | 107 |
| Port Republic, Va., U.S. | B4 | 123 |
| Port Rexton, Newf. | D5 | 72 |
| Port Richey, Fl., U.S. | D4 | 86 |
| Port Rowan, Ont. | E4 | 73 |
| Port Royal, Ky., U.S. | B4 | 94 |
| Port Royal, Pa., U.S. | E7 | 115 |
| Port Royal, S.C., U.S. | G6 | 117 |
| Port Royal, Va., U.S. | B5 | 123 |
| Port Royal Island, i., S.C., U.S. | G6 | 117 |
| Port Royal Sound, strt., S.C., U.S. | G6 | 117 |
| Portrush, N. Ire., U.K. | B5 | 11 |
| Port Said (Būr Saʿīd), Eg. | B3 | 38 |
| Port Saint Johns, Transkei | D4 | 49 |
| Port-Saint-Louis [-du-Rhône], Fr. | F6 | 16 |
| Port Saint Lucie, Fl., U.S. | E6 | 86 |
| Port Salerno, Fl., U.S. | E6 | 86 |
| Portsalon, Ire. | B4 | 11 |
| Port Sanilac, Mi., U.S. | E8 | 99 |
| Port Saunders, Newf. | C3 | 72 |
| Port Sewall, Fl., U.S. | E6 | 86 |
| Port Shepstone, S. Afr. | D5 | 49 |
| Portsmouth, Dom. | I14 | 64 |
| Portsmouth, Eng., U.K. | E6 | 10 |
| Portsmouth, Ia., U.S. | C2 | 92 |
| Portsmouth, N.H., U.S. | D5 | 106 |
| Portsmouth, Oh., U.S. | D3 | 112 |
| Portsmouth, R.I., U.S. | E6 | 116 |
| Portsmouth, Va., U.S. | D6 | 123 |
| Portsmouth Naval Shipyard, mil., Me., U.S. | D5 | 106 |
| Portsoy, Scot., U.K. | C6 | 13 |
| Port Stanley, Ont. | E3 | 73 |
| Port Sudan (Būr Sūdān), Sud. | B4 | 47 |
| Port Sulphur, La., U.S. | E6 | 95 |
| Port-sur-Saône, Fr. | B2 | 20 |
| Port Talbot (Afan), Wales, U.K. | C4 | 12 |
| Porttipahdan Reservoir, res., Fin. | C12 | 14 |
| Port Tobacco Village, Md., U.S. | C3 | 97 |
| Port Townsend, Wa., U.S. | A3 | 124 |
| Portugal, ctry., Eur. | C1 | 22 |
| Portugal Cove South, Newf. | E5 | 72 |
| Portugalete, Spain | A4 | 22 |
| Portuguesa, state, Ven. | B4 | 60 |
| Portuguesa, stm., Ven. | B4 | 60 |
| Portumna, Ire. | D3 | 11 |
| Port Union, Newf. | D5 | 72 |
| Porvenir, Chile | h11 | 54 |
| Porz, W. Ger. | C2 | 19 |
| Posadas, Arg. | E4 | 55 |
| Posadas, Spain | D3 | 22 |
| Poschiavo, Switz. | D9 | 21 |
| Posen, Il., U.S. | k9 | 90 |
| Posen, Mi., U.S. | C7 | 99 |
| Posey, co., In., U.S. | H2 | 91 |
| Poseyville, In., U.S. | H2 | 91 |
| Poshekhonye-Volodarsk, Sov. Un. | B12 | 27 |
| Poso, Indon. | F6 | 34 |
| Poso, Lake, l., Indon. | F6 | 34 |
| Posong, S. Kor. | I3 | 33 |
| Posse, Braz. | A3 | 56 |
| Pössneck, E. Ger. | C6 | 19 |
| Post, Or., U.S. | C6 | 114 |
| Post, Tx., U.S. | C2 | 120 |
| Poste-de-la-Baleine, Que. | g11 | 74 |
| Post Falls, Id., U.S. | B2 | 89 |
| Postmasburg, S. Afr. | C3 | 49 |
| Post Mills, Vt., U.S. | D4 | 122 |
| Postojna, Yugo. | C1 | 24 |
| Potaro Landing, Guy. | A3 | 59 |
| Potawatomi Indian Reservation, Ks., U.S. | C8 | 93 |
| Potchefstroom, S. Afr. | C4 | 49 |
| Poteau, Ok., U.S. | B7 | 113 |
| Poteau Mountain, mtn., U.S. | C1 | 81 |
| Poteet, Tx., U.S. | E3 | 120 |
| Potenza, Italy | D5 | 23 |
| Potenza, stm., Italy | C4 | 23 |
| Potgietersrus, S. Afr. | B5 | 49 |
| Poth, Tx., U.S. | E3 | 120 |
| Potholes Reservoir, res., Wa., U.S. | B6 | 124 |
| Poti, Sov. Un. | G17 | 8 |
| Poti, stm., Braz. | C2 | 57 |
| Potiskum, Nig. | D7 | 45 |
| Potlatch, Id., U.S. | B2 | 89 |
| Potlatch, stm., Id., U.S. | B2 | 89 |
| Potomac, Il., U.S. | C6 | 90 |
| Potomac, Md., U.S. | B3 | 97 |
| Potomac, stm., U.S. | D3 | 103 |
| Potomac, North Branch, stm., U.S. | m12 | 125 |
| Potomac, South Branch, stm., W.V., U.S. | B6 | 125 |
| Potomac, South Branch, North Fork, stm., W.V., U.S. | C5 | 125 |
| Potomac, South Branch, South Fork, stm., W.V., U.S. | B6 | 125 |
| Potomac Heights, Md., U.S. | C3 | 97 |
| Potomac Park, Md., U.S. | k13 | 97 |
| Potosí, Bol. | C2 | 55 |
| Potosi, Mo., U.S. | D7 | 102 |
| Potosí, dept., Bol. | D2 | 55 |
| Potrerillos, Chile | B3 | 54 |
| Potrero, Cerro el, mtn., S.A. | B6 | 18 |
| Potsdam, E. Ger. | B6 | 18 |
| Potsdam, N.Y., U.S. | f10 | 109 |
| Pottawatomie, co., Ks., U.S. | C7 | 93 |
| Pottawatomie, co., Ok., U.S. | B4 | 113 |
| Pottawatomie Creek, stm., U.S. | D8 | 93 |
| Pottawattamie, co., Ia., U.S. | C2 | 92 |
| Potter, Ar., U.S. | C1 | 81 |

| Name | Map Ref. | Page |
|---|---|---|

| Potter, Ks., U.S. | C8 | 93 |
| Potter, Ne., U.S. | C2 | 104 |
| Potter, Wi., U.S. | h9 | 126 |
| *Potter, co., Pa., U.S.* | C6 | 115 |
| *Potter, co., S.D., U.S.* | B6 | 118 |
| *Potter, co., Tx., U.S.* | B2 | 120 |
| Potter Hill, R.I., U.S. | F1 | 116 |
| Potter Place, N.H., U.S. | D3 | 106 |
| Potters Mills, Pa., U.S. | E6 | 115 |
| Pottersville, Mo., U.S. | E5 | 102 |
| Pottersville, N.J., U.S. | B3 | 107 |
| Pottersville, N.Y., U.S. | D7 | 109 |
| Potter Valley, Ca., U.S. | C2 | 82 |
| Potterville, Ga., U.S. | D2 | 87 |
| Potts Camp, Ms., U.S. | A4 | 101 |
| *Potts Creek, stm., U.S.* | C2 | 123 |
| Pottstown, Pa., U.S. | F10 | 115 |
| Pottsville, Ar., U.S. | B2 | 81 |
| Pottsville, Pa., U.S. | E9 | 115 |
| Pottsville, Tx., U.S. | D3 | 120 |
| Potwin, Ks., U.S. | E6 | 93 |
| Pouce Coupe, B.C. | B7 | 69 |
| Pouch Cove, Newf. | E5 | 72 |
| Poughkeepsie, Ar., U.S. | A4 | 81 |
| Poughkeepsie, N.Y., U.S. | D7 | 109 |
| Poulan, Ga., U.S. | E3 | 87 |
| Poulsbo, Wa., U.S. | B3 | 124 |
| Poultney, Vt., U.S. | D2 | 122 |
| *Poultney, stm., Vt., U.S.* | D2 | 122 |
| Pound, Va., U.S. | e9 | 123 |
| Pound, Wi., U.S. | C5 | 126 |
| *Pound Gap, U.S.* | C7 | 94 |
| Pouso Alegre, Braz. | C3 | 56 |
| Poutasi, W. Sam. | G12 | 52 |
| Pouthisat, Camb. | C2 | 34 |
| Pouxeux, Fr. | A2 | 20 |
| Považská Bystrica, Czech. | *D5 | 26 |
| Povenets, Sov. Un. | C16 | 8 |
| *Poverty Bay, b., N.Z.* | M16 | 51 |
| Póvoa de Varzim, Port. | B1 | 22 |
| Povorino, Sov. Un. | C2 | 28 |
| *Povorotnyy, Cape, c., Sov. Un.* | E6 | 33 |
| Povungnituk, Que. | f11 | 74 |
| Powassan, Ont. | A5 | 73 |
| Poway, Ca., U.S. | F5 | 82 |
| *Powder, stm., U.S.* | A6 | 76 |
| *Powder, stm., Or., U.S.* | C9 | 114 |
| *Powder, Middle Fork, stm., Wy., U.S.* | C6 | 127 |
| *Powder, North Fork, stm., Wy., U.S.* | C6 | 127 |
| *Powder, South Fork, stm., Wy., U.S.* | C6 | 127 |
| Powderhorn, Co., U.S. | C3 | 83 |
| Powder River, Wy., U.S. | C6 | 127 |
| *Powder River, co., Mt., U.S.* | E11 | 103 |
| *Powder River Pass, Wy., U.S.* | B5 | 127 |
| Powder Springs, Ga., U.S. | h8 | 87 |
| Powderville, Mt., U.S. | E11 | 103 |
| *Powder Wash, Co., U.S.* | A2 | 83 |
| Powe, Mo., U.S. | E7 | 102 |
| Powell, Mo., U.S. | E3 | 102 |
| Powell, Oh., U.S. | B2 | 112 |
| Powell, Pa., U.S. | C9 | 115 |
| Powell, Tn., U.S. | m13 | 119 |
| Powell, Tx., U.S. | C4 | 120 |
| Powell, Wy., U.S. | B4 | 127 |
| *Powell, co., Ky., U.S.* | C6 | 94 |
| *Powell, co., Mt., U.S.* | D4 | 103 |
| *Powell, stm., U.S.* | C10 | 119 |
| *Powell, Lake, res., U.S.* | F5 | 121 |
| *Powell, Mount, mtn., Co., U.S.* | B4 | 83 |
| Powell Butte, Or., U.S. | C5 | 114 |
| Powellhurst, Or., U.S. | *B4 | 114 |
| *Powell Mountain, mtn., U.S.* | C10 | 119 |
| *Powell Mountain, mtn., N.M., U.S.* | B1 | 108 |
| *Powell Park, reg., Co., U.S.* | A2 | 83 |
| Powell River, B.C. | E5 | 69 |
| Powellsville, N.C., U.S. | A6 | 110 |
| Powellton, W.V., U.S. | C3 | 125 |
| Powellville, Md., U.S. | D7 | 97 |
| Powelton, Ga., U.S. | C4 | 87 |
| Power, Mt., U.S. | C5 | 103 |
| *Power, co., Id., U.S.* | G5 | 89 |
| *Power Head, c., Ire.* | F3 | 11 |
| Powers, Mi., U.S. | C3 | 99 |
| Powers, Or., U.S. | E2 | 114 |
| Powers Lake, N.D., U.S. | A3 | 111 |
| Powersville, Mo., U.S. | A4 | 102 |
| Powerview, Man. | D3 | 70 |
| *Poweshiek, co., Ia., U.S.* | C5 | 92 |
| Powhatan, Al., U.S. | B4 | 78 |
| Powhatan, Ar., U.S. | A4 | 81 |
| Powhatan, La., U.S. | C2 | 95 |
| Powhatan, Va., U.S. | C5 | 123 |
| *Powhatan, co., Va., U.S.* | C5 | 123 |
| Powhatan Point, Oh., U.S. | C5 | 112 |
| Powhattan, Ks., U.S. | C8 | 93 |
| Pownal, Me., U.S. | g7 | 96 |
| Pownal, Vt., U.S. | F2 | 122 |
| Pownal Center, Me., U.S. | g7 | 96 |
| Pownal Center, Vt., U.S. | F2 | 122 |
| *Powys, co., Wales, U.K.* | B4 | 12 |
| Poxoréo, Braz. | B2 | 56 |
| *Poyang Hu, l., China* | F8 | 31 |
| Poyarkovo, Sov. Un. | A8 | 32 |
| Poydras, La., U.S. | *E6 | 95 |
| Poyen, Ar., U.S. | C3 | 81 |
| *Poygan, Lake, l., Wi., U.S.* | D5 | 126 |
| Poynette, Wi., U.S. | E4 | 126 |
| Poynor, Mo., U.S. | E7 | 102 |
| Poyntzpass, N. Ire., U.K. | C5 | 11 |
| Poy Sippi, Wi., U.S. | D4 | 126 |
| Požarevac, Yugo. | C5 | 24 |
| Poza Rica de Hidalgo, Mex. | m15 | 63 |
| Poznań, Pol. | B4 | 26 |
| Pozo Almonte, Chile | D2 | 55 |
| Pozoblanco, Spain | C3 | 22 |
| Pozo Colorado, Para. | D4 | 55 |
| *Pozo Redondo Mountains, mts., U.S.* | E3 | 80 |
| Pozos, Mex. | m13 | 63 |
| Pozuelo de Alarcón, Spain | p17 | 22 |
| Pozuelos, Ven. | A5 | 60 |
| Pozuzo, Peru | D2 | 58 |
| Pozzallo, Italy | F5 | 23 |
| Pozzuoli, Italy | D5 | 23 |
| Prachatice, Czech. | E9 | 19 |
| Prachin Buri, Thai. | C2 | 34 |
| Prachuap Khiri Khan, Thai. | G3 | 34 |
| Praco, Al., U.S. | f6 | 78 |
| *Prácticos, Punta de c., Cuba* | D5 | 64 |
| Prades, Fr. | F5 | 16 |
| *Prado Flood Control Basin, Ca., U.S.* | n13 | 82 |
| Præstø, Den. | C6 | 15 |
| Praga (part of Warsaw), Pol. | k14 | 26 |
| Prague (Praha), Czech. | C3 | 26 |
| Prague, Ne., U.S. | C9 | 104 |
| Prague, Ok., U.S. | B5 | 113 |
| Prainha, Braz. | C4 | 59 |
| Prairie, Al., U.S. | C2 | 78 |
| Prairie, Ms., U.S. | B5 | 101 |
| *Prairie, co., Ar., U.S.* | C4 | 81 |
| *Prairie, co., Mt., U.S.* | D11 | 103 |
| *Prairie, stm., Mn., U.S.* | C5 | 100 |
| *Prairie, stm., Wi., U.S.* | C4 | 126 |
| *Prairie Bayou, stm., Ar., U.S.* | g7 | 81 |
| Prairie City, Il., U.S. | C3 | 90 |
| Prairie City, Ia., U.S. | C4 | 92 |
| Prairie City, Or., U.S. | C8 | 114 |
| Prairie City, S.D., U.S. | B3 | 118 |
| Prairie Creek, In., U.S. | F3 | 91 |
| *Prairie Creek Reservoir, res., In., U.S.* | D7 | 91 |
| *Prairie Dog Creek, stm., U.S.* | C3 | 93 |
| Prairie Du Chien, Wi., U.S. | E2 | 126 |
| Prairie Du Rocher, Il., U.S. | E3 | 90 |
| Prairie du Sac, Wi., U.S. | E4 | 126 |
| Prairie Farm, Wi., U.S. | C2 | 126 |
| Prairie Grove, Ar., U.S. | B1 | 81 |
| Prairie Hill, Mo., U.S. | B5 | 102 |
| Prairie Home, Mo., U.S. | C5 | 102 |
| Prairie Home, Ne., U.S. | h11 | 104 |
| Prairie Point, Ms., U.S. | B5 | 101 |
| Prairie River, Sask. | E4 | 75 |
| *Prairies, Lake of the, res., Can.* | F5 | 75 |
| *Prairies, Rivière des, stm., Que.* | p19 | 74 |
| Prairieton, In., U.S. | F3 | 91 |
| Prairie View, Ar., U.S. | B2 | 81 |
| Prairie View, Ks., U.S. | C4 | 93 |
| Prairie View, Tx., U.S. | D5 | 120 |
| Prairie Village, Ks., U.S. | m16 | 93 |
| Prairieville, La., U.S. | h10 | 95 |
| Pralognan-la-Vanoise, Fr. | D2 | 20 |
| Pran Buri, Thai. | C2 | 34 |
| Praszka, Pol. | C5 | 26 |
| Prata, Braz. | B3 | 56 |
| Pratāpgarh, India | E5 | 37 |
| *Prater Mountain, mtn., Wy., U.S.* | C2 | 127 |
| Prato, Italy | C3 | 23 |
| Prats-de-Mollo, Fr. | F5 | 16 |
| Pratt, Ks., U.S. | E5 | 93 |
| Pratt, W.V., U.S. | *C3 | 125 |
| *Pratt, co., Ks., U.S.* | E5 | 93 |
| Prattsburg, N.Y., U.S. | C3 | 109 |
| Prattsville, Ar., U.S. | C3 | 81 |
| Prattsville, N.Y., U.S. | C6 | 109 |
| Prattville, Al., U.S. | C3 | 78 |
| Prattville, Mi., U.S. | G6 | 99 |
| Pravdinsk, Sov. Un. | A6 | 26 |
| Pravia, Spain | A2 | 22 |
| Pray, Mt., U.S. | E6 | 103 |
| Preble, In., U.S. | C7 | 91 |
| *Preble, co., Oh., U.S.* | C1 | 112 |
| Predazzo, Italy | C7 | 20 |
| Preeceville, Sask. | F4 | 75 |
| Preetz, W. Ger. | D4 | 15 |
| *Pregel, stm., Sov. Un.* | D3 | 27 |
| *Pregolya, stm., Sov. Un.* | A6 | 26 |
| Prelate, Sask. | G1 | 75 |
| Premana, Italy | D7 | 21 |
| Premont, Tx., U.S. | F3 | 120 |
| Prémontré, Fr. | E3 | 17 |
| Premosello, Italy | D5 | 21 |
| Prenjasi, Alb. | B3 | 25 |
| Prenter, W.V., U.S. | C3 | 125 |
| Prentice, Wi., U.S. | C3 | 126 |
| Prentiss, Me., U.S. | C4 | 96 |
| Prentiss, Ms., U.S. | D4 | 101 |
| *Prentiss, co., Ms., U.S.* | A5 | 101 |
| Prenzlau, E. Ger. | B6 | 18 |
| Přerov, Czech. | D4 | 26 |
| Prescott, Ont. | C9 | 73 |
| Prescott, Az., U.S. | C3 | 80 |
| Prescott, Ar., U.S. | D2 | 81 |
| Prescott, Ia., U.S. | C3 | 92 |
| Prescott, Ks., U.S. | D9 | 93 |
| Prescott, Mi., U.S. | D7 | 99 |
| Prescott, Wa., U.S. | C7 | 124 |
| *Prescott, co., Ont.* | B10 | 73 |
| Presho, S.D., U.S. | D5 | 118 |
| Presidencia Roque Sáenz Peña, Arg. | E3 | 55 |
| Presidente Epitácio, Braz. | C2 | 56 |
| *Presidente Hayes, dept., Para.* | D4 | 55 |
| Presidente Olegário, Braz. | B3 | 56 |
| Presidente Prudente, Braz. | C2 | 56 |
| *Presidential Range, mts., N.H., U.S.* | B4 | 106 |
| *Presidents Island, i., Tn., U.S.* | e8 | 119 |
| Presidio, Tx., U.S. | p12 | 120 |
| *Presidio, co., Tx., U.S.* | o12 | 120 |
| *Presidio of San Francisco, mil., Ca., U.S.* | h8 | 82 |
| Presnja, Bul. | D8 | 24 |
| Prešov, Czech. | D6 | 26 |
| *Prespa, Lake, l., Eur.* | E5 | 24 |
| Presque Isle, Me., U.S. | B5 | 96 |
| Presque Isle, Wi., U.S. | C7 | 99 |
| *Presque Isle, co., Mi., U.S.* | C6 | 99 |
| Pressath, W. Ger. | D6 | 19 |
| Pressbaum, Austl. | G16 | 19 |
| Prestatyn, Wales, U.K. | A4 | 12 |
| Presteigne, Wales, U.K. | B4 | 12 |
| Přeštice, Czech. | D2 | 19 |
| Preston, Austl. | *G8 | 50 |
| Preston, Eng., U.K. | D5 | 10 |
| Preston, Ct., U.S. | C8 | 84 |
| Preston, Ga., U.S. | D2 | 87 |
| Preston, Id., U.S. | G7 | 89 |
| Preston, Ia., U.S. | B7 | 92 |
| Preston, Ks., U.S. | E5 | 93 |
| Preston, Md., U.S. | C6 | 97 |
| Preston, Mn., U.S. | G6 | 100 |
| Preston, Mo., U.S. | D4 | 102 |
| Preston, Ok., U.S. | B6 | 113 |
| *Preston, co., W.V., U.S.* | B5 | 125 |
| *Preston Peak, mtn., Ca., U.S.* | B2 | 82 |
| Prestonsburg, Ky., U.S. | C7 | 94 |
| *Prestrud Inlet, b., Ant.* | B33 | 7 |
| Prestwick, Scot., U.K. | C4 | 10 |
| Pretoria, S. Afr. | C4 | 49 |
| *Prettyboy Reservoir, res., Md., U.S.* | A4 | 97 |
| Pretty Prairie, Ks., U.S. | E5 | 93 |
| Préveza, Grc. | E3 | 25 |
| Prewitt, N.M., U.S. | B1 | 108 |
| *Prewitt Reservoir, res., Co., U.S.* | A7 | 83 |
| Prey Veng, Camb. | G6 | 35 |
| *Pribilof Islands, is., Ak., U.S.* | D5 | 79 |
| Priboj, Yugo. | D4 | 24 |
| Příbram, Czech. | D3 | 26 |
| Price, Md., U.S. | B6 | 97 |
| Price, Tx., U.S. | C5 | 120 |
| Price, Ut., U.S. | D5 | 121 |
| *Price, co., Wi., U.S.* | C3 | 126 |
| *Price, stm., Ut., U.S.* | D5 | 121 |
| Price Creek, In., U.S. | F3 | 91 |
| Pricedale, Ms., U.S. | C5 | 101 |
| *Price Inlet, b., S.C., U.S.* | k12 | 117 |
| Priceville, Ont. | C4 | 73 |
| Prichard, Al., U.S. | E1 | 78 |
| Prichard, W.V., U.S. | C2 | 125 |
| Priddy, Tx., U.S. | D3 | 120 |
| Priego [de Córdoba], Spain | D3 | 22 |
| Prien, La., U.S. | *D2 | 95 |
| *Priest Lake, l., Id., U.S.* | A2 | 89 |
| *Priestley, Mount, mtn., B.C.* | B3 | 69 |
| Priest Rapids Dam, Wa., U.S. | C6 | 124 |
| *Priest Rapids Lake, res., Wa., U.S.* | C6 | 124 |
| Prievidza, Czech. | *D5 | 26 |
| Prijedor, Yugo. | C3 | 24 |
| Prijepolje, Yugo. | D4 | 24 |
| Prikumsk, Sov. Un. | E2 | 28 |
| Prilep, Yugo. | E5 | 24 |
| Prilly, Switz. | C2 | 21 |
| Priluki, Sov. Un. | F9 | 27 |
| *Prim, Point, c., P.E.I.* | C6 | 71 |
| Primate, Sask. | E1 | 75 |
| *Primero, stm., Arg.* | A4 | 54 |
| Primghar, Ia., U.S. | A2 | 92 |
| Primolano, Italy | D7 | 20 |
| Primorsk, Sov. Un. | A6 | 26 |
| Primorsko-Akhtarsk, Sov. Un. | H12 | 27 |
| Primrose, Ne., U.S. | C7 | 104 |
| Primrose, R.I., U.S. | B3 | 116 |
| *Primrose Lake, l., Can.* | B6 | 68 |
| Prince, Sask. | E1 | 75 |
| *Prince, co., P.E.I.* | C5 | 71 |
| *Prince, Lake, res., Va., U.S.* | k14 | 123 |
| Prince Albert, Sask. | D3 | 75 |
| *Prince Albert Mountains, mts., Ant.* | B29 | 7 |
| Prince Albert National Park, Sask. | C2 | 75 |
| *Prince Albert Sound, strt., N.W. Ter.* | B9 | 66 |
| *Prince Alfred, Cape, c., N.W. Ter.* | B8 | 66 |
| *Prince Charles Foreland, i., Nor.* | B14 | 128 |
| *Prince Charles Island, i., N.W. Ter.* | C17 | 66 |
| *Prince Charles Mountains, mts., Ant.* | B19 | 7 |
| *Prince Edward, co., Ont.* | C7 | 73 |
| *Prince Edward, co., Va., U.S.* | C4 | 123 |
| *Prince Edward Island, prov., Can.* | C6 | 71 |
| Prince Edward Island National Park, P.E.I. | C6 | 71 |
| *Prince Edward Islands, is., Afr.* | J23 | 2 |
| Prince Frederick, Md., U.S. | C4 | 97 |
| Prince George, B.C. | C6 | 69 |
| Prince George, Va., U.S. | C5 | 123 |
| *Prince George, co., Va., U.S.* | C5 | 123 |
| *Prince Georges, co., Md., U.S.* | C4 | 97 |
| *Prince of Wales, i., Austl.* | B7 | 50 |
| *Prince of Wales, Cape, c., Ak., U.S.* | B6 | 79 |
| *Prince of Wales Island, i., N.W. Ter.* | B13 | 66 |
| *Prince of Wales Island, i., Ak., U.S.* | n23 | 79 |
| *Prince of Wales Strait, strt., N.W. Ter.* | B9 | 66 |
| *Prince Olav Coast, Ant.* | C17 | 7 |
| *Prince Patrick Island, i., N.W. Ter.* | m27 | 66 |
| *Prince Regent Inlet, b., N.W. Ter.* | B14 | 66 |
| Prince Rupert, B.C. | B2 | 69 |
| Princess Isabel, Braz. | C3 | 57 |
| Princes Lakes, In., U.S. | F5 | 91 |
| Princes Risborough, Eng., U.K. | C7 | 12 |
| Princess Anne, Md., U.S. | D6 | 97 |
| *Princess Astrid Coast, Ant.* | B14 | 7 |
| *Princess Charlotte Bay, b., Austl.* | B7 | 50 |
| *Princess Martha Coast, Ant.* | B11 | 7 |
| *Princess Ragnhild Coast, Ant.* | B15 | 7 |
| *Princess Royal Channel, strt., B.C.* | C3 | 69 |
| *Princess Royal Island, i., B.C.* | C3 | 69 |
| Princes Town, Trin. | O23 | 65 |
| Princeton, Newf. | D5 | 72 |
| Princeton, B.C. | E7 | 69 |
| Princeton, Ca., U.S. | C2 | 82 |
| Princeton, Fl., U.S. | G6 | 86 |
| Princeton, Il., U.S. | B4 | 90 |
| Princeton, In., U.S. | H2 | 91 |
| Princeton, Ia., U.S. | C7 | 92 |
| Princeton, Ks., U.S. | D8 | 93 |
| Princeton, Ky., U.S. | C2 | 94 |
| Princeton, La., U.S. | B2 | 95 |
| Princeton, Me., U.S. | C5 | 96 |
| Princeton, Ma., U.S. | B4 | 98 |
| Princeton, Mn., U.S. | E5 | 100 |
| Princeton, Mo., U.S. | A4 | 102 |
| Princeton, N.J., U.S. | C3 | 107 |
| Princeton, N.C., U.S. | B4 | 110 |
| Princeton, Or., U.S. | D7 | 114 |
| Princeton, S.C., U.S. | C3 | 117 |
| Princeton, Tx., U.S. | C4 | 120 |
| Princeton, Wi., U.S. | E4 | 126 |
| Princeton, W.V., U.S. | D3 | 125 |
| *Princeton, Mount, mtn., Co., U.S.* | C4 | 83 |
| Princeton Junction, N.J., U.S. | C3 | 107 |
| Princeville, Que. | C6 | 74 |
| Princeville, Il., U.S. | C4 | 90 |
| Princeville, N.C., U.S. | B5 | 110 |
| Prince William, N.B. | D2 | 71 |
| *Prince William, co., Va., U.S.* | B5 | 123 |
| *Prince William Sound, strt., Ak., U.S.* | g18 | 79 |
| *Príncipe, i., S. Tom./Pr.* | E1 | 46 |
| *Príncipe Channel, strt., B.C.* | C3 | 69 |
| Prineville, Or., U.S. | C6 | 114 |
| *Prineville Reservoir, res., Or., U.S.* | C6 | 114 |
| Pringle, S.D., U.S. | D2 | 118 |
| Prinsburg, Mn., U.S. | F3 | 100 |
| Prinzapolka, Nic. | E8 | 63 |
| *Prinzapolka, stm., Nic.* | D6 | 62 |
| Prior Lake, Mn., U.S. | F5 | 100 |
| Priozersk, Sov. Un. | A8 | 27 |
| Pripyat, Sov. Un. | F7 | 27 |
| *Pripyat (Pripet), stm., Sov. Un.* | E7 | 27 |
| Prishib, Sov. Un. | B4 | 39 |
| Priština, Yugo. | D5 | 24 |
| Pritchett, Co., U.S. | D8 | 83 |
| *Pritchards Island, i., S.C., U.S.* | G6 | 117 |
| Pritchett, Tx., U.S. | C5 | 120 |
| Pritzerbe, E. Ger. | F6 | 15 |
| Pritzwalk, E. Ger. | B6 | 18 |
| Privas, Fr. | E6 | 16 |
| *Privert, Lac, l., Que.* | g8 | 72 |
| Privolnoye, Sov. Un. | H9 | 27 |
| Prizren, Yugo. | D5 | 24 |
| Prizzi, Italy | F4 | 23 |
| Probolinggo, Indon. | G4 | 34 |
| Procious, W.V., U.S. | m13 | 125 |
| Procter, B.C. | E9 | 69 |
| Proctor, Mn., U.S. | D6 | 100 |
| Proctor, Mt., U.S. | C2 | 103 |
| Proctor, Ok., U.S. | B7 | 113 |
| Proctor, Tx., U.S. | D3 | 120 |
| Proctor, Vt., U.S. | D2 | 122 |
| Proctor, W.V., U.S. | g8 | 125 |
| *Proctor Lake, res., Tx., U.S.* | C3 | 120 |
| Proctorsville, Vt., U.S. | E3 | 122 |
| Proctorville, N.C., U.S. | C3 | 110 |
| Proctorville, Oh., U.S. | D3 | 112 |
| Proença-a-Nova, Port. | C2 | 22 |
| Progreso, Mex. | C7 | 63 |
| Prokhladnyy, Sov. Un. | E2 | 28 |
| Prokopyevsk, Sov. Un. | D11 | 29 |
| Prokuplje, Yugo. | D5 | 24 |
| Prole, Ia., U.S. | f8 | 92 |
| Proletarsk, Sov. Un. | H13 | 27 |
| Proletarsk, Sov. Un. | q21 | 27 |
| Prome (Pye), Burma | E10 | 36 |
| Promise City, Ia., U.S. | D4 | 92 |
| Promissão, Braz. | C3 | 56 |
| *Promontory Mountains, mts., Ut., U.S.* | B3 | 121 |
| Pronsfeld, W. Ger. | D6 | 17 |
| Prophetstown, Il., U.S. | B4 | 90 |
| Proprià, Braz. | D3 | 57 |
| *Prorer Wiek, b., E. Ger.* | D7 | 15 |
| Prorva, Sov. Un. | D4 | 28 |
| Proserpine, Austl. | D8 | 50 |
| *Prosna, stm., Pol.* | C5 | 26 |
| Prosotsáni, Grc. | B4 | 25 |
| Prospect, N.S. | E6 | 71 |
| Prospect, Ct., U.S. | C4 | 84 |
| Prospect, In., U.S. | G4 | 91 |
| Prospect, Ky., U.S. | g11 | 94 |
| Prospect, Oh., U.S. | B2 | 112 |
| Prospect, Or., U.S. | E4 | 114 |
| Prospect, Pa., U.S. | E1 | 115 |
| Prospect, Tn., U.S. | B4 | 119 |
| Prospect, Va., U.S. | C4 | 123 |
| Prospect Harbor, Me., U.S. | D4 | 96 |
| Prospect Heights, Il., U.S. | *h9 | 90 |
| Prospect Hill, N.C., U.S. | A3 | 110 |
| *Prospect Hill, mtn., Or., U.S.* | k11 | 114 |
| *Prospect Hill, hill, Ma., U.S.* | g10 | 98 |
| Prospect Park, N.J., U.S. | B4 | 107 |
| Prospect Park, Pa., U.S. | p20 | 115 |
| Prospect Plains, N.J., U.S. | C4 | 107 |
| Prosperity, S.C., U.S. | C4 | 117 |
| Prosperity, W.V., U.S. | n13 | 125 |
| Prosser, Ne., U.S. | D7 | 104 |
| Prosser, Wa., U.S. | C5 | 124 |
| Prostějov, Czech. | D4 | 26 |
| Prostki, Pol. | B7 | 26 |
| Protem, Mo., U.S. | E4 | 102 |
| Protivín, Ia., U.S. | A5 | 92 |
| Proton Station, Ont. | C4 | 73 |
| Prouts Neck, Me., U.S. | g7 | 96 |
| Provadiya, Bul. | D8 | 24 |
| Provençal, La., U.S. | C2 | 95 |
| *Provence, hist. reg., Fr.* | F7 | 16 |
| Providence, Fl., U.S. | G4 | 86 |
| Providence, Ky., U.S. | C2 | 94 |
| Providence, R.I., U.S. | C4 | 116 |
| Providence, Ut., U.S. | B4 | 121 |
| *Providence, co., R.I., U.S.* | C3 | 116 |
| *Providence, stm., R.I., U.S.* | C5 | 116 |
| Providence Bay, Ont. | B2 | 73 |
| Providence Forge, Va., U.S. | C5 | 123 |
| *Providence Point, c., R.I., U.S.* | D7 | 116 |
| *Providencia, Isla de, i., Col.* | D7 | 62 |
| *Province Lake, l., N.H., U.S.* | C5 | 106 |
| Provincetown, Ma., U.S. | B7 | 98 |
| Provins, Fr. | C5 | 16 |
| Provo, S.D., U.S. | D2 | 118 |
| Provo, Ut., U.S. | C4 | 121 |
| *Provo, stm., Ut., U.S.* | C4 | 121 |
| Provost, Alta. | C5 | 68 |
| *Prowers, co., Co., U.S.* | D8 | 83 |
| Pruden, Tn., U.S. | C10 | 119 |
| Prudence Island, R.I., U.S. | E5 | 116 |
| Prudenville, Mi., U.S. | D6 | 99 |
| Prudhoe Bay, Ak., U.S. | A10 | 79 |
| *Prudhoe Bay, b., Ak., U.S.* | A10 | 79 |
| Prud'homme, Sask. | E3 | 75 |
| Prudnik, Pol. | C4 | 26 |
| Prüm, W. Ger. | C3 | 18 |
| Pruszków, Pol. | B6 | 26 |
| *Prut, stm., Eur.* | H9 | 27 |
| Pružany, Sov. Un. | E5 | 27 |
| *Prydz Bay, b., Ant.* | C20 | 7 |
| Pryor, Mt., U.S. | E8 | 103 |
| Pryor, Ok., U.S. | A6 | 113 |
| *Pryor Mountains, mts., Mt., U.S.* | E8 | 103 |
| Przasnysz, Pol. | B6 | 26 |
| Przedbórz, Pol. | C5 | 26 |
| *Przemsza, stm., Pol.* | g10 | 26 |
| Przemyśl, Pol. | D7 | 26 |
| Przeworsk, Pol. | C7 | 26 |
| Przewóz, Pol. | B9 | 19 |
| Przhevalsk, Sov. Un. | C9 | 29 |
| Psakhná, Grc. | C4 | 25 |
| *Psará, i., Grc.* | C5 | 25 |
| Psary, Pol. | g10 | 26 |
| *Psel, stm., Sov. Un.* | G9 | 27 |
| Pskov, Sov. Un. | D5 | 29 |
| *Pskov, Lake, l., Sov. Un.* | D5 | 29 |
| Pszczyna, Pol. | D5 | 26 |
| Pszów, Pol. | h10 | 26 |
| *Ptich, stm., Sov. Un.* | E7 | 27 |
| Ptolemaís, Grc. | B3 | 25 |
| Ptuj, Yugo. | B2 | 24 |
| Puako, Hi., U.S. | D6 | 88 |
| Puán, Arg. | B4 | 54 |
| Pu'apu'a, W. Sam. | F11 | 52 |
| Pucallpa, Peru | C3 | 58 |
| Pucheng, China | K8 | 32 |
| Pucheng, China | G6 | 32 |
| Puchón, S. Kor. | *H3 | 33 |
| Puck, Pol. | A5 | 26 |
| *Puckaway Lake, l., Wi., U.S.* | E4 | 126 |
| Puckett, Ms., U.S. | C4 | 101 |
| Pudasjärvi, Fin. | E12 | 14 |
| Pudozh, Sov. Un. | A11 | 27 |
| *Puebla, state, Mex.* | D5 | 63 |
| Puebla de Don Fadrique, Spain | D4 | 22 |
| Puebla [de Zaragoza], Mex. | D5 | 63 |
| Pueblo, Co., U.S. | C6 | 83 |
| *Pueblo, co., Co., U.S.* | C6 | 83 |
| *Pueblo Colorado Wash, val., Az., U.S.* | B6 | 80 |
| Pueblo Hundido, Chile | E1 | 55 |
| Pueblo Libre, Peru | *D2 | 58 |
| *Pueblo Mountain, mtn., Or., U.S.* | E8 | 114 |
| *Pueblo Mountains, mts., Or., U.S.* | E8 | 114 |
| Pueblo Nuevo (part of Panamá), Pan. | k11 | 62 |
| Pueblo Nuevo, Ven. | A4 | 60 |
| *Pueblo Reservoir, res., Co., U.S.* | C6 | 83 |
| Puebloviejo, Ec. | B2 | 58 |
| Puenteareas, Spain | A1 | 22 |
| Puente-Ceso, Spain | A1 | 22 |
| Puentedeume, Spain | A1 | 22 |
| Puente-Genil, Spain | D3 | 22 |
| *Pueo Point, c., Hi., U.S.* | B1 | 88 |
| *Puerca, Punta, c., P.R.* | B4 | 65 |
| *Puerco, stm., U.S.* | C6 | 80 |
| *Puerco, Rio, stm., N.M., U.S.* | B2 | 108 |
| Puerto Acosta, Bol. | C2 | 55 |
| Puerto Aisén, Chile | D2 | 54 |
| Puerto Alegre, Bol. | B3 | 55 |
| Puerto Armuelles, Pan. | F6 | 62 |
| Puerto Asís, Col. | C2 | 60 |
| Puerto Ayacucho, Ven. | D4 | 60 |
| Puerto Baquerizo Moreno, Ec. | g6 | 58 |
| Puerto Barrios, Guat. | D7 | 63 |
| Puerto Belgrano, Arg. | B4 | 54 |
| Puerto Bermúdez, Peru | D3 | 58 |
| Puerto Berrío, Col. | B3 | 60 |
| Puerto Bolívar, Ec. | B1 | 58 |
| Puerto Cabello, Ven. | A4 | 60 |
| Puerto Cabezas, Nic. | E8 | 63 |
| Puerto Carreño, Col. | B4 | 60 |
| Puerto Casado, Para. | D4 | 55 |
| Puerto Chicama, Peru | C2 | 58 |
| Puerto Colombia, Col. | A3 | 60 |
| Puerto Constanza, Arg. | f7 | 54 |
| Puerto Cortés, Hond. | D7 | 63 |
| Puerto Cumarebo, Ven. | A4 | 60 |
| Puerto de la Cruz, Spain | m13 | 22 |
| Puerto del Rosario, Spain | m15 | 22 |
| Puerto del Son, Spain | A1 | 22 |
| Puerto de Luna, N.M., U.S. | C5 | 108 |
| Puerto Deseado, Arg. | D3 | 54 |
| Puerto Eten, Peru | C2 | 58 |
| Puerto Francisco de Orellana, Ec. | B2 | 58 |
| Puerto Guaraní, Para. | *B2 | 55 |
| Puerto Heath, Bol. | B2 | 55 |
| Puerto Inírida, Col. | C4 | 60 |
| Puerto Jiménez, C.R. | F6 | 62 |
| Puerto la Cruz, Ven. | A5 | 60 |
| Puerto Leguízamo, Col. | D3 | 60 |
| Puerto Limón, Col. | C3 | 60 |
| Puerto Lobos, Arg. | C3 | 54 |
| Puerto López, Col. | C3 | 60 |
| Puerto Madryn, Arg. | C3 | 54 |
| Puerto Maldonado, Peru | D4 | 58 |
| Puerto México see Coatzacoalcos, Mex. | D6 | 63 |
| Puerto Mineral, Arg. | C2 | 55 |
| Puerto Montt, Chile | C2 | 54 |
| Puerto Morazán, Nic. | G4 | 62 |
| Puerto Nariño, Col. | C4 | 60 |
| Puerto Natales, Chile | D2 | 54 |
| Puerto Padre, Cuba | D5 | 64 |
| Puerto Páez, Ven. | B4 | 60 |
| Puerto Peñasco, Mex. | A2 | 63 |
| Puerto Pilón, Pan. | k11 | 62 |
| Puerto Pinasco, Para. | D4 | 55 |
| Puerto Pirámides, Arg. | C4 | 54 |
| Puerto Plata, Dom. Rep. | E8 | 64 |
| Puerto Portillo, Peru | C3 | 58 |
| Puerto Presidente Stroessner, Para. | E5 | 55 |
| Puerto Princesa, Phil. | D5 | 34 |
| Puerto Real, Spain | *D2 | 22 |
| *Puerto Rico, ctry., N.A.* | G11 | 64 |
| Puerto Saavedra, Chile | *D2 | 54 |
| Puerto Sastre, Para. | D4 | 55 |
| Puerto Siles, Bol. | B2 | 55 |
| Puerto Suárez, Bol. | C4 | 55 |
| Puerto Tejada, Col. | C2 | 60 |
| Puerto Toledo, Col. | C3 | 60 |
| Puerto Vallarta, Mex. | C3 | 63 |
| Puerto Varas, Chile | C2 | 54 |
| Puerto Victoria, Peru | C3 | 58 |
| Puerto Viejo, C.R. | F6 | 62 |
| Puerto Villamizar, Col. | B3 | 60 |
| Puerto Visser, Arg. | D3 | 54 |
| Puerto Wilches, Col. | B3 | 60 |
| Pugachev, Sov. Un. | F4 | 28 |
| *Puget Sound, strt., Wa., U.S.* | B3 | 124 |
| *Puget Sound Naval Shipyard, mil., Wa., U.S.* | e10 | 124 |
| Pugwash, N.S. | D6 | 71 |
| Puhi, Hi., U.S. | B2 | 88 |
| Puhsi, China | B2 | 33 |
| Pujehun, S.L. | E2 | 45 |
| Pujili, Ec. | A2 | 58 |
| Puká, Alb. | B3 | 25 |
| *Pukaki, Lake, l., N.Z.* | M15 | 51 |
| Pukalani, Hi., U.S. | C5 | 88 |
| Pukaskwa National Park, Ont. | o18 | 73 |
| *Pukeashun Mountain, mtn., B.C.* | D8 | 69 |
| Pukekohe, N.Z. | L15 | 51 |
| Pukou, China | H8 | 32 |
| *Puksubaek, Mount, mtn., N. Kor.* | *F3 | 33 |
| Pukwana, S.D., U.S. | D6 | 118 |
| Pula, Italy | E2 | 23 |
| Pula, Yugo. | C1 | 24 |
| Pulacayo, Bol. | D2 | 55 |
| Pulaski, Il., U.S. | F4 | 90 |
| Pulaski, In., U.S. | C4 | 91 |
| Pulaski, Ms., U.S. | C4 | 101 |
| Pulaski, N.Y., U.S. | B4 | 109 |
| Pulaski, Tn., U.S. | B4 | 119 |
| Pulaski, Va., U.S. | C2 | 123 |
| Pulaski, Wi., U.S. | D5 | 126 |
| *Pulaski, co., Ar., U.S.* | C3 | 81 |
| *Pulaski, co., Ga., U.S.* | D3 | 87 |
| *Pulaski, co., Il., U.S.* | F4 | 90 |
| *Pulaski, co., In., U.S.* | B4 | 91 |
| *Pulaski, co., Ky., U.S.* | C5 | 94 |
| *Pulaski, co., Mo., U.S.* | D5 | 102 |
| *Pulaski, co., Va., U.S.* | C2 | 123 |
| Puławy, Pol. | C6 | 26 |
| Pulheim, W. Ger. | *C3 | 18 |
| Pullman, Mi., U.S. | F4 | 99 |
| Pullman, Wa., U.S. | C8 | 124 |
| Pullman, W.V., U.S. | B4 | 125 |
| *Pulog, Mount, mtn., Phil.* | B6 | 34 |
| Pulozero, Sov. Un. | C15 | 14 |
| *Puma Lake, l., China* | C13 | 37 |
| Pumphrey, Md., U.S. | h11 | 97 |
| *Pumpkin Buttes, mtn., Wy., U.S.* | C7 | 127 |
| *Pumpkin Creek, stm., Mt., U.S.* | E11 | 103 |
| *Pumpkin Creek, stm., Ne., U.S.* | C2 | 104 |
| Pumpville, Tx., U.S. | E2 | 120 |
| *Puná, Isla, i., Ec.* | B1 | 58 |
| Punakha, Bhu. | C8 | 36 |
| Punat, Yugo. | C2 | 24 |
| Punata, Bol. | C2 | 55 |
| Punchaw, B.C. | C6 | 69 |
| Pune, India | E5 | 36 |
| *Pungo Lake, l., N.C., U.S.* | B6 | 110 |
| Pungsan, N. Kor. | F4 | 33 |
| Punia, Zaire | B4 | 48 |
| *Punjab, state, India* | B5 | 36 |
| *Punjab, prov., Pak.* | B5 | 36 |
| Punnichy, Sask. | F3 | 75 |
| Puno, Peru | E3 | 58 |
| *Puno, dept., Peru* | E3 | 58 |
| Punta Alta, Arg. | B4 | 54 |
| Punta Arenas, Chile | h11 | 54 |
| Punta de Díaz, Chile | E1 | 55 |
| Punta del Este, Ur. | E2 | 56 |
| Punta de Piedras, Ven. | A5 | 60 |
| Punta de Vacas, Arg. | A3 | 54 |
| Punta Gorda, Belize | D7 | 63 |
| Punta Gorda, Fl., U.S. | F4 | 86 |
| *Punta Gorda, Bahía de, b., Nic.* | E8 | 63 |
| Punta Moreno, Peru | C2 | 58 |
| Puntarenas, C.R. | E5 | 62 |
| Punto Fijo, Ven. | A3 | 60 |
| *Puntzi Lake, l., B.C.* | C5 | 69 |
| Punxsutawney, Pa., U.S. | E4 | 115 |
| Puposky, Mn., U.S. | C4 | 100 |
| Puquio, Peru | D3 | 58 |
| *Pur, stm., Sov. Un.* | C10 | 29 |
| Pūranpur, India | C8 | 37 |
| *Purari, stm., Pap. N. Gui.* | k11 | 50 |
| Purcell, Mo., U.S. | D3 | 102 |
| Purcell, Ok., U.S. | B4 | 113 |
| *Purcell Mountains, mts., N.A.* | | |
| Purcellville, Va., U.S. | A5 | 123 |
| *Purdham Hill, mtn., Ar., U.S.* | h10 | 81 |
| Purdin, Mo., U.S. | B4 | 102 |
| Purdum, Ne., U.S. | B5 | 104 |
| Purdy, Mo., U.S. | E4 | 102 |
| Purépero, Mex. | n12 | 63 |
| *Purgatoire, stm., Co., U.S.* | D7 | 83 |
| *Purgatoire Peak, mtn., Co., U.S.* | D5 | 83 |
| Puri, India | E8 | 36 |
| Purmerend, Neth. | B4 | 17 |
| Pūrna, India | B4 | 36 |
| *Pūrna, stm., India* | H6 | 37 |
| Purnia, India | C8 | 36 |
| Purple Springs, Alta. | E5 | 68 |
| *Purús, stm., S.A.* | B4 | 58 |
| Puruliya, India | D8 | 36 |
| Purvis, Ms., U.S. | D4 | 101 |
| Purwakarta, Indon. | *G3 | 34 |
| Purwokerto, Indon. | *G3 | 34 |
| Puryear, Tn., U.S. | A3 | 119 |
| Puryŏng-dong, N. Kor. | F4 | 33 |
| Pusan, S. Kor. | D10 | 31 |
| *Pushaw Lake, l., Me., U.S.* | D4 | 96 |
| Pushkin, Sov. Un. | B4 | 27 |
| Pushkino, Sov. Un. | C11 | 27 |
| *Pushmataha, co., Ok., U.S.* | C6 | 113 |
| Pushthrough, Newf. | E3 | 72 |
| *Pusiano, Lago di, l., Italy* | E7 | 21 |
| Püspökladány, Hung. | B5 | 24 |
| Pustelnik, Pol. | k14 | 26 |
| Pustynya, Sov. Un. | B8 | 28 |
| Putao, Burma | C10 | 36 |
| Puteaux, Fr. | g9 | 16 |
| Putian, China | F8 | 31 |
| Putilovo, Sov. Un. | s32 | 14 |
| *Puting, Cape, c., Indon.* | F4 | 34 |
| Putnam, Ct., U.S. | B8 | 84 |
| Putnam, Tx., U.S. | C3 | 120 |
| *Putnam, co., Fl., U.S.* | C5 | 86 |
| *Putnam, co., Ga., U.S.* | C3 | 87 |
| *Putnam, co., Il., U.S.* | B4 | 90 |
| *Putnam, co., In., U.S.* | E4 | 91 |
| *Putnam, co., Mo., U.S.* | A4 | 102 |
| *Putnam, co., N.Y., U.S.* | D7 | 109 |
| *Putnam, co., Oh., U.S.* | B1 | 112 |
| *Putnam, co., Tn., U.S.* | C8 | 119 |
| *Putnam, co., W.V., U.S.* | C3 | 125 |
| Putnam Station, N.Y., U.S. | B7 | 109 |
| Putnamville, In., U.S. | E4 | 91 |
| Putnamville, Vt., U.S. | C3 | 122 |
| Putney, Ga., U.S. | E2 | 87 |
| Putney, S.D., U.S. | B7 | 118 |
| Putney, Vt., U.S. | F3 | 122 |
| Putre, Chile | C2 | 55 |
| Puttalam, Sri L. | G6 | 36 |
| Putte, Neth. | C4 | 17 |
| Püttlingen, W. Ger. | D1 | 19 |
| *Putumayo, dept., Col.* | C2 | 60 |
| *Putumayo (Içá), stm., S.A.* | D3 | 58 |
| Pütürge, Tur. | C12 | 40 |
| Puʻukoholā Heiau National Historic Site, hist., Hi., U.S. | D6 | 88 |
| Puukolii, Hi., U.S. | *C5 | 88 |
| *Puulavesi, l., Fin.* | G12 | 14 |
| Puunene, Hi., U.S. | C5 | 88 |
| Puurs, Bel. | C4 | 17 |
| Puxico, Mo., U.S. | E7 | 102 |
| Puyallup, Wa., U.S. | B3 | 124 |

Name  Map Ref.  Page

Puyallup, stm., Wa., U.S. ... C3 124
Puyang, China ... G6 32
Puyehue, Chile ... C2 54
Puyo, Ec. ... B2 58
Pūzak, Hāmūn-e, l., Afg. ... F10 39
Pwani, prov., Tan. ... C6 48
Pweto, Zaire ... C4 48
Pwllheli, Wales, U.K. ... D4 10
Pyaozero, l., Sov. Un. ... D14 14
Pyapon, Burma ... E10 36
Pyasina, stm., Sov. Un. ... B12 29
Pyatigorsk, Sov. Un. ... E2 28
Pyatt, Ar., U.S. ... A3 81
Pyhäjärvi, l., Fin. ... G10 14
Pyinmana, Burma ... E10 36
Pyland, Ms., U.S. ... B4 101
Pyles Fork, stm., W.V., U.S. ... h10 125
Pymatuning Reservoir, res., U.S. ... C1 115
Pyŏngchang, S. Kor. ... H4 33
Pyŏngtaek, S. Kor. ... H3 33
Pyŏngyang, N. Kor. ... D10 31
Pyote, Tx., U.S. ... D1 120
Pyramid Lake, l., Nv., U.S. ... C2 105
Pyramid Lake Indian Reservation, Nv., U.S. ... D2 105
Pyramid Mountains, mts., N.M., U.S. ... E1 108
Pyramid Peak, mtn., N.M., U.S. ... E1 108
Pyramid Peak, mtn., Wy., U.S. ... C2 127
Pyramids, hist., Eg. ... C3 38
Pyrenees, mts., Eur. ... A6 22
Pyrites, N.Y., U.S. ... f9 109
Pyrmont, In., U.S. ... D4 91
Pyrzyce, Pol. ... B3 26
Pyskowice, Pol. ... g9 26
Pytalovo, Sov. Un. ... C6 27
Pyu, Burma ... E10 36

**Q**
Qabātiyah, Isr. Occ. ... B7 41
Qā'emshahr, Iran ... C6 39
Qā'en, Iran ... E9 39
Qahar Youyi Zhongqi, China . D5 32
Qaidam Pendi (Tsaidam Basin), China ... D3 31
Qalamshah, Eg. ... H8 40
Qalāt, Afg. ... B4 36
Qal'at Bīshah, Sau. Ar. ... C4 38
Qal' at Şāliḥ, Iraq ... F3 39
Qal' at Sukkar, Iraq ... F3 39
Qal'eh-ye Now, Afg. ... D11 39
Qallābāt, Sud. ... C4 47
Qalqīlya, Isr. Occ. ... B6 41
Qalyūb, Eg. ... D3 41
Qamdo, China ... E4 31
Qamea, l., Fiji ... H16 52
Qamīnīs, Libya ... C4 43
Qānā, Leb. ... A7 41
Qandahār see Kandahar, Afg. . B4 36
Qandala, Som. ... C6 47
Qārah, Egypt ... H6 40
Qardho, Som. ... D6 47
Qareh, stm., Iran ... D5 39
Qārūn, Birkat, l., Eg. ... D6 43
Qaryat Abu Nujaym, Libya ... C3 43
Qaşr al Farāfirah, Eg. ... C2 38
Qaşr Banī Walīd, Libya ... C2 43
Qasr el Boukhari, Alg. ... B5 44
Qaşr-e Shīrīn, Iran ... D2 39
Qa'ţabah, Yemen ... D4 38
Qatar, ctry., Asia ... C5 38
Qattara Depression, depr., Eg. ... C2 38
Qawz Rajab, Sud. ... B4 47
Qazvīn, Iran ... B4 38
Qeshm, Iran ... H8 39
Qeshm, i., Iran ... C5 38
Qezel Owzan, stm., Iran ... C4 39
Qian'an, China ... D8 32
Qianjiang, China ... J3 32
Qianshan, China ... I7 32
Qiantang Jiang, stm., China . J8 32
Qianxian, China ... G3 32
Qianyang, China ... F7 31
Qiaojia, China ... F5 31
Qichun, China ... I6 31
Qiemo, China ... A8 36
Qijiang, China ... J2 32
Qila Lādgasht, Pak. ... C3 36
Qila Saifullāh, Pak. ... B2 37
Qilian Shan, mts., China ... D4 31
Qimen, China ... J7 32
Qinā, Eg. ... C3 38
Qing'an, China ... C3 33
Qingdao (Tsingtao), China .. D9 31
Qinghai Hu, l., China ... D4 31
Qingjian, China ... D7 31
Qingjiang, China ... J6 32
Qingliu, China ... F8 31
Qingpu, China ... E9 31
Qingyang, China ... D6 31
Qingyuan, China ... C11 32
Qingyun, China ... F7 32
Qing Zang Gaoyuan (Plateau of Tibet), plat., China ... G11 30
Qin He, stm., China ... G5 32
Qinhuangdao, China ... D8 31
Qin Ling (Tsinling Shan), mts., China ... E6 31
Qinxian, China ... F5 32
Qinyang, China ... G5 32
Qinzhou, China ... B8 35
Qiongshan, China ... B4 34
Qiongzhou Haixia, strt., China B8 35
Qiqian, China ... A9 31
Qiqihar (Tsitsihar), China ... B9 31
Qiryat Ata, Isr. ... B7 41
Qiryat Gat, Isr. ... C6 41
Qiryat Mal'akhi, Isr. ... C6 41
Qiryat Ono, Isr. ... g10 41
Qiryat Shemona, Isr. ... A7 41
Qiryat Yam, Isr. ... B7 41
Qishn, Yemen ... D6 38
Qishon, stm., Isr. ... B7 41
Qitai, China ... A4 36
Qitaihe, China ... *B11 31
Qiyang, China ... F7 31
Qīzān, Sau. Ar. ... D4 38
Qnadsa, Alg. ... C4 44
Qom, Iran ... B5 38
Qom, stm., Iran ... E5 39
Qomemiyyut (Talbiya) (part of Jerusalem), Isr. ... m14 41
Qomsheh, Iran ... E5 39
Quabbin Reservoir, res., Ma., U.S. ... B3 98
Quaco Head, c., N.B. ... D4 71
Quaddick, Ct., U.S. ... B8 84
Quaddick Reservoir, res., Ct., U.S. ... B8 84
Quail Oaks, Va., U.S. ... n18 123
Quakenbrück, W. Ger. ... B3 18

Quaker City, Oh., U.S. ... C4 112
Quaker Hill, Ct., U.S. ... D7 84
Quakertown, N.J., U.S. ... B3 107
Quakertown, Pa., U.S. ... F11 115
Qualicum Beach, B.C. ... E5 69
Quality, Ky., U.S. ... C3 94
Quamba, Mn., U.S. ... E5 100
Quanah, Tx., U.S. ... B3 120
Quang Ngai, Viet. ... B3 34
Quang Trach, Viet. ... D7 35
Quang Tri, Viet. ... B3 34
Quannapowitt, Lake, l., Ma., U.S. ... f11 98
Quantico, Md., U.S. ... D6 97
Quantico, Va., U.S. ... B5 123
Quantico Marine Corps Air Station, mil., Va., U.S. ... B5 123
Quantico Station, Va., U.S. ... *B5 123
Quanzhou, China ... F7 31
Quanzhou, China ... G8 31
Quapaw, Ok., U.S. ... A7 113
Qu'Appelle, Sask. ... G4 75
Qu'Appelle, stm., Can. ... G4 75
Quarai, Braz. ... E1 56
Quaraí, stm., S.A. ... E1 56
Quarles Mountains, mts., Indon. ... F5 34
Quarryville, N.B. ... C4 71
Quarryville, Ct., U.S. ... B6 84
Quarryville, Pa., U.S. ... G9 115
Quartz Hill, Ca., U.S. ... *E4 82
Quartz Mountain, mtn., Or., U.S. ... D4 114
Quartzsite, Az., U.S. ... D1 80
Quasqueton, Ia., U.S. ... B6 92
Quassapaug, Lake, l., Ct., U.S. ... C3 84
Quatre, Isle, i., St. Vin. ... V26 65
Quatsino Sound, strt., B.C. .. D3 69
Quay, N.M., U.S. ... C6 108
Quay, Ok., U.S. ... A5 113
Quay, co., N.M., U.S. ... C6 108
Qūchān, Iran ... B5 38
Quealy, Wy., U.S. ... E3 127
Québec, co., Que. ... C6 74
Québec, co., Que. ... B5 74
Quebec, prov., Can. ... C5 74
Quebeck, Tn., U.S. ... D8 119
Quechee, Vt., U.S. ... D4 122
Quechee Gorge, val., Vt., U.S. D4 122
Quecreek, Pa., U.S. ... F3 115
Quedlinburg, E. Ger. ... C5 18
Queen, stm., R.I., U.S. ... E3 116
Queen, Cape, c., N.W. Ter. .. D17 66
Queen Alexandra Range, mts., Ant. ... A29 7
Queen Anne, co., Md., U.S. .. C6 97
Queen Annes, co., Md., U.S. . B5 97
Queen Bess, Mount, mtn., B.C. ... D5 69
Queenborough [-in-Sheppey], Eng., U.K. ... E7 10
Queen Charlotte, B.C. ... C1 69
Queen Charlotte Islands, is., B.C. ... C1 69
Queen Charlotte Mountains, mts., B.C. ... C1 69
Queen Charlotte Sound, strt., B.C. ... n17 69
Queen Charlotte Strait, strt., B.C. ... D4 69
Queen City, Mo., U.S. ... A5 102
Queen City, Tx., U.S. ... C5 120
Queen Creek, Az., U.S. ... m9 80
Queen Elizabeth Islands, is., N.W. Ter. ... k30 66
Queen Fabiola Mountains, mts., Ant. ... B16 7
Queen Mary Coast, Ant. ... C22 7
Queen Maud Gulf, b., N.W. Ter. ... C12 66
Queen Maud Land, reg., Ant. . B15 7
Queen Maud Mountains, mts., Ant. ... A31 7
Queens, co., N.B. ... D4 71
Queens, co., N.B. ... E4 71
Queens, co., P.E.I. ... C6 71
Queens, co., N.Y., U.S. ... E7 109
Queensborough, Ont. ... C7 73
Queensborough, Wa., U.S. ... *B3 124
Queensferry, Scot., U.K. ... E5 13
Queensferry see South Queensferry, Scot., U.K. .. E5 13
Queen Shoals, W.V., U.S. ... C3 125
Queensland, Ga., U.S. ... E3 87
Queensland, state, Austl. ... D7 50
Queensport, N.S. ... D8 71
Queens Sound, strt., B.C. ... D3 69
Queenstown, Austl. ... o15 50
Queenstown, Alta. ... D4 68
Queenstown, N.B. ... D3 71
Queenstown, N.Z. ... P12 51
Queenstown, S. Afr. ... D4 49
Queenstown, Md., U.S. ... C5 97
Queen Victoria Sea, Eur. ... A5 29
Queets, Wa., U.S. ... B1 124
Queguay Grande, stm., Ur. .. E1 56
Queimadas, Braz. ... D3 57
Queimadinhas, Braz. ... A4 56
Queixada, Braz. ... B4 56
Quela, Ang. ... C2 48
Quelelevu, i., Fiji ... H16 52
Quelimane, Moz. ... A6 49
Quemado, N.M., U.S. ... C1 108
Quemado, Tx., U.S. ... E2 120
Quemado de Güines, Cuba .. C3 64
Quemú Quemú, Arg. ... B4 54
Quenemo, Ks., U.S. ... D8 93
Quentin, Ms., U.S. ... D3 101
Quepos, C.R. ... F5 62
Quequén, Arg. ... B5 54
Querémaro, Mex. ... C4 63
Querétaro, Mex. ... C5 63
Querétaro, state, Mex. ... C5 63
Querfurt, E. Ger. ... B6 19
Quers, Fr. ... A1 21
Quesada, Spain ... D4 22
Queshan, China ... H6 32
Quesnel, B.C. ... C6 69
Quesnel, stm., B.C. ... C6 69
Quesnel Lake, l., B.C. ... C7 69
Questa, N.M., U.S. ... A4 108
Quetena, Bol. ... D2 55
Quetico Provincial Park, Ont. . o17 73
Quetta, Pak. ... B4 36
Quevedo, Ec. ... B2 58
Quezaltenango, Guat. ... E6 63
Quezaltepeque, El Sal. ... D3 62
Quezon City, Phil. ... C6 34
Quibala, Ang. ... D1 48
Quibdó, Col. ... B2 60
Quibell, Ont. ... E5 70
Quiberon, Fr. ... D2 16
Quiberon Peninsula, pen., Fr. . D2 16
Quicksand Pond, l., R.I., U.S. E6 116

Quicksburg, Va., U.S. ... B4 123
Quidnessett, R.I., U.S. ... E4 116
Quidnick, R.I., U.S. ... D3 116
Quidnick Reservoir, res., R.I., U.S. ... D2 116
Quiindy, Para. ... E4 55
Quilá, Mex. ... C3 63
Quilcene, Wa., U.S. ... B3 124
Quilengues, Ang. ... D1 48
Quileute Indian Reservation, Wa., U.S. ... B1 124
Quilino, Arg. ... F3 55
Quillagua, Chile ... D2 55
Quillan, Fr. ... F5 16
Quill Lake, Sask. ... E3 75
Quillota, Chile ... A2 54
Quilmes, Arg. ... g7 54
Quilon, India ... G6 36
Quilpie, Austl. ... E7 50
Quilpué, Chile ... A2 54
Quilty, Ire. ... E2 11
Quimbele, Ang. ... C2 48
Quimby, Ia., U.S. ... B2 92
Quimby, Me., U.S. ... B4 96
Quimili, Arg. ... E3 55
Quimper, Fr. ... C1 16
Quimperlé, Fr. ... D2 16
Quinaby, Or., U.S. ... B4 114
Quinault, Wa., U.S. ... B2 124
Quinault, Lake, l., Wa., U.S. . B2 124
Quinault Indian Reservation, Wa., U.S. ... B1 124
Quince Orchard, Md., U.S. ... *B3 97
Quincy, Ca., U.S. ... C3 82
Quincy, Fl., U.S. ... B2 86
Quincy, Il., U.S. ... D2 90
Quincy, In., U.S. ... F4 91
Quincy, Ks., U.S. ... E8 93
Quincy, Ky., U.S. ... B6 94
Quincy, Ma., U.S. ... B5 98
Quincy, Mi., U.S. ... G6 99
Quincy, Mo., U.S. ... C4 102
Quincy, Oh., U.S. ... B2 112
Quincy, Or., U.S. ... A3 114
Quincy, Wa., U.S. ... B6 124
Quincy Bay, b., Ma., U.S. ... g12 98
Quindío, dept., Col. ... C2 60
Quinebaug, Ct., U.S. ... A8 84
Quinebaug, stm., Ct., U.S. ... C8 84
Quines, Arg. ... A3 54
Quinga, Moz. ... A7 49
Quinhagak, Ak., U.S. ... D7 79
Qui Nhon, Viet. ... C3 34
Quinlan, Ok., U.S. ... A2 113
Quinlan, Tx., U.S. ... C4 120
Quinn, stm., Nv., U.S. ... B3 105
Quinn Canyon Range, mts., Nv., U.S. ... F6 105
Quinnesec, Mi., U.S. ... C3 99
Quinnipiac, stm., Ct., U.S. ... D4 84
Quinnville, R.I., U.S. ... B4 116
Quinter, Ks., U.S. ... C3 93
Quintero, Chile ... A2 54
Quinton, Sask. ... F3 75
Quinton, Ky., U.S. ... D5 94
Quinton, N.J., U.S. ... D2 107
Quinton, Ok., U.S. ... B6 113
Quinton, W.V., U.S. ... C4 125
Quinwood, W.V., U.S. ... C4 125
Quipapá, Braz. ... C7 57
Quipungo, Ang. ... D1 48
Quirauk Mountain, mtn., Md., U.S. ... A2 97
Quirindi, Austl. ... E8 51
Quirinópolis, Braz. ... B2 56
Quiriquire, Ven. ... B5 60
Quiroga, Spain ... A2 22
Quirpon Island, i., Newf. ... C4 72
Quissanga, Moz. ... D7 48
Quitaque, Tx., U.S. ... B2 120
Quita Sueño Bank, Col. ... C7 62
Quitman, Ar., U.S. ... B3 81
Quitman, Ga., U.S. ... F3 87
Quitman, La., U.S. ... B3 95
Quitman, Ms., U.S. ... C5 101
Quitman, Mo., U.S. ... A2 102
Quitman, Tx., U.S. ... C5 120
Quitman, co., Ga., U.S. ... E1 87
Quitman, co., Ms., U.S. ... A3 101
Quitman Mountains, mts., Tx., U.S. ... o12 120
Quito, Ec. ... B2 58
Quixadá, Braz. ... B3 57
Quixeramobim, Braz. ... C3 57
Qulin, Mo., U.S. ... E7 102
Quoi, i., Micron. ... Q18 52
Quonnipaug Lake, l., Ct., U.S. D5 84
Quonochontaug, R.I., U.S. ... G2 116
Quonochontaug Pond, l., R.I., U.S. ... G2 116
Quonset Point, c., R.I., U.S. .. E4 116
Quorn, Austl. ... F2 51
Qurayyah, Wādī, val., Eg. ... D6 41
Qūş, Eg. ... C3 38
Quşrah, Isr. Occ. ... g12 41
Quthing, Leso. ... D4 49
Quxian, China ... E6 31
Quxian, China ... F8 31
Quzhou, China ... *F8 31

**R**
Raab (Rába), stm., Eur. ... B2 24
Raabs [an der Thaya], Aus. . D7 18
Raahe, Fin. ... E11 14
Raalte, Neth. ... B6 17
Raasay, i., Scot., U.K. ... C2 13
Rab, i., Yugo. ... B2 24
Raba, Indon. ... G5 34
Rába (Raab), stm., Eur. ... B2 24
Rabastens, Fr. ... F4 16
Rabat, Mor. ... B3 44
Rabaul, Pap. N. Gui. ... h13 50
Rabbit Creek, stm., S.D., U.S. B4 118
Rabbit Ears Pass, Co., U.S. .. A4 83
Rabbit Nash, Ky., U.S. ... k13 94
Rabbit Lake, Sask. ... D2 75
Rabi, i., Fiji ... H16 52
Rābigh, Sau. Ar. ... C3 38
Rabun, Al., U.S. ... B3 78
Rabun, co., Ga., U.S. ... B3 87
Rabun Bald, mtn., Ga., U.S. . B3 87
Rača, Yugo. ... C5 24

Raceland, Ky., U.S. ... B7 94
Raceland, La., U.S. ... E5 95
Race Point, c., Ma., U.S. ... B7 98
Race Pond, Ga., U.S. ... F4 87
Rach Gia, Viet. ... C2 34
Racibórz, Pol. ... C5 26
Racine, Mn., U.S. ... G6 100
Racine, Mo., U.S. ... E3 102
Racine, Oh., U.S. ... D4 112
Racine, W.V., U.S. ... C3 125
Racine, Wi., U.S. ... F6 126
Racine, co., Wi., U.S. ... F5 126
Racine Dam, U.S. ... C3 125
Račinevci, Czech. ... n17 26
Racket, Mo., U.S. ... C4 102
Raco, Mi., U.S. ... B6 99
Rădăuţi, Rom. ... B7 24
Radbuza, stm., Czech. ... D8 19
Radcliff, Ky., U.S. ... C4 94
Radcliff, N.D., U.S. ... C3 112
Radcliffe, Ia., U.S. ... B4 92
Råde, Nor. ... p28 14
Radeberg, E. Ger. ... C6 18
Radebeul, E. Ger. ... B8 19
Radersburg, Mt., U.S. ... D5 103
Radford, Va., U.S. ... C2 123
Rādhanpur, India ... F3 37
Radisson, Sask. ... E2 75
Radisson, Wi., U.S. ... C2 126
Radium, Ks., U.S. ... D5 93
Radium, Mn., U.S. ... B2 100
Radium Hot Springs, B.C. ... D9 69
Radium Springs, N.M., U.S. . E3 108
Radix, Point, c., Trin. ... O24 65
Radley, Ks., U.S. ... *E9 93
Radnice, Czech. ... D8 19
Radnor, In., U.S. ... C4 91
Radnor, Oh., U.S. ... B2 112
Radnor Township, Pa., J.S. . *F11 115
Radom, Pol. ... C6 26
Radom, Il., U.S. ... E4 90
Radomir, Bul. ... D6 24
Radomsko, Pol. ... C5 26
Radomyshl, Sov. Un. ... F7 27
Radoviš, Yugo. ... E6 24
Radstadt, Aus. ... E6 18
Radville, Sask. ... H3 75
Radway, Alta. ... B4 68
Radzionków, Pol. ... g9 26
Radzymin, Pol. ... k14 26
Radzyń [Podlaski], Pol. ... C7 26
Rae, N.W. Ter. ... D9 66
Rāe Bareli, India ... C7 36
Raeford, N.C., U.S. ... C3 110
Raesfeld, W. Ger. ... B1 19
Raeside, Lake, l., Austl. ... E3 50
Rae Strait, strt., N.W. Ter. ... C14 66
Raeville, Ne., U.S. ... C7 104
Rafaela, Arg. ... A4 54
Rafaḥ, Isr. Occ. ... G10 40
Rafaï, Cen. Afr. Rep. ... D4 46
Rafḥā', Sau. Ar. ... C4 38
Rafsanjān, Iran ... F8 39
Raft, stm., Id., U.S. ... G5 89
Raft River Mountains, mts., Ut., U.S. ... B2 121
Raga, Sud. ... D2 47
Ragan, Ne., U.S. ... D6 104
Ragay, Phil. ... p14 34
Ragay Gulf, b., Phil. ... p14 34
Ragged Island, i., Me., U.S. .. E4 96
Ragged Island Range, is., Bah. ... C6 64
Ragged Island, i., Me., U.S. .. C3 96
Ragged Top Mountain, mtn., Wy., U.S. ... E7 127
Raghza, Pak. ... B4 36
Ragland, Al., U.S. ... B3 78
Raglesville, In., U.S. ... G4 91
Ragley, La., U.S. ... D2 95
Rago, Ks., U.S. ... E5 93
Ragsdale, In., U.S. ... G3 91
Ragunda, Swe. ... F7 14
Ragusa, Italy ... F5 23
Rahad al Bardī, Sud. ... C1 47
Rahden, W. Ger. ... F2 15
Rahīmyār Khān, Pak. ... C5 36
Rahway, N.J., U.S. ... B4 107
Rahway, stm., N.J., U.S. ... k7 107
Rāichūr, India ... E4 36
Raiford, Fl., U.S. ... B4 86
Raigarh, India ... D7 37
Railroad Valley, val., Nv., U.S. E6 105
Raimbault, stm., Que. ... A5 74
Rainbow Bridge National Monument, Ut., U.S. ... F5 121
Rainbow City, Pan. ... k11 62
Rainbow City, Al., U.S. ... *A3 78
Rainbow Falls, wtfl., Tn., U.S. D10 119
Rainbow Flowage, res., Wi., U.S. ... C4 126
Rainbow Lake, l., Me., U.S. .. C3 96
Rainelle, W.V., U.S. ... D4 125
Rainier, Or., U.S. ... A4 114
Rainier, Wa., U.S. ... C3 124
Rainier, Mount, mtn., Wa., U.S. ... C4 124
Rains, co., Tx., U.S. ... C5 120
Rainsboro, Oh., U.S. ... C2 112
Rainsville, In., U.S. ... D4 91
Rainy, stm., N.A. ... B5 100
Rainy Lake, l., N.A. ... B5 100
Rainy Lake, l., Mn., U.S. ... B5 100
Rainy River, Ont. ... o16 73
Rainy River, dept., Ont. ... o16 73
Raipur, India ... D7 36
Ra'īs, Sau. Ar. ... D3 38
Raismes, Fr. ... A5 16
Raja, Cape, c., Indon. ... F8 34
Rājahmundry, India ... E7 36
Rājang, stm., Malay. ... E5 34
Rājapālaiyam, India ... *G6 36
Rājasthān, state, India ... C5 36
Rājkot, India ... D5 36
Rājpīpla, India ... D3 37
Rājshāhi, Bngl. ... D8 36
Rakaia, stm., N.Z. ... O13 51
Raka Zangbo, stm., China ... C11 37
Rake, Ia., U.S. ... A4 92
Rakhov, Sov. Un. ... A7 24
Rakkestad, Nor. ... p29 14
Rakovník, Czech. ... C2 26
Rakvere, Sov. Un. ... B6 27
Raleigh, Newf. ... C4 72
Raleigh, Il., U.S. ... F5 90
Raleigh, Ms., U.S. ... C4 101
Raleigh, N.C., U.S. ... B4 110
Raleigh, N.D., U.S. ... C4 111
Raleigh, W.V., U.S. ... D3 125
Raleigh, co., W.V., U.S. ... D3 125
Raleigh Bay, b., N.C., U.S. .. C6 110
Raleigh Hills, Or., U.S. ... *B4 114

Ralls, Tx., U.S. ... C2 120
Ralls, co., Mo., U.S. ... B6 102
Ralph, Al., U.S. ... B2 78
Ralph, Mi., U.S. ... B3 99
Ralph, S.D., U.S. ... B2 118
Ralston, Ia., U.S. ... B3 92
Ralston, Ok., U.S. ... A5 113
Ralston, Pa., U.S. ... D8 115
Ralston, Tn., U.S. ... A3 119
Ralston, Wy., U.S. ... B4 127
Ralston Valley, val., Nv., U.S. . E4 105
Ram, stm., Alta. ... C3 68
Rama, Sask. ... F4 75
Rama, Isr. ... B7 41
Rama, Nic. ... E8 63
Ramādī Barrage, Iraq ... F14 40
Ramah, Co., U.S. ... B6 83
Ramah, N.M., U.S. ... B1 108
Ramah Indian Reservation, N.M., U.S. ... C1 108
Rām Allāh, Isr. Occ. ... C7 41
Ramapo, stm., N.J., U.S. ... A4 107
Ramapo Mountains, mts., N.J., U.S. ... A4 107
Ramat Gan, Isr. ... B6 41
Ramat ḤaKovesh, Isr. ... g10 41
Ramat HaSharon, Isr. ... g10 41
Rambervillers, Fr. ... C7 16
Rambleton Acres, De., U.S. .. *B3 85
Ramblewood, N.J., U.S. ... D3 107
Rambouillet, Fr. ... C4 16
Ramea, Newf. ... E3 72
Ramea Islands, is., Newf. ... E3 72
Ramenskoye, Sov. Un. ... D12 27
Ramer, Al., U.S. ... C3 78
Ramer, Tn., U.S. ... B3 119
Ramey, Pa., U.S. ... E5 115
Rāmgangā, stm., India ... D7 37
Rāmhormoz, Iran ... F4 39
Ramirez, Tx., U.S. ... F3 120
Ramiriquí, Col. ... C6 60
Ramla, Isr. ... C6 41
Ramm, Jabal, mtn., Jord. ... H10 40
Ramnäs, Swe. ... t34 14
Ramon, Har, mtn., Isr. ... D6 41
Ramon, Naḥal, val., Isr. ... D6 41
Ramona, Ca., U.S. ... F5 82
Ramona, Ks., U.S. ... D6 93
Ramona, Ok., U.S. ... A6 113
Ramona, S.D., U.S. ... C8 118
Ramor, Lough, l., Ire. ... B4 11
Rampart, Ak., U.S. ... B9 79
Rampart Range, mts., Co., U.S. ... B5 83
Rāmpur, India ... C6 36
Rāmpur, India ... D7 37
Ramsay, l., Mi., U.S. ... n12 99
Ramsay, Ont. ... h12 73
Ramseur, N.C., U.S. ... B3 110
Ramsey, I. of Man ... C2 10
Ramsey, Il., U.S. ... D4 90
Ramsey, N.J., U.S. ... A4 107
Ramsey, co., Mn., U.S. ... E5 100
Ramsey, co., N.D., U.S. ... A7 111
Ramsgate, Eng., U.K. ... E7 10
Ramshorn Peak, mtn., Mt., U.S. ... E5 103
Ramshorn Peak, mtn., Wy., U.S. ... C3 127
Ramu, stm., Pap. N. Gui. ... k11 50
Rānāghāt, India ... F12 37
Ranau, Lake, l., Indon. ... F2 34
Ranburne, Al., U.S. ... B4 78
Rancagua, Chile ... A2 54
Ranchería, Braz. ... C2 56
Rancheria Rock, mtn., Or., U.S. ... C6 114
Ranchester, Wy., U.S. ... B5 127
Rānchi, India ... D8 36
Ranchito, N.M., U.S. ... A4 108
Rancho Cordova, Ca., U.S. .. *C3 82
Rancho Mirage, Ca., U.S. ... *F5 82
Rancho Palos Verdes, Ca., U.S. ... n12 82
Rancho Rinconado, Ca., U.S. *k8 82
Rancho Santa Fe, Ca., U.S. .. o15 82
Ranchos de Taos, N.M., U.S. A4 108
Ranco, Lago, l., Chile ... C2 54
Rancocas, N.J., U.S. ... C3 107
Rancocas Creek, stm., N.J., U.S. ... C3 107
Rancocas Creek, South Branch, stm., N.J., U.S. .. D3 107
Rancocas Woods, N.J., U.S. . D3 107
Rand, Co., U.S. ... A4 83
Rand, W.V., U.S. ... C3 125
Randalia, Ia., U.S. ... B6 92
Randall, Ia., U.S. ... B4 92
Randall, Ks., U.S. ... C5 93
Randall, Mn., U.S. ... D4 100
Randall, co., Tx., U.S. ... B1 120
Randallstown, Md., U.S. ... B4 97
Randalstown, N. Ire., U.K. ... C3 11
Randazzo, Italy ... F5 23
Randers, Den. ... I4 14
Randle, Wa., U.S. ... C4 124
Randleman, N.C., U.S. ... B3 110
Randlett, Ok., U.S. ... D3 113
Randlett, Ut., U.S. ... C6 121
Randolph, Az., U.S. ... E4 80
Randolph, Ia., U.S. ... D2 92
Randolph, Ks., U.S. ... C7 93
Randolph, Ma., U.S. ... B5 98
Randolph, Mn., U.S. ... F5 100
Randolph, Ms., U.S. ... B4 101
Randolph, Ne., U.S. ... B8 104
Randolph, N.Y., U.S. ... C2 109
Randolph, Oh., U.S. ... A4 112
Randolph, Ut., U.S. ... B4 121
Randolph, Vt., U.S. ... D3 122
Randolph, Wi., U.S. ... E4 126
Randolph, co., Al., U.S. ... B4 78
Randolph, co., Ar., U.S. ... A4 81
Randolph, co., Ga., U.S. ... E2 87
Randolph, co., Il., U.S. ... E4 90
Randolph, co., In., U.S. ... D8 91
Randolph, co., Mo., U.S. ... B5 102
Randolph, co., N.C., U.S. ... B3 110
Randolph, co., W.V., U.S. ... C5 125
Randolph Air Force Base, mil., Tx., U.S. ... h7 120
Randolph Center, Vt., U.S. ... D3 122
Randolph Hills, Md., U.S. ... B3 97
Random Island, i., Newf. ... D4 72
Random Lake, Wi., U.S. ... E6 126
Randow, stm., E. Ger. ... B7 18
Randsburg, Ca., U.S. ... E5 82
Randwick, Austl. ... *F9 50
Ranfurly, Alta. ... C5 68
Rangaunu Bay, b., N.Z. ... K14 51
Rangeley, Me., U.S. ... D2 96

Rangeley Lake, l., Me., U.S. . D2 96
Rangely, Co., U.S. ... A2 83
Ranger, Ga., U.S. ... B2 87
Ranger, Tx., U.S. ... C3 120
Ranger, W.V., U.S. ... C2 125
Rangia, India ... *G6 36
Rangiora, N.Z. ... O14 51
Rangitata, stm., N.Z. ... O13 51
Rangoon (Yangon), Burma .. E10 36
Rangpur, Bngl. ... C8 36
Ranier, Mn., U.S. ... B5 100
Rankin, Il., U.S. ... C6 90
Rankin, Pa., U.S. ... k14 115
Rankin, Tx., U.S. ... D2 120
Rankin, co., Ms., U.S. ... C4 101
Ranong, Thai. ... H3 35
Ransom, Il., U.S. ... B5 90
Ransom, Ks., U.S. ... D4 93
Ransom, Pa., U.S. ... m17 115
Ransom, co., N.D., U.S. ... C8 111
Ransomville, N.Y., U.S. ... B2 109
Ranson, W.V., U.S. ... B7 125
Rantauprapat, Indon. ... K3 35
Rantekombola, mtn., Indon. . F6 34
Rantoul, Il., U.S. ... C5 90
Rantoul, Ks., U.S. ... D8 93
Ranum, Den. ... B3 18
Raohe, China ... B11 31
Raon [-l'Étape], Fr. ... A2 21
Raoui, Erg er, des., Alg. ... D4 44
Raoul, Ga., U.S. ... B3 87
Rapallo, Italy ... B2 23
Rāpch, stm., Iran ... I9 39
Rapelje, Mt., U.S. ... E7 103
Raphine, Va., U.S. ... C3 123
Raphoe, Ire. ... C4 11
Rapid, stm., Mn., U.S. ... B4 100
Rapid, North Branch, stm., Mn., U.S. ... B4 100
Rapid City, Man. ... D1 70
Rapid City, Mi., U.S. ... D5 99
Rapid City, S.D., U.S. ... C2 118
Rapides, co., La., U.S. ... C3 95
Rapid River, Mi., U.S. ... C4 99
Rapids City, Il., U.S. ... B3 90
Rappahannock, co., Va., U.S. B4 123
Rappahannock, stm., Va., U.S. B5 123
Rappahannock Academy, Va., U.S. ... B5 123
Rapperswil, Switz. ... B6 21
Räpti, stm., Asia ... C6 36
Ra's al 'Ayn, Syria ... D13 40
Ra's al Khaymah, U.A.E. ... C5 38
Ra's al Unūf, Libya ... C3 43
Ra's an Naqb, Jord. ... C3 41
Ra's Gharib, Eg. ... D6 43
Rashad, Sud. ... C3 47
Rāshayyā, Leb. ... F10 41
Rashīd (Rosetta), Eg. ... H3 40
Rāshidah, Ma'tan, well, Libya H3 43
Rashkov, Sov. Un. ... B9 24
Rasht, Iran ... B4 38
Raška, Yugo. ... D5 24
Raška, stm., Yugo. ... D5 24
Raso, Cabo, c., Arg. ... C3 54
Raspberry Peak, mtn., Ar., U.S. ... C1 81
Rasskazovo, Sov. Un. ... E13 27
Ra's Tannūrah, Sau. Ar. ... C5 38
Rastatt, W. Ger. ... D3 18
Rastede, W. Ger. ... C2 18
Rastibonne Monastery, Isr. .. m14 41
Raszyn, Pol. ... m13 26
Rat, stm., Man. ... A2 70
Rat, stm., Man. ... E3 70
Ratchaburi, Thai. ... C1 34
Ratcliff, Ar., U.S. ... B2 81
Ratekau, W. Ger. ... B4 18
Rathbun, Ia., U.S. ... D5 92
Rathbun Lake, res., Ia., U.S. . D5 92
Rathdrum, Ire. ... E5 11
Rathdrum, Id., U.S. ... B2 89
Rathenow, E. Ger. ... C6 18
Rathfriland, N. Ire., U.K. ... C4 11
Rathkeale, Ire. ... E3 11
Rathlin Island, i., N. Ire., U.K. A5 11
Rathlin Sound, strt., N. Ire., U.K. ... B5 11
Ráth Luirc, Ire. ... E3 11
Rathmore, Ire. ... E2 11
Rathmullen, Ire. ... B4 11
Rathowen, Ire. ... C4 11
Rathwell, Man. ... E2 70
Ratingen, W. Ger. ... B1 19
Ratio, Ar., U.S. ... C5 81
Rat Islands, is., Ak., U.S. ... E3 79
Rat Lake, l., Man. ... A2 70
Rat Lake, l., Man. ... B4 70
Ratnāgiri, India ... E3 36
Ratner, Sask. ... A3 75
Raton, N.M., U.S. ... A5 108
Raton Pass, N.M., U.S. ... A5 108
Rattan, Ok., U.S. ... C6 113
Rattenburg, Aus. ... E5 18
Rattlesnake Creek, stm., Ks., U.S. ... E4 93
Rattlesnake Creek, stm., Oh., U.S. ... C2 112
Rattlesnake Creek, stm., Wa., U.S. ... C6 124
Rattlesnake Flat, pl., Wa., U.S. C7 124
Rattlesnake Hills, hills, Wa., U.S. ... C6 124
Rattlesnake Hills, hills, Wy., U.S. ... D5 127
Rattlesnake Mountain, mtn., Ct., U.S. ... C4 84
Rattling Brook, Newf. ... D3 72
Rattray Head, c., Scot., U.K. . C7 13
Rättvik, Swe. ... G6 14
Ratzeburg, W. Ger. ... E4 15

| Name | Map Ref. | Page |
|---|---|---|
| Ratzeburger, l., Eur. | E4 | 15 |
| Raub, Malay. | K4 | 35 |
| Raub, In., U.S. | C3 | 91 |
| Raub, N.D., U.S. | B3 | 111 |
| Rauch, Arg. | B5 | 54 |
| Rauer, i., Nor. | p28 | 14 |
| Raufarhöfn, Ice. | m25 | 14 |
| Raukumara, mtn., N.Z. | L17 | 51 |
| Rauland, Nor. | H2 | 14 |
| Rauma, Fin. | G9 | 14 |
| Raurkela, India | F10 | 37 |
| Rausu, Mount, mtn., Japan | D12 | 33 |
| Rautalampi, Fin. | F12 | 14 |
| Ravalli, Mt., U.S. | C2 | 103 |
| Ravalli, co., Mt., U.S. | D2 | 103 |
| Ravanna, Ar., U.S. | D1 | 81 |
| Ravanna, Mo., U.S. | A4 | 102 |
| Rãvar, Iran | B5 | 38 |
| Rava-Russkaya, Sov. Un. | F4 | 27 |
| Raven, i., U.S. | e10 | 123 |
| Ravena, N.Y., U.S. | C7 | 109 |
| Ravendale, Ca., U.S. | B3 | 82 |
| Ravenden, Ar., U.S. | A4 | 81 |
| Ravenden Springs, Ar., U.S. | A4 | 81 |
| Ravenel, S.C., U.S. | k11 | 117 |
| Ravenglass, Eng., U.K. | F5 | 13 |
| Ravenna, Italy | B4 | 23 |
| Ravenna, Ky., U.S. | C6 | 94 |
| Ravenna, Mi., U.S. | E5 | 99 |
| Ravenna, Ne., U.S. | C7 | 104 |
| Ravenna, Oh., U.S. | A4 | 112 |
| Raven Park, reg., Co., U.S. | A2 | 83 |
| Raven Rock, N.J., U.S. | C2 | 107 |
| Ravensburg, W. Ger. | E4 | 18 |
| Ravenscrag, Sask. | H1 | 75 |
| Ravenscroft, Tn., U.S. | D8 | 119 |
| Ravensdale, Wa., U.S. | f12 | 124 |
| Ravensthorpe, Austl. | F3 | 50 |
| Ravenswood, In., U.S. | k10 | 91 |
| Ravenswood, W.V., U.S. | C3 | 125 |
| Ravensworth, Ont. | B5 | 73 |
| Ravenwood, Mo., U.S. | A3 | 102 |
| Rãvi, stm., Asia | B4 | 37 |
| Ravia, Ok., U.S. | C5 | 113 |
| Ravinia, S.D., U.S. | D7 | 118 |
| Rãwalpindi, Pak. | B5 | 36 |
| Rãwalpindi Cantonment, Pak. | *B5 | 36 |
| Rawa Mazowiecka, Pol. | C6 | 26 |
| Rawãndūz, Iraq | D15 | 40 |
| Rawdon, Que. | C4 | 74 |
| Rawd Sãlim, Bi'r, well, Eg. | D5 | 41 |
| Rawhide Creek, stm., Wy., U.S. | D8 | 127 |
| Rawicz, Pol. | C4 | 26 |
| Rawlings, Md., U.S. | k13 | 97 |
| Rawlings, Va., U.S. | D5 | 123 |
| Rawlinna, Austl. | F4 | 50 |
| Rawlins, Wy., U.S. | E5 | 127 |
| Rawlins, co., Ks., U.S. | C2 | 93 |
| Rawson, Arg. | C3 | 54 |
| Rawson, Arg. | g6 | 54 |
| Rawson, N.D., U.S. | B2 | 111 |
| Rawson, Oh., U.S. | B2 | 112 |
| Rawsonville, Vt., U.S. | E3 | 122 |
| Ray, In., U.S. | A8 | 91 |
| Ray, Mn., U.S. | B5 | 100 |
| Ray, N.D., U.S. | A2 | 111 |
| Ray, co., Mo., U.S. | B3 | 102 |
| Ray, Cape, c., Newf. | E2 | 72 |
| Raya, mtn., Indon. | F4 | 34 |
| Raya, i., Indon. | J1 | 35 |
| Rãyagarha, India | H9 | 37 |
| Raychikhinsk, Sov. Un. | B4 | 33 |
| Ray City, Ga., U.S. | E3 | 87 |
| Raygorodka, Sov. Un. | q22 | 27 |
| Rayle, Ga., U.S. | C4 | 87 |
| Raymond, Alta. | E4 | 68 |
| Raymond, Ca., U.S. | D4 | 82 |
| Raymond, Il., U.S. | D4 | 90 |
| Raymond, In., U.S. | F7 | 91 |
| Raymond, Ks., U.S. | D5 | 93 |
| Raymond, Me., U.S. | E2 | 96 |
| Raymond, Mn., U.S. | E3 | 100 |
| Raymond, Ms., U.S. | C3 | 101 |
| Raymond, Mt., U.S. | B12 | 103 |
| Raymond, Ne., U.S. | D9 | 104 |
| Raymond, N.H., U.S. | D4 | 106 |
| Raymond, S.D., U.S. | C8 | 118 |
| Raymond, Wa., U.S. | C2 | 124 |
| Raymond Terrace, Austl. | F8 | 51 |
| Raymondville, Mo., U.S. | D6 | 102 |
| Raymondville, N.Y., U.S. | f10 | 109 |
| Raymondville, Tx., U.S. | F4 | 120 |
| Raymore, Sask. | F3 | 75 |
| Raymore, Mo., U.S. | C3 | 102 |
| Rayne, La., U.S. | D3 | 95 |
| Rayner Glacier, ice, Ant. | C17 | 7 |
| Raynesford, Mt., U.S. | C6 | 103 |
| Raynham, Ma., U.S. | C5 | 98 |
| Raynham Center, Ma., U.S. | C5 | 98 |
| Rayón, Mex. | B2 | 63 |
| Rayong, Thai. | F4 | 35 |
| Rayside-Balfour, Ont. | *p19 | 73 |
| Raytown, Mo., U.S. | h11 | 102 |
| Rayville, La., U.S. | B4 | 95 |
| Rayville, Mo., U.S. | B3 | 102 |
| Razan, Iran | D4 | 39 |
| Razgrad, Bul. | D8 | 24 |
| Razlog, Bul. | E6 | 24 |
| Razorback Mountain, mtn., B.C. | D5 | 69 |
| Re, i., Viet. | E8 | 35 |
| Ré, Île de, i., Fr. | D3 | 16 |
| Rea, Mo., U.S. | A3 | 102 |
| Rea, Lough, l., Ire. | D3 | 11 |
| Reader, Ar., U.S. | D2 | 81 |
| Reader, W.V., U.S. | B4 | 125 |
| Reader Lake, l., Man. | C1 | 70 |
| Readfield, Me., U.S. | D3 | 96 |
| Reading, Eng., U.K. | E6 | 10 |
| Reading, Ks., U.S. | D8 | 93 |
| Reading, Ma., U.S. | A5 | 98 |
| Reading, Mi., U.S. | G6 | 99 |
| Reading, Mn., U.S. | G3 | 100 |
| Reading, Oh., U.S. | C1 | 112 |
| Reading, Pa., U.S. | F10 | 115 |
| Reading, Vt., U.S. | E3 | 122 |
| Reading Center, N.Y., U.S. | C4 | 109 |
| Readland, Ar., U.S. | D4 | 81 |
| Readlyn, Sask. | H3 | 75 |
| Readlyn, Ia., U.S. | B5 | 92 |
| Readsboro, Vt., U.S. | F3 | 122 |
| Readstown, Wi., U.S. | E3 | 126 |
| Readyville, Tn., U.S. | B5 | 119 |
| Reagan, Tn., U.S. | B3 | 119 |
| Reagan, co., Tx., U.S. | D2 | 120 |
| Real, Cordillera, mts., S.A. | C2 | 55 |
| Realicó, Arg. | B4 | 54 |
| Realitos, Tx., U.S. | F3 | 120 |
| Reamstown, Pa., U.S. | F9 | 115 |
| Reardan, Wa., U.S. | B8 | 124 |
| Reasnor, Ia., U.S. | C4 | 92 |
| Reata, Mex. | B4 | 63 |
| Reaville, N.J., U.S. | C3 | 107 |
| Reay, Scot., U.K. | B5 | 13 |
| Rebecca, Ga., U.S. | E3 | 87 |
| Rebersburg, Pa., U.S. | E7 | 115 |
| Rebiana, well, Libya | E4 | 43 |
| Rebiana Sand Sea, des., Libya | E3 | 43 |
| Reboly, Sov. Un. | F14 | 14 |
| Rebun Island, i., Japan | D10 | 33 |
| Recalde, Arg. | B4 | 54 |
| Recanati, Italy | C4 | 23 |
| Recherche, Archipelago of the, is., Austl. | F3 | 50 |
| Rechitsa, Sov. Un. | E8 | 27 |
| Recife, Braz. | C4 | 57 |
| Recinto, Chile | B2 | 54 |
| Recklinghausen, W. Ger. | C3 | 18 |
| Recluse, Wy., U.S. | B7 | 127 |
| Recogne, Bel. | E5 | 17 |
| Reconquista, Arg. | E4 | 55 |
| Recovery, Ga., U.S. | F2 | 87 |
| Recreo, Arg. | E2 | 55 |
| Rector, Ar., U.S. | A5 | 81 |
| Red, stm., N.A. | A8 | 76 |
| Red, stm., U.S. | D9 | 76 |
| Red, stm., Ky., U.S. | C6 | 94 |
| Red, stm., Tn., U.S. | A4 | 119 |
| Red, Elm Fork, stm., U.S. | B2 | 113 |
| Red, North Fork, stm., U.S. | B1 | 113 |
| Red, Salt Fork, stm., U.S. | C2 | 113 |
| Red, South Fork, stm., U.S. | A5 | 119 |
| Red, West Fork, stm., U.S. | A4 | 119 |
| Red Bank, N.J., U.S. | C4 | 107 |
| Red Bank, S.C., U.S. | D5 | 117 |
| Red Bank, Tn., U.S. | D8 | 119 |
| Red Banks, Ms., U.S. | A4 | 101 |
| Red Bay, Newf. | C3 | 72 |
| Red Bay, Al., U.S. | A1 | 78 |
| Redbay, Fl., U.S. | u16 | 86 |
| Red Bay, b., N. Ire., U.K. | B6 | 11 |
| Redberry Lake, l., Sask. | E2 | 75 |
| Redbird, Oh., U.S. | A4 | 112 |
| Redbird, Ok., U.S. | B6 | 113 |
| Red Bird, stm., Ky., U.S. | C6 | 94 |
| Red Bluff, Ca., U.S. | B2 | 82 |
| Red Bluff Lake, res., U.S. | o12 | 120 |
| Red Boiling Springs, Tn., U.S. | C8 | 119 |
| Red Bud, Il., U.S. | E4 | 90 |
| Red Butte, mtn., Ut., U.S. | B2 | 121 |
| Red Buttes Village, Wy., U.S. | C4 | 100 |
| Redby, Mn., U.S. | C4 | 100 |
| Redcar, Eng., U.K. | F7 | 13 |
| Red Cedar, stm., Wi., U.S. | C2 | 126 |
| Red Cedar Lake, l., Wi., U.S. | C2 | 126 |
| Redcliff, Alta. | D5 | 68 |
| Redcliff, Co., U.S. | B4 | 83 |
| Red Cliff, Wi., U.S. | B3 | 126 |
| Redcliffe, Austl. | E9 | 50 |
| Red Cliff Indian Reservation, Wi., U.S. | B2 | 126 |
| Red Cloud, Ne., U.S. | D7 | 104 |
| Redcloud Peak, mtn., Co., U.S. | D3 | 83 |
| Red Creek, N.Y., U.S. | B4 | 109 |
| Red Creek, stm., Ms., U.S. | E4 | 101 |
| Red Cross Lake, l., Man. | B5 | 70 |
| Red Deer, Alta. | C4 | 68 |
| Red Deer, stm., Can. | D4 | 68 |
| Red Deer, stm., Can. | E4 | 75 |
| Red Deer Lake, l., Man. | C1 | 70 |
| Reddell, La., U.S. | D3 | 95 |
| Red Desert, Wy., U.S. | E4 | 127 |
| Reddick, Fl., U.S. | C4 | 86 |
| Reddick, Il., U.S. | B5 | 90 |
| Redding, Ct., U.S. | D2 | 84 |
| Redding, Ia., U.S. | D3 | 92 |
| Redding Ridge, Ct., U.S. | D2 | 84 |
| Reddish Knob, mtn., U.S. | C5 | 125 |
| Redditch, Eng., U.K. | B6 | 12 |
| Redditt, Ont. | E4 | 70 |
| Rede, stm., Eng., U.K. | E6 | 13 |
| Redenção, Braz. | B5 | 57 |
| Redeye, stm., Mn., U.S. | D3 | 100 |
| Red Feather Lakes, Co., U.S. | A5 | 83 |
| Redfield, Ar., U.S. | C3 | 81 |
| Redfield, Ia., U.S. | C3 | 92 |
| Redfield, Ks., U.S. | E9 | 93 |
| Redfield, N.Y., U.S. | B5 | 109 |
| Redfield, S.D., U.S. | C7 | 118 |
| Redford, Mi., U.S. | *F7 | 99 |
| Redford, N.Y., U.S. | f11 | 109 |
| Redford, Tx., U.S. | p12 | 120 |
| Redgranite, Wi., U.S. | D4 | 126 |
| Redhill, Eng., U.K. | m12 | 10 |
| Red Hook, N.Y., U.S. | C7 | 109 |
| Redhouse, Ky., U.S. | C5 | 94 |
| Red House, Va., U.S. | C4 | 123 |
| Red House, W.V., U.S. | C3 | 125 |
| Redig, S.D., U.S. | B2 | 118 |
| Red Indian Lake, l., Newf. | D3 | 72 |
| Red Island, i., Newf. | E4 | 72 |
| Red Jacket, W.V., U.S. | D2 | 125 |
| Redkey, In., U.S. | D7 | 91 |
| Red Lake, Ont. | o16 | 73 |
| Red Lake, co., Mn., U.S. | C2 | 100 |
| Red Lake, l., Az., U.S. | B1 | 80 |
| Red Lake Falls, Mn., U.S. | C2 | 100 |
| Red Lake Indian Reservation, Mn., U.S. | B3 | 100 |
| Redlands, Ca., U.S. | E5 | 82 |
| Red Level, Al., U.S. | D3 | 78 |
| Red Lick, Ms., U.S. | D3 | 101 |
| Red Lion, Pa., U.S. | G8 | 115 |
| Red Lodge, Mt., U.S. | E7 | 103 |
| Red Mill Pond, l., De., U.S. | F5 | 85 |
| Redmon, Il., U.S. | D6 | 90 |
| Redmond, Or., U.S. | C5 | 114 |
| Redmond, Ut., U.S. | E4 | 121 |
| Redmond, Wa., U.S. | e11 | 124 |
| Red Mountain, mtn., U.S. | E5 | 82 |
| Red Mountain, mtn., Al., U.S. | B3 | 78 |
| Red Mountain, mtn., Ca., U.S. | B2 | 82 |
| Red Mountain, mtn., Mt., U.S. | C4 | 103 |
| Red Mountain Pass, Co., U.S. | D3 | 83 |
| Rednitz, stm., W. Ger. | D5 | 18 |
| Red Oak, Ga., U.S. | h7 | 87 |
| Red Oak, Ia., U.S. | D2 | 92 |
| Red Oak, N.C., U.S. | A5 | 110 |
| Red Oak, Ok., U.S. | C6 | 113 |
| Red Oak, Tx., U.S. | n10 | 120 |
| Red Oak, Va., U.S. | D4 | 123 |
| Red Oak Mill, N.Y., U.S. | *D7 | 109 |
| Red Oaks Mill, N.Y., U.S. | h9 | 95 |
| Redland, Ky., U.S. | e9 | 94 |
| Reds Grove, Md., U.S. | C6 | 97 |
| Redon, Fr. | D4 | 87 |
| Redonda Islands, is., B.C. | D5 | 69 |
| Redondela, Spain | A1 | 22 |
| Redondo, Port. | C2 | 22 |
| Redondo, Wa., U.S. | f11 | 124 |
| Redondo Beach, Ca., U.S. | n12 | 82 |
| Redoubt Volcano, vol., Ak., U.S. | g15 | 79 |
| Redowl, S.D., U.S. | C3 | 118 |
| Red Pass, B.C. | C8 | 69 |
| Red Peak, mtn., Co., U.S. | B4 | 83 |
| Red Pheasant, Sask. | E1 | 75 |
| Red Rapids, N.B. | C2 | 71 |
| Red River, N.M., U.S. | A4 | 108 |
| Red River, co., La., U.S. | B2 | 95 |
| Red River, co., Tx., U.S. | C5 | 120 |
| Red Rock, B.C. | C6 | 69 |
| Red Rock, Az., U.S. | E4 | 80 |
| Red Rock, N.M., U.S. | E1 | 108 |
| Red Rock, Ok., U.S. | A4 | 113 |
| Red Rock, Tx., U.S. | E4 | 120 |
| Red Rock, stm., Mt., U.S. | F4 | 103 |
| Red Rock, Lake, res., Ia., U.S. | C4 | 92 |
| Red Sea | C3 | 38 |
| Red Shirt, S.D., U.S. | D3 | 118 |
| Red Springs, N.C., U.S. | C3 | 110 |
| Redstone, B.C. | C6 | 69 |
| Redstone, Co., U.S. | B3 | 83 |
| Redstone, Mt., U.S. | B12 | 103 |
| Redstone, N.H., U.S. | B4 | 106 |
| Red Sucker, stm., Man. | B5 | 70 |
| Red Sucker Lake, l., Man. | B5 | 70 |
| Red Table Mountain, mts., Co., U.S. | B4 | 83 |
| Redvale, Co., U.S. | C2 | 83 |
| Redvers, Sask. | H5 | 75 |
| Redwater, Alta. | C4 | 68 |
| Redwater, stm., Mt., U.S. | C11 | 103 |
| Red Willow, Alta. | C4 | 68 |
| Red Willow, co., Ne., U.S. | D5 | 104 |
| Redwillow, stm., Can. | B7 | 69 |
| Red Willow Creek, stm., Ne., U.S. | D5 | 104 |
| Redwine, Ky., U.S. | C6 | 94 |
| Red Wing, Co., U.S. | D5 | 83 |
| Red Wing, Mn., U.S. | F6 | 100 |
| Redwood, Ms., U.S. | C3 | 101 |
| Redwood, N.Y., U.S. | A5 | 109 |
| Redwood, Ut., U.S. | *C4 | 121 |
| Redwood, co., Mn., U.S. | F3 | 100 |
| Redwood, stm., Mn., U.S. | F3 | 100 |
| Redwood City, Ca., U.S. | D2 | 82 |
| Redwood Falls, Mn., U.S. | F3 | 100 |
| Redwood National Park, Ca., U.S. | B2 | 82 |
| Redwood Valley, Ca., U.S. | C2 | 82 |
| Red see Yuan Jiang, stm., Asia | G5 | 36 |
| Ree, Lough, l., Ire. | D2 | 10 |
| Reece, Ks., U.S. | E7 | 93 |
| Reece City, Al., U.S. | A3 | 78 |
| Reed, Ok., U.S. | C2 | 113 |
| Reed City, Mi., U.S. | E5 | 99 |
| Reeder, N.D., U.S. | C3 | 111 |
| Reed Lake, l., Man. | B1 | 70 |
| Reed Lake, l., Sask. | G2 | 75 |
| Reedley, Ca., U.S. | D4 | 82 |
| Reedpoint, W.V., U.S. | E7 | 103 |
| Reeds Beach, N.J., U.S. | E3 | 107 |
| Reedsburg, Wi., U.S. | E3 | 126 |
| Reeds Peak, mtn., N.M., U.S. | D2 | 108 |
| Reedsport, Or., U.S. | D2 | 114 |
| Reeds Spring, Mo., U.S. | E4 | 102 |
| Reedsville, Oh., U.S. | C4 | 112 |
| Reedsville, Pa., U.S. | E6 | 115 |
| Reedsville, W.V., U.S. | B5 | 125 |
| Reedsville, Wi., U.S. | D6 | 126 |
| Reedurban, Oh., U.S. | *B4 | 112 |
| Reedville, Va., U.S. | C6 | 123 |
| Reedy, W.V., U.S. | C3 | 125 |
| Reedy, stm., S.C., U.S. | C3 | 117 |
| Reedy Lake, l., Fl., U.S. | E5 | 86 |
| Reefton, N.Z. | O13 | 51 |
| Reelfoot Lake, l., Tn., U.S. | A2 | 119 |
| Reelsville, In., U.S. | E4 | 91 |
| Reere Island, i., Marsh Is. | P18 | 52 |
| Reese, Mi., U.S. | E7 | 99 |
| Reese, stm., Nv., U.S. | C4 | 105 |
| Reese Air Force Base, mil., Tx., U.S. | C1 | 120 |
| Reese Station, Oh., U.S. | m11 | 112 |
| Reeseville, Wi., U.S. | E5 | 126 |
| Reeth, Eng., U.K. | F7 | 13 |
| Reeves, La., U.S. | D2 | 95 |
| Reeves, co., Tx., U.S. | o13 | 120 |
| Reevesville, Il., U.S. | F5 | 90 |
| Reevesville, S.C., U.S. | E6 | 117 |
| Reform, Al., U.S. | B1 | 78 |
| Reform, Ms., U.S. | B4 | 101 |
| Refresco, Chile | E2 | 55 |
| Reftele, Swe. | A7 | 15 |
| Refuge Cove, B.C. | D5 | 69 |
| Refugio, Tx., U.S. | E4 | 120 |
| Refugio, co., Tx., U.S. | E4 | 120 |
| Rega, stm., Pol. | B3 | 26 |
| Regan, N.D., U.S. | B5 | 111 |
| Regen, W. Ger. | E8 | 19 |
| Regen, stm., W. Ger. | D6 | 18 |
| Regensburg, W. Ger. | D6 | 18 |
| Regent, Man. | E1 | 70 |
| Regent, N.D., U.S. | C3 | 111 |
| Reggâne, Alg. | D5 | 44 |
| Reggio di Calabria, Italy | E5 | 23 |
| Reggio nell'Emilia, Italy | B3 | 23 |
| Reghin, Rom. | B7 | 24 |
| Regina, Sask. | G3 | 75 |
| Régina, Fr. Gu. | B4 | 59 |
| Regina, Mt., U.S. | C9 | 103 |
| Regina Beach, Sask. | G3 | 75 |
| Register, Ga., U.S. | E5 | 87 |
| Regna, Swe. | u33 | 14 |
| Regnitz, stm., W. Ger. | D5 | 19 |
| Reguengos de Monsaraz, Port. | C2 | 22 |
| Rehau, W. Ger. | C7 | 19 |
| Rehavya (part of Jerusalem), Isr. | m14 | 41 |
| Rehe, E. Ger. | E5 | 15 |
| Rehoboth, Nmb. | B2 | 49 |
| Rehoboth, Ma., U.S. | C5 | 98 |
| Rehoboth, N.M., U.S. | B1 | 108 |
| Rehoboth Bay, b., De., U.S. | F5 | 85 |
| Rehoboth Beach, De., U.S. | F5 | 85 |
| Rehovot, Isr. | C6 | 41 |
| Reichenbach, E. Ger. | C6 | 18 |
| Reichenbach, Switz. | A4 | 20 |
| Reid, Mount, mtn., Ak., U.S. | n24 | 79 |
| Reid, Peak, mtn., Sask. | G1 | 75 |
| Reidland, Ky., U.S. | e9 | 94 |
| Reids Grove, Md., U.S. | C6 | 97 |
| Reidsville, Ga., U.S. | D4 | 87 |
| Reidsville, N.C., U.S. | A3 | 110 |
| Reidville, S.C., U.S. | B3 | 117 |
| Reigate, Eng., U.K. | E6 | 10 |
| Reina Adelaida, Archipiélago, is., Chile | E2 | 54 |
| Reinach, Switz. | B5 | 21 |
| Reinbeck, Ia., U.S. | B5 | 92 |
| Reindeer, stm., Sask. | B4 | 75 |
| Reindeer, i., Man. | C3 | 70 |
| Reindeer Lake, l., Can. | m8 | 75 |
| Reinersville, Oh., U.S. | C4 | 112 |
| Reinfeld, W. Ger. | E4 | 15 |
| Reinosa, Spain | A3 | 22 |
| Reinosa see Reynosa, Mex. | B5 | 63 |
| Reisterstown, Md., U.S. | B4 | 97 |
| Reit im Winkl, W. Ger. | B8 | 20 |
| Reitz, S. Afr. | C4 | 49 |
| Rekarne, Swe. | t34 | 14 |
| Reliance, De., U.S. | F3 | 85 |
| Reliance, S.D., U.S. | D6 | 118 |
| Reliance, Tn., U.S. | D9 | 119 |
| Reliance, Wy., U.S. | E3 | 127 |
| Remada, Tun. | C7 | 44 |
| Remagen, W. Ger. | C2 | 19 |
| Remanso, Braz. | C2 | 57 |
| Rembert, S.C., U.S. | C6 | 117 |
| Rembertów (part of Warsaw), Pol. | k14 | 26 |
| Rembrandt, Ia., U.S. | B2 | 92 |
| Remecó, Arg. | B4 | 54 |
| Remedios, Cuba | C4 | 64 |
| Remedios, Pan. | F7 | 62 |
| Remer, Mn., U.S. | C5 | 100 |
| Remerton, Ga., U.S. | F3 | 87 |
| Remeshk, Iran | H9 | 39 |
| Remington, In., U.S. | C3 | 91 |
| Remington, Va., U.S. | B5 | 123 |
| Rémire, Fr. Gu. | B4 | 59 |
| Remlap, Al., U.S. | B3 | 78 |
| Remmel Dam, U.S. | g8 | 81 |
| Remmel, stm., W. Ger. | E4 | 19 |
| Remscheid, W. Ger. | C3 | 18 |
| Remsen, Ia., U.S. | B2 | 92 |
| Remsen, N.Y., U.S. | B5 | 109 |
| Remus, Mi., U.S. | E5 | 99 |
| Rena Lara, Ms., U.S. | A3 | 101 |
| Renault, Il., U.S. | E3 | 90 |
| Renco, Ks., U.S. | k15 | 93 |
| Rencontre East, Newf. | E4 | 72 |
| Rend Lake, res., Il., U.S. | E5 | 90 |
| Rendsburg, W. Ger. | A4 | 18 |
| Renedo, Spain | A4 | 22 |
| Renens, Switz. | C2 | 21 |
| Renews [-Cappahayden], Newf. | E5 | 72 |
| Renforth, N.B. | D4 | 71 |
| Renfrew, Ont. | B8 | 73 |
| Renfrew, S.C., U.S. | B3 | 117 |
| Renfrew, co., Ont. | B7 | 73 |
| Renfrow, Ok., U.S. | A4 | 113 |
| Rengo, Chile | A2 | 54 |
| Reni, Sov. Un. | C9 | 24 |
| Renick, Mo., U.S. | B5 | 102 |
| Renick, W.V., U.S. | D4 | 125 |
| Renish Point, c., Scot., U.K. | C2 | 13 |
| Renmark, Austl. | F7 | 50 |
| Renner, S.D., U.S. | D9 | 118 |
| Rennerod, W. Ger. | C3 | 19 |
| Rennert, N.C., U.S. | C3 | 110 |
| Rennes, Fr. | C3 | 16 |
| Rennick Bay, b., Ant. | C29 | 7 |
| Rennick Glacier, ice, Ant. | B29 | 7 |
| Rennie, Man. | E4 | 70 |
| Reno, Mn., U.S. | G7 | 100 |
| Reno, Nv., U.S. | D2 | 105 |
| Reno, Oh., U.S. | C4 | 112 |
| Reno, co., Ks., U.S. | E5 | 93 |
| Reno, stm., Italy | B3 | 23 |
| Reno Hill, mtn., Wy., U.S. | D6 | 127 |
| Renous, N.B. | C4 | 71 |
| Renovo, Pa., U.S. | D6 | 115 |
| Renown, Sask. | F3 | 75 |
| Renshou, China | E8 | 31 |
| Rensselaer, In., U.S. | C3 | 91 |
| Rensselaer, N.Y., U.S. | C7 | 109 |
| Rensselaer, co., N.Y., U.S. | C7 | 109 |
| Rensselaer Falls, N.Y., U.S. | f9 | 109 |
| Rensselaerville, N.Y., U.S. | C6 | 109 |
| Rentiesville, Ok., U.S. | B6 | 113 |
| Renton, Wa., U.S. | C3 | 124 |
| Rentz, Ga., U.S. | D4 | 87 |
| Renville, Mn., U.S. | F3 | 100 |
| Renville, co., Mn., U.S. | F4 | 100 |
| Renville, co., N.D., U.S. | A4 | 111 |
| Renwick, Ia., U.S. | B4 | 92 |
| Repentigny, Que. | D4 | 74 |
| Repton, Al., U.S. | D2 | 78 |
| Republic, Ks., U.S. | C6 | 93 |
| Republic, Mi., U.S. | B3 | 99 |
| Republic, Mo., U.S. | D4 | 102 |
| Republic, Wa., U.S. | A7 | 124 |
| Republic, co., Ks., U.S. | C6 | 93 |
| Republican, stm., U.S. | C6 | 93 |
| Republican, North Fork, stm., U.S. | A8 | 83 |
| Republican, South Fork, stm., U.S. | E4 | 104 |
| Republican City, Ne., U.S. | D6 | 104 |
| Repulse Bay, N.W. Ter. | C15 | 66 |
| Repulse Bay, b., Austl. | D8 | 50 |
| Requena, Spain | C5 | 22 |
| Requena, Peru | B11 | 40? |
| Resadiye, Tur. | B11 | 40 |
| Resang, Cape, c., Malay. | E2 | 34 |
| Rescue, Va., U.S. | k14 | 123 |
| Reserve, Sask. | E4 | 75 |
| Reserve, Ks., U.S. | C8 | 93 |
| Reserve, La., U.S. | h10 | 95 |
| Reserve, N.M., U.S. | D1 | 108 |
| Reserve, Wi., U.S. | B2 | 126 |
| Reservoir Pond, l., Ma., U.S. | h11 | 98 |
| Reshef, Isr. | g10 | 41 |
| Resistencia, Arg. | E4 | 55 |
| Resita, Rom. | C5 | 24 |
| Resko, Pol. | B3 | 26 |
| Resolute, N.W. Ter. | B16 | 66 |
| Resolution Island, i., N.W. Ter. | D20 | 66 |
| Resplendor, Braz. | B4 | 56 |
| Resthaven Mountain, mtn., Alta. | C1 | 68 |
| Restigouche, co., N.B. | B2 | 71 |
| Restigouche, stm., Can. | B2 | 71 |
| Restingué, Punta, c., Pan. | G7 | 62 |
| Resülhinzir, c., Tur. | D10 | 40 |
| Reszel, Pol. | a6 | 26 |
| Retalhuleu, Guat. | E6 | 63 |
| Retamito, Arg. | A3 | 54 |
| Rethel, Fr. | C6 | 16 |
| Rethimnon, Grc. | E5 | 40 |
| Retie, Bel. | C5 | 17 |
| Retlaw, Alta. | D4 | 68 |
| Retsof, N.Y., U.S. | C3 | 109 |
| Reubens, Id., U.S. | *C2 | 89 |
| Reuland, Bel. | D6 | 17 |
| Reunion, dep., Afr. | H24 | 2 |
| Reus, Spain | B6 | 22 |
| Reuss, stm., Switz. | B5 | 21 |
| Reuterstadt Stavenhagen, E. Ger. | E6 | 15 |
| Reutlingen, W. Ger. | D4 | 18 |
| Reutte, Aus. | E5 | 18 |
| Reva, S.D., U.S. | B2 | 118 |
| Revda, Sov. Un. | B5 | 28 |
| Revel, Fr. | F5 | 16 |
| Revelo, Ky., U.S. | D5 | 94 |
| Revelstoke, B.C. | D8 | 69 |
| Revelstoke, Lake, res., B.C. | D8 | 69 |
| Reventazón, Peru | C1 | 58 |
| Revenue, Sask. | E1 | 75 |
| Revere, Ma., U.S. | g11 | 98 |
| Revere, Mn., U.S. | F3 | 100 |
| Revere, Mo., U.S. | A6 | 102 |
| Revigny [-sur-Ornain], Fr. | F4 | 17 |
| Revillagigedo, Islas, is., Mex. | D2 | 63 |
| Revillagigedo Island, i., Ak., U.S. | n24 | 79 |
| Revillo, S.D., U.S. | B9 | 118 |
| Revin, Fr. | C6 | 16 |
| Revloc, Pa., U.S. | F4 | 115 |
| Řevnice, Czech. | o17 | 26 |
| Rew, Pa., U.S. | C4 | 115 |
| Rewa, India | D7 | 36 |
| Reward, Sask. | E1 | 75 |
| Rewari, India | C6 | 36 |
| Rewey, Wi., U.S. | F3 | 126 |
| Rex, Ga., U.S. | h8 | 87 |
| Rex, Mount, mtn., Ant. | B5 | 7 |
| Rexburg, Id., U.S. | F7 | 89 |
| Rexdale, Alta. | D6 | 68 |
| Rexford, Ks., U.S. | C3 | 93 |
| Rexford, Mt., U.S. | B1 | 103 |
| Rexhame, Ma., U.S. | h13 | 98 |
| Rexton, N.B. | C5 | 71 |
| Rexton, Mi., U.S. | B5 | 99 |
| Rey, Bouba, Cam. | D2 | 46 |
| Reydell, Ar., U.S. | C4 | 81 |
| Reyes, Point, c., Ca., U.S. | C2 | 82 |
| Reyhanlı, Tur. | A5 | 40 |
| Reykjavík, Ice. | n22 | 14 |
| Reynaud, Sask. | E3 | 75 |
| Reyno, Ar., U.S. | A5 | 81 |
| Reynolds, Ga., U.S. | D2 | 87 |
| Reynolds, Il., U.S. | B3 | 90 |
| Reynolds, In., U.S. | C4 | 91 |
| Reynolds, Ne., U.S. | D8 | 104 |
| Reynolds, N.D., U.S. | B8 | 111 |
| Reynolds, co., Mo., U.S. | D6 | 102 |
| Reynoldsburg, Oh., U.S. | C3 | 112 |
| Reynoldsville, Pa., U.S. | D4 | 115 |
| Reynosa (Reinosa), Mex. | A5 | 63 |
| Rezã'īyeh see Orūmīyeh, Iran | B4 | 38 |
| Rézé, Fr. | D3 | 16 |
| Rēzekne, Sov. Un. | C6 | 27 |
| Rezina, Sov. Un. | B9 | 24 |
| Rezzato, Italy | — | — |
| Rhaetian Alps, mts., Eur. | A3 | 23 |
| Rhame, N.D., U.S. | C2 | 111 |
| Rhea, co., Tn., U.S. | D9 | 119 |
| Rheda-Wiedenbrück, W. Ger. | B3 | 18 |
| Rheden, Neth. | A7 | 16 |
| Rhein, Sask. | F5 | 75 |
| Rheine, W. Ger. | B3 | 18 |
| Rheinfelden, Switz. | A4 | 21 |
| Rheinhausen, W. Ger. | B1 | 19 |
| Rheinland, hist. reg., W. Ger. | C2 | 19 |
| Rheinland-Pfalz, state, W. Ger. | C2 | 19 |
| Rheinsberg, E. Ger. | B5 | 20 |
| Rheinwaldhorn, mtn., Switz. | C5 | 20 |
| Rhenen, Neth. | C6 | 17 |
| Rheydt, W. Ger. | C6 | 17 |
| Rhiconich, Scot., U.K. | B4 | 13 |
| Rhin Canal, E. Ger. | B5 | 15 |
| Rhine, Ga., U.S. | D3 | 87 |
| Rhine, stm., Eur. | C3 | 18 |
| Rhinebeck, N.Y., U.S. | C7 | 109 |
| Rhineland, Mo., U.S. | C6 | 102 |
| Rhinelander, Wi., U.S. | C4 | 126 |
| Rhinow, E. Ger. | F6 | 15 |
| Rhir, Cap, c., Mor. | C3 | 44 |
| Rhode Island, state, U.S. | D3 | 116 |
| Rhode Island, i., R.I., U.S. | E5 | 116 |
| Rhode Island Sound, strt., U.S. | D6 | 116 |
| Rhodell, W.V., U.S. | D3 | 125 |
| Rhodes, Mi., U.S. | E6 | 99 |
| Rhodes, S. Afr. | D3 | 49 |
| Rhodes see Ródhos, i., Grc. | D7 | 40 |
| Rhodesia see Zimbabwe, ctry., Afr. | A5 | 49 |
| Rhodes Peak, mtn., Id., U.S. | C4 | 89 |
| Rhodes Point, Md., U.S. | E5 | 97 |
| Rhodhiss, N.C., U.S. | B1 | 110 |
| Rhodope Mountains, mts., Eur. | E7 | 24 |
| Rhome, Tx., U.S. | m9 | 120 |
| Rhondda, Wales, U.K. | E5 | 13 |
| Rhône, stm., Eur. | B3 | 21 |
| Rhône au Rhin, Canal du, Fr. | A3 | 20 |
| Rhum, i., Scot., U.K. | B3 | 10 |
| Rhum, Sound of, strt., Scot., U.K. | B3 | 10 |
| Rhyl, Wales, U.K. | D5 | 10 |
| Rhymney, Wales, U.K. | E5 | 13 |
| Riacho de Santana, Braz. | A4 | 56 |
| Rialma, Braz. | B4 | 56 |
| Rialto, Ca., U.S. | m14 | 82 |
| Rianjo, Spain | A1 | 22 |
| Riau Islands, is., Indon. | E2 | 34 |
| Riaza, stm., Spain | B3 | 22 |
| Ribadavia, Spain | A1 | 22 |
| Ribadeo, Spain | A2 | 22 |
| Ribadesella, Spain | A3 | 22 |
| Ribas do Rio Pardo, Braz. | C1 | 56 |
| Ribauè, Moz. | D6 | 48 |
| Ribble, stm., Eng., U.K. | C2 | 15 |
| Ribe, Den. | C2 | 15 |
| Ribe, co., Den. | C2 | 15 |
| Ribeauvillé, Fr. | C7 | 16 |
| Ribeira, stm., Braz. | C3 | 56 |
| Ribeira, Braz. | A4 | 56 |
| Ribeira Branco, Braz. | n7 | 66 |
| Ribeirão Bonito, Braz. | m7 | 56 |
| Ribeirão do Pombal, Braz. | B4 | 56 |
| Ribeirão Preto, Braz. | C3 | 56 |
| Ribera, Italy | B2 | 23 |
| Ribera, N.M., U.S. | B4 | 108 |
| Ribérac, Fr. | E5 | 16 |
| Riberalta, Bol. | B2 | 55 |
| Ribnitz-Damgarten, E. Ger. | A5 | 20 |
| Ribstone, Alta. | C5 | 68 |
| Ribstone, stm., Alta. | C5 | 68 |
| Říčany, Czech. | o18 | 26 |
| Riccione, Italy | E4 | 23 |
| Rice, Mn., U.S. | E4 | 100 |
| Rice, Va., U.S. | C4 | 123 |
| Rice, co., Ks., U.S. | D5 | 93 |
| Rice, co., Mn., U.S. | F5 | 100 |
| Riceboro, Ga., U.S. | E5 | 87 |
| Rice Creek, stm., Mn., U.S. | m12 | 100 |
| Rice Lake, Wi., U.S. | C2 | 126 |
| Rice Lake, l., Ont. | C6 | 73 |
| Rice Lake, l., Mn., U.S. | D5 | 100 |
| Rices Landing, Pa., U.S. | G1 | 115 |
| Riceton, Sask. | G3 | 75 |
| Riceville, Ia., U.S. | A5 | 92 |
| Riceville, Tn., U.S. | D9 | 119 |
| Rich, Ms., U.S. | A3 | 101 |
| Rich, co., Ut., U.S. | B4 | 121 |
| Rich, Cape, c., Ont. | C4 | 73 |
| Richard, Sask. | E2 | 75 |
| Richard City, Tn., U.S. | D8 | 119 |
| Richards, Mo., U.S. | D3 | 102 |
| Richards, Tx., U.S. | D5 | 120 |
| Richards-Gebaur Air Force Base, mil., Mo., U.S. | C3 | 102 |
| Richard's Harbour, Newf. | E3 | 72 |
| Richardson, Sask. | G3 | 75 |
| Richardson, Ky., U.S. | C7 | 94 |
| Richardson, Tx., U.S. | n10 | 120 |
| Richardson, co., Ne., U.S. | D10 | 104 |
| Richardson Lakes, l., Me., U.S. | D2 | 96 |
| Richardson Mountains, mts., Can. | | |
| Richardson Park, De., U.S. | *B3 | 85 |
| Richards Spur, Ok., U.S. | C3 | 113 |
| Richardton, N.D., U.S. | C3 | 111 |
| Richburg, Pa., U.S. | *F11 | 115 |
| Richburg, N.Y., U.S. | C2 | 109 |
| Richburg, S.C., U.S. | B5 | 117 |
| Rich Creek, Va., U.S. | C2 | 123 |
| Richdale, Alta. | D5 | 68 |
| Riche, Pointe, c., Newf. | C3 | 72 |
| Richelieu, co., Que. | D4 | 74 |
| Richer, Man. | E3 | 70 |
| Richey, Mt., U.S. | C11 | 103 |
| Richfield, Id., U.S. | F4 | 89 |
| Richfield, Ks., U.S. | E2 | 93 |
| Richfield, Mn., U.S. | F5 | 100 |
| Richfield, Ne., U.S. | g12 | 104 |
| Richfield, N.C., U.S. | B2 | 110 |
| Richfield, Pa., U.S. | E7 | 115 |
| Richfield, Ut., U.S. | E3 | 121 |
| Richfield, Wi., U.S. | m11 | 126 |
| Richfield Springs, N.Y., U.S. | C5 | 109 |
| Richford, N.Y., U.S. | C4 | 109 |
| Richford, Vt., U.S. | B3 | 122 |
| Rich Fountain, Mo., U.S. | C6 | 102 |
| Rich Hill, Mo., U.S. | C3 | 102 |
| Richibucto, N.B. | C5 | 71 |
| Rich Lake, Alta. | B5 | 68 |
| Richland, Ga., U.S. | D2 | 87 |
| Richland, In., U.S. | I3 | 91 |
| Richland, Mi., U.S. | F5 | 99 |
| Richland, Mo., U.S. | D5 | 102 |
| Richland, N.J., U.S. | E3 | 107 |
| Richland, N.Y., U.S. | B4 | 109 |
| Richland, Or., U.S. | C9 | 114 |
| Richland, S.D., U.S. | C9 | 118 |
| Richland, Wa., U.S. | C6 | 124 |
| Richland, co., Il., U.S. | E5 | 90 |
| Richland, co., La., U.S. | B4 | 95 |
| Richland, co., Mt., U.S. | C12 | 103 |
| Richland, co., N.D., U.S. | C8 | 111 |
| Richland, co., Oh., U.S. | B3 | 112 |
| Richland, co., S.C., U.S. | D6 | 117 |
| Richland, co., Wi., U.S. | E3 | 126 |
| Richland Balsam, mtn., N.C., U.S. | f10 | 110 |
| Richland Center, Wi., U.S. | E3 | 126 |
| Richland Creek, stm., Tn., U.S. | B5 | 119 |
| Richland Hills, Tx., U.S. | *C4 | 120 |
| Richlands, N.C., U.S. | C5 | 110 |
| Richlands, Va., U.S. | e10 | 123 |
| Richland Springs, Tx., U.S. | D3 | 120 |
| Richlandtown, Pa., U.S. | F11 | 115 |
| Richlea, Sask. | F1 | 75 |
| Richmond, Austl. | D7 | 50 |
| Richmond, B.C. | E6 | 69 |
| Richmond, Ont. | B9 | 73 |
| Richmond, P.E.I. | C6 | 71 |
| Richmond, Que. | D5 | 74 |
| Richmond, N.Z. | N14 | 51 |
| Richmond, S. Afr. | H5 | 49 |
| Richmond (part of London), Eng., U.K. | C7 | 12 |
| Richmond, Ca., U.S. | h7 | 82 |
| Richmond, Il., U.S. | A5 | 90 |
| Richmond, In., U.S. | E8 | 91 |
| Richmond, Ks., U.S. | D8 | 93 |
| Richmond, Ky., U.S. | C6 | 94 |
| Richmond, Me., U.S. | D3 | 96 |
| Richmond, Mi., U.S. | F8 | 99 |
| Richmond, Mn., U.S. | E4 | 100 |
| Richmond, Mo., U.S. | B4 | 102 |
| Richmond, Oh., U.S. | B5 | 112 |
| Richmond, Tx., U.S. | E5 | 120 |
| Richmond, Ut., U.S. | B4 | 121 |
| Richmond, Va., U.S. | C5 | 123 |
| Richmond, Vt., U.S. | C2 | 122 |
| Richmond, co., Ga., U.S. | C4 | 87 |
| Richmond, co., N.Y., U.S. | E6 | 109 |
| Richmond, co., N.C., U.S. | C3 | 110 |
| Richmond, co., Va., U.S. | C6 | 123 |
| Richmond Beach, Wa., U.S. | B3 | 124 |
| Richmond Dale, Oh., U.S. | C3 | 112 |
| Richmond Heights, Fl., U.S. | s13 | 86 |
| Richmond Heights, Mo., U.S. | f13 | 102 |
| Richmond Heights, Oh., U.S. | *g9 | 112 |
| Richmond Highlands, Wa., U.S. | B3 | 124 |
| Richmond Hill, Ont. | D5 | 73 |
| Richmond Hill, Ga., U.S. | E5 | 87 |
| Richmond National Battlefield Park, Va., U.S. | n18 | 123 |
| Richmond Park, Eng., U.K. | *m12 | 10 |
| Richmondville, N.Y., U.S. | C6 | 109 |
| Richmound, Sask. | G1 | 75 |
| Rich Mountain, mtn., U.S. | C1 | 81 |
| Rich Mountain, mtn., Va., U.S. | C1 | 123 |
| Rich Mountain, mtn., W.V., U.S. | C5 | 125 |
| Rich Square, N.C., U.S. | A5 | 110 |
| Richthofen, Mount, mtn., Co., U.S. | A5 | 83 |
| Richton, Ms., U.S. | D5 | 101 |
| Richton Park, Il., U.S. | *m9 | 91 |
| Richvalley, In., U.S. | C6 | 91 |

| Name | Map Ref. | Page |
|---|---|---|
| Richview, Il., U.S. | E4 | 90 |
| Richville, Mi., U.S. | E7 | 99 |
| Richville, Mn., U.S. | D7 | 100 |
| Richville, N.Y., U.S. | f9 | 109 |
| Richwood, Ky., U.S. | k13 | 94 |
| Richwood, Oh., U.S. | B2 | 112 |
| Richwood, W.V., U.S. | C4 | 125 |
| Richwoods, Mo., U.S. | C7 | 102 |
| Rickenbacker Air Force Base, mil., Oh., U.S. | m11 | 112 |
| Ricketts, Ia., U.S. | B2 | 92 |
| Rickman, Tn., U.S. | C8 | 119 |
| Rickmansworth, Eng., U.K. | k12 | 10 |
| Rickreall, Or., U.S. | C3 | 114 |
| Rico, Co., U.S. | D2 | 83 |
| Riddle, Id., U.S. | G2 | 89 |
| Riddle, N.C., U.S. | A6 | 110 |
| Riddle, Or., U.S. | E3 | 114 |
| Riddle Mountain, mtn., Or., U.S. | D8 | 114 |
| Riddlesburg, Pa., U.S. | F5 | 115 |
| Rideau, stm., Ont. | B9 | 73 |
| Riderwood, Al., U.S. | C1 | 78 |
| Ridge, N.Y., U.S. | *n16 | 109 |
| Ridgebury, Ct., U.S. | D1 | 84 |
| Ridgecrest, Ca., U.S. | E5 | 82 |
| Ridgecrest, N.C., U.S. | f10 | 110 |
| Ridgecrest, Wa., U.S. | *B3 | 124 |
| Ridgedale, Sask. | D3 | 75 |
| Ridgedale, Mo., U.S. | E4 | 102 |
| Ridge Farm, Il., U.S. | D6 | 90 |
| Ridgefield, Ct., U.S. | D2 | 84 |
| Ridgefield, N.J., U.S. | h8 | 107 |
| Ridgefield, Wa., U.S. | D3 | 124 |
| Ridgefield Park, N.J., U.S. | B4 | 107 |
| Ridgeland, Ms., U.S. | C3 | 101 |
| Ridgeland, S.C., U.S. | G6 | 117 |
| Ridgeland, Wi., U.S. | C2 | 126 |
| Ridgeley, W.V., U.S. | B6 | 125 |
| Ridgely, Md., U.S. | C6 | 97 |
| Ridgely, Tn., U.S. | A2 | 119 |
| Ridgeside, Tn., U.S. | h11 | 119 |
| Ridge Spring, S.C., U.S. | D4 | 117 |
| Ridgetop, Tn., U.S. | A5 | 119 |
| Ridgetown, Ont. | E3 | 73 |
| Ridgeview, S.D., U.S. | B5 | 118 |
| Ridgeview, W.V., U.S. | C3 | 125 |
| Ridgeview, Man. | E3 | 70 |
| Ridgeville, Ga., U.S. | E5 | 87 |
| Ridgeville, In., U.S. | D7 | 91 |
| Ridgeville, S.C., U.S. | E7 | 117 |
| Ridgeville Corners, Oh., U.S. | A1 | 112 |
| Ridgeway, Al., U.S. | A6 | 92 |
| Ridgeway, Mi., U.S. | F7 | 99 |
| Ridgeway, Mo., U.S. | A4 | 102 |
| Ridgeway, N.J., U.S. | C4 | 107 |
| Ridgeway, Oh., U.S. | B2 | 112 |
| Ridgeway, S.C., U.S. | C6 | 117 |
| Ridgeway, Va., U.S. | D3 | 123 |
| Ridgeway, Wi., U.S. | E4 | 126 |
| Ridgewood, N.J., U.S. | B4 | 107 |
| Ridgewood Park, Ct., U.S. | D7 | 84 |
| Ridgway, Co., U.S. | C3 | 83 |
| Ridgway, Il., U.S. | F5 | 90 |
| Ridgway, Pa., U.S. | D4 | 115 |
| Riding Mountain, hills, Man. | D1 | 70 |
| Riding Mountain National Park, Man. | D1 | 70 |
| Ridley Park, Pa., U.S. | p20 | 115 |
| Ridley Township, Pa., U.S. | *G11 | 115 |
| Ridott, Il., U.S. | A4 | 90 |
| Ried [im Innkreis], Aus. | D6 | 18 |
| Riehen, Switz. | A4 | 21 |
| Rienza, stm., Italy | C7 | 20 |
| Rienzi, Ms., U.S. | A5 | 101 |
| Riesa, E. Ger. | C6 | 18 |
| Riesco, Isla, i., Chile | h11 | 54 |
| Riesel, Tx., U.S. | D4 | 120 |
| Rieth, Or., U.S. | B8 | 114 |
| Rieti, Italy | C4 | 23 |
| Riffe Lake, res., Wa., U.S. | C3 | 124 |
| Rifle, Co., U.S. | B3 | 83 |
| Rifle, stm., Mi., U.S. | D6 | 99 |
| Rift Valley, prov., Kenya | A6 | 48 |
| Rift Valley, val., Afr. | *F9 | 42 |
| Rīga, Sov. Un. | D5 | 29 |
| Rīga, Gulf of, b., Sov. Un. | C4 | 27 |
| Rīgān, Iran | C5 | 38 |
| Rīgān, Iran | G9 | 39 |
| Rigaud, Que. | D3 | 74 |
| Rigby, Id., U.S. | F7 | 89 |
| Rīgestān, reg., Afg. | B4 | 36 |
| Riggins, Id., U.S. | D2 | 89 |
| Riggisberg, Switz. | C3 | 21 |
| Rigi, mtn., Switz. | B4 | 20 |
| Rigili, i., Marsh Is. | S18 | 52 |
| Rigney, Fr. | B1 | 21 |
| Rigo, Pap. N. Gui. | k12 | 50 |
| Rigolet, Newf. | A2 | 72 |
| Riihimäki, Fin. | G11 | 14 |
| Riiser-Larsen Peninsula, pen., Ant. | C16 | 7 |
| Rijeka (Fiume), Yugo. | C2 | 24 |
| Rijssen, Neth. | B6 | 17 |
| Riley, In., U.S. | F3 | 91 |
| Riley, Ks., U.S. | C7 | 93 |
| Riley, Ky., U.S. | C4 | 94 |
| Riley, Or., U.S. | D7 | 114 |
| Riley, co., Ks., U.S. | C7 | 93 |
| Riley, Mount, mtn., N.M., U.S. | F2 | 108 |
| Rillito, Az., U.S. | E4 | 80 |
| Rilly-la-Montagne, Fr. | E4 | 17 |
| Rímac, Peru | *D2 | 58 |
| Rimavská Sobota, Czech. | D6 | 26 |
| Rimbey, Alta. | C3 | 68 |
| Rimbo, Swe. | t36 | 14 |
| Rimella, Italy | E5 | 21 |
| Rimersburg, Pa., U.S. | D3 | 115 |
| Rimini, Italy | B4 | 23 |
| Rîmnicu-Sărat, Rom. | C8 | 24 |
| Rîmnicu-Vîlcea, Rom. | C7 | 24 |
| Rimouski, Que. | A9 | 74 |
| Rimouski, co., Que. | A9 | 74 |
| Rimouski, stm., Que. | A9 | 74 |
| Rimouski-Est, Que. | A9 | 74 |
| Rimrock, Az., U.S. | C4 | 80 |
| Rimrock Lake, res., Wa., U.S. | C4 | 124 |
| Rinard, Il., U.S. | E5 | 90 |
| Rinard, Ia., U.S. | B3 | 92 |
| Rincon, Ga., U.S. | D5 | 87 |
| Rincon, N.M., U.S. | E2 | 108 |
| Rincón, Bahía de, b., P.R. | C3 | 65 |
| Rinconada, Arg. | D2 | 55 |
| Rincón del Bonete, Lago Artificial de, res., Ur. | E1 | 56 |
| Rincón de Romos, Mex. | k12 | 63 |
| Rincon Mountains, mts., Az., U.S. | E5 | 80 |
| Rindge, N.H., U.S. | E2 | 106 |
| Riner, Va., U.S. | C2 | 123 |
| Rineyville, Ky., U.S. | C4 | 94 |
| Ringas, India | D5 | 37 |
| Ringe, Den. | C4 | 15 |
| Ringelheim, W. Ger. | A5 | 19 |
| Ringel Spitze, mtn., Switz. | C7 | 21 |

| Name | Map Ref. | Page |
|---|---|---|
| Ringerike, Nor. | *G4 | 14 |
| Ringgold, Ga., U.S. | B1 | 87 |
| Ringgold, La., U.S. | B2 | 95 |
| Ringgold, Md., U.S. | A2 | 97 |
| Ringgold, Ne., U.S. | C5 | 104 |
| Ringgold, Tx., U.S. | C4 | 120 |
| Ringgold, co., Ia., U.S. | D3 | 92 |
| Ringgold Isles, is., Fiji | H16 | 52 |
| Ringim, Nig. | D6 | 45 |
| Ringkøbing, Den. | I3 | 14 |
| Ringkøbing, co., Den. | B2 | 15 |
| Ringkøbing Fjord, Den. | B2 | 15 |
| Ringling, Mt., U.S. | D6 | 103 |
| Ringling, Ok., U.S. | C4 | 113 |
| Ringoes, N.J., U.S. | C3 | 107 |
| Ringold, Ok., U.S. | C6 | 113 |
| Ringos Mills, Ky., U.S. | B6 | 94 |
| Ringsaker, Nor. | G4 | 14 |
| Ringsjön, l., Swe. | C7 | 15 |
| Ringsön, i., Swe. | u35 | 14 |
| Ringsted, Den. | C5 | 15 |
| Ringsted, Ia., U.S. | A3 | 92 |
| Ringvassøya, i., Nor. | C8 | 14 |
| Ringville, Ire. | E4 | 11 |
| Ringwood, N.J., U.S. | A4 | 107 |
| Ringwood, Ok., U.S. | A3 | 113 |
| Riñihue, Chile | B2 | 54 |
| Rinjani, mtn., Indon. | G5 | 34 |
| Rinnes, Ben, mtn., Scot., U.K. | C5 | 13 |
| Rinns Point, c., Scot., U.K. | E2 | 13 |
| Rinteln, W. Ger. | A4 | 19 |
| Rio, Fl., U.S. | E6 | 86 |
| Rio, Il., U.S. | B3 | 90 |
| Rio, W.V., U.S. | B6 | 125 |
| Rio, Wi., U.S. | E4 | 126 |
| Rio Arriba, co., N.M., U.S. | A2 | 108 |
| Riobamba, Ec. | B2 | 58 |
| Rio Benito, Eq. Gui. | E1 | 46 |
| Río Blanco, co., Co., U.S. | B2 | 83 |
| Rio Branco, Braz. | A2 | 55 |
| Rio Branco, Braz. | E2 | 56 |
| Rio Branco do Sul, Braz. | D3 | 56 |
| Rio Brilhante, Braz. | C2 | 56 |
| Rio Bueno, Chile | C2 | 54 |
| Rio Caribe, Ven. | A5 | 60 |
| Rio Chico, Ven. | A4 | 60 |
| Rio Claro, Braz. | C3 | 56 |
| Rio Claro, Trin. | O23 | 65 |
| Rio Colorado, Arg. | B4 | 54 |
| Rio Cuarto, Arg. | A4 | 54 |
| Rio de Janeiro, Braz. | C4 | 56 |
| Rio de Janeiro, state, Braz. | C4 | 56 |
| Rio de Jesús, Pan. | G7 | 62 |
| Rio Dell, Ca., U.S. | B1 | 82 |
| Rio Del Mar, Ca., U.S. | *D3 | 82 |
| Rio de Oro, Col. | B3 | 60 |
| Rio do Prado, Braz. | B4 | 56 |
| Rio do Sul, Braz. | D3 | 56 |
| Río Gallegos, Arg. | E3 | 54 |
| Río Grande, Arg. | h12 | 54 |
| Rio Grande, Braz. | E2 | 56 |
| Río Grande, Mex. | C4 | 63 |
| Rio Grande, N.J., U.S. | E3 | 107 |
| Rio Grande, Oh., U.S. | D3 | 112 |
| Rio Grande, co., Co., U.S. | D4 | 83 |
| Rio Grande City, Tx., U.S. | F3 | 120 |
| Rio Grande do Norte, state, Braz. | C3 | 57 |
| Rio Grande do Sul, state, Braz. | D2 | 56 |
| Rio Grande Reservoir, res., Co., U.S. | D3 | 83 |
| Ríohacha, Col. | A3 | 60 |
| Río Hato, Pan. | F7 | 62 |
| Rio Hondo, Mex. | h9 | 63 |
| Rio Hondo, Tx., U.S. | F4 | 120 |
| Rioja, Peru | C2 | 58 |
| Riolândia, Braz. | B3 | 56 |
| Rio Linda, Ca., U.S. | *C3 | 82 |
| Riom, Fr. | E5 | 16 |
| Rio Maior, Port. | C1 | 22 |
| Rio Mayo, Arg. | D2 | 54 |
| Rio Mulatos, Bol. | C2 | 55 |
| Rion, S.C., U.S. | C5 | 117 |
| Riondel, B.C. | E9 | 69 |
| Rio Negro, Braz. | D3 | 56 |
| Río Negro, prov., Arg. | C3 | 54 |
| Rionero in Vulture, Italy | D5 | 23 |
| Rio Pardo, Braz. | D2 | 56 |
| Rio Pardo de Minas, Braz. | B4 | 56 |
| Rio Pomba, Braz. | g6 | 56 |
| Rio Preto da Eva, Braz. | C3 | 59 |
| Rio Primero, Arg. | A4 | 54 |
| Rio Rancho, N.M., U.S. | B3 | 108 |
| Riosucio, Col. | B2 | 60 |
| Riosucio, Col. | B2 | 60 |
| Rio Tercero, Arg. | A4 | 54 |
| Rio Verde, Braz. | B2 | 56 |
| Rioverde, Mex. | m13 | 63 |
| Rio Verde de Mato Grosso, Braz. | B2 | 56 |
| Rio Vermelho, Braz. | B4 | 56 |
| Rio Vista, Ca., U.S. | C3 | 82 |
| Rioz, Fr. | B1 | 21 |
| Ripley, Ont. | C3 | 73 |
| Ripley, Eng., U.K. | A6 | 12 |
| Ripley, Ca., U.S. | F6 | 82 |
| Ripley, Il., U.S. | C3 | 90 |
| Ripley, Me., U.S. | D3 | 96 |
| Ripley, Ms., U.S. | A5 | 101 |
| Ripley, N.Y., U.S. | C1 | 109 |
| Ripley, Oh., U.S. | D2 | 112 |
| Ripley, Ok., U.S. | A5 | 113 |
| Ripley, Tn., U.S. | B2 | 119 |
| Ripley, W.V., U.S. | C3 | 125 |
| Ripley, co., In., U.S. | F7 | 91 |
| Ripley, co., Mo., U.S. | E7 | 102 |
| Riplinger, Wi., U.S. | *D3 | 126 |
| Ripogenus Pond, l., Me., U.S. | C3 | 96 |
| Ripoll, Spain | A7 | 22 |
| Ripon, Que. | D2 | 74 |
| Ripon, Eng., U.K. | C6 | 10 |
| Ripon, Ca., U.S. | C3 | 82 |
| Ripon, Wi., U.S. | E5 | 126 |
| Ripples, N.B. | C3 | 71 |
| Rippey, Ia., U.S. | C3 | 92 |
| Rippowam, stm., Ct., U.S. | E1 | 84 |
| Ripton, Vt., U.S. | D2 | 122 |
| Ririe, Id., U.S. | F7 | 89 |
| Ririe Lake, res., Id., U.S. | F7 | 89 |
| Risaralda, dept., Col. | B2 | 60 |
| Risco, Mo., U.S. | E8 | 102 |
| Rishiri Island, i., Japan | D10 | 33 |
| Rishon LeZiyyon, Isr. | C4 | 41 |
| Rising City, Ne., U.S. | C8 | 104 |
| Rising Star, Tx., U.S. | C3 | 120 |
| Rising Sun, De., U.S. | D3 | 85 |
| Rising Sun, In., U.S. | G8 | 91 |
| Risingsun, Oh., U.S. | e9 | 92 |
| Rising Sun, Md., U.S. | A5 | 97 |
| Risingsun, Oh., U.S. | A2 | 112 |
| Risle, stm., Fr. | C4 | 16 |
| Rison, Ar., U.S. | D3 | 81 |

| Name | Map Ref. | Page |
|---|---|---|
| Rison, Md., U.S. | C3 | 97 |
| Risör, Nor. | H3 | 14 |
| Ritchey, Mo., U.S. | E3 | 102 |
| Ritchie, co., W.V., U.S. | B3 | 125 |
| Ritidian Point, c., Guam | L10 | 52 |
| Ritscher Upland, plat., Ant. | B12 | 7 |
| Ritter, Or., U.S. | C7 | 114 |
| Ritter, Mount, mtn., Ca., U.S. | D4 | 82 |
| Rittman, Oh., U.S. | B4 | 112 |
| Ritzville, Wa., U.S. | B7 | 124 |
| Rivadavia, Arg. | A3 | 54 |
| Rivadavia, Arg. | A4 | 54 |
| Rivadavia, Arg. | D3 | 55 |
| Rivarolo [del Garda], Italy | B3 | 23 |
| Rivanna, stm., Va., U.S. | C4 | 123 |
| Rivare, In., U.S. | C8 | 91 |
| Rive-de-Gier, Fr. | E6 | 16 |
| Rivera, Arg. | B4 | 54 |
| Rivera, Ur. | E1 | 56 |
| Riverbank, Ca., U.S. | D3 | 82 |
| River Cess, Lib. | E4 | 44 |
| Riverdale, Ca., U.S. | D4 | 82 |
| Riverdale, Ga., U.S. | *C2 | 87 |
| Riverdale, Il., U.S. | k9 | 90 |
| Riverdale, Ia., U.S. | g11 | 92 |
| Riverdale, Ks., U.S. | E6 | 93 |
| Riverdale, Md., U.S. | C4 | 97 |
| Riverdale, Ne., U.S. | D6 | 104 |
| Riverdale, N.J., U.S. | B4 | 107 |
| Riverdale, N.D., U.S. | B4 | 111 |
| Riverdale, Ut., U.S. | *B3 | 121 |
| Riverdale, Va., U.S. | D4 | 123 |
| River Edge, N.J., U.S. | h8 | 107 |
| River Falls, Al., U.S. | D3 | 78 |
| River Falls, Wi., U.S. | D1 | 126 |
| River Forest, Il., U.S. | k9 | 90 |
| River Grove, Il., U.S. | k9 | 90 |
| Riverhaven, In., U.S. | B7 | 91 |
| Riverhead, N.Y., U.S. | n16 | 109 |
| River Hebert, N.S. | D5 | 71 |
| River Heights, Ut., U.S. | B4 | 121 |
| River Hills, Wi., U.S. | m12 | 126 |
| Riverhurst, Sask. | G2 | 75 |
| River John, N.S. | D6 | 71 |
| River Jordan, B.C. | h11 | 69 |
| River Oaks, Tx., U.S. | *n9 | 120 |
| River of Ponds, Newf. | C3 | 72 |
| River Pines, Ma., U.S. | f10 | 98 |
| Riverport, N.S. | E5 | 71 |
| River Ridge, La., U.S. | k11 | 95 |
| River Road, Or., U.S. | C3 | 114 |
| River Rouge, Mi., U.S. | p15 | 99 |
| Rivers, Man. | D1 | 70 |
| Rivers, Lake of the, l., Sask. | H3 | 75 |
| Riversdale, N.S. | D6 | 71 |
| Riverside, Al., U.S. | B3 | 78 |
| Riverside, Ca., U.S. | F5 | 82 |
| Riverside, Ct., U.S. | D3 | 84 |
| Riverside, Ga., U.S. | E3 | 87 |
| Riverside, Il., U.S. | k9 | 90 |
| Riverside, Ia., U.S. | C6 | 92 |
| Riverside, N.J., U.S. | C3 | 107 |
| Riverside, Or., U.S. | D8 | 114 |
| Riverside, Pa., U.S. | E8 | 115 |
| Riverside, Ut., U.S. | B3 | 121 |
| Riverside, Wy., U.S. | E6 | 127 |
| Riverside, co., Ca., U.S. | F5 | 82 |
| Riverside-Albert, N.B. | D5 | 71 |
| Riverside Reservoir, res., Co., U.S. | A6 | 83 |
| Rivers Inlet, b., B.C. | D4 | 69 |
| River Sioux, Ia., U.S. | C1 | 92 |
| Riverton, Man. | D3 | 70 |
| Riverton, N.Z. | Q12 | 51 |
| Riverton, Ct., U.S. | B3 | 84 |
| Riverton, Il., U.S. | D4 | 90 |
| Riverton, Ia., U.S. | D2 | 92 |
| Riverton, Ks., U.S. | E9 | 93 |
| Riverton, La., U.S. | B3 | 95 |
| Riverton, Mn., U.S. | D4 | 100 |
| Riverton, Ne., U.S. | D7 | 104 |
| Riverton, N.J., U.S. | C3 | 107 |
| Riverton, Ut., U.S. | C4 | 121 |
| Riverton, Vt., U.S. | C3 | 122 |
| Riverton, Wy., U.S. | C4 | 127 |
| Riverton Heights, Wa., U.S. | f11 | 124 |
| River Vale, N.J., U.S. | h8 | 107 |
| River View, Al., U.S. | C4 | 78 |
| Riverview, Fl., U.S. | p11 | 86 |
| Riverview, Mi., U.S. | p15 | 99 |
| Rives, Mo., U.S. | E7 | 102 |
| Rives Junction, Mi., U.S. | F6 | 99 |
| Rivesville, W.V., U.S. | B4 | 125 |
| Riviera, Az., U.S. | B1 | 80 |
| Riviera, Tx., U.S. | F4 | 120 |
| Riviera Beach, Fl., U.S. | F6 | 86 |
| Riviera Beach, Md., U.S. | B4 | 97 |
| Rivière-à-Pierre, Que. | B5 | 74 |
| Rivière-Bleue, Que. | B9 | 74 |
| Rivière-du-Loup, Que. | B8 | 74 |
| Rivière-du-Loup, co., Que. | B8 | 74 |
| Rivière-Ouelle, Que. | B7 | 74 |
| Rivière-Trois-Pistoles, Que. | A8 | 74 |
| Rivière-Verte, N.B. | B1 | 71 |
| Rivière-Verte, Que. | B8 | 74 |
| Rivulet, Mt., U.S. | D2 | 103 |
| Rixford, Pa., U.S. | C4 | 115 |
| Rixie's, Nv., U.S. | *C5 | 105 |
| Riyadh (Ar Riyāḍ), Sau. Ar. | C4 | 38 |
| Rize, Tur. | B13 | 40 |
| Rizhao, China | E6 | 31 |
| Rizzuto, Cape, c., Italy | E6 | 23 |
| Rjukan, Nor. | G3 | 14 |
| Roachdale, In., U.S. | E4 | 91 |
| Roads, Oh., U.S. | C3 | 112 |
| Roadstown, N.J., U.S. | E2 | 107 |
| Roan Cliffs, clf., U.S. | B1 | 83 |
| Roan Creek, stm., Co., U.S. | B2 | 83 |
| Roane, co., Tn., U.S. | D9 | 119 |
| Roane, co., W.V., U.S. | C3 | 125 |
| Roan High Knob, mtn., U.S. | C11 | 119 |
| Roan Mountain, Tn., U.S. | C11 | 119 |
| Roann, In., U.S. | C6 | 91 |
| Roanne, Fr. | D6 | 16 |
| Roanoke, Al., U.S. | B4 | 78 |
| Roanoke, Il., U.S. | C4 | 90 |
| Roanoke, In., U.S. | C7 | 91 |
| Roanoke, Tx., U.S. | D3 | 120 |
| Roanoke, Va., U.S. | C3 | 123 |
| Roanoke, W.V., U.S. | C4 | 125 |

| Name | Map Ref. | Page |
|---|---|---|
| Roanoke, co., Va., U.S. | C2 | 123 |
| Roanoke, stm., U.S. | A5 | 110 |
| Roanoke Island, i., N.C., U.S. | B7 | 110 |
| Roanoke Rapids, N.C., U.S. | A5 | 110 |
| Roanoke Rapids Lake, res., U.S. | A5 | 110 |
| Roan Plateau, plat., U.S. | B2 | 83 |
| Roaring Branch, Pa., U.S. | C8 | 115 |
| Roaring Fork, stm., Co., U.S. | C4 | 83 |
| Roaring Spring, Pa., U.S. | F5 | 115 |
| Roaring Springs, Tx., U.S. | C2 | 120 |
| Roaringwater Bay, b., Ire. | F2 | 11 |
| Roark, Ky., U.S. | C6 | 94 |
| Roatán, Hond. | D7 | 63 |
| Roba, Al., U.S. | C4 | 78 |
| Robards, Ky., U.S. | C2 | 94 |
| Robb, Alta. | C2 | 68 |
| Robbin, Mn., U.S. | B1 | 100 |
| Robbins, Il., U.S. | k9 | 90 |
| Robbins, N.C., U.S. | B3 | 110 |
| Robbins, Tn., U.S. | C9 | 119 |
| Robbinsdale, Mn., U.S. | m12 | 100 |
| Robbinston, Me., U.S. | C5 | 96 |
| Robbinsville, N.J., U.S. | C3 | 107 |
| Robbinsville, N.C., U.S. | f9 | 110 |
| Robbs, Il., U.S. | F5 | 90 |
| Robe, stm., Ire. | D2 | 11 |
| Robeline, La., U.S. | C2 | 95 |
| Robersonville, N.C., U.S. | B5 | 110 |
| Robert, La., U.S. | D5 | 95 |
| Roberta, Ga., U.S. | D2 | 87 |
| Roberts, Id., U.S. | F6 | 89 |
| Roberts, Il., U.S. | C5 | 90 |
| Roberts, Mt., U.S. | E7 | 103 |
| Roberts, Wi., U.S. | C1 | 126 |
| Roberts, co., S.D., U.S. | B8 | 118 |
| Roberts, co., Tx., U.S. | B2 | 120 |
| Roberts, Cape, c., Ont. | A2 | 73 |
| Roberts, Point, c., Wa., U.S. | A2 | 124 |
| Robert's Arm, Newf. | D4 | 72 |
| Roberts Creek Mountain, mtn., Nv., U.S. | D5 | 105 |
| Robertsdale, Al., U.S. | E2 | 78 |
| Robertsdale, Pa., U.S. | F5 | 115 |
| Robert S. Kerr Reservoir, res., Ok., U.S. | B6 | 113 |
| Roberts Mountain, mtn., Ak., U.S. | C6 | 79 |
| Roberts Mountain, mtn., Wy., U.S. | D3 | 127 |
| Robertson, S. Afr. | D3 | 49 |
| Robertson, Wy., U.S. | E2 | 127 |
| Robertson, co., Ky., U.S. | B5 | 94 |
| Robertson, co., Tn., U.S. | A5 | 119 |
| Robertson, co., Tx., U.S. | D4 | 120 |
| Robertson, Lac, l., Que. | C2 | 72 |
| Robertson Bay, b., Ant. | B29 | 7 |
| Robertsonville, Que. | C6 | 74 |
| Robertstown, Aust. | F7 | 50 |
| Robertville, Que. | C6 | 74 |
| Roberval, Que. | A5 | 74 |
| Robeson, co., N.C., U.S. | C3 | 110 |
| Robersonia, Pa., U.S. | F9 | 115 |
| Robinhood, Mo., U.S. | g8 | 102 |
| Robins, Ia., U.S. | B6 | 92 |
| Robins, Oh., U.S. | C4 | 112 |
| Robins Air Force Base, mil., Ga., U.S. | D3 | 87 |
| Robinson, Il., U.S. | D6 | 90 |
| Robinson, Ks., U.S. | C8 | 93 |
| Robinson, Me., U.S. | B5 | 96 |
| Robinson, N.D., U.S. | B6 | 111 |
| Robinson, Pa., U.S. | *F13 | 115 |
| Ròbinson Crusoe, Isla, i., Chile | G3 | 53 |
| Robinson Fork, stm., W.V., U.S. | k9 | 125 |
| Robinson Fork, stm., W.V., U.S. | m14 | 125 |
| Robinson Mountain, mtn., Ar., U.S. | A1 | 81 |
| Robinsons, Newf. | D2 | 72 |
| Robinsonville, Ms., U.S. | A3 | 101 |
| Robinvale, Austl. | F7 | 50 |
| Roblin, Man. | D1 | 70 |
| Roblin, stm., Man. | A5 | 70 |
| Roboré, Bol. | C4 | 55 |
| Robsart, Sask. | H1 | 75 |
| Robson, B.C. | E9 | 69 |
| Robson, Mount, mtn., B.C. | C8 | 69 |
| Robstown, Tx., U.S. | F4 | 120 |
| Roby, Mo., U.S. | D5 | 102 |
| Roby, Tx., U.S. | C2 | 120 |
| Roca, Ne., U.S. | h11 | 104 |
| Roca, Cape, c., Port. | f9 | 22 |
| Rocafuerte, Ec. | B1 | 58 |
| Rocafuerte, Peru | A2 | 59 |
| Rocanville, Sask. | G5 | 75 |
| Rocas, Átol das, atoll, Braz. | B4 | 57 |
| Rocca Massima, Italy | h9 | 23 |
| Roccastrada, Italy | C3 | 23 |
| Rocha, Ur. | E2 | 56 |
| Rochdale, Eng., U.K. | D5 | 10 |
| Rochdale, Ma., U.S. | B4 | 98 |
| Rochechouart, Fr. | E4 | 16 |
| Rochedo, Braz. | B6 | 16 |
| Rochefort, Bel. | E3 | 16 |
| Rochefort, Fr. | E3 | 16 |
| Roche Harbor, Wa., U.S. | A2 | 124 |
| Rochelle, Ga., U.S. | E3 | 87 |
| Rochelle, Il., U.S. | B4 | 90 |
| Rochelle, Tx., U.S. | D3 | 120 |
| Rochelle, Va., U.S. | B4 | 123 |
| Roche-Percée, Sask. | H4 | 75 |
| Rocheport, Mo., U.S. | C5 | 102 |
| Rochester, Alta. | B4 | 68 |
| Rochester, Eng., U.K. | J13 | 10 |
| Rochester, Il., U.S. | D4 | 90 |
| Rochester, In., U.S. | B5 | 91 |
| Rochester, Ky., U.S. | C3 | 94 |
| Rochester, Ma., U.S. | C6 | 98 |
| Rochester, Mi., U.S. | F7 | 99 |
| Rochester, Mn., U.S. | F6 | 100 |
| Rochester, N.H., U.S. | D5 | 106 |
| Rochester, N.Y., U.S. | B3 | 109 |
| Rochester, Oh., U.S. | E1 | 115 |
| Rochester, Tx., U.S. | C3 | 120 |
| Rochester, Vt., U.S. | D3 | 122 |
| Rochester, Wa., U.S. | C3 | 124 |
| Rochester, Wi., U.S. | n11 | 126 |
| Rochester Hills, Mi., U.S. | *F7 | 99 |
| Rochester Mountain, mtn., Vt., U.S. | D3 | 122 |
| Rockwell, co., Tx., U.S. | C4 | 120 |
| Rochford, S.D., U.S. | C2 | 118 |
| Rochfort Bridge, Alta. | C3 | 68 |
| Rochfortbridge, Ire. | D4 | 11 |
| Rochikarai Island, i., Marsn Is. | P18 | 52 |
| Rochlitz, E. Ger. | B7 | 19 |

| Name | Map Ref. | Page |
|---|---|---|
| Rociada, N.M., U.S. | B4 | 108 |
| Rock, Ks., U.S. | E7 | 93 |
| Rock, Ma., U.S. | *C6 | 98 |
| Rock, Mi., U.S. | B3 | 99 |
| Rock, co., Mn., U.S. | G2 | 100 |
| Rock, co., Ne., U.S. | B6 | 104 |
| Rock, co., Wi., U.S. | F4 | 126 |
| Rock, stm., U.S. | B3 | 99 |
| Rock, stm., U.S. | A1 | 92 |
| Rockaway, N.J., U.S. | B3 | 107 |
| Rockaway, Or., U.S. | B3 | 114 |
| Rockaway Beach, Mo., U.S. | E4 | 102 |
| Rock Bay, B.C. | D5 | 69 |
| Rock Bluff, Fl., U.S. | B2 | 86 |
| Rockbridge, Il., U.S. | D3 | 90 |
| Rockbridge, Oh., U.S. | C3 | 112 |
| Rockbridge, co., Va., U.S. | C3 | 123 |
| Rockcastle, co., Ky., U.S. | C5 | 94 |
| Rockcastle, stm., Ky., U.S. | C5 | 94 |
| Rock Creek, B.C. | E8 | 69 |
| Rock Creek, Ks., U.S. | k14 | 93 |
| Rock Creek, Mn., U.S. | E6 | 100 |
| Rock Creek, Oh., U.S. | A5 | 112 |
| Rock Creek, stm., N.A. | H2 | 75 |
| Rock Creek, stm., Il., U.S. | B7 | 90 |
| Rock Creek, stm., Il., U.S. | h14 | 124 |
| Rock Creek, stm., Ks., U.S. | g10 | 93 |
| Rock Creek, stm., Ne., U.S. | g11 | 104 |
| Rock Creek, stm., Nv., U.S. | C5 | 105 |
| Rock Creek, stm., Or., U.S. | B6 | 114 |
| Rock Creek, stm., Wa., U.S. | B8 | 124 |
| Rock Creek, stm., Wa., U.S. | D5 | 124 |
| Rock Creek, stm., Wy., U.S. | E6 | 127 |
| Rock Creek Butte, mtn., Or., U.S. | C8 | 114 |
| Rockdale, Austl. | *F9 | 50 |
| Rockdale, Il., U.S. | B5 | 90 |
| Rockdale, Ia., U.S. | B7 | 92 |
| Rockdale, Md., U.S. | B4 | 97 |
| Rockdale, Tn., U.S. | B4 | 119 |
| Rockdale, Tx., U.S. | D4 | 120 |
| Rockdale, co., Ga., U.S. | C2 | 87 |
| Rockefeller Plateau, plat., Ant. | A35 | 7 |
| Rock Elm, Wi., U.S. | D1 | 126 |
| Rock Falls, Il., U.S. | B4 | 90 |
| Rock Falls, Ia., U.S. | A4 | 92 |
| Rockfield, Ky., U.S. | D3 | 94 |
| Rockfield, Wi., U.S. | m11 | 126 |
| Rockford, Al., U.S. | C3 | 78 |
| Rockford, Il., U.S. | A4 | 90 |
| Rockford, Ia., U.S. | A5 | 92 |
| Rockford, Mn., U.S. | E5 | 100 |
| Rockford, Oh., U.S. | B1 | 112 |
| Rockford, Tn., U.S. | D10 | 119 |
| Rockford, Wa., U.S. | B8 | 124 |
| Rockglen, Sask. | H3 | 75 |
| Rock Hall, Md., U.S. | B5 | 97 |
| Rockham, S.D., U.S. | C7 | 118 |
| Rockhampton, Austl. | D9 | 50 |
| Rockhaven, Sask. | E1 | 75 |
| Rock Hill, Mo., U.S. | *f13 | 102 |
| Rock Hill, S.C., U.S. | B5 | 117 |
| Rockhill Furnace, Pa., U.S. | F6 | 115 |
| Rockholds, Ky., U.S. | D5 | 94 |
| Rockingham, Ga., U.S. | E4 | 87 |
| Rockingham, N.C., U.S. | C3 | 110 |
| Rockingham, Vt., U.S. | E4 | 122 |
| Rockingham, co., N.H., U.S. | D4 | 106 |
| Rockingham, co., N.C., U.S. | A3 | 110 |
| Rockingham, co., Va., U.S. | B4 | 123 |
| Rock Island, Que. | D5 | 74 |
| Rock Island, Il., U.S. | B3 | 90 |
| Rock Island, Ok., U.S. | B7 | 113 |
| Rock Island, co., Il., U.S. | B3 | 90 |
| Rock Island, i., Fl., U.S. | C3 | 86 |
| Rock Island, i., Wi., U.S. | C7 | 126 |
| Rock Lake, l., Man. | E2 | 70 |
| Rocklake, N.D., U.S. | A6 | 111 |
| Rock Lake, l., Man. | B8 | 124 |
| Rockland, Ont. | B9 | 73 |
| Rockland, Id., U.S. | G6 | 89 |
| Rockland, Me., U.S. | D3 | 96 |
| Rockland, Ma., U.S. | B6 | 98 |
| Rockland, Mi., U.S. | m12 | 99 |
| Rockland, N.Y., U.S. | D6 | 109 |
| Rockland, co., N.Y., U.S. | D6 | 109 |
| Rocklands Reservoir, res., Austl. | H3 | 51 |
| Rockledge, Fl., U.S. | D6 | 86 |
| Rockledge, Pa., U.S. | o20 | 115 |
| Rocklin, Ca., U.S. | C3 | 82 |
| Rockmart, Ga., U.S. | B1 | 87 |
| Rock Mountain, mtn., Al., U.S. | B2 | 78 |
| Rock Mountain, mtn., Co., U.S. | D3 | 83 |
| Rock Point, Md., U.S. | D4 | 97 |
| Rockport, Ar., U.S. | g8 | 81 |
| Rockport, Il., U.S. | D2 | 90 |
| Rockport, In., U.S. | I3 | 91 |
| Rockport, Ky., U.S. | C3 | 94 |
| Rockport, Ma., U.S. | A6 | 98 |
| Rockport, Me., U.S. | D3 | 96 |
| Rockport, N.J., U.S. | B3 | 107 |
| Rockport, Tx., U.S. | E4 | 120 |
| Rockport, Wa., U.S. | A4 | 124 |
| Rock Rapids, Ia., U.S. | A1 | 92 |
| Rock River, Wy., U.S. | E7 | 127 |
| Rock Run, Al., U.S. | B4 | 78 |
| Rock Springs, Mt., U.S. | D10 | 103 |
| Rocksprings, Tx., U.S. | D2 | 120 |
| Rock Springs, Wi., U.S. | E4 | 126 |
| Rockstone, Guy. | A3 | 59 |
| Rockton, Il., U.S. | A4 | 90 |
| Rockton, Pa., U.S. | D4 | 115 |
| Rock Valley, Ia., U.S. | A1 | 92 |
| Rockvale, Co., U.S. | C5 | 83 |
| Rockvale, Tn., U.S. | B5 | 119 |
| Rockville, Ct., U.S. | B6 | 84 |
| Rockville, In., U.S. | E3 | 91 |
| Rockville, Md., U.S. | B3 | 97 |
| Rockville, Mn., U.S. | E4 | 100 |
| Rockville, Mo., U.S. | C3 | 102 |
| Rockville, Ne., U.S. | C7 | 104 |
| Rockville, R.I., U.S. | D1 | 116 |
| Rockville, Ut., U.S. | F2 | 121 |
| Rockville Centre, N.Y., U.S. | n15 | 109 |
| Rockwall, co., Tx., U.S. | C4 | 120 |
| Rockwell, N.C., U.S. | B2 | 110 |
| Rockwell City, Ia., U.S. | B3 | 92 |
| Rockwell Park, N.C., U.S. | B2 | 110 |
| Rockwood, Ont. | D4 | 73 |

| Name | Map Ref. | Page |
|---|---|---|
| Rockwood, Al., U.S. | A2 | 78 |
| Rockwood, Il., U.S. | F4 | 90 |
| Rockwood, Me., U.S. | C3 | 96 |
| Rockwood, Mi., U.S. | F7 | 99 |
| Rockwood, Pa., U.S. | *B4 | 114 |
| Rockwood, Pa., U.S. | G3 | 115 |
| Rockwood, Tn., U.S. | D9 | 119 |
| Rockwood, Tx., U.S. | D3 | 120 |
| Rocky, Ok., U.S. | B2 | 113 |
| Rocky, stm., Alta. | C2 | 68 |
| Rocky, stm., N.C., U.S. | B2 | 110 |
| Rocky, stm., S.C., U.S. | C2 | 117 |
| Rocky, East Branch, stm., Oh., U.S. | h9 | 112 |
| Rocky, West Branch, stm., Oh., U.S. | h9 | 112 |
| Rocky Bay, b., Newf. | B4 | 72 |
| Rocky Boys Indian Reservation, Mt., U.S. | B7 | 103 |
| Rocky Comfort, Mo., U.S. | E3 | 102 |
| Rocky Coulee, val., Wa., U.S. | B6 | 124 |
| Rocky Creek, Fl., U.S. | *o10 | 86 |
| Rockyford, Alta. | D4 | 68 |
| Rocky Ford, Co., U.S. | C7 | 83 |
| Rocky Ford, Ga., U.S. | D5 | 87 |
| Rocky Fork Lake, l., Oh., U.S. | C2 | 112 |
| Rocky Gap, Va., U.S. | C1 | 123 |
| Rocky Harbour, Newf. | D3 | 72 |
| Rocky Hill, Ct., U.S. | C5 | 84 |
| Rocky Hill, Ky., U.S. | C3 | 94 |
| Rocky Lake, l., Man. | B1 | 70 |
| Rocky Lake, l., Me., U.S. | D5 | 96 |
| Rocky Mount, N.C., U.S. | B5 | 110 |
| Rocky Mount, Va., U.S. | D3 | 123 |
| Rocky Mountain, mtn., Mt., U.S. | C4 | 103 |
| Rocky Mountain House, Alta. | C3 | 68 |
| Rocky Mountain National Park, Co., U.S. | A5 | 83 |
| Rocky Mountains, mts., N.A. | C9 | 61 |
| Rocky Point, N.Y., U.S. | *n16 | 109 |
| Rocky Point, N.C., U.S. | C4 | 110 |
| Rocroi, Fr. | B6 | 16 |
| Roda, Va., U.S. | f9 | 123 |
| Rodach, W. Ger. | C5 | 19 |
| Rodanthe, N.C., U.S. | B7 | 110 |
| Rodarte, N.M., U.S. | *A4 | 108 |
| Rødby, Den. | D5 | 15 |
| Rødbyhavn, Den. | D5 | 15 |
| Rødding, Den. | C3 | 15 |
| Roddickton, Newf. | C3 | 72 |
| Rødding, Den. | D9 | 119 |
| Roddy, Tn., U.S. | C3 | 15 |
| Rodeo, Ca., U.S. | *g8 | 82 |
| Rodeo, N.M., U.S. | F1 | 108 |
| Roderfield, W.V., U.S. | D3 | 125 |
| Roderick Island, i., B.C. | C3 | 69 |
| Rodessa, La., U.S. | B2 | 95 |
| Rodewisch, E. Ger. | E2 | 19 |
| Rodney, Ont. | E3 | 73 |
| Rodman, Ia., U.S. | A3 | 92 |
| Rodman, N.Y., U.S. | B5 | 109 |
| Rodney, Ont. | E3 | 73 |
| Rodney, Ms., U.S. | D2 | 101 |
| Rodney, Cape, c., Ak., U.S. | C6 | 79 |
| Rodney Pond, l., Newf. | D4 | 72 |
| Rodney Village, De., U.S. | D3 | 85 |
| Roduco, N.C., U.S. | A6 | 110 |
| Roe, Ar., U.S. | C4 | 81 |
| Roebling, N.J., U.S. | C3 | 107 |
| Roebourne, Austl. | D3 | 50 |
| Roebuck, S.C., U.S. | B4 | 117 |
| Roebuck Bay, b., Austl. | C4 | 50 |
| Roeland Park, Ks., U.S. | k16 | 93 |
| Roermond, Neth. | B6 | 16 |
| Roeselare (Roulers), Bel. | B3 | 16 |
| Roessleville, N.Y., U.S. | *C7 | 109 |
| Roes Welcome Sound, strt., N.W. Ter. | D15 | 66 |
| Roetgen, W. Ger. | C6 | 17 |
| Roff, Ok., U.S. | C5 | 113 |
| Rogachev, Sov. Un. | E8 | 27 |
| Rogagua, Laguna, l., Bol. | B2 | 55 |
| Rogáguado, Laguna, l., Bol. | B2 | 55 |
| Roganville, Tx., U.S. | D6 | 120 |
| Rogatica, Yugo. | B2 | 24 |
| Roger Mills, co., Ok., U.S. | B2 | 113 |
| Rogers, Ar., U.S. | A1 | 81 |
| Rogers, Ct., U.S. | B8 | 84 |
| Rogers, Mn., U.S. | C5 | 100 |
| Rogers, N.M., U.S. | D6 | 108 |
| Rogers, N.D., U.S. | B4 | 111 |
| Rogers, Oh., U.S. | B5 | 112 |
| Rogers, Tx., U.S. | D4 | 120 |
| Rogers, co., Ok., U.S. | A6 | 113 |
| Rogers, Mount, mtn., Va., U.S. | f10 | 123 |
| Rogers City, Mi., U.S. | C7 | 99 |
| Rogers Lake, res., Ct., U.S. | D6 | 84 |
| Rogerson, Id., U.S. | G4 | 89 |
| Rogers Pass, Mt., U.S. | C4 | 103 |
| Rogersville, N.B. | C4 | 71 |
| Rogersville, Al., U.S. | A2 | 78 |
| Rogersville, Mo., U.S. | D4 | 102 |
| Rogersville, Pa., U.S. | G1 | 115 |
| Rogersville, Tn., U.S. | C10 | 119 |
| Roggen, Co., U.S. | A6 | 83 |
| Rogozhina, Alb. | B2 | 24 |
| Rogozno, Pol. | B3 | 26 |
| Rogue, stm., Or., U.S. | E2 | 114 |
| Rogue River, Or., U.S. | E3 | 114 |
| Rohnert Park, Ca., U.S. | *C2 | 82 |
| Rohrersville, Md., U.S. | B2 | 97 |
| Rohri Canal, Pak. | D2 | 37 |
| Rohtak, India | D6 | 37 |
| Rohwer, Ar., U.S. | D4 | 81 |
| Roi Et, Thai. | B3 | 34 |
| Roi Island, i., Marsh Is. | S17 | 52 |
| Roissy-en-France, Fr. | g11 | 17 |
| Rojas, Arg. | A4 | 54 |
| Rojo, Cabo, c., Mex. | m15 | 63 |
| Rojo, Cabo, c., P.R. | H11 | 64 |
| Rokan, stm., Indon. | L4 | 35 |
| Rokeby, Sask. | F4 | 75 |
| Rokel, stm., S.L. | G2 | 44 |
| Rokitno, Sov. Un. | F6 | 27 |
| Rokycany, Czech. | C1 | 26 |
| Roland, Man. | E3 | 70 |
| Roland, Ar., U.S. | C3 | 81 |
| Roland, Ia., U.S. | B4 | 92 |
| Roland, Ok., U.S. | B7 | 113 |
| Roland, Lake, res., Md., U.S. | g11 | 97 |
| Rolesville, N.C., U.S. | B4 | 110 |
| Rolette, N.D., U.S. | A6 | 111 |
| Rolette, co., N.D., U.S. | A5 | 111 |
| Rolfe, Ia., U.S. | B3 | 92 |

| Name | Map Ref. | Page |
|---|---|---|
| Roll, Az., U.S. | E2 | 80 |
| Roll, In., U.S. | C7 | 91 |
| Roll, Ok., U.S. | B2 | 113 |
| Rolla, B.C. | B7 | 69 |
| Rolla, Ar., U.S. | C3 | 81 |
| Rolla, Ks., U.S. | E2 | 93 |
| Rolla, Mo., U.S. | D6 | 102 |
| Rolla, N.D., U.S. | A6 | 111 |
| Rolle, Switz. | E3 | 18 |
| Rolleville, Bah. | C6 | 64 |
| Rollingbay, Wa., U.S. | e10 | 124 |
| Rolling Fork, Ms., U.S. | C3 | 101 |
| Rolling Fork, stm., Ar., U.S. | C1 | 81 |
| Rolling Fork, stm., Ky., U.S. | C4 | 94 |
| Rolling Hills Estates, Ca., U.S. | *n12 | 82 |
| Rolling Meadows, Il., U.S. | h8 | 90 |
| Rollingstone, Mn., U.S. | F7 | 100 |
| Rollins, Mt., U.S. | C2 | 103 |
| Rollinsford, N.H., U.S. | D5 | 106 |
| Rolvsøya, i., Nor. | B10 | 14 |
| Roma, Austl. | E8 | 50 |
| Roma, Alta. | A2 | 68 |
| Roma, Tx., U.S. | F3 | 120 |
| Romain, Cape, c., S.C., U.S. | F9 | 117 |
| Romaine, stm., Can. | h9 | 72 |
| Roman, Rom. | B8 | 24 |
| Romania, ctry., Eur. | C7 | 24 |
| Roman Nose Mountain, mtn., Md., U.S. | m12 | 97 |
| Roman Nose Mountain, mtn., Or., U.S. | D3 | 114 |
| Romano, Cape, c., Fl., U.S. | G5 | 86 |
| Romano, Cayo, i., Cuba | C5 | 64 |
| Romanshorn, Switz. | A7 | 21 |
| Romans [-sur-Isère], Fr. | E6 | 16 |
| Romanzof, Cape, c., Ak., U.S. | C6 | 79 |
| Romanzof Mountains, mts., Ak., U.S. | B11 | 79 |
| Romayor, Tx., U.S. | D5 | 120 |
| Rombauer, Mo., U.S. | E7 | 102 |
| Rome (Roma), Italy | D4 | 23 |
| Rome, Ga., U.S. | B1 | 87 |
| Rome, Il., U.S. | C4 | 90 |
| Rome, In., U.S. | I4 | 91 |
| Rome, Ia., U.S. | D6 | 92 |
| Rome, Ms., U.S. | B3 | 101 |
| Rome, N.Y., U.S. | B5 | 109 |
| Rome, Oh., U.S. | D3 | 112 |
| Rome, Pa., U.S. | C9 | 115 |
| Rome City, In., U.S. | B7 | 91 |
| Romema (part of Jerusalem), Isr. | m14 | 41 |
| Romeo, In., U.S. | D4 | 83 |
| Romeo, Mi., U.S. | F7 | 99 |
| Romeoville, Il., U.S. | k8 | 90 |
| Romeville, La., U.S. | h10 | 95 |
| Romford (part of London), Eng., U.K. | k13 | 10 |
| Romilly, Fr. | C5 | 16 |
| Romita, Mex. | m13 | 63 |
| Romney, In., U.S. | D4 | 91 |
| Romney, W.V., U.S. | B6 | 125 |
| Romny, Sov. Un. | F9 | 27 |
| Rømø, i., Den. | C2 | 15 |
| Romona, In., U.S. | F4 | 91 |
| Romont, Switz. | C2 | 21 |
| Romorantin, Fr. | D4 | 16 |
| Rompin, stm., Malay. | K5 | 35 |
| Romsey, Eng., U.K. | D6 | 12 |
| Romulus, Mi., U.S. | p15 | 99 |
| Romulus, N.Y., U.S. | C4 | 109 |
| Romunun, i., Micron. | Q18 | 52 |
| Romurikku Island, i., Marsh Is. | P18 | 52 |
| Ron, Viet. | D7 | 35 |
| Ron, Cape, c., Viet. | C7 | 35 |
| Rona, i., Scot., U.K. | C3 | 13 |
| Rona, i., Scot., U.K. | A3 | 13 |
| Ronald, Wa., U.S. | B4 | 124 |
| Ronan, Mt., U.S. | C2 | 103 |
| Roncador, Serra do, plat., Braz. | E4 | 59 |
| Roncador Bank, Col. | D7 | 62 |
| Ronceverte, W.V., U.S. | D4 | 125 |
| Ronciglione, Italy | C4 | 23 |
| Ronda, Spain | D3 | 22 |
| Ronda, N.C., U.S. | A2 | 110 |
| Rønde, Den. | B4 | 15 |
| Ronde Island, i., Gren. | W25 | 65 |
| Rondo, Ar., U.S. | C5 | 81 |
| Rondônia, state, Braz. | E2 | 59 |
| Rondonópolis, Braz. | B2 | 56 |
| Roneys Point, W.V., U.S. | f8 | 125 |
| Ronge, Lac la, l., Sask. | B3 | 75 |
| Rongjiang, China | L3 | 32 |
| Rongxian, China | G7 | 31 |
| Ronkiti Harbor, b., Micron. | Q17 | 52 |
| Ronkonkoma, N.Y., U.S. | *n15 | 109 |
| Rønne, Den. | J6 | 14 |
| Rønne, stm., Swe. | B6 | 15 |
| Ronneby, E. Ger. | C7 | 19 |
| Ronne Entrance, b., Ant. | B5 | 7 |
| Ronne Ice Shelf, ice, Ant. | B6 | 7 |
| Ronse, Bel. | B5 | 16 |
| Ronuro, stm., Braz. | E4 | 59 |
| Roodepoort-Maraisburg, S. Afr. | *C4 | 49 |
| Roodeschool, Neth. | A6 | 17 |
| Roodhouse, Il., U.S. | D3 | 90 |
| Roof Butte, mtn., Az., U.S. | A6 | 80 |
| Rooks, co., Ks., U.S. | C4 | 93 |
| Roopville, Ga., U.S. | C1 | 87 |
| Roosendaal, Neth. | B6 | 16 |
| Roosevelt, Az., U.S. | D4 | 80 |
| Roosevelt, Mn., U.S. | B3 | 100 |
| Roosevelt, N.J., U.S. | C4 | 107 |
| Roosevelt, N.Y., U.S. | *n15 | 109 |
| Roosevelt, Ok., U.S. | C2 | 113 |
| Roosevelt, Tx., U.S. | D2 | 120 |
| Roosevelt, Ut., U.S. | C5 | 121 |
| Roosevelt, Wa., U.S. | D5 | 124 |
| Roosevelt, co., Mt., U.S. | B11 | 103 |
| Roosevelt, co., N.M., U.S. | C6 | 108 |
| Roosevelt, stm., Braz. | D2 | 59 |
| Roosevelt Campobello International Park, N.A. | E3 | 71 |
| Roosevelt Island, i., Ant. | B32 | 7 |
| Roosevelt Park, Mi., U.S. | F4 | 99 |
| Root, stm., Mn., U.S. | G7 | 100 |
| Root, stm., Wi., U.S. | n12 | 126 |
| Rootstown, Oh., U.S. | A4 | 112 |
| Ropczyce, Pol. | C6 | 26 |
| Roper, N.C., U.S. | B6 | 110 |
| Roper, stm., Austl. | B5 | 50 |
| Ropesville, Tx., U.S. | C1 | 120 |
| Roque Bluffs, Me., U.S. | D5 | 96 |
| Roquefort, Fr. | E3 | 16 |
| Roquetas, Spain | B6 | 22 |
| Rora Head, c., Scot., U.K. | B5 | 13 |
| Roraima, terr., Braz. | A2 | 59 |
| Roraima, Mount, mtn., S.A. | A2 | 59 |
| Rorke Lake, l., Can. | B5 | 70 |
| Rorketon, Man. | D2 | 70 |
| Røros, Nor. | F4 | 14 |
| Rorschach, Switz. | E4 | 18 |
| Rosa, La., U.S. | D3 | 95 |
| Rosa, Monte, mtn., Eur. | B1 | 23 |
| Rosa, Punta, c., Mex. | B3 | 63 |
| Rosales, Phil. | o13 | 34 |
| Rosalia, Ks., U.S. | E7 | 93 |
| Rosalia, Wa., U.S. | B8 | 124 |
| Rosalie, Ne., U.S. | B9 | 104 |
| Rosalind, Alta. | C4 | 68 |
| Rosamond, Ca., U.S. | E4 | 82 |
| Rosamond, Il., U.S. | D4 | 90 |
| Rosamorada, Mex. | k11 | 63 |
| Rosario, Arg. | A4 | 54 |
| Rosário, Braz. | B2 | 57 |
| Rosario, Mex. | C3 | 63 |
| Rosario, Para. | D4 | 55 |
| Rosario, Ur. | E1 | 56 |
| Rosario, Phil. | p13 | 34 |
| Rosario, [Villa del], Ven. | A3 | 60 |
| Rosario de la Frontera, Arg. | E3 | 55 |
| Rosário do Sul, Braz. | E5 | 55 |
| Rosário Oeste, Braz. | A1 | 56 |
| Rosati, Mo., U.S. | C6 | 102 |
| Rosburg, Wa., U.S. | C2 | 124 |
| Roscoe, Il., U.S. | A5 | 90 |
| Roscoe, Mn., U.S. | E4 | 100 |
| Roscoe, Mo., U.S. | D4 | 102 |
| Roscoe, Mt., U.S. | E7 | 103 |
| Roscoe, Ne., U.S. | C4 | 104 |
| Roscoe, N.Y., U.S. | D6 | 109 |
| Roscoe, Pa., U.S. | F2 | 115 |
| Roscoe, S.D., U.S. | B6 | 118 |
| Roscoe, Tx., U.S. | C2 | 120 |
| Roscoe Glacier, ice, Ant. | C22 | 7 |
| Roscommon, Ire. | D2 | 10 |
| Roscommon, Mi., U.S. | D6 | 99 |
| Roscommon, co., Ire. | D3 | 11 |
| Roscommon, co., Mi., U.S. | D6 | 99 |
| Roscrea, Ire. | D3 | 10 |
| Rose, Ne., U.S. | B6 | 104 |
| Rose, Ok., U.S. | A6 | 113 |
| Rose, Mount, mtn., Nv., U.S. | D2 | 105 |
| Roseau, Dom. | I14 | 64 |
| Roseau, Mn., U.S. | B3 | 100 |
| Roseau, co., Mn., U.S. | B3 | 100 |
| Roseau, stm., N.A. | E3 | 70 |
| Roseau, South Fork, stm., Mn., U.S. | B3 | 100 |
| Rosebery, B.C. | D9 | 69 |
| Rose-Blanche [-Harbour le Cou], Newf. | E2 | 72 |
| Roseboro, N.C., U.S. | C4 | 110 |
| Rosebud, Alta. | D4 | 68 |
| Rose Bud, Ar., U.S. | B3 | 81 |
| Rosebud, Mo., U.S. | C6 | 102 |
| Rosebud, Mt., U.S. | D10 | 103 |
| Rosebud, S.D., U.S. | D5 | 118 |
| Rosebud, Tx., U.S. | D4 | 120 |
| Rosebud, co., Mt., U.S. | D10 | 103 |
| Rosebud, stm., Alta. | D4 | 68 |
| Rosebud Creek, stm., Mt., U.S. | E10 | 103 |
| Rosebud Indian Reservation, S.D., U.S. | D5 | 118 |
| Roseburg, Or., U.S. | D3 | 114 |
| Rosebush, Mi., U.S. | E6 | 99 |
| Rose City, Mi., U.S. | D6 | 99 |
| Rose Creek, stm., N.A. | G6 | 100 |
| Rosedale, Alta. | D4 | 68 |
| Rosedale, B.C. | f14 | 69 |
| Rosedale, In., U.S. | E3 | 91 |
| Rosedale, Md., U.S. | g11 | 97 |
| Rosedale, Ms., U.S. | B2 | 101 |
| Rosedale, Ok., U.S. | C4 | 113 |
| Rosedale, Tn., U.S. | C9 | 119 |
| Rosedale, W.V., U.S. | C4 | 125 |
| Rosedale Colony, S.D., U.S. | *D8 | 118 |
| Rose Farm, Oh., U.S. | C3 | 112 |
| Rosegin, N.D., U.S. | B4 | 111 |
| Rosehearty, Scot., U.K. | C6 | 13 |
| Rose Hill, Il., U.S. | D5 | 90 |
| Rose Hill, Ia., U.S. | C5 | 92 |
| Rose Hill, Ks., U.S. | E6 | 93 |
| Rose Hill, Ms., U.S. | C4 | 101 |
| Rose Hill, N.C., U.S. | C4 | 110 |
| Rose Hill, Va., U.S. | *B5 | 123 |
| Roseisle, Man. | E2 | 70 |
| Roseland, Ca., U.S. | *C2 | 82 |
| Roseland, Fl., U.S. | E6 | 86 |
| Roseland, In., U.S. | A5 | 91 |
| Roseland, La., U.S. | D5 | 95 |
| Roseland, Ne., U.S. | D7 | 104 |
| Roseland, N.J., U.S. | *B4 | 107 |
| Roseland, Oh., U.S. | B3 | 112 |
| Roselawn, In., U.S. | B3 | 91 |
| Roselle, Il., U.S. | k8 | 90 |
| Roselle, N.J., U.S. | k8 | 107 |
| Roselle Park, N.J., U.S. | k7 | 107 |
| Rose Lynn, Alta. | D5 | 68 |
| Rosemark, Tn., U.S. | B2 | 119 |
| Rosemary, Alta. | D5 | 68 |
| Rosemead, Ca., U.S. | *m15 | 82 |
| Rosemère, Que. | p19 | 74 |
| Rosemont, Ca., U.S. | *C3 | 82 |
| Rosemont, N.J., U.S. | C3 | 107 |
| Rosemont, W.V., U.S. | k10 | 125 |
| Rosemount, Mn., U.S. | F5 | 100 |
| Rosenberg, Tx., U.S. | E5 | 120 |
| Rosendale, Mo., U.S. | A3 | 102 |
| Rosendale, N.Y., U.S. | D6 | 109 |
| Rosendale, Wi., U.S. | E5 | 126 |
| Rosenfeld, Man. | E3 | 70 |
| Rosenhayn, N.J., U.S. | E2 | 107 |
| Rosenheim, W. Ger. | E5 | 19 |
| Rose Peak, mtn., Az., U.S. | D6 | 80 |
| Rosepine, La., U.S. | D2 | 95 |
| Rose Point, c., B.C. | B2 | 69 |
| Rose Prairie, B.C. | A7 | 69 |
| Roseto, Pa., U.S. | E11 | 115 |
| Rosetown, Sask. | F1 | 75 |
| Rosetta Branch, stm., Eg. | D2 | 41 |
| Rosetta Mouth, stm., Eg. | B3 | 41 |
| Rosetta see Rashīd, Eg. | B3 | 38 |
| Rose Valley, Sask. | E4 | 75 |
| Rosevear, Alta. | C2 | 68 |
| Roseville, Ca., U.S. | C3 | 82 |
| Roseville, Il., U.S. | C3 | 90 |
| Roseville, Mi., U.S. | o16 | 99 |
| Roseville, Mn., U.S. | m12 | 100 |
| Roseville, Oh., U.S. | C4 | 112 |
| Rosewood, Il., U.S. | E4 | 90 |
| Rosewood, Oh., U.S. | B2 | 112 |
| Rosewood Heights, Il., U.S. | *C3 | 90 |
| Rosharon, Tx., U.S. | r14 | 120 |
| Rosh Ha' Ayin, Isr. | B6 | 41 |
| Rosholt, S.D., U.S. | B9 | 118 |
| Rosholt, Wi., U.S. | D4 | 126 |
| Rosh Pinna, Isr. | B7 | 41 |
| Rosie, Ar., U.S. | B4 | 81 |
| Rosier, Ga., U.S. | D4 | 87 |
| Rosières-en-Santerre, Fr. | C5 | 16 |
| Rosignano Marittimo, Italy | C3 | 23 |
| Rosignol, Guy. | A3 | 59 |
| Roșiorii de Vede, Rom. | C7 | 24 |
| Roskilde, Den. | C6 | 15 |
| Roskilde, co., Den. | C6 | 15 |
| Roslavl, Sov. Un. | E9 | 27 |
| Roslyn, Pa., U.S. | o21 | 115 |
| Roslyn, S.D., U.S. | B8 | 118 |
| Roslyn, Wa., U.S. | B4 | 124 |
| Roslyn Heights, N.Y., U.S. | h13 | 109 |
| Rosman, N.C., U.S. | f10 | 110 |
| Ross, N.Z. | O13 | 51 |
| Ross, Mn., U.S. | B3 | 100 |
| Ross, N.D., U.S. | A3 | 111 |
| Ross, Oh., U.S. | C1 | 112 |
| Ross, co., Oh., U.S. | C2 | 112 |
| Ross, Mount, mtn., N.Z. | N15 | 51 |
| Rossa, Switz. | D7 | 21 |
| Rossano, Italy | E6 | 23 |
| Ross Barnett Reservoir, res., Ms., U.S. | C3 | 101 |
| Rossburg, Oh., U.S. | B1 | 112 |
| Rossburn, Man. | D1 | 70 |
| Ross Carbery, Ire. | F2 | 11 |
| Rosseau, Ont. | B5 | 73 |
| Rosseau, Lake, l., Ont. | B5 | 73 |
| Rossendale, Man. | E2 | 70 |
| Rosser, Tx., U.S. | n10 | 120 |
| Rosses Bay, b., Ire. | B3 | 11 |
| Rosses Point, Ire. | C3 | 11 |
| Rossford, Oh., U.S. | A2 | 112 |
| Ross Ice Shelf, ice, Ant. | A31 | 7 |
| Rossie, N.Y., U.S. | f9 | 109 |
| Rossignol, Lake, l., N.S. | E4 | 71 |
| Rossinière, Switz. | D3 | 21 |
| Ross Island, i., Ant. | B29 | 7 |
| Ross Island, i., Man. | B3 | 70 |
| Rossiter, Pa., U.S. | E4 | 115 |
| Ross Lake, res., N.A. | A4 | 124 |
| Ross Lake National Recreation Area, Wa., U.S. | A5 | 124 |
| Rossland, B.C. | E9 | 69 |
| Rosslare, Ire. | E5 | 11 |
| Rosslau, E. Ger. | B7 | 19 |
| Rosslea, N. Ire., U.K. | C4 | 11 |
| Rossmoor, Ca., U.S. | *n12 | 82 |
| Rosso, Maur. | C1 | 45 |
| Ross-on-Wye, Eng., U.K. | C5 | 12 |
| Rossosh, Sov. Un. | F12 | 27 |
| Ross River, Yukon | D6 | 66 |
| Ross Sea, Ant. | B31 | 7 |
| Rosston, Ar., U.S. | D2 | 81 |
| Rosston, Ok., U.S. | A2 | 113 |
| Ross Township, Pa., U.S. | *E1 | 115 |
| Rossville, Ga., U.S. | B1 | 87 |
| Rossville, Il., U.S. | C6 | 90 |
| Rossville, In., U.S. | D4 | 91 |
| Rossville, Ks., U.S. | C8 | 93 |
| Rossville, Ok., U.S. | B5 | 113 |
| Rossville, Tn., U.S. | B2 | 119 |
| Rossway, N.S. | E4 | 71 |
| Rosthern, Sask. | E2 | 75 |
| Rostock, E. Ger. | A6 | 18 |
| Rostov, Sov. Un. | C12 | 27 |
| Rostov-na-Donu, Sov. Un. | E6 | 29 |
| Roșul Pass, Rom. | C7 | 24 |
| Roswell, Ga., U.S. | B2 | 87 |
| Roswell, Id., U.S. | F2 | 89 |
| Roswell, N.M., U.S. | D5 | 108 |
| Roswell, S.D., U.S. | C8 | 118 |
| Rota, Spain | D2 | 22 |
| Rotan, Tx., U.S. | C2 | 120 |
| Rotenburg, W. Ger. | B4 | 18 |
| Rotenburg [an der Fulda], W. Ger. | B4 | 19 |
| Roth, W. Ger. | D6 | 19 |
| Roth, N.D., U.S. | A5 | 111 |
| Rothaar Mountains, mts., W. Ger. | C4 | 18 |
| Rothbury, Eng., U.K. | E7 | 13 |
| Rothbury, Mi., U.S. | E4 | 99 |
| Röthenbach [bei Sankt Wolfgang], W. Ger. | D6 | 19 |
| Röthenbach im Emmental, Switz. | C4 | 21 |
| Rothenburg, E. Ger. | B9 | 19 |
| Rothenburg [ob der Tauber], W. Ger. | D5 | 18 |
| Rothenthurm, Switz. | B6 | 21 |
| Rother, stm., Eng., U.K. | D6 | 12 |
| Rothera, sci., Ant. | A6 | 7 |
| Rotherham, Eng., U.K. | C6 | 12 |
| Rothes, Scot., U.K. | D5 | 13 |
| Rothesay, N.B. | D4 | 71 |
| Rothesay, Scot., U.K. | C4 | 10 |
| Rothsay, Mn., U.S. | D2 | 100 |
| Rothschild, Wi., U.S. | D4 | 126 |
| Rothville, Pa., U.S. | F9 | 115 |
| Rothville, Mo., U.S. | B4 | 102 |
| Rothwell, Eng., U.K. | D6 | 12 |
| Roto, Austl. | F5 | 51 |
| Rotondella, Italy | D6 | 23 |
| Rotondo, Monte, mtn., Fr. | m23 | 16a |
| Rotorua, N.Z. | M16 | 51 |
| Rott, stm., W. Ger. | E8 | 19 |
| Rottenburg, W. Ger. | E4 | 19 |
| Rottenmann, Aus. | E7 | 18 |
| Rotterdam, Neth. | C6 | 16 |
| Rotterdam, N.Y., U.S. | C6 | 109 |
| Rottumeroog, i., Neth. | A6 | 17 |
| Rottweil, W. Ger. | D4 | 18 |
| Roubaix, Fr. | B5 | 16 |
| Roubideau Creek, stm., Co., U.S. | C2 | 83 |
| Roudnice [nad Labem], Czech. | n17 | 26 |
| Rouen, Fr. | C4 | 16 |
| Rouge, stm., Que. | D3 | 74 |
| Rougemont, Fr. | B2 | 20 |
| Rougemont, N.C., U.S. | A3 | 110 |
| Rough, stm., Ky., U.S. | C3 | 94 |
| Rough River Lake, res., Ky., U.S. | C3 | 94 |
| Rougon, La., U.S. | D4 | 95 |
| Rouleau, Sask. | G3 | 75 |
| Roulers see Roeselare, Bel. | C2 | 16 |
| Roulette, Pa., U.S. | C5 | 115 |
| Round, stm., Newf. | E3 | 72 |
| Roundhead, Oh., U.S. | B2 | 112 |
| Round Hill, Alta. | C4 | 68 |
| Round Hill, N.S. | E4 | 71 |
| Round Island, i., Ms., U.S. | g8 | 101 |
| Round Island Passage, strt., Fiji | H14 | 52 |
| Round Lake, Mn., U.S. | G3 | 100 |
| Round Lake, N.Y., U.S. | C7 | 109 |
| Round Lake, l., Ont. | G4 | 73 |
| Round Lake, l., Ont. | B7 | 73 |
| Round Lake Beach, Il., U.S. | h8 | 90 |
| Round Mound, hill, Ks., U.S. | D4 | 93 |
| Round Mountain, Nv., U.S. | E4 | 105 |
| Round Mountain, Tx., U.S. | D3 | 120 |
| Round Mountain, mtn., Austl. | F9 | 50 |
| Round Oak, Ga., U.S. | C3 | 87 |
| Round Pond, l., Newf. | D4 | 72 |
| Round Pond, Me., U.S. | E3 | 96 |
| Round Pond, l., Newf. | D4 | 72 |
| Round Rock, Az., U.S. | A6 | 80 |
| Round Rock, Tx., U.S. | D4 | 120 |
| Round Spring, Mo., U.S. | D6 | 102 |
| Roundstone, Ire. | D2 | 11 |
| Round Top Hill, mtn., Ma., U.S. | B2 | 98 |
| Roundup, Mt., U.S. | D8 | 103 |
| Round Valley Indian Reservation, Ca., U.S. | C2 | 82 |
| Round Valley Reservoir, res., N.J., U.S. | B3 | 107 |
| Rousay, i., Scot., U.K. | A5 | 10 |
| Rouses Point, N.Y., U.S. | f11 | 109 |
| Rouseville, Pa., U.S. | D2 | 115 |
| Routon, Tn., U.S. | A3 | 119 |
| Routt, co., Co., U.S. | A3 | 83 |
| Rouville, co., Que. | D4 | 74 |
| Rouyn, Que. | k11 | 74 |
| Rouzerville, Pa., U.S. | G6 | 115 |
| Rovaniemi, Fin. | D11 | 14 |
| Rovato, Italy | B2 | 23 |
| Rovenki, Sov. Un. | G12 | 27 |
| Rovenki, Sov. Un. | G12 | 27 |
| Rover, Ar., U.S. | C2 | 81 |
| Rover, Tn., U.S. | B5 | 119 |
| Roveredo, Switz. | D7 | 21 |
| Rovereto, Italy | B3 | 23 |
| Rovigo, Italy | B3 | 23 |
| Rovinj, Yugo. | C1 | 24 |
| Rovno, Sov. Un. | D5 | 29 |
| Rovnoye, Sov. Un. | F16 | 27 |
| Row, Ok., U.S. | A7 | 113 |
| Rowan, Ia., U.S. | B4 | 92 |
| Rowan, co., Ky., U.S. | B6 | 94 |
| Rowan, co., N.C., U.S. | B2 | 110 |
| Rowan Lake, l., Ont. | E5 | 70 |
| Rowan's Ravine Provincial Park, Sask. | G3 | 75 |
| Rowe, Ma., U.S. | A2 | 98 |
| Rowe, N.M., U.S. | B4 | 108 |
| Rowena, S.D., U.S. | D9 | 118 |
| Rowena, Tx., U.S. | D2 | 120 |
| Rowesville, S.C., U.S. | E6 | 117 |
| Rowland, Ky., U.S. | C5 | 94 |
| Rowland, N.C., U.S. | C3 | 110 |
| Rowland, Pa., U.S. | D11 | 115 |
| Rowland Heights, Ca., U.S. | *n13 | 82 |
| Rowlesburg, W.V., U.S. | B5 | 125 |
| Rowlett, Tx., U.S. | *n9 | 120 |
| Rowletts, Ky., U.S. | C4 | 94 |
| Rowley, Alta. | D4 | 68 |
| Rowley, Ia., U.S. | B6 | 92 |
| Rowley, Ma., U.S. | A6 | 98 |
| Rowley Shoals, rf., Austl. | C2 | 50 |
| Roxabell, Oh., U.S. | C2 | 112 |
| Roxana, De., U.S. | G5 | 85 |
| Roxas (Capiz), Phil. | C6 | 34 |
| Roxboro, N.C., U.S. | A4 | 110 |
| Roxburgh, N.Z. | P12 | 51 |
| Roxbury, Ct., U.S. | C2 | 84 |
| Roxbury, Ks., U.S. | D6 | 93 |
| Roxbury, Me., U.S. | D2 | 96 |
| Roxbury, N.Y., U.S. | C6 | 109 |
| Roxbury, Vt., U.S. | C3 | 122 |
| Roxie, Ms., U.S. | D2 | 101 |
| Roxobel, N.C., U.S. | A5 | 110 |
| Roxton, Tx., U.S. | C5 | 120 |
| Roxton Falls, Que. | D5 | 74 |
| Roxton Pond, Que. | D5 | 74 |
| Roy, La., U.S. | B2 | 95 |
| Roy, Mt., U.S. | C8 | 103 |
| Roy, N.M., U.S. | B6 | 108 |
| Roy, Ut., U.S. | B3 | 121 |
| Roy, Wa., U.S. | C3 | 124 |
| Roya, Peña, mtn., Spain | B5 | 22 |
| Royal, Ar., U.S. | C2 | 81 |
| Royal, Ia., U.S. | A2 | 92 |
| Royal, Ne., U.S. | B7 | 104 |
| Royal, N.C., U.S. | B6 | 110 |
| Royal, Tn., U.S. | B5 | 119 |
| Royal, stm., Me., U.S. | g7 | 96 |
| Royal Canal, Ire. | C4 | 11 |
| Royal Center, In., U.S. | C4 | 91 |
| Royale, Isle, i., Mi., U.S. | h9 | 99 |
| Royal Gorge, val., Co., U.S. | C5 | 83 |
| Royal Leamington Spa, Eng., U.K. | D6 | 10 |
| Royal Oak, B.C. | h12 | 69 |
| Royal Oak, Md., U.S. | C5 | 97 |
| Royal Oak, Mi., U.S. | *F7 | 99 |
| Royal Oak, Mi., U.S. | o15 | 99 |
| Royal Pines, N.C., U.S. | f10 | 110 |
| Royalston, Ma., U.S. | A3 | 98 |
| Royalton, Il., U.S. | F4 | 90 |
| Royalton, In., U.S. | k9 | 91 |
| Royalton, Ky., U.S. | C6 | 94 |
| Royalton, Mn., U.S. | E4 | 100 |
| Royalton, Vt., U.S. | D3 | 122 |
| Royalton, Wi., U.S. | D5 | 126 |
| Royalty, Tx., U.S. | D1 | 120 |
| Royan, Fr. | D3 | 16 |
| Royersford, Pa., U.S. | F10 | 115 |
| Royerton, In., U.S. | D7 | 91 |
| Royse City, Tx., U.S. | C4 | 120 |
| Royston, B.C. | E5 | 69 |
| Royston, Ga., U.S. | B3 | 87 |
| Royston, Eng., U.K. | D6 | 10 |
| Rozel, Ks., U.S. | D4 | 93 |
| Rozet, Wy., U.S. | B7 | 127 |
| Rožňava, Czech. | F21 | 19 |
| Rtishchevo, Sov. Un. | E14 | 27 |
| Ruapehu, Mount, mtn., N.Z. | M15 | 51 |
| Rub' al Khali, des., Sau. Ar. | C5 | 38 |
| Rubiataba, Braz. | C4 | 59 |
| Rubidoux, Ca., U.S. | n14 | 82 |
| Rubim, Braz. | D8 | 59 |
| Rubonia, Fl., U.S. | p10 | 86 |
| Rubottom, Ok., U.S. | D4 | 113 |
| Rubtsovsk, Sov. Un. | C10 | 28 |
| Ruby, Ak., U.S. | C8 | 79 |
| Ruby, S.C., U.S. | B7 | 117 |
| Ruby, Va., U.S. | C3 | 105 |
| Ruby Dome, mtn., Nv., U.S. | C6 | 105 |
| Ruby Lake, l., Nv., U.S. | C6 | 105 |
| Ruby Mountains, mts., Nv., U.S. | C6 | 105 |
| Ruby Range, mts., Co., U.S. | C3 | 83 |
| Ruby Range, mts., Mt., U.S. | E4 | 103 |
| Rubys Inn, Ut., U.S. | F3 | 121 |
| Ruby Valley, Nv., U.S. | C6 | 105 |
| Ruchi, i., Marsh Is. | S18 | 52 |
| Rucker, Tn., U.S. | B5 | 119 |
| Ruda, stm., Pol. | g9 | 26 |
| Ruda Śląska, Pol. | g9 | 26 |
| Rūdbār, Afg. | B3 | 36 |
| Rudd, Ia., U.S. | A5 | 92 |
| Ruddell, Sask. | E2 | 75 |
| Ruddels Mills, Ky., U.S. | B5 | 94 |
| Rüdesheim, W. Ger. | C3 | 18 |
| Rudkøbing, Den. | D4 | 15 |
| Rudnichnyy, Sov. Un. | B4 | 28 |
| Rudnyy, Sov. Un. | *D9 | 29 |
| Rudolf, Lake, l., Afr. | A6 | 48 |
| Rudolstadt, E. Ger. | C5 | 18 |
| Rudy, Ar., U.S. | B1 | 81 |
| Rudyard, Mi., U.S. | B6 | 99 |
| Rudyard, Mt., U.S. | B6 | 103 |
| Rue, Fr. | D9 | 12 |
| Ruel, Ont. | A4 | 73 |
| Rueil-Malmaison, Fr. | g9 | 16 |
| Ruelle, Fr. | E4 | 16 |
| Rueun, Switz. | C7 | 21 |
| Rufā'ah, Sud. | E6 | 47 |
| Ruffec, Fr. | C4 | 16 |
| Ruffin, N.C., U.S. | A3 | 110 |
| Ruffin, S.C., U.S. | E6 | 117 |
| Rufiji, stm., Tan. | C6 | 48 |
| Rufino, Arg. | A4 | 54 |
| Rufisque, Sen. | D1 | 45 |
| Rufus Woods Lake, res., Wa., U.S. | B6 | 124 |
| Rugao, China | H9 | 32 |
| Rugby, Eng., U.K. | B6 | 12 |
| Rugby, N.D., U.S. | A6 | 111 |
| Rugeley, Eng., U.K. | B6 | 12 |
| Rügen, i., E. Ger. | A6 | 18 |
| Rugged Mountain, mtn., B.C. | D4 | 69 |
| Rugozero, Sov. Un. | E15 | 14 |
| Ruhengeri, Rw. | B4 | 48 |
| Ruhla, E. Ger. | C5 | 19 |
| Rühland, E. Ger. | B8 | 19 |
| Ruhr, stm., W. Ger. | C4 | 18 |
| Rui'an, China | F9 | 31 |
| Ruidosa, Tx., U.S. | p12 | 120 |
| Ruidoso, N.M., U.S. | D4 | 108 |
| Ruidoso Downs, N.M., U.S. | D4 | 108 |
| Ruijiyoru, i., Marsh Is. | S18 | 52 |
| Rujki Island, i., Marsh Is. | P18 | 52 |
| Rukoji Pass, strt., Marsh Is. | P18 | 52 |
| Rukuruku Bay, b., Fiji | H15 | 52 |
| Rukwa, prov., Tan. | C5 | 48 |
| Rukwa, Lake, l., Tan. | C5 | 48 |
| Ruleton, Ks., U.S. | C2 | 93 |
| Rule, Tx., U.S. | C3 | 120 |
| Rule Creek, stm., Co., U.S. | D7 | 83 |
| Ruleville, Ms., U.S. | B3 | 101 |
| Rulo, Ne., U.S. | D10 | 104 |
| Rum, stm., Mn., U.S. | D5 | 100 |
| Ruma, Yugo. | C4 | 24 |
| Rumbek, Sud. | D2 | 47 |
| Rumbling Bridge, Scot., U.K. | C4 | 13 |
| Rumburk, Czech. | C9 | 19 |
| Rum Cay, i., Bah. | C6 | 64 |
| Rum Creek, stm., W.V., U.S. | n12 | 125 |
| Rumely, Mi., U.S. | B3 | 99 |
| Rumford, Me., U.S. | D2 | 96 |
| Rumilly, Fr. | D1 | 20 |
| Rummah, Wādī ar, val., Sau. Ar. | C4 | 38 |
| Rummānah, Eg. | C4 | 41 |
| Rumney, N.H., U.S. | C3 | 106 |
| Rumney Depot, N.H., U.S. | C3 | 106 |
| Rumoi, Japan | E10 | 33 |
| Rumonge, Bur. | B5 | 48 |
| Rump Mountain, mtn., Me., U.S. | C1 | 96 |
| Rumsey, Alta. | D4 | 68 |
| Rumson, N.J., U.S. | C4 | 107 |
| Rumstick Point, c., R.I., U.S. | D5 | 116 |
| Runan, China | H6 | 32 |
| Runcorn, Eng., U.K. | A5 | 12 |
| Rung, i., Camb. | E4 | 120 |
| Rungwa, Tan. | C5 | 48 |
| Rungwe, Tan. | C5 | 48 |
| Runnells, Ia., U.S. | C4 | 92 |
| Runnels, co., Tx., U.S. | D2 | 120 |
| Runnemede, N.J., U.S. | D2 | 107 |
| Runtu, Nmb. | A2 | 49 |
| Ruoqiang, China | D3 | 31 |
| Ruo Shui, stm., China | C5 | 31 |
| Rupanco, Chile | E2 | 54 |
| Rupat, i., Indon. | L4 | 35 |
| Rupea, Rom. | C7 | 24 |
| Rupert, Id., U.S. | G5 | 89 |
| Rupert, Vt., U.S. | E2 | 122 |
| Rupert, W.V., U.S. | D4 | 125 |
| Rupert, Rivière de, stm., Que. | h11 | 74 |
| Rupununi, dept., Guy. | B3 | 59 |
| Rupununi, stm., Guy. | B3 | 59 |
| Rural Hall, N.C., U.S. | A2 | 110 |
| Rural Retreat, Va., U.S. | D1 | 123 |
| Rurrenabaque, Bol. | B2 | 56 |
| Rusagonis, N.B. | D3 | 71 |
| Rusape, Zimb. | A5 | 49 |
| Ruṣayriṣ, Khazzān ar, res., Afr. | C3 | 47 |
| Rush, Ire. | C5 | 11 |
| Rush, co., In., U.S. | E7 | 91 |
| Rush, co., Ks., U.S. | D4 | 93 |
| Rush, stm., Mn., U.S. | F4 | 100 |
| Rush, stm., Wi., U.S. | D1 | 126 |
| Rush Center, Ks., U.S. | D4 | 93 |
| Rush City, Mn., U.S. | E6 | 100 |
| Rush Creek, stm., Co., U.S. | C7 | 83 |
| Rush Creek, stm., Ne., U.S. | C3 | 104 |
| Rush Creek, stm., Oh., U.S. | B3 | 112 |
| Rushden, Eng., U.K. | B7 | 12 |
| Rushford, N.Y., U.S. | C2 | 109 |
| Rushford, Mn., U.S. | G7 | 100 |
| Rushmere, Va., U.S. | h14 | 123 |
| Rushmore, Mn., U.S. | G3 | 100 |
| Rush Springs, Ok., U.S. | C4 | 113 |
| Rushsylvania, Oh., U.S. | B2 | 112 |
| Rushville, Il., U.S. | C3 | 90 |
| Rushville, In., U.S. | E7 | 91 |
| Rushville, Mo., U.S. | B2 | 102 |
| Rushville, Ne., U.S. | B3 | 104 |
| Rushville, Oh., U.S. | C3 | 112 |
| Rusk, Tx., U.S. | D5 | 120 |
| Rusk, co., Tx., U.S. | C5 | 120 |
| Rusk, co., Wi., U.S. | C2 | 126 |
| Ruskin, Fl., U.S. | E4 | 86 |
| Ruskin, Ne., U.S. | D8 | 104 |
| Ruso, N.D., U.S. | B5 | 111 |
| Russas, Braz. | B3 | 57 |
| Russell, Man. | D1 | 70 |
| Russell, Ont. | B9 | 73 |
| Russell, Ar., U.S. | B4 | 81 |
| Russell, Fl., U.S. | m8 | 86 |
| Russell, Ia., U.S. | D4 | 92 |
| Russell, Ks., U.S. | D5 | 93 |
| Russell, Ky., U.S. | B7 | 94 |
| Russell, Ma., U.S. | B2 | 98 |
| Russell, Mn., U.S. | F3 | 100 |
| Russell, N.Y., U.S. | f9 | 109 |
| Russell, N.D., U.S. | A5 | 111 |
| Russell, Pa., U.S. | C3 | 115 |
| Russell, co., Ont. | B9 | 73 |
| Russell, co., Al., U.S. | C4 | 78 |
| Russell, co., Ks., U.S. | D5 | 93 |
| Russell, co., Ky., U.S. | D4 | 94 |
| Russell, co., Va., U.S. | f9 | 123 |
| Russell, Mount, mtn., Ak., U.S. | f16 | 79 |
| Russell Cave National Monument, Al., U.S. | A4 | 78 |
| Russell Fork, stm., U.S. | C7 | 94 |
| Russell Lake, l., Alta. | A3 | 68 |
| Russell Lake, l., Man. | A1 | 70 |
| Russell Springs, Ks., U.S. | D2 | 93 |
| Russell Springs, Ky., U.S. | C4 | 94 |
| Russellville, Al., U.S. | A2 | 78 |
| Russellville, Ar., U.S. | B2 | 81 |
| Russellville, Il., U.S. | E6 | 90 |
| Russellville, In., U.S. | E4 | 91 |
| Russellville, Ky., U.S. | D3 | 94 |
| Russellville, Mo., U.S. | C5 | 102 |
| Russellville, Oh., U.S. | D2 | 112 |
| Russellville, Or., U.S. | *B4 | 114 |
| Russellville, S.C., U.S. | E8 | 117 |
| Russellville, Tn., U.S. | C10 | 119 |
| Rüsselsheim, W. Ger. | D3 | 19 |
| Russia, Oh., U.S. | B1 | 112 |
| Russian Soviet Federative Socialist Republic, state, Sov. Un. | C12 | 29 |
| Russiaville, In., U.S. | D5 | 91 |
| Russum, Ms., U.S. | D2 | 101 |
| Rustad, Mn., U.S. | D2 | 100 |
| Rustavi, Sov. Un. | B15 | 40 |
| Rustburg, Va., U.S. | C3 | 123 |
| Rustenburg, S. Afr. | C4 | 49 |
| Ruston, La., U.S. | B3 | 95 |
| Ruston, Wa., U.S. | B3 | 124 |
| Ruswil, Switz. | B4 | 21 |
| Ruszów, Pol. | B10 | 19 |
| Rutana, Bdi. | B4 | 48 |
| Rute, Spain | D3 | 22 |
| Ruth, Mi., U.S. | E8 | 99 |
| Ruth, Ms., U.S. | D3 | 101 |
| Ruth, Nv., U.S. | D6 | 105 |
| Ruth, N.C., U.S. | f11 | 110 |
| Ruth, W.V., U.S. | m12 | 125 |
| Rutherford, N.J., U.S. | B4 | 107 |
| Rutherford, Tn., U.S. | A3 | 119 |
| Rutherford, co., N.C., U.S. | B1 | 110 |
| Rutherford, co., Tn., U.S. | B5 | 119 |
| Rutherfordton, N.C., U.S. | B1 | 110 |
| Rutherglen, Ont. | A5 | 73 |
| Rutherglen, Scot., U.K. | E4 | 13 |
| Rutherglen, N.M., U.S. | A3 | 108 |
| Ruthilda, Sask. | F1 | 75 |
| Ruthin, Wales, U.K. | A4 | 12 |
| Ruthton, Mn., U.S. | F2 | 100 |
| Ruthven, Ont. | F2 | 73 |
| Ruthven, Ia., U.S. | A3 | 92 |
| Rüti, Switz. | B4 | 21 |
| Rutland, B.C. | E8 | 69 |
| Rutland, Il., U.S. | C4 | 90 |
| Rutland, Ia., U.S. | B3 | 92 |
| Rutland, Ma., U.S. | B4 | 98 |
| Rutland, N.D., U.S. | C8 | 111 |
| Rutland, Oh., U.S. | C3 | 112 |
| Rutland, Vt., U.S. | D2 | 122 |
| Rutland, co., Vt., U.S. | D2 | 122 |
| Rutland Station, Sask. | E1 | 75 |
| Rutledge, Al., U.S. | D3 | 78 |
| Rutledge, Ga., U.S. | C3 | 87 |
| Rutledge, Mn., U.S. | D6 | 100 |
| Rutledge, Tn., U.S. | C10 | 119 |
| Rutshuru, Zaire | B5 | 48 |
| Rutter, Ont. | A4 | 73 |
| Ruvo [di Puglia], Italy | D6 | 23 |
| Ruvu, Tan. | C6 | 48 |
| Ruvuma, prov., Tan. | D6 | 48 |
| Ruvuma, stm., Afr. | D6 | 48 |
| Ruwenzori, mts., Afr. | A4 | 48 |
| Ruza, Sov. Un. | D11 | 27 |
| Ruzayevka, Sov. Un. | D15 | 27 |
| Ružomberok, Czech. | f16 | 26 |
| Rwanda, ctry., Afr. | B5 | 48 |
| Ryā, stm., Den. | A3 | 15 |
| Ryan, Ok., U.S. | C4 | 113 |
| Ryan Creek, stm., Al., U.S. | A3 | 78 |
| Ryan Park, Wy., U.S. | E6 | 127 |
| Ryan Peak, mtn., Id., U.S. | F4 | 89 |
| Ryazan, Sov. Un. | D12 | 27 |
| Ryazhsk, Sov. Un. | E13 | 27 |
| Rybachye, Sov. Un. | D15 | 29 |
| Rybatskoye (part of Leningrad), Sov. Un. | s31 | 14 |
| Rybinsk see Andropov, Sov. Un. | D6 | 29 |
| Rybinsk Reservoir, res., Sov. Un. | D6 | 29 |
| Rybnik, Pol. | B9 | 24 |
| Rychnov [nad Kněžnou], Czech. | B9 | 19 |
| Rycroft, Alta. | B1 | 68 |
| Ryde, Austl. | *F9 | 50 |
| Ryde, Eng., U.K. | D6 | 12 |
| Ryder, N.D., U.S. | B4 | 111 |
| Ryderwood, Wa., U.S. | C2 | 124 |
| Rye, Eng., U.K. | D6 | 12 |
| Rye, N.H., U.S. | D5 | 106 |
| Rye, N.Y., U.S. | h13 | 109 |
| Rye Beach, N.H., U.S. | D5 | 106 |
| Rye Patch Dam, Nv., U.S. | C3 | 105 |
| Ryegate, Mt., U.S. | D7 | 103 |
| Ryegate, Vt., U.S. | C4 | 122 |
| Rye Brook, N.Y., U.S. | *D7 | 109 |
| Rye Patch Reservoir, res., Nv., U.S. | C3 | 105 |
| Ryerson, Sask. | H5 | 75 |
| Rygge, Nor. | p28 | 14 |

| Name | Map Ref. | Page |
|---|---|---|
| Ryley, Alta. | C4 | 68 |
| Rylsk, Sov. Un. | F10 | 27 |
| Rynda, Sov. Un. | C17 | 14 |
| Ryomgård, Den. | B4 | 15 |
| Ryōtsu, Japan | G9 | 33 |
| Rypin, Pol. | B5 | 26 |
| Rysy, mtn., Eur. | *D6 | 26 |
| Ryukyu Islands, is., Japan | F10 | 31 |
| Rzadza, stm., Pol. | k14 | 26 |
| Rzepin, Pol. | B3 | 26 |
| Rzeszów, Pol. | C6 | 26 |
| Rzhev, Sov. Un. | C10 | 27 |

**S**

| Name | Map Ref. | Page |
|---|---|---|
| Saale, stm., Eur. | C5 | 18 |
| Saaler Bodden, b., E. Ger. | D6 | 15 |
| Saalfeld, E. Ger. | C5 | 18 |
| Saalfelden, Aus. | B8 | 20 |
| Saanen, Switz. | D3 | 21 |
| Saar, hist. reg., W. Ger. | D3 | 18 |
| Saar, stm., Eur. | E6 | 17 |
| Saarbrücken, W. Ger. | D3 | 18 |
| Saarburg, W. Ger. | E6 | 17 |
| Saaremaa, i., Sov. Un. | B4 | 27 |
| Saarland, state, W. Ger. | E6 | 17 |
| Saarlouis, W. Ger. | D3 | 18 |
| Saas-Almagell, Switz. | D4 | 21 |
| Saas-Fee, Switz. | D4 | 21 |
| Saavedra, Arg. | B4 | 54 |
| Saba, i., Neth. Ant. | H13 | 64 |
| Šabac, Yugo. | C4 | 24 |
| Sabadell, Spain | B7 | 22 |
| Sabae, Japan | n15 | 33 |
| Sabael, N.Y., U.S. | B6 | 109 |
| Sabah (North Borneo), state, Malay. | D5 | 34 |
| Sa'bah, Qārat as, Libya | D3 | 43 |
| Sabana, Archipiélago de, is., Cuba | C3 | 64 |
| Sabana de la Mar, Dom. Rep. | E9 | 64 |
| Sabanagrande, Hond. | D4 | 62 |
| Sabanalarga, Col. | A3 | 60 |
| Sabaneta, Puntan, c., N. Mar. Is. | C8 | 52 |
| Sabang, Indon. | k11 | 34 |
| Sabará, Braz. | B4 | 56 |
| Sābarmati, stm., India | D5 | 36 |
| Sabastīyah, Isr. Occ. | f11 | 41 |
| Sabattus, Me., U.S. | D2 | 96 |
| Sabattus Pond, l., Me., U.S. | D2 | 96 |
| Sabaudia, Italy | D4 | 23 |
| Sabbathday Pond, l., Me., U.S. | g7 | 96 |
| Sabetha, Ks., U.S. | C8 | 93 |
| Sabhah, Libya | D2 | 43 |
| Sabillasville, Md., U.S. | A3 | 97 |
| Sabin, Mn., U.S. | D2 | 100 |
| Sabina, Oh., U.S. | C2 | 112 |
| Sabinal, Tx., U.S. | E3 | 120 |
| Sabinas, Mex. | B4 | 63 |
| Sabinas Hidalgo, Mex. | B4 | 63 |
| Sabine, W.V., U.S. | D3 | 125 |
| Sabine, co., La., U.S. | C2 | 95 |
| Sabine, co., Tx., U.S. | D6 | 120 |
| Sabine, stm., U.S. | D6 | 120 |
| Sabine, Mount, mtn., Ant. | B29 | 7 |
| Sabine Lake, l., U.S. | E2 | 95 |
| Sabine Pass, Tx., U.S. | E6 | 120 |
| Sabine Pass, strt., U.S. | E2 | 95 |
| Sabinópolis, Braz. | B4 | 56 |
| Sabinsville, Pa., U.S. | C7 | 115 |
| Sablé, Fr. | D3 | 16 |
| Sable, Cape, c., N.S. | H19 | 63 |
| Sable, Cape, c., Fl., U.S. | G5 | 86 |
| Sable Island, i., N.S. | F10 | 71 |
| Sable River, N.S. | F4 | 71 |
| Sabon Birni, Nig. | D6 | 45 |
| Sabor, stm., Port. | B2 | 22 |
| Şabrātah, Libya | *C2 | 43 |
| Sabrina Coast, Ant. | C25 | 7 |
| Sabula, Ia., U.S. | B7 | 92 |
| Sabula, Mo., U.S. | D7 | 102 |
| Sabzevār, Iran | B5 | 38 |
| Sac, co., Ia., U.S. | B2 | 92 |
| Sac, stm., Mo., U.S. | D4 | 102 |
| Sacaba, Bol. | C2 | 55 |
| Sacajawea, Lake, res., Wa., U.S. | C7 | 124 |
| Sacajawea Peak, mtn., Or., U.S. | B9 | 114 |
| Sacandaga Lake, l., N.Y., U.S. | B6 | 109 |
| Sac and Fox Indian Reservation, Ia., U.S. | C5 | 92 |
| Sacaton, Az., U.S. | D4 | 80 |
| Sacavém, Port. | f9 | 22 |
| Sac City, Ia., U.S. | B2 | 92 |
| Săcele, Rom. | C7 | 24 |
| Sachem Head, Ct., U.S. | E5 | 84 |
| Sachigo Lake, l., Ont. | C5 | 70 |
| Sachse, Tx., U.S. | n10 | 120 |
| Sachs Harbour, N.W. Ter. | B8 | 66 |
| Sachuest Point, c., R.I., U.S. | F6 | 116 |
| Sacile, Italy | D8 | 20 |
| Sackets Harbor, N.Y., U.S. | B4 | 109 |
| Säckingen, W. Ger. | A4 | 21 |
| Sackville, N.B. | D5 | 71 |
| Saclay, Fr. | h9 | 16 |
| Saco, Ia., U.S. | D4 | 78 |
| Saco, Me., U.S. | E2 | 96 |
| Saco, Mt., U.S. | B9 | 103 |
| Saco, co., U.S. | E2 | 96 |
| Saco, East Branch, stm., N.H., U.S. | B4 | 106 |
| Sacramento, Ca., U.S. | C3 | 82 |
| Sacramento, Ky., U.S. | C2 | 94 |
| Sacramento, N.M., U.S. | E4 | 108 |
| Sacramento, co., Ca., U.S. | C3 | 82 |
| Sacramento, stm., Ca., U.S. | C3 | 82 |
| Sacramento, stm., N.M., U.S. | E4 | 108 |
| Sacramento Mountains, mts., N.M., U.S. | D4 | 108 |
| Sacramento Valley, val., Az., U.S. | B1 | 80 |
| Sacramento Valley, val., Ca., U.S. | C2 | 82 |
| Sacré-Coeur-Saguenay, Que. | A8 | 74 |
| Sacred Heart, Mn., U.S. | F3 | 100 |
| Sacrofano, Italy | g8 | 23 |
| Sacul, Tx., U.S. | D5 | 120 |
| Şa'dah, Yemen | C6 | 38 |
| Šadani, Tan. | C6 | 48 |
| Saddle (Burnt), mtn., Alta. | B1 | 68 |
| Saddle, mtn., N.J., U.S. | h8 | 107 |
| Saddleback Mountain, mtn., Az., U.S. | k8 | 80 |
| Saddleback Mountain, mtn., Me., U.S. | D2 | 96 |
| Saddleback Mountain, mtn., Me., U.S. | B4 | 96 |
| Saddle Ball Mountain, mtn., Ma., U.S. | A1 | 98 |
| Saddle Brook, N.J., U.S. | h8 | 107 |
| Saddlebunch Keys, is., Fl., U.S. | H5 | 86 |
| Saddle Mountain, mtn., Or., U.S. | B3 | 114 |
| Saddle Mountains, mts., Wa., U.S. | C5 | 124 |
| Saddle River, N.J., U.S. | A4 | 107 |
| Saddlestring, Wy., U.S. | B6 | 127 |
| Sadieville, Ky., U.S. | B5 | 94 |
| Sadiya, India | C10 | 36 |
| Sado, stm., Port. | C1 | 22 |
| Sado Island, i., Japan | D12 | 31 |
| Sadorus, Il., U.S. | D5 | 90 |
| Sadská, Czech. | n18 | 26 |
| Sæby, Den. | A4 | 15 |
| Saegertown, Pa., U.S. | C1 | 115 |
| Safājah, Bûr, well, Egypt | H9 | 41 |
| Safety Harbor, Fl., U.S. | E4 | 86 |
| Saffell, Ar., U.S. | B4 | 81 |
| Safford, Al., U.S. | C2 | 78 |
| Safford, Az., U.S. | E6 | 80 |
| Saffron Walden, Eng., U.K. | B8 | 12 |
| Safi, Mor. | C3 | 44 |
| Safīd Kūh, Selseleh-ye, mts., Afg. | D12 | 39 |
| Safonovo, Sov. Un. | D9 | 27 |
| Safranbolu, Tur. | B9 | 40 |
| Safune, W. Sam. | F11 | 52 |
| Safune Bay, b., W. Sam. | F11 | 52 |
| Saga, China | C8 | 36 |
| Sagadahoc, co., Me., U.S. | E3 | 96 |
| Sagaing, Burma | D10 | 36 |
| Sagamihara, Japan | *l9 | 33 |
| Sagami Sea, b., Japan | n18 | 33 |
| Sagamore, Ma., U.S. | C6 | 98 |
| Sagamore, Pa., U.S. | E2 | 115 |
| Sagamore Beach, Ma., U.S. | *C6 | 98 |
| Sagamore Hills, Oh., U.S. | h9 | 112 |
| Sagan, stm., Swe. | t34 | 14 |
| Saganaga Lake, l., Mn., U.S. | B7 | 100 |
| Sagar, India | D6 | 36 |
| Sagara, Japan | o17 | 33 |
| Saggart, Ire. | D5 | 11 |
| Sag Harbor, N.Y., U.S. | m16 | 109 |
| Saginaw, Al., U.S. | B3 | 78 |
| Saginaw, Mi., U.S. | E7 | 99 |
| Saginaw, Or., U.S. | D3 | 114 |
| Saginaw, Tx., U.S. | n9 | 120 |
| Saginaw, co., Mi., U.S. | E6 | 99 |
| Saginaw Bay, b., Mi., U.S. | E7 | 99 |
| Sagiz, Sov. Un. | D4 | 28 |
| Sagiz, stm., Sov. Un. | D5 | 28 |
| Sagle, Id., U.S. | A2 | 89 |
| Sagleipie, Lib. | E3 | 45 |
| Saglek Bay, b., Newf. | f9 | 72 |
| Sagola, Mi., U.S. | B2 | 99 |
| Saguache, Co., U.S. | C4 | 83 |
| Saguache, co., Co., U.S. | C4 | 83 |
| Saguache Creek, stm., Co., U.S. | C4 | 83 |
| Sagua de Tánamo, Cuba | D6 | 64 |
| Sagua la Grande, Cuba | C3 | 64 |
| Saguaro Lake, res., Az., U.S. | k10 | 80 |
| Saguaro National Monument, Az., U.S. | E5 | 80 |
| Saguaro National Monument (Tucson Mountain Section), Az., U.S. | E4 | 80 |
| Saguenay, co., Que. | A8 | 74 |
| Saguenay, stm., Que. | A7 | 74 |
| Sagunto, Spain | C5 | 22 |
| Sahāb, Jord. | C8 | 41 |
| Sahagún, Col. | B2 | 60 |
| Sahand, Kūh-e, mtn., Iran | C3 | 39 |
| Sahara, des., Afr. | D6 | 42 |
| Sahāranpur, India | C6 | 36 |
| Sāhīwal (Montgomery), Pak. | B5 | 36 |
| Sahuaripa, Mex. | B3 | 63 |
| Sahuarita, Az., U.S. | F5 | 80 |
| Sahuayo [de Díaz], Mex. | m12 | 63 |
| Said, Sov. Un. | E6 | 28 |
| Saïda, Alg. | C5 | 44 |
| Saidpur, Bngl. | C8 | 36 |
| Saigō, Japan | H6 | 33 |
| Saigon see Ho Chi Minh City, Viet. | C3 | 34 |
| Saiki, Japan | J5 | 33 |
| Sailor Springs, Il., U.S. | E5 | 90 |
| Saimaa, l., Fin. | G13 | 14 |
| Saint Abb's Head, c., Scot., U.K. | E6 | 13 |
| Saint-Adelphe, Que. | C5 | 74 |
| Saint Adolphe, Man. | E3 | 70 |
| Saint-Affrique, Fr. | F5 | 16 |
| Saint-Agapit, Que. | C6 | 74 |
| Sainte Agathe, Me., U.S. | A4 | 96 |
| Sainte-Agathe, Que. | C6 | 74 |
| Sainte-Agathe-des-Monts, Que. | C3 | 74 |
| Sainte-Agnès-de-Dundee, Que. | D3 | 74 |
| Sainte-Aimé (Massueville), Que. | D5 | 74 |
| Saint-Alban, Que. | C5 | 74 |
| Saint Alban's, Newf. | E4 | 72 |
| Saint Albans, Eng., U.K. | C6 | 12 |
| Saint Albans, Me., U.S. | D3 | 96 |
| Saint Albans, Vt., U.S. | B2 | 122 |
| Saint Albans, W.V., U.S. | C3 | 125 |
| Saint Albans Bay, Vt., U.S. | B2 | 122 |
| Saint Albert, Alta. | C4 | 68 |
| Saint-Alexandre [-de-Kamouraska], Que. | B8 | 74 |
| Saint-Alexis-des-Monts, Que. | C4 | 74 |
| Saint-Alphonse [de-Granby], Que. | D5 | 74 |
| Saint-Amand-Mont-Rond, Fr. | D5 | 16 |
| Saint-Amant, Fr. | h10 | 16 |
| Saint-Amarin, Fr. | B3 | 20 |
| Saint-Ambroise, Que. | A6 | 74 |
| Saint-Anaclet, Que. | A9 | 74 |
| Saint-André-Avellin, Que. | D2 | 74 |
| Saint-André-Est, Que. | D3 | 74 |
| Saint Andrew Bay, b., Fl., U.S. | u16 | 86 |
| Saint Andrews, Newf. | E3 | 72 |
| Saint Andrews, Scot., U.K. | B5 | 10 |
| Saint Andrews, S.C., U.S. | F7 | 117 |
| Saint Andrews, S.C., U.S. | C5 | 117 |
| Saint Andrews, Tn., U.S. | D8 | 119 |
| Saint Andrews Bay, b., Scot., U.K. | D6 | 13 |
| Saint Andrew Sound, strt., Ga., U.S. | F5 | 87 |
| Sainte-Angèle [-de-Monnoir], Que. | D4 | 74 |
| Saint-Anicet, Que. | D3 | 74 |
| Saint Ann, Mo., U.S. | *f13 | 102 |
| Saint Anna, Wi., U.S. | k9 | 126 |
| Sainte-Anne, Guad. | H14 | 64 |
| Saint Anne, Il., U.S. | B6 | 90 |
| Sainte-Anne, stm., Que. | B6 | 74 |
| Sainte-Anne, Lac, l., Alta. | C3 | 68 |
| Saint-Anselme, Que. | C7 | 74 |
| Saint Ansgar, Ia., U.S. | A5 | 92 |
| Saint Anthony, Newf. | C4 | 72 |
| Saint Anthony, Id., U.S. | F7 | 89 |
| Saint Anthony, In., U.S. | H4 | 91 |
| Saint Anthony, Mn., U.S. | *E5 | 100 |
| Saint Anthony, N.D., U.S. | C5 | 111 |
| Saint Antoine, N.B. | C5 | 71 |
| Saint-Antoine [-de-Tilly], Que. | C6 | 74 |
| Saint-Antoine [-sur-Richelieu], Que. | D4 | 74 |
| Saint-Antonin, Que. | B8 | 74 |
| Saint-Apollinaire, Que. | C6 | 74 |
| Saint-Apolline, Que. | C7 | 74 |
| Saint Arnaud, Austl. | H4 | 51 |
| Saint-Arsène, Que. | B8 | 74 |
| Saint Arthur, N.B. | B3 | 71 |
| Saint-Athanase, Que. | B8 | 74 |
| Saint-Aubert, Que. | B7 | 74 |
| Saint-Augustin, Que. | o17 | 74 |
| Saint-Augustin, stm., Can. | C2 | 72 |
| Saint Augustine, Fl., U.S. | C5 | 86 |
| Saint-Augustine-Nord-Ouest, stm., Que. | C2 | 72 |
| Saint Augustin-Saguenay, Que. | C2 | 72 |
| Saint Austell, Eng., U.K. | D3 | 12 |
| Saint-Avold, Fr. | C7 | 16 |
| Saint-Barbe, Que. | D3 | 74 |
| Saint-Barnabé-Nord, Que. | C5 | 74 |
| Saint-Barnabé-Sud, Que. | D5 | 74 |
| Saint-Barthélemy, Que. | C4 | 74 |
| Saint-Barthélemy, i., Guad. | H13 | 64 |
| Saint Basile, N.B. | B1 | 71 |
| Saint Basile [-Sud], Que. | C6 | 74 |
| Saint-Béatrix, Que. | C4 | 74 |
| Saint Bees Head, c., Eng., U.K. | C5 | 10 |
| Saint Benedict, Sask. | E3 | 75 |
| Saint Benedict, Ks., U.S. | C7 | 93 |
| Saint Benoît, Ia., U.S. | h12 | 114 |
| Saint-Benoît-Labre, Que. | C7 | 74 |
| Saint-Benoît, Que. | C6 | 74 |
| Saint Bernard, Al., U.S. | A3 | 78 |
| Saint Bernard, La., U.S. | E6 | 95 |
| Saint Bernard, Ne., U.S. | C8 | 104 |
| Saint Bernard, Oh., U.S. | o13 | 112 |
| Saint Bernard, co., La., U.S. | E6 | 95 |
| Saint Bernice, In., U.S. | E2 | 91 |
| Saint Bethlehem, Tn., U.S. | A4 | 119 |
| Saint-Blandine, Que. | A9 | 74 |
| Saint-Bonaventure, Que. | D5 | 74 |
| Saint Boswells, Sask. | G2 | 75 |
| Saint Brendan's, Newf. | D5 | 72 |
| Saint Bride, Mount, mtn., Alta. | D3 | 68 |
| Saint Bride's, Newf. | E4 | 72 |
| Saint Brides Bay, b., Wales, U.K. | E4 | 10 |
| Saint-Brieuc, Fr. | C2 | 16 |
| Saint Brieux, Sask. | E3 | 75 |
| Saint-Brigide [-d'Iberville], Que. | D4 | 74 |
| Sainte-Brigitte [-des-Saults], Que. | C5 | 74 |
| Saint-Bruno, Que. | A6 | 74 |
| Saint-Calais, Fr. | D4 | 16 |
| Saint-Calixte, Que. | D4 | 74 |
| Saint-Camille, Que. | D6 | 74 |
| Saint-Camille-d'Aumonc, Que. | C3 | 74 |
| Saint-Casimir, Que. | C5 | 74 |
| Saint Catharine, Ky., U.S. | C4 | 94 |
| Saint Catharines, Ont. | D5 | 73 |
| Sainte-Catherine, Que. | C6 | 74 |
| Saint Catherine, Lake, l., Vt., U.S. | E2 | 122 |
| Saint Catherine, Mount, mtn., Gren. | W25 | 65 |
| Saint Catherines Island, i., Ga., U.S. | E5 | 87 |
| Saint Catherine's Point, c., Eng., U.K. | D6 | 12 |
| Saint Catherines Sound, strt., Ga., U.S. | E5 | 87 |
| Sainte-Cécile [-de-Frontenac], Que. | D7 | 74 |
| Saint-Célestin (Annaville), Que. | C5 | 74 |
| Saint-Césaire, Que. | D4 | 74 |
| Saint-Chamond, Fr. | E6 | 16 |
| Saint Charles, Id., U.S. | G7 | 89 |
| Saint Charles, Il., U.S. | B5 | 90 |
| Saint Charles, Ky., U.S. | C2 | 94 |
| Saint Charles, Md., U.S. | *C4 | 97 |
| Saint Charles, Mn., U.S. | G6 | 100 |
| Saint Charles, Mo., U.S. | C7 | 102 |
| Saint Charles, S.D., U.S. | D6 | 118 |
| Saint Charles, Va., U.S. | f8 | 123 |
| Saint Charles, co., La., U.S. | E5 | 95 |
| Saint Charles, co., Mo., U.S. | C7 | 102 |
| Saint Charles, Cape, c., Newf. | *B7 | 72 |
| Saint Charles Mesa, Co., U.S. | *D6 | 83 |
| Saint-Chély-d'Apcher, Fr. | E5 | 16 |
| Saint Christopher (Saint Kitts)-Nevis, ctry., N.A. | H13 | 64 |
| Saint-Chrysostome, Que. | D4 | 74 |
| Saint Clair, Mi., U.S. | F8 | 99 |
| Saint Clair, Mn., U.S. | F5 | 100 |
| Saint Clair, Mo., U.S. | C6 | 102 |
| Saint Clair, Pa., U.S. | E9 | 115 |
| Saint Clair, co., Al., U.S. | B3 | 78 |
| Saint Clair, co., Il., U.S. | E3 | 90 |
| Saint Clair, co., Mi., U.S. | F8 | 99 |
| Saint Clair, co., Mo., U.S. | C4 | 102 |
| Saint Clair, stm., N.A. | E2 | 73 |
| Saint Clair, Lake, l., N.A. | E2 | 73 |
| Sainte-Claire, Que. | C7 | 74 |
| Saint Clair Shores, Mi., U.S. | p16 | 99 |
| Saint Clairsville, Oh., U.S. | B5 | 112 |
| Saint Claude, Man. | E2 | 70 |
| Saint-Claude, Que. | D6 | 74 |
| Saint-Claude, Fr. | D6 | 16 |
| Saint-Clément, Que. | B8 | 74 |
| Saint Clements Creek, stm., Md., U.S. | D4 | 97 |
| Saint-Clothilde, Que. | D5 | 74 |
| Saint-Cloud, Fr. | g9 | 16 |
| Saint Cloud, Fl., U.S. | D5 | 86 |
| Saint Cloud, Mn., U.S. | E4 | 100 |
| Saint Cloud, Wi., U.S. | E5 | 126 |
| Saint-Coeur-de-Marie, Que. | A6 | 74 |
| Saint-Côme, Que. | C4 | 74 |
| Saint-Constant, Que. | q19 | 74 |
| Saint Croix, N.B. | D2 | 71 |
| Sainte-Croix, Que. | C6 | 74 |
| Sainte-Croix, Switz. | C2 | 20 |
| Saint Croix, co., Wi., U.S. | C1 | 126 |
| Saint Croix, i., V.I.U.S. | H12 | 64 |
| Saint Croix, stm., N.A. | C5 | 96 |
| Saint Croix, stm., U.S. | C1 | 126 |
| Saint Croix, Lake, l., U.S. | D1 | 126 |
| Saint Croix Falls, Wi., U.S. | C1 | 126 |
| Saint Croix Stream, stm., Me., U.S. | B4 | 96 |
| Saint-Cuthbert, Que. | C4 | 74 |
| Saint-Cyrille [-de-L'Islet], Que. | B7 | 74 |
| Saint-Cyrille [-de-Wendover], Que. | D5 | 74 |
| Saint-Cyr [-sur-Loire], Fr. | D4 | 16 |
| Saint-Damase, Que. | D4 | 74 |
| Saint-Damase-des-Aulnaies, Que. | B7 | 74 |
| Saint-Damien-de-Brandon, Que. | C4 | 74 |
| Saint-Damien [-de-Buckland], Que. | C7 | 74 |
| Saint David, Az., U.S. | F5 | 80 |
| Saint David, Il., U.S. | C3 | 90 |
| Saint David, Me., U.S. | A4 | 96 |
| Saint-David-de-l'Auberivière, Que. | n17 | 74 |
| Saint-David [-d'Yamaska], Que. | D5 | 74 |
| Saint David's, Newf. | D2 | 72 |
| Saint David's, Wales, U.K. | C2 | 12 |
| Saint David's Head, c., Wales, U.K. | E4 | 10 |
| Saint David's Island, i., Ber. | o21 | 64 |
| Saint-Denis, Que. | D4 | 74 |
| Saint-Denis, Fr. | C5 | 16 |
| Saint-Denis, Reu. | H24 | 2 |
| Saint-Denis [-de-la-Bouteillerie], Que. | B8 | 74 |
| Saint-Didace, Que. | C4 | 74 |
| Saint-Dié, Fr. | C7 | 16 |
| Saint-Dizier, Fr. | C6 | 16 |
| Saint-Dominique, Que. | D5 | 74 |
| Saint-Dominique, Que. | q18 | 74 |
| Saint-Donat-de-Montcalm, Que. | C3 | 74 |
| Saint Donatus, Ia., U.S. | B7 | 92 |
| Saint-Édouard [-de-Napierville], Que. | q19 | 74 |
| Saint Edward, Ne., U.S. | C8 | 104 |
| Sainte-Edwidge, Que. | D6 | 74 |
| Saint Eleanor's, P.E.I. | C6 | 71 |
| Saint Elias, Cape, c., Ak. U.S. | D11 | 79 |
| Saint Elias Mountains, mts., N.A. | C11 | 79 |
| Sainte-Élie, Fr. Gu. | B4 | 59 |
| Sainte-Élisabeth, Que. | C4 | 74 |
| Saint Elizabeth, Mo., U.S. | C5 | 102 |
| Saint Elmo, Al., U.S. | E1 | 78 |
| Saint Elmo, Il., U.S. | D5 | 90 |
| Saint-Éloi, Que. | A8 | 74 |
| Sainte-Émélie-de-l'Énergie, Que. | C4 | 74 |
| Saint-Éphrem [-de-Tring], Que. | C7 | 74 |
| Saint-Esprit, Que. | D4 | 74 |
| Saint-Étienne, Fr. | E6 | 16 |
| Saint-Étienne [-de-Beauharnois], Que. | q19 | 74 |
| Sainte-Eulalie, Que. | C5 | 74 |
| Sainte-Euphémie, Que. | B9 | 74 |
| Sainte-Eusèbe, Que. | B8 | 74 |
| Saint-Eustache, Que. | D4 | 74 |
| Saint-Fabien, Que. | A9 | 74 |
| Sainte-Famille, Que. | C7 | 74 |
| Sainte-Famille-d'Aumonc, Que. | C3 | 74 |
| Saint-Faustin, Que. | C3 | 74 |
| Saint-Félicien, Que. | A5 | 74 |
| Saint-Félix-de-Valois, Que. | C4 | 74 |
| Saint-Ferdinand (Bernierville), Que. | C6 | 74 |
| Saint-Ferréol [-les-Neiges], Que. | B7 | 74 |
| Saint-Fidèle, Que. | B7 | 74 |
| Saint Fintan's, Newf. | D2 | 72 |
| Saint-Flavien, Que. | C6 | 74 |
| Saint-Florent, Fr. | D5 | 16 |
| Saint Florian, Al., U.S. | A2 | 78 |
| Saint-Fortunat, Que. | D6 | 74 |
| Saint Francis, Ks., U.S. | C2 | 93 |
| Saint Francis, Me., U.S. | A4 | 96 |
| Saint Francis, Mn., U.S. | E5 | 100 |
| Saint Francis, S.D., U.S. | D5 | 118 |
| Saint Francis, Wi., U.S. | n12 | 126 |
| Saint Francis, co., Ar., U.S. | B5 | 81 |
| Saint Francis, stm., N.A. | B8 | 74 |
| Saint Francis, Cape, c., Newf. | E5 | 72 |
| Saint Francisville, La., U.S. | D4 | 95 |
| Saint Francisville, Il., U.S. | E6 | 90 |
| Saint François, Guad. | Q9 | 65 |
| Saint-François, co., Mo. U.S. | D7 | 102 |
| Saint-François, Lac, l., Que. | D6 | 74 |
| Saint-Françoise, Que. | B8 | 74 |
| Saint François Mountains, hills, Mo., U.S. | D7 | 102 |
| Saint-François-Xavier [-de-Brompton], Que. | D5 | 74 |
| Saint Froid Lake, l., Me., U.S. | B4 | 96 |
| Saint-Fulgence, Que. | A7 | 74 |
| Saint Gabriel, La., U.S. | h9 | 95 |
| Saint-Gédéon, Que. | D7 | 74 |
| Saint George, Austl. | E8 | 50 |
| Saint George, Ber. | o20 | 64 |
| Saint George, N.B. | D3 | 71 |
| Saint George, Ont. | D4 | 73 |
| Saint George, Ga., U.S. | F4 | 87 |
| Saint George, Ks., U.S. | C7 | 93 |
| Saint George, Me., U.S. | D3 | 96 |
| Saint George, S.C., U.S. | E6 | 117 |
| Saint George, Ut., U.S. | F2 | 121 |
| Saint George, Cape, c., Newf. | D2 | 72 |
| Saint George, Cape, c., Fl., U.S. | C1 | 86 |
| Saint George Island, Md., U.S. | D4 | 97 |
| Saint George Island, i., Ak., U.S. | D6 | 79 |
| Saint George Island, i., Fl., U.S. | C2 | 86 |
| Saint-Georges, Bel. | D5 | 17 |
| Saint-Georges, Newf. | D2 | 72 |
| Saint-Georges, Fr. Gu. | B4 | 59 |
| Saint-Georges, De., U.S. | B3 | 85 |
| Saint Georges, Gren. | J14 | 64 |
| Saint George's Bay, b., Newf. | D2 | 72 |
| Saint George's Bay, b., N.S. | D8 | 71 |
| Saint George's Cathedral, Isr. Occ. | m14 | 41 |
| Saint George's Channel, strt., Eur. | E3 | 10 |
| Saint George's Island, i., Ber. | o20 | 64 |
| Saint-Gérard, Que. | D6 | 74 |
| Saint Germain, Wi., U.S. | C4 | 126 |
| Saint-Germain, Forêt de, Fr. | g9 | 16 |
| Saint-Germain-de-Kamouraska, Que. | B8 | 74 |
| Saint-Germain-en-Laye, Fr. | g9 | 16 |
| Saint-Gervais, Que. | C7 | 74 |
| Saint-Gervais-les-Bains, Fr. | D2 | 20 |
| Saint-Gilles (Sint-Gillis), Bel. | *D4 | 17 |
| Saint-Gilles, Que. | C6 | 74 |
| Saint-Gilles-Croix-de-Vie, Fr. | D3 | 16 |
| Saint-Gilles-du-Gard, Fr. | F6 | 16 |
| Saint-Girons, Fr. | F4 | 16 |
| Saint-Gobain, Fr. | C5 | 16 |
| Saint Gotthard Tunnel, Switz. | E4 | 18 |
| Saint Govan's Head, c., Wales, U.K. | C3 | 12 |
| Saint-Grégoire (Larochelle), Que. | C5 | 74 |
| Saint Gregor, Sask. | E3 | 75 |
| Saint Gregory, Mount, mtn., Newf. | D2 | 72 |
| Saint-Guillaume-d'Upton, Que. | D5 | 74 |
| Saint Helen, Lake, l., Mi., U.S. | D6 | 99 |
| Saint Helena, Ca., U.S. | C2 | 82 |
| Saint Helena, co., La., U.S. | D5 | 95 |
| Saint Helena, dep., Afr. | H5 | 42 |
| Saint Helena Island, i., S.C., U.S. | G6 | 117 |
| Saint Helena Sound, strt., S.C., U.S. | G7 | 117 |
| Sainte-Hélène [-de-Kamouraska], Que. | B8 | 74 |
| Saint Helens, Eng., U.K. | A5 | 12 |
| Saint Helens, Or., U.S. | B4 | 114 |
| Saint Helens, Mount, vol., Wa., U.S. | C3 | 124 |
| Saint Helier, Jersey | F5 | 10 |
| Sainte-Hénédine, Que. | C7 | 74 |
| Saint-Henri [-de-Lévis], Que. | C6 | 74 |
| Saint Henry, Oh., U.S. | B1 | 112 |
| Saint-Herménégilde, Que. | D6 | 74 |
| Saint Hilaire, Mn., U.S. | B2 | 100 |
| Saint-Hilaire-Dorset, Que. | D7 | 74 |
| Saint-Hilarion, Que. | B7 | 74 |
| Saint-Hippolyte, Fr. | B2 | 21 |
| Saint-Honoré, Que. | A7 | 74 |
| Saint-Honoré-de-Témiscouata, Que. | B8 | 74 |
| Saint-Hubert, Bel. | D5 | 17 |
| Saint-Hubert-de-Témiscouata, Que. | B8 | 74 |
| Saint-Hugues, Que. | D5 | 74 |
| Saint-Hyacinthe, Que. | D5 | 74 |
| Saint-Hyacinthe, co., Que. | D4 | 74 |
| Saint Ignace, N.B. | C5 | 71 |
| Saint Ignace, Mi., U.S. | C6 | 99 |
| Saint Ignatius, Guy. | B3 | 59 |
| Saint Ignatius, Mt., U.S. | C2 | 103 |
| Saint Inigoes, Md., U.S. | D5 | 97 |
| Saint-Irénée, Que. | B7 | 74 |
| Saint Isidore, N.B. | B4 | 71 |
| Saint-Isidore-d'Auckland, Que. | D6 | 74 |
| Saint Isidore de Prescott, Ont. | B10 | 73 |
| Saint Ives, Eng., U.K. | B7 | 12 |
| Saint Ives, Eng., U.K. | E1 | 12 |
| Saint Jacob, Il., U.S. | E4 | 90 |
| Saint Jacobs, Ont. | D4 | 73 |
| Saint-Jacques, N.B. | B1 | 71 |
| Saint-Jacques, Que. | D4 | 74 |
| Saint-Jacques-le-Mineur, Que. | q20 | 74 |
| Saint James, La., U.S. | h10 | 95 |
| Saint James, Mn., U.S. | G4 | 100 |
| Saint James, Mo., U.S. | D6 | 102 |
| Saint James, N.Y., U.S. | *n15 | 109 |
| Saint James, co., La., U.S. | h10 | 95 |
| Saint James City, Fl., U.S. | F5 | 86 |
| Saint James, Cape, c., B.C. | D2 | 69 |
| Saint-Jean, Que. | D4 | 74 |
| Saint-Jean, Lac, l., Que. | A5 | 74 |
| Saint Jean Baptiste, Man. | E3 | 70 |
| Saint-Jean-Chrysostome, Que. | o17 | 74 |
| Saint-Jean-d'Angély, Fr. | E4 | 16 |
| Saint-Jean-de-Dieu, Que. | A8 | 74 |
| Saint-Jean-de-Luz, Fr. | F2 | 16 |
| Saint-Jean-de-Matha, Que. | C4 | 74 |
| Saint-Jean-Port-Joli, Que. | B7 | 74 |
| Saint-Jérôme, Que. | D3 | 74 |
| Saint Jo, Tx., U.S. | C4 | 120 |
| Saint-Joachim, Que. | B7 | 74 |
| Saint-Joachim-de-Courval, Que. | D5 | 74 |
| Saint Joe, Ar., U.S. | A3 | 81 |
| Saint Joe, stm., Id., U.S. | B3 | 89 |
| Saint John, N.B. | D3 | 71 |
| Saint John, In., U.S. | B3 | 91 |
| Saint John, Ks., U.S. | E5 | 93 |
| Saint John, Me., U.S. | A4 | 96 |
| Saint John, N.D., U.S. | A6 | 111 |
| Saint John, Wa., U.S. | B8 | 124 |
| Saint John, co., N.B. | D3 | 71 |
| Saint John, i., V.I.U.S. | G12 | 64 |
| Saint John, stm., N.A. | G19 | 66 |
| Saint John, Cape, c., Newf. | D4 | 72 |
| Saint John, Southeast Branch, stm., N.A. | B2 | 96 |
| Saint John Bay, b., Newf. | C3 | 72 |
| Saint John Island, i., Newf. | C3 | 72 |
| Saint John's, Antig. | H14 | 64 |
| Saint John's, Newf. | E5 | 72 |
| Saint Johns, Az., U.S. | C6 | 80 |
| Saint Johns, Mi., U.S. | F6 | 99 |
| Saint Johns, Mo., U.S. | *f13 | 102 |
| Saint Johns, Oh., U.S. | B1 | 112 |
| Saint Johns, co., Fl., U.S. | C5 | 86 |
| Saint Johnsbury, Vt., U.S. | C4 | 122 |
| Saint Johnsbury Center, Vt., U.S. | C4 | 122 |
| Saint John's Point, c., Ire. | C3 | 11 |
| Saint John's Point, c., N. Ire., U.K. | C6 | 11 |
| Saint Johnsville, N.Y., U.S. | B6 | 109 |
| Saint John the Baptist, co., La., U.S. | D5 | 95 |
| Saint Jones, stm., De., U.S. | D4 | 85 |
| Saint Joseph, N.B. | D5 | 71 |
| Saint Joseph, Dom. | I14 | 64 |
| Saint Joseph, Il., U.S. | C5 | 90 |
| Saint Joseph, La., U.S. | C4 | 95 |
| Saint Joseph, Mi., U.S. | F4 | 99 |
| Saint Joseph, Mn., U.S. | E4 | 100 |
| Saint Joseph, Mo., U.S. | B3 | 102 |
| Saint Joseph, Tn., U.S. | B4 | 119 |
| Saint Joseph, co., In., U.S. | A5 | 91 |
| Saint Joseph, co., Mi., U.S. | G5 | 99 |
| Saint Joseph, Lac, l., Ont. | o17 | 73 |
| Saint Joseph, Lake, l., Ont. | o17 | 73 |
| Saint Joseph Bay, b., Fl., U.S. | C1 | 86 |
| Saint-Joseph-de-Beauce, Que. | C7 | 74 |
| Saint-Joseph-de-la-Rive, Que. | B7 | 74 |
| Saint-Joseph-du-Lac, Que. | p18 | 74 |
| Saint Joseph Point, c., Fl., U.S. | v16 | 86 |
| Saint Joseph Sound, strt., Fl., U.S. | o10 | 86 |
| Saint-Jovite, Que. | C3 | 74 |
| Saint-Julien [-en-Genevois], Fr. | D1 | 21 |
| Sainte-Julienne, Que. | D4 | 74 |
| Sainte-Julie-Station, Que. | C6 | 74 |
| Saint Just, Eng., U.K. | D2 | 12 |
| Saint-Just-en-Chaussée, Fr. | E2 | 17 |
| Sainte-Justine, Que. | C7 | 74 |
| Sainte-Justine [-de-Newton], Que. | D3 | 74 |
| Saint-Lambert [-de-Lévis], Que. | C6 | 74 |
| Saint Landry, La., U.S. | D3 | 95 |
| Saint Landry, co., La., U.S. | D3 | 95 |
| Saint-Laurent, Man. | D3 | 70 |
| Saint-Laurent, Que. | p19 | 74 |
| Saint-Laurent-Blangy, Fr. | D2 | 17 |
| Saint-Laurent-de-la-Salanque, Fr. | F5 | 16 |
| Saint-Laurent [-du-Maroni], Fr. Gu. | A4 | 59 |
| Saint Laurent [du Maroni], ter., Fr. Gu. | B4 | 59 |
| Saint-Laurent-en-Grandvaux, Fr. | C1 | 20 |
| Saint Lawrence, Austl. | D8 | 50 |
| Saint Lawrence, Newf. | E4 | 72 |
| Saint Lawrence, S.D., U.S. | C7 | 118 |
| Saint Lawrence, co., N.Y., U.S. | A5 | 109 |
| Saint Lawrence, stm., N.A. | G19 | 66 |
| Saint Lawrence, Cape, c., N.S. | B9 | 71 |
| Saint Lawrence, Gulf of, b., Can. | G20 | 66 |
| Saint Lawrence Island, i., Ak., U.S. | C5 | 79 |
| Saint Lawrence Islands National Park, Ont. | C9 | 73 |
| Saint Lazare, Man. | D1 | 70 |
| Saint Lazare, Que. | q18 | 74 |
| Saint Leo, Fl., U.S. | D4 | 86 |
| Saint-Léon, Que. | C5 | 74 |
| Saint-Léonard, N.B. | B2 | 71 |
| Saint Leonard, Md., U.S. | C4 | 97 |
| Saint-Léonard [-d'Aston], Que. | C5 | 74 |
| Saint-Léonard-de-Portneuf, Que. | C6 | 74 |
| Saint Lewis, Newf. | B3 | 72 |
| Saint Lewis Sound, strt., Newf. | B4 | 72 |
| Saint-Liboire, Que. | D5 | 74 |
| Saint-Lô, Fr. | C3 | 16 |
| Saint Louis, P.E.I. | C5 | 71 |
| Saint Louis, Sask. | E3 | 75 |
| Saint-Louis, Guad. | R9 | 65 |
| Saint-Louis, Sen. | C1 | 45 |
| Saint Louis, Mi., U.S. | E6 | 99 |
| Saint Louis, Mo., U.S. | C7 | 102 |
| Saint Louis, Ok., U.S. | B5 | 113 |
| Saint Louis, co., Mn., U.S. | C6 | 100 |
| Saint Louis, co., Mo., U.S. | C7 | 102 |
| Saint Louis, stm., U.S. | D6 | 100 |
| Saint Louis Bay, b., Ms., U.S. | f7 | 101 |
| Saint Louis Crossing, In., U.S. | F6 | 91 |
| Saint-Louis-de-Bonsecours, Que. | D5 | 74 |
| Saint-Louis-de-Gonzague, Que. | D3 | 74 |
| Saint-Louis-de-Kent, N.B. | C5 | 71 |
| Saint-Louis-du-Ha! Ha!, Que. | B8 | 74 |
| Sainte-Louise, Que. | B7 | 74 |
| Saint Louis Park, Mn., U.S. | n12 | 100 |
| Saint Louisville, Oh., U.S. | B3 | 112 |
| Saint-Loup-sur-Semouse, Fr. | B2 | 20 |
| Saint-Luc, Que. | D4 | 74 |
| Saint-Luc, Switz. | D3 | 21 |
| Saint Lucas, Ia., U.S. | A6 | 92 |
| Saint Lucia, ctry., N.A. | J14 | 64 |
| Saint Lucia, Cape, c., S. Afr. | C5 | 49 |
| Saint Lucia Channel, strt., N.A. | I14 | 64 |
| Saint Lucie, Fl., U.S. | E6 | 86 |
| Saint Lucie, co., Fl., U.S. | E6 | 86 |
| Saint Lucie Canal, Fl., U.S. | F6 | 86 |
| Saint-Lucie-de-Beauregard, Que. | C7 | 74 |
| Saint Lucie Inlet, b., Fl., U.S. | E6 | 86 |

| Name | Map Ref. | Page |
|---|---|---|
| Saint-Ludger, Que. | D7 | 74 |
| Sainte-Madeleine, Que. | D4 | 74 |
| Sainte-Magloire, Que. | C7 | 74 |
| Saint Magnus Bay, b., Scot., U.K. | g10 | 10 |
| Saint-Maixent-l'École, Fr. | D3 | 16 |
| Sainte-Malachie, Que. | C7 | 74 |
| Saint Malo, Man. | E3 | 70 |
| Saint-Malo, Fr. | C2 | 16 |
| Saint Malo, Gulf of, b., Fr. | C2 | 16 |
| Saint-Mandé, Fr. | g10 | 16 |
| Saint-Marc, Que. | D4 | 74 |
| Saint-Marc, Haiti | E7 | 64 |
| Saint-Marc [-des-Carrières], Que. | C5 | 74 |
| Saint-Marcel-de-L'Islet, Que. | C7 | 74 |
| Saint-Marcellin, Fr. | E6 | 16 |
| Saint Margaret Bay, b., Newf. | C3 | 72 |
| Saint Margaret's Hope, Scot., U.K. | B6 | 13 |
| Sainte-Marguerite, stm., Que. | h8 | 72 |
| Sainte-Marguerite, stm., Que. | A7 | 74 |
| Sainte-Marguerite-de-Dorchester, Que. | C7 | 74 |
| Sainte-Marguerite Nord-Est, stm., Que. | A7 | 74 |
| Sainte-Marie, Que. | C5 | 74 |
| Sainte-Marie, Que. | C6 | 74 |
| Sainte-Marie, Mart. | S11 | 65 |
| Sainte Marie, Il., U.S. | E5 | 90 |
| Sainte-Marie, Cap, c., Madag. | i8 | 49 |
| Sainte-Marie-aux-Mines, Fr. | A3 | 20 |
| Sainte Maries, Id., U.S. | B2 | 89 |
| Sainte Marie-sur-Mer, N.B. | B5 | 71 |
| Saint Mark, Ks., U.S. | g11 | 93 |
| Saint Marks, Fl., U.S. | B2 | 86 |
| Sainte-Marthe, Que. | D3 | 74 |
| Saint-Martin, Fr. | D3 | 16 |
| Saint Martin, co., La., U.S. | D4 | 95 |
| Saint Martin, i., N.A. | G13 | 64 |
| Saint Martin, stm., Md., U.S. | D7 | 97 |
| Saint Martin, Lake, l., Man. | D2 | 70 |
| Saint-Martin-Boulogne, Fr. | D9 | 12 |
| Sainte-Martine, Que. | D4 | 74 |
| Saint Martin Island, i., Mi., U.S. | C4 | 99 |
| Saint Martins, N.B. | D4 | 71 |
| Saint Martin Station, Man. | D2 | 70 |
| Saint Martinville, La., U.S. | D4 | 95 |
| Saint-Martory, Fr. | F4 | 16 |
| Saint Mary, Ky., U.S. | C4 | 94 |
| Saint Mary, Mo., U.S. | D8 | 102 |
| Saint Mary, co., La., U.S. | E4 | 95 |
| Saint Mary, stm., B.C. | E2 | 68 |
| Saint Mary, stm., N.A. | E4 | 68 |
| Saint Mary-of-the-Woods, In., U.S. | E3 | 91 |
| Saint Mary Peak, mtn., Austl. | F6 | 50 |
| Saint Mary Reservoir, res., Alta. | E4 | 68 |
| Saint Mary's, Newf. | E5 | 72 |
| Saint Mary's, Ont. | D3 | 73 |
| Saint Marys, Ak., U.S. | C7 | 79 |
| Saint Marys, Ga., U.S. | F5 | 87 |
| Saint Marys, In., U.S. | A5 | 91 |
| Saint Marys, Ks., U.S. | C7 | 93 |
| Saint Marys, Oh., U.S. | B1 | 112 |
| Saint Marys, Pa., U.S. | D4 | 115 |
| Saint Marys, W.V., U.S. | B3 | 125 |
| Saint Marys, co., Md., U.S. | D4 | 97 |
| Saint Marys, stm., N.S. | D8 | 71 |
| Saint Marys, stm., U.S. | F5 | 87 |
| Saint Marys, stm., U.S. | C8 | 91 |
| Saint Marys, stm., Md., U.S. | D5 | 97 |
| Saint Mary's, Cape, c., Newf. | E4 | 72 |
| Saint Marys, Cape, c., N.S. | E3 | 71 |
| Saint Mary's Bay, b., Newf. | E5 | 72 |
| Saint Marys Bay, b., N.S. | E3 | 71 |
| Saint Marys City, Md., U.S. | D5 | 97 |
| Saint Marys Entrance, strt., Ga., U.S. | F5 | 87 |
| Saint-Mathieu, Que. | q19 | 74 |
| Saint-Mathieu, Que. | A9 | 74 |
| Saint Matthew Island, i., Ak., U.S. | C5 | 79 |
| Saint Matthews, Ky., U.S. | B4 | 94 |
| Saint Matthews, S.C., U.S. | D6 | 117 |
| Saint-Maur-des-Fossés, Fr. | g10 | 16 |
| Saint-Maurice, Que. | C5 | 74 |
| Saint-Maurice, Switz. | C3 | 20 |
| Saint-Maurice, La., U.S. | C3 | 95 |
| Saint-Maurice, co., Que. | C4 | 74 |
| Saint-Maurice, stm., Que. | C5 | 74 |
| Saint Meinrad, In., U.S. | H4 | 91 |
| Sainte-Mélanie, Que. | C4 | 74 |
| Saint-Memmie, Fr. | F4 | 17 |
| Sainte-Menehould, Fr. | C6 | 16 |
| Saint-Méthode [-de-Frontenac], Que. | C6 | 74 |
| Saint Michael, Alta. | C4 | 68 |
| Saint Michael, Ak., U.S. | C7 | 79 |
| Saint Michael, Mn., U.S. | E5 | 100 |
| Saint Michael, N.D., U.S. | B7 | 111 |
| Saint Michaels, Az., U.S. | B6 | 80 |
| Saint Michaels, Md., U.S. | C5 | 97 |
| Saint Michaels Bay, b., Newf. | B4 | 72 |
| Saint-Michel, Fr. | E4 | 17 |
| Saint-Michel, Fr. | D2 | 20 |
| Saint-Michel [-de-Bellechasse], Que. | C7 | 74 |
| Saint-Michel-de-Napierville, Que. | q19 | 74 |
| Saint-Michel-des-Saints, Que. | C4 | 74 |
| Saint-Mihiel, Fr. | C6 | 16 |
| Saint-Modeste, Que. | B8 | 74 |
| Sainte-Monique [-de-Nicolet], Que. | C5 | 74 |
| Saint-Nazaire, Que. | D5 | 74 |
| Saint-Nazaire, Fr. | D2 | 16 |
| Saint-Nazaire [-de-Buckland], Que. | C7 | 74 |
| Saint-Nazaire-de-Chicoutimi, Que. | A6 | 74 |
| Saint Nazianz, Wi., U.S. | D6 | 126 |
| Saint Neots, Eng., U.K. | B7 | 12 |
| Sainte-Nérée, Que. | C7 | 74 |
| Saint-Nicolas, Que. | o17 | 74 |
| Saint-Nicolas-de-Port, Fr. | F6 | 17 |
| Saint-Nicolas see Sint-Niklaas, Bel. | B6 | 16 |
| Saint-Odilon, Que. | C7 | 74 |
| Saint Olaf, Ia., U.S. | B6 | 92 |
| Saint-Omer, Fr. | B5 | 16 |
| Saint Onge, S.D., U.S. | C2 | 118 |
| Saintonge, hist. reg., Fr. | E3 | 16 |
| Saint-Ouen, Fr. | g10 | 16 |
| Saint-Ours, Que. | D4 | 74 |
| Saint-Pacôme, Que. | B8 | 74 |
| Saint-Pamphile, Que. | C8 | 74 |
| Saint Paris, Oh., U.S. | B2 | 112 |
| Saint-Pascal, Que. | B8 | 74 |
| Saint Patrice, Lac, l., Que. | A7 | 73 |
| Saint Paul, Alta. | B5 | 68 |
| Saint Paul, Ak., U.S. | D5 | 79 |
| Saint Paul, Ar., U.S. | B2 | 81 |
| Saint Paul, In., U.S. | F6 | 91 |
| Saint Paul, Ks., U.S. | E8 | 93 |
| Saint Paul, Mn., U.S. | F5 | 100 |
| Saint Paul, Mo., U.S. | f12 | 102 |
| Saint Paul, Ne., U.S. | C7 | 104 |
| Saint Paul, Or., U.S. | h12 | 114 |
| Saint Paul, S.C., U.S. | D7 | 117 |
| Saint Paul, Va., U.S. | f9 | 123 |
| Saint-Paul, stm., Can. | C3 | 72 |
| Saint-Paul, stm., Lib. | E2 | 45 |
| Saint-Paul, Île, i., F.S.A.T. | I2 | 2 |
| Saint-Paul-de-Chester, Que. | D6 | 74 |
| Saint-Paul-de-la-Croix, Que. | B8 | 74 |
| Saint-Paul-de-Montminy, Que. | C7 | 74 |
| Saint-Paul-du-Nord, Que. | A8 | 74 |
| Saint Pauls, N.C., U.S. | C4 | 110 |
| Saint Paul Island, i., N.S. | B9 | 71 |
| Saint Paul Island, i., Ak., U.S. | D5 | 79 |
| Saint Paul Park, Mn., U.S. | n12 | 100 |
| Sainte-Perpétue-de-L'Islet, Que. | B8 | 74 |
| Saint Peter, Il., U.S. | E5 | 90 |
| Saint Peter, Ks., U.S. | C3 | 93 |
| Saint Peter, Mn., U.S. | F5 | 100 |
| Saint Peter Port, Guernsey | F5 | 10 |
| Saint Peters, N.S. | D9 | 71 |
| Saint Peters, In., U.S. | F7 | 91 |
| Saint Peters, Mo., U.S. | C7 | 102 |
| Saint Peters Bay, P.E.I. | C7 | 71 |
| Saint Petersburg, Fl., U.S. | E4 | 86 |
| Saint Petersburg, Pa., U.S. | D2 | 115 |
| Saint Petersburg Beach, Fl., U.S. | p10 | 86 |
| Saint-Philémon, Que. | C7 | 74 |
| Saint Philip, In., U.S. | I2 | 91 |
| Saint-Philippe [-de-Laprairie], Que. | D4 | 74 |
| Saint-Philippe-de-Néri, Que. | B8 | 74 |
| Saint Phillips Island, i., S.C. | G6 | 117 |
| Saint-Pie, Que. | D5 | 74 |
| Saint-Pierre, Mart. | I14 | 64 |
| Saint-Pierre, i., St. P./M. | E3 | 72 |
| Saint-Pierre, St. P./M. | E3 | 72 |
| Saint-Pierre, Lac, l., Que. | C5 | 74 |
| Saint Pierre and Miquelon, dep., N.A. | E5 | 72 |
| Saint-Pierre-d'Albigny, Fr. | D2 | 20 |
| Saint-Pierre-en-Port, Fr. | E8 | 12 |
| Saint-Pierre-Jolys, Man. | E3 | 70 |
| Saint-Pierre-Montmagny, Que. | C7 | 74 |
| Saint-Placide, Que. | p18 | 74 |
| Saint-Pol-de-Léon, Fr. | C2 | 16 |
| Saint-Pol-sur-Mer, Fr. | C2 | 17 |
| Saint-Pol [-sur-Ternoise], Fr. | B5 | 16 |
| Saint-Pourçain, Fr. | D5 | 16 |
| Saint-Prime, Que. | A5 | 74 |
| Saint-Prosper, Que. | C5 | 74 |
| Saint-Prosper-de-Dorchester, Que. | C7 | 74 |
| Saint Quentin, N.B. | B2 | 71 |
| Saint-Quentin, Fr. | C5 | 16 |
| Saint-Raphaël, Fr. | F7 | 16 |
| Saint-Raphaël, Fr. | F7 | 16 |
| Saint-Raphaël-sur-Mer, N.B. | B5 | 71 |
| Saint-Raymond, Que. | C6 | 74 |
| Saint-Rédempteur, Que. | o17 | 74 |
| Saint Regis, Mt., U.S. | C1 | 103 |
| Saint Regis, stm., N.Y., U.S. | f10 | 109 |
| Saint Regis, West Branch, stm., N.Y., U.S. | f10 | 109 |
| Saint Regis Falls, N.Y., U.S. | f10 | 109 |
| Saint-Rémi-d'Amherst, Que. | C3 | 74 |
| Saint-Rémi [-de-Tingwick], Que. | D6 | 74 |
| Saint-Roch [-de-Richelieu], Que. | D4 | 74 |
| Saint-Roch-des-Aulnaies, Que. | B7 | 74 |
| Sainte-Rose, Guad. | H14 | 64 |
| Sainte Rose, La., U.S. | k11 | 95 |
| Sainte Rose du Lac, Man. | D2 | 70 |
| Saintes, Fr. | E3 | 16 |
| Saintes, Île des, is., Guad. | R8 | 65 |
| Sainte-Sabine-de-Bellechasse, Que. | C7 | 74 |
| Saint Samuel, Que. | D7 | 74 |
| Saint Sanford, Man. | E3 | 70 |
| Saint Sauveur, N.B. | B4 | 71 |
| Saint-Sauveur-des-Monts, Que. | D3 | 74 |
| Sainte-Savine, Fr. | C6 | 16 |
| Saint-Sébastien, Que. | D7 | 74 |
| Saint-Sébastien, Cap, c., Madag. | f9 | 49 |
| Saint-Sébastien [-sur-Loire], Fr. | D4 | 16 |
| Saint-Sever, Fr. | F3 | 16 |
| Saint-Séverin-de-Beauce, Que. | C6 | 74 |
| Saint Shotts, Newf. | E5 | 72 |
| Saint-Siméon, Que. | B8 | 74 |
| Saint-Simon-de-Rimouski, Que. | A8 | 74 |
| Saint Simons Island, Ga., U.S. | E5 | 87 |
| Saint Simons Island, i., Ga., U.S. | E5 | 87 |
| Saint Simons Sound, strt., Ga., U.S. | E5 | 87 |
| Sainte-Sixte, Que. | D2 | 74 |
| Sainte-Sophie [-de-Lévrard], Que. | C5 | 74 |
| Sainte-Sophie [-de-Mégantic], Que. | C6 | 74 |
| Saint Stephen, N.B. | D2 | 71 |
| Saint Stephen, S.C., U.S. | E8 | 117 |
| Saint Stephens, Al., U.S. | D1 | 78 |
| Saint Stephens, N.C., U.S. | *B1 | 110 |
| Saint Stephen's Church, Isr. Occ. | m14 | 41 |
| Saint Stephen's Gate, hist., Isr. Occ. | m14 | 41 |
| Saint-Sylvère, Que. | C5 | 74 |
| Saint-Sylvestre, Que. | C6 | 74 |
| Saint Tammany, co., La., U.S. | D5 | 95 |
| Saint-Théodore, Que. | C4 | 74 |
| Saint-Théophile, Que. | C7 | 74 |
| Sainte-Thérèse, Que. | D4 | 74 |
| Saint Thomas, Ont. | E3 | 73 |
| Saint Thomas, Mo., U.S. | C5 | 102 |
| Saint Thomas, N.D., U.S. | A8 | 111 |
| Saint Thomas, Pa., U.S. | G6 | 115 |
| Saint Thomas, i., V.I.U.S. | G12 | 64 |
| Saint-Thomas [-de-Joliette], Que. | C4 | 74 |
| Saint-Timothée, Que. | q18 | 74 |
| Sainte-Tite, Que. | C5 | 74 |
| Sainte-Tite-des-Caps, Que. | B7 | 74 |
| Saint-Tropez, Fr. | F7 | 16 |
| Sainte-Ubalde, Que. | C5 | 74 |
| Saint-Urbain-de-Charlevoix, Que. | B7 | 74 |
| Saint-Urbain [-de-Châteauguay], Que. | q19 | 74 |
| Saint-Valère, Que. | C5 | 74 |
| Saint-Valérien, Que. | D5 | 74 |
| Saint-Valéry-en-Caux, Fr. | E8 | 12 |
| Saint-Valéry-sur-Somme, Fr. | B4 | 16 |
| Saint-Vallier, Que. | C7 | 74 |
| Saint-Vallier, Fr. | E6 | 16 |
| Saint-Victor, Que. | C7 | 74 |
| Sainte-Véronique, Que. | C3 | 74 |
| Saint Vincent, Mn., U.S. | B1 | 100 |
| Saint Vincent, i., St. Vin. | U26 | 65 |
| Saint-Vincent, Cap, c., Madag. | h8 | 49 |
| Saint Vincent, Gulf, b., Austl. | G6 | 50 |
| Saint Vincent and the Grenadines, ctry., N.A. | J14 | 64 |
| Saint Vincent Island, i., Fl., U.S. | C1 | 86 |
| Saint Vincent Passage, strt., N.A. | J14 | 64 |
| Saint Vincent's [-Saint Stephens-Peter's River], Newf. | E5 | 72 |
| Saint-Vith, Bel. | D6 | 17 |
| Saint Vrain, N.M., U.S. | C6 | 108 |
| Saint Walburg, Sask. | D1 | 75 |
| Saint Wendells, In., U.S. | H2 | 91 |
| Saint Williams, Ont. | E4 | 73 |
| Saint Xavier, Mt., U.S. | E9 | 103 |
| Saint-Yrieix-la-Perche, Fr. | E4 | 16 |
| Saint-Zacharie, Que. | C7 | 74 |
| Saint-Zéphirin, Que. | C5 | 74 |
| Saipan, i., N. Mar. Is. | E8 | 6 |
| Saipan Channel, strt., N. Mar. Is. | D7 | 52 |
| Saipan International Airport, N. Mar. Is. | D7 | 52 |
| Sairecábur, Cerro, mtn., S.A. | D2 | 55 |
| Sai Yok, Thai. | F5 | 35 |
| Sajama, Nevado, mtn., Bol. | C2 | 55 |
| Saka, Kenya | B6 | 48 |
| Sa Kaeo, Thai. | F5 | 35 |
| Sakai, Japan | o14 | 33 |
| Sakākah, Sau. Ar. | C4 | 38 |
| Sakakawea, Lake, res., N.D., U.S. | B3 | 111 |
| Sakami, Lac, l., Que. | F17 | 66 |
| Sakania, Zaire | D4 | 48 |
| Sakaraha, Madag. | h8 | 49 |
| Sakarya, stm., Tur. | B4 | 40 |
| Sakashita, Japan | n16 | 33 |
| Sakata, Japan | D12 | 31 |
| Sakchu, N. Kor. | F2 | 33 |
| Sakhalin, i., Sov. Un. | D17 | 29 |
| Šakiai, Sov. Un. | A7 | 26 |
| Sakishima Islands, is., Japan | G9 | 31 |
| Sakmara, stm., Sov. Un. | C5 | 28 |
| Sakon Nakhon, Thai. | B2 | 34 |
| Sakonnet, stm., R.I., U.S. | E6 | 116 |
| Sakonnet Point, c., R.I., U.S. | F6 | 116 |
| Saksköbing, Den. | D5 | 15 |
| Sakti, India | D7 | 36 |
| Sal, stm., Sov. Un. | H14 | 27 |
| Sal, Point, c., Ca., U.S. | E3 | 82 |
| Saladas, Arg. | B5 | 54 |
| Saladillo, Arg. | B5 | 54 |
| Saladino, Italy | D5 | 23 |
| Salado, stm., Arg. | B4 | 54 |
| Salado, stm., Arg. | B3 | 54 |
| Salado, stm., Arg. | F3 | 55 |
| Salado, stm., Mex. | B4 | 63 |
| Salado, Arroyo, stm., Arg. | C2 | 55 |
| Salado, Rio, stm., N.M., U.S. | C2 | 108 |
| Salaga, Ghana | E4 | 45 |
| Sala'ilua, W. Sam. | F11 | 52 |
| Sala'ilua Bay, b., W. Sam. | F11 | 52 |
| Şalālah, Oman | D5 | 38 |
| Salamá, Guat. | C2 | 62 |
| Salamá, Hond. | E7 | 63 |
| Salamanca, Chile | A2 | 54 |
| Salamanca, Mex. | m13 | 63 |
| Salamanca, Spain | B3 | 22 |
| Salamanca, N.Y., U.S. | C2 | 109 |
| Salamat, Bahr, stm., Chad | C3 | 46 |
| Salamaua, Pap. N. Gui. | k12 | 50 |
| Salamina, Col. | D4 | 25 |
| Salamís, Grc. | h10 | 25 |
| Salamis, i., Grc. | h10 | 25 |
| Salamonia, Indon. | D8 | 91 |
| Salamonie, stm., In., U.S. | C6 | 91 |
| Salamonie Lake, res., In., U.S. | C6 | 91 |
| Salani, W. Sam. | G12 | 52 |
| Salar de Pocitos, Arg. | D2 | 55 |
| Salas, Spain | A2 | 22 |
| Salatiga, Indon. | *G4 | 34 |
| Salavat, Sov. Un. | C5 | 28 |
| Salaverry, Peru | C2 | 58 |
| Salavina, Arg. | B3 | 54 |
| Salawati, i., Indon. | F8 | 34 |
| Sala y Gómez, Isla, i., Chile | H15 | 6 |
| Salbris, Fr. | D5 | 16 |
| Salcantay, Nevado, mtn., Peru | D3 | 58 |
| Salcedo, Ec. | B2 | 58 |
| Saldanha, S. Afr. | D2 | 49 |
| Saldus, Sov. Un. | C4 | 27 |
| Sale, Austl. | I6 | 51 |
| Sale City, Ga., U.S. | E2 | 87 |
| Sale Creek, Tn., U.S. | D8 | 119 |
| Salée, Rivière, strt., Guad. | Q8 | 65 |
| Salekhard, Sov. Un. | C9 | 29 |
| Salem, India | F6 | 36 |
| Salem, Al., U.S. | C4 | 78 |
| Salem, Ar., U.S. | A4 | 81 |
| Salem, Ct., U.S. | D7 | 84 |
| Salem, Il., U.S. | E5 | 90 |
| Salem, In., U.S. | G5 | 91 |
| Salem, Ia., U.S. | D6 | 92 |
| Salem, Ky., U.S. | e9 | 94 |
| Salem, Ma., U.S. | A6 | 98 |
| Salem, Mi., U.S. | p14 | 99 |
| Salem, Mo., U.S. | D6 | 102 |
| Salem, N.H., U.S. | E4 | 106 |
| Salem, N.J., U.S. | D2 | 107 |
| Salem, N.Y., U.S. | B7 | 109 |
| Salem, Oh., U.S. | B5 | 112 |
| Salem, Or., U.S. | C4 | 114 |
| Salem, S.C., U.S. | B2 | 117 |
| Salem, S.D., U.S. | D8 | 118 |
| Salem, Va., U.S. | C2 | 123 |
| Salem, W.V., U.S. | B4 | 125 |
| Salem, Wi., U.S. | n11 | 126 |
| Salem, co., N.J., U.S. | D2 | 107 |
| Salem, stm., N.J., U.S. | D2 | 107 |
| Salem, Lake, l., Vt., U.S. | B4 | 122 |
| Salemburg, N.C., U.S. | B4 | 110 |
| Salemi, Italy | F4 | 23 |
| Salen, Scot., U.K. | D3 | 13 |
| Salen, Scot., U.K. | D3 | 13 |
| Salerno, Italy | D5 | 23 |
| Salerno, Gulf of, b., Italy | D5 | 23 |
| Salfit, Isr. Occ. | B7 | 41 |
| Salford, Eng., U.K. | D5 | 10 |
| Salgótarján, Hung. | A4 | 24 |
| Salgueiro, Braz. | C3 | 57 |
| Salida, Co., U.S. | C5 | 83 |
| Salies-de-Béarn, Fr. | F3 | 16 |
| Salihli, Tur. | C7 | 25 |
| Salima, Mwi. | D5 | 48 |
| Ṣalīmah, Wāḥat, well, Sud. | A2 | 47 |
| Salin, Burma | B1 | 35 |
| Salina, Ks., U.S. | D6 | 93 |
| Salina, Ok., U.S. | A6 | 80 |
| Salina, Ut., U.S. | E4 | 121 |
| Salina, i., Italy | E5 | 23 |
| Salina Cruz, Mex. | D5 | 63 |
| Salinas, Braz. | B4 | 56 |
| Salinas, Ec. | B1 | 58 |
| Salinas, Ca., U.S. | D3 | 82 |
| Salinas, stm., Ca., U.S. | D3 | 82 |
| Salinas, Cape, c., Spain | C7 | 22 |
| Salinas, Pampa de las, pl., Arg. | A3 | 54 |
| Salinas de Garci Mendoza, Bol. | C2 | 55 |
| Salinas National Monument, N.M., U.S. | C3 | 108 |
| Salinas Peak, mtn., N.M., U.S. | D3 | 95 |
| Saline, La., U.S. | B3 | 95 |
| Saline, co., Ar., U.S. | C3 | 81 |
| Saline, co., Il., U.S. | F5 | 90 |
| Saline, co., Ks., U.S. | D6 | 93 |
| Saline, co., Mo., U.S. | C4 | 81 |
| Saline, co., Ne., U.S. | D8 | 104 |
| Saline, stm., Ar., U.S. | C1 | 81 |
| Saline, stm., Ar., U.S. | D4 | 81 |
| Saline, stm., Il., U.S. | F5 | 90 |
| Saline, North Fork, stm., Il., U.S. | F5 | 90 |
| Saline, South Fork, stm., Ar., U.S. | f8 | 81 |
| Saline Bayou, stm., La., U.S. | B3 | 95 |
| Saline Lake, res., La., U.S. | C3 | 95 |
| Salineno, Tx., U.S. | F3 | 120 |
| Salines, Point, c., Gren. | W25 | 65 |
| Salines, Pointe des, c., Mart. | T11 | 65 |
| Salineville, Oh., U.S. | B5 | 112 |
| Salinópolis, Braz. | B1 | 57 |
| Salisbury, Austl. | *F6 | 50 |
| Salisbury, N.B. | C4 | 71 |
| Salisbury, Eng., U.K. | E6 | 10 |
| Salisbury, Ct., U.S. | B2 | 84 |
| Salisbury, Md., U.S. | D6 | 97 |
| Salisbury, Ma., U.S. | A6 | 98 |
| Salisbury, Mo., U.S. | B5 | 102 |
| Salisbury, N.H., U.S. | D3 | 106 |
| Salisbury, N.C., U.S. | B2 | 110 |
| Salisbury, Pa., U.S. | G3 | 115 |
| Salisbury, Vt., U.S. | D2 | 122 |
| Salisbury Center, N.Y., U.S. | B6 | 109 |
| Salisbury see Harare, Zimb. | A5 | 49 |
| Salisbury Heights, N.H., U.S. | D3 | 106 |
| Salisbury Island, i., N.W. Ter. | D17 | 66 |
| Salisbury Plain, pl., Eng., U.K. | C6 | 12 |
| Salish Mountains, mts., Mt., U.S. | B2 | 103 |
| Salitpa, Al., U.S. | D1 | 78 |
| Salix, Ia., U.S. | B1 | 92 |
| Salkehatchie, stm., S.C., U.S. | E5 | 117 |
| Salkum, Wa., U.S. | C3 | 124 |
| Salladasburg, Pa., U.S. | D7 | 115 |
| Sallanches, Fr. | D2 | 20 |
| Salley, S.C., U.S. | D5 | 117 |
| Salliqueló, Arg. | B4 | 54 |
| Sallis, Ms., U.S. | B4 | 101 |
| Sallisaw, Ok., U.S. | B7 | 113 |
| Salluit, Que. | f11 | 74 |
| Sallūm, Khalīj as, b., Afr. | B9 | 128 |
| Salm, i., Sov. Un. | B9 | 128 |
| Salmās, Iran | D3 | 41 |
| Salmo, B.C. | E9 | 69 |
| Salmon, Id., U.S. | E5 | 89 |
| Salmon, stm., B.C. | B6 | 69 |
| Salmon, stm., N.B. | C4 | 71 |
| Salmon, stm., N.B. | B2 | 71 |
| Salmon, stm., N.A. | f10 | 109 |
| Salmon, stm., Id., U.S. | D3 | 89 |
| Salmon, Middle Fork, stm., Id., U.S. | E4 | 89 |
| Salmon, South Fork, stm., Id., U.S. | E3 | 89 |
| Salmon-Bay, Que. | C3 | 72 |
| Salmon Creek, Wa., U.S. | D3 | 124 |
| Salmon Creek Reservoir, res., Id., U.S. | G4 | 89 |
| Salmon Falls, stm., U.S. | D5 | 106 |
| Salmon Falls Creek, stm., U.S. | G4 | 89 |
| Salmon Mountain, mtn., N.H., U.S. | f7 | 106 |
| Salmon Mountains, mts., Ca., U.S. | B2 | 82 |
| Salmon Peak, mtn., Tx., U.S. | E2 | 120 |
| Salmon River, Ont. | D7 | 73 |
| Salmon River Mountains, mts., Id., U.S. | E3 | 89 |
| Salmon River Reservoir, res., N.Y., U.S. | B5 | 109 |
| Salmon Valley, B.C. | B6 | 69 |
| Salo, Fin. | G10 | 14 |
| Salò, Italy | D6 | 20 |
| Salol, Mn., U.S. | B3 | 100 |
| Salome, Az., U.S. | D2 | 80 |
| Salon-de-Provence, Fr. | F6 | 16 |
| Salonika see Thessaloníki, Grc. | B4 | 25 |
| Salonika, Gulf of see Thermaïkós Kólpos, b., Grc. | B4 | 25 |
| Salonta, Rom. | B5 | 24 |
| Salsette, i., India | H4 | 37 |
| Salsk, Sov. Un. | H13 | 27 |
| Salsomaggiore Terme, Italy | D2 | 20 |
| Salt, stm., Ky., U.S. | C4 | 94 |
| Salt, stm., Mo., U.S. | B6 | 102 |
| Salt, Middle Fork, stm., Mo., U.S. | B5 | 102 |
| Salt, North Fork, stm., Mo., U.S. | B5 | 102 |
| Salt, South Fork, stm., Mo., U.S. | B5 | 102 |
| Salta, Arg. | D2 | 55 |
| Salta, prov., Arg. | D2 | 55 |
| Saltash, Eng., U.K. | D3 | 12 |
| Saltburn-by-the-Sea, Eng., U.K. | F8 | 13 |
| Salt Cay, i., Bah. | m18 | 64 |
| Saltcoats, Sask. | F4 | 75 |
| Saltcoats, Scot., U.K. | E4 | 13 |
| Salt Creek, stm., Il., U.S. | C4 | 90 |
| Salt Creek, stm., Ne., U.S. | h11 | 104 |
| Salt Creek, stm., N.M., U.S. | D5 | 108 |
| Salt Creek, stm., Oh., U.S. | C3 | 112 |
| Salt Creek, stm., Wy., U.S. | C6 | 127 |
| Salter Path, N.C., U.S. | C6 | 110 |
| Salters, S.C., U.S. | D8 | 117 |
| Saltese, Mt., U.S. | C1 | 103 |
| Salt Fork, Ok., U.S. | A4 | 113 |
| Salt Fork Lake, res., Oh., U.S. | B4 | 112 |
| Saltholm, i., Den. | C6 | 15 |
| Saltillo, Mex. | B4 | 63 |
| Saltillo, In., U.S. | G5 | 91 |
| Saltillo, Pa., U.S. | F6 | 115 |
| Saltillo, Ms., U.S. | A5 | 101 |
| Saltillo, Tn., U.S. | B3 | 119 |
| Salt Lake, l., Hi., U.S. | g10 | 88 |
| Salt Lake, l., N.M., U.S. | E6 | 108 |
| Salt Lake City, Ut., U.S. | C4 | 121 |
| Salt Lick, Ky., U.S. | B6 | 94 |
| Salto, Braz. | m8 | 56 |
| Salto, Ur. | E1 | 56 |
| Salto Grande, Braz. | C3 | 56 |
| Saltonstall, Lake, l., Ct., U.S. | D4 | 84 |
| Salt Point, c., Ca., U.S. | C2 | 82 |
| Saltpond, Ghana | E4 | 45 |
| Salt River Indian Reservation, Az., U.S. | k9 | 80 |
| Salt River Range, mts., Wy., U.S. | D2 | 127 |
| Salt Rock, W.V., U.S. | C2 | 125 |
| Saltsburg, Pa., U.S. | F3 | 115 |
| Saltsjöbaden (part of Nacka), Swe. | t36 | 14 |
| Saltspring Island, i., B.C. | E6 | 69 |
| Salt Springs, Fl., U.S. | C5 | 86 |
| Saltville, Va., U.S. | f10 | 123 |
| Saltwater, Wa., U.S. | *B3 | 124 |
| Salt Wells Creek, stm., Wy., U.S. | E4 | 127 |
| Salud, Pan. | k10 | 62 |
| Saluda, N.C., U.S. | f10 | 110 |
| Saluda, S.C., U.S. | C4 | 117 |
| Saluda, Va., U.S. | C6 | 123 |
| Saluda, co., S.C., U.S. | C4 | 117 |
| Saluda, stm., S.C., U.S. | C4 | 117 |
| Saluda Dam, S.C., U.S. | C5 | 117 |
| Salūr, India | E7 | 36 |
| Salus, Ar., U.S. | B1 | 81 |
| Saluvia, Pa., U.S. | F5 | 115 |
| Saluzzo, Italy | B1 | 23 |
| Salvador, Braz. | D3 | 57 |
| Salvador, Sask. | E1 | 75 |
| Salvador, Lake, l., La., U.S. | E5 | 95 |
| Salvage, Newf. | D5 | 72 |
| Salvatierra, Mex. | m13 | 63 |
| Salvisa, Ky., U.S. | C5 | 94 |
| Salwa Bay, b., Asia | I5 | 39 |
| Salween (Thanlwin), stm., Asia | D10 | 36 |
| Salyān, Nepal | C9 | 37 |
| Salyany, Sov. Un. | F3 | 28 |
| Salyer, Ca., U.S. | B2 | 82 |
| Salyersville, Ky., U.S. | C6 | 94 |
| Salym Marsh, sw., Sov. Un. | B8 | 29 |
| Salzach, stm., Eur. | E6 | 18 |
| Salzburg, Aus. | E6 | 18 |
| Salzburg, state, Aus. | E6 | 18 |
| Salzgitter, W. Ger. | B5 | 18 |
| Salzwedel, E. Ger. | B5 | 18 |
| Sama [de Langreo], Spain | A3 | 22 |
| Samaipata, Bol. | C3 | 55 |
| Samalá, stm., Guat. | D6 | 63 |
| Samālūt, Eg. | D6 | 43 |
| Samana, Dom. Rep. | E9 | 64 |
| Samaná, Bahía de, b., Dom. Rep. | E9 | 64 |
| Samana Cay, i., Bah. | B8 | 64 |
| Samandaği, Tur. | D10 | 40 |
| Samani, Japan | E11 | 33 |
| Samaniego, Col. | C2 | 60 |
| Samannūd, Eg. | D3 | 43 |
| Samar, Isr. | E6 | 41 |
| Samar, i., Phil. | C7 | 34 |
| Samara, stm., Sov. Un. | C4 | 28 |
| Samarai, Pap. N. Gui. | m13 | 50 |
| Samarga, Sov. Un. | C9 | 33 |
| Samariapo, Ven. | B6 | 60 |
| Samarinda, Indon. | F6 | 34 |
| Samarkand, Sov. Un. | F9 | 29 |
| Sämarrā', Iraq | E14 | 40 |
| Sämarrā' Barrage, Iraq | E14 | 40 |
| Samataiuta, W. Sam. | F11 | 52 |
| Samatan, Fr. | F4 | 16 |
| Samawi, Phil. | C6 | 34 |
| Sambalpur, India | D7 | 36 |
| Sambar, Cape, c., Indon. | F4 | 34 |
| Sambas, Indon. | E3 | 34 |
| Sambava, Madag. | f10 | 49 |
| Sambhal, India | C7 | 37 |
| Sambhar, India | D5 | 37 |
| Sambor, Sov. Un. | G4 | 27 |
| Samborombón, Bahía, b., Arg. | B5 | 54 |
| Sambre, stm., Eur. | C4 | 17 |
| Samch'ŏk, S. Kor. | H4 | 33 |
| Samch'ŏk, S. Kor. | I4 | 33 |
| Samch'ung, Tai. | *F9 | 31 |
| Same, Tan. | B6 | 48 |
| Samedan, Switz. | C5 | 20 |
| Sammamish Lake, l., Wa., U.S. | e11 | 124 |
| Samnorwood, Tx., U.S. | B2 | 120 |
| Samnū, Libya | B8 | 47 |
| Samoa, dep., Oceania | B1 | 82 |
| Samokov, Bul. | D6 | 24 |
| Sámos, Grc. | D6 | 25 |
| Sámos, i., Grc. | D6 | 25 |
| Samosir, i., Indon. | E1 | 34 |
| Samoth, Il., U.S. | F5 | 90 |
| Samothrace see Samothráki, i., Grc. | B5 | 40 |
| Samothráki (Samothrace), i., Grc. | B5 | 40 |
| Sampaloc Point, c., Phil. | o13 | 34 |
| Sampit, stm., S.C., U.S. | E9 | 117 |
| Sampit, Indon. | F4 | 34 |
| Sampson, co., N.C., U.S. | B4 | 110 |
| Sampwe, Zaire | C4 | 48 |
| Sam Rayburn Reservoir, res., Tx., U.S. | D5 | 120 |
| Samsang, China | B9 | 37 |
| Samsø, i., Den. | C3 | 15 |
| Samsø Bælt, strt., Den. | D3 | 15 |
| Samson, Al., U.S. | D3 | 78 |
| Samsun, Tur. | B11 | 40 |
| Samtown, La., U.S. | *C3 | 95 |
| Samtredia, Sov. Un. | A14 | 40 |
| Samuels, Id., U.S. | A2 | 89 |
| Samui, i., Thai. | H4 | 35 |
| Samus, Sov. Un. | D25 | 8 |
| Samut Sakhon, Thai. | C2 | 34 |
| San, Mali | D4 | 45 |
| San, stm., Asia | F7 | 35 |
| San, stm., Eur. | C7 | 26 |
| Sana, prov., Yemen | D4 | 38 |
| Sanaag, prov., Som. | C6 | 47 |
| San Acacia, N.M., U.S. | C3 | 108 |
| San Acacio, Co., U.S. | C5 | 83 |
| Sanaga, stm., Cam. | E2 | 46 |
| San Agustín, Col. | C2 | 60 |
| San Agustin, Cape, c., Phil. | D7 | 34 |
| San Agustin, Plains of, pl., N.M., U.S. | C2 | 108 |
| San Agustín de Valle Fértil, Arg. | A3 | 54 |
| San Ambrosio, Isla, i., Chile | F3 | 53 |
| Sanana, i., Indon. | F7 | 34 |
| Sanandaj, Iran | B4 | 38 |
| San Andreas, Ca., U.S. | C3 | 82 |
| San Andrés, Col. | D7 | 62 |
| San Andrés, Isla de, i., Col. | D7 | 62 |
| San Andrés de Giles, Arg. | g7 | 54 |
| San Andres Mountains, mts., N.M., U.S. | E3 | 108 |
| San Andres Peak, mtn., N.M., U.S. | E3 | 108 |
| San Andrés Tetepilco (part of Mexico City), Mex. | h9 | 63 |
| San Andrés y Providencia, dept., Col. | *D7 | 62 |
| San Angelo, Tx., U.S. | D2 | 120 |
| San Anselmo, Ca., U.S. | h7 | 82 |
| San Antonio, Arg. | D2 | 55 |
| San Antonio, Chile | A2 | 54 |
| San Antonio, Chile | E2 | 55 |
| San Antonio, N. Mar. Is. | D7 | 52 |
| San Antonio, Phil. | o13 | 34 |
| San Antonio, Fl., U.S. | D4 | 86 |
| San Antonio, N.M., U.S. | k8 | 108 |
| San Antonio, Tx., U.S. | E3 | 120 |
| San Antonio, Cabo, c., Arg. | B5 | 54 |
| San Antonio, Cabo, c., Cuba | D1 | 64 |
| San Antonio Abad, Spain | C6 | 22 |
| San Antonio Bay, b., Tx., U.S. | E4 | 120 |
| San Antonio de Areco, Arg. | g7 | 54 |
| San Antonio de los Baños, Cuba | C2 | 64 |
| San Antonio de los Cobres, Arg. | D2 | 55 |
| San Antonio Mountain, mtn., N.M., U.S. | A3 | 108 |
| San Antonio Oeste, Arg. | C4 | 54 |
| Sanarate, Guat. | C2 | 62 |
| Sanatorium, Ms., U.S. | D4 | 101 |
| San Augustine, Tx., U.S. | D5 | 120 |
| San Augustine, co., Tx., U.S. | D5 | 120 |
| San Bartolomeo [in Galdo], Italy | D5 | 23 |
| San Benedetto del Tronto, Italy | C4 | 23 |
| San Benito, Tx., U.S. | F4 | 120 |
| San Benito, co., Ca., U.S. | D3 | 82 |
| San Benito Mountain, mtn., Ca., U.S. | D3 | 82 |
| San Bernardino, Switz. | D7 | 21 |
| San Bernardino, Ca., U.S. | E5 | 82 |
| San Bernardino, co., Ca., U.S. | E5 | 82 |
| San Bernardo, Chile | A2 | 54 |
| San Blas, Mex. | m11 | 63 |
| San Blas, Cape, c., Fl., U.S. | v16 | 86 |
| San Blas, Cordillera de, mts., Pan. | F8 | 62 |
| San Bonifacio, Italy | D7 | 20 |
| San Borja, Bol. | B2 | 55 |
| San Borja, Braz. | A2 | 54 |
| Sanborn, Mn., U.S. | F3 | 100 |
| Sanborn, N.D., U.S. | C7 | 111 |
| Sanborn, Wi., U.S. | B3 | 126 |
| Sanborn, co., S.D., U.S. | D7 | 118 |
| Sanbornton, N.H., U.S. | D3 | 106 |
| Sanbornville, N.H., U.S. | C4 | 106 |
| San Bruno, Ca., U.S. | h8 | 82 |
| San Candido, Italy | C8 | 20 |
| San Carlos, Arg. | A3 | 54 |
| San Carlos, Chile | B2 | 54 |
| San Carlos, Mex. | B4 | 63 |
| San Carlos, Nic. | F5 | 63 |
| San Carlos, Phil. | o13 | 34 |
| San Carlos, Az., U.S. | D5 | 80 |
| San Carlos, Ven. | B4 | 60 |
| San Carlos del Zulia, Ven. | B3 | 60 |
| San Carlos de Río Negro, Ven. | C4 | 60 |
| San Carlos Indian Reservation, Az., U.S. | D5 | 80 |
| San Carlos Lake, res., Az., U.S. | D5 | 80 |
| San Cataldo, Italy | F4 | 23 |
| Sancerre, Fr. | D5 | 16 |
| Sanch'ung, Tai. | *F9 | 31 |
| San Ciro de Acosta, Mex. | m14 | 63 |
| San Clemente, Spain | C4 | 22 |
| San Clemente Island, i., Ca., U.S. | F4 | 82 |
| San Cristóbal, Arg. | A4 | 54 |
| San Cristóbal, Dom. Rep. | E8 | 64 |
| San Cristóbal, i., Sol.Is. | A4 | 108 |
| San Cristóbal, i., Sol.Is. | G9 | 6 |
| San Cristóbal, Isla (Chatham), i., Ec. | g6 | 58 |
| San Cristóbal, Volcán, vol., Nic. | D4 | 62 |
| San Cristóbal de las Casas, Mex. | D6 | 63 |
| Sancti-Spíritus, Cuba | D6 | 64 |
| Sancti-Spíritus, prov., Cuba | C4 | 64 |
| Sandusky, Sask. | G1 | 75 |
| Sancy, Puy de, mtn., Fr. | E5 | 16 |
| Sand, stm., Alta. | B5 | 68 |
| Sanda, Japan | o14 | 33 |
| Sand Island, i., Scot., U.K. | D5 | 8 |
| Sandakan, Malay. | D6 | 34 |
| Sandcut Cove, Fl., U.S. | *F6 | 86 |
| San Daniele del Friuli, Italy | D7 | 20 |
| Sandaré, Mali | D2 | 45 |
| Sanday, i., Scot., U.K. | A5 | 10 |
| Sandbach, Eng., U.K. | D10 | 13 |
| Sanday Sound, strt., Scot., U.K. | A6 | 13 |
| Sandborn, In., U.S. | G3 | 91 |
| Sand Brook, N.J., U.S. | *C3 | 107 |

Sand Coulee, Mt., U.S. — C5 103
Sand Creek, Wi., U.S. — C2 126
Sand Creek, stm., In., U.S. — F6 91
Sand Creek, stm., Ks., U.S. — g12 93
Sand Creek, stm., Wy., U.S. — C7 127
Sand Draw, Wy., U.S. — *D4 127
Sande, Nor. — p28 14
Sandefjord, Nor. — p28 14
Sanders, Az., U.S. — B6 80
Sanders, Ky., U.S. — B5 94
Sanders, Mt., U.S. — D9 103
Sanders, co., Mt., U.S. — C1 103
Sanderson, Tx., U.S. — D1 120
Sandersville, Ga., U.S. — D4 87
Sandersville, Ms., U.S. — D4 101
Sandfly Lake, l., Sask. — B2 75
Sandford, In., U.S. — E2 91
Sand Fork, W.V., U.S. — C4 125
Sandhammaren, c., Swe. — C8 15
Sand Hill, Ms., U.S. — h13 101
Sand Hill, Ms., U.S. — D5 101
Sandhill, Ms., U.S. — C4 101
Sand Hill, stm., Newf. — B3 72
Sand Hill, stm., Mn., U.S. — C2 100
Sandi, India — C7 36
Sandia, Peru — D4 58
Sandia, N.M., U.S. — *B3 109
Sandia, Tx., U.S. — E4 120
Sandia Crest, mtn., N.M., U.S. — k8 108
Sandia Indian Reservation, N.M., U.S. — k7 108
Sandia Mountains, mts., N.M., U.S. — k8 108
Sandia Park, N.M., U.S. — k8 108
San Diego, Ca., U.S. — F5 82
San Diego, Tx., U.S. — F3 120
San Diego, co., Ca., U.S. — F5 82
San Diego, stm., Ca., U.S. — o15 82
San Diego, Cabo, c., Arg. — h12 54
San Diego Naval Station, mil., Ca., U.S. — o15 82
San Diego Naval Training Center, mil., Ca., U.S. — o15 82
Sandikli, Tur. — C8 40
Sandilands, Man. — E3 70
San Dimas, Mex. — C3 63
San Dimas, Ca., U.S. — *m13 82
Sand Island, i., Mid. Is. — K3 52
Sand Island, i., Hi., U.S. — g10 88
Sand Island, i., Wi., U.S. — B3 126
Sand Islet, i., Mid. Is. — J3 52
Sand Key, i., Fl., U.S. — E4 86
Sand Lake, Mi., U.S. — E5 99
Sandlick Creek, stm., W.V., U.S. — n13 125
Sand Mountain, mtn., U.S. — A3 94
Sandnes, Nor. — H1 14
Sandoa, Zaire — C3 44
Sandomierz, Pol. — C6 26
Sandon, B.C. — D9 69
Sandoná, Col. — C2 60
San Donà di Piave, Italy — B4 23
Sandoval, Il., U.S. — E4 90
Sandoval, co., N.M., U.S. — B2 108
Sandover, stm., Austl. — D6 50
Sandoway, Burma — E9 36
Sandown, Eng., U.K. — D6 12
Sandown, N.H., U.S. — E4 106
Sand Point, Ont. — B8 73
Sand Point, Ak., U.S. — D7 79
Sandpoint, Id., U.S. — A2 89
Sands, Mi., U.S. — B3 99
Sands Key, i., Fl., U.S. — s3 86
Sandspit, B.C. — C2 69
Sand Springs, Mt., U.S. — C9 103
Sand Springs, Ok., U.S. — A5 113
Sandston, Va., U.S. — m18 123
Sandstone, Austl. — E2 50
Sandstone, Mn., U.S. — D6 100
Sandstone, W.V., U.S. — D4 125
Sandtown, De., U.S. — D3 85
Sandusky, Mi., U.S. — E8 99
Sandusky, N.Y., U.S. — C2 109
Sandusky, Oh., U.S. — A3 112
Sandusky, co., Oh., U.S. — A2 112
Sandusky, stm., Oh., U.S. — B2 112
Sandusky Bay, b., Oh., U.S. — A3 112
Sandvig (part of Allinge-Sandvig), Den. — C8 15
Sandviken, Swe. — G7 14
Sandwich, Il., U.S. — B5 90
Sandwich, Ma., U.S. — C7 98
Sandwich, N.H., U.S. — C4 106
Sandwich Bay, b., Newf. — B3 72
Sandwich Range, mts., N.H., U.S. — C3 106
Sandwick, B.C. — E5 69
Sandwith, Sask. — D1 75
Sandy, Or., U.S. — B4 114
Sandy, Ut., U.S. — C4 121
Sandy, stm., Me., U.S. — D2 96
Sandy Bay Mountain, mtn., Me., U.S. — C2 96
Sandy Brook, stm., Ct., U.S. — A3 84
Sandy Cape, c., Austl. — D9 50
Sandy Creek, N.Y., U.S. — B4 109
Sandy Creek, stm., Oh., U.S. — B4 112
Sandy Creek, stm., Ok., U.S. — C2 113
Sandy Hook, Ct., U.S. — D2 84
Sandy Hook, Ky., U.S. — B6 94
Sandy Hook, Md., U.S. — B2 97
Sandy Hook, Ms., U.S. — D4 101
Sandy Hook, spit, N.J., U.S. — C5 107
Sandy Lake, i., S.C., U.S. — D9 117
Sandy Lake, Man. — D1 70
Sandy Lake, Pa., U.S. — D1 115
Sandy Lake, l., Newf. — n16 73
Sandy Lake, l., Ont. — n16 73
Sandy Lake, l., Sask. — B2 75
Sandy Neck, pen., Ma., U.S. — C7 98
Sandy Point, Me., U.S. — D4 96
Sandy Point, c., Trin. — M24 65
Sandy Point, c., R.I., U.S. — h7 116
Sandy Point, c., V.I.U.S. — B3 64
Sandy Pond, l., N.Y., U.S. — g10 98
Sandy Ridge, Al., U.S. — C3 78
Sandy Ridge, N.C., U.S. — A2 110
Sandy Ridge, Pa., U.S. — E5 115
Sandy Ridge, mtn., Va., U.S. — e9 123
Sandy Springs, Ga., U.S. — h8 87
Sandy Springs, S.C., U.S. — B2 117
Sandyville, W.V., U.S. — C3 125
San Elizario, Tx., U.S. — o11 120
San Enrique, Arg. — B4 54
San Estanislao, Para. — D4 55
San Esteban, Hond. — D7 63
San Felice sul Panaro, Italy — E7 23
San Felipe, Col. — A2 54
San Felipe, Mex. — m13 63
San Felipe, Ven. — A4 60
San Felipe, Punta, c., Mex. — A2 63
San Felipe Indian Reservation, N.M., U.S. — k8 108

San Felipe Pueblo, N.M., U.S. — B3 108
San Feliu de Guixols, Spain — B7 22
San Félix, Isla, i., Chile — F2 53
San Fernando, Arg. — A5 54
San Fernando, Chile — A2 54
San Fernando, Mex. — C5 63
San Fernando, Phil. — B6 34
San Fernando, Phil. — o13 34
San Fernando, Spain — D2 22
San Fernando, Trin. — K14 64
San Fernando, Ca., U.S. — m12 82
San Fernando de Apure, Ven. — B4 60
San Fernando de Atabapo, Ven. — C4 60
San Fernando de Henares, Spain — p17 22
San Fidel, N.M., U.S. — B2 108
Sanford, Co., U.S. — D5 83
Sanford, Fl., U.S. — D5 86
Sanford, Me., U.S. — E2 96
Sanford, Mi., U.S. — E6 99
Sanford, Ms., U.S. — D4 101
Sanford, N.C., U.S. — B3 110
Sanford, Tx., U.S. — B2 120
Sanford, Mount, mtn., Ak., U.S. — C11 79
San Francisco, Arg. — A4 54
San Francisco, Col. — C2 60
San Francisco, Ca., U.S. — D2 82
San Francisco, co., Ca., U.S. — D2 82
San Francisco, stm., U.S. — D6 80
San Francisco, Paso de, S.A. — E2 55
San Francisco Bay, b., Ca., U.S. — h8 82
San Francisco de Borja, Mex. — B3 63
San Francisco del Oro, Mex. — B3 63
San Francisco del Rincón, Mex. — m13 63
San Francisco de Macorís, Dom. Rep. — E8 64
San Francisco Gotera, El Sal. — D3 62
San Francisco Mountains, mts., Ut., U.S. — E2 121
San Francisco Solano, Punta, c., Col. — B2 60
San Gabriel, Ec. — A2 58
San Gabriel, Ca., U.S. — m12 82
San Gabriel, Punta, c., Mex. — B2 63
San Gabriel Chilac, Mex. — D5 63
San Gabriel Mountains, mts., Ca., U.S. — m12 82
San Gallan, Isla, i., Peru — D2 58
Sangamner, India — H5 37
Sangamon, co., Il., U.S. — D4 90
Sangamon, stm., Il., U.S. — C3 90
Sangatte, Fr. — D9 12
Sangay, Volcán, vol., Ec. — B2 58
Sange-e Māsheh, Afg. — E13 39
Sanger, Ca., U.S. — D4 82
Sanger, Tx., U.S. — C4 120
Sangerhausen, E. Ger. — C5 18
Sangerville, Me., U.S. — C3 96
Sanggau, Indon. — E4 34
San Giacomo Pass, Eur. — D5 21
Sangihe, i., Indon. — E7 34
San Gil, Col. — B3 60
San Gimignano, Italy — C3 23
San Giovanni in Fiore, Italy — E6 23
San Giovanni in Persiceto, Italy — E7 20
Sangju, S. Kor. — H4 33
Sāngli, India — *E5 36
Sangmélima, Cam. — E2 46
San Gorgonio Mountain, mtn., Ca., U.S. — E5 82
Sangre de Cristo Mountains, mts., U.S. — C6 76
San Gregorio, Ca., U.S. — k8 82
San Gregorio, Ur. — E1 56
Sangre Grande, Trin. — N23 65
Sangro, stm., Italy — D5 23
Sangrūr, India — B5 37
Sanguango, Alta. — C3 68
Sangue, Rio do, stm., Braz. — B4 55
Sangüesa, Spain — A5 22
Sanguinara, stm., Italy — h8 23
Sanhedriyya (part of Jerusalem), Isr. — m14 41
Sanibel, Fl., U.S. — F4 86
Sanibel Island, i., Fl., U.S. — F4 86
San Ignacio, Belize — B3 62
San Ignacio, Bol. — B2 55
San Ignacio, Bol. — C3 55
San Ignacio, Mex. — B2 63
San Ignacio, Para. — E4 55
Sanilac, co., Mi., U.S. — E8 99
San Ildefonso, Cape, c., Phil. — B6 34
San Ildefonso [o la Granja], Spain — B3 22
San Ildefonso Peninsula, pen., Phil. — n14 34
Sanish, N.D., U.S. — B3 111
San Isidro, Arg. — g7 54
San Isidro, Peru — *D2 58
San Isidro, Tx., U.S. — F3 120
San Isidro [del General], C.R. — F6 62
Sanitz, E. Ger. — D6 15
Sanīyah, Hawr as, l., Iraq — E3 39
San Jacinto, Ca., U.S. — F5 82
San Jacinto, co., Tx., U.S. — D5 120
San Jacinto, stm., Tx., U.S. — r14 120
San Jacinto Peak, mtn., Ca., U.S. — F5 82
San Javier, Arg. — A4 54
San Javier, Bol. — C3 55
San Javier [de Loncomilla], Chile — B2 54
San Jerónimo, Serranía de, mts., Col. — B2 60
San Jerónimo Lídice (part of Mexico City), Mex. — h9 63
San Joaquín, Para. — D4 55
San Joaquin, co., Ca., U.S. — D3 82
San Joaquin, stm., Ca., U.S. — D3 82
San Joaquin Valley, val., Ca., U.S. — D3 82
San Jon, N.M., U.S. — B6 108
San Jorge, Golfo, b., Arg. — F3 53
San Jose, Belize — B3 62
San Jose, C.R. — F8 62
San Jose, Guat. — E6 63
San Jose, N. Mar. Is. — E7 52
San Jose, N. Mar. Is. — D7 52
San Jose, Phil. — C6 34
San Jose, Az., U.S. — E6 80
San Jose, Il., U.S. — C4 90
San Jose, N.M., U.S. — B4 108

San José, dept., Ur. — g8 54
San Jose, stm., B.C. — D7 69
San José, stm., Ur. — g8 54
Sanmen Bay, b., China — J9 32
San José [de Chiquitos], Bol. — C3 55
San José de Feliciano, Arg. — A5 54
San José de Guanipa (El Tigrito), Ven. — B5 60
San José de Jachal, Arg. — F2 55
San José del Boquerón, Arg. — E3 55
San José del Cabo, Mex. — C3 63
San José del Guaviare, Col. — C2 60
San José de los Molinos, Peru — D2 58
San José de Mayo, Ur. — E1 56
San José de Ocuné, Col. — C3 60
San Jose Island, i., Tx., U.S. — E4 120
San Juan, Arg. — A3 55
San Juan, Phil. — p13 34
San Juan, Phil. — n13 34
San Juan, P.R. — G11 64
San Juan, Co., U.S. — D6 83
San Juan, Tx., U.S. — F3 120
San Juan, co., Co., U.S. — D3 83
San Juan, co., N.M., U.S. — A1 108
San Juan, co., Ut., U.S. — F5 121
San Juan, co., Wa., U.S. — A2 124
San Juan, stm., Arg. — A3 54
San Juan, stm., B.C. — g11 69
San Juan, stm., Col. — C2 60
San Juan, stm., N.A. — E8 63
San Juan, stm., U.S. — C6 76
San Juan, Cabezas de, c., P.R. — B4 65
San Juan Bautista, Para. — E4 55
San Juan Capistrano, Ca., U.S. — F5 82
San Juan de Aragón (part of Mexico City), Mex. — h9 63
San Juan de Colón, Ven. — B3 60
San Juan [de la Maguana], Dom. Rep. — E8 64
San Juan de Lima, Punta, c., Mex. — D4 63
San Juan del Norte, Nic. — E8 63
San Juan de los Cayos, Ven. — A4 60
San Juan de los Lagos, Mex. — m12 63
San Juan de los Morros, Ven. — B4 60
San Juan del Río, Mex. — m13 63
San Juan del Sur, Nic. — E7 63
San Juan Island, i., Wa., U.S. — A2 124
San Juan Mountains, mts., Co., U.S. — D3 83
San Juan Nepomuceno, Col. — D2 58
San Juan Pueblo, N.M., U.S. — *A3 108
San Juan y Martínez, Cuba — C2 64
San Julián, Arg. — D3 54
San Justo, Arg. — A4 54
Sankarani, stm., Afr. — D3 45
Sankt Anton [am Arlberg], Aus. — B6 20
Sankt Blasien, W. Ger. — B4 20
Sankt Gallen, Switz. — E4 18
Sankt Gallen, state, Switz. — B5 20
Sankt Gallenkirch, Aus. — B8 21
Sankt Georgen [im Attergau], Aus. — B9 20
Sankt Goarshausen, W. Ger. — C2 19
Sankt Johann [in Tirol], Aus. — B8 20
Sankt Margrethen, Switz. — B8 21
Sankt Michaelisdonn, W. Ger. — E3 15
Sankt Moritz, Switz. — E4 18
Sankt Olof, Swe. — C8 15
Sankt Pölten, Aus. — D7 18
Sankt Veit [an der Glan], Aus. — E7 18
Sankt Wendel, W. Ger. — D2 19
Sankuru, stm., Zaire — B3 48
San Leandro, Ca., U.S. — h8 82
San Lorenzo, Arg. — A4 54
San Lorenzo, Ec. — A2 58
San Lorenzo, Hond. — D4 62
San Lorenzo, P.R. — B2 65
San Lorenzo, stm., N.M., U.S. — E2 108
San Lorenzo, Cerro, mtn., S.A. — D2 54
San Lorenzo de El Escorial, Spain — B3 22
Sanlúcar [de Barrameda], Spain — D2 22
San Lucas, Bol. — D2 55
San Lucas, Mex. — C2 63
San Lucas, Cabo, c., Mex. — C3 63
San Lucas, Serranía de, mts., Col. — B3 60
San Luis, Arg. — A3 54
San Luis, Cuba — D6 64
San Luis, Guat. — D7 63
San Luis, Az., U.S. — E3 80
San Luis, Co., U.S. — D5 83
San Luis, prov., Arg. — A3 54
San Luis, stm., Mex. — h9 63
San Luis, Point, c., Ca., U.S. — E3 82
San Luis Creek, stm., Co., U.S. — C5 83
San Luis de la Paz, Mex. — m13 63
San Luis Jilotepeque, Guat. — D3 62
San Luis Obispo, Ca., U.S. — E3 82
San Luis Obispo, co., Ca., U.S. — E3 82
San Luis Pass, strt., Tx., U.S. — r14 120
San Luis Peak, mtn., Co., U.S. — D4 83
San Luis Potosí, Mex. — F5 63
San Luis Potosí, state, Mex. — A5 54
San Luis Río Colorado, Mex. — A2 63
San Luis Valley, val., Co., U.S. — D4 83
San Manuel, Az., U.S. — E5 80
San Marco [in Lamis], Italy — D5 23
San Marcos, Col. — B2 60
San Marcos, Guat. — D2 62
San Marcos, Mex. — C5 63
San Marcos, Ca., U.S. — F5 82
San Marcos, Tx., U.S. — E4 120
San Marcos, stm., Tx., U.S. — h8 120
San Marcos, Punta, c., Mex. — B2 63
San Marcos de Colón, Hond. — D7 63
San Marino, Ca., U.S. — m12 82
San Marino, ctry., Eur. — E6 4
San Martín, Arg. — A3 54
San Martín, Col. — C3 60
San Martín, dept., Peru — C2 58
San Martín, Lago (Lago O'Higgins), l., S.A. — D2 54
San Martín de la Vega, Spain — p17 22
San Martín de los Andes, Arg. — D2 54
San Martino di Castrozza, Italy — C7 20
San Mateo, Spain — B2 22
San Mateo, Ca., U.S. — h8 82
San Mateo, Fl., U.S. — C5 86
San Mateo, N.M., U.S. — B2 108
San Mateo, co., Ca., U.S. — D2 82
San Mateo, Cabo, c., Ec. — B1 58
San Mateo Mountains, mts., N.M., U.S. — D2 108
San Mateo Mountains, mts., N.M., U.S. — B2 108

San Matías, Bol. — C4 55
San Matías, Golfo, b., Arg. — C4 54
Sanmenxia, China — E7 31
San Miguel, El Sal. — E7 63
San Miguel, Pan. — F8 62
San Miguel, Az., U.S. — F4 80
San Miguel, Ca., U.S. — E3 82
San Miguel, N.M., U.S. — E3 108
San Miguel, co., Co., U.S. — D2 83
San Miguel, co., N.M., U.S. — B5 108
San Miguel, stm., Bol. — C3 55
San Miguel, stm., S.A. — C2 60
San Miguel, stm., Co., U.S. — C2 83
San Miguel, Golfo de, b., Pan. — F8 62
San Miguel de Allende, Mex. — m13 63
San Miguel de Tucumán, Arg. — E2 55
San Miguel Island, i., Ca., U.S. — E3 82
San Miguelito, Pan. — *F8 62
San Miguel Mountains, mts., Co., U.S. — D2 83
Sanming, China — K7 32
Sannār, Sud. — C3 47
San Narciso, Phil. — o13 34
San Narciso, Phil. — p14 34
Sannar Dam, Sud. — C3 47
San Nicolás [de los Arroyos], Arg. — A4 54
San Nicolás de los Garzas, Mex. — *B4 63
San Nicolas Island, i., Ca., U.S. — F4 82
Sanniquellie, Lib. — E3 45
Sannois, Fr. — g10 16
Sano, Japan — m18 33
Sanok, Pol. — D7 26
San Onofre, Col. — B2 60
San Pablo, Phil. — o13 34
San Pablo, Ca., U.S. — *h8 82
San Pablo, Co., U.S. — D5 83
San Pablo, stm., Bol. — C3 55
San Pablo Bay, b., Ca., U.S. — g8 82
San Patricio, co., Tx., U.S. — E4 120
San Patricio, Bayou, stm., La., U.S. — C2 95
San Pedrillo, Punta, c., C.R. — F6 62
San Pedro, Arg. — A5 54
San Pedro, Arg. — D3 55
San Pedro, Bol. — B3 55
San Pedro, Chile — D2 55
San Pedro, Para. — D4 55
San Pedro, N.M., U.S. — *B3 108
San Pedro, dept., Para. — D4 55
San Pedro, stm., Mex. — k11 63
San Pedro, stm., N.A. — B2 62
San Pedro, stm., Az., U.S. — E5 80
San Pedro, Punta, c., Chile — E1 55
San Pedro de Atacama, Chile — D2 55
San Pedro [de Buena Vista], Bol. — C2 55
San Pedro de las Colonias, Mex. — B4 63
San Pedro de Lloc, Peru — B2 58
San Pedro de Macorís, Dom. Rep. — E9 64
San Pedro Mártir, Sierra de, mts., Mex. — A1 63
San Pedro Peaks, mts., N.M., U.S. — A3 108
San Pedro Sula, Hond. — D7 63
San Pedro Tlaquepaque see Tlaquepaque, Mex. — m12 63
Sanpete, co., Ut., U.S. — D4 121
San Pierre, In., U.S. — B4 91
San Pietro, i., Italy — E2 23
San Pitch Mountains, mts., Ut., U.S. — D4 121
Sanpoil, stm., Wa., U.S. — A7 124
Sanpoil, West Fork, stm., Wa., U.S. — A7 124
Sanquhar, Scot., U.K. — E5 13
San Quintín, Phil. — o13 34
San Rafael, Arg. — A3 54
San Rafael, Ca., U.S. — D2 82
San Rafael, N.M., U.S. — B2 108
San Rafael, Ven. — A3 60
San Rafael, stm., Ut., U.S. — D5 121
San Rafael Desert, des., Ut., U.S. — E5 121
San Rafael Knob, mtn., Ut., U.S. — E5 121
San Rafael Mountains, mts., Ca., U.S. — E4 82
San Rafael Swell, plat., Ut., U.S. — E5 121
San Ramón, Peru — D2 58
San Ramon, Ca., U.S. — h9 82
San Ramón, Ur. — g9 54
San Ramón de la Nueva Orán, Arg. — D3 55
San Remo, Italy — E2 23
San Remo, N.Y., U.S. — *n15 109
San Román, Arg. — A2 54
San Roque, N. Mar. Is. — D8 52
San Roque, Spain — D3 22
San Rosendo, Chile — B2 54
San Saba, Tx., U.S. — D3 120
San Saba, co., Tx., U.S. — D3 120
San Saba, stm., Tx., U.S. — D3 120
San Salvador, El Sal. — E7 63
San Salvador (Watling Island), i., Bah. — B6 64
San Salvador, Isla (James), i., Ec. — g5 58
San Salvador de Jujuy, Arg. — D2 55
Sansanné-Mango, Togo — D5 45
Sans Bois Mountains, mts., Ok., U.S. — B6 113
San Sebastián (part of San José), C.R. — F5 62
San Sebastián, Spain — A4 22
San Sebastián, Cabo, c., Arg. — h12 54
San Sebastián de los Reyes, Spain — o17 22
Sansepolcro, Italy — C4 23
San Severo, Italy — D5 23
San Simeon, Ca., U.S. — E3 82
San Simon, stm., Az., U.S. — E6 80
Sans Souci, S.C., U.S. — *B3 117
Santa, Peru — C2 58
Santa, Id., U.S. — B2 89
Santa, stm., Peru — C2 58
Santa Ana, Bol. — B2 55
Santa Ana, Bol. — B3 55
Santa Ana, Ec. — B1 58
Santa Ana, El Sal. — E7 63
Santa Ana, Mex. — A2 63
Santa Ana, Peru — D3 58
Santa Ana, Ca., U.S. — F5 82

Santa Ana, Ven. — B5 60
Santa Ana, stm., Ca., U.S. — n13 82
Santa Ana Indian Reservation, N.M., U.S. — h7 108
Santa Ana Mountains, mts., Ca., U.S. — n13 82
Santa Ana Pueblo, N.M., U.S. — B3 108
Santa Anita (part of Mexico City), Mex. — h9 63
Santa Anna, Tx., U.S. — D3 120
Santa Bárbara, Braz. — B4 56
Santa Bárbara, Chile — B2 54
Santa Bárbara, Hond. — C3 62
Santa Barbara, Mex. — B3 63
Santa Barbara, Ca., U.S. — E4 82
Santa Barbara, co., Ca., U.S. — E3 82
Santa Barbara Channel, strt., Ca., U.S. — E3 82
Santa Bárbara d'Oeste, Braz. — m8 56
Santa Barbara Island, i., Ca., U.S. — F4 82
Santa Catalina, Arg. — D2 55
Santa Catalina, Gulf of, b., Ca., U.S. — F5 82
Santa Catalina Island, i., Ca., U.S. — F4 82
Santa Catalina Mountains, mts., Az., U.S. — E5 80
Santa Catarina, Mex. — *B4 63
Santa Catarina, state, Braz. — D2 56
Santa Catarina, Ilha de, i., Braz. — D3 56
Santa Clara, Cuba — C4 64
Santa Clara, Ca., U.S. — D2 82
Santa Clara, N.Y., U.S. — f10 109
Santa Clara, Or., U.S. — *C3 114
Santa Clara, Ut., U.S. — F2 121
Santa Clara, co., Ca., U.S. — D3 82
Santa Clara, stm., Ca., U.S. — E4 82
Santa Clara Pueblo, N.M., U.S. — *B3 108
Santa Claus, In., U.S. — H4 91
Santa Clotilde, Peru — B3 58
Santa Coloma de Farnés, Spain — B7 22
Santa Coloma [de Gramanet], Spain — B7 22
Santa Croce, Cape, c., Italy — F5 23
Santa Cruz, Arg. — E3 54
Santa Cruz, Bol. — C3 55
Santa Cruz, Braz. — C3 57
Santa Cruz, Chile — A2 54
Santa Cruz, C.R. — E7 63
Santa Cruz, N.M., U.S. — *B3 108
Santa Cruz, Phil. — o13 34
Santa Cruz, Phil. — o12 34
Santa Cruz, stm., N.A. — B2 62
Santa Cruz, Ca., U.S. — D2 82
Santa Cruz, N.M., U.S. — B3 108
Santa Cruz, co., Az., U.S. — F5 80
Santa Cruz, co., Ca., U.S. — D2 82
Santa Cruz, prov., Arg. — D3 54
Santa Cruz, dept., Bol. — C3 55
Santa Cruz, stm., Arg. — E2 54
Santa Cruz, stm., Az., U.S. — E4 80
Santa Cruz, Isla (Indefatigable Island), i., Ec. — g5 58
Santa Cruz de la Palma, Spain — m13 22
Santa Cruz del Quiché, Guat. — C2 62
Santa Cruz del Sur, Cuba — D5 64
Santa Cruz de Tenerife, Spain — m13 22
Santa Cruz do Rio Pardo, Braz. — C3 56
Santa Cruz (do Sul), Braz. — D2 56
Santa Cruz Island, i., Ca., U.S. — F4 82
Santa Cruz Islands, is., Sol.Is. — G10 6
Santa Cruz Mountains, mts., Ca., U.S. — k8 82
Santa Elena, Ec. — B1 58
Santa Elena, Bahía de, b., C.R. — B1 58
Santa Elena, Cabo, c., C.R. — E7 63
Santa Elena, Punta, c., Ec. — B1 58
Santa Elena de Uairén, Ven. — C5 60
Santa Eugenia, Spain — A1 22
Santa Eulalia del Río, Spain — C6 22
Santa Fe, Arg. — A4 54
Santa Fe (part of Mexico City), Mex. — h9 63
Santa Fe, Pan. — F7 62
Santa Fe, Spain — D3 22
Santa Fe, N.M., U.S. — B4 108
Santa Fe, Oh., U.S. — B1 112
Santa Fe, Tn., U.S. — B4 119
Santa Fe, Tx., U.S. — r14 120
Santa Fe, prov., Arg. — A4 54
Santa Fe, co., N.M., U.S. — B3 108
Santa Fe, stm., N.M., U.S. — h8 108
Santa Fe, stm., Fl., U.S. — g5 58
Santa Fe Baldy, mtn., N.M., U.S. — B4 108
Santa Fe Springs, Ca., U.S. — *n12 82
Santa Filomena, Braz. — C1 57
Santai, China — E6 31
Santa Inés, Isla, i., Chile — h11 54
Santa Isabel, Arg. — B3 54
Santa Isabel, P.R. — C3 65
Santa Isabel, Pico de, mtn., Eq. Gui. — *E1 46
Santa Isabel de Sihuas, Peru — E3 58
Santa Isabel do Rio Negro, Braz. — C2 59
Santa Isabel see Malabo, Eq. Gui.
Santa Lucía, Cuba — D6 64
Santa Lucía, stm., Ur. — g8 54
Santa Lucia Range, mts., Ca., U.S. — E3 82
Santa Magdalena, Isla, i., Mex. — B2 63
Santa Margarita, Ca., U.S. — E3 82
Santa Margarita, Isla de, i., Mex. — C2 63
Santa María [Capua Vetere], Italy — H9 23
Santa María Colotepec, Mex. — D5 63
Santa María de la Vitória, Braz. — B3 57
Santa María del Oro, Mex. — B3 63
Santa María di Leuca, Cape, c., Italy — E7 23
Santa Maria Mountains, mts., Az., U.S. — C3 80
Santa Marta, Col. — A3 60

Santa Marta, Spain — C2 22
Santa Marta Grande, Cabo de, c., Braz. — D3 56
Santa Monica, Ca., U.S. — m12 82
Santan, Az., U.S. — m9 80
Santana, Braz. — D2 57
Santana, Port. — h12 27
Santana, Coxilha de, hills, S.A. — E2 56
Santana do Cariri, Braz. — C3 57
Santana do Ipanema, Braz. — E1 57
Santana do Livramento, Braz. — E1 56
Santander, Col. — C2 60
Santander, Spain — A4 22
Santander, dept., Col. — B3 60
Santander Jiménez, Mex. — C5 63
Sant'Angelo Romano, Italy — g9 23
Santanilla, Islas, is., Hond. — B6 62
Santanoni Peak, mtn., N.Y., U.S. — A6 109
Sant'Antioco, i., Italy — E2 23
Sant'Anthony, Spain — C7 22
Santa Paula, Ca., U.S. — E4 82
Santaquin, Ut., U.S. — D4 121
Santarém, Braz. — C4 59
Santarém, Port. — C1 22
Santaren Channel, strt., Bah. — B4 64
Santa Rita, Braz. — C4 57
Santa Rita, Guam — M9 52
Santa Rita, Mt., U.S. — B4 103
Santa Rita, Ven. — A3 60
Santa Rita do Weil, Braz. — B4 59
Santa Rita Park, Ca., U.S. — D3 82
Santa Rosa, Arg. — A3 54
Santa Rosa, Arg. — A3 54
Santa Rosa, Bol. — B2 55
Santa Rosa, Braz. — B2 56
Santa Rosa, Col. — C4 60
Santa Rosa, Ec. — B2 58
Santa Rosa, Ca., U.S. — C2 82
Santa Rosa, Mo., U.S. — B3 102
Santa Rosa, N.M., U.S. — C5 108
Santa Rosa, co., Fl., U.S. — u14 86
Santa Rosa, Mount, hill, Guam — L10 52
Santa Rosa Beach, Fl., U.S. — u15 86
Santa Rosa de Aguán, Hond. — C5 62
Santa Rosa de Copán, Hond. — C3 62
Santa Rosa de Osos, Col. — B2 60
Santa Rosa [de Río Primero], Arg. — A4 54
Santa Rosa Island, i., Ca., U.S. — F3 82
Santa Rosa Island, i., Fl., U.S. — u14 86
Santa Rosalía, Mex. — B2 63
Santa Rosa Range, mts., Nv., U.S. — B4 105
Santa Teresa Gallura, Italy — D2 23
Santa Úrsula Coapa (part of Mexico City), Mex. — h9 63
Santa Venetia, Ca., U.S. — *D2 82
Santa Vitória do Palmar, Braz. — E2 56
Santa Ynez, Ca., U.S. — E3 82
Santee, Ca., U.S. — o16 82
Santee, Ne., U.S. — B8 104
Santee, stm., S.C., U.S. — E8 117
Santee Dam, S.C., U.S. — E7 117
Santee Indian Reservation, Ne., U.S. — B8 104
Sant'Eufemia, Gulf of, b., Italy — E6 23
Santiago, Braz. — D2 56
Santiago, Chile — A2 54
Santiago, Mex. — C3 63
Santiago, Pan. — F7 62
Santiago, Para. — E4 55
Santiago, Phil. — n13 34
Santiago, stm., S.A. — B2 58
Santiago, Cape, c., Phil. — p13 34
Santiago de Cao, Peru — C2 58
Santiago [de Compostela], Spain — A1 22
Santiago de Cuba, Cuba — E6 64
Santiago de Cuba, prov., Cuba — D6 64
Santiago del Estero, Arg. — E3 55
Santiago del Estero, prov., Arg. — E3 55
Santiago [de los Caballeros], Dom. Rep. — E8 64
Santiago de Machaca, Bol. — G5 54
Santiago Island, i., Phil. — n12 34
Santiago Ixcuintla, Mex. — m12 63
Santiago Papasquiaro, Mex. — B3 63
Santiago Peak, mtn., Ca., U.S. — n13 82
Santiago Reservoir, res., Ca., U.S. — n13 82
Santiam Pass, Or., U.S. — C4 114
Säntis, mtn., Switz. — B7 21
Santo, Tx., U.S. — C3 120
Santo Amaro, Braz. — B3 57
Santo Amaro, Ilha de, i., Braz. — m8 56
Santo Anastácio, Braz. — D2 56
Santo Ângelo, Braz. — B2 56
Santo Antônio, Braz. — C3 57
Santo Antônio, Ponta de, c., Braz. — E3 57
Santo Antônio de Jesus, Braz. — B3 57
Santo Antônio do Içá, Braz. — D4 60
Santo Corazón, Bol. — G7 54
Santo Domingo, Dom. Rep. — E9 64
Santo Domingo, Nic. — E8 63
Santo Domingo, stm., Mex. — n15 63
Santo Domingo de la Calzada, Spain — A4 22
Santo Domingo de los Colorados, Ec. — B2 58
Santo Domingo Indian Reservation, N.M., U.S. — h8 108
Santo Domingo Pueblo, N.M., U.S. — B3 108
Santoríni see Thíra, i., Grc.
Santos, Braz. — D3 56
Santos Dumont, Braz. — u4 56
Santo Tomás, Nic. — D5 63
Santo Tomás, Peru — D3 58
Santo Tomás, Mex. — B2 63
Santo Tomé, Arg. — E4 55
Santuit, R.I., U.S. — *C7 98
San Valentín, Cerro, mtn., Chile — D2 54
San Vicente, El Sal. — E7 63
San Vicente, N. Mar. Is. — D7 52
San Vicente de Alcántara, Spain — C2 22
San Vicente de Cañete, Peru — D2 58
San Vicente de la Barquera, Spain — A3 22
San Vicente del Caguán, Col. — C3 60
San Vicente Reservoir, res., Ca., U.S. — o16 82
San Vito al Tagliamento, Italy — B4 23
San Xavier Indian Reservation, Az., U.S. — E4 80

| Name | Map Ref. | Page |
|---|---|---|
| San Ygnacio, Tx., U.S. | F3 | 120 |
| San Ysidro, N.M., U.S. | B3 | 108 |
| Sanza Pombo, Ang. | C2 | 48 |
| Sanzhan, China | B3 | 33 |
| São Bento do Sul, Braz. | D3 | 56 |
| São Bento do Una, Braz. | k5 | 57 |
| São Bernardo do Campo, Braz. | C3 | 56 |
| São Borja, Braz. | D1 | 56 |
| São Carlos, Braz. | C3 | 56 |
| São Cristóvão, Braz. | D3 | 57 |
| São Domingos, Braz. | A3 | 56 |
| São Félix do Araguaia, Braz. | E4 | 59 |
| São Félix do Xingu, Braz. | D4 | 59 |
| São Fidélis, Braz. | B4 | 56 |
| São Francisco, Braz. | B4 | 56 |
| São Francisco, stm., Braz. | C3 | 57 |
| São Francisco do Sul, Braz. | D3 | 56 |
| São Gabriel, Braz. | E2 | 56 |
| São Gabriel da Cachoeira, Braz. | D4 | 60 |
| São Gotardo, Braz. | B3 | 56 |
| Sao Hill, Tan. | C6 | 48 |
| São Jerônimo, Braz. | E2 | 56 |
| São Jerônimo, Serra de, plat., Braz. | B2 | 56 |
| São João da Barra, Braz. | C4 | 56 |
| São João da Boa Vista, Braz. | C3 | 56 |
| São João da Ponte, Braz. | B4 | 56 |
| São João das Lampas, Port. | f9 | 22 |
| São João del Rei, Braz. | h5 | 57 |
| São João do Cariri, Braz. | C2 | 57 |
| São João do Piauí, Braz. | C3 | 57 |
| São João Nepomuceno, Braz. | C4 | 56 |
| São Joaquim, Braz. | D3 | 56 |
| São Joaquim National Park, Braz. | D2 | 56 |
| São Jorge, i., Port. | g8 | 44 |
| São José de Mipibu, Braz. | h6 | 57 |
| São José do Barreiro, Braz. | h5 | 56 |
| São José do Rio Pardo, Braz. | k8 | 56 |
| São José do Rio Preto, Braz. | C3 | 56 |
| São José dos Campos, Braz. | C3 | 56 |
| São José dos Pinhais, Braz. | D3 | 56 |
| São Leopoldo, Braz. | D2 | 56 |
| São Lourenço, Braz. | C3 | 56 |
| São Lourenço, stm., Braz. | B1 | 56 |
| São Lourenço do Sul, Braz. | E2 | 56 |
| São Luís, Braz. | B2 | 57 |
| São Luís de Quitunde, Braz. | k6 | 57 |
| São Luís Gonzaga, Braz. | D2 | 56 |
| São Manuel, Braz. | C3 | 56 |
| São Manuel, stm., Braz. | D3 | 59 |
| São Mateus, Braz. | E3 | 57 |
| São Miguel, i., Port. | h9 | 44 |
| São Miguel Arcanjo, Braz. | m7 | 56 |
| São Miguel dos Campos, Braz. | k5 | 57 |
| Saona, Isla, i., Dom. Rep. | E9 | 64 |
| Saône, stm., Fr. | D6 | 16 |
| São Paulo, Braz. | C3 | 56 |
| São Paulo, state, Braz. | C3 | 56 |
| São Paulo de Olivença, Braz. | D4 | 60 |
| São Pedro, Braz. | m8 | 56 |
| São Pedro do Piauí, Braz. | C2 | 57 |
| São Raimundo Nonato, Braz. | C2 | 57 |
| São Romão, Braz. | B3 | 56 |
| São Roque, Braz. | m8 | 56 |
| São Roque, Cabo de, c., Braz. | C3 | 57 |
| Saorre, Mount, mtn., N.W. Ter. | D16 | 66 |
| São Sebastião, Ilha de, i., Braz. | C3 | 56 |
| São Sebastião, Ponta, c., Moz. | B6 | 49 |
| São Sebastião do Caí, Braz. | D2 | 56 |
| São Sebastião do Paraíso, Braz. | C3 | 56 |
| São Sepé, Braz. | E2 | 56 |
| São Simão, Braz. | C3 | 56 |
| São Tomé, S. Tom./P. | E1 | 46 |
| São Tomé, i., S. Tom./P. | E1 | 46 |
| São Tomé, Cabo de, c., Braz. | C4 | 56 |
| São Tomé, Pico de, mtn., S. Tom./P. | *E1 | 46 |
| Sao Tome and Principe, ctry., Afr. | E1 | 46 |
| Saoura, Oued, val., Alg. | D4 | 44 |
| São Vicente, Braz. | C3 | 56 |
| São Vicente, Port. | h11 | 22 |
| São Vicente do Sul, Braz. | D2 | 56 |
| Sápai, Grc. | B5 | 25 |
| Sapele, Nig. | E6 | 45 |
| Sapello, N.M., U.S. | B4 | 108 |
| Sapelo Island, i., Ga., U.S. | E5 | 87 |
| Sapelo Sound, strt., Ga., U.S. | E5 | 87 |
| Sapinero, Co., U.S. | C3 | 83 |
| Sapitwa, mtn., Mwi. | E6 | 48 |
| Saposoa, Peru | C2 | 58 |
| Sapozhok, Sov. Un. | E13 | 27 |
| Sappa Creek, stm., U.S. | E5 | 104 |
| Sappa Creek, Middle Fork, stm., Ks., U.S. | C2 | 93 |
| Sappa Creek, South Fork, stm., Ks., U.S. | C3 | 93 |
| Sappemeer (part of Hoogezand), Neth. | A6 | 17 |
| Sapphire Mountains, mts., Mt., U.S. | D3 | 103 |
| Sappington, Mo., U.S. | f13 | 102 |
| Sapporo, Japan | C13 | 31 |
| Sapri, Italy | D5 | 23 |
| Sapulpa, Ok., U.S. | B5 | 113 |
| Saqqârah, Eg. | E3 | 41 |
| Saqqez, Iran | C3 | 39 |
| Saquarema, Braz. | C4 | 56 |
| Saquena, Peru | B3 | 58 |
| Saráb, Iran | C3 | 39 |
| Sarābiyûm, Eg. | D4 | 41 |
| Saraburi, Thai. | E4 | 35 |
| Saragossa, Tx., U.S. | D1 | 120 |
| Saragossa, Al., U.S. | B2 | 78 |
| Sarah, Ms., U.S. | A3 | 101 |
| Sarajevo, Yugo. | D4 | 24 |
| Sarakhs, Iran | C10 | 39 |
| Saraktash, Sov. Un. | E20 | 8 |
| Saraland, Al., U.S. | E1 | 78 |
| Saramacca, dept., Sur. | B3 | 59 |
| Saranac, Mi., U.S. | F5 | 99 |
| Saranac, N.Y., U.S. | f11 | 109 |
| Saranac, stm., N.Y., U.S. | F11 | 109 |
| Saranac Inn, N.Y., U.S. | f10 | 109 |
| Saranac Lake, N.Y., U.S. | f10 | 109 |
| Saranac Lakes, l., N.Y., U.S. | f10 | 109 |
| Saranda, Alb. | C3 | 40 |
| Sarandí, Braz. | D2 | 56 |
| Sarandí del Yi, Ur. | E1 | 56 |
| Sarandí Grande, Ur. | E1 | 56 |
| Sarangani Bay, b., Phil. | D6 | 34 |
| Sarangarh, India | D6 | 36 |
| Saranley, Som. | E5 | 47 |
| Saransk, Sov. Un. | D1 | 28 |
| Sarapuí, Braz. | m8 | 56 |
| Sarapul, Sov. Un. | B4 | 28 |
| Sarasota, Fl., U.S. | E4 | 86 |
| Sarasota, co., Fl., U.S. | E4 | 86 |
| Sarasota Bay, b., Fl., U.S. | E4 | 86 |
| Sarata, Sov. Un. | B9 | 24 |
| Saratoga, Ar., U.S. | D2 | 81 |
| Saratoga, Ca., U.S. | k8 | 82 |
| Saratoga, In., U.S. | D8 | 91 |
| Saratoga, Ia., U.S. | A5 | 92 |
| Saratoga, N.C., U.S. | B5 | 110 |
| Saratoga, Tx., U.S. | D5 | 120 |
| Saratoga, Wy., U.S. | E6 | 127 |
| Saratoga, co., N.Y., U.S. | B7 | 109 |
| Saratoga Lake, l., N.Y., U.S. | C7 | 109 |
| Saratoga National Historical Park, N.Y., U.S. | B7 | 109 |
| Saratoga Springs, i., U.S. | *E4 | 86 |
| Saratoga Springs, N.Y., U.S. | B7 | 109 |
| Saratov, Sov. Un. | D7 | 29 |
| Sarāvān, Iran | H11 | 39 |
| Saravan, Laos | E7 | 35 |
| Sarawak, state, Malay. | E4 | 34 |
| Saray, Tur. | B6 | 25 |
| Saudi Arabia, ctry., Asia | C4 | 38 |
| Sauêruiná, stm., Braz. | B4 | 55 |
| Saufley Field Naval Air Station, mil., Fl., U.S. | u14 | 86 |
| Sarca, stm., Italy | D6 | 20 |
| Sarcelles, Fr. | g10 | 16 |
| Sarcoxie, Mo., U.S. | D3 | 102 |
| Sārda, stm., Asia | C8 | 37 |
| Sardalas, Libya | D2 | 43 |
| Sardina, Col. | C4 | 60 |
| Sardinia, Oh., U.S. | C2 | 112 |
| Sardinia, i., Italy | D3 | 23 |
| Sardis, B.C. | f14 | 69 |
| Sardis, Al., U.S. | C2 | 78 |
| Sardis, Ga., U.S. | D5 | 87 |
| Sardis, Ky., U.S. | B6 | 94 |
| Sardis, Ms., U.S. | A4 | 101 |
| Sardis, Oh., U.S. | C5 | 112 |
| Sardis, Ok., U.S. | C6 | 113 |
| Sardis, Tn., U.S. | B3 | 119 |
| Sardis Lake, res., Ms., U.S. | A4 | 101 |
| Sarektjåkkå, mtn., Swe. | D7 | 14 |
| Sar-e Pol, Afg. | C12 | 39 |
| Sarepta, La., U.S. | B2 | 95 |
| Sarepta, Ms., U.S. | A4 | 101 |
| Sargans, Switz. | B5 | 20 |
| Sargeant, Mn., U.S. | G6 | 100 |
| Sargent, Ga., U.S. | C2 | 87 |
| Sargent, Ne., U.S. | C6 | 104 |
| Sargent, co., N.D., U.S. | C8 | 111 |
| Sargents, Co., U.S. | C4 | 83 |
| Sargodha, Pak. | *B5 | 36 |
| Sarh (Fort-Archambault), Chad | D3 | 46 |
| Sarhad, Afg. | k17 | 39 |
| Sārī, Iran | C6 | 39 |
| Saría, i., Grc. | E6 | 25 |
| Sarıkamış, Tur. | B14 | 40 |
| Sarina, Austl. | D8 | 50 |
| Sarine, stm., Switz. | C3 | 20 |
| Sariñena, Spain | B5 | 22 |
| Sarita, Tx., U.S. | F4 | 120 |
| Sariwòn, N. Kor. | G2 | 33 |
| Sark, i., Guernsey | F5 | 10 |
| Sarkand, Sov. Un. | F24 | 8 |
| Şarkışla, Tur. | C11 | 40 |
| Şarköy, Tur. | B6 | 40 |
| Şarlat, Fr. | E4 | 16 |
| Sarles, N.D., U.S. | A6 | 111 |
| Sarmiento, Arg. | D3 | 54 |
| Sarmiento, Cerro, mtn., Chile | h11 | 54 |
| Särna, Swe. | G5 | 14 |
| Sarnen, Switz. | C4 | 20 |
| Sarnen, Lake, l., Switz. | C4 | 20 |
| Sarnia, Ont. | E2 | 73 |
| Sarny, Sov. Un. | F6 | 27 |
| Sárö, Swe. | A5 | 15 |
| Sarona, Wi., U.S. | C2 | 126 |
| Saronic Gulf, b., Grc. | D4 | 25 |
| Saronno, Italy | B2 | 23 |
| Saronville, Ne., U.S. | D8 | 104 |
| Saros, Gulf of, b., Tur. | B6 | 25 |
| Sárospatak, Hung. | A5 | 24 |
| Sárova, Sov. Un. | D14 | 27 |
| Šar Planina, mts., Yugo. | E5 | 24 |
| Sarpsborg, Nor. | p29 | 14 |
| Sarpy, co., Ne., U.S. | C9 | 104 |
| Sarrebourg, Fr. | F7 | 17 |
| Sarreguemines, Fr. | C7 | 16 |
| Sarre-Union, Fr. | F7 | 17 |
| Sarria, Spain | A2 | 22 |
| Sarsfield, Ont. | h13 | 73 |
| Sarstún, stm., N.A. | C3 | 62 |
| Sartell, Mn., U.S. | E4 | 100 |
| Sartène, Fr. | m23 | 23 |
| Sarthe, stm., Fr. | D3 | 16 |
| Sartrouville, Fr. | g9 | 16 |
| Sarufutsu, Japan | D11 | 31 |
| Sárvár, Hung. | B3 | 24 |
| Sarvestān, Iran | G6 | 39 |
| Saruysu, stm., Sov. Un. | D7 | 28 |
| Sarzana, Italy | B2 | 23 |
| Sasabe, Az., U.S. | F4 | 80 |
| Sasakwa, Ok., U.S. | C5 | 113 |
| Sasaginnigak Lake, l., Man. | D4 | 70 |
| Sasarām, India | D7 | 36 |
| Sasebo, Japan | E10 | 31 |
| Saskatchewan, prov., Can. | E3 | 75 |
| Saskatchewan, stm., Can. | F12 | 66 |
| Saskatoon, Sask. | E2 | 75 |
| Sasovo, Sov. Un. | D13 | 27 |
| Sassafras, Tx., U.S. | k7 | 120 |
| Sassafras, stm., Md., U.S. | B5 | 97 |
| Sassafras Mountain, mtn., U.S. | A2 | 117 |
| Sassandra, I.C. | F3 | 45 |
| Sassandra, stm., I.C. | E3 | 45 |
| Sassari, Italy | D2 | 23 |
| Sasser, Ga., U.S. | E2 | 87 |
| Sasso Marconi, Italy | E7 | 20 |
| Sassuolo, Italy | E6 | 20 |
| Sastown, Lib. | F3 | 45 |
| Sastre, Arg. | A4 | 54 |
| Sasu-ri, N. Kor. | F3 | 33 |
| Sasykkol, Lake, l., Sov. Un. | D10 | 28 |
| Satah Mountain, mtn., B.C. | C5 | 69 |
| Satanta, Ks., U.S. | E3 | 93 |
| Satartia, Ms., U.S. | C3 | 101 |
| Sātāra, India | I4 | 37 |
| Satatna, W. Sam. | F11 | 52 |
| Satawal, i., Micron. | E5 | 52 |
| Satilla, stm., Ga., U.S. | E5 | 87 |
| Satevo, Mex. | C7 | 63 |
| Satinka, stm., Eng., U.K. | B9 | 12 |
| Satipo, Peru | D3 | 58 |
| Satirlar, Tur. | D7 | 25 |
| Satka, Sov. Un. | D8 | 28 |
| Sátmäla Range, mts., India | H7 | 37 |
| Satna, India | E8 | 37 |
| Sátoraljaújhely, Hung. | A5 | 24 |
| Sátpura Range, mts., India | D6 | 36 |
| Satrup, W. Ger. | D3 | 15 |
| Satsop, Wa., U.S. | B2 | 124 |
| Satsuma, Al., U.S. | E1 | 78 |
| Satsuma, Fl., U.S. | C5 | 86 |
| Sattahip, Thai. | F4 | 35 |
| Sattler, Tx., U.S. | h7 | 120 |
| Satu Mare, Rom. | B6 | 24 |
| Satun, Thai. | I4 | 35 |
| Satupa'itea, W. Sam. | F11 | 52 |
| Saturna Island, i., B.C. | E6 | 69 |
| Satus Creek, stm., Wa., U.S. | C5 | 124 |
| Sauce, Arg. | A5 | 54 |
| Sauceda Mountains, mts., Az., U.S. | E3 | 80 |
| Saucier, Ms., U.S. | E4 | 101 |
| Saucillo, Mex. | B3 | 63 |
| Sauda, Nor. | H2 | 14 |
| Saugatuck, Mi., U.S. | F4 | 99 |
| Saugatuck, stm., Ct., U.S. | D2 | 84 |
| Saugatucket, stm., R.I., U.S. | F4 | 116 |
| Saugatuck Reservoir, res., Ct., U.S. | D2 | 84 |
| Saugerties, N.Y., U.S. | C7 | 109 |
| Saugus, Ca., U.S. | *E4 | 82 |
| Saugus, Ma., U.S. | B5 | 98 |
| Saugus, stm., Ma., U.S. | g11 | 98 |
| Sauk, co., Wi., U.S. | E4 | 126 |
| Sauk, stm., Mn., U.S. | E4 | 100 |
| Sauk, stm., Wa., U.S. | A4 | 124 |
| Sauk Centre, Mn., U.S. | E4 | 100 |
| Sauk City, Wi., U.S. | E4 | 126 |
| Sauk Rapids, Mn., U.S. | E4 | 100 |
| Sauk Village, Il., U.S. | *m9 | 90 |
| Saukville, Wi., U.S. | E6 | 126 |
| Saül, Fr. Gu. | B4 | 59 |
| Saulgrub, W. Ger. | B7 | 20 |
| Saulnierville, N.S. | E3 | 71 |
| Saulsbury, Tn., U.S. | B2 | 119 |
| Saulston, N.C., U.S. | B5 | 110 |
| Sault-au-Mouton, Que. | A8 | 74 |
| Sault Sainte Marie, Ont. | p18 | 73 |
| Sault Sainte Marie, Mi., U.S. | B6 | 99 |
| Saulx [-de-Vesoul], Fr. | A1 | 21 |
| Saumâtre, Étang, l., Haiti | E7 | 64 |
| Saumlaki, Indon. | G8 | 34 |
| Saunders, co., Ne., U.S. | C9 | 104 |
| Saundersville, R.I., U.S. | E4 | 116 |
| Saundersville, Tn., U.S. | g10 | 119 |
| Saunemin, Il., U.S. | C5 | 90 |
| Saurimo, Ang. | C3 | 48 |
| Sausalito, Ca., U.S. | D2 | 82 |
| Sauveterre, Fr. | E5 | 16 |
| Savá, Hond. | C4 | 62 |
| Sava, stm., Yugo. | C2 | 24 |
| Savage, Md., U.S. | B4 | 97 |
| Savage, Mn., U.S. | *F5 | 100 |
| Savage, Ms., U.S. | A3 | 101 |
| Savage, Mt., U.S. | C12 | 103 |
| Savage, stm., Md., U.S. | k12 | 97 |
| Savai'i, i., W. Sam. | G11 | 6 |
| Savalou, Benin | E5 | 45 |
| Savanna, Il., U.S. | A3 | 90 |
| Savanna, Ok., U.S. | C6 | 113 |
| Savannah, Ga., U.S. | D5 | 87 |
| Savannah, Mo., U.S. | B3 | 102 |
| Savannah, N.Y., U.S. | B3 | 109 |
| Savannah, Oh., U.S. | B3 | 112 |
| Savannah, stm., U.S. | F5 | 117 |
| Savannah River Plant, sci., S.C., U.S. | E4 | 117 |
| Savanna Lake, l., Md., U.S. | D6 | 97 |
| Savanna-la-Mar, Jam. | E4 | 64 |
| Savannakhet, Laos | D6 | 35 |
| Save, stm., Afr. | B5 | 49 |
| Săveni, Rom. | B8 | 24 |
| Saverne, Fr. | C7 | 16 |
| Saverton, Mo., U.S. | B6 | 102 |
| Savery, Wy., U.S. | E5 | 127 |
| Savigliano, Italy | B1 | 23 |
| Savigny [-sur-Orge], Fr. | F2 | 17 |
| Saville Dam, l., Ct., U.S. | B4 | 84 |
| Savoie, dept., Fr. | D2 | 20 |
| Savona, B.C. | D7 | 69 |
| Savona, Italy | B2 | 23 |
| Savona, N.Y., U.S. | C3 | 109 |
| Savonlinna, Fin. | G13 | 14 |
| Savoonga, Ak., U.S. | C5 | 79 |
| Savoy, Ma., U.S. | A1 | 98 |
| Savran, Sov. Un. | G8 | 27 |
| Savsjö, Swe. | A8 | 15 |
| Savur, Tur. | D13 | 40 |
| Savusavu Bay, b., Fiji | H15 | 52 |
| Savu Sea, Indon. | G6 | 34 |
| Sawahlunto, Indon. | F2 | 34 |
| Sawākin (part of Port Sudan), Sud. | B4 | 47 |
| Sawanhalok, Thai. | B1 | 34 |
| Sawatch Range, mts., Co., U.S. | B4 | 83 |
| Sawdā', Jabal as, hills, Libya | D3 | 43 |
| Sawdirī, Sud. | C2 | 47 |
| Sawel Mountain, mtn., N. Ire., U.K. | C4 | 11 |
| Sawhāj, Eg. | D6 | 43 |
| Sawknah, Libya | D3 | 43 |
| Sawl, Eg. | E3 | 41 |
| Sawmill, Az., U.S. | B6 | 80 |
| Sawnee Mountain, mtn., Ga., U.S. | B2 | 87 |
| Sawn Lake, l., Alta. | A3 | 68 |
| Sawtooth Mountains, mts., Id., U.S. | F4 | 89 |
| Sawtooth National Recreation Area, Id., U.S. | E3 | 89 |
| Sawtooth Ridge, mtn., Wa., U.S. | A5 | 124 |
| Sawyer, Ks., U.S. | E5 | 93 |
| Sawyer, Mi., U.S. | G4 | 99 |
| Sawyer, Mn., U.S. | D6 | 100 |
| Sawyer, N.D., U.S. | A4 | 111 |
| Sawyer, Ok., U.S. | C6 | 113 |
| Sawyer, co., Wi., U.S. | C2 | 126 |
| Sawyers Hill, hill, Newf. | E5 | 72 |
| Sawyerville, Que. | D6 | 74 |
| Saxe, Va., U.S. | D4 | 123 |
| Saxis, U.S. | C7 | 123 |
| Saxmundham, Eng., U.K. | I13 | 12 |
| Saxon, W.V., U.S. | n13 | 125 |
| Saxon, Wi., U.S. | B3 | 126 |
| Saxonburg, Pa., U.S. | E2 | 115 |
| Saxony, hist. reg., E. Ger. | C6 | 18 |
| Saxony-Anhalt, hist. reg., E. Ger. | B6 | 19 |
| Saxton, Ky., U.S. | D5 | 94 |
| Saxton, Pa., U.S. | F5 | 115 |
| Saxtons, stm., Vt., U.S. | E3 | 122 |
| Saxtons River, Vt., U.S. | E3 | 122 |
| Say, Niger | D5 | 45 |
| Sayan, Peru | D2 | 58 |
| Sayan Mountains, mts., Asia | D12 | 29 |
| Saybrook, Il., U.S. | C5 | 90 |
| Saybrook Manor, Ct., U.S. | D6 | 84 |
| Saybrook Point, Ct., U.S. | D6 | 84 |
| Şaydā (Sidon), Leb. | B3 | 38 |
| Saydel, Ia., U.S. | e8 | 92 |
| Sayhūt, Yemen | D5 | 38 |
| Saylesville, R.I., U.S. | B4 | 116 |
| Saylorsburg, Pa., U.S. | E11 | 115 |
| Saylorville, Ia., U.S. | e8 | 92 |
| Saylorville Lake, res., Ia., U.S. | C4 | 92 |
| Sayner, Wi., U.S. | C4 | 126 |
| Sayre, Ok., U.S. | B2 | 113 |
| Sayre, Pa., U.S. | C8 | 115 |
| Sayreton, Al., U.S. | B3 | 78 |
| Sayreville, N.J., U.S. | C4 | 107 |
| Sayre Usa, Mong. | C6 | 31 |
| Sayula, Laguna de, l., Mex. | m12 | 63 |
| Say'ün, Yemen | D4 | 38 |
| Sayville, N.Y., U.S. | n15 | 109 |
| Sayward, B.C. | D5 | 69 |
| Sazani, i., Alb. | B2 | 25 |
| Sázava, Czech. | o18 | 26 |
| Sázava, stm., Czech. | D3 | 26 |
| Sazliyka, stm., Bul. | A3 | 90 |
| Scafell Pikes, mtn., Eng., U.K. | F5 | 13 |
| Scales Mound, Il., U.S. | A3 | 90 |
| Scalp Level, Pa., U.S. | F4 | 115 |
| Scaly Mountain, N.C., U.S. | f9 | 110 |
| Scammon, Ks., U.S. | E9 | 93 |
| Scammon Bay, Ak., U.S. | C6 | 79 |
| Scandia, Alta. | D4 | 68 |
| Scandia, Ks., U.S. | C6 | 93 |
| Scandicci, Italy | C3 | 23 |
| Scandinavia, Wi., U.S. | D4 | 126 |
| Scanlon, Mn., U.S. | D6 | 100 |
| Scansano, Italy | C3 | 23 |
| Scanzano, Italy | D6 | 23 |
| Scapa, Alta. | D5 | 68 |
| Scapa Flow, b., Scot., U.K. | A5 | 10 |
| Scapegoat Mountain, mtn., Mt., U.S. | C3 | 103 |
| Scappoose, Or., U.S. | B4 | 114 |
| Scarba, i., Scot., U.K. | D3 | 13 |
| Scarboro, Ga., U.S. | D5 | 87 |
| Scarborough, Ont. | m15 | 73 |
| Scarborough, Trin. | K14 | 64 |
| Scarborough, Eng., U.K. | C6 | 10 |
| Scarborough, Me., U.S. | E2 | 96 |
| Scarbro, W.V., U.S. | n13 | 125 |
| Scariff Island, i., Ire. | F1 | 11 |
| Scariff, Ire. | E3 | 11 |
| Scarsdale, N.Y., U.S. | h13 | 109 |
| Scartaglin, Ire. | E2 | 11 |
| Scarth, Man. | E1 | 70 |
| Scarville, Ia., U.S. | A4 | 92 |
| Scauri, Italy | F4 | 23 |
| Sceaux, Fr. | g10 | 16 |
| Scenic, S.D., U.S. | D3 | 118 |
| Sceptre, Sask. | G1 | 75 |
| Schaal, l., Eur. | B5 | 18 |
| Schaefferstown, Pa., U.S. | *F9 | 115 |
| Schaerbeek (Schaarbeek), Bel. | *D4 | 17 |
| Schaffer, Mi., U.S. | C3 | 99 |
| Schaffhausen, Switz. | A4 | 18 |
| Schaffhausen, state, Switz. | B4 | 20 |
| Schagen, Neth. | B4 | 17 |
| Schaghticoke, N.Y., U.S. | C7 | 109 |
| Schaller, Ia., U.S. | B2 | 92 |
| Schangnau, Switz. | C4 | 21 |
| Schärding, Aus. | E8 | 19 |
| Scharnhörn, i., W. Ger. | E2 | 15 |
| Schaumburg, Il., U.S. | h8 | 90 |
| Schefferville, Que. | h13 | 74 |
| Schell City, Mo., U.S. | C3 | 102 |
| Schell Creek Range, mts., Nv., U.S. | D7 | 105 |
| Schellsburg, Pa., U.S. | F4 | 115 |
| Schenectady, N.Y., U.S. | C7 | 109 |
| Schenectady, co., N.Y., U.S. | C6 | 109 |
| Schenefeld, W. Ger. | B5 | 18 |
| Schenevus, N.Y., U.S. | C6 | 109 |
| Scherer, Lake, res., Ga., U.S. | B3 | 91 |
| Schererville, In., U.S. | B3 | 91 |
| Scherfede, W. Ger. | B8 | 18 |
| Schertz, Tx., U.S. | h7 | 120 |
| Scheveningen (part of The Hague), Neth. | B4 | 17 |
| Schiedam, Neth. | B4 | 17 |
| Schiermonnikoog, i., Neth. | A6 | 17 |
| Schifferstadt, W. Ger. | D3 | 19 |
| Schiller Park, Il., U.S. | k9 | 90 |
| Schilpario, Italy | C7 | 20 |
| Schiltigheim, Fr. | C7 | 16 |
| Schio, Italy | C3 | 23 |
| Schkeuditz, E. Ger. | B7 | 19 |
| Schladming, Aus. | E8 | 19 |
| Schlater, Ms., U.S. | B3 | 101 |
| Schlei, b., W. Ger. | D3 | 15 |
| Schleicher, co., Tx., U.S. | D2 | 120 |
| Schleiz, E. Ger. | C7 | 18 |
| Schleswig, W. Ger. | A4 | 18 |
| Schleswig, Ia., U.S. | B2 | 92 |
| Schleswig-Holstein, state, W. Ger. | D3 | 15 |
| Schleswig-Holstein, hist. reg., W. Ger. | A4 | 18 |
| Schley, Va., U.S. | C6 | 123 |
| Schley, co., Ga., U.S. | D2 | 87 |
| Schlitz, W. Ger. | C4 | 19 |
| Schloss Neuhaus, W. Ger. | C4 | 18 |
| Schlüchtern, W. Ger. | C4 | 19 |
| Schmalkalden, E. Ger. | C5 | 18 |
| Schmölln, E. Ger. | C7 | 19 |
| Schnackenburg, W. Ger. | B6 | 18 |
| Schneeberg, E. Ger. | C7 | 19 |
| Schneeberg, mtn., W. Ger. | C4 | 19 |
| Schneider, In., U.S. | B3 | 91 |
| Schoenchen, Ks., U.S. | D4 | 93 |
| Schofield, Wi., U.S. | D4 | 126 |
| Schofield Barracks, mil., Hi., U.S. | g9 | 88 |
| Scott, i., Ant. | C31 | 7 |
| Schoharie, N.Y., U.S. | C6 | 109 |
| Schoharie, co., N.Y., U.S. | C6 | 109 |
| Schoharie Creek, stm., N.Y., U.S. | C6 | 109 |
| Scholls, Or., U.S. | h12 | 114 |
| Schönbach, Aus. | D7 | 19 |
| Schönebeck, E. Ger. | B6 | 18 |
| Schöneck, E. Ger. | C7 | 19 |
| Schongau, W. Ger. | E5 | 18 |
| Schöningen, W. Ger. | A5 | 19 |
| Schoodic Lake, l., Me., U.S. | C4 | 96 |
| Schoolcraft, Mi., U.S. | F5 | 99 |
| Schoolcraft, co., Mi., U.S. | B4 | 99 |
| Schooleys Mountain, mtn., N.J., U.S. | B3 | 107 |
| Schoonhoven, Neth. | C4 | 17 |
| Schopfheim, W. Ger. | B3 | 20 |
| Schorndorf, W. Ger. | E4 | 19 |
| Schoten, Bel. | C4 | 17 |
| Schötmar, W. Ger. | A3 | 19 |
| Schouten Islands, is., Indon. | F9 | 34 |
| Schramberg, W. Ger. | D4 | 18 |
| Schriever, La., U.S. | E5 | 95 |
| Schrobenhausen, W. Ger. | D5 | 18 |
| Schroeder, Mn., U.S. | C8 | 100 |
| Schroon Lake, N.Y., U.S. | B7 | 109 |
| Schroon Lake, l., N.Y., U.S. | B7 | 109 |
| Schuchk, Az., U.S. | E3 | 80 |
| Schuchuli, Az., U.S. | E3 | 80 |
| Schuler, Alta. | D5 | 68 |
| Schulenburg, Tx., U.S. | E4 | 120 |
| Schulte, Ks., U.S. | g12 | 93 |
| Schulter, Ok., U.S. | B6 | 113 |
| Schüpfheim, Switz. | C4 | 21 |
| Schurz, Nv., U.S. | E3 | 105 |
| Schussen, stm., W. Ger. | C4 | 21 |
| Schüttorf, W. Ger. | A2 | 19 |
| Schuyler, Ne., U.S. | C8 | 104 |
| Schuyler, Va., U.S. | C4 | 123 |
| Schuyler, co., Il., U.S. | C3 | 90 |
| Schuyler, co., Mo., U.S. | A5 | 102 |
| Schuyler, co., N.Y., U.S. | C4 | 109 |
| Schuyler Lake, N.Y., U.S. | C5 | 109 |
| Schuylerville, N.Y., U.S. | B7 | 109 |
| Schuylkill, co., Pa., U.S. | E9 | 115 |
| Schuylkill, stm., Pa., U.S. | F10 | 115 |
| Schuylkill Haven, Pa., U.S. | E9 | 115 |
| Schwabach, W. Ger. | D5 | 18 |
| Schwäbische Alb, mts., W. Ger. | E4 | 19 |
| Schwäbisch Gmünd, W. Ger. | D4 | 18 |
| Schwäbisch Hall, W. Ger. | D4 | 18 |
| Schwabmünchen, W. Ger. | A6 | 20 |
| Schwanden, Switz. | C4 | 18 |
| Schwandorf, W. Ger. | D6 | 18 |
| Schwaner Mountains, mts., Indon. | F4 | 34 |
| Schwarmstedt, W. Ger. | B4 | 19 |
| Schwarza, stm., W. Ger. | A5 | 19 |
| Schwarze Elster, stm., E. Ger. | B8 | 19 |
| Schwarzenbach [an der Saale], W. Ger. | C6 | 19 |
| Schwarzenbek, W. Ger. | B5 | 18 |
| Schwarzenberg, E. Ger. | C7 | 19 |
| Schwarzenfeld, W. Ger. | D7 | 19 |
| Schwarzheide, E. Ger. | B8 | 19 |
| Schwaz, Aus. | E5 | 18 |
| Schwedt, E. Ger. | B7 | 18 |
| Schweinfurt, W. Ger. | C5 | 18 |
| Schwerin, E. Ger. | B6 | 18 |
| Schwerin, Lake, l., E. Ger. | B5 | 18 |
| Schwetzingen, W. Ger. | *C4 | 18 |
| Schwyz, Switz. | E4 | 18 |
| Schwyz, state, Switz. | B4 | 20 |
| Sciacca, Italy | F4 | 23 |
| Science Hill, Ky., U.S. | C5 | 94 |
| Scilly, Isles of, is., Eng., U.K. | F3 | 10 |
| Scio, N.Y., U.S. | C3 | 109 |
| Scio, Oh., U.S. | B4 | 112 |
| Scio, Or., U.S. | C4 | 114 |
| Sciota, Il., U.S. | C3 | 90 |
| Scioto, co., Oh., U.S. | D2 | 112 |
| Scioto, stm., Oh., U.S. | B3 | 112 |
| Scioto Furnace, Oh., U.S. | D3 | 112 |
| Scipio, In., U.S. | F6 | 91 |
| Scipio, Ok., U.S. | B6 | 113 |
| Scipio, Ut., U.S. | D3 | 121 |
| Scircleville, In., U.S. | D5 | 91 |
| Scituate, Ma., U.S. | B6 | 98 |
| Scituate Reservoir, res., R.I., U.S. | C3 | 116 |
| Scobey, Ms., U.S. | D2 | 83 |
| Scobey, Mt., U.S. | B11 | 103 |
| Scofield, Ut., U.S. | D4 | 121 |
| Scofield Reservoir, res., Ut., U.S. | D4 | 121 |
| Scollard, Alta. | D4 | 68 |
| Scone, Austl. | F8 | 51 |
| Scooba, Ms., U.S. | C5 | 101 |
| Scopus, Mount, mtn., Isr. | m14 | 41 |
| Scoresbysund, Grnld. | B17 | 128 |
| Scotch Plains, N.J., U.S. | B4 | 107 |
| Scotchtown, N.Y., U.S. | *D6 | 109 |
| Scotia, Ont. | B5 | 73 |
| Scotia, Ca., U.S. | B1 | 82 |
| Scotia, N.Y., U.S. | C7 | 109 |
| Scotia, S.C., U.S. | F5 | 117 |
| Scotland, Ont. | D4 | 73 |
| Scotland, Ar., U.S. | B3 | 81 |
| Scotland, Ga., U.S. | D4 | 87 |
| Scotland, S.D., U.S. | D8 | 118 |
| Scotland, Tx., U.S. | C3 | 120 |
| Scotland, co., Mo., U.S. | A5 | 102 |
| Scotland, co., N.C., U.S. | C3 | 110 |
| Scotland, ter., U.K. | C6 | 8 |
| Scotland Neck, N.C., U.S. | A5 | 110 |
| Scotlandville, La., U.S. | D4 | 95 |
| Scotrun, Pa., U.S. | D11 | 115 |
| Scotsburn, N.S. | D6 | 71 |
| Scotstown, Que. | D6 | 74 |
| Scott, Sask. | E1 | 75 |
| Scott, Ar., U.S. | C3 | 81 |
| Scott, La., U.S. | D3 | 95 |
| Scott, Oh., U.S. | B1 | 112 |
| Scott, co., Ar., U.S. | C1 | 81 |
| Scott, co., Il., U.S. | D3 | 90 |
| Scott, co., In., U.S. | G6 | 91 |
| Scott, co., Ia., U.S. | C7 | 92 |
| Scott, co., Ks., U.S. | D3 | 93 |
| Scott, co., Ky., U.S. | B5 | 94 |
| Scott, co., Mn., U.S. | F5 | 100 |
| Scott, co., Ms., U.S. | C4 | 101 |
| Scott, co., Mo., U.S. | E8 | 102 |
| Scott, co., Tn., U.S. | C9 | 119 |
| Scott, co., Va., U.S. | f9 | 123 |
| Scott, i., Ant. | B29 | 7 |
| Scott, Cape, c., B.C. | D3 | 69 |
| Scott, Mount, mtn., Ok., U.S. | C3 | 113 |
| Scott, Mount, mtn., Or., U.S. | E4 | 114 |
| Scott Air Force Base, mil., Il., U.S. | E4 | 90 |
| Scott City, Ks., U.S. | D3 | 93 |
| Scott City, Mo., U.S. | D8 | 102 |
| Scottdale, Ga., U.S. | h8 | 87 |
| Scottdale, Pa., U.S. | F2 | 115 |
| Scott Glacier, ice, Ant. | C23 | 7 |
| Scott Glacier, ice, Ant. | A33 | 7 |
| Scott Islands, is., B.C. | D3 | 69 |
| Scott Lake, Fl., U.S. | *G6 | 86 |
| Scott Mountain, mtn., Id., U.S. | E3 | 89 |
| Scott Peak, mtn., Id., U.S. | E6 | 89 |
| Scott Reef, rf., Austl. | B3 | 50 |
| Scott Reservoir, res., N.C., U.S. | A1 | 110 |
| Scotts, Mi., U.S. | F5 | 99 |
| Scottsbluff, Ne., U.S. | C2 | 104 |
| Scotts Bluff, co., Ne., U.S. | C2 | 104 |
| Scotts Bluff National Monument, U.S. | C2 | 104 |
| Scottsboro, Al., U.S. | A3 | 78 |
| Scottsburg, In., U.S. | G6 | 91 |
| Scottsburg, Or., U.S. | D3 | 114 |
| Scottsdale, Az., U.S. | D4 | 80 |
| Scotts Hill, N.C., U.S. | C5 | 110 |
| Scotts Hill, Tn., U.S. | B3 | 119 |
| Scotts Mills, Or., U.S. | B4 | 114 |
| Scotts Mountain, mtn., N.J., U.S. | B2 | 107 |
| Scottsville, Ky., U.S. | D3 | 94 |
| Scottsville, Ar., U.S. | C6 | 93 |
| Scottsville, N.Y., U.S. | B3 | 109 |
| Scottsville, Va., U.S. | C4 | 123 |
| Scott Township, Pa., U.S. | *k13 | 115 |
| Scottville, Il., U.S. | D3 | 90 |
| Scottville, Mi., U.S. | E4 | 99 |
| Scourie, Scot., U.K. | B3 | 13 |
| Scout Lake, Sask. | H3 | 75 |
| Scow Bay, Ak., U.S. | m23 | 79 |
| Scraggly Lake, l., Me., U.S. | B4 | 96 |
| Scranton, Ar., U.S. | B2 | 81 |
| Scranton, Ia., U.S. | B3 | 92 |
| Scranton, Ks., U.S. | D8 | 93 |
| Scranton, Ky., U.S. | C6 | 94 |
| Scranton, N.C., U.S. | B6 | 110 |
| Scranton, N.D., U.S. | C2 | 111 |
| Scranton, Pa., U.S. | D10 | 115 |
| Scranton, S.C., U.S. | D8 | 117 |
| Screven, Ga., U.S. | E4 | 87 |
| Screven, co., Ga., U.S. | D5 | 87 |
| Scribner, Ne., U.S. | C9 | 104 |
| Scridain, Loch, b., Scot., U.K. | E3 | 13 |
| Scrivia, stm., Italy | C4 | 18 |
| Scugog, Lake, l., Ont. | C6 | 73 |
| Sculville, Il., U.S. | D3 | 107 |
| Scunthorpe, Eng., U.K. | D6 | 10 |
| Scuol (Schuls), Switz. | E5 | 18 |
| Scurry, Tx., U.S. | C2 | 120 |
| Scurry, co., Tx., U.S. | C2 | 120 |
| Scutari see Shkodra, Alb. | A2 | 40 |
| Scyrene, Al., U.S. | D2 | 78 |
| Scyros see Skíros, i., Grc. | C5 | 40 |
| Seaboard, N.C., U.S. | A5 | 110 |
| Seabreeze, De., U.S. | F5 | 85 |
| Sea Bright, N.J., U.S. | C5 | 107 |
| Seabrook, Md., U.S. | *C4 | 97 |
| Seabrook, N.H., U.S. | E5 | 106 |
| Seabrook, Tx., U.S. | r14 | 120 |
| Seabrook Beach, N.H., U.S. | E5 | 106 |
| Seabrook Island, i., S.C., U.S. | F7 | 117 |
| Sea Cliff, N.Y., U.S. | *E7 | 109 |
| Seadrift, Tx., U.S. | E4 | 120 |
| Seaford, De., U.S. | F3 | 85 |
| Seaford, N.Y., U.S. | *E7 | 109 |
| Seaford, Va., U.S. | h15 | 123 |
| Seaforth, Ont. | D3 | 73 |
| Seaforth, Mn., U.S. | F3 | 100 |
| Sea Girt, N.J., U.S. | C4 | 107 |
| Seagoville, Tx., U.S. | n10 | 120 |
| Seagram Lakes, l., Sask. | E1 | 75 |
| Seagrave, Ont. | C6 | 73 |
| Seagraves, Tx., U.S. | C1 | 120 |
| Seagrove, N.C., U.S. | B3 | 110 |
| Seaham, Eng., U.K. | F7 | 13 |
| Seahouses, Eng., U.K. | E7 | 13 |
| Sea Isle City, N.J., U.S. | E3 | 107 |
| Seal, stm., Man. | f8 | 70 |
| Seal Beach, Ca., U.S. | *n12 | 82 |
| Seal Cove, N.B. | E3 | 71 |
| Seal Cove, Newf. | D3 | 72 |
| Seale, Al., U.S. | C4 | 78 |
| Sealevel, N.C., U.S. | C6 | 110 |
| Seal Harbor, Me., U.S. | D4 | 96 |
| Seal Lake, l., Newf. | g9 | 72 |
| Seal Point, b., P.E.I. | C5 | 71 |
| Seal Rock, Or., U.S. | C2 | 114 |
| Sealston, Va., U.S. | B5 | 123 |
| Sealy, Tx., U.S. | E4 | 120 |
| Seama, N.M., U.S. | B2 | 108 |
| Seaman, Oh., U.S. | D2 | 112 |
| Seaman Range, mts., Nv., U.S. | F6 | 105 |
| Seanor, Pa., U.S. | F4 | 115 |
| Searchlight, Nv., U.S. | H7 | 105 |
| Searcy, Ar., U.S. | B4 | 81 |
| Searcy, co., Ar., U.S. | B3 | 81 |
| Searight, Pa., U.S. | G2 | 115 |
| Searles, Al., U.S. | B3 | 78 |
| Searles, Mn., U.S. | F4 | 100 |
| Searles Lake, l., Ca., U.S. | E5 | 82 |
| Searsboro, Ia., U.S. | C5 | 92 |
| Searsmont, Me., U.S. | D3 | 96 |
| Sears Falls, wtfl., Ne., U.S. | B5 | 104 |
| Searsport, Me., U.S. | D4 | 96 |
| Seaside, Or., U.S. | *D3 | 114 |
| Seaside, Ca., U.S. | D3 | 82 |
| Seaside Heights, N.J., U.S. | D4 | 107 |
| Seaside Park, N.J., U.S. | D4 | 107 |
| Seaton, Eng., U.K. | D4 | 12 |
| Seat Pleasant, Md., U.S. | C4 | 97 |
| Seattle, Wa., U.S. | B3 | 124 |
| Seattle-Tacoma International Airport, Wa., U.S. | f11 | 124 |
| Sea View, Wa., U.S. | *H13 | 98 |
| Seaview, Wa., U.S. | C1 | 124 |
| Seaville, N.J., U.S. | E3 | 107 |
| Seaward Roads, strt., Mid. Is. | J3 | 52 |
| Seba Beach, Alta. | C3 | 68 |
| Sébaco, Nic. | *E2 | 96 |
| Sebago Lake, Me., U.S. | E2 | 96 |
| Sebago Estates, Me., U.S. | g8 | 96 |
| Sebastian, Fl., U.S. | E6 | 86 |
| Sebastian, co., Ar., U.S. | B1 | 81 |
| Sebastian, Cape, c., Or., U.S. | E2 | 114 |
| Sebastián Vizcaíno, Bahía, b., Mex. | B2 | 63 |

| Name | Map Ref. | Page |
|---|---|---|
| Sebasticook Lake, l., Me., U.S. | D3 | 96 |
| Sebastopol, Ca., U.S. | C2 | 82 |
| Sebastopol, Ms., U.S. | C4 | 101 |
| Sebatik Island, i., Asia | E5 | 34 |
| Sebderat, Eth. | B4 | 47 |
| Sebec, Me., U.S. | C3 | 96 |
| Sebec Lake, l., Me., U.S. | C3 | 96 |
| Sebeka, Mn., U.S. | D3 | 100 |
| Sebeş, Rom. | C6 | 24 |
| Sebewaing, Mi., U.S. | E7 | 99 |
| Şebinkarahisar, Tur. | B12 | 40 |
| Šebnitz, E. Ger. | C7 | 18 |
| Seboeis, Me., U.S. | C4 | 96 |
| Seboeis, stm., Me., U.S. | B4 | 96 |
| Seboeis Lake, l., Me., U.S. | C4 | 96 |
| Seboomook Lake, l., Me., U.S. | C3 | 96 |
| Seboyeta, N.M., U.S. | B2 | 108 |
| Sebree, Ky., U.S. | C2 | 94 |
| Sebrell, Va., U.S. | D5 | 123 |
| Sebring, Fl., U.S. | E5 | 86 |
| Sebring, Oh., U.S. | B4 | 112 |
| Sebringville, Ont. | D3 | 73 |
| Secaucus, N.J., U.S. | h8 | 107 |
| Secchia, stm., Italy | B3 | 23 |
| Sechelt, B.C. | E6 | 69 |
| Sechura, Peru | C1 | 58 |
| Sechura, Bahía de, b., Peru | C1 | 58 |
| Sechura, Desierto de, des., Peru | C1 | 58 |
| Seclin, Fr. | D3 | 17 |
| Seco, Ky., U.S. | C7 | 94 |
| Second Lake, l., N.H., U.S. | f7 | 106 |
| Second Mesa, Az., U.S. | B5 | 80 |
| Secor, Il., U.S. | C4 | 90 |
| Secretan, Sask. | G2 | 75 |
| Secretary, Md., U.S. | C6 | 97 |
| Secretary Island, i., N.Z. | P11 | 51 |
| Secret Lake, l., R.I., U.S. | E4 | 116 |
| Section, Al., U.S. | A4 | 78 |
| Sector Popular (part of Mexico City), Mex. | h9 | 63 |
| Security, Co., U.S. | C6 | 83 |
| Sedalia, Alta. | D5 | 68 |
| Sedalia, Co., U.S. | B6 | 83 |
| Sedalia, In., U.S. | D4 | 91 |
| Sedalia, Ky., U.S. | f9 | 94 |
| Sedalia, Mo., U.S. | C4 | 102 |
| Sedalia, Oh., U.S. | C2 | 112 |
| Sedan, Fr. | C6 | 16 |
| Sedan, Ks., U.S. | E7 | 93 |
| Sedan, Mn., U.S. | E3 | 100 |
| Sedan, N.M., U.S. | A6 | 108 |
| Sedbergh, Eng., U.K. | F6 | 13 |
| Sederot, Isr. | C6 | 41 |
| Sedgewick, Alta. | C5 | 68 |
| Sedgewick, Mount, mtn., N.M., U.S. | B1 | 108 |
| Sedgewickville, Mo., U.S. | D8 | 102 |
| Sedgwick, Ar., U.S. | B5 | 81 |
| Sedgwick, Co., U.S. | A8 | 83 |
| Sedgwick, Ks., U.S. | E6 | 93 |
| Sedgwick, Me., U.S. | D4 | 96 |
| Sedgwick, co., Co., U.S. | A8 | 83 |
| Sedgwick, co., Ks., U.S. | E6 | 93 |
| Sédhiou, Sen. | D1 | 45 |
| Sedillo Hill, N.M., U.S. | k8 | 108 |
| Sedlčany, Czech. | D9 | 19 |
| Sedley, Sask. | G3 | 75 |
| Sedley, Va., U.S. | D6 | 123 |
| Sedom, Isr. | C7 | 41 |
| Sedona, Az., U.S. | C4 | 80 |
| Sedot Yam, Isr. | B6 | 41 |
| Sedro Woolley, Wa., U.S. | A3 | 124 |
| Sedrun, Switz. | C6 | 21 |
| Seebe, Alta. | D3 | 68 |
| Seeber, stm., Can. | C5 | 70 |
| Seebert, W.V., U.S. | C4 | 125 |
| Seehausen, E. Ger. | F5 | 15 |
| Seeheim, Nmb. | C2 | 49 |
| Seeis, Nmb. | B2 | 49 |
| Seekonk, Ma., U.S. | C5 | 98 |
| Seekonk, stm., R.I., U.S. | C4 | 116 |
| Seeley, Ca., U.S. | F6 | 82 |
| Seeley Lake, Mt., U.S. | C3 | 103 |
| Seeleys Bay, Ont. | C8 | 73 |
| Seelow, E. Ger. | F8 | 15 |
| Seelyville, In., U.S. | F3 | 91 |
| Seelyville, Pa., U.S. | C11 | 115 |
| Sées, Fr. | C4 | 16 |
| Seesen, W. Ger. | B5 | 19 |
| Seez, stm., Switz. | C7 | 21 |
| Sefadu, S.L. | E2 | 45 |
| Seferihisar, Tur. | C6 | 25 |
| Sefid, stm., Iran | C4 | 39 |
| Sefid Ābeh, Iran | F10 | 39 |
| Segamat, Malay. | K5 | 35 |
| Segbwema, S.L. | E2 | 45 |
| Segesta, hist., Italy | F4 | 23 |
| Segezha, Sov. Un. | F16 | 14 |
| Segorbe, Spain | C5 | 22 |
| Ségou, Mali | D3 | 45 |
| Segovia, Spain | B3 | 22 |
| Segozero, l., Sov. Un. | F15 | 14 |
| Segré, Fr. | D3 | 16 |
| Segre, stm., Eur. | B6 | 22 |
| Segreganset, Ma., U.S. | C5 | 98 |
| Seguam Island, i., Ak., U.S. | E5 | 79 |
| Seguam Pass, strt., Ak., U.S. | E5 | 79 |
| Séguédine, Niger | B7 | 45 |
| Séguéla, I.C. | E3 | 45 |
| Seguin, Tx., U.S. | E4 | 120 |
| Seguin Falls, Ont. | B5 | 73 |
| Segundo, Co., U.S. | D6 | 83 |
| Segura, stm., Spain | C5 | 22 |
| Sehnkwehn, Lib. | E3 | 45 |
| Sehore, India | F6 | 37 |
| Sehwān, Pak. | D1 | 37 |
| Seibert, Co., U.S. | B8 | 83 |
| Seiling, Ok., U.S. | A3 | 113 |
| Seille, stm., Fr. | F6 | 17 |
| Seinäjoki, Fin. | F10 | 14 |
| Seine, stm., Fr. | C4 | 16 |
| Seine, Bay of the, est., Fr. | C3 | 16 |
| Seine-et-Marne, dept., Fr. | F3 | 17 |
| Seixal, Port. | f9 | 22 |
| Sejerby, Den. | C5 | 15 |
| Sejerø, i., Den. | C5 | 15 |
| Sejerø Bugt, b., Den. | C5 | 15 |
| Sekenke, Tan. | B5 | 48 |
| Seki, Japan | o15 | 33 |
| Sekiu, Wa., U.S. | A1 | 124 |
| Sekondi-Takoradi, Ghana | F4 | 45 |
| Sekota, Eth. | C4 | 47 |
| Selah, Wa., U.S. | C5 | 124 |
| Selangor, state, Malay. | K4 | 35 |
| Selanovtsi, Bul. | D7 | 24 |
| Selaru, i., Indon. | G8 | 34 |
| Selatan, Cape, c., Indon. | F4 | 34 |
| Selatpanjang, Indon. | L5 | 35 |
| Selawik, Ak., U.S. | B7 | 79 |
| Selawik Lake, l., Ak., U.S. | B7 | 79 |
| Selayar, i., Indon. | G6 | 34 |
| Selb, W. Ger. | C6 | 18 |
| Selbourne, Cape, c., Ant. | g40 | 7 |
| Selbu, Nor. | F4 | 14 |
| Selby, Eng., U.K. | A6 | 12 |
| Selby, S.D., U.S. | B5 | 118 |
| Selbyville, De., U.S. | G5 | 85 |
| Selbyville, W.V., U.S. | C4 | 125 |
| Selde, Den. | B3 | 15 |
| Selden, Ks., U.S. | C3 | 93 |
| Selden, N.Y., U.S. | *n15 | 109 |
| Seldovia, Ak., U.S. | D9 | 79 |
| Seldus, Mn., U.S. | D3 | 100 |
| Selenga, stm., Asia | B5 | 31 |
| Selenge, stm., Asia | B5 | 31 |
| Selenter, l., W. Ger. | D4 | 15 |
| Sélestat, Fr. | C7 | 16 |
| Selfridge, N.D., U.S. | C5 | 111 |
| Sélibaby, Maur. | C2 | 45 |
| Seligenstadt, W. Ger. | C3 | 19 |
| Seliger, Lake, l., Sov. Un. | C9 | 27 |
| Seligman, Az., U.S. | B3 | 80 |
| Seligman, Mo., U.S. | E4 | 102 |
| Selinsgrove, Pa., U.S. | E8 | 115 |
| Selizharovo, Sov. Un. | C9 | 27 |
| Selkirk, Man. | D3 | 70 |
| Selkirk, Ont. | E5 | 73 |
| Selkirk, Scot., U.K. | C5 | 10 |
| Selkirk, Pic la, mtn., Haiti | E8 | 64 |
| Selkirk Mountains, mts., N.A. | D9 | 69 |
| Selleck, Wa., U.S. | B4 | 124 |
| Seller Lake, l., Man. | B4 | 70 |
| Sellers, Al., U.S. | C3 | 78 |
| Sellers, S.C., U.S. | C9 | 117 |
| Sellersburg, In., U.S. | H6 | 91 |
| Sellersville, Pa., U.S. | F11 | 115 |
| Sells, Az., U.S. | F4 | 80 |
| Selm, W. Ger. | B2 | 19 |
| Selma, N.S. | D6 | 71 |
| Selma, Al., U.S. | C2 | 78 |
| Selma, Ar., U.S. | D4 | 81 |
| Selma, Ca., U.S. | D4 | 82 |
| Selma, In., U.S. | D7 | 91 |
| Selma, N.C., U.S. | B4 | 110 |
| Selma, Or., U.S. | E3 | 114 |
| Selmer, Tn., U.S. | B3 | 119 |
| Selsey, Eng., U.K. | D7 | 12 |
| Selsey Bill, c., Eng., U.K. | D7 | 12 |
| Selva, Arg. | E3 | 55 |
| Selvagens, Ilhas, is., Port. | m14 | 22 |
| Selvas, for., Braz. | D4 | 53 |
| Selway, stm., Id., U.S. | C3 | 89 |
| Selway, Mount, mtn., B.C. | A6 | 69 |
| Selwyn, Mount, mtn., B.C. | A6 | 69 |
| Selwyn Lake, l., Can. | k8 | 75 |
| Selwyn Mountains, mts., Can. | D6 | 66 |
| Selz, N.D., U.S. | B6 | 111 |
| Seman, Al., U.S. | C3 | 78 |
| Semani, stm., Alb. | B2 | 25 |
| Semans, Sask. | F3 | 75 |
| Semara, W. Sah. | D2 | 44 |
| Semarang, Indon. | G4 | 34 |
| Semenovka, Sov. Un. | E9 | 27 |
| Semeru, mtn., Indon. | G4 | 34 |
| Seminary, Ms., U.S. | D4 | 101 |
| Seminoe Dam, Wy., U.S. | D6 | 127 |
| Seminoe Mountains, mts., Wy., U.S. | D6 | 127 |
| Seminoe Reservoir, res., Wy., U.S. | D6 | 127 |
| Seminole, Al., U.S. | C3 | 78 |
| Seminole, Ok., U.S. | B5 | 113 |
| Seminole, Tx., U.S. | C1 | 120 |
| Seminole, co., Fl., U.S. | D5 | 86 |
| Seminole, co., Ga., U.S. | F2 | 87 |
| Seminole, co., Ok., U.S. | B5 | 113 |
| Seminole, Lake, res., U.S. | F2 | 87 |
| Seminole Park, Fl., U.S. | *p10 | 86 |
| Semipalatinsk, Sov. Un. | D11 | 29 |
| Semisopochnoi Island, i., Ak., U.S. | E3 | 79 |
| Semitau, Indon. | E4 | 34 |
| Semiyarskoye, Sov. Un. | C9 | 28 |
| Semliki, stm., Afr. | A5 | 48 |
| Semmens Lake, l., Man. | B4 | 70 |
| Semmering Pass, Aus. | E7 | 18 |
| Semmes, Al., U.S. | E1 | 78 |
| Semnān, Iran | B5 | 38 |
| Semois, stm., Eur. | E5 | 17 |
| Semonov, Sov. Un. | D17 | 8 |
| Semora, N.C., U.S. | A3 | 110 |
| Sempach, Switz. | B5 | 21 |
| Sempacher Lake, l., Switz. | B4 | 20 |
| Semur-en-Auxois, Fr. | D6 | 16 |
| Sen, stm., Camb. | F6 | 35 |
| Sena, N.M., U.S. | B4 | 108 |
| Senachwine Lake, l., Il., U.S. | B4 | 90 |
| Senador Pompeu, Braz. | C3 | 57 |
| Sena Madureira, Braz. | C4 | 58 |
| Senanga, Zam. | E3 | 48 |
| Senate, Sask. | H1 | 75 |
| Senath, Mo., U.S. | E7 | 102 |
| Senatobia, Ms., U.S. | A4 | 101 |
| Sendai, Japan | K5 | 33 |
| Sendai, Japan | D13 | 31 |
| Sendai Bay, b., Japan | G10 | 33 |
| Seneca, Il., U.S. | B5 | 90 |
| Seneca, Ks., U.S. | C7 | 93 |
| Seneca, Mo., U.S. | E3 | 102 |
| Seneca, Ne., U.S. | B5 | 104 |
| Seneca, Or., U.S. | C8 | 114 |
| Seneca, Pa., U.S. | D2 | 115 |
| Seneca, S.C., U.S. | B2 | 117 |
| Seneca, S.D., U.S. | B6 | 118 |
| Seneca, Wi., U.S. | E3 | 126 |
| Seneca, co., N.Y., U.S. | C4 | 109 |
| Seneca, co., Oh., U.S. | A2 | 112 |
| Seneca Falls, N.Y., U.S. | C4 | 109 |
| Seneca Lake, l., N.Y., U.S. | C4 | 109 |
| Senecaville, Oh., U.S. | C4 | 112 |
| Senecaville Lake, res., Oh., U.S. | C4 | 112 |
| Seneffe, Bel. | D4 | 17 |
| Senegal, ctry., Afr. | D2 | 45 |
| Sénégal, stm., Afr. | C2 | 45 |
| Senetosa, Point, c., Italy | D2 | 23 |
| Seney, Mi., U.S. | B5 | 99 |
| Senftenberg, E. Ger. | C6 | 18 |
| Senga Hill, Zam. | B6 | 48 |
| Sênggê Zangbo, stm., China | B7 | 36 |
| Senguerr, stm., Arg. | D2 | 53 |
| Senhor do Bonfim, Braz. | C4 | 57 |
| Senigallia, Italy | C4 | 23 |
| Senj, Yugo. | C7 | 14 |
| Senja, i., Nor. | C7 | 14 |
| Senlac, Sask. | E1 | 75 |
| Senlis, Fr. | C5 | 16 |
| Senneterre, Que. | k11 | 74 |
| Senoia, Ga., U.S. | C2 | 87 |
| Sens, Fr. | C5 | 16 |
| Senta, Yugo. | C5 | 24 |
| Sentery, Zaire | C4 | 48 |
| Sentinel, Ok., U.S. | B2 | 113 |
| Sentinel Butte, N.D., U.S. | C2 | 111 |
| Sentinel Butte, mtn., N.D., U.S. | C2 | 111 |
| Sentinel Peak, mtn., B.C. | B6 | 69 |
| Sentinel Range, mts., Ant. | B4 | 7 |
| Senzu, Japan | n17 | 33 |
| Seo de Urgel, Spain | A6 | 22 |
| Seongnam, S. Kor. | *H3 | 33 |
| Seoni, India | F7 | 37 |
| Seoul (Sŏul), S. Kor. | D10 | 31 |
| Sepik, stm., Pap. N. Gui. | h11 | 50 |
| Sept-Îles (Seven Islands), Que. | h13 | 74 |
| Sepulga, stm., Al., U.S. | D3 | 78 |
| Sequatchie, Tn., U.S. | D8 | 119 |
| Sequatchie, co., Tn., U.S. | D8 | 119 |
| Sequatchie, stm., Tn., U.S. | D8 | 119 |
| Sequim, Wa., U.S. | A2 | 124 |
| Sequoia National Park, Ca., U.S. | D4 | 82 |
| Sequoia National Park, Ca., U.S. | D4 | 82 |
| Sequoyah, co., Ok., U.S. | B7 | 113 |
| Serafimovich, Sov. Un. | G14 | 27 |
| Serafina, N.M., U.S. | B4 | 108 |
| Seraing, Bel. | B6 | 16 |
| Serang, Indon. | G3 | 34 |
| Serasan, i., Indon. | k8 | 35 |
| Serbia, hist. reg., Yugo. | D5 | 24 |
| Serdo, Eth. | C5 | 47 |
| Serdobsk, Sov. Un. | E15 | 27 |
| Sered', Czech. | D4 | 26 |
| Şereflikoçhisar, Tur. | C9 | 40 |
| Seremban, Malay. | E2 | 34 |
| Serengeti Plain, pl., Tan. | B5 | 48 |
| Serenje, Zam. | D5 | 48 |
| Sergeant, Pa., U.S. | C4 | 115 |
| Sergeant Bluff, Ia., U.S. | B1 | 92 |
| Sergeantsville, N.J., U.S. | C3 | 107 |
| Sergino, Sov. Un. | C22 | 8 |
| Sergipe, state, Braz. | D5 | 57 |
| Seria, Bru. | E4 | 34 |
| Sérifos, i., Grc. | D5 | 25 |
| Serina, Italy | C4 | 23 |
| Seringapatam Reef, rf., Austl. | B3 | 50 |
| Serinhaém, Braz. | k6 | 57 |
| Serio, stm., Italy | E4 | 21 |
| Serles, Tn., U.S. | B3 | 119 |
| Sernyĭ Zavod, Sov. Un. | B9 | 39 |
| Serón, Spain | D4 | 22 |
| Serov, Sov. Un. | D9 | 29 |
| Serowe, Bots. | B4 | 49 |
| Serpa, Port. | D2 | 22 |
| Serpentine Lakes, l., Austl. | E4 | 50 |
| Serpents Mouth, strt. | K14 | 64 |
| Serpukhov, Sov. Un. | D6 | 29 |
| Serra dos Órgãos National Park, Braz. | h6 | 56 |
| Sérrai, Grc. | B4 | 40 |
| Serrana Bank, Col. | C7 | 62 |
| Serra Negra, Braz. | m8 | 56 |
| Serranilla Bank, Col. | C8 | 62 |
| Serranópolis, Braz. | B2 | 56 |
| Serra Talhada, Braz. | C3 | 57 |
| Serres, Fr. | E1 | 20 |
| Serres, Braz. | A3 | 54 |
| Serrinha, Braz. | D3 | 57 |
| Sêrro, Braz. | B4 | 56 |
| Sertã, Port. | C1 | 22 |
| Sertânia, Braz. | C3 | 57 |
| Sertãozinho, Braz. | k8 | 56 |
| Serua, i., Indon. | G8 | 34 |
| Serui, Indon. | F9 | 34 |
| Serule, Bots. | B4 | 49 |
| Sérvia, Grc. | B4 | 25 |
| Sêrxü, China | E4 | 31 |
| Sese Islands, is., Ug. | B5 | 48 |
| Sesfontein, Nmb. | A1 | 49 |
| Sesheke, Zam. | E3 | 48 |
| Sesia, stm., Italy | B2 | 23 |
| Sesser, Il., U.S. | E4 | 90 |
| Sessums, Ms., U.S. | B5 | 101 |
| Sesto [Fiorentino], Italy | C3 | 23 |
| Šeštokai, Sov. Un. | A7 | 26 |
| Sesto San Giovanni, Italy | D5 | 20 |
| Sestriere, Italy | D1 | 23 |
| Sestri Levante, Italy | B2 | 23 |
| Sestroretsk, Sov. Un. | A8 | 27 |
| Setana, Japan | E9 | 33 |
| Sète, Fr. | F5 | 16 |
| Sete Guedas National Park, Braz. | C2 | 56 |
| Sete Lagoas, Braz. | B4 | 56 |
| Seth, W.V., U.S. | C3 | 125 |
| Seto, Japan | I8 | 33 |
| Seton Portage, B.C. | D6 | 69 |
| Seto Sea, Japan | I6 | 33 |
| Settat, Mor. | C3 | 44 |
| Sette Cama, Gabon | F1 | 46 |
| Settee Lake, l., Sask. | B3 | 75 |
| Setting Lake, l., Man. | B2 | 70 |
| Settle, Eng., U.K. | F6 | 13 |
| Setúbal, Port. | C1 | 22 |
| Setúbal, Bay of, b., Port. | C1 | 22 |
| Seul, Lac, l., Ont. | o16 | 73 |
| Seul Choix Point, c., Mi., U.S. | C5 | 99 |
| Seurre, Fr. | E6 | 16 |
| Sevan, Lake, l., Sov. Un. | E6 | 29 |
| Sevastopol, Sov. Un. | E6 | 29 |
| Seven Devils Lake, res., Ar., U.S. | D1 | 81 |
| Seven Devils Mountains, mts., Id., U.S. | D2 | 89 |
| Seven Heads, c., Ire. | F3 | 11 |
| Seven Hills, Oh., U.S. | h9 | 112 |
| Seven Islands Bay, b., Newf. | f9 | 72 |
| Seven Mile, Oh., U.S. | C1 | 112 |
| Seven Mile Beach, N.J., U.S. | E3 | 107 |
| Sevenoaks, Eng., U.K. | m13 | 12 |
| Seven Oaks, S.C., U.S. | *C5 | 117 |
| Seven Persons, Alta. | E5 | 68 |
| Seven Sisters Peaks, mts., B.C. | B3 | 69 |
| Seven Springs, N.C., U.S. | B5 | 110 |
| Seventy Mile House, B.C. | D7 | 69 |
| Severance, Co., U.S. | A6 | 83 |
| Severance, Ks., U.S. | C8 | 93 |
| Severance, N.H., U.S. | D3 | 106 |
| Severka, stm., Sov. Un. | n18 | 27 |
| Severn, Md., U.S. | B4 | 97 |
| Severn, N.C., U.S. | A5 | 110 |
| Severn, stm., Ont. | o17 | 73 |
| Severn, stm., U.K. | E3 | 12 |
| Severn, Mouth of the, mth., U.K. | C5 | 12 |
| Severna Park, Md., U.S. | *B4 | 97 |
| Severnaya Zemlya, is., Sov. Un. | B11 | 29 |
| Severn River, Md., U.S. | *B4 | 97 |
| Severnoe, stm., Switz. | C3 | 21 |
| Severočeský, prov., Czech. | C9 | 19 |
| Severodonetsk, Sov. Un. | q21 | 27 |
| Severodvinsk, Sov. Un. | C16 | 8 |
| Severomorsk, Sov. Un. | C15 | 14 |
| Severouralsk, Sov. Un. | C21 | 8 |
| Severy, Ks., U.S. | E7 | 93 |
| Sevier, Ut., U.S. | E3 | 121 |
| Sevier, co., Ar., U.S. | D1 | 81 |
| Sevier, co., Tn., U.S. | D10 | 119 |
| Sevier, co., Ut., U.S. | E4 | 121 |
| Sevier, stm., Ut., U.S. | D3 | 121 |
| Sevier, East Fork, stm. Ut., U.S. | F3 | 121 |
| Sevier Bridge Reservoir, res., Ut., U.S. | D4 | 121 |
| Sevier Desert, des., Ut., U.S. | D3 | 121 |
| Sevier Lake, l., Ut., U.S. | E2 | 121 |
| Sevierville, Tn., U.S. | D10 | 119 |
| Sevilla, Col. | C2 | 60 |
| Sevilla, Spain | D5 | 22 |
| Seville, Fl., U.S. | C5 | 86 |
| Seville, Ga., U.S. | E3 | 87 |
| Seville, Oh., U.S. | A4 | 112 |
| Sevlievo, Bul. | D7 | 24 |
| Sevran, Fr. | g11 | 16 |
| Sèvre, stm., Fr. | E8 | 16 |
| Sèvre Niortaise, stm., Fr. | D3 | 16 |
| Sèvres, Fr. | g9 | 16 |
| Sewal, Ia., U.S. | D4 | 92 |
| Sewanee, Tn., U.S. | D8 | 119 |
| Seward, Ak., U.S. | C10 | 79 |
| Seward, Ks., U.S. | D5 | 93 |
| Seward, Ne., U.S. | D8 | 104 |
| Seward, N.Y., U.S. | C6 | 109 |
| Seward, Ok., U.S. | B4 | 113 |
| Seward, Pa., U.S. | F3 | 115 |
| Seward, co., Ks., U.S. | E3 | 93 |
| Seward, co., Ne., U.S. | D8 | 104 |
| Seward Peninsula, pen., Ak., U.S. | B7 | 79 |
| Sewaren, N.J., U.S. | k7 | 107 |
| Sewell, Chile | A2 | 54 |
| Sewell, N.J., U.S. | D2 | 107 |
| Sewen, Fr. | D6 | 16 |
| Sewickley, Pa., U.S. | E1 | 115 |
| Sexsmith, Alta. | B1 | 68 |
| Sextonville, Wi., U.S. | E3 | 126 |
| Seychelles, ctry., Afr. | G24 | 2 |
| Seydişehir, Tur. | D8 | 40 |
| Seydisfjördur, Ice. | n26 | 14 |
| Seyhan (Sarus), stm., Tur. | C10 | 40 |
| Seylac, Som. | C5 | 47 |
| Seym, stm., Sov. Un. | F9 | 27 |
| Seymchan, Sov. Un. | C18 | 29 |
| Seymour, i., Grnld. | B16 | 128 |
| Seymour, Austl. | H5 | 51 |
| Seymour, Ct., U.S. | D3 | 84 |
| Seymour, Il., U.S. | C5 | 90 |
| Seymour, In., U.S. | G6 | 91 |
| Seymour, Ia., U.S. | D4 | 92 |
| Seymour, Mo., U.S. | D5 | 102 |
| Seymour, Tn., U.S. | D10 | 119 |
| Seymour, Tx., U.S. | C3 | 120 |
| Seymour, Wi., U.S. | D5 | 126 |
| Seymour, Lake, l., Vt., U.S. | B4 | 122 |
| Seymour Inlet, b., B.C. | D4 | 69 |
| Seymour Johnson Air Force Base, mil., N.C., U.S. | B5 | 110 |
| Seymour Lake, l., Vt., U.S. | B4 | 122 |
| Seymourville, La., U.S. | h9 | 95 |
| Sézanne, Fr. | C5 | 16 |
| Sezimbra, Port. | C1 | 22 |
| Sezze, Italy | D4 | 23 |
| Sfax, Tun. | C7 | 44 |
| Shaanxi, prov., China | D6 | 31 |
| Shabbona, Il., U.S. | B5 | 90 |
| Shabeellaha Dhexe, prov., Som. | E6 | 47 |
| Shabeellaha Hoose, prov., Som. | E5 | 47 |
| Shabeelle (Shebele), stm., Afr. | E5 | 47 |
| Shabogamo Lake, l., Newf. | h8 | 72 |
| Shabunda, Zaire | B4 | 48 |
| Shabwah, Yemen | B6 | 47 |
| Shache, China | F10 | 29 |
| Shackelford, co., Tx., U.S. | C3 | 120 |
| Shackleton, Sask. | G1 | 75 |
| Shackleton Glacier, ice, Ant. | A31 | 7 |
| Shackleton Ice Shelf, ice, Ant. | C23 | 7 |
| Shackleton Range, mts., Ant. | A10 | 7 |
| Shadehill, S.D., U.S. | B3 | 118 |
| Shadehill Dam, S.D., U.S. | B3 | 118 |
| Shadehill Reservoir, res., S.D. | B3 | 118 |
| Shades Creek, stm., Al., U.S. | g7 | 78 |
| Shades Mountain, mtn., Al., U.S. | g7 | 78 |
| Shadow Mountain National Recreation Area, Co., U.S. | A4 | 83 |
| Shadrinsk, Sov. Un. | B6 | 28 |
| Shady Cove, Or., U.S. | E4 | 114 |
| Shady Dale, Ga., U.S. | C3 | 87 |
| Shady Grove, Al., U.S. | D3 | 78 |
| Shady Grove, Fl., U.S. | B3 | 86 |
| Shady Grove, Ky., U.S. | e10 | 94 |
| Shady Point, Ok., U.S. | B7 | 113 |
| Shady Rest, Ct., U.S. | *D2 | 84 |
| Shady Side, Md., U.S. | C4 | 97 |
| Shadyside, Oh., U.S. | C5 | 112 |
| Shady Spring, W.V., U.S. | D3 | 125 |
| Shady Valley, Tn., U.S. | C12 | 119 |
| Shafer, Lake, l., In., U.S. | C4 | 91 |
| Shafer Butte, mtn., Id., U.S. | F2 | 89 |
| Shafter, Ca., U.S. | E4 | 82 |
| Shafter, Nv., U.S. | C7 | 105 |
| Shafter, Tx., U.S. | p12 | 120 |
| Shaftesbury, Eng., U.K. | C5 | 12 |
| Shaftsbury, Vt., U.S. | F2 | 122 |
| Shaftsbury Center, Vt., U.S. | F2 | 122 |
| Shagamu, Nig. | *E5 | 45 |
| Shageluk, Ak., U.S. | C8 | 79 |
| Shag Harbour, N.S. | F4 | 71 |
| Shaguotun, China | D9 | 32 |
| Shah Alam, Malay. | *K4 | 35 |
| Shahbanou Farah Dam, Iran | C4 | 36 |
| Shāhdādkot, Pak. | D1 | 37 |
| Shahdol, India | F6 | 37 |
| Shāhgarh, India | D3 | 37 |
| Shāhhāt, Libya | C2 | 39 |
| Shāhī, i., U.S. | C4 | 36 |
| Shāhjahānpur, India | D7 | 37 |
| Shāh Jūy, Afg. | E13 | 39 |
| Shāhpur, India | C4 | 36 |
| Shāhpur, Pak. | C4 | 36 |
| Shāhpura, India | D7 | 37 |
| Shahrak, Afg. | D12 | 39 |
| Shahr-e Bābak, Iran | E5 | 39 |
| Shahr-e Kord, Iran | C4 | 36 |
| Shāhrūd, Iran | B5 | 38 |
| Shāhrūd see Emāmshahr, Iran | | |
| Shakawe, Bots. | A3 | 49 |
| Shakhrisyabz, Sov. Un. | B13 | 39 |
| Shakhty, Sov. Un. | E7 | 29 |
| Shakhunya, Sov. Un. | D17 | 8 |
| Shaki, Nig. | E5 | 45 |
| Shakopee, Mn., U.S. | F5 | 100 |
| Shakotan, Cape, c., Japan | E10 | 33 |
| Shaktoolik, Ak., U.S. | C7 | 79 |
| Shala, Lake, l., Eth. | D4 | 47 |
| Shalath, B.C. | D6 | 69 |
| Shaler Mountains, mts., N.W. Ter. | B10 | 66 |
| Shaler Township, Pa., U.S. | *E2 | 115 |
| Shalkar, Lake, l., Sov. Un. | C4 | 28 |
| Shallmar, Md., U.S. | m12 | 97 |
| Shallotte, N.C., U.S. | C4 | 110 |
| Shallotte Inlet, b., N.C., U.S. | D4 | 110 |
| Shallowater, Tx., U.S. | C2 | 120 |
| Shallow Lake, Ont. | C3 | 73 |
| Shallow Water, Ks., U.S. | D3 | 93 |
| Sham, Mount, mtn., Oman | C5 | 38 |
| Shamattawa, Man. | B5 | 70 |
| Shambat, Sud. | B3 | 47 |
| Shambaugh, Ia., U.S. | D2 | 92 |
| Shambe, Sud. | D3 | 47 |
| Shāmil, Iran | H8 | 39 |
| Shamokin, Pa., U.S. | E8 | 115 |
| Shamokin Dam, Pa., U.S. | E8 | 115 |
| Shamrock, Sask. | G2 | 75 |
| Shamrock, Fl., U.S. | C3 | 86 |
| Shamrock, Ok., U.S. | B5 | 113 |
| Shamrock, Tx., U.S. | B2 | 120 |
| Shamva, Zimb. | A5 | 49 |
| Shandaken, N.Y., U.S. | C6 | 109 |
| Shandĭ, Sud. | B3 | 47 |
| Shandon, Ca., U.S. | E3 | 82 |
| Shandon, Oh., U.S. | n12 | 112 |
| Shandong, prov., China | D8 | 31 |
| Shandong Bandao, pen., China | D9 | 31 |
| Shangdu, China | D5 | 32 |
| Shanghai, China | E9 | 31 |
| Shangnan, China | H4 | 32 |
| Shangqiu, China | E8 | 31 |
| Shangrao, China | F8 | 31 |
| Shangshui, China | A2 | 54 |
| Shangsi, China | A7 | 35 |
| Shangzhi, China | H4 | 32 |
| Shanhaiguan, China | D8 | 31 |
| Shaniko, Or., U.S. | B6 | 114 |
| Shannock, R.I., U.S. | F2 | 116 |
| Shannon, Ga., U.S. | B1 | 87 |
| Shannon, Il., U.S. | A4 | 90 |
| Shannon, Ms., U.S. | A5 | 101 |
| Shannon, co., Mo., U.S. | D6 | 102 |
| Shannon, co., S.D., U.S. | D3 | 118 |
| Shannon, i., Grnld. | B16 | 128 |
| Shannon, Lake, l., Wa., U.S. | A4 | 124 |
| Shannon Airport, Ire. | E3 | 11 |
| Shannon City, Ia., U.S. | D3 | 92 |
| Shannontown, S.C., U.S. | D7 | 117 |
| Shanshan, China | C3 | 31 |
| Shantar Islands, is., Sov. Un. | D16 | 29 |
| Shantou (Swatow), China | G8 | 31 |
| Shantung see Shandong, prov., China | D8 | 31 |
| Shantung Peninsula see Shandong Bandao, pen., China | D9 | 31 |
| Shanwa, Tan. | B5 | 48 |
| Shanxi, prov., China | D7 | 31 |
| Shaobo, China | H8 | 32 |
| Shaoguan, China | G7 | 31 |
| Shaowu, China | K7 | 32 |
| Shaoxing, China | F9 | 31 |
| Shaoyang, China | F7 | 31 |
| Shap, Eng., U.K. | F6 | 13 |
| Shapinsay, i., Scot., U.K. | *A2 | 78 |
| Shapio Lake, l., Newf. | g9 | 72 |
| Shapki, Sov. Un. | s32 | 14 |
| Shapleigh, Me., U.S. | *E2 | 96 |
| Shaqqah, Bi'r ash, well, Egypt | G5 | 40 |
| Sharafkhāneh, Iran | B2 | 39 |
| Sharangad, Mong. | B2 | 32 |
| Sharbatāt, Ra's ash-, c., Oman | D5 | 38 |
| Sharbot Lake, Ont. | C8 | 73 |
| Shari, Japan | E12 | 33 |
| Sharīṭah, Ra's, c., Oman | H8 | 39 |
| Shark Bay, b., Austl. | E1 | 50 |
| Sharkey, co., Ms., U.S. | C3 | 101 |
| Shark Point, c., Fl., U.S. | H5 | 86 |
| Sharktooth Mountain, mtn., B.C. | E7 | 66 |
| Sharm ash Shaykh, Eg. | D2 | 38 |
| Sharon, Ct., U.S. | B2 | 84 |
| Sharon, Ks., U.S. | E5 | 93 |
| Sharon, Ma., U.S. | B5 | 98 |
| Sharon, N.H., U.S. | E3 | 106 |
| Sharon, N.D., U.S. | B8 | 111 |
| Sharon, Ok., U.S. | A2 | 113 |
| Sharon, Pa., U.S. | D1 | 115 |
| Sharon, S.C., U.S. | A5 | 117 |
| Sharon, Tn., U.S. | A3 | 119 |
| Sharon, Vt., U.S. | D3 | 122 |
| Sharon, Wi., U.S. | F5 | 126 |
| Sharon, W.V., U.S. | m13 | 125 |
| Sharon Grove, Ky., U.S. | D2 | 94 |
| Sharon Hill, Pa., U.S. | p20 | 115 |
| Sharon Park, Oh., U.S. | n12 | 112 |
| Sharon Springs, Ks., U.S. | D2 | 93 |
| Sharon Springs, N.Y., U.S. | C6 | 109 |
| Sharon Valley, Ct., U.S. | B2 | 84 |
| Sharonville, Oh., U.S. | n13 | 112 |
| Sharp, co., Ar., U.S. | A4 | 81 |
| Sharpe, Lake, res., S.D., U.S. | C6 | 118 |
| Sharpes, Fl., U.S. | D6 | 86 |
| Sharpley, Bl., U.S. | h7 | 85 |
| Sharpsburg, Ga., U.S. | C2 | 87 |
| Sharpsburg, Ia., U.S. | D3 | 92 |
| Sharpsburg, Ky., U.S. | B6 | 94 |
| Sharpsburg, Md., U.S. | B2 | 97 |
| Sharpsburg, N.C., U.S. | B5 | 110 |
| Sharpsburg, Pa., U.S. | k14 | 115 |
| Sharps Chapel, Tn., U.S. | C10 | 119 |
| Sharpsville, In., U.S. | D5 | 91 |
| Sharpsville, Pa., U.S. | D1 | 115 |
| Sharptown, Md., U.S. | C6 | 97 |
| Sharptown, N.J., U.S. | D2 | 107 |
| Sharp Top Mountain, mtn., | C2 | 81 |
| Sharya, Sov. Un. | D7 | 8 |
| Shashi, China | E8 | 31 |
| Shashke, Sov. Un. | n14 | 100 |
| Shasta, co., Ca., U.S. | B2 | 82 |
| Shasta, Mount, vol., Ca., U.S. | B2 | 82 |
| Shasta Lake, l., Ca., U.S. | B2 | 82 |
| Shatney Mountain, mtn., N.H., U.S. | f7 | 106 |
| Shatsk, Sov. Un. | D13 | 27 |
| Shattuck, Ok., U.S. | A2 | 113 |
| Shattuckville, Ma., U.S. | A2 | 98 |
| Shatura, Sov. Un. | D12 | 27 |
| Shauck, Oh., U.S. | B3 | 112 |
| Shaunavon, Sask. | H1 | 75 |
| Shaw, Ms., U.S. | B3 | 101 |
| Shaw, Or., U.S. | k12 | 114 |
| Shaw Air Force Base, mil., S.C., U.S. | D7 | 117 |
| Shawanaga, Ont. | B4 | 73 |
| Shawangunk Mountains, mts., N.Y., U.S. | D6 | 109 |
| Shawano, Wi., U.S. | D5 | 126 |
| Shawano, co., Wi., U.S. | D5 | 126 |
| Shawano Lake, l., Wi., U.S. | D5 | 126 |
| Shawboro, N.C., U.S. | A6 | 110 |
| Shawbridge, Que. | D3 | 74 |
| Shawinigan, Que. | C5 | 74 |
| Shawinigan-Sud, Que. | C5 | 74 |
| Shawmut, Mt., U.S. | D7 | 103 |
| Shawnee, Ga., U.S. | D5 | 87 |
| Shawnee, Co., U.S. | B5 | 83 |
| Shawnee, Ks., U.S. | k16 | 93 |
| Shawnee, Oh., U.S. | C3 | 112 |
| Shawnee, Ok., U.S. | B5 | 113 |
| Shawnee, Wy., U.S. | D7 | 127 |
| Shawnee, co., Ks., U.S. | D8 | 93 |
| Shawnee Hills, Oh., U.S. | B2 | 112 |
| Shawneetown, Il., U.S. | F5 | 90 |
| Shawsheen, stm., Ma., U.S. | f11 | 98 |
| Shawsville, Va., U.S. | C2 | 123 |
| Shawville, Que. | B8 | 73 |
| Shaxian, China | F8 | 31 |
| Shayang, China | I5 | 32 |
| Shay Gap, Austl. | D3 | 50 |
| Shaykh Miskīn, Syria | B8 | 41 |
| Shchekino, Sov. Un. | D11 | 27 |
| Shchelkovo, Sov. Un. | n18 | 27 |
| Shchetovo, Sov. Un. | q22 | 27 |
| Shchigry, Sov. Un. | F11 | 27 |
| Shchors, Sov. Un. | F9 | 27 |
| Shchuchinsk, Sov. Un. | C8 | 28 |
| Shchurovo, Sov. Un. | n18 | 27 |
| Shebele (Shabeelle), stm., Afr. | D5 | 47 |
| Sheberghān, Afg. | A4 | 36 |
| Sheboygan, Wi., U.S. | E6 | 126 |
| Sheboygan, co., Wi., U.S. | E5 | 126 |
| Sheboygan Falls, Wi., U.S. | E6 | 126 |
| Shedden, Ont. | E3 | 73 |
| Shediac, N.B. | C5 | 71 |
| Sheekh, Som. | D6 | 47 |
| Sheelin, Lough, l., Ire. | D3 | 10 |
| Sheenjek, stm., Ak., U.S. | B11 | 79 |
| Sheep Creek, stm., Alta. | C1 | 68 |
| Sheep Haven, b., Ire. | B4 | 11 |
| Sheep Mountain, mtn., Az., U.S. | E1 | 80 |
| Sheep Mountain, mtn., Wy., U.S. | C2 | 127 |
| Sheep Mountain, mtn., Wy., U.S. | B5 | 127 |
| Sheep Peak, mtn., Nv., U.S. | G6 | 105 |
| Sheep Range, mts., Nv., U.S. | F2 | 105 |
| Sheep's Head, c., Ire. | F2 | 11 |
| Sheeps Heaven Mountain, mtn., Ma., U.S. | A1 | 98 |
| Sheerness, Alta. | D5 | 68 |
| Sheerness, Eng., U.K. | C8 | 12 |
| Sheet Harbour, N.S. | E7 | 71 |
| Shefar'am, Isr. | B7 | 41 |
| Shefayim, Isr. | g10 | 41 |
| Sheffield, Eng., U.K. | D6 | 10 |
| Sheffield, Al., U.S. | A2 | 78 |
| Sheffield, Ia., U.S. | B4 | 92 |
| Sheffield, Ma., U.S. | B1 | 98 |
| Sheffield, Pa., U.S. | C3 | 115 |
| Sheffield, Tx., U.S. | D2 | 120 |
| Sheffield, Vt., U.S. | B4 | 122 |
| Sheffield Lake, Oh., U.S. | A3 | 112 |
| Sheffield Lake, l., Newf. | D3 | 72 |
| Shefford, co., Que. | D5 | 74 |
| Sheguiandah, Ont. | B3 | 73 |
| Sheho, Sask. | F3 | 75 |
| Shehuen, stm., Arg. | D2 | 54 |
| Sheila, N.B. | B5 | 71 |
| Shekhūpura, Pak. | C5 | 36 |
| Shelagski, Cape, c., Sov. Un. | B33 | 29 |
| Shelagyote Peak, mtn., B.C. | B4 | 69 |
| Shelbiana, Ky., U.S. | C7 | 94 |
| Shelbina, Mo., U.S. | B5 | 102 |
| Shelburn, In., U.S. | F3 | 91 |
| Shelburne, N.S. | F4 | 71 |
| Shelburne, Ont. | C4 | 73 |
| Shelburne, Vt., U.S. | C2 | 122 |
| Shelburne, co., N.S. | F4 | 71 |
| Shelburne Falls, Ma., U.S. | A2 | 98 |
| Shelburne Falls, Vt., U.S. | C2 | 122 |
| Shelburne Pond, l., Vt., U.S. | C2 | 122 |
| Shelby, Al., U.S. | B3 | 78 |
| Shelby, Ia., U.S. | C2 | 92 |
| Shelby, Mi., U.S. | E4 | 99 |
| Shelby, Ms., U.S. | B3 | 101 |
| Shelby, Mt., U.S. | B5 | 103 |
| Shelby, Ne., U.S. | C8 | 104 |
| Shelby, N.C., U.S. | B1 | 110 |
| Shelby, Oh., U.S. | B3 | 112 |
| Shelby, co., Al., U.S. | B3 | 78 |
| Shelby, co., Il., U.S. | D5 | 90 |
| Shelby, co., In., U.S. | E6 | 91 |
| Shelby, co., Ia., U.S. | C2 | 92 |
| Shelby, co., Ky., U.S. | B4 | 94 |
| Shelby, co., Mo., U.S. | B5 | 102 |
| Shelby, co., Oh., U.S. | B1 | 112 |
| Shelby, co., Tn., U.S. | B2 | 119 |
| Shelby, co., Tx., U.S. | D5 | 120 |
| Shelby, Lake, res., Il., U.S. | e8 | 90 |
| Sheldahl, Ia., U.S. | C4 | 92 |
| Sheldon, Il., U.S. | C6 | 90 |
| Sheldon, Ia., U.S. | A2 | 92 |
| Sheldon, Mo., U.S. | D3 | 102 |
| Sheldon, N.D., U.S. | C8 | 111 |
| Sheldon, S.C., U.S. | F6 | 117 |
| Sheldon, Tx., U.S. | r14 | 120 |
| Sheldon, Wi., U.S. | C2 | 126 |
| Sheldon Springs, Vt., U.S. | B3 | 122 |
| Shelekhov, Gulf of, b., Sov. Un. | D17 | 29 |
| Shelikof Strait, strt., Ak., U.S. | D9 | 79 |
| Shell, Wy., U.S. | B5 | 127 |
| Shell, stm., Man. | D1 | 70 |
| Shell, Loch, b., Scot., U.K. | C2 | 75 |
| Shellbrook, Sask. | D2 | 75 |
| Shell Creek, Tn., U.S. | C11 | 119 |

| Name | Map Ref. | Page |
|---|---|---|
| Shell Creek, stm., U.S. | A2 | 83 |
| Shell Creek, stm., Wy., U.S. | B5 | 127 |
| Shelley, B.C. | C6 | 69 |
| Shelley, Id., U.S. | F6 | 89 |
| Shellharbour, Austl. | G8 | 51 |
| Shell Lake, Sask. | D2 | 75 |
| Shell Lake, Wi., U.S. | C2 | 126 |
| Shell Lake, l., Mn., U.S. | D3 | 100 |
| Shell Lake, l., Wi., U.S. | C2 | 126 |
| Shellman, Ga., U.S. | E2 | 87 |
| Shellman Bluff, Ga., U.S. | E5 | 87 |
| Shellmouth, Man. | D1 | 70 |
| Shellpot Creek, stm., De., U.S. | h7 | 85 |
| Shell Rock, Ia., U.S. | B5 | 92 |
| Shell Rock, stm., Ia., U.S. | B5 | 92 |
| Shell Rock, West Fork, stm., Ia., U.S. | B5 | 92 |
| Shellsburg, Ia., U.S. | B6 | 92 |
| Shelly, Mn., U.S. | C2 | 100 |
| Shelly Mountain, mtn., Id., U.S. | F5 | 89 |
| Shelter Harbor, R.I., U.S. | G2 | 116 |
| Shelter Island, N.Y., U.S. | m16 | 109 |
| Shelton, Ct., U.S. | D3 | 84 |
| Shelton, Ne., U.S. | D7 | 104 |
| Shelton, Wa., U.S. | B2 | 124 |
| Shemogue, N.B. | C5 | 71 |
| Shemya Air Force Base, mil., Ak., U.S. | E2 | 79 |
| Shenandoah, Ia., U.S. | D2 | 92 |
| Shenandoah, Pa., U.S. | E9 | 115 |
| Shenandoah, Va., U.S. | B4 | 123 |
| Shenandoah, co., Va., U.S. | B4 | 123 |
| Shenandoah, stm., U.S. | A5 | 123 |
| Shenandoah, North Fork, stm., Va., U.S. | B4 | 123 |
| Shenandoah, South Fork, stm., Va., U.S. | B4 | 123 |
| Shenandoah Mountain, mtn., U.S. | B3 | 123 |
| Shenandoah National Park, Va., U.S. | B4 | 123 |
| Shenandoah Valley, val., U.S. | B4 | 123 |
| Shenango River Lake, res., U.S. | D1 | 115 |
| Shengxian, China | J9 | 32 |
| Shenipsit Lake, l., Ct., U.S. | B6 | 84 |
| Shenmu, China | D7 | 31 |
| Shenqiu, China | H6 | 32 |
| Shensi see Shaanxi, prov., China | D6 | 31 |
| Shenyang, China | C9 | 31 |
| Sheopur, India | E6 | 37 |
| Shepard, Alta. | D4 | 68 |
| Shepard Island, i., Ant. | B35 | 7 |
| Shepardsville, In., U.S. | E3 | 91 |
| Shepaug, stm., Ct., U.S. | C2 | 84 |
| Shepaug Dam, Ct., U.S. | D2 | 84 |
| Shepaug Reservoir, res., Ct., U.S. | C2 | 84 |
| Shepetovka, Sov. Un. | F6 | 27 |
| Shepherd, Mi., U.S. | E6 | 99 |
| Shepherd, Mt., U.S. | E8 | 103 |
| Shepherd, Tx., U.S. | D5 | 120 |
| Shepherdstown, W.V., U.S. | B7 | 125 |
| Shepherdsville, Ky., U.S. | C4 | 94 |
| Sheppard Air Force Base, mil., Tx., U.S. | C3 | 120 |
| Shepparton, Austl. | G8 | 50 |
| Sheppey, Isle of, i., Eng., U.K. | C8 | 12 |
| Shepton, Pa., U.S. | E9 | 115 |
| Shepton Mallet, Eng., U.K. | C5 | 12 |
| Sheqi, China | H5 | 32 |
| Sherabad, Sov. Un. | C13 | 29 |
| Sherard, Ms., U.S. | A3 | 101 |
| Sherborn, Ma., U.S. | h10 | 98 |
| Sherborne, Eng., U.K. | D5 | 12 |
| Sherbro Island, i., S.L. | E2 | 45 |
| Sherbrooke, N.S. | D8 | 71 |
| Sherbrooke, Que. | D6 | 74 |
| Sherbrooke, co., Que. | D5 | 74 |
| Sherbrooke Lake, l., N.S. | E5 | 71 |
| Sherburn, Mn., U.S. | G4 | 100 |
| Sherburne, N.Y., U.S. | C5 | 109 |
| Sherburne, co., Mn., U.S. | E5 | 100 |
| Shercock, Ire. | C5 | 11 |
| Shereshevo, Sov. Un. | B8 | 26 |
| Sheridan, Ar., U.S. | C3 | 81 |
| Sheridan, Co., U.S. | *B6 | 83 |
| Sheridan, Il., U.S. | B5 | 90 |
| Sheridan, In., U.S. | D5 | 91 |
| Sheridan, Ky., U.S. | e9 | 94 |
| Sheridan, Me., U.S. | B4 | 96 |
| Sheridan, Mi., U.S. | E5 | 99 |
| Sheridan, Mo., U.S. | A3 | 102 |
| Sheridan, Or., U.S. | B3 | 114 |
| Sheridan, Wy., U.S. | B6 | 127 |
| Sheridan, co., Ks., U.S. | C3 | 93 |
| Sheridan, co., Mt., U.S. | B12 | 103 |
| Sheridan, co., Ne., U.S. | B3 | 104 |
| Sheridan, co., N.D., U.S. | B5 | 111 |
| Sheridan, co., Wy., U.S. | B5 | 127 |
| Sheridan, Mount, mtn., Wy., U.S. | B2 | 127 |
| Sheridan Beach, Wa., U.S. | *B3 | 124 |
| Sheridan Gardens, Wy., U.S. | *B6 | 127 |
| Sheridan Lake, Co., U.S. | C8 | 83 |
| Sheringham, Eng., U.K. | D7 | 10 |
| Sherman, Ct., U.S. | C2 | 84 |
| Sherman, Me., U.S. | C4 | 96 |
| Sherman, Ms., U.S. | A5 | 101 |
| Sherman, Mo., U.S. | f12 | 102 |
| Sherman, N.Y., U.S. | C1 | 109 |
| Sherman, S.D., U.S. | D9 | 118 |
| Sherman, Tx., U.S. | C4 | 120 |
| Sherman, co., Ks., U.S. | C2 | 93 |
| Sherman, co., Ne., U.S. | C6 | 104 |
| Sherman, co., Or., U.S. | B6 | 114 |
| Sherman, co., Tx., U.S. | A2 | 120 |
| Sherman Mills, Me., U.S. | C4 | 96 |
| Sherman Mountain, mtn., Ar., U.S. | A2 | 81 |
| Sherman Reservoir, res., Ne., U.S. | C7 | 104 |
| Sherman Station, Me., U.S. | C4 | 96 |
| Sherpur, Bngl. | E12 | 37 |
| Sherrard, Il., U.S. | B3 | 90 |
| Sherrelwood, Co., U.S. | *D6 | 127 |
| Sherridon, Man. | B1 | 70 |
| Sherrill, Ar., U.S. | C4 | 81 |
| Sherrill, N.Y., U.S. | B5 | 109 |
| Sherrodsville, Oh., U.S. | B4 | 112 |
| 's Hertogenbosch, Neth. | B6 | 16 |
| Sherwood, P.E.I. | C6 | 71 |
| Sherwood, Ar., U.S. | C3 | 81 |
| Sherwood, Ms., U.S. | B5 | 101 |
| Sherwood, N.D., U.S. | A4 | 111 |
| Sherwood, Oh., U.S. | A1 | 112 |
| Sherwood, Tn., U.S. | h12 | 114 |
| Sherwood, Wi., U.S. | h9 | 126 |
| Sherwood Manor, Ct., U.S. | A5 | 84 |
| Sherwood Park, Alta. | C4 | 68 |
| Sherwood Park, De., U.S. | i7 | 85 |
| Shetek, Lake, l., Mn., U.S. | G3 | 100 |
| Shetland Islands, is., Scot., U.K. | g10 | 10 |
| Shetucket, stm., Ct., U.S. | C7 | 84 |
| Shevchenko, Sov. Un. | E8 | 29 |
| Shevlin, Mn., U.S. | C3 | 100 |
| Shevut 'Am, Isr. | f10 | 41 |
| Shewa, prov., Eth. | D4 | 47 |
| Shewa Gimira, Eth. | D4 | 47 |
| Shexian, China | J8 | 32 |
| Sheyenne, N.D., U.S. | B6 | 111 |
| Sheyenne, stm., N.D., U.S. | C8 | 111 |
| Sheyenne Lake, res., N.D., U.S. | B5 | 111 |
| Sheykhābād, Afg. | D14 | 39 |
| Shiawassee, co., Mi., U.S. | F6 | 99 |
| Shibām, Yemen | D4 | 38 |
| Shibecha, Japan | E12 | 33 |
| Shibata, Japan | H9 | 33 |
| Shibetsu, Japan | D11 | 33 |
| Shibetsu, Japan | E12 | 33 |
| Shibīn al Kawm, Eg. | D3 | 41 |
| Shibīn al Qanāṭir, Eg. | D3 | 41 |
| Shicheng, China | K7 | 32 |
| Shickley, Ne., U.S. | D8 | 104 |
| Shickshinny, Pa., U.S. | D9 | 115 |
| Shidao, China | F10 | 32 |
| Shideler, In., U.S. | D7 | 91 |
| Shiderty, stm., Sov. Un. | C8 | 28 |
| Shidler, Ok., U.S. | A5 | 113 |
| Shiel, Loch, l., Scot., U.K. | D3 | 13 |
| Shieldaig, Scot., U.K. | C3 | 13 |
| Shields, Ks., U.S. | D3 | 93 |
| Shields, N.D., U.S. | C4 | 111 |
| Shihezi, China | C2 | 31 |
| Shijiazhuang, China | D7 | 31 |
| Shikārpur, Pak. | C4 | 36 |
| Shikohābād, India | D7 | 37 |
| Shikoku, i., Japan | E11 | 31 |
| Shiliguri, India | C8 | 36 |
| Shilka, Sov. Un. | D14 | 29 |
| Shilka, Sov. Un. | A8 | 31 |
| Shilka, stm., Sov. Un. | D14 | 29 |
| Shillington, Pa., U.S. | F10 | 115 |
| Shillong, India | G13 | 36 |
| Shiloh, Ga., U.S. | D2 | 87 |
| Shiloh, N.J., U.S. | E2 | 107 |
| Shiloh, N.C., U.S. | A6 | 110 |
| Shiloh, Oh., U.S. | B3 | 112 |
| Shiloh, Pa., U.S. | *G8 | 115 |
| Shiloh, Tn., U.S. | B3 | 119 |
| Shiloh, Tn., U.S. | A4 | 119 |
| Shiloh National Military Park, Tn., U.S. | B3 | 119 |
| Shimabara, Japan | J5 | 33 |
| Shimada, Japan | o17 | 33 |
| Shimanovsk, Sov. Un. | D15 | 29 |
| Shimber Berris, mtn., Som. | C6 | 47 |
| Shimen, China | F7 | 31 |
| Shimizu, Japan | I9 | 33 |
| Shimla, India | B6 | 36 |
| Shimoda, Japan | o17 | 33 |
| Shimodate, Japan | m19 | 33 |
| Shimoga, India | F6 | 36 |
| Shimo Island, i., Japan | J4 | 33 |
| Shimonoseki, Japan | E11 | 31 |
| Shimotsuma, Japan | m18 | 33 |
| Shin, Loch, l., Scot., U.K. | A4 | 10 |
| Shinall Mountain, mtn., Ar., U.S. | h10 | 81 |
| Shinano, stm., Japan | H9 | 33 |
| Shindand, Afg. | D2 | 36 |
| Shiner, Tx., U.S. | E4 | 120 |
| Shingbwiyang, Burma | C10 | 34 |
| Shinglehouse, Pa., U.S. | C5 | 115 |
| Shingleton, Mi., U.S. | B4 | 99 |
| Shingū, Japan | J8 | 33 |
| Shinjō, Japan | G10 | 33 |
| Shinkolobwe, Zaire | D4 | 48 |
| Shinnston, W.V., U.S. | G4 | 31 |
| Shin Pond, Me., U.S. | B4 | 96 |
| Shinshiro, Japan | o16 | 33 |
| Shinyanga, Tan. | B5 | 48 |
| Shinyanga, prov., Tan. | B5 | 48 |
| Shiocton, Wi., U.S. | D5 | 126 |
| Shiogama, Japan | G10 | 33 |
| Shiojiri, Japan | m16 | 33 |
| Shioya, Cape, c., Japan | H10 | 33 |
| Ship Bottom, N.J., U.S. | D4 | 107 |
| Ship Cove, Newf. | E4 | 72 |
| Ship Harbour, N.S. | E7 | 71 |
| Ship Island, i., Ms., U.S. | E5 | 101 |
| Ship Island Pass, strt., Ms., U.S. | g7 | 101 |
| Shipki Pass, Bul. | D7 | 24 |
| Shipki Pass, India | B7 | 37 |
| Shipley, Eng., U.K. | G7 | 13 |
| Shipman, Sask. | D3 | 75 |
| Shipman, Il., U.S. | D4 | 90 |
| Shipman, Va., U.S. | C4 | 123 |
| Shippegan, N.B. | B5 | 71 |
| Shippensburg, Pa., U.S. | F6 | 115 |
| Shippenville, Pa., U.S. | D2 | 115 |
| Shiprock, N.M., U.S. | A1 | 108 |
| Ship Rock, mtn., N.M., U.S. | A1 | 108 |
| Shipshewana, In., U.S. | A6 | 91 |
| Shipyard, Belize | D3 | 63 |
| Shiquan, China | E6 | 31 |
| Shirase Glacier, ice, Ant. | B16 | 7 |
| Shirbīn, Eg. | C3 | 41 |
| Shire, stm., Afr. | E5 | 48 |
| Shiretoko, Cape, c., Japan | D12 | 33 |
| Shiribetsu, Mount, mtn., Japan | E10 | 33 |
| Shiriya, Cape, c., Japan | F10 | 33 |
| Shīr Kūh, mtn., Iran | F7 | 39 |
| Shirley, Ar., U.S. | B3 | 81 |
| Shirley, Il., U.S. | C4 | 90 |
| Shirley, In., U.S. | E6 | 91 |
| Shirley, Ma., U.S. | A4 | 98 |
| Shirley, N.Y., U.S. | *n16 | 109 |
| Shirley, W.V., U.S. | k9 | 125 |
| Shirley Basin, Wy., U.S. | D6 | 127 |
| Shirley Center, Ma., U.S. | A4 | 98 |
| Shirley Mills, Me., U.S. | C3 | 96 |
| Shirley Mountains, mts., Wy., U.S. | D6 | 127 |
| Shirleysburg, Pa., U.S. | F6 | 115 |
| Shiroishi, Japan | H10 | 33 |
| Shirotori, Japan | n15 | 33 |
| Shīrvān, Iran | C8 | 39 |
| Shishaldin Volcano, vol., Ak., U.S. | E7 | 79 |
| Shishmaref, Ak., U.S. | B6 | 79 |
| Shishou, China | J5 | 32 |
| Shitara, Japan | n16 | 33 |
| Shively, Ky., U.S. | B4 | 94 |
| Shivpuri, India | E6 | 37 |
| Shivwits, Ut., U.S. | F2 | 121 |
| Shivwits Plateau, plat., Az., U.S. | A2 | 80 |
| Shiyan, China | *E7 | 31 |
| Shizuishan, China | D6 | 31 |
| Shizuoka, Japan | E12 | 31 |
| Shkhara, Mount, mtn., Sov. Un. | *E7 | 29 |
| Shkodra (Scutari), Alb. | A2 | 40 |
| Shkotovo, Sov. Un. | E6 | 33 |
| Shoal, stm., U.S. | C1 | 70 |
| Shoal Creek, stm., U.S. | B4 | 119 |
| Shoal Harbour, Newf. | D4 | 72 |
| Shoal Lake, Man. | D1 | 70 |
| Shoal Lake, l., Can. | E4 | 70 |
| Shoals, In., U.S. | G4 | 91 |
| Shoals, Isles of, is., Me., U.S. | E2 | 96 |
| Shoalwater, Cape, c., Wa., U.S. | C1 | 124 |
| Shobonier, Il., U.S. | E4 | 90 |
| Shoe Cove, Newf. | D4 | 72 |
| Shoemakersville, Pa., U.S. | F10 | 115 |
| Sholes, Ne., U.S. | B8 | 104 |
| Shomolu, Nig. | *E5 | 45 |
| Shongaloo, La., U.S. | B2 | 95 |
| Shongopovi, Az., U.S. | B5 | 80 |
| Shonkin, Mt., U.S. | C6 | 103 |
| Shonto, Az., U.S. | A5 | 80 |
| Shooting Creek, N.C., U.S. | f9 | 110 |
| Shop Springs, Tn., U.S. | A5 | 119 |
| Shoreacres, B.C. | E9 | 69 |
| Shore Acres, Ma., U.S. | h13 | 98 |
| Shore Acres, N.J., U.S. | C4 | 107 |
| Shore Acres, R.I., U.S. | E4 | 116 |
| Shoreham, Mi., U.S. | F4 | 99 |
| Shoreham, Vt., U.S. | D2 | 122 |
| Shoreview, Mn., U.S. | m12 | 100 |
| Shorewood, Il., U.S. | k8 | 90 |
| Shorewood, Mn., U.S. | n11 | 100 |
| Shorewood, Wi., U.S. | E6 | 126 |
| Shorewood Hills, Wi., U.S. | *E4 | 126 |
| Short Beach, Ct., U.S. | D4 | 84 |
| Shorter, Al., U.S. | C4 | 78 |
| Shorterville, Al., U.S. | D4 | 78 |
| Short Falls, N.H., U.S. | D4 | 106 |
| Short Mountain, mtn., Tn., U.S. | D8 | 119 |
| Shortsville, N.Y., U.S. | C3 | 109 |
| Shoshone, Ca., U.S. | E5 | 82 |
| Shoshone, Id., U.S. | G4 | 89 |
| Shoshone, co., Id., U.S. | B2 | 89 |
| Shoshone, stm., Wy., U.S. | B4 | 127 |
| Shoshone, North Fork, stm., Wy., U.S. | B3 | 127 |
| Shoshone, South Fork, stm., Wy., U.S. | B3 | 127 |
| Shoshone Falls, wtfl., Id., U.S. | G4 | 89 |
| Shoshone Lake, l., Wy., U.S. | B2 | 127 |
| Shoshone Mountains, mts., Nv., U.S. | E4 | 105 |
| Shoshone Peak, mtn., Nv., U.S. | G5 | 105 |
| Shoshone Range, mts., Nv., U.S. | C5 | 105 |
| Shoshong, Bots. | B4 | 49 |
| Shoshoni, Wy., U.S. | C4 | 127 |
| Shostka, Sov. Un. | F9 | 27 |
| Shouldice, Alta. | D4 | 68 |
| Shouns, Tn., U.S. | C12 | 119 |
| Shoup, Id., U.S. | D4 | 89 |
| Showell, Md., U.S. | D7 | 97 |
| Show Low, Az., U.S. | C5 | 80 |
| Shpola, Sov. Un. | G8 | 27 |
| Shreve, Oh., U.S. | B3 | 112 |
| Shreveport, La., U.S. | B2 | 95 |
| Shrewsbury, Eng., U.K. | D5 | 10 |
| Shrewsbury, Ma., U.S. | B4 | 98 |
| Shrewsbury, Mo., U.S. | *f13 | 102 |
| Shrewsbury, N.J., U.S. | C4 | 107 |
| Shrewsbury, Pa., U.S. | G8 | 115 |
| Shrīrangapattana, India | F6 | 36 |
| Shropshire (Salop), co., Eng., U.K. | B5 | 12 |
| Shrule, Ire. | D2 | 11 |
| Shuangcheng, China | B10 | 31 |
| Shuangjiang, China | G4 | 31 |
| Shuangliao, China | C9 | 31 |
| Shuangshan, China | C10 | 32 |
| Shuangyang, China | C11 | 32 |
| Shuangyashan, China | B11 | 31 |
| Shubenacadie, N.S. | D6 | 71 |
| Shubenacadie Lake, l., N.S. | E6 | 71 |
| Shubert, Ne., U.S. | D10 | 104 |
| Shubrā al Khaymah, Eg. | C6 | 43 |
| Shubrā Khīt, Eg. | C2 | 41 |
| Shubuta, Ms., U.S. | D5 | 101 |
| Shucheng, China | I7 | 32 |
| Shueib Dam, Jord. | h13 | 41 |
| Shuʻfāṭ, Isr. Occ. | h11 | 41 |
| Shujāābād, Pak. | C3 | 37 |
| Shuksan, Mount, mtn., Wa., U.S. | A4 | 124 |
| Shulan, China | C12 | 31 |
| Shulaps Peak, mtn., B.C. | D6 | 69 |
| Shule He, stm., China | *C5 | 31 |
| Shulerville, S.C., U.S. | E8 | 117 |
| Shullsburg, Wi., U.S. | F3 | 126 |
| Shumagin Islands, is., Ak., U.S. | E7 | 79 |
| Shumaykh, Libya | C2 | 43 |
| Shumen, Bul. | D8 | 24 |
| Shumerlya, Sov. Un. | D16 | 27 |
| Shumikha, Sov. Un. | B6 | 28 |
| Shumway, Il., U.S. | D5 | 90 |
| Shunchang, China | K7 | 32 |
| Shungnak, Ak., U.S. | B8 | 79 |
| Shuoxian, China | H7 | 32 |
| Shuoxian, China | E5 | 32 |
| Shuqrah, Yemen | D4 | 38 |
| Shuqualak, Ms., U.S. | C5 | 101 |
| Shūr, stm., Iran | D5 | 39 |
| Shūr, stm., Iran | F7 | 39 |
| Shuri, Japan | O5 | 52 |
| Shurugwi, Zimb. | A5 | 49 |
| Shushan, N.Y., U.S. | B7 | 109 |
| Shūshtar, Iran | E4 | 39 |
| Shuswap, stm., B.C. | D8 | 69 |
| Shuswap Lake, l., B.C. | D8 | 69 |
| Shutesbury, Ma., U.S. | B3 | 98 |
| Shuwak, Sud. | C4 | 47 |
| Shuwaykah, Isr. Occ. | f11 | 41 |
| Shuya, Japan | N6 | 52 |
| Shuzenji, Japan | o17 | 33 |
| Shwebo, Burma | D2 | 35 |
| Shwegyin, Burma | D2 | 35 |
| Siālkot, Pak. | A5 | 36 |
| Siam, Gulf of see Thailand, Gulf of, b., Asia | C2 | 34 |
| Siam see Thailand, ctry., Asia | B2 | 34 |
| Sian see Xi'an, China | E8 | 31 |
| Siantan, i., Indon. | K7 | 35 |
| Siásconset, Ma., U.S. | D8 | 98 |
| Siátista, Grc. | B3 | 25 |
| Šiauliai, Sov. Un. | E7 | 22 |
| Sibay, Sov. Un. | C5 | 28 |
| Sibbald, Alta. | D5 | 68 |
| Šibenik, Yugo. | D2 | 24 |
| Siberia, In., U.S. | H4 | 91 |
| Siberia, reg., Sov. Un. | C13 | 29 |
| Sibert, Ky., U.S. | C6 | 94 |
| Siberut, i., Indon. | F1 | 34 |
| Sibi, Pak. | C4 | 36 |
| Sibiryakov, i., Sov. Un. | B7 | 128 |
| Sibiti, Congo | B1 | 48 |
| Sibiu, Rom. | C7 | 24 |
| Sibley, Il., U.S. | C5 | 90 |
| Sibley, Ia., U.S. | A2 | 92 |
| Sibley, La., U.S. | B2 | 95 |
| Sibley, Mo., U.S. | h11 | 102 |
| Sibley, N.D., U.S. | B8 | 111 |
| Sibley, co., Mn., U.S. | F4 | 100 |
| Sibolga, Indon. | E1 | 34 |
| Sibsāgar, India | C9 | 36 |
| Sibu, Malay. | E4 | 34 |
| Sibuatan, mtn., Indon. | m11 | 34 |
| Sibutu Island, i., Phil. | E5 | 34 |
| Sibutu Passage, strt., Asia | E5 | 34 |
| Sibuyan Sea, Phil. | C6 | 34 |
| Sicamous, B.C. | D8 | 69 |
| Si Chang, i., Thai. | F4 | 35 |
| Sichomovi, Az., U.S. | B5 | 80 |
| Sichuan, prov., China | E5 | 31 |
| Sicily, i., Italy | F4 | 23 |
| Sicily Island, La., U.S. | C4 | 95 |
| Sicklerville, N.J., U.S. | D3 | 107 |
| Sicuani, Peru | D3 | 58 |
| Sidamo, prov., Eth. | E4 | 47 |
| Sideling Hill, mtn., Md., U.S. | A1 | 97 |
| Sideling Hill Creek, stm., Md., U.S. | A1 | 97 |
| Sidell, Il., U.S. | D6 | 90 |
| Siderno Marina, Italy | E6 | 23 |
| Sídheros, Ákra, c., Grc. | E6 | 40 |
| Sidhirókastron, Grc. | B4 | 40 |
| Sidi Barrānī, Eg. | C5 | 43 |
| Sidi bel Abbès, Alg. | B4 | 44 |
| Sidi Bennour, Mor. | C3 | 44 |
| Sidi Ifni, Mor. | D2 | 44 |
| Sidi Kacem, Mor. | *C3 | 44 |
| Sidikalang, Indon. | m11 | 34 |
| Sīdī Muḥammad, 'Ayn, well, Libya | H3 | 40 |
| Sīdī Sālim, Eg. | C2 | 41 |
| Sidi Slimane, Mor. | *C3 | 44 |
| Sidlaw Hills, hills, Scot., U.K. | D5 | 13 |
| Sidley, Mount, mtn., Ant. | B36 | 7 |
| Sidmouth, Eng., U.K. | D4 | 12 |
| Sidnaw, Mi., U.S. | B2 | 99 |
| Sidney, B.C. | E6 | 69 |
| Sidney, Man. | E2 | 70 |
| Sidney, Ar., U.S. | A4 | 81 |
| Sidney, Il., U.S. | C5 | 90 |
| Sidney, Ia., U.S. | D2 | 92 |
| Sidney, Mt., U.S. | C12 | 103 |
| Sidney, Ne., U.S. | C3 | 104 |
| Sidney, N.J., U.S. | B3 | 107 |
| Sidney, N.Y., U.S. | C5 | 109 |
| Sidney, Oh., U.S. | B1 | 112 |
| Sidney Center, N.Y., U.S. | C5 | 109 |
| Sidney Lanier, Lake, res., Ga., U.S. | B2 | 87 |
| Sidon, Ms., U.S. | B3 | 101 |
| Sidonia, Tn., U.S. | A3 | 119 |
| Sidon see Ṣaydā, Leb. | B3 | 38 |
| Sidorovka, Sov. Un. | D25 | 8 |
| Sidra, Gulf of (Khalīj Surt), b., Libya | C3 | 43 |
| Sidrolândia, Braz. | C2 | 56 |
| Siedlce, Pol. | B7 | 26 |
| Sieg, stm., W. Ger. | C3 | 18 |
| Siegburg, W. Ger. | C3 | 18 |
| Siegen, W. Ger. | C4 | 18 |
| Sieglar, W. Ger. | C2 | 19 |
| Siegle, La., U.S. | *B3 | 95 |
| Siemianowice Śląskie, Pol. | g10 | 26 |
| Siemiatycze, Pol. | B7 | 26 |
| Siemréab, Camb. | C2 | 34 |
| Siena, Italy | C3 | 23 |
| Sieper, La., U.S. | C3 | 95 |
| Sieradz, Pol. | A3 | 21 |
| Sierck, Spain | B5 | 22 |
| Sierra, co., Ca., U.S. | C3 | 82 |
| Sierra, co., N.M., U.S. | D2 | 108 |
| Sierra Blanca, Tx., U.S. | o12 | 120 |
| Sierra Blanca Peak, mtn., N.M., U.S. | D4 | 108 |
| Sierra City, Ca., U.S. | C3 | 82 |
| Sierra Colorada, Arg. | E3 | 54 |
| Sierra Estrella, mts., Az., U.S. | m8 | 80 |
| Sierra Gorda, Chile | A3 | 54 |
| Sierra Leone, ctry., Afr. | E2 | 45 |
| Sierra Madre, Ca., U.S. | m12 | 82 |
| Sierra Mojada, Mex. | B4 | 63 |
| Sierra Nevada (Great Bolivar) National Park, Ven. | B3 | 60 |
| Sierraville, Ca., U.S. | C3 | 82 |
| Sierra Vista, Az., U.S. | F5 | 80 |
| Sierre, Switz. | C3 | 21 |
| Siesta Key, Fl., U.S. | *E4 | 86 |
| Siesta Key, i., Fl., U.S. | E4 | 86 |
| Siewierz, Pol. | g10 | 26 |
| Sífnos, i., Grc. | C5 | 40 |
| Sifton, Man. | D1 | 70 |
| Sigatoka, Fiji | n14 | 52 |
| Sigean, Fr. | F5 | 16 |
| Sigel, Il., U.S. | D5 | 90 |
| Sigel, Pa., U.S. | D3 | 115 |
| Sighetu Marmaţiei, Rom. | B6 | 24 |
| Sighişoara, Rom. | C7 | 24 |
| Sighty Crag, mtn., Eng., U.K. | E6 | 13 |
| Sigli, Indon. | k11 | 34 |
| Siglufjördur, Ice. | m23 | 14 |
| Sigmaringen, W. Ger. | A5 | 20 |
| Signachi, Sov. Un. | B15 | 40 |
| Signal Mountain, Tn., U.S. | D8 | 119 |
| Signal Mountain, mtn., Az., U.S. | F2 | 121 |
| Signal Peak, mtn., Az., U.S. | D2 | 80 |
| Signal Peak, mtn., Ut., U.S. | F2 | 121 |
| Signal Mountain, mtn., Vt., U.S. | C4 | 122 |
| Signal Mountain, mtn., Va., U.S. | g11 | 123 |
| Signy-l'Abbaye, Fr. | E4 | 17 |
| Sigourney, Ia., U.S. | C5 | 92 |
| Sigsbee, Ga., U.S. | E3 | 87 |
| Sigtuna, Swe. | t35 | 14 |
| Siguatepeque, Hond. | G4 | 63 |
| Sigüenza, Spain | B4 | 22 |
| Siguiri, Gui. | D3 | 45 |
| Sigurd, Ut., U.S. | E4 | 121 |
| Sihanoukville see Kampong Saom, Camb. | C2 | 34 |
| Sihl Lake, l., Switz. | B6 | 21 |
| Sihuas, Peru | C2 | 58 |
| Sīʼīr, Isr. Occ. | C7 | 41 |
| Siirt, Tur. | D13 | 40 |
| Siis, i., Micron. | Q18 | 52 |
| Sikar, India | C6 | 36 |
| Sikasso, Mali | D3 | 45 |
| Sikes, La., U.S. | B3 | 95 |
| Sikeston, Mo., U.S. | E8 | 102 |
| Sikhote-Alin Mountains, mts., Sov. Un. | E16 | 29 |
| Sikiá, Grc. | C5 | 40 |
| Sikinos, i., Grc. | D5 | 40 |
| Sikkim, state, India | C8 | 36 |
| Siklós, Hung. | C4 | 24 |
| Sil, stm., Spain | A2 | 22 |
| Silandro, Italy | A3 | 23 |
| Silang, Phil. | o13 | 34 |
| Silao, Mex. | m13 | 63 |
| Silas, Al., U.S. | D1 | 78 |
| Silat Aẕ Ẕahr, Isr. Occ. | f11 | 41 |
| Silchar, India | D9 | 36 |
| Şile, Tur. | B7 | 40 |
| Siler City, N.C., U.S. | B3 | 110 |
| Silerton, Tn., U.S. | B3 | 119 |
| Silesia, Mt., U.S. | E8 | 103 |
| Silesia, hist. reg., Pol. | C4 | 26 |
| Siletz, Or., U.S. | C3 | 114 |
| Siletz, stm., Or., U.S. | C3 | 114 |
| Silex, Mo., U.S. | B6 | 102 |
| Silgarhi-Doti, Nepal | C8 | 37 |
| Silica, Oh., U.S. | e6 | 112 |
| Silifke, Tur. | D9 | 40 |
| Siling Co, l., China | D8 | 36 |
| Silisili, Mount, mtn., W. Sam. | F11 | 52 |
| Silistra, Bul. | C8 | 24 |
| Silivri, Tur. | B7 | 40 |
| Siljan, Swe. | p27 | 14 |
| Siljan, l., Swe. | G6 | 14 |
| Silkeborg, Den. | B3 | 15 |
| Sillery, Que. | n17 | 74 |
| Silloth, Eng., U.K. | F5 | 13 |
| Sil Nakaya, Az., U.S. | E4 | 80 |
| Siloam, Ga., U.S. | C3 | 87 |
| Siloam Springs, Ar., U.S. | A1 | 81 |
| Silsbee, Tx., U.S. | D5 | 120 |
| Silsby Lake, l., Man. | B4 | 70 |
| Silton, Sask. | G3 | 75 |
| Šilutė, Sov. Un. | A6 | 26 |
| Silva, Mo., U.S. | D7 | 102 |
| Silva, N.D., U.S. | A6 | 111 |
| Silva Jardim, Braz. | h6 | 56 |
| Sílvânia, Braz. | B5 | 56 |
| Silver, S.C., U.S. | D7 | 117 |
| Silver Bay, Mn., U.S. | C7 | 100 |
| Silver Bow, co., Mt., U.S. | E4 | 103 |
| Silver City, Ia., U.S. | C2 | 92 |
| Silver City, Ms., U.S. | B3 | 101 |
| Silver City, Nv., U.S. | D2 | 105 |
| Silver City, N.M., U.S. | E1 | 108 |
| Silver City, S.D., U.S. | C2 | 118 |
| Silver Cliff, Co., U.S. | C5 | 83 |
| Silver Creek, Ga., U.S. | B1 | 87 |
| Silver Creek, Ms., U.S. | D3 | 101 |
| Silver Creek, Ne., U.S. | C8 | 104 |
| Silver Creek, N.Y., U.S. | C1 | 109 |
| Silver Creek, stm., Ne., U.S. | g11 | 104 |
| Silver Creek, stm., Or., U.S. | D7 | 114 |
| Silverdale, Ks., U.S. | E7 | 93 |
| Silverdale, Wa., U.S. | B3 | 124 |
| Silver Fork, Ut., U.S. | *C4 | 121 |
| Silver Gate, Mt., U.S. | E7 | 103 |
| Silver Grove, Ky., U.S. | h14 | 94 |
| Silver Hill, Md., U.S. | f9 | 97 |
| Silver Island Mountains, mts., Ut., U.S. | C2 | 121 |
| Silver Lake, Ks., U.S. | C8 | 93 |
| Silver Lake, Mn., U.S. | F4 | 100 |
| Silver Lake, N.H., U.S. | C4 | 106 |
| Silver Lake, Or., U.S. | D5 | 114 |
| Silver Lake, Wi., U.S. | F5 | 126 |
| Silver Lake, l., Ont. | E4 | 70 |
| Silver Lake, l., De., U.S. | A3 | 92 |
| Silver Lake, l., Me., U.S. | C2 | 106 |
| Silver Lake, l., N.H., U.S. | C3 | 106 |
| Silver Lake, l., N.H., U.S. | D1 | 114 |
| Silver Lake, l., Wa., U.S. | g13 | 124 |
| Silvermine, Ire. | E3 | 11 |
| Silver Peak Range, mts., Nv., U.S. | F4 | 105 |
| Silverpeak, Nv., U.S. | F4 | 105 |
| Silver Plume, Co., U.S. | *B5 | 83 |
| Silver Point, Tn., U.S. | C8 | 119 |
| Silver Run, Md., U.S. | A3 | 97 |
| Silver Spring, Md., U.S. | C3 | 97 |
| Silver Springs, Fl., U.S. | C4 | 86 |
| Silver Springs, Nv., U.S. | D2 | 105 |
| Silver Springs, N.Y., U.S. | C2 | 109 |
| Silver Star, Mt., U.S. | E4 | 103 |
| Silver Star Mountain, mtn., Wa., U.S. | A5 | 124 |
| Silverstreet, S.C., U.S. | C4 | 117 |
| Silverthrone Mountain, mtn., B.C. | D4 | 69 |
| Silvertip Mountain, mtn., Mt., U.S. | C3 | 103 |
| Silverton, B.C. | E9 | 69 |
| Silverton, Co., U.S. | D3 | 83 |
| Silverton, Id., U.S. | B3 | 89 |
| Silverton, N.J., U.S. | C4 | 107 |
| Silverton, Oh., U.S. | o13 | 112 |
| Silverton, Or., U.S. | B4 | 114 |
| Silverton, Tx., U.S. | B2 | 120 |
| Silves, Port. | D1 | 22 |
| Silvia, Col. | B3 | 60 |
| Silvies, stm., Or., U.S. | D7 | 114 |
| Silvis, Il., U.S. | B3 | 90 |
| Silwān (part of Jerusalem), Isr. Occ. | h11 | 41 |
| Simanggang, Malay. | E4 | 34 |
| Simao, China | G5 | 31 |
| Simav, Tur. | B7 | 40 |
| Simav, stm., Tur. | B7 | 25 |
| Simcoe, Ont. | E4 | 73 |
| Simcoe, co., Ont. | C4 | 73 |
| Simcoe, Lake, l., Ont. | C5 | 73 |
| Simdega, India | F10 | 37 |
| Simeulue, i., Indon. | m11 | 34 |
| Simferopol, Sov. Un. | E9 | 29 |
| Sími, i., Grc. | D6 | 25 |
| Similan Islands, is., Thai. | H2 | 35 |
| Similkameen, stm., N.A. | E7 | 69 |
| Simití, Col. | B3 | 60 |
| Simi Valley, Ca., U.S. | E4 | 82 |
| Simla, Co., U.S. | B6 | 83 |
| Simleu Silvaniei, Rom. | B6 | 24 |
| Simme, stm., Switz. | C3 | 21 |
| Simmern, W. Ger. | D2 | 19 |
| Simmesport, La., U.S. | D4 | 95 |
| Simmie, Sask. | H1 | 75 |
| Simmons, Mo., U.S. | D5 | 102 |
| Simms, Mt., U.S. | C5 | 103 |
| Simms Point, c., Bah. | m16 | 64 |
| Simms Stream, stm., N.H., U.S. | g7 | 106 |
| Simonette, stm., Alta. | B1 | 68 |
| Simonhouse Lake, l., Man. | B1 | 70 |
| Simonstorp (part of Norrköping), Swe. | u34 | 14 |
| Simonstown (Simonstad), S. Afr. | D2 | 49 |
| Simonsville, Vt., U.S. | E3 | 122 |
| Simoom Sound, B.C. | D4 | 69 |
| Simpang-kiri, stm., Indon. | K2 | 35 |
| Simplício Mendes, Braz. | C4 | 57 |
| Simplon Pass, Switz. | C4 | 20 |
| Simplon Tunnel, Eur. | A2 | 23 |
| Simpson, Sask. | F3 | 75 |
| Simpson, Il., U.S. | F5 | 90 |
| Simpson, Ks., U.S. | C6 | 93 |
| Simpson, La., U.S. | C3 | 95 |
| Simpson, Mn., U.S. | G6 | 100 |
| Simpson, N.C., U.S. | B5 | 110 |
| Simpson, Ok., U.S. | C5 | 113 |
| Simpson, Pa., U.S. | C11 | 115 |
| Simpson, W.V., U.S. | k10 | 125 |
| Simpson, co., Ky., U.S. | D3 | 94 |
| Simpson, co., Ms., U.S. | D4 | 101 |
| Simpson Creek, stm., W.V., U.S. | k10 | 125 |
| Simpson Desert, des., Austl. | E6 | 50 |
| Simpson Peninsula, pen., N.W. Ter. | C15 | 66 |
| Simpsonville, Ky., U.S. | B4 | 94 |
| Simpsonville, S.C., U.S. | B3 | 117 |
| Simrishamn, Swe. | J6 | 14 |
| Sims, Ar., U.S. | C2 | 81 |
| Sims, Il., U.S. | E5 | 90 |
| Sims, Tx., U.S. | D5 | 120 |
| Sims, N.C., U.S. | B4 | 110 |
| Simsboro, La., U.S. | B3 | 95 |
| Simsbury, Ct., U.S. | B4 | 84 |
| Sims Chapel, Al., U.S. | D1 | 78 |
| Simunjan, Malay. | E4 | 34 |
| Sinabang, Indon. | K2 | 35 |
| Sinai, S.D., U.S. | C8 | 118 |
| Sinaia, Rom. | C7 | 24 |
| Sinai Peninsula, pen., Eg. | C3 | 38 |
| Sinajana, Guam | L10 | 52 |
| Sinaloa, state, Mex. | B3 | 63 |
| Sinaloa [de Leyva], Mex. | B3 | 63 |
| Sinan, China | F6 | 31 |
| Sinanju, N. Kor. | G3 | 33 |
| Sinarū, Eg. | E2 | 41 |
| Sīnāwan, Libya | C2 | 43 |
| Sincan, Tur. | *C9 | 40 |
| Sinçé, Col. | B2 | 60 |
| Sincelejo, Col. | B2 | 60 |
| Sinclair, Man. | E1 | 70 |
| Sinclair, Me., U.S. | A4 | 96 |
| Sinclair, Wy., U.S. | E5 | 127 |
| Sinclair, Lake, res., Ga., U.S. | C3 | 87 |
| Sinclair's Bay, b., Scot., U.K. | B5 | 13 |
| Sinclairville, N.Y., U.S. | C1 | 109 |
| Sind, prov., Pak. | C4 | 36 |
| Sind, stm., India | D7 | 37 |
| Sindal, Den. | A4 | 15 |
| Sindara, Gabon | F2 | 46 |
| Sindelfingen, W. Ger. | C7 | 40 |
| Sindirgi, Tur. | C7 | 40 |
| Sinel'nikovo, Sov. Un. | G10 | 27 |
| Sines, Port. | D1 | 22 |
| Sinfra, I.C. | E3 | 45 |
| Singapore, Sing. | E3 | 34 |
| Singapore, ctry., Asia | E3 | 34 |
| Singapore Strait, strt., Asia | L5 | 35 |
| Singaraja, Indon. | G5 | 34 |
| Singer, (Hohentwiel), W. Ger. | B4 | 20 |
| Singer, La., U.S. | D2 | 95 |
| Singhampton, Ont. | C4 | 73 |
| Singida, Tan. | B5 | 48 |
| Singida, prov., Tan. | C5 | 48 |
| Singitic Gulf, b., Grc. | B4 | 25 |
| Singkawang, Indon. | E3 | 34 |
| Singkep, i., Indon. | F2 | 34 |
| Singleton, Austl. | F8 | 51 |
| Sinhŭng, N. Kor. | F3 | 33 |
| Siniscola, Italy | C3 | 23 |
| Sinj, Yugo. | D2 | 24 |
| Sinjai, Indon. | G6 | 34 |
| Sinjil, Isr. Occ. | g12 | 41 |
| Sinkāt, Sud. | B4 | 47 |
| Sinkiang see Xinjiang Uygur, prov., China | C2 | 31 |
| Sinking Creek, stm., Ky., U.S. | C4 | 94 |
| Sinking Spring, Oh., U.S. | C2 | 112 |
| Sinks Grove, W.V., U.S. | D4 | 125 |
| Sinnamahoning, Pa., U.S. | D5 | 115 |
| Sinnamahoning Creek, stm., Pa., U.S. | D5 | 115 |
| Sinnamahoning Creek, First Fork, stm., Pa., U.S. | D5 | 115 |
| Sînnicolau Mare, Rom. | B5 | 24 |
| Sinnūris, Eg. | A10 | 40 |
| Sinop, N. Kor. | F4 | 33 |
| Sinp'o, N. Kor. | F4 | 33 |
| Sintaluta, Sask. | G4 | 75 |
| Sint-Amandsberg (part of Gent), Bel. | E4 | 34 |
| Sintang, Indon. | E4 | 34 |
| Sint Christoffelberg, hill, Neth. Ant. | H18 | 65 |
| Sint Eustatius, i., Neth. Ant. | H13 | 64 |
| Sint Helenabaai, b., S. Afr. | D2 | 49 |
| Sint Jacobiparochie, Neth. | B6 | 16 |
| Sint Kruis, Neth. Ant. | H18 | 65 |
| Sint-Lenaarts, Bel. | B6 | 16 |
| Sint Marie, Kaap, c., Neth. Ant. | H17 | 65 |
| Sint Nicolaas, Aruba | H17 | 65 |
| Sint-Niklaas (Saint-Nicolas), Bel. | B6 | 16 |
| Sinton, Tx., U.S. | E4 | 120 |
| Sintra, Port. | f9 | 22 |
| Sint-Truiden, Bel. | B7 | 25 |
| Sinú, stm., Col. | B2 | 60 |
| Sinŭiju, N. Kor. | G3 | 33 |
| Sinyavino, Sov. Un. | s32 | 14 |
| Sinzig, W. Ger. | C2 | 19 |
| Sion, Switz. | C3 | 21 |
| Sioux, co., Ia., U.S. | A1 | 92 |
| Sioux, co., Ne., U.S. | B2 | 104 |
| Sioux, co., N.D., U.S. | C4 | 111 |
| Sioux Center, Ia., U.S. | A1 | 92 |
| Sioux City, Ia., U.S. | B1 | 92 |

| Name | Map Ref. | Page |
|---|---|---|
| Sioux Falls, S.D., U.S. | D9 | 118 |
| Sioux Lookout, Ont. | o17 | 73 |
| Sioux Rapids, Ia., U.S. | B2 | 92 |
| Sipanok Channel, mth., Sask. | D4 | 75 |
| Siparia, Trin. | O22 | 65 |
| Siping, China | C9 | 31 |
| Sipiwesk Lake, l., Man. | B3 | 70 |
| Siple, sci., Ant. | | 7 |
| Siple, Mount, mtn., Ant. | B36 | 7 |
| Siple Coast, Ant. | A33 | 7 |
| Sipsey, Al., U.S. | B2 | 78 |
| Sipsey, stm., Al., U.S. | B2 | 78 |
| Sipsey Fork, stm., Al., U.S. | A2 | 78 |
| Sipura, i., Indon. | F1 | 34 |
| Siquirres, C.R. | E6 | 62 |
| Siquisique, Ven. | A4 | 60 |
| Şīr Abū Nu'Ayr, i., U.A.E. | I7 | 39 |
| Siracusa (Syracuse), Italy | F5 | 23 |
| Sirāiganj, Bngl. | D8 | 36 |
| Sir Alexander, Mount, mtn., B.C. | C7 | 69 |
| Sirdar, B.C. | E9 | 69 |
| Sir Douglas, Mount, mtn., Can. | D3 | 68 |
| Sir Edward Pellew Group, is., Austl. | C6 | 50 |
| Siren, Wi., U.S. | C1 | 126 |
| Siret, Rom. | B8 | 24 |
| Siret, stm., Eur. | B8 | 24 |
| Sirḥān, Wādī as, val., Asia | C7 | 43 |
| Sirik, cape, c., Malay. | E4 | 34 |
| Sirina, i., Grc. | D6 | 25 |
| Sir James MacBrien, Mount, mtn., N.W. Ter. | D7 | 66 |
| Sīrjān, Iran | G7 | 39 |
| Sirmans, Fl., U.S. | B3 | 86 |
| Sirmione, Italy | D6 | 20 |
| Sironj, India | E6 | 37 |
| Síros, i., Grc. | D5 | 25 |
| Sirpur, India | H7 | 37 |
| Sirr, Munkhaţ as, well, Eg. | D5 | 41 |
| Sirrī, i., Iran | I7 | 39 |
| Sirsa, India | C6 | 36 |
| Sir Sandford, Mount, mtn., B.C. | D9 | 69 |
| Širvintos, Sov. Un. | A8 | 26 |
| Sir-Wilfrid, Mont, mtn., Que. | C2 | 74 |
| Sir Wilfrid Laurier, Mount, mtn., B.C. | C8 | 69 |
| Sisak, Yugo. | C3 | 24 |
| Si Sa Ket, Thai. | B2 | 34 |
| Sishui, China | G7 | 32 |
| Sisib Lake, l., Man. | B1 | 70 |
| Siskiyou, co., Ca., U.S. | B2 | 82 |
| Siskiyou Mountains, mts., U.S. | F3 | 114 |
| Siskiyou Pass, Or., U.S. | E4 | 114 |
| Sisquoc, Ca., U.S. | E3 | 82 |
| Sissach, Switz. | B4 | 21 |
| Sisseton, S.D., U.S. | B8 | 118 |
| Sisseton Indian Reservation, U.S. | B8 | 118 |
| Sissiboo, stm., N.S. | E4 | 71 |
| Sisson Branch Reservoir, res., N.B. | B2 | 71 |
| Sissonville, W.V., U.S. | C3 | 125 |
| Šīstān, reg., Asia | D8 | 39 |
| Sister Bay, Wi., U.S. | C6 | 126 |
| Sisterdale, Tx., U.S. | E3 | 120 |
| Sisteron, Fr. | E6 | 16 |
| Sisters, Or., U.S. | C5 | 114 |
| Sistersville, W.V., U.S. | B4 | 125 |
| Sītāpur, India | C7 | 36 |
| Sitía, Grc. | E6 | 40 |
| Sitio da Abadia, Braz. | A3 | 56 |
| Sitionuevo, Col. | A3 | 60 |
| Sitka, Ak., U.S. | D12 | 79 |
| Sitka National Historical Park, Ak., U.S. | m22 | 79 |
| Sitka Sound, strt., Ak., U.S. | m22 | 79 |
| Sittard, Neth. | D5 | 17 |
| Sittoung, stm., Burma | E10 | 36 |
| Sittwe (Akyab), Burma | D9 | 36 |
| Siuna, Nic. | D5 | 62 |
| Siuri, India | D8 | 36 |
| Sivas, Tur. | C11 | 40 |
| Siverek, Tur. | D12 | 40 |
| Siwah, Eg. | C2 | 38 |
| Siwalik Range, mts., India | B6 | 36 |
| Six-Fours-la-Plage, Fr. | F6 | 16 |
| Sixian, China | H7 | 32 |
| Si see Xi Jiang, stm., China | G7 | 31 |
| Six Mile, S.C., U.S. | B2 | 117 |
| Sixmile Creek, stm., Fl., U.S. | n8 | 86 |
| Sixmilecross, N. Ire., U.K. | C4 | 11 |
| Sixt, Fr. | D2 | 21 |
| Sizhan, China | B2 | 33 |
| Sjælland, i., Den. | J4 | 14 |
| Sjællands Odde, pen., Den. | B5 | 15 |
| Sjenica, Yugo. | D5 | 24 |
| Sjöbo, Swe. | C7 | 15 |
| Skælskør, Den. | C5 | 15 |
| Skærbæk, Den. | C2 | 15 |
| Skagen, Den. | A4 | 15 |
| Skagerrak, strt., Eur. | I3 | 14 |
| Skagit, co., Wa., U.S. | A4 | 124 |
| Skagit, stm., N.A. | A3 | 69 |
| Skagway, Ak., U.S. | D12 | 79 |
| Skälderviken, b., Swe. | B6 | 15 |
| Skalka Reservoir, res., Czech. | C7 | 19 |
| Skamania, Wa., U.S. | D3 | 124 |
| Skamania, co., Wa., U.S. | D3 | 124 |
| Skamokawa, Wa., U.S. | C2 | 124 |
| Skanderborg, Den. | B3 | 15 |
| Skaneateles, N.Y., U.S. | C4 | 109 |
| Skaneateles Lake, l., N.Y., U.S. | C4 | 109 |
| Skanee, Mi., U.S. | B2 | 99 |
| Skånes-Fagerhult, Swe. | B7 | 15 |
| Skanör, Swe. | C6 | 15 |
| Skántzoura, i., Grc. | C5 | 25 |
| Skara, Swe. | H5 | 14 |
| Skarven, l., Swe. | t35 | 14 |
| Skarżysko-Kamienna, Pol. | C6 | 26 |
| Skawa, stm., Pol. | h11 | 26 |
| Skawina, Pol. | D5 | 26 |
| Skedee, Ok., U.S. | A5 | 113 |
| Skeena, stm., B.C. | F7 | 66 |
| Skeena Mountains, mts., B.C. | E7 | 66 |
| Skegness, Eng., U.K. | D7 | 10 |
| Skeldon, Guy. | A3 | 59 |
| Skeleton Lake, l., Ont. | B5 | 73 |
| Skellefteå, Swe. | E9 | 14 |
| Skellefteälven, stm., Swe. | E8 | 14 |
| Skellytown, Tx., U.S. | B2 | 120 |
| Skelton, W.V., U.S. | n13 | 125 |
| Skelton Glacier, ice, Ant. | f40 | 7 |
| Skene, Ms., U.S. | B3 | 101 |
| Skerries, Ire. | D5 | 11 |
| Skerry, Stack, rock, Scot., U.K. | A4 | 13 |
| Skhmatárion, Grc. | g11 | 25 |
| Skiathos, Grc. | C5 | 25 |
| Skíathos, i., Grc. | C4 | 25 |
| Skiatook, Ok., U.S. | A5 | 113 |
| Skiatook Reservoir, res., Ok., U.S. | A5 | 113 |
| Skibbereen, Ire. | E2 | 10 |
| Skibby, Den. | C5 | 15 |
| Skiddaw, mtn., Eng., U.K. | F5 | 13 |
| Skidegate, B.C. | C2 | 69 |
| Skidegate Inlet, b., B.C. | C2 | 69 |
| Skidmore, Mo., U.S. | A2 | 102 |
| Skidmore, Tx., U.S. | E4 | 120 |
| Skien, Nor. | H3 | 14 |
| Skierniewice, Pol. | C6 | 26 |
| Skiff, Alta. | E5 | 68 |
| Skihist Mountain, mtn., B.C. | D7 | 69 |
| Skikda (Philippeville), Alg. | B6 | 44 |
| Skillet Fork, stm., Il., U.S. | E5 | 90 |
| Skillman, N.J., U.S. | C3 | 107 |
| Skipperville, Al., U.S. | D4 | 78 |
| Skipton, Eng., U.K. | G7 | 13 |
| Skíros, Grc. | C5 | 40 |
| Skíros (Scyros), i., Grc. | C5 | 40 |
| Skive, Den. | B3 | 15 |
| Skjern, Den. | C2 | 15 |
| Skjern Å, stm., Den. | C2 | 15 |
| Skoczów, Pol. | h9 | 26 |
| Škofja Loka, Yugo. | B2 | 24 |
| Skokie, Il., U.S. | A6 | 90 |
| Skokomish Indian Reservation, Wa., U.S. | B2 | 124 |
| Skole, Sov. Un. | D7 | 26 |
| Skópelos, i., Grc. | C4 | 40 |
| Skopin, Sov. Un. | E12 | 27 |
| Skopje, Yugo. | B3 | 15 |
| Skørping, Den. | B3 | 15 |
| Skotovataya, Sov. Un. | q20 | 27 |
| Skotselv, Nor. | p27 | 14 |
| Skövde, Swe. | H5 | 14 |
| Skovorodino, Sov. Un. | D15 | 29 |
| Skowhegan, Me., U.S. | D3 | 96 |
| Skownan, Man. | D2 | 70 |
| Skradin, Yugo. | D2 | 24 |
| Skreen, Ire. | C3 | 11 |
| Skull, Ire. | F2 | 11 |
| Skull Valley, Az., U.S. | C3 | 80 |
| Skull Valley, val., Ut., U.S. | C3 | 121 |
| Skull Valley Indian Reservation, Ut., U.S. | C3 | 121 |
| Skuna, stm., Ms., U.S. | B4 | 101 |
| Skunk, stm., Ia., U.S. | D6 | 92 |
| Skurup, Swe. | C7 | 15 |
| Skvira, Sov. Un. | G7 | 27 |
| Skwentna, Ak., U.S. | g16 | 79 |
| Skwentna, stm., Ak., U.S. | g15 | 79 |
| Skwierzyna (Schwerin), Pol. | B3 | 10 |
| Skye, Island of, i., Scot., U.K. | B4 | 124 |
| Skykomish, Wa., U.S. | B4 | 124 |
| Skykomish, stm., Wa., U.S. | B4 | 124 |
| Sky Lake, Fl., U.S. | *D5 | 86 |
| Skyland, Nv., U.S. | D2 | 105 |
| Skyland, N.C., U.S. | f10 | 110 |
| Skylight, Ky., U.S. | g11 | 94 |
| Skylight Mountain, mtn., Ar., U.S. | B1 | 81 |
| Skyline, Al., U.S. | A3 | 78 |
| Skyring, Seno, strt., Chile | h11 | 54 |
| Skyway, Co., U.S. | C6 | 83 |
| Skyway, Wa., U.S. | *f11 | 124 |
| Slackwood, N.J., U.S. | *C3 | 107 |
| Slade, Ky., U.S. | C6 | 94 |
| Slagelse, Den. | C5 | 15 |
| Slagle, La., U.S. | C2 | 95 |
| Slane, Ire. | D5 | 11 |
| Slaney, stm., Ire. | E5 | 11 |
| Slangerup, Den. | C5 | 15 |
| Slánic, Rom. | C7 | 24 |
| Slaný, Czech. | n17 | 26 |
| Slapout, Ok., U.S. | A1 | 113 |
| Slapy, Czech. | o17 | 26 |
| Slater Reservoir, res., Czech. | D9 | 19 |
| Slater, Ia., U.S. | A3 | 83 |
| Slater, Ia., U.S. | C4 | 92 |
| Slater, Mo., U.S. | B4 | 102 |
| Slater, S.C., U.S. | A3 | 117 |
| Slatersville, R.I., U.S. | A3 | 116 |
| Slatersville Reservoir, res., R.I., U.S. | B3 | 116 |
| Slate Spring, Ms., U.S. | B4 | 101 |
| Slatina, Rom. | C7 | 24 |
| Slatington, Pa., U.S. | E10 | 115 |
| Slaton, Tx., U.S. | C2 | 120 |
| Slaughter, La., U.S. | D4 | 95 |
| Slaughter Beach, De., U.S. | D5 | 85 |
| Slaughters, Ky., U.S. | C2 | 94 |
| Slave, stm., Can. | D10 | 66 |
| Slave Lake, Alta. | B3 | 68 |
| Slavgorod, Sov. Un. | D10 | 29 |
| Slavonia, hist. reg., Yugo. | C3 | 24 |
| Slavonska Požega, Yugo. | C3 | 24 |
| Slavonski Brod, Yugo. | C4 | 24 |
| Slavsk, Sov. Un. | A6 | 26 |
| Slavyanoserbsk, Sov. Un. | q21 | 27 |
| Slavyansk, Sov. Un. | G11 | 27 |
| Slavyansk-na-Kubani, Sov. Un. | I12 | 27 |
| Sławków, Pol. | g10 | 26 |
| Slayden, Ms., U.S. | A4 | 101 |
| Slaydenville, De., U.S. | A4 | 101 |
| Slayton, Mn., U.S. | G3 | 100 |
| Slaytonville, De., U.S. | E3 | 85 |
| Sleaford, Eng., U.K. | A7 | 12 |
| Slea Head, c., Ire. | E1 | 11 |
| Sleat, Point of, c., Scot., U.K. | C2 | 13 |
| Sleat, Sound of, strt., Scot., U.K. | C3 | 13 |
| Sledge, Ms., U.S. | A3 | 101 |
| Sled Lake, l., Sask. | C2 | 75 |
| Sleeping Bear Dunes National Lakeshore, Mi., U.S. | D4 | 99 |
| Sleeping Bear Point, c., Mi., U.S. | D4 | 99 |
| Sleepy Creek, W.V., U.S. | B6 | 125 |
| Sleepy Eye, Mn., U.S. | F4 | 100 |
| Sleepy Point, c., Fiji | H15 | 52 |
| Sleetmute, Ak., U.S. | C8 | 79 |
| Slemp, Ky., U.S. | C6 | 94 |
| Slick, Ok., U.S. | B5 | 113 |
| Slick Rock, Co., U.S. | C2 | 83 |
| Slidell, La., U.S. | D6 | 95 |
| Slide Mountain, mtn., N.Y., U.S. | D6 | 109 |
| Sliderock Mountain, mtn., Mt., U.S. | D3 | 103 |
| Slieve Aughty Mountains, mts., Ire. | D3 | 11 |
| Slievecallan, hill, Ire. | E2 | 11 |
| Slieve Mish Mountains, mts., Ire. | E2 | 11 |
| Slievenamon, Ire. | E4 | 11 |
| Sligo, Ire. | C2 | 10 |
| Sligo, Pa., U.S. | D3 | 115 |
| Sligo Bay, b., Ire. | C2 | 10 |
| Slim Buttes, mtn., S.D., U.S. | B2 | 118 |

| Name | Map Ref. | Page |
|---|---|---|
| Slinger, Wi., U.S. | E5 | 126 |
| Slippery Rock, Pa., U.S. | D1 | 115 |
| Sliven, Bul. | D8 | 24 |
| Slivenec, Czech. | n17 | 26 |
| Sloan, Ia., U.S. | B1 | 92 |
| Sloan, Nv., U.S. | H6 | 105 |
| Sloan, N.Y., U.S. | C2 | 109 |
| Sloans Valley, Ky., U.S. | D5 | 94 |
| Sloat, Ca., U.S. | C3 | 82 |
| Sloatsburg, N.Y., U.S. | *D6 | 109 |
| Slobodskoy, Sov. Un. | B4 | 29 |
| Slobozia, Rom. | C8 | 24 |
| Slocan, B.C. | E9 | 69 |
| Slocan Lake, l., B.C. | E9 | 69 |
| Slocomb, Al., U.S. | D4 | 78 |
| Slocum, R.I., U.S. | E3 | 116 |
| Slonim, Sov. Un. | E5 | 27 |
| Slope, co., N.D., U.S. | C2 | 111 |
| Slough, Eng., U.K. | k11 | 10 |
| Slovak, Ar., U.S. | C4 | 81 |
| Slovakia, hist. reg., Czech. | D5 | 26 |
| Slovan, Pa., U.S. | F1 | 115 |
| Slovenia, hist. reg., Yugo. | C2 | 24 |
| Šlubice, Pol. | A9 | 19 |
| Sluch, stm., Sov. Un. | F6 | 27 |
| Slunj, Yugo. | C2 | 24 |
| Słupca, Pol. | B4 | 26 |
| Stupia, stm., Pol. | A4 | 26 |
| Słupsk, Pol. | A4 | 26 |
| Slutsk, Sov. Un. | E6 | 27 |
| Slyne Head, c., Ire. | D1 | 10 |
| Slyudyanka, Sov. Un. | D13 | 29 |
| Smackover, Ar., U.S. | D3 | 81 |
| Smackover Creek, stm., Ar., U.S. | D3 | 81 |
| Smålandsfarvandet, strt., Den. | C5 | 15 |
| Small Point, Me., U.S. | g8 | 96 |
| Small Point, c., Me., U.S. | g8 | 96 |
| Smallwood Reservoir, res., Newf. | g8 | 72 |
| Smarr, Ga., U.S. | D3 | 87 |
| Smarts Mountain, mtn., N.H., U.S. | C2 | 106 |
| Smartt, Tn., U.S. | D8 | 119 |
| Smeaton, Sask. | D3 | 75 |
| Smečno, Czech. | n17 | 26 |
| Smederevo, Yugo. | C5 | 24 |
| Smela, Sov. Un. | G8 | 27 |
| Smelterville, Id., U.S. | B2 | 89 |
| Smethport, Pa., U.S. | C5 | 115 |
| Smethwick (Warley), Eng., U.K. | D5 | 10 |
| Smíchov (part of Prague), Czech. | n17 | 26 |
| Smicksburg, Pa., U.S. | E3 | 115 |
| Smidovich, Sov. Un. | B6 | 33 |
| Smiley, Sask. | F1 | 75 |
| Smiley, Tx., U.S. | E4 | 120 |
| Smirnovo, Sov. Un. | H11 | 27 |
| Smith, Alta. | B3 | 68 |
| Smith, Nv., U.S. | E2 | 105 |
| Smith, co., Ks., U.S. | C5 | 93 |
| Smith, co., Ms., U.S. | C4 | 101 |
| Smith, co., Tn., U.S. | A5 | 119 |
| Smith, co., Tx., U.S. | C5 | 120 |
| Smith, stm., N.A. | D6 | 103 |
| Smith, stm., Mt., U.S. | D5 | 103 |
| Smith, Cape, c., Ont. | B3 | 73 |
| Smith and Sayles Reservoir, res., R.I., U.S. | B2 | 116 |
| Smith Bay, b., Ak., U.S. | A9 | 79 |
| Smithboro, Il., U.S. | E4 | 90 |
| Smithburg, W.V., U.S. | B4 | 125 |
| Smith Canyon, val., Co., U.S. | D7 | 83 |
| Smith Center, Ks., U.S. | C5 | 93 |
| Smithdale, Ms., U.S. | D3 | 101 |
| Smithers, B.C. | B4 | 69 |
| Smithers, W.V., U.S. | C3 | 125 |
| Smithfield, Il., U.S. | C3 | 90 |
| Smithfield, Me., U.S. | D3 | 96 |
| Smithfield, Ne., U.S. | D6 | 104 |
| Smithfield, N.C., U.S. | B4 | 110 |
| Smithfield, Oh., U.S. | B5 | 112 |
| Smithfield, Ut., U.S. | B4 | 121 |
| Smithfield, Va., U.S. | D6 | 123 |
| Smithfield, W.V., U.S. | k9 | 125 |
| Smith Island, i., B.A.T. | C6 | 7 |
| Smith Island, i., Md., U.S. | D5 | 97 |
| Smith Island, i., Va., U.S. | C7 | 123 |
| Smithland, Ia., U.S. | B2 | 92 |
| Smithland, Ky., U.S. | e9 | 94 |
| Smithmill, Pa., U.S. | E5 | 115 |
| Smith Mills, Ky., U.S. | C2 | 94 |
| Smith Mountain Lake, res., Va., U.S. | C3 | 123 |
| Smith Peak, mtn., Id., U.S. | A2 | 89 |
| Smith Peninsula, pen., Ant. | B6 | 7 |
| Smith Point, c., N.S. | D6 | 71 |
| Smith Point, c., Ma., U.S. | D7 | 98 |
| Smith Point, c., Va., U.S. | C6 | 123 |
| Smith River, Ca., U.S. | B1 | 82 |
| Smiths, Al., U.S. | C4 | 78 |
| Smiths Md., U.S. | A2 | 97 |
| Smiths Cove, N.S. | E4 | 71 |
| Smiths Falls, Ont. | C8 | 73 |
| Smiths Ferry, Id., U.S. | E3 | 89 |
| Smiths Grove, Ky., U.S. | C3 | 94 |
| Smithshire, Il., U.S. | C3 | 90 |
| Smithsonia, Ga., U.S. | C3 | 87 |
| Smith Sound, strt., B.C. | D4 | 69 |
| Smithton, Austl. | o15 | 50 |
| Smithton, Il., U.S. | E4 | 90 |
| Smithton, Mo., U.S. | C4 | 102 |
| Smith Town, Ky., U.S. | C6 | 94 |
| Smithtown, N.Y., U.S. | n15 | 109 |
| Smithville, Ar., U.S. | A4 | 81 |
| Smithville, Ga., U.S. | E2 | 87 |
| Smithville, Ms., U.S. | A5 | 101 |
| Smithville, Mo., U.S. | B3 | 102 |
| Smithville, N.H., U.S. | B3 | 106 |
| Smithville, Oh., U.S. | B4 | 112 |
| Smithville, Tn., U.S. | C7 | 119 |
| Smithville, Tx., U.S. | D4 | 120 |
| Smithville, W.V., U.S. | B3 | 125 |
| Smithville Flats, N.Y., U.S. | C5 | 109 |
| Smithville Lake, res., Mo., U.S. | C3 | 108 |
| Smoaks, S.C., U.S. | E6 | 117 |
| Smoke Tran, Viet. | | |
| Smok̠erun, Pa., U.S. | E5 | 115 |
| Smoke, Cape, c., N.S. | C9 | 71 |
| Smokey Dome, mtn., Id., U.S. | F4 | 89 |
| Smoky, stm., Alta. | B1 | 68 |
| Smoky Cape, c., Austl. | E9 | 51 |
| Smoky Hill, stm., U.S. | *D5 | 93 |
| Smoky Hill, North Fork, stm., U.S. | C7 | 113 |
| Smoky Junction, Tn., U.S. | C9 | 119 |
| Smoky Lake, Alta. | B4 | 68 |

| Name | Map Ref. | Page |
|---|---|---|
| Smoky Mountains, mts., Id., U.S. | F4 | 89 |
| Smøla, i., Nor. | F2 | 14 |
| Smolan, Ks., U.S. | D6 | 93 |
| Smolensk, Sov. Un. | D6 | 29 |
| Smolyan, Bul. | E7 | 24 |
| Smoot, Wy., U.S. | D2 | 127 |
| Smooth Rock Falls, Ont. | o19 | 73 |
| Smoothstone, stm., Sask. | B2 | 75 |
| Smoothstone Lake, l., Sask. | C2 | 75 |
| Smyadovo, Bul. | D8 | 24 |
| Smygehamn, Swe. | C7 | 15 |
| Smyrna, De., U.S. | C3 | 85 |
| Smyrna, Ga., U.S. | C2 | 87 |
| Smyrna, N.Y., U.S. | C5 | 109 |
| Smyrna, S.C., U.S. | A5 | 117 |
| Smyrna, Tn., U.S. | B5 | 119 |
| Smyrna, stm., De., U.S. | C3 | 85 |
| Smyrna see İzmir, Tur. | | |
| Smyrna Mills, Me., U.S. | B4 | 96 |
| Smyth, co., Va., U.S. | f10 | 123 |
| Smythe, Mount, mtn., B.C. | E8 | 66 |
| Snaefell, mtn., I. of Man | A4 | 76 |
| Snake, stm., U.S. | D5 | 100 |
| Snake, stm., U.S. | B1 | 100 |
| Snake, stm., Ne., U.S. | B4 | 104 |
| Snake Creek, stm., Ne., U.S. | B2 | 104 |
| Snake Falls, wtfl., Ne., U.S. | B2 | 104 |
| Snake Indian, stm., Alta. | C1 | 68 |
| Snake Mountain, mtn., U.S. | A10 | 119 |
| Snake Mountain, mtn., Vt., U.S. | C2 | 122 |
| Snake Range, mts., Nv., U.S. | E7 | 105 |
| Snake River Plain, pl., Id., U.S. | F2 | 89 |
| Snake River Range, mts., U.S. | C2 | 127 |
| Snake Valley, val., U.S. | D2 | 121 |
| Snares Islands, is., N.Z. | R11 | 51 |
| Sneads, Fl., U.S. | B2 | 86 |
| Sneads Ferry, N.C., U.S. | C5 | 110 |
| Snedsted, Den. | B2 | 15 |
| Sneedville, Tn., U.S. | C10 | 119 |
| Sneek, Neth. | A6 | 16 |
| Sneem, Ire. | E2 | 11 |
| Snelling, S.C., U.S. | E5 | 117 |
| Snellville, Ga., U.S. | *h8 | 87 |
| Snezhnoye, Sov. Un. | q21 | 27 |
| Sniardwy, Lake, l., Pol. | B6 | 26 |
| Snipe Keys, is., Fl., U.S. | H5 | 86 |
| Snipe Lake, l., Alta. | B2 | 68 |
| Snizort, Loch, b., Scot., U.K. | C2 | 13 |
| Snøhetta, mtn., Nor. | F3 | 14 |
| Snohomish, Wa., U.S. | B3 | 124 |
| Snohomish, co., Wa., U.S. | A4 | 124 |
| Snoqualmie, Wa., U.S. | B4 | 124 |
| Snoqualmie, stm., Wa., U.S. | B4 | 124 |
| Snoqualmie Pass, Wa., U.S. | B4 | 124 |
| Snøtinden, mtn., Nor. | D5 | 14 |
| Snov, stm., Sov. Un. | F8 | 27 |
| Snover, Mi., U.S. | E8 | 99 |
| Snow, Ok., U.S. | C6 | 113 |
| Snowbank Lake, l., Mr., U.S. | B7 | 100 |
| Snow Camp, N.C., U.S. | B3 | 110 |
| Snowden, Sask. | D3 | 75 |
| Snowdon, mtn., Wales U.K. | D4 | 10 |
| Snowdoun, Al., U.S. | C3 | 78 |
| Snowflake, Man. | E2 | 70 |
| Snowflake, Az., U.S. | C5 | 80 |
| Snow Hill, Al., U.S. | C2 | 78 |
| Snow Hill, Md., U.S. | D3 | 81 |
| Snow Hill, Md., U.S. | D7 | 97 |
| Snow Hill, N.C., U.S. | B5 | 110 |
| Snowking Mountain, mtn., Wa., U.S. | A4 | 124 |
| Snow Lake, Man. | B1 | 70 |
| Snow Lake, Ar., U.S. | C4 | 81 |
| Snowmass, Co., U.S. | B4 | 83 |
| Snowmass Mountain, mtn., Co., U.S. | B3 | 83 |
| Snow Mountain, mtn., Me., U.S. | C2 | 96 |
| Snow Mills, Il., U.S. | A7 | 124 |
| Snow Road Station, Ont. | C8 | 73 |
| Snow Shoe, Pa., U.S. | D6 | 115 |
| Snowshoe Lake, l., Me., U.S. | B4 | 96 |
| Snowshoe Peak, Mt., U.S. | B1 | 103 |
| Snow Water Lake, l., Nv., U.S. | C7 | 105 |
| Snowville, N.H., U.S. | C4 | 106 |
| Snowville, Ut., U.S. | B3 | 121 |
| Snow Water Lake, l., Nv., U.S. | *C2 | 123 |
| Snowy, Austl. | H7 | 51 |
| Snowy Mountain, mtn., N.Y., U.S. | B6 | 109 |
| Snowy Mountains, mts., Austl. | G8 | 50 |
| Snowyside Peak, mtn., Id., U.S. | F4 | 89 |
| Snyatyn, Sov. Un. | A7 | 24 |
| Snyder, Ar., U.S. | D4 | 81 |
| Snyder, Co., U.S. | A7 | 83 |
| Snyder, Ne., U.S. | C9 | 104 |
| Snyder, Ok., U.S. | C3 | 113 |
| Snyder, Tx., U.S. | C2 | 120 |
| Snyder, co., Pa., U.S. | E7 | 115 |
| Snyder Knob, mtn., W.V., U.S. | C5 | 125 |
| Soacha, Col. | *C3 | 60 |
| Soalala, Madag. | g9 | 49 |
| Soap Lake, Wa., U.S. | B6 | 124 |
| Soar, stm., Eng., U.K. | C5 | 10 |
| Soatá, Col. | B3 | 60 |
| Soay, i., Scot., U.K. | C2 | 13 |
| Sobat, stm., Sud. | D3 | 47 |
| Soběslav, Czech. | D4 | 18 |
| Sobieski, Mn., U.S. | E4 | 100 |
| Sobieski, Wi., U.S. | D5 | 126 |
| Sobinka, Sov. Un. | D13 | 27 |
| Sobral, Braz. | D4 | 57 |
| Sobti, well, Mali | A4 | 45 |
| Socastee, S.C., U.S. | D9 | 117 |
| Sochaczew, Pol. | B6 | 26 |
| Sochaux, Fr. | E6 | 21 |
| Sochi, Sov. Un. | I14 | 27 |
| Social Circle, Ga., U.S. | C3 | 87 |
| Social Hill, Ar., U.S. | C3 | 81 |
| Society Hill, S.C., U.S. | C8 | 117 |
| Society Islands, is., Fr. Poly. | H12 | 6 |
| Socompa, Paso de, p., S.A. | A2 | 55 |
| Socorro, Braz. | m8 | 56 |
| Socorro, Col. | B3 | 60 |
| Socorro, N.M., U.S. | D2 | 108 |
| Socorro, co., N.M., U.S. | D2 | 108 |
| Socotra (Suquṭrā), i., Yemen | D5 | 38 |
| Soc Trang, Viet. | | |
| Socuéllamos, Spain | C3 | 22 |
| Soda Creek, B.C. | C6 | 69 |
| Sodankylä, Fin. | D12 | 14 |
| Soda Springs, Id., U.S. | G7 | 89 |
| Sodaville, Or., U.S. | C4 | 114 |
| Soddy-Daisy, Tn., U.S. | D8 | 119 |
| Söderhamn, Swe. | G7 | 14 |
| Söderköping, Swe. | H7 | 14 |
| Södertälje, Swe. | t35 | 14 |
| Sodo, Eth. | D4 | 47 |

| Name | Map Ref. | Page |
|---|---|---|
| Sodus, N.Y., U.S. | B3 | 109 |
| Sodus Point, N.Y., U.S. | B4 | 109 |
| Soest, W. Ger. | C4 | 18 |
| Sofádhes, Grc. | C4 | 25 |
| Sofala, dept., Moz. | A5 | 49 |
| Sofia (Sofiya), Bul. | D6 | 24 |
| Sofia, stm., Madag. | g9 | 49 |
| Sofiyevka, Sov. Un. | G9 | 27 |
| Sogamoso, Col. | B3 | 60 |
| Sögel, W. Ger. | B9 | 18 |
| Sognafjorden, Nor. | G1 | 14 |
| Söğüt, Tur. | C8 | 25 |
| Soham, N.M., U.S. | B4 | 108 |
| Soignies, Bel. | D4 | 16 |
| Sointula, B.C. | D4 | 69 |
| Soissons, Fr. | C5 | 16 |
| Sokal, Sov. Un. | F5 | 27 |
| Sökche, S. Kor. | C13 | 33 |
| Söke, Tur. | D6 | 25 |
| Sokehs Passage, strt., Micron. | Q17 | 52 |
| Sokhondo, Mount, mtn., Sov. Un. | E14 | 29 |
| Sokodé, Togo | E5 | 45 |
| Sokol, Sov. Un. | B13 | 27 |
| Sokółka, Pol. | B7 | 26 |
| Sokolo, Mali | D2 | 45 |
| Sokolov, Czech. | C7 | 19 |
| Sokołów [Podlaski], Pol. | B7 | 26 |
| Sokoto, Nig. | D6 | 45 |
| Sol, Pico do, mtn., Braz. | C4 | 56 |
| Sola, stm., Pol. | h10 | 26 |
| Solana, Fl., U.S. | *F5 | 86 |
| Solana Beach, Ca., U.S. | *F5 | 82 |
| Solander Island, i., N.Z. | Q11 | 51 |
| Solano, Phil. | n13 | 34 |
| Solano, N.M., U.S. | B5 | 108 |
| Solano, co., Ca., U.S. | C3 | 82 |
| Solāpur, India | E5 | 36 |
| Solbad Hall [in Tirol], Aus. | F26 | 8 |
| Soldatovo, Sov. Un. | F26 | 8 |
| Soldier, Ks., U.S. | C8 | 93 |
| Soldier, Ks., U.S. | B6 | 94 |
| Soldier Creek, S.D., U.S. | *D5 | 118 |
| Soldier Creek, stm., Ks., U.S. | C8 | 93 |
| Soldier Key, i., Fl., U.S. | s3 | 86 |
| Soldier Pond, Me., U.S. | A4 | 96 |
| Soldier Summit, Ut., U.S. | D5 | 121 |
| Soldotna, Ak., U.S. | g16 | 79 |
| Soledad, Col. | A3 | 60 |
| Soledad, Ca., U.S. | D3 | 82 |
| Soledad, Ven. | B5 | 60 |
| Soledad Diez Gutiérrez, Mex. | *C4 | 63 |
| Soleduck, stm., Wa., U.S. | B1 | 124 |
| Solen, N.D., U.S. | C5 | 111 |
| Solesmes, Fr. | B3 | 17 |
| Solihull, Eng., U.K. | B6 | 12 |
| Solikamsk, Sov. Un. | D8 | 29 |
| Sol-Iletsk, Sov. Un. | C5 | 28 |
| Soliman, Tun. | F3 | 23 |
| Solingen, W. Ger. | C6 | 18 |
| Sollas, Scot., U.K. | C1 | 13 |
| Sollefteå, Swe. | F7 | 14 |
| Sollentuna, Swe. | *H8 | 14 |
| Söller, Spain | p28 | 14 |
| Sollihögda, Nor. | p28 | 14 |
| Solna, Swe. | H7 | 14 |
| Solomon, Az., U.S. | E6 | 80 |
| Solomon, Ks., U.S. | D6 | 93 |
| Solomon, stm., Ks., U.S. | C6 | 93 |
| Solomon, North Fork, stm., Ks., U.S. | C4 | 93 |
| Solomon, South Fork, stm., Ks., U.S. | C4 | 93 |
| Solomon Islands, ctry., Oc. | G9 | 6 |
| Solomons, Md., U.S. | C4 | 97 |
| Solomon Sea, Oc. | k12 | 50 |
| Solon, China | B9 | 31 |
| Solon, Ia., U.S. | C6 | 92 |
| Solon, Me., U.S. | D3 | 96 |
| Solon, Oh., U.S. | A4 | 112 |
| Solon Mills, Il., U.S. | h8 | 90 |
| Solon Springs, Wi., U.S. | B2 | 126 |
| Solothurn, Switz. | E3 | 20 |
| Solothurn, state, Switz. | B3 | 20 |
| Solovyevsk, Sov. Un. | D15 | 29 |
| Solsberry, In., U.S. | F4 | 91 |
| Šolta, i., Yugo. | D2 | 24 |
| Soltau, W. Ger. | B4 | 18 |
| Solvay, N.Y., U.S. | B4 | 109 |
| Sölvesborg, Swe. | B8 | 15 |
| Solway, Mn., U.S. | C3 | 100 |
| Solway Firth, est., U.K. | C5 | 10 |
| Solwezi, Zam. | C5 | 49 |
| Soma, Tur. | D6 | 25 |
| Somalia, ctry., Afr. | D6 | 47 |
| Sombor, Yugo. | C4 | 24 |
| Sombra, Ont. | E2 | 73 |
| Sombrerete, Mex. | D4 | 63 |
| Sombrero Channel, strt., India | Q19 | 36 |
| Sombrio, Braz. | C4 | 56 |
| Somerdale, N.J., U.S. | D2 | 107 |
| Somers, Ct., U.S. | B6 | 84 |
| Somers, Ia., U.S. | B3 | 92 |
| Somers, Mt., U.S. | B2 | 103 |
| Somers, Wi., U.S. | F6 | 126 |
| Somers, Ber. | | |
| Somerset, Man. | E2 | 70 |
| Somerset, Co., U.S. | C3 | 83 |
| Somerset, Ky., U.S. | C5 | 94 |
| Somerset, Ma., U.S. | C5 | 98 |
| Somerset, Oh., U.S. | C3 | 112 |
| Somerset, Pa., U.S. | F3 | 115 |
| Somerset, Tx., U.S. | k7 | 120 |
| Somerset, Wi., U.S. | C1 | 126 |
| Somerset, co., Eng., U.K. | C5 | 12 |
| Somerset, co., Me., U.S. | C2 | 96 |
| Somerset, co., Md., U.S. | D6 | 97 |
| Somerset, co., N.J., U.S. | B3 | 107 |
| Somerset, co., Pa., U.S. | G3 | 115 |
| Somerset East, S. Afr. | D4 | 49 |
| Somerset Island, i., N.W. Ter. | B14 | 66 |
| Somerset Reservoir, res., Vt., U.S. | E3 | 122 |
| Somers Point, N.J., U.S. | E3 | 107 |
| Somersworth, N.H., U.S. | D5 | 106 |
| Somerton, Az., U.S. | E1 | 80 |
| Somerville, Al., U.S. | A3 | 78 |
| Somerville, Ma., U.S. | B5 | 98 |
| Somerville, N.J., U.S. | B3 | 107 |
| Somerville, Tn., U.S. | B2 | 119 |
| Somerville, Tx., U.S. | D4 | 120 |
| Somerville Lake, res., Tx., U.S. | D4 | 120 |
| Someş (Szamos), stm., Eur. | B6 | 24 |
| Someş, dept., Fr. | B2 | 17 |
| Somme, stm., Fr. | B4 | 16 |

| Name | Map Ref. | Page |
|---|---|---|
| Sommepy [-Tahure], Fr. | E4 | 17 |
| Sömmerda, E. Ger. | B6 | 19 |
| Sommesous, Fr. | F4 | 17 |
| Somonauk, Il., U.S. | B5 | 90 |
| Somosomo, Fiji | H16 | 52 |
| Somosomo Strait, strt., Fiji | H15 | 52 |
| Somoto, Nic. | E7 | 63 |
| Sompeta, India | H10 | 37 |
| Somuncurá, Meseta de, plat., Arg. | C3 | 54 |
| Son, India | D7 | 36 |
| Soná, Pan. | F7 | 62 |
| Sönchön, N. Kor. | G2 | 33 |
| Soncino, Italy | D5 | 20 |
| Sønder, stm., Den. | D3 | 15 |
| Sønderborg, Den. | D3 | 15 |
| Sønderho, Den. | C2 | 15 |
| Sønderjylland, co., Den. | D3 | 15 |
| Sønder Omme, Den. | C2 | 15 |
| Sondershausen, E. Ger. | B5 | 18 |
| Sondervig, Den. | B2 | 15 |
| Sondheimer, La., U.S. | B4 | 95 |
| Sondrio, Italy | A3 | 23 |
| Sonepur, India | D7 | 36 |
| Sonestown, Pa., U.S. | D8 | 115 |
| Song, Nig. | E7 | 45 |
| Song Cau, Viet. | F8 | 35 |
| Songea, Tan. | D6 | 48 |
| Songhua Jiang, stm., China | B10 | 31 |
| Songjiang, China | E9 | 31 |
| Sŏngjin see Kimchaek, N. Kor. | C10 | 31 |
| Songkan, China | J2 | 32 |
| Songkhla, Thai. | D2 | 34 |
| Songnim (Kyŏmipo), N. Kor. | G2 | 33 |
| Songololo, Zaire | C1 | 48 |
| Songtao, China | J3 | 32 |
| Sonid Youqi, China | C5 | 32 |
| Sonid Zuoqi, China | C5 | 32 |
| Son La, Viet. | B5 | 35 |
| Sonmiāni, Pak. | C4 | 36 |
| Sonmiāni Bay, b., Pak. | I13 | 39 |
| Sonneberg, E. Ger. | C5 | 18 |
| Sonningdale, Sask. | E2 | 75 |
| Sono, Rio do, stm., Braz. | C1 | 57 |
| Sonobe, Japan | n14 | 33 |
| Sonoita, Mex. | A2 | 63 |
| Sonoita, Az., U.S. | F5 | 80 |
| Sonoma, Ca., U.S. | C2 | 82 |
| Sonoma, co., Ca., U.S. | C2 | 82 |
| Sonoma Peak, mtn., Nv., U.S. | C4 | 105 |
| Sonoma Range, mts., Nv., U.S. | C4 | 105 |
| Sonora, Ca., U.S. | D3 | 82 |
| Sonora, Ky., U.S. | C4 | 94 |
| Sonora, Oh., U.S. | C4 | 112 |
| Sonora, Tx., U.S. | D2 | 120 |
| Sonora, state, Mex. | B3 | 63 |
| Sonqor, Iran | D3 | 39 |
| Sonsón, Col. | B3 | 60 |
| Sonsonate, El Sal. | E7 | 63 |
| Sontag, Ms., U.S. | D3 | 101 |
| Sonthofen, W. Ger. | A9 | 21 |
| Sonyea, N.Y., U.S. | C3 | 109 |
| Sooke, B.C. | E6 | 69 |
| Soo Locks, N.A. | B6 | 99 |
| Sopchoppy, Fl., U.S. | B2 | 86 |
| Soper, Ok., U.S. | C6 | 113 |
| Soperton, Ga., U.S. | D4 | 87 |
| Sophia, N.C., U.S. | B3 | 110 |
| Sophia, W.V., U.S. | D3 | 125 |
| Sopot, Pol. | A5 | 26 |
| Sopron, Hung. | B3 | 24 |
| Soquel, Ca., U.S. | *D3 | 82 |
| Sor, stm., Port. | C1 | 22 |
| Sora, Italy | D4 | 23 |
| Sòrak, Mount, mtn., S. Kor. | G4 | 33 |
| Sorata, Bol. | C2 | 55 |
| Sorbas, Spain | D4 | 22 |
| Sorel, Que. | C4 | 74 |
| Sorell, Cape, c., Austl. | o15 | 50 |
| Sorento, Il., U.S. | E4 | 90 |
| Soreq, stm., Isr. | h10 | 41 |
| Soresina, Italy | D15 | 29 |
| Soria, Spain | B4 | 22 |
| Soriano, Ur. | f7 | 54 |
| Soriano, dept., Ur. | f8 | 54 |
| Sorø, Den. | C5 | 15 |
| Sorocaba, Braz. | B7 | 56 |
| Sorochinsk, Sov. Un. | G7 | 27 |
| Soroki, Sov. Un. | F8 | 34 |
| Sorong, Indon. | A5 | 48 |
| Soroti, Ug. | B10 | 14 |
| Sørøya, i., Nor. | C1 | 22 |
| Sorrento, Italy | D5 | 23 |
| Sorrento, Fl., U.S. | D5 | 86 |
| Sorris Sorris, Nmb. | B1 | 49 |
| Sør Rondane Mountains, mts., Ant. | B15 | 7 |
| Sorsogon, Phil. | C6 | 34 |
| Sortavala, Sov. Un. | A8 | 27 |
| Sorum, S.D., U.S. | B3 | 118 |
| Sörumsand, Nor. | p29 | 14 |
| Sösan, S. Kor. | H3 | 33 |
| Sosnogorsk, Sov. Un. | C19 | 27 |
| Sosnowka, Sov. Un. | E13 | 27 |
| Sosnowiec, Pol. | C5 | 26 |
| Soso, Ms., U.S. | D4 | 101 |
| Sosva, Sov. Un. | C21 | 27 |
| Sottern, l., Swe. | t33 | 14 |
| Sotteville-lès-Rouen, Fr. | C4 | 16 |
| Souanké, Congo | A1 | 48 |
| Soubré, I.C. | E3 | 45 |
| Soucook, stm., N.H., U.S. | D4 | 106 |
| Soudan, Austl. | C6 | 50 |
| Souderton, Pa., U.S. | F11 | 115 |
| Soufli, Grc. | B6 | 25 |
| Soufrière, St. Luc. | J14 | 65 |
| Soufrière, mtn., St. Vin. | U26 | 65 |
| Souhegan, stm., N.H., U.S. | E3 | 106 |
| Soulac, Fr. | D3 | 16 |
| Soulanges, co., Que. | | |
| Sound Beach, N.Y., U.S. | *n16 | 109 |
| Sounding Creek, stm., Alta. | D5 | 68 |
| Sounding Lake, l., Alta. | D5 | 68 |
| Sound View, Ct., U.S. | D6 | 84 |
| Sources, Mount aux, mtn., Afr. | C4 | 49 |
| Soure, Braz. | C5 | 59 |
| Souris, Man. | E1 | 70 |
| Souris, P.E.I. | C7 | 71 |
| Souris, Mn., U.S. | A5 | 111 |
| Souris, Ind., U.S. | A7 | 76 |
| Souris, Ia., U.S. | D4 | 120 |
| Sourlake, Tx., U.S. | D5 | 120 |
| Sourland Mountain, hill, N.J., U.S. | C3 | 107 |
| Souss, Oued, val., Mor. | C3 | 44 |
| Sousa, Braz. | C3 | 57 |

| Name | Map Ref. | Page |
|---|---|---|

Sousse, Tun. B7 44
Soustons, Fr. F3 16
South, stm., Ont. B5 73
South, stm., Ga., U.S. h8 87
South, stm., Ia., U.S. C4 92
South, stm., N.C., U.S. C4 110
South Acworth, N.H., U.S. D2 106
South Addison, Me., U.S. D5 96
South Africa, ctry., Afr. C4 49
South Amboy, N.J., U.S. C4 107
South America, cont. E5 53
South Amherst, Ma., U.S. B2 98
South Amherst, Oh., U.S. A3 112
Southampton, N.B. D2 71
Southampton, N.S. D5 71
Southampton, Ont. C3 73
Southampton, Eng., U.K. E6 10
Southampton, Ma., U.S. B2 98
Southampton, N.Y., U.S. n16 109
Southampton, co., Va., U.S. D5 123
Southampton, Cape, c., N.W. Ter. D16 66
Southampton Island, i., N.W. Ter. D16 66
South Andaman, i., India F9 36
South Anna, stm., Va., U.S. C5 123
Southard, Ok., U.S. A3 113
South Ashburnham, Ma., U.S. A4 98
South Ashland, Ma., U.S. A2 98
South Aulatsivik Island, i., Newf. g9 72
South Australia, state, Austl. E5 50
Southaven, Ms., U.S. A3 101
South Bald Mountain, mtn., Co., U.S. A5 83
South Baldy, mtn., N.M., U.S. D2 108
Southbank, B.C. C5 69
South Barnstead, N.H., U.S. D4 106
South Barre, Ma., U.S. B3 98
South Barre, Vt., U.S. C3 122
South Barrule, hill, I. of Man F4 13
South Bay, Fl., U.S. F6 86
South Bay, b., Ont. B3 73
Southbeach, Or., U.S. C2 114
South Belmar, N.J., U.S. C4 107
South Beloit, Il., U.S. A4 90
South Bend, In., U.S. A5 91
South Bend, Ne., U.S. h12 104
South Bend, Tx., U.S. C3 120
South Bend, Wa., U.S. C2 124
South Bentinck Arm, b., B.C. C4 69
South Berwick, Me., U.S. E2 96
South Bethany, De., U.S. F5 85
South Bethlehem, N.Y., U.S. C7 109
South Bloomfield, Oh., U.S. C3 112
South Boardman, Mi., U.S. D5 99
South Bolton, Que. D5 74
Southborough, Ma., U.S. B4 98
South Boston, Va., U.S. D4 123
South Bound Brook, N.J., U.S. B3 107
South Bradenton, Fl., U.S. *E4 86
South Branch, Newf. E2 72
South Branch, Mi., U.S. D7 99
South Branch Lake, l., Me., U.S. C4 96
South Branch Mountain, mtn., W.V., U.S. B6 125
Southbridge, Ma., U.S. B3 98
South Bristol, Me., U.S. E3 96
South Britain, Ct., U.S. D3 84
South Broadway, Ma., U.S. C5 124
South Brookfield, N.S. E5 71
South Bruny, i., Austl. o15 50
South Burlington, Vt., U.S. C2 122
Southbury, Ct., U.S. D3 84
South Byfield, Ma., U.S. A6 98
South Byron, N.Y., U.S. B2 109
South Canaan, Pa., U.S. D11 115
South Cape, c., Nor. B13 32
South Carolina, state, U.S. D6 117
South Carver, Ma., U.S. C6 98
South Channel, strt., Marsh Is. S18 52
South Charleston, Oh., U.S. C2 112
South Charleston, W.V., U.S. C3 125
South Charlestown, N.H., U.S. D2 106
South Chatham, Ma., U.S. C7 98
South Chatham, N.H., U.S. B4 106
South Chicago Heights, Il., U.S. m9 90
South China, Me., U.S. D3 96
South China Sea, Asia H14 30
South Cle Elum, Wa., U.S. B5 124
South Coffeyville, Ok., U.S. a6 113
South Colby, Wa., U.S. e10 124
South Colton, N.Y., U.S. f10 109
South Congaree, S.C., U.S. D5 117
South Connellsville, Pa., U.S. G2 115
South Corning, N.Y., U.S. C3 109
South Cottonwood, Ut., U.S. *C4 121
South Dakota, state, U.S. C5 118
South Danville, N.H., U.S. E4 106
South Dayton, N.Y., U.S. C1 109
South Daytona, Fl., U.S. C5 86
South Decatur, Ga., U.S. *h8 87
South Deerfield, Ma., U.S. B2 98
South Deerfield, N.H., U.S. D4 106
South Deer Isle, Me., U.S. D4 96
South Dennis, Ma., U.S. C7 98
South Dennis, N.J., U.S. E3 107
South Dorset, Vt., U.S. E2 122
South Dos Palos, Ca., U.S. D3 82
South Downs, plat., Eng., U.K. E6 10
South Dum Dum, India F12 37
South Duxbury, Ma., U.S. B6 98
Southeast Cape, c., Ak., U.S. C6 79
Southeast Pass, strt., La., U.S. E7 95
Southeast Point, c., R.I., U.S. h7 116
South Effingham, N.H., U.S. C5 106
South Egremont, Ma., U.S. B1 98
South Elgin, Il., U.S. B5 90
South El Monte, Ca., U.S. *m12 82
Southend-on-Sea, Eng., U.K. E7 10
Southern, prov., Mwi. E6 48
Southern, prov., Zam. E4 48
Southern Alps, mts., N.Z. O13 51
Southern Bug, stm., Sov. Un. H8 27
Southern Cross, Austl. F2 50
Southern Indian Lake, l., Man. f8 70
Southern Pines, N.C., U.S. B3 110
Southern Uplands, plat., Scot., U.K. C5 10
Southern Ute Indian Reservation, Co., U.S. D2 83
South Esk, stm., Scot., U.K. d10 13
South Euclid, Oh., U.S. g9 112
Southey, Sask. G3 75
South Fabius, stm., Mo., U.S. A5 102
South Fallsburg, N.Y., U.S. D6 109
South Farmingdale, N.Y., U.S. *n15 109
Southfield, Ma., U.S. B1 98

Southfield, Mi., U.S. o15 99
South Flevoland, reg., Neth. B5 17
South Fork, Sask. H1 75
South Fork, stm., U.S. D4 83
South Fork, Pa., U.S. F4 115
South Fort George, B.C. C6 69
South Foster, R.I., U.S. C2 116
South Fox Island, i., Mi., U.S. C5 99
South Freeport, Me., U.S. g7 96
South Fulton, Tn., U.S. A3 119
South Gastonia, N.C., U.S. B1 110
South Gate, Ca., U.S. n12 82
Southgate, Fl., U.S. *E4 86
Southgate, Ky., U.S. h14 94
South Gate, Md., U.S. *B4 97
Southgate, Mi., U.S. p15 99
South Gifford, Mo., U.S. A5 102
South Glastonbury, Ct., U.S. C5 84
Southglenn, Co., U.S. *B6 83
South Glens Falls, N.Y., U.S. B7 109
South Grafton, Ma., U.S. B4 98
South Grand, stm., Mo., U.S. C3 102
South Greenfield, Mo., U.S. D4 102
South Gulf of Évvoia, b., Grc. g11 25
South Hackensack, N.J., U.S. *B4 107
South Hadley, Ma., U.S. B2 98
South Hadley Falls, Ma., U.S. B2 98
South Hamilton, Ma., U.S. A6 98
South Hampton, N.H., U.S. E5 106
South Hanover, Ma., U.S. h12 98
South Harpswell, Me., U.S. g7 96
South Harwich, Ma., U.S. C7 98
South Haven, In., U.S. A3 91
South Haven, Ks., U.S. E6 93
South Haven, Mi., U.S. F4 99
South Heart, N.D., U.S. C3 111
South Heart, stm., Alta. B2 68
South Hero, Vt., U.S. B2 122
South Hero Island, i., Vt., U.S. B2 122
South Hill, N.Y., U.S. *C4 109
South Hill, Va., U.S. D4 123
South Hingham, Ma., U.S. h12 98
South Holland, Il., U.S. k9 90
South Holland (Zuid-Holland), prov., Neth. B4 17
South Holston Lake, res., U.S. A9 119
South Hooksett, N.H., U.S. D4 106
South Hopkinton, R.I., U.S. F1 116
South Houston, Tx., U.S. r14 120
South Huntington, N.Y., U.S. *n15 109
South Hutchinson, Ks., U.S. f11 93
South Indian Lake, Man. A2 70
Southington, Ct., U.S. C4 84
South International Falls, Mn., U.S. B5 100
South Island, i., Micron. Q18 52
South Island, i., N.Z. O13 51
South Island, i., S.C., U.S. E9 117
South Jacksonville, Il., U.S. D3 90
South Jordan, Ut., U.S. C3 121
South Junction, Man. E4 70
South Kenosha, Wi., U.S. F6 126
South Kensington, Md., U.S. *B3 97
South Kent, Ct., U.S. C2 84
South Killingly, Ct., U.S. B8 84
South Komelik, Az., U.S. F4 80
South Laguna, Ca., U.S. *F5 82
South Lake Tahoe, Ca., U.S. C4 82
South Lancaster, Ma., U.S. B4 98
South Laramie, Wy., U.S. *E7 127
South Laurel, Md., U.S. B4 97
South Lebanon, Me., U.S. E2 96
South Lebanon, Oh., U.S. C1 112
South Lincoln, Vt., U.S. C3 122
South Londonderry, Vt., U.S. E3 122
South Loup, stm., Ne., U.S. C6 104
South Lunenburg, Vt., U.S. C5 122
South Lyme, Ct., U.S. D6 84
South Lyndeborough, N.H., U.S. E3 106
South Lyon, Mi., U.S. F7 99
South Magnetawan, Ont. B4 73
South Magnetic Pole, Ant. C26 7
South Manitou Island, i., Mi., U.S. C4 99
South Mansfield, La., U.S. B2 95
South Marsh Island, i., Md. D5 97
South Medford, Or., U.S. E4 114
South Merrimack, N.H., U.S. E3 106
South Miami, Fl., U.S. G6 86
South Miami Heights, Fl., U.S. s13 86
South Middleboro, Ma., U.S. C6 98
South Milford, In., U.S. A7 91
South Mills, N.C., U.S. A6 110
South Milwaukee, Wi., U.S. F6 126
Southminster, Eng., U.K. C8 12
South Modesto, Ca., U.S. *D3 82
South Molton, Eng., U.K. C4 12
Southmont, N.C., U.S. B2 110
South Montrose, Pa., U.S. C10 115
South Moose Lake, l., Man. C1 70
South Mountain, Pa., U.S. G7 115
South Mountain, mtn., U.S. B2 97
South Mountain, mtn., Id. G2 89
South Mountain, mtn., N.M. k8 108
South Mountains, mts., Az., U.S. m8 80
South Mountains, mts., N.C. B1 110
South Naknek, Ak., U.S. D8 79
South Negril Point, c., Jam. E4 64
South New Berlin, N.Y., U.S. C5 109
South Newbury, N.H., U.S. D2 106
South Newbury, Vt., U.S. C4 122
South Newfane, Vt., U.S. F3 122
South New River Canal, Fl., U.S. r3 86
South Northfield, Vt., U.S. C3 122
South Nyack, N.Y., U.S. *D7 109
South Ogden, Ut., U.S. B4 121
Southold, N.Y., U.S. m16 109
South Orange, N.J., U.S. B4 107
South Orkney Islands, is., B.A.T. C8 7
South Orrington, Me., U.S. D4 96
South Otselic, N.Y., U.S. C5 109
South Paris, Me., U.S. D2 96
South Park, val., Co., U.S. B5 83
South Pasadena, Ca., U.S. *m12 82
South Pass, Wy., U.S. D4 127
South Pass, strt., Marsh Is. S17 52
South Pass City, Wy., U.S. D4 127
South Patrick Shores, Fl., U.S. D6 86
South Peacham, Vt., U.S. C4 122
South Pekin, Il., U.S. C4 90
South Pittsburg, Tn., U.S. D8 119

South Plainfield, N.J., U.S. B4 107
South Platte, stm., U.S. B7 76
South Point, c., Austl. I6 51
South Point, c., Barb. K20 65
South Point, c., Mi., U.S. D7 99
South Point, c., Newf. C4 72
South Pole, Ant. A7 7
South Pomfret, Vt., U.S. D3 122
Southport (Gold Coast), Austl. E9 50
Southport, Eng., U.K. D5 10
Southport, Fl., U.S. u16 86
Southport, In., U.S. E5 91
Southport, N.Y., U.S. C4 109
Southport, N.C., U.S. D4 110
South Portland, Me., U.S. E2 96
South Portsmouth, Ky., U.S. B6 94
South Poultney, Vt., U.S. E2 122
South Prairie, Wa., U.S. B3 124
South Range, Mi., U.S. A2 99
South Range, Wi., U.S. B2 126
South Reading, Vt., U.S. E3 122
South Renovo, Pa., U.S. D6 115
South River, Ont. B5 73
South River, N.J., U.S. C4 107
South River, b., Md., U.S. C4 97
South Ronaldsay, i., Scot., U.K. A5 10
South Royalston, Ma., U.S. A3 98
South Royalton, Vt., U.S. D3 122
South Rustico, P.E.I. C6 71
South Ryegate, Vt., U.S. C4 122
South Salem, Oh., U.S. C2 112
South Salt Lake, Ut., U.S. *C4 121
South Sandwich Islands, is., S.A. D10 7
South San Francisco, Ca., U.S. h8 82
South San Gabriel, Ca., U.S. *m12 82
South San Jose Hills, Ca., U.S. *m13 82
South Saskatchewan, stm., Can. F11 66
South Seaville, N.J., U.S. E3 107
South Setauket, N.Y., U.S. *n15 109
South Shetland Islands, is., B.A.T. C7 7
South Shields, Eng., U.K. C6 10
South Shore, Mo., U.S. f12 102
South Shore, S.D., U.S. B9 118
Southside, Al., U.S. B3 78
Southside, N.C., U.S. B1 110
Southside, Tn., U.S. A4 119
Southside Place, Tx., U.S. r14 120
South Sioux City, Ne., U.S. B9 104
South Slocan, B.C. E9 69
South Solon, Oh., U.S. C2 112
South Sound, strt., N.B. D2 11
South Spicer Island, i., N.W. Ter. C17 66
South Sterling, Pa., U.S. D11 115
South Stony Brook, N.Y., U.S. n15 109
South St. Paul, Mn., U.S. n12 100
South Strafford, Vt., U.S. D4 122
South Streator, Il., U.S. B5 90
South Sumter, S.C., U.S. *D7 117
South Superior, Wy., U.S. E4 127
South Sutton, N.H., U.S. D3 106
South Swansea, Ma., U.S. C5 98
South Tamworth, N.H., U.S. C4 106
South Taranaki Bight, N.Z. M15 51
South Toms River, N.J., U.S. D4 107
South Torrington, Wy., U.S. D8 127
South Tucson, Az., U.S. E5 80
South Tunnel, Tn., U.S. A5 119
South Twin Lake, l., Newf. D4 72
South Twin Mountain, mtn., N.H., U.S. B3 106
South Tyne, stm., Eng., U.K. G6 13
South Uist, i., Scot., U.K. B3 10
South Valley Stream, N.Y., U.S. *n15 109
South Van Buren, Mo., U.S. E6 102
South Venice, Fl., U.S. E4 86
South Ventana Cone, vol., Ca., U.S. D3 82
South Vienna, Oh., U.S. C2 112
South Wabasca Lake, l., Alta. B4 68
South Wadesboro, N.C., U.S. C2 110
South Wallingford, Vt., U.S. E3 122
South Walpole, Ma., U.S. h10 98
South Waterford, Me., U.S. D2 96
South Waverly, Pa., U.S. C8 115
South Wayne, Wi., U.S. F4 126
South Weare, N.H., U.S. D3 106
South Webster, Oh., U.S. D3 112
South Wellfleet, Ma., U.S. C8 98
South Wellington, B.C. f12 69
Southwest, Pa., U.S. F3 115
South West Africa see Namibia, dep., Afr. B2 49
South West Bay, b., Bah. n16 64
South Westbury, N.Y., U.S. n15 109
South West Cape, c., Austl. o15 50
Southwest Cape, c., N.Z. Q11 51
Southwest Channel, strt., Fl., U.S. E4 86
South West City, Mo., U.S. E3 102
Southwest Harbor, Me., U.S. D4 96
Southwest Head, c., N.B. E3 71
Southwest Miramichi, stm., N.B. C3 71
Southwest Mountains, mts., Va., U.S. B4 123
Southwest Pass, strt., La., U.S. E4 95
Southwest Pass, strt., La., U.S. F6 95
Southwest Passage, strt., Marsh Is. S18 52
Southwest Point, c., R.I., U.S. h7 116
South Weymouth Naval Air Station, Ma., U.S. h12 98
South Whitley, In., U.S. B6 91
South Whittier, Ca., U.S. *n13 82
Southwick, Id., U.S. C2 89
Southwick, Ma., U.S. B2 98
South Williamson, Ky., U.S. C7 94
South Williamsport, Pa., U.S. D7 115
South Willington, Ct., U.S. B6 84
South Wilmington, Il., U.S. B5 90
South Windham, Ct., U.S. C7 84
South Windham, Me., U.S. E2 96
South Windsor, Ct., U.S. B5 84
South Wolfeboro, N.H., U.S. C4 106
South Wolf Island, i., Newf. B4 72
Southwood, Ct., U.S. C5 84
Southwood Acres, Ct., U.S. A5 84
South Woodbury, Vt., U.S. C4 122
South Woodstock, Ct., U.S. B8 84
South Woodstock, Vt., U.S. D3 122
South Yarmouth, Ma., U.S. C7 98

South Yorkshire, co., Eng., U.K. A6 12
South Yuba City, Ca., U.S. *C3 82
South Zanesville, Oh., U.S. C3 112
Soverato, Italy E6 23
Sovereign, Sask. F2 75
Sovetsk (Tilsit), Sov. Un. D3 27
Sovetskaya Gavan, Sov. Un. H16 29
Sovetskaya Gavan, Sov. Un. B10 33
Soviet Union, ctry., Asia D11 29
Soweto, S. Afr. C4 49
Soyo, Ang. C1 48
Sōya, Cape, c., Japan D10 33
Sozh, stm., Sov. Un. E8 27
Sozopol, Bul. D8 24
Spa, Bel. B6 16
Spada, Ar., U.S. B2 81
Spadra, Ar., U.S. B2 81
Spain, ctry., Eur. B4 22
Spalding, Austl. F2 51
Spalding, Sask. E3 75
Spalding, Eng., U.K. D6 10
Spalding, Id., U.S. C2 89
Spalding, Ne., U.S. C7 104
Spalding, co., Ga., U.S. C2 87
Spanaway, Wa., U.S. B3 124
Spangle, Wa., U.S. B8 124
Spangler, Pa., U.S. E4 115
Spaniard's Bay, Newf. E5 72
Spanish, Ont. A2 73
Spanish, stm., Ont. A2 73
Spanishburg, W.V., U.S. D3 125
Spanish Fork, Ut., U.S. C4 121
Spanish Fort, Al., U.S. E2 78
Spanish North Africa, dep., Afr. *B4 44
Spanish Peak, mtn., Or., U.S. C7 114
Spanish Ranch, Ca., U.S. C3 82
Spanish Town, Jam. F5 64
Sparkman, Ar., U.S. D3 81
Sparks, Ga., U.S. E3 87
Sparks, Ne., U.S. B5 104
Sparks, Nv., U.S. D2 105
Sparks, Ok., U.S. B5 113
Sparland, Il., U.S. B4 90
Sparr, Fl., U.S. C4 86
Sparreholm, Swe. t34 14
Sparrows Point, Md., U.S. B5 97
Sparta, see Spárti, Grc. D4 40
Sparta, Il., U.S. E4 90
Sparta, Ga., U.S. C4 87
Sparta, Ky., U.S. B5 94
Sparta, Mi., U.S. E5 99
Sparta, N.J., U.S. A3 107
Sparta, N.C., U.S. A1 110
Sparta, Oh., U.S. B3 112
Sparta, Tn., U.S. D8 119
Sparta, Wa., U.S. B8 124
Sparta, Wi., U.S. E3 126
Sparta Mountains, mts., N.J., U.S. B3 107
Spartanburg, In., U.S. D8 91
Spartanburg, S.C., U.S. B4 117
Spartanburg, co., S.C., U.S. B3 117
Spartansburg, Pa., U.S. C2 115
Spárti (Sparta), Grc. D4 40
Spartivento, Cape, c., Italy F5 23
Spartivento, Cape, c., Italy E2 23
Sparwood, B.C. E10 69
Spas-Demensk, Sov. Un. D10 27
Spassk-Dalniy, Sov. Un. E16 29
Spassk-Ryazanskiy, Sov. Un. D13 27
Spáta, Grc. h11 25
Spátha, Ákra, c., Grc. E4 40
Spatha, Grc. D4 40
Spearfish, S.D., U.S. C2 118
Spearhill, Man. D2 70
Spearman, Tx., U.S. A2 120
Spearsville, La., U.S. B3 95
Spearville, Ks., U.S. E4 93
Spectacle Pond, l., Me., U.S. B4 96
Spedden, Alta. B5 68
Spednic Lake, l., N.A. C5 96
Speed, In., U.S. H6 91
Speed, Ks., U.S. C4 93
Speed, N.C., U.S. B5 110
Speedway, In., U.S. E5 91
Speedwell, Tn., U.S. C10 119
Speedwell, Va., U.S. D1 123
Speers, Sask. E2 75
Speigner, Al., U.S. C3 78
Speight, Ky., U.S. C7 94
Spelter, W.V., U.S. k10 125
Spenard (part of Anchorage), Ak., U.S. g17 79
Spencer, Id., U.S. E6 89
Spencer, In., U.S. F4 91
Spencer, Ia., U.S. A2 92
Spencer, Ma., U.S. B4 98
Spencer, Ne., U.S. B7 104
Spencer, N.Y., U.S. C4 109
Spencer, N.C., U.S. B2 110
Spencer, Oh., U.S. A3 112
Spencer, Ok., U.S. B4 113
Spencer, S.D., U.S. D8 118
Spencer, Tn., U.S. D8 119
Spencer, W.V., U.S. C3 125
Spencer, co., In., U.S. H4 91
Spencer, co., Ky., U.S. B4 94
Spencer, Cape, c., Ak., U.S. k21 79
Spencer Gulf, b., Austl. F6 50
Spencer Lake, l., Me., U.S. C2 96
Spencerport, N.Y., U.S. B3 109
Spencers Bridge, B.C. D7 69
Spencerville, Ont. C9 73
Spencerville, Md., U.S. B4 97
Spencerville, Oh., U.S. B1 112
Spennymoor, Eng., U.K. F7 13
Sperling, Man. E3 70
Sperry, Ia., U.S. D6 92
Sperry, Ok., U.S. A6 113
Sperryville, Va., U.S. B4 123
Spesutie Island, i., Md., U.S. B5 97
Spey, stm., Scot., U.K. D5 10
Speyer, W. Ger. D4 18
Sphinx, hist., Eg. C6 42
Spiceland, In., U.S. E7 91
Spicer, Mn., U.S. E4 100
Spider Lake, l., Wi., U.S. B2 126
Spiekeroog, W. Ger. A7 17

Spiekeroog, i., W. Ger. B3 18
Spiez, Switz. C4 21
Spigno Monferrato, Italy E4 20
Spijkenisse, Neth. *C4 17
Spillville, Ia., U.S. A6 92
Spinazzola, Italy D6 23
Spindale, N.C., U.S. B1 110
Spink, S.D., U.S. E9 118
Spink, co., S.D., U.S. C7 118
Spink Colony, S.D., U.S. C7 118
Spirit Lake, Ia., U.S. A2 92
Spirit Lake, Id., U.S. A2 89
Spirit Lake, l., Wa., U.S. C3 124
Spirit River, Alta. A1 68
Spirit River Flowage, res., Wi., U.S. C4 126
Spiritwood, Sask. D2 75
Spiritwood, N.D., U.S. C7 111
Spiro, Ok., U.S. B7 113
Spišská Nová Ves, Czech. D6 26
Spit Island, i., Mid. Is. K3 52
Spitsbergen, i., Nor. B13 128
Spittal, Aus. E6 18
Spivey, Ks., U.S. E5 93
Split, Yugo. D3 23
Split, Cape, c., N.S. D5 71
Split Lake, l., Man. A4 70
Split Rock Creek, stm., U.S. G2 100
Splügen, Switz. C5 20
Splügen Pass, Eur. C5 20
Spofford, N.H., U.S. E2 106
Spofford, Tx., U.S. E3 120
Spofford Lake, l., N.H., U.S. E2 106
Spokane, La., U.S. C4 95
Spokane, Wa., U.S. B8 124
Spokane, co., Wa., U.S. B8 124
Spokane, stm., Wa., U.S. B8 124
Spokane, Mount, mtn., Wa., U.S. B8 124
Spokane Indian Reservation, Wa., U.S. B8 124
Spöl, stm., Eur. C4 23
Spoleto, Italy C4 23
Spondin, Alta. D5 68
Spoon, stm., Il., U.S. C3 90
Spooner, Wi., U.S. C2 126
Spooner Lake, l., Wi., U.S. C2 126
Spotswood, N.J., U.S. C4 107
Spotsylvania, Va., U.S. B5 123
Spotsylvania, co., Va., U.S. B5 123
Spotted Island, i., Newf. B4 72
Spottsville, Ky., U.S. C2 94
Sprague, Man. E4 70
Sprague, Al., U.S. C3 78
Sprague, Ne., U.S. D9 104
Sprague, Wa., U.S. B8 124
Sprague, stm., Or., U.S. E5 114
Sprague Lake, l., Wa., U.S. B7 124
Sprague River, Or., U.S. E5 114
Spragueville, Ia., U.S. B7 92
Spragueville, N.Y., U.S. A5 109
Spragueville, R.I., U.S. B3 116
Sprakensehl, W. Ger. F4 15
Spratly Island, i., Asia A4 34
Spray, Or., U.S. C7 114
Spread Eagle, Wi., U.S. C6 126
Spreckelsville, Hi., U.S. *C5 88
Spree, stm., Eur. C7 18
Spremberg, E. Ger. C7 18
Sprigg, W.V., U.S. D2 125
Spring, Tx., U.S. q14 120
Spring, stm., Ar., U.S. A4 81
Spring, South Fork, stm., U.S. A4 81
Spring Arbor, Mi., U.S. F6 99
Spring Bay, b., Il., U.S. C4 90
Springboro, Oh., U.S. C1 112
Springboro, Pa., U.S. C1 115
Springbrook, Ont. C7 73
Springbrook, Wi., U.S. C2 126
Spring Brook, N.D., U.S. A2 111
Spring Brook, stm., Pa., U.S. n18 115
Spring City, Pa., U.S. F10 115
Spring City, Tn., U.S. D9 119
Spring City, Ut., U.S. D4 121
Spring Coulee, Alta. E4 68
Spring Creek, Tn., U.S. B3 119
Spring Creek, stm., Ne., U.S. B4 104
Spring Creek, stm., Ga., U.S. F2 87
Spring Creek, stm., Nv., U.S. C4 105
Spring Creek, stm., N.D., U.S. B3 111
Spring Creek Colony, S.D. (—)

Springfield, Lake, res., Il., U.S. D4 90
Springfield Township, Pa., U.S. *F11 115
Springfontein, S. Afr. D4 49
Spring Garden, Al., U.S. B4 78
Spring Garden, Pa., U.S. *G8 115
Spring Glen, Ut., U.S. D5 121
Spring Green, Wi., U.S. E3 126
Spring Grove, Il., U.S. h8 90
Spring Grove, In., U.S. E8 91
Spring Grove, Mn., U.S. G7 100
Spring Grove, Pa., U.S. G8 115
Springhill, N.S. D5 71
Spring Hill, Ar., U.S. D2 81
Spring Hill, Ct., U.S. B7 84
Spring Hill, Fl., U.S. D4 86
Spring Hill, In., U.S. k10 91
Spring Hill, Ia., U.S. f8 92
Spring Hill, Ks., U.S. D9 93
Spring Hill, La., U.S. A2 95
Spring Hill, Tn., U.S. B5 119
Springhill Junction, N.S. D5 71
Spring Hope, N.C., U.S. B4 110
Springhouse, B.C. D6 69
Spring Lake, i., S.C., U.S. G6 117
Spring Lake, Fl., U.S. D4 86
Spring Lake, Mi., U.S. E4 99
Spring Lake, N.J., U.S. C4 107
Spring Lake, N.C., U.S. B4 110
Spring Lake, Ut., U.S. C4 121
Spring Lake, l., Me., U.S. C2 96
Spring Lake, res., U.S. B3 90
Spring Lake Heights, N.J., U.S. C4 107
Spring Lake Park, Mn., U.S. *E5 100
Spring Lick, Ky., U.S. C3 94
Spring Mills, Pa., U.S. E6 115
Spring Mountains, mts., Nv., U.S. G6 105
Spring Place, Ga., U.S. B2 87
Springport, In., U.S. D7 91
Springport, Mi., U.S. F6 99
Springs, S. Afr. C4 49
Springside, Sask. F4 75
Springvale, Austl. A3 51
Springvale, Ga., U.S. E2 87
Springvale, Me., U.S. E2 96
Spring Valley, Sask. H3 75
Spring Valley, Ca., U.S. o16 82
Spring Valley, Il., U.S. B4 90
Spring Valley, Mn., U.S. G6 100
Spring Valley, N.Y., U.S. g12 109
Spring Valley, Oh., U.S. C1 112
Spring Valley, Wi., U.S. D1 126
Springview, Ne., U.S. B6 104
Springville, Al., U.S. B3 78
Springville, Ia., U.S. B6 92
Springville, N.Y., U.S. C2 109
Springville, Tn., U.S. A3 119
Springville, Ut., U.S. C4 121
Springwater, Sask. F1 75
Springwater, N.Y., U.S. C3 109
Spruce, Mi., U.S. D7 99
Spruce Brook, Newf. D2 72
Spruce Creek, Pa., U.S. E5 115
Sprucedale, Ont. B5 73
Spruce Fork, stm., W.V., U.S. m12 125
Spruce Grove, Alta. C4 68
Spruce Knob, mtn., W.V., U.S. C6 125
Spruce Knob-Seneca Rocks National Recreation Area, W.V., U.S. C5 125
Spruce Lake, Sask. D1 75
Spruce Mountain, mtn., Az., U.S. C3 80
Spruce Mountain, mtn., Nv., U.S. C7 105
Spruce Pine, Al., U.S. A2 78
Spruce Pine, N.C., U.S. f10 110
Spruce Run Reservoir, res., N.J., U.S. B3 107
Spruga, Switz. D6 21
Spur, Tx., U.S. C2 120
Spurfield, Alta. B3 68
Spurgeon, In., U.S. H3 91
Spurn Head, c., Eng., U.K. A8 12
Spurr, Mount, mtn., Ak., U.S. g15 79
Spy Hill, Sask. G5 75
Squamish, B.C. E6 69
Squam Lake, l., N.H., U.S. C4 106
Squam Mountains, mts., N.H., U.S. C3 106
Squantum, Ma., U.S. B5 98
Squa Pan Lake, l., Me., U.S. B4 96
Squapan Lake, l., Me., U.S. B4 96
Square Islands, Newf. B4 72
Square Lake, l., Me., U.S. B4 96
Squatec, Que. B9 74
Squaw Cap Mountain, mtn., N.B. B3 71
Squaw Harbor, Ak., U.S. D7 79
Squaw Hill, mtn., Wy., U.S. E7 127
Squaw Lake, Mn., U.S. C4 100
Squaw Peak, mtn., Mt., U.S. C2 103
Squaw Rapids, Sask. D4 75
Squibnocket Point, c., Ma. D6 98
Squillace, Gulf of, b., Italy E6 23
Squire, W.V., U.S. D3 125
Squires, Mo., U.S. E5 102
Squirrel, Id., U.S. E7 89
Srbobran, Yugo. C3 24
Srednekolymsk, Sov. Un. C18 29
Sredniy Vasyugan, Sov. Un. D24 37
Śrem, Pol. B4 24
Sremska Mitrovica, Yugo. C3 24
Sremski Karlovci, Yugo. C3 24
Srepok, stm., Asia C3 34
Sretensk, Sov. Un. G13 29
Sri Lanka, ctry., Asia G7 36
Srīnagar, India B5 36
Środa Śląska, Pol. B5 24
Środa [Wielkopolska], Pol. B4 24
Staatsburg, N.Y., U.S. D7 109
Stab, Ky., U.S. C4 94
Stack Reservoir, res., R.I. C2 116
Stack's Mountains, mts., Ire. *E2 11
Stacy, Ar., U.S. B5 81
Stacy, N.C., U.S. C6 110
Stacyville, Ia., U.S. A5 92
Stacyville, Me., U.S. B4 96
Stade, W. Ger. B9 15
Stadskanaal, Neth. B6 17
Stadthagen, W. Ger. A4 19
Stadtkyll, W. Ger. D6 17
Stadtlohn, W. Ger. B1 19
Stadtroda, E. Ger. C6 18

| Name | Map Ref. | Page |
|---|---|---|
| Stäfa, Switz. | B6 | 21 |
| Staffa, i., Scot., U.K. | D2 | 13 |
| Stafford, Eng., U.K. | D5 | 10 |
| Stafford, Ct., U.S. | B6 | 84 |
| Stafford, Ks., U.S. | E5 | 93 |
| Stafford, N.Y., U.S. | C2 | 109 |
| Stafford, Oh., U.S. | C4 | 112 |
| Stafford, Ok., U.S. | B2 | 113 |
| Stafford, Va., U.S. | B5 | 123 |
| Stafford, co., Ks., U.S. | D5 | 93 |
| Stafford, co., Va., U.S. | B5 | 123 |
| Stafford Pond, l., R.I., U.S. | D6 | 116 |
| Staffordshire, co., Eng., U.K. | B5 | 12 |
| Stafford Springs, Ct., U.S. | B6 | 84 |
| Staffordsville, Ky., U.S. | C7 | 94 |
| Staffordville, Ct., U.S. | B6 | 84 |
| Staffordville, N.J., U.S. | D4 | 107 |
| Staines, Eng., U.K. | m11 | 10 |
| Stains, Fr. | g10 | 16 |
| Stairs Mountain, mtn., N.H., U.S. | B4 | 106 |
| Stakhanov, Sov. Un. | G12 | 27 |
| Stålboga, Swe. | t34 | 14 |
| Stalden, Switz. | D4 | 21 |
| Staley, N.C., U.S. | B3 | 110 |
| Stalin (Kuçovë), Alb. | B2 | 25 |
| Stalingrad, see Volgograd, Sov. Un. | E7 | 29 |
| Stalinogród see Katowice, Pol. | C5 | 26 |
| Stall Lake, Man. | F13 | 66 |
| Stallworthy, Cape, c., N.W. Ter. | k33 | 66 |
| Stalowa Wola, Pol. | C7 | 26 |
| Stalwart, Sask. | F3 | 75 |
| Stalwart, Mi., U.S. | B6 | 99 |
| Stambaugh, Mi., U.S. | B2 | 99 |
| Stamford, Eng., U.K. | B7 | 12 |
| Stamford, Ct., U.S. | E1 | 84 |
| Stamford, Ne., U.S. | D6 | 104 |
| Stamford, N.Y., U.S. | C6 | 109 |
| Stamford, Tx., U.S. | C3 | 120 |
| Stamford, Vt., U.S. | F2 | 122 |
| Stamford, Lake, res., Tx., U.S. | C3 | 120 |
| Stamping Ground, Ky., U.S. | B5 | 94 |
| Stampriet, Nmb. | B2 | 49 |
| Stamps, Ar., U.S. | D2 | 81 |
| Stanaford, W.V., U.S. | D3 | 125 |
| Stanardsville, Va., U.S. | B4 | 123 |
| Stanberry, Mo., U.S. | A3 | 102 |
| Stanchfield, Mn., U.S. | E5 | 100 |
| Standard, Alta. | D4 | 68 |
| Standard, Il., U.S. | B4 | 90 |
| Standard, La., U.S. | C3 | 95 |
| Standerton, S. Afr. | C4 | 49 |
| Standing Rock, Al., U.S. | B4 | 78 |
| Standing Rock, N.M., U.S. | B1 | 108 |
| Standing Rock Indian Reservation, U.S. | B4 | 118 |
| Standish, Me., U.S. | E2 | 96 |
| Standish, Mi., U.S. | E7 | 99 |
| Standish, N.Y., U.S. | f11 | 109 |
| Stanfield, Az., U.S. | E3 | 80 |
| Stanfield, Or., U.S. | B7 | 114 |
| Stanford, Ca., U.S. | *k8 | 82 |
| Stanford, Il., U.S. | C4 | 90 |
| Stanford, In., U.S. | F4 | 91 |
| Stanford, Ky., U.S. | C5 | 94 |
| Stanford, Mt., U.S. | C6 | 103 |
| Stangelville, Wi., U.S. | D6 | 126 |
| Stanger, S. Afr. | C5 | 49 |
| Stanhope, Que. | D6 | 74 |
| Stanhope, Eng., U.K. | F6 | 13 |
| Stanhope, Ia., U.S. | B4 | 92 |
| Stanhope, N.J., U.S. | B3 | 107 |
| Staniard Creek, Bah. | B5 | 64 |
| Stanislaus, co., Ca., U.S. | D3 | 82 |
| Stanisławów, Pol. | k15 | 26 |
| Stanke Dimitrov (Dupnitsa), Bul. | D6 | 24 |
| Stanley, N.B. | C3 | 71 |
| Stanley, Falk. Is. | I5 | 53 |
| Stanley, Id., U.S. | E4 | 89 |
| Stanley, Ks., U.S. | D9 | 93 |
| Stanley, Ky., U.S. | C2 | 94 |
| Stanley, La., U.S. | C2 | 95 |
| Stanley, N.M., U.S. | B4 | 108 |
| Stanley, N.C., U.S. | B1 | 110 |
| Stanley, N.D., U.S. | A3 | 111 |
| Stanley, Va., U.S. | B4 | 123 |
| Stanley, Wi., U.S. | D3 | 126 |
| Stanley, co., S.D., U.S. | C5 | 118 |
| Stanley Falls see Boyoma Falls, wtfl., Zaire | A4 | 48 |
| Stanleytown, Va., U.S. | D3 | 123 |
| Stanleyville, N.C., U.S. | A2 | 110 |
| Stanleyville see Kisangani, Zaire | A4 | 48 |
| Stanly, co., N.C., U.S. | B2 | 110 |
| Stanmore, Alta. | D5 | 68 |
| Stann Creek, Belize | D7 | 63 |
| Stans, Switz. | C4 | 20 |
| Stansbury Mountains, mts., Ut., U.S. | C3 | 121 |
| Stansbury Park, Ut., U.S. | *C3 | 121 |
| Stanstead, Que. | D5 | 74 |
| Stanstead, co., Que. | D5 | 74 |
| Stanthorpe, Austl. | E9 | 50 |
| Stanton, Al., U.S. | C3 | 78 |
| Stanton, Ca., U.S. | *n13 | 82 |
| Stanton, Ia., U.S. | D2 | 92 |
| Stanton, Ky., U.S. | C6 | 94 |
| Stanton, Mi., U.S. | E5 | 99 |
| Stanton, Mo., U.S. | C6 | 102 |
| Stanton, Ne., U.S. | C8 | 104 |
| Stanton, N.J., U.S. | B3 | 107 |
| Stanton, N.D., U.S. | B4 | 111 |
| Stanton, Tn., U.S. | B2 | 119 |
| Stanton, Tx., U.S. | C2 | 120 |
| Stanton, co., Ks., U.S. | E2 | 93 |
| Stanton, co., Ne., U.S. | C8 | 104 |
| Stantonsburg, N.C., U.S. | B5 | 110 |
| Stantonville, Tn., U.S. | B3 | 119 |
| Stanwood, Ia., U.S. | C6 | 92 |
| Stanwood, Mi., U.S. | E5 | 99 |
| Stanwood, Wa., U.S. | A3 | 124 |
| Staplehurst, Ne., U.S. | D8 | 104 |
| Staples, Mn., U.S. | D4 | 100 |
| Staples, Tx., U.S. | H8 | 120 |
| Stapleton, Al., U.S. | E2 | 78 |
| Stapleton, Ga., U.S. | C4 | 87 |
| Stapleton, Ne., U.S. | C5 | 104 |
| Star, Id., U.S. | F2 | 89 |
| Star, Ms., U.S. | C3 | 101 |
| Star, N.C., U.S. | B3 | 110 |
| Star, Tx., U.S. | D3 | 120 |
| Starachowice, Pol. | C6 | 26 |
| Staraya Russa, Sov. Un. | C8 | 27 |
| Stara Zagora, Bul. | D7 | 24 |
| Starbuck, Man. | E3 | 70 |
| Starbuck, Mn., U.S. | E3 | 100 |
| Starbuck, Wa., U.S. | C7 | 124 |
| Starbuck Island, i., Kir. | G12 | 6 |
| Star City, Sask. | E3 | 75 |
| Star City, Ar., U.S. | D4 | 81 |
| Star City, In., U.S. | C4 | 91 |
| Star City, W.V., U.S. | B5 | 125 |
| Starford, Pa., U.S. | E4 | 115 |
| Stargard [Szczeciński], Pol. | B3 | 26 |
| Stargo, Az., U.S. | D6 | 80 |
| Staritsa, Sov. Un. | C10 | 27 |
| Stark, Ks., U.S. | E8 | 93 |
| Stark, N.H., U.S. | A4 | 106 |
| Stark, co., Il., U.S. | B4 | 90 |
| Stark, co., N.D., U.S. | C3 | 111 |
| Stark, co., Oh., U.S. | B4 | 112 |
| Starke, Fl., U.S. | C4 | 86 |
| Starke, co., In., U.S. | B4 | 91 |
| Starkey, Va., U.S. | C3 | 123 |
| Starks, La., U.S. | D2 | 95 |
| Starksboro, Vt., U.S. | C2 | 122 |
| Starkville, Co., U.S. | D6 | 83 |
| Starkville, Ms., U.S. | B5 | 101 |
| Starkville, N.Y., U.S. | C6 | 109 |
| Starkweather, N.D., U.S. | A7 | 111 |
| Starlight, Pa., U.S. | C11 | 115 |
| Starnberg, W. Ger. | B7 | 20 |
| Starnberger See, l., W. Ger. | E5 | 18 |
| Starobelsk, Sov. Un. | G12 | 27 |
| Starodub, Sov. Un. | E9 | 27 |
| Starokonstantinov, Sov. Un. | H12 | 27 |
| Starominskaya, Sov. Un. | H12 | 27 |
| Star Peak, mtn., Nv., U.S. | C3 | 105 |
| Star Prairie, Wi., U.S. | C1 | 126 |
| Starr, S.C., U.S. | C2 | 117 |
| Starr, co., Tx., U.S. | F3 | 120 |
| Startex, S.C., U.S. | B3 | 117 |
| Start Point, c., Eng., U.K. | E5 | 10 |
| Starý Plzenec, Czech. | D8 | 19 |
| Staryy Oskol, Sov. Un. | F11 | 27 |
| Stassfurt, E. Ger. | C5 | 18 |
| Staszów, Pol. | C6 | 26 |
| State Center, Ia., U.S. | B4 | 92 |
| State College, Pa., U.S. | E6 | 115 |
| State Line, In., U.S. | D2 | 91 |
| State Line, Ma., U.S. | B1 | 98 |
| State Line, Ms., U.S. | D5 | 101 |
| Stateline, Nv., U.S. | E2 | 105 |
| State Road, N.C., U.S. | A2 | 110 |
| Statesboro, Ga., U.S. | D5 | 87 |
| Statesville, N.C., U.S. | B2 | 110 |
| Statham, Ga., U.S. | C3 | 87 |
| Stathelle, Nor. | p27 | 14 |
| Staten Island, i., N.Y., U.S. | k12 | 109 |
| Statue of Liberty National Monument, N.J., U.S. | k8 | 107 |
| Staufen, W. Ger. | B3 | 20 |
| Staunton, Il., U.S. | D4 | 90 |
| Staunton, In., U.S. | F3 | 91 |
| Staunton, Va., U.S. | B3 | 123 |
| Stave Lake, l., B.C. | f13 | 69 |
| Staveley, Eng., U.K. | A6 | 12 |
| Stavelot, Bel. | D5 | 17 |
| Stavely, Alta. | D4 | 68 |
| Stavenisse, Neth. | C4 | 17 |
| Staveren, Neth. | B5 | 17 |
| Stavropol, Sov. Un. | E7 | 29 |
| Stawell, Austl. | H4 | 51 |
| Stayner, Ont. | C4 | 73 |
| Stayton, Or., U.S. | C4 | 114 |
| Stead, N.M., U.S. | A6 | 108 |
| Steamboat Canyon, Az., U.S. | B6 | 80 |
| Steamboat Mountain, mtn., Mt., U.S. | C4 | 103 |
| Steamboat Mountain, mtn., Wy., U.S. | E4 | 127 |
| Steamboat Rock, Ia., U.S. | B4 | 92 |
| Steamboat Springs, Co., U.S. | A4 | 83 |
| Stearns, Ky., U.S. | D5 | 94 |
| Stearns, co., Mn., U.S. | E4 | 100 |
| Stearns Brook, stm., N.H., U.S. | A4 | 106 |
| Stebbins, Ak., U.S. | C7 | 79 |
| Steblev, Sov. Un. | G8 | 27 |
| Štěchovice, Czech. | o17 | 26 |
| Štěchovice, Czech. | o17 | 26 |
| Stecker, Ok., U.S. | C3 | 113 |
| Stecoah, N.C., U.S. | f9 | 110 |
| Steele, Al., U.S. | B3 | 78 |
| Steele, Mo., U.S. | E8 | 102 |
| Steele, N.D., U.S. | C6 | 111 |
| Steele, co., Mn., U.S. | F5 | 100 |
| Steele, co., N.D., U.S. | B8 | 111 |
| Steele, Mount, mtn., Wy., U.S. | E6 | 127 |
| Steele City, Ne., U.S. | D8 | 104 |
| Steeleville, Il., U.S. | E4 | 90 |
| Steelton, Pa., U.S. | F8 | 115 |
| Steelville, Mo., U.S. | D6 | 102 |
| Steen, Mn., U.S. | G2 | 100 |
| Steenbergen, Neth. | C4 | 17 |
| Steens, Ms., U.S. | B5 | 101 |
| Steens Mountain, mts., Or., U.S. | E8 | 114 |
| Steenwijk, Neth. | B6 | 17 |
| Steep Falls, Me., U.S. | E2 | 96 |
| Steephill Lake, l., Sask. | B4 | 75 |
| Steep Point, c., Austl. | E1 | 50 |
| Steep Rock, Man. | D2 | 70 |
| Steep Rock Lake, Ont. | o17 | 73 |
| Ştefăneşti, Rom. | B8 | 24 |
| Ştefanie, Lake, l., Afr. | E4 | 47 |
| Stefansson Island, i., N.W. Ter. | B11 | 66 |
| Steffisburg, Switz. | C4 | 21 |
| Steger, Il., U.S. | B6 | 90 |
| Stehekin, Wa., U.S. | A5 | 124 |
| Steilacoom, Wa., U.S. | f10 | 124 |
| Steinach, Aus. | B7 | 20 |
| Stein [am Rhein], Switz. | E4 | 21 |
| Steinauer, Ne., U.S. | D9 | 104 |
| Steinbach, Man. | E3 | 70 |
| Steinbach-Hallenberg, E. Ger. | C5 | 19 |
| Steinfort, Lux. | E5 | 17 |
| Steinhatchee, Fl., U.S. | C3 | 86 |
| Steinhatchee, stm., Fl., U.S. | C3 | 86 |
| Steinhausen, Nmb. | B2 | 49 |
| Steinheim, W. Ger. | F3 | 15 |
| Steinkjer, Nor. | E4 | 14 |
| Stella, Ont. | C8 | 73 |
| Stella, Ky., U.S. | f9 | 94 |
| Stella, Mo., U.S. | E3 | 102 |
| Stella, Ne., U.S. | D10 | 104 |
| Stellarton, N.S. | D7 | 71 |
| Stello, mtn., Italy | C5 | 20 |
| Stem, N.C., U.S. | A4 | 110 |
| Stenay, Fr. | E5 | 17 |
| Stendal, E. Ger. | B5 | 18 |
| Stendal, In., U.S. | H3 | 91 |
| Stenen, Sask. | F4 | 75 |
| Stenness, Loch of, l., Scot., U.K. | A5 | 13 |
| Stepanakert, Sov. Un. | F3 | 28 |
| Stephan, S.D., U.S. | C6 | 118 |
| Stephen, Mn., U.S. | B2 | 100 |
| Stephens, Ar., U.S. | D2 | 81 |
| Stephens, Ga., U.S. | C3 | 87 |
| Stephens, co., Ga., U.S. | B3 | 87 |
| Stephens, co., Ok., U.S. | C4 | 113 |
| Stephens, co., Tx., U.S. | C3 | 120 |
| Stephens, Port, b., Austl. | F9 | 51 |
| Stephensburg, N.J., U.S. | B3 | 107 |
| Stephens City, Va., U.S. | A4 | 123 |
| Stephens Knob, hill, Ky., U.S. | D5 | 94 |
| Stephens Lake, res., Man. | A4 | 70 |
| Stephenson, Mi., U.S. | C3 | 99 |
| Stephenson, co., Il., U.S. | A4 | 90 |
| Stephenson, Mount, mtn., Ant. | C6 | 7 |
| Stephens Passage, strt., Ak., U.S. | m23 | 79 |
| Stephensport, Ky., U.S. | C3 | 94 |
| Stephenville, Newf. | D2 | 72 |
| Stephenville, Tx., U.S. | C3 | 120 |
| Stephenville Crossing, Newf. | D2 | 72 |
| Stepnica, Pol. | E8 | 15 |
| Stepnyak, Sov. Un. | C8 | 28 |
| Steppes, plat., Sov. Un. | C8 | 28 |
| Step Pyramid, hist., Egypt | E3 | 41 |
| Steps Point, c., Am. Sam. | G13 | 52 |
| Steptoe, Nv., U.S. | D7 | 105 |
| Steptoe, Wa., U.S. | B8 | 124 |
| Sterkstroom, S. Afr. | D4 | 49 |
| Sterling, Ak., U.S. | g16 | 79 |
| Sterling, Co., U.S. | A7 | 83 |
| Sterling, Ct., U.S. | C8 | 84 |
| Sterling, Ga., U.S. | E5 | 87 |
| Sterling, Il., U.S. | B4 | 90 |
| Sterling, Ks., U.S. | D5 | 93 |
| Sterling, Ma., U.S. | B4 | 98 |
| Sterling, Mi., U.S. | D6 | 99 |
| Sterling, Ne., U.S. | D9 | 104 |
| Sterling, N.D., U.S. | C5 | 111 |
| Sterling, Ok., U.S. | C3 | 113 |
| Sterling, Ut., U.S. | D4 | 121 |
| Sterling, Va., U.S. | A5 | 123 |
| Sterling, co., Tx., U.S. | D2 | 120 |
| Sterling City, Tx., U.S. | D2 | 120 |
| Sterling Heights, Mi., U.S. | o15 | 99 |
| Sterling Reservoir, res., Co., U.S. | A6 | 83 |
| Sterling Run, Pa., U.S. | D5 | 115 |
| Sterlington, La., U.S. | B3 | 95 |
| Sterlitamak, Sov. Un. | D8 | 29 |
| Sternberg, E. Ger. | E5 | 15 |
| Šternberk, Czech. | D4 | 26 |
| Sterrett, Al., U.S. | B3 | 78 |
| Stetson, Me., U.S. | D4 | 96 |
| Stetson Mountain, mtn., Me., U.S. | C4 | 96 |
| Stetsonville, Wi., U.S. | C3 | 126 |
| Stettin Lagoon, b., Eur. | B7 | 18 |
| Stettin see Szczecin, Pol. | B3 | 26 |
| Stettler, Alta. | C4 | 68 |
| Steuben, Me., U.S. | D5 | 96 |
| Steuben, Mi., U.S. | B4 | 99 |
| Steuben, Wi., U.S. | E3 | 126 |
| Steuben, co., In., U.S. | A7 | 91 |
| Steuben, co., N.Y., U.S. | C3 | 109 |
| Steubenville, Oh., U.S. | B5 | 112 |
| Stevenage, Eng., U.K. | C7 | 12 |
| Stevens, co., Ks., U.S. | E2 | 93 |
| Stevens, co., Mn., U.S. | E3 | 100 |
| Stevens, co., Wa., U.S. | A7 | 124 |
| Stevens Creek Dam, U.S. | C4 | 87 |
| Stevenson, Al., U.S. | A4 | 78 |
| Stevenson, Ct., U.S. | D3 | 84 |
| Stevenson, Wa., U.S. | D4 | 124 |
| Stevenson, stm., Man. | C4 | 70 |
| Stevenson Lake, l., Man. | C4 | 70 |
| Stevenson Mountain, mtn., Ar., U.S. | B1 | 81 |
| Stevens Pass, Wa., U.S. | B4 | 124 |
| Stevens Peak, mtn., Id., U.S. | B3 | 89 |
| Stevens Point, Wi., U.S. | D4 | 126 |
| Stevens Pottery, Ga., U.S. | D3 | 87 |
| Stevens Village, Ak., U.S. | B10 | 79 |
| Stevensville, Md., U.S. | C5 | 97 |
| Stevensville, Mi., U.S. | F4 | 99 |
| Stevensville, Mt., U.S. | D2 | 103 |
| Stevensville, Pa., U.S. | C9 | 115 |
| Steward, Il., U.S. | B4 | 90 |
| Stewardson, Il., U.S. | D5 | 90 |
| Stewart, B.C. | B3 | 69 |
| Stewart, Al., U.S. | C2 | 78 |
| Stewart, Mn., U.S. | F4 | 100 |
| Stewart, Ms., U.S. | B4 | 101 |
| Stewart, Oh., U.S. | C4 | 112 |
| Stewart, Tn., U.S. | A4 | 119 |
| Stewart, co., Ga., U.S. | D2 | 87 |
| Stewart, stm., Yukon | D5 | 66 |
| Stewart Island, i., N.Z. | Q11 | 51 |
| Stewart Mountain, mtn., Az., U.S. | k9 | 80 |
| Stewarton, Scot., U.K. | F8 | 13 |
| Stewarts Point, Nv., U.S. | G7 | 105 |
| Stewartstown, N. Ire., U.K. | C5 | 11 |
| Stewartstown, N.H., U.S. | f6 | 106 |
| Stewartstown, Pa., U.S. | G8 | 115 |
| Stewartstown Hollow, N.H., U.S. | g7 | 106 |
| Stewartsville, In., U.S. | H2 | 91 |
| Stewartsville, Mo., U.S. | B3 | 102 |
| Stewartsville, N.J., U.S. | B2 | 107 |
| Stewart Valley, Sask. | G2 | 75 |
| Stewartville, Mn., U.S. | G6 | 100 |
| Steynsburg, S. Afr. | D4 | 49 |
| Steyr, Aus. | D5 | 19 |
| Stickney, Il., U.S. | *k9 | 90 |
| Stickney, S.D., U.S. | D7 | 118 |
| Stif (Sétif), Alg. | B6 | 44 |
| Stigler, Ok., U.S. | B6 | 113 |
| Stikine, stm., N.A. | E6 | 66 |
| Stikine, stm., Ak., U.S. | D13 | 79 |
| Stilesville, In., U.S. | E4 | 91 |
| Stilis, Grc. | C4 | 25 |
| Stillaguamish, North Fork, stm., Wa., U.S. | A4 | 124 |
| Stillaguamish, South Fork, stm., Wa., U.S. | A4 | 124 |
| Stillhouse Hollow Lake, res., Tx., U.S. | D4 | 120 |
| Stillman Valley, Il., U.S. | A4 | 90 |
| Stillmore, Ga., U.S. | D4 | 87 |
| Still Pond, Md., U.S. | B5 | 97 |
| Still River, Ct., U.S. | B4 | 98 |
| Stillwater, B.C. | E5 | 69 |
| Stillwater, Mn., U.S. | E6 | 100 |
| Stillwater, N.Y., U.S. | C7 | 109 |
| Stillwater, Ok., U.S. | A4 | 113 |
| Stillwater, Ok., U.S. | D9 | 115 |
| Stillwater, co., Mt., U.S. | E7 | 103 |
| Stillwater Range, mts., Nv., U.S. | D3 | 105 |
| Stillwater Reservoir, res., N.Y., U.S. | B5 | 109 |
| Stillwater Reservoir, res., R.I., U.S. | B3 | 116 |
| Stillwell, Ga., U.S. | D5 | 87 |
| Stillwell, In., U.S. | A4 | 91 |
| Stilson, Ga., U.S. | D5 | 87 |
| Stilwell, Ks., U.S. | D9 | 93 |
| Stilwell, Ok., U.S. | B7 | 113 |
| Stimson, Mount, mtn., Mt., U.S. | B3 | 103 |
| Stinear Nunataks, mtn., Ant. | C19 | 7 |
| Stine Mountain, mtn., Mt., U.S. | C6 | 7 |
| Stinesville, In., U.S. | F4 | 91 |
| Stinking Lake, l., N.M., U.S. | A3 | 108 |
| Stinnett, Tx., U.S. | B2 | 120 |
| Stinson Lake, N.H., U.S. | C3 | 106 |
| Ştip, Yugo. | E6 | 24 |
| Stirling, Austl. | F2 | 50 |
| Stirling, Alta. | E4 | 68 |
| Stirling, Ont. | C7 | 73 |
| Stirling, Scot., U.K. | B5 | 10 |
| Stirling City, Ca., U.S. | C3 | 82 |
| Stirrat, W.V., U.S. | D3 | 125 |
| Stirum, N.D., U.S. | C8 | 111 |
| Stites, Id., U.S. | C3 | 89 |
| Stittsville, Ont. | B9 | 73 |
| Stjørdalshalsen, Nor. | F4 | 14 |
| Stockach, W. Ger. | A7 | 21 |
| Stockbridge, Ga., U.S. | C2 | 87 |
| Stockbridge, Ma., U.S. | B1 | 98 |
| Stockbridge, Mi., U.S. | F6 | 99 |
| Stockbridge, Vt., U.S. | D3 | 122 |
| Stockbridge, Wi., U.S. | D5 | 126 |
| Stockbridge-Munsee Indian Reservation, Wi., U.S. | D5 | 126 |
| Stockdale, Oh., U.S. | D3 | 112 |
| Stockdale, Tx., U.S. | E4 | 120 |
| Stockerau, Aus. | D8 | 18 |
| Stockertown, Pa., U.S. | E11 | 115 |
| Stockett, Mt., U.S. | C5 | 103 |
| Stockham, Ne., U.S. | D8 | 104 |
| Stockholm, Sask. | G4 | 75 |
| Stockholm, Swe. | H8 | 14 |
| Stockholm, Me., U.S. | A4 | 96 |
| Stockholm, N.J., U.S. | A3 | 107 |
| Stockholm, S.D., U.S. | B9 | 118 |
| Stockholm, Wi., U.S. | D1 | 126 |
| Stockland, Il., U.S. | C6 | 90 |
| Stockley, De., U.S. | F4 | 85 |
| Stockport, Eng., U.K. | D5 | 10 |
| Stockport, Ia., U.S. | D6 | 92 |
| Stockport, Oh., U.S. | C4 | 112 |
| Stockton, Man. | E2 | 70 |
| Stockton, Al., U.S. | E2 | 78 |
| Stockton, Ca., U.S. | D3 | 82 |
| Stockton, Ga., U.S. | F4 | 87 |
| Stockton, Il., U.S. | A3 | 90 |
| Stockton, Ks., U.S. | C4 | 93 |
| Stockton, Md., U.S. | D7 | 97 |
| Stockton, Mo., U.S. | D4 | 102 |
| Stockton, N.J., U.S. | C3 | 107 |
| Stockton, N.Y., U.S. | C1 | 109 |
| Stockton, Ut., U.S. | C3 | 121 |
| Stockton Island, i., Wi., U.S. | B3 | 126 |
| Stockton Lake, res., Mo., U.S. | D4 | 102 |
| Stockton-on-Tees, Eng., U.K. | F7 | 13 |
| Stockton Plateau, plat., Tx., U.S. | D1 | 120 |
| Stockton Springs, Me., U.S. | D4 | 96 |
| Stockville, Ne., U.S. | D5 | 104 |
| Stockwell, In., U.S. | D4 | 91 |
| Stod, Czech. | D8 | 19 |
| Stoddard, N.H., U.S. | D2 | 106 |
| Stoddard, Wi., U.S. | E2 | 126 |
| Stoddard, co., Mo., U.S. | E8 | 102 |
| Stoeckl, Mount, mtn., N.A. | A2 | 69 |
| Stoer, Point of, c., Scot., U.K. | A3 | 13 |
| Stoke-Centre, Que. | D6 | 74 |
| Stoke-on-Trent, Eng., U.K. | D5 | 10 |
| Stokes, N.C., U.S. | B5 | 110 |
| Stokes, co., N.C., U.S. | A2 | 110 |
| Stokes, Mount, mtn., N.Z. | N15 | 51 |
| Stokesdale, N.C., U.S. | A3 | 110 |
| Stokesley, Eng., U.K. | F7 | 13 |
| Stokke, Nor. | p28 | 14 |
| Stolac, Yugo. | D3 | 24 |
| Stolberg, W. Ger. | C3 | 18 |
| Stolbovaya, Sov. Un. | n17 | 27 |
| Stolbovoy, i., Sov. Un. | B11 | 28 |
| Stolberg, E. Ger. | C7 | 18 |
| Stollings, W.V., U.S. | n12 | 125 |
| Stolzenau, W. Ger. | F3 | 15 |
| Stone, Id., U.S. | G6 | 89 |
| Stone, Ky., U.S. | C7 | 94 |
| Stone, co., Ar., U.S. | B3 | 81 |
| Stone, co., Ms., U.S. | E4 | 101 |
| Stone, co., Mo., U.S. | E4 | 102 |
| Stoneboro, Pa., U.S. | D1 | 115 |
| Stone City, Ia., U.S. | B6 | 92 |
| Stone Corral Lake, l., Or., U.S. | E7 | 114 |
| Stonefort, Il., U.S. | F5 | 90 |
| Stonega, Va., U.S. | f9 | 123 |
| Stoneham, Co., U.S. | A7 | 83 |
| Stoneham, Ma., U.S. | g11 | 98 |
| Stone Harbor, N.J., U.S. | E3 | 107 |
| Stonehaven, N.B. | B4 | 71 |
| Stonehaven, Scot., U.K. | B6 | 10 |
| Stonehenge, Austl. | A4 | 51 |
| Stone Lake, Wi., U.S. | C2 | 126 |
| Stone Mountain, Ga., U.S. | C2 | 87 |
| Stone Mountain, mtn., Ga., U.S. | C2 | 87 |
| Stone Mountain, mtn., Vt., U.S. | B5 | 122 |
| Stone Mountains, mts., U.S. | A1 | 110 |
| Stoner, B.C. | C6 | 69 |
| Stoner, Co., U.S. | D2 | 83 |
| Stoner, Ia., U.S. | A3 | 106 |
| Stones River National Battlefield, hist., Tn., U.S. | B5 | 119 |
| Stoneville, Ms., U.S. | B3 | 101 |
| Stoneville, N.C., U.S. | A3 | 110 |
| Stoneville, S.D., U.S. | C3 | 118 |
| Stonewall, Man. | D3 | 70 |
| Stonewall, La., U.S. | B2 | 95 |
| Stonewall, Ms., U.S. | C5 | 101 |
| Stonewall, Ok., U.S. | C5 | 113 |
| Stonewall, co., Tx., U.S. | C2 | 120 |
| Stonewall Jackson Lake, res., W.V., U.S. | k10 | 125 |
| Stonewood, W.V., U.S. | k10 | 125 |
| Stoney Creek, Ont. | D5 | 73 |
| Stonington, Co., U.S. | D8 | 83 |
| Stonington, Ct., U.S. | D8 | 84 |
| Stonington, Il., U.S. | D4 | 90 |
| Stonington, Me., U.S. | D4 | 96 |
| Stono, stm., S.C., U.S. | k11 | 117 |
| Stono Inlet, b., S.C., U.S. | F8 | 117 |
| Stony Beach, Sask. | G3 | 75 |
| Stony Brook, N.Y., U.S. | n15 | 109 |
| Stony Brook, stm., N.J., U.S. | C3 | 107 |
| Stony Creek, Ct., U.S. | D5 | 84 |
| Stony Creek, N.Y., U.S. | B7 | 109 |
| Stony Creek, Va., U.S. | D5 | 123 |
| Stony Creek, stm., Va., U.S. | C5 | 123 |
| Stony Island, i., Newf. | B4 | 72 |
| Stony Lake, l., Ont. | C6 | 73 |
| Stony Mountain, Man. | D3 | 70 |
| Stony Plain, Alta. | C3 | 68 |
| Stony Point, N.Y., U.S. | *D7 | 109 |
| Stony Point, N.C., U.S. | B1 | 110 |
| Stony Rapids, Sask. | m7 | 75 |
| Stony Ridge, Oh., U.S. | e6 | 112 |
| Stör, stm., W. Ger. | B2 | 15 |
| Storå, stm., Den. | B2 | 15 |
| Stora Lulevatten, l., Swe. | D8 | 14 |
| Stora Sundby, Swe. | t34 | 14 |
| Storavan, l., Swe. | E8 | 14 |
| Storden, Mn., U.S. | F3 | 100 |
| Store Bælt, strt., Den. | C4 | 15 |
| Store Heddinge, Den. | J5 | 14 |
| Storey, co., Nv., U.S. | D2 | 105 |
| Storkow, E. Ger. | A8 | 19 |
| Storla, S.D., U.S. | D7 | 118 |
| Storm Lake, Ia., U.S. | B2 | 92 |
| Storm Lake, l., Ia., U.S. | B2 | 92 |
| Storm Mountain, mtn., Ak., U.S. | h16 | 79 |
| Stormont, co., Ont. | B10 | 73 |
| Stornoway, Sask. | F4 | 75 |
| Stornoway, Scot., U.K. | A3 | 10 |
| Storozhinets, Sov. Un. | G5 | 27 |
| Storrs, Ct., U.S. | B7 | 84 |
| Storsjö, Swe. | F5 | 14 |
| Storsjön, l., Swe. | F6 | 14 |
| Storstrøm, co., Den. | D5 | 15 |
| Storthoaks, Sask. | H5 | 75 |
| Storuman, Swe. | E7 | 14 |
| Storuman, l., Swe. | E7 | 14 |
| Story, Ar., U.S. | C2 | 81 |
| Story, Wy., U.S. | B6 | 127 |
| Story, co., Ia., U.S. | B4 | 92 |
| Story City, Ia., U.S. | B4 | 92 |
| Stotesbury, Mo., U.S. | D3 | 102 |
| Stotts City, Mo., U.S. | D4 | 102 |
| Stottville, N.Y., U.S. | C7 | 109 |
| Stoughton, Sask. | H4 | 75 |
| Stoughton, Ma., U.S. | B5 | 98 |
| Stoughton, Wi., U.S. | F4 | 126 |
| Stour, stm., Eng., U.K. | D4 | 101 |
| Stour, stm., Eng., U.K. | E6 | 10 |
| Stourbridge, Eng., U.K. | B5 | 12 |
| Stourport-on-Severn, Eng., U.K. | B3 | 101 |
| Stout, Oh., U.S. | D2 | 112 |
| Stoutland, Mo., U.S. | D5 | 102 |
| Stoutsville, Mo., U.S. | B6 | 102 |
| Stoutsville, Oh., U.S. | C3 | 112 |
| Stovall, Ga., U.S. | D2 | 87 |
| Stovall, Ms., U.S. | A3 | 101 |
| Stovall, N.C., U.S. | A4 | 110 |
| Stove Creek, Sask. | E4 | 75 |
| Stover, Mo., U.S. | C5 | 102 |
| Støvring, Den. | B3 | 15 |
| Stow, Me., U.S. | D2 | 96 |
| Stow, Ma., U.S. | B5 | 98 |
| Stow, Oh., U.S. | A4 | 112 |
| Stow Creek, stm., N.J., U.S. | D2 | 107 |
| Stowe, Pa., U.S. | F10 | 115 |
| Stowe, Vt., U.S. | C3 | 122 |
| Stowe Township, Pa., U.S. | *k13 | 115 |
| Stowmarket, Eng., U.K. | B8 | 12 |
| Stoyoma Mountain, mtn., B.C. | E7 | 69 |
| Stoystown, Pa., U.S. | F4 | 115 |
| Strabane, N. Ire., U.K. | C5 | 11 |
| Strabane, Pa., U.S. | F1 | 115 |
| Strachur, Scot., U.K. | D3 | 13 |
| Stradbally, Ire. | D4 | 11 |
| Stradone, Ire. | D4 | 11 |
| Strafford, Mo., U.S. | D4 | 102 |
| Strafford, N.H., U.S. | D4 | 106 |
| Strafford, Vt., U.S. | D4 | 122 |
| Strafford, co., N.H., U.S. | D4 | 106 |
| Straffordville, Ont. | E4 | 73 |
| Straight, Ok., U.S. | e9 | 113 |
| Strakonice, Czech. | D2 | 26 |
| Straldzha, Bul. | D8 | 24 |
| Stralsund, E. Ger. | A6 | 18 |
| Strand, S. Afr. | C2 | 49 |
| Strandburg, S.D., U.S. | B9 | 118 |
| Strandby, Den. | A3 | 15 |
| Strandhill, Ire. | C3 | 11 |
| Strandquist, Mn., U.S. | B2 | 100 |
| Strang, Ne., U.S. | D8 | 104 |
| Strang, Ok., U.S. | A6 | 113 |
| Stranger Creek, stm., Ks., U.S. | k15 | 93 |
| Strangford, N. Ire., U.K. | C6 | 11 |
| Strangford Lough, l., N. Ire., U.K. | C6 | 11 |
| Strängnäs, Swe. | t35 | 14 |
| Strängsjö, Swe. | u34 | 14 |
| Stranraer, Sask. | F1 | 75 |
| Stranraer, Scot., U.K. | E6 | 86 |
| Strasbourg, Sask. | F3 | 75 |
| Strasbourg, Fr. | C7 | 16 |
| Strasburg, E. Ger. | E6 | 15 |
| Strasburg, Co., U.S. | B6 | 83 |
| Strasburg, Il., U.S. | D5 | 90 |
| Strasburg, Mo., U.S. | C3 | 102 |
| Strasburg, N.D., U.S. | C5 | 111 |
| Strasburg, Oh., U.S. | B4 | 112 |
| Strasburg, Pa., U.S. | G9 | 115 |
| Strasburg, Va., U.S. | B4 | 123 |
| Strasswalchen, Aus. | D7 | 18 |
| Stratford, Ont. | D3 | 73 |
| Stratford, N.Z. | M15 | 51 |
| Stratford, Ct., U.S. | E3 | 84 |
| Stratford, Ia., U.S. | B4 | 92 |
| Stratford, N.J., U.S. | D2 | 107 |
| Stratford, N.Y., U.S. | B6 | 109 |
| Stratford, Ok., U.S. | C5 | 113 |
| Stratford, S.D., U.S. | B7 | 118 |
| Stratford, Tx., U.S. | A1 | 120 |
| Stratford, Wi., U.S. | D3 | 126 |
| Stratford Centre, Que. | D6 | 74 |
| Stratford Landing, Va., U.S. | *B5 | 123 |
| Stratford Point, c., Ct., U.S. | E3 | 84 |
| Stratford-upon-Avon, Eng., U.K. | D5 | 10 |
| Stratham, N.H., U.S. | D5 | 106 |
| Strathaven, Scot., U.K. | E4 | 13 |
| Strathclair, Man. | D1 | 70 |
| Strathclyde, prov., Scot., U.K. | E4 | 13 |
| Strathcona, Ont. | C8 | 73 |
| Strathcona, Mn., U.S. | B2 | 100 |
| Strathcona Provincial Park, B.C. | E5 | 69 |
| Strathlorne, N.S. | C8 | 71 |
| Strathmere, N.J., U.S. | E3 | 107 |
| Strathmore, Alta. | D4 | 68 |
| Strathmore, Ca., U.S. | D4 | 82 |
| Strathmore, N.J., U.S. | C4 | 107 |
| Strathroy, Ont. | E3 | 73 |
| Strathy Point, c., Scot., U.K. | C2 | 82 |
| Strattanville, Pa., U.S. | D3 | 115 |
| Stratton, Co., U.S. | B8 | 83 |
| Stratton, Me., U.S. | C2 | 96 |
| Stratton, Ne., U.S. | D4 | 104 |
| Stratton, Oh., U.S. | B5 | 112 |
| Stratton Meadows, Co., U.S. | C6 | 83 |
| Stratton Mountain, mtn., Vt., U.S. | E3 | 122 |
| Straubing, W. Ger. | D6 | 18 |
| Straubville, N.D., U.S. | C8 | 111 |
| Straughn, In., U.S. | E7 | 91 |
| Strausberg, E. Ger. | F7 | 15 |
| Strausstown, Pa., U.S. | F9 | 115 |
| Strawberry, Ar., U.S. | A5 | 81 |
| Strawberry, stm., Ar., U.S. | A4 | 81 |
| Strawberry, stm., Ut., U.S. | C5 | 121 |
| Strawberry Mountain, mtn., Or., U.S. | C8 | 114 |
| Strawberry Plains, Tn., U.S. | C10 | 119 |
| Strawberry Point, Ia., U.S. | B6 | 92 |
| Strawberry Point, c., Ma., U.S. | B6 | 98 |
| Strawberry Range, mts., Or., U.S. | C8 | 114 |
| Strawberry Reservoir, res., Ut., U.S. | C4 | 121 |
| Strawn, Il., U.S. | C5 | 90 |
| Strawn, Ks., U.S. | D8 | 93 |
| Strawn, Tx., U.S. | C3 | 120 |
| Strážnice, Czech. | D4 | 26 |
| Streamstown, Alta. | C5 | 68 |
| Streamwood, Il., U.S. | *h8 | 90 |
| Streator, Il., U.S. | B5 | 90 |
| Středočeský, prov., Czech. | D9 | 19 |
| Streeter, N.D., U.S. | C6 | 111 |
| Streetman, Tx., U.S. | D4 | 120 |
| Streetsboro, Oh., U.S. | *A4 | 112 |
| Streetsville, Ont. | m14 | 73 |
| Strehaia, Rom. | C6 | 24 |
| Strelka, Sov. Un. | D27 | 8 |
| Strelka-Chunya, Sov. Un. | C13 | 29 |
| Stresa, Italy | D4 | 20 |
| Stříbro, Czech. | D8 | 19 |
| Strichen, Scot., U.K. | C6 | 13 |
| Strimón (Struma), stm., Eur. | B4 | 25 |
| Strimón, Gulf of, b., Grc. | B4 | 25 |
| Stringer, Ms., U.S. | D4 | 101 |
| Stringtown, Ok., U.S. | C5 | 113 |
| Stringtown, Ky., U.S. | B5 | 94 |
| Strofádhes, is., Grc. | D3 | 25 |
| Stroh, In., U.S. | A7 | 91 |
| Strokestown, Ire. | D3 | 11 |
| Stromboli, i., Italy | E5 | 23 |
| Strome, Alta. | C4 | 68 |
| Stromeferry, Scot., U.K. | C3 | 13 |
| Stromness, Scot., U.K. | B5 | 13 |
| Stromsburg, Ne., U.S. | C8 | 104 |
| Stronach, Mi., U.S. | D4 | 99 |
| Strong, Ar., U.S. | D3 | 81 |
| Strong, Me., U.S. | D2 | 96 |
| Strong, stm., Ms., U.S. | C4 | 101 |
| Strong City, Ks., U.S. | D7 | 93 |
| Strong City, Ok., U.S. | B2 | 113 |
| Strongfield, Sask. | F2 | 75 |
| Stronghurst, Il., U.S. | C3 | 90 |
| Strongs, Mi., U.S. | B6 | 99 |
| Strongsville, Oh., U.S. | A4 | 112 |
| Stronsay, i., Scot., U.K. | A5 | 10 |
| Stronsay Firth, sirt., Scot., U.K. | A6 | 13 |
| Strontian, Scot., U.K. | D3 | 13 |
| Stroud, Eng., U.K. | C5 | 12 |
| Stroud, Ok., U.S. | B5 | 113 |
| Stroudsburg, Pa., U.S. | E11 | 115 |
| Stroudwater, stm., Me., U.S. | g7 | 96 |
| Struble, Ia., U.S. | B1 | 92 |
| Struer, Den. | I3 | 14 |
| Struga, Yugo. | E5 | 24 |
| Strule, stm., N. Ire., U.K. | C5 | 11 |
| Struma (Strimón), stm., Eur. | B4 | 25 |
| Strumble Head, c., Wales, U.K. | B2 | 12 |
| Strumica, Yugo. | E6 | 24 |
| Strunk, Ky., U.S. | D5 | 94 |
| Struthers, Oh., U.S. | A5 | 112 |
| Stryama, stm., Bul. | D7 | 24 |
| Stryker, Mt., U.S. | B2 | 103 |
| Stryker, Oh., U.S. | A1 | 112 |
| Strykersville, N.Y., U.S. | C2 | 109 |
| Stryy, Sov. Un. | G4 | 27 |
| Stryy, stm., Sov. Un. | D7 | 26 |
| Strzegom, Pol. | C4 | 26 |
| Strzelce Krajeńskie, Pol. | B3 | 26 |
| Strzelce [Opolskie], Pol. | C5 | 26 |
| Strzelecki Creek, stm., Austl. | E7 | 50 |
| Strzelin, Pol. | C4 | 26 |
| Strzelno, Pol. | B5 | 26 |
| Strzemieszyce, Pol. | g10 | 26 |
| Stuart, Fl., U.S. | E6 | 86 |
| Stuart, Ia., U.S. | C3 | 92 |
| Stuart, Ne., U.S. | B6 | 104 |
| Stuart, Ok., U.S. | C5 | 113 |
| Stuart, Va., U.S. | D2 | 123 |
| Stuart, B.C. | B5 | 69 |
| Stuart, Mount, mtn., U.S. | B5 | 124 |
| Stuart Lake, l., B.C. | B5 | 69 |
| Stuarts Draft, Va., U.S. | B3 | 123 |
| Stub Hill, mtn., N.H., U.S. | f7 | 106 |
| Studley, Ks., U.S. | C4 | 93 |
| Stühlingen, W. Ger. | A5 | 21 |
| Stull, stm., Can. | B5 | 70 |
| Stull Lake, l., Can. | B5 | 70 |
| Stump Creek, Pa., U.S. | D4 | 115 |
| Stump Lake, l., N.D., U.S. | B7 | 111 |
| Stump Pond, res., R.I., U.S. | C4 | 116 |
| Stumptown, W.V., U.S. | C4 | 125 |
| Stumpy Point, N.C., U.S. | B7 | 110 |
| Stupart, stm., Man. | B3 | 70 |
| Stupino, Sov. Un. | D11 | 27 |
| Sturbridge, Ma., U.S. | B3 | 98 |
| Sturgeon, Mo., U.S. | B5 | 102 |
| Sturgeon, stm., Sask. | D2 | 75 |
| Sturgeon Bay, Wi., U.S. | D6 | 126 |
| Sturgeon Bay, b., Man. | C2 | 70 |
| Sturgeon Falls, Ont. | A5 | 73 |
| Sturgeon Lake, Alta. | B2 | 68 |
| Sturgeon Lake, l., Alta. | B2 | 68 |
| Sturgeon Lake, l., Ont. | C6 | 73 |
| Sturgeon Lake, l., Sask. | D2 | 75 |

| Name | Map Ref. | Page |
|---|---|---|
| Sturgeon Landing, Sask. | C5 | 75 |
| Sturgeon-weir, stm., Sask. | C4 | 75 |
| Sturgis, Sask. | F4 | 75 |
| Sturgis, Ky., U.S. | e10 | 94 |
| Sturgis, Mi., U.S. | G5 | 99 |
| Sturgis, Ms., U.S. | B4 | 101 |
| Sturgis, S.D., U.S. | C2 | 118 |
| Sturt Creek, stm., Austl. | C4 | 50 |
| Sturt Desert, des., Austl. | D3 | 51 |
| Sturtevant, Wi., U.S. | F6 | 126 |
| Stutsman, co., N.D., U.S. | B6 | 111 |
| Stutterheim, S. Afr. | D4 | 49 |
| Stuttgart, W. Ger. | D4 | 18 |
| Stuttgart, Ar., U.S. | C4 | 81 |
| Stuttgart, Ks., U.S. | C4 | 93 |
| Styr, stm., Sov. Un. | F5 | 27 |
| Styria, hist. reg., Aus. | E7 | 18 |
| Subarnarekha, stm., India | F11 | 37 |
| Subi, i., Indon. | K8 | 35 |
| Subiaco, Ar., U.S. | B2 | 81 |
| Subic, Phil. | o13 | 34 |
| Subic Bay, b., Phil. | o13 | 34 |
| Sublette, Il., U.S. | B4 | 90 |
| Sublette, Ks., U.S. | E3 | 93 |
| Sublette, co., Wy., U.S. | D2 | 127 |
| Sublett Range, mts., Id., U.S. | G6 | 89 |
| Sublimity, Or., U.S. | C4 | 114 |
| Subotica, Yugo. | B4 | 24 |
| Sucarnoochee, stm., Al., U.S. | C1 | 78 |
| Succasunna, N.J., U.S. | B3 | 107 |
| Success, Sask. | G1 | 75 |
| Success, Ar., U.S. | A5 | 81 |
| Success, Mo., U.S. | D5 | 102 |
| Success, Mount, mtn., N.H., U.S. | B4 | 106 |
| Suceava, Rom. | B8 | 24 |
| Suceava, stm., Rom. | B8 | 24 |
| Sucha [Beskidzka], Pol. | F5 | 27 |
| Suchdol, Czech. | n17 | 26 |
| Suches, Ar., U.S. | B2 | 87 |
| Suchitoto, El Sal. | D3 | 62 |
| Süchow see Xuzhou, China | E8 | 31 |
| Suck, stm., Ire. | D2 | 10 |
| Sucre, Bol. | C2 | 55 |
| Sucre, state, Ven. | A5 | 60 |
| Sucre, dept., Col. | B2 | 60 |
| Sucuaro, Col. | C4 | 60 |
| Sucuriú, stm., Braz. | C2 | 56 |
| Sucy-en-Brie, Fr. | g11 | 16 |
| Sudan, Tx., U.S. | B1 | 120 |
| Sudan, ctry., Afr. | C2 | 47 |
| Sudan, reg., Afr. | E7 | 42 |
| Sudbury, Ont. | A4 | 73 |
| Sudbury, Eng., U.K. | B8 | 12 |
| Sudbury, Ma., U.S. | B5 | 98 |
| Sudbury, Vt., U.S. | D2 | 122 |
| Sudbury, dept., Ont. | p19 | 73 |
| Sudbury, stm., Ma., U.S. | B5 | 98 |
| Sudbury Center, Ma., U.S. | g10 | 98 |
| Sudbury Reservoir, res., Ma., U.S. | g10 | 98 |
| Suddie, Guy. | A3 | 59 |
| Süderbrarup, W. Ger. | D3 | 15 |
| Suderburg, W. Ger. | B5 | 18 |
| Sudetes, mts., Eur. | C4 | 26 |
| Sudlersville, Md., U.S. | B6 | 97 |
| Süd-Nord Canal, W. Ger. | B7 | 17 |
| Sudogda, Sov. Un. | D13 | 27 |
| Sudr, 'Ayn, well, Eg. | E5 | 41 |
| Sudzha, Sov. Un. | F10 | 27 |
| Sue, stm., Sud. | D2 | 47 |
| Sueca, Spain | C5 | 22 |
| Suez (As Suways), Eg. | C3 | 38 |
| Suez, Gulf of, b., Eg. | C3 | 38 |
| Suez Canal, Eg. | B3 | 38 |
| Suffern, N.Y., U.S. | D6 | 109 |
| Suffield, Alta. | D5 | 68 |
| Suffield, Ct., U.S. | B5 | 84 |
| Suffolk, Va., U.S. | C7 | 103 |
| Suffolk, co., Eng., U.K. | D6 | 123 |
| Suffolk, co., Eng., U.K. | B8 | 12 |
| Suffolk, co., Ma., U.S. | B5 | 98 |
| Suffolk, co., N.Y., U.S. | n15 | 109 |
| Sugar, stm., U.S. | F4 | 126 |
| Sugar, stm., N.H., U.S. | D2 | 106 |
| Sugar, North Branch, stm., N.H., U.S. | D2 | 106 |
| Sugar City, Co., U.S. | C7 | 83 |
| Sugar City, Id., U.S. | F7 | 89 |
| Sugar Creek, Mo., U.S. | h11 | 102 |
| Sugarcreek, Pa., U.S. | D2 | 115 |
| Sugar Creek, stm., In., U.S. | F6 | 91 |
| Sugar Creek, stm., Oh., U.S. | E3 | 91 |
| Sugar Creek, stm., U.S. | C2 | 112 |
| Sugar Creek, stm., U.S. | C8 | 115 |
| Sugar Grove, N.C., U.S. | A1 | 110 |
| Sugar Grove, Oh., U.S. | C3 | 112 |
| Sugargrove, Pa., U.S. | C3 | 115 |
| Sugar Grove, Va., U.S. | D1 | 123 |
| Sugar Grove, W.V., U.S. | C5 | 125 |
| Sugar Hill, Ga., U.S. | B2 | 87 |
| Sugar Hill, N.H., U.S. | B3 | 106 |
| Sugar Island, i., Mi., U.S. | B6 | 99 |
| Sugar Land, Tx., U.S. | E5 | 120 |
| Sugarland Run, Va., U.S. | A5 | 123 |
| Sugar Loaf, Ca., U.S. | C3 | 123 |
| Sugar Loaf, mtn., Braz. | h6 | 56 |
| Sugarloaf, mtn., N.H., U.S. | A4 | 106 |
| Sugarloaf, hill, Oh., U.S. | A4 | 112 |
| Sugarloaf Mountain, mtn., Me., U.S. | C2 | 96 |
| Sugar Loaf Mountain, mtn., Md., U.S. | B3 | 97 |
| Sugarloaf Mountain, mtn., Mt., U.S. | C4 | 103 |
| Sugar Loaf Mountain, mtn., Ok., U.S. | B7 | 113 |
| Sugarloaf Point, c., Austl. | F9 | 51 |
| Sugar Mountain, mtn., Mi., U.S. | k9 | 99 |
| Sugar Notch, Pa., U.S. | n17 | 115 |
| Sugartown, La., U.S. | D2 | 95 |
| Sugar Valley, Ga., U.S. | B1 | 87 |
| Sugden, Ok., U.S. | C4 | 113 |
| Suggi Lake, l., Sask. | C4 | 75 |
| Suggsville, Al., U.S. | D2 | 78 |
| Şuḥār, Oman | C5 | 38 |
| Sühbaatar, Mong. | A6 | 31 |
| Suhl, E. Ger. | C5 | 18 |
| Suiattle, stm., Wa., U.S. | A4 | 124 |
| Suibin, China | A5 | 33 |
| Suichuan, China | F7 | 31 |
| Suide, China | C11 | 31 |
| Suifenhe, China | C11 | 31 |
| Suihua, China | B10 | 31 |
| Suijiang, China | F5 | 31 |
| Suileng, China | C3 | 33 |
| Suining, China | E6 | 31 |
| Suipacha, Arg. | g7 | 54 |
| Suipacha, Bol. | D2 | 55 |
| Suippes, Fr. | E4 | 17 |
| Suir, stm., Ire. | D3 | 11 |
| Suisun City, Ca., U.S. | *C2 | 82 |
| Suit, N.C., U.S. | f8 | 110 |
| Suita, Japan | *l7 | 33 |
| Suitland, Md., U.S. | C4 | 97 |
| Suixian, China | E7 | 31 |
| Suixian, China | G6 | 32 |
| Suizhong, China | D9 | 32 |
| Sukabumi, Indon. | G3 | 34 |
| Sukadana, Indon. | F3 | 34 |
| Sukaraja, Indon. | F4 | 34 |
| Sukarnapura see Jayapura, Indon. | F10 | 34 |
| Sukhaya Tunguska, Sov. Un. | B26 | 8 |
| Sukhobuzimskoye, Sov. Un. | D27 | 8 |
| Sukhona, stm., Sov. Un. | C7 | 29 |
| Sukhothai, Thai. | B1 | 34 |
| Sukhumi, Sov. Un. | G17 | 8 |
| Sukkur, Pak. | C4 | 36 |
| Sukumo, Japan | J6 | 33 |
| Sukunka, stm., B.C. | B7 | 69 |
| Sula, Mt., U.S. | E3 | 103 |
| Sula, stm., Sov. Un. | F9 | 27 |
| Sulaiman Range, mts., Pak. | C4 | 36 |
| Sulaco, stm., Hond. | C4 | 62 |
| Sula Islands, is., Indon. | F7 | 34 |
| Sula Sgeir, i., Scot., U.K. | A2 | 13 |
| Sulecin, Pol. | B3 | 26 |
| Sulejówek, Pol. | m14 | 26 |
| Sulina, Rom. | C9 | 24 |
| Sulitelma, mtn., Eur. | D7 | 14 |
| Sullana, Peru | B1 | 58 |
| Sulligent, Al., U.S. | B1 | 78 |
| Sullivan, Il., U.S. | D5 | 90 |
| Sullivan, In., U.S. | F3 | 91 |
| Sullivan, Ky., U.S. | C2 | 94 |
| Sullivan, Mo., U.S. | C6 | 102 |
| Sullivan, N.H., U.S. | D2 | 106 |
| Sullivan, Oh., U.S. | A3 | 112 |
| Sullivan, Wi., U.S. | E5 | 126 |
| Sullivan, co., In., U.S. | F3 | 91 |
| Sullivan, co., Mo., U.S. | A4 | 102 |
| Sullivan, co., N.H., U.S. | D2 | 106 |
| Sullivan, co., N.Y., U.S. | D6 | 109 |
| Sullivan, co., Pa., U.S. | D9 | 115 |
| Sullivan, co., Tn., U.S. | C11 | 119 |
| Sullivan Lake, l., Alta. | D5 | 68 |
| Sullivans Island, S.C., U.S. | k12 | 117 |
| Sully, Ia., U.S. | C5 | 92 |
| Sully, co., S.D., U.S. | C5 | 118 |
| Sulmona, Italy | C4 | 23 |
| Sulphide, Ont. | C7 | 73 |
| Sulphur, Ky., U.S. | B4 | 94 |
| Sulphur, La., U.S. | D2 | 95 |
| Sulphur, Ok., U.S. | C5 | 113 |
| Sulphur, stm., Alta. | C1 | 68 |
| Sulphur, stm., U.S. | D2 | 81 |
| Sulphur Rock, Ar., U.S. | B4 | 81 |
| Sulphur Spring Range, mts., Nv., U.S. | C5 | 105 |
| Sulphur Springs, Ar., U.S. | A1 | 81 |
| Sulphur Springs, In., U.S. | D7 | 91 |
| Sulphur Springs, Mo., U.S. | g13 | 102 |
| Sulphur Springs, Oh., U.S. | B3 | 112 |
| Sulphur Springs, Tx., U.S. | C5 | 120 |
| Sulphur Springs Valley, val., Az., U.S. | E6 | 80 |
| Sultan, Wa., U.S. | B4 | 124 |
| Sultānpur, India | D9 | 37 |
| Sulu Archipelago, is., Phil. | D6 | 34 |
| Sulu Sea, Asia | D5 | 34 |
| Sulūq, Libya | C4 | 43 |
| Sulzbach, W. Ger. | D2 | 19 |
| Sulzbach-Rosenberg, W. Ger. | D6 | 19 |
| Sulzberger Bay, b., Ant. | B33 | 7 |
| Sumas, Wa., U.S. | A3 | 124 |
| Sumatra, Mt., U.S. | B2 | 86 |
| Sumatra, Mt., U.S. | D9 | 103 |
| Sumatra (Sumatera), i., Indon. | F2 | 34 |
| Sumava Resorts, In., U.S. | B3 | 91 |
| Sumba, i., Indon. | G6 | 34 |
| Sumba, stm., Sov. Un. | B7 | 39 |
| Sumbawa, i., Indon. | G5 | 34 |
| Sumbawa Besar, Indon. | G5 | 34 |
| Sumbawanga, Tan. | C5 | 48 |
| Sumbay, Peru | E3 | 58 |
| Sumbe (Ngunza), Ang. | D1 | 48 |
| Sumburgh Head, c., Scot., U.K. | h10 | 10 |
| Sümeg, Hung. | B3 | 24 |
| Sumenep, Indon. | G4 | 34 |
| Sumgait, Sov. Un. | A4 | 39 |
| Sumiswald, Switz. | B4 | 21 |
| Sumiton, Al., U.S. | B2 | 78 |
| Summerberry, Sask. | G4 | 75 |
| Summerdale, Al., U.S. | E2 | 78 |
| Summerfield, Fl., U.S. | C4 | 86 |
| Summerfield, Ks., U.S. | C7 | 93 |
| Summerfield, La., U.S. | B3 | 95 |
| Summerfield, Mo., U.S. | C6 | 102 |
| Summerfield, N.C., U.S. | A3 | 110 |
| Summerfield, Oh., U.S. | C4 | 112 |
| Summerford, Newf. | D4 | 72 |
| Summerhill, Pa., U.S. | F4 | 115 |
| Summer Hill, Il., U.S. | D3 | 90 |
| Summer Island, i., Mi., U.S. | C4 | 99 |
| Summer Lake, l., Or., U.S. | E6 | 114 |
| Summerland, B.C. | E8 | 69 |
| Summerland Key, Fl., U.S. | H5 | 86 |
| Summers, co., W.V., U.S. | D4 | 125 |
| Summer Shade, Ky., U.S. | D4 | 94 |
| Summerside, P.E.I. | C6 | 71 |
| Summersville, Ky., U.S. | C4 | 94 |
| Summersville, Mo., U.S. | D6 | 102 |
| Summersville, W.V., U.S. | C4 | 125 |
| Summersville Lake, res., W.V., U.S. | C4 | 125 |
| Summerton, S.C., U.S. | D7 | 117 |
| Summertown, Ga., U.S. | D4 | 87 |
| Summertown, Tn., U.S. | B4 | 119 |
| Summerville, Ga., U.S. | B1 | 87 |
| Summerville, Or., U.S. | B8 | 114 |
| Summerville, Pa., U.S. | D3 | 115 |
| Summerville, S.C., U.S. | E7 | 117 |
| Summit, Ar., U.S. | A3 | 81 |
| Summit, Il., U.S. | k9 | 90 |
| Summit, Ms., U.S. | D3 | 101 |
| Summit, N.J., U.S. | B4 | 107 |
| Summit, R.I., U.S. | D2 | 116 |
| Summit, Tn., U.S. | h11 | 119 |
| Summit, Ut., U.S. | F3 | 121 |
| Summit, co., Co., U.S. | B4 | 83 |
| Summit, co., Oh., U.S. | A4 | 112 |
| Summit, co., Ut., U.S. | C5 | 121 |
| Summit, mtn., N.Z. | N16 | 51 |
| Summit Hill, Pa., U.S. | E10 | 115 |
| Summit Lake, B.C. | B6 | 69 |
| Summit Lake, l., Ia., U.S. | C3 | 92 |
| Summit Lake Indian Reservation, Nv., U.S. | B2 | 105 |
| Summit Mountain, mtn., Nv., U.S. | D5 | 105 |
| Summit Peak, mtn., Co., U.S. | D4 | 83 |
| Summit Point, W.V., U.S. | B7 | 125 |
| Summit Station, Oh., U.S. | k11 | 112 |
| Summitville, Co., U.S. | D4 | 83 |
| Summitville, In., U.S. | D6 | 91 |
| Summitville, Tn., U.S. | D8 | 119 |
| Summum, Il., U.S. | C3 | 90 |
| Sumner, Ga., U.S. | E3 | 87 |
| Sumner, Il., U.S. | E6 | 90 |
| Sumner, Ia., U.S. | B5 | 92 |
| Sumner, Ms., U.S. | B3 | 101 |
| Sumner, Mo., U.S. | B4 | 102 |
| Sumner, Ne., U.S. | D6 | 104 |
| Sumner, Ok., U.S. | A4 | 113 |
| Sumner, Wa., U.S. | B3 | 124 |
| Sumner, co., Ks., U.S. | E6 | 93 |
| Sumner, co., Tn., U.S. | A5 | 119 |
| Sumner Lake, res., N.M., U.S. | C5 | 108 |
| Sumner Strait, strt., Ak., U.S. | m23 | 79 |
| Sumoto, Japan | I7 | 33 |
| Šumperk, Czech. | D4 | 26 |
| Sumpter, Or., U.S. | C8 | 114 |
| Sumrall, Ms., U.S. | D4 | 101 |
| Sumter, Ga., U.S. | E2 | 87 |
| Sumter, S.C., U.S. | D7 | 117 |
| Sumter, co., Al., U.S. | C1 | 78 |
| Sumter, co., Fl., U.S. | D4 | 86 |
| Sumter, co., Ga., U.S. | D2 | 87 |
| Sumter, co., S.C., U.S. | D7 | 117 |
| Sumterville, Al., U.S. | C1 | 78 |
| Sumy, Sov. Un. | D6 | 29 |
| Sun, La., U.S. | D6 | 95 |
| Sun, stm., Mt., U.S. | C4 | 103 |
| Sunapee, N.H., U.S. | D2 | 106 |
| Sunapee Lake, l., N.H., U.S. | D2 | 106 |
| Sunapee Mountain, mtn., N.H., U.S. | D2 | 106 |
| Sunart, Loch, in., Scot., U.K. | D3 | 13 |
| Sunbright, Tn., U.S. | C9 | 119 |
| Sunburg, Mn., U.S. | E3 | 100 |
| Sunburst, Mt., U.S. | B5 | 103 |
| Sunbury, N.C., U.S. | A6 | 110 |
| Sunbury, Oh., U.S. | B3 | 112 |
| Sunbury, Pa., U.S. | E8 | 115 |
| Sunbury, co., N.B. | D3 | 71 |
| Sunchales, Arg. | A4 | 54 |
| Suncho Corral, Arg. | E3 | 55 |
| Sunchon, N. Kor. | G2 | 33 |
| Sunchon, S. Kor. | I3 | 33 |
| Sun City, Az., U.S. | k8 | 80 |
| Sun City, Ca., U.S. | *F5 | 82 |
| Sun City, Fl., U.S. | p10 | 86 |
| Sun City, Ks., U.S. | E5 | 93 |
| Sun City Center, Fl., U.S. | *E4 | 86 |
| Suncook, N.H., U.S. | D4 | 106 |
| Suncook, stm., N.H., U.S. | D4 | 106 |
| Suncook Lakes, l., N.H., U.S. | D4 | 106 |
| Sundance, Wy., U.S. | B8 | 127 |
| Sundance Mountain, mtn., Wy., U.S. | B8 | 127 |
| Sundarbans, reg., Asia | D8 | 36 |
| Sunda Strait, strt., Indon. | G3 | 34 |
| Sunday Strait, strt., Austl. | C3 | 50 |
| Sundbyberg, Swe. | t35 | 14 |
| Sunderland, Ont. | C5 | 73 |
| Sunderland, Eng., U.K. | C6 | 10 |
| Sunderland, Md., U.S. | C4 | 97 |
| Sunderland, Ma., U.S. | B2 | 98 |
| Sunderland, Vt., U.S. | E2 | 122 |
| Sundown, Man. | E3 | 70 |
| Sundown, Tx., U.S. | C1 | 120 |
| Sundre, Alta. | D3 | 68 |
| Sundridge, Ont. | B5 | 73 |
| Sunds, Den. | B3 | 15 |
| Sundsvall, Swe. | F7 | 14 |
| Sunfield, Mi., U.S. | F5 | 99 |
| Sunflower, Ms., U.S. | B3 | 101 |
| Sunflower, co., Ms., U.S. | B3 | 101 |
| Sunflower, Mount, mtn., Ks., U.S. | C2 | 93 |
| Sungaiguntung, Indon. | E2 | 34 |
| Sungaipenuh, Indon. | F2 | 34 |
| Sungai Petani, Malay. | J4 | 35 |
| Sungari Reservoir see, China | E3 | 33 |
| Sungari see Songhua Jiang, stm., China | B10 | 31 |
| Sungurlu, Tur. | B10 | 40 |
| Sunland Park, N.M., U.S. | F3 | 108 |
| Sunlight Creek, stm., Wy., U.S. | B3 | 127 |
| Sunman, In., U.S. | F7 | 91 |
| Sunne, Swe. | H5 | 14 |
| Sunnybrae, N.S. | D7 | 71 |
| Sunnybrook, Alta. | C4 | 68 |
| Sunny Isles, Fl., U.S. | *G6 | 86 |
| Sunnyland, Fl., U.S. | q11 | 86 |
| Sunnymead, Ca., U.S. | *F5 | 82 |
| Sunnynook, Alta. | D5 | 68 |
| Sunnyside, Newf. | E5 | 72 |
| Sunnyside, Ca., U.S. | h9 | 82 |
| Sunnyside, Fl., U.S. | u16 | 86 |
| Sunnyside, Ut., U.S. | D5 | 121 |
| Sunnyside, Wa., U.S. | C5 | 124 |
| Sunny South, Al., U.S. | D2 | 78 |
| Sunnyvale, Ca., U.S. | k8 | 82 |
| Sunnyvale, Tx., U.S. | n10 | 120 |
| Sunol, Ca., U.S. | h9 | 82 |
| Sunol, Ne., U.S. | C3 | 104 |
| Sun Prairie, Wi., U.S. | E4 | 126 |
| Sunray, Ok., U.S. | C4 | 113 |
| Sunray, Tx., U.S. | A2 | 120 |
| Sunrise, Fl., U.S. | *r13 | 86 |
| Sunrise, Wy., U.S. | D8 | 127 |
| Sunrise Manor, Nv., U.S. | G6 | 105 |
| Sunrise Mountain, mtn., N.J., U.S. | A3 | 107 |
| Sun River, Mt., U.S. | C5 | 103 |
| Sunset, Fl., U.S. | *G6 | 86 |
| Sunset, La., U.S. | D3 | 95 |
| Sunset, Me., U.S. | D4 | 96 |
| Sunset, Tx., U.S. | C4 | 120 |
| Sunset, Ut., U.S. | B4 | 121 |
| Sunset Beach, Hi., U.S. | f9 | 88 |
| Sunset Crater National Monument, Az., U.S. | B4 | 80 |
| Sunset Hill, hill, Ct., U.S. | k9 | 90 |
| Sunset Lake, l., Vt., U.S. | D2 | 122 |
| Sunset Park, Ut., U.S. | *G2 | 121 |
| Sunshine, Austl. | *G7 | 50 |
| Sunshine, Ak., U.S. | f16 | 79 |
| Sunshine, Me., U.S. | D4 | 96 |
| Sunspot, N.M., U.S. | E4 | 108 |
| Suntar, Sov. Un. | C14 | 29 |
| Suntaug Lake, l., Ma., U.S. | f11 | 98 |
| Suntrana, Ak., U.S. | C10 | 79 |
| Sun Valley, Id., U.S. | F4 | 89 |
| Sun Valley, Nv., U.S. | D2 | 105 |
| Sunyani, Ghana | E4 | 45 |
| Suo Sea, Japan | J5 | 33 |
| Suoyarvi, Sov. Un. | F15 | 14 |
| Superb, Sask. | F1 | 75 |
| Superior, Co., U.S. | B5 | 83 |
| Superior, Ia., U.S. | A3 | 92 |
| Superior, Mt., U.S. | C2 | 103 |
| Superior, Ne., U.S. | D7 | 104 |
| Superior, Wi., U.S. | B1 | 126 |
| Superior, Wy., U.S. | E4 | 127 |
| Superior, Lake, l., N.A. | A10 | 76 |
| Superstition Mountains, mts., Az., U.S. | m10 | 80 |
| Suphan Buri, Thai. | E4 | 35 |
| Supi Oidak, Az., U.S. | F4 | 80 |
| Supply, N.C., U.S. | C4 | 110 |
| Supreme, La., U.S. | k9 | 95 |
| Supung Reservoir, res., Asia | F2 | 33 |
| Sūq ash Shuyūkh, Iraq | F3 | 39 |
| Suquamish, Wa., U.S. | B3 | 124 |
| Sur, Point, c., Ca., U.S. | D3 | 82 |
| Sur, stm., Sov. Un. | D16 | 27 |
| Surabaya, Indon. | G4 | 34 |
| Surakarta, Indon. | G4 | 34 |
| Surakhany, Sov. Un. | E4 | 28 |
| Surany, Czech. | D5 | 26 |
| Surat, Austl. | C7 | 51 |
| Surat, India | D5 | 36 |
| Sūratgarh, India | C4 | 37 |
| Surat Thani, Thai. | D1 | 34 |
| Surazh, Sov. Un. | E9 | 27 |
| Surco, Peru | *D2 | 58 |
| Surendranagar, India | F3 | 37 |
| Suresnes, Fr. | g9 | 16 |
| Suretka, C.R. | F6 | 62 |
| Surettes Island, N.S. | F4 | 71 |
| Surf City, N.J., U.S. | D4 | 107 |
| Surfside, Fl., U.S. | s13 | 86 |
| Surfside Beach, S.C., U.S. | D10 | 117 |
| Surgères, Fr. | D3 | 16 |
| Surgoinsville, Tn., U.S. | C11 | 119 |
| Surgut, Sov. Un. | C4 | 28 |
| Surgut, Sov. Un. | C10 | 29 |
| Suriāpet, India | I7 | 37 |
| Suribachi, Mount, hill, Japan | P17 | 52 |
| Surigao, Phil. | D7 | 34 |
| Suriname, dept., Sur. | A3 | 59 |
| Suriname, ctry., S.A. | B3 | 59 |
| Suring, Wi., U.S. | D5 | 126 |
| Surkhan Darya, stm., Sov. Un. | C13 | 39 |
| Surprise, Az., U.S. | k8 | 80 |
| Surprise, Ne., U.S. | C8 | 104 |
| Surquillo, Peru | *D2 | 58 |
| Surrency, Ga., U.S. | E4 | 87 |
| Surrey, N.D., U.S. | A4 | 111 |
| Surrey, co., Eng., U.K. | C7 | 12 |
| Surry, Me., U.S. | D4 | 96 |
| Surry, Va., U.S. | C6 | 123 |
| Surry, co., N.C., U.S. | A2 | 110 |
| Surry, co., Va., U.S. | C6 | 123 |
| Surry Mountain Lake, res., N.H., U.S. | D2 | 106 |
| Sursee, Switz. | B5 | 21 |
| Surt, Libya | C3 | 43 |
| Sürüç, Tur. | D12 | 40 |
| Suruga Bay, b., Japan | o17 | 33 |
| Susa, Italy | B1 | 23 |
| Susaki, Japan | J6 | 33 |
| Sušac, i., Yugo. | D3 | 24 |
| Sušak (part of Rijeka), Yugo. | C2 | 24 |
| Susak, i., Yugo. | C2 | 24 |
| Susanino, Sov. Un. | s31 | 14 |
| Susank, Ks., U.S. | D5 | 93 |
| Susanville, Ca., U.S. | B3 | 82 |
| Sušice, Czech. | D2 | 26 |
| Susitna, stm., Ak., U.S. | C10 | 79 |
| Susoh, Indon. | K2 | 35 |
| Susong, China | I7 | 32 |
| Susquehanna, Pa., U.S. | C10 | 115 |
| Susquehanna, co., Pa., U.S. | C10 | 115 |
| Susquehanna, stm., U.S. | A5 | 97 |
| Susquehanna, West Branch, stm., Pa., U.S. | D5 | 115 |
| Susques, Arg. | D2 | 54 |
| Sussex, N.B. | D4 | 71 |
| Sussex, N.J., U.S. | A3 | 107 |
| Sussex, Wi., U.S. | m11 | 126 |
| Sussex, co., De., U.S. | F4 | 85 |
| Sussex, co., N.J., U.S. | A3 | 107 |
| Sussex, co., Va., U.S. | D5 | 123 |
| Sussex Shores, De., U.S. | F5 | 85 |
| Sustut, stm., B.C. | A4 | 69 |
| Susulatna, Tur. | C7 | 40 |
| Sutcliffe, Nv., U.S. | D2 | 105 |
| Sutherland, Ia., U.S. | B2 | 92 |
| Sutherland, S. Afr. | D4 | 49 |
| Sutherland, Ut., U.S. | D3 | 121 |
| Sutherland Springs, Tx., U.S. | k7 | 120 |
| Sutlej (Langqên Zangbo), stm., Asia | B6 | 36 |
| Sutter, co., Ca., U.S. | C3 | 82 |
| Sutter Creek, Ca., U.S. | C3 | 82 |
| Suttle, Ut., U.S. | C2 | 78 |
| Sutton, Que. | D5 | 74 |
| Sutton, Ak., U.S. | g17 | 79 |
| Sutton, Ma., U.S. | B4 | 98 |
| Sutton, Ne., U.S. | D8 | 104 |
| Sutton, N.H., U.S. | D3 | 106 |
| Sutton, Vt., U.S. | B4 | 122 |
| Sutton, W.V., U.S. | C4 | 125 |
| Sutton, co., Tx., U.S. | D2 | 120 |
| Sutton Coldfield, Eng., U.K. | B6 | 12 |
| Sutton in Ashfield, Eng., U.K. | B6 | 10 |
| Sutton Lake, res., W.V., U.S. | C4 | 125 |
| Suttons Bay, Mi., U.S. | D5 | 99 |
| Sutton, Pa., N.J., U.S. | C4 | 113 |
| Suttsu, Japan | E10 | 33 |
| Sutwik Island, i., Ak., U.S. | D8 | 79 |
| Suva, Fiji | I15 | 52 |
| Suva Harbour, b., Fiji | I15 | 52 |
| Suwa, Japan | m17 | 33 |
| Suwałki, Pol. | A6 | 26 |
| Suwanee, Ga., U.S. | B2 | 87 |
| Suwannee, co., Fl., U.S. | B3 | 86 |
| Suwannee, stm., U.S. | C3 | 86 |
| Suwannee Lake, l., Man. | A1 | 70 |
| Suwannee Sound, strt., Fl., U.S. | C3 | 86 |
| Suwanose, i., Japan | L4 | 33 |
| Suwayliḥ, Jord. | B7 | 41 |
| Suwaylimah, Thamilat, well, Eg. | D6 | 41 |
| Suwaymah, Jord. | D4 | 41 |
| Suwŏn, S. Kor. | H3 | 33 |
| Suxian, China | H7 | 32 |
| Suyo, Peru | B1 | 58 |
| Suzhou, China | E9 | 31 |
| Suzu, Cape, c., Japan | H8 | 33 |
| Suzuka, Japan | o15 | 33 |
| Suzzara, Italy | E6 | 20 |
| Svalbard, ter., Nor. | B13 | 128 |
| Svalöv, Swe. | C3 | 15 |
| Svaneke, Den. | C8 | 15 |
| Svärtagård, Swe. | u35 | 14 |
| Svartån, stm., Swe. | t34 | 14 |
| Svatovo, Sov. Un. | G12 | 27 |
| Svay Rieng, Camb. | C3 | 34 |
| Svedala, Swe. | C7 | 15 |
| Svedrup i., Sov. Un. | B7 | 128 |
| Sveg, Swe. | F6 | 14 |
| Svendborg, Den. | C4 | 15 |
| Svene, Nor. | p27 | 14 |
| Svenljunga, Swe. | A7 | 15 |
| Svensen, Or., U.S. | A3 | 114 |
| Svenstrup, Den. | B3 | 15 |
| Sverdlovsk, Sov. Un. | q22 | 27 |
| Sverdlovsk, Sov. Un. | D9 | 29 |
| Sverdrup Islands, is., N.W. Ter. | B13 | 66 |
| Svetlaya, Sov. Un. | C9 | 33 |
| Svetlograd, Sov. Un. | I14 | 27 |
| Svicha, stm., Sov. Un. | D8 | 27 |
| Svilajnac, Yugo. | C5 | 24 |
| Svilengrad, Bul. | E8 | 24 |
| Svindal, Nor. | p29 | 14 |
| Svinninge, Den. | C5 | 15 |
| Svir, stm., Sov. Un. | A10 | 27 |
| Svirstroy, Sov. Un. | A9 | 27 |
| Svishtov, Bul. | D7 | 24 |
| Svitavy, Czech. | D4 | 26 |
| Svobodnyy, Sov. Un. | B8 | 31 |
| Svobodnyy, Cape, c., Sov. Un. | C11 | 33 |
| Svyatoy Nos, Cape, c., Sov. Un. | B16 | 29 |
| Swadlincote, Eng., U.K. | B6 | 12 |
| Swaffham, Eng., U.K. | B8 | 12 |
| Swain, co., N.C., U.S. | f9 | 110 |
| Swain Mountain, mtn., Ar., U.S. | A2 | 81 |
| Swain Reefs, rf., Austl. | D9 | 50 |
| Swainsboro, Ga., U.S. | D4 | 87 |
| Swakopmund, Nmb. | B1 | 49 |
| Swale, stm., Eng., U.K. | C6 | 10 |
| Swaledale, Ia., U.S. | B4 | 92 |
| Swalwell, Alta. | D4 | 68 |
| Swampscott, Ma., U.S. | B6 | 98 |
| Swan, i., Al., U.S. | B3 | 68 |
| Swan, stm., Alta. | B3 | 68 |
| Swan, stm., Can. | C1 | 70 |
| Swan Creek, Il., U.S. | C3 | 90 |
| Swan Creek, Ut., U.S. | B4 | 121 |
| Swan Creek, stm., Oh., U.S. | e6 | 112 |
| Swandale, W.V., U.S. | m14 | 125 |
| Swan Hill, Austl. | G7 | 50 |
| Swan Hills, Alta. | B3 | 68 |
| Swan Hills, hills, Alta. | B3 | 68 |
| Swanington, In., U.S. | C3 | 91 |
| Swan Lake, Man. | E2 | 70 |
| Swanlake, Id., U.S. | G6 | 89 |
| Swan Lake, l., Man. | B3 | 101 |
| Swan Lake, l., Man. | C1 | 70 |
| Swan Lake, l., Me., U.S. | D4 | 96 |
| Swan Lake, l., Ne., U.S. | C3 | 104 |
| Swanley, Eng., U.K. | C7 | 12 |
| Swannanoa, N.C., U.S. | f10 | 110 |
| Swan Peak, mtn., Mt., U.S. | C3 | 103 |
| Swanquarter, N.C., U.S. | B6 | 110 |
| Swan Range, mts., Mt., U.S. | C3 | 103 |
| Swan River, Man. | C1 | 70 |
| Swansboro, N.C., U.S. | C5 | 110 |
| Swansea, Wales, U.K. | J9 | 12 |
| Swansea, Il., U.S. | E4 | 90 |
| Swansea, Ma., U.S. | C5 | 98 |
| Swansea, S.C., U.S. | D5 | 117 |
| Swansea Bay, b., Wales, U.K. | C4 | 12 |
| Swansea Center, N.H., U.S. | C2 | 98 |
| Swans Island, Me., U.S. | D4 | 96 |
| Swanson, Sask. | F2 | 75 |
| Swanson Lake, res., Ne., U.S. | D4 | 104 |
| Swanton, Md., U.S. | m12 | 97 |
| Swanton, Oh., U.S. | A2 | 112 |
| Swanton, Vt., U.S. | B2 | 122 |
| Swan Valley, Id., U.S. | F7 | 89 |
| Swanville, Mn., U.S. | E4 | 100 |
| Swanwick, Eng., U.K. | B6 | 10 |
| Swanwyck Estates, De., U.S. | *B3 | 85 |
| Swanzey Center, N.H., U.S. | E2 | 106 |
| Swarthmore, Pa., U.S. | p20 | 115 |
| Swartswood, N.J., U.S. | A3 | 107 |
| Swartswood Lake, l., N.J., U.S. | A3 | 107 |
| Swartz, La., U.S. | B4 | 95 |
| Swartz Creek, Mi., U.S. | F7 | 99 |
| Swatara, Mn., U.S. | D5 | 100 |
| Swatara Township, Pa., U.S. | *F8 | 115 |
| Swatow see Shantou, China | G8 | 31 |
| Swayzee, In., U.S. | C6 | 91 |
| Swaziland, ctry., Afr. | D5 | 49 |
| Swea City, Ia., U.S. | A3 | 92 |
| Sweatman, Ms., U.S. | B4 | 101 |
| Swedeborg, Mo., U.S. | D5 | 102 |
| Sweden, ctry., Eur. | F6 | 14 |
| Swedesboro, N.J., U.S. | D2 | 107 |
| Swedesburg, Ia., U.S. | C6 | 92 |
| Sweeny, Tx., U.S. | r14 | 120 |
| Sweet, Id., U.S. | F2 | 89 |
| Sweet Briar, Va., U.S. | C3 | 123 |
| Sweetgrass, Mt., U.S. | B5 | 103 |
| Sweet Grass, co., Mt., U.S. | E7 | 103 |
| Sweet Home, Ar., U.S. | C3 | 81 |
| Sweet Home, Or., U.S. | C4 | 114 |
| Sweet Home, Tx., U.S. | E4 | 120 |
| Sweetser, In., U.S. | C6 | 91 |
| Sweet Springs, Mo., U.S. | C4 | 102 |
| Sweet Springs, W.V., U.S. | D4 | 125 |
| Sweetwater, Fl., U.S. | *s13 | 86 |
| Sweetwater, Ok., U.S. | B2 | 113 |
| Sweetwater, Tn., U.S. | D9 | 119 |
| Sweetwater, co., Wy., U.S. | E3 | 127 |
| Sweetwater Creek, Fl., U.S. | p10 | 86 |
| Sweetwater Creek, stm., U.S. | B1 | 113 |
| Sweetwater Station, Wy., U.S. | D4 | 127 |
| Swellendam, S. Afr. | D3 | 49 |
| Swenson, Tx., U.S. | C2 | 120 |
| Swepsonville, N.C., U.S. | A3 | 110 |
| Świdnica, Pol. | C4 | 26 |
| Świdwin, Pol. | B3 | 26 |
| Świebodzice, Pol. | C3 | 26 |
| Świebodzin, Pol. | B3 | 26 |
| Świecie, Pol. | B5 | 26 |
| Świętokrzyskie, Góry, mts., Pol. | C5 | 26 |
| Swift, Mn., U.S. | B3 | 100 |
| Swift, co., Mn., U.S. | E3 | 100 |
| Swift, stm., N.H., U.S. | B4 | 106 |
| Swift Creek, stm., N.C., U.S. | B5 | 110 |
| Swift Creek, stm., Va., U.S. | n17 | 123 |
| Swift Creek Reservoir, res., Wa., U.S. | C3 | 124 |
| Swift Current, Sask. | G2 | 75 |
| Swiftcurrent Creek, stm., Sask. | H1 | 75 |
| Swift Diamond, stm., N.H., U.S. | g7 | 106 |
| Swifton, Ar., U.S. | B4 | 81 |
| Swiftown, Ms., U.S. | B3 | 101 |
| Swiftwater, N.H., U.S. | B3 | 106 |
| Swilly, Lough, b., Ire. | B4 | 11 |
| Swinburne, Cape, c., N.W. Ter. | B13 | 66 |
| Swindle Island, i., B.C. | C3 | 69 |
| Swindon, Eng., U.K. | E6 | 10 |
| Swinford, Ire. | D3 | 11 |
| Swink, Co., U.S. | C7 | 83 |
| Swink, Ok., U.S. | C6 | 113 |
| Swinomish Indian Reservation, Wa., U.S. | A3 | 124 |
| Świnoujście, Pol. | B3 | 26 |
| Swisher, Ia., U.S. | C6 | 92 |
| Swisher, co., Tx., U.S. | B2 | 120 |
| Swiss, W.V., U.S. | C3 | 125 |
| Swisshome, Or., U.S. | C3 | 114 |
| Swissvale, Pa., U.S. | I14 | 115 |
| Switz City, In., U.S. | F3 | 91 |
| Switzer, W.V., U.S. | D3 | 125 |
| Switzerland, Fl., U.S. | m8 | 86 |
| Switzerland, S.C., U.S. | C5 | 117 |
| Switzerland, co., In., U.S. | G7 | 91 |
| Switzerland, ctry., Eur. | E4 | 18 |
| Swords, Ire. | D5 | 11 |
| Swords, Ga., U.S. | C3 | 87 |
| Swoyerville, Pa., U.S. | D10 | 115 |
| Sycamore, Al., U.S. | B3 | 78 |
| Sycamore, Ga., U.S. | E3 | 87 |
| Sycamore, Il., U.S. | B5 | 90 |
| Sycamore, Ks., U.S. | E8 | 93 |
| Sycamore, Mo., U.S. | E5 | 102 |
| Sycamore, Oh., U.S. | B2 | 112 |
| Sycamore, S.C., U.S. | E5 | 117 |
| Sycamore Creek, stm., Tn., U.S. | A4 | 119 |
| Sycamore Creek, stm., W.V., U.S. | m13 | 125 |
| Sychevka, Sov. Un. | D10 | 27 |
| Syców, Pol. | C4 | 26 |
| Sydenham, Ont. | C8 | 73 |
| Sydney, Austl. | F9 | 50 |
| Sydney, N.S. | C9 | 71 |
| Sydney Mines, N.S. | C9 | 71 |
| Sykeston, N.D., U.S. | B6 | 111 |
| Sykesville, Md., U.S. | B4 | 97 |
| Sykesville, N.J., U.S. | C3 | 107 |
| Sykesville, Pa., U.S. | D4 | 115 |
| Syktyvkar, Sov. Un. | E2 | 70 |
| Sylacauga, Al., U.S. | B3 | 78 |
| Sylamore, Ar., U.S. | B3 | 81 |
| Sylhet, Bngl. | D9 | 36 |
| Sylling, Nor. | p28 | 14 |
| Sylt, i., W. Ger. | A4 | 18 |
| Sylva, N.C., U.S. | f9 | 110 |
| Sylvan, Pa., U.S. | G5 | 115 |
| Sylvan Grove, Ks., U.S. | C6 | 93 |
| Sylvan Hills, Pa., U.S. | h10 | 91 |
| Sylvania, Sask. | E3 | 75 |
| Sylvania, Al., U.S. | A4 | 78 |
| Sylvania, Ga., U.S. | D5 | 87 |
| Sylvania, Oh., U.S. | A2 | 112 |
| Sylvania, Pa., U.S. | C8 | 115 |
| Sylvan Lake, Alta. | C3 | 68 |
| Sylvan Lake, Mi., U.S. | o15 | 99 |
| Sylvan Lake, l., In., U.S. | B7 | 91 |
| Sylvan Pass, Wy., U.S. | B2 | 127 |
| Sylvarena, Ms., U.S. | C4 | 101 |
| Sylvester, Ga., U.S. | E3 | 87 |
| Sylvester, Tx., U.S. | C2 | 120 |
| Sylvester, Mount, hill, Newf. | D4 | 72 |
| Sylvia, Ks., U.S. | E5 | 93 |
| Sylvia, Tn., U.S. | A4 | 119 |
| Sym, stm., Sov. Un. | C26 | 8 |
| Symmes Creek, stm., Oh., U.S. | D3 | 112 |
| Symsonia, Ky., U.S. | f9 | 94 |
| Syosset, N.Y., U.S. | *E7 | 109 |
| Syracuse, In., U.S. | B6 | 91 |
| Syracuse, Ks., U.S. | E2 | 93 |
| Syracuse, Mo., U.S. | C5 | 102 |
| Syracuse, Ne., U.S. | D9 | 104 |
| Syracuse, N.Y., U.S. | B4 | 109 |
| Syracuse, Ut., U.S. | B3 | 121 |
| Syracuse see Siracusa, Italy | F5 | 23 |
| Syr Darya, stm., Sov. Un. | B9 | 39 |
| Syria, ctry., Asia | B3 | 38 |
| Syriam, Burma | F4 | 34 |
| Syrian Desert, des., Asia | B3 | 38 |
| Syros see Ermoúpolis, Grc. | D5 | 24 |
| Sysladobsis Lake, l., Me., U.S. | C4 | 96 |
| Sysola, Sov. Un. | C19 | 8 |
| Syurkum, Cape, c., Sov. Un. | A10 | 39 |
| Syzran, Sov. Un. | D7 | 29 |
| Szabadszállás, Hung. | B4 | 24 |
| Szamos (Someş), stm., Eur. | B6 | 24 |
| Szamotuły, Pol. | B4 | 26 |
| Szarvas, Hung. | B4 | 24 |
| Szczakowa (part of Jaworzno), Pol. | g10 | 27 |
| Szczebrzeszyn, Pol. | C7 | 26 |
| Szczecin (Stettin), Pol. | B3 | 26 |
| Szczecinek, Pol. | B4 | 26 |
| Szczuczyn, Pol. | B7 | 26 |
| Szczytno, Pol. | B6 | 26 |
| Szechwan see Sichuan, prov., China | E5 | 31 |
| Szeged, Hung. | B5 | 24 |
| Székesfehérvár, Hung. | B4 | 24 |
| Szekszárd, Hung. | B4 | 24 |
| Szentendre, Hung. | B4 | 24 |
| Szentes, Hung. | B5 | 24 |
| Szigetvár, Hung. | B3 | 24 |
| Szolnok, Hung. | B5 | 24 |
| Szombathely, Hung. | B3 | 24 |
| Szprotawa, Pol. | C3 | 26 |
| Sztum, Pol. | B5 | 26 |
| Szubin, Pol. | B4 | 26 |
| Szydłowiec, Pol. | C6 | 26 |
| Szymanów, Pol. | m12 | 26 |

**T**

| Taal, Phil. | p13 | 34 |
| Taal, Lake, l., Phil. | p13 | 34 |
| Tab, Iran | D3 | 91 |
| Tabar Islands, is., Pap. N. Gui. | h13 | 50 |
| Tabarka, Tun. | F2 | 23 |
| Tabas, Iran | E8 | 39 |
| Tabasco, state, Mex. | D6 | 63 |
| Tabas Masina, Iran | E10 | 39 |
| Tabatinga, Braz. | k7 | 56 |

| Name | Map Ref. | Page |
|---|---|---|

Tabayin, Burma — A1 35
Tabbys Peak, mtn., Ut., U.S. — C3 121
Tabelbala, Alg. — D4 44
Taber, Alta. — E4 68
Tabernacle, N.J., U.S. — D3 107
Tabernas, Spain — D4 22
Tabernash, Co., U.S. — B5 83
Taberville, Mo., U.S. — C4 102
Tabik Island, i., Marsh Is. — S17 52
Tabiona, Ut., U.S. — C5 121
Tabiteuea, Kir. — R18 52
Tabla, Cerro de la, mtn., P.R. — B3 65
Tablas, Cabo, c., Chile — A2 54
Tablas Island, i., Phil. — C6 34
Table Bay, b., Newf. — B3 72
Table Bay, b., S. Afr. — D2 49
Table Grove, Il., U.S. — C3 90
Table Head, c., Newf. — B4 72
Table Mountain, mtn., Newf. — E2 72
Table Mountain, mtn., Az., U.S. — E5 80
Table Rock, Ne., U.S. — D9 104
Table Rock Lake, res., U.S. — E4 102
Table Top, mtn., Az., U.S. — E3 80
Taboada, Spain — A2 22
Tábor, Czech. — D3 26
Tabor, Ia., U.S. — D2 92
Tabor, Mn., U.S. — B2 100
Tabor, S.D., U.S. — E8 118
Tabor, Mount, mtn., Isr. — B7 41
Tabora, Tan. — C5 48
Tabora, prov., Tan. — C5 48
Tabor City, N.C., U.S. — C4 110
Tabou, I.C. — F3 45
Tabrīz, Iran — B4 38
Tabuaeran Island (Fanning Island), atoll, Kir. — F12 6
Tabūk, Sau. Ar. — C3 38
Tabusintac, stm., N.B. — B4 71
Täby, Swe. — *H8 14
Tacámbaro de Codallos, Mex. — n13 63
Tacheng, China — B1 31
Tachie, B.C. — B5 69
Tachiiwa Point, c., Japan — P17 52
Tachikawa, Japan — n18 33
Táchira, state, Ven. — B3 60
Tachov, Czech. — D2 26
Tacloban, Phil. — C7 34
Tacna, Peru — E3 58
Tacna, Az., U.S. — E1 80
Tacna, dept., Peru — E3 58
Tacoma, Co., U.S. — D3 83
Tacoma, Wa., U.S. — B3 124
Taconic, Ct., U.S. — A2 84
Taconic Range, mts., U.S. — A1 98
Taconite, Mn., U.S. — C5 100
Tacoronte, Spain — m13 22
Tacuarembo, Ur. — E1 56
Tacuatí, Para. — D4 55
Tad, W.V., U.S. — m13 125
Tademaït, Plateau du, plat., Alg. — D5 44
Tadjoura, Dji. — C5 47
Tadoule Lake, l., Man. — f8 70
Tadoussac, Que. — A8 74
T'aebaek-Sanmaek, mts., Asia — H4 33
Taegu, S. Kor. — D10 31
Taejŏn, S. Kor. — D10 31
Tafalla, Spain — A5 22
Tafí Viejo, Arg. — E2 55
Tafo, Ghana — *E4 45
Taft, Ca., U.S. — E4 82
Taft, La., U.S. — k11 95
Taft, Ok., U.S. — B6 113
Taft, Tn., U.S. — B5 119
Taft, Tx., U.S. — F4 120
Taftan, Kūh-e, mtn., Iran — G10 39
Taftsville, Vt., U.S. — D4 122
Tafuna International Airport, Am. Sam. — G13 52
Taganrog, Sov. Un. — H12 27
Taganrog, Gulf of, b., Sov. Un. — H12 27
Tagaytay, Phil. — o13 34
Tagbilaran, Phil. — D6 34
Taghmon, Ire. — E5 11
Taghrīfat, Libya — D3 43
Tagliamento, stm., Italy — C8 20
Tagolo Point, c., Phil. — D6 34
Taguan Point, c., Guam — L10 52
Taguatinga, Braz. — D1 57
Tagus, N.D., U.S. — A4 111
Tagus (Tejo) (Tajo), stm., Eur. — C1 22
Tahan, mtn., Malay. — E2 34
Tahat, mtn., Alg. — E6 44
Tahgong, Puntan, c., N. Mar. Is. — D7 52
Tahiti, i., Fr. Poly. — H13 6
Tahlequah, Ok., U.S. — B7 113
Ṭaḥmā wa Minshāt 'Abd as Sayyid, Eg. — E3 41
Tahoe, Lake, l., U.S. — E1 105
Tahoe City, Ca., U.S. — C3 82
Tahoka, Tx., U.S. — C2 120
Taholah, Wa., U.S. — B1 124
Tahoma, Ca., U.S. — C3 82
Tahoua, Niger — D6 45
Tahquamenon, stm., Mi., U.S. — B5 99
Tahsis, B.C. — E4 69
Ṭaḥṭā, Eg. — C3 38
Tahtsa Lake, l., B.C. — C4 69
Tahtsa Peak, mtn., B.C. — C4 69
Tahuya, Wa., U.S. — B2 124
Taï, I.C. — A3 45
Tai'an, China — D10 32
Tai'an, China — F7 32
Taiban, N.M., U.S. — C5 108
Taibus Qi, China — D6 32
T'aichung, Tai. — G9 31
Taigu, China — F5 32
Taihape, N.Z. — M15 51
Taiho, Japan — N6 52
Tai Hu, l., China — E8 31
Tailai, China — A10 32
Tailem Bend, Austl. — G6 50
Tailevu Point, c., Fiji — H15 52
Tain, Scot., U.K. — B4 10
T'ainan, Tai. — G9 31
Taínaron, Ákra, c., Grc. — D4 40
Taining, China — K7 32
Taiobeiras, Braz. — B4 56
Taipei, Tai. — G9 31
Taiping, Malay. — E2 34
Taipu, Braz. — g6 57
Taira see Iwaki, Japan — H10 33
Taishun, China — K8 32
Taitao, Península de, pen., Chile — D2 54
T'aitung, Tai. — G9 31
Taivalkoski, Fin. — E13 14
Taiwan, ctry., Asia — G9 31
Taiwan Strait, strt., Asia — G8 31
Taiyiba, Isr. — B7 41
Taiyuan, China — D7 31

Taizhao, China — E3 31
Taizhou, China — H8 32
Ta'izz, Yemen — D4 38
Tajarhī, Libya — E2 43
Tajimi, Japan — I8 33
Tajique, N.M., U.S. — C3 108
Tajumulco, Volcán, vol., Guat. — C2 62
Tajuña, stm., Spain — B4 22
Tājūrā', Libya — C2 43
Tak, Thai. — B1 34
Takabanare Island, i., Japan — O6 52
Takahe, Mount, mtn., Ant. — B1 7
Takaka, N.Z. — N14 51
Takamatsu, Japan — E11 31
Takaoka, Japan — H8 33
Takapuna, N.Z. — L15 51
Takara Island, i., Japan — L4 33
Takasaki, Japan — H9 33
Takashippu, Japan — O5 52
Takatō, Japan — n17 33
Takatsuki, Japan — o14 33
Takaw, Burma — B3 35
Takayama, Japan — H8 33
Takefu, Japan — n15 33
Take Islands see Tok Islands, is., Asia — H5 33
Takengon, Indon. — J2 35
Tākestān, Iran — C4 39
Takev, Camb. — G6 35
Takhta-Bazar, Sov. Un. — D11 39
Takhtakupyr, Sov. Un. — E6 28
Takigawa, Japan — E10 33
Takijuq Lake, l., N.W. Ter. — C10 66
Takilma, Or., U.S. — E3 114
Takishiri Island, i., Japan — D10 33
Takla Lake, l., B.C. — B5 69
Taklamakan Shamo, des., China — F11 29
Takoma Park, Md., U.S. — f8 97
Takotna, Ak., U.S. — C8 79
Takpocha, Okso, mtn., N. Mar. Is. — D7 52
Taku, stm., N.A. — k23 79
Taku Pa, Thai. — H3 35
Taku Glacier, ice, Ak., U.S. — k22 79
Takut, Burma — A3 35
Talā, Eg. — D2 41
Tala, Mex. — m12 63
Tala, Ur. — E1 56
Talagante, Chile — A2 54
Talakan, Sov. Un. — B6 33
Talala, Ok., U.S. — A6 113
Talanga, Hond. — C4 62
Talara, Peru — B1 58
Talas, Sov. Un. — E8 28
Talasea, Pap. N. Gui. — k13 50
Talata Mafara, Nig. — D6 45
Talaud Islands, is., Indon. — E7 34
Talavera de la Reina, Spain — C3 22
Talawdī, Sud. — C3 47
Talbert, Ky., U.S. — C6 94
Talbot, In., U.S. — D3 91
Talbot, co., Ga., U.S. — D2 87
Talbot, co., Md., U.S. — C5 97
Talbot Island, i., Fl., U.S. — B5 86
Talbot Lake, l., Man. — B2 70
Talbotton, Ga., U.S. — D2 87
Talbragar, stm., Austl. — B6 51
Talca, Chile — B2 54
Talcahuano, Chile — B2 54
Tālcher, India — D8 36
Talco, Tx., U.S. — C5 120
Talcott, W.V., U.S. — D4 125
Talcottville, N.Y., U.S. — B5 109
Taldy-Kurgan, Sov. Un. — D9 28
Talent, Or., U.S. — E4 114
Talesh, Iran — C4 39
Taliabu, i., Indon. — F6 34
Taliaferro, co., Ga., U.S. — C4 87
Talica, Sov. Un. — B6 28
Talihina, Ok., U.S. — C6 113
Talim Island, i., Phil. — o13 34
Tali Post, Sud. — D3 47
Talisay, Phil. — o14 34
Talisheek, La., U.S. — D6 95
Talish Mountains, mts., Asia — B4 39
Talkeetna, Ak., U.S. — C10 79
Talkeetna Mountains, mts., Ak., U.S. — f17 79
Talkhā, Eg. — C3 41
Talking Rock, Ga., U.S. — B2 87
Tall, Isr. Occ. — g11 41
Talladega, Al., U.S. — B3 78
Talladega, co., Al., U.S. — B3 78
Talladega Mountain, mtn., Al., U.S. — B3 78
Talladega Springs, Al., U.S. — B3 78
Talla Bena, La., U.S. — B4 95
Tallahala Creek, stm., Ms., U.S. — D4 101
Tallahassee, Fl., U.S. — B2 86
Tallahatchie, co., Ms., U.S. — B3 101
Tallahatchie, stm., Ms., U.S. — B3 101
Tall al Abyaḍ, Syria — B3 38
Tallangatta, Austl. — H6 51
Tallapoosa, Ga., U.S. — C1 87
Tallapoosa, Mo., U.S. — E8 102
Tallapoosa, co., Al., U.S. — C4 78
Tallapoosa, stm., Al., U.S. — C3 78
Tallard, Fr. — E2 20
Tallassee, Al., U.S. — C4 78
Talleyville, De., U.S. — A3 85
Tall Kalakh, Syria — E11 40
Tallmadge, Oh., U.S. — A4 112
Tallow, Ire. — E3 11
Tallula, Il., U.S. — D4 90
Tallulah, La., U.S. — B4 95
Talmage, Sask. — H4 75
Talmage, Ks., U.S. — C6 93
Talmage, Ne., U.S. — D9 104
Talnoye, Sov. Un. — G8 27
Talofofo, Guam — M10 52
Talofofo Bay, b., Guam — M10 52
Taloga, Ok., U.S. — A3 113
Talon, Lake, l., Ont. — A5 73
Talowah, Ms., U.S. — D4 101
Talpa de Allende, Mex. — m11 63
Talsi, Sov. Un. — C4 27
Talsint, Chile — E1 55
Tama, Ia., U.S. — C5 92
Tama, co., Ia., U.S. — B5 92
Tamacuari, Pico, mtn., S.A. — C5 60
Tamaha, Ok., U.S. — B7 113
Tamale, Ghana — F4 45
Tamalpais, Mount, mtn., Ca., U.S. — h7 82

Tamalpais Valley, Ca., U.S. — *D2 82
Taman, Sov. Un. — I11 27
Tamana, Mount, hill, Trin. — O23 65
Tamanar, Mor. — C3 44
Tamano, Japan — I6 33
Tamaqua, Pa., U.S. — E10 115
Tamar, stm., Eng., U.K. — D3 12
Tamarac, Fl., U.S. — *r13 86
Tamarack, Mn., U.S. — D5 100
Tamarite [de Litera], Spain — B6 22
Tamaroa, Il., U.S. — E4 90
Tamassee, S.C., U.S. — B1 117
Tamaulipas, state, Mex. — C5 63
Tamazula de Gordiano, Mex. — n12 63
Tamazulapan [del Progreso], Mex. — o15 63
Tamazunchale, Mex. — C5 63
Tambach, Kenya — A6 48
Tambacounda, Sen. — D2 45
Tambaú, Braz. — k8 56
També, Braz. — C3 57
Tambelan Besar, i., Indon. — L7 35
Tambelan Islands, is., Indon. — E3 34
Tambo, Austl. — B6 51
Tambo, stm., Peru — E3 58
Tambo, stm., Peru — D3 58
Tambo Grande, Peru — B1 58
Tambohorano, Madag. — g8 49
Tambov, Sov. Un. — D7 29
Tambre, stm., Spain — A1 22
Tambura, Sud. — D2 47
Tamchaket, Maur. — C2 45
Tamdybulak, Sov. Un. — E6 28
Tame, Col. — B3 60
Tâmega, stm., Port. — B2 22
Tamel Aike, Arg. — D2 54
Tamenghest, Alg. — E5 44
Tamenghest, Oued, val., Alg. — E5 44
Tamgué, Massif du, mts., Gui. — D2 45
Tamiahua, Mex. — C5 63
Tamiahua, Laguna de, b., Mex. — C5 63
Tamiami, Fl., U.S. — *G6 86
Tamiami Canal, Fl., U.S. — G6 86
Tamil Nadu (Madras), state, India — G6 36
Tamina, Tx., U.S. — D5 120
Tamins, Switz. — C7 21
Tamiš, stm., Eur. — C5 24
Tam Ky, Viet. — E8 35
Tamms, Il., U.S. — F4 90
Tamo, Ar., U.S. — C4 81
Tamora, Ne., U.S. — D8 104
Tampa, Fl., U.S. — E4 86
Tampa, Ks., U.S. — D6 93
Tampa Bay, b., Fl., U.S. — E4 86
Tampere, Fin. — G10 14
Tampico, Mex. — C5 63
Tampico, Il., U.S. — B4 90
Tampico, In., U.S. — G6 91
Tams, W.V., U.S. — D3 125
Tamsagbulag, Mong. — B8 31
Tamshiyacu, Peru — B3 58
Tamuning, Guam — L10 52
Tamworth, Austl. — F9 50
Tamworth, Ont. — C8 73
Tamworth, Eng., U.K. — B6 12
Tamworth, N.H., U.S. — C4 106
Tana, Chile — C2 55
Tana, stm., Eur. — B12 14
Tana, stm., Kenya — B7 48
Tana, Lake, l., Eth. — C4 47
Tanabe, Japan — J7 33
Tanabi, Braz. — C3 56
Tanacross, Ak., U.S. — C11 79
Tanafjorden, Nor. — B13 14
Tanaga Island, i., Ak., U.S. — E4 79
Tanahbala, i., Indon. — F1 34
Tanahgrogot, Indon. — F5 34
Tanahmasa, i., Indon. — F1 34
Tanankpur, India — C8 37
Tanami, Austl. — C5 50
Tan An, Viet. — G7 35
Tanana, Ak., U.S. — B9 79
Tanana, stm., Ak., U.S. — C10 79
Tananarive see Antananarivo, Madag. — g9 49
Tanapag, N. Mar. Is. — D8 52
Tanapag, Lagunan, b., N. Mar. Is. — D7 52
Tanaro, stm., Italy — B2 23
Tanauanella, Italy — D2 23
Tanavuso Point, c., Fiji — H15 52
Tancheng, China — G8 32
Tanchŏn, N. Kor. — F3 33
Tancook Island, N.S. — E5 71
Tānda, India — C8 37
Tāndārei, Rom. — C4 24
Tandil, Arg. — D5 54
Tando Adam, Pak. — E2 37
Tandou Lake, l., Austl. — F3 51
Tanega Island, i., Japan — E11 31
Tanegashima Strait, strt., Japan — K5 33
Taney, co., Mo., U.S. — E4 102
Taneycomo, Lake, res., Mo., U.S. — E4 102
Taneytown, Md., U.S. — A3 97
Taneyville, Mo., U.S. — E4 102
Tanezrouft, des., Afr. — E4 44
Tanga, Tan. — B7 48
Tanga, prov., Tan. — B6 48
Tanganyika, Lake, l., Afr. — C4 48
Tangent, Or., U.S. — C3 114
Tangerhütte, E. Ger. — A6 19
Tangermünde, E. Ger. — B5 18
Tangier (Tanger), Mor. — B3 44
Tangier, Va., U.S. — C7 123
Tangier Island, i., Va., U.S. — C7 123
Tangier Sound, strt., Md., U.S. — D6 97
Tangipahoa, co., La., U.S. — D5 95
Tangipahoa, stm., La., U.S. — D5 95
Tanglewood, Fl., U.S. — *F5 86
Tangra Yumco, l., China — D8 31
Tangshan, China — D8 31
Tanguiéta, Benin — F5 45
Tanguisson Point, c., Guam — L10 52
Tangwang He, stm., China — B10 31
Tangyuan, China — B12 31
Taninges, Fr. — C2 20
Tanjore see Thanjāvūr, India — F5 36
Tanjung, Indon. — F5 34
Tanjungbalai, Indon. — E1 34
Tanjungkarang-Telukbetung, Indon. — G3 34

Tanjungpandan, Indon. — F3 34
Tanjungselor, Indon. — E5 34
Tānk, Pak. — B5 36
Tännäs, Swe. — F5 14
Tanner, Al., U.S. — A3 78
Tanner, W.V., U.S. — C4 125
Tanner, Mount, mtn., B.C. — E8 69
Tannersville, N.Y., U.S. — C6 109
Tannis Bugt, b., Den. — A4 15
Tannu-Ola Mountains, mts., Asia — A3 31
Tânout, Niger — C6 45
Tanpok, stm., Fr. Gu. — B4 59
Tanque Verde, Az., U.S. — E5 80
Tanța, Eg. — B3 38
Tantallon, Sask. — G5 75
Tantani, mtn., Peru — E3 58
Tantoyuca, Mex. — m14 63
Tanum (Tanumshede), Swe. — C5 14
Tanzania, ctry., Afr. — C5 48
Tao, i., Thai. — H3 35
Tao'an, China — B9 31
Tao'er He, stm., China — B9 31
Taopi, Mn., U.S. — G6 100
Taormina, Italy — C5 23
Taos, Mo., U.S. — C5 102
Taos, N.M., U.S. — A4 108
Taos, co., N.M., U.S. — A4 108
Taos Pueblo, N.M., U.S. — A4 108
Taoudenni, Mali — B4 45
Taoyuan, China — C2 55
Tapacarí, Bol. — C2 55
Tapachula, Mex. — E6 63
Tapaga, Cape, c., W. Sam. — G12 52
Tapajós, stm., Braz. — C3 59
Tapaktuan, Indon. — m11 34
Tapalquén, Arg. — B5 54
Tapanahony, stm., Sur. — B5 59
Tapanui, N.Z. — P12 51
Tapauá, Braz. — D2 59
Tapauá, stm., Braz. — D2 59
Tapejara, Braz. — D2 59
Taperoá, Braz. — h5 57
Tapeta, Lib. — E3 45
Tāpi, stm., India — D5 36
Tapirapé, stm., Braz. — E4 59
Tapoco, N.C., U.S. — f9 110
Tappahannock, Va., U.S. — C6 123
Tappan, N.Y., U.S. — g13 109
Tappan, Lake, res., N.J., U.S. — g9 107
Tappan, Lake, res., Oh., U.S. — B4 112
Tappen, N.D., U.S. — C6 111
Tapuaenuku, mtn., N.Z. — N14 51
Taputapu, Cape, c., Am. Sam. — G13 52
Taqâțu' Hayyâ, Sud. — B4 47
Taquara, Braz. — D2 56
Taquari, stm., Braz. — D2 56
Taquari, stm., Braz. — B1 56
Taquaritinga, Braz. — k7 56
Taquaritinga do Norte, Braz. — h5 57
Tar, stm., N.C., U.S. — B10 103
Tara, Ont. — C3 73
Tara, Sov. Un. — D10 29
Tara, stm., Sov. Un. — B9 29
Tara, stm., Yugo. — D4 24
Tara, Hill of, hist., Ire. — D5 11
Tarabai, Braz. — C2 56
Tara Hills, Ca., U.S. — *h8 82
Tarakan, Indon. — E5 34
Tarakliya, Sov. Un. — C9 24
Tarancón, Spain — B4 22
Taransay, i., Scot., U.K. — C1 13
Taranto, Italy — E6 23
Taranto, Gulf of, b., Italy — E6 23
Tarapacá, Col. — D4 60
Tarapacá, prov., Chile — C2 55
Tarapoto, Peru — B2 58
Tarare, Fr. — E6 16
Tarascon-sur-Ariège, Fr. — F8 16
Tarascon-sur-Rhône, Fr. — F6 16
Tarasp, Switz. — C7 21
Tarata, Bol. — C2 55
Tarata, Peru — E3 58
Tarauacá, Braz. — C3 58
Tarauacá, stm., Braz. — C3 58
Tarawa, atoll, Kir. — F10 6
Tarawera, N.Z. — M16 51
Tarazit, Massif de, mts., Niger — C6 45
Tarazona, Spain — B5 22
Tarazona [de la Mancha], Spain — C5 22
Tarbagatay Range, mts., Asia — D10 28
Tarbat Ness, c., Scot., U.K. — B5 10
Tarbela, Vt., U.S. — E3 122
Tarbert, Ire. — E2 11
Tarbert, Scot., U.K. — C2 13
Tarbes, Fr. — F4 16
Tarboro, Ga., U.S. — B5 87
Tarboro, N.C., U.S. — B5 110
Tarbū, Libya — D3 43
Tarcenay, Fr. — C7 20
Tarcento, Italy — C9 20
Taree, Austl. — F5 50
Tarentum, Pa., U.S. — E2 115
Tarfawi, Bi'r, well, Sud. — A3 47
Tarfaya, Mor. — D2 44
Tarfside, Scot., U.K. — D6 13
Targhee Pass, U.S. — F7 89
Tarhūnah, Libya — C2 43
Tarifa, Spain — D3 22
Tarifa, Point, c., Spain — D3 22
Tarija, Bol. — D3 55
Tarija, dept., Bol. — D3 55
Tarim, stm., China — E11 29
Tarim Pendi, des., China — E11 30
Tarkastad, S. Afr. — H5 49
Tarkiln, R.I., U.S. — B3 116
Tarkio, Mo., U.S. — A2 102
Tarko-Sale, Sov. Un. — C24 8
Tarkwa, Ghana — E4 45
Tarlac, Phil. — B6 34
Tarland, Scot., U.K. — C6 13
Tarlton, Oh., U.S. — C3 112
Tarm, Den. — C2 15
Tarma, Peru — D2 58
Tärn, stm., Fr. — F4 16
Tärnaby, Swe. — D8 14
Tarnobrzeg, Pol. — C5 26
Tarnopol, Sask. — E3 75
Tárnov, N.D., U.S. — B8 104
Tarnów, Pol. — C5 26
Tarnowskie Góry, Pol. — C5 26
Taro, stm., Italy — B2 23
Taroom, Austl. — E8 50
Taroudant, Mor. — D3 44
Tarp, W. Ger. — D3 15
Tarpey, Ca., U.S. — D4 82

Tarpley, Tx., U.S. — E3 120
Tarpon, co., Fl., U.S. — o10 86
Tarpon Springs, Fl., U.S. — D4 86
Tarqui, Peru — B2 58
Tarquinia, Italy — C3 23
Tarragona, Spain — B6 22
Tarrant, co., Tx., U.S. — C4 120
Tarrant City, Al., U.S. — B3 78
Tarrasa, Spain — B7 22
Tárrega, Spain — B6 22
Tarry, Ar., U.S. — C4 81
Tarryall Creek, stm., Co., U.S. — B5 83
Tarryall Mountains, mts., Co., U.S. — B5 83
Tarrytown, Fl., U.S. — D4 86
Tarrytown, Ga., U.S. — D4 87
Tarrytown, N.Y., U.S. — D7 109
Tårs, Den. — A4 15
Tarsus, Tur. — D10 40
Tartagal, Arg. — D3 55
Tartu, Sov. Un. — D5 29
Tartuguan Point, c., Guam — M10 52
Ṭarṭūs, Syria — E10 40
Țărut, i., Sau. Ar. — H5 39
Tarutung, Indon. — L3 35
Tarver, Ga., U.S. — F4 87
Tarves, Scot., U.K. — C6 13
Tasaral, Sov. Un. — D8 28
Tasāwah, Libya — D2 43
Taseko Lakes, l., B.C. — D6 69
Taseko Mountain, mtn., B.C. — D6 69
Tashauz, Sov. Un. — E6 28
Tashkent, Sov. Un. — E8 28
Tash-Kumyr, Sov. Un. — E9 28
Tasikmalaya, Indon. — G3 34
Tåsinge, i., Den. — I8 15
Taskan, Sov. Un. — B10 40
Taşköprü, Tur. — N14 51
Tasman Bay, b., N.Z. — o15 50
Tasmania, state, Austl. — o15 50
Tasman Peninsula, pen., Austl. — I9 6
Tasman Sea, Oc. — D9 119
Tasso, Tn., U.S. — H4 91
Taswell, In., U.S. — B4 24
Tata, Hung. — B4 24
Tatabánya, Hung. — D6 71
Tatamagouche, N.S. — D17 29
Tatarsk, Sov. Un. — D9 29
Tatar Strait, strt., Sov. Un. — F3 75
Tate, Sask. — B2 87
Tate, co., Ms., U.S. — A4 101
Tateville, Ky., U.S. — D5 94
Tateyama, Japan — I9 33
Tathlina Lake, l., N.W. Ter. — D9 66
Tatitlek, Ak., U.S. — C10 79
Tatla Lake, l., B.C. — D5 69
Tatlayoko Lake, B.C. — f9 70
Tatnam, Cape, c., Man. — D4 36
Tatta, Pak. — A7 12
Tattersall, Eng., U.K. — D4 87
Tattnall, co., Ga., U.S. — C3 56
Tatui, Braz. — D6 108
Tatum, N.M., U.S. — B5 117
Tatum, Tx., U.S. — A2 119
Tatumville, Tn., U.S. — C14 40
Tatvan, Tur. — C2 57
Tauá, Braz. — D4 56
Taubaté, Braz. — D4 19
Tauber, stm., W. Ger. — B7 19
Tauberbischofsheim, W. Ger. — C9 20
Taucha, E. Ger. — A4 101
Tauern Tunnel, Aus. — D3 11
Taughmaconnell, Ire. — D6 102
Taum Sauk Mountain, mtn., Mo., U.S. — C3 49
Taung, Boph. — D10 36
Taungdwingyi, Burma — D10 36
Taunggyi, Burma — E3 12
Taunton, Eng., U.K. — C5 98
Taunton, Ma., U.S. — F2 100
Taunton, Mn., U.S. — C5 98
Taunton, stm., Ma., U.S. — D3 107
Taunton Lakes, N.J., U.S. — C3 19
Taunus, mts., W. Ger. — D4 27
Taupo, Lake, l., N.Z. — L16 51
Tauragė, Sov. Un. — C4 74
Taureau, Réservoir, res., Que. — E6 23
Taurianova, Italy — C4 40
Taurus Mountains, mts., Tur. — B5 22
Tauste, Spain — D8 21
Tavannes, Switz. — D5 86
Tavares, Fl., U.S. — C4 40
Tavas, Tur. — D9 29
Tavda, Sov. Un. — D9 29
Tavda, stm., Sov. Un. — G7 86
Tavernier, Fl., U.S. — H16 52
Taveuni, i., Fiji — D2 22
Tavira, Port. — D3 73
Tavistock, Ont. — D5 12
Tavistock, Eng., U.K. — C9 28
Tavolzhan, Sov. Un. — F2 35
Tavoy, Point, c., Burma — C7 40
Tavşanlı, Tur. — D4 12
Tawe, stm., Eng., U.K. — C4 120
Tawakoni, Lake, res., Tx., U.S. — D7 99
Tawas City, Mi., U.S. — D7 99
Tawas Lake, l., Mi., U.S. — C4 68
Tawatinaw, Alta. — E5 34
Tawau, Malay. — C3 12
Tawe, stm., Wales, U.K. — D6 34
Tawitawi Group, is., Phil. — D6 34
Tawi-Tawi Island, i., Phil. — B4 47
Tawkar, Sud. — A3 11
Tawny, Ire. — C3 43
Tāwurghā', Libya — D5 63
Taxco de Alarcón, Mex. — B5 10
Tay, stm., Scot., U.K. — g7 96
Tay, Firth of, est., Scot., U.K. — B4 10
Tay, Loch, l., Scot., U.K. — B3 58
Tayabamba, Peru — f12 41
Tayasīr, Isr. Occ. — k9 126
Taycheedah, Wi., U.S. — B11 29
Tayga, Sov. Un. — A7 69
Taylor, B.C. — A6 80
Taylor, Az., U.S. — p15 99
Taylor, Mi., U.S. — C9 104
Taylor, Ne., U.S. — C6 111
Taylor, N.D., U.S. — D10 115
Taylor, Pa., U.S. — D4 120
Taylor, Tx., U.S. — D3 126
Taylor, Wi., U.S. — D2 87
Taylor, co., Fl., U.S. — B2 86
Taylor, co., Ga., U.S. — D2 92
Taylor, co., Ia., U.S. — C4 94
Taylor, co., Ky., U.S. — C3 120
Taylor, co., Tx., U.S. — B4 125
Taylor, co., W.V., U.S. — C3 126
Taylor, co., Wi., U.S. — B2 70
Taylor, stm., Man. — C4 83
Taylor, stm., Co., U.S. — O13 51
Taylor, Mount, mtn., N.Z. — B2 108
Taylor, Mount, mtn., N.M., U.S. — B2 108
Taylor Knob, hill, Tn., U.S. — B3 78
Taylor Mill, Ky., U.S. — k14 94
Taylor Mountain, mtn., Id., U.S. — E4 89
Taylor Park Reservoir, res., Co., U.S. — C4 83
Taylor Ridge, mtn., Ga., U.S. — B1 87
Taylors, S.C., U.S. — B3 117
Taylors Bridge, De., U.S. — C3 85
Taylors Falls, Mn., U.S. — E6 100
Taylors Island, Md., U.S. — D5 97
Taylors Island, i., Md., U.S. — D5 97
Taylorsport, Ky., U.S. — h13 94
Taylor Springs, Il., U.S. — D4 90
Taylorsville, Ga., U.S. — B2 87
Taylorsville, In., U.S. — F6 91
Taylorsville, Ky., U.S. — B4 94
Taylorsville, Ms., U.S. — D4 101
Taylorsville, N.C., U.S. — B1 110
Taylorsville, Ut., U.S. — *C4 121
Taylorville, Il., U.S. — D4 90
Taymā', Sau. Ar. — D7 43
Taymyr Lake, l., Sov. Un. — B13 29
Taymyr Peninsula, pen., Sov. Un. — B12 29
Tay Ninh, Viet. — G7 35
Tayport, Scot., U.K. — D6 13
Taytay, Phil. — D12 29
Taytsy, Sov. Un. — s31 14
Taz, stm., Sov. Un. — C11 29
Taza, Mor. — C4 44
Taz Bay, b., Sov. Un. — C7 128
Tazerbo, well, Libya — D4 43
Tazewell, Ga., U.S. — D2 87
Tazewell, Tn., U.S. — C10 119
Tazewell, Va., U.S. — e10 123
Tazewell, co., Il., U.S. — C4 90
Tazewell, co., Va., U.S. — e10 123
Tazrouk, Alg. — E6 44
Tbessa, Alg. — B6 44
Tbilisi, Sov. Un. — I7 29
Tchentlo Lake, l., B.C. — B5 69
Tchibanga, Gabon — F2 46
Tchien, Lib. — E3 45
Tchula, Ms., U.S. — B3 101
Tczew, Pol. — A5 26
Tea, S.D., U.S. — D9 118
Tea, stm., Braz. — D4 60
Teachey, N.C., U.S. — C4 110
Tea Creek, stm., Sask. — C2 75
Teague, Tx., U.S. — D4 120
Teakean Butte, mtn., Id., U.S. — C2 89
Te Anau, Lake, l., N.Z. — P11 51
Teaneck, N.J., U.S. — h8 107
Teangue, Scot., U.K. — D3 13
Teapa, Mex. — D6 63
Tearaght, i., Ire. — E1 11
Tearinbai, Kir. — R18 52
Teasdale, Ut., U.S. — E4 121
Teaticket, Ma., U.S. — C7 98
Tea Tree Gully, Austl. — *F6 50
Te Awamutu, N.Z. — M15 51
Tebbetts, Mo., U.S. — C6 102
Tebicuary, stm., Para. — E4 55
Tebingtinggi, Indon. — E1 34
Tecalitlán, Mex. — n12 63
Tecate, Mex. — D4 95
Teche, Bayou, stm., La., U.S. — C9 24
Techirghiol, Rom. — C2 54
Tecolotito, N.M., U.S. — m15 63
Tecolutla, stm., Mex. — m15 63
Tecomán, Mex. — D4 63
Tecopa, Ca., U.S. — E5 82
Tecpan de Galeana, Mex. — D4 63
Tecuala, Mex. — C8 24
Tecuci, Rom. — E2 73
Tecumseh, Ont. — E2 73
Tecumseh, Ks., U.S. — k14 93
Tecumseh, Mi., U.S. — D9 104
Tecumseh, Ne., U.S. — D9 104
Tecumseh, Mount, N.H., U.S. — C3 106
Tecumseh, Ok., U.S. — B5 113
Ted Geddaar Dabole, Som. — E5 47
Tedzhen, Sov. Un. — C10 39
Teec Nos Pos, Az., U.S. — A6 80
Teegarden, In., U.S. — B5 91
Tees, Alta. — C4 68
Tees, stm., Eng., U.K. — C6 12
Teeside see Middlesbrough, Eng., U.K. — C6 10
Teeswater, Ont. — C3 73
Tefé, Braz. — C2 59
Tefé, stm., Braz. — C2 59
Tefé, Lago de, l., Braz. — C2 59
Tefenni, Tur. — D3 40
Tefft, In., U.S. — B4 91
Tegal, Indon. — G3 34
Tegelen, Neth. — C6 17
Tegernsee, l., W. Ger. — D9 21
Teghra, India — C4 37
Teglio, Italy — D9 21
Tegucigalpa, Hond. — E7 63
Teguise, Spain — m15 22
Tehachapi, Ca., U.S. — E4 82
Tehachapi Mountains, mts., Ca., U.S. — E4 82
Tehama, co., Ca., U.S. — B2 82
Tehek Lake, l., N.W. Ter. — C13 66
Tehrān, Iran — B5 39
Tehuacán, Mex. — D5 63
Tehuantepec, Golfo de, b., Mex. — D6 63
Tehuitzingo, Mex. — n13 63
Teide, Pico de, mtn., Spain — m13 22
Teifi, stm., Wales, U.K. — B3 12
Teignmouth, Eng., U.K. — C8 103
Teiteirupuchi, i., Marsh Is. — S18 52
Tekamah, Ne., U.S. — C9 104
Tekapo, Lake, l., N.Z. — O13 51
Tekax de Álvaro Obregón, Mex. — C7 63
Tekeli, Sov. Un. — E9 28
Tekes, stm., Afr. — B6 47
Tekirdağ, Tur. — H10 40
Tekkali, India — C8 36
Tekoa, Wa., U.S. — B8 124
Tekonsha, Mi., U.S. — F5 99
Tekro, well, Chad — E4 47
Te Kuiti, N.Z. — M15 51
Tel, stm., India — H10 37
Tela, Hond. — D7 63

| Name | Map Ref. | Page |
|---|---|---|
| Telavi, Sov. Un. | E3 | 28 |
| Tel Aviv-Yafo (Tel Aviv-Jaffa), Isr. | B3 | 38 |
| Telde, Spain | m14 | 22 |
| Telegraph Creek, B.C. | m16 | 69 |
| Telén, Arg. | B3 | 54 |
| Teleneshty, Sov. Un. | B9 | 24 |
| Teleorman, hist. reg., Rom. | C7 | 24 |
| Telephone, Tx., U.S. | C4 | 120 |
| Télérthéba, Djebel, mtn., Alg. | E6 | 44 |
| Telescope Peak, mtn., Ca., U.S. | D5 | 82 |
| Telfair, co., Ga., U.S. | E4 | 87 |
| Telford, Eng., U.K. | B5 | 12 |
| Telford, Pa., U.S. | F11 | 115 |
| Telford, Tn., U.S. | C11 | 119 |
| Telfs, Aus. | B7 | 20 |
| Télimélé, Gui. | D2 | 45 |
| Telkwa, B.C. | B4 | 69 |
| Tell, Tx., U.S. | B2 | 120 |
| Tell City, In., U.S. | I4 | 91 |
| Teller, Ak., U.S. | B6 | 79 |
| Teller, co., Co., U.S. | C5 | 83 |
| Tellico Plains, Tn., U.S. | D9 | 119 |
| Telluride, Co., U.S. | D3 | 83 |
| Tel Mond, Isr. | B6 | 41 |
| Telogia, Fl., U.S. | B2 | 86 |
| Telok Anson (Teluk Intan), Malay. | E2 | 34 |
| Teloloapan, Mex. | D5 | 63 |
| Telos Lake, l., Me., U.S. | B3 | 96 |
| Telsen, Arg. | C3 | 54 |
| Tema, Ghana | E5 | 45 |
| Temax, Mex. | C7 | 63 |
| Tembo, Zaire | C2 | 48 |
| Temecula, Ca., U.S. | F5 | 82 |
| Temelli, Tur. | C8 | 40 |
| Temirtau, Sov. Un. | E26 | 8 |
| Temirtau, Sov. Un. | D10 | 29 |
| Témiscaming, Que. | G17 | 66 |
| Témiscouata, Que. | B9 | 74 |
| Témiscouata, Lac, l., Que. | B9 | 74 |
| Te-Moak Indian Reservation, Nv., U.S. | C6 | 105 |
| Temora, Austl. | G6 | 51 |
| Temósachic, Mex. | B3 | 63 |
| Tempe, Az., U.S. | D4 | 80 |
| Tempe Downs, Austl. | D5 | 50 |
| Temperance, Mi., U.S. | G7 | 99 |
| Temperance, stm., Mn., U.S. | C8 | 100 |
| Temperanceville, Va., U.S. | C7 | 123 |
| Tempio Pausania, Italy | D2 | 23 |
| Temple, Ga., U.S. | C1 | 87 |
| Temple, Mi., U.S. | D5 | 99 |
| Temple, N.H., U.S. | E3 | 106 |
| Temple, Ok., U.S. | C3 | 113 |
| Temple, Pa., U.S. | F10 | 115 |
| Temple, Tx., U.S. | D4 | 120 |
| Temple City, Ca., U.S. | *m12 | 82 |
| Temple Hill, Ky., U.S. | D4 | 94 |
| Templemore, Ire. | E4 | 11 |
| Temple Terrace, Fl., U.S. | o11 | 86 |
| Templeton, In., U.S. | C3 | 91 |
| Templeton, Ia., U.S. | C3 | 92 |
| Templeton, Ma., U.S. | A3 | 98 |
| Templeton, Pa., U.S. | E3 | 115 |
| Templeville, Md., U.S. | B6 | 97 |
| Templin, E. Ger. | B6 | 18 |
| Tempoal, stm., Mex. | m14 | 63 |
| Temryuk, Sov. Un. | I11 | 27 |
| Temuco, Chile | B2 | 54 |
| Temuka, N.Z. | P13 | 51 |
| Temwen, i., Micron. | Q17 | 52 |
| Tena, Ec. | B2 | 58 |
| Tenafly, N.J., U.S. | B5 | 107 |
| Tenaha, Tx., U.S. | D5 | 120 |
| Tenakee Springs, Ak., U.S. | D12 | 79 |
| Tenāli, India | *E7 | 36 |
| Tenancingo [de Degollado], Mex. | D5 | 63 |
| Tenango del Valle, Mex. | n14 | 63 |
| Tenant Mountain, mtn., N.Y., U.S. | B6 | 109 |
| Tenants Harbor, Me., U.S. | D3 | 96 |
| Tenasserim, Burma | F10 | 36 |
| Tenay, Fr. | E6 | 16 |
| Tenby, Wales, U.K. | C3 | 12 |
| Tendaho, Eth. | C5 | 47 |
| Tende, Fr. | E7 | 16 |
| Ten Degree Channel, strt., India | G9 | 36 |
| Tendoy, Id., U.S. | E5 | 89 |
| Tendre, Mont, mtn., Switz. | C2 | 20 |
| Ténéré, des., Niger | C7 | 45 |
| Tenerife, i., Spain | m13 | 22 |
| Ténès, Alg. | B5 | 44 |
| Teng, stm., Burma | B2 | 35 |
| Tengah Islands, is., Indon. | G5 | 34 |
| Tengchong, China | F4 | 31 |
| Tengiz, Lake, l., Sov. Un. | D9 | 29 |
| Tengxian, China | G7 | 32 |
| Tenino, Wa., U.S. | C3 | 124 |
| Tenke, Zaire | D4 | 48 |
| Tenkiller Ferry Lake, res., Ok., U.S. | B6 | 113 |
| Tenkodogo, Burkina | F5 | 45 |
| Ten Mile, Tn., U.S. | D9 | 119 |
| Tenmile, Ut., U.S. | B5 | 116 |
| Tenmile Creek, stm., W.V., U.S. | k10 | 125 |
| Ten Mile Lake, l., Newf. | C3 | 72 |
| Tenmile Lake, l., Mn., U.S. | D4 | 100 |
| Tennant, Ia., U.S. | C2 | 92 |
| Tennant Creek, Austl. | C5 | 50 |
| Tennent, N.J., U.S. | C4 | 107 |
| Tennessee, state, U.S. | B5 | 119 |
| Tennessee, stm., U.S. | D10 | 76 |
| Tennessee City, Tn., U.S. | A4 | 119 |
| Tennessee Pass, Co., U.S. | B4 | 83 |
| Tennessee Ridge, Tn., U.S. | A4 | 119 |
| Tennga, Ga., U.S. | B1 | 87 |
| Tennille, Ga., U.S. | D4 | 87 |
| Tennyson, In., U.S. | H3 | 91 |
| Tenosique [de Pino Suárez], Mex. | D6 | 63 |
| Tenryū, stm., Japan | n16 | 33 |
| Tensas, co., La., U.S. | B4 | 95 |
| Tensas, stm., La., U.S. | B4 | 95 |
| Tensaw, stm., Al., U.S. | E2 | 78 |
| Tensed, Id., U.S. | B2 | 89 |
| Ten Sleep, Wy., U.S. | B5 | 127 |
| Tenstrike, Mn., U.S. | C4 | 100 |
| Tenterfield, Austl. | E9 | 50 |
| Ten Thousand Islands, is., Fl., U.S. | G5 | 86 |
| Teocaltiche, Mex. | C4 | 63 |
| Teófilo Otoni, Braz. | E8 | 57 |
| Tepa, Indon. | G7 | 34 |
| Tepalcatepec, Mex. | n12 | 63 |
| Tepalcatepec, stm., Mex. | n12 | 63 |
| Tepatitlán [de Morelos], Mex. | C4 | 63 |
| Tepeji del Río, Mex. | n14 | 63 |
| Tepelena, Alb. | B2 | 25 |
| Tepepan (part of Mexico City), Mex. | h9 | 63 |
| Tepic, Mex. | C4 | 63 |
| Teplice, Czech. | C2 | 26 |
| Teplice, Czech. | C2 | 26 |
| Tepoca, Cabo, c., Mex. | A2 | 63 |
| Tequila, Mex. | m12 | 63 |
| Ter, stm., Spain | A7 | 22 |
| Téra, Niger | D5 | 45 |
| Teraina Island (Washington Island), i., Kir. | F12 | 6 |
| Teramo, Italy | C4 | 23 |
| Ter Apel, Neth. | B7 | 17 |
| Tercan, Tur. | C13 | 40 |
| Terceira, i., Port. | g9 | 44 |
| Tercero, stm., Arg. | A4 | 54 |
| Terebovlya, Sov. Un. | G5 | 27 |
| Terek, stm., Sov. Un. | G18 | 8 |
| Terek Pass, Sov. Un. | G23 | 8 |
| Terekty, Sov. Un. | D7 | 28 |
| Terence Bay, N.S. | E6 | 71 |
| Terenggau, state, Malay. | J5 | 35 |
| Terenos, Braz. | C2 | 56 |
| Teresina, Braz. | C2 | 57 |
| Teresópolis, Braz. | C4 | 56 |
| Terezník, Fr. | E3 | 17 |
| Terhune, In., U.S. | D5 | 91 |
| Teriberka, Sov. Un. | C16 | 14 |
| Terlingua, Tx., U.S. | D1 | 120 |
| Terlton, Ok., U.S. | A5 | 113 |
| Termez, Sov. Un. | F9 | 29 |
| Termini Imerese, Italy | F4 | 23 |
| Términos, Laguna de, b., Mex. | D6 | 63 |
| Termoli, Italy | C5 | 23 |
| Ternate, Indon. | E7 | 34 |
| Ternate, i., Indon. | E7 | 34 |
| Terneuzen, Neth. | B5 | 16 |
| Terney, Sov. Un. | D8 | 33 |
| Terni, Italy | C4 | 23 |
| Ternopol, Sov. Un. | G5 | 27 |
| Terpeniya Bay, b., Sov. Un. | B11 | 33 |
| Terpeniye, Cape, c., Sov. Un. | B12 | 33 |
| Terra Alta, W.V., U.S. | B5 | 125 |
| Terrace, B.C. | B3 | 69 |
| Terrace, Mn., U.S. | E3 | 100 |
| Terrace Bay, Ont. | G15 | 66 |
| Terracina, Italy | D4 | 23 |
| Terral, Ok., U.S. | D4 | 113 |
| Terra Nova, Newf. | D4 | 72 |
| Terra Nova National Park, Newf. | D4 | 72 |
| Terra Rica, Braz. | C2 | 56 |
| Terrasson, Fr. | G8 | 16 |
| Terrebonne, Bayou, stm., La., U.S. | k10 | 95 |
| Terrebonne, Que. | D4 | 74 |
| Terrebonne, co., La., U.S. | E5 | 95 |
| Terrebonne, co., Que. | C3 | 74 |
| Terrebonne, co., La., U.S. | E5 | 95 |
| Terrebonne Bay, b., La., U.S. | E5 | 95 |
| Terre Haute, In., U.S. | F3 | 91 |
| Terre Hill, Pa., U.S. | F9 | 115 |
| Terrell, N.C., U.S. | B2 | 110 |
| Terrell, Tx., U.S. | C4 | 120 |
| Terrell, co., Ga., U.S. | E2 | 87 |
| Terrell, co., Tx., U.S. | D1 | 120 |
| Terrell Hills, Tx., U.S. | k7 | 120 |
| Terrenceville, Newf. | E4 | 72 |
| Terri, Mont, mtn., Switz. | F6 | 89 |
| Terril, Ia., U.S. | A3 | 92 |
| Terror, Mount, mtn., Ant. | e38 | 7 |
| Terry, Ms., U.S. | C3 | 101 |
| Terry, Mt., U.S. | D11 | 103 |
| Terry, co., Tx., U.S. | C1 | 120 |
| Terry Peak, mtn., S.D., U.S. | C2 | 118 |
| Terrytown, Ne., U.S. | C2 | 104 |
| Terryville, Ct., U.S. | C3 | 84 |
| Terryville, N.Y., U.S. | *n15 | 109 |
| Tersakkan, stm., Sov. Un. | C7 | 28 |
| Terschelling, i., Neth. | A6 | 16 |
| Terskey-Alatau Range, mts., Sov. Un. | E9 | 28 |
| Teruel, Spain | E5 | 22 |
| Teruel, Spain | B5 | 22 |
| Terutao, i., Thai. | I3 | 35 |
| Terwagne, Bel. | D5 | 17 |
| Tešanj, Yugo. | D3 | 24 |
| Tescott, Ks., U.S. | C6 | 93 |
| Teseney, Eth. | B4 | 47 |
| Teshekpuk Lake, l., Ak., U.S. | A9 | 79 |
| Teshie, Ghana | *E5 | 45 |
| Teshio, Japan | D10 | 33 |
| Tesiyn, stm., Asia | B4 | 31 |
| Teslin, Yukon | D6 | 66 |
| Teslin Lake, l., Can. | D6 | 66 |
| Tessalit, Mali | B5 | 45 |
| Tessaoua, Niger | F7 | 45 |
| Tessier, Sask. | F2 | 75 |
| Tessin, E. Ger. | D5 | 15 |
| Test, stm., Eng., U.K. | E6 | 12 |
| Tesuque, N.M., U.S. | B4 | 108 |
| Tesuque Pueblo, N.M., U.S. | B4 | 108 |
| Tetachuck Lake, l., B.C. | C5 | 69 |
| Tetagouche, stm., N.B. | B3 | 71 |
| Tetas, Punta, c., Chile | F3 | 53 |
| Tetbury, Eng., U.K. | C5 | 12 |
| Tete, dept., Moz. | E5 | 48 |
| Tête-à-la-Baleine, Que. | C2 | 72 |
| Tête Jaune Cache, B.C. | C8 | 69 |
| Teteven, E. Ger. | B6 | 18 |
| Teteven, Bul. | D7 | 24 |
| Tetlin, Ak., U.S. | C11 | 79 |
| Teton, Id., U.S. | F7 | 89 |
| Teton, co., Id., U.S. | F7 | 89 |
| Teton, co., Mt., U.S. | C4 | 103 |
| Teton, stm., Mt., U.S. | C5 | 103 |
| Tetonia, Id., U.S. | F7 | 89 |
| Teton Pass, Wy., U.S. | C2 | 127 |
| Teton Range, mts., Wy., U.S. | C2 | 127 |
| Teton Village, Wy., U.S. | C2 | 127 |
| Tétouan, Mor. | A4 | 44 |
| Tetovo, Yugo. | E4 | 24 |
| Tettnang, W. Ger. | A8 | 21 |
| Teuchern, E. Ger. | B7 | 19 |
| Teuco, stm., Arg. | D3 | 53 |
| Teufen, Switz. | B7 | 21 |
| Teulada, Italy | E2 | 23 |
| Teúl de González Ortega, Mex. | m12 | 63 |
| Teulon, Man. | D3 | 70 |
| Teuri Island, i., Japan | D10 | 33 |
| Teutopolis, Il., U.S. | D5 | 90 |
| Teviot, stm., Scot., U.K. | F6 | 13 |
| Tevriz, Sov. Un. | D7 | 28 |
| Te Waewae Bay, b., N.Z. | Q11 | 51 |
| Tewantin-Noosa, Austl. | E9 | 50 |
| Tewkesbury, Eng., U.K. | C5 | 12 |
| Tewksbury, Ma., U.S. | A5 | 98 |
| Texada Island, i., B.C. | E5 | 69 |
| Texanna, Ok., U.S. | B6 | 113 |
| Texarkana, Ar., U.S. | D1 | 81 |
| Texarkana, Tx., U.S. | C5 | 120 |
| Texas, co., Mo., U.S. | D5 | 102 |
| Texas, co., Ok., U.S. | e9 | 113 |
| Texas, state, U.S. | D3 | 120 |
| Texcaltitlán, Mex. | n14 | 63 |
| Texcoco, Lago de. l., Mex. | g10 | 63 |
| Texcoco [de Mora], Mex. | n14 | 63 |
| Texel, i., Neth. | A6 | 16 |
| Texhoma, Ok., U.S. | e9 | 113 |
| Texhoma, Tx., U.S. | A2 | 120 |
| Texico, N.M., U.S. | C6 | 108 |
| Texline, Tx., U.S. | A1 | 120 |
| Texola, Ok., U.S. | B2 | 113 |
| Texoma, Lake, res., U.S. | D5 | 113 |
| Texon, Tx., U.S. | D2 | 120 |
| Teywarah, Afg. | E12 | 39 |
| Teziutlán, Mex. | D5 | 63 |
| Tezpur, India | C9 | 36 |
| Tezzeron Lake, l., B.C. | B5 | 69 |
| Thabana Ntlenyana, mtn., Leso. | C4 | 49 |
| Thacker, W.V., U.S. | D2 | 125 |
| Thackeray, Il., U.S. | E5 | 90 |
| Thackerville, Ok., U.S. | D4 | 113 |
| Thai Binh, Viet. | B7 | 35 |
| Thailand, ctry., Asia | C2 | 34 |
| Thailand, Gulf of, b., Asia | C2 | 34 |
| Thai Nguyen, Viet. | B6 | 35 |
| Thai, Pak. | C4 | 39 |
| Thale, E. Ger. | B5 | 18 |
| Thale Luang, b., Thai. | I4 | 35 |
| Thalia, Tx., U.S. | C3 | 120 |
| Thame, Eng., U.K. | C7 | 12 |
| Thames, N.Z. | L15 | 51 |
| Thames, stm., Ont. | E3 | 73 |
| Thames, stm., Eng., U.K. | E6 | 10 |
| Thames, stm., Ct., U.S. | D7 | 84 |
| Thames, Firth of, b., N.Z. | L15 | 51 |
| Thamesville, Ont. | E3 | 73 |
| Thāna, India | H4 | 37 |
| Thanh Hoa, Viet. | B6 | 35 |
| Thanjāvūr, India | F6 | 36 |
| Thann, Fr. | D7 | 16 |
| Thannhausen, W. Ger. | A6 | 20 |
| Thaon[-les-Vosges], Fr. | C7 | 16 |
| Thar Desert (Great Indian Desert), des., India | E10 | 36 |
| Tharrawaddy, Burma | E10 | 36 |
| Thásos, Grc. | B5 | 25 |
| Thásos, i., Grc. | B5 | 40 |
| Thatcher, Az., U.S. | E6 | 80 |
| Thatcher, Id., U.S. | G7 | 89 |
| Thaton, Burma | E10 | 36 |
| Thawville, Il., U.S. | C5 | 90 |
| Thaxton, Ms., U.S. | A4 | 101 |
| Thayer, Il., U.S. | D4 | 90 |
| Thayer, Ia., U.S. | C3 | 92 |
| Thayer, In., U.S. | B3 | 91 |
| Thayer, Ks., U.S. | E8 | 93 |
| Thayer, Mo., U.S. | E6 | 102 |
| Thayer, Ne., U.S. | D8 | 104 |
| Thayer, W.V., U.S. | n13 | 125 |
| Thayer, co., Ne., U.S. | D8 | 104 |
| Thayetmyo, Burma | D1 | 127 |
| Thayne, Wy., U.S. | B2 | 35 |
| Thazi, Burma | C7 | 34 |
| Thealka, Ky., U.S. | E3 | 80 |
| Theba, Az., U.S. | A2 | 72 |
| The Backway, b., Newf. | B5 | 194 |
| The Barrens, plat., Tn., U.S. | F4 | 90 |
| The Bells, Il., U.S. | C3 | 38 |
| Thebes, hist., Eg. | C4 | 25 |
| Thebes see Thívai, Grc. | B6 | 64 |
| The Bight, Bah. | E5 | 13 |
| The Cheviot, mtn., Eng., U.K. | C5 | 10 |
| The Cheviot Hills, hills, U.K. | F2 | 75 |
| The Colony, Tx., U.S. | B5 | 114 |
| The Coteau, hills, Sask. | E4 | 108 |
| The Dalles, Or., U.S. | D3 | 73 |
| The Dells, val., Wi., U.S. | F2 | 122 |
| The Dome, mtn., Vt., U.S. | F8 | 51 |
| The Entrance, Austl. | G6 | 86 |
| The Everglades, sw., Fl., U.S. | k13 | 50 |
| The Father, mtn., Pap. N. Gui. | G3 | 75 |
| The Fens, sw., Eng., U.K. | B3 | 83 |
| The Fishing Lake, l., Sask. | B3 | 106 |
| The Flat Tops, mts., Co., U.S. | g12 | 98 |
| The Flume, wtfl., N.H., U.S. | A6 | 16 |
| The Graves, is., Ma., U.S. | E2 | 114 |
| The Hague ('s Gravenhage), Neth. | E1 | 21 |
| The Heads, c., Or., U.S. | C2 | 20 |
| The Hummocks, R.I., U.S. | B6 | 116 |
| The Landes, reg., Fr. | E3 | 16 |
| The Little Minch, strt., Scot., U.K. | B3 | 10 |
| Thelma, N.C., U.S. | A5 | 110 |
| Thelon, stm., N.W. Ter. | D12 | 66 |
| Tetas, Punta, c., Chile | | |
| The Minch, strt., Scot., U.K. | B3 | 10 |
| The Narrows, strt., Wa., U.S. | f10 | 124 |
| The Naze, c., Nor. | I2 | 14 |
| The Naze, c., Eng., U.K. | C9 | 12 |
| The Oa, pen., Scot., U.K. | E2 | 13 |
| Theodore, Austl. | D9 | 50 |
| Theodore, Sask. | F4 | 75 |
| Theodore, Al., U.S. | E1 | 78 |
| Theodore Roosevelt Lake, res., Az., U.S. | D4 | 80 |
| Theodore Roosevelt National Park (South Unit), N.D., U.S. | C2 | 111 |
| Theodore Roosevelt National Park (North Unit), N.D., U.S. | B2 | 111 |
| Theodosia, Mo., U.S. | E5 | 102 |
| Theológos, Grc. | B7 | 24 |
| The Palisades, clf., N.J., U.S. | h9 | 107 |
| The Pas, Man. | C1 | 70 |
| The Peak, mtn., N.J., U.S. | A1 | 10 |
| The Pinnacle, hill, Ct., U.S. | B4 | 84 |
| The Pinnacle, hill, Mo., U.S. | B7 | 102 |
| The Plains, Oh., U.S. | C3 | 112 |
| The Plains, Va., U.S. | B5 | 123 |
| Thérain, stm., Fr. | C5 | 17 |
| Theresa, N.Y., U.S. | A5 | 109 |
| Theresa, Wi., U.S. | E5 | 126 |
| Thermaïkós Kólpos (Gulf of Salonika), b., Grc. | B4 | 40 |
| Thermopolis, Wy., U.S. | C5 | 25 |
| The Rock, Ga., U.S. | D2 | 87 |
| The Rockies, mts., U.S. | C3 | 84 |
| Theron Mountains, mts., Ant. | B10 | 7 |
| The Solent, strt., Eng., U.K. | D6 | 12 |
| The Sound see Øresund, strt., Eur. | J5 | 14 |
| Thessalon, Ont. | p19 | 73 |
| Thessaloniki (Salonika), Grc. | B4 | 40 |
| Thessaly, hist. reg., Grc. | C4 | 25 |
| The Storr, mtn., Scot., U.K. | C2 | 13 |
| Theta, Tn., U.S. | B4 | 119 |
| Thetford, Eng., U.K. | D7 | 10 |
| Thetford, Vt., U.S. | D4 | 122 |
| Thetford Center, Vt., U.S. | D4 | 122 |
| Thetford Mines, Que. | C6 | 74 |
| The Thimbles, is., Ct., U.S. | E5 | 84 |
| The Village, Ok., U.S. | B4 | 113 |
| The Village of India, Oh., U.S. | *C1 | 112 |
| The Wash, b., Eng., U.K. | D7 | 10 |
| The Wolds, hills, Eng., U.K. | A5 | 12 |
| The Woodlands, Tx., U.S. | *E5 | 120 |
| Thibar, Tun. | F2 | 23 |
| Thibaudeau, Man. | A4 | 70 |
| Thibodaux, La., U.S. | E5 | 95 |
| Thicket Portage, Man. | B3 | 70 |
| Thickwood Hills, hills, Sask. | E2 | 75 |
| Thief, stm., Mn., U.S. | B3 | 100 |
| Thief Lake, l., Mn., U.S. | B3 | 100 |
| Thief River Falls, Mn., U.S. | B2 | 100 |
| Thief Rock Cove, Newf. | D2 | 72 |
| Three Sisters, mtn., Or., U.S. | C5 | 114 |
| Thielsen, Mount, mtn., Or., U.S. | D4 | 114 |
| Thiene, Italy | D7 | 20 |
| Thiensville, Wi., U.S. | E6 | 126 |
| Thiers, Fr. | E5 | 16 |
| Thiès, Sen. | D1 | 45 |
| Thika, Kenya | B6 | 48 |
| Thimbu see Thimphu, Bhu. | C8 | 36 |
| Thimphu (Thimbu), Bhu. | C8 | 36 |
| Thingangyun, Burma | *E10 | 36 |
| Thionville, Fr. | C7 | 16 |
| Thíra, i., Grc. | D5 | 40 |
| Third Lake, l., N.H., U.S. | f7 | 106 |
| Thirsk, Eng., U.K. | F7 | 13 |
| Thisted, Den. | B2 | 15 |
| Thívai (Thebes), Grc. | C4 | 25 |
| Tho Chu, i., Viet. | H5 | 35 |
| Tholen, Neth. | C4 | 17 |
| Thomas, Ok., U.S. | B3 | 113 |
| Thomas, Ia., U.S. | f11 | 124 |
| Thomas, W.V., U.S. | B5 | 125 |
| Thomas, co., Ga., U.S. | F3 | 87 |
| Thomas, co., Ks., U.S. | C2 | 93 |
| Thomas, co., Ne., U.S. | C5 | 104 |
| Thomasboro, Il., U.S. | C5 | 90 |
| Thomaston, Al., U.S. | C2 | 78 |
| Thomaston, Ct., U.S. | C3 | 84 |
| Thomaston, Ga., U.S. | D2 | 87 |
| Thomaston, Me., U.S. | D3 | 96 |
| Thomaston Reservoir, res., Ct., U.S. | C3 | 84 |
| Thomastown, Ire. | E4 | 11 |
| Thomastown, Ms., U.S. | C4 | 101 |
| Thomasville, Al., U.S. | D2 | 78 |
| Thomasville, Ga., U.S. | F3 | 87 |
| Thomasville, Mo., U.S. | E6 | 102 |
| Thomasville, N.C., U.S. | B2 | 110 |
| Thomasville, Tn., U.S. | A4 | 119 |
| Thomlinson, Mount, mtn., B.C. | B4 | 69 |
| Thompson, Man. | B3 | 70 |
| Thompson, Ct., U.S. | B8 | 84 |
| Thompson, Ia., U.S. | A4 | 92 |
| Thompson, Mi., U.S. | C4 | 99 |
| Thompson, Mo., U.S. | B6 | 102 |
| Thompson, N.D., U.S. | B8 | 111 |
| Thompson, Oh., U.S. | A4 | 112 |
| Thompson, Pa., U.S. | C10 | 115 |
| Thompson, Ut., U.S. | E6 | 121 |
| Thompson, stm., B.C. | D7 | 69 |
| Thompson, stm., U.S. | A4 | 102 |
| Thompson Creek, stm., Ms., U.S. | D5 | 101 |
| Thompson Falls, Mt., U.S. | C1 | 103 |
| Thompson Island, i., Ma., U.S. | g11 | 98 |
| Thompson Lake, l., Me., U.S. | D2 | 96 |
| Thompson Peak, mtn., Ca., U.S. | B2 | 82 |
| Thompson Peak, mtn., N.M., U.S. | h9 | 108 |
| Thompson Reservoir, res., Or., U.S. | E5 | 114 |
| Thompsons Station, Tn., U.S. | B5 | 119 |
| Thompsontown, Pa., U.S. | E7 | 115 |
| Thompsonville, Mi., U.S. | F5 | 90 |
| Thomson, Ga., U.S. | C4 | 87 |
| Thomson, Il., U.S. | B3 | 90 |
| Thomson, Mn., U.S. | D6 | 100 |
| Thomson, stm., Austl. | D7 | 50 |
| Thomson's Falls, Kenya | A6 | 48 |
| Thônes, Fr. | E1 | 21 |
| Thonon-les-Bains, Fr. | C2 | 20 |
| Thonotosassa, Fl., U.S. | D4 | 86 |
| Thorburn, N.S. | D7 | 71 |
| Thoreau, N.M., U.S. | B1 | 108 |
| Thorhild, Alta. | B4 | 68 |
| Thornbury, Ar., U.S. | E5 | 81 |
| Thornbury, Ont. | C4 | 73 |
| Thorndale, Ont. | D3 | 73 |
| Thorndale, Tx., U.S. | D4 | 120 |
| Thorndike, Me., U.S. | D3 | 96 |
| Thorndike, Ma., U.S. | B3 | 98 |
| Thornfield, Mo., U.S. | E5 | 102 |
| Thornhill, Man. | E2 | 70 |
| Thornhill, Scot., U.K. | D5 | 13 |
| Thornton, Ar., U.S. | D3 | 81 |
| Thornton, Co., U.S. | B6 | 83 |
| Thornton, Ia., U.S. | A4 | 92 |
| Thornton, Il., U.S. | k9 | 90 |
| Thornton, Ms., U.S. | B3 | 101 |
| Thornton, N.H., U.S. | C3 | 106 |
| Thornton, Tx., U.S. | D4 | 120 |
| Thornton, W.V., U.S. | k11 | 125 |
| Thornton Gap, Va., U.S. | B4 | 123 |
| Thorntonville, Tx., U.S. | D1 | 120 |
| Thornville, Oh., U.S. | C3 | 112 |
| Thornwood, N.Y., U.S. | *m15 | 109 |
| Thornwood, W.V., U.S. | C5 | 125 |
| Thorny Mountain, mtn., Mo., U.S. | D6 | 102 |
| Thorofare, N.J., U.S. | D2 | 107 |
| Thorold, Ont. | D5 | 73 |
| Thorp, Wa., U.S. | B5 | 124 |
| Thorp, Wi., U.S. | D3 | 126 |
| Thorsby, Al., U.S. | C3 | 78 |
| Thousand Islands, is., N.Y., U.S. | A4 | 109 |
| Thousand Lake Mountain, mtn., Ut., U.S. | E4 | 121 |
| Thousand Oaks, Ca., U.S. | *E4 | 82 |
| Thousand Springs Creek, stm., U.S. | B7 | 105 |
| Thrace, hist. reg., Eur. | B6 | 25 |
| Thrapston, Eng., U.K. | B7 | 12 |
| Thrashers, Ms., U.S. | A5 | 101 |
| Three Bridges, N.J., U.S. | B3 | 107 |
| Three Fingered Jack, mtn., Or. | C5 | 114 |
| Three Forks, Mt., U.S. | E5 | 103 |
| Three Hills, Alta. | D4 | 68 |
| Three Kings Islands, is., N.Z. | K14 | 51 |
| Three Lakes, Wi., U.S. | C4 | 126 |
| Three Mile Bay, N.Y., U.S. | A4 | 109 |
| Three Mile Plains, N.S. | E5 | 71 |
| Three Nunataks, mtn., Ant. | g41 | 7 |
| Three Oaks, Mi., U.S. | G4 | 99 |
| Threepoint Lake, l., Man. | B3 | 70 |
| Three Points, Cape, c., Ghana | F4 | 45 |
| Three Rivers, Ma., U.S. | B3 | 98 |
| Three Rivers, Mi., U.S. | G5 | 99 |
| Three Rivers, Ms., U.S. | E5 | 101 |
| Three Rivers, Tx., U.S. | E3 | 120 |
| Three Rock Cove, Newf. | D2 | 72 |
| Three Springs, Pa., U.S. | F6 | 115 |
| Throckmorton, Tx., U.S. | C3 | 120 |
| Throop, Pa., U.S. | m18 | 115 |
| Thu, i., Viet. | G8 | 35 |
| Thu Dau Mot, Viet. | G7 | 35 |
| Thule (Qaanaaq), Grnld. | B14 | 61 |
| Thun, Switz. | E3 | 18 |
| Thun, Lake, l., Switz. | E3 | 18 |
| Thunder Bay, Ont. | o17 | 73 |
| Thunder Bay, dept., Ont. | o17 | 73 |
| Thunder Bay, b., Mi., U.S. | D7 | 99 |
| Thunder Bay, stm., Mi., U.S. | D6 | 99 |
| Thunder Bay, North Branch, stm., Mi., U.S. | | |
| Thunderbird, Lake, res., Ok., U.S. | B4 | 113 |
| Thunderbolt, Ga., U.S. | D5 | 87 |
| Thunder Butte, S.D., U.S. | B4 | 118 |
| Thunder Butte, mtn., S.D., U.S. | B4 | 118 |
| Thunder Butte Creek, stm., S.D., U.S. | B3 | 118 |
| Thunder Hawk, S.D., U.S. | B4 | 118 |
| Thung Song, Thai. | H3 | 35 |
| Thur, stm., Switz. | A6 | 21 |
| Thurgau, state, Switz. | B5 | 20 |
| Thüringer Wald, mts., E. Ger. | C5 | 18 |
| Thuringia, hist. reg., E. Ger. | C5 | 18 |
| Thurles, Ire. | D3 | 10 |
| Thurlow Dam, Al., U.S. | C4 | 78 |
| Thurman, Ia., U.S. | D2 | 92 |
| Thurman, Oh., U.S. | D3 | 112 |
| Thurmont, Md., U.S. | A3 | 97 |
| Thuro, i., Den. | C4 | 15 |
| Thursday Island, Austl. | B7 | 50 |
| Thurso, Que. | D2 | 74 |
| Thurso, Scot., U.K. | A5 | 10 |
| Thurso, stm., Scot., U.K. | B5 | 13 |
| Thurston, Ne., U.S. | B9 | 104 |
| Thurston, co., Ne., U.S. | B9 | 104 |
| Thurston, co., Wa., U.S. | C2 | 124 |
| Thurston Island, i., Ant. | B7 | 7 |
| Thusis, Switz. | E4 | 18 |
| Thwaites Iceburg Tongue, ice, Ant. | B2 | 7 |
| Thyborøn, Den. | B2 | 15 |
| Thyborøn Kanal, strt., Den. | B2 | 15 |
| Tiahuanaco, Bol. | C2 | 55 |
| Tiancang, China | C5 | 31 |
| Tianjin (Tientsin), China | D8 | 31 |
| Tianjun, China | I5 | 32 |
| Tianmen, China | E8 | 32 |
| Tianshui, China | E8 | 31 |
| Tianzhen, China | D6 | 32 |
| Tibagi, Braz. | A6 | 113 |
| Tibati, Cam. | C2 | 56 |
| Tibbie, Al., U.S. | D1 | 78 |
| Tibbie, Pic de, mtn., Gui. | E8 | 31 |
| Tiber (Tevere), stm., Italy | C4 | 23 |
| Tiberias (Teverya), Isr. | F10 | 40 |
| Tibesti (mtes), Chad | A3 | 46 |
| Tibet (Xizang), prov., China | E8 | 31 |
| Tibni, Niger | E2 | 40 |
| Tibooburra, Austl. | E7 | 50 |
| Tiburón, Isla, i., Mex. | *h8 | 82 |
| Tice, Fl., U.S. | F5 | 86 |
| Tichfield, Sask. | F2 | 75 |
| Tichitt, Maur. | C3 | 45 |
| Tichnor, Ar., U.S. | C4 | 81 |
| Ticino, state, Switz. | E5 | 18 |
| Ticino, stm., Eur. | B2 | 23 |
| Ticomán (part of Mexico City), Mex. | g9 | 63 |
| Ticonderoga, N.Y., U.S. | B7 | 109 |
| Ticul, Mex. | C7 | 63 |
| Tide Head, N.B. | B3 | 71 |
| Tidikelt, pl., Alg. | D5 | 44 |
| Tidioute, Pa., U.S. | C3 | 115 |
| Tidjikdja, Maur. | C2 | 45 |
| Tidore, i., Indon. | E7 | 34 |
| Tiel, Neth. | C5 | 17 |
| Tielì, Sen. | C2 | 45 |
| Tieli, China | *B10 | 31 |
| Tieling, China | C11 | 31 |
| Tielmes de Tajuña, Spain | p18 | 22 |
| Tielt, Bel. | B3 | 17 |
| Tien Shan, mts., Asia | E10 | 30 |
| Tien Yen, Viet. | B7 | 35 |
| Tientsin see Tianjin, China | D8 | 31 |
| Tierp, Swe. | G7 | 14 |
| Tierra Amarilla, Chile | E1 | 55 |
| Tierra Amarilla, N.M., U.S. | A3 | 108 |
| Tierra Blanca, Mex. | *D5 | 63 |
| Tierra del Fuego, Antártida e Islas del Atlántico Sur, ter., Arg. | h12 | 54 |
| Tierra del Fuego, Isla Grande de, i., S.A. | h12 | 54 |
| Tie Plant, Ms., U.S. | B4 | 101 |
| Tie Siding, Wy., U.S. | E7 | 127 |
| Tietê, Braz. | G5 | 57 |
| Tietê, stm., Braz. | C5 | 56 |
| Tieton, Wa., U.S. | C5 | 124 |
| Tieton, stm., Wa., U.S. | C4 | 124 |
| Tieton Dam, Wa., U.S. | C4 | 124 |
| Tiffany Mountain, mtn., Wa., U.S. | A6 | 124 |
| Tiff City, Mo., U.S. | E3 | 102 |
| Tiffin, Ia., U.S. | C6 | 92 |
| Tiffin, Oh., U.S. | A2 | 112 |
| Tiffin, stm., Oh., U.S. | A1 | 112 |
| Tiflis see Tbilisi, Sov. Un. | E7 | 29 |
| Tift, co., Ga., U.S. | E3 | 87 |
| Tifton, Ga., U.S. | E3 | 87 |
| Tigard, Or., U.S. | h12 | 114 |
| Tiger, Ga., U.S. | B3 | 87 |
| Tigerton, Wi., U.S. | D4 | 126 |
| Tigerville, S.C., U.S. | A3 | 117 |
| Tighnabruaich, Scot., U.K. | E3 | 13 |
| Tigil, Sov. Un. | D18 | 29 |
| Tignall, Ga., U.S. | C4 | 87 |
| Tignère, Cam. | D2 | 46 |
| Tignish, P.E.I. | C5 | 71 |
| Tigray (Tigre), prov., Eth. | g7 | 54 |
| Tigre, Arg. | B2 | 58 |
| Tigre, stm., Peru | B3 | 60 |
| Tigre, stm., Ven. | B5 | 60 |
| Tigrett, Tn., U.S. | B2 | 119 |
| Tigris (Dicle), stm., Asia | B4 | 38 |
| Tiguabos, Cuba | D6 | 64 |
| Tiguentourine, Alg. | D6 | 44 |
| Tih, Jabal at, plat., Eg. | E5 | 41 |
| Tihert, Alg. | C2 | 44 |
| Tihuatlán, Mex. | m15 | 63 |
| Tijeras, N.M., U.S. | B3 | 108 |
| Tiji, Libya | C2 | 43 |
| Tijuana, Mex. | A1 | 63 |
| Tijucas, Braz. | D5 | 56 |
| Tikal, hist., Guat. | D7 | 63 |
| Tikamgarh, India | E7 | 37 |
| Tikhoretsk, Sov. Un. | I13 | 27 |
| Tikhvin, Sov. Un. | B9 | 27 |
| Tikrīt, Iraq | E14 | 40 |
| Tiksi, Sov. Un. | B15 | 29 |
| Tilamuta, Indon. | E6 | 34 |
| Tilarán, C.R. | E5 | 62 |
| Tilburg, Neth. | B6 | 16 |
| Tilbury, Ont. | E2 | 73 |
| Tilbury, Eng., U.K. | m13 | 12 |
| Tilcara, Arg. | D2 | 55 |
| Tilden, Il., U.S. | E4 | 90 |
| Tilden, Ne., U.S. | B8 | 104 |
| Tilden, Tx., U.S. | E3 | 120 |
| Tilemsi, Vallée du, val., Mali | C5 | 45 |
| Tilford, S.D., U.S. | C2 | 118 |
| Tilghman, Md., U.S. | C5 | 97 |
| Tilghman Island, i., Md., U.S. | C5 | 97 |
| Tilimsen (Tlemcen), Alg. | C4 | 44 |
| Tiline, Ky., U.S. | e9 | 94 |
| Till, stm., Eng., U.K. | E6 | 13 |
| Tillabéry, Niger | D5 | 45 |
| Tillamook, Or., U.S. | B3 | 114 |
| Tillamook, co., Or., U.S. | B3 | 114 |
| Tillar, Ar., U.S. | D4 | 81 |
| Tillatoba, Ms., U.S. | A3 | 101 |
| Tillberga (part of Västerås), Swe. | t34 | 14 |
| Tillery, Lake, res., N.C., U.S. | B2 | 110 |
| Tilley, Alta. | D5 | 68 |
| Tillman, S.C., U.S. | G5 | 117 |
| Tillman, co., Ok., U.S. | C2 | 113 |
| Tillmans Corner, Al., U.S. | E1 | 78 |
| Tillson, N.Y., U.S. | D6 | 109 |
| Tillsonburg, Ont. | E4 | 73 |
| Tilly, Fr. | B3 | 81 |
| Tillyfourie, Scot., U.K. | C6 | 13 |
| Tilpa, Austl. | E5 | 51 |
| Tilrhemt, Alg. | C5 | 44 |
| Tilston, Man. | E1 | 70 |
| Tilton, Il., U.S. | C6 | 90 |
| Tilton, N.H., U.S. | D3 | 106 |
| Tiltonsville, Oh., U.S. | B5 | 112 |
| Tim, co., U.S. | F11 | 27 |
| Timaná, Col. | C2 | 60 |
| Timaru, N.Z. | P13 | 51 |
| Timashevsk, Sov. Un. | I12 | 27 |
| Timbalier Bay, b., La., U.S. | E5 | 95 |
| Timbalier Island, i., La., U.S. | E5 | 95 |
| Timbaúba, Braz. | h6 | 57 |
| Timbédra, Maur. | C3 | 45 |
| Timber, Or., U.S. | B3 | 114 |
| Timbered Knob, mtn., Mo., U.S. | E5 | 102 |
| Timberlake, N.C., U.S. | A3 | 110 |
| Timberlake, Va., U.S. | C3 | 123 |
| Timberville, Va., U.S. | B4 | 123 |
| Timblin, Pa., U.S. | D3 | 115 |
| Timbo, Gui. | E2 | 45 |
| Timbuktu see Tombouctou, Mali | C4 | 45 |
| Timerzit, Mor. | C3 | 90 |
| Timewell, Il., U.S. | C3 | 90 |
| Timimoun, Alg. | C5 | 44 |
| Timiris, Cap, c., Maur. | C1 | 45 |
| Timiskaming, dept., U.S. | o19 | 73 |
| Timişoara, Rom. | C5 | 24 |
| Timken, Ks., U.S. | D4 | 93 |
| Timmendorfer Strand, W. Ger. | E4 | 15 |
| Timmins, Ont. | o19 | 73 |
| Timmonsville, S.C., U.S. | C8 | 117 |
| Timms Hill, hill, Wi., U.S. | C3 | 126 |
| Timnath, Co., U.S. | A5 | 83 |
| Timok, stm., Eur. | C5 | 24 |
| Timor, i., Indon. | G7 | 34 |
| Timor Sea | B4 | 50 |
| Timpanogos Cave National Monument, Ut., U.S. | C4 | 121 |
| Timpas Creek, stm., Co., U.S. | D7 | 83 |
| Timpson, Tx., U.S. | D5 | 120 |
| Timrå, Swe. | E11 | 14 |
| Timsān, Lake, l., Eg. | D4 | 41 |
| Tims Ford Lake, res., Tn., U.S. | B5 | 119 |
| Tin, Ra's at, c., Libya | B4 | 102 |
| Tina, Ven. | B4 | 60 |
| Tinaca Point, c., Phil. | D7 | 34 |
| Tinahely, Ire. | E5 | 11 |
| Tinaquillo, Ven. | C3 | 60 |
| Tindouf, Alg. | D3 | 44 |
| Tineo, Spain | A2 | 22 |
| Tinghert, Ḥammādat, plat. | D2 | 43 |
| Tingo María, Peru | C2 | 58 |
| Tingréla, C.R. | D3 | 45 |
| Tingri, China | C11 | 37 |
| Tinghert, Plateau du (Ḥammādat Tinghert), plat., Afr. | D6 | 44 |
| Tingley, Ia., U.S. | D3 | 92 |
| Tingmerkpuk Mountain, mtn., Ak., U.S. | B7 | 79 |

| Name | Map Ref. | Page |
|---|---|---|
| Tingsryd, Swe. | B8 | 15 |
| Tinguipaya, Bol. | C2 | 55 |
| Tingwick, Que. | D6 | 74 |
| Tinian, i., N. Mar. Is. | F8 | 6 |
| Tinian Harbor, b., N. Mar. Is. | E7 | 52 |
| Tinizong, Switz. | C8 | 21 |
| Tinker Air Force Base, mil., Ok., U.S. | B4 | 113 |
| Tinkerville, N.H., U.S. | B3 | 106 |
| Tinkisso, stm., Gui. | D2 | 45 |
| Tinley Park, Il., U.S. | k9 | 90 |
| Tinnie, N.M., U.S. | D4 | 108 |
| Tinniswood, Mount, mtn., B.C. | D6 | 69 |
| Tinogasta, Arg. | E2 | 55 |
| Tínos, Grc. | D5 | 40 |
| Tínos, i., Grc. | D5 | 40 |
| Tinqueux, Fr. | E3 | 17 |
| Tinsley, Ms., U.S. | C3 | 101 |
| Tinsman, Ar., U.S. | D3 | 81 |
| Tinsukia, India | C10 | 36 |
| Tintah, Mn., U.S. | D2 | 100 |
| Tintigny, Bel. | E5 | 17 |
| Tintina, Arg. | E3 | 55 |
| Tintinara, Austl. | G3 | 51 |
| Tinton Falls, N.J., U.S. | C4 | 107 |
| Ti-n-Zaouatene, Alg. | E5 | 44 |
| Tio, Eth. | C5 | 47 |
| Tioga, Il., U.S. | C2 | 90 |
| Tioga, La., U.S. | C3 | 95 |
| Tioga, N.D., U.S. | A3 | 111 |
| Tioga, Pa., U.S. | C7 | 115 |
| Tioga, W.V., U.S. | C4 | 125 |
| Tioga, co., N.Y., U.S. | C4 | 109 |
| Tioga, co., Pa., U.S. | C7 | 115 |
| Tioga, stm., Pa., U.S. | B7 | 115 |
| Tiogue Lake, res., R.I., U.S. | D3 | 116 |
| Tioman, i., Malay. | K6 | 35 |
| Tiona, Pa., U.S. | C3 | 115 |
| Tione di Trento, Italy | C6 | 20 |
| Tionesta, Pa., U.S. | D3 | 115 |
| Tionesta Creek, stm., Pa., U.S. | C3 | 115 |
| Tionesta Lake, res., Pa., U.S. | D3 | 115 |
| Tioughnioga, stm., N.Y., U.S. | C4 | 109 |
| Tipler, Wi., U.S. | C5 | 126 |
| Tiplersville, Ms., U.S. | A5 | 101 |
| Tippah, co., Ms., U.S. | A5 | 101 |
| Tippah, stm., Ms., U.S. | A4 | 101 |
| Tipp City, Oh., U.S. | C1 | 112 |
| Tippecanoe, In., U.S. | B5 | 91 |
| Tippecanoe, co., In., U.S. | D4 | 91 |
| Tippecanoe, stm., In., U.S. | C4 | 91 |
| Tipperary, Ire. | D2 | 10 |
| Tipperary, co., Ire. | E4 | 11 |
| Tippo, Ms., U.S. | B3 | 101 |
| Tipton, Ca., U.S. | D4 | 82 |
| Tipton, In., U.S. | D5 | 91 |
| Tipton, Ia., U.S. | C6 | 92 |
| Tipton, Ks., U.S. | C5 | 93 |
| Tipton, Mo., U.S. | C5 | 102 |
| Tipton, Ok., U.S. | C2 | 113 |
| Tipton, Tn., U.S. | B2 | 119 |
| Tipton, co., In., U.S. | D5 | 91 |
| Tipton, co., Tn., U.S. | B2 | 119 |
| Tipton, Mount, mtn., Az., U.S. | B1 | 80 |
| Tiptonville, Tn., U.S. | A2 | 119 |
| Tip Top, Ky., U.S. | C6 | 94 |
| Tiptop, Va., U.S. | C1 | 123 |
| Tip Top Mountain, mtn., Ont. | o18 | 73 |
| Tiquisate, Guat. | C2 | 62 |
| Tira, Isr. | B6 | 41 |
| Tīrān, Jazīrat, i., Sau. Ar. | I10 | 40 |
| Tirana (Tiranë), Alb. | B2 | 40 |
| Tiranë see Tirana, Alb. | B2 | 40 |
| Tirano, Italy | A3 | 23 |
| Tiraque, Bol. | C2 | 55 |
| Tiraspol, Sov. Un. | H7 | 27 |
| Tirat Karmel, Isr. | B6 | 41 |
| Tirat Zevi, Isr. | B7 | 41 |
| Tire, Tur. | C6 | 40 |
| Tirebolu, Tur. | B12 | 40 |
| Tiree, i., Scot., U.K. | B3 | 10 |
| Tire Hill, Pa., U.S. | F4 | 115 |
| Tîrgoviște, Rom. | C7 | 24 |
| Tîrgu-Frumos, Rom. | B8 | 24 |
| Tîrgu-Jiu, Rom. | C6 | 24 |
| Tîrgu-Neamţ, Rom. | B8 | 24 |
| Tîrgu-Ocna, Rom. | C8 | 24 |
| Tîrgu-Secuiesc, Rom. | B8 | 24 |
| Tirich Mīr, mtn., Pak. | A5 | 36 |
| Tiriro, Gui. | D3 | 45 |
| Tirlyanskiy, Sov. Un. | E20 | 8 |
| Tîrnava Mică, stm., Rom. | B7 | 24 |
| Tîrnăveni, Rom. | B7 | 24 |
| Tírnavos, Grc. | C4 | 25 |
| Tiro, Oh., U.S. | B3 | 112 |
| Tirol (Tyrol), state, Aus. | B7 | 20 |
| Tirol, hist. reg., Aus. | E5 | 18 |
| Tiros, Braz. | B3 | 56 |
| Tirschenreuth, W. Ger. | D7 | 19 |
| Tirso, stm., Italy | D2 | 23 |
| Tirstrup, Den. | B4 | 15 |
| Tiruchchirāppalli (Trichinopoly), India | F6 | 36 |
| Tirunelveli (Tinnevelly), India | G6 | 36 |
| Tiruppur, India | *F6 | 36 |
| Tisa (Tisza), stm., Eur. | C5 | 24 |
| Tisaren, l., Swe. | t33 | 14 |
| Tisch Mills, Wi., U.S. | h10 | 126 |
| Tisdale, Sask. | E3 | 75 |
| Tishomingo, Ms., U.S. | A5 | 101 |
| Tishomingo, Ok., U.S. | C5 | 113 |
| Tishomingo, co., Ms., U.S. | A5 | 101 |
| Tiskilwa, Il., U.S. | B4 | 90 |
| Tisnaren, l., Swe. | u33 | 14 |
| Tissemsilt, Alg. | B5 | 44 |
| Tīsta, stm., Asia | D12 | 37 |
| Tisvildeleje, Den. | B6 | 15 |
| Tisza (Tisa), stm., Eur. | B5 | 24 |
| Tiszafüred, Hung. | B5 | 24 |
| Tiszakécske, Hung. | B5 | 24 |
| Titicaca, Lake, l., S.A. | E4 | 58 |
| Titograd, Yugo. | D4 | 24 |
| Titonka, Ia., U.S. | A3 | 92 |
| Titovo Užice, Yugo. | D4 | 24 |
| Titov Veles, Yugo. | E5 | 24 |
| Titule, Zaire | A4 | 48 |
| Titus, co., Tx., U.S. | C5 | 120 |
| Titusville, Fl., U.S. | D6 | 86 |
| Titusville, N.J., U.S. | C3 | 107 |
| Titusville, Pa., U.S. | C2 | 115 |
| Tivaouane, Sen. | C1 | 45 |
| Tiverton, N.S. | E3 | 71 |
| Tiverton, Ont. | C3 | 73 |
| Tiverton, Eng., U.K. | E5 | 10 |
| Tiverton, R.I., U.S. | D6 | 116 |
| Tiverton Four Corners, R.I., U.S. | E6 | 116 |
| Tivoli, Italy | D4 | 23 |
| Tivoli, N.Y., U.S. | C7 | 109 |
| Tivoli, Tx., U.S. | E4 | 120 |
| Tixtla [de Guerrero], Mex. | o14 | 63 |
| Tizapán [part of Mexico City], Mex. | h9 | 63 |
| Tizard Bank, atoll, Asia | C4 | 34 |
| Tizimín, Mex. | C7 | 63 |
| Tizi-Ouzou, Alg. | B5 | 44 |
| Tiznit, Mor. | D3 | 44 |
| Tjeukemeer, l., Neth. | B5 | 17 |
| Tlacolula [de Matamoros], Mex. | D5 | 63 |
| Tlacotalpan, Mex. | D5 | 63 |
| Tlacotepec, Mex. | o13 | 63 |
| Tláhuac [part of Mexico City], Mex. | h9 | 63 |
| Tlahualilo de Zaragoza, Mex. | B4 | 63 |
| Tlalnepantla, stm., Mex. | g9 | 63 |
| Tlalnepantla [de Comonfort], Mex. | g9 | 63 |
| Tlalpan [part of Mexico City], Mex. | h9 | 63 |
| Tlaltenango [de Sánchez Román], Mex. | C4 | 63 |
| Tlaltenco [part of Mexico City], Mex. | h9 | 63 |
| Tlapa, Mex. | o14 | 63 |
| Tlapacoyan, Mex. | n15 | 63 |
| Tlapaneco, stm., Mex. | o14 | 63 |
| Tlaquepaque (San Pedro Tlaquepaque), Mex. | m12 | 63 |
| Tlaxcala, state, Mex. | D5 | 63 |
| Tlaxcala [de Xicohténcatl], Mex. | D5 | 63 |
| Tlaxco [de Morelos], Mex. | n14 | 63 |
| Tlaxiaco, Mex. | D5 | 63 |
| Tłuszcz, Pol. | k14 | 26 |
| Tmassah, Libya | D3 | 43 |
| Toadlena, N.M., U.S. | A1 | 108 |
| Toamasina, Madag. | g9 | 49 |
| Toamasina, prov., Madag. | g9 | 49 |
| Toano, Va., U.S. | C6 | 123 |
| Toano Range, mts., Nv., U.S. | C7 | 105 |
| Toast, N.C., U.S. | A2 | 110 |
| Toay, Arg. | B4 | 54 |
| Toba, Japan | o15 | 33 |
| Toba, stm., B.C. | D5 | 69 |
| Toba, Lake, l., Indon. | E1 | 34 |
| Tobacco Root Mountains, mts., Mt., U.S. | E5 | 103 |
| Tobago, i., Trin. | K14 | 64 |
| Tobago Cays, is., St. Vin. | V26 | 65 |
| Toba Inlet, b., B.C. | D5 | 69 |
| Tobarra, Spain | C5 | 22 |
| Tobaru, Japan | O5 | 52 |
| Tobercurry, Ire. | C3 | 11 |
| Tobermory, Ont. | B3 | 73 |
| Tobermory, Scot., U.K. | D2 | 13 |
| Tobias, Ne., U.S. | D8 | 104 |
| Tobiishi Point, c., Japan | P17 | 52 |
| Tobi Island, i., Japan | G9 | 33 |
| Tobin, Mount, mtn., Nv., U.S. | C4 | 105 |
| Tobin Lake, l., Austl. | D4 | 50 |
| Tobin Lake, l., Sask. | D4 | 75 |
| Tobin Range, mts., Nv., U.S. | C4 | 105 |
| Tobins Harbor, Mi., U.S. | h10 | 99 |
| Tobique, stm., N.B. | B2 | 71 |
| Tobol, Sov. Un. | C6 | 28 |
| Tobol, stm., Sov. Un. | D9 | 29 |
| Tobolsk, Sov. Un. | D9 | 29 |
| Tobruk see Ṭubruq, Libya | C4 | 43 |
| Toby, Mount, mtn., Ma., U.S. | B2 | 98 |
| Tobyhanna, Pa., U.S. | D11 | 115 |
| Tocantinópolis, Braz. | C1 | 57 |
| Tocantins, stm., Braz. | D6 | 53 |
| Tocantins National Park, Braz. | A3 | 56 |
| Toccoa, Ga., U.S. | B3 | 87 |
| Toccoa, stm., Ga., U.S. | B2 | 87 |
| Toccoa Falls, Ga., U.S. | B3 | 87 |
| Toccopola, Ms., U.S. | A4 | 101 |
| Toce, stm., Italy | C4 | 20 |
| Tochcha Lake, l., B.C. | B5 | 69 |
| Tochigi, Japan | H9 | 33 |
| Toco, Chile | D2 | 55 |
| Toco, Trin. | N24 | 65 |
| Tocoa, Hond. | C4 | 62 |
| Tocopilla, Chile | D1 | 55 |
| Tocsin, In., U.S. | C7 | 91 |
| Tocumen, Pan. | F8 | 62 |
| Tocumwal, Austl. | G5 | 51 |
| Tocuyo, stm., Ven. | A4 | 60 |
| Todd, N.C., U.S. | A1 | 110 |
| Todd, co., Ky., U.S. | D3 | 94 |
| Todd, co., Mn., U.S. | D4 | 100 |
| Todd, co., S.D., U.S. | D5 | 118 |
| Todd Estates, De., U.S. | *B3 | 85 |
| Toddville, Md., U.S. | D5 | 97 |
| Toddy Pond, l., Me., U.S. | D4 | 96 |
| Todi, Italy | C4 | 23 |
| Tödi, mtn., Switz. | C4 | 20 |
| Todoga, Cape, c., Japan | G11 | 33 |
| Todos Santos, Bol. | C2 | 55 |
| Todos Santos, Mex. | C2 | 63 |
| Todos Santos, Baía de, b., Braz. | D3 | 57 |
| Todtnau, W. Ger. | B3 | 20 |
| Toe Head, c., Ire. | F2 | 11 |
| Toe Head, c., Scot., U.K. | C1 | 13 |
| Tofield, Alta. | C4 | 68 |
| Tofino, B.C. | E5 | 69 |
| Tofte, Mn., U.S. | C8 | 100 |
| Toftlund, Den. | C3 | 15 |
| Togdheer, prov., Som. | D6 | 47 |
| Togiak, Ak., U.S. | D7 | 79 |
| Togian Islands, is., Indon. | F6 | 34 |
| Togo, Sask. | F5 | 75 |
| Togo, ctry., Afr. | E5 | 45 |
| Togtoh, China | D4 | 32 |
| Togwottee Pass, Wy., U.S. | C2 | 127 |
| Tohakum Peak, mtn., Nv., U.S. | C2 | 105 |
| Tohatchi, N.M., U.S. | B1 | 108 |
| Tohopekaliga, Lake, l., Fl., U.S. | D5 | 86 |
| Toi, Cape, c., Japan | K5 | 33 |
| To Island, i., Japan | I9 | 33 |
| Toivola, Mn., U.S. | C6 | 100 |
| Toiyabe Range, mts., Nv., U.S. | D4 | 105 |
| Tojo, Japan | G6 | 33 |
| Tokachi, Mount, mtn., Japan | E11 | 33 |
| Tokaj, Hung. | A5 | 24 |
| Tokara Islands, is., Japan | F10 | 31 |
| Tokara Strait, strt., Japan | K5 | 33 |
| Tokat, Tur. | B11 | 40 |
| Tōkchŏn, N. Kor. | G3 | 33 |
| Tokeland, Wa., U.S. | C2 | 124 |
| Tokelau, dep., Oc. | G11 | 6 |
| Tokio, Wa., U.S. | C2 | 81 |
| Tokio, N.D., U.S. | B7 | 111 |
| Tokio, Tx., U.S. | C1 | 120 |
| Tok Point, c., Wake I. | A1 | 52 |
| Tok Islands (Take Islands), is., Asia | H5 | 33 |
| Tokmak, Sov. Un. | H10 | 27 |
| Tokmak, Sov. Un. | E9 | 28 |
| Tokoroa, N.Z. | M15 | 51 |
| Tokuno Island, i., Japan | F10 | 31 |
| Tokushima, Japan | E11 | 31 |
| Tokuyama, Japan | J5 | 33 |
| Tōkyō, Japan | D12 | 31 |
| Tōkyō Bay, b., Japan | n18 | 33 |
| Tol, i., Micron. | Q18 | 52 |
| Tolar, N.M., U.S. | C6 | 108 |
| Tolbukhin (Dobrich), Bul. | D8 | 24 |
| Toleak Point, c., Wa., U.S. | B1 | 124 |
| Toledo, Braz. | C2 | 56 |
| Toledo, Ont. | C8 | 73 |
| Toledo, Spain | C3 | 22 |
| Toledo, Il., U.S. | D5 | 90 |
| Toledo, Ia., U.S. | B5 | 92 |
| Toledo, Oh., U.S. | A2 | 112 |
| Toledo, Or., U.S. | C3 | 114 |
| Toledo, Wa., U.S. | C3 | 124 |
| Toledo, Montes de, mts., Spain | C3 | 22 |
| Toledo Bend Reservoir, res., U.S. | C2 | 95 |
| Toler, Ky., U.S. | C7 | 94 |
| Tolga, Alg. | B7 | 44 |
| Toliara, Madag. | h8 | 49 |
| Toliara, prov., Madag. | h8 | 49 |
| Tolima, dept., Col. | C2 | 60 |
| Tolima, Nevado del, mtn., Col. | C2 | 60 |
| Tolimán, Mex. | m14 | 63 |
| Tolitoli, Indon. | E6 | 34 |
| Tolken, l., Swe. | A6 | 15 |
| Tolland, Ct., U.S. | B6 | 84 |
| Tolland, co., Ct., U.S. | B6 | 84 |
| Tollense, l., E. Ger. | E7 | 15 |
| Tollense, stm., E. Ger. | E7 | 15 |
| Tollesboro, Ky., U.S. | B6 | 94 |
| Tolleson, Az., U.S. | m8 | 80 |
| Tollette, Ar., U.S. | D2 | 81 |
| Tolley, N.D., U.S. | A4 | 111 |
| Tollhouse, Ca., U.S. | D4 | 82 |
| Tolloche, Arg. | E3 | 55 |
| Tolmezzo, Italy | A4 | 23 |
| Tolmin, Yugo. | B1 | 24 |
| Tolna, Hung. | B4 | 24 |
| Tolna, N.D., U.S. | B7 | 111 |
| Tolo, Gulf of, b., Indon. | F6 | 34 |
| Tolono, Il., U.S. | D5 | 90 |
| Tolosa, Spain | A4 | 22 |
| Tolovana Park, Or., U.S. | B3 | 114 |
| Tolsta Head, c., Scot., U.K. | C2 | 13 |
| Tolstoi, Man. | E3 | 70 |
| Tolstoy, S.D., U.S. | B6 | 118 |
| Toltén, Chile | B2 | 54 |
| Tolt Reservoir, res., Wa., U.S. | B4 | 124 |
| Tolú, Col. | B2 | 60 |
| Tolu, Ky., U.S. | e9 | 94 |
| Toluca, Il., U.S. | C4 | 90 |
| Toluca, Nevado de, vol., Mex. | n14 | 63 |
| Toluca [de Lerdo], Mex. | n14 | 63 |
| Tolyatti, Sov. Un. | C3 | 28 |
| Tom, Ok., U.S. | D7 | 113 |
| Tom, Mount, hill, Ct., U.S. | C2 | 84 |
| Tomah, Wi., U.S. | E3 | 126 |
| Tomahawk, Wi., U.S. | C4 | 126 |
| Tomahawk Lake, l., Wi., U.S. | C4 | 126 |
| Tomakomai, Japan | E10 | 33 |
| Tomakovka, Sov. Un. | H10 | 27 |
| Tomanivi, mtn., Fiji | H15 | 52 |
| Tomar, Port. | C1 | 22 |
| Tomari, Sov. Un. | E17 | 29 |
| Tomaszów Lubelski, Pol. | C7 | 26 |
| Tomaszów Mazowiecki, Pol. | C6 | 26 |
| Tomatlán, Mex. | D3 | 63 |
| Tomato, Ar., U.S. | B6 | 81 |
| Tomave, Bol. | C2 | 55 |
| Tombador, Serra do, plat., Braz. | B4 | 55 |
| Tomball, Tx., U.S. | D5 | 120 |
| Tombigbee, stm., U.S. | D1 | 78 |
| Tomboco, Ang. | C1 | 48 |
| Tombouctou (Timbuktu), Mali | C4 | 45 |
| Tombstone, Az., U.S. | F5 | 80 |
| Tombstone Mountain, mtn., Yukon | D5 | 66 |
| Tombua (Porto Alexandre), Ang. | E1 | 48 |
| Tomé, Chile | B2 | 54 |
| Tome, N.M., U.S. | C3 | 108 |
| Tomelilla, Swe. | C7 | 15 |
| Tomelloso, Spain | C4 | 22 |
| Tom Green, co., Tx., U.S. | D2 | 120 |
| Tomichi Creek, stm., Co., U.S. | C4 | 83 |
| Tomini, Gulf of, b., Indon. | E6 | 34 |
| Tominian, Mali | C4 | 45 |
| Tomintoul, Scot., U.K. | C5 | 13 |
| Tomkins Cove, N.Y., U.S. | D6 | 109 |
| Tommot, Sov. Un. | D15 | 29 |
| Tom Nevers Head, c., Ma., U.S. | D8 | 98 |
| Tomnolen, Ms., U.S. | B4 | 101 |
| Tomo, stm., Col. | B4 | 60 |
| Tomobe, Japan | m19 | 33 |
| Tomori, Japan | O5 | 52 |
| Tompkins, Sask. | G1 | 75 |
| Tompkins, co., N.Y., U.S. | C4 | 109 |
| Tompkinsville, Ky., U.S. | D4 | 94 |
| Tompkinsville, Md., U.S. | D4 | 97 |
| Tom Price, Austl. | D2 | 50 |
| Toms, stm., N.J., U.S. | C4 | 107 |
| Toms, Ridgeway Branch, stm., N.J., U.S. | C4 | 107 |
| Toms Creek, Va., U.S. | f9 | 123 |
| Tomsk, Sov. Un. | D11 | 29 |
| Toms River, N.J., U.S. | C4 | 107 |
| Tonalá, Mex. | D6 | 63 |
| Tonalea, Az., U.S. | A5 | 80 |
| Tonantins, Braz. | D3 | 60 |
| Tonasket, Wa., U.S. | A6 | 124 |
| Tonate, Fr. Gu. | C8 | 60 |
| Tonawanda, N.Y., U.S. | B2 | 109 |
| Tonawanda Indian Reservation, N.Y., U.S. | B2 | 109 |
| Tonbridge, Eng., U.K. | E13 | 12 |
| Tondano, Indon. | E6 | 34 |
| Tønder, Den. | D2 | 15 |
| Tone, stm., Japan | n19 | 33 |
| Tonekābon, Iran | C8 | 39 |
| Toney, Al., U.S. | A3 | 78 |
| Tonga, ctry., Oc. | H11 | 6 |
| Tonganoxie, Ks., U.S. | C8 | 93 |
| Tongbei, China | B12 | 33 |
| Tongcheng, China | I7 | 32 |
| Tongchuan, China | E9 | 32 |
| Tongeren, Bel. | D5 | 17 |
| Tongguan, China | E10 | 32 |
| Tonghai, China | B4 | 34 |
| Tonghua, China | C13 | 33 |
| Tongjiang, China | I2 | 32 |
| Tongjiang, China | B13 | 33 |
| Tongliao, China | C11 | 33 |
| Tongling, China | E11 | 32 |
| Tongoy, Chile | F1 | 55 |
| Tongren, China | F8 | 32 |
| Tongue, Scot., U.K. | B4 | 13 |
| Tongue, stm., Mt., U.S. | E10 | 103 |
| Tongue, stm., Tx., U.S. | p13 | 120 |
| Tongue, Kyle of, b., Scot., U.K. | B4 | 13 |
| Tongyu, China | B10 | 32 |
| Tongzi, China | J2 | 32 |
| Tonica, Il., U.S. | B4 | 90 |
| Tónichi, Mex. | B3 | 63 |
| Tonj, Sud. | D2 | 47 |
| Tönjum, Nor. | G2 | 14 |
| Tonk, India | C6 | 36 |
| Tonkawa, Ok., U.S. | A4 | 113 |
| Tonkin, hist. reg., Viet. | B6 | 35 |
| Tonkin, Gulf of, b., Asia | B3 | 34 |
| Tonle Sap, l., Camb. | C2 | 35 |
| Tonneins, Fr. | E4 | 16 |
| Tonnerre, Fr. | D5 | 16 |
| Tönning, W. Ger. | D2 | 15 |
| Tonoloway Ridge, mtn., Md., U.S. | A1 | 97 |
| Tonopah, Az., U.S. | D3 | 80 |
| Tonopah, Nv., U.S. | E4 | 105 |
| Tonosí, Pan. | F7 | 62 |
| Tönsberg, Nor. | H4 | 14 |
| Tontitown, Ar., U.S. | A1 | 81 |
| Tonto, stm., Mex. | n15 | 63 |
| Tonto Basin, Az., U.S. | D4 | 80 |
| Tontogany, Oh., U.S. | f6 | 112 |
| Tonto National Monument, Az., U.S. | D4 | 80 |
| Tonto Natural Bridge, Az., U.S. | C4 | 80 |
| Tony, Wi., U.S. | C3 | 126 |
| Tooele, Ut., U.S. | C3 | 121 |
| Tooele, co., Ut., U.S. | C2 | 121 |
| Toole, co., Mt., U.S. | B5 | 103 |
| Toombs, co., Ga., U.S. | D4 | 87 |
| Toomsboro, Ga., U.S. | D3 | 87 |
| Toomsuba, Ms., U.S. | C5 | 101 |
| Toomyvara, Ire. | E3 | 11 |
| Toone, Tn., U.S. | B3 | 119 |
| Toormakeady, Ire. | C2 | 11 |
| Toowoomba, Austl. | E9 | 50 |
| Topawa, Az., U.S. | F4 | 80 |
| Topaz, Ca., U.S. | C4 | 82 |
| Topeka, In., U.S. | A6 | 91 |
| Topeka, Ks., U.S. | C8 | 93 |
| Topinabee, Mi., U.S. | C6 | 99 |
| Topki, Sov. Un. | B11 | 28 |
| Topley, B.C. | B4 | 69 |
| Toplica, stm., Yugo. | D5 | 24 |
| Topocalma, Punta, c., Chile | A2 | 54 |
| Topock, Az., U.S. | C1 | 80 |
| Topol'čany, Czech. | D5 | 26 |
| Topolnitsa, stm., Bul. | D7 | 24 |
| Topolobampo, Mex. | B3 | 63 |
| Topolovgrad, Bul. | D8 | 24 |
| Toponas, Co., U.S. | A4 | 83 |
| Topozero, l., Sov. Un. | E14 | 14 |
| Toppenish, Wa., U.S. | C5 | 124 |
| Toppenish Ridge, mtn., Wa., U.S. | C5 | 124 |
| Top Pond, l., Newf. | E3 | 72 |
| Topsfield, Me., U.S. | C5 | 96 |
| Topsfield, Ma., U.S. | A6 | 98 |
| Topsham, Me., U.S. | E3 | 96 |
| Topsham, Vt., U.S. | C4 | 122 |
| Topton, N.C., U.S. | f9 | 110 |
| Topton, Pa., U.S. | F10 | 115 |
| Toquerville, Ut., U.S. | F2 | 121 |
| Toquima Range, mts., Nv., U.S. | E5 | 105 |
| Torbali, Tur. | C6 | 40 |
| Torbat-e Ḥeydarīyeh, Iran | D9 | 39 |
| Torbat-e Jām, Iran | D10 | 39 |
| Torbay, Newf. | E5 | 72 |
| Tor Bay, b., Eng., U.K. | D4 | 12 |
| Torbert, Mount, mtn., Ak., U.S. | g15 | 79 |
| Torbrook, N.S. | E5 | 71 |
| Torcello, Italy | D8 | 20 |
| Torch, stm., Sask. | D4 | 75 |
| Torch Lake, l., Mi., U.S. | D5 | 99 |
| Torekov, Swe. | B6 | 15 |
| Torez, Sov. Un. | q21 | 27 |
| Torgau, E. Ger. | C6 | 18 |
| Torhout, Bel. | B5 | 16 |
| Toride, Japan | n19 | 33 |
| Tori Island, i., Japan | J4 | 33 |
| Torit, Sud. | E3 | 47 |
| Tormes, stm., Spain | B3 | 22 |
| Tornado Mountain, mtn., Can. | E3 | 68 |
| Tornealven, stm., Eur. | D10 | 14 |
| Torneträsk, l., Swe. | C9 | 14 |
| Torngat Mountains, mts., Can. | f8 | 72 |
| Tornillo, Tx., U.S. | o11 | 120 |
| Tornio, Fin. | D10 | 14 |
| Tornquist, Arg. | B4 | 54 |
| Toro, Spain | C2 | 22 |
| Torö, Swe. | u35 | 14 |
| Törökszentmiklós, Hung. | B5 | 24 |
| Toronto, Ont. | D5 | 73 |
| Toronto, Ks., U.S. | E8 | 93 |
| Toronto, Oh., U.S. | B5 | 112 |
| Toronto, S.D., U.S. | C9 | 118 |
| Toronto Lake, res., Ks., U.S. | E7 | 93 |
| Toro Peak, mtn., Ca., U.S. | F5 | 82 |
| Toropets, Sov. Un. | C8 | 27 |
| Tororo, Ug. | D3 | 48 |
| Toro Rumi, mtn., Peru | D3 | 58 |
| Torote, stm., Spain | o18 | 22 |
| Torpsbruk, Swe. | A8 | 15 |
| Torquay, Sask. | H4 | 75 |
| Torquay, Eng., U.K. | E5 | 12 |
| Torrance, Ont. | C5 | 73 |
| Torrance, Ca., U.S. | n12 | 82 |
| Torrance, co., N.M., U.S. | C3 | 108 |
| Torre Annunziata, Italy | D5 | 23 |
| Torre de Cerredo, mtn., Spain | A3 | 22 |
| Torre del Greco, Italy | D5 | 23 |
| Torredonjimeno, Spain | D3 | 22 |
| Torrejón de Ardoz, Spain | p18 | 22 |
| Torrejoncillo, Spain | C2 | 22 |
| Torrelavega, Spain | A3 | 22 |
| Torremaggiore, Italy | D5 | 23 |
| Torrens, Lake, l., Austl. | F6 | 50 |
| Torreón, Mex. | B4 | 63 |
| Torre-Pacheco, Spain | D5 | 22 |
| Torres, Braz. | B5 | 54 |
| Torres Novas, Port. | C1 | 22 |
| Torres Strait, strt., Austl. | B8 | 50 |
| Torres Vedras, Port. | C1 | 22 |
| Torrevieja, Spain | D5 | 22 |
| Torrey, Ut., U.S. | E4 | 121 |
| Torridge, stm., Eng., U.K. | D4 | 12 |
| Torridon, Loch, b., Scot., U.K. | D3 | 13 |
| Torriglia, Italy | E5 | 20 |
| Torrijos, Spain | C2 | 22 |
| Torrington, Alta. | D4 | 68 |
| Torrington, Ct., U.S. | B3 | 84 |
| Torrington, Wy., U.S. | D8 | 127 |
| Torrinha, Braz. | m7 | 56 |
| Torrox, Spain | D4 | 22 |
| Tors Cove, Newf. | E5 | 72 |
| Torshälla (part of Eskilstuna), Swe. | t34 | 14 |
| Tórshavn, Faer. Is. | C7 | 8 |
| Tortilla Flat, Az., U.S. | D4 | 80 |
| Tortola, i., V.I., Br. | G12 | 64 |
| Tortona, Italy | E5 | 20 |
| Tortosa, Spain | B6 | 22 |
| Tortosa, Cape, c., Spain | B6 | 22 |
| Tortue, Île de la, i., Haiti | D7 | 64 |
| Tortugas, Golfo de, b., Col. | C12 | 119 |
| Torugart Pass, Asia | E9 | 28 |
| Torun, Pol. | B5 | 26 |
| Torup, Swe. | B7 | 15 |
| Tory Hill, Ont. | C6 | 73 |
| Tory Island, i., Ire. | C2 | 10 |
| Torysa, stm., Czech. | D6 | 26 |
| Tory Sound, strt., Ire. | B3 | 11 |
| Torzhok, Sov. Un. | C10 | 27 |
| Torzym, Pol. | A10 | 19 |
| Tosa-shimizu, Japan | J6 | 33 |
| Tosno, Sov. Un. | B8 | 27 |
| Tostado, Arg. | E3 | 55 |
| Toston, Mt., U.S. | D5 | 103 |
| Tosya, Tur. | B10 | 40 |
| Toszek, Pol. | g9 | 26 |
| Totagatic, stm., Wi., U.S. | B2 | 126 |
| Totana, Spain | D5 | 22 |
| Toteng, Bots. | B3 | 49 |
| Totíu, i., Micron. | Q18 | 52 |
| Tótkomlós, Hung. | B5 | 24 |
| Totma, Sov. Un. | B2 | 28 |
| Totness, Sur. | A3 | 59 |
| Toto, Guam | L10 | 52 |
| Totolapan (part of Mexico City), Mex. | h9 | 63 |
| Totoras, N.M., U.S. | A4 | 108 |
| Totonicapán, Guat. | E6 | 63 |
| Totora Palca, Bol. | C2 | 55 |
| Totowa, N.J., U.S. | B4 | 107 |
| Totoya Island, i., Fiji | I16 | 52 |
| Totson Mountain, mtn., Ak., U.S. | D2 | 79 |
| Totten Glacier, ice, Ant. | C24 | 7 |
| Tottenham, Austl. | F6 | 51 |
| Tottenham, Ont. | C5 | 73 |
| Tottenham (part of London), Eng., U.K. | k12 | 10 |
| Tottori, Japan | D11 | 31 |
| Totz, Ky., U.S. | D6 | 94 |
| Touba, I.C. | E3 | 45 |
| Touba, Sen. | D1 | 45 |
| Toubkal, Jbel, mtn., Mor. | C3 | 44 |
| Touchet, Wa., U.S. | C7 | 124 |
| Touchet, stm., Wa., U.S. | C7 | 124 |
| Touchwood Lake, l., Man. | B4 | 70 |
| Toucy, Fr. | D5 | 16 |
| Touggourt, Alg. | B7 | 44 |
| Touhy, Ne., U.S. | C9 | 104 |
| Touisset, Ma., U.S. | C5 | 98 |
| Toul, Fr. | D6 | 16 |
| Toulépleu, I.C. | E3 | 45 |
| Toulon, Fr. | F6 | 16 |
| Toulon, Il., U.S. | B4 | 90 |
| Toulouse, Fr. | F4 | 16 |
| Toungo, Nig. | G8 | 45 |
| Toungoo, Burma | E10 | 36 |
| Touraine, hist. reg., Fr. | D4 | 16 |
| Tourcoing, Fr. | B5 | 16 |
| Tourlaville, Fr. | C3 | 16 |
| Tournai (Doornik), Bel. | D3 | 17 |
| Tournon, Fr. | E6 | 16 |
| Tournus, Fr. | D6 | 16 |
| Touros, Braz. | C3 | 57 |
| Tours, Fr. | D4 | 16 |
| Tourville, Que. | B8 | 74 |
| Touside, Pic, mtn., Chad | A3 | 46 |
| Toussaint Creek, stm., Oh., U.S. | f7 | 112 |
| Toutle, North Fork, stm., Wa., U.S. | C3 | 124 |
| Tovar, Ven. | B9 | 118 |
| Tovarkovskiy, Sov. Un. | E12 | 27 |
| Towai, N.Z. | D4 | 90 |
| Towanda, Il., U.S. | C5 | 90 |
| Towanda, Ks., U.S. | E7 | 93 |
| Towanda, Pa., U.S. | C9 | 115 |
| Towanda Creek, stm., Pa., U.S. | C8 | 115 |
| Towaoc, Co., U.S. | D2 | 83 |
| Tower, Mi., U.S. | C6 | 99 |
| Tower, Mn., U.S. | C6 | 100 |
| Tower City, N.D., U.S. | C8 | 111 |
| Tower City, Pa., U.S. | E8 | 115 |
| Tower Hill, Il., U.S. | D5 | 90 |
| Tower Hill, hill, Ber. | p20 | 64 |
| Towle, Ca., U.S. | C3 | 82 |
| Town and Country, Wa., U.S. | *B8 | 124 |
| Town Creek, Al., U.S. | A2 | 78 |
| Town Creek Manor, Md., U.S. | D5 | 97 |
| Towner, N.D., U.S. | A5 | 111 |
| Towner, co., N.D., U.S. | A6 | 111 |
| Townley, Al., U.S. | B2 | 78 |
| Town 'n Country, Fl., U.S. | *E4 | 86 |
| Town of Tonawanda, N.Y., U.S. | C2 | 109 |
| Towns, co., Ga., U.S. | B3 | 87 |
| Townsend, De., U.S. | C3 | 85 |
| Townsend, Ma., U.S. | A4 | 98 |
| Townsend, Mt., U.S. | D5 | 103 |
| Townsend, Tn., U.S. | D10 | 119 |
| Townsend, Vt., U.S. | E3 | 122 |
| Townshend Reservoir, res., Vt., U.S. | E3 | 122 |
| Townsville, Austl. | C8 | 50 |
| Townville, S.C., U.S. | B2 | 117 |
| Towraz̄ī, Afg. | H4 | 36 |
| Towson, Md., U.S. | B4 | 97 |
| Toxey, Al., U.S. | D1 | 78 |
| Toyah, Tx., U.S. | o13 | 120 |
| Toyahvale, Tx., U.S. | o13 | 120 |
| Toyama, Japan | D12 | 31 |
| Toyama Bay, b., Japan | H8 | 33 |
| Toyohashi, Japan | I8 | 33 |
| Toyonaka, Japan | o14 | 33 |
| Toyooka, Japan | n16 | 33 |
| Toyota, Japan | I7 | 33 |
| Tracy, Que. | C4 | 74 |
| Tracy, Ca., U.S. | D3 | 82 |
| Tracy, Ia., U.S. | C5 | 92 |
| Tracy, Mn., U.S. | F3 | 100 |
| Tracy, Mo., U.S. | B3 | 102 |
| Tracy City, Tn., U.S. | D8 | 119 |
| Tracys Creek, stm., Md., U.S. | C4 | 97 |
| Tracyton, Wa., U.S. | e10 | 124 |
| Tradate, Italy | E6 | 21 |
| Trade Lake, l., Sask. | B4 | 75 |
| Tradewater, stm., Ky., U.S. | C2 | 94 |
| Trading Post, Ks., U.S. | D9 | 93 |
| Traer, Ks., U.S. | C3 | 93 |
| Traer, Ia., U.S. | B5 | 92 |
| Trafalgar, Cape, c., Spain | D2 | 22 |
| Trafford, Pa., U.S. | k14 | 115 |
| Trafford, Lake, l., Fl., U.S. | F5 | 86 |
| Traiguén, Chile | B2 | 54 |
| Trail, B.C. | E9 | 69 |
| Trail, Mn., U.S. | C3 | 100 |
| Trail, Or., U.S. | E4 | 114 |
| Trail City, S.D., U.S. | B5 | 118 |
| Trail Creek, In., U.S. | A4 | 91 |
| Traill, co., N.D., U.S. | B8 | 111 |
| Traill, i., Grnld. | B16 | 128 |
| Trail Ridge, mtn., U.S. | F4 | 87 |
| Traipu, Braz. | C3 | 57 |
| Trairí, stm., Braz. | h6 | 57 |
| Tralee, Ire. | D2 | 10 |
| Tralee Bay, b., Ire. | E2 | 11 |
| Tramelan [-Dessus], Switz. | B3 | 21 |
| Tramore, Ire. | E4 | 11 |
| Trampas, N.M., U.S. | A4 | 108 |
| Tramping Lake, l., Sask. | E1 | 75 |
| Tramping Lake, l., Sask. | E1 | 75 |
| Tranås, Swe. | H6 | 14 |
| Trancão, stm., Port. | f9 | 22 |
| Trancas, Arg. | E2 | 55 |
| Trancoso, Port. | B2 | 22 |
| Tranemo, Swe. | A7 | 15 |
| Trang, Thai. | D1 | 34 |
| Trangan, i., Indon. | G8 | 34 |
| Trani, Italy | D6 | 23 |
| Trannim, Plateau du, plat., Laos | C5 | 35 |
| Tranquillity, N.J., U.S. | B3 | 107 |
| Tranquillity, Ca., U.S. | D3 | 82 |
| Transkei, ctry., Afr. | H4 | 49 |
| Transvaal, prov., S. Afr. | B4 | 49 |
| Transylvania, La., U.S. | B4 | 95 |
| Transylvania, co., N.C., U.S. | f10 | 110 |
| Transylvania, hist. reg., Rom. | B6 | 24 |
| Transylvanian Alps, mts., Rom. | C7 | 24 |
| Trapani, Italy | E4 | 23 |
| Trap Mountain, mtn., Ar., U.S. | g7 | 81 |
| Trappe, Md., U.S. | C5 | 97 |
| Trapper Creek, stm., Md., U.S. | D7 | 97 |
| Trapper Peak, mtn., Mt., U.S. | E2 | 103 |
| Traralgon, Austl. | G8 | 50 |
| Traunstein, W. Ger. | B7 | 15 |
| Traun, stm., Aus. | D7 | 18 |
| Traunreut, Mi., U.S. | B4 | 99 |
| Trauik Lake, l., Aus. | E6 | 18 |
| Trave, stm., Eur. | E4 | 15 |
| Travelers Rest, S.C., U.S. | B3 | 117 |
| Travers, Alta. | D4 | 68 |
| Travers, Switz. | C2 | 21 |
| Traverse, co., Mn., U.S. | E2 | 100 |
| Traverse City, Mi., U.S. | D5 | 99 |
| Traverspine, stm., Newf. | B1 | 72 |
| Travers Reservoir, res., Alta. | D4 | 68 |
| Travis, co., Tx., U.S. | D4 | 120 |
| Tra Vinh, Viet. | H7 | 35 |
| Travis Air Force Base, mil., Ca., U.S. | C2 | 82 |
| Travnik, Yugo. | C3 | 24 |
| Tray Mountain, mtn., Ga., U.S. | B3 | 87 |
| Treadway, Tn., U.S. | C10 | 119 |
| Treasure, co., Mt., U.S. | D9 | 103 |
| Treasure Island, Fl., U.S. | *p10 | 86 |
| Treasure Island Naval Station, mil., Ca., U.S. | h8 | 82 |
| Trebbia, stm., Italy | E5 | 20 |
| Trebel, stm., E. Ger. | E6 | 15 |
| Třebíč, Czech. | D3 | 19 |
| Trebišov, Czech. | D6 | 26 |
| Trebloc, Ms., U.S. | B5 | 101 |
| Treble Mountain, mtn., B.C. | B5 | 69 |
| Třeboň, Czech. | D14 | 19 |
| Trece Martires, Phil. | o13 | 34 |
| Trees, La., U.S. | E9 | 93 |
| Tregaron, Wales, U.K. | D5 | 10 |
| Tregarva, Sask. | G3 | 75 |
| Trego, Wi., U.S. | C2 | 126 |
| Trego, co., Ks., U.S. | D4 | 93 |
| Tréguier, Fr. | C2 | 16 |
| Treherne, Man. | E2 | 70 |
| Treig, Loch, res., Scot., U.K. | D4 | 13 |
| Treinta y Tres, Uru. | C6 | 54 |
| Treis, W. Ger. | C2 | 18 |
| Trelew, Arg. | E3 | 53 |
| Trelleborg, Swe. | J5 | 14 |
| Tremadog Bay, b., Wales, U.K. | D4 | 12 |
| Tremblant, Mont, mtn., Que. | C3 | 74 |
| Trembleur Lake, l., B.C. | g11 | 69 |
| Trementina, N.M., U.S. | B5 | 108 |
| Tremiti Islands, is., Italy | C5 | 23 |
| Tremont, Il., U.S. | C4 | 90 |
| Tremont, Ms., U.S. | A5 | 101 |
| Tremont, Pa., U.S. | E9 | 115 |
| Tremont City, Oh., U.S. | B2 | 112 |
| Tremonton, Ut., U.S. | B3 | 121 |
| Třemošná, Czech. | D2 | 19 |
| Trempealeau, Wi., U.S. | D2 | 126 |
| Trempealeau, co., Wi., U.S. | D2 | 126 |
| Trempealeau, stm., Wi., U.S. | D2 | 126 |
| Trenary, Mi., U.S. | B4 | 99 |
| Trenche, stm., Que. | B5 | 74 |
| Trent, S.D., U.S. | D9 | 118 |
| Trent, Tx., U.S. | C2 | 120 |
| Trent, stm., Eng., U.K. | D6 | 10 |

| Name | Map Ref. | Page |
|---|---|---|
| Trent, stm., N.C., U.S. | B5 | 110 |
| Trente et un Milles, Lac des, l., Que. | C2 | 74 |
| Trentino-Alto Adige, prov., Italy | C7 | 20 |
| Trento (Trent), Italy | A3 | 23 |
| Trenton, N.S. | D7 | 71 |
| Trenton, Ont. | C7 | 73 |
| Trenton, Al., U.S. | A3 | 78 |
| Trenton, Fl., U.S. | C4 | 86 |
| Trenton, Ga., U.S. | B1 | 87 |
| Trenton, Il., U.S. | E4 | 90 |
| Trenton, Ky., U.S. | D2 | 94 |
| Trenton, Mi., U.S. | F7 | 99 |
| Trenton, Mo., U.S. | A4 | 102 |
| Trenton, Ne., U.S. | D4 | 104 |
| Trenton, N.J., U.S. | C3 | 107 |
| Trenton, N.C., U.S. | B5 | 110 |
| Trenton, N.D., U.S. | A2 | 111 |
| Trenton, Oh., U.S. | C1 | 112 |
| Trenton, S.C., U.S. | D4 | 117 |
| Trenton, Tn., U.S. | B3 | 119 |
| Trenton, Tx., U.S. | C4 | 120 |
| Trenton, Ut., U.S. | B4 | 121 |
| Trepassey, Newf. | E5 | 72 |
| Trepassey Bay, b., Newf. | E5 | 72 |
| Tres Algarrobos, Arg. | B4 | 54 |
| Tres Árboles, Ur. | E1 | 56 |
| Tres Arroyos, Arg. | B4 | 54 |
| Tres Cerros, Arg. | D3 | 54 |
| Tresckow, Pa., U.S. | E10 | 115 |
| Três Corações, Braz. | C3 | 56 |
| Tres Esquinas, Col. | C2 | 60 |
| Treshnish Point, c., Scot., U.K. | D2 | 13 |
| Tres Irmãos, Serra dos, hills, Braz. | D2 | 59 |
| Treska, stm., Yugo. | E5 | 24 |
| Três Lagoas, Braz. | C2 | 56 |
| Três Marias, Represa, res., Braz. | B3 | 56 |
| Tres Piedras, N.M., U.S. | A4 | 108 |
| Tres Puntas, Cabo, c., Arg. | D3 | 54 |
| Três Rios, Braz. | h6 | 56 |
| Tres Ritos, N.M., U.S. | A4 | 108 |
| Trestle Creek, Id., U.S. | A2 | 89 |
| Treuchtlingen, W. Ger. | F5 | 19 |
| Treuenbrietzen, E. Ger. | A7 | 19 |
| Treutlen, co., Ga., U.S. | D4 | 87 |
| Treviglio, Italy | B2 | 23 |
| Trévillers, Fr. | B2 | 21 |
| Treviño, Spain | A4 | 22 |
| Treviso, Italy | B4 | 23 |
| Trevlac, In., U.S. | F5 | 91 |
| Trevor, Wi., U.S. | n11 | 126 |
| Trevorton, Pa., U.S. | E8 | 115 |
| Trevose, Pa., U.S. | o22 | 115 |
| Trevose Head, c., Eng., U.K. | D2 | 12 |
| Treynor, Ia., U.S. | C2 | 92 |
| Treysa, W. Ger. | C4 | 19 |
| Trezevant, Tn., U.S. | A3 | 119 |
| Trhové Sviny, Czech. | E9 | 19 |
| Triadelphia, W.V., U.S. | A4 | 125 |
| Triadelphia Reservoir, res., Md., U.S. | B3 | 97 |
| Triánda, Grc. | D7 | 25 |
| Triangle, Va., U.S. | B5 | 123 |
| Triaucourt [-en-Argonne], Fr. | F5 | 17 |
| Tribbett, Ms., U.S. | B3 | 101 |
| Tribbey, Ok., U.S. | B4 | 113 |
| Tribune, Sask. | H4 | 75 |
| Tribune, Ks., U.S. | D2 | 93 |
| Trichinopoly see Tiruchchirāppalli, India | F6 | 36 |
| Trichūr, India | F6 | 36 |
| Tri City, Or., U.S. | E3 | 114 |
| Tridell, Ut., U.S. | C6 | 121 |
| Trident, Mt., U.S. | E5 | 103 |
| Trident Peak, mtn., Nv., U.S. | B3 | 105 |
| Trier, W. Ger. | D3 | 18 |
| Trieste, Italy | B4 | 23 |
| Trieste, Gulf of, b., Eur. | B4 | 23 |
| Trigg, co., Ky., U.S. | D2 | 94 |
| Triglav, mtn., Yugo. | B1 | 24 |
| Trigo Mountains, mts., Az., U.S. | D1 | 80 |
| Trigueros, Spain | D2 | 22 |
| Trikala, Grc. | C3 | 40 |
| Trikhonís, Lake l., Grc. | C3 | 25 |
| Trikora Peak, mtn., Indon. | F9 | 34 |
| Tri Lakes, In., U.S. | B7 | 91 |
| Trilby, Fl., U.S. | D4 | 86 |
| Trilla, Il., U.S. | D5 | 90 |
| Trillick, N. Ire., U.K. | C4 | 11 |
| Trim, Ire. | D5 | 11 |
| Trimble, Mo., U.S. | B3 | 102 |
| Trimble, Tn., U.S. | A2 | 119 |
| Trimble, co., Ky., U.S. | B4 | 94 |
| Trimont, Mn., U.S. | G4 | 100 |
| Trimountain, Mi., U.S. | A2 | 99 |
| Trinchera, Co., U.S. | D5 | 83 |
| Trinchera Creek, stm., Co., U.S. | D5 | 83 |
| Trincomalee, Sri L. | G7 | 36 |
| Trindade, i., Braz. | H8 | 5 |
| Třinec, Czech. | *D5 | 26 |
| Tring Jonction, Que. | C6 | 74 |
| Trinidad, Bol. | B3 | 55 |
| Trinidad, Cuba | B3 | 60 |
| Trinidad, Col. | D6 | 83 |
| Trinidad, Tx., U.S. | C4 | 120 |
| Trinidad, Ur. | E1 | 56 |
| Trinidad, i., Trin. | K14 | 64 |
| Trinidad, Bahía, b., Pan. | k11 | 62 |
| Trinidad, Isla, i., Arg. | B4 | 54 |
| Trinidad and Tobago, ctry., N.A. | K14 | 64 |
| Trinity Head, c., Ca., U.S. | B1 | 82 |
| Trinity, Newf. | D5 | 72 |
| Trinity, Newf. | D5 | 72 |
| Trinity, Al., U.S. | A2 | 78 |
| Trinity, N.C., U.S. | *B3 | 110 |
| Trinity, co., Ca., U.S. | B2 | 82 |
| Trinity, co., Tx., U.S. | D5 | 120 |
| Trinity, stm., Ca., U.S. | B2 | 82 |
| Trinity, East Fork, stm., Tx., U.S. | n10 | 120 |
| Trinity, Elm Fork, stm., Tx., U.S. | m10 | 120 |
| Trinity, South Fork, stm., Ca., U.S. | B2 | 82 |
| Trinity, West Fork, stm., Tx., U.S. | n9 | 120 |
| Trinity Bay, b., Newf. | D5 | 72 |
| Trinity Center, Ca., U.S. | B2 | 82 |
| Trinity Islands, is., Ak., U.S. | D9 | 79 |
| Trinity Mountain, mtn., Id., U.S. | F3 | 89 |
| Trinity Mountains, mts., Ca., U.S. | B2 | 82 |
| Trinity Peak, mtn., Nv., U.S. | C3 | 105 |
| Trinity Range, mts., Nv., U.S. | C3 | 105 |
| Trinity Springs, In., U.S. | G4 | 91 |
| Trino, Italy | B2 | 23 |
| Trinway, Oh., U.S. | B3 | 112 |
| Trio, S.C., U.S. | E8 | 117 |
| Trion, Ga., U.S. | B1 | 87 |
| Triplett, Mo., U.S. | B4 | 102 |
| Tripoli (Tarābulus), Leb. | B3 | 38 |
| Tripoli (Tarābulus), Libya | C2 | 43 |
| Tripoli, Ia., U.S. | B5 | 92 |
| Tripoli, Wi., U.S. | C4 | 126 |
| Tripolis, Grc. | D4 | 40 |
| Tripolitania (Tarābulus), hist. reg., Libya | C3 | 43 |
| Tripp, S.D., U.S. | D8 | 118 |
| Tripp, co., S.D., U.S. | D6 | 118 |
| Tripura, state, India | D9 | 36 |
| Trisanna, stm., Aus. | B9 | 21 |
| Trischen, i., W. Ger. | A4 | 18 |
| Tristan da Cunha, is., St. Hel. | I9 | 5 |
| Triste, Golfo, b., Ven. | A4 | 60 |
| Triumph, La., U.S. | E6 | 95 |
| Triune, Tn., U.S. | B5 | 119 |
| Triunfo, Braz. | C3 | 57 |
| Trivandrum, India | G6 | 36 |
| Trnava, Czech. | D4 | 26 |
| Trobriand Islands, is., Pap. N. Gui. | k13 | 50 |
| Trochu, Alta. | D4 | 68 |
| Trogir, Yugo. | D3 | 24 |
| Trögstad, Nor. | p29 | 14 |
| Troisdorf, W. Ger. | C2 | 19 |
| Trois-Pistoles, Que. | A8 | 74 |
| Trois-Rivières, Que. | C5 | 74 |
| Trois-Rivières-Ouest, Que. | C5 | 74 |
| Trois-Saumons, Que. | B7 | 74 |
| Troisvierges, Lux. | D6 | 17 |
| Troitsk, Sov. Un. | D9 | 29 |
| Troitskoye, Sov. Un. | B8 | 33 |
| Trollhättan, Swe. | H5 | 14 |
| Trollheimen, Nor. | p28 | 14 |
| Trombetas, stm., Braz. | C3 | 59 |
| Trombly, Mi., U.S. | B3 | 99 |
| Tromper Wiek, b., E. Ger. | D7 | 15 |
| Tromsö, Nor. | C8 | 14 |
| Trona, Ca., U.S. | E5 | 82 |
| Tronador, Monte, mtn., S.A. | C2 | 54 |
| Trondheim, Nor. | F4 | 14 |
| Trondheimsfjorden, Nor. | F3 | 14 |
| Troon, Scot., U.K. | F4 | 13 |
| Trooper, Pa., U.S. | *F11 | 115 |
| Tropea, Italy | F5 | 23 |
| Trophy Mountain, mtn., B.C. | D8 | 69 |
| Tropic, Ut., U.S. | F3 | 121 |
| Trosa, Swe. | u35 | 14 |
| Trosky, Mtn., U.S. | G2 | 100 |
| Trossachs, Sask. | H3 | 75 |
| Trostan, mtn., N. Ire., U.K. | B5 | 11 |
| Trotters, N.D., U.S. | B2 | 111 |
| Trotwood, Oh., U.S. | C1 | 112 |
| Troup, Tx., U.S. | C5 | 120 |
| Troup, co., Ga., U.S. | C1 | 87 |
| Trousdale, Ks., U.S. | E4 | 93 |
| Trousdale, co., Tn., U.S. | A5 | 119 |
| Trousers Lake, l., N.B. | B3 | 71 |
| Trout, La., U.S. | C3 | 95 |
| Trout, stm., Alta. | A3 | 68 |
| Trout, stm., Fl., U.S. | m8 | 86 |
| Trout, stm., Vt., U.S. | B3 | 122 |
| Trout Creek, Ont. | B5 | 73 |
| Trout Creek, Mi., U.S. | n12 | 99 |
| Trout Creek, Mt., U.S. | C1 | 103 |
| Trout Creek, Ut., U.S. | D2 | 121 |
| Trout Creek Pass, Co., U.S. | C5 | 83 |
| Troutdale, Me., U.S. | C3 | 96 |
| Troutdale, Or., U.S. | *B4 | 114 |
| Troutdale, Va., U.S. | D1 | 123 |
| Trout Lake, Mi., U.S. | B6 | 99 |
| Trout Lake, Wa., U.S. | D4 | 124 |
| Trout Lake, l., N.W. Ter. | D9 | 66 |
| Trout Lake, l., Ont. | o16 | 73 |
| Trout Lake, l., Ont. | A5 | 73 |
| Trout Lake, l., Wi., U.S. | B4 | 126 |
| Troutman, Ga., U.S. | E2 | 87 |
| Troutman, N.C., U.S. | B2 | 110 |
| Trout Peak, mtn., Wy., U.S. | B3 | 127 |
| Trout River, Newf. | D2 | 72 |
| Trout Run, Pa., U.S. | D7 | 115 |
| Troutville, Va., U.S. | C3 | 123 |
| Trouville [-sur-Mer], Fr. | C4 | 16 |
| Trowbridge, Eng., U.K. | E5 | 10 |
| Troy, Al., U.S. | D4 | 78 |
| Troy, Id., U.S. | C2 | 89 |
| Troy, Il., U.S. | E4 | 90 |
| Troy, Ks., U.S. | C8 | 93 |
| Troy, Mi., U.S. | o15 | 99 |
| Troy, Mo., U.S. | C7 | 102 |
| Troy, Mt., U.S. | B1 | 103 |
| Troy, N.H., U.S. | E2 | 106 |
| Troy, N.Y., U.S. | C7 | 109 |
| Troy, N.C., U.S. | B3 | 110 |
| Troy, Oh., U.S. | B1 | 112 |
| Troy, Ok., U.S. | C5 | 113 |
| Troy, Pa., U.S. | C8 | 115 |
| Troy, S.C., U.S. | D3 | 117 |
| Troy, Tn., U.S. | A2 | 119 |
| Troy, Vt., U.S. | B4 | 122 |
| Troy, W.V., U.S. | B4 | 125 |
| Troyes, Fr. | C6 | 16 |
| Troy Grove, Il., U.S. | B4 | 90 |
| Troy Mills, Ia., U.S. | B6 | 92 |
| Troy Peak, mtn., Nv., U.S. | E6 | 105 |
| Truax, Sask. | H3 | 75 |
| Trubchevsk, Sov. Un. | E9 | 27 |
| Trubschachen, Switz. | C4 | 21 |
| Truchas, N.M., U.S. | A4 | 108 |
| Truchas Peak, mtn., N.M., U.S. | B4 | 108 |
| Truckee, Ca., U.S. | C3 | 82 |
| Truckee, stm., U.S. | D2 | 105 |
| Trujillo, Hond. | D7 | 63 |
| Trujillo, Peru | C2 | 58 |
| Trujillo, Spain | C3 | 22 |
| Trujillo, state, Ven. | B3 | 60 |
| Trujillo, Ven. | B3 | 60 |
| Truk, is., Micron. | F9 | 6 |
| Truk International Airport, Micron. | Q18 | 52 |
| Truk Lagoon, b., Micron. | Q18 | 52 |
| Trumann, Ar., U.S. | B5 | 81 |
| Trumansburg, N.Y., U.S. | C4 | 109 |
| Trumbull, Ct., U.S. | E3 | 84 |
| Trumbull, Ne., U.S. | D7 | 104 |
| Trumbull, co., Oh., U.S. | A5 | 112 |
| Trumbull, Mount, mtn., Az., U.S. | A2 | 80 |
| Trún, Bul. | D6 | 24 |
| Truro, N.S. | D6 | 71 |
| Truro, Eng., U.K. | E4 | 10 |
| Truro, Ia., U.S. | C4 | 92 |
| Truro, Ma., U.S. | C7 | 98 |
| Truscott, Tx., U.S. | C3 | 120 |
| Truskmore, mtn., Ire. | C3 | 11 |
| Trussville, Al., U.S. | B3 | 78 |
| Trustom Pond, l., R.I., U.S. | G3 | 116 |
| Trust Territory of the Pacific Islands see Pacific Islands, Trust Territory of the, dep., Oc. | F9 | 6 |
| Truth or Consequences (Hot Springs), N.M., U.S. | D2 | 108 |
| Trutnov, Czech. | C3 | 26 |
| Truxton, Az., U.S. | B2 | 80 |
| Truxton, Mo., U.S. | B6 | 102 |
| Truxton, N.Y., U.S. | C4 | 109 |
| Tryon, N.C., U.S. | f10 | 110 |
| Tryon, Ok., U.S. | B5 | 113 |
| Trysil, Nor. | G5 | 14 |
| Trzcianka, Pol. | B4 | 26 |
| Trzebiatów, Pol. | A3 | 26 |
| Trzebinia, Pol. | C5 | 26 |
| Trzebnica, Pol. | C4 | 26 |
| Tsagaan Tologoy Hiid, Mong. | C2 | 32 |
| Tsaidam Basin see Qaidam Pendi, China | D3 | 31 |
| Tsakir, Sov. Un. | A5 | 31 |
| Tsala Apopka Lake, l., Fl., U.S. | D4 | 86 |
| Tsaratanana, Madag. | g9 | 49 |
| Tsast Bogd Mountain, mtn., Mong. | B3 | 31 |
| Tsau, Bots. | B3 | 49 |
| Tsavo, Kenya | B6 | 48 |
| Tschetter Colony, S.D., U.S. | D8 | 118 |
| Tschida, Lake, res., N.D., U.S. | C4 | 111 |
| Tselinograd, Sov. Un. | D10 | 29 |
| Tsentralnyy, Sov. Un. | D26 | 8 |
| Tsetserleg, Mong. | B5 | 31 |
| Tshabong, Bots. | C3 | 49 |
| Tshane, Bots. | B3 | 49 |
| Tshela, Zaire | B1 | 48 |
| Tshikapa, Zaire | C3 | 48 |
| Tshilongo, Zaire | D4 | 48 |
| Tshimbo, Zaire | C4 | 48 |
| Tshofa, Zaire | C4 | 48 |
| Tshuapa, stm., Zaire | B3 | 48 |
| Tshukudu, Bots. | B3 | 49 |
| Tshwaane, Bots. | B3 | 49 |
| Tsiafajavona, mtn., Madag. | g9 | 49 |
| Tsihombe, Madag. | i9 | 49 |
| Tsimlyansk Reservoir, res., Sov. Un. | E7 | 29 |
| Tsinan see Jinan, China | D8 | 31 |
| Tsinghai see Qinghai, prov., China | D4 | 31 |
| Tsingtao see Qingdao, China | D9 | 31 |
| Tsinling Shan see Qin Ling, mts., China | E6 | 31 |
| Tsintsabis, Nmb. | A2 | 49 |
| Tsiroanomandidy, Madag. | g9 | 49 |
| Tsitsihar see Qiqihar, China | B9 | 31 |
| Tsitsutl Peak, mtn., B.C. | C5 | 69 |
| Tsivory, Madag. | h9 | 49 |
| Tskhinvali, Sov. Un. | E2 | 28 |
| Tsna, stm., Sov. Un. | E13 | 27 |
| Tsodilo Hill, hill, Bots. | A3 | 49 |
| Tsogttsetsiy, Mong. | C1 | 32 |
| Tsu, Japan | i8 | 33 |
| Tsuchiura, Japan | H10 | 33 |
| Tsugaru Strait, strt., Japan | F10 | 33 |
| Tsuken Island, i., Japan | O5 | 52 |
| Tsulukidze, Sov. Un. | A14 | 40 |
| Tsumeb, Nmb. | A2 | 49 |
| Tsumis Park, Nmb. | B2 | 49 |
| Tsun Wan, H.K. | *G7 | 31 |
| Tsuruga, Japan | i8 | 33 |
| Tsuruoka, Japan | G9 | 33 |
| Tsushima, Japan | n15 | 33 |
| Tsu Shima, is., Japan | E10 | 31 |
| Tsuyama, Japan | I6 | 33 |
| Tua, stm., Port. | B2 | 22 |
| Tual, Indon. | G8 | 34 |
| Tualatin, Or., U.S. | *h12 | 114 |
| Tualatin, stm., Or., U.S. | h11 | 114 |
| Tuam, Ire. | D2 | 10 |
| Tuamotu Archipelago, is., Fr. Poly. | H13 | 6 |
| Tuangku, i., Indon. | K2 | 35 |
| Tuapse, Sov. Un. | G16 | 8 |
| Tuasivi, W. Sam. | F11 | 52 |
| Tuasivi, Cape, c., W. Sam. | F11 | 52 |
| Tuatapere, N.Z. | Q11 | 51 |
| Tubac, Az., U.S. | F4 | 80 |
| Tuba City, Az., U.S. | A4 | 80 |
| Tubarão, Braz. | D3 | 56 |
| Tubas, Isr. Occ. | B7 | 41 |
| Tuberose, Sask. | G1 | 75 |
| Tübingen, W. Ger. | D4 | 18 |
| Tubruq (Tobruk), Libya | C4 | 43 |
| Tubuai Islands, is., Fr. Poly. | H13 | 6 |
| Tucacas, Ven. | A4 | 60 |
| Tucannon, stm., Wa., U.S. | C8 | 124 |
| Tucannon Canyon, val., Wa., U.S. | C8 | 124 |
| Tucano, Braz. | D3 | 57 |
| Tuchola, Pol. | B4 | 26 |
| Tuckahoe, N.J., U.S. | E3 | 107 |
| Tuckahoe, N.Y., U.S. | h13 | 109 |
| Tuckahoe, stm., N.J., U.S. | E3 | 107 |
| Tuckahoe Creek, stm., Md., U.S. | C6 | 97 |
| Tucker, Ar., U.S. | C3 | 81 |
| Tucker, Ga., U.S. | h8 | 87 |
| Tucker, co., W.V., U.S. | B5 | 125 |
| Tucker Island, i., N.J., U.S. | E4 | 107 |
| Tuckerman, Ar., U.S. | B4 | 81 |
| Tuckernuck Island, i., Ma., U.S. | D7 | 98 |
| Tuckers Crossing, Ms., U.S. | D4 | 101 |
| Tuckerton, N.J., U.S. | E4 | 107 |
| Tucson, Az., U.S. | E5 | 80 |
| Tucumán, prov., Arg. | B2 | 54 |
| Tucumcari, N.M., U.S. | B6 | 108 |
| Tucumcari Mountain, mtn., N.M., U.S. | B6 | 108 |
| Tucupita, Ven. | B6 | 60 |
| Tucuruí, Braz. | C5 | 59 |
| Tudela, Spain | A5 | 22 |
| Tudmur (Palmyra), Syria | E12 | 41 |
| Tufi, Pap. N. Gui. | k12 | 50 |
| Tuftonboro, N.H., U.S. | C4 | 106 |
| Tugaloo Lake, res., U.S. | B1 | 117 |
| Tugaske, Sask. | G3 | 75 |
| Tug Fork, stm., U.S. | C2 | 125 |
| Tuguegarao, Phil. | B7 | 34 |
| Tuira, stm., Pan. | G9 | 62 |
| Tukangbesi Islands, is., Indon. | G6 | 34 |
| Tükrah, Libya | C4 | 43 |
| Tuktoyaktuk, N.W. Ter. | C6 | 66 |
| Tukums, Sov. Un. | C4 | 27 |
| Tukuyu, Tan. | C5 | 48 |
| Tukwila, Wa., U.S. | f11 | 124 |
| Tula, Ms., U.S. | B4 | 101 |
| Tula, Sov. Un. | D6 | 29 |
| Tula de Allende, Mex. | m14 | 63 |
| Tulalip Indian Reservation, Wa., U.S. | A3 | 124 |
| Tulancingo, Mex. | C5 | 63 |
| Tulare, Ca., U.S. | D4 | 82 |
| Tulare, S.D., U.S. | C7 | 118 |
| Tulare, co., Ca., U.S. | D4 | 82 |
| Tulare Lake, l., Ca., U.S. | D4 | 82 |
| Tularosa, N.M., U.S. | D3 | 108 |
| Tularosa Mountains, mts., N.M., U.S. | D1 | 108 |
| Tularosa Valley, val., N.M., U.S. | E3 | 108 |
| Tulbagh, S. Afr. | D2 | 49 |
| Tulcán, Ec. | A2 | 58 |
| Tulcea, Rom. | C9 | 24 |
| Tulchin, Sov. Un. | G7 | 27 |
| Tulelake, Ca., U.S. | B3 | 82 |
| Tule Lake Sump, sw., Ca., U.S. | B3 | 82 |
| Tule River Indian Reservation, Ca., U.S. | E4 | 82 |
| Tuleta, Tx., U.S. | E4 | 120 |
| Tule Valley, val., Ut., U.S. | D2 | 121 |
| Tuli, Zimb. | B4 | 49 |
| Tulia, Tx., U.S. | B2 | 120 |
| Tulla, Ire. | E3 | 11 |
| Tullahassee, Ok., U.S. | B6 | 113 |
| Tullahoma, Tn., U.S. | B5 | 119 |
| Tullamore, Ire. | D3 | 10 |
| Tulle, Fr. | D4 | 16 |
| Tullins, Fr. | E6 | 16 |
| Tulln, Aus. | D8 | 18 |
| Tullos, La., U.S. | C3 | 95 |
| Tullow, Ire. | E5 | 11 |
| Tully, N.Y., U.S. | C4 | 109 |
| Tully, Austl. | A4 | 49 |
| Tulmaythah, Libya | C4 | 43 |
| Tuloma, stm., Sov. Un. | B15 | 8 |
| Tulot, Ar., U.S. | B5 | 81 |
| Tulsa, Ok., U.S. | A6 | 113 |
| Tulsa, co., Ok., U.S. | B6 | 113 |
| Tulsequah, B.C. | E6 | 66 |
| Tulsk, Ire. | D3 | 11 |
| Tuluá, Col. | C2 | 60 |
| Tulun, Sov. Un. | D13 | 29 |
| Tulungagung, Indon. | G4 | 34 |
| Tulu Welel, mtn., Eth. | D4 | 47 |
| Tuma, stm., Nic. | D5 | 62 |
| Tumaco, Col. | C2 | 60 |
| Tumacacori National Monument, Az., U.S. | F4 | 80 |
| Tumaco, Ensenada de, b., Col. | C2 | 60 |
| Tumalo, Or., U.S. | C5 | 114 |
| Tumatumari, Guy. | A3 | 59 |
| Tumba, Lac, l., Zaire | B2 | 48 |
| Tumbarumba, Austl. | G7 | 51 |
| Tumbaya, Arg. | D2 | 55 |
| Tumbes, Peru | B1 | 58 |
| Tumbes, dept., Peru | B1 | 58 |
| Tumble Mountain, mtn., Mt., U.S. | E7 | 103 |
| Tumbler Ridge, B.C. | B7 | 69 |
| Tumbling Shoals, Ar., U.S. | B3 | 81 |
| Tumen, China | C10 | 31 |
| Tumen Jiang, stm., Asia | C10 | 31 |
| Tumeremo, Ven. | B6 | 60 |
| Tumkūr, India | F6 | 36 |
| Tummin, stm., Sov. Un. | A10 | 33 |
| Tumon Bay, b., Guam | L10 | 52 |
| Tumtum, Wa., U.S. | B8 | 124 |
| Tumu, Ghana | D4 | 45 |
| Tumuc-Humac Mountains, mts., S.A. | B3 | 59 |
| Tumut, Austl. | G7 | 51 |
| Tumwater, Wa., U.S. | B3 | 124 |
| Tunapuna, Trin. | N23 | 65 |
| Tunas de Zaza, Cuba | D4 | 60 |
| Tunaycha, l., Sov. Un. | C11 | 33 |
| Tunbridge, Vt., U.S. | D4 | 122 |
| Tunbridge Wells see Royal Tunbridge Wells, Eng., U.K. | J13 | 7 |
| Tunduru, Tan. | D7 | 48 |
| Tundzha, stm., Eur. | D8 | 24 |
| Tunga, stm., India | F6 | 36 |
| Tungla, Nic. | D6 | 62 |
| Tungurahua, prov., Ec. | B2 | 58 |
| Tuni, India | I9 | 37 |
| Tunica, La., U.S. | D4 | 95 |
| Tunica, Ms., U.S. | A3 | 101 |
| Tunica, co., Ms., U.S. | A3 | 101 |
| Tunis, Tun. | B7 | 44 |
| Tunis, Gulf of, b., Tun. | F3 | 23 |
| Tunisia, ctry., Afr. | C5 | 44 |
| Tunis Mills, Md., U.S. | C5 | 97 |
| Tunja, Col. | B2 | 58 |
| Tunkhannock, Pa., U.S. | C10 | 115 |
| Tunk Lake, l., Me., U.S. | D4 | 96 |
| Tunnel Hill, Ga., U.S. | B1 | 87 |
| Tunnel Springs, Al., U.S. | D2 | 78 |
| Tunnelton, In., U.S. | G5 | 91 |
| Tunnelton, W.V., U.S. | B5 | 125 |
| Tunø, i., Den. | C4 | 15 |
| Tunp Range, mts., Wy., U.S. | D2 | 127 |
| Tunungayualok Island, i., Newf. | g9 | 72 |
| Tunuyán, Arg. | A3 | 54 |
| Tunuyán, stm., Arg. | A3 | 54 |
| Tunxi, China | F5 | 31 |
| Tuolumne, Ca., U.S. | D3 | 82 |
| Tuolumne, co., Ca., U.S. | D3 | 82 |
| Tuolumne, stm., Ca., U.S. | D3 | 82 |
| Tupã, Braz. | G12 | 29 |
| Tupanciretã, Braz. | D2 | 56 |
| Tupelo, Ms., U.S. | A5 | 101 |
| Tupelo, Ok., U.S. | C5 | 113 |
| Tupik, Sov. Un. | D13 | 29 |
| Tupiza, Bol. | D2 | 55 |
| Tupman, Ca., U.S. | E4 | 82 |
| Tupper, B.C. | B7 | 69 |
| Tupper Lake, N.Y., U.S. | A6 | 109 |
| Tupper Lake, l., N.Y., U.S. | A6 | 109 |
| Tuppers Plains, Oh., U.S. | C4 | 112 |
| Tupperville, Ont. | E2 | 73 |
| Tupungato, Arg. | A3 | 54 |
| Tupungato, Cerro, mtn., S.A. | A3 | 54 |
| Tuquan, China | B11 | 31 |
| Túquerres, Col. | C2 | 60 |
| Tura, Sov. Un. | C12 | 29 |
| Tura, stm., Sov. Un. | D9 | 29 |
| Tura, India | H14 | 36 |
| Turan Lowland, pl., Sov. Un. | E5 | 28 |
| Turayf, Sau. Ar. | B3 | 38 |
| Turbaco, Col. | A2 | 60 |
| Turbat, Pak. | C3 | 36 |
| Turbenthal, Switz. | B6 | 21 |
| Turbo, Col. | B2 | 60 |
| Turbotville, Pa., U.S. | D8 | 115 |
| Turda, Rom. | B6 | 24 |
| Turek, Pol. | B5 | 26 |
| Turgay, Sov. Un. | E9 | 29 |
| Turgay, stm., Sov. Un. | D6 | 28 |
| Türgen Mountain, mtn., Mong. | B3 | 31 |
| Türgovishte, Bul. | C8 | 24 |
| Turgutlu, Tur. | C6 | 40 |
| Turhal, Tur. | *B11 | 27 |
| Turia, stm., Spain | C5 | 22 |
| Turiaçu, Braz. | B1 | 57 |
| Turiaçu, stm., Braz. | A5 | 60 |
| Turin, Alta. | E4 | 68 |
| Turin (Torino), Italy | B1 | 23 |
| Turin, Ga., U.S. | C2 | 87 |
| Turin, Ia., U.S. | B1 | 92 |
| Turin, N.Y., U.S. | B5 | 109 |
| Turinsk, Sov. Un. | B6 | 28 |
| Turiy Rog, Sov. Un. | D5 | 33 |
| Turkestan, Sov. Un. | E8 | 28 |
| Türkeve, Hung. | B5 | 24 |
| Turkey, N.C., U.S. | B4 | 110 |
| Turkey, Tx., U.S. | B2 | 120 |
| Turkey, ctry., Asia | C10 | 40 |
| Turkey, stm., Ia., U.S. | B6 | 92 |
| Turkey Creek, La., U.S. | D3 | 95 |
| Turkey Creek, stm., Ne., U.S. | D8 | 104 |
| Turkey Creek, stm., Ok., U.S. | A3 | 113 |
| Turkey Point, c., Md., U.S. | B5 | 97 |
| Turkmen S.S.R., state, Sov. Un. | F8 | 29 |
| Turk Mine, Zimb. | A4 | 49 |
| Turks and Caicos Islands, dep., N.A. | D8 | 64 |
| Turks Island Passage, strt., T./C. Is. | D8 | 64 |
| Turku (Åbo), Fin. | G10 | 14 |
| Turkwel, stm., Kenya | A6 | 48 |
| Turley, Ok., U.S. | A6 | 113 |
| Turlock, Ca., U.S. | D3 | 82 |
| Turmalina, Braz. | D6 | 57 |
| Turmus 'Ayyā, Isr. Occ. | B7 | 41 |
| Turnagain, Cape, c., N.Z. | E26 | 8 |
| Turneffe Islands, is., Belize | D7 | 63 |
| Turner, Ar., U.S. | C4 | 81 |
| Turner, Me., U.S. | D2 | 96 |
| Turner, Mi., U.S. | D7 | 99 |
| Turner, Mt., U.S. | B8 | 103 |
| Turner, Or., U.S. | C4 | 114 |
| Turner, co., Ga., U.S. | E3 | 87 |
| Turner, co., S.D., U.S. | D8 | 118 |
| Turner Mountain, hill, Ct., U.S. | C1 | 84 |
| Turners Falls, Ma., U.S. | A2 | 98 |
| Turner Valley, Alta. | D3 | 68 |
| Turnhout, Bel. | B6 | 16 |
| Turnor Lake, l., Sask. | m7 | 75 |
| Turnov, Czech. | C3 | 26 |
| Turnu-Măgurele, Rom. | E26 | 8 |
| Turon, Ks., U.S. | E5 | 93 |
| Turpan, China | C2 | 31 |
| Turpan Pendi, China | C2 | 31 |
| Turpin, Ok., U.S. | e10 | 113 |
| Turquino, Pico, mtn., Cuba | E5 | 64 |
| Turrell, Ar., U.S. | B5 | 81 |
| Turret Peak, mtn., Az., U.S. | C4 | 80 |
| Turriff, Scot., U.K. | C6 | 13 |
| Turshiz see Kāshmar, Iran | E9 | 29 |
| Turtkul, Sov. Un. | E9 | 29 |
| Turtle, stm., Ont. | E5 | 93 |
| Turtle Creek, N.B. | D5 | 71 |
| Turtle Creek, stm., Pa., U.S. | k14 | 115 |
| Turtle Flambeau Flowage, res., Wi., U.S. | B3 | 126 |
| Turtleford, Sask. | D1 | 75 |
| Turtle Lake, N.D., U.S. | B5 | 111 |
| Turtle Lake, Wi., U.S. | C1 | 126 |
| Turtle Lake, l., Sask. | D1 | 75 |
| Turtle Mountain Indian Reservation, N.D., U.S. | A6 | 111 |
| Turtle Mountains, hills, N.A. | A5 | 111 |
| Turton, S.D., U.S. | B7 | 118 |
| Turukhansk, Sov. Un. | C11 | 29 |
| Turya, stm., Sov. Un. | E5 | 93 |
| Tuscaloosa, Al., U.S. | B2 | 78 |
| Tuscaloosa, co., Al., U.S. | B2 | 78 |
| Tuscany (Toscana), prov., Italy | C4 | 23 |
| Tuscarawas, co., Oh., U.S. | B4 | 112 |
| Tuscarawas, stm., Oh., U.S. | B4 | 112 |
| Tuscarora Indian Reservation, N.Y., U.S. | B2 | 109 |
| Tuscarora Mountain, mtn., Pa., U.S. | F6 | 115 |
| Tuscarora Mountains, mts., Nv., U.S. | D5 | 105 |
| Tuscola, Il., U.S. | D5 | 90 |
| Tuscola, Ms., U.S. | C5 | 101 |
| Tuscola, co., Mi., U.S. | C3 | 120 — |
| Tusculum, hist., Italy | h9 | 23 |
| Tuscumbia, Al., U.S. | A2 | 78 |
| Tuscumbia, Mo., U.S. | C5 | 102 |
| Tushka, Ok., U.S. | C6 | 113 |
| Tuskahoma, Ok., U.S. | C6 | 113 |
| Tuskegee, Al., U.S. | C4 | 78 |
| Tusket, N.S. | F4 | 71 |
| Tusket, stm., N.S. | E4 | 71 |
| Tustin, Ca., U.S. | *n13 | 82 |
| Tustin, Mi., U.S. | D5 | 99 |
| Tustumena Lake, l., Ak., U.S. | g16 | 79 |
| Tutayev, Sov. Un. | C12 | 27 |
| Tuthill, S.D., U.S. | D4 | 118 |
| Tuticorin, India | G6 | 36 |
| Tutrakan, Bul. | C8 | 24 |
| Tuttle, N.D., U.S. | B6 | 111 |
| Tuttle, Ok., U.S. | B4 | 113 |
| Tuttle Creek Dam, Ks., U.S. | C7 | 93 |
| Tuttle Creek Lake, res., Ks., U.S. | C7 | 93 |
| Tuttlingen, W. Ger. | E4 | 18 |
| Tutubu, Tan. | C5 | 48 |
| Tutuila, i., Am. Sam. | G13 | 52 |
| Tututepec, Mex. | n15 | 63 |
| Tutupaca, Volcán, vol., Peru | E3 | 58 |
| Tututalak Mountain, mtn., Ak., U.S. | B7 | 79 |
| Tuttwiler, Ms., U.S. | A3 | 101 |
| Tuvalu, ctry., Oc. | G10 | 6 |
| Tuve, Sov. Un. | E13 | 37 |
| Tuvuca, i., Fiji | H16 | 52 |
| Tuwayq, Jabal, mts., Sau. Ar. | C4 | 38 |
| Tuxedo, N.C., U.S. | f10 | 110 |
| Tuxedo Park, De., U.S. | i7 | 85 |
| Tuxford, Sask. | G3 | 75 |
| Tuxpan, Mex. | n12 | 63 |
| Tuxpan, Mex. | C3 | 63 |
| Tuxpan, stm., Mex. | m15 | 63 |
| Tuxpan de Rodríguez Cano, Mex. | C5 | 63 |
| Tuxtepec, Mex. | n15 | 63 |
| Tuxtla Gutiérrez, Mex. | D6 | 63 |
| Túy, Spain | A1 | 22 |
| Tuyen Quang, Viet. | F8 | 35 |
| Tuymazy, Sov. Un. | D8 | 29 |
| Tuy Hoa, Viet. | F8 | 35 |
| Tüysärkän, Iran | D4 | 39 |
| Tuz, Lake, l., Tur. | C9 | 40 |
| Tuzigoot National Monument, Az., U.S. | C4 | 80 |
| Tuz Khurmātū, Iraq | E15 | 40 |
| Tuzla, Yugo. | C4 | 24 |
| Tweed, Ont. | C7 | 73 |
| Tweed, stm., U.K. | C5 | 10 |
| Tweedsmuir Provincial Park, B.C. | C4 | 69 |
| Tweedy Mountain, mtn., Mt., U.S. | E4 | 103 |
| Twelve Mile, In., U.S. | C5 | 91 |
| Twelve Mile Lake, l., Sask. | H2 | 75 |
| Twelvepole Creek, stm., W.V., U.S. | C2 | 125 |
| Twelvepole Creek, East Fork, stm., W.V., U.S. | D2 | 125 |
| Twelvepole Creek, West Fork, stm., W.V., U.S. | D2 | 125 |
| Twentymile Creek, stm., W.V., U.S. | C3 | 125 |
| Twentynine Palms, Ca., U.S. | E5 | 82 |
| Twentynine Palms Base, Ca., U.S. | *E5 | 82 |
| Twentynine Palms Marine Corps Base, mil., Ca., U.S. | E5 | 82 |
| Twig, Mn., U.S. | D6 | 100 |
| Twiggs, co., Ga., U.S. | D3 | 87 |
| Twillingate, Newf. | D4 | 72 |
| Twin Bridges, Mt., U.S. | E4 | 103 |
| Twin Brooks, S.D., U.S. | B9 | 118 |
| Twin Buttes, mtn., Or., U.S. | C4 | 114 |
| Twin Buttes Reservoir, res., Tx., U.S. | D2 | 120 |
| Twin City, Ga., U.S. | D4 | 87 |
| Twin Creek, stm., Oh., U.S. | C1 | 112 |
| Twin Falls, Id., U.S. | G4 | 89 |
| Twin Falls, co., Id., U.S. | G4 | 89 |
| Twin Lakes, Co., U.S. | B4 | 83 |
| Twin Lakes, Ga., U.S. | F3 | 87 |
| Twin Lakes, Wi., U.S. | F5 | 126 |
| Twin Lakes, l., Ct., U.S. | A2 | 84 |
| Twin Lakes, l., Ia., U.S. | B3 | 92 |
| Twin Lakes, l., Me., U.S. | C4 | 96 |
| Twin Lakes Mountain, mtn., N.Y., U.S. | B6 | 109 |
| Twin Mountains, N.H., U.S. | B3 | 106 |
| Twin Mountains, mts., Wy., U.S. | E7 | 127 |
| Twin Peaks, mts., Id., U.S. | E4 | 89 |
| Twin Rivers, N.J., U.S. | C4 | 107 |
| Twin Rocks, Pa., U.S. | F4 | 115 |
| Twinsburg, Oh., U.S. | A4 | 112 |
| Twin Valley, Mn., U.S. | C2 | 100 |
| Twisp, Wa., U.S. | A5 | 124 |
| Twist, Ar., U.S. | B5 | 81 |
| Two Butte Creek, stm., Co., U.S. | D8 | 83 |
| Two Buttes, Co., U.S. | D8 | 83 |
| Two Creeks, Man. | D1 | 70 |
| Twodot, Mt., U.S. | D6 | 103 |
| Twoforks, stm., Sask. | C2 | 75 |
| Two Harbors, Mn., U.S. | C7 | 100 |
| Two Hills, Alta. | C5 | 68 |
| Two Mile Beach, N.J., U.S. | F3 | 107 |
| Two Prairie, Bayou, stm., Ar., U.S. | h11 | 81 |
| Two Rivers, Wi., U.S. | D6 | 126 |
| Two Rivers, North Branch, stm., Mn., U.S. | B2 | 100 |
| Two Rivers, South Branch, stm., Mn., U.S. | B2 | 100 |
| Tyachev, Sov. Un. | D7 | 26 |
| Tyaskin, Md., U.S. | D6 | 97 |
| Tybee Island, Ga., U.S. | g9 | 26 |
| Tychy, Pol. | g9 | 26 |
| Tye River, Va., U.S. | C4 | 123 |
| Tygart Lake, res., W.V., U.S. | B5 | 125 |
| Tygart River, Falls of the, wtfl., W.V., U.S. | k10 | 125 |
| Tygarts Creek, stm., Ky., U.S. | B7 | 94 |
| Tygart Valley, stm., W.V., U.S. | B4 | 125 |
| Tyger, stm., S.C., U.S. | B4 | 117 |
| Tygh Valley, Or., U.S. | B5 | 114 |
| Tyler, Mn., U.S. | F2 | 100 |
| Tyler, Pa., U.S. | D4 | 115 |
| Tyler, Tx., U.S. | C5 | 120 |
| Tyler, co., Tx., U.S. | D5 | 120 |
| Tyler, co., W.V., U.S. | B4 | 125 |
| Tyler, Lake, res., Tx., U.S. | C5 | 120 |
| Tyler Branch, stm., Vt., U.S. | B3 | 122 |
| Tyler Heights, W.V., U.S. | C3 | 125 |
| Tylersburg, Pa., U.S. | E7 | 115 |
| Tylerville, Pa., U.S. | E7 | 115 |
| Tylertown, Ms., U.S. | D3 | 101 |
| Tymochtee Creek, stm., Oh., U.S. | B2 | 112 |
| Tym, stm., Sov. Un. | C25 | 8 |
| Tynagh, Ire. | D3 | 11 |
| Tynda, Man. | D3 | 11 |
| Tyndall, S.D., U.S. | E8 | 118 |
| Tyndall Air Force Base, mil., Fl., U.S. | u16 | 86 |
| Tyndinskiy, Sov. Un. | D14 | 29 |
| Tyndrum, Scot., U.K. | E4 | 13 |
| Tyne, stm., Scot., U.K. | E6 | 13 |
| Tyne and Wear, co., Eng., U.K. | E7 | 13 |
| Tynemouth, Eng., U.K. | C6 | 10 |
| Týnec, Czech. | o18 | 26 |
| Tyner, In., U.S. | B5 | 91 |
| Tyner, N.C., U.S. | A6 | 110 |
| Tyner, Tn., U.S. | h11 | 119 |
| Tyngsboro, Ma., U.S. | A5 | 98 |
| Týn nad Vltavou, Czech. | F14 | 9 |
| Tynset, Nor. | F4 | 14 |
| Tyonek, Ak., U.S. | g17 | 79 |
| Tyre (Sūr), Leb. | B3 | 38 |
| Tyre, Ks., U.S. | D8 | 93 |
| Tyrma, Sov. Un. | A6 | 33 |
| Tyro, Ks., U.S. | E8 | 93 |

| Name | Map Ref. | Page |
|---|---|---|
| Tyrone, Ky., U.S. | B5 | 94 |
| Tyrone, N.M., U.S. | E1 | 108 |
| Tyrone, Ok., U.S. | e9 | 113 |
| Tyrone, Pa., U.S. | E5 | 115 |
| Tyronza, Ar., U.S. | B5 | 81 |
| Tyrrell, co., N.C., U.S. | B6 | 110 |
| Tyrrell, Lake, l., Austl. | G4 | 51 |
| Tyrrhenian Sea, Eur. | D3 | 23 |
| Tysons Corner, Va., U.S. | *B5 | 123 |
| Ty Ty, Ga., U.S. | E3 | 87 |
| Ty Ty Creek, stm., Ga., U.S. | E3 | 87 |
| Tyub-Karagan Peninsula, pen., Sov. Un. | E4 | 28 |
| Tyukalinsk, Sov. Un. | B8 | 28 |
| Tyuleniy Island, i., Sov. Un. | B12 | 33 |
| Tyumen, Sov. Un. | D9 | 29 |
| Tyuratam, Sov. Un. | D6 | 28 |
| Tyvan, Sask. | G4 | 75 |
| Tywyn, Wales, U.K. | B3 | 12 |
| Tzaneen, S. Afr. | B5 | 49 |
| **U** | | |
| Uatumã, stm., Braz. | C3 | 59 |
| Uaupés (Vaupés), stm., S.A. | C4 | 59 |
| Ubá, Braz. | C4 | 56 |
| Ubaíra, Braz. | D3 | 57 |
| Ubaitaba, Braz. | D3 | 57 |
| Ubangi (Oubangui), stm., Afr. | A2 | 48 |
| Ubaye, stm., Fr. | E2 | 20 |
| Ubayyid, Wādī al, val., Asia | B4 | 38 |
| Ube, Japan | E11 | 31 |
| Úbeda, Spain | C4 | 22 |
| Uberaba, Braz. | B3 | 56 |
| Uberlândia, Braz. | B3 | 56 |
| Überlingen, W. Ger. | E4 | 18 |
| Ubiaja, Nig. | E6 | 45 |
| Ubly, Mi., U.S. | E8 | 99 |
| Ubombo, S. Afr. | C5 | 49 |
| Ubon Ratchathani, Thai. | B2 | 34 |
| Uborka, Sov. Un. | D7 | 33 |
| Ubort, stm., Sov. Un. | F6 | 27 |
| Ubrique, Spain | D3 | 22 |
| Ubundu (Ponthierville), Zaire | B4 | 48 |
| Ucayali, dept., Peru | *C3 | 58 |
| Ucayali, stm., Peru | C3 | 58 |
| Uccle, Bel. | B6 | 16 |
| Ucharal, Sov. Un. | D10 | 28 |
| Uchiura Bay, b., Japan | E10 | 33 |
| Uchiza, Peru | C2 | 58 |
| Uchoa, Braz. | C3 | 56 |
| Uckange, Fr. | E6 | 17 |
| Ucluelet, B.C. | E5 | 69 |
| Ucon, Id., U.S. | F7 | 89 |
| Udagamandalam, India | F6 | 36 |
| Udaipur, India | D5 | 36 |
| Udall, Ks., U.S. | E6 | 93 |
| Udall, Mo., U.S. | E5 | 102 |
| Udaquiola, Arg. | B5 | 54 |
| Uddevalla, Swe. | H4 | 14 |
| Uden, Neth. | C5 | 17 |
| Udgīr, India | H6 | 37 |
| Udhampur, India | B6 | 36 |
| Udine, Italy | A4 | 23 |
| Udon Thani, Thai. | B2 | 34 |
| Udot, i., Micron. | Q18 | 52 |
| Udu Point, c., Fiji | H16 | 52 |
| Uecker, stm., E. Ger. | B6 | 18 |
| Ueckermünde, E. Ger. | B6 | 18 |
| Ueda, Japan | H9 | 33 |
| Uehling, Ne., U.S. | C9 | 104 |
| Uele, stm., Zaire | A3 | 48 |
| Uelen, Sov. Un. | C21 | 29 |
| Uelkal, Sov. Un. | C21 | 29 |
| Uelsen, W. Ger. | B6 | 17 |
| Uelzen, W. Ger. | B5 | 18 |
| Ueno, Japan | o15 | 33 |
| Uere, stm., Zaire | A4 | 48 |
| Uesslingen, Switz. | A6 | 21 |
| Uetendorf, Switz. | C4 | 21 |
| Uetersen, W. Ger. | E3 | 15 |
| Ufa, Sov. Un. | D8 | 29 |
| Ufa, stm., Sov. Un. | B5 | 28 |
| Uffenheim, W. Ger. | D5 | 19 |
| Ugab, stm., Nmb. | B2 | 49 |
| Ugalla, stm., Tan. | C5 | 48 |
| Uganda, ctry., Afr. | A5 | 48 |
| Ugashik, Ak., U.S. | D8 | 79 |
| Ugashik Lakes, l., Ak., U.S. | D8 | 79 |
| Ugep, Nig. | E6 | 45 |
| Ugine, Fr. | D2 | 20 |
| Uglegorsk, Sov. Un. | B13 | 31 |
| Uglich, Sov. Un. | C12 | 27 |
| Ugra, stm., Sov. Un. | D10 | 27 |
| Ugúrchin, Bul. | D7 | 24 |
| Uh, stm., Eur. | D7 | 26 |
| Uherské Hradiště, Czech. | D4 | 26 |
| Úhlava, stm., Czech. | D8 | 19 |
| Ühlingen, W. Ger. | A5 | 21 |
| Uhlman Lake, l., Man. | A2 | 70 |
| Uhrichsville, Oh., U.S. | B4 | 112 |
| Unřiňěves, Czech. | n18 | 26 |
| Uig, Scot., U.K. | C2 | 13 |
| Uig, Scot., U.K. | C2 | 13 |
| Uíge, Ang. | C2 | 48 |
| Uíge, dept., Ang. | C2 | 48 |
| Uijŏngbu, S. Kor. | H3 | 33 |
| Uiju, N. Kor. | C9 | 31 |
| Uil, Sov. Un. | D4 | 28 |
| Uil, stm., Sov. Un. | D4 | 28 |
| Uinkaret Plateau, plat., Az., U.S. | A2 | 80 |
| Uinta, co., Wy., U.S. | E2 | 127 |
| Uinta, stm., Ut., U.S. | C5 | 121 |
| Uintah, Ut., U.S. | *B4 | 121 |
| Uintah, co., Ut., U.S. | D6 | 121 |
| Uintah and Ouray Indian Reservation, Ut., U.S. | C5 | 121 |
| Uinta Mountains, mts., Ut., U.S. | C5 | 121 |
| Uitenhage, S. Afr. | D4 | 49 |
| Uithuizen, Neth. | A6 | 17 |
| Uivak, Cape, c., Newf. | f9 | 72 |
| Uji, Islands, is., Japan | K4 | 33 |
| Ujiji, Tan. | B4 | 48 |
| Uji-yamada see Ise, Japan | I8 | 33 |
| Ujjain, India | D6 | 36 |
| Ujungpandang (Makasar), Indon. | G5 | 34 |
| Uka, Japan | N6 | 52 |
| Uka, Sov. Un. | D19 | 29 |
| Ukerewe, i., Tan. | B5 | 48 |
| Ukhta, Sov. Un. | c8 | 29 |
| Ukiah, Ca., U.S. | C2 | 82 |
| Ukiah, Or., U.S. | B8 | 114 |
| Ukmergė, Sov. Un. | D5 | 27 |
| Ukraine, state, Sov. Un. | E5 | 29 |
| Uku, Japan | D1 | 43 |
| Ulaangom, Mong. | B3 | 31 |
| Ulak Island, i., Ak., U.S. | E4 | 79 |
| Ulan Bator (Ulaanbaatar), Mong. | B6 | 31 |
| Ulan-Ude, Sov. Un. | D13 | 29 |
| Ulba, Sov. Un. | E25 | 8 |
| Ulchin, S. Kor. | H4 | 33 |
| Ulcinj, Yugo. | E4 | 24 |
| Uldza, stm., Asia | B7 | 31 |
| Ulen, Mn., U.S. | C2 | 100 |
| Ulen, In., U.S. | D5 | 91 |
| Ulfborg, Den. | B2 | 15 |
| Ulhāsnagar, India | *E5 | 36 |
| Uliastay, Mong. | B4 | 31 |
| Ulindi, stm., Zaire | B4 | 48 |
| Ulla, Sov. Un. | D7 | 27 |
| Ulla, stm., Spain | A1 | 22 |
| Ulladulla, Austl. | G8 | 51 |
| Ullapool, Scot., U.K. | B4 | 10 |
| Ullared, Swe. | A6 | 15 |
| Ullin, Il., U.S. | F4 | 90 |
| Ullswater, l., Eng., U.K. | F6 | 13 |
| Ullŭng Island, i., S. Kor. | H5 | 33 |
| Ulm, W. Ger. | D4 | 18 |
| Ulm, Ar., U.S. | C4 | 81 |
| Ulm, Mt., U.S. | C5 | 103 |
| Ulman, Mo., U.S. | C5 | 102 |
| Ulricehamn, Swe. | I5 | 14 |
| Ulsan, S. Kor. | I4 | 33 |
| Ulster, Pa., U.S. | C9 | 115 |
| Ulster, co., N.Y., U.S. | D6 | 109 |
| Ulster, hist. reg., Eur. | C4 | 11 |
| Ulúa, stm., Hond. | C3 | 62 |
| Ulubat Lake, l., Tur. | B7 | 25 |
| Uluborlu, Tur. | C8 | 40 |
| Uludağ, mtn., Tur. | B7 | 40 |
| Ulukışla, Tur. | C8 | 40 |
| Ulungur He, stm., China | B2 | 31 |
| Ulva, i., Scot., U.K. | D2 | 13 |
| Ulverstone, Austl. | o15 | 50 |
| Ulyanovka, Sov. Un. | s31 | 14 |
| Ulyanovsk, Sov. Un. | D7 | 29 |
| Ulysses, Ks., U.S. | E2 | 93 |
| Ulysses, Ne., U.S. | C8 | 104 |
| Ulysses, Pa., U.S. | C6 | 115 |
| Ulzburg, W. Ger. | E3 | 15 |
| Uman, Sov. Un. | G8 | 27 |
| Umarkot, Pak. | C4 | 36 |
| Umatac Bay, b., Guam | M9 | 52 |
| Umatilla, Fl., U.S. | D5 | 86 |
| Umatilla, co., Or., U.S. | B8 | 114 |
| Umatilla, Or., U.S. | B7 | 114 |
| Umatilla Indian Reservation, Or., U.S. | B8 | 114 |
| Umba, Sov. Un. | D16 | 14 |
| Umbagog Lake, l., U.S. | A4 | 106 |
| Umboi, i., Pap. N. Gui. | k12 | 50 |
| Umbrail Pass, Eur. | C9 | 21 |
| Umbria, prov., Italy | C4 | 23 |
| Umbuzeiro, Braz. | C3 | 57 |
| Umcolcus Lake, l., Me., U.S. | B4 | 96 |
| Umeå, Swe. | F9 | 14 |
| Umeälven, stm., Swe. | E8 | 14 |
| Umhausen, Aus. | B6 | 20 |
| Umlazi, S. Afr. | *C5 | 49 |
| Umm el Fahm, Isr. | B7 | 41 |
| Umm Kaddadah, Sud. | C2 | 47 |
| Umm Lajj, Sau. Ar. | C3 | 38 |
| Umm Ruwābah, Sud. | C4 | 47 |
| Umnak Island, i., Ak., U.S. | E6 | 79 |
| Umniati, stm., Zimb. | A4 | 49 |
| Umpire, Ar., U.S. | C1 | 81 |
| Umpqua, stm., Or., U.S. | D3 | 114 |
| Umpqua, stm., Or., U.S. | D3 | 114 |
| Umrāniye, Yemen | B5 | 47 |
| Umsaskis Lake, l., Me., U.S. | B3 | 96 |
| Umtanum Ridge, mtn., Wa., U.S. | C5 | 124 |
| Umtata, Transkei | D4 | 49 |
| Umuahia, Nig. | E6 | 45 |
| Umzinto, S. Afr. | D5 | 49 |
| Una, stm., Yugo. | C2 | 24 |
| Unadilla, Ga., U.S. | D3 | 87 |
| Unadilla, Ne., U.S. | h12 | 104 |
| Unadilla, N.Y., U.S. | C5 | 109 |
| Unadilla, stm., N.Y., U.S. | C5 | 109 |
| Unaí, Braz. | B3 | 56 |
| Unaka, N.C., U.S. | f8 | 110 |
| Unaka Mountains, mts., U.S. | C11 | 119 |
| Unalakleet, Ak., U.S. | C7 | 79 |
| Unalaska Island, i., Ak., U.S. | E6 | 79 |
| 'Unayzah, Sau. Ar. | C4 | 38 |
| Uncasville, Ct., U.S. | D7 | 84 |
| Uncia, Bol. | C2 | 55 |
| Uncompahgre, stm., Co., U.S. | C3 | 83 |
| Uncompahgre Butte, mtn., Co., U.S. | C2 | 83 |
| Uncompahgre Mountains, mts., Co., U.S. | C3 | 83 |
| Uncompahgre Peak, mtn., Co., U.S. | C3 | 83 |
| Uncompahgre Plateau, plat., Co., U.S. | C2 | 83 |
| Underhill Center, Vt., U.S. | B3 | 122 |
| Underwood, Al., U.S. | B3 | 78 |
| Underwood, In., U.S. | G6 | 91 |
| Underwood, Ia., U.S. | C2 | 92 |
| Underwood, Mn., U.S. | D3 | 100 |
| Underwood, N.D., U.S. | B4 | 111 |
| Underwood, Wa., U.S. | D4 | 124 |
| Unecha, Sov. Un. | E9 | 27 |
| Uneiuxi, stm., Braz. | D4 | 60 |
| Unezhma, Sov. Un. | F17 | 14 |
| Ungarie, Austl. | F6 | 51 |
| Ungava, Péninsule d', pen., Que. | g12 | 74 |
| Ungava Bay, b., Can. | E19 | 16 |
| União, Braz. | D2 | 57 |
| União da Vitória, Braz. | D2 | 56 |
| União dos Palmares, Braz. | C3 | 57 |
| Unije, i., Yugo. | C2 | 24 |
| Unimak Island, i., Ak., U.S. | E6 | 79 |
| Unimak Pass, strt., Ak., U.S. | E6 | 79 |
| Unini, stm., Braz. | C2 | 59 |
| Union, Ar., U.S. | A4 | 81 |
| Union, Ct., U.S. | B7 | 84 |
| Union, Il., U.S. | A5 | 90 |
| Union, Ia., U.S. | H3 | 91 |
| Union, Ky., U.S. | k13 | 94 |
| Union, Me., U.S. | h10 | 95 |
| Union, Ms., U.S. | D3 | 96 |
| Union, Mo., U.S. | C6 | 102 |
| Union, Ne., U.S. | D10 | 104 |
| Union, N.H., U.S. | D4 | 106 |
| Union, N.J., U.S. | *B4 | 107 |
| Union, N.C., U.S. | A5 | 110 |
| Union, N.D., U.S. | A8 | 111 |
| Union, Oh., U.S. | *C1 | 112 |
| Union, Or., U.S. | B9 | 114 |
| Union, S.C., U.S. | B4 | 117 |
| Union, Ut., U.S. | *C4 | 121 |
| Union, Wa., U.S. | B2 | 124 |
| Union, W.V., U.S. | D4 | 125 |
| Union, co., Ar., U.S. | D3 | 81 |
| Union, co., Fl., U.S. | B4 | 86 |
| Union, co., Ga., U.S. | B2 | 87 |
| Union, co., Il., U.S. | F4 | 90 |
| Union, co., In., U.S. | E8 | 91 |
| Union, co., Ia., U.S. | C3 | 92 |
| Union, co., Ky., U.S. | C2 | 94 |
| Union, co., La., U.S. | B3 | 95 |
| Union, co., Ms., U.S. | A4 | 101 |
| Union, co., N.J., U.S. | B4 | 107 |
| Union, co., N.M., U.S. | A6 | 108 |
| Union, co., N.C., U.S. | B2 | 110 |
| Union, co., Oh., U.S. | B2 | 112 |
| Union, co., Or., U.S. | B8 | 114 |
| Union, co., Pa., U.S. | E7 | 115 |
| Union, co., S.C., U.S. | B4 | 117 |
| Union, co., S.D., U.S. | E9 | 118 |
| Union, co., Tn., U.S. | C10 | 119 |
| Union, West Branch, stm., Me., U.S. | D4 | 96 |
| Union Bay, B.C. | E5 | 69 |
| Union Beach, N.J., U.S. | C4 | 107 |
| Union Bridge, Md., U.S. | A3 | 97 |
| Union Center, S.D., U.S. | C3 | 118 |
| Union Center, Wi., U.S. | E3 | 126 |
| Union Church, Ms., U.S. | D3 | 101 |
| Union City, Ca., U.S. | h8 | 82 |
| Union City, Ga., U.S. | C2 | 87 |
| Union City, In., U.S. | D8 | 91 |
| Union City, Mi., U.S. | F5 | 99 |
| Union City, N.J., U.S. | h8 | 107 |
| Union City, Oh., U.S. | B1 | 112 |
| Union City, Ok., U.S. | B4 | 113 |
| Union City, Pa., U.S. | C2 | 115 |
| Union City, Tn., U.S. | A2 | 119 |
| Union Creek, Or., U.S. | E4 | 114 |
| Uniondale, In., U.S. | C7 | 91 |
| Uniondale, N.Y., U.S. | *E7 | 109 |
| Union Dale, Pa., U.S. | C10 | 115 |
| Unión de Reyes, Cuba | C3 | 64 |
| Union de Tula, Mex. | n11 | 63 |
| Union Flat Creek, stm., Wa., U.S. | C8 | 124 |
| Union Furnace, Oh., U.S. | C3 | 112 |
| Union Gap, Wa., U.S. | C5 | 124 |
| Union Grove, Wi., U.S. | F5 | 126 |
| Union Hall, Va., U.S. | D3 | 123 |
| Union Island, i., St. Vin. | V26 | 65 |
| Union Lake, Mi., U.S. | *o15 | 99 |
| Union Lake, l., N.J., U.S. | E2 | 107 |
| Union Mills, In., U.S. | C6 | 88 |
| Union Mills, N.C., U.S. | B4 | 110 |
| Union Mills, Md., U.S. | A3 | 97 |
| Union Park, Fl., U.S. | *D5 | 86 |
| Union Pier, Mi., U.S. | G4 | 99 |
| Union Point, Ga., U.S. | C3 | 87 |
| Union Springs, Al., U.S. | C4 | 78 |
| Union Springs, N.Y., U.S. | C4 | 109 |
| Union Star, Mo., U.S. | B3 | 102 |
| Uniontown, Al., U.S. | C2 | 78 |
| Uniontown, Ks., U.S. | E9 | 93 |
| Uniontown, Ky., U.S. | C2 | 94 |
| Uniontown, Md., U.S. | A3 | 97 |
| Uniontown, Oh., U.S. | B4 | 112 |
| Uniontown, Pa., U.S. | G2 | 115 |
| Uniontown, Wa., U.S. | C8 | 124 |
| Union Village, R.I., U.S. | B3 | 116 |
| Union Village, Vt., U.S. | D4 | 122 |
| Union Village Reservoir, res., Vt., U.S. | D4 | 122 |
| Unionville, Ct., U.S. | B4 | 84 |
| Unionville, Il., U.S. | F5 | 90 |
| Unionville, Ia., U.S. | D5 | 92 |
| Unionville, Me., U.S. | D5 | 96 |
| Unionville, Mo., U.S. | A4 | 102 |
| Unionville, Nv., U.S. | C3 | 105 |
| Unionville, N.C., U.S. | B2 | 110 |
| Unionville, Tn., U.S. | B5 | 119 |
| Unionville, Va., U.S. | B5 | 123 |
| Unionville Center, Oh., U.S. | B2 | 112 |
| Unisan, Phil. | p13 | 34 |
| United, Pa., U.S. | F3 | 115 |
| United Arab Emirates, ctry., Asia | C5 | 38 |
| United Kingdom, ctry., Eur. | C5 | 10 |
| United Nations Headquarters, N.Y., U.S. | h12 | 109 |
| United Pueblos Indian Reservations, N.M., U.S. | A3 | 108 |
| United States, ctry., N.A. | C8 | 76 |
| United States Air Force Academy, mil., Co., U.S. | B6 | 83 |
| United States Military Academy, mil., N.Y., U.S. | C6 | 109 |
| United States Naval Academy, mil., Md., U.S. | C4 | 97 |
| Unity, Sask. | E1 | 75 |
| Unity, Il., U.S. | F4 | 90 |
| Unity, Me., U.S. | D3 | 96 |
| Unity, N.H., U.S. | D2 | 106 |
| Unity Pond, l., Me., U.S. | D3 | 96 |
| Unity Reservoir, res., Or., U.S. | C8 | 114 |
| Unityville, S.D., U.S. | D8 | 118 |
| Universal, In., U.S. | E3 | 91 |
| Universal City, Tx., U.S. | *E3 | 120 |
| Universales, Montes, mts., Spain | B5 | 22 |
| University City, Mo., U.S. | C7 | 102 |
| University Gardens, N.Y., U.S. | *n15 | 109 |
| University Heights, In., U.S. | C6 | 91 |
| University Heights, Oh., U.S. | h9 | 112 |
| University Park, Ia., U.S. | C5 | 92 |
| University Park, N.M., U.S. | E3 | 108 |
| University Park, Tx., U.S. | n10 | 120 |
| University Place, Wa., U.S. | f10 | 124 |
| Upata, Ven. | B5 | 60 |
| Upatoi Creek, stm., Ga., U.S. | D2 | 87 |
| Upemba, Lac, l., Zaire | C4 | 48 |
| Upernavik, Grnld. | B15 | 61 |
| Upham, N.D., U.S. | A5 | 111 |
| Upía, stm., Col. | C3 | 60 |
| Upington, S. Afr. | C3 | 49 |
| Upland, Ca., U.S. | E5 | 82 |
| Upland, In., U.S. | D7 | 91 |
| Upland, Ne., U.S. | D7 | 104 |
| Upolu, i., W. Sam. | G11 | 6 |
| Upolu Point, c., Hi., U.S. | C6 | 88 |
| Upper, prov., Ghana | D4 | 45 |
| Upper Ammonoosuc, stm., N.H., U.S. | A4 | 106 |
| Upper Arlington, Oh., U.S. | B2 | 112 |
| Upper Arrow Lake, res., B.C. | D9 | 69 |
| Upper Black Eddy, Pa., U.S. | E11 | 115 |
| Upper Blackville, N.B. | C4 | 71 |
| Upper Chichester Township, Pa., U.S. | *G11 | 115 |
| Upperco, Md., U.S. | A4 | 97 |
| Upper Darby, Pa., U.S. | G11 | 115 |
| Upper Dublin Township, Pa., U.S. | *F11 | 115 |
| Upper Fairmount, Md., U.S. | D6 | 97 |
| Upper Fraser, B.C. | B7 | 69 |
| Upper Frenchville, Me., U.S. | A4 | 96 |
| Upper Gagetown, N.B. | D3 | 71 |
| Upper Ganges Canal, India | C6 | 37 |
| Upper Gloucester, Me., U.S. | E2 | 96 |
| Upper Graniteville, Vt., U.S. | C4 | 122 |
| Upper Greenwood Lake, N.J., U.S. | A4 | 107 |
| Upper Humber, stm., Newf. | D3 | 72 |
| Upper Indian Pond, l., Newf. | D3 | 72 |
| Upper Iowa, stm., Ia., U.S. | A5 | 92 |
| Upper Island Cove, Newf. | E5 | 72 |
| Upper Jay, N.Y., U.S. | f11 | 109 |
| Upper Kapuas Mountains, mts., Asia | E4 | 34 |
| Upper Kent, N.B. | C2 | 71 |
| Upper Klamath Lake, l., Or., U.S. | E4 | 114 |
| Upper Manitou Lake, l., Ont. | E5 | 70 |
| Upper Marlboro, Md., U.S. | C4 | 97 |
| Upper Merion Township, Pa., U.S. | *F11 | 115 |
| Upper Moreland Township, Pa., U.S. | *F11 | 115 |
| Upper Musquodoboit, N.S. | D7 | 71 |
| Upper New York Bay, b., U.S. | k8 | 107 |
| Upper Providence Township, Pa., U.S. | *G11 | 115 |
| Upper Red Lake, l., Mn., U.S. | B4 | 100 |
| Upper Saddle River, N.J., U.S. | A4 | 107 |
| Upper Saint Clair, Pa., U.S. | *F1 | 115 |
| Upper Sandusky, Oh., U.S. | B2 | 112 |
| Upper Sheila, N.B. | B5 | 71 |
| Upper Silesia, hist. reg., Pol. | g9 | 26 |
| Upper Southampton Township, Pa., U.S. | *F11 | 115 |
| Upper Strasburg, Pa., U.S. | F6 | 115 |
| Upperville, Va., U.S. | B5 | 123 |
| Upper Volta see Burkina Faso, ctry., Afr. | D4 | 45 |
| Upper Wilson Pond, l., Me., U.S. | C3 | 96 |
| Upper Woods Harbour, N.S. | F4 | 71 |
| Uppsala, Swe. | H7 | 14 |
| Upright, Cape, c., Ak., U.S. | C5 | 79 |
| Upsala, Mn., U.S. | E4 | 100 |
| Upsalquitch, N.B. | B3 | 71 |
| Upshur, co., Tx., U.S. | C5 | 120 |
| Upshur, co., W.V., U.S. | C4 | 125 |
| Upson, Wi., U.S. | B3 | 126 |
| Upson, co., Ga., U.S. | D2 | 87 |
| Upton, Que. | D5 | 74 |
| Upton, Ky., U.S. | C4 | 94 |
| Upton, Me., U.S. | D1 | 96 |
| Upton, Ma., U.S. | B4 | 98 |
| Upton, Wy., U.S. | B8 | 127 |
| Upton, co., Tx., U.S. | D2 | 120 |
| Urabá, Golfo de, b., Col. | B2 | 60 |
| Uracoa, Ven. | B5 | 60 |
| Urad Qianqi, China | D3 | 32 |
| Ural, stm., Sov. Un. | D8 | 29 |
| Ural Mountains, mts., Sov. Un. | D8 | 29 |
| Uralsk, Sov. Un. | D8 | 29 |
| Urandi, Braz. | A4 | 56 |
| Urania, La., U.S. | C3 | 95 |
| Uranium City, Sask. | m7 | 75 |
| Uraricoera, Braz. | B5 | 60 |
| Uraricoera, stm., Braz. | B2 | 59 |
| Urasoe, Japan | O5 | 52 |
| Ura-Tyube, Sov. Un. | H22 | 8 |
| Uravan, Co., U.S. | C2 | 83 |
| Urawa, Japan | I9 | 33 |
| Urbana, Il., U.S. | C5 | 90 |
| Urbana, Ia., U.S. | B6 | 92 |
| Urbana, Mo., U.S. | D4 | 102 |
| Urbana, Oh., U.S. | B2 | 112 |
| Urbancrest, Oh., U.S. | m10 | 112 |
| Urbandale, Ia., U.S. | C4 | 92 |
| Urbank, Mn., U.S. | D3 | 100 |
| Urbanna, Va., U.S. | C6 | 123 |
| Urbino, Italy | C4 | 23 |
| Urcos, Peru | D3 | 58 |
| Urdaneta, Phil. | o13 | 34 |
| Urdzhar, Sov. Un. | D10 | 28 |
| Ures, stm., Eng., U.K. | F7 | 13 |
| Ures, Mex. | B3 | 63 |
| Ure, Tur. | D12 | 40 |
| Urga, Sov. Un. | E6 | 29 |
| Urgench, Sov. Un. | E6 | 29 |
| Uri, state, Switz. | C3 | 21 |
| Uriah, Al., U.S. | D2 | 78 |
| Uribia, Col. | A3 | 60 |
| Urich, Mo., U.S. | C4 | 102 |
| Urique, Mex. | B3 | 63 |
| Uritsk (part of Leningrad), Sov. Un. | s31 | 14 |
| Urk, Neth. | B5 | 17 |
| Urla, Tur. | C6 | 25 |
| Urlingford, Ire. | E4 | 11 |
| Urmia, Lake, l., Iran | B4 | 38 |
| Urmia see Orūmīyeh, Iran | B4 | 38 |
| Uroyán, Montañas de, mts., P.R. | f10 | 64 |
| Urr, stm., Scot., U.K. | F5 | 13 |
| Urrao, Col. | B2 | 60 |
| Ursa, Il., U.S. | C2 | 90 |
| Ursina, Pa., U.S. | G3 | 115 |
| Ursine, Nv., U.S. | *F7 | 105 |
| Ursus (part of Warsaw), Pol. | m13 | 26 |
| Uruaçu, Braz. | A4 | 56 |
| Uruana, Braz. | B11 | 40 |
| Uruapan [del Progreso], Mex. | D4 | 63 |
| Urubamba, Peru | D3 | 58 |
| Urubamba, stm., Peru | D3 | 58 |
| Urubu, stm., Braz. | C3 | 59 |
| Urucará, Braz. | C3 | 59 |
| Uruçuí, Braz. | C2 | 57 |
| Urucuituba, Braz. | C3 | 59 |
| Urucuia, stm., Braz. | B3 | 56 |
| Uruguaiana, Braz. | D1 | 56 |
| Uruguay, ctry., S.A. | E1 | 56 |
| Uruguay (Uruguai), stm., S.A. | E1 | 56 |
| Urumchi see Ürümqi, China | C2 | 31 |
| Ürümqi (Urumchi), China | C2 | 31 |
| Uruno Point, c., Guam | L10 | 52 |
| Urusha, Sov. Un. | D15 | 29 |
| Urutaí, Braz. | B3 | 56 |
| Uryu, stm., Japan | D11 | 33 |
| Uryupinsk, Sov. Un. | F14 | 27 |
| Urzhum, Sov. Un. | B3 | 28 |
| Urziceni, Rom. | C8 | 24 |
| Usa, stm., Sov. Un. | B20 | 8 |
| Uşak, Tur. | C7 | 40 |
| Usakos, Nmb. | B2 | 49 |
| Usedom, E. Ger. | E7 | 15 |
| Usedom, i., Eur. | E8 | 15 |
| Ushaki, Sov. Un. | s32 | 14 |
| Ushibuka, Japan | J4 | 33 |
| Ushtobe, Sov. Un. | D9 | 28 |
| Ushuaia, Arg. | h12 | 54 |
| Usingen, W. Ger. | C3 | 19 |
| Usk, B.C. | B3 | 69 |
| Usk, Wa., U.S. | A8 | 124 |
| Uslar, W. Ger. | D8 | 19 |
| Úslava, stm., Czech. | D8 | 19 |
| Usman, Sov. Un. | E12 | 27 |
| Usolye-Sibirskoye, Sov. Un. | D13 | 29 |
| Uspenskiy, Sov. Un. | D9 | 28 |
| Usquepaug, R.I., U.S. | F3 | 116 |
| Ussel, Fr. | E5 | 16 |
| Ussuri (Wusuli), stm., Asia | B11 | 31 |
| Ussuriysk, Sov. Un. | E16 | 29 |
| Ust-Bolsheretsk, Sov. Un. | D18 | 29 |
| Uster, Switz. | B4 | 21 |
| Ustica, i., Italy | E4 | 23 |
| Ústí nad Labem, Czech. | C3 | 26 |
| Ustinov see Izhevsk, Sov. Un. | D8 | 29 |
| Ust-Ishim, Sov. Un. | B8 | 28 |
| Ustka, Pol. | A4 | 26 |
| Ust-Kamchatsk, Sov. Un. | D19 | 29 |
| Ust-Kamenogorsk, Sov. Un. | E11 | 29 |
| Ust-Kut, Sov. Un. | D13 | 29 |
| Ust-Maya, Sov. Un. | C16 | 29 |
| Ust-Olenek, Sov. Un. | B14 | 29 |
| Ust-Shchugor, Sov. Un. | C9 | 28 |
| Ust-Srednekan, Sov. Un. | C18 | 29 |
| Ust-Tsilma, Sov. Un. | C8 | 29 |
| Ust-Tym, Sov. Un. | D11 | 28 |
| Ust-Urt Plateau, plat., Sov. Un. | E8 | 29 |
| Ust-Usa, Sov. Un. | C8 | 29 |
| Ustyuzhna, Sov. Un. | B11 | 27 |
| Usu, China | C1 | 31 |
| Usulután, El Sal. | E7 | 63 |
| Usumacinta, stm., N.A. | D6 | 63 |
| Utah, co., Ut., U.S. | C4 | 121 |
| Utah, state, U.S. | D4 | 121 |
| Utah Lake, l., Ut., U.S. | C4 | 121 |
| Utajärvi, Fin. | E12 | 14 |
| Ute, Ia., U.S. | B2 | 92 |
| Ute Creek, stm., N.M., U.S. | A6 | 108 |
| Ute Mountain Indian Reservation, Co., U.S. | D2 | 83 |
| Ute Park, N.M., U.S. | A5 | 108 |
| Ute Reservoir, res., N.M., U.S. | B6 | 108 |
| Utete, Tan. | C6 | 48 |
| Uthai Thani, Thai. | B1 | 34 |
| Utica, Il., U.S. | B5 | 90 |
| Utica, In., U.S. | H6 | 91 |
| Utica, Ky., U.S. | C2 | 94 |
| Utica, Ms., U.S. | C3 | 101 |
| Utica, Mo., U.S. | B4 | 102 |
| Utica, Ne., U.S. | D8 | 104 |
| Utica, N.Y., U.S. | B5 | 109 |
| Utica, Oh., U.S. | B3 | 112 |
| Utica, S.D., U.S. | D8 | 118 |
| Utiel, Spain | C5 | 22 |
| Utikuma Lake, l., Alta. | B3 | 68 |
| Utö, i., Swe. | u36 | 14 |
| Utopia, Tx., U.S. | E3 | 120 |
| Utopia, Lake, l., N.B. | D3 | 71 |
| Utrata, stm., Pol. | m11 | 26 |
| Utrecht, Neth. | A4 | 16 |
| Utrecht, prov., Neth. | B5 | 17 |
| Utrera, Spain | D3 | 22 |
| Utsjoki, Fin. | B12 | 14 |
| Utsunomiya, Japan | D12 | 31 |
| Uttaradit, Thai. | B2 | 34 |
| Uttar Pradesh, state, India | C6 | 36 |
| Uttoxeter, Eng., U.K. | B6 | 12 |
| Utuado, P.R. | B2 | 65 |
| Utulei, Am. Sam. | F13 | 52 |
| Uusikaupunki, Fin. | G9 | 14 |
| Uvá, Col. | C3 | 60 |
| Uvalda, Ga., U.S. | D4 | 87 |
| Uvalde, Tx., U.S. | E3 | 120 |
| Uvalde, co., Tx., U.S. | E3 | 120 |
| Uvarovo, Sov. Un. | E14 | 27 |
| Úvaly, Czech. | n18 | 26 |
| Uverite Point, c., Fiji | H14 | 52 |
| Uvinza, Tan. | C5 | 48 |
| Uvira, Zaire | B5 | 48 |
| Uvs Lake, l., Asia | A3 | 31 |
| Uwajima, Japan | J6 | 31 |
| Uwayl, Sud. | D2 | 47 |
| 'Uwaynāt, Jabal al, mtn., Afr. | C2 | 47 |
| Uwharrie, stm., N.C., U.S. | B3 | 110 |
| Uxbridge (part of London), Eng., U.K. | k12 | 10 |
| Uxbridge, Ma., U.S. | B4 | 98 |
| Uxbridge, Ont. | C5 | 73 |
| Uxmal, hist., Mex. | D7 | 63 |
| Uyar, Sov. Un. | D27 | 8 |
| Uyo, Nig. | *E6 | 45 |
| Uyuni, Bol. | C2 | 55 |
| Uyuni, Salar de, pl., Bol. | C2 | 55 |
| Uzbek S.S.R., state, Sov. Un. | E9 | 29 |
| Uzès, Fr. | E6 | 16 |
| Uzh, stm., Sov. Un. | F7 | 27 |
| Uzhgorod, Sov. Un. | F3 | 27 |
| Uzlovaya, Sov. Un. | E11 | 27 |
| Uzunköprü, Tur. | B8 | 40 |
| Uzwil, Switz. | B7 | 21 |
| **V** | | |
| Vaal, stm., S. Afr. | C4 | 49 |
| Vaals, Neth. | D5 | 17 |
| Vaasa, Fin. | F9 | 14 |
| Vác, Hung. | B4 | 26 |
| Vaca Key, i., Fl., U.S. | H5 | 86 |
| Vacaria, Braz. | D2 | 56 |
| Vacaville, Ca., U.S. | C3 | 82 |
| Vacha, E. Ger. | C5 | 19 |
| Vacherie, La., U.S. | h10 | 95 |
| Vader, Wa., U.S. | C3 | 124 |
| Vadis, W.V., U.S. | B4 | 125 |
| Vadito, N.M., U.S. | A4 | 108 |
| Vadnais Heights, Mn., U.S. | *m12 | 100 |
| Vado, N.M., U.S. | E3 | 108 |
| Vadodara, India | D5 | 36 |
| Vadsø, Nor. | B13 | 14 |
| Vaduz, Liech. | E4 | 18 |
| Vagay, Sov. Un. | B7 | 28 |
| Vaggeryd, Swe. | A8 | 15 |
| Vagnhärad, Swe. | u35 | 14 |
| Vagos, Port. | B1 | 22 |
| Váh, stm., Czech. | D4 | 26 |
| Vahsel Bay, b., Ant. | B9 | 7 |
| Vaiden, Ms., U.S. | B4 | 101 |
| Vaigai, stm., India | G6 | 36 |
| Vaihingen, W. Ger. | E7 | 15 |
| Vail, Az., U.S. | E5 | 80 |
| Vail, Co., U.S. | B4 | 83 |
| Vail, Ia., U.S. | B2 | 92 |
| Vail Homes, N.J., U.S. | *C4 | 107 |
| Vailoa see Palauli, W. Sam. | F11 | 52 |
| Vails, N.J., U.S. | B2 | 107 |
| Vaitele Bay, b., W. Sam. | F12 | 52 |
| Vākhān, reg., Afg. | k17 | 39 |
| Vakhrushev, Sov. Un. | B11 | 33 |
| Valais, state, Switz. | C3 | 20 |
| Valatie, N.Y., U.S. | C7 | 109 |
| Val-Barrette, Que. | C2 | 74 |
| Val-Bélair, Que. | n17 | 74 |
| Valcartier-Village, Que. | C6 | 74 |
| Valcheta, Arg. | E3 | 54 |
| Valcourt, Que. | D5 | 74 |
| Valdagno, Italy | D7 | 20 |
| Valdai Hills, hills, Sov. Un. | C9 | 27 |
| Val-David, Que. | C2 | 74 |
| Valday, Sov. Un. | C9 | 27 |
| Valdemarsvik, Swe. | H7 | 14 |
| Valdemorillo, Spain | o16 | 22 |
| Valdepeñas, Spain | C4 | 22 |
| Valderaduey, stm., Spain | A3 | 22 |
| Valders, Wi., U.S. | D6 | 126 |
| Valdés, Península, pen., Arg. | C4 | 54 |
| Valdese, N.C., U.S. | B1 | 110 |
| Valdez, Ak., U.S. | C10 | 79 |
| Valdez, N.M., U.S. | A4 | 108 |
| Valdilecha, Spain | p18 | 22 |
| Valdivia, Chile | B2 | 54 |
| Valdivia, Col. | B2 | 60 |
| Valdobbiadene, Italy | D7 | 20 |
| Val-d'Or, Que. | k11 | 74 |
| Valdosta, Ga., U.S. | F3 | 87 |
| Vale, Nor. | p28 | 14 |
| Vale, Or., U.S. | D9 | 114 |
| Vale, S.D., U.S. | C2 | 118 |
| Vale, Tn., U.S. | A3 | 119 |
| Valemount, B.C. | C8 | 69 |
| Valença, Braz. | C4 | 56 |
| Valença, Port. | A1 | 22 |
| Valença do Piauí, Braz. | C2 | 57 |
| Valence, Fr. | E6 | 16 |
| Valencia, Spain | C5 | 22 |
| Valencia, Az., U.S. | m7 | 80 |
| Valencia, Ca., U.S. | *E4 | 82 |
| Valencia, Pa., U.S. | E2 | 115 |
| Valencia, Ven. | A4 | 60 |
| Valencia, co., N.M., U.S. | C3 | 108 |
| Valencia, hist. reg., Spain | C5 | 22 |
| Valencia [de Alcántara], Spain | C2 | 22 |
| Valencia Heights, S.C., U.S. | D6 | 117 |
| Valencia Island, i., Ire. | E1 | 11 |
| Valenciennes, Fr. | B5 | 16 |
| Valentigney, Fr. | D7 | 16 |
| Valentine, Ne., U.S. | B5 | 104 |
| Valentine, Tx., U.S. | o12 | 120 |
| Valhalla, N.Y., U.S. | *g13 | 109 |
| Valhermoso Springs, Al., U.S. | A3 | 78 |
| Valier, Il., U.S. | F4 | 90 |
| Valier, Mt., U.S. | B4 | 103 |
| Valier, Pa., U.S. | E4 | 115 |
| Valkenswaard, Neth. | C5 | 17 |
| Valki, Sov. Un. | G10 | 27 |
| Valladolid, Ec. | B2 | 58 |
| Valladolid, Mex. | C7 | 63 |
| Valladolid, Spain | B3 | 22 |
| Vallåkra, Swe. | C6 | 15 |
| Vallauris, Fr. | F7 | 16 |
| Vall de Uxó, Spain | C5 | 22 |
| Vallecas, Spain | B4 | 22 |
| Vallecito Reservoir, res., Co., U.S. | D3 | 83 |
| Vallecitos, N.M., U.S. | A3 | 108 |
| Vallée-Jonction, Que. | C7 | 74 |
| Vallegrande, Bol. | C2 | 55 |
| Vallejo, Ca., U.S. | C2 | 82 |
| Vallenar, Chile | B2 | 54 |
| Valletta, Malta | *H11 | 23 |
| Valle Vista, Ca., U.S. | *F5 | 82 |
| Valley, Ne., U.S. | C9 | 104 |
| Valley, Wa., U.S. | A8 | 124 |
| Valley, co., Id., U.S. | E3 | 89 |
| Valley, co., Mt., U.S. | B10 | 103 |
| Valley, co., Ne., U.S. | C6 | 104 |
| Valley Bend, W.V., U.S. | C5 | 125 |
| Valley Center, Ks., U.S. | E6 | 93 |
| Valley Center, Sask. | F2 | 93 |
| Valley City, Il., U.S. | D3 | 90 |
| Valley City, N.D., U.S. | C8 | 111 |
| Valley City, Oh., U.S. | A4 | 112 |
| Valley Cottage, N.Y., U.S. | g13 | 109 |
| Valley Creek, stm., Al., U.S. | g6 | 78 |
| Valley East, Ont. | p19 | 73 |
| Valley Falls, Ks., U.S. | C8 | 93 |
| Valley Falls, Or., U.S. | E6 | 114 |
| Valley Falls, R.I., U.S. | B4 | 116 |
| Valley Farms, Az., U.S. | E4 | 80 |
| Valleyfield (part of Badger's Quay-Valleyfield-Pool's Island), Newf. | D5 | 72 |

| Name | Map Ref. | Page |
|---|---|---|
| Valleyford, Wa., U.S. | B8 | 124 |
| Valley Forge, Pa., U.S. | o20 | 115 |
| Valley Grove, W.V., U.S. | A4 | 125 |
| Valley Head, Al., U.S. | A4 | 78 |
| Valley Head, W.V., U.S. | C4 | 125 |
| Valley Lee, Md., U.S. | D4 | 97 |
| Valley Mills, Tx., U.S. | D4 | 120 |
| Valley Park, Ms., U.S. | C3 | 101 |
| Valley Park, Mo., U.S. | f12 | 102 |
| Valley Ridge, W.V., U.S. | *B3 | 124 |
| Valley Spring, Tx., U.S. | D3 | 120 |
| Valley Springs, Ar., U.S. | A3 | 81 |
| Valley Springs, S.D., U.S. | D9 | 118 |
| Valley Station, Ky., U.S. | g11 | 94 |
| Valley Stream, N.Y., U.S. | n15 | 109 |
| Valleyview, Alta. | B2 | 68 |
| Valley View, Ky., U.S. | C5 | 94 |
| Valley View, Pa., U.S. | E8 | 115 |
| Valley View, Tx., U.S. | C4 | 120 |
| Valliant, Ok., U.S. | D6 | 113 |
| Vallo della Lucania, Italy | D5 | 23 |
| Vallonia, In., U.S. | G5 | 91 |
| Vallorbe, Switz. | E3 | 18 |
| Valls, Spain | B6 | 22 |
| Vallscreek, W.V., U.S. | D3 | 125 |
| Val Marie, Sask. | H2 | 75 |
| Valmeyer, Il., U.S. | E3 | 90 |
| Valmiera, Sov. Un. | C5 | 27 |
| Valmont, Que. | C5 | 74 |
| Valmontone, Italy | h9 | 23 |
| Valmora, N.M., U.S. | B5 | 108 |
| Val-Morin, Que. | C3 | 74 |
| Valmy, Nv., U.S. | C4 | 105 |
| Valognes, Fr. | C3 | 16 |
| Valois, N.Y., U.S. | C4 | 109 |
| Valona see Vlora, Alb. | | |
| Valparaíso, Sask. | E3 | 75 |
| Valparaíso, Chile | A2 | 54 |
| Valparaíso, Mex. | C4 | 63 |
| Valparaiso, Fl., U.S. | u15 | 86 |
| Valparaiso, In., U.S. | B3 | 91 |
| Valparaiso, Ne., U.S. | C9 | 104 |
| Valparaíso, prov., Chile | A2 | 54 |
| Val-Racine, Que. | D6 | 74 |
| Valréas, Fr. | E6 | 16 |
| Vals, Cape, c., Indon. | G9 | 34 |
| Val-Saint-Michel, Que. | n17 | 74 |
| Valsetz, Or., U.S. | C3 | 114 |
| Vals Platz, Switz. | C7 | 21 |
| Valtournanche, Italy | E4 | 21 |
| Valuyki, Sov. Un. | F12 | 27 |
| Val Verda, Ut., U.S. | C4 | 121 |
| Val Verde, co., Tx., U.S. | E2 | 120 |
| Valverde del Camino, Spain | D2 | 22 |
| Vamdrup, Den. | C3 | 15 |
| Vamori, Az., U.S. | F4 | 80 |
| Van, Tur. | C14 | 40 |
| Van, Tx., U.S. | C5 | 120 |
| Van, W.V., U.S. | n12 | 125 |
| Van, Lake, l., Tur. | C14 | 40 |
| Vanadium, N.M., U.S. | E1 | 108 |
| Van Alstyne, Tx., U.S. | C4 | 120 |
| Vananda, B.C. | E5 | 69 |
| Van-Bruyssel, Que. | B5 | 74 |
| Van Buren, Ar., U.S. | B1 | 81 |
| Van Buren, In., U.S. | C6 | 91 |
| Van Buren, Me., U.S. | A5 | 96 |
| Van Buren, Mo., U.S. | E6 | 102 |
| Van Buren, Oh., U.S. | A2 | 112 |
| Van Buren, co., Ar., U.S. | B3 | 81 |
| Van Buren, co., Ia., U.S. | D6 | 92 |
| Van Buren, co., Mi., U.S. | F4 | 99 |
| Van Buren, co., Tn., U.S. | D8 | 119 |
| Vance, Ms., U.S. | A3 | 101 |
| Vance, S.C., U.S. | E7 | 117 |
| Vance, co., N.C., U.S. | A4 | 110 |
| Vance Air Force Base, mil., Ok., U.S. | A3 | 113 |
| Vanceboro, Me., U.S. | C5 | 96 |
| Vanceboro, N.C., U.S. | B5 | 110 |
| Vanceburg, Ky., U.S. | B6 | 94 |
| Vancleave, Ms., U.S. | E5 | 101 |
| Vancleve, Ky., U.S. | C6 | 94 |
| Vancorum, Co., U.S. | C2 | 83 |
| Vancouver, B.C. | E6 | 69 |
| Vancouver, Wa., U.S. | D3 | 124 |
| Vancouver Island, i., B.C. | E4 | 69 |
| Vancouver Island Ranges, mts., B.C. | D4 | 69 |
| Vandalia, Il., U.S. | E4 | 90 |
| Vandalia, Mo., U.S. | B6 | 102 |
| Vandalia, Mt., U.S. | B10 | 103 |
| Vandalia, Oh., U.S. | *C1 | 112 |
| Vandemere, N.C., U.S. | B6 | 110 |
| Vandenberg Air Force Base, mil., Ca., U.S. | E3 | 82 |
| Vandenberg Village, Ca., U.S. | *E3 | 82 |
| Vander, N.C., U.S. | B4 | 110 |
| Vanderbilt, Mi., U.S. | C6 | 99 |
| Vanderbilt, Pa., U.S. | F2 | 115 |
| Vanderbilt, Tx., U.S. | E4 | 120 |
| Vanderbilt Peak, mtn., N.M., U.S. | E1 | 108 |
| Vanderburgh, co., In., U.S. | H2 | 91 |
| Vandercook Lake, Mi., U.S. | *F6 | 99 |
| Vandergrift, Pa., U.S. | E2 | 115 |
| Vanderhoof, B.C. | C5 | 69 |
| Vanderpool, Tx., U.S. | E3 | 120 |
| Vandervoort, Ar., U.S. | C1 | 81 |
| Vanderwagen, N.M., U.S. | B1 | 108 |
| Van Diemen, Cape, c., Austl. | B5 | 50 |
| Van Diemen Gulf, b., Austl. | B5 | 50 |
| Vandiver, Al., U.S. | B3 | 78 |
| Vandling, Pa., U.S. | C11 | 115 |
| Vanduser, Mo., U.S. | E8 | 102 |
| Vandyne, Wi., U.S. | k9 | 126 |
| Vanegas, Mex. | C4 | 63 |
| Vänern, l., Swe. | H5 | 14 |
| Vanga, Kenya | B6 | 48 |
| Vangaindrano, Madag. | h9 | 49 |
| Vanguard, Sask. | H2 | 75 |
| Van Horn, Tx., U.S. | o12 | 120 |
| Van Horne, Ia., U.S. | B5 | 92 |
| Vanier, Ont. | h12 | 73 |
| Vanimo, Pap. N. Gui. | h11 | 50 |
| Vankleek Hill, Ont. | B10 | 73 |
| Van Kull, Kill, stm., N.J., U.S. | k8 | 107 |
| Van Lear, Ky., U.S. | C7 | 94 |
| Vanleer, Tn., U.S. | A4 | 119 |
| Vanlue, Oh., U.S. | B2 | 112 |
| Van Meter, Ia., U.S. | C4 | 92 |
| Vanna, Ga., U.S. | B3 | 87 |
| Vanndale, Ar., U.S. | B5 | 81 |
| Vannes, Fr. | D2 | 16 |
| Vanoss, Ok., U.S. | C5 | 113 |
| Van Phong Bay, b., Viet. | F8 | 35 |
| Van Rees Mountains, mts., Indon. | F9 | 34 |
| Vanrhynsdorp, S. Afr. | D2 | 49 |
| Vansant, Va., U.S. | e9 | 123 |
| Vanscoy, Sask. | E2 | 75 |
| Vantaa (Vanda), Fin. | *G11 | 14 |
| Vantage, Sask. | H2 | 75 |
| Van Tassell, Wy., U.S. | D8 | 127 |
| Vanua Balavu, i., Fiji | H16 | 52 |
| Vanua Levu, i., Fiji | H15 | 52 |
| Vanuatu, ctry., Oc. | H10 | 6 |
| Vanua Vatu, i., Fiji | I16 | 52 |
| Vanves, Fr. | g10 | 16 |
| Vanvleck, Tx., U.S. | r14 | 120 |
| Van Vleet, Ms., U.S. | B5 | 101 |
| Van Wert, Ga., U.S. | C1 | 87 |
| Van Wert, Ia., U.S. | D4 | 92 |
| Van Wert, Oh., U.S. | B1 | 112 |
| Van Wert, co., Oh., U.S. | B1 | 112 |
| Van Wyck, S.C., U.S. | B6 | 117 |
| Vanzant, Mo., U.S. | E5 | 102 |
| Varallo, Italy | D4 | 23 |
| Varāmīn, Iran | D5 | 39 |
| Vārānasi (Benares), India | C7 | 36 |
| Varangerfjorden, Nor. | B14 | 14 |
| Varano, Lake, b., Italy | D5 | 23 |
| Varazdin, Yugo. | B3 | 24 |
| Varazze, Italy | B2 | 23 |
| Varberg, Swe. | I5 | 14 |
| Vardaman, Ms., U.S. | B4 | 101 |
| Vardar (Axiós), stm., Eur. | B4 | 40 |
| Varde, Den. | C2 | 15 |
| Varde Å, stm., Den. | C2 | 15 |
| Vardenis, Sov. Un. | B15 | 40 |
| Vardø, Nor. | B14 | 14 |
| Varel, W. Ger. | B4 | 18 |
| Varena, Sov. Un. | A8 | 26 |
| Varennes, Que. | D4 | 74 |
| Varennes, Fr. | D5 | 16 |
| Vareš, Yugo. | C4 | 24 |
| Varese, Italy | B2 | 23 |
| Varese, Lake, l., Italy | E6 | 21 |
| Varginha, Braz. | C3 | 56 |
| Vári, Grc. | h11 | 25 |
| Varina, Ia., U.S. | B3 | 92 |
| Varina, Va., U.S. | C5 | 123 |
| Varjão, Braz. | B3 | 56 |
| Varkaus, Fin. | F12 | 14 |
| Varkhān, stm., Afg. | E12 | 39 |
| Varna (Stalin), Bul. | D8 | 24 |
| Varna, Ont. | D3 | 73 |
| Varna, Il., U.S. | B4 | 90 |
| Varnado, La., U.S. | D6 | 95 |
| Värnamo, Swe. | I6 | 14 |
| Varney, Ont. | C4 | 73 |
| Varnsdorf, Czech. | C3 | 26 |
| Varnville, S.C., U.S. | F5 | 117 |
| Värö, Swe. | A6 | 15 |
| Várpalota, Hung. | B4 | 24 |
| Vars, Ont. | h13 | 73 |
| Varysburg, N.Y., U.S. | C2 | 109 |
| Várzea da Palma, Braz. | D2 | 56 |
| Várzea Grande, Braz. | B4 | 56 |
| Varzi, Italy | E5 | 20 |
| Varzuga, stm., Sov. Un. | D17 | 14 |
| Vashon, Wa., U.S. | B3 | 124 |
| Vashon, Point, c., Wa., U.S. | E11 | 124 |
| Vashon Island, i., Wa., U.S. | f11 | 124 |
| Vasilkov, Sov. Un. | F8 | 27 |
| Vass, N.C., U.S. | B3 | 110 |
| Vassalboro, Me., U.S. | *D3 | 96 |
| Vassar, Man. | E4 | 70 |
| Vassar, Ks., U.S. | D8 | 93 |
| Vassar, Mi., U.S. | E7 | 99 |
| Vassouras, Braz. | h6 | 56 |
| Västerås, Swe. | H7 | 14 |
| Västerhaninge, Swe. | t36 | 14 |
| Västervik, Swe. | I7 | 14 |
| Vasto, Italy | C5 | 23 |
| Vasyugan, stm., Sov. Un. | B9 | 28 |
| Vaternish Point, c., Scot., U.K. | C2 | 13 |
| Vatican City, ctry., Eur. | D4 | 23 |
| Vaticano, Cape, c., Italy | E5 | 23 |
| Vatnajökull, ice, Ice. | n24 | 14 |
| Vatomandry, Madag. | g9 | 49 |
| Vatra Dornei, Rom. | B7 | 24 |
| Vättern, l., Swe. | H6 | 14 |
| Vatulele, i., Fiji | I14 | 52 |
| Vatu Vara, i., Fiji | H16 | 52 |
| Vaucluse, S.C., U.S. | D4 | 117 |
| Vaucouleurs, Fr. | F5 | 17 |
| Vaud, state, Switz. | C2 | 20 |
| Vaudreuil, Que. | D3 | 74 |
| Vaudreuil, co., Que. | D3 | 74 |
| Vaughan, Ont. | D5 | 73 |
| Vaughan, Ms., U.S. | C3 | 101 |
| Vaughan, N.C., U.S. | A4 | 110 |
| Vaughan, W.V., U.S. | m13 | 125 |
| Vaughn, Mt., U.S. | C5 | 103 |
| Vaughn, N.M., U.S. | C4 | 108 |
| Vaughn, Or., U.S. | C3 | 114 |
| Vaughnsville, Oh., U.S. | B1 | 112 |
| Vaupés, dept., Col. | C3 | 60 |
| Vaupés (Uaupés), stm., S.A. | C3 | 60 |
| Vauvillers, Fr. | B2 | 20 |
| Vauxhall, Alta. | D4 | 68 |
| Vavoua, I.C. | E3 | 45 |
| Vawn, Sask. | D1 | 75 |
| Vaxholm, Swe. | t36 | 14 |
| Växjö, Swe. | I6 | 14 |
| Våxtorp, Swe. | B7 | 15 |
| Váyia, Grc. | g10 | 25 |
| Veazie, Me., U.S. | D4 | 96 |
| Veblen, S.D., U.S. | B8 | 118 |
| Vechta, W. Ger. | F2 | 15 |
| Vechte, stm., Eur. | A7 | 16 |
| Veckholm, Swe. | t35 | 14 |
| Veddige, Swe. | A6 | 15 |
| Vedea, stm., Rom. | C7 | 24 |
| Vedia, Arg. | A4 | 54 |
| Veedersburg, In., U.S. | D3 | 91 |
| Veendam, Neth. | A6 | 17 |
| Vega, i., Nor. | E4 | 14 |
| Vega Alta, P.R. | B3 | 65 |
| Vegreville, Alta. | C4 | 68 |
| Veguita, N.M., U.S. | C3 | 108 |
| Veinticinco de Mayo, Arg. | B3 | 54 |
| Veinticinco de Mayo, Arg. | A3 | 54 |
| Vejen, Den. | C3 | 15 |
| Vejer [de la Frontera], Spain | D5 | 22 |
| Vejle, Den. | J3 | 14 |
| Vejprty, Czech. | C2 | 26 |
| Velarde, N.M., U.S. | A4 | 108 |
| Velas, Cabo de la, c., Col. | A3 | 60 |
| Velásquez, Braz. | B3 | 56 |
| Velbert, W. Ger. | B2 | 19 |
| Velda Rose Estates, Az., U.S. | k9 | 80 |
| Velden, W. Ger. | A8 | 20 |
| Velebit Mountains, mts., Yugo. | C2 | 24 |
| Velestínon, Grc. | C4 | 25 |
| Vélez, Col. | B3 | 60 |
| Vélez Blanco, Spain | D4 | 22 |
| Vélez-Málaga, Spain | D3 | 22 |
| Vélez Rubio, Spain | D4 | 22 |
| Velhas, Rio das, stm., Braz. | B4 | 56 |
| Velika Morava, stm., Yugo. | C5 | 24 |
| Velikaya, stm., Sov. Un. | C7 | 27 |
| Velikaya Lepetikha, Sov. Un. | H10 | 27 |
| Velikiye Luki, Sov. Un. | C8 | 27 |
| Velikiy Ustyug, Sov. Un. | C7 | 29 |
| Veliko Tŭrnovo, Bul. | D7 | 24 |
| Vélingara, Sen. | D2 | 45 |
| Vélingara, Sen. | D2 | 45 |
| Velizh, Sov. Un. | D8 | 27 |
| Velké Meziříčí, Czech. | D4 | 26 |
| Velletri, Italy | D4 | 23 |
| Vellinge, Swe. | C7 | 15 |
| Vellore, India | F6 | 36 |
| Velma, Ok., U.S. | C4 | 113 |
| Velpen, In., U.S. | H3 | 91 |
| Velsen (part of IJmuiden), Neth. | B4 | 17 |
| Velsk, Sov. Un. | C7 | 29 |
| Veltrusy, Czech. | n17 | 26 |
| Velva, N.D., U.S. | A5 | 111 |
| Velvary, Czech. | n17 | 26 |
| Vemb, Den. | B2 | 15 |
| Ven, i., Swe. | C6 | 15 |
| Venaco, Fr. | C2 | 23 |
| Venado Tuerto, Arg. | A4 | 54 |
| Venango, Ne., U.S. | D3 | 104 |
| Venango, Pa., U.S. | C1 | 115 |
| Venango, co., Pa., U.S. | D2 | 115 |
| Venceslau Brás, Braz. | C3 | 56 |
| Venda, ctry., Afr. | B5 | 49 |
| Vendôme, Fr. | D4 | 16 |
| Vendrell, Spain | B6 | 22 |
| Venedocia, Oh., U.S. | B1 | 112 |
| Venedy, Il., U.S. | E4 | 90 |
| Veneta, Or., U.S. | C3 | 114 |
| Veneta, Laguna, b., Italy | D8 | 20 |
| Venetia (Veneto), prov., Italy | A3 | 23 |
| Venetie, Ak., U.S. | B10 | 79 |
| Veneto, prov., Italy | D7 | 20 |
| Venev, Sov. Un. | D12 | 27 |
| Venezuela, ctry., S.A. | B4 | 60 |
| Venezuela, Golfo de, b., S.A. | A3 | 60 |
| Veniaminof, Mount, mtn., Ak., U.S. | D8 | 79 |
| Venice, Alta. | B4 | 68 |
| Venice (Venezia), Italy | B4 | 23 |
| Venice, Fl., U.S. | E4 | 86 |
| Venice, Il., U.S. | E3 | 90 |
| Venice, La., U.S. | E6 | 95 |
| Venice, Ne., U.S. | g12 | 104 |
| Venice, Ut., U.S. | E4 | 121 |
| Venice, Gulf of, b., Eur. | B4 | 23 |
| Venice Gardens, Fl., U.S. | *E4 | 86 |
| Vénissieux, Fr. | E6 | 16 |
| Venlo, Neth. | B7 | 16 |
| Venn, Sask. | F3 | 75 |
| Vennachar, Ont. | B7 | 73 |
| Venø, i., Den. | B2 | 15 |
| Vent, stm., Sov. Un. | C6 | 20 |
| Venta, stm., Sov. Un. | C3 | 27 |
| Ventana, Az., U.S. | E3 | 80 |
| Ventimiglia, Italy | C1 | 23 |
| Ventnor, Ont. | C9 | 73 |
| Ventnor, Eng., U.K. | D6 | 12 |
| Ventnor City, N.J., U.S. | E4 | 107 |
| Venton, Md., U.S. | D6 | 97 |
| Ventoux, Mont, mtn., Fr. | E6 | 16 |
| Ventry, Ire. | E1 | 11 |
| Ventspils, Sov. Un. | C3 | 27 |
| Ventuari, stm., Ven. | C4 | 60 |
| Ventura (San Buenaventura), Ca., U.S. | E4 | 82 |
| Ventura, Ia., U.S. | A4 | 92 |
| Ventura, co., Ca., U.S. | E4 | 82 |
| Venturia, N.D., U.S. | D6 | 111 |
| Venus, Fl., U.S. | E5 | 86 |
| Venus, Pa., U.S. | D2 | 115 |
| Venus, Tx., U.S. | n9 | 120 |
| Venustiano Carranza, Mex. | D6 | 63 |
| Vera, Arg. | E3 | 55 |
| Vera, Spain | D5 | 22 |
| Vera, Ok., U.S. | A6 | 113 |
| Vera, Tx., U.S. | C3 | 120 |
| Vera Cruz, In., U.S. | C7 | 91 |
| Veracruz [Llave], Mex. | H10 | 63 |
| Veracruz [Llave], Mex. | D5 | 63 |
| Veradale, Wa., U.S. | *B8 | 124 |
| Veranópolis, Braz. | D2 | 56 |
| Verāval, India | D5 | 36 |
| Verbania, Italy | D4 | 20 |
| Verbena, Al., U.S. | C3 | 78 |
| Vercel, Fr. | B1 | 21 |
| Vercelli, Italy | B2 | 23 |
| Verchères, Que. | D4 | 74 |
| Verchères, co., Que. | D4 | 74 |
| Verda, Ky., U.S. | D6 | 94 |
| Verde, stm., Braz. | B4 | 56 |
| Verde, stm., Braz. | C2 | 56 |
| Verde, stm., Mex. | m14 | 63 |
| Verde, stm., Mex. | m12 | 63 |
| Verde, stm., Para. | D4 | 55 |
| Verde, stm., Az., U.S. | C4 | 80 |
| Verde, Point, c., Newf. | E4 | 72 |
| Verde Island, i., Phil. | p13 | 34 |
| Verde Island Passage, strt., Phil. | p13 | 34 |
| Verdel, Ne., U.S. | B7 | 104 |
| Verden, W. Ger. | B5 | 18 |
| Verdi, Nv., U.S. | D2 | 105 |
| Verdigre, Ne., U.S. | B7 | 104 |
| Verdigris, Ok., U.S. | A6 | 113 |
| Verdi Peak, mtn., Nv., U.S. | C6 | 105 |
| Verdon, stm., Fr. | E7 | 16 |
| Verdun, Que. | p19 | 74 |
| Verdun, Fr. | C6 | 16 |
| Verdunville, W.V., U.S. | *D2 | 125 |
| Vereeniging, S. Afr. | C4 | 49 |
| Vereshchagino, Sov. Un. | D19 | 8 |
| Vergara, Ur. | E2 | 56 |
| Vergas, Mn., U.S. | D3 | 100 |
| Vergennes, Il., U.S. | F4 | 90 |
| Vergennes, Vt., U.S. | C2 | 122 |
| Vergigny, Sask. | F4 | 75 |
| Verín, Spain | C3 | 22 |
| Verísimo Sarmento see Camissombo, Ang. | C3 | 48 |
| Veríssimo, Braz. | B3 | 56 |
| Verkhniy Baskunchak, Sov. Un. | D3 | 28 |
| Verkhniy Ufaley, Sov. Un. | B6 | 28 |
| Verkhnyaya Tura, Sov. Un. | D21 | 8 |
| Verkhoyansk, Sov. Un. | C16 | 29 |
| Verkhoyansk Mountains, mts., Sov. Un. | C15 | 29 |
| Verlo, Sask. | G1 | 75 |
| Vermilion, Alta. | C5 | 68 |
| Vermilion, Il., U.S. | D6 | 90 |
| Vermilion, Oh., U.S. | A3 | 112 |
| Vermilion, co., Il., U.S. | C6 | 90 |
| Vermilion, co., In., U.S. | D2 | 91 |
| Vermilion, co., La., U.S. | E3 | 95 |
| Vermilion, stm., Il., U.S. | C5 | 90 |
| Vermilion, stm., Il., U.S. | B5 | 90 |
| Vermilion, stm., La., U.S. | E3 | 95 |
| Vermilion, stm., Mn., U.S. | B6 | 100 |
| Vermilion, stm., Oh., U.S. | A3 | 112 |
| Vermilion Bay, Ont. | E5 | 70 |
| Vermilion Bay, b., La., U.S. | E3 | 95 |
| Vermilion Lake, l., Mn., U.S. | C6 | 100 |
| Vermilion Pass, Can. | D2 | 68 |
| Vermilion Range, hills, Mn., U.S. | C6 | 100 |
| Vermillion, Ks., U.S. | C7 | 93 |
| Vermillion, S.D., U.S. | E9 | 118 |
| Vermillion, co., In., U.S. | E2 | 91 |
| Vermillion, East Fork, stm., S.D., U.S. | D8 | 118 |
| Vermillion Bluffs, clf., Co., U.S. | A2 | 83 |
| Vermillion Creek, stm., Co., U.S. | A2 | 83 |
| Vermillon, stm., Que. | B4 | 74 |
| Vermont, Il., U.S. | C3 | 90 |
| Vermont, state, U.S. | D3 | 122 |
| Vermontville, Mi., U.S. | F5 | 99 |
| Vernal, Ut., U.S. | C6 | 121 |
| Vernalis, Ca., U.S. | h10 | 82 |
| Verndale, Mn., U.S. | D3 | 100 |
| Verner, Ont. | A4 | 73 |
| Verneuil, Fr. | C4 | 16 |
| Verneukpan, pl., S. Afr. | D3 | 49 |
| Vernon, B.C. | D8 | 69 |
| Vernon, Al., U.S. | B1 | 78 |
| Vernon, Az., U.S. | C6 | 80 |
| Vernon, Co., U.S. | B8 | 83 |
| Vernon, Ct., U.S. | *B6 | 84 |
| Vernon, Fl., U.S. | u16 | 86 |
| Vernon, In., U.S. | G6 | 91 |
| Vernon, Ok., U.S. | B6 | 113 |
| Vernon, Tn., U.S. | B4 | 119 |
| Vernon, Tx., U.S. | B3 | 120 |
| Vernon, Vt., U.S. | F3 | 122 |
| Vernon, co., La., U.S. | C2 | 95 |
| Vernon, co., Mo., U.S. | D3 | 102 |
| Vernon, co., Wi., U.S. | E3 | 126 |
| Vernon, Lake, l., Ont. | B5 | 73 |
| Vernon Bridge, P.E.I. | C7 | 71 |
| Vernon Center, Mn., U.S. | G4 | 100 |
| Vernon Hill, Va., U.S. | D3 | 123 |
| Vernon Hills, Il., U.S. | h9 | 90 |
| Vernonia, Or., U.S. | B3 | 114 |
| Vernon River, P.E.I. | C7 | 71 |
| Vero Beach, Fl., U.S. | E6 | 86 |
| Véroia, Grc. | B4 | 40 |
| Verona, Ont. | C8 | 73 |
| Verona, Italy | A3 | 23 |
| Verona, Il., U.S. | B5 | 90 |
| Verona, Ky., U.S. | B5 | 94 |
| Verona, Ms., U.S. | A5 | 101 |
| Verona, Mo., U.S. | E4 | 102 |
| Verona, N.J., U.S. | B4 | 107 |
| Verona, N.C., U.S. | C5 | 110 |
| Verona, N.D., U.S. | C7 | 111 |
| Verona, Oh., U.S. | C1 | 112 |
| Verona, Pa., U.S. | k14 | 115 |
| Verona, Tn., U.S. | B5 | 119 |
| Verona, Wi., U.S. | F4 | 126 |
| Verónica, Arg. | g8 | 54 |
| Verret, N.B. | B1 | 71 |
| Verret, Lake, l., La., U.S. | E4 | 95 |
| Verrières-le-Buisson, Fr. | h10 | 16 |
| Versailles, Fr. | C5 | 16 |
| Versailles, Ct., U.S. | C7 | 84 |
| Versailles, Il., U.S. | D3 | 90 |
| Versailles, In., U.S. | F7 | 91 |
| Versailles, Ky., U.S. | B5 | 94 |
| Versailles, Mo., U.S. | C5 | 102 |
| Versailles, Oh., U.S. | B1 | 112 |
| Versmold, W. Ger. | D4 | 18 |
| Versoix, Switz. | C2 | 20 |
| Vert, Cap, c., Sen. | E4 | 42 |
| Verte, stm., Que. | B8 | 74 |
| Verte, Île, i., Que. | A9 | 74 |
| Verton, Fr. | D9 | 12 |
| Vertou, Fr. | E5 | 16 |
| Vertus, Fr. | F4 | 17 |
| Verviers, Bel. | C5 | 16 |
| Vervins, Fr. | B5 | 16 |
| Verwall Group, mts., Aus. | D2 | 20 |
| Verwood, Sask. | H3 | 75 |
| Verzasca, stm., Switz. | C6 | 16 |
| Verzenay, Fr. | C6 | 16 |
| Verzy, Fr. | E6 | 16 |
| Veseleyville, N.D., U.S. | A8 | 111 |
| Veselí nad Lužnicí, Czech. | D9 | 19 |
| Veseloye, Sov. Un. | H10 | 27 |
| Vesoul, Fr. | B1 | 21 |
| Vesoul, Fr. | E6 | 16 |
| Vesper, Ks., U.S. | C5 | 93 |
| Vesta, C.R. | G6 | 64 |
| Vesta, Mn., U.S. | F3 | 100 |
| Vestaburg, Mi., U.S. | E6 | 99 |
| Vestal, N.Y., U.S. | C4 | 109 |
| Vestal Center, N.Y., U.S. | C4 | 109 |
| Vestavia Hills, Al., U.S. | g7 | 78 |
| Vestby, Nor. | p28 | 14 |
| Vesterålen, is., Nor. | D10 | 14 |
| Vesterø Havn, Den. | A4 | 15 |
| Vestervig, Den. | B2 | 15 |
| Vestfjorden, Nor. | D9 | 14 |
| Vestmannaeyjar, Ice. | o22 | 14 |
| Vestsjælland, co., Den. | C3 | 15 |
| Vesuvius, vol., Italy | D5 | 23 |
| Vesuvius, Va., U.S. | C3 | 123 |
| Veszprém, Hung. | B3 | 24 |
| Vésztő, Hung. | B11 | 24 |
| Vetal, S.D., U.S. | D4 | 118 |
| Veteran, Alta. | D5 | 68 |
| Veteran, Wy., U.S. | E8 | 127 |
| Vetlanda, Swe. | I6 | 14 |
| Vetluga, stm., Sov. Un. | B8 | 28 |
| Vetovo, Bul. | D8 | 24 |
| Vetren, Bul. | D7 | 24 |
| Veurne, Bel. | C2 | 17 |
| Vevay, In., U.S. | G7 | 91 |
| Vevey, Switz. | C2 | 20 |
| Veynes, Fr. | E6 | 16 |
| Veyo, Ut., U.S. | F2 | 121 |
| Veyrier-du-Lac, Fr. | E1 | 21 |
| Vézère, stm., Fr. | E4 | 16 |
| Vezirköprü, Tur. | B10 | 40 |
| Viacha, Bol. | C2 | 55 |
| Viadana, Italy | B3 | 23 |
| Viamão, Braz. | B2 | 57 |
| Vian, Ok., U.S. | B7 | 113 |
| Viana, Braz. | B2 | 57 |
| Viana do Bollo, Spain | A2 | 22 |
| Viana do Alentejo, Port. | C1 | 22 |
| Viana do Castelo, Port. | B1 | 22 |
| Vianen, Neth. | C5 | 17 |
| Viangchan (Vientiane), Laos | B2 | 34 |
| Vianópolis, Braz. | B3 | 56 |
| Viar, stm., Spain | D3 | 22 |
| Viareggio, Italy | C3 | 23 |
| Vibank, Sask. | G4 | 75 |
| Viborg, Den. | B3 | 15 |
| Viborg, S.D., U.S. | D8 | 118 |
| Viborg, co., Den. | B3 | 15 |
| Vibo Valentia, Italy | E6 | 23 |
| Viburnum, Mo., U.S. | D6 | 102 |
| Vic, Fr. | F4 | 16 |
| Vicálvaro, Spain | p17 | 22 |
| Vicco, Ky., U.S. | C6 | 94 |
| Vicente, Point, c., Ca., U.S. | n12 | 82 |
| Vicenza, Italy | B3 | 23 |
| Viceroy, Sask. | H3 | 75 |
| Vich, Spain | B7 | 22 |
| Vichada, dept., Col. | C4 | 60 |
| Vichada, stm., Col. | C4 | 60 |
| Vichuga, Sov. Un. | C13 | 27 |
| Vichuquén, Chile | A2 | 54 |
| Vichy, Fr. | D5 | 16 |
| Vichy, Mo., U.S. | C6 | 102 |
| Vici, Ok., U.S. | A2 | 113 |
| Vick, Ar., U.S. | D3 | 81 |
| Vick, La., U.S. | C3 | 95 |
| Vickery, Oh., U.S. | A3 | 112 |
| Vicksburg, In., U.S. | F3 | 91 |
| Vicksburg, Mi., U.S. | F5 | 99 |
| Vicksburg, Ms., U.S. | C3 | 101 |
| Vicksburg National Military Park, Ms., U.S. | C3 | 101 |
| Viçosa, Braz. | C4 | 56 |
| Viçosa, Braz. | C3 | 57 |
| Viçosa do Ceará, Braz. | B2 | 57 |
| Vicosoprano, Switz. | D8 | 21 |
| Vicovaro, Italy | g9 | 23 |
| Vic [-sur-Seille], Fr. | F6 | 17 |
| Victor, Co., U.S. | C5 | 83 |
| Victor, Id., U.S. | F7 | 89 |
| Victor, Ia., U.S. | C5 | 92 |
| Victor, Mt., U.S. | D2 | 103 |
| Victor, N.Y., U.S. | C3 | 109 |
| Victor, S.D., U.S. | B9 | 118 |
| Victor Harbor, Austl. | G6 | 50 |
| Victoria, Arg. | A4 | 54 |
| Victoria, B.C. | E6 | 69 |
| Victoria, Newf. | E5 | 72 |
| Victoria, P.E.I. | C6 | 71 |
| Victoria, Chile | B2 | 54 |
| Victoria, Gren. | W25 | 65 |
| Victoria (Hong Kong), H.K. | G7 | 31 |
| Victoria, Malay. | D6 | 32 |
| Victoria, Phil. | o13 | 34 |
| Victoria, Il., U.S. | B3 | 90 |
| Victoria, Ks., U.S. | D4 | 93 |
| Victoria, Ms., U.S. | A4 | 101 |
| Victoria, Mo., U.S. | C7 | 102 |
| Victoria, Tn., U.S. | D8 | 119 |
| Victoria, Tx., U.S. | E4 | 120 |
| Victoria, Va., U.S. | D4 | 123 |
| Victoria, state, Austl. | G7 | 50 |
| Victoria, co., N.B. | B2 | 71 |
| Victoria, co., Ont. | C6 | 73 |
| Victoria, co., Tx., U.S. | E4 | 120 |
| Victoria, stm., Newf. | D3 | 72 |
| Victoria, Lake, l., Afr. | B5 | 48 |
| Victoria, Lake, l., Austl. | F3 | 51 |
| Victoria, Mount, mtn., Burma | D9 | 36 |
| Victoria, Mount, mtn., Pap. N. Gui. | k12 | 50 |
| Victoria Beach, Man. | D3 | 70 |
| Victoria Island, i., N.W. Ter. | B10 | 66 |
| Victoria Lake, res., Newf. | D3 | 72 |
| Victoria Land, reg., Ant. | B28 | 7 |
| Victoria Falls, Zimb. | A4 | 49 |
| Victoria Falls, wtfl., Afr. | A4 | 49 |
| Victoria Harbour, Ont. | C5 | 73 |
| Victoria Peak, mtn., Belize | B3 | 62 |
| Victoria Road, Ont. | C6 | 73 |
| Victoria Strait, strt., N.W. Ter. | C12 | 66 |
| Victoriaville, Que. | C6 | 74 |
| Victoria West, S. Afr. | D3 | 49 |
| Victorino, Ven. | C4 | 60 |
| Victorville, Ca., U.S. | E5 | 82 |
| Victory, Wi., U.S. | E2 | 126 |
| Vicuña, Chile | F1 | 55 |
| Vicuña Mackenna, Arg. | A4 | 54 |
| Vida, Or., U.S. | C4 | 114 |
| Vidal, Ca., U.S. | E6 | 82 |
| Vidalia, Ga., U.S. | D4 | 87 |
| Vidalia, La., U.S. | C4 | 95 |
| Vidigueira, Port. | C2 | 22 |
| Vidin, Bul. | C5 | 24 |
| Vidisha, India | B6 | 36 |
| Vidor, Tx., U.S. | D5 | 120 |
| Vidora, Sask. | H1 | 75 |
| Viechtach, W. Ger. | D7 | 19 |
| Viedma, Arg. | D4 | 54 |
| Viedma, Lago, l., Arg. | F2 | 53 |
| Vieja, Sierra, mts., Tx., U.S. | o12 | 120 |
| Viejo, Cerro el, mtn., Col. | B3 | 60 |
| Vielsalm, Bel. | D5 | 17 |
| Vienna (Wien), Aus. | D5 | 123 |
| Vienna, Ga., U.S. | D3 | 87 |
| Vienna, Il., U.S. | F5 | 90 |
| Vienna, Md., U.S. | D6 | 97 |
| Vienna, Mo., U.S. | C6 | 102 |
| Vienna, N.J., U.S. | B3 | 107 |
| Vienna, S.D., U.S. | C8 | 118 |
| Vienna, Va., U.S. | B5 | 123 |
| Vienna, W.V., U.S. | B3 | 125 |
| Vienne, Fr. | E6 | 16 |
| Vienne, stm., Fr. | D4 | 16 |
| Vientiane see Viangchan, Laos | | |
| Vieques, P.R. | B5 | 65 |
| Vieques, Isla de, i., P.R. | G12 | 64 |
| Vieques, Pasaje de, strt., P.R. | B5 | 65 |
| Viersen, W. Ger. | C6 | 17 |
| Vierzon, Fr. | D5 | 16 |
| Viesca, Mex. | B4 | 63 |
| Vieste, Italy | D6 | 23 |
| Vietnam, ctry., Asia | B3 | 34 |
| Viet Tri, Viet. | B6 | 35 |
| Vieux Desert, Lac, l., Wi., U.S. | B4 | 126 |
| Vieux Fort, St. Luc. | J14 | 64 |
| Vieux-Fort, Pointe du, c., Guad. | R8 | 65 |
| View Park, Ca., U.S. | *m12 | 82 |
| Vigan, Phil. | m6 | 34 |
| Vigevano, Italy | B2 | 23 |
| Vignola, Italy | E6 | 20 |
| Vigo, Spain | A1 | 22 |
| Vigo, co., In., U.S. | F3 | 91 |
| Vigsø Bugt, b., Den. | A2 | 15 |
| Vihowa, Pak. | B5 | 36 |
| Vijayawāda (Bezwada), India | E7 | 36 |
| Vik, Ice. | o23 | 14 |
| Vikersund, Nor. | p27 | 14 |
| Viking, Alta. | C5 | 68 |
| Viking, Mn., U.S. | B2 | 100 |
| Vila Alferes Chamusca, Moz. | B5 | 49 |
| Vila Bela de Santíssima Trinidade, Braz. | B4 | 55 |
| Vila da Maganja, Moz. | A6 | 49 |
| Vila de Manica, Moz. | A5 | 49 |
| Vila de Rei, Port. | C1 | 22 |
| Vila de Sena, Moz. | A6 | 49 |
| Vila do Conde, Port. | B1 | 22 |
| Vila Fontes, Moz. | A6 | 49 |
| Vilafranca del Penedés, Spain | B6 | 22 |
| Vila Franca de Xira, Port. | C1 | 22 |
| Vilaine, stm., Fr. | D2 | 16 |
| Vila Nova de Gaia, Port. | B1 | 22 |
| Vila Nova de Foz Côa, Port. | B2 | 22 |
| Vila Nova de Milfontes, Port. | D1 | 22 |
| Vila Real, Port. | B2 | 22 |
| Vila Real de Santo António, Port. | D2 | 22 |
| Vilas, Co., U.S. | D8 | 83 |
| Vilas, S.D., U.S. | C8 | 118 |
| Vilas, co., Wi., U.S. | B4 | 126 |
| Vila São Luis, Braz. | B3 | 59 |
| Vila Vasco da Gama, Moz. | D5 | 48 |
| Vila Velha, Braz. | C4 | 56 |
| Vila Viçosa, Port. | C2 | 22 |
| Vildbjerg, Den. | B2 | 15 |
| Vildo, In., U.S. | B2 | 119 |
| Vilhelmina, Swe. | E7 | 14 |
| Vilhena, Braz. | B3 | 55 |
| Vilia, Grc. | g10 | 25 |
| Viljandi, Sov. Un. | C5 | 27 |
| Vilkaviškis, Sov. Un. | A7 | 26 |
| Vilkitskiy, i., Sov. Un. | B7 | 128 |
| Vilkovo, Sov. Un. | I7 | 27 |
| Villa Abecia, Bol. | D2 | 55 |
| Villa Adriana, hist., Italy | h9 | 23 |
| Villa Ahumada, Mex. | A3 | 63 |
| Villa Ángela, Arg. | E3 | 55 |
| Villa Aroma, Bol. | C2 | 55 |
| Villa Bella, Bol. | B2 | 55 |
| Villablino, Spain | A2 | 22 |
| Villacañas, Spain | C4 | 22 |
| Villacarrillo, Spain | C4 | 22 |
| Villach, Aus. | E6 | 18 |
| Villacidro, Italy | E2 | 23 |
| Villa Clara, prov., Cuba | C3 | 64 |
| Villa Constitución, Arg. | A4 | 54 |
| Villa Cuauhtémoc, Mex. | k15 | 63 |
| Villa de Arriaga, Mex. | m13 | 63 |
| Villa de Cura, Ven. | B3 | 60 |
| Villa Delgado, El Sal. | *D3 | 62 |
| Villa del Rosario, Ven. | B5 | 63 |
| Villa de Méndez, Mex. | B5 | 63 |
| Villa Dolores, Arg. | A3 | 54 |
| Villa Eufronio Viscarra, Bol. | C2 | 55 |
| Villafranca del Bierzo, Spain | A2 | 22 |
| Villafranca de los Barros, Spain | C2 | 22 |
| Villafranca [di Verona], Italy | B3 | 23 |
| Villa Frontera, Mex. | B4 | 63 |
| Villa García, Mex. | k13 | 63 |
| Villagarcía, Spain | A1 | 22 |
| Village, Va., U.S. | C6 | 123 |
| Village Creek, stm., Al., U.S. | f7 | 78 |
| Village Springs, Al., U.S. | B3 | 78 |
| Villa González, Mex. | C5 | 63 |
| Villa Grove, Il., U.S. | D5 | 90 |
| Villa Grove, Il., U.S. | D5 | 90 |
| Villaguay, Arg. | A5 | 54 |
| Villa Hayes, Para. | E4 | 55 |
| Villahermosa, Mex. | D6 | 63 |
| Villa Hills, Ky., U.S. | *A5 | 94 |
| Villa Huidobro, Arg. | A3 | 54 |
| Villa Iris, Arg. | B4 | 54 |
| Villajoyosa, Spain | C5 | 22 |
| Villa María, Arg. | A4 | 54 |
| Villa María Grande, Arg. | A5 | 54 |
| Villa Mazán, Arg. | E2 | 55 |
| Villa Montes, Bol. | D3 | 55 |
| Villanova, Col. | A3 | 60 |
| Villa Nueva, N.M., U.S. | C4 | 108 |
| Villanueva de Córdoba, Spain | C3 | 22 |
| Villanueva del Arzobispo, Spain | C4 | 22 |
| Villanueva de la Serana, Spain | C3 | 22 |
| Villanueva de los Infantes, Spain | C4 | 22 |
| Villanueva [del Río y Minas], Spain | D2 | 22 |
| Villanueva y Geltrú, Spain | B6 | 22 |
| Villa Obregón (part of Mexico City), Mex. | h9 | 63 |
| Villa Ocampo, Arg. | E4 | 55 |
| Villa Oliva, Para. | E4 | 55 |
| Villa Ojo de Agua, Arg. | E3 | 55 |
| Villa Park, Il., U.S. | k8 | 90 |
| Villaputzu, Italy | E3 | 23 |
| Villard, Mn., U.S. | E3 | 100 |
| Villa Rica, Ga., U.S. | C2 | 87 |
| Villa Rica, Para. | F4 | 55 |
| Villa Ridge, Mo., U.S. | C7 | 102 |
| Villarrica, Chile | B2 | 54 |
| Villarrobledo, Spain | C4 | 22 |
| Villars-le-Terroir, Switz. | D3 | 21 |
| Villa San Martín (Loreto), Arg. | E3 | 55 |
| Villa Unión, Arg. | E2 | 55 |

| Name | Ref. | Page |
|---|---|---|
| Villa Unión, Mex. | B4 | 63 |
| Villa Unión, Mex. | C3 | 63 |
| Villa Valeria, Arg. | A4 | 54 |
| Villaverde, Spain | p17 | 22 |
| Villavicencio, Col. | C3 | 60 |
| Villaviciosa, Spain | A3 | 22 |
| Villefranche [-sur-Saône], Fr. | E5 | 16 |
| Villefranche [-sur-Saône], Fr. | D6 | 16 |
| Villegreen, Co., U.S. | D7 | 83 |
| Villejuif, Fr. | g10 | 16 |
| Ville Marie, Que. | G17 | 66 |
| Villemomble, Fr. | g11 | 16 |
| Villena, Spain | C5 | 22 |
| Villenauxe-la-Grande, Fr. | F3 | 17 |
| Villeneuve-le-Roi, Fr. | h10 | 16 |
| Villeneuve-d'Ascq, Fr. | *B5 | 16 |
| Villeneuve [-lès-Avignon], Fr. | F6 | 16 |
| Villeneuve-Saint-Georges, Fr. | h10 | 16 |
| Villeneuve-sur-Lot, Fr. | E4 | 16 |
| Villeneuve-sur-Yonne, Fr. | C5 | 16 |
| Villepinte, Fr. | g11 | 16 |
| Ville Platte, La., U.S. | D3 | 95 |
| Villeroy, Que. | C6 | 74 |
| Villers-Bretonneux, Fr. | E2 | 17 |
| Villers-Cotterêts, Fr. | C5 | 16 |
| Villersexel, Fr. | A1 | 21 |
| Villers-Outréaux, Fr. | D3 | 17 |
| Villers-Semeuse, Fr. | E4 | 17 |
| Villerupt, Fr. | C6 | 16 |
| Ville Saint-Georges, Que. | C7 | 74 |
| Villeta, Para. | E4 | 55 |
| Villeurbanne, Fr. | E6 | 16 |
| Villingen-Schwenningen, W. Ger. | D4 | 18 |
| Villisca, Ia., U.S. | D3 | 92 |
| Vilna, Alta. | B5 | 68 |
| Vilnius, Sov. Un. | D5 | 29 |
| Vilonia, Ar., U.S. | B3 | 81 |
| Vilppula, Fin. | F11 | 14 |
| Vils, stm., W. Ger. | E7 | 19 |
| Vils, stm., W. Ger. | D6 | 19 |
| Vilsbiburg, W. Ger. | E7 | 19 |
| Vilseck, W. Ger. | D6 | 19 |
| Vilshofen, W. Ger. | E8 | 19 |
| Vilvoorde, Bel. | B6 | 16 |
| Vilyuy, stm., Sov. Un. | C15 | 29 |
| Vilyuysk, Sov. Un. | C15 | 29 |
| Vimianzo, Spain | A1 | 22 |
| Vimmerby, Swe. | I6 | 14 |
| Vimperk, Czech. | D2 | 26 |
| Vimy Ridge, Ar., U.S. | k10 | 81 |
| Vina, Al., U.S. | A1 | 78 |
| Vina, Ca., U.S. | C2 | 82 |
| Viña del Mar, Chile | A2 | 54 |
| Vinalhaven, Me., U.S. | D4 | 96 |
| Vinalhaven Island, i., Me., U.S. | D4 | 96 |
| Vinaroz, Spain | B6 | 22 |
| Vincennes, Fr. | g10 | 16 |
| Vincennes, In., U.S. | G2 | 91 |
| Vincennes Bay, b., Ant. | C23 | 7 |
| Vincent, Al., U.S. | B3 | 78 |
| Vincent, Oh., U.S. | C4 | 112 |
| Vincent, Tx., U.S. | C2 | 120 |
| Vincentown, N.J., U.S. | D3 | 107 |
| Vinces, Ec. | B2 | 58 |
| Vinchina, Arg. | E2 | 55 |
| Vinchina, stm., Arg. | E2 | 55 |
| Vinco, Ok., U.S. | B4 | 113 |
| Vindelälven, stm., Swe. | E8 | 14 |
| Vindeln, Swe. | E8 | 14 |
| Vinderup, Den. | B2 | 15 |
| Vindhya Range, mts., India | D6 | 36 |
| Vine Brook, stm., Ma., U.S. | g11 | 98 |
| Vinegar Hill, mtn., Or., U.S. | C8 | 114 |
| Vine Grove, Ky., U.S. | C4 | 94 |
| Vineland, N.J., U.S. | E2 | 107 |
| Vinemont, Al., U.S. | A3 | 78 |
| Vineyard Haven, Ma., U.S. | D6 | 98 |
| Vineyard Sound, strt., Ma., U.S. | D6 | 98 |
| Vingåker, Swe. | t33 | 14 |
| Vinh, Viet. | B3 | 34 |
| Vinhais, Port. | B2 | 22 |
| Vinh Long, Viet. | C3 | 34 |
| Vining, Ks., U.S. | C6 | 93 |
| Vining, Mn., U.S. | D3 | 100 |
| Vinita, Ok., U.S. | A6 | 113 |
| Vinkovci, Yugo. | C4 | 24 |
| Vinland, Ks., U.S. | m15 | 93 |
| Vinnitsa, Sov. Un. | E5 | 29 |
| Vinson, Ok., U.S. | C2 | 113 |
| Vinson Massif, mtn., Ant. | B4 | 7 |
| Vinton, Ia., U.S. | B5 | 92 |
| Vinton, La., U.S. | D2 | 95 |
| Vinton, Oh., U.S. | D3 | 112 |
| Vinton, Va., U.S. | C3 | 123 |
| Vinton, co., Oh., U.S. | C3 | 112 |
| Vintondale, Pa., U.S. | F4 | 115 |
| Viola, Ar., U.S. | A4 | 81 |
| Viola, De., U.S. | D3 | 85 |
| Viola, Id., U.S. | C1 | 89 |
| Viola, Il., U.S. | B3 | 90 |
| Viola, Ks., U.S. | E6 | 93 |
| Viola, N.Y., U.S. | *D6 | 109 |
| Viola, Tn., U.S. | D8 | 119 |
| Viola, Wi., U.S. | E3 | 126 |
| Violet, La., U.S. | k12 | 95 |
| Vipiteno, Italy | C7 | 20 |
| Virden, Man. | E1 | 70 |
| Virden, Il., U.S. | D4 | 90 |
| Virden, N.M., U.S. | E1 | 108 |
| Vire, Fr. | C3 | 16 |
| Vire, stm., Fr. | D4 | 16 |
| Viren, l., Swe. | t34 | 14 |
| Virgem da Lapa, Braz. | B4 | 56 |
| Vírgenes, Cabo, c., S.A. | F3 | 54 |
| Virgil, Ks., U.S. | E7 | 93 |
| Virgil, N.Y., U.S. | C4 | 109 |
| Virgil, S.D., U.S. | C7 | 118 |
| Virgilina, Va., U.S. | D4 | 123 |
| Virgin, Ut., U.S. | F2 | 121 |
| Virgin, stm., U.S. | G8 | 105 |
| Virgin Gorda, i., V.I., Br. | G12 | 64 |
| Virginia, Ire. | D4 | 11 |
| Virginia, S. Afr. | C4 | 49 |
| Virginia, Al., U.S. | g6 | 78 |
| Virginia, Il., U.S. | D3 | 90 |
| Virginia, Ne., U.S. | D9 | 104 |
| Virginia, state, U.S. | C4 | 123 |
| Virginia Beach, Va., U.S. | D7 | 123 |
| Virginia City, Mt., U.S. | E5 | 103 |
| Virginia City, Nv., U.S. | D2 | 105 |
| Virginia Peak, mtn., Nv., U.S. | D2 | 105 |
| Virgin Islands, dep., N.A. | G12 | 64 |
| Virgin Islands, is., N.A. | B6 | 65 |
| Virgin Mountains, mts., U.S. | A1 | 80 |
| Virginópolis, Braz. | B5 | 56 |
| Virgin Passage, strt., N.A. | B5 | 65 |
| Virgolândia, Braz. | B5 | 56 |
| Virochey, Camb. | C3 | 34 |
| Viroflay, Fr. | g9 | 16 |
| Víron, Grc. | *D4 | 25 |
| Viroqua, Wi., U.S. | E3 | 126 |
| Virovitica, Yugo. | C3 | 24 |
| Virpazar, Yugo. | D4 | 24 |
| Virrat, Fin. | F10 | 14 |
| Virserum, Swe. | I6 | 14 |
| Virton, Bel. | E5 | 17 |
| Virú, Peru | C2 | 58 |
| Vis, Yugo. | D3 | 24 |
| Vis, i., Yugo. | D3 | 24 |
| Visalia, Ca., U.S. | D4 | 82 |
| Visalia, Ky., U.S. | k14 | 94 |
| Visayan Sea, Phil. | C6 | 34 |
| Visby, Swe. | I8 | 14 |
| Viscount Melville Sound, strt., N.W. Ter. | B11 | 66 |
| Visé, Bel. | D5 | 17 |
| Višegrad, Yugo. | D4 | 24 |
| Viseu, Braz. | B1 | 57 |
| Viseu, Port. | B2 | 22 |
| Vishākhapatnam (Vizagapatam), India | E7 | 36 |
| Vishera, stm., Sov. Un. | A5 | 28 |
| Viskan, stm., Swe. | A6 | 15 |
| Vislanda, Swe. | B8 | 15 |
| Viso, Mount, mtn., Italy | B1 | 23 |
| Visoko, Yugo. | D4 | 24 |
| Visp, Switz. | E3 | 18 |
| Vista, Man. | D1 | 70 |
| Vista, Ca., U.S. | F5 | 82 |
| Vista, Mo., U.S. | D4 | 102 |
| Vista, Nv., U.S. | *D2 | 105 |
| Vista Alegre, Braz. | C4 | 60 |
| Vistonís, Lake, l., Grc. | B5 | 25 |
| Vistula, In., U.S. | A6 | 91 |
| Vistula Lagoon, b., Eur. | A5 | 26 |
| Vistula see Wisła, stm., Pol. | B5 | 26 |
| Vit, stm., Bul. | D7 | 24 |
| Vita, Man. | E3 | 70 |
| Vitanovac, Yugo. | D5 | 24 |
| Vitarte, Peru | D2 | 58 |
| Vitebsk, Sov. Un. | D6 | 29 |
| Viterbo, Italy | C4 | 23 |
| Vitichi, Bol. | D2 | 55 |
| Viti Levu, i., Fiji | H14 | 52 |
| Viti Levu Bay, b., Fiji | H15 | 52 |
| Vitim, Sov. Un. | D14 | 29 |
| Vitim, stm., Sov. Un. | D14 | 29 |
| Vitória, Braz. | C4 | 54 |
| Vitória, Braz. | C4 | 54 |
| Vitória, Spain | A4 | 22 |
| Vitória [de Santo Antão], Braz. | C3 | 57 |
| Vitória do Mearim, Braz. | B2 | 57 |
| Vitória Quebrangulo, Braz. | k5 | 57 |
| Vitré, Fr. | C3 | 16 |
| Vitry-le-François, Fr. | C6 | 16 |
| Vitry [-sur-Seine], Fr. | g10 | 16 |
| Vittel, Fr. | C6 | 16 |
| Vittoria, Ont. | E4 | 73 |
| Vittoria, Italy | F5 | 23 |
| Vittorio Veneto, Italy | B4 | 23 |
| Vivero, Spain | A2 | 22 |
| Vivian, La., U.S. | B2 | 95 |
| Vivian, S.D., U.S. | D5 | 118 |
| Vivian Park, Ut., U.S. | C4 | 121 |
| Vivoratá, Arg. | B5 | 54 |
| Viwa, i., Fiji | H14 | 52 |
| Vize, Tur. | B6 | 40 |
| Vizianagaram, India | E7 | 36 |
| Vizille, Fr. | E6 | 16 |
| Vižinj, Rom. | C8 | 24 |
| Vizzini, Italy | F5 | 23 |
| Vladimiro-Aleksandrovskoye, Sov. Un. | C11 | 31 |
| Vladimirovo, Sov. Un. | B12 | 33 |
| Vladimir-Volynskiy, Sov. Un. | F5 | 27 |
| Vladivostok, Sov. Un. | E16 | 29 |
| Vlasenica, Yugo. | C4 | 24 |
| Vlašim, Czech. | D9 | 19 |
| Vlasotince, Yugo. | D6 | 24 |
| Vlčany, Czech. | D4 | 26 |
| Vlieland, i., Neth. | A6 | 16 |
| Vlissingen, Neth. | B5 | 16 |
| Vlkava, Czech. | n18 | 26 |
| Vlora (Valona), Alb. | B2 | 40 |
| Vlotho, W. Ger. | A3 | 19 |
| Vltava, stm., Czech. | D3 | 26 |
| Voca, Tx., U.S. | D3 | 120 |
| Vodlozero, l., Sov. Un. | F17 | 14 |
| Vodňany, Czech. | D9 | 19 |
| Voghera, Italy | B2 | 23 |
| Vohenstrauss, W. Ger. | D7 | 19 |
| Vohibinany, Madag. | g9 | 49 |
| Vohimarina, Madag. | f9 | 49 |
| Vohipeno, Madag. | h9 | 49 |
| Voi, Kenya | B6 | 48 |
| Voinjama, Lib. | E3 | 45 |
| Voiron, Fr. | E6 | 16 |
| Voisin, Lac, l., Sask. | C2 | 75 |
| Voitsberg, Aus. | E7 | 18 |
| Vojens, Den. | C3 | 15 |
| Vokhma, Sov. Un. | B3 | 28 |
| Volborg, Mt., U.S. | E11 | 103 |
| Volcano, Hi., U.S. | D6 | 88 |
| Volcano Island, i., Phil. | o13 | 34 |
| Volcano Islands, is., Japan | E8 | 6 |
| Volcano Islands see Kazan-rettō, is., Japan | F11 | 27 |
| Volchansk, Sov. Un. | B7 | 33 |
| Volda, Nor. | G6 | 34 |
| Volga, Ia., U.S. | B6 | 92 |
| Volga, S.D., U.S. | C9 | 118 |
| Volga, W.V., U.S. | B4 | 125 |
| Volga, stm., Sov. Un. | E7 | 29 |
| Volga Plateau, plat., Sov. Un. | C3 | 28 |
| Volga, stm., Sov. Un. | H13 | 27 |
| Volgodonsk, Sov. Un. | H13 | 27 |
| Volgograd (Stalingrad), Sov. Un. | E7 | 29 |
| Volgograd Reservoir, res., Sov. Un. | D7 | 29 |
| Volin, S.D., U.S. | E8 | 118 |
| Volkach, W. Ger. | D5 | 19 |
| Volkhov, stm., Sov. Un. | B9 | 27 |
| Völklingen, W. Ger. | D1 | 19 |
| Volkovysk, Sov. Un. | D5 | 27 |
| Vollenhove, Neth. | B5 | 17 |
| Volney, Va., U.S. | D1 | 123 |
| Volnovakha, Sov. Un. | H11 | 27 |
| Volo, Il., U.S. | h8 | 90 |
| Volochayevka Vtoraya, Sov. Un. | B7 | 33 |
| Volodarskiy, Sov. Un. | G6 | 27 |
| Volodarskiy (part of Leningrad), Sov. Un. | s31 | 14 |
| Volodarskoye, Sov. Un. | C7 | 28 |
| Vologda, Sov. Un. | D7 | 29 |
| Vólos, Grc. | C4 | 40 |
| Vólos, Gulf of see Pagasitikós Kólpos, b., Grc. | C4 | 40 |
| Volsk, Sov. Un. | C3 | 28 |
| Volta, prov., Ghana | E5 | 45 |
| Volta, Lake, res., Ghana | E5 | 45 |
| Voltaire, N.D., U.S. | A5 | 111 |
| Volta Noire (Black Volta), stm., Afr. | D4 | 45 |
| Volta Redonda, Braz. | C4 | 56 |
| Volterra, Italy | C3 | 23 |
| Voltri, Italy | B2 | 23 |
| Volturno, stm., Italy | D5 | 23 |
| Voluntown, Ct., U.S. | C8 | 84 |
| Volusia, co., Fl., U.S. | C5 | 86 |
| Vólvi, Lake, l., Grc. | B4 | 25 |
| Volzhskiy, Sov. Un. | G15 | 27 |
| Vombsjön, l., Swe. | C7 | 15 |
| Vona, Co., U.S. | B8 | 83 |
| Vonda, Sask. | E2 | 75 |
| Von Frank Mountain, mtn., Ak., U.S. | C9 | 79 |
| Vónitsa, Grc. | C3 | 25 |
| Vonore, Tn., U.S. | D9 | 119 |
| Von Ormy, Tx., U.S. | k7 | 120 |
| Vopnafjördur, Ice. | n25 | 14 |
| Vorarlberg, state, Aus. | B5 | 20 |
| Vorderrhein, stm., Switz. | C7 | 21 |
| Vorderthal, Switz. | B6 | 21 |
| Vordingborg, Den. | C5 | 15 |
| Vorkuta, Sov. Un. | C9 | 29 |
| Vorona, stm., Sov. Un. | E14 | 27 |
| Voronezh, Sov. Un. | D6 | 29 |
| Voronezh, stm., Sov. Un. | E12 | 27 |
| Voronezh, stm., Sov. Un. | C16 | 14 |
| Voroshilovgrad, Sov. Un. | E6 | 29 |
| Vorskla, stm., Sov. Un. | G10 | 27 |
| Vørterkaka Nunatak, mtn., Ant. | B15 | 7 |
| Vosburg, S. Afr. | D3 | 49 |
| Vosges, dept., Fr. | A2 | 20 |
| Vosges, mts., Fr. | C7 | 16 |
| Voskresensk, Sov. Un. | n18 | 27 |
| Voss, Nor. | G2 | 14 |
| Voss, N.D., U.S. | A8 | 111 |
| Vossburg, Ms., U.S. | D5 | 101 |
| Vossevangen, Switz. | B11 | 33 |
| Vostok, sci., Ant. | B23 | 7 |
| Vostok Island, i., Kir. | G12 | 6 |
| Votaw, Tx., U.S. | D5 | 120 |
| Votice, Czech. | D9 | 19 |
| Votkinsk, Sov. Un. | B4 | 28 |
| Vouga, stm., Port. | B1 | 22 |
| Vouliagméni, Grc. | h11 | 25 |
| Vouvray, Fr. | D4 | 16 |
| Vouziers, Fr. | C6 | 16 |
| Voyageurs National Park, Mn., U.S. | B5 | 100 |
| Voyeykov Ice Shelf, ice, Ant. | C25 | 7 |
| Vozhega, Sov. Un. | A13 | 27 |
| Voznesensk, Sov. Un. | H8 | 27 |
| Voznesenskoye, Sov. Un. | A8 | 33 |
| Voznesenye, Sov. Un. | A10 | 27 |
| Vrå, Den. | A3 | 15 |
| Vranje, Yugo. | D5 | 24 |
| Vratsa, Bul. | D6 | 24 |
| Vrbas, Yugo. | C4 | 24 |
| Vrbas, stm., Yugo. | C3 | 24 |
| Vrchlabí, Czech. | C3 | 26 |
| Vrede, S. Afr. | C4 | 49 |
| Vredenburgh, Al., U.S. | D2 | 78 |
| Vreed en Hoop, Guy. | A3 | 59 |
| Vrena, Swe. | u34 | 14 |
| Vrezenveen, Neth. | B6 | 17 |
| Vrigstad, Swe. | A8 | 15 |
| Vrin, Switz. | C7 | 21 |
| Vršac, Yugo. | C5 | 24 |
| Vršovice (part of Prague), Czech. | n17 | 26 |
| Vrútky, Czech. | D5 | 26 |
| Vryburg, S. Afr. | C3 | 49 |
| Vryheid, S. Afr. | C5 | 49 |
| Všetaty, Czech. | n18 | 26 |
| Vsetín, Czech. | D5 | 26 |
| Vsevidof, Mount, mtn., Ak., U.S. | E6 | 79 |
| Vsevolozhsk, Sov. Un. | r31 | 14 |
| Vuaqava, i., Fiji | I16 | 52 |
| Vúcha, stm., Bul. | E7 | 24 |
| Vuda Point, c., Fiji | H14 | 52 |
| Vukovar, Yugo. | C4 | 24 |
| Vulcan, Alta. | D4 | 68 |
| Vulcan, Mi., U.S. | C3 | 99 |
| Vulcan, stm., Czech. | D3 | 26 |
| Vulcano, i., Italy | E5 | 23 |
| Vúlchedrúma, Bul. | D6 | 24 |
| Vung Tau, Viet. | G7 | 35 |
| Vung Tau, Cape, c., Viet. | G7 | 35 |
| Vunidawa, Fiji | H15 | 52 |
| Vuoloyarvi, Sov. Un. | r31 | 14 |
| Vuya Point, c., Fiji | H15 | 52 |
| Vyartsilya, Sov. Un. | F14 | 14 |
| Vyatka, stm., Sov. Un. | D7 | 29 |
| Vyatskiye Polyany, Sov. Un. | B4 | 28 |
| Vyazemskiy, Sov. Un. | C7 | 33 |
| Vyazma, Sov. Un. | D10 | 27 |
| Vyazniki, Sov. Un. | C14 | 27 |
| Vyborg, Sov. Un. | C5 | 29 |
| Vychegda, stm., Sov. Un. | C18 | 8 |
| Vygozero, l., Sov. Un. | F16 | 14 |
| Vyksa, Sov. Un. | D14 | 27 |
| Vyritsa, Sov. Un. | s31 | 14 |
| Výrovka, stm., Czech. | n19 | 26 |
| Vyshniy Volochek, Sov. Un. | C10 | 27 |
| Vyškov, Czech. | D4 | 26 |
| Vysočany (part of Prague), Czech. | n17 | 26 |
| Vysoká, Czech. | n18 | 26 |
| Vysoké Mýto, Czech. | D4 | 26 |
| Vyšší Brod, Czech. | E9 | 19 |
| Vytegra, Sov. Un. | C6 | 29 |

## W

| Name | Ref. | Page |
|---|---|---|
| Wa, Ghana | D4 | 45 |
| Waal, stm., Neth. | B6 | 16 |
| Waalwijk, Neth. | B5 | 16 |
| Waawaa, Puu, mtn., Hi., U.S. | D6 | 88 |
| Wabasca, Alta. | B4 | 68 |
| Wabasca, stm., Alta. | H1 | 68 |
| Wabash, In., U.S. | C6 | 91 |
| Wabash, co., Il., U.S. | E6 | 90 |
| Wabash, co., In., U.S. | C6 | 91 |
| Wabash, stm., U.S. | H2 | 91 |
| Wabasha, Mn., U.S. | F6 | 100 |
| Wabasha, co., Mn., U.S. | F6 | 100 |
| Wabasso, Fl., U.S. | E6 | 86 |
| Wabasso, Mn., U.S. | F3 | 100 |
| Wabaunsee, Ks., U.S. | C7 | 93 |
| Wabaunsee, co., Ks., U.S. | D7 | 93 |
| Wabbaseka, Ar., U.S. | C4 | 81 |
| Wabeno, Wi., U.S. | C5 | 126 |
| Wabigoon, Ont. | E5 | 70 |
| Wabigoon Lake, l., Ont. | E5 | 70 |
| Wabowden, Man. | B2 | 70 |
| Wabrzeźno, Pol. | B5 | 26 |
| Wabuk, Newf. | h8 | 72 |
| Wabuska, Nv., U.S. | D2 | 105 |
| Waccamaw, stm., U.S. | D9 | 117 |
| Waccamaw, Lake, l., N.C., U.S. | C4 | 110 |
| Waccasassa Bay, b., Fl., U.S. | C4 | 86 |
| Wachapreague, Va., U.S. | C7 | 123 |
| Wachusett Mountain, mtn., Ma., U.S. | B4 | 98 |
| Wachusett Reservoir, res., Ma., U.S. | B4 | 98 |
| Wacissa, Fl., U.S. | B3 | 86 |
| Wacker, Il., U.S. | A3 | 90 |
| Waco, Ga., U.S. | C1 | 87 |
| Waco, Ky., U.S. | g12 | 93 |
| Waco, Ne., U.S. | D8 | 104 |
| Waco, N.C., U.S. | B1 | 110 |
| Waco, Tx., U.S. | D4 | 120 |
| Waco Lake, res., Tx., U.S. | D4 | 120 |
| Waconda Lake, res., Ks., U.S. | C5 | 93 |
| Waconia, Mn., U.S. | F5 | 100 |
| Waddān, Libya | D3 | 43 |
| Waddān, Jabal, mtn., Libya | D3 | 43 |
| Waddell, Az., U.S. | D3 | 80 |
| Wadden Zee, Neth. | A6 | 16 |
| Waddington, N.Y., U.S. | f9 | 109 |
| Waddington, Mount, mtn., B.C. | D5 | 69 |
| Waddy, Ky., U.S. | B4 | 94 |
| Wade, N.C., U.S. | B4 | 110 |
| Wade, Ok., U.S. | D5 | 113 |
| Wade, Mount, mtn., Ant. | A32 | 7 |
| Wade Hampton, S.C., U.S. | *B3 | 117 |
| Wadena, Sask. | F4 | 75 |
| Wadena, In., U.S. | C3 | 91 |
| Wadena, Ia., U.S. | B6 | 92 |
| Wadena, Mn., U.S. | D4 | 100 |
| Wadena, co., Mn., U.S. | D4 | 100 |
| Wädenswil, Switz. | B4 | 20 |
| Wadesboro, N.C., U.S. | C2 | 110 |
| Wadesville, In., U.S. | H2 | 91 |
| Wadham Islands, is., Newf. | D5 | 72 |
| Wadhwan see Surendranagar, India | F3 | 37 |
| Wādī al Jayb (Ha Arava), val., Asia | G10 | 40 |
| Wādī al Jōz (part of Jerusalem), Isr. Occ. | m14 | 41 |
| Wading, West Branch, stm., N.J., U.S. | D3 | 107 |
| Wading River, N.J., U.S. | D4 | 107 |
| Wading River, N.Y., U.S. | n16 | 109 |
| Wadley, Al., U.S. | B4 | 78 |
| Wadley, Ga., U.S. | D4 | 87 |
| Wad Madanī, Sud. | C3 | 47 |
| Wadmalaw Island, i., S.C., U.S. | F7 | 117 |
| Wadowice, Pol. | D5 | 26 |
| Wadsworth, Al., U.S. | C3 | 78 |
| Wadsworth, Il., U.S. | h9 | 90 |
| Wadsworth, Nv., U.S. | D2 | 105 |
| Wadsworth, Oh., U.S. | A4 | 112 |
| Waelder, Tx., U.S. | E4 | 120 |
| Wagarville, Al., U.S. | D1 | 78 |
| Wagener, S.C., U.S. | D5 | 117 |
| Wageningen, Sur. | A3 | 59 |
| Wager Bay, b., N.W. Ter. | C15 | 66 |
| Wagga, Sask. | B4 | 47 |
| Wagga Wagga, Austl. | G8 | 50 |
| Waggaman, La., U.S. | k11 | 95 |
| Waggoner, Il., U.S. | D4 | 90 |
| Wagner, Mt., U.S. | B8 | 103 |
| Wagner, S.D., U.S. | D7 | 118 |
| Wagners Lake, Ne., U.S. | *C8 | 104 |
| Wagoner, Ok., U.S. | B6 | 113 |
| Wagoner, co., Ok., U.S. | B6 | 113 |
| Wagon Mound, N.M., U.S. | A5 | 108 |
| Wagontire Mountain, mtn., Or., U.S. | D7 | 114 |
| Wagram, N.C., U.S. | C3 | 110 |
| Wagrowiec, Pol. | B4 | 26 |
| Waha, Libya | D3 | 43 |
| Wahai, Indon. | F7 | 34 |
| Wah Cantonment, Pak. | *B5 | 36 |
| Wahiawa, Hi., U.S. | B3 | 88 |
| Wahiawa Reservoir, res., Hi., U.S. | g9 | 88 |
| Wahkiakum, co., Wa., U.S. | C2 | 124 |
| Wahkon, Mn., U.S. | D5 | 100 |
| Wahlern, Switz. | C3 | 21 |
| Wahoo, Ne., U.S. | C9 | 104 |
| Wahoo Creek, stm., Ne., U.S. | g11 | 104 |
| Wahpeton, N.D., U.S. | C9 | 111 |
| Wah Wah Mountains, mts., Ut., U.S. | E2 | 121 |
| Wahweap Creek, stm., Ut., U.S. | F4 | 121 |
| Waialua, Hi., U.S. | B3 | 88 |
| Waialua Bay, b., Hi., U.S. | B3 | 88 |
| Waianae, Hi., U.S. | B3 | 88 |
| Waianae Range, mts., Hi., U.S. | f9 | 88 |
| Waiau, stm., N.Z. | O14 | 51 |
| Waiblingen, W. Ger. | E4 | 18 |
| Waigeo, i., Indon. | F8 | 34 |
| Waihee, Hi., U.S. | C5 | 88 |
| Wai Islands, is., Camb | H5 | 35 |
| Waikabubak, Indon. | G6 | 34 |
| Waikato, stm., N.Z. | L15 | 51 |
| Waikelo, Indon. | G5 | 34 |
| Waikerie, Austl. | F7 | 50 |
| Waikiki Beach, Hi., U.S. | g10 | 88 |
| Wailagi Lala, i., Fiji | H16 | 52 |
| Wailea, Hi., U.S. | C6 | 88 |
| Wailua, Hi., U.S. | A2 | 88 |
| Wailuku, Hi., U.S. | C5 | 88 |
| Wailuku, stm., Hi., U.S. | D6 | 88 |
| Waimanalo, Hi., U.S. | g11 | 88 |
| Waimanalo Bay, b., Hi., U.S. | g11 | 88 |
| Waimate, N.Z. | P13 | 51 |
| Waimea, Hi., U.S. | A2 | 88 |
| Waimea, Hi., U.S. | D6 | 88 |
| Waimea Bay, b., Hi., U.S. | f9 | 88 |
| Waini Point, c., Guy. | A3 | 59 |
| Wainunu Bay, b., Fiji | H15 | 52 |
| Wainwright, Alta. | C5 | 68 |
| Wainwright, Ak., U.S. | A8 | 79 |
| Wainwright, Oh., U.S. | B4 | 112 |
| Wainwright, Ok., U.S. | B6 | 113 |
| Waiohinu, Hi., U.S. | D6 | 88 |
| Waipahu, Hi., U.S. | B3 | 88 |
| Waipara, N.Z. | O14 | 51 |
| Waipawa, N.Z. | M16 | 51 |
| Waipio Acres, Hi., U.S. | g9 | 88 |
| Waipio Peninsula, pen., Hi., U.S. | g10 | 88 |
| Waipukurau, N.Z. | N16 | 51 |
| Wairau, stm., N.Z. | N14 | 51 |
| Wairoa, N.Z. | M16 | 51 |
| Waitaki, stm., N.Z. | P13 | 51 |
| Waitara, N.Z. | M15 | 51 |
| Waite, Me., U.S. | C5 | 96 |
| Waite Park, Mn., U.S. | E4 | 100 |
| Waiteville, W.V., U.S. | D4 | 125 |
| Waits, stm., Vt., U.S. | C4 | 122 |
| Waitsburg, Wa., U.S. | C7 | 124 |
| Waitsfield, Vt., U.S. | C3 | 122 |
| Waits River, Vt., U.S. | C4 | 122 |
| Waitville, Sask. | E3 | 75 |
| Waiwo, Indon. | F8 | 34 |
| Wajima, Japan | H8 | 33 |
| Wajir, Kenya | A7 | 48 |
| Waka, Eth. | D4 | 47 |
| Waka, Tx., U.S. | A2 | 120 |
| Waka, Zaire | A3 | 48 |
| Wakarusa, In., U.S. | A5 | 91 |
| Wakarusa, Ks., U.S. | D8 | 93 |
| Wakarusa, stm., Ks., U.S. | D8 | 93 |
| Wakasa Bay, b., Japan | I7 | 33 |
| Wakatipu, Lake, l., N.Z. | P12 | 51 |
| Wakaw, Sask. | E3 | 75 |
| Wakaya, i., Fiji | H15 | 52 |
| Wakayama, Japan | E12 | 31 |
| Wake, co., N.C., U.S. | B4 | 110 |
| Wa Keeney, Ks., U.S. | C4 | 93 |
| Wakefield, Que. | D2 | 74 |
| Wakefield, Eng., U.K. | A6 | 12 |
| Wakefield, Ks., U.S. | C6 | 93 |
| Wakefield, La., U.S. | D4 | 95 |
| Wakefield, Ma., U.S. | B5 | 98 |
| Wakefield, Mi., U.S. | n12 | 99 |
| Wakefield, Ne., U.S. | B9 | 104 |
| Wakefield, N.H., U.S. | C4 | 106 |
| Wakefield, Oh., U.S. | D2 | 112 |
| Wakefield, R.I., U.S. | F3 | 116 |
| Wakefield, Va., U.S. | D6 | 123 |
| Wakema, Burma | D1 | 35 |
| Wakeman, Oh., U.S. | A3 | 112 |
| Wakenda, Mo., U.S. | B4 | 102 |
| Wakita, Ok., U.S. | A4 | 113 |
| Wakkanai, Japan | B13 | 31 |
| Wakkerstroom, S. Afr. | C5 | 49 |
| Wakonda, S.D., U.S. | D8 | 118 |
| Wakopa, Man. | E2 | 70 |
| Wakpala, S.D., U.S. | B5 | 118 |
| Wakuach, Lac, l., Que. | g8 | 72 |
| Waku Kungo, Ang. | D2 | 48 |
| Wakulla, Fl., U.S. | B2 | 86 |
| Wakulla, co., Fl., U.S. | B2 | 86 |
| Walachia, hist. reg., Rom. | C7 | 24 |
| Walbourg, Fr. | F7 | 17 |
| Walbridge, Oh., U.S. | e6 | 112 |
| Wałbrzych (Waldenburg), Pol. | C3 | 26 |
| Walchen Lake, l., W. Ger. | B7 | 20 |
| Walcott, Ar., U.S. | A5 | 81 |
| Walcott, Ia., U.S. | C7 | 92 |
| Walcott, N.D., U.S. | C9 | 111 |
| Walcott, Wy., U.S. | E6 | 118 |
| Walcott, Lake, res., Id., U.S. | G5 | 89 |
| Walcz, Pol. | B3 | 26 |
| Wald, Switz. | B6 | 21 |
| Waldbröl, W. Ger. | C2 | 19 |
| Walden, Ont. | A3 | 73 |
| Walden, Co., U.S. | A4 | 83 |
| Walden, N.Y., U.S. | D6 | 109 |
| Walden, Vt., U.S. | C4 | 122 |
| Waldenburg, Ar., U.S. | B5 | 81 |
| Waldenburg see Wałbrzych, Pol. | C3 | 26 |
| Walden Heights, Vt., U.S. | C4 | 122 |
| Walden Pond, l., Ma., U.S. | g10 | 98 |
| Walden Ridge, mtn., Tn., U.S. | D8 | 119 |
| Waldheim, Sask. | E2 | 75 |
| Waldheim, E. Ger. | C7 | 19 |
| Waldkappel, W. Ger. | B5 | 19 |
| Waldkirchen, W. Ger. | E8 | 19 |
| Waldmünchen, W. Ger. | D7 | 19 |
| Waldnaab, stm., W. Ger. | D6 | 19 |
| Waldo, B.C. | E10 | 69 |
| Waldo, Ar., U.S. | D2 | 81 |
| Waldo, Fl., U.S. | C4 | 86 |
| Waldo, Ks., U.S. | C5 | 93 |
| Waldo, Me., U.S. | D3 | 96 |
| Waldo, Oh., U.S. | B2 | 112 |
| Waldo, Wi., U.S. | E6 | 126 |
| Waldo, co., Me., U.S. | D3 | 96 |
| Waldo Lake, l., Ma., U.S. | h11 | 98 |
| Waldo Lake, l., Or., U.S. | D4 | 114 |
| Waldorf, Md., U.S. | C4 | 97 |
| Waldorf, Mn., U.S. | G5 | 100 |
| Waldport, Or., U.S. | C2 | 114 |
| Waldron, Sask. | G4 | 75 |
| Waldron, Ar., U.S. | C1 | 81 |
| Waldron, In., U.S. | F6 | 91 |
| Waldron, Mi., U.S. | G6 | 99 |
| Waldron, Mo., U.S. | h10 | 102 |
| Waldsassen, W. Ger. | C7 | 19 |
| Waldshut, W. Ger. | E4 | 18 |
| Waldwick, N.J., U.S. | A4 | 107 |
| Walen, Lake, l., Switz. | B5 | 20 |
| Walenstadt, Switz. | B6 | 21 |
| Wales, Ak., U.S. | B6 | 79 |
| Wales, N.D., U.S. | A7 | 111 |
| Wales, Ut., U.S. | D4 | 121 |
| Wales, Wi., U.S. | *E5 | 126 |
| Wales, ter., U.K. | D5 | 10 |
| Waleska, Ga., U.S. | B2 | 87 |
| Walford, Ia., U.S. | C6 | 92 |
| Walgett, Austl. | E8 | 50 |
| Walgreen Coast, Ant. | B2 | 7 |
| Walhalla, Mi., U.S. | E4 | 99 |
| Walhalla, N.D., U.S. | A8 | 111 |
| Walhalla, S.C., U.S. | B1 | 117 |
| Walhonding, stm., Oh., U.S. | B3 | 112 |
| Walikale, Zaire | B4 | 48 |
| Walker, co., Al., U.S. | B2 | 78 |
| Walker, co., Ga., U.S. | B1 | 87 |
| Walker, co., Tx., U.S. | D5 | 120 |
| Walker, Mn., U.S. | C4 | 100 |
| Walker Lake, l., Man. | B3 | 70 |
| Walker Lake, l., Nv., U.S. | E3 | 105 |
| Walker Mill, Md., U.S. | *C4 | 97 |
| Walker Mountain, mtn., Ga., U.S. | B3 | 87 |
| Walker Mountain, mtn., Va., U.S. | C1 | 123 |
| Walker River Indian Reservation, Nv., U.S. | D3 | 105 |
| Walker Springs, Al., U.S. | D2 | 78 |
| Walkersville, Md., U.S. | B3 | 97 |
| Walkersville, W.V., U.S. | C4 | 125 |
| Walkerton, Ont. | C3 | 73 |
| Walkerton, In., U.S. | B5 | 91 |
| Walkertown, N.C., U.S. | A2 | 110 |
| Walkerville, Mt., U.S. | D4 | 103 |
| Wall, S.D., U.S. | D3 | 118 |
| Wallace, N.S. | D6 | 71 |
| Wallace, Ont. | B6 | 73 |
| Wallace, Id., U.S. | B3 | 89 |
| Wallace, In., U.S. | E3 | 91 |
| Wallace, Ks., U.S. | D2 | 93 |
| Wallace, Mi., U.S. | C3 | 99 |
| Wallace, Ne., U.S. | D4 | 104 |
| Wallace, N.Y., U.S. | C3 | 109 |
| Wallace, N.C., U.S. | C5 | 110 |
| Wallace, S.D., U.S. | C8 | 118 |
| Wallace, W.V., U.S. | B4 | 125 |
| Wallace, co., Ks., U.S. | D2 | 93 |
| Wallaceburg, Ont. | E2 | 73 |
| Wallacetown, Ont. | E3 | 73 |
| Wallace Lake, res., La., U.S. | B2 | 95 |
| Walland, Tn., U.S. | D10 | 119 |
| Wallaroo, Austl. | F6 | 50 |
| Wallasey, Eng., U.K. | C5 | 10 |
| Walla Walla, Wa., U.S. | C7 | 124 |
| Walla Walla, co., Wa., U.S. | C7 | 124 |
| Walla Walla, stm., Wa., U.S. | C7 | 124 |
| Walldürn, W. Ger. | D4 | 19 |
| Walled Lake, Mi., U.S. | o15 | 99 |
| Wallen, In., U.S. | B7 | 91 |
| Wallenpaupack, Lake, l., Pa., U.S. | D11 | 115 |
| Wallen Ridge, mtn., Tn., U.S. | C10 | 119 |
| Waller, Tx., U.S. | q14 | 120 |
| Waller, co., Tx., U.S. | E4 | 120 |
| Wallingford, Eng., U.K. | C6 | 12 |
| Wallingford, Ct., U.S. | D4 | 84 |
| Wallingford, Vt., U.S. | E3 | 122 |
| Walling Mountain, mtn., Ma., U.S. | B1 | 98 |
| Wallington, N.J., U.S. | h8 | 107 |
| Wallis, Tx., U.S. | E4 | 120 |
| Wallis and Futuna, dep., Oc. | G11 | 6 |
| Wallis Sands, N.H., U.S. | D5 | 106 |
| Wallkill, N.Y., U.S. | D6 | 109 |
| Wallkill, stm., N.Y., U.S. | D6 | 109 |
| Wall Lake, Ia., U.S. | B2 | 92 |
| Wall Lake, l., Ia., U.S. | B4 | 92 |
| Walloomsac, stm., U.S. | F2 | 122 |
| Walloon Lake, l., Mi., U.S. | C6 | 99 |
| Wallowa, Or., U.S. | B9 | 114 |
| Wallowa, co., Or., U.S. | B9 | 114 |
| Wallowa Mountains, mts., Or., U.S. | B9 | 114 |
| Wallpack Center, N.J., U.S. | A3 | 107 |
| Walls, Ms., U.S. | A3 | 101 |
| Wallsburg, Ut., U.S. | C4 | 121 |
| Wallsend, Eng., U.K. | C6 | 11 |
| Wallula, Wa., U.S. | C7 | 124 |
| Wallula, Lake, res., U.S. | C7 | 124 |
| Wallum Lake, l., U.S. | A1 | 116 |
| Walney, Isle of, i., Eng., U.K. | C5 | 10 |
| Walnut, Ca., U.S. | *m13 | 82 |
| Walnut, Il., U.S. | B4 | 90 |
| Walnut, Ia., U.S. | C2 | 92 |
| Walnut, Ks., U.S. | E8 | 93 |
| Walnut, Ms., U.S. | A5 | 101 |
| Walnut, N.C., U.S. | f10 | 110 |
| Walnut, stm., Ks., U.S. | E6 | 93 |
| Walnut Bottom, Pa., U.S. | F7 | 115 |
| Walnut Canyon National Monument, Az., U.S. | B4 | 80 |
| Walnut Cove, N.C., U.S. | A2 | 110 |
| Walnut Creek, Ca., U.S. | h8 | 82 |
| Walnut Creek, stm., Ks., U.S. | D4 | 93 |
| Walnut Creek West, Ca., U.S. | *D2 | 82 |
| Walnut Grove, Al., U.S. | A3 | 78 |
| Walnut Grove, Ca., U.S. | C3 | 82 |
| Walnut Grove, Ms., U.S. | C4 | 101 |
| Walnut Grove, Mo., U.S. | D4 | 102 |
| Walnut Hill, Fl., U.S. | u14 | 86 |
| Walnut Hill, hill, Ma., U.S. | g7 | 98 |
| Walnut Mountain, hill, Ct., U.S. | B3 | 84 |
| Walnut Park, Ca., U.S. | *n12 | 82 |
| Walnutport, Pa., U.S. | E10 | 115 |
| Walnut Ridge, Ar., U.S. | A5 | 81 |
| Walpole, Sask. | H5 | 75 |
| Walpole, Ma., U.S. | B5 | 98 |
| Walpole, N.H., U.S. | D2 | 106 |
| Walsall, Eng., U.K. | D6 | 10 |
| Walsenburg, Co., U.S. | D6 | 83 |
| Walsh, Alta. | E5 | 68 |
| Walsh, Co., U.S. | D8 | 83 |
| Walsh, co., N.D., U.S. | A8 | 111 |
| Walsingham, Cape, c., N.W. Ter. | C20 | 66 |
| Walston, Pa., U.S. | E4 | 115 |
| Walter Bathurst, Cape, c., N.W. Ter. | B17 | 66 |
| Walterboro, S.C., U.S. | F6 | 117 |
| Walter F. George Dam, U.S. | D4 | 78 |
| Walter F. George Lake, res., U.S. | D4 | 78 |
| Walterhill, Tn., U.S. | B5 | 119 |
| Walters, Ok., U.S. | C3 | 113 |
| Walthall, Ms., U.S. | B4 | 101 |
| Walthall, co., Ms., U.S. | D3 | 101 |
| Waltham, Que. | C1 | 74 |
| Waltham, Ma., U.S. | g10 | 98 |
| Waltham, Mn., U.S. | G6 | 100 |
| Walthill, Ne., U.S. | B9 | 104 |
| Walthourville, Ga., U.S. | E5 | 87 |
| Walton, Ont. | D3 | 73 |
| Walton, In., U.S. | C5 | 91 |

Name — Map Ref. — Page


Walton, Ks., U.S. D6 93
Walton, Ky., U.S. B5 94
Walton, Ne., U.S. h11 104
Walton, N.Y., U.S. C5 109
Walton, W.V., U.S. C3 125
*Walton, co., Fl., U.S.* u15 86
*Walton, co., Ga., U.S.* C3 87
Waltonville, Il., U.S. E4 90
Walvisbaai (Walvis Bay), S. Afr. B1 49
Walvis Bay see Walvisbaai, S. Afr. B1 49
Walworth, N.Y., U.S. B3 109
Walworth, Wi., U.S. F5 126
*Walworth, co., S.D., U.S.* B5 118
*Walworth, co., Wi., U.S.* F5 126
Wamac, Il., U.S. E4 90
Wamba, Nig. E6 45
Wamba, Zaire A4 48
*Wamba, stm., Afr.* C2 48
Wamego, Ks., U.S. C7 93
Wamesit, Ma., U.S. A5 98
*Wami, stm., Tan.* C6 48
Wamic, Or., U.S. B5 114
Wampsville, N.Y., U.S. B5 109
Wampum, Pa., U.S. E1 115
Wamsutter, Wy., U.S. E5 127
Wāna, Pak. B4 36
Wanaka, N.Z. P12 51
*Wanaka, Lake, l., N.Z.* P12 51
Wanakena, N.Y., U.S. A6 109
Wanamie, Pa., U.S. D9 115
Wanamingo, Mn., U.S. F6 100
Wan'an, China K6 32
*Wanapitei, stm., Ont.* A4 73
*Wanapum Dam, Wa., U.S.* C6 124
*Wanapum Lake, res., Wa., U.S.* B6 124
Wanaque, N.J., U.S. A4 107
*Wanaque Reservoir, res., N.J., U.S.* A4 107
Wanatah, In., U.S. B4 91
Wanblee, S.D., U.S. D4 118
Wanchese, N.C., U.S. B7 110
Wanda, Mn., U.S. F3 100
Wandering River, Alta. B4 68
Wando, S. Kor. I3 33
Wando, S.C., U.S. F8 117
*Wando, stm., S.C., U.S.* F8 117
Wandoan, Austl. C7 51
Wando Woods, S.C., U.S. k11 117
Wandsworth (part of London), Eng., U.K. m12 10
Wanette, Ok., U.S. C4 113
*Wang, stm., Thai.* D3 35
Wanganui, N.Z. M15 51
Wangaratta, Austl. G8 50
Wangen [im Allgäu], W. Ger. B5 20
*Wangerooge, i., W. Ger.* B3 18
Wangkui, China A12 32
Wangqing, China C10 31
Wanham, Alta. B1 68
Wanilla, Ms., U.S. D3 101
*Wanipigow, stm., Can.* D4 70
*Wankie National Park, Zimb.* A4 49
Wann, Ne., U.S. g12 104
Wann, Ok., U.S. A6 113
Wannaska, Mn., U.S. B3 100
Wanship, Ut., U.S. C4 121
Wantage, Eng., U.K. C6 12
Wantagh, N.Y., U.S. *E7 109
Wanup, Ont. A4 73
Wanxian, China E6 31
Wanzai, China J6 32
Wapakoneta, Oh., U.S. B1 112
Wapanucka, Ok., U.S. C5 113
Wapato, Wa., U.S. C5 124
*Wapawekka Hills, hills, Sask.* C3 75
*Wapawekka Lake, l., Sask.* C3 75
Wapella, Sask. G5 75
Wapella, Il., U.S. C5 90
Wapello, Ia., U.S. C6 92
*Wapello, co., Ia., U.S.* C5 92
*Wapisu Lake, l., Man.* B2 70
Wapiti, Wy., U.S. B3 127
*Wapiti, stm., Can.* B1 68
*Wapiti Ridge, mtn., Wy., U.S.* B3 127
Wappapello, Mo., U.S. E7 102
*Wappapello, Lake, res., Mo., U.S.* D7 102
Wappingers Falls, N.Y., U.S. D7 109
*Wapsipinicon, stm., Ia., U.S.* B6 92
Wapske, N.B. C2 71
*Wapus Lake, l., Sask.* A4 75
Wapwallopen, Pa., U.S. D9 115
Wāqid, Eg. D2 41
Waqqāş, Jord. B7 41
Waquoit, Ma., U.S. C6 98
War, W.V., U.S. D3 125
*Waramaug, Lake, l., Ct., U.S.* C2 84
Warangal, India E6 36
Warba, Mn., U.S. C5 100
Warburg, Alta. C3 68
Warburg, W. Ger. B4 19
Warburton, Austl. H5 51
*Warburton Creek, stm., Austl.* E6 50
Ward, Al., U.S. C1 78
Ward, Ar., U.S. B4 81
Ward, Co., U.S. *A5 83
Ward, S.C., U.S. D4 117
Ward, S.D., U.S. C9 118
*Ward, co., N.D., U.S.* A4 111
*Ward, co., Tx., U.S.* D1 120
*Ward, Mount, mtn., Ant.* B6 7
Wardell, Mo., U.S. E8 102
Warden, Alta. C4 68
Warden, Que. D5 74
Warden, La., U.S. B4 95
Warden, Wa., U.S. C6 124
Wardensville, W.V., U.S. B6 125
*Warder, l., W. Ger.* E4 15
Wardha, India D6 36
*Wardha, stm., India* D6 36
*Ward Hill, hill, Scot., U.K.* B5 13
Wardlow, Alta. D5 68
*Ward Mountain, mtn., Mt., U.S.* D2 103
Wardner, B.C. E10 69
Wardner, Id., U.S. B2 89
Wardsboro, Vt., U.S. E3 122
Wardsville, Ont. E3 73
Wardville, Ok., U.S. C5 113
Ware, Ma., U.S. B3 98
*Ware, co., Ga., U.S.* E4 87
*Ware, stm., Ma., U.S.* B3 98
War Eagle, W.V., U.S. D3 125
*War Eagle Creek, stm., Ar., U.S.* A2 81
*War Eagle Mountain, mtn., Id., U.S.* G2 89
Wareham, Eng., U.K. D5 12
Wareham, Ma., U.S. C6 98
Warehouse Point, Ct., U.S. B5 84
Waren, E. Ger. B6 18
Waren, Indon. F9 34
Warendorf, W. Ger. B2 19
Waresboro, Ga., U.S. E4 87
Ware Shoals, S.C., U.S. C3 117
Waretown, N.J., U.S. D4 107
Warfield, B.C. E9 69
Warfield, Ky., U.S. C7 94
Warfield, Va., U.S. D5 123
Warfordsburg, Pa., U.S. G5 115
Wargla, Alg. C6 44
Warin, E. Ger. E5 15
Waring, Tx., U.S. E3 120
Wark, Eng., U.K. E6 13
Warkworth, Ont. C7 73
Warkworth, N.Z. L15 51
Warley see Smethwick, Eng., U.K. D5 10
Warman, Sask. E2 75
Warman, Mn., U.S. D5 100
Warmbad, Nmb. C2 49
Warmbad, S. Afr. B4 49
Warm Beach, Wa., U.S. A3 124
Warminster, Eng., U.K. C5 12
Warminster, Pa., U.S. F11 115
Warm Lake, Id., U.S. E3 89
Warm River, Id., U.S. E7 89
Warm Springs, Ar., U.S. A4 81
Warm Springs, Ga., U.S. D2 87
Warm Springs, Nv., U.S. E5 105
Warm Springs, Or., U.S. C5 114
Warm Springs, Va., U.S. B3 123
*Warm Springs Indian Reservation, Or., U.S.* C5 114
*Warm Springs Reservoir, res., Or., U.S.* D8 114
Warnemünde (part of Rostock), E. Ger. A6 18
Warner, Alta. E4 68
Warner, N.H., U.S. D3 106
Warner, Oh., U.S. C4 112
Warner, Ok., U.S. B6 113
Warner, S.D., U.S. B7 118
*Warner, stm., N.H., U.S.* D3 106
*Warner Mountain, mtn., Ma., U.S.* B1 98
*Warner Mountains, mts., Ca., U.S.* B3 82
*Warner Peak, mtn., Or., U.S.* E7 114
Warner Robins, Ga., U.S. D3 87
Warner Springs, Ca., U.S. F5 82
Warnes, Bol. C3 55
*Warnow, stm., E. Ger.* B5 18
*Warpath, stm., Man.* C2 70
Warracknabeal, Austl. H4 51
Warr Acres, Ok., U.S. B4 113
Warragul, Austl. I5 51
*Warrego, stm., Austl.* E8 50
Warren, Austl. E6 51
Warren, Ont. A4 73
Warren, Ar., U.S. D3 81
Warren, Ct., U.S. C2 84
Warren, Id., U.S. D3 89
Warren, Il., U.S. A4 90
Warren, In., U.S. C7 91
Warren, Me., U.S. D3 96
Warren, Ma., U.S. B3 98
Warren, Mi., U.S. F7 99
Warren, Mn., U.S. B2 100
Warren, N.H., U.S. C3 106
Warren, N.Y., U.S. C6 109
Warren, Oh., U.S. A5 112
Warren, Ok., U.S. C2 113
Warren, Or., U.S. B4 114
Warren, Pa., U.S. C3 115
Warren, R.I., U.S. D5 116
Warren, Tx., U.S. D5 120
Warren, Vt., U.S. C3 122
*Warren, co., Ga., U.S.* C4 87
*Warren, co., Il., U.S.* C3 90
*Warren, co., In., U.S.* D3 91
*Warren, co., Ia., U.S.* C4 92
*Warren, co., Ky., U.S.* C3 94
*Warren, co., Ms., U.S.* C3 101
*Warren, co., Mo., U.S.* C6 102
*Warren, co., N.J., U.S.* B3 107
*Warren, co., N.Y., U.S.* B7 109
*Warren, co., N.C., U.S.* A4 110
*Warren, co., Oh., U.S.* C1 112
*Warren, co., Pa., U.S.* C3 115
*Warren, co., Tn., U.S.* D8 119
*Warren, co., Va., U.S.* B4 123
*Warren, stm., U.S.* D5 116
Warren Center, Pa., U.S. C9 115
Warrendale, Pa., U.S. h13 115
Warren Park, In., U.S. k10 91
*Warren Peaks, mts., Wy., U.S.* B8 127
Warrenpoint, N. Ire., U.K. C5 11
Warren Point, R.I., U.S. F6 116
Warrens, Wi., U.S. D3 126
Warrensburg, Il., U.S. D4 90
Warrensburg, Mo., U.S. C4 102
Warrensburg, N.Y., U.S. B7 109
Warrensburg, Tn., U.S. C10 119
Warrensville, Pa., U.S. D8 115
Warrensville Heights, Oh., U.S. h9 112
Warrenton, S. Afr. C3 49
Warrenton, Ga., U.S. C4 87
Warrenton, Mo., U.S. C6 102
Warrenton, N.C., U.S. A4 110
Warrenton, Or., U.S. A3 114
Warrenton, Va., U.S. B5 123
Warrenville, Ct., U.S. B7 84
Warrenville, Il., U.S. k8 90
Warrenville, S.C., U.S. D4 117
Warri, Nig. E6 45
*Warrick, co., In., U.S.* H3 91
Warrington, Eng., U.K. D5 10
Warrington, Fl., U.S. u14 86
Warrington, Pa., U.S. *F11 115
Warrior, Al., U.S. B3 78
*Warrior Mountain, mtn., Md., U.S.* k13 97
*Warrior Reservoir, res., Al., U.S.* C2 78
Warriors Mark, Pa., U.S. E5 115
Warrnambool, Austl. G7 50
Warroad, Mn., U.S. B3 100
Warsaw, Ont. C6 73
Warsaw (Warszawa), Pol. B6 26
Warsaw, Il., U.S. C2 90
Warsaw, In., U.S. B6 91
Warsaw, Ky., U.S. B5 94
Warsaw, Mo., U.S. C4 102
Warsaw, N.Y., U.S. C2 109
Warsaw, N.C., U.S. B4 110
Warsaw, N.D., U.S. A8 111
Warsaw, Oh., U.S. B3 112
Warsaw, Va., U.S. C6 123
Warspite, Alta. B4 68
Warstein, W. Ger. B3 19
Warta, Pol. C5 26
*Warta, stm., Pol.* B3 26
Wartburg, Tn., U.S. C9 119
Warth, Aus. B6 20
Warthen, Ga., U.S. C4 87
Wartime, Sask. F1 75
Wartrace, Tn., U.S. B5 119
Warwick, Austl. D8 51
Warwick, Ont. D3 73
Warwick, Que. D6 74
Warwick, Eng., U.K. D6 10
Warwick, Ga., U.S. E3 87
Warwick, Md., U.S. B6 97
Warwick, Ma., U.S. A3 98
Warwick, N.Y., U.S. D6 109
Warwick, N.D., U.S. B7 111
Warwick, Ok., U.S. B4 113
Warwick, Pa., U.S. F10 115
Warwick, R.I., U.S. D4 116
*Warwick Dam, Ga., U.S.* E3 87
*Warwickshire, co., Eng., U.K.* B6 12
Wasaga Beach, Ont. C4 73
*Wasatch, co., Ut., U.S.* C4 121
*Wasatch Plateau, plat., Ut., U.S.* D4 121
*Wasatch Range, mts., U.S.* B5 76
*Wascana Creek, stm., Sask.* G3 75
Wasco, Ca., U.S. E4 82
Wasco, Or., U.S. B6 114
*Wasco, co., Or., U.S.* B5 114
Waseca, Sask. D1 75
Waseca, Mn., U.S. F5 100
*Waseca, co., Mn., U.S.* F5 100
*Washademoak Lake, l., N.B.* D4 71
Washago, Ont. C5 73
*Washakie, co., Wy., U.S.* C4 127
*Washakie Needles, mts., Wy., U.S.* C3 127
Washburn, Il., U.S. C4 90
Washburn, Ia., U.S. B5 92
Washburn, Me., U.S. B4 96
Washburn, Mo., U.S. E4 102
Washburn, N.D., U.S. B5 111
Washburn, Tn., U.S. C10 119
Washburn, Wi., U.S. B3 126
*Washburn, co., Wi., U.S.* C2 126
*Washburn, Mount, mtn., Wy., U.S.* B2 127
Wāshīm, India G6 37
Washington, Ar., U.S. D2 81
Washington, Ct., U.S. C2 84
Washington, D.C., U.S. C3 97
Washington, Ga., U.S. C4 87
Washington, Il., U.S. C4 90
Washington, In., U.S. G3 91
Washington, Ia., U.S. C6 92
Washington, Ks., U.S. C6 93
Washington, Ky., U.S. B6 94
Washington, La., U.S. D3 95
Washington, Ma., U.S. B1 98
Washington, Ms., U.S. D2 101
Washington, Mo., U.S. C6 102
Washington, Ne., U.S. g12 104
Washington, N.H., U.S. D2 106
Washington, N.J., U.S. B3 107
Washington, N.C., U.S. B5 110
Washington, Ok., U.S. B4 113
Washington, Pa., U.S. F1 115
Washington, Tn., U.S. D9 119
Washington, Ut., U.S. F2 121
Washington, Vt., U.S. C4 122
Washington, Va., U.S. B4 123
Washington, W.V., U.S. B3 125
*Washington, co., Al., U.S.* D1 78
*Washington, co., Ar., U.S.* A1 81
*Washington, co., Co., U.S.* B7 83
*Washington, co., Fl., U.S.* u16 86
*Washington, co., Ga., U.S.* C4 87
*Washington, co., Id., U.S.* E2 89
*Washington, co., Il., U.S.* E4 90
*Washington, co., In., U.S.* G5 91
*Washington, co., Ia., U.S.* C6 92
*Washington, co., Ks., U.S.* C6 93
*Washington, co., Ky., U.S.* C4 94
*Washington, co., La., U.S.* D5 95
*Washington, co., Me., U.S.* D5 96
*Washington, co., Md., U.S.* A2 97
*Washington, co., Mn., U.S.* E6 100
*Washington, co., Ms., U.S.* B3 101
*Washington, co., Mo., U.S.* D7 102
*Washington, co., Ne., U.S.* C9 104
*Washington, co., N.Y., U.S.* B7 109
*Washington, co., N.C., U.S.* B6 110
*Washington, co., Oh., U.S.* C4 112
*Washington, co., Ok., U.S.* A6 113
*Washington, co., Or., U.S.* B3 114
*Washington, co., Pa., U.S.* F1 115
*Washington, co., R.I., U.S.* E2 116
*Washington, co., Tn., U.S.* C11 119
*Washington, co., Tx., U.S.* D4 120
*Washington, co., Ut., U.S.* F2 121
*Washington, co., Vt., U.S.* C3 122
*Washington, co., Va., U.S.* f9 123
*Washington, co., Wi., U.S.* E5 126
*Washington, state, U.S.* B5 124
*Washington, Cape, c., Fiji* I14 52
*Washington, Lake, l., Fl., U.S.* D6 86
*Washington, Lake, l., Mn., U.S.* E4 100
*Washington, Lake, l., Ms., U.S.* B3 101
*Washington, Lake, l., Wa., U.S.* e11 124
*Washington, Mount, mtn., N.H., U.S.* B4 106
Washington Court House, Oh., U.S. C2 112
Washington Crossing, N.J., U.S. C3 107
Washington Depot, Ct., U.S. C2 84
*Washington Island, i., Wi., U.S.* C7 126
*Washington Island see Teraina Island, i., Kir.* F12 6
Washington Park, Fl., U.S. *F6 86
Washington Park, Il., U.S. E3 90
Washington Terrace, Ut., U.S. B4 121
Washington Township, N.J., U.S. *B4 107
Washingtonville, Pa., U.S. D8 115
Washita, Ok., U.S. B3 113
*Washita, co., Ok., U.S.* B2 113
*Washita, stm., Ok., U.S.* C4 113
*Washoe, co., Nv., U.S.* C2 105
Washoe City, Nv., U.S. D2 105
Washougal, Wa., U.S. D3 124
*Washow Bay, b., Man.* D3 70
Washta, Ia., U.S. B2 92
*Washtenaw, co., Mi., U.S.* F7 99
Washtucna, Wa., U.S. C7 124
Wasilków, Pol. B7 26
Wasilla, Ak., U.S. C10 79
Wasioja, Mn., U.S. F6 100
Waskada, Man. E1 70
Waskaganish, Que. h11 74
*Waskaiowaka Lake, l., Man.* A3 70
Waskatenau, Alta. B4 68
*Waskesiu Lake, l., Sask.* D2 75
Waskish, Mn., U.S. B4 100
Waskom, Tx., U.S. C5 120
Waspam, Nic. C5 62
*Wasque Point, c., Ma., U.S.* D7 98
*Wassaw Sound, strt., Ga., U.S.* E6 87
Wassenaar, Neth. B4 17
Wasseralfingen, W. Ger. E5 19
Wasserburg [am Inn], W. Ger. D6 18
*Wasserkuppe, mtn., W. Ger.* C4 19
*Wass Lake, l., Man.* C4 70
Wasson, Il., U.S. F5 90
*Wassookeag, Lake, l., Me., U.S.* C3 96
*Wassuk Range, mts., Nv., U.S.* E3 105
Wassy-sur-Blaise, Fr. F4 17
Wasta, S.D., U.S. C3 118
Waswanipi, Que. o20 73
Wataga, Il., U.S. B3 90
Watampone, Indon. F6 34
*Watapi Lake, l., Sask.* B6 68
*Watatic, Mount, mtn., Ma., U.S.* A4 98
Watauga, S.D., U.S. B4 118
Watauga, Tn., U.S. C11 119
Watauga, Tx., U.S. *n9 120
*Watauga, co., N.C., U.S.* A1 110
*Watauga, stm., Tn., U.S.* C12 119
*Watauga Lake, res., Tn., U.S.* C12 119
*Watchaug Pond, l., R.I., U.S.* F2 116
Watchet, Eng., U.K. C4 12
Watch Hill, R.I., U.S. G1 116
*Watch Hill Point, c., R.I., U.S.* G1 116
Watchung, N.J., U.S. B4 107
Waterboro, Me., U.S. E2 96
Waterbury, Ct., U.S. C3 84
Waterbury, Ne., U.S. B9 104
Waterbury, Vt., U.S. C3 122
Waterbury Center, Vt., U.S. C3 122
*Waterbury Reservoir, res., Vt., U.S.* C3 122
Waterdown, Ont. D5 73
*Wateree, stm., S.C., U.S.* D6 117
*Wateree Lake, res., S.C., U.S.* C6 117
Waterfall, Ak., U.S. n23 79
Waterflow, N.M., U.S. A1 108
Waterford, Ont. E4 73
Waterford, P.E.I. C5 71
Waterford, Ire. D3 10
Waterford, Ct., U.S. D7 84
Waterford, In., U.S. A4 91
Waterford, Ky., U.S. g12 94
Waterford, Mi., U.S. *F7 99
Waterford, Ms., U.S. A4 101
Waterford, N.Y., U.S. C7 109
Waterford, Oh., U.S. C4 112
Waterford, Pa., U.S. C2 115
Waterford, Va., U.S. A5 123
Waterford, Wi., U.S. F5 126
*Waterford, co., Ire.* E4 11
*Waterford Harbour, b., Ire.* E5 11
Waterford Mills, In., U.S. A6 91
Waterford Works, N.J., U.S. D3 107
Watergrasshill, Ire. E3 11
*Waterhen Lake, l., Man.* C2 70
Waterloo, Bel. D4 17
Waterloo, Ont. D4 73
Waterloo, Que. D5 74
Waterloo, S.L. E2 45
Waterloo, Al., U.S. A1 78
Waterloo, Ar., U.S. D2 81
Waterloo, Il., U.S. E3 90
Waterloo, In., U.S. B7 91
Waterloo, Ia., U.S. B5 92
Waterloo, Ks., U.S. g11 93
Waterloo, Mt., U.S. E4 103
Waterloo, Ne., U.S. g12 104
Waterloo, N.Y., U.S. C4 109
Waterloo, Or., U.S. C4 114
Waterloo, S.C., U.S. C3 117
Waterloo, Wi., U.S. E5 126
*Waterloo, co., Ont.* D4 73
Waterman, Il., U.S. B5 90
Waterman Four Corners, R.I., U.S. C3 116
*Waterman Reservoir, res., R.I., U.S.* B3 116
Waterport, N.Y., U.S. B2 109
Waterproof, La., U.S. C4 95
Waters, Mi., U.S. D6 99
Watersmeet, Mi., U.S. n12 99
*Waterton, stm., N.A.* E4 68
*Waterton-Glacier International Peace Park, N.A.* B3 103
*Waterton Lakes National Park, Alta.* E3 68
Waterton Park, Alta. E4 68
Watertown, Ct., U.S. C3 84
Watertown, Fl., U.S. B4 86
Watertown, Ma., U.S. g11 98
Watertown, N.Y., U.S. B5 109
Watertown, Oh., U.S. C4 112
Watertown, S.D., U.S. C8 118
Watertown, Tn., U.S. A5 119
Watertown, Wi., U.S. E5 126
Water Valley, Ky., U.S. f9 94
Water Valley, Ms., U.S. A4 101
Water Valley, Tx., U.S. D2 120
Water View, Va., U.S. C6 123
Water Village, N.H., U.S. C4 106
Waterville, N.S. D5 71
Waterville, Ire. F1 11
Waterville, Ia., U.S. A6 92
Waterville, Ks., U.S. C7 93
Waterville, Me., U.S. D3 96
Waterville, Ma., U.S. A3 98
Waterville, Mn., U.S. F5 100
Waterville, N.Y., U.S. C5 109
Waterville, Oh., U.S. A2 112
Waterville, Pa., U.S. D7 115
Waterville, Vt., U.S. B3 122
Waterville, Wa., U.S. B5 124
Waterville Valley, N.H., U.S. C3 106
Watervliet, Bel. C3 17
Watervliet, Mi., U.S. F4 99
Watervliet, N.Y., U.S. C7 109
Watford, Ont. E3 73
Watford, Eng., U.K. k12 10
Watford City, N.D., U.S. B2 111
Watha, N.C., U.S. C5 110
Wathena, Ks., U.S. C9 93
Watino, Alta. B2 68
Watkins, Co., U.S. *B6 83
Watkins, Ia., U.S. C6 92
Watkins, Mn., U.S. E4 100
Watkins Glen, N.Y., U.S. C4 109
Watkinsville, Ga., U.S. C3 87
Watonga, Ok., U.S. B3 113
*Watonwan, co., Mn., U.S.* F4 100
*Watonwan, stm., Mn., U.S.* G4 100
Watou, Bel. D2 17
Watova, Ok., U.S. A6 113
Watrous, Sask. F3 75
Watrous, N.M., U.S. B5 108
Watsa, Zaire A4 48
Watseka, Il., U.S. C6 90
Watson, Sask. E3 75
Watson, Ar., U.S. D4 81
Watson, Il., U.S. D5 90
Watson, In., U.S. H6 91
Watson, Mn., U.S. E3 100
Watson, Mo., U.S. A2 102
Watson, Ok., U.S. C7 113
Watson Chapel, Ar., U.S. C3 81
Watson Lake, Yukon D7 66
Watsontown, Pa., U.S. D8 115
Watsonville, Ca., U.S. D3 82
Watten, Fr. D10 12
Watten, Fr. D2 17
*Watten, Loch, l., Scot., U.K.* B5 13
Wattenberg, Co., U.S. A6 83
*Wattensaw Bayou, stm., Ar., U.S.* C4 81
Watton, Mi., U.S. B2 99
Wattrelos, Fr. B5 16
Watts (part of Los Angeles), Ca., U.S. n12 82
Watts, Ok., U.S. A7 113
Watts Bar Dam, Tn., U.S. D9 119
*Watts Bar Dam, Tn., U.S.* D9 119
*Watts Bar Lake, res., Tn., U.S.* D9 119
Wattsburg, Pa., U.S. B2 115
Wattsville, Al., U.S. B3 78
Wattsville, S.C., U.S. B4 117
Wattwil, Switz. B5 20
Watu, Zaire B3 48
*Watubela Islands, is., Indon.* F8 34
*Watuppa Pond, l., Ma., U.S.* C5 98
Waubamik, Ont. B4 73
Waubaushene, Ont. C5 73
Waubay, S.D., U.S. B8 118
*Waubay Lake, l., S.D., U.S.* B8 118
Waubun, Mn., U.S. C3 100
Wauchope, Austl. E9 51
Wauchope, Sask. H5 75
Wauchula, Fl., U.S. E5 86
Waucoma, Ia., U.S. A5 92
Wauconda, Il., U.S. h8 90
Wauconda, Wa., U.S. A6 124
Waugh, Man. E4 70
*Waugh Mountain, mtn., Id., U.S.* D4 89
Waukau, Wi., U.S. E5 126
Waukee, Ia., U.S. C4 92
Waukeenah, Fl., U.S. B3 86
Waukegan, Il., U.S. A6 90
Waukesha, Wi., U.S. F5 126
*Waukesha, co., Wi., U.S.* E5 126
*Waukewan, Lake, l., N.H., U.S.* C3 106
Waukomis, Ok., U.S. A4 113
Waukon, Ia., U.S. A6 92
Wauna, Wa., U.S. f10 124
Waunakee, Wi., U.S. E4 126
Wauneta, Ne., U.S. D4 104
*Waungumbaug Lake, l., Ct., U.S.* B6 84
Waupaca, Wi., U.S. D4 126
*Waupaca, co., Wi., U.S.* D5 126
Waupun, Wi., U.S. E5 126
Wauregan, Ct., U.S. C8 84
Waurika, Ok., U.S. C4 113
*Waurika Lake, res., Ok., U.S.* C3 113
Wausa, Ne., U.S. B8 104
Wausau, Fl., U.S. u16 86
Wausau, Wi., U.S. D4 126
*Wausau, Lake, res., Wi., U.S.* D4 126
Wausaukee, Wi., U.S. C6 126
Wauseon, Oh., U.S. A1 112
*Waushara, co., Wi., U.S.* D4 126
Wautoma, Wi., U.S. D4 126
Wauwatosa, Wi., U.S. m12 126
Wauzeka, Wi., U.S. E3 126
Waveland, In., U.S. E3 91
Waveland, Ms., U.S. E4 101
*Waveney, stm., Eng., U.K.* D7 10
Waverley, Austl. *F9 50
Waverley, Austl. *G8 50
Waverley, N.S. E6 71
Waverly, Al., U.S. C4 78
Waverly, Ga., U.S. E5 87
Waverly, Il., U.S. D4 90
Waverly, In., U.S. E5 91
Waverly, Ia., U.S. B5 92
Waverly, Ks., U.S. D8 93
Waverly, Ky., U.S. C2 94
Waverly, Mi., U.S. *F6 99
Waverly, Mn., U.S. E5 100
Waverly, Mo., U.S. B4 102
Waverly, Ne., U.S. D9 104
Waverly, N.Y., U.S. C4 109
Waverly, Oh., U.S. C3 112
Waverly, Tn., U.S. A4 119
Waverly, Va., U.S. C5 123
Waverly, W.V., U.S. B3 125
Waverly Hall, Ga., U.S. D2 87
Wavre, Bel. D4 17
Wāw, Sud. D2 47
Wawa, Ont. o18 73
Wawa, Nig. E5 45
*Wawa, stm., Nic.* C6 62
Wawaka, In., U.S. B7 91
Wāw al Kabīr, Libya D3 43
Wawanesa, Man. E2 70
*Wawasee, Lake, l., In., U.S.* B6 91
*Wawayanda Lake, l., N.J., U.S.* A4 107
*Wawayanda Mountain, mtn., U.S.* A4 107
Waweig, N.B. D2 71
Wawota, Sask. H4 75
Waxahachie, Tx., U.S. C4 120
Waxhaw, N.C., U.S. C2 110
Waxweiler, W. Ger. D6 17
*Waya, i., Fiji* H14 52
*Wayagamac, Lac, l., Que.* B5 74
Wayan, Id., U.S. G7 89
Waycross, Ga., U.S. E4 87
Wayland, Ia., U.S. C6 92
Wayland, Ky., U.S. C7 94
Wayland, Ma., U.S. g10 98
Wayland, Mi., U.S. F5 99
Wayland, Mo., U.S. A6 102
Wayland, N.Y., U.S. C3 109
Wayland Springs, Tn., U.S. B4 119
Waylyn, S.C., U.S. k12 117
Waymart, Pa., U.S. C11 115
Wayne, Alta. D4 68
Wayne, Mi., U.S. p15 99
Wayne, Ne., U.S. B8 104
Wayne, N.J., U.S. B4 107
Wayne, N.Y., U.S. C3 109
Wayne, Oh., U.S. A2 112
Wayne, Ok., U.S. C4 113
Wayne, Pa., U.S. F11 115
Wayne, W.V., U.S. C2 125
*Wayne, co., Ga., U.S.* E5 87
*Wayne, co., Il., U.S.* E5 90
*Wayne, co., In., U.S.* E7 91
*Wayne, co., Ia., U.S.* D4 92
*Wayne, co., Ky., U.S.* D5 94
*Wayne, co., Mi., U.S.* F7 99
*Wayne, co., Ms., U.S.* D5 101
*Wayne, co., Mo., U.S.* D7 102
*Wayne, co., Ne., U.S.* B8 104
*Wayne, co., N.Y., U.S.* B3 109
*Wayne, co., N.C., U.S.* B4 110
*Wayne, co., Oh., U.S.* B4 112
*Wayne, co., Pa., U.S.* C11 115
*Wayne, co., Tn., U.S.* B4 119
*Wayne, co., Ut., U.S.* E4 121
*Wayne, co., W.V., U.S.* C2 125
Wayne City, Il., U.S. E5 90
Waynesboro, Ga., U.S. C4 87
Waynesboro, Ms., U.S. D5 101
Waynesboro, Pa., U.S. G6 115
Waynesboro, Tn., U.S. B4 119
Waynesboro, Va., U.S. B4 123
Waynesburg, Ky., U.S. C5 94
Waynesburg, Oh., U.S. B4 112
Waynesburg, Pa., U.S. G1 115
Waynesville, Ga., U.S. E5 87
Waynesville, Il., U.S. C4 90
Waynesville, Mo., U.S. D5 102
Waynesville, N.C., U.S. f10 110
Waynesville, Oh., U.S. C1 112
Waynetown, In., U.S. D3 91
Waynewood, Va., U.S. g12 123
Waynoka, Ok., U.S. A3 113
Wayside, Ks., U.S. E8 93
Wayside, Ms., U.S. B2 101
Wayside, Tx., U.S. B2 120
Wayside, Wi., U.S. h10 126
Wayzata, Mn., U.S. n11 100
*We, i., Indon.* J1 35
*Weakley, co., Tn., U.S.* A3 119
Weare, N.H., U.S. D3 106
Weatherby, Mo., U.S. B3 102
Weatherford, Ok., U.S. B3 113
Weatherford, Tx., U.S. C4 120
Weatherly, Pa., U.S. E10 115
Weatogue, Ct., U.S. B4 84
Weaubleau, Mo., U.S. D4 102
Weaver, Al., U.S. B4 78
*Weaver Lake, l., Man.* C3 70
*Weaver Mountains, mts., Az., U.S.* C3 80
Weaverville, Ca., U.S. B2 82
Weaverville, N.C., U.S. f10 110
Webb, Sask. G1 75
Webb, Al., U.S. D4 78
Webb, Ia., U.S. B2 92
Webb, Ms., U.S. B3 101
*Webb, co., Tx., U.S.* F3 120
*Webb Air Force Base, mil., Tx., U.S.* C2 120
Webb City, Ar., U.S. B2 81
Webb City, Mo., U.S. D3 102
Webb City, Ok., U.S. A5 113
Webber, Ks., U.S. C5 93
*Webber Lake, l., Man.* B5 70
Webbers Falls, Ok., U.S. B6 113
Webberville, Mi., U.S. F6 99
*Webb Hill, hill, Ma., U.S.* B3 98
*Webb Lake, l., Me., U.S.* D2 96
Webbville, Ky., U.S. B7 94
Webbwood, Ont. A3 73
*Weber, co., Ut., U.S.* B4 121
*Weber, Mount, mtn., B.C.* B3 69
Weber City, Va., U.S. f9 123
Webster, Alta. B1 68
Webster, Fl., U.S. D4 86
Webster, In., U.S. E8 91
Webster, Ia., U.S. C5 92
Webster, Ma., U.S. B4 98
Webster, Mn., U.S. F5 100
Webster, N.H., U.S. D3 106
Webster, N.Y., U.S. B3 109
Webster, N.D., U.S. A7 111
Webster, Oh., U.S. B1 112
Webster, Pa., U.S. F2 115
Webster, S.D., U.S. B8 118
Webster, Tx., U.S. r14 120
Webster, Wi., U.S. C1 126
*Webster, co., Ga., U.S.* D2 87
*Webster, co., Ia., U.S.* B3 92
*Webster, co., Ky., U.S.* C2 94
*Webster, co., La., U.S.* B2 95
*Webster, co., Ms., U.S.* B4 101
*Webster, co., Mo., U.S.* D5 102
*Webster, co., Ne., U.S.* D7 104
*Webster, co., W.V., U.S.* C4 125
Webster City, Ia., U.S. B4 92
Webster Groves, Mo., U.S. f13 102
Webster Mills, Pa., U.S. G5 115
*Webster Reservoir, res., Ks., U.S.* C4 93
Webster Springs, W.V., U.S. C4 125
Websterville, Vt., U.S. C4 122
Wecota, S.D., U.S. B6 118
Weda, Indon. E7 34
*Weddell Sea, Ant.* C9 7
Wedderburn, Or., U.S. E2 114
Wedgefield, S.C., U.S. D6 117
Wedgeport, N.S. F4 71
Wedgewood, Mo., U.S. f13 102
Wedowee, Al., U.S. B4 78
Wedron, Il., U.S. B5 90
Weed, Ca., U.S. B2 82
Weed, N.M., U.S. E4 108
Weed Heights, Nv., U.S. E2 105
Weedon, Que. D6 74
*Weed Patch Hill, hill, In., U.S.* F5 91
Weedsport, N.Y., U.S. B4 109
Weedville, Pa., U.S. D5 115
Weehawken, N.J., U.S. h8 107
Weekapaug, R.I., U.S. G1 116
Weekes, Sask. E4 75
Weeksbury, Ky., U.S. C7 94
Weekstown, N.J., U.S. D3 107
Weeksville, N.C., U.S. A6 110
Weems, Va., U.S. C6 123
Weener, W. Ger. A7 17
Weeping Water, Ne., U.S. D9 104
*Weeping Water Creek, stm., Ne., U.S.* h12 104
Weert, Neth. B6 16
Weesen, Switz. B7 21
Weesp, Neth. B5 17
Weferlingen, E. Ger. A6 19
Wegdahl, Mn., U.S. F3 100
Weggis, Switz. B5 21
Węgorzewo, Pol. A6 26
Węgrów, Pol. B7 26
Wehr, W. Ger. A4 21
Weichang, China C8 31
Weida, E. Ger. C7 19
Weiden, W. Ger. D6 18
Weidman, Mi., U.S. E6 99
Weifang, China D8 31
Weigelstown, Pa., U.S. *G8 115
Weihai, China D9 31
*Wei He, stm., China* E6 31
Weilburg, W. Ger. C3 19
Weiler, W. Ger. A8 21
Weilheim, W. Ger. E5 18

Weimar, E. Ger. C5 18
Weimar, Tx., U.S. E4 120
Weinan, China E6 31
Weinböhla, E. Ger. B8 19
Weiner, Ar., U.S. B5 81
Weinert, Tx., U.S. C3 120
Weinfelden, Switz. A7 21
Weingarten, W. Ger. D3 19
Weingarten, W. Ger. A8 21
Weinheim, W. Ger. D4 18
Weinsberg, W. Ger. D4 19
Weipa, Austl. B7 50
Weippe, Id., U.S. C3 89
Weir, Que. D3 74
Weir, Ks., U.S. E9 93
Weir, Ky., U.S. C2 94
Weir, stm., Man. A4 70
Weir, i., Fl., U.S. C5 86
Weirdale, Sask. D3 75
Weir River, Man. A4 70
Weirsdale, Fl., U.S. D5 86
Weirton, W.V., U.S. A4 125
Weisburg, In., U.S. F7 91
Weiser, Id., U.S. E2 89
Weiser, stm., Id., U.S. E2 89
Weishan Lake, I., China G7 32
Weishi, China G6 32
Weisner Mountain, hill, Al., U.S. A4 78
Weisse Elster, stm., E. Ger. B7 19
Weissenburg, W. Ger. D5 18
Weissenburg, Switz. C3 21
Weissenfels, E. Ger. B6 19
Weissenhorn, W. Ger. A6 20
Weissen Lake, I., Aus. C9 20
Weissert, Ne., U.S. C6 104
Weisshorn, mtn., Switz. C3 20
Weiss Lake, res., U.S. A4 78
Weisswasser, E. Ger. B9 19
Weitra, Aus. E9 19
Weixi, China F4 31
Weizhou Dao, i., China B8 35
Wejherowo, Pol. A5 26
Wekiva Springs, Fl., U.S. *D5 86
Wekusko Lake, I., Man. B2 70
Welaka, Fl., U.S. C5 86
Welch, Ok., U.S. A6 113
Welch, Tx., U.S. C1 120
Welch, W.V., U.S. D3 125
Welches, Or., U.S. B5 114
Welcome, La., U.S. h10 95
Welcome, Mn., U.S. G4 100
Welcome, S.C., U.S. B3 117
Weld, Me., U.S. D2 96
Weld, co., Co., U.S. A6 83
Welda, Ks., U.S. D8 93
Welden, W. Ger. E5 19
Weldon, Sask. D3 75
Weldon, Ar., U.S. B4 81
Weldon, Ca., U.S. C5 90
Weldon, Ia., U.S. D4 92
Weldon, N.C., U.S. A5 110
Weldon, Tx., U.S. D5 120
Weldona, Co., U.S. A7 83
Weldon Spring, Mo., U.S. f12 102
Weleetka, Ok., U.S. B5 113
Welega, prov., Eth. D4 47
Welkom, S. Afr. C4 49
Welland, Ont. E5 73
Welland, stm., Eng., U.K. D6 10
Wellandport, Ont. D5 73
Wellborn, Fl., U.S. B4 86
Wellborn, Tx., U.S. D4 120
Wellersburg, Pa., U.S. G4 115
Welles Harbor, b., Mid. Is. K3 52
Wellesley, Ont. D4 73
Wellesley, Ma., U.S. B5 98
Wellesley Islands, is., Austl. C6 50
Wellfleet, Ma., U.S. C7 98
Wellfleet, Ne., U.S. D5 104
Wellford, S.C., U.S. B3 117
Wellin, Bel. D5 17
Welling, Ok., U.S. B7 113
Wellingborough, Eng., U.K. D6 12
Wellington, Austl. F7 51
Wellington, B.C. f11 69
Wellington, Ont. D7 73
Wellington, N.Z. N15 51
Wellington, S. Afr. D2 49
Wellington, Eng., U.K. B5 12
Wellington, Eng., U.K. C4 12
Wellington, Al., U.S. B4 78
Wellington, Co., U.S. A5 83
Wellington, Il., U.S. C6 90
Wellington, Ks., U.S. E6 93
Wellington, Me., U.S. C3 96
Wellington, Mo., U.S. B4 102
Wellington, Nv., U.S. E2 105
Wellington, Oh., U.S. A3 112
Wellington, Tx., U.S. B2 120
Wellington, Ut., U.S. D5 121
Wellington, co., Ont. D4 73
Wellington, Isla, i., Chile D2 54
Wellington Channel, strt., N.W. Ter. m33 66
Wellington Station, N.S. E6 71
Wellington Station, P.E.I. C5 71
Wellman, Ia., U.S. C6 92
Wellman, Tx., U.S. C1 120
Wellpinit, Wa., U.S. B8 124
Wells, B.C. C7 69
Wells, Eng., U.K. C5 12
Wells, Ks., U.S. C6 93
Wells, Mi., U.S. C3 99
Wells, Mn., U.S. G5 100
Wells, Nv., U.S. B7 105
Wells, N.Y., U.S. B6 109
Wells, Tx., U.S. D5 120
Wells, Vt., U.S. E2 122
Wells, co., In., U.S. C7 91
Wells, co., N.D., U.S. B6 111
Wells, stm., Vt., U.S. C4 122
Wells, Lake, I., Austl. E3 50
Wells Beach, Me., U.S. E2 96
Wellsboro, In., U.S. B4 91
Wellsboro, Pa., U.S. C7 115
Wellsburg, Ia., U.S. B5 92
Wellsburg, N.Y., U.S. C4 109
Wellsburg, W.V., U.S. A4 125
Wellsford, Ks., U.S. E4 93
Wells Gray Provincial Park, B.C. C8 69
Wells Lake, I., Man. A1 70
Wells-next-the-Sea, Eng., U.K. D7 10
Wells River, Vt., U.S. C4 122
Wells Tannery, Pa., U.S. F5 115
Wellston, Mi., U.S. D5 99
Wellston, Oh., U.S. C3 112
Wellston, Ok., U.S. B4 113
Wellsville, Ks., U.S. D8 93
Wellsville, Mo., U.S. B6 102
Wellsville, N.Y., U.S. C3 109

Wellsville, Oh., U.S. B5 112
Wellsville, Pa., U.S. F8 115
Wellsville, Ut., U.S. B4 121
Wells see Wells-next-the-Sea, Eng., U.K. D7 10
Welzow, E. Ger. B9 19
Wem, Eng., U.K. B5 12
Wellton, Az., U.S. E1 80
Welo, prov., Eth. C5 47
Wels, Aus. D7 18
Welsh, La., U.S. D3 95
Welshpool, Wales, U.K. D5 10
Welton, Ia., U.S. C7 92
Welty, Ok., U.S. B5 113
Welwitschia, Nmb. B1 49
Welwyn, Sask. G5 75
Welwyn Garden City, Eng., U.K. k12 10
Wembere, stm., Tan. B3 48
Wembley, Alta. B1 68
Wemding, W. Ger. E5 19
Wemme, Or., U.S. B5 114
Wenasoga, Ms., U.S. A3 101
Wenatchee, Wa., U.S. B5 124
Wenatchee, stm., Wa., U.S. B5 124
Wenatchee Lake, I., Wa., U.S. B5 124
Wenatchee Mountains, mts., Wa., U.S. B5 124
Wenchang, China C9 35
Wenchi, Ghana E4 45
Wenchou see Wenzhou, China F9 31
Wendel, Ca., U.S. B3 82
Wendel, W.V., U.S. k10 125
Wendell, Id., U.S. G4 89
Wendell, Ma., U.S. A3 98
Wendell, Mn., U.S. D2 100
Wendell, N.C., U.S. B4 110
Wenden, Az., U.S. D2 80
Wendeng, China F10 32
Wendo, Eth. D4 47
Wendover, Nv., U.S. C7 105
Wendover, Ut., U.S. C1 121
Wenham Lake, I., Ma., U.S. A6 98
Wenham Swamp, sw., Ma., U.S. f12 98
Wenji Gefersa, Eth. *D4 47
Wenlock, stm., Austl. B7 50
Wenona, Il., U.S. B4 90
Wenona, Md., U.S. D6 97
Wenonah, N.J., U.S. D2 107
Wenshan, China F7 31
Wentworth, Austl. F7 51
Wentworth, N.S. D6 71
Wentworth, N.H., U.S. C3 106
Wentworth, N.C., U.S. A3 110
Wentworth, S.D., U.S. C8 118
Wentworth, Wi., U.S. B2 126
Wentworth, co., Ont. D4 73
Wentworth, Lake, I., N.H., U.S. C4 106
Wentzville, Mo., U.S. C7 102
Wenzhou (Wenchou), China F9 31
Weohyakapka, Lake, I., Fl., U.S. E5 86
Weott, Ca., U.S. B2 82
Wepener, S. Afr. C4 49
Wequetequock, Ct., U.S. D8 84
Werbomont, Bel. D5 17
Werda, E. Ger. C6 18
Werdau, E. Ger. A7 19
Werdohl, W. Ger. B2 19
Werfen, Aus. E6 18
Werl, W. Ger. B2 19
Wernberg, W. Ger. D6 18
Werne, W. Ger. B2 19
Werneuchen, E. Ger. B8 18
Wernigerode, E. Ger. C5 18
Werra, stm., Eur. C4 18
Wertach, stm., W. Ger. D5 18
Wertheim, W. Ger. D4 19
Wertingen, W. Ger. E5 19
Wervik, Bel. D3 17
Wesco, Mo., U.S. D6 102
Wesel, W. Ger. C3 18
Weser, stm., W. Ger. B4 18
Weskan, Ks., U.S. D2 93
Weslaco, Tx., U.S. F4 120
Weslemkoon Lake, I., Ont. C7 73
Wesley, Ar., U.S. A2 81
Wesley, Ga., U.S. D4 87
Wesley, Me., U.S. D5 96
Wesleyville, Newf. D5 72
Wesleyville, Pa., U.S. B2 115
Wesselburen, W. Ger. B6 18
Wesserunsett Lake, I., Me., U.S. D3 96
Wessington, S.D., U.S. C7 118
Wessington Springs, S.D., U.S. C7 118
Wesson, Ar., U.S. D3 81
Wesson, Ms., U.S. D3 101
West, Ms., U.S. B4 101
West, Tx., U.S. D4 120
West, stm., P.E.I. C6 71
West, stm., Ct., U.S. D5 84
West, stm., Ma., U.S. h9 98
West, stm., Vt., U.S. E3 122
West Abington, Ma., U.S. h12 98
West Acton, Ma., U.S. g10 98
West Alexander, Pa., U.S. F1 115
West Alexandria, Oh., U.S. C1 112
West Allis, Wi., U.S. m11 126
Westalton, Mo., U.S. f13 102
West Alton, N.H., U.S. C4 106
West Amityville, N.Y., U.S. n15 109
West Andover, Ma., U.S. A5 98
West Arichat, N.S. D8 71
West Athens, Ca., U.S. *n12 82
West Athens, Me., U.S. D3 96
West Augusta, Va., U.S. B3 123
West Babylon, N.Y., U.S. *E7 109
West Baden Springs, In., U.S. G4 91
West Baldwin, Me., U.S. E2 96
Westbank, B.C. E8 69
West Bank, ter., Isr. Occ. B7 41
West Barnet, Vt., U.S. C4 122
West Barnstable, Ma., U.S. C7 98
West Barrington, R.I., U.S. C5 116
West Baton Rouge, co., La., U.S. D4 95
West Bay, Newf. A3 72
West Bay, b., N.S. D8 71
West Bay, b., Fl., U.S. u16 86
West Bay, b., Fl., U.S. u16 86
West Bay, b., Tx., U.S. r15 120
West Bay Shore, N.Y., U.S. *n15 109

West Bend, Sask. F4 75
West Bend, Ia., U.S. B3 92
West Bend, Wi., U.S. E5 126
West Bengal, state, India F11 37
West Berkshire, Vt., U.S. B3 122
West Berlin, N.J., U.S. D3 107
West Berlin see Berlin (West), W. Ger. B6 18
West Bethel, Me., U.S. D2 96
West Billerica, Ma., U.S. f10 98
West Blocton, Al., U.S. B2 78
West Bloomfield, N.Y., U.S. C3 109
West Bloomfield Township, Mi., U.S. *F7 99
Westboro, Mo., U.S. A2 102
Westboro, Wi., U.S. C3 126
Westborough, Ma., U.S. B4 98
Westbourne, Man. D2 70
West Bountiful, Ut., U.S. C4 121
West Bowdoin, Me., U.S. f7 96
West Boylston, Ma., U.S. B4 98
West Bradenton, Fl., U.S. *E4 86
West Branch, Ia., U.S. C6 92
West Branch, Mi., U.S. D6 99
West Branch Reservoir, res., Ct., U.S. B3 84
West Brentwood, N.H., U.S. E4 106
West Bridgewater, Ma., U.S. B5 98
West Bridgewater, Vt., U.S. D3 122
West Bromwich, Eng., U.K. D6 10
Westbrook, Me., U.S. E2 96
Westbrook, Mn., U.S. F3 100
Westbrook, Tx., U.S. C2 120
West Brookfield, Ma., U.S. B3 98
Westbrook, Il., U.S. B4 90
Westbrookville, N.Y., U.S. D6 109
West Burke, Vt., U.S. B5 122
West Burlington, Ia., U.S. D6 92
Westbury, N.Y., U.S. *n15 109
West Buxton, Me., U.S. E2 96
Westby, Mt., U.S. B12 103
Westby, Wi., U.S. E3 126
West Cache Creek, stm., Ok., U.S. C3 113
West Caldwell, N.J., U.S. B4 107
West Campton, N.H., U.S. C3 106
West Canaan, N.H., U.S. C2 106
West Canada Creek, stm., N.Y., U.S. B6 109
West Cape Howe, c., Austl. G2 50
West Cape May, N.J., U.S. F3 107
West Carroll, co., La., U.S. B4 95
West Carrollton, Oh., U.S. C1 112
West Carry Pond, I., Me., U.S. C2 96
West Carson, Ca., U.S. *n12 82
West Carthage, N.Y., U.S. B5 109
West Castleton, Vt., U.S. D2 122
West Charleston, Vt., U.S. B4 122
West Chatham, Ma., U.S. C8 98
West Chazy, N.Y., U.S. f11 109
Westchester, Fl., U.S. *s13 86
Westchester, Il., U.S. k9 90
West Chester, Ia., U.S. C6 92
West Chester, Oh., U.S. n13 112
West Chester, Pa., U.S. G10 115
Westchester, co., N.Y., U.S. D7 109
West Chesterfield, N.H., U.S. E1 106
Westchester Station, N.S. D6 71
West Chicago, Il., U.S. k8 90
West Chop, c., Ma., U.S. D6 98
West City, Il., U.S. F5 90
Westcliffe, Co., U.S. C5 83
West Coffeyville, Ks., U.S. E8 93
West College Corner, In., U.S. E8 91
West Columbia, S.C., U.S. D5 117
West Columbia, Tx., U.S. E5 120
West Compton, Ca., U.S. *F4 82
West Concord, Ma., U.S. B5 98
West Concord, Mn., U.S. F6 100
West Concord, N.C., U.S. B2 110
Westconnaug Reservoir, res., R.I., U.S. C2 116
West Cornwall, Ct., U.S. B2 84
West Cote Blanche Bay, b., La., U.S. E4 95
West Covina, Ca., U.S. m13 82
West Creek, N.J., U.S. D4 107
West Crossett, Ar., U.S. D4 81
West Cumberland, Me., U.S. E2 96
West Cummington, Ma., U.S. B2 98
West Danby, N.Y., U.S. C4 109
West Danville, Vt., U.S. C4 122
West Decatur, Pa., U.S. E5 115
West Dennis, Ma., U.S. C7 98
West Des Moines, Ia., U.S. C4 92
West Dover, Vt., U.S. F3 122
West Dudley, Ma., U.S. B4 98
West Dummerston, Vt., U.S. F3 122
West Elk Mountains, mts., Co., U.S. C3 83
West Elk Peak, mtn., Co., U.S. C3 83
West Elkton, Oh., U.S. C1 112
West Elmira, N.Y., U.S. *C4 109
West Elwood, In., U.S. D6 91
West Eminence, Mo., U.S. D6 102
West Emma Creek, stm., Ks., U.S. D6 93
West End, Bah. A4 64
Westend, Ca., U.S. E5 82
West End, N.C., U.S. B3 110
West Enfield, Me., U.S. C4 96
West Enosburg, Vt., U.S. B3 122
West Epping, N.H., U.S. D4 106
Westerkappeln, W. Ger. A2 19
Westerland, W. Ger. A4 18
Westerly, R.I., U.S. F1 116
Western, Ne., U.S. D8 104
Western, prov., Ghana E4 45
Western, prov., Kenya A5 48
Western, prov., Zam. D3 48
Western Australia, state, Austl. D3 50
Western Channel, strt., Asia I4 33
Western Desert, des., Eg. C2 38
Western Dvina (Daugava), stm., Sov. Un. D7 27
Western Ghâts, mts., India E5 36
Western Grove, Ar., U.S. A3 81
Western Head, c., Newf. D2 72
Western Head, c., N.S. F5 71
Western Hills, Co., U.S. *B6 83
Western Island, i., Newf. C4 72
Western Isles, prov., Scot., U.K. A3 13
Westernport, Md., U.S. m12 97
Westernport Reservoir, res., Md., U.S. k12 97
Western Sahara, dep., Afr. D2 44
Western Samoa, ctry., Oc. G11 6
Western Shore, N.S. E5 71

Western Springs, Il., U.S. k9 90
Westerschelde, est., Neth. B5 16
Westerstede, W. Ger. A7 17
Westervelt, Il., U.S. D5 90
Westerville, Ne., U.S. C6 104
Westerville, Oh., U.S. B3 112
Westerwald, mts., W. Ger. C4 18
West Fairlee, Vt., U.S. D4 122
West Fairview, Pa., U.S. *F8 115
Westfall, Ks., U.S. D5 93
West Falmouth, Ma., U.S. C6 98
West Fargo, N.D., U.S. C9 111
West Farmington, Me., U.S. D2 96
West Farmington, Oh., U.S. A5 112
West Feliciana, co., La., U.S. D4 95
Westfield, N.B. D3 71
Westfield, Il., U.S. D6 90
Westfield, In., U.S. D5 91
Westfield, Ma., U.S. B2 98
Westfield, N.J., U.S. B4 107
Westfield, N.Y., U.S. C1 109
Westfield, N.C., U.S. A2 110
Westfield, Pa., U.S. C6 115
Westfield, Vt., U.S. B4 122
Westfield, Wi., U.S. E4 126
Westfield, stm., Ma., U.S. B2 98
Westfield Center, Oh., U.S. A4 112
Westfir, Or., U.S. D4 114
West Flanders, prov., Bel. C3 17
Westford, Ct., U.S. B7 84
Westford, Ma., U.S. f10 98
Westford, Vt., U.S. B2 122
West Fork, Ar., U.S. B1 81
West Fork, stm., W.V., U.S. B4 125
West Frankfort, Il., U.S. F5 90
West Freehold, N.J., U.S. *C4 107
West Friendship, Md., U.S. B4 97
West Frisian Islands, is., Neth. A6 16
Westgate, Fl., U.S. F6 86
Westgate, Ia., U.S. B6 92
West Gate, Va., U.S. *B5 123
West Gate of Lomond, Va., U.S. *B5 123
West Germany see Germany, Federal Republic of, ctry., Eur. C4 18
West Glacier, Mt., U.S. B3 103
West Glamorgan, co., Wales, U.K. C4 12
West Glens Falls, N.Y., U.S. *B7 109
West Glocester, R.I., U.S. B1 116
West Gorham, Me., U.S. g7 96
West Goshen, Ct., U.S. B3 84
West Gouldsboro, Me., U.S. D4 96
West Granby, Ct., U.S. B4 84
West Granville, Ma., U.S. B2 98
West Green, Ga., U.S. E4 87
West Greene, Al., U.S. C1 78
West Greenville, R.I., U.S. B3 116
West Groton, Ma., U.S. A4 98
West Grove, Ia., U.S. D5 92
West Grove, Pa., U.S. G10 115
West Halifax, Vt., U.S. F3 122
West Hamlin, W.V., U.S. C2 125
West Hampstead, N.H., U.S. E4 106
Westhampton, Ma., U.S. B2 98
West Hanover, Ma., U.S. h12 98
West Harrison, In., U.S. F8 91
West Hartford, Ct., U.S. B4 84
West Hartford, Vt., U.S. D4 122
West Hatfield, Ma., U.S. B2 98
West Haven, Ct., U.S. D4 84
West Haven, Or., U.S. *B4 114
West Haven, Ut., U.S. *B3 121
West Haverstraw, N.Y., U.S. *D7 109
West Hazleton, Pa., U.S. E9 115
West Helena, Ar., U.S. C5 81
West Hempstead, N.Y., U.S. *k13 109
West Hickory, Pa., U.S. C3 115
West Hill Reservoir, res., Ma., U.S. B4 98
Westhoff, Tx., U.S. E4 120
West Hollywood, Ca., U.S. *m12 82
Westhope, N.D., U.S. A4 111
West Hopkinton, N.H., U.S. D3 106
West Huntington, N.Y., U.S. *n15 109
West Hyannisport, Ma., U.S. C7 98
West Ice Shelf, ice, Ant. C21 7
West Indies, is. A3 53
West Island, i., Ant. C6 7
West Islip, N.Y., U.S. *E7 109
West Jefferson, N.C., U.S. A1 110
West Jefferson, Oh., U.S. C2 112
West Jersey, Il., U.S. B4 90
West Jordan, Ut., U.S. C4 121
West Kennebunk, Me., U.S. E2 96
West Kingston, R.I., U.S. F3 116
West Lafayette, In., U.S. D4 91
West Lafayette, Oh., U.S. B4 112
Westlake, La., U.S. D2 95
Westlake, Oh., U.S. h9 112
Westlake, Or., U.S. D2 114
Westlake Village, Ca., U.S. *E4 82
Westland, Mi., U.S. F7 99
West Laramie, Wy., U.S. E7 127
West Lawn, Pa., U.S. F10 115
West Lebanon, In., U.S. D3 91
West Lebanon, N.H., U.S. D2 106
West Leisenring, Pa., U.S. G2 115
West Leyden, N.Y., U.S. B5 109
West Liberty, Ia., U.S. C6 92
West Liberty, Ky., U.S. C6 94
West Liberty, Oh., U.S. B2 112
West Liberty, W.V., U.S. f8 125
West Lima, Wi., U.S. E3 126
West Lincoln, Ne., U.S. D9 104
West Long Branch, N.J. C4 107
West Lorne, Ont. E3 73
West Louisville, Ky., U.S. C2 94
West Manchester, Oh., U.S. C1 112
West Mansfield, Oh., U.S. B2 112
West Marion, N.C., U.S. f10 110
Westmeath, Ont. B8 73
Westmeath, co., Ire. D4 11

West Medway, Ma., U.S. B5 98
West Melbourne, Fl., U.S. *D6 86
West Memphis, Ar., U.S. B5 81
Westmere, N.Y., U.S. *C7 109
West Miami, Fl., U.S. s13 86
West Middlesex, Pa., U.S. D1 115
West Middleton, In., U.S. D5 91
West Mifflin, Pa., U.S. F2 115
West Milford, N.J., U.S. A4 107
West Milton, Oh., U.S. C1 112
West Milton, Vt., U.S. D8 115
West Milwaukee, Wi., U.S. m12 126
West Mineral, Ks., U.S. E9 93
Westminster (part of London), Eng., U.K. k12 10
Westminster, Ca., U.S. n12 82
Westminster, Co., U.S. B5 83
Westminster, Md., U.S. A4 97
Westminster, Ma., U.S. A4 98
Westminster, S.C., U.S. B1 117
Westminster, Vt., U.S. E4 122
Westminster West, Vt., U.S. E3 122
West Modesto, Ca., U.S. *D3 82
West Monroe, La., U.S. B3 95
Westmont, Ca., U.S. n12 82
Westmont, Il., U.S. k9 90
Westmont, N.J., U.S. D2 107
Westmont, Pa., U.S. F4 115
West Monterey, Pa., U.S. D2 115
Westmoreland, Ks., U.S. C7 93
Westmoreland, N.H., U.S. E2 106
Westmoreland, Tn., U.S. A5 119
Westmoreland, co., Pa., U.S. F2 115
Westmoreland, co., Va., U.S. B6 123
Westmorland, Ca., U.S. F6 82
Westmorland, co., N.B. C4 71
West Mountain, mtn., Ar., U.S. f7 81
West Mountain, mtn., N.Y., U.S. B6 109
West Mountain, mtn., Vt., U.S. B5 122
West Muncie, In., U.S. D7 91
West Musquash Lake, I., Me., U.S. C5 96
West Mystic, Ct., U.S. D8 84
West Newbury, Ma., U.S. A6 98
West Newbury, Vt., U.S. C4 122
West Newfield, Me., U.S. E2 96
West Newton, Pa., U.S. F2 115
West New York, N.J., U.S. h8 107
West Nicholson, Zimb. B4 49
West Nishnabotna, stm., Ia., U.S. C2 92
West Norriton, Pa., U.S. o20 115
West Nottingham, N.H., U.S. D4 106
West Nyack, N.Y., U.S. *D7 109
West Olive, Mi., U.S. F7 99
Weston, Co., U.S. D6 83
Weston, Ct., U.S. E2 84
Weston, Ga., U.S. E2 87
Weston, Id., U.S. G7 89
Weston, Il., U.S. C5 90
Weston, Ma., U.S. g10 98
Weston, Mo., U.S. B3 102
Weston, Ne., U.S. C9 104
Weston, Or., U.S. B8 114
Weston, W.V., U.S. B4 125
Weston, Wy., U.S. B7 127
Weston, co., Wy., U.S. C8 127
Weston (part of York), Ont. m14 73
Weston-super-Mare, Eng., U.K. C4 10
West Orange, N.J., U.S. B4 107
West Ossipee, N.H., U.S. C4 106
Westover, Al., U.S. B3 78
Westover, Md., U.S. D6 97
Westover, Tn., U.S. B3 119
Westover Air Force Base, mil., Ma., U.S. B3 98
West Palm Beach, Fl., U.S. F6 86
West Paris, Me., U.S. D2 96
West Park, N.Y., U.S. D7 109
West Pasco, Wa., U.S. *C6 124
West Paterson, N.J., U.S. *B4 107
West Pawlet, Vt., U.S. E2 122
West Pearl, stm., La., U.S. D6 95
West Pelham, Ma., U.S. *B2 98
West Pelzer, S.C., U.S. B3 117
West Pembroke, Me., U.S. D5 96
West Pensacola, Fl., U.S. u14 86
West Peoria, Il., U.S. C4 90
West Peru, Me., U.S. D2 96
West Peterborough, N.H., U.S. E3 106
Westphalia, In., U.S. G3 91
Westphalia, Ks., U.S. D8 93
Westphalia, Mi., U.S. F6 99
Westphalia, hist. reg., W. Ger. C3 18
West Pittsburg, Ca., U.S. *g9 82
West Pittsburg, Pa., U.S. E1 115
West Pittston, Pa., U.S. m17 115
West Plains, Mo., U.S. E6 102
West Plymouth, N.H., U.S. C3 106
West Point, Al., U.S. A3 78
West Point, Ca., U.S. C3 82
West Point, Ga., U.S. C1 87
West Point, Il., U.S. C2 90
West Point, In., U.S. D4 91
West Point, Ia., U.S. D6 92
West Point, Ky., U.S. C4 94
West Point, Ms., U.S. B5 101
West Point, Ne., U.S. C9 104
West Point, N.Y., U.S. D7 109
West Point, Va., U.S. C6 123
West Point Lake, res., U.S. C1 87
West Portsmouth, Oh., U.S. D2 112
West Prairie, stm., Alta. B2 68

West Pubnico, N.S. F4 71
West Puente Valley, Ca., U.S. *m13 82
West Quoddy Head, c., Me., U.S. D6 96
Westray, i., Scot., U.K. A5 13
Westray Firth, strt., Scot., U.K. A5 13
West Reading, Pa., U.S. F10 115
West Redding, Ct., U.S. D2 84
Westrheiderfehn, W. Ger. A7 17
West Ridge, Ar., U.S. B5 81
West Rindge, N.H., U.S. E2 106
West River, Md., U.S. C4 97
West Road, stm., B.C. C5 69
West Rumney, N.H., U.S. C3 106
West Rupert, Vt., U.S. E2 122
West Rutland, Vt., U.S. D2 122
West Rye, N.H., U.S. D5 106
West Sacramento, Ca., U.S. *C3 82
West Saint Modeste, Newf. C3 72
West Saint Paul, Mn., U.S. n12 100
West Salem, Il., U.S. E5 90
West Salem, Oh., U.S. B3 112
West Salem, Wi., U.S. E2 126
West Salt Creek, stm., Co., U.S. B2 83
West Sayville, N.Y., U.S. *n15 109
West Scarborough, Me., U.S. E2 96
West Seneca, N.Y., U.S. C2 109
West Siberian Lowland, pl., Sov. Un. C10 29
Westside, Ia., U.S. B2 92
West Simsbury, Ct., U.S. B4 84
West Slope, Or., U.S. g12 114
West Spanish Peak, mtn., Co., U.S. D6 83
West Spit, spit, Marsh Is. S18 52
West Springfield, Ma., U.S. B2 98
West Springfield, N.H., U.S. D2 106
West Springfield, Va., U.S. g12 123
West Stafford, Ct., U.S. B6 84
West Stockbridge, Ma., U.S. B1 98
West Suffield, Ct., U.S. B5 84
West Sullivan, Me., U.S. D4 96
West Sumner, Me., U.S. D2 96
West Sunbury, Pa., U.S. E2 115
West Sussex, co., Eng., U.K. D7 12
West Swanzey, N.H., U.S. E2 106
West Terre Haute, In., U.S. F3 91
West-Terschelling, Neth. A5 17
West Thompson Lake, res., Ct., U.S. B8 84
West Thornton, N.H., U.S. C3 106
West Tisbury, Ma., U.S. D6 98
West Topsham, Vt., U.S. C4 122
West Townsend, Ma., U.S. A4 98
West Townsend, Vt., U.S. E3 122
West Union, Il., U.S. D6 90
West Union, Ia., U.S. B6 92
West Union, Oh., U.S. D2 112
West Union, S.C., U.S. B1 117
West Union, W.V., U.S. B4 125
West Unity, Oh., U.S. A1 112
West University Place, Tx., U.S. r14 120
West Upton, Ma., U.S. B4 98
Westvale, N.Y., U.S. *B4 109
West Valley, N.Y., U.S. C2 109
West Valley City, Ut., U.S. C4 121
West Vancouver, B.C. f12 69
West Van Lear, Ky., U.S. C7 94
Westview, Fl., U.S. *G6 86
West View, Pa., U.S. h13 115
Westville, N.S. D7 71
Westville, Fl., U.S. u16 86
Westville, Il., U.S. C6 90
Westville, In., U.S. A4 91
Westville, N.H., U.S. E4 106
Westville, N.J., U.S. D2 107
Westville, Ok., U.S. A7 113
Westville, Pa., U.S. D1 115
Westville, S.C., U.S. C6 117
Westville Lake, res., Ma., U.S. B3 98
West Virginia, state, U.S. C4 125
West Walker, stm., U.S. E2 105
Wardsboro, Vt., U.S. E3 122
West Wareham, Ma., U.S. C6 98
West Warren, Ma., U.S. B3 98
West Warwick, R.I., U.S. D3 116
West Webster, N.Y., U.S. *B3 109
Westwego, La., U.S. k11 95
West Whittier, Ca., U.S. *n12 82
West Willington, Ct., U.S. B6 84
West Willow, Mi., U.S. *F7 99
West Wilton, N.H., U.S. E3 106
West Winfield, N.Y., U.S. C5 109
West Winfield, Pa., U.S. E2 115
Westwold, B.C. D8 69
Westwood, Ca., U.S. B3 82
Westwood, Ks., U.S. k16 93
Westwood, Ma., U.S. B5 98
Westwood, Mi., U.S. *F5 99
Westwood, N.J., U.S. B4 107
Westwood Lakes, Fl., U.S. s13 86
West Woodstock, Vt., U.S. D3 122
West Wyalong, Austl. F8 51
West Wyoming, Pa., U.S. n17 115
West Yarmouth, Ma., U.S. C7 98
West Yellowstone, Mt., U.S. F5 103
West York, Il., U.S. D6 90
West York, Pa., U.S. G8 115
West Yorkshire, co., Eng., U.K. *G7 13
Wetar, i., Indon. G7 33
Wetaskiwin, Alta. C4 68
Wete, Tan. C6 48
Wethersfield, Ct., U.S. C5 84
Wetmore, Co., U.S. C5 83
Wetmore, Ks., U.S. C8 93
Wetmore, Mi., U.S. B4 99
Wetonka, S.D., U.S. B7 118
Wettingen, Switz. B5 21
Wetumka, Ok., U.S. B5 113
Wetumpka, Al., U.S. C3 78
Wetzel, co., W.V., U.S. B4 125
Wetzlar, W. Ger. C4 18
Wewahitchka, Fl., U.S. B1 86
Wewak, Pap. N. Gui. h11 50
Wewela, S.D., U.S. E6 118
Wewoka, Ok., U.S. B5 113
Wexford, Ire. E5 11
Wexford, co., Ire. D5 11
Wexford, co., Mi., U.S. D5 99
Wexford Harbour, b., Ire. E5 11
Weyakwin, Lake, I., Sask. C2 75
Weyanoke, La., U.S. D4 95
Weyauwega, Wi., U.S. D5 126

| Name | Map Ref. | Page |
|---|---|---|

Weybridge, Eng., U.K. — m12 10
Weyburn, Sask. — H4 75
Weyerhaeuser, Wi., U.S. — C2 126
Weyers Cave, Va., U.S. — A3 123
Weymouth, N.S. — E4 71
Weymouth, Ma., U.S. — B6 98
Weymouth, N.J., U.S. — D3 107
Weymouth [and Melcombe Regis], Eng., U.K. — E5 10
Weymouth Bay, b., Eng., U.K. — E5 10
Whakatane, N.Z. — L16 51
Whalan, Mn., U.S. — G7 100
Whales, Bay of, b., Ant. — B32 7
Whaleysville, Md., U.S. — D7 97
Whalom, Ma., U.S. — A4 98
Whangarei, N.Z. — K15 51
Wharfe, stm., Eng., U.K. — D6 10
Wharton, N.J., U.S. — B3 107
Wharton, Oh., U.S. — B2 112
Wharton, Tx., U.S. — E4 120
Wharton, W.V., U.S. — n12 125
Wharton, co., Tx., U.S. — E4 120
Whataroa, N.Z. — O13 51
What Cheer, Ia., U.S. — C5 92
Whatcom, co., Wa., U.S. — A4 124
Whatcom, Lake, l., Wa., U.S. — A3 124
Whately, Ma., U.S. — B2 98
Whatley, Al., U.S. — D2 78
Wheatcroft, Ky., U.S. — C2 94
Wheatfield, In., U.S. — B3 91
Wheatland, Ca., U.S. — C3 82
Wheatland, Ia., U.S. — G3 91
Wheatland, Ia., U.S. — C7 92
Wheatland, Mo., U.S. — D4 102
Wheatland, N.D., U.S. — C8 111
Wheatland, Pa., U.S. — D1 115
Wheatland, Wy., U.S. — D8 127
Wheatland, co., Mt., U.S. — D7 103
Wheatland Reservoir, res., Wy., U.S. — E7 127
Wheatley, Ont. — E2 73
Wheatley, Ar., U.S. — C4 81
Wheaton, Il., U.S. — B5 90
Wheaton, Ks., U.S. — C7 93
Wheaton, Md., U.S. — B3 97
Wheaton, Mn., U.S. — E2 100
Wheaton, Mo., U.S. — E3 102
Wheat Ridge, Co., U.S. — B5 83
Wheelbarrow Peak, mtn., Nv., U.S. — F5 105
Wheeler, Al., U.S. — A2 78
Wheeler, Ar., U.S. — A1 81
Wheeler, Il., U.S. — D5 90
Wheeler, In., U.S. — B3 91
Wheeler, Ks., U.S. — C2 93
Wheeler, Ms., U.S. — A5 101
Wheeler, Or., U.S. — B3 114
Wheeler, Tx., U.S. — B2 120
Wheeler, Wi., U.S. — C2 126
Wheeler, co., Ga., U.S. — D4 87
Wheeler, co., Ne., U.S. — C7 104
Wheeler, co., Or., U.S. — C6 114
Wheeler, co., Tx., U.S. — B2 120
Wheeler Air Force Base, mil., Hi., U.S. — g9 88
Wheeler Dam, Al., U.S. — A2 78
Wheeler Lake, res., Al., U.S. — A2 78
Wheeler Peak, mtn., Ca., U.S. — C4 82
Wheeler Peak, mtn., Nv., U.S. — E7 105
Wheeler Peak, mtn., N.M., U.S. — A4 108
Wheelersburg, Oh., U.S. — D3 112
Wheeling, Il., U.S. — h9 90
Wheeling, Mo., U.S. — B4 102
Wheeling, W.V., U.S. — A4 125
Wheeling Creek, stm., W.V., U.S. — f8 125
Wheelock, N.D., U.S. — A2 111
Wheelock, Vt., U.S. — B4 122
Wheelock Mountain, mtn., Vt., U.S. — B4 122
Wheelockville, Ma., U.S. — *B4 98
Wheelon, Ut., U.S. — *B3 121
Wheelright, Ky., U.S. — C7 94
Wheelwright, Ma., U.S. — B3 98
Whelen Springs, Ar., U.S. — D2 81
Whernside, mtn., Eng., U.K. — F6 13
Whetstone, stm., U.S. — E2 100
Whickham, Eng., U.K. — F7 13
Whidbey Island, i., Wa., U.S. — A3 124
Whidbey Island Naval Air Station, mil., Wa., U.S. — A3 124
Whigham, Ga., U.S. — F2 87
Whigville, Ct., U.S. — C4 84
Whipholt, Mn., U.S. — C4 100
Whipple, W.V., U.S. — n13 125
Whiskey Gap, Alta. — E4 68
Whiskey Peak, mtn., Wy., U.S. — D5 127
Whiskeytown-Shasta-Trinity National Recreation Area, Ca., U.S. — B2 82
Whisky Chitto Creek, stm., La., U.S. — C2 95
Whistler, B.C. — D6 69
Whitacres, Ct., U.S. — A5 84
Whitakers, N.C., U.S. — A5 110
Whitbourne, Newf. — E5 72
Whitby, Ont. — D6 73
Whitby, Eng., U.K. — C6 10
Whitchurch, Eng., U.K. — B5 12
Whitchurch-Stouffville, Ont. — D5 73
Whitcombe, Mount, mtn., N.Z. — O13 51
Whitcomb Mountain, mtn., N.H., U.S. — A4 106
White, Ga., U.S. — B2 87
White, S.D., U.S. — C9 118
White, co., Ar., U.S. — B4 81
White, co., Ga., U.S. — B3 87
White, co., Il., U.S. — E5 90
White, co., In., U.S. — C4 91
White, co., Tn., U.S. — D8 119
White, stm., B.C. — D3 68
White, stm., U.S. — C4 81
White, stm., U.S. — D5 118
White, stm., U.S. — C7 121
White, stm., Az., U.S. — D5 80
White, stm., In., U.S. — H2 91
White, stm., Mi., U.S. — E4 99
White, stm., Nv., U.S. — E6 105
White, stm., Tx., U.S. — C2 120
White, stm., Vt., U.S. — D4 122
White, stm., Wa., U.S. — B4 124
White, East Fork, stm., In., U.S. — G5 91
White Lake, l., Austl. — D4 50
White Bay, b., Newf. — D3 72
White Bear, Sask. — G1 75
White Bear, stm., Newf. — E3 72
White Bear Islands, is., Newf. — A3 72
White Bear Lake, Mn., U.S. — E5 100
White Bear Lake, l., Newf. — A2 72
White Bear Lake, l., Sask. — H4 75
White Bird, Id., U.S. — D2 89

White Bluff, Tn., U.S. — A4 119
White Breast Creek, stm., Ia., U.S. — C4 92
White Butte, mtn., N.D., U.S. — C2 111
White Cap Mountain, mtn., Me., U.S. — C3 96
White Castle, La., U.S. — D4 95
White Center, Wa., U.S. — e11 124
White City, Fl., U.S. — C1 86
White City, Ks., U.S. — D7 93
White City, Or., U.S. — E4 114
White City, Ut., U.S. — *C4 121
White Clay Creek, stm., U.S. — A3 104
White Clay Creek, stm., De., U.S. — B3 85
White Cliffs, Austl. — E4 51
White Cloud, Ks., U.S. — C8 93
White Cloud, Mi., U.S. — E5 99
Whitecourt, Alta. — B3 68
White Creek, stm., U.S. — E2 122
Whiteday, stm., W.V., U.S. — h10 125
White Deer, Pa., U.S. — D8 115
White Deer, Tx., U.S. — B2 120
White Earth, Mn., U.S. — C3 100
White Earth, N.D., U.S. — A3 111
White Earth Indian Reservation, Mn., U.S. — C3 100
White Earth Lake, l., Mn., U.S. — C3 100
Whiteface, Tx., U.S. — C1 120
Whiteface, stm., Mn., U.S. — C6 100
Whiteface Mountain, mtn., N.Y., U.S. — f10 109
White Face Mountain, mtn., Vt., U.S. — B3 122
Whitefathers, N.Y., U.S. — f10 109
Whitefield, Me., U.S. — *D3 96
Whitefield, N.H., U.S. — B3 106
Whitefield, Ok., U.S. — B6 113
Whitefish, Mt., U.S. — B2 103
Whitefish Bay, Wi., U.S. — m12 126
Whitefish Bay, b., Mi., U.S. — B6 99
Whitefish Falls, Ont. — A3 73
Whitefish Lake, l., Alta. — B4 68
Whitefish Lake, l., Mn., U.S. — D4 100
Whitefish Point, Mi., U.S. — A3 99
Whitefish Range, mts., Mt., U.S. — B2 103
Whiteford, Md., U.S. — A5 97
White Fox, Sask. — D3 75
White Fox, stm., Sask. — D3 75
White Gull Creek, stm., Sask. — D3 75
Whitehall, Ire. — E4 11
Whitehall, Al., U.S. — C3 78
Whitehall, Ar., U.S. — C3 81
Whitehall, Ga., U.S. — C3 87
Whitehall, Il., U.S. — D3 90
Whitehall, La., U.S. — D5 95
Whitehall, Md., U.S. — A4 97
Whitehall, Mi., U.S. — E4 99
Whitehall, N.Y., U.S. — B7 109
Whitehall, Oh., U.S. — m11 112
Whitehall, Pa., U.S. — *E11 115
Whitehall, Pa., U.S. — *k14 115
Whitehall, S.C., U.S. — F6 117
Whitehall, Wi., U.S. — D2 126
Whitehall Reservoir, res., Ma., U.S. — h9 98
Whitehaven, Eng., U.K. — C5 10
Whitehaven, Md., U.S. — D6 97
Whitehead, N. Ire., U.K. — C6 11
White Heath, Il., U.S. — C5 90
Whitehorn, Point, c., Wa., U.S. — A3 124
Whitehorse, Yukon — D5 66
White Horse, N.J., U.S. — C3 107
Whitehorse, S.D., U.S. — B5 118
White Horse Beach, Ma., U.S. — C6 98
Whitehouse, Scot., U.K. — C6 13
Whitehouse, Oh., U.S. — A2 112
White House, Tn., U.S. — A5 119
White House Station, N.J., U.S. — B3 107
White Island, i., Ant. — C17 7
White Island, i., Ant. — f38 7
White Island Shores, Ma., U.S. — C6 98
White Knob Mountains, mts., Id., U.S. — F5 89
White Lake, Ont. — B8 73
White Lake, S.D., U.S. — D7 118
White Lake, Wi., U.S. — C5 126
White Lake, l., Ont. — B8 73
White Lake, l., La., U.S. — E3 95
Whitelaw, Alta. — A1 68
Whitelaw, Wi., U.S. — h10 126
White Meadow Lake, N.J., U.S. — B3 107
White Mesa Natural Bridge, Az., U.S. — A4 80
White Mills, Pa., U.S. — C11 115
White Mountain, Ak., U.S. — C7 79
White Mountain Peak, mtn., Ca., U.S. — D4 82
White Mountains, mts., U.S. — D4 82
White Mountains, mts., N.H., U.S. — B3 106
Whitemouth, Man. — E4 70
Whitemouth, stm., Man. — E4 70
Whitemouth Lake, l., Man. — E4 70
Whitemud, stm., Alta. — A2 68
White Nile (Al Baḥr al Abyaḍ), stm., Sud. — C3 47
White Nile Dam, Sud. — B3 47
White Oak, N.C., U.S. — E8 87
White Oak, N.C., U.S. — C4 110
White Oak, Oh., U.S. — o12 112
White Oak, Ok., U.S. — A6 113
White Oak, Pa., U.S. — *k14 115
White Oak, S.C., U.S. — C5 117
White Oak Creek, stm., Oh., U.S. — D2 112
Whiteoak Creek, stm., Tn., U.S. — A4 119
White Oak Lake, res., Ar., U.S. — D2 81
White Oak Mountain, mtn., Ar., U.S. — B2 81
White Owl, S.D., U.S. — C3 118
White Pass, N.A. — D12 79
White Pigeon, Mi., U.S. — G5 99
White Pine, Mi., U.S. — m12 99
White Pine, Tn., U.S. — C10 119
White Pine, co., Nv., U.S. — D6 105
White Plains, Al., U.S. — B4 78
White Plains, Ga., U.S. — C3 87
White Plains, Ky., U.S. — C2 94

White Plains, Md., U.S. — C4 97
White Plains, N.Y., U.S. — D7 109
White Plains, N.C., U.S. — A2 110
White Pond, S.C., U.S. — E5 117
White River, S.D., U.S. — D5 118
White River Junction, Vt., U.S. — D4 122
White River Plateau, plat., Co., U.S. — B3 83
White Rock, B.C. — f13 69
White Rock, N.M., U.S. — *B3 108
White Rock, R.I., U.S. — F1 116
White Rock, S.C., U.S. — C5 117
White Rock, Ut., U.S. — B9 118
White Rock Creek, stm., Ks., U.S. — C5 93
Whiterocks, Ut., U.S. — C6 121
White Russia, see Byelorussia, state, Sov. Un. — D5 29
Whitesail Lake, l., B.C. — C4 69
White Salmon, Wa., U.S. — D4 124
White Salmon, stm., Wa., U.S. — D4 124
Whitesand, stm., Sask. — F4 75
Whitesand Bay, b., Eng., U.K. — D3 12
White Sands Missile Range, mil., N.M., U.S. — E3 108
White Sands National Monument, N.M., U.S. — E3 108
Whitesboro, N.J., U.S. — E3 107
Whitesboro, N.Y., U.S. — B5 109
Whitesboro, Ok., U.S. — C7 113
Whitesboro, Tx., U.S. — C4 120
Whitesburg, Ga., U.S. — C2 87
Whitesburg, Ky., U.S. — C7 94
Whites City, N.M., U.S. — E5 108
Whites Creek, stm., Tn., U.S. — g10 119
White Sea, Sov. Un. — C6 29
White Settlement, Tx., U.S. — *n9 120
Whiteshell Provincial Park, Man. — D4 70
Whiteshore Lake, l., Sask. — E1 75
Whiteside, Mo., U.S. — B6 102
Whiteside, Tn., U.S. — D8 119
Whiteside, co., Il., U.S. — B3 90
Whiteson, Or., U.S. — B3 114
White Springs, Fl., U.S. — B4 86
Whitestone, Ga., U.S. — B2 87
White Stone, Va., U.S. — C6 123
White Stone Lake, l., Man. — A3 70
Whitestown, In., U.S. — C5 91
White Sulphur Springs, Mt., U.S. — D6 103
White Sulphur Springs, W.V., U.S. — D4 125
Whitesville, De., U.S. — G4 85
Whitesville, Ky., U.S. — C3 94
Whitesville, N.Y., U.S. — C3 109
Whitesville, W.V., U.S. — D3 125
White Swan, Wa., U.S. — C5 124
Whiteswan Lakes, l., Sask. — C3 75
Whitetail, Mt., U.S. — B11 103
White Tank Mountains, mts., Az., U.S. — k7 80
Whiteville, N.C., U.S. — C4 110
Whiteville, Tn., U.S. — B2 119
White Volta, stm., Afr. — D4 45
Whitewater, Man. — E1 70
Whitewater, Co., U.S. — C2 83
Whitewater, Ks., U.S. — E6 93
Whitewater, Mo., U.S. — D8 102
Whitewater, Mt., U.S. — B9 103
Whitewater, Wi., U.S. — F5 126
Whitewater, stm., U.S. — F7 91
Whitewater, stm., Ks., U.S. — E6 93
Whitewater, East Fork, stm., U.S. — E8 91
Whitewater, West Branch, stm., Ks., U.S. — g12 93
Whitewater Baldy, mtn., N.M., U.S. — D1 108
Whitewater Bay, b., Fl., U.S. — G6 86
White Woman Creek, stm., Ks., U.S. — D2 93
Whitewood, Sask. — G4 75
Whitewood, S.D., U.S. — C2 118
Whitewright, Tx., U.S. — C4 120
Whitfield, Al., U.S. — C1 78
Whitfield, co., Ga., U.S. — B2 87
Whitfield Estates, Fl., U.S. — q10 86
Whithorn, Scot., U.K. — C4 10
Whiting, In., U.S. — A3 91
Whiting, Ia., U.S. — B1 92
Whiting, Ks., U.S. — C8 93
Whiting, Me., U.S. — D5 96
Whiting, N.J., U.S. — D4 107
Whiting, Vt., U.S. — D2 122
Whiting, Wi., U.S. — D4 126
Whiting Bay, Scot., U.K. — E3 13
Whiting Field Naval Air Station, mil., Fl., U.S. — u14 86
Whitingham, Vt., U.S. — F3 122
Whitinsville, Ma., U.S. — B4 98
Whitkow, Sask. — E2 75
Whitla, Alta. — E5 68
Whitlash, Mt., U.S. — B5 103
Whitley, co., In., U.S. — B6 91
Whitley, co., Ky., U.S. — D5 94
Whitley City, Ky., U.S. — D5 94
Whitlock, Tn., U.S. — A3 119
Whitman, Ma., U.S. — B6 98
Whitman, Ne., U.S. — B4 104
Whitman, N.D., U.S. — A7 111
Whitman, W.V., U.S. — D2 125
Whitman, co., Wa., U.S. — B8 124
Whitmans Pond, l., Ma., U.S. — h12 98
Whitman Square, N.J., U.S. — D2 107
Whitmell, Va., U.S. — D3 123
Whitmire, S.C., U.S. — C5 117
Whitmore Lake, Mi., U.S. — p14 99
Whitmore Mountains, mts., Ant. — A2 7
Whitmore Village, Hi., U.S. — f9 88
Whitney, Ont. — B6 73
Whitney, Ne., U.S. — B2 104
Whitney, Pa., U.S. — F3 115
Whitney, S.C., U.S. — B4 117
Whitney, Tx., U.S. — D4 120
Whitney, Lake, res., Tx., U.S. — D4 120
Whitney, Mount, mtn., Ca., U.S. — D4 82
Whitney Point, N.Y., U.S. — C5 109
Whitney Point Lake, res., N.Y., U.S. — C5 109
Whitneyville, Plateau, U.S. — D5 96
Whitsett, N.C., U.S. — A3 110
Whitstable, Eng., U.K. — C9 12
Whitt, Tx., U.S. — C3 120
Whittemore, Ia., U.S. — A3 92
Whittemore, Mi., U.S. — D7 99

Whitten, Ia., U.S. — B4 92
Whittier, Ak., U.S. — C10 79
Whittier, Ca., U.S. — F4 82
Whittier, N.H., U.S. — C4 106
Whittier, N.C., U.S. — f9 110
Whittlesey, Eng., U.K. — B7 12
Whittlesey, Mount, hill, Wi., U.S. — B3 126
Whitwell, Tn., U.S. — D8 119
Wholdaia Lake, l., N.W. Ter. — D12 66
Whyalla, Austl. — F6 50
Whycocomagh, N.S. — D8 71
Wiarton, Ont. — C3 73
Wiau Lake, l., Alta. — B5 68
Wiawso, Ghana — E4 45
Wiay, i., Scot., U.K. — C1 13
Wibaux, Mt., U.S. — D12 103
Wibaux, co., Mt., U.S. — D12 103
Wiborg, Ky., U.S. — D5 94
Wichita, Ks., U.S. — E6 93
Wichita, co., Ks., U.S. — D2 93
Wichita, co., Tx., U.S. — B3 120
Wichita Falls, Tx., U.S. — C3 120
Wichita Mountains, mts., Ok., U.S. — C3 113
Wick, Scot., U.K. — A5 10
Wickatunk, N.J., U.S. — C4 107
Wickenburg, Az., U.S. — D3 80
Wickes, Ar., U.S. — C1 81
Wickes, Mt., U.S. — D4 103
Wickett, Tx., U.S. — D1 120
Wickham, Que. — D5 74
Wickiup Reservoir, res., Or., U.S. — E5 114
Wickliffe, Ky., U.S. — f8 94
Wickliffe, Oh., U.S. — *A5 112
Wickliffe, Oh., U.S. — A4 112
Wicklow, Ire. — D10 11
Wicklow, co., Ire. — E5 11
Wicklow Head, c., Ire. — E6 11
Wicklow Mountains, mts., Ire. — D10 11
Wicomico, co., Md., U.S. — D6 97
Wicomico, stm., Md., U.S. — D6 97
Wiconisco, Pa., U.S. — E8 115
Widefield, Co., U.S. — C6 83
Widen, W.V., U.S. — C4 125
Widener, Ar., U.S. — B5 81
Widerøe, Mount, mtn., Ant. — B15 7
Wide Ruins, Az., U.S. — B6 80
Widnes, Eng., U.K. — A5 12
Widuchowa, Pol. — B11 15
Wiebelskirchen, W. Ger. — D2 19
Wielen, Pol. — C6 26
Wieliczka, Pol. — F6 15
Wieluń, Pol. — C5 26
Wiener Neustadt, Aus. — E8 18
Wieprz, stm., Pol. — C7 26
Wieprzanka, stm., Pol. — h10 26
Wiergate, Tx., U.S. — D6 120
Wiesau, W. Ger. — D7 19
Wiesbaden, W. Ger. — C4 18
Wiese, stm., W. Ger. — A4 21
Wiesenburg, E. Ger. — A7 19
Wiesental, W. Ger. — D3 19
Wiesloch, W. Ger. — D3 19
Wigan, Eng., U.K. — A5 12
Wiggins, Co., U.S. — A6 83
Wiggins, Ms., U.S. — E4 101
Wiggins Peak, mtn., Wy., U.S. — C3 127
Wight, Isle of, i., Eng., U.K. — E6 10
Wigton, Eng., U.K. — F5 13
Wigtown, Scot., U.K. — C4 10
Wigtown Bay, b., Scot., U.K. — C4 10
Wijhe, Neth. — B6 17
Wikieup, Az., U.S. — C2 80
Wikwemikong, Ont. — B3 73
Wil, Switz. — B6 21
Wilayah Persekutuan (Federal Territory), ter., Malay. — *K4 35
Wilbar, N.C., U.S. — A1 110
Wilbarger, co., Tx., U.S. — B3 120
Wilber, Ne., U.S. — D9 104
Wilberforce, Ont. — B6 73
Wilberforce, Oh., U.S. — C2 112
Wilbraham, Ma., U.S. — B3 98
Wilbur, Or., U.S. — D3 114
Wilbur, Wa., U.S. — B7 124
Wilburn, Ar., U.S. — B4 81
Wilburton, Ok., U.S. — C6 113
Wilcannia, Austl. — F7 50
Wilcox, Sask. — G3 75
Wilcox, Ne., U.S. — D6 104
Wilcox, Pa., U.S. — C4 115
Wilcox, co., Al., U.S. — D2 78
Wilcox, co., Ga., U.S. — E3 87
Wilcox, Mount, mtn., Ma., U.S. — B1 98
Wilczek, i., Sov. Un. — A8 28
Wild, stm., U.S. — B4 106
Wild Ammonoosuc, stm., N.H., U.S. — B3 106
Wildbad [im Schwarzwald], W. Ger. — E3 19
Wild Horse, Alta. — E5 68
Wildcat Creek, stm., In., U.S. — D4 91
Wildcat Creek, South Fork, stm., In., U.S. — D4 91
Wildcat Top, mtn., Tn., U.S. — D10 119
Wilder, Ky., U.S. — h14 94
Wilder, Vt., U.S. — D4 122
Wilder Dam, U.S. — D4 122
Wildersville, Tn., U.S. — B3 119
Wildervank (part of Veendam), Neth. — A7 16
Wilderville, Or., U.S. — E3 114
Wildeshausen, W. Ger. — F2 15
Wildhaus, Switz. — B7 21
Wildhay, stm., Alta. — C2 68
Wildhorn, mtn., Switz. — D3 21
Wild Horse, Co., U.S. — C7 83
Wildhorse Creek, stm., Ok., U.S. — C4 113
Wild Horse Reservoir, res., Nv., U.S. — B6 105
Wildomar, Tx., U.S. — B1 120
Wild Rice, stm., Mn., U.S. — C2 100
Wild Rice, stm., N.D., U.S. — C8 111
Wild Rice, South Branch, stm., Mn., U.S. — C2 100
Wildrose, Mn., U.S. — A2 111
Wild Rose, Wi., U.S. — D4 126
Wildspitze, mtn., Aus. — C5 24
Wildsville, La., U.S. — C4 95
Wildwood, Alta. — C3 68
Wildwood, Fl., U.S. — D4 86
Wildwood, Il., U.S. — h9 90
Wildwood, N.J., U.S. — F3 107
Wildwood Crest, N.J., U.S. — *C4 107
Wiley, Co., U.S. — C8 83
Wiley, Wa., U.S. — C5 124
Wilgesburg, Ky., U.S. — C4 94
Wilhelm, Mount, mtn., Pap. N. Gui. — k12 50
Wilhelmina Gebergte, mts., Sur. — B3 59

Wilhelm-Pieck-Stadt Guben, E. Ger. — C7 18
Wilhelmshaven, W. Ger. — B4 18
Wilhoit, Az., U.S. — C3 80
Wilkau [-Hasslau], E. Ger. — C7 19
Wilkes, co., Ga., U.S. — C4 87
Wilkes, co., N.C., U.S. — A1 110
Wilkes-Barre, Pa., U.S. — D10 115
Wilkesboro, N.C., U.S. — A1 110
Wilkes Island, i., Wake I. — D12 66
Wilkes Land, reg., Ant. — B25 7
Wilkeson, Wa., U.S. — B3 124
Wilkesville, Oh., U.S. — C3 112
Wilkie, Sask. — E1 75
Wilkin, co., Mn., U.S. — D2 100
Wilkinsburg, Pa., U.S. — F2 115
Wilkinson, In., U.S. — E6 91
Wilkinson, Ms., U.S. — D1 101
Wilkinson, W.V., U.S. — D3 125
Wilkinson, co., Ga., U.S. — D3 87
Wilkinson, co., Ms., U.S. — D2 101
Wilkins Sound, strt., Ant. — B5 7
Wilkins Township, Pa., U.S. — *F2 115
Will, co., Il., U.S. — B6 90
Willacoochee, Ga., U.S. — E3 87
Willacy, co., Tx., U.S. — F4 120
Willamette, stm., Or., U.S. — C3 114
Willamette, Middle Fork, stm., Or., U.S. — D4 114
Willamette Pass, Or., U.S. — D4 114
Willamina, Or., U.S. — B3 114
Willangee, Austl. — E3 51
Willapa, Wa., U.S. — C2 124
Willapa Bay, b., Wa., U.S. — C1 124
Willard, Ks., U.S. — C8 93
Willard, Ky., U.S. — B7 94
Willard, Mo., U.S. — D4 102
Willard, N.M., U.S. — C3 108
Willard, N.Y., U.S. — C4 109
Willard, Oh., U.S. — A3 112
Willard, Ut., U.S. — B3 121
Willard, Wi., U.S. — D3 126
Willard Bay, b., Ut., U.S. — B3 121
Willards, Md., U.S. — D7 97
Willard Stream, stm., Vt., U.S. — B5 122
Willcox, Az., U.S. — E6 80
Willcox Playa, l., Az., U.S. — E5 80
Willemstad, Neth. — C4 17
Willemstad, Neth. Ant. — H19 65
Willet, N.Y., U.S. — C5 109
Willette, Tn., U.S. — C8 119
William "Bill" Dannelly Reservoir, res., Al., U.S. — C2 78
William Lane, l., Tx., U.S. — C2 70
William P. Lane, Jr. Memorial Bridge, Md., U.S. — B5 97
Williams, Az., U.S. — B3 80
Williams, In., U.S. — G4 91
Williams, Ia., U.S. — B4 92
Williams, Mn., U.S. — B4 100
Williams, S.C., U.S. — E6 117
Williams, co., N.D., U.S. — A2 111
Williams, co., Oh., U.S. — A1 112
Williams, stm., Vt., U.S. — E3 122
Williams Air Force Base, mil., Az., U.S. — D4 80
Williams Bay, Wi., U.S. — F5 126
Williamsburg, Ont. — C9 73
Williamsburg, Co., U.S. — *C5 83
Williamsburg, In., U.S. — E8 91
Williamsburg, Ks., U.S. — D8 93
Williamsburg, Ky., U.S. — D5 94
Williamsburg, Md., U.S. — C6 97
Williamsburg, Mi., U.S. — D5 99
Williamsburg, Oh., U.S. — C1 112
Williamsburg, Pa., U.S. — F5 115
Williamsburg, Va., U.S. — C6 123
Williamsburg, W.V., U.S. — D4 125
Williamsburg, co., S.C., U.S. — D8 117
Williamsfield, Il., U.S. — C3 90
Williams Fork, stm., Co., U.S. — A3 83
Williams Harbour, Newf. — B3 72
Williams Lake, B.C. — C6 69
Williams Mountain, mtn., Ok., U.S. — C7 113
Williamson, Ia., U.S. — C4 92
Williamson, N.Y., U.S. — B3 109
Williamson, W.V., U.S. — D2 125
Williamson, co., Il., U.S. — F5 90
Williamson, co., Tn., U.S. — B5 119
Williamson, co., Tx., U.S. — D4 120
Williamson, Mount, mtn., Ca., U.S. — *D4 82
Williamsport, Newf. — D3 72
Williamsport, In., U.S. — D3 91
Williamsport, Md., U.S. — A2 97
Williamsport, Oh., U.S. — C2 112
Williamsport, Pa., U.S. — D8 115
Williamsport, Tn., U.S. — B4 119
Williamston, Mi., U.S. — F6 99
Williamston, N.C., U.S. — B5 110
Williamston, S.C., U.S. — B3 117
Williamstown, Ont. — B10 73
Williamstown, Ks., U.S. — k15 93
Williamstown, Ky., U.S. — B5 94
Williamstown, Ma., U.S. — A1 98
Williamstown, N.J., U.S. — D3 107
Williamstown, N.Y., U.S. — B5 109
Williamstown, Pa., U.S. — E8 115
Williamstown, Vt., U.S. — C4 122
Williamstown, W.V., U.S. — B3 125
Williamsville, Il., U.S. — D4 90
Williamsville, Mo., U.S. — E7 102
Williamsville, N.Y., U.S. — C2 109
Williamsville, Vt., U.S. — F3 122
Williford, Ar., U.S. — A4 81
Willimantic, Ct., U.S. — C7 84
Willimantic Reservoir, res., Ct., U.S. — C7 84
Willingboro, N.J., U.S. — C3 107
Willingdon, Alta. — C4 68
Willis, Tx., U.S. — D5 120
Willisburg, Ky., U.S. — C4 94
Willis Island, i., Newf. — p14 99
Williston, S. Afr. — D3 49
Williston, Fl., U.S. — C4 86
Williston, N.C., U.S. — C6 110

Williston, N.D., U.S. — A2 111
Williston, S.C., U.S. — E5 117
Williston, Tn., U.S. — B2 119
Williston, Vt., U.S. — C2 122
Williston Basin, U.S. — B2 111
Williston Lake, res., B.C. — B6 69
Willisville, Il., U.S. — F4 90
Willis Wharf, Va., U.S. — C7 123
Willits, Ca., U.S. — C2 82
Willmar, Sask. — H4 75
Willmar, Mn., U.S. — E3 100
Willmore Wilderness Park, Alta. — C1 68
Willoughby, Austl. — *F9 50
Willoughby, Oh., U.S. — A4 112
Willoughby, Lake, l., Vt., U.S. — B4 122
Willoughby Hills, Oh., U.S. — A4 112
Willow, Ak., U.S. — g17 79
Willow, Ar., U.S. — C3 81
Willow, Ok., U.S. — B2 113
Willow, stm., B.C. — C6 69
Willow Branch, In., U.S. — E6 91
Willowbrook, Sask. — F4 75
Willow Brook, Ca., U.S. — *n12 82
Willowbrook, Il., U.S. — *B6 89
Willow Bunch, Sask. — H3 75
Willow Bunch Lake, l., Sask. — H3 75
Willow City, N.D., U.S. — A5 111
Willow City, Tx., U.S. — D3 120
Willow Creek, Mt., U.S. — E5 103
Willow Creek, stm., Alta. — D4 68
Willow Creek, stm., U.S. — E5 105
Willow Creek, stm., Ut., U.S. — D6 121
Willow Creek, stm., Wy., U.S. — C6 127
Willow Glen, La., U.S. — C3 95
Willow Grove, De., U.S. — D3 85
Willow Grove, Pa., U.S. — F11 115
Willow Grove Naval Air Station, mil., Pa., U.S. — F11 115
Willow Hill, Il., U.S. — E5 90
Willow Hill, Pa., U.S. — F6 115
Willowick, Oh., U.S. — A4 112
Willow Island, Ne., U.S. — D5 104
Willow Lake, S.D., U.S. — C8 118
Willowmore, S. Afr. — D4 49
Willow Reservoir, res., Wi., U.S. — C3 126
Willow River, B.C. — B6 69
Willow River, Mn., U.S. — D6 100
Willow River, De., U.S. — i7 85
Willow Run, Mi., U.S. — p14 99
Willows, Sask. — H3 75
Willows, Ca., U.S. — C2 82
Willow Springs, Mo., U.S. — E6 102
Willsboro, N.Y., U.S. — f11 109
Wills Hill, hill, Ma., U.S. — f11 98
Willshire, Oh., U.S. — B1 112
Wills Mountain, mtn., U.S. — k13 97
Willston, Va., U.S. — B5 123
Wilmar, Ar., U.S. — D4 81
Wilmer, Al., U.S. — E1 78
Wilmer, Tx., U.S. — n10 120
Wilmerding, Pa., U.S. — k14 115
Wilmersdorf, E. Ger. — E7 15
Wilmette, Il., U.S. — A6 90
Wilmington, Austl. — F2 51
Wilmington, De., U.S. — B3 85
Wilmington, Il., U.S. — B5 90
Wilmington, Ma., U.S. — A5 98
Wilmington, N.Y., U.S. — f11 109
Wilmington, N.C., U.S. — C5 110
Wilmington, Oh., U.S. — C2 112
Wilmington, Vt., U.S. — F3 122
Wilmington Island, Ga., U.S. — *E5 87
Wilmington Manor, De., U.S. — i7 85
Wilmington Manor Gardens, De., U.S. — *B3 85
Wilmont, Mn., U.S. — G3 100
Wilmore, Ks., U.S. — E4 93
Wilmore, Ky., U.S. — C5 94
Wilmore, Pa., U.S. — F4 115
Wilmot, N.S. — E4 71
Wilmot, Ar., U.S. — D4 81
Wilmot, Oh., U.S. — B4 112
Wilmot, S.D., U.S. — B9 118
Wilmot Flat, N.H., U.S. — D3 106
Wilmslow, Eng., U.K. — A5 12
Wilno, Ont. — B7 73
Wilsall, Mt., U.S. — E6 103
Wilsey, Ks., U.S. — D7 93
Wilson, Ar., U.S. — B5 81
Wilson, Ks., U.S. — D5 93
Wilson, La., U.S. — D4 95
Wilson, Mi., U.S. — C3 99
Wilson, N.Y., U.S. — B2 109
Wilson, N.C., U.S. — B5 110
Wilson, Ok., U.S. — C4 113
Wilson, stm., Austl. — E4 51
Wilson, Mount, mtn., Ca., U.S. — m12 82
Wilson, Mount, mtn., Co., U.S. — D2 83
Wilson, Mount, mtn., Nv., U.S. — E7 105
Wilson, Mount, mtn., Or., U.S. — B5 114
Wilson Creek, Wa., U.S. — B6 124
Wilson Creek, stm., Wa., U.S. — B5 124
Wilson Dam, Al., U.S. — A2 78
Wilson Lake, res., Al., U.S. — A2 78
Wilson Lake, res., Ks., U.S. — D4 93
Wilson Piedmont Glacier, ice, Ant. — e39 7
Wilsons, Va., U.S. — C5 123
Wilsons Beach, N.B. — E3 71
Wilsons Mills, Me., U.S. — D1 96
Wilsons Mills, N.C., U.S. — B4 110
Wilsons Promontory, c., Austl. — G8 50
Wilsonville, Al., U.S. — B3 78
Wilsonville, Ct., U.S. — A8 84
Wilsonville, Il., U.S. — D5 104
Wilsonville, Ne., U.S. — h12 114
Wilstedt, W. Ger. — E3 15
Wilster, W. Ger. — B3 15
Wilton, Al., U.S. — B3 78
Wilton, Ar., U.S. — E2 84
Wilton, Ia., U.S. — C6 92
Wilton, Me., U.S. — D2 96
Wilton, Mn., U.S. — C3 100
Wilton, N.H., U.S. — E3 106
Wilton, N.Y., U.S. — B7 109
Wilton, N.D., U.S. — B5 111

| Name | Map Ref. | Page |
|---|---|---|
| Wilton, Wi., U.S. | E3 | 126 |
| Wilton Center, N.H., U.S. | E3 | 106 |
| Wilton Manors, Fl., U.S. | *r13 | 86 |
| Wiltshire, co., Eng., U.K. | C6 | 12 |
| Wiltz, Lux. | C6 | 16 |
| Wiluna, Austl. | E3 | 50 |
| Wimapedi, stm., Man. | B2 | 70 |
| Wimauma, Fl., U.S. | E4 | 86 |
| Wimbledon (part of London), Eng., U.K. | m12 | 10 |
| Wimbledon, N.D., U.S. | B7 | 111 |
| Wimborne, Alta. | D4 | 68 |
| Wimborne Minster, Eng., U.K. | D6 | 12 |
| Wimico, Lake, l., Fl., U.S. | C1 | 86 |
| Winagami Lake, l., Alta. | B2 | 68 |
| Winamac, In., U.S. | B4 | 91 |
| Winburg, S. Afr. | C4 | 49 |
| Winburne, Pa., U.S. | E5 | 115 |
| Wincheck Pond, l., R.I., U.S. | E1 | 116 |
| Winchell Mountain, mtn., Ma., U.S. | B2 | 98 |
| Winchendon, Ma., U.S. | A3 | 98 |
| Winchendon Springs, Ma., U.S. | A3 | 98 |
| Winchester, Ont. | B9 | 73 |
| Winchester, Eng., U.K. | E6 | 10 |
| Winchester, Ar., U.S. | D4 | 81 |
| Winchester, Id., U.S. | C2 | 89 |
| Winchester, Il., U.S. | D3 | 90 |
| Winchester, In., U.S. | D8 | 91 |
| Winchester, Ks., U.S. | k15 | 93 |
| Winchester, Ky., U.S. | C5 | 94 |
| Winchester, Ma., U.S. | g11 | 98 |
| Winchester, Ms., U.S. | D5 | 101 |
| Winchester, Mo., U.S. | A6 | 102 |
| Winchester, Nv., U.S. | G6 | 105 |
| Winchester, N.H., U.S. | E2 | 106 |
| Winchester, Oh., U.S. | D2 | 112 |
| Winchester, Tn., U.S. | B5 | 119 |
| Winchester, Va., U.S. | A4 | 123 |
| Winchester Bay, Or., U.S. | D2 | 114 |
| Winchester Center, Ct., U.S. | B3 | 84 |
| Wind, stm., Wy., U.S. | D4 | 124 |
| Wind, stm., Wy., U.S. | C4 | 127 |
| Windber, Pa., U.S. | F4 | 115 |
| Wind Cave National Park, S.D., U.S. | D2 | 118 |
| Wind Creek, stm., Wy., U.S. | C7 | 127 |
| Windcrest, Tx., U.S. | *E3 | 120 |
| Winder, Ga., U.S. | C3 | 87 |
| Windermere, B.C. | D10 | 69 |
| Windermere, Ont. | B5 | 73 |
| Windermere, Eng., U.K. | C5 | 10 |
| Windermere, l., Eng., U.K. | F6 | 13 |
| Windfall, Alta. | B2 | 68 |
| Windfall, In., U.S. | D6 | 91 |
| Windgap, Pa., U.S. | E11 | 115 |
| Windham, Ct., U.S. | C7 | 84 |
| Windham, Mt., U.S. | C6 | 103 |
| Windham, N.Y., U.S. | C6 | 109 |
| Windham, Oh., U.S. | A4 | 112 |
| Windham, co., Ct., U.S. | B7 | 84 |
| Windham, co., Vt., U.S. | F3 | 122 |
| Windham Center, Me., U.S. | *E2 | 96 |
| Windhoek, Nmb. | B2 | 49 |
| Windigo, stm., Que. | B4 | 74 |
| Winding Stair Mountain, mts., Ok., U.S. | C6 | 113 |
| Wind Lake, Wi., U.S. | F5 | 126 |
| Wind Lake, l., Wi., U.S. | n11 | 126 |
| Windmill Point, c., Va., U.S. | C6 | 123 |
| Windom, Ks., U.S. | D6 | 93 |
| Windom, Mn., U.S. | G3 | 100 |
| Windom Peak, mtn., Co., U.S. | D3 | 83 |
| Window Rock, Az., U.S. | B6 | 80 |
| Wind Point, Wi., U.S. | n12 | 126 |
| Wind Ridge, Pa., U.S. | G1 | 115 |
| Wind River Indian Reservation, Wy., U.S. | C4 | 127 |
| Wind River Peak, mtn., Wy., U.S. | D3 | 127 |
| Wind River Range, mts., Wy., U.S. | C3 | 127 |
| Windsbach, W. Ger. | D5 | 19 |
| Windsor, Newf. | D4 | 72 |
| Windsor, N.S. | E5 | 71 |
| Windsor, Ont. | E1 | 73 |
| Windsor, Que. | D5 | 74 |
| Windsor (New Windsor), Eng., U.K. | E6 | 10 |
| Windsor, Co., U.S. | A6 | 83 |
| Windsor, Ct., U.S. | B5 | 84 |
| Windsor, Il., U.S. | D5 | 90 |
| Windsor, Ma., U.S. | A1 | 98 |
| Windsor, Mo., U.S. | C4 | 102 |
| Windsor, N.J., U.S. | C3 | 107 |
| Windsor, N.C., U.S. | B6 | 110 |
| Windsor, Pa., U.S. | G8 | 115 |
| Windsor, S.C., U.S. | E4 | 117 |
| Windsor, Vt., U.S. | E4 | 122 |
| Windsor, co., Vt., U.S. | D6 | 123 |
| Windsor, co., Vt., U.S. | D3 | 122 |
| Windsor Heights, Ia., U.S. | e8 | 92 |
| Windsor Hills, Ca., U.S. | *n12 | 82 |
| Windsor Locks, Ct., U.S. | B5 | 84 |
| Windsorville, Ct., U.S. | B5 | 84 |
| Windthorst, Sask. | G4 | 75 |
| Windthorst, Tx., U.S. | C3 | 120 |
| Windward Islands, is., N.A. | I14 | 64 |
| Windward Passage, strt., N.A. | E7 | 64 |
| Windygates, Man. | E2 | 70 |
| Windy Hill, S.C., U.S. | C8 | 117 |
| Windy Hills, Ga., U.S. | *B3 | 85 |
| Windy Lake, l., Sask. | C4 | 75 |
| Windy Peak, mtn., Wa., U.S. | A6 | 124 |
| Windy Point, c., Newf. | C4 | 72 |
| Winefred, stm., Alta. | B5 | 68 |
| Winefred Lake, l., Alta. | B5 | 68 |
| Winfall, N.C., U.S. | A6 | 110 |
| Winfield, Alta. | C3 | 68 |
| Winfield, Al., U.S. | B2 | 78 |
| Winfield, Ia., U.S. | C6 | 92 |
| Winfield, Ks., U.S. | E7 | 93 |
| Winfield, Md., U.S. | B3 | 97 |
| Winfield, N.J., U.S. | k7 | 107 |
| Winfield, Tn., U.S. | C9 | 119 |
| Winfield, W.V., U.S. | C3 | 125 |
| Winfred, S.D., U.S. | D8 | 118 |
| Wing, N.D., U.S. | D3 | 78 |
| Wing, Ar., U.S. | C2 | 81 |
| Wing, N.D., U.S. | B5 | 111 |
| Wing, stm., Mn., U.S. | *D3 | 100 |
| Wingate, In., U.S. | D3 | 91 |
| Wingate, Md., U.S. | D5 | 97 |
| Wingate, N.C., U.S. | C2 | 110 |
| Winger, Mn., U.S. | C3 | 100 |
| Wingham, Ont. | D3 | 73 |
| Wingo, Ky., U.S. | f9 | 94 |
| Winifred, Mt., U.S. | C7 | 103 |
| Winifreda, Arg. | B4 | 54 |
| Winifrede, W.V., U.S. | m12 | 125 |
| Winigan, Mo., U.S. | A5 | 102 |

| Winisk, Ont. | n18 | 73 |
| Winisk, stm., Ont. | n18 | 73 |
| Winisk Lake, l., Ont. | n18 | 73 |
| Wink, Tx., U.S. | D1 | 120 |
| Winkelman, Az., U.S. | E5 | 80 |
| Winkler, Man. | E3 | 70 |
| Winkler, co., Tx., U.S. | D1 | 120 |
| Winlaw, B.C. | E9 | 69 |
| Winlock, Wa., U.S. | C3 | 124 |
| Winn, Me., U.S. | C4 | 96 |
| Winn, Mi., U.S. | E6 | 99 |
| Winn, co., La., U.S. | C3 | 95 |
| Winnabow, N.C., U.S. | C4 | 110 |
| Winneba, Ghana | E4 | 45 |
| Winnebago, Il., U.S. | A4 | 90 |
| Winnebago, Mn., U.S. | G4 | 100 |
| Winnebago, Ne., U.S. | B9 | 104 |
| Winnebago, co., Il., U.S. | A4 | 90 |
| Winnebago, co., Ia., U.S. | A4 | 92 |
| Winnebago, co., Wi., U.S. | D5 | 126 |
| Winnebago, stm., Ia., U.S. | A4 | 92 |
| Winnebago, Lake, l., Wi., U.S. | E5 | 126 |
| Winnebago Indian Reservation, Ne., U.S. | B9 | 104 |
| Winneconne, Wi., U.S. | D5 | 126 |
| Winnemucca, Nv., U.S. | C4 | 105 |
| Winnemucca Lake, l., Nv., U.S. | C2 | 105 |
| Winnesboug, Fr. | C7 | 16 |
| Winnetka, Il., U.S. | A6 | 90 |
| Winnetoon, Ne., U.S. | B8 | 104 |
| Winnett, Mt., U.S. | C8 | 103 |
| Winnfield, La., U.S. | C3 | 95 |
| Winnibigoshish, Lake, l., Mn., U.S. | C4 | 100 |
| Winnipeg, Man. | E3 | 70 |
| Winnipeg, Lake, l., Man. | C3 | 70 |
| Winnipegosis, Man. | D2 | 70 |
| Winnipegosis, Lake, l., Man. | C2 | 70 |
| Winnipesaukee, N.H., U.S. | C4 | 106 |
| Winnipesaukee, Lake, l., N.H., U.S. | C4 | 106 |
| Winnisquam, N.H., U.S. | C3 | 106 |
| Winnisquam Lake, l., N.H., U.S. | C3 | 106 |
| Winnsboro, La., U.S. | B4 | 95 |
| Winnsboro, S.C., U.S. | C5 | 117 |
| Winnsboro, Tx., U.S. | C5 | 120 |
| Winnsboro Mills, S.C., U.S. | C5 | 117 |
| Winona, Ont. | C2 | 93 |
| Winona, Mi., U.S. | B2 | 99 |
| Winona, Mn., U.S. | F7 | 100 |
| Winona, Mo., U.S. | D6 | 102 |
| Winona, N.H., U.S. | C3 | 106 |
| Winona, Oh., U.S. | C8 | 124 |
| Winona, W.V., U.S. | C4 | 125 |
| Winona, co., Mn., U.S. | F7 | 100 |
| Winona Lake, In., U.S. | B6 | 91 |
| Winona Lake, l., Vt., U.S. | C2 | 122 |
| Winooski, Vt., U.S. | C2 | 122 |
| Winooski, stm., Vt., U.S. | C3 | 122 |
| Winooski, North Branch, stm., Vt., U.S. | C3 | 122 |
| Winschoten, Neth. | A7 | 16 |
| Winsford, Eng., U.K. | A5 | 12 |
| Winside, Ne., U.S. | B8 | 104 |
| Winslow, Az., U.S. | C5 | 80 |
| Winslow, Ar., U.S. | B1 | 81 |
| Winslow, Il., U.S. | A4 | 90 |
| Winslow, In., U.S. | H3 | 91 |
| Winslow, Me., U.S. | D3 | 96 |
| Winslow, Ne., U.S. | C9 | 104 |
| Winslow, N.J., U.S. | D3 | 107 |
| Winsted, Ct., U.S. | B3 | 84 |
| Winsted, Mn., U.S. | F4 | 100 |
| Winston, Fl., U.S. | D4 | 86 |
| Winston, Mo., U.S. | B3 | 102 |
| Winston, Mt., U.S. | D5 | 103 |
| Winston, N.M., U.S. | D2 | 108 |
| Winston, Or., U.S. | D3 | 114 |
| Winston, co., Al., U.S. | A2 | 78 |
| Winston, co., Ms., U.S. | B4 | 101 |
| Winston-Salem, N.C., U.S. | A2 | 110 |
| Winstonville, Ms., U.S. | B3 | 101 |
| Winsum, Neth. | A6 | 17 |
| Winter, Sask. | E1 | 75 |
| Winter, Wi., U.S. | C2 | 126 |
| Winter Beach, Fl., U.S. | E6 | 86 |
| Winter Garden, Fl., U.S. | D5 | 86 |
| Winter Harbor, Me., U.S. | D4 | 96 |
| Winter Harbour, B.C. | D3 | 69 |
| Winter Haven, Fl., U.S. | D5 | 86 |
| Wintering Lake, l., Man. | B3 | 70 |
| Winter Park, Co., U.S. | B5 | 83 |
| Winter Park, Fl., U.S. | D5 | 86 |
| Winter Park, N.C., U.S. | C5 | 110 |
| Winterpock, Va., U.S. | C5 | 123 |
| Winterport, Me., U.S. | D4 | 96 |
| Winter Ridge, mtn., Or., U.S. | E6 | 114 |
| Winters, Ca., U.S. | C2 | 82 |
| Winters, Tx., U.S. | D3 | 120 |
| Winterset, Ia., U.S. | C3 | 92 |
| Winter Springs, Fl., U.S. | *D5 | 86 |
| Wintersville, Oh., U.S. | B5 | 112 |
| Winterswijk, Neth. | C6 | 17 |
| Winterthur, Switz. | E4 | 18 |
| Winterthur, De., U.S. | h7 | 85 |
| Winterton, Newf. | E5 | 72 |
| Winterville, Ga., U.S. | C3 | 87 |
| Winterville, Me., U.S. | B4 | 96 |
| Winterville, Ms., U.S. | B2 | 101 |
| Winterville, N.C., U.S. | B5 | 110 |
| Winthrop, Ar., U.S. | D1 | 81 |
| Winthrop, Ia., U.S. | D5 | 84 |
| Winthrop, Me., U.S. | D6 | 98 |
| Winthrop, Mn., U.S. | F4 | 100 |
| Winthrop, N.Y., U.S. | f10 | 109 |
| Winthrop, Wa., U.S. | A5 | 124 |
| Winthrop, co., Ia., U.S. | h10 | 98 |
| Winthrop Harbor, Il., U.S. | A6 | 90 |
| Winton, Austl. | D8 | 50 |
| Winton, Bah. | m18 | 64 |
| Winton, Mn., U.S. | C7 | 100 |
| Winton, N.C., U.S. | A6 | 110 |
| Wintzenheim, Fr. | A3 | 20 |
| Winyah Bay, b., S.C., U.S. | E9 | 117 |
| Wiota, Ia., U.S. | C3 | 92 |
| Wirātnagar, Nepal | C8 | 36 |
| Wirral, N.B. | D3 | 71 |
| Wirt, Mn., U.S. | C5 | 100 |
| Wirt, co., W.V., U.S. | B3 | 125 |
| Wirtz, Va., U.S. | C3 | 123 |
| Wisbech, Eng., U.K. | D7 | 10 |

| Wiscasset, Me., U.S. | D3 | 96 |
| Wisconsin, state, U.S. | D4 | 126 |
| Wisconsin, stm., Wi., U.S. | E3 | 126 |
| Wisconsin, Lake, res., Wi., U.S. | E4 | 126 |
| Wisconsin Dells, Wi., U.S. | E4 | 126 |
| Wisconsin Rapids, Wi., U.S. | D4 | 126 |
| Wisdom, Mt., U.S. | E3 | 103 |
| Wise, N.C., U.S. | A4 | 110 |
| Wise, Va., U.S. | f9 | 123 |
| Wise, co., Tx., U.S. | C4 | 120 |
| Wise, co., Va., U.S. | e9 | 123 |
| Wiseman, Ak., U.S. | B9 | 79 |
| Wise River, Mt., U.S. | E4 | 103 |
| Wiseton, Sask. | F2 | 75 |
| Wishart, Sask. | F3 | 75 |
| Wishart, Mo., U.S. | D4 | 102 |
| Wishaw, Scot., U.K. | E5 | 13 |
| Wishek, N.D., U.S. | C6 | 111 |
| Wishram, Wa., U.S. | D4 | 124 |
| Wisła (Vistula), stm., Pol. | B5 | 26 |
| Wisłok, stm., Pol. | C7 | 26 |
| Wisłoka, stm., Pol. | D6 | 26 |
| Wismar, E. Ger. | B5 | 18 |
| Wismar Bucht, b., E. Ger. | D5 | 15 |
| Wisner, La., U.S. | C4 | 95 |
| Wisner, Ne., U.S. | C9 | 104 |
| Wissant, Fr. | D9 | 12 |
| Wissembourg, Fr. | C7 | 16 |
| Wissota, Lake, res., Wi., U.S. | D2 | 126 |
| Wister, Ok., U.S. | C7 | 113 |
| Wister Lake, res., Ok., U.S. | C7 | 113 |
| Witbank, S. Afr. | C4 | 49 |
| Witchekan Lake, l., Sask. | D2 | 75 |
| Witham, Eng., U.K. | C8 | 12 |
| Witham, stm., Eng., U.K. | A7 | 12 |
| Withamsville, Oh., U.S. | C1 | 112 |
| Withee, Wi., U.S. | D3 | 126 |
| Witherbee, N.Y., U.S. | A7 | 109 |
| Witherspoon, Mount, mtn., Ak., U.S. | g18 | 79 |
| Withlacoochee, stm., U.S. | B3 | 86 |
| Withlacoochee, stm., Fl., U.S. | C4 | 86 |
| Withrow, Wa., U.S. | B6 | 124 |
| Witless Bay, Newf. | E5 | 72 |
| Witney, Eng., U.K. | C6 | 12 |
| Witry-lès-Reims, Fr. | E4 | 17 |
| Witt, Il., U.S. | D4 | 90 |
| Witt, Tn., U.S. | C10 | 119 |
| Witten, W. Ger. | B2 | 19 |
| Witten, S.D., U.S. | D5 | 118 |
| Witten, l., W. Ger. | D3 | 15 |
| Wittenberg, E. Ger. | C6 | 18 |
| Wittenberg, Wi., U.S. | D4 | 126 |
| Wittenberge, E. Ger. | B5 | 18 |
| Wittenheim, Fr. | B3 | 20 |
| Wittingen, W. Ger. | B5 | 18 |
| Wittlich, W. Ger. | D3 | 18 |
| Wittman, Md., U.S. | C5 | 97 |
| Wittmann, Az., U.S. | D3 | 80 |
| Wittmund, W. Ger. | A7 | 17 |
| Wittstock, E. Ger. | B6 | 18 |
| Witu Islands, is., Pap. N. Gui. | h12 | 50 |
| Witvlei, Nmb. | B2 | 49 |
| Witzenhausen, W. Ger. | B4 | 19 |
| Wiveliscombe, Eng., U.K. | C4 | 12 |
| Wixòn, N. Kor. | F3 | 33 |
| Wixom, Mi., U.S. | o14 | 99 |
| Wixom Lake, res., Mi., U.S. | E6 | 99 |
| Wkra, stm., Pol. | B6 | 26 |
| Władowo, Pol. | A5 | 26 |
| Włocławek, Pol. | B5 | 26 |
| Włodawa, Pol. | C7 | 26 |
| Włoszczowa, Pol. | C5 | 26 |
| Woburn, Que. | D7 | 74 |
| Woburn, In., U.S. | H3 | 91 |
| Woburn, Ma., U.S. | B5 | 98 |
| Woburn, Ia., U.S. | k9 | 90 |
| Wodzisław Śląski, Pol. | *C5 | 26 |
| Woerden, Neth. | B4 | 17 |
| Wohlen, Switz. | B5 | 21 |
| Wohlthat Mountains, mts., Ant. | B14 | 7 |
| Woito, Ont. | B7 | 73 |
| Wokam, i., Indon. | G8 | 34 |
| Woking, Alta. | B1 | 68 |
| Woking, Eng., U.K. | m11 | 10 |
| Wokingham, Eng., U.K. | C7 | 12 |
| Wolbach, Ne., U.S. | C7 | 104 |
| Wolcott, Co., U.S. | B4 | 83 |
| Wolcott, Ct., U.S. | C4 | 84 |
| Wolcott, In., U.S. | C3 | 91 |
| Wolcott, N.Y., U.S. | B4 | 109 |
| Wolcott, Vt., U.S. | B4 | 122 |
| Wolcottville, In., U.S. | A7 | 91 |
| Woldegk, E. Ger. | E7 | 15 |
| Wolf, Ok., U.S. | B5 | 113 |
| Wolf, Wy., U.S. | B5 | 127 |
| Wolf, stm., Ms., U.S. | E4 | 101 |
| Wolf, stm., Tn., U.S. | e9 | 119 |
| Wolf, stm., Wi., U.S. | C5 | 126 |
| Wolf, Isla, i., Ec. | f5 | 58 |
| Wolf, North Fork, stm., Tn., U.S. | B2 | 119 |
| Wolf, Volcán, vol., Ec. | f5 | 58 |
| Wolf Creek, Mt., U.S. | C4 | 103 |
| Wolf Creek, Or., U.S. | E3 | 114 |
| Wolf Creek, stm., U.S. | A2 | 113 |
| Wolf Creek, stm., Ia., U.S. | B5 | 92 |
| Wolf Creek, stm., Mi., U.S. | D7 | 99 |
| Wolf Creek, stm., Mt., U.S. | C7 | 103 |
| Wolf Creek, stm., W.V., U.S. | m13 | 125 |
| Wolf Creek Pass, Co., U.S. | D3 | 83 |
| Wolfe, co., Que. | D6 | 74 |
| Wolfe, co., Ky., U.S. | C6 | 94 |
| Wolfeboro, N.H., U.S. | C4 | 106 |
| Wolfeboro Falls, N.H., U.S. | C4 | 106 |
| Wolfe City, Tx., U.S. | C4 | 120 |
| Wolfegg, W. Ger. | A8 | 21 |
| Wolfen, E. Ger. | B7 | 18 |
| Wolfenbüttel, W. Ger. | B5 | 18 |
| Wolfenschiessen, Switz. | C5 | 21 |
| Wolfhagen, W. Ger. | B4 | 19 |
| Wolf Island, Mo., U.S. | E8 | 102 |
| Wolf Lake, Il., U.S. | F4 | 90 |
| Wolf Lake, Mi., U.S. | E4 | 99 |
| Wolf Lake, l., U.S. | k9 | 90 |
| Wolf Lake, l., Alta. | B5 | 68 |
| Wolf Mountain, mtn., Ak., U.S. | B9 | 79 |
| Wolford, N.D., U.S. | A6 | 111 |
| Wolf Point, Mt., U.S. | B11 | 103 |
| Wolfratshausen, W. Ger. | B7 | 20 |
| Wolfsberg, Aus. | E7 | 18 |
| Wolfsville, Md., U.S. | A2 | 97 |
| Wolf Swamp, sw., N.C., U.S. | B5 | 110 |
| Wolf Trap, Va., U.S. | *B5 | 123 |
| Wolfville, N.S. | D5 | 71 |
| Wolgast, E. Ger. | A6 | 18 |
| Wolhusen, Switz. | B4 | 20 |
| Wolin, Pol. | E8 | 15 |
| Wolin, i., Pol. | E8 | 15 |
| Wollaston, Cape, c., N.W. Ter. | B9 | 66 |

| Wollaston, Islas, is., Chile | k12 | 54 |
| Wollaston Lake, l., Sask. | m8 | 75 |
| Wollongong, Austl. | F9 | 50 |
| Wolmaransstad, S. Afr. | C4 | 49 |
| Wolmirstedt, E. Ger. | A6 | 19 |
| Wołomin, Pol. | k14 | 26 |
| Wołów, Pol. | C4 | 26 |
| Wolseley, Sask. | G4 | 75 |
| Wolsey, S.D., U.S. | C7 | 118 |
| Wolsztyn, Pol. | B4 | 26 |
| Wolverhampton, Eng., U.K. | D5 | 10 |
| Wolverine, Mi., U.S. | C6 | 99 |
| Wolverton, Eng., U.K. | D6 | 10 |
| Wolverton, Mn., U.S. | D2 | 100 |
| Womack Hill, Al., U.S. | D1 | 78 |
| Woman Lake, l., Mn., U.S. | D4 | 100 |
| Womelsdorf, Pa., U.S. | F9 | 115 |
| Wonalancet, N.H., U.S. | C4 | 106 |
| Wonder Lake, Il., U.S. | A5 | 90 |
| Wonderland, Ca., U.S. | B3 | 82 |
| Wonewoc, Wi., U.S. | E3 | 126 |
| Wŏnju, S. Kor. | H3 | 33 |
| Wonotobo Vallen, wtfl., Sur. | B3 | 59 |
| Wonowon, B.C. | A7 | 69 |
| Wŏnsan, N. Kor. | D10 | 31 |
| Wonthaggi, Austl. | G8 | 50 |
| Wood, N.C., U.S. | A4 | 110 |
| Wood, Pa., U.S. | F5 | 115 |
| Wood, S.D., U.S. | D5 | 118 |
| Wood, co., Oh., U.S. | A2 | 112 |
| Wood, co., Tx., U.S. | C5 | 120 |
| Wood, co., W.V., U.S. | B3 | 125 |
| Wood, co., Wi., U.S. | D3 | 126 |
| Wood, stm., B.C. | C8 | 69 |
| Wood, stm., Sask. | H2 | 75 |
| Wood, stm., R.I., U.S. | F2 | 116 |
| Wood, stm., Wy., U.S. | C3 | 127 |
| Wood, Mount, mtn., Mt., U.S. | E7 | 103 |
| Woodall Mountain, mtn., Ms., U.S. | A5 | 101 |
| Woodberry, Ar., U.S. | D3 | 81 |
| Woodbine, Ga., U.S. | F5 | 87 |
| Woodbine, Il., U.S. | A3 | 90 |
| Woodbine, Ia., U.S. | C2 | 92 |
| Woodbine, Ks., U.S. | D7 | 93 |
| Woodbine, Ky., U.S. | D5 | 94 |
| Woodbine, Md., U.S. | B3 | 97 |
| Woodbine, N.J., U.S. | E3 | 107 |
| Woodboro, Wi., U.S. | C4 | 126 |
| Woodbourne, N.Y., U.S. | D6 | 109 |
| Woodbourne, Oh., U.S. | *C1 | 112 |
| Woodbridge, Eng., U.K. | B9 | 12 |
| Woodbridge, Ct., U.S. | D3 | 84 |
| Woodbridge, Va., U.S. | B5 | 123 |
| Woodbridge [Township], N.J., U.S. | B4 | 107 |
| Wood Buffalo National Park, Can. | E10 | 66 |
| Woodburn, In., U.S. | B8 | 91 |
| Woodburn, Ia., U.S. | C4 | 92 |
| Woodburn, Ky., U.S. | D3 | 94 |
| Woodbury, Ct., U.S. | C3 | 84 |
| Woodbury, Ga., U.S. | D2 | 87 |
| Woodbury, Ky., U.S. | C3 | 94 |
| Woodbury, Mn., U.S. | F6 | 100 |
| Woodbury, N.J., U.S. | D2 | 107 |
| Woodbury, N.Y., U.S. | *E7 | 109 |
| Woodbury, Pa., U.S. | F5 | 115 |
| Woodbury, Tn., U.S. | B5 | 119 |
| Woodbury, co., Ia., U.S. | B1 | 92 |
| Woodbury Mountain, mtn., Vt., U.S. | C4 | 122 |
| Woodcliff, Ga., U.S. | D5 | 87 |
| Woodcliff Lake, N.J., U.S. | g8 | 107 |
| Woodcliff Lake, l., N.J., U.S. | g8 | 107 |
| Wood Dale, Il., U.S. | k9 | 90 |
| Wood End, spit, Ma., U.S. | B7 | 98 |
| Woodenhawk, De., U.S. | E3 | 85 |
| Woodfibre, B.C. | E6 | 69 |
| Woodfield, S.C., U.S. | C6 | 117 |
| Woodford, Ire. | D3 | 11 |
| Woodford, S.C., U.S. | D5 | 117 |
| Woodford, co., Il., U.S. | C4 | 90 |
| Woodford, co., Ky., U.S. | B5 | 94 |
| Woodfords, Ca., U.S. | C4 | 82 |
| Woodhaven, Mi., U.S. | *F7 | 99 |
| Woodhull, Il., U.S. | B3 | 90 |
| Woodhull, N.Y., U.S. | C3 | 109 |
| Woodlake, Ca., U.S. | D4 | 82 |
| Wood Lake, Mn., U.S. | F3 | 100 |
| Wood Lake, Ne., U.S. | B5 | 104 |
| Woodlake, N.C., U.S. | B3 | 110 |
| Wood Lake, l., Sask. | B4 | 75 |
| Woodland, Al., U.S. | B4 | 78 |
| Woodland, Ca., U.S. | C3 | 82 |
| Woodland, Me., U.S. | C5 | 96 |
| Woodland, Mn., U.S. | D6 | 100 |
| Woodland, N.C., U.S. | A5 | 110 |
| Woodland, Pa., U.S. | D5 | 115 |
| Woodland, Wa., U.S. | D3 | 124 |
| Woodland Acres, Co., U.S. | D6 | 83 |
| Woodland Beach, De., U.S. | C4 | 85 |
| Woodland Mills, Tn., U.S. | A2 | 119 |
| Woodland Park, Co., U.S. | C5 | 83 |
| Woodlawn, Ont. | h11 | 73 |
| Woodlawn, Il., U.S. | E4 | 90 |
| Woodlawn, Ky., U.S. | e9 | 94 |
| Woodlawn, Md., U.S. | g10 | 97 |
| Woodlawn, Oh., U.S. | n13 | 112 |
| Woodlawn, Tn., U.S. | A4 | 119 |
| Woodlawn, Va., U.S. | D2 | 123 |
| Woodleaf, N.C., U.S. | B2 | 110 |
| Woodlynne, N.J., U.S. | *D2 | 107 |
| Woodman, Wi., U.S. | E3 | 126 |
| Woodmere, N.H., U.S. | E2 | 106 |
| Woodmere, N.Y., U.S. | *k13 | 109 |
| Woodmont, Ct., U.S. | E4 | 84 |
| Woodmoor, Md., U.S. | B4 | 97 |
| Wood Mountain, mtn., Sask. | H2 | 75 |
| Woodport, N.J., U.S. | B3 | 107 |
| Woodridge, Man. | E3 | 70 |
| Woodridge, Il., U.S. | k8 | 90 |
| Wood-Ridge, N.J., U.S. | h8 | 107 |
| Wood River, Il., U.S. | E3 | 90 |
| Wood River, Ne., U.S. | D7 | 104 |
| Wood River Junction, R.I. | | |
| Wounded Knee, S.D., U.S. | D3 | 118 |
| Wounta, Nic. | H6 | 64 |
| Wowoni, i., Indon. | F7 | 34 |
| Woy Woy, Austl. | F9 | 50 |
| Woźniki, Pol. | f10 | 26 |
| Wrangel Island, i., Sov. Un. | B21 | 29 |
| Wrangell, Ak., U.S. | D13 | 79 |
| Wrangell, Mount, mtn., Ak., U.S. | f19 | 79 |
| Wrangell Island, i., Ak., U.S. | m24 | 79 |
| Wrangell Mountains, mts., N.A. | D4 | 66 |

| Woods, Lake, res., Tn., U.S. | B5 | 119 |
| Woods, Lake of the, l., N.A. | E4 | 70 |
| Woodsboro, Md., U.S. | A3 | 97 |
| Woodsboro, Tx., U.S. | E4 | 120 |
| Woods Cross, Ut., U.S. | C4 | 121 |
| Woodsdale, N.C., U.S. | A4 | 110 |
| Woodsfield, Oh., U.S. | C4 | 112 |
| Woods Hole, Ma., U.S. | C6 | 98 |
| Woodside, Austl. | I6 | 51 |
| Woodside, Ca., U.S. | *k8 | 82 |
| Woodside, De., U.S. | D3 | 85 |
| Woodside, Ut., U.S. | E4 | 121 |
| Wood's Island, Newf. | D2 | 72 |
| Woodson, Ar., U.S. | C3 | 81 |
| Woodson, Il., U.S. | D3 | 90 |
| Woodson, co., Ks., U.S. | E8 | 93 |
| Woodstock, N.B. | C2 | 71 |
| Woodstock, Ont. | D4 | 73 |
| Woodstock, Al., U.S. | B2 | 78 |
| Woodstock, Ct., U.S. | B8 | 84 |
| Woodstock, Ga., U.S. | B2 | 87 |
| Woodstock, Il., U.S. | A5 | 90 |
| Woodstock, Md., U.S. | B4 | 97 |
| Woodstock, Mn., U.S. | F2 | 100 |
| Woodstock, N.H., U.S. | C3 | 106 |
| Woodstock, N.Y., U.S. | C6 | 109 |
| Woodstock, Oh., U.S. | B2 | 112 |
| Woodstock, Vt., U.S. | D3 | 122 |
| Woodstock, Va., U.S. | B4 | 123 |
| Woodstock Valley, Ct., U.S. | B7 | 84 |
| Woodston, Ks., U.S. | C4 | 93 |
| Woodstown, N.J., U.S. | D2 | 107 |
| Woodsville, N.H., U.S. | B2 | 106 |
| Woodville, Austl. | *F6 | 50 |
| Woodville, Ont. | C5 | 73 |
| Woodville, N.Z. | N15 | 51 |
| Woodville, Fl., U.S. | B2 | 86 |
| Woodville, Ga., U.S. | C3 | 87 |
| Woodville, Ms., U.S. | D2 | 101 |
| Woodville, Oh., U.S. | A2 | 112 |
| Woodville, Tx., U.S. | D5 | 120 |
| Woodward, Al., U.S. | B3 | 78 |
| Woodward, Ia., U.S. | C4 | 92 |
| Woodward, Ok., U.S. | A2 | 113 |
| Woodward, co., Ok., U.S. | A2 | 113 |
| Woodwards Cove, N.B. | E3 | 71 |
| Woodway, Tx., U.S. | *D4 | 120 |
| Woodway, Va., U.S. | f9 | 123 |
| Woodworth, La., U.S. | C3 | 95 |
| Woodworth, N.D., U.S. | B6 | 111 |
| Woody, co., Can. | C1 | 70 |
| Wooldridge, Mo., U.S. | C5 | 102 |
| Wooler, Eng., U.K. | E6 | 13 |
| Woolford, Md., U.S. | C5 | 97 |
| Woollahra, Austl. | *F9 | 50 |
| Woolmarket, Ms., U.S. | E5 | 101 |
| Woolper Creek, stm., Ky., U.S. | h13 | 94 |
| Woolrich, Pa., U.S. | D7 | 115 |
| Woolsey Peak, mtn., Az., U.S. | D3 | 80 |
| Woolstock, Ia., U.S. | B4 | 92 |
| Woolwich, Me., U.S. | g8 | 96 |
| Woomera, Austl. | F7 | 50 |
| Woonsocket, R.I., U.S. | A3 | 116 |
| Woonsocket, S.D., U.S. | C7 | 118 |
| Woonsocket Reservoir Number Three, res., R.I., U.S. | B3 | 116 |
| Wooster, Ar., U.S. | B3 | 81 |
| Wooster, Oh., U.S. | B4 | 112 |
| Woosung, Il., U.S. | B4 | 90 |
| Woqooyi Galbeed, prov., Som. | C5 | 47 |
| Worb, Switz. | C4 | 20 |
| Worbis, E. Ger. | B5 | 19 |
| Worcester, S. Afr. | D2 | 49 |
| Worcester, Eng., U.K. | D5 | 10 |
| Worcester, Ma., U.S. | B4 | 98 |
| Worcester, N.Y., U.S. | C6 | 109 |
| Worcester, Vt., U.S. | C3 | 122 |
| Worcester, co., Md., U.S. | D7 | 97 |
| Worcester, co., Ma., U.S. | A3 | 98 |
| Worcester Mountains, mts., Vt., U.S. | C3 | 122 |
| Worden, Il., U.S. | E4 | 90 |
| Worden, Mt., U.S. | E8 | 103 |
| Worden, Or., U.S. | E5 | 114 |
| Worden Pond, l., R.I., U.S. | F3 | 116 |
| Wordsworth, Sask. | H4 | 75 |
| Workington, Eng., U.K. | A6 | 12 |
| Worksop, Eng., U.K. | A6 | 12 |
| Workum, Neth. | B5 | 17 |
| Worland, Mo., U.S. | C3 | 102 |
| Worland, Wy., U.S. | B5 | 127 |
| Worley, Id., U.S. | B2 | 89 |
| Wormerveer, Neth. | B4 | 17 |
| Worms, W. Ger. | D4 | 18 |
| Worms, Ne., U.S. | C7 | 104 |
| Worms Head, c., Wales, U.K. | C4 | 12 |
| Woronoco, Ma., U.S. | B2 | 98 |
| Worth, Il., U.S. | k9 | 90 |
| Worth, Mo., U.S. | A3 | 102 |
| Worth, co., Ga., U.S. | E3 | 87 |
| Worth, co., Ia., U.S. | A4 | 92 |
| Worth, co., Mo., U.S. | A3 | 102 |
| Wortham, Tx., U.S. | D4 | 120 |
| Worthing, Eng., U.K. | E6 | 10 |
| Worthing, S.D., U.S. | D9 | 118 |
| Worthington, In., U.S. | F4 | 91 |
| Worthington, Ky., U.S. | B7 | 94 |
| Worthington, Ma., U.S. | B2 | 98 |
| Worthington, Mn., U.S. | G3 | 100 |
| Worthington, Oh., U.S. | B2 | 112 |
| Worthington, Pa., U.S. | E2 | 115 |
| Worthington, W.V., U.S. | k10 | 125 |
| Worthington Knob, mtn., Tn., U.S. | D8 | 119 |
| Worthington Peak, mtn., Nv., U.S. | F6 | 105 |
| Worthington Springs, Fl., U.S. | B4 | 86 |
| Worthville, Ky., U.S. | B4 | 94 |
| Worthville, N.C., U.S. | B3 | 110 |
| Worton, Md., U.S. | B5 | 97 |
| Wostok, Alta. | C4 | 68 |
| Wotton, Que. | D6 | 74 |
| Woubrugge, Neth. | D8 | 17 |
| Wrangell Mountains, mts., Ak., U.S. | C11 | 79 |
| Wrangell-Saint Elias National Park, Ak., U.S. | C11 | 79 |
| Wrath, Cape, c., Scot., U.K. | A4 | 10 |
| Wray, Co., U.S. | A8 | 83 |
| Wray, Ga., U.S. | E3 | 87 |
| Wren, Oh., U.S. | B1 | 112 |
| Wrens, Ga., U.S. | C4 | 87 |
| Wrenshall, Mn., U.S. | D6 | 100 |
| Wrentham, Alta. | E4 | 68 |
| Wrentham, Ma., U.S. | B5 | 98 |
| Wrexham, Wales, U.K. | D5 | 10 |
| Wriezen, E. Ger. | B7 | 18 |
| Wright, Al., U.S. | A2 | 78 |
| Wright, Ar., U.S. | C3 | 81 |
| Wright, Fl., U.S. | *u15 | 86 |
| Wright, Ia., U.S. | C5 | 92 |
| Wright, Ks., U.S. | E4 | 93 |
| Wright, co., Ia., U.S. | B4 | 92 |
| Wright, co., Mn., U.S. | E4 | 100 |
| Wright, co., Mo., U.S. | D5 | 102 |
| Wright, Mount, mtn., Mt., U.S. | C4 | 103 |
| Wright Brothers National Memorial, hist., N.C., U.S. | A7 | 110 |
| Wright City, Mo., U.S. | C6 | 102 |
| Wright City, Ok., U.S. | C6 | 113 |
| Wright-Patterson Air Force Base, mil., Oh., U.S. | C1 | 112 |
| Wrightson, Mount, mtn., Az., U.S. | F5 | 80 |
| Wrightstown, N.J., U.S. | C3 | 107 |
| Wrightstown, Wi., U.S. | D5 | 126 |
| Wrightsville, Ar., U.S. | C3 | 81 |
| Wrightsville, Ga., U.S. | D4 | 87 |
| Wrightsville, Pa., U.S. | F8 | 115 |
| Wrightsville Beach, N.C., U.S. | C5 | 110 |
| Wrightsville Reservoir, res., Vt., U.S. | C4 | 122 |
| Wrightwood, Ca., U.S. | E5 | 82 |
| Wrigley, N.W. Ter. | D8 | 66 |
| Wrigley, Tn., U.S. | B4 | 119 |
| Wrigley Gulf, b., Ant. | B36 | 7 |
| Wrocław (Breslau), Pol. | C4 | 26 |
| Wrong Lake, l., Man. | C3 | 70 |
| Wroxeter, Ont. | D3 | 73 |
| Wroxham, Eng., U.K. | B9 | 12 |
| Wroxton, Sask. | F5 | 75 |
| Września, Pol. | B4 | 26 |
| Wschowa, Pol. | C4 | 26 |
| Wuchang, China | D3 | 33 |
| Wuchou see Wuzhou, China | G7 | 31 |
| Wuchuan, China | J3 | 32 |
| Wuchuan, China | D4 | 32 |
| Wuchuan, China | D3 | 32 |
| Wuda, China | D6 | 31 |
| Wudaoliang, China | C1 | 70 |
| Wudu, China | E6 | 31 |
| Wufeng, China | I4 | 32 |
| Wugang, China | F7 | 31 |
| Wuhai, China | E2 | 32 |
| Wuhan, China | E7 | 31 |
| Wuhe, China | H7 | 32 |
| Wuhu, China | E8 | 31 |
| Wu Jiang, stm., China | F6 | 31 |
| Wukari, Nig. | G7 | 45 |
| Wum, Cam. | D2 | 46 |
| Wümme, stm., W. Ger. | E3 | 15 |
| Wunnumin, W. Ger. | A4 | 19 |
| Wupatki National Monument, Az., U.S. | B4 | 80 |
| Wuppertal, W. Ger. | C3 | 18 |
| Wurtsboro, N.Y., U.S. | D6 | 109 |
| Wurtsmith Air Force Base, mil., Mi., U.S. | D7 | 99 |
| Württemberg, hist. reg., W. Ger. | D4 | 18 |
| Würzburg, W. Ger. | D4 | 18 |
| Wurzen, E. Ger. | C6 | 18 |
| Wushan, China | E8 | 31 |
| Wuskwatim Lake, l., Man. | B2 | 70 |
| Wusong, China | I9 | 32 |
| Wusuli (Ussuri), stm., Asia | B11 | 31 |
| Wutongqiao, China | F5 | 31 |
| Wuwei, China | D5 | 31 |
| Wuwei, China | I7 | 32 |
| Wuxi, China | E9 | 31 |
| Wuxing, China | E9 | 31 |
| Wuyi, China | F6 | 32 |
| Wuyiling, China | B10 | 31 |
| Wuyuan, China | C6 | 31 |
| Wuzhan, China | A3 | 33 |
| Wuzhi Peak, mtn., China | B3 | 34 |
| Wuzhong, China | E6 | 31 |
| Wuzhou (Wuchou), China | G7 | 31 |
| Wyaconda, Mo., U.S. | A6 | 102 |
| Wyaconda, stm., Mo., U.S. | A6 | 102 |
| Wyalusing, Pa., U.S. | C9 | 115 |
| Wyandanch, N.Y., U.S. | *n15 | 109 |
| Wyandot, co., Oh., U.S. | B2 | 112 |
| Wyandotte, Mi., U.S. | F7 | 99 |
| Wyandotte, co., Ks., U.S. | C9 | 93 |
| Wyandra, Austl. | E6 | 51 |
| Wyanet, Il., U.S. | B4 | 90 |
| Wyarno, Wy., U.S. | B6 | 127 |
| Wyatt, In., U.S. | A5 | 91 |
| Wyatt, Mo., U.S. | E8 | 102 |
| Wyckoff, N.J., U.S. | *A4 | 107 |
| Wyco, W.V., U.S. | D3 | 125 |
| Wye, stm., U.K. | C5 | 12 |
| Wyebridge, Ont. | C5 | 73 |
| Wye Mills, Md., U.S. | C5 | 97 |
| Wyevale, Ont. | C5 | 73 |
| Wyeville, Wi., U.S. | D3 | 126 |
| Wykoff, Mn., U.S. | G6 | 100 |
| Wylie, Lake, res., U.S. | A5 | 117 |
| Wylliesburg, Va., U.S. | C4 | 123 |
| Wyman, Me., U.S. | C2 | 96 |
| Wyman Lake, res., Me., U.S. | C3 | 96 |
| Wymark, Sask. | G2 | 75 |
| Wymondham, Eng., U.K. | B9 | 12 |
| Wymore, Ne., U.S. | D9 | 104 |
| Wynbring, Austl. | A2 | 119 |
| Wyndel, B.C. | E9 | 69 |
| Wyndmere, N.D., U.S. | C8 | 111 |
| Wynne, Ar., U.S. | B5 | 81 |
| Wynne, Wi., U.S. | B5 | 81 |
| Wynnewood, Ok., U.S. | C4 | 113 |
| Wynona, Ok., U.S. | A5 | 113 |
| Wynot, Ne., U.S. | B8 | 104 |
| Wynyard, Austl. | o15 | 50 |
| Wynyard, Sask. | F3 | 75 |
| Wyocena, Wi., U.S. | E4 | 126 |
| Wyodak, Wy., U.S. | B7 | 127 |
| Wyola, Mt., U.S. | E9 | 103 |
| Wyoming, De., U.S. | D3 | 85 |
| Wyoming, Il., U.S. | B4 | 90 |
| Wyoming, Ia., U.S. | B6 | 92 |
| Wyoming, Mi., U.S. | F5 | 99 |
| Wyoming, Mn., U.S. | E6 | 100 |

| Name | Map Ref. | Page |
|---|---|---|
| Wyoming, N.Y., U.S. | C2 | 109 |
| Wyoming, Oh., U.S. | o13 | 112 |
| Wyoming, Pa., U.S. | n17 | 115 |
| Wyoming, R.I., U.S. | E2 | 116 |
| *Wyoming, co., N.Y., U.S.* | C2 | 109 |
| *Wyoming, co., Pa., U.S.* | D9 | 115 |
| *Wyoming, co., W.V., U.S.* | D3 | 125 |
| *Wyoming, state, U.S.* | C5 | 127 |
| *Wyoming Peak, mtn., Wy., U.S.* | D2 | 127 |
| *Wyoming Range, mts., Wy., U.S.* | D2 | 127 |
| Wyomissing, Pa., U.S. | F10 | 115 |
| Wyrzysk, Pol. | B4 | 26 |
| *Wysocking Bay, b., N.C., U.S.* | B7 | 110 |
| Wysokie Mazowieckie, Pol. | B7 | 26 |
| Wyszków, Pol. | B6 | 26 |
| *Wythe, co., Va., U.S.* | D1 | 123 |
| Wytheville, Va., U.S. | D1 | 123 |
| Wytopitlock, Me., U.S. | C4 | 96 |
| *Wyvis, Ben, mtn., Scot., U.K.* | C4 | 13 |
| **X** | | |
| Xaafuun, Som. | C7 | 47 |
| Xainza, China | B8 | 36 |
| Xai-Xai (João Belo), Moz. | C5 | 49 |
| Xalin, Som. | D6 | 47 |
| Xambioá, Braz. | D5 | 59 |
| Xam Nua, Laos | A2 | 34 |
| Xangongo, Ang. | E1 | 48 |
| Xánthi, Grc. | B5 | 40 |
| *Xapecó, stm., Braz.* | D2 | 56 |
| Xapuri, Braz. | D5 | 55 |
| Xarardheere, Som. | E6 | 47 |
| *Xau, I., Bots.* | B3 | 49 |
| Xbonil, Mex. | D6 | 63 |
| Xcalak, Mex. | D7 | 63 |
| Xenia, Il., U.S. | E5 | 90 |
| Xenia, Oh., U.S. | C2 | 112 |
| Xiaguan, China | F5 | 31 |
| Xiajiang, China | F8 | 31 |
| Xiajin, China | F6 | 32 |
| Xiamen (Amoy), China | G8 | 31 |
| Xi'an (Sian), China | E6 | 31 |
| Xiangfan, China | E7 | 31 |
| *Xiang Jiang, stm., China* | J5 | 32 |
| Xiangkhoang, Laos | B2 | 34 |
| Xiangtan, China | F7 | 31 |
| Xiangxiang, China | K5 | 32 |
| Xianning, China | J6 | 32 |
| Xianyang, China | E6 | 31 |
| Xianyou, China | F8 | 31 |
| *Xiao Hinggan Ling (Lesser Khingan Range), mts., China* | B10 | 31 |
| Xiapu, China | F9 | 31 |
| Xichang, China | F5 | 31 |
| Xifeng, China | C11 | 31 |
| Xigazê, China | C8 | 36 |
| *Xi Jiang, stm., China* | G7 | 31 |
| Xilitla, Mex. | m14 | 63 |
| Xin Barag Zuoqi, China | B8 | 31 |
| Xinbin, China | D11 | 32 |
| Xincai, China | H6 | 32 |
| Xingcheng, China | D9 | 32 |
| Xinghua, China | H8 | 32 |
| *Xingkai Hu (Lake Khanka), l., Asia* | B11 | 31 |
| Xingtai, China | D7 | 31 |
| *Xingu, stm., Braz.* | C4 | 59 |
| Xinhua, China | K4 | 32 |
| Xining, China | D5 | 31 |
| Xinjiang, China | G4 | 32 |
| *Xinjiang Uygur, prov., China* | C2 | 31 |
| Xinjin, China | D9 | 31 |
| Xinmin, China | C9 | 31 |
| Xinning, China | K4 | 32 |
| Xintai, China | *D8 | 31 |
| Xinwen, China | G7 | 32 |
| Xinxian, China | D7 | 31 |
| Xinxiang, China | D9 | 31 |
| Xinyang, China | E7 | 31 |
| Xinye, China | H5 | 32 |
| *Xinyi He, stm., China* | G8 | 32 |
| Xinzhou, China | D7 | 31 |
| Xique-Xique, Braz. | D2 | 57 |
| Xishui, China | I6 | 32 |
| Xi Ujimqin Qi, China | B7 | 32 |
| Xiushui, China | J6 | 32 |
| *Xixabangma Mountain, mtn., Asia* | C8 | 36 |
| Xixian, China | F4 | 32 |
| *Xizang see Tibet, prov., China* | E3 | 31 |
| Xochimilco (part of Mexico City), Mex. | h9 | 63 |
| Xuancheng, China | I8 | 32 |
| Xuanhua, China | C2 | 31 |
| Xuchang, China | E7 | 31 |
| Xuddun, Som. | D6 | 47 |
| Xuddur, Som. | E5 | 47 |
| Xuguit Qi (Yakeshi), China | *B9 | 31 |
| Xunhe, China | B4 | 33 |
| Xunke, China | B4 | 33 |
| Xupu, China | K4 | 32 |
| Xuwen, China | H8 | 32 |
| Xuyi, China | H6 | 32 |
| *Xuy Nong, is., Viet.* | B7 | 34 |
| Xuyong, China | F6 | 31 |
| Xuzhou (Süchow), China | E8 | 31 |
| **Y** | | |
| Ya'an, China | F5 | 31 |
| Ya'bad, Isr. Occ. | B7 | 41 |
| Yabassi, Cam. | E2 | 46 |
| *Yabbenohr Island, i., Marsh Is.* | S17 | 52 |
| Yablis, Nic. | C6 | 62 |
| *Yablonovy Mountains, mts., Sov. Un.* | D14 | 29 |
| Yabu, Japan | N5 | 52 |
| Yabucoa, P.R. | B4 | 65 |
| *Yacata, i., Fiji* | H16 | 52 |
| Yachats, Or., U.S. | C2 | 114 |
| Yacheng, China | D3 | 34 |
| *Yaco (Iaco), stm., S.A.* | D3 | 58 |
| Yacolt, Wa., U.S. | D3 | 124 |
| Yacuiba, Bol. | D3 | 55 |
| Yad Eli'ezer, Isr. | h10 | 41 |
| *Yadkin, co., N.C., U.S.* | A2 | 110 |
| *Yadkin, stm., N.C., U.S.* | A2 | 110 |
| Yadkinville, N.C., U.S. | A2 | 110 |
| Yad Mordekhay, Isr. | D12 | 41 |
| Yadong, China | D12 | 37 |
| *Yadua, i., Fiji* | H15 | 52 |
| *Yagasa Cluster, is., Fiji* | I16 | 52 |
| Yagoua, Cam. | C3 | 46 |
| Yaguajay, Cuba | C4 | 64 |
| *Yaguas, stm., Peru* | D3 | 58 |
| Yahk, B.C. | E9 | 69 |
| Yahuma, Zaire | A3 | 48 |
| *Yainax Butte, mtn., Or., U.S.* | E5 | 114 |
| Yaizu, Japan | o17 | 33 |
| Yakima, Wa., U.S. | C5 | 124 |
| *Yakima, co., Wa., U.S.* | C4 | 124 |
| *Yakima, stm., Wa., U.S.* | C6 | 124 |
| Yakima Indian Reservation, Wa., U.S. | C5 | 124 |
| *Yakima Ridge, mtn., Wa., U.S.* | C5 | 124 |
| *Yakima Valley, val., Wa., U.S.* | C5 | 124 |
| Yako, Burkina | D4 | 45 |
| *Yakobi Island, i., Ak., U.S.* | m21 | 79 |
| Yakoma, Zaire | A3 | 48 |
| *Yaku Island, i., Japan* | E11 | 31 |
| Yakutat, Ak., U.S. | D12 | 79 |
| *Yakutat Bay, b., Ak., U.S.* | D11 | 79 |
| Yakutsk, Sov. Un. | C15 | 29 |
| Yala, Thai. | D2 | 34 |
| Yalaha, Fl., U.S. | D5 | 86 |
| Yale, B.C. | E7 | 69 |
| Yale, Il., U.S. | D5 | 90 |
| Yale, Ia., U.S. | C3 | 92 |
| Yale, Mi., U.S. | E8 | 99 |
| Yale, Ok., U.S. | A5 | 113 |
| Yale, S.D., U.S. | C8 | 118 |
| Yale, Va., U.S. | D5 | 123 |
| *Yale, Mount, mtn., Co., U.S.* | C5 | 83 |
| *Yale Lake, res., Wa., U.S.* | D3 | 124 |
| Yalinga, Cen. Afr. Rep. | D4 | 46 |
| *Yallahs Hill, hill, Jam.* | F15 | 65 |
| *Yalobusha, co., Ms., U.S.* | A4 | 101 |
| *Yalobusha, stm., Ms., U.S.* | B4 | 101 |
| *Yalong Jiang, stm., China* | E5 | 31 |
| Yalova, Tur. | B5 | 40 |
| Yalta, Sov. Un. | I10 | 27 |
| Yalu, China | B9 | 31 |
| *Yalu Jiang, stm., Asia* | C9 | 31 |
| Yalutorovsk, Sov. Un. | B7 | 28 |
| Yalvaç, Tur. | C8 | 40 |
| Yamachiche, Que. | C5 | 74 |
| Yamagata, Japan | D13 | 31 |
| Yamaguchi, Japan | I5 | 33 |
| *Yamal Peninsula, pen., Sov. Un.* | B9 | 29 |
| *Yamantau, Mount, mtn., Sov. Un.* | D8 | 29 |
| Yamaska (Saint-Michel), Que. | C5 | 74 |
| *Yamaska, co., Que.* | C5 | 74 |
| Yambio, Sud. | E2 | 47 |
| Yambol, Bul. | D8 | 24 |
| *Yamdena, i., Indon.* | G9 | 34 |
| Yamethin, Burma | D10 | 36 |
| Yamhill, Or., U.S. | h11 | 114 |
| *Yamhill, co., Or., U.S.* | B3 | 114 |
| Yamkino, Sov. Un. | n18 | 27 |
| *Yamma Yamma, Lake, l., Austl.* | E7 | 50 |
| Yamoussoukro, I.C. | E3 | 45 |
| Yampa, Co., U.S. | A4 | 83 |
| *Yampa, stm., Co., U.S.* | A2 | 83 |
| *Yampa Plateau, plat., U.S.* | A1 | 83 |
| Yamparáez, Bol. | C2 | 55 |
| *Yamsay Mountain, mtn., Or., U.S.* | E5 | 114 |
| Yamsk, Sov. Un. | D18 | 29 |
| *Yamuna, stm., India* | C7 | 36 |
| *Yamzho Yumco, l., China* | C9 | 36 |
| *Yana, stm., Sov. Un.* | C16 | 29 |
| Yanac, Austl. | H3 | 51 |
| Yanam, India | E7 | 36 |
| Yan'an, China | D6 | 31 |
| Yanaoca, Peru | D3 | 58 |
| Yanaul, Sov. Un. | D20 | 8 |
| Yanbu' al Bahr, Sau. Ar. | C3 | 38 |
| *Yancey, co., N.C., U.S.* | f10 | 110 |
| Yanceyville, N.C., U.S. | A3 | 110 |
| Yancheng, China | *E9 | 31 |
| Yancheng, China | H9 | 32 |
| Yancheng, China | H5 | 32 |
| Yanco Creek, Sask. | E3 | 75 |
| Yanfolila, Mali | D3 | 45 |
| Yangambi, Zaire | A4 | 48 |
| Yangbajain, China | B13 | 37 |
| *Yangchou see Yangzhou, China* | E8 | 31 |
| Yangchun, China | G7 | 31 |
| Yangdök, N. Kor. | G3 | 33 |
| Yangiyul, Sov. Un. | G22 | 8 |
| Yangjiang, China | G7 | 31 |
| Yangquan, China | D7 | 31 |
| *Yangtze (Chang Jiang), stm., China* | E8 | 31 |
| Yangxian, China | H2 | 32 |
| Yangyang, S. Kor. | G4 | 33 |
| Yangzhou (Yangchou), China | E8 | 31 |
| Yanji, China | C10 | 31 |
| Yankeetown, Fl., U.S. | C4 | 86 |
| Yankeetown, In., U.S. | I3 | 91 |
| Yankton, S.D., U.S. | E8 | 118 |
| *Yankton, co., S.D., U.S.* | D8 | 118 |
| Yanonge, Zaire | A3 | 48 |
| Yanqi, China | C2 | 31 |
| Yanshan, China | E7 | 32 |
| Yanshi, China | G5 | 32 |
| Yanshou, China | D4 | 33 |
| Yantai, China | D9 | 31 |
| *Yantic, stm., Ct., U.S.* | C7 | 84 |
| Yantley, Al., U.S. | C1 | 78 |
| *Yantra, stm., Bul.* | D7 | 24 |
| Yanush, Ok., U.S. | C6 | 113 |
| Yanzhou, China | D8 | 31 |
| Yao, Chad | C2 | 46 |
| Yao, Japan | *I7 | 33 |
| Yaosca, Nic. | D5 | 62 |
| Yaoundé, Cam. | E2 | 46 |
| *Yap, i., Micron.* | F8 | 6 |
| *Yapen, i., Indon.* | F9 | 34 |
| Yaphank, N.Y., U.S. | *n16 | 109 |
| *Yaqeta, i., Fiji* | H14 | 52 |
| *Yaqui, stm., Mex.* | B3 | 63 |
| Yar, Sov. Un. | B4 | 28 |
| *Yaracuy, state, Ven.* | A4 | 60 |
| Yaraka, Austl. | D7 | 50 |
| Yardville, N.J., U.S. | C3 | 107 |
| *Yarí, stm., Col.* | C5 | 60 |
| Yaritagua, Ven. | A4 | 60 |
| Yarkovo, Sov. Un. | B7 | 28 |
| Yarmouth, N.S. | F3 | 71 |
| Yarmouth, Ia., U.S. | C6 | 92 |
| Yarmouth, Me., U.S. | E2 | 96 |
| Yarmouth, Ma., U.S. | C7 | 98 |
| *Yarmouth, co., N.S.* | E2 | 71 |
| Yarmouth Port, Ma., U.S. | *C7 | 98 |
| Yarnell, Az., U.S. | C3 | 80 |
| Yaroslavl, Sov. Un. | F18 | 14 |
| *Yarqon, stm., Isr.* | B6 | 41 |
| Yarram, Austl. | I6 | 51 |
| Yarrow, B.C. | f13 | 69 |
| Yarrowsburg, Md., U.S. | B2 | 97 |
| Yartsevo, Sov. Un. | C27 | 8 |
| Yartsevo, Sov. Un. | D9 | 27 |
| Yarumal, Col. | B2 | 60 |
| *Yasawa, i., Fiji* | H14 | 52 |
| *Yasawa Group, is., Fiji* | H14 | 52 |
| Yashi, Nig. | D6 | 45 |
| Yasinovataya, Sov. Un. | q20 | 27 |
| Yasinya, Sov. Un. | A7 | 24 |
| Yasothon, Thai. | E6 | 35 |
| Yass, Austl. | F8 | 50 |
| Yata, Bol. | B5 | 55 |
| *Yates, co., N.Y., U.S.* | C3 | 109 |
| Yatesboro, Pa., U.S. | E3 | 115 |
| Yates Center, Ks., U.S. | E8 | 93 |
| Yates City, Il., U.S. | C3 | 90 |
| Yatesville, Ga., U.S. | D2 | 87 |
| *Yathkyed Lake, l., N.W. Ter.* | D13 | 66 |
| *Yatsuga, Mount, mtn., Japan* | m17 | 33 |
| Yatsushiro, Japan | J5 | 33 |
| *Yatsushiro Sea, Japan* | J4 | 33 |
| Yauca, Peru | E3 | 58 |
| Yauco, P.R. | E2 | 65 |
| *Yauco, Embalse de, res., P.R.* | B2 | 65 |
| Yauli, Peru | D2 | 58 |
| Yaupi, Ec. | B2 | 58 |
| Yauri, Peru | D3 | 58 |
| Yautepec, Mex. | n14 | 63 |
| Yauyos, Peru | D2 | 58 |
| *Yavapai, co., Az., U.S.* | C3 | 80 |
| *Yavarí (Javari), stm., S.A.* | B3 | 58 |
| Yavatmāl, India | G7 | 37 |
| *Yavi, Cerro, mtn., Ven.* | B4 | 60 |
| Yaviza, Pan. | F9 | 62 |
| Yavne, Isr. | C4 | 41 |
| Yavorov, Sov. Un. | G4 | 27 |
| Yawatahama, Japan | J6 | 33 |
| *Yawgoog Pond, l., R.I., U.S.* | E1 | 116 |
| Yaxian, China | B3 | 34 |
| Yazd (Yezd), Iran | B5 | 38 |
| *Yazoo, co., Ms., U.S.* | C3 | 101 |
| *Yazoo, stm., Ms., U.S.* | C3 | 101 |
| Yazoo City, Ms., U.S. | C3 | 101 |
| *Ybbs, stm., Aus.* | D7 | 18 |
| *Yding Skovhøj, hill, Den.* | D3 | 14 |
| Ye, Burma | E10 | 36 |
| Yeadon, Pa., U.S. | p21 | 115 |
| Yeager, Ok., U.S. | B5 | 113 |
| Yeagertown, Pa., U.S. | E6 | 115 |
| Yebbi Bou, Chad | A3 | 46 |
| Yecla, Spain | C5 | 22 |
| Yeddo, In., U.S. | D3 | 91 |
| Yefremov, Sov. Un. | E12 | 27 |
| Yegindybulak, Sov. Un. | D9 | 28 |
| Yegoryevsk, Sov. Un. | D12 | 27 |
| *Yeguas, Punta, c., P.R.* | B4 | 65 |
| Yehud, Isr. | g10 | 41 |
| Yei, Sud. | E3 | 47 |
| Yekaterinoslavka, Sov. Un. | A4 | 33 |
| Yelabuga, Indon. | D19 | 8 |
| Yelabuga, Sov. Un. | B7 | 33 |
| Yelan, Sov. Un. | F14 | 29 |
| Yelan-Kolenovskiy, Sov. Un. | F13 | 27 |
| Yelanskoye, Sov. Un. | C15 | 29 |
| Yelets, Sov. Un. | D6 | 29 |
| Yélimané, Mali | C2 | 45 |
| *Yell, co., Ar., U.S.* | B2 | 81 |
| *Yell, i., Scot., U.K.* | g10 | 11 |
| Yellandu, India | I8 | 37 |
| Yellow, U.S. | u15 | 86 |
| *Yellow, stm., Ga., U.S.* | h8 | 87 |
| *Yellow, stm., In., U.S.* | B4 | 91 |
| *Yellow, stm., Wi., U.S.* | D3 | 126 |
| *Yellow, stm., Wi., U.S.* | C3 | 126 |
| Yellow Creek, Sask. | E3 | 75 |
| *Yellow Creek, stm., Tn., U.S.* | A4 | 119 |
| Yellow Grass, Sask. | H3 | 75 |
| Yellowhead Pass, Can. | C1 | 68 |
| *Yellow see Huang He, stm., China* | D8 | 31 |
| Yellow Jacket, Co., U.S. | D2 | 83 |
| *Yellowjacket Mountains, mts., Id., U.S.* | E4 | 89 |
| Yellowknife, N.W. Ter. | D10 | 66 |
| *Yellow Lake, l., Wi., U.S.* | C1 | 126 |
| *Yellow Medicine, co., Mn., U.S.* | F2 | 100 |
| Yellow Pine, Al., U.S. | D1 | 78 |
| Yellow Pine, Id., U.S. | E3 | 89 |
| *Yellow Sea, Asia* | D9 | 31 |
| Yellow Springs, Md., U.S. | B3 | 97 |
| Yellow Springs, Oh., U.S. | C2 | 112 |
| *Yellowstone, co., Mt., U.S.* | D8 | 103 |
| *Yellowstone, stm., U.S.* | D10 | 103 |
| *Yellowstone, Clarks Fork, stm., U.S.* | F7 | 103 |
| *Yellowstone Lake, l., Wy., U.S.* | B2 | 127 |
| Yellowstone National Park, Wy., U.S. | B2 | 127 |
| *Yellowstone National Park, co., Mt., U.S.* | E6 | 103 |
| Yellowstone National Park, U.S. | B2 | 127 |
| Yellville, Ar., U.S. | A3 | 81 |
| Yelm, Wa., U.S. | C3 | 124 |
| Yelnya, Sov. Un. | D9 | 27 |
| *Yeltes, stm., Spain* | D2 | 22 |
| *Yelverton Bay, b., N.W. Ter.* | k35 | 66 |
| Yelwa, Nig. | D6 | 45 |
| Yemanzhelinsk, Sov. Un. | C6 | 28 |
| Yemassee, S.C., U.S. | F6 | 117 |
| *Yemen, ctry., Asia* | D4 | 38 |
| Yen Bai, Viet. | B6 | 35 |
| Yendéré, Burkina | D4 | 45 |
| Yendi, Ghana | E4 | 45 |
| *Yenice, stm., Tur.* | B9 | 40 |
| *Yenisei Ridge, mts., Sov. Un.* | D27 | 8 |
| Yeniseysk, Sov. Un. | D12 | 29 |
| *Yentna, stm., Ak., U.S.* | f16 | 79 |
| *Yeo Lake, l., Austl.* | E3 | 50 |
| Yeoman, In., U.S. | C4 | 91 |
| *Yeotmal see Yavatmāl, India* | G7 | 37 |
| Yeovil, Eng., U.K. | E5 | 13 |
| *Yeránia Óri, mts., Grc.* | g10 | 25 |
| Yerbas Buena, Chile | E1 | 55 |
| *Yermūk, Nahr al, stm., Asia* | B7 | 41 |
| Yerevan, Sov. Un. | E7 | 29 |
| Yerington, Nv., U.S. | E2 | 105 |
| *Yerington Indian Reservation, Nv., U.S.* | D2 | 105 |
| Yermakovskoye, Sov. Un. | E27 | 8 |
| Yermentau, Sov. Un. | C8 | 28 |
| Yermo, Ca., U.S. | E5 | 82 |
| Yermolayevo, Sov. Un. | C5 | 28 |
| Yerres, Fr. | h10 | 16 |
| *Yerres, stm., Fr.* | F2 | 17 |
| Yerseke, Neth. | C4 | 17 |
| Yershov, Sov. Un. | C3 | 28 |
| *Yerupaja, Nevado, mtn., Peru* | D2 | 58 |
| Yeso, N.M., U.S. | C5 | 108 |
| Yessentuki, Sov. Un. | G17 | 8 |
| Yessey, Sov. Un. | C13 | 29 |
| Yeste, Spain | C4 | 22 |
| Yetter, Ia., U.S. | B3 | 92 |
| *Yeu, Île d', i., Fr.* | D2 | 16 |
| Yevlakh, Sov. Un. | E3 | 28 |
| Yevpatoriya, Sov. Un. | I9 | 27 |
| Yexian, China | F8 | 32 |
| *Yeya, stm., Sov. Un.* | H12 | 27 |
| Yeysk, Sov. Un. | H12 | 27 |
| *Yezd see Yazd, Iran* | B5 | 38 |
| *Yi, stm., Ur.* | E1 | 56 |
| Yibin, China | F5 | 31 |
| Yichang, China | E7 | 31 |
| Yicheng, China | I5 | 32 |
| Yichuan, China | D7 | 31 |
| Yichun, China | B10 | 31 |
| Yichun, China | K6 | 32 |
| Yidu, China | I4 | 32 |
| Yidu, China | F8 | 32 |
| Yigo, Guam | L10 | 52 |
| Yilan, China | B10 | 31 |
| Yiliang, China | D4 | 33 |
| Yinchuan, China | D6 | 31 |
| Yingde, China | G7 | 31 |
| *Ying He, stm., China* | E8 | 31 |
| Yingkou, China | C9 | 31 |
| Yingshang, China | H7 | 32 |
| Yingxian, China | E5 | 32 |
| Yining, China | E11 | 29 |
| *Yin Mountains, mts., China* | D4 | 32 |
| Yirga Alem, Eth. | D4 | 47 |
| Yirol, Sud. | D3 | 47 |
| Yishan, China | G6 | 31 |
| Yithion, Grc. | D4 | 40 |
| Yitong, China | C11 | 32 |
| Yixian, China | D9 | 32 |
| Yixing, China | I8 | 32 |
| Yiyang, China | F7 | 31 |
| *Ylig Bay, b., Guam* | M10 | 52 |
| *Ylikitka, l., Fin.* | D13 | 14 |
| *Ymers, i., Grnld.* | B16 | 128 |
| Ymir, B.C. | E9 | 69 |
| Yoakum, Tx., U.S. | E4 | 120 |
| *Yoakum, co., Tx., U.S.* | C1 | 120 |
| *Yockanookany, stm., Ms., U.S.* | C4 | 101 |
| *Yocona, stm., Ms., U.S.* | A4 | 101 |
| Yoder, In., U.S. | C7 | 91 |
| Yoder, Ks., U.S. | g11 | 93 |
| Yoder, Wy., U.S. | E8 | 127 |
| Yogyakarta, Indon. | G4 | 34 |
| Yoho National Park, B.C. | D9 | 69 |
| Yoichi, Japan | E10 | 33 |
| *Yojoa, Lago de, l., Hond.* | C3 | 62 |
| Yokadouma, Cam. | E2 | 46 |
| Yokkaichi, Japan | E12 | 31 |
| Yoko, Cam. | D2 | 46 |
| *Yokote Island, i., Japan* | L4 | 33 |
| Yokohama, Japan | D12 | 31 |
| Yokoshiba, Japan | n19 | 33 |
| Yokosuka, Japan | D12 | 31 |
| Yokote, Japan | G10 | 33 |
| Yola, Nig. | E7 | 45 |
| *Yolo, co., Ca., U.S.* | C2 | 82 |
| Yolyn, W.V., U.S. | n12 | 125 |
| *Yom, stm., Thai.* | B1 | 34 |
| Yomba Indian Reservation, Nv., U.S. | D4 | 105 |
| Yona, Guam | M10 | 52 |
| Yonabaru, Japan | O5 | 52 |
| *Yonaha Mountain, hill, Japan* | N6 | 52 |
| Yoncalla, Or., U.S. | D3 | 114 |
| Yonezawa, Japan | H10 | 33 |
| Yong'an, China | F8 | 31 |
| Yŏngan, N. Kor. | F4 | 33 |
| Yonges Island, S.C., U.S. | F7 | 117 |
| Yonghŭng, N. Kor. | G3 | 33 |
| *Yŏngil Bay, b., S. Kor.* | H4 | 33 |
| Yongji, China | G4 | 32 |
| Yongnian, China | D9 | 31 |
| Yongshou, China | G2 | 32 |
| Yongshun, China | F6 | 31 |
| Yongxiu, China | J6 | 32 |
| Yonkers, N.Y., U.S. | E7 | 109 |
| *Yonne, stm., Fr.* | D5 | 16 |
| Yopal, Col. | B2 | 60 |
| Yorba Linda, Ca., U.S. | *n13 | 82 |
| York, Austl. | F2 | 50 |
| York, Ont. | D5 | 73 |
| York, Eng., U.K. | D6 | 10 |
| York, Al., U.S. | C1 | 78 |
| York, Il., U.S. | D6 | 90 |
| York, In., U.S. | A8 | 91 |
| York, Me., U.S. | E2 | 96 |
| York, N.D., U.S. | A6 | 111 |
| York, Pa., U.S. | G8 | 115 |
| York, S.C., U.S. | B5 | 117 |
| *York, co., N.B.* | C3 | 71 |
| *York, co., Me., U.S.* | E2 | 96 |
| *York, co., Ne., U.S.* | D8 | 104 |
| *York, co., Pa., U.S.* | G8 | 115 |
| *York, co., S.C., U.S.* | A5 | 117 |
| *York, co., Va., U.S.* | C6 | 123 |
| *York, Cape, c., Austl.* | B7 | 50 |
| *York, Kap, c., Grnld.* | B14 | 61 |
| York Beach, Me., U.S. | E2 | 96 |
| *Yorke Peninsula, pen., Austl.* | F6 | 50 |
| Yorketown, N.J., U.S. | *C4 | 107 |
| York Factory, Man. | *C4 | 107 |
| York Harbor, Me., U.S. | E2 | 96 |
| York Haven, Pa., U.S. | F8 | 115 |
| Yorklyn, De., U.S. | A3 | 85 |
| *York Point, c., Newf.* | C4 | 72 |
| Yorkshire, N.Y., U.S. | C2 | 109 |
| York Springs, Pa., U.S. | F7 | 115 |
| Yorkton, Sask. | F4 | 75 |
| Yorktown, In., U.S. | D6 | 91 |
| Yorktown, Tx., U.S. | E4 | 120 |
| Yorktown, Va., U.S. | C6 | 123 |
| Yorktown Heights, N.Y., U.S. | *D7 | 109 |
| Yorktown Manor, R.I., U.S. | C3 | 116 |
| Yorkville, Il., U.S. | B5 | 90 |
| Yorkville, N.Y., U.S. | B5 | 109 |
| Yorkville, Oh., U.S. | B5 | 112 |
| Yorkville, Tn., U.S. | A2 | 119 |
| Yoro, Hond. | C4 | 62 |
| Yorosso, Mali | D4 | 45 |
| Yoseki, Zaire | A3 | 48 |
| Yosemite, Ky., U.S. | C5 | 94 |
| Yosemite National Park, Ca., U.S. | D4 | 82 |
| Yosemite National Park, Ca., U.S. | D4 | 82 |
| Yoshkar-Ola, Sov. Un. | B3 | 28 |
| Yost, Ut., U.S. | B2 | 121 |
| Yost Lake, Ok., U.S. | A5 | 113 |
| Yosu, S. Kor. | I3 | 33 |
| Yotala, Bol. | C2 | 55 |
| Yotvata, Isr. | E7 | 41 |
| Youbou, B.C. | g11 | 69 |
| Youghal, Ire. | D2 | 10 |
| *Youghal Bay, b., Ire.* | E3 | 10 |
| *Youghiogheny, stm., U.S.* | F2 | 115 |
| *Youghiogheny River Lake, res., U.S.* | G3 | 115 |
| *You Jiang, stm., China* | G6 | 31 |
| Youkounkoun, Gui. | D2 | 45 |
| Young, Austl. | G9 | 51 |
| Young, Sask. | F3 | 75 |
| Young, Az., U.S. | C5 | 80 |
| Young, Ur. | E1 | 56 |
| *Young, co., Tx., U.S.* | C3 | 120 |
| Young America, In., U.S. | C5 | 91 |
| Young Harris, Ga., U.S. | B3 | 87 |
| *Youngs, Lake, l., Wa., U.S.* | f11 | 124 |
| Youngs Creek, In., U.S. | H4 | 91 |
| Youngs Point, Ont. | C6 | 73 |
| Youngstown, Alta. | D5 | 68 |
| Youngstown, Fl., U.S. | B1 | 86 |
| Youngstown, N.Y., U.S. | B1 | 109 |
| Youngstown, Oh., U.S. | A5 | 112 |
| Youngsville, La., U.S. | D3 | 95 |
| Youngsville, N.C., U.S. | A4 | 110 |
| Youngsville, N.M., U.S. | A3 | 108 |
| Youngsville, Pa., U.S. | C3 | 115 |
| Youngtown, Az., U.S. | k8 | 80 |
| Youngwood, Pa., U.S. | F2 | 115 |
| Youssoufia, Mor. | C3 | 44 |
| Youxi, China | K8 | 32 |
| Youyang, China | J3 | 32 |
| Youyu, China | C7 | 31 |
| Yozgat, Tur. | C10 | 40 |
| Ypacaraí, Para. | D13 | 14 |
| *Ypané, stm., Para.* | D4 | 55 |
| *Ypres see Ieper, Bel.* | B5 | 16 |
| Ypsilanti, Mi., U.S. | F7 | 99 |
| Ypsilanti, N.D., U.S. | C7 | 111 |
| Yreka, Ca., U.S. | B2 | 82 |
| Yssingeaux, Fr. | E6 | 16 |
| Ystad, Swe. | J5 | 14 |
| *Ythan, stm., Scot., U.K.* | C6 | 13 |
| *Yu'alliq, Jabal, mtn., Eg.* | D5 | 41 |
| Yuan'an, China | E2 | 32 |
| Yuanjiang, China | G5 | 31 |
| *Yuan Jiang (Red), stm., Asia* | G5 | 36 |
| *Yuan Jiang (Red), stm., China* | G5 | 36 |
| Yuanling, China | F7 | 31 |
| Yuanping, China | D9 | 31 |
| Yuanshi, China | F6 | 32 |
| *Yuba, co., Ca., U.S.* | C3 | 82 |
| *Yuba, stm., Ca., U.S.* | C3 | 82 |
| Yuba City, Ca., U.S. | C3 | 82 |
| Yūbari, Japan | E10 | 33 |
| Yucaipa, Ca., U.S. | *E5 | 82 |
| *Yucatán, state, Mex.* | C7 | 63 |
| *Yucatan Channel, strt., N.A.* | C7 | 63 |
| Yucca, Az., U.S. | C1 | 80 |
| *Yucca Lake, l., Nv., U.S.* | F5 | 105 |
| *Yucca Mountain, mtn., Nv., U.S.* | G5 | 105 |
| Yucca Valley, Ca., U.S. | *E5 | 82 |
| Yucheng, China | F7 | 32 |
| Yuci, China | D9 | 31 |
| Yudu, China | J5 | 32 |
| Yueqing, China | G8 | 31 |
| Yueyang, China | F7 | 31 |
| *Yug, stm., Sov. Un.* | A3 | 28 |
| *Yugoslavia, ctry., Eur.* | C4 | 24 |
| Yuhuan, China | J9 | 32 |
| Yukhnov, Sov. Un. | D10 | 27 |
| Yukon, Ok., U.S. | B4 | 113 |
| Yukon, W.V., U.S. | D3 | 125 |
| *Yukon, prov., Can.* | C7 | 66 |
| *Yukon, stm., N.A.* | C9 | 79 |
| *Yule Bay, b., Ant.* | B29 | 7 |
| Yulee, Fl., U.S. | B5 | 86 |
| Yuli, Nig. | E7 | 45 |
| Yulin, China | G7 | 31 |
| Yulin, China | B3 | 34 |
| Yulin, China | D6 | 31 |
| Yuma, Az., U.S. | E1 | 80 |
| Yuma, Co., U.S. | A8 | 83 |
| Yuma, Mi., U.S. | D5 | 99 |
| *Yuma, co., Az., U.S.* | E1 | 80 |
| *Yuma, co., Co., U.S.* | A8 | 83 |
| *Yuma Desert, des., Az., U.S.* | E1 | 80 |
| Yuma Marine Corps Air Station, mil., Az., U.S. | E1 | 80 |
| Yumbi, Zaire | B4 | 48 |
| Yumen, China | C4 | 31 |
| Yumenzhen, China | C4 | 31 |
| Yuna, Japan | N6 | 52 |
| *Yuna, stm., Dom. Rep.* | E9 | 64 |
| Yuncheng, China | F4 | 32 |
| *Yungas, reg., Bol.* | C2 | 55 |
| Yungay, Chile | D2 | 55 |
| Yungay, Peru | C2 | 58 |
| *Yun Gui Plateau, plat., China* | F5 | 31 |
| Yunhe, China | J8 | 32 |
| *Yunjinghong see Jinghong, China* | B5 | 34 |
| *Yunnan, prov., China* | F5 | 31 |
| *Yunnan Plateau see Yun Gui Plateau, plat., China* | F5 | 31 |
| Yunta, Austl. | F2 | 51 |
| Yunxian, China | E8 | 31 |
| Yunxiao, China | K7 | 32 |
| *Yura, stm., Bol.* | C2 | 55 |
| Yurécuaro, Mex. | m12 | 63 |
| Yurga, Sov. Un. | D25 | 8 |
| Yurimaguas, Peru | B2 | 58 |
| Yurino, Sov. Un. | C16 | 27 |
| Yuriria, Mex. | m13 | 63 |
| *Yurochi Island, i., Marsh Is.* | P18 | 52 |
| Yuryevets, Sov. Un. | C6 | 29 |
| Yuryev-Polskiy, Sov. Un. | C12 | 27 |
| Yuscarán, Hond. | D3 | 62 |
| Yushan, China | J8 | 32 |
| *Yü Shan, mtn., Tai.* | M9 | 31 |
| Yushu, China | G7 | 31 |
| Yutan, Ne., U.S. | C9 | 104 |
| Yutian, China | C9 | 36 |
| Yuty, Para. | E4 | 55 |
| Yuwang, China | F3 | 32 |
| Yuxian, China | E6 | 32 |
| Yuyao, China | J9 | 32 |
| Yuzha, Sov. Un. | C13 | 27 |
| Yuzhno-Sakhalinsk, Sov. Un. | E17 | 29 |
| Yuzhnoye, Sov. Un. | C11 | 33 |
| Yverdon, Switz. | E3 | 18 |
| Yvetot, Fr. | C4 | 16 |
| Yvonand, Switz. | C2 | 21 |
| Yzeure, Fr. | D5 | 16 |
| **Z** | | |
| Zaanstad, Neth. | A6 | 16 |
| Zabīd, Yemen | D4 | 38 |
| Ząbki, Pol. | k14 | 26 |
| Ząbkowice, Pol. | g10 | 26 |
| Ząbkowice 95[Śląskie], Pol. | C4 | 26 |
| Zābol, Iran | B6 | 38 |
| Zāboli, Iran | H10 | 39 |
| Zabré, Burkina | D4 | 45 |
| Zabrze, Pol. | C5 | 26 |
| Zacapa, Guat. | C3 | 64 |
| Zacapu, Mex. | n13 | 63 |
| Zacatecas, Mex. | C4 | 63 |
| *Zacatecas, state, Mex.* | C4 | 63 |
| Zacatecoluca, El Sal. | D3 | 62 |
| Zachary, La., U.S. | D4 | 95 |
| Zacoalco [de Torres], Mex. | C4 | 63 |
| Zacualpan, Mex. | m14 | 63 |
| Zacualtipán, Mex. | m14 | 63 |
| Zadar, Yugo. | C2 | 24 |
| *Zadetkale, i., Burma* | G3 | 35 |
| *Zadetkyi, i., Burma* | H3 | 35 |
| Zadonsk, Sov. Un. | E12 | 27 |
| *Zafer, Cape, c., N. Cyp.* | E10 | 40 |
| Zafra, Spain | C2 | 22 |
| Zafra, Ok., U.S. | C7 | 113 |
| Żagań, Pol. | C3 | 26 |
| Zaghouan, Tun. | B7 | 44 |
| Zagorá, Grc. | C4 | 25 |
| Zagora, Mor. | C3 | 44 |
| Zagorsk, Sov. Un. | C12 | 27 |
| Zagreb, Yugo. | C2 | 24 |
| *Zagros Mountains, mts., Iran* | E3 | 39 |
| Zähedān, Iran | C6 | 38 |
| Zahl, N.D., U.S. | A2 | 111 |
| Zahlah, Leb. | F10 | 40 |
| Zahna, E. Ger. | B7 | 19 |
| *Zailiyskiy Alatau Mountains, mts., Sov. Un.* | E9 | 28 |
| *Zaire, dept., Ang.* | C1 | 48 |
| *Zaire, ctry., Afr.* | B3 | 48 |
| *Zaire Basin (Congo Basin), Afr.* | B3 | 48 |
| Zaječar, Yugo. | D6 | 24 |
| Zaka, Zimb. | B5 | 49 |
| Zakataly, Sov. Un. | B16 | 40 |
| Zākhū, Iraq | D14 | 40 |
| Zákinthos, Grc. | D3 | 40 |
| *Zákinthos (Zante), i., Grc.* | D3 | 40 |
| Zakopane, Pol. | D5 | 26 |
| Zakroczym, Pol. | B6 | 26 |
| *Zala, stm., Hung.* | B3 | 24 |
| Zalaegerszeg, Hung. | B3 | 24 |
| Zalamea de la Serana, Spain | C3 | 22 |
| Zalamea la Real, Spain | D2 | 22 |
| Zalău, Rom. | B6 | 24 |
| Zaleski, Oh., U.S. | C3 | 112 |
| Zalewo, Pol. | B5 | 26 |
| Zalingei, Sud. | C1 | 47 |
| Zalma, Mo., U.S. | D7 | 102 |
| Zaltbommel, Neth. | C4 | 17 |
| Zama, Ms., U.S. | C4 | 101 |
| *Zambales Mountains, mts., Phil.* | o13 | 34 |
| Zambezi (Balovale), Zam. | D3 | 48 |
| *Zambezi, stm., Afr.* | H8 | 42 |
| *Zambézia, dept., Moz.* | A6 | 49 |
| *Zambia, ctry., Afr.* | D5 | 48 |
| Zamboanga, Phil. | D6 | 34 |
| Zambrano, Col. | B3 | 60 |
| Zambrów, Pol. | B7 | 26 |
| Zamora, Ec. | B2 | 58 |
| Zamora, Spain | B3 | 22 |
| *Zamora-Chinchipe, prov., Ec.* | B2 | 58 |
| Zamora de Hidalgo, Mex. | C4 | 63 |
| Zamość, Pol. | C7 | 26 |
| *Zamzam, Wādī, val., Libya* | B8 | 44 |
| Zanaga, Congo | B1 | 48 |
| Zandvoort, Neth. | A4 | 17 |
| Zanesville, In., U.S. | C7 | 91 |
| Zanesville, Oh., U.S. | C4 | 112 |
| Zanjān, Iran | B4 | 38 |
| *Zanpa Cape, c., Japan* | O5 | 52 |
| *Zante see Zákinthos, i., Grc.* | D3 | 40 |
| *Zanzibar, i., Tan.* | C6 | 48 |
| Zanzibar, Tan. | C6 | 48 |
| Zaozhuang, China | G5 | 31 |
| Zap, N.D., U.S. | B4 | 111 |
| *Zapadna Morava, stm., Yugo.* | D5 | 24 |
| *Západočeský, prov., Czech.* | D8 | 19 |
| Zapala, Arg. | B2 | 54 |
| Zapata, Tx., U.S. | F3 | 120 |
| *Zapata, co., Tx., U.S.* | F3 | 120 |
| *Zapata, Península de, pen., Cuba* | C3 | 64 |
| Zapatoca, Col. | B3 | 60 |
| Zapopan, Mex. | m12 | 63 |
| Zaporozhye, Sov. Un. | E6 | 29 |
| Zapotillo, Ec. | B1 | 58 |
| Zara, Tur. | C11 | 40 |
| Zaragoza, Mex. | B3 | 63 |
| Zaragoza, Mex. | k13 | 63 |
| Zaragoza, Spain | B5 | 22 |
| Zarand, Iran | E9 | 39 |
| Zaraysk, Sov. Un. | D12 | 27 |
| Zaraza, Ven. | B4 | 60 |
| *Zard Küh, mtn., Iran* | E5 | 39 |
| *Zarembo Island, i., Ak., U.S.* | m23 | 79 |
| Zarephath, N.J., U.S. | B3 | 107 |
| Zaria, Nig. | D6 | 45 |
| *Zarqā', Nahr az, stm., Jord.* | B7 | 41 |
| Zarrentin, E. Ger. | B5 | 19 |
| Zarrīn Shahr, Iran | E5 | 39 |
| Zaruma, Ec. | B2 | 58 |
| Zarumilla, Peru | B1 | 58 |
| Zary, Pol. | C3 | 26 |
| Zarzal, Col. | C2 | 60 |
| Zarzis, Tun. | B8 | 44 |
| Zasenbeck, W. Ger. | F4 | 15 |
| Zasieki, Pol. | C3 | 26 |
| Zásmuky, Czech. | o19 | 19 |
| Zastavna, Sov. Un. | A7 | 24 |
| Zastron, S. Afr. | D4 | 49 |
| Žatec, Czech. | C3 | 19 |
| Zator, Pol. | h10 | 26 |
| *Zavala, co., Tx., U.S.* | E3 | 120 |
| Zavitinsk, Sov. Un. | D15 | 29 |
| Zavodo-Petrovskiy, Sov. Un. | B7 | 28 |
| Zawiercie, Pol. | C5 | 26 |
| Zawilah, Libya | D3 | 43 |

| Name | Map Ref. | Page |
|------|----------|------|
| Zāwiyat Masūs, Libya | C4 | 43 |
| Zawr, Ra's az, c., Sau. Ar. | H4 | 39 |
| Zaysan, Sov. Un. | E11 | 29 |
| Zaysan, Lake, l., Sov. Un. | E11 | 29 |
| Zaza, stm., Cuba | C4 | 64 |
| Zbraslav, Czech. | o17 | 26 |
| Žd'ár [nad Sazavou], Czech. | D3 | 26 |
| Zdice, Czech. | o16 | 26 |
| Zdolbunov, Sov. Un. | F6 | 27 |
| Zduńska Wola, Pol. | C5 | 26 |
| Zealandia, Sask. | F2 | 75 |
| Zearing, Ia., U.S. | B4 | 92 |
| Zeballos, B.C. | D4 | 69 |
| Zebla, mtn., Tun. | F2 | 23 |
| Zebrzydowice, Pol. | h9 | 26 |
| Zebulon, Ga., U.S. | C2 | 87 |
| Zebulon, Ky., U.S. | C7 | 94 |
| Zebulon, N.C., U.S. | B4 | 110 |
| Zeebrugge (part of Brugge), Bel. | B5 | 16 |
| Zeeland, Mi., U.S. | F5 | 99 |
| Zeeland, N.D., U.S. | D6 | 111 |
| Zeeland, prov., Neth. | C3 | 17 |
| Zeerust, S. Afr. | C4 | 49 |
| Zefat (Safad), Isr. | F10 | 40 |
| Zegrze, Pol. | k14 | 26 |
| Zehdenick, E. Ger. | B6 | 18 |
| Zeigler, Il., U.S. | F4 | 90 |
| Zeil, Mount, mtn., Austl. | D5 | 50 |
| Zeist, Neth. | A6 | 16 |
| Zeitz, E. Ger. | C6 | 18 |
| Zekiah Swamp Run, stm., Md., U.S. | D4 | 97 |
| Żelechów, Pol. | C6 | 26 |
| Zelenodolsk, Sov. Un. | B3 | 28 |
| Zelenogorsk, Sov. Un. | A7 | 27 |
| Zelenograd, Sov. Un. | C11 | 27 |
| Železná Ruda, Czech. | D8 | 19 |
| Zelienople, Pa., U.S. | E1 | 115 |
| Zell, S.D., U.S. | C7 | 118 |
| Zella-Mehlis, E. Ger. | C5 | 18 |
| Zell am Ziller, Aus. | B7 | 20 |
| Zeller Lake, l., Aus. | B8 | 20 |
| Zelma, Sask. | F3 | 75 |
| Zelzate, Bel. | C3 | 17 |
| Zembra, i., Tun. | F3 | 23 |
| Zemetchino, Sov. Un. | E14 | 27 |
| Zemio, Cen. Afr. Rep. | D5 | 46 |
| Zenda, Ks., U.S. | E5 | 93 |
| Zendeh Jān, Afg. | D10 | 39 |
| Zenica, Yugo. | C3 | 24 |
| Zenith, Ks., U.S. | E5 | 93 |
| Zenith, Wa., U.S. | f11 | 124 |
| Zenon Park, Sask. | D4 | 75 |
| Zenobia Peak, mtn., Co., U.S. | A2 | 83 |
| Zeona, S.D., U.S. | B3 | 118 |
| Zephyr, Tx., U.S. | D3 | 120 |
| Zephyr Cove, Nv., U.S. | E2 | 105 |
| Zephyrhills, Fl., U.S. | D4 | 86 |
| Zerbst, E. Ger. | C6 | 18 |
| Zereh, Gowd-e, depr., Afg. | C3 | 36 |
| Zermatt, Switz. | C3 | 20 |
| Zernez, Switz. | C6 | 20 |
| Zeta, stm., Yugo. | D4 | 24 |
| Zeulenroda, E. Ger. | C6 | 19 |
| Zeven, W. Ger. | E3 | 15 |
| Zevenaar, Neth. | C6 | 17 |
| Zevgolation, Grc. | D3 | 25 |
| Zeya, Sov. Un. | D15 | 29 |
| Zeya, stm., Sov. Un. | D15 | 29 |
| Zeya Reservoir, res., Sov. Un. | f15 | 29 |
| Zgierz, Pol. | C5 | 26 |
| Zgorzelec, Pol. | C3 | 26 |
| Zhanatas, Sov. Un. | E7 | 28 |
| Zhangbei, China | D6 | 32 |
| Zhangiztobe, Sov. Un. | D10 | 28 |
| Zhangjiakou, China | C7 | 31 |
| Zhangwu, China | C10 | 32 |
| Zhangye, China | D5 | 31 |
| Zhangzhou (Changchou), China | G8 | 31 |
| Zhanjiang, China | G7 | 31 |
| Zhanyu, China | B10 | 32 |
| Zhao'an, China | G8 | 31 |
| Zhaodong, China | A11 | 32 |
| Zhaoqing, China | G7 | 31 |
| Zhaotong, China | F5 | 31 |
| Zhaoxing, China | C5 | 33 |
| Zhaoyuan, China | B11 | 32 |
| Zhaozhou, China | D2 | 33 |
| Zhari Namco, l., China | B8 | 36 |
| Zharkamys, Sov. Un. | D5 | 28 |
| Zhashui, China | H3 | 32 |
| Zhaxigang, China | A7 | 37 |
| Zhdanov see Mariupol, Sov. Un. | E6 | 29 |
| Zhecheng, China | G6 | 32 |
| Zhejiang, prov., China | F9 | 31 |
| Zhelaniya, Cape, c., Sov. Un. | B9 | 29 |
| Zhen'an, China | H3 | 32 |
| Zhenba, China | H2 | 32 |
| Zheng'an, China | J2 | 32 |
| Zhenglan Qi, China | C6 | 32 |
| Zhengyangguan, China | H7 | 32 |
| Zhengzhou (Chengchou), China | E7 | 31 |
| Zhenjiang, China | E8 | 31 |
| Zhenlai, China | B10 | 32 |
| Zhenping, China | I3 | 32 |
| Zhenyuan, China | K3 | 32 |
| Zhidachov, Sov. Un. | D8 | 26 |
| Zhidan, China | D6 | 31 |
| Zhigansk, Sov. Un. | C15 | 29 |
| Zhigulevsk, Sov. Un. | K3 | 27 |
| Zhilaya Kosa, Sov. Un. | D4 | 28 |
| Zhilevo, Sov. Un. | o18 | 27 |
| Zhitomir, Sov. Un. | D5 | 29 |
| Zhizdra, Sov. Un. | E10 | 27 |
| Zhmerinka, Sov. Un. | G7 | 27 |
| Zhob, Pak. | B4 | 36 |
| Zhob, stm., Pak. | B2 | 37 |
| Zhongba, China | C7 | 36 |
| Zhongdian, China | F5 | 31 |
| Zhongwei, China | D6 | 31 |
| Zhongxian, China | E6 | 31 |
| Zhongxiang, China | I5 | 32 |
| Zhoukou, China | *E7 | 32 |
| Zhoushan Qundao, is., China | E9 | 31 |
| Zhuanghe, China | E10 | 32 |
| Zhucheng, China | F8 | 32 |
| Zhuji, China | J9 | 32 |
| Zhukovskiy, Sov. Un. | n18 | 27 |
| Zhumadian, China | H6 | 32 |
| Zhuoxian, China | E6 | 32 |
| Zhushan, China | E7 | 31 |
| Zhuzhou, China | F7 | 31 |
| Zia Indian Reservation, N.M., U.S. | h7 | 108 |
| Zia Pueblo, N.M., U.S. | *B3 | 108 |
| Ziebach, co., S.D., U.S. | C4 | 118 |
| Zielona Góra, Pol. | C3 | 26 |
| Zierikzee, Neth. | C3 | 17 |
| Ziesar, E. Ger. | A7 | 19 |
| Ziftā, Eg. | D3 | 41 |
| Zigazinskiy, Sov. Un. | C5 | 28 |
| Zigey, Chad | C3 | 46 |
| Zigong, China | F5 | 31 |
| Zigui, China | E7 | 31 |
| Ziguinchor, Sen. | D1 | 45 |
| Zikhron Ya'aqov, Isr. | B6 | 41 |
| Zile, Tur. | B10 | 40 |
| Žilina, Czech. | D5 | 26 |
| Zillah, Libya | D3 | 43 |
| Zillah, Wa., U.S. | C5 | 124 |
| Ziller, stm., Aus. | B7 | 20 |
| Zilwaukee, Mi., U.S. | E7 | 99 |
| Zima, Sov. Un. | D13 | 29 |
| Zimapán, Mex. | C5 | 63 |
| Zimba, Zam. | E4 | 48 |
| Zimbabwe, ctry., Afr. | A5 | 49 |
| Zimmerman, Mn., U.S. | E5 | 100 |
| Zimnicea, Rom. | D7 | 24 |
| Zin, Naḥal, val., Isr. | D7 | 41 |
| Zinc, Ar., U.S. | A3 | 81 |
| Zincville, Ok., U.S. | A7 | 113 |
| Zinder, Niger | D6 | 45 |
| Zingst, E. Ger. | D6 | 15 |
| Zion, Il., U.S. | A6 | 90 |
| Zion, N.J., U.S. | C3 | 107 |
| Zion, S.C., U.S. | C9 | 117 |
| Zion Gate, hist., Isr. Occ. | m14 | 41 |
| Zion National Park, Ut. U.S. | F3 | 121 |
| Zion Reservoir, res., Az., U.S. | C6 | 80 |
| Zionsville, In., U.S. | E5 | 91 |
| Zionville, N.C., U.S. | A1 | 110 |
| Zipaquirá, Col. | B3 | 60 |
| Zirándaro, Mex. | n13 | 63 |
| Zirkel, Mount, mtn., Cc., U.S. | A4 | 83 |
| Zirndorf, W. Ger. | D5 | 19 |
| Zistersdorf, Aus. | D8 | 18 |
| Zitácuaro, Mex. | n13 | 63 |
| Zittau, E. Ger. | C7 | 18 |
| Ziwa Magharibi, prov., Tan. | B5 | 48 |
| Ziway, Lake, l., Eth. | D4 | 47 |
| Ziyang, China | E6 | 31 |
| Ziyuan, China | K4 | 32 |
| Žižkov (part of Prague), Czech. | n17 | 26 |
| Zlatograd, Bul. | E7 | 24 |
| Zlatoust, Sov. Un. | D9 | 29 |
| Złoczew, Pol. | C5 | 26 |
| Zlonice, Czech. | n17 | 26 |
| Złotoryja, Pol. | C3 | 26 |
| Złotów, Pol. | B4 | 26 |
| Zlynka, Sov. Un. | E8 | 27 |
| Zmeinogorsk, Sov. Un. | C10 | 28 |
| Znamenka, Sov. Un. | G9 | 27 |
| Żnin, Pol. | B4 | 26 |
| Znojmo, Czech. | D4 | 26 |
| Zoetermeer, Neth. | *B4 | 17 |
| Zofingen, Switz. | B4 | 21 |
| Zogno, Italy | E8 | 21 |
| Zográfos, Grc. | *D4 | 25 |
| Zohreh, stm., Iran | F5 | 39 |
| Zolfo Springs, Fl., U.S. | E5 | 86 |
| Zolochev, Sov. Un. | G5 | 27 |
| Zolotonosha, Sov. Un. | G9 | 27 |
| Zolotoy, Cape, c., Sov. Un. | B12 | 31 |
| Zomba, Mwi. | E6 | 48 |
| Zomergem, Bel. | C3 | 17 |
| Zongo, Zaire | A2 | 48 |
| Zonguldak, Tur. | B8 | 40 |
| Zörbig, E. Ger. | B7 | 19 |
| Zorita, Spain | C3 | 22 |
| Zorritos, Peru | B1 | 58 |
| Zortman, Mt., U.S. | C8 | 103 |
| Żory, Pol. | g9 | 26 |
| Zossen, E. Ger. | B6 | 18 |
| Zottegem, Bel. | D3 | 17 |
| Zouar, Chad | A3 | 46 |
| Zoutkamp, Neth. | A6 | 17 |
| Zreigat, Bir, well, Maur. | B3 | 45 |
| Zrenjanin (Petrovgrad), Yugo. | C5 | 24 |
| Zrmanja, stm., Yugo. | C2 | 24 |
| Zschopau, E. Ger. | C8 | 19 |
| Zuata, stm., Ven. | B4 | 60 |
| Zubtsov, Sov. Un. | C10 | 27 |
| Zuénoula, I.C. | E3 | 45 |
| Zuera, Spain | B5 | 22 |
| Zug, Switz. | E4 | 18 |
| Zug, W. Sah. | E2 | 44 |
| Zug, state, Switz. | B4 | 20 |
| Zug, Lake, l., Switz. | E4 | 18 |
| Zugdidi, Sov. Un. | A13 | 40 |
| Zugspitze, mtn., Eur. | B6 | 20 |
| Zuider Zee see IJsselmeer, l., Neth. | A6 | 16 |
| Zulia, state, Ven. | B3 | 60 |
| Zülpich, W. Ger. | C1 | 19 |
| Zumbi, Ponta do, c., Braz. | C3 | 26 |
| Zumbo, Moz. | A5 | 49 |
| Zumbro, stm., Mn., U.S. | F6 | 100 |
| Zumbro Falls, Mn., U.S. | F6 | 100 |
| Zumbrota, Mn., U.S. | F6 | 100 |
| Zumpango, Mex. | n14 | 63 |
| Zungeru, Nig. | E6 | 45 |
| Zunhua, China | C8 | 31 |
| Zuni, N.M., U.S. | B1 | 108 |
| Zuni, Va., U.S. | k14 | 123 |
| Zuni, stm., U.S. | C6 | 80 |
| Zuni Indian Reservation, N.M., U.S. | B1 | 108 |
| Zuni Mountains, mts., N.M., U.S. | B1 | 108 |
| Zunyi, China | F6 | 31 |
| Zuoquan, China | F5 | 32 |
| Zuqar, i., Yemen | C5 | 47 |
| Zúqar, Ont. | D3 | 73 |
| Zürich, Switz. | E4 | 18 |
| Zurich, Ks., U.S. | C4 | 93 |
| Zürich, state, Switz. | B4 | 20 |
| Zürich, Lake, l., Switz. | E4 | 18 |
| Zuru, Nig. | D6 | 45 |
| Zusam, stm., W. Ger. | E5 | 19 |
| Zussdorf, W. Ger. | A7 | 21 |
| Zutphen, Neth. | C6 | 17 |
| Zuwārah, Libya | C2 | 43 |
| Zuwayzā, Jord. | C7 | 41 |
| Zuyevka, Sov. Un. | B4 | 28 |
| Zvenigorodka, Sov. Un. | G8 | 27 |
| Zvishavane, Zimb. | B5 | 49 |
| Zvolen, Czech. | D5 | 26 |
| Zvornik, Yugo. | C4 | 24 |
| Zwartsluis, Neth. | B6 | 17 |
| Zweibrücken, W. Ger. | D3 | 18 |
| Zweisimmen, Switz. | B7 | 19 |
| Zwenkau, E. Ger. | B7 | 19 |
| Zwettl, Aus. | D7 | 18 |
| Zwickau, E. Ger. | C6 | 18 |
| Zwickauer Mulde, stm., E. Ger. | C7 | 19 |
| Zwingle, Ia., U.S. | B7 | 92 |
| Zwischenahn, W. Ger. | A7 | 17 |
| Zwolle, Neth. | A7 | 16 |
| Zwolle, La., U.S. | C2 | 95 |
| Zylks, La., U.S. | A1 | 95 |
| Żyrardów, Pol. | B6 | 26 |
| Zyryanovsk, Sov. Un. | D10 | 28 |
| Żywiec, Pol. | D5 | 26 |

# WORLD POLITICAL INFORMATION

This table lists the area, population, population density, form of government, political status, capital and predominant languages for every country in the world.

The populations are estimates for January 1, 1990 made by Rand McNally on the basis of official data, United Nations estimates, and other available information. Area figures include inland water.

The political units listed in the table are categorized by political status, as follows:

A–independent countries; B–internally independent political entities which are under the protection of other countries in matters of defense and foreign affairs; C–colonies and other dependent political units; D–the major administrative subdivisions of Australia, Canada, China, the Soviet Union, the United Kingdom, and the United States. For comparison, the table also includes the continents and the world.

All footnotes to this table appear on page 228.

| Country, Division or Region English (Conventional) | Area in sq. mi. | Estimated Population 1/1/90 | Pop. per sq. mi. | Form of Government and Political Status | | Capital | Predominant Languages |
|---|---|---|---|---|---|---|---|
| Afars and Issas *see* Djibouti | — | — | — | | | | |
| † Afghanistan | 251,826 | 15,210,000 | 60 | Socialist republic | A | Kabul (Kābol) | Dari, Pashto, Uzbek, Turkmen |
| Africa | 11,700,000 | 648,300,000 | 55 | | | | |
| † Alabama | 51,704 | 4,203,000 | 81 | State (U.S.) | D | Montgomery | English |
| Alaska | 591,004 | 543,000 | 0.9 | State (U.S.) | D | Juneau | English, indigenous languages |
| † Albania | 11,100 | 3,233,000 | 291 | Socialist republic | A | Tirana | Albanian, Greek |
| Alberta | 255,287 | 2,475,000 | 9.7 | Province (Canada) | D | Edmonton | English |
| † Algeria | 919,595 | 24,880,000 | 27 | Socialist republic | A | Algiers (El Djazaïr) | Arabic, Berber dialects, French |
| American Samoa | 77 | 44,000 | 571 | Unincorporated territory (U.S.) | C | Pago Pago | Samoan, English |
| Andorra | 175 | 51,000 | 291 | Coprincipality (Spanish and French protection) | B | Andorra | Spanish, French |
| † Angola | 481,354 | 8,668,000 | 18 | Socialist republic | A | Luanda | Portuguese, indigenous languages |
| Anguilla | 35 | 7,000 | 200 | Dependent territory (U.K. protection) | B | The Valley | English |
| Anhui | 53,668 | 53,840,000 | 1,003 | Province (China) | D | Hefei | Chinese (Mandarin) |
| Antarctica | 5,400,000 | (1) | | | | | |
| † Antigua and Barbuda | 171 | 79,000 | 462 | Parliamentary state | A | St. Johns | English, local dialects |
| † Argentina | 1,073,400 | 32,680,000 | 30 | Republic | A | Buenos Aires | Spanish, English, Italian, German, French |
| Arizona | 114,002 | 3,577,000 | 31 | State (U.S.) | D | Phoenix | English |
| Arkansas | 53,191 | 2,451,000 | 46 | State (U.S.) | D | Little Rock | English |
| Armenia | 11,506 | 3,324,000 | 289 | Soviet socialist republic (Soviet Union) | D | Yerevan | Armenian, Azerbaijani, Russian |
| Aruba | 75 | 63,000 | 840 | Self-governing territory (Netherlands protection) | B | Oranjestad | Dutch, Papiamento, English, Spanish |
| Ascension | 34 | 1,300 | 38 | Dependency (St. Helena) | C | Georgetown | English |
| Asia | 17,300,000 | 3,156,100,000 | 182 | | | | |
| † Australia | 2,966,155 | 16,950,000 | 5.7 | Federal parliamentary state | A | Canberra | English, indigenous languages |
| Australian Capital Territory | 927 | 280,000 | 302 | Territory (Australia) | D | Canberra | English |
| † Austria | 32,377 | 7,644,000 | 236 | Federal republic | A | Vienna (Wien) | German |
| Azerbaijan | 33,436 | 7,081,000 | 212 | Soviet socialist republic (Soviet Union) | D | Baku | Azerbaijani, Russian, Armenian |
| † Bahamas | 5,380 | 251,000 | 47 | Parliamentary state | A | Nassau | English, Creole |
| † Bahrain | 267 | 478,000 | 1,790 | Monarchy | A | Manama | Arabic, English, Farsi, Urdu |
| † Bangladesh | 55,598 | 107,510,000 | 1,934 | Islamic republic | A | Dhaka | Bangla, English |
| † Barbados | 166 | 255,000 | 1,536 | Parliamentary state | A | Bridgetown | English |
| Beijing | 6,487 | 10,045,000 | 1,548 | Autonomous city (China) | D | Beijing (Peking) | Chinese (Mandarin) |
| † Belgium | 11,783 | 9,877,000 | 838 | Constitutional monarchy | A | Brussels (Bruxelles) | Dutch (Flemish), French, German |
| † Belize | 8,866 | 189,000 | 21 | Parliamentary state | A | Belmopan | English, Spanish, Garifuna, Mayan |
| † Benin | 43,475 | 4,667,000 | 107 | Socialist republic | A | Porto-Novo and Cotonou | French, Fon, Adja, indigenous languages |
| Bermuda | 21 | 57,000 | 2,714 | Dependent territory (U.K.) | C | Hamilton | English |
| † Bhutan | 17,954 | 1,550,000 | 86 | Monarchy (Indian protection) | B | Thimphu | Dzongkha, Tibetan and Nepalese dialects |
| † Bolivia | 424,165 | 7,298,000 | 17 | Republic | A | La Paz and Sucre | Spanish, Quechua, Aymara |
| Bophuthatswana(2) | 15,641 | 2,251,000 | 144 | National state (South African protection) | B | Mmabatho | Tswana |
| † Botswana | 224,711 | 1,280,000 | 5.7 | Republic | A | Gaborone | English, Tswana |
| † Brazil | 3,286,488 | 148,980,000 | 45 | Federal republic | A | Brasília | Portuguese, Spanish, English, French |
| British Columbia | 365,948 | 3,011,000 | 8.2 | Province (Canada) | D | Victoria | English |
| British Indian Ocean Territory | 23 | (1) | — | Dependent territory (U.K.) | C | | English |
| † Brunei | 2,226 | 253,000 | 114 | Monarchy | A | Bandar Seri Begawan | Malay, English, Chinese |
| † Bulgaria | 42,823 | 9,015,000 | 211 | Socialist republic | A | Sofia (Sofiya) | Bulgarian |
| † Burkina Faso | 105,869 | 9,019,000 | 85 | Provisional military government | A | Ouagadougou | French, indigenous languages |
| † Burma (Myanmar) | 261,228 | 40,865,000 | 156 | Provisional military government | A | Rangoon (Yangon) | Burmese, indigenous languages |
| † Burundi | 10,745 | 5,380,000 | 501 | Provisional military government | A | Bujumbura | French, Kirundi, Swahili |
| † Byelorussia | 80,155 | 10,290,000 | 128 | Soviet socialist republic (Soviet Union) | D | Minsk | Byelorussian, Russian |
| California | 158,704 | 28,815,000 | 182 | State (U.S.) | D | Sacramento | English |
| † Cambodia | 69,898 | 8,153,000 | 117 | Socialist republic | A | Phnum Pénh (Phnom Penh) | Khmer, French |
| † Cameroon | 183,569 | 11,580,000 | 63 | Republic | A | Yaoundé | English, French, indigenous languages |
| † Canada | 3,849,674 | 26,415,000 | 6.9 | Federal parliamentary state | A | Ottawa | English, French, indigenous languages |
| † Cape Verde | 1,557 | 370,000 | 238 | Republic | A | Praia | Portuguese, Crioulo |
| Cayman Islands | 100 | 25,000 | 250 | Dependent territory (U.K.) | C | Georgetown | English |
| † Central African Republic | 240,535 | 2,843,000 | 12 | Republic | A | Bangui | French, Sango, Arabic, indigenous languages |
| Ceylon *see* Sri Lanka | — | — | — | | | | |
| † Chad | 495,755 | 4,984,000 | 10 | Republic | A | N'Djamena | Arabic, French, indigenous languages |
| Channel Islands | 75 | 138,000 | 1,840 | Dependent territory (U.K.) | C | | English, French |
| † Chile | 292,135 | 13,140,000 | 45 | Republic | A | Santiago | Spanish |
| † China (excl. Taiwan) | 3,689,631 | 1,092,100,000 | 296 | Socialist republic | A | Beijing (Peking) | Chinese dialects |
| Christmas Island | 52 | 2,000 | 38 | External territory (Australia) | C | The Settlement | English, Chinese, Malay |
| Ciskei(2) | 2,996 | 1,268,000 | 423 | National state (South African protection) | B | Bisho | English, Xhosa, Afrikaans |
| Cocos (Keeling) Islands | 5.4 | 600 | 111 | Part of Australia | | | English, Cocos-Malay, Malay |
| † Colombia | 440,831 | 30,860,000 | 70 | Republic | A | Bogotá | Spanish |
| Colorado | 104,094 | 3,402,000 | 33 | State (U.S.) | D | Denver | English |
| † Comoros (excl. Mayotte) | 863 | 452,000 | 524 | Federal Islamic republic | A | Moroni | Arabic, French, Swahili, Malagasy |
| † Congo | 132,047 | 2,267,000 | 17 | Socialist republic | A | Brazzaville | French, indigenous languages |
| Connecticut | 5,019 | 3,302,000 | 658 | State (U.S.) | D | Hartford | English |
| Cook Islands | 91 | 18,000 | 198 | Self-governing territory (New Zealand protection) | B | Avarua | English, Malay-Polynesian languages |
| † Costa Rica | 19,730 | 2,958,000 | 150 | Republic | A | San José | Spanish |
| † Cuba | 42,804 | 10,640,000 | 249 | Socialist republic | A | Havana (La Habana) | Spanish |
| † Cyprus | 2,276 | 524,000 | 230 | Republic | A | Nicosia (Levkosía) | Greek, English |
| † Cyprus, North(3) | 1,295 | 173,000 | 134 | Republic | A | Nicosia (Lefkoşa) | Turkish |
| † Czechoslovakia | 49,382 | 15,670,000 | 317 | Federal republic | A | Prague (Praha) | Czech, Slovak, Hungarian |
| Delaware | 2,045 | 650,000 | 318 | State (U.S.) | D | Dover | English |
| † Denmark | 16,638 | 5,135,000 | 309 | Constitutional monarchy | A | Copenhagen (København) | Danish |
| District of Columbia | 69 | 625,000 | 9,058 | Federal district (U.S.) | D | Washington | English |
| † Djibouti | 8,958 | 333,000 | 37 | Republic | A | Djibouti | French, Somali, Afar, Arabic |
| † Dominica | 305 | 86,000 | 282 | Republic | A | Roseau | English, French |
| † Dominican Republic | 18,704 | 7,094,000 | 379 | Republic | A | Santo Domingo | Spanish |
| † Ecuador | 109,484 | 10,650,000 | 97 | Republic | A | Quito | Spanish, Quechua, indigenous languages |
| † Egypt | 386,662 | 52,830,000 | 137 | Socialist republic | A | Cairo (Al Qāhirah) | Arabic |
| Ellis Islands *see* Tuvalu | — | — | — | | | | |
| † El Salvador | 8,124 | 5,260,000 | 647 | Republic | A | San Salvador | Spanish, Nahua |
| England | 50,363 | 47,730,000 | 948 | Administrative division (U.K.) | D | London | English |
| † Equatorial Guinea | 10,831 | 357,000 | 33 | Republic | A | Malabo | Spanish, indigenous languages, English |
| Estonia | 17,413 | 1,590,000 | 91 | Soviet socialist republic (Soviet Union) | D | Tallinn | Estonian, Russian |
| † Ethiopia | 483,123 | 49,628,000 | 103 | Socialist republic | A | Addis Ababa | Amharic, Tigrinya, Orominga, Arabic |
| Europe | 3,800,000 | 688,000,000 | 181 | | | | |
| † Faeroe Islands | 540 | 47,000 | 87 | Self-governing territory (Danish protection) | C | Tórshavn | Danish, Faroese |
| Falkland Islands(4) | 4,700 | 2,000 | 0.4 | Dependent territory (U.K.) | C | Stanley | English |
| † Fiji | 7,078 | 720,000 | 102 | Republic | A | Suva | English, Fijian, Hindustani |
| † Finland | 130,559 | 4,985,000 | 38 | Republic | A | Helsinki (Helsingfors) | Finnish, Swedish, Lapp |
| Florida | 58,668 | 12,610,000 | 215 | State (U.S.) | D | Tallahassee | English |
| † France (excl. Overseas Departments) | 211,208 | 56,210,000 | 266 | Republic | A | Paris | French |
| French Guiana | 35,135 | 96,000 | 2.7 | Overseas department (France) | C | Cayenne | French |
| French Polynesia | 1,544 | 194,000 | 126 | Overseas territory (France) | C | Papeete | French, Tahitian, Chinese |
| Fujian | 46,332 | 28,395,000 | 613 | Province (China) | D | Fuzhou | Chinese dialects |
| † Gabon | 103,347 | 1,065,000 | 10 | Republic | A | Libreville | French, Fang, indigenous languages |

225

# World Political Information

| Country, Division or Region English (Conventional) | Area in sq. mi. | Estimated Population 1/1/90 | Pop. per sq. mi. | Form of Government and Political Status | | Capital | Predominant Languages |
|---|---|---|---|---|---|---|---|
| † Gambia | 4,361 | 805,000 | 185 | Republic | A | Banjul | English, Malinke, Wolof, Fula, indigenous languages |
| Gansu | 173,746 | 21,405,000 | 123 | Province (China) | D | Lanzhou | Chinese (Mandarin), Mongolian, Tibetan dialects |
| Georgia | 58,914 | 6,504,000 | 110 | State (U.S.) | D | Atlanta | English |
| Georgia | 26,911 | 5,491,000 | 204 | Soviet socialist republic (Soviet Union) | D | Tbilisi | Georgian, Russian, Armenian |
| † German Democratic Republic (East Germany) | 41,828 | 16,740,000 | 400 | Socialist republic | A | Berlin (East) | German |
| † Germany, Federal Republic of (West Germany) | 96,028 | 61,460,000 | 640 | Federal republic | A | Bonn | German |
| † Ghana | 92,098 | 14,160,000 | 154 | Provisional military government | A | Accra | English, Akan, indigenous languages |
| Gibraltar | 2.3 | 31,000 | 13,478 | Dependent territory (U.K.) | C | Gibraltar | English, Spanish |
| Gilbert Islands see Kiribati | — | — | — | | | | |
| † Great Britain see United Kingdom | | | | | | | |
| † Greece | 50,962 | 10,010,000 | 196 | Republic | A | Athens (Athinai) | Greek |
| Greenland | 840,004 | 57,000 | 0.1 | Self-governing territory (Danish protection) | B | Godthåb | Danish, Greenlandic, Inuit dialects |
| † Grenada | 133 | 97,000 | 729 | Parliamentary state | A | St. George's | English, French |
| Guadeloupe (incl. Dependencies) | 687 | 346,000 | 504 | Overseas department (France) | C | Basse-Terre | French, Creole |
| Guam | 209 | 154,000 | 737 | Unincorporated territory (U.S.) | C | Agana | English, Chamorro, Filipino dialects |
| Guangdong | 68,726 | 58,970,000 | 858 | Province (China) | D | Guangzhou (Canton) | Chinese dialects, Miao-Yao |
| Guangxi Zhuangzu | 91,236 | 40,735,000 | 446 | Autonomous region (China) | D | Nanning | Chinese dialects, Thai, Miao-Yao |
| † Guatemala | 42,042 | 9,059,000 | 215 | Republic | A | Guatemala | Spanish, indigenous languages |
| Guernsey (incl. Dependencies) | 30 | 57,000 | 1,900 | Bailiwick (Channel Islands) | C | St. Peter Port | English, French |
| † Guinea | 94,926 | 7,178,000 | 76 | Provisional military government | A | Conakry | French, indigenous languages |
| † Guinea-Bissau | 13,948 | 986,000 | 71 | Republic | A | Bissau | Portuguese, Crioulo, indigenous languages |
| Guizhou | 65,637 | 31,125,000 | 474 | Province (China) | D | Guiyang | Chinese (Mandarin), Thai, Miao-Yao |
| † Guyana | 83,000 | 765,000 | 9.2 | Republic | A | Georgetown | English, indigenous languages |
| Hainan | 13,127 | 6,553,000 | 499 | Province (China) | D | Haikou | Chinese, Min, Tai |
| † Haiti | 10,714 | 6,456,000 | 603 | Provisional military government | A | Port-au-Prince | Creole, French |
| Hawaii | 6,473 | 1,126,000 | 174 | State (U.S.) | D | Honolulu | English, Hawaiian, Japanese |
| Hebei | 73,359 | 57,990,000 | 790 | Province (China) | D | Shijiazhuang | Chinese (Mandarin) |
| Heilongjiang | 181,082 | 34,400,000 | 190 | Province (China) | D | Harbin | Chinese dialects, Mongolian, Tungus |
| Henan | 64,479 | 80,800,000 | 1,253 | Province (China) | D | Zhengzhou | Chinese (Mandarin) |
| Holland see Netherlands | — | — | — | | | | |
| † Honduras | 43,277 | 5,039,000 | 116 | Republic | A | Tegucigalpa | Spanish, indigenous |
| Hong Kong | 414 | 5,888,000 | 14,222 | Dependent territory (U.K.) | C | Victoria (Hong Kong) | Chinese (Cantonese), English |
| Hubei | 72,356 | 51,550,000 | 712 | Province (China) | D | Wuhan | Chinese dialects |
| Hunan | 81,081 | 58,860,000 | 726 | Province (China) | D | Changsha | Chinese dialects, Miao-Yao |
| † Hungary | 35,920 | 10,565,000 | 294 | Republic | A | Budapest | Hungarian |
| † Iceland | 39,769 | 254,000 | 6.4 | Republic | A | Reykjavík | Icelandic |
| Idaho | 83,566 | 1,026,000 | 12 | State (U.S.) | D | Boise | English |
| Illinois | 57,872 | 11,780,000 | 204 | State (U.S.) | D | Springfield | English |
| † India (incl. part of Jammu and Kashmir) | 1,237,062 | 841,750,000 | 680 | Federal republic | A | New Delhi | English, Hindi, Hindustani, indigenous languages |
| Indiana | 36,417 | 5,653,000 | 155 | State (U.S.) | D | Indianapolis | English |
| † Indonesia | 741,101 | 189,460,000 | 256 | Republic | A | Jakarta | Indonesian, Javanese, Sundanese, other indigenous languages |
| Inner Mongolia (Nei Monggol) | 456,759 | 20,970,000 | 46 | Autonomous region (China) | D | Hohhot | Mongolian |
| Iowa | 56,275 | 2,877,000 | 51 | State (U.S.) | D | Des Moines | English |
| † Iran | 636,296 | 55,280,000 | 87 | Islamic republic | A | Tehrān | Farsi, Turkish, Kurdish, Arabic, English, French |
| † Iraq | 169,235 | 17,745,000 | 105 | Republic | A | Baghdād | Arabic, Kurdish, Assyrian, Armenian |
| † Ireland | 27,137 | 3,536,000 | 130 | Republic | A | Dublin (Baile Átha Cliath) | English, Irish Gaelic |
| Isle of Man | 221 | 67,000 | 303 | Self-governing territory (U.K. protection) | B | Douglas | English, Manx Gaelic |
| † Israel (excl. Occupied Areas) | 8,019 | 4,460,000 | 556 | Republic | A | Jerusalem (Yerushalayim) | Hebrew, Arabic, English, Yiddish |
| Israeli Occupied Areas(5) | 2,947 | 1,876,000 | 637 | None | | | Arabic, Hebrew, English |
| † Italy | 116,324 | 57,625,000 | 495 | Republic | A | Rome (Roma) | Italian |
| † Ivory Coast | 124,518 | 11,845,000 | 95 | Republic | A | Abidjan and Yamoussoukro(6) | French, indigenous languages |
| † Jamaica | 4,244 | 2,386,000 | 562 | Parliamentary state | A | Kingston | English, Creole |
| † Japan | 145,870 | 123,350,000 | 846 | Constitutional monarchy | A | Tōkyō | Japanese |
| Jersey | 45 | 81,000 | 1,800 | Bailiwick (Channel Islands) | C | St. Helier | English, French |
| Jiangsu | 39,614 | 64,760,000 | 1,635 | Province (China) | D | Nanjing (Nanking) | Chinese dialects |
| Jiangxi | 64,325 | 36,260,000 | 564 | Province (China) | D | Nanchang | Chinese dialects |
| Jilin | 72,201 | 23,915,000 | 331 | Province (China) | D | Changchun | Chinese (Mandarin), Mongolian, Korean |
| † Jordan (excl. West Bank) | 35,135 | 3,011,000 | 86 | Constitutional monarchy | A | 'Ammān | Arabic |
| Kansas | 82,282 | 2,527,000 | 31 | State (U.S.) | D | Topeka | English |
| Kazakh S.S.R. | 1,049,156 | 16,675,000 | 16 | Soviet socialist republic (Soviet Union) | D | Alma-Ata | Kazakh, Russian, German, Ukrainian |
| Kentucky | 40,414 | 3,802,000 | 94 | State (U.S.) | D | Frankfort | English |
| † Kenya | 224,961 | 25,350,000 | 113 | Republic | A | Nairobi | English, Swahili, indigenous languages |
| Kirghiz S.S.R. | 76,641 | 4,335,000 | 57 | Soviet socialist republic (Soviet Union) | D | Frunze | Kirghiz, Russian, Uzbek |
| Kiribati | 280 | 70,000 | 250 | Republic | A | Bairiki | English, Gilbertese |
| Korea, North | 46,540 | 22,790,000 | 490 | Socialist republic | A | Pyŏngyang | Korean |
| Korea, South | 38,230 | 42,590,000 | 1,114 | Republic | A | Seoul (Sŏul) | Korean |
| † Kuwait | 6,880 | 1,971,000 | 286 | Constitutional monarchy | A | Kuwait | Arabic, English |
| † Laos | 91,429 | 3,980,000 | 44 | Socialist republic | A | Viangchan (Vientiane) | Lao, French, Thai, indigenous languages |
| Latvia | 24,595 | 2,717,000 | 110 | Soviet socialist republic (Soviet Union) | D | Rīga | Latvian, Russian |
| † Lebanon | 4,015 | 3,377,000 | 841 | Republic | A | Beirut (Bayrūt) | Arabic, French, Armenian, English |
| † Lesotho | 11,720 | 1,772,000 | 151 | Constitutional monarchy | A | Maseru | English, Sesotho, Zulu, Xhosa |
| Liaoning | 56,255 | 38,440,000 | 683 | Province (China) | D | Shenyang (Mukden) | Chinese (Mandarin), Mongolian |
| † Liberia | 38,250 | 2,670,000 | 70 | Republic | A | Monrovia | English, indigenous languages |
| † Libya | 679,362 | 4,143,000 | 6.1 | Socialist republic | A | Tripoli (Ṭarābulus) | Arabic |
| Liechtenstein | 62 | 28,000 | 452 | Constitutional monarchy | A | Vaduz | German |
| Lithuania(7) | 25,174 | 3,728,000 | 148 | Soviet socialist republic (Soviet Union) | D | Vilnius | Lithuanian, Russian, Polish |
| Louisiana | 47,750 | 4,503,000 | 94 | State (U.S.) | D | Baton Rouge | English |
| † Luxembourg | 998 | 381,000 | 382 | Constitutional monarchy | A | Luxembourg | French, Luxembourgish, German, English |
| Macao | 6.6 | 454,000 | 68,788 | Chinese territory under Portuguese administration | C | Macao | Portuguese, Chinese (Cantonese) |
| † Madagascar | 226,658 | 11,615,000 | 51 | Republic | A | Antananarivo | Malagasy, French |
| Maine | 33,265 | 1,226,000 | 37 | State (U.S.) | D | Augusta | English |
| † Malawi | 45,747 | 8,335,000 | 182 | Republic | A | Lilongwe | Chichewa, English, Tombuka |
| † Malaysia | 129,251 | 17,480,000 | 135 | Federal constitutional monarchy | A | Kuala Lumpur | Malay, Chinese dialects, English, Tamil |
| † Maldives | 115 | 211,000 | 1,835 | Republic | A | Male | Divehi |
| † Mali | 478,767 | 9,293,000 | 19 | Republic | A | Bamako | French, Bambara, indigenous languages |
| † Malta | 122 | 347,000 | 2,844 | Republic | A | Valletta | English, Maltese |
| Manitoba | 250,947 | 1,115,000 | 4.4 | Province (Canada) | D | Winnipeg | English |
| Marshall Islands | 70 | 43,000 | 614 | Republic (U.S. protection) | B | Majuro (island) | English, Malay-Polynesian languages, Japanese |
| Martinique | 425 | 347,000 | 816 | Overseas department (France) | C | Fort-de-France | French, Creole |
| Maryland | 10,461 | 4,703,000 | 450 | State (U.S.) | D | Annapolis | English |
| Massachusetts | 8,286 | 5,954,000 | 719 | State (U.S.) | D | Boston | English |
| † Mauritania | 395,956 | 2,008,000 | 5.1 | Provisional military government | A | Nouakchott | Arabic, French, indigenous languages |
| † Mauritius (incl. Dependencies) | 788 | 1,105,000 | 1,402 | Parliamentary state | A | Port Louis | English, Creole, French, Bhojpuri |
| Mayotte(8) | 144 | 82,000 | 569 | Territorial collectivity (France) | C | Dzaoudzi and Mamoudzou(6) | French, Swahili (Mahorian) |
| † Mexico | 756,066 | 85,090,000 | 113 | Federal republic | A | Mexico City (Ciudad de México) | Spanish, indigenous languages |
| Michigan | 97,107 | 9,431,000 | 97 | State (U.S.) | D | Lansing | English |
| Micronesia, Federated States of | 271 | 90,000 | 332 | Republic (U.S. protection) | B | Kolonia | English, Malay-Polynesian languages |
| Midway Islands | 2.0 | 500 | 250 | Unincorporated territory (U.S.) | C | | English |
| Minnesota | 86,614 | 4,378,000 | 51 | State (U.S.) | D | St. Paul | English |
| Mississippi | 47,691 | 2,702,000 | 57 | State (U.S.) | D | Jackson | English |

226

| Country, Division or Region English (Conventional) | Area in sq. mi. | Estimated Population 1/1/90 | Pop. per sq. mi. | Form of Government and Political Status | | Capital | Predominant Languages |
|---|---|---|---|---|---|---|---|
| Missouri | 69,697 | 5,253,000 | 75 | State (U.S.) | D | Jefferson City | English |
| Moldavia | 13,012 | 4,365,000 | 335 | Soviet socialist republic (Soviet Union) | D | Kishinev | Moldavian, Russian, Ukrainian |
| Monaco | 0.7 | 29,000 | 41,429 | Constitutional monarchy | A | Monaco | French, English, Italian, Monegasque |
| † Mongolia | 604,250 | 2,155,000 | 3.6 | Socialist republic | A | Ulan Bator (Ulaanbaatar) | Khalkha Mongol, Kazakh, Russian, Chinese |
| Montana | 147,045 | 825,000 | 5.6 | State (U.S.) | D | Helena | English |
| Montserrat | 39 | 12,000 | 308 | Dependent territory (U.K.) | C | Plymouth | English |
| † Morocco (excl. Western Sahara) | 172,414 | 25,930,000 | 150 | Constitutional monarchy | A | Rabat | Arabic, Berber dialects, French |
| † Mozambique | 308,642 | 15,535,000 | 50 | Socialist republic | A | Maputo | Portuguese, indigenous languages |
| Namibia (excl. Walvis Bay) | 317,818 | 1,386,000 | 4.4 | Republic | A | Windhoek | Afrikaans, English, German, indigenous languages |
| Nauru | 8.1 | 9,000 | 1,111 | Republic | A | Yaren District | Nauruan, English |
| Nebraska | 77,350 | 1,626,000 | 21 | State (U.S.) | D | Lincoln | English |
| † Nepal | 56,827 | 18,930,000 | 333 | Constitutional monarchy | A | Kathmandu (Kāṭmāṇḍaū) | Nepali, Maithili, Bhojpuri, other indigenous languages |
| † Netherlands | 16,133 | 14,825,000 | 919 | Constitutional monarchy | A | Amsterdam and The Hague ('s-Gravenhage) | Dutch |
| Netherlands Antilles | 309 | 207,000 | 670 | Self-governing territory (Netherlands protection) | B | Willemstad | Dutch, Papiamento, English, Spanish |
| Nevada | 110,562 | 1,076,000 | 9.7 | State (U.S.) | D | Carson City | English |
| New Brunswick | 28,355 | 740,000 | 26 | Province (Canada) | D | Fredericton | English, French |
| New Caledonia | 7,358 | 153,000 | 21 | Overseas territory (France) | C | Nouméa | French, Malay-Polynesian languages |
| Newfoundland | 156,649 | 592,000 | 3.8 | Province (Canada) | D | St. John's | English |
| New Hampshire | 9,278 | 1,101,000 | 119 | State (U.S.) | D | Concord | English |
| New Hebrides see Vanuatu | — | — | — | | | | |
| † New Jersey | 7,787 | 7,830,000 | 1,006 | State (U.S.) | D | Trenton | English |
| New Mexico | 121,594 | 1,551,000 | 13 | State (U.S.) | D | Santa Fe | English, Spanish |
| New South Wales | 309,500 | 5,823,000 | 19 | State (Australia) | D | Sydney | English |
| New York | 52,737 | 18,185,000 | 345 | State (U.S.) | D | Albany | English |
| † New Zealand | 103,519 | 3,408,000 | 33 | Parliamentary state | A | Wellington | English, Maori |
| † Nicaragua | 50,193 | 3,555,000 | 71 | Republic | A | Managua | Spanish, English, indigenous languages |
| † Niger | 489,191 | 7,609,000 | 16 | Provisional military government | A | Niamey | French, Hausa, Djerma, indigenous languages |
| † Nigeria | 356,669 | 111,010,000 | 311 | Provisional military government | A | Lagos and Abuja[6] | English, Hausa, Fulani, Yorbua, Ibo, indigenous languages |
| Ningxia Huizu | 25,637 | 4,368,000 | 170 | Autonomous region (China) | D | Yinchuan | Chinese (Mandarin) |
| Niue | 102 | 1,600 | 16 | Self-governing territory (New Zealand protection) | B | Alofi | English, Malay-Polynesian languages |
| Norfolk Island | 14 | 1,900 | 136 | External territory (Australia) | C | Kingston | English, Norfolk |
| North America | 9,400,000 | 423,600,000 | 45 | | | | |
| † North Carolina | 52,669 | 6,604,000 | 125 | State (U.S.) | D | Raleigh | English |
| North Dakota | 70,702 | 699,000 | 9.9 | State (U.S.) | D | Bismarck | English |
| Northern Ireland | 5,452 | 1,588,000 | 291 | Administrative division (U.K.) | D | Belfast | English |
| Northern Mariana Islands | 184 | 24,000 | 130 | Commonwealth (U.S. protection) | B | Saipan (island) | English, Malay-Polynesian languages |
| Northern Territory | 519,771 | 158,000 | 0.3 | Territory (Australia) | D | Darwin | English, indigenous languages |
| Northwest Territories | 1,322,910 | 55,000 | — | Territory (Canada) | D | Yellowknife | English, indigenous languages |
| † Norway (incl. Svalbard and Jan Mayen) | 149,412 | 4,202,000 | 28 | Constitutional monarchy | A | Oslo | Norwegian, Lapp |
| Nova Scotia | 21,425 | 909,000 | 42 | Province (Canada) | D | Halifax | English |
| Oceania (incl. Australia) | 3,300,000 | 26,300,000 | 8.0 | | | | |
| † Ohio | 44,786 | 11,005,000 | 246 | State (U.S.) | D | Columbus | English |
| Oklahoma | 69,957 | 3,352,000 | 48 | State (U.S.) | D | Oklahoma City | English |
| † Oman | 82,030 | 1,325,000 | 16 | Monarchy | A | Mascāt (Muscat) | Arabic, English, Baluchi, Urdu, Indian dialects |
| Ontario | 412,581 | 9,495,000 | 23 | Province (Canada) | D | Toronto | English |
| Oregon | 97,076 | 2,777,000 | 29 | State (U.S.) | D | Salem | English |
| Pacific Islands, Trust Territory of the | 196 | 15,000 | 77 | United Nations trusteeship (U.S. administration) | B | Saipan (island) | English, Palauan |
| † Pakistan (incl. part of Jammu and Kashmir) | 339,732 | 112,360,000 | 331 | Federal Islamic republic | A | Islāmābād | English, Urdu, Punjabi, Pashto, Sindhi, Saraiki |
| Palau (Belau) | 196 | 15,000 | 77 | Part of Trust Territory of the Pacific Islands | B | Koror | English, Palauan |
| † Panama | 29,762 | 2,396,000 | 81 | Republic | A | Panamá | Spanish, English, indigenous languages |
| † Papua New Guinea | 178,704 | 3,653,000 | 20 | Parliamentary state | A | Port Moresby | English, Motu, Pidgin, indigenous languages |
| † Paraguay | 157,048 | 4,221,000 | 27 | Republic | A | Asunción | Spanish, Guarani |
| Pennsylvania | 46,047 | 12,155,000 | 264 | State (U.S.) | D | Harrisburg | English |
| † Peru | 496,225 | 22,085,000 | 45 | Republic | A | Lima | Quechua, Spanish, Aymara |
| † Philippines | 115,831 | 60,835,000 | 525 | Republic | A | Manila | English, Pilipino, Tagalog, Cebuano |
| Pitcairn (incl. Dependencies) | 19 | 60 | 3.2 | Dependent territory (U.K.) | C | Adamstown | English, Tahitian |
| † Poland | 120,728 | 37,840,000 | 313 | Republic | A | Warsaw (Warszawa) | Polish |
| † Portugal | 35,516 | 10,495,000 | 296 | Republic | A | Lisbon (Lisboa) | Portuguese |
| Prince Edward Island | 2,185 | 132,000 | 60 | Province (Canada) | D | Charlottetown | English |
| Puerto Rico | 3,515 | 3,368,000 | 958 | Commonwealth (U.S. protection) | B | San Juan | Spanish, English |
| † Qatar | 4,416 | 417,000 | 94 | Monarchy | A | Doha (Ad Dawḥah) | Arabic, English |
| Qinghai | 277,994 | 4,259,000 | 15 | Province (China) | D | Xining | Tibetan dialects, Mongolian, Turkish dialects, Chinese (Mandarin) |
| Quebec | 594,860 | 6,815,000 | 11 | Province (Canada) | D | Québec | French, English |
| Queensland | 666,876 | 2,843,000 | 4.3 | State (Australia) | D | Brisbane | English |
| Reunion | 969 | 590,000 | 609 | Overseas department (France) | C | Saint-Denis | French, Creole |
| Rhode Island | 1,212 | 1,001,000 | 826 | State (U.S.) | D | Providence | English |
| Rhodesia see Zimbabwe | — | — | — | | | | |
| † Romania | 91,699 | 23,210,000 | 253 | Socialist republic | A | Bucharest (Bucureşti) | Romanian, Hungarian, German |
| Russian Soviet Federative Socialist Republic | 6,592,849 | 148,550,000 | 23 | Soviet socialist republic (Soviet Union) | D | Moscow (Moskva) | Russian, Tatar, Ukrainian |
| † Rwanda | 10,169 | 7,463,000 | 734 | Republic | A | Kigali | French, Kinyarwanda |
| † St. Christopher-Nevis | 104 | 46,000 | 442 | Parliamentary state | A | Basseterre | English |
| St. Helena (incl. Dependencies) | 162 | 7,600 | 47 | Dependent territory (U.K.) | C | Jamestown | English |
| † St. Lucia | 238 | 151,000 | 634 | Parliamentary state | A | Castries | English, French |
| St. Pierre and Miquelon | 93 | 6,800 | 73 | Territorial collectivity (France) | C | Saint-Pierre | French |
| † St. Vincent and the Grenadines | 150 | 114,000 | 760 | Parliamentary state | A | Kingstown | English, French |
| San Marino | 24 | 24,000 | 1,000 | Republic | A | San Marino | Italian |
| † Sao Tome and Principe | 372 | 123,000 | 331 | Republic | A | São Tomé | Portuguese, indigenous languages |
| Saskatchewan | 251,866 | 1,051,000 | 4.2 | Province (Canada) | D | Regina | English |
| † Saudi Arabia | 830,000 | 14,645,000 | 18 | Monarchy | A | Riyadh (Ar Riyāḍ) | Arabic |
| Scotland | 30,414 | 5,150,000 | 169 | Administrative division (U.K.) | D | Edinburgh | English, Scots Gaelic |
| † Senegal | 75,955 | 7,367,000 | 97 | Republic | A | Dakar | French, Wolof, indigenous languages |
| † Seychelles | 175 | 69,000 | 394 | Republic | A | Victoria | English, French, Creole |
| Shaanxi | 79,151 | 31,450,000 | 397 | Province (China) | D | Xi'an (Sian) | Chinese (Mandarin) |
| Shandong | 59,074 | 80,380,000 | 1,361 | Province (China) | D | Jinan | Chinese (Mandarin) |
| Shanghai | 2,394 | 12,780,000 | 5,338 | Autonomous city (China) | D | Shanghai | Chinese (Wu) |
| Shanxi | 60,232 | 27,410,000 | 455 | Province (China) | D | Taiyuan | Chinese (Mandarin) |
| Sichuan | 220,078 | 106,590,000 | 484 | Province (China) | D | Chengdu | Chinese (Mandarin), Tibetan dialects, Miao-Yao |
| † Sierra Leone | 27,925 | 4,116,000 | 147 | Republic | A | Freetown | English, Krio, indigenous languages |
| † Singapore | 246 | 2,710,000 | 11,016 | Republic | A | Singapore | Chinese (Mandarin), English, Malay, Tamil |
| † Solomon Islands | 10,954 | 312,000 | 28 | Parliamentary state | A | Honiara | English, Malay-Polynesian languages |
| † Somalia | 246,201 | 8,332,000 | 34 | Socialist republic | A | Mogadishu (Muqdisho) | Arabic, Somali, English, Italian |
| † South Africa (incl. Walvis Bay) | 433,680 | 36,790,000 | 85 | Republic | A | Pretoria, Cape Town, and Bloemfontein | Afrikaans, English, Zulu, Xhosa, other indigenous languages |
| South America | 6,900,000 | 293,700,000 | 43 | | | | |
| † South Australia | 379,925 | 1,437,000 | 3.8 | State (Australia) | D | Adelaide | English |
| South Carolina | 31,116 | 3,552,000 | 114 | State (U.S.) | D | Columbia | English |

# World Political Information

| Country, Division or Region English (Conventional) | Area in sq. mi. | Estimated Population 1/1/90 | Pop. per sq. mi. | Form of Government and Political Status | Capital | Predominant Languages |
|---|---|---|---|---|---|---|
| **South Dakota** | 77,120 | 725,000 | 9.4 | State (U.S.) D | Pierre | English |
| **South Georgia and the South Sandwich Islands** | 1,450 | (1) | — | Dependent territory (U.K.) C | | English |
| **† Soviet Union** | 8,600,387 | 289,010,000 | 34 | Federal socialist republic A | Moscow (Moskva) | Russian and other Slavic languages, various ethnic languages |
| **† Spain** | 194,885 | 39,520,000 | 203 | Constitutional monarchy A | Madrid | Spanish (Castilian), Catalan, Galician, Basque |
| **Spanish North Africa**[9] | 12 | 100,000 | 8,333 | Five possessions (Spain) C | | Spanish, Arabic, Berber dialects |
| **Spanish Sahara *see* Western Sahara** | — | — | — | | | |
| **† Sri Lanka** | 24,962 | 16,935,000 | 678 | Socialist republic A | Colombo and Sri Jayawardenapura | English, Sinhala, Tamil |
| **† Sudan** | 967,500 | 24,775,000 | 26 | Provisional military government A | Khartoum (Al Kharṭūm) | Arabic, indigenous, English |
| **† Suriname** | 63,251 | 405,000 | 6.4 | Republic A | Paramaribo | Dutch, Sranan Tongo, English, Hindustani, Javanese |
| **† Swaziland** | 6,704 | 787,000 | 117 | Monarchy A | Mbabane and Lobamba[6] | English, siSwati |
| **† Sweden** | 173,732 | 8,503,000 | 49 | Constitutional monarchy A | Stockholm | Swedish |
| **Switzerland** | 15,943 | 6,623,000 | 415 | Federal republic A | Bern (Berne) | German, French, Italian, Romansch |
| **† Syria** | 71,498 | 11,915,000 | 167 | Socialist republic A | Damascus (Dimashq) | Arabic, Kurdish, Armenian, Aramaic, Circassian |
| **Taiwan** | 13,900 | 20,345,000 | 1,464 | Republic A | T'aipei | Chinese dialects |
| **Tajik S.S.R.** | 55,251 | 5,144,000 | 93 | Soviet socialist republic (Soviet Union) D | Dushanbe | Tajik, Uzbek, Russian |
| **† Tanzania** | 364,900 | 25,220,000 | 69 | Republic A | Dar es Salaam and Dodoma[6] | English, Swahili, indigenous languages |
| **Tasmania** | 26,178 | 456,000 | 17 | State (Australia) D | Hobart | English |
| **Tennessee** | 42,143 | 5,003,000 | 119 | State (U.S.) D | Nashville | English |
| **Texas** | 266,805 | 17,060,000 | 64 | State (U.S.) D | Austin | English, Spanish |
| **† Thailand** | 198,115 | 55,925,000 | 282 | Constitutional monarchy A | Bangkok (Krung Thep) | Thai, indigenous languages |
| **Tianjin (Tientsin)** | 4,363 | 8,409,000 | 1,927 | Autonomous city (China) D | Tianjin (Tientsin) | Chinese (Mandarin) |
| **Tibet (Xizang)** | 471,045 | 2,075,000 | 4.4 | Autonomous region (China) D | Lhasa | Tibetan dialects |
| **† Togo** | 21,925 | 3,508,000 | 160 | Republic A | Lomé | French, indigenous languages |
| **Tokelau** | 4.6 | 1,700 | 370 | Island territory (New Zealand) C | | English, Tokelauan |
| **Tonga** | 290 | 97,000 | 334 | Constitutional monarchy A | Nuku'alofa | Tongan, English |
| **Transkei**[2] | 16,816 | 3,636,000 | 216 | National state (South African protection) B | Umtata | Xhosa, Afrikaans |
| **† Trinidad and Tobago** | 1,980 | 1,248,000 | 630 | Republic A | Port of Spain | English, Hindi, French, Spanish |
| **Tristan da Cunha** | 40 | 300 | 7.5 | Dependency (St. Helena) C | Edinburgh | English |
| **† Tunisia** | 63,170 | 8,079,000 | 128 | Republic A | Tunis | Arabic, French |
| **† Turkey** | 300,948 | 54,075,000 | 180 | Republic A | Ankara | Turkish, Kurdish, Arabic |
| **Turkmen S.S.R.** | 188,456 | 3,555,000 | 19 | Soviet socialist republic (Soviet Union) D | Ashkhabad | Turkmen, Russian, Uzbek, Kazakh |
| **Turks and Caicos Islands** | 166 | 11,000 | 66 | Dependent territory (U.K.) C | Grand Turk | English |
| **Tuvalu** | 10 | 8,800 | 880 | Parliamentary state A | Funafuti | Tuvaluan, English |
| **† Uganda** | 93,104 | 17,300,000 | 186 | Provisional military government A | Kampala | English, Luganda, Swahili, indigenous languages |
| **† Ukraine** | 233,090 | 52,110,000 | 224 | Soviet socialist republic (Soviet Union) D | Kiev | Ukrainian, Russian |
| **† United Arab Emirates** | 32,278 | 2,183,000 | 68 | Federation of monarchs A | Abu Dhabi (Abū Ẓaby) | Arabic, English, Farsi, Hindi, Urdu |
| **† United Kingdom** | 94,248 | 57,335,000 | 608 | Constitutional monarchy A | London | English, Welsh, Gaelic |
| **† United States** | 3,679,245 | 250,150,000 | 68 | Federal republic A | Washington | English, Spanish |
| **Upper Volta *see* Burkina Faso** | — | — | — | | | |
| **† Uruguay** | 68,500 | 3,120,000 | 46 | Republic A | Montevideo | Spanish |
| **Utah** | 84,902 | 1,726,000 | 20 | State (U.S.) D | Salt Lake City | English |
| **Uzbek S.S.R.** | 172,742 | 20,055,000 | 116 | Soviet socialist republic (Soviet Union) D | Tashkent | Uzbek, Russian, Kazakh, Tajik, Tatar |
| **† Vanuatu** | 4,706 | 158,000 | 34 | Republic A | Port-Vila | Bislama, English, French |
| **Vatican City** | 0.2 | 800 | 4,000 | Ecclesiastical city-state A | Vatican City | Italian, Latin |
| **Venda**[2] | 2,393 | 588,000 | 246 | National state (South African protection) B | Thohoyandou | Afrikaans, English, Venda |
| **† Venezuela** | 352,145 | 19,485,000 | 55 | Federal republic A | Caracas | Spanish, indigenous |
| **Vermont** | 9,614 | 563,000 | 59 | State (U.S.) D | Montpelier | English |
| **Victoria** | 87,877 | 4,355,000 | 50 | State (Australia) D | Melbourne | English |
| **† Vietnam** | 127,242 | 65,475,000 | 515 | Socialist republic A | Hanoi (Ha Noi) | Vietnamese, French, Chinese, English, indigenous languages |
| **Virginia** | 40,763 | 6,104,000 | 150 | State (U.S.) D | Richmond | English |
| **Virgin Islands (U.S.)** | 133 | 114,000 | 857 | Unincorporated territory (U.S.) C | Charlotte Amalie | English, Spanish, Creole |
| **Virgin Islands, British** | 59 | 13,000 | 220 | Dependent territory (U.K.) C | Road Town | English |
| **Wake Island** | 3.0 | 300 | 100 | Unincorporated territory (U.S.) C | | English |
| **Wales** | 8,019 | 2,867,000 | 358 | Administrative division (U.K.) D | Cardiff | English, Welsh Gaelic |
| **Wallis and Futuna** | 98 | 16,000 | 163 | Overseas territory (France) C | Mata-Utu | French, Uvean, Futunan |
| **Washington** | 68,139 | 4,678,000 | 69 | State (U.S.) D | Olympia | English |
| **Western Australia** | 975,101 | 1,598,000 | 1.6 | State (Australia) D | Perth | English |
| **Western Sahara** | 102,703 | 196,000 | 1.9 | Occupied by Morocco C | El Aaiún | Arabic |
| **† Western Samoa** | 1,093 | 184,000 | 168 | Constitutional monarchy A | Apia | English, Samoan |
| **West Virginia** | 24,236 | 1,926,000 | 79 | State (U.S.) D | Charleston | English |
| **Wisconsin** | 66,213 | 4,903,000 | 74 | State (U.S.) D | Madison | English |
| **Wyoming** | 97,808 | 500,000 | 5.1 | State (U.S.) D | Cheyenne | English |
| **Xinjiang Uygur** | 617,764 | 14,305,000 | 23 | Autonomous region (China) D | Ürümqi | Turkish dialects, Mongolian, Tungus, English |
| **† Yemen** | 205,356 | 13,019,000 | 63 | Islamic republic A | Ṣan'ā' | Arabic |
| **† Yugoslavia** | 98,766 | 23,765,000 | 241 | Federal socialist republic A | Belgrade (Beograd) | Macedonian, Serbo-Croatian, Slovene, Albanian, Hungarian |
| **Yukon Territory** | 186,661 | 25,000 | 0.1 | Territory (Canada) D | Whitehorse | English, Inuktitut, indigenous languages |
| **Yunnan** | 152,124 | 35,710,000 | 235 | Province (China) D | Kunming | Chinese (Mandarin), Tibetan dialects, Khmer, Miao-Yao |
| **† Zaire** | 905,568 | 35,165,000 | 39 | Republic A | Kinshasa | French, Kikongo, Lingala, Swahili, Tshiluba |
| **† Zambia** | 290,586 | 7,995,000 | 28 | Republic A | Lusaka | English, Bemba, Nyanja, Tonga, indigenous languages |
| **Zhejiang** | 39,305 | 42,045,000 | 1,070 | Province (China) D | Hangzhou | Chinese dialects |
| **† Zimbabwe** | 150,873 | 9,252,000 | 61 | Republic A | Harare (Salisbury) | English, ChiShona, SiNdebele |
| **WORLD** | 57,800,000 | 5,236,000,000 | 91 | | | |

† Member of the United Nations (1989).
(1) No permanent population.
(2) Bophuthatswana, Ciskei, Transkei, and Venda are not recognized by the United Nations.
(3) North Cyprus unilaterally declared its independence from Cyprus in 1983.
(4) Claimed by Argentina.
(5) Includes West Bank, Golan Heights, and Gaza Strip.
(6) Future capital.
(7) Lithuania unilaterally declared its independence from the Soviet Union in 1990.
(8) Claimed by Comoros.
(9) Comprises Ceuta, Melilla, and several small islands.

# WORLD GEOGRAPHICAL INFORMATION

## GENERAL

**MOVEMENTS OF THE EARTH**

The earth makes one complete revolution around the sun every 365 days, 5 hours, 48 minutes, and 46 seconds.

The earth makes one complete rotation on its axis in 23 hours, 56 minutes and 4 seconds.

The earth revolves in its orbit around the sun at a speed of 66,700 miles per hour.

The earth rotates on its axis at an equatorial speed of more than 1,000 miles per hour.

**MEASUREMENTS OF THE EARTH**

Estimated age of the earth, at least 4.6 billion years.

Equatorial diameter of the earth, 7,926.38 miles.

Polar diameter of the earth, 7,899.80 miles.

Mean diameter of the earth, 7,917.52 miles.

Equatorial circumference of the earth, 24,901.46 miles.

Polar circumference of the earth, 24,855.34 miles.

Difference between equatorial and polar circumferences of the earth, 46.12 miles.

Weight of the earth, 6,600,000,000,000,000,000,000 tons, or 6,600 billion billion tons.

**THE EARTH'S SURFACE**

Total area of the earth, 197,000,000 square miles.

Total land area of the earth (including inland water and Antarctica), 57,800,000 square miles.

Highest point on the earth's surface, Mt. Everest, Asia, 29,028 feet.

Lowest point on the earth's land surface, shores of the Dead Sea, Asia, –1,322 feet below sea level.

Greatest known depth of the ocean, the Mariana Trench, southwest of Guam, Pacific Ocean, 35,810 feet.

**THE EARTH'S INHABITANTS**

Population of the earth is estimated to be 5,236,000,000 (January 1, 1990).

Estimated population density of the earth, 91 per square mile.

**EXTREMES OF TEMPERATURE AND RAINFALL OF THE EARTH**

Highest temperature ever recorded, 136° F. at Al' 'Azīzīyah, Libya, Africa, on September 13, 1922.

Lowest temperature ever recorded, –129° F. at Vostok, Antarctica on July 21, 1983.

Highest mean annual temperature, 94° F. at Dallol, Ethiopia.

Lowest mean annual temperature, –70° F. at Plateau Station, Antarctica.

The greatest local average annual rainfall is at Mt. Waialeale, Kauai, Hawaii, 460 inches.

The greatest 24-hour rainfall, 74 inches, is at Cilaos, Reunion Island, March 15-16, 1952.

The lowest local average annual rainfall is at Arica, Chile, .03 inches.

The longest dry period, over 14 years, is at Arica, Chile, October 1903 to January 1918.

## THE CONTINENTS

| CONTINENT | Area (sq. mi.) | Estimated Population Jan. 1, 1990 | Population per sq. mi. | Mean Elevation (feet) | Highest Elevation (Feet) | Lowest Elevation (Feet) | Highest Recorded Temperature | Lowest Recorded Temperature |
|---|---|---|---|---|---|---|---|---|
| North America | 9,400,000 | 423,600,000 | 45 | 2,000 | Mt. McKinley, Alaska, United States, 20,320 | Death Valley, California, United States 282 below sea level | Death Valley, California 134° F | Northice, Greenland –87° F |
| South America | 6,900,000 | 293,700,000 | 43 | 1,800 | Cerro Aconcagua, Argentina 22,831 | Salinas Chicas, Argentina 138 below sea level | Rivadavia, Argentina 120° F | Sarmiento, Argentina –27° F |
| Europe | 3,800,000 | 688,000,000 | 181 | 980 | Mt. Elbrus, Soviet Union 18,510 | Caspian Sea, Soviet Union-Iran 92 below sea level | Sevilla, Spain 122° F | Ust-Shchugor, Soviet Union –67° F |
| Asia | 17,300,000 | 3,156,100,000 | 182 | 3,000 | Mt. Everest, China-Nepal 29,028 | Dead Sea, Israel-Jordan 1,322 below sea leve | Tirat Zevi, Israel 129° F | Oymyakon and Verkhoyansk, Soviet Union –90° F |
| Africa | 11,700,000 | 648,300,000 | 55 | 1,900 | Kilimanjaro, Tanzania 19,340 | Lac Assal, Djibouti 509 below sea level | Al 'Azīzīyah, Libya 136° F | Ifrane, Morocco –11° F |
| Oceania, incl. Australia | 3,300,000 | 26,300,000 | 8.0 | .... | Mt. Wilhelm, Papua New Guinea 14,793 | Lake Eyre, South Australia 52 below sea level | Cloncurry, Queensland, Australia 128° F | Charlotte Pass, New South Wales, Australia –8° F |
| Australia | 2,966,155 | 16,950,000 | 5.7 | 1,000 | Mt. Kosciusko, New South Wales 7,310 | Lake Eyre, South Australia 52 below sea level | Cloncurry, Queensland 128° F | Charlotte Pass, New South Wales –8° F |
| Antarctica | 5,400,000 | Uninhabited | .... | 6,000 | Vinson Massif 16,864 | sea level | Vanda Station 59° F | Vostok –129° F |
| World | 57,800,000 | 5,236,000,000 | 91 | .... | Mt. Everest, China-Nepal 29,028 | Dead Sea, Israel-Jordan 1,322 below sea leve | Al 'Azīzīyah, Libya 136° F | Vostok, Antarctica –129° |

## HISTORICAL POPULATIONS *

| AREA | 1650 | 1750 | 1800 | 1850 | 1900 | 1914 | 1920 | 1939 | 1950 | 1990 |
|---|---|---|---|---|---|---|---|---|---|---|
| North America | 5,000,000 | 5,000,000 | 13,000,000 | 39,000,000 | 106,000,000 | 141,000,000 | 147,000,000 | 186,000,000 | 219,000,000 | 423,600,000 |
| South America | 8,000,000 | 7,000,000 | 12,000,000 | 20,000,000 | 38,000,000 | 55,000,000 | 61,000,000 | 90,000,000 | 111,000,000 | 293,700,000 |
| Europe | 100,000,000 | 140,000,000 | 190,000,000 | 265,000,000 | 400,000,000 | 470,000,000 | 453,000,000 | 526,000,000 | 530,000,000 | 688,000,000 |
| Asia | 335,000,000 | 476,000,000 | 593,000,000 | 754,000,000 | 932,000,000 | 1,006,000,000 | 1,000,000,000 | 1,247,000,000 | 1,418,000,000 | 3,156,100,000 |
| Africa | 100,000,000 | 95,000,000 | 90,000,000 | 95,000,000 | 118,000,000 | 130,000,000 | 140,000,000 | 170,000,000 | 199,000,000 | 648,300,000 |
| Oceania, incl. Australia | 2,000,000 | 2,000,000 | 2,000,000 | 2,000,000 | 6,000,000 | 8,000,000 | 9,000,000 | 11,000,000 | 13,000,000 | 26,300,000 |
| Australia | | | | | 4,000,000 | 5,000,000 | 6,000,000 | 7,000,000 | 8,000,000 | 16,950,000 |
| World | 550,000,000 | 725,000,000 | 900,000,000 | 1,175,000,000 | 1,600,000,000 | 1,810,000,000 | 1,810,000,000 | 2,230,000,000 | 2,490,000,000 | 5,236,000,000 |

* Figures prior to 1990 are rounded to the nearest million.    Figures in italics represent very rough estimates.

## LARGEST COUNTRIES : POPULATION

| | | Population 1/1/90 |
|---|---|---|
| 1 | China (excl. Taiwan) | 1,092,100,000 |
| 2 | India (incl. part of Jammu and Kashmir) | 841,750,000 |
| 3 | Soviet Union | 289,010,000 |
| 4 | United States | 250,150,000 |
| 5 | Indonesia | 189,460,000 |
| 6 | Brazil | 148,980,000 |
| 7 | Japan | 123,350,000 |
| 8 | Pakistan (incl. part of Jammu and Kashmir) | 112,360,000 |
| 9 | Nigeria | 111,010,000 |
| 10 | Bangladesh | 107,510,000 |
| 11 | Mexico | 85,090,000 |
| 12 | Vietnam | 65,475,000 |
| 13 | Germany, Federal Republic of (West Germany) | 61,460,000 |
| 14 | Philippines | 60,835,000 |
| 15 | Italy | 57,625,000 |
| 16 | United Kingdom | 57,335,000 |
| 17 | France | 56,210,000 |
| 18 | Thailand | 55,925,000 |
| 19 | Iran | 55,280,000 |
| 20 | Turkey | 54,075,000 |
| 21 | Egypt | 52,830,000 |
| 22 | Ethiopia | 49,628,000 |
| 23 | Korea, South | 42,590,000 |
| 24 | Burma | 40,865,000 |
| 25 | Spain | 39,520,000 |

## LARGEST COUNTRIES : AREA

| | | Area (sq. mi.) |
|---|---|---|
| 1 | Soviet Union | 8,600,387 |
| 2 | Canada | 3,849,674 |
| 3 | China (excl. Taiwan) | 3,689,631 |
| 4 | United States | 3,679,245 |
| 5 | Brazil | 3,286,488 |
| 6 | Australia | 2,966,155 |
| 7 | India (incl. part of Jammu and Kashmir) | 1,237,062 |
| 8 | Argentina | 1,073,400 |
| 9 | Sudan | 967,500 |
| 10 | Algeria | 919,595 |
| 11 | Zaire | 905,568 |
| 12 | Greenland | 840,004 |
| 13 | Saudi Arabia | 830,000 |
| 14 | Mexico | 756,066 |
| 15 | Indonesia | 741,101 |
| 16 | Libya | 679,362 |
| 17 | Iran | 636,296 |
| 18 | Mongolia | 604,250 |
| 19 | Peru | 496,225 |
| 20 | Chad | 495,755 |
| 21 | Niger | 489,191 |
| 22 | Ethiopia | 483,123 |
| 23 | Angola | 481,354 |
| 24 | Mali | 478,767 |
| 25 | Colombia | 440,831 |
| 26 | South Africa | 433,680 |
| 27 | Bolivia | 424,165 |
| 28 | Mauritania | 395,956 |
| 29 | Egypt | 386,662 |
| 30 | Tanzania | 364,900 |
| 31 | Nigeria | 356,669 |

# World Geographical Information

## PRINCIPAL MOUNTAINS

### NORTH AMERICA

Height (feet)

| | |
|---|---|
| McKinley, Mt., Δ Alaska (Δ United States; Δ North America) | 20,320 |
| Logan, Mt., Δ Canada (Δ Yukon; Δ St. Elias Mts.) | 19,524 |
| Orizaba, Pico de, Δ Mexico | 18,406 |
| St. Elias, Mt., Alaska—Canada | 18,008 |
| Popocatépetl, Volcán, Mexico | 17,930 |
| Foraker, Mt., Alaska | 17,400 |
| Iztaccíhuatl, Mexico | 17,159 |
| Lucania, Mt., Canada | 17,147 |
| Fairweather, Mt., Alaska—Canada (Δ British Columbia) | 15,300 |
| Whitney, Mt., Δ California | 14,491 |
| Elbert, Mt., Δ Colorado (Δ Rocky Mts.) | 14,433 |
| Massive, Mt., Colorado | 14,421 |
| Harvard, Mt., Colorado | 14,420 |
| Rainier, Mt., Δ Washington (Δ Cascade Range) | 14,410 |
| Williamson, Mt., California | 14,375 |
| Blanca Pk., Colorado (Δ Sangre de Cristo Mts.) | 14,345 |
| La Plata Pk., Colorado | 14,336 |
| Uncompahgre Pk., Colorado (Δ San Juan Mts.) | 14,309 |
| Grays Pk., Colorado (Δ Front Range) | 14,270 |
| Evans, Mt., Colorado | 14,264 |
| Longs Pk., Colorado | 14,255 |
| Wrangell, Mt., Alaska | 14,163 |
| Shasta, Mt., California | 14,162 |
| Pikes Pk., Colorado | 14,110 |
| Colima, Nevado de, Mexico | 13,911 |
| Tajumulco, Volcán, Δ Guatemala (Δ Central America) | 13,846 |
| Gannett Pk., Δ Wyoming | 13,804 |
| Mauna Kea, Δ Hawaii | 13,796 |
| Grand Teton Mtn., Wyoming | 13,770 |
| Mauna Loa, Hawaii | 13,679 |
| Kings Pk,, Δ Utah | 13,528 |
| Cloud Pk., Wyoming (Δ Bighorn Mts.) | 13,167 |
| Wheeler Pk., Δ New Mexico | 13,161 |
| Boundary Pk., Δ Nevada | 13,143 |
| Waddington, Mt., Canada (Δ Coast Mts.) | 13,104 |
| Robson, Mt., Canada (Δ Canadian Rockies) | 12,972 |
| Granite Pk., Δ Montana | 12,799 |
| Borah Pk., Δ Idaho | 12,662 |
| Humphreys Pk., Δ Arizona | 12,633 |
| Chirripó, Cerro, Δ Costa Rica | 12,533 |
| Columbia, Mt., Canada (Δ Alberta) | 12,294 |
| Adams, Mt., Washington | 12,276 |
| Gunnbjørn Mtn., Δ Greenland | 12,139 |
| San Gorgonio Mtn., California | 11,499 |
| Barú, Volcán, Δ Panama | 11,411 |
| Hood, Mt., Δ Oregon | 11,235 |
| Lassen Pk., California | 10,457 |
| Duarte, Pico, Δ Dominican Rep. (Δ West Indies) | 10,417 |
| Haleakala Crater, Hawaii (Δ Maui) | 10,023 |
| Paricutín, Mexico | 9,213 |
| El Pital, Cerro, Δ El Salvador—Honduras | 8,957 |
| La Selle, Pic, Δ Haiti | 8,773 |
| Guadalupe Pk., Δ Texas | 8,749 |
| Olympus, Mt., Washington (Δ Olympic Mts.) | 7,965 |
| Blue Mountain Pk., Δ Jamaica | 7,402 |
| Harney Pk., Δ South Dakota (Δ Black Hills) | 7,242 |
| Mitchell, Mt., Δ North Carolina (Δ Appalachian Mts.) | 6,684 |
| Clingmans Dome, North Carolina—Δ Tennessee (Δ Great Smoky Mts.) | 6,643 |
| Turquino, Pico, Δ Cuba | 6,542 |
| Washington, Mt., Δ New Hampshire (Δ White Mts.) | 6,288 |
| Rogers, Mt., Δ Virginia | 5,729 |
| Marcy, Mt., Δ New York (Δ Adirondack Mts.) | 5,344 |
| Katahdin, Mt., Δ Maine | 5,268 |
| Kawaikini, Hawaii (Δ Kauai) | 5,243 |
| Spruce Knob, Δ West Virginia | 4,862 |
| Pelée, Montagne, Δ Martinique | 4,583 |
| Mansfield, Mt., Δ Vermont (Δ Green Mts.) | 4,393 |
| Punta, Cerro de, Δ Puerto Rico | 4,389 |
| Black Mtn., Δ Kentucky—Virginia | 4,145 |
| Kaala, Hawaii (Δ Oahu) | 4,040 |

### SOUTH AMERICA

| | |
|---|---|
| Aconcagua, Cerro, Δ Argentina (Δ Andes Mts.; Δ South America) | 22,831 |
| Ojos del Salado, Nevado, Argentina—Δ Chile | 22,615 |
| Illimani, Nevado, Δ Bolivia | 22,579 |
| Bonete, Cerro, Argentina | 22,546 |
| Pissis, Monte, Argentina | 22,241 |
| Huascarán, Nevado, Δ Peru | 22,123 |
| Llullaillaco, Volcán, Argentina—Chile | 22,110 |
| Yerupaja, Nevado, Peru | 21,765 |
| Tupungato, Cerro, Argentina—Chile | 21,490 |
| Sajama, Nevado, Bolivia | 21,463 |
| Illampu, Nevado, Bolivia | 20,873 |
| Chimborazo, Δ Ecuador | 20,702 |
| Antofalla, Volcán, Argentina | 20,013 |
| Cotopaxi, Ecuador | 19,347 |
| Misti, Volcán, Peru | 19,101 |
| Cristóbal Colón, Pico, Δ Colombia | 19,028 |
| Huila, Nevado del, Colombia (Δ Cordillera Central) | 18,865 |
| Bolívar, Pico, Δ Venezuela | 16,427 |
| Fitzroy, Monte (Cerro Chaltel), Argentina—Chile | 11,073 |
| Neblina, Pico da, Δ Brazil—Venezuela | 9,888 |

### EUROPE

| | |
|---|---|
| Elbrus, Mt., Soviet Union (Δ Caucasus Mts.; Δ Europe) | 18,510 |
| Dykh—Tau, Mt., Soviet Union | 17,073 |
| Shkhara, Mt., Soviet Union | 16,512 |
| Blanc, Mont (Monte Bianco), Δ France—Δ Italy (Δ Alps) | 15,771 |
| Rosa, Monte (Dufourspitze), Italy—Δ Switzerland | 15,203 |
| Weisshorn, Switzerland | 14,780 |
| Matterhorn, Italy—Switzerland | 14,692 |
| Finsteraarhorn, Switzerland | 14,022 |
| Jungfrau, Switzerland | 13,642 |
| Écrins, Barre des, France | 13,458 |
| Viso, Mt., Italy (Δ Cottian Alps) | 12,602 |
| Grossglockner, Δ Austria | 12,457 |
| Teide, Pico de, Δ Spain (Δ Canary Is.) | 12,198 |
| Mulhacén, Δ Spain (continental) | 11,411 |
| Aneto, Pico de, Spain (Δ Pyrenees) | 11,168 |
| Perdido (Perdu), Spain | 11,007 |
| Etna, Mt., Italy (Δ Sicily) | 10,902 |
| Zugspitze, Austria—Δ Germany, Fed. Rep. of | 9,718 |
| Musala, Δ Bulgaria | 9,596 |
| Olympus, Mt., Δ Greece | 9,570 |
| Corno Grande, Italy (Δ Apennines) | 9,554 |
| Triglav, Δ Yugoslavia | 9,393 |
| Korab, Δ Albania—Yugoslavia | 9,026 |
| Cinto, Monte, France (Δ Corsica) | 8,878 |
| Gerlachovka, Δ Czechoslovakia (Δ Carpathian Mts.) | 8,711 |
| Moldoveanu, Δ Romania | 8,343 |
| Rysy, Czechoslovakia—Δ Poland | 8,199 |
| Glittertinden, Δ Norway (Δ Scandinavia) | 8,110 |
| Parnassós, Greece | 8,061 |
| Ida, Mount, Greece (Δ Crete) | 8,058 |
| Pico, Ponta do, Δ Portugal (Δ Azores Is.) | 7,713 |
| Hvannadalshnúkur, Δ Iceland | 6,952 |
| Kebnekaise, Δ Sweden | 6,926 |
| Estrêla, Serra da, Δ Portugal (continental) | 6,539 |
| Narodnaya, Mt., Soviet Union (Δ Ural Mts.) | 6,217 |
| Sancy, Puy de, France (Δ Massif Central) | 6,184 |
| La Marmora, Punta, Italy (Δ Sardinia) | 6,017 |
| Hekla, Mt., Iceland | 4,892 |
| Nevis, Ben, Δ United Kingdom (Δ Scotland) | 4,406 |
| Haltia, Δ Finland—Norway | 4,357 |
| Vesuvius, Italy | 4,190 |
| Snowdon, United Kingdom (Δ Wales) | 3,560 |
| Carrauntoohil, Δ Ireland | 3,406 |
| Kékes, Δ Hungary | 3,327 |
| Scafell Pikes, United Kingdom (Δ England) | 3,210 |

### ASIA

| | |
|---|---|
| Everest, Mt., Δ China—Δ Nepal (Δ Tibet; Δ Himalayas; Δ Asia; Δ World) | 29,028 |
| K2 (Godwin Austen/Qogir Feng), China—Δ Pakistan (Δ Kashmir; Δ Karakoram Range) | 28,250 |
| Kānchenjunga, Δ India—Nepal | 28,208 |
| Makālu, China—Nepal | 27,825 |
| Dhawalāgiri, Nepal | 26,810 |
| Nānga Parbat, Pakistan | 26,660 |
| Annapurna, Nepal | 26,504 |
| Gasherbrum, China—Pakistan | 26,470 |
| Xixabangma Mtn. (Gosainthan), China | 26,286 |
| Nanda Devi, India | 25,645 |
| Kāmet, China—India | 25,446 |
| Namjagbarwa Feng, China | 25,446 |
| Muztag, China (Δ Kunlun Shan) | 25,338 |
| Tirich Mīr, Pakistan (Δ Hindu Kush) | 25,230 |
| Gongga Shan, China | 24,790 |
| Kula Kangri, Δ Bhutan | 24,784 |
| Muztagata, China | 24,757 |
| Communism Pk., Δ Soviet Union (Δ Pamir Mts.) | 24,590 |
| Nowshāk, Δ Afghanistan—Pakistan | 24,557 |
| Pobedy, Pk., China—Soviet Union | 24,406 |
| Chomo Lhāri, Bhutan—China | 23,996 |
| Lenin Pk., Soviet Union | 23,406 |
| Api, Nepal | 23,399 |
| Kangrinboqê Mtn., China | 22,028 |
| Hkakabo Razi, Δ Burma | 19,296 |
| Demavend, Mt., Δ Iran | 18,386 |
| Fūlādī, Kūh-e, Afghanistan | 16,847 |
| Ararat, Mt., Δ Turkey | 16,804 |
| Jaya Pk., Δ Indonesia (Δ New Guinea) | 16,503 |
| Klyuchevskaya Sopka, Soviet Union (Δ Kamchatka Peninsula) | 15,584 |
| Trikora Pk., Indonesia | 15,584 |
| Belukha, Mt., Soviet Union | 14,783 |
| Kinabalu, Mt., Δ Malaysia (Δ Borneo) | 13,455 |
| Türgen Mtn., Mongolia | 13,051 |
| Yu Shan, Δ Taiwan | 12,959 |
| Erciyes Mtn., Turkey | 12,848 |
| Kerinci, Indonesia (Δ Sumatra) | 12,467 |
| Fuji, Mt., Δ Japan (Δ Honshu) | 12,388 |
| Rinjani, Indonesia (Δ Lombok) | 12,224 |
| Semeru, Indonesia (Δ Java) | 12,060 |
| Nabi Shuayb, Mt., Δ Yemen (Δ Arabian Peninsula) | 12,008 |
| Rantekombola, Indonesia (Δ Celebes) | 11,335 |
| Slamet, Indonesia | 11,247 |
| Fan Si Pan, Δ Vietnam | 10,312 |
| Sham, Mt., Δ Oman | 9,957 |
| Apo, Mt., Δ Philippines (Δ Mindanao) | 9,692 |
| Pulog, Mt., Philippines (Δ Luzon) | 9,626 |
| Bia, Mt., Δ Laos | 9,249 |
| Hermon, Mt., Lebanon—Δ Syria | 9,232 |
| Paektu, Mt., Δ North Korea—China | 9,003 |
| Inthanon, Mt., Δ Thailand | 8,530 |
| Pidurutalagala, Δ Sri Lanka | 8,281 |
| Mayon Volcano, Philippines | 8,077 |
| Asahi, Mt., Japan (Δ Hokkaido) | 7,513 |
| Tahan, Malaysia (Δ Malaya) | 7,174 |
| Ólimbos, Δ Cyprus | 6,401 |
| Halla, Mt., Δ South Korea | 6,398 |
| Aoral, Mt., Δ Cambodia | 5,948 |
| Kujū, Mt., Japan (Δ Kyushu) | 5,866 |
| Ramm, Jabal, Δ Jordan | 5,755 |
| Meron, Mt., Δ Israel | 3,963 |
| Carmel, Mt., Israel | 1,791 |

### AFRICA

| | |
|---|---|
| Kilimanjaro, Δ Tanzania (Δ Africa) | 19,340 |
| Kirinyaga (Mt. Kenya), Δ Kenya | 17,058 |
| Margherita Pk., Δ Uganda—Δ Zaire | 16,763 |
| Ras Dashen Terara, Δ Ethiopia | 15,158 |
| Meru, Mt., Tanzania | 14,978 |
| Karisimbi, Volcan, Δ Rwanda—Zaire | 14,787 |
| Elgon, Mt., Kenya—Uganda | 14,178 |
| Toubkal, Jbel, Δ Morocco (Δ Atlas Mts.) | 13,665 |
| Cameroun, Mont, Δ Cameroon | 13,353 |
| Ntlenyana, Thabana, Δ Lesotho | 11,425 |
| eNjesuthi, Δ South Africa | 11,306 |
| Koussi, Emi, Δ Chad (Δ Tibesti Mts.) | 11,204 |
| Kinyeti, Δ Sudan | 10,456 |
| Santa Isabel, Pico de, Δ Equatorial Guinea (Δ Bioko) | 9,869 |
| Tahat, Δ Algeria (Δ Ahaggar Mts.) | 9,541 |
| Maromokotro, Δ Madagascar | 9,436 |
| Kātrīnā, Jabal, Δ Egypt | 8,668 |
| São Tomé, Pico de, Δ Sao Tome | 6,640 |

### OCEANIA

| | |
|---|---|
| Wilhelm, Mt., Δ Papua New Guinea | 14,793 |
| Giluwe, Mt., Papua New Guinea | 14,331 |
| Bangeta, Mt., Papua New Guinea | 13,520 |
| Victoria, Mt., Papua New Guinea (Δ Owen Stanley Range) | 13,240 |
| Cook, Mt., Δ New Zealand (Δ South Island) | 12,349 |
| Ruapehu, Mt., New Zealand (Δ North Island) | 9,177 |
| Balbi, Papua New Guinea (Δ Solomon Is.) | 9,000 |
| Egmont, Mt., New Zealand | 8,260 |
| Orohena, Mont, Δ French Polynesia (Δ Tahiti) | 7,352 |
| Kosciusko, Mt., Δ Australia (Δ New South Wales) | 7,310 |
| Silisili, Mt., Δ Western Samoa | 6,096 |
| Panié, Mont, Δ New Caledonia | 5,341 |
| Ossa, Mt., Australia (Δ Tasmania) | 5,305 |
| Bartle Frere, Mt., Australia (Δ Queensland) | 5,285 |
| Woodroffe, Mt., Australia (Δ South Australia) | 4,721 |
| Sinewit, Mt., Papua New Guinea (Δ Bismarck Archipelago) | 4,462 |
| Tomanivi (Victoria), Δ Fiji (Δ Viti Levu) | 4,341 |
| Meharry, Mt., Australia (Δ Western Australia) | 4,104 |
| Ayers Rock, Australia | 2,844 |

### ANTARCTICA

| | |
|---|---|
| Vinson Massif, Δ Antarctica | 16,864 |
| Kirkpatrick, Mt. | 14,856 |
| Markham,Mt. | 14,275 |
| Jackson, Mt. | 13,750 |
| Sidley, Mt. | 13,717 |
| Wade, Mt. | 13,399 |

Δ *Highest mountain in state, country, range, or region named.*

## OCEANS, SEAS AND GULFS

| | Area (sq. mi.) | Greatest Depth (ft.) | | Area (sq. mi.) | Greatest Depth (ft.) | | Area (sq. mi.) | Greatest Depth (ft.) |
|---|---|---|---|---|---|---|---|---|
| Pacific Ocean | 63,800,000 | 35,810 | South China Sea | 1,331,000 | 18,241 | Okhotsk, Sea of | 619,000 | 11,063 |
| Atlantic Ocean | 31,800,000 | 28,232 | Caribbean Sea | 1,063,000 | 25,197 | Norwegian Sea | 597,000 | 13,189 |
| Indian Ocean | 28,900,000 | 23,376 | Mediterranean Sea | 967,000 | 16,470 | Mexico, Gulf of | 596,000 | 14,370 |
| Arctic Ocean | 5,400,000 | 17,881 | Bering Sea | 876,000 | 13,438 | Hudson Bay | 475,000 | 850 |
| Arabian Sea | 1,492,000 | 19,029 | Bengal, Bay of | 839,000 | 17,251 | Greenland Sea | 465,000 | 15,899 |

## PRINCIPAL LAKES

| | Area (sq. mi.) | | Area (sq. mi.) | | Area (sq. mi.) |
|---|---|---|---|---|---|
| Caspian Sea, Iran—Soviet Union (salt) | 143,240 | Ladoga, L., Soviet Union | 6,833 | Nettilling Lake, Canada | 2,140 |
| Superior, L., Canada—United States | 31,700 | Chad, L., Cameroon—Chad—Nigeria | 6,300 | Winnipegosis, L., Canada | 2,075 |
| Victoria, L., Kenya—Tanzania—Uganda | 26,820 | Onega, L., Soviet Union | 3,753 | Bangweulu, L., Zambia | 1,930 |
| Aral Sea, Soviet Union (salt) | 24,700 | Eyre, L., Australia (salt) | Δ 3,700 | Nipigon, L. Canada | 1,872 |
| Huron, L., Canada—United States | 23,000 | Titicaca, Lago, Bolivia—Peru | 3,200 | Urmia, L., Iran (salt) | Δ 1,815 |
| Michigan, L., United States | 22,300 | Nicaragua, Lago, de Nicaragua | 3,150 | Manitoba, L., Canada | 1,785 |
| Tanganyika. L., Burundi—Tanzania—Zaire—Zambia | 12,350 | Mai-Ndombe, Lac, Zaire | Δ 3,100 | Woods, Lake of the, Canada—United States | 1,727 |
| Baikal, L., Soviet Union | 12,200 | Athabasca, L., Canada | 3,064 | Kyoga, L., Uganda | 1,710 |
| Great Bear Lake, Canada | 12,095 | Reindeer Lake, Canada | 2,568 | Great Salt Lake, United States (salt) | 1,680 |
| Nyasa, L., Malawi—Mozambique—Tanzania | 11,150 | Tonle Sap, Cambodia | Δ 2,500 | Mweru, L., Zaire—Zambia | 1,680 |
| Great Slave Lake, Canada | 11,030 | Rudolf, L., Ethiopia—Kenya (salt) | 2,473 | Gairdner, L., Australia (salt) | Δ 1,700 |
| Erie, L., Canada—United States | 9,910 | Issyk-Kul, L., Soviet Union (salt) | 2,425 | Peipus, L., Soviet Union | 1,660 |
| Winnipeg, L., Canada | 9,416 | Torrens, L., Australia (salt) | 2,300 | Qinghai Hu, China (salt) | 1,650 |
| Ontario, L., Canada—United States | 7,540 | Albert, L., Uganda—Zaire | 2,160 | Khanka, L., (Xingkai Hu) China—Soviet Union | 1,618 |
| Balkhash, L., Soviet Union | Δ 7,100 | Vänern, Sweden | 2,156 | Van, Lake, Turkey (salt) | 1,420 |

Δ Due to seasonal fluctuations in water level, areas of these lakes vary considerably.

## PRINCIPAL RIVERS

| | Length (miles) | | Length (miles) | | Length (miles) |
|---|---|---|---|---|---|
| Nile, Africa | 4,145 | Euphrates, Asia | 1,510 | Brazos, North America | 900 |
| Amazon—Ucayali, South America | 4,000 | Ural, Asia | 1,509 | Salado, South America | 900 |
| Yangtze (Chang Jiang), Asia | 3,900 | Arkansas, North America | 1,459 | Oka, Europe | 900 |
| Mississippi—Missouri, North America | 3,740 | Colorado, North America (U.S.—Mexico) | 1,450 | Darling, Australia | 864 |
| Huang He (Yellow), Asia | 3,395 | Aldan, Asia | 1,412 | Fraser, North America | 851 |
| Ob—Irtysh, Asia | 3,362 | Araguaia, South America | 1,400 | Parnaíba, South America | 850 |
| Río de la Plata—Paraná, South America | 3,030 | Dnepr, Europe | 1,400 | Colorado, North America (Texas) | 840 |
| Congo (Zaïre), Africa | 2,900 | Syr Darya, Asia | 1,370 | Dnestr, Europe | 840 |
| Paraná, South America | 2,800 | Kasai, Africa | 1,338 | Rhine, Europe | 820 |
| Amur—Argun, Asia | 2,761 | Tarim He, Asia | 1,328 | Saint Lawrence, North America | 800 |
| Amur (Heilong Jiang), Asia | 2,744 | Kolyma, Asia | 1,323 | Narmada, Asia | 800 |
| Lena, Asia | 2,700 | Ayeyarwady (Irrawaddy), Asia | 1,300 | Ottawa, North America | 790 |
| Mackenzie, North America | 2,635 | Negro, South America | 1,300 | Athabasca, North America | 765 |
| Mekong, Asia | 2,600 | Orange, Africa | 1,300 | Northern Donets, Europe | 735 |
| Niger, Africa | 2,600 | Red, North America | 1,270 | Pecos, North America | 735 |
| Yenisey, Asia | 2,543 | Juruá, South America | 1,250 | Green, North America | 730 |
| Missouri—Red Rock, North America | 2,533 | Xingu, South America | 1,230 | Elbe (Labe), Europe | 720 |
| Mississippi, North America | 2,348 | Ucayali, South America | 1,220 | White, North America (Ar.—Mo.) | 720 |
| Murray—Darling, Australia | 2,330 | Saskatchewan—Bow, North America | 1,205 | Cumberland, North America | 720 |
| Missouri, North America | 2,315 | Columbia, North America | 1,200 | James, North America (N./S. Dakota) | 710 |
| Volga, Europe | 2,194 | Peace, North America | 1,195 | Gambia, Africa | 680 |
| Madeira, South America | 2,013 | Tigris, Asia | 1,180 | Yellowstone, North America | 671 |
| São Francisco, South America | 1,988 | Don, Europe | 1,162 | Tennessee, North America | 652 |
| Grande, Rio, North America | 1,885 | Songhua Jiang, Asia | 1,140 | Gila, North America | 630 |
| Purús, South America | 1,860 | Pechora, Europe | 1,124 | Wisła (Vistula), Europe | 630 |
| Indus, Asia | 1,800 | Kama, Europe | 1,122 | Loire, Europe | 625 |
| Danube, Europe | 1,776 | Angara, Asia | 1,105 | Tagus (Tejo) (Tajo), Europe | 625 |
| Yukon, North America | 1,770 | Limpopo, Africa | 1,100 | North Platte, North America | 618 |
| Brahmaputra, Asia | 1,770 | Snake, North America | 1,038 | Albany, North America | 610 |
| Salween (Nu Jiang) (Thanlwin), Asia | 1,750 | Uruguay (Uruguai), South America | 1,025 | Tisza (Tisa), Europe | 607 |
| Zambezi, Africa | 1,700 | Churchill, North America | 1,000 | Ouachita, North America | 605 |
| Vilyuy, Asia | 1,647 | Marañón, South America | 1,000 | Back, North America | 605 |
| Tocantins, South America | 1,640 | Tobol, Asia | 989 | Cimarron, North America | 600 |
| Paraguay (Paraguai), South America | 1,610 | Ohio, North America | 981 | Sava, Europe | 585 |
| Orinoco, South America | 1,600 | Magdalena, South America | 950 | Nemunas (Neman), Europe | 582 |
| Amu Darya, Asia | 1,578 | Roosevelt, South America | 950 | Branco, South America | 580 |
| Murray, Australia | 1,566 | Xiang Jiang, Asia | 930 | Meuse, Europe | 575 |
| Ganges, Asia | 1,560 | Godāvari, Asia | 930 | Oder (Odra), Europe | 565 |
| Pilcomayo, South America | 1,550 | Canadian, North America | 906 | Rhône, Europe | 500 |

## PRINCIPAL ISLANDS

| | Area (sq. mi.) | | Area (sq. mi.) | | Area (sq. mi.) |
|---|---|---|---|---|---|
| Greenland, North America | 840,000 | Sakhalin, Soviet Union | 29,500 | New Caledonia, Oceania | 6,252 |
| New Guinea, Asia—Oceania | 309,000 | Hispaniola, North America | 29,400 | Timor, Indonesia | 5,743 |
| Borneo (Kalimantan), Asia | 287,300 | Banks I., Canada | 27,038 | Flores, Indonesia | 5,502 |
| Madagascar, Africa | 226,500 | Tasmania, Austl. | 26,200 | Samar, Philippines | 5,100 |
| Baffin I., Canada | 195,928 | Sri Lanka, Asia | 24,900 | Negros, Philippines | 4,907 |
| Sumatra (Sumatera), Indonesia | 182,860 | Devon I., Canada | 21,331 | Palawan, Philippines | 4,550 |
| Honshū, Japan | 89,176 | Tierra del Fuego, Isla Grande de, South America | 18,600 | Panay, Philippines | 4,446 |
| Great Britain, United Kingdom | 88,795 | Kyūshū, Japan | 17,129 | Jamaica, North America | 4,200 |
| Victoria I., Canada | 83,897 | Melville I., Canada | 16,274 | Hawaii, United States | 4,034 |
| Ellesmere I., Canada | 75,767 | Southampton I., Canada | 15,913 | Cape Breton I., Canada | 3,981 |
| Celebes (Sulawesi), Indonesia | 73,057 | Spitsbergen, Norway | 15,260 | Mindoro, Philippines | 3,759 |
| South I., New Zealand | 57,870 | New Britain, Papua New Guinea | 14,093 | Kodiak I., United States | 3,670 |
| Java (Jawa) Indonesia | 51,038 | Taiwan, Asia | 13,900 | Bougainville, Papua New Guinea | 3,600 |
| Ceram, Indonesia | 45,801 | Hainan I., China | 13,100 | Cyprus, Asia | 3,572 |
| North I., New Zealand | 44,274 | Prince of Wales I., Canada | 12,872 | New Ireland, Papua New Guinea | 3,500 |
| Cuba, North America | 42,800 | Vancouver I., Canada | 12,079 | Puerto Rico, North America | 3,500 |
| Newfoundland, Canada | 42,031 | Sicily, Italy | 9,926 | Corsica, France | 3,367 |
| Luzon, Philippines | 40,420 | Somerset I., Canada | 9,570 | Crete, Greece | 3,189 |
| Iceland, Europe | 39,800 | Sardinia, Italy | 9,301 | Wrangel I., Soviet Union | 2,800 |
| Mindanao, Philippines | 36,537 | Shikoku, Japan | 7,258 | Leyte, Philippines | 2,785 |
| Ireland, Europe | 32,600 | North East Land, Norway | 6,350 | Guadalcanal, Solomon Is. | 2,060 |
| Hokkaidō, Japan | 32,245 | | | Long I., United States | 1,377 |
| Novaya Zemlya, Soviet Union | 31,900 | | | | |

# WORLD METROPOLITAN AREAS

This table lists the major metropolitan areas of the world according to their estimated population on January 1, 1989. For convenience in reference, the areas are grouped by major region, and the number of areas in each region and size group is given.

The metropolitan areas are listed alphabetically within population classifications. Altogether these 282 metropolitan areas have an estimated 1989 population of about 811,000,000, or 15.6 percent of the world total. The 33 metropolitan areas of 5 million or more account for about 338,000,000 population.

For ease of comparison, each metropolitan area has been defined by Rand McNally according to consistent rules. A metropolitan area includes a central city, neighboring communities linked to it by continuous built-up areas, and more distant communities if the bulk of their population is supported by commuters to the central city. Some metropolitan areas have more than one central city, for example Tōkyō-Yokohama or San Francisco-Oakland-San Jose.

| POPULATION CLASSIFICATION | UNITED STATES and CANADA | LATIN AMERICA | EUROPE (excl. Soviet Union) | SOVIET UNION | WEST ASIA | EAST ASIA | AFRICA and OCEANIA |
|---|---|---|---|---|---|---|---|
| Over 15,000,000 (6) | New York, U.S. | Mexico City, Mex. São Paulo, Brazil | | | | Ōsaka-Kōbe-Kyōto, Japan Seoul, Kor. S. Tōkyō-Yokohama, Japan | |
| 10,000,000-15,000,000 (9) | Los Angeles, U.S. | Buenos Aires, Arg. Rio de Janeiro, Brazil | London, Eng. Paris, France | Moscow | Bombay, India Calcutta, India | | Cairo, Egypt |
| 5,000,000-10,000,000 (18) | Chicago, U.S. Philadelphia-Trenton-Wilmington, U.S. San Francisco-Oakland-San Jose, U.S. | Lima, Peru | | Leningrad | Delhi-New Delhi, India İstanbul, Tur. Karāchi, Pak. Madras, India Tehrān, Iran | Bangkok (Krung Thep), Thai. Beijing (Peking), China Jakarta, Indon. Manila, Phil. Shanghai, China T'aipei, Taiwan Tianjin (Tientsin), China Victoria (Hong Kong), Hong Kong | |
| 3,000,000-5,000,000 (38) | Boston, U.S. Dallas-Fort Worth, U.S. Detroit, U.S.-Windsor, Can. Houston, U.S. Miami-Fort Lauderdale, U.S. Toronto, Can. Washington, U.S. | Belo Horizonte, Brazil Bogotá, Col. Caracas, Ven. Guadalajara, Mex. Santiago, Chile | Athens, Greece Barcelona, Spain Berlin, Ger. Essen-Dortmund-Duisburg (The Ruhr), F.R. Ger. Madrid, Spain Milan, Italy Rome, Italy | | Baghdād, Iraq Bangalore, India Dhaka (Dacca), Bngl. Hyderābād, India Lahore, Pak. | Guangzhou (Canton), China Ho Chi Minh City (Saigon), Viet. Nagoya, Japan Pusan, Kor. S. Rangoon (Yangoon), Burma Shenyang, China Singapore, Sing. Wuhan, China | Alexandria, Egypt Johannesburg, S. Afr. Kinshasa, Zaire Lagos, Nigeria Melbourne, Austl. Sydney, Austl. |
| 2,000,000-3,000,000 (49) | Atlanta, U.S. Baltimore, U.S. Cleveland, U.S. Minneapolis-St. Paul, U.S. Montréal, Can. Phoenix, U.S. Pittsburgh, U.S. St. Louis, U.S. San Diego, U.S.-Tijuana, Mex. Seattle-Tacoma, U.S. | Fortaleza, Brazil Havana, Cuba Medellín, Col. Monterrey, Mex. Porto Alegre, Brazil Recife, Brazil Salvador, Brazil | Birmingham, Eng. Brussels, Bel. Bucharest, Rom. Budapest, Hung. Hamburg, F.R. Ger. Katowice-Bytom-Gliwice, Pol. Lisbon, Port. Manchester, Eng. Naples, Italy Warsaw, Pol. | Baku Donetsk-Makeyevka Gorkiy Kiev Tashkent | Ahmadābād, India Ankara, Tur. Colombo, Sri Lan. Kānpur, India Pune (Poona), India | Bandung, Indon. Chongqing (Chungking), China Harbin, China Kuala Lumpur, Malay. Nanjing (Nanking), China Sapporo-Otaru, Japan Surabaya, Indon. Taegu, Kor. S. Xi'an (Sian), China | Algiers, Alg. Cape Town, S. Afr. Casablanca, Mor. |
| 1,500,000-2,000,000 (57) | Cincinnati, U.S. Denver, U.S. | Brasília, Brazil Cali, Col. Curitiba, Brazil Guayaquil, Ec. Montevideo, Ur. San Juan, P.R. Santo Domingo, Dom. Rep. | Amsterdam, Neth. Belgrade, Yugo. Cologne, F.R. Ger. Copenhagen, Den. Frankfurt am Main, F.R. Ger. Glasgow, Scot. Leeds-Bradford, Eng. Liverpool, Eng. Munich, F.R. Ger. Stuttgart, F.R. Ger. Turin, Italy Vienna, Aus. | Dnepropetrovsk Kharkov Kuybyshev Minsk Novosibirsk Sverdlovsk | 'Ammān, Jordan Beirut, Leb. Chittagong, Bngl. Damascus, Syria İzmir, Tur. Jiddah, Sau. Ar. Kuwait (Al Kuwayt), Kuwait Mashhad, Iran Nāgpur, India Riyadh, Sau. Ar. Tel Aviv-Yafo, Isr. | Changchun, China Chengdu (Chengtu), China Dalian (Dairen), China Fukuoka, Japan Hanoi, Viet. Hiroshima-Kure, Japan Jinan (Tsinan), China Kaohsiung, Taiwan Kitakyūshū-Shimonoseki, Japan Medan, Indon. Pyŏngyang, Kor. N. Semarang, Indon. Taiyuan, China | Abidjan, I.C. Addis Ababa, Eth. Dakar, Sen. Dar es Salaam, Tan. Durban, S. Afr. Khartoum-Omdurman, Sudan |
| 1,000,000-1,500,000 (105) | Buffalo-Niagara Falls, U.S.-St. Catharines-Niagara Falls, Can. Columbus, U.S. El Paso, U.S.-Ciudad Juárez, Mex. Hartford-New Britain, U.S. Indianapolis, U.S. Kansas City, U.S. Milwaukee, U.S. New Orleans, U.S. Portland, U.S. Riverside-San Bernardino, U.S. Sacramento, U.S. St. Petersburg-Clearwater, U.S. San Antonio, U.S. Vancouver, Can. | Barranquilla, Col. Belém, Brazil Campinas, Brazil Córdoba, Arg. Goiânia, Brazil Guatemala, Guat. La Paz, Bol. Maracaibo, Ven. Puebla, Mex. Quito, Ec. Rosario, Arg. Santos, Brazil | Antwerp, Bel. Dublin, Ire. Düsseldorf, F.R. Ger. Hannover, F.R. Ger. Lille-Roubaix, France Łódź, Pol. Lyon, France Mannheim, F.R. Ger. Marseille, France Newcastle-Sunderland, Eng. Nürnberg, F.R. Ger. Porto, Port. Prague, Czech. Rotterdam, Neth. Sofia, Bul. Stockholm, Swe. Valencia, Spain | Alma-Ata Chelyabinsk Kazan Odessa Omsk Perm Rīga Rostov-na-Donu Saratov Tbilisi Ufa Volgograd Yerevan | Aleppo, Syria Āsānsol, India Coimbatore, India Eşfahān, Iran Faisalabad, Pak. Indore, India Jaipur, India Kabul (Kābol), Afg. Lucknow, India Madurai, India Patna, India Rāwalpindi-Islāmābād, Pak. Sūrat, India Tabrīz, Iran Vārānasi (Benares), India | Anshan, China Baotou, China Changsha, China Fushun, China Guiyang, China Hangzhou (Hangchou), China Jilin (Kirin), China Kunming, China Kwangju, Kor. S. Lanzhou (Lanchou), China Nanchang, China Palembang, Indon. Qingdao (Tsingtao), China Qiqihar (Tsitsihar), China Sendai, Japan Shijiazhuang, China Tangshan, China Ujungpandang (Makasar), Indon. Ürümqi, China Zhengzhou (Chengchou), China | Accra, Ghana Adelaide, Austl. Brisbane, Austl. Douala, Cam. Harare, Zimb. Ibadan, Nigeria Luanda, Ang. Maputo, Moz. Nairobi, Kenya Perth, Austl. Pretoria, S. Afr. Rabat-Salé, Mor. Tripoli, Libya Tunis, Tun. |
| Total by Region (282) | 38 | 36 | 48 | 26 | 43 | 61 | 30 |

# WORLD POPULATIONS

This table includes every urban center of 50,000 or more population in the world (excluding the United States), as well as many other important or well-known cities and towns. The table also lists major political subdivisions (states, provinces, etc.) of many countries.

The population figures are all from recent censuses (designated C) or official estimates (designated E), except for a few cities for which only unofficial estimates are available (designated UE). The date of the census or estimate is specified for each country. Individual exceptions are dated in parentheses.

For many cities, a second population figure is given accompanied by a star (★). The starred population refers to the city's entire metropolitan area, including suburbs. These metropolitan areas have been defined by Rand McNally, following consistent rules to facilitate comparisons among the urban centers of various countries. Where a place is part of the metropolitan area of another city, that city's name is specified in parentheses preceded by (★). Some important places that are considered to be secondary central cities of their areas are designated by (★★) preceding the name of the metropolitan area's main city. A population preceded by a triangle (⏶) refers to an entire municipality, commune, or other district, which includes rural areas in addition to the urban center itself. The names of capital cities appear in CAPITALS; the largest city in each country is designated by the symbol (•).

For more recent population totals for countries, see the Rand McNally population estimates in the World Political Information table. For lists of the largest metropolitan areas, see the World Metropolitan Areas and United States Metropolitan Areas tables.

### AFGHANISTAN / Afghānestān

1984 E 17,672,000

*Cities and Towns*

Andkhvoy (1981 E) 13,469
Baghlān (1982 E) 41,000
Chārīkār (1981 E) 22,994
Ghaznī (1981 E) 31,196
Herāt 160,000
Jalālābād (1982 E) 58,000
• KABUL (KĀBOL) 1,179,000
Kandahar (Qandahār) 203,000
Khānābād (1981 E) 27,482
Kholm (1981 E) 28,788
Kondūz (1982 E) 57,000
Lashkar Gāh (1981 E) 22,147
Mazār-e Sharīf 118,000
Meymaneh (1981 E) 39,218
Pol-e Khomrī (1981 E) 31,888
Sheberghān (1981 E) 19,475
Tāloqān (1981 E) 20,429

### ALBANIA / Shqipëri

1983 E 2,841,300

*Cities and Towns*

Berati (Berat) 36,600
Durrësi (Durrës) 72,400
Elbasani (Elbasan) 69,900
Fieri (Fier) 37,000
Gjirokastra (Gjirokastër) 21,400
Kavaja (Kavajë) 22,500
Korça (Korçë) 57,100
Lushnja (Lushnje) 24,200
Shkodra (Scutari) 71,200
Stalin (Kuçovë) 18,900
• TIRANA (TIRANË) (1984 E) 210,800
Vlora (Valona) 61,100

### ALGERIA / Djazaïr

1987 C 23,038,942

*Cities and Towns*

Adrar 28,580
Aflou 29,890
Aïn Benian (★ Algiers) 34,084
Aïn Defla 25,251
Aïn el Beïda 61,997
Aïn Fekroun 25,432
Aïn M'lila 33,345
Aïn Oussera 44,270
Aïn Sefra 23,799
Aïn Témouchent 47,479
Aïn Touta 28,915
• ALGIERS (EL DJAZAÏR) (★ 2,547,983) 1,507,241
Annaba (Bône) 305,526
Arzew 35,784
Bab Ezzouar (★ Algiers) 55,211
Barika 56,488
Batna 181,601
Béchar (Colomb-Béchar) 107,311
Bejaïa (Bougie) 114,534
Beni Saf 29,921
Beskra (Biskra) 128,281
Bir el Ater 33,364
Birkhadem (★ Algiers) 28,217
Bordj Bou Arreridj 84,264
Bordj el Kiffan (★ Algiers) 61,035
Bordj Menaïel 28,520
Boufarik 41,305
Bougara 29,650
Bouïra 36,550
Bou Saâda 66,688
Chelghoum-el Aïd 29,896
Cherchell 18,727
Cheria 32,953
Constantine (Qacentina) 440,842
Douéra 11,873
Ech Cheliff (Orléansville) 129,976
El Affroun 23,247
El Beyyadh 41,119
El Boulaïda (Blida) 170,935
El Djelfa 84,207
El Eulma 67,933
El Ghazawet 24,936
El Grara 33,912
El Kroub 36,924
El Menia 30,413
El Qoll 21,113
El Wad 70,073
Frenda 30,640
Ghardaïa 89,415
Ghilizane 80,091
Guelma 77,821
Hadjout 24,251
Hamma Bouziane 29,203
Hassi Bahbah 34,176
Jijel 62,793
Khemis Miliana 55,335
Khenchla 69,743
Koléa 33,115
Ksar Chellala 27,058
Laghouat 67,214
Lakhdaria 28,023
Larbaa 35,896
Lemdiyya (Médéa) 85,195
Maghnia 52,275
Mechriyya 39,145
Melyana 27,183
Messaad 47,460
Mestghanem (Mostaganem) 114,037
Mila 33,456
Mohammadia 42,123
Mouaskar (Mascara) 64,691
M'Sila 65,805
Oran (Wahran) 628,558
Oued Rhiou 27,056
Oued Zenati 17,772
Ouenza 36,096
Ouled Djellal 28,438
Oum el Bouaghi 34,257
Qasr el Boukhari 39,003
Reghaïa 26,542
Rouiba 16,435
Saïda 80,825
Sedrata 31,464
Sidi Aïssa 31,455
Sidi bel Abbès 152,778
Sidi Moussa 25,074
Sig 42,197
Skikda (Philippeville) 128,747
Sougueur 38,407
Souk Ahras 83,015
Sour el Ghozlane 24,527
Stif (Sétif) 170,182
Tbessa 107,559
Tihert 95,821
Tilimsen 126,882
Tissemsilt 26,250
Tizi-Ouzou 61,163
Touggourt 70,645
Wargla (Ouargla) 81,721

### AMERICAN SAMOA / Amerika Samoa

1980 C 32,279

*Cities and Towns*

• PAGO PAGO 3,075

### ANDORRA

1982 C 38,051

*Cities and Towns*

• ANDORRA 14,928

### ANGOLA

1986 E 8,981,000

*Cities and Towns*

Benguela (1983 E) 155,000
Cabinda (1970 C) 21,124
Huambo (Nova Lisboa) (1983 E) 203,000
Lobito (1983 E) 150,000
• LUANDA 1,082,000
Lubango (1984 E) 105,000
Malanje (1970 C) 31,599
Namibe (Moçâmedes) (1981 E) 100,000

### ANGUILLA

1984 C 6,680

*Cities and Towns*

South Hill 961
• THE VALLEY 1,042

### ANTIGUA AND BARBUDA

1977 E 72,000

*Cities and Towns*

• SAINT JOHN'S 24,359

### ARGENTINA

1980 C 27,947,446

*Cities and Towns*

Alm (★ Buenos Aires) 331,919
Alta Gracia 30,668
Avellaneda (★ Buenos Aires) 334,145
Azul 44,062
Bahía Blanca 223,818
Balcarce 29,406
Bell Ville 26,494
Berazategui (★ Buenos Aires) 201,862
Berisso (★ Buenos Aires) 66,152
Bragado 27,406
• BUENOS AIRES (★ 10,750,000) 2,922,829
Campana (★ Buenos Aires) 54,832
Cañada de Gómez 24,569
Caseros (Tres de Febrero) (★ Buenos Aires) 345,424
Casilda 23,074
Chacabuco 26,860
Chivilcoy 44,579
Cipolletti 40,268
Comodoro Rivadavia 96,817
Concepción 29,355
Concepción del Uruguay 46,247
Concordia 94,222
Córdoba (★ 1,070,000) 993,055
Coronel Rosales 56,620
Corrientes 180,612
Cruz del Eje 23,255
Curuzú Cuatiá 24,962
Cutral-Có 25,911
Ensenada (★ Buenos Aires) 41,323
Esquel 17,277
Esteban Echeverría (★ Buenos Aires) 188,923
Florencio Varela (★ Buenos Aires) 173,452
Formosa 93,603
General Pico 30,173
General Roca 38,419
General San Martín (★ Buenos Aires) 385,625
General Sarmiento (San Miguel) (★ Buenos Aires) 502,926
Godoy Cruz (★ Mendoza) 142,408
Goya 47,395
Gualeguay 25,075
Gualeguaychú 51,400
Guaymallén (★ Mendoza) 164,670
Junín 62,458
La Banda (★★ Santiago del Estero) 46,837
Lanús (★ Buenos Aires) 466,980
La Plata (★★ Buenos Aires) 477,175
La Rioja 67,043
Las Heras (★ Mendoza) 101,579
Lomas de Zamora (★ Buenos Aires) 510,130
Luján (★ Buenos Aires) 48,377
Maipú 7,247
Mar del Plata 414,696
Mendoza (★ 650,000) 119,088
Mercedes (★ Buenos Aires) 41,484
Mercedes 50,992
Merlo (★ Buenos Aires) 292,587
Moreno (★ Buenos Aires) 194,440
Morón (★ Buenos Aires) 598,420
Necochea 51,069
Neuquén 90,089
Olavarría 64,097
Paraná 161,638
Pergamino 68,612
Pilar (★ Buenos Aires) 84,429
Posadas 143,889
Presidencia Roque Sáenz Peña 49,341
Quilmes (★ Buenos Aires) 446,587
Rafaela 53,273
Reconquista 33,106
Resistencia 220,104
Río Cuarto 110,254
Río Tercero 34,745
Rosario (★ 1,045,000) 938,120
Salta 260,744
San Carlos de Bariloche 48,980
San Carlos de Bolívar 16,426
San Fernando (★ Buenos Aires) 133,624
San Fernando del Valle de Catamarca (★ 90,000) 78,799
San Francisco (★ 58,536) 51,932
San Isidro (★ Buenos Aires) 289,170
San Juan (★ 300,000) 118,046
San Justo (La Matanza) (★ Buenos Aires) 949,566
San Lorenzo (★ Rosario) 96,891
San Luis 70,999
San Miguel de Tucumán (★ 525,000) 392,888
San Nicolás [de los Arroyos] 98,495
San Pedro 27,386
San Pedro [de Jujuy] 37,101
San Rafael 70,959
San Ramón de la Nueva Orán 32,910
San Salvador de Jujuy 124,950
Santa Fe 292,165
Santiago del Estero (★ 200,000) 148,758
Santo Tomé 35,840
San Vicente (★ Buenos Aires) 55,803
Tafí Viejo 26,660
Tandil 79,429
Tartagal 31,556
Tigre (★ Buenos Aires) 206,349
Trelew 52,372
Tres Arroyos 41,265
Ushuaia 11,029
Venado Tuerto 47,501
Vicente López (★ Buenos Aires) 291,072
Victoria 18,894
Viedma 24,346
Villa Ángela 25,744
Villa Carlos Paz 29,655
Villa Constitución 36,425
Villa Krause (★ San Juan) 66,693
Villa María 67,560
Zárate 67,143

*Provinces*

Buenos Aires 10,865,408
Catamarca 207,717
Chaco 701,392
Chubut 263,116
Córdoba 2,407,754
Corrientes 661,454
Distrito Federal 2,922,829
Entre Ríos 908,313
Formosa 295,887
Jujuy 410,008
La Pampa 208,260
La Rioja 164,217
Mendoza 1,196,228
Misiones 588,977
Neuquén 243,850
Río Negro 383,354
Salta 662,870
San Juan 465,976
San Luis 214,416
Santa Cruz 114,941
Santa Fe 2,465,546
Santiago del Estero 594,920
Tierra del Fuego, Antártida e Islas del Atlántico Sur (Ter.) 27,358
Tucumán 972,655

### ARUBA

1987 E 64,763

*Cities and Towns*

• ORANJESTAD 19,800

### AUSTRALIA

1986 C 15,602,156

*Cities and Towns*

Adelaide (★ 977,721) 14,157
Albany 13,258
Albury (★ 62,697) 38,704
Alice Springs 22,759
Altona (★ Melbourne) 32,838
Armadale (★ Perth) 41,248
Armidale 19,525
Ashfield (★ Sydney) 40,401
Auburn (★ Sydney) 47,147
Ballarat (★ 75,210) 34,806
Bankstown (★ Sydney) 151,570
Bathurst 24,460
Bendigo (★ 62,380) 30,704
Berwick (★ Melbourne) 48,677
Blacktown (★ Sydney) 192,442
Blue Mountains (★ Sydney) 63,866
Botany (★ Sydney) 34,271
Box Hill (★ Melbourne) 45,785
Brighton (★ Melbourne) 33,195
Brisbane (★ 1,149,401) 705,755
Broadmeadows (★ Melbourne) 101,144
Broken Hill 24,460
Brunswick (★ Melbourne) 41,362
Bunbury 23,031
Bundaberg (★ 42,036) 31,421
Burnside (★ Adelaide) 37,198
Burwood (★ Sydney) 28,556
Cairns (★ 74,358) 42,227
Camberwell (★ Melbourne) 83,792
Campbelltown (★ Adelaide) 43,352
Campbelltown (★ Sydney) 121,297
CANBERRA (★ 271,362) 247,194
Canning (★ Perth) 60,736
Canterbury (★ Sydney) 128,502
Caulfield (★ Melbourne) 67,718
Cessnock (★★ Newcastle) 41,733
Chelsea (★ Melbourne) 25,803
Coburg (★ Melbourne) 52,885
Cockburn (★ Perth) 40,711
Croydon (★ Melbourne) 40,096
Dandenong (★ Melbourne) 56,461
Darwin (★ 72,937) 66,131
Devonport 24,417
Doncaster and Templestowe (★ Melbourne) 99,269
Drummoyne (★ Sydney) 30,605
Dubbo 30,918
Elizabeth (★ Adelaide) 30,687
Enfield (★ Adelaide) 63,528
Essendon (★ Melbourne) 53,977
Fairfield (★ Sydney) 153,522
Footscray (★ Melbourne) 47,330
Frankston (★ Melbourne) 83,819
Fremantle (★ Perth) 22,709
Gawler 11,354
Geelong (★ 139,792) 13,441
Geraldton 18,801
Glenorchy (★ Hobart) 40,883
Gosford 109,278
Gosnells (★ Perth) 60,610
Goulburn 21,552
Grafton 16,647
Hawthorn (★ Melbourne) 29,623
Heidelberg (★ Melbourne) 61,917
Hobart (★ 175,082) 47,356
Holroyd (★ Sydney) 78,237
Horsham 12,174
Hurstville (★ Sydney) 63,219
Ipswich (★ Brisbane) 71,861
Kalgoorlie (★ 22,232) 10,087
Keilor (★ Melbourne) 93,327
Knox (★ Melbourne) 104,207
Kogarah (★ Sydney) 45,949
Lake Macquarie (★ Newcastle) 153,540
Launceston (★ 88,486) 61,492
Leichhardt (★ Sydney) 56,303
Lismore 37,053
Liverpool (★ Sydney) 93,215
Logan (★ Brisbane) 117,191
Mackay (★ 48,725) 22,199
Maitland (★ Newcastle) 44,315
Malvern (★ Melbourne) 41,777
Manly (★ Sydney) 35,730
Marion (★ Adelaide) 69,695
Marrickville (★ Sydney) 81,647
Maryborough 7,705
Melbourne (★ 2,832,893) 60,828
Melville (★ Perth) 67,131
Mitcham (★ Adelaide) 61,213
Moe 16,999
Moorabbin (★ Melbourne) 95,291
Mordialloc (★ Melbourne) 26,817
Morwell 16,387
Mosman (★ Sydney) 25,781
Mount Gambier (★ 25,858) 18,729
Mount Isa 23,927
Murray Bridge 11,893
Newcastle (★ 405,089) 129,490
Noarlunga (★ Adelaide) 69,809
Northcote (★ Melbourne) 48,552
North Sydney (★ Sydney) 49,927
Nunawading (★ Melbourne) 93,482
Oakleigh (★ Melbourne) 55,764
Orange 31,710
Parramatta (★ Sydney) 130,783
Penrith (★ Sydney) 135,342
Perth (★ 994,472) 79,409
Port Adelaide (★ Adelaide) 37,296
Port Augusta 15,621
Port Lincoln 11,943
Port Pirie 14,597
Prahran (★ Melbourne) 43,051
Preston (★ Melbourne) 80,551
Queanbeyan (★ Canberra) 22,698
Randwick (★ Sydney) 115,620
Redcliffe (★ Brisbane) 44,933
Richmond (★ Melbourne) 23,275
Ringwood (★ Melbourne) 40,289
Rockdale (★ Sydney) 83,350
Rockhampton (★ 59,056) 56,742

C Census. E Official estimate. UE Unofficial estimate.
• Largest city in country.
★ Population or designation of metropolitan area, including suburbs (see headnote).
⏶ Population of an entire municipality, commune, or district, including rural area.

Rockingham 30,635
Ryde (★ Sydney) 89,252
Saint Kilda (★ Melbourne) 45,889
Sale 13,559
Salisbury (★ Adelaide) 96,618
Sandringham (★ Melbourne) 30,416
Shellharbour (★ Wollongong) 43,872
Shepparton (★ 37,086) 24,744
Shoalhaven 55,980
South Barwon (★ Geelong) 38,019
South Perth (★ Perth) 32,626
Southport (★ 215,663) 130,304
Springvale (★ Melbourne) 83,385
Stirling (★ Perth) 164,687
Sunshine (★ Melbourne) 94,413
• Sydney (★ 3,364,858) 86,311
Tamworth 33,321
Taree (Greater Taree) 35,921
Tea Tree Gully (★ Adelaide) 73,838
Thuringowa 30,104
Toowoomba 73,390
Townsville (★ 106,416) 82,809
Unley (★ Adelaide) 36,195
Wagga Wagga 49,401
Wangaratta 16,598
Wanneroo (★ Perth) 126,053
Warrnambool 22,706
Waverley (★ Melbourne) 122,935
Waverley (★ Sydney) 59,847
West Torrens (★ Adelaide) 43,639
Whyalla 27,102
Willoughby (★ Sydney) 51,893
Wollongong (★ 225,178) 167,863
Woodville (★ Adelaide) 79,886
Woollahra (★ Sydney) 51,057

*States*

Australian Capital Territory (Ter.) 249,407
New South Wales 5,401,881
Northern Territory (Ter.) 154,848
Queensland 2,587,315
South Australia 1,345,945
Tasmania 436,353
Victoria 4,019,478
Western Australia 1,406,929

## AUSTRIA / Österreich

1981 C 7,555,338

*Cities and Towns*

Amstetten (★ 30,000) 21,989
Baden [bei Wien] (★ Vienna) 23,140
Bad Ischl 12,970
Braunau [am Inn] 16,318
Bregenz (★ 73,000) 24,561
Bruck [an der Mur] (★ 52,000) 15,068
Dornbirn 38,641
Feldkirch (★ 52,000) 23,745
Gmunden (★ 27,000) 12,653
Graz (★ 325,000) 243,166
Hallein (★ Salzburg) 15,377
Hohenems (★ 31,000) 12,666
Innsbruck (★ 185,000) 117,287
Kapfenberg (★★ Bruck an der Mur) 25,716
Kitzbühel 7,840
Klagenfurt (★ 115,000) 87,321
Klosterneuburg (★ Vienna) 22,975
Knittelfeld (★ 59,000) 14,136
Krems [an der Donau] (★ 37,000) 23,056
Kufstein (★ 20,000) 13,118
Leoben (★ 52,000) 31,989
Leonding (★ Linz) 19,389
Lienz (★ 17,000) 11,661
Linz (★ 335,000) 199,910
Lustenau 17,401
Mödling (★ Vienna) 19,276
Mürzzuschlag (★ 16,000) 10,751
Neunkirchen (★ 45,000) 10,764
Salzburg (★ 220,000) 139,426
Sankt Pölten (★ 67,000) 50,419
Sankt Veit [an der Glan] 12,007
Solbad Hall [in Tirol] (★ Innsbruck) 12,614
Spittal (★ 24,000) 14,736
Steyr (★ 65,000) 38,942
Stockerau (★ Vienna) 12,679
Ternitz (★★ Neunkirchen) 16,120
Traun (★ Linz) 21,464
• VIENNA (WIEN) (★ 1,875,000) (1988 E) 1,480,688
Villach (★ 65,000) 52,692
Vöcklabruck (★ 48,000) 11,019
Voitsberg (★ 37,000) 10,945
Wels (★ 76,000) 51,060
Wiener Neustadt (★ 62,000) 35,006
Wolfsberg (★ 39,000) 28,097

*States*

1988 ESTIMATE

Burgenland 267,120
Kärnten (Carinthia) 541,900
Niederösterreich (Lower Austria) 1,427,636
Oberösterreich (Upper Austria) 1,297,171
Salzburg 463,422
Steiermark (Styria) 1,180,625
Tirol (Tyrol) 613,205
Vorarlberg 314,649
Wien (Vienna) 1,480,688

## BAHAMAS

1982 E 218,000

*Cities and Towns*

Freeport 25,000
Matthew Town (1980 C) 939
• NASSAU 135,000
West End (1980 C) 1,834

## BAHRAIN / Al Baḩrayn

1981 C 350,798

*Cities and Towns*

Al Muḩarraq (★ Manama) 57,688
• MANAMA (★ 224,643) 115,054

## BANGLADESH

1981 C 87,119,965

*Cities and Towns*

Barisāl 172,905
Begumganj 69,623
Bhairab Bāzār 63,563
Bogra 68,749
Brāhmanbāria 87,570
Chāndpur 85,656
Chittagong (★ 1,391,877) 980,000
Chuādānga 76,000
Comilla 184,132
• DHAKA (DACCA) (★ 3,430,312) 2,365,695
Dinājpur 96,718
Farīdpur 66,579
Gopālpur 31,725
Gulshan (★ Dhaka) 215,444
Jamālpur 91,815
Jessore 148,927
Jhenida 47,953
Khulna 648,359
Kishorganj 52,302
Kurīgrām 47,641
Kushtia 74,892
Mādārīpur 63,917
Mīrpur (★ Dhaka) 349,031
Mymensingh (Nasirābād) 190,991
Naogaon 52,975
Nārāyanganj (★★ Dhaka) 405,562
Narsingdi 76,841
Nawābganj 87,724
Netrakona 37,455
Noākhāli 59,065
Pābna 109,065
Pārbatipur 18,979
Patuākhāli 48,121
Rājshāhi (Rampur Boalia) 253,740
Rangpur 153,174
Saidpur 126,608
Sātkhira 52,156
Sherpur 48,214
Sirājganj 106,774
Sītākunda (★ Chittagong) 237,520
Sylhet 168,371
Tangail 77,518
Tongi (★ Dhaka) 94,580

## BARBADOS

1980 C 244,228

*Cities and Towns*

• BRIDGETOWN (★ 115,000) 7,466

## BELGIUM / Belgique / België

1987 E 9,864,751

*Cities and Towns*

Aalst (Alost) (★ Brussels) 77,113
Anderlecht (★ Brussels) 88,849
Antwerp (Antwerpen) (Anvers) (★ 1,100,000) 479,748
Arlon (▲ 22,208) 16,600
Ath (Aat) (▲ 23,535) 14,200
Auderghem (★ Brussels) 29,063
Bastogne (▲ 11,699) 6,900
Berchem-Sainte-Agathe (Sint-Agatha-Berchem) (★ Brussels) 18,942
Binche 32,647
Braine-l'Alleud (★ Brussels) 31,070
Brasschaat (★ Antwerp) 33,372
Brugge (Bruges) (★ 223,000) 117,755
• BRUSSELS (BRUXELLES) (BRUSSEL) (★ 2,385,000) 136,920
Charleroi (★ 480,000) 209,395
Châtelet (★ Charleroi) 37,351
Dendermonde 42,389
Edegem (★ Antwerp) 23,595
Eeklo 19,211
Etterbeek (★ Brussels) 44,240
Eupen 16,967
Evere (★ Brussels) 30,303
Forest (Vorst) (★ Brussels) 48,266
Ganshoren (★ Brussels) 20,629
Geel (▲ 31,981) 17,600
Genk (★★ Hasselt) 61,391
Gent (Ghent) (Gand) (★ 465,000) 233,856
Geraardsbergen (Grammont) (▲ 30,079) 14,800
Halle (Hal) (★ Brussels) 32,332
Hamme 22,694
Harelbeke (★ Kortrijk) 25,491
Hasselt (★ 290,000) 65,563
Herentals 24,162
Herstal (★ Liège) 36,849
Huy (▲ 17,230) 12,500
Ieper (Ypres) (▲ 34,757) 21,200
Ixelles (Elseue) (★ Brussels) 76,241
Izegem 26,377
Jette (★ Brussels) 38,623
Knokke [-Heist] 30,618
Kortrijk (Courtrai) (★ 202,000) 76,216
La Louvière (★ 147,000) 76,340
Leuven (Louvain) (★ 173,000) 84,583
Liège (Luik) (★ 750,000) 200,891
Lier (Lierre) (★ Antwerp) 30,867
Lokeren 34,256
Maasmechelen (Mechelen) 33,432
Mechelen (Malines) (★ 121,000) 75,808
Menen 32,804
Mol (▲ 30,179) 17,000
Molenbeek Saint-Jean (Sint-Jans-Molenbeek) (★ Brussels) 69,764
Mons (Bergen) (★ 242,000) 89,697
Mortsel (★ Antwerp) 26,085
Mouscron (Moeskroen) (★ Lille, France) 53,713
Namur (Namen) (★ 147,000) 102,670
Nivelles (Nijvel) 22,130
Oostende (Ostende) (★ 122,000) 68,318
Oudenaarde (Audenarde) (▲ 27,233) 26,926
Roeselare (Roulers) 51,963
Ronse (Renaix-Gleiche) 23,981
Saint-Gilles (Sint-Gillis) (★ Brussels) 42,482
Schaerbeek (Schaarbeek) (★ Brussels) 104,919
Schoten (★ Antwerp) 30,785
Seraing (★ Liège) 61,731
Sint-Niklaas (Saint-Nicolas) 68,082
Sint-Truiden (Saint-Trond) (▲ 36,612) 17,300
Soignies (Zinnik) (▲ 23,407) 11,600
Spa 9,645
Tienen (Tirlemont) 31,900
Tongeren (Tongres) (▲ 29,643) 18,600
Tournai (Doornik) (▲ 66,998) 44,900
Turnhout 37,462
Uccle (Ukkel) (★ Brussels) 75,876
Verviers (★ 101,000) 53,498
Veurne (Furnes) (▲ 11,284) 7,500
Vilvoorde (★ Brussels) 32,895
Waregem 33,945
Waterloo (★ Brussels) 25,232
Woluwe-Saint-Lambert (Sint-Lambrechts-Woluwe) (★ Brussels) 47,887
Woluwe-Saint-Pierre (Sint-Pieters-Woluwe) (★ Brussels) 39,492
Zottegem (▲ 24,596) 12,700

*Provinces*

Antwerp (Antwerpen) (Anvers) 1,585,163
Brabant 2,219,272
East Flanders (Oost-Vlaanderen) (Flandre Orientale) 1,328,931
Hainaut (Henegouwen) 1,274,034
Liège (Luik) 991,089
Limburg (Limbourg) 734,382
Luxembourg (Luxemburg) 225,563
Namur (Namen) 413,621
West Flanders (West-Vlaanderen) (Flandre Occidentale) 1,092,696

## BELIZE

1985 E 166,400

*Cities and Towns*

• Belize City 47,000
BELMOPAN 4,500
Corozal 10,000
Orange Walk 9,600
Punta Gorda (1980 C) 2,219
San Ignacio (1980 C) 5,553
Stann Creek 7,700

## BENIN / Bénin

1984 E 3,825,000

*Cities and Towns*

Abomey 53,000
• Cotonou 478,000
Natitingou (1975 E) 51,000
Ouidah (1979 E) 53,000
Parakou 92,000
PORTO-NOVO 164,000

## BERMUDA

1985 E 56,000

*Cities and Towns*

• HAMILTON (★ 15,000) 1,676
Saint George 1,707

## BHUTAN / Druk-Yul

1982 E 1,333,000

*Cities and Towns*

• THIMPHU 12,000

## BOLIVIA

1985 E 6,429,226

*Cities and Towns*

Cobija 4,989
Cochabamba 317,251
• LA PAZ 992,592
Oruro 178,393
Potosí 113,380
Santa Cruz 441,717
SUCRE 86,609
Tarija 60,621
Trinidad 40,288

*Departments*

Beni 239,810
Chuquisaca 462,904
Cochabamba 979,171
La Paz 2,091,429
Oruro 412,756
Pando 46,933
Potosí 878,232
Santa Cruz 1,047,964
Tarija 270,027

## BOPHUTHATSWANA

1982 E 1,347,000

*Cities and Towns*

• Ga-Rankuwa (1980 C) 48,300
Mabopane (1970 C) 22,559
Mafikeng (★ 16,000) (1980 C) 6,500
MMABATHO (★ Mafikeng) (1977 E) 9,062

## BOTSWANA

1986 E 1,127,900

*Cities and Towns*

Francistown 43,837
• GABORONE (GABERONES) 95,163
Kanye (1982 E) 22,000
Lobatse 23,832
Mahalatswe (1982 E) 19,000
Mochudi (1982 E) 20,000
Molepolole (1982 E) 19,000
Selebi Phikwe 41,382

## BRAZIL / Brasil

1985 E 135,564,395

*Cities and Towns*

Alagoinhas (▲ 116,959) 87,500
Alegrete (▲ 71,898) 56,700
Alvorada 105,730
Americana 156,030
Anápolis 225,840
Andradina 45,888
Apucarana (▲ 92,812) 73,700
Aracaju 360,013
Araçatuba 129,304
Araguari (▲ 96,035) 84,300
Arapiraca (▲ 147,879) 91,400
Araraquara (▲ 145,042) 87,500
Araras (▲ 71,652) 59,900
Araxá 61,418
Assis (▲ 74,238) 63,100
Bagé (▲ 106,155) 70,800
Barbacena (▲ 99,337) 80,200
Barra do Piraí (▲ 71,931) 55,700
Barra Mansa (★ Volta Redonda) 149,200
Barretos 80,202
Bauru 220,105
Bayeux (★ João Pessoa) 67,182
Belém (★ 1,200,000) 1,116,578
Belford Roxo (★ Rio de Janeiro) 340,700
Belo Horizonte (★ 2,950,000) 2,114,429
Betim (★ Belo Horizonte) 96,810
Blumenau 192,074
Boa Vista 66,028
Botucatu (▲ 71,139) 62,600
Bragança Paulista (▲ 105,099) 76,300
BRASÍLIA 1,567,709
Caçapava (▲ 64,213) 56,600
Cachoeira do Sul (▲ 91,492) 58,900
Cachoeirinha (★ Porto Alegre) 73,117
Cachoeiro de Itapemirim (▲ 138,156) 95,000
Campina Grande 279,929
Campinas (★ 1,125,000) 841,016
Campo Grande 384,398
Campos (▲ 366,716) 187,900
Campos Elyseos (★ Rio de Janeiro) 188,200
Canoas (★ Porto Alegre) 261,222
Carapicuíba (★ São Paulo) 265,856
Carazinho (▲ 62,108) 48,500
Cariacica (★ Vitória) 74,300
Caruaru (▲ 190,794) 152,100
Cascavel (▲ 200,485) 123,100
Castanhal (▲ 89,703) 71,200
Catanduva (▲ 80,309) 71,400
Caucaia (★ Fortaleza) 78,500
Cavaleiro (★ Recife) 106,600
Caxias (▲ 148,230) 66,300
Caxias do Sul 266,809
Chapecó (▲ 100,997) 64,200
Coelho da Rocha (★ Rio de Janeiro) 164,400
Colatina (▲ 106,260) 58,600
Colombo (★ Curitiba) 65,900
Conselheiro Lafaiete 77,958
Contagem (★ Belo Horizonte) 152,700
Corumbá (▲ 80,666) 65,800
Crato (▲ 86,371) 52,700
Criciúma (▲ 128,410) 85,900
Cruz Alta (▲ 71,817) 58,300
Cruzeiro 63,918
Cubatão (★ Santos) 98,322
Cuiabá (▲ 279,651) 220,400
Curitiba (★ 1,700,000) 1,279,205
Diadema (★ São Paulo) 320,187
Divinópolis 139,940
Dourados (▲ 123,757) 89,200
Duque de Caxias (★ Rio de Janeiro) 353,200
Embu (★ São Paulo) 119,791
Erexim (▲ 70,709) 54,300
Esteio (★ Porto Alegre) 58,964
Feira de Santana (▲ 355,201) 278,600
Ferraz de Vasconcelos (★ São Paulo) 68,831
Florianópolis (★ 365,000) 178,400
Fortaleza (★ 1,825,000) 1,582,414
Foz do Iguaçu (▲ 182,101) 124,900
Franca 182,820
Garanhuns 73,100
Goiânia (★ 990,000) 923,333
Governador Valadares (▲ 216,957) 192,300
Guaratinguetá (▲ 93,534) 80,400
Guarujá (★ Santos) 83,500
Guarulhos (★ São Paulo) 571,700
Ijuí (▲ 82,064) 64,400
Ilhéus (▲ 145,810) 79,400
Imperatriz (▲ 235,453) 119,500
Ipatinga (★ 270,000) 149,100
Ipiíba (★ Rio de Janeiro) 116,200
Itabira (▲ 81,771) 66,300
Itabuna (▲ 167,543) 142,200
Itajaí 104,232
Itajubá (▲ 69,675) 61,500
Itapecerica da Serra (★ São Paulo) 65,500
Itapetininga (▲ 105,512) 76,700
Itapevi (★ São Paulo) 66,825
Itaquaquecetuba (★ São Paulo) 91,366
Itaquari (★ Vitória) 163,900
Itaúna 61,446
Itu (▲ 92,786) 77,900
Ituiutaba (▲ 85,365) 74,900
Itumbiara (▲ 78,844) 57,200
Jaboatão (★ Recife) 82,900
Jacareí 149,061
Jandira 45,069
Jaú (▲ 92,547) 74,500
Jequié (▲ 127,070) 92,100
João Pessoa (Paraíba) (★ 550,000) 348,500
Joinville 302,877
Juazeiro (★ Petrolina) 78,600
Juazeiro do Norte 159,806
Juiz de Fora 349,720

C Census. E Official estimate. UE Unofficial estimate.
• Largest city in country.

★ Population or designation of metropolitan area, including suburbs (see headnote).
▲ Population of an entire municipality, commune, or district, including rural area.

| | |
|---|---|
| Jundiaí (▲ 313,652) | 268,900 |
| Lajes (▲ 143,246) | 103,600 |
| Lavras | 52,100 |
| Limeira | 186,986 |
| Linhares (▲ 122,453) | 53,400 |
| Londrina (▲ 346,676) | 296,400 |
| Lorena | 63,230 |
| Luziânia (▲ 98,408) | 71,400 |
| Macapá (▲ 168,839) | 109,400 |
| Maceió | 482,195 |
| Manaus | 809,914 |
| Marabá (▲ 133,559) | 92,700 |
| Marília (▲ 136,187) | 116,100 |
| Maringá | 196,871 |
| Mauá (★ São Paulo) | 269,321 |
| Mesquita (★ Rio de Janeiro) | 161,300 |
| Mogi das Cruzes (★ São Paulo) | 144,800 |
| Mogi-Guaçu (▲ 91,994) | 81,800 |
| Mogi-Mirim (▲ 63,313) | 52,300 |
| Monjolo (★ Rio de Janeiro) | 113,900 |
| Montes Claros (▲ 214,472) | 183,500 |
| Mossoró (▲ 158,723) | 128,300 |
| Muriaé (▲ 80,466) | 57,600 |
| Muribeca dos Guararapes (★ Recife) | 171,200 |
| Natal | 510,106 |
| Neves (★ Rio de Janeiro) | 163,600 |
| Nilópolis (★ Rio de Janeiro) | 112,800 |
| Niterói (★ Rio de Janeiro) | 441,684 |
| Nova Friburgo (▲ 143,529) | 103,500 |
| Nova Iguaçu (★ Rio de Janeiro) | 592,800 |
| Novo Hamburgo (★ Porto Alegre) | 167,744 |
| Olinda (★ Recife) | 316,600 |
| Osasco (★ São Paulo) | 591,568 |
| Ourinhos (▲ 65,841) | 58,100 |
| Paranaguá (▲ 94,809) | 82,300 |
| Paranavaí (▲ 75,511) | 60,900 |
| Parnaíba (▲ 116,206) | 90,200 |
| Parque Industrial (★ Belo Horizonte) | 228,400 |
| Passo Fundo (▲ 137,843) | 117,500 |
| Passos (▲ 79,393) | 65,500 |
| Patos | 74,298 |
| Patos de Minas (▲ 99,027) | 69,000 |
| Paulo Afonso (▲ 86,182) | 75,300 |
| Pelotas (▲ 277,730) | 210,300 |
| Petrolina (★ 225,000) | 92,100 |
| Petrópolis (★ Rio de Janeiro) | 170,300 |
| Pindamonhangaba (▲ 86,990) | 64,100 |
| Pinheirinho (★ Curitiba) | 51,600 |
| Piracicaba (▲ 252,079) | 211,000 |
| Poá (★ São Paulo) | 66,006 |
| Poços de Caldas | 100,004 |
| Ponta Grossa | 223,154 |
| Porto Alegre (★ 2,600,000) | 1,272,121 |
| Porto Velho (▲ 202,011) | 152,700 |
| Pouso Alegre (▲ 65,958) | 58,300 |
| Praia Grande (★ Santos) | 67,800 |
| Presidente Prudente | 155,883 |
| Queimados (★ Rio de Janeiro) | 113,700 |
| Recife (★ 2,625,000) | 1,287,623 |
| Ribeirão Preto | 383,125 |
| Rio Branco (▲ 145,486) | 109,800 |
| Rio Claro | 129,859 |
| Rio de Janeiro (★ 10,150,000) | 5,603,388 |
| Rio Grande | 164,221 |
| Rio Verde (▲ 92,954) | 59,400 |
| Rondonópolis (▲ 101,642) | 65,500 |
| Salvador (★ 2,050,000) | 1,804,438 |
| Santa Bárbara d'Oeste | 95,818 |
| Santa Cruz [do Sul] (▲ 115,288) | 60,300 |
| Santa Maria (▲ 196,827) | 163,900 |
| Santana do Livramento | 60,100 |
| Santarém (▲ 226,618) | 120,800 |
| Santa Rita (★ João Pessoa) | 60,100 |
| Santo André (★ São Paulo) | 635,129 |
| Santo Ângelo (▲ 107,559) | 57,700 |
| Santos (★ 1,065,000) | 460,100 |
| São Bernardo [do Campo] (★ São Paulo) | 562,485 |
| São Caetano do Sul (★ São Paulo) | 171,005 |
| São Carlos | 140,383 |
| São Gonçalo (★ Rio de Janeiro) | 262,400 |
| São João da Boa Vista (▲ 61,653) | 50,400 |
| São João del Rei (▲ 74,385) | 61,400 |
| São João de Meriti (★ Rio de Janeiro) | 241,700 |
| São José do Rio Preto | 229,221 |
| São José dos Campos | 372,578 |
| São José dos Pinhais (★ Curitiba) | 64,100 |
| São Leopoldo (★ Porto Alegre) | 114,065 |
| São Lourenço da Mata (★ Recife) | 65,936 |
| São Luís (★ 600,000) | 227,900 |
| • São Paulo (★ 15,175,000) | 10,063,110 |
| São Vicente (★ Santos) | 239,778 |
| Sapucaia do Sul (★ Porto Alegre) | 91,820 |
| Sete Lagoas | 121,418 |
| Sete Pontes (★ Rio de Janeiro) | 72,300 |
| Sobral (▲ 112,275) | 69,400 |
| Sorocaba | 327,468 |
| Suzano (★ São Paulo) | 128,924 |
| Taboão da Serra (★ São Paulo) | 122,112 |
| Tatuí (▲ 69,358) | 56,000 |
| Taubaté | 205,120 |
| Teófilo Otoni (▲ 126,265) | 82,700 |
| Teresina (★ 525,000) | 425,300 |
| Teresópolis (▲ 115,859) | 92,600 |
| Timon (★ Teresina) | 68,300 |
| Tubarão (▲ 82,082) | 70,400 |
| Uberaba | 244,875 |
| Uberlândia | 312,024 |
| Uruguaiana (▲ 105,862) | 91,500 |
| Varginha | 74,630 |
| Vicente de Carvalho (★ Santos) | 102,700 |
| Vila Velha (Espírito Santo) (★ Vitória) | 91,900 |
| Vitória (★ 735,000) | 201,500 |
| Vitória da Conquista (▲ 198,150) | 145,800 |
| Vitória de Santo Antão (▲ 100,450) | 67,800 |
| Volta Redonda (★ 375,000) | 219,267 |

*States*

| | |
|---|---|
| Acre | 366,103 |
| Alagoas | 2,224,238 |
| Amapá (Ter.) | 217,027 |
| Amazonas | 1,739,540 |
| Bahia | 10,654,453 |
| Ceará | 5,890,414 |
| Distrito Federal | 1,567,709 |
| Espírito Santo | 2,287,888 |
| Fernando de Noronha (Ter.) | 1,294 |
| Goiás | 4,437,483 |
| Maranhão | 4,655,123 |
| Mato Grosso | 1,486,111 |
| Mato Grosso do Sul | 1,592,489 |
| Minas Gerais | 14,609,062 |
| Pará | 4,318,420 |
| Paraíba | 3,008,534 |
| Paraná | 8,130,905 |
| Pernambuco | 6,742,169 |
| Piauí | 2,419,502 |
| Rio de Janeiro | 12,695,417 |
| Rio Grande do Norte | 2,111,947 |
| Rio Grande do Sul | 8,471,943 |
| Rondônia | 908,938 |
| Roraima (Ter.) | 102,491 |
| Santa Catarina | 4,085,847 |
| São Paulo | 29,541,863 |
| Sergipe | 1,297,485 |

## BRUNEI

1981 C 192,832

*Cities and Towns*

| | |
|---|---|
| • BANDAR SERI BEGAWAN (BRUNEI) (★ 64,000) | 22,777 |
| Seria | 23,415 |

## BULGARIA / Bâlgarija

1986 E 9,913,000

*Cities and Towns*

| | |
|---|---|
| Asenovgrad (1985 E) | 47,143 |
| Blagoevgrad (Gorna Dzhumaya) | 67,766 |
| Burgas | 186,369 |
| Dimitrovgrad | 54,898 |
| Gabrovo | 81,688 |
| Gorna Oryakhovitsa (1985 E) | 40,704 |
| Kazanlŭk | 61,780 |
| Khaskovo | 89,273 |
| Kŭrdzhali | 56,906 |
| Kyustendil | 54,773 |
| Lom (1985 E) | 32,121 |
| Lovech (1985 E) | 48,862 |
| Mikhaylovgrad | 53,529 |
| Pazardzhik | 79,198 |
| Pernik (Dimitrovo) | 96,277 |
| Pleven | 132,206 |
| Plovdiv | 349,148 |
| Razgrad | 51,277 |
| Ruse | 186,428 |
| Shumen (Kolarovgrad) | 102,886 |
| Silistra | 54,627 |
| Sliven | 104,345 |
| Smolyan (1985 E) | 31,539 |
| • SOFIA (SOFIYA) (★ 1,205,000) | 1,119,152 |
| Stanke Dimitrov (1985 E) | 42,153 |
| Stara Zagora | 153,538 |
| Svishtov (1985 E) | 30,550 |
| Tolbukhin (Dobrich) | 110,471 |
| Tŭrgovishte (1985 E) | 46,522 |
| Varna | 303,071 |
| Veliko Tŭrnovo (Tŭrnovo) | 70,610 |
| Vidin | 63,813 |
| Vratsa | 77,934 |
| Yambol | 92,321 |

*Provinces*

1985 ESTIMATE

| | |
|---|---|
| Blagoevgrad | 346,266 |
| Burgas | 449,314 |
| Gabrovo | 175,120 |
| Khaskovo | 301,249 |
| Kŭrdzhali | 302,578 |
| Kyustendil | 190,410 |
| Lovech | 202,708 |
| Mikhaylovgrad | 223,292 |
| Pazardzhik | 326,315 |
| Pernik | 174,419 |
| Pleven | 362,130 |
| Plovdiv | 754,393 |
| Razgrad | 198,007 |
| Ruse | 304,443 |
| Shumen | 254,789 |
| Silistra | 174,052 |
| Sliven | 239,479 |
| Smolyan | 164,223 |
| Sofiya | 305,251 |
| Sofiya (Sofia) (city) | 1,199,405 |
| Stara Zagora | 411,506 |
| Tolbukhin | 257,298 |
| Tŭrgovishte | 171,167 |
| Varna | 464,701 |
| Veliko Tŭrnovo | 339,120 |
| Vidin | 166,388 |
| Vratsa | 287,841 |
| Yambol | 203,754 |

## BURKINA FASO

1985 C 7,964,705

*Cities and Towns*

| | |
|---|---|
| Bobo Dioulasso | 228,668 |
| Koudougou | 51,926 |
| • OUAGADOUGOU | 441,514 |
| Ouahigouya | 38,902 |

## BURMA / Myanmar

1983 C 35,306,189

*Cities and Towns*

| | |
|---|---|
| Bago | 150,447 |
| Chauk (1953 C) | 24,466 |
| Dawei (1970 E) | 53,000 |
| Henzada (1970 E) | 85,000 |
| Mandalay | 532,895 |
| Mawlamyine | 219,991 |
| Meiktila (1953 C) | 25,180 |
| Mergui (1953 C) | 33,697 |
| Monywa | 106,873 |
| Myaungmya (1953 C) | 24,532 |
| Myingyan (1970 E) | 65,000 |
| Myitkyinā (1953 C) | 12,833 |
| Pakokku (1953 C) | 30,943 |
| Pathein | 144,092 |
| Prome (Pyè) (1970 E) | 65,000 |
| • RANGOON (YANGON) (★ 2,800,000) | 2,458,712 |
| Sagaing (1953 C) | 15,439 |
| Sittwe (Akyab) | 107,607 |
| Taunggyi | 107,907 |
| Thaton (1953 C) | 38,047 |
| Toungoo (1953 C) | 31,589 |
| Yenangyaung (1953 C) | 24,416 |

## BURUNDI

1986 E 4,782,000

*Cities and Towns*

| | |
|---|---|
| • BUJUMBURA | 273,000 |
| Bururi (1979 E) | 7,800 |
| Gitega | 95,000 |
| Muyinga (1982 E) | 5,400 |

## CAMEROON / Cameroun

1986 E 10,446,000

*Cities and Towns*

| | |
|---|---|
| Bafoussam (1985 E) | 89,000 |
| Bamenda (1985 E) | 72,000 |
| • Douala | 1,029,731 |
| Foumban (1985 E) | 50,000 |
| Garoua (1985 E) | 96,000 |
| Kumba (1985 E) | 67,000 |
| Limbe (Victoria) (1976 C) | 27,016 |
| Maroua | 103,653 |
| Ngaoundéré (1985 E) | 61,000 |
| Nkongsamba | 123,149 |
| YAOUNDÉ | 653,670 |

## CAMBODIA / Kâmpŭchéa

1986 E 7,492,000

*Cities and Towns*

| | |
|---|---|
| Batdambang (1962 C) | 38,780 |
| Kampong Cham (1971 E) | 35,000 |
| Kampong Saom (1981 E) | 53,000 |
| • PHNUM PENH | 700,000 |

## CANADA

1986 C 25,354,064

## CANADA: ALBERTA

1986 C 2,375,278

*Cities and Towns*

| | |
|---|---|
| Banff (1981 C) | 4,208 |
| Calgary (★ 671,326) | 636,104 |
| Camrose | 12,968 |
| Edmonton (★ 785,465) | 573,982 |
| Fort McMurray (★ 48,497) | 34,949 |
| Fort Saskatchewan (★ Edmonton) | 11,983 |
| Grande Prairie | 26,471 |
| Jasper (1981 C) | 3,269 |
| Leduc | 13,126 |
| Lethbridge | 58,841 |
| Lloydminster, Alta. and Sask. prov. | 17,356 |
| Medicine Hat (★ 50,734) | 41,804 |
| Red Deer | 54,425 |
| Saint Albert (★ Edmonton) | 36,710 |
| Sherwood Park (★ Edmonton) (1981 C) | 29,285 |
| Spruce Grove | 11,918 |

## CANADA: BRITISH COLUMBIA

1986 C 2,889,207

*Cities and Towns*

| | |
|---|---|
| Burnaby (★ Vancouver) | 145,161 |
| Campbell River (1981 C) | 15,370 |
| Chilliwack (★ 50,288) | 41,337 |
| Courtenay (★ 37,553) | 9,631 |
| Cranbrook | 15,893 |
| Dawson Creek | 10,544 |
| Esquimalt (★ Victoria) | 15,972 |
| Fort Saint John | 13,355 |
| Kamloops | 61,773 |
| Kelowna (★ 89,730) | 61,213 |
| Kitimat (★ Terrace) | 11,196 |
| Langley (★ Vancouver) | 16,557 |
| Matsqui (★ 88,420) | 51,449 |
| Nanaimo (★ 60,420) | 49,029 |
| New Westminster (★ Vancouver) | 39,972 |
| North Vancouver (★ Vancouver) | 35,698 |
| Oak Bay (★ Victoria) | 17,065 |
| Penticton (★ 38,966) | 23,588 |
| Port Alberni (★ 26,134) | 18,241 |
| Port Coquitlam (★ Vancouver) | 29,115 |
| Port Moody (★ Vancouver) | 15,754 |
| Powell River (★ 18,374) | 12,440 |
| Prince George | 67,621 |
| Prince Rupert (★ 17,581) | 15,755 |
| Richmond (★ Vancouver) | 108,492 |
| Terrace (★ 17,390) | 10,532 |
| Trail (★ 20,257) | 7,948 |
| Vancouver (★ 1,380,729) | 431,147 |
| Vernon (★ 42,802) | 20,241 |
| Victoria (★ 255,547) | 66,303 |
| West Vancouver (★ Vancouver) | 36,266 |
| White Rock (★ Vancouver) | 14,387 |

## CANADA: MANITOBA

1986 C 1,071,232

*Cities and Towns*

| | |
|---|---|
| Brandon | 38,708 |
| Churchill (1981 C) | 1,186 |
| Flin Flon, Man. and Sask. prov. (★ 9,211) | 7,591 |
| Portage la Prairie | 13,198 |
| Selkirk | 10,013 |
| Thompson (★ 14,729) | 14,701 |
| Winnipeg (★ 625,304) | 594,551 |

## CANADA: NEW BRUNSWICK

1986 C 710,422

*Cities and Towns*

| | |
|---|---|
| Bathurst (★ 34,895) | 14,683 |
| Campbellton (★ 17,418) | 9,077 |
| Edmundston (★ 22,614) | 11,497 |
| Fredericton (★ 65,768) | 44,352 |
| Moncton (★ 102,084) | 55,468 |
| Oromocto | 9,656 |
| Riverview (★ Moncton) | 15,638 |
| Saint John (★ 121,265) | 76,381 |

## CANADA: NEWFOUNDLAND

1986 C 568,349

*Cities and Towns*

| | |
|---|---|
| Carbonear (★ 13,082) | 5,337 |
| Channel-Port-aux-Basques | 5,901 |
| Conception Bay South (★ Saint John's) | 15,531 |
| Corner Brook (★ 33,730) | 22,719 |
| Gander (★ 10,899) | 10,207 |
| Grand Falls (★ 25,612) | 9,121 |
| Happy Valley-Goose Bay | 7,248 |
| Kilbride (★ Saint John's) (1981 C) | 5,014 |
| Labrador City (★ 11,301) | 8,664 |
| Marystown | 6,660 |
| Mount Pearl (★ Saint John's) | 20,293 |
| Saint John's (★ 161,901) | 96,216 |
| Saint John's Metropolitan Area (★ Saint John's) | 6,254 |
| Stephenville | 7,994 |
| Windsor (★ Grand Falls) | 5,545 |

## CANADA: NORTHWEST TERRITORIES

1986 C 52,238

*Cities and Towns*

| | |
|---|---|
| Eskimo Point | 1,189 |
| Fort Smith | 2,460 |
| Hay River | 2,964 |
| Inuvik | 3,389 |
| Iqaluit (1981 C) | 2,333 |
| Pine Point | 1,558 |
| Rae | 1,378 |
| Rankin Inlet | 1,374 |
| Yellowknife | 11,753 |

## CANADA: NOVA SCOTIA

1986 C 873,199

*Cities and Towns*

| | |
|---|---|
| Dartmouth (★ Halifax) | 65,243 |
| Glace Bay (★★ Sydney) | 20,467 |
| Halifax (★ 295,990) | 113,577 |
| Kentville | 5,208 |
| Louisbourg | 1,355 |
| New Glasgow (★ 38,737) | 10,022 |
| Sydney (★ 119,470) | 27,754 |
| Sydney Mines | 8,063 |
| Truro (★ 41,516) | 12,124 |

## CANADA: ONTARIO

1986 C 9,113,515

*Cities and Towns*

| | |
|---|---|
| Ajax (★ Toronto) | 36,550 |
| Ancaster (★ Hamilton) | 17,264 |
| Aurora (★ Toronto) | 20,905 |
| Barrie (★ 67,703) | 48,287 |
| Belleville (★ 87,530) | 36,041 |
| Brampton (★ Toronto) | 188,498 |
| Brantford (★ 90,521) | 76,146 |
| Brockville (★ 37,115) | 20,880 |
| Burlington (★ Hamilton) | 116,675 |
| Caledon (★ Toronto) | 29,666 |
| Cambridge (Galt) (★★ Kitchener) | 79,920 |
| Chatham | 42,211 |
| Cobourg | 13,197 |
| Collingwood | 12,172 |
| Cornwall (★ 51,719) | 46,425 |
| Dundas (★ Hamilton) | 20,118 |
| Dunnville | 11,589 |
| East Gwillimbury | 14,644 |
| East York (★ Toronto) | 101,085 |
| Elliot Lake (★ 19,071) | 17,984 |
| Etobicoke (★ Toronto) | 302,973 |
| Fergus | 6,372 |
| Fort Erie | 23,253 |
| Gloucester (★ Ottawa) | 89,810 |
| Grimsby (★ Hamilton) | 16,956 |
| Guelph (★ 85,962) | 78,235 |
| Haileybury (★ 14,781) | 4,820 |
| Haldimand | 17,701 |
| Halton Hills | 35,570 |
| Hamilton (★ 557,029) | 306,728 |
| Hawkesbury (★ 11,064) | 9,710 |
| Huntsville | 12,131 |
| Kanata (★ Ottawa) | 27,519 |
| Kapuskasing | 11,378 |
| Kenora (★ 15,456) | 9,621 |
| Kingston (★ 122,350) | 55,050 |
| Kirkland Lake | 11,604 |
| Kitchener (★ 311,195) | 150,604 |
| Leamington | 12,828 |
| Lincoln | 14,391 |
| Lindsay (★ 17,913) | 14,455 |
| London (★ 342,302) | 269,140 |
| Markham (★ Toronto) | 114,597 |
| Midland (★ 35,003) | 12,092 |
| Milton | 32,037 |
| Mississauga (★ Toronto) | 374,005 |
| Nanticoke | 20,202 |
| Nepean (★ Ottawa) | 95,490 |
| Newcastle | 34,073 |
| Newmarket (★ Toronto) | 34,923 |

C Census. E Official estimate. UE Unofficial estimate.
• Largest city in country.

★ Population or designation of metropolitan area, including suburbs (see headnote).
▲ Population of an entire municipality, commune, or district, including rural area.

Niagara Falls (★★ Saint Catharines) 72,107
Niagara-on-the-Lake (★ Saint Catharines) 12,494
Nickel Centre (★ Sudbury) 11,469
North Bay (★ 57,422) 50,623
North York (★ Toronto) 556,297
Oakville (★ Toronto) 87,107
Orangeville 14,440
Orillia (★ 31,252) 24,077
Oshawa (★ 203,543) 123,651
OTTAWA (★ 819,263) 300,763
Owen Sound (★ 27,364) 19,804
Pelham (★ Saint Catharines) 12,137
Pembroke (★ 22,560) 14,131
Petawawa 5,580
Peterborough (★ 87,083) 61,049
Pickering (★ Toronto) 48,959
Port Colborne (★ Saint Catharines) 18,281
Rayside-Balfour (★ Sudbury) 14,231
Richmond Hill (★ Toronto) 46,766
Saint Catharines (★ 343,258) 123,455
Saint Thomas 28,851
Sarnia (★ 85,700) 49,033
Sault Sainte Marie (★ 84,617) 80,905
Scarborough (★ Toronto) 484,676
Simcoe 14,290
Smiths Falls 9,163
Stoney Creek (★ Hamilton) 43,554
Stratford 26,451
Sudbury (★ 148,877) 88,717
Thorold (★ Saint Catharines) 16,131
Thunder Bay (★ 122,217) 112,272
Tillsonburg 10,745
Timmins 46,657
• Toronto (★ 3,427,168) 612,289
Trenton 15,311
Valley East (★ Sudbury) 19,233
Vanier (Eastview) (★ Ottawa) 18,426
Vaughan (Woodbridge) (★ Toronto) 65,058
Walden (★ Sudbury) 9,442
Wallaceburg 11,367
Waterloo (★ Kitchener) 58,718
Welland (★★ Saint Catharines) 45,054
Whitby (★ Oshawa) 45,819
Whitchurch-Stouffville (★ Toronto) 15,135
Windsor (★ 253,988) 193,111
Woodstock 26,386
York (★ Toronto) 135,401

## CANADA: PRINCE EDWARD ISLAND

1986 C 126,646

***Cities and Towns***

Charlottetown (★ 53,868) 15,776
Summerside (★ 15,614) 8,020

## CANADA: QUEBEC / Québec

1986 C 6,540,276

***Cities and Towns***

Alma (★ 29,977) 25,923
Ancienne-Lorette (Notre-Dame-de-Lorette) (★ Québec) 13,747
Anjou (★ Montréal) 36,916
Asbestos 6,961
Aylmer East (★ Ottawa) 28,976
Baie-Comeau (★ 33,047) 26,244
Beaconsfield (★ Montréal) 19,301
Beauport (★ Québec) 62,869
Bécancour 10,472
Beloeil (★ Montréal) 17,958
Blainville (★ Montréal) 16,175
Boisbriand (★ Montréal) 14,360
Boucherville (★ Montréal) 31,116
Brossard (★ Montréal) 57,441
Cap-de-la-Madeleine (★ Trois-Rivières) 32,800
Chambly (★ Montréal) 12,869
Charlesbourg (★ Québec) 68,996
Châteauguay (★ Montréal) 37,865
Chibougamau 9,922
Chicoutimi (★ 158,468) 61,083
Côte-Saint-Luc (★ Montréal) 28,582
Cowansville (★ 12,114) 11,643
Dolbeau (★ 15,288) 8,554
Dollard-des-Ormeaux (★ Montréal) 43,089
Dorval (★ Montréal) 17,354
Drummondville (★ 56,283) 36,020
Gaspé 17,350
Gatineau (★ Ottawa) 81,244
Granby (★ 51,176) 38,508
Grand-Mère (★ Shawinigan) 14,582
Greenfield Park (★ Montréal) 18,290
Hauterive (★ Baie-Comeau) (1981 C) 13,995
Hull (★ Ottawa) 58,722
Joliette (★ 34,897) 16,845
Jonquière (★★ Chicoutimi) 58,467
Kirkland (★ Montréal) 13,376
La Baie 20,753
Lachine (★ Montréal) 34,906
Lachute 11,586
La Prairie (★ Montréal) 11,072
LaSalle (★ Montréal) 75,621
La Tuque (★ 13,468) 10,723
Lauzon (★ Québec) 13,620
Laval (★ Montréal) 284,164
Lévis (★ Québec) 18,310
Longueuil (★ Montréal) 125,441
Loretteville (★ Québec) 14,335
Magog (★ 18,738) 13,530
Mascouche (★ Montréal) 21,285
Matane (★ 15,361) 13,243
Mirabel 13,875
Montmagny 11,958
Montréal (★ 2,921,357) 1,015,420
Montréal-Nord (★ Montréal) 90,303
Mont-Royal (★ Montréal) 18,350
Mont-Saint-Hilaire (★ Montréal) 10,588
Outremont (★ Montréal) 23,080
Pierrefonds (★ Montréal) 39,605
Pointe-Claire (★ Montréal) 26,026
Québec (★ 603,267) 164,580
Repentigny (★ Montréal) 40,778
Rimouski (★ 46,210) 29,672
Rivière-du-Loup (★ 22,471) 13,321
Roberval 11,448
Rouyn (★ 36,495) 17,319
Saint-Bruno-de-Montarville (★ Montréal) 23,103
Saint-Eustache (★ Montréal) 32,226
Sainte-Foy (★ Québec) 69,615
Saint-Hubert (★ Montréal) 66,218
Saint-Hyacinthe (★ 48,303) 38,603
Saint-Jean-sur-Richelieu (★ 59,958) 34,745
Saint-Jérôme (★ 44,048) 23,316
Sainte-Julie (★ Montréal) 15,502
Saint-Lambert (★ Montréal) 20,030
Saint-Laurent (★ Montréal) 67,002
Saint-Léonard (★ Montréal) 75,947
Sainte-Thérèse-de-Blainville (★ Montréal) 19,336
Salaberry-de-Valleyfield (★ 38,797) 27,942
Sept-Îles (Seven Islands) (★ 28,050) 25,637
Shawinigan (★ 61,965) 21,470
Shawinigan-Sud (★ Shawinigan) 11,412
Sherbrooke (★ 129,960) 74,438
Sillery (★ Québec) 12,784
Sorel (★ 46,096) 19,522
Terrebonne (★ Montréal) 31,310
Thetford Mines (★ 31,940) 18,561
Tracy (★ Sorel) 12,546
Trois-Rivières (★ 128,888) 50,122
Trois-Rivières-Ouest (★ Trois-Rivières) 15,538
Val-Bélair (★ Québec) 13,105
Val-d'Or (★ 27,178) 22,252
Vanier (Québec-Ouest) (★ Québec) 10,208
Verdun (★ Montréal) 60,246
Victoriaville (★ 38,003) 21,587
Ville-Saint-Georges (★ 21,022) 11,723
Westmount (★ Montréal) 20,011

## CANADA: SASKATCHEWAN

1986 C 1,010,198

***Cities and Towns***

Lloydminster, Sask. and Alta. prov. 17,356
Moose Jaw (★ 37,219) 35,073
North Battleford (★ 18,709) 14,876
Prince Albert (★ 40,841) 33,686
Regina (★ 186,521) 175,064
Saskatoon (★ 200,665) 177,641
Swift Current 15,666
Yorkton (★ 18,525) 15,574

## CANADA: YUKON

1986 C 23,504

***Cities and Towns***

Dawson 896
Faro 400
Whitehorse 15,199

## CAPE VERDE / Cabo Verde

1980 C 296,093

***Cities and Towns***

Mindelo 36,265
• PRAIA 37,480

## CAYMAN ISLANDS

1987 E 23,000

***Cities and Towns***

• GEORGETOWN 11,500

## CENTRAL AFRICAN REPUBLIC / République centrafricaine

1984 E 2,517,000

***Cities and Towns***

Bambari (1982 E) 35,000
• BANGUI 473,817
Berbérati (1982 E) 40,000
Bossangoa (1982 E) 36,000
Bouar (1982 E) 48,000

## CHAD / Tchad

1979 E 4,405,000

***Cities and Towns***

Abéché 54,000
Kélo 27,000
Koumra 27,000
Moundou 66,000
• N'DJAMENA (FORT-LAMY) 303,000
Sarh (Fort-Archambault) 65,000

## CHILE

1982 C 11,329,736

***Cities and Towns***

Angol 31,005
Antofagasta 185,486
Arica 139,320
Calama 81,684
Cauquenes 23,908
Cerrillos (★ Santiago) 67,013
Cerro Navia (★ Santiago) 137,777
Chillán 118,163
Chuquicamata 16,891
Concepción (★ 675,000) 267,891
Conchalí (★ Santiago) 157,884
Copiapó 69,045
Coquimbo 62,186
Coronel (★ Concepción) 65,918
Curicó 60,550
El Bosque (★ Santiago) 143,717
Estación Central (★ Santiago) 147,918
Huechuraba (★ Santiago) 56,313
Independencia (★ Santiago) 86,724
Iquique 110,153
La Calera 38,322
La Cisterna (★ Santiago) 95,863
La Florida (★ Santiago) 191,883
La Granja (★ Santiago) 109,168
La Pintana (★ Santiago) 73,932
La Reina (★ Santiago) 80,452
Las Condes (★ Santiago) 175,735
La Serena 83,283
La Unión 16,925
Lebu 16,952
Limache 22,711
Linares 46,433
Lo Barnechea (★ Santiago) 24,258
Lo Espejo (★ Santiago) 124,462
Lo Prado (★ Santiago) 103,575
Los Andes 34,613
Los Ángeles 70,529
Lota (★ Concepción) 47,133
Macul (★ Santiago) 113,100
Maipú (★ Santiago) 114,117
Melipilla 33,654
Ñuñoa (★ Santiago) 168,919
Osorno 95,286
Ovalle 43,023
Parral 21,221
Pedro Aguirre Cerda (★ Santiago) 145,207
Peñalolén (★ Santiago) 137,298
Penco (★ Concepción) 30,939
Providencia (★ Santiago) 115,449
Pudahuel (★ Santiago) 97,578
Puente Alto (★ Santiago) 109,239
Puerto Aisén 9,176
Puerto Montt 84,410
Puerto Natales 14,250
Punta Arenas 95,332
Quillota 44,824
Quilpué (★ Valparaíso) 84,136
Quinta Normal (★ Santiago) 128,989
Rancagua 139,925
Recoleta (★ Santiago) 164,292
Renca (★ Santiago) 93,928
San Antonio 61,486
San Bernardo (★ Santiago) 117,132
San Carlos 21,919
San Felipe 31,656
San Fernando 32,432
San Joaquín (★ Santiago) 123,904
San Miguel (★ Santiago) 88,764
San Ramón (★ Santiago) 99,410
• SANTIAGO (★ 4,100,000) 232,667
Talca 128,544
Talcahuano (★★ Concepción) 202,368
Temuco 157,297
Tocopilla 21,883
Tomé (★ Concepción) 34,107
Valdivia 100,046
Vallenar 38,375
Valparaíso (★ 675,000) 265,355
Victoria 19,743
Villa Alemana (★ Valparaíso) 55,766
Viña del Mar (★ Valparaíso) 244,899
Vitacura (★ Santiago) 72,038

***Regions***

1984 ESTIMATE

Aisén del General Carlos Ibáñez del Campo 71,369
Antofagasta 338,219
Atacama 214,718
Biobío 1,569,431
Coquimbo 439,938
La Araucanía 677,951
Libertador General Bernardo O'Higgins 589,347
Los Lagos 904,557
Magallanes y Antártica Chilena 117,401
Maule 739,329
Metropolitana 4,722,528
Tarapacá 266,428
Valparaíso 1,326,834

## CHINA / Zhongguo

1987 E 1,057,210,000

***Cities and Towns***

Abagnar Qi (Xilin Hot) (▲ 100,700) (1986 E) 71,700
Acheng (1985 E) 100,304
Aksu (▲ 345,900) (1986 E) 143,100
Altay (▲ 141,700) (1986 E) 62,800
Anci (Langfang) (▲ 522,800) (1986 E) 122,100
Anda (▲ 425,500) (1986 E) 130,200
Ankang (1985 E) 89,188
Anlu (1985 E) 35,199
Anqing (▲ 433,900) (1986 E) 213,200
Anqiu (1985 E) 18,969
Anshan 1,300,000
Anshun (▲ 214,700) (1986 E) 128,800
Anyang (▲ 541,900) (1986 E) 361,200
Arxan (1985 E) 36,343
Baicheng (▲ 282,000) (1986 E) 198,600
Baiquan (1985 E) 50,996
Baiyin (▲ 301,900) (1986 E) 157,100
Baoding (▲ 535,100) (1986 E) 423,200
Baoji (▲ 359,500) (1986 E) 286,200
Baoqing (1985 E) 38,364
Baoshan (▲ 688,400) (1986 E) 52,300
Baotou 1,120,000
Baoying (1985 E) 50,479
Bayan (1985 E) 42,299
Bei'an (▲ 440,500) (1986 E) 199,500
Beihai (▲ 175,900) (1986 E) 119,000
BEIJING (PEKING) (▲ 6,450,000) 5,970,000
Beipiao (▲ 603,700) (1986 E) 180,900
Bengbu (▲ 612,600) (1986 E) 403,900
Benxi (Xiaoshi) (1985 E) 29,442
Benxi 840,000
Bijie (1985 E) 54,871
Binhai (Dongkan) (1985 E) 37,565
Binxian (Binzhou) (▲ 177,900) (1986 E) 86,700
Binxian (Beizhen) (1982 C) 127,326
Bo'ai (Qinghua) (1985 E) 25,471
Bole (Bortala) (▲ 137,300) (1986 E) 41,400
Boli (1985 E) 61,990
Bose (▲ 271,400) (1986 E) 82,000
Boshan (1975 UE) 100,000
Boxian (Bozhou) (1985 E) 63,222
Boxing (1982 C) 57,554
Boyang (1985 E) 60,688
Butha Qi (▲ 389,500) (1986 E) 111,300
Cangshan (Bianzhuang) (1982 C) 79,334
Cangzhou (▲ 293,600) (1986 E) 196,700
Chaihe (1985 E) 40,328
Changchun (▲ 1,910,000) 1,740,000
Changde (▲ 220,800) (1986 E) 178,200
Changge (1982 C) 67,002
Changji (▲ 233,400) (1986 E) 110,500
Changle (1982 C) 43,092
Changli (1985 E) 29,966
Changqing (1982 C) 65,094
Changsha 1,190,000
Changshou (1985 E) 51,923
Changshu (Yushan) (▲ 998,000) (1986 E) 281,300
Changtu (1985 E) 49,937
Changyi (1982 C) 64,513
Changzhi (▲ 463,400) (1986 E) 273,000
Changzhou (1986 E) 522,700
Chao'an (▲ 1,214,500) (1986 E) 265,400
Chaoxian (▲ 739,500) (1986 E) 116,800
Chaoyang (Miancheng), Guangdong prov. (1985 E) 85,968
Chaoyang, Liaoning prov. (▲ 318,900) (1986 E) 180,300
Chengde (▲ 330,400) (1986 E) 226,600
Chengdu (Chengtu) (▲ 2,640,000) 1,810,000
Chenghai (1985 E) 50,631
Chengwu (1982 C) 43,244
Chenxian (Chenzhou) (▲ 191,900) (1986 E) 143,500
Chifeng (Ulanhad) (▲ 882,900) (1986 E) 299,000
Chiping (1982 C) 44,036
Chongqing (Chungking) (▲ 2,830,000) 2,450,000
Chuxian (▲ 365,000) (1986 E) 113,300
Chuxiong (Lucheng) (▲ 379,400) (1986 E) 67,700
Da'an (Dalai) (1985 E) 70,552
Dachangzhen (1975 UE) 50,000
Dalian (Lüda) (Dairen) 1,680,000
Dandong (Antung) (1986 E) 579,800
Danyang (1985 E) 48,449
Daqing (Anda) (▲ 850,000) 620,000
Dashiqiao (1985 E) 68,898
Dashitou (1985 E) 45,550
Datong (▲ 1,020,000) 790,000
Datong (Qiaotou) (1985 E) 55,529
Dawa (1985 E) 142,581
Daxian (▲ 209,400) (1986 E) 142,000
Daxing (Huangcun) (1985 E) 39,271
Dehui (1985 E) 60,247
Dengfeng (1982 C) 49,746
Dengxian (1985 E) 32,130
Deqing (1982 C) 48,726
Deyang (▲ 753,400) (1986 E) 184,800
Dezhou (▲ 276,200) (1986 E) 161,300
Didao (1975 UE) 50,000
Dinghai (1985 E) 50,161
Dingshuzhen (1985 E) 46,373
Dingtao (1982 C) 44,955
Dingxian (1985 E) 40,037
Dongchuan (Xincun) (▲ 275,100) (1986 E) 67,400
Dongfeng (1985 E) 44,747
Dongguan (Guancheng) (▲ 1,208,500) (1986 E) 254,900
Dongjingcheng (1985 E) 40,531
Dongming (1982 C) 44,660
Dongning (1985 E) 29,937
Dongshan (1985 E) 37,023
Dongsheng (▲ 121,300) (1986 E) 57,500
Dongtai (1985 E) 65,788
Dongying (▲ 514,400) (1986 E) 178,100
Dorbod (Taikang) (1985 E) 34,100
Dukou (▲ 551,200) (1986 E) 380,200
Dunhua (▲ 448,000) (1986 E) 217,100
Duyun (▲ 386,600) (1986 E) 123,800
Echeng (▲ 938,000) (1986 E) 217,400
Enshi (▲ 679,000) (1986 E) 84,300
Erenhot (1986 E) 7,200
Ergun Zuoqi (Genhe) (1985 E) 55,970
Fanjiatun (1985 E) 33,035
Feixian (1982 C) 73,246
Fengcheng, Liaoning prov. (1985 E) 66,745
Fengzhen (1985 E) 38,267
Fenyang (1985 E) 30,222
Foshan (▲ 312,700) (1986 E) 243,500
Fu'an (1985 E) 31,077
Fujin (1985 E) 60,948
Fuling (▲ 973,500) (1986 E) 166,300
Fushan (1982 C) 43,685
Fushun 1,270,000
Fuxian (Wafangdian) (▲ 960,700) (1986 E) 246,200
Fuxin 690,000

C Census. E Official estimate. UE Unofficial estimate.
• Largest city in country.

★ Population or designation of metropolitan area, including suburbs (see headnote).
▲ Population of an entire municipality, commune, or district, including rural area.

Fuxin (1985 E) .... 36,438
Fuyang (▲ 195,200) (1986 E) .... 143,400
Fuyu, Heilongjiang prov. (1985 E) .... 48,670
Fuyu, Jilin prov. (1985 E) .... 98,373
Fuzhou (Fuchou) (▲ 1,210,000) .... 890,000
Fuzhou (▲ 171,800) (1986 E) .... 106,700
Gaixian (Gaizhou) (1985 E) .... 67,587
Ganhe (1985 E) .... 48,128
Gannan (1985 E) .... 38,623
Ganzhou (Kanchow) (▲ 346,000) (1986 E) .... 191,600
Gaomi (1985 E) .... 34,542
Gaoqing (Tianzhen) (1982 C) .... 70,411
Gaoyou (1985 E) .... 57,844
Gaozhou (1985 E) .... 41,919
Gejiu (▲ 341,700) (1986 E) .... 193,600
Golmud (1986 E) .... 60,300
Gongchangling (1982 C) .... 49,281
Gongxi (1985 E) .... 24,612
Gongxian (Xiaoyi) (1985 E) .... 22,669
Guanghan (Luocheng) (1985 E) .... 47,577
Guangyuan (Jialing) (▲ 805,500) (1986 E) .... 162,200
Guangzhou (Canton) (▲ 3,360,000) .... 3,050,000
Guanxian (1982 C) .... 49,782
Guanxian (Guankou) (1985 E) .... 65,039
Gucheng (1985 E) .... 27,643
Guichi (Chizhou) (1985 E) .... 36,623
Guilin (Kweilin) (▲ 457,500) (1986 E) .... 324,200
Guixian (Guicheng) (1985 E) .... 61,970
Guiyang (▲ 1,400,000) .... 1,010,000
Gushi (1985 E) .... 38,152
Haicheng (▲ 984,800) (1986 E) .... 210,700
Haifeng (Haicheng) (1985 E) .... 50,401
Haikang (Leizhou) (1985 E) .... 24,422
Haikou (▲ 289,600) (1986 E) .... 209,200
Hailar (1986 E) .... 180,000
Hailin (1985 E) .... 58,909
Hailong (Meihekou) (▲ 534,200) (1986 E) .... 117,500
Hailun (1985 E) .... 83,448
Haimen (1985 E) .... 46,341
Haining (Xiashi) (1985 E) .... 43,426
Haiyang (Dongcun) (1982 C) .... 77,098
Hami (▲ 270,300) (1986 E) .... 146,400
Hancheng (▲ 304,200) (1986 E) .... 66,600
Handan (▲ 1,010,000) .... 850,000
Hangu (1975 UE) .... 100,000
Hangzhou (Hangchou) .... 1,270,000
Hanzhong (▲ 415,000) (1986 E) .... 151,700
Harbin (Haerhpin) .... 2,670,000
Hebi (▲ 321,600) (1986 E) .... 158,500
Hechi (Jinchengjiang) (▲ 266,800) (1986 E) .... 74,400
Hechuan (1985 E) .... 65,237
Hefei (▲ 900,000) .... 720,000
Hegang (1986 E) .... 588,300
Heihe (Aihui) (▲ 135,000) (1986 E) .... 76,700
Heishan (1985 E) .... 39,271
Helong (1985 E) .... 62,665
Hengshui (▲ 286,500) (1986 E) .... 83,100
Hengyang (▲ 601,300) (1986 E) .... 419,200
Hepu (Lianzhou) (1985 E) .... 42,524
Heshan (▲ 109,600) (1986 E) .... 42,000
Hexian (Babu) (1985 E) .... 34,298
Heyuan (Yuancheng) (1985 E) .... 43,124
Heze (Caozhou) (▲ 1,001,500) (1986 E) .... 115,400
Hohhot (Kweisui) (▲ 810,000) .... 650,000
Honghu (Xindi) (1985 E) .... 44,057
Hongjiang (▲ 67,000) (1986 E) .... 54,300
Horinger (1986 E) .... 29,900
Horqin Youyi Qianqi (Ulan Hot) (▲ 192,100) (1986 E) .... 129,100
Hotan (▲ 122,800) (1986 E) .... 71,700
Houma (▲ 158,500) (1986 E) .... 67,000
Huadian (1985 E) .... 75,183
Huai'an (Huaicheng) (1985 E) .... 65,673
Huaibei (▲ 447,200) (1986 E) .... 252,100
Huaide (Gongzhuling) (▲ 899,400) (1986 E) .... 187,600
Huaihua (▲ 427,100) (1986 E) .... 102,000
Huainan (Hwainan) (▲ 1,090,000) .... 690,000
Huaiyang (Huizu) (1985 E) .... 35,679
Huaiyin (Wangying) (▲ 382,500) (1986 E) .... 201,700
Huanan (1985 E) .... 66,596
Huangchuan (1985 E) .... 45,574
Huanggang (Huangzhou) (1982 C) .... 65,961
Huangnihe (1985 E) .... 33,072
Huangshi (1986 E) .... 451,900
Huangyan (1985 E) .... 39,284
Huanren (1985 E) .... 33,345
Huantai (Suozhen) (1982 C) .... 44,903
Huayun (Huarong) (▲ 313,500) (1986 E) .... 81,000
Huilai (Huicheng) (1985 E) .... 30,671
Huinan (Chaoyang) (1985 E) .... 52,429
Huixian (1985 E) .... 25,031
Huizhou (▲ 182,100) (1986 E) .... 117,000
Hulan (1985 E) .... 74,989
Hunjiang (▲ 687,700) (1986 E) .... 442,600
Huzhou (▲ 964,400) (1986 E) .... 208,500
Jiading (1985 E) .... 60,718
Jiamusi (▲ 557,700) (1986 E) .... 429,800
Ji'an (▲ 184,300) (1986 E) .... 132,200
Jiangdu (1985 E) .... 32,638
Jiangjin (1985 E) .... 44,378
Jiangling (Jingzhou) (1985 E) .... 77,887
Jiangmen (▲ 231,700) (1986 E) .... 168,800
Jiangyin (Chengjiang) (1985 E) .... 66,476
Jiangyou (Zhongba) (1985 E) .... 72,663
Jian'ou (1985 E) .... 55,180
Jianping (Yebaishou) (1985 E) .... 39,690
Jianyang (Jiancheng) (1985 E) .... 45,977
Jiaohe (1985 E) .... 51,504
Jiaojiang (▲ 385,200) (1986 E) .... 82,300
Jiaoxian (1985 E) .... 51,869
Jiaozuo (▲ 509,900) (1986 E) .... 335,400
Jiawang (1975 UE) .... 50,000
Jiaxing (▲ 686,500) (1986 E) .... 210,200
Jiayuguan (▲ 102,100) (1986 E) .... 73,800
Jiazi (1985 E) .... 46,073
Jidong (1985 E) .... 38,948
Jieshi (1985 E) .... 37,502
Jiexiu (1985 E) .... 51,300
Jieyang (Rongcheng) (1985 E) .... 98,531
Jilin (Kirin) .... 1,170,000
Jimo (1985 E) .... 22,845
Jinan (Tsinan) .... 1,460,000
Jinchang (Baijiazui) (▲ 136,000) (1986 E) .... 90,500
Jincheng (▲ 612,700) (1986 E) .... 99,900
Jingdezhen (▲ 569,700) (1986 E) .... 304,000
Jinghong (Yunjinghong) (1985 E) .... 28,029
Jingmen (▲ 946,500) (1986 E) .... 227,000
Jinhua (▲ 799,900) (1986 E) .... 147,800
Jining, Inner Mongolia prov. (1986 E) .... 163,300
Jining, Shandong prov. (▲ 765,700) (1986 E) .... 222,600
Jinshi (▲ 219,700) (1986 E) .... 73,700
Jinxi (▲ 634,300) (1986 E) .... 223,100
Jinxian (Jinzhou) (1985 E) .... 95,761
Jinzhou (▲ 790,000) .... 690,000
Jishou (▲ 194,500) (1986 E) .... 59,500
Jishu (1985 E) .... 75,587
Jiujiang (▲ 382,300) (1986 E) .... 248,500
Jiuquan (Suzhou) (▲ 269,900) (1986 E) .... 56,300
Jiutai (1985 E) .... 63,021
Jixi (Chihsi) (▲ 820,000) .... 700,000
Jixian (1985 E) .... 59,725
Jixian (Fulitun) (1985 E) .... 35,705
Juancheng (1982 C) .... 54,110
Junan (Shizilu) (1982 C) .... 90,222
Junxian (Danjiang) (▲ 423,400) (1986 E) .... 97,000
Juxian (1982 C) .... 51,666
Kaifeng (▲ 629,100) (1986 E) .... 458,800
Kaili (▲ 342,100) (1986 E) .... 96,600
Kaiping (Sanbu) (1985 E) .... 54,145
Kaiyuan (▲ 342,100) (1986 E) .... 96,600
Kaiyuan (1985 E) .... 85,762
Karamay (1986 E) .... 185,300
Kashi (Kaxgar) (▲ 194,500) (1986 E) .... 146,300
Keshan (1985 E) .... 65,088
Korla (▲ 219,000) (1986 E) .... 129,400
Kunming (Yünnanfu) (▲ 1,520,000) .... 1,280,000
Kunshan (Yushan) (1985 E) .... 44,645
Kuqa (1985 E) .... 63,847
Kuytun (1986 E) .... 60,200
Laiwu (▲ 1,041,800) (1986 E) .... 143,500
Laixi (Shuiji) (1982 C) .... 41,117
Laiyang (1985 E) .... 42,813
Langxiang (1985 E) .... 64,658
Lanxi (▲ 606,800) (1986 E) .... 70,500
Lanxi (1985 E) .... 53,236
Lanzhou (Lanchou) (▲ 1,390,000) .... 1,270,000
Laohekou (Guanghua) (▲ 420,000) (1986 E) .... 104,400
Lechang (1986 E) .... 56,913
Leiyang (1985 E) .... 27,572
Lengshuijiang (▲ 277,600) (1986 E) .... 101,700
Lengshuitan (▲ 362,000) (1986 E) .... 60,900
Leping (1985 E) .... 45,620
Leshan (▲ 972,300) (1986 E) .... 307,300
Lhasa (▲ 107,700) (1986 E) .... 84,400
Lianxian (Lianzhou) (1985 E) .... 34,720
Lianyungang (▲ 459,400) (1986 E) .... 288,000
Liaocheng (▲ 724,300) (1986 E) .... 119,000
Liaoyang (▲ 576,900) (1986 E) .... 442,600
Liaoyuan (1986 E) .... 370,400
Lihu (1985 E) .... 30,204
Lijiang Naxi (Dayan) (1985 E) .... 36,939
Liling (▲ 856,300) (1986 E) .... 107,100
Linfen (▲ 530,100) (1986 E) .... 157,600
Lingling (Yongzhou) (▲ 515,300) (1986 E) .... 72,700
Lingxian (1982 C) .... 40,617
Lingyuan (1985 E) .... 66,825
Linhai (1985 E) .... 52,653
Linhe (▲ 365,900) (1986 E) .... 99,800
Linkou (1985 E) .... 52,936
Linqing (▲ 603,000) (1986 E) .... 87,000
Linqu (1982 C) .... 84,196
Linru (1985 E) .... 21,403
Linxia (▲ 150,200) (1986 E) .... 72,900
Linyi (▲ 1,365,000) (1986 E) .... 190,000
Linying (1982 C) .... 44,516
Lishi (1985 E) .... 32,083
Lishu (1985 E) .... 40,838
Lishui (1985 E) .... 42,004
Liuhe (1985 E) .... 42,695
Liujiachang (1985 E) .... 25,296
Liupanshui (Shuicheng) (▲ 2,216,500) (1986 E) .... 363,500
Liuzhou .... 660,000
Liyang (Licheng) (1985 E) .... 43,974
Longhai (Shima) (1985 E) .... 40,817
Longjiang (1985 E) .... 51,156
Longyan (▲ 378,500) (1986 E) .... 114,500
Loudi (▲ 254,300) (1986 E) .... 84,200
Lu'an (▲ 163,400) (1986 E) .... 122,600
Luanchuan (1982 C) .... 40,297
Lufeng (Donghai) (1985 E) .... 53,015
Luhe (Lucheng) (1985 E) .... 45,183
Lujiang (1985 E) .... 32,021
Luohe (▲ 159,100) (1986 E) .... 102,300
Luoyang (▲ 1,060,000) .... 740,000
Lushan (1985 E) .... 22,205
Luzhou (Luchou) (▲ 360,300) (1986 E) .... 237,800
Ma'anshan (▲ 367,000) (1986 E) .... 258,900
Manzhouli (1986 E) .... 116,600
Maoming (▲ 434,900) (1986 E) .... 118,600
Meizhou (▲ 740,600) (1986 E) .... 169,100
Mengjin (1982 C) .... 41,706
Mengxian (1982 C) .... 45,599
Mengyin (1982 C) .... 70,602
Mianduhe (1982 C) .... 46,629
Mianyang (Xiantao), Hubei prov. (1985 E) .... 41,008
Mianyang, Sichuan prov. (▲ 848,500) (1986 E) .... 233,900
Mingshui (1985 E) .... 42,956
Minhang (1975 UE) .... 60,000
Mishan (1985 E) .... 54,919
Mixian (1982 C) .... 64,776
Mudanjiang .... 630,000
Muling (Bamiantong) (1985 E) .... 38,638
Muling (1985 E) .... 30,416
Naizishan (1985 E) .... 51,982
Nancha (1975 UE) .... 50,000
Nanchang (▲ 1,190,000) .... 1,030,000
Nanchang (Liantang) (1985 E) .... 37,661
Nanchong (▲ 238,100) (1986 E) .... 158,000
Nanjing (Nanking) .... 2,290,000
Nanning (▲ 960,000) .... 690,000
Nanpiao (1982 C) .... 67,274
Nanping (▲ 420,800) (1986 E) .... 157,100
Nantong (▲ 411,000) (1986 E) .... 308,800
Nanxiong (1985 E) .... 33,424
Nanyang (▲ 294,800) (1986 E) .... 199,400
Nanzhang (1985 E) .... 22,398
Nehe (1985 E) .... 49,725
Neihuang (1982 C) .... 56,039
Neijiang (▲ 298,500) (1986 E) .... 191,100
Nenjiang (1985 E) .... 59,276
Ning'an (1985 E) .... 49,334
Ningbo (▲ 1,030,000) .... 560,000
Ningde (1985 E) .... 36,529
Ningyang (1982 C) .... 55,424
Nong'an (1985 E) .... 55,966
Orogen Zizhiqi (Alihe) (1985 E) .... 48,042
Orqohan (1982 C) .... 44,875
Panshan (▲ 343,100) (1986 E) .... 248,100
Panshi (1985 E) .... 59,270
Panyu (Shiqiao) (1985 E) .... 46,705
Penglai (1985 E) .... 21,502
Pengxian (Tianpeng) (1985 E) .... 41,190
Pingdingshan (▲ 819,900) (1986 E) .... 363,200
Pingdu (1985 E) .... 23,362
Pingliang (▲ 362,500) (1986 E) .... 85,400
Pingnan (1985 E) .... 22,601
Pingxiang, Guangxi Zhuangzu prov. (▲ 81,100) (1986 E) .... 14,600
Pingxiang, Jiangxi prov. (▲ 1,286,700) (1986 E) .... 368,700
Pingyao (1985 E) .... 34,007
Pingyi (1982 C) .... 89,373
Pingyin (1982 C) .... 62,827
Potou (▲ 456,100) (1986 E) .... 59,000
Puqi (1985 E) .... 65,239
Putian (▲ 265,400) (1986 E) .... 64,600
Putuo (Shenjiamen) (1985 E) .... 50,962
Puyang (▲ 1,086,100) (1986 E) .... 131,000
Qian Gorlos (Qianguozhen) (1985 E) .... 79,494
Qianyang (Anjiang) (1985 E) .... 38,836
Qihe (Yancheng) (1982 C) .... 43,556
Qilimiao (1985 E) .... 48,692
Qing'an (1985 E) .... 41,990
Qingdao (Tsingtao) .... 1,270,000
Qinggang (1985 E) .... 43,075
Qingjiang (Zhangshu), Jiangxi prov. (1985 E) .... 42,698
Qingjiang, Jiangsu prov. (▲ 246,617) (1982 C) .... 150,000
Qingyuan (Qingcheng) (1985 E) .... 51,756
Qinhuangdao (★ 436,000) .... 307,500
Qinzhou (▲ 923,400) (1986 E) .... 97,100
Qiqihar (Tsitsihar) (▲ 1,300,000) .... 1,150,000
Qitaihe (▲ 309,900) (1986 E) .... 166,400
Qixia (1982 C) .... 54,158
Qixian (1982 C) .... 53,041
Qizhou (1982 C) .... 48,010
Quanyang (1985 E) .... 36,623
Quanzhou (▲ 436,000) (1986 E) .... 157,000
Qujing (▲ 758,000) (1986 E) .... 135,000
Quzhou (▲ 704,800) (1986 E) .... 124,000
Raoping (Huanggang) (1985 E) .... 54,831
Rizhao (▲ 970,300) (1986 E) .... 93,300
Roncheng (Yatou) (1982 C) .... 52,878
Rugao (Rucheng) (1985 E) .... 50,643
Rui'an (1985 E) .... 57,993
Sandu (1985 E) .... 37,804
Sanmenxia (▲ 150,000) (1986 E) .... 79,000
Sanming (▲ 214,300) (1986 E) .... 144,900
Shache (Yarkant) (1985 E) .... 45,331
Shahe (Dalian) (1985 E) .... 29,943
• Shanghai (★ 9,300,000) .... 7,100,000
Shangqiu (Zhuji) (▲ 199,400) (1986 E) .... 135,400
Shangrao (▲ 142,500) (1986 E) .... 113,000
Shangshui (1982 C) .... 50,191
Shangzhi (1985 E) .... 41,326
Shanhetun (1985 E) .... 42,148
Shantou (Swatow) (▲ 770,000) .... 550,000
Shanwei (1985 E) .... 61,234
Shanxian (1985 E) .... 31,197
Shaoguan (1986 E) .... 363,100
Shaowu (▲ 266,700) (1986 E) .... 81,400
Shaoxing (▲ 250,900) (1986 E) .... 167,100
Shaoyang (▲ 465,900) (1986 E) .... 218,600
Shashi (1986 E) .... 253,700
Shengfang (1982 C) .... 45,999
Shenqiu (Huaidian) (1985 E) .... 29,311
Shenxian (1982 C) .... 50,208
Shenyang (Mukden) (▲ 4,290,000) .... 3,840,000
Shenzhen (▲ 231,900) (1986 E) .... 189,600
Shiguaigou (1975 UE) .... 50,000
Shihezi (▲ 549,300) .... 304,700
Shijiazhuang .... 1,190,000
Shijiusuo (1985 E) .... 22,660
Shilong (1985 E) .... 39,189
Shiyan (▲ 332,600) (1986 E) .... 227,300
Shizuishan (▲ 317,400) (1986 E) .... 225,500
Shouguang (1982 C) .... 83,400
Shuangcheng (1985 E) .... 91,163
Shuangfeng (1985 E) .... 34,456
Shuangliao (1985 E) .... 67,326
Shuangyashan (1986 E) .... 427,300
Shulan (1986 E) .... 50,582
Shunde (Daliang) (1985 E) .... 50,262
Shuyang (Shucheng) (1985 E) .... 42,053
Simao (1985 E) .... 36,891
Siping (▲ 357,800) (1986 E) .... 280,100
Sishui (1982 C) .... 82,990
Siyang (Zhongxing) (1985 E) .... 31,090
Songjiang (1985 E) .... 71,864
Songjianghe (1985 E) .... 53,023
Suifenhe (▲ 21,700) (1986 E) .... 13,900
Suihua (▲ 732,100) (1986 E) .... 200,400
Suileng (1985 E) .... 68,399
Suining (▲ 1,174,900) (1986 E) .... 118,500
Suixian (Suizhou) (▲ 1,281,600) (1986 E) .... 187,700
Suqian (Sucheng) (1985 E) .... 50,742
Suxian (Suzhou) (▲ 218,600) (1986 E) .... 123,300
Suzhou (Soochow) .... 720,000
Tacheng (Qoqek) (▲ 119,000) (1986 E) .... 40,000
Tai'an (▲ 1,325,400) (1986 E) .... 215,900
Tailai (1985 E) .... 44,866
Taishan (Taicheng) (1985 E) .... 48,759
Taixian (Jiangyan) (1985 E) .... 45,156
Taixing (1985 E) .... 40,580
Taiyuan (▲ 1,930,000) .... 1,660,000
Taizhou (▲ 210,800) .... 143,200
Tancheng (1982 C) .... 61,857
Tangshan (▲ 1,410,000) .... 1,060,000
Tao'an (Taonan) (1985 E) .... 76,269
Tengxian (1985 E) .... 53,254
Tianjin (Tientsin) (▲ 5,460,000) .... 4,880,000
Tianmen (1985 E) .... 42,706
Tianshui (Beidaobu) (▲ 186,460) (1985 E) .... 38,595
Tianshui (▲ 953,200) (1986 E) .... 209,500
Tiefa (▲ 146,367) (1982 C) .... 60,000
Tieli (1985 E) .... 102,527
Tieling (▲ 454,100) (1986 E) .... 326,100
Tongchuan (▲ 393,200) (1986 E) .... 268,900
Tonghua (▲ 367,400) (1986 E) .... 290,200
Tongliao (▲ 253,100) (1986 E) .... 190,100
Tongling (▲ 216,400) (1986 E) .... 182,900
Tongren (1985 E) .... 50,307
Tongxian (Tongzhou) (1985 E) .... 97,168
Tongyu (Kaitong) (1985 E) .... 47,781
Tumen (▲ 99,700) (1986 E) .... 77,600
Tunxi (▲ 104,500) (1986 E) .... 61,800
Turpan (▲ 196,800) (1986 E) .... 52,300
Ürümqi (Urumchi) .... 1,040,000
Wangkui (1985 E) .... 52,021
Wangqing (1985 E) .... 61,237
Wanxian (▲ 280,800) (1986 E) .... 138,700
Weifang (▲ 1,042,200) (1986 E) .... 312,500
Weihai (▲ 220,800) (1986 E) .... 83,000
Weihe (1985 E) .... 30,226
Weinan (▲ 699,400) (1986 E) .... 111,300
Weishan (Xiazhen) (1982 C) .... 57,932
Weixian (Hanting) (1982 C) .... 50,180
Wenling (1985 E) .... 20,273
Wenxian (1982 C) .... 44,781
Wenzhou (▲ 530,600) (1986 E) .... 372,200
Wuchang (1985 E) .... 64,403
Wuchuan (Meilü) (1985 E) .... 44,146
Wuhai (1986 E) .... 266,000
Wuhan (Hankow) .... 3,490,000
Wuhu (▲ 502,200) (1986 E) .... 396,000
Wulian (Hongning) (1982 C) .... 51,718
Wuqing (Yangcun) (1985 E) .... 24,225
Wusong (1982 C) .... 64,017
Wuwei (Liangzhou) (▲ 804,000) (1986 E) .... 115,500
Wuxi .... 860,000
Wuzhong (▲ 402,400) (1986 E) .... 48,600
Wuzhou (Wuchou) (▲ 261,500) (1986 E) .... 194,800
Xiaguan (▲ 395,800) (1986 E) .... 112,100
Xiamen (Amoy) (▲ 546,400) (1986 E) .... 343,700
Xi'an (Sian) (▲ 2,390,000) .... 2,050,000

C Census. E Official estimate. UE Unofficial estimate.
• Largest city in country.
★ Population or designation of metropolitan area, including suburbs (see headnote).
▲ Population of an entire municipality, commune, or district, including rural area.

Xiangfan (▲ 421,200) (1986 E) 314,900
Xiangtan (Siangtan) (▲ 511,100) (1986 E) 389,500
Xiangxiang (1985 E) 38,509
Xiangyin (1985 E) 37,830
Xianning (▲ 402,200) (1986 E) 122,200
Xianyang (Sienyang) (▲ 641,800) (1986 E) 285,900
Xiaogan (▲ 1,204,400) (1986 E) 125,500
Xiaoshan (1985 E) 63,074
Xichang (▲ 161,000) (1986 E) 105,000
Xifeng (▲ 229,500) (1986 E) 37,200
Xihua (1985 C) 40,022
Xin'an (1982 C) 46,823
Xinghua (Xinxing) (1985 E) 75,573
Xinglongzhen (1982 C) 52,961
Xingning (Xingcheng) (1985 E) 42,983
Xingtai (▲ 350,800) (1986 E) 265,600
Xingyi (1985 E) 36,416
Xinhua (1985 E) 33,260
Xinhui (Huicheng) (1985 E) 77,381
Xining 610,000
Xinjin (Pulandian) (1985 E) 43,196
Xinmin (1985 E) 47,900
Xintai (▲ 1,157,300) (1986 E) 171,400
Xinwen (Suncun) (1975 UE) 50,000
Xinxian (▲ 398,600) (1986 E) 74,200
Xinxiang (▲ 540,500) (1986 E) 411,000
Xinyang (▲ 234,200) (1986 E) 169,100
Xinyu (▲ 610,600) (1986 E) 140,200
Xiuyan (1985 E) 46,087
Xuancheng (1985 E) 52,387
Xuanhua (1975 UE) 140,000
Xuanwei (1982 C) 70,081
Xuchang (▲ 247,200) (1986 E) 167,800
Xuguit Qi (Yakeshi) (1986 E) 390,000
Xuzhou 840,000
Ya'an (▲ 277,600) (1986 E) 89,200
Yan'an (▲ 259,800) (1986 E) 86,700
Yancheng (▲ 1,251,400) (1986 E) 258,400
Yangcheng (1982 C) 57,255
Yanggu (1982 C) 45,839
Yangjiang (Jiangcheng) (1986 E) 91,433
Yangjiazhangzi (1985 E) 44,916
Yangquan (▲ 478,900) (1986 E) 295,100
Yangzhou (▲ 417,300) (1986 E) 321,500
Yanji (Longjing) (1985 E) 55,035
Yanji (▲ 216,900) (1986 E) 175,000
Yanling (1982 C) 52,679
Yanshou (1985 E) 34,294
Yantai (▲ 717,300) (1986 E) 327,000
Yanzhou (1985 E) 48,972
Yaxian (Sanya) (▲ 321,700) (1986 E) 70,500
Yexian (1985 E) 26,543
Yi'an (1986 E) 54,253
Yibin (▲ 636,500) (1986 E) 218,800
Yichang (Ichang) (1986 E) 410,500
Yichuan (1982 C) 58,914
Yichun, Heilongjiang prov. 830,000
Yichun, Jiangxi prov. (▲ 770,200) (1986 E) 132,600
Yidu (1985 E) 54,838
Yilan (1985 E) 50,436
Yima (▲ 84,800) (1986 E) 53,700
Yimianpo (1985 E) 23,518
Yinan (Jiehu) (1982 C) 67,803
Yinchuan (▲ 396,900) (1986 E) 268,200
Yingcheng (1985 E) 59,072
Yingkou (▲ 480,000) (1986 E) 366,900
Yingtan (▲ 116,200) (1986 E) 64,500
Yining (Gulja) (▲ 232,000) (1986 E) 153,200
Yishan (Qingyuan) (1985 E) 39,447
Yiyang (▲ 365,000) (1986 E) 155,300
Yiyuan (Nanma) (1982 C) 53,800
Yong'an (▲ 269,000) (1986 E) 105,100
Yongchuan (1985 E) 70,444
Yuci (▲ 420,700) (1986 E) 171,000
Yueyang (▲ 411,300) (1986 E) 239,500
Yulin, Guangxi Zhuangzu prov. (▲ 1,228,800) (1986 E) 115,600
Yulin, Shaanxi prov. (1985 E) 51,610
Yumen (Laojunmiao) (▲ 160,100) (1986 E) 84,300
Yuncheng, Shandong prov. (1982 C) 54,262
Yuncheng, Shansi prov. (▲ 434,900) (1986 E) 87,000
Yunxiao (1985 E) 32,701
Yunyang (1982 C) 54,903
Yushu (1985 E) 57,222
Yutai (Guting) (1982 C) 41,990
Yuxi (▲ 291,500) (1986 E) 47,400
Yuxian (1985 E) 40,271
Yuyao (▲ 772,700) (1986 E) 169,700
Zaoyang (1985 E) 30,446
Zaozhuang (▲ 1,592,000) (1986 E) 292,200
Zhangjiakou (▲ 626,500) (1986 E) 492,800
Zhangye (▲ 394,200) (1986 E) 73,000
Zhangzhou (Changchou) (▲ 310,400) (1986 E) 159,400
Zhanhua (Fuguo) (1982 C) 48,193
Zhanjiang (▲ 920,900) (1986 E) 335,500
Zhao'an (1985 E) 42,047
Zhaodong (1985 E) 99,836
Zhaoqing (▲ 187,600) (1986 E) 145,700
Zhaotong (▲ 546,600) (1986 E) 77,500
Zhaoyuan (1985 E) 42,426
Zhaoyuan (1982 C) 56,389
Zhaozhou (1985 E) 38,500
Zhengzhou (Chengchou) (▲ 1,610,000) 1,170,000
Zhenjiang (Chinkiang) (1986 E) 412,400
Zhenlai (1985 E) 40,928
Zhongshan (Shiqizhen) (▲ 1,059,700) (1986 E) 238,700
Zhoucun (1975 UE) 50,000
Zhoukou (▲ 220,400) (1986 E) 110,500
Zhuanghe (1985 E) 42,502
Zhucheng (1985 E) 32,852
Zhuhai (▲ 155,000) (1986 E) 88,800
Zhumadian (▲ 149,500) (1986 E) 99,400
Zhuoxian (Zhouzhou) (1985 E) 54,523
Zhuzhou (▲ 499,600) (1986 E) 344,800
Zibo (Zhangdian) (▲ 2,330,000) 830,000
Zigong (▲ 909,300) (1986 E) 361,700
Zixing (▲ 334,300) (1986 E) 97,100
Ziyang (1985 E) 57,349
Zouping (1982 C) 49,274
Zouxian (1985 E) 61,578
Zunyi (▲ 347,600) (1986 E) 236,600

*Political Divisions*

Anhui 52,170,000
Beijing (Peking) (Auton. City) 9,750,000
Fujian 27,490,000
Gansu 20,710,000
Guangdong 63,460,000
Guangxi Zhuangzu (Auton. Region) 39,460,000
Guizhou (Kweichow) 30,080,000
Hainan
Hebei 56,170,000
Heilongjiang 33,320,000
Henan (Honan) 78,080,000
Hubei (Hupeh) 49,890,000
Hunan 56,960,000
Inner Mongolia (Nei Mongol) 20,290,000
Jiangsu (Kiangsu) 62,700,000
Jiangxi 35,090,000
Jilin 23,150,000
Liaoning 37,260,000
Ningxia Huizu 4,240,000
Qinghai 4,120,000
Shaanxi (Shensi) 30,430,000
Shandong 77,760,000
Shanghai (Municipality) 12,320,000
Shanxi 26,550,000
Sichuan 103,200,000
Tianjin (Tientsin) (Municipality) 8,190,000
Xinjiang Uygur 13,840,000
Xizang (Tibet) (Auton. Region) 2,030,000
Yunnan 34,560,000
Zhejiang (Chekiang) 40,700,000

### CISKEI

1986 E 882,200

*Cities and Towns*

BISHO 2,850
• Mdantsane (★ East London, S. Afr.) 242,823
Zwelitsha (★ King William's Town, S. Afr.) 30,760

### COLOMBIA

1985 C 27,867,326

*Cities and Towns*

Apartadó 29,151
Armenia 187,130
Armero 20,962
Barrancabermeja 137,406
Barranquilla (★ 1,140,000) 899,781
Bello (★ Medellín) 212,861
• BOGOTÁ (★ 4,260,000) 3,982,941
Bucaramanga (★ 550,000) 352,326
Buenaventura 160,342
Buga 82,992
Caldas (★ Medellín) 36,203
Cali (★ 1,400,000) 1,350,565
Cartagena 531,426
Cartago 97,791
Ciénaga 56,860
Cúcuta (★ 445,000) 379,478
Dos Quebradas (★ Pereira) 101,480
Duitama 56,390
Envigado (★ Medellín) 91,391
Espinal 37,563
Facatativá 44,331
Florencia 66,430
Florida 30,040
Floridablanca (★ Bucaramanga) 143,824
Girardot 70,078
Ibagué 292,965
Ipiales 45,419
Itagüí (★ Medellín) 137,623
La Dorada 48,572
Líbano 23,703
Lorica 24,264
Magangué 49,160
Maicao 46,033
Malambo (★ Barranquilla) 52,584
Manizales (★ 330,000) 299,352
Medellín (★ 2,095,000) 1,468,089
Montería 157,466
Neiva 194,556
Ocaña 51,443
Palmira 175,186
Pamplona 34,213
Pasto 197,407
Pereira (★ 390,000) 233,271
Piedecuesta 34,646
Planeta Rica 24,238
Popayán 141,964
Puerto Berrío 21,414
Quibdó 47,950
Ríohacha 46,667
Ríonegro 28,706
Sabanalarga 35,786
Santa Marta 177,922
Santa Rosa de Cabal 37,112
Sevilla 31,309
Sincelejo 120,537
Soacha (★ Bogotá) 109,051
Sogamoso 64,437
Soledad (★ Barranquilla) 165,791
Sonsón 15,535
Tuluá 99,721
Tumaco 45,456
Tunja 93,792
Valledupar 142,771
Villa Rosario (★ Cúcuta) 63,615
Villavicencio 178,685
Yumbo (★ Cali) 43,508
Zipaquirá 45,676

*Departments*

Amazonas (Comisaría) 30,327
Antioquia 3,888,067
Arauca (intendencia) 70,085
Atlántico 1,428,601
Bolívar 1,197,623
Boyacá 1,097,618
Caldas 838,094
Caquetá 214,473
Casanare (intendencia) 110,253
Cauca 795,838
Cesar 584,631
Chocó 242,768
Córdoba 913,636
Cundinamarca 1,382,360
Distrito Especial (Bogotá) 3,982,941
Guainía (comisaría) 9,214
Guajira 255,310
Guaviare (comisaría) 35,305
Huila 647,756
Magdalena 769,141
Meta 412,312
Nariño 1,019,098
Norte de Santander 883,884
Putumayo (intendencia) 119,815
Quindío 377,860
Risaralda 625,451
San Andrés y Providencia (intendencia) 35,936
Santander 1,438,226
Sucre 529,059
Tolima 1,051,852
Valle del Cauca 2,847,087
Vaupés (Comisaría) 18,935
Vichada (comisaría) 13,770

### COMOROS / Comores / Al Qumur

1980 C 346,992

*Cities and Towns*

• MORONI 20,112
Mutsamudu 14,000

### CONGO (PEOPLE'S REPUBLIC OF THE CONGO)

1984 C 1,912,429

*Cities and Towns*

• BRAZZAVILLE 585,812
Jacob 36,540
Loubomo 49,134
Pointe-Noire 294,203

### COOK ISLANDS

1981 C 17,753

*Cities and Towns*

• AVARUA 9,525

### COSTA RICA

1984 C 2,416,809

*Cities and Towns*

Alajuela (▲ 34,556) 29,273
Cartago 23,928
Cinco Esquinas 27,140
Desamparados (★ San José) 43,352
Guadalupe (★ San José) 25,506
Heredia 21,440
Ipís (★ San José) 25,586
Limón (▲ 52,602) 33,925
Puntarenas 29,224
• SAN JOSÉ (★ 670,000) 241,464
San Juan (★ San José) 22,415
San Pedro (★ San José) 24,519
San Vicente (★ San José) 24,661

### CUBA

1981 C 9,723,605

*Cities and Towns*

Amancio Rodríguez 21,097
Artemisa 33,907
Banes 31,237
Baracoa 35,754
Bayamo (1985 E) 105,302
Cabaiguán 26,460
Caibarién 31,872
Camagüey (1985 E) 260,782
Cárdenas 59,352
Ciego de Avila (1985 E) 80,500
Cienfuegos (1985 E) 109,304
Colón 34,744
Contramaestre 22,168
Florida 39,482
Guanajay 20,548
Guantánamo (1985 E) 174,383
Güines 41,591
Güira de Melena 21,088
• HAVANA (LA HABANA) (★ 2,125,000) (1987 E) 2,036,800
Holguín (1985 E) 194,728
Jobabo 14,895
Jovellanos 20,635
Manzanillo 87,830
Matanzas (1985 E) 105,382
Mayarí 21,076
Moa 26,893
Morón 39,779
Nueva Gerona (1985 E) 34,400
Nuevitas 34,869
Palma Soriano 55,851
Pinar del Río (1985 E) 100,906
Placetas 37,310
Puerto Padre 23,310
Ranchuelo (▲ 60,829) 14,700
Remedios (▲ 47,347) 16,200
Sagua de Tánamo 15,435
Sagua la Grande 42,291
San Antonio de los Baños (★ Havana) 27,488
Sancti-Spiritus (1985 E) 75,600
San José de las Lajas 26,917
San Luis 24,347
Santa Clara (1985 E) 178,278
Santiago de Cuba (1985 E) 358,764
Trinidad 32,935
Vertientes 22,432
Victoria de las Tunas (1985 E) 91,400

### CYPRUS / Kípros / Kıbrıs

1982 C 512,097

*Cities and Towns*

Lárnax (Larnaca) (★ 48,330) 35,823
Lemesós (Limassol) (★ 107,161) 74,782
• NICOSIA (LEVKOSÍA) (★ 185,000) 48,221
Páfos (★ 20,824) 13,124

### CYPRUS, NORTH / Kuzey Kıbrıs

1985 E 160,287

*Cities and Towns*

Gazimağusa (Famagusta) 19,428
• NICOSIA (LEFKOŞA) 37,400

### CZECHOSLOVAKIA / Československo

1989 E 15,624,021

*Cities and Towns*

Banská Bystrica 85,327
Bardejov 30,157
Beroun 24,018
Bratislava 435,499
Břeclav 26,141
Brno (★ 450,000) 389,892
Česká Lípa 39,047
České Budějovice (Budweis) (★ 114,000) 97,340
Český Těšín (★★ Třinec) 28,647
Cheb 31,600
Chomutov (★ 80,000) 56,715
Děčín (★ 72,000) 56,200
Frýdek-Místek (★ Ostrava) 65,481
Gottwaldov (Zlín) (★ 124,000) 86,742
Havířov (★ Ostrava) 92,279
Havlíčkův Brod 25,157
Hlohovec 23,499
Hodonín 33,449
Hradec Králové (★ 113,000) 100,454
Humenné 34,636
Jablonec [nad Nisou] (★★ Liberec) 46,200
Jihlava 53,987
Karlovy Vary (Carlsbad) 55,907
Karviná (★★ Ostrava) 71,742
Kladno (★ 88,500) 73,180
Kolín 32,036
Komárno 37,569
Košice 232,253
Krnov 25,976
Kroměříž (★ 38,500) 29,396
Levice 32,951
Liberec (★ 175,000) 103,752
Liptovský Mikuláš 30,449
Litoměřice 26,322
Litvínov (★★ Most) 30,344
Louny 25,994
Lučenec 29,783
Mariánské Lázně (Marienbad) 18,513
Martin 65,218
Michalovce 38,242
Mladá Boleslav 48,600
Most (★ 135,000) 69,557
Náchod 21,751
Nitra 89,306
Nové Zámky 41,718
Nový Jičín 32,917
Olomouc (★ 126,000) 106,662
Opava (★ 77,500) 63,084
Orlová (★ Ostrava) 36,233
Ostrava (★ 760,000) 330,614
Ostrov 19,566
Pardubice 95,668
Partizánske 26,255
Piešťany 33,667
Písek 29,395
Plzeň (Pilsen) (★ 210,000) 174,635
Poprad 50,300
Považská Bystrica 39,569
• PRAGUE (PRAHA) (★ 1,325,000) 1,211,106
Přerov 51,800
Prešov 87,396
Příbram 40,110
Prievidza 51,200
Prostějov 51,900
Ružomberok 29,509
Sokolov (★ 36,000) 28,382
Spišská Nová Ves 44,600
Šumperk 36,940
Tábor (★ 55,500) 35,703
Teplice (★ 94,000) 55,756
Topoľčany 37,259
Třebíč 38,847
Trenčín 56,843
Třinec (★ 87,500) 45,600
Trnava 72,200
Trutnov 31,640
Uherské Hradiště 38,871
Ústí nad Labem (★ 115,000) 105,854
Valašské Meziříčí 26,786
Vsetín 31,944
Žďár nad Sazavou 26,759
Žilina 96,418
Znojmo 37,364
Zvolen 41,800

*Republics*

Česká Socialistická Republika 10,360,480
Slovenská Socialistická Republika 5,263,541

*Regions*

Bratislava (city) 435,499
Jihočeský 697,785
Jihomoravský 2,058,530
Praha (Prague) (city) 1,211,106

C Census. E Official estimate. UE Unofficial estimate.
• Largest city in country.

★ Population or designation of metropolitan area, including suburbs (see headnote).
▲ Population of an entire municipality, commune, or district, including rural area.

Severočeský 1,190,606
Severomoravský 1,969,991
Středočeský 1,122,023
Stredoslovenský 1,608,192
Východočeský 1,240,847
Východoslovenský 1,494,084
Západočeský 869,592
Západoslovenský 1,725,766

*Historic Provinces*

Bohemia (Čechy) 6,331,959
Moravia (Morava) 4,028,521
Sloviakia (Slovensko) 5,263,541

**DENMARK / Danmark**

1988 E 5,129,254

*Cities and Towns*

Åbenrå (▲ 21,363) 15,500
Albertslund (★ Copenhagen) 29,001
Ålborg (▲ 154,739) 113,800
Århus (▲ 258,028) 199,700
Ballerup (★ Copenhagen) 45,791
Brøndby (★ Copenhagen) 34,704
• COPENHAGEN (KØBENHAVN) (★ 1,685,000) 468,704
Esbjerg (▲ 81,385) 71,800
Fredericia (▲ 45,970) 28,300
Frederiksberg (★ Copenhagen) 85,814
Frederikshavn (▲ 35,531) 25,336
Gentofte (★ Copenhagen) 65,467
Gladsakse (★ Copenhagen) 61,424
Glostrup (★ Copenhagen) 19,896
Greve (★ Copenhagen) 45,121
Haderslev (▲ 30,208) 19,500
Helsingør (Elsinore) (★ Copenhagen) 56,607
Herlev (★ Copenhagen) 27,068
Herning (▲ 56,191) 28,900
Hillerød (★ Copenhagen) 25,300
Hjørring (▲ 34,426) 23,658
Høje Tåstrup (★ Copenhagen) 44,266
Holbæk (▲ 30,860) 21,300
Holstebro (▲ 38,256) 29,300
Horsens (▲ 54,776) 46,900
Hvidovre (★ Copenhagen) 49,332
Køge (★ Copenhagen) 30,400
Kolding (▲ 57,043) 42,000
Lyngby (Kongens Lyngby) [-Tårbæk] (★ Copenhagen) 49,601
Middelfart (▲ 18,468) 12,100
Næstved (▲ 45,132) 38,000
Nakskov 16,229
Nykøbing Falster (▲ 25,121) 18,800
Odense (▲ 174,016) 138,400
Randers 61,155
Ringsted (▲ 28,445) 17,000
Rødovre (★ Copenhagen) 35,787
Rønne 15,397
Roskilde (★ Copenhagen) 39,700
Silkeborg (▲ 47,917) 33,775
Skagen (▲ 13,890) 11,653
Skive (▲ 26,854) 19,500
Slagelse (▲ 34,022) 29,000
Søllerød (★ Copenhagen) 31,253
Sønderborg 27,793
Svendborg (▲ 40,623) 25,800
Tårnby (★ Copenhagen) 39,829
Thisted (▲ 29,781) 12,363
Vejle (▲ 50,817) 44,800
Viborg (▲ 39,631) 29,400
Vordingborg (▲ 19,947) 8,800

*Counties*

Århus 591,993
Bornholm 46,642
Fredericksberg (City) 85,814
Frederiksborg 339,914
Fyn 457,070
København (City) 468,704
København 605,127
Nordjylland 483,675
Ribe 217,973
Ringkøbing 266,554
Roskilde 215,164
Sønderjylland 250,132
Storstrøm 257,161
Vejle 329,590
Vestsjælland 282,775
Viborg 230,966

**DJIBOUTI**

1976 E 226,000

*Cities and Towns*

• DJIBOUTI 120,000

**DOMINICA**

1984 E 77,000

*Cities and Towns*

• ROSEAU 9,348

**DOMINICAN REPUBLIC / República Dominicana**

1981 C 5,647,977

*Cities and Towns*

Azua 31,481
Bajos de Haina 33,135
Baní 36,705
Barahona 49,334
Bonao 44,486
La Romana 91,571
La Vega 52,432
Mao (Valverde) 33,527
Moca 31,176
Puerto Plata 45,348
Salvaleón de Higüey 33,501
San Cristóbal 58,520
San Francisco de Macorís 64,906
San Juan [de La Maguana] 49,764
San Pedro de Macorís 78,562
Santiago [de los Caballeros] 278,638
• SANTO DOMINGO 1,313,172

**ECUADOR**

1982 C 8,050,630

*Cities and Towns*

Alfaro (★ Guayaquil) 51,023
Ambato 100,454
Azogues 14,548
Babahoyo 42,266
Chone 33,839
Cuenca 157,213
Esmeraldas 91,382
Guaranda 13,685
• Guayaquil (★ 1,255,000) 1,204,532
Ibarra 53,428
Jipijapa 27,146
Latacunga 28,764
Loja 71,652
Machala 108,156
Manta 103,609
Milagro 77,010
Pasaje 26,224
Portoviejo 102,628
Quevedo 67,023
QUITO (★ 1,050,000) 890,355
Riobamba 75,455
Santo Domingo de los Colorados 69,235
Tulcán 30,985

*Provinces*

Azuay 443,044
Bolívar 141,566
Cañar 174,674
Carchi 125,452
Chimborazo 320,268
Cotopaxi 279,765
El Oro 337,818
Esmeraldas 247,311
Galápagos (Ter.) 6,119
Guayas 2,047,001
Imbabura 245,745
Loja 358,952
Los Ríos 457,065
Manabí 858,780
Morona-Santiago 70,217
Napo 115,110
Pastaza 31,779
Pichincha 1,376,831
Tungurahua 324,286
Zamora-Chinchipe 46,691
Zones in dispute with Peru 42,156

**EGYPT / Miṣr**

1986 C 48,205,049

*Cities and Towns*

Abnūb 48,519
Abū Kabīr 69,509
Abū Tīj 48,711
Akhmīm 70,602
Al 'Arīsh 67,638
Al Badārī 34,858
Al Badrashayn 40,159
Alexandria (Al Iskandarīyah) (★ 3,350,000) 2,917,327
Al Fashn 43,347
Al Fayyūm 212,523
Al Ghurdaqah 22,801
Al Ḥawāmidīyah (★ Cairo) 73,060
Al Karnak 20,842
Al Khārijah 38,544
Al Madīnah al Fikrīyah 45,629
Al Maḥallah al Kubrā 358,844
Al Manshāh 37,788
Al Manṣūrah (El Mansura) (★ 375,000) 316,870
Al Manzilah 55,090
Al Maṭarīyah 74,554
Al Minyā 179,136
Al Qanāṭir al Khayrīyah 48,909
Al Qaṣr 5,263
Al Quṣayr 19,997
Al Qūṣīyah 42,175
Armant 54,650
Ashmūn 54,450
Ash Shuhadā' 34,695
As Sallūm 3,601
As Sinbillāwayn 60,285
Aswān 191,461
Asyūṭ 273,191
Az Zaqāzīq 245,496
Bahtīm (★ Cairo) 275,807
Banhā 115,571
Banī Mazār 47,964
Banī Suwayf 151,813
Bibā 40,668
Bilbays 96,540
Bilqās Qism Awwal 73,162
Biyalā 47,781
Būlāq ad Dakrūr (★ Cairo) 148,787
Būsh 54,482
• CAIRO (AL QĀHIRAH) (★ 9,300,000) 6,052,836
Damanhūr 190,840
Dayr Mawās 25,518
Dayrūṭ 44,498
Dishnā 37,978
Disūq 78,119
Dumyāṭ (Damietta) 89,498
Fāqūs 48,625
Fuwah 46,014
Giheina al Gharbiya 34,395
Giza (Al Jīzah) (★ Cairo) 1,870,508
Ḥawsh'Īsā (1980 C) 53,619
Hihyā 29,334
Idfū 45,737
Idkū 70,729
Ismailia (Al Ismā'īlīyah) (★ 235,000) 212,567
Isnā 43,055
Jirjā 70,899
Kafr ad Dawwār (★ Alexandria) 195,102
Kafr ash Shaykh 102,910
Kafr az Zayyāt 58,061
Kafr Salīm (★ Alexandria) 2,956
Kawm Umbū 52,131
Luxor (Al Uqṣur) 125,404
Maghāghah 50,807
Mallawī 99,062
Manfalūṭ 52,644
Marsā Maṭrūḥ 43,192
Minūf 69,883
Minyā al Qamḥ 45,871
Mīt Ghamr (★ 100,000) 92,253
Nafīshah (★ Al Ismā'īlīyah) 46,188
Naj'Ḥammādī 28,493
Port Said (Būr Sa'īd) 399,793
Qalyūb 86,684
Qinā 119,794
Qūṣ 42,467
Ra's Gharib 20,617
Rashīd (Rosetta) 52,014
Rummānah 50,014
Samālūt 62,404
Samannūd 41,670
Sāqiyat Makkī 51,062
Sawhāj 132,965
Shibīn al Kawm 132,751
Shibīn al Qanāṭir 35,519
Shirbīn 40,441
Shubrā al Khaymah (★ Cairo) 710,794
Sīdī Barrānī 19,359
Sīdī Sālim 31,674
Sinnūris 55,323
Sīwah 7,329
Suez (As Suways) 326,820
Ṭahṭā 58,516
Talā 38,584
Ṭalkhā (★ Al Manṣūrah) 55,757
Ṭanṭā 334,505
Ṭimā 47,223
Warrāq al 'Arab (★ Cairo) 127,108
Ziftā (★★ Mīt Ghamr) 69,050

**EL SALVADOR**

1985 E 5,337,896

*Cities and Towns*

Ahuachapán 20,376
Chalchuapa (▲ 62,340) 26,158
Cojutepeque 32,043
Cuscatancingo (★ San Salvador) 27,638
Ilopango (★ San Salvador) 31,294
La Unión (▲ 56,063) 27,917
Mejicanos (★ San Salvador) 91,465
Nueva San Salvador (★ San Salvador) 53,688
Quezaltepeque (▲ 44,496) 18,887
San Marcos (★ San Salvador) 37,202
San Miguel 88,520
• SAN SALVADOR (★ 920,000) 462,652
Santa Ana 137,879
San Vicente 27,205
Sonsonate 48,436
Soyapango (★ San Salvador) 60,000
Usulután 32,172
Villa Delgado (★ San Salvador) 67,684
Zacatecoluca 26,646

**EQUATORIAL GUINEA / Guinea Ecuatorial**

1983 C 300,000

*Cities and Towns*

Bata 24,100
• MALABO 30,710

**ETHIOPIA / Ityopiya**

1984 C 42,019,418

*Cities and Towns*

• ADDIS ABABA (★ 1,500,000) 1,412,575
Adwa 13,823
Akaki Beseka (★ Addis Ababa) 54,146
Akordat 5,948
Aseb 30,385
Asela 36,720
Asmara 275,385
Awasa 36,169
Bahir Dar 54,800
Debre Birhan 25,753
Debre Markos 39,808
Debre Zeyit 51,143
Dese 68,848
Dire Dawa 98,104
Gonder 68,958
Harer 62,160
Jima 60,992
Keren 26,149
Massawa (Mitsiwa) 15,441
Mekele 61,583
Nazret 76,284
Nekemte 28,824
Sashemene 31,531
Wenji Gefersa 35,420

**FAEROE ISLANDS / Føroyar**

1988 E 47,653

*Cities and Towns*

• TÓRSHAVN 14,547

**FALKLAND ISLANDS**

1986 C 1,916

*Cities and Towns*

• STANLEY 1,200

**FIJI**

1986 C 715,375

*Cities and Towns*

Lautoka (★ 39,057) 28,728
• SUVA (★ 141,273) 69,665

**FINLAND / Suomi**

1988 E 4,938,602

*Cities and Towns*

Borgå (Porvoo) 19,858
Espoo (Esbo) (★ Helsinki) 164,569
Hämeenlinna 42,486
• HELSINKI (HELSINGFORS) (★ 900,000) 490,034
Hyvinkää 39,185
Iisalmi (▲ 23,695) 17,000
Imatra 34,566
Jakobstad (Pietarsaari) 20,118
Järvenpää (★ Helsinki) 29,001
Joensuu 47,099
Jyväskylä (★ 89,000) 65,719
Kajaani 36,056
Kemi 25,984
Kerava (★ Helsinki) 26,829
Kokkola (Gamlakarleby) 34,599
Kotka 57,745
Kouvola (★ 55,000) 31,933
Kuopio 78,916
Kuusankoski (★★ Kouvola) 21,888
Lahti (★ 109,000) 74,300
Lappeenranta (▲ 53,780) 47,400
Mariehamn (Maarianhamina) 9,966
Mikkeli 31,728
Nokia (★ Tampere) 21,900
Oulu (★ 112,000) 98,582
Pori 77,395
Rauma 30,757
Riihimäki 24,674
Rovaniemi 32,911
Salo 20,838
Savonlinna (▲ 28,510) 24,500
Seinäjoki 26,837
Tampere (★ 241,000) 170,533
Turku (Åbo) (★ 221,000) 160,456
Vaasa (Vasa) 53,737
Vantaa (Vanda) (★ Helsinki) 149,063
Varkaus (▲ 24,791) 19,200

*Provinces*

Ahvenanmaa (Åland) 23,761
Häme 681,550
Keski-Suomi 248,441
Kuopio 255,705
Kymi 337,254
Lappi 200,174
Mikkeli 207,927
Oulu (Uleåborg) 433,715
Pohjois-Karjala 176,699
Turku-Pori 714,196
Uusimaa (Nyland) 1,214,775
Vaasa (Vasa) 444,405

**FRANCE**

1982 C 54,334,871

*Cities and Towns*

Abbeville 24,915
Agen (★ 58,288) 31,593
Aigues-Mortes 4,472
Aix-en-Provence (★ 126,552) 121,327
Aix-les-Bains (★ 31,680) 23,451
Ajaccio 54,089
Albi (★ 60,181) 45,947
Alençon (★ 43,101) 31,608
Alès (★ 70,180) 43,268
Alfortville (★ Paris) 36,231
Amiens (★ 154,498) 131,332
Angers (★ 195,859) 136,038
Angoulême (★ 103,552) 46,197
Annecy (★ 112,632) 49,965
Antibes (★★ Cannes) 62,859
Antony (★ Paris) 54,610
Arcachon (★ 39,931) 13,293
Argenteuil (★ Paris) 95,347
Arles (★ 52,547) 37,571
Armentières (★ 59,000) 24,834
Arras (★ 80,477) 41,736
Asnières [-sur-Seine] (★ Paris) 71,077
Athis-Mons (★ Paris) 28,496
Aubervilliers (★ Paris) 67,719
Auch (▲ 23,258) 20,273
Aulnay-sous-Bois (★ Paris) 75,996
Aurillac (★ 35,829) 30,963
Autun 20,587
Auxerre (★ 42,126) 38,741
Avignon (★ 174,264) 89,132
Avranches (★ 14,889) 9,468
Bagneux (★ Paris) 40,385
Bagnolet (★ Paris) 32,557
Barentin (★ 19,499) 12,364
Bar-le-Duc 18,471
Bastia (★ 50,596) 44,020
Bayeux 14,721
Bayonne (★ 127,477) 41,381
Beauvais (★ 55,817) 52,365
Belfort (★ 76,221) 51,206
Besançon (★ 120,772) 113,283
Béthune (★ 258,383) 25,508
Béziers (★ 81,347) 76,647
Biarritz (★★ Bayonne) 26,598
Blois (★ 61,049) 47,243
Bobigny (★ Paris) 42,723
Bois-Colombes (★ Paris) 23,780
Bondy (★ Paris) 44,301
Bordeaux (★ 640,012) 208,159
Boulogne-Billancourt (★ Paris) 102,582
Boulogne-sur-Mer (★ 98,566) 47,653
Bourg [-en-Bresse] (★ 53,463) 41,098
Bourges (★ 92,202) 76,432
Brest (★ 201,145) 156,060
Briançon (★ 13,123) 9,710
Brive [-la-Gaillarde] (★ 64,301) 51,511
Bron (★ Lyon) 40,638
Bruay [-en-Artois] (★★ Béthune) 22,893
Caen (★ 183,526) 114,068
Cagnes-sur-Mer (★ Nice) 35,214
Cahors 19,707
Calais (★ 100,823) 76,527
Caluire [-et-Cuire] (★ Lyon) 41,931
Cambrai (★ 49,581) 35,272
Cannes (★ 295,525) 72,259
Carcassonne 41,153
Carmaux (★ 19,422) 12,113
Castres (★ 46,891) 45,578
Châlons-sur-Marne (★ 63,061) 51,137
Chalon-sur-Saône (★ 78,064) 56,194
Chambéry (★ 96,163) 53,427
Chamonix [-Mont-Blanc] (★ 10,512) 7,406
Champigny-sur-Marne (★ Paris) 76,176
Chantilly (★ 28,128) 10,065
Charleville-Mézières (★ 67,694) 58,667
Chartres (★ 77,795) 37,119
Châteauroux (★ 66,851) 51,942
Château-Thierry (★ 22,696) 14,557
Châtellerault 35,838
Châtenay-Malabry (★ Paris) 28,580

C Census. E Official estimate. UE Unofficial estimate.
• Largest city in country.

★ Population or designation of metropolitan area, including suburbs (see headnote).
▲ Population of an entire municipality, commune, or district, including rural area.

Châtillon (★ Paris) 24,834
Chatou (★ Paris) 28,437
Chaumont 27,554
Chauny (★ 20,078) 13,435
Chelles (★ Paris) 41,838
Cherbourg (★ 85,485) 28,442
Chinon (▲ 8,622) 6,032
Choisy-le-Roi (★ Paris) 35,476
Cholet 55,524
Clamart (★ Paris) 48,353
Clermont-Ferrand (★ 256,189) 147,361
Clichy (★ Paris) 46,895
Cognac (★ 31,189) 20,660
Colmar (★ 82,468) 62,483
Colombes (★ Paris) 78,777
Compiègne (★ 62,778) 40,384
Concarneau (★ 23,893) 15,747
Corbeil [-Essonnes] (★ Paris) 37,846
Courbevoie (★ Paris) 59,830
Coutances 9,930
Creil (★ 82,505) 34,709
Créteil (★ Paris) 71,693
Dax (★ 33,475) 18,648
Deauville 4,682
Decazeville (★ 21,925) 8,804
Denain (★★ Valenciennes) 21,825
Dieppe (★ 41,812) 35,957
Dijon (★ 215,865) 140,942
Dinard (★ 15,838) 9,590
Dives-sur-Mer (★ 11,204) 5,508
Dôle (★ 31,546) 26,889
Douai (★ 202,366) 42,576
Douarnenez 17,653
Drancy (★ Paris) 60,183
Dreux (★ 44,706) 33,379
Dunkerque (★ 195,705) 73,120
Elbeuf (★ 51,083) 17,224
Épernay (★ 34,355) 27,668
Épinal (★ 51,495) 37,818
Épinay [-sur-Seine] (★ Paris) 50,314
Étaples (★ 22,701) 11,292
Eu (★ 20,506) 8,588
Évreux (★ 54,654) 46,045
Évry (★ Paris) 29,471
Falaise 8,597
Fécamp 21,436
Foix 9,282
Fontaine (★ Grenoble) 22,827
Fontainebleau (★ 35,629) 15,679
Fontenay [-sous-Bois] (★ Paris) 52,627
Forbach (★ 99,606) 27,187
Fougères 24,362
Fréjus (★ 60,289) 31,662
Gagny (★ Paris) 34,861
Gap (▲ 30,676) 21,874
Garges-lès-Gonesse (★ Paris) 40,182
Gennevilliers (★ Paris) 45,396
Givors (★ Lyon) 20,544
Granville (★ 17,890) 13,546
Grasse (★★ Cannes) 24,553
Grenoble (★ 392,021) 156,637
Guebwiller (★ 25,427) 10,689
Guéret 15,720
Hagondange (★ 119,669) 9,091
Haguenau (★ 32,403) 26,629
Hayange (★★ Thionville) 17,848
Hendaye 10,572
Hénin-Beaumont (Hénin-Liétard) (★★ Lens) 26,037
Houilles (★ Paris) 29,537
Hyères (★★ Toulon) 32,191
Issy [-les-Moulineaux] (★ Paris) 45,772
Ivry-sur-Seine (★ Paris) 55,699
Jœuf (★ Hagondange) 9,016
La Baule-Escoublac (★ Saint-Nazaire) 14,553
La Ciotat (★ 39,956) 31,727
La Courneuve (★ Paris) 33,537
La Garenne-Colombes (★ Paris) 20,990
La Grand'Combe (★ 13,743) 8,329
Lambersart (★ Lille) 28,520
Laon 26,682
La Rochelle (★ 102,143) 75,840
La Roche-sur-Yon 45,098
La Seyne [-sur-Mer] (★ Toulon) 57,659
Laval (★ 55,984) 50,360
Le Blanc-Mesnil (★ Paris) 47,037
Le Creusot (★ 44,389) 32,149
Le Grand-Quevilly (★ Rouen) 31,650
Le Havre (★ 254,595) 199,388
Le Mans (★ 191,080) 147,697
Lens (★ 327,383) 38,244
Le Perreux-sur-Marne (★ Paris) 27,647
Le Puy [-en-Velay] (★ 42,382) 24,064
Les Sables-d'Olonne (★ 32,436) 16,100
Levallois-Perret (★ Paris) 53,500
Le Vésinet (★ Paris) 17,272
L'Haÿ-les-Roses (★ Paris) 29,568
Libourne (★ 26,992) 22,119
Liévin (★ Lens) 33,096
Lille (★ 1,020,000) 168,424
Limoges (★ 171,689) 140,400
Lisieux (★ 29,063) 24,940
Livry-Gargan (★ Paris) 32,778
Loches (▲ 6,772) 5,847
Lomme (★ Lille) 28,281
Longwy (★ 77,000) 17,338
Lons-le-Saunier (★ 26,410) 20,105
Lorient (★ 104,025) 62,554
Lourdes 17,425
Lunéville 21,468
Lyon (★ 1,275,000) 413,095
Mâcon (★ 47,274) 38,404
Maisons-Alfort (★ Paris) 51,065
Maisons-Laffitte (★ Paris) 22,595
Malakoff (★ Paris) 32,553
Mantes [-la-Jolie] (★ 170,265) 43,564
Marcq-en-Baroeul (★ Lille) 35,278
Marignane (★ Marseille) 31,109
Marseille (★ 1,225,000) 874,436
Martigues (★ Marseille) 31,157
Massy (★ Paris) 40,135
Maubeuge (★ 105,714) 36,061
Mazamet (★ 26,676) 12,840
Meaux (★ 55,797) 45,005
Melun (★ 82,479) 35,005
Mende 10,929
Menton (★★ Monaco, Monaco) 25,072
Mérignac (★ Bordeaux) 51,306
Metz (★ 186,437) 114,232
Meudon (★ Paris) 48,450
Millau 21,695
Montargis (★ 51,954) 16,110
Montauban (▲ 50,682) 36,758
Montbéliard (★ 128,194) 31,836
Montceau-les-Mines (★ 51,290) 26,925
Mont-de-Marsan (★ 33,616) 27,326
Montélimar (★ 38,292) 29,161
Montereau [-faut-Yonne] (★ 26,663) 19,413
Montigny [-lès-Metz] (★ Metz) 22,114
Montluçon (★ 67,963) 49,912
Montmorency (★ Paris) 20,798
Montpellier (★ 221,307) 197,231
Montreuil [-sous-Bois] (★ Paris) 93,368
Montrouge (★ Paris) 38,517
Morlaix (★ 27,829) 15,558
Moulins (★ 43,082) 25,159
Moyeuvre [-Grande] (★ Hagondange) 10,287
Mulhouse (★ 220,613) 112,157
Nancy (★ 306,982) 96,317
Nanterre (★ Paris) 88,578
Nantes (★ 464,857) 240,539
Narbonne 41,565
Neuilly [-sur-Seine] (★ Paris) 64,170
Nevers (★ 59,274) 43,013
Nice (★ 449,496) 337,085
Nîmes (★ 132,343) 124,220
Niort (★ 61,959) 58,203
Nogent [-sur-Marne] (★ Paris) 24,630
Noisy-le-Grand (★ Paris) 40,585
Noisy-le-Sec (★ Paris) 36,880
Noyon 14,041
Orange (▲ 26,499) 18,727
Orléans (★ 220,478) 102,710
Orly (★ Paris) 23,766
Oullins (★ Lyon) 27,168
Oyonnax (★ 28,107) 22,739
Palaiseau (★ Paris) 28,369
Pantin (★ Paris) 43,553
Paray-le-Monial 10,639
• PARIS (★ 9,775,000) (1987 E) 2,078,900
Pau (★ 131,265) 83,790
Périgueux (★ 59,716) 32,916
Perpignan (★ 137,915) 111,669
Pessac (★ Bordeaux) 50,267
Poissy (★ Paris) 36,389
Poitiers (★ 103,204) 79,350
Pont-à-Mousson (★ 22,661) 14,942
Pontoise (★ Paris) 28,434
Port-de-Bouc 20,106
Privas (★ 14,108) 10,345
Puteaux (★ Paris) 36,117
Quimper 56,907
Reims (★ 199,388) 194,656
Rennes (★ 234,418) 117,234
Rezé (★ Nantes) 33,562
Riom (★ 23,316) 18,346
Rive-de-Gier (★★ Saint-Chamond) 15,806
Roanne (★ 81,786) 48,705
Rochefort (★ 35,122) 26,167
Rodez (★ 37,953) 24,368
Romans [-sur-Isère] (★ 47,083) 33,152
Rosny-sous-Bois (★ Paris) 36,970
Roubaix (★★ Lille) 101,602
Rouen (★ 379,879) 101,945
Royan (★ 28,327) 17,540
Rueil-Malmaison (★ Paris) 63,412
Saint-Avold (★ 26,543) 12,389
Saint-Brieuc (★ 83,900) 48,563
Saint-Chamond (★ 82,059) 40,267
Saint-Cyr-l'École (★ Paris) 14,996
Saint-Denis (★ Paris) 90,829
Saint-Dié (★ 27,708) 23,759
Saint-Dizier 35,189
Saint-Étienne (★ 317,228) 204,955
Saint-Étienne-du-Rouvray (★ Rouen) 32,444
Saint-Germain-en-Laye (★ Paris) 38,499
Saint-Jean-de-Luz (★ 23,868) 12,769
Saint-Lô (★ 27,656) 23,212
Saint-Malo 46,347
Saint-Martin-d'Hères (★ Grenoble) 35,188
Saint-Maur-des-Fossés (★ Paris) 80,811
Saint-Nazaire (★ 130,271) 68,348
Saint-Omer (★ 53,748) 15,415
Saint-Ouen (★ Paris) 43,606
Saint-Quentin (★ 71,887) 63,567
Saintes 25,471
Saint-Tropez (▲ 6,213) 4,961
Salon-de-Provence (★ 41,091) 34,846
Sarcelles (★ Paris) 53,630
Sarreguemines 24,763
Sartrouville (★ Paris) 46,197
Saumur 32,149
Savigny-sur-Orge (★ Paris) 32,502
Schiltigheim (★ Strasbourg) 29,574
Sedan (★ 30,871) 23,477
Senlis 14,514
Sens (★ 35,178) 26,602
Sète (★ 58,865) 39,545
Sèvres (★ Paris) 20,208
Soissons (★ 47,305) 30,213
Sotteville-lès-Rouen (★ Rouen) 30,558
Stains (★ Paris) 36,079
Strasbourg (★ 400,000) 248,712
Suresnes (★ Paris) 35,187
Tarbes (★ 78,056) 51,422
Thann (★ 28,406) 7,788
Thionville (★ 138,034) 40,573
Thonon-les-Bains (★ 45,372) 27,161
Toul (★ 22,878) 17,406
Toulon (★ 410,393) 179,423
Toulouse (★ 541,271) 347,995
Tourcoing (★★ Lille) 96,908
Tours (★ 262,786) 132,209
Trouville [-sur-Mer] (★ 18,533) 6,008
Troyes (★ 125,240) 63,581
Tulle 18,880
Valence (★ 106,041) 66,356
Valenciennes (★ 349,505) 40,276
Vannes 42,178
Vanves (★ Paris) 22,868
Vénissieux (★ Lyon) 64,804
Verdun (★ 26,944) 21,516
Versailles (★ Paris) 91,494
Vesoul (★ 26,592) 18,412
Vichy (★ 63,501) 30,527
Vienne (★ 41,019) 28,294
Vierzon 34,209
Villefranche-sur-Mer (★ Nice) 7,363
Villefranche [-sur-Saône] (★ 50,143) 28,881
Villejuif (★ Paris) 52,448
Villemomble (★ Paris) 27,571
Villeneuve-d'Ascq (★ Lille) 59,527
Villeneuve-Saint-Georges (★ Paris) 28,119
Villeurbanne (★ Lyon) 115,960
Vincennes (★ Paris) 42,870
Viry-Châtillon (★ Paris) 30,224
Vitry-le-François (★ 21,192) 18,261
Vitry-sur-Seine (★ Paris) 85,263
Voiron (★ 33,492) 18,911
Wattrelos (★ Lille) 44,626

***Departments***

1987 ESTIMATE

Ain 453,200
Aisne 532,600
Allier 364,500
Alpes-de-Haute-Provence (Basses-Alpes) 125,900
Alpes-Maritimes 907,200
Ardèche 274,500
Ardennes 297,900
Ariège 136,100
Aube 294,600
Aude 288,800
Aveyron 276,100
Bas-Rhin 941,600
Belfort, Territoire de 130,000
Bouches-du-Rhône 1,754,500
Calvados 608,000
Cantal 159,600
Charente 342,500
Charente-Maritime 522,500
Cher 322,700
Corrèze 238,900
Corse-du-Sud 111,400
Côte-d'Or 485,300
Côtes-du-Nord 541,700
Creuse 135,700
Deux-Sèvres 346,000
Dordogne 379,200
Doubs 478,800
Drôme 412,200
Essonne 1,042,600
Eure 490,200
Eure-et-Loir 378,800
Finistère 834,200
Gard 566,000
Gers 175,200
Gironde 1,161,700
Haute-Corse 134,600
Haute-Garonne 858,800
Haute-Loire 209,100
Haute-Marne 207,600
Hautes-Alpes 108,700
Haute-Saône 234,100
Haute-Savoie 535,200
Hautes-Pyrénées 232,300
Haute-Vienne 360,100
Haut-Rhin 663,800
Hauts-de-Seine 1,371,300
Hérault 769,200
Ille-et-Vilaine 777,900
Indre 238,300
Indre-et-Loire 524,600
Isère 982,700
Jura 245,100
Landes 308,600
Loire 739,200
Loire-Atlantique 1,032,600
Loiret 568,900
Loir-et-Cher 300,600
Lot 154,700
Lot-et-Garonne 304,300
Lozère 72,400
Maine-et-Loire 707,600
Manche 476,600
Marne 557,700
Mayenne 280,400
Meurthe-et-Moselle 709,000
Meuse 197,600
Morbihan 609,400
Moselle 1,030,500
Nièvre 235,400
Nord 2,507,200
Oise 695,600
Orne 294,800
Paris 2,078,900
Pas-de-Calais 1,424,300
Puy-de-Dôme 596,000
Pyrénées-Atlantiques (Basses Pyrénées) 569,800
Pyrénées-Orientales 357,200
Rhône 1,443,600
Saône-et-Loire 571,000
Sarthe 515,400
Savoie 334,200
Seine-et-Marne 975,400
Seine-Maritime 1,209,400
Seine-Saint-Denis 1,343,700
Somme 548,200
Tarn 341,500
Tarn-et-Garonne 194,900
Val-de-Marne 1,198,600
Val-d'Oise 985,900
Var 754,800
Vaucluse 461,400
Vendée 506,600
Vienne 380,500
Vosges 389,900
Yonne 318,900
Yvelines 1,262,900

***Historic Regions***

1987 ESTIMATE

Alsace 1,605,300
Aquitaine 2,723,600
Auvergne 1,329,200
Basse-Normandie 1,379,400
Bourgogne 1,610,600
Bretagne 2,763,100
Centre 2,333,800
Champagne-Ardenne 1,357,900
Corse (Corsica) 246,000
Franche-Comté 1,088,000
Haute-Normandie 1,699,600
Île-de-France 10,259,400
Languedoc-Roussillon 2,053,600
Limousin 734,700
Lorraine 2,326,900
Midi-Pyrénées 2,369,500
Nord-Pas-de-Calais 3,931,500
Pays de la Loire 3,042,500
Picardie 1,776,400
Poitou-Charentes 1,591,500
Provence-Alpes-Côte D'Azur 4,112,500
Rhône-Alpes 5,174,800

## FRENCH GUIANA / Guyane française

1982 C 73,022

***Cities and Towns***

• CAYENNE 38,091
Kourou 7,061
Saint-Laurent [-du-Maroni] (▲ 6,971) 4,500

## FRENCH POLYNESIA / Polynésie française

1983 C 166,753

***Cities and Towns***

• PAPEETE (★ 80,000) 23,496

## GABON

1985 E 1,312,000

***Cities and Towns***

Franceville 58,800
Lambaréné 49,500
• LIBREVILLE 235,700
Port-Gentil 124,400

## GAMBIA

1983 C 696,000

***Cities and Towns***

• BANJUL (BATHURST) (★ 95,000) 44,536
Brikama 20,208

## GERMAN DEMOCRATIC REPUBLIC (EAST GERMANY) / Deutsche Demokratische Republik

1987 E 16,639,877

***Cities and Towns***

Altenburg 53,602
Annaberg-Buchholz 26,002
Apolda 28,230
Arnstadt 30,207
Aschersleben 34,166
Aue 27,935
Bautzen 52,354
• BERLIN (EAST) (★★ Berlin) 1,236,248
Bernburg 40,834
Bitterfeld (★ 105,000) 20,869
Blankenburg 19,279
Borna 24,397
Brandenburg 94,755
Burg bei Magdeburg 28,359
Coswig (★ Dresden) 27,590
Cottbus 126,592
Crimmitschau 24,440
Delitzsch 27,636
Dessau (★ 140,000) 103,538
Döbeln 27,706
Dresden (★ 670,000) 519,810
Eberswalde [-Finow] 54,566
Eilenburg 21,931
Eisenach 49,534
Eisenhüttenstadt 51,729
Eisleben 26,484
Erfurt 217,134
Falkensee (★ Berlin) 23,024
Finsterwalde 23,857
Forst [Lausitz] 26,501
Frankfurt [an der Oder] 86,441
Freiberg 50,415
Freital (★ Dresden) 43,092
Fürstenwalde [Spree] 35,282
Gera 132,319
Glauchau 28,309
Görlitz 78,856
Gotha 57,423
Greifswald 67,298
Greiz 34,858
Güstrow 38,971
Halberstadt 47,017
Halle (★ 475,000) 236,148
Halle-Neustadt (★ Halle) 93,477
Heidenau (★ Dresden) 19,133
Henningsdorf bei Berlin (★ Berlin) 26,574
Hettstedt 21,861
Hoyerswerda 69,113
Ilmenau 29,338
Jena 107,610
Karl-Marx-Stadt (Chemnitz) (★ 450,000) 313,799
Köthen 34,617
Lauchhammer 24,391
Leipzig (★ 700,000) 550,641
Limbach-Oberfrohna (★ Karl-Marx-Stadt) 22,059
Lübbenau 20,815
Luckenwalde 26,761
Ludwigsfelde 22,290
Magdeburg (★ 400,000) 288,975
Markkleeberg (★ Leipzig) 19,240
Meerane 21,879
Meiningen 25,823
Meissen 37,757
Merseburg (★★ Halle) 46,188
Mühlhausen (Thomas-Müntzer-Stadt) 43,046
Naumburg [an der Saale] 32,100
Neubrandenburg 87,235
Neuruppin 26,934
Neustrelitz 27,300
Nordhausen 47,681
Oranienburg (★ Berlin) 28,667
Parchim 23,454
Pirna 46,991
Plauen 77,514
Potsdam (★ Berlin) 141,231
Prenzlau 23,642
Quedlinburg 29,168
Radebeul (★ Dresden) 33,757
Rathenow 31,302
Reichenbach 24,749
Riesa 49,108
Rostock 249,349
Rudolstadt 32,264
Saalfeld 33,453
Salzwedel 23,163
Sangerhausen 33,064
Sassnitz 14,077
Schmalkalden 17,409
Schneeberg 22,105
Schönebeck 45,155
Schwedt 51,753
Schwerin 128,328
Senftenberg 32,428
Sömmerda 23,398
Sondershausen 24,178
Sonneberg 28,152
Spremberg 24,815
Stassfurt 27,372
Stendal 47,880
Stralsund 75,857
Strausberg (★ Berlin) 27,527
Suhl 55,295
Tangermünde 11,720
Torgau 22,749
Waren 24,318
Weimar 63,910
Weissenfels 38,763

C Census. E Official estimate. UE Unofficial estimate.
• Largest city in country.

★ Population or designation of metropolitan area, including suburbs (see headnote).
▲ Population of an entire municipality, commune, or district, including rural area.

| | |
|---|---|
| Weisswasser | 36,472 |
| Werdau | 19,451 |
| Wernigerode | 36,499 |
| Wilhelm-Pieck-Stadt Guben | 34,665 |
| Wismar | 58,066 |
| Wittenberge | 30,389 |
| Wittenberg [Lutherstadt] | 53,670 |
| Wolfen (★★ Bitterfeld) | 43,606 |
| Wurzen | 19,330 |
| Zeitz | 42,985 |
| Zerbst | 18,717 |
| Zittau | 39,305 |
| Zwickau (★ 165,000) | 120,923 |

***Districts***

| | |
|---|---|
| Berlin, [East] (city) | 1,236,248 |
| Cottbus | 883,591 |
| Dresden | 1,768,990 |
| Erfurt | 1,235,785 |
| Frankfurt | 710,634 |
| Gera | 739,856 |
| Halle | 1,783,987 |
| Karl-Marx-Stadt | 1,866,321 |
| Leipzig | 1,371,427 |
| Magdeburg | 1,249,636 |
| Neubrandenburg | 620,057 |
| Potsdam | 1,121,640 |
| Rostock | 909,550 |
| Schwerin | 592,519 |
| Suhl | 549,636 |

**GERMANY, FEDERAL REPUBLIC OF (WEST GERMANY) / Bundesrepublik Deutschland**

| | |
|---|---|
| 1987 E | 61,140,461 |

***Cities and Towns***

| | |
|---|---|
| Aachen (★ 535,000) | 239,170 |
| Aalen (★ 80,000) | 63,337 |
| Achern | 20,667 |
| Achim (★ Bremen) | 28,122 |
| Ahaus | 29,604 |
| Ahlen | 51,895 |
| Ahrensburg (★ Hamburg) | 27,203 |
| Albstadt | 45,973 |
| Alfeld (Leine) | 22,453 |
| Alsdorf (★ Aachen) | 45,925 |
| Altena | 22,103 |
| Amberg | 43,348 |
| Andernach (★★ Neuwied) | 26,520 |
| Ansbach | 37,451 |
| Arnsberg | 74,641 |
| Aschaffenburg (★ 145,000) | 59,646 |
| Augsburg (★ 405,000) | 245,962 |
| Aurich | 35,063 |
| Backnang | 29,695 |
| Baden-Baden | 49,257 |
| Bad Harzburg (★ Goslar) | 23,701 |
| Bad Hersfeld | 27,239 |
| Bad Homburg vor der Höhe (★ Frankfurt am Main) | 51,081 |
| Bad Honnef am Rhein (★ Bonn) | 20,495 |
| Bad Kissingen | 21,092 |
| Bad Kreuznach | 39,713 |
| Bad Nauheim (★ Frankfurt am Main) | 26,521 |
| Bad Neuenahr-Ahrweiler | 24,749 |
| Bad Oeynhausen | 43,237 |
| Bad Oldesloe | 20,775 |
| Bad Reichenhall | 17,506 |
| Bad Salzuflen (★★ Herford) | 51,187 |
| Bad Vilbel (★ Frankfurt am Main) | 24,984 |
| Balingen | 29,917 |
| Bamberg (★ 120,000) | 69,591 |
| Barsinghausen (★ Hannover) | 32,521 |
| Bayreuth (★ 90,000) | 72,326 |
| Beckum | 36,542 |
| Bensheim | 33,537 |
| Berchtesgaden | 8,051 |
| Bergheim (Erft) (★ Cologne) | 54,413 |
| Bergisch Gladbach (★ Cologne) | 101,776 |
| Bergkamen (★ Essen) | 47,912 |
| Berlin (West) (★ 3,825,000) | 1,879,225 |
| Biberach [an der Riss] | 28,015 |
| Bielefeld (★ 515,000) | 299,360 |
| Bietigheim-Bissingen (★ Stuttgart) | 35,618 |
| Bingen am Rhein | 22,138 |
| Böblingen (★ Stuttgart) | 41,485 |
| Bocholt | 66,443 |
| Bochum (★★ Essen) | 381,216 |
| BONN (★ 570,000) | 291,439 |
| Borken | 33,696 |
| Bornheim (★ Bonn) | 36,168 |
| Bottrop (★ Essen) | 112,256 |
| Brake | 16,862 |
| Bramsche | 23,648 |
| Braunschweig (Brunswick) (★ 330,000) | 247,836 |
| Bremen (★ 800,000) | 521,976 |
| Bremerhaven (★ 190,000) | 132,194 |
| Bretten | 23,668 |
| Brilon | 24,565 |
| Bruchsal | 36,549 |
| Brühl (★ Cologne) | 40,680 |
| Buchholz in der Nordheide (★ Hamburg) | 30,870 |
| Bückeburg | 20,409 |
| Bünde | 38,360 |
| Burgdorf (★ Hannover) | 28,674 |
| Butzbach | 21,252 |
| Buxtehude (★ Hamburg) | 32,474 |
| Calw | 22,401 |
| Castrop-Rauxel (★ Essen) | 76,110 |
| Celle | 70,245 |
| Cloppenburg | 22,008 |
| Coburg | 44,412 |
| Coesfeld | 31,584 |
| Cologne (Köln) (★ 1,760,000) | 914,336 |
| Crailsheim | 25,097 |
| Cuxhaven | 56,076 |
| Dachau (★ Munich) | 32,871 |
| Darmstadt (★ 305,000) | 133,572 |
| Datteln (★ Essen) | 36,276 |
| Deggendorf | 30,243 |
| Delmenhorst (★★ Bremen) | 70,512 |
| Detmold | 66,660 |
| Dietzenbach (★ Frankfurt am Main) | 27,127 |
| Dillingen / Saar (★ Saarlouis) | 20,061 |
| Dinkelsbühl | 10,520 |
| Dinslaken (★ Essen) | 61,330 |
| Ditzingen (★ Stuttgart) | 22,196 |
| Dormagen (★ Cologne) | 57,513 |
| Dorsten (★ Essen) | 74,115 |
| Dortmund (★★ Essen) | 568,164 |
| Dreieich (★ Frankfurt am Main) | 38,082 |
| Duderstadt | 22,815 |
| Duisburg (★★ Essen) | 514,628 |
| Dülmen | 40,136 |
| Düren (★ 110,000) | 84,100 |
| Düsseldorf (★ 1,190,000) | 560,572 |
| Eckernförde | 24,470 |
| Einbeck | 27,440 |
| Elmshorn | 41,467 |
| Emden | 49,557 |
| Emmendingen | 25,111 |
| Emmerich | 29,075 |
| Emsdetten | 31,121 |
| Ennepetal (★ Essen) | 33,744 |
| Erftstadt (★ Cologne) | 45,010 |
| Erkelenz | 36,865 |
| Erkrath (★ Düsseldorf) | 45,204 |
| Erlangen (★★ Nürnberg) | 100,200 |
| Eschwege | 22,893 |
| Eschweiler (★★ Aachen) | 53,082 |
| Espelkamp | 21,725 |
| • Essen (★ 4,950,000) | 615,421 |
| Esslingen am Neckar (★ Stuttgart) | 86,886 |
| Ettlingen (★ Karlsruhe) | 37,081 |
| Euskirchen | 45,676 |
| Fellbach (★ Stuttgart) | 39,819 |
| Filderstadt (★ Stuttgart) | 37,355 |
| Flensburg (★ 103,000) | 85,714 |
| Forchheim | 28,808 |
| Frankenthal (★ Mannheim) | 44,269 |
| Frankfurt [am Main] (★ 1,855,000) | 592,411 |
| Frechen (★ Cologne) | 42,327 |
| Freiburg [im Breisgau] (★ 225,000) | 186,156 |
| Freising | 36,209 |
| Friedberg (★ Augsburg) | 25,562 |
| Friedrichshafen | 52,064 |
| Fulda (★ 79,000) | 54,131 |
| Fürstenfeldbruck (★ Munich) | 31,458 |
| Fürth (★★ Nürnberg) | 98,203 |
| Gaggenau | 27,915 |
| Ganderkesee (★ Bremen) | 26,233 |
| Garbsen (★ Hannover) | 57,541 |
| Garmisch-Partenkirchen | 27,701 |
| Geesthacht (★ Hamburg) | 25,495 |
| Geislingen an der Steige (★ Göppingen) | 26,164 |
| Geldern | 27,239 |
| Gelsenkirchen (★★ Essen) | 283,560 |
| Georgsmarienhütte (★ Osnabrück) | 30,636 |
| Germering (★ Munich) | 35,565 |
| Gevelsberg (★ Essen) | 30,444 |
| Giessen (★ 160,000) | 71,095 |
| Gifhorn | 34,501 |
| Gladbeck (★ Essen) | 76,625 |
| Goch | 28,477 |
| Göppingen (★ 155,000) | 51,416 |
| Goslar (★ 84,000) | 49,034 |
| Göttingen | 133,796 |
| Greven | 28,753 |
| Grevenbroich (★ Düsseldorf) | 57,463 |
| Gronau (★ Enschede, Netherlands) | 39,858 |
| Gummersbach | 48,359 |
| Gütersloh (★★ Bielefeld) | 79,432 |
| Haan (★ Wuppertal) | 27,838 |
| Hagen (★★ Essen) | 206,070 |
| Haltern (★ Essen) | 32,158 |
| Hamburg (★ 2,225,000) | 1,571,267 |
| Hameln (★ 72,000) | 55,390 |
| Hamm | 165,957 |
| Hanau [am Main] (★★ Frankfurt am Main) | 85,217 |
| Hannover (★ 1,000,000) | 505,718 |
| Hattingen (★ Essen) | 54,964 |
| Heide | 20,652 |
| Heidelberg (★★ Mannheim) | 136,227 |
| Heidenheim an der Brenz (★ 89,000) | 47,611 |
| Heilbronn (★ 230,000) | 111,713 |
| Heiligenhaus (★ Essen) | 28,514 |
| Heinsberg | 36,638 |
| Helmstedt | 25,471 |
| Hemer | 31,486 |
| Hennef (★ Siegburg) | 30,236 |
| Heppenheim (★ Mannheim) | 24,028 |
| Herdecke (★ Essen) | 24,703 |
| Herford (★ 120,000) | 59,495 |
| Herne (★ Essen) | 171,274 |
| Herrenberg (★ Stuttgart) | 26,072 |
| Herten (★ Essen) | 67,829 |
| Herzogenrath (★ Aachen) | 43,326 |
| Hilden (★ Düsseldorf) | 53,820 |
| Hildesheim (★ 140,000) | 100,558 |
| Hof | 50,623 |
| Hofheim am Taunus (★ Frankfurt am Main) | 33,985 |
| Holzminden | 20,978 |
| Homburg (★★ Zweibrücken) | 40,836 |
| Höxter | 31,506 |
| Hückelhoven | 35,629 |
| Hürth (★ Cologne) | 51,286 |
| Husum | 23,795 |
| Ibbenbüren | 42,664 |
| Idar-Oberstein | 33,980 |
| Ingolstadt (★ 138,000) | 92,593 |
| Iserlohn | 89,466 |
| Itzehoe | 31,727 |
| Jüchen (★ Mönchengladbach) | 20,479 |
| Jülich | 30,156 |
| Kaarst (★ Düsseldorf) | 39,321 |
| Kaiserslautern (★ 138,000) | 96,766 |
| Kamen (★ Essen) | 44,509 |
| Kamp-Lintfort (★ Essen) | 36,596 |
| Karlsruhe (★ 485,000) | 268,309 |
| Kassel (★ 360,000) | 185,370 |
| Kaufbeuren | 41,475 |
| Kehl (★ Strasbourg, France) | 28,768 |
| Kelkheim (★ Frankfurt am Main) | 26,961 |
| Kempen (★ Essen) | 31,882 |
| Kempten [in Allgäu] | 56,950 |
| Kerpen (★ Cologne) | 55,158 |
| Kiel (★ 335,000) | 243,626 |
| Kirchheim unter Teck (★ Stuttgart) | 34,000 |
| Kleve (Cleves) | 44,725 |
| Koblenz (★ 180,000) | 110,277 |
| Königswinter (★ Bonn) | 33,685 |
| Konstanz | 70,539 |
| Korbach | 22,213 |
| Kornwestheim (★ Stuttgart) | 26,956 |
| Korschenbroich (★ Düsseldorf) | 27,427 |
| Krefeld (★★ Essen) | 216,598 |
| Kreuztal (★ Siegen) | 28,989 |
| Kulmbach | 27,364 |
| Laatzen (★ Hannover) | 36,884 |
| Lage | 32,207 |
| Lahnstein (★ Koblenz) | 18,086 |
| Lahr / Schwarzwald | 34,566 |
| Lampertheim (★ Mannheim) | 30,660 |
| Landau in der Pfalz | 35,284 |
| Landshut | 57,067 |
| Langen (★ Frankfurt am Main) | 29,302 |
| Langenfeld (Rheinland) (★ Düsseldorf) | 45,463 |
| Langenhagen (★ Hannover) | 46,630 |
| Leer | 30,075 |
| Lehrte (★ Hannover) | 39,238 |
| Leinfelden-Echterdingen (★ Stuttgart) | 35,349 |
| Lemgo | 39,108 |
| Lengerich | 20,182 |
| Lennestadt | 25,985 |
| Leonberg (★ Stuttgart) | 40,235 |
| Leverkusen (★ Cologne) | 154,703 |
| Limburg [an der Lahn] | 28,905 |
| Lindau (Bodensee) | 23,053 |
| Lingen | 45,722 |
| Lippstadt | 60,141 |
| Lohmar (★ Siegburg) | 25,334 |
| Löhne | 36,209 |
| Lörrach (★ Basel, Switzerland) | 41,198 |
| Lübeck (★ 260,000) | 209,159 |
| Lüdenscheid | 73,442 |
| Ludwigsburg (★ Stuttgart) | 76,898 |
| Ludwigshafen am Rhein (★★ Mannheim) | 152,162 |
| Lüneburg | 59,497 |
| Lünen (★ Essen) | 84,352 |
| Maintal (★ Frankfurt am Main) | 36,589 |
| Mainz (★★ Wiesbaden) | 189,005 |
| Mannheim (★ 1,400,000) | 294,648 |
| Marburg [an der Lahn] | 77,114 |
| Marl (★ Essen) | 87,766 |
| Meerbusch (★ Düsseldorf) | 49,158 |
| Melle | 39,862 |
| Memmingen | 37,284 |
| Menden | 52,175 |
| Meppen | 29,087 |
| Merzig | 29,228 |
| Meschede | 29,313 |
| Mettmann (★ Düsseldorf) | 36,297 |
| Minden (★ 125,000) | 75,384 |
| Moers (★ Essen) | 95,407 |
| Mönchengladbach (★ 410,000) | 255,087 |
| Monheim (★ Düsseldorf) | 40,838 |
| Mörfelden-Walldorf (★ Frankfurt am Main) | 29,406 |
| Mülheim [am der Ruhr] (★ Essen) | 170,392 |
| Münden | 24,215 |
| Munich (München) (★ 1,955,000) | 1,274,716 |
| Münster | 267,628 |
| Neckarsulm (★ Heilbronn) | 21,891 |
| Nettetal | 37,123 |
| Neuburg [an der Donau] | 24,267 |
| Neu-Isenburg (★ Frankfurt am Main) | 35,170 |
| Neukirchen-Vluyn (★ Essen) | 25,391 |
| Neumarkt [in der Oberpfalz] | 32,059 |
| Neumünster | 77,877 |
| Neunkirchen [Saar] (★ 135,000) | 49,536 |
| Neuss (★ Düsseldorf) | 143,832 |
| Neustadt am Rübenberge (★ Hannover) | 37,893 |
| Neustadt [an der Weinstrasse] | 48,391 |
| Neu-Ulm (★ Ulm) | 46,409 |
| Neuwied (★ 150,000) | 58,263 |
| Niederkassel (★ Bonn) | 27,734 |
| Nienburg | 29,827 |
| Norden | 23,553 |
| Nordenham (★★ Bremerhaven) | 28,817 |
| Norderstedt (★ Hamburg) | 68,724 |
| Nordhorn | 48,015 |
| Nördlingen | 18,084 |
| Northeim | 30,638 |
| Nürnberg (Nuremberg) (★ 1,030,000) | 467,392 |
| Nürtingen (★ Stuttgart) | 35,858 |
| Oberammergau | 4,664 |
| Oberhausen (★★ Essen) | 221,542 |
| Oberursel (★ Frankfurt am Main) | 38,781 |
| Oelde | 26,991 |
| Oer-Erkenschwick (★ Essen) | 27,306 |
| Offenbach am Main (★ Frankfurt am Main) | 107,078 |
| Offenburg | 50,468 |
| Oldenburg | 139,256 |
| Olpe | 22,371 |
| Osnabrück (★ 270,000) | 153,776 |
| Osterode am Harz | 26,990 |
| Ostfildern (★ Stuttgart) | 28,384 |
| Overath (★ Cologne) | 23,169 |
| Paderborn | 110,296 |
| Papenburg | 28,652 |
| Passau | 52,733 |
| Peine | 45,576 |
| Pforzheim (★ 220,000) | 104,452 |
| Pinneberg (★ Hamburg) | 35,615 |
| Pirmasens | 46,077 |
| Plettenberg | 27,568 |
| Porta Westfalica (★ Minden) | 33,200 |
| Pulheim (★ Cologne) | 47,673 |
| Rastatt | 37,595 |
| Ratingen (★ Düsseldorf) | 89,161 |
| Ravensburg (★ 75,000) | 43,245 |
| Recklinghausen (★ Essen) | 117,585 |
| Regensburg (★ 205,000) | 123,821 |
| Reinbek (★ Hamburg) | 25,315 |
| Remagen (★ Bonn) | 14,270 |
| Remscheid (★★ Wuppertal) | 121,005 |
| Rendsburg | 30,647 |
| Reutlingen (★ 160,000) | 97,920 |
| Rheda-Wiedenbrück (★ Bielefeld) | 37,684 |
| Rheinberg (★ Essen) | 26,192 |
| Rheine | 70,412 |
| Rheinfelden | 27,145 |
| Rietberg | 23,479 |
| Rinteln | 25,377 |
| Rodgau (★ Frankfurt am Main) | 37,319 |
| Rosenheim | 53,168 |
| Rösrath (★ Cologne) | 21,450 |
| Rothenburg [ob der Tauber] | 11,171 |
| Rottenburg am Neckar | 33,601 |
| Rottweil | 23,297 |
| Rüsselsheim (★★ Wiesbaden) | 57,303 |
| Saarbrücken (★ 385,000) | 184,353 |
| Saarlouis (★ 115,000) | 37,411 |
| Salzgitter | 105,392 |
| Sankt Augustin (★ Bonn) | 51,105 |
| Sankt Ingbert | 40,455 |
| Sankt Wendel | 26,278 |
| Schleswig | 28,291 |
| Schmallenberg | 24,429 |
| Schorndorf (★ Stuttgart) | 34,722 |
| Schwabach (★ Nürnberg) | 35,627 |
| Schwäbisch Gmünd | 56,137 |
| Schwäbisch Hall | 30,942 |
| Schwandorf | 26,368 |
| Schweinfurt (★ 110,000) | 50,568 |
| Schwelm (★ Wuppertal) | 29,831 |
| Schwerte (★ Essen) | 48,456 |
| Seelze (★ Hannover) | 29,469 |
| Seesen | 21,648 |
| Seevetal (★ Hamburg) | 37,258 |
| Selb | 20,044 |
| Selm (★ Essen) | 25,641 |
| Siegburg (★ 170,000) | 34,085 |
| Siegen (★ 200,000) | 107,319 |
| Sindelfingen (★ Stuttgart) | 55,715 |
| Singen (Hohentwiel) | 41,454 |
| Sinsheim | 27,716 |
| Soest | 42,028 |
| Solingen (★★ Wuppertal) | 158,401 |
| Speyer | 42,865 |
| Springe | 29,042 |
| Stade | 42,979 |
| Stadthagen | 22,251 |
| Steinfurt | 31,432 |
| Stolberg (★★ Aachen) | 56,421 |
| Straubing | 41,622 |
| Stuhr (★ Bremen) | 26,966 |
| Stuttgart (★ 1,925,000) | 565,486 |
| Sulzbach-Rosenberg | 17,638 |
| Sulzbach [Saar] (★ Saarbrücken) | 19,591 |
| Sundern [Sauerland] | 25,223 |
| Taunusstein (★ Wiesbaden) | 26,178 |
| Trier (★ 125,000) | 93,076 |
| Troisdorf (★★ Siegburg) | 61,832 |
| Tübingen | 76,122 |
| Tuttlingen | 30,780 |
| Uelzen | 35,093 |
| Ulm (★ 210,000) | 100,745 |
| Unna (★ Essen) | 59,587 |
| Vaihingen an der Enz (★ Stuttgart) | 22,920 |
| Varel | 23,859 |
| Vechta | 24,220 |
| Velbert (★ Essen) | 88,573 |
| Verden | 24,172 |
| Viernheim (★ Mannheim) | 29,076 |
| Viersen (★★ Mönchengladbach) | 78,124 |
| Villingen-Schwenningen | 76,155 |
| Voerde (★ Essen) | 33,534 |
| Völklingen (★★ Saarbrücken) | 43,146 |
| Waiblingen (★ Stuttgart) | 45,062 |
| Walsrode | 22,669 |
| Waltrop (★ Essen) | 27,427 |
| Warburg | 21,790 |
| Warendorf | 33,545 |
| Warstein | 27,616 |
| Wedel (★ Hamburg) | 30,534 |
| Wegberg (★ Mönchengladbach) | 24,626 |
| Weiden [in der Oberpfalz] | 41,807 |
| Weil am Rhein (★ Basel, Switzerland) | 26,038 |
| Weingarten (★ Ravensburg) | 22,187 |
| Weinheim (★ Mannheim) | 40,616 |
| Werdohl | 20,336 |
| Werl | 26,025 |
| Wermelskirchen (★ Wuppertal) | 33,871 |
| Werne an der Lippe (★ Essen) | 28,303 |
| Wesel | 54,604 |
| Wesseling (★ Cologne) | 30,356 |
| Wetter (★ Essen) | 28,737 |
| Wetzlar (★ 105,000) | 50,284 |
| Wiesbaden (★ 795,000) | 266,542 |
| Wilhelmshaven (★ 135,000) | 94,896 |
| Willich (★ Essen) | 39,990 |
| Winsen (Luhe) (★ Hamburg) | 27,406 |
| Witten (★ Essen) | 102,232 |
| Wolfenbüttel (★★ Braunschweig) | 48,623 |
| Wolfsburg | 121,951 |
| Worms (★★ Mannheim) | 72,045 |
| Wunstorf (★ Hannover) | 37,344 |
| Wuppertal (★ 830,000) | 374,217 |
| Würselen (★ Aachen) | 33,592 |
| Würzburg (★ 210,000) | 127,050 |
| Zweibrücken (★ 105,000) | 32,722 |

***States***

| | |
|---|---|
| Baden-Württemberg | 9,326,780 |
| Bayern (Bavaria) | 11,026,490 |
| Berlin, [West] (city) | 1,879,225 |
| Bremen | 654,170 |
| Hamburg | 1,571,267 |
| Hessen (Hesse) | 5,543,657 |
| Niedersachsen (Lower Saxony) | 7,196,127 |
| Nordrhein-Westfalen (North Rhinewestphalia) | 16,676,501 |
| Rheinland-Pfalz (Rhineland-Palatinate) | 3,611,437 |
| Saarland | 1,042,135 |
| Schleswig-Holstein | 2,612,672 |

***Districts***

| | |
|---|---|
| Arnsberg | 3,564,601 |
| Berlin, [West] (city) | 1,879,225 |
| Braunschweig | 1,593,212 |
| Bremen | 654,170 |
| Darmstadt | 3,405,524 |
| Detmold | 1,787,042 |
| Düsseldorf | 5,034,721 |
| Freiburg | 1,891,169 |
| Giessen | 966,909 |
| Hamburg | 1,571,267 |
| Hannover | 2,008,858 |
| Karlsruhe | 2,410,098 |
| Kassel | 1,171,224 |
| Koblenz | 1,346,018 |
| Köln | 3,887,576 |
| Lüneburg | 1,469,236 |
| Mittelfranken | 1,521,262 |
| Münster | 2,402,561 |
| Niederbayern | 1,017,984 |
| Oberbayern | 3,736,358 |
| Oberfranken | 1,037,245 |
| Oberpfalz | 963,034 |
| Rheinhessen-Pfalz | 1,797,847 |
| Saarland | 1,042,135 |
| Schleswig-Holstein | 2,612,672 |
| Schwaben | 1,548,811 |
| Stuttgart | 3,490,434 |
| Trier | 467,572 |
| Tübingen | 1,535,079 |
| Unterfranken | 1,201,796 |
| Weser-Ems | 2,124,821 |

C Census. E Official estimate. UE Unofficial estimate.
• Largest city in country.

★ Population or designation of metropolitan area, including suburbs (see headnote).
▲ Population of an entire municipality, commune, or district, including rural area.

### GHANA

1984 C 12,205,574

*Cities and Towns*

• ACCRA (★ 1,250,000) 859,640
Ashiaman (★ Accra) 49,427
Bawku 33,900
Bolgatanga 31,547
Cape Coast 86,620
Ho 37,231
Keta 12,666
Koforidua 54,400
Kumasi (★ 600,000) 348,880
Nkawkaw 34,068
Nsawam 31,900
Obuasi 60,146
Oda 24,384
Sekondi (★ 175,352) 32,355
Tafo (★ Kumasi) 50,432
Takoradi (★★ Sekondi) 61,527
Tamale (★ 168,091) 136,828
Tarkwa 21,971
Tema (★★ Accra) 99,608
Teshie (★ Accra) 62,954
Wa 35,993
Winneba 26,218
Yendi 30,733

### GIBRALTAR

1987 E 30,000

*Cities and Towns*

• GIBRALTAR 30,000

### GREECE / Ellás

1981 C 9,740,417

*Cities and Towns*

Agrínion (★ 45,087) 35,774
Aiyáleo (★ Athens) 81,906
Aíyion (Aegion) (★ 25,723) 20,955
Akharnaí (Acharnae) 40,185
Alexandroúpolis 34,535
Amaliás 14,698
Amaroúsion (★ Athens) 48,151
Ampelókipoi (★ Thessaloníki) 40,033
Árgos 20,702
Árta 18,283
• ATHENS (ATHÍNAI) (★ 3,027,331) 885,737
Ayía Paraskeví (★ Athens) 32,904
Ayía Varvára (★ Athens) 29,259
Áyioi Anáryiroi (★ Athens) 30,320
Áyios Dhimítrios (★ Athens) 51,421
Dháfni (★ Athens) 26,887
Dráma 36,109
Édhessa (Edessa) 16,054
Elevsís (Eleusis) 20,320
Ermoúpolis (Syros) (★ 16,595) 13,876
Flórina (Phlorina) 12,562
Galátsion (★ Athens) 50,096
Glifádha (★ Athens) 44,018
Ilioúpolis (★ Athens) 69,560
Ioánnina 44,829
Iráklion (★ Athens) 37,833
Iráklion (Canadia) (★ 110,958) 102,398
Kaisarianí (★ Athens) 28,972
Kalámai (★ 43,235) 42,075
Kalamariá (★ Thessaloníki) 51,676
Kallithéa (★ Athens) 117,319
Kardhítsa 27,291
Kastoría 17,133
Kateríni (★ 39,895) 38,404
Kavála 56,375
Keratsínion (★ Athens) 74,179
Kérkira (Corfu) 33,561
Khaïdhárion (★ Athens) 47,396
Khalándrion (★ Athens) 54,320
Khalkís (Chalcis) 44,867
Khaniá (Canea) (★ 61,976) 47,451
Khíos (Chios) (★ 29,742) 24,070
Kholargós (★ Athens) 31,703
Kifisiá (★ Athens) 31,876
Komotiní 34,051
Koridhallós (★ Athens) 61,313
Kórinthos (Corinth) 22,658
Kozáni 30,994
Lamía 41,667
Lárisa 102,048
Levádhia (Lebadea) 16,864
Mégara 17,719
Mitilíni (Mytilene) 24,115
Návplion (Nauplia) 10,609
Néa Ionía (★ Athens) 59,202
Néa Liósia (★ Athens) 72,427
Neápolis (★ Thessaloníki) 31,464
Néa Smírni (★ Athens) 67,408
Níkaia (★ Athens) 90,368
Palaión Fáliron (★ Athens) 53,273
Pátrai (Patras) (★ 154,596) 142,163
Peristérion (★ Athens) 140,858
Piraiévs (Piraeus) (★★ Athens) 196,389
Pírgos (Pyrgos) 21,958
Ródhos (Rhodes) 40,392
Salamís 20,437
Sérrai 45,213
Spárti (Sparta) (★ 14,388) 12,975
Thessaloníki (Salonika) (★ 706,180) 406,413
Thívai (Thebes) 18,712
Tríkala 40,857
Trípolis (Tripolitza) 21,311
Véroia 37,087
Víron (★ Athens) 57,880
Vólos (★ 107,407) 71,378
Xánthi 31,541
Zográfos (★ Athens) 84,548

### GREENLAND / Kalaallit Nunaat / Grønland

1989 E 55,171

*Cities and Towns*

Angmagssalik 2,861
Egedesminde 3,601
Godhavn 1,143
• GODTHÅB (NUUK) 12,426
Holsteinsborg 5,024
Julianehåb 3,514
Sukkertoppen 4,024
Thule 849

### GRENADA

1981 C 89,088

*Cities and Towns*

• SAINT GEORGE'S (★ 25,000) 4,788

### GUADELOUPE

1982 C 328,400

*Cities and Towns*

BASSE-TERRE (★ 26,600) 13,656
Capesterre (▲ 17,472) 7,572
Les Abymes (★ Pointe-à-Pitre) 56,165
• Pointe-à-Pitre (★ 83,000) 25,310

### GUAM

1980 C 105,979

*Cities and Towns*

• AGANA (★ 44,000) 896
Tamuning (★ Agana) 8,862

### GUATEMALA

1981 C 6,054,227

*Cities and Towns*

Amatitlán 20,407
Antigua Guatemala 15,801
Chimaltenango 14,967
Chiquimula 18,965
Coatepeque 19,307
Cobán 14,152
Escuintla 36,931
• GUATEMALA (★ 1,100,000) 754,243
Huehuetenango 12,422
Mazatenango 20,918
Puerto Barrios 24,235
Quezaltenango 62,719
Retalhuleu 22,001
Tiquisate 12,096
Zacapa 12,482

### GUERNSEY

1986 C 55,482

*Cities and Towns*

• SAINT PETER PORT (★ 36,000) 16,085

### GUINEA / Guinée

1986 E 6,225,000

*Cities and Towns*

• CONAKRY 800,000
Kankan 100,000
Kindia 80,000
Labé 110,000
Mamou (1983 C) 35,748
Nzérékoré (1983 C) 55,356
Siguiri (1983 C) 37,361

### GUINEA-BISSAU / Guiné-Bissau

1979 C 777,214

*Cities and Towns*

• BISSAU 109,486

### GUYANA

1983 E 918,000

*Cities and Towns*

• GEORGETOWN (★ 188,000) 78,500
Linden (1980 C) 30,043
New Amsterdam (1982 E) 20,000

### HAITI / Haïti

1982 C 5,053,791

*Cities and Towns*

Cap-Haïtien (1986 E) 70,500
Gonaïves (1986 E) 36,500
Jacmel 13,730
Jérémie 18,493
Les Cayes (1986 E) 36,500
Pétionville (★ Port-au-Prince) 35,333
• PORT-AU-PRINCE (★ 760,000) 684,284
Port-de-Paix 15,540
Saint-Marc 24,165

### HONDURAS

1986 E 4,514,000

*Cities and Towns*

Choluteca 60,700
Comayagua 30,100
Danlí 18,800
El Progreso 58,300
Juticalpa 13,900
La Ceiba 63,800
La Lima (1974 C) 14,631
Puerto Cortés 40,900
San Pedro Sula 399,700
• TEGUCIGALPA 604,600
Tela 27,200

### HONG KONG

1986 C 5,395,997

*Cities and Towns*

Kowloon (★★ Victoria) 774,781
Kwai Chung (★ Victoria) 131,362
New Kowloon (Xinjiulong) (★★ Victoria) 1,526,910
Sha Tin (★ Victoria) 355,810
Sheung Shui 87,206
Tai Po 119,679
Tsun Wan (★ Victoria) 514,241
Tuen Mun (★ Victoria) 262,458
• VICTORIA (HONG KONG) (XIANGGANG) (★ 4,770,000) 1,175,860
Yuen Long 75,740

### HUNGARY / Magyarország

1989 E 10,589,000

*Cities and Towns*

Ajka 34,390
Baja 40,426
Békés (▲ 22,140) 18,200
Békéscsaba (▲ 70,978) 61,700
• BUDAPEST (★ 2,565,000) 2,113,645
Cegléd (▲ 39,574) 32,400
Csongrád (▲ 20,449) 17,900
Debrecen 219,251
Dunakeszi (★ Budapest) 29,148
Dunaújváros 62,386
Eger 67,252
Érd (★ Budapest) 48,037
Esztergom 32,303
Gödöllő (★ Budapest) 30,261
Gyöngyös 36,420
Győr 131,503
Gyula (▲ 36,025) 30,900
Hajdúböszörmény (▲ 30,799) 27,500
Hajdúszoboszló 24,494
Hatvan 24,816
Hódmezővásárhely (▲ 53,311) 44,600
Jászberény (▲ 30,001) 24,200
Kaposvár 76,834
Karcag 24,473
Kazincbarcika 39,233
Kecskemét (▲ 106,869) 85,400
Kiskunfélegyháza (▲ 34,889) 26,500
Kiskunhalas (▲ 31,991) 23,100
Komló 32,845
Makó 28,178
Miskolc 207,826
Mohács (▲ 21,081) 17,800
Mosonmagyaróvár 29,779
Nagykanizsa 55,023
Nagykőrös (▲ 26,193) 20,500
Nyíregyháza (▲ 119,333) 92,500
Orosháza (▲ 36,475) 31,900
Ózd 44,617
Paks 26,240
Pápa 34,412
Pécs 183,082
Salgótarján 48,785
Sopron 57,107
Szeged 189,484
Székesfehérvár 113,935
Szekszárd 39,005
Szentes (▲ 34,950) 30,700
Szolnok 81,907
Szombathely 87,997
Tata 25,931
Tatabánya 76,455
Törökszentmiklós (▲ 23,973) 20,900
Vác 36,070
Várpalota 28,095
Veszprém 66,280
Zalaegerszeg 63,785

*Counties*

Bács-Kiskun 552,000
Baranya 251,000
Békés 413,000
Borsod-Abaúj-Zemplén 564,000
Budapest (Independent city) 2,114,000
Csongrád 267,000
Debrecen (city) 219,000
Fejér 426,000
Győr (city) 132,000
Győr-Sopron 294,000
Hajdú-Bihar 330,000
Heves 336,000
Komárom 320,000
Miskolc (city) 208,000
Nógrád 227,000
Pécs (city) 183,000
Pest 990,000
Somogy 348,000
Szabolcs-Szatmár 564,000
Szeged (city) 189,000
Szolnok 426,000
Tolna 262,000
Vas 276,000
Veszprém 386,000
Zala 310,000

### ICELAND / Ísland

1987 E 247,357

*Cities and Towns*

Akureyri 13,856
Hafnarfjörður (★ Reykjavík) 13,780
Keflavík 7,133
Kópavogur (★ Reykjavík) 15,037
• REYKJAVÍK (★ 137,941) 93,425

### INDIA / Bhārat

1981 C 685,184,692

*Cities and Towns*

Abohar 86,334
Achalpur (Ellichpur) 81,186
Ādilābād 53,482
Adityapur (★ Jamshedpur) 53,421
Ādoni 108,939
Agartala 132,186
Āgra (★ 747,318) 694,191
Ahmadābād (★ 2,400,000) 2,059,725
Ahmadnagar (★ 181,210) 143,937
Aijal 74,493
Ajmer 375,593
Akola 225,412
Akot 51,936
Alandur (★ Madras) 97,449
Alīgarh 320,861
Alīpur Duār (★ 71,573) 45,324
Allahābād (★ 650,070) 616,051
Alleppey 169,940
Almora (★ 22,705) 20,758
Alwar 145,795
Amalner 67,516
Ambāla (★ 233,110) 104,565
Ambāla Sadar (★ Ambāla) 80,741
Ambarnāth (★ Bombay) 96,347
Ambāsamudram (★ 52,591) 29,761
Ambattur (★ Madras) 115,901
Āmbūr 66,042
Amrāvati (Amraoti) 261,404
Amreli (★ 58,241) 56,598
Amritsar 594,844
Amroha 112,682
Anakāpalle 73,179
Ānand 83,936
Anantapur 119,531
Ara 125,111
Arakkonam 59,405
Arcot (★ 94,363) 38,836
Arni 49,365
Aruppukkottai 72,245
Āsānsol (★ 1,050,000) 183,375
Ashoknagar-Kalyangarh (★ Hābra) 55,176
Āttūr 50,517
Aurangābād (★ 316,421) 284,607
Avadi (★ Madras) 124,701
Āzamgarh 66,523
Badagara 64,174
Bāgalkot 67,858
Baharampur (★ 102,311) 92,889
Bahraich 99,889
Baidyabāti (★ Calcutta) 70,573
Bālāghāt (★ 53,183) 49,564
Balāngīr 54,943
Bāleshwar 65,779
Ballarpur 61,398
Ballia 61,704
Bālly (★ Calcutta) 147,735
Bālly (★ Calcutta) 54,859
Balrāmpur 46,058
Bālurghāt (★ 112,621) 104,646
Bānda 72,379
Bangalore (★ 2,950,000) 2,476,355
Bangaon 69,885
Bānkura 94,954
Bānsbāria (★ Calcutta) 77,020
Bānswāra (★ 48,070) 46,749
Bāpatla 55,347
Bārākpur (★ Calcutta) 115,253
Baranagar (★ Calcutta) 170,343
Bārāsat (★ Calcutta) 66,504
Barauni 56,366
Baraut 46,292
Barddhamān 167,364
Bareilly (★ 449,425) 386,734
Bāripada (★ 52,989) 40,314
Bārmer 55,554
Bārsi 72,537
Basīrhāt 81,040
Basti 69,357
Batala (★ 101,966) 87,135
Bathinda (★ 127,363) 124,453
Beāwar 89,998
Begusarai (★ 68,305) 56,633
Behāla (South Suburban) (★ Calcutta) 378,765
Bela (Pratapgarh) 49,932
Belgaum (★ 300,372) 274,430
Bellary 201,579
Bettiah 72,167
Betūl 46,293
Bhadrak 60,600
Bhadrāvati (★ 130,606) 53,551
Bhadrāvati New Town (★★ Bhadrāvati) 77,055
Bhadreswar (★ Calcutta) 58,858
Bhāgalpur 225,062
Bhandāra 56,025
Bharatpur 105,274
Bharūch (★ 120,524) 110,070
Bhātpāra (★ Calcutta) 260,761
Bhavāni (★ 80,472) 28,898
Bhāvnagar (★ 308,642) 307,121
Bhilai (Bhilainagar) (★ 490,214) 290,090
Bhīlwāra 122,625
Bhīmavaram 101,894
Bhind 74,515
Bhiwandi (★ Bombay) 115,298
Bhiwāni 101,277
Bhopāl 671,018
Bhubaneshwar 219,211
Bhuj (★ 70,211) 69,693
Bhusāwal (★ 132,142) 123,133
Bīdar 78,856
Bihār 151,343
Bijāpur 147,313
Bijnor 56,713
Bīkāner (★ 287,712) 253,174
Bilāspur (★ 187,104) 147,218
Bīr (Bhir) 80,287
Birlapur (★ 50,831) 20,470
Birnagar (★ 67,066) 14,581
Bishnupur 47,529
Bodhan 50,807
Bodināyakkanūr 59,168
Bokāro Steel City (★ 264,480) 224,099
Bombay (★ 9,950,000) 8,243,405
Botād 50,274
Brahmapur 162,550
Brajrajnagar 54,033
Budaun 93,004
Budge Budge (★ Calcutta) 66,424
Bulandshahr 103,436
Būndi (★ 48,027) 47,736
Burhānpur 140,896
• Calcutta (★ 11,100,000) 3,305,006
Calicut (Kozhikode) (★ 546,058) 394,447
Cannanore (★ 157,797) 60,904
Chākdaha 59,308
Chakradharpur (★ 44,532) 29,272
Chālisgaon 59,342
Champdāni (★ Calcutta) 76,138
Chandannagar (Chandernagore) (★ Calcutta) 101,925
Chandausi 66,970
Chandīgarh (★ 422,841) 373,789
Chandrapur 115,777
Changanācheri 51,955
Channapatna 50,725
Chhapra 111,564
Chhatarpur 51,959
Chhindwāra 75,178

C Census. E Official estimate. UE Unofficial estimate.
• Largest city in country.

★ Population or designation of metropolitan area, including suburbs (see headnote).
▲ Population of an entire municipality, commune, or district, including rural area.

Chidambaram (★ 62,543) 55,920
Chikmagalūr 60,582
Chilakalūrupet 61,645
Chīrāla 72,040
Chitradurga 74,580
Chittaranjan (★ 61,045) 50,748
Chittoor 86,230
Chūru (★ 62,070) 61,811
Cochin (★ 685,836) 513,249
Coimbatore (★ 965,000) 704,514
Coonoor (★ 92,242) 44,750
Cuddalore 127,625
Cuddapah 103,125
Cuttack (★ 327,412) 269,950
Dabgram 76,402
Dabhoi 44,357
Dabra 33,421
Dāhod (★ 82,256) 55,256
Dalhousie (★ 4,189) 2,936
Dāltenganj 51,952
Damān 21,003
Damoh (★ 76,758) 75,573
Dānāpur (★ Patna) 58,684
Darbhanga 176,301
Darjeeling 57,603
Datia 49,386
Dāvangere 196,621
Dehra Dūn (★ 293,010) 211,416
Dehra Dūn Cantonment (★ Dehra Dūn) 43,566
Dehri 90,409
Delhi (★ 7,200,000) 4,884,234
Delhi Cantonment (★ Delhi) 85,166
Deoband 51,270
Deoghar (★ 59,120) 52,904
Deolāli (★★ Nāsik) 77,666
Deolāli Cantonment (★ Nāsik) 57,745
Deoria 55,720
Dewās 83,465
Dhamtari 55,797
Dhanbād (★ 825,000) 120,221
Dhār 48,870
Dharmapuri 51,223
Dharmavaram 50,969
Dhorāji (★ 77,716) 76,556
Dhrāngadhra 51,280
Dhuburi (★ 45,580) (1971 C) 36,503
Dhule 210,759
Dibrugarh (1971 C) 80,348
Digboi (★ 32,388) (1971 C) 16,538
Dindigul 164,103
Dombivli (★ Bombay) 103,222
Dum-Dum (★ Calcutta) 33,604
Durg (★★ Bhilai) 114,637
Durgāpur 311,798
Dwārka 21,375
Elūru (Ellore) 168,154
Erode (★ 275,999) 142,252
Etah 53,784
Etāwah 112,174
Faizābād (Fyzabad) (★ 143,167) 101,873
Farīdābād New Township (★ Delhi) 330,864
Farrukhābād (★ 160,796) 145,793
Fatehpur, Rājasthān state 51,084
Fatehpur, Uttar Pradesh state 84,831
Fatehpur Sīkri 17,908
Fīrozābād 202,338
Fīrozpur (Ferozepore) (★ 105,840) 61,162
Gadag 117,368
Gandhidham (★ 61,489) 61,415
Gāndhinagar 62,443
Gangāvathi 58,735
Garden Reach (★ Calcutta) 191,107
Gārulia (★ Calcutta) 57,061
Gaya 247,075
Ghāziābād (★ 287,170) 271,730
Ghāzīpur 60,725
Giridīh 65,444
Godhra (★ 86,228) 85,784
Gonda 70,847
Gondal (★ 66,818) 66,096
Gondia 100,423
Gorakhpur (★ 307,501) 290,814
Gudivāda 80,198
Gudiyāttam (★ 80,674) 75,044
Gulbarga 221,325
Guna (★ 64,659) 60,255
Guntakal 84,599
Guntūr 367,699
Gurgaon (★ 100,877) 89,115
Guruvayur (★ 59,467) 17,858
Guwāhāti (★ 200,377) (1971 C) 123,783
Gwalior (★ 555,862) 539,015
Hābra (★ 129,610) 74,434
Hājīpur 62,520
Haldwāni 77,300
Hālisahar (★ Calcutta) 95,579
Hānsi 50,365
Hanumangarh 60,071
Hāora (★ Calcutta) 744,429
Hāpur 102,837
Hardoi 67,259
Haridwār (★ 145,946) 114,180
Hassan 71,534
Hāthras 92,962
Hazārībāg 80,155
Hindupur 55,901
Hinganghāt 59,075
Hisār (★ 137,369) 131,309
Hooghly-Chinsura (★ Calcutta) 125,193
Hoshiārpur 85,648
Hospet (★ 115,351) 90,572
Hubli-Dhārwār 527,108
Hyderābād (★ 2,750,000) 2,187,262
Ichalkaranji 133,751
Imphāl 156,622
Indore (★ 850,000) 829,327
Ingrāj Bāzār (English Bāzār) 79,010
Itārsi (★ 69,619) 62,499
Jabalpur (★ 757,303) 614,162
Jabalpur Cantonment (★ Jabalpur) 61,026
Jadabpur (★ Calcutta) 251,968
Jagādhri (★★ Yamunānagar) 43,102
Jagdalpur (★ 63,632) 51,286
Jagtiāl 53,213
Jaipur (★ 1,025,000) 977,165
Jalandhar (★ 441,552) 408,186
Jālgaon 145,335
Jālna 122,276
Jalpāiguri 61,743
Jamālpur 78,356
Jammu (★ 223,361) 206,135
Jamnagar (Navanagar) (★ 317,362) 277,615
Jamshedpur (★ 669,580) 438,385
Jangaon 70,727
Jaora (★ 47,548) 47,129
Jaridih Bazar (★ 101,946) 46,477
Jaunpur 105,140
Jaypur 53,981
Jetpur (★ 63,074) 62,806
Jhānsi (★ 284,141) 246,172
Jharia (★★ Dhanbād) 57,496
Jhārsuguda 54,859
Jīnd 56,748
Jodhpur 506,345
Jorhāt (★ 70,674) (1971 C) 30,247
Jūnāgadh (★ 120,416) 118,646
Kadaiyanallūr 60,306
Kadiri 52,774
Kaithal 58,385
Kākināda (Cocanada) 226,409
Kālol (★ Ahmadābād) 69,946
Kalyān (★ Bombay) 136,052
Kāmārhāti (★ Calcutta) 234,951
Kambam 50,340
Kamptee (★ Nāgpur) 67,364
Kānchipuram (Conjeeveram) (★ 145,254) 130,926
Kānchrāpāra (★ Calcutta) 88,798
Kānpur (★ 1,875,000) 1,481,789
Kānpur Cantonment (★ Kānpur) 90,311
Kapūrthala 50,300
Karād 54,364
Kāraikkudi (★ 100,141) 66,993
Karīmnagar 86,125
Karnāl 132,107
Karūr (★ 93,810) 72,692
Kāsganj 61,402
Kashīpur 51,773
Katihār (★ 122,005) 104,781
Kātwa (★ 44,430) 32,890
Kāvali 48,119
Kayankulam (Kayamkulam) 61,327
Kerkend (★ Dhānbād) 75,186
Khambhāt 68,791
Khāmgaon 61,992
Khammam 98,757
Khandwa 114,725
Khanna 53,761
Kharagpur (★ 232,575) 150,475
Kharagpur Railway Settlement (★ Kharagpur) 82,100
Khargone 52,749
Khurja 67,119
Kirkee Cantonment (★ Pune) 80,835
Kishanganj 51,790
Kishangarh 62,032
Koch Bihār (★ 80,101) 62,127
Kohīma 34,340
Kolār 65,834
Kolār Gold Fields (★ 144,385) 77,679
Kolhāpur (★ 351,392) 340,625
Konnagar (★ Calcutta) 51,211
Korba 83,387
Kota 358,241
Kot Kapūra 47,550
Kottagūdem 94,894
Kottayam 64,431
Kovilpatti 63,964
Krishnagiri 48,335
Krishnanagar 98,141
Kulti (★★ Asansol) 41,323
Kumba-konam (★ 141,794) 132,832
Kundla (★ 51,431) 49,740
Kurasia (★ 53,015) 12,963
Kurichi (★ Coimbatore) 48,936
Kurnool 206,362
Lakhīmpur 61,003
Lātūr 111,986
Leh 8,718
Lucknow (★ 1,060,000) 895,721
Lucknow Cantonment (★ Lucknow) 59,614
Ludhiāna 607,052
Machilīpatnam 138,530
Madanapalle 54,938
Madgaon (Margao) (★ 64,858) 53,076
Madras (★ 4,475,000) 3,276,622
Madurai (★ 960,000) 820,891
Mahbūbnagar 87,503
Mahesāna (★ 73,024) 72,872
Mahuva (★ 56,072) 53,625
Mainpuri 58,928
Mālegaon 245,883
Māler Kotla 65,756
Malkajgiri (★ Hyderābād) 65,776
Mandsaur 77,603
Mandya 100,285
Mangalore (★ 306,078) 172,252
Mango (★ Jamshedpur) 67,284
Manjeri 53,959
Manmād 51,439
Mannārgudi 51,738
Mathura (Muttra) (★ 160,995) 147,493
Maunath Bhanjan 86,326
Māyūram 67,675
Medinīpur 86,118
Meerut (★ 536,615) 417,395
Meerut Cantonment (★ Meerut) 94,210
Melappālaiyam (★ Tirunelveli) 57,683
Mettuppālaiyam 59,537
Mhow Cantonment (★ 76,037) 70,130
Miraj (★★ Sāngli) 105,455
Mirzāpur 127,787
Modinagar (★ 87,665) 78,243
Moga 80,272
Mokāma 51,047
Morādābād (★ 345,350) 330,051
Morbi 73,327
Morena 69,864
Mormugão 69,684
Motihāri (★ 63,212) 57,911
Muktsar 50,941
Munger 129,260
Murwāra (Katni) (★ 123,017) 77,862
Muzaffarnagar 171,816
Muzaffarpur 190,416
Mysore (★ 479,081) 441,754
Nabadwīp (★ 129,800) 109,108
Nadiād 142,689
Nāgappattinam (★ 90,650) 82,828
Nāgaur 48,005
Nāgda 56,602
Nāgercoil 171,648
Nagīna 50,405
Nāgpur (★ 1,302,066) 1,219,461
Naihāti (★ Calcutta) 114,607
Naini Tāl (★ 26,093) 24,835
Najībābād 55,109
Nalgonda 62,458
Nānded 191,269
Nandurbār 65,394
Nandyāl 88,185
Nangi (★ Calcutta) 54,035
Narasapur 46,033
Narasaraopet 67,032
Nāshik (★ 429,034) 262,428
Navsāri (★ 129,266) 106,793
Nawābganj (★ 62,216) 51,518
Neemuch (★ 68,853) 65,860
Nellore 237,065
NEW DELHI (★★ Delhi) 273,036
Neyveli (★ 98,866) 88,000
Nizāmābād 183,061
North Barrackpore (★ Calcutta) 81,758
North Dum Dum (★ Calcutta) 96,418
Nowgong (1971 C) 56,537
Ongole 85,302
Orai 66,397
Outer Burnpur (★ Asansol) 86,803
Pālakollu 46,146
Pālanpur 61,262
Pālayankottai (★★ Tirunelveli) 87,302
Pālghāt (★ 117,986) 111,245
Pāli 91,568
Pallavaram (★ Madras) 83,901
Palni (★ 68,389) 64,444
Palwal 47,328
Panaji (★ 77,226) 43,165
Pānchur (★ Calcutta) 51,223
Pandharpur 64,380
Pānihāti (★ Calcutta) 205,718
Pānīpat 137,927
Panruti 43,042
Paramagudi 61,149
Parbhani 109,364
Parli 48,946
Pātan 79,196
Pathānkot 110,039
Patiāla (★ 206,254) 205,141
Patna (★ 1,025,000) 776,371
Pattukkottai 49,484
Periyakulam 44,310
Petlād 47,020
Phagwāra (★ 75,961) 72,499
Pīlībhīt 88,548
Pimpri-Chinchwad (★ Pune) 220,966
Pollāchi (★ 114,971) 82,354
Pondicherry (★ 251,420) 162,636
Ponmalai (★ Tiruchchirāppalli) 55,995
Ponnāni 43,226
Ponnur 50,206
Porbandar (★ 133,307) 115,182
Port Blair 49,634
Proddatūr 107,070
Pudukkottai 87,952
Pune (★ 1,775,000) 1,203,351
Pune Cantonment (★ Pune) 85,986
Puri 100,942
Pūrnia (★ 109,875) 91,144
Puruliya 73,904
Quilon (★ 167,598) 137,943
Rabkavi Banhatti 51,693
Rāe Bareli 89,697
Rāichūr 124,762
Raiganj (★ 66,705) 60,343
Raigarh (★ 69,791) 68,060
Raipur 338,245
Rājahmundry (★ 268,370) 203,358
Rājapālaiyam 101,640
Rajhara-Jharandalli 55,307
Rājkot 445,076
Rāj Nāndgaon 86,367
Rājpur (★ 60,734) 43,985
Rājpura 58,645
Rāmanāthapuram 45,719
Ramgarh [Cantonment] (★ 65,268) 41,257
Rāmpur 204,610
Rānāghāt (★ 83,744) 58,356
Rānchi (★ 502,771) 489,626
Rānībennur 58,118
Rānīganj (★ 119,101) 48,702
Ratlām (★ 155,578) 142,319
Ratnāgiri 47,036
Raurkela (★ 322,610) 206,821
Raurkela Civil Township (★ Raurkela) 96,000
Rewa 100,641
Rewāri 51,562
Rishra (★ Calcutta) 81,001
Robertson Pet (★ Kolār Gold Fields) 61,099
Rohtak 166,767
Roorkee (★ 79,076) 61,851
Sāgar (★ 207,479) 160,392
Sahāranpur 295,355
Saharsa 57,580
Sahijpur Bogha (★ Ahmadābād) 65,327
Salem (★ 518,615) 361,394
Sambalpur (★ 162,214) 110,282
Sambhal 108,232
Sāngli (★ 268,988) 152,339
Sardarnagar (★ Ahmadābād) 50,128
Sardārshahr (★ 56,388) 55,473
Sāsarām 73,457
Sātāra 83,336
Satna (★ 96,667) 90,476
Saunda (★ 99,990) 70,780
Sawai Mādhopur (★ 59,083) 28,139
Secunderābād Cantonment (★ Hyderābād) 135,994
Sehore 52,190
Seoni 54,017
Serampore (★ Calcutta) 127,304
Shahdol (★ 49,631) 44,342
Shāhjahānpur (★ 205,095) 185,396
Shāmli 51,850
Shāntipur 82,980
Shikohābād 47,083
Shiliguri 154,378
Shillong (★ 174,703) 109,244
Shimla 70,604
Shimoga 151,783
Shivpuri 75,738
Shrirampur 55,491
Sidhpur (★ 52,706) 51,953
Sīkar 102,970
Silchar (1971 C) 52,596
Sindri (★★ Dhānbād) 70,645
Sirsa 89,068
Sītāpur 101,210
Sivakāsi (★ 83,072) 59,827
Siwān 51,284
Solāpur (★ 514,860) 511,103
Sonīpat 109,369
South Dum Dum (★ Calcutta) 230,266
Sri Gangānagar (Gangānagar) 123,692
Srīkākulam 68,145
Srikalahasti 51,306
Srīnagar (★ 606,002) 594,775
Srīrangam (★ Tiruchchirāppalli) 64,241
Srīvilliputtūr 61,458
Sūjāngarh 55,546
Sultānpur 48,782
Sūrat (★ 913,806) 776,583
Surendranagar (★ 130,602) 89,619
Tādepallegūdem 62,574
Tādpatri 53,920
Tāmbaram (★ Madras) 86,923
Tānda 54,474
Tanuku 53,618
Tellicherry (★ 98,704) 75,561
Tenāli 119,257
Tenkāsi 49,214
Thāna (★ Bombay) 309,897
Thānesar 49,052
Thanjāvūr 184,015
Theni-Allinagaram 53,018
Tindivanam 56,520
Tinsukia (1971 C) 54,911
Tiruchchirāppalli (Trichinopoly) (★ 609,548) 362,045
Tiruchendūr (★ 68,884) 24,233
Tiruchengodu 53,941
Tirunelveli (Tinnevelly) (★ 323,344) 128,850
Tirupati 115,292
Tiruppattūr 52,422
Tiruppur (★ 215,859) 165,223
Tiruvannāmalai 89,462
Tiruvottiyūr (★ Madras) 134,014
Titāgarh (★ Calcutta) 104,534
Tonk 77,653
Trichūr (★ 170,122) 77,923
Trivandrum (★ 520,125) 483,086
Tumkūr 108,670
Tuticorin (★ 250,677) 192,949
Udagamandalam 78,277
Udaipur 232,588
Udamalpet 54,852
Udgīr 50,564
Ujjain (★ 282,203) 278,454
Ulhāsnagar (★ Bombay) 273,668
Unnāo 75,983
Upleta 54,907
Uttarpara-Kotrung (★ Calcutta) 79,598
Vadodara (★ 744,881) 734,473
Valparai 115,452
Valsad (Bulsar) (★ Bombay) 54,017
Vāniyambādi (★ 75,042) 59,107
Vārānasi (Benares) (★ 925,000) 708,647
Vasai (Bassein) (★ 52,398) 34,940
Vellore (★ 274,041) 174,247
Verāval (★ 105,307) 85,048
Vidisha 65,521
Vijayawāda (Bezwada) (★ 543,008) 454,577
Vikramasingapuram 49,319
Villupuram 77,091
Viramgām 48,275
Virudunagar 68,047
Vishākhapatnam (Vizagapatam) (★ 603,630) 565,321
Visnagar 46,631
Vizianagaram 114,806
Warangal 335,150
Wardha 88,495
Yamunānagar (★ 160,424) 109,304
Yavatmāl 89,071
Yemmiganur 50,701

***States***

Andaman and Nicobar Islands (Ter.) 188,741
Andhra Pradesh 53,549,673
Arunachal Pradesh 631,839
Assam 19,896,843
Bihār 69,914,734
Chandīgarh (Ter.) 451,610
Dādra and Nagar Haveli (Ter.) 103,676
Damān and Diu (Ter.) 79,981
Delhi (Ter.) 6,220,406
Goa 1,007,749
Gujarat 34,085,799
Haryana 12,922,618
Himachal Pradesh 4,280,818
Jammu and Kashmir 5,987,389
Karnataka (Mysore) 37,135,714
Kerala 25,453,680
Lakshadweep (Ter.) 40,249
Madhya Pradesh 52,178,844
Mahārāshtra 62,784,171
Manipur 1,420,953
Meghalaya 1,335,819
Mizoram 493,757
Nāgāland 774,930
Orissa 26,370,271
Pondicherry (Ter.) 604,471
Punjab 16,788,915
Rājasthān 34,261,862
Sikkim 316,385
Tamil Nadu (Madras) 48,408,077
Tripura 2,053,058
Uttar Pradesh 110,862,013
West Bengal 54,580,647

## INDONESIA

1980 C 147,490,298

***Cities and Towns***

Amahai (1961 C) 18,256
Ambon (▲ 207,702) 111,914
Balikpapan (▲ 279,852) 208,040
Banda Aceh (Kutaraja) 71,868
Bandung (★ 1,800,000) 1,461,407
Bangil 42,241
Bangkalan 34,947
Banjarmasin 380,884
Bantul 12,268
Banyuwangi 90,378
Batang 49,328
Baubau 17,771
Bekasi (★ Jakarta) 144,290
Bengkulu (▲ 64,733) 32,478
Binjai 71,444
Blitar (★ 100,000) 78,503
Blora 31,978
Bogor (★ 560,000) 246,946
Bojonegoro 57,483
Bondowoso 35,496
Brebes 40,971
Bukittinggi (▲ 70,691) 55,577
Ciamis 18,897
Cianjur 105,655
Cibinong 87,580
Cikampek 46,124
Cilacap 127,017
Ciledug 43,959
Cimahi (★ Bandung) (1971 C) 72,367
Ciparay 66,854
Cirebon (★ 275,000) 223,504
Denpasar 159,233
Depok (★ Jakarta) 126,693
Dili (▲ 67,039) 6,890
Dumai 44,644
Ende 27,074
Garut 145,624
Genteng 59,481
Gorontalo (▲ 97,610) 63,554

C Census. E Official estimate. UE Unofficial estimate.
• Largest city in country.
★ Population or designation of metropolitan area, including suburbs (see headnote).
▲ Population of an entire municipality, commune, or district, including rural area.

Gresik 86,418
Indramayu 32,273
• JAKARTA (★ 8,600,000) (1985 E) 7,885,000
Jambi (▲ 230,046) 155,761
Jayapura 60,641
Jember 171,284
Jepara 30,315
Jombang 58,800
Kandangan 13,498
Kebumen 44,139
Kediri (▲ 221,830) 176,261
Kendari 42,999
Kisaran 58,129
Klangenang 64,013
Klaten 117,560
Kotabumi 40,090
Krawang 72,195
Kualakapuas 15,685
Kudus 154,478
Kuningan 32,702
Kupang 84,587
Lahat 25,972
Langsa 16,426
Lawang 28,647
Lhokseumawe 22,611
Lumajang 58,495
Madiun (★ 180,000) 150,562
Magelang (★ 160,000) 123,358
Magetan 23,517
Majalaya 87,474
Majalengka 19,294
Majene 31,016
Malang 511,780
Manado 217,091
Martapura 26,405
Mataram 210,485
Medan 1,373,747
Metro 42,387
Mojokerto 68,849
Muncar 47,009
Muntilan 43,090
Nganjuk 33,916
Ngawi 20,887
Padang (▲ 480,607) 296,675
Padangpanjang (▲ 34,443) 13,661
Padangsidempuan 56,984
Palangkaraya (▲ 60,447) 51,686
Palembang 786,607
Palopo 44,611
Palu 41,779
Pamekasan 39,026
Pangkalpinang 90,078
Pare 47,262
Parepare (▲ 86,360) 62,865
Pasuruan (★ 125,000) 95,864
Pati 50,159
Payakumbuh (▲ 78,789) 24,567
Pekalongan (★ 260,000) 132,413
Pekanbaru 186,199
Pemalang 72,663
Pematangsiantar (★ 175,000) 150,296
Perabumulih 43,846
Pinrang 21,263
Ponorogo 55,523
Pontianak 304,490
Praya 22,087
Pringsewu 56,115
Probolinggo 100,296
Purbolinggo 41,997
Purwakarta 61,995
Purwokerto 143,787
Purworejo 38,276
Raba 39,921
Rangkasbitung 18,674
Rantauprapat 25,043
Rembang 27,850
Salatiga 85,740
Samarinda (▲ 264,012) 182,473
Sampit 16,377
Semarang 1,024,940
Serang 78,209
Sibolga 59,466
Sidoarjo 56,090
Singaraja 53,368
Singkawang 58,693
Situbondo 58,299
Solok (▲ 31,700) 6,976
Sorong 52,041
Sragen 39,349
Subang 52,041
Sukabumi (★ 225,000) 109,898
Sumedang 42,549
Sumenep 48,705
Surabaya 2,027,913
Surakarta (★ 575,000) 469,532
Taman 64,358
Tangerang 97,091
Tanjungbalai 41,776
Tanjungkarang-Telukbetung (★ 375,000) 284,167
Tanjungpandan 33,433
Tanjungpinang 36,999
Tarakan 46,657
Tasikmalaya 192,267
Tebingtinggi (▲ 92,068) 69,569
Tegal (★ 340,000) 131,440
Tembilahan 52,140
Tuban 48,558
Tulungagung 91,585
Ujungpandang (Makasar) 708,465
Watampone 37,869
Yogyakarta (★ 510,000) 394,965

*Provinces*

Aceh 2,611,271
Bali 2,469,930
Bengkulu 768,064
Irian Jaya 1,173,875
Jakarta Raya (Greater Jakarta) 6,503,449
Jambi 1,445,994
Jawa Barat (West Java) 27,453,525
Jawa Tengah (Central Java) 25,372,889
Jawa Timur (East Java) 29,188,852
Kalimantan Barat (West Borneo) 2,486,068
Kalimantan Selatan (South Borneo) 2,064,649
Kalimantan Tengah (Central Borneo) 954,353
Kalimantan Timur (East Borneo) 1,218,016
Lampung 4,624,785
Maluku (Moluccas) 1,411,006
Nusa Tenggara Barat (West Nusa Tenggara) 2,724,664
Nusa Tenggara Timur (East Nusa Tenggara) 2,737,166
Riau 2,168,535
Sulawesi Selatan (South Celebes) 6,062,212
Sulawesi Tengah (Central Celebes) 1,289,635
Sulawesi Tenggara (Tenggara Celebes) 942,302
Sulawesi Utara (North Celebes) 2,115,384
Sumatera Barat (West Sumatra) 3,406,816
Sumatera Selatan (South Sumatra) 4,629,801
Sumatera Utara (North Sumatra) 8,360,894
Timor Timur 555,350
Yogyakarta 2,750,813

### IRAN / Īrān

1986 C 49,445,010

*Cities and Towns*

Ābādān (1976 C) 296,081
Ābādeh (1982 E) 45,000
Abhar (1982 E) 31,000
Āghā Jārī (1982 E) 64,000
Ahar (1982 E) 52,000
Ahvāz 579,826
Āmol 118,242
Andīmeshk (1982 E) 53,000
Arāk 265,349
Ardabīl 281,973
Bābol 115,320
Bākhtarān (Kermānshāh) 560,514
Bam (1982 E) 46,000
Bandar-e ‘Abbās 201,642
Bandar-e Anzalī (Bandar-e Pahlavī) (1982 E) 83,000
Bandar-e Būshehr 120,787
Bandar-e Khomeynī (Bandar-e Shāhpūr) (1982 E) 47,000
Bandar-e Māhshahr (1982 E) 88,000
Behbahān (1982 E) 84,000
Behshahr (1982 E) 45,000
Bīrjand (1982 E) 68,000
Bojnūrd (1982 E) 82,000
Borāzjān (1982 E) 53,000
Borūjerd 183,879
Dezfūl 151,420
Do Gonbadān (1982 E) 47,000
Do Rūd (1982 E) 52,000
Emāmshahr (Shāhrūd) (1982 E) 68,000
Eṣfahān (Isfahan) 986,753
Eslāmābād (1982 E) 71,000
Eslamshahr (★ Tehrān) 215,129
Fasā (1982 E) 67,000
Gonbad-e Qābūs (1982 E) 75,000
Gorgān 139,430
Hamadān 272,499
Īlām (1982 E) 75,000
Jahrom (1982 E) 68,000
Karaj (★ Tehrān) 275,100
Kāshān 138,599
Kāshmar (1982 E) 40,000
Kāzerūn (1982 E) 63,000
Kermān 257,284
Khomeynīshahr (Homāyūnshahr) 104,647
Khorramābād 208,592
Khorramshahr (1976 C) 146,709
Khvoy 115,343
Lāhījān (1982 E) 35,000
Mahābād (1982 E) 63,000
Malāyer 103,640
Marāgheh 100,679
Marand (1982 E) 59,000
Marv Dasht (1982 E) 72,000
Mashhad (Meshed) 1,463,508
Masjed-e Soleymān 104,787
Miāndoāb (1982 E) 52,000
Mīāneh (1982 E) 57,000
Nahāvand (1982 E) 45,000
Najafābād 129,058
Neyshābūr 109,258
Orūmīyeh (Reẕā'īyeh) 300,746
Qā'emshahr (Shāhī) 109,288
Qazvīn 248,591
Qom 543,139
Qomsheh (1982 E) 67,000
Qūchān (1982 E) 61,000
Rafsanjān (1982 E) 61,000
Rāmhormoz (1982 E) 53,000
Rasht 290,897
Robāṭ Karīm (1982 E) 40,000
Sabzevār 129,103
Salmās (1982 E) 44,000
Sanandaj 204,537
Saqqez (1982 E) 76,000
Sārī 141,020
Sāveh (1982 E) 46,000
Semnān (1982 E) 54,000
Shahr-e Kord (1982 E) 63,000
Shīrāz 848,289
Sīrjān (1982 E) 67,000
Tabrīz 971,482
• TEHRĀN (★ 6,400,000) 6,042,584
Torbat-e Ḥeydarīyeh (1982 E) 62,000
Varāmīn (1982 E) 51,000
Yazd 230,483
Zābol (1982 E) 58,000
Zāhedān 281,923
Zanjān 215,261
Zarrīn Shahr (1982 E) 69,000

### IRAQ / Al ‘Irāq

1985 E 15,584,987

*Cities and Towns*

Ad Dīwānīyah (1970 E) 62,300
Al ‘Amārah 131,758
Al Fallūjah (1965 C) 38,072
Al Ḥillah (Hilla) 215,249
Al Kūfah (1965 C) 30,862
Al Kūt (Kūt al Imāra) (1965 C) 42,116
An Najaf 242,603
An Nāṣirīyah 138,842
Ar Ramādī 137,388
As Samāwah (1965 C) 33,473
As Sulaymānīyah 279,424
Az Zubayr (1965 C) 41,408
• BAGHDĀD (1987 C) 3,841,268
Ba‘qūbah 114,516
Basra (Al Baṣrah) 616,700
Irbīl 333,903
Karbalā' 184,574
Kirkūk (1970 E) 207,900
Mosul (Al Mawṣil) 570,926
Sāmarrā' (1965 C) 24,746
Tall ‘Afar (1965 C) 36,837

### IRELAND / Éire

1986 C 3,540,643

*Cities and Towns*

An Uaimh (Navan) (★ 11,929) 3,660
Arklow (Inbhear Mór) 8,388
Athlone (Áth Luain) (★ 15,571) 8,815
Balbriggan (★ 7,555) 5,680
Bray (Brí Chualann) (★ Dublin) 24,686
Carlow (Ceatharlach) (★ 13,816) 11,509
Castlebar (Caisleán an Bharraigh) (★ 7,645) 6,349
Clonmel (Cluain Meala) (★ 15,517) 11,759
Cobh (★ 8,282) 6,369
Cork (Corcaigh) (★ 173,694) 133,271
Drogheda (Droichead Átha) (★ 24,681) 24,086
Droichead Nua (★ 11,503) 5,983
• DUBLIN (BAILE ÁTHA CLIATH) (★ 1,140,000) 502,749
Dundalk (Dún Dealgan) (★ 30,608) 26,669
Dún Laoghaire (★ Dublin) 54,715
Ennis (Inis) (★ 15,547) 5,917
Enniscorthy (Inis Coirthe) (★ 7,753) 4,483
Galway (Gaillimh) 47,104
Kilkenny (Cill Choinnigh) (★ 17,537) 8,969
Killarney (Cill Áirne) (★ 10,189) 7,837
Leixlip (★ Dublin) 11,938
Letterkenny (★ 9,809) 6,691
Limerick (Luimneach) (★ 76,557) 56,279
Lucan (★ Dublin) 12,259
Mallow (Mala) (★ 7,685) 6,488
Monaghan (Muineachán) (★ 6,284) 6,075
Mullingar (Muileann Cearr) (★ 12,127) 8,077
Naas (Nás na Ríogh) (★ Dublin) 10,017
Nenagh (Aonach Urmhumhan) (★ 5,777) 5,483
Port Laoise (Portlaoghise) (★ 8,384) 3,773
Shannon 8,005
Sligo (Sligeach) (★ 18,018) 17,259
Swords (★ Dublin) 15,312
Thurles (Durlas éile) (★ 7,338) 7,049
Tipperary (Tiobrad Árann) (★ 5,209) 5,033
Tralee (Tráighlí) (★ 17,620) 17,109
Tuam (Tuaim) (★ 6,039) 4,109
Tullamore (Tulach Mhór) (★ 9,442) 8,484
Waterford (Port Láirge) (★ 41,054) 39,529
Wexford (Loch Garman) (★ 15,365) 10,336

*Counties*

Carlow 40,988
Cavan 53,965
Clare 91,344
Cork 412,735
Donegal 129,664
Dublin 1,021,449
Galway 178,552
Kerry 124,159
Kildare 116,247
Kilkenny 73,186
Laois 53,284
Leitrim 27,035
Limerick 164,569
Longford 31,496
Louth 91,810
Mayo 115,184
Meath 103,881
Monaghan 52,379
Offaly 59,835
Roscommon 54,592
Sligo 56,046
Tipperary 136,619
Waterford 91,151
Westmeath 63,379
Wexford 102,552
Wicklow 94,542

*Historic Provinces*

Connaught 431,409
Leinster 1,852,649
Munster 1,020,577
Ulster 236,008

### ISLE OF MAN

1986 C 64,282

*Cities and Towns*

Castletown 3,019
• DOUGLAS (★ 28,500) 20,368
Peel 3,660
Ramsey 5,778

### ISRAEL / Yisra'el / Isrā'īl

1989 E 4,386,000

*Cities and Towns*

‘Afula 24,500
‘Akko (★ Haifa) 37,200
Ashdod 74,700
Ashqelon 56,300
Bat Yam (★ Tel Aviv-Yafo) 133,100
Be'er Sheva‘ 113,200
Bene Beraq (★ Tel Aviv-Yafo) 109,400
Dimona 25,000
Elat (Elath) 24,700
Giv'atayim (★ Tel Aviv-Yafo) 45,600
Hadera 41,600
Haifa (Hefa) (★ 435,000) 222,600
Herzliyya (★ Tel Aviv-Yafo) 71,600
Hod HaSharon (★ Tel Aviv-Yafo) 24,500
Holon (★ Tel Aviv-Yafo) 146,100
• JERUSALEM (YERUSHALAYIM) (AL-QUDS) (★ 490,000) 493,500
Karmi'el (Carmiel) 20,100
Kefar Sava (★ Tel Aviv-Yafo) 54,800
Lod (Lydda) (★ Tel Aviv-Yafo) 41,300
Nahariyya 28,800
Nazareth (Nazerat) (★ 74,000) 50,600
Nazerat ‘Illit (★ Nazareth) 24,900
Nes Ziyyona (★ Tel Aviv-Yafo) 18,600
Netanya (★ Tel Aviv-Yafo) 117,800
Or Yehuda (★ Tel Aviv-Yafo) 20,000
Petah Tiqwa (★ Tel Aviv-Yafo) 133,600
Qiryat Atta (★ Haifa) 35,500
Qiryat Bialik (★ Haifa) 32,600
Qiryat Gat 27,400
Qiryat Motzkin (★ Haifa) 30,000
Qiryat Ono (★ Tel Aviv-Yafo) 22,200
Qiryat Shemona 15,400
Qiryat Yam (★ Haifa) 31,800
Ra'ananna (★ Tel Aviv-Yafo) 49,400
Ramat Gan (★ Tel Aviv-Yafo) 115,700
Ramat HaSharon (★ Tel Aviv-Yafo) 36,100
Ramla (★ Tel Aviv-Yafo) 44,500
Rehovot (★ Tel Aviv-Yafo) 72,500
Rishon leZiyyon (★ Tel Aviv-Yafo) 123,800
Tayibe 20,000
• Tel Aviv-Yafo (Tel Aviv-Jaffa) (★ 1,670,000) 317,800
Tiberias (Teverya) 31,200
Tirat Karmel (★ Haifa) 14,600
Umm el Fahm 23,800
Yavne (★ Tel Aviv-Yafo) 20,800
Zefat 16,400

*Districts*

Central 949,400
Haifa 605,000
Jerusalem 544,200
Northern 722,200
Southern 533,000
Tel Aviv 1,032,200

### ISRAELI OCCUPIED TERRITORIES

1989 E 1,574,700

*Cities and Towns*

Bethlehem (Bayt Lahm) (1971 E) 25,000
• Gaza (Ghazzah) (1967 C) 118,272
Hebron (Al Khalīl) (1971 E) 43,000
Jabālyah (1967 C) 43,604
Janīn (1971 E) 20,000
Jericho (Arīḥā) (1967 C) 6,829
Jerusalem (Al-Quds) (★ Jerusalem, Israel) (1976 E) 90,000
Khān Yūnus (1967 C) 52,997
Nābulus (1971 E) 64,000
Rafah (1967 C) 49,812

*Territories*

Gaza Strip 591,700
Golan Heights 24,300
West Bank 958,700

### ITALY / Italia

1987 E 57,290,519

*Cities and Towns*

Abano Terme (▲ 17,044) 14,000
Acerra (★ Naples) 39,067
Acireale 46,997
Adrano 35,066
Afragola (★ Naples) 59,397
Agrigento (▲ 54,600) 41,200
Alassio 12,204
Alba (▲ 30,932) 25,500
Albano Laziale (★ Rome) 29,967
Alberobello (▲ 10,309) 8,700
Alcamo 43,072
Alessandria (▲ 96,014) 76,100
Alghero 39,795
Altamura 54,784
Amalfi (▲ 6,026) 4,400
Ancona 104,409
Andria 88,348
Anzio 30,806
Aosta 36,856
Arezzo (▲ 91,681) 74,200
Ascoli Piceno (▲ 53,281) 43,600
Assisi (▲ 24,492) 4,700
Asti (▲ 75,459) 63,600
Augusta 39,735
Avellino 56,407
Aversa (★ Naples) 57,827
Avezzano 35,966
Avola 31,809
Bagheria 43,725
Barcellona [Pozzo di Gotto] (▲ 39,295) 34,400
Bari (★ 475,000) 362,524
Barletta 86,954
Bassano del Grappa (▲ 38,666) 33,900
Battipaglia (▲ 43,845
Belluno (▲ 36,157) 28,200
Benevento (▲ 65,661) 54,400
Bergamo (★ 345,000) 118,959
Biella 51,788
Bisceglie 47,771
Bitonto 51,962
Bollate (★ Milan) 42,921
Bologna (★ 525,000) 432,406
Bolzano (Bozen) 101,515
Bordighera (▲ 11,511) 10,100
Brescia 199,286
Bressanone (▲ 16,466) 12,800
Bresso (★ Milan) 31,570
Brindisi 92,280
Busto Arsizio (★ Milan) 78,056
Cagliari (★ 305,000) 220,574
Caltagirone 38,331
Caltanissetta 62,352
Camaiore (▲ 30,836) 24,500
Campobasso (▲ 50,801) 44,000
Canicattì 34,009
Canosa [di Puglia] 31,003
Cantù 36,349
Capannori 44,084
Capua (▲ 18,966) 15,500
Carbonia (▲ 33,495) 26,167
Carpi (▲ 60,614) 49,500
Carrara (★★ Massa) 69,229
Casale Monferrato (▲ 40,408) 35,800
Cascina 35,781
Caserta 65,974
Casoria (★ Naples) 54,100
Cassino (▲ 33,927) 24,200
Castel Gandolfo (★ Rome) 6,918

C Census. E Official estimate. UE Unofficial estimate.
• Largest city in country.

★ Population or designation of metropolitan area, including suburbs (see headnote).
▲ Population of an entire municipality, commune, or district, including rural area.

Castellammare di Stabia (★ Naples) 68,491
Castelvetrano 31,809
Catania (★ 550,000) 372,486
Catanzaro 102,558
Cattolica 15,735
Cava de'Tirreni (★ Salerno) 52,028
Cefalù 14,322
Cerignola 53,463
Cesano Maderno (★ Milan) 31,338
Cesena (▲ 90,012) 72,600
Cesenatico (▲ 20,123) 15,700
Chiavari 29,103
Chieri 30,981
Chieti 55,827
Chioggia (▲ 53,744) 47,000
Chivasso (▲ 25,884) 21,600
Ciampino (★ Rome) 32,524
Cinisello Balsamo (★ Milan) 78,917
Cittadella (▲ 17,783) 12,400
Città di Castello (▲ 38,159) 21,800
Civitanova Marche (▲ 36,648) 28,500
Civitavecchia 50,806
Collegno (★ Turin) 49,334
Cologno Monzese (★ Milan) 52,554
Como (★ 165,000) 91,738
Conegliano 36,074
Corato 42,704
Corsico (★ Milan) 40,908
Cortina d'Ampezzo (▲ 7,738) 6,800
Cortona (▲ 22,679) 3,200
Cosenza (★ 150,000) 106,026
Crema 33,784
Cremona 76,979
Crotone (▲ 61,005) 53,600
Cuneo (▲ 55,878) 47,900
Desio (★ Milan) 33,357
Domodossola 19,902
Eboli (▲ 33,413) 26,000
Empoli (▲ 43,940) 33,200
Enna 29,124
Ercolano (Resina) (★ Naples) 62,783
Erice (▲ 28,878) 24,300
Este (▲ 17,931) 14,900
Faenza (▲ 54,622) 40,300
Fano (▲ 54,442) 42,700
Fasano (▲ 37,705) 24,400
Favara 32,357
Fermo (▲ 35,168) 17,600
Ferrara (▲ 143,950) 113,300
Fiesole (★ Florence) 3,900
Florence (Firenze) (★ 640,000) 425,835
Foggia 155,051
Foligno (▲ 53,568) 42,500
Forlì (▲ 110,482) 91,200
Francavilla Fontana 34,439
Frascati (★ Rome) 19,593
Frattamaggiore (★ Naples) 37,740
Frosinone 46,814
Gaeta 24,154
Gallarate (★ Milan) 46,857
Gela 79,378
Genoa (Genova) (★ 805,000) 727,427
Giugliano in Campania (★ Naples) 51,187
Gorizia 40,187
Gravina [in Puglia] 38,088
Grosseto (▲ 70,592) 56,400
Grottaglie 30,169
Grugliasco (★ Turin) 27,500
Gubbio (▲ 32,354) 14,100
Guidonia [Montecelio] (★ Rome) 11,700
Iesi (Jesi) 40,855
Iglesias (▲ 30,390) 26,500
Imola (▲ 61,587) 48,200
Imperia 41,481
Isernia (▲ 21,083) 17,700
Ivrea 26,624
L'Aquila (▲ 66,438) 42,200
La Spezia (★ 185,000) 108,937
Latina (▲ 98,479) 67,800
Lecce 100,981
Lecco 48,844
Legnago (▲ 26,890) 23,100
Legnano (★ Milan) 48,711
Lentini 30,855
Licata 42,484
Limbiate (★ Milan) 32,308
Lissone (★ Milan) 30,676
Livorno (Leghorn) 174,065
Lodi 42,460
Loreto (▲ 10,528) 6,400
Lucca 88,024
Lucera 34,479
Lugo (▲ 33,282) 20,900
Macerata (▲ 43,719) 34,400
Maddaloni (▲ 36,223) 32,400
Magenta 23,625
Manduria 32,443
Manfredonia 57,707
Mantova (▲ 56,817) 49,000
Marino (★ Rome) 33,105
Marsala 80,468
Martina [Franca] (▲ 44,663) 36,300
Massa (★ 145,000) 66,872
Matera 52,819
Mazara del Vallo 47,628
Merano 33,323
Messina 268,896
Mestre (★ Venice) 189,700

• Milan (Milano) (★ 3,750,000) 1,495,260
Milazzo 32,016
Modena 176,880
Modica (▲ 49,550) 36,100
Molfetta 64,519
Moncalieri (★ Turin) 62,306
Monfalcone 28,629
Monopoli (▲ 46,257) 35,600
Monreale (▲ 26,636) 20,700
Montecatini Terme (▲ 21,063) 18,700
Montepulciano (▲ 14,094) 3,400
Monte Sant'Angelo 16,379
Monza (★ Milan) 122,064
Naples (Napoli) (★ 2,875,000) 1,204,211
Nardò 30,135
Nettuno 33,145
Nicastro (Lamezia Terme) (▲ 67,562) 52,100
Nichelino (★ Turin) 46,260
Nocera Inferiore 48,151
Nola (▲ 32,675) 25,300
Novara 102,742
Novi Ligure 30,848
Nuoro 37,542
Oristano (▲ 31,890) 25,900
Orvieto (▲ 22,386) 7,300
Otranto 5,077
Paderno Dugnano (★ Milan) 42,099
Padova (★ 270,000) 225,769
Pagani 32,961
Palermo 723,732
Parma 175,842
Partinico 28,966
Paternò 45,513
Pavia 82,065
Perugia (▲ 146,713) 106,700
Pesaro (▲ 90,336) 78,700
Pescara 131,027
Piacenza 105,626
Piazza Armerina 22,300
Pietrasanta (▲ 25,404) 20,400
Pinerolo 36,288
Piombino 38,266
Pisa 104,384
Pistoia (▲ 90,689) 76,800
Poggibonsi (▲ 26,553) 22,800
Pompei (★ Naples) 16,200
Pontedera (▲ 27,325) 20,700
Pordenone 50,825
Portici (★ Naples) 76,302
Portoferraio (▲ 11,587) 8,700
Portofino (▲ 664) 560
Potenza (▲ 67,114) 57,600
Pozzuoli (★ Naples) 65,000
Prato (★ 215,000) 164,595
Quartu Sant' Elena 52,838
Ragusa 67,748
Rapallo 29,451
Ravello (▲ 2,373) 1,300
Ravenna (▲ 136,016) 86,500
Reggio di Calabria 178,821
Reggio nell'Emilia (▲ 130,086) 107,300
Rho (★ Milan) 50,876
Riccione 32,193
Rieti (▲ 43,921) 34,300
Rimini (▲ 130,698) 114,600
Riva [del Garda] 13,171
Rivoli (★ Turin) 50,786
ROME (ROMA) (★ 3,175,000) 2,815,457
Rosignano Marittimo (▲ 29,827) 2,200
Rovereto 33,017
Rovigo (▲ 52,594) 41,400
Salerno (★ 250,000) 154,848
Salsomaggiore Terme (▲ 17,713) 14,800
San Benedetto del Tronto 45,397
San Donà di Piave (▲ 32,775) 24,300
San Gimignano (▲ 7,175) 3,900
San Giorgio a Cremano (★ Naples) 63,656
San Remo 60,797
San Severo 55,239
Santa Maria [Capua Vetere] 32,610
Sarno 31,160
Saronno 37,963
Sassari 120,152
Sassuolo 39,234
Savona (★ 112,000) 62,300
Scandicci (★ Florence) 54,367
Schio (▲ 36,187) 30,900
Sciacca 39,539
Senigallia (▲ 40,814) 28,000
Seregno (★ Milan) 37,988
Sesto [Fiorentino] (★ Florence) 46,355
Sesto San Giovanni (★ Milan) 91,624
Sestri Levante 21,218
Settimo Torinese (★ Turin) 45,430
Siena 59,712
Siracusa 122,857
Sondrio (▲ 22,914) 20,100
Sora (▲ 26,876) 21,300
Sorrento (★ 45,000) 17,722
Spoleto (▲ 37,932) 22,000
Sulmona 24,540
Taormina (▲ 10,606) 7,300
Taranto 244,997
Taurianova (▲ 16,911) 13,000
Teramo (▲ 52,378) 36,000
Termini Imerese 26,440
Terni (▲ 111,157) 94,500
Terracina (▲ 38,528) 28,600
Tivoli (★ Rome) 31,100

Todi (▲ 16,976) 6,200
Torre Annunziata (★ Naples) 57,508
Torre del Greco (★ Naples) 105,066
Torremaggiore 17,489
Tortona (▲ 28,541) 25,000
Trani 47,872
Trapani (▲ 73,083) 63,000
Trento (▲ 100,202) 81,500
Treviglio 25,413
Treviso 85,083
Trieste 239,031
Turin (Torino) (★ 1,550,000) 1,035,565
Udine (★ 126,000) 100,211
Urbino (▲ 15,639) 8,000
Varese 88,353
Velletri 43,899
Venice (Venezia) (★ 420,000) 88,700
Verbania 31,299
Vercelli 51,008
Verona 259,151
Viareggio (▲ 59,146) 50,300
Vibo Valentia (▲ 33,216) 19,900
Vicenza 110,449
Vigevano 62,671
Villa San Giovanni 12,780
Viterbo (▲ 59,267) 47,900
Vittoria 54,795
Vittorio Veneto (▲ 29,584) 25,500
Voghera 41,524

### *Regions*

Abruzzi 1,254,129
Basilicata (Lucania) 620,260
Calabria 2,139,301
Campania 5,690,431
Emilia-Romagna 3,931,014
Friuli-Venezia-Giulia 1,214,557
Lazio (Latium) 5,116,125
Liguria 1,758,961
Lombardia (Lombardy) 8,876,787
Marche (Marches) 1,426,965
Molise 334,195
Piemonte (Piedmont) 4,389,430
Puglia (Apulia) 4,026,151
Sardegna (Sardinia) 1,643,789
Sicilia (Sicily) 5,112,073
Toscana (Tuscany) 3,571,538
Trentino-Alto Adige 880,237
Umbria 817,852
Valle d'Aosta 113,855
Veneto (Venetia) 4,372,869

### *Provinces*

Agrigento 488,768
Alessandria 452,493
Ancona 438,045
Aosta 113,855
Arezzo 313,396
Ascoli Piceno 358,827
Asti 211,041
Avellino 447,822
Bari 1,515,742
Belluno 216,763
Benevento 298,159
Bergamo 912,688
Bologna 917,016
Bolzano 435,377
Brescia 1,030,360
Brindisi 406,162
Cagliari 759,076
Caltanissetta 294,247
Campobasso 240,753
Caserta 803,438
Catania 1,060,527
Catanzaro 771,585
Chieti 382,765
Como 783,881
Cosenza 777,000
Cremona 328,613
Cuneo 547,116
Enna 197,701
Ferrara 372,240
Firenze (Florence) 1,197,310
Foggia 699,624
Forlì 608,159
Frosinone 478,931
Genova (Genoa) 1,006,711
Gorizia 141,215
Grosseto 220,170
Imperia 222,067
Isernia 93,442
L'Aquila 298,299
La Spezia 236,625
Latina 463,141
Lecce 808,294
Livorno 345,175
Lucca 382,882
Macerata 294,759
Mantova 372,802
Massa-Carrara 205,001
Matera 207,899
Messina 687,776
Milano (Milan) 3,978,658
Modena 595,610
Napoli (Naples) 3,087,246
Novara 501,706
Nuoro 277,107
Oristano 159,551
Padova 816,226
Palermo 1,249,005
Parma 396,491
Pavia 501,470
Perugia 591,166
Pesaro e Urbino 335,334
Pescara 293,669
Piacenza 273,606
Pisa 388,620
Pistoia 265,509
Pordenone 276,102
Potenza 412,361
Ragusa 287,927
Ravenna 353,375
Reggio di Calabria 590,716
Reggio nell'Emilia 414,517
Rieti 145,475
Roma (Rome) 3,752,360
Rovigo 250,734
Salerno 1,053,766
Sassari 448,055
Savona 293,558
Siena 253,475
Siracusa 409,509
Sondrio 176,120
Taranto 596,329
Teramo 279,396
Terni 226,686
Torino (Turin) 2,292,068
Trapani 436,613
Trento 444,860
Treviso 731,893
Trieste 269,878
Udine 527,362
Varese 792,195
Venezia (Venice) 837,170
Vercelli 385,006
Verona 782,754
Vicenza 737,329
Viterbo 276,218

## IVORY COAST / Côte d'Ivoire

1983 E 9,300,000

### *Cities and Towns*

Abengourou (1975 C) 31,239
• ABIDJAN 1,950,000
Agboville (1975 C) 27,192
Bouaké 275,000
Daloa 70,000
Danané (1975 C) 19,872
Dimbokro (1975 C) 30,986
Divo (1975 C) 37,896
Gagnoa (1975 C) 42,362
Grand-Bassam (1975 C) 25,808
Korhogo 125,000
Man 55,000
YAMOUSSOUKRO 80,000

## JAMAICA

1982 C 2,190,357

### *Cities and Towns*

• KINGSTON (★ 770,000) 586,930
Mandeville 34,502
May Pen 40,962
Montego Bay 70,265
Ocho Rios 7,777
Port Antonio 12,285
Portmore (★ Kingston) 73,426
Savanna-la-Mar 14,912
Spanish Town (★ Kingston) 89,097

## JAPAN / Nihon

1985 C 121,048,923

### *Cities and Towns*

Abashiri 44,283
Abiko (★ Tōkyō) 111,659
Ageo (★ Tōkyō) 178,587
Aioi 39,868
Aizu-wakamatsu 118,140
Akashi (★ Ōsaka) 263,363
Akigawa (★ Tōkyō) 45,735
Akishima (★ Tōkyō) 97,543
Akita 296,400
Akō 52,374
Amagasaki (★ Ōsaka) 509,115
Amagi (▲ 43,575) 33,600
Anan (▲ 60,749) 48,100
Anjō 133,059
Annaka (▲ 44,601) 34,500
Aomori 294,045
Arao (★ Ōmuta) 62,570
Arida (▲ 35,401) 29,600
Asahikawa 363,631
Asaka (★ Tōkyō) 94,431
Ashibetsu (▲ 30,017) 25,500
Ashikaga 167,656
Ashiya (★ Ōsaka) 87,127
Atami 49,374
Atsugi (★ Tōkyō) 175,600
Ayabe (▲ 41,903) 31,800
Ayase (★ Tōkyō) 71,152
Beppu 134,775
Bibai (▲ 37,414) 29,400
Bisai (★ Nagoya) 56,234
Bizen 32,243
Chiba (★ Tōkyō) 788,930
Chichibu 61,013
Chigasaki (★ Tōkyō) 185,030
Chikugo (▲ 43,359) 35,600
Chikushino (★ Fukuoka) 63,242
Chino (▲ 47,273) 38,300
Chiryū (★ Nagoya) 50,506
Chita (★ Nagoya) 70,013
Chitose 73,610
Chōfu (★ Tōkyō) 191,071
Chōshi 87,883
Daitō (★ Ōsaka) 122,441
Dazaifu (★ Fukuoka) 57,737
Ebetsu (★ Sapporo) 90,328
Ebina (★ Tōkyō) 93,159
Ena (▲ 35,356) 30,700
Eniwa 48,305
Fuchū 47,798
Fuchū (★ Tōkyō) 201,972
Fuchū 48,833
Fuji (★ 370,000) 214,448
Fujieda (★ Shizuoka) 111,985
Fujiidera (★ Ōsaka) 65,252
Fujimi (★ Tōkyō) 85,697
Fujinomiya (★★ Fuji) 112,642
Fujioka (▲ 57,082) 46,900
Fujisawa (★ Tōkyō) 328,387
Fuji-yoshida 54,796
Fukaya (▲ 89,121) 71,600
Fukuchiyama (▲ 65,995) 56,200
Fukui 250,261
Fukuoka (★ 1,750,000) 1,160,440
Fukuroi (▲ 49,480) 40,700
Fukushima 270,762
Fukuyama 360,261
Funabashi (★ Tōkyō) 506,966
Furukawa (▲ 60,718) 48,400
Fussa (★ Tōkyō) 51,478
Futtsu (▲ 56,777) 48,200
Gamagōri 85,580
Gifu 411,743
Ginowan 69,206
Gobō (▲ 30,450) 24,800
Gose (★ Ōsaka) 36,693
Gosen (▲ 40,261) 33,000
Goshogawara (▲ 49,543) 34,500
Gotemba 74,882
Gushikawa 51,351
Gyōda 79,359
Habikino (★ Ōsaka) 111,394
Hachinohe 241,430
Hachiōji (★ Tōkyō) 426,654
Hadano (★ Tōkyō) 141,803
Hagi 52,740
Hakodate 319,194
Hamada 51,071
Hamakita 77,228
Hamamatsu 514,118
Hanamaki (▲ 69,886) 54,500
Handa (★ Nagoya) 92,883
Hannō (★ Tōkyō) 66,550
Hanyū (▲ 51,504) 44,700
Haramachi (▲ 48,411) 40,200
Hashima 59,760
Hasuda (★ Tōkyō) 53,991
Hatogaya (★ Tōkyō) 55,424
Hatsukaichi (★ Hiroshima) 52,020
Hekinan 63,778
Higashihiroshima (★ Hiroshima) 84,717
Higashikurume (★ Tōkyō) 110,079
Higashimatsuyama 70,426
Higashimurayama (★ Tōkyō) 123,798
Higashine (▲ 41,874) 30,400
Higashiōsaka (★ Ōsaka) 522,805
Higashiyamato (★ Tōkyō) 69,881
Hikari (★ Tokuyama) 49,246
Hikone 94,204
Himeji (★ 660,000) 452,917
Himi (▲ 62,112) 52,300
Hino (★ Tōkyō) 156,031
Hirakata (★ Ōsaka) 382,257
Hiratsuka (★ Tōkyō) 229,990
Hirosaki (▲ 176,082) 134,800
Hiroshima (★ 1,575,000) 1,044,118
Hisai 39,134
Hita (▲ 65,730) 57,900
Hitachi 206,074
Hitoyoshi (▲ 42,292) 35,600
Hōfu 118,067
Hondo (▲ 42,641) 35,800
Honjō, Saitama pref. 56,495
Hōya (★ Tōkyō) 9,156
Hyūga 59,163
Ibara 37,212
Ibaraki (★ Ōsaka) 250,463
Ichihara (★ Tōkyō) 237,617
Ichikawa (★ Tōkyō) 397,822
Ichinomiya (★★ Nagoya) 257,388
Ichinoseki (▲ 60,941) 49,200
Iida (▲ 92,401) 65,000
Iizuka (★ 110,000) 81,868
Ikeda (★ Ōsaka) 101,683
Ikoma (★ Ōsaka) 86,293
Imabari 125,115
Imaichi (▲ 53,113) 44,000
Imari (▲ 62,044) 50,700
Ina (▲ 59,010) 48,600
Inagi (★ Tōkyō) 50,766
Inazawa (★ Nagoya) 94,479
Innoshima (▲ 37,239) 32,100
Inuyama (★ Nagoya) 68,723
Iruma (★ Tōkyō) 118,603
Isahaya 88,376
Ise (Uji-yamada) 105,455
Isehara (★ Tōkyō) 7,776
Isesaki 112,459
Ishigaki (▲ 41,177) 34,600
Ishinomaki 122,674
Ishioka (▲ 49,059) 41,400
Itami (★ Ōsaka) 182,731
Itō 70,197
Itoigawa (▲ 35,797) 27,700
Itoman (▲ 45,921) 37,000
Iwai (▲ 42,177) 29,100
Iwaki (Taira) 350,569
Iwakuni 111,833
Iwakura (★ Nagoya) 42,508
Iwamizawa 81,664
Iwanuma (▲ 36,519) 31,800
Iwata 80,810
Iwatsuki (★ Tōkyō) 100,903
Iyo-mishima 38,603
Izumi (★ Sendai) 124,216
Izumi (▲ 40,084) 30,500

C Census. E Official estimate. UE Unofficial estimate.
• Largest city in country.

★ Population or designation of metropolitan area, including suburbs (see headnote).
▲ Population of an entire municipality, commune, or district, including rural area.

| | |
|---|---|
| Izumi (★ Ōsaka) | 137,641 |
| Izumi-ōtsu (★ Ōsaka) | 67,755 |
| Izumi-sano (★ Ōsaka) | 91,563 |
| Izumo (▲ 80,749) | 68,000 |
| Joetsu | 130,659 |
| Jōyō (★ Ōsaka) | 81,850 |
| Kadoma (★ Ōsaka) | 140,590 |
| Kaga | 68,630 |
| Kagoshima | 530,502 |
| Kainan (★ Wakayama) | 50,779 |
| Kaizuka (★ Ōsaka) | 79,591 |
| Kakamigahara | 124,464 |
| Kakegawa (▲ 68,724) | 55,600 |
| Kakogawa (★ Ōsaka) | 227,311 |
| Kamagaya (★ Tōkyō) | 85,705 |
| Kamaishi | 60,007 |
| Kamakura (★ Tōkyō) | 175,495 |
| Kameoka | 76,207 |
| Kameyama | 35,510 |
| Kamifukuoka (★ Tōkyō) | 57,638 |
| Kamo | 35,959 |
| Kanazawa | 430,481 |
| Kani (★ Nagoya) | 69,630 |
| Kanonji (▲ 45,569) | 38,300 |
| Kanoya (▲ 76,029) | 60,200 |
| Kanuma (▲ 88,078) | 73,200 |
| Karatsu (▲ 78,744) | 70,100 |
| Kariya (★ Nagoya) | 112,403 |
| Karuizawa | 15,050 |
| Kasai | 52,107 |
| Kasaoka (▲ 60,598) | 53,500 |
| Kashihara (★ Ōsaka) | 112,888 |
| Kashiwa (★ Tōkyō) | 273,128 |
| Kashiwara (★ Ōsaka) | 73,252 |
| Kashiwazaki (▲ 86,020) | 73,350 |
| Kasuga (★ Fukuoka) | 75,555 |
| Kasugai (★ Nagoya) | 256,990 |
| Kasukabe (★ Tōkyō) | 171,890 |
| Katano (★ Ōsaka) | 64,205 |
| Katsuta | 102,763 |
| Kawachi-nagano (★ Ōsaka) | 91,313 |
| Kawagoe (★ Tōkyō) | 285,437 |
| Kawaguchi (★ Tōkyō) | 403,015 |
| Kawanishi (★ Ōsaka) | 136,376 |
| Kawanoe | 38,538 |
| Kawasaki (★ Tōkyō) | 1,088,624 |
| Kazo (▲ 50,537) | 41,200 |
| Kazuno (▲ 44,499) | 32,600 |
| Kesennuma | 68,137 |
| Kimitsu (▲ 84,310) | 71,900 |
| Kiryū | 131,267 |
| Kisarazu | 120,201 |
| Kishiwada (★ Ōsaka) | 185,731 |
| Kita-ibaraki | 51,035 |
| Kitakami (▲ 56,741) | 46,200 |
| Kitakyūshū (★ 1,525,000) | 1,056,402 |
| Kitami | 107,281 |
| Kitamoto (★ Tōkyō) | 58,114 |
| Kiyose (★ Tōkyō) | 65,066 |
| Kobayashi (▲ 40,976) | 27,300 |
| Kōbe (★★ Ōsaka) | 1,410,834 |
| Kōchi | 312,241 |
| Kodaira (★ Tōkyō) | 158,673 |
| Kōfu | 202,405 |
| Koga (★ Tōkyō) | 57,541 |
| Koganei (★ Tōkyō) | 104,642 |
| Kokubu (▲ 40,931) | 33,000 |
| Kokubunji (★ Tōkyō) | 95,467 |
| Komae (★ Tōkyō) | 73,784 |
| Komaki (★ Nagoya) | 113,284 |
| Komatsu | 106,041 |
| Komatsushima (▲ 43,998) | 38,300 |
| Komoro (▲ 43,705) | 33,900 |
| Kōnan (★ Nagoya) | 92,049 |
| Kōnosu (★ Tōkyō) | 60,565 |
| Kōriyama | 301,673 |
| Kosai | 41,371 |
| Koshigaya (★ Tōkyō) | 253,479 |
| Kōshoku (▲ 36,849) | 30,500 |
| Kudamatsu (★★ Tokuyama) | 54,445 |
| Kuki (★ Tōkyō) | 58,636 |
| Kumagaya | 143,496 |
| Kumamoto | 555,719 |
| Kunitachi (★ Tōkyō) | 64,881 |
| Kurashiki | 413,632 |
| Kurayoshi (▲ 52,351) | 43,000 |
| Kure (★★ Hiroshima) | 226,488 |
| Kurobe (▲ 36,135) | 31,400 |
| Kuroishi (▲ 40,501) | 28,500 |
| Kuroiso (▲ 49,742) | 39,800 |
| Kurume | 222,847 |
| Kusatsu (★ Ōsaka) | 87,542 |
| Kushiro | 214,541 |
| Kuwana (★ Nagoya) | 94,731 |
| Kyōto (★★ Ōsaka) | 1,479,218 |
| Machida (★ Tōkyō) | 321,188 |
| Maebashi | 277,319 |
| Maizuru | 98,775 |
| Marugame | 74,272 |
| Masuda (▲ 54,049) | 46,200 |
| Matsubara (★ Ōsaka) | 136,455 |
| Matsudo (★ Tōkyō) | 427,473 |
| Matsue | 140,005 |
| Matsumoto | 197,340 |
| Matsuyama | 426,658 |
| Matsuzaka | 116,886 |
| Mihara | 85,975 |
| Miki (★ Ōsaka) | 74,527 |
| Minamata (▲ 36,520) | 31,700 |
| Minamiashigara | 41,706 |
| Minō (★ Ōsaka) | 114,770 |
| Minokamo | 41,700 |
| Misato (★ Tōkyō) | 107,964 |
| Misawa (▲ 41,425) | 34,500 |
| Mishima (★★ Numazu) | 99,600 |
| Mitaka (★ Tōkyō) | 166,252 |
| Mito | 228,985 |
| Mitsuke (▲ 42,546) | 37,400 |
| Miura (★ Tōkyō) | 50,471 |
| Miyako | 61,654 |
| Miyakonojō (▲ 132,098) | 107,600 |
| Miyazaki | 279,114 |
| Miyoshi (▲ 38,968) | 31,500 |
| Mizunami | 40,078 |
| Mizusawa (▲ 57,257) | 47,900 |
| Mobara | 76,929 |
| Mōka (▲ 57,261) | 43,500 |
| Mombetsu | 32,163 |
| Moriguchi (★ Ōsaka) | 159,400 |
| Morioka | 235,469 |
| Moriyama | 53,052 |
| Mukō (★ Ōsaka) | 52,216 |
| Munakata | 60,971 |
| Murakami | 33,325 |
| Muroran (★ 195,000) | 136,208 |
| Musashi-murayama (★ Tōkyō) | 60,930 |
| Musashino (★ Tōkyō) | 138,783 |
| Mutsu | 49,292 |
| Nabari | 56,474 |
| Nagahama | 55,531 |
| Nagano | 336,973 |
| Nagaoka | 183,756 |
| Nagaokakyō (★ Ōsaka) | 75,242 |
| Nagareyama (★ Tōkyō) | 124,682 |
| Nagasaki | 449,382 |
| Nago (▲ 49,038) | 40,800 |
| Nagoya (★ 4,800,000) | 2,116,381 |
| Naha | 303,674 |
| Nakama (★ Kitakyūshū) | 50,294 |
| Nakatsu | 66,260 |
| Nakatsugawa | 53,277 |
| Nanao | 50,582 |
| Nankoku (▲ 47,554) | 36,700 |
| Nara (★ Ōsaka) | 327,702 |
| Narashino (★ Tōkyō) | 136,365 |
| Narita | 77,181 |
| Naruto | 64,329 |
| Natori (★ Sendai) | 43,200 |
| Naze | 49,765 |
| Nemuro | 40,675 |
| Neyagawa (★ Ōsaka) | 258,228 |
| Nichinan (▲ 51,966) | 44,900 |
| Niigata | 475,630 |
| Niihama | 132,184 |
| Niitsu (▲ 63,846) | 55,600 |
| Niiza (★ Tōkyō) | 129,287 |
| Nikkō | 21,705 |
| Nishinomiya (★ Ōsaka) | 421,267 |
| Nishio | 91,930 |
| Nishiwaki | 38,770 |
| Nobeoka | 136,381 |
| Noboribetsu (★ Muroran) | 58,370 |
| Noda (★ Tōkyō) | 105,937 |
| Nōgata | 64,479 |
| Noshiro (▲ 59,170) | 50,400 |
| Numata (▲ 47,179) | 38,400 |
| Numazu (★ 495,000) | 210,490 |
| Obihiro | 162,932 |
| Ōbu (★ Nagoya) | 66,696 |
| Ōda (▲ 38,242) | 29,400 |
| Ōdate (▲ 71,794) | 60,900 |
| Odawara | 185,941 |
| Ōfunato | 39,300 |
| Oga (▲ 36,949) | 30,900 |
| Ōgaki | 145,910 |
| Ogōri | 43,811 |
| Ōita | 390,096 |
| Ojiya (▲ 44,204) | 35,200 |
| Ōkawa | 47,837 |
| Okaya | 61,747 |
| Okayama | 572,479 |
| Okazaki | 284,996 |
| Okegawa (★ Tōkyō) | 61,499 |
| Okinawa | 101,210 |
| Ōmagari (▲ 41,545) | 32,500 |
| Ōme (★ Tōkyō) | 110,828 |
| Ōmi-hachiman (★ Ōsaka) | 63,791 |
| Ōmiya (★ Tōkyō) | 373,022 |
| Ōmura | 69,472 |
| Ōmuta (★ 225,000) | 159,424 |
| Ono | 45,686 |
| Ōno (▲ 41,926) | 33,500 |
| Onoda (★ Ube) | 46,364 |
| Ōnojō (★ Fukuoka) | 69,435 |
| Onomichi | 100,640 |
| Ōsaka (★ 16,450,000) | 2,636,249 |
| Ōta | 133,670 |
| Ōtake | 34,760 |
| Otaru (★★ Sapporo) | 172,486 |
| Ōtawara (▲ 49,542) | 37,000 |
| Ōtsu (★ Ōsaka) | 234,551 |
| Ōtsuki | 34,914 |
| Owari-asahi (★ Nagoya) | 57,415 |
| Oyabe (▲ 36,711) | 31,000 |
| Oyama (▲ 134,242) | 113,100 |
| Rumoi | 35,542 |
| Ryōtsu (▲ 20,412) | 14,700 |
| Ryūgasaki (▲ 48,857) | 40,400 |
| Sabae | 61,452 |
| Saga | 168,252 |
| Sagamihara (★ Tōkyō) | 482,778 |
| Saijō | 56,516 |
| Saiki | 54,708 |
| Sakado (★ Tōkyō) | 87,586 |
| Sakai (★ Ōsaka) | 818,271 |
| Sakaide | 66,087 |
| Sakaiminato | 37,351 |
| Sakata | 101,392 |
| Saku (▲ 59,974) | 48,400 |
| Sakura (★ Tōkyō) | 121,213 |
| Sakurai | 58,894 |
| Sanda (▲ 40,716) Ōsaka) | 34,300 |
| Sanjō | 86,325 |
| Sano | 80,753 |
| Sapporo (★ 1,900,000) | 1,542,979 |
| Sasebo | 250,633 |
| Satte | 51,462 |
| Sawara (▲ 49,784) | 36,800 |
| Sayama (★ Ōsaka) | 50,246 |
| Sayama (★ Tōkyō) | 144,366 |
| Seki | 64,149 |
| Sendai, Kagoshima pref. (▲ 71,444) | 57,800 |
| Sendai, Miyagi pref. (★ 1,175,000) | 700,254 |
| Sennan (★ Ōsaka) | 60,059 |
| Seto | 124,623 |
| Settsu (★ Ōsaka) | 86,332 |
| Shibata (▲ 77,219) | 62,800 |
| Shibukawa | 47,814 |
| Shijōnawate (★ Ōsaka) | 50,352 |
| Shiki (★ Tōkyō) | 58,935 |
| Shimabara (▲ 46,061) | 39,500 |
| Shimada (▲ 72,388) | 63,200 |
| Shimizu (★★ Shizuoka) | 242,166 |
| Shimminato (★ Takaoka) | 41,707 |
| Shimodate (▲ 63,958) | 52,400 |
| Shimonoseki (★★ Kitakyūshū) | 269,169 |
| Shingū | 38,231 |
| Shinjō (▲ 43,033) | 33,500 |
| Shinnayō | 33,895 |
| Shiogama (★ Sendai) | 61,825 |
| Shiojiri (▲ 55,960) | 44,500 |
| Shirakawa (▲ 44,678) | 39,100 |
| Shiroishi (▲ 42,262) | 34,300 |
| Shizuoka (★ 975,000) | 468,362 |
| Sōja (▲ 51,240) | 43,500 |
| Sōka (★ Tōkyō) | 194,205 |
| Suita (★ Ōsaka) | 348,948 |
| Sukagawa (▲ 58,786) | 44,100 |
| Sukumo (▲ 26,255) | 21,500 |
| Sumoto (▲ 44,563) | 38,500 |
| Susono (★ Numazu) | 45,149 |
| Suwa | 52,329 |
| Suzaka (▲ 53,611) | 44,500 |
| Suzuka | 164,936 |
| Tachikawa (★ Tōkyō) | 146,523 |
| Tagajō (★ Sendai) | 54,436 |
| Tagawa | 59,727 |
| Tajimi (★ Nagoya) | 84,829 |
| Takahama | 31,270 |
| Takaishi (★ Ōsaka) | 66,974 |
| Takamatsu | 326,999 |
| Takaoka (★ 220,000) | 175,780 |
| Takarazuka (★ Ōsaka) | 194,273 |
| Takasago (★ Ōsaka) | 91,434 |
| Takasaki | 231,766 |
| Takatsuki (★ Ōsaka) | 348,784 |
| Takayama | 65,033 |
| Takefu | 69,148 |
| Takehara (▲ 36,286) | 32,000 |
| Takikawa | 52,004 |
| Tama (★ Tōkyō) | 122,135 |
| Tamana (▲ 46,115) | 35,900 |
| Tamano | 76,954 |
| Tanabe (▲ 70,835) | 59,800 |
| Tanashi (★ Tōkyō) | 71,331 |
| Tatebayashi | 75,141 |
| Tateyama (▲ 56,035) | 47,100 |
| Tatsuno (★ Himeji) | 41,157 |
| Tendō (▲ 55,123) | 42,800 |
| Tenri | 69,129 |
| Tenryū (▲ 25,008) | 21,900 |
| Toba | 28,363 |
| Tochigi | 86,290 |
| Toda (★ Tōkyō) | 76,960 |
| Tōkai (★ Nagoya) | 95,278 |
| Tōkamachi (▲ 48,005) | 39,700 |
| Toki | 65,308 |
| Tokoname (★ Nagoya) | 53,077 |
| Tokorozawa (★ Tōkyō) | 275,168 |
| Tokushima | 257,884 |
| Tokuyama (★ 250,000) | 112,638 |
| • TŌKYŌ (★ 27,700,000) | 8,354,615 |
| Tomakomai | 158,061 |
| Tomioka (▲ 48,551) | 37,400 |
| Tondabayashi (★ Ōsaka) | 102,619 |
| Toride (★ Tōkyō) | 78,608 |
| Tosa-shimizu (▲ 23,014) | 20,600 |
| Tosu | 55,791 |
| Tottori | 137,060 |
| Towada (▲ 61,295) | 46,000 |
| Toyama | 314,111 |
| Toyoake (★ Nagoya) | 57,969 |
| Toyohashi | 322,142 |
| Toyokawa | 107,430 |
| Toyonaka (★ Ōsaka) | 413,213 |
| Toyooka | 47,712 |
| Toyosaka (▲ 44,534) | 35,100 |
| Toyota | 308,111 |
| Tsu | 150,690 |
| Tsubame | 44,651 |
| Tsuchiura | 120,175 |
| Tsuru | 33,158 |
| Tsuruga | 65,670 |
| Tsuruoka | 100,200 |
| Tsushima (★ Nagoya) | 58,735 |
| Tsuyama | 86,837 |
| Ube (★ 230,000) | 174,855 |
| Ueda | 116,178 |
| Ueno (▲ 60,812) | 51,800 |
| Uji (★ Ōsaka) | 165,411 |
| Uozu | 49,825 |
| Urasoe | 81,611 |
| Urawa (★ Tōkyō) | 377,235 |
| Urayasu (★ Tōkyō) | 93,756 |
| Usa (▲ 52,217) | 39,500 |
| Ushiku | 51,926 |
| Usuki (▲ 39,719) | 34,200 |
| Utsunomiya | 405,375 |
| Uwajima | 71,381 |
| Wakayama (★ 495,000) | 401,352 |
| Wakkanai | 51,854 |
| Wakō (★ Tōkyō) | 55,212 |
| Warabi (★ Tōkyō) | 70,408 |
| Yachiyo (★ Tōkyō) | 142,184 |
| Yaizu (★ Shizuoka) | 108,558 |
| Yamagata | 245,158 |
| Yamaguchi | 124,213 |
| Yamato (★ Tōkyō) | 177,669 |
| Yamato-kōriyama (★ Ōsaka) | 89,624 |
| Yamato-takada (★ Ōsaka) | 65,223 |
| Yame (▲ 40,286) | 33,000 |
| Yanagawa (▲ 44,942) | 38,000 |
| Yanai (▲ 37,414) | 30,800 |
| Yao (★ Ōsaka) | 276,394 |
| Yashio (★ Tōkyō) | 67,635 |
| Yatsushiro (▲ 108,790) | 88,700 |
| Yawata (★ Ōsaka) | 72,356 |
| Yawatahama (▲ 41,600) | 33,000 |
| Yōkaichi | 39,744 |
| Yokkaichi | 263,001 |
| Yokohama (★★ Tōkyō) | 2,992,926 |
| Yokosuka (★ Tōkyō) | 427,116 |
| Yokote (▲ 43,266) | 34,800 |
| Yonago | 131,792 |
| Yonezawa | 93,721 |
| Yono (★ Tōkyō) | 71,597 |
| Yotsukaidō (★ Tōkyō) | 67,008 |
| Yūbari | 31,665 |
| Yūki (▲ 52,283) | 40,200 |
| Yukuhashi | 65,527 |
| Yuzawa (▲ 37,079) | 28,000 |
| Zama (★ Tōkyō) | 100,000 |
| Zentsūji | 33,900 |
| Zushi (★ Tōkyō) | 57,656 |

*Prefectures*

| | |
|---|---|
| Aichi | 6,455,172 |
| Akita | 1,254,032 |
| Aomori | 1,524,448 |
| Chiba | 5,148,163 |
| Ehime | 1,529,983 |
| Fukui | 817,633 |
| Fukuoka | 4,719,259 |
| Fukushima | 2,080,304 |
| Gifu | 2,028,536 |
| Gumma | 1,921,259 |
| Hiroshima | 2,819,200 |
| Hokkaidō | 5,679,439 |
| Hyōgo | 5,278,050 |
| Ibaraki | 2,725,005 |
| Ishikawa | 1,152,325 |
| Iwate | 1,433,611 |
| Kagawa | 1,022,569 |
| Kagoshima | 1,819,270 |
| Kanagawa | 7,431,974 |
| Kōchi | 839,784 |
| Kumamoto | 1,837,747 |
| Kyōto | 2,586,574 |
| Mie | 1,747,311 |
| Miyagi | 2,176,295 |
| Miyazaki | 1,175,543 |
| Nagano | 2,136,927 |
| Nagasaki | 1,593,968 |
| Nara | 1,304,866 |
| Niigata | 2,478,470 |
| Ōita | 1,250,214 |
| Okayama | 1,916,906 |
| Okinawa | 1,179,097 |
| Ōsaka | 8,668,095 |
| Saga | 880,013 |
| Saitama | 5,863,678 |
| Shiga | 1,155,844 |
| Shimane | 794,629 |
| Shizuoka | 3,574,692 |
| Tochigi | 1,866,066 |
| Tokushima | 834,889 |
| Tōkyō | 11,829,363 |
| Tottori | 616,024 |
| Toyama | 1,118,369 |
| Wakayama | 1,087,206 |
| Yamagata | 1,261,662 |
| Yamaguchi | 1,601,627 |
| Yamanashi | 832,832 |

## JERSEY

| | |
|---|---|
| 1986 C | 80,212 |

*Cities and Towns*

| | |
|---|---|
| • SAINT HELIER (★ 46,500) | 27,083 |

## JORDAN / Al Urdunn

| | |
|---|---|
| 1986 E | 2,796,100 |

*Cities and Towns*

| | |
|---|---|
| Al Buq'ah | 57,860 |
| Al Karak | 15,700 |
| Al Mafraq | 27,980 |
| • 'AMMĀN (★ 1,250,000) | 833,500 |
| Aqaba (Al 'Aqabah) | 37,360 |
| Ar Ramthā | 35,470 |
| Ar Ruṣayfah (★ 'Ammān) | 65,560 |
| As Salṭ | 42,690 |
| Az Zarqā' | 285,000 |
| Irbid | 150,000 |
| Ma'ān | 14,720 |
| Ma'dabā | 36,150 |
| Ṣuwayliḥ | 31,340 |

## KENYA

| | |
|---|---|
| 1989 E | 24,506,000 |

*Cities and Towns*

| | |
|---|---|
| Eldoret (1979 C) | 50,503 |
| Kakamega (1979 C) | 32,025 |
| Kisumu (1984 E) | 167,100 |
| Machakos (1983 E) | 92,300 |
| Meru (1979 C) | 72,049 |
| Mombasa (1985 E) | 442,369 |
| • NAIROBI | 1,286,200 |
| Nakuru (1984 E) | 101,700 |
| Nyeri (1979 C) | 35,753 |
| Thika (1979 C) | 41,324 |

## KIRIBATI

| | |
|---|---|
| 1985 C | 63,883 |

*Cities and Towns*

| | |
|---|---|
| BAIRIKI | 2,086 |
| • Bikenibeu | 4,293 |

## KOREA, NORTH / Chosŏn-minjujuŭi-inmin-konghwaguk

| | |
|---|---|
| 1981 E | 18,317,000 |

*Cities and Towns*

| | |
|---|---|
| Aoji-ri (1944 C) | 39,616 |
| Chŏngjin | 490,000 |
| Haeju (1983 E) | 213,000 |
| Hamhŭng (1970 E) | 150,000 |
| Hŭngnam (1976 E) | 260,000 |
| Kaesŏng | 259,000 |
| Kanggye (1967 E) | 130,000 |
| Kilchu (1944 C) | 30,026 |
| Kimchaek (Sŏngjin) (1967 E) | 265,000 |
| Najin (1944 C) | 34,338 |
| Nampo (Chinnampo) | 241,000 |
| Ongjin (1949 C) | 32,965 |
| Pukchŏng (1944 C) | 30,709 |
| • PYŎNGYANG (★ 1,600,000) | 1,283,000 |
| Sariwŏn (1944 C) | 42,957 |
| Sinŭiju | 305,000 |
| Songnim (1944 C) | 53,035 |
| Tanchŏn (1944 C) | 32,761 |
| Wŏnsan | 398,000 |

*Provinces*

1982 ESTIMATE

| | |
|---|---|
| Chagang-do (Jagang) | 1,020,000 |
| Chŏngjin | 720,000 |
| Hamgyŏng-namdo (South Hamgyeong) | 2,400,000 |
| Hamgyŏng-pukto (North Hamgyeong) | 1,110,000 |
| Hwanghae-namdo (South Hwanghae) | 1,770,000 |
| Hwanghae-pukto (North Hwanghae) | 1,350,000 |
| Kaesŏng (Gaeseong) (City) | 330,000 |
| Kangwŏn-do (Gangweon) | 1,350,000 |
| Nampo | 660,000 |
| P'yŏngan-namdo (South Pyeongan) | 2,490,000 |
| P'yŏngan-pukto (North Pyeongan) | 2,160,000 |
| P'yŏngyang (Pyeongyang) | 2,520,000 |
| Yanggang-do | 570,000 |

## KOREA, SOUTH / Taehan-min'guk

| | |
|---|---|
| 1985 C | 40,448,486 |

*Cities and Towns*

| | |
|---|---|
| Andong | 114,216 |
| Anyang (★ Seoul) | 361,577 |
| Changwŏn (★ Masan) | 173,508 |
| Chechŏn | 102,274 |
| Cheju | 202,911 |
| Chinhae | 121,341 |
| Chinju | 227,309 |
| Chŏnan | 170,196 |
| Chŏngju | 79,323 |
| Chŏngju, Ch'ungch'ŏng Pukto prov. | 350,256 |
| Chŏnju | 426,473 |
| Chunchŏn | 162,988 |
| Chungju | 113,331 |
| Chungmu | 87,459 |
| Inchŏn (★★ Seoul) (1989 E) | 1,604,000 |
| Iri | 192,269 |
| Kangnŭng | 132,897 |
| Kimchŏn | 77,254 |
| Kimhae | 77,903 |
| Kumi | 142,094 |
| Kŭmsŏng | 58,897 |
| Kunsan | 185,649 |
| Kwangju (1989 E) | 1,165,000 |
| Kwangmyŏng (★ Seoul) | 219,611 |
| Kyŏngju | 127,544 |
| Masan (★ 625,000) | 448,746 |
| Mokpo | 236,085 |
| Namwŏn | 61,447 |
| Pohang | 260,691 |
| Puchŏn (★ Seoul) | 456,292 |
| Pusan (★ 3,800,000) (1989 E) | 3,754,000 |
| Pyŏngtaek (▲ 180,513) | 63,400 |
| Samchŏnpo | 62,466 |
| Sangju (▲ 180,575) | 28,300 |
| Seongnam (★ Seoul) | 447,692 |
| • SEOUL (SŎUL) (★ 15,850,000) (1989 E) | 10,513,000 |
| Sŏgwipo | 82,311 |
| Sŏkcho | 69,501 |
| Songjŏng (▲ 136,612) | 35,300 |
| Songtan | 66,357 |
| Sunchŏn (▲ 116,323) | 121,958 |

C Census. E Official estimate. UE Unofficial estimate.
• Largest city in country.

★ Population or designation of metropolitan area, including suburbs (see headnote).
▲ Population of an entire municipality, commune, or district, including rural area.

Suwŏn (★ Seoul) 430,752
Taebaek 113,997
Taegu (1989 C) 2,206,000
Taejŏn 866,148
Tongduchŏn 68,633
Tonghae 91,691
Ŭijŏngbu (★ Seoul) 162,700
Ulsan 551,014
Wŏnju 151,165
Yŏngchŏn 52,811
Yŏngju 84,742
Yŏsu 171,933

*Provinces*

1989 ESTIMATE

Cheju Do (Jeju) 505,000
Chŏlla Namdo (South Jeonia) 2,540,000
Chŏlla Pukto (North Jeonia) 2,118,000
Ch'ungch'ŏng Namdo (South Chungcheong) 3,008,000
Ch'ungch'ŏng Pukto (North Chungcheong) 1,356,000
Inchŏn (City) 1,604,000
Kangwŏn Do (Gangweon) 1,663,000
Kwangju 1,165,000
Kyŏnggi Do (Gyeonggi) 5,466,000
Kyŏngsang Namdo (South Gyeongsang) 3,636,000
Kyŏngsang Pukto (North Gyeongsang) 2,846,000
Pusan (Busan) (City) 3,754,000
Sŏul (Seoul) (City) 10,513,000
Taegu (City) 2,206,000

### KUWAIT / Al Kuwayt

1985 C 1,697,301

*Cities and Towns*

Abraq Khīţān (★ Kuwait) 45,120
Aḥmadī (★ 285,000) 26,899
Al Farwānīyah (★ Kuwait) 68,701
Al Fuḥayḥīl (★ Aḥmadī) 50,081
Al Jahrah (★ Kuwait) 111,222
Ar Rumaythīyah (★ Kuwait) 39,058
As Sālimīyah (★ Kuwait) 153,359
Aş Şulaybīyah (★ Kuwait) 51,314
Ḩawallī (★ Kuwait) 145,126
Jaleeb al Shuyūkh (★ Kuwait) 114,771
• KUWAIT (AL KUWAYT) (★ 1,375,000) 44,335
Salwa and Messellah (★ Kuwait) 24,948
South Khīţān (★ Kuwait) 69,256
Subahiya (★ Aḥmadī) 60,787
Umm al Himan (★ Aḥmadī) 31,588

### LAOS / Lao

1985 C 3,584,803

*Cities and Towns*

Louangphrabang (1975 E) 46,000
Pakxe (1975 E) 47,000
Savannakhet (1975 E) 53,000
• VIENTIANE (VIANGCHAN) 377,409

### LEBANON / Al Lubnān

1982 E 2,637,000

*Cities and Towns*

Ba'labakk 24,000
• BEIRUT (BAYRŪT) (★ 1,675,000) 509,000
Jūniyah 29,000
Şaydā (Sidon) 105,000
Tripoli (Ţarābulus) 198,000
Tyre (Şūr) (1970 E) 12,500
Zaḩlah 45,000

### LESOTHO

1986 C 1,577,536

*Cities and Towns*

• MASERU 109,382

### LIBERIA

1986 E 2,221,000

*Cities and Towns*

Buchanan (1981 E) 30,000
• MONROVIA 465,000

### LIBYA / Lībīya

1984 C 3,637,488

*Cities and Towns*

Benghazi (Banghāzī) 435,886
Darnah 62,179
Misrātah 131,031
• TRIPOLI (ŢARĀBULUS) 990,697
Ţubruq (Tobruk) 75,282
Zāwiyat al Bayḍā' (Beida) 67,120

### LIECHTENSTEIN

1989 E 28,181

*Cities and Towns*

• VADUZ 4,919

### LUXEMBOURG

1985 E 366,000

*Cities and Towns*

Differdange (1981 C) 8,588
Dudelange (1981 C) 14,074
Esch-sur-Alzette (★ 83,000) (1981 C) 25,142
• LUXEMBOURG (★ 133,000) 76,130

### MACAO / Macau

1987 E 429,000

*Cities and Towns*

• MACAO 429,000

### MADAGASCAR / Madagasikara

1984 E 9,731,000

*Cities and Towns*

• ANTANANARIVO (1985 E) 663,000
Antsirabe (▲ 95,000) 50,100
Antsiranana 100,000
Fianarantsoa 130,000
Mahajanga 85,000
Manakara (1975 C) 20,037
Marovoay (1975 C) 16,303
Toamasina 100,000
Toliara 55,000

### MALAWI / Malaŵi

1987 C 7,982,607

*Cities and Towns*

• Blantyre 331,588
LILONGWE 233,973
Mzuzu 44,238
Zomba 42,878

### MALAYSIA

1980 C 13,136,109

*Cities and Towns*

Alor Setar 69,435
Ayer Itam (★ George Town) 35,550
Batu Pahat 64,727
Bukit Mertajam 28,675
Butterworth (★★ George Town) 77,982
George Town (Pinang) (★ 495,000) 248,241
Ipoh 293,849
Johor Baharu (★ Singapore) 246,395
Kajang 29,301
Kampar 24,626
Kelang 192,080
Keluang 50,315
Kota Baharu 167,872
Kota Kinabalu (Jesselton) 55,997
• KUALA LUMPUR (★ 1,475,000) 919,610
Kuala Terengganu 180,296
Kuantan 131,547
Kuching 72,555
Kulim 26,817
Melaka (Malacca) 87,494
Miri 52,125
Muar (Bandar Maharani) 65,151
Petaling Jaya (★ Kuala Lumpur) 207,805
Port Dickson 24,389
Sandakan 70,420
Segamat 34,008
Seremban 132,911
Sibu 85,231
Sungai Petani 45,343
Taiping 146,000
Tawau 43,200
Telok Anson (Teluk Intan) 49,148

*States*

Johor 1,580,423
Kedah 1,077,815
Kelantan 859,270
Melaka 446,769
Negeri Sembilan 551,442
Pahang 768,801
Perak 1,743,655
Perlis 144,782
Pinang 900,772
Sabah (North Borneo) 955,712
Sarawak 1,235,553
Selangor 1,426,250
Terengganu 525,255
Wilayah Persekutuan (Federal Territory) 919,610

### MALDIVES

1985 C 181,453

*Cities and Towns*

• MALE 46,334

### MALI

1987 C 7,620,225

*Cities and Towns*

• BAMAKO 646,163
Djénné (1976 C) 10,275
Gao 54,874
Goundam (1976 C) 10,468
Kati 34,092
Kayes 48,216
Kita 22,629
Koulikoro 20,354
Koutiala 48,010
Mopti 73,979
Nioro du Sahel 17,197
San 30,688
Ségou 88,877
Sikasso 73,050
Tombouctou (Timbuktu) 31,925

### MALTA

1987 E 343,334

*Cities and Towns*

Birkirkara (★ Valletta) 20,300
Ħamrun (★ Valletta) 13,651
Qormi (★ Valletta) 18,413
Rabat (Victoria), Gozo I. 5,922
Sliema (★ Valletta) 13,650
• VALLETTA (★ 215,000) 9,263

### MARTINIQUE

1982 C 328,566

*Cities and Towns*

• FORT-DE-FRANCE (★ 116,017) 99,844
Le Lamentin (▲ 26,367) 7,207
Saint-Pierre 5,438
Schœlcher (★ Fort-de-France) 18,094

### MAURITANIA / Mauritanie / Mūrītāniyā

1987 E 2,007,000

*Cities and Towns*

Aleg (1962 C) 1,360
Atar (1986 E) 19,000
'Ayoûn el'Atroûs (1962 C) 4,877
Fdérik (1976 C) 18,000
Kaédi (1986 E) 20,000
Kiffa (1976 C) 10,700
Néma (1962 C) 3,893
Nouadhibou (1986 E) 24,400
• NOUAKCHOTT 285,000
Rosso (1986 E) 18,500
Zouîrât (1986 E) 22,000

### MAURITIUS

1987 E 1,008,864

*Cities and Towns*

Beau Bassin-Rose Hill (★ Port Louis) 93,125
Curepipe (★ Port Louis) 64,243
• PORT LOUIS (★ 420,000) 139,730
Quatre Bornes (★ Port Louis) 65,480
Vacoas-Phoenix (★ Port Louis) 55,667

### MAYOTTE

1985 E 67,205

*Cities and Towns*

• DZAOUDZI (★ 6,979) 5,865

### MEXICO / México

1980 C 67,395,826

*Cities and Towns*

Acámbaro 38,224
Acaponeta 15,272
Acapulco [de Juárez] 301,902
Acayucan 32,398
Actopan 16,215
Agua Dulce 27,242
Agua Prieta 28,862
Aguascalientes 293,152
Alvarado 22,633
Ameca 25,946
Amecameca [de Juárez] 23,508
Apatzingán 55,522
Apizaco 30,498
Arandas 19,835
Arriaga 17,848
Atlixco 53,207
Atotonilco el Alto 21,276
Autlán de Navarro 27,926
Caborca 33,696
Cadereyta Jiménez 26,539
Campeche 128,434
Cananea 19,551
Cancún 33,273
Cárdenas, Michoacán state 26,217
Cárdenas, Tabasco state 34,078
Celaya 141,675
Cerro Azul 29,082
Chetumal 56,709
Chihuahua 385,603
Chilpancingo [de los Bravos] 67,498
Cholula [de Rivadabia] (★ Puebla de Zaragoza) 26,748
Ciudad Acuña 38,898
Ciudad Camargo 29,433
Ciudad del Carmen 72,489
Ciudad de Naucalpan de Juárez (★ Mexico City) 723,723
Ciudad de Valles 65,609
Ciudad Guzmán 60,938
Ciudad Hidalgo 32,311
Ciudad Ixtepec 13,302
Ciudad Jiménez 23,786
Ciudad Juárez (★★ El Paso, Tex., U.S.A.) 544,496
Ciudad Lerdo (★ Torreón) 33,470
Ciudad Madero (★ Tampico) 132,444
Ciudad Mante 70,647
Ciudad Melchor Múzquiz 22,115
Ciudad Mendoza (★ Orizaba) 25,330
Ciudad Obregón 165,572
Ciudad Serdán 12,824
Ciudad Victoria 140,161
Coatepec 28,499
Coatzacoalcos 127,170
Colima 86,044
Comalcalco 25,021
Comitán [de Domínguez] 27,374
Córdoba 99,972
Cortazar 35,330
Cosamaloapan [de Carpio] 29,457
Cuauhtémoc 43,546
Cuautla 24,153
Cuernavaca 192,770
Culiacán 304,826
Delicias 65,504
Dolores Hidalgo 23,143
Durango 257,915
Ecatepec de Morelos (★ Mexico City) 741,821
El Grullo 16,595
Empalme 31,555
Encarnación de Díaz 14,795
Ensenada 120,483
Escuinapa [de Hidalgo] 20,247
Etzatlán 10,309
Fortín de las Flores 14,046
Fresnillo [de González Echeverría] 56,066
Garza García (★ Monterrey) 81,974
Gómez Palacio (★★ Torreón) 116,967
Guadalajara (★ 2,325,000) 1,626,152
Guadalupe (★ Monterrey) 370,524
Guadalupe 25,395
Guamúchil 36,308
Guanajuato 48,981
Guasave (1970 C) 26,080
Guaymas 54,826
Hermosillo 297,175
Heroica Nogales 65,603
Hidalgo del Parral 75,590
Huajuapan de León 16,743
Huamantla 21,944
Huatabampo 22,635
Huauchinango 25,776
Huixtla 21,578
Iguala 66,005
Irapuato 170,138
Izúcar de Matamoros 27,714
Jacona de Plancarte 29,955
Jalapa Enríquez 204,594
Jalostotitlán 13,031
Jerez de García Salinas 28,629
Jiquilpan de Juárez 22,149
Jojutla 21,243
Juchitán [de Zaragoza] 38,801
La Barca 20,889
Lagos de Moreno 44,223
La Paz 91,453
La Piedad [Cavadas] 47,441
Las Choapas 35,807
León [de los Aldamas] 593,002
Linares 33,012
Loma Bonita 24,344
Los Mochis 122,531
Los Reyes [de Salgado] 23,633
Magdalena 13,618
Manzanillo 39,088
Martínez de la Torre 25,837
Matamoros (★★ Brownsville, Tex., U.S.A.) 188,745
Matamoros [de la Laguna] (★ Torreón) 28,175
Matehuala 41,550
Matías Romero 15,092
Mazatlán 199,830
Meoqui 14,859
Mérida 400,142
Mexicali (★ 365,000) 341,559
• MEXICO CITY (CIUDAD DE MÉXICO) (★ 14,100,000) 8,831,079
Minatitlán 106,765
Mineral del Monte 8,605
Monclova 115,786
Montemorelos 28,342
Monterrey (★ 2,015,000) 1,090,009
Morelia 297,544
Moroleón 37,500
Motul [de Felipe Carrillo Puerto] 15,919
Múgica 21,239
Navojoa 62,901
Netzahualcóyotl (★ Mexico City) 1,341,230
Nogales (★ Orizaba) 22,499
Nueva Casas Grandes 28,514
Nueva Rosita 33,121
Nuevo Laredo (★★ Laredo, Tex., U.S.A.) 201,731
Oaxaca [de Juárez] 154,223
Ocotlán 48,931
Ojinaga 18,162
Orizaba (★ 215,000) 114,848
Pachuca [de Soto] 110,351
Pánuco 26,652
Papantla [de Olarte] 43,935
Parras de la Fuente 23,453
Pátzcuaro 32,902
Pénjamo 17,307
Piedras Negras 67,455
Poza Rica de Hidalgo 166,799
Progreso 24,257
Puebla [de Zaragoza] (★ 1,055,000) 835,759
Puerto Vallarta 38,645
Puruándiro 17,535
Querétaro 215,976
Reynosa 194,693
Río Bravo 55,236
Ríoverde 30,267
Romita 14,492
Rosario 12,171
Sabinas 27,413
Sabinas Hidalgo 23,187
Sahuayo [de Díaz] 43,258
Salamanca 96,703
Salina Cruz 40,010
Saltillo 284,937
Salvatierra 28,878
San Andrés Tuxtla 40,412
San Cristóbal de las Casas 42,026
San Francisco del Oro 10,813
San Francisco del Rincón 40,943
San Juan de los Lagos 26,204
San Juan del Río 27,204
San Juan Teotihuacán (★ Mexico City) 6,815
San Luis de la Paz 19,306
San Luis Potosí (★ 470,000) 362,371
San Luis Río Colorado 76,684
San Martín Texmelucan 36,712
San Miguel de Allende 30,003
San Miguel el Alto 13,949
San Nicolás de los Garzas (★ Monterrey) 280,696
San Pedro de las Colonias 35,879
Santa Ana Chiautempan 13,204
Santa Bárbara 14,894
Santa Catarina (★ Monterrey) 87,673
Santa Cruz de Juventino Rosas 20,436
Santa Inés Zacatelco (★ Puebla de Zaragoza) 19,421
Santa Rosalía 8,221
Santiago Ixcuintla 17,516
Sayula 17,809

C Census. E Official estimate. UE Unofficial estimate.
• Largest city in country.

★ Population or designation of metropolitan area, including suburbs (see headnote).
▲ Population of an entire municipality, commune, or district, including rural area.

Silao 32,248
Soledad Díez Gutiérrez (★ San Luis Potosí) 49,173
Sombrerete 13,562
Tala 19,680
Tamazula de Gordiano 14,080
Tamazunchale 12,863
Tampico (★ 435,000) 267,957
Tangancícuaro [de Arista] 14,433
Tantoyuca 19,552
Tapachula 85,766
Taxco de Alarcón 36,315
Tecate 23,909
Tecomán 46,371
Tecuala 14,755
Tehuacán 79,547
Tehuantepec 22,019
Teocaltiche 16,559
Tepatitlán [de Morelos] 41,813
Tepic 145,741
Tequila 15,514
Texcoco [de Mora] (★ Mexico City) 30,593
Teziutlán 25,119
Ticul 18,255
Tierra Blanca 31,653
Tijuana (★★ San Diego, Calif., U.S.A.) 429,500
Tizimín 26,305
Tlalnepantla [de Comonfort] (★ Mexico City) 778,173
Tlapacoyan 14,000
Tlaquepaque (★ Guadalajara) 133,500
Tlaxcala [de Xicohténcatl] 14,437
Toluca [de Lerdo] 199,778
Tonalá 19,013
Torreón (★ 575,000) 328,086
Tula de Allende 18,744
Tulancingo 53,400
Tuxpan 24,476
Tuxpan de Rodríguez Cano 56,037
Tuxtepec 29,060
Tuxtla Gutiérrez 131,096
Umán 10,273
Unión de Tula 7,670
Uriangato 19,845
Uruapan [del Progreso] 122,828
Valladolid 28,201
Valle de Santiago 37,645
Valle Hermoso 27,966
Venustiano Carranza 8,546
Veracruz [Llave] (★ 385,000) 284,822
Vicente Guerrero (★ Orizaba) (1970 C) 11,688
Vicente Guerrero (★ Puebla de Zaragoza) 27,589
Villa Flores 20,313
Villa Frontera 32,568
Villahermosa 158,216
Xicotepec de Juárez 18,473
Yautepec 17,899
Yurécuaro 16,123
Yuriria 14,960
Zaachila 8,474
Zacapu 39,570
Zacatecas 80,088
Zacatepec 18,042
Zacoalco [de Torres] 13,105
Zamora de Hidalgo 86,998
Zapopan (★ Guadalajara) 345,390
Zapotiltic 14,552
Zihuatanejo (1970 C) 4,879
Zitácuaro 47,520
Zumpango 19,389

*States*

Aguascalientes 519,439
Baja California Norte 1,177,886
Baja California Sur 215,139
Campeche 420,553
Chiapas 2,084,717
Chihuahua 2,005,477
Coahuila 1,557,265
Colima 346,293
Distrito Federal (Federal District) 8,831,079
Durango 1,182,320
Guanajuato 3,006,110
Guerrero 2,109,513
Hidalgo 1,547,493
Jalisco 4,371,998
México 7,564,335
Michoacán 2,868,824
Morelos 947,089
Nayarit 726,120
Nuevo León 2,513,044
Oaxaca 2,369,076
Puebla 3,347,685
Querétaro 739,605
Quintana Roo 225,985
San Luis Potosí 1,673,893
Sinaloa 1,849,879
Sonora 1,513,731
Tabasco 1,062,961
Tamaulipas 1,924,484
Tlaxcala 556,597
Veracruz 5,387,680
Yucatán 1,063,733
Zacatecas 1,136,830

**MONACO**

1982 C 27,063

*Cities and Towns*

• MONACO (★ 87,000) 27,063

**MONGOLIA / Mongol Ard Uls**

1987 E 1,966,000

*Cities and Towns*

Choybalsan (1979 C) 29,800
Darhan (1985 E) 69,800
Erdene (1985 E) 42,900
• ULAN BATOR (ULAANBAATAR) 511,100

**MONTSERRAT**

1980 C 11,606

*Cities and Towns*

• PLYMOUTH 1,568

**MOROCCO / Al Maghrib**

1982 C 20,419,555

*Cities and Towns*

Agadir 110,479
Al Hoceima 41,662
Beni Mellal 95,003
Berkane 60,490
Berrechid (★ Casablanca) 29,738
• Casablanca (Dar el Beida) (★ 2,475,000) 2,139,204
Dcheïra 39,760
El Jadida (Mazagan) 81,455
El Kelaa des Srarhna 33,353
Essaouira (Mogador) 42,035
Fès (Fez) (★ 535,000) 448,823
Fkih Ben Salah 47,540
Jerada 43,016
Kenitra 188,194
Khemisset 58,925
Khenifra 38,840
Khouribga 127,181
Ksar el Kebir 73,541
Ksar es Souk 27,040
Larache 63,893
Marrakech (★ 535,000) 439,728
Meknès (★ 375,000) 319,783
Mohammedia (Fedala) (★ Casablanca) 105,120
Nador 62,040
Ouarzazate 17,227
Oued Zem 58,744
Ouezzane 40,485
Oujda 260,082
RABAT (★ 980,000) 518,616
Safi 197,309
Salé (★★ Rabat) 289,391
Sefrou 38,833
Settat 65,203
Sidi Ifni 16,188
Sidi Kacem 55,833
Sidi Slimane 50,457
Tangier (Tanger) (★ 370,000) 266,346
Tan-Tan 41,451
Taourirt 32,667
Taroudant 35,848
Taza 77,216
Temara (★ Rabat) 48,644
Tétouan 199,615
Youssoufia 42,195

**MOZAMBIQUE / Moçambique**

1980 C 12,130,000

*Cities and Towns*

Beira 230,744
Chimoio (Vila Pery) 74,372
Inhambane 54,990
Lichinga 39,487
• MAPUTO (LOURENÇO MARQUES) (1987 E) 1,006,765
Nacala 80,426
Nampula (1986 E) 183,000
Pemba 42,962
Quelimane 62,174
Tete 48,064
Xai-Xai (João Belo) 44,164

**NAMIBIA**

1981 C 1,033,196

*Cities and Towns*

Gobabis 5,528
Keetmanshoop 11,502
Lüderitz 4,748
Mariental 5,367
Otjiwarongo 9,087
Rehoboth 12,378
Swakopmund 12,219
Tsumeb 11,269
• WINDHOEK (1984 E) 120,000

**NAURU / Naoero**

1987 E 8,000

**NEPAL / Nepāl**

1981 C 15,022,839

*Cities and Towns*

Bhaktapur 48,472
Bīrganj 43,642
Dharān Bāzār 42,146
• KATHMANDU (KĀTHMĀNDAU) (★ 320,000) 235,160
Mahendranagar 43,834
Nepālganj 34,015
Pokharā 46,642
Wirātnagar 93,544

**NETHERLANDS / Nederland**

1986 E 14,529,430

*Cities and Towns*

Aalsmeer 21,293
Alkmaar (★ 121,000) 86,509
Almelo 62,421
Alphen aan den Rijn 55,812
Amersfoort (★ 130,158) 89,596
Amstelveen (★ Amsterdam) 68,090
• AMSTERDAM (★ 1,860,000) 679,140
Apeldoorn 145,773
Arnhem (★ 294,085) 127,968
Assen 47,462
Bergen op Zoom 46,103
Beverwijk (★ Amsterdam) 34,889
Breda (★ 154,565) 119,174
Brunssum (★ Heerlen) 29,726
Bussum (★ Amsterdam) 32,706
Capelle aan den IJssel (▲ 54,862) 41,100
Castricum (★ Amsterdam) 22,815
De Bilt (★ Utrecht) 31,470
Delft (★★ The Hague) 87,440
Delfzijl 24,320
Den Helder 63,231
Deventer 64,806
Doetinchem (▲ 40,406) 30,400
Dordrecht (★ 200,396) 106,968
Drachten (Smallingerland) (▲ 50,635) 40,400
Edam [-Volendam] (★ Amsterdam) 24,158
Ede (▲ 88,866) 46,700
Eindhoven (★ 376,185) 190,839
Emmen (▲ 91,775) 36,400
Enschede (★ 288,000) 144,048
Etten-Leur (▲ 31,465) 26,900
Geldrop (★ Eindhoven) 26,051
Geleen (★ 177,243) 34,292
Goes 31,422
Gorinchem 28,003
Gouda 60,927
Groningen (★ 207,060) 168,006
Haarlem (★ Amsterdam) 149,776
Haarlemmermeer (★ Amsterdam) (1984 E) 11,400
Harderwijk 33,195
Harlingen 16,320
Heemstede (★ Amsterdam) 26,106
Heerenveen (▲ 37,304) 20,700
Heerlen (★ 266,617) 93,871
Helmond 63,043
Hengelo (★★ Enschede) 76,694
Hilversum (★ Amsterdam) 86,125
Hoogeveen (▲ 45,233) 34,200
Hoorn 52,720
IJmuiden (Velsen) (★ Amsterdam) 57,157
Kampen 32,230
Katwijk aan Zee 38,882
Kerkrade (★ Heerlen) 52,885
Leeuwarden 84,966
Leiden (★ 178,731) 105,262
Lelystad (▲ 57,952) 15,100
Maassluis (★ Rotterdam) 32,770
Maastricht (★ 158,915) 114,579
Meppel 22,923
Middelburg 39,105
Nieuwegein (★ Utrecht) 55,644
Nijmegen (★ 238,187) 147,182
Oldenzaal 29,128
Oss 50,343
Papendrecht (★ Dordrecht) 26,492
Purmerend (★ Amsterdam) 50,664
Renkum (★ Arnhem) 12,500
Ridderkerk (★ Rotterdam) 46,419
Rijswijk (★ The Hague) 48,886
Roermond 38,307
Roosendaal 57,385
Rotterdam (★ 1,110,000) 571,372
Schiedam (★ Rotterdam) 69,078
's-Hertogenbosch (★ 189,067) 89,039
Sittard (★★ Geleen) 44,037
Sliedrecht 22,696
Sneek 29,504
Soest (★ Amersfoort) 40,562
Spijkenisse (★ Rotterdam) 60,221
Tegelen (★ Venlo) 18,565
Terneuzen (▲ 35,250) 22,200
THE HAGUE ('s-GRAVENHAGE) (★ 770,000) 443,961
Tiel 30,251
Tilburg (★ 223,043) 153,703
Utrecht (★ 511,195) 229,933
Veendam 28,323
Veenendaal 44,866
Veldhoven (★ Eindhoven) 36,492
Venlo (★ 87,000) 63,475
Vlaardingen (★ Rotterdam) 75,536
Vlissingen (Flushing) (▲ 45,339) 26,000
Voorburg (★ The Hague) 41,433
Vught (★ 's-Hertogenbosch) 23,347
Waalwijk 28,581
Wageningen 32,358
Wassenaar (★ The Hague) 26,513
Weert (▲ 39,542) 28,700
Winschoten 20,286
Woerden 26,955
Zaandam (Zaanstad) (★ Amsterdam) 128,248
Zeist (★ Utrecht) 59,743
Zoetermeer (★ The Hague) 82,334
Zutphen 31,298
Zwijndrecht (★★ Dordrecht) 40,182
Zwolle 88,438

*Provinces*

Drenthe 431,997
Flevoland 177,334
Friesland 598,068
Gelderland 1,761,492
Groningen 560,029
Limburg 1,088,331
North Brabant (Noord-Brabant) 2,124,656
North Holland (Noord-Holland) 2,322,708
Overijssel 998,751
South Holland (Zuid-Holland) 3,164,652
Utrecht 944,372
Zeeland 355,781

**NETHERLANDS ANTILLES / Nederlandse Antillen**

1984 E 178,744

*Cities and Towns*

Kralendijk (1981 C) 1,270
• WILLEMSTAD (★ 130,000) (1981 C) 31,883

*Political Divisions*

Bonaire 10,001
Curacao 147,481
Saba 977
Sint Eustatius 1,638
Sint Maarten 18,647

**NEW CALEDONIA / Nouvelle-Calédonie**

1983 C 145,368

*Cities and Towns*

• NOUMÉA (★ 83,000) 60,112

**NEW ZEALAND**

1986 C 3,307,084

*Cities and Towns*

• Auckland (★ 850,000) 149,046
Birkenhead (★ Auckland) 22,582
Blenheim (★ 22,681) 18,308
Christchurch (★ 320,000) 168,200
Dunedin (★ 109,000) 76,964
East Coast Bays (★ Auckland) 31,325
Gisborne (★ 32,238) 30,020
Hamilton (★ 101,814) 94,511
Hastings (★★ Napier) 37,658
Invercargill (★ 52,807) 48,197
Kapiti (★ Wellington) 17,357
Levin (★ 18,962) 15,368
Lower Hutt (★ Wellington) 63,862
Manukau (★ Auckland) 177,248
Masterton (★ 20,145) 18,511
Mount Albert (★ Auckland) 27,579
Mount Eden (★ Auckland) 18,877
Mount Roskill (★ Auckland) 35,158
Mount Wellington (★ Auckland) 20,397
Napier (★ 107,060) 49,428
Nelson (★ 44,593) 34,274
New Plymouth (★ 47,384) 36,865
Palmerston North (★ 67,405) 60,503
Papakura (★ Auckland) 23,357
Papatoetoe (★ Auckland) 21,883
Porirua (★ Wellington) 43,213
Rotorua (★ 52,001) 40,597
Takapuna (★ Auckland) 69,419
Tauranga (★ 59,435) 41,611
Timaru (★ 28,621) 27,757
Tokoroa (★ 18,193) 17,628
Upper Hutt (★ Wellington) 31,130
Wainuiomata (★ Wellington) 18,810
Waitemata (★ Auckland) 96,365
Wanganui (★ 40,758) 38,084
WELLINGTON (★ 350,000) 137,495
Whangarei (★ 44,043) 40,179

**NICARAGUA**

1985 E 3,272,100

*Cities and Towns*

Bluefields (1981 E) 20,608
Chinandega 75,000
Granada (1981 E) 64,642
León 101,000
• MANAGUA 682,000
Masaya 75,000
Matagalpa 68,000
Rivas (1981 E) 18,360

**NIGER**

1988 C 7,250,383

*Cities and Towns*

Agadez 50,164
Arlit 31,993
Birni Nkonni 29,948
Dosso 27,092
Maradi 112,965
• NIAMEY 398,265
Tahoua 51,607
Zinder 120,892

**NIGERIA**

1987 E 101,907,000

*Cities and Towns*

Aba 239,800
Abakaliki 56,800
Abeokuta 341,300
Ado-Ekiti 287,000
Afikpo 65,790
Agege 83,810
Akure 129,600
Amaigbo 53,690
Apomu 49,570
Aramoko 48,280
Asaba 47,410
Awka 88,800
Azare 50,020
Bauchi 68,840
Benin City 183,200
Bida 100,200
Birnin Kebbi 48,250
Calabar 139,800
Deba 110,600
Dukku 52,880
Ede 245,200
Effon-Alaiye 122,300
Ejigbo 84,570
Emure-Ekiti 58,750
Enugu 252,500
Epe 80,560
Erin-Oshogbo 59,940
Eruwa 49,140
Fiditi 49,440
Garko 46,400
Gboko 49,390
Gbongan 53,990
Gombe 86,120
Gusau 126,200
Ibadan 1,144,000
Idah 50,550
Idanre 56,080
Ife 237,000
Ifon-Oshogbo 65,980
Igbasa-Odo 48,040
Igboho 85,230
Igbo-Ora 68,060
Igede-Ekiti 56,570
Ihiala 73,240
Ijebu Igbo 78,680
Ijebu Ode 124,900
Ijero-Ekiti 76,420
Ikare 112,500
Ikerre 195,400
Ikire 94,450
Ikirun 144,900
Ikole 71,860
Ikorodu 147,700
Ikot Ekpene 69,440
Ila 210,800
Ilawe-Ekiti 147,300
Ilesha 302,100
Ilobu 159,000
Ilorin 380,000
Inisa 95,630
Ipoti-Ekiti 53,220
Ise-Ekiti 82,580
Iseyin 173,500
Iwo 289,100

C Census. E Official estimate. UE Unofficial estimate.
• Largest city in country.

★ Population or designation of metropolitan area, including suburbs (see headnote).
▲ Population of an entire municipality, commune, or district, including rural area.

Jega (1985 E) 47,000
Jimeta 66,130
Jos 164,700
Kaduna 273,200
Kano 538,300
Katsina 165,000
Kaura Namoda 52,910
Keffi 57,790
Kishi 77,210
Kumo 118,200
Lafia 97,810
Lafiagi 57,580
• LAGOS (★ 3,800,000) 1,213,000
Lalupon 56,130
Lere 49,670
Lokoja 45,550
Maiduguri 255,100
Makurdi 98,350
Minna 109,300
Mubi 51,190
Mushin (★ Lagos) 266,100
Nembe 45,600
Nguru 78,770
Nsukka 47,760
Ode-Ekiti 48,910
Offa 157,500
Ogbomosho 582,900
Oka 114,400
Oke-Mesi 55,040
Okwe 52,550
Olupona 65,720
Ondo 135,300
Onitsha 298,200
Opobo 64,620
Oron 62,260
Oshogbo 380,800
Owerri (1982 E) 52,670
Owo 146,600
Oyan 50,930
Oyo 204,700
Pindiga 64,130
Port Harcourt 327,300
Potiskum 56,490
Sapele 111,200
Shagamu 93,610
Shaki 139,000
Shomolu (★ Lagos) 120,700
Sokoto 163,700
Ugep 81,910
Umuahia 52,550
Uyo 60,500
Warri 100,700
Zaria 302,800

## NIUE

1986 C 2,531

*Cities and Towns*

• ALOFI 811

## NORWAY / Norge

1985 E 4,153,000

*Cities and Towns*

Ålesund 35,000
Arendal (★ 22,500) (1983 E) 11,743
Asker (★ Oslo) 37,800
Bærum (★ Oslo) 83,000
Bergen (★ 239,000) 207,374
Bodø 34,000
Drammen (★ 73,000) 50,700
Fredrikstad (★ 52,000) (1983 E) 27,618
Gjøvik (1983 E) 26,077
Halden (1983 E) 26,223
Hamar (★ 28,000) (1983 E) 15,837
Hammerfest (1983 E) 7,208
Harstad (1983 E) 21,765
Haugesund (★ 31,000) (1983 E) 27,043
Kongsberg (1983 E) 20,629
Kristiansand 62,200
Kristiansund (1983 E) 17,895
Larvik (★ 19,000) (1983 E) 8,226
Lillehammer (1983 E) 21,954
Molde (1983 E) 21,057
Moss (★ 30,000) (1983 E) 24,967
Narvik (1983 E) 19,080
• OSLO (★ 720,000) 447,304
Porsgrunn (★★ Skien) 31,400
Ringerike (1983 E) 26,839
Sandefjord 35,000
Sandnes (★ Stavanger) 39,700
Sarpsborg (★ 41,500) (1983 E) 12,143
Skien (★ 77,981) 46,700
Stavanger (★ 132,000) 94,200
Steinkjer (1983 E) 20,694
Tønsberg (★ 37,500) (1983 E) 8,921
Tromsø 47,800
Trondheim 134,019
Vadsø (1983 E) 5,995

*Counties*

1984 ESTIMATE

Akershus 386,400
Aust-Agder 94,200
Buskerud 219,300
Finnmark 76,700
Hedmark 187,000
Hordaland 397,500
Møre og Romsdal 237,400
Nordland 243,600
Nord-Trøndelag 126,900
Oppland 182,100
Oslo 447,304
Østfold 235,000
Rogaland 320,200
Sogn og Fjordane 106,200
Sør-Trøndelag 246,400
Telemark 162,300
Troms 147,100
Vest-Agder 139,800
Vestfold 190,500

## OMAN / ʻUmān

1981 E 919,000

*Cities and Towns*

• MASQAṬ (MUSCAT) 50,000
Maṭraḥ (1971 E) 14,000
Nazwá (1980 E) 25,000
Ṣuḥār (1980 E) 20,000
Ṣūr (1980 E) 30,000

## PACIFIC ISLANDS, TRUST TERRITORY OF THE

1980 C 132,929

*Cities and Towns*

Garapan 2,063
• Jarej-Uliga-Delap 8,583
Kolonia 5,549
Koror 6,222

*Political Divisions*

Federated States of Micronesia 73,160
Marshall Islands 30,873
Northern Mariana Islands 16,780
Palau (Belau) 12,116

## PAKISTAN / Pākistān

1981 C 84,253,644

*Cities and Towns*

Abbottābād (★ 65,996) 32,188
Ahmadpur East 56,979
Attock (★ 39,986) 26,233
Bahāwalnagar 74,533
Bahāwalpur (★ 180,263) 152,009
Bannu (★ 43,210) 35,170
Bhakkar 41,934
Chārsadda 62,530
Chīchāwatni 50,241
Chiniot 105,559
Chishtiān Mandi 61,959
Dādu 39,298
Daska 55,555
Dera Ghāzi Khān 102,007
Dera Ismāīl Khān (★ 68,145) 64,358
Drigh Road Cantonment (★ Karāchi) 56,742
Faisalabad (Lyallpur) 1,104,209
Gojra 68,000
Gujrānwāla (★ 658,753) 600,993
Gujrānwāla Cantonment (★ Gujrānwāla) 57,760
Gujrāt 155,058
Gwādar 17,000
Hāfizābād 83,464
Hyderābād (★ 800,000) 702,539
Hyderābād Cantonment (★ Hyderābād) 48,990
ISLĀMĀBĀD (★★ Rāwalpindi) 204,364
Jacobābād 79,365
Jarānwāla 69,459
Jhang Sadar 195,558
Jhelum (★ 106,462) 92,646
Kamālia 61,107
Kāmoke 71,097
• Karāchi (★ 5,300,000) 4,901,627
Karāchi Cantonment (★ Karāchi) 181,981
Kasūr 155,523
Khairpur 61,447
Khānewāl 89,090
Khānpur 70,589
Khāriān (★ 51,506) 16,042
Khushāb 56,274
Kohāt (★ 77,604) 55,832
Lahore (★ 3,025,000) 2,707,215
Lahore Cantonment (★ Lahore) 245,474
Lārkāna 123,890
Leiah 51,482
Malir Cantonment (★ Karāchi) 47,588
Mandi Būrewāla 86,311
Mardān (★ 147,977) 141,842
Miānwāli 59,159
Mingāora 88,078
Mīrpur Khās 124,371
Multān (★ 732,070) 696,316
Muzaffargarh 53,000
Nawābshāh 102,139
Nowshera (★ 74,913) 38,875
Okāra (★ 153,483) 127,455
Pākpattan 69,820
Peshāwar (★ 566,248) 506,896
Peshāwar Cantonment (★ Peshāwar) 59,352
Quetta (★ 285,719) 244,842
Rahīmyār Khān (★ 132,635) 119,036
Rāwalpindi (★ 1,040,000) 457,091
Rāwalpindi Cantonment (★ Rāwalpindi) 337,752
Sādiqābad 63,935
Sāhīwal (Montgomery) 150,954
Sargodha (★ 291,362) 231,895
Sargodha Cantonment (★ Sargodha) 59,467
Shekhūpura 141,168
Shikārpur 88,138
Shorkot (★ 50,568) 18,533
Siālkot (★ 302,009) 258,147
Sibi 23,043
Sukkur 190,551
Tando Ādam 62,744
Turbat 52,337
Vihāri 53,799
Wāh Cantonment 122,335
Wazīrābād 62,725

## PANAMA / Panamá

1980 C 1,795,012

*Cities and Towns*

Balboa (★ Panamá) 1,904
Colón (★ 88,000) (1982 E) 64,763
David 49,472
La Chorrera 37,566
La Concepción 10,823
• PANAMÁ (★ 625,000) (1984 E) 424,204
Puerto Armuelles 12,562
San Miguelito (★ Panamá) (1984 E) 200,584
Santiago 24,205

## PAPUA NEW GUINEA

1984 E 3,239,000

*Cities and Towns*

Lae 73,400
Madang 23,700
• PORT MORESBY 144,300
Rabaul (1980 C) 14,954
Wewak 22,100

## PARAGUAY

1985 E 3,279,000

*Cities and Towns*

• ASUNCIÓN (★ 700,000) 477,100
Caacupé (1972 C) 7,278
Concepción (1984 E) 25,000
Coronel Oviedo (1982 C) 21,782
Encarnación (1984 E) 31,000
Fernando de la Mora (★ Asunción) 80,000
Lambaré (★ Asunción) 84,000
Luque (★ Asunción) (1972 C) 13,921
Paraguarí (1972 C) 5,036
Pedro Juan Caballero (1982 C) 37,331
Pilar (1982 C) 13,135
Puerto Presidente Stroessner 64,000
San Lorenzo (★ Asunción) (1982 C) 74,632
Villa Hayes (1972 C) 4,749
Villarrica (1982 C) 21,203

*Departments*

Alto Paraguay 10,100
Alto Paraná 255,000
Amambay 69,400
Asunción (Distrito Federal) 477,100
Boquerón 12,000
Caaguazú 333,000
Caazapá 111,400
Canendiyu 77,100
Central 572,500
Chaco 300
Concepción 143,000
Cordillera 194,000
Guairá 149,600
Itapúa 284,500
Misiones 80,100
Ñeembucú 69,500
Nueva Asunción 200
Paraguarí 201,900
Presidente Hayes 27,800
San Pedro 210,500

## PERU / Perú

1981 C 17,031,221

*Cities and Towns*

Abancay 19,863
Arequipa (★ 446,942) 108,023
Ayacucho (★ 69,533) 57,432
Barranco (★ Lima) 46,478
Barrio Obrero Industrial (★ Lima) 404,856
Breña (★ Lima) 112,398
Cajamarca 62,259
Callao (★★ Lima) 264,133
Cerro de Pasco (★ 66,373) 55,597
Chachapoyas 11,853
Chiclayo (★ 279,527) 213,095
Chimbote 223,341
Chincha Alta 41,369
Chorrillos (★ Lima) 141,881
Chosica 65,139
Chulucanas (▲ 63,163) 35,000
Cuzco (★ 184,550) 89,563
Huacho 43,398
Huancavelica 21,137
Huancayo (★ 164,954) 84,845
Huánuco 61,812
Huaraz 44,814
Ica 114,786
Iquitos 178,738
Jesús María (★ Lima) 83,179
Juliaca 87,651
Lambayeque (▲ 30,784) 24,000
La Oroya 34,940
La Victoria (★ Lima) 270,778
• LIMA (★ 4,608,010) 371,122
Lince (★ Lima) 80,456
Magdalena del Mar (★ Lima) 55,535
Miraflores (★ Lima) 103,453
Moyobamba 14,376
Pisco 55,604
Piura (★ 207,934) 144,609
Pucallpa 112,263
Pueblo Libre (★ Lima) 83,985
Puerto Maldonado 12,693
Puno 67,397
Rímac (★ Lima) 184,484
San Isidro (★ Lima) 71,203
Sullana 89,037
Surco (★ Lima) 146,636
Surquillo (★ Lima) 134,158
Tacna 97,173
Talara 57,351
Trujillo (★ 354,301) 202,469
Tumbes 47,936
Vitarte (★ Lima) 145,504

*Departments*

Amazonas 254,560
Ancash 818,289
Apurímac 323,346
Arequipa 706,580
Ayacucho 503,392
Cajamarca 1,045,569
Callao (Province) 443,413
Cuzco (Cusco) 832,504
Huancavelica 346,797
Huánuco 484,780
Ica 433,897
Junín 852,238
La Libertad 962,949
Lambayeque 674,442
Lima 4,745,877
Loreto 445,368
Madre de Dios 33,007
Moquegua 101,610
Pasco 213,125
Piura 1,125,865
Puno 890,258
San Martín 319,751
Tacna 143,085
Tumbes 103,839
Ucayali 200,669

## PHILIPPINES / Pilipinas

1980 C 48,098,460

*Cities and Towns*

Angeles (1984 E) 213,305
Angono 26,571
Antipolo (▲ 68,912) 54,117
Bacolod (1984 E) 287,830
Bacoor (★ Manila) 90,364
Baguio (1984 E) 133,726
Bais (▲ 49,301) 8,225
Balagtas 28,654
Baliuag 70,555
Basista 17,191
Batangas (▲ 143,570) 24,678
Binalbagan (▲ 49,428) 21,589
Biñan (★ Manila) 83,684
Binangonan 80,980
Bislig (▲ 81,615) 49,498
Bocaue 49,693
Bulan (▲ 60,911) 14,234
Butuan (▲ 172,489) (1984 E) 74,900
Cabanatuan (▲ 153,899) (1984 E) 67,300
Cadiz (▲ 129,632) 25,215
Cagayan de Oro (▲ 275,938) (1984 E) 207,000
Cainta (★ Manila) 59,025
Calamba (▲ 121,175) 72,359
Calapan (▲ 67,370) 16,435
Calbayog (▲ 113,954) (1984 E) 15,000
Caloocan (★ Manila) (1984 E) 524,624
Calumpit 45,454
Carmona (★ Manila) 65,014
Catarman (▲ 59,021) 17,714
Catbalogan (▲ 58,737) 23,739
Cavite (★ 175,000) 87,666
Cebu (★ 600,000) (1984 E) 552,155
Cordoba 16,455
Cotabato 83,871
Daet (▲ 54,789) 27,812
Dagupan (1984 E) 103,401
Davao (▲ 610,375) 408,775
Digos (▲ 70,065) 26,919
Dinagat 36,726
Dipolog (▲ 61,919) 26,211
Dumaguete 63,411
Escalante (▲ 71,293) 19,639
General Santos (Dadiangas) (▲ 183,255) (1984 E) 115,600
Gingoog (▲ 79,937) 20,128
Guagua 72,609
Guiguinto 27,751
Ilagan (▲ 79,336) 12,168
Iligan (▲ 181,865) (1984 E) 23,300
Iloilo (1984 E) 263,422
Iriga (▲ 66,113) 18,252
Isabela (Basilan) (▲ 49,891) 11,491
Jolo 52,429
Kawit (★ Cavite) 39,368
Koronadal (▲ 80,566) 33,526
La Carlota (▲ 45,812) 20,943
Laoag (▲ 69,648) 32,357
Lapu-Lapu 98,723
Las Piñas (★ Manila) (1984 E) 190,364
Legaspi (▲ 108,864) (1984 E) 56,600
Lingayen (▲ 65,187) 19,367
Lipa (▲ 133,540) (1984 E) 25,200
Lucena (1984 E) 124,355
Maasin (▲ 59,731) 11,151
Mabalacat (▲ 80,966) 54,988
Macabebe 45,830
Makati (★ Manila) (1984 E) 408,991
Malabon (★ Manila) (1984 E) 212,930
Malaybalay (▲ 60,779) 14,018
Malolos 95,699
Manaoag 36,742
Mandaluyong (★ Manila) (1984 E) 226,670
Mandaue (★ Cebu) (1984 E) 137,300
Mangaldan 50,434
• MANILA (★ 6,800,000) (1984 E) 1,728,441
Marawi 53,812
Marikina (★ Manila) (1984 E) 248,183
Mati (▲ 78,178) 19,400
Meycauayan (★ Manila) 83,579
Muntinglupa (★ Manila) (1984 E) 172,421
Naga 90,712
Navotas (★ Manila) (1984 E) 146,899
Noveleta (★ Cavite) 14,460
Olongapo (1984 E) 173,701
Ormoc (▲ 116,474) (1984 E) 15,600
Ozamiz (▲ 77,832) 25,827
Pagadian (▲ 80,861) 39,561
Parañaque (★ Manila) (1984 E) 252,791
Pasay (★ Manila) (1984 E) 320,889
Pasig (★ Manila) (1984 E) 318,853
Puerto Princesa (▲ 60,234) 34,003
Pulilan 38,110
Quezon City (★ Manila) (1984 E) 1,326,035
Rosario (★ Cavite) 33,312
Roxas (Capiz) (▲ 81,183) 19,399
Sagay (▲ 99,118) 43,662
San Carlos (▲ 107,080) (1984 E) 26,300
San Fernando 110,891
San Juan del Monte (★ Manila) (1984 E) 139,126
San Pablo (▲ 143,023) (1984 E) 74,500
San Pedro 74,556
Santa Cruz 60,620
Santa Rosa (★ Manila) 64,325
Santo Tomas, Pampanga prov. 24,951
Santo Tomas, Pangasinan prov. 8,946
Silay (▲ 111,131) 37,173
Surigao (▲ 79,745) 28,482
Tacloban (1984 E) 117,243
Tagaytay (▲ 16,322) 3,678
Tagbilaran 42,683
Tagig (★ Manila) (1984 E) 130,719
Tagum (▲ 86,201) 35,785
Talisay (▲ 53,624) 26,463
Tarlac (▲ 175,691) 38,205
Taytay (★ Manila) 75,328
Toledo (▲ 102,565) (1984 E) 8,900
Trece Martires (▲ 8,579) 1,455
Tuguegarao (▲ 73,507) 30,107
Valenzuela (★ Manila) (1984 E) 275,725
Victorias (▲ 55,959) 27,407
Vigan 33,483
Zamboanga (▲ 379,194) (1984 E) 91,300

C Census. E Official estimate. UE Unofficial estimate.
• Largest city in country.

★ Population or designation of metropolitan area, including suburbs (see headnote).
▲ Population of an entire municipality, commune, or district, including rural area.

## PITCAIRN

| | |
|---|---|
| 1988 C | 59 |

*Cities and Towns*

| | |
|---|---|
| • ADAMSTOWN | 59 |

## POLAND / Polska

| | |
|---|---|
| 1988 E | 37,663,800 |

*Cities and Towns*

| | |
|---|---|
| Augustów | 27,900 |
| Będzin (★ Katowice) | 77,300 |
| Bełchatów | 54,900 |
| Biała Podlaska | 49,700 |
| Białogard | 23,700 |
| Białystok | 259,600 |
| Bielawa (★★ Dzierżoniów) | 34,100 |
| Bielsko-Biała | 177,700 |
| Bochnia | 28,200 |
| Bolesławiec (Bunzlau) | 43,300 |
| Brzeg (Brieg) | 37,700 |
| Bydgoszcz | 372,600 |
| Bytom (★★ Katowice) | 239,800 |
| Chełm | 62,700 |
| Chojnice | 36,500 |
| Chorzów (★★ Katowice) | 138,200 |
| Chrzanów | 40,400 |
| Ciechanów | 41,000 |
| Cieszyn | 36,900 |
| Czechowice-Dziedzice | 35,100 |
| Czeladź (★ Katowice) | 38,000 |
| Częstochowa | 252,900 |
| Dąbrowa Górnicza (★ Katowice) | 140,000 |
| Dębica | 42,700 |
| Dzierżoniów (Reichenbach) (★ 89,000) | 37,800 |
| Elbląg (Elbing) | 121,800 |
| Ełk (Lyck) | 45,300 |
| Gdańsk (Danzig) (★ 909,000) | 469,100 |
| Gdynia (★★ Gdańsk) | 249,500 |
| Giżycko | 29,000 |
| Gliwice (Gleiwitz) (★★ Katowice) | 211,300 |
| Głogów | 70,100 |
| Gniezno | 70,000 |
| Gorzów [Wielkopolski] | 119,500 |
| Grodzisk Mazowiecki (★ Warsaw) | 25,200 |
| Grudziądz | 98,300 |
| Inowrocław | 74,600 |
| Jarosław | 41,700 |
| Jasło | 35,900 |
| Jastrzębie-Zdrój | 102,200 |
| Jaworzno (★ Katowice) | 97,500 |
| Jelenia Góra (Hirschberg) | 92,500 |
| Kalisz | 105,300 |
| Kamienna Góra (Landeshut) | 23,300 |
| • Katowice (★ 2,778,000) | 368,600 |
| Kędzierzyn-Koźle | 72,900 |
| Kętrzyn | 29,600 |
| Kielce | 208,100 |
| Kłodzko (Glatz) | 29,500 |
| Knurów (★ Katowice) | 45,600 |
| Kołobrzeg (Kolberg) | 43,100 |
| Konin | 78,100 |
| Kościan | 23,100 |
| Koszalin (Köslin) | 104,700 |
| Kraków (★ 828,000) | 744,900 |
| Kraśnik | 35,800 |
| Krosno | 47,300 |
| Krotoszyn | 27,000 |
| Kutno | 47,400 |
| Kwidzyn (Marienwerder) | 36,200 |
| Lębork | 32,900 |
| Legionowo (★ Warsaw) | 47,600 |
| Legnica (Liegnitz) | 100,700 |
| Leszno | 56,300 |
| Łódź (★ 1,061,000) | 844,900 |
| Łomża | 54,800 |
| Łowicz | 29,500 |
| Lubań | 23,300 |
| Lubin | 77,600 |
| Lublin (★ 389,000) | 333,000 |
| Lubliniec | 24,700 |
| Łuków | 29,600 |
| Malbork (Marienburg) | 38,200 |
| Mielec | 56,900 |
| Mikołów (★ Katowice) | 36,800 |
| Mińsk Mazowiecki | 34,000 |
| Mława | 26,800 |
| Mysłowice (★ Katowice) | 91,900 |
| Myszków | 32,300 |
| Nowa Ruda | 26,600 |
| Nowa Sól | 42,700 |
| Nowy Sącz | 73,200 |
| Nowy Targ | 31,300 |
| Nysa (Neisse) | 45,800 |
| Oława | 31,400 |
| Oleśnica | 36,400 |
| Olkusz | 37,700 |
| Olsztyn (Allenstein) | 154,900 |
| Opole (Oppeln) | 128,200 |
| Ostróda (Osterode) | 32,500 |
| Ostrołęka | 46,900 |
| Ostrowiec [Świętokrzyski] | 75,500 |
| Ostrów Wielkopolski | 70,400 |
| Oświęcim | 45,500 |
| Otwock (★ Warsaw) | 44,700 |
| Pabianice (★ Łódź) | 73,600 |
| Piaseczno (★ Warsaw) | 24,500 |
| Piekary Śląskie (★ Katowice) | 69,400 |
| Piła (Schneidemühl) | 69,700 |
| Piotrków [Trybunalski] | 80,200 |
| Płock | 117,600 |
| Poznań (★ 672,000) | 585,900 |
| Prudnik | 24,600 |
| Pruszków (★ Warsaw) | 53,700 |
| Przemyśl | 67,200 |
| Pszczyna | 39,100 |
| Puławy | 51,200 |
| Racibórz (Ratibor) | 62,500 |
| Radom | 221,800 |
| Radomsko | 49,600 |
| Ruda Śląska (★ Katowice) | 167,900 |
| Rumia (★ Gdańsk) | 36,100 |
| Rybnik | 141,000 |
| Rzeszów | 147,300 |
| Sanok | 37,500 |
| Siedlce | 68,400 |
| Siemianowice Śląskie (★ Katowice) | 82,200 |
| Sieradz | 39,500 |
| Skarżysko-Kamienna | 49,500 |
| Skierniewice | 42,600 |
| Słupsk (Stolp) | 96,200 |
| Sochaczew | 37,400 |
| Sopot (Zoppot) (★ Gdańsk) | 49,700 |
| Sosnowiec (★★ Katowice) | 259,600 |
| Stalowa Wola | 68,800 |
| Starachowice | 56,000 |
| Stargard [Szczeciński] | 68,500 |
| Starogard [Gdański] | 46,900 |
| Suwałki | 55,900 |
| Świdnica (Schweidnitz) | 61,900 |
| Świdnik (★ Lublin) | 38,800 |
| Świecie | 26,000 |
| Świętochłowice (★ Katowice) | 60,900 |
| Świnoujście (Swinemünde) | 44,100 |
| Szczecin (Stettin) (★ 449,000) | 396,600 |
| Szczecinek | 39,200 |
| Szczytno (Ortelsburg) | 26,200 |
| Tarnobrzeg | 44,700 |
| Tarnów | 118,400 |
| Tarnowskie Góry (★ Katowice) | 74,300 |
| Tczew | 59,000 |
| Tomaszów Mazowiecki | 67,400 |
| Toruń | 197,000 |
| Trzebinia | 20,900 |
| Turek | 28,000 |
| Tychy (★ Katowice) | 187,800 |
| Wałbrzych (Waldenburg) (★ 207,000) | 141,100 |
| Wałcz | 26,200 |
| WARSAW (WARSZAWA) (★ 2,323,000) | 1,671,400 |
| Wejherowo | 46,500 |
| Włocławek | 119,200 |
| Wodzisław Śląski | 111,500 |
| Wołomin (★ Warsaw) | 35,300 |
| Wrocław (Breslau) | 640,200 |
| Września | 26,300 |
| Zabrze (Hindenburg) (★★ Katowice) | 199,400 |
| Żagań (Sagan) | 27,000 |
| Zakopane | 30,100 |
| Zamość | 58,400 |
| Żary (Sorau) | 39,700 |
| Zawiercie | 56,100 |
| Zduńska Wola | 43,800 |
| Zgierz (★ Łódź) | 56,200 |
| Zgorzelec | 35,900 |
| Zielona Góra (Grünberg) | 113,300 |
| Żory | 65,300 |
| Żyrardów (★ Warsaw) | 40,900 |
| Żywiec | 30,100 |

*Voivodships*

| | |
|---|---|
| Biała Podlaska | 300,300 |
| Białystok | 678,100 |
| Bielsko-Biała | 881,400 |
| Bydgoszcz | 1,093,500 |
| Chełm | 242,900 |
| Ciechanów | 421,200 |
| Częstochowa | 770,300 |
| Elbląg | 470,800 |
| Gdańsk | 1,416,000 |
| Gorzów Wielkopolski | 488,600 |
| Jelenia Góra | 513,200 |
| Kalisz | 701,900 |
| Katowice | 3,957,600 |
| Kielce | 1,113,900 |
| Konin | 462,400 |
| Koszalin | 496,500 |
| Kraków | 1,215,300 |
| Krosno | 481,600 |
| Legnica | 499,700 |
| Leszno | 379,400 |
| Łódź | 1,149,300 |
| Łomża | 341,200 |
| Lublin | 994,100 |
| Nowy Sącz | 676,300 |
| Olsztyn | 735,800 |
| Opole | 1,022,000 |
| Ostrołęka | 388,300 |
| Piła | 470,900 |
| Piotrków Trybunalski | 637,600 |
| Płock | 512,000 |
| Poznań | 1,311,900 |
| Przemyśl | 399,100 |
| Radom | 734,800 |
| Rzeszów | 700,400 |
| Siedlce | 640,500 |
| Sieradz | 403,000 |
| Skierniewice | 412,300 |
| Słupsk | 402,000 |
| Suwałki | 456,400 |
| Szczecin | 955,000 |
| Tarnobrzeg | 585,500 |
| Tarnów | 649,100 |
| Toruń | 647,600 |
| Wałbrzych | 738,900 |
| Warszawa | 2,425,900 |
| Włocławek | 427,500 |
| Wrocław | 1,119,600 |
| Zamość | 489,400 |
| Zielona Góra | 652,800 |

## PORTUGAL

| | |
|---|---|
| 1981 C | 9,833,014 |

*Cities and Towns*

| | |
|---|---|
| Agualva-Cacém (★ Lisbon) | 34,341 |
| Águas Santas (★ Porto) | 26,523 |
| Algés (★ Lisbon) | 20,377 |
| Algueirão-Mem Martins (★ Lisbon) | 28,154 |
| Almada (★ Lisbon) | 42,607 |
| Amadora (★ Lisbon) | 95,518 |
| Angra do Heroísmo, Azores Is. | 12,292 |
| Aveiro | 28,625 |
| Baixa da Banheira (★ Lisbon) | 21,358 |
| Barreiro (★ Lisbon) | 50,863 |
| Beja | 19,643 |
| Braga | 63,033 |
| Bragança | 14,181 |
| Castelo Branco | 21,256 |
| Coimbra | 74,616 |
| Cova da Piedade (★ Lisbon) | 28,251 |
| Covilhã | 21,807 |
| Damaia (★ Lisbon) | 23,261 |
| Évora | 34,851 |
| Faro | 27,974 |
| Funchal, Madeira Is. | 44,111 |
| Guimarães | 21,947 |
| Horta, Azores Is. | 5,749 |
| Laranjeiro (★ Lisbon) | 20,374 |
| • LISBON (LISBOA) (★ 2,250,000) | 807,167 |
| Matosinhos (★ Porto) | 26,404 |
| Montijo (★ Lisbon) | 23,017 |
| Moscavide (★ Lisbon) | 17,797 |
| Odivelas (★ Lisbon) | 38,322 |
| Oeiras (★ Lisbon) | 32,529 |
| Olhão | 20,080 |
| Ponta Delgada, Azores Is. | 21,187 |
| Portimão | 19,605 |
| Porto (Oporto) (★ 1,225,000) | 327,368 |
| Póvoa de Varzim | 23,729 |
| Queluz (★ Lisbon) | 42,241 |
| Sacavém (★ Lisbon) | 24,116 |
| Santarém | 19,761 |
| Setúbal | 77,885 |
| Sintra (★ Lisbon) | 9,322 |
| Vila do Conde | 20,613 |
| Vila Nova de Gaia (★ Porto) | 62,469 |
| Viseu | 20,070 |

*Districts*

| | |
|---|---|
| Açores (Azores) (Auton. Region) | 243,410 |
| Aveiro | 622,988 |
| Beja | 188,420 |
| Braga | 708,924 |
| Bragança | 184,252 |
| Castelo Branco | 234,230 |
| Coimbra | 436,324 |
| Évora | 180,277 |
| Faro | 323,534 |
| Guarda | 205,631 |
| Leiria | 420,229 |
| Lisboa (Lisbon) | 2,069,467 |
| Madeira (Auton. Region) | 252,844 |
| Portalegre | 142,905 |
| Porto | 1,562,287 |
| Santarém | 454,123 |
| Setúbal | 658,326 |
| Viana do Castelo | 256,814 |
| Vila Real | 264,381 |
| Viseu | 423,648 |

## PUERTO RICO

| | |
|---|---|
| 1980 C | 3,196,520 |

*Cities and Towns*

| | |
|---|---|
| Adjuntas (▲ 18,786) | 5,239 |
| Aguadilla (★ 152,793) | 22,039 |
| Aibonito (▲ 22,167) | 9,331 |
| Arecibo (★ 160,336) | 48,779 |
| Bayamón (★ San Juan) | 185,087 |
| Caguas (★ San Juan) | 87,214 |
| Carolina (★ San Juan) | 147,835 |
| Cataño (★ San Juan) | 26,243 |
| Cayey (▲ 41,099) San Juan) | 23,305 |
| Coamo (▲ 30,822) | 12,851 |
| Corozal (★ San Juan) | 5,889 |
| Fajardo (▲ 32,087) San Juan) | 26,928 |
| Guánica (▲ 18,799) | 9,628 |
| Guayama (▲ 40,183) | 21,097 |
| Guayanilla (▲ 21,050) | 6,163 |
| Guaynabo (★ San Juan) | 65,075 |
| Humacao (★ San Juan) | 19,147 |
| Isabela (★ Aguadilla) | 12,087 |
| Manatí (★ San Juan) | 17,347 |
| Mayagüez (★ 200,464) | 82,968 |
| Ponce (★ 232,551) | 161,739 |
| San Germán (★ Mayagüez) | 13,054 |
| • SAN JUAN (★ 1,775,260) | 424,600 |
| San Sebastián (▲ 35,690) | 10,619 |
| Trujillo Alto (★ San Juan) | 41,141 |
| Utuado (▲ 34,505) | 11,113 |
| Vega Alta (★ San Juan) | 10,582 |
| Vega Baja (★ San Juan) | 18,233 |
| Yabucoa (▲ 31,425) | 6,797 |
| Yauco (▲ 37,742) | 14,594 |

## QATAR / Qaṭar

| | |
|---|---|
| 1986 C | 369,079 |

*Cities and Towns*

| | |
|---|---|
| Ar Rayyān (★ Doha) | 91,996 |
| • DOHA (AD DAWḤAH) (★ 310,000) | 217,294 |

## REUNION / Réunion

| | |
|---|---|
| 1982 C | 515,814 |

*Cities and Towns*

| | |
|---|---|
| Le Port (▲ 30,131) | 26,000 |
| • SAINT-DENIS (▲ 109,072) | 84,400 |
| Saint-Pierre (▲ 58,412) | 28,000 |

## ROMANIA / România

| | |
|---|---|
| 1986 E | 22,823,479 |

*Cities and Towns*

| | |
|---|---|
| Aiud | 29,250 |
| Alba Iulia | 66,100 |
| Alexandria | 52,802 |
| Arad | 187,744 |
| Bacău | 179,877 |
| Baia-Mare | 139,704 |
| Bîrlad | 70,365 |
| Bistriţa | 77,267 |
| Blaj | 23,438 |
| Borşa | 29,494 |
| Botoşani | 108,775 |
| Brăila | 235,620 |
| Braşov | 351,493 |
| • BUCHAREST (BUCUREŞTI) (★ 2,250,000) | 1,989,823 |
| Buzău | 136,080 |
| Călăraşi | 69,350 |
| Caracal | 36,963 |
| Caransebeş | 32,787 |
| Carei | 27,727 |
| Cîmpia Turzii | 28,342 |
| Cîmpina | 39,032 |
| Cîmpulung | 41,895 |
| Cluj-Napoca | 310,017 |
| Codlea | 24,039 |
| Constanţa | 327,676 |
| Craiova | 281,044 |
| Cugir | 33,325 |
| Curtea-de-Argeş | 30,019 |
| Dej | 39,229 |
| Deva | 77,976 |
| Dorohoi | 29,721 |
| Drobeta-Turnu-Severin | 99,366 |
| Făgăraş | 41,851 |
| Feteşti | 32,504 |
| Focşani | 86,411 |
| Galaţi | 295,372 |
| Gheorghe Gheorghiu-Dej | 52,329 |
| Giurgiu | 68,002 |
| Hunedoara | 88,514 |
| Huşi | 28,963 |
| Iaşi | 313,060 |
| Lugoj | 53,665 |
| Lupeni | 30,949 |
| Mangalia | 38,803 |
| Medgidia | 48,409 |
| Mediaş | 72,816 |
| Miercurea Ciuc | 46,494 |
| Moineşti | 23,004 |
| Odorheiu Secuiesc | 41,071 |
| Olteniţa | 29,367 |
| Oradea | 213,846 |
| Paşcani | 36,420 |
| Petrila (★ Petroşani) | 26,468 |
| Petroşani (★ 74,000) | 49,131 |
| Piatra-Neamţ | 109,393 |
| Piteşti | 157,190 |
| Ploieşti (★ 300,000) | 234,886 |
| Rădăuţi | 28,740 |
| Reghin | 36,423 |
| Reşiţa | 105,914 |
| Rîmnicu-Sărat | 36,501 |
| Rîmnicu-Vîlcea | 96,051 |
| Roman | 72,415 |
| Roşiorii de Vede | 35,622 |
| Săcele | 33,502 |
| Satu Mare | 130,082 |
| Sebeş | 30,793 |
| Sfîntu Gheorghe | 67,587 |
| Sibiu | 177,511 |
| Sighetu Marmaţiei | 43,274 |
| Sighişoara | 36,775 |
| Slatina | 76,714 |
| Slobozia | 46,324 |
| Suceava | 96,317 |
| Tecuci | 44,075 |
| Timişoara | 325,272 |
| Tîrgovişte | 91,990 |
| Tîrgu-Jiu | 87,693 |
| Tîrgu Mureş | 158,998 |
| Tîrnăveni | 29,341 |
| Tulcea | 86,336 |
| Turda | 61,594 |
| Turnu-Măgurele | 35,094 |
| Vaslui | 65,070 |
| Vulcan | 34,117 |
| Zalău | 57,283 |
| Zărneşti | 26,773 |

## RWANDA

| | |
|---|---|
| 1983 E | 5,762,000 |

*Cities and Towns*

| | |
|---|---|
| Butare | 30,000 |
| • KIGALI | 181,600 |

## SAINT CHRISTOPHER-NEVIS

| | |
|---|---|
| 1980 C | 44,404 |

*Cities and Towns*

| | |
|---|---|
| • BASSETERRE | 14,725 |
| Charlestown | 1,771 |

## SAINT HELENA

| | |
|---|---|
| 1987 C | 5,644 |

*Cities and Towns*

| | |
|---|---|
| • JAMESTOWN | 1,413 |

## SAINT LUCIA

| | |
|---|---|
| 1987 E | 142,342 |

*Cities and Towns*

| | |
|---|---|
| • CASTRIES | 53,933 |

## SAINT PIERRE AND MIQUELON / Saint-Pierre-et-Miquelon

| | |
|---|---|
| 1982 C | 6,041 |

*Cities and Towns*

| | |
|---|---|
| • SAINT-PIERRE | 5,371 |

## SAINT VINCENT AND THE GRENADINES

| | |
|---|---|
| 1987 E | 112,589 |

*Cities and Towns*

| | |
|---|---|
| • KINGSTOWN (★ 28,936) | 19,028 |

## SAN MARINO

| | |
|---|---|
| 1988 E | 22,304 |

*Cities and Towns*

| | |
|---|---|
| • SAN MARINO | 4,137 |

## SAO TOME AND PRINCIPE / São Tomé e Príncipe

| | |
|---|---|
| 1970 C | 73,631 |

*Cities and Towns*

| | |
|---|---|
| • SÃO TOMÉ | 17,380 |

## SAUDI ARABIA / Al 'Arabīyah as Su'ūdīyah

| | |
|---|---|
| 1980 E | 9,229,000 |

*Cities and Towns*

| | |
|---|---|
| Abhā (1974 C) | 30,150 |
| Ad Dammām | 200,000 |
| Al Hufūf (Hofuf) (1974 C) | 101,271 |
| Al Khubar (1974 C) | 48,817 |
| Al Mubarraz (1974 C) | 54,325 |
| Aṭ Ṭā'if | 300,000 |
| Aẓ Ẓahrān (Dhahran) (1974 UE) | 25,000 |
| Buraydah (1974 C) | 69,940 |
| Ḥā'il (1974 C) | 40,502 |
| • Jiddah | 1,300,000 |
| Khamīs Mushayṭ (1974 C) | 49,581 |

C Census. E Official estimate. UE Unofficial estimate.
• Largest city in country.

★ Population or designation of metropolitan area, including suburbs (see headnote).
▲ Population of an entire municipality, commune, or district, including rural area.

Mecca (Makkah) 550,000
Medina (Al Madīnah) 290,000
Najran (1974 C) 47,501
Qīzān (1974 C) 32,812
RIYADH (AR RIYĀḌ) 1,250,000
Tabūk (1974 C) 74,825

**SENEGAL / Sénégal**

1985 E 6,566,988

***Cities and Towns***

• DAKAR 1,428,084
Diourbel 76,409
Kaolack 132,386
Kolda 42,180
Louga 49,436
Saint-Louis 91,485
Tambacounda 44,510
Thiès 156,200
Ziguinchor 106,460

**SEYCHELLES**

1984 E 64,718

***Cities and Towns***

• VICTORIA 23,000

**SIERRA LEONE**

1985 C 3,515,812

***Cities and Towns***

Bo 59,768
• FREETOWN (★ 525,000) 469,776
Kenema 52,473
Koidu 82,474
Lunsar 16,073
Makeni 49,038
Port Loko 15,248

**SINGAPORE**

1988 E 2,631,000

***Cities and Towns***

• SINGAPORE (★ 3,000,000) 2,631,000

**SOLOMON ISLANDS**

1986 C 285,176

***Cities and Towns***

• HONIARA 30,413

**SOMALIA / Soomaaliya**

1984 E 5,423,000

***Cities and Towns***

Berbera 65,000
Hargeysa 70,000
Kismaayo 70,000
Marka 60,000
• MOGADISHU (MUQDISHO) 600,000

**SOUTH AFRICA / Suid-Afrika**

1985 C 23,385,645

***Cities and Towns***

Alberton (★ Johannesburg) 66,155
Alexandra (★ Johannesburg) 67,276
Aliwal North 5,399
Atlantis (★ Cape Town) 29,524
Atteridgeville (★ Pretoria) 73,439
Beaufort West (★ 24,487) 18,979
Bellville (★ Cape Town) 68,915
Benoni (★ Johannesburg) 94,926
Bethal (★ 23,510) 8,721
Bethlehem (★ 35,301) 12,871
Bloemfontein (★ 235,000) 104,381
Boksburg (★ Johannesburg) 110,832
Botshabelo (★ Bloemfontein) 95,625
Brakpan (★ Johannesburg) 46,416
CAPE TOWN (KAAPSTAD) (★ 1,790,000) 776,617
Carletonville (★ 120,499) 97,874
Clermont (★ Durban) 27,136
Constantia (★ Cape Town) 25,749
Cradock (★ 22,930) 10,911
Daveyton (★ Johannesburg) 99,056
De Aar (★ 22,484) 17,540
Diepmeadow (★ Johannesburg) 192,682
Dobsonville (★ Johannesburg) 38,166
Duduza (★ Johannesburg) 27,649
Dundee 9,737
Durban (★ 1,550,000) 634,301
East London (Oos-Londen) (★ 320,000) 85,699
Edendale (★ Pietermaritzburg) 47,001
Edenvale (★ Johannesburg) 30,699
Elsies River (★ Cape Town) 70,067
Empumalanga (★ Durban) 47,938
Ermelo (★ 32,047) 12,746
Evaton (★ Vereeniging) 52,559
Ezakheni 27,277
Galeshewe (★ Kimberley) 63,238
George (★ 55,935) 41,920
Germiston (★★ Johannesburg) 116,718
Goodwood (★ Cape Town) 33,451
Graaff-Reinet (★ 23,758) 18,106
Grahamstown (★ 48,452) 19,188
Grassy Park (★ Cape Town) 50,193
Guguletu (★ Cape Town) 63,893
Harrismith 4,518
Ikageng (★ Potchefstroom) 35,099
Imbali (★ Pietermaritzburg) 27,866
• Johannesburg (★ 3,650,000) 632,369
Jouberton (★ Klerksdorp) 33,180
Kagiso (★ Johannesburg) 50,647
Katlehong (★ Johannesburg) 137,745
Kayamnandi (★ Port Elizabeth) 220,548
Kempton Park (★ Johannesburg) 87,721
Kimberley (★ 145,000) 74,061
King William's Town (★ 48,300) 16,123
Klerksdorp (★ 205,000) 48,947
Kraaifontein (★ Cape Town) 29,431
Kroonstad (★ 65,165) 22,886
Krugersdorp (★ Johannesburg) 73,767
Kwaguqa (★ Witbank) 35,387
Kwa Makuta (★ Durban) 71,378
Kwa Mashu (★ Durban) 111,593
Kwanobuhle (★ Port Elizabeth) 52,376
Kwathema (★ Johannesburg) 78,640
Ladysmith (★ 31,670) 25,102
Langa (★ Cape Town) 22,998
Lekoa (Shapeville) (★ Vereeniging) 218,392
Madadeni (★ Newcastle) 65,832
Mamelodi (★ Pretoria) 127,033
Mangaung (★ Bloemfontein) 79,851
Middelburg (★ 44,762) 25,627
Mohlakeng (★ Johannesburg) 27,706
Mosselbaai (★ 22,180) 20,404
Nelspruit (★ 40,300) 15,519
Newcastle (★ 155,000) 34,931
Nigel (★ Johannesburg) 27,138
Ntuzuma (★ Durban) 61,834
Nyanga (★ Cape Town) 148,882
Odendaalsrus (★★ Welkom) 8,819
Orkney (★★ Klerksdorp) 19,431
Oudtshoorn (★ 37,112) 34,124
Ozisweni (★ Newcastle) 51,934
Paarl (★★ Cape Town) 63,671
Parow (★ Cape Town) 60,294
Parys (★ 22,320) 7,345
Phalaborwa (★ 29,740) 9,284
Pietermaritzburg (★ 230,000) 133,809
Pietersburg (★ 62,804) 29,909
Pinetown (★ Durban) 55,770
Port Elizabeth (★ 690,000) 272,844
Potchefstroom (★ 78,865) 43,766
Potgietersrus (★ 22,140) 8,195
PRETORIA (★ 960,000) 443,059
Queenstown (★ 32,699) 17,996
Randburg (★ Johannesburg) 74,347
Randfontein (★ Johannesburg) 43,763
Rhini (★ Grahamstown) 29,264
Roodepoort-Maraisburg (★ Johannesburg) 141,764
Rustenburg 37,712
Sandton (★ Johannesburg) 86,089
Sasolburg (★★ Vereeniging) 29,310
Seeisoville (★ Kroonstad) 42,279
Seshego (★ Pietersburg) 32,895
Soshanguve (★ Pretoria) 68,598
Soweto (★ Johannesburg) 521,948
Springs (★ Johannesburg) 68,235
Standerton (★ 31,728) 15,301
Stellenbosch (★★ Cape Town) 38,602
Stilfontein (★★ Klerksdorp) 13,782
Strand (★ Cape Town) 28,474
Tembisa (★ Johannesburg) 149,282
Thabong (★ Welkom) 43,470
Tokoza (★ Johannesburg) 44,589
Tsakane (★ Johannesburg) 42,280
Uitenhage (★★ Port Elizabeth) 54,987
Umlazi (★ Durban) 194,933
Upington (★ 40,463) 32,182
Vanderbijlpark (★★ Vereeniging) 59,865
Vereeniging (★ 525,000) 60,584
Verwoerdburg (★ Pretoria) 49,891
Virginia (★ 65,000) 17,624
Vosloosrus (★ Johannesburg) 52,061
Vredenburg-Saldanha 26,091
Vryburg (★ 20,993) 10,071
Vryheid (★ 18,680) 12,313
Walvisbaai (Walvis Bay) (★ 16,607) 9,687
Welkom (★ 215,000) 54,488
Westonaria (★ Johannesburg) 46,523
Westville (★ Durban) 24,933
Witbank (★ 77,171) 41,784
Worcester (★ 54,007) 46,043

***Provinces***

Cape 5,041,137
Natal 5,892,033
Orange Free State 1,958,462
Transvaal 10,494,013

**SOVIET UNION / Sovetskiy Soyuz**

1989 C 286,717,000

***Cities and Towns***

Abakan 154,000
Abay (1974 E) 41,000
Abdulino (1974 E) 25,000
Abovyan (1987 E) 53,000
Achinsk 122,000
Agryz (1974 E) 19,000
Akhtubinsk (1987 E) 53,000
Akhtyrka (1974 E) 43,000
Aktyubinsk 253,000
Alapajevsk (1987 E) 51,000
Alatyr (1974 E) 46,000
Aleksandriya 103,000
Aleksandrov (1987 E) 66,000
Aleksin (1987 E) 72,000
Aleysk (1974 E) 37,000
Ali-Bayramly (1987 E) 51,000
Alma-Ata (★ 1,190,000) 1,128,000
Almalyk 114,000
Almetyevsk 129,000
Alytus (1987 E) 71,000
Amursk (1987 E) 54,000
Anapa (1974 E) 30,000
Andizhan 293,000
Angarsk 266,000
Angren 131,000
Antratsit (★★ Krasnyy Luch) (1987 E) 70,000
Anzhero-Sudzhensk 108,000
Apatity (1987 E) 80,000
Apsheronsk (1974 E) 33,000
Aralsk (1974 E) 39,000
Arkalyk (1987 E) 71,000
Arkhangelsk 416,000
Armavir 161,000
Arsenyev (1987 E) 67,000
Artem (1987 E) 73,000
Artemovsk (1987 E) 91,000
Artemovskiy (1974 E) 38,000
Arzamas 109,000
Asbest (1987 E) 83,000
Asha (1974 E) 38,000
Ashkhabad 398,000
Asino (1974 E) 31,000
Astrakhan 509,000
Atbasar (1974 E) 39,000
Atkarsk (1974 E) 30,000
Avdeyevka (★ Donetsk) (1974 E) 33,000
Ayaguz (1974 E) 40,000
Azov (1987 E) 81,000
Baku (★ 2,020,000) 1,150,000
Balakhna (★ Gorkiy) (1974 E) 37,000
Balakleya (1974 E) 31,000
Balakovo 198,000
Balashikha (★ Moscow) 136,000
Balashov (1987 E) 99,000
Balkhash (1987 E) 84,000
Barabinsk (1974 E) 37,000
Baranovichi 159,000
Barnaul (★ 665,000) 602,000
Bataysk (★ Rostov-na-Donu) (1987 E) 98,000
Batumi 136,000
Bayram-Ali (1974 E) 36,000
Bekabad (Begovat) (1987 E) 80,000
Belaya Kalitva (1974 E) 35,000
Belaya Tserkov 197,000
Belebey (1987 E) 51,000
Belgorod 300,000
Belgorod-Dnestrovskiy (1987 E) 54,000
Belogorsk (1987 E) 71,000
Belorechensk (1974 E) 38,000
Beloretsk (1987 E) 75,000
Belovo (1987 E) 118,000
Beltsy 159,000
Bendery 130,000
Berdichev (1987 E) 89,000
Berdsk (★ Novosibirsk) (1987 E) 77,000
Berdyansk 132,000
Berezniki 201,000
Berezovskiy (1987 E) 51,000
Bezhetsk (1974 E) 30,000
Birobidzan (1987 E) 82,000
Biysk 233,000
Blagoveshchensk 206,000
Bobruysk 223,000
Bogoroditsk (1974 E) 32,000
Bogorodsk (★ Gorkiy) (1974 E) 37,000
Bologoye (1974 E) 34,000
Bor (★ Gorkiy) (1987 E) 65,000
Borislav (1974 E) 36,000
Borisoglebsk (1987 E) 69,000
Borisov 144,000
Borispol (1974 E) 36,000
Borovichi (1987 E) 64,000
Boyarka (★ Kiev) (1974 E) 31,000
Bratsk 255,000
Brest 258,000
Brovary (★ Kiev) (1987 E) 73,000
Bryanka (★ Stakhanov) (1987 E) 65,000
Bryansk 452,000
Budennovsk (1987 E) 54,000
Bugulma (1987 E) 88,000
Buguruslan (1987 E) 53,000
Bukhara 224,000
Buy (1974 E) 28,000
Buynaksk (1987 E) 53,000
Buzuluk (1987 E) 82,000
Chapayevsk (1987 E) 87,000
Chardzhou 161,000
Chaykovskij (1987 E) 83,000
Chebarkul (1974 E) 42,000
Cheboksary 420,000
Chekhov (1987 E) 57,000
Chelyabinsk (★ 1,325,000) 1,143,000
Cheremkhovo (1987 E) 73,000
Cherepovets 310,000
Cherkassy 290,000
Cherkessk 113,000
Chernigov 296,000
Chernogorsk (1987 E) 80,000
Chernovtsy 257,000
Chernyakhovsk (Insterburg) (1974 E) 34,000
Chervonograd (1987 E) 71,000
Chimkent 393,000
Chirchik (★ Tashkent) 156,000
Chistopol (1987 E) 65,000
Chita 366,000
Chu (1974 E) 35,000
Chusovoy (1987 E) 59,000
Chust (1974 E) 31,000
Daugavpils 127,000
Debaltsevo (1983 E) 37,000
Denau (1987 E) 53,000
Derbent (1987 E) 83,000
Dimitrov (★★ Krasnoarmeysk) (1987 E) 62,000
Dimitrovgrad (Melekess) 124,000
Dmitrov (1987 E) 64,000
Dneprodzerzhinsk (★★ Dnepropetrovsk) 282,000
Dnepropetrovsk (★ 1,600,000) 1,179,000
Dobropolye (1974 E) 31,000
Dolgoprudnyy (★ Moscow) (1987 E) 71,000
Domodedovo (★ Moscow) (1987 E) 51,000
Donetsk, Donetsk oblast (★ 2,200,000) 1,110,000
Donetsk, Rostov oblast (1974 E) 42,000
Donskoy (★ Novomoskovsk) (1974 E) 34,000
Drogobych (1987 E) 76,000
Druzhkovka (★ Kramatorsk) (1987 E) 70,000
Dubna (1987 E) 64,000
Dushanbe 595,000
Dzerzhinsk (★ Gorlovka) (1974 E) 46,000
Dzerzhinsk (★ Gorkiy) 285,000
Dzhalal-Abad (1987 E) 74,000
Dzhambul 307,000
Dzhankoy (1987 E) 51,000
Dzhetygara (1974 E) 39,000
Dzhezkazgan 109,000
Dzhizak 102,000
Echmiadzin (★ Yerevan) (1987 E) 53,000
Ekibastuz 135,000
Elektrostal 153,000
Elista (1987 E) 85,000
Engels (★★ Saratov) 182,000
Fastov (1987 E) 55,000
Feodosiya (1987 E) 83,000
Fergana 200,000
Frolovo (1974 E) 38,000
Frunze 616,000
Fryazino (★ Moscow) (1987 E) 52,000
Furmanov (1974 E) 41,000
Gatchina (★ Leningrad) (1987 E) 81,000
Gelendzhik (1974 E) 31,000
Geokchay (1974 E) 30,000
Georgiu-Dez (Liski) (1987 E) 54,000
Georgiyevsk (1987 E) 62,000
Glazov 104,000
Glukhov (1974 E) 30,000
Gomel 500,000
Gori (1987 E) 62,000
Gorkiy (Gorki) (★ 2,025,000) 1,438,000
Gorlovka (★ 710,000) 337,000
Gorno-Altaysk (1974 E) 39,000
Gorodets (1974 E) 35,000
Grodno 270,000
Groznyy 401,000
Gryazi (1974 E) 42,000
Gubakha (1974 E) 32,000
Gubkin (1987 E) 75,000
Gudermes (1974 E) 34,000
Gukovo (1987 E) 72,000
Gulistan (1987 E) 51,000
Guryev 149,000
Gus-Khrustalnyy (1987 E) 75,000
Ilichevsk (★ Odessa) (1987 E) 52,000
Ingulets (1974 E) 35,000
Inta (1987 E) 58,000
Irbit (1987 E) 53,000
Irkutsk 626,000
Ishim (1987 E) 65,000
Ishimbay (1987 E) 67,000
Iskitim (1987 E) 69,000
Ivano-Frankovsk 214,000
Ivanovo 481,000
Ivanteyevka (★ Moscow) (1987 E) 53,000
Izhevsk (Ustinov) 635,000
Izmail (1987 E) 90,000
Izyum (1987 E) 63,000
Jelgava (1987 E) 72,000
Jurmala (★ Rīga) (1987 E) 65,000
Kachkanar (1974 E) 38,000
Kafan (1974 E) 31,000
Kagan (1974 E) 38,000
Kagul (1974 E) 31,000
Kakhovka (1974 E) 35,000
Kalinin 451,000
Kaliningrad (★ Moscow) 160,000
Kaliningrad (Königsberg) 401,000
Kaluga 312,000
Kalush (1987 E) 67,000
Kamenets-Podolskiy 102,000
Kamenka (1974 E) 32,000
Kamen-na-Obi (1974 E) 40,000
Kamensk-Shakhtinskiy (1987 E) 75,000
Kamensk-Uralskiy 209,000
Kamyshin 122,000
Kamyshlov (1974 E) 31,000
Kanash (1987 E) 53,000
Kandalaksha (1974 E) 43,000
Kansk 110,000
Kapsukas (1974 E) 33,000
Kara-Balty (1987 E) 55,000
Karaganda 614,000
Karpinsk (1974 E) 37,000
Karshi 156,000
Kartaly (1974 E) 44,000
Kashira (1974 E) 42,000
Kasimov (1974 E) 34,000
Kaspiysk (1987 E) 61,000
Kattakurgan (1987 E) 63,000
Kaunas 423,000
Kazan (★ 1,140,000) 1,094,000
Kemerovo 520,000
Kentau (1987 E) 60,000
Kerch 174,000
Khabarovsk 601,000
Khanty-Mansiysk (1974 E) 26,000
Kharkov (★ 1,940,000) 1,611,000
Khartsyzsk (★ Donetsk) (1987 E) 69,000
Khasavyurt (1987 E) 74,000
Kherson 355,000
Khimki (★ Moscow) 133,000
Khmelnitskiy 237,000
Khodzheyli (1987 E) 55,000
Kholmsk (1987 E) 50,000
Kiev (Kiyev) (★ 2,900,000) 2,587,000
Kimovsk (1974 E) 44,000
Kimry (1987 E) 61,000
Kinel (1974 E) 40,000
Kineshma 105,000
Kirishi (1987 E) 51,000
Kirov 441,000
Kirovabad 278,000
Kirovakan (1987 E) 169,000
Kirovo-Chepetsk (1987 E) 89,000
Kirovograd 269,000
Kirovsk (★ Stakhanov) (1974 E) 40,000
Kirovsk (1974 E) 40,000
Kiselevsk (★★ Prokopyevsk) 128,000
Kishinev 665,000
Kislovodsk 114,000
Kizel (1974 E) 42,000
Klaipėda (Memel) 204,000
Klimovsk (★ Moscow) (1987 E) 57,000
Klin (1987 E) 95,000
Klintsy (1987 E) 72,000
Kohtla-Järve (1987 E) 78,000
Kokand 182,000
Kokchetav 137,000
Kolchugino (1974 E) 43,000
Kolomna 162,000
Kolomyya (1987 E) 63,000
Kolpino (★ Leningrad) 142,000
Kommunarsk (★ Stakhanov) 126,000
Komsomolsk-na-Amure 315,000
Konakovo (1974 E) 33,000
Kondopoga (1974 E) 32,000
Konotop (1987 E) 93,000

C Census. E Official estimate. UE Unofficial estimate.
• Largest city in country.

★ Population or designation of metropolitan area, including suburbs (see headnote).
▲ Population of an entire municipality, commune, or district, including rural area.

Konstantinovka 108,000
Kopeysk (★ Chelyabinsk) (1987 E) 99,000
Korkino (1981 E) 63,000
Korosten (1987 E) 72,000
Korsakov (1974 E) 40,000
Kostroma 278,000
Kotelnich (1974 E) 31,000
Kotlas (1987 E) 69,000
Kotovsk (1974 E) 39,000
Kovel (1987 E) 66,000
Kovrov 160,000
Kramatorsk (★ 465,000) 198,000
Krasnoarmeysk (★ 175,000) (1987 E) 70,000
Krasnodar 620,000
Krasnodon (1987 E) 52,000
Krasnogorsk (★ Moscow) (1987 E) 89,000
Krasnokamensk (1987 E) 70,000
Krasnokamsk (1987 E) 58,000
Krasnoturinsk (1987 E) 66,000
Krasnoufimsk (1974 E) 40,000
Krasnouralsk (1974 E) 40,000
Krasnovodsk (1987 E) 59,000
Krasnoyarsk 912,000
Krasnyy Luch (★ 250,000) 113,000
Krasnyy Sulin (1974 E) 43,000
Kremenchug 236,000
Krivoy Rog 713,000
Kronshtadt (★ Leningrad) (1970 C) 39,477
Kropotkin (1987 E) 73,000
Krymsk (Krymskaya) (1983 E) 50,000
Kstovo (★ Gorkiy) (1987 E) 64,000
Kuba (1974 E) 19,000
Kulebaki (1974 E) 46,000
Kulyab (1987 E) 71,000
Kumertau (1987 E) 62,000
Kungur (1987 E) 83,000
Kupyansk (1974 E) 34,000
Kurgan 356,000
Kurganinsk (1974 E) 38,000
Kurgan-Tyube (1987 E) 55,000
Kursk 424,000
Kushva (1974 E) 43,000
Kustanay 224,000
Kutaisi 235,000
Kuybyshev (★ 1,505,000) 1,257,000
Kuybyshev (1987 E) 51,000
Kuznetsk (1987 E) 98,000
Kyshtym (1974 E) 39,000
Kyzyl (1987 E) 80,000
Kyzyl-Kiya (1974 E) 33,000
Kzyl-Orda 153,000
Labinsk (1987 E) 58,000
Leninabad 160,000
Leninakan 120,000
Leningrad (★ 5,825,000) 4,456,000
Leninogorsk, Tatarskaya Auton. S. S. R. (1987 E) 69,000
Leninogorsk, Vostochno-Kazakhstanskaya oblast' (1987 E) 61,000
Leninsk (1974 E) 31,000
Leninsk-Kuznetskiy 165,000
Lenkoran (1974 E) 38,000
Lesozavodsk (1974 E) 38,000
Lida (1987 E) 81,000
Liepāja 114,000
Lipetsk 450,000
Lisichansk (★ 410,000) 127,000
Livny (1987 E) 51,000
Lobnya (★ Moscow) (1987 E) 59,000
Lomonosov (★ Leningrad) (1980 E) 46,000
Lozovaya (1987 E) 68,000
Lubny (1987 E) 58,000
Luga (1974 E) 35,000
Lutsk 198,000
Lvov 790,000
Lysva (1987 E) 77,000
Lytkarino (★ Moscow) (1987 E) 51,000
Lyubertsy (★ Moscow) 165,000
Lyubotin (1974 E) 33,000
Lyudinovo (1974 E) 36,000
Magadan 152,000
Magnitogorsk 440,000
Makeyevka (★★ Donetsk) 430,000
Makhachkala 315,000
Marganets (1987 E) 55,000
Margilan 125,000
Mariinsk (1974 E) 40,000
Mariupol 517,000
Mary (1987 E) 89,000
Maykop 149,000
Mednogorsk (1974 E) 36,000
Melitopol 174,000
Mezhdurechensk 107,000
Miass 168,000
Michurinsk 109,000
Mikhaylovka (1987 E) 58,000
Millerovo (1974 E) 37,000
Mineralnyye Vody (1987 E) 75,000
Mingechaur (1987 E) 78,000
Minsk (★ 1,650,000) 1,589,000
Minusinsk (1987 E) 72,000
Mogilev 356,000
Molodechno (1987 E) 87,000
Monchegorsk (1987 E) 65,000
Morshansk (1987 E) 51,000
• MOSCOW (MOSKVA) (★ 13,100,000) 8,769,000
Mozdok (1974 E) 33,000
Mozhga (1974 E) 41,000
Mozyr 101,000
Mtsensk (1974 E) 34,000
Mukachevo (1987 E) 88,000
Murmansk 468,000
Murom 124,000
Myski (1974 E) 38,000
Mytishchi (★ Moscow) 154,000
Naberezhnyye Chelny 501,000
Nakhichevan (1987 E) 51,000
Nakhodka 165,000
Nalchik 235,000
Namangan 308,000
Naro-Fominsk (1987 E) 60,000
Narva (1987 E) 81,000
Navoy 107,000
Nazarovo (1987 E) 63,000
Nebit-Dag (1987 E) 85,000
Neftekamsk 107,000
Nefteyugansk (1987 E) 86,000
Neryungri (1987 E) 68,000
Nevinnomyssk 121,000
Nevyansk (1974 E) 31,000
Nezhin (1987 E) 81,000
Nikolayev 503,000
Nikolayevsk [-na-Amure] (1974 E) 33,000
Nikolskiy (1987 E) 64,000
Nikopol 158,000
Nizhnekamsk 191,000
Nizhneudinsk (1974 E) 42,000
Nizhnevartovsk 242,000
Nizhniy Tagil 440,000
Noginsk 123,000
Norilsk 174,000
Novaya Kakhovka (1987 E) 53,000
Novgorod 229,000
Novoaltaysk (★ Barnaul) (1987 E) 51,000
Novocheboksarsk 115,000
Novocherkassk 187,000
Novodvinsk (1987 E) 50,000
Novoekonomicheskoye (★★ Krasnoarmeysk) (1970 C) 31,214
Novograd-Volynskiy (1987 E) 52,000
Novokazalinsk (1970 C) 34,815
Novokuybyshevsk (★ Kuybyshev) 113,000
Novokuznetsk 600,000
Novomoskovsk, Dnepropetrovsk oblast (1987 E) 76,000
Novomoskovsk, Tula oblast (★ 365,000) 146,000
Novopolotsk (1987 E) 90,000
Novorossiysk 186,000
Novoshakhtinsk 106,000
Novosibirsk (★ 1,600,000) 1,436,000
Novotroitsk 106,000
Novovolynsk (1987 E) 54,000
Novozybkov (1974 E) 39,000
Novyy Urengoy (1987 E) 79,000
Noyabrsk (1987 E) 77,000
Nukus 169,000
Obninsk 100,000
Odessa (★ 1,185,000) 1,115,000
Odintsovo (★ Moscow) 125,000
Okha (1974 E) 31,000
Oktyabr'sk (1974 E) 33,000
Oktyabrskiy 105,000
Omsk (★ 1,175,000) 1,148,000
Ordzhonikidze 300,000
Orekhovo-Zuyevo (★ 205,000) 137,000
Orel 337,000
Orenburg 547,000
Orsha 123,000
Orsk 271,000
Osh 213,000
Osinniki (1987 E) 63,000
Otradnyy (1974 E) 46,000
Panevėžys 126,000
Pärnu (1987 E) 53,000
Partizansk (Suchan) (1974 E) 49,000
Pavlodar 331,000
Pavlograd 131,000
Pavlovo (1987 E) 72,000
Pavlovskiy Posad (1987 E) 71,000
Pechora (1987 E) 64,000
Penza 543,000
Pereslavl-Zalesskiy (1974 E) 33,000
Perevalsk (★ Stakhanov) (1974 E) 32,000
Perm (★ 1,160,000) 1,091,000
Pervomaysk (1987 E) 79,000
Pervomaysk (★ Stakhanov) (1974 E) 46,000
Pervouralsk 142,000
Petrodvorets (★ Leningrad) (1987 E) 77,000
Petropavlovsk 241,000
Petropavlovsk [-Kamchatskiy] 269,000
Petrovsk (1974 E) 34,000
Petrozavodsk 270,000
Pinsk 119,000
Podolsk (★ Moscow) 210,000
Polevskoy (1987 E) 71,000
Polotsk (1987 E) 80,000
Poltava 315,000
Poti (1977 E) 54,000
Priluki (1987 E) 73,000
Prokhladnyy (1987 E) 53,000
Prokopyevsk (★ 410,000) 274,000
Przhevalsk (1987 E) 64,000
Pskov 204,000
Pugachev (1974 E) 35,000
Pushkin (★ Leningrad) (1987 E) 97,000
Pushkino (1987 E) 74,000
Pyatigorsk 129,000
Ramenskoye (1987 E) 86,000
Rasskazovo (1974 E) 40,000
Razdan (1987 E) 56,000
Rechitsa (1987 E) 71,000
Reutov (★ Moscow) (1987 E) 68,000
Revda (1987 E) 66,000
Rēzekne (1974 E) 34,000
Rezh (1974 E) 34,000
Rīga (★ 1,005,000) 915,000
Rodniki (1974 E) 30,000
Romny (1987 E) 53,000
Roslavl (1987 E) 61,000
Rossosh (1987 E) 55,000
Rostov (1974 E) 31,000
Rostov-na-Donu (★ 1,165,000) 1,020,000
Rovenki (1987 E) 68,000
Rovno 228,000
Rtishchevo (1974 E) 41,000
Rubezhnoye (★★ Lisichansk) (1987 E) 72,000
Rubtsovsk 172,000
Rudnyy 124,000
Rustavi (★ Tbilisi) 159,000
Ruzayevka (1987 E) 53,000
Ryazan 515,000
Rybachye (1974 E) 33,000
Rybinsk 252,000
Rybnitsa (1987 E) 58,000
Rzhev (1987 E) 70,000
Safonovo (1987 E) 56,000
Salavat 150,000
Salsk (1987 E) 62,000
Samarkand 366,000
Saran (1987 E) 64,000
Saransk 312,000
Sarapul 111,000
Saratov (★ 1,155,000) 905,000
Satka (1974 E) 44,000
Segezha (1974 E) 33,000
Semipalatinsk 334,000
Serdobsk (1974 E) 37,000
Serov 104,000
Serpukhov 144,000
Sevastopol 356,000
Severodonetsk (★★ Lisichansk) 131,000
Severodvinsk (Molotovsk) 249,000
Severomorsk (1987 E) 55,000
Shadrinsk (1987 E) 87,000
Shakhtersk (★★ Torez) (1987 E) 73,000
Shakhtinsk (1987 E) 62,000
Shakhty 224,000
Shchekino (1987 E) 70,000
Shchelkovo (★ Moscow) 109,000
Shchuchinsk (1987 E) 53,000
Shebekino (1974 E) 36,000
Sheki (Nukha) (1987 E) 54,000
Shepetovka (1974 E) 42,000
Shevchenko 159,000
Shostka (1987 E) 87,000
Shumerlya (1974 E) 35,000
Shuya (1987 E) 72,000
Šiauliai 145,000
Sibay (1974 E) 40,000
Simferopol 344,000
Slantsy (1974 E) 42,000
Slavyansk (★★ Kramatorsk) 135,000
Slavyansk-na-Kubani (1987 E) 57,000
Slobodskoy (1974 E) 36,000
Slutsk (1987 E) 55,000
Smela (1987 E) 76,000
Smolensk 341,000
Snezhnoye (★ Torez) (1987 E) 68,000
Sochi 337,000
Sokol (1974 E) 48,000
Soligorsk (1987 E) 92,000
Solikamsk 110,000
Solnechnogorsk (★ Moscow) (1987 E) 53,000
Solntsevo (★ Moscow) (1984 E) 62,000
Sosnovyy Bor (1987 E) 56,000
Sovetsk (Tilsit) (1974 E) 40,000
Spassk-Dalniy (1987 E) 60,000
Stakhanov (Kadiyevka) (★ 610,000) 112,000
Staraya Russa (1974 E) 37,000
Staryy Oskol 174,000
Stavropol 318,000
Sterlitamak 248,000
Stryy (1987 E) 63,000
Stupino (1987 E) 73,000
Sukhumi 121,000
Sumgait (★ Baku) 231,000
Sumy 291,000
Surgut 248,000
Suzdal (1959 C) 9,000
Sverdlovsk (★ 1,620,000) 1,367,000
Sverdlovsk (1987 E) 84,000
Svetlogorsk (1987 E) 68,000
Svetlovodsk (Kremges) (1987 E) 55,000
Svobodnyy (1987 E) 78,000
Syktyvkar 233,000
Syzran 174,000
Taganrog 291,000
Taldy-Kurgan 119,000
Talgar (1974 E) 35,000
Tallinn 482,000
Talnakh (1987 E) 54,000
Tambov 305,000
Tartu 114,000
Tashauz 112,000
Tashkent (★ 2,325,000) 2,073,000
Tatarsk (1974 E) 31,000
Tavda (1974 E) 47,000
Tayshet (1974 E) 35,000
Tbilisi (★ 1,460,000) 1,260,000
Temirtau 212,000
Termez (1987 E) 72,000
Ternopol 205,000
Teykovo (1974 E) 42,000
Tikhoretsk (1987 E) 67,000
Tikhvin (1987 E) 70,000
Tiraspol 182,000
Tobolsk (1987 E) 82,000
Tokmak (1987 E) 71,000
Tokmak (1974 E) 39,000
Tolyatti (Stavropol) 630,000
Tomsk 502,000
Topki (1974 E) 30,000
Torez (Chistyakovo) (★ 290,000) (1987 E) 88,000
Torzhok (1987 E) 51,000
Troitsk (1987 E) 91,000
Tselinograd (Akmolinsk) 277,000
Tskhinvali (1975 E) 34,000
Tuapse (1987 E) 64,000
Tula (★ 640,000) 540,000
Tulun (1987 E) 56,000
Turkestan (1987 E) 77,000
Tuymazy (1987 E) 54,000
Tynda (1987 E) 61,000
Tyumen 477,000
Ufa (★ 1,100,000) 1,083,000
Uglich (1974 E) 37,000
Ukhta 111,000
Ulan-Ude 353,000
Ulyanovsk 625,000
Uman (1987 E) 89,000
Uralsk 200,000
Ura-Tyube (1974 E) 36,000
Urgench 128,000
Uryupinsk (1974 E) 39,000
Usolye-Sibirskoye 107,000
Ussuriysk 162,000
Ust-Ilimsk 109,000
Ust-Kamenogorsk 324,000
Ust-Kut (1987 E) 58,000
Ust'-Labinsk (1974 E) 38,000
Uzhgorod 117,000
Uzlovaya (1987 E) 63,000
Valuyki (1974 E) 30,000
Velikiye Luki 114,000
Velikiy Ustyug (1974 E) 38,000
Ventspils (1987 E) 52,000
Verkhniy Ufaley (1974 E) 38,000
Verkhnyaya Pyshma (★ Sverdlovsk) (1974 E) 40,000
Verkhnyaya Salda (1987 E) 56,000
Vichuga (1987 E) 51,000
Vidnoye (1974 E) 40,000
Vilnius 582,000
Vinnitsa 374,000
Vitebsk 350,000
Vladimir 350,000
Vladivostok 648,000
Volgodonsk 176,000
Volgograd (Stalingrad) (★ 1,360,000) 999,000
Volkhov (1987 E) 51,000
Vologda 283,000
Volsk (1987 E) 66,000
Volzhsk (1987 E) 60,000
Volzhskiy (★ Volgograd) 269,000
Vorkuta 116,000
Voronezh 887,000
Voroshilovgrad (Lugansk) 497,000
Voskresensk (1987 E) 80,000
Votkinsk 103,000
Voznesensk (1974 E) 39,000
Vyatskiye Polyany (1974 E) 35,000
Vyazma (1987 E) 57,000
Vyazniki (1974 E) 44,000
Vyborg (1987 E) 81,000
Vyksa (1987 E) 60,000
Vyshniy Volochek (1987 E) 70,000
Yakutsk 187,000
Yalta (1987 E) 89,000
Yangiyul (1987 E) 71,000
Yaroslavl 633,000
Yartsevo (1974 E) 39,000
Yasinovataya (1974 E) 39,000
Yefremov (1987 E) 58,000
Yegoryevsk (1987 E) 73,000
Yelabuga (1974 E) 35,000
Yelets 120,000
Yemanzhelinsk (1974 E) 34,000
Yenakiyevo (★★ Gorlovka) 121,000
Yerevan (★ 1,315,000) 1,199,000
Yermak (1974 E) 40,000
Yessentuki (1987 E) 84,000
Yevpatoriya 108,000
Yeysk (1987 E) 77,000
Yoshkar-Ola 242,000
Yurga (1987 E) 92,000
Yuzhno-Sakhalinsk 157,000
Yuzhno-Uralsk (1974 E) 37,000
Zagorsk 115,000
Zaporozhye 884,000
Zavolzhye (1974 E) 38,000
Zelenograd (★ Moscow) 158,000
Zel'onodol'sk (1987 E) 93,000
Zhanatas (1987 E) 53,000
Zheleznodorozhnyy (★ Moscow) (1987 E) 90,000
Zheleznogorsk (1987 E) 81,000
Zheltyye Vody (1987 E) 61,000
Zhigulevsk (1977 E) 50,000
Zhitomir 292,000
Zhlobin (1987 E) 52,000
Zhmerinka (1974 E) 38,000
Zhodino (1987 E) 51,000
Zhukovskiy 101,000
Zima (1987 E) 51,000
Zlatoust 208,000
Zugdidi (1974 E) 41,000
Zyryanovsk (1987 E) 55,000

***Republics***

Armenia 3,283,000
Azerbaijan S.S.R. 7,029,000
Byelorussia (White Russia) 10,200,000
Estonia 1,573,000
Georgia 5,449,000
Kazakh S.S.R. 16,538,000
Kirghiz S.S.R. 4,291,000
Latvia 2,681,000
Lithuania 3,690,000
Moldavia 4,341,000
Russian Soviet Federative Socialist Republic 147,386,000
Tajik S.S.R. 5,112,000
Turkmen S.S.R. 3,534,000
Ukraine 51,704,000
Uzbek S.S.R. 19,906,000

## SPAIN / España

1987 E 38,606,576

***Cities and Towns***

Águilas 23,162
Albacete 125,764
Alcalá [de Guadaira] 50,567
Alcalá de Henares (★ Madrid) 145,320
Alcalá la Real (▲ 20,410) 12,184
Alcantarilla 27,454
Alcázar de San Juan 26,302
Alcira 40,234
Alcobendas (★ Madrid) 71,542
Alcorcón (★ Madrid) 138,448
Alcoy 66,312
Algeciras 97,601
Algemesí 25,195
Algorta (Guecho) (▲ 78,672) 37,800
Alicante 258,004
Almadén (1981 C) 9,521
Almendralejo 25,137
Almería 154,911
Andújar (▲ 36,027) 31,400
Antequera (▲ 40,844) 31,900
Aranjuez 37,079
Arcos de la Frontera (▲ 26,915) 19,300
Arizgoiti (Basauri) (★ Bilbao) 45,600
Arrecife, Canary Is. 33,272
Ávila 44,221
Avilés (★ 131,000) 86,858
Badajoz (▲ 120,240) 104,500
Badalona (★ Barcelona) 224,233
Baracaldo (★ Bilbao) 114,090
Barcelona (★ 4,040,000) 1,703,744
Baza 20,682
Benidorm 34,831
Bilbao (★ 985,000) 382,413
Burgos 158,857
Burjasot (★ Valencia) 35,024
Burriana 25,369
Cabra (▲ 20,181) 17,900
Cáceres 69,770
Cádiz (★ 240,000) 156,113
Camas (★ Sevilla) 25,427
Carmona 24,029
Cartagena (▲ 169,036) 68,500
Castellón de la Plana 128,664
Cerdanyola de Vallés (★ Barcelona) 42,700
Chiclana [de la Frontera] 42,226
Cieza 30,419
Ciudad Real 55,072
Colmenar Viejo 30,328
Córdoba 298,372
Cornellá (★ Barcelona) 86,971
Coslada (★ Madrid) 65,598
Cuenca 41,407
Daimiel (1981 C) 16,260
Don Benito (▲ 28,829) 24,100
Dos Hermanas (▲ 67,330) 59,600
Écija (▲ 35,434) 30,600
Éibar 34,545
Elche (▲ 177,629) 156,000
Elda 56,189
El Ferrol [del Caudillo] (★ 129,000) 86,329
El Puerto de Santa María (▲ 61,032) 48,900
Esplugas Llobregat (★ Barcelona) 47,598
Figueras 32,035
Fuenlabrada (★ Madrid) 122,752
Gandía (▲ 51,092) 44,700
Gavá (★ Barcelona) 33,076
Gerona (▲ 67,447) 30,200
Getafe (★ Madrid) 132,786
Gijón 258,759
Granada 256,800
Granollers (★ Barcelona) 48,380
Guadalajara 59,492
Guadix (▲ 20,286) 16,500
Guernica y Luno (▲ 17,836) (1981 C) 12,214
Hellín (▲ 24,487) 19,000
Hospitalet (★ Barcelona) 277,688
Huelva 135,938
Huesca 40,949
Ibiza 27,685
Igualada 31,107
Irún 54,301

C Census. E Official estimate. UE Unofficial estimate.
• Largest city in country.

★ Population or designation of metropolitan area, including suburbs (see headnote).
▲ Population of an entire municipality, commune, or district, including rural area.

Jaén 103,698
Játiva 24,237
Jerez de la Frontera (▲ 179,349) 153,100
La Coruña 242,437
La Línea 59,260
La Orotava, Canary Is. (▲ 35,528) 11,500
Las Palmas de Gran Canaria, Canary Is. (▲ 358,272) 312,000
Leganés (★ Madrid) 167,748
León (★ 159,000) 135,521
Lérida (▲ 108,207) 90,200
Linares (▲ 57,401) 57,526
Logroño 116,273
Loja (▲ 21,883) 14,000
Lorca (▲ 65,458) 26,300
Lucena (▲ 31,243) 25,800
Lugo (▲ 77,043) 67,200
• MADRID (★ 4,650,000) 3,100,507
Mahón 22,028
Málaga 566,330
Manacor 24,397
Manresa 65,285
Marbella (▲ 75,351) 44,900
Martos (▲ 22,036) 16,800
Mataró 100,189
Mérida 52,225
Mieres (▲ 57,532) 26,500
Miranda de Ebro 35,892
Mislata (★ Valencia) 35,815
Mollet 38,568
Morón de la Frontera 28,653
Móstoles (★ Madrid) 176,993
Motril (▲ 44,882) 37,700
Murcia (▲ 305,278) 145,600
Olot (▲ 24,892) 18,573
Onteniente 29,162
Orense 103,397
Orihuela (▲ 45,938) 20,300
Oviedo (▲ 186,363) 165,600
Palencia 75,951
Palma [de Mallorca] (▲ 306,840) 242,900
Pamplona 178,666
Parla (★ Madrid) 64,546
Peñarroya-Pueblonuevo (1981 C) 13,219
Plasencia 32,902
Ponferrada (▲ 59,399) 33,600
Pontevedra (▲ 67,314) 40,000
Portugalete (★ Bilbao) 58,117
Prat de Llobregat (★ Barcelona) 63,411
Priego [de Córdoba] (▲ 20,788) 14,200
Puente-Genil (▲ 26,961) 24,000
Puerto de la Cruz, Canary Is. 25,418
Puertollano 51,755
Rentería (★ San Sebastián) 43,653
Reus 81,816
Ronda (▲ 32,556) 25,600
Rota (▲ 21,583) 18,900
Rubí (★ Barcelona) 47,069
Sabadell (★ Barcelona) 187,506
Sagunto (▲ 55,957) 19,400
Salamanca 155,612
Sama [de Langreo] (▲ 53,889) 9,800
San Adrián de Besós (★ Barcelona) 34,673
San Baudilio de Llobregat (★ Barcelona) 76,008
San Cristóbal de la Laguna, Canary Is. (▲ 107,593) 25,000
San Felíu de Llobregat 37,626
San Fernando (★★ Cádiz) 80,791
Sanlúcar [de Barrameda] (▲ 53,566) 37,300
San Sebastián (★ 285,000) 176,586
San Sebastián de los Reyes (★ Madrid) 50,531
Santa Coloma [de Gramanet] (★ Barcelona) 135,310
Santa Cruz de Tenerife, Canary Is. 211,209
Santander (▲ 187,222) 163,700
Santiago [de Compostela] (▲ 86,818) 67,800
Santurce-Antiguo (★ Bilbao) 52,480
Segovia 53,849
Sestao (★ Bilbao) 38,217
Sevilla (Seville) (★ 945,000) 655,435
Soria 31,507
Sueca 24,400
Talavera de la Reina 67,680
Tarragona (▲ 107,356) 62,200
Tarrasa (★ Barcelona) 160,245
Telde, Canary Is. (▲ 75,106) 18,300
Teruel 27,475
Toledo 58,297
Tolosa (▲ 18,894) (1981 C) 13,015
Tomelloso 28,344
Torrejón de Ardoz (★ Madrid) 81,658
Torrelavega (▲ 58,885) 28,600
Torrente (★ Valencia) 54,739
Tortosa (▲ 28,862) 19,300
Totana (▲ 18,394) (1981 C) 15,420
Úbeda 30,720
Utrera (▲ 41,021) 35,500
Valdepeñas 25,337
Valencia (★ 1,270,000) 732,491
Valladolid 329,206
Vall de Uxó 27,565
Vélez-Málaga (▲ 51,132) 31,600
Vich 28,609
Vigo (▲ 262,560) 173,800
Viladecáns 45,423
Villanueva y Geltrú 45,258
Villarreal [de los Infantes] (▲ 37,035) 33,100
Villarrobledo 20,829
Villena 30,428
Vitoria 200,742
Zamora 60,708
Zaragoza (Saragossa) 575,317

*Regions*

Andalusia 6,842,464
Aragón 1,185,840
Asturias 1,115,016
Baleares 700,307
Canarias (Canary Is.) 1,479,549
Cantabria 524,844
Castilla-La Mancha 1,680,780
Castilla-León 2,592,287
Cataluña 6,000,522
Extremadura 1,092,398
Galicia 2,858,130
La Rioja 260,964
Madrid 4,846,100
Murcia 1,013,647
Navarra 516,872
País Vasco 2,142,631
Palencia 189,898
Valencia 3,754,225

*Provinces*

Alava 268,863
Albacete 346,793
Alicante 1,226,657
Almería 446,200
Asturias 1,115,016
Ávila 182,634
Badajoz 670,051
Baleares 700,307
Barcelona 4,629,176
Burgos 359,711
Cáceres 422,347
Cádiz 1,052,419
Cantabria (Santander) 524,844
Castellón 439,266
Ciudad Real 485,639
Córdoba 753,102
Cuenca 213,812
Gerona 492,028
Granada 788,187
Guadalajara 146,669
Guipúzcoa 691,410
Huelva 436,813
Huesca 210,257
Jaén 650,844
La Coruña 1,116,398
La Rioja 260,964
Las Palmas 761,793
León 532,890
Lérida 352,350
Lugo 406,123
Madrid 4,846,100
Málaga 1,160,739
Murcia 1,013,647
Navarra 516,872
Orense 432,714
Pontevedra 902,895
Salamanca 362,477
Santa Cruz de Tenerife 717,756
Segovia 151,036
Sevilla 1,554,160
Soria 97,915
Tarragona 526,968
Teruel 149,423
Toledo 487,867
Valencia 2,088,302
Valladolid 493,486
Vizcaya 1,182,358
Zamora 222,240
Zaragosa 826,160

## SPANISH NORTH AFRICA / Plazas de Soberanía en el Norte de África

1987 E 118,380

*Cities and Towns*

• Ceuta 65,141
Melilla 53,239

## SRI LANKA

1985 E 15,837,000

*Cities and Towns*

Anuradhapura 46,000
Badulla 44,000
Battaramulla (★ Colombo) (1981 C) 56,535
Batticaloa 47,000
• COLOMBO (★ 2,050,000) 664,000
Dalugama (★ Colombo) (1981 C) 47,723
Dehiwala-Mount Lavinia (★ Colombo) 188,000
Galle 102,000
Jaffna 138,000
Kalutara 47,000
Kandy 125,000
Kegalla (1981 C) 15,000
Kelaniya (★ Colombo) (1981 C) 36,738
Kolonnawa (★ Colombo) (1981 C) 41,005
Kotikawatta (★ Colombo) (1981 C) 48,262
Kotte (★ Colombo) 102,000
Kurunegala 44,000
Maharagama (★ Colombo) (1981 C) 49,765
Matale 57,000
Matara (1981 C) 39,000
Moratuwa (★ Colombo) 138,000
Negombo 76,000
Puttalam (1981 C) 21,000
Ratnapura 51,000
Trincomalee 51,000

## SUDAN / As Sūdān

1983 C 20,564,364

*Cities and Towns*

Al Junaynah (1973 C) 35,424
Al Qaḍārif (1973 C) 66,465
An Nuhūd (1973 C) 26,002
'Aṭbarah 73,000
Barbar (1973 C) 11,303
El Fasher (1973 C) 51,932
El Obeid (Al Ubayyiḍ) 140,000
Jūbā (1973 C) 56,737
Kassalā 143,000
• KHARTOUM (AL KHARṬŪM) (★ 1,450,000) 476,218
Khartoum North (Al Kharṭūm Baḥrī) (★ Khartoum) 341,146
Kūstī (1973 C) 65,257
Malakāl (1973 C) 34,898
Nyala (1973 C) 59,852
Omdurman (Umm Durmān) (★★ Khartoum) 526,287
Port Sudan (Būr Sūdān) 206,727
Sannār (1973 C) 28,546
Sinjah (1973 C) 19,452
Ṭawkar (1973 C) 13,394
Umm Ruwābah (1973 C) 19,713
Wad Madanī 141,000
Wāw (1973 C) 52,752

## SURINAME

1988 E 392,000

*Cities and Towns*

• PARAMARIBO 241,000
Wanica 55,000

## SWAZILAND

1986 C 712,131

*Cities and Towns*

LOBAMBA
Manzini (★ 30,000) 18,084
• MBABANE 38,290

## SWEDEN / Sverige

1988 E 8,414,083

*Cities and Towns*

Alingsås (▲ 32,051) 20,900
Ängelholm (▲ 32,443) 18,600
Arvika (▲ 26,532) 13,600
Avesta (▲ 24,731) 17,300
Boden (▲ 29,117) 18,800
Bollnäs (▲ 27,659) 13,000
Borås 100,395
Borlänge 45,990
Enköping (▲ 33,290) 18,900
Eskilstuna 88,508
Eslöv (▲ 26,566) 13,900
Falkenberg (▲ 36,095) 16,100
Falun (▲ 52,202) 33,500
Gällivare (▲ 22,908) 7,600
Gävle (▲ 87,474) 67,000
Göteborg (Gothenburg) (★ 710,894) 431,521
Halmstad (▲ 77,942) 50,000
Härnösand (▲ 27,252) 19,200
Hässleholm (▲ 48,493) 16,000
Helsingborg 106,982
Huddinge (★ Stockholm) 71,910
Hudiksvall (▲ 37,568) 14,800
Järfälla (★ Stockholm) 56,563
Jönköping 108,962
Kalmar (▲ 54,915) 31,000
Karlshamn (▲ 31,429) 17,700
Karlskoga 34,395
Karlskrona (▲ 58,650) 31,700
Karlstad 74,892
Katrineholm (▲ 31,884) 21,600
Kiruna 26,551
Köping (▲ 26,280) 19,100
Kristianstad (▲ 70,180) 31,200
Kristinehamn (▲ 26,061) 19,700
Kungsbacka (▲ 50,804) 14,500
Landskrona 35,371
Lidingö (★ Stockholm) 38,818
Lidköping (▲ 35,082) 21,400
Lindesberg (▲ 24,446) 8,300
Linköping 118,602
Ljungby (▲ 27,199) 13,500
Ludvika (▲ 29,414) 16,400
Luleå 66,719
Lund (★★ Malm320) 84,342
Malmö (★ 445,000) 230,838
Mariestad (▲ 24,465) 15,700
Mjölby (▲ 25,828) 12,300
Mölndal (★ Göteborg) 50,549
Motala (▲ 41,444) 29,400
Nacka (★ Stockholm) 61,084
Nässjö (▲ 30,739) 17,000
Norrköping 119,001
Norrtälje (▲ 43,140) 13,700
Nyköping (▲ 64,428) 28,300
Örebro 119,066
Örnsköldsvik (▲ 59,248) 29,400
Oskarshamn (▲ 27,351) 18,600
Östersund (▲ 56,914) 41,200
Partille (★ Göteborg) 29,604
Piteå (▲ 38,828) 16,300
Ronneby (▲ 28,988) 11,600
Sandviken 39,876
Skellefteå (▲ 74,091) 30,000
Skövde (▲ 46,438) 30,000
Söderhamn (▲ 29,709) 13,400
Södertälje (★ Stockholm) 80,263
Sollefteå (▲ 25,184) 9,200
Sollentuna (★ Stockholm) 49,757
Solna (★ Stockholm) 50,450
• STOCKHOLM (★ 1,449,972) 666,810
Sundbyberg (★ Stockholm) 30,569
Sundsvall (▲ 92,721) 50,200
Täby (★ Stockholm) 55,661
Trelleborg (▲ 34,362) 22,200
Trollhättan 49,914
Tumba (Botkyrka) (★ Stockholm) 67,536
Uddevalla (▲ 46,257) 30,500
Umeå (▲ 86,816) 56,600
Upplands Väsby (★ Stockholm) 35,023
Uppsala 159,962
Vänersborg (▲ 35,948) 20,700
Varberg (▲ 47,040) 21,100
Värnamo (▲ 30,894) 23,800
Västerås 117,563
Västervik (▲ 39,558) 20,800
Växjö (★ 67,350) 44,500
Vetlanda (▲ 27,727) 12,100
Visby (Gotland) (▲ 56,269) 20,100

*Counties*

Älvsborg 430,129
Blekinge 149,600
Gävleborg 286,907
Göteborg och Bohus 726,325
Gotland 56,269
Halland 244,377
Jämtland 133,389
Jönköping 302,475
Kalmar 237,356
Kopparberg 283,330
Kristianstad 281,907
Kronoberg 174,116
Malmöhus 757,643
Norrbotten 260,833
Örebro 269,341
Östergötland 395,580
Skaraborg 270,847
Södermanland 250,073
Stockholm 1,606,157
Uppsala 257,739
Värmland 279,402
Västerbotten 245,703
Västernorrland 260,332
Västmanland 254,253

*Historic Provinces*

Ångermanland 155,632
Blekinge 149,600
Bohuslän 237,749
Dalarna 283,845
Dalsland 55,769
Gästrikland 145,476
Gotland 56,269
Halland 248,567
Hälsingland 142,344
Härjedalen 11,430
Jämtland 115,779
Lappland 114,348
Medelpad 123,855
Närke 173,174
Norrbotten 192,638
Öland 23,924
Östergötland 392,674
Skåne 1,037,834
Småland 699,690
Södermanland 982,985
Uppland 1,152,482
Värmland 324,131
Västerbotten 185,147
Västergötland 1,125,461
Västmanland 283,280

## SWITZERLAND / Schweiz / Suisse / Svizzera

1987 E 6,523,413

*Cities and Towns*

Aarau (★ 57,900) 15,750
Adliswil (★ Zürich) 15,848
Allschwil (★ Basel) 18,339
Altdorf 8,163
Appenzell 4,914
Arbon (★ 41,100) 12,292
Arosa 2,399
Baar (★ Zug) 15,481
Baden (★ 70,700) 14,058
Basel (Bâle) (★ 575,000) 173,160
Bellinzona (★ 36,500) 16,886
BERN (BERNE) (★ 298,800) 137,134
Biel (Bienne) (★ 81,900) 51,341
Bülach 13,292
Burgdorf 15,072
Château d'Oex 2,797
Chiasso (★ 38,600) 8,687
Chur (Coire) (★ 42,500) 30,740
Davos 10,377
Delémont 11,298
Einsiedeln 9,973
Emmen (★ Luzern) 23,451
Frauenfeld 18,944
Fribourg (Freiburg) (★ 56,800) 33,935
Geneva (Genève) (★ 460,000) 160,645
Glarus 5,593
Grenchen (★ 23,800) 15,705
Grindelwald 3,560
Herisau (★★ Sankt Gallen) 14,947
Illnau [-Effretikon] (★ Zürich) 14,624
Interlaken 4,899
Köniz (★ Bern) 35,664
Kreuzlingen (★ 22,200) 16,149
Kriens (★ Luzern) 21,327
La Chaux-de-Fonds 35,726
Langenthal 13,868
Lausanne (★ 259,900) 124,206
Lauterbrunnen 2,829
Le Locle 10,953
Liestal (★ Basel) 12,161
Locarno (★ 42,350) 14,473
Lugano (★ 94,800) 27,462
Luzern (Lucerne) (★ 159,500) 59,904
Martigny 12,359
Meiringen 4,000
Monthey 11,809
Montreux (★★ Vevey) 18,970
Morges (★ Lausanne) 13,565
Neuchâtel (Neuenburg) (★ 65,900) 32,650
Nyon 13,587
Olten (★ 43,450) 17,800
Riehen (★ Basel) 20,054
Rorschach (★★ Arbon) 9,325
Sankt Gallen (Saint-Gall) (★ 125,000) 72,910
Sankt Moritz 5,335
Sarnen 7,980
Schaffhausen (★ 53,000) 33,826
Schwyz 12,350
Sierre 13,063
Sion 23,504
Solothurn (Soleure) (★ 56,800) 15,499
Stans 5,969
Thun (Thoune) (★ 77,200) 37,074
Uster 25,227
Vernier (★ Genève) 27,426
Vevey (★ 63,100) 15,021
Wädenswil 19,084
Wettingen (★ Baden) 17,799
Wil (★ 23,200) 16,124
Winterthur (★ 107,400) 84,548
Wohlen 11,553
Yverdon (Iferten) (★ 21,500) 21,004
Zermatt 3,929
Zug (Zoug) (★ 67,100) 21,569
• Zürich (★ 860,000) 349,549

*Cantons*

Aargau 472,685
Appenzell Ausser-Rhoden 49,342
Appenzell Inner-Rhoden 13,137
Basel-Land 225,836
Basel-Stadt 194,340
Bern (Berne) 925,463
Fribourg (Freiburg) 194,645
Genève 363,550
Glarus 36,580
Graubünden (Grisons) 166,494
Jura 64,711
Luzern (Lucerne) 306,132
Neuchâtel 156,216
Nidwalden 31,041
Obwalden 27,594
Sankt Gallen 403,931
Schaffhausen 69,781
Schwyz 103,358
Solothurn 219,458
Thurgau 192,439
Ticino (Tessin) 277,220
Uri 33,456
Valais (Wallis) 232,550
Vaud (Waadt) 550,336
Zug (Zoug) 81,634
Zürich 1,131,484

## SYRIA / As Sūrīyah

1987 E 10,969,000

*Cities and Towns*

Aleppo (Ḥalab) 1,216,000
Al Ḥasakah (1981 C) 73,426

C Census. E Official estimate. UE Unofficial estimate.
• Largest city in country.
★ Population or designation of metropolitan area, including suburbs (see headnote).
▲ Population of an entire municipality, commune, or district, including rural area.

# World Populations

Al Qāmishlī (1988 E) ... 126,236
Ar Raqqah ... 126,700
As Suwaydā' (1981 C) ...43,414
• DAMASCUS (DIMASHQ)
(★ 1,850,000) (1988 E) ... 1,326,000
Dar'ā (1981 C) ...49,534
Dārayyā (1988 E) ...53,204
Dayr az Zawr (1986 E) ... 106,500
Dūmā (★ Damascus)
(1988 E) ...66,130
Hajar Aswad (1988 E) ...36,820
Hamāh ... 214,000
Hims (Homs) ... 431,000
Idlib (1981 C) ...51,682
Jaramānah (★ Damascus)
(1988 E) ...96,681
Kābir as Saghīr (1988 E) ...47,728
Latakia (Al Lādhiqīyah) ... 241,000
Madīnat ath Thawrah
(1988 E) ...58,151
Manbij (1988 E) ...36,085
Salamīyah (1988 E) ...46,844
Tartūs (1981 C) ...52,589

## TAIWAN / T'aiwan

1988 E ... 19,672,612

### Cities and Towns

Changhua (▲ 206,603) ... 158,400
Chiai ... 254,875
Chilung (Keelung) ... 348,541
Chungho (★ T'aipei) ... 343,389
Chungli (Chunli) ... 247,639
Chutung ... 104,797
Fengshan
(Kaohsiunghsien)
(★ Kaohsiung) ... 276,259
Fengyüan
(T'aichunghsien)
(▲ 144,434) ... 115,300
Hsichih (★ T'aipei)
(1980 C) ...70,031
Hsinchu ... 309,899
Hsinchuang (★ T'aipei) ... 259,001
Hsintien (★ T'aipei) ... 205,094
Hualien ... 106,658
Ilan (▲ 81,751) (1980 C) ...70,900
Kangshan (1980 C) ...78,049
Kaohsiung (★ 1,845,000) ... 1,342,797
Lotung (1980 C) ...57,925
Lukang (Luchiang)
(1980 C) ...72,019
Makung (▲ 55,678)
(1980 C) ... 23,000
Miaoli (1980 C) ...81,500
Nant'ou (1980 C) ...84,038
Panch'iao (T'aipeihsien)
(★ T'aipei) ... 506,220
P'ingchen (★ T'aipei) ... 134,925
P'ingtung (▲ 204,990) ... 167,600
Quemoy (Chinmen)
(▲ 51,958) (1980 C) ...14,000
Sanch'ung (★ T'aipei) ... 362,171
Shulin (★ T'aipei)
(1980 C) ...75,700
Tach'i (1980 C) ...67,209
T'aichung ... 715,107
T'ainan ... 656,927
• T'AIPEI (★ 6,130,000) ... 2,637,100
T'aitung (★ 109,358) ...79,800
Tanshui (★ T'aipei)
(1980 C) ... 28,000
T'aoyüan ... 220,255
T'oufen (1980 C) ...66,536
T'uch'eng (★ T'aipei) ...70,500
Yangmei (1980 C) ...84,353
Yüanlin (▲ 116,936) ...51,300
Yungho (★ T'aipei) ... 242,252
Yungkang (▲ 114,904) ...59,600

## TANZANIA

1984 E ... 21,062,000

### Cities and Towns

Arusha ...69,000
• DAR ES SALAAM ... 1,300,000
Dodoma ...54,000
Iringa ...67,000
Kigoma (1978 C) ...50,044
Mbeya ...93,000
Morogoro ...72,000
Moshi ...62,000
Mtwara (1978 C) ...48,510
Musoma (1978 C) ...32,658
Mwanza (1978 C) ... 110,611
Singida (1987 C) ...29,252
Tabora ...87,000
Tanga ... 121,000
Ujiji (1967 C) ...21,369
Zanzibar (1980 E) ... 119,000

## THAILAND / Prathet Thai

1986 E ...52,969,204

### Cities and Towns

• BANGKOK (KRUNG
THEP) (★ 6,450,000) ... 5,468,915
Ban Phai ...36,393
Ban Pong ...24,749
Buri Ram ...29,402
Chachoengsao ...43,117

Chanthaburi ...37,885
Chiang Mai ... 157,843
Chiang Rai ...37,847
Chon Buri ...48,203
Hat Yai (Ban Hat Yai) ... 131,302
Hua Hin ...31,889
Kalasin ...32,436
Kanchanaburi ...33,616
Khon Kaen ... 130,773
Lampang ...47,493
Lop Buri ...39,447
Maha Sarakham ...37,547
Nakhon Pathom ...45,284
Nakhon Phanom ...32,700
Nakhon Ratchasima ... 206,758
Nakhon Sawan ... 101,498
Nakhon Si Thammarat ...72,558
Narathiwat ...38,066
Nong Khai ...24,024
Nonthaburi (★ Bangkok) ...40,502
Pattani ...38,775
Pattaya ...49,548
Phatthalung ...33,075
Phayao ...24,457
Phetchabun ...27,955
Phetchaburi ...34,268
Phitsanulok ...75,804
Phra Nakhon Si
Ayutthaya ...60,511
Phuket ...47,430
Ratchaburi ...43,239
Rayong ...42,594
Roi Et ...33,994
Sakon Nakhon ...23,454
Samut Prakan
(★ Bangkok) ...69,218
Samut Sakhon ...53,274
Samut Songkhram ...35,477
Saraburi ...57,364
Songkhla ...84,738
Suphan Buri ...25,581
Surat Thani (Ban Don) ...41,473
Surin ...40,044
Trang ...47,065
Ubon Ratchathani ... 100,145
Udon Thani ...82,706
Uttaradit ...32,884
Warin Chamrap ...30,721
Yala ...64,695

## TOGO

1981 C ... 2,702,945

### Cities and Towns

Atakpamé ...24,377
Lama-Kara ...28,480
• LOMÉ (1984 E) ... 400,000
Palimé ...27,669
Sokodé ...48,098
Tsévié ...20,247

## TOKELAU

1986 C ... 1,690

## TONGA

1986 C ...94,535

### Cities and Towns

• NUKU'ALOFA ...21,265

## TRANSKEI

1982 E ... 2,400,000

### Cities and Towns

• UMTATA (1978 E) ...30,000

## TRINIDAD AND TOBAGO

1980 C ... 1,055,763

### Cities and Towns

Arima ...24,112
Barataria ...14,983
Chaguanas ...6,112
Morvant ...25,416
Point Fortin ...6,538
• PORT OF SPAIN
(★ 370,000) (1982 E) ...59,649
Princes Town ...8,288
San Fernando (★ 75,000) ...33,395
Sangre Grande ...8,948
Scarborough ...6,057
Tunapuna (★ Port of
Spain) ...10,251

## TUNISIA / Tunisie / Tunis

1984 C ... 6,975,450

### Cities and Towns

Ariana (★ Tunis) ...98,655
Bardo (★ Tunis) ...65,669
Béja ...46,708
Ben Arous (★ Tunis) ...52,105
Bizerte ...94,509
El Kairouan ...72,254
El Kasserine ...47,606
El Kef ...34,519
El Mahdia ...36,828
Gabès ...92,258
Gafsa ...60,970
Hammamet ...30,441
Hammam Lif (★ Tunis) ...47,009
Houmt Essouk (Djerba) ...92,269
Jendouba (Souk el Arba) ...23,249
Kalaa Kebira
(★★ Sousse) ...31,406
La Goulette (★ Tunis) ...61,609
La Marsa (★ Tunis) ...38,319
Manouba (★ Tunis) ...31,758
Médenine ...26,602
Menzel Bourguiba ...51,399
Monastir ...35,546
Msaken ...41,217
Nabeul (★ 75,000) ...39,531
Rades (★ Tunis) ...30,218
Sfax (★ 310,000) ... 231,911
Sousse (★ 160,000) ...83,509
Tataouine ...30,371
• TUNIS (★ 1,225,000) ... 596,654
Zarzis ...49,063

## TURKEY / Türkiye

1985 C ...50,664,458

### Cities and Towns

Adana ... 777,554
Adapazarı ... 152,291
Afyonkarahisar ...87,033
Ağrı (Karaköse) ...54,942
Akhisar ...68,553
Aksaray ...81,056
Akşehir ...45,320
Alaşehir ...29,484
Amasya ...53,431
ANKARA (★ 2,400,000) ... 2,235,035
Antakya (Antioch) ... 107,821
Antalya ... 261,114
Artvin ...18,720
Aydın ...90,449
Bafra ...53,482
Balıkesir ... 149,989
Bandırma ...70,137
Batman ... 110,036
Bayburt ...28,068
Bergama ...38,849
Bilecik ...18,506
Bingöl ...34,024
Bitlis ...36,073
Bolu ...50,288
Bolvadin ...35,509
Burdur ...53,995
Bursa ... 612,510
Çanakkale ...48,059
Çankırı ...41,420
Çarşamba ...34,519
Ceyhan ...72,624
Çorlu ...59,107
Çorum ...96,725
Denizli ... 169,130
Diyarbakır ... 305,940
Doğubeyazıt ...31,134
Dörtyol ...30,722
Düzce ...45,077
Düziçi ...35,750
Edirne ...86,909
Edremit ...30,159
Elazığ ... 182,296
Elbistan ...48,756
Erciş ...36,582
Ereğli, Konya prov. ...68,749
Ereğli, Zonguldak prov. ...54,837
Ergani ...33,209
Erzincan ...82,616
Erzurum ... 246,053
Eskişehir ... 366,765
Gaziantep ... 478,635
Gebze (★ İstanbul) ...92,592
Gelibolu (Gallipoli) ...16,715
Gemlik ...36,693
Giresun ...55,887
Gölcük ...56,087
Gümüşhane ...22,067
Hakkâri ...20,754
içel (Mersin) ... 314,350
İnegöl ...54,569
İskenderun (Alexandretta) ... 152,096
Isparta ... 101,215
• İstanbul (★ 5,750,000) ... 5,475,982
İzmir (Smyrna)
(★ 1,550,000) ... 1,489,772
İzmit (Kocaeli) ... 233,338
Kadirli ...47,609
Kahramanmaraş (Maraş) ... 210,371
Karabük ...94,818
Karaman ...64,735
Kars ...69,293
Kastamonu ...46,986
Kayseri ... 373,937
Keşan ...34,518
Kilimli (★ Zonguldak) ...34,748
Kilis ...59,876
Kırıkhan ...52,780
Kırıkkale ... 208,018
Kırklareli ...40,881
Kırşehir ...64,754
Kızıltepe ...40,852

Konya ... 439,181
Kozan ...50,324
Kozlu (★ Zonguldak) ...35,691
Kütahya ... 118,773
Lüleburgaz ...43,420
Malatya ... 243,138
Manisa ... 127,012
Mardin ...44,085
Merzifon ...37,027
Muğla ...31,279
Muş ...42,159
Mustafakemalpaşa ...33,904
Nazilli ...77,627
Nevşehir ...50,204
Niğde ...49,068
Nizip ...50,067
Nusaybin ...45,178
Ödemiş ...47,475
Ordu ...80,828
Osmaniye ... 103,824
Polatlı ...52,737
Reyhanlı ...37,471
Rize ...50,221
Salihli ...63,759
Samsun ... 240,674
Seydişehir ...37,226
Siirt ...53,884
Silvan (Miyafarkin) ...45,825
Sincan (★ Ankara) ...50,869
Sivas ... 198,553
Siverek ...48,333
Söke ...44,556
Soma ...39,088
Suluova (Suluca) ...32,717
Tarsus ... 146,502
Tatvan ...51,906
Tavşanlı ...30,506
Tekirdağ ...63,215
Tire ...35,044
Tokat ...73,008
Trabzon ... 142,008
Tunceli ...18,471
Turgutlu ...65,740
Turhal ...60,097
Ünye ...35,508
Urfa ... 194,969
Uşak ...88,267
Uzunköprü ...33,878
Van ... 110,653
Viranşehir ...45,329
Yalova ...53,857
Yarımca ...48,420
Yozgat ...43,686
Zile ...37,097
Zonguldak (★ 210,000) ... 117,879

## TURKS AND CAICOS ISLANDS

1980 C ... 7,436

### Cities and Towns

• GRAND TURK ... 3,146

## TUVALU

1979 C ... 7,349

### Cities and Towns

• FUNAFUTI ... 2,191

## UGANDA

1980 C ... 12,636,179

### Cities and Towns

Entebbe ...21,289
Fort Portal (Kabarole) ...26,806
Gulu ...14,958
Jinja (1982 E) ...55,000
• KAMPALA (1982 E) ... 460,000
Masaka ...29,123
Mbale ...28,039
Mbarara ...23,255
Tororo ...16,707

## UNITED ARAB EMIRATES / Al Imārāt al 'Arabīyah al Muttahidah

1980 C ... 980,000

### Cities and Towns

ABU DHABI (ABŪ ZABY) ... 242,975
'Ajmān (1968 C) ... 3,725
Al 'Ayn ... 101,663
Al Fujayrah (1968 C) ... 2,001
Ash Shāriqah ... 125,149
• Dubai (Dubayy) ... 265,702
Ra's al Khaymah ...42,000
Umm al Qaywayn
(1968 C) ... 2,928

## UNITED KINGDOM

1981 C ...55,678,079

### Political Divisions

England ...46,220,955
Northern Ireland ... 1,578,500
Scotland ... 5,117,146
Wales ... 2,790,462

## UNITED KINGDOM: ENGLAND

1981 C ...46,220,955

### Cities and Towns

Abingdon (★ Oxford) ...29,130
Accrington
(★★ Blackburn) ...36,459
Aldershot (Rushmoor)
(★ London) ...53,665
Altrincham
(★ Manchester) ...39,528
Andover ...30,632
Arnold (★ Nottingham) ...37,721
Ashford ...45,198
Ashington ...27,786
Ashton-in-Makerfield
(★ Manchester) ...28,517
Ashton-under-Lyne
(★ Manchester) ...43,605
Aylesbury ...51,999
Banbury ...37,463
Banstead and Tadworth
(★ London) ...35,360
Barnsley ...76,783
Barnstaple ...24,490
Barrow-in-Furness ...50,174
Basildon (★ London) ...94,800
Basingstoke ...73,027
Bath ...84,283
Batley (★ Leeds) ...45,582
Battle ... 4,662
Bebington (★ Liverpool) ...62,618
Bedford (North
Bedfordshire) ...75,632
Bedlington ...15,074
Beeston and Stapleford
(Broxtowe)
(★ Nottingham) ...64,785
Benfleet (★ London) ...50,783
Bentley ...34,273
Berkhamsted (★ London) ...16,874
Berwick-upon-Tweed ...12,772
Bexhill-on-Sea ...34,625
Billericay (★ London) ...30,397
Billingham
(★ Middlesbrough) ...36,855
Birkenhead (★ Liverpool) ...99,075
Birmingham
(★ 2,675,000) ... 1,013,995
Bishop Auckland ...23,560
Bishop's Stortford
(★ London) ...22,535
Blackburn (★ 221,900) ... 109,564
Blackpool (★ 280,000) ... 146,297
Bletchley ...37,903
Blyth ...35,101
Bodmin ...11,992
Bognor Regis ...50,323
Bolton (★★ Manchester) ... 143,960
Bootle ...70,860
Borehamwood
(★ London) ...28,426
Boston ...33,908
Bournemouth
(★ 315,000) ... 142,829
Bracknell (★ London) ...52,257
Bradford (★★ Leeds) ... 293,336
Bradford-on-Avon ... 8,921
Braintree ...30,975
Bredbury and Romiley
(★ Manchester) ...28,600
Brentwood (★ London) ...51,212
Bridgwater ...30,782
Bridlington ...28,426
Brighouse (★ Leeds) ...32,597
Brighton (★ 420,000) ... 134,581
Bristol (★ 630,000) ... 413,861
Bromsgrove
(★ Birmingham) ...24,576
Broxtowe see Beeston
and Stapleford
Burgess Hill ...23,577
Burnham-on-Sea /
Highbridge ...17,022
Burnley (★ 160,000) ...76,365
Burntwood
(★ Birmingham) ...28,938
Burton upon Trent ...59,040
Bury (★ Manchester) ...61,785
Bury Saint Edmunds ...30,563
Buxton ...19,502
Camberley see Frimley
and Camberley
Camborne [-Redruth]
(Kerrier) ...34,262
Cambridge ...87,111
Cannock (★ Birmingham) ...54,503
Canterbury ...34,546
Canvey (★ London) ...35,243
Carlisle ...72,206
Carlton (★ Nottingham) ...46,053
Castleford (★ Leeds) ...39,308
Caterham and
Warlingham (Tandridge)
(★ London) ...30,331
Chadderton
(★ Manchester) ...33,512
Chalfont Saint Giles ... 5,216
Chatham (★ London) ...65,835
Cheadle and Gatley
(★ Manchester) ...59,478
Chelmsford (★ London) ...91,109
Cheltenham ...87,188

C Census.　　E Official estimate.　　UE Unofficial estimate.
• Largest city in country.

★ Population or designation of metropolitan area, including suburbs (see headnote).
▲ Population of an entire municipality, commune, or district, including rural area.

Chertsey (★ London) 10,198
Chesham (★ London) 20,883
Cheshunt (★ London) 49,616
Chester 80,154
Chesterfield (★ 127,000) 73,352
Chester-le-Street (★ Newcastle upon Tyne) 34,776
Chichester 26,050
Chippenham 21,325
Chipping Sodbury (★ Bristol) 26,882
Chorley (★★ Preston) 33,465
Christchurch (★ Bournemouth) 32,854
Cirencester 13,491
Clacton-on-Sea 39,618
Cleckheaton and Liversedge (★ Leeds) 26,340
Cleethorpes (★ Grimsby) 33,238
Clevedon 17,875
Coalville 28,831
Colchester 87,476
Consett (★ Newcastle upon Tyne) 22,409
Corby 48,704
Coventry (★ 645,000) 318,718
Cowes 16,134
Cramlington (★ Newcastle upon Tyne) 25,324
Crawley (★ London) 80,113
Crewe 59,097
Crosby (★ Liverpool) 54,103
Darlington 85,519
Dartford (★ London) 62,032
Dartmouth 5,282
Darwen (★ Blackburn) 30,883
Deal 26,311
Denton (★ Manchester) 37,784
Derby (★ 275,000) 218,026
Dewsbury (★★ Leeds) 49,612
Doncaster 74,727
Dorchester 13,734
Dorking (★ London) 14,602
Dover 33,461
Dronfield (★ Sheffield) 22,641
Dudley (★★ Birmingham) 186,513
Dunstable (★ Luton) 48,436
Durham 38,105
Eastbourne 86,715
East Grinstead (★ London) 23,867
Eastleigh (★ Southampton) 58,585
East Retford 19,308
Eccles (★ Manchester) 37,497
Ellesmere Port (★ Liverpool) 65,829
Ely 9,006
Epsom [and Ewell] (★ London) 65,830
Esher / Molesey (★ London) 46,688
Eston and South Bank (★ Middlesbrough) 37,694
Eton see Windsor / Eton
Evesham 15,069
Exeter 88,235
Exmouth 28,037
Falmouth 17,810
Fareham / Portchester (★ Portsmouth) 55,563
Farnborough (★ London) 48,063
Farnham (★ London) 34,541
Farnworth (★ Manchester) 25,591
Faversham 15,914
Felixstowe 24,207
Felling (★ Newcastle upon Tyne) 36,377
Fleet (★ London) 27,406
Fleetwood (★★ Blackpool) 27,899
Folkestone 42,949
Formby (Shepway) (★ Liverpool) 26,852
Frimley and Camberley (Surrey Heath) (★ London) 45,108
Frome 19,678
Gainsborough 20,326
Gateshead (★ Newcastle upon Tyne) 91,429
Gillingham (★ London) 92,531
Glastonbury 6,751
Glossop / Hollingworth (★ Manchester) 29,923
Gloucester (★ 115,000) 106,526
Golborne (★ Manchester) 20,633
Goole 19,394
Gosforth (★ Newcastle upon Tyne) 25,128
Gosport (★ Portsmouth) 69,664
Grantham 30,700
Gravesend (Gravesham) (★ London) 53,450
Grays (★ London) 45,881
Greasby / Moreton (★ Liverpool) 56,410
Great Malvern 30,153
Great Sankey 26,222
Great Yarmouth 54,777
Grimsby (Great Grimsby) (★ 145,000) 91,532
Guildford (★ London) 61,509
Guiseley / Yeadon (★ Leeds) 30,811
Halesowen (★ Birmingham) 57,533
Halifax 76,675
Harlow (★ London) 79,150
Harpenden (★ London) 28,589
Harrogate 63,637
Hartlepool (★★ Middlesbrough) 91,749
Harwich 17,245
Haslemere (★ London) 10,544
Hastings 74,979
Hatfield 33,174
Havant (★ Portsmouth) 50,098
Haverhill 16,970
Haywards Heath 27,958
Hazel Grove and Bramhall (★ Manchester) 40,819
Heanor 21,863
Hemel Hempstead (Dacorum) (★ London) 80,110
Hemsworth 9,608
Henley-on-Thames 10,910
Hereford 48,277
Herne Bay 26,523
Hertford (★ London) 21,350
Heswall (★ Liverpool) 31,037
Hexham 8,914
Heywood (★ Manchester) 29,639
High Wycombe (Wycombe) (▲ 156,800) 69,575
Hinckley (★★ Coventry) 35,510
Hitchin 33,480
Hoddesdon (★ London) 37,960
Horsham (★ London) 38,356
Houghton-le-Spring (★ Newcastle upon Tyne) 35,337
Hove (★ Brighton) 65,587
Hucknall (★ Nottingham) 27,463
Huddersfield (Kirklees) (▲ 377,400) 147,825
Huntingdon 14,395
Huyton-with-Roby (★ Liverpool) 62,011
Hyde (★ Manchester) 30,461
Hythe 13,118
Ilkeston (★ Nottingham) 34,683
Ipswich 129,661
Jarrow (★ Newcastle upon Tyne) 31,345
Keighley (★ Leeds) 49,188
Kendal 23,710
Kenilworth (★ Coventry) 18,782
Keswick 4,777
Kettering 44,758
Kidderminster 50,385
Kidsgrove (★ Stoke-on-Trent) 27,999
King's Lynn 37,323
Kingston upon Hull (★ 350,000) 322,144
Kingswood (★ Bristol) 54,736
Kirkby (★ Liverpool) 52,825
Kirkby in Ashfield (★ Mansfield) 26,098
Lancaster 43,902
Leatherhead (Mole Valley) (★ London) 42,399
Leeds (★ 1,540,000) 445,242
Leek 18,495
Leicester (★ 495,000) 324,394
Leigh (★ Manchester) 42,627
Leighton Buzzard 29,554
Letchworth 31,146
Lewes 14,499
Leyland (★ Preston) 36,694
Lichfield 25,408
Lincoln 79,980
Littlehampton 46,028
Liverpool (★ 1,525,000) 538,809
• LONDON (★ 11,100,000) 6,574,009
Longbenton / Backworth (★ Newcastle upon Tyne) 36,780
Long Eaton (★ Nottingham) 42,285
Loughborough (Charnwood) 44,895
Loughton (★ London) 39,162
Lowestoft (Waveney) 59,430
Ludlow 7,496
Luton (★ 220,000) 163,209
Lymington 11,614
Lytham Saint Anne's (Fylde) (★ Blackpool) 39,559
Macclesfield 47,525
Maidenhead (★ London) 59,809
Maidstone 86,067
Manchester (★ 2,775,000) 437,612
Mangotsfield (★ Bristol) 28,664
Mansfield (★ 198,000) 71,325
Margate 53,137
Market Harborough 15,852
Marlborough 5,330
Matlock 13,706
Melton Mowbray 23,379
Middlesbrough (Teesside) (★ 580,000) 158,516
Middleton (★ Manchester) 51,373
Milton Keynes 36,886
Morecambe (★★ Lancaster) 41,432
Morley (★ Leeds) 44,652
Nelson (★★ Burnley) 30,449
Newark-on-Trent 33,143
Newburn (★ Newcastle upon Tyne) 43,713
Newbury 31,488
Newcastle-under-Lyme (★★ Stoke-on-Trent) 73,208
Newcastle upon Tyne (★ 1,300,000) 199,064
Newmarket 15,861
Newport 19,758
Newton Abbot 20,567
Newton Aycliffe 24,375
Newtown 8,906
Northampton 154,172
North Shields (★ Newcastle upon Tyne) 41,519
Northwich 32,664
Norwich (★ 230,000) 169,814
Nottingham (★ 655,000) 273,300
Nuneaton (★★ Coventry) 60,337
Oadby (★ Leicester) 18,331
Oakengates / Donnington 26,890
Oakham 7,914
Oldbury / Smethwick (★ Birmingham) 153,268
Oldham (★★ Manchester) 107,095
Ormskirk (★ Liverpool) 22,308
Oxford (★ 230,000) 113,847
Paignton (★ Torquay) 39,565
Penrith 12,086
Penzance 18,501
Peterborough 113,404
Peterlee 31,405
Plymouth (★ 290,000) 238,583
Pontefract (★ Leeds) 28,621
Poole (★★ Bournemouth) 122,815
Portsmouth (★ 485,000) 174,218
Prescot (★ Liverpool) 40,191
Preston (★ 250,000) 166,675
Prestwich (★ Manchester) 31,854
Pudsey (★ Leeds) 31,943
Radcliffe (★ Manchester) 27,664
Ramsgate 36,678
Rawtenstall 21,247
Rayleigh (★ London) 28,574
Reading (★ 200,000) 194,727
Redcar (★ Middlesbrough) 35,373
Redditch (★ Birmingham) 61,639
Reigate / Redhill (★ London) 48,241
Rickmansworth (★ London) 15,960
Ripon 13,036
Rochdale (★★ Manchester) 97,292
Rotherham (★★ Sheffield) 122,374
Royal Leamington Spa (★★ Coventry) 56,552
Royal Tunbridge Wells 57,699
Rugby 59,039
Runcorn (★ Liverpool) 63,995
Rushden 22,394
Ryde 19,384
Rye 4,127
Saint Albans (★ London) 76,709
Saint Austell 20,267
Saint Helens 114,397
Sale (★ Manchester) 57,872
Salford (★ Manchester) 96,525
Salisbury 36,890
Sandwich 4,184
Scarborough 36,665
Scunthorpe 79,043
Seaford 16,367
Seaham (★ Newcastle upon Tyne) 21,807
Selby 12,224
Sevenoaks (★ London) 24,493
Sheffield (★ 710,000) 470,685
Shipley (★ Leeds) 28,815
Shoreham-by-Sea (★ Brighton) 20,562
Shrewsbury 57,731
Sittingbourne 35,893
Skelmersdale (★ Manchester) 42,611
Slough (★ London) 106,341
Solihull (★ Birmingham) 93,940
Sompting / Lancing (★ Brighton) 25,585
Southampton (★ 415,000) 211,321
Southend-on-Sea (★ London) 155,720
Southport (Sefton) (★★ Liverpool) 88,596
South Shields (★★ Newcastle) 86,488
Spalding 18,182
Spennymoor 18,563
Stafford 60,915
Staines (Spelthorne) (★ London) 51,949
Stamford 16,127
Stanford le Hope / Corringham (★ London) 32,150
Stanley (★ Newcastle) 20,058
Stapleford see Beeston and Stapleford
Stevenage 74,757
Stockport (★ Manchester) 135,489
Stockton-on-Tees (★★ Middlesbrough) 86,699
Stoke-on-Trent (★ 440,000) 272,446
Stourbridge (★ Birmingham) 55,136
Stratford-upon-Avon 20,941
Stretford (★ Manchester) 47,522
Strood (★ London) 32,822
Stroud 37,791
Sudbury 17,723
Sunbury (★ London) 28,240
Sunderland (★★ Newcastle) 195,064
Surrey Heath see Frimley and Camberley
Sutton Coldfield (★ Birmingham) 102,572
Sutton in Ashfield (Ashfield) (★★ Mansfield) 39,536
Swadlincote 33,667
Swindon 127,348
Swinton and Pendlebury (★ Manchester) 44,416
Tamworth 63,260
Taunton 47,793
Telford 28,645
Tewkesbury 9,454
Thetford 19,529
Thornaby-on-Tees (★ Middlesbrough) 26,319
Thornton / Cleveleys (★ Blackpool) 26,697
Tiverton 14,745
Todmorden 11,936
Tonbridge (★ London) 34,407
Torquay (Torbay) (★ 112,400) 54,430
Trowbridge 27,299
Truro 17,852
Tyldesley (★ Manchester) 27,773
Tynemouth (★ Newcastle upon Tyne) 17,877
Ulverston 11,976
Urmston (★ Manchester) 43,706
Wakefield (★★ Leeds) 74,764
Walkden (★ Manchester) 39,413
Wallasey (★ Liverpool) 62,465
Wallsend (★ Newcastle upon Tyne) 44,542
Walsall (★★ Birmingham) 177,923
Walton and Weybridge (★ London) 50,031
Warlingham see Caterham and Warlingham
Warrington 81,366
Warwick (★★ Coventry) 21,701
Washington (★ Newcastle upon Tyne) 48,856
Waterlooville (★ Portsmouth) 57,296
Watford (★ London) 109,503
Wellingborough 38,598
Wells 9,252
Welwyn Garden City (★ London) 40,665
West Bridgford (★ Nottingham) 27,463
West Bromwich (★ Birmingham) 153,725
Weston-super-Mare 60,821
Weybridge see Walton and Weybridge
Weymouth 38,384
Whitby 12,982
Whitefield (★ Manchester) 27,715
Whitehaven 27,512
Whitley Bay (★ Newcastle upon Tyne) 36,040
Whitstable 26,227
Widnes 55,973
Wigan (★★ Manchester) 88,725
Wigston (★ Leicester) 32,373
Wilmslow (★ Manchester) 28,827
Winchester 34,127
Windermere 6,835
Windsor / [Eton] (★ London) 30,832
Winsford 26,548
Woking / [Byfleet] (★ London) 92,667
Wokingham 30,344
Wolverhampton (★★ Birmingham) 263,501
Worcester 75,466
Workington 25,978
Worksop 34,551
Worthing (★★ Brighton) 90,687
Yeovil 36,114
York (★ 145,000) 123,126

### *Counties*

Avon 909,408
Bedfordshire 504,986
Berkshire 675,153
Buckinghamshire 565,992
Cambridgeshire 575,177
Cheshire 926,293
Cleveland 565,775
Cornwall and Isles of Scilly 430,506
Cumbria 483,427
Derby 906,929
Devon 952,000
Dorset 591,990
Durham 604,728
East Sussex 652,568
Essex 1,469,065
Gloucestershire 499,351
Greater London 6,696,008
Greater Manchester 2,594,778
Hampshire 1,456,367
Hereford and Worcester 630,218
Hertfordshire 954,535
Humberside 847,666
Isle of Wight 118,192
Kent 1,463,055
Lancashire 1,372,118
Leicestershire 842,577
Lincolnshire 547,560
Merseyside 1,513,070
Norfolk 693,490
Northamptonshire 527,532
Northumberland 299,905
North Yorkshire 666,610
Nottinghamshire 982,631
Oxfordshire 515,079
Shropshire 375,610
Somerset 424,988
South Yorkshire 1,301,813
Staffordshire 1,012,320
Suffolk 596,354
Surrey 999,393
Tyne and Wear 1,143,245
Warwickshire 473,620
West Midlands 2,644,634
West Sussex 658,562
West Yorkshire 2,037,510
Wiltshire 518,167

## UNITED KINGDOM: NORTHERN IRELAND

1987 E 1,575,200

### *Cities and Towns*

Antrim (1981 C) 22,342
Armagh (1981 C) 12,700
Ballymena (1981 C) 28,166
Bangor (North Down) (★ Belfast) 70,700
Belfast (★ 685,000) 303,800
Castlereagh (★ Belfast) 57,900
Enniskillen (1981 C) 10,429
Larne (1981 C) 18,224
Lisburn (★ Belfast) (1981 C) 40,391
Londonderry (Derry) (★ 97,200) 97,500
Lurgan (★ 63,000) (1981 C) 20,991
Newry (1981 C) 19,426
Newtownabbey (★ Belfast) 72,300
Newtownards (1981 C) 20,531
Omagh (1981 C) 14,627
Portadown (★★ Lurgan) (1981 C) 21,333

## UNITED KINGDOM: SCOTLAND

1981 C 5,035,315

### *Cities and Towns*

Aberdeen 186,757
Airdrie (★ Glasgow) 45,320
Alexandria (★ Glasgow) 25,947
Alloa 26,378
Arbroath 23,934
Ardrossan (★★ Irvine) 11,386
Ayr (★ 100,000) 48,493
Bearsden (★ Glasgow) 27,146
Bellshill (★ Glasgow) 39,713
Clydebank (★ Glasgow) 51,832
Coatbridge 50,831
Cumbernauld (★ Glasgow) 47,517
Dumbarton (★ Glasgow) 23,345
Dumfries 31,307
Dundee 172,294
Dunfermline (★ 125,817) 52,105
East Kilbride (★ Glasgow) 70,454
Edinburgh (★ 630,000) 408,822
Elgin 18,702
Falkirk (★ 148,171) 36,372
Forfar 12,652
Giffnock (★ Glasgow) 33,585
Glasgow (★ 1,800,000) 754,586
Glenrothes (★★ Kirkcaldy) 33,639
Grangemouth (★★ Falkirk) 21,744
Greenock (★ 101,000) 58,436
Hamilton (★ Glasgow) 51,666
Hawick 16,213
Helensburgh (★ Glasgow) 16,432
Inverness 38,204
Irvine (★ 94,000) 32,507
Johnstone (★ Glasgow) 42,731
Kilmarnock (★ 84,000) 51,799
Kirkcaldy (★ 148,171) 46,356
Kirkintilloch (★ Glasgow) 33,024
Kirkwall 5,867
Lerwick 7,149
Livingston 38,671
Montrose 12,127
Motherwell (★ Glasgow) 30,616
Oban 7,476
Paisley (★ Glasgow) 84,330
Perth 41,916
Peterhead 16,804
Port Glasgow 22,636
Prestwick (★ Ayr) 13,355
Saint Andrews 10,525
Stirling (★ 61,000) 36,640
Stonehouse 5,092
Stranraer 10,766
Thurso 8,828
Wick 7,770
Wishaw (★ Glasgow) 37,717

### *Regions*

Borders 99,248
Central 273,078
Dumfries and Galloway 145,078
Fife 326,480
Grampian 470,596
Highland 200,030
Lothian 735,892
Orkney (island area) 18,906
Shetland (island area) 26,716
Strathclyde 2,397,827
Tayside 391,529
Western Isles (island area) 31,766

## UNITED KINGDOM: WALES

1981 C 2,790,462

C Census. E Official estimate. UE Unofficial estimate.
• Largest city in country.
★ Population or designation of metropolitan area, including suburbs (see headnote).
▲ Population of an entire municipality, commune, or district, including rural area.

*Cities and Towns*

Aberdare (Cynon Valley) 31,617
Aberdare / Brynmawr 28,239
Aberystwyth 10,290
Bangor 12,244
Bargoed (★ Newport) 15,321
Barry (Vale of Glamorgan) (★ Cardiff) 44,443
Brecon 7,166
Bridgend 31,008
Caernarfon 9,271
Caerphilly (★ Cardiff) 28,681
Cardiff (★ 625,000) 262,313
Carmarthen 13,860
Colwyn Bay 27,002
Cwmbran (★ Newport) 44,592
Ebbw Vale (Blaenau Gwent) 21,048
Flint 11,411
Llandudno 13,202
Llanelli 45,336
Merthyr Tydfil 38,893
Milford Haven 13,883
Monmouth 7,379
Neath (★★ Swansea) 48,687
Newport (★ 310,000) 115,896
Pembroke 7,049
Pontypool (★★ Newport) 36,064
Pontypridd (Taff-Ely) (★ Cardiff) 29,465
Port Talbot (Afan) (★ 130,000) 40,078
Prestatyn 16,246
Rhondda (★★ Cardiff) 70,980
Rhyl (Rhuddlan) 23,130
Swansea (★ 275,000) 172,433
Wrexham 39,929

*Counties*

Clwyd 390,173
Dyfed 329,977
Gwent 439,684
Gwynedd 230,468
Mid Glamorgan 537,866
Powys 110,467
South Glamorgan 384,633
West Glamorgan 367,194

## URUGUAY

1985 C 2,940,200

*Cities and Towns*

Artigas 31,200
Canelones 15,800
Durazno 26,500
Florida 26,200
Fray Bentos 18,800
La Paz (★ Montevideo) 17,200
Las Piedras (★ Montevideo) 61,300
Maldonado 32,300
Melo 39,600
Mercedes 33,300
Minas 33,700
• MONTEVIDEO (★ 1,550,000) 1,246,500
Pando (★ Montevideo) 21,000
Paysandú 75,200
Punta del Este 6,500
Rivera 55,400
Rocha 25,200
Salto 77,400
San Carlos 20,000
San José de Mayo 32,100
Santa Lucía 15,600
Tacuarembó 38,600
Treinta y Tres 27,500
Trinidad 16,500

*Departments*

Artigas 68,994
Canelones 359,913
Cerro Largo 77,985
Colonia 112,348
Durazno 53,864
Flores 24,381
Florida 65,873
Lavalleja 61,241
Maldonado 92,618
Montevideo 1,303,942
Paysandú 103,487
Río Negro 48,590
Rivera 83,801
Rocha 66,440
Salto 105,617
San José 88,020
Soriano 79,042
Tacuarembó 82,809
Treinta y Tres 46,599

## VANUATU

1986 C 140,154

*Cities and Towns*

• PORT-VILA (★ 18,000) 14,184

## VATICAN CITY / Città del Vaticano

1987 E 752

## VENDA

1985 C 459,819

*Cities and Towns*

Makwarela 3,712
• Shayandima 4,853
THOHOYANDOU 3,641

## VENEZUELA

1981 C 14,516,735

*Cities and Towns*

Acarigua 91,662
Altagracia de Orituco 31,582
Anaco 43,607
Araure 41,747
Bachaquero (1971 C) 17,896
Barcelona 156,461
Barinas 110,462
Barquisimeto 497,635
Baruta (★ Caracas) 200,063
Boconó 18,906
Cabimas 140,435
Cagua 53,704
Calabozo 61,995
• CARACAS (★ 3,600,000) 1,816,901
Caripito 18,172
Carora 58,694
Carúpano 64,579
Catia La Mar (★ Caracas) 87,916
Chacao (★ Caracas) 72,703
Charallave 29,410
Chivacoa 27,500
Ciudad Bolívar 182,941
Ciudad Guayana (Santo Tomé de Guayana) 314,497
Ciudad Ojeda 83,565
Coro 96,339
Cumaná 179,814
El Hatillo 27,999
El Limón 65,122
El Tigre 73,595
El Tocuyo 22,854
El Vigía 40,753
Guacara 72,727
Guanare 64,025
Guarenas (★ Caracas) 101,742
Guatire 37,827
Güigüe 27,662
La Guaira (★ Caracas) 21,815
La Victoria 70,828
Los Dos Caminos (★ Caracas) 63,346
Los Teques (★ Caracas) 112,857
Machiques 27,242
Maiquetía (★ Caracas) 66,056
Maracaibo 890,643
Maracay 322,560
Mariara 47,242
Maturín 154,976
Mérida 143,209
Morón 33,973
Ocumare del Tuy 40,666
Palo Negro 27,789
Petare (★ Caracas) 395,715
Porlamar 51,079
Pozuelos 80,342
Puerto Cabello 71,759
Puerto la Cruz 53,881
Punto Fijo 71,114
San Antonio del Táchira 26,939
San Carlos 37,892
San Carlos del Zulia 31,437
San Cristóbal 198,793
San Felipe 57,526
San Fernando de Apure 57,308
San José de Guanipa (El Tigrito) 35,689
San Juan de los Morros 57,219
San Mateo 22,841
Santa Teresa 34,460
Trujillo 31,774
Tucupita 27,299
Turmero 111,186
Upata 33,238
Valencia 616,224
Valera 102,068
Valle de la Pascua 55,761
Villa de Cura 39,228
Yaritagua 31,936

*States*

Amazonas (Ter.) 45,667
Anzoátegui 683,717
Apure 188,187
Aragua 891,623
Barinas 326,166
Bolívar 668,340
Carabobo 1,062,268
Cojedes 133,991
Delta Amacuro (Ter.) 56,720
Dependencias Federales (Ter.) 850
Distrito Federal (Federal District) 2,070,742
Falcón 503,896
Guárico 393,467
Lara 945,064
Mérida 459,361
Miranda 1,421,442
Monagas 388,536
Nueva Esparta 197,198
Portuguesa 424,984
Sucre 585,698
Táchira 660,234
Trujillo 433,735
Yaracuy 300,597
Zulia 1,674,252

## VIETNAM / Viet Nam

1979 C 52,741,766

*Cities and Towns*

Bac Giang 54,506
Bac Lieu (1967 E) 41,700
Bac Ninh 38,097
Ben Tre 28,672
Bien Hoa 187,254
Bien Son 29,482
Buon Me Thuot 71,815
Ca Mau 67,484
Cam Pha 76,697
Cam Ranh (1973 E) 118,111
Can Tho 182,856
Cao Bang 26,741
Chau Doc 45,245
Da Lat 87,136
Da Nang 318,653
Dong Ha 28,796
Dong Hoi 39,521
Ha Dong 37,378
Hai Duong 54,579
Hai Phong (▲ 1,279,067) 385,210
HANOI (HA NOI) (★ 1,500,000) 897,500
Hoa Binh 51,187
• Ho Chi Minh City (Thanh Pho Ho Chi Minh) (★ 3,100,000) 2,700,849
Hoi An 23,490
Hon Gai 114,573
Hue 165,710
Kon Tum 28,378
Lang Son 20,204
Lao Cai 18,618
Long Xuyen 112,485
Minh Hai 72,517
My Tho 101,493
Nam Dinh 160,179
Nha Trang 172,663
Phan Rang (1967 E) 21,900
Phan Thiet 75,241
Phu Tho 22,273
Play Cu 58,088
Qui Nhon 127,211
Rach Gia 81,075
Sa Dec 73,104
Soc Trang 74,967
Soc Trang (1967 E) 40,300
Son La 14,810
Tam Ky (1971 E) 18,100
Tan An 43,364
Tay Ninh 32,151
Thai Binh 79,566
Thai Nguyen 138,023
Thanh Hoa 72,646
Thu Dau Mot 40,759
Tra Vinh 44,020
Tuyen Quang 22,279
Tuy Hoa 46,617
Uong Bi 34,400
Viet Tri 72,108
Vinh 159,753
Vinh Long 71,505
Vinh Yen 9,590
Vung Tau 81,694
Yen Bai 40,017

## VIRGIN ISLANDS, BRITISH

1980 C 12,034

*Cities and Towns*

• ROAD TOWN 2,479

## VIRGIN ISLANDS OF THE UNITED STATES

1980 C 96,569

*Cities and Towns*

• CHARLOTTE AMALIE (★ 32,000) 11,842

## WALLIS AND FUTUNA / Wallis et Futuna

1983 E 12,408

*Cities and Towns*

• MATA-UTU 815
Ono (1976 C) 624

## WESTERN SAHARA

1982 E 142,000

*Cities and Towns*

• EL AAIÚN (LA'YOUN) 93,875

## WESTERN SAMOA / Samoa i Sisifo

1981 C 156,349

*Cities and Towns*

• APIA 33,170

## YEMEN / Al Yaman

1990 E 15,267,000

*Cities and Towns*

Aden ('Adan) (★ 318,000) (1984 E) 176,100
Al Mukallā (1984 E) 58,000
Dhamār (1981 C) 30,367
Hodeida (Al Ḥudaydah) (1986 C) 155,110
• ṢAN'Ā' (1986 C) 427,150
Say'ūn (1984 E) 25,400
Ta'izz (1986 C) 178,043

## YUGOSLAVIA / Jugoslavija

1987 E 23,417,188

*Cities and Towns*

Banja Luka (▲ 193,890) 130,900
Bečej (1971 C) 26,470
• BELGRADE (BEOGRAD) (★ 1,400,000) 1,130,000
Bihać (1971 C) 24,026
Bijeljina (1971 C) 24,722
Bitola (▲ 143,090) 76,200
Bor (1971 C) 29,039
Brčko (1971 C) 25,422
Čačak (1971 C) 38,170
Celje (1971 C) 31,788
Cetinje (1971 C) 11,892
Đakovica (1971 C) 29,638
Dubrovnik (1971 C) 31,106
Karlovac (1971 C) 47,532
Kikinda (1971 C) 37,487
Kosovska Mitrovica (1971 C) 42,241
Kragujevac (▲ 171,609) 94,800
Kraljevo (1971 C) 27,817
Kranj (1971 C) 27,209
Kruševac (1971 C) 29,469
Kumanovo (1971 C) 46,406
Leskovac (1971 C) 44,255
Ljubljana (▲ 316,607) 233,200
Maribor (▲ 187,651) 107,400
Mostar (1971 C) 47,606
Nikšić (1971 C) 28,547
Niš (▲ 240,219) 168,400
Novi Pazar (1971 C) 29,072
Novi Sad (▲ 266,772) 176,000
Ohrid (1971 C) 26,370
Osijek (▲ 162,490) 106,800
Pančevo (★ Belgrade) 62,700
Peć (1971 C) 42,113
Pirot (1971 C) 29,228
Požarevac (1971 C) 33,121
Prilep (1971 C) 48,242
Priština (▲ 244,830) 125,400
Prizren (1971 C) 41,661
Pula (1971 C) 47,414
Rijeka (▲ 199,282) 166,400
Šabac (1971 C) 42,307
Sarajevo (▲ 479,688) 341,200
Šibenik (1971 C) 30,090
Sisak (1971 C) 38,421
Skopje (▲ 547,214) 444,900
Slavonski Brod (1971 C) 38,762
Smederevo (1971 C) 40,289
Sombor (1971 C) 43,971
Split 191,074
Sremska Mitrovica (1971 C) 31,921
Štip (1971 C) 27,289
Subotica (▲ 153,306) 100,500
Svetozarevo (1971 C) 27,542
Tetovo (1971 C) 35,792
Titograd (▲ 145,163) 82,500
Titovo Užice (1971 C) 34,312
Titov Veles (1971 C) 36,026
Tuzla (▲ 129,967) 67,300
Valjevo (1971 C) 26,367
Varaždin (1971 C) 34,270
Vinkovci (1971 C) 29,072
Vranje (1971 C) 25,685
Vršac (1971 C) 34,231
Vukovar (1971 C) 30,149
Zadar (1971 C) 43,187
Zagreb 697,925
Zenica (▲ 144,869) 67,500
Zrenjanin (▲ 140,009) 65,400

*Republics*

Bosnia-Hercegovina (Bosna i Hercegovina) 4,400,464
Croatia (Hrvatska) 4,673,517
Macedonia (Makedonija) 2,064,581
Montenegro (Crna Gora) 625,882
Serbia (Srbija) 9,716,138
Slovenia (Slovenija) 1,936,606

## ZAIRE / Zaïre

1984 C 29,671,407

*Cities and Towns*

Bandundu 63,189
Beni 73,319
Boma 88,556
Bukavu 171,064
Bumba 46,823
Bunia 46,224
Butembo 78,633
Gandajika 60,263
Gemena 62,641
Goma 76,745
Ilebo 48,831
Isiro 78,871
Kabalo 38,787
Kabinda 81,752
Kalemie (Albertville) 70,694
Kalima 22,716
Kamina 5,970
Kananga (Luluabourg) 290,898
Kikwit 146,784
Kindu 68,044
• KINSHASA (LÉOPOLDVILLE) (1986 E) 3,000,000
Kisangani (Stanleyville) 282,650
Kolwezi 201,382
Likasi (Jadotville) 194,465
Lisala 40,471
Lubumbashi (Élisabethville) 543,268
Matadi 144,742
Mbandaka (Coquilhatville) 125,263
Mbanza-Ngungu 43,900
Mbuji-Mayi (Bakwanga) 423,363
Mwene-Ditu 72,567
Tshikapa 105,484
Yangambi 53,726

## ZAMBIA

1980 C 5,661,801

*Cities and Towns*

Chililabombwe (Bancroft) (★ 56,582) 25,900
Chingola 130,872
Kabwe (Broken Hill) 127,420
Kalulushi 53,383
Kitwe (★ 283,962) 207,500
Livingstone 61,296
Luanshya (★ 113,422) 61,600
• LUSAKA 535,830
Mufulira (★ 138,824) 77,100
Ndola 250,490

## ZIMBABWE

1982 C 7,539,000

*Cities and Towns*

Bulawayo 413,814
Chinhoyi 24,322
Chitungwiza (★ Harare) 172,556
Gweru 78,918
• HARARE (SALISBURY) (★ 890,000) 656,011
Hwange 39,202
Kadoma 44,613
Kwekwe 47,607
Masvingo (Nyanda) 30,642
Mutare 69,621
Zvishavane 26,758

C Census. E Official estimate. UE Unofficial estimate.
• Largest city in country.

★ Population or designation of metropolitan area, including suburbs (see headnote).
▲ Population of an entire municipality, commune, or district, including rural area.

# UNITED STATES GEOGRAPHICAL INFORMATION

## GENERAL

### ELEVATION

The highest elevation in the United States is Mount McKinley, Alaska, 20,320 feet.

The lowest elevation in the United States is in Death Valley, California, 282 feet below sea level.

The average elevation of the United States is 2,500 feet.

### EXTREMITIES

| Direction | Location | Latitude | Longitude |
|---|---|---|---|
| North | Point Barrow, Ak. | 71° 23'N. | 156° 29'W. |
| South | Ka Lae (point) Hi. | 18° 56'N. | 155° 41'W. |
| East | West Quoddy Head, Me. | 44° 49'N. | 66° 57'W. |
| West | Cape Wrangell, Ak. | 52° 55'N. | 172° 27'E. |

The two places in the United States separated by the greatest distance are Kure Island, Hawaii, and Elliot Key, Florida. These points are 5,852 miles apart.

### LENGTH OF BOUNDARIES

The total length of the Canadian boundary of the United States is 5,525 miles.

The total length of the Mexican boundary of the United States is 1,933 miles.

The total length of the Atlantic coastline of the United States is 2,069 miles.

The total length of the Pacific and Arctic coastline of the United States is 8,683 miles.

The total length of the Gulf of Mexico coastline of the United States is 1,631 miles.

The total length of all coastlines and land boundaries of the United States is 19,841 miles.

The total length of the tidal shoreline and land boundaries of the United States is 96,091 miles.

### GEOGRAPHIC CENTERS

The geographic center of the United States (including Alaska and Hawaii) is in Butte County, South Dakota at 44° 58'N., 103° 46'W.

The geographic center of North America is in North Dakota, a few miles west of Devils Lake, at 48° 10'N., 100° 10'W.

### EXTREMES OF TEMPERATURE

The highest temperature ever recorded in the United States was 134° F., at Greenland Ranch, Death Valley, California, on July 10, 1913.

The lowest temperature ever recorded in the United States was -80° F., at Prospect Creek, Alaska, on January 23, 1971.

### PRECIPITATION

The average annual precipitation for the United States is approximately 29 inches.

Hawaii is the wettest state, with an average annual rainfall of 82 inches. Nevada, with an average annual rainfall of 9 inches, is the driest state.

The greatest local average annual rainfall in the United States is at Mt. Waialeale, Kauai, Hawaii, 460 inches.

The greatest 24-hour rainfall in the United States, 43 inches at Alvin, Texas, July 25-26, 1979.

The lowest local average annual rainfall in the United States is at Death Valley, California, 1.63 inches.

The longest dry period in the United States, 767 days, is at Bagdad, California, October 3, 1912 to November 8, 1914.

Heavy snowfall records include 76 inches in 24 hours at Silver Lake, Colorado, April 14-15, 1921; 189 inches in one storm at Mt. Shasta Ski Bowl, California, February 13-19, 1959.

The greatest seasonal snowfall, 1,122 inches, more than 93 feet, at Paradise Ranger Station, Washington, during the winter of 1971-72.

## TERRITORIAL ACQUISITION AND POPULATION MOVEMENT

### TERRITORIAL ACQUISITIONS

| Accession | Date | Area (sq. mi.) | Cost in Dollars |
|---|---|---|---|
| Original territory of the Thirteen States | 1790 | 888,685 | |
| Purchase of Louisiana Territory, from France | 1803 | 827,192 | $11,250,000 |
| By treaty with Spain: Florida | 1819 | 58,560 | 5,000,000 |
| Other areas | 1819 | 13,443 | |
| Annexation of Texas | 1845 | 390,144 | |
| Oregon Territory, by treaty with Great Britain | 1846 | 285,580 | |
| Mexican Cession | 1848 | 529,017 | $15,000,000 |
| Gadsden Purchase, from Mexico | 1853 | 29,640 | $10,000,000 |
| Purchase of Alaska, from Russia | 1867 | 586,412 | 7,200,000 |
| Annexation of Hawaiian Islands | 1898 | 6,450 | |
| Puerto Rico, by treaty with Spain | 1899 | 3,435 | |
| Guam, by treaty with Spain | 1899 | 212 | |
| American Samoa, by treaty with Great Britain and Germany | 1900 | 76 | |
| Virgin Islands, by purchase from Denmark | 1917 | 133 | $25,000,000 |

Note: The Philippines, ceded by Spain in 1898 for $20,000,000 were a territorial possession of the United States from 1898 to 1946. On July 4, 1946 they became the independent Republic of the Philippines.

Note: The Canal Zone, ceded by Panama in 1903 for $10,000,000 was a territory of the United States from 1903 to 1979. As a result of treaties signed in 1977, sovereignty over the Canal Zone reverted to Panama in 1979.

### WESTWARD MOVEMENT OF CENTER OF POPULATION

| Year | U.S. Population Total at Census | Approximate Location |
|---|---|---|
| 1790 | 3,929,214 | 23 miles east of Baltimore, Md. |
| 1800 | 5,308,483 | 18 miles west of Baltimore, Md. |
| 1810 | 7,239,881 | 40 miles northwest of Washington, D.C. |
| 1820 | 9,638,453 | 16 miles east of Moorefield, W. Va. |
| 1830 | 12,866,020 | 19 miles southwest of Moorefield, W. Va. |
| 1840 | 17,069,453 | 16 miles south of Clarksburg, W. Va. |
| 1850 | 23,191,876 | 23 miles southeast of Parkersburg, W. Va. |
| 1860 | 31,443,321 | 20 miles southeast of Chillicothe, Ohio |
| 1870 | 39,818,449 | 48 miles northeast of Cincinnati, Ohio |
| 1880 | 50,155,783 | 8 miles southwest of Cincinnati, Ohio |
| 1890 | 62,947,714 | 20 miles east of Columbus, Ind. |
| 1900 | 75,994,575 | 6 miles southeast of Columbus, Ind. |
| 1910 | 91,972,266 | Bloomington, Ind. |
| 1920 | 105,710,620 | 8 miles southeast of Spencer, Ind. |
| 1930 | 122,775,046 | 3 miles northeast of Linton, Ind. |
| 1940 | 131,669,275 | 2 miles southeast of Carlisle, Ind. |
| 1950 | 150,697,361 | 8 miles northwest of Olney, Ill. |
| 1960 | 179,323,175 | 6 miles northwest of Centralia, Ill. |
| 1970 | 204,816,296 | 5 miles southeast of Mascoutah, Ill. |
| 1980 | 226,549,010 | 1/4 mile west of DeSoto, Mo. |

## STATE AREAS AND POPULATIONS

| STATE | Land Area square miles | Water Area* square miles | Total Area* square miles | Area Rank land area | 1980 Resident Population | 1980 Population per square mile | 1970 Population | 1960 Population | 1950 Population | Population Rank 1980 | Population Rank 1970 | Population Rank 1960 |
|---|---|---|---|---|---|---|---|---|---|---|---|---|
| Alabama | 50,766 | 938 | 51,704 | 28 | 3,893,978 | 77 | 3,444,165 | 3,266,740 | 3,061,743 | 22 | 21 | 19 |
| Alaska | 570,833 | 20,171 | 591,004 | 1 | 401,851 | 0.7 | 302,173 | 226,167 | 128,643 | 50 | 50 | 50 |
| Arizona | 113,510 | 492 | 114,002 | 6 | 2,718,425 | 24 | 1,772,482 | 1,302,161 | 749,587 | 29 | 33 | 35 |
| Arkansas | 52,082 | 1,109 | 53,191 | 27 | 2,286,419 | 44 | 1,923,295 | 1,786,272 | 1,909,511 | 33 | 32 | 31 |
| California | 156,297 | 2,407 | 158,704 | 3 | 23,667,837 | 151 | 19,953,134 | 15,717,204 | 10,586,223 | 1 | 1 | 2 |
| Colorado | 103,598 | 496 | 104,094 | 8 | 2,889,735 | 28 | 2,207,259 | 1,753,947 | 1,325,089 | 28 | 30 | 33 |
| Connecticut | 4,872 | 147 | 5,019 | 48 | 3,107,576 | 638 | 3,032,217 | 2,535,234 | 2,007,280 | 25 | 24 | 25 |
| Delaware | 1,933 | 112 | 2,045 | 49 | 594,317 | 307 | 548,104 | 446,292 | 318,085 | 47 | 46 | 46 |
| District of Columbia | 63 | 6 | 69 | . . | 638,432 | 10,134 | 756,510 | 763,956 | 802,178 | . . | . . | . . |
| Florida | 54,157 | 4,511 | 58,668 | 26 | 9,746,421 | 180 | 6,789,443 | 4,951,560 | 2,771,305 | 7 | 9 | 10 |
| Georgia | 58,060 | 854 | 58,914 | 21 | 5,463,087 | 94 | 4,589,575 | 3,943,116 | 3,444,578 | 13 | 15 | 16 |
| Hawaii | 6,427 | 46 | 6,473 | 47 | 964,691 | 150 | 769,913 | 632,772 | 499,794 | 39 | 40 | 43 |
| Idaho | 82,413 | 1,153 | 83,566 | 11 | 944,038 | 11 | 713,008 | 667,191 | 588,637 | 41 | 42 | 42 |
| Illinois | 55,646 | 2,226 | 57,872 | 24 | 11,427,414 | 205 | 11,113,976 | 10,081,158 | 8,712,176 | 5 | 5 | 4 |
| Indiana | 35,936 | 481 | 36,417 | 38 | 5,490,260 | 153 | 5,193,669 | 4,662,498 | 3,934,224 | 12 | 11 | 11 |
| Iowa | 55,965 | 310 | 56,275 | 23 | 2,913,808 | 52 | 2,825,041 | 2,757,537 | 2,621,073 | 27 | 25 | 24 |
| Kansas | 81,783 | 499 | 82,282 | 13 | 2,364,236 | 29 | 2,249,071 | 2,178,611 | 1,905,299 | 32 | 28 | 28 |
| Kentucky | 39,674 | 740 | 40,414 | 37 | 3,660,257 | 92 | 3,219,311 | 3,038,156 | 2,944,806 | 23 | 23 | 22 |
| Louisiana | 44,520 | 3,230 | 47,750 | 33 | 4,206,098 | 94 | 3,643,180 | 3,257,022 | 2,683,516 | 19 | 20 | 20 |
| Maine | 30,995 | 2,270 | 33,265 | 39 | 1,125,030 | 36 | 993,663 | 969,265 | 913,774 | 38 | 38 | 36 |
| Maryland | 9,838 | 623 | 10,461 | 42 | 4,216,941 | 429 | 3,922,399 | 3,100,689 | 2,343,001 | 18 | 18 | 21 |
| Massachusetts | 7,826 | 460 | 8,286 | 45 | 5,737,081 | 733 | 5,689,170 | 5,148,578 | 4,690,514 | 11 | 10 | 9 |
| Michigan | 56,959 | 40,148 | 97,107 | 22 | 9,262,070 | 163 | 8,875,083 | 7,823,194 | 6,371,766 | 8 | 7 | 7 |
| Minnesota | 79,548 | 7,066 | 86,614 | 14 | 4,075,970 | 51 | 3,805,069 | 3,413,864 | 2,982,483 | 21 | 19 | 18 |
| Mississippi | 47,234 | 457 | 47,691 | 31 | 2,520,631 | 53 | 2,216,912 | 2,178,141 | 2,178,914 | 31 | 29 | 29 |
| Missouri | 68,945 | 752 | 69,697 | 18 | 4,916,759 | 71 | 4,677,399 | 4,319,813 | 3,954,653 | 15 | 13 | 13 |
| Montana | 145,388 | 1,657 | 147,045 | 4 | 786,690 | 5.4 | 694,409 | 674,767 | 591,024 | 44 | 43 | 41 |
| Nebraska | 76,639 | 711 | 77,350 | 15 | 1,569,825 | 20 | 1,483,791 | 1,411,330 | 1,325,510 | 35 | 35 | 34 |
| Nevada | 109,895 | 667 | 110,562 | 7 | 800,493 | 7.3 | 488,738 | 285,278 | 160,083 | 43 | 47 | 49 |
| New Hampshire | 8,992 | 286 | 9,278 | 44 | 920,610 | 102 | 737,681 | 606,921 | 533,242 | 42 | 41 | 45 |
| New Jersey | 7,468 | 319 | 7,787 | 46 | 7,365,011 | 986 | 7,168,164 | 6,066,782 | 4,835,329 | 9 | 8 | 8 |
| New Mexico | 121,336 | 258 | 121,594 | 5 | 1,303,445 | 11 | 1,016,000 | 951,023 | 681,187 | 37 | 37 | 37 |
| New York | 47,379 | 5,358 | 52,737 | 30 | 17,558,072 | 371 | 18,241,266 | 16,782,304 | 14,830,192 | 2 | 1 | 1 |
| North Carolina | 48,843 | 3,826 | 52,669 | 29 | 5,881,385 | 120 | 5,082,059 | 4,556,155 | 4,061,929 | 10 | 12 | 12 |
| North Dakota | 69,299 | 1,403 | 70,702 | 17 | 652,717 | 9.4 | 617,761 | 632,446 | 619,636 | 46 | 45 | 44 |
| Ohio | 41,004 | 3,782 | 44,786 | 35 | 10,797,624 | 263 | 10,652,017 | 9,706,397 | 7,946,627 | 6 | 6 | 5 |
| Oklahoma | 68,656 | 1,301 | 69,957 | 19 | 3,025,495 | 44 | 2,559,253 | 2,328,284 | 2,233,351 | 26 | 27 | 27 |
| Oregon | 96,187 | 889 | 97,076 | 10 | 2,633,149 | 27 | 2,091,385 | 1,768,687 | 1,521,341 | 30 | 31 | 32 |
| Pennsylvania | 44,892 | 1,155 | 46,047 | 32 | 11,864,751 | 264 | 11,793,909 | 11,319,366 | 10,498,012 | 4 | 3 | 3 |
| Rhode Island | 1,054 | 158 | 1,212 | 50 | 947,154 | 899 | 949,723 | 859,488 | 791,896 | 40 | 39 | 39 |
| South Carolina | 30,207 | 909 | 31,116 | 40 | 3,122,814 | 103 | 2,590,516 | 2,382,594 | 2,117,027 | 24 | 26 | 26 |
| South Dakota | 75,956 | 1,164 | 77,120 | 16 | 690,768 | 9.1 | 666,257 | 680,514 | 652,740 | 45 | 44 | 40 |
| Tennessee | 41,154 | 989 | 42,143 | 34 | 4,591,120 | 112 | 3,924,164 | 3,567,089 | 3,291,718 | 17 | 17 | 17 |
| Texas | 262,015 | 4,790 | 266,805 | 2 | 14,227,574 | 54 | 11,196,730 | 9,579,677 | 7,711,194 | 3 | 4 | 6 |
| Utah | 82,076 | 2,826 | 84,902 | 12 | 1,461,037 | 18 | 1,059,273 | 890,627 | 688,862 | 36 | 36 | 38 |
| Vermont | 9,273 | 341 | 9,614 | 43 | 511,456 | 55 | 444,732 | 389,881 | 377,747 | 48 | 48 | 47 |
| Virginia | 39,700 | 1,063 | 40,763 | 36 | 5,346,797 | 135 | 4,648,494 | 3,966,949 | 3,318,680 | 14 | 14 | 14 |
| Washington | 66,512 | 1,627 | 68,139 | 20 | 4,132,204 | 62 | 3,409,169 | 2,853,214 | 2,378,963 | 20 | 22 | 23 |
| West Virginia | 24,124 | 112 | 24,236 | 41 | 1,950,258 | 81 | 1,744,237 | 1,860,421 | 2,005,552 | 34 | 34 | 30 |
| Wisconsin | 54,424 | 11,789 | 66,213 | 25 | 4,705,642 | 86 | 4,417,933 | 3,951,777 | 3,434,575 | 16 | 16 | 15 |
| Wyoming | 96,988 | 820 | 97,808 | 9 | 469,557 | 4.8 | 332,416 | 330,066 | 290,529 | 49 | 49 | 48 |
| United States | 3,539,341 | 139,904 | 3,679,245 | . . | 226,549,010 | 64 | 203,235,298 | 179,323,175 | 151,325,798 | . . | . . | . . |

*Includes the United States area of the Great Lakes.

# United States Geographical Information

# UNITED STATES GENERAL INFORMATION

| STATE | CAPITAL | LARGEST CITY | ENTERED UNION AS STATE — Date of Entry | Rank of Entry | GREATEST MEASUREMENT — N-S (miles) | GREATEST MEASUREMENT — E-W (miles) | HIGHEST POINT — Location | HIGHEST POINT — Altitude (feet) | STATE FLOWER | STATE BIRD | STATE NICKNAME |
|---|---|---|---|---|---|---|---|---|---|---|---|
| Alabama | Montgomery | Birmingham | Dec. 14, 1819 | 22 | 330 | 200 | Cheaha Mountain | 2,407 | Camellia | Yellowhammer | Yellowhammer |
| Alaska | Juneau | Anchorage | Jan. 3, 1959 | 49 | 1,332 | 2,250 | Mt. McKinley | 20,320 | Forget-me-not | Willow Ptarmigan | Last Frontier |
| Arizona | Phoenix | Phoenix | Feb. 14, 1912 | 48 | 390 | 335 | Humphreys Peak | 12,633 | Saguaro Cactus | Cactus Wren | Grand Canyon |
| Arkansas | Little Rock | Little Rock | June 15, 1836 | 25 | 240 | 275 | Magazine Mtn. | 2,753 | Apple Blossom | Mockingbird | Land of Opportunity |
| California | Sacramento | Los Angeles | Sept. 9, 1850 | 31 | 800 | 375 | Mt. Whitney | 14,491 | Golden Poppy | California Valley Quail | Golden |
| Colorado | Denver | Denver | Aug. 1, 1876 | 38 | 270 | 380 | Mt. Elbert | 14,433 | Rocky Mountain Columbine | Lark Bunting | Centennial |
| Connecticut★ | Hartford | Bridgeport | Jan. 9, 1788 | 5 | 75 | 90 | S. slope of Mt. Frissell | 2,380 | Mountain Laurel | Robin | Constitution |
| Delaware★ | Dover | Wilmington | Dec. 7, 1787 | 1 | 95 | 35 | Ebright Road, New Castle Co. | 442 | Peach Blossom | Blue Hen Chicken | First |
| District of Columbia★ | Washington | Washington | March 3, 1791 | ...... | 15 | 15 | Tenleytown | 410 | American Beauty Rose | Wood Thrush | |
| Florida | Tallahassee | Jacksonville | March 3, 1845 | 27 | 460 | 400 | N. boundary, Walton Co. | 345 | Orange Blossom | Mockingbird | Sunshine |
| Georgia★ | Atlanta | Atlanta | Jan. 2, 1788 | 4 | 315 | 250 | Brasstown Bald | 4,784 | Cherokee Rose | Brown Thrasher | Peach |
| Hawaii | Honolulu | Honolulu | Aug. 21, 1959 | 50 | 655 | 1,600 | Mauna Kea | 13,796 | Red Hibiscus | Nene (Hawaiian Goose) | Aloha |
| Idaho | Boise | Boise | July 3, 1890 | 43 | 480 | 305 | Borah Peak | 12,662 | Syringa | Mountain Bluebird | Gem |
| Illinois | Springfield | Chicago | Dec. 3, 1818 | 21 | 380 | 205 | Charles Mound | 1,235 | Violet | Cardinal | Prairie |
| Indiana | Indianapolis | Indianapolis | Dec. 11, 1816 | 19 | 265 | 160 | Near Spartanburg | 1,257 | Peony | Cardinal | Hoosier |
| Iowa | Des Moines | Des Moines | Dec. 28, 1846 | 29 | 205 | 310 | N.W. corner, Osceola Co. | 1,670 | Wild Rose | Eastern Goldfinch | Hawkeye |
| Kansas | Topeka | Wichita | Jan. 29, 1861 | 34 | 205 | 410 | Mt. Sunflower | 4,039 | Sunflower | Western Meadowlark | Sunflower |
| Kentucky | Frankfort | Louisville | June 1, 1792 | 15 | 175 | 350 | Black Mountain | 4,145 | Goldenrod | Kentucky Cardinal | Bluegrass |
| Louisiana | Baton Rouge | New Orleans | April 30, 1812 | 18 | 275 | 300 | Driskill Mountain | 535 | Magnolia | Pelican | Pelican |
| Maine | Augusta | Portland | March 15, 1820 | 23 | 310 | 210 | Mt. Katahdin | 5,268 | Pinecone and Tassel | Chickadee | Pine Tree |
| Maryland★ | Annapolis | Baltimore | April 28, 1788 | 7 | 120 | 200 | Backbone Mountain | 3,360 | Black-eyed Susan | Baltimore Oriole | Free |
| Massachusetts★ | Boston | Boston | Feb. 6, 1788 | 6 | 110 | 190 | Mt. Greylock | 3,491 | Mayflower | Chickadee | Bay |
| Michigan | Lansing | Detroit | Jan. 26, 1837 | 26 | 400 | 310 | Mt. Arvon | 1,979 | Apple Blossom | Robin | Wolverine |
| Minnesota | St. Paul | Minneapolis | May 11, 1858 | 32 | 400 | 350 | Eagle Mountain | 2,301 | Lady's-slipper | Loon | Gopher |
| Mississippi | Jackson | Jackson | Dec. 10, 1817 | 20 | 340 | 180 | Woodall Mountain | 806 | Magnolia | Mockingbird | Magnolia |
| Missouri | Jefferson City | St. Louis | Aug. 10, 1821 | 24 | 280 | 300 | Taum Sauk Mountain | 1,772 | Hawthorn | Bluebird | Show Me |
| Montana | Helena | Billings | Nov. 8, 1889 | 41 | 315 | 570 | Granite Peak | 12,799 | Bitterroot | Western Meadowlark | Big Sky Country |
| Nebraska | Lincoln | Omaha | March 1, 1867 | 37 | 210 | 415 | S.W. corner, Kimball Co. | 5,426 | Goldenrod | Western Meadowlark | Cornhusker |
| Nevada | Carson City | Las Vegas | Oct. 31, 1864 | 36 | 485 | 315 | Boundary Peak | 13,143 | Shrub Sagebrush | Mountain Bluebird | Silver |
| New Hampshire★ | Concord | Manchester | June 21, 1788 | 9 | 185 | 90 | Mt. Washington | 6,288 | Purple Lilac | Purple Finch | Granite |
| New Jersey★ | Trenton | Newark | Dec. 18, 1787 | 3 | 166 | 70 | High Point | 1,803 | Purple Violet | Eastern Goldfinch | Garden |
| New Mexico | Santa Fe | Albuquerque | Jan. 6, 1912 | 47 | 390 | 350 | Wheeler Peak | 13,161 | Yucca | Roadrunner | Land of Enchantment |
| New York★ | Albany | New York | July 26, 1788 | 11 | 310 | 330 | Mt. Marcy | 5,344 | Rose | Bluebird | Empire |
| North Carolina★ | Raleigh | Charlotte | Nov. 21, 1789 | 12 | 200 | 520 | Mt. Mitchell | 6,684 | Dogwood | Cardinal | Tar Heel |
| North Dakota | Bismarck | Fargo | Nov. 2, 1889 | 39 | 210 | 360 | White Butte | 3,506 | Wild Prairie Rose | Western Meadowlark | Flickertail |
| Ohio | Columbus | Cleveland | March 1, 1803 | 17 | 230 | 205 | Campbell Hill | 1,550 | Scarlet Carnation | Cardinal | Buckeye |
| Oklahoma | Oklahoma City | Oklahoma City | Nov. 16, 1907 | 46 | 210 | 460 | Black Mesa | 4,973 | Mistletoe | Scissor-tailed Flycatcher | Sooner |
| Oregon | Salem | Portland | Feb. 14, 1859 | 33 | 290 | 375 | Mt. Hood | 11,235 | Oregon Grape | Western Meadowlark | Beaver |
| Pennsylvania★ | Harrisburg | Philadelphia | Dec. 12, 1787 | 2 | 180 | 310 | Mt. Davis | 3,213 | Mountain Laurel | Ruffed Grouse | Keystone |
| Rhode Island★ | Providence | Providence | May 29, 1790 | 13 | 50 | 35 | Jerimoth Hill | 812 | Violet | Rhode Island Red | Little Rhody |
| South Carolina★ | Columbia | Columbia | May 23, 1788 | 8 | 215 | 285 | Sassafras Mountain | 3,560 | Yellow Jessamine | Carolina Wren | Palmetto |
| South Dakota | Pierre | Sioux Falls | Nov. 2, 1889 | 40 | 240 | 360 | Harney Peak | 7,242 | Pasque | Ring-necked Pheasant | Coyote |
| Tennessee | Nashville | Memphis | June 1, 1796 | 16 | 120 | 430 | Clingmans Dome | 6,643 | Iris | Mockingbird | Volunteer |
| Texas | Austin | Houston | Dec. 29, 1845 | 28 | 710 | 760 | Guadalupe Peak | 8,749 | Bluebonnet | Mockingbird | Lone Star |
| Utah | Salt Lake City | Salt Lake City | Jan. 4, 1896 | 45 | 345 | 275 | Kings Peak | 13,528 | Sego Lily | Sea Gull | Beehive |
| Vermont | Montpelier | Burlington | March 4, 1791 | 14 | 155 | 90 | Mt. Mansfield | 4,393 | Red Clover | Hermit Thrush | Green Mountain |
| Virginia★ | Richmond | Norfolk | June 25, 1788 | 10 | 205 | 425 | Mt. Rogers | 5,729 | American Dogwood | Cardinal | Old Dominion |
| Washington | Olympia | Seattle | Nov. 11, 1889 | 42 | 230 | 340 | Mt. Rainier | 14,410 | Rhododendron | Willow Goldfinch | Evergreen |
| West Virginia | Charleston | Charleston | June 20, 1863 | 35 | 200 | 225 | Spruce Knob | 4,862 | Rhododendron | Cardinal | Mountain |
| Wisconsin | Madison | Milwaukee | May 29, 1848 | 30 | 300 | 290 | Timms Hill | 1,952 | Violet | Robin | Badger |
| Wyoming | Cheyenne | Casper | July 10, 1890 | 44 | 275 | 365 | Gannett Peak | 13,804 | Indian Paintbrush | Meadowlark | Equality |
| United States | Washington, D.C. | New York | ...... | ...... | ...... | 365 | Mt. McKinley, Alaska | 20,320 | | Bald Eagle | |

★One of the Thirteen Original States

# UNITED STATES POPULATION BY STATE OR COLONY, 1650–1980

| STATES | 1650 | 1700 | 1750 | 1770 | 1790 | 1800 | 1820 | 1840 | 1860 | 1880 | 1900 | 1920 | 1940 | 1950 | 1960 | 1970 | 1980 |
|---|---|---|---|---|---|---|---|---|---|---|---|---|---|---|---|---|---|
| Alabama | | | | | | | 127,901 | 590,756 | 964,201 | 1,262,505 | 1,828,697 | 2,348,174 | 2,832,961 | 3,061,743 | 3,266,740 | 3,444,165 | 3,893,978 |
| Alaska | | | | | | | | | | 33,426 | 63,592 | 55,036 | 72,524 | 128,643 | 226,167 | 302,173 | 401,851 |
| Arizona | | | | | | | | | | 40,440 | 122,931 | 334,162 | 499,261 | 749,587 | 1,302,161 | 1,772,482 | 2,718,425 |
| Arkansas | | | | | | | 14,273 | 97,574 | 435,450 | 802,525 | 1,311,564 | 1,752,204 | 1,949,387 | 1,909,511 | 1,786,272 | 1,923,295 | 2,286,419 |
| California | | | | | | | | | 379,994 | 864,694 | 1,485,053 | 3,426,861 | 6,907,387 | 10,586,223 | 15,717,204 | 19,953,134 | 23,667,837 |
| Colorado | | | | | | | | | 34,277 | 194,327 | 539,700 | 939,629 | 1,123,296 | 1,325,089 | 1,753,947 | 2,207,259 | 2,889,735 |
| Connecticut | 4,139 | 25,970 | 111,280 | 183,881 | 237,946 | 251,002 | 275,248 | 309,978 | 460,147 | 622,700 | 908,420 | 1,380,631 | 1,709,242 | 2,007,280 | 2,535,234 | 3,032,217 | 3,107,576 |
| Delaware | 185 | 2,470 | 28,704 | 35,496 | 59,096 | 64,273 | 72,749 | 78,085 | 112,216 | 146,608 | 184,735 | 223,003 | 266,505 | 318,085 | 446,292 | 548,104 | 594,317 |
| District of Columbia | | | | | | 8,144 | 23,336 | 33,745 | 75,080 | 177,624 | 278,718 | 437,571 | 663,091 | 802,178 | 763,956 | 756,510 | 638,432 |
| Florida | | | | | | | | 54,477 | 140,424 | 269,493 | 528,542 | 968,470 | 1,897,414 | 2,771,305 | 4,951,560 | 6,789,443 | 9,746,421 |
| Georgia | | | 5,200 | 23,375 | 82,548 | 162,686 | 340,989 | 691,392 | 1,057,286 | 1,542,180 | 2,216,331 | 2,895,832 | 3,123,723 | 3,444,578 | 3,943,116 | 4,589,575 | 5,463,087 |
| Hawaii | | | | | | | | | | | 154,001 | 255,881 | 422,770 | 499,794 | 632,772 | 769,913 | 964,691 |
| Idaho | | | | | | | | | | 32,610 | 161,772 | 431,866 | 524,873 | 588,637 | 667,191 | 713,008 | 944,038 |
| Illinois | | | | | | | 55,211 | 476,183 | 1,711,951 | 3,077,871 | 4,821,550 | 6,485,280 | 7,897,241 | 8,712,176 | 10,081,158 | 11,113,976 | 11,427,414 |
| Indiana | | | | | | 5,641 | 147,178 | 685,866 | 1,350,428 | 1,978,301 | 2,516,462 | 2,930,390 | 3,427,796 | 3,934,224 | 4,662,498 | 5,193,669 | 5,490,260 |
| Iowa | | | | | | | | 43,112 | 674,913 | 1,624,615 | 2,231,853 | 2,404,021 | 2,538,268 | 2,621,073 | 2,757,537 | 2,825,041 | 2,913,808 |
| Kansas | | | | | | | | | 107,206 | 996,096 | 1,470,495 | 1,769,257 | 1,801,028 | 1,905,299 | 2,178,611 | 2,249,071 | 2,364,236 |
| Kentucky | | | | 15,700 | 73,677 | 220,955 | 564,317 | 779,828 | 1,155,684 | 1,648,690 | 2,147,174 | 2,416,630 | 2,845,627 | 2,944,806 | 3,038,156 | 3,219,311 | 3,660,257 |
| Louisiana | | | | | | | 153,407 | 352,411 | 708,002 | 939,946 | 1,381,625 | 1,798,509 | 2,363,880 | 2,683,516 | 3,257,022 | 3,643,180 | 4,206,098 |
| Maine[4] | | | | 31,257 | 96,540 | 151,719 | 298,335 | 501,793 | 628,279 | 648,936 | 694,466 | 768,014 | 847,226 | 913,774 | 969,265 | 993,663 | 1,125,030 |
| Maryland | 4,504 | 29,604 | 141,073 | 202,599 | 319,728 | 341,548 | 407,350 | 470,019 | 687,049 | 934,943 | 1,188,044 | 1,449,661 | 1,821,244 | 2,343,001 | 3,100,689 | 3,922,399 | 4,216,941 |
| Massachusetts[4] | 16,603 | 55,941 | 188,000 | 235,308 | 378,787 | 422,845 | 523,287 | 737,699 | 1,231,066 | 1,783,085 | 2,805,346 | 3,852,356 | 4,316,721 | 4,690,514 | 5,148,578 | 5,689,170 | 5,737,081 |
| Michigan | | | | | | | 8,896 | 212,267 | 749,113 | 1,636,937 | 2,420,982 | 3,668,412 | 5,256,106 | 6,371,766 | 7,823,194 | 8,875,083 | 9,262,070 |
| Minnesota | | | | | | | | | 172,023 | 780,773 | 1,751,394 | 2,387,125 | 2,792,300 | 2,982,483 | 3,413,864 | 3,805,069 | 4,075,970 |
| Mississippi | | | | | | 8,850 | 75,448 | 375,651 | 791,305 | 1,131,597 | 1,551,270 | 1,790,618 | 2,183,796 | 2,178,914 | 2,178,141 | 2,216,912 | 2,520,631 |
| Missouri | | | | | | | 66,586 | 383,702 | 1,182,012 | 2,168,380 | 3,106,665 | 3,404,055 | 3,784,664 | 3,954,653 | 4,319,813 | 4,677,399 | 4,916,759 |
| Montana | | | | | | | | | | 39,159 | 243,329 | 548,889 | 559,456 | 591,024 | 674,767 | 694,409 | 786,690 |
| Nebraska | | | | | | | | | 28,841 | 452,402 | 1,066,300 | 1,296,372 | 1,315,834 | 1,325,510 | 1,411,330 | 1,483,791 | 1,569,825 |
| Nevada | | | | | | | | | 6,857 | 62,266 | 42,335 | 77,407 | 110,247 | 160,083 | 285,278 | 488,738 | 800,493 |
| New Hampshire | 1,305 | 4,958 | 27,505 | 62,396 | 141,885 | 183,858 | 244,161 | 284,574 | 326,073 | 346,991 | 411,588 | 443,083 | 491,524 | 533,242 | 606,921 | 737,681 | 920,610 |
| New Jersey | | 14,010 | 71,393 | 117,431 | 184,139 | 211,149 | 277,575 | 373,306 | 672,035 | 1,131,116 | 1,883,669 | 3,155,900 | 4,160,165 | 4,835,329 | 6,066,782 | 7,168,164 | 7,365,011 |
| New Mexico | | | | | | | | | 93,516 | 119,565 | 195,310 | 360,350 | 531,818 | 681,187 | 951,023 | 1,016,000 | 1,303,445 |
| New York | 4,116 | 19,107 | 76,696 | 162,920 | 340,120 | 589,051 | 1,372,812 | 2,428,921 | 3,880,735 | 5,082,871 | 7,268,894 | 10,385,227 | 13,479,142 | 14,830,192 | 16,782,304 | 18,241,266 | 17,558,072 |
| North Carolina | | 10,720 | 72,984 | 197,200 | 393,751 | 478,103 | 638,829 | 753,419 | 992,622 | 1,399,750 | 1,893,810 | 2,559,123 | 3,571,623 | 4,061,929 | 4,556,155 | 5,082,059 | 5,881,385 |
| North Dakota[3] | | | | | | | | | | 36,909 | 319,146 | 646,872 | 641,935 | 619,636 | 632,446 | 617,761 | 652,717 |
| Ohio[3] | | | | | | 45,365 | 581,434 | 1,519,467 | 2,339,511 | 3,198,062 | 4,157,545 | 5,759,394 | 6,907,612 | 7,946,627 | 9,706,397 | 10,652,017 | 10,797,624 |
| Oklahoma[5] | | | | | | | | | | | 790,391 | 2,028,283 | 2,336,434 | 2,233,351 | 2,328,284 | 2,559,253 | 3,025,495 |
| Oregon | | | | | | | | | 52,465 | 174,768 | 413,536 | 783,389 | 1,089,684 | 1,521,341 | 1,768,687 | 2,091,385 | 2,633,149 |
| Pennsylvania | | 17,950 | 119,666 | 240,057 | 434,373 | 602,365 | 1,049,458 | 1,724,033 | 2,906,215 | 4,282,891 | 6,302,115 | 8,720,017 | 9,900,180 | 10,498,012 | 11,319,366 | 11,793,909 | 11,864,751 |
| Rhode Island | 785 | 5,894 | 33,226 | 58,196 | 68,825 | 69,122 | 83,059 | 108,830 | 174,620 | 276,531 | 428,556 | 604,397 | 713,346 | 791,896 | 859,488 | 949,723 | 947,154 |
| South Carolina | | 5,704 | 64,000 | 124,244 | 249,073 | 345,591 | 502,741 | 594,398 | 703,708 | 995,577 | 1,340,316 | 1,683,724 | 1,899,804 | 2,117,027 | 2,382,594 | 2,590,516 | 3,122,814 |
| South Dakota[3] | | | | | | | | | | 98,268 | 401,570 | 636,547 | 642,961 | 652,740 | 680,514 | 666,257 | 690,768 |
| Tennessee | | | | 1,000 | 35,691 | 105,602 | 422,823 | 829,210 | 1,109,801 | 1,542,359 | 2,020,616 | 2,337,885 | 2,915,841 | 3,291,718 | 3,567,089 | 3,924,164 | 4,591,120 |
| Texas | | | | | | | | | 604,215 | 1,591,749 | 3,048,710 | 4,663,228 | 6,414,824 | 7,711,194 | 9,579,677 | 11,196,730 | 14,227,574 |
| Utah | | | | | | | | | 40,273 | 143,963 | 276,749 | 449,396 | 550,310 | 688,862 | 890,627 | 1,059,273 | 1,461,037 |
| Vermont | | | | 10,000 | 85,425 | 154,465 | 235,981 | 291,948 | 315,098 | 332,286 | 343,641 | 352,428 | 359,231 | 377,747 | 389,881 | 444,732 | 511,456 |
| Virginia[6] | 18,731 | 58,560 | 231,033 | 447,016 | 691,737 | 807,557 | 938,261 | 1,025,227 | 1,219,630 | 1,512,565 | 1,854,184 | 2,309,187 | 2,677,773 | 3,318,680 | 3,966,949 | 4,648,494 | 5,346,797 |
| Washington | | | | | | | | | 11,594 | 75,116 | 518,103 | 1,356,621 | 1,736,191 | 2,378,963 | 2,853,214 | 3,409,169 | 4,132,204 |
| West Virginia[6] | | | | | 55,873 | 78,592 | 136,808 | 224,537 | 376,688 | 618,457 | 958,800 | 1,463,701 | 1,901,974 | 2,005,552 | 1,860,421 | 1,744,237 | 1,950,258 |
| Wisconsin | | | | | | | | 30,945 | 775,881 | 1,315,497 | 2,069,042 | 2,632,067 | 3,137,587 | 3,434,575 | 3,951,777 | 4,417,933 | 4,705,642 |
| Wyoming | | | | | | | | | | 20,789 | 92,531 | 194,402 | 250,742 | 290,529 | 330,066 | 332,416 | 469,557 |
| **Total[1]** | 50,368 | 250,888 | 1,170,760 | 2,148,076 | 3,929,214 | 5,308,483 | 9,638,453 | 17,069,453[2] | 31,443,321 | 50,189,209 | 76,212,168 | 106,021,537 | 132,164,569 | 151,325,798 | 179,323,175 | 203,235,298 | 226,549,010 |

1 All figures prior to 1890 exclude uncivilized Indians. Figures for 1650 through 1770 include only the British colonies that later became the United States. No areas are included prior to their annexation to the United States. However, many of the figures refer to territories prior to their admission as States. U.S. total includes Alaska from 1880 through 1970 and Hawaii from 1900 through 1970.

2 U.S. total for 1840 includes 6,100 persons on public ships in service of the United States, not credited to any State.

3 South Dakota figure for 1860 represents entire Dakota Territory; North and South Dakota figures for 1880 are for the parts of Dakota Territory which later constituted the respective States.

4 Maine figures for 1770 through 1800 are for that area of Massachusetts which became the State of Maine in 1820. Massachusetts figures exclude Maine from 1770 through 1800, but include it from 1650 through 1750. Massachusetts figure for 1650 also includes population of Plymouth (1,566), a separate colony until 1691.

5 Oklahoma figure for 1900 includes population of Indian Territory (392,060).

6 West Virginia figures for 1790 through 1860 are for that area of Virginia which became West Virginia in 1863. These figures are excluded from the figures for Virginia from 1790 through 1860.

# UNITED STATES METROPOLITAN AREAS

This table ranks the largest cities of the United States according to their metropolitan area populations. The Ranally Metropolitan Area (RMA) populations reflect Rand McNally's exclusive definition of metropolitan areas. Each RMA includes one or more central cities, as well as socially and economically integrated surrounding areas. The populations of RMAs that are partly in Canada or Mexico are for the United States parts only. The table also indicates central city populations and compares the latest available data to the previous census. Populations are rounded totals. 1980 populations reflect final census data.

| 1980 Rank | Metropolitan Area | Metropolitan Area Population Census 4/1/80 | Census 4/1/70 | % Change 1970–80 | City Population Census 4/1/80 | % Change 1970–80 |
|---|---|---|---|---|---|---|
| 1 | New York, NY-NJ-CT | 16,800,900 | 17,483,900 | −3.9 | 7,400,800 | −10.6 |
| | New York, NY | | | | 7,071,600 | −10.4 |
| | Newark, NJ | | | | 329,200 | −13.8 |
| 2 | Los Angeles, CA | 9,763,600 | 8,672,500 | 12.6 | 2,968,600 | 5.6 |
| 3 | Chicago, IL-IN-WI | 7,717,100 | 7,577,900 | 1.8 | 3,005,100 | −10.8 |
| 4 | Philadelphia-Trenton-Wilmington, PA-NJ-DE-MD | 5,208,600 | 5,322,200 | −2.1 | 1,850,500 | −13.3 |
| | Philadelphia, PA | | | | 1,688,200 | −13.4 |
| | Trenton, NJ | | | | 92,100 | −12.1 |
| | Wilmington, NJ | | | | 70,200 | −12.7 |
| 5 | San Francisco-Oakland-San Jose, CA | 4,683,200 | 4,278,600 | 9.5 | 1,647,700 | 7.2 |
| | San Francisco, CA | | | | 679,000 | −5.1 |
| | Oakland, CA | | | | 339,300 | −6.2 |
| | San Jose, CA | | | | 629,400 | 36.9 |
| 6 | Detroit, MI-CAN | 4,445,800 | 4,526,100 | −1.8 | 1,310,500 | −18.8 |
| | Detroit, MI | | | | 1,202,500 | −20.6 |
| | Ann Arbor, MI | | | | 108,000 | 7.3 |
| 7 | Boston, MA-NH | 3,971,700 | 3,939,000 | .8 | 899,000 | −8.1 |
| | Boston, MA | | | | 563,000 | −12.2 |
| | Lowell, MA | | | | 92,400 | −1.9 |
| | Lawrence, MA | | | | 63,200 | −5.5 |
| | Haverhill, MA | | | | 46,900 | 1.7 |
| | Brockton, MA | | | | 95,200 | 7.0 |
| | Salem, MA | | | | 38,300 | −5.7 |
| 8 | Washington, DC-MD-VA | 3,221,400 | 2,992,600 | 7.6 | 638,400 | −15.6 |
| 9 | Miami-Ft. Lauderdale, FL | 2,827,300 | 1,973,500 | 43.3 | 500,200 | 5.4 |
| | Miami, FL | | | | 346,900 | 3.6 |
| | Ft. Lauderdale, FL | | | | 153,300 | 9.8 |
| 10 | Houston, TX | 2,755,100 | 1,903,300 | 44.8 | 1,595,100 | 29.3 |
| 11 | Dallas-Ft. Worth, TX | 2,727,300 | 2,187,500 | 24.7 | 1,289,300 | 4.1 |
| | Dallas, TX | | | | 904,100 | 7.1 |
| | Ft. Worth, TX | | | | 385,200 | −2.1 |
| 12 | Pittsburgh, PA | 2,218,800 | 2,350,300 | −5.6 | 424,000 | −18.5 |
| 13 | Cleveland, OH | 2,218,400 | 2,360,600 | −6.0 | 573,800 | −23.6 |
| 14 | St. Louis, MO-IL | 2,203,000 | 2,285,900 | −3.6 | 452,800 | −27.2 |
| 15 | Seattle-Tacoma, WA | 2,077,100 | 1,823,500 | 13.9 | 706,700 | −4.3 |
| | Seattle, WA | | | | 493,800 | −7.0 |
| | Tacoma, WA | | | | 158,500 | 2.7 |
| 16 | Minneapolis-St. Paul, MN-WI | 2,012,400 | 1,857,500 | 8.3 | 641,200 | −13.9 |
| | Minneapolis, MN | | | | 371,000 | −14.6 |
| | St. Paul, MN | | | | 270,200 | −12.8 |
| 17 | Atlanta, GA | 1,962,500 | 1,543,200 | 27.2 | 425,000 | −14.1 |
| 18 | Baltimore, MD | 1,960,400 | 1,900,300 | 3.2 | 786,700 | −13.1 |
| 19 | San Diego, CA-MEX | 1,648,500 | 1,227,700 | 34.3 | 875,500 | 25.5 |
| 20 | Phoenix, AZ | 1,482,400 | 955,300 | 55.2 | 790,000 | 35.2 |
| 21 | Cincinnati, OH-KY-IN | 1,480,100 | 1,448,400 | 2.2 | 385,500 | −15.0 |
| 22 | Denver, CO | 1,405,300 | 1,083,600 | 29.7 | 492,400 | −4.3 |
| 23 | Milwaukee, WI | 1,374,700 | 1,388,900 | −1.0 | 636,300 | −11.3 |
| 24 | Kansas City, MO-KS | 1,272,400 | 1,228,700 | 3.6 | 448,000 | −11.7 |
| 25 | Portland, OR-WA | 1,227,200 | 997,100 | 23.1 | 368,100 | −3.1 |
| 26 | New Orleans, LA | 1,185,000 | 1,045,300 | 13.4 | 557,900 | −6.0 |
| 27 | Buffalo, NY-CAN | 1,155,200 | 1,266,700 | −8.8 | 357,900 | −22.7 |
| 28 | Indianapolis, IN | 1,072,500 | 1,022,500 | 4.9 | 700,800 | −6.2 |
| 29 | Hartford-New Britain, CT | 1,013,600 | 999,800 | 1.4 | 210,200 | −12.9 |
| | Hartford, CT | | | | 136,400 | −13.7 |
| | New Britain, CT | | | | 73,800 | −11.5 |
| 30 | San Antonio, TX | 968,200 | 818,300 | 18.3 | 786,000 | 20.1 |
| 31 | Columbus, OH | 963,600 | 906,500 | 6.3 | 565,000 | 4.6 |
| 32 | Providence-Warwick, RI-MA | 921,100 | 910,100 | 1.3 | 245,100 | −6.7 |
| | Providence, RI | | | | 156,800 | −12.5 |
| | Warwick, RI | | | | 88,300 | 5.5 |
| 33 | Louisville, KY-IN | 891,400 | 853,000 | 4.5 | 298,700 | −17.4 |
| 34 | Sacramento, CA | 866,400 | 698,100 | 24.1 | 275,700 | 7.2 |
| 35 | Memphis, TN-AR-MS | 852,900 | 779,200 | 9.5 | 646,200 | 3.6 |
| 36 | St. Petersburg-Clearwater, FL | 852,300 | 561,800 | 51.7 | 324,100 | 20.8 |
| | St. Petersburg, FL | | | | 238,600 | 10.4 |
| | Clearwater, FL | | | | 85,500 | 64.1 |
| 37 | Rochester, NY | 816,200 | 811,700 | .6 | 241,700 | −18.1 |
| 38 | Norfolk-Virginia Beach, VA | 795,600 | 725,800 | 9.6 | 529,200 | 10.2 |
| | Norfolk, VA | | | | 267,000 | −13.3 |
| | Virginia Beach, VA | | | | 262,200 | 52.4 |
| 39 | Riverside-San Bernardino, CA | 768,300 | 628,800 | 22.2 | 289,400 | 17.2 |
| | Riverside, CA | | | | 170,600 | 21.8 |
| | San Bernardino, CA | | | | 118,800 | 11.1 |
| 40 | Dayton, OH | 768,200 | 797,200 | −3.6 | 193,500 | −20.4 |
| 41 | Honolulu, HI | 762,600 | 630,500 | 21.0 | 365,000 | 12.3 |
| 42 | Birmingham, AL | 747,400 | 690,100 | 8.3 | 286,800 | −4.7 |
| 43 | Oklahoma City, OK | 742,000 | 627,300 | 18.3 | 403,500 | 9.6 |
| 44 | Albany-Schenectady-Troy, NY | 729,100 | 717,200 | 1.7 | 226,300 | −11.8 |
| | Albany, NY | | | | 101,700 | −12.2 |
| | Schenectady, NY | | | | 68,000 | −12.8 |
| | Troy, NY | | | | 56,600 | −10.0 |
| 45 | Richmond, VA | 690,600 | 621,900 | 11.0 | 219,200 | −12.1 |
| 46 | Salt Lake City, UT | 682,400 | 510,200 | 33.8 | 163,000 | −7.0 |
| 47 | Jacksonville, FL | 635,900 | 561,700 | 13.2 | 540,900 | 7.3 |
| 48 | Nashville, TN | 633,900 | 537,800 | 17.9 | 455,700 | 7.0 |
| 49 | Orlando, FL | 619,300 | 410,900 | 50.7 | 128,300 | 29.6 |
| 50 | Akron, OH | 614,100 | 635,200 | −3.3 | 237,200 | −13.9 |
| 51 | Toledo, OH-MI | 595,500 | 589,000 | 1.1 | 354,600 | −7.4 |
| 52 | Tampa, FL | 594,500 | 454,600 | 30.8 | 271,600 | −2.2 |
| 53 | Tulsa, OK | 567,100 | 459,400 | 23.4 | 360,900 | −9.2 |
| 54 | Omaha, NE | 538,600 | 512,400 | 5.1 | 322,100 | −7.1 |
| 55 | Allentown-Bethlehem, PA-NJ | 529,000 | 499,500 | 5.9 | 174,200 | −4.1 |
| | Allentown, PA | | | | 103,800 | −5.6 |
| | Bethlehem, PA | | | | 70,400 | −3.2 |
| 56 | Flint, MI | 521,200 | 502,000 | 3.8 | 159,600 | −17.4 |
| 57 | Syracuse, NY | 518,600 | 521,200 | − .5 | 170,100 | −13.8 |
| 58 | Grand Rapids, MI | 503,800 | 454,300 | 10.9 | 181,800 | −8.0 |
| 59 | New Haven, CT | 500,500 | 488,700 | 2.4 | 126,100 | −8.4 |
| 60 | Youngstown-Warren, OH-PA | 499,600 | 507,900 | −1.6 | 172,000 | −15.9 |
| | Youngstown, OH | | | | 115,400 | −18.1 |
| | Warren, OH | | | | 56,600 | −10.9 |
| 61 | Tuscon, AZ | 495,600 | 331,000 | 49.7 | 336,500 | 28.0 |
| 62 | Scranton–Wilkes-Barre, PA | 492,700 | 500,700 | −1.6 | 139,700 | −13.6 |
| | Scranton, PA | | | | 88,100 | −14.2 |
| | Wilkes-Barre, PA | | | | 51,600 | −12.4 |
| 63 | Knoxville-Marysville-Oak Ridge, TN | 490,000 | 419,400 | 16.8 | 220,200 | 1.6 |
| | Knoxville, TN | | | | 175,000 | .2 |
| | Marysville, TN | | | | 17,500 | 26.8 |
| | Oak Ridge, TN | | | | 27,700 | −2.1 |
| 64 | Springfield, MA | 485,900 | 498,400 | −2.5 | 152,300 | −7.1 |
| 65 | El Paso, TX-MEX | 482,700 | 360,100 | 34.0 | 425,300 | 32.0 |
| 66 | Charlotte, NC | 479,200 | 416,800 | 15.0 | 315,500 | 30.7 |
| 67 | Las Vegas, NV | 453,800 | 267,800 | 69.5 | 164,700 | 30.9 |
| 68 | Albuquerque, NM | 453,200 | 331,100 | 36.9 | 332,300 | 35.9 |
| 69 | Bridgeport, CT | 438,500 | 443,700 | −1.2 | 142,500 | −8.9 |
| 70 | Baton Rouge, LA | 434,400 | 328,800 | 32.1 | 238,900 | 44.0 |
| 71 | Austin, TX | 430,200 | 299,700 | 43.5 | 345,900 | 36.4 |
| 72 | Worcester, MA | 402,900 | 399,700 | .8 | 161,800 | −8.4 |
| 73 | Harrisburg, PA | 396,300 | 362,900 | 9.2 | 53,300 | −21.7 |
| 74 | Greensboro-High Point, NC | 392,400 | 347,800 | 12.8 | 219,400 | 5.8 |
| | Greensboro, NC | | | | 155,600 | 8.0 |
| | High Point, NC | | | | 63,800 | .9 |
| 75 | Fresno, CA | 389,500 | 314,100 | 24.0 | 235,800 | 42.3 |
| 76 | Little Rock, AR | 382,000 | 312,300 | 22.3 | 167,700 | 26.6 |
| 77 | Columbia, SC | 375,900 | 296,700 | 26.7 | 101,200 | −10.8 |
| 78 | Wichita, KS | 372,200 | 353,600 | 5.3 | 279,800 | 1.2 |
| 79 | Saginaw-Bay City-Midland, MI | 362,700 | 353,600 | 2.6 | 156,400 | −11.3 |
| | Saginaw, MI | | | | 77,500 | −15.6 |
| | Bay City, MI | | | | 41,600 | −15.7 |
| | Midland, MI | | | | 37,300 | 6.0 |
| 80 | Mobile, AL | 361,900 | 318,300 | 13.7 | 200,500 | 5.5 |
| 81 | Chattanooga, TN-GA | 359,200 | 316,400 | 13.5 | 169,700 | 41.5 |
| 82 | West Palm Beach, FL | 356,000 | 233,300 | 52.6 | 63,300 | 10.3 |
| 83 | Lansing, MI | 352,600 | 319,100 | 10.5 | 130,400 | − .8 |
| 84 | Charleston, SC | 352,000 | 274,400 | 28.3 | 69,900 | 4.5 |
| 85 | Beaumont-Port Arthur, TX | 346,300 | 324,000 | 6.9 | 179,400 | 2.6 |
| | Beaumont, TX | | | | 118,100 | .5 |
| | Port Arthur, TX | | | | 61,300 | 6.8 |
| 86 | Greenville, SC | 328,500 | 265,900 | 23.5 | 58,200 | −5.2 |
| 87 | Davenport-Rock Island-Moline, IA-IL | 320,400 | 304,000 | 5.4 | 196,500 | .8 |
| | Davenport, IA | | | | 103,300 | 4.9 |
| | Rock Island, IL | | | | 46,800 | −6.8 |
| | Moline, IL | | | | 46,400 | −1.1 |
| 88 | Peoria, IL | 319,700 | 301,800 | 5.9 | 124,200 | −2.2 |
| 89 | Newport News-Hampton, VA | 314,600 | 299,100 | 5.2 | 267,500 | 3.3 |
| | Newport News, VA | | | | 194,900 | 4.8 |
| | Hampton, VA | | | | 122,600 | 1.5 |
| 90 | Canton-Massillon, OH | 311,200 | 311,100 | .3 | 123,700 | −13.3 |
| | Canton, OH | | | | 93,100 | −15.4 |
| | Massillon, OH | | | | 30,600 | −5.8 |
| 91 | Des Moines, IA | 308,000 | 273,800 | 12.5 | 191,000 | −5.2 |
| 92 | Jackson, MS | 306,900 | 245,200 | 25.2 | 202,900 | 31.8 |
| 93 | Spokane, WA-ID | 303,200 | 258,200 | 17.4 | 171,300 | .5 |
| 94 | Colorado Springs, CO | 301,500 | 252,300 | 19.5 | 214,800 | 58.5 |
| 95 | Madison, WI | 294,300 | 263,600 | 11.6 | 170,600 | − .7 |
| 96 | Oxnard-Ventura, CA | 294,200 | 222,800 | 32.0 | 186,200 | 44.1 |
| | Oxnard, CA | | | | 108,200 | 52.0 |
| | Ventura, CA | | | | 78,000 | 34.5 |
| 97 | Shreveport, LA-TX | 292,500 | 260,000 | 12.5 | 205,800 | 13.0 |
| 98 | Fort Wayne, IN | 284,300 | 270,700 | 5.0 | 172,300 | −3.4 |
| 99 | Raleigh, NC | 282,800 | 216,900 | 30.4 | 150,300 | 22.4 |
| 100 | Sarasota-Bradenton, FL | 281,900 | 187,400 | 50.4 | 79,100 | 29.2 |
| | Sarasota, FL | | | | 48,900 | 21.6 |
| | Bradenton, FL | | | | 30,200 | 43.8 |
| 101 | Rockford, IL | 280,700 | 281,400 | − .3 | 139,700 | −5.2 |
| 102 | South Bend, IN-MI | 279,500 | 279,600 | .0 | 109,700 | −12.7 |
| 103 | Winston-Salem, NC | 278,400 | 236,700 | 17.6 | 138,600 | 3.7 |
| 104 | Huntington, WV-KY-OH | 273,900 | 256,600 | 6.7 | 63,700 | −14.7 |
| 105 | Corpus Christi, TX | 272,000 | 237,800 | 14.4 | 231,100 | 13.0 |
| 106 | Lexington, KY | 255,600 | 212,000 | 20.6 | 204,200 | 88.9 |
| 107 | Augusta, GA-SC | 251,100 | 211,900 | 18.5 | 47,500 | −20.7 |
| 108 | New London-Norwich, CT-RI | 250,800 | 242,600 | 3.4 | 66,900 | −8.7 |
| | New London, CT | | | | 28,800 | −8.9 |
| | Norwich, CT | | | | 38,100 | −8.6 |
| 109 | Pensacola, FL | 250,200 | 210,000 | 19.1 | 57,600 | −3.2 |
| 110 | Erie, PA-NY | 248,800 | 235,900 | 5.5 | 119,100 | −7.9 |
| 111 | Bakersfield, CA | 245,100 | 198,800 | 23.3 | 105,700 | 52.1 |
| 112 | Reading, PA | 245,100 | 239,500 | 2.3 | 78,700 | −10.2 |
| 113 | Kalamazoo, MI | 240,800 | 222,500 | 8.2 | 79,700 | −6.9 |
| 114 | Fayetteville, NC | 236,200 | 202,700 | 16.5 | 59,500 | 11.2 |
| 115 | Charleston, WV | 236,300 | 244,500 | −3.4 | 64,000 | −10.5 |
| 116 | Columbus, GA-AL | 233,400 | 231,000 | 1.0 | 169,400 | 1.7 |
| 117 | Binghamton, NY-PA | 230,600 | 238,700 | −3.4 | 55,900 | −12.8 |
| 118 | Melbourne, FL | 227,500 | 155,600 | 46.2 | 46,200 | 15.7 |
| 119 | Macon, GA | 227,400 | 203,200 | 11.9 | 116,900 | −4.5 |
| 120 | Lancaster, PA | 227,200 | 206,600 | 10.0 | 54,700 | −5.2 |
| 121 | Montgomery, AL | 225,000 | 182,000 | 23.6 | 177,900 | 33.4 |
| 122 | Utica-Rome, NY | 224,000 | 246,700 | −9.2 | 119,400 | −15.6 |
| | Utica, NY | | | | 75,600 | −17.3 |
| | Rome, NY | | | | 43,800 | −12.6 |
| 123 | Evansville, IN-KY | 223,900 | 209,900 | 6.7 | 130,500 | −6.0 |
| 124 | Eugene, OR | 218,100 | 172,100 | 26.7 | 105,700 | 33.8 |
| 125 | Ogden, UT | 217,300 | 172,000 | 26.3 | 64,400 | −7.3 |
| 126 | Roanoke, VA | 216,000 | 196,000 | 10.2 | 100,200 | 8.8 |
| 127 | Provo, UT | 215,200 | 135,700 | 58.6 | 74,100 | 39.5 |
| 128 | York, PA | 213,300 | 194,400 | 9.7 | 44,600 | −11.3 |
| 129 | Stockton, CA | 213,000 | 182,700 | 16.6 | 149,800 | 36.2 |
| 130 | Savannah, GA | 212,800 | 194,700 | 9.3 | 141,700 | 19.8 |
| 131 | McAllen, TX | 207,600 | 127,800 | 62.4 | 66,300 | 76.3 |
| 132 | Waterbury, CT | 205,000 | 196,100 | 4.5 | 103,300 | −4.4 |
| 133 | Durham-Chapel Hill, NC | 203,100 | 170,000 | 19.5 | 132,900 | 9.3 |
| | Durham, NC | | | | 100,500 | 5.3 |
| | Chapel Hill, NC | | | | 32,400 | 23.7 |
| 134 | Lubbock, TX | 198,100 | 270,700 | 16.1 | 174,000 | −16.7 |
| 135 | Biloxi-Gulfport, MS | 196,900 | 164,900 | −19.4 | 89,000 | −8.6 |
| | Biloxi, MS | | | | 49,300 | 1.6 |
| | Gulfport, MS | | | | 39,700 | −18.8 |
| 136 | Portland, ME | 193,800 | 171,900 | 12.7 | 61,600 | −5.4 |
| 137 | Springfield, MO | 192,600 | 157,300 | 22.4 | 133,100 | 10.8 |
| 138 | Poughkeepsie, NY | 191,700 | 172,000 | 11.5 | 29,800 | −6.9 |
| 139 | Huntsville, AL | 189,600 | 178,700 | 6.1 | 142,500 | 2.3 |
| 140 | Anchorage, AK | 184,300 | 130,000 | 41.8 | 174,400 | 262.6 |
| 141 | Modesto, CA | 183,800 | 132,700 | 38.5 | 107,000 | 17.3 |
| 142 | Daytona Beach, FL | 178,800 | 122,700 | 45.8 | 54,200 | 19.6 |
| 143 | Lincoln, NE | 176,500 | 152,900 | 15.4 | 171,900 | 15.0 |
| 144 | Reno, NV | 176,200 | 109,900 | 60.3 | 100,800 | 38.3 |
| 145 | Salem, OR | 175,300 | 129,200 | 35.7 | 89,200 | 29.8 |
| 146 | Spartanburg, SC | 172,100 | 148,200 | 16.1 | 43,800 | −1.6 |
| 147 | Atlantic City, NJ | 170,700 | 156,300 | 9.2 | 40,200 | −16.1 |
| 148 | Santa Barbara, CA | 170,300 | 149,900 | 13.6 | 74,400 | 6.0 |
| 149 | Portsmouth-Dover-Rochester, NH-ME | 170,200 | 144,500 | 17.8 | 70,300 | 9.0 |
| | Portsmouth, NH | | | | 26,300 | 2.3 |
| | Dover, NH | | | | 22,400 | 7.2 |
| | Rochester, NH | | | | 21,600 | 20.7 |
| 150 | Johnstown, PA | 168,400 | 171,300 | −1.7 | 35,500 | −16.5 |
| 151 | Wheeling, WV, OH | 168,200 | 168,500 | − .2 | 43,100 | −10.6 |

# UNITED STATES POPULATIONS AND ZIP CODES

The following alphabetical list shows populations for all counties and nearly 15,000 selected cities and towns in the United States. ZIP codes are shown for all of the cities listed in the table. The state abbreviation following each name is that used by the United States Postal Service.

ZIP codes are listed for cities and towns after the state abbreviations. For each city with more than one ZIP code, the range of numbers assigned to the city is shown: For example, the ZIP code range for Chicago is 60601-99, and this indicates that the numbers between 60601 and 60699 are valid Chicago ZIP codes. ZIP codes are not listed for counties.

Populations for cities and towns appear as *italics* after the ZIP codes, and populations for counties appear after the state abbreviations. These populations are either 1980 census figures or, where census data are not available, estimates created by Rand McNally & Company. City populations are for central cities, not metropolitan areas. For New England, 1980 census populations are given for incorporated cities. Estimates are used for unincorporated places that are not treated separately by the census. 'Town' (or 'township') populations are not included unless the town is considered to be primarily urban and contains only one commonly used placename.

Counties are identified by a square symbol (□).

**Abbreviations for State Names**

| | | | | | | | |
|---|---|---|---|---|---|---|---|
| **AK** | Alaska | **IA** | Iowa | **MS** | Mississippi | **PA** | Pennsylvania |
| **AL** | Alabama | **ID** | Idaho | **MT** | Montana | **RI** | Rhode Island |
| **AR** | Arkansas | **IL** | Illinois | **NC** | North Carolina | **SC** | South Carolina |
| **AZ** | Arizona | **IN** | Indiana | **ND** | North Dakota | **SD** | South Dakota |
| **CA** | California | **KS** | Kansas | **NE** | Nebraska | **TN** | Tennessee |
| **CO** | Colorado | **KY** | Kentucky | **NH** | New Hampshire | **TX** | Texas |
| **CT** | Connecticut | **LA** | Louisiana | **NJ** | New Jersey | **UT** | Utah |
| **DC** | District of Columbia | **MA** | Massachusetts | **NM** | New Mexico | **VA** | Virginia |
| | | **MD** | Maryland | **NV** | Nevada | **VT** | Vermont |
| **DE** | Delaware | **ME** | Maine | **NY** | New York | **WA** | Washington |
| **FL** | Florida | **MI** | Michigan | **OH** | Ohio | **WI** | Wisconsin |
| **GA** | Georgia | **MN** | Minnesota | **OK** | Oklahoma | **WV** | West Virginia |
| **HI** | Hawaii | **MO** | Missouri | **OR** | Oregon | **WY** | Wyoming |

## A

Abbeville, AL 36310 • *3,155*
Abbeville, GA 31001 • *985*
Abbeville, LA 70510 • *12,391*
Abbeville, SC 29620 • *5,833*
Abbeville □, SC • *22,627*
Abbotsford, WI 54405 • *1,901*
Abbott Run Valley, RI 02864 • *1,300*
Abbottstown, PA 17301 • *689*
Aberdeen, ID 83210 • *1,528*
Aberdeen, MD 21001 • *11,533*
Aberdeen, MS 39730 • *7,184*
Aberdeen, NC 28315 • *1,945*
Aberdeen, OH 45101 • *1,566*
Aberdeen, SD 57401 • *25,851*
Aberdeen, WA 98520 • *18,739*
Abernathy, TX 79311 • *2,904*
Abilene, KS 67410 • *6,572*
Abilene, TX 79601-99 • *98,315*
Abingdon, IL 61410 • *4,210*
Abingdon, VA 24210 • *4,318*
Abington, MA 02351 • *13,517*
Abington, PA 19001 • *7,900*
Abita Springs, LA 70420 • *1,072*
Absarokee, MT 59001 • *750*
Absecon, NJ 08201 • *6,859*
Academia, OH 43050 • *1,447*
Acadia □, LA • *56,427*
Accomack □, VA • *31,268*
Ackerman, MS 39735 • *1,598*
Ackley, IA 50601 • *1,900*
Acton, CA 93510 • *900*
Acton, MA 01720 • *2,500*
Acushnet, MA 02743 • *6,400*
Acworth, GA 30101 • *3,648*
Ada, MN 56510 • *1,971*
Ada, OH 45810 • *5,669*
Ada, OK 74820 • *15,902*
Ada □, ID • *173,036*
Adair, IA 50002 • *883*
Adair □, IA • *9,509*
Adair □, KY • *15,233*
Adair □, MO • *24,870*
Adair □, OK • *18,575*
Adairsville, GA 30103 • *1,739*
Adairville, KY 42202 • *1,105*
Adams, MA 01220 • *10,381*
Adams, MN 55909 • *797*
Adams, NY 13605 • *1,701*
Adams, WI 53910 • *1,744*
Adams □, CO • *245,944*
Adams □, ID • *3,347*
Adams □, IL • *71,622*
Adams □, IN • *29,619*
Adams □, IA • *5,731*
Adams □, MS • *38,035*
Adams □, NE • *30,656*
Adams □, ND • *3,584*
Adams □, OH • *24,328*
Adams □, PA • *68,292*
Adams □, WA • *13,267*
Adams □, WI • *13,457*
Adams Center, NY 13606 • *800*
Adams City, CO 80022 • *2,200*
Adamston, NJ 08723 • *1,300*
Adamstown, PA 19501 • *1,119*
Adamsville, AL 35005 • *2,498*
Adamsville, TN 38310 • *1,453*
Addis, LA 70710 • *1,320*
Addison, AL 35540 • *746*
Addison, CT 06033 • *1,100*
Addison, IL 60101 • *29,826*
Addison, NY 14801 • *2,028*
Addison, TX 75001 • *5,553*
Addison □, VT • *29,406*
Addyston, OH 45001 • *1,195*
Adel, GA 31620 • *5,592*
Adel, IA 50003 • *2,846*
Adelanto, CA 92301 • *2,164*
Adena, OH 43901 • *1,062*
Adobe Acres, NM 87105 • *3,400*
Adrian, GA 31002 • *756*
Adrian, MI 49221 • *21,186*
Adrian, MN 56110 • *1,336*
Adrian, MO 64720 • *1,484*
Advance, MO 63730 • *1,054*
Affton, MO 63123 • *23,181*
Afton, IA 50830 • *985*
Afton, MN 55001 • *2,550*
Afton, NY 13730 • *982*
Afton, OK 74331 • *1,174*
Afton, WY 83110 • *1,481*
Agate Beach, OR 97365 • *700*
Agawam, MA 01001 • *10,300*
Agency, IA 52530 • *657*
Agua Fria, NM 87501 • *850*
Aguilar, CO 81020 • *624*
Ahoskie, NC 27910 • *4,887*
Ahwahnee, CA 93601 • *900*
Aiea, HI 96701 • *15,200*
Aiken, SC 29801 • *14,978*
Aiken □, SC • *105,625*
Ainsworth, NE 69210 • *2,256*
Air Park West, NE 68524 • *3,100*
Aitkin, MN 56431 • *1,770*
Aitkin □, MN • *13,404*
Ajo, AZ 85321 • *5,189*
Akron, AL 35441 • *604*
Akron, CO 80720 • *1,716*
Akron, IN 46910 • *1,045*
Akron, IA 51001 • *1,517*
Akron, NY 14001 • *2,971*
Akron, OH 44301-99 • *237,177*
Akron, PA 17501 • *3,471*
Alabaster, AL 35007 • *7,079*
Alachua, FL 32615 • *3,561*
Alachua □, FL • *151,348*
Alamance □, NC • *99,319*
Alameda, CA 94501 • *63,852*
Alameda, NM 87114 • *7,800*
Alameda □, CA • *1,105,379*
Alamo, GA 30411 • *993*
Alamo, TN 38001 • *2,615*
Alamo, TX 78516 • *5,831*
Alamogordo, NM 88310 • *24,024*
Alamo Heights, TX 78209 • *6,252*
Alamosa, CO 81101 • *6,830*
Alamosa □, CO • *11,799*
Alamosa East, CO 81101 • *1,175*
Alapaha, GA 31622 • *771*
Albany, CA 94706 • *15,130*
Albany, GA 31701-08 • *74,550*
Albany, IL 61230 • *1,014*
Albany, IN 47320 • *2,625*
Albany, KY 42602 • *2,083*
Albany, LA 70711 • *857*
Albany, MN 56307 • *1,569*
Albany, MO 64402 • *2,152*
Albany, NY 12201-99 • *101,727*
Albany, OH 45710 • *905*
Albany, OR 97321 • *26,678*
Albany, TX 76430 • *2,450*
Albany, WI 53502 • *1,051*
Albany □, NY • *285,909*
Albany □, WY • *29,062*
Albemarle, NC 28001 • *15,110*
Albemarle □, VA • *55,783*
Albert City, IA 50510 • *818*
Albert Lea, MN 56007 • *19,200*
Albertson, NY 11507 • *11,200*
Albertville, AL 35950 • *12,039*
Albia, IA 52531 • *4,184*
Albion, IL 62806 • *2,285*
Albion, IN 46701 • *1,637*
Albion, IA 50005 • *739*
Albion, MI 49224 • *11,059*
Albion, NE 68620 • *1,997*
Albion, NY 14411 • *4,897*
Albion, PA 16401 • *1,818*
Albion, RI 02802 • *1,200*
Albion, WA 99102 • *631*
Albuquerque, NM 87101-99 • *331,767*
Alburtis, PA 18011 • *1,428*
Alcalde, NM 87511 • *800*
Alcester, SD 57001 • *885*
Alcoa, TN 37701 • *6,870*
Alcona □, MI • *9,740*
Alcorn □, MS • *33,036*
Alda, NE 68810 • *601*
Alden, IA 50006 • *953*
Alden, MN 56009 • *687*
Alden, NY 14004 • *2,488*
Alden, PA 18634 • *800*
Alderson, WV 24910 • *1,375*
Aledo, IL 61231 • *3,881*
Aledo, TX 76008 • *1,027*
Alex, OK 73002 • *769*
Alexander □, IL • *12,264*
Alexander □, NC • *24,999*
Alexander City, AL 35010 • *13,807*
Alexander Mills, NC 28043 • *643*
Alexandria, IN 46001 • *6,028*
Alexandria, KY 41001 • *4,735*
Alexandria, LA 71301-03 • *51,565*
Alexandria, MN 56308 • *7,608*
Alexandria, TN 37012 • *689*
Alexandria, VA 22301-99 • *103,217*
Alexandria Bay, NY 13607 • *1,265*
Alexis, IL 61412 • *1,076*
Alfalfa □, OK • *7,077*
Alfred, NY 14802 • *4,967*
Alger, OH 45812 • *992*
Alger □, MI • *9,225*
Algoma, WI 54201 • *3,656*
Algona, IA 50511 • *6,289*
Algona, WA 98002 • *1,467*
Algonac, MI 48001 • *4,412*
Algonquin, IL 60102 • *5,834*
Algood, TN 38501 • *2,406*
Alhambra, CA 91801-99 • *64,615*
Alhambra, IL 62001 • *643*
Alice, TX 78332 • *20,961*
Aliceville, AL 35442 • *3,207*
Aliquippa, PA 15001 • *17,094*
Allamakee □, IA • *15,108*
Allardt, TN 38504 • *654*
Allegan, MI 49010 • *4,576*
Allegan □, MI • *81,555*
Allegany, NY 14706 • *2,078*
Allegany □, MD • *80,548*
Allegany □, NY • *51,742*
Alleghany □, NC • *9,587*
Alleghany □, VA • *14,333*
Allegheny □, PA • *1,450,085*
Allen, OK 74825 • *998*
Allen, TX 75002 • *8,314*
Allen □, IN • *294,335*
Allen □, KS • *1,564*
Allen □, KY • *14,128*
Allen □, LA • *21,390*
Allen □, OH • *112,241*
Allendale, IL 62410 • *613*
Allendale, NJ 07401 • *5,901*
Allendale, SC 29810 • *4,400*
Allendale □, SC • *10,700*
Allenhurst, GA 31301 • *606*
Allenhurst, NJ 07711 • *912*
Allen Park, MI 48101 • *34,196*
Allentown, NJ 08501 • *1,962*
Allentown, PA 18101-99 • *103,758*
Allerton, IA 50008 • *670*
Alliance, NE 69301 • *9,920*
Alliance, NC 28509 • *616*
Alliance, OH 44601 • *24,315*
Allison, IA 50602 • *1,132*
Allison, PA 15413 • *1,040*
Allison Park, PA 15101 • *5,600*
Allouez, WI 54301 • *13,753*
Alloway, NJ 08001 • *1,370*
Allyn, WA 98524 • *900*
Alma, AR 72921 • *2,755*
Alma, GA 31510 • *3,819*
Alma, KS 66401 • *925*
Alma, MI 48801 • *9,652*
Alma, NE 68920 • *1,369*
Alma, WI 54610 • *876*
Almont, MI 48003 • *1,857*
Aloha, OR 97007 • *10,000*
Alondra, CA 90249 • *12,096*
Alpaugh, CA 93201 • *900*
Alpena, MI 49707 • *12,214*
Alpena □, MI • *32,315*
Alpha, IL 61413 • *815*
Alpha, NJ 08865 • *2,644*
Alpharetta, GA 30201 • *3,128*
Alpine, NJ 07620 • *1,549*
Alpine, TX 79830 • *5,465*
Alpine, UT 84003 • *2,649*
Alpine □, CA • *1,097*
Alsip, IL 60658 • *17,134*
Alta, IA 51002 • *1,720*
Altadena, CA 91001 • *40,983*
Altamont, IL 62411 • *2,389*
Altamont, KS 67330 • *1,054*
Altamont, NY 12009 • *1,292*
Altamont, OR 97601 • *19,805*
Altamont, TN 37301 • *679*
Altamonte Springs, FL 32701 • *22,028*
Altavista, VA 24517 • *3,849*
Altheimer, AR 72004 • *1,231*
Alto, GA 30510 • *618*
Alto, TX 75925 • *1,203*
Alton, IL 62002 • *34,171*
Alton, IA 51003 • *986*
Alton, MO 65606 • *721*
Alton, NH 03809 • *900*
Altona, IL 61414 • *610*
Alton Bay, NH 03810 • *900*
Altoona, AL 35952 • *928*
Altoona, FL 32702 • *1,300*
Altoona, IA 50009 • *5,764*
Altoona, PA 16601-03 • *57,078*
Altoona, WI 54720 • *4,393*
Alturas, CA 96101 • *3,025*
Altus, OK 73521 • *23,101*
Alum Rock, CA 95127 • *17,471*
Alva, FL 33920 • *1,200*
Alva, OK 73717 • *6,416*
Alvarado, TX 76009 • *2,701*
Alvin, TX 77511 • *16,515*
Alvord, TX 76225 • *874*
Ama, LA 70031 • *875*
Amador □, CA • *19,314*
Amagansett, NY 11930 • *1,800*
Amanda, OH 43102 • *720*
Amarillo, TX 79101-99 • *149,230*
Ambler, PA 19002 • *6,628*
Amboy, IL 61310 • *2,377*
Amboy, MN 56010 • *606*
Ambridge, PA 15003 • *9,575*
Amelia, LA 70340 • *3,612*
Amelia, OH 45102 • *1,108*
Amelia □, VA • *8,405*
Amelia Court House, VA 23002 • *700*
Amenia, NY 12501 • *1,157*
American Falls, ID 83211 • *3,626*
American Fork, UT 84003 • *12,693*
Americus, GA 31709 • *16,120*
Americus, KS 66835 • *915*
Amery, WI 54001 • *2,404*
Ames, IA 50010 • *45,775*
Amesbury, MA 01913 • *13,971*
Amherst, MA 01002 • *26,300*
Amherst, NH 03031 • *750*
Amherst, NY 14226 • *66,100*
Amherst, OH 44001 • *10,638*
Amherst, TX 79312 • *971*
Amherst, VA 24521 • *1,135*
Amherst, WI 54406 • *701*
Amherst □, VA • *29,122*
Amherstdale, WV 25607 • *800*
Amite, LA 70422 • *4,301*
Amite □, MS • *13,369*
Amity, AR 71921 • *859*
Amity, OR 97101 • *1,092*
Amityville, NY 11701 • *9,076*
Ammon, ID 83401 • *4,669*
Amory, MS 38821 • *7,307*
Amsterdam, NY 12010 • *21,872*
Amsterdam, OH 43903 • *783*
Anacoco, LA 71403 • *820*
Anaconda, MT 59711 • *12,518*
Anacortes, WA 98221 • *9,013*
Anadarko, OK 73005 • *6,378*
Anaheim, CA 92801-99 • *219,494*
Anahola, HI 96703 • *915*
Anahuac, TX 77514 • *1,840*
Anamosa, IA 52205 • *4,958*
Anandale, LA 71301 • *2,000*
Anawalt, WV 24808 • *652*
Anchorage, AK 99501-40 • *174,431*
Anchorage, KY 40223 • *1,726*
Andalusia, AL 36420 • *10,415*
Andalusia, IL 61232 • *1,238*
Anderson, CA 96007 • *7,381*
Anderson, IN 46011-18 • *64,695*
Anderson, MO 64831 • *1,237*
Anderson, SC 29621-24 • *27,965*
Anderson □, KS • *8,749*
Anderson □, KY • *12,567*
Anderson □, SC • *133,235*
Anderson □, TN • *67,346*
Anderson □, TX • *38,381*
Andover, IL 61233 • *612*
Andover, KS 67002 • *2,801*
Andover, MA 01810 • *8,445*
Andover, MN 55303 • *9,387*
Andover, NY 14806 • *1,120*
Andover, OH 44003 • *1,205*
Andrew □, MO • *13,980*
Andrews, IN 46702 • *1,243*
Andrews, NC 28901 • *1,621*
Andrews, SC 29510 • *3,129*
Andrews, TX 79714 • *11,061*
Andrews □, TX • *13,323*
Androscoggin □, ME • *99,657*
Angelica, NY 14709 • *982*
Angelina □, TX • *64,172*
Angels Camp, CA 95222 • *2,302*
Angier, NC 27501 • *1,709*
Angleton, TX 77515 • *13,929*
Angola, IN 46703 • *5,486*
Angola, NY 14006 • *2,292*
Anguilla, MS 38721 • *950*
Anita, IA 50020 • *1,153*
Ankeny, IA 50021 • *15,429*
Anna, IL 62906 • *5,408*
Anna, OH 45302 • *1,038*
Annalee Heights, VA 22042 • *1,750*
Anna Maria, FL 33501 • *1,537*
Annandale, MN 55302 • *1,568*
Annandale, NJ 08801 • *1,040*
Annandale, VA 22003 • *35,300*
Annapolis, MD 21401-99 • *31,740*
Ann Arbor, MI 48103-09 • *107,966*
Annawan, IL 61234 • *908*
Anne Arundel □, MD • *370,775*
Anniston, AL 36201-05 • *29,523*
Annville, PA 17003 • *4,493*
Anoka, MN 55303 • *15,634*
Anoka □, MN • *195,998*
Ansley, NE 68814 • *644*
Anson, ME 04911 • *900*
Anson, TX 79501 • *2,831*
Anson □, NC • *25,649*
Ansonia, CT 06401 • *19,039*
Ansonia, OH 45303 • *1,267*
Ansonville, NC 28007 • *794*
Ansted, WV 25812 • *1,952*
Antelope □, NE • *8,675*
Anthon, IA 51004 • *687*
Anthony, FL 32617 • *1,200*
Anthony, KS 67003 • *2,661*
Anthony, NM 88021 • *3,285*
Anthony, RI 02816 • *4,500*
Antigo, WI 54409 • *8,653*
Antioch, CA 94509 • *42,683*
Antioch, IL 60002 • *4,419*
Antlers, OK 74523 • *2,989*
Anton, TX 79313 • *1,180*
Antonito, CO 81120 • *1,103*
Antrim, NH 03440 • *1,142*
Antrim □, MI • *16,194*
Antwerp, NY 13608 • *749*
Antwerp, OH 45813 • *1,765*
Apache, OK 73006 • *1,560*
Apache □, AZ • *52,108*
Apache Junction, AZ 85220 • *9,935*
Apalachicola, FL 32320 • *2,565*
Apalachin, NY 13732 • *1,233*
Apex, NC 27502 • *2,847*
Aplington, IA 50604 • *1,027*
Apollo, PA 15613 • *2,212*
Apopka, FL 32703 • *6,019*
Appalachia, VA 24216 • *2,418*
Appanoose □, IA • *15,511*
Apple Creek, OH 44606 • *741*
Applegate, OR 97530 • *800*
Appleton, MN 56208 • *1,842*
Appleton, WI 54911-19 • *58,913*
Appleton City, MO 64724 • *1,257*
Apple Valley, CA 92307 • *14,305*
Apple Valley, MN 55124 • *21,818*
Applewood, CO 80401 • *7,200*
Appleyard, WA 98801 • *1,500*
Appling □, GA • *15,565*
Appomattox, VA 24522 • *1,345*
Appomattox □, VA • *11,971*
Aptos, CA 95003 • *7,039*
Aquebogue, NY 11931 • *1,300*
Arab, AL 35016 • *5,967*
Arabi, LA 70032 • *10,248*
Aragon, GA 30104 • *855*
Aransas □, TX • *14,260*
Aransas Pass, TX 78336 • *7,173*
Arapaho, OK 73620 • *851*
Arapahoe, NE 68922 • *1,107*
Arapahoe □, CO • *293,621*
Arbuckle, CA 95912 • *1,306*
Arbyrd, MO 63821 • *704*
Arcade, CA 95821 • *37,600*
Arcade, NY 14009 • *2,052*
Arcadia, CA 91006 • *45,994*
Arcadia, FL 33821 • *6,002*
Arcadia, IN 46030 • *1,801*
Arcadia, LA 71001 • *3,403*
Arcadia, MO 63621 • *683*
Arcadia, SC 29320 • *2,088*
Arcadia, WI 54612 • *2,109*
Arcanum, OH 45304 • *2,002*
Arcata, CA 95521 • *12,850*
Archbald, PA 18403 • *6,295*
Archbold, OH 43502 • *3,318*
Archdale, NC 27263 • *5,326*
Archer, FL 32618 • *1,230*
Archer □, TX • *7,266*
Archer City, TX 76351 • *1,862*
Archie, MO 64725 • *753*
Archuleta □, CO • *3,664*
Arco, ID 83213 • *1,241*
Arcola, IL 61910 • *2,714*
Arden, CA 95825 • *49,130*
Arden Hills, MN 55112 • *8,012*
Ardmore, AL 35739 • *1,096*
Ardmore, IN 46628 • *3,400*
Ardmore, MD 20706 • *900*
Ardmore, OK 73401 • *23,689*
Ardmore, PA 19003 • *13,600*
Ardmore, TN 38449 • *835*
Ardsley, NY 10502 • *4,183*
Arenac □, MI • *14,706*
Argenta, IL 62501 • *994*
Argos, IN 46501 • *1,547*
Argyle, MN 56713 • *741*
Argyle, WI 53504 • *720*
Ariton, AL 36311 • *844*
Arizona Sunsites, AZ 85625 • *900*
Arjay, KY 40902 • *650*
Arkadelphia, AR 71923 • *10,005*
Arkansas □, AR • *24,175*
Arkansas City, AR 71630 • *668*
Arkansas City, KS 67005 • *13,201*
Arkoma, OK 74901 • *2,175*
Arkport, NY 14807 • *811*
Arkwright, RI 02816 • *1,500*
Arlington, GA 31713 • *1,572*
Arlington, KS 67514 • *631*
Arlington, LA 70808 • *850*
Arlington, MA 02174 • *48,219*
Arlington, MN 55307 • *1,779*
Arlington, NE 68002 • *1,117*
Arlington, NC 28642 • *872*
Arlington, NY 12603 • *11,203*
Arlington, OH 45814 • *1,187*
Arlington, SD 57212 • *991*
Arlington, TN 38002 • *1,778*
Arlington, TX 76010-19 • *160,113*
Arlington, VT 05250 • *800*
Arlington, VA 22201-99 • *152,599*
Arlington, WA 98223 • *3,282*
Arlington □, VA • *152,599*
Arlington Heights, IL 60004-08 • *66,116*
Arma, KS 66712 • *1,676*
Armada, MI 48005 • *1,392*
Armijo, NM 87105 • *18,900*
Armonk, NY 10504 • *5,900*
Armour, SD 57313 • *819*
Armstrong, IA 50514 • *1,153*
Armstrong □, PA • *77,768*
Armstrong □, TX • *1,994*
Arnaudville, LA 70512 • *1,679*
Arnett, OK 73832 • *714*
Arnold, CA 95223 • *2,385*
Arnold, MN 55803 • *1,350*
Arnold, MO 63010 • *19,141*
Arnold, NE 69120 • *813*
Arnold, PA 15068 • *6,853*
Arnolds Park, IA 51331 • *1,051*
Aroma Park, IL 60910 • *673*
Aroostook □, ME • *91,331*
Arp, TX 75750 • *939*
Arrowhead Village, NJ 08723 • *3,100*
Arroyo Grande, CA 93420 • *11,290*
Artesia, CA 90701 • *14,301*
Artesia, NM 88210 • *10,385*
Arthur, IL 61911 • *2,122*
Arthur □, NE • *513*
Arundel Village, MD 21225 • *5,300*

United States Populations and ZIP Codes

Arvada, CO 80001–05 • 84,576
Arvin, CA 93203 • 6,863
Arvonia, VA 23004 • 700
Asbury Park, NJ 07712 • 17,015
Ascension □, LA • 50,068
Ashaway, RI 02804 • 1,747
Ashburn, GA 31714 • 4,766
Ashburnham, MA 01430 • 1,150
Ashdown, AR 71822 • 4,218
Ashe □, NC • 22,325
Asheboro, NC 27203 • 15,252
Asher, OK 74826 • 659
Asherton, TX 78827 • 1,574
Asheville, NC 28801–99 • 53,583
Ashford, AL 36312 • 2,165
Ash Grove, MO 65604 • 1,157
Ashkum, IL 60911 • 735
Ashland, AL 36251 • 2,052
Ashland, CA 94541 • 13,893
Ashland, IL 62612 • 1,351
Ashland, KS 67831 • 1,096
Ashland, KY 41101 • 27,064
Ashland, ME 04732 • 800
Ashland, MA 01721 • 9,165
Ashland, MO 65010 • 1,021
Ashland, NE 68003 • 2,274
Ashland, NH 03217 • 1,479
Ashland, OH 44805 • 20,326
Ashland, OR 97520 • 14,943
Ashland, PA 17921 • 4,235
Ashland, VA 23005 • 4,640
Ashland, WI 54806 • 9,115
Ashland □, OH • 46,178
Ashland □, WI • 16,783
Ashland City, TN 37015 • 2,329
Ashley, IL 62808 • 658
Ashley, IN 46705 • 841
Ashley, ND 58413 • 1,192
Ashley, OH 43003 • 1,057
Ashley, PA 18706 • 3,512
Ashley □, AR • 26,538
Ashmore, IL 61912 • 883
Ashtabula, OH 44004 • 23,449
Ashtabula □, OH • 104,215
Ashton, ID 83420 • 1,219
Ashton, IL 61006 • 1,140
Ashton, MD 20861 • 1,010
Ashton, RI 02864 • 875
Ashville, AL 35953 • 1,489
Ashville, OH 43103 • 2,046
Ashwaubenon, WI 54304 • 14,486
Asotin, WA 99402 • 943
Asotin □, WA • 16,823
Aspen, CO 81611 • 3,678
Aspen Hill, MD 20906 • 9,800
Aspermont, TX 79502 • 1,357
Aspinwall, PA 15215 • 3,284
Assinippi, MA 02339 • 1,400
Assonet, MA 02702 • 900
Assumption, IL 62510 • 1,283
Assumption □, LA • 22,084
Aston, PA 19014 • 6,900
Astor, FL 32002 • 950
Astoria, IL 61501 • 1,370
Astoria, OR 97103 • 9,998
Atascadero, CA 93422 • 16,232
Atascosa □, TX • 25,055
Atchison, KS 66002 • 11,407
Atchison □, KS • 18,397
Atchison □, MO • 8,605
Atco, NJ 08004 • 2,100
Athena, OR 97813 • 965
Athens, AL 35611 • 14,558
Athens, GA 30601–13 • 42,549
Athens, IL 62613 • 1,371
Athens, MI 49011 • 960
Athens, NY 12015 • 1,738
Athens, OH 45701 • 19,743
Athens, PA 18810 • 3,622
Athens, TN 37303 • 12,080
Athens, TX 75751 • 10,197
Athens, WV 24712 • 1,147
Athens, WI 54411 • 988
Athens □, OH • 56,399
Atherton, CA 94025 • 7,797
Athol, MA 01331 • 10,634
Atkins, AR 72823 • 3,002
Atkinson, IL 61235 • 1,138
Atkinson, NE 68713 • 1,521
Atkinson, NH 03811 • 900
Atkinson □, GA • 6,141
Atlanta, GA 30301–99 • 425,022
Atlanta, IL 61723 • 1,807
Atlanta, IN 46031 • 657
Atlanta, MI 49709 • 650
Atlanta, NY 14808 • 750
Atlanta, TX 75551 • 6,272
Atlantic, IA 50022 • 7,789
Atlantic, NC 28511 • 900
Atlantic □, NJ • 194,119
Atlantic Beach, FL 32233 • 7,847
Atlantic City, NJ 08401–99 • 40,199
Atlantic Highlands, NJ 07716 • 4,950
Atmore, AL 36502 • 8,789
Atoka, OK 74525 • 3,409
Atoka, TN 38004 • 691
Atoka □, OK • 12,748
Attala □, MS • 19,865
Attalla, AL 35954 • 7,737
Attapulgus, GA 31715 • 623
Attica, IN 47918 • 3,841
Attica, KS 67009 • 730
Attica, NY 14011 • 2,659
Attica, OH 44807 • 865
Attleboro, MA 02703 • 34,196
Atwater, CA 95301 • 17,530
Atwater, MN 56209 • 1,128
Atwood, IL 61913 • 1,464
Atwood, KS 67730 • 1,665
Atwood, TN 38220 • 1,143
Auberry, CA 93602 • 1,100
Auburn, AL 36830 • 28,471
Auburn, CA 95603 • 7,540
Auburn, GA 30203 • 692
Auburn, IL 62615 • 3,616
Auburn, IN 46706 • 8,122
Auburn, KS 66402 • 890
Auburn, KY 42206 • 1,467
Auburn, ME 04210 • 23,128
Auburn, MA 01501 • 14,845
Auburn, MI 48611 • 1,921
Auburn, NE 68305 • 3,482
Auburn, NY 13021 • 32,548
Auburn, PA 17922 • 999
Auburn, WA 98002–03 • 26,417
Auburndale, FL 33823 • 6,501
Auburndale, WI 54412 • 641
Auburn Heights, MI 48057 • 4,000
Audrain □, MO • 26,458
Audubon, IA 50025 • 2,841
Audubon, NJ 08106 • 9,533
Audubon □, IA • 8,559
Auglaize □, OH • 42,554
Au Gres, MI 48703 • 768
Augusta, AR 72006 • 3,496
Augusta, GA 30901–99 • 47,532
Augusta, IL 62311 • 764
Augusta, KS 67010 • 6,968
Augusta, KY 41002 • 1,455
Augusta, ME 04330 • 21,819
Augusta, MI 49012 • 893
Augusta, WI 54722 • 1,560
Augusta □, VA • 53,732
Aulander, NC 27805 • 1,214
Ault, CO 80610 • 1,056
Aumsville, OR 97325 • 1,432
Aurelia, IA 51005 • 1,143
Aurora, CO 80010–17 • 158,588
Aurora, IL 60504–07 • 81,293
Aurora, IN 47001 • 3,816
Aurora, MN 55705 • 2,670
Aurora, MO 65605 • 6,437
Aurora, NE 68818 • 3,717
Aurora, NC 27806 • 698
Aurora, NY 13026 • 926
Aurora, OH 44202 • 8,177
Aurora, UT 84620 • 874
Aurora □, SD • 3,628
Au Sable, MI 48750 • 1,240
Au Sable Forks, NY 12912 • 2,100
Austell, GA 30001 • 3,939
Austin, IN 47102 • 4,857
Austin, MN 55912 • 23,020
Austin, PA 16720 • 740
Austin, TX 78701–99 • 345,496
Austin □, TX • 17,726
Austintown, OH 44512 • 33,636
Austinville, VA 24312 • 800
Autauga □, AL • 32,259
Autaugaville, AL 36003 • 843
Auxier, KY 41602 • 900
Auxvasse, MO 65231 • 858
Ava, IL 62907 • 811
Ava, MO 65608 • 2,761
Avalon, CA 90704 • 2,022
Avalon, NJ 08202 • 2,162
Avalon, PA 15202 • 6,240
Avella, PA 15312 • 1,109
Avenal, CA 93204 • 4,137
Avenel, MD 20783 • 5,600
Avenel, NJ 07001 • 11,500
Averill Park, NY 12018 • 1,500
Avery □, NC • 14,409
Avilla, IN 46710 • 1,272
Avis, PA 17721 • 1,718
Aviston, IL 62216 • 846
Avoca, IA 51521 • 1,650
Avoca, NY 14809 • 1,144
Avoca, PA 18641 • 3,536
Avocado Heights, CA 91746 • 11,721
Avon, CT 06001 • 1,434
Avon, IL 61415 • 1,019
Avon, MA 02322 • 5,026
Avon, MN 56310 • 804
Avon, NY 14414 • 3,006
Avon, OH 44011 • 7,241
Avon by the Sea, NJ 07717 • 2,337
Avondale, AZ 85323 • 8,168
Avondale, CO 81022 • 800
Avondale, LA 70094 • 6,699
Avondale, MO 64117 • 612
Avondale, OH 45404 • 5,000
Avondale, PA 19311 • 891
Avondale Estates, GA 30002 • 1,313
Avon Lake, OH 44012 • 13,222
Avonmore, PA 15618 • 1,234
Avon Park, FL 33825 • 8,026
Avoyelles □, LA • 41,393
Axtell, NE 68924 • 602
Ayden, NC 28513 • 4,361
Ayer, MA 01432–33 • 6,993
Aynor, SC 29511 • 643
Azalea Park, FL 32807 • 8,304
Azle, TX 76020 • 5,822
Aztec, NM 87410 • 5,512
Azusa, CA 91702 • 29,380

## B

Babbitt, MN 55706 • 2,435
Babbitt, NV 89416 • 1,800
Babson Park, FL 33827 • 950
Babylon, NY 11702–04 • 12,388
Baca □, CO • 5,419
Bacon □, GA • 9,379
Baconton, GA 31716 • 763
Bad Axe, MI 48413 • 3,184
Baden, PA 15005 • 5,318
Badger, IA 50516 • 653
Badin, NC 28009 • 1,514
Bagdad, AZ 86321 • 2,331
Bagdad, FL 32530 • 1,479
Bagley, MN 56621 • 1,321
Bailey, NC 27807 • 685
Bailey □, TX • 8,168
Bailey Island, ME 04003 • 650
Baileys Crossroads, VA 22041 • 4,600
Bainbridge, GA 31717 • 10,553
Bainbridge, IN 46105 • 644
Bainbridge, NY 13733 • 1,603
Bainbridge, OH 45612 • 1,042
Baird, TX 79504 • 1,696
Bairdford, PA 15006 • 950
Baker, CA 92309 • 650
Baker, LA 70714 • 12,865
Baker, MT 59313 • 2,354
Baker, OR 97814 • 9,471
Baker □, FL • 15,289
Baker □, GA • 3,808
Baker □, OR • 16,134
Bakersfield, CA 93301–99 • 105,735
Bakerstown, PA 15007 • 1,000
Bala-Cynwyd, PA 19004 • 8,600
Balaton, MN 56115 • 752
Balch Springs, TX 75180 • 13,746
Bald Knob, AR 72010 • 2,756
Baldwin, FL 32234 • 1,526
Baldwin, GA 30511 • 1,080
Baldwin, LA 70514 • 2,644
Baldwin, MI 49304 • 674
Baldwin, NY 11510 • 35,100
Baldwin, PA 15234 • 24,712
Baldwin, SC 29706 • 700
Baldwin, WI 54002 • 1,620
Baldwin □, AL • 78,556
Baldwin □, GA • 34,686
Baldwin City, KS 66006 • 2,829
Baldwin Park, CA 91706 • 50,554
Baldwinsville, NY 13027 • 6,446
Baldwinville, MA 01436 • 1,709
Baldwyn, MS 38824 • 3,427
Balfour, NC 28706 • 1,772
Ball, LA 71405 • 3,405
Ballard □, KY • 8,798
Ballardvale, MA 01810 • 1,300
Ball Ground, GA 30107 • 640
Ballinger, TX 76821 • 4,207
Ballston Spa, NY 12020 • 4,711
Ballwin, MO 63011 • 12,656
Bally, PA 19503 • 1,051
Balmville, NY 12550 • 3,214
Balsam Lake, WI 54810 • 749
Baltic, CT 06330 • 1,500
Baltic, SD 57003 • 679
Baltimore, MD 21201–99 • 786,775
Baltimore, OH 43105 • 2,689
Baltimore □, MD • 655,615
Baltimore Highlands, MD 21227 • 6,750
Bamberg, SC 29003 • 3,672
Bamberg □, SC • 18,118
Bancroft, IA 50517 • 1,082
Bancroft, MI 48414 • 618
Bandera, TX 78003 • 947
Bandera □, TX • 7,084
Bandon, OR 97411 • 2,311
Bangor, ME 04401 • 31,643
Bangor, MI 49013 • 2,001
Bangor, PA 18013 • 5,006
Bangor, WI 54614 • 1,012
Bangor Township, MI 48706 • 17,494
Bangs, TX 76823 • 1,716
Banks □, GA • 8,702
Banner □, NE • 918
Banner Elk, NC 28604 • 1,087
Banning, CA 92220 • 14,020
Bannock □, ID • 65,421
Bantam, CT 06750 • 860
Baraboo, WI 53913 • 8,081
Baraga, MI 49908 • 1,055
Baraga □, MI • 8,484
Barataria, LA 70036 • 1,123
Barber □, KS • 6,548
Barberton, OH 44203 • 29,751
Barbour □, AL • 24,756
Barbour □, WV • 16,639
Barboursville, WV 25504 • 2,871
Barbourville, KY 40906 • 3,333
Bardstown, KY 40004 • 6,155
Bardwell, KY 42023 • 988
Bargersville, IN 46106 • 1,647
Bar Harbor, ME 04609 • 2,685
Barker Heights, NC 28739 • 1,267
Barling, AR 72923 • 3,761
Barlow, KY 42024 • 746
Bar Mills, ME 04004 • 825
Barnegat, NJ 08005 • 1,012
Barnegat Light, NJ 08006 • 619
Barnes □, ND • 13,960
Barnesboro, PA 15714 • 2,741
Barnesville, GA 30204 • 4,887
Barnesville, MN 56514 • 2,207
Barnesville, OH 43713 • 4,633
Barnhart, MO 63012 • 800
Barnsdall, OK 74002 • 1,501
Barnstable, MA 02630 • 2,033
Barnstable □, MA • 147,925
Barnwell, SC 29812 • 5,572
Barnwell □, SC • 19,868
Baroda, MI 49101 • 627
Barrackville, WV 26559 • 1,815
Barre, MA 01005 • 1,136
Barre, VT 05641 • 9,824
Barren □, KY • 34,009
Barrett, WV 25013 • 800
Barrington, IL 60010 • 9,029
Barrington, NJ 08007 • 7,418
Barrington, RI 02806 • 16,174
Barron, WI 54812 • 2,595
Barron □, WI • 38,730
Barron Lake, MI 49120 • 1,600
Barrow, AK 99723 • 2,207
Barrow □, GA • 21,354
Barry, IL 62312 • 1,487
Barry □, MI • 45,781
Barry □, MO • 24,408
Barstow, CA 92311 • 17,690
Barstow, TX 79719 • 637
Bartholomew □, IN • 65,088
Bartlesville, OK 74003–06 • 34,568
Bartlett, IL 60103 • 13,254
Bartlett, NH 03812 • 700
Bartlett, TN 38134 • 17,170
Bartlett, TX 76511 • 1,567
Barton, MD 21521 • 617
Barton, OH 43905 • 1,039
Barton, VT 05822 • 1,062
Barton □, KS • 31,343
Barton □, MO • 11,292
Bartonville, IL 61607 • 6,137
Bartow, FL 33830 • 14,780
Bartow □, GA • 40,760
Barview, OR 97420 • 1,462
Basehor, KS 66007 • 1,483
Basile, LA 70515 • 2,635
Basin, WY 82410 • 1,349
Baskin, FL 34648 • 800
Basking Ridge, NJ 07920 • 4,800
Bassett, NE 68714 • 1,009
Bassett, VA 24055 • 2,950
Bass Lake, IN 46534 • 1,500
Bastrop, LA 71220 • 15,527
Bastrop, TX 78602 • 3,789
Bastrop □, TX • 24,726
Batavia, IL 60510 • 12,574
Batavia, NY 14020 • 16,703
Batavia, OH 45103 • 1,896
Bates □, MO • 15,873
Batesburg, SC 29006 • 4,023
Batesville, AR 72501 • 8,263
Batesville, IN 47006 • 4,152
Batesville, MS 38606 • 4,692
Batesville, TX 78829 • 800
Bath, ME 04530 • 10,246
Bath, NY 14810 • 6,042
Bath, PA 18014 • 1,953
Bath, SC 29816 • 2,242
Bath □, KY • 10,025
Bath □, VA • 5,860
Baton Rouge, LA 70801–99 • 219,419
Batson, TX 77519 • 650
Battleboro, NC 27809 • 632
Battle Creek, IA 51006 • 919
Battle Creek, MI 49014–17 • 56,339
Battle Creek, NE 68715 • 948
Battle Ground, IN 47920 • 812
Battle Ground, WA 98604 • 2,774
Battle Lake, MN 56515 • 708
Battle Mountain, NV 89820 • 2,755
Baudette, MN 56623 • 1,170
Bawcomville, LA 71291 • 2,500
Baxley, GA 31513 • 3,586
Baxter, IA 50028 • 951
Baxter, MN 56401 • 2,625
Baxter, TN 38544 • 1,411
Baxter □, AR • 27,409
Baxter Springs, KS 66713 • 4,730
Bay, AR 72411 • 1,605
Bay □, FL • 97,740
Bay □, MI • 119,881
Bayard, IA 50029 • 637
Bayard, NE 69334 • 1,435
Bayard, NM 88023 • 3,036
Bayberry, NY 13088 • 5,900
Bayboro, NC 28515 • 759
Bay City, MI 48706–08 • 41,593
Bay City, OR 97107 • 986
Bay City, TX 77414 • 17,837
Bayfield, CO 81122 • 724
Bayfield, WI 54814 • 778
Bayfield □, WI • 13,822
Bay Head, NJ 08742 • 1,340
Baylor □, TX • 4,919
Bay Minette, AL 36507 • 7,455
Bayonne, NJ 07002 • 65,047
Bayou George, FL 32401 • 1,500
Bayou Goula, LA 70716 • 800
Bayou La Batre, AL 36509 • 2,005
Bay Port, MI 48720 • 800
Bayport, MN 55003 • 2,932
Bayport, NY 11705 • 8,900
Bay Ridge, MD 21403 • 1,989
Bay Saint Louis, MS 39520 • 7,891
Bay Shore, NY 11706 • 31,200
Bayshore Gardens, FL 34207 • 14,945
Bayside, WI 53217 • 4,724
Bay Springs, MS 39422 • 1,884
Baytown, TX 77520–22 • 56,923
Bayview, AL 35005 • 830
Bay View, MI 49770 • 1,000
Bay Village, OH 44140 • 17,846
Bayville, NJ 08721 • 900
Bayville, NY 11709 • 7,034
Beach, IL 60085 • 4,650
Beach, ND 58621 • 1,381
Beach City, OH 44608 • 1,083
Beach Haven, NJ 08008 • 1,714
Beachwood, NJ 08722 • 7,687
Beachwood, OH 44122 • 9,983
Beacon, NY 12508 • 12,937
Beacon Falls, CT 06403 • 1,500
Beadle □, SD • 19,195
Beallsville, OH 43716 • 601
Bear, DE 19701 • 950
Bearden, AR 71720 • 1,191
Beardstown, IL 62618 • 6,338
Bear Lake □, ID • 6,931
Bear Town, MS 39648 • 1,277
Beatrice, NE 68310 • 12,891
Beatty, NV 89003 • 900
Beattyville, KY 41311 • 1,068
Beaufort, NC 28516 • 3,826
Beaufort, SC 29902 • 8,634
Beaufort □, NC • 40,355
Beaufort □, SC • 65,364
Beaumont, CA 92223 • 6,818
Beaumont, MS 39423 • 1,112
Beaumont, TX 77701–99 • 118,102
Beauregard □, LA • 29,692
Beaver, OK 73932 • 1,939
Beaver, PA 15009 • 5,441
Beaver, UT 84713 • 1,792
Beaver, WV 25813 • 1,400
Beaver □, OK • 6,806
Beaver □, PA • 204,441
Beaver □, UT • 4,378
Beaver City, NE 68926 • 775
Beavercreek, OH 45385 • 31,589
Beaverdale, PA 15921 • 1,579
Beaver Dam, KY 42320 • 3,185
Beaver Dam, WI 53916 • 14,149
Beaver Falls, PA 15010 • 12,525
Beaverhead □, MT • 8,186
Beaver Meadows, PA 18216 • 1,078
Beaver Springs, PA 17812 • 725
Beaverton, MI 48612 • 1,025
Beaverton, OR 97005–07 • 30,582
Beavertown, PA 17813 • 853
Beckemeyer, IL 62219 • 1,119
Becker, MN 55308 • 601
Becker □, MN • 29,336
Beckham □, OK • 19,243
Beckley, WV 25801 • 20,492
Beckville, TX 75631 • 945
Bedford, IN 47421 • 14,410
Bedford, IA 50833 • 1,692
Bedford, KY 40006 • 835
Bedford, MA 01730 • 13,067
Bedford, NH 03102 • 1,300
Bedford, OH 44146 • 15,056
Bedford, PA 15522 • 3,326
Bedford, TX 76021–22 • 20,821
Bedford, VA 24523 • 5,991
Bedford □, PA • 46,784
Bedford □, TN • 27,916
Bedford □, VA • 34,927
Bedford Heights, OH 44146 • 13,214
Bedford Hills, NY 10507 • 3,200
Bee □, TX • 26,030
Beebe, AR 72012 • 3,599
Beech Creek, PA 16822 • 760
Beecher, IL 60401 • 2,024
Beecher, MI 48505 • 17,178
Beech Grove, IN 46107 • 13,196
Beech Island, SC 29841 • 1,300
Beemer, NE 68716 • 853
Bee Ridge, FL 34233 • 3,313
Beersheba Springs, TN 37305 • 643
Beeville, TX 78102 • 14,574
Beggs, OK 74421 • 1,428
Bel Air, MD 21014 • 7,814
Bel Aire, KS 67220 • 2,650
Bel Aire Estates, CT 06355 • 900
Belcamp, MD 21017 • 650
Belchertown, MA 01007 • 2,531
Belcourt, ND 58316 • 1,803
Belding, MI 48809 • 5,634
Belen, NM 87002 • 5,617
Belfast, ME 04915 • 6,243
Belfast, NC 27530 • 950
Belfast, NY 14711 • 900
Belfield, ND 58622 • 1,274
Belford, NJ 07718 • 6,000
Belfry, KY 41514 • 900
Belgium, WI 53004 • 892
Belgrade, MN 56312 • 805
Belgrade, MT 59714 • 2,336
Belhaven, NC 27810 • 2,430
Belington, WV 26250 • 2,038
Belknap □, NH • 42,884
Bell, CA 90201 • 25,450
Bell □, KY • 34,330
Bell □, TX • 157,820
Bellair, FL 32073 • 5,200
Bellaire, MI 49615 • 1,063
Bellaire, OH 43906 • 8,241
Bellaire, TX 77401 • 14,950
Bellamy, AL 36901 • 750
Bella Vista, AR 72712 • 2,589
Bellbrook, OH 45305 • 5,174
Belle, MO 65013 • 1,233
Belle, WV 25015 • 1,621
Belleair, FL 33516 • 5,200
Belle Center, OH 43310 • 930
Belle Chasse, LA 70037 • 5,412
Bellefontaine, OH 43311 • 11,888
Bellefontaine Neighbors, MO 63137 • 12,082
Bellefonte, DE 19809 • 1,279
Bellefonte, PA 16823 • 6,300
Belle Fourche, SD 57717 • 4,692
Belle Glade, FL 33430 • 16,535
Belle Isle, FL 32809 • 2,848
Belle Meade, TN 37205 • 3,182
Belle Plaine, IA 52208 • 2,903
Belle Plaine, KS 67013 • 1,706
Belle Plaine, MN 56011 • 2,754
Belle Rose, LA 70341 • 700
Belle Vernon, PA 15012 • 1,489
Belleview, FL 32620 • 1,913
Belle View, VA 22307 • 3,500
Belleville, IL 62220–25 • 41,580
Belleville, KS 66935 • 2,805
Belleville, MI 48111 • 3,366
Belleville, NJ 07109 • 35,367
Belleville, PA 17004 • 1,817
Belleville, WI 53508 • 1,302
Bellevue, ID 83313 • 1,016
Bellevue, IA 52031 • 2,450
Bellevue, KY 41073 • 7,678
Bellevue, MI 49021 • 1,289
Bellevue, NE 68005 • 21,813
Bellevue, OH 44811 • 8,187
Bellevue, PA 15202 • 10,128
Bellevue, WA 98004–09 • 73,903
Bellflower, CA 90706 • 53,441
Bell Gardens, CA 90201 • 34,117
Bellingham, MA 02019 • 14,300
Bellingham, WA 98225–27 • 45,794
Bellmawr, NJ 08031 • 13,721
Bellmead, TX 76705 • 7,569
Bellmore, NY 11710 • 18,431
Bellows Falls, VT 05101 • 3,456
Bellport, NY 11713 • 2,809
Bells, TN 38006 • 1,571
Bellville, OH 44813 • 1,714
Bellville, TX 77418 • 2,860
Bellwood, IL 60104 • 19,811
Bellwood, PA 16617 • 2,114
Belmar, NJ 07719 • 6,771
Belmond, IA 50421 • 2,505
Belmont, CA 94002 • 24,505
Belmont, MA 02178 • 26,100
Belmont, MS 38827 • 1,420
Belmont, NH 03220 • 900
Belmont, NC 28012 • 4,607
Belmont, NY 14813 • 1,024
Belmont, OH 43718 • 714
Belmont, WV 26134 • 887
Belmont, WI 53510 • 826
Belmont □, OH • 82,569
Bel-Nor, MO 63133 • 2,047
Beloit, KS 67420 • 4,367
Beloit, OH 44609 • 1,093
Beloit, WI 53511 • 35,207
Beloit North, WI 53511 • 5,912
Belpre, OH 45714 • 7,193
Belt, MT 59412 • 825
Belton, MO 64012 • 12,708
Belton, SC 29627 • 5,312
Belton, TX 76513 • 10,660
Beltrami □, MN • 30,982
Beltsville, MD 20705 • 12,760
Belvedere, SC 29841 • 6,859
Belvedere Park, GA 30032 • 17,766
Belvidere, DE 19804 • 1,100
Belvidere, IL 61008 • 15,176
Belvidere, NJ 07823 • 2,475
Belzoni, MS 39038 • 2,982
Bement, IL 61813 • 1,770
Bemidji, MN 56601 • 10,949
Bemis, TN 38314 • 1,883
Benavides, TX 78341 • 1,978
Benbrook, TX 76126 • 13,579
Bend, OR 97701–09 • 17,263

Benedict, MD 20612 • 700
Benewah □, ID • 8,292
Benham, KY 40807 • 936
Ben Hill □, GA • 16,000
Benicia, CA 94510 • 15,376
Benkelman, NE 69021 • 1,235
Benld, IL 62009 • 1,638
Bennett, CO 80102 • 942
Bennett □, SD • 3,044
Bennettsville, SC 29512 • 8,774
Bennington, NE 68007 • 631
Bennington, VT 05201 • 9,349
Bennington □, VT • 33,345
Bennion, UT 84107 • 950
Bensenville, IL 60106 • 16,124
Bensley, VA 23234 • 3,300
Benson, AZ 85602 • 4,190
Benson, MN 56215 • 3,656
Benson, NC 27504 • 2,792
Benson □, ND • 7,944
Bent □, CO • 5,945
Bentleyville, PA 15314 • 2,525
Benton, AR 72015 • 17,717
Benton, IL 62812 • 7,778
Benton, KS 67017 • 609
Benton, KY 42025 • 3,700
Benton, LA 71006 • 1,864
Benton, MO 63736 • 674
Benton, PA 17814 • 981
Benton, TN 37307 • 1,115
Benton, WI 53803 • 983
Benton □, AR • 78,115
Benton □, IN • 10,218
Benton □, IA • 23,649
Benton □, MN • 25,187
Benton □, MS • 8,153
Benton □, MO • 12,183
Benton □, OR • 68,211
Benton □, TN • 14,901
Benton □, WA • 109,444
Benton City, WA 99320 • 1,980
Benton Harbor, MI 49022 • 14,707
Benton Heights, MI 49022 • 6,787
Bentonville, AR 72712 • 8,756
Benwood, WV 26031 • 1,994
Benzie □, MI • 11,205
Berea, KY 40403 • 8,226
Berea, OH 44017 • 19,567
Berea, SC 29611 • 7,500
Beresford, SD 57004 • 1,865
Bergen, NY 14416 • 976
Bergen □, NJ • 845,385
Bergenfield, NJ 07621 • 25,568
Bergholz, OH 43908 • 914
Bergland, MI 49910 • 700
Berkeley, CA 94701–99 • 103,328
Berkeley, IL 60162 • 5,467
Berkeley, MO 63134 • 15,922
Berkeley, RI 02864 • 930
Berkeley □, SC • 94,727
Berkeley □, WV • 46,775
Berkeley Heights, NJ 07922 • 12,549
Berkeley Springs, WV 25411 • 789
Berkley, MI 48072 • 18,637
Berks □, PA • 312,509
Berkshire □, MA • 145,110
Berlin, CT 06037 • 2,000
Berlin, MD 21811 • 2,162
Berlin, NH 03570 • 13,084
Berlin, NJ 08009 • 5,786
Berlin, NY 12022 • 850
Berlin, OH 44610 • 800
Berlin, PA 15530 • 1,999
Berlin, WI 54923 • 5,478
Berlin Heights, OH 44814 • 756
Bernalillo, NM 87004 • 3,012
Bernalillo □, NM • 419,700
Bernardston, MA 01337 • 700
Bernardsville, NJ 07924 • 6,715
Berne, IN 46711 • 3,300
Bernice, LA 71222 • 1,956
Bernie, MO 63822 • 1,975
Bernville, PA 19506 • 798
Berrien □, GA • 13,525
Berrien □, MI • 171,276
Berrien Springs, MI 49103 • 2,042
Berry, AL 35546 • 916
Berry Hill, TN 37204 • 1,113
Berryville, AR 72616 • 2,966
Berryville, VA 22611 • 1,752
Berthoud, CO 80513 • 2,362
Bertie □, NC • 21,024
Bertram, TX 78605 • 824
Bertrand, MI 49120 • 5,000
Bertrand, MO 63823 • 688
Bertrand, NE 68927 • 775
Berwick, LA 70342 • 4,466
Berwick, ME 03901 • 2,378
Berwick, PA 18603 • 11,850
Berwyn, IL 60402 • 46,849
Berwyn, PA 19312 • 9,300
Bessemer, AL 35020–23 • 31,729
Bessemer, MI 49911 • 2,553
Bessemer, PA 16112 • 1,293
Bessemer City, NC 28016 • 4,787
Bethalto, IL 62010 • 8,630
Bethany, CT 06525 • 890
Bethany, IL 61914 • 1,550
Bethany, MO 64424 • 3,095
Bethany, OK 73008 • 22,130
Bethany, WV 26032 • 1,336
Bethel, AK 99559 • 3,576
Bethel, CT 06801 • 8,755
Bethel, ME 04217 • 1,225
Bethel, NC 27812 • 1,825
Bethel, OH 45106 • 2,231
Bethel, VT 05032 • 1,016
Bethel Acres, OK 74801 • 747
Bethel Park, PA 15102 • 34,755
Bethel Springs, TN 38315 • 873
Bethesda, MD 20814–17 • 63,022
Bethesda, OH 43719 • 1,429
Bethlehem, CT 06751 • 1,762
Bethlehem, NH 03574 • 700
Bethlehem, PA 18015–18 • 70,419
Bethpage, NY 11714 • 29,900
Betsy Layne, KY 41605 • 900
Bettendorf, IA 52722 • 27,381
Bettsville, OH 44815 • 752
Beulah, ND 58523 • 2,908
Beulaville, NC 28518 • 1,060

Beverly, MA 01915 • 37,655
Beverly, NJ 08010 • 2,919
Beverly, OH 45715 • 1,471
Beverly Hills, CA 90210–13 • 32,367
Beverly Hills, MI 48009 • 11,598
Beverly Shores, IN 46301 • 864
Bexar □, TX • 988,798
Bexley, OH 43209 • 13,405
Bibb □, AL • 15,723
Bibb □, GA • 150,256
Bibb City, GA 31904 • 667
Bicknell, IN 47512 • 4,713
Biddeford, ME 04005 • 19,638
Bienville □, LA • 16,387
Big Bear City, CA 92314 • 3,500
Big Bend, WI 53103 • 1,345
Big Creek, CA 93605 • 700
Big Flats, NY 14814 • 2,500
Bigfork, MT 59911 • 1,080
Biggs, CA 95917 • 1,413
Big Horn □, MT • 11,096
Big Horn □, WY • 11,896
Big Lake, MN 55309 • 2,210
Big Lake, TX 76932 • 3,404
Biglerville, PA 17307 • 991
Big Pine, CA 93513 • 1,510
Bigpoint, MS 39567 • 900
Big Rapids, MI 49307 • 14,361
Big Run, PA 15715 • 822
Big Sandy, MT 59520 • 835
Big Sandy, TN 38221 • 650
Big Sandy, TX 75755 • 1,258
Big Spring, TX 79720 • 24,804
Big Stone □, MN • 7,716
Big Stone City, SD 57216 • 672
Big Stone Gap, VA 24219 • 4,748
Big Timber, MT 59011 • 1,690
Big Wells, TX 78830 • 939
Billerica, MA 01821 • 6,400
Billings, MO 65610 • 911
Billings, MT 59101–99 • 66,842
Billings, OK 74630 • 632
Billings □, ND • 1,138
Billings Heights, MT 59105 • 8,480
Biloxi, MS 39530–34 • 49,311
Biltmore Forest, NC 28803 • 1,499
Bingen, WA 98605 • 644
Binger, OK 73009 • 791
Bingham, ME 04920 • 1,074
Bingham □, ID • 36,489
Binghamton, NY 13901–99 • 55,860
Biola, CA 93606 • 800
Birch Run, MI 48415 • 1,196
Birch Tree, MO 65438 • 622
Birchwood City, MD 20745 • 8,000
Birchwood Park, DE 19711 • 1,500
Bird Island, MN 55310 • 1,372
Birdsboro, PA 19508 • 3,481
Birmingham, AL 35201–99 • 286,799
Birmingham, MI 48008–12 • 21,689
Birnamwood, WI 54414 • 688
Biron, WI 54494 • 698
Bisbee, AZ 85603 • 7,154
Biscayne Gardens, FL 33168 • 13,000
Biscayne Park, FL 33161 • 3,088
Biscoe, NC 27209 • 1,334
Bishop, CA 93514 • 3,333
Bishop, TX 78343 • 3,706
Bishopville, SC 29010 • 3,429
Bismarck, IL 61814 • 750
Bismarck, MO 63624 • 1,625
Bismarck, ND 58501 • 44,485
Biwabik, MN 55708 • 1,428
Bixby, OK 74008 • 6,969
Black Creek, WI 54106 • 1,097
Black Diamond, WA 98010 • 1,170
Blackduck, MN 56630 • 653
Black Eagle, MT 59414 • 1,100
Black Earth, WI 53515 • 1,145
Blackfoot, ID 83221 • 10,065
Blackford □, IN • 15,570
Black Forest, CO 80908 • 3,372
Black Hawk, SD 57718 • 1,608
Black Hawk □, IA • 137,961
Black Jack, MO 63031 • 5,293
Black Lick, PA 15716 • 1,074
Blacklick Estates, OH 43227 • 11,223
Black Mountain, NC 28711 • 4,083
Black Oak, IN 46406 • 10,000
Black River, NY 13612 • 1,384
Black River Falls, WI 54615 • 3,434
Black Rock, AR 72415 • 848
Blacksburg, SC 29702 • 1,873
Blacksburg, VA 24060 • 30,638
Blackshear, GA 31516 • 3,222
Blackstone, MA 01504 • 5,100
Blackstone, VA 23824 • 3,624
Blackville, SC 29817 • 2,840
Blackwell, OK 74631 • 8,400
Blackwood, NJ 08012 • 5,219
Bladen □, NC • 30,491
Bladenboro, NC 28320 • 1,428
Bladensburg, MD 20710 • 7,691
Blades, DE 19973 • 664
Blaine, ME 04734 • 620
Blaine, MN 55433 • 28,558
Blaine, TN 37709 • 1,147
Blaine, WA 98230 • 2,363
Blaine □, ID • 9,841
Blaine □, MT • 6,999
Blaine □, NE • 867
Blaine □, OK • 13,443
Blair, NE 68008 • 6,418
Blair, OK 73526 • 1,092
Blair, WI 54616 • 1,142
Blair □, PA • 136,621
Blairstown, IA 52209 • 695
Blairsville, PA 15717 • 4,166
Blakely, GA 31723 • 5,880
Blakely, PA 18447 • 7,438
Blanchard, LA 71009 • 1,128
Blanchard, OK 73010 • 1,688
Blanchard, PA 16826 • 750
Blanchardville, WI 53516 • 803
Blanchester, OH 45107 • 3,202
Blanco, TX 78606 • 1,179
Blanco □, TX • 4,681
Bland, MO 65014 • 662
Bland □, VA • 6,349
Blandburg, PA 16619 • 775
Blandford, MA 01008 • 800

Blanding, UT 84511 • 3,118
Blandinsville, IL 61420 • 886
Blanford, IN 47831 • 700
Blasdell, NY 14219 • 3,288
Blauvelt, NY 10913 • 5,426
Blawnox, PA 15238 • 1,653
Bleckley □, GA • 10,767
Bledsoe □, TN • 9,478
Blende, CO 81006 • 1,500
Blennerhassett, WV 26101 • 2,200
Blessing, TX 77419 • 950
Blissfield, MI 49228 • 3,107
Block Island, RI 02807 • 620
Bloomdale, OH 44817 • 744
Bloomer, WI 54724 • 3,342
Bloomfield, CT 06002 • 7,400
Bloomfield, IN 47424 • 2,705
Bloomfield, IA 52537 • 2,849
Bloomfield, KY 40008 • 954
Bloomfield, MO 63825 • 1,795
Bloomfield, NE 68718 • 1,393
Bloomfield, NJ 07003 • 47,792
Bloomfield, NM 87413 • 4,881
Bloomfield Hills, MI 48013 • 3,985
Bloomingburg, OH 43106 • 869
Bloomingdale, GA 31302 • 1,855
Bloomingdale, IL 60108 • 12,659
Bloomingdale, NJ 07403 • 7,867
Bloomingdale, NY 12913 • 608
Bloomingdale, TN 37660 • 9,000
Blooming Grove, TX 76626 • 823
Blooming Prairie, MN 55917 • 1,969
Bloomington, CA 92316 • 6,674
Bloomington, IL 61701 • 44,189
Bloomington, IN 47401 • 52,044
Bloomington, MN 55420 • 81,831
Bloomington, TX 77951 • 1,750
Bloomington, WI 53804 • 743
Bloomsburg, PA 17815 • 11,717
Bloomsbury, NJ 08804 • 864
Bloomville, OH 44818 • 1,019
Blossburg, PA 16912 • 1,757
Blossom, TX 75416 • 1,487
Blount □, AL • 36,459
Blount □, TN • 77,770
Blountstown, FL 32424 • 2,632
Blountsville, AL 35031 • 1,509
Blountville, TN 37617 • 2,554
Blowing Rock, NC 28605 • 1,337
Blue Ash, OH 45242 • 9,506
Blue Earth, MN 56013 • 4,132
Blue Earth □, MN • 52,314
Bluefield, VA 24605 • 5,946
Bluefield, WV 24701 • 16,060
Blue Grass, IA 52726 • 1,377
Blue Hill, ME 04614 • 700
Blue Hill, NE 68930 • 883
Blue Hills, CT 06002 • 6,600
Blue Island, IL 60406 • 21,855
Blue Lake, CA 95525 • 1,201
Blue Mound, IL 62513 • 1,338
Blue Mountain, MS 38610 • 867
Blue Rapids, KS 66411 • 1,280
Blue Ridge, GA 30513 • 1,376
Blue Ridge, VA 24064 • 1,200
Blue Ridge Summit, PA 17214 • 800
Blue Springs, MO 64015 • 25,927
Bluewell, WV 24701 • 1,000
Bluff City, TN 37618 • 1,121
Bluffdale, UT 84065 • 1,300
Bluff Park, AL 35226 • 12,000
Bluffs, IL 62621 • 821
Bluffton, IN 46714 • 8,705
Bluffton, OH 45817 • 3,310
Bluford, IL 62814 • 728
Bly, OR 97622 • 750
Blythe, CA 92225 • 6,805
Blytheville, AR 72315 • 23,844
Boalsburg, PA 16827 • 950
Boardman, OH 44512 • 39,161
Boardman, OR 97818 • 1,261
Boaz, AL 35957 • 7,151
Bobtown, PA 15315 • 1,055
Boca Grande, FL 33921 • 1,200
Boca Raton, FL 33431–34 • 49,505
Boerne, TX 78006 • 3,229
Bogalusa, LA 70427 • 16,976
Bogart, GA 30622 • 819
Bogata, TX 75417 • 1,508
Boger City, NC 28092 • 2,252
Bogota, NJ 07603 • 8,344
Bohemia, NY 11716 • 9,800
Boiling Springs, NC 28017 • 2,381
Boiling Springs, PA 17007 • 1,521
Boise, ID 83701–99 • 102,160
Boise □, ID • 2,999
Boise City, OK 73933 • 1,761
Boissevain, VA 24606 • 900
Bokchito, OK 74726 • 628
Bokeelia, FL 33922 • 900
Boling, TX 77420 • 1,000
Bolingbrook, IL 60439 • 37,261
Bolivar, MO 65613 • 5,919
Bolivar, NY 14715 • 1,345
Bolivar, OH 44612 • 989
Bolivar, PA 15923 • 706
Bolivar, TN 38008 • 6,597
Bolivar, WV 25425 • 672
Bolivar □, MS • 45,965
Bollinger □, MO • 10,301
Bolton, MS 39041 • 664
Bolton Landing, NY 12814 • 1,500
Bon Air, VA 23235 • 13,000
Bonaire, GA 31005 • 800
Bond □, IL • 16,224
Bondsville, MA 01009 • 1,906
Bonduel, WI 54107 • 1,160
Bondurant, IA 50035 • 1,283
Bonham, TX 75418 • 7,338
Bon Homme □, SD • 8,059
Bonifay, FL 32425 • 2,534
Bonita Springs, FL 33923 • 3,400
Bonneauville, PA 17325 • 920
Bonner □, ID • 24,163
Bonners Ferry, ID 83805 • 1,906
Bonner Springs, KS 66012 • 6,266
Bonne Terre, MO 63628 • 3,797
Bonneville □, ID • 65,980
Bonney Lake, WA 98390 • 5,328
Bonnie Doone, NC 28303 • 5,950
Bono, AR 72416 • 967

Booker, TX 79005 • 1,219
Boomer, WV 25031 • 1,100
Boone, IA 50036 • 12,602
Boone, NC 28607 • 10,191
Boone □, AR • 26,067
Boone □, IL • 28,630
Boone □, IN • 36,446
Boone □, IA • 26,184
Boone □, KY • 45,842
Boone □, MO • 100,376
Boone □, NE • 7,391
Boone □, WV • 30,447
Booneville, AR 72927 • 3,718
Booneville, MS 38829 • 6,199
Boonsboro, MD 21713 • 1,908
Boonton, NJ 07005 • 8,620
Boonville, CA 95415 • 1,000
Boonville, IN 47601 • 6,300
Boonville, MO 65233 • 6,959
Boonville, NC 27011 • 1,028
Boonville, NY 13309 • 2,344
Boothbay Harbor, ME 04538 • 2,207
Boothwyn, PA 19061 • 7,100
Borden □, TX • 859
Bordentown, NJ 08505 • 4,441
Borger, TX 79007 • 15,837
Boron, CA 93516 • 2,040
Borrego Springs, CA 92004 • 1,405
Boscobel, WI 53805 • 2,662
Bosque □, TX • 13,401
Bossert Estates, NJ 08505 • 2,800
Bossier □, LA • 80,721
Bossier City, LA 71111–13 • 50,817
Boston, GA 31626 • 1,424
Boston, MA 02101–99 • 562,994
Boston Heights, OH 44236 • 781
Boswell, IN 47921 • 810
Boswell, OK 74727 • 702
Boswell, PA 15531 • 1,480
Botetourt □, VA • 23,270
Bothell, WA 98011–12 • 7,943
Botkins, OH 45306 • 1,372
Bottineau, ND 58318 • 2,829
Bottineau □, ND • 9,239
Boulder, CO 80301–99 • 76,685
Boulder, MT 59632 • 1,441
Boulder □, CO • 189,625
Boulder City, NV 89005 • 9,590
Boulder Hill, IL 60538 • 9,333
Boulevard Heights, MD 20743 • 1,700
Boundary □, ID • 7,289
Bound Brook, NJ 08805 • 9,710
Bountiful, UT 84010 • 32,877
Bourbon, IN 46504 • 1,522
Bourbon, MO 65441 • 1,259
Bourbon □, KS • 15,969
Bourbon □, KY • 19,405
Bourbonnais, IL 60914 • 13,280
Bourg, LA 70343 • 2,073
Bourne, MA 02532 • 800
Boutte, LA 70039 • 1,200
Bovey, MN 55709 • 813
Bovina, TX 79009 • 1,499
Bowdle, SD 57428 • 644
Bowdon, GA 30108 • 1,743
Bowie, MD 20715–16 • 33,695
Bowie, TX 76230 • 5,610
Bowie □, TX • 75,301
Bowling Green, FL 33834 • 2,310
Bowling Green, KY 42101 • 40,450
Bowling Green, MO 63334 • 3,022
Bowling Green, OH 43402 • 25,728
Bowling Green, SC 29703 • 850
Bowling Green, VA 22427 • 665
Bowman, GA 30624 • 890
Bowman, ND 58623 • 2,071
Bowman, SC 29018 • 1,137
Bowman □, ND • 4,229
Bowmanstown, PA 18030 • 1,078
Bow Mar, CO 80120 • 930
Box Butte □, NE • 13,696
Box Elder, SD 57719 • 3,186
Box Elder □, UT • 33,222
Boxford, MA 01921 • 1,841
Boyce, LA 71409 • 1,198
Boyceville, WI 54725 • 862
Boyd, TX 76023 • 889
Boyd, WI 54726 • 660
Boyd □, KY • 55,513
Boyd □, NE • 3,331
Boyden, IA 51234 • 708
Boyertown, PA 19512 • 3,979
Boykins, VA 23827 • 791
Boyle, MS 38730 • 888
Boyle □, KY • 25,066
Boylston, MA 01505 • 950
Boyne City, MI 49712 • 3,348
Boynton Beach, FL 33435–37 • 35,624
Boys Ranch, TX 79010 • 650
Boys Town, NE 68010 • 622
Bozeman, MT 59715 • 21,645
Braceville, IL 60407 • 721
Bracken □, KY • 7,738
Brackenridge, PA 15014 • 4,297
Brackettville, TX 78832 • 1,676
Braddock, PA 15104 • 5,634
Braddock Heights, MD 21714 • 4,223
Bradenton, FL 34201–10 • 30,170
Bradenville, PA 15620 • 1,200
Bradford, AR 72020 • 950
Bradford, IL 61421 • 924
Bradford, OH 45308 • 2,166
Bradford, PA 16701 • 11,211
Bradford, RI 02808 • 1,354
Bradford, TN 38316 • 1,146
Bradford, VT 05033 • 831
Bradford □, FL • 20,023
Bradford □, PA • 62,919
Bradfordwoods, PA 15015 • 1,264
Bradley, AR 71826 • 790
Bradley, FL 33835 • 1,108
Bradley, IL 60915 • 11,008
Bradley, ME 04411 • 625
Bradley, WV 25818 • 1,200
Bradley □, AR • 13,803
Bradley □, TN • 67,547
Bradley Beach, NJ 07720 • 4,772
Bradner, OH 43406 • 1,175
Bradshaw, MD 21021 • 800
Bradshaw, WV 24817 • 628
Brady, TX 76825 • 5,969

Braham, MN 55006 • 1,015
Braidwood, IL 60408 • 3,429
Brainerd, MN 56401 • 11,489
Braintree, MA 02184 • 36,337
Bramwell, WV 24715 • 989
Branch □, MI • 40,188
Branchville, SC 29432 • 1,769
Brandenburg, KY 40108 • 1,831
Brandon, FL 33511 • 29,100
Brandon, MS 39042 • 9,626
Brandon, SC 29611 • 2,170
Brandon, SD 57005 • 2,589
Brandon, VT 05733 • 1,925
Brandon, WI 53919 • 862
Brandywine, MD 20613 • 1,319
Branford, CT 06405 • 5,438
Branford, FL 32008 • 622
Branford Hills, CT 06405 • 2,200
Branford Point, CT 06405 • 700
Branson, MO 65616 • 2,550
Brant Lake, NY 12815 • 700
Brantley, AL 36009 • 1,151
Brantley □, GA • 8,701
Brant Rock, MA 02020 • 1,500
Bratenahl, OH 44108 • 1,485
Brattleboro, VT 05301 • 8,596
Brawley, CA 92227 • 14,946
Braxton □, WV • 13,894
Braymer, MO 64624 • 986
Brazil, IN 47834 • 7,852
Brazoria, TX 77422 • 3,025
Brazoria □, TX • 169,587
Brazos □, TX • 93,588
Brea, CA 92621 • 27,913
Breathitt □, KY • 17,004
Breaux Bridge, LA 70517 • 5,922
Breckenridge, CO 80424 • 818
Breckenridge, MI 48615 • 1,495
Breckenridge, MN 56520 • 3,909
Breckenridge, TX 76024 • 6,921
Breckenridge Hills, MO 63114 • 5,666
Breckinridge □, KY • 16,861
Brecksville, OH 44141 • 10,132
Breese, IL 62230 • 3,516
Bremen, GA 30110 • 3,966
Bremen, IN 46506 • 3,565
Bremen, OH 43107 • 1,432
Bremer □, IA • 24,820
Bremerton, WA 98310–15 • 36,208
Bremond, TX 76629 • 1,025
Brenham, TX 77833 • 10,966
Brent, AL 35034 • 2,862
Brent, FL 32503 • 4,100
Brenton, WV 24818 • 800
Brentwood, CA 94513 • 4,434
Brentwood, MD 20722 • 2,988
Brentwood, MO 63144 • 8,209
Brentwood, NY 11717 • 48,800
Brentwood, OH 45231 • 5,508
Brentwood, PA 15227 • 11,861
Brentwood, SC 29405 • 2,000
Brentwood, TN 37027 • 9,431
Breton Woods, NJ 08723 • 1,300
Brevard, NC 28712 • 5,323
Brevard □, FL • 272,959
Brewer, ME 04412 • 9,017
Brewster, MA 02631 • 1,744
Brewster, NY 10509 • 1,650
Brewster, OH 44613 • 2,321
Brewster, WA 98812 • 1,337
Brewster □, TX • 7,573
Brewton, AL 36426 • 6,680
Briarcliff, PA 19036 • 9,300
Briarcliff Manor, NY 10510 • 7,115
Briceville, TN 37710 • 800
Brick, NJ 08723–24 • 3,200
Bridge City, LA 70094 • 2,500
Bridgehampton, NY 11932 • 950
Bridgeport, AL 35740 • 2,974
Bridgeport, CA 93517 • 900
Bridgeport, CT 06601–99 • 142,546
Bridgeport, IL 62417 • 2,281
Bridgeport, MI 48722 • 3,500
Bridgeport, NE 69336 • 1,668
Bridgeport, NJ 08014 • 900
Bridgeport, OH 43912 • 2,642
Bridgeport, PA 19405 • 4,843
Bridgeport, TX 76026 • 3,737
Bridgeport, WA 98813 • 1,174
Bridgeport, WV 26330 • 6,604
Bridger, MT 59014 • 724
Bridgeton, MO 63044 • 18,445
Bridgeton, NJ 08302 • 18,795
Bridgetown, OH 45211 • 11,460
Bridgeview, IL 60455 • 14,155
Bridgeville, DE 19933 • 1,238
Bridgeville, PA 15017 • 6,154
Bridgewater, MA 02324 • 6,781
Bridgewater, NJ 08807 • 5,800
Bridgewater, SD 57319 • 653
Bridgewater, VA 22812 • 3,289
Bridgman, MI 49106 • 2,235
Bridgton, ME 04009 • 1,639
Brielle, NJ 08730 • 4,068
Brigantine, NJ 08203 • 8,318
Brigham City, UT 84302 • 15,596
Brighton, AL 35020 • 5,308
Brighton, CO 80601 • 12,773
Brighton, IL 62012 • 2,364
Brighton, IA 52540 • 804
Brighton, MI 48116 • 4,268
Brighton, NY 14610 • 35,776
Brighton, TN 38011 • 976
Brilliant, AL 35548 • 871
Brilliant, OH 43913 • 1,751
Brillion, WI 54110 • 2,907
Brimfield, IL 61517 • 890
Brinkley, AR 72021 • 4,909
Briscoe □, TX • 2,579
Bristol, CT 06010 • 57,370
Bristol, FL 32321 • 1,044
Bristol, IN 46507 • 1,203
Bristol, NH 03222 • 1,258
Bristol, PA 19007 • 10,867
Bristol, RI 02809 • 20,128
Bristol, TN 37620 • 23,986
Bristol, VT 05443 • 1,793
Bristol, VA 24201 • 19,042
Bristol □, MA • 474,641
Bristol □, RI • 46,942
Bristow, OK 74010 • 4,702

# United States Populations and ZIP Codes

Britt, IA 50423 • 2,185
Britton, MI 49229 • 693
Britton, SD 57430 • 1,590
Broadalbin, NY 12025 • 1,415
Broad Brook, CT 06016 • 7,879
Broadmoor, CO 80906 • 1,900
Broadus, MT 59317 • 712
Broadview, IL 60153 • 8,618
Broadview Heights, OH 44141 • 10,920
Broadview Park, FL 33314 • 6,022
Broadwater □, MT • 3,267
Broadway, NC 27505 • 908
Broadway, VA 22815 • 1,234
Brockport, NY 14420 • 9,776
Brockton, MA 02401–99 • 95,172
Brockway, PA 15824 • 2,376
Brocton, NY 14716 • 1,416
Broderick, CA 95605 • 9,900
Brodhead, KY 40409 • 686
Brodhead, WI 53520 • 3,153
Broken Arrow, OK 74012–14 • 35,761
Broken Bow, NE 68822 • 3,979
Broken Bow, OK 74728 • 3,965
Bronson, FL 32621 • 853
Bronson, MI 49028 • 2,271
Bronte, TX 76933 • 983
Bronx □, NY • 1,168,972
Bronxville, NY 10708 • 6,267
Brook, IN 47922 • 926
Brooke □, WV • 31,117
Brookfield, CT 06804 • 1,000
Brookfield, IL 60513 • 19,395
Brookfield, MA 01506 • 1,037
Brookfield, MO 64628 • 5,555
Brookfield, VA 22021 • 2,500
Brookfield, WI 53005 • 34,035
Brookfield Center, CT 06805 • 900
Brookhaven, MS 39601 • 10,800
Brookhaven, PA 19015 • 7,912
Brookhaven, WV 26505 • 1,200
Brookings, OR 97415 • 3,384
Brookings, SD 57006 • 14,951
Brookings □, SD • 24,332
Brookland, AR 72417 • 840
Brooklawn, NJ 08030 • 2,133
Brooklet, GA 30415 • 1,035
Brookline, MA 02146 • 55,062
Brooklyn, CT 06234 • 900
Brooklyn, IN 46111 • 889
Brooklyn, IA 52211 • 1,509
Brooklyn, MI 49230 • 1,110
Brooklyn, MS 39425 • 800
Brooklyn, OH 44144 • 12,342
Brooklyn, SC 29720 • 1,800
Brooklyn, WI 53521 • 627
Brooklyn Center, MN 55429 • 31,230
Brooklyn Park, MD 21225 • 11,508
Brooklyn Park, MN 55443 • 43,332
Brookneal, VA 24528 • 1,454
Brook Park, OH 44142 • 26,195
Brookport, IL 62910 • 1,128
Brookridge, CO 80120 • 1,200
Brooks, KY 40109 • 1,344
Brooks □, GA • 15,255
Brooks □, TX • 8,428
Brookshire, TX 77423 • 2,175
Brookside, AL 35036 • 1,409
Brookside, DE 19713 • 15,255
Brookston, IN 47923 • 1,701
Brooksville, FL 34601–02 • 5,582
Brooksville, KY 41004 • 680
Brooksville, MS 39739 • 1,038
Brookville, IN 47012 • 2,874
Brookville, MA 02343 • 950
Brookville, NY 11545 • 3,290
Brookville, OH 45309 • 4,322
Brookville, PA 15825 • 4,568
Brookwood, NJ 08527 • 4,000
Broomall, PA 19008 • 23,642
Broome □, NY • 213,648
Broomfield, CO 80020 • 20,730
Brooten, MN 56316 • 647
Broussard, LA 70518 • 2,923
Broward □, FL • 1,018,200
Browardale, FL 33311 • 7,571
Browerville, MN 56438 • 693
Brown □, IL • 5,411
Brown □, IN • 12,377
Brown □, KS • 11,955
Brown □, MN • 28,645
Brown □, NE • 4,377
Brown □, OH • 31,920
Brown □, SD • 36,962
Brown □, TX • 33,057
Brown □, WI • 175,280
Brown City, MI 48416 • 1,163
Brown Deer, WI 53209 • 12,921
Brownfield, TX 79316 • 10,387
Brownfields, LA 70811 • 1,800
Browning, MT 59417 • 1,226
Brownsburg, IN 46112 • 6,242
Brownsdale, MN 55918 • 691
Browns Mills, NJ 08015 • 10,568
Brownstown, IL 62418 • 708
Brownstown, IN 47220 • 2,704
Brownstown, PA 15906 • 800
Browns Valley, MN 56219 • 887
Brownsville, FL 33142 • 18,058
Brownsville, KY 42210 • 674
Brownsville, LA 71291 • 3,000
Brownsville, OR 97327 • 1,261
Brownsville, PA 15417 • 4,043
Brownsville, TN 38012 • 9,307
Brownsville, TX 78520–26 • 84,997
Brownton, MN 55312 • 697
Brownville, NY 13615 • 1,099
Brownville Junction, ME 04415 • 775
Brownwood, TX 76801 • 19,396
Broxton, GA 31519 • 1,117
Broyhill Park, VA 22042 • 3,600
Bruce, MS 38915 • 2,208
Bruce, WI 54819 • 905
Bruceton, TN 38317 • 1,579
Bruceville, IN 47516 • 646
Brule □, SD • 5,245
Brundidge, AL 36010 • 3,213
Brunswick, GA 31520 • 17,605
Brunswick, ME 04011 • 10,990
Brunswick, MD 21716 • 4,572
Brunswick, MO 65236 • 1,272
Brunswick, OH 44212 • 28,104
Brunswick □, NC • 35,777
Brunswick □, VA • 15,632
Brush, CO 80723 • 4,082
Brusly, LA 70719 • 1,762
Bryan, OH 43506 • 7,879
Bryan, TX 77801–06 • 44,337
Bryan □, GA • 10,175
Bryan □, OK • 30,535
Bryans Road, MD 20616 • 3,739
Bryant, AR 72022 • 2,682
Bryantville, MA 02327 • 1,500
Bryn Mawr, PA 19010 • 9,500
Bryn Mawr, WA 98178 • 2,100
Bryson City, NC 28713 • 1,556
Buchanan, GA 30113 • 1,019
Buchanan, MI 49107 • 5,142
Buchanan, VA 24066 • 1,205
Buchanan □, IA • 22,900
Buchanan □, MO • 87,888
Buchanan □, VA • 37,989
Buckatunna, MS 39322 • 700
Buckeye, AZ 85326 • 3,434
Buckeye Lake, OH 43008 • 2,521
Buckhannon, WV 26201 • 6,820
Buckhorn, AZ 85205 • 4,000
Buckingham □, VA • 11,751
Buckley, IL 60918 • 604
Buckley, WA 98321 • 3,143
Bucklin, KS 67834 • 786
Bucklin, MO 64631 • 713
Bucknell Manor, VA 22307 • 2,350
Buckner, MO 64016 • 2,848
Bucks □, PA • 479,211
Bucksport, ME 04416 • 2,853
Bucksport, SC 29527 • 1,125
Bucyrus, OH 44820 • 13,433
Buda, IL 61314 • 668
Bude, MS 39630 • 1,092
Buechel, KY 40218 • 6,912
Buena, NJ 08310 • 3,642
Buena, WA 98921 • 800
Buena Park, CA 90620–24 • 64,165
Buena Vista, CO 81211 • 2,075
Buena Vista, FL 34691 • 3,000
Buena Vista, GA 31803 • 1,544
Buena Vista, VA 24416 • 6,717
Buena Vista □, IA • 20,774
Buffalo, IA 52728 • 1,569
Buffalo, MN 55313 • 4,560
Buffalo, MO 65622 • 2,217
Buffalo, NY 14201–99 • 357,870
Buffalo, OH 43722 • 800
Buffalo, OK 73834 • 1,381
Buffalo, SC 29321 • 1,641
Buffalo, TX 75831 • 1,507
Buffalo, WV 25033 • 1,034
Buffalo, WI 54622 • 894
Buffalo, WY 82834 • 3,799
Buffalo □, NE • 34,797
Buffalo □, SD • 1,795
Buffalo □, WI • 14,309
Buffalo Center, IA 50424 • 1,233
Buffalo Grove, IL 60089 • 22,230
Buffalo Lake, MN 55314 • 782
Buford, GA 30518 • 6,578
Buhl, ID 83316 • 3,629
Buhl, MN 55713 • 1,284
Buhler, KS 67522 • 1,188
Buies Creek, NC 27506 • 1,939
Bullhead City, AZ 86430 • 5,000
Bullitt □, KY • 43,346
Bulloch □, GA • 35,785
Bullock □, AL • 10,596
Bullock Creek, MI 48640 • 900
Bulls Gap, TN 37711 • 821
Bull Shoals, AR 72619 • 1,312
Buna, TX 77612 • 1,900
Bunche Park, FL 33054 • 4,000
Buncombe □, NC • 160,934
Bunker, MO 63629 • 673
Bunker Hill, IL 62014 • 1,700
Bunker Hill, IN 46914 • 984
Bunker Hill, OR 97420 • 1,555
Bunker Hill, WV 25309 • 800
Bunkie, LA 71322 • 5,364
Bunnell, FL 32010 • 1,816
Buras, LA 70041 • 2,600
Burbank, CA 91501–99 • 84,625
Burbank, IL 60459 • 28,462
Burbank, WA 99323 • 700
Bureau □, IL • 39,114
Burgaw, NC 28425 • 1,738
Burgettstown, PA 15021 • 1,867
Burgin, KY 40310 • 1,008
Burien, WA 98166 • 14,250
Burkburnett, TX 76354 • 10,668
Burke, SD 57523 • 859
Burke, VA 22015 • 1,500
Burke □, GA • 19,349
Burke □, NC • 72,504
Burke □, ND • 3,822
Burke City, MO 63135 • 2,600
Burkesville, KY 42717 • 2,051
Burkeville, VA 23922 • 606
Burleigh □, ND • 54,811
Burleson, TX 76028 • 11,734
Burleson □, TX • 12,313
Burley, ID 83318 • 8,761
Burlingame, CA 94010 • 26,173
Burlingame, KS 66413 • 1,239
Burlington, CO 80807 • 3,107
Burlington, IN 46915 • 680
Burlington, IA 52601 • 29,529
Burlington, KS 66839 • 2,901
Burlington, MA 01803 • 23,486
Burlington, NJ 08016 • 10,246
Burlington, NC 27215 • 37,266
Burlington, ND 58722 • 762
Burlington, VT 05401 • 37,712
Burlington, WA 98233 • 3,894
Burlington, WI 53105 • 8,385
Burlington □, NJ • 362,542
Burlington Beach, IN 46383 • 900
Burlington Junction, MO 64428 • 657
Burnet, TX 78611 • 3,410
Burnet □, TX • 17,803
Burnett □, WI • 12,340
Burney, CA 96013 • 3,187
Burnham, PA 17009 • 2,457
Burns, OR 97720 • 3,579
Burns, TN 37029 • 777
Burns Flat, OK 73624 • 2,431
Burnside, KY 42519 • 775
Burnsville, MN 55337 • 35,674
Burnsville, MS 38833 • 889
Burnsville, NC 28714 • 1,452
Burnt Hills, NY 12027 • 2,000
Burr Oak, MI 49030 • 853
Burrton, KS 67020 • 976
Burt, IA 50522 • 689
Burt □, NE • 8,813
Burton, MI 48509 • 29,976
Burton, OH 44021 • 1,401
Burwell, NE 68823 • 1,383
Bushnell, FL 33513 • 983
Bushnell, IL 61422 • 3,811
Butler, AL 36904 • 1,882
Butler, GA 31006 • 1,959
Butler, IN 46721 • 2,509
Butler, KY 41006 • 663
Butler, MO 64730 • 4,107
Butler, NJ 07405 • 7,616
Butler, OH 44822 • 991
Butler, PA 16001 • 17,026
Butler, WI 53007 • 2,059
Butler □, AL • 21,680
Butler □, IA • 17,668
Butler □, KS • 44,782
Butler □, KY • 11,064
Butler □, MO • 37,693
Butler □, NE • 9,330
Butler □, OH • 258,787
Butler □, PA • 147,912
Butner, NC 27509 • 4,240
Butte, MT 59701 • 37,205
Butte □, CA • 143,851
Butte □, ID • 3,342
Butte □, SD • 8,372
Butterfield, MN 56120 • 634
Buttonwillow, CA 93206 • 1,350
Butts □, GA • 13,665
Buxton, NC 27920 • 700
Buzzards Bay, MA 02532 • 3,375
Byers, CO 80103 • 1,100
Byesville, OH 43723 • 2,572
Byfield, MA 01922 • 950
Byhalia, MS 38611 • 757
Bylas, AZ 85530 • 1,175
Byng, OK 74820 • 833
Byrdstown, TN 38549 • 884
Byron, CA 94514 • 900
Byron, GA 31008 • 1,661
Byron, IL 61010 • 2,035
Byron, MN 55920 • 1,715
Byron, WY 82412 • 633

## C

Cabarrus □, NC • 85,895
Cabell □, WV • 106,835
Cabin Creek, WV 25035 • 900
Cabin John, MD 20818 • 1,500
Cabool, MO 65689 • 2,090
Cabot, AR 72023 • 4,806
Cache, OK 73527 • 1,661
Cache □, UT • 57,176
Caddo, OK 74729 • 923
Caddo □, LA • 252,358
Caddo □, OK • 30,905
Cadillac, MI 49601 • 10,199
Cadiz, KY 42211 • 1,661
Cadiz, OH 43907 • 4,058
Cadott, WI 54727 • 1,247
Cahaba Heights, AL 35243 • 3,800
Cahokia, IL 62206 • 18,904
Cairnbrook, PA 15924 • 800
Cairo, GA 31728 • 8,777
Cairo, IL 62914 • 5,931
Cairo, NE 68824 • 737
Cairo, NY 12413 • 725
Calabasas, CA 91302 • 900
Calais, ME 04619 • 4,262
Calaveras □, CA • 20,710
Calavo Gardens, CA 92041 • 6,100
Calcasieu □, LA • 167,223
Calcutta, OH 43920 • 1,121
Caldwell, ID 83605 • 17,699
Caldwell, KS 67022 • 1,401
Caldwell, NJ 07006 • 7,624
Caldwell, OH 43724 • 1,935
Caldwell, TX 77836 • 2,953
Caldwell □, KY • 13,473
Caldwell □, LA • 10,761
Caldwell □, MO • 8,660
Caldwell □, NC • 67,746
Caldwell □, TX • 23,637
Caledonia, MI 49316 • 722
Caledonia, MN 55921 • 2,691
Caledonia, NY 14423 • 2,188
Caledonia, OH 43314 • 759
Caledonia □, VT • 25,808
Calera, AL 35040 • 2,035
Calera, OK 74730 • 1,390
Calexico, CA 92231 • 14,412
Calhoun, GA 30701 • 5,563
Calhoun, KY 42327 • 1,080
Calhoun □, AL • 119,761
Calhoun □, AR • 6,079
Calhoun □, FL • 9,294
Calhoun □, GA • 5,717
Calhoun □, IL • 5,867
Calhoun □, IA • 13,542
Calhoun □, MI • 141,557
Calhoun □, MS • 15,664
Calhoun □, SC • 12,206
Calhoun □, TX • 19,574
Calhoun □, WV • 8,250
Calhoun City, MS 38916 • 2,033
Calhoun Falls, SC 29628 • 2,491
Calico Rock, AR 72519 • 1,046
Caliente, NV 89008 • 982
Califon, NJ 07830 • 1,023
California, MO 65018 • 3,381
California, PA 15419 • 5,703
Calion, AR 71724 • 638
Calipatria, CA 92233 • 2,636
Calistoga, CA 94515 • 3,879
Callahan, FL 32011 • 869
Callahan, KS 67209 • 900
Callahan □, TX • 10,992
Callaway, FL 32401 • 7,154
Callaway □, MO • 32,252
Calloway □, KY • 30,031
Calmar, IA 52132 • 1,053
Calumet, MI 49913 • 1,013
Calumet □, WI • 30,867
Calumet City, IL 60409 • 39,697
Calumet Park, IL 60643 • 8,788
Calvert, TX 77837 • 1,732
Calvert □, MD • 34,638
Calvert City, KY 42029 • 2,388
Calverton, MD 20705 • 7,649
Calverton Park, MO 63136 • 1,717
Calwa, CA 93725 • 6,640
Calypso, NC 28325 • 689
Camanche, IA 52730 • 4,725
Camarillo, CA 93010 • 37,797
Camas, WA 98607 • 5,681
Camas □, ID • 818
Cambria, CA 93428 • 3,061
Cambria, WI 53923 • 680
Cambria □, PA • 183,263
Cambrian Park, CA 95124 • 4,000
Cambridge, IL 61238 • 2,217
Cambridge, IA 50046 • 732
Cambridge, MD 21613 • 11,703
Cambridge, MA 02138 • 95,322
Cambridge, MN 55008 • 3,287
Cambridge, NE 69022 • 1,206
Cambridge, NY 12816 • 1,820
Cambridge, OH 43725 • 13,573
Cambridge, WI 53523 • 844
Cambridge City, IN 47327 • 2,407
Cambridge Springs, PA 16403 • 2,102
Camden, AL 36726 • 2,406
Camden, AR 71701 • 15,356
Camden, DE 19934 • 1,757
Camden, IN 46917 • 618
Camden, ME 04843 • 3,743
Camden, NJ 08101–99 • 84,910
Camden, NY 13316 • 2,667
Camden, OH 45311 • 1,971
Camden, SC 29020 • 7,462
Camden, TN 38320 • 3,279
Camden □, GA • 13,371
Camden □, MO • 20,017
Camden □, NJ • 471,650
Camden □, NC • 5,829
Camdenton, MO 65020 • 2,303
Cameron, LA 70631 • 1,736
Cameron, MO 64429 • 4,519
Cameron, TX 76520 • 5,721
Cameron, WV 26033 • 1,474
Cameron, WI 54822 • 1,115
Cameron □, LA • 9,336
Cameron □, PA • 6,674
Cameron □, TX • 209,727
Camilla, GA 31730 • 5,414
Camino, CA 95709 • 900
Cammack Village, AR 72207 • 920
Camp □, TX • 9,275
Campbell, CA 95008 • 26,910
Campbell, FL 32741 • 2,941
Campbell, MO 63933 • 2,134
Campbell, OH 44405 • 11,619
Campbell □, KY • 83,317
Campbell □, SD • 2,243
Campbell □, TN • 34,923
Campbell □, VA • 45,424
Campbell □, WY • 24,367
Campbellsburg, IN 47108 • 695
Campbellsburg, KY 40011 • 714
Campbellsport, WI 53010 • 1,740
Campbellsville, KY 42718 • 8,715
Camp Hill, AL 36850 • 1,628
Camp Hill, PA 17011 • 8,422
Camp Point, IL 62320 • 1,285
Camp Springs, MD 20748 • 2,500
Campti, LA 71411 • 1,069
Camp Verde, AZ 86322 • 1,125
Camp Wood, TX 78833 • 728
Canaan, CT 06018 • 1,160
Canadensis, PA 18325 • 800
Canadian, TX 79014 • 3,491
Canadian □, OK • 56,452
Canajoharie, NY 13317 • 2,412
Canal Fulton, OH 44614 • 3,481
Canal Point, FL 33438 • 950
Canal Winchester, OH 43110 • 2,749
Canandaigua, NY 14424 • 10,419
Canaseraga, NY 14822 • 700
Canastota, NY 13032 • 4,773
Canby, MN 56220 • 2,143
Canby, OR 97013 • 7,659
Candler □, GA • 7,518
Candlewood Isle, CT 06812 • 750
Candlewood Shores, CT 06804 • 1,950
Cando, ND 58324 • 1,496
Candor, NC 27229 • 868
Candor, NY 13743 • 917
Caney, KS 67333 • 2,284
Caneyville, KY 42721 • 642
Canfield, OH 44406 • 5,535
Canisteo, NY 14823 • 2,679
Canistota, SD 57012 • 626
Cannelton, IN 47520 • 2,373
Cannelton, WV 25036 • 750
Cannon □, TN • 10,234
Cannon Beach, OR 97110 • 1,187
Cannondale, CT 06897 • 1,300
Cannon Falls, MN 55009 • 2,653
Canon, GA 30520 • 704
Canon City, CO 81212 • 13,037
Canonsburg, PA 15317 • 10,459
Canton, CT 06019 • 1,680
Canton, GA 30114 • 3,601
Canton, IL 61520 • 14,626
Canton, KS 67428 • 926
Canton, MA 02021 • 18,182
Canton, MI 48187 • 5,000
Canton, MS 39046 • 11,116
Canton, MO 63435 • 2,435
Canton, NC 28716 • 4,631
Canton, NY 13617 • 7,055
Canton, OH 44701–99 • 93,077
Canton, OK 73724 • 854
Canton, PA 17724 • 1,959
Canton, SD 57013 • 2,886
Canton, TX 75103 • 2,845
Cantonment, FL 32533 • 3,200
Canute, OK 73626 • 676
Canutillo, TX 79835 • 2,000
Canyon, TX 79015 • 10,724
Canyon □, ID • 83,756
Canyon City, OR 97820 • 639
Canyon Lake, TX 78130 • 6,000
Canyonville, OR 97417 • 1,288
Capac, MI 48014 • 1,377
Cape Canaveral, FL 32920 • 5,733
Cape Charles, VA 23310 • 1,512
Cape Coral, FL 33904 • 32,103
Cape Elizabeth, ME 04107 • 7,838
Cape Girardeau, MO 63701 • 34,361
Cape Girardeau □, MO • 58,837
Cape May, NJ 08204 • 4,853
Cape May □, NJ • 82,266
Cape May Court House, NJ 08210 • 3,597
Cape Vincent, NY 13618 • 785
Capitan, NM 88316 • 762
Capitola, CA 95010 • 9,095
Capitol Heights, IA 50317 • 815
Capitol Heights, MD 20743 • 3,271
Capron, IL 61012 • 678
Captain Cook, HI 96704 • 2,008
Captiva, FL 33924 • 1,200
Caraway, AR 72419 • 1,165
Carbon □, MT • 8,099
Carbon □, PA • 53,285
Carbon □, UT • 22,179
Carbon □, WY • 21,896
Carbondale, CO 81623 • 2,084
Carbondale, IL 62901 • 26,414
Carbondale, KS 66414 • 1,518
Carbondale, PA 18407 • 11,255
Carbon Hill, AL 35549 • 2,452
Cardiff-By-The-Sea, CA 92007 • 10,054
Cardington, OH 43315 • 1,665
Cardwell, MO 63829 • 831
Carencro, LA 70520 • 3,712
Caretta, WV 24821 • 950
Carey, OH 43316 • 3,674
Caribou, ME 04736 • 9,916
Caribou □, ID • 8,695
Carle Place, NY 11514 • 6,300
Carleton, MI 48117 • 2,786
Carlin, NV 89822 • 1,232
Carlinville, IL 62626 • 5,439
Carlisle, AR 72024 • 2,567
Carlisle, IN 47838 • 717
Carlisle, IA 50047 • 3,073
Carlisle, KY 40311 • 1,757
Carlisle, OH 45005 • 4,276
Carlisle, PA 17013 • 18,314
Carlisle □, KY • 5,487
Carl Junction, MO 64834 • 3,937
Carlsbad, CA 92008 • 35,490
Carlsbad, NM 88220 • 25,496
Carlstadt, NJ 07072 • 6,166
Carlton, MN 55718 • 862
Carlton, OR 97111 • 1,302
Carlton □, MN • 29,936
Carlyle, IL 62231 • 3,388
Carmel, CA 93923 • 4,707
Carmel, IN 46032 • 18,272
Carmel, NY 10512 • 3,395
Carmi, IL 62821 • 6,264
Carmichael, CA 95608 • 43,108
Carmichaels, PA 15320 • 630
Carnation, WA 98014 • 913
Carnegie, OK 73015 • 2,016
Carnegie, PA 15106 • 10,099
Carney, OK 74832 • 622
Carneys Point, NJ 08069 • 7,574
Carnot, PA 15108 • 5,400
Caro, MI 48723 • 4,317
Carol City, FL 33055 • 47,349
Caroleen, NC 28019 • 1,000
Carolina, WV 26563 • 650
Carolina Beach, NC 28428 • 2,000
Caroline □, MD • 23,143
Caroline □, VA • 17,904
Carol Stream, IL 60188 • 15,472
Carpentersville, IL 60110 • 23,272
Carpinteria, CA 93013 • 10,835
Carrabelle, FL 32322 • 1,304
Carrboro, NC 27510 • 7,336
Carrier Mills, IL 62917 • 2,268
Carrington, ND 58421 • 2,641
Carrizo Springs, TX 78834 • 6,886
Carrizozo, NM 88301 • 1,222
Carroll, IA 51401 • 9,705
Carroll, OH 43112 • 641
Carroll □, AR • 16,203
Carroll □, GA • 56,346
Carroll □, IL • 18,779
Carroll □, IN • 19,722
Carroll □, IA • 22,951
Carroll □, KY • 9,270
Carroll □, MD • 96,356
Carroll □, MS • 9,776
Carroll □, MO • 12,131
Carroll □, NH • 27,931
Carroll □, OH • 25,598
Carroll □, TN • 28,285
Carroll □, VA • 27,270
Carrollton, AL 35447 • 1,104
Carrollton, GA 30117 • 14,078
Carrollton, IL 62016 • 2,816
Carrollton, KY 41008 • 3,967
Carrollton, MI 48724 • 7,482
Carrollton, MO 64633 • 4,700
Carrollton, OH 44615 • 3,065
Carrollton, TX 75006–08 • 40,595
Carrolltown, PA 15722 • 1,395
Carrville, AL 36023 • 820
Carson, CA 90745 • 81,221
Carson, IA 51525 • 716
Carson, WA 98610 • 950
Carson □, TX • 6,672
Carson City, MI 48811 • 1,229
Carson City, NV 89701 • 32,022
Carsonville, MI 48419 • 622
Carter □, KY • 25,060
Carter □, MO • 5,428
Carter □, MT • 1,799
Carter □, OK • 43,610
Carter □, TN • 50,205
Carteret, NJ 07008 • 20,598
Carteret □, NC • 41,092
Carter Lake, IA 51510 • 3,438
Cartersville, GA 30120 • 9,247
Carterville, IL 62918 • 3,445

Carterville, MO 64835 • 1,973
Carthage, IL 62321 • 2,978
Carthage, IN 46115 • 886
Carthage, MS 39051 • 3,453
Carthage, MO 64836 • 11,104
Carthage, NC 28327 • 925
Carthage, NY 13619 • 3,643
Carthage, TN 37030 • 2,672
Carthage, TX 75633 • 6,447
Caruthersville, MO 63830 • 7,958
Carver, MA 02330 • 650
Carver, MN 55315 • 642
Carver □, MN • 37,046
Carver Ranch Estates, FL 33023 • 5,600
Carville, LA 70721 • 1,037
Cary, IL 60013 • 6,640
Cary, NC 27511 • 21,763
Caryville, FL 32427 • 633
Caryville, TN 37714 • 2,039
Casa Grande, AZ 85222 • 14,971
Casas Adobes, AZ 85704 • 5,300
Cascade, ID 83611 • 945
Cascade, IA 52033 • 1,912
Cascade, MT 59421 • 773
Cascade, WI 53011 • 615
Cascade □, MT • 80,696
Cascade Locks, OR 97014 • 838
Caseville, MI 48725 • 851
Casey, IL 62420 • 3,026
Casey □, KY • 14,818
Cashion, AZ 85329 • 3,014
Cashmere, WA 98815 • 2,240
Cashton, WI 54619 • 827
Casper, WY 82601–15 • 51,016
Caspian, MI 49915 • 1,038
Cass □, IL • 15,084
Cass □, IN • 40,936
Cass □, IA • 16,932
Cass □, MI • 49,499
Cass □, MN • 21,050
Cass □, MO • 51,029
Cass □, NE • 20,297
Cass □, ND • 88,247
Cass □, TX • 29,430
Cassadaga, NY 14718 • 821
Cass City, MI 48726 • 2,258
Casselberry, FL 32707–08 • 15,247
Casselton, ND 58012 • 1,661
Cassia □, ID • 19,427
Cass Lake, MN 56633 • 1,001
Cassopolis, MI 49031 • 1,933
Cassville, MO 65625 • 2,091
Cassville, WI 53806 • 1,270
Castalia, OH 44824 • 973
Castanea, PA 17726 • 1,204
Castile, NY 14427 • 1,135
Castleberry, AL 36432 • 847
Castle Dale, UT 84513 • 1,910
Castle Hayne, NC 28429 • 1,087
Castle Hills, DE 19720 • 1,950
Castle Park, CA 92011 • 6,300
Castle Point, MO 63136 • 6,500
Castle Rock, CO 80104 • 3,921
Castle Rock, WA 98611 • 2,162
Castle Shannon, PA 15234 • 10,164
Castleton on Hudson, NY 12033 • 1,627
Castro □, TX • 10,556
Castro Valley, CA 94546 • 44,011
Castroville, CA 95012 • 4,396
Castroville, TX 78009 • 1,821
Caswell □, NC • 20,705
Catahoula □, LA • 12,287
Catalina Foothills, AZ 85718 • 1,500
Catasauqua, PA 18032 • 6,711
Cataumet, MA 02534 • 800
Catawba □, NC • 105,208
Catawissa, PA 17820 • 1,568
Cathedral City, CA 92234 • 4,130
Cathlamet, WA 98612 • 635
Catlettsburg, KY 41129 • 3,005
Catlin, IL 61817 • 2,226
Catonsville, MD 21228 • 33,208
Catoosa, OK 74015 • 1,561
Catoosa □, GA • 36,991
Catron □, NM • 2,720
Catskill, NY 12414 • 4,718
Cattaraugus, NY 14719 • 1,200
Cattaraugus □, NY • 85,697
Cavalier, ND 58220 • 1,505
Cavalier □, ND • 7,636
Cave City, AR 72521 • 1,634
Cave City, KY 42127 • 2,098
Cave Creek, AZ 85331 • 1,589
Cave Junction, OR 97523 • 1,023
Cave Spring, GA 30124 • 883
Cave Spring, VA 24018 • 6,300
Cavetown, MD 21720 • 1,533
Cawker City, KS 67430 • 640
Cawood, KY 40815 • 800
Cayce, SC 29033 • 11,701
Cayuga, IN 47928 • 1,258
Cayuga □, NY • 79,894
Cayuga Heights, NY 14850 • 3,170
Cazenovia, NY 13035 • 2,599
Cecil, PA 15321 • 900
Cecil □, MD • 60,430
Cedar □, IA • 18,635
Cedar □, MO • 11,894
Cedar □, NE • 11,375
Cedar Bluff, AL 35959 • 1,129
Cedar Bluff, TN 37722 • 1,200
Cedar Bluffs, NE 68015 • 632
Cedarburg, WI 53012 • 9,005
Cedar City, UT 84720 • 10,972
Cedar Crest, NM 87008 • 900
Cedaredge, CO 81413 • 1,184
Cedar Falls, IA 50613 • 36,322
Cedar Grove, NJ 07009 • 12,600
Cedar Grove, WV 25039 • 1,479
Cedar Grove, WI 53013 • 1,420
Cedar Hill, MO 63016 • 1,512
Cedar Hill, TX 75104 • 6,849
Cedar Hills, OR 97225 • 8,000
Cedarhurst, NY 11516 • 6,162
Cedar Key, FL 32625 • 700
Cedar Knolls, NJ 07927 • 3,000
Cedar Lake, IN 46303 • 8,754
Cedar Rapids, IA 52401–99 • 110,243
Cedar Springs, MI 49319 • 2,615
Cedartown, GA 30125 • 8,619
Cedar Vale, KS 67024 • 848
Cedarville, CA 96104 • 950
Cedarville, IL 61013 • 766
Cedarville, NJ 08311 • 990
Cedarville, OH 45314 • 2,799
Celina, OH 45822 • 9,137
Celina, TN 38551 • 1,580
Celina, TX 75009 • 1,520
Celoron, NY 14720 • 1,405
Cement, OK 73017 • 884
Cementon, PA 18052 • 1,200
Center, CO 81125 • 1,630
Center, MO 63436 • 669
Center, ND 58530 • 900
Center, TX 75935 • 5,827
Centerbrook, CT 06409 • 900
Centerburg, OH 43011 • 1,275
Centereach, NY 11720 • 34,600
Centerfield, UT 84622 • 653
Center Hill, FL 33514 • 751
Center Line, MI 48015 • 9,293
Center Moriches, NY 11934 • 4,000
Center Point, AL 35215 • 23,317
Center Point, IA 52213 • 1,591
Centerville, IN 47330 • 2,284
Centerville, IA 52544 • 6,558
Centerville, MA 02632 • 3,640
Centerville, OH 45459 • 18,886
Centerville, PA 15417 • 4,207
Centerville, SD 57014 • 892
Centerville, TN 37033 • 2,824
Centerville, TX 75833 • 799
Centerville, UT 84014 • 8,069
Central, NM 88026 • 1,968
Central, SC 29630 • 1,914
Central City, IL 62801 • 1,505
Central City, IA 52214 • 1,067
Central City, KY 42330 • 5,214
Central City, NE 68826 • 3,083
Central City, PA 15926 • 1,496
Central Falls, RI 02863 • 16,995
Central Heights, AZ 85501 • 1,500
Centralia, IL 62801 • 15,126
Centralia, MO 65240 • 3,537
Centralia, WA 98531 • 11,555
Central Islip, NY 11722 • 26,000
Central Lake, MI 49622 • 895
Central Park, WA 98520 • 2,900
Central Point, OR 97502 • 6,357
Central Square, NY 13036 • 1,418
Central Valley, CA 96019 • 3,424
Central Valley, NY 10917 • 1,200
Central Village, CT 06332 • 1,200
Centre, AL 35960 • 2,351
Centre □, PA • 112,760
Centre City, NJ 08051 • 2,500
Centre Hall, PA 16828 • 1,233
Centreville, AL 35042 • 2,504
Centreville, IL 62207 • 9,747
Centreville, MD 21617 • 2,018
Centreville, MI 49032 • 1,202
Centreville, MS 39631 • 1,844
Centreville, VA 22020 • 950
Centuria, WI 54824 • 711
Century, FL 32535 • 1,805
Ceredo, WV 25507 • 2,255
Ceres, CA 95307 • 13,281
Ceresco, NE 68017 • 836
Cerritos, CA 90701 • 53,020
Cerro Gordo, IL 61818 • 1,553
Cerro Gordo □, IA • 48,458
Chadbourn, NC 28431 • 1,975
Chadron, NE 69337 • 5,933
Chadwick, IL 61014 • 631
Chadwicks, NY 13319 • 1,500
Chaffee, MO 63740 • 3,241
Chaffee □, CO • 13,227
Chaffin, MA 01520 • 3,700
Chagrin Falls, OH 44022 • 4,335
Chalfonte, DE 19810 • 2,200
Challis, ID 83226 • 758
Chalmette, LA 70043 • 33,847
Chama, NM 87520 • 1,090
Chamberlain, SD 57325 • 2,258
Chambers □, AL • 39,191
Chambers □, TX • 18,538
Chambersburg, PA 17201 • 16,174
Chamblee, GA 30341 • 7,137
Champaign, IL 61820–21 • 58,133
Champaign □, IL • 168,392
Champaign □, OH • 33,649
Champion, OH 44481 • 5,270
Champlain, NY 12919 • 1,410
Champlin, MN 55316 • 9,006
Chandler, AZ 85224 • 29,673
Chandler, IN 47610 • 3,043
Chandler, OK 74834 • 2,926
Chandler, TX 75758 • 1,308
Chandler Heights, AZ 85227 • 750
Chandlerville, IL 62627 • 842
Chanhassen, MN 55317 • 6,359
Channahon, IL 60410 • 3,734
Channel Lake, IL 60002 • 1,613
Channelview, TX 77530 • 16,000
Chantilly, VA 22021 • 950
Chanute, KS 66720 • 10,506
Chapel Hill, NC 27514 • 32,421
Chapel Hill, TN 37034 • 861
Chapel Square, VA 22003 • 2,000
Chapin, IL 62628 • 648
Chapman, KS 67431 • 1,255
Chapmanville, WV 25508 • 1,164
Chappaqua, NY 10514 • 5,100
Chappell, NE 69129 • 1,095
Chardon, OH 44024 • 4,434
Charenton, LA 70523 • 950
Chariton, IA 50049 • 4,987
Chariton □, MO • 10,489
Charleroi, PA 15022 • 5,717
Charles □, MD • 72,751
Charles City, IA 50616 • 8,778
Charles City □, VA • 6,692
Charles Mix □, SD • 9,680
Charleston, AR 72933 • 1,748
Charleston, IL 61920 • 19,355
Charleston, MS 38921 • 2,878
Charleston, MO 63834 • 5,230
Charleston, OR 97420 • 700
Charleston, SC 29401–25 • 69,510
Charleston, TN 37310 • 756
Charleston, WV 25301–99 • 63,968
Charleston □, SC • 276,974
Charlestown, IN 47111 • 5,596
Charlestown, MD 21914 • 720
Charlestown, NH 03603 • 1,294
Charlestown, RI 02813 • 1,200
Charles Town, WV 25414 • 2,857
Charlevoix, MI 49720 • 3,296
Charlevoix □, MI • 19,907
Charlotte, MI 48813 • 8,251
Charlotte, NC 28201–99 • 314,447
Charlotte, TN 37036 • 788
Charlotte, TX 78011 • 1,443
Charlotte □, FL • 58,460
Charlotte □, VA • 12,266
Charlotte Hall, MD 20622 • 1,000
Charlotte Harbor, FL 33980 • 2,084
Charlottesville, VA 22901–10 • 39,916
Charlton □, GA • 7,343
Charlton City, MA 01508 • 1,100
Charmco, WV 25958 • 800
Charter Oak, IA 51439 • 615
Chase, KS 67524 • 753
Chase, MD 21027 • 700
Chase □, KS • 3,309
Chase □, NE • 4,758
Chase City, VA 23924 • 2,749
Chaska, MN 55318 • 8,346
Chassell, MI 49916 • 700
Chateaugay, NY 12920 • 869
Chatfield, MN 55923 • 2,055
Chatham, IL 62629 • 5,597
Chatham, LA 71226 • 714
Chatham, MA 02633 • 1,922
Chatham, NJ 07928 • 8,537
Chatham, NY 12037 • 2,001
Chatham, VA 24531 • 1,390
Chatham □, GA • 202,226
Chatham □, NC • 33,415
Chatom, AL 36518 • 1,122
Chatsworth, GA 30705 • 2,493
Chatsworth, IL 60921 • 1,187
Chattahoochee, FL 32324 • 5,332
Chattahoochee □, GA • 21,732
Chattanooga, TN 37401–99 • 169,558
Chattaroy, WV 25667 • 1,200
Chattooga □, GA • 21,856
Chaumont, NY 13622 • 620
Chauncey, OH 45719 • 1,050
Chautauqua □, KS • 5,016
Chautauqua □, NY • 146,925
Chauvin, LA 70344 • 3,338
Chaves □, NM • 51,103
Chazy, NY 12921 • 800
Cheatham □, TN • 21,616
Chebanse, IL 60922 • 1,191
Cheboygan, MI 49721 • 5,106
Cheboygan □, MI • 20,649
Checotah, OK 74426 • 3,454
Cheektowaga, NY 14225 • 100,400
Chehalis, WA 98532 • 6,100
Chelan, WA 98816 • 2,802
Chelan □, WA • 45,061
Chelmsford, MA 01824 • 31,174
Chelsea, MA 02150 • 25,431
Chelsea, MI 48118 • 3,816
Chelsea, OK 74016 • 1,754
Chelsea Estates, DE 19720 • 1,500
Cheltenham, PA 19012 • 7,700
Chelyan, WV 25035 • 800
Chemung □, NY • 97,656
Chenango □, NY • 49,344
Chenango Bridge, NY 13745 • 2,600
Cheney, KS 67025 • 1,404
Cheney, WA 99004 • 7,630
Cheneyville, LA 71325 • 865
Chenoa, IL 61726 • 1,847
Chenoweth, OR 97058 • 2,820
Chepachet, RI 02814 • 900
Cheraw, SC 29520 • 5,654
Cheriton, VA 23316 • 695
Cherokee, AL 35616 • 1,589
Cherokee, IA 51012 • 7,004
Cherokee, KS 66724 • 775
Cherokee, OK 73728 • 2,105
Cherokee □, AL • 18,760
Cherokee □, GA • 51,699
Cherokee □, IA • 16,238
Cherokee □, KS • 22,304
Cherokee □, NC • 18,933
Cherokee □, OK • 30,684
Cherokee □, SC • 40,983
Cherokee □, TX • 38,127
Cherokee Village, AR 72525 • 3,200
Cherry □, NE • 6,758
Cherry Creek, NY 14723 • 677
Cherry Hill, NJ 08002–03 • 68,785
Cherry Hills Village, CO 80110 • 5,127
Cherryvale, KS 67335 • 2,769
Cherry Valley, AR 72324 • 729
Cherry Valley, IL 61016 • 946
Cherry Valley, MA 01611 • 1,400
Cherry Valley, NY 13320 • 684
Cherryville, NC 28021 • 4,844
Chesaning, MI 48616 • 2,656
Chesapeake, OH 45619 • 1,370
Chesapeake, VA 23320–25 • 114,486
Chesapeake, WV 25315 • 2,364
Chesapeake Beach, MD 20732 • 1,408
Chesapeake City, MD 21915 • 899
Cheshire, CT 06410 • 5,722
Cheshire, MA 01225 • 1,100
Cheshire □, NH • 62,116
Chesilhurst, NJ 08089 • 1,590
Chesnee, SC 29323 • 1,069
Chester, CA 96020 • 1,756
Chester, CT 06412 • 1,388
Chester, IL 62233 • 8,401
Chester, MA 01011 • 750
Chester, MT 59522 • 963
Chester, NJ 07930 • 1,433
Chester, NY 10918 • 1,910
Chester, PA 19013–16 • 45,794
Chester, SC 29706 • 6,820
Chester, VA 23831 • 7,000
Chester, WV 26034 • 3,297
Chester □, PA • 316,660
Chester □, SC • 30,148
Chester □, TN • 12,727
Chesterfield, IN 46017 • 2,701
Chesterfield, SC 29709 • 1,432
Chesterfield □, SC • 38,161
Chesterfield □, VA • 141,372
Chesterton, IN 46304 • 8,531
Chestertown, MD 21620 • 3,300
Chestertown, NY 12817 • 750
Chester Township, PA 19013 • 5,687
Chestnut Hill Estates, DE 19713 • 2,000
Cheswick, PA 15024 • 2,336
Chetek, WI 54728 • 1,931
Chetopa, KS 67336 • 1,751
Cheverly, MD 20785 • 5,751
Cheviot, OH 45211 • 9,888
Chevy Chase, MD 20815 • 12,232
Chewelah, WA 99109 • 1,888
Cheyenne, OK 73628 • 1,207
Cheyenne, WY 82001–09 • 47,283
Cheyenne □, CO • 2,153
Cheyenne □, KS • 3,678
Cheyenne □, NE • 10,057
Cheyenne Canon, CO 80907 • 1,100
Cheyenne Wells, CO 80810 • 950
Chicago, IL 60601–99 • 3,005,072
Chicago Heights, IL 60411 • 37,026
Chicago Ridge, IL 60415 • 13,473
Chickamauga, GA 30707 • 2,232
Chickasaw, AL 36611 • 7,402
Chickasaw □, IA • 15,437
Chickasaw □, MS • 17,853
Chickasha, OK 73018 • 15,828
Chico, CA 95926 • 26,603
Chico, TX 76030 • 890
Chico, WA 98310 • 750
Chicopee, GA 30501 • 900
Chicopee, MA 01013–22 • 55,112
Chicora, PA 16025 • 1,192
Chicot □, AR • 17,793
Chiefland, FL 32626 • 1,986
Childersburg, AL 35044 • 5,084
Childress, TX 79201 • 5,817
Childress □, TX • 6,950
Chilhowie, VA 24319 • 1,269
Chili Center, NY 14624 • 5,300
Chillicothe, IL 61523 • 6,176
Chillicothe, MO 64601 • 9,089
Chillicothe, OH 45601 • 23,420
Chillicothe, TX 79225 • 1,052
Chillum, MD 20783 • 14,900
Chiloquin, OR 97624 • 778
Chilton, WI 53014 • 2,965
Chilton □, AL • 30,612
Chimayo, NM 87522 • 1,993
China Grove, NC 28023 • 2,081
Chincoteague, VA 23336 • 1,607
Chinle, AZ 86503 • 2,815
Chino, CA 91710 • 40,165
Chinook, MT 59523 • 1,660
Chinook, WA 98614 • 650
Chino Valley, AZ 86323 • 2,858
Chipley, FL 32428 • 3,330
Chippewa □, MI • 29,029
Chippewa □, MN • 14,941
Chippewa □, WI • 52,127
Chippewa Falls, WI 54729 • 12,270
Chisago □, MN • 25,717
Chisago City, MN 55013 • 1,634
Chisholm, ME 04239 • 1,796
Chisholm, MN 55719 • 5,930
Chittenango, NY 13037 • 4,290
Chittenden □, VT • 115,534
Chocowinity, NC 27817 • 644
Choctaw, OK 73020 • 7,520
Choctaw □, AL • 16,839
Choctaw □, MS • 8,996
Choctaw □, OK • 17,203
Choteau, MT 59422 • 1,798
Choudrant, LA 71227 • 809
Chouteau, OK 74337 • 1,559
Chouteau □, MT • 6,092
Chowan □, NC • 12,558
Chowchilla, CA 93610 • 5,122
Chrisman, IL 61924 • 1,413
Christian □, IL • 36,446
Christian □, KY • 66,878
Christian □, MO • 22,402
Christiana, PA 17509 • 1,183
Christiansburg, VA 24073 • 10,345
Christmas, FL 32709 • 1,200
Christopher, IL 62822 • 3,086
Christoval, TX 76935 • 700
Chubbuck, ID 83202 • 7,052
Chula Vista, CA 92010–12 • 83,927
Church Hill, TN 37642 • 4,110
Churchill, OH 44505 • 7,700
Churchill □, NV • 13,917
Church Point, LA 70525 • 4,599
Churchton, MD 20733 • 800
Churchville, NY 14428 • 1,399
Churubusco, IN 46723 • 1,638
Cibecue, AZ 85911 • 950
Cibola □, NM • 30,102
Cicero, IL 60650 • 61,232
Cicero, IN 46034 • 2,557
Cimarron, KS 67835 • 1,491
Cimarron, NM 87714 • 888
Cimarron □, OK • 3,648
Cincinnati, OH 45201–99 • 385,457
Cinnaminson, NJ 08077 • 16,072
Circle, MT 59215 • 931
Circle Pines, MN 55014 • 3,321
Circleville, OH 43113 • 11,700
Cisco, TX 76437 • 4,517
Cisne, IL 62823 • 705
Cissna Park, IL 60924 • 825
Citra, FL 32627 • 1,500
Citronelle, AL 36522 • 2,841
Citrus □, FL • 54,703
Citrus Heights, CA 95610 • 85,911
City of Commerce, CA 90040 • 10,509
City View, SC 29611 • 1,662
Clackamas, OR 97015 • 3,250
Clackamas □, OR • 241,911
Claflin, KS 67525 • 764
Claiborne, LA 71291 • 2,000
Claiborne □, LA • 17,095
Claiborne □, MS • 12,279
Claiborne □, TN • 24,595
Clair-Mel City, FL 33619 • 7,000
Clairton, PA 15025 • 12,188
Clallam □, WA • 51,648
Clanton, AL 35045 • 5,832
Clara City, MN 56222 • 1,574
Clare, MI 48617 • 3,300
Clare □, MI • 23,822
Claremont, CA 91711 • 30,950
Claremont, NH 03743 • 14,557
Claremont, NC 28610 • 880
Claremore, OK 74017 • 12,085
Clarence, IA 52216 • 1,001
Clarence, LA 71414 • 612
Clarence, MO 63437 • 1,147
Clarendon, AR 72029 • 2,361
Clarendon, PA 16313 • 776
Clarendon, TX 79226 • 2,220
Clarendon □, SC • 27,464
Clarendon Hills, IL 60514 • 6,870
Clarinda, IA 51632 • 5,458
Clarion, IA 50525 • 3,060
Clarion, PA 16214 • 6,198
Clarion □, PA • 43,362
Clarissa, MN 56440 • 663
Clark, NJ 07066 • 16,699
Clark, SD 57225 • 1,351
Clark □, AR • 23,326
Clark □, ID • 798
Clark □, IL • 16,913
Clark □, IN • 88,838
Clark □, KS • 2,599
Clark □, KY • 28,322
Clark □, MO • 8,493
Clark □, NV • 463,087
Clark □, OH • 150,236
Clark □, SD • 4,894
Clark □, WA • 192,227
Clark □, WI • 32,910
Clarkdale, AZ 86324 • 1,512
Clarke □, AL • 27,702
Clarke □, GA • 74,498
Clarke □, IA • 8,612
Clarke □, MS • 16,945
Clarke □, VA • 9,965
Clarkesville, GA 30523 • 1,348
Clarkfield, MN 56223 • 1,171
Clarks, LA 71415 • 931
Clarksboro, NJ 08020 • 800
Clarksburg, WV 26301 • 22,371
Clarksdale, MS 38614 • 21,137
Clarks Grove, MN 56016 • 620
Clarks Hill, IN 47930 • 653
Clarkson, KY 42726 • 666
Clarkson, NE 68629 • 817
Clarks Summit, PA 18411 • 5,272
Clarkston, GA 30021 • 4,539
Clarkston, MI 48016 • 968
Clarkston, WA 99403 • 6,903
Clarksville, AR 72830 • 5,237
Clarksville, IN 47130 • 15,164
Clarksville, IA 50619 • 1,424
Clarksville, TN 37040–43 • 54,777
Clarksville, TX 75426 • 4,917
Clarksville, VA 23927 • 1,468
Clarkton, MO 63837 • 1,228
Clarkton, NC 28433 • 664
Clatskanie, OR 97016 • 1,648
Clatsop □, OR • 32,489
Claude, TX 79019 • 1,112
Clawson, MI 48017 • 15,103
Claxton, GA 30417 • 2,694
Clay, KY 42404 • 1,356
Clay, WV 25043 • 940
Clay □, AL • 13,703
Clay □, AR • 20,616
Clay □, FL • 67,052
Clay □, GA • 3,553
Clay □, IL • 15,283
Clay □, IN • 24,862
Clay □, IA • 19,576
Clay □, KS • 9,802
Clay □, KY • 22,752
Clay □, MN • 49,327
Clay □, MS • 21,082
Clay □, MO • 136,488
Clay □, NE • 8,106
Clay □, NC • 6,619
Clay □, SD • 13,689
Clay □, TN • 7,676
Clay □, TX • 9,582
Clay □, WV • 11,265
Clay Center, KS 67432 • 4,948
Clay Center, NE 68933 • 962
Clay City, IL 62824 • 1,038
Clay City, IN 47841 • 883
Clay City, KY 40312 • 1,276
Claymont, DE 19702 • 10,022
Claypool, AZ 85532 • 2,362
Claysburg, PA 16625 • 1,516
Claysville, PA 15323 • 1,029
Clayton, AL 36016 • 1,589
Clayton, DE 19938 • 1,216
Clayton, GA 30525 • 1,838
Clayton, IL 62324 • 889
Clayton, IN 46118 • 703
Clayton, LA 71326 • 1,204
Clayton, MO 63105 • 14,273
Clayton, NJ 08312 • 6,013
Clayton, NM 88415 • 2,968
Clayton, NC 27520 • 4,091
Clayton, NY 13624 • 1,816
Clayton, OK 74536 • 833
Clayton □, GA • 150,357
Clayton □, IA • 21,098
Clear Creek □, CO • 7,308
Clearfield, KY 40313 • 1,250
Clearfield, PA 16830 • 7,580
Clearfield, UT 84015 • 17,982
Clearfield □, PA • 83,578
Clearlake, CA 95422 • 13,300
Clear Lake, IA 50428 • 7,458
Clear Lake, SD 57226 • 1,310
Clearlake, WA 98235 • 900
Clear Lake, WI 54005 • 899
Clear Lake City, TX 77062 • 8,700
Clear Lake Shores, TX 77565 • 755
Clearwater, FL 34615–25 • 85,528
Clearwater, KS 67026 • 1,684
Clearwater, SC 29822 • 3,967
Clearwater □, ID • 10,390
Clearwater □, MN • 8,761
Cleburne, TX 76031 • 19,218
Cleburne □, AL • 12,595
Cleburne □, AR • 16,909
Cle Elum, WA 98922 • 1,773
Cleland Heights, DE 19805 • 1,500
Clementon, NJ 08021 • 5,764

United States Populations and ZIP Codes

Clemmons, NC 27012 • 7,401
Clemson, SC 29631 • 8,118
Clendenin, WV 25045 • 1,373
Cleona, PA 17042 • 2,003
Clermont, FL 32711 • 5,461
Clermont, IA 52135 • 602
Clermont □, OH • 128,483
Cleveland, GA 30528 • 1,578
Cleveland, MN 56017 • 699
Cleveland, MS 38732 • 14,524
Cleveland, NY 13042 • 855
Cleveland, OH 44101–99 • 573,822
Cleveland, OK 74020 • 2,972
Cleveland, TN 37311–12 • 26,415
Cleveland, TX 77327 • 5,977
Cleveland, WI 53015 • 1,270
Cleveland □, AR • 7,868
Cleveland □, NC • 83,435
Cleveland □, OK • 133,173
Cleveland Heights, OH 44118 • 56,438
Cleves, OH 45002 • 2,094
Clewiston, FL 33440 • 5,219
Cliffside Park, NJ 07010 • 21,464
Cliffwood Beach, NJ 07735 • 6,300
Clifton, AZ 85533 • 4,245
Clifton, CO 81520 • 5,223
Clifton, IL 60927 • 1,390
Clifton, KS 66937 • 695
Clifton, NJ 07011–15 • 74,388
Clifton, SC 29324 • 800
Clifton, TN 38425 • 773
Clifton, TX 76634 • 3,063
Clifton Forge, VA 24422 • 5,046
Clifton Heights, PA 19018 • 7,320
Clifton Knolls, NY 12065 • 4,000
Clifton Springs, NY 14432 • 2,039
Climax, MI 49034 • 619
Clinch □, GA • 6,660
Clinchco, VA 24226 • 1,000
Clint, TX 79836 • 1,314
Clinton, AR 72031 • 1,284
Clinton, CT 06413 • 11,195
Clinton, IL 61727 • 8,014
Clinton, IN 47842 • 5,267
Clinton, IA 52732 • 32,828
Clinton, KY 42031 • 1,720
Clinton, LA 70722 • 1,919
Clinton, ME 04927 • 1,305
Clinton, MD 20735 • 16,438
Clinton, MA 01510 • 12,771
Clinton, MI 49236 • 2,342
Clinton, MN 56225 • 622
Clinton, MS 39056 • 14,660
Clinton, MO 64735 • 8,366
Clinton, NJ 08809 • 1,910
Clinton, NC 28328 • 7,552
Clinton, NY 13323 • 2,107
Clinton, OK 73601 • 8,796
Clinton, SC 29325 • 8,596
Clinton, TN 37716 • 5,245
Clinton, UT 84015 • 5,777
Clinton, WA 98236 • 2,000
Clinton, WI 53525 • 1,751
Clinton □, IL • 32,617
Clinton □, IN • 31,545
Clinton □, IA • 57,122
Clinton □, KY • 9,321
Clinton □, MI • 55,893
Clinton □, MO • 15,916
Clinton □, NY • 80,750
Clinton □, OH • 34,603
Clinton □, PA • 38,971
Clinton Township, MI 48043 • 72,400
Clintonville, WI 54929 • 4,567
Clintwood, VA 24228 • 1,369
Clio, AL 36017 • 1,224
Clio, MI 48420 • 2,669
Clio, SC 29525 • 1,031
Clive, IA 50053 • 6,064
Cloquet, MN 55720 • 11,142
Closter, NJ 07624 • 8,164
Cloud □, KS • 12,494
Clover, SC 29710 • 3,451
Cloverdale, CA 95425 • 3,989
Cloverdale, IN 46120 • 1,357
Cloverdale, VA 24077 • 850
Cloverleaf, TX 77015 • 11,800
Cloverport, KY 40111 • 1,585
Clovis, CA 93612 • 33,021
Clovis, NM 88101 • 31,194
Clute, TX 77531 • 9,577
Clyde, KS 66938 • 909
Clyde, NC 28721 • 1,008
Clyde, NY 14433 • 2,491
Clyde, OH 43410 • 5,489
Clyde, TX 79510 • 2,562
Clymer, PA 15728 • 1,761
Coachella, CA 92236 • 9,129
Coahoma, TX 79511 • 1,069
Coahoma □, MS • 36,918
Coal □, OK • 6,041
Coal City, IL 60416 • 3,028
Coaldale, PA 18218 • 2,762
Coal Fork, WV 25306 • 900
Coalgate, OK 74538 • 2,001
Coal Grove, OH 45638 • 2,602
Coal Hill, AR 72832 • 859
Coalinga, CA 93210 • 6,593
Coalmont, TN 37313 • 625
Coalport, PA 16627 • 739
Coalton, OH 45621 • 639
Coalville, UT 84017 • 1,031
Coalwood, WV 24824 • 1,100
Coatesville, PA 19320 • 10,698
Coats, NC 27521 • 1,385
Cobb □, GA • 297,718
Cobden, IL 62920 • 1,210
Cobleskill, NY 12043 • 5,272
Coburg, OR 97401 • 699
Cochise □, AZ • 85,686
Cochituate, MA 01778 • 6,126
Cochran, GA 31014 • 5,121
Cochran □, TX • 4,825
Cochranton, PA 16314 • 1,240
Cocke □, TN • 28,792
Cockeysville, MD 21030 • 17,013
Cockrell Hill, TX 75211 • 3,262
Cocoa, FL 32922–27 • 16,096
Cocoa Beach, FL 32931 • 10,926
Cocoa West, FL 32922 • 6,432
Coconino □, AZ • 75,008
Coconut Creek, FL 33060 • 6,288
Codington □, SD • 20,885
Cody, WY 82414 • 6,790
Coeburn, VA 24230 • 2,625
Coeur d'Alene, ID 83814 • 20,054
Coffee □, AL • 38,533
Coffee □, GA • 26,894
Coffee □, TN • 38,311
Coffeen, IL 62017 • 842
Coffeeville, MS 38922 • 1,129
Coffey □, KS • 9,370
Coffeyville, KS 67337 • 15,185
Coggon, IA 52218 • 639
Cohasset, MA 02025 • 5,300
Cohocton, NY 14826 • 902
Cohoes, NY 12047 • 18,144
Cokato, MN 55321 • 2,056
Coke □, TX • 3,196
Colbert, OK 74733 • 1,122
Colbert □, AL • 54,519
Colby, KS 67701 • 5,544
Colby, WI 54421 • 1,496
Colchester, CT 06415 • 3,190
Colchester, IL 62326 • 1,729
Cold Spring, KY 41076 • 2,117
Cold Spring, MN 56320 • 2,294
Cold Spring, NJ 08204 • 850
Cold Spring Harbor, NY 11724 • 5,490
Coldwater, KS 67029 • 989
Coldwater, MI 49036 • 9,461
Coldwater, MS 38618 • 1,505
Coldwater, OH 45828 • 4,220
Cole □, MO • 56,663
Colebrook, NH 03576 • 1,131
Cole Camp, MO 65325 • 1,022
Coleman, FL 33521 • 1,022
Coleman, MI 48618 • 1,429
Coleman, TX 76834 • 5,960
Coleman, WI 54112 • 852
Coleman □, TX • 10,439
Coleraine, MN 55722 • 1,116
Coleridge, NE 68727 • 673
Coles □, IL • 52,260
Colfax, CA 95713 • 981
Colfax, IL 61728 • 920
Colfax, IN 46035 • 823
Colfax, IA 50054 • 2,234
Colfax, LA 71417 • 1,680
Colfax, WA 99111 • 2,780
Colfax, WI 54730 • 1,149
Colfax □, NE • 9,890
Colfax □, NM • 13,667
College, AK 99701 • 800
Collegedale, TN 37315 • 1,500
College Park, GA 30337 • 24,632
College Park, MD 20740 • 23,614
College Place, WA 99324 • 5,771
College Station, AR 72053 • 4,000
College Station, TX 77840 • 37,272
Collegeville, IN 47978 • 1,059
Collegeville, PA 19426 • 3,406
Colleton □, SC • 31,776
Colleyville, TX 76034 • 6,700
Collier □, FL • 85,971
Collierville, TN 38017 • 7,839
Collin □, TX • 144,576
Collingdale, PA 19023 • 9,539
Collingswood, NJ 08108 • 15,838
Collingsworth □, TX • 4,648
Collins, GA 30421 • 639
Collins, MS 39428 • 2,131
Collins Park, DE 19720 • 2,850
Collinsville, AL 35961 • 1,383
Collinsville, CT 06022 • 2,555
Collinsville, IL 62234 • 19,613
Collinsville, OK 74021 • 3,556
Collinsville, VA 24078 • 7,400
Collinwood, TN 38450 • 1,064
Colmar Manor, MD 20722 • 1,286
Colo, IA 50056 • 808
Coloma, MI 49038 • 1,833
Colon, MI 49040 • 1,190
Colonia, NJ 07067 • 20,900
Colonial Beach, VA 22443 • 2,474
Colonial Heights, TN 37663 • 6,744
Colonial Heights, VA 23834 • 16,509
Colonial Park, PA 17109 • 10,000
Colonie, NY 12212 • 8,869
Colorado □, TX • 18,823
Colorado City, CO 81019 • 950
Colorado City, TX 79512 • 5,405
Colorado Springs, CO 80901–99 • 214,821
Colquitt, GA 31737 • 2,065
Colquitt □, GA • 35,376
Colstrip, MT 59323 • 1,476
Colter Bay, WY 83001 • 2,000
Colton, CA 92324 • 15,201
Colton, SD 57018 • 757
Columbia, AL 36319 • 881
Columbia, CA 95310 • 950
Columbia, IL 62236 • 4,269
Columbia, KY 42728 • 3,710
Columbia, LA 71418 • 687
Columbia, MD 21045–46 • 52,518
Columbia, MS 39429 • 7,733
Columbia, MO 65201–18 • 62,061
Columbia, NC 27925 • 758
Columbia, PA 17512 • 10,466
Columbia, SC 29201–99 • 100,385
Columbia, TN 38401 • 26,571
Columbia □, AR • 26,644
Columbia □, FL • 35,399
Columbia □, GA • 40,118
Columbia □, NY • 59,487
Columbia □, OR • 35,646
Columbia □, PA • 61,967
Columbia □, WA • 4,057
Columbia □, WI • 43,222
Columbia City, IN 46725 • 5,091
Columbia City, OR 97018 • 678
Columbia Falls, MT 59912 • 3,112
Columbia Heights, MN 55421 • 20,029
Columbiana, AL 35051 • 2,655
Columbiana, OH 44408 • 4,987
Columbiana □, OH • 113,572
Columbiaville, MI 48421 • 953
Columbus, GA 31901–99 • 169,441
Columbus, IN 47201–03 • 30,614
Columbus, KS 66725 • 3,426
Columbus, MS 39701–04 • 27,383
Columbus, MT 59019 • 1,439
Columbus, NE 68601 • 17,328
Columbus, NJ 08022 • 700
Columbus, NC 28722 • 727
Columbus, OH 43201–99 • 565,032
Columbus, TX 78934 • 3,923
Columbus, WI 53925 • 4,049
Columbus □, NC • 51,037
Columbus Grove, OH 45830 • 2,313
Columbus Junction, IA 52738 • 1,429
Colusa, CA 95932 • 4,075
Colusa □, CA • 12,791
Colver, PA 15927 • 1,175
Colville, WA 99114 • 4,510
Colwich, KS 67030 • 935
Comal □, TX • 36,446
Comanche, OK 73529 • 1,937
Comanche, TX 76442 • 4,075
Comanche □, KS • 2,554
Comanche □, OK • 112,456
Comanche □, TX • 12,617
Combined Locks, WI 54113 • 2,573
Combs, KY 41729 • 700
Comer, GA 30629 • 930
Comfort, TX 78013 • 950
Commack, NY 11725 • 24,300
Commerce, GA 30529 • 4,092
Commerce, OK 74339 • 2,556
Commerce, TX 75428 • 8,136
Commerce City, CO 80022 • 16,234
Common Fence Point, RI 02871 • 850
Como, MS 38619 • 1,378
Compton, CA 90220–24 • 81,286
Comstock, MI 49041 • 5,310
Concho □, TX • 2,915
Concord, CA 94518–24 • 103,255
Concord, MA 01742 • 6,400
Concord, MI 49237 • 900
Concord, MO 63851 • 20,896
Concord, NH 03301–06 • 30,400
Concord, NC 28025 • 16,942
Concordia, KS 66901 • 6,847
Concordia, MO 64020 • 2,129
Concordia □, LA • 22,981
Condon, OR 97823 • 783
Conecuh □, AL • 15,884
Conejos □, CO • 7,794
Conemaugh, PA 15909 • 2,128
Confluence, PA 15424 • 968
Congers, NY 10920 • 5,000
Conklin, NY 13748 • 1,900
Conneaut, OH 44030 • 13,835
Conneaut Lake, PA 16316 • 767
Conneautville, PA 16406 • 971
Connell, WA 99326 • 1,981
Connellsville, PA 15425 • 10,319
Connersville, IN 47331 • 17,023
Conover, NC 28613 • 4,245
Conrad, IA 50621 • 1,133
Conrad, MT 59425 • 3,074
Conroe, TX 77301–05 • 18,034
Conshohocken, PA 19428 • 8,475
Constantia, NY 13044 • 900
Constantine, MI 49042 • 1,680
Continental, OH 45831 • 1,179
Contoocook, NH 03229 • 1,499
Contra Costa □, CA • 656,380
Converse, IN 46919 • 1,279
Converse, SC 29329 • 1,173
Converse □, WY • 14,069
Convoy, OH 45832 • 1,140
Conway, AR 72032 • 20,375
Conway, FL 32809 • 16,000
Conway, MO 65632 • 601
Conway, NH 03818 • 1,781
Conway, NC 27820 • 678
Conway, PA 15027 • 2,747
Conway, SC 29526 • 10,240
Conway □, AR • 19,505
Conway Springs, KS 67031 • 1,313
Conyers, GA 30207–08 • 6,567
Cook, MN 55723 • 800
Cook □, GA • 13,490
Cook □, IL • 5,253,655
Cook □, MN • 4,092
Cooke □, TX • 27,656
Cookeville, TN 38501 • 20,535
Cooleemee, NC 27014 • 1,448
Coolidge, AZ 85228 • 6,851
Coolidge, GA 31738 • 736
Coolidge, TX 76635 • 810
Coolville, OH 45723 • 649
Coon Rapids, IA 50058 • 1,448
Coon Rapids, MN 55433 • 35,826
Coon Valley, WI 54623 • 758
Cooper, TX 75432 • 2,338
Cooper □, MO • 14,643
Cooper City, FL 33328 • 10,140
Cooper Road, LA 71107 • 10,000
Coopersburg, PA 18036 • 2,595
Cooperstown, ND 58425 • 1,308
Cooperstown, NY 13326 • 2,342
Cooperstown, PA 16317 • 644
Coopersville, MI 49404 • 2,889
Coos □, NH • 35,147
Coos □, OR • 64,047
Coosa □, AL • 11,377
Coosada, AL 36020 • 980
Coos Bay, OR 97420 • 14,424
Copake, NY 12516 • 700
Copalis Beach, WA 98535 • 800
Copan, OK 74022 • 960
Copeland, FL 33926 • 700
Copenhagen, NY 13626 • 656
Copiague, NY 11726 • 21,000
Copiah □, MS • 26,503
Coplay, PA 18037 • 3,130
Copperas Cove, TX 76522 • 19,469
Copperton, UT 84006 • 850
Coquille, OR 97423 • 4,481
Coral, PA 15731 • 700
Coral Gables, FL 33134 • 43,241
Coralville, IA 52241 • 7,687
Coram, NY 11727 • 5,400
Coraopolis, PA 15108 • 7,308
Corbin, KY 40701 • 8,075
Corcoran, CA 93212 • 6,454
Corcoran, MN 55340 • 4,252
Cordaville, MA 01772 • 1,384
Cordele, GA 31015 • 11,184
Cordell, OK 73632 • 3,301
Cordova, AL 35550 • 3,123
Cordova, AK 99574 • 1,879
Cordova, IL 61242 • 697
Cordova, NC 28330 • 1,200
Corfu, NY 14036 • 689
Corinna, ME 04928 • 950
Corinth, MS 38834 • 13,839
Corinth, NY 12822 • 2,702
Cornelia, GA 30531 • 3,203
Cornelius, NC 28031 • 1,460
Cornelius, OR 97113 • 4,462
Cornell, IL 61319 • 603
Cornell, WI 54732 • 1,583
Cornersville, TN 37047 • 722
Corning, AR 72422 • 3,650
Corning, CA 96021 • 4,745
Corning, IA 50841 • 1,939
Corning, NY 14830 • 12,953
Corning, OH 43730 • 789
Cornville, AZ 86325 • 800
Cornwall, PA 17016 • 2,653
Cornwall On Hudson, NY 12520 • 3,164
Cornwells Heights, PA 19020 • 8,700
Corona, CA 91720 • 37,791
Coronado, CA 92118 • 18,790
Corpus Christi, TX 78401–99 • 231,999
Correctionville, IA 51016 • 935
Corrigan, TX 75939 • 1,770
Corriganville, MD 21524 • 1,020
Corry, PA 16407 • 7,149
Corsica, SD 57328 • 644
Corsicana, TX 75110 • 21,712
Corson □, SD • 5,196
Corte Madera, CA 94925 • 8,074
Cortez, CO 81321 • 7,095
Cortez, FL 34215 • 1,450
Cortland, IL 60112 • 1,019
Cortland, NY 13045 • 20,138
Cortland, OH 44410 • 5,011
Cortland □, NY • 48,820
Corunna, MI 48817 • 3,206
Corvallis, OR 97330–33 • 40,960
Corydon, IN 47112 • 2,724
Corydon, IA 50060 • 1,818
Corydon, KY 42406 • 874
Coryell □, TX • 56,767
Coshocton, OH 43812 • 13,405
Coshocton □, OH • 36,024
Cosmopolis, WA 98537 • 1,575
Costa Mesa, CA 92626–27 • 82,562
Costilla □, CO • 3,071
Cottage Grove, MN 55016 • 18,994
Cottage Grove, OR 97424 • 7,148
Cotter, AR 72626 • 920
Cottle □, TX • 2,947
Cotton □, OK • 7,338
Cottondale, AL 35453 • 2,300
Cottondale, FL 32431 • 1,056
Cotton Plant, AR 72036 • 1,323
Cottonport, LA 71327 • 1,911
Cotton Valley, LA 71018 • 1,445
Cottonwood, AL 36320 • 1,352
Cottonwood, AZ 86326 • 4,550
Cottonwood, CA 96022 • 1,553
Cottonwood, ID 83522 • 941
Cottonwood, MN 56229 • 924
Cottonwood, UT 84121 • 11,554
Cottonwood □, MN • 14,854
Cottonwood Falls, KS 66845 • 954
Cottonwood Heights, UT 84121 • 18,000
Cotuit, MA 02635 • 1,300
Cotulla, TX 78014 • 3,912
Coudersport, PA 16915 • 2,791
Coulee Dam, WA 99116 • 1,412
Coulterville, IL 62237 • 1,118
Council, ID 83612 • 917
Council Bluffs, IA 51501 • 56,449
Council Grove, KS 66846 • 2,381
Country Club Hills, IL 60477 • 14,676
Country Homes, WA 99218 • 3,850
Countryside, IL 60525 • 6,538
Coupeville, WA 98239 • 1,006
Courtland, VA 23837 • 976
Coushatta, LA 71019 • 2,084
Covedale, OH 45238 • 6,530
Covelo, CA 95428 • 1,448
Coventry, CT 06238 • 3,769
Coventry, DE 19720 • 830
Coventry, RI 02816 • 8,000
Covina, CA 91722–24 • 33,751
Covington, GA 30209 • 10,586
Covington, IN 47932 • 2,883
Covington, KY 41011–19 • 49,563
Covington, LA 70433 • 7,892
Covington, OH 45318 • 2,610
Covington, OK 73730 • 715
Covington, TN 38019 • 6,065
Covington, VA 24426 • 9,063
Covington □, AL • 36,850
Covington □, MS • 15,927
Cowan, TN 37318 • 1,790
Cowden, IL 62422 • 623
Cowen, WV 26206 • 723
Coweta, OK 74429 • 4,554
Coweta □, GA • 39,268
Cowley □, KS • 36,824
Cowlitz □, WA • 79,548
Cowpens, SC 29330 • 2,023
Coxsackie, NY 12051 • 2,786
Cozad, NE 69130 • 4,453
Crab Orchard, KY 40419 • 843
Crab Orchard, TN 37723 • 1,065
Crab Orchard, WV 25827 • 1,900
Crabtree, PA 15624 • 1,021
Crafton, PA 15205 • 7,623
Craig, CO 81625 • 8,133
Craig □, OK • 15,014
Craig □, VA • 3,948
Craighead □, AR • 63,239
Craigmont, ID 83523 • 617
Craigsville, VA 24430 • 845
Craigsville, WV 26205 • 900
Cramerton, NC 28032 • 1,869
Cranbury, NJ 08512 • 1,255
Crandall, TX 75114 • 831
Crandon, WI 54520 • 1,969
Crane, AZ 85364 • 2,400
Crane, MO 65633 • 1,185
Crane, TX 79731 • 3,622
Crane □, TX • 4,600
Cranesville, PA 16410 • 703
Cranford, NJ 07016 • 24,573
Cranston, RI 02910 • 71,992
Craven □, NC • 71,043
Crawford, NE 69339 • 1,315
Crawford □, AR • 36,892
Crawford □, GA • 7,684
Crawford □, IL • 20,818
Crawford □, IN • 9,820
Crawford □, IA • 18,935
Crawford □, KS • 37,916
Crawford □, MI • 9,465
Crawford □, MO • 18,300
Crawford □, OH • 50,075
Crawford □, PA • 88,869
Crawford □, WI • 16,556
Crawfordsville, AR 72327 • 685
Crawfordsville, IN 47933 • 13,325
Crawfordville, FL 32327 • 1,110
Creal Springs, IL 62922 • 845
Creede, CO 81130 • 610
Creedmoor, NC 27522 • 1,641
Creek □, OK • 59,016
Creighton, NE 68729 • 1,341
Creighton, PA 15030 • 1,658
Crenshaw, MS 38621 • 1,019
Crenshaw □, AL • 14,110
Creola, AL 36525 • 1,652
Cresaptown, MD 21502 • 4,645
Crescent, OK 73028 • 1,651
Crescent, OR 97733 • 700
Crescent City, CA 95531 • 3,075
Crescent City, FL 32012 • 1,722
Crescent City, IL 60928 • 641
Crescent Springs, KY 41016 • 1,951
Cresco, IA 52136 • 3,860
Cresskill, NJ 07626 • 7,609
Cresson, PA 16630 • 2,184
Cressona, PA 17929 • 1,810
Crested Butte, CO 81224 • 959
Cresthaven, FL 33064 • 2,400
Crest Hill, IL 60435 • 9,252
Crestline, OH 44827 • 5,406
Creston, IA 50801 • 8,429
Creston, OH 44217 • 1,828
Crestview, FL 32536 • 7,617
Crestview, HI 96797 • 1,000
Crestwood, IL 60445 • 10,852
Crestwood, MO 63126 • 12,815
Crestwood Village, NJ 08759 • 7,965
Creswell, OR 97426 • 1,770
Crete, IL 60417 • 5,417
Crete, NE 68333 • 4,872
Creve Coeur, IL 61611 • 6,851
Creve Coeur, MO 63141 • 11,757
Crewe, VA 23930 • 2,325
Cricket, NC 28659 • 2,307
Cridersville, OH 45806 • 1,843
Cripple Creek, CO 80813 • 655
Crisfield, MD 21817 • 2,924
Crisp □, GA • 19,489
Crittenden □, AR • 49,499
Crittenden □, KY • 9,207
Crivitz, WI 54114 • 1,041
Crocker, MO 65452 • 979
Crockett, CA 94525 • 2,900
Crockett, TX 75835 • 7,405
Crockett □, TN • 14,941
Crockett □, TX • 4,608
Crofton, KY 42217 • 823
Crofton, MD 21114 • 12,009
Crofton, NE 68730 • 948
Croghan, NY 13327 • 703
Cromona, KY 41810 • 700
Cromwell, CT 06416 • 10,100
Crook □, OR • 13,091
Crook □, WY • 5,308
Crookston, MN 56716 • 8,628
Crooksville, OH 43731 • 2,766
Crosby, MN 56441 • 2,218
Crosby, ND 58730 • 1,469
Crosby, TX 77532 • 1,450
Crosby □, TX • 8,859
Crosbyton, TX 79322 • 2,289
Cross □, AR • 20,434
Cross City, FL 32628 • 2,154
Crossett, AR 71635 • 6,706
Cross Hill, SC 29332 • 604
Crosslake, MN 56442 • 1,064
Cross Lanes, WV 25313 • 3,500
Cross Mill, NC 28752 • 1,200
Cross Plains, TN 37049 • 655
Cross Plains, TX 76443 • 1,240
Cross Plains, WI 53528 • 2,156
Crossville, AL 35962 • 1,222
Crossville, IL 62827 • 944
Crossville, TN 38555 • 6,394
Croswell, MI 48422 • 2,073
Crothersville, IN 47229 • 1,747
Croton-on-Hudson, NY 10520 • 6,889
Crouse, NC 28033 • 900
Crow Agency, MT 59022 • 750
Crowder, MS 38622 • 789
Crowell, TX 79227 • 1,509
Crowley, LA 70526 • 16,036
Crowley, TX 76036 • 5,852
Crowley □, CO • 2,988
Crown Point, IN 46307 • 16,455
Crown Point, LA 70072 • 1,016
Crown Point, NE 68122 • 700
Crownpoint, NM 87313 • 1,134
Crown Point, NY 12928 • 900
Crow Wing □, MN • 41,722
Croydon, PA 19020 • 10,000
Crozet, VA 22932 • 1,433
Crucible, PA 15325 • 800
Crystal, MN 55428 • 25,543
Crystal Bay, NV 89402 • 1,200
Crystal Beach, FL 34681 • 1,450
Crystal City, MO 63019 • 3,618
Crystal City, TX 78839 • 8,334
Crystal Falls, MI 49920 • 1,965
Crystal Lake, FL 33803 • 6,827
Crystal Lake, IL 60014 • 18,590
Crystal Lawns, IL 60435 • 2,800
Crystal Manor, IL 60014 • 750
Crystal River, FL 32629 • 2,778
Crystal Springs, FL 33524 • 800
Crystal Springs, MS 39059 • 4,902
Cuba, IL 61427 • 1,648
Cuba, MO 65453 • 2,120

Cuba, NM 87013 • 609
Cuba, NY 14727 • 1,739
Cuba City, WI 53807 • 2,129
Cucamonga, CA 91730 • 55,250
Cudahy, CA 90201 • 17,984
Cudahy, WI 53110 • 19,547
Cuero, TX 77954 • 7,124
Culberson □, TX • 3,315
Culbertson, MT 59218 • 887
Culbertson, NE 69024 • 767
Cullen, LA 71021 • 1,869
Cullman, AL 35055 • 13,084
Cullman □, AL • 61,642
Culloden, WV 25510 • 1,500
Cullom, IL 60929 • 608
Cullowhee, NC 28723 • 2,000
Culpeper, VA 22701 • 6,621
Culpeper □, VA • 22,620
Culver, IN 46511 • 1,601
Culver City, CA 90230–32 • 38,139
Cumberland, KY 40823 • 3,712
Cumberland, MD 21502 • 25,933
Cumberland, NC 28331 • 900
Cumberland, WI 54829 • 1,983
Cumberland □, IL • 11,062
Cumberland □, KY • 7,289
Cumberland □, ME • 215,789
Cumberland □, NJ • 132,866
Cumberland □, NC • 247,160
Cumberland □, PA • 178,541
Cumberland □, TN • 28,676
Cumberland □, VA • 7,881
Cumberland Center, ME 04021 • 2,015
Cumberland Foreside, ME 04110 • 1,000
Cumberland Hill, RI 02864 • 5,421
Cuming □, NE • 11,664
Cumming, GA 30130 • 2,094
Cupertino, CA 95014 • 34,265
Currituck □, NC • 11,089
Curry □, NM • 42,019
Curry □, OR • 16,992
Curtice, OH 43412 • 800
Curtis, NE 69025 • 1,014
Curtisville, PA 15032 • 1,337
Curwensville, PA 16833 • 3,116
Cushing, OK 74023 • 7,720
Cusseta, GA 31805 • 1,218
Custer, SD 57730 • 1,830
Custer □, CO • 1,528
Custer □, ID • 3,385
Custer □, MT • 13,109
Custer □, NE • 13,877
Custer □, OK • 25,995
Custer □, SD • 6,000
Cut Bank, MT 59427 • 3,688
Cutchogue, NY 11935 • 1,000
Cuthbert, GA 31740 • 4,340
Cutler Ridge, FL 33157 • 20,886
Cutlerville, MI 49508 • 8,256
Cut Off, LA 70345 • 5,049
Cuyahoga □, OH • 1,498,400
Cuyahoga Falls, OH 44221–24 • 43,890
Cygnet, OH 43413 • 646
Cynthiana, IN 47612 • 874
Cynthiana, KY 41031 • 5,881
Cypress, CA 90630 • 40,391
Cypress, TX 77429 • 700
Cypress Quarters, FL 34972 • 1,479
Cyril, OK 73029 • 1,220

## D

Dacono, CO 80514 • 2,321
Dacula, GA 30211 • 1,577
Dade □, FL • 1,625,781
Dade □, GA • 12,318
Dade □, MO • 7,383
Dade City, FL 33525 • 4,923
Dadeville, AL 36853 • 3,263
Daggett, CA 92327 • 650
Daggett □, UT • 769
Dahlonega, GA 30533 • 2,844
Daingerfield, TX 75638 • 3,030
Daisetta, TX 77533 • 1,177
Dakota □, MN • 194,279
Dakota □, NE • 16,573
Dakota City, IA 50529 • 1,072
Dakota City, NE 68731 • 1,440
Dale, IN 47523 • 1,693
Dale □, AL • 47,821
Dale City, VA 22193 • 23,000
Daleville, AL 36322 • 4,250
Daleville, IN 47334 • 2,000
Dalhart, TX 79022 • 6,854
Dallam □, TX • 6,531
Dallas, GA 30132 • 2,508
Dallas, NC 28034 • 3,340
Dallas, OR 97338 • 8,530
Dallas, PA 18612 • 2,679
Dallas, TX 75201–99 • 904,078
Dallas □, AL • 53,981
Dallas □, AR • 10,515
Dallas □, IA • 29,513
Dallas □, MO • 12,096
Dallas □, TX • 1,556,390
Dallas Center, IA 50063 • 1,360
Dallas City, IL 62330 • 1,408
Dallastown, PA 17313 • 3,949
Dalton, GA 30720 • 20,939
Dalton, MA 01226 • 6,797
Dalton, OH 44618 • 1,357
Dalton, PA 18414 • 1,383
Dalton Gardens, ID 83814 • 1,795
Daly City, CA 94014–17 • 78,519
Dalzell, IL 61320 • 824
Damariscotta, ME 04543 • 950
Damascus, MD 20872 • 4,129
Damascus, VA 24236 • 1,330
Damon, TX 77430 • 700
Dana, IN 47847 • 803
Danbury, CT 06810–17 • 60,470
Danbury, TX 77534 • 1,357
Dandridge, TN 37725 • 1,383
Dane □, WI • 323,545
Dania, FL 33004 • 11,811
Daniels □, MT • 2,835
Danielson, CT 06239 • 4,553
Dannemora, NY 12929 • 3,770
Dansville, NY 14437 • 4,979
Dante, VA 24237 • 1,200
Danvers, IL 61732 • 921
Danvers, MA 01923 • 24,100
Danville, AR 72833 • 1,698
Danville, CA 94526 • 26,000
Danville, IL 61832–33 • 38,985
Danville, IN 46122 • 4,220
Danville, IA 52623 • 994
Danville, KY 40422 • 12,942
Danville, OH 43014 • 1,127
Danville, PA 17821 • 5,239
Danville, VA 24541–43 • 45,642
Danville, WV 25053 • 727
Daphne, AL 36526 • 3,406
Darby, PA 19023 • 11,513
Darbydale, OH 43123 • 825
Dardanelle, AR 72834 • 3,621
Dare □, NC • 13,377
Darien, CT 06820 • 18,892
Darien, GA 31305 • 1,731
Darien, IL 60559 • 14,536
Darien, WI 53114 • 1,152
Darke □, OH • 55,096
Darley Woods, DE 19810 • 1,400
Darlington, IN 47940 • 811
Darlington, SC 29532 • 7,989
Darlington, WI 53530 • 2,300
Darlington □, SC • 62,717
Darrington, WA 98241 • 1,064
Dassel, MN 55325 • 1,066
Dauphin, PA 17018 • 901
Dauphin □, PA • 232,317
Davenport, FL 33837 • 1,509
Davenport, IA 52801–99 • 103,264
Davenport, OK 74026 • 974
Davenport, WA 99122 • 1,559
David City, NE 68632 • 2,514
Davidson, NC 28036 • 3,241
Davidson □, NC • 113,162
Davidson □, TN • 477,811
Davidsville, PA 15928 • 900
Davie, FL 33329 • 20,877
Davie □, NC • 24,599
Daviess □, IN • 27,836
Daviess □, KY • 85,949
Daviess □, MO • 8,905
Davis, CA 95616 • 36,640
Davis, OK 73030 • 2,782
Davis, WV 26260 • 979
Davis □, IA • 9,104
Davis □, UT • 146,540
Davison, MI 48423 • 6,087
Davison □, SD • 17,820
Davy, WV 24828 • 882
Dawes □, NE • 9,609
Dawson, GA 31742 • 5,699
Dawson, MN 56232 • 1,901
Dawson, PA 15428 • 661
Dawson, TX 76639 • 747
Dawson □, GA • 4,774
Dawson □, MT • 11,805
Dawson □, NE • 22,304
Dawson □, TX • 16,184
Dawson Springs, KY 42408 • 3,275
Day □, SD • 8,133
Dayton, IN 47941 • 781
Dayton, IA 50530 • 941
Dayton, KY 41074 • 6,979
Dayton, MD 21036 • 700
Dayton, MN 55327 • 4,070
Dayton, NJ 08810 • 900
Dayton, OH 45401–99 • 193,444
Dayton, OR 97114 • 1,409
Dayton, PA 16222 • 648
Dayton, TN 37321 • 5,913
Dayton, TX 77535 • 4,908
Dayton, VA 22821 • 1,017
Dayton, WA 99328 • 2,565
Dayton, WY 82836 • 701
Daytona Beach, FL 32014–23 • 54,176
Dayville, CT 06241 • 1,100
Deadwood, SD 57732 • 2,035
Deaf Smith □, TX • 21,165
Deal, NJ 07723 • 1,952
Deale, MD 20751 • 3,008
Dearborn, MI 48120–26 • 90,660
Dearborn □, IN • 34,291
Dearborn Heights, MI 48127 • 67,706
De Baca □, NM • 2,454
De Bary, FL 32713 • 4,980
Debolt, NE 68152 • 800
Decatur, AL 35601–03 • 42,002
Decatur, AR 72722 • 1,013
Decatur, GA 30030–38 • 18,404
Decatur, IL 62521–26 • 94,081
Decatur, IN 46733 • 8,649
Decatur, MI 49045 • 1,915
Decatur, MS 39327 • 1,148
Decatur, NE 68020 • 723
Decatur, TN 37322 • 1,069
Decatur, TX 76234 • 4,104
Decatur □, GA • 25,495
Decatur □, IN • 23,841
Decatur □, IA • 9,794
Decatur □, KS • 4,509
Decatur □, TN • 10,857
Decaturville, TN 38329 • 1,004
Decherd, TN 37324 • 2,233
Deckerville, MI 48427 • 887
Decorah, IA 52101 • 7,991
Dedham, MA 02026 • 25,298
Deep River, CT 06417 • 2,495
Deepwater, NJ 08023 • 650
Deer Creek, IL 61733 • 688
Deerfield, IL 60015 • 17,430
Deerfield, MI 49238 • 957
Deerfield, WI 53531 • 1,466
Deerfield Beach, FL 33441 • 39,193
Deer Lodge, MT 59722 • 4,023
Deer Lodge □, MT • 12,518
Deer Park, NY 11729 • 33,400
Deer Park, OH 45236 • 6,745
Deer Park, TX 77536 • 22,648
Deer Park, WA 99006 • 2,140
Deer River, MN 56636 • 907
Defiance, OH 43512 • 16,810
Defiance □, OH • 39,987
De Forest, WI 53532 • 3,367
De Funiak Springs, FL 32433 • 5,563
De Graff, OH 43318 • 1,358
De Kalb, IL 60115 • 33,099
De Kalb, MS 39328 • 1,159
De Kalb, TX 75559 • 2,217
De Kalb □, AL • 53,658
De Kalb □, GA • 483,024
De Kalb □, IL • 74,624
De Kalb □, IN • 33,606
De Kalb □, MO • 8,222
De Kalb □, TN • 13,589
Delafield, WI 53018 • 4,083
Del Aire, CA 90250 • 3,900
Delanco, NJ 08075 • 3,730
De Land, FL 32720–24 • 15,354
Delano, CA 93215 • 16,491
Delano, MN 55328 • 2,480
Delavan, IL 61734 • 1,973
Delavan, WI 53115 • 5,684
Delavan Lake, WI 53115 • 2,124
Delaware, OH 43015 • 18,780
Delaware □, IN • 128,587
Delaware □, IA • 18,933
Delaware □, NY • 46,824
Delaware □, OH • 53,840
Delaware □, OK • 23,946
Delaware □, PA • 555,007
Delaware City, DE 19706 • 1,858
Delbarton, WV 25670 • 981
Delcambre, LA 70528 • 2,216
Del City, OK 73115 • 28,523
De Leon, TX 76444 • 2,478
De Leon Springs, FL 32028 • 1,669
Delevan, NY 14042 • 1,113
Delhi, LA 71232 • 3,290
Delhi, NY 13753 • 3,374
Delhi Hills, OH 45238 • 7,650
Dell Rapids, SD 57022 • 2,389
Dellslow, WV 26531 • 700
Dellwood, MO 63136 • 6,200
Del Mar, CA 92014 • 5,017
Delmar, DE 19940 • 948
Delmar, IA 52037 • 633
Delmar, MD 21875 • 1,232
Delmar, NY 12054 • 8,900
Del Norte, CO 81132 • 1,709
Del Norte □, CA • 18,217
Del Park Manor, DE 19808 • 1,700
Delphi, IN 46923 • 3,042
Delphos, OH 45833 • 7,314
Delran, NJ 08075 • 10,065
Delray Beach, FL 33444–47 • 34,325
Del Rio, TX 78840 • 30,034
Delta, CO 81416 • 3,931
Delta, OH 43515 • 2,831
Delta, PA 17314 • 692
Delta, UT 84624 • 1,930
Delta □, CO • 21,225
Delta □, MI • 38,947
Delta □, TX • 4,839
Delta Junction, AK 99737 • 945
Deltona, FL 32725 • 4,868
Demarest, NJ 07627 • 4,963
Deming, NM 88030 • 9,964
Demopolis, AL 36732 • 7,678
Demorest, GA 30535 • 1,130
Demotte, IN 46310 • 2,559
Denham Springs, LA 70726 • 8,563
Denison, IA 51442 • 6,675
Denison, TX 75020 • 23,884
Denmark, SC 29042 • 4,434
Denmark, WI 54208 • 1,475
Dennis, MA 02638 • 900
Dennison, OH 44621 • 3,398
Dennis Port, MA 02639 • 2,570
Denny Terrace, SC 29203 • 1,885
Dent □, MO • 14,517
Denton, MD 21629 • 1,927
Denton, NC 27239 • 949
Denton, TX 76201–06 • 48,063
Denton □, TX • 143,126
Dentsville, SC 29204 • 5,000
Denver, CO 80201–99 • 492,365
Denver, IA 50622 • 1,647
Denver, PA 17517 • 2,018
Denver □, CO • 492,365
Denver City, TX 79323 • 4,704
Denville, NJ 07834 • 14,045
De Pere, WI 54115 • 14,892
Depew, NY 14043 • 19,819
Depew, OK 74028 • 682
Depoe Bay, OR 97341 • 723
Deport, TX 75435 • 724
Deposit, NY 13754 • 1,897
Depue, IL 61322 • 1,873
De Queen, AR 71832 • 4,594
De Quincy, LA 70633 • 3,966
Derby, CT 06418 • 12,346
Derby, KS 67037 • 9,786
Derby, NY 14047 • 1,200
Derby Line, VT 05830 • 874
De Ridder, LA 70634 • 11,057
Derma, MS 38839 • 793
Dermott, AR 71638 • 4,731
Derry, NH 03038 • 12,248
Derry, PA 15627 • 3,072
Des Allemands, LA 70030 • 2,920
Des Arc, AR 72040 • 2,001
Deschutes □, OR • 62,142
Desert Hot Springs, CA 92240 • 5,941
Desha, AR 72527 • 750
Desha □, AR • 19,760
Deshler, NE 68340 • 997
Deshler, OH 43516 • 1,870
Desloge, MO 63601 • 2,934
De Smet, SD 57231 • 1,237
Des Moines, IA 50301–99 • 191,003
Des Moines, WA 98188 • 7,378
Des Moines □, IA • 46,203
De Soto, IL 62924 • 1,589
De Soto, IA 50069 • 1,035
De Soto, KS 66018 • 2,061
De Soto, MO 63020 • 5,993
De Soto, TX 75115 • 15,538
De Soto □, FL • 19,039
De Soto □, LA • 25,727
De Soto □, MS • 53,930
Despard, WV 26301 • 1,200
Des Peres, MO 63131 • 8,254
Des Plaines, IL 60016–18 • 53,568
Destin, FL 32541 • 3,672
Destrehan, LA 70047 • 2,382
Detroit, MI 48201–99 • 1,203,339
Detroit, TX 75436 • 805
Detroit Lakes, MN 56501 • 7,106
Deuel □, NE • 2,462
Deuel □, SD • 5,289
De Valls Bluff, AR 72041 • 738
Devils Lake, ND 58301 • 7,442
Devine, TX 78016 • 3,756
Devola, OH 45750 • 2,708
Devon, PA 19333 • 6,700
Devonshire, DE 19810 • 1,800
Dewar, OK 74431 • 1,048
Dewey, OK 74029 • 3,545
Dewey □, OK • 5,922
Dewey □, SD • 5,366
Dewey Beach, DE 19971 • 1,500
Deweyville, TX 77614 • 950
De Witt, AR 72042 • 3,928
De Witt, IA 52742 • 4,512
De Witt, MI 48820 • 3,165
De Witt, NE 68341 • 642
De Witt, NY 13214 • 10,032
De Witt □, IL • 18,108
De Witt □, TX • 18,903
Dexter, IA 50070 • 678
Dexter, ME 04930 • 3,118
Dexter, MI 48130 • 1,524
Dexter, MO 63841 • 7,043
Dexter, NM 88230 • 882
Dexter, NY 13634 • 1,053
Diamond Bar, CA 91765 • 28,045
Diamond Hill, RI 02864 • 1,150
Diamond Lake, IL 60060 • 1,503
Diamond Springs, CA 95619 • 2,287
Diamondville, WY 83116 • 1,000
Diaz, AR 72043 • 1,192
D'Iberville, MS 39532 • 9,000
Diboll, TX 75941 • 5,227
Dickens □, TX • 3,539
Dickenson □, VA • 19,806
Dickey □, ND • 7,207
Dickeyville, WI 53808 • 1,156
Dickinson, ND 58601 • 15,924
Dickinson, TX 77539 • 7,505
Dickinson □, IA • 15,629
Dickinson □, KS • 20,175
Dickinson □, MI • 25,341
Dickson, OK 73401 • 996
Dickson, TN 37055 • 7,040
Dickson □, TN • 30,037
Dickson City, PA 18519 • 6,699
Dierks, AR 71833 • 1,249
Dieterich, IL 62424 • 633
Dighton, KS 67839 • 1,390
Dighton, MA 02715 • 900
Dike, IA 50624 • 987
Dillard, OR 97432 • 1,000
Dill City, OK 73641 • 649
Dilley, TX 78017 • 2,579
Dillingham, AK 99576 • 914
Dillon, MT 59725 • 3,976
Dillon, SC 29536 • 7,060
Dillon □, SC • 31,083
Dillonvale, OH 43917 • 912
Dillsboro, IN 47018 • 1,038
Dillsburg, PA 17019 • 1,733
Dillwyn, VA 23936 • 637
Dilworth, MN 56529 • 2,585
Dimmit □, TX • 11,367
Dimmitt, TX 79027 • 5,019
Dimondale, MI 48821 • 1,008
Dinuba, CA 93618 • 9,907
Dinwiddie □, VA • 22,602
Dishman, WA 99213 • 9,900
District Heights-Forestville, MD 20747 • 6,799
Divernon, IL 62530 • 1,081
Divide □, ND • 3,494
Dix, IL 62830 • 3,198
Dixfield, ME 04224 • 1,725
Dix Hills, NY 11746 • 10,500
Dixie □, FL • 7,751
Dixon, CA 95620 • 7,541
Dixon, IL 61021 • 15,701
Dixon, MO 65459 • 1,402
Dixon □, NE • 7,137
Dixonville, PA 15734 • 900
Dobbs Ferry, NY 10522 • 10,053
Dobson, NC 27017 • 1,222
Docena, AL 35060 • 1,140
Dock Junction, GA 31520 • 6,189
Doddridge □, WV • 7,433
Dodge, NE 68633 • 815
Dodge □, GA • 16,955
Dodge □, MN • 14,773
Dodge □, NE • 35,847
Dodge □, WI • 75,064
Dodge Center, MN 55927 • 1,816
Dodge City, KS 67801 • 18,001
Dodgeville, WI 53533 • 3,458
Doerun, GA 31744 • 1,062
Doe Run, MO 63637 • 900
Dolgeville, NY 13329 • 2,602
Dollar Bay, MI 49922 • 900
Dolomite, AL 35061 • 2,400
Dolores, CO 81323 • 802
Dolores □, CO • 1,658
Dolton, IL 60419 • 24,766
Dona Ana □, NM • 96,340
Donaldsonville, LA 70346 • 7,901
Donalsonville, GA 31745 • 3,320
Doneraile, SC 29532 • 1,276
Dongola, IL 62926 • 886
Doniphan, MO 63935 • 1,921
Doniphan, NE 68832 • 696
Doniphan □, KS • 9,268
Donley □, TX • 4,075
Donna, TX 78537 • 9,952
Donnellson, IA 52625 • 972
Donora, PA 15033 • 7,524
Doolittle, MO 65401 • 701
Dooly □, GA • 10,826
Door □, WI • 25,029
Dora, AL 35062 • 2,327
Doraville, GA 30340 • 7,414
Dorchester, NE 68343 • 611
Dorchester, WI 54425 • 613
Dorchester □, MD • 30,623
Dorchester □, SC • 58,761
Dormont, PA 15216 • 11,275
Dorothy Pond, MA 01527 • 1,900
Dorris, CA 96023 • 836
Dorsey, MD 21227 • 1,186
Dothan, AL 36301–03 • 48,750
Double Springs, AL 35553 • 1,057
Dougherty □, GA • 100,718
Douglas, AZ 85607 • 13,058
Douglas, GA 31533 • 10,980
Douglas, MI 49406 • 948
Douglas, WY 82633 • 6,030
Douglas □, CO • 25,153
Douglas □, GA • 54,573
Douglas □, IL • 19,774
Douglas □, KS • 67,640
Douglas □, MN • 27,839
Douglas □, MO • 11,594
Douglas □, NE • 397,038
Douglas □, NV • 19,421
Douglas □, OR • 93,748
Douglas □, SD • 4,181
Douglas □, WA • 22,144
Douglas □, WI • 44,421
Douglass, KS 67039 • 1,450
Douglasville, GA 30133–35 • 7,641
Dousman, WI 53118 • 1,153
Dove Creek, CO 81324 • 826
Dover, AR 72837 • 948
Dover, DE 19901 • 23,507
Dover, FL 33527 • 2,354
Dover, MA 02030 • 2,051
Dover, NH 03820 • 22,377
Dover, NJ 07801 • 14,681
Dover, OH 44622 • 11,782
Dover, PA 17315 • 1,910
Dover, TN 37058 • 1,197
Dover-Foxcroft, ME 04426 • 2,974
Dover Plains, NY 12522 • 800
Dowagiac, MI 49047 • 6,307
Dow City, IA 51528 • 616
Downers Grove, IL 60515–17 • 42,572
Downey, CA 90240–42 • 82,602
Downey, ID 83234 • 645
Downieville, CA 95936 • 950
Downingtown, PA 19335 • 7,650
Downs, KS 67437 • 1,324
Downsville, NY 13755 • 950
Dows, IA 50071 • 771
Doyle, CA 96109 • 900
Doylestown, OH 44230 • 2,493
Doylestown, PA 18901 • 8,717
Doyline, LA 71023 • 801
Dracut, MA 01826 • 21,249
Drain, OR 97435 • 1,148
Drakesboro, KY 42337 • 798
Drakes Branch, VA 23937 • 617
Draper, UT 84020 • 5,521
Drayton, ND 58225 • 1,082
Drayton, SC 29333 • 1,443
Drayton Plains, MI 48020 • 18,000
Dreamland Villa, AZ 85205 • 3,200
Dresden, OH 43821 • 1,646
Dresden, TN 38225 • 2,256
Dresser, WI 54009 • 670
Drew, MS 38737 • 2,528
Drew □, AR • 17,910
Drexel, MO 64742 • 908
Drexel, NC 28619 • 1,392
Drexel, OH 45427 • 2,250
Drexel Hill, PA 19026 • 29,600
Driggs, ID 83422 • 727
Dripping Springs, TX 78620 • 606
Driscoll, TX 78351 • 648
Drumright, OK 74030 • 3,162
Drybranch, WV 25061 • 700
Dryden, MI 48428 • 650
Dryden, NY 13053 • 1,761
Dry Ridge, KY 41035 • 1,250
Duarte, CA 91010 • 16,766
Dubach, LA 71235 • 1,161
Dublin, CA 94568 • 19,000
Dublin, GA 31021 • 16,083
Dublin, IN 47335 • 979
Dublin, OH 43017 • 3,855
Dublin, PA 18917 • 1,565
Dublin, TX 76446 • 2,723
Dublin, VA 24084 • 2,368
Du Bois, PA 15801 • 9,290
Dubois, WY 82513 • 1,067
Dubois □, IN • 34,238
Duboistown, PA 17701 • 1,218
Dubuque, IA 52001 • 62,321
Dubuque □, IA • 93,745
Duchesne, UT 84021 • 1,677
Duchesne □, UT • 12,565
Duck Hill, MS 38925 • 706
Dudley, MA 01570 • 3,700
Duenweg, MO 64841 • 703
Due West, SC 29639 • 1,366
Dugger, IN 47848 • 1,118
Duke Center, PA 16729 • 900
Dukes □, MA • 8,942
Dulce, NM 87528 • 1,648
Duluth, GA 30136 • 2,956
Duluth, MN 55801–99 • 92,811
Dumas, AR 71639 • 6,091
Dumas, TX 79029 • 12,194
Dumfries, VA 22026 • 3,214
Dumont, IA 50625 • 815
Dumont, NJ 07628 • 18,334
Dunaire, GA 30032 • 5,400
Dunbar, PA 15431 • 1,369
Dunbar, WV 25064 • 9,285
Duncan, AZ 85534 • 603
Duncan, OK 73533 • 22,517
Duncan, SC 29334 • 1,259
Duncan Falls, OH 43734 • 1,200
Duncannon, PA 17020 • 1,645
Duncansville, PA 16635 • 1,355
Duncanville, TX 75116 • 27,781
Dundalk, MD 21222 • 71,293
Dundee, FL 33838 • 2,227
Dundee, IL 60118 • 3,551
Dundee, MI 48131 • 2,575
Dundee, NY 14837 • 1,556
Dundee, OR 97115 • 1,223
Dundy □, NE • 2,861
Dunedin, FL 34698 • 30,203
Dunellen, NJ 08812 • 6,593
Dunkerton, IA 50626 • 718
Dunkirk, IN 47336 • 3,180
Dunkirk, NY 14048 • 15,310
Dunkirk, OH 45836 • 954
Dunklin □, MO • 36,324
Dunlap, IL 61525 • 824

Dunlap, IN 46514 • 2,500
Dunlap, IA 51529 • 1,374
Dunlap, TN 37327 • 3,681
Dunleith, DE 19801 • 2,700
Dunlo, PA 15930 • 950
Dunmore, PA 18512 • 16,781
Dunn, NC 28334 • 8,962
Dunn □, ND • 4,627
Dunn □, WI • 34,314
Dunnellon, FL 32630 • 1,427
Dunn Loring Woods, VA 22180 • 2,800
Dunseith, ND 58329 • 625
Dunsmuir, CA 96025 • 2,253
Dunstable, MA 01827 • 900
Dunwoody, GA 30338 • 5,100
Du Page □, IL • 658,829
Duplin □, NC • 40,952
Dupont, CO 80024 • 2,000
Dupont, PA 18641 • 3,460
Dupont City, WV 25015 • 900
Dupont Manor, DE 19901 • 1,059
Duquesne, PA 15110 • 10,094
Du Quoin, IL 62832 • 6,594
Durand, IL 61024 • 1,073
Durand, MI 48429 • 4,241
Durand, WI 54736 • 2,047
Durango, CO 81301 • 11,649
Durant, IA 52747 • 1,583
Durant, MS 39063 • 2,889
Durant, OK 74701 • 11,972
Durham, CA 95938 • 950
Durham, CT 06422 • 2,641
Durham, NH 03824 • 8,448
Durham, NC 27701-99 • 100,538
Durham □, NC • 152,785
Duryea, PA 18642 • 5,415
Dushore, PA 18614 • 692
Duson, LA 70529 • 1,253
Dutchess □, NY • 245,055
Duval □, FL • 571,003
Duval □, TX • 12,517
Duxbury, MA 02332 • 1,685
Dwight, IL 60420 • 4,146
Dyer, AR 72935 • 608
Dyer, IN 46311 • 9,555
Dyer, TN 38330 • 2,419
Dyer □, TN • 34,663
Dyersburg, TN 38024 • 15,856
Dyersville, IA 52040 • 3,825
Dysart, IA 52224 • 1,355

## E

Eads, CO 81036 • 878
Eagan, MN 55121 • 20,700
Eagar, AZ 85925 • 2,791
Eagle, CO 81631 • 950
Eagle, ID 83616 • 2,620
Eagle, NE 68347 • 832
Eagle, WI 53119 • 1,008
Eagle □, CO • 13,320
Eagle Grove, IA 50533 • 4,324
Eagle Lake, MN 56024 • 1,470
Eagle Lake, TX 77434 • 3,921
Eagle Lake, WI 53139 • 1,000
Eagle Pass, TX 78852 • 21,407
Eagle Point, OR 97524 • 2,764
Eagle River, WI 54521 • 1,326
Earle, AR 72331 • 3,517
Earlham, IA 50072 • 1,140
Earlimart, CA 93219 • 4,578
Earlington, KY 42410 • 2,011
Earlville, IL 60518 • 1,382
Earlville, IA 52041 • 844
Earlville, NY 13332 • 985
Early, IA 50535 • 670
Early □, GA • 13,158
Earth, TX 79031 • 1,512
Easley, SC 29640 • 14,264
East Acton, MA 01720 • 1,200
East Alton, IL 62024 • 7,096
East Aurora, NY 14052 • 6,803
East Bangor, PA 18013 • 955
East Bank, WV 25067 • 1,155
East Barre, VT 05649 • 900
East Baton Rouge □, LA • 366,191
East Bend, NC 27018 • 602
East Berlin, CT 06023 • 900
East Berlin, PA 17316 • 1,054
East Bernard, TX 77435 • 1,700
East Bernstadt, KY 40729 • 700
East Bethel, MN 55005 • 6,626
East Billerica, MA 01821 • 2,900
Eastborough, KS 67206 • 854
East Brady, PA 16028 • 1,153
East Brewster, MA 02631 • 700
East Brewton, AL 36426 • 3,012
East Bridgewater, MA 02333 • 3,300
East Brookfield, MA 01515 • 1,443
East Brooklyn, CT 06239 • 1,251
East Brunswick, NJ 08816 • 37,711
East Butler, PA 16029 • 799
East Canaan, CT 06024 • 800
East Carbon, UT 84520 • 1,942
East Carroll □, LA • 11,772
East Chelmsford, MA 01824 • 2,900
Eastchester, NY 10709 • 22,600
East Chicago, IN 46312 • 39,786
East Chicago Heights, IL 60411 • 5,347
East Cleveland, OH 44112 • 36,957
East Dennis, MA 02641 • 800
East Detroit, MI 48021 • 38,280
East Douglas, MA 01516 • 1,683
East Dubuque, IL 61025 • 2,194
East Falmouth, MA 02536 • 5,181
East Feliciana □, LA • 19,015
East Flat Rock, NC 28726 • 3,365
East Fultonham, OH 43735 • 650
East Gaffney, SC 29340 • 4,092
East Galesburg, IL 61430 • 928
Eastgate, WA 98004 • 5,300
East Glenville, NY 12302 • 11,800
East Grand Forks, MN 56721 • 8,537
East Grand Rapids, MI 49506 • 10,914
East Greenville, PA 18041 • 2,456
East Greenwich, RI 02818 • 10,211
East Half Hollow Hills, NY 11746 • 9,691
Eastham, MA 02642 • 1,100
East Hampden, ME 04401 • 950
East Hampstead, NH 03826 • 900
East Hampton, CT 06424 • 2,152
Easthampton, MA 01027 • 15,580
East Hampton, NY 11937 • 1,886
East Hanover, NJ 07936 • 9,319
East Hartford, CT 06108 • 52,563
East Haven, CT 06512 • 25,028
East Helena, MT 59635 • 1,647
East Hills, NY 11576 • 7,160
East Islip, NY 11730 • 13,700
East Jordan, MI 49727 • 2,185
Eastlake, OH 44094 • 22,104
Eastland, TX 76448 • 3,747
Eastland □, TX • 19,480
East Lansing, MI 48823 • 51,392
East Las Vegas, NV 89112 • 6,449
East Liverpool, OH 43920 • 16,687
East Longmeadow, MA 01028 • 12,905
East Los Angeles, CA 90022 • 110,017
East Lyme, CT 06333 • 700
Eastman, GA 31023 • 5,330
East Marion, NY 11939 • 900
East Meadow, NY 11554 • 47,300
East Millbury, MA 01527 • 1,000
East Millinocket, ME 04430 • 2,361
East Moline, IL 61244 • 20,907
East Naples, FL 33962 • 9,000
East Newark, NJ 07029 • 1,923
East Newnan, GA 30263 • 1,499
East Norriton, PA 19401 • 12,711
East Northport, NY 11731 • 22,200
East Olympia, WA 98506 • 700
Easton, MD 21601 • 7,536
Easton, PA 18042 • 26,027
Eastondale, MA 02375 • 900
East Orange, NJ 07017-19 • 77,690
East Orleans, MA 02643 • 1,200
Eastover, SC 29044 • 899
East Palatka, FL 32031 • 1,613
East Palestine, OH 44413 • 5,306
East Palo Alto, CA 94303 • 18,191
East Patchogue, NY 11772 • 8,300
East Pea Ridge, WV 25705 • 1,900
East Peoria, IL 61611 • 22,385
East Pepperell, MA 01463 • 2,212
East Petersburg, PA 17520 • 3,600
East Pittsburgh, PA 15112 • 2,493
Eastpoint, FL 32328 • 1,246
East Point, GA 30344 • 37,486
Eastport, ME 04631 • 1,982
Eastport, NY 11941 • 1,308
East Prairie, MO 63845 • 3,713
East Providence, RI 02914 • 50,980
East Quogue, NY 11942 • 1,200
East Randolph, NY 14730 • 655
East Ridge, TN 37412 • 21,236
East River, CT 06443 • 1,800
East Rochester, NY 14445 • 7,596
East Rockaway, NY 11518 • 10,917
East Rockingham, NC 28379 • 5,190
East Rutherford, NJ 07073 • 7,849
East Saint Louis, IL 62201-08 • 55,200
Eastside, OR 97420 • 1,601
Eastsound, WA 98245 • 900
East Sparta, OH 44626 • 868
East Spencer, NC 28039 • 2,150
East Stroudsburg, PA 18301 • 8,039
East Sudbury, MA 01776 • 1,500
East Tawas, MI 48730 • 2,584
East Templeton, MA 01438 • 980
East Troy, WI 53120 • 2,385
East Tustin, CA 92705 • 10,000
East Vestal, NY 13902 • 5,300
East View, WV 26301 • 1,618
East Walpole, MA 02032 • 4,900
East Wareham, MA 02538 • 1,000
East Washington, PA 15301 • 2,241
East Wenatchee, WA 98801 • 1,640
East Windsor, NJ 08520 • 15,000
Eastwood, MI 49001 • 7,186
Eastwood Hills, UT 84106 • 1,200
Eaton, CO 80615 • 1,932
Eaton, IN 47338 • 1,804
Eaton, OH 45320 • 6,839
Eaton □, MI • 88,337
Eaton Rapids, MI 48827 • 4,510
Eatonton, GA 31024 • 4,833
Eatontown, NJ 07724 • 12,703
Eatonville, WA 98328 • 998
Eau Claire, WI 54701-03 • 51,509
Eau Claire □, WI • 78,805
Ebensburg, PA 15931 • 4,096
Eccles, WV 25836 • 1,100
Echo, OR 97826 • 624
Echols □, GA • 2,297
Eckhart Mines, MD 21528 • 1,333
Eckman, WV 24829 • 700
Eclectic, AL 36024 • 1,124
Economy, PA 15005 • 9,538
Ecorse, MI 48229 • 14,447
Ecru, MS 38841 • 687
Ector □, TX • 115,374
Edcouch, TX 78538 • 3,092
Eddy □, NM • 47,855
Eddy □, ND • 3,554
Eddystone, PA 19013 • 2,555
Eddyville, IA 52553 • 1,116
Eddyville, KY 42038 • 1,949
Eden, NC 27288 • 15,672
Eden, NY 14057 • 3,000
Eden, TX 76837 • 1,294
Eden Prairie, MN 55344 • 16,263
Edenton, NC 27932 • 5,357
Eden Valley, MN 55329 • 763
Edgar, NE 68935 • 705
Edgar, WI 54426 • 1,194
Edgar □, IL • 21,725
Edgard, LA 70049 • 680
Edgartown, MA 02539 • 1,138
Edgecombe □, NC • 55,988
Edgefield, SC 29824 • 2,713
Edgefield □, SC • 17,528
Edgeley, ND 58433 • 843
Edgemere, MD 21222 • 7,800
Edgemont, SD 57735 • 1,468
Edgemoor, DE 19802 • 7,397
Edgerton, KS 66021 • 1,214
Edgerton, MN 56128 • 1,123
Edgerton, OH 43517 • 1,813
Edgerton, WI 53534 • 4,335
Edgewater, AL 35224 • 1,400
Edgewater, CO 80214 • 4,766
Edgewater, FL 32032 • 6,726
Edgewater, MD 21037 • 800
Edgewater, NJ 07020 • 4,628
Edgewater Park, NJ 08010 • 9,273
Edgewood, IN 46011 • 2,215
Edgewood, IA 52042 • 900
Edgewood, KY 41017 • 7,230
Edgewood, MD 21040 • 19,455
Edgewood, OH 44004 • 3,099
Edgewood, PA 15218 • 4,382
Edgewood, WA 98371 • 1,800
Edgeworth, PA 15143 • 1,738
Edina, MN 55424 • 46,073
Edina, MO 63537 • 1,520
Edinboro, PA 16412 • 6,324
Edinburg, IL 62531 • 1,231
Edinburg, TX 78539 • 24,075
Edinburg, VA 22824 • 752
Edinburgh, IN 46124 • 4,856
Edison, GA 31746 • 1,128
Edison, NJ 08817-20 • 70,193
Edmond, OK 73034 • 34,637
Edmonds, WA 98020 • 27,679
Edmondson Heights, MD 21207 • 5,000
Edmonson □, KY • 9,962
Edmonton, KY 42129 • 1,401
Edmore, MI 48829 • 1,176
Edmunds □, SD • 5,159
Edna, TX 77957 • 5,650
Edon, OH 43518 • 947
Edwards, MS 39066 • 1,515
Edwards □, IL • 7,961
Edwards □, KS • 4,271
Edwards □, TX • 2,033
Edwardsburg, MI 49112 • 1,135
Edwardsville, IL 62025 • 12,480
Edwardsville, KS 66113 • 3,364
Edwardsville, PA 18704 • 5,729
Effingham, IL 62401 • 11,270
Effingham, KS 66023 • 634
Effingham □, GA • 18,327
Effingham □, IL • 30,944
Egg Harbor City, NJ 08215 • 4,618
Egypt, MA 02066 • 1,100
Ehrenberg, AZ 85334 • 900
Ekalaka, MT 59324 • 620
Elaine, AR 72333 • 991
Elba, AL 36323 • 4,355
Elba, NY 14058 • 750
Elberfeld, IN 47613 • 640
Elbert □, CO • 6,850
Elbert □, GA • 18,758
Elberton, GA 30635 • 5,686
Elbow Lake, MN 56531 • 1,358
Elburn, IL 60119 • 1,224
El Cajon, CA 92020-22 • 73,892
El Campo, TX 77437 • 10,462
El Centro, CA 92243 • 23,996
El Cerrito, CA 94530 • 22,731
Eldon, IA 52554 • 1,255
Eldon, MO 65026 • 4,342
Eldora, IA 50627 • 3,063
El Dorado, AR 71730 • 25,270
Eldorado, GA 31794 • 1,000
Eldorado, IL 62930 • 5,198
El Dorado, KS 67042 • 10,510
Eldorado, OK 73537 • 688
Eldorado, TX 76936 • 2,061
El Dorado □, CA • 85,812
El Dorado Springs, MO 64744 • 3,868
Eldred, PA 16731 • 965
Eldridge, IA 52748 • 3,279
Eleanor, WV 25070 • 1,282
Electra, TX 76360 • 3,755
El Encanto Heights, CA 93117 • 7,700
Elgin, IL 60120 • 63,981
Elgin, IA 52141 • 702
Elgin, MN 55932 • 667
Elgin, NE 68636 • 807
Elgin, ND 58533 • 930
Elgin, OK 73538 • 1,003
Elgin, OR 97827 • 1,701
Elgin, SC 29720 • 900
Elgin, TX 78621 • 4,535
Elida, OH 45807 • 1,349
Eliot, ME 03903 • 2,450
Elizabeth, CO 80107 • 789
Elizabeth, GA 30060 • 1,700
Elizabeth, IL 61028 • 772
Elizabeth, NJ 07201-99 • 106,201
Elizabeth, WV 26143 • 856
Elizabeth City, NC 27909 • 13,784
Elizabethton, TN 37643 • 12,431
Elizabethtown, IN 47232 • 603
Elizabethtown, KY 42701 • 15,380
Elizabethtown, NC 28337 • 3,551
Elizabethtown, NY 12932 • 650
Elizabethtown, PA 17022 • 8,233
Elizabethville, PA 17023 • 1,531
El Jebel, CO 81628 • 900
Elk □, KS • 3,918
Elk □, PA • 38,338
Elkader, IA 52043 • 1,688
Elk City, ID 83525 • 670
Elk City, OK 73644 • 9,579
Elk Grove, CA 95624 • 10,059
Elk Grove Village, IL 60007 • 28,907
Elkhart, IN 46514-17 • 41,305
Elkhart, KS 67950 • 2,243
Elkhart, TX 75839 • 1,317
Elkhart □, IN • 137,330
Elkhart Lake, WI 53020 • 1,054
Elk Horn, IA 51531 • 746
Elkhorn, NE 68022 • 1,344
Elkhorn, WV 24831 • 700
Elkhorn, WI 53121 • 4,605
Elkhorn City, KY 41522 • 1,446
Elkin, NC 28621 • 2,858
Elkins, WV 26241 • 8,536
Elkins Park, PA 19117 • 14,000
Elkland, PA 16920 • 1,974
Elk Mound, WI 54739 • 737
Elko, NV 89801 • 8,758
Elko □, NV • 17,269
Elk Point, SD 57025 • 1,661
Elk Rapids, MI 49629 • 1,504
Elkridge, MD 21227 • 2,100
Elk River, MN 55330 • 6,785
Elkton, KY 42220 • 1,815
Elkton, MD 21921 • 6,468
Elkton, MI 48731 • 953
Elkton, SD 57026 • 632
Elkton, VA 22827 • 1,520
Elkview, WV 25071 • 1,486
Elkville, IL 62932 • 973
Ellaville, GA 31806 • 1,684
Ellendale, ND 58436 • 1,967
Ellensburg, WA 98926 • 11,752
Ellenton, FL 34222 • 1,561
Ellenville, NY 12428 • 4,405
Ellerbe, NC 28338 • 1,415
Ellerslie, MD 21529 • 1,150
Ellettsville, IN 47429 • 3,328
Ellicott City, MD 21043 • 4,000
Ellicottville, NY 14731 • 713
Ellijay, GA 30540 • 1,507
Ellington, CT 06029 • 1,000
Ellington, MO 63638 • 1,215
Ellinwood, KS 67526 • 2,508
Elliott, MS 38926 • 1,200
Elliott □, KY • 6,908
Ellis, KS 67637 • 2,062
Ellis □, KS • 26,098
Ellis □, OK • 5,596
Ellis □, TX • 59,743
Elliston, VA 24087 • 750
Ellisville, MS 39437 • 4,652
Ellisville, MO 63011 • 6,233
Elloree, SC 29047 • 909
Ellport, PA 16117 • 1,290
Ellsworth, KS 67439 • 2,465
Ellsworth, ME 04605 • 5,179
Ellsworth, MN 56129 • 629
Ellsworth, PA 15331 • 1,228
Ellsworth, WI 54011 • 2,143
Ellsworth □, KS • 6,640
Ellwood City, PA 16117 • 9,998
Elma, IA 50628 • 714
Elma, WA 98541 • 2,720
Elm City, NC 27822 • 1,561
Elm Creek, NE 68836 • 862
Elmer, NJ 08318 • 1,569
Elm Grove, WI 53122 • 6,735
Elmhurst, IL 60126 • 44,276
Elmhurst, PA 18416 • 953
Elmira, NY 14901-99 • 35,327
El Mirage, AZ 85335 • 4,307
Elmira Heights, NY 14903 • 4,279
Elmont, NY 11003 • 30,000
El Monte, CA 91731-35 • 79,494
Elmora, PA 15737 • 950
Elmore, MN 56027 • 882
Elmore, OH 43416 • 1,271
Elmore □, AL • 43,390
Elmore □, ID • 21,565
Elm Springs, AR 72728 • 781
Elmwood, IL 61529 • 2,117
Elmwood, MA 02337 • 750
Elmwood, WI 54740 • 885
Elmwood Park, IL 60635 • 24,016
Elmwood Park, NJ 07407 • 18,377
Elmwood Place, OH 45216 • 2,840
Elnora, IN 47529 • 756
Eloise, FL 33880 • 1,408
Elon College, NC 27244 • 2,873
Eloy, AZ 85231 • 6,240
El Paso, IL 61738 • 2,676
El Paso, TX 79901-99 • 425,259
El Paso □, CO • 309,424
El Paso □, TX • 479,899
El Portal, CA 95318 • 850
El Portal, FL 33138 • 2,055
El Prado, NM 87529 • 700
Elrama, PA 15038 • 800
El Reno, OK 73036 • 15,486
El Rio, CA 93030 • 5,674
Elroy, WI 53929 • 1,504
Elsa, TX 78543 • 5,061
Elsah, IL 62028 • 990
Elsberry, MO 63343 • 1,272
El Segundo, CA 90245 • 13,752
Elsie, MI 48831 • 1,022
Elsinore, UT 84724 • 612
Elsmere, DE 19805 • 6,493
Elsmere, KY 41018 • 7,203
Elsmere, NY 12054 • 5,500
El Sobrante, CA 94803 • 10,535
Elton, LA 70532 • 1,450
El Toro, CA 92630 • 38,153
Elvins, MO 63601 • 1,548
Elwood, IN 46036 • 10,867
Elwood, KS 66024 • 1,275
Elwood, NE 68937 • 716
Elwood, NJ 08217 • 900
Elwood, NY 11731 • 15,400
Ely, MN 55731 • 4,820
Ely, NV 89301 • 4,882
Elyria, OH 44035-39 • 57,538
Elysburg, PA 17824 • 1,337
Emanuel □, GA • 20,795
Emerson, GA 30137 • 1,110
Emerson, NE 68733 • 874
Emerson, NJ 07630 • 7,793
Emery □, UT • 11,451
Eminence, KY 40019 • 2,260
Eminence, MO 65466 • 614
Emlenton, PA 16373 • 807
Emmaus, PA 18049 • 11,001
Emmet □, IA • 13,336
Emmet □, MI • 22,992
Emmetsburg, IA 50536 • 4,621
Emmett, ID 83617 • 4,605
Emmitsburg, MD 21727 • 1,552
Emmons □, ND • 5,877
Emory, TX 75440 • 813
Empire, LA 70050 • 630
Emporia, KS 66801 • 25,287
Emporia, VA 23847 • 4,840
Emporium, PA 15834 • 2,837
Emsworth, PA 15202 • 3,074
Encampment, WY 82325 • 611
Encinal, TX 78019 • 704
Encinitas, CA 92024 • 10,796
Enderlin, ND 58027 • 1,151
Endicott, NY 13760 • 14,457
Endwell, NY 13760 • 15,999
Enfield, CT 06082 • 8,151
Enfield, IL 62835 • 890
Enfield, NH 03748 • 1,581
Enfield, NC 27823 • 2,995
England, AR 72046 • 3,081
Engleside, VA 22309 • 21,400
Englewood, CO 80110-12 • 30,021
Englewood, FL 34223-24 • 10,242
Englewood, NJ 07631-32 • 23,701
Englewood, OH 45322 • 11,329
Englewood, TN 37329 • 1,840
Englewood Cliffs, NJ 07632 • 5,698
English, IN 47118 • 633
Englishtown, NJ 07726 • 976
Enid, OK 73701 • 50,363
Enka, NC 28728 • 5,567
Ennis, MT 59729 • 660
Ennis, TX 75119 • 12,110
Enoch, UT 84720 • 678
Enola, PA 17025 • 3,600
Enon, OH 45323 • 2,597
Enoree, SC 29335 • 1,107
Enosburg Falls, VT 05450 • 1,207
Ensley, FL 32504 • 2,200
Enterprise, AL 36330 • 18,033
Enterprise, KS 67441 • 839
Enterprise, MS 39330 • 607
Enterprise, OR 97828 • 2,003
Enterprise, UT 84725 • 905
Enterprise, WV 26568 • 950
Enumclaw, WA 98022 • 5,427
Ephraim, UT 84627 • 2,810
Ephrata, PA 17522 • 11,095
Ephrata, WA 98823 • 5,359
Epping, NH 03042 • 1,384
Epps, LA 71237 • 672
Epworth, IA 52045 • 1,380
Equality, IL 62934 • 831
Erath, LA 70533 • 2,133
Erath □, TX • 22,560
Erdenheim, PA 19118 • 3,300
Erial, NJ 08081 • 900
Erick, OK 73645 • 1,375
Erie, CO 80516 • 1,254
Erie, IL 61250 • 1,725
Erie, KS 66733 • 1,415
Erie, MI 48133 • 700
Erie, PA 16501-99 • 119,123
Erie □, NY • 1,015,472
Erie □, OH • 79,655
Erie □, PA • 279,780
Erin, TN 37061 • 1,614
Erlanger, KY 41018 • 14,433
Erma, NJ 08204 • 1,200
Errol Heights, OR 97266 • 7,800
Erwin, NC 28339 • 2,828
Erwin, TN 37650 • 4,739
Escalante, UT 84726 • 652
Escalon, CA 95320 • 3,127
Escambia □, AL • 38,440
Escambia □, FL • 233,794
Escanaba, MI 49829 • 14,355
Escatawpa, MS 39552 • 5,367
Escondido, CA 92025-27 • 64,355
Eskridge, KS 66423 • 603
Esmeralda □, NV • 777
Esmond, RI 02917 • 3,500
Espanola, NM 87532 • 6,803
Esparto, CA 95627 • 1,303
Espy, PA 17815 • 1,652
Essex, CT 06426 • 2,501
Essex, IA 51638 • 1,001
Essex, MD 21221 • 39,614
Essex, MA 01929 • 1,490
Essex, VT 05451 • 800
Essex □, MA • 633,632
Essex □, NJ • 851,116
Essex □, NY • 36,176
Essex □, VT • 6,313
Essex □, VA • 8,864
Essex Fells, NJ 07021 • 2,363
Essex Junction, VT 05452 • 7,033
Essexville, MI 48732 • 4,378
Estacada, OR 97023 • 1,419
Estancia, NM 87016 • 830
Estelline, SD 57234 • 719
Estell Manor, NJ 08319 • 848
Estero, FL 33928 • 950
Estes Park, CO 80517 • 2,703
Estherville, IA 51334 • 7,518
Estherwood, LA 70534 • 691
Estill, SC 29918 • 2,308
Estill □, KY • 14,495
Estill Springs, TN 37330 • 1,324
Etna, CA 96027 • 754
Etna, PA 15223 • 4,534
Etowah, TN 37331 • 3,758
Etowah □, AL • 103,057
Ettrick, VA 23803 • 4,000
Euclid, OH 44117 • 59,999
Eudora, AR 71640 • 3,840
Eudora, KS 66025 • 2,934
Eufaula, AL 36027 • 12,097
Eufaula, OK 74432 • 3,159
Eugene, OR 97401-05 • 105,624
Eulaton, AL 36201 • 1,869
Euless, TX 76039-40 • 24,002
Eunice, LA 70535 • 12,479
Eunice, NM 88231 • 2,970
Eupora, MS 39744 • 2,048
Eureka, CA 95501 • 24,153
Eureka, IL 61530 • 4,306
Eureka, KS 67045 • 3,425
Eureka, MO 63025 • 3,862
Eureka, MT 59917 • 1,119
Eureka, SC 29706 • 1,627
Eureka, SD 57437 • 1,360
Eureka, UT 84628 • 670
Eureka □, NV • 1,198
Eureka Springs, AR 72632 • 1,989
Eustis, FL 32726 • 9,453
Eutaw, AL 35462 • 2,444
Eutawville, SC 29048 • 615
Evangeline □, LA • 33,343
Evans, CO 80620 • 5,063
Evans, GA 30809 • 800
Evans □, GA • 8,428
Evans City, PA 16033 • 2,299
Evansdale, IA 50707 • 4,798
Evans Mills, NY 13637 • 651
Evanston, IL 60201-99 • 73,706
Evanston, WY 82930 • 6,421
Evansville, IL 62242 • 863
Evansville, IN 47701-99 • 130,496
Evansville, WI 53536 • 2,835
Evansville, WY 82636 • 2,335

Evart, MI 49631 • 1,945
Evarts, KY 40828 • 1,234
Eveleth, MN 55734 • 5,042
Everett, MA 02149 • 37,195
Everett, PA 15537 • 1,828
Everett, WA 98201–07 • 54,413
Evergreen, AL 36401 • 4,171
Evergreen, CO 80439 • 6,376
Evergreen Park, IL 60642 • 22,260
Everly, IA 51338 • 796
Everman, TX 76140 • 5,387
Everson, PA 15631 • 1,032
Everson, WA 98247 • 898
Ewa, HI 96706 • 2,637
Ewa Beach, HI 96706–07 • 14,369
Ewing Township, NJ 08618 • 34,842
Excelsior Springs, MO 64024 • 10,424
Exeter, CA 93221 • 5,606
Exeter, NE 68351 • 807
Exeter, NH 03833 • 8,947
Exeter, PA 18643 • 5,493
Exira, IA 50076 • 978
Exmore, VA 23350 • 1,300
Experiment, GA 30212 • 3,000
Export, PA 15632 • 1,143
Eyota, MN 55934 • 1,244

# F

Fabens, TX 79838 • 3,500
Factoryville, PA 18419 • 924
Fairbank, IA 50629 • 980
Fairbanks, AK 99701 • 22,645
Fair Bluff, NC 28439 • 1,095
Fairborn, OH 45324 • 29,702
Fairburn, GA 30213 • 3,466
Fairbury, IL 61739 • 3,544
Fairbury, NE 68352 • 5,265
Fairchance, PA 15436 • 2,106
Fairdale, KY 40118 • 7,315
Fairfax, AL 36854 • 3,776
Fairfax, CA 94930 • 7,391
Fairfax, DE 19803 • 2,850
Fairfax, IA 52228 • 683
Fairfax, MN 55332 • 1,405
Fairfax, MO 64446 • 835
Fairfax, OK 74637 • 1,949
Fairfax, SC 29827 • 2,154
Fairfax, VA 22030–39 • 19,390
Fairfax □, VA • 596,901
Fairfield, AL 35064 • 13,242
Fairfield, CA 94533 • 58,099
Fairfield, CT 06430 • 54,849
Fairfield, IL 62837 • 5,954
Fairfield, IA 52556 • 9,428
Fairfield, ME 04937 • 3,169
Fairfield, MT 59436 • 650
Fairfield, NJ 07006 • 7,987
Fairfield, OH 45014 • 30,777
Fairfield, TX 75840 • 3,505
Fairfield □, CT • 807,143
Fairfield □, OH • 93,678
Fairfield □, SC • 20,700
Fairfield Bay, AR 72088 • 1,000
Fairgrove, MI 48733 • 691
Fair Grove, MO 65648 • 863
Fair Grove, NC 27360 • 1,500
Fairhaven, MA 02719 • 15,759
Fair Haven, MI 48023 • 900
Fair Haven, NJ 07701 • 5,679
Fair Haven, NY 13064 • 976
Fair Haven, VT 05743 • 2,819
Fairhope, AL 36532 • 7,286
Fairland, IN 46126 • 900
Fairland, OK 74343 • 1,073
Fair Lawn, NJ 07410 • 32,229
Fairlawn, OH 44313 • 6,100
Fairlawn, VA 24141 • 2,000
Fairlea, WV 24902 • 1,200
Fairless Hills, PA 19030 • 12,500
Fairmont, IL 60441 • 2,600
Fairmont, MN 56031 • 11,506
Fairmont, NE 68354 • 767
Fairmont, NC 28340 • 2,658
Fairmont, WV 26554 • 23,863
Fairmount, GA 30139 • 842
Fairmount, IL 61841 • 851
Fairmount, IN 46928 • 3,286
Fairmount, NY 13219 • 8,700
Fairmount Heights, MD 20743 • 1,616
Fair Oaks, CA 95628 • 20,235
Fair Oaks, GA 30060 • 8,486
Fairoaks, PA 15003 • 1,854
Fair Plain, MI 49022 • 8,289
Fairport, NY 14450 • 5,970
Fairport Harbor, OH 44077 • 3,357
Fairton, NJ 08320 • 1,107
Fairview, MT 59221 • 1,366
Fairview, NJ 07022 • 10,519
Fairview, NY 12601 • 8,517
Fairview, OK 73737 • 3,370
Fairview, OR 97024 • 1,749
Fairview, PA 16415 • 1,855
Fairview, TN 37062 • 3,648
Fairview, UT 84629 • 916
Fairview, WV 26570 • 759
Fairview Heights, IL 62208 • 12,414
Fairview Park, IN 47842 • 1,545
Fairview Park, OH 44126 • 19,311
Fairview Shores, FL 32804 • 6,100
Fairway, KS 66205 • 4,619
Faison, NC 28341 • 636
Falconer, NY 14733 • 2,778
Falcon Heights, MN 55113 • 5,291
Falcon Heights, OR 97601 • 1,389
Falfurrias, TX 78355 • 6,103
Falkville, AL 35622 • 1,310
Fall Branch, TN 37656 • 1,340
Fallbrook, CA 92028 • 14,041
Fall City, WA 98024 • 1,600
Fall Creek, WI 54742 • 1,148
Fall Mountain Lake, CT 06786 • 730
Fallon, NV 89406 • 4,262
Fallon □, MT • 3,763
Fall River, MA 02720–26 • 92,574
Fall River, WI 53932 • 850
Fall River □, SD • 8,439
Fall River Mills, CA 96028 • 900
Falls □, TX • 17,946
Falls Church, VA 22040–48 • 9,515
Falls City, NE 68355 • 5,374
Falls City, OR 97344 • 804
Falls Creek, PA 15840 • 1,208
Fallston, MD 21047 • 5,572
Fallston, NC 28042 • 614
Falmouth, KY 41040 • 2,482
Falmouth, ME 04105 • 6,853
Falmouth, MA 02540–41 • 4,200
Falmouth, VA 22403 • 970
Fannin □, GA • 14,748
Fannin □, TX • 24,285
Fanwood, NJ 07023 • 7,767
Fargo, ND 58102–99 • 61,383
Far Hills, NJ 07931 • 677
Faribault, MN 55021 • 16,241
Faribault □, MN • 19,714
Farley, IA 52046 • 1,287
Farmer City, IL 61842 • 2,252
Farmers Branch, TX 75234 • 24,863
Farmersburg, IN 47850 • 1,240
Farmersville, CA 93223 • 5,544
Farmersville, IL 62533 • 686
Farmersville, TX 75031 • 2,360
Farmerville, LA 71241 • 3,768
Farmingdale, ME 04345 • 2,014
Farmingdale, NJ 07727 • 1,348
Farmingdale, NY 11735 • 7,946
Farmington, AR 72730 • 1,283
Farmington, CT 06032 • 2,000
Farmington, IL 61531 • 3,118
Farmington, IA 52626 • 869
Farmington, ME 04938 • 3,583
Farmington, MI 48024 • 11,022
Farmington, MN 55024 • 4,370
Farmington, MO 63640 • 8,270
Farmington, NH 03835 • 3,284
Farmington, NM 87401 • 31,222
Farmington, UT 84025 • 4,691
Farmington Hills, MI 48018 • 58,056
Farmingville, NY 11738 • 5,700
Farmland, IN 47340 • 1,560
Farmville, NC 27828 • 4,707
Farmville, VA 23901 • 6,067
Farragut, IA 51639 • 603
Farrell, PA 16121 • 8,645
Farwell, MI 48622 • 804
Farwell, TX 79325 • 1,354
Faulk □, SD • 3,327
Faulkland Heights, DE 19808 • 1,650
Faulkner □, AR • 46,192
Faulkton, SD 57438 • 981
Fauquier □, VA • 35,889
Fayette, AL 35555 • 5,287
Fayette, IA 52142 • 1,515
Fayette, MS 39069 • 2,033
Fayette, MO 65248 • 2,983
Fayette, OH 43521 • 1,222
Fayette □, AL • 18,809
Fayette □, GA • 29,043
Fayette □, IL • 22,167
Fayette □, IN • 28,272
Fayette □, IA • 25,488
Fayette □, KY • 204,165
Fayette □, OH • 27,467
Fayette □, PA • 159,417
Fayette □, TN • 25,305
Fayette □, TX • 18,832
Fayette □, WV • 57,863
Fayetteville, AR 72701–03 • 36,608
Fayetteville, GA 30214 • 2,715
Fayetteville, NC 28301–08 • 59,507
Fayetteville, PA 17222 • 2,449
Fayetteville, TN 37334 • 7,559
Fayetteville, WV 25840 • 2,366
Fayville, MA 01745 • 1,000
Feasterville, PA 19047 • 6,900
Federal Heights, CO 80221 • 7,846
Federalsburg, MD 21632 • 1,952
Federal Way, WA 98003 • 17,850
Feeding Hills, MA 01030 • 8,500
Felicity, OH 45120 • 929
Fellowship, NJ 08057 • 1,900
Fellsmere, FL 32948 • 1,161
Felton, CA 95018 • 4,000
Fennimore, WI 53809 • 2,212
Fennville, MI 49408 • 934
Fenton, MI 48430 • 8,098
Fentress □, TN • 14,826
Ferdinand, IN 47532 • 2,192
Fergus □, MT • 13,076
Fergus Falls, MN 56537 • 12,519
Ferguson, KY 42533 • 1,009
Ferguson, MO 63135 • 24,740
Fernandina Beach, FL 32034 • 7,224
Fern Creek, KY 40291 • 16,866
Ferndale, CA 95536 • 1,367
Ferndale, MD 21061 • 2,600
Ferndale, MI 48220 • 26,227
Ferndale, PA 15905 • 2,204
Ferndale, WA 98248 • 3,855
Fernley, NV 89408 • 1,200
Fernwood, ID 83830 • 680
Ferriday, LA 71334 • 4,472
Ferris, TX 75125 • 2,228
Ferron, UT 84523 • 1,718
Ferry □, WA • 5,811
Ferry Farms, VA 22401 • 1,300
Fertile, MN 56540 • 869
Fessenden, ND 58438 • 761
Festus, MO 63028 • 7,574
Fieldale, VA 24089 • 1,400
Field Crest Estates, CT 06355 • 1,200
Fig Garden, CA 93704 • 9,000
Filer, ID 83328 • 1,645
Fillmore, CA 93015 • 9,602
Fillmore, UT 84631 • 2,083
Fillmore □, MN • 21,930
Fillmore □, NE • 7,920
Findlay, IL 62534 • 868
Findlay, OH 45840 • 35,594
Finley, ND 58230 • 718
Finley, TN 38030 • 1,014
Finney □, KS • 23,825
Fircrest, WA 98466 • 5,477
Firebaugh, CA 93622 • 3,740
Firestone, CO 80520 • 1,204
Fisher, IL 61843 • 1,572
Fisher □, TX • 5,891
Fishers, IN 46038 • 2,008
Fishersville, VA 22939 • 700
Fishing Creek, MD 21634 • 650
Fishkill, NY 12524 • 1,555
Fiskdale, MA 01518 • 1,859
Fitchburg, MA 01420 • 39,580
Fitzgerald, GA 31750 • 10,187
Five Points, NM 87105 • 5,500
Flagler □, FL • 10,913
Flagler Beach, FL 32036 • 2,208
Flagtown, NJ 08821 • 800
Flanagan, IL 61740 • 978
Flanders, NJ 07836 • 6,000
Flandreau, SD 57028 • 2,114
Flathead □, MT • 51,966
Flat Lick, KY 40935 • 700
Flatonia, TX 78941 • 1,070
Flat River, MO 63601 • 4,443
Flat Rock, MI 48134 • 6,853
Flat Rock, NC 28731 • 1,200
Flatwoods, KY 41139 • 8,354
Fleetwood, PA 19522 • 3,422
Fleming □, KY • 12,323
Fleming-Neon, KY 41816 • 1,195
Flemingsburg, KY 41041 • 2,835
Flemington, NJ 08822 • 4,132
Flemington, PA 17745 • 1,416
Fletcher, NC 28732 • 700
Fletcher, OK 73541 • 1,074
Flint, MI 48501–99 • 159,611
Flint City, AL 35601 • 673
Flippin, AR 72634 • 1,072
Flomaton, AL 36441 • 1,882
Floodwood, MN 55736 • 648
Flora, IL 62839 • 5,379
Flora, IN 46929 • 2,303
Flora, MS 39071 • 1,507
Florala, AL 36442 • 2,165
Floral City, FL 32636 • 1,181
Floral Park, NY 11001–05 • 16,805
Florence, AL 35630–33 • 37,029
Florence, AZ 85232 • 3,391
Florence, CA 90001 • 38,000
Florence, CO 81226 • 2,987
Florence, KS 66851 • 729
Florence, KY 41042 • 15,586
Florence, MS 39073 • 1,111
Florence, NJ 08518 • 5,000
Florence, OR 97439 • 4,411
Florence, SC 29501–03 • 29,176
Florence, TX 76527 • 744
Florence □, SC • 110,163
Florence □, WI • 4,172
Floresville, TX 78114 • 4,381
Florham Park, NJ 07932 • 9,359
Florida, NY 10921 • 1,947
Florida City, FL 33034 • 6,174
Florien, LA 71429 • 964
Florin, CA 95828 • 16,523
Florissant, MO 63031–34 • 55,372
Flossmoor, IL 60422 • 8,423
Flourtown, PA 19031 • 5,200
Flower Hill, NY 11050 • 4,558
Flowery Branch, GA 30542 • 755
Flowood, MS 39208 • 943
Floyd □, GA • 79,800
Floyd □, IN • 61,205
Floyd □, IA • 19,597
Floyd □, KY • 48,764
Floyd □, TX • 9,834
Floyd □, VA • 11,563
Floydada, TX 79235 • 4,193
Flushing, MI 48433 • 8,624
Flushing, OH 43977 • 1,266
Fluvanna □, VA • 10,244
Foard □, TX • 2,158
Folcroft, PA 19032 • 8,231
Foley, AL 36535 • 4,003
Foley, MN 56329 • 1,606
Folkston, GA 31537 • 2,243
Follansbee, WV 26037 • 3,994
Folly Beach, SC 29439 • 1,478
Folsom, CA 95630 • 11,003
Folsom, NJ 08037 • 1,892
Folsom, PA 19033 • 7,600
Fonda, IA 50540 • 863
Fonda, NY 12068 • 1,006
Fond du Lac, WI 54935 • 35,863
Fond du Lac □, WI • 88,964
Fontana, CA 92335 • 37,107
Fontana, WI 53125 • 1,764
Fontanelle, IA 50846 • 805
Foothill Farms, CA 95841 • 13,700
Footville, WI 53537 • 794
Ford □, IL • 15,265
Ford □, KS • 24,315
Ford City, CA 93268 • 3,392
Ford City, PA 16226 • 3,923
Fordoche, LA 70732 • 676
Fords, NJ 08863 • 12,600
Fords Prairie, WA 98531 • 2,000
Fordyce, AR 71742 • 5,175
Foreman, AR 71836 • 1,377
Forest, MS 39074 • 5,229
Forest, OH 45843 • 1,633
Forest □, PA • 5,072
Forest □, WI • 9,044
Forest Acres, SC 29206 • 6,071
Forest City, IA 50436 • 4,270
Forest City, NC 28043 • 7,688
Forest City, PA 18421 • 1,924
Forest Grove, OR 97116 • 11,499
Forest Hill, TX 76119 • 11,684
Forest Hills, PA 15221 • 8,198
Forest Knolls, CA 94933 • 2,000
Forest Lake, MN 55025 • 4,596
Forest Park, GA 30050 • 18,782
Forest Park, IL 60130 • 15,177
Forest Park, LA 71291 • 1,500
Forest Park, OH 45240 • 18,675
Forestville, MD 20747 • 16,401
Forestville, NY 14062 • 804
Forgan, OK 73938 • 611
Forge Village, MA 01886 • 1,400
Forked River, NJ 08731 • 1,422
Forks, WA 98331 • 3,060
Forman, ND 58032 • 629
Forney, TX 75126 • 2,483
Forrest, IL 61741 • 1,246
Forrest □, MS • 66,018
Forrest City, AR 72335 • 13,803
Forreston, IL 61030 • 1,384
Forsyth, GA 31029 • 4,624
Forsyth, IL 62535 • 1,072
Forsyth, MO 65653 • 1,010
Forsyth, MT 59327 • 2,553
Forsyth □, GA • 27,958
Forsyth □, NC • 243,683
Fort Ashby, WV 26719 • 1,200
Fort Atkinson, WI 53538 • 9,785
Fort Bend □, TX • 130,846
Fort Benton, MT 59442 • 1,693
Fort Bragg, CA 95437 • 5,019
Fort Branch, IN 47648 • 2,504
Fort Calhoun, NE 68023 • 641
Fort Cobb, OK 73038 • 760
Fort Collins, CO 80521–26 • 65,092
Fort Covington, NY 12937 • 1,200
Fort Davis, TX 79734 • 850
Fort Defiance, AZ 86504 • 3,431
Fort Deposit, AL 36032 • 1,519
Fort Dodge, IA 50501 • 29,423
Fort Edward, NY 12828 • 3,561
Fort Fairfield, ME 04742 • 2,282
Fort Gaines, GA 31751 • 1,260
Fort Gay, WV 25514 • 886
Fort Gibson, OK 74434 • 2,477
Fort Hall, ID 83203 • 900
Fort Howard, MD 21052 • 1,050
Fort Kent, ME 04743 • 2,375
Fort Lauderdale, FL 33301–99 • 153,279
Fort Lee, NJ 07024 • 32,449
Fort Loramie, OH 45845 • 977
Fort Loudon, PA 17224 • 900
Fort Lupton, CO 80621 • 4,251
Fort Madison, IA 52627 • 13,520
Fort McKinley, OH 45426 • 11,536
Fort Meade, FL 33841 • 5,546
Fort Mill, SC 29715 • 4,162
Fort Mitchell, KY 41017 • 7,297
Fort Morgan, CO 80701 • 8,768
Fort Myers, FL 33901–19 • 36,638
Fort Myers Beach, FL 33931 • 5,753
Fort Ogden, FL 33842 • 900
Fort Oglethorpe, GA 30742 • 5,443
Fort Payne, AL 35967 • 11,485
Fort Pierce, FL 34950–54 • 33,802
Fort Pierre, SD 57532 • 1,789
Fort Plain, NY 13339 • 2,555
Fort Recovery, OH 45846 • 1,370
Fort Scott, KS 66701 • 8,893
Fort Shawnee, OH 45806 • 4,541
Fort Smith, AR 72901–16 • 71,626
Fort Stockton, TX 79735 • 8,688
Fort Sumner, NM 88119 • 1,421
Fort Thomas, KY 41075 • 16,012
Fort Totten, ND 58335 • 750
Fort Towson, OK 74735 • 789
Fortuna, CA 95540 • 7,591
Fort Valley, GA 31030 • 9,000
Fortville, IN 46040 • 2,787
Fort Walton Beach, FL 32548 • 20,829
Fort Washington, PA 19034 • 4,500
Fort Washington Forest, MD 20744 • 1,800
Fort Wayne, IN 46801–99 • 172,028
Fort Wingate, NM 87316 • 900
Fort Worth, TX 76101–99 • 385,164
Fort Wright, KY 41011 • 4,481
Fort Yates, ND 58538 • 771
Forty Fort, PA 18704 • 5,590
Fort Yukon, AK 99740 • 619
Fosston, MN 56542 • 1,599
Foster □, ND • 4,611
Foster Brook, PA 16701 • 950
Foster City, CA 94404 • 23,287
Foster Village, HI 96818 • 3,700
Fostoria, OH 44830 • 15,743
Fouke, AR 71837 • 614
Fountain, CO 80817 • 8,324
Fountain □, IN • 19,033
Fountain City, IN 47341 • 839
Fountain City, WI 54629 • 963
Fountain Hill, PA 18015 • 4,805
Fountain Inn, SC 29644 • 4,226
Fountain Place, LA 70811 • 9,200
Fountain Valley, CA 92708 • 55,080
Four Corners, OR 97301 • 11,331
Four Oaks, NC 27524 • 1,049
Fowler, CA 93625 • 2,496
Fowler, CO 81039 • 1,227
Fowler, IN 47944 • 2,319
Fowler, MI 48835 • 1,021
Fowlerville, MI 48836 • 2,289
Foxboro, MA 02035 • 5,697
Fox Chapel, PA 15238 • 5,049
Fox Lake, IL 60020 • 6,831
Fox Lake, WI 53933 • 1,373
Fox Point, WI 53217 • 7,649
Fox River Grove, IL 60021 • 2,515
Foxworth, MS 39483 • 1,000
Frackville, PA 17931 • 5,308
Framingham, MA 01701 • 65,113
Francesville, IN 47946 • 944
Francisco, IN 47649 • 612
Frankenmuth, MI 48734 • 3,753
Frankford, DE 19945 • 828
Frankfort, IL 60423 • 4,357
Frankfort, IN 46041 • 15,168
Frankfort, KS 66427 • 1,038
Frankfort, KY 40601 • 25,973
Frankfort, MI 49635 • 1,603
Frankfort, NY 13340 • 2,995
Frankfort, OH 45628 • 1,008
Franklin, GA 30217 • 711
Franklin, IL 62638 • 645
Franklin, IN 46131 • 11,563
Franklin, KY 42134 • 7,738
Franklin, LA 70538 • 9,584
Franklin, MA 02038 • 18,217
Franklin, NE 68939 • 1,167
Franklin, NH 03235 • 7,901
Franklin, NJ 07416 • 4,486
Franklin, NC 28734 • 2,640
Franklin, OH 45005 • 10,711
Franklin, PA 16323 • 8,146
Franklin, TN 37064 • 12,407
Franklin, TX 77856 • 1,349
Franklin, VA 23851 • 7,308
Franklin, WV 26807 • 780
Franklin, WI 53132 • 16,871
Franklin □, AL • 28,350
Franklin □, AR • 14,705
Franklin □, FL • 7,661
Franklin □, GA • 15,185
Franklin □, ID • 8,895
Franklin □, IL • 43,201
Franklin □, IN • 19,612
Franklin □, IA • 13,036
Franklin □, KS • 22,062
Franklin □, KY • 41,830
Franklin □, LA • 24,141
Franklin □, ME • 27,447
Franklin □, MA • 64,317
Franklin □, MS • 8,208
Franklin □, MO • 71,233
Franklin □, NE • 4,377
Franklin □, NC • 30,055
Franklin □, NY • 44,929
Franklin □, OH • 869,126
Franklin □, PA • 113,629
Franklin □, TN • 31,983
Franklin □, TX • 6,893
Franklin □, VT • 34,788
Franklin □, VA • 35,740
Franklin □, WA • 35,025
Franklin Grove, IL 61031 • 965
Franklin Lakes, NJ 07417 • 8,769
Franklin Park, IL 60131 • 17,507
Franklin Park, PA 15143 • 6,135
Franklin Square, NY 11010 • 32,800
Franklinton, LA 70438 • 4,119
Franklinton, NC 27525 • 1,394
Franklinville, NJ 08322 • 900
Franklinville, NC 27248 • 607
Franklinville, NY 14737 • 1,887
Frankston, TX 75763 • 1,255
Frankton, IN 46044 • 2,080
Fraser, MI 48026 • 14,560
Frazee, MN 56544 • 1,284
Frazeysburg, OH 43822 • 1,025
Frazier Park, CA 93225 • 1,444
Frederic, WI 54837 • 1,039
Frederica, DE 19946 • 864
Frederick, CO 80530 • 855
Frederick, MD 21701 • 28,086
Frederick, OK 73542 • 6,153
Frederick □, MD • 114,792
Frederick □, VA • 34,150
Fredericksburg, IA 50630 • 1,075
Fredericksburg, PA 17026 • 750
Fredericksburg, TX 78624 • 6,412
Fredericksburg, VA 22401–05 • 15,322
Fredericktown, MO 63645 • 4,036
Fredericktown, OH 43019 • 2,299
Fredericktown, PA 15333 • 1,067
Fredonia, AZ 86022 • 1,040
Fredonia, KS 66736 • 3,047
Fredonia, NY 14063 • 11,126
Fredonia, PA 16124 • 712
Fredonia, WI 53021 • 1,437
Freeborn □, MN • 36,329
Freeburg, IL 62243 • 2,989
Freeburg, PA 17827 • 643
Freedom, CA 95019 • 6,416
Freedom, PA 15042 • 2,272
Freehold, NJ 07728 • 10,020
Freeland, MI 48623 • 1,364
Freeland, PA 18224 • 4,285
Freelandville, IN 47535 • 680
Freeman, SD 57029 • 1,462
Freemansburg, PA 18017 • 1,879
Freeport, FL 32439 • 669
Freeport, IL 61032 • 26,266
Freeport, ME 04032 • 1,906
Freeport, NY 11520 • 38,272
Freeport, PA 16229 • 2,381
Freeport, TX 77541 • 13,444
Freer, TX 78357 • 3,213
Freestone □, TX • 14,830
Fremont, CA 94536–39 • 131,945
Fremont, IN 46737 • 1,180
Fremont, IA 52561 • 730
Fremont, MI 49412 • 3,672
Fremont, NE 68025 • 23,979
Fremont, NC 27830 • 1,736
Fremont, OH 43420 • 17,834
Fremont □, CO • 28,676
Fremont □, ID • 10,813
Fremont □, IA • 9,401
Fremont □, WY • 38,992
French Island, WI 54601 • 3,000
French Lick, IN 47432 • 2,265
French Settlement, LA 70733 • 761
Frenchtown, NJ 08825 • 1,573
Frenchville, ME 04745 • 615
Fresno, CA 93701–99 • 217,289
Fresno □, CA • 514,229
Frewsburg, NY 14738 • 2,000
Friars Point, MS 38631 • 1,400
Friday Harbor, WA 98250 • 1,200
Fridley, MN 55432 • 30,228
Friedens, PA 18080 • 900
Friend, NE 68359 • 1,079
Friendship, NY 14739 • 1,285
Friendship, TN 38034 • 763
Friendship, WI 53934 • 744
Friendsville, TN 37737 • 694
Friendswood, TX 77546 • 10,719
Fries, VA 24330 • 758
Frio □, TX • 13,785
Friona, TX 79035 • 3,809
Frisco, CO 80443 • 1,221
Frisco City, AL 36445 • 1,424
Fritch, TX 79036 • 2,299
Frontenac, KS 66762 • 2,586
Frontier □, NE • 3,647
Front Royal, VA 22630 • 11,126
Frostburg, MD 21532 • 7,715
Frostproof, FL 33843 • 2,995
Fruita, CO 81521 • 2,810
Fruit Heights, UT 84037 • 2,728
Fruitland, ID 83619 • 2,559
Fruitland, MD 21826 • 2,694
Fruitland, NM 87416 • 700
Fruitland Park, FL 32731 • 2,259
Fruitport, MI 49415 • 1,143
Fruitvale, WA 98902 • 3,600
Fruitville, FL 34232 • 3,070
Fryeburg, ME 04037 • 1,644
Fulda, MN 56131 • 1,308
Fullerton, CA 92631–35 • 102,034
Fullerton, NE 68638 • 1,506
Fulton, AL 36446 • 606
Fulton, IL 61252 • 3,936

# United States Populations and ZIP Codes

Fulton, KY 42041 • 3,137
Fulton, MI 49052 • 750
Fulton, MS 38843 • 3,238
Fulton, MO 65251 • 11,046
Fulton, NY 13069 • 13,312
Fulton □, AR • 9,975
Fulton □, GA • 589,904
Fulton □, IL • 43,687
Fulton □, IN • 19,335
Fulton □, KY • 8,971
Fulton □, NY • 55,153
Fulton □, OH • 37,751
Fulton □, PA • 12,842
Fultondale, AL 35068 • 6,217
Funkstown, MD 21734 • 1,103
Fuquay-Varina, NC 27526 • 3,110
Furnas □, NE • 6,486
Fyffe, AL 35971 • 1,305

## G

Gabbs, NV 89409 • 811
Gadsden, AL 35901–05 • 47,565
Gadsden, TN 38337 • 683
Gadsden □, FL • 41,565
Gaffney, SC 29340 • 13,453
Gage, OK 73843 • 667
Gage □, NE • 24,456
Gahanna, OH 43230 • 18,001
Gaines □, TX • 13,150
Gainesboro, TN 38562 • 1,119
Gainesville, FL 32601–14 • 81,371
Gainesville, GA 30501–06 • 15,280
Gainesville, MO 65655 • 707
Gainesville, TX 76240 • 14,081
Gaithersburg, MD 20877–79 • 26,424
Galatia, IL 62935 • 1,042
Galax, VA 24333 • 6,524
Galena, AK 99741 • 765
Galena, IL 61036 • 3,876
Galena, KS 66739 • 3,587
Galena Park, TX 77547 • 9,879
Galesburg, IL 61401 • 35,305
Galesburg, MI 49053 • 1,822
Gales Ferry, CT 06335 • 1,191
Galesville, WI 54630 • 1,239
Galeton, PA 16922 • 1,462
Galeville, NY 13088 • 5,600
Galien, MI 49113 • 692
Galion, OH 44833 • 12,391
Gallatin, MO 64640 • 2,063
Gallatin, TN 37066 • 17,191
Gallatin □, IL • 7,590
Gallatin □, KY • 4,842
Gallatin □, MT • 42,865
Gallaway, TN 38036 • 804
Gallia □, OH • 30,098
Galliano, LA 70354 • 5,159
Gallipolis, OH 45631 • 5,576
Gallitzin, PA 16641 • 2,315
Gallup, NM 87301 • 18,167
Galt, CA 95632 • 5,514
Galva, IL 61434 • 3,185
Galva, KS 67443 • 651
Galveston, IN 46932 • 1,822
Galveston, TX 77550–53 • 61,902
Galveston □, TX • 195,940
Gambier, OH 43022 • 2,056
Gambrills, MD 21054 • 650
Ganado, AZ 86505 • 1,200
Ganado, TX 77962 • 1,770
Gang Mills, NY 14870 • 1,258
Gantt, SC 29605 • 1,600
Gap, PA 17527 • 1,022
Garber, OK 73738 • 1,215
Garberville, CA 95440 • 1,200
Garden □, NE • 2,802
Gardena, CA 90247–49 • 45,165
Garden City, AL 35070 • 655
Garden City, GA 31408 • 6,895
Garden City, ID 83704 • 4,571
Garden City, KS 67846 • 18,256
Garden City, MI 48135 • 35,640
Garden City, MO 64747 • 1,021
Garden City, NY 11530 • 22,927
Garden City Park, NY 11040 • 5,200
Gardendale, AL 35071 • 7,928
Garden Grove, CA 92640–45 • 123,307
Garden Home, OR 97223 • 5,500
Garden Plain, KS 67050 • 775
Gardiner, ME 04345 • 6,485
Gardner, IL 60424 • 1,322
Gardner, KS 66030 • 2,392
Gardner, MA 01440 • 17,900
Gardnerville, NV 89410 • 2,800
Garfield, NJ 07026 • 26,803
Garfield □, CO • 22,514
Garfield □, MT • 1,656
Garfield □, NE • 2,363
Garfield □, OK • 62,820
Garfield □, UT • 3,673
Garfield □, WA • 2,468
Garfield Heights, OH 44125 • 34,938
Garfield Park, DE 19720 • 1,000
Garibaldi, OR 97118 • 999
Garland, AR 71839 • 660
Garland, NC 28441 • 885
Garland, TX 75040–43 • 138,857
Garland, UT 84312 • 1,405
Garland □, AR • 70,531
Garnavillo, IA 52049 • 723
Garner, IA 50438 • 2,908
Garner, NC 27529 • 10,073
Garnett, KS 66032 • 3,310
Garrard □, KY • 10,853
Garretson, SD 57030 • 963
Garrett, IN 46738 • 4,751
Garrett □, MD • 26,498
Garrett Park, MD 20896 • 2,800
Garrettsville, OH 44231 • 1,769
Garrison, KY 41141 • 650
Garrison, MD 21055 • 750
Garrison, ND 58540 • 1,830
Garrison, NY 10524 • 650
Garrison, TX 75946 • 1,059
Garvin □, OK • 27,856
Garwin, IA 50632 • 626
Garwood, NJ 07027 • 4,752
Gary, IN 46401–99 • 151,953
Gary, WV 24836 • 2,233
Garysburg, NC 27831 • 1,434
Garyville, LA 70051 • 2,856
Garza □, TX • 5,336
Gas City, IN 46933 • 6,370
Gasconade □, MO • 13,181
Gasport, NY 14067 • 950
Gassaway, WV 26624 • 1,225
Gassville, AR 72635 • 859
Gaston, IN 47342 • 1,150
Gaston, NC 27832 • 883
Gaston, SC 29053 • 960
Gaston □, NC • 162,568
Gastonia, NC 28052–54 • 47,333
Gate City, VA 24251 • 2,494
Gates, NY 14624 • 29,756
Gates, TN 38037 • 729
Gates □, NC • 8,875
Gatesville, TX 76528 • 6,260
Gatlinburg, TN 37738 • 3,210
Gauley Bridge, WV 25085 • 1,177
Gautier, MS 39553 • 8,917
Gaylord, MI 49735 • 3,011
Gaylord, MN 55334 • 1,933
Gays Mills, WI 54631 • 627
Gearhart, OR 97138 • 967
Geary, OK 73040 • 1,700
Geary □, KS • 29,852
Geauga □, OH • 74,474
Geistown, PA 15904 • 3,304
Gem □, ID • 11,972
Genesee, ID 83832 • 791
Genesee, MI 48437 • 950
Genesee □, MI • 450,449
Genesee □, NY • 59,400
Geneseo, IL 61254 • 6,373
Geneseo, NY 14454 • 6,746
Geneva, AL 36340 • 4,866
Geneva, IL 60134 • 9,881
Geneva, IN 46740 • 1,430
Geneva, NE 68361 • 2,400
Geneva, NY 14456 • 15,133
Geneva, OH 44041 • 6,655
Geneva □, AL • 24,253
Geneva-on-the-Lake, OH 44041 • 1,634
Genoa, IL 60135 • 3,276
Genoa, NE 68640 • 1,090
Genoa, OH 43430 • 2,213
Genoa City, WI 53128 • 1,202
Genola, UT 84655 • 630
Gentry, AR 72734 • 1,468
Gentry □, MO • 7,887
George, IA 51237 • 1,241
George □, MS • 15,297
Georgetown, CA 95634 • 2,000
Georgetown, CO 80444 • 830
Georgetown, CT 06829 • 1,834
Georgetown, DE 19947 • 1,710
Georgetown, GA 31754 • 935
Georgetown, IL 61846 • 4,220
Georgetown, IN 47122 • 1,494
Georgetown, KY 40324 • 10,972
Georgetown, MA 01833 • 2,600
Georgetown, OH 45121 • 3,467
Georgetown, SC 29440 • 10,144
Georgetown, TX 78626 • 9,468
Georgetown □, SC • 42,461
George West, TX 78022 • 2,627
Georgiana, AL 36033 • 1,993
Gerald, MO 63037 • 921
Geraldine, AL 35974 • 911
Gerber, CA 96035 • 950
Gering, NE 69341 • 7,760
Germantown, IL 62245 • 1,191
Germantown, MD 20874 • 9,721
Germantown, OH 45327 • 5,015
Germantown, TN 38138 • 21,482
Germantown, WI 53022 • 10,729
Geronimo, OK 73543 • 726
Gervais, OR 97026 • 799
Gettysburg, PA 17325 • 7,194
Gettysburg, SD 57442 • 1,623
Geyserville, CA 95441 • 950
Giants Neck, CT 06357 • 1,150
Gibbon, MN 55335 • 787
Gibbon, NE 68840 • 1,531
Gibbstown, NJ 08027 • 5,676
Gibsland, LA 71028 • 1,354
Gibson, GA 30810 • 730
Gibson □, IN • 33,156
Gibson □, TN • 49,467
Gibsonburg, OH 43431 • 2,479
Gibson City, IL 60936 • 3,498
Gibsonia, PA 15044 • 2,065
Gibsonton, FL 33534 • 3,700
Gibsonville, NC 27249 • 2,865
Giddings, TX 78942 • 3,950
Gideon, MO 63848 • 1,240
Gifford, FL 32960 • 6,240
Gifford, IL 61847 • 848
Gig Harbor, WA 98335 • 2,429
Gila □, AZ • 37,080
Gila Bend, AZ 85337 • 1,585
Gilbert, AZ 85234 • 5,717
Gilbert, IA 50105 • 805
Gilbert, LA 71336 • 800
Gilbert, MN 55741 • 2,721
Gilbert, OR 97266 • 4,000
Gilbert, WV 25621 • 757
Gilbertsville, PA 19525 • 900
Gilbertville, IA 50634 • 740
Gilbertville, MA 01031 • 1,029
Gilchrist □, FL • 5,767
Gilcrest, CO 80623 • 1,025
Giles □, TN • 24,625
Giles □, VA • 17,810
Gillespie, IL 62033 • 3,740
Gillespie □, TX • 13,532
Gillett, AR 72055 • 927
Gillett, WI 54124 • 1,356
Gillette, WY 82716 • 12,134
Gilliam □, OR • 2,057
Gilman, IL 60938 • 1,913
Gilman, IA 50106 • 642
Gilmer, TX 75644 • 5,167
Gilmer □, GA • 11,110
Gilmer □, WV • 8,334
Gilmore City, IA 50541 • 626
Gilpin □, CO • 2,441
Gilroy, CA 95020 • 21,641
Girard, IL 62640 • 2,246
Girard, KS 66743 • 2,888
Girard, OH 44420 • 12,517
Girard, PA 16417 • 2,615
Girardville, PA 17935 • 2,268
Glacier □, MT • 10,628
Gladbrook, IA 50635 • 970
Glades □, FL • 5,992
Glade Spring, VA 24340 • 1,722
Gladewater, TX 75647 • 6,548
Gladstone, MI 49837 • 4,533
Gladstone, MO 64118 • 24,990
Gladstone, NJ 07934 • 2,038
Gladstone, OR 97027 • 9,500
Gladwin, MI 48624 • 2,479
Gladwin □, MI • 19,957
Glandorf, OH 45848 • 746
Glasco, KS 67445 • 710
Glasco, NY 12432 • 1,169
Glascock □, GA • 2,382
Glasford, IL 61533 • 1,201
Glasgow, KY 42141 • 12,958
Glasgow, MO 65254 • 1,336
Glasgow, MT 59230 • 4,455
Glasgow, VA 24555 • 1,259
Glasgow, WV 25086 • 1,031
Glasgow Village, MO 63137 • 7,200
Glassboro, NJ 08028 • 14,574
Glasscock □, TX • 1,304
Glassport, PA 15045 • 6,242
Glastonbury, CT 06033 • 7,049
Gleason, TN 38229 • 1,335
Glen Allen, VA 23060 • 1,100
Glen Alpine, NC 28628 • 645
Glen Avon, CA 92509 • 8,444
Glen Burnie, MD 21061 • 30,000
Glen Carbon, IL 62034 • 5,197
Glencoe, AL 35905 • 4,648
Glencoe, IL 60022 • 9,200
Glencoe, MN 55336 • 4,396
Glen Cove, NY 11542 • 24,618
Glendale, AZ 85301–11 • 97,172
Glendale, CA 91201–99 • 139,060
Glendale, CO 80222 • 2,496
Glendale, MS 39401 • 1,329
Glendale, MO 63122 • 6,035
Glendale, OH 45246 • 2,368
Glendale, OR 97442 • 712
Glendale, SC 29346 • 1,049
Glen Dale, WV 26038 • 1,971
Glendale, WI 53209 • 13,882
Glendale Heights, IL 60139 • 23,163
Glendale Heights, WV 26038 • 700
Glendive, MT 59330 • 5,978
Glendola, NJ 07719 • 2,300
Glendora, CA 91740 • 38,500
Glendora, NJ 08029 • 5,632
Glen Ellyn, IL 60137 • 23,717
Glen Gardner, NJ 08826 • 834
Glenham, NY 12527 • 2,720
Glen Head, NY 11545 • 6,800
Glen Lyon, PA 18617 • 3,408
Glenmora, LA 71433 • 1,479
Glenn □, CA • 21,350
Glenns Ferry, ID 83623 • 1,374
Glennville, GA 30427 • 4,144
Glenolden, PA 19036 • 7,633
Glenpool, OK 74033 • 2,706
Glen Raven, NC 27215 • 2,755
Glen Ridge, NJ 07028 • 7,855
Glen Rock, NJ 07452 • 11,497
Glen Rock, PA 17327 • 1,662
Glenrock, WY 82637 • 2,736
Glen Rose, TX 76043 • 2,075
Glens Falls, NY 12801 • 15,897
Glenshaw, PA 15116 • 14,000
Glenside, PA 19038 • 17,400
Glen Ullin, ND 58631 • 1,125
Glenview, IL 60025 • 32,060
Glenville, MN 56036 • 851
Glenville, WV 26351 • 2,155
Glenwood, AR 71943 • 1,402
Glenwood, FL 32722 • 950
Glenwood, GA 30428 • 824
Glenwood, IL 60425 • 10,538
Glenwood, IA 51534 • 5,280
Glenwood, MN 56334 • 2,523
Glenwood, VA 24541 • 1,000
Glenwood City, WI 54013 • 950
Glenwood Farms, VA 23223 • 3,200
Glenwood Springs, CO 81601 • 4,637
Glidden, IA 51443 • 1,076
Glide, OR 97443 • 900
Globe, AZ 85501 • 6,886
Gloster, MS 39638 • 1,726
Gloucester, MA 01930 • 27,768
Gloucester, VA 23061 • 900
Gloucester □, NJ • 199,917
Gloucester □, VA • 20,107
Gloucester City, NJ 08030 • 13,121
Gloucester Point, VA 23062 • 850
Glouster, OH 45732 • 2,211
Gloversville, NY 12078 • 17,836
Gloverville, SC 29828 • 2,619
Gluck, SC 29621 • 650
Glyndon, MD 21071 • 1,100
Glyndon, MN 56547 • 882
Glynn □, GA • 54,981
Gnadenhutten, OH 44629 • 1,320
Gobles, MI 49055 • 816
Goddard, KS 67052 • 1,427
Godfrey, IL 62035 • 2,600
Godley, TX 76044 • 614
Goffstown, NH 03045 • 2,500
Gogebic □, MI • 19,686
Golconda, IL 62938 • 960
Gold Bar, WA 98251 • 794
Gold Beach, OR 97444 • 1,515
Golden, CO 80401–19 • 12,237
Golden Beach, FL 34292 • 612
Golden City, MO 64748 • 900
Goldendale, WA 98620 • 3,575
Golden Meadow, LA 70357 • 2,282
Golden Valley, MN 55427 • 22,775
Golden Valley □, MT • 1,026
Golden Valley □, ND • 2,391
Goldfield, IA 50542 • 789
Gold Hill, OR 97525 • 904
Goldsboro, NC 27530 • 31,871
Goldsby, OK 73093 • 603
Goldthwaite, TX 76844 • 1,783
Goleta, CA 93117 • 28,100
Golf Manor, OH 45237 • 4,317
Goliad, TX 77963 • 1,990
Goliad □, TX • 5,193
Gonzales, CA 93926 • 2,891
Gonzales, LA 70737 • 7,287
Gonzales, TX 78629 • 7,152
Gonzales □, TX • 16,949
Gonzalez, FL 32560 • 6,084
Goochland □, VA • 11,761
Goodhue, MN 55027 • 657
Goodhue □, MN • 38,749
Gooding, ID 83330 • 2,949
Gooding □, ID • 11,874
Goodland, FL 33933 • 1,000
Goodland, IN 47948 • 1,200
Goodland, KS 67735 • 5,708
Goodlettsville, TN 37072 • 8,327
Goodman, MS 39079 • 1,285
Goodman, MO 64843 • 1,030
Good Pine, LA 71342 • 900
Goodview, MN 55987 • 2,567
Goodwater, AL 35072 • 1,895
Goodwell, OK 73939 • 1,186
Goodyear, AZ 85323 • 2,747
Goose Creek, SC 29445 • 17,811
Gordo, AL 35466 • 2,112
Gordon, GA 31031 • 2,768
Gordon, NE 69343 • 2,167
Gordon □, GA • 30,070
Gordonsville, TN 38563 • 893
Gordonsville, VA 22942 • 1,421
Goreville, IL 62939 • 978
Gorham, ME 04038 • 4,052
Gorham, NH 03581 • 2,180
Gorham, NY 14461 • 800
Gorman, TX 76454 • 1,258
Goshen, IN 46526 • 19,665
Goshen, NY 10924 • 4,874
Goshen, OH 45122 • 1,400
Goshen □, WY • 12,040
Gosnell, AR 72319 • 3,215
Gosper □, NE • 2,140
Gosport, IN 47433 • 729
Gothenburg, NE 69138 • 3,479
Gould, AR 71643 • 1,671
Goulds, FL 33170 • 7,078
Gouverneur, NY 13642 • 4,285
Gove □, KS • 3,726
Gowanda, NY 14070 • 2,713
Gower, MO 64454 • 1,276
Gowrie, IA 50543 • 1,089
Grabill, IN 46741 • 658
Grace, ID 83241 • 1,216
Graceville, FL 32440 • 2,918
Graceville, MN 56240 • 780
Grady □, GA • 19,845
Grady □, OK • 39,490
Graettinger, IA 51342 • 923
Grafton, IL 62037 • 1,024
Grafton, MA 01519 • 2,000
Grafton, ND 58237 • 5,293
Grafton, OH 44044 • 2,231
Grafton, VA 23692 • 900
Grafton, WV 26354 • 6,845
Grafton, WI 53024 • 8,381
Grafton □, NH • 65,806
Graham, CA 90002 • 10,600
Graham, NC 27253 • 8,674
Graham, TX 76046 • 9,170
Graham □, AZ • 22,862
Graham □, KS • 3,995
Graham □, NC • 7,217
Grainger □, TN • 16,751
Grain Valley, MO 64029 • 1,327
Grambling, LA 71245 • 4,226
Gramercy, LA 70052 • 3,211
Granbury, TX 76048 • 3,332
Granby, CO 80446 • 963
Granby, CT 06035 • 1,192
Granby, MA 01033 • 1,302
Granby, MO 64844 • 1,908
Grand □, CO • 7,475
Grand □, UT • 8,241
Grand Bay, AL 36541 • 3,185
Grand Blanc, MI 48439 • 6,848
Grand Caillou, LA 70360 • 1,400
Grand Canyon, AZ 86023 • 1,348
Grand Coteau, LA 70541 • 1,165
Grand Coulee, WA 99133 • 1,180
Grandfalls, TX 79742 • 635
Grandfield, OK 73546 • 1,445
Grand Forks, ND 58201 • 43,765
Grand Forks □, ND • 66,100
Grand Gorge, NY 12434 • 800
Grand Haven, MI 49417 • 11,763
Grand Island, NE 68801 • 33,180
Grand Isle, LA 70358 • 1,982
Grand Isle □, VT • 4,613
Grand Junction, CO 81501–05 • 27,956
Grand Junction, IA 50107 • 970
Grand Ledge, MI 48837 • 6,920
Grand Marais, MN 55604 • 1,289
Grand Meadow, MN 55936 • 965
Grand Mound, IA 52751 • 674
Grand Prairie, TX 75050–52 • 71,462
Grand Rapids, MI 49501–99 • 181,843
Grand Rapids, MN 55744 • 7,934
Grand Rapids, OH 43522 • 962
Grand Ridge, IL 61325 • 684
Grand Saline, TX 75140 • 2,709
Grand Terrace, CA 92324 • 8,498
Grand Tower, IL 62942 • 748
Grand Traverse □, MI • 54,899
Grandview, IN 47615 • 670
Grandview, MO 64030 • 24,502
Grandview, WA 98930 • 5,615
Grandview Heights, OH 43212 • 7,420
Grandville, MI 49418 • 12,412
Granger, IA 50109 • 619
Granger, TX 76530 • 1,236
Granger, WA 98932 • 1,812
Grangeville, ID 83530 • 3,666
Granite, OK 73547 • 1,617
Granite, UT 84070 • 650
Granite □, MT • 2,700
Granite City, IL 62040 • 36,815
Granite Falls, MN 56241 • 3,451
Granite Falls, NC 28630 • 2,580
Granite Falls, WA 98252 • 911
Granite Park, UT 84106 • 5,554
Granite Quarry, NC 28072 • 1,294
Graniteville, MA 01886 • 1,000
Graniteville, SC 29829 • 1,158
Graniteville, VT 05654 • 1,800
Grant, AL 35747 • 632
Grant, FL 32949 • 900
Grant, MI 49327 • 683
Grant, NE 69140 • 1,270
Grant □, AR • 13,008
Grant □, IN • 80,934
Grant □, KS • 6,977
Grant □, KY • 13,308
Grant □, LA • 16,703
Grant □, MN • 7,171
Grant □, NE • 877
Grant □, NM • 26,204
Grant □, ND • 4,274
Grant □, OK • 6,518
Grant □, OR • 8,210
Grant □, SD • 9,013
Grant □, WA • 48,522
Grant □, WV • 10,210
Grant □, WI • 51,736
Grant City, MO 64456 • 1,068
Grant Park, IL 60940 • 1,038
Grants, NM 87020 • 11,439
Grantsburg, WI 54840 • 1,153
Grants Pass, OR 97526–27 • 15,032
Grantsville, UT 84029 • 4,419
Grantsville, WV 26147 • 788
Grant Town, WV 26574 • 987
Grantville, GA 30220 • 1,110
Granville, IL 61326 • 1,537
Granville, NY 12832 • 2,696
Granville, OH 43023 • 3,851
Granville, WV 26534 • 992
Granville □, NC • 34,043
Grapeland, TX 75844 • 1,634
Grapevine, KY 42431 • 900
Grapevine, TX 76051 • 11,801
Grasonville, MD 21638 • 1,910
Grasselli, AL 35211 • 2,400
Grassflat, PA 16839 • 750
Grass Lake, IL 60002 • 2,191
Grass Lake, MI 49240 • 962
Grass Valley, CA 95945–49 • 6,697
Gratiot □, MI • 40,448
Gratis, OH 45330 • 809
Gratz, PA 17030 • 678
Graves □, KY • 34,049
Gravette, AR 72736 • 1,218
Gray, GA 31032 • 2,145
Gray, KY 40734 • 750
Gray, LA 70359 • 4,000
Gray, ME 04039 • 900
Gray □, KS • 5,138
Gray □, TX • 26,386
Gray Court, SC 29645 • 988
Grayling, MI 49738 • 1,792
Graylyn Crest, DE 19810 • 5,000
Grays Harbor □, WA • 66,314
Grayslake, IL 60030 • 5,260
Grayson, KY 41143 • 3,423
Grayson □, KY • 20,854
Grayson □, TX • 89,796
Grayson □, VA • 16,579
Graysville, AL 35073 • 2,642
Graysville, TN 37338 • 1,380
Grayville, IL 62844 • 2,313
Great Barrington, MA 01230 • 3,150
Great Bend, KS 67530 • 16,608
Great Bend, PA 18821 • 740
Great Falls, MT 59401–06 • 56,725
Great Falls, SC 29055 • 2,601
Great Neck, NY 11020–24 • 5,604
Great Neck Estates, NY 11021 • 2,936
Greece, NY 14616 • 63,700
Greeley, CO 80631–39 • 53,006
Greeley □, KS • 1,845
Greeley □, NE • 3,462
Green, OR 97470 • 3,897
Green □, KY • 11,043
Green □, WI • 30,012
Green Acres, DE 19803 • 1,200
Greenacres, WA 99016 • 3,650
Greenacres City, FL 33463 • 8,843
Green Bay, WI 54301–99 • 87,899
Greenbelt, MD 20770 • 17,332
Greenbriar, VA 22033 • 6,000
Greenbrier, AR 72058 • 1,423
Green Brier, TN 37073 • 3,180
Greenbrier □, WV • 37,665
Green Brook, NJ 08812 • 4,500
Greenbush, MN 56726 • 817
Greencastle, IN 46135 • 8,403
Greencastle, PA 17225 • 3,679
Green City, MO 63545 • 719
Green Cove Springs, FL 32043 • 4,154
Greendale, IN 47025 • 3,795
Greendale, WI 53129 • 16,928
Greene, IA 50636 • 1,332
Greene, NY 13778 • 1,747
Greene □, AL • 11,021
Greene □, AR • 30,744
Greene □, GA • 11,391
Greene □, IL • 16,661
Greene □, IN • 30,416
Greene □, IA • 12,119
Greene □, MS • 9,827
Greene □, MO • 185,302
Greene □, NC • 16,117
Greene □, NY • 40,861
Greene □, OH • 129,769
Greene □, PA • 40,476
Greene □, TN • 54,422
Greene □, VA • 7,625
Greeneville, TN 37743 • 14,097
Greenfield, CA 93927 • 4,181
Greenfield, IL 62044 • 1,090
Greenfield, IN 46140 • 11,299
Greenfield, IA 50849 • 2,243
Greenfield, MA 01301 • 14,198
Greenfield, MO 65661 • 1,394
Greenfield, OH 45123 • 5,150
Greenfield, TN 38230 • 2,109
Greenfield, WI 53220 • 31,467
Greenfield Plaza, IA 50315 • 2,100
Green Forest, AR 72638 • 1,609
Green Harbor, MA 02041 • 2,002
Greenhills, OH 45218 • 4,927
Green Island, NY 12183 • 2,696
Green Lake, WI 54941 • 1,208
Green Lake □, WI • 18,370

Greenland, AR 72737 • 622
Greenlawn, NY 11740 • 8,600
Greenlee □, AZ • 11,406
Green Manorville, CT 06082 • 3,250
Green Mountain Falls, CO 80819 • 607
Greenock, PA 15047 • 2,800
Greenport, NY 11944 • 2,073
Green River, UT 84525 • 1,048
Green River, WY 82935 • 12,807
Green Rock, IL 61241 • 3,324
Greensboro, AL 36744 • 3,248
Greensboro, GA 30642 • 2,985
Greensboro, MD 21639 • 1,253
Greensboro, NC 27401–99 • 155,642
Greensburg, IN 47240 • 9,254
Greensburg, KS 67054 • 1,885
Greensburg, KY 42743 • 2,377
Greensburg, LA 70441 • 662
Greensburg, PA 15601 • 17,558
Green Springs, OH 44836 • 1,568
Greensville □, VA • 10,903
Greentown, IN 46936 • 2,265
Green Tree, PA 15220 • 5,722
Greenup, IL 62428 • 1,655
Greenup, KY 41144 • 1,386
Greenup □, KY • 39,132
Green Valley, AZ 85614 • 7,999
Green Valley, IL 61534 • 768
Greenview, IL 62642 • 830
Greenville, AL 36037 • 7,807
Greenville, CA 95947 • 1,537
Greenville, FL 32331 • 1,096
Greenville, GA 30222 • 1,213
Greenville, IL 62246 • 5,271
Greenville, KY 42345 • 4,631
Greenville, ME 04441 • 1,640
Greenville, MI 48838 • 8,019
Greenville, MS 38701–03 • 40,613
Greenville, NH 03048 • 1,447
Greenville, NC 27834 • 35,740
Greenville, NY 10583 • 5,500
Greenville, OH 45331 • 12,999
Greenville, PA 16125 • 7,730
Greenville, RI 02828 • 7,576
Greenville, SC 29601–16 • 58,242
Greenville, TX 75401 • 22,161
Greenville □, SC • 287,913
Greenwich, CT 06830 • 59,578
Greenwich, NY 12834 • 1,955
Greenwich, OH 44837 • 1,458
Greenwood, AR 72936 • 3,317
Greenwood, IN 46142 • 19,327
Greenwood, LA 71033 • 1,043
Greenwood, MS 38930 • 20,115
Greenwood, MO 64034 • 1,315
Greenwood, PA 16601 • 1,700
Greenwood, SC 29646 • 21,613
Greenwood, WI 54437 • 1,124
Greenwood □, KS • 8,764
Greenwood □, SC • 57,847
Greenwood Lake, NY 10925 • 2,809
Greenwood Village, CO 80110 • 5,729
Greer, SC 29651 • 10,525
Greer □, OK • 7,028
Gregg □, TX • 99,495
Gregory, SD 57533 • 1,503
Gregory □, SD • 6,015
Greilickville, MI 49684 • 1,000
Grenada, MS 38901 • 12,641
Grenada □, MS • 21,043
Gresham, OR 97030 • 33,005
Gresham Park, GA 30316 • 6,232
Gretna, FL 32332 • 1,448
Gretna, LA 70053 • 20,615
Gretna, NE 68028 • 1,609
Gretna, VA 24557 • 1,255
Greybull, WY 82426 • 2,277
Gridley, CA 95948 • 3,982
Gridley, IL 61744 • 1,246
Griffin, GA 30223 • 20,728
Griffith, IN 46319 • 17,026
Grifton, NC 28530 • 2,179
Griggs □, ND • 3,714
Griggsville, IL 62340 • 1,301
Grimes, IA 50111 • 1,973
Grimes □, TX • 13,580
Grindall Creek, VA 23234 • 1,900
Grinnell, IA 50112 • 8,868
Griswold, IA 51535 • 1,176
Groesbeck, OH 45239 • 9,594
Groesbeck, TX 76642 • 3,373
Groom, TX 79039 • 736
Grosse Ile, MI 48138 • 9,320
Grosse Pointe, MI 48236 • 5,901
Grosse Pointe Park, MI 48236 • 13,639
Grosse Pointe Woods, MI 48236 • 18,886
Grosse Tete, LA 70740 • 749
Grossmont, CA 92041 • 2,600
Grosvenor Dale, CT 06246 • 700
Groton, CT 06340 • 10,086
Groton, MA 01450 • 1,264
Groton, NY 13073 • 2,313
Groton, SD 57445 • 1,230
Groton Long Point, CT 06340 • 800
Grottoes, VA 24441 • 1,369
Grove, OK 74344 • 3,378
Grove City, FL 34224 • 2,587
Grove City, OH 43123 • 16,816
Grove City, PA 16127 • 8,162
Grove Hill, AL 36451 • 1,912
Groveland, FL 32736 • 1,992
Groveland, MA 01834 • 4,300
Groveport, OH 43125 • 3,286
Grover City, CA 93433 • 8,827
Groves, TX 77619 • 17,090
Groveton, NH 03582 • 1,389
Groveton, TX 75845 • 1,262
Groveton, VA 22306 • 6,800
Groveton Gardens, VA 22303 • 2,800
Grovetown, GA 30813 • 3,384
Groveville, NJ 08620 • 1,200
Gruetli-Laager, TN 37339 • 2,000
Grulla, TX 78548 • 1,442
Grundy, VA 24614 • 1,699
Grundy □, IL • 30,582
Grundy □, IA • 14,366
Grundy □, MO • 11,959
Grundy □, TN • 13,787
Grundy Center, IA 50638 • 2,880
Gruver, TX 79040 • 1,216
Guadalupe, AZ 85283 • 4,506
Guadalupe, CA 93434 • 3,629
Guadalupe □, NM • 4,496
Guadalupe □, TX • 46,708
Gualala, CA 95445 • 700
Guernsey, WY 82214 • 1,512
Guernsey □, OH • 42,024
Gueydan, LA 70542 • 1,695
Guilford, CT 06437 • 2,555
Guilford, ME 04443 • 1,235
Guilford □, NC • 317,154
Guin, AL 35563 • 2,418
Gulf □, FL • 10,658
Gulf Breeze, FL 32561 • 5,478
Gulf Gate Estates, FL 34231 • 9,428
Gulfport, FL 33737 • 11,180
Gulfport, MS 39501–03 • 39,676
Gulf Shores, AL 36542 • 1,349
Gunnison, CO 81230 • 5,785
Gunnison, MS 38746 • 708
Gunnison, UT 84634 • 1,255
Gunnison □, CO • 10,689
Guntersville, AL 35976 • 7,041
Gurdon, AR 71743 • 2,707
Gurley, AL 35748 • 735
Gurnee, IL 60031 • 7,179
Gustine, CA 95322 • 3,142
Guthrie, KY 42234 • 1,361
Guthrie, OK 73044 • 10,312
Guthrie, WV 25312 • 800
Guthrie □, IA • 11,983
Guthrie Center, IA 50115 • 1,713
Guttenberg, IA 52052 • 2,428
Guttenberg, NJ 07093 • 7,340
Guymon, OK 73942 • 8,492
Guyton, GA 31312 • 749
Gwinhurst, DE 19809 • 1,400
Gwinn, MI 49841 • 1,408
Gwinner, ND 58040 • 725
Gwinnett □, GA • 166,903
Gypsum, CO 81637 • 743

## H

Haakon □, SD • 2,794
Habersham □, GA • 25,020
Hacienda Heights, CA 91745 • 49,422
Hackberry, LA 70645 • 800
Hackensack, NJ 07601–08 • 36,039
Hackettstown, NJ 07840 • 8,850
Hackleburg, AL 35564 • 883
Haddock, GA 31033 • 700
Haddonfield, NJ 08033 • 12,337
Haddon Heights, NJ 08035 • 8,361
Hadley, MA 01035 • 890
Hadlock, WA 98339 • 950
Hagan, GA 30429 • 880
Hagerman, ID 83332 • 602
Hagerman, NM 88232 • 936
Hagerstown, IN 47346 • 1,950
Hagerstown, MD 21740 • 34,132
Hahira, GA 31632 • 1,534
Hahnville, LA 70057 • 2,947
Haiku, HI 96708 • 619
Hailey, ID 83333 • 2,109
Haileyville, OK 74546 • 832
Haines, AK 99827 • 993
Haines City, FL 33844 • 10,799
Haines Falls, NY 12436 • 700
Hainesport, NJ 08036 • 900
Halawa Heights, HI 96701 • 7,000
Hale □, AL • 15,604
Hale □, TX • 37,592
Hale Center, TX 79041 • 2,297
Haledon, NJ 07508 • 6,607
Haleiwa, HI 96712 • 2,412
Hales Corners, WI 53130 • 7,110
Halethorpe, MD 21227 • 20,163
Haleyville, AL 35565 • 5,306
Half Hollow Hills, NY 11746 • 12,800
Half Moon Bay, CA 94019 • 7,282
Halfway, MD 21740 • 8,659
Halifax, MA 02338 • 900
Halifax, PA 17032 • 909
Halifax, VA 24558 • 772
Halifax □, NC • 55,286
Halifax □, VA • 30,599
Haliimaile, HI 96768 • 741
Hall □, GA • 75,649
Hall □, NE • 47,690
Hall □, TX • 5,594
Hallandale, FL 33009 • 36,517
Hallettsville, TX 77964 • 2,865
Hallie, WI 54729 • 1,200
Hallock, MN 56728 • 1,405
Hallowell, ME 04347 • 2,502
Halls, TN 38040 • 2,444
Halls Crossroads, TN 37918 • 1,600
Hallstead, PA 18822 • 1,280
Hallsville, MO 65255 • 624
Hallsville, TX 75650 • 1,556
Halsey, OR 97348 • 693
Halstad, MN 56548 • 690
Halstead, KS 67056 • 1,994
Haltom City, TX 76117 • 29,014
Hamblen □, TN • 49,300
Hamburg, AR 71646 • 3,394
Hamburg, IA 51640 • 1,597
Hamburg, NJ 07419 • 1,832
Hamburg, NY 14075 • 10,582
Hamburg, PA 19526 • 4,011
Hamden, CT 06514 • 51,071
Hamden, OH 45634 • 1,010
Hamel, MN 55340 • 2,623
Hamersville, OH 45130 • 688
Hamilton, AL 35570 • 5,093
Hamilton, IL 62341 • 3,509
Hamilton, MA 01936 • 1,000
Hamilton, MI 49419 • 800
Hamilton, MO 64644 • 1,582
Hamilton, MT 59840 • 2,661
Hamilton, NC 27840 • 638
Hamilton, NY 13346 • 3,725
Hamilton, OH 45011–26 • 63,189
Hamilton, TX 76531 • 3,189
Hamilton □, FL • 8,761
Hamilton □, IL • 9,172
Hamilton □, IN • 82,027
Hamilton □, IA • 17,862
Hamilton □, KS • 2,514
Hamilton □, NE • 9,301
Hamilton □, NY • 5,034
Hamilton □, OH • 873,224
Hamilton □, TN • 287,740
Hamilton □, TX • 8,297
Hamilton City, CA 95951 • 800
Hamilton Square, NJ 08690 • 10,000
Ham Lake, MN 55303 • 7,832
Hamler, OH 43524 • 625
Hamlet, IN 46532 • 738
Hamlet, NC 28345 • 4,720
Hamlin, TX 79520 • 3,248
Hamlin, WV 25523 • 1,219
Hamlin □, SD • 5,261
Hammon, OK 73650 • 866
Hammond, IN 46320–27 • 93,714
Hammond, LA 70401–03 • 15,043
Hammond, WI 54015 • 991
Hammondsport, NY 14840 • 1,065
Hammonton, NJ 08037 • 12,298
Hampden, ME 04444 • 2,300
Hampden, MA 01036 • 700
Hampden □, MA • 443,018
Hampden Highlands, ME 04444 • 1,540
Hampshire, IL 60140 • 1,735
Hampshire □, MA • 138,813
Hampshire □, WV • 14,867
Hampstead, MD 21074 • 1,293
Hampstead, NC 28443 • 700
Hampton, AR 71744 • 1,627
Hampton, GA 30228 • 2,059
Hampton, IA 50441 • 4,630
Hampton, NH 03842 • 6,779
Hampton, NJ 08827 • 1,614
Hampton, SC 29924 • 3,143
Hampton, TN 37658 • 2,236
Hampton, VA 23660–70 • 122,617
Hampton □, SC • 18,159
Hampton Bays, NY 11946 • 3,550
Hampton Beach, NH 03842 • 900
Hamtramck, MI 48212 • 21,300
Hana, HI 96713 • 643
Hanahan, SC 29410 • 13,224
Hanamaulu, HI 96715 • 3,227
Hanapepe, HI 96716 • 1,417
Hanceville, AL 35077 • 2,220
Hancock, MD 21750 • 1,887
Hancock, MI 49930 • 5,122
Hancock, MN 56244 • 877
Hancock, NY 13783 • 1,526
Hancock □, GA • 9,466
Hancock □, IL • 23,877
Hancock □, IN • 43,939
Hancock □, IA • 13,833
Hancock □, KY • 7,742
Hancock □, ME • 41,781
Hancock □, MS • 24,537
Hancock □, OH • 64,581
Hancock □, TN • 6,887
Hancock □, WV • 41,053
Hand □, SD • 4,948
Handley, WV 25102 • 633
Hanford, CA 93230 • 20,958
Hankinson, ND 58041 • 1,158
Hanna, WY 82327 • 2,288
Hanna City, IL 61536 • 1,361
Hannibal, MO 63401 • 18,811
Hannibal, NY 13074 • 680
Hannibal, OH 43931 • 650
Hanover, IL 61041 • 1,069
Hanover, IN 47243 • 4,054
Hanover, KS 66945 • 802
Hanover, MA 02339 • 2,500
Hanover, MN 55341 • 647
Hanover, NH 03755 • 6,861
Hanover Township, NJ • 11,846
Hanover, OH 43055 • 926
Hanover, PA 17331 • 14,890
Hanover □, VA • 50,398
Hanover Center, MA 02339 • 1,000
Hanover Park, IL 60103 • 28,850
Hansen, ID 83334 • 1,078
Hansford □, TX • 6,209
Hanson, MA 02341 • 2,120
Hanson □, SD • 3,415
Hapeville, GA 30354 • 6,166
Happy, TX 79042 • 674
Happy Camp, CA 96039 • 1,110
Happy Valley, NM 88220 • 630
Happy Valley, OR 97236 • 1,499
Harahan, LA 70123 • 11,384
Haralson □, GA • 18,422
Harbor, OR 97415 • 2,856
Harbor Beach, MI 48441 • 2,000
Harborcreek, PA 16421 • 800
Harbor Springs, MI 49740 • 1,567
Hardee □, FL • 19,379
Hardeeville, SC 29927 • 1,250
Hardeman □, TN • 23,873
Hardeman □, TX • 6,368
Hardin, IL 62047 • 1,107
Hardin, MO 64035 • 688
Hardin, MT 59034 • 3,300
Hardin □, IL • 5,383
Hardin □, IA • 21,776
Hardin □, KY • 88,917
Hardin □, OH • 32,719
Hardin □, TN • 22,280
Hardin □, TX • 40,721
Harding, MA 02052 • 950
Harding □, NM • 1,090
Harding □, SD • 1,700
Hardinsburg, KY 40143 • 2,211
Hardwick, GA 31034 • 6,000
Hardwick, VT 05843 • 1,476
Hardy, AR 72542 • 643
Hardy □, WV • 10,030
Harford □, MD • 145,930
Hargill, TX 78549 • 800
Harker Heights, TX 76543 • 7,345
Harkers Island, NC 28531 • 1,901
Harlan, IN 46743 • 1,000
Harlan, IA 51537 • 5,357
Harlan, KY 40831 • 3,024
Harlan □, KY • 41,889
Harlan □, NE • 4,292
Harlem, FL 33440 • 2,669
Harlem, GA 30814 • 1,485
Harlem, MT 59526 • 1,023
Harleyville, SC 29448 • 606
Harlingen, TX 78550–52 • 43,543
Harlowton, MT 59036 • 1,181
Harmon □, OK • 4,519
Harmony, IN 47853 • 613
Harmony, MN 55939 • 1,133
Harmony, PA 16037 • 1,334
Harmony, RI 02829 • 800
Harmony Hills, DE 19711 • 1,350
Harnett □, NC • 59,570
Harney □, OR • 8,314
Harper, KS 67058 • 1,823
Harper □, KS • 7,778
Harper □, OK • 4,715
Harpersville, AL 35078 • 934
Harper Woods, MI 48225 • 16,361
Harrah, OK 73045 • 2,897
Harriman, TN 37748 • 8,303
Harrington, DE 19952 • 2,405
Harrington Park, NJ 07640 • 4,532
Harris, MN 55032 • 678
Harris, RI 02816 • 1,000
Harris □, GA • 15,464
Harris □, TX • 2,409,547
Harrisburg, AR 72432 • 1,921
Harrisburg, IL 62946 • 10,410
Harrisburg, OR 97446 • 1,881
Harrisburg, PA 17101–99 • 53,264
Harrison, AR 72601 • 9,567
Harrison, MI 48625 • 1,700
Harrison, NJ 07029 • 12,242
Harrison, NY 10528 • 23,046
Harrison, OH 45030 • 5,855
Harrison, TN 37341 • 6,206
Harrison □, IN • 27,276
Harrison □, IA • 16,348
Harrison □, KY • 15,166
Harrison □, MS • 157,665
Harrison □, MO • 9,890
Harrison □, OH • 18,152
Harrison □, TX • 52,265
Harrison □, WV • 77,710
Harrisonburg, LA 71340 • 610
Harrisonburg, VA 22801 • 19,671
Harrisonville, MO 64701 • 6,372
Harristown, IL 62537 • 1,456
Harrisville, NY 13648 • 937
Harrisville, PA 16038 • 1,033
Harrisville, RI 02830 • 1,224
Harrisville, UT 84404 • 1,371
Harrisville, WV 26362 • 1,673
Harrodsburg, KY 40330 • 7,265
Hart, MI 49420 • 1,888
Hart, TX 79043 • 1,008
Hart □, GA • 18,585
Hart □, KY • 15,402
Hartford, AL 36344 • 2,647
Hartford, AR 72938 • 613
Hartford, CT 06101–99 • 136,392
Hartford, IL 62048 • 1,887
Hartford, IA 50118 • 761
Hartford, KY 42347 • 2,512
Hartford, MI 49057 • 2,493
Hartford, SD 57033 • 1,207
Hartford, WI 53027 • 7,046
Hartford □, CT • 807,766
Hartford City, IN 47348 • 7,622
Hartington, NE 68739 • 1,730
Hartland, ME 04943 • 1,041
Hartland, WI 53029 • 5,559
Hartley, IA 51346 • 1,700
Hartley □, TX • 3,987
Hartsdale, NY 10530 • 12,226
Hartselle, AL 35640 • 8,858
Hartshorne, OK 74547 • 2,380
Hartsville, SC 29550 • 7,631
Hartsville, TN 37074 • 2,674
Hartville, OH 44632 • 1,772
Hartwell, GA 30643 • 4,855
Harvard, IL 60033 • 5,126
Harvard, MA 01451 • 900
Harvard, NE 68944 • 1,217
Harvey, IL 60426 • 35,810
Harvey, LA 70058 • 15,000
Harvey, MI 49855 • 1,341
Harvey, ND 58341 • 2,527
Harvey □, KS • 30,531
Harwich, MA 02645 • 1,000
Harwich Port, MA 02646 • 1,900
Harwinton, CT 06791 • 3,293
Harwood, MA 01460 • 900
Harwood Heights, IL 60656 • 8,228
Hasbrouck Heights, NJ 07604 • 12,166
Haskell, AR 72015 • 1,074
Haskell, OK 74436 • 1,953
Haskell, TX 79521 • 3,782
Haskell □, KS • 3,814
Haskell □, OK • 11,010
Haskell □, TX • 7,725
Haslett, MI 48840 • 7,025
Hastings, FL 32045 • 636
Hastings, MI 49058 • 6,418
Hastings, MN 55033 • 12,827
Hastings, NE 68901 • 23,045
Hastings, PA 16646 • 1,574
Hastings-On-Hudson, NY 10706 • 8,573
Hatboro, PA 19040 • 7,579
Hatch, NM 87937 • 1,028
Hatfield, MA 01038 • 1,251
Hatfield, PA 19440 • 2,533
Hatteras, NC 27943 • 700
Hattiesburg, MS 39401–02 • 40,829
Hatton, ND 58240 • 787
Haubstadt, IN 47639 • 1,389
Haughton, LA 71037 • 1,510
Hauppauge, NY 11788 • 14,200
Hauser, OR 97459 • 630
Hauula, HI 96717 • 2,997
Havana, FL 32333 • 2,782
Havana, IL 62644 • 4,277
Havelock, NC 28532 • 17,718
Haven, KS 67543 • 1,125
Haverford Township, PA 19041 • 5,800
Haverhill, MA 01830 • 46,865
Haverstraw, NY 10927 • 8,800
Havertown, PA 19083 • 36,000
Haviland, KS 67059 • 770
Havre, MT 59501 • 10,891
Havre de Grace, MD 21078 • 8,763
Havre North, MT 59501 • 1,073
Hawaii □, HI • 92,053
Hawaiian Gardens, CA 90716 • 10,548
Hawarden, IA 51023 • 2,722
Hawesville, KY 42348 • 1,036
Hawi, HI 96719 • 795
Hawkins □, TN • 43,751
Hawkinsville, GA 31036 • 4,372
Hawk Run, PA 16840 • 750
Hawley, MN 56549 • 1,634
Hawley, PA 18428 • 1,181
Hawley, TX 79525 • 679
Haworth, NJ 07641 • 3,509
Haw River, NC 27258 • 1,858
Hawthorne, CA 90250 • 56,447
Hawthorne, FL 32640 • 1,303
Hawthorne, NV 89415 • 3,741
Hawthorne, NJ 07506 • 18,200
Hawthorne, NY 10532 • 4,900
Haxtun, CO 80731 • 1,014
Hayden, AZ 85235 • 1,205
Hayden, CO 81639 • 1,720
Hayden, ID 83835 • 2,586
Haydenville, MA 01039 • 900
Hayes, LA 70646 • 830
Hayes □, NE • 1,356
Hayesville, OR 97303 • 9,213
Hayfield, MN 55940 • 1,243
Hayfield, VA 22310 • 2,200
Hayfork, CA 96041 • 1,788
Haynesville, LA 71038 • 3,454
Hays, KS 67601 • 16,301
Hays, NC 28635 • 900
Hays □, TX • 40,594
Hay Springs, NE 69347 • 794
Haysville, KS 67060 • 8,006
Hayti, MO 63851 • 3,964
Hayti Heights, MO 63851 • 1,023
Hayward, CA 94540–46 • 94,342
Hayward, WI 54843 • 1,698
Hayward Addition, SD 57106 • 725
Haywood □, NC • 46,495
Haywood □, TN • 20,318
Hazard, KY 41701 • 5,371
Hazardville, CT 06082 • 5,436
Hazel Crest, IL 60429 • 13,973
Hazel Dell, WA 98665 • 6,000
Hazel Green, AL 35750 • 1,503
Hazel Green, WI 53811 • 1,282
Hazel Park, MI 48030 • 20,914
Hazelwood, MO 63042–45 • 12,935
Hazelwood, NC 28738 • 1,811
Hazen, AR 72064 • 1,636
Hazen, ND 58545 • 2,365
Hazlehurst, GA 31539 • 4,249
Hazlehurst, MS 39083 • 4,437
Hazlet, NJ 07730 • 28,013
Hazleton, IA 50641 • 877
Hazleton, PA 18201 • 27,318
Headland, AL 36345 • 3,327
Healdsburg, CA 95448 • 7,217
Healdton, OK 73438 • 3,769
Heard □, GA • 6,520
Hearne, TX 77859 • 5,418
Heath, OH 43056 • 6,969
Heath Springs, SC 29058 • 979
Hebbronville, TX 78361 • 4,079
Heber City, UT 84032 • 4,362
Heber Springs, AR 72543 • 4,589
Hebron, IL 60034 • 786
Hebron, IN 46341 • 2,696
Hebron, MD 21830 • 714
Hebron, NE 68370 • 1,906
Hebron, ND 58638 • 1,078
Hebron, OH 43025 • 2,035
Hector, MN 55342 • 1,252
Hedges, FL 32097 • 900
Hedrick, IA 52563 • 847
Heflin, AL 36264 • 3,014
Hegins, PA 17938 • 900
Heidelberg, MS 39439 • 1,098
Heilwood, PA 15745 • 700
Helena, AL 35080 • 2,130
Helena, AR 72342 • 9,598
Helena, GA 31037 • 1,390
Helena, MT 59601 • 23,938
Helena, OK 73741 • 710
Hellam, PA 17406 • 1,428
Hellertown, PA 18055 • 6,025
Helmetta, NJ 08828 • 955
Helotes, TX 78023 • 1,409
Helper, UT 84526 • 2,724
Hemet, CA 92343–44 • 22,454
Hemingford, NE 69348 • 1,023
Hemingway, SC 29554 • 853
Hemlock, MI 48626 • 1,362
Hemphill, TX 75948 • 1,353
Hemphill □, TX • 5,304
Hempstead, NY 11550–54 • 40,404
Hempstead, TX 77445 • 3,456
Hempstead □, AR • 23,635
Henagar, AL 35978 • 1,188
Henderson, KY 42420 • 24,834
Henderson, LA 70517 • 1,560
Henderson, MN 56044 • 739
Henderson, NE 68371 • 1,072
Henderson, NV 89015 • 24,363
Henderson, NC 27536 • 13,522
Henderson, TN 38340 • 4,449
Henderson, TX 75652 • 11,473
Henderson, WV 25106 • 604
Henderson □, IL • 9,114
Henderson □, KY • 40,849
Henderson □, NC • 58,580
Henderson □, TN • 21,390
Henderson □, TX • 42,606
Henderson's Point, MS 39571 • 1,114
Hendersonville, NC 28739 • 6,862
Hendersonville, TN 37075 • 26,561
Hendricks, MN 56136 • 737
Hendricks □, IN • 69,804
Hendry □, FL • 18,599
Henlawson, WV 25624 • 950
Hennepin, IL 61327 • 716
Hennepin □, MN • 941,411
Hennessey, OK 73742 • 2,287
Henniker, NH 03242 • 1,538
Henning, MN 56551 • 832
Henning, TN 38041 • 638
Henrico □, VA • 180,735
Henrietta, NC 28076 • 1,412
Henrietta, NY 14467 • 1,200
Henrietta, TX 76365 • 3,149
Henry, IL 61537 • 2,740
Henry □, AL • 15,302

# United States Populations and ZIP Codes

Henry □, GA • 36,309
Henry □, IL • 57,968
Henry □, IN • 53,336
Henry □, IA • 18,890
Henry □, KY • 12,740
Henry □, MO • 19,672
Henry □, OH • 28,383
Henry □, TN • 28,656
Henry □, VA • 57,654
Henryetta, OK 74437 • 6,432
Henryville, IN 47126 • 1,132
Hephzibah, GA 30815 • 1,452
Heppner, OR 97836 • 1,498
Herculaneum, MO 63048 • 2,293
Hercules, CA 94547 • 5,963
Hereford, TX 79045 • 15,853
Herington, KS 67449 • 2,930
Heritage Village, CT 06488 • 5,200
Herkimer, NY 13350 • 8,383
Herkimer □, NY • 66,714
Hermann, MO 65041 • 2,695
Hermansville, MI 49847 • 700
Hermantown, MN 55811 • 6,759
Herminie, PA 15637 • 1,100
Hermiston, OR 97838 • 9,408
Hermitage, PA 16148 • 16,365
Hermosa Beach, CA 90254 • 18,070
Hernando, FL 32642 • 1,653
Hernando, MS 38632 • 2,969
Hernando □, FL • 44,469
Herndon, VA 22070–71 • 11,449
Heron Lake, MN 56137 • 783
Herrin, IL 62948 • 10,708
Herscher, IL 60941 • 1,214
Hershey, NE 69143 • 633
Hershey, PA 17033 • 9,000
Hertford, NC 27944 • 1,941
Hertford □, NC • 23,368
Hesperia, CA 92345 • 13,540
Hesperia, MI 49421 • 876
Hessmer, LA 71341 • 743
Hesston, KS 67062 • 3,013
Hettinger, ND 58639 • 1,739
Hettinger □, ND • 4,275
Heuvelton, NY 13654 • 777
Hewitt, TX 76643 • 5,247
Hewlett, NY 11557 • 6,880
Heyburn, ID 83336 • 2,889
Heyworth, IL 61745 • 1,598
Hialeah, FL 33010–16 • 145,254
Hiawatha, IA 52233 • 4,825
Hiawatha, KS 66434 • 3,702
Hibbing, MN 55746 • 21,193
Hickman, KY 42050 • 2,894
Hickman, NE 68372 • 687
Hickman □, KY • 6,065
Hickman □, TN • 15,151
Hickory, MS 39332 • 670
Hickory, NC 28601 • 20,757
Hickory □, MO • 6,367
Hickory Hills, IL 60457 • 13,778
Hicksville, NY 11801–99 • 43,245
Hicksville, OH 43526 • 3,929
Hico, TX 76457 • 1,375
Hico, WV 25854 • 700
Hidalgo, TX 78557 • 2,288
Hidalgo □, NM • 6,049
Hidalgo □, TX • 283,323
Hiddenite, NC 28636 • 800
Higbee, MO 65257 • 817
Higganum, CT 06441 • 1,660
Higgins, TX 79046 • 702
Higginsville, MO 64037 • 4,595
High Bridge, NJ 08829 • 3,435
Highland, CA 92346 • 10,400
Highland, IL 62249 • 7,122
Highland, IN 46322 • 25,935
Highland, KS 66035 • 954
Highland, MI 48031 • 1,000
Highland, NY 12528 • 2,184
Highland, WI 53543 • 860
Highland □, OH • 33,477
Highland □, VA • 2,937
Highland Falls, NY 10928 • 4,187
Highland Heights, OH 44124 • 5,739
Highland Lakes, NJ 07422 • 2,888
Highland Park, IL 60035 • 30,611
Highland Park, MI 48203 • 27,909
Highland Park, NJ 08904 • 13,396
Highland Park, TX 75205 • 8,909
Highlands, NJ 07732 • 5,187
Highlands, NC 28741 • 653
Highlands, TX 77562 • 4,450
Highlands □, FL • 47,526
Highland Springs, VA 23075 • 7,500
Highmore, SD 57345 • 1,055
High Point, NC 27260–64 • 63,808
High Ridge, MO 63049 • 900
High Rolls Mountain Park, NM 88325 • 650
High Spire, PA 17034 • 2,959
High Springs, FL 32643 • 2,491
Hightstown, NJ 08520 • 4,581
Highview, KY 40228 • 13,286
Highwood, IL 60040 • 5,452
Hilbert, WI 54129 • 1,176
Hildale, UT 86021 • 1,009
Hill □, MT • 17,985
Hill □, TX • 25,024
Hill City, KS 67642 • 2,028
Hillcrest, IL 61068 • 818
Hillcrest, NY 10977 • 5,357
Hillcrest Center, CA 93306 • 30,000
Hillcrest Heights, MD 20748 • 17,021
Hilliard, FL 32046 • 1,869
Hilliard, OH 43026 • 8,008
Hillsboro, IL 62049 • 4,408
Hillsboro, KS 67063 • 2,717
Hillsboro, MO 63050 • 1,508
Hillsboro, NH 03244 • 1,797
Hillsboro, ND 58045 • 1,600
Hillsboro, OH 45133 • 6,356
Hillsboro, OR 97123–24 • 27,664
Hillsboro, TX 76645 • 7,397
Hillsboro, WI 54634 • 1,263
Hillsborough, CA 94010 • 10,372
Hillsborough, NC 27278 • 3,019
Hillsborough □, FL • 646,960
Hillsborough □, NH • 276,608
Hillsdale, IL 61257 • 731
Hillsdale, MI 49242 • 7,432
Hillsdale, NJ 07642 • 10,495
Hillsdale □, MI • 42,071
Hillside, IL 60162 • 8,279
Hillside, NJ 07205 • 21,440
Hillside Heights, DE 19711 • 800
Hillsville, PA 16132 • 915
Hillsville, VA 24343 • 2,123
Hillview, KY 40229 • 5,196
Hilo, HI 96720 • 35,269
Hilton, NY 14468 • 4,151
Hilton Head Island, SC 29928 • 11,344
Hima, KY 40951 • 700
Hinckley, IL 60520 • 1,447
Hinckley, MN 55037 • 963
Hindman, KY 41822 • 876
Hinds □, MS • 250,998
Hines, OR 97738 • 1,632
Hinesville, GA 31313 • 11,309
Hingham, MA 02043 • 12,800
Hinkley, CA 92347 • 700
Hinsdale, IL 60521 • 16,726
Hinsdale, MA 01235 • 950
Hinsdale, NH 03451 • 1,546
Hinsdale □, CO • 408
Hinton, IA 51024 • 659
Hinton, OK 73047 • 1,432
Hinton, WV 25951 • 4,622
Hiram, GA 30141 • 1,030
Hiram, OH 44234 • 1,360
Hitchcock, TX 77563 • 6,655
Hitchcock □, NE • 4,079
Hitchcock Lake, CT 06716 • 1,600
Hitchins, KY 41146 • 700
Hoagland, IN 46745 • 650
Hobart, IN 46342 • 22,987
Hobart, OK 73651 • 4,735
Hobbs, NM 88240 • 29,153
Hobe Sound, FL 33455 • 6,822
Hoboken, NJ 07030 • 42,460
Hockessin, DE 19707 • 950
Hocking □, OH • 24,304
Hockley □, TX • 23,230
Hodge, LA 71247 • 708
Hodgeman □, KS • 2,269
Hodgenville, KY 42748 • 2,531
Hoffman, MN 56339 • 631
Hoffman Estates, IL 60195 • 37,272
Hogansville, GA 30230 • 3,362
Hohenwald, TN 38462 • 3,922
Ho-Ho-Kus, NJ 07423 • 4,129
Hoisington, KS 67544 • 3,678
Hokah, MN 55941 • 686
Hoke □, NC • 20,383
Hokes Bluff, AL 35903 • 3,216
Holbrook, AZ 86025 • 5,785
Holbrook, MA 02343 • 11,140
Holbrook, NY 11741 • 12,800
Holcomb, KS 67851 • 816
Holcomb, MO 63852 • 632
Holden, MA 01520 • 3,900
Holden, MO 64040 • 2,195
Holden, WV 25625 • 1,600
Holden Heights, FL 32805 • 8,000
Holdenville, OK 74848 • 5,469
Holdingford, MN 56340 • 635
Holdrege, NE 68949 • 5,624
Holgate, OH 43527 • 1,315
Holiday, FL 34690 • 15,400
Holladay, UT 84117 • 22,189
Holland, IN 47541 • 683
Holland, MI 49423 • 26,281
Holland, NY 14080 • 1,000
Holland, OH 43528 • 1,048
Holland, TX 76534 • 863
Hollandale, MS 38748 • 4,336
Holley, NY 14470 • 1,882
Holliday, TX 76366 • 1,349
Hollidaysburg, PA 16648 • 5,892
Hollins, VA 24019 • 11,000
Hollis, OK 73550 • 2,958
Hollister, CA 95023 • 11,488
Hollister, MO 65672 • 1,439
Holliston, MA 01746 • 12,622
Holloway Terrace, DE 19720 • 1,000
Hollow Rock, TN 38342 • 955
Hollsopple, PA 15935 • 900
Holly, CO 81047 • 969
Holly, MI 48442 • 4,874
Holly Grove, AR 72069 • 754
Holly Hill, FL 32017 • 9,953
Holly Hill, SC 29059 • 1,785
Holly Springs, GA 30142 • 687
Holly Springs, MS 38635 • 7,285
Holly Springs, NC 27540 • 688
Hollywood, AL 35752 • 1,110
Hollywood, FL 33020–29 • 121,323
Hollywood, SC 29449 • 729
Holmdel, NJ 07733 • 800
Holmen, WI 54636 • 2,411
Holmes □, FL • 14,723
Holmes □, MS • 22,970
Holmes □, OH • 29,416
Holstein, IA 51025 • 1,477
Holt, AL 35404 • 4,300
Holt, FL 32564 • 780
Holt, MI 48842 • 10,097
Holt □, MO • 6,882
Holt □, NE • 13,552
Holton, KS 66436 • 3,132
Holtville, CA 92250 • 4,399
Holualoa, HI 96725 • 1,243
Holyoke, CO 80734 • 2,092
Holyoke, MA 01040 • 44,678
Homecroft, IN 46227 • 831
Homedale, ID 83628 • 2,078
Home Gardens, CA 91720 • 5,783
Homeland, GA 31537 • 683
Home Place, IN 46240 • 2,000
Homer, AK 99603 • 2,209
Homer, GA 30547 • 734
Homer, IL 61849 • 1,279
Homer, LA 71040 • 4,307
Homer, MI 49245 • 1,791
Homer, NY 13077 • 3,635
Homer City, PA 15748 • 2,248
Homerville, GA 31634 • 3,112
Homestead, FL 33030–35 • 20,668
Homestead, PA 15120 • 5,092
Hometown, IL 60456 • 5,324
Homewood, AL 35209 • 21,412
Homewood, IL 60430 • 19,724
Homewood, OH 45015 • 2,550
Hominy, OK 74035 • 3,130
Homosassa, FL 32646 • 1,426
Honaker, VA 24260 • 1,475
Hondo, TX 78861 • 6,057
Honea Path, SC 29654 • 4,114
Honeoye Falls, NY 14472 • 2,410
Honesdale, PA 18431 • 5,128
Honey Brook, PA 19344 • 1,164
Honey Grove, TX 75446 • 1,973
Honeypot Glen, CT 06410 • 900
Honeyville, UT 84314 • 915
Honokaa, HI 96727 • 1,936
Honolulu, HI 96801–99 • 365,048
Honolulu □, HI • 762,565
Hood □, TX • 17,714
Hood River, OR 97031 • 4,329
Hood River □, OR • 15,835
Hoodsport, WA 98548 • 900
Hooker, OK 73945 • 1,788
Hooker □, NE • 990
Hooksett, NH 03106 • 1,868
Hoonah, AK 99829 • 680
Hooper, NE 68031 • 932
Hooper Bay, AK 99604 • 627
Hoopeston, IL 60942 • 6,411
Hoosick Falls, NY 12090 • 3,609
Hoover, AL 35216 • 19,792
Hooverson Heights, WV 26037 • 1,500
Hooversville, PA 15936 • 863
Hopatcong, NJ 07843 • 15,531
Hope, AR 71801 • 10,290
Hope, IN 47246 • 2,185
Hopedale, IL 61747 • 913
Hopedale, MA 01747 • 3,905
Hopedale, OH 43976 • 857
Hopelawn, NJ 08861 • 12,600
Hope Mills, NC 28348 • 5,412
Hope Valley, RI 02832 • 1,414
Hopewell, NJ 08525 • 2,001
Hopewell, VA 23860 • 23,397
Hopewell Junction, NY 12533 • 2,055
Hopkins, MN 55343–45 • 15,336
Hopkins, MO 64461 • 634
Hopkins, SC 29061 • 1,600
Hopkins □, KY • 46,174
Hopkins □, TX • 25,247
Hopkinsville, KY 42240 • 27,318
Hopkinton, IA 52237 • 774
Hopkinton, MA 01748 • 2,542
Hopland, CA 95449 • 900
Hopwood, PA 15445 • 2,190
Hoquiam, WA 98550 • 9,719
Horatio, AR 71842 • 989
Horicon, WI 53032 • 3,584
Horine, MO 63070 • 850
Hornell, NY 14843 • 10,234
Hornersville, MO 63855 • 704
Horn Lake, MS 38637 • 4,326
Horry □, SC • 101,419
Horse Cave, KY 42749 • 2,045
Horseheads, NY 14845 • 7,348
Horseshoe Bend, ID 83629 • 700
Horsham, PA 19044 • 6,000
Horton, KS 66439 • 2,130
Hortonville, WI 54944 • 2,016
Hosford, FL 32334 • 700
Hospers, IA 51238 • 655
Hotchkiss, CO 81419 • 849
Hotevilla, AZ 86030 • 700
Hot Spring □, AR • 26,819
Hot Springs, MT 59845 • 601
Hot Springs see Truth or Consequences, NM • 5,219
Hot Springs, NC 28743 • 678
Hot Springs, SD 57747 • 4,742
Hot Springs □, WY • 5,710
Hot Springs National Park, AR 71901–13 • 35,781
Houghton, MI 49931 • 7,512
Houghton, NY 14744 • 1,620
Houghton □, MI • 37,872
Houghton Lake, MI 48629 • 1,500
Houghton Lake Heights, MI 48630 • 2,449
Houlka, MS 38850 • 710
Houlton, ME 04730 • 5,730
Houma, LA 70360–64 • 32,602
Housatonic, MA 01236 • 1,314
Houston, MN 55943 • 1,057
Houston, MS 38851 • 3,747
Houston, MO 65483 • 2,157
Houston, PA 15342 • 1,568
Houston, TX 77001–99 • 1,595,138
Houston □, AL • 74,632
Houston □, GA • 77,605
Houston □, MN • 18,382
Houston □, TN • 6,871
Houston □, TX • 22,299
Houtzdale, PA 16651 • 1,222
Hoven, SD 57450 • 615
Howard, KS 67349 • 965
Howard, PA 16841 • 838
Howard, SD 57349 • 1,169
Howard, WI 54303 • 8,240
Howard □, AR • 13,459
Howard □, IN • 86,896
Howard □, IA • 11,114
Howard □, MD • 118,572
Howard □, MO • 10,008
Howard □, NE • 6,773
Howard □, TX • 33,142
Howard City, MI 49329 • 1,118
Howard Lake, MN 55349 • 1,240
Howards Grove-Millersville, WI 53081 • 1,838
Howell, MI 48843 • 6,976
Howell □, MO • 28,807
Howells, NE 68641 • 677
Howland, ME 04448 • 1,602
Hoxie, AR 72433 • 2,961
Hoxie, KS 67740 • 1,462
Hoyt Lakes, MN 55750 • 3,186
Huachuca City, AZ 85616 • 1,661
Hubbard, IA 50122 • 852
Hubbard, OH 44425 • 9,245
Hubbard, OR 97032 • 1,640
Hubbard, TX 76648 • 1,676
Hubbard □, MN • 14,098
Hubbell, MI 49934 • 1,278
Huber Heights, OH 45424 • 35,480
Huber South, OH 45439 • 4,800
Huckleberry Hill, CT 06001 • 700
Hudson, CO 80642 • 698
Hudson, FL 34667 • 5,799
Hudson, IL 61748 • 929
Hudson, IA 50643 • 2,267
Hudson, MA 01749 • 9,714
Hudson, MI 49247 • 2,545
Hudson, NH 03051 • 6,248
Hudson, NC 28638 • 2,888
Hudson, NY 12534 • 7,986
Hudson, OH 44236 • 4,615
Hudson, WI 54016 • 5,434
Hudson □, NJ • 556,972
Hudson Falls, NY 12839 • 7,419
Hudson Lake, IN 46552 • 1,347
Hudsonville, MI 49426 • 4,844
Hudspeth □, TX • 2,728
Huerfano □, CO • 6,440
Hueytown, AL 35023 • 13,478
Hughes, AR 72348 • 1,919
Hughes □, OK • 14,338
Hughes □, SD • 14,220
Hughesville, MD 20637 • 1,208
Hughesville, PA 17737 • 2,174
Hugo, CO 80821 • 776
Hugo, MN 55038 • 3,771
Hugo, OK 74743 • 7,172
Hugoton, KS 67951 • 3,165
Huguley, AL 36854 • 2,947
Hulbert, OK 74441 • 633
Hull, IA 51239 • 1,714
Hull, MA 02045 • 9,714
Humansville, MO 65674 • 907
Humble, TX 77338–39 • 6,729
Humboldt, IA 50548 • 4,794
Humboldt, KS 66748 • 2,230
Humboldt, NE 68376 • 1,176
Humboldt, TN 38343 • 10,209
Humboldt □, CA • 108,514
Humboldt □, IA • 12,246
Humboldt □, NV • 9,434
Humeston, IA 50123 • 671
Hummels Wharf, PA 17831 • 750
Humphrey, AR 72073 • 872
Humphrey, NE 68642 • 799
Humphreys □, MS • 13,931
Humphreys □, TN • 15,957
Hungry Horse, MT 59919 • 900
Hunt □, TX • 55,248
Hunterdon □, NJ • 87,361
Huntertown, IN 46748 • 1,265
Huntingburg, IN 47542 • 5,376
Huntingdon, PA 16652 • 7,042
Huntingdon, TN 38344 • 3,962
Huntingdon □, PA • 42,253
Huntingdon Valley, PA 19006 • 10,400
Huntington, AR 72940 • 662
Huntington, IN 46750 • 16,202
Huntington, MA 01050 • 950
Huntington, NJ 08865 • 700
Huntington, NY 11743 • 12,601
Huntington, TX 75949 • 1,672
Huntington, UT 84528 • 2,316
Huntington, WV 25701–99 • 63,684
Huntington □, IN • 35,596
Huntington Bay, NY 11743 • 1,783
Huntington Beach, CA 92646–49 • 170,505
Huntington Park, CA 90255 • 46,223
Huntington Station, NY 11746 • 30,300
Huntington Woods, MI 48070 • 6,937
Huntland, TN 37345 • 983
Huntley, IL 60142 • 1,646
Huntsville, AL 35801–99 • 142,513
Huntsville, AR 72740 • 1,394
Huntsville, MO 65259 • 1,657
Huntsville, TX 77340 • 23,936
Hurley, NM 88043 • 1,616
Hurley, NY 12443 • 4,081
Hurley, WI 54534 • 2,015
Hurlock, MD 21643 • 1,690
Huron, OH 44839 • 7,123
Huron, SD 57350 • 13,000
Huron □, MI • 36,459
Huron □, OH • 54,608
Hurricane, UT 84737 • 2,361
Hurricane, WV 25526 • 3,751
Hurst, IL 62949 • 938
Hurst, TX 76053–54 • 31,420
Hurt, VA 24563 • 1,481
Hurtsboro, AL 36860 • 752
Hustisford, WI 53034 • 874
Hutchins, TX 75141 • 2,837
Hutchinson, KS 67501–05 • 40,284
Hutchinson, MN 55350 • 9,244
Hutchinson □, SD • 9,350
Hutchinson □, TX • 26,304
Hutsonville, IL 62433 • 705
Huttig, AR 71747 • 976
Hutto, TX 78634 • 659
Huxley, IA 50124 • 1,884
Hyannis, MA 02601 • 8,000
Hyannis Port, MA 02647 • 1,150
Hyattsville, MD 20780–88 • 12,709
Hybla Valley, VA 22306 • 4,350
Hyde, PA 16843 • 1,791
Hyde □, NC • 5,873
Hyde □, SD • 2,069
Hyde Park, NY 12538 • 2,805
Hyde Park, UT 84318 • 1,495
Hydetown, PA 16328 • 760
Hydro, OK 73048 • 938
Hymera, IN 47855 • 1,054
Hyndman, PA 15545 • 1,106
Hyrum, UT 84319 • 3,952

## I

Iaeger, WV 24844 • 833
Iberia, MO 65486 • 852
Iberia □, LA • 63,752
Iberville □, LA • 32,159
Ida, MI 48140 • 1,000
Ida □, IA • 8,908
Ida Grove, IA 51445 • 2,285
Idaho □, ID • 14,769
Idaho Falls, ID 83401–15 • 39,590
Idaho Springs, CO 80452 • 2,077
Idalou, TX 79329 • 2,348
Idaville, IN 47950 • 625
Ideal, GA 31041 • 619
Ider, AL 35981 • 698
Ignacio, CO 81137 • 667
Ilion, NY 13357 • 9,450
Illiopolis, IL 62539 • 1,118
Illmo, MO 63780 • 1,368
Ilwaco, WA 98624 • 604
Imboden, AR 72434 • 661
Imlay City, MI 48444 • 2,495
Immokalee, FL 33934 • 11,038
Imperial, CA 92251 • 3,451
Imperial, MO 63052 • 950
Imperial, NE 69033 • 1,941
Imperial, PA 15126 • 2,385
Imperial, TX 79743 • 750
Imperial □, CA • 92,110
Imperial Beach, CA 92032 • 22,689
Incline Village, NV 89450 • 4,500
Independence, CA 93526 • 1,000
Independence, IA 50644 • 6,392
Independence, KS 67301 • 10,598
Independence, KY 41051 • 7,998
Independence, LA 70443 • 1,684
Independence, MO 64050–58 • 111,806
Independence, OH 44131 • 6,607
Independence, OR 97351 • 4,024
Independence, VA 24348 • 1,112
Independence, WI 54747 • 1,180
Independence □, AR • 30,147
Indiana, PA 15701 • 16,051
Indiana □, PA • 92,281
Indianapolis, IN 46201–99 • 700,807
Indian Harbour Beach, FL 32937 • 5,967
Indian Head, MD 20640 • 1,381
Indian Heights, IN 46901 • 4,277
Indian Hills, CO 80454 • 900
Indian Mound Beach, MA 02532 • 800
Indian Neck, CT 06405 • 2,200
Indianola, IA 50125 • 10,843
Indianola, MS 38751 • 8,221
Indianola, NE 69034 • 856
Indian Ridge Estates, AZ 85715 • 2,300
Indian River □, FL • 59,896
Indian Rocks Beach, FL 34635 • 3,717
Indian Springs, NV 89018 • 900
Indiantown, FL 34956 • 3,383
Indian Trail, NC 28079 • 811
Indio, CA 92201 • 21,611
Inez, TX 77968 • 900
Ingalls, IN 46048 • 909
Ingalls Park, IL 60431 • 3,500
Ingham □, MI • 275,520
Ingleside, TX 78362 • 5,436
Inglewood, CA 90301–99 • 94,245
Ingram, PA 15205 • 4,346
Inkom, ID 83245 • 830
Inkster, MI 48141 • 35,190
Inman, KS 67546 • 947
Inman, SC 29349 • 1,554
Inniswold, LA 70809 • 1,800
Inola, OK 74036 • 1,550
Institute, WV 25112 • 1,500
Intercession City, FL 33848 • 950
Interlachen, FL 32148 • 848
Interlaken, NY 14847 • 685
International Falls, MN 56649 • 5,611
Inver Grove Heights, MN 55075 • 17,171
Inverness, CA 94937 • 1,400
Inverness, FL 32650 • 4,095
Inverness, MS 38753 • 1,034
Inwood, FL 33880 • 6,668
Inwood, IA 51240 • 755
Inwood, NY 11696 • 8,200
Inwood, WV 25428 • 800
Inyo □, CA • 17,895
Inyokern, CA 93527 • 900
Iola, KS 66749 • 6,938
Iola, WI 54945 • 957
Iona, ID 83427 • 1,072
Ione, CA 95640 • 2,207
Ionia, MI 48846 • 5,920
Ionia □, MI • 51,815
Iosco □, MI • 28,349
Iota, LA 70543 • 1,326
Iowa, LA 70647 • 2,437
Iowa □, IA • 15,429
Iowa □, WI • 19,802
Iowa City, IA 52240 • 50,508
Iowa Falls, IA 50126 • 6,174
Iowa Park, TX 76367 • 6,184
Ipava, IL 61441 • 661
Ipswich, MA 01938 • 4,548
Ipswich, SD 57451 • 1,153
Iraan, TX 79744 • 1,358
Iredell □, NC • 82,538
Irion □, TX • 1,386
Irmo, SC 29063 • 3,957
Iron □, MI • 13,635
Iron □, MO • 11,084
Iron □, UT • 17,349
Iron □, WI • 6,730
Irondale, AL 35210 • 6,510
Irondequoit, NY 14617 • 57,648
Iron Gate, VA 24448 • 620
Ironia, NJ 07845 • 900
Iron Mountain, MI 49801 • 8,341
Iron Ridge, WI 53035 • 766
Iron River, MI 49935 • 2,426
Iron River, WI 54847 • 650
Ironton, MO 63650 • 1,743
Ironton, OH 45638 • 14,290
Ironwood, MI 49938 • 7,741
Iroquois □, IL • 32,976
Irrigon, OR 97844 • 700
Irvine, CA 92714 • 62,134
Irvine, KY 40336 • 2,889
Irving, IL 62051 • 612
Irving, TX 75060–63 • 109,943
Irvington, IL 62848 • 789
Irvington, KY 40146 • 1,409
Irvington, NJ 07111 • 61,493
Irvington, NY 10533 • 5,774
Irvona, PA 16656 • 644
Irwin, PA 15642 • 4,995
Irwin □, GA • 8,988
Irwinton, GA 31042 • 841
Isabella, PA 15447 • 700
Isabella □, MI • 54,110
Isanti, MN 55040 • 858

Isanti □, MN • 23,600
Iselin, NJ 08830 • 16,500
Ishpeming, MI 49849 • 7,538
Islamorada, FL 33036 • 1,441
Island □, WA • 44,048
Island Falls, ME 04747 • 650
Island Heights, NJ 08732 • 1,575
Island Park, NY 11558 • 4,847
Island Park, RI 02871 • 1,000
Island Pond, VT 05846 • 1,216
Isla Vista, CA 93117 • 16,700
Isle of Palms, SC 29451 • 3,421
Isle of Wight □, VA • 21,603
Isleta, NM 87022 • 1,246
Isleton, CA 95641 • 914
Islington, MA 02090 • 5,100
Islip, NY 11751 • 12,100
Islip Terrace, NY 11752 • 5,200
Isola, MS 38754 • 834
Issaquah, WA 98027 • 5,536
Issaquena □, MS • 2,513
Italy, TX 76651 • 1,306
Itasca, IL 60143 • 7,129
Itasca, TX 76055 • 1,600
Itasca □, MN • 43,069
Itawamba □, MS • 20,518
Ithaca, MI 48847 • 2,950
Ithaca, NY 14850 • 28,732
Itta Bena, MS 38941 • 2,904
Iuka, MS 38852 • 2,846
Iva, SC 29655 • 1,369
Ivanhoe, MN 56142 • 761
Ivoryton, CT 06442 • 950
Ivywild, CO 80906 • 4,000
Izard □, AR • 10,768

## J

Jacinto City, TX 77029 • 8,953
Jack □, TX • 7,408
Jackman, ME 04945 • 800
Jacksboro, TN 37757 • 1,722
Jacksboro, TX 76056 • 4,000
Jackson, AL 36545 • 6,073
Jackson, CA 95642 • 2,331
Jackson, GA 30233 • 4,133
Jackson, KY 41339 • 2,651
Jackson, LA 70748 • 3,133
Jackson, MI 49201–04 • 39,739
Jackson, MN 56143 • 3,797
Jackson, MS 39201–99 • 202,895
Jackson, MO 63755 • 7,827
Jackson, NC 27845 • 720
Jackson, OH 45640 • 6,675
Jackson, SC 29831 • 1,771
Jackson, TN 38301–05 • 49,131
Jackson, WI 53037 • 1,817
Jackson, WY 83001 • 4,511
Jackson □, AL • 51,407
Jackson □, AR • 21,646
Jackson □, CO • 1,863
Jackson □, FL • 39,154
Jackson □, GA • 25,343
Jackson □, IL • 61,649
Jackson □, IN • 36,523
Jackson □, IA • 22,503
Jackson □, KS • 11,644
Jackson □, KY • 11,996
Jackson □, LA • 17,321
Jackson □, MI • 151,495
Jackson □, MN • 13,690
Jackson □, MS • 118,015
Jackson □, MO • 629,266
Jackson □, NC • 25,811
Jackson □, OH • 30,592
Jackson □, OK • 30,356
Jackson □, OR • 132,456
Jackson □, SD • 3,437
Jackson □, TN • 9,398
Jackson □, TX • 13,352
Jackson □, WV • 25,794
Jackson □, WI • 16,831
Jackson Center, OH 45334 • 1,310
Jacksonville, AL 36265 • 9,735
Jacksonville, AR 72076 • 27,589
Jacksonville, FL 32201–99 • 540,920
Jacksonville, IL 62650 • 20,284
Jacksonville, NC 28540 • 18,237
Jacksonville, OH 45740 • 651
Jacksonville, OR 97530 • 2,030
Jacksonville, TX 75766 • 12,264
Jacksonville Beach, FL 32250 • 15,462
Jaffrey, NH 03452 • 2,684
Jal, NM 88252 • 2,675
Jamesburg, NJ 08831 • 4,114
James City, NC 28560 • 700
James City □, VA • 22,763
James Island, SC 29412 • 24,124
Jamesport, MO 64648 • 651
Jamestown, CA 95327 • 2,206
Jamestown, IN 46147 • 924
Jamestown, KY 42629 • 1,441
Jamestown, NC 27282 • 2,148
Jamestown, ND 58401 • 16,280
Jamestown, NY 14701 • 35,775
Jamestown, OH 45335 • 1,702
Jamestown, PA 16134 • 854
Jamestown, RI 02835 • 4,040
Jamestown, TN 38556 • 2,364
Jamesville, NC 27846 • 604
Jamul, CA 92035 • 1,826
Janesville, CA 96114 • 1,200
Janesville, IA 50647 • 840
Janesville, MN 56048 • 1,897
Janesville, WI 53545–47 • 51,071
Jarratt, VA 23867 • 614
Jarrettsville, MD 21084 • 1,485
Jasmine Estates, FL 34668 • 3,500
Jasonville, IN 47438 • 2,497
Jasper, AL 35501 • 11,894
Jasper, FL 32052 • 2,093
Jasper, GA 30143 • 1,556
Jasper, IN 47546 • 9,097
Jasper, MN 56144 • 731
Jasper, MO 64755 • 1,012
Jasper, TN 37347 • 2,633
Jasper, TX 75951 • 6,959
Jasper □, GA • 7,553
Jasper □, IL • 11,318
Jasper □, IN • 26,138
Jasper □, IA • 36,425
Jasper □, MS • 17,265
Jasper □, MO • 86,958
Jasper □, SC • 14,504
Jasper □, TX • 30,781
Jay, FL 32565 • 633
Jay, OK 74346 • 2,100
Jay □, IN • 23,239
Jayton, TX 79528 • 638
Jeanerette, LA 70544 • 6,511
Jeannette, PA 15644 • 13,106
Jeff Davis □, GA • 11,473
Jeff Davis □, TX • 1,647
Jefferson, GA 30549 • 1,820
Jefferson, IA 50129 • 4,854
Jefferson, LA 70121 • 15,550
Jefferson, MA 01522 • 800
Jefferson, NC 28640 • 1,086
Jefferson, OH 44047 • 2,952
Jefferson, OR 97352 • 1,702
Jefferson, PA 15025 • 8,643
Jefferson, SC 29718 • 651
Jefferson, TX 75657 • 2,643
Jefferson, WI 53549 • 5,647
Jefferson □, AL • 671,324
Jefferson □, AR • 90,718
Jefferson □, CO • 371,753
Jefferson □, FL • 10,703
Jefferson □, GA • 18,403
Jefferson □, ID • 15,304
Jefferson □, IL • 36,558
Jefferson □, IN • 30,419
Jefferson □, IA • 16,316
Jefferson □, KS • 15,207
Jefferson □, KY • 684,565
Jefferson □, LA • 454,592
Jefferson □, MS • 9,181
Jefferson □, MO • 146,183
Jefferson □, MT • 7,029
Jefferson □, NE • 9,817
Jefferson □, NY • 88,151
Jefferson □, OH • 91,564
Jefferson □, OK • 8,183
Jefferson □, OR • 11,599
Jefferson □, PA • 48,303
Jefferson □, TN • 31,284
Jefferson □, TX • 250,938
Jefferson □, WA • 15,965
Jefferson □, WV • 30,302
Jefferson □, WI • 66,152
Jefferson City, MO 65101 • 33,619
Jefferson City, TN 37760 • 5,612
Jefferson Davis □, LA • 32,168
Jefferson Davis □, MS • 13,846
Jefferson Farms, DE 19720 • 2,400
Jefferson Manor, VA 22303 • 2,550
Jeffersontown, KY 40299 • 15,795
Jefferson Village, VA 22042 • 2,800
Jeffersonville, GA 31044 • 1,473
Jeffersonville, IN 47130 • 21,220
Jeffersonville, KY 40337 • 1,528
Jeffersonville, OH 43128 • 1,252
Jeffrey, WV 25114 • 900
Jellico, TN 37762 • 2,798
Jemez Pueblo, NM 87024 • 1,503
Jemison, AL 35085 • 1,828
Jena, LA 71342 • 4,375
Jenison, MI 49428 • 16,330
Jenkins, KY 41537 • 3,271
Jenkins □, GA • 8,841
Jenkintown, PA 19046 • 4,942
Jenks, OK 74037 • 5,876
Jenners, PA 15546 • 800
Jennings, FL 32053 • 749
Jennings, LA 70546 • 12,401
Jennings, MO 63136 • 17,026
Jennings □, IN • 22,854
Jennings Lodge, OR 97222 • 3,000
Jensen Beach, FL 34957–58 • 6,639
Jerauld □, SD • 2,929
Jericho, NY 11753 • 14,200
Jericho, VT 05465 • 1,340
Jermyn, PA 18433 • 2,411
Jerome, FL 33926 • 675
Jerome, ID 83338 • 6,891
Jerome, PA 15937 • 1,158
Jerome □, ID • 14,840
Jersey □, IL • 20,538
Jersey City, NJ 07301–99 • 223,532
Jersey Shore, PA 17740 • 4,631
Jerseyville, IL 62052 • 7,506
Jessamine □, KY • 26,065
Jessup, MD 20794 • 4,288
Jessup, PA 18434 • 4,974
Jesup, GA 31545 • 9,418
Jesup, IA 50648 • 2,343
Jetmore, KS 67854 • 862
Jewell, IA 50130 • 1,145
Jewell □, KS • 5,241
Jewett, OH 43986 • 972
Jewett City, CT 06351 • 3,294
Jim Hogg □, TX • 5,168
Jim Thorpe, PA 18229 • 5,263
Jim Wells □, TX • 36,498
Joanna, SC 29351 • 1,839
Jo Daviess □, IL • 23,520
John Day, OR 97845 • 2,012
Johnsburg, IL 60050 • 900
Johnson, KS 67855 • 1,244
Johnson, VT 05656 • 1,393
Johnson □, AR • 17,423
Johnson □, GA • 8,660
Johnson □, IL • 9,624
Johnson □, IN • 77,240
Johnson □, IA • 81,717
Johnson □, KS • 270,269
Johnson □, KY • 24,432
Johnson □, MO • 39,059
Johnson □, NE • 5,285
Johnson □, TN • 13,745
Johnson □, TX • 67,649
Johnson □, WY • 6,700
Johnsonburg, PA 15845 • 3,938
Johnson City, NY 13790 • 17,126
Johnson City, TN 37601–04 • 39,753
Johnson City, TX 78636 • 872
Johnson Creek, WI 53038 • 1,136
Johnsonville, SC 29555 • 1,421
Johnston, IA 50131 • 2,617
Johnston, RI 02919 • 24,907
Johnston, SC 29832 • 2,624
Johnston □, NC • 70,599
Johnston □, OK • 10,356
Johnston City, IL 62951 • 3,873
Johnstown, CO 80534 • 1,535
Johnstown, NY 12095 • 9,360
Johnstown, OH 43031 • 3,158
Johnstown, PA 15901–15 • 35,496
Joiner, AR 72350 • 725
Joliet, IL 60431–36 • 77,956
Jones, OK 73049 • 2,270
Jones □, GA • 16,579
Jones □, IA • 20,401
Jones □, MS • 61,912
Jones □, NC • 9,705
Jones □, SD • 1,463
Jones □, TX • 17,268
Jonesboro, AR 72401 • 31,530
Jonesboro, GA 30236 • 4,132
Jonesboro, IL 62952 • 1,842
Jonesboro, IN 46938 • 2,279
Jonesboro, LA 71251 • 5,061
Jonesboro, TN 37659 • 2,829
Jonesburg, MO 63351 • 614
Jones Creek, TX 77541 • 2,634
Jones Mill, AR 72105 • 850
Jonesport, ME 04649 • 1,050
Jonestown, MS 38639 • 1,231
Jonestown, PA 17038 • 814
Jonesville, LA 71343 • 2,828
Jonesville, MI 49250 • 2,172
Jonesville, NC 28642 • 1,752
Jonesville, SC 29353 • 1,201
Jonesville, VA 24263 • 874
Joplin, MO 64801 • 39,023
Joppa, MD 21085 • 11,348
Jordan, MN 55352 • 2,663
Jordan, NY 13080 • 1,371
Joseph, OR 97846 • 999
Joseph City, AZ 86032 • 900
Josephine □, OR • 58,855
Joshua, TX 76058 • 1,470
Joshua Tree, CA 92252 • 2,083
Jourdanton, TX 78026 • 2,743
Joyce, LA 71440 • 900
Juab □, UT • 5,530
Judith Basin □, MT • 2,646
Judsonia, AR 72081 • 2,025
Julesburg, CO 80737 • 1,528
Julian, CA 92036 • 1,320
Julian, WV 25529 • 700
Junction, TX 76849 • 2,593
Junction City, AR 71749 • 813
Junction City, KS 66441 • 19,305
Junction City, KY 40440 • 2,045
Junction City, LA 71749 • 727
Junction City, OH 43748 • 754
Junction City, OR 97448 • 3,320
Juneau, AK 99801 • 19,528
Juneau, WI 53039 • 2,045
Juneau □, WI • 21,039
June Lake, CA 93529 • 900
Juniata, NE 68955 • 703
Juniata □, PA • 19,188
Juniata Terrace, PA 17044 • 631
Jupiter, FL 33458 • 9,868
Justice, IL 60458 • 10,552
Justin, TX 76247 • 920

## K

Kaaawa, HI 96730 • 959
Kadoka, SD 57543 • 832
Kahaluu, HI 96744 • 2,925
Kahoka, MO 63445 • 2,101
Kahuku, HI 96731 • 935
Kahului, HI 96732 • 12,978
Kailua, HI 96734 • 35,812
Kailua Kona, HI 96740 • 4,751
Kalaheo, HI 96741 • 2,500
Kalama, WA 98625 • 1,216
Kalamazoo, MI 49001–09 • 79,722
Kalamazoo □, MI • 212,378
Kalawao □, HI • 144
Kalispell, MT 59901 • 10,648
Kalkaska, MI 49646 • 1,654
Kalkaska □, MI • 10,952
Kalona, IA 52247 • 1,862
Kamas, UT 84036 • 1,064
Kamiah, ID 83536 • 1,478
Kamuela (Waimea), HI 96743 • 1,179
Kanab, UT 84741 • 2,148
Kanabec □, MN • 12,161
Kanawha, IA 50447 • 756
Kanawha □, WV • 231,414
Kandiyohi □, MN • 36,763
Kane, PA 16735 • 4,916
Kane □, IL • 278,405
Kane □, UT • 4,024
Kaneohe, HI 96744 • 29,919
Kankakee, IL 60901 • 30,141
Kankakee □, IL • 102,926
Kannapolis, NC 28081 • 34,564
Kanopolis, KS 67454 • 729
Kansas, IL 61933 • 791
Kansas City, KS 66101–99 • 161,148
Kansas City, MO 64101–99 • 448,159
Kapaa, HI 96746 • 4,467
Kaplan, LA 70548 • 5,016
Karlstad, MN 56732 • 934
Karnak, IL 62956 • 646
Karnes □, TX • 13,593
Karnes City, TX 78118 • 3,296
Karns, TN 37921 • 1,173
Kasota, MN 56050 • 739
Kasson, MN 55944 • 2,827
Kathleen, FL 33849 • 1,866
Katy, TX 77449–50 • 5,660
Kauai □, HI • 39,082
Kaufman, TX 75142 • 4,658
Kaufman □, TX • 39,029
Kaukauna, WI 54130 • 11,310
Kaumakani, HI 96747 • 888
Kaunakakai, HI 96748 • 2,231
Kay □, OK • 49,852
Kayenta, AZ 86033 • 3,343
Kaysville, UT 84037 • 9,811
Keaau, HI 96749 • 775
Kealakekua, HI 96750 • 1,033
Kealia, HI 96751 • 700
Keansburg, NJ 07734 • 10,613
Kearney, MO 64060 • 1,433
Kearney, NE 68847 • 21,158
Kearney □, NE • 7,053
Kearns, UT 84118 • 21,353
Kearny, AZ 85237 • 2,646
Kearny, NJ 07032 • 35,735
Kearny □, KS • 3,435
Keego Harbor, MI 48033 • 3,083
Keene, NH 03431 • 21,449
Keene, TX 76059 • 3,013
Keeseville, NY 12944 • 2,025
Keewatin, MN 55753 • 1,443
Keiser, AR 72351 • 962
Keith □, NE • 9,364
Keithsburg, IL 61442 • 936
Keizer, OR 97303 • 18,592
Kekaha, HI 96752 • 3,260
Keller, TX 76248 • 4,156
Kellogg, ID 83837 • 3,417
Kellogg, IA 50135 • 654
Kelly Lake, MN 55754 • 900
Kellyville, OK 74039 • 960
Kelseyville, CA 95451 • 1,567
Kelso, WA 98626 • 11,129
Kemmerer, WY 83101 • 3,273
Kemp, TX 75143 • 1,035
Kemper □, MS • 10,148
Kenai, AK 99611 • 4,324
Kenansville, FL 32739 • 700
Kenansville, NC 28349 • 931
Kenbridge, VA 23944 • 1,352
Kendall, FL 33156 • 51,000
Kendall □, IL • 37,202
Kendall □, TX • 10,635
Kendall Park, NJ 08824 • 7,419
Kendallville, IN 46755 • 7,299
Kenedy, TX 78119 • 4,356
Kenedy □, TX • 543
Kenesaw, NE 68956 • 854
Kenilworth, IL 60043 • 2,708
Kenilworth, NJ 07033 • 8,221
Kenly, NC 27542 • 1,433
Kenmare, ND 58746 • 1,456
Kenmawr, PA 15136 • 5,100
Kenmore, NY 14217 • 18,474
Kenmore, WA 98028 • 7,900
Kennebec □, ME • 109,889
Kennebunk, ME 04043 • 3,294
Kennebunkport, ME 04046 • 1,685
Kennedale, TX 76060 • 2,594
Kennedy, AL 35574 • 604
Kennedy Heights, LA 70094 • 2,000
Kenner, LA 70062–65 • 66,382
Kennesaw, GA 30144 • 5,095
Kennett, MO 63857 • 10,145
Kennett Square, PA 19348 • 4,715
Kennewick, WA 99336–37 • 34,397
Kennydale, WA 98055 • 1,000
Keno, OR 97627 • 900
Kenosha, WI 53140–42 • 77,685
Kenosha □, WI • 123,137
Kenova, WV 25530 • 4,454
Ken Rock, IL 61109 • 5,945
Kensett, AR 72082 • 1,751
Kensington, CA 94707 • 5,342
Kensington, CT 06037 • 7,502
Kensington, KS 66951 • 681
Kensington, MD 20895 • 1,822
Kent, OH 44240 • 26,164
Kent, WA 98031–32 • 23,152
Kent □, DE • 98,219
Kent □, MD • 16,695
Kent □, MI • 444,506
Kent □, RI • 154,163
Kent □, TX • 1,145
Kent City, MI 49330 • 860
Kentland, IN 47951 • 1,936
Kenton, OH 43326 • 8,605
Kenton, TN 38233 • 1,551
Kenton □, KY • 137,058
Kentwood, LA 70444 • 2,667
Kentwood, MI 49508 • 30,438
Kenvil, NJ 07847 • 3,000
Kenvir, KY 40847 • 950
Kenwood, OH 45236 • 9,928
Kenyon, MN 55946 • 1,529
Keokea, HI 96790 • 900
Keokuk, IA 52632 • 13,536
Keokuk □, IA • 12,921
Keosauqua, IA 52565 • 1,003
Keota, IA 52248 • 1,034
Keota, OK 74941 • 661
Kerens, TX 75144 • 1,582
Kerhonkson, NY 12446 • 1,243
Kerkhoven, MN 56252 • 761
Kermit, TX 79745 • 8,015
Kermit, WV 25674 • 705
Kern □, CA • 403,089
Kernersville, NC 27284 • 6,802
Kernville, CA 93238 • 1,660
Kerr □, TX • 28,780
Kerrville, TX 78028 • 15,276
Kersey, CO 80644 • 913
Kershaw, SC 29067 • 1,993
Kershaw □, SC • 39,015
Ketchikan, AK 99901 • 7,198
Ketchum, ID 83340 • 2,200
Kettering, OH 45429 • 61,186
Kettle Falls, WA 99141 • 1,087
Kettleman City, CA 93239 • 1,051
Kewanee, IL 61443 • 14,508
Kewanna, IN 46939 • 711
Kewaskum, WI 53040 • 2,381
Kewaunee, WI 54216 • 2,801
Kewaunee □, WI • 19,539
Keweenaw □, MI • 1,963
Keya Paha □, NE • 1,301
Key Largo, FL 33037 • 7,447
Keyport, NJ 07735 • 7,413
Keyser, WV 26726 • 6,569
Keystone, IA 52249 • 618
Keystone, WV 24852 • 902
Keystone Heights, FL 32656 • 1,056
Keysville, VA 23947 • 704
Keytesville, MO 65261 • 689
Key West, FL 33040 • 24,382
Kezar Falls, ME 04047 • 900
Kidder □, ND • 3,833
Kiefer, OK 74041 • 912
Kiel, WI 53042 • 3,083
Kiester, MN 56051 • 670
Kihei, HI 96753 • 5,644
Kilauea, HI 96754 • 895
Kilgore, TX 75662 • 11,006
Killbuck, OH 44637 • 937
Killdeer, ND 58640 • 790
Killeen, TX 76541–46 • 46,296
Killen, AL 35645 • 747
Killian, LA 70462 • 611
Kilmarnock, VA 22482 • 945
Kilmichael, MS 39747 • 906
Kiln, MS 39556 • 650
Kimball, MN 55353 • 651
Kimball, NE 69145 • 3,120
Kimball, SD 57355 • 752
Kimball, WV 24853 • 871
Kimball □, NE • 4,882
Kimberly, AL 35091 • 1,043
Kimberly, ID 83341 • 2,307
Kimberly, WV 25118 • 800
Kimberly, WI 54136 • 5,881
Kimble □, TX • 4,063
Kincaid, IL 62540 • 1,591
Kincaid, WV 25119 • 700
Kinder, LA 70648 • 2,603
Kinderhook, NY 12106 • 1,377
King, NC 27021 • 5,000
King, WI 54946 • 750
King □, TX • 425
King □, WA • 1,269,749
King and Queen □, VA • 5,968
King City, CA 93930 • 5,495
King City, MO 64463 • 1,063
Kingfield, ME 04947 • 700
Kingfisher, OK 73750 • 4,245
Kingfisher □, OK • 14,187
King George □, VA • 10,543
Kingman, AZ 86401 • 9,257
Kingman, KS 67068 • 3,563
Kingman □, KS • 8,960
King of Prussia, PA 19406 • 18,200
Kings, MS 39180 • 1,165
Kings □, CA • 73,738
Kings □, NY • 2,230,936
Kingsburg, CA 93631 • 5,115
Kingsbury □, SD • 6,679
Kingsford, MI 49801 • 5,290
Kingsland, GA 31548 • 2,008
Kingsland, TX 78639 • 1,600
Kingsley, IA 51028 • 1,209
Kingsley, MI 49649 • 664
Kings Mountain, NC 28086 • 9,080
Kings Park, VA 22151 • 4,450
Kings Park West, VA 22030 • 5,000
Kings Point, NY 11024 • 5,234
Kingsport, TN 37660–65 • 32,027
Kingston, GA 30145 • 733
Kingston, ID 83839 • 1,000
Kingston, IL 60145 • 618
Kingston, MA 02364 • 4,405
Kingston, NH 03848 • 900
Kingston, NJ 08528 • 900
Kingston, NY 12401 • 24,481
Kingston, OH 45644 • 1,208
Kingston, OK 73439 • 1,171
Kingston, PA 18704 • 15,681
Kingston, RI 02881 • 5,419
Kingston, TN 37763 • 4,441
Kingston Springs, TN 37082 • 1,017
Kingstown, MD 21620 • 1,192
Kingstree, SC 29556 • 4,147
Kingsville, MD 21087 • 2,824
Kingsville, OH 44048 • 1,243
Kingsville, TX 78363 • 28,808
King William □, VA • 9,334
Kingwood, WV 26537 • 2,877
Kinloch, MO 63140 • 4,455
Kinmundy, IL 62854 • 945
Kinnelon, NJ 07405 • 7,770
Kinney □, TX • 2,279
Kinsey, AL 36301 • 1,239
Kinsley, KS 67547 • 2,074
Kinsman, OH 44428 • 800
Kinston, AL 36453 • 604
Kinston, NC 28501 • 25,234
Kiowa, KS 67070 • 1,409
Kiowa, OK 74553 • 866
Kiowa □, CO • 1,936
Kiowa □, KS • 4,046
Kiowa □, OK • 12,711
Kirby, TX 78280 • 6,435
Kirbyville, TX 75956 • 1,972
Kirkersville, OH 43033 • 626
Kirkland, IL 60146 • 1,155
Kirkland, WA 98033–34 • 18,779
Kirklin, IN 46050 • 662
Kirksville, MO 63501 • 17,167
Kirkwood, IL 61447 • 1,008
Kirkwood, MO 63122 • 27,987
Kirtland, NM 87417 • 2,358
Kirtland, OH 44094 • 5,969
Kissimmee, FL 32741–43 • 15,487
Kistler, WV 25628 • 750
Kit Carson □, CO • 7,599
Kitsap □, WA • 147,152
Kittanning, PA 16201 • 5,432
Kittery, ME 03904 • 5,465
Kittery Point, ME 03905 • 1,260
Kittitas, WA 98934 • 782
Kittitas □, WA • 24,877
Kittson □, MN • 6,672
Klamath, CA 95548 • 850
Klamath □, OR • 59,117
Klamath Falls, OR 97601–03 • 16,661
Kleberg □, TX • 33,358
Klein, TX 77379 • 9,000
Klemme, IA 50449 • 620
Klickitat, WA 98628 • 700
Klickitat □, WA • 15,822
Knightdale, NC 27545 • 985
Knights Landing, CA 95645 • 1,000
Knightstown, IN 46148 • 2,325
Knightsville, IN 47857 • 763
Knob Noster, MO 65336 • 2,040
Knollwood, WV 25302 • 700
Knott □, KY • 17,940
Knox, IN 46534 • 3,674
Knox, PA 16232 • 1,364
Knox □, IL • 61,607
Knox □, IN • 41,838
Knox □, KY • 30,239
Knox □, ME • 32,941

United States Populations and ZIP Codes

Knox □, MO • 5,508
Knox □, NE • 11,457
Knox □, OH • 46,304
Knox □, TN • 319,694
Knox □, TX • 5,329
Knox City, TX 79529 • 1,546
Knoxville, IL 61448 • 3,432
Knoxville, IA 50138 • 8,143
Knoxville, PA 16928 • 650
Knoxville, TN 37901–99 • 175,045
Kodiak, AK 99615 • 4,756
Kohler, WI 53044 • 1,651
Kokomo, IN 46901–02 • 47,808
Koloa, HI 96756 • 1,457
Konawa, OK 74849 • 1,711
Koochiching □, MN • 17,571
Koontz Lake, IN 46574 • 1,436
Kooskia, ID 83539 • 784
Kootenai □, ID • 59,770
Koppel, PA 16136 • 1,146
Kosciusko, MS 39090 • 7,415
Kosciusko □, IN • 59,555
Kossuth □, IA • 21,891
Kotzebue, AK 99752 • 2,054
Kountze, TX 77625 • 2,716
Kouts, IN 46347 • 1,619
Krebs, OK 74554 • 1,754
Kremmling, CO 80459 • 1,296
Kress, TX 79052 • 783
Krotz Springs, LA 70750 • 1,374
Kula, HI 96790 • 1,300
Kulpmont, PA 17834 • 3,675
Kuna, ID 83634 • 1,767
Kurtistown, HI 96760 • 1,200
Kutztown, PA 19530 • 4,040
Kyle, TX 78640 • 2,093

## L

Labadieville, LA 70372 • 2,138
La Belle, FL 33935 • 2,287
La Belle, MO 63447 • 845
Labette □, KS • 25,682
La Canada Flintridge, CA 91011 • 20,153
Lac du Flambeau, WI 54538 • 900
La Center, KY 42056 • 1,044
Lacey, WA 98503 • 13,940
Lackawanna, NY 14218 • 22,701
Lackawanna □, PA • 227,908
Laclede □, MO • 24,323
Lacombe, LA 70445 • 5,146
Lacon, IL 61540 • 2,135
Laconia, NH 03246 • 15,575
La Conner, WA 98257 • 633
Lacoochee, FL 33537 • 1,720
Lac Qui Parle □, MN • 10,592
La Crescent, MN 55947 • 4,311
La Crescenta, CA 91214 • 12,500
La Crosse, IN 46348 • 713
La Crosse, KS 67548 • 1,618
La Crosse, VA 23950 • 734
La Crosse, WI 54601–03 • 48,347
La Crosse □, WI • 91,056
La Cygne, KS 66040 • 1,025
Ladd, IL 61329 • 1,337
Laddonia, MO 63352 • 726
Ladera Heights, CA 90045 • 6,647
Ladoga, IN 47954 • 1,151
Ladonia, TX 75449 • 761
Ladson, SC 29456 • 13,246
Lady Lake, FL 32659 • 1,193
Ladysmith, WI 54848 • 3,826
La Farge, WI 54639 • 746
Lafayette, AL 36862 • 3,647
Lafayette, CA 94549 • 20,879
Lafayette, CO 80026 • 8,985
Lafayette, GA 30728 • 6,517
Lafayette, IN 47901–07 • 43,011
Lafayette, LA 70501–09 • 81,961
Lafayette, NC 28304 • 4,100
Lafayette, OR 97127 • 1,215
La Fayette, RI 02852 • 680
Lafayette, TN 37083 • 3,808
Lafayette □, AR • 10,213
Lafayette □, FL • 4,035
Lafayette □, LA • 150,017
Lafayette □, MS • 31,030
Lafayette □, MO • 29,925
Lafayette □, WI • 17,412
Lafayette Hill, PA 19444 • 6,600
Lafayette Southwest, LA 70501 • 5,500
La Feria, TX 78559 • 3,495
Lafitte, LA 70067 • 1,312
La Follette, TN 37766 • 8,198
La Fontaine, IN 46940 • 946
Lafourche □, LA • 82,483
La France, SC 29656 • 800
Lagonda, LA 70380 • 5,805
La Grande, OR 97850 • 11,354
La Grange, GA 30240 • 24,204
La Grange, IL 60525 • 15,445
Lagrange, IN 46761 • 2,164
La Grange, KY 40031 • 2,971
La Grange, MO 63448 • 1,217
La Grange, NC 28551 • 3,147
Lagrange, OH 44050 • 1,258
La Grange, TX 78945 • 3,768
Lagrange □, IN • 25,550
La Grange Highlands, IL 60525 • 7,100
La Grange Park, IL 60525 • 13,359
Laguna, NM 87026 • 800
Laguna Beach, CA 92651–53 • 17,901
Laguna Hills, CA 92653 • 16,400
La Habra, CA 90631 • 45,232
Lahaina, HI 96761 • 6,095
La Harpe, IL 61450 • 1,471
La Harpe, KS 66751 • 687
Laie, HI 96762 • 4,643
Laingsburg, MI 48848 • 1,145
La Jara, CO 81140 • 858
La Junta, CO 81050 • 8,338
Lake □, CA • 36,366
Lake □, CO • 8,830
Lake □, FL • 104,870
Lake □, IL • 440,372
Lake □, IN • 522,965
Lake □, MI • 7,711
Lake □, MN • 13,043
Lake □, MT • 19,056
Lake □, OH • 212,801
Lake □, OR • 7,532
Lake □, SD • 10,724
Lake □, TN • 7,455
Lake Alfred, FL 33850 • 3,134
Lake Andes, SD 57356 • 1,029
Lake Arrowhead, CA 92352 • 2,500
Lake Arthur, LA 70549 • 3,615
Lake Barcroft, VA 22041 • 2,250
Lake Benton, MN 56149 • 869
Lake Bluff, IL 60044 • 4,434
Lake Butler, FL 32054 • 1,830
Lake Charles, LA 70601–11 • 75,226
Lake City, AR 72437 • 1,842
Lake City, FL 32055 • 9,257
Lake City, IA 51449 • 2,006
Lake City, MI 49651 • 843
Lake City, MN 55041 • 4,505
Lake City, PA 16423 • 2,384
Lake City, SC 29560 • 6,731
Lake City, TN 37769 • 2,335
Lake Crystal, MN 56055 • 2,078
Lake Delta, NY 13440 • 2,400
Lake Delton, WI 53940 • 1,158
Lake Elmo, MN 55042 • 5,296
Lake Elsinore, CA 92330 • 5,982
Lake Erie Beach, NY 14006 • 3,500
Lakefield, MN 56150 • 1,845
Lake Forest, FL 33023 • 5,400
Lake Forest, IL 60045 • 15,245
Lake Geneva, WI 53147 • 5,612
Lake George, NY 12845 • 1,047
Lake Grove, NY 11755 • 9,692
Lake Hamilton, AR 71913 • 1,054
Lake Havasu City, AZ 86403 • 15,909
Lake Helen, FL 32744 • 2,047
Lake Hiawatha, NJ 07034 • 14,000
Lake Hughes, CA 93532 • 800
Lakehurst, NJ 08733 • 2,908
Lake in the Hills, IL 60102 • 5,651
Lake Jackson, TX 77566 • 19,102
Lake Katrine, NY 12449 • 1,092
Lakeland, FL 33801–07 • 50,455
Lakeland, GA 31635 • 2,647
Lake Linden, MI 49945 • 1,181
Lake Luzerne, NY 12846 • 1,000
Lake Magdalene, FL 33612 • 13,331
Lake Mary, FL 32746 • 2,853
Lake Mills, IA 50450 • 2,281
Lake Mills, WI 53551 • 3,670
Lakemont, PA 16602 • 1,500
Lakemore, OH 44250 • 2,744
Lake Nebagamon, WI 54849 • 780
Lake Odessa, MI 48849 • 2,171
Lake Of The Woods □, MN • 3,764
Lake Orion, MI 48035 • 2,907
Lake Oswego, OR 97034 • 22,527
Lake Park, FL 33403 • 6,909
Lake Park, IA 51347 • 1,123
Lake Park, MN 56554 • 716
Lake Placid, FL 33852 • 963
Lake Placid, NY 12946 • 2,490
Lakeport, CA 95453 • 3,675
Lake Preston, SD 57249 • 789
Lake Providence, LA 71254 • 6,361
Lake Ridge, VA 22191 • 6,500
Lake Ronkonkoma, NY 11779 • 9,600
Lake Shore, MD 21122 • 2,100
Lakeshore, MS 39558 • 800
Lakeside, AZ 85929 • 1,333
Lakeside, CA 92040 • 23,921
Lakeside, CT 06488 • 900
Lakeside, OH 43440 • 950
Lakeside, OR 97449 • 1,453
Lakeside, VA 23228 • 29,400
Lakeside Park, KY 41017 • 3,038
Lake Station, IN 46405 • 14,294
Lake Station, OK 74127 • 800
Lake Stevens, WA 98258 • 1,660
Lake Telemark, NJ 07866 • 1,216
Lakeview, GA 30741 • 5,403
Lake View, IA 51450 • 1,291
Lakeview, MI 48850 • 1,139
Lake View, NY 14085 • 4,600
Lakeview, OH 43331 • 1,089
Lakeview, OR 97630 • 2,770
Lake View, SC 29563 • 939
Lake Villa, IL 60046 • 1,462
Lake Village, AR 71653 • 3,088
Lake Village, IN 46349 • 650
Lakeville, CT 06039 • 1,200
Lakeville, IN 46536 • 629
Lakeville, MA 02346 • 1,948
Lakeville, MN 55044 • 14,790
Lakeville, NY 14480 • 950
Lake Waccamaw, NC 28450 • 1,133
Lake Wales, FL 33853 • 8,466
Lake Wissota, WI 54729 • 1,419
Lakewood, CA 90712–16 • 74,654
Lakewood, CO 80215 • 113,808
Lakewood, IA 50211 • 900
Lakewood, NJ 08701 • 22,863
Lakewood, NY 14750 • 3,941
Lakewood, OH 44107 • 61,963
Lakewood Center, WA 98499 • 51,300
Lake Worth, FL 33460–67 • 27,048
Lake Zurich, IL 60047 • 8,225
Lakin, KS 67860 • 1,823
Lakota, ND 58344 • 963
La Luz, NM 88337 • 1,194
Lamar, AR 72846 • 708
Lamar, CO 81052 • 7,713
Lamar, MO 64759 • 4,053
Lamar, PA 16848 • 650
Lamar, SC 29069 • 1,333
Lamar □, AL • 16,453
Lamar □, GA • 12,215
Lamar □, MS • 23,821
Lamar □, TX • 42,156
La Marque, TX 77568 • 15,372
Lamb □, TX • 18,669
Lambert, MS 38643 • 1,624
Lamberton, MN 56152 • 1,032
Lambertville, MI 48144 • 6,341
Lambertville, NJ 08530 • 4,044
La Mesa, CA 92041 • 50,308
La Mesa, NM 88044 • 900
Lamesa, TX 79331 • 11,790
La Mirada, CA 90638 • 40,986
La Moille, IL 61330 • 734
Lamoille □, VT • 16,767
Lamoni, IA 50140 • 2,705
Lamont, CA 93241 • 9,616
La Monte, MO 65337 • 1,054
La Moure, ND 58458 • 1,077
La Moure □, ND • 6,473
Lampasas, TX 76550 • 6,165
Lampasas □, TX • 12,005
Lanai City, HI 96763 • 2,092
Lanark, IL 61046 • 1,483
Lanark Village, FL 32323 • 650
Lancaster, CA 93534–39 • 48,027
Lancaster, KY 40444 • 3,365
Lancaster, MA 01523 • 900
Lancaster, MO 63548 • 855
Lancaster, NH 03584 • 2,134
Lancaster, NY 14086 • 13,056
Lancaster, OH 43130 • 34,953
Lancaster, PA 17601–99 • 54,725
Lancaster, SC 29720 • 9,703
Lancaster, TX 75146 • 14,807
Lancaster, WI 53813 • 4,076
Lancaster □, NE • 192,884
Lancaster □, PA • 362,346
Lancaster □, SC • 53,361
Lancaster □, VA • 10,129
Lander, WY 82520 • 7,867
Lander □, NV • 4,076
Landis, NC 28088 • 2,092
Lando, SC 29724 • 850
Landrum, SC 29356 • 2,141
Lane □, KS • 2,472
Lane □, OR • 275,226
Lanesboro, MA 01237 • 950
Lanesboro, MN 55949 • 923
Lanett, AL 36863 • 6,897
Langdale, AL 36854 • 2,034
Langdon, ND 58249 • 2,335
Langeloth, PA 15054 • 950
Langhorne, PA 19047 • 1,697
Langlade □, WI • 19,978
Langley, SC 29834 • 1,714
Langley, WA 98260 • 650
Langley Park, MD 20787 • 11,100
Lanham, MD 20706 • 7,300
Lanier □, GA • 5,654
Lannon, WI 53046 • 987
Lanoka Harbor, NJ 08734 • 700
Lansdale, PA 19446 • 16,526
Lansdowne, MD 21227 • 10,000
Lansdowne, PA 19050 • 11,891
L'Anse, MI 49946 • 2,500
Lansford, PA 18232 • 4,466
Lansing, IL 60438 • 29,039
Lansing, IA 52151 • 1,181
Lansing, KS 66043 • 5,307
Lansing, MI 48901–99 • 130,414
Lantana, FL 33462 • 8,048
Laona, WI 54541 • 700
La Palma, CA 90623 • 15,399
Lapaz, IN 46537 • 651
La Paz □, AZ • 12,557
Lapeer, MI 48446 • 6,198
Lapeer □, MI • 70,038
Lapel, IN 46051 • 1,881
La Pine, OR 97739 • 900
La Place, LA 70068 • 16,112
La Plata, MD 20646 • 2,484
La Plata, MO 63549 • 1,423
La Plata □, CO • 27,195
Laporte, CO 80535 • 900
La Porte, IN 46350 • 21,796
La Porte, TX 77571 • 16,836
La Porte □, IN • 108,632
La Porte City, IA 50651 • 2,324
La Pryor, TX 78872 • 1,000
La Puente, CA 91744–49 • 30,882
Lapwai, ID 83540 • 1,043
Laramie, WY 82070 • 24,410
Laramie □, WY • 68,649
Larchmont, NY 10538 • 6,308
Larchmont North, NY 10538 • 11,500
Larchwood, IA 51241 • 701
Laredo, TX 78040–44 • 91,449
Largo, FL 34640–44 • 58,977
Larimer □, CO • 149,184
Larimore, ND 58251 • 1,524
Larkspur, CA 94939 • 11,064
Larksville, PA 18704 • 4,410
Larned, KS 67550 • 4,811
Larose, LA 70373 • 5,234
La Rue, OH 43332 • 861
Larue □, KY • 11,922
La Salle, CO 80645 • 1,929
La Salle, IL 61301 • 10,347
La Salle □, IL • 112,033
La Salle □, LA • 17,004
La Salle □, TX • 5,514
Las Animas, CO 81054 • 2,818
Las Animas □, CO • 14,897
Las Cruces, NM 88001–08 • 45,086
Lassen □, CA • 21,661
Las Vegas, NV 89101–99 • 164,674
Las Vegas, NM 87701 • 14,322
Latah □, ID • 28,749
Latham, NY 12110 • 8,000
Lathrop, MO 64465 • 1,732
Latimer □, OK • 9,840
Laton, CA 93242 • 1,100
Latrobe, PA 15650 • 10,799
Latta, SC 29565 • 1,804
Lattimer Mines, PA 18234 • 650
Lauderdale, MS 39335 • 750
Lauderdale □, AL • 80,546
Lauderdale □, MS • 77,285
Lauderdale □, TN • 24,555
Lauderdale Lakes, FL 33313 • 25,426
Lauderhill, FL 33313 • 37,271
Laughlintown, PA 15655 • 750
Laurel, DE 19956 • 3,052
Laurel, FL 34272 • 1,500
Laurel, IN 47024 • 819
Laurel, MD 20707–08 • 12,103
Laurel, MS 39440 • 21,897
Laurel, MT 59044 • 5,481
Laurel, NE 68745 • 1,031
Laurel, VA 23060 • 1,500
Laurel □, KY • 38,982
Laurel Bay, SC 29902 • 5,238
Laureldale, PA 19605 • 4,047
Laurel Hill, FL 32567 • 610
Laurel Hill, NC 28351 • 2,314
Laurel Run, PA 18702 • 725
Laurence Harbor, NJ 08879 • 5,000
Laurens, IA 50554 • 1,606
Laurens, SC 29360 • 10,587
Laurens □, GA • 36,990
Laurens □, SC • 52,214
Laurinburg, NC 28352 • 11,480
Laurium, MI 49913 • 2,678
Lavaca, AR 72941 • 1,092
Lavaca □, TX • 19,004
La Vale, MD 21502 • 5,500
Lavallette, NJ 08735 • 2,072
La Vergne, TN 37086 • 5,495
La Verkin, UT 84745 • 1,174
La Verne, CA 91750 • 23,508
Laverne, OK 73848 • 1,563
La Vernia, TX 78121 • 632
La Veta, CO 81055 • 611
La Vista, GA 30329 • 5,200
La Vista, NE 68128 • 9,588
Lavonia, GA 30553 • 2,024
Lawai, HI 96765 • 950
Lawndale, CA 90260 • 23,460
Lawnside, NJ 08045 • 3,042
Lawrence, IN 46226 • 25,591
Lawrence, KS 66044–46 • 52,738
Lawrence, MA 01840–45 • 63,175
Lawrence, MI 49064 • 903
Lawrence, NY 11559 • 6,175
Lawrence, PA 15055 • 970
Lawrence □, AL • 30,170
Lawrence □, AR • 18,447
Lawrence □, IL • 17,807
Lawrence □, IN • 42,472
Lawrence □, KY • 14,121
Lawrence □, MS • 12,518
Lawrence □, MO • 28,973
Lawrence □, OH • 63,849
Lawrence □, PA • 107,150
Lawrence □, SD • 18,339
Lawrence □, TN • 34,110
Lawrenceburg, IN 47025 • 4,403
Lawrenceburg, KY 40342 • 5,167
Lawrenceburg, TN 38464 • 10,184
Lawrence Park, PA 16511 • 4,584
Lawrenceville, GA 30245 • 8,928
Lawrenceville, IL 62439 • 5,652
Lawrenceville, NJ 08648 • 1,800
Lawrenceville, VA 23868 • 1,484
Lawson, MO 64062 • 1,688
Lawsonia, MD 21817 • 1,687
Lawtell, LA 70550 • 1,014
Lawtey, FL 32058 • 692
Lawton, MI 49065 • 1,558
Lawton, OK 73501–05 • 80,054
Layton, UT 84041 • 26,393
Laytonville, CA 95454 • 1,096
Lea □, NM • 55,993
Leachville, AR 72438 • 1,882
Lead, SD 57754 • 4,330
Leadville, CO 80461 • 3,879
Leadwood, MO 63653 • 1,371
Leaf River, IL 61047 • 637
League City, TX 77573 • 16,578
Leake □, MS • 18,790
Leakesville, MS 39451 • 1,120
Lealman, FL 33714 • 19,875
Leary, GA 31762 • 783
Leavenworth, KS 66048 • 33,656
Leavenworth, WA 98826 • 1,522
Leavenworth □, KS • 54,809
Leavittsburg, OH 44430 • 2,220
Leawood, KS 66206 • 13,360
Lebanon, IL 62254 • 3,245
Lebanon, IN 46052 • 11,456
Lebanon, KY 40033 • 6,590
Lebanon, MO 65536 • 9,507
Lebanon, NH 03766 • 11,134
Lebanon, NJ 08833 • 820
Lebanon, OH 45036 • 9,636
Lebanon, OR 97355 • 10,413
Lebanon, PA 17042 • 25,711
Lebanon, TN 37087 • 11,872
Lebanon, VA 24266 • 3,206
Lebanon □, PA • 108,582
Lebanon Junction, KY 40150 • 1,581
Lebec, CA 93243 • 900
Lebo, KS 66856 • 966
Le Center, MN 56057 • 1,967
Le Claire, IA 52753 • 2,899
Lecompte, LA 71346 • 1,661
Ledgewood, NJ 07852 • 1,100
Lee, MA 01238 • 2,140
Lee □, AL • 76,283
Lee □, AR • 15,539
Lee □, FL • 205,266
Lee □, GA • 11,684
Lee □, IL • 36,328
Lee □, IA • 43,106
Lee □, KY • 7,754
Lee □, MS • 57,061
Lee □, NC • 36,718
Lee □, SC • 18,929
Lee □, TX • 10,952
Lee □, VA • 25,956
Leechburg, PA 15656 • 2,682
Leedom Estates, DE 19720 • 1,300
Leeds, AL 35094 • 8,638
Leeds, ND 58346 • 678
Leelanau □, MI • 14,007
Lee Park, PA 18702 • 3,900
Leesburg, FL 32748–49 • 13,191
Leesburg, GA 31763 • 1,301
Leesburg, IN 46538 • 629
Leesburg, NJ 08327 • 700
Leesburg, OH 45135 • 1,019
Leesburg, VA 22075 • 8,357
Lees Summit, MO 64063 • 28,741
Leesville, LA 71446 • 9,054
Leesville, SC 29070 • 2,296
Leeton, MO 64761 • 604
Leetonia, OH 44431 • 2,121
Leetsdale, PA 15056 • 1,604
Lee Vining, CA 93541 • 900
Leflore □, MS • 41,525
Le Flore □, OK • 40,698
Lefors, TX 79054 • 829
Leggett, CA 95455 • 700
Le Grand, CA 95333 • 1,500
Le Grand, IA 50142 • 921
Lehi, UT 84043 • 6,848
Lehigh, IA 50557 • 654
Lehigh □, PA • 272,349
Lehigh Acres, FL 33936 • 9,604
Lehighton, PA 18235 • 5,826
Leicester, MA 01524 • 3,400
Leighton, AL 35646 • 1,218
Leipsic, OH 45856 • 2,171
Leisure City, FL 33033 • 17,905
Leitchfield, KY 42754 • 4,533
Leland, IL 60531 • 775
Leland, MS 38756 • 6,667
Le Mars, IA 51031 • 8,276
Lemay, MO 63125 • 35,424
Lemhi □, ID • 7,460
Lemmon, SD 57638 • 1,871
Lemmon Valley, NV 89501 • 2,000
Lemon Grove, CA 92045 • 20,780
Lemont, IL 60439 • 5,640
Lemont, PA 16851 • 2,613
Lemoore, CA 93245 • 8,832
Lena, IL 61048 • 2,295
Lenawee □, MI • 89,948
Lenexa, KS 66215 • 18,639
Lennox, CA 90304 • 18,445
Lennox, SD 57039 • 1,827
Lenoir, NC 28645 • 13,748
Lenoir □, NC • 59,819
Lenoir City, TN 37771 • 5,446
Lenox, GA 31637 • 965
Lenox, IA 50851 • 1,338
Lenox, MA 01240 • 2,668
Leo, IN 46765 • 800
Leola, SD 57456 • 645
Leominster, MA 01453 • 34,508
Leon, IA 50144 • 2,094
Leon, KS 67074 • 667
Leon □, FL • 148,655
Leon □, TX • 9,594
Leonard, TX 75452 • 1,421
Leonardo, NJ 07737 • 3,600
Leonardtown, MD 20650 • 1,448
Leonia, NJ 07605 • 8,027
Leon Valley, TX 78268 • 9,088
Leonville, LA 70551 • 1,143
Leoti, KS 67861 • 1,869
Lepanto, AR 72354 • 1,964
Le Roy, IL 61752 • 2,870
Le Roy, KS 66857 • 701
Le Roy, MN 55951 • 930
Le Roy, NY 14482 • 4,900
Leslie, MI 49251 • 2,110
Leslie, SC 29730 • 1,102
Leslie □, KY • 14,882
Lester, WV 25865 • 626
Lester Prairie, MN 55354 • 1,229
Le Sueur, MN 56058 • 3,763
Le Sueur □, MN • 23,434
Letcher □, KY • 30,687
Leto, FL 33614 • 9,003
Leucadia, CA 92024 • 9,478
Levelland, TX 79336–38 • 13,809
Levittown, NY 11756 • 65,400
Levittown, PA 19053–59 • 17,420
Levy □, FL • 19,870
Lewes, DE 19958 • 2,197
Lewis □, ID • 4,118
Lewis □, KY • 14,545
Lewis □, MO • 10,901
Lewis □, NY • 25,035
Lewis □, TN • 9,700
Lewis □, WA • 56,025
Lewis □, WV • 18,813
Lewis And Clark □, MT • 43,039
Lewisburg, KY 42256 • 972
Lewisburg, OH 45338 • 1,450
Lewisburg, PA 17837 • 5,407
Lewisburg, TN 37091 • 8,760
Lewisburg, WV 24901 • 3,065
Lewisport, KY 42351 • 1,832
Lewis Run, PA 16738 • 677
Lewiston, ID 83501 • 27,986
Lewiston, ME 04240 • 40,481
Lewiston, MN 55952 • 1,226
Lewiston, NY 14092 • 3,326
Lewiston, UT 84320 • 1,438
Lewiston Woodville, NC 27849 • 671
Lewistown, IL 61542 • 2,758
Lewistown, MT 59457 • 7,104
Lewistown, PA 17044 • 9,830
Lewisville, AR 71845 • 1,476
Lewisville, TX 75067 • 24,273
Lexington, AL 35648 • 884
Lexington, IL 61753 • 1,806
Lexington, KY 40501–99 • 204,165
Lexington, MA 02173 • 29,479
Lexington, MI 48450 • 765
Lexington, MS 39095 • 2,628
Lexington, MO 64067 • 5,063
Lexington, NE 68850 • 7,040
Lexington, NC 27292 • 15,711
Lexington, OH 44904 • 3,823
Lexington, OK 73051 • 1,731
Lexington, SC 29072 • 2,131
Lexington, TN 38351 • 5,934
Lexington, TX 78947 • 1,065
Lexington, VA 24450 • 7,292
Lexington □, SC • 140,353
Lexington Park, MD 20653 • 10,361
Libby, MT 59923 • 2,748
Liberal, KS 67901 • 14,911
Liberal, MO 64762 • 701
Liberty, IN 47353 • 1,844
Liberty, KY 42539 • 2,206
Liberty, MS 39645 • 669
Liberty, MO 64068 • 16,251
Liberty, NC 27298 • 1,997
Liberty, NY 12754 • 4,293
Liberty, SC 29657 • 3,167
Liberty, TX 77575 • 7,945
Liberty □, FL • 4,260
Liberty □, GA • 37,583
Liberty □, MT • 2,329
Liberty □, TX • 47,088
Liberty Acres, CA 90250 • 4,600
Liberty Center, OH 43532 • 1,111
Liberty Corner, NJ 07938 • 800
Liberty Lake, WA 99019 • 900
Libertyville, IL 60048 • 16,520
Libuse, LA 71348 • 700
Licking, MO 65542 • 1,272
Licking □, OH • 120,981

Lidgerwood, ND 58053 • 971
Liftwood, DE 19803 • 800
Lighthouse Point, FL 33064 • 11,488
Ligonier, IN 46767 • 3,134
Ligonier, PA 15658 • 1,917
Lihue, HI 96766 • 4,000
Lilbourn, MO 63862 • 1,463
Lilburn, GA 30247 • 3,765
Lillington, NC 27546 • 1,948
Lilly, PA 15938 • 1,462
Lilly Grove, WV 24740 • 1,700
Lima, NY 14485 • 2,025
Lima, OH 45801–09 • 47,381
Limestone, ME 04750 • 1,334
Limestone □, AL • 46,005
Limestone □, TX • 20,224
Limon, CO 80828 • 1,805
Lincoln, AL 35096 • 2,081
Lincoln, AR 72744 • 1,422
Lincoln, CA 95648 • 4,132
Lincoln, ID 83401 • 700
Lincoln, IL 62656 • 16,327
Lincoln, KS 67455 • 1,599
Lincoln, ME 04457 • 3,524
Lincoln, MA 01773 • 3,300
Lincoln, MO 65338 • 819
Lincoln, NE 68501–99 • 171,932
Lincoln □, AR • 13,369
Lincoln □, CO • 4,663
Lincoln □, GA • 6,716
Lincoln □, ID • 3,436
Lincoln □, KS • 4,145
Lincoln □, KY • 19,053
Lincoln □, LA • 39,763
Lincoln □, ME • 25,691
Lincoln □, MN • 8,207
Lincoln □, MS • 30,174
Lincoln □, MO • 22,193
Lincoln □, MT • 17,752
Lincoln □, NE • 36,455
Lincoln □, NV • 3,732
Lincoln □, NM • 10,997
Lincoln □, NC • 42,372
Lincoln □, OK • 26,601
Lincoln □, OR • 35,264
Lincoln □, SD • 13,942
Lincoln □, TN • 26,483
Lincoln □, WA • 9,604
Lincoln □, WV • 23,675
Lincoln □, WI • 26,555
Lincoln □, WY • 12,177
Lincoln Acres, CA 92047 • 1,800
Lincoln City, OR 97367 • 5,469
Lincoln Heights, OH 45215 • 5,259
Lincoln Park, CO 81212 • 3,426
Lincoln Park, GA 30286 • 1,755
Lincoln Park, MI 48146 • 45,105
Lincoln Park, NJ 07035 • 8,806
Lincolnshire, IL 60069 • 4,151
Lincolnton, GA 30817 • 1,406
Lincolnton, NC 28092 • 4,879
Lincoln Village, CA 95207 • 6,476
Lincoln Village, OH 43228 • 10,548
Lincolnville, SC 29483 • 808
Lincolnwood, IL 60645 • 11,921
Lincroft, NJ 07738 • 4,100
Linda, CA 95901 • 10,225
Lindale, GA 30147 • 2,958
Lindale, TX 75771 • 2,180
Linden, AL 36748 • 2,773
Linden, IN 47955 • 700
Linden, MI 48451 • 2,174
Linden, NJ 07036 • 37,836
Linden, TN 37096 • 1,087
Linden, TX 75563 • 2,443
Lindenhurst, IL 60046 • 6,220
Lindenhurst, NY 11757 • 26,919
Lindenwold, NJ 08021 • 18,196
Lindon, UT 84062 • 2,796
Lindsay, CA 93247 • 6,924
Lindsay, OK 73052 • 3,454
Lindsborg, KS 67456 • 3,155
Lindstrom, MN 55045 • 1,972
Linesville, PA 16424 • 1,198
Lineville, AL 36266 • 2,257
Linglestown, PA 17112 • 3,000
Linn, MO 65051 • 1,211
Linn □, IA • 169,775
Linn □, KS • 8,234
Linn □, MO • 15,495
Linn □, OR • 89,495
Lino Lakes, MN 55014 • 4,966
Linthicum Heights, MD 21090 • 7,457
Linton, IN 47441 • 6,315
Linton, ND 58552 • 1,561
Linwood, MA 01525 • 1,100
Linwood, NJ 08221 • 6,144
Linworth, OH 43085 • 650
Lipscomb, AL 35020 • 3,741
Lipscomb □, TX • 3,766
Lisbon, IA 52253 • 1,458
Lisbon, ME 04250 • 1,200
Lisbon, NH 03585 • 1,151
Lisbon, ND 58054 • 2,283
Lisbon, OH 44432 • 3,159
Lisbon Center, ME 04251 • 625
Lisbon Falls, ME 04252 • 4,370
Lisle, IL 60532 • 13,625
Lisman, AL 36912 • 638
Litchfield, CT 06759 • 1,489
Litchfield, IL 62056 • 7,204
Litchfield, MI 49252 • 1,353
Litchfield, MN 55355 • 5,904
Litchfield □, CT • 156,769
Litchfield Park, AZ 85340 • 3,657
Lithia Springs, GA 30057 • 9,145
Lithonia, GA 30058 • 2,637
Lititz, PA 17543 • 7,590
Little Canada, MN 55110 • 7,102
Little Chute, WI 54140 • 7,907
Little Falls, MN 56345 • 7,250
Little Falls, NJ 07424 • 11,496
Little Falls, NY 13365 • 6,156
Little Ferry, NJ 07643 • 9,399
Littlefield, TX 79339 • 7,409
Littlefork, MN 56653 • 918
Little Hocking, OH 45742 • 800
Little Lake, MI 49833 • 900
Little River □, AR • 13,952
Little Rock, AR 72201–99 • 158,461
Little Silver, NJ 07739 • 5,548
Littlestown, PA 17340 • 2,870
Littleton, CO 80120–27 • 28,631
Littleton, MA 01460 • 3,109
Littleton, NH 03561 • 4,480
Littleton, NC 27850 • 820
Little Valley, NY 14755 • 1,203
Littleville, AL 35653 • 1,262
Live Oak, CA 95953 • 3,103
Live Oak, FL 32060 • 6,732
Live Oak, TX 78233 • 8,183
Live Oak □, TX • 9,606
Live Oak Manor, LA 70094 • 1,500
Livermore, CA 94550 • 48,349
Livermore, KY 42352 • 1,672
Livermore Falls, ME 04254 • 2,441
Liverpool, PA 17045 • 809
Liverpool, TX 77577 • 602
Livingston, AL 35470 • 3,187
Livingston, CA 95334 • 5,326
Livingston, IL 62058 • 949
Livingston, LA 70754 • 1,260
Livingston, MT 59047 • 6,994
Livingston, NJ 07039 • 28,040
Livingston, TN 38570 • 3,372
Livingston, TX 77351 • 4,928
Livingston, WI 53554 • 642
Livingston □, IL • 41,381
Livingston □, KY • 9,219
Livingston □, LA • 58,806
Livingston □, MI • 100,289
Livingston □, MO • 15,739
Livingston □, NY • 57,006
Livingston Manor, NY 12758 • 1,522
Livonia, LA 70755 • 980
Livonia, MI 48150–54 • 104,814
Livonia, NY 14487 • 1,238
Llangollen Estates, DE 19720 • 870
Llano, TX 78643 • 3,071
Llano □, TX • 10,144
Lloyd Harbor, NY 11743 • 3,405
Loami, IL 62661 • 770
Lobelville, TN 37097 • 993
Loch Lomond, VA 22110 • 2,300
Lockesburg, AR 71846 • 616
Lockhart, FL 32810 • 10,571
Lockhart, TX 78644 • 7,953
Lock Haven, PA 17745 • 9,617
Lockland, OH 45215 • 4,292
Lockney, TX 79241 • 2,334
Lockport, IL 60441 • 9,170
Lockport, LA 70374 • 2,424
Lockport, NY 14094 • 24,844
Lockwood, MO 65682 • 971
Lockwood, MT 59101 • 1,600
Locust, NJ 07760 • 700
Locust, NC 28097 • 1,590
Locust Grove, GA 30248 • 1,479
Locust Grove, NY 11791 • 11,648
Locust Grove, OK 74352 • 1,179
Lodge Grass, MT 59050 • 771
Lodi, CA 95240 • 35,221
Lodi, NJ 07644 • 23,956
Lodi, OH 44254 • 2,942
Lodi, WI 53555 • 1,959
Logan, IA 51546 • 1,540
Logan, KS 67646 • 720
Logan, NM 88426 • 735
Logan, OH 43138 • 6,557
Logan, UT 84321 • 26,844
Logan, WV 25601 • 3,029
Logan □, AR • 20,144
Logan □, CO • 19,800
Logan □, IL • 31,802
Logan □, KS • 3,478
Logan □, KY • 24,138
Logan □, NE • 983
Logan □, ND • 3,493
Logan □, OH • 39,155
Logan □, OK • 26,881
Logan □, WV • 50,679
Logansport, IN 46947 • 17,731
Logansport, LA 71049 • 1,565
Loganville, GA 30249 • 1,841
Loganville, PA 17342 • 1,020
Log Lane Village, CO 80701 • 709
Lolo, MT 59847 • 2,418
Loma Linda, CA 92354 • 10,694
Lomax, IL 61454 • 601
Lombard, IL 60148 • 36,897
Lometa, TX 76853 • 666
Lomira, WI 53048 • 1,446
Lomita, CA 90717 • 18,807
Lompoc, CA 93436 • 26,267
Lonaconing, MD 21539 • 1,420
London, AR 72847 • 859
London, KY 40741 • 4,002
London, OH 43140 • 6,958
Londonderry, NH 03053 • 950
Londontowne, MD 21037 • 3,500
Lone Grove, OK 73443 • 3,369
Lone Pine, CA 93545 • 1,684
Lone Tree, IA 52755 • 1,014
Lone Wolf, OK 73655 • 613
Long □, GA • 4,524
Long Bar Harbor, MD 21009 • 700
Long Beach, CA 90801–99 • 361,334
Long Beach, IN 46360 • 2,262
Long Beach, MD 20685 • 900
Long Beach, MS 39560 • 7,967
Long Beach, NY 11561 • 34,073
Long Beach, WA 98631 • 1,199
Longboat Key, FL 34228 • 4,843
Long Branch, NJ 07740 • 29,819
Longbranch, WA 98351 • 900
Long Lake, IL 60041 • 2,201
Longmeadow, MA 01106 • 16,301
Longmont, CO 80501 • 42,942
Longport, NJ 08403 • 1,249
Long Prairie, MN 56347 • 2,859
Long Valley, NJ 07853 • 1,682
Long View, KY 42701 • 650
Long View, NC 28601 • 3,587
Longview, TX 75601–08 • 62,762
Longview, WA 98632 • 31,052
Longwood, FL 32750 • 10,029
Lonoke, AR 72086 • 4,128
Lonoke □, AR • 34,518
Lonsdale, MN 55046 • 1,160
Lonsdale, RI 02865 • 4,100
Loogootee, IN 47553 • 3,100
Lookout Mountain, TN 37350 • 1,886
Loon Lake, WA 99148 • 650
Lorain, OH 44052–55 • 75,416
Lorain □, OH • 274,909
Loraine, TX 79532 • 929
Lordsburg, NM 88045 • 3,195
Loreauville, LA 70552 • 860
Lorenzo, TX 79343 • 1,394
Loretto, KY 40037 • 954
Loretto, PA 15940 • 1,395
Loretto, TN 38469 • 1,612
Lorida, FL 33857 • 620
Loris, SC 29569 • 2,193
Lorman, MS 39096 • 650
Los Alamitos, CA 90720 • 11,529
Los Alamos, CA 93440 • 950
Los Alamos, NM 87544 • 11,039
Los Alamos □, NM • 17,599
Los Altos, CA 94022 • 25,769
Los Altos Hills, CA 94022 • 7,421
Los Angeles, CA 90001–99 • 2,966,850
Los Angeles □, CA • 7,477,503
Los Banos, CA 93635 • 10,341
Los Fresnos, TX 78566 • 2,173
Los Gatos, CA 95030 • 26,906
Los Lunas, NM 87031 • 3,525
Los Molinos, CA 96055 • 1,241
Los Nietos, CA 90606 • 7,100
Los Padillas, NM 87105 • 2,500
Los Ranchos de Albuquerque, NM 87107 • 2,702
Lost Creek, WV 26385 • 604
Lost Hills, CA 93249 • 800
Lott, TX 76656 • 865
Loudon, TN 37774 • 3,943
Loudon □, TN • 28,553
Loudonville, NY 12211 • 9,000
Loudonville, OH 44842 • 2,945
Loudoun □, VA • 57,427
Loughman, FL 33858 • 800
Louisa, KY 41230 • 1,832
Louisa, VA 23093 • 932
Louisa □, IA • 12,055
Louisa □, VA • 17,825
Louisburg, KS 66053 • 1,744
Louisburg, NC 27549 • 3,238
Louise, TX 77455 • 900
Louisiana, MO 63353 • 4,261
Louisville, AL 36048 • 791
Louisville, CO 80027 • 5,593
Louisville, GA 30434 • 2,823
Louisville, IL 62858 • 1,166
Louisville, KY 40201–99 • 298,840
Louisville, MS 39339 • 7,323
Louisville, NE 68037 • 1,022
Louisville, OH 44641 • 7,996
Loup □, NE • 859
Loup City, NE 68853 • 1,368
Love □, OK • 7,469
Loveland, CO 80537 • 30,244
Loveland, OH 45140 • 9,106
Loveland Park, OH 45140 • 1,653
Lovell, WY 82431 • 2,447
Lovelock, NV 89419 • 1,680
Lovely, KY 41231 • 700
Loves Park, IL 61111 • 13,192
Lovettsville, VA 22080 • 613
Lovilia, IA 50150 • 637
Loving, NM 88256 • 1,355
Loving □, TX • 91
Lovington, IL 61937 • 1,313
Lovington, IA 50322 • 850
Lovington, NM 88260 • 9,727
Lowden, IA 52255 • 717
Lowell, AR 72745 • 1,078
Lowell, IN 46356 • 5,827
Lowell, MA 01850–54 • 92,418
Lowell, MI 49331 • 3,707
Lowell, NC 28098 • 2,917
Lowell, OH 45744 • 729
Lowell, OR 97452 • 661
Lowellville, OH 44436 • 1,558
Lower Burrell, PA 15068 • 13,200
Lower Paia, HI 96779 • 1,500
Lowmoor, VA 24457 • 700
Lowndes □, AL • 13,253
Lowndes □, GA • 67,972
Lowndes □, MS • 57,304
Lowry City, MO 64763 • 676
Lowville, NY 13367 • 3,364
Loxley, AL 36551 • 804
Loyal, WI 54446 • 1,252
Loyall, KY 40854 • 1,210
Loyalton, CA 96118 • 1,030
Lubbock, TX 79401–99 • 173,979
Lubbock □, TX • 211,651
Lubec, ME 04652 • 990
Lucama, NC 27851 • 1,070
Lucas, OH 44843 • 753
Lucas □, IA • 10,313
Lucas □, OH • 471,741
Lucasville, OH 45648 • 3,349
Luce □, MI • 6,659
Lucedale, MS 39452 • 2,429
Lucerne, CA 95458 • 1,767
Lucernemines, PA 15754 • 1,380
Lucerne Valley, CA 92356 • 1,300
Luck, WI 54853 • 997
Luckey, OH 43443 • 895
Ludington, MI 49431 • 8,937
Ludlow, KY 41016 • 4,959
Ludlow, MA 01056 • 18,150
Ludlow, PA 16333 • 800
Ludlow, VT 05149 • 1,352
Ludowici, GA 31316 • 1,286
Lufkin, TX 75901 • 28,562
Lugoff, SC 29078 • 2,909
Lukachukai, AZ 86507 • 1,049
Lula, GA 30554 • 857
Luling, LA 70070 • 4,006
Luling, TX 78648 • 5,039
Lumber City, GA 31549 • 1,426
Lumberport, WV 26386 • 939
Lumberton, MS 39455 • 2,217
Lumberton, NJ 08048 • 700
Lumberton, NC 28358 • 18,241
Lumpkin, GA 31815 • 1,335
Lumpkin □, GA • 10,762
Luna □, NM • 15,585
Luna Pier, MI 48157 • 1,443
Lunenburg, MA 01462 • 1,789
Lunenburg □, VA • 12,124
Luray, VA 22835 • 3,584
Lusk, WY 82225 • 1,650
Lutcher, LA 70071 • 4,730
Lutesville, MO 63762 • 865
Luther, OK 73054 • 1,159
Lutherville-Timonium, MD 21093 • 17,854
Luttrell, TN 37779 • 962
Lutz, FL 33549 • 5,555
Luverne, AL 36049 • 2,639
Luverne, MN 56156 • 4,568
Luxemburg, WI 54217 • 1,040
Luxora, AR 72358 • 1,739
Luzerne, PA 18709 • 3,703
Luzerne □, PA • 343,079
Lycoming □, PA • 118,416
Lyford, TX 78569 • 1,618
Lykens, PA 17048 • 2,181
Lyle, WA 98635 • 700
Lyman, SC 29365 • 1,067
Lyman, WY 82937 • 2,284
Lyman □, SD • 3,864
Lynch, KY 40855 • 1,614
Lynchburg, OH 45142 • 1,205
Lynchburg, TN 37352 • 668
Lynchburg, VA 24501–15 • 66,743
Lynden, WA 98264 • 4,022
Lyndhurst, NJ 07071 • 20,326
Lyndhurst, OH 44124 • 18,092
Lyndon, IL 61261 • 777
Lyndon, KS 66451 • 1,132
Lyndon, KY 40222 • 1,553
Lyndonville, NY 14098 • 916
Lyndonville, VT 05851 • 1,401
Lyndora, PA 16045 • 1,900
Lynn, IN 47355 • 1,250
Lynn, MA 01901–10 • 78,471
Lynn □, TX • 8,605
Lynne Acres, MD 21207 • 7,700
Lynnfield, MA 01940 • 11,267
Lynn Garden, TN 37665 • 7,213
Lynn Haven, FL 32444 • 6,239
Lynnwood, WA 98036–37 • 22,641
Lynwood, CA 90262 • 48,548
Lyon □, IA • 12,896
Lyon □, KS • 35,108
Lyon □, KY • 6,490
Lyon □, MN • 25,207
Lyon □, NV • 13,594
Lyon Mountain, NY 12952 • 950
Lyons, CO 80540 • 1,137
Lyons, GA 30436 • 4,203
Lyons, IL 60534 • 9,925
Lyons, IN 47443 • 782
Lyons, KS 67554 • 4,134
Lyons, MI 48851 • 708
Lyons, NE 68038 • 1,214
Lyons, NY 14489 • 4,160
Lyons, OR 97358 • 877
Lyons Falls, NY 13368 • 755
Lytle, TX 78052 • 1,920

## M

Mabank, TX 75147 • 1,443
Mabel, MN 55954 • 861
Maben, MS 39750 • 855
Mableton, GA 30059 • 20,200
Mabscott, WV 25871 • 1,668
Mabton, WA 98935 • 1,248
McAdoo, PA 18237 • 2,940
McAlester, OK 74501 • 17,255
McAlisterville, PA 17049 • 650
McAllen, TX 78501–04 • 66,281
McAlmont, AR 72117 • 1,600
McAlpine, MD 21043 • 2,500
McArthur, OH 45651 • 1,912
McBee, SC 29101 • 774
McCall, ID 83638 • 2,188
McCamey, TX 79752 • 2,436
McCammon, ID 83250 • 770
McCandless, PA 15237 • 26,250
McCaysville, GA 30555 • 1,219
McClain □, OK • 20,291
McCleary, WA 98557 • 1,419
MacClenny, FL 32063 • 3,851
McCloud, CA 96057 • 1,656
McClure, IL 62957 • 700
McClure, OH 43534 • 694
McClure, PA 17841 • 1,024
McClusky, ND 58463 • 658
McColl, SC 29570 • 2,677
McComas, WV 24735 • 800
McComb, MS 39648 • 12,331
McComb, OH 45858 • 1,608
McCone □, MT • 2,702
McConnellsburg, PA 17233 • 1,178
McConnelsville, OH 43756 • 2,018
McCook, NE 69001 • 8,404
McCook □, SD • 6,444
McCormick, SC 29835 • 1,725
McCormick □, SC • 7,797
McCracken □, KY • 61,310
McCreary □, KY • 15,634
McCrory, AR 72101 • 1,942
McCulloch □, TX • 8,735
McCurtain □, OK • 36,151
McDonald □, MO • 14,917
McDonough, GA 30253 • 2,778
McDonough □, IL • 37,467
McDowell □, NC • 35,135
McDowell □, WV • 49,899
McDuffie □, GA • 18,546
Macedon, NY 14502 • 1,400
Macedonia, OH 44056 • 6,571
McEwen, TN 37101 • 1,352
McFarland, CA 93250 • 5,151
McFarland, WI 53558 • 3,783
McGehee, AR 71654 • 5,671
McGill, NV 89318 • 1,419
McGraw, NY 13101 • 1,188
McGregor, IA 52157 • 945
McGregor, TX 76657 • 4,513
McGuffey, OH 45859 • 646
McHenry, IL 60050 • 11,949
McHenry □, IL • 147,897
McHenry □, ND • 7,858
Machias, ME 04654 • 1,277
Machias, NY 14101 • 700
McIntosh, MN 56556 • 681
McIntosh □, GA • 8,046
McIntosh □, ND • 4,800
McIntosh □, OK • 15,562
McKean □, PA • 50,635
McKee, KY 40447 • 759
McKeesport, PA 15130–35 • 31,012
McKees Rocks, PA 15136 • 8,742
McKenzie, AL 36456 • 605
McKenzie, TN 38201 • 5,405
McKenzie □, ND • 7,132
Mackinac □, MI • 10,178
Mackinaw, IL 61755 • 1,354
Mackinaw City, MI 49701 • 820
McKinley □, NM • 56,536
McKinleyville, CA 95521 • 7,772
McKinney, TX 75069 • 16,256
McLain, MS 39456 • 688
McLaughlin, SD 57642 • 754
McLean, IL 61754 • 836
McLean, TX 79057 • 1,160
McLean, VA 22101–03 • 22,000
McLean □, IL • 119,149
McLean □, KY • 10,090
McLean □, ND • 12,383
McLeansboro, IL 62859 • 2,960
McLennan □, TX • 170,755
McLeod □, MN • 29,657
McLoud, OK 74851 • 4,061
McLouth, KS 66054 • 700
McMechen, WV 26040 • 2,402
McMinn □, TN • 41,878
McMinnville, OR 97128 • 14,080
McMinnville, TN 37110 • 10,683
McMullen □, TX • 789
McNairy □, TN • 22,525
McNary, AZ 85930 • 1,320
McNeil, AR 71752 • 725
McNulty, OR 97051 • 1,805
Macomb, IL 61455 • 19,863
Macomb □, MI • 694,600
Macon, GA 31201–99 • 116,896
Macon, IL 62544 • 1,300
Macon, MS 39341 • 2,396
Macon, MO 63552 • 5,680
Macon □, AL • 26,829
Macon □, GA • 14,003
Macon □, IL • 131,375
Macon □, MO • 16,313
Macon □, NC • 20,178
Macon □, TN • 15,700
Macoupin □, IL • 49,384
McPherson, KS 67460 • 11,753
McPherson □, KS • 26,855
McPherson □, NE • 593
McPherson □, SD • 4,027
McQueeney, TX 78123 • 950
McRae, AR 72102 • 641
McRae, GA 31055 • 3,409
McRoberts, KY 41835 • 1,106
McSherrystown, PA 17344 • 2,764
Macungie, PA 18062 • 1,899
McVeigh, KY 41546 • 800
McVille, ND 58254 • 626
Madawaska, ME 04756 • 4,165
Maddock, ND 58348 • 677
Madeira, OH 45243 • 9,341
Madelia, MN 56062 • 2,130
Madera, CA 93637–39 • 21,732
Madera, PA 16661 • 900
Madera □, CA • 63,116
Madill, OK 73446 • 3,173
Madison, AL 35758 • 4,057
Madison, AR 72359 • 1,238
Madison, CT 06443 • 2,069
Madison, FL 32340 • 3,487
Madison, GA 30650 • 2,954
Madison, IL 62060 • 5,915
Madison, IN 47250 • 12,472
Madison, KS 66860 • 1,099
Madison, ME 04950 • 2,788
Madison, MN 56256 • 2,212
Madison, MS 39110 • 2,241
Madison, MO 65263 • 656
Madison, NE 68748 • 1,950
Madison, NJ 07940 • 15,357
Madison, NC 27025 • 2,806
Madison, OH 44057 • 2,291
Madison, SD 57042 • 6,210
Madison, WV 25130 • 3,228
Madison, WI 53701–99 • 170,616
Madison □, AL • 196,966
Madison □, AR • 11,373
Madison □, FL • 14,894
Madison □, GA • 17,747
Madison □, ID • 19,480
Madison □, IL • 247,661
Madison □, IN • 139,336
Madison □, IA • 12,597
Madison □, KY • 53,352
Madison □, LA • 15,975
Madison □, MS • 41,613
Madison □, MO • 10,725
Madison □, MT • 5,448
Madison □, NE • 31,382
Madison □, NC • 16,827
Madison □, NY • 65,150
Madison □, OH • 33,004
Madison □, TN • 74,546
Madison □, TX • 10,649
Madison □, VA • 10,232
Madison Heights, MI 48071 • 35,375
Madison Heights, VA 24572 • 3,500
Madisonville, KY 42431 • 16,979
Madisonville, LA 70447 • 799
Madisonville, TN 37354 • 2,884
Madisonville, TX 77864 • 3,660
Madras, OR 97741 • 2,235
Madrid, IA 50156 • 2,281
Madrid, NY 13660 • 800
Maeser, UT 84078 • 2,216
Magalia, CA 95954 • 950
Magazine, AR 72943 • 799
Magdalena, NM 87825 • 1,022
Magee, MS 39111 • 3,497
Magna, UT 84044 • 13,138
Magnolia, AR 71753 • 11,909
Magnolia, MS 39652 • 2,461
Magnolia, NJ 08049 • 4,881
Magnolia, OH 44643 • 986
Magnolia, TX 77355 • 867
Magoffin □, KY • 13,515

# United States Populations and ZIP Codes

Mahanoy City, PA 17948 • 6,167
Mahaska □, IA • 22,867
Mahnomen, MN 56557 • 1,283
Mahnomen □, MN • 5,535
Mahomet, IL 61853 • 1,986
Mahoning □, OH • 289,487
Mahopac, NY 10541 • 5,265
Mahwah, NJ 07430 • 7,500
Maiden, NC 28650 • 2,574
Maili, HI 96792 • 5,026
Maine, NY 13802 • 700
Maitland, FL 32751 • 8,763
Maize, KS 67101 • 1,294
Major □, OK • 8,772
Makaha, HI 96792 • 7,905
Makakilo City, HI 96706 • 7,691
Makawao, HI 96788 • 1,066
Makaweli, HI 96769 • 700
Malabar, FL 32950 • 1,118
Malad City, ID 83252 • 1,915
Malaga, NJ 08328 • 950
Malakoff, TX 75148 • 2,082
Malden, MA 02148 • 53,386
Malden, MO 63863 • 6,096
Malden, WV 25306 • 950
Malheur □, OR • 26,896
Malibu, CA 90265 • 10,000
Malone, FL 32445 • 897
Malone, NY 12953 • 7,668
Malta, IL 60150 • 995
Malta, MT 59538 • 2,367
Malta, OH 43758 • 956
Malvern, AR 72104 • 10,163
Malvern, IA 51551 • 1,244
Malvern, OH 44644 • 1,032
Malvern, PA 19355 • 2,999
Malverne, NY 11565 • 9,262
Mamaroneck, NY 10543 • 17,616
Mammoth, AZ 85618 • 1,906
Mammoth, WV 25132 • 750
Mammoth Lakes, CA 93546 • 3,000
Mammoth Spring, AR 72554 • 1,158
Mamou, LA 70554 • 3,194
Man, WV 25635 • 1,333
Manahawkin, NJ 08050 • 1,467
Manasquan, NJ 08736 • 5,354
Manassa, CO 81141 • 945
Manassas, VA 22110–11 • 15,438
Manassas Park, VA 22111 • 6,524
Manatee □, FL • 148,442
Manawa, WI 54949 • 1,205
Mancelona, MI 49659 • 1,432
Manchaug, MA 01526 • 1,000
Manchester, CT 06040 • 49,761
Manchester, GA 31816 • 4,796
Manchester, IA 52057 • 4,942
Manchester, KY 40962 • 1,838
Manchester, MD 21102 • 1,830
Manchester, MA 01944 • 5,424
Manchester, MI 48158 • 1,686
Manchester, MO 63011 • 6,191
Manchester, NH 03101–99 • 90,936
Manchester, NY 14504 • 1,698
Manchester, OH 45144 • 2,223
Manchester, PA 17345 • 2,027
Manchester, TN 37355 • 7,250
Manchester Center, VT 05255 • 1,719
Mancos, CO 81328 • 870
Mandan, ND 58554 • 15,513
Mandeville, AR 75501 • 700
Mandeville, LA 70448 • 6,076
Mangham, LA 71259 • 867
Mangum, OK 73554 • 3,833
Manhasset, NY 11030 • 8,530
Manhattan, KS 66502 • 32,644
Manhattan, MT 59741 • 988
Manhattan Beach, CA 90266 • 31,542
Manheim, PA 17545 • 5,015
Manila, AR 72442 • 2,553
Manilla, IA 51454 • 1,020
Manistee, MI 49660 • 7,566
Manistee □, MI • 23,019
Manistique, MI 49854 • 3,962
Manito, IL 61546 • 1,869
Manitou Beach, MI 49779 • 4,500
Manitou Springs, CO 80829 • 4,475
Manitowoc, WI 54220 • 32,547
Manitowoc □, WI • 82,918
Mankato, KS 66956 • 1,205
Mankato, MN 56001 • 28,651
Manlius, NY 13104 • 5,241
Manly, IA 50456 • 1,496
Mannford, OK 74044 • 1,610
Manning, IA 51455 • 1,609
Manning, SC 29102 • 4,746
Mannington, WV 26582 • 3,036
Manomet, MA 02345 • 950
Manor, TX 78653 • 1,044
Manorhaven, NY 11050 • 5,384
Mansfield, AR 72944 • 1,000
Mansfield, IL 61854 • 921
Mansfield, LA 71052 • 6,485
Mansfield, MA 02048 • 6,786
Mansfield, MO 65704 • 1,423
Mansfield, OH 44901–99 • 53,927
Mansfield, PA 16933 • 3,322
Mansfield, TX 76063 • 8,102
Mansfield Center, CT 06250 • 1,043
Manson, IA 50563 • 1,924
Mansura, LA 71350 • 2,074
Mantachie, MS 38855 • 732
Manteca, CA 95336 • 24,925
Manteno, IL 60950 • 3,155
Manteo, NC 27954 • 902
Manti, UT 84642 • 2,080
Manton, MI 49663 • 1,212
Mantorville, MN 55955 • 705
Mantua, NJ 08051 • 1,900
Mantua, OH 44255 • 1,041
Mantua Hills, VA 22030 • 1,550
Manvel, TX 77578 • 3,549
Manville, NJ 08835 • 11,278
Manville, RI 02838 • 3,100
Many, LA 71449 • 3,988
Many Farms, AZ 86538 • 1,364
Maple Bluff, WI 53704 • 1,351
Maple Grove, MN 55369 • 20,525
Maple Heights, OH 44137 • 29,735
Maple Lake, MN 55358 • 1,132
Maple Plain, MN 55359 • 1,421
Maple Rapids, MI 48853 • 683
Maple Shade, NJ 08052 • 20,525
Maplesville, AL 36750 • 754
Mapleton, IA 51034 • 1,495
Mapleton, MN 56065 • 1,516
Mapleton, OR 97453 • 900
Mapleton, UT 84663 • 2,726
Maple Valley, WA 98038 • 900
Mapleville, RI 02839 • 900
Maplewood, MN 55109 • 26,990
Maplewood, MO 63143 • 10,960
Maplewood, NJ 07040 • 22,950
Maquoketa, IA 52060 • 6,313
Marana, AZ 85653 • 1,674
Marathon, FL 33050 • 7,508
Marathon, NY 13803 • 1,046
Marathon, TX 79842 • 750
Marathon, WI 54448 • 1,552
Marathon □, WI • 111,270
Marble, MN 55764 • 757
Marble, NC 28905 • 700
Marble Cliff, OH 43212 • 630
Marble Falls, TX 78654 • 3,252
Marblehead, MA 01945 • 20,126
Marblehead, OH 43440 • 679
Marble Hill, MO 63764 • 601
Marbury, MD 20658 • 1,189
Marceline, MO 64658 • 2,938
Marcellus, MI 49067 • 1,134
Marco, FL 33937 • 4,679
Marcus, IA 51035 • 1,206
Marcus Hook, PA 19061 • 2,638
Marengo, IL 60152 • 4,361
Marengo, IN 47140 • 892
Marengo, IA 52301 • 2,308
Marengo □, AL • 25,047
Marfa, TX 79843 • 2,466
Margaret, AL 35112 • 757
Margaretville, NY 12455 • 755
Margate, FL 33063 • 35,900
Margate, MD 21061 • 4,800
Margate City, NJ 08402 • 9,179
Marianna, AR 72360 • 6,220
Marianna, FL 32446 • 7,006
Maricopa, AZ 85239 • 900
Maricopa, CA 93252 • 946
Maricopa □, AZ • 1,509,262
Mariemont, OH 45227 • 3,295
Marienville, PA 16239 • 900
Maries □, MO • 7,551
Marietta, GA 30060–69 • 30,829
Marietta, OH 45750 • 16,467
Marietta, OK 73448 • 2,494
Marietta, SC 29661 • 900
Marin □, CA • 222,592
Marina, CA 93933 • 20,647
Marina del Rey, CA 90292 • 8,065
Marine, IL 62061 • 957
Marine City, MI 48039 • 4,414
Marinette, WI 54143 • 11,965
Marinette □, WI • 39,314
Maringouin, LA 70757 • 1,291
Marion, AL 36756 • 4,467
Marion, AR 72364 • 2,996
Marion, CT 06444 • 800
Marion, IL 62959 • 14,031
Marion, IN 46952–53 • 35,874
Marion, IA 52302 • 19,474
Marion, KS 66861 • 1,951
Marion, KY 42064 • 3,392
Marion, LA 71260 • 989
Marion, MA 02738 • 1,438
Marion, MI 49665 • 816
Marion, MS 39342 • 771
Marion, NC 28752 • 3,684
Marion, NY 14505 • 950
Marion, OH 43302 • 37,040
Marion, PA 17235 • 900
Marion, SC 29571 • 7,700
Marion, SD 57043 • 830
Marion, VA 24354 • 7,029
Marion, WI 54950 • 1,348
Marion □, AL • 30,041
Marion □, AR • 11,334
Marion □, FL • 122,488
Marion □, GA • 5,297
Marion □, IL • 43,523
Marion □, IN • 765,233
Marion □, IA • 29,669
Marion □, KS • 13,522
Marion □, KY • 17,910
Marion □, MS • 25,708
Marion □, MO • 28,638
Marion □, OH • 67,974
Marion □, OR • 204,692
Marion □, SC • 34,179
Marion □, TN • 24,416
Marion □, TX • 10,360
Marion □, WV • 65,789
Marionville, MO 65705 • 1,920
Mariposa, CA 95338 • 1,150
Mariposa □, CA • 11,108
Marissa, IL 62257 • 2,568
Marked Tree, AR 72365 • 3,201
Markesan, WI 53946 • 1,446
Markham, IL 60426 • 15,172
Markham, TX 77456 • 1,100
Markle, IN 46770 • 975
Marks, MS 38646 • 2,260
Marksville, LA 71351 • 5,113
Marlboro, NJ 07746 • 5,700
Marlboro, NY 12542 • 1,580
Marlboro, VA 23224 • 950
Marlboro □, SC • 31,634
Marlborough, CT 06447 • 1,039
Marlborough, MA 01752 • 30,617
Marlborough, NH 03455 • 1,231
Marlene Village, OR 97005 • 1,500
Marlette, MI 48453 • 1,761
Marley, MD 21061 • 4,800
Marlin, TX 76661 • 7,099
Marlinton, WV 24954 • 1,352
Marlow, OK 73055 • 5,017
Marlowe, WV 25419 • 700
Marlton, NJ 08053 • 9,411
Marmaduke, AR 72443 • 1,168
Marmet, WV 25315 • 2,196
Maroa, IL 61756 • 1,760
Marquette, KS 67464 • 639
Marquette, MI 49855 • 23,288
Marquette □, MI • 74,101
Marquette □, WI • 11,672
Marquette Heights, IL 61554 • 3,386
Marrero, LA 70072 • 36,548
Marrtown, WV 26101 • 900
Mars, PA 16046 • 1,803
Marseilles, IL 61341 • 4,766
Marshall, AR 72650 • 1,595
Marshall, IL 62441 • 3,655
Marshall, MI 49068 • 7,201
Marshall, MN 56258 • 11,161
Marshall, MO 65340 • 12,781
Marshall, NC 28753 • 809
Marshall, TX 75670 • 24,921
Marshall, WI 53559 • 2,363
Marshall □, AL • 65,622
Marshall □, IL • 14,479
Marshall □, IN • 39,155
Marshall □, IA • 41,652
Marshall □, KS • 12,787
Marshall □, KY • 25,637
Marshall □, MN • 13,027
Marshall □, MS • 29,296
Marshall □, OK • 10,550
Marshall □, SD • 5,404
Marshall □, TN • 19,698
Marshall □, WV • 41,608
Marshallton, DE 19808 • 3,950
Marshalltown, IA 50158 • 26,938
Marshallville, GA 31057 • 1,540
Marshallville, OH 44645 • 788
Marshfield, MA 02050 • 4,421
Marshfield, MO 65706 • 3,871
Marshfield, WI 54449 • 18,290
Marshfield Hills, MA 02051 • 2,308
Mars Hill, ME 04758 • 1,500
Mars Hill, NC 28754 • 2,126
Marshville, NC 28103 • 2,011
Marsing, ID 83639 • 786
Marston, MO 63866 • 742
Mart, TX 76664 • 2,324
Martin, KY 41649 • 827
Martin, SD 57551 • 1,018
Martin, TN 38237 • 8,898
Martin □, FL • 64,014
Martin □, IN • 11,001
Martin □, KY • 13,925
Martin □, MN • 24,687
Martin □, NC • 25,948
Martin □, TX • 4,684
Martinez, CA 94553 • 22,582
Martinez, GA 30907 • 16,472
Martinsburg, PA 16662 • 2,231
Martinsburg, WV 25401 • 13,063
Martins Ferry, OH 43935 • 9,331
Martinsville, IL 62442 • 1,298
Martinsville, IN 46151 • 11,311
Martinsville, VA 24112 • 18,149
Marvell, AR 72366 • 1,724
Maryland City, MD 20707 • 6,250
Maryland Heights, MO 63043 • 5,676
Marysville, CA 95901 • 9,898
Marysville, KS 66508 • 3,670
Marysville, MI 48040 • 7,345
Marysville, OH 43040 • 7,414
Marysville, PA 17053 • 2,452
Marysville, WA 98270 • 5,080
Maryville, KY 40229 • 6,000
Maryville, MO 64468 • 9,558
Maryville, TN 37801 • 17,480
Masaryktown, FL 34609 • 800
Mascot, TN 37806 • 2,203
Mascoutah, IL 62258 • 4,962
Mason, MI 48854 • 6,019
Mason, OH 45040 • 8,692
Mason, TX 76856 • 2,153
Mason, WV 25260 • 1,432
Mason □, IL • 19,492
Mason □, KY • 17,765
Mason □, MI • 26,365
Mason □, TX • 3,683
Mason □, WA • 31,184
Mason □, WV • 27,045
Mason City, IL 62664 • 2,719
Mason City, IA 50401 • 30,144
Masontown, PA 15461 • 4,909
Masontown, WV 26542 • 1,052
Massac □, IL • 14,990
Massapequa, NY 11758 • 27,500
Massapequa Park, NY 11762 • 19,779
Massena, NY 13662 • 12,851
Massillon, OH 44646 • 30,557
Mastic, NY 11950 • 5,200
Mastic Beach, NY 11951 • 5,200
Masury, OH 44438 • 1,836
Matador, TX 79244 • 1,052
Matagorda, TX 77457 • 850
Matagorda □, TX • 37,828
Matamoras, PA 18336 • 2,111
Matawan, NJ 07747 • 8,837
Matewan, WV 25678 • 822
Matfield, MA 02379 • 700
Mather, PA 15346 • 860
Matherville, IL 61263 • 793
Mathews, LA 70375 • 900
Mathews, VA 23109 • 650
Mathews □, VA • 7,995
Mathis, TX 78368 • 5,667
Mathiston, MS 39752 • 632
Matoaca, VA 23803 • 2,000
Matoaka, WV 24736 • 613
Mattapoisett, MA 02739 • 3,159
Mattawamkeag, ME 04459 • 750
Matteson, IL 60443 • 10,223
Matthews, IN 46957 • 745
Matthews, NC 28105 • 1,648
Mattituck, NY 11952 • 1,200
Mattoon, IL 61938 • 19,055
Mattydale, NY 13211 • 8,292
Maud, OK 74854 • 1,444
Maugansville, MD 21767 • 1,707
Maui □, HI • 70,847
Mauldin, SC 29662 • 8,143
Maumee, OH 43537 • 15,747
Maunaloa, HI 96770 • 633
Maunawili, HI 96734 • 2,200
Maury □, TN • 51,095
Maury City, TN 38050 • 989
Mauston, WI 53948 • 3,284
Maverick □, TX • 31,398
Maxton, NC 28364 • 2,711
Maxwell, CA 95955 • 800
Maxwell, IA 50161 • 783
Maxwell Acres, WV 26041 • 1,000
Maybeury, WV 24861 • 700
Mayer, AZ 86333 • 950
Mayes □, OK • 32,261
Mayesville, SC 29104 • 663
Mayfield, KY 42066 • 10,705
Mayfield, NY 12117 • 944
Mayfield, PA 18433 • 1,812
Mayfield Heights, OH 44124 • 21,550
Mayflower, AR 72106 • 1,381
Maynard, MA 01754 • 9,590
Maynardville, TN 37807 • 924
Mayo, FL 32066 • 891
Mayo, MD 21106 • 1,500
Mayo, SC 29368 • 900
Mayodan, NC 27027 • 2,627
May Park, OR 97850 • 1,466
Mays Landing, NJ 08330 • 2,054
Maysville, GA 30558 • 619
Maysville, KY 41056 • 7,983
Maysville, MO 64469 • 1,187
Maysville, NC 28555 • 877
Maysville, OK 73057 • 1,396
Mayville, MI 48744 • 958
Mayville, ND 58257 • 2,255
Mayville, NY 14757 • 1,626
Mayville, WI 53050 • 4,333
Maywood, CA 90270 • 21,810
Maywood, IL 60153 • 27,998
Maywood, NJ 07607 • 9,895
Maywood Park, OR 97220 • 1,083
Mazeppa, MN 55956 • 680
Mazomanie, WI 53560 • 1,248
Mazon, IL 60444 • 828
Mead, WA 99021 • 1,400
Meade, KS 67864 • 1,777
Meade □, KS • 4,788
Meade □, KY • 22,854
Meade □, SD • 20,717
Meadow Lands, PA 15347 • 1,200
Meadowood, DE 19711 • 2,260
Meadville, PA 16335 • 15,544
Meagher □, MT • 2,154
Mebane, NC 27302 • 2,782
Mecca, CA 92254 • 1,698
Mechanic Falls, ME 04256 • 2,616
Mechanicsburg, OH 43044 • 1,792
Mechanicsburg, PA 17055 • 9,487
Mechanicsville, IA 52306 • 1,166
Mechanicsville, VA 23111 • 9,000
Mechanicville, NY 12118 • 5,500
Mecklenburg □, NC • 404,270
Mecklenburg □, VA • 29,444
Mecosta □, MI • 36,961
Medaryville, IN 47957 • 731
Medfield, MA 02052 • 6,108
Medford, MA 02155 • 58,076
Medford, MN 55049 • 775
Medford, NJ 08055 • 1,448
Medford, NY 11763 • 5,000
Medford, OK 73759 • 1,419
Medford, OR 97501–04 • 39,603
Medford, WI 54451 • 4,035
Medford Lakes, NJ 08055 • 4,958
Media, PA 19063–65 • 6,119
Mediapolis, IA 52637 • 1,685
Medical Lake, WA 99022 • 3,600
Medicine Bow, WY 82329 • 953
Medicine Lodge, KS 67104 • 2,384
Medina, NY 14103 • 6,392
Medina, OH 44256 • 15,268
Medina, TN 38355 • 687
Medina, WA 98039 • 3,220
Medina □, OH • 113,150
Medina □, TX • 23,164
Medora, IN 47260 • 853
Medway, MA 02053 • 4,300
Meeker, CO 81641 • 2,356
Meeker, OK 74855 • 1,032
Meeker □, MN • 20,594
Mehlville, MO 63129 • 22,900
Meigs, GA 31765 • 1,231
Meigs □, OH • 23,641
Meigs □, TN • 7,431
Meiners Oaks, CA 93023 • 5,600
Melbourne, AR 72556 • 1,619
Melbourne, FL 32901–19 • 46,536
Melbourne, IA 50162 • 732
Melbourne, KY 41059 • 628
Melbourne Beach, FL 32951 • 2,713
Melcher, IA 50163 • 953
Mellen, WI 54546 • 1,046
Mellette □, SD • 2,249
Melrose, FL 32666 • 1,700
Melrose, MA 02176 • 30,055
Melrose, MN 56352 • 2,409
Melrose, NM 88124 • 649
Melrose Park, FL 33312 • 5,725
Melrose Park, IL 60160–65 • 20,735
Melville, LA 71353 • 1,764
Melville, NY 11747 • 10,250
Melvin, KY 41650 • 700
Melvindale, MI 48122 • 12,322
Memphis, FL 34221 • 5,501
Memphis, MI 48041 • 1,171
Memphis, MO 63555 • 2,105
Memphis, TN 38101–99 • 646,174
Memphis, TX 79245 • 3,352
Mena, AR 71953 • 5,154
Menahga, MN 56464 • 980
Menan, ID 83434 • 605
Menands, NY 12204 • 4,012
Menard, TX 76859 • 1,697
Menard □, IL • 11,700
Menard □, TX • 2,346
Menasha, WI 54952 • 14,728
Mendenhall, MS 39114 • 2,533
Mendham, NJ 07945 • 4,899
Mendocino, CA 95460 • 1,008
Mendocino □, CA • 66,738
Mendon, IL 62351 • 979
Mendon, MA 01756 • 900
Mendon, MI 49072 • 951
Mendon, OH 45862 • 749
Mendon, UT 84325 • 663
Mendota, CA 93640 • 5,038
Mendota, IL 61342 • 7,134
Mendota Heights, MN 55118 • 7,288
Menifee □, KY • 5,117
Menlo, GA 30731 • 611
Menlo Park, CA 94025 • 26,369
Menno, SD 57045 • 793
Menominee, MI 49858 • 10,099
Menominee □, MI • 26,201
Menominee □, WI • 3,373
Menomonee Falls, WI 53051 • 27,845
Menomonie, WI 54751 • 12,769
Mentone, IN 46539 • 973
Mentor, OH 44060 • 42,065
Mentor-on-the-Lake, OH 44060 • 7,919
Mequon, WI 53092 • 16,193
Meraux, LA 70075 • 4,100
Merced, CA 95340 • 36,499
Merced □, CA • 134,558
Mercedes, TX 78570 • 11,851
Mercer, PA 16137 • 2,532
Mercer, WI 54547 • 1,250
Mercer □, IL • 19,286
Mercer □, KY • 19,011
Mercer □, MO • 4,685
Mercer □, NJ • 307,863
Mercer □, ND • 9,404
Mercer □, OH • 38,334
Mercer □, PA • 128,299
Mercer □, WV • 73,942
Mercer Island, WA 98040 • 21,522
Mercersburg, PA 17236 • 1,617
Mercerville, NJ 08619 • 15,500
Merchantville, NJ 08109 • 3,972
Meredith, NH 03253 • 1,202
Meredosia, IL 62665 • 1,272
Meriden, CT 06450 • 57,118
Meriden, KS 66512 • 707
Meridian, ID 83642 • 6,658
Meridian, MS 39301–05 • 46,577
Meridian, PA 16001 • 2,400
Meridian, TX 76665 • 1,330
Meridian Hills, IN 46260 • 1,801
Meridianville, AL 35759 • 1,403
Merion Station, PA 19066 • 7,400
Meriwether □, GA • 21,229
Merkel, TX 79536 • 2,493
Mermentau, LA 70556 • 771
Merriam, KS 66203 • 10,794
Merrick, NY 11566 • 26,400
Merrick □, NE • 8,945
Merrifield, VA 22116 • 2,100
Merrill, IA 51038 • 737
Merrill, MI 48637 • 851
Merrill, OR 97633 • 809
Merrill, WI 54452 • 9,578
Merrillville, IN 46410 • 27,677
Merrimac, MA 01860 • 2,300
Merrimack, NH 03054 • 1,200
Merrimack □, NH • 98,302
Merritt Island, FL 32952–54 • 30,708
Mer Rouge, LA 71261 • 802
Merryville, LA 70653 • 1,286
Merton, WI 53056 • 1,045
Mertzon, TX 76941 • 687
Mesa, AZ 85201–08 • 152,453
Mesa □, CO • 81,530
Mescalero, NM 88340 • 1,259
Mesilla, NM 88046 • 2,029
Mesquite, NV 89024 • 700
Mesquite, TX 75149–50 • 67,053
Metairie, LA 70001–11 • 164,160
Metamora, IL 61548 • 2,482
Metcalfe, MS 38760 • 952
Metcalfe □, KY • 9,484
Methuen, MA 01844 • 36,701
Metlakatla, AK 99926 • 1,056
Metropolis, IL 62960 • 7,171
Metter, GA 30439 • 3,531
Metuchen, NJ 08840 • 13,762
Metzger, OR 97223 • 5,544
Mexia, TX 76667 • 7,094
Mexico, IN 46958 • 850
Mexico, ME 04257 • 3,207
Mexico, MO 65265 • 12,276
Mexico, NY 13114 • 1,621
Meyersdale, PA 15552 • 2,581
Miami, AZ 85539 • 2,716
Miami, FL 33101–99 • 346,865
Miami, OK 74354 • 14,237
Miami, TX 79059 • 813
Miami □, IN • 39,820
Miami □, KS • 21,618
Miami □, OH • 90,381
Miami Beach, FL 33139 • 96,298
Miamisburg, OH 45342 • 15,304
Miami Shores, FL 33153 • 9,244
Miami Springs, FL 33166 • 12,350
Miamitown, OH 45041 • 650
Micanopy, FL 32667 • 737
Micco, FL 32958 • 3,585
Michigan Center, MI 49254 • 5,244
Michigan City, IN 46360 • 36,850
Middleboro, MA 02346 • 7,012
Middlebourne, WV 26149 • 941
Middleburg, FL 32068 • 2,500
Middleburg, NY 12122 • 1,358
Middleburg, PA 17842 • 1,357
Middleburg, VA 22117 • 619
Middleburgh, NY 12122 • 1,358
Middleburg Heights, OH 44130 • 16,218
Middlebury, CT 06762 • 3,900
Middlebury, IN 46540 • 1,665
Middlebury, VT 05753 • 5,591
Middlefield, OH 44062 • 1,997
Middle Point, OH 45863 • 709
Middleport, NY 14105 • 1,995
Middleport, OH 45760 • 2,971
Middle River, MD 21220 • 26,756
Middlesboro, KY 40965 • 12,251
Middlesex, NJ 08846 • 13,480
Middlesex, NC 27557 • 837
Middlesex □, CT • 129,017
Middlesex □, MA • 1,367,034
Middlesex □, NJ • 595,893
Middlesex □, VA • 7,719
Middleton, ID 83644 • 1,901
Middleton, MA 01949 • 4,135
Middleton, WI 53562 • 11,848
Middletown, CA 95461 • 2,000
Middletown, CT 06457 • 39,040
Middletown, DE 19709 • 2,946
Middletown, IN 47356 • 2,978
Middletown, MD 21769 • 1,748
Middletown, NJ 07718 • 61,615
Middletown, NY 10940 • 21,454
Middletown, OH 45042–43 • 43,719

Middletown, PA 17057 • *10,122*
Middletown, RI 02840 • *3,350*
Middletown, VA 22645 • *841*
Middleville, MI 49333 • *1,797*
Middleville, NY 13406 • *647*
Midfield, AL 35228 • *6,203*
Midland, MD 21542 • *601*
Midland, MI 48640 • *37,250*
Midland, PA 15059 • *4,310*
Midland, TX 79701–11 • *70,525*
Midland □, MI • *73,578*
Midland □, TX • *82,636*
Midland City, AL 36350 • *1,903*
Midland Park, KS 67216 • *1,350*
Midland Park, NJ 07432 • *7,381*
Midland Park, SC 29405 • *1,300*
Midlothian, IL 60445 • *14,274*
Midlothian, TX 76065 • *3,219*
Midlothian, VA 23113 • *1,000*
Midvale, OH 44653 • *654*
Midvale, UT 84047 • *10,146*
Midville, GA 30441 • *670*
Midway, KY 40347 • *1,445*
Midway, OR 97233 • *19,000*
Midway, PA 15060 • *1,187*
Midway, UT 84049 • *1,194*
Midwest, WY 82643 • *638*
Midwest City, OK 73110 • *49,559*
Mifflin, PA 17058 • *648*
Mifflin □, PA • *46,908*
Mifflinburg, PA 17844 • *3,151*
Mifflintown, PA 17059 • *783*
Mifflinville, PA 18631 • *1,074*
Milaca, MN 56353 • *2,104*
Milam □, TX • *22,732*
Milan, GA 31060 • *1,115*
Milan, IL 61264 • *6,264*
Milan, IN 47031 • *1,566*
Milan, MI 48160 • *4,182*
Milan, MO 63556 • *1,947*
Milan, NM 87021 • *3,747*
Milan, OH 44846 • *1,569*
Milan, TN 38358 • *8,083*
Milbank, SD 57252 • *4,120*
Mildred, PA 18632 • *800*
Miles, TX 76861 • *720*
Milesburg, PA 16853 • *1,309*
Miles City, MT 59301 • *9,602*
Milford, CT 06460 • *49,101*
Milford, DE 19963 • *5,366*
Milford, IL 60953 • *1,716*
Milford, IN 46542 • *1,153*
Milford, IA 51351 • *2,076*
Milford, ME 04461 • *1,688*
Milford, MA 01757 • *23,390*
Milford, MI 48042 • *5,041*
Milford, NE 68405 • *2,108*
Milford, NH 03055 • *6,289*
Milford, NJ 08848 • *1,368*
Milford, OH 45150 • *5,232*
Milford, PA 18337 • *1,143*
Milford, UT 84751 • *1,293*
Milford Center, OH 43045 • *764*
Mililani Town, HI 96789 • *20,351*
Millard □, UT • *8,970*
Millbrae, CA 94030 • *20,058*
Millbrook, AL 36054 • *3,101*
Millbrook, NY 12545 • *1,343*
Millburn, NJ 07041 • *19,543*
Millbury, MA 01527 • *5,700*
Millbury, OH 43447 • *955*
Mill City, OR 97360 • *1,565*
Millcreek, UT 84109 • *24,150*
Mill Creek, WV 26280 • *801*
Millcreek Township, PA 16505 • *44,303*
Milldale, CT 06467 • *1,100*
Milledgeville, GA 31061 • *12,176*
Milledgeville, IL 61051 • *1,209*
Mille Lacs □, MN • *18,430*
Millen, GA 30442 • *3,988*
Miller, SD 57362 • *1,931*
Miller □, AR • *37,766*
Miller □, GA • *7,038*
Miller □, MO • *18,532*
Millersburg, IN 46543 • *809*
Millersburg, KY 40348 • *987*
Millersburg, OH 44654 • *3,247*
Millersburg, PA 17061 • *2,770*
Millers Falls, MA 01349 • *1,101*
Millersport, OH 43046 • *844*
Millersville, PA 17551 • *7,668*
Millerton, NY 12546 • *1,013*
Mill Grove, MO 64673 • *850*
Mill Hall, PA 17751 • *1,744*
Millheim, PA 16854 • *800*
Milligan College, TN 37682 • *1,200*
Milliken, CO 80543 • *1,506*
Millington, MI 48746 • *1,237*
Millington, TN 38053 • *20,236*
Millinocket, ME 04462 • *7,567*
Millis, MA 02054 • *3,777*
Millport, AL 35576 • *1,287*
Millry, AL 36558 • *956*
Mills, WY 82644 • *2,139*
Mills □, IA • *13,406*
Mills □, TX • *4,477*
Millsboro, DE 19966 • *1,233*
Millsboro, PA 15348 • *900*
Millstadt, IL 62260 • *2,736*
Milltown, IN 47145 • *1,006*
Milltown, NJ 08850 • *7,136*
Milltown, WI 54858 • *732*
Millvale, PA 15209 • *4,772*
Mill Valley, CA 94941 • *12,967*
Millville, MA 01529 • *1,764*
Millville, NJ 08332 • *24,815*
Millville, OH 45013 • *809*
Millville, PA 17846 • *975*
Millville, UT 84326 • *848*
Millwood, WA 99212 • *1,717*
Milnor, ND 58060 • *716*
Milo, IA 50166 • *778*
Milo, ME 04463 • *2,255*
Milpitas, CA 95035 • *37,820*
Milroy, IN 46156 • *900*
Milroy, PA 17063 • *1,575*
Milstead, GA 30207 • *1,157*
Milton, DE 19968 • *1,359*
Milton, FL 32570 • *7,206*
Milton, IN 47357 • *729*
Milton, KY 40045 • *718*
Milton, MA 02186 • *25,860*
Milton, NH 03851 • *1,000*
Milton, PA 17847 • *6,730*
Milton, VT 05468 • *1,411*
Milton, WA 98354 • *3,162*
Milton, WV 25541 • *2,178*
Milton, WI 53563 • *4,092*
Milton-Freewater, OR 97862 • *5,086*
Milwaukee, WI 53201–99 • *636,236*
Milwaukee □, WI • *964,988*
Milwaukie, OR 97222 • *17,931*
Mimosa Park, LA 70070 • *3,737*
Mims, FL 32754 • *7,583*
Minatare, NE 69356 • *969*
Minco, OK 73059 • *1,489*
Minden, LA 71055 • *15,084*
Minden, NE 68959 • *2,939*
Minden, NV 89423 • *1,300*
Minden, WV 25879 • *800*
Mine Hill, NJ 07801 • *3,250*
Mineola, NY 11501 • *20,757*
Mineola, TX 75773 • *4,346*
Miner, MO 63801 • *1,182*
Miner □, SD • *3,739*
Mineral □, CO • *804*
Mineral □, MT • *3,675*
Mineral □, NV • *6,217*
Mineral □, WV • *27,234*
Mineral City, OH 44656 • *884*
Mineral Point, WI 53565 • *2,259*
Mineral Springs, AR 71851 • *936*
Mineral Wells, TX 76067 • *14,468*
Minersville, PA 17954 • *5,635*
Minerva, OH 44657 • *4,549*
Minetto, NY 13115 • *900*
Mineville, NY 12956 • *1,000*
Mingo □, WV • *37,336*
Mingo Junction, OH 43938 • *4,834*
Minidoka □, ID • *19,718*
Minier, IL 61759 • *1,261*
Minneapolis, KS 67467 • *2,075*
Minneapolis, MN 55401–99 • *370,951*
Minnehaha □, SD • *109,435*
Minneola, KS 67865 • *712*
Minneota, MN 56264 • *1,470*
Minnesota Lake, MN 56068 • *744*
Minnetonka, MN 55345 • *38,683*
Minocqua, WI 54548 • *900*
Minonk, IL 61760 • *2,039*
Minooka, IL 60447 • *1,565*
Minot, MA 02055 • *800*
Minot, ND 58701 • *32,843*
Minquadale, DE 19720 • *1,700*
Minster, OH 45865 • *2,557*
Mint Hill, NC 28212 • *7,915*
Minturn, CO 81645 • *1,060*
Mio, MI 48647 • *1,500*
Mira Loma, CA 91752 • *8,707*
Miramar, FL 33023 • *32,813*
Misenheimer, NC 28109 • *1,250*
Mishawaka, IN 46544–45 • *40,201*
Mishicot, WI 54228 • *1,503*
Missaukee □, MI • *10,009*
Mission, KS 66222 • *8,643*
Mission, SD 57555 • *748*
Mission, TX 78572 • *22,653*
Mission Hills, KS 66205 • *3,904*
Mission Viejo, CA 92691 • *50,666*
Mississippi □, AR • *59,517*
Mississippi □, MO • *15,726*
Mississippi State, MS 39762 • *4,595*
Missoula, MT 59801–12 • *33,388*
Missoula □, MT • *76,016*
Missouri City, TX 77459 • *24,533*
Missouri Valley, IA 51555 • *3,107*
Mitchell, IL 62040 • *1,500*
Mitchell, IN 47446 • *4,641*
Mitchell, NE 69357 • *1,956*
Mitchell, SD 57301 • *13,916*
Mitchell □, GA • *21,114*
Mitchell □, IA • *12,329*
Mitchell □, KS • *8,117*
Mitchell □, NC • *14,428*
Mitchell □, TX • *9,088*
Mitchellville, IA 50169 • *1,530*
Moab, UT 84532 • *5,333*
Moberly, MO 65270 • *13,418*
Mobile, AL 36601–99 • *200,452*
Mobile □, AL • *364,980*
Mobridge, SD 57601 • *4,174*
Mocanaqua, PA 18655 • *990*
Mocksville, NC 27028 • *2,637*
Moclips, WA 98562 • *700*
Modesto, CA 95350–56 • *106,602*
Modoc □, CA • *8,610*
Moenkopi, AZ 86045 • *900*
Moffat □, CO • *13,133*
Mogadore, OH 44260 • *4,190*
Mohall, ND 58761 • *1,049*
Mohave □, AZ • *55,865*
Mohave Valley, AZ 86440 • *750*
Mohawk, MI 49950 • *950*
Mohawk, NY 13407 • *2,956*
Mohnton, PA 19540 • *2,156*
Mojave, CA 93501 • *2,886*
Mokelumne Hill, CA 95245 • *950*
Mokena, IL 60448 • *4,578*
Molalla, OR 97038 • *2,992*
Moline, IL 61265 • *46,278*
Moline, MI 49335 • *800*
Molino, FL 32577 • *1,456*
Momence, IL 60954 • *3,297*
Monaca, PA 15061 • *7,661*
Monahans, TX 79756 • *8,397*
Monarch Mills, SC 29379 • *2,353*
Moncks Corner, SC 29461 • *3,699*
Mondovi, WI 54755 • *2,545*
Monee, IL 60449 • *993*
Monessen, PA 15062 • *11,928*
Monett, MO 65708 • *6,148*
Monette, AR 72447 • *1,165*
Monfort Heights, OH 45239 • *9,745*
Moniteau □, MO • *12,068*
Monmouth, IL 61462 • *10,706*
Monmouth, OR 97361 • *5,594*
Monmouth □, NJ • *503,173*
Monmouth Beach, NJ 07750 • *3,318*
Monmouth Junction, NJ 08852 • *2,579*
Mono □, CA • *8,577*
Monon, IN 47959 • *1,540*
Monona, IA 52159 • *1,530*
Monona, WI 53716 • *8,809*
Monona □, IA • *11,692*
Monongah, WV 26554 • *1,132*
Monongahela, PA 15063 • *5,950*
Monongalia □, WV • *75,024*
Monroe, CT 06468 • *760*
Monroe, GA 30655 • *8,854*
Monroe, IN 46772 • *739*
Monroe, IA 50170 • *1,875*
Monroe, LA 71201–12 • *57,597*
Monroe, MI 48161 • *23,531*
Monroe, NC 28110 • *12,639*
Monroe, NY 10950 • *5,996*
Monroe, OH 45050 • *4,256*
Monroe, UT 84754 • *1,476*
Monroe, WA 98272 • *2,869*
Monroe, WI 53566 • *10,027*
Monroe □, AL • *22,651*
Monroe □, AR • *14,052*
Monroe □, FL • *63,188*
Monroe □, GA • *14,610*
Monroe □, IL • *20,117*
Monroe □, IN • *98,785*
Monroe □, IA • *9,209*
Monroe □, KY • *12,353*
Monroe □, MI • *134,659*
Monroe □, MS • *36,404*
Monroe □, MO • *9,716*
Monroe □, NY • *702,238*
Monroe □, OH • *17,382*
Monroe □, PA • *69,409*
Monroe □, TN • *28,700*
Monroe □, WV • *12,873*
Monroe □, WI • *35,074*
Monroe Center, CT 06468 • *6,950*
Monroe City, MO 63456 • *2,557*
Monroe Park, DE 19807 • *1,250*
Monroeton, PA 18832 • *677*
Monroeville, AL 36460 • *5,674*
Monroeville, IN 46773 • *1,372*
Monroeville, OH 44847 • *1,329*
Monroeville, PA 15146 • *30,977*
Monrovia, CA 91016 • *30,531*
Monsey, NY 10952 • *7,400*
Monson, MA 01057 • *2,167*
Montague, CA 96064 • *1,285*
Montague, MA 01351 • *900*
Montague, MI 49437 • *2,332*
Montague □, TX • *17,410*
Mont Alto, PA 17237 • *1,592*
Montandon, PA 17850 • *650*
Montauk, NY 11954 • *1,300*
Mont Belvieu, TX 77580 • *1,730*
Montcalm □, MI • *47,555*
Montclair, CA 91763 • *22,628*
Montclair, NJ 07042–44 • *38,321*
Mont Clare, PA 19453 • *1,274*
Monteagle, TN 37356 • *1,126*
Montebello, CA 90640 • *52,929*
Montecito, CA 93108 • *9,300*
Montegut, LA 70377 • *800*
Montello, WI 53949 • *1,273*
Monterey, CA 93940 • *27,558*
Monterey, TN 38574 • *2,610*
Monterey □, CA • *290,444*
Monterey Park, CA 91754 • *54,338*
Montesano, WA 98563 • *3,247*
Montevallo, AL 35115 • *3,965*
Montevideo, MN 56265 • *5,845*
Monte Vista, CO 81144 • *3,902*
Montezuma, GA 31063 • *4,830*
Montezuma, IN 47862 • *1,352*
Montezuma, IA 50171 • *1,485*
Montezuma, KS 67867 • *730*
Montezuma □, CO • *16,510*
Montfort, WI 53569 • *616*
Montgomery, AL 36101–99 • *177,857*
Montgomery, IL 60538 • *3,369*
Montgomery, LA 71454 • *843*
Montgomery, MN 56069 • *2,349*
Montgomery, NY 12549 • *2,316*
Montgomery, OH 45242 • *10,088*
Montgomery, PA 17752 • *1,653*
Montgomery, WV 25136 • *3,104*
Montgomery □, AL • *197,038*
Montgomery □, AR • *7,771*
Montgomery □, GA • *7,011*
Montgomery □, IL • *31,686*
Montgomery □, IN • *35,501*
Montgomery □, IA • *13,413*
Montgomery □, KS • *42,281*
Montgomery □, KY • *20,046*
Montgomery □, MD • *579,053*
Montgomery □, MS • *13,366*
Montgomery □, MO • *11,537*
Montgomery □, NC • *22,469*
Montgomery □, NY • *53,439*
Montgomery □, OH • *571,697*
Montgomery □, PA • *643,621*
Montgomery □, TN • *83,342*
Montgomery □, TX • *128,487*
Montgomery □, VA • *63,516*
Montgomery City, MO 63361 • *2,101*
Montgomery Creek, CA 96065 • *800*
Montgomery Village, MD 20879 • *16,600*
Monticello, AR 71655 • *8,259*
Monticello, FL 32344 • *2,994*
Monticello, GA 31064 • *2,382*
Monticello, IL 61856 • *4,753*
Monticello, IN 47960 • *5,162*
Monticello, IA 52310 • *3,641*
Monticello, KY 42633 • *5,677*
Monticello, MN 55362 • *2,830*
Monticello, MS 39654 • *1,834*
Monticello, NY 12701 • *6,306*
Monticello, UT 84535 • *1,929*
Monticello, WI 53570 • *1,021*
Montmorenci, SC 29839 • *900*
Montmorency □, MI • *7,492*
Montour □, PA • *16,675*
Montour Falls, NY 14865 • *1,791*
Montoursville, PA 17754 • *5,403*
Montpelier, ID 83254 • *3,107*
Montpelier, IN 47359 • *1,995*
Montpelier, OH 43543 • *4,431*
Montpelier, VT 05602 • *8,241*
Montreal, WI 54550 • *887*
Montreat, NC 28757 • *741*
Montrose, AL 36559 • *1,200*
Montrose, AR 71658 • *641*
Montrose, CO 81401 • *8,722*
Montrose, IA 52639 • *1,038*
Montrose, MI 48457 • *1,706*
Montrose, PA 18801 • *1,980*
Montrose, VA 23231 • *2,200*
Montrose □, CO • *24,352*
Montvale, NJ 07645 • *7,318*
Montville, CT 06353 • *1,711*
Montville, NJ 07045 • *2,700*
Monument, CO 80132 • *690*
Monument Beach, MA 02553 • *1,500*
Monument Heights, VA 23226 • *3,100*
Moodus, CT 06469 • *1,179*
Moody, TX 76557 • *1,385*
Moody □, SD • *6,692*
Moody Beach, ME 04054 • *3,000*
Moonachie, NJ 07074 • *2,706*
Moon Run, PA 15136 • *700*
Moorcroft, WY 82721 • *1,014*
Moore, OK 73160 • *35,063*
Moore □, NC • *50,505*
Moore □, TN • *4,510*
Moore □, TX • *16,575*
Moorefield, WV 26836 • *2,257*
Moore Haven, FL 33471 • *1,250*
Mooreland, OK 73852 • *1,383*
Moorestown, NJ 08057 • *15,596*
Mooresville, IN 46158 • *5,349*
Mooresville, NC 28115 • *8,575*
Moorhead, MN 56560 • *29,998*
Moorhead, MS 38761 • *2,358*
Mooringsport, LA 71060 • *911*
Moose Lake, MN 55767 • *1,408*
Moosic, PA 18507 • *6,068*
Moosup, CT 06354 • *3,308*
Mora, MN 55051 • *2,890*
Mora, NM 87732 • *900*
Mora □, NM • *4,205*
Moraga, CA 94556 • *15,014*
Moraine, OH 45439 • *5,325*
Moran, KS 66755 • *643*
Moravia, IA 52571 • *706*
Moravia, NY 13118 • *1,582*
Moreauville, LA 71355 • *853*
Morehead, KY 40351 • *7,789*
Morehead City, NC 28557 • *4,359*
Morehouse, MO 63868 • *1,220*
Morehouse □, LA • *34,803*
Morenci, AZ 85540 • *1,200*
Morenci, MI 49256 • *2,110*
Morgan, MN 56266 • *975*
Morgan, UT 84050 • *1,896*
Morgan □, AL • *90,231*
Morgan □, CO • *22,513*
Morgan □, GA • *11,572*
Morgan □, IL • *37,502*
Morgan □, IN • *51,999*
Morgan □, KY • *12,103*
Morgan □, MO • *13,807*
Morgan □, OH • *14,241*
Morgan □, TN • *16,604*
Morgan □, UT • *4,917*
Morgan □, WV • *10,711*
Morgan City, LA 70380 • *16,114*
Morganfield, KY 42437 • *3,781*
Morgan Hill, CA 95037 • *17,060*
Morganton, NC 28655 • *13,763*
Morgantown, IN 46160 • *897*
Morgantown, KY 42261 • *2,000*
Morgantown, MS 39120 • *3,445*
Morgantown, PA 19543 • *800*
Morgantown, WV 26505 • *27,605*
Morganville, NJ 07751 • *900*
Morganza, LA 70759 • *846*
Moriarty, NM 87035 • *1,276*
Morley, MO 63767 • *745*
Morningdale, MA 01530 • *1,150*
Morning Sun, IA 52640 • *959*
Morocco, IN 47963 • *1,348*
Moroni, UT 84646 • *1,086*
Morrill, NE 69358 • *1,097*
Morrill □, NE • *6,085*
Morrilton, AR 72110 • *7,355*
Morris, AL 35116 • *623*
Morris, IL 60450 • *8,833*
Morris, MN 56267 • *5,367*
Morris, NY 13808 • *681*
Morris, OK 74445 • *1,288*
Morris □, KS • *6,419*
Morris □, NJ • *407,630*
Morris □, TX • *14,629*
Morrison, IL 61270 • *4,605*
Morrison, OK 73061 • *671*
Morrison □, MN • *29,311*
Morrison City, TN 37660 • *2,032*
Morrisonville, IL 62546 • *1,208*
Morrisonville, NY 12962 • *1,500*
Morris Plains, NJ 07950 • *5,305*
Morristown, IN 46161 • *989*
Morristown, MN 55052 • *639*
Morristown, NJ 07960 • *16,614*
Morristown, TN 37814 • *19,683*
Morrisville, NY 13408 • *2,707*
Morrisville, PA 19067 • *9,845*
Morrisville, VT 05661 • *2,074*
Morro Bay, CA 93442 • *9,064*
Morrow, GA 30260 • *3,791*
Morrow, OH 45152 • *1,254*
Morrow □, OH • *26,480*
Morrow □, OR • *7,519*
Morse, LA 70559 • *835*
Morton, IL 61550 • *14,178*
Morton, MS 39117 • *3,303*
Morton, TX 79346 • *2,674*
Morton, WA 98356 • *1,264*
Morton □, KS • *3,454*
Morton □, ND • *25,177*
Morton Grove, IL 60053 • *23,747*
Mortons Gap, KY 42440 • *1,201*
Morven, NC 28119 • *765*
Moscow, ID 83843 • *16,513*
Moscow, PA 18444 • *1,536*
Moses Lake, WA 98837 • *10,629*
Mosheim, TN 37818 • *1,539*
Mosinee, WI 54455 • *3,015*
Moss Bluff, LA 70611 • *7,004*
Moss Point, MS 39563 • *18,998*
Motley □, TX • *1,950*
Mott, ND 58646 • *1,315*
Moulton, AL 35650 • *3,197*
Moulton, IA 52572 • *762*
Moultrie, GA 31768 • *15,708*
Moultrie □, IL • *14,546*
Mound, MN 55364 • *9,280*
Mound Bayou, MS 38762 • *2,917*
Mound City, IL 62963 • *1,102*
Mound City, KS 66056 • *755*
Mound City, MO 64470 • *1,447*
Moundridge, KS 67107 • *1,453*
Mounds, IL 62964 • *1,669*
Mounds, OK 74047 • *1,086*
Mounds View, MN 55432 • *12,593*
Moundsville, WV 26041 • *12,419*
Moundville, AL 35474 • *1,310*
Mountainair, NM 87036 • *1,170*
Mountainaire, AZ 86001 • *700*
Mountain Brook, AL 35223 • *19,718*
Mountain City, GA 30562 • *701*
Mountain City, TN 37683 • *2,125*
Mountain Dale, NY 12763 • *1,200*
Mountain Grove, MO 65711 • *3,974*
Mountain Home, AR 72653 • *8,066*
Mountain Home, ID 83647 • *7,540*
Mountain Iron, MN 55768 • *4,134*
Mountain Lake, MN 56159 • *2,277*
Mountain Lake Park, MD 21550 • *1,597*
Mountain Lakes, NJ 07046 • *4,153*
Mountain Pine, AR 71956 • *1,068*
Mountainside, NJ 07092 • *7,118*
Mountain View, AR 72560 • *2,147*
Mountain View, CA 94040–43 • *58,655*
Mountain View, CO 80521 • *1,294*
Mountain View, MO 65548 • *1,664*
Mountain View, NM 87105 • *1,900*
Mountain View, OK 73062 • *1,189*
Mountain View, WY 82601 • *1,500*
Mountain View, WY 82939 • *628*
Mount Airy, GA 30563 • *670*
Mount Airy, MD 21771 • *2,450*
Mount Airy, NC 27030 • *6,862*
Mount Angel, OR 97362 • *2,876*
Mount Arlington, NJ 07856 • *4,251*
Mount Ayr, IA 50854 • *1,938*
Mount Carmel, IL 62863 • *8,908*
Mount Carmel, OH 45244 • *900*
Mount Carmel, PA 17851 • *8,190*
Mount Carroll, IL 61053 • *1,936*
Mount Clare, WV 26408 • *900*
Mount Clemens, MI 48043–46 • *18,806*
Mount Dora, FL 32757 • *5,883*
Mount Ephraim, NJ 08059 • *4,863*
Mount Freedom, NJ 07970 • *1,621*
Mount Gay, WV 25637 • *1,650*
Mount Gilead, NC 27306 • *1,423*
Mount Gilead, OH 43338 • *2,911*
Mount Healthy, OH 45231 • *7,562*
Mount Holly, NJ 08060 • *10,818*
Mount Holly, NC 28120 • *4,530*
Mount Holly Springs, PA 17065 • *2,068*
Mount Hope, KS 67108 • *791*
Mount Hope, WV 25880 • *1,849*
Mount Horeb, WI 53572 • *3,251*
Mount Ida, AR 71957 • *1,023*
Mount Jackson, VA 22842 • *1,419*
Mount Jewett, PA 16740 • *1,053*
Mount Joy, PA 17552 • *5,680*
Mount Juliet, TN 37122 • *2,879*
Mount Kisco, NY 10549 • *8,025*
Mountlake Terrace, WA 98043 • *16,534*
Mount Lebanon, PA 15228 • *34,414*
Mount Morris, IL 61054 • *2,989*
Mount Morris, MI 48458 • *3,246*
Mount Morris, NY 14510 • *3,039*
Mount Olive, AL 35117 • *1,900*
Mount Olive, IL 62069 • *2,357*
Mount Olive, MS 39119 • *993*
Mount Olive, NC 28365 • *4,876*
Mount Orab, OH 45154 • *1,573*
Mount Penn, PA 19606 • *3,025*
Mount Pleasant, IA 52641 • *7,322*
Mount Pleasant, MI 48858 • *23,746*
Mount Pleasant, NC 28124 • *1,210*
Mount Pleasant, PA 15666 • *5,354*
Mount Pleasant, SC 29464 • *14,209*
Mount Pleasant, TN 38474 • *3,375*
Mount Pleasant, TX 75455 • *11,003*
Mount Pleasant, UT 84647 • *2,049*
Mount Pocono, PA 18344 • *1,237*
Mount Prospect, IL 60056 • *52,634*
Mount Pulaski, IL 62548 • *1,783*
Mountrail □, ND • *7,679*
Mount Rainier, MD 20712 • *7,361*
Mount Savage, MD 21545 • *1,640*
Mount Shasta, CA 96067 • *2,837*
Mount Sterling, IL 62353 • *2,186*
Mount Sterling, KY 40353 • *5,820*
Mount Sterling, OH 43143 • *1,623*
Mount Union, PA 17066 • *3,101*
Mount Vernon, AL 36560 • *1,038*
Mount Vernon, GA 30445 • *1,737*
Mount Vernon, IL 62864 • *17,193*
Mount Vernon, IN 47620 • *7,656*
Mount Vernon, IA 52314 • *3,325*
Mount Vernon, KY 40456 • *2,334*
Mount Vernon, MO 65712 • *3,341*
Mount Vernon, NY 10550–59 • *66,713*
Mount Vernon, OH 43050 • *14,323*
Mount Vernon, TX 75457 • *2,025*
Mount Vernon, WA 98273 • *13,009*
Mount Victory, OH 43340 • *667*
Mount Washington, KY 40047 • *3,997*
Mount Wolf, PA 17347 • *1,517*
Mount Zion, IL 62549 • *4,563*
Moville, IA 51039 • *1,273*
Moweaqua, IL 62550 • *1,922*
Mower □, MN • *40,390*
Moxee City, WA 98936 • *687*
Moyock, NC 27958 • *700*
Muenster, TX 76252 • *1,408*
Muhlenberg □, KY • *32,238*
Muir, MI 48860 • *698*
Mukilteo, WA 98275 • *1,426*
Mukwonago, WI 53149 • *4,014*
Mulberry, AR 72947 • *1,444*
Mulberry, FL 33860 • *2,932*
Mulberry, IN 46058 • *1,225*
Mulberry, KS 66756 • *647*
Mulberry, NC 28659 • *1,210*
Mulberry, OH 45150 • *800*
Mulberry Grove, IL 62262 • *707*
Muldraugh, KY 40155 • *1,752*
Muldrow, OK 74948 • *2,538*

United States Populations and ZIP Codes

Muleshoe, TX 79347 • *4,842*
Mullan, ID 83846 • *1,269*
Mullen, NE 69152 • *720*
Mullens, WV 25882 • *2,919*
Mullica Hill, NJ 08062 • *1,050*
Mullins, SC 29574 • *6,068*
Multnomah □, OR • *562,640*
Mulvane, KS 67110 • *4,254*
Muncie, IN 47302–06 • *77,216*
Muncy, PA 17756 • *2,700*
Munday, TX 76371 • *1,738*
Mundelein, IL 60060 • *17,053*
Munford, TN 38058 • *2,336*
Munfordville, KY 42765 • *1,783*
Munhall, PA 15120 • *14,535*
Munising, MI 49862 • *3,083*
Munster, IN 46321 • *20,671*
Murdo, SD 57559 • *723*
Murfreesboro, AR 71958 • *1,883*
Murfreesboro, NC 27855 • *3,007*
Murfreesboro, TN 37130 • *32,845*
Murphy, MO 63026 • *8,121*
Murphy, NC 28906 • *2,070*
Murphys, CA 95247 • *950*
Murphysboro, IL 62966 • *9,866*
Murray, IA 50174 • *703*
Murray, KY 42071 • *14,248*
Murray, UT 84107 • *25,750*
Murray □, GA • *19,685*
Murray □, MN • *11,507*
Murray □, OK • *12,147*
Murrayville, IL 62668 • *712*
Murrells Inlet, SC 29576 • *950*
Murrysville, PA 15668 • *16,036*
Muscatine, IA 52761 • *23,467*
Muscatine □, IA • *40,436*
Muscle Shoals, AL 35662 • *8,911*
Muscoda, WI 53573 • *1,331*
Muscogee □, GA • *170,108*
Muscoy, CA 92405 • *6,188*
Muse, PA 15350 • *1,358*
Muskego, WI 53150 • *15,277*
Muskegon, MI 49440–45 • *40,823*
Muskegon □, MI • *157,589*
Muskegon Heights, MI 49444 • *14,611*
Muskingum □, OH • *83,340*
Muskogee, OK 74401–03 • *40,011*
Muskogee □, OK • *66,939*
Musselshell □, MT • *4,428*
Mustang, OK 73064 • *7,496*
Myerstown, PA 17067 • *3,131*
Myrtle Beach, SC 29577–79 • *18,446*
Myrtle Creek, OR 97457 • *3,365*
Myrtle Grove, FL 32506 • *14,238*
Myrtle Point, OR 97458 • *2,859*
Mystic, CT 06355 • *2,333*
Mystic, IA 52574 • *665*

## N

Naalehu, HI 96772 • *1,168*
Nabnasset, MA 01886 • *4,800*
Naches, WA 98937 • *644*
Naco, AZ 85620 • *800*
Nacogdoches, TX 75961 • *27,149*
Nacogdoches □, TX • *46,786*
Nags Head, NC 27959 • *1,020*
Nahant, MA 01908 • *3,947*
Nahunta, GA 31553 • *951*
Nampa, ID 83651 • *25,112*
Nanakuli, HI 96792 • *8,185*
Nance □, NE • *4,740*
Nanticoke, PA 18634 • *13,044*
Nantucket, MA 02554 • *3,229*
Nantucket □, MA • *5,087*
Nanty Glo, PA 15943 • *3,936*
Nanuet, NY 10954 • *8,300*
Napa, CA 94558–59 • *50,879*
Napa □, CA • *99,199*
Napanoch, NY 12458 • *800*
Napavine, WA 98565 • *611*
Naperville, IL 60540 • *42,601*
Naples, FL 33940–42 • *17,581*
Naples, NY 14512 • *1,225*
Naples, TX 75568 • *1,908*
Napoleon, ND 58561 • *1,103*
Napoleon, OH 43545 • *8,614*
Napoleonville, LA 70390 • *829*
Nappanee, IN 46550 • *4,694*
Naranja, FL 33032 • *5,000*
Narberth, PA 19072 • *4,496*
Narragansett, RI 02882 • *3,342*
Narrows, VA 24124 • *2,516*
Narrowsburg, NY 12764 • *700*
Naselle, WA 98638 • *900*
Nash, TX 75569 • *2,022*
Nash □, NC • *67,153*
Nashua, IA 50658 • *1,846*
Nashua, NH 03060–63 • *67,865*
Nashville, AR 71852 • *4,554*
Nashville, GA 31639 • *4,831*
Nashville, IL 62263 • *3,186*
Nashville, IN 47448 • *705*
Nashville, MI 49073 • *1,628*
Nashville, NC 27856 • *3,033*
Nashville, TN 37201–99 • *455,651*
Nashwauk, MN 55769 • *1,419*
Nassau, NY 12123 • *1,285*
Nassau □, FL • *32,894*
Nassau □, NY • *1,321,582*
Nassau Shores, NY 11758 • *5,500*
Nassawadox, VA 23413 • *630*
Natalbany, LA 70451 • *700*
Natalia, TX 78059 • *1,264*
Natchez, MS 39120 • *22,015*
Natchitoches, LA 71457 • *16,664*
Natchitoches □, LA • *39,863*
Natick, MA 01760 • *29,461*
National City, CA 92050 • *48,772*
National Park, NJ 08063 • *3,552*
Natrona □, WY • *71,856*
Natrona Heights, PA 15065 • *13,252*
Natural Bridge, NY 13665 • *650*
Naturita, CO 81422 • *819*
Naugatuck, CT 06770 • *26,456*
Nautilus Park, CT 06340 • *6,500*
Nauvoo, IL 62354 • *1,133*
Navajo □, AZ • *67,629*
Navarre, OH 44662 • *1,343*
Navarro □, TX • *35,323*
Navasota, TX 77868 • *5,971*
Navesink, NJ 07752 • *1,500*
Naylor, MO 63953 • *602*
Nazareth, KY 40048 • *700*
Nazareth, PA 18064 • *5,443*
Neah Bay, WA 98357 • *1,000*
Nebraska City, NE 68410 • *7,127*
Necedah, WI 54646 • *773*
Nederland, CO 80466 • *1,212*
Nederland, TX 77627 • *16,855*
Nedrow, NY 13120 • *3,000*
Needham, MA 02192 • *27,901*
Needles, CA 92363 • *4,120*
Needville, TX 77461 • *1,417*
Neenah, WI 54956 • *22,432*
Neffs, OH 43940 • *1,106*
Neffsville, PA 17601 • *1,300*
Negaunee, MI 49866 • *5,189*
Negley, OH 44441 • *900*
Neillsville, WI 54456 • *2,780*
Nekoosa, WI 54457 • *2,519*
Neligh, NE 68756 • *1,893*
Nelson, NE 68961 • *733*
Nelson □, KY • *27,584*
Nelson □, ND • *5,233*
Nelson □, VA • *12,204*
Nelsonville, OH 45764 • *4,567*
Nemacolin, PA 15351 • *1,273*
Nemaha □, KS • *11,211*
Nemaha □, NE • *8,367*
Neodesha, KS 66757 • *3,414*
Neoga, IL 62447 • *1,736*
Neola, IA 51559 • *839*
Neopit, WI 54150 • *1,122*
Neosho, MO 64850 • *9,493*
Neosho □, KS • *18,967*
Nephi, UT 84648 • *3,285*
Neptune, NJ 07753 • *28,366*
Neptune Beach, FL 32233 • *5,248*
Neptune City, NJ 07753 • *5,276*
Nesconset, NY 11767 • *8,300*
Nescopeck, PA 18635 • *1,768*
Neshoba □, MS • *23,789*
Nesquehoning, PA 18240 • *3,346*
Ness □, KS • *4,498*
Ness City, KS 67560 • *1,769*
Netcong, NJ 07857 • *3,557*
Nettleton, MS 38858 • *1,911*
Nevada, IA 50201 • *5,912*
Nevada, MO 64772 • *9,044*
Nevada, OH 44849 • *945*
Nevada □, AR • *11,097*
Nevada □, CA • *51,645*
Nevada City, CA 95959 • *2,431*
New Albany, IN 47150 • *37,103*
New Albany, MS 38652 • *7,072*
New Albin, IA 52160 • *609*
Newark, AR 72562 • *1,128*
Newark, CA 94560 • *32,126*
Newark, DE 19711–13 • *25,247*
Newark, IL 60541 • *798*
Newark, NJ 07101–99 • *329,248*
Newark, NY 14513 • *10,017*
Newark, OH 43055 • *41,200*
Newark Valley, NY 13811 • *1,190*
New Athens, IL 62264 • *1,937*
Newaygo, MI 49337 • *1,271*
Newaygo □, MI • *34,917*
New Baden, IL 62265 • *2,476*
New Baltimore, MI 48047 • *5,439*
New Baltimore, NY 12124 • *700*
New Bedford, MA 02740–48 • *98,478*
New Bedford, PA 16140 • *900*
Newberg, OR 97132 • *10,394*
New Berlin, IL 62670 • *834*
New Berlin, NY 13411 • *1,392*
New Berlin, PA 17855 • *783*
New Berlin, WI 53151 • *30,529*
New Bern, NC 28560 • *14,557*
Newbern, TN 38059 • *2,794*
Newberry, FL 32669 • *1,826*
Newberry, MI 49868 • *2,120*
Newberry, SC 29108 • *9,866*
Newberry □, SC • *31,242*
Newberry Springs, CA 92365 • *900*
New Bethlehem, PA 16242 • *1,441*
New Bloomfield, PA 17068 • *1,109*
New Boston, IL 61272 • *731*
New Boston, MI 48164 • *1,200*
New Boston, OH 45662 • *3,188*
New Boston, TX 75570 • *4,628*
New Braunfels, TX 78130 • *22,402*
New Bremen, OH 45869 • *2,393*
New Brighton, MN 55112 • *23,269*
New Brighton, PA 15066 • *7,364*
New Britain, CT 06050–53 • *73,840*
New Brockton, AL 36351 • *1,392*
New Brunswick, NJ 08901–99 • *41,442*
New Buffalo, MI 49117 • *2,821*
Newburg, MO 65550 • *743*
Newburg, WI 53060 • *783*
Newburgh, IN 47630 • *2,906*
Newburgh, NY 12550 • *23,438*
Newburgh Heights, OH 44105 • *2,678*
Newbury, MA 01950 • *900*
Newburyport, MA 01950 • *15,900*
New Canaan, CT 06840 • *17,931*
New Carlisle, IN 46552 • *1,439*
New Carlisle, OH 45344 • *6,498*
New Carrollton, MD 20784 • *12,632*
New Cassel, NY 11590 • *8,817*
New Castle, AL 35119 • *1,000*
New Castle, DE 19720 • *4,907*
New Castle, IN 47362 • *20,056*
New Castle, KY 40050 • *832*
New Castle, NH 03854 • *975*
Newcastle, OK 73065 • *3,076*
New Castle, PA 16101–08 • *33,621*
Newcastle, TX 76372 • *688*
Newcastle, WY 82701 • *3,596*
New Castle □, DE • *398,115*
New City, NY 10956 • *30,800*
Newcomb, NY 12852 • *800*
Newcomerstown, OH 43832 • *3,986*
New Concord, OH 43762 • *1,860*
New Cumberland, PA 17070 • *8,051*
New Cumberland, WV 26047 • *1,752*
New Egypt, NJ 08533 • *2,111*
Newell, IA 50568 • *913*
Newell, SD 57760 • *638*
Newell, WV 26050 • *1,900*
New Ellenton, SC 29809 • *2,628*
Newellton, LA 71357 • *1,726*
New England, ND 58647 • *825*
New Fairfield, CT 06812 • *2,150*
Newfane, NY 14108 • *2,700*
Newfield, NJ 08344 • *1,563*
Newfields, NH 03856 • *700*
New Florence, MO 63363 • *731*
New Florence, PA 15944 • *855*
Newfoundland, NJ 07435 • *900*
New Franklin, MO 65274 • *1,228*
New Freedom, PA 17349 • *2,205*
New Glarus, WI 53574 • *1,763*
Newhall, CA 91321 • *12,029*
Newhall, IA 52315 • *899*
New Hampton, IA 50659 • *3,940*
New Hanover □, NC • *103,471*
New Harmony, IN 47631 • *945*
New Hartford, CT 06057 • *1,310*
New Hartford, IA 50660 • *764*
New Haven, CT 06501–99 • *126,109*
New Haven, IN 46774 • *6,714*
New Haven, KY 40051 • *926*
New Haven, MI 48048 • *1,871*
New Haven, MO 63068 • *1,581*
New Haven, WV 25265 • *1,723*
New Haven □, CT • *761,337*
New Holland, GA 30501 • *800*
New Holland, OH 43145 • *783*
New Holland, PA 17557 • *4,147*
New Holstein, WI 53061 • *3,412*
New Hope, AL 35760 • *1,546*
New Hope, MN 55428 • *23,087*
New Hope, PA 18938 • *1,473*
New Hudson, MI 48165 • *800*
New Hyde Park, NY 11040 • *9,801*
New Iberia, LA 70560 • *32,766*
Newington, CT 06111 • *28,841*
New Johnsonville, TN 37134 • *1,824*
New Kensington, PA 15068 • *17,660*
New Kent □, VA • *8,781*
Newkirk, OK 74647 • *2,413*
New Knoxville, OH 45871 • *760*
Newland, NC 28657 • *722*
New Lebanon, NY 12125 • *800*
New Lenox, IL 60451 • *5,792*
New Lexington, OH 43764 • *5,179*
New Lisbon, WI 53950 • *1,390*
Newllano, LA 71461 • *2,213*
New London, CT 06320 • *28,842*
New London, IA 52645 • *2,043*
New London, MN 56273 • *812*
New London, MO 63459 • *1,161*
New London, NH 03257 • *1,335*
New London, OH 44851 • *2,449*
New London, WI 54961 • *6,210*
New London □, CT • *238,409*
New Lothrop, MI 48460 • *646*
New Madison, OH 45346 • *1,008*
New Madrid, MO 63869 • *3,204*
New Madrid □, MO • *22,945*
Newman, CA 95360 • *2,785*
Newman, IL 61942 • *1,079*
Newman Grove, NE 68758 • *930*
Newmanstown, PA 17073 • *1,532*
New Market, IN 47965 • *608*
Newmarket, NH 03857 • *3,749*
New Market, TN 37820 • *1,216*
New Market, VA 22844 • *1,118*
New Martinsville, WV 26155 • *7,109*
New Matamoras, OH 45767 • *1,172*
New Miami, OH 45011 • *2,980*
New Milford, CT 06776 • *5,186*
New Milford, NJ 07646 • *16,876*
New Milford, PA 18834 • *1,040*
Newnan, GA 30263–65 • *11,449*
New Orleans, LA 70101–99 • *557,927*
New Oxford, PA 17350 • *1,921*
New Palestine, IN 46163 • *749*
New Paltz, NY 12561 • *4,938*
New Paris, IN 46553 • *1,062*
New Paris, OH 45347 • *1,709*
New Philadelphia, OH 44663 • *16,883*
New Philadelphia, PA 17959 • *1,341*
New Plymouth, ID 83655 • *1,186*
Newport, AR 72112 • *8,339*
Newport, DE 19804 • *1,167*
Newport, IN 47966 • *704*
Newport, KY 41071–76 • *21,587*
Newport, ME 04953 • *1,748*
Newport, MI 48166 • *900*
Newport, MN 55055 • *3,323*
Newport, NH 03773 • *4,388*
Newport, NC 28570 • *1,883*
Newport, NY 13416 • *746*
Newport, OH 45768 • *950*
Newport, OR 97365 • *7,519*
Newport, PA 17074 • *1,600*
Newport, RI 02840 • *29,259*
Newport, TN 37821 • *7,580*
Newport, VT 05855 • *4,756*
Newport, WA 99156 • *1,665*
Newport □, RI • *81,383*
Newport Beach, CA 92660–63 • *62,556*
Newport Hills, WA 98006 • *6,000*
Newport News, VA 23601–07 • *144,903*
New Port Richey, FL 34652–56 • *11,196*
New Prague, MN 56071 • *2,952*
New Preston, CT 06777 • *1,209*
New Providence, NJ 07974 • *12,426*
New Richland, MN 56072 • *1,263*
New Richmond, OH 45157 • *2,769*
New Richmond, WI 54017 • *4,306*
New Roads, LA 70760 • *3,924*
New Rochelle, NY 10801–99 • *70,794*
New Rockford, ND 58356 • *1,791*
New Salem, ND 58563 • *1,081*
New Sarpy, LA 70078 • *2,249*
New Sharon, IA 50207 • *1,225*
New Smyrna Beach, FL 32069 • *13,557*
New Straitsville, OH 43766 • *937*
New Tazewell, TN 37825 • *1,677*
Newton, AL 36352 • *1,540*
Newton, GA 31770 • *711*
Newton, IL 62448 • *3,186*
Newton, IA 50208 • *15,292*
Newton, KS 67114 • *16,332*
Newton, MA 02158 • *83,622*
Newton, MS 39345 • *3,708*
Newton, NJ 07860 • *7,748*
Newton, NC 28658 • *7,624*
Newton, TX 75966 • *1,620*
Newton, UT 84327 • *623*
Newton □, AR • *7,756*
Newton □, GA • *34,489*
Newton □, IN • *14,844*
Newton □, MS • *19,944*
Newton □, MO • *40,555*
Newton □, TX • *13,254*
Newton Falls, OH 44444 • *4,960*
Newtown, CT 06470 • *2,022*
New Town, ND 58763 • *1,335*
Newtown, OH 45244 • *1,817*
Newtown Square, PA 19073 • *11,775*
New Ulm, MN 56073 • *13,755*
New Vienna, OH 45159 • *1,133*
Newville, AL 36353 • *814*
Newville, PA 17241 • *1,370*
New Washington, OH 44854 • *1,213*
New Washoe City, NV 89701 • *2,543*
New Waterford, OH 44445 • *1,314*
New Waverly, TX 77358 • *824*
New Whiteland, IN 46184 • *4,502*
New Wilmington, PA 16142 • *2,774*
New Windsor, IL 61465 • *863*
New Windsor, MD 21776 • *799*
New Windsor, NY 12550 • *8,803*
New York, NY 10001–99 • *7,071,639*
New York □, NY • *1,428,285*
New York Mills, MN 56567 • *972*
Nez Perce □, ID • *33,220*
Niagara, WI 54151 • *2,079*
Niagara □, NY • *227,354*
Niagara Falls, NY 14301–99 • *71,384*
Niantic, CT 06357 • *3,151*
Nibley, UT 84321 • *1,036*
Niceville, FL 32578 • *8,543*
Nicholas □, KY • *7,157*
Nicholas □, WV • *28,126*
Nicholasville, KY 40356 • *10,319*
Nicholls, GA 31554 • *1,114*
Nichols, NY 13812 • *613*
Nichols, SC 29581 • *606*
Nichols Hills, OK 73116 • *4,171*
Nicholson, PA 18446 • *945*
Nickerson, KS 67561 • *1,292*
Nicollet, MN 56074 • *709*
Nicollet □, MN • *26,929*
Nicoma Park, OK 73066 • *2,588*
Nikishka, AK 99635 • *1,109*
Niland, CA 92257 • *1,042*
Niles, IL 60648 • *30,363*
Niles, MI 49120 • *13,115*
Niles, OH 44446 • *23,088*
Ninety Six, SC 29666 • *2,249*
Niobrara □, WY • *2,924*
Niota, TN 37826 • *765*
Nipomo, CA 93444 • *5,247*
Niskayuna, NY 12309 • *17,471*
Nisswa, MN 56468 • *1,391*
Nitro, WV 25143 • *8,074*
Nixa, MO 65714 • *2,662*
Nixon, TX 78140 • *2,008*
Noank, CT 06340 • *1,406*
Noble, IL 62868 • *832*
Noble, OK 73068 • *3,497*
Noble □, IN • *35,443*
Noble □, OH • *11,310*
Noble □, OK • *11,573*
Nobles □, MN • *21,840*
Noblesville, IN 46060 • *12,056*
Nocatee, FL 33864 • *1,300*
Nocona, TX 76255 • *2,992*
Nodaway □, MO • *21,996*
Noel, MO 64854 • *1,161*
Nogales, AZ 85621 • *15,683*
Nokomis, FL 34275 • *3,108*
Nokomis, IL 62075 • *2,656*
Nolan □, TX • *17,359*
Nome, AK 99762 • *2,301*
Nora Springs, IA 50458 • *1,572*
Norborne, MO 64668 • *931*
Norco, CA 91760 • *21,126*
Norco, LA 70079 • *4,416*
Norcross, GA 30071 • *3,317*
Norfolk, CT 06058 • *1,500*
Norfolk, NE 68701 • *19,449*
Norfolk, NY 13667 • *1,379*
Norfolk, VA 23501–99 • *266,979*
Norfolk □, MA • *606,587*
Norland, FL 33169 • *19,471*
Norlina, NC 27563 • *901*
Norma, NJ 08347 • *800*
Normal, AL 35762 • *5,000*
Normal, IL 61761 • *35,672*
Norman, OK 73069–71 • *68,020*
Norman □, MN • *9,379*
Normandy, MO 63121 • *5,174*
Normangee, TX 77871 • *636*
Norman Park, GA 31771 • *757*
Norphlet, AR 71759 • *756*
Norridge, IL 60656 • *16,483*
Norridgewock, ME 04957 • *1,318*
Norris, SC 29667 • *903*
Norris, TN 37828 • *1,374*
Norris City, IL 62869 • *1,515*
Norristown, PA 19401–09 • *34,684*
North, SC 29112 • *1,304*
North Abington, MA 02351 • *4,700*
North Acton, MA 01720 • *900*
North Adams, MA 01247 • *18,063*
North Albany, OR 97321 • *4,499*
North Amherst, MA 01059 • *5,616*
North Amityville, NY 11701 • *11,936*
Northampton, MA 01060 • *29,286*
Northampton, PA 18067 • *8,240*
Northampton □, NC • *22,584*
Northampton □, PA • *225,418*
Northampton □, VA • *14,625*
North Andover, MA 01845 • *20,129*
North Andrews Gardens, FL 33308 • *8,967*
North Apollo, PA 15673 • *1,487*
North Arlington, NJ 07032 • *16,587*
North Atlanta, GA 30319 • *22,800*
North Attleboro, MA 02760–63 • *21,095*
North Augusta, SC 29841 • *13,593*
North Aurora, IL 60542 • *5,205*
North Babylon, NY 11703 • *23,000*
North Baltimore, OH 45872 • *3,127*
North Beach, MD 20714 • *1,504*
North Bellmore, NY 11710 • *23,600*
North Belmont, NC 28012 • *5,000*
North Bend, NE 68649 • *1,368*
North Bend, OR 97459 • *9,779*
North Bend, PA 17760 • *700*
North Bend, WA 98045 • *1,701*
North Bennington, VT 05257 • *1,635*
North Bergen, NJ 07047 • *47,019*
North Berwick, ME 03906 • *1,436*
North Billerica, MA 01862 • *6,700*
Northborough, MA 01532 • *5,670*
North Braddock, PA 15104 • *8,711*
North Branch, MI 48461 • *896*
North Branch, MN 55056 • *1,597*
North Branch, NH 03440 • *800*
North Branch, NJ 08876 • *2,500*
North Branford, CT 06471 • *5,200*
Northbridge, MA 01534 • *3,321*
Northbrook, IL 60062 • *30,778*
Northbrook, OH 45231 • *8,357*
North Brookfield, MA 01535 • *2,677*
North Brunswick, NJ 08902 • *22,220*
North Caldwell, NJ 07006 • *5,832*
North Canton, OH 44720 • *14,228*
North Cape May, NJ 08204 • *4,029*
North Carrollton, MS 38947 • *859*
North Carver, MA 02355 • *700*
North Charleston, SC 29406 • *62,534*
North Chicago, IL 60064 • *38,774*
North City, WA 98155 • *6,200*
North Cohasset, MA 02025 • *900*
North College Hill, OH 45239 • *11,114*
North Collins, NY 14111 • *1,496*
North Conway, NH 03860 • *2,184*
North Corbin, KY 40701 • *1,000*
North Creek, NY 12853 • *950*
North Crossett, AR 71635 • *3,513*
North Dartmouth, MA 02747 • *6,000*
North Decatur, GA 30033 • *11,830*
North Dighton, MA 02764 • *1,174*
North Druid Hills, GA 30033 • *8,700*
North Eagle Butte, SD 57625 • *1,354*
North East, MD 21901 • *1,469*
North East, PA 16428 • *4,568*
North Eastham, MA 02651 • *1,318*
Northeast Henrietta, NY 14534 • *12,000*
North Easton, MA 02356 • *6,100*
North English, IA 52316 • *990*
North Enid, OK 73701 • *992*
North Fair Oaks, CA 94025 • *10,294*
North Falmouth, MA 02556 • *1,800*
Northfield, IL 60093 • *5,807*
Northfield, MA 01360 • *1,182*
Northfield, MN 55057 • *12,562*
Northfield, NH 03276 • *1,340*
Northfield, NJ 08225 • *7,795*
Northfield, OH 44067 • *3,913*
Northfield, VT 05663 • *2,033*
North Fond du Lac, WI 54935 • *3,844*
Northford, CT 06472 • *2,800*
North Fork, CA 93643 • *950*
North Fort Myers, FL 33903 • *17,200*
North Freedom, WI 53951 • *616*
Northglenn, CO 80233 • *29,847*
North Grafton, MA 01536 • *3,400*
North Great River, NY 11722 • *12,400*
North Grosvenordale, CT 06255 • *1,856*
North Gulfport, MS 39501 • *6,660*
North Haledon, NJ 07508 • *8,177*
North Hampton, NH 03862 • *1,000*
North Hanover, MA 02339 • *900*
North Haven, CT 06473 • *22,080*
North Highlands, CA 95660 • *37,825*
North Hudson, WI 54016 • *2,218*
North Industry, OH 44707 • *3,250*
North Judson, IN 46366 • *1,653*
North Kansas City, MO 64116 • *4,507*
North Kingstown, RI 02852 • *3,100*
North Kingsville, OH 44068 • *2,939*
North La Junta, CO 81050 • *1,076*
Northlake, IL 60164 • *12,166*
North Las Vegas, NV 89030 • *42,739*
North Lauderdale, FL 33068 • *18,653*
North Lewisburg, OH 43060 • *1,072*
North Liberty, IN 46554 • *1,211*
North Liberty, IA 52317 • *2,046*
North Lima, OH 44452 • *900*
North Lindenhurst, NY 11757 • *11,400*
North Little Rock, AR 72114–19 • *64,288*
North Logan, UT 84321 • *2,258*
North Manchester, IN 46962 • *5,998*
North Mankato, MN 56001 • *9,145*
North Massapequa, NY 11758 • *23,100*
North Merrick, NY 11566 • *13,650*
North Merrydale, LA 70812 • *3,500*
North Miami, FL 33161 • *36,553*
North Miami Beach, FL 33162 • *36,481*
North Middletown, KY 40357 • *637*
North Muskegon, MI 49445 • *4,024*
North Myrtle Beach, SC 29582 • *3,960*
North Naples, FL 33940 • *7,950*
North New Hyde Park, NY 11040 • *16,100*
North Oaks, CA 91350 • *5,800*
North Ogden, UT 84404 • *9,309*
North Olmsted, OH 44070 • *36,486*
North Omaha, NE 68112 • *1,100*
North Oxford, MA 01537 • *1,550*
North Palm Beach, FL 33408 • *11,344*
North Park, IL 61111 • *15,806*
North Patchogue, NY 11772 • *8,000*
North Pembroke, MA 02358 • *2,215*
North Plainfield, NJ 07060 • *19,108*
North Plains, OR 97133 • *715*
North Platte, NE 69101 • *24,509*
Northport, AL 35476 • *14,291*
North Port, FL 34287 • *6,205*
Northport, MI 49670 • *611*
Northport, NY 11768 • *7,651*
North Prairie, WI 53153 • *938*
North Providence, RI 02911 • *18,220*
North Reading, MA 01864 • *11,455*
North Richland Hills, TX 76118 • *30,592*
Northridge, OH 45502 • *5,559*
North Ridgeville, OH 44039 • *21,522*
North Riverside, IL 60546 • *6,764*
North Rose, NY 14516 • *700*
North Royalton, OH 44133 • *17,671*
North Salt Lake, UT 84054 • *5,548*
North Scituate, MA 02060 • *4,100*

North Sioux City, SD 57049 • *1,992*
North Springfield, VT 05150 • *750*
North Springfield, VA 22151 • *8,631*
North Star, DE 19711 • *650*
North St. Paul, MN 55109 • *11,921*
North Stratford, NH 03590 • *650*
North Sudbury, MA 01776 • *1,700*
North Swansea, MA 02777 • *950*
North Swanzey, NH 03431 • *950*
North Syracuse, NY 13212 • *7,970*
North Tarrytown, NY 10591 • *7,994*
North Terre Haute, IN 47805 • *1,500*
North Tewksbury, MA 01876 • *1,400*
North Tonawanda, NY 14120 • *35,760*
North Troy, VT 05859 • *717*
North Truro, MA 02652 • *700*
North Tunica, MS 38676 • *1,026*
Northumberland, PA 17857 • *3,636*
Northumberland □, PA • *100,381*
Northumberland □, VA • *9,828*
North Uxbridge, MA 01538 • *1,400*
Northvale, NJ 07647 • *5,046*
North Valley Stream, NY 11580 • *14,881*
North Vassalboro, ME 04962 • *850*
North Vernon, IN 47265 • *5,768*
North Versailles, PA 15137 • *13,294*
Northville, MI 48167 • *5,698*
Northville, NY 12134 • *1,304*
North Wales, PA 19454 • *3,391*
North Walpole, NH 03609 • *950*
North Wantagh, NY 11793 • *15,117*
North Warren, PA 16365 • *1,360*
North Webster, IN 46555 • *709*
North Wildwood, NJ 08260 • *4,714*
North Wilkesboro, NC 28659 • *3,260*
North Wilmington, MA 01887 • *4,200*
North Windham, CT 06256 • *750*
North Windham, ME 04062 • *5,492*
Northwood, IA 50459 • *2,193*
Northwood, ND 58267 • *1,240*
Northwood, OH 43619 • *5,495*
Northwoods, MO 63121 • *5,831*
North York, PA 17404 • *1,755*
Norton, KS 67654 • *3,400*
Norton, MA 02766 • *2,035*
Norton, OH 44203 • *12,242*
Norton, VA 24273 • *4,757*
Norton □, KS • *6,689*
Norton Shores, MI 49441 • *22,025*
Nortonville, KS 66060 • *692*
Nortonville, KY 42442 • *1,336*
Norwalk, CA 90650 • *85,286*
Norwalk, CT 06850–57 • *77,767*
Norwalk, IA 50211 • *2,676*
Norwalk, OH 44857 • *14,358*
Norway, IA 52318 • *633*
Norway, ME 04268 • *2,653*
Norway, MI 49870 • *2,919*
Norwell, MA 02061 • *800*
Norwich, CT 06360 • *38,074*
Norwich, NY 13815 • *8,082*
Norwich, VT 05055 • *1,000*
Norwood, MA 02062 • *29,711*
Norwood, MN 55368 • *1,219*
Norwood, NJ 07648 • *4,413*
Norwood, NC 28128 • *1,818*
Norwood, NY 13668 • *1,902*
Norwood, OH 45212 • *26,342*
Norwood, PA 19074 • *6,647*
Norwoodville, IA 50317 • *1,400*
Notasulga, AL 36866 • *876*
Nottoway □, VA • *14,666*
Novato, CA 94947 • *43,916*
Novi, MI 48050 • *22,525*
Novinger, MO 63559 • *626*
Nowata, OK 74048 • *4,270*
Nowata □, OK • *11,486*
Noxen, PA 18636 • *800*
Noxubee □, MS • *13,212*
Nuckolls □, NE • *6,726*
Nucla, CO 81424 • *1,027*
Nueces □, TX • *268,215*
Nunda, NY 14517 • *1,169*
Nuremberg, PA 18241 • *800*
Nutley, NJ 07110 • *28,998*
Nutter Fort, WV 26301 • *2,078*
Nutting Lake, MA 01865 • *2,400*
Nyack, NY 10960 • *6,428*
Nye □, NV • *9,048*
Nyssa, OR 97913 • *2,862*

# O

Oak Bluffs, MA 02557 • *1,984*
Oak Brook, IL 60521 • *6,641*
Oak Creek, CO 80467 • *929*
Oak Creek, WI 53154 • *16,932*
Oakdale, CA 95361 • *8,474*
Oakdale, GA 30080 • *800*
Oakdale, LA 71463 • *7,155*
Oakdale, MN 55119 • *12,123*
Oakdale, NY 11769 • *7,800*
Oakdale, PA 15071 • *1,955*
Oakes, ND 58474 • *2,112*
Oakfield, NY 14125 • *1,791*
Oakfield, WI 53065 • *990*
Oak Forest, IL 60452 • *26,096*
Oak Grove, KY 42262 • *2,088*
Oak Grove, LA 71263 • *2,214*
Oak Grove, OR 97267 • *11,640*
Oak Harbor, OH 43449 • *2,678*
Oak Harbor, WA 98277 • *12,271*
Oak Hill, FL 32759 • *938*
Oak Hill, MI 49660 • *1,000*
Oak Hill, OH 45656 • *1,713*
Oak Hill, WV 25901 • *7,120*
Oakhurst, NJ 07755 • *4,600*
Oakhurst, OK 74050 • *2,000*
Oakland, CA 94601–99 • *339,337*
Oakland, FL 32760 • *658*
Oakland, IL 61943 • *1,035*
Oakland, IA 51560 • *1,552*
Oakland, ME 04963 • *3,387*
Oakland, MD 21550 • *1,994*
Oakland, NE 68045 • *1,393*
Oakland, NJ 07436 • *13,443*
Oakland, OR 97462 • *886*
Oakland, PA 18847 • *734*
Oakland □, MI • *1,011,793*
Oakland City, IN 47660 • *3,301*
Oakland Park, FL 33334 • *23,035*
Oak Lawn, IL 60453–59 • *60,590*
Oaklawn, KS 67216 • *4,200*
Oakley, ID 83346 • *663*
Oakley, KS 67748 • *2,343*
Oaklyn, NJ 08107 • *4,223*
Oakman, AL 35579 • *770*
Oakmont, PA 15139 • *7,039*
Oak Park, IL 60301–99 • *54,887*
Oak Park, MI 48237 • *31,537*
Oak Ridge, NC 27310 • *950*
Oakridge, OR 97463 • *3,729*
Oak Ridge, TN 37830 • *27,662*
Oaks, PA 19456 • *700*
Oakton, VA 22124 • *900*
Oaktown, IN 47561 • *776*
Oak Valley, NJ 08090 • *7,000*
Oakville, CT 06779 • *8,737*
Oakville, MO 63129 • *1,100*
Oakwood, GA 30566 • *723*
Oakwood, IL 61858 • *1,627*
Oakwood, OH 45419 • *3,786*
Oakwood, OH 45873 • *886*
Oakwood, TX 75855 • *606*
Oberlin, KS 67749 • *2,387*
Oberlin, LA 70655 • *1,764*
Oberlin, OH 44074 • *8,660*
Obetz, OH 43207 • *3,095*
Obion, TN 38240 • *1,282*
Obion □, TN • *32,781*
Oblong, IL 62449 • *1,840*
O'Brien □, IA • *16,972*
Ocala, FL 32670–78 • *37,170*
Ocean, NJ 07755 • *23,570*
Ocean □, NJ • *346,038*
Oceana, WV 24870 • *2,143*
Oceana □, MI • *22,002*
Ocean Bluff, MA 02065 • *2,500*
Ocean City, FL 32548 • *5,582*
Ocean City, MD 21842 • *4,946*
Ocean City, NJ 08226 • *13,949*
Ocean Gate, NJ 08740 • *1,385*
Ocean Grove, MA 02777 • *4,000*
Ocean Grove, NJ 07756 • *4,200*
Ocean Park, WA 98640 • *1,500*
Ocean Port, NJ 07757 • *5,888*
Oceanside, CA 92054–56 • *76,698*
Oceanside, NY 11572 • *36,400*
Ocean Springs, MS 39564 • *14,504*
Ochiltree □, TX • *9,588*
Ochlocknee, GA 31773 • *627*
Ocilla, GA 31774 • *3,436*
Ocoee, FL 32761 • *7,803*
Oconee □, GA • *12,427*
Oconee □, SC • *48,611*
Oconomowoc, WI 53066 • *9,909*
Oconto, WI 54153 • *4,505*
Oconto □, WI • *28,947*
Oconto Falls, WI 54154 • *2,500*
Odebolt, IA 51458 • *1,299*
Odell, IL 60460 • *1,083*
Odem, TX 78370 • *2,363*
Odenton, MD 21113 • *7,500*
Odenville, AL 35120 • *724*
Odessa, FL 33556 • *950*
Odessa, MO 64076 • *3,088*
Odessa, NY 14869 • *613*
Odessa, TX 79760–68 • *90,027*
Odessa, WA 99159 • *1,009*
Odin, IL 62870 • *1,285*
Odon, IN 47562 • *1,463*
O'Donnell, TX 79351 • *1,200*
Oelwein, IA 50662 • *7,564*
O'Fallon, IL 62269 • *12,241*
O'Fallon, MO 63366 • *8,677*
Ogallala, NE 69153 • *5,638*
Ogden, IL 61859 • *818*
Ogden, IA 50212 • *1,953*
Ogden, KS 66517 • *1,804*
Ogden, UT 84401–99 • *64,407*
Ogdensburg, NJ 07439 • *2,737*
Ogdensburg, NY 13669 • *12,375*
Ogemaw □, MI • *16,436*
Ogle □, IL • *46,338*
Oglesby, IL 61348 • *3,979*
Oglethorpe, GA 31068 • *1,305*
Oglethorpe □, GA • *8,929*
Ogunquit, ME 03907 • *1,492*
Ohatchee, AL 36271 • *860*
Ohio □, IN • *5,114*
Ohio □, KY • *21,765*
Ohio □, WV • *61,389*
Ohio City, OH 45874 • *881*
Ohioville, PA 15059 • *4,217*
Oil City, LA 71061 • *1,323*
Oil City, PA 16301 • *13,881*
Oildale, CA 93308 • *23,382*
Oilton, OK 74052 • *1,244*
Ojai, CA 93023 • *6,816*
Okaloosa □, FL • *109,920*
Okanogan, WA 98840 • *2,302*
Okanogan □, WA • *30,639*
Okarche, OK 73762 • *1,064*
Okauchee, WI 53069 • *1,800*
Okauchee Lake, WI 53058 • *1,400*
Okawville, IL 62271 • *1,337*
Okeechobee, FL 34972–74 • *4,225*
Okeechobee □, FL • *20,264*
Okeene, OK 73763 • *1,601*
Okemah, OK 74859 • *3,381*
Okemos, MI 48864 • *8,882*
Okfuskee □, OK • *11,125*
Oklahoma □, OK • *568,933*
Oklahoma City, OK 73101–99 • *403,136*
Oklawaha, FL 32679 • *1,200*
Okmulgee, OK 74447 • *16,263*
Okmulgee □, OK • *39,169*
Okolona, KY 40219 • *20,039*
Okolona, MS 38860 • *3,409*
Oktibbeha □, MS • *36,018*
Ola, AR 72853 • *1,121*
Olanta, SC 29114 • *699*
Olathe, CO 81425 • *1,262*
Olathe, KS 66061–62 • *37,258*
Olcott, NY 14126 • *1,650*
Old Bethpage, NY 11804 • *7,160*
Old Bridge, NJ 08857 • *12,500*
Oldenburg, IN 47036 • *770*
Old Forge, NY 13420 • *950*
Old Forge, PA 18518 • *9,304*
Old Fort, NC 28762 • *752*
Oldham □, KY • *27,795*
Oldham □, TX • *2,283*
Oldham Village, MA 02359 • *900*
Old Orchard Beach, ME 04064 • *6,291*
Old Saybrook, CT 06475 • *1,857*
Oldsmar, FL 34677 • *2,608*
Old Tappan, NJ 07675 • *4,168*
Old Town, ME 04468 • *8,422*
Olean, NY 14760 • *18,207*
Oley, PA 19547 • *700*
Olin, IA 52320 • *735*
Olive Branch, MS 38654 • *2,067*
Olive Hill, KY 41164 • *2,539*
Olivehurst, CA 95961 • *8,929*
Oliver, PA 15472 • *1,500*
Oliver □, ND • *2,495*
Oliver Springs, TN 37840 • *3,659*
Olivet, MI 49076 • *1,604*
Olivette, MO 63132 • *7,985*
Olivia, MN 56277 • *2,802*
Olla, LA 71465 • *1,603*
Olmito, TX 78575 • *1,500*
Olmos Park, TX 78212 • *2,069*
Olmsted □, MN • *92,006*
Olmsted Falls, OH 44138 • *5,868*
Olney, IL 62450 • *9,026*
Olney, MD 20832 • *10,000*
Olney, TX 76374 • *4,060*
Olton, TX 79064 • *2,235*
Olustee, OK 73560 • *721*
Olympia, WA 98501–07 • *27,447*
Olympia Heights, FL 33165 • *33,112*
Olyphant, PA 18447 • *5,204*
Omaha, NE 68101–99 • *313,911*
Omak, WA 98841 • *4,007*
Omar, WV 25638 • *950*
Omega, GA 31775 • *996*
Omro, WI 54963 • *2,763*
Onaga, KS 66521 • *752*
Onalaska, WI 54650 • *9,249*
Onamia, MN 56359 • *691*
Onancock, VA 23417 • *1,461*
Onarga, IL 60955 • *1,269*
Onawa, IA 51040 • *3,283*
Onaway, MI 49765 • *1,084*
Oneco, FL 34264 • *6,417*
Oneida, IL 61467 • *765*
Oneida, NY 13421 • *10,810*
Oneida, OH 45042 • *1,650*
Oneida, TN 37841 • *3,717*
Oneida □, ID • *3,258*
Oneida □, NY • *253,466*
Oneida □, WI • *31,216*
O'Neill, NE 68763 • *4,049*
Oneonta, AL 35121 • *4,824*
Oneonta, NY 13820 • *14,933*
Onida, SD 57564 • *851*
Onondaga □, NY • *463,920*
Onset, MA 02558 • *1,493*
Onslow □, NC • *112,784*
Onsted, MI 49265 • *670*
Ontario, CA 91761–62 • *88,820*
Ontario, NY 14519 • *750*
Ontario, OH 44862 • *4,123*
Ontario, OR 97914 • *8,814*
Ontario □, NY • *88,909*
Ontonagon, MI 49953 • *2,182*
Ontonagon □, MI • *9,861*
Oolitic, IN 47451 • *1,495*
Oologah, OK 74053 • *798*
Ooltewah, TN 37363 • *900*
Oostburg, WI 53070 • *1,647*
Opal Cliffs, CA 95010 • *5,041*
Opa-Locka, FL 33054–56 • *14,460*
Opelika, AL 36801 • *21,896*
Opelousas, LA 70570 • *18,903*
Opp, AL 36467 • *7,204*
Opportunity, WA 99214 • *17,600*
Oquawka, IL 61469 • *1,533*
Oracle, AZ 85623 • *2,484*
Oradell, NJ 07649 • *8,658*
Oran, MO 63771 • *1,266*
Orange, CA 92667–69 • *91,450*
Orange, CT 06477 • *13,237*
Orange, MA 01364 • *3,942*
Orange, NJ 07050–52 • *31,136*
Orange, TX 77630 • *23,628*
Orange, VA 22960 • *2,631*
Orange □, CA • *1,932,709*
Orange □, FL • *471,016*
Orange □, IN • *18,677*
Orange □, NC • *77,055*
Orange □, NY • *259,603*
Orange □, TX • *83,838*
Orange □, VT • *22,739*
Orange □, VA • *18,063*
Orangeburg, SC 29115 • *14,933*
Orangeburg □, SC • *82,276*
Orange City, FL 32763 • *2,795*
Orange City, IA 51041 • *4,588*
Orange Grove, MS 39501 • *2,700*
Orange Grove, TX 78372 • *1,212*
Orange Lake, FL 32681 • *950*
Orangevale, CA 95662 • *20,585*
Orangeville, UT 84537 • *1,309*
Orchard City, CO 81410 • *1,914*
Orchard Homes, MT 59801 • *4,000*
Orchard Mesa, CO 81501 • *4,876*
Orchard Park, NY 14127 • *3,671*
Orchards, WA 98662 • *3,950*
Orchard Valley, WY 82001 • *800*
Orcutt, CA 93455 • *1,500*
Ord, NE 68862 • *2,658*
Ordway, CO 81063 • *1,135*
Oreana, IL 62554 • *999*
Ore City, TX 75683 • *1,050*
Oregon, IL 61061 • *3,559*
Oregon, MO 64473 • *901*
Oregon, OH 43616 • *18,675*
Oregon, WI 53575 • *3,876*
Oregon □, MO • *10,238*
Oregon City, OR 97045 • *14,673*
Oreland, PA 19075 • *9,000*
Orem, UT 84057–59 • *52,399*
Orfordville, WI 53576 • *1,143*
Orient, NY 11957 • *800*
Orinda, CA 94563 • *16,825*
Orion, IL 61273 • *2,013*
Oriskany, NY 13424 • *1,680*
Oriskany Falls, NY 13425 • *802*
Orland, CA 95963 • *4,031*
Orlando, FL 32801–99 • *128,291*
Orland Park, IL 60462 • *23,045*
Orleans, CA 95556 • *900*
Orleans, IN 47452 • *2,161*
Orleans, MA 02653 • *1,811*
Orleans, VT 05860 • *983*
Orleans □, LA • *557,927*
Orleans □, NY • *38,496*
Orleans □, VT • *23,440*
Ormond Beach, FL 32074 • *21,378*
Ormond By The Sea, FL 32074 • *7,665*
Orofino, ID 83544 • *3,711*
Oro Grande, CA 92368 • *900*
Orono, ME 04473 • *10,578*
Orono, MN 55323 • *6,845*
Oroville, CA 95965 • *8,683*
Oroville, WA 98844 • *1,483*
Orrick, MO 64077 • *922*
Orrville, OH 44667 • *7,511*
Orting, WA 98360 • *1,787*
Ortonville, MI 48462 • *1,190*
Ortonville, MN 56278 • *2,550*
Orwell, OH 44076 • *1,067*
Orwigsburg, PA 17961 • *2,700*
Osage, IA 50461 • *3,718*
Osage □, KS • *15,319*
Osage □, MO • *12,014*
Osage □, OK • *39,327*
Osage Beach, MO 65065 • *1,992*
Osage City, KS 66523 • *2,667*
Osakis, MN 56360 • *1,355*
Osawatomie, KS 66064 • *4,459*
Osborne, KS 67473 • *2,120*
Osborne □, KS • *5,959*
Osbornsville, NJ 08723 • *800*
Osburn, ID 83849 • *2,220*
Osceola, AR 72370 • *8,881*
Osceola, IN 46561 • *1,990*
Osceola, IA 50213 • *3,750*
Osceola, MO 64776 • *841*
Osceola, NE 68651 • *975*
Osceola, WI 54020 • *1,581*
Osceola □, FL • *49,287*
Osceola □, IA • *8,371*
Osceola □, MI • *18,928*
Osceola Mills, PA 16666 • *1,466*
Oscoda, MI 48750 • *2,431*
Oscoda □, MI • *6,858*
Osgood, IN 47037 • *1,554*
Oshkosh, NE 69154 • *1,057*
Oshkosh, WI 54901–04 • *50,016*
Oskaloosa, IA 52577 • *10,989*
Oskaloosa, KS 66066 • *1,092*
Osmond, NE 68765 • *871*
Osprey, FL 34229 • *1,660*
Osseo, MN 55369 • *2,974*
Osseo, WI 54758 • *1,474*
Ossian, IN 46777 • *1,945*
Ossian, IA 52161 • *829*
Ossining, NY 10562 • *20,196*
Osteen, FL 32764 • *900*
Osterville, MA 02655 • *1,799*
Oswego, IL 60543 • *3,021*
Oswego, KS 67356 • *2,218*
Oswego, NY 13126 • *19,793*
Oswego □, NY • *113,901*
Otay, CA 92010 • *6,400*
Oteen, NC 28805 • *2,200*
Otego, NY 13825 • *1,089*
Otero □, CO • *22,567*
Otero □, NM • *44,665*
Othello, WA 99344 • *4,454*
Otho, IA 50569 • *692*
Otis Orchards, WA 99027 • *1,000*
Otisville, MI 48463 • *682*
Otoe □, NE • *15,183*
Otsego, MI 49078 • *3,802*
Otsego □, MI • *14,993*
Otsego □, NY • *59,075*
Ottawa, IL 61350 • *18,166*
Ottawa, KS 66067 • *11,016*
Ottawa, OH 45875 • *3,874*
Ottawa □, KS • *5,971*
Ottawa □, MI • *157,174*
Ottawa □, OH • *40,076*
Ottawa □, OK • *32,870*
Ottawa Hills, OH 43606 • *4,065*
Otterbein, IN 47970 • *1,118*
Otter Tail □, MN • *51,937*
Ottoville, OH 45876 • *833*
Ottumwa, IA 52501 • *27,381*
Ouachita □, AR • *30,541*
Ouachita □, LA • *139,241*
Ouray, CO 81427 • *684*
Ouray □, CO • *1,925*
Outagamie □, WI • *128,730*
Overbrook, KS 66524 • *930*
Overland, MO 63114 • *19,620*
Overland Park, KS 66204 • *81,784*
Overlea, MD 21206 • *6,200*
Overton, NE 68863 • *633*
Overton, NV 89040 • *1,111*
Overton, TX 75684 • *2,430*
Overton □, TN • *17,575*
Ovid, MI 48866 • *1,712*
Ovid, NY 14521 • *666*
Owasso, OK 74055 • *6,149*
Owatonna, MN 55060 • *18,632*
Owego, NY 13827 • *4,364*
Owen, WI 54460 • *998*
Owen □, IN • *15,841*
Owen □, KY • *8,924*
Owensboro, KY 42301 • *54,450*
Owens Cross Roads, AL 35763 • *804*
Owensville, IN 47665 • *1,261*
Owensville, MO 65066 • *2,241*
Owensville, OH 45160 • *858*
Owenton, KY 40359 • *1,341*
Owings Mills, MD 21117 • *9,526*
Owingsville, KY 40360 • *1,419*
Owosso, MI 48867 • *16,455*
Owsley □, KY • *5,709*
Owyhee, NV 89832 • *700*
Owyhee □, ID • *8,272*
Oxford, AL 36203 • *8,939*
Oxford, CT 06483 • *900*
Oxford, GA 30267 • *1,750*
Oxford, IN 47971 • *1,327*
Oxford, IA 52322 • *676*
Oxford, KS 67119 • *1,125*
Oxford, ME 04270 • *625*
Oxford, MD 21654 • *754*
Oxford, MA 01540 • *6,369*
Oxford, MI 48051 • *2,746*
Oxford, MS 38655 • *9,882*
Oxford, NE 68967 • *1,109*
Oxford, NJ 07863 • *1,587*
Oxford, NC 27565 • *7,603*
Oxford, NY 13830 • *1,765*
Oxford, OH 45056 • *17,655*
Oxford, PA 19363 • *3,633*
Oxford □, ME • *48,968*
Oxnard, CA 93030–39 • *108,195*
Oxon Hill, MD 20745 • *8,100*
Oyster Bay, NY 11771 • *7,200*
Ozark, AL 36360 • *13,188*
Ozark, AR 72949 • *3,597*
Ozark, MO 65721 • *2,980*
Ozark □, MO • *7,961*
Ozaukee □, WI • *66,981*
Ozona, FL 34660 • *1,200*
Ozona, TX 76943 • *2,864*

# P

Paauilo, HI 96776 • *755*
Paauilo, HI 96776 • *755*
Pace, FL 32570 • *5,006*
Pacific, MO 63069 • *4,410*
Pacific, WA 98047 • *2,261*
Pacific □, WA • *17,237*
Pacifica, CA 94044 • *36,866*
Pacific Beach, WA 98571 • *1,000*
Pacific City, OR 97135 • *1,500*
Pacific Grove, CA 93950 • *15,755*
Pacific Palisades, HI 96782 • *9,500*
Packwood, WA 98361 • *1,150*
Pacolet, SC 29372 • *1,556*
Pacolet Mills, SC 29373 • *1,051*
Paddock Lake, WI 53168 • *2,207*
Paden City, WV 26159 • *3,671*
Paducah, KY 42001 • *29,315*
Paducah, TX 79248 • *2,216*
Page, AZ 86040 • *4,907*
Page □, IA • *19,063*
Page □, VA • *19,401*
Pageland, SC 29728 • *2,720*
Page Manor, OH 45431 • *9,300*
Pagosa Springs, CO 81147 • *1,331*
Pahala, HI 96777 • *1,619*
Pahoa, HI 96778 • *923*
Pahokee, FL 33476 • *6,346*
Pahrump, NV 89041 • *1,000*
Paia, HI 96779 • *1,000*
Paincourtville, LA 70391 • *2,004*
Painesdale, MI 49955 • *650*
Painesville, OH 44077 • *16,391*
Painted Post, NY 14870 • *2,196*
Paintsville, KY 41240 • *3,815*
Pajarito, NM 87105 • *2,000*
Palacios, TX 77465 • *4,667*
Palatine, IL 60067 • *32,166*
Palatka, FL 32077 • *10,175*
Palestine, AR 72372 • *976*
Palestine, IL 62451 • *1,718*
Palestine, TX 75801 • *15,948*
Palisade, CO 81526 • *1,551*
Palisades Park, NJ 07650 • *13,732*
Palm Bay, FL 32905 • *18,560*
Palm Beach, FL 33480 • *9,729*
Palm Beach □, FL • *576,863*
Palm Beach Gardens, FL 33410 • *6,102*
Palmdale, CA 93550 • *12,277*
Palm Desert, CA 92260 • *11,801*
Palmer, AK 99645 • *2,141*
Palmer, MA 01069 • *3,854*
Palmer, MI 49871 • *900*
Palmer, MS 39401 • *2,765*
Palmer, TN 37365 • *1,027*
Palmer, TX 75152 • *1,187*
Palmer Lake, CO 80133 • *1,130*
Palmer Park, MD 20785 • *7,986*
Palmerton, PA 18071 • *5,455*
Palmetto, FL 34221 • *8,637*
Palmetto, GA 30268 • *2,086*
Palm Harbor, FL 34683–85 • *5,215*
Palm Springs, CA 92262–64 • *32,366*
Palm Springs, FL 33460 • *8,166*
Palmyra, IL 62674 • *864*
Palmyra, IN 47164 • *692*
Palmyra, MO 63461 • *3,469*
Palmyra, NJ 08065 • *7,085*
Palmyra, NY 14522 • *3,729*
Palmyra, PA 17078 • *7,228*
Palmyra, WI 53156 • *1,515*
Palo Alto, CA 94301–99 • *55,225*
Palo Alto □, IA • *12,721*
Palo Pinto □, TX • *24,062*
Palos Heights, IL 60463 • *11,096*
Palos Hills, IL 60465 • *16,654*
Palos Park, IL 60464 • *3,150*
Palos Verdes Estates, CA 90274 • *14,376*
Palouse, WA 99161 • *1,005*
Pamlico □, NC • *10,398*
Pampa, TX 79065 • *21,396*
Pamplico, SC 29583 • *1,213*
Pana, IL 62557 • *6,040*
Panacea, FL 32346 • *950*
Panama, IL 62077 • *637*
Panama, OK 74951 • *1,425*
Panama City, FL 32401–10 • *33,346*
Panama City Beach, FL 32407 • *2,148*
Pandora, OH 45877 • *977*
Pangburn, AR 72121 • *673*
Panguitch, UT 84759 • *1,343*
Panhandle, TX 79068 • *2,226*
Panola □, MS • *28,164*
Panola □, TX • *20,724*
Panora, IA 50216 • *1,211*
Panthersville, GA 30032 • *11,366*
Paola, KS 66071 • *4,557*
Paoli, IN 47454 • *3,637*
Paoli, PA 19301 • *6,100*
Paonia, CO 81428 • *1,425*
Papaikou, HI 96781 • *1,567*
Papillion, NE 68046 • *6,399*
Paradis, LA 70080 • *800*
Paradise, CA 95969 • *22,571*
Paradise, NV 89109 • *45,000*
Paradise, PA 17963 • *900*

## United States Populations and ZIP Codes

Paradise Hills, NM 87114 • *5,096*
Paradise Valley, AZ 85253 • *11,085*
Paradise Valley, WY 82601 • *2,300*
Paragould, AR 72450 • *15,248*
Paramount, CA 90723 • *36,407*
Paramount, MD 21740 • *1,878*
Paramus, NJ 07652 • *26,474*
Parchment, MI 49004 • *1,817*
Pardeeville, WI 53954 • *1,594*
Paris, AR 72855 • *3,991*
Paris, ID 83261 • *707*
Paris, IL 61944 • *9,885*
Paris, KY 40361 • *7,935*
Paris, MO 65275 • *1,598*
Paris, TN 38242 • *10,728*
Paris, TX 75460 • *25,498*
Park □, CO • *5,333*
Park □, MT • *12,869*
Park □, WY • *21,639*
Park City, KS 67219 • *3,778*
Park City, KY 42160 • *614*
Park City, UT 84060 • *2,823*
Parke □, IN • *16,372*
Parker, AZ 85344 • *2,542*
Parker, FL 32401 • *4,298*
Parker, PA 16049 • *808*
Parker, SD 57053 • *999*
Parker □, TX • *44,609*
Parker City, IN 47368 • *1,414*
Parkersburg, IA 50665 • *1,968*
Parkersburg, WV 26101–05 • *39,967*
Parkers Prairie, MN 56361 • *917*
Parkesburg, PA 19365 • *2,578*
Park Falls, WI 54552 • *3,192*
Park Forest, IL 60466 • *26,222*
Park Forest South, IL 60466 • *6,245*
Park Hills, KY 41015 • *3,500*
Parkin, AR 72373 • *2,035*
Parkland, WA 98444 • *22,300*
Park Layne, OH 45431 • *5,372*
Park Rapids, MN 56470 • *2,976*
Park Ridge, IL 60068 • *38,704*
Park Ridge, NJ 07656 • *8,515*
Park River, ND 58270 • *1,844*
Parkrose, OR 97230 • *21,103*
Parksley, VA 23421 • *979*
Parkston, SD 57366 • *1,545*
Parkville, MD 21234 • *35,159*
Parkville, MO 64152 • *1,997*
Parkwater, WA 99211 • *4,850*
Parkway, CA 95823 • *12,000*
Parkwood, NC 27707 • *3,420*
Parlier, CA 93648 • *2,902*
Parma, ID 83660 • *1,820*
Parma, MI 49269 • *873*
Parma, MO 63870 • *1,081*
Parma, OH 44129 • *92,548*
Parma Heights, OH 44130 • *23,112*
Parmer □, TX • *11,038*
Parowan, UT 84761 • *1,836*
Parrish, AL 35580 • *1,583*
Parrish, FL 34219 • *950*
Parshall, ND 58770 • *1,059*
Parsippany, NJ 07054 • *8,000*
Parsons, KS 67357 • *12,898*
Parsons, TN 38363 • *2,422*
Parsons, WV 26287 • *1,937*
Pasadena, CA 91101–99 • *118,072*
Pasadena, MD 21122 • *3,900*
Pasadena, TX 77501–07 • *112,560*
Pascagoula, MS 39567 • *29,318*
Pasco, WA 99301 • *18,425*
Pasco □, FL • *193,661*
Pascoag, RI 02859 • *3,807*
Paso Robles, CA 93446 • *9,163*
Pasquotank □, NC • *28,462*
Passaic, NJ 07055 • *52,463*
Passaic □, NJ • *447,585*
Pass Christian, MS 39571 • *5,014*
Patagonia, AZ 85624 • *980*
Pataskala, OH 43062 • *2,284*
Patchogue, NY 11772 • *11,291*
Paterson, NJ 07501–99 • *137,970*
Patoka, IL 62875 • *662*
Patoka, IN 47666 • *832*
Patrick □, VA • *17,647*
Patten, ME 04765 • *1,057*
Patterson, GA 31557 • *763*
Patterson, LA 70392 • *4,693*
Patterson, NY 12563 • *950*
Patton, PA 16668 • *2,441*
Paul, ID 83347 • *940*
Paulding, OH 45879 • *2,754*
Paulding □, GA • *26,110*
Paulding □, OH • *21,302*
Paulina, LA 70763 • *980*
Paullina, IA 51046 • *1,224*
Paulsboro, NJ 08066 • *6,944*
Pauls Valley, OK 73075 • *5,664*
Pavo, GA 31778 • *830*
Pawcatuck, CT 06379 • *5,216*
Paw Creek, NC 28130 • *1,700*
Pawhuska, OK 74056 • *4,771*
Pawleys Island, SC 29585 • *2,200*
Pawling, NY 12564 • *1,996*
Pawnee, IL 62558 • *2,577*
Pawnee, OK 74058 • *1,688*
Pawnee □, KS • *8,065*
Pawnee □, NE • *3,937*
Pawnee □, OK • *15,310*
Pawnee City, NE 68420 • *1,156*
Pawpaw, IL 61353 • *839*
Paw Paw, MI 49079 • *3,211*
Paw Paw, WV 25434 • *644*
Pawtucket, RI 02860–65 • *71,204*
Paxton, FL 32538 • *659*
Paxton, IL 60957 • *4,258*
Paxton, MA 01612 • *1,800*
Payette, ID 83661 • *5,448*
Payette □, ID • *15,825*
Payne, OH 45880 • *1,399*
Payne □, OK • *62,435*
Paynesville, MN 56362 • *2,140*
Payson, AZ 85541 • *5,068*
Payson, IL 62360 • *1,065*
Payson, UT 84651 • *8,246*
Peabody, KS 66866 • *1,474*
Peabody, MA 01960 • *45,976*
Peace Dale, RI 02883 • *3,100*
Peach □, GA • *19,151*
Peach Orchard, GA 30906 • *14,000*
Peachtree City, GA 30269 • *6,429*
Pea Ridge, AR 72751 • *1,488*
Pearisburg, VA 24134 • *2,128*
Pearl, MS 39208 • *18,580*
Pearland, TX 77581 • *13,248*
Pearl City, HI 96782 • *33,000*
Pearl City, IL 61062 • *661*
Pearl River, LA 70452 • *1,693*
Pearl River, NY 10965 • *17,146*
Pearl River □, MS • *33,795*
Pearsall, TX 78061 • *7,383*
Pearson, GA 31642 • *1,827*
Pecatonica, IL 61063 • *1,732*
Peck, MI 48466 • *606*
Pecos, NM 87552 • *885*
Pecos, TX 79772 • *12,855*
Pecos □, TX • *14,618*
Peculiar, MO 64078 • *1,571*
Pedricktown, NJ 08067 • *900*
Peebles, OH 45660 • *1,790*
Peekskill, NY 10566 • *18,236*
Pe Ell, WA 98572 • *617*
Pegram, TN 37143 • *1,081*
Pekin, IL 61554 • *33,967*
Pekin, IN 47165 • *1,125*
Pelahatchie, MS 39145 • *1,445*
Pelham, AL 35124 • *6,759*
Pelham, GA 31779 • *4,306*
Pelham, NY 10803 • *6,848*
Pelham Manor, NY 10803 • *6,130*
Pelican Rapids, MN 56572 • *1,867*
Pella, IA 50219 • *8,349*
Pell City, AL 35125 • *6,616*
Pell Lake, WI 53157 • *1,400*
Pemberton, NJ 08068 • *1,198*
Pemberville, OH 43450 • *1,321*
Pembina, ND 58271 • *673*
Pembina □, ND • *10,399*
Pembroke, GA 31321 • *1,400*
Pembroke, KY 42266 • *636*
Pembroke, MA 02359 • *1,800*
Pembroke, NC 28372 • *2,698*
Pembroke, VA 24136 • *1,302*
Pembroke Pines, FL 33024 • *35,776*
Pemiscot □, MO • *24,987*
Pen Argyl, PA 18072 • *3,388*
Penasco, NM 87553 • *900*
Penbrook, PA 17103 • *3,006*
Pender, NE 68047 • *1,318*
Pender □, NC • *22,262*
Pendleton, IN 46064 • *2,130*
Pendleton, OR 97801 • *14,521*
Pendleton, SC 29670 • *3,154*
Pendleton □, KY • *10,989*
Pendleton □, WV • *7,910*
Pendley Hills, GA 30032 • *5,800*
Pend Oreille □, WA • *8,580*
Penfield, NY 14526 • *9,600*
Peninsula, OH 44264 • *604*
Penn Acres, DE 19720 • *1,950*
Penney Farms, FL 32079 • *630*
Penn Hills, PA 15235 • *57,632*
Pennington, NJ 08534 • *2,109*
Pennington □, MN • *15,258*
Pennington □, SD • *70,361*
Pennington Gap, VA 24277 • *1,716*
Pennsauken, NJ 08110 • *33,775*
Pennsboro, WV 26415 • *1,652*
Pennsburg, PA 18073 • *2,339*
Penns Grove, NJ 08069 • *5,760*
Pennsville, NJ 08070 • *12,467*
Penn Valley, PA 19072 • *6,100*
Pennville, IN 47369 • *805*
Penn Yan, NY 14527 • *5,242*
Penobscot □, ME • *137,015*
Pensacola, FL 32501–23 • *57,619*
Pentwater, MI 49449 • *1,165*
Peoria, AZ 85345 • *12,307*
Peoria, IL 61601–99 • *124,160*
Peoria □, IL • *200,466*
Peoria Heights, IL 61613 • *7,453*
Peotone, IL 60468 • *2,832*
Pepeekeo, HI 96783 • *1,800*
Pepin, WI 54759 • *890*
Pepin □, WI • *7,477*
Pepperell, MA 01463 • *2,076*
Pepper Pike, OH 44124 • *6,177*
Pequabuck, CT 06781 • *1,400*
Pequannock, NJ 07440 • *13,776*
Pequot Lakes, MN 56472 • *681*
Percy, IL 62272 • *1,053*
Perdido, AL 36562 • *1,100*
Perham, MN 56573 • *2,086*
Perkasie, PA 18944 • *5,241*
Perkins, OK 74059 • *1,762*
Perkins □, NE • *3,637*
Perkins □, SD • *4,700*
Perkinston, MS 39573 • *650*
Perl-Mack, CO 80221 • *6,002*
Perquimans □, NC • *9,486*
Perrine, FL 33157 • *16,129*
Perris, CA 92370 • *6,827*
Perry, FL 32347 • *8,254*
Perry, GA 31069 • *9,453*
Perry, IA 50220 • *7,053*
Perry, KS 66073 • *907*
Perry, MI 48872 • *2,051*
Perry, MO 63462 • *836*
Perry, NY 14530 • *4,198*
Perry, OH 44081 • *961*
Perry, OK 73077 • *5,796*
Perry, UT 84302 • *1,084*
Perry □, AL • *15,012*
Perry □, AR • *7,266*
Perry □, IL • *21,714*
Perry □, IN • *19,346*
Perry □, KY • *33,763*
Perry □, MS • *9,864*
Perry □, MO • *16,784*
Perry □, OH • *31,032*
Perry □, PA • *35,718*
Perry □, TN • *6,111*
Perry Hall, MD 21128 • *13,455*
Perry Heights, OH 44646 • *9,206*
Perryman, MD 21130 • *1,819*
Perrysburg, OH 43551 • *10,215*
Perrysburg Heights, OH 43551 • *650*
Perrysville, OH 44864 • *836*
Perrysville, PA 15237 • *5,300*
Perryton, TX 79070 • *7,991*
Perryville, AR 72126 • *1,058*
Perryville, KY 40468 • *841*
Perryville, MD 21903 • *2,018*
Perryville, MO 63775 • *7,343*
Pershing □, NV • *3,408*
Person □, NC • *29,164*
Perth Amboy, NJ 08861–63 • *38,951*
Peru, IL 61354 • *10,886*
Peru, IN 46970 • *13,764*
Peru, NE 68421 • *998*
Peru, NY 12972 • *1,300*
Peshastin, WA 98847 • *900*
Peshtigo, WI 54157 • *2,807*
Pesotum, IL 61863 • *651*
Petal, MS 39465 • *8,476*
Petaluma, CA 94952 • *33,834*
Peterborough, NH 03458 • *2,100*
Petersburg, AK 99833 • *2,821*
Petersburg, IL 62675 • *2,419*
Petersburg, IN 47567 • *2,987*
Petersburg, MI 49270 • *1,222*
Petersburg, OH 44454 • *950*
Petersburg, TN 37144 • *681*
Petersburg, TX 79250 • *1,633*
Petersburg, VA 23803–05 • *41,055*
Petersburg, WV 26847 • *2,084*
Peterstown, WV 24963 • *648*
Petersville, AL 35633 • *2,000*
Petoskey, MI 49770 • *6,097*
Petroleum □, MT • *655*
Petrolia, TX 76377 • *755*
Petros, TN 37845 • *1,286*
Pettis □, MO • *36,378*
Pevely, MO 63070 • *2,732*
Pewaukee, WI 53072 • *4,637*
Pewee Valley, KY 40056 • *982*
Pharr, TX 78577 • *21,381*
Phelps, KY 41553 • *1,120*
Phelps, NY 14532 • *2,004*
Phelps, WI 54554 • *700*
Phelps □, MO • *33,633*
Phelps □, NE • *9,769*
Phenix City, AL 36867 • *26,928*
Philadelphia, MS 39350 • *6,434*
Philadelphia, NY 13673 • *855*
Philadelphia, PA 19101–99 • *1,688,210*
Philadelphia □, PA • *1,688,210*
Phil Campbell, AL 35581 • *1,549*
Philip, SD 57567 • *1,088*
Philippi, WV 26416 • *3,194*
Philipsburg, MT 59858 • *1,138*
Philipsburg, PA 16866 • *3,533*
Phillips, ME 04966 • *700*
Phillips, TX 79007 • *3,000*
Phillips, WI 54555 • *1,522*
Phillips □, AR • *34,772*
Phillips □, CO • *4,542*
Phillips □, KS • *7,406*
Phillips □, MT • *5,367*
Phillipsburg, KS 67661 • *3,229*
Phillipsburg, NJ 08865 • *16,647*
Philmont, NY 12565 • *1,539*
Philo, IL 61864 • *973*
Philo, OH 43771 • *799*
Philomath, OR 97370 • *2,673*
Phoenicia, NY 12464 • *700*
Phoenix, AZ 85001–99 • *789,704*
Phoenix, IL 60426 • *2,850*
Phoenix, NY 13135 • *2,357*
Phoenix, OR 97535 • *2,309*
Phoenixville, PA 19460 • *14,165*
Piatt □, IL • *16,581*
Picayune, MS 39466 • *10,361*
Picher, OK 74360 • *2,180*
Pickaway □, OH • *43,662*
Pickens, MS 39146 • *1,386*
Pickens, SC 29671 • *3,199*
Pickens □, AL • *21,481*
Pickens □, GA • *11,652*
Pickens □, SC • *79,292*
Pickerington, OH 43147 • *3,917*
Pickett □, TN • *4,358*
Pico Rivera, CA 90660 • *53,387*
Picture Rocks, PA 17762 • *615*
Piedmont, AL 36272 • *5,544*
Piedmont, CA 94611 • *10,498*
Piedmont, MO 63957 • *2,359*
Piedmont, OK 73078 • *2,016*
Piedmont, SC 29673 • *2,992*
Piedmont, WV 26750 • *1,491*
Pierce, CO 80650 • *878*
Pierce, ID 83546 • *1,060*
Pierce, NE 68767 • *1,535*
Pierce □, GA • *11,897*
Pierce □, NE • *8,481*
Pierce □, ND • *6,166*
Pierce □, WA • *485,667*
Pierce □, WI • *31,149*
Pierce City, MO 65723 • *1,391*
Pierceton, IN 46562 • *1,086*
Pierre, SD 57501 • *11,973*
Pierre Part, LA 70339 • *3,153*
Pierson, FL 32080 • *1,085*
Pierz, MN 56364 • *1,018*
Pigeon, MI 48755 • *1,247*
Pigeon Cove, MA 01966 • *1,700*
Pigeon Forge, TN 37863 • *1,822*
Piggott, AR 72454 • *3,762*
Pike □, AL • *28,050*
Pike □, AR • *10,373*
Pike □, GA • *8,937*
Pike □, IL • *18,896*
Pike □, IN • *13,465*
Pike □, KY • *81,123*
Pike □, MS • *36,173*
Pike □, MO • *17,568*
Pike □, OH • *22,802*
Pike □, PA • *18,271*
Pike Lake, MN 55811 • *1,004*
Pikesville, MD 21208 • *20,000*
Piketon, OH 45661 • *1,726*
Pikeville, KY 41501 • *4,756*
Pikeville, NC 27863 • *662*
Pikeville, TN 37367 • *2,085*
Pilgrim Gardens, PA 19026 • *8,400*
Pilot Grove, MO 65276 • *745*
Pilot Knob, MO 63663 • *722*
Pilot Mountain, NC 27041 • *1,090*
Pilot Point, TX 76258 • *2,211*
Pilot Rock, OR 97868 • *1,630*
Pima, AZ 85543 • *1,599*
Pima □, AZ • *531,443*
Pimmit Hills, VA 22043 • *7,200*
Pinal □, AZ • *90,918*
Pinardville, NH 03045 • *4,500*
Pinckard, AL 36371 • *771*
Pinckney, MI 48169 • *1,390*
Pinckneyville, IL 62274 • *3,319*
Pinconning, MI 48650 • *1,430*
Pine □, MN • *19,871*
Pine Bluff, AR 71601–13 • *56,636*
Pinebluff, NC 28373 • *935*
Pine Bluffs, WY 82082 • *1,077*
Pine Bridge, CT 06403 • *870*
Pine Bush, NY 12566 • *1,200*
Pine Castle, FL 32809 • *9,992*
Pine City, MN 55063 • *2,489*
Pinedale, WY 82941 • *1,066*
Pine Grove, PA 17963 • *2,244*
Pine Grove Mills, PA 16868 • *900*
Pine Hill, NJ 08021 • *8,684*
Pine Hills, FL 32808 • *26,000*
Pinehurst, MA 01866 • *6,588*
Pinehurst, NJ 08201 • *1,500*
Pinehurst, NC 28374 • *3,421*
Pine Island, MN 55963 • *1,986*
Pine Island, NY 10969 • *950*
Pine Knot, KY 42635 • *1,389*
Pine Lake, GA 30072 • *901*
Pine Lake, MA 01776 • *800*
Pine Lawn, MO 63120 • *6,662*
Pine Level, NC 27568 • *953*
Pinellas □, FL • *728,531*
Pinellas Park, FL 34665–66 • *32,811*
Pine Mountain, GA 31822 • *984*
Pine Orchard, CT 06405 • *1,500*
Pine Plains, NY 12567 • *950*
Pine Point, ME 04074 • *700*
Pine Prairie, LA 70576 • *734*
Pine Rest, MA 01776 • *900*
Pine Ridge, SD 57770 • *3,059*
Pine River, MN 56474 • *881*
Pinetop, AZ 85935 • *1,527*
Pinetops, NC 27864 • *1,465*
Pine Valley, CA 92062 • *950*
Pineville, KY 40977 • *2,599*
Pineville, LA 71360 • *12,034*
Pineville, NC 28134 • *1,525*
Pineville, WV 24874 • *1,140*
Pinewald, NJ 08721 • *900*
Pinewood, FL 33168 • *7,900*
Pinewood, SC 29125 • *689*
Piney Point, MD 20674 • *900*
Piney View, WV 25906 • *800*
Pink Hill, NC 28572 • *644*
Pinole, CA 94564 • *14,253*
Pinson, AL 35126 • *1,600*
Pioche, NV 89043 • *700*
Pioneer, OH 43554 • *1,133*
Piper, KS 66109 • *730*
Piper City, IL 60959 • *905*
Pipestone, MN 56164 • *4,887*
Pipestone □, MN • *11,690*
Piqua, OH 45356 • *20,480*
Pirtleville, AZ 85626 • *1,425*
Piscataquis □, ME • *17,634*
Piscataway, NJ 08854 • *42,223*
Pisgah, AL 35765 • *699*
Pisgah, OH 45069 • *1,000*
Pisgah Forest, NC 28768 • *1,899*
Pismo Beach, CA 93449 • *5,364*
Pitcairn, PA 15140 • *4,175*
Pitkin, LA 70656 • *750*
Pitkin □, CO • *10,338*
Pitman, NJ 08071 • *9,744*
Pitt □, NC • *90,146*
Pittsboro, IN 46167 • *891*
Pittsboro, NC 27312 • *1,332*
Pittsburg, CA 94565 • *33,034*
Pittsburg, IL 62974 • *605*
Pittsburg, KS 66762 • *18,770*
Pittsburg, KY 40755 • *620*
Pittsburg, TX 75686 • *4,245*
Pittsburg □, OK • *40,524*
Pittsburgh, PA 15201–99 • *423,959*
Pittsfield, IL 62363 • *4,170*
Pittsfield, ME 04967 • *3,117*
Pittsfield, MA 01201 • *51,974*
Pittsfield, NH 03263 • *1,584*
Pittsford, VT 05763 • *666*
Pittston, PA 18640–44 • *9,930*
Pittsville, WI 54466 • *810*
Pittsylvania □, VA • *66,147*
Piute □, UT • *1,329*
Pixley, CA 93256 • *2,488*
Placentia, CA 92670 • *35,041*
Placer □, CA • *117,247*
Placerville, CA 95667 • *6,739*
Placida, FL 33946 • *700*
Plain, WI 53577 • *676*
Plain City, OH 43064 • *2,102*
Plain City, UT 84404 • *2,379*
Plain Dealing, LA 71064 • *1,213*
Plainfield, CT 06374 • *2,799*
Plainfield, IL 60544 • *3,767*
Plainfield, IN 46168 • *9,191*
Plainfield, NJ 07060–63 • *45,555*
Plainfield, WI 54966 • *813*
Plainfield Heights, MI 49505 • *5,000*
Plains, GA 31780 • *651*
Plains, KS 67869 • *1,044*
Plains, MT 59859 • *1,116*
Plains, PA 18705 • *6,606*
Plains, TX 79355 • *1,457*
Plainsboro, NJ 08536 • *800*
Plainview, AR 72857 • *752*
Plainview, MN 55964 • *2,416*
Plainview, NE 68769 • *1,483*
Plainview, NY 11803 • *32,300*
Plainview, TX 79072 • *22,187*
Plainville, CT 06062 • *16,401*
Plainville, KS 67663 • *2,458*
Plainville, MA 02762 • *4,953*
Plainwell, MI 49080 • *3,751*
Plaistow, NH 03865 • *1,800*
Plankinton, SD 57368 • *644*
Plano, IL 60545 • *4,875*
Plano, TX 75074–75 • *72,331*
Plantation, FL 33317 • *48,653*
Plant City, FL 33566 • *17,064*
Plantersville, AL 36758 • *650*
Plantersville, MS 38862 • *920*
Plantsite, AZ 85540 • *1,500*
Plantsville, CT 06479 • *5,700*
Plaquemine, LA 70764 • *7,521*
Plaquemines □, LA • *26,049*
Platte, SD 57369 • *1,334*
Platte □, MO • *46,341*
Platte □, NE • *28,852*
Platte □, WY • *11,975*
Platte City, MO 64079 • *2,114*
Platteville, CO 80651 • *1,662*
Platteville, WI 53818 • *9,580*
Plattsburg, MO 64477 • *2,095*
Plattsburgh, NY 12901 • *21,057*
Plattsmouth, NE 68048 • *6,295*
Pleasant Gap, PA 16823 • *1,773*
Pleasant Garden, NC 27313 • *1,991*
Pleasant Grove, AL 35127 • *7,102*
Pleasant Grove, UT 84062 • *10,833*
Pleasant Hill, CA 94523 • *25,124*
Pleasant Hill, IL 62366 • *1,112*
Pleasant Hill, IA 50301 • *3,493*
Pleasant Hill, LA 71065 • *776*
Pleasant Hill, MO 64080 • *3,301*
Pleasant Hill, OH 45359 • *1,051*
Pleasant Hills, PA 15236 • *9,374*
Pleasanton, CA 94566 • *35,160*
Pleasanton, KS 66075 • *1,303*
Pleasanton, TX 78064 • *6,346*
Pleasant Plains, IL 62677 • *688*
Pleasants □, WV • *8,236*
Pleasant Valley, IA 52767 • *750*
Pleasant Valley, MO 64068 • *1,545*
Pleasant Valley, NY 12569 • *1,372*
Pleasant Valley, OH 45601 • *650*
Pleasant View, CO 80401 • *4,500*
Pleasant View, UT 84404 • *3,983*
Pleasant View, WI 54615 • *700*
Pleasantville, IA 50225 • *1,531*
Pleasantville, NJ 08232 • *13,435*
Pleasantville, NY 10570 • *6,749*
Pleasantville, OH 43148 • *780*
Pleasantville, PA 16341 • *1,099*
Pleasure Beach, CT 06385 • *1,356*
Pleasure Ridge Park, KY 40258 • *27,332*
Pleasureville, KY 40057 • *837*
Plentywood, MT 59254 • *2,476*
Plover, WI 54467 • *5,310*
Plum, PA 15239 • *25,390*
Plumas □, CA • *17,340*
Plumerville, AR 72127 • *785*
Plummer, ID 83851 • *634*
Plymouth, CT 06782 • *1,000*
Plymouth, FL 32768 • *2,700*
Plymouth, IL 62367 • *649*
Plymouth, IN 46563 • *7,693*
Plymouth, MA 02360 • *7,232*
Plymouth, MI 48170 • *9,986*
Plymouth, MN 55441 • *31,615*
Plymouth, NH 03264 • *3,628*
Plymouth, NC 27962 • *4,571*
Plymouth, OH 44865 • *1,939*
Plymouth, PA 18651 • *7,605*
Plymouth, WI 53073 • *6,027*
Plymouth □, IA • *24,743*
Plymouth □, MA • *405,437*
Plymouth Meeting, PA 19462 • *6,000*
Plymouth Valley, PA 19401 • *8,200*
Poca, WV 25159 • *1,142*
Pocahontas, AR 72455 • *5,995*
Pocahontas, IL 62275 • *866*
Pocahontas, IA 50574 • *2,352*
Pocahontas, VA 24635 • *708*
Pocahontas □, IA • *11,369*
Pocahontas □, WV • *9,919*
Pocasset, MA 02559 • *2,000*
Pocatalico, WV 25320 • *900*
Pocatello, ID 83201–09 • *46,340*
Pocola, OK 74902 • *3,268*
Pocomoke City, MD 21851 • *3,558*
Poinsett □, AR • *27,032*
Point Clear, AL 36564 • *1,812*
Pointe Coupee □, LA • *24,045*
Point Independence, MA 02532 • *700*
Point Lookout, MO 65726 • *900*
Point Marion, PA 15474 • *1,642*
Point Pleasant, NJ 08742 • *17,747*
Point Pleasant, WV 25550 • *5,682*
Point Pleasant Beach, NJ 08742 • *5,415*
Point Roberts, WA 98281 • *750*
Poipu, HI 96756 • *685*
Pojoaque Valley, NM 87501 • *900*
Polk, PA 16342 • *1,884*
Polk □, AR • *17,007*
Polk □, FL • *321,652*
Polk □, GA • *32,386*
Polk □, IA • *303,170*
Polk □, MN • *34,844*
Polk □, MO • *18,822*
Polk □, NE • *6,320*
Polk □, NC • *12,984*
Polk □, OR • *45,203*
Polk □, TN • *13,602*
Polk □, TX • *24,407*
Polk □, WI • *32,351*
Polk City, IA 50226 • *1,658*
Polkton, NC 28135 • *762*
Polo, IL 61064 • *2,643*
Polson, MT 59860 • *2,798*
Pomeroy, IA 50575 • *895*
Pomeroy, OH 45769 • *2,728*
Pomeroy, WA 99347 • *1,716*
Pomona, CA 91766–69 • *92,742*
Pomona, KS 66076 • *868*
Pomona, NJ 08240 • *2,358*
Pomona Park, FL 32081 • *791*
Pompano Beach, FL 33060–69 • *52,618*
Pompano Beach Highlands, FL 33064 • *9,000*
Pompton Lakes, NJ 07442 • *10,660*
Ponca, NE 68770 • *1,057*
Ponca City, OK 74601–04 • *26,238*
Ponchatoula, LA 70454 • *5,469*
Pond Creek, OK 73766 • *949*
Pondera □, MT • *6,731*
Ponte Vedra Beach, FL 32082 • *1,700*
Pontiac, IL 61764 • *11,227*
Pontiac, MI 48053–59 • *76,715*
Pontotoc, MS 38863 • *4,723*
Pontotoc □, MS • *20,918*
Pontotoc □, OK • *32,598*
Pooler, GA 31322 • *2,543*

Poolesville, MD 20837 • 3,428
Pope □, AR • 39,021
Pope □, IL • 4,404
Pope □, MN • 11,657
Poplar, MT 59255 • 995
Poplar Bluff, MO 63901 • 17,139
Poplar Grove, IL 61065 • 818
Poplarville, MS 39470 • 2,562
Poquonock, CT 06064 • 900
Poquonock Bridge, CT 06340 • 2,549
Poquoson, VA 23662 • 8,726
Portage, IN 46368 • 27,409
Portage, MI 49081 • 38,157
Portage, PA 15946 • 3,510
Portage, WI 53901 • 7,896
Portage □, OH • 135,856
Portage □, WI • 57,420
Portage Lakes, OH 44319 • 11,310
Portageville, MO 63873 • 3,470
Portal, GA 30450 • 694
Portales, NM 88130 • 9,940
Port Allegany, PA 16743 • 2,593
Port Allen, LA 70767 • 6,114
Port Angeles, WA 98362 • 17,311
Port Aransas, TX 78373 • 1,968
Port Arthur, TX 77640–43 • 61,251
Port Austin, MI 48467 • 839
Port Barre, LA 70577 • 2,625
Port Bolivar, TX 77650 • 1,600
Port Byron, IL 61275 • 1,289
Port Byron, NY 13140 • 1,400
Port Carbon, PA 17965 • 2,576
Port Charlotte, FL 33952 • 25,770
Port Chester, NY 10573 • 23,565
Port Clinton, OH 43452 • 7,223
Port Deposit, MD 21904 • 664
Port Dickinson, NY 13901 • 1,974
Port Edwards, WI 54469 • 2,077
Porter, IN 46304 • 2,988
Porter, OK 74454 • 642
Porter, TX 77365 • 5,000
Porter □, IN • 119,816
Porterdale, GA 30270 • 1,451
Porterville, CA 93257 • 19,707
Port Ewen, NY 12466 • 2,600
Port Gibson, MS 39150 • 2,371
Port Henry, NY 12974 • 1,450
Port Hueneme, CA 93041 • 17,803
Port Huron, MI 48060 • 33,981
Port Isabel, TX 78578 • 3,769
Port Jefferson, NY 11777 • 6,731
Port Jefferson Station, NY 11776 • 7,500
Port Jervis, NY 12771 • 8,699
Portland, AR 71663 • 701
Portland, CT 06480 • 8,383
Portland, IN 47371 • 7,074
Portland, ME 04101–99 • 61,572
Portland, MI 48875 • 3,963
Portland, ND 58274 • 627
Portland, OR 97201–99 • 366,383
Portland, TN 37148 • 4,030
Portland, TX 78374 • 12,023
Port Lavaca, TX 77979 • 10,911
Port Leyden, NY 13433 • 740
Port Matilda, PA 16870 • 647
Port Monmouth, NJ 07758 • 3,600
Port Neches, TX 77651 • 13,944
Port Norris, NJ 08349 • 1,730
Port O'Connor, TX 77982 • 1,500
Portola, CA 96122 • 1,885
Port Orange, FL 32019 • 18,756
Port Orchard, WA 98366 • 4,787
Port Orford, OR 97465 • 1,061
Port Reading, NJ 07064 • 4,300
Port Republic, NJ 08241 • 837
Port Richey, FL 34668–69 • 2,165
Port Royal, PA 17082 • 835
Port Royal, SC 29935 • 2,977
Port Saint Joe, FL 32456 • 4,027
Port Saint Lucie, FL 34952 • 14,690
Port Salerno, FL 34992 • 4,511
Portsmouth, NH 03801 • 26,254
Portsmouth, OH 45662 • 25,943
Portsmouth, RI 02871 • 4,300
Portsmouth, VA 23701–99 • 104,577
Port Sulphur, LA 70083 • 3,318
Port Townsend, WA 98368 • 6,067
Portville, NY 14770 • 1,136
Port Vue, PA 15133 • 5,316
Port Washington, NY 11050 • 15,923
Port Washington, OH 43837 • 622
Port Washington, WI 53074 • 8,612
Port Wentworth, GA 31407 • 3,947
Porum, OK 74455 • 668
Posen, IL 60469 • 4,642
Posey □, IN • 26,414
Poseyville, IN 47633 • 1,247
Post, TX 79356 • 3,961
Post Falls, ID 83854 • 5,736
Postville, IA 52162 • 1,475
Poteau, OK 74953 • 7,089
Poteet, TX 78065 • 3,086
Poth, TX 78147 • 1,461
Potlatch, ID 83855 • 819
Potomac, IL 61865 • 874
Potomac, MD 20854 • 22,800
Potomac Heights, MD 20640 • 2,456
Potomac Park, MD 21502 • 1,250
Potosi, MO 63664 • 2,528
Potosi, WI 53820 • 736
Potsdam, NY 13676 • 10,635
Pottawatomie □, KS • 14,782
Pottawatomie □, OK • 55,239
Pottawattamie □, IA • 86,561
Potter □, PA • 17,726
Potter □, SD • 3,674
Potter □, TX • 98,637
Potter Valley, CA 95469 • 1,500
Pottstown, PA 19464 • 22,729
Pottsville, PA 17901 • 18,195
Poughkeepsie, NY 12601–99 • 29,757
Poulan, GA 31781 • 818
Poulsbo, WA 98370 • 3,453
Poultney, VT 05764 • 1,554
Pound, VA 24279 • 1,086
Poway, CA 92064 • 33,300
Powder River □, MT • 2,520
Powder Springs, GA 30073 • 3,381
Powell, WY 82435 • 5,310
Powell □, KY • 11,101
Powell □, MT • 6,958
Powellhurst, OR 97236 • 9,000
Powellton, WV 25161 • 1,200
Power □, ID • 6,844
Powers, OR 97466 • 819
Poweshiek □, IA • 19,306
Powhatan □, VA • 13,062
Powhatan Point, OH 43942 • 2,181
Poynette, WI 53955 • 1,447
Prague, OK 74864 • 2,208
Prairie □, AR • 10,140
Prairie □, MT • 1,836
Prairie City, IA 50228 • 1,278
Prairie City, OR 97869 • 1,106
Prairie du Chien, WI 53821 • 5,859
Prairie Du Rocher, IL 62277 • 701
Prairie du Sac, WI 53578 • 2,145
Prairie Grove, AR 72753 • 1,708
Prairie View, TX 77446 • 3,993
Prairie Village, KS 66208 • 24,657
Pratt, KS 67124 • 6,885
Pratt, WV 25162 • 821
Pratt □, KS • 10,275
Prattsburg, NY 14873 • 750
Prattville, AL 36067 • 18,647
Preble □, OH • 38,223
Premont, TX 78375 • 2,984
Prentice, WI 54556 • 605
Prentiss, MS 39474 • 1,465
Prentiss □, MS • 24,025
Prescott, AZ 86301 • 20,055
Prescott, AR 71857 • 4,103
Prescott, WI 54021 • 2,654
Presho, SD 57568 • 760
Presidio, TX 79845 • 1,100
Presidio □, TX • 5,188
Presque Isle, ME 04769 • 11,172
Presque Isle □, MI • 14,267
Preston, ID 83263 • 3,759
Preston, IA 52069 • 1,120
Preston, MN 55965 • 1,478
Preston □, WV • 30,460
Prestonsburg, KY 41653 • 4,011
Pretty Prairie, KS 67570 • 655
Price, TX 75687 • 650
Price, UT 84501 • 9,086
Price □, WI • 15,788
Prichard, AL 36610 • 39,541
Priest River, ID 83856 • 1,639
Primghar, IA 51245 • 1,050
Prince Edward □, VA • 16,456
Prince Frederick, MD 20678 • 1,805
Prince George □, VA • 25,733
Prince Georges □, MD • 665,071
Princes Lakes, IN 46164 • 937
Princess Anne, MD 21853 • 1,499
Princeton, FL 33032 • 5,300
Princeton, IL 61356 • 7,342
Princeton, IN 47670 • 8,976
Princeton, IA 52768 • 965
Princeton, KY 42445 • 7,073
Princeton, ME 04668 • 800
Princeton, MN 55371 • 3,146
Princeton, MO 64673 • 1,264
Princeton, NJ 08540 • 12,035
Princeton, NC 27569 • 1,034
Princeton, WV 24740 • 7,493
Princeton, WI 54968 • 1,479
Princeton Junction, NJ 08550 • 2,419
Princeville, IL 61559 • 1,712
Princeville, NC 27886 • 1,508
Prince William □, VA • 144,703
Prineville, OR 97754 • 5,276
Prior Lake, MN 55372 • 7,284
Proctor, MN 55810 • 3,180
Proctor, VT 05765 • 1,998
Proctorville, OH 45669 • 975
Prophetstown, IL 61277 • 2,141
Prospect, CT 06712 • 6,807
Prospect, KY 40059 • 1,981
Prospect, OH 43342 • 1,159
Prospect, OR 97536 • 1,200
Prospect, PA 16052 • 1,016
Prospect Heights, IL 60070 • 11,808
Prospect Park, NJ 07508 • 5,142
Prospect Park, PA 19076 • 6,593
Prosperity, SC 29127 • 803
Prosperity, WV 25909 • 1,000
Prosser, WA 99350 • 3,896
Protection, KS 67127 • 684
Provencal, LA 71468 • 695
Providence, KY 42450 • 4,434
Providence, RI 02901–99 • 156,804
Providence, UT 84332 • 2,675
Providence □, RI • 571,349
Provincetown, MA 02657 • 3,536
Provo, UT 84601–04 • 74,108
Prowers □, CO • 13,070
Prudenville, MI 48651 • 1,000
Pryor, OK 74361 • 8,483
Pueblo, CO 81001–19 • 101,686
Pueblo □, CO • 125,972
Puhi, HI 96766 • 991
Pukalani, HI 96788 • 3,950
Pulaski, NY 13142 • 2,415
Pulaski, TN 38478 • 7,184
Pulaski, VA 24301 • 10,106
Pulaski, WI 54162 • 1,875
Pulaski □, AR • 340,613
Pulaski □, GA • 8,950
Pulaski □, IL • 8,840
Pulaski □, IN • 13,258
Pulaski □, KY • 45,803
Pulaski □, MO • 42,011
Pulaski □, VA • 35,229
Pullman, WA 99163 • 23,579
Pumphrey, MD 21227 • 3,300
Punta Gorda, FL 33950–55 • 6,797
Punxsutawney, PA 15767 • 7,479
Purcell, OK 73080 • 4,638
Purcellville, VA 22132 • 1,567
Purdy, MO 65734 • 928
Purvis, MS 39475 • 2,256
Puryear, TN 38251 • 624
Pushmataha □, OK • 11,773
Putnam, CT 06260 • 6,855
Putnam □, FL • 50,549
Putnam □, GA • 10,295
Putnam □, IL • 6,085
Putnam □, IN • 29,163
Putnam □, MO • 6,092
Putnam □, NY • 77,193
Putnam □, OH • 32,991
Putnam □, TN • 47,690
Putnam □, WV • 38,181
Putney, GA 31782 • 650
Putney, VT 05346 • 1,100
Puxico, MO 63960 • 833
Puyallup, WA 98371–73 • 18,251

## Q

Quail Oaks, VA 23234 • 1,700
Quaker City, OH 43773 • 698
Quaker Hill, CT 06375 • 2,052
Quakertown, PA 18951 • 8,867
Quanah, TX 79252 • 3,890
Quantico, VA 22134 • 621
Quapaw, OK 74363 • 1,097
Quarryville, PA 17566 • 1,558
Quay □, NM • 10,577
Queen Annes □, MD • 25,508
Queen City, MO 63561 • 783
Queen City, TX 75572 • 1,748
Queen Creek, AZ 85242 • 900
Queens □, NY • 1,891,325
Questa, NM 87556 • 1,202
Quidnessett, RI 02852 • 3,300
Quidnick, RI 02816 • 2,300
Quilcene, WA 98376 • 950
Quincy, CA 95971 • 2,700
Quincy, FL 32351 • 8,591
Quincy, IL 62301 • 42,554
Quincy, MA 02169 • 84,743
Quincy, MI 49082 • 1,569
Quincy, OH 43343 • 633
Quincy, WA 98848 • 3,525
Quinebaug, CT 06262 • 1,088
Quinlan, TX 75474 • 1,002
Quinnesec, MI 49876 • 900
Quinter, KS 67752 • 951
Quinton, OK 74561 • 1,228
Quitaque, TX 79255 • 696
Quitman, GA 31643 • 5,188
Quitman, MS 39355 • 2,632
Quitman, TX 75783 • 1,893
Quitman □, GA • 2,357
Quitman □, MS • 12,636
Quonochontaug, RI 02808 • 1,000

## R

Rabun □, GA • 10,466
Raceland, KY 41169 • 1,970
Raceland, LA 70394 • 6,302
Racine, OH 45771 • 908
Racine, WV 25165 • 650
Racine, WI 53401–99 • 85,725
Racine □, WI • 173,132
Radcliff, KY 40160 • 14,519
Radford, VA 24141 • 13,225
Raeford, NC 28376 • 3,630
Ragland, AL 35131 • 1,807
Rahway, NJ 07065–67 • 26,723
Rainbow City, AL 35901 • 6,299
Rainelle, WV 25962 • 1,983
Rainier, OR 97048 • 1,655
Rainier, WA 98576 • 891
Rains □, TX • 4,839
Rainsville, AL 35986 • 3,907
Raleigh, MS 39153 • 998
Raleigh, NC 27601–99 • 150,255
Raleigh, WV 25911 • 900
Raleigh □, WV • 86,821
Raleigh Hills, OR 97225 • 6,500
Ralls, TX 79357 • 2,422
Ralls □, MO • 8,984
Ralston, NE 68127 • 5,143
Rambleton Acres, DE 19720 • 1,500
Ramblewood, NJ 08054 • 6,475
Ramona, CA 92065 • 8,173
Ramsay, MI 49959 • 1,068
Ramseur, NC 27316 • 1,162
Ramsey, IL 62080 • 1,058
Ramsey, MN 55303 • 10,093
Ramsey, NJ 07446 • 12,899
Ramsey □, MN • 459,784
Ramsey □, ND • 13,048
Ranchester, WY 82839 • 655
Rancho Cordova, CA 95670 • 42,881
Rancho Mirage, CA 92270 • 6,281
Rancho Palos Verdes, CA 90274 • 36,577
Rancho Rinconado, CA 95014 • 5,100
Rancho Santa Fe, CA 92067 • 4,014
Ranchos de Taos, NM 87557 • 1,411
Rancocas Woods, NJ 08060 • 1,400
Rand, WV 25306 • 2,500
Randall □, TX • 75,062
Randallstown, MD 21133 • 20,500
Randleman, NC 27317 • 2,156
Randolph, ME 04345 • 1,834
Randolph, MA 02368 • 22,218
Randolph, NE 68771 • 1,106
Randolph, NY 14772 • 1,398
Randolph, OH 44265 • 800
Randolph, UT 84064 • 659
Randolph, VT 05060 • 2,217
Randolph, WI 53956 • 1,691
Randolph □, AL • 20,075
Randolph □, AR • 16,834
Randolph □, GA • 9,599
Randolph □, IL • 35,652
Randolph □, IN • 29,997
Randolph □, MO • 25,460
Randolph □, NC • 91,728
Randolph □, WV • 28,734
Random Lake, WI 53075 • 1,287
Rangeley, ME 04970 • 700
Rangely, CO 81648 • 2,113
Ranger, TX 76470 • 3,142
Rankin, IL 60960 • 727
Rankin, PA 15104 • 2,892
Rankin, TX 79778 • 1,216
Rankin □, MS • 69,427
Ransom □, ND • 6,698
Ransomville, NY 14131 • 1,500
Ranson, WV 25438 • 2,471
Rantoul, IL 61866 • 20,161
Raoul, GA 30510 • 1,400
Rapid City, SD 57701–08 • 46,492
Rapides □, LA • 135,282
Rapid River, MI 49878 • 700
Rapids City, IL 61278 • 1,058
Rappahannock □, VA • 6,093
Raritan, NJ 08869 • 6,128
Rathdrum, ID 83858 • 1,369
Raton, NM 87740 • 8,225
Ravalli □, MT • 22,493
Raven, VA 24639 • 1,880
Ravena, NY 12143 • 3,091
Ravenel, SC 29470 • 1,655
Ravenna, KY 40472 • 793
Ravenna, MI 49451 • 951
Ravenna, NE 68869 • 1,296
Ravenna, OH 44266 • 11,987
Ravenswood, WV 26164 • 4,126
Rawlins, WY 82301 • 11,547
Rawlins □, KS • 4,105
Ray, ND 58849 • 766
Ray □, MO • 21,378
Ray City, GA 31645 • 658
Raymond, IL 62560 • 957
Raymond, MN 56282 • 723
Raymond, MS 39154 • 1,967
Raymond, NH 03077 • 1,192
Raymond, WA 98577 • 2,991
Raymondville, TX 78580 • 9,493
Raymore, MO 64083 • 3,154
Rayne, LA 70578 • 9,066
Raynham, MA 02767 • 2,124
Raynham Center, MA 02768 • 3,776
Raytown, MO 64133 • 31,759
Rayville, LA 71269 • 4,610
Reader, WV 26167 • 700
Reading, MA 01867 • 22,678
Reading, MI 49274 • 1,203
Reading, OH 45215 • 12,843
Reading, PA 19601–99 • 78,686
Readlyn, IA 50668 • 858
Reagan □, TX • 4,135
Real □, TX • 2,469
Reamstown, PA 17567 • 1,050
Rector, AR 72461 • 2,336
Red Bank, NJ 07701 • 12,031
Red Bank, TN 37415 • 13,299
Red Bay, AL 35582 • 3,232
Redbird, OH 44057 • 1,600
Red Bluff, CA 96080 • 9,490
Red Boiling Springs, TN 37150 • 1,173
Red Bud, IL 62278 • 2,850
Red Cloud, NE 68970 • 1,300
Red Creek, NY 13143 • 645
Reddick, FL 32686 • 657
Redding, CA 96001–03 • 41,995
Redding, CT 06875 • 950
Redfield, AR 72132 • 745
Redfield, IA 50233 • 959
Redfield, SD 57469 • 3,027
Redford, MI 48239 • 58,441
Redgranite, WI 54970 • 976
Red Hook, NY 12571 • 1,692
Red Jacket, WV 25692 • 1,000
Redkey, IN 47373 • 1,537
Red Lake □, MN • 5,471
Red Lake Falls, MN 56750 • 1,732
Redlands, CA 92373–74 • 43,619
Red Lion, PA 17356 • 5,824
Red Lodge, MT 59068 • 1,896
Redmond, OR 97756 • 6,452
Redmond, UT 84652 • 619
Redmond, WA 98052–53 • 23,318
Red Oak, GA 30272 • 1,200
Red Oak, IA 51566 • 6,810
Red Oak, OK 74563 • 676
Red Oak, TX 75154 • 1,882
Red Oaks, LA 70815 • 2,000
Redondo Beach, CA 90277–78 • 57,102
Red River □, LA • 10,433
Red River □, TX • 16,101
Red Springs, NC 28377 • 3,607
Red Willow □, NE • 12,615
Red Wing, MN 55066 • 13,736
Redwood, UT 84119 • 2,000
Redwood □, MN • 19,341
Redwood City, CA 94061–65 • 54,951
Redwood Falls, MN 56283 • 5,210
Redwood Valley, CA 95470 • 1,300
Reece City, AL 35954 • 718
Reed City, MI 49677 • 2,221
Reedley, CA 93654 • 11,071
Reedsburg, WI 53959 • 5,038
Reedsport, OR 97467 • 4,984
Reedsville, PA 17084 • 950
Reedsville, WI 54230 • 1,134
Reedurban, OH 44710 • 6,650
Reese, MI 48757 • 1,645
Reeseville, WI 53579 • 649
Reeves □, TX • 15,801
Reform, AL 35481 • 2,245
Refugio, TX 78377 • 3,898
Refugio □, TX • 9,289
Rehoboth Beach, DE 19971 • 1,730
Reidland, KY 42001 • 3,730
Reidsville, GA 30453 • 2,296
Reidsville, NC 27320 • 12,492
Reinbeck, IA 50669 • 1,808
Reisterstown, MD 21136 • 19,385
Remington, IN 47977 • 1,268
Remsen, IA 51050 • 1,592
Remsen, NY 13438 • 621
Reno, NV 89501–99 • 100,756
Reno, OH 45773 • 850
Reno □, KS • 64,983
Renovo, PA 17764 • 1,812
Rensselaer, IN 47978 • 4,944
Rensselaer, NY 12144 • 9,047
Rensselaer □, NY • 151,966
Renton, WA 98055–57 • 30,612
Renville, MN 56284 • 1,493
Renville □, MN • 20,401
Renville □, ND • 3,608
Republic, MI 49879 • 1,000
Republic, MO 65738 • 4,485
Republic, OH 44867 • 656
Republic, PA 15475 • 1,500
Republic, WA 99166 • 1,018
Republic □, KS • 7,569
Reserve, LA 70084 • 7,288
Reston, VA 22090 • 32,000
Revere, MA 02151 • 42,423
Revloc, PA 15948 • 800
Rex, GA 30273 • 700
Rexburg, ID 83440 • 11,559
Reynolds, GA 31076 • 1,298
Reynolds, IL 61279 • 701
Reynolds, IN 47980 • 632
Reynolds □, MO • 7,230
Reynoldsburg, OH 43068 • 20,661
Reynoldsville, PA 15851 • 3,016
Rhea □, TN • 24,235
Rhinebeck, NY 12572 • 2,542
Rhinelander, WI 54501 • 7,873
Rhodhiss, NC 28667 • 727
Rialto, CA 92376 • 37,474
Rib Lake, WI 54470 • 945
Rice □, KS • 11,900
Rice □, MN • 46,087
Rice Lake, WI 54868 • 7,691
Riceville, IA 50466 • 919
Rich □, UT • 2,100
Richardson, TX 75080–85 • 72,496
Richardson □, NE • 11,315
Richardton, ND 58652 • 699
Rich Creek, VA 24147 • 746
Richfield, MN 55423 • 37,851
Richfield, UT 84701 • 5,482
Richfield Springs, NY 13439 • 1,561
Richford, VT 05476 • 1,471
Rich Hill, MO 64779 • 1,471
Richland, GA 31825 • 1,802
Richland, MO 65556 • 1,922
Richland, NJ 08350 • 800
Richland, WA 99352 • 33,578
Richland □, IL • 17,587
Richland □, LA • 22,187
Richland □, MT • 12,243
Richland □, ND • 19,207
Richland □, OH • 131,205
Richland □, SC • 269,735
Richland □, WI • 17,476
Richland Center, WI 53581 • 4,997
Richlands, NC 28574 • 825
Richlands, VA 24641 • 5,796
Richlandtown, PA 18955 • 1,180
Richmond, CA 94801–99 • 74,676
Richmond, IL 60071 • 1,068
Richmond, IN 47374 • 41,349
Richmond, KY 40475 • 21,705
Richmond, ME 04357 • 1,578
Richmond, MI 48062 • 3,536
Richmond, MN 56368 • 867
Richmond, MO 64085 • 5,499
Richmond, TX 77469 • 9,692
Richmond, UT 84333 • 1,705
Richmond, VT 05477 • 865
Richmond, VA 23201–99 • 219,214
Richmond □, GA • 181,629
Richmond □, NC • 45,481
Richmond □, NY • 352,121
Richmond □, VA • 6,952
Richmond Beach, WA 98160 • 8,000
Richmond Dale, OH 45673 • 650
Richmond Heights, FL 33156 • 8,577
Richmond Heights, MO 63117 • 11,516
Richmond Heights, OH 44143 • 10,095
Richmond Highlands, WA 98133 • 20,300
Richmond Hill, GA 31324 • 1,177
Richmondville, NY 12149 • 792
Rich Square, NC 27869 • 1,057
Richton, MS 39476 • 1,205
Richton Park, IL 60471 • 9,403
Richwood, OH 43344 • 2,181
Richwood, WV 26261 • 3,568
Riddle, OR 97469 • 1,265
Ridgecrest, CA 93555 • 15,929
Ridgecrest, WA 98155 • 7,000
Ridge Farm, IL 61870 • 1,096
Ridgefield, CT 06877 • 6,066
Ridgefield, NJ 07657 • 10,294
Ridgefield, WA 98642 • 1,062
Ridgefield Park, NJ 07660 • 12,738
Ridgeland, MS 39157 • 5,461
Ridgeland, SC 29936 • 1,143
Ridgeley, WV 26753 • 994
Ridgely, MD 21660 • 933
Ridgely, TN 38080 • 1,775
Ridgemont, NY 14626 • 8,500
Ridge Spring, SC 29129 • 969
Ridgetop, TN 37152 • 1,225
Ridgeville, IN 47380 • 933
Ridgeville, SC 29472 • 603
Ridgeway, VA 24148 • 858
Ridgewood, NJ 07450–52 • 25,208
Ridgway, IL 62979 • 1,245
Ridgway, PA 15853 • 5,604
Ridley Park, PA 19078 • 7,889
Riesel, TX 76682 • 691
Rifle, CO 81650 • 3,215
Rigby, ID 83442 • 2,624
Riley, KS 66531 • 779
Riley □, KS • 63,505
Rimersburg, PA 16248 • 1,096
Rincon, GA 31326 • 1,988
Ringgold, GA 30736 • 1,882
Ringgold, LA 71068 • 1,655
Ringgold □, IA • 6,112
Ringling, OK 73456 • 1,561
Ringoes, NJ 08551 • 650
Ringwood, NJ 07456 • 12,625
Rio, FL 34957 • 1,205
Rio, WI 53960 • 785
Rio Arriba □, NM • 29,282
Rio Blanco □, CO • 6,255
Rio Dell, CA 95562 • 2,687
Rio Grande, NJ 08242 • 2,016
Rio Grande, OH 45674 • 864
Rio Grande □, CO • 10,511
Rio Grande City, TX 78582 • 7,000
Rio Hondo, TX 78583 • 1,673
Rio Linda, CA 95673 • 7,359
Rio Rancho, NM 87124 • 12,000
Rio Vista, CA 94571 • 3,142
Ripley, MS 38663 • 4,271
Ripley, NY 14775 • 1,000
Ripley, OH 45167 • 2,174
Ripley, TN 38063 • 6,366
Ripley, WV 25271 • 3,464
Ripley □, IN • 24,398
Ripley □, MO • 12,458
Ripon, WI 54971 • 7,111
Rising Star, TX 76471 • 1,204

Rising Sun, IN 47040 • *2,478*
Rising Sun, MD 21911 • *1,160*
Risingsun, OH 43457 • *698*
Rison, AR 71665 • *1,325*
Ritchie □, WV • *11,442*
Rittman, OH 44270 • *6,063*
Ritzville, WA 99169 • *1,800*
Riverbank, CA 95367 • *5,695*
Riverdale, CA 93656 • *1,866*
Riverdale, GA 30274 • *7,121*
Riverdale, IL 60627 • *13,233*
Riverdale, MD 20737 • *4,748*
Riverdale, NJ 07457 • *2,530*
Riverdale, UT 84401 • *6,031*
River Edge, NJ 07661 • *11,111*
River Falls, AL 36476 • *669*
River Falls, WI 54022 • *9,019*
River Forest, IL 60305 • *12,392*
River Grove, IL 60171 • *10,368*
Riverhaven, IN 46802 • *700*
Riverhead, NY 11901 • *7,400*
River Heights, UT 84321 • *1,211*
River Hills, WI 53217 • *1,642*
River Oaks, TX 76114 • *6,890*
River Pines, MA 01821 • *3,700*
River Ridge, LA 70123 • *17,146*
River Road, OR 97404 • *10,370*
River Rouge, MI 48218 • *12,912*
Riverside, AL 35135 • *849*
Riverside, CA 92501–99 • *170,591*
Riverside, IL 60546 • *9,236*
Riverside, IA 52327 • *826*
Riverside, NJ 08075 • *7,941*
Riverside, PA 17868 • *2,266*
Riverside □, CA • *663,199*
Riverton, IL 62561 • *2,783*
Riverton, NJ 08077 • *3,068*
Riverton, UT 84065 • *7,293*
Riverton, WY 82501 • *9,247*
Riverton Heights, WA 98188 • *33,500*
River Vale, NJ 07675 • *9,489*
River View, AL 36854 • *1,314*
Riverview, FL 33569 • *3,200*
Riverview, MI 48192 • *14,569*
Rivesville, WV 26588 • *1,327*
Riviera, AZ 86442 • *4,500*
Riviera Beach, FL 33404 • *26,489*
Riviera Beach, MD 21122 • *5,600*
Riviera Beach, NJ 08723 • *2,000*
Roachdale, IN 46172 • *958*
Roane □, TN • *48,425*
Roane □, WV • *15,952*
Roan Mountain, TN 37687 • *1,108*
Roanoke, AL 36274 • *5,896*
Roanoke, IL 61561 • *2,001*
Roanoke, IN 46783 • *891*
Roanoke, TX 76262 • *910*
Roanoke, VA 24001–50 • *100,220*
Roanoke □, VA • *72,945*
Roanoke Rapids, NC 27870 • *14,702*
Roaring Spring, PA 16673 • *2,962*
Robbins, IL 60472 • *8,853*
Robbins, NC 27325 • *1,256*
Robbinsdale, MN 55422 • *14,422*
Robbinsville, NC 28771 • *1,370*
Robersonville, NC 27871 • *1,981*
Roberta, GA 31078 • *859*
Robert Lee, TX 76945 • *1,202*
Roberts, WI 54023 • *833*
Roberts □, SD • *10,911*
Roberts □, TX • *1,187*
Robertsdale, AL 36567 • *2,306*
Robertson □, KY • *2,265*
Robertson □, TN • *37,021*
Robertson □, TX • *14,653*
Robeson □, NC • *101,610*
Robins, IA 52328 • *726*
Robinson, IL 62454 • *7,285*
Robinson, PA 15949 • *660*
Robinson, TX 76706 • *6,074*
Robstown, TX 78380 • *12,100*
Roby, TX 79543 • *814*
Rochdale, MA 01542 • *1,105*
Rochelle, GA 31079 • *1,626*
Rochelle, IL 61068 • *8,982*
Rochelle Park, NJ 07662 • *5,603*
Rochester, IL 62563 • *2,488*
Rochester, IN 46975 • *5,050*
Rochester, MI 48063–64 • *7,203*
Rochester, MN 55901–04 • *57,890*
Rochester, NH 03867 • *21,560*
Rochester, NY 14601–99 • *241,741*
Rochester, PA 15074 • *4,759*
Rochester, WA 98579 • *900*
Rochester, WI 53167 • *746*
Rock □, MN • *10,703*
Rock □, NE • *2,383*
Rock □, WI • *139,420*
Rockaway, NJ 07866 • *6,852*
Rockaway, OR 97136 • *906*
Rockbridge □, VA • *17,911*
Rockcastle □, KY • *13,973*
Rock Creek, MN 55067 • *890*
Rock Creek, OH 44084 • *652*
Rockdale, IL 60436 • *1,913*
Rockdale, MD 21207 • *4,200*
Rockdale, TX 76567 • *5,611*
Rockdale □, GA • *36,747*
Rock Falls, IL 61071 • *10,633*
Rockford, IL 61101–99 • *139,712*
Rockford, IA 50468 • *1,012*
Rockford, MI 49341 • *3,324*
Rockford, MN 55373 • *2,408*
Rockford, OH 45882 • *1,245*
Rock Hall, MD 21661 • *1,511*
Rock Hill, MO 63124 • *5,702*
Rock Hill, SC 29730 • *35,344*
Rockingham, NC 28379 • *8,300*
Rockingham □, NH • *190,345*
Rockingham □, NC • *83,426*
Rockingham □, VA • *57,038*
Rock Island, IL 61201 • *46,928*
Rock Island □, IL • *165,968*
Rockland, ME 04841 • *7,919*
Rockland, MA 02370 • *15,695*
Rockland □, NY • *259,530*
Rockledge, FL 32955 • *11,877*
Rockledge, PA 19111 • *2,538*
Rocklin, CA 95677 • *7,344*
Rockmart, GA 30153 • *3,645*
Rockport, IN 47635 • *2,590*
Rockport, ME 04856 • *1,000*
Rockport, MA 01966 • *4,600*
Rock Port, MO 64482 • *1,511*
Rockport, TX 78382 • *3,686*
Rock Rapids, IA 51246 • *2,693*
Rocksprings, TX 78880 • *1,317*
Rock Springs, WY 82901 • *19,458*
Rockton, IL 61072 • *2,313*
Rock Valley, IA 51247 • *2,706*
Rockville, IN 47872 • *2,785*
Rockville, MD 20850–58 • *43,811*
Rockville Centre, NY 11570 • *25,412*
Rockwall, TX 75087 • *5,939*
Rockwall □, TX • *14,528*
Rockwell, IA 50469 • *1,039*
Rockwell, NC 28138 • *1,339*
Rockwell City, IA 50579 • *2,276*
Rockwell Park, NC 28213 • *2,600*
Rockwood, MI 48173 • *3,346*
Rockwood, OR 97233 • *11,000*
Rockwood, PA 15557 • *1,058*
Rockwood, TN 37854 • *5,767*
Rocky Creek, FL 33615 • *7,800*
Rocky Ford, CO 81067 • *4,804*
Rocky Hill, CT 06067 • *14,559*
Rocky Hill, NJ 08553 • *717*
Rocky Mount, NC 27801 • *41,283*
Rocky Mount, VA 24151 • *4,198*
Rocky Ripple, IN 46208 • *778*
Rocky River, OH 44116 • *21,084*
Rodeo, CA 94572 • *8,286*
Roderfield, WV 24881 • *1,100*
Rodney Village, DE 19901 • *1,100*
Roebling, NJ 08554 • *3,600*
Roebuck, SC 29376 • *1,088*
Roeland Park, KS 66203 • *7,962*
Roessleville, NY 12205 • *5,476*
Roff, OK 74865 • *729*
Roger Mills □, OK • *4,799*
Rogers, AR 72756 • *17,429*
Rogers, MN 55374 • *652*
Rogers, TX 76569 • *1,242*
Rogers □, OK • *46,436*
Rogers City, MI 49779 • *3,923*
Rogersville, AL 35652 • *1,224*
Rogersville, MO 65742 • *741*
Rogersville, TN 37857 • *4,368*
Rogue River, OR 97537 • *1,308*
Rohnert Park, CA 94928 • *22,965*
Roland, IA 50236 • *1,005*
Roland, OK 74954 • *1,472*
Rolette, ND 58366 • *667*
Rolette □, ND • *12,177*
Rolfe, IA 50581 • *796*
Rolla, MO 65401 • *13,303*
Rolla, ND 58367 • *1,538*
Rollingbay, WA 98061 • *700*
Rolling Fork, MS 39159 • *2,590*
Rolling Hills Estates, CA 90274 • *7,701*
Rolling Meadows, IL 60008 • *20,167*
Rollinsford, NH 03869 • *1,173*
Roma, TX 78584 • *3,384*
Rome, GA 30161 • *29,654*
Rome, IL 61562 • *2,744*
Rome, NY 13440 • *43,826*
Rome City, IN 46784 • *1,319*
Romeo, MI 48065 • *3,509*
Romeoville, IL 60441 • *15,519*
Romney, WV 26757 • *2,094*
Romulus, MI 48174 • *24,857*
Ronan, MT 59864 • *1,530*
Ronceverte, WV 24970 • *2,312*
Ronkonkoma, NY 11779 • *20,200*
Roodhouse, IL 62082 • *2,364*
Rooks □, KS • *7,006*
Roosevelt, NJ 08555 • *835*
Roosevelt, NY 11575 • *15,000*
Roosevelt, UT 84066 • *3,842*
Roosevelt □, MT • *10,467*
Roosevelt □, NM • *15,695*
Roosevelt Park, MI 49441 • *4,015*
Rootstown, OH 44272 • *650*
Roper, NC 27970 • *795*
Rosamond, CA 93560 • *2,869*
Roscoe, IL 61073 • *1,388*
Roscoe, PA 15477 • *1,123*
Roscoe, TX 79545 • *1,628*
Roscommon, MI 48653 • *834*
Roscommon □, MI • *16,374*
Roseau, MN 56751 • *2,272*
Roseau □, MN • *12,574*
Roseboro, NC 28382 • *1,227*
Rosebud, TX 76570 • *2,076*
Rosebud □, MT • *9,899*
Roseburg, OR 97470 • *16,644*
Rose City, MI 48654 • *661*
Rosedale, IN 47874 • *744*
Rosedale, MD 21237 • *19,956*
Rosedale, MS 38769 • *2,793*
Rose Hill, KS 67133 • *1,557*
Rose Hill, NC 28458 • *1,508*
Rose Hill, VA 24281 • *800*
Roseland, CA 95407 • *7,915*
Roseland, FL 32957 • *1,607*
Roseland, IN 46635 • *832*
Roseland, LA 70456 • *1,346*
Roseland, NJ 07068 • *5,330*
Roseland, OH 44906 • *3,000*
Roselle, IL 60172 • *16,948*
Roselle, NJ 07203 • *20,641*
Roselle Park, NJ 07204 • *13,377*
Rosemead, CA 91770 • *42,604*
Rosemount, MN 55068 • *5,083*
Rosenberg, TX 77471 • *17,995*
Rosendale, WI 54974 • *725*
Rosenhayn, NJ 08352 • *750*
Rosepine, LA 70659 • *953*
Roseto, PA 18013 • *1,484*
Roseville, CA 95678 • *24,347*
Roseville, IL 61473 • *1,254*
Roseville, MI 48066 • *54,311*
Roseville, MN 55113 • *35,820*
Roseville, OH 43777 • *1,915*
Rosewood Heights, IL 62024 • *5,085*
Rosiclare, IL 62982 • *1,441*
Roslyn, PA 19001 • *13,400*
Roslyn, WA 98941 • *938*
Roslyn Heights, NY 11577 • *7,270*
Ross, OH 45061 • *2,767*
Ross □, OH • *65,004*
Rossford, OH 43460 • *5,978*
Rossiter, PA 15772 • *750*
Rossmoor, CA 90720 • *10,457*
Rossville, GA 30741 • *3,851*
Rossville, IL 60963 • *1,363*
Rossville, IN 46065 • *1,148*
Rossville, KS 66533 • *1,045*
Roswell, GA 30075–77 • *23,337*
Roswell, NM 88201 • *39,676*
Rotan, TX 79546 • *2,284*
Rothschild, WI 54474 • *3,338*
Rothsville, PA 17543 • *1,318*
Rotterdam, NY 12303 • *24,800*
Roulette, PA 16746 • *1,100*
Round Lake, IL 60073 • *2,644*
Round Lake, NY 12151 • *791*
Round Lake Beach, IL 60073 • *12,921*
Round Rock, TX 78664 • *12,740*
Roundup, MT 59072 • *2,119*
Rouses Point, NY 12979 • *2,266*
Rouseville, PA 16344 • *734*
Routt □, CO • *13,404*
Rouzerville, PA 17250 • *1,371*
Rowan □, KY • *19,049*
Rowan □, NC • *99,186*
Rowland, NC 28383 • *1,841*
Rowland Heights, CA 91748 • *28,252*
Rowlesburg, WV 26425 • *966*
Rowlett, TX 75088 • *7,522*
Rowley, MA 01969 • *1,321*
Roxboro, NC 27573 • *7,532*
Roxbury, NY 12474 • *700*
Roxton, TX 75477 • *735*
Roy, UT 84067 • *19,694*
Royal Center, IN 46978 • *908*
Royal Oak, MI 48067–73 • *70,893*
Royal Pines, NC 28704 • *2,041*
Royalton, IL 62983 • *1,320*
Royalton, MN 56373 • *660*
Royersford, PA 19468 • *4,243*
Royerton, IN 47302 • *650*
Royse City, TX 75089 • *1,566*
Royston, GA 30662 • *2,404*
Rubidoux, CA 92509 • *13,200*
Rudyard, MI 49780 • *900*
Rugby, ND 58368 • *3,335*
Ruidoso, NM 88345 • *4,260*
Ruidoso Downs, NM 88346 • *949*
Rule, TX 79547 • *1,015*
Ruleville, MS 38771 • *3,332*
Rumford, ME 04276 • *6,256*
Rumson, NJ 07760 • *7,623*
Runge, TX 78151 • *1,244*
Runnels □, TX • *11,872*
Runnemede, NJ 08078 • *9,461*
Rupert, ID 83350 • *5,476*
Rupert, WV 25984 • *1,276*
Rural Hall, NC 27045 • *1,336*
Rural Retreat, VA 24368 • *1,083*
Rush □, IN • *19,604*
Rush □, KS • *4,516*
Rush City, MN 55069 • *1,198*
Rushford, MN 55971 • *1,478*
Rush Springs, OK 73082 • *1,451*
Rushsylvania, OH 43347 • *610*
Rushville, IL 62681 • *3,348*
Rushville, IN 46173 • *6,113*
Rushville, NE 69360 • *1,217*
Rusk, TX 75785 • *4,681*
Rusk □, TX • *41,382*
Rusk □, WI • *15,589*
Ruskin, FL 33570 • *5,117*
Russell, KS 67665 • *5,427*
Russell, KY 41169 • *3,824*
Russell, MA 01071 • *650*
Russell, PA 16345 • *800*
Russell □, AL • *47,356*
Russell □, KS • *8,868*
Russell □, KY • *13,708*
Russell □, VA • *31,761*
Russell Springs, KY 42642 • *1,831*
Russellville, AL 35653 • *8,195*
Russellville, AR 72801 • *14,031*
Russellville, KY 42276 • *7,520*
Russellville, MO 65074 • *667*
Russellville, OR 97216 • *6,500*
Russellville, TN 37860 • *1,069*
Russiaville, IN 46979 • *973*
Ruston, LA 71270 • *20,585*
Ruston, WA 98407 • *612*
Ruth, NV 89319 • *735*
Rutherford, NJ 07070–75 • *19,068*
Rutherford, TN 38369 • *1,378*
Rutherford □, NC • *53,787*
Rutherford □, TN • *84,058*
Rutherfordton, NC 28139 • *3,434*
Ruthven, IA 51358 • *769*
Rutland, MA 01543 • *2,312*
Rutland, OH 45775 • *635*
Rutland, VT 05701 • *18,436*
Rutland □, VT • *58,347*
Rutledge, GA 30663 • *694*
Rutledge, TN 37861 • *1,058*
Ryan, OK 73565 • *1,083*
Rye, NH 03870 • *800*
Rye, NY 10580 • *15,083*

## S

Sabattus, ME 04280 • *1,234*
Sabetha, KS 66534 • *2,286*
Sabina, OH 45169 • *2,799*
Sabinal, TX 78881 • *1,827*
Sabine □, LA • *25,280*
Sabine □, TX • *8,702*
Sabine Pass, TX 77655 • *900*
Sabula, IA 52070 • *824*
Sac □, IA • *14,118*
Sacaton, AZ 85247 • *1,951*
Sac City, IA 50583 • *3,000*
Sachse, TX 75040 • *1,640*
Sackets Harbor, NY 13685 • *1,017*
Saco, ME 04072 • *12,921*
Sacramento, CA 95801–99 • *275,741*
Sacramento □, CA • *783,381*
Sacred Heart, MN 56285 • *666*
Saddle Brook, NJ 07662 • *14,084*
Saddle River, NJ 07458 • *2,763*
Saegertown, PA 16433 • *942*
Safety Harbor, FL 34695 • *6,461*
Safford, AZ 85546 • *7,010*
Sagadahoc □, ME • *28,795*
Sagamore, MA 02561 • *1,152*
Sagamore, PA 16250 • *850*
Sagamore Beach, MA 02562 • *800*
Sagamore Hills, OH 44067 • *4,700*
Sag Harbor, NY 11963 • *2,581*
Saginaw, MI 48601–08 • *77,508*
Saginaw, TX 76179 • *5,736*
Saginaw □, MI • *228,059*
Saguache, CO 81149 • *656*
Saguache □, CO • *3,935*
Saint Albans, VT 05478 • *7,308*
Saint Albans, WV 25177 • *12,402*
Saint Andrews, SC 29407 • *9,908*
Saint Andrews, SC 29210 • *20,245*
Saint Ann, MO 63074 • *15,523*
Saint Anne, IL 60964 • *1,421*
Saint Ansgar, IA 50472 • *1,100*
Saint Anthony, ID 83445 • *3,212*
Saint Augustine, FL 32084–86 • *11,985*
Saint Bernard, LA 70085 • *720*
Saint Bernard, OH 45217 • *5,396*
Saint Bernard □, LA • *64,097*
Saint Bernice, IN 47875 • *900*
Saint Charles, IL 60174 • *17,492*
Saint Charles, MI 48655 • *2,276*
Saint Charles, MN 55972 • *2,184*
Saint Charles, MO 63301–03 • *37,379*
Saint Charles □, LA • *37,259*
Saint Charles □, MO • *144,107*
Saint Clair, MI 48079 • *4,780*
Saint Clair, MN 56080 • *655*
Saint Clair, MO 63077 • *3,485*
Saint Clair, PA 17970 • *4,037*
Saint Clair □, AL • *41,205*
Saint Clair □, IL • *267,531*
Saint Clair □, MI • *138,802*
Saint Clair □, MO • *8,622*
Saint Clair Shores, MI 48080–82 • *76,210*
Saint Clairsville, OH 43950 • *5,452*
Saint Cloud, FL 32769 • *7,840*
Saint Cloud, MN 56301 • *42,566*
Saint Croix □, WI • *43,262*
Saint Croix Falls, WI 54024 • *1,497*
Saint David, AZ 85630 • *950*
Saint David, IL 61563 • *786*
Saint Edward, NE 68660 • *891*
Saint Elmo, IL 62458 • *1,611*
Saint Francis, KS 67756 • *1,610*
Saint Francis, MN 55070 • *1,184*
Saint Francis, SD 57572 • *766*
Saint Francis, WI 53207 • *10,042*
Saint Francis □, AR • *30,858*
Saint Francisville, IL 62460 • *1,040*
Saint Francisville, LA 70775 • *1,471*
Saint Francois □, MO • *42,600*
Sainte Genevieve, MO 63670 • *4,481*
Sainte Genevieve □, MO • *15,180*
Saint George, SC 29477 • *2,134*
Saint George, UT 84770 • *11,350*
Saint Helena, CA 94574 • *4,898*
Saint Helena □, LA • *9,827*
Saint Helens, OR 97051 • *7,064*
Saint Henry, OH 45883 • *1,596*
Saint Ignace, MI 49781 • *2,632*
Saint Ignatius, MT 59865 • *877*
Saint Jacob, IL 62281 • *792*
Saint James, MN 56081 • *4,346*
Saint James, MO 65559 • *3,328*
Saint James, NY 11780 • *11,000*
Saint James □, LA • *21,495*
Saint James City, FL 33956 • *1,298*
Saint Jo, TX 76265 • *1,071*
Saint John, IN 46373 • *3,974*
Saint John, KS 67576 • *1,501*
Saint Johns, AZ 85936 • *3,368*
Saint Johns, MI 48879 • *7,376*
Saint Johns, MO 63114 • *7,854*
Saint Johns □, FL • *51,303*
Saint Johnsbury, VT 05819 • *7,150*
Saint Johnsville, NY 13452 • *1,974*
Saint John the Baptist □, LA • *31,924*
Saint Joseph, IL 61873 • *1,900*
Saint Joseph, LA 71366 • *1,687*
Saint Joseph, MI 49085 • *9,622*
Saint Joseph, MN 56374 • *2,994*
Saint Joseph, MO 64501–08 • *76,691*
Saint Joseph, TN 38481 • *897*
Saint Joseph □, IN • *241,617*
Saint Joseph □, MI • *56,083*
Saint Landry □, LA • *84,128*
Saint Lawrence □, NY • *114,254*
Saint Leo, FL 33574 • *917*
Saint Louis, MI 48880 • *4,107*
Saint Louis, MO 63101–99 • *453,085*
Saint Louis □, MN • *222,229*
Saint Louis □, MO • *973,896*
Saint Louis Park, MN 55426 • *42,931*
Saint Lucie □, FL • *87,182*
Saint Maries, ID 83861 • *2,794*
Saint Martin □, LA • *40,214*
Saint Martinville, LA 70582 • *7,965*
Saint Mary □, LA • *64,253*
Saint Mary-of-the-Woods, IN 47876 • *650*
Saint Marys, GA 31558 • *3,596*
Saint Marys, IN 46556 • *1,700*
Saint Marys, KS 66536 • *1,598*
Saint Marys, OH 45885 • *8,414*
Saint Marys, PA 15857 • *6,417*
Saint Marys, WV 26170 • *2,219*
Saint Marys □, MD • *59,895*
Saint Marys City, MD 20686 • *900*
Saint Matthews, KY 40207 • *13,519*
Saint Matthews, SC 29135 • *2,496*
Saint Michael, MN 55376 • *1,519*
Saint Michaels, MD 21663 • *1,301*
Saint Nazianz, WI 54232 • *738*
Saint Paris, OH 43072 • *1,742*
Saint Paul, IN 47272 • *976*
Saint Paul, KS 66771 • *746*
Saint Paul, MN 55101–99 • *270,230*
Saint Paul, MO 63366 • *607*
Saint Paul, NE 68873 • *2,094*
Saint Paul, VA 24283 • *973*
Saint Paul Park, MN 55071 • *4,864*
Saint Pauls, NC 28384 • *1,639*
Saint Peter, MN 56082 • *9,056*
Saint Peters, MO 63376 • *15,700*
Saint Petersburg, FL 33701–99 • *238,647*
Saint Petersburg Beach, FL 33736 • *9,354*
Saint Regis Falls, NY 12980 • *950*
Saint Rose, LA 70087 • *2,800*
Saint Simons Island, GA 31522 • *6,566*
Saint Stephen, SC 29479 • *1,850*
Saint Tammany □, LA • *110,869*
Saint Thomas, PA 17252 • *700*
Salamanca, NY 14779 • *6,890*
Sale Creek, TN 37373 • *900*
Salem, AR 72576 • *1,424*
Salem, IL 62881 • *7,813*
Salem, IN 47167 • *5,290*
Salem, KY 42078 • *833*
Salem, MA 01970 • *38,220*
Salem, MO 65560 • *4,454*
Salem, NH 03079 • *11,500*
Salem, NJ 08079 • *6,959*
Salem, NY 12865 • *959*
Salem, OH 44460 • *12,869*
Salem, OR 97301–14 • *89,233*
Salem, SD 57058 • *1,486*
Salem, UT 84653 • *2,233*
Salem, VA 24153 • *23,958*
Salem, WV 26426 • *2,706*
Salem, WI 53168 • *1,000*
Salem □, NJ • *64,676*
Salemburg, NC 28385 • *742*
Salida, CO 81201 • *4,870*
Salina, KS 67401 • *41,843*
Salina, OK 74365 • *1,115*
Salina, UT 84654 • *1,992*
Salinas, CA 93901–15 • *80,479*
Saline, MI 48176 • *6,483*
Saline □, AR • *53,161*
Saline □, IL • *28,448*
Saline □, KS • *48,905*
Saline □, MO • *24,919*
Saline □, NE • *13,131*
Salineville, OH 43945 • *1,629*
Salisbury, CT 06068 • *900*
Salisbury, MD 21801 • *16,429*
Salisbury, MA 01950 • *3,265*
Salisbury, MO 65281 • *1,975*
Salisbury, NC 28144 • *22,677*
Salisbury, PA 15558 • *817*
Sallisaw, OK 74955 • *6,403*
Salmon, ID 83467 • *3,308*
Salmon Creek, WA 98665 • *1,950*
Saltillo, MS 38866 • *1,271*
Salt Lake □, UT • *619,066*
Salt Lake City, UT 84101–99 • *163,697*
Salt Rock, WV 25559 • *900*
Saltsburg, PA 15681 • *964*
Salt Springs, FL 32627 • *1,500*
Saltville, VA 24370 • *2,376*
Saluda, NC 28773 • *607*
Saluda, SC 29138 • *2,752*
Saluda □, SC • *16,150*
Salyer, CA 95563 • *950*
Salyersville, KY 41465 • *1,352*
Samoa, CA 95564 • *850*
Samoset, FL 34208 • *5,747*
Sampson □, NC • *49,687*
Samson, AL 36477 • *2,402*
Samtown, LA 71301 • *4,125*
Samuels, ID 83862 • *650*
San Andreas, CA 95249 • *1,564*
San Angelo, TX 76901–09 • *73,240*
San Anselmo, CA 94960 • *12,067*
San Antonio, TX 78201–99 • *786,023*
Sanatorium, MS 39112 • *700*
San Augustine, TX 75972 • *2,930*
San Augustine □, TX • *8,785*
San Benito, TX 78586 • *17,988*
San Benito □, CA • *25,005*
San Bernardino, CA 92401–99 • *118,794*
San Bernardino □, CA • *895,016*
Sanborn, IA 51248 • *1,398*
Sanborn □, SD • *3,213*
Sanbornville, NH 03872 • *800*
San Bruno, CA 94066 • *35,417*
San Carlos, AZ 85550 • *2,668*
San Carlos, CA 94070 • *24,710*
San Clemente, CA 92672 • *27,325*
Sanders □, MT • *8,675*
Sanderson, TX 79848 • *1,300*
Sandersville, GA 31082 • *6,137*
Sandersville, MS 39477 • *800*
Sand Hill, MA 02066 • *1,750*
San Diego, CA 92101–99 • *875,538*
San Diego, TX 78384 • *5,225*
San Diego □, CA • *1,861,846*
San Dimas, CA 91773 • *24,014*
Sandoval, IL 62882 • *1,734*
Sandoval □, NM • *34,799*
Sand Point, AK 99661 • *625*
Sandpoint, ID 83864 • *4,460*
Sand Springs, OK 74063 • *13,121*
Sandston, VA 23150 • *4,500*
Sandstone, MN 55072 • *1,594*
Sandusky, MI 48471 • *2,071*
Sandusky, OH 44870 • *31,360*
Sandusky □, OH • *63,267*
Sandwich, IL 60548 • *5,244*
Sandwich, MA 02563 • *1,784*
Sandy, OR 97055 • *2,905*
Sandy, UT 84070 • *52,210*
Sandy Creek, NY 13145 • *765*
Sandy Hook, CT 06482 • *950*
Sandy Hook, KY 41171 • *627*
Sandy Lake, PA 16145 • *779*
Sandy Springs, GA 30328 • *20,300*
Sandy Springs, SC 29677 • *1,100*
San Elizario, TX 79849 • *1,100*
San Felipe Pueblo, NM 87001 • *1,465*
San Fernando, CA 91340–46 • *17,731*
Sanford, CO 81151 • *687*
Sanford, FL 32771 • *23,176*
Sanford, ME 04073 • *10,268*
Sanford, MI 48657 • *864*
Sanford, NC 27330 • *14,773*
San Francisco, CA 94101–99 • *678,974*
San Francisco □, CA • *678,974*
San Gabriel, CA 91775–78 • *30,072*
Sangamon □, IL • *176,070*
Sanger, CA 93657 • *12,542*
Sanger, TX 76266 • *2,574*

Sanibel, FL 33957 • 3,363
Sanilac □, MI • 40,789
San Isidro, TX 78588 • 700
San Jacinto, CA 92383 • 7,098
San Jacinto □, TX • 11,434
San Joaquin □, CA • 347,342
San Jose, CA 95101-99 • 629,546
San Jose, IL 62682 • 784
San Juan, TX 78589 • 7,608
San Juan □, CO • 833
San Juan □, NM • 81,433
San Juan □, UT • 12,253
San Juan □, WA • 7,838
San Juan Capistrano, CA 92675 • 18,959
San Leandro, CA 94577-79 • 63,952
San Lorenzo, CA 94580 • 20,545
San Luis, CO 81152 • 842
San Luis Obispo, CA 93401 • 34,252
San Luis Obispo □, CA • 155,435
San Manuel, AZ 85631 • 5,443
San Marcos, CA 92069 • 17,479
San Marcos, TX 78666 • 23,420
San Marino, CA 91108 • 13,307
San Mateo, CA 94401-99 • 77,640
San Mateo, FL 32088 • 950
San Mateo □, CA • 587,329
San Miguel, CA 93451 • 800
San Miguel □, CO • 3,192
San Miguel □, NM • 22,751
San Pablo, CA 94806 • 19,750
San Patricio □, TX • 58,013
Sanpete □, UT • 14,620
San Rafael, CA 94901-15 • 44,700
San Remo, NY 11754 • 8,700
San Saba, TX 76877 • 2,847
San Saba □, TX • 6,204
Santa Ana, CA 92701-99 • 204,023
Santa Anna, TX 76878 • 1,535
Santa Barbara, CA 93101-99 • 74,414
Santa Barbara □, CA • 298,694
Santa Clara, CA 95050-55 • 87,700
Santa Clara, OR 97401 • 11,288
Santa Clara, UT 84765 • 1,091
Santa Clara □, CA • 1,295,071
Santa Cruz, CA 95060-66 • 41,483
Santa Cruz □, AZ • 20,459
Santa Cruz □, CA • 188,141
Santa Fe, NM 87501-09 • 48,953
Santa Fe, TX 77510 • 6,172
Santa Fe □, NM • 75,360
Santa Fe Springs, CA 90670 • 14,520
Santa Margarita, CA 93453 • 1,200
Santa Maria, CA 93454-56 • 39,685
Santa Monica, CA 90401-99 • 88,314
Santa Paula, CA 93060 • 20,552
Santaquin, UT 84655 • 2,175
Santa Rosa, CA 95401-07 • 83,320
Santa Rosa, NM 88435 • 2,469
Santa Rosa □, FL • 55,988
Santa Rosa Beach, FL 32459 • 950
Santa Ynez, CA 93460 • 3,335
Santee, CA 92071 • 40,313
Santo Domingo Pueblo, NM 87052 • 2,082
San Ygnacio, TX 78067 • 900
Sappington, MO 63126 • 11,388
Sapulpa, OK 74066 • 15,853
Saraland, AL 36571 • 9,833
Saranac, MI 48881 • 1,421
Saranac Lake, NY 12983 • 5,578
Sarasota, FL 34230-43 • 48,868
Sarasota □, FL • 202,251
Saratoga, CA 95070 • 29,261
Saratoga, TX 77585 • 1,000
Saratoga, WY 82331 • 2,410
Saratoga □, NY • 153,759
Saratoga Springs, NY 12866 • 23,906
Sarcoxie, MO 64862 • 1,381
Sardinia, OH 45171 • 826
Sardis, GA 30456 • 1,180
Sardis, MS 38666 • 2,278
Sarepta, LA 71071 • 831
Sargent, GA 30275 • 700
Sargent, NE 68874 • 828
Sargent □, ND • 5,512
Sarpy □, NE • 86,015
Sartell, MN 56377 • 3,427
Satanta, KS 67870 • 1,117
Satellite Beach, FL 32937 • 9,163
Satsuma, AL 36572 • 3,822
Satsuma, FL 32189 • 950
Saugatuck, MI 49453 • 1,079
Saugerties, NY 12477 • 3,882
Saugus, CA 91350 • 16,283
Saugus, MA 01906 • 24,746
Sauk □, WI • 43,469
Sauk Centre, MN 56378 • 3,709
Sauk City, WI 53583 • 2,703
Sauk Rapids, MN 56379 • 5,793
Sauk Village, IL 60411 • 10,906
Saukville, WI 53080 • 3,494
Saunders □, NE • 18,716
Sausalito, CA 94965 • 7,338
Savage, MD 20763 • 2,928
Savanna, IL 61074 • 4,529
Savanna, OK 74565 • 828
Savannah, GA 31401-99 • 141,390
Savannah, MO 64485 • 4,184
Savannah, NY 13146 • 640
Savannah, TN 38372 • 6,992
Savona, NY 14879 • 932
Savoy, IL 61874 • 2,126
Sawyer □, WI • 12,843
Saxon, SC • 1,200
Saxonburg, PA 16056 • 1,336
Saybrook, IL 61770 • 882
Saybrook Manor, CT 06475 • 1,140
Saydel, IA 50313 • 4,200
Saylesville, RI 02865 • 3,200
Saylorville, IA 50313 • 780
Sayre, OK 73662 • 3,177
Sayre, PA 18840 • 6,951
Sayreville, NJ 08872 • 29,969
Sayville, NY 11782 • 15,300
Scalp Level, PA 15963 • 1,186
Scanlon, MN 55720 • 1,050
Scappoose, OR 97056 • 3,213
Scarborough, ME 04074 • 2,280
Scarsdale, NY 10583 • 17,650
Schaefferstown, PA 17088 • 800

Schaghticoke, NY 12154 • 677
Schaller, IA 51053 • 832
Schaumburg, IL 60194 • 53,305
Schenectady, NY 12301-99 • 67,972
Schenectady □, NY • 149,946
Schenevus, NY 12155 • 625
Schererville, IN 46375 • 13,209
Schertz, TX 78154 • 7,262
Schiller Park, IL 60176 • 11,458
Schleicher □, TX • 2,820
Schleswig, IA 51461 • 868
Schley □, GA • 3,433
Schofield, WI 54476 • 2,226
Schoharie, NY 12157 • 1,016
Schoharie □, NY • 29,710
Schoolcraft, MI 49087 • 1,359
Schoolcraft □, MI • 8,575
Schram City, IL 62049 • 708
Schroon Lake, NY 12870 • 1,000
Schulenburg, TX 78956 • 2,469
Schuyler, NE 68661 • 4,151
Schuyler □, IL • 8,365
Schuyler □, MO • 4,979
Schuyler □, NY • 17,686
Schuylerville, NY 12871 • 1,256
Schuylkill □, PA • 160,630
Schuylkill Haven, PA 17972 • 5,977
Science Hill, KY 42553 • 655
Scio, OH 43988 • 1,003
Scioto □, OH • 84,545
Scituate, MA 02066 • 5,351
Scobey, MT 59263 • 1,382
Scotch Plains, NJ 07076 • 20,774
Scotia, CA 95565 • 1,200
Scotia, NY 12302 • 7,280
Scotland, SD 57059 • 1,022
Scotland □, MO • 5,415
Scotland □, NC • 32,273
Scotland Neck, NC 27874 • 2,834
Scotlandville, LA 70807 • 15,113
Scott, LA 70583 • 2,239
Scott □, AR • 9,685
Scott □, IL • 6,142
Scott □, IN • 20,422
Scott □, IA • 160,022
Scott □, KS • 5,782
Scott □, KY • 21,813
Scott □, MN • 43,784
Scott □, MS • 24,556
Scott □, MO • 39,647
Scott □, TN • 19,259
Scott □, VA • 25,068
Scott City, KS 67871 • 4,154
Scott City, MO 63780 • 4,630
Scottdale, GA 30079 • 8,777
Scottdale, PA 15683 • 5,833
Scottsbluff, NE 69361 • 14,156
Scotts Bluff □, NE • 38,344
Scottsboro, AL 35768 • 14,758
Scottsburg, IN 47170 • 5,068
Scottsdale, AZ 85251-71 • 88,622
Scotts Hill, TN 38374 • 668
Scotts Valley, CA 95066 • 6,891
Scottsville, KY 42164 • 4,278
Scottsville, NY 14546 • 1,789
Scott Township, PA 15106 • 20,413
Scottville, MI 49454 • 1,241
Scranton, IA 51462 • 748
Scranton, KS 66537 • 664
Scranton, PA 18501-99 • 88,117
Scranton, SC 29591 • 861
Screven, GA 31560 • 872
Screven □, GA • 14,043
Scribner, NE 68057 • 1,011
Scurry □, TX • 18,192
Seaboard, NC 27876 • 687
Sea Bright, NJ 07760 • 1,812
Seabrook, MD 20706 • 7,100
Seabrook, NH 03874 • 700
Seabrook, NJ 08302 • 1,411
Seabrook, TX 77586 • 4,670
Sea Cliff, NY 11579 • 5,364
Seadrift, TX 77983 • 1,277
Seaford, DE 19973 • 5,256
Seaford, NY 11783 • 17,150
Seaford, VA 23696 • 1,700
Sea Girt, NJ 08750 • 2,650
Seagoville, TX 75159 • 7,304
Seagraves, TX 79359 • 2,596
Sea Isle City, NJ 08243 • 2,644
Seal Beach, CA 90740 • 25,975
Seal Rock, OR 97376 • 800
Sealy, TX 77474 • 3,875
Seaman, OH 45679 • 1,039
Searcy, AR 72143 • 13,612
Searcy □, AR • 8,847
Searsport, ME 04974 • 1,348
Seaside, CA 93955 • 36,567
Seaside, OR 97138 • 5,193
Seaside Heights, NJ 08751 • 1,802
Seaside Park, NJ 08752 • 1,795
Seat Pleasant, MD 20743 • 5,217
Seattle, WA 98101-99 • 493,846
Sebastian, FL 32958 • 2,831
Sebastian □, AR • 95,172
Sebastopol, CA 95472 • 5,595
Sebeka, MN 56477 • 774
Sebewaing, MI 48759 • 2,046
Sebree, KY 42455 • 1,516
Sebring, FL 33870 • 8,736
Sebring, OH 44672 • 5,078
Secaucus, NJ 07094 • 13,719
Section, AL 35771 • 821
Security, CO 80911 • 11,000
Sedalia, MO 65301 • 20,927
Sedan, KS 67361 • 1,579
Sedgwick, KS 67135 • 1,471
Sedgwick □, CO • 3,266
Sedgwick □, KS • 367,088
Sedona, AZ 86336 • 5,368
Sedro Woolley, WA 98284 • 6,110
Seekonk, MA 02771 • 12,269
Seeley, CA 92273 • 1,058
Seeley Lake, MT 59868 • 800
Seelyville, IN 47878 • 1,374
Seguin, TX 78155 • 17,854
Seiling, OK 73663 • 1,103
Selah, WA 98942 • 4,500
Selby, SD 57472 • 884
Selbyville, DE 19975 • 1,251
Selden, NY 11784 • 24,100

Seligman, AZ 86337 • 950
Selinsgrove, PA 17870 • 5,227
Sellersburg, IN 47172 • 3,211
Sellersville, PA 18960 • 3,143
Sells, AZ 85634 • 1,864
Selma, AL 36701 • 26,684
Selma, CA 93662 • 10,942
Selma, IN 47383 • 1,056
Selma, NC 27576 • 4,762
Selmer, TN 38375 • 3,979
Seminole, OK 74868 • 8,590
Seminole, TX 79360 • 6,080
Seminole □, FL • 179,752
Seminole □, GA • 9,057
Seminole □, OK • 27,473
Seminole Park, FL 34647 • 8,000
Semmes, AL 36575 • 1,200
Senath, MO 63876 • 1,728
Senatobia, MS 38668 • 5,013
Seneca, IL 61360 • 2,098
Seneca, KS 66538 • 2,389
Seneca, MO 64865 • 1,853
Seneca, PA 16346 • 980
Seneca, SC 29678 • 7,436
Seneca □, NY • 33,733
Seneca □, OH • 61,901
Seneca Falls, NY 13148 • 7,466
Senoia, GA 30276 • 900
Sentinel, OK 73664 • 1,016
Sequatchie □, TN • 8,605
Sequim, WA 98382 • 3,013
Sequoyah □, OK • 30,749
Sergeant Bluff, IA 51054 • 2,416
Sesser, IL 62884 • 2,238
Seth, WV 25181 • 650
Seven Hills, OH 44131 • 13,650
Seven Mile, OH 45062 • 841
Severn, MD 21144 • 20,147
Severna Park, MD 21146 • 21,253
Sevier □, AR • 14,060
Sevier □, TN • 41,418
Sevier □, UT • 14,727
Sevierville, TN 37862 • 4,556
Seville, FL 32090 • 800
Seville, OH 44273 • 1,568
Sewanee, TN 37375 • 2,218
Seward, AK 99664 • 1,843
Seward, NE 68434 • 5,713
Seward, PA 15954 • 675
Seward □, KS • 17,071
Seward □, NE • 15,789
Sewaren, NJ 07077 • 2,300
Sewell, NJ 08080 • 1,900
Sewickley, PA 15143 • 4,778
Seymour, CT 06483 • 13,434
Seymour, IN 47274 • 15,050
Seymour, IA 52590 • 1,036
Seymour, MO 65746 • 1,535
Seymour, TX 76380 • 3,657
Seymour, WI 54165 • 2,530
Seymourville, LA 70764 • 2,891
Shabbona, IL 60550 • 851
Shackelford □, TX • 3,915
Shady Cove, OR 97539 • 1,097
Shady Side, MD 20764 • 2,877
Shadyside, OH 43947 • 4,315
Shady Spring, WV 25918 • 1,000
Shafter, CA 93263 • 7,010
Shaftsbury, VT 05262 • 700
Shaker Heights, OH 44122 • 32,487
Shakopee, MN 55379 • 9,941
Shallotte, NC 28459 • 680
Shallowater, TX 79363 • 1,932
Shamokin, PA 17872 • 10,357
Shamokin Dam, PA 17876 • 1,622
Shamrock, TX 79079 • 2,834
Shandon, CA 93461 • 800
Shannon, GA 30172 • 2,040
Shannon, IL 61078 • 938
Shannon, MS 38868 • 680
Shannon □, MO • 7,885
Shannon □, SD • 11,323
Shannontown, SC 29150 • 7,900
Sharkey □, MS • 7,964
Sharon, CT 06069 • 900
Sharon, MA 02067 • 13,601
Sharon, PA 16146 • 19,057
Sharon, TN 38255 • 1,134
Sharon, WI 53585 • 1,280
Sharon Hill, PA 19079 • 6,221
Sharon Springs, KS 67758 • 982
Sharonville, OH 45241 • 10,108
Sharp □, AR • 14,607
Sharpes, FL 32959 • 1,250
Sharpley, DE 19803 • 1,700
Sharpsburg, MD 21782 • 721
Sharpsburg, NC 27878 • 997
Sharpsburg, PA 15215 • 4,351
Sharpsville, IN 46068 • 617
Sharpsville, PA 16150 • 5,375
Sharptown, MD 21861 • 654
Shasta □, CA • 115,715
Shattuck, OK 73858 • 1,759
Shaw, MS 38773 • 2,461
Shawano, WI 54166 • 7,013
Shawano □, WI • 35,928
Shawmut, AL 36854 • 2,284
Shawnee, KS 66203 • 29,653
Shawnee, OH 43782 • 924
Shawnee, OK 74801 • 26,506
Shawnee □, KS • 154,916
Shawneetown, IL 62984 • 1,841
Sheboygan, WI 53081 • 48,085
Sheboygan □, WI • 100,935
Sheboygan Falls, WI 53085 • 5,253
Sheffield, AL 35660-62 • 11,903
Sheffield, IL 61361 • 1,130
Sheffield, IA 50475 • 1,224
Sheffield, MA 01257 • 1,100
Sheffield, PA 16347 • 1,564
Sheffield Lake, OH 44054 • 10,484
Shelbina, MO 63468 • 2,169
Shelburn, IN 47879 • 1,259
Shelburne Falls, MA 01370 • 2,046
Shelby, IN 46377 • 700
Shelby, IA 51570 • 665
Shelby, MI 49455 • 1,624
Shelby, MS 38774 • 2,540
Shelby, MT 59474 • 3,142
Shelby, NE 68662 • 724
Shelby, NC 28150 • 15,310

Shelby, OH 44875 • 9,646
Shelby □, AL • 66,298
Shelby □, IL • 23,923
Shelby □, IN • 39,887
Shelby □, IA • 15,043
Shelby □, KY • 23,328
Shelby □, MO • 7,826
Shelby □, OH • 43,089
Shelby □, TN • 777,113
Shelby □, TX • 23,084
Shelby City, KY 40422 • 700
Shelbyville, IL 62565 • 5,259
Shelbyville, IN 46176 • 14,989
Shelbyville, KY 40065 • 5,329
Shelbyville, MO 63469 • 645
Shelbyville, TN 37160 • 13,530
Sheldon, IL 60966 • 1,215
Sheldon, IA 51201 • 5,003
Sheldon, TX 77028 • 2,800
Shelley, ID 83274 • 3,300
Shell Lake, WI 54871 • 1,135
Shellman, GA 31786 • 1,254
Shell Rock, IA 50670 • 1,478
Shellsburg, IA 52332 • 771
Shelter Island, NY 11964 • 1,000
Shelton, CT 06484 • 31,314
Shelton, NE 68876 • 1,046
Shelton, WA 98584 • 7,629
Shenandoah, IA 51601 • 6,274
Shenandoah, PA 17976 • 7,589
Shenandoah, VA 22849 • 1,861
Shenandoah □, VA • 27,559
Shepherd, MI 48883 • 1,534
Shepherd, TX 77371 • 1,674
Shepherdstown, WV 25443 • 1,791
Shepherdsville, KY 40165 • 4,454
Sheppton, PA 18248 • 650
Sherborn, MA 01770 • 950
Sherburn, MN 56171 • 1,275
Sherburne, NY 13460 • 1,561
Sherburne □, MN • 29,908
Sheridan, AR 72150 • 3,042
Sheridan, CO 80110 • 5,377
Sheridan, IL 60551 • 719
Sheridan, IN 46069 • 2,200
Sheridan, MI 48884 • 664
Sheridan, MT 59749 • 646
Sheridan, OR 97378 • 2,249
Sheridan, WY 82801 • 15,146
Sheridan □, KS • 3,544
Sheridan □, MT • 5,414
Sheridan □, NE • 7,544
Sheridan □, ND • 2,819
Sheridan □, WY • 25,048
Sherman, NY 14781 • 775
Sherman, TX 75090 • 30,413
Sherman □, KS • 7,759
Sherman □, NE • 4,226
Sherman □, OR • 2,172
Sherman □, TX • 3,174
Sherrard, IL 61281 • 811
Sherrelwood, CO 80221 • 11,450
Sherrill, NY 13461 • 2,830
Sherwood, AR 72116 • 10,406
Sherwood, OH 43556 • 915
Sherwood, OR 97140 • 2,386
Sherwood Manor, CT 06082 • 6,303
Sherwood Park, DE 19808 • 2,300
Shiawassee □, MI • 71,140
Shickshinny, PA 18655 • 1,192
Shidler, OK 74652 • 708
Shillington, PA 19607 • 5,601
Shiloh, NJ 79363 • 604
Shiloh, OH 44878 • 857
Shiner, TX 77984 • 2,213
Shinglehouse, PA 16748 • 1,310
Shinnston, WV 26431 • 3,059
Shiocton, WI 54170 • 805
Ship Bottom, NJ 08008 • 1,427
Shippensburg, PA 17257 • 5,261
Shiprock, NM 87420 • 7,237
Shirley, IN 47384 • 919
Shirley, MA 01464 • 1,630
Shirley, NY 11967 • 8,200
Shively, KY 40216 • 16,819
Shoals, IN 47581 • 967
Shoemakersville, PA 19555 • 1,391
Shore Acres, MA 02066 • 1,200
Shore Acres, NJ 08723 • 1,300
Shoreham, MI 49085 • 742
Shoreview, MN 55112 • 17,300
Shorewood, IL 60435 • 4,714
Shorewood, MN 55331 • 4,646
Shorewood, WI 53211 • 14,327
Shorewood Hills, WI 53705 • 1,837
Short Beach, CT 06405 • 1,200
Shortsville, NY 14548 • 1,669
Shoshone, ID 83352 • 1,242
Shoshone □, ID • 19,226
Shoshoni, WY 82649 • 879
Show Low, AZ 85901 • 4,298
Shreve, OH 44676 • 1,608
Shreveport, LA 71101-10 • 205,820
Shrewsbury, MA 01545 • 22,674
Shrewsbury, MO 63119 • 5,077
Shrewsbury, NJ 07701 • 2,962
Shrewsbury, PA 17361 • 2,688
Shubuta, MS 39360 • 626
Shullsburg, WI 53586 • 1,484
Sibley, IA 51249 • 3,051
Sibley, LA 71073 • 1,211
Sibley □, MN • 15,448
Sicily Island, LA 71368 • 691
Sicklerville, NJ 08081 • 850
Sidell, IL 61876 • 625
Sidney, IL 61877 • 886
Sidney, IA 51652 • 1,308
Sidney, MT 59270 • 5,726
Sidney, NE 69162 • 6,010
Sidney, NY 13838 • 4,861
Sidney, OH 45365 • 17,657
Siegle, LA 71291 • 1,400
Sierra □, CA • 3,073
Sierra □, NM • 8,454
Sierra Blanca, TX 79851 • 900
Sierra City, CA 96125 • 800
Sierra Madre, CA 91024 • 10,837
Sierra Vista, AZ 85635 • 24,937
Signal Hill, CA 90806 • 5,734
Signal Mountain, TN 37377 • 5,818
Sigourney, IA 52591 • 2,330

Sikeston, MO 63801 • 17,431
Siler City, NC 27344 • 4,446
Siletz, OR 97380 • 1,001
Siloam Springs, AR 72761 • 7,940
Silsbee, TX 77656 • 7,684
Silt, CO 81652 • 923
Silver Bay, MN 55614 • 2,917
Silver Bow □, MT • 38,092
Silver City, NM 88061 • 9,887
Silver Creek, NY 14136 • 3,088
Silverdale, WA 98383 • 1,500
Silver Grove, KY 41085 • 1,260
Silverhill, AL 36576 • 624
Silver Hill, MD 20746 • 2,400
Silver Lake, KS 66539 • 1,350
Silver Lake, MA 01887 • 3,400
Silver Lake, MN 55381 • 698
Silver Lake, WI 53170 • 1,598
Silver Spring, MD 20901-99 • 64,100
Silver Springs, FL 32688 • 1,082
Silver Springs, NY 14550 • 801
Silverton, CO 81433 • 794
Silverton, ID 83867 • 750
Silverton, NJ 08753 • 7,236
Silverton, OH 45236 • 6,172
Silverton, OR 97381 • 5,168
Silverton, TX 79257 • 918
Silview, DE 19804 • 1,650
Silvis, IL 61282 • 7,130
Simi Valley, CA 93065 • 77,500
Simmesport, LA 71369 • 2,293
Simpson, PA 18407 • 2,200
Simpson □, KY • 14,673
Simpson □, MS • 23,441
Simpsonville, KY 40067 • 642
Simpsonville, SC 29681 • 9,037
Simsbury, CT 06070 • 5,488
Sinclairville, NY 14782 • 772
Sinton, TX 78387 • 6,044
Sioux □, IA • 30,813
Sioux □, NE • 1,845
Sioux □, ND • 3,620
Sioux Center, IA 51250 • 4,588
Sioux City, IA 51101-11 • 82,003
Sioux Falls, SD 57101-99 • 81,343
Sioux Rapids, IA 50585 • 897
Sipsey, AL 35584 • 678
Siren, WI 54872 • 896
Siskiyou □, CA • 39,732
Sisseton, SD 57262 • 2,789
Sisters, OR 97759 • 696
Sistersville, WV 26175 • 2,367
Sitka, AK 99835 • 7,803
Skagit □, WA • 64,138
Skagway, AK 99840 • 768
Skamania □, WA • 7,919
Skaneateles, NY 13152 • 2,789
Skellytown, TX 79080 • 899
Skiatook, OK 74070 • 3,596
Skidmore, TX 78389 • 800
Skokie, IL 60076-77 • 60,278
Skowhegan, ME 04976 • 6,517
Skyland, NC 28776 • 2,200
Skyland, CO 80906 • 3,600
Skyway, WA 98178 • 12,500
Slackwood, NJ 08638 • 8,100
Slater, IA 50244 • 1,312
Slater, MO 65349 • 2,492
Slater, SC 29683 • 1,000
Slatersville, RI 02876 • 2,000
Slatington, PA 18080 • 4,277
Slaton, TX 79364 • 6,804
Slaughter, LA 70777 • 729
Slayton, MN 56172 • 2,420
Sledge, MS 38670 • 699
Sleepy Eye, MN 56085 • 3,581
Slickville, PA 15684 • 1,066
Slidell, LA 70458-61 • 26,718
Sligo, PA 16255 • 798
Slinger, WI 53086 • 1,612
Slippery Rock, PA 16057 • 3,047
Sloan, IA 51055 • 978
Sloan, NY 14225 • 4,529
Sloatsburg, NY 10974 • 3,154
Slocomb, AL 36375 • 2,153
Slope □, ND • 1,157
Slovan, PA 15078 • 900
Smackover, AR 71762 • 2,453
Smelterville, ID 83868 • 776
Smethport, PA 16749 • 1,797
Smith □, KS • 5,947
Smith □, MS • 15,077
Smith □, TN • 14,935
Smith □, TX • 128,366
Smith Center, KS 66967 • 2,240
Smithers, WV 25186 • 1,482
Smithfield, NC 27577 • 7,288
Smithfield, OH 43948 • 1,308
Smithfield, PA 15478 • 1,084
Smithfield, UT 84335 • 4,993
Smithfield, VA 23430 • 3,718
Smith River, CA 95567 • 1,000
Smiths, AL 36877 • 900
Smithsburg, MD 21783 • 833
Smiths Grove, KY 42171 • 767
Smithton, IL 62285 • 1,447
Smithtown, NY 11787 • 23,000
Smithville, GA 31787 • 867
Smithville, MS 38870 • 866
Smithville, MO 64089 • 1,873
Smithville, OH 44677 • 1,467
Smithville, TN 37166 • 3,839
Smithville, TX 78957 • 3,470
Smyrna, DE 19977 • 4,750
Smyrna, GA 30080 • 20,312
Smyrna, TN 37167 • 8,839
Smyth □, VA • 33,366
Sneads, FL 32460 • 1,690
Sneedville, TN 37869 • 1,110
Snellville, GA 30278 • 8,514
Snohomish, WA 98290 • 5,294
Snohomish □, WA • 337,720
Snoqualmie, WA 98065 • 1,370
Snowflake, AZ 85937 • 3,510
Snow Hill, MD 21863 • 2,192
Snow Hill, NC 28580 • 1,374
Snow Shoe, PA 16874 • 852
Snyder, OK 73566 • 1,848
Snyder, TX 79549 • 12,705
Snyder □, PA • 33,584
Soap Lake, WA 98851 • 1,196

# United States Populations and ZIP Codes

Socastee, SC 29577 • 1,082
Social Circle, GA 30279 • 2,591
Society Hill, SC 29593 • 848
Socorro, NM 87801 • 7,173
Socorro □, NM • 12,566
Soda Springs, ID 83276 • 4,051
Soddy-Daisy, TN 37379 • 8,388
Sodus, NY 14551 • 1,790
Sodus Point, NY 14555 • 1,334
Solana, FL 33950 • 1,408
Solana Beach, CA 92075 • 13,047
Solano □, CA • 235,203
Soldiers Grove, WI 54655 • 622
Soldotna, AK 99669 • 2,320
Soledad, CA 93960 • 5,928
Solomon, KS 67480 • 1,018
Solon, IA 52333 • 969
Solon, OH 44139 • 14,341
Solvay, NY 13209 • 7,140
Somerdale, NJ 08083 • 5,900
Somers, CT 06071 • 1,643
Somers, MT 59932 • 800
Somerset, KY 42501 • 10,649
Somerset, MA 02725 • 18,813
Somerset, NJ 08873 • 21,731
Somerset, OH 43783 • 1,432
Somerset, PA 15501 • 6,474
Somerset, TX 78069 • 1,102
Somerset, WI 54025 • 860
Somerset □, ME • 45,046
Somerset □, MD • 19,188
Somerset □, NJ • 203,129
Somerset □, PA • 81,243
Somers Point, NJ 08244 • 10,330
Somersville, CT 06072 • 750
Somersworth, NH 03878 • 10,350
Somerton, AZ 85350 • 5,761
Somervell □, TX • 4,154
Somerville, MA 02143 • 77,372
Somerville, NJ 08876 • 11,973
Somerville, TN 38068 • 2,264
Somerville, TX 77879 • 1,814
Somonauk, IL 60552 • 1,344
Sonoma, CA 95476 • 6,054
Sonoma □, CA • 299,681
Sonora, CA 95370 • 3,247
Sonora, TX 76950 • 3,856
Soperton, GA 30457 • 2,981
Sophia, WV 25921 • 1,216
Soquel, CA 95073 • 6,212
Sorento, IL 62086 • 677
Sorrento, FL 32776 • 950
Sorrento, LA 70778 • 1,197
Soudan, MN 55782 • 950
Souderton, PA 18964 • 6,657
Sound Beach, NY 11789 • 5,400
Sourlake, TX 77659 • 1,807
South Acton, MA 01720 • 4,600
South Amboy, NJ 08879 • 8,322
South Amherst, MA 01002 • 4,861
South Amherst, OH 44001 • 1,848
Southampton, NY 11968 • 4,000
Southampton, PA 18966 • 9,500
Southampton □, VA • 18,731
South Ashburnham, MA 01466 • 1,123
Southaven, MS 38671 • 16,071
South Barre, VT 05670 • 1,301
South Bay, FL 33493 • 3,886
South Belmar, NJ 07719 • 1,566
South Beloit, IL 61080 • 4,088
South Bend, IN 46601–99 • 109,727
South Bend, WA 98586 • 1,686
South Berwick, ME 03908 • 2,120
South Bloomfield, OH 43103 • 934
Southborough, MA 01772 • 1,600
South Boston, VA 24592 • 7,093
South Bound Brook, NJ 08880 • 4,331
Southbridge, MA 01550 • 16,665
South Broadway, WA 98902 • 3,620
South Burlington, VT 05401 • 10,679
Southbury, CT 06488 • 900
South Charleston, OH 45368 • 1,682
South Charleston, WV 25303 • 15,968
South Chatham, MA 02659 • 950
South Chicago Heights, IL 60411 • 3,932
South Coffeyville, OK 74072 • 873
South Congaree, SC 29169 • 2,113
South Connellsville, PA 15425 • 2,296
South Corning, NY 14830 • 1,195
South Dartmouth, MA 02748 • 7,000
South Dayton, NY 14138 • 661
South Daytona, FL 32021 • 11,252
South Decatur, GA 30037 • 28,100
South Deerfield, MA 01373 • 1,926
South Dennis, MA 02660 • 1,500
South Dos Palos, CA 93665 • 850
South Duxbury, MA 02332 • 2,985
South Easton, MA 02375 • 1,400
South Elgin, IL 60177 • 5,970
South El Monte, CA 91733 • 16,623
Southern Pines, NC 28387 • 8,620
South Euclid, OH 44121 • 25,713
South Fallsburg, NY 12779 • 1,590
South Farmingdale, NY 11735 • 20,500
Southfield, MI 48034 • 75,568
South Fork, PA 15956 • 1,401
South Fulton, TN 38257 • 2,735
South Gastonia, NC 28052 • 2,000
South Gate, CA 90280 • 66,784
Southgate, KY 41071 • 2,833
Southgate, MI 48195 • 32,058
South Glastonbury, CT 06073 • 1,600
Southglenn, CO 80122 • 3,800
South Glens Falls, NY 12801 • 3,714
South Grafton, MA 01560 • 3,000
South Hackensack, NJ 07606 • 2,229
South Hadley, MA 01075 • 8,900
South Hadley Falls, MA 01075 • 5,600
South Hamilton, MA 01982 • 2,900
South Hanover, MA 02339 • 950
South Harwich, MA 02661 • 900
South Haven, IN 46383 • 6,679
South Haven, MI 49090 • 5,943
South Hill, VA 23970 • 4,347
South Hingham, MA 02043 • 5,200
South Holland, IL 60473 • 24,977
South Hooksett, NH 03106 • 1,200
South Houston, TX 77587 • 13,293
South Huntington, NY 11746 • 9,115
South Hutchinson, KS 67505 • 2,226

Southington, CT 06489 • 17,400
South International Falls, MN 56679 • 2,806
South Jacksonville, IL 62650 • 3,382
South Jordan, UT 84065 • 7,492
South Kenosha, WI 53140 • 875
South Lake Tahoe, CA 95705 • 20,681
South Lancaster, MA 01561 • 2,329
South Laramie, WY 82070 • 1,500
South Laurel, MD 20707 • 8,500
South Lebanon, OH 45065 • 2,700
South Lyon, MI 48178 • 5,214
South Mansfield, LA 71052 • 1,463
South Medford, OR 97501 • 2,898
South Miami, FL 33143 • 10,944
South Miami Heights, FL 33157 • 18,000
South Mills, NC 27976 • 800
South Milwaukee, WI 53172 • 21,069
South Modesto, CA 95350 • 12,492
Southmont, NC 27351 • 700
South Nyack, NY 10960 • 3,602
South Ogden, UT 84403 • 11,366
Southold, NY 11971 • 2,030
South Orange, NJ 07079 • 15,864
South Paris, ME 04281 • 2,128
South Pasadena, CA 91030 • 22,681
South Patrick Shores, FL 32937 • 9,816
South Pekin, IL 61564 • 1,243
South Pittsburg, TN 37380 • 3,636
South Plainfield, NJ 07080 • 20,521
Southport, FL 32409 • 1,992
Southport, IN 46217 • 2,266
Southport, NC 28461 • 2,824
Southport, NY 14904 • 8,700
South Portland, ME 04106 • 22,712
South Range, MI 49963 • 861
South Renovo, PA 17764 • 663
South River, NJ 08882 • 14,361
South Royalton, VT 05068 • 700
South Salt Lake, UT 84115 • 9,884
South San Francisco, CA 94080 • 49,393
South San Gabriel, CA 91770 • 5,421
Southside, AL 35901 • 5,141
Southside Place, TX 77005 • 1,366
South Sioux City, NE 68776 • 9,339
South Stony Brook, NY 11790 • 15,329
South St. Paul, MN 55075 • 21,235
South Streator, IL 61364 • 2,334
South Swansea, MA 02777 • 1,700
South Toms River, NJ 08757 • 3,954
South Tucson, AZ 85725 • 6,554
South Valley Stream, NY 11581 • 6,600
South Venice, FL 34293 • 8,075
South Walpole, MA 02071 • 1,600
South Waverly, PA 14892 • 1,176
South Webster, OH 45682 • 886
Southwest, PA 15685 • 700
South Westbury, NY 11590 • 10,700
Southwest Harbor, ME 04679 • 1,052
South Whitley, IN 46787 • 1,575
South Whittier, CA 90605 • 43,815
Southwick, MA 01077 • 1,200
South Williamson, KY 41503 • 1,016
South Williamsport, PA 17701 • 6,581
South Wilmington, IL 60474 • 747
South Windham, CT 06266 • 1,399
South Windham, ME 04082 • 1,366
South Windsor, CT 06074 • 10,200
Southwood, CO 80120 • 2,600
Southwood Acres, CT 06082 • 9,779
South Woodstock, CT 06267 • 1,319
South Yarmouth, MA 02664 • 7,525
South Zanesville, OH 43701 • 1,739
Spalding, NE 68665 • 645
Spalding □, GA • 47,899
Spanaway, WA 98387 • 5,940
Spangler, PA 15775 • 2,399
Spanish Fork, UT 84660 • 9,825
Spanish Fort, AL 36527 • 3,415
Spanish Lake, MO 63138 • 20,632
Sparkman, AR 71763 • 622
Sparks, GA 31647 • 1,353
Sparks, NV 89431–33 • 40,780
Sparks, OK 74869 • 772
Sparland, IL 61565 • 624
Sparr, FL 32690 • 1,100
Sparta, GA 31087 • 1,745
Sparta, IL 62286 • 4,957
Sparta, MI 49345 • 3,373
Sparta, MO 65753 • 743
Sparta, NJ 07871 • 8,498
Sparta, NC 28675 • 1,687
Sparta, TN 38583 • 4,864
Sparta, WI 54656 • 6,934
Spartanburg, SC 29301–18 • 43,826
Spartanburg □, SC • 201,861
Spavinaw, OK 74366 • 623
Spearfish, SD 57783 • 5,251
Spearman, TX 79081 • 3,413
Spearville, KS 67876 • 693
Speed, IN 47172 • 650
Speedway, IN 46224 • 12,641
Spencer, IN 47460 • 2,732
Spencer, IA 51301 • 11,726
Spencer, MA 01562 • 6,350
Spencer, NC 28159 • 2,938
Spencer, NY 14883 • 863
Spencer, OH 44275 • 764
Spencer, TN 38585 • 1,126
Spencer, WV 25276 • 2,799
Spencer, WI 54479 • 1,754
Spencer □, IN • 19,361
Spencer □, KY • 5,929
Spencerport, NY 14559 • 3,424
Spencerville, MD 20868 • 1,100
Spencerville, OH 45887 • 2,184
Sperry, OK 74073 • 1,276
Spiceland, IN 47385 • 940
Spicer, MN 56288 • 909
Spindale, NC 28160 • 4,246
Spink □, SD • 9,201
Spirit Lake, ID 83869 • 834
Spirit Lake, IA 51360 • 3,976
Spiro, OK 74959 • 2,221
Spokane, WA 99201–99 • 171,300
Spokane □, WA • 341,835
Spooner, WI 54801 • 2,365
Spotswood, NJ 08884 • 7,840
Spotsylvania □, VA • 34,435

Sprague, WV 25926 • 900
Spring, TX 77373 • 3,000
Springboro, OH 45066 • 4,962
Spring City, PA 19475 • 3,389
Spring City, TN 37381 • 1,951
Spring City, UT 84662 • 671
Springdale, AR 72764 • 23,458
Springdale, OH 45246 • 10,111
Springdale, PA 15144 • 4,418
Springdale, SC 29169 • 2,985
Springer, NM 87747 • 1,657
Springer, OK 73458 • 679
Springerville, AZ 85938 • 1,452
Springfield, CO 81073 • 1,657
Springfield, FL 32401 • 7,220
Springfield, GA 31329 • 1,075
Springfield, IL 62701–99 • 100,054
Springfield, KY 40069 • 3,179
Springfield, MA 01101–99 • 152,319
Springfield, MI 49015 • 5,917
Springfield, MN 56087 • 2,303
Springfield, MO 65801–99 • 133,116
Springfield, NE 68059 • 782
Springfield, NJ 07081 • 13,955
Springfield, OH 45501–99 • 72,563
Springfield, OR 97477–78 • 41,621
Springfield, PA 19064 • 25,326
Springfield, SC 29146 • 604
Springfield, SD 57062 • 1,377
Springfield, TN 37172 • 10,814
Springfield, VT 05156 • 5,603
Springfield, VA 22150–61 • 12,500
Spring Glen, UT 84526 • 800
Spring Green, WI 53588 • 1,265
Spring Grove, MN 55974 • 1,275
Spring Grove, PA 17362 • 1,832
Spring Hill, FL 34606 • 6,468
Spring Hill, KS 66083 • 2,005
Springhill, LA 71075 • 6,516
Spring Hill, TN 37174 • 989
Spring Hope, NC 27882 • 1,254
Spring Lake, MI 49456 • 2,731
Spring Lake, NJ 07762 • 4,215
Spring Lake, NC 28390 • 6,273
Spring Lake Heights, NJ 07762 • 5,424
Springport, MI 49284 • 675
Springvale, ME 04083 • 2,940
Spring Valley, CA 92077–78 • 40,191
Spring Valley, IL 61362 • 5,822
Spring Valley, MN 55975 • 2,616
Spring Valley, NY 10977 • 20,537
Spring Valley, WI 54767 • 982
Springville, AL 35146 • 1,476
Springville, IA 52336 • 1,165
Springville, NY 14141 • 4,285
Springville, UT 84663 • 12,101
Spruce Pine, NC 28777 • 2,282
Spur, TX 79370 • 1,690
Squire, WV 24884 • 900
Staatsburg, NY 12580 • 950
Stafford, KS 67578 • 1,425
Stafford, VA 22554 • 650
Stafford □, KS • 5,694
Stafford □, VA • 40,470
Stafford Springs, CT 06076 • 3,392
Staffordsville, KY 41256 • 700
Stambaugh, MI 49964 • 1,442
Stamford, CT 06901–99 • 102,453
Stamford, NY 12167 • 1,240
Stamford, TX 79553 • 4,542
Stamps, AR 71860 • 2,859
Stanaford, WV 25927 • 1,000
Stanberry, MO 64489 • 1,387
Standish, MI 48658 • 1,264
Stanfield, AZ 85272 • 900
Stanfield, OR 97875 • 1,568
Stanford, CA 94305 • 11,045
Stanford, IL 61774 • 720
Stanford, KY 40484 • 2,764
Stanhope, NJ 07874 • 3,638
Stanislaus □, CA • 265,900
Stanley, NC 28164 • 2,341
Stanley, ND 58784 • 1,631
Stanley, VA 22851 • 1,204
Stanley, WI 54768 • 2,095
Stanley □, SD • 2,533
Stanleytown, VA 24168 • 650
Stanleyville, NC 27045 • 5,039
Stanly □, NC • 48,517
Stanton, CA 90680 • 23,723
Stanton, IA 51573 • 747
Stanton, KY 40380 • 2,691
Stanton, MI 48888 • 1,315
Stanton, NE 68779 • 1,603
Stanton, ND 58571 • 623
Stanton, TX 79782 • 2,314
Stanton □, KS • 2,339
Stanton □, NE • 6,549
Stantonsburg, NC 27883 • 920
Stanwood, IA 52337 • 705
Stanwood, WA 98292 • 1,646
Staples, MN 56479 • 2,887
Stapleton, AL 36578 • 900
Star, NC 27356 • 816
Starbuck, MN 56381 • 1,224
Star City, AR 71667 • 2,066
Star City, WV 26505 • 1,464
Stargo, AZ 85540 • 1,038
Stark □, IL • 7,389
Stark □, ND • 23,697
Stark □, OH • 378,823
Starke, FL 32091 • 5,306
Starke □, IN • 21,997
Starks, LA 70661 • 780
Starkville, MS 39759 • 15,169
Starr □, TX • 27,266
Startex, SC 29377 • 1,006
State Center, IA 50247 • 1,292
State College, PA 16801–05 • 36,130
Stateline, NV 89449 • 1,500
State Line, PA 17263 • 700
Statenville, GA 31648 • 650
State Road, NC 28676 • 800
Statesboro, GA 30458 • 14,866
Statesville, NC 28677 • 18,622
Statham, GA 30666 • 1,101
Staunton, IL 62088 • 4,744
Staunton, IN 47881 • 607
Staunton, VA 24401 • 21,857
Stayton, OR 97383 • 4,396
Steamboat Springs, CO 80487 • 5,098

Stearns, KY 42647 • 1,557
Stearns □, MN • 108,161
Steele, AL 35987 • 795
Steele, MO 63877 • 2,419
Steele, ND 58482 • 796
Steele □, MN • 30,328
Steele □, ND • 3,106
Steeleville, IL 62288 • 2,240
Steelton, PA 17113 • 6,484
Steelville, MO 65565 • 1,470
Steger, IL 60475 • 9,269
Steilacoom, WA 98388 • 4,886
Steinhatchee, FL 32359 • 800
Stephen, MN 56757 • 898
Stephens, AR 71764 • 1,366
Stephens □, GA • 21,763
Stephens □, OK • 43,419
Stephens □, TX • 9,926
Stephens City, VA 22655 • 1,179
Stephenson, MI 49887 • 967
Stephenson □, IL • 49,536
Stephenville, TX 76401 • 11,881
Sterling, AK 99672 • 919
Sterling, CO 80751 • 11,385
Sterling, IL 61081 • 16,281
Sterling, KS 67579 • 2,312
Sterling, MA 01564 • 1,200
Sterling, OK 73567 • 702
Sterling, VA 22170 • 12,000
Sterling □, TX • 1,206
Sterling City, TX 76951 • 915
Sterling Heights, MI 48077 • 108,999
Sterlington, LA 71280 • 1,400
Steuben □, IN • 24,694
Steuben □, NY • 99,217
Steubenville, OH 43952 • 26,400
Stevens □, KS • 4,736
Stevens □, MN • 11,322
Stevens □, WA • 28,979
Stevenson, AL 35772 • 2,568
Stevenson, WA 98648 • 1,172
Stevens Point, WI 54481 • 22,970
Stevensville, MI 49127 • 1,268
Stevensville, MT 59870 • 1,207
Stewardson, IL 62463 • 745
Stewart, MN 55385 • 616
Stewart □, GA • 5,896
Stewart □, TN • 8,665
Stewartstown, PA 17363 • 1,072
Stewartsville, MO 64490 • 832
Stewartsville, NJ 08886 • 900
Stewartville, MN 55976 • 3,925
Stickney, IL 60402 • 5,893
Stigler, OK 74462 • 2,630
Stillman Valley, IL 61084 • 961
Stillwater, MN 55082 • 12,290
Stillwater, NY 12170 • 1,572
Stillwater, OK 74074–78 • 38,268
Stillwater □, MT • 5,598
Stilwell, OK 74960 • 2,369
Stilwell, OK 74960 • 2,369
Stinnett, TX 79083 • 2,222
Stirling, NJ 07980 • 2,000
Stockbridge, GA 30281 • 2,103
Stockbridge, MA 01262 • 1,109
Stockbridge, MI 49285 • 1,213
Stockdale, TX 78160 • 1,265
Stockertown, PA 18083 • 661
Stockton, CA 95201–12 • 149,779
Stockton, IL 61085 • 1,872
Stockton, KS 67669 • 1,825
Stockton, MO 65785 • 1,432
Stockton, NJ 08559 • 643
Stoddard, WI 54658 • 762
Stoddard □, MO • 29,009
Stokes □, NC • 33,086
Stokesdale, NC 27357 • 1,070
Stollings, WV 25646 • 900
Stone □, AR • 9,022
Stone □, MS • 9,716
Stone □, MO • 15,587
Stoneboro, PA 16153 • 1,177
Stoneham, MA 02180 • 21,424
Stone Harbor, NJ 08247 • 1,187
Stone Mountain, GA 30086–88 • 4,867
Stoneville, NC 27048 • 1,054
Stonewall, LA 71078 • 1,175
Stonewall, MS 39363 • 1,345
Stonewall, OK 74871 • 672
Stonewall □, TX • 2,406
Stonewood, WV 26301 • 2,058
Stonington, CT 06378 • 1,228
Stonington, IL 62567 • 1,184
Stonington, ME 04681 • 700
Stony Brook, NY 11790 • 6,600
Stony Creek, CT 06405 • 700
Stony Point, NC 28678 • 1,150
Stony Point, NY 10980 • 8,270
Storey □, NV • 1,503
Storm Lake, IA 50588 • 8,814
Storrs, CT 06268 • 11,394
Story, WY 82842 • 700
Story □, IA • 72,326
Story City, IA 50248 • 2,762
Stottville, NY 12172 • 1,300
Stoughton, MA 02072 • 26,710
Stoughton, WI 53589 • 7,589
Stover, MO 65078 • 1,041
Stow, MA 01775 • 1,100
Stow, OH 44224 • 25,303
Stowe, PA 19464 • 4,038
Stowe Township, PA 15136 • 10,119
Strabane, PA 15363 • 1,900
Strafford, MO 65757 • 1,121
Strafford □, NH • 85,408
Strasburg, CO 80136 • 1,105
Strasburg, ND 58573 • 623
Strasburg, OH 44680 • 2,091
Strasburg, PA 17579 • 1,999
Strasburg, VA 22657 • 2,311
Stratford, CA 93266 • 850
Stratford, CT 06497 • 50,541
Stratford, IA 50249 • 806
Stratford, NJ 08084 • 8,005
Stratford, OK 74872 • 1,459
Stratford, TX 79084 • 1,917
Stratford, WI 54484 • 1,385
Stratford Landing, VA 22308 • 2,650
Strathmore, CA 93267 • 1,221
Strathmore, NJ 07747 • 7,674
Stratton, CO 80836 • 705

Stratton Meadows, CO 80906 • 6,223
Strawberry Point, IA 52076 • 1,463
Strawn, TX 76475 • 694
Streamwood, IL 60103 • 23,456
Streator, IL 61364 • 14,795
Streetsboro, OH 44241 • 9,055
Stringtown, OK 74569 • 1,047
Stromsburg, NE 68666 • 1,290
Strong, AR 71765 • 785
Strong, ME 04983 • 700
Strong City, KS 66869 • 675
Stronghurst, IL 61480 • 865
Strongsville, OH 44136 • 28,577
Stroud, OK 74079 • 3,148
Stroudsburg, PA 18360 • 5,148
Strum, WI 54770 • 944
Struthers, OH 44471 • 13,624
Stryker, OH 43557 • 1,423
Stuart, FL 34994–97 • 9,467
Stuart, IA 50250 • 1,650
Stuart, NE 68780 • 641
Stuart, VA 24171 • 1,131
Stuarts Draft, VA 24477 • 950
Sturbridge, MA 01566 • 1,891
Sturgeon, MO 65284 • 901
Sturgeon Bay, WI 54235 • 8,847
Sturgis, KY 42459 • 2,293
Sturgis, MI 49091 • 9,468
Sturgis, SD 57785 • 5,184
Sturtevant, WI 53177 • 4,130
Stutsman □, ND • 24,154
Stuttgart, AR 72160 • 10,941
Subiaco, AR 72865 • 744
Sublette, KS 67877 • 1,293
Sublette □, WY • 4,548
Sublimity, OR 97385 • 1,077
Succasunna, NJ 07876 • 9,000
Sudan, TX 79371 • 1,091
Sudbury, MA 01776 • 2,200
Sudbury Center, MA 01776 • 2,900
Suffern, NY 10901 • 10,794
Suffield, CT 06078 • 1,122
Suffolk, VA 23434–38 • 47,621
Suffolk □, MA • 650,142
Suffolk □, NY • 1,284,231
Sugar City, ID 83448 • 1,022
Sugar Creek, MO 64054 • 4,305
Sugarcreek, PA 16323 • 5,954
Sugargrove, PA 16350 • 630
Sugar Hill, GA 30518 • 2,473
Sugar Land, TX 77478–79 • 8,826
Sugarland Run, VA 22170 • 4,500
Sugar Loaf, VA 24018 • 6,000
Sugar Notch, PA 18706 • 1,191
Suisun City, CA 94585 • 11,087
Suitland, MD 20746 • 24,800
Sulligent, AL 35586 • 2,130
Sullivan, IL 61951 • 4,526
Sullivan, IN 47882 • 4,774
Sullivan, MO 63080 • 5,461
Sullivan □, IN • 21,107
Sullivan □, MO • 7,434
Sullivan □, NH • 36,063
Sullivan □, NY • 65,155
Sullivan □, PA • 6,349
Sullivan □, TN • 143,968
Sullivans Island, SC 29482 • 1,867
Sully, IA 50251 • 828
Sully □, SD • 1,990
Sulphur, LA 70663 • 19,709
Sulphur, OK 73086 • 5,516
Sulphur Springs, TX 75482 • 12,804
Sultan, WA 98294 • 1,578
Sumas, WA 98295 • 712
Sumiton, AL 35148 • 2,815
Summerfield, NC 27358 • 1,680
Summers □, WV • 15,875
Summersville, WV 26651 • 2,972
Summerton, SC 29148 • 1,173
Summerville, GA 30747 • 4,878
Summerville, PA 15864 • 830
Summerville, SC 29483 • 6,706
Summit, IL 60501 • 10,110
Summit, MS 39666 • 1,753
Summit, NJ 07901 • 21,071
Summit, TN 37363 • 1,500
Summit □, CO • 8,848
Summit □, OH • 524,472
Summit □, UT • 10,198
Summit Hill, PA 18250 • 3,418
Summitville, IN 46070 • 1,085
Sumner, IL 62466 • 1,238
Sumner, IA 50674 • 2,335
Sumner, WA 98390 • 4,936
Sumner □, KS • 24,928
Sumner □, TN • 85,790
Sumrall, MS 39482 • 1,197
Sumter, SC 29150–52 • 24,890
Sumter □, AL • 16,908
Sumter □, FL • 24,272
Sumter □, GA • 29,360
Sumter □, SC • 88,243
Sunapee, NH 03782 • 900
Sunbury, OH 43074 • 2,101
Sunbury, PA 17801 • 12,292
Sun City, AZ 85351 • 40,505
Sun City, CA 92381 • 6,500
Sun City, FL 33586 • 700
Suncook, NH 03275 • 4,698
Sundance, WY 82729 • 1,087
Sundown, TX 79372 • 1,511
Sunflower, MS 38778 • 1,027
Sunflower □, MS • 34,844
Sunland Park, NM 88063 • 3,377
Sunman, IN 47041 • 924
Sunnyland, FL 34233 • 650
Sunnymead, CA 92388 • 11,554
Sunnyside, UT 84539 • 611
Sunnyside, WA 98944 • 9,225
Sunnyvale, CA 94086–88 • 106,618
Sunol, CA 94586 • 750
Sun Prairie, WI 53590 • 12,931
Sunray, TX 79086 • 1,952
Sunrise, FL 33313 • 39,681
Sunrise Manor, NV 89110 • 44,155
Sunset, LA 70584 • 2,300
Sunset, UT 84015 • 5,733
Sunset Beach, HI 96712 • 800
Sunset Park, KS 67217 • 1,050
Sun Valley, NV 89433 • 8,822
Superior, AZ 85273 • 4,600

Superior, MT 59872 • 1,054
Superior, NE 68978 • 2,502
Superior, WI 54880 • 29,571
Suquamish, WA 98392 • 1,500
Surf City, NJ 08008 • 1,571
Surfside, FL 33154 • 3,763
Surfside Beach, SC 29577 • 2,522
Surgoinsville, TN 37873 • 1,536
Surprise, AZ 85345 • 3,723
Surrey, ND 58785 • 999
Surry □, NC • 59,449
Surry □, VA • 6,046
Susanville, CA 96130 • 6,520
Susquehanna, PA 18847 • 1,994
Susquehanna □, PA • 37,876
Sussex, NJ 07461 • 2,418
Sussex, WI 53089 • 3,482
Sussex □, DE • 97,983
Sussex □, NJ • 116,119
Sussex □, VA • 10,874
Sutherland, IA 51058 • 897
Sutherland, NE 69165 • 1,238
Sutherlin, OR 97479 • 4,560
Sutter □, CA • 52,246
Sutter Creek, CA 95685 • 1,705
Sutton, NE 68979 • 1,416
Sutton, WV 26601 • 1,192
Sutton □, TX • 5,130
Sutton Park, NJ 07836 • 2,500
Suwanee, GA 30174 • 1,026
Suwannee □, FL • 22,287
Svensen, OR 97103 • 650
Swain □, NC • 10,283
Swainsboro, GA 30401 • 7,602
Swampscott, MA 01907 • 13,837
Swannanoa, NC 28778 • 5,586
Swansboro, NC 28584 • 976
Swansea, IL 62221 • 5,347
Swansea, MA 02777 • 750
Swansea, SC 29160 • 888
Swanton, OH 43558 • 3,424
Swanton, VT 05488 • 2,520
Swanwyck Estates, DE 19720 • 1,700
Swanzey Center, NH 03431 • 700
Swarthmore, PA 19081 • 5,950
Swartz Creek, MI 48473 • 5,013
Swayzee, IN 46986 • 1,127
Swea City, IA 50590 • 813
Swedesboro, NJ 08085 • 2,031
Sweeny, TX 77480 • 3,538
Sweet Briar, VA 24595 • 900
Sweet Grass □, MT • 3,216
Sweet Home, AR 72164 • 1,100
Sweet Home, OR 97386 • 6,921
Sweetser, IN 46987 • 944
Sweet Springs, MO 65351 • 1,694
Sweetwater, TN 37874 • 4,725
Sweetwater, TX 79556 • 12,242
Sweetwater □, WY • 41,723
Sweetwater Creek, FL 33614 • 18,000
Swepsonville, NC 27359 • 900
Swift □, MN • 12,920
Swifton, AR 72471 • 859
Swink, CO 81077 • 668
Swisher, IA 52338 • 654
Swisher □, TX • 9,723
Swissvale, PA 15218 • 11,345
Switzer, WV 25647 • 1,000
Switzerland, FL 32043 • 2,400
Switzerland □, IN • 7,153
Swoyerville, PA 18704 • 5,795
Sycamore, AL 35149 • 900
Sycamore, IL 60178 • 9,219
Sycamore, OH 44882 • 1,059
Sykesville, MD 21784 • 1,712
Sykesville, PA 15865 • 1,537
Sylacauga, AL 35150 • 12,708
Sylva, NC 28779 • 1,699
Sylvan Beach, NY 13157 • 1,243
Sylvan Hills, AR 72116 • 2,900
Sylvania, AL 35988 • 1,156
Sylvania, GA 30467 • 3,352
Sylvania, OH 43560 • 15,527
Sylvan Lake, MI 48053 • 1,949
Sylvester, GA 31791 • 5,860
Syosset, NY 11791 • 10,200
Syracuse, IN 46567 • 2,579
Syracuse, KS 67878 • 1,654
Syracuse, NE 68446 • 1,638
Syracuse, NY 13201–99 • 170,105
Syracuse, OH 45779 • 946
Syracuse, UT 84041 • 3,702

## T

Tabor, IA 51653 • 1,088
Tabor City, NC 28463 • 2,710
Tacoma, WA 98401–99 • 158,501
Taft, CA 93268 • 5,316
Taft, TX 78390 • 3,686
Tahlequah, OK 74464 • 9,708
Tahoe City, CA 95730 • 1,300
Tahoka, TX 79373 • 3,262
Taholah, WA 98587 • 800
Takoma Park, MD 20912 • 16,231
Talbot □, GA • 6,536
Talbot □, MD • 25,604
Talbotton, GA 31827 • 1,140
Talco, TX 75487 • 751
Talent, OR 97540 • 2,577
Taliaferro □, GA • 2,032
Talihina, OK 74571 • 1,387
Talladega, AL 35160 • 19,128
Talladega □, AL • 73,826
Tallahassee, FL 32301–17 • 81,548
Tallahatchie □, MS • 17,157
Tallapoosa, GA 30176 • 2,647
Tallapoosa □, AL • 38,676
Tallassee, AL 36078 • 4,763
Talleyville, DE 19803 • 6,880
Tallmadge, OH 44278 • 15,269
Tallula, IL 62688 • 681
Tallulah, LA 71282 • 11,634
Tama, IA 52339 • 2,968
Tama □, IA • 19,533
Tamaqua, PA 18252 • 8,843
Tamarac, FL 33321 • 29,376
Tamaroa, IL 62888 • 885
Tamina, TX 77302 • 900
Tamms, IL 62988 • 826
Tampa, FL 33601–99 • 271,523
Tampico, IL 61283 • 966
Taney □, MO • 20,467
Taneytown, MD 21787 • 2,618
Tangier, VA 23440 • 771
Tangipahoa □, LA • 80,698
Tannersville, NY 12485 • 685
Taos, MO 65101 • 759
Taos, NM 87571 • 3,369
Taos □, NM • 19,456
Taos Pueblo, NM 87571 • 1,030
Tappahannock, VA 22560 • 1,821
Tappan, NY 10983 • 6,100
Tara Hills, CA 94564 • 6,000
Tarboro, NC 27886 • 8,634
Tarentum, PA 15084 • 6,419
Tariffville, CT 06081 • 1,324
Tarkio, MO 64491 • 2,375
Tarpey, CA 93727 • 4,000
Tarpon Springs, FL 34689–91 • 13,251
Tarrant □, TX • 860,880
Tarrant City, AL 35217 • 8,148
Tarrytown, NY 10591 • 10,648
Tate, GA 30177 • 900
Tate □, MS • 20,119
Tateville, KY 42558 • 725
Tattnall □, GA • 18,134
Tatum, NM 88267 • 896
Taunton, MA 02780 • 45,001
Tavares, FL 32778 • 4,103
Tavernier, FL 33070 • 1,834
Tawas City, MI 48763 • 1,967
Taylor, AZ 85939 • 1,915
Taylor, AR 71861 • 657
Taylor, MI 48180 • 77,568
Taylor, PA 18517 • 7,246
Taylor, TX 76574 • 10,619
Taylor □, FL • 16,532
Taylor □, GA • 7,902
Taylor □, IA • 8,353
Taylor □, KY • 21,178
Taylor □, TX • 110,932
Taylor □, WV • 16,584
Taylor □, WI • 18,817
Taylor Mill, KY 41015 • 4,509
Taylors, SC 29687 • 12,100
Taylors Falls, MN 55084 • 623
Taylor Springs, IL 62089 • 671
Taylorsville, IN 47280 • 1,247
Taylorsville, KY 40071 • 801
Taylorsville, MS 39168 • 1,387
Taylorsville, NC 28681 • 1,103
Taylorsville, UT 84107 • 17,448
Taylorville, IL 62568 • 11,386
Tazewell, TN 37879 • 2,090
Tazewell, VA 24651 • 4,468
Tazewell □, IL • 132,078
Tazewell □, VA • 50,511
Tchula, MS 39169 • 1,931
Tea, SD 57064 • 729
Teague, TX 75860 • 3,390
Teaneck, NJ 07666 • 39,007
Teaticket, MA 02536 • 2,000
Tecumseh, MI 49286 • 7,320
Tecumseh, NE 68450 • 1,926
Tecumseh, OK 74873 • 5,123
Tehachapi, CA 93561 • 4,126
Tehama □, CA • 38,888
Tekamah, NE 68061 • 1,886
Tekoa, WA 99033 • 854
Tekonsha, MI 49092 • 755
Telfair □, GA • 11,445
Telford, PA 18969 • 3,507
Tell City, IN 47586 • 8,704
Teller □, CO • 8,034
Tellico Plains, TN 37385 • 698
Telluride, CO 81435 • 1,047
Temecula, CA 92390 • 1,783
Tempe, AZ 85281–89 • 106,743
Temperance, MI 48182 • 3,500
Temple, GA 30179 • 1,520
Temple, OK 73568 • 1,339
Temple, PA 19560 • 1,486
Temple, TX 76501–08 • 42,354
Temple City, CA 91780 • 28,972
Temple Terrace, FL 33617 • 11,097
Templeton, MA 01468 • 900
Templeton, PA 16259 • 700
Tenafly, NJ 07670 • 13,552
Tenaha, TX 75974 • 1,005
Tenino, WA 98589 • 1,280
Tennessee Ridge, TN 37178 • 1,325
Tennille, GA 31089 • 1,709
Tensas □, LA • 8,525
Terra Alta, WV 26764 • 1,946
Terral, OK 73569 • 604
Terrebonne, OR 97760 • 900
Terrebonne □, LA • 94,393
Terre Haute, IN 47801–12 • 61,125
Terre Hill, PA 17581 • 1,217
Terrell, TX 75160 • 13,269
Terrell □, GA • 12,017
Terrell □, TX • 1,595
Terrell Hills, TX 78209 • 4,644
Terry, MS 39170 • 655
Terry, MT 59349 • 929
Terry □, TX • 14,581
Terrytown, NE 69341 • 727
Terryville, CT 06786 • 5,234
Terryville, NY 11776 • 5,900
Tesuque, NM 87574 • 1,014
Teton □, ID • 2,897
Teton □, MT • 6,491
Teton □, WY • 9,355
Teutopolis, IL 62467 • 1,414
Tewksbury, MA 01876 • 11,500
Texarkana, AR 75502 • 21,459
Texarkana, TX 75501–07 • 31,271
Texas □, MO • 21,070
Texas □, OK • 17,727
Texas City, TX 77590–91 • 41,403
Texhoma, OK 73949 • 785
Texico, NM 88135 • 958
Thatcher, AZ 85552 • 3,374
Thayer, IL 62689 • 759
Thayer, MO 65791 • 2,211
Thayer □, NE • 7,582
The Colony, TX 75056 • 11,586
The Dalles, OR 97058 • 10,820
Theodore, AL 36582 • 6,392
The Plains, OH 45780 • 2,044
Theresa, NY 13691 • 827
Theresa, WI 53091 • 766
Thermopolis, WY 82443 • 3,852
The Village, OK 73120 • 11,049
Thibodaux, LA 70301–02 • 15,810
Thief River Falls, MN 56701 • 9,105
Thiensville, WI 53092 • 3,341
Thomas, OK 73669 • 1,515
Thomas, WV 26292 • 747
Thomas □, GA • 38,098
Thomas □, KS • 8,451
Thomas □, NE • 973
Thomasboro, IL 61878 • 1,242
Thomaston, AL 36783 • 679
Thomaston, CT 06787 • 3,500
Thomaston, GA 30286 • 9,682
Thomaston, ME 04861 • 2,348
Thomasville, AL 36784 • 4,387
Thomasville, GA 31792 • 18,463
Thomasville, NC 27360 • 14,144
Thompson, IA 50478 • 668
Thompson, ND 58278 • 785
Thompson Falls, MT 59873 • 1,478
Thompsonville, IL 62890 • 610
Thomson, GA 30824 • 7,001
Thomson, IL 61285 • 911
Thonotosassa, FL 33592 • 1,500
Thoreau, NM 87323 • 1,099
Thorndale, TX 76577 • 1,300
Thorndike, MA 01079 • 1,000
Thornton, AR 71766 • 711
Thornton, CO 80229 • 40,343
Thorntonville, TX 79756 • 717
Thorntown, IN 46071 • 1,468
Thornville, OH 43076 • 838
Thornwood, NY 10594 • 5,400
Thorofare, NJ 08086 • 1,400
Thorp, WI 54771 • 1,635
Thorsby, AL 35171 • 1,422
Thousand Oaks, CA 91359–63 • 77,072
Three Bridges, NJ 08887 • 650
Three Forks, MT 59752 • 1,247
Three Oaks, MI 49128 • 1,774
Three Rivers, MA 01080 • 3,322
Three Rivers, MI 49093 • 7,015
Three Rivers, TX 78071 • 2,133
Throckmorton, TX 76083 • 1,174
Throckmorton □, TX • 2,053
Throop, PA 18512 • 4,166
Thunderbolt, GA 31404 • 2,165
Thurmont, MD 21788 • 2,934
Thurston □, NE • 7,186
Thurston □, WA • 124,264
Tiburon, CA 94920 • 6,685
Tice, FL 33905 • 6,645
Ticonderoga, NY 12883 • 2,938
Tidioute, PA 16351 • 844
Tierra Amarilla, NM 87575 • 800
Tiffin, OH 44883 • 19,549
Tift □, GA • 32,862
Tifton, GA 31794 • 13,749
Tigard, OR 97223 • 14,286
Tigerton, WI 54486 • 865
Tignall, GA 30668 • 733
Tilden, IL 62292 • 1,025
Tilden, NE 68781 • 1,012
Tilghman, MD 21671 • 900
Tillamook, OR 97141 • 3,981
Tillamook □, OR • 21,164
Tillman □, OK • 12,398
Tillmans Corner, AL 36619 • 5,000
Tillson, NY 12486 • 1,300
Tilton, IL 61833 • 2,405
Tilton, NH 03276 • 1,230
Tiltonsville, OH 43963 • 1,750
Timber Lake, SD 57656 • 660
Timberlake, VA 24502 • 2,700
Timberville, VA 22853 • 1,510
Timmonsville, SC 29161 • 2,112
Timpson, TX 75975 • 1,164
Tinley Park, IL 60477 • 26,171
Tinton Falls, NJ 07724 • 7,740
Tioga, LA 71477 • 1,200
Tioga, ND 58852 • 1,597
Tioga □, NY • 49,812
Tioga □, PA • 40,973
Tionesta, PA 16353 • 659
Tippah □, MS • 18,739
Tipp City, OH 45371 • 5,595
Tippecanoe □, IN • 121,702
Tipton, CA 93272 • 1,185
Tipton, IN 46072 • 5,004
Tipton, IA 52772 • 3,055
Tipton, MO 65081 • 2,155
Tipton, OK 73570 • 1,475
Tipton □, IN • 16,819
Tipton □, TN • 32,930
Tiptonville, TN 38079 • 2,438
Tire Hill, PA 15959 • 750
Tishomingo, OK 73460 • 3,212
Tishomingo □, MS • 18,434
Tiskilwa, IL 61368 • 990
Titonka, IA 50480 • 607
Titus □, TX • 21,442
Titusville, FL 32780–83 • 31,910
Titusville, NJ 08560 • 900
Titusville, PA 16354 • 6,884
Tiverton, RI 02878 • 7,653
Tivoli, NY 12583 • 711
Toano, VA 23168 • 750
Toast, NC 27049 • 2,339
Tobyhanna, PA 18466 • 700
Toccoa, GA 30577 • 9,104
Todd □, KY • 11,874
Todd □, MN • 24,991
Todd □, SD • 7,328
Todd Estates, DE 19713 • 2,050
Tohatchi, NM 87325 • 1,011
Toledo, IL 62468 • 1,284
Toledo, IA 52342 • 2,445
Toledo, OH 43601–99 • 354,635
Toledo, OR 97391 • 3,151
Toledo, WA 98591 • 637
Tolland □, CT • 114,823
Tollesboro, KY 41189 • 808
Tolleson, AZ 85353 • 4,433
Tolono, IL 61880 • 2,434
Toluca, IL 61369 • 1,471
Tomah, WI 54660 • 7,204
Tomahawk, WI 54487 • 3,527
Tomball, TX 77375 • 3,996
Tombstone, AZ 85638 • 1,632
Tom Green □, TX • 84,784
Tomkins Cove, NY 10986 • 700
Tompkins □, NY • 87,085
Tompkinsville, KY 42167 • 4,366
Toms River, NJ 08753–59 • 7,465
Tonasket, WA 98855 • 985
Tonawanda, NY 14150 • 18,693
Tonganoxie, KS 66086 • 1,864
Tonica, IL 61370 • 695
Tonkawa, OK 74653 • 3,524
Tonopah, NV 89049 • 1,952
Tontitown, AR 72770 • 615
Tooele, UT 84074 • 14,335
Tooele □, UT • 26,033
Toole □, MT • 5,559
Toombs □, GA • 22,592
Toomsboro, GA 31090 • 673
Topeka, IN 46571 • 876
Topeka, KS 66601–99 • 115,266
Toppenish, WA 98948 • 6,517
Topsfield, MA 01983 • 2,647
Topsham, ME 04086 • 4,657
Topton, PA 19562 • 1,818
Toronto, OH 43964 • 6,934
Torrance, CA 90501–99 • 129,881
Torrance □, NM • 7,491
Torrington, CT 06790 • 30,987
Torrington, WY 82240 • 5,441
Totowa, NJ 07512 • 11,448
Touisset, MA 02777 • 1,300
Toulon, IL 61483 • 1,390
Towaco, NJ 07082 • 1,400
Towanda, IL 61776 • 630
Towanda, KS 67144 • 1,332
Towanda, PA 18848 • 3,526
Tower, MN 55790 • 640
Tower City, PA 17980 • 1,667
Tower Hill, IL 62571 • 715
Town and Country, WA 99210 • 7,100
Town Creek, AL 35672 • 1,201
Town Creek Manor, MD 20653 • 900
Towner, ND 58788 • 867
Towner □, ND • 4,052
Town of Tonawanda, NY 14223 • 78,100
Towns □, GA • 5,638
Townsend, MA 01469 • 1,266
Townsend, MT 59644 • 1,587
Towson, MD 21204 • 51,083
Tracy, CA 95376 • 18,428
Tracy, MN 56175 • 2,478
Tracy City, TN 37387 • 1,356
Tracyton, WA 98393 • 1,600
Traer, IA 50675 • 1,703
Trafford, PA 15085 • 3,662
Trail Creek, IN 46360 • 2,581
Traill □, ND • 9,624
Tranquillity, CA 93668 • 950
Transylvania □, NC • 23,417
Trappe, MD 21673 • 739
Travelers Rest, SC 29690 • 3,017
Traverse □, MN • 5,542
Traverse City, MI 49684 • 15,516
Travis □, TX • 419,573
Treasure □, MT • 981
Treasure Island, FL 33740 • 6,316
Trego □, KS • 4,165
Tremont, IL 61568 • 2,096
Tremont, PA 17981 • 1,796
Tremonton, UT 84337 • 3,464
Trempealeau, WI 54661 • 956
Trempealeau □, WI • 26,158
Trenton, FL 32693 • 1,131
Trenton, GA 30752 • 1,636
Trenton, IL 62293 • 2,504
Trenton, MI 48183 • 22,762
Trenton, MO 64683 • 6,811
Trenton, NE 69044 • 796
Trenton, NJ 08601–99 • 92,124
Trenton, OH 45067 • 6,401
Trenton, TN 38382 • 4,601
Trenton, TX 75490 • 691
Tresckow, PA 18254 • 1,146
Treutlen □, GA • 6,087
Trevorton, PA 17881 • 2,196
Trevose, PA 19047 • 7,000
Treynor, IA 51575 • 981
Trezevant, TN 38258 • 921
Triadelphia, WV 26059 • 1,461
Triangle, VA 22172 • 3,050
Tribune, KS 67879 • 955
Tri City, OR 97457 • 3,439
Trigg □, KY • 9,384
Tri Lakes, IN 46725 • 1,356
Trilby, FL 33593 • 950
Trimble, TN 38259 • 722
Trimble □, KY • 6,253
Trimont, MN 56176 • 805
Trinidad, CO 81082 • 9,663
Trinidad, TX 75163 • 1,130
Trinity, AL 35673 • 1,328
Trinity, TX 75862 • 2,620
Trinity □, CA • 11,858
Trinity □, TX • 9,450
Trinity Center, CA 96091 • 650
Trion, GA 30753 • 1,732
Tripoli, IA 50676 • 1,280
Tripp, SD 57376 • 804
Tripp □, SD • 7,268
Triumph, LA 70041 • 1,600
Trona, CA 93562 • 1,400
Trotwood, OH 45426 • 7,802
Troup, TX 75789 • 1,911
Troup □, GA • 50,003
Trousdale □, TN • 6,137
Troutdale, OR 97060 • 5,908
Troutman, NC 28166 • 1,360
Troy, AL 36081 • 12,945
Troy, ID 83871 • 820
Troy, IL 62294 • 3,772
Troy, KS 66087 • 1,240
Troy, MI 48084 • 67,102
Troy, MO 63379 • 2,624
Troy, MT 59935 • 1,088
Troy, NH 03465 • 1,318
Troy, NC 27371 • 2,702
Troy, NY 12180–83 • 56,638
Troy, OH 45373 • 19,086
Troy, PA 16947 • 1,381
Troy, SC 29848 • 705
Troy, TN 38260 • 1,093
Truckee, CA 95734 • 2,389
Truman, MN 56088 • 1,392
Trumann, AR 72472 • 6,405
Trumansburg, NY 14886 • 1,722
Trumbull, CT 06611 • 32,989
Trumbull □, OH • 241,863
Trussville, AL 35173 • 3,507
Truth or Consequences (Hot Springs), NM 87901 • 5,219
Tryon, NC 28782 • 1,796
Tualatin, OR 97062 • 7,483
Tuba City, AZ 86045 • 5,041
Tuckahoe, NJ 08250 • 650
Tuckahoe, NY 10707 • 6,076
Tucker, GA 30084 • 18,200
Tucker □, WV • 8,675
Tuckerman, AR 72473 • 2,078
Tuckerton, NJ 08087 • 2,472
Tucson, AZ 85701–99 • 330,537
Tucumcari, NM 88401 • 6,765
Tukwila, WA 98188 • 3,578
Tulare, CA 93274 • 22,526
Tulare □, CA • 245,738
Tularosa, NM 88352 • 2,536
Tulelake, CA 96134 • 783
Tulia, TX 79088 • 5,033
Tullahoma, TN 37388 • 15,800
Tullos, LA 71479 • 776
Tully, NY 13159 • 1,049
Tulsa, OK 74101–99 • 360,919
Tulsa □, OK • 470,593
Tumwater, WA 98502 • 6,705
Tunica, MS 38676 • 1,361
Tunica □, MS • 9,652
Tunkhannock, PA 18657 • 2,144
Tunnel Hill, GA 30755 • 936
Tuolumne, CA 95379 • 1,708
Tuolumne □, CA • 33,928
Tupelo, MS 38801 • 23,905
Tupper Lake, NY 12986 • 4,478
Turbotville, PA 17772 • 675
Turkey, TX 79261 • 644
Turley, OK 74156 • 6,336
Turlock, CA 95380 • 26,287
Turner, OR 97392 • 1,116
Turner □, GA • 9,510
Turner □, SD • 9,255
Turners Falls, MA 01376 • 4,711
Turrell, AR 72384 • 1,041
Turtle Creek, PA 15145 • 6,959
Turtle Lake, ND 58575 • 802
Turtle Lake, WI 54889 • 762
Tuscaloosa, AL 35401–06 • 75,211
Tuscaloosa □, AL • 137,541
Tuscarawas □, OH • 84,614
Tuscola, IL 61953 • 3,839
Tuscola, TX 79562 • 660
Tuscola □, MI • 56,961
Tuscumbia, AL 35674 • 9,137
Tuskegee, AL 36083 • 13,327
Tustin, CA 92680 • 32,317
Tuttle, OK 73089 • 3,051
Tutwiler, MS 38963 • 1,174
Tuxedo, NC 28784 • 950
Tuxedo Park, DE 19804 • 1,700
Twentynine Palms, CA 92277 • 7,465
Twiggs □, GA • 9,354
Twin City, GA 30471 • 1,402
Twin Falls, ID 83301 • 26,209
Twin Falls □, ID • 52,927
Twin Knolls, AZ 85207 • 4,700
Twin Lakes, GA 31636 • 800
Twin Lakes, WI 53181 • 3,474
Twin Rivers, NJ 08520 • 7,742
Twin Rocks, PA 15960 • 700
Twinsburg, OH 44087 • 7,632
Twin Valley, MN 56584 • 907
Twisp, WA 98856 • 911
Two Harbors, MN 55616 • 4,039
Two Rivers, WI 54241 • 13,354
Tybee Island, GA 31328 • 2,240
Tyler, MN 56178 • 1,353
Tyler, TX 75701–12 • 70,508
Tyler □, TX • 16,223
Tyler □, WV • 11,320
Tyler Heights, WV 25312 • 3,200
Tylertown, MS 39667 • 1,976
Tyndall, SD 57066 • 1,253
Tyrone, NM 88065 • 950
Tyrone, OK 73951 • 928
Tyrone, PA 16686 • 6,346
Tyronza, AR 72386 • 777
Tyrrell □, NC • 3,975
Ty Ty, GA 31795 • 618

## U

Ubly, MI 48475 • 862
Ucon, ID 83454 • 833
Udall, KS 67146 • 891
Uhrichsville, OH 44683 • 6,130
Uinta □, WY • 13,021
Uintah □, UT • 20,506
Ukiah, CA 95482 • 12,035
Uleta, FL 33164 • 10,000
Ulster □, NY • 158,158
Ulysses, KS 67880 • 4,653
Ulysses, PA 16948 • 654
Umatilla, FL 32784 • 1,872
Umatilla, OR 97882 • 3,199
Umatilla □, OR • 58,861
Unadilla, GA 31091 • 1,566
Unadilla, NY 13849 • 1,367
Unalakleet, AK 99684 • 623
Uncasville, CT 06382 • 1,597
Underwood, AL 35630 • 750
Underwood, ND 58576 • 1,329
Unicoi □, TN • 16,362
Union, IL 60180 • 622
Union, KY 41091 • 601
Union, MS 39365 • 1,931
Union, MO 63084 • 5,506
Union, NJ 07083 • 50,184
Union, OH 45322 • 5,219
Union, OR 97883 • 2,062
Union, SC 29379 • 10,523
Union, UT 84047 • 3,100
Union, WV 24983 • 743
Union □, AR • 48,573

Union □, FL • 10,166
Union □, GA • 9,390
Union □, IL • 17,765
Union □, IN • 6,860
Union □, IA • 13,858
Union □, KY • 17,821
Union □, LA • 21,167
Union □, MS • 21,741
Union □, NJ • 504,094
Union □, NM • 4,725
Union □, NC • 70,380
Union □, OH • 29,536
Union □, OR • 23,921
Union □, PA • 32,870
Union □, SC • 30,764
Union □, SD • 10,938
Union □, TN • 11,707
Union Beach, NJ 07735 • 6,354
Union Bridge, MD 21791 • 927
Union City, CA 94587 • 39,406
Union City, GA 30291 • 4,780
Union City, IN 47390 • 3,908
Union City, MI 49094 • 1,667
Union City, NJ 07087 • 55,593
Union City, OH 45390 • 1,716
Union City, PA 16438 • 3,623
Union City, TN 38261 • 10,436
Uniondale, NY 11553 • 24,500
Union Gap, WA 98903 • 3,184
Union Grove, WI 53182 • 3,517
Union Lake, MI 48085 • 12,000
Union Pier, MI 49129 • 1,039
Union Point, GA 30669 • 1,750
Union Springs, AL 36089 • 4,431
Union Springs, NY 13160 • 1,201
Uniontown, AL 36786 • 2,112
Uniontown, KY 42461 • 1,169
Uniontown, OH 44685 • 1,450
Uniontown, PA 15401 • 14,510
Union Village, RI 02895 • 2,400
Unionville, CT 06085 • 4,900
Unionville, MO 63565 • 2,178
United, PA 15689 • 950
Universal City, TX 78148 • 10,720
University City, MO 63130 • 42,738
University Gardens, NY 11020 • 5,400
University Heights, IA 52240 • 1,069
University Heights, OH 44118 • 15,401
University Park, IA 52595 • 645
University Park, NM 88003 • 4,383
University Park, TX 75205 • 22,254
University Place, WA 98465 • 13,620
Upland, CA 91786 • 47,647
Upland, IN 46989 • 3,335
Upper Arlington, OH 43221 • 35,648
Upper Darby, PA 19082–84 • 50,200
Upper Greenwood Lake, NJ 07421 • 2,734
Upper Marlboro, MD 20772 • 828
Upper Saddle River, NJ 07458 • 7,958
Upper Saint Clair, PA 15241 • 19,023
Upper Sandusky, OH 43351 • 5,967
Upshur □, TX • 28,595
Upshur □, WV • 23,427
Upson □, GA • 25,998
Upton, KY 42784 • 731
Upton, MA 01568 • 1,500
Upton, WY 82730 • 1,193
Upton □, TX • 4,619
Urania, LA 71480 • 849
Uravan, CO 81436 • 800
Urbana, IL 61801 • 35,978
Urbana, OH 43078 • 10,762
Urbancrest, OH 43123 • 880
Urbandale, IA 50322 • 17,869
Utah □, UT • 218,106
Utica, IL 61373 • 1,067
Utica, IN 47130 • 644
Utica, MI 48077–78 • 5,282
Utica, MS 39175 • 865
Utica, NE 68456 • 689
Utica, NY 13501–99 • 75,632
Utica, OH 43080 • 2,238
Uvalda, GA 30473 • 646
Uvalde, TX 78801 • 14,178
Uvalde □, TX • 22,441
Uxbridge, MA 01569 • 3,500

## V

Vacaville, CA 95688 • 43,367
Vacherie, LA 70090 • 2,169
Vadnais Heights, MN 55110 • 5,111
Vaiden, MS 39176 • 924
Vail, CO 81657 • 2,261
Vail Homes, NJ 07724 • 900
Valatie, NY 12184 • 1,492
Valders, WI 54245 • 984
Valdese, NC 28690 • 3,364
Valdez, AK 99686 • 3,079
Valdosta, GA 31601–05 • 37,596
Vale, OR 97918 • 1,558
Valencia, AZ 85326 • 1,300
Valencia □, NM • 31,013
Valencia Heights, SC 29205 • 5,328
Valentine, NE 69201 • 2,829
Valhalla, NY 10595 • 6,600
Valier, IL 62891 • 729
Valier, MT 59486 • 640
Valinda, CA 91744 • 18,700
Vallejo, CA 94590–92 • 80,303
Valley, NE 68064 • 1,716
Valley □, ID • 5,604
Valley □, MT • 10,250
Valley □, NE • 5,633
Valley Center, KS 67147 • 3,300
Valley City, ND 58072 • 7,774
Valley Cottage, NY 10989 • 6,007
Valley Falls, KS 66088 • 1,189
Valley Falls, RI 02864 • 10,892
Valley Forge, PA 19481 • 950
Valley Head, AL 35989 • 609
Valley Mills, TX 76689 • 1,236
Valley Park, MO 63088 • 3,232
Valley Springs, SD 57068 • 801
Valley Station, KY 40272 • 20,000
Valley Stream, NY 11580–83 • 35,769
Valley View, PA 17983 • 1,585
Valliant, OK 74764 • 927
Vallscreek, WV 24890 • 900
Valmeyer, IL 62295 • 898
Valparaiso, FL 32580 • 6,142
Valparaiso, IN 46383 • 22,247
Val Verda, UT 84010 • 6,422
Val Verde □, TX • 35,910
Van, TX 75790 • 1,881
Van Alstyne, TX 75095 • 1,860
Van Buren, AR 72956 • 12,020
Van Buren, IN 46991 • 935
Van Buren, ME 04785 • 3,282
Van Buren, MO 63965 • 850
Van Buren □, AR • 13,357
Van Buren □, IA • 8,626
Van Buren □, MI • 66,814
Van Buren □, TN • 4,728
Vance □, NC • 36,748
Vanceboro, NC 28586 • 833
Vanceburg, KY 41179 • 1,939
Vancleave, MS 39564 • 1,330
Vancouver, WA 98660–68 • 42,834
Vandalia, IL 62471 • 5,338
Vandalia, MO 63382 • 3,170
Vandalia, OH 45377 • 13,161
Vander, NC 28301 • 1,671
Vanderbilt, PA 15486 • 689
Vanderbilt, TX 77991 • 750
Vanderburgh □, IN • 167,515
Vandercook Lake, MI 49203 • 4,975
Vandergrift, PA 15690 • 6,823
Van Horn, TX 79855 • 2,772
Van Horne, IA 52346 • 682
Van Lear, KY 41265 • 2,035
Van Meter, IA 50261 • 747
Van Vleck, TX 77482 • 1,300
Van Wert, OH 45891 • 11,035
Van Wert □, OH • 30,458
Van Zandt □, TX • 31,426
Vardaman, MS 38878 • 1,009
Varina, VA 23231 • 2,000
Varnville, SC 29944 • 1,948
Vass, NC 28394 • 828
Vassar, MI 48768 • 2,727
Vaughn, MT 59487 • 2,270
Vaughn, NM 88353 • 737
Veazie, ME 04401 • 1,610
Veedersburg, IN 47987 • 2,261
Vega, TX 79092 • 900
Velda Rose Estates, AZ 85201 • 2,250
Velma, OK 73091 • 831
Velva, ND 58790 • 1,101
Venango □, PA • 64,444
Veneta, OR 97487 • 2,449
Venice, FL 34292–93 • 12,153
Venice, IL 62090 • 3,480
Ventnor City, NJ 08406 • 11,704
Ventura (San Buenaventura), CA 93001–09 • 74,393
Ventura, IA 50482 • 614
Ventura □, CA • 529,174
Verda, KY 40828 • 1,132
Verden, OK 73092 • 625
Verdi, NV 89439 • 800
Verdigre, NE 68783 • 617
Verdunville, WV 25649 • 950
Vergennes, VT 05491 • 2,273
Vermilion, OH 44089 • 11,012
Vermilion □, IL • 95,222
Vermilion □, LA • 48,458
Vermillion, SD 57069 • 10,136
Vermillion □, IN • 18,229
Vermont, IL 61484 • 885
Vermontville, MI 49096 • 832
Vernal, UT 84078 • 6,600
Vernon, AL 35592 • 2,609
Vernon, CT 06066 • 27,974
Vernon, FL 32462 • 885
Vernon, TX 76384 • 12,695
Vernon □, LA • 53,475
Vernon □, MO • 19,806
Vernon □, WI • 25,642
Vernon Hills, IL 60061 • 9,827
Vernonia, OR 97064 • 1,785
Vero Beach, FL 32960–64 • 16,176
Verona, MS 38879 • 2,497
Verona, NJ 07044 • 14,166
Verona, PA 15147 • 3,179
Verona, WI 53593 • 3,336
Versailles, IN 47042 • 1,560
Versailles, KY 40383 • 6,427
Versailles, MO 65084 • 2,406
Versailles, OH 45380 • 2,384
Vestal, NY 13850 • 6,000
Vestal Center, NY 13850 • 900
Vestavia Hills, AL 35216 • 15,722
Vevay, IN 47043 • 1,343
Vian, OK 74962 • 1,521
Viborg, SD 57070 • 812
Viburnum, MO 65566 • 836
Vici, OK 73859 • 845
Vicksburg, MI 49097 • 2,224
Vicksburg, MS 39180 • 25,434
Victor, IA 52347 • 1,046
Victor, NY 14564 • 2,370
Victoria, KS 67671 • 1,328
Victoria, MS 38679 • 950
Victoria, TX 77901–04 • 50,695
Victoria, VA 23974 • 2,004
Victoria □, TX • 68,807
Victorville, CA 92392 • 14,220
Vidalia, GA 30474 • 10,393
Vidalia, LA 71373 • 5,936
Vidor, TX 77662 • 11,834
Vidor, TX 77662 • 12,117
Vienna, GA 31092 • 2,886
Vienna, IL 62995 • 1,420
Vienna, VA 22180 • 15,469
Vienna, WV 26105 • 11,618
View Park, CA 90043 • 5,900
Vigo □, IN • 112,385
Vilas □, WI • 16,535
Villa Grove, IL 61956 • 2,707
Villanova, PA 19085 • 6,600
Villa Park, CA 92667 • 7,137
Villa Park, IL 60181 • 23,185
Villa Rica, GA 30180 • 3,420
Villas, NJ 08251 • 5,909
Ville Platte, LA 70586 • 9,201
Villisca, IA 50864 • 1,434
Vilonia, AR 72173 • 736
Vinalhaven, ME 04863 • 900
Vincennes, IN 47591 • 20,857
Vincent, AL 35178 • 1,652
Vincentown, NJ 08088 • 800
Vine Grove, KY 40175 • 3,583
Vineland, NJ 08360 • 53,753
Vinemont, AL 35179 • 615
Vineyard Haven, MA 02568 • 1,704
Vinita, OK 74301 • 6,740
Vinton, IA 52349 • 5,040
Vinton, LA 70668 • 3,631
Vinton, VA 24179 • 8,027
Vinton □, OH • 11,584
Vintondale, PA 15961 • 697
Viola, IL 61486 • 1,144
Viola, WI 54664 • 696
Violet, LA 70092 • 6,000
Virden, IL 62690 • 3,899
Virginia, AL 35020 • 700
Virginia, IL 62691 • 1,825
Virginia, MN 55792 • 11,056
Virginia Beach, VA 23450–65 • 262,199
Viroqua, WI 54665 • 3,716
Visalia, CA 93277–79 • 49,729
Vista, CA 92083–84 • 35,834
Vivian, LA 71082 • 4,146
Volcano, HI 96785 • 900
Volga, SD 57071 • 1,221
Volusia □, FL • 258,762

## W

Wabash, IN 46992 • 12,985
Wabash □, IL • 13,713
Wabash □, IN • 36,640
Wabasha, MN 55981 • 2,372
Wabasha □, MN • 19,335
Wabasso, FL 32970 • 2,157
Wabasso, MN 56293 • 745
Wabaunsee □, KS • 6,867
Wabeno, WI 54566 • 700
Waco, TX 76701–99 • 101,261
Waconia, MN 55387 • 2,638
Waddington, NY 13694 • 980
Wadena, MN 56482 • 4,699
Wadena □, MN • 14,192
Wadesboro, NC 28170 • 4,206
Wading River, NY 11792 • 2,500
Wadley, GA 30477 • 2,438
Wadsworth, IL 60083 • 1,104
Wadsworth, OH 44281 • 15,166
Waelder, TX 78959 • 942
Wagener, SC 29164 • 903
Wagner, SD 57380 • 1,453
Wagoner, OK 74467 • 6,191
Wagoner □, OK • 41,801
Wagram, NC 28396 • 617
Wahiawa, HI 96786 • 16,911
Wahkiakum □, WA • 3,832
Wahoo, NE 68066 • 3,555
Wahpeton, ND 58075 • 9,064
Waialua, HI 96791 • 4,051
Waianae, HI 96792 • 5,000
Waikapu, HI 96793 • 698
Wailua, HI 96746 • 1,587
Wailuku, HI 96793 • 10,260
Waimanalo, HI 96795 • 3,562
Waimea, HI 96796 • 1,569
Waipahu, HI 96797 • 29,139
Waipio Acres, HI 96786 • 4,091
Waite Park, MN 56387 • 3,496
Waitsburg, WA 99361 • 1,035
Wakarusa, IN 46573 • 1,281
Wake □, NC • 301,327
Wa Keeney, KS 67672 • 2,388
Wakefield, KS 67487 • 803
Wakefield, MA 01880 • 24,895
Wakefield, MI 49968 • 2,591
Wakefield, NE 68784 • 1,125
Wakefield, RI 02879–83 • 3,400
Wakefield, VA 23888 • 1,355
Wake Forest, NC 27587 • 3,780
Wakeman, OH 44889 • 906
Wakulla □, FL • 10,887
Walbridge, OH 43465 • 2,900
Walcott, IA 52773 • 1,425
Walden, CO 80480 • 947
Walden, NY 12586 • 5,659
Waldo, AR 71770 • 1,685
Waldo, FL 32694 • 993
Waldo □, ME • 28,414
Waldoboro, ME 04572 • 1,195
Waldorf, MD 20601 • 9,782
Waldport, OR 97394 • 1,274
Waldron, AR 72958 • 2,642
Waldron, IN 46182 • 800
Waldwick, NJ 07463 • 10,802
Walhalla, ND 58282 • 1,429
Walhalla, SC 29691 • 3,977
Walker, IA 52352 • 733
Walker, LA 70785 • 2,957
Walker, MI 49504 • 15,088
Walker, MN 56484 • 970
Walker □, AL • 68,660
Walker □, GA • 56,470
Walker □, TX • 41,789
Walkersville, MD 21793 • 2,212
Walkerton, IN 46574 • 2,051
Walkertown, NC 27051 • 2,100
Walkerville, MT 59701 • 887
Wall, SD 57790 • 770
Wallace, ID 83873 • 1,736
Wallace, NC 28466 • 2,903
Wallace, WV 26448 • 900
Wallace □, KS • 2,045
Walla Walla, WA 99362 • 25,618
Walla Walla □, WA • 47,435
Walled Lake, MI 48088 • 4,748
Wallen, IN 46806 • 1,200
Waller, TX 77484 • 1,241
Waller □, TX • 19,798
Wallingford, CT 06492 • 37,274
Wallingford, VT 05773 • 1,141
Wallington, NJ 07057 • 10,741
Wallis, TX 77485 • 1,138
Wallkill, NY 12589 • 1,849
Wall Lake, IA 51466 • 892
Wallowa, OR 97885 • 847
Wallowa □, OR • 7,273
Walnut, CA 91789 • 12,478
Walnut, IL 61376 • 1,513
Walnut, IA 51577 • 897
Walnut Cove, NC 27052 • 1,147
Walnut Creek, CA 94595–98 • 53,643
Walnut Grove, MN 56180 • 753
Walnut Park, CA 90255 • 11,811
Walnutport, PA 18088 • 2,007
Walnut Ridge, AR 72476 • 4,152
Walpole, MA 02081 • 5,274
Walpole, NH 03608 • 700
Walsenburg, CO 81089 • 3,945
Walsh, CO 81090 • 884
Walsh □, ND • 15,371
Walterboro, SC 29488 • 6,209
Walters, OK 73572 • 2,778
Walthall □, MS • 13,761
Waltham, MA 02154 • 58,200
Walthill, NE 68067 • 847
Walthourville, GA 31333 • 905
Walton, IN 46994 • 1,202
Walton, KY 41094 • 1,651
Walton, NY 13856 • 3,329
Walton □, FL • 21,300
Walton □, GA • 31,211
Walworth, WI 53184 • 1,607
Walworth □, SD • 7,011
Walworth □, WI • 71,507
Wamac, IL 62801 • 1,665
Wamego, KS 66547 • 3,159
Wamesit, MA 01876 • 2,700
Wampum, PA 16157 • 851
Wamsutter, WY 82336 • 681
Wanamingo, MN 55983 • 717
Wanaque, NJ 07465 • 10,025
Wanatah, IN 46390 • 879
Wanchese, NC 27981 • 1,105
Wando Woods, SC 29405 • 5,253
Wantagh, NY 11793 • 22,300
Wapakoneta, OH 45895 • 8,402
Wapato, WA 98951 • 3,307
Wapella, IL 61777 • 768
Wapello, IA 52653 • 2,011
Wapello □, IA • 40,241
Wappingers Falls, NY 12590 • 5,110
War, WV 24892 • 2,158
Ward, AR 72176 • 981
Ward □, ND • 58,392
Ward □, TX • 13,976
Warden, WA 98857 • 1,479
Ware, MA 01082 • 6,806
Ware □, GA • 37,180
Wareham, MA 02571 • 2,473
Warehouse Point, CT 06088 • 1,850
Ware Shoals, SC 29692 • 2,370
Waretown, NJ 08758 • 1,175
Warminster, PA 18974 • 35,543
Warner, NH 03278 • 700
Warner, OK 74469 • 1,310
Warner Robins, GA 31093 • 39,893
Warr Acres, OK 73132 • 9,940
Warren, AR 71671 • 7,646
Warren, IL 61087 • 1,595
Warren, IN 46792 • 1,254
Warren, MA 01083 • 1,548
Warren, MI 48089–93 • 161,134
Warren, MN 56762 • 2,105
Warren, OH 44481–86 • 56,629
Warren, OR 97053 • 800
Warren, PA 16365 • 12,146
Warren, RI 02885 • 10,640
Warren □, GA • 6,583
Warren □, IL • 21,943
Warren □, IN • 8,976
Warren □, IA • 34,878
Warren □, KY • 71,828
Warren □, MS • 51,627
Warren □, MO • 14,900
Warren □, NJ • 84,429
Warren □, NC • 16,232
Warren □, NY • 54,854
Warren □, OH • 99,276
Warren □, PA • 47,449
Warren □, TN • 32,653
Warren □, VA • 21,200
Warrendale, PA 15086 • 800
Warren Park, IN 46219 • 1,803
Warrensburg, IL 62573 • 1,372
Warrensburg, MO 64093 • 13,807
Warrensburg, NY 12885 • 2,743
Warrensville Heights, OH 44122 • 16,565
Warrenton, GA 30828 • 2,172
Warrenton, MO 63383 • 3,219
Warrenton, NC 27589 • 908
Warrenton, OR 97146 • 2,493
Warrenton, VA 22186 • 3,907
Warrenville, IL 60555 • 7,519
Warrenville, SC 29851 • 1,029
Warrick □, IN • 41,474
Warrington, FL 32507 • 15,792
Warrior, AL 35180 • 3,260
Warroad, MN 56763 • 1,216
Warsaw, IL 62379 • 1,842
Warsaw, IN 46580 • 10,647
Warsaw, KY 41095 • 1,328
Warsaw, MO 65355 • 1,494
Warsaw, NC 28398 • 2,910
Warsaw, NY 14569 • 3,619
Warsaw, OH 43844 • 765
Warsaw, VA 22572 • 771
Wartburg, TN 37887 • 761
Warwick, NY 10990 • 4,320
Warwick, RI 02886–89 • 87,123
Wasatch □, UT • 8,523
Wasco, CA 93280 • 9,613
Wasco □, OR • 21,732
Waseca, MN 56093 • 8,219
Waseca □, MN • 18,448
Washakie □, WY • 9,496
Washburn, IL 61570 • 1,206
Washburn, IA 50706 • 1,400
Washburn, ME 04786 • 1,221
Washburn, ND 58577 • 1,767
Washburn, WI 54891 • 2,080
Washburn □, WI • 13,174
Washington, DC 20001–99 • 638,432
Washington, GA 30673 • 4,662
Washington, IL 61571 • 10,364
Washington, IN 47501 • 11,325
Washington, IA 52353 • 6,584
Washington, KS 66968 • 1,488
Washington, KY 41096 • 624
Washington, LA 70589 • 1,266
Washington, MS 39190 • 900
Washington, MO 63090 • 9,251
Washington, NJ 07882 • 6,429
Washington, NC 27889 • 8,418
Washington, PA 15301 • 18,363
Washington, UT 84780 • 3,092
Washington □, AL • 16,821
Washington □, AR • 100,494
Washington □, CO • 5,304
Washington □, FL • 14,509
Washington □, GA • 18,842
Washington □, ID • 8,803
Washington □, IL • 15,472
Washington □, IN • 21,932
Washington □, IA • 20,141
Washington □, KS • 8,543
Washington □, KY • 10,764
Washington □, LA • 44,207
Washington □, ME • 34,963
Washington □, MD • 113,086
Washington □, MN • 113,571
Washington □, MS • 72,344
Washington □, MO • 17,983
Washington □, NE • 15,508
Washington □, NC • 14,801
Washington □, NY • 54,795
Washington □, OH • 64,266
Washington □, OK • 48,113
Washington □, OR • 245,860
Washington □, PA • 217,074
Washington □, RI • 93,317
Washington □, TN • 88,755
Washington □, TX • 21,998
Washington □, UT • 26,065
Washington □, VT • 52,393
Washington □, VA • 46,487
Washington □, WI • 84,848
Washington Court House, OH 43160 • 12,682
Washington Park, IL 62204 • 8,223
Washington Terrace, UT 84403 • 8,212
Washington Township, NJ 07675 • 9,550
Washita □, OK • 13,798
Washoe □, NV • 193,623
Washougal, WA 98671 • 3,834
Washtenaw □, MI • 264,748
Wasilla, AK 99687 • 1,559
Waskom, TX 75692 • 1,821
Wataga, IL 61488 • 996
Watauga, TX 76148 • 10,284
Watauga □, NC • 31,666
Watchung, NJ 07060 • 5,290
Waterbury, CT 06701–49 • 103,266
Waterbury, VT 05676 • 1,892
Waterford, CT 06385 • 2,736
Waterford, MI 48095 • 64,250
Waterford, NY 12188 • 2,405
Waterford, PA 16441 • 1,568
Waterford, WI 53185 • 2,051
Waterloo, IL 62298 • 4,646
Waterloo, IN 46793 • 1,951
Waterloo, IA 50701–99 • 75,985
Waterloo, NY 13165 • 5,303
Waterloo, WI 53594 • 2,393
Waterman, IL 60556 • 943
Waterproof, LA 71375 • 1,339
Watersmeet, MI 49969 • 700
Watertown, CT 06795 • 6,000
Watertown, MA 02172 • 34,384
Watertown, NY 13601 • 27,861
Watertown, SD 57201 • 15,649
Watertown, TN 37184 • 1,300
Watertown, WI 53094 • 18,113
Water Valley, MS 38965 • 4,147
Waterville, KS 66548 • 694
Waterville, ME 04901 • 17,779
Waterville, MN 56096 • 1,717
Waterville, NY 13480 • 1,672
Waterville, OH 43566 • 3,884
Waterville, WA 98858 • 908
Watervliet, MI 49098 • 1,867
Watervliet, NY 12189 • 11,354
Watford City, ND 58854 • 2,119
Wathena, KS 66090 • 1,418
Watkins, MN 55389 • 757
Watkins Glen, NY 14891 • 2,440
Watkinsville, GA 30677 • 1,240
Watonga, OK 73772 • 4,139
Watonwan □, MN • 12,361
Watseka, IL 60970 • 5,543
Watson Chapel, AR 71601 • 900
Watsontown, PA 17777 • 2,366
Watsonville, CA 95076 • 23,663
Wattsville, SC 29360 • 1,324
Waubay, SD 57273 • 675
Wauchula, FL 33873 • 2,986
Wauconda, IL 60084 • 5,688
Waukee, IA 50263 • 2,227
Waukegan, IL 60085–87 • 67,653
Waukesha, WI 53186–88 • 50,365
Waukesha □, WI • 280,080
Waukomis, OK 73773 • 1,551
Waukon, IA 52172 • 3,983
Waunakee, WI 53597 • 3,866
Wauneta, NE 69045 • 746
Waupaca, WI 54981 • 4,472
Waupaca □, WI • 42,831
Waupun, WI 53963 • 8,132
Wauregan, CT 06387 • 900
Waurika, OK 73573 • 2,258
Wausa, NE 68786 • 647
Wausau, WI 54401 • 32,426
Wausaukee, WI 54177 • 648
Wauseon, OH 43567 • 6,173
Waushara □, WI • 18,526
Wautoma, WI 54982 • 1,629
Wauwatosa, WI 53213 • 51,308
Waveland, MS 39576 • 4,186
Waverly, IL 62692 • 1,537
Waverly, IA 50677 • 8,444
Waverly, KS 66871 • 671
Waverly, MO 64096 • 941
Waverly, NE 68462 • 1,726
Waverly, NY 14892 • 4,738
Waverly, OH 45690 • 4,603
Waverly, TN 37185 • 4,405
Waverly, VA 23890 • 2,284
Waverly Hall, GA 31831 • 913
Waxahachie, TX 75165 • 14,624
Waxhaw, NC 28173 • 1,208

Waycross, GA 31501 • *19,371*
Wayland, IA 52654 • *720*
Wayland, KY 41666 • *601*
Wayland, MA 01778 • *5,500*
Wayland, MI 49348 • *2,023*
Wayland, NY 14572 • *1,846*
Waylyn, SC 29405 • *2,400*
Waymart, PA 18472 • *1,248*
Wayne, MI 48184 • *21,159*
Wayne, NE 68787 • *5,240*
Wayne, NJ 07470 • *46,474*
Wayne, OH 43466 • *894*
Wayne, OK 73095 • *621*
Wayne, PA 19087 • *8,900*
Wayne, WV 25570 • *1,495*
Wayne □, GA • *20,750*
Wayne □, IL • *18,059*
Wayne □, IN • *76,058*
Wayne □, IA • *8,199*
Wayne □, KY • *17,022*
Wayne □, MI • *2,337,891*
Wayne □, MS • *19,135*
Wayne □, MO • *11,277*
Wayne □, NE • *9,858*
Wayne □, NC • *97,054*
Wayne □, NY • *84,581*
Wayne □, OH • *97,408*
Wayne □, PA • *35,237*
Wayne □, TN • *13,946*
Wayne □, UT • *1,911*
Wayne □, WV • *46,021*
Wayne City, IL 62895 • *1,132*
Waynesboro, GA 30830 • *5,760*
Waynesboro, MS 39367 • *5,349*
Waynesboro, PA 17268 • *9,726*
Waynesboro, TN 38485 • *2,109*
Waynesboro, VA 22980 • *15,329*
Waynesburg, OH 44688 • *1,160*
Waynesburg, PA 15370 • *4,482*
Waynesville, MO 65583 • *2,879*
Waynesville, NC 28786 • *6,765*
Waynesville, OH 45068 • *1,796*
Waynetown, IN 47990 • *915*
Waynewood, VA 22308 • *4,500*
Waynoka, OK 73860 • *1,377*
Wayzata, MN 55391 • *3,621*
Weakley □, TN • *32,896*
Weatherford, OK 73096 • *9,640*
Weatherford, TX 76086 • *12,049*
Weatherly, PA 18255 • *2,891*
Weatogue, CT 06089 • *2,249*
Weaver, AL 36277 • *2,765*
Weaverville, CA 96093 • *2,787*
Weaverville, NC 28787 • *1,495*
Webb, MS 38966 • *782*
Webb □, TX • *99,258*
Webb City, MO 64870 • *7,309*
Webberville, MI 48892 • *1,535*
Weber □, UT • *144,616*
Weber City, VA 24251 • *1,543*
Webster, FL 33597 • *856*
Webster, MA 01570 • *14,480*
Webster, NY 14580 • *5,499*
Webster, PA 15087 • *800*
Webster, SD 57274 • *2,417*
Webster, TX 77598 • *2,405*
Webster, WI 54893 • *610*
Webster □, GA • *2,341*
Webster □, IA • *45,953*
Webster □, KY • *14,832*
Webster □, LA • *43,631*
Webster □, MS • *10,300*
Webster □, MO • *20,414*
Webster □, NE • *4,858*
Webster □, WV • *12,245*
Webster City, IA 50595 • *8,572*
Webster Groves, MO 63119 • *23,097*
Webster Springs, WV 26288 • *939*
Wedgewood, MO 63031 • *5,700*
Wedowee, AL 36278 • *908*
Weed, CA 96094 • *2,879*
Weed Heights, NV 89447 • *650*
Weedsport, NY 13166 • *1,952*
Weehawken, NJ 07087 • *13,168*
Weeksbury, KY 41667 • *700*
Weeping Water, NE 68463 • *1,109*
Weimar, TX 78962 • *2,128*
Weiner, AR 72479 • *750*
Weippe, ID 83553 • *828*
Weir, KS 66781 • *705*
Weirsdale, FL 32695 • *1,500*
Weirton, WV 26062 • *25,371*
Weiser, ID 83672 • *4,771*
Welch, OK 74369 • *697*
Welch, WV 24801 • *3,885*
Welcome, MN 56181 • *855*
Welcome, SC 29611 • *6,922*
Weld □, CO • *123,438*
Weldon, NC 27890 • *1,844*
Weleetka, OK 74880 • *1,195*
Wellesley, MA 02181 • *27,209*
Wellfleet, MA 02667 • *950*
Wellford, SC 29385 • *2,143*
Wellington, CO 80549 • *1,215*
Wellington, KS 67152 • *8,212*
Wellington, MO 64097 • *780*
Wellington, OH 44090 • *4,146*
Wellington, TX 79095 • *3,043*
Wellington, UT 84542 • *1,406*
Wellman, IA 52356 • *1,125*
Wells, ME 04090 • *850*
Wells, MI 49894 • *1,100*
Wells, MN 56097 • *2,777*
Wells, NV 89835 • *1,218*
Wells, TX 75976 • *926*
Wells □, IN • *25,401*
Wells □, ND • *6,979*
Wellsboro, PA 16901 • *3,805*
Wellsburg, IA 50680 • *761*
Wellsburg, NY 14894 • *647*
Wellsburg, WV 26070 • *3,963*
Wellston, OH 45692 • *6,016*
Wellston, OK 74881 • *802*
Wellsville, KS 66092 • *1,612*
Wellsville, MO 63384 • *1,546*
Wellsville, NY 14895 • *5,769*
Wellsville, OH 43968 • *5,095*
Wellsville, UT 84339 • *1,952*
Wellton, AZ 85356 • *911*
Welsh, LA 70591 • *3,515*
Wenatchee, WA 98801 • *17,257*

Wendell, ID 83355 • *1,974*
Wendell, NC 27591 • *2,222*
Wendover, UT 84083 • *1,099*
Wenham, MA 01984 • *3,897*
Wenona, IL 61377 • *1,025*
Wenonah, NJ 08090 • *2,303*
Wentzville, MO 63385 • *3,193*
Wequetequock, CT 02891 • *800*
Weslaco, TX 78596 • *19,331*
Wesleyville, PA 16510 • *3,998*
Wessington Springs, SD 57382 • *1,203*
Wesson, MS 39191 • *1,313*
West, TX 76691 • *2,485*
West Abington, MA 02351 • *2,000*
West Acton, MA 01720 • *5,800*
West Alexandria, OH 45381 • *1,313*
West Allis, WI 53214 • *63,982*
West Amityville, NY 11758 • *6,470*
West Andover, MA 01810 • *3,700*
West Athens, CA 90247 • *8,531*
West Babylon, NY 11704 • *32,500*
West Baden Springs, IN 47469 • *796*
West Barrington, RI 02806 • *3,700*
West Baton Rouge □, LA • *19,086*
West Bay Shore, NY 11706 • *8,900*
West Bend, IA 50597 • *941*
West Bend, WI 53095 • *21,484*
West Berlin, NJ 08091 • *3,300*
West Billerica, MA 01862 • *2,000*
West Blocton, AL 35184 • *1,147*
Westborough, MA 01581 • *13,619*
West Bountiful, UT 84087 • *3,556*
West Boylston, MA 01583 • *3,500*
West Branch, IA 52358 • *1,867*
West Branch, MI 48661 • *1,785*
West Bridgewater, MA 02379 • *2,100*
Westbrook, CT 06498 • *2,035*
Westbrook, ME 04092 • *14,976*
Westbrook, MN 56183 • *978*
West Brookfield, MA 01585 • *1,423*
West Burlington, IA 52655 • *3,371*
Westbury, NY 11590 • *13,871*
Westby, WI 54667 • *1,797*
West Caldwell, NJ 07006 • *11,407*
West Cape May, NJ 08204 • *1,091*
West Carroll □, LA • *12,922*
West Carrollton, OH 45449 • *13,148*
West Carson, CA 90502 • *17,997*
West Carthage, NY 13619 • *1,824*
West Chatham, MA 02669 • *1,398*
West Chazy, NY 12992 • *700*
Westchester, FL 33144 • *20,000*
Westchester, IL 60153 • *17,730*
West Chester, PA 19380–82 • *17,435*
Westchester □, NY • *866,599*
West Chicago, IL 60185 • *12,550*
West City, IL 62812 • *886*
West College Corner, IN 45003 • *614*
West Columbia, SC 29169 • *10,409*
West Columbia, TX 77486 • *4,109*
West Concord, MA 01742 • *5,331*
West Concord, MN 55985 • *762*
West Concord, NC 28025 • *5,859*
West Covina, CA 91790–93 • *80,291*
West Crossett, AR 71635 • *1,466*
West Cumberland, ME 04021 • *800*
West Dennis, MA 02670 • *2,030*
West Des Moines, IA 50265 • *21,894*
West Elmira, NY 14905 • *5,901*
West End, NC 27376 • *900*
Westerly, RI 02891 • *14,093*
Western Hills, CO 80221 • *6,000*
Westernport, MD 21562 • *2,706*
Western Springs, IL 60558 • *12,876*
Westerville, OH 43081 • *23,414*
West Fairview, PA 17025 • *1,426*
West Falmouth, MA 02574 • *1,200*
West Fargo, ND 58078 • *10,099*
West Feliciana □, LA • *12,186*
Westfield, IL 62474 • *733*
Westfield, IN 46074 • *2,783*
Westfield, MA 01085 • *36,465*
Westfield, NJ 07090–92 • *30,447*
Westfield, NY 14787 • *3,446*
Westfield, PA 16950 • *1,268*
Westfield, WI 53964 • *1,033*
Westfield Center, OH 44251 • *791*
Westford, MA 01886 • *1,000*
West Fork, AR 72774 • *1,526*
West Frankfort, IL 62896 • *9,437*
Westgate, FL 34205 • *2,100*
West Groton, MA 01472 • *950*
West Grove, PA 19390 • *1,820*
Westham, VA 23229 • *3,600*
West Hamlin, WV 25571 • *643*
West Hanover, MA 02339 • *1,600*
West Hartford, CT 06107 • *61,306*
West Haven, CT 06516 • *53,184*
West Haven, OR 97225 • *3,400*
West Haverstraw, NY 10993 • *9,181*
West Hazleton, PA 18201 • *4,871*
West Helena, AR 72390 • *11,367*
West Hempstead, NY 11552 • *26,500*
West Hollywood, CA 90069 • *35,703*
Westhope, ND 58793 • *741*
West Huntington, NY 11743 • *6,170*
West Hyannisport, MA 02672 • *1,200*
West Islip, NY 11795 • *29,533*
West Jefferson, NC 28694 • *822*
West Jefferson, OH 43162 • *4,448*
West Jordan, UT 84084 • *27,192*
West Kingston, RI 02892 • *700*
West Lafayette, IN 47906 • *21,247*
West Lafayette, OH 43845 • *2,225*
Westlake, LA 70669 • *5,246*
Westlake, OH 44145 • *19,483*
Westland, MI 48185 • *84,603*
West Laramie, WY 82070 • *2,000*
West Lawn, PA 19609 • *1,686*
West Lebanon, IN 47991 • *946*
West Leisenring, PA 15489 • *700*
West Liberty, IA 52776 • *2,723*
West Liberty, KY 41472 • *1,381*
West Liberty, OH 43357 • *1,653*
West Liberty, WV 26074 • *744*
West Linn, OR 97068 • *12,956*
West Long Branch, NJ 07764 • *7,380*
West Mansfield, OH 43358 • *716*
West Marion, NC 28752 • *1,596*
West Medway, MA 02053 • *2,269*
West Melbourne, FL 32901 • *5,078*

West Memphis, AR 72301 • *28,138*
Westmere, NY 12203 • *5,500*
West Miami, FL 33174 • *6,076*
West Middlesex, PA 16159 • *1,064*
West Mifflin, PA 15122 • *26,552*
West Milford, NJ 07480 • *1,600*
West Milton, OH 45383 • *4,119*
West Milton, PA 17886 • *775*
West Milwaukee, WI 53214 • *3,535*
Westminster, CA 92683 • *71,133*
Westminster, CO 80030 • *50,211*
Westminster, MD 21157 • *8,808*
Westminster, MA 01473 • *950*
Westminster, SC 29693 • *3,114*
West Modesto, CA 95351 • *6,135*
West Monroe, LA 71291 • *14,993*
Westmont, CA 90044 • *27,916*
Westmont, IL 60559 • *16,718*
Westmont, NJ 08108 • *5,700*
Westmont, PA 15905 • *6,113*
Westmoreland, TN 37186 • *1,754*
Westmoreland □, PA • *392,294*
Westmoreland □, VA • *14,041*
Westmorland, CA 92281 • *1,590*
West Mystic, CT 06388 • *3,364*
West Newbury, MA 01985 • *950*
West Newton, PA 15089 • *3,387*
West New York, NJ 07093 • *39,194*
West Norriton, PA 19401 • *14,034*
Weston, CT 06883 • *1,200*
Weston, MA 02193 • *11,169*
Weston, MO 64098 • *1,440*
Weston, OH 43569 • *1,708*
Weston, OR 97886 • *719*
Weston, WV 26452 • *6,250*
Weston, WI 54476 • *3,400*
Weston □, WY • *7,106*
West Orange, NJ 07052 • *39,400*
Westover, WV 26505 • *4,884*
West Palm Beach, FL 33401–18 • *63,305*
West Park, NY 12493 • *700*
West Paterson, NJ 07424 • *11,293*
West Pelzer, SC 29669 • *944*
West Pensacola, FL 32505 • *24,571*
West Peoria, IL 61604 • *5,219*
Westphalia, MI 48894 • *896*
West Pittsburg, CA 94565 • *6,000*
West Pittsburg, PA 16160 • *950*
West Pittston, PA 18643 • *5,980*
West Plains, MO 65775 • *7,741*
West Point, CA 95255 • *1,500*
West Point, GA 31833 • *4,294*
West Point, IA 52656 • *1,133*
West Point, KY 40177 • *1,339*
West Point, MS 39773 • *8,811*
West Point, NE 68788 • *3,609*
West Point, NY 10996 • *8,000*
West Point, UT 84015 • *2,170*
West Point, VA 23181 • *2,726*
Westport, CT 06880 • *25,290*
Westport, IN 47283 • *1,450*
Westport, IN 47283 • *1,450*
Westport, MA 02790 • *1,850*
Westport, NY 12993 • *613*
Westport, WA 98595 • *1,954*
West Portsmouth, OH 45662 • *4,095*
West Puente Valley, CA 91744 • *20,445*
West Reading, PA 19611 • *4,507*
West Rutland, VT 05777 • *2,351*
West Sacramento, CA 95691 • *10,875*
West Saint Paul, MN 55118 • *18,527*
West Salem, IL 62476 • *1,145*
West Salem, OH 44287 • *1,357*
West Salem, WI 54669 • *3,276*
West Sayville, NY 11796 • *5,000*
West Scarborough, ME 04074 • *700*
West Seneca, NY 14224 • *51,210*
West Simsbury, CT 06092 • *2,140*
West Slope, OR 97225 • *5,364*
West Springfield, MA 01089 • *27,042*
West Springfield, VA 22152 • *16,000*
West Stockbridge, MA 01266 • *800*
West Swanzey, NH 03469 • *1,022*
West Terre Haute, IN 47885 • *2,806*
West Townsend, MA 01474 • *700*
West Union, IA 52175 • *2,783*
West Union, OH 45693 • *2,791*
West Union, WV 26456 • *1,090*
West Unity, OH 43570 • *1,639*
West University Place, TX 77005 • *12,010*
West Upton, MA 01587 • *1,000*
Westvale, NY 13219 • *7,300*
West Valley City, UT 84120 • *72,511*
West Van Lear, KY 41268 • *900*
West View, PA 15229 • *7,648*
Westville, IL 61883 • *3,573*
Westville, IN 46391 • *2,887*
Westville, NH 03865 • *700*
Westville, NJ 08093 • *4,786*
Westville, OK 74965 • *1,049*
West Wareham, MA 02576 • *1,837*
West Warren, MA 01092 • *1,200*
West Warwick, RI 02893 • *27,026*
West Webster, NY 14580 • *10,600*
Westwego, LA 70094 • *12,663*
West Whittier, CA 90606 • *13,800*
West Winfield, NY 13491 • *979*
Westwood, CA 96137 • *2,081*
Westwood, KS 66205 • *1,783*
Westwood, KY 41101 • *5,973*
Westwood, MA 02090 • *6,500*
Westwood, MI 49007 • *8,519*
Westwood, NJ 07675 • *10,714*
Westwood Lakes, FL 33165 • *11,478*
West Wyoming, PA 18644 • *3,288*
West Yarmouth, MA 02673 • *3,882*
West Yellowstone, MT 59758 • *735*
West York, PA 17404 • *4,526*
Wethersfield, CT 06109 • *26,013*
Wetumka, OK 74883 • *1,725*
Wetumpka, AL 36092 • *4,341*
Wetzel □, WV • *21,874*
Wewahitchka, FL 32465 • *1,742*
Wewoka, OK 74884 • *5,480*
Wexford □, MI • *25,102*
Weyauwega, WI 54983 • *1,549*
Weymouth, MA 02188 • *55,601*
Whalom, MA 01420 • *1,400*
Wharton, NJ 07885 • *5,485*

Wharton, TX 77488 • *9,033*
Wharton □, TX • *40,242*
What Cheer, IA 50268 • *803*
Whatcom □, WA • *106,701*
Wheatfield, IN 46392 • *755*
Wheatland, CA 95692 • *1,474*
Wheatland, IA 52777 • *840*
Wheatland, PA 16161 • *1,132*
Wheatland, WY 82201 • *5,816*
Wheatland □, MT • *2,359*
Wheaton, IL 60187–89 • *43,043*
Wheaton, MD 20902 • *48,600*
Wheaton, MN 56296 • *1,969*
Wheat Ridge, CO 80033 • *30,293*
Wheeler, TX 79096 • *1,584*
Wheeler □, GA • *5,155*
Wheeler □, NE • *1,060*
Wheeler □, OR • *1,513*
Wheeler □, TX • *7,137*
Wheelersburg, OH 45694 • *4,796*
Wheeling, IL 60090 • *23,266*
Wheeling, WV 26003 • *43,070*
Wheelwright, KY 41669 • *865*
Whitacres, CT 06082 • *2,500*
Whitakers, NC 27891 • *924*
White □, AR • *50,835*
White □, GA • *10,120*
White □, IL • *17,864*
White □, IN • *23,867*
White □, TN • *19,567*
White Bear Lake, MN 55110 • *22,538*
White Bluff, TN 37187 • *2,055*
White Castle, LA 70788 • *2,160*
White Center, WA 98126 • *19,700*
White City, FL 32465 • *725*
White City, OR 97503 • *5,445*
White City, UT 84070 • *1,180*
White Cloud, MI 49349 • *1,101*
White Deer, TX 79097 • *1,210*
Whitefield, NH 03598 • *1,005*
Whitefish, MT 59937 • *3,703*
Whitefish Bay, WI 53217 • *14,930*
White Hall, AR 71602 • *2,214*
White Hall, IL 62092 • *2,935*
Whitehall, MI 49461 • *2,856*
Whitehall, MT 59759 • *1,030*
Whitehall, NY 12887 • *3,241*
Whitehall, OH 43213 • *21,299*
Whitehall, PA 15227 • *15,143*
Whitehall, WI 54773 • *1,530*
White Haven, PA 18661 • *1,921*
White Horse, NJ 08610 • *10,098*
White Horse Beach, MA 02381 • *800*
Whitehouse, OH 43571 • *2,137*
White House, TN 37188 • *2,225*
White House Station, NJ 08889 • *1,019*
White Island Shores, MA 02538 • *950*
Whitelaw, WI 54247 • *649*
White Meadow Lake, NJ 07866 • *8,429*
White Oak, OH 45239 • *4,900*
White Oak, PA 15131 • *9,480*
White Pigeon, MI 49099 • *1,478*
White Pine, MI 49971 • *1,400*
White Pine, TN 37890 • *1,900*
White Pine □, NV • *8,167*
White Plains, KY 42464 • *859*
White Plains, MD 20695 • *5,167*
White Plains, NY 10601–99 • *46,999*
Whiteriver, AZ 85941 • *1,400*
White River Junction, VT 05001 • *2,582*
White Salmon, WA 98672 • *1,853*
Whitesboro, NJ 08252 • *900*
Whitesboro, NY 13492 • *4,460*
Whitesboro, TX 76273 • *3,197*
Whitesburg, GA 30185 • *775*
Whitesburg, KY 41858 • *1,525*
White Settlement, TX 76108 • *13,508*
Whiteside □, IL • *65,970*
White Springs, FL 32096 • *781*
White Sulphur Springs, MT 59645 • *1,302*
White Sulphur Springs, WV 24986 • *3,371*
Whitesville, KY 42378 • *788*
Whitesville, WV 25209 • *689*
Whiteville, NC 28472 • *5,565*
Whiteville, TN 38075 • *1,270*
Whitewater, KS 67154 • *751*
Whitewater, WI 53190 • *11,520*
Whitewood, SD 57793 • *821*
Whitewright, TX 75491 • *1,760*
Whitfield □, GA • *65,789*
Whitfield Estates, FL 34243 • *3,000*
Whiting, IN 46394 • *5,630*
Whiting, IA 51063 • *734*
Whiting, NJ 08759 • *700*
Whiting, WI 54481 • *2,050*
Whitinsville, MA 01588 • *5,379*
Whitley □, IN • *26,215*
Whitley □, KY • *33,396*
Whitley City, KY 42653 • *1,683*
Whitman, MA 02382 • *13,534*
Whitman, WV 25652 • *950*
Whitman □, WA • *40,103*
Whitman Square, NJ 08012 • *2,600*
Whitmire, SC 29178 • *2,038*
Whitmore Lake, MI 48189 • *2,920*
Whitmore Village, HI 96786 • *2,318*
Whitney, SC 29303 • *1,800*
Whitney, TX 76692 • *1,631*
Whitney Point, NY 13862 • *1,093*
Whittemore, IA 50598 • *647*
Whittier, CA 90601–12 • *69,717*
Whitwell, TN 37397 • *1,783*
Wibaux, MT 59353 • *782*
Wibaux □, MT • *1,476*
Wichita, KS 67201–99 • *279,835*
Wichita □, KS • *3,041*
Wichita □, TX • *121,082*
Wichita Falls, TX 76301–11 • *94,201*
Wickenburg, AZ 85358 • *3,535*
Wickett, TX 79788 • *689*
Wickliffe, KY 42087 • *1,034*
Wickliffe, OH 44515 • *8,800*
Wicomico □, MD • *64,540*
Wiconisco, PA 17097 • *1,236*
Widefield, CO 80911 • *7,500*
Wiggins, MS 39577 • *3,205*
Wilbarger □, TX • *15,931*
Wilber, NE 68465 • *1,624*
Wilberforce, OH 45384 • *2,512*

Wilbraham, MA 01095 • *3,379*
Wilbur, WA 99185 • *1,122*
Wilburton, OK 74578 • *2,996*
Wilcox, PA 15870 • *900*
Wilcox □, AL • *14,755*
Wilcox □, GA • *7,682*
Wilder, ID 83676 • *1,260*
Wilder, VT 05088 • *1,461*
Wild Rose, WI 54984 • *741*
Wildwood, FL 32785 • *2,665*
Wildwood, NJ 08260 • *4,913*
Wildwood Crest, NJ 08260 • *4,149*
Wilkes □, GA • *10,951*
Wilkes □, NC • *58,657*
Wilkes-Barre, PA 18701–99 • *51,551*
Wilkesboro, NC 28697 • *2,335*
Wilkin □, MN • *8,454*
Wilkinsburg, PA 15221 • *23,669*
Wilkinson, WV 25653 • *700*
Wilkinson □, GA • *10,368*
Wilkinson □, MS • *10,021*
Will □, IL • *324,460*
Willacoochee, GA 31650 • *1,166*
Willacy □, TX • *17,495*
Willamina, OR 97396 • *1,749*
Willard, MO 65781 • *1,799*
Willard, NY 14588 • *700*
Willard, OH 44890 • *5,720*
Willard, UT 84340 • *1,241*
Willcox, AZ 85643 • *3,243*
Williams, AZ 86046 • *2,266*
Williams, CA 95987 • *1,655*
Williams □, ND • *22,237*
Williams □, OH • *36,369*
Williams Bay, WI 53191 • *1,763*
Williamsburg, IA 52361 • *2,033*
Williamsburg, KY 40769 • *5,560*
Williamsburg, MA 01096 • *950*
Williamsburg, OH 45176 • *1,952*
Williamsburg, PA 16693 • *1,400*
Williamsburg, VA 23185 • *9,870*
Williamsburg □, SC • *38,226*
Williamson, NY 14589 • *1,991*
Williamson, WV 25661 • *5,219*
Williamson □, IL • *56,538*
Williamson □, TN • *58,108*
Williamson □, TX • *76,507*
Williamsport, IN 47993 • *1,747*
Williamsport, MD 21795 • *2,153*
Williamsport, OH 43164 • *792*
Williamsport, PA 17701 • *33,401*
Williamston, MI 48895 • *2,981*
Williamston, NC 27892 • *6,159*
Williamston, SC 29697 • *4,310*
Williamstown, KY 41097 • *2,502*
Williamstown, MA 01267 • *4,798*
Williamstown, NJ 08094 • *5,768*
Williamstown, PA 17098 • *1,664*
Williamstown, VT 05679 • *650*
Williamstown, WV 26187 • *3,095*
Williamsville, IL 62693 • *996*
Williamsville, NY 14221 • *6,017*
Willimantic, CT 06226 • *14,652*
Willingboro, NJ 08046 • *39,912*
Willis, TX 77378 • *1,674*
Williston, FL 32696 • *2,240*
Williston, ND 58801 • *13,336*
Williston, SC 29853 • *3,173*
Williston Park, NY 11596 • *8,216*
Willisville, IL 62997 • *628*
Willits, CA 95490 • *4,008*
Willmar, MN 56201 • *15,895*
Willoughby, OH 44094 • *19,329*
Willoughby Hills, OH 44092 • *8,612*
Willow Brook, CA 90222 • *30,845*
Willow Grove, PA 19090 • *21,300*
Willowick, OH 44094 • *17,834*
Willow Run, DE 19805 • *1,950*
Willow Run, MI 48197 • *6,400*
Willows, CA 95988 • *4,777*
Willow Springs, IL 60480 • *4,147*
Willow Springs, MO 65793 • *2,215*
Willsboro, NY 12996 • *950*
Willston, VA 22044 • *2,500*
Wilmar, AR 71675 • *747*
Wilmer, TX 75172 • *2,367*
Wilmerding, PA 15148 • *2,421*
Wilmette, IL 60091 • *28,229*
Wilmington, DE 19801–99 • *70,195*
Wilmington, IL 60481 • *4,424*
Wilmington, MA 01887 • *17,471*
Wilmington, NC 28401–06 • *44,000*
Wilmington, OH 45177 • *10,431*
Wilmington Manor, DE 19720 • *2,000*
Wilmington Manor Gardens, DE 19720 • *1,600*
Wilmore, KY 40390 • *3,787*
Wilmot, AR 71676 • *1,227*
Wilson, AR 72395 • *1,115*
Wilson, KS 67490 • *978*
Wilson, LA 70789 • *656*
Wilson, NC 27893 • *34,424*
Wilson, NY 14172 • *1,259*
Wilson, OK 73463 • *1,585*
Wilson, PA 18042 • *7,564*
Wilson □, KS • *12,128*
Wilson □, NC • *63,132*
Wilson □, TN • *56,064*
Wilson □, TX • *16,756*
Wilsonville, AL 35186 • *914*
Wilsonville, IL 62093 • *608*
Wilsonville, OR 97070 • *2,920*
Wilton, AL 35187 • *642*
Wilton, CT 06897 • *6,500*
Wilton, IA 52778 • *2,502*
Wilton, ME 04294 • *2,262*
Wilton, NH 03086 • *1,310*
Wilton, ND 58579 • *950*
Wilton Manors, FL 33334 • *12,742*
Wimauma, FL 33598 • *1,477*
Winamac, IN 46996 • *2,370*
Winburne, PA 16879 • *650*
Winchendon, MA 01475 • *4,030*
Winchester, IL 62694 • *1,716*
Winchester, IN 47394 • *5,659*
Winchester, KY 40391 • *15,216*
Winchester, MA 01890 • *20,701*
Winchester, NV 89101 • *19,728*
Winchester, NH 03470 • *1,732*
Winchester, OH 45697 • *1,080*
Winchester, TN 37398 • *5,821*

# United States Populations and ZIP Codes

Winchester, VA 22601 • 20,217
Winchester Bay, OR 97467 • 900
Windber, PA 15963 • 5,585
Windcrest, TX 78239 • 5,332
Winder, GA 30680 • 6,705
Windfall, IN 46076 • 911
Windgap, PA 18091 • 2,651
Windham, CT 06280 • 700
Windham, OH 44288 • 3,721
Windham □, CT • 92,312
Windham □, VT • 36,933
Wind Lake, WI 53185 • 2,400
Windom, MN 56101 • 4,666
Window Rock, AZ 86515 • 2,230
Wind Point, WI 53402 • 1,695
Windsor, CO 80550 • 4,277
Windsor, CT 06095 • 17,517
Windsor, IL 61957 • 1,228
Windsor, MO 65360 • 3,058
Windsor, NC 27983 • 2,126
Windsor, PA 17366 • 1,205
Windsor, VT 05089 • 4,084
Windsor, VA 23487 • 985
Windsor □, VT • 51,030
Windsor Forest, GA 31406 • 7,288
Windsor Heights, IA 50311 • 5,474
Windsor Hills, CA 90052 • 6,200
Windsor Locks, CT 06096 • 12,190
Windy Hill, SC 29501 • 1,605
Windy Hills, DE 19711 • 1,300
Winfall, NC 27985 • 634
Winfield, AL 35594 • 3,781
Winfield, IA 52659 • 1,042
Winfield, KS 67156 • 10,736
Winfield, IL 07036 • 1,785
Wingate, NC 28174 • 2,615
Wingo, KY 42088 • 606
Winifrede, WV 25214 • 800
Wink, TX 79789 • 1,182
Winkelman, AZ 85292 • 1,060
Winkler □, TX • 9,944
Winlock, WA 98596 • 1,052
Winn □, LA • 17,253
Winnebago, IL 61088 • 1,644
Winnebago, MN 56098 • 1,869
Winnebago, NE 68071 • 902
Winnebago □, IL • 250,884
Winnebago □, IA • 13,010
Winnebago □, WI • 131,772
Winneconne, WI 54986 • 1,935
Winnemucca, NV 89445 • 4,140
Winner, SD 57580 • 3,472
Winneshiek □, IA • 21,876
Winnetka, IL 60093 • 12,772
Winnfield, LA 71483 • 7,311
Winnsboro, LA 71295 • 5,921
Winnsboro, SC 29180 • 2,919
Winnsboro, TX 75494 • 3,458
Winnsboro Mills, SC 29180 • 1,890
Winona, MN 55987 • 25,075
Winona, MS 38967 • 6,177
Winona, MO 65588 • 1,050
Winona □, MN • 46,256
Winona Lake, IN 46590 • 2,827
Winooski, VT 05404 • 6,318
Winslow, AZ 86047 • 7,921
Winslow, IN 47598 • 1,017
Winslow, ME 04901 • 5,903
Winslow, WA 98110 • 2,196
Winsted, CT 06098 • 8,092
Winsted, MN 55395 • 1,522
Winston, FL 33803 • 5,500
Winston, OR 97496 • 3,359
Winston □, AL • 21,953
Winston □, MS • 19,474
Winston-Salem, NC 27101–99 • 131,885
Winter Beach, FL 32971 • 700
Winter Garden, FL 32787 • 6,789

Winter Harbor, ME 04693 • 900
Winter Haven, FL 33880–88 • 21,119
Winter Park, FL 32789–93 • 22,339
Winter Park, NC 28401 • 4,504
Winterport, ME 04496 • 1,126
Winters, CA 95694 • 2,652
Winters, TX 79567 • 3,061
Winterset, IA 50273 • 4,021
Winter Springs, FL 32708 • 10,475
Wintersville, OH 43952 • 4,724
Winterville, GA 30683 • 621
Winterville, NC 28590 • 2,052
Winthrop, IA 50682 • 767
Winthrop, ME 04364 • 3,264
Winthrop, MA 02152 • 19,294
Winthrop, MN 55396 • 1,376
Winthrop Harbor, IL 60096 • 5,431
Winton, NC 27986 • 825
Wirt □, WV • 4,922
Wiscasset, ME 04578 • 1,350
Wisconsin Dells, WI 53965 • 2,521
Wisconsin Rapids, WI 54494 • 17,995
Wise, VA 24293 • 3,894
Wise □, TX • 26,575
Wise □, VA • 43,863
Wishek, ND 58495 • 1,345
Wishram, WA 98673 • 675
Wisner, LA 71378 • 1,424
Wisner, NE 68791 • 1,335
Withamsville, OH 45245 • 3,650
Witherbee, NY 12998 • 1,000
Witt, IL 62094 • 1,205
Wittenberg, WI 54499 • 997
Wittmann, AZ 85361 • 700
Wixom, MI 48096 • 6,705
Wolcott, CT 06716 • 5,500
Wolcott, IN 47995 • 923
Wolcott, NY 14590 • 1,496
Wolcottville, IN 46795 • 890
Wolfe □, KY • 6,698
Wolfeboro, NH 03894 • 1,800
Wolfe City, TX 75496 • 1,594
Wolf Lake, MI 49442 • 3,876
Wolf Point, MT 59201 • 3,074
Womelsdorf, PA 19567 • 1,827
Wonder Lake, IL 60097 • 752
Wonewoc, WI 53968 • 842
Wood □, OH • 107,372
Wood □, TX • 24,697
Wood □, WV • 93,648
Wood □, WI • 72,799
Woodbine, GA 31569 • 910
Woodbine, IA 51579 • 1,463
Woodbine, NJ 08270 • 2,809
Woodbourne, NY 12788 • 1,155
Woodbridge, CT 06525 • 7,600
Woodbridge, NJ 07095 • 16,400
Woodbridge, VA 22191–99 • 35,000
Woodburn, IN 46797 • 1,002
Woodburn, OR 97071 • 11,196
Woodbury, CT 06798 • 1,299
Woodbury, GA 30293 • 1,738
Woodbury, MN 55119 • 10,297
Woodbury, NJ 08096 • 10,353
Woodbury, TN 37190 • 2,160
Woodbury □, IA • 100,884
Woodcliff Lake, NJ 07675 • 5,644
Wood Dale, IL 60191 • 11,251
Woodfield, SC 29206 • 9,588
Woodford □, IL • 33,320
Woodford □, KY • 17,778
Woodhaven, MI 48183 • 10,902
Woodhull, IL 61490 • 901
Woodlake, CA 93286 • 4,343
Woodland, CA 95695 • 30,235
Woodland, GA 31836 • 664
Woodland, ME 04694 • 1,363

Woodland, NC 27897 • 861
Woodland, WA 98674 • 2,341
Woodland Acres, CO 81069 • 800
Woodland Park, CO 80863 • 2,634
Woodlawn, KY 42001 • 1,200
Woodlawn, MD 21207 • 8,000
Woodlawn, OH 45215 • 2,715
Woodlyn, PA 19094 • 6,000
Woodlynne, NJ 08107 • 2,578
Woodmere, NY 11598 • 19,700
Woodmont, CT 06460 • 1,797
Woodmoor, MD 21207 • 7,600
Woodridge, IL 60517 • 22,561
Wood-Ridge, NJ 07075 • 7,929
Wood River, IL 62095 • 12,446
Wood River, NE 68883 • 1,334
Woodruff, SC 29388 • 5,171
Woodruff, WI 54568 • 900
Woodruff □, AR • 11,222
Woods □, OK • 10,923
Woodsboro, TX 78393 • 1,974
Woods Cross, UT 84087 • 4,263
Woodsfield, OH 43793 • 3,145
Woods Hole, MA 02543 • 1,080
Woodside, CA 94062 • 5,291
Woodson □, KS • 4,600
Woodstock, GA 30188 • 2,699
Woodstock, IL 60098 • 11,725
Woodstock, MD 21163 • 700
Woodstock, NY 12498 • 1,073
Woodstock, VT 05091 • 1,178
Woodstock, VA 22664 • 2,627
Woodstown, NJ 08098 • 3,250
Woodsville, NH 03785 • 1,195
Woodville, FL 32362 • 1,768
Woodville, MS 39669 • 1,512
Woodville, OH 43469 • 2,050
Woodville, TX 75979 • 2,821
Woodville, WI 54028 • 725
Woodward, IA 50276 • 1,212
Woodward, OK 73801 • 13,610
Woodward □, OK • 21,172
Woodway, TX 76710 • 7,091
Woolmarket, MS 39532 • 670
Woolrich, PA 17779 • 700
Woonsocket, RI 02895 • 45,914
Woonsocket, SD 97385 • 799
Wooster, OH 44691 • 19,289
Worcester, MA 01601–99 • 161,799
Worcester, NY 12197 • 950
Worcester □, MD • 30,889
Worcester □, MA • 646,352
Worden, IL 62097 • 953
Worland, WY 82401 • 6,391
Worth, IL 60482 • 11,592
Worth □, GA • 18,064
Worth □, IA • 9,075
Worth □, MO • 3,008
Wortham, TX 76693 • 1,187
Worthington, IN 47471 • 1,574
Worthington, KY 41183 • 1,948
Worthington, MN 56187 • 10,243
Worthington, OH 43085 • 15,016
Worthington, PA 16262 • 760
Wrangell, AK 99929 • 2,184
Wray, CO 80758 • 2,131
Wrens, GA 30833 • 2,415
Wrentham, MA 02093 • 1,400
Wright □, IA • 16,319
Wright □, MN • 58,681
Wright □, MO • 16,188
Wright City, MO 63390 • 1,179
Wright City, OK 74766 • 1,168
Wrightstown, NJ 08562 • 3,031
Wrightstown, WI 54180 • 1,169
Wrightsville, AR 72183 • 1,100
Wrightsville, GA 31096 • 2,526
Wrightsville, PA 17368 • 2,365

Wrightsville Beach, NC 28480 • 2,910
Wrightwood, CA 92397 • 2,511
Wurtsboro, NY 12790 • 1,128
Wyalusing, PA 18853 • 716
Wyandanch, NY 11798 • 17,900
Wyandot □, OH • 22,651
Wyandotte, MI 48192 • 34,006
Wyandotte □, KS • 172,335
Wyanet, IL 61379 • 1,069
Wyckoff, NJ 07481 • 15,500
Wymore, NE 68466 • 1,841
Wyncote, PA 19095 • 5,300
Wyndmoor, PA 19118 • 5,800
Wynne, AR 72396 • 7,805
Wynnewood, OK 73098 • 2,615
Wynnewood, PA 19096 • 7,700
Wynona, OK 74084 • 780
Wyoming, DE 19934 • 960
Wyoming, IL 61491 • 1,614
Wyoming, IA 52362 • 702
Wyoming, MI 49509 • 59,616
Wyoming, MN 55092 • 1,559
Wyoming, OH 45215 • 8,282
Wyoming, PA 18644 • 3,655
Wyoming □, NY • 39,895
Wyoming □, PA • 26,433
Wyoming □, WV • 35,993
Wyomissing, PA 19610 • 6,551
Wythe □, VA • 25,522
Wytheville, VA 24382 • 7,135

## X

Xenia, OH 45385 • 24,653

## Y

Yadkin □, NC • 28,439
Yadkinville, NC 27055 • 2,216
Yakima, WA 98901–09 • 49,826
Yakima □, WA • 172,508
Yalaha, FL 32797 • 950
Yale, MI 48097 • 1,814
Yale, OK 74085 • 1,652
Yalobusha □, MS • 13,139
Yamhill, OR 97148 • 690
Yamhill □, OR • 55,332
Yancey □, NC • 14,934
Yanceyville, NC 27379 • 1,511
Yankton, SD 57078 • 12,011
Yankton □, SD • 18,952
Yardley, PA 19067 • 2,533
Yardville, NJ 08620 • 8,400
Yarmouth, ME 04096 • 2,421
Yarmouth, MA 02675 • 900
Yarmouth Port, MA 02675 • 2,490
Yarnell, AZ 85362 • 950
Yates □, NY • 21,459
Yatesboro, PA 16263 • 700
Yates Center, KS 66783 • 1,998
Yates City, IL 61572 • 860
Yavapai □, AZ • 68,145
Yazoo □, MS • 27,349
Yazoo City, MS 39194 • 12,092
Yeadon, PA 19050 • 11,727
Yeagertown, PA 17099 • 1,363
Yell □, AR • 17,026
Yellow Medicine □, MN • 13,653
Yellow Springs, OH 45387 • 4,077
Yellowstone □, MT • 108,035
Yellowstone National Park □, MT • 275
Yellville, AR 72687 • 1,044
Yelm, WA 98597 • 1,294
Yemassee, SC 29945 • 789
Yerington, NV 89447 • 2,021
Yermo, CA 92398 • 1,092
Yoakum, TX 77995 • 6,148

Yoakum □, TX • 8,299
Yolo □, CA • 113,374
Yoncalla, OR 97499 • 805
Yonkers, NY 10701–99 • 195,351
Yorba Linda, CA 92686 • 28,254
York, AL 36925 • 3,392
York, ME 03909 • 3,130
York, NE 68467 • 7,723
York, PA 17401–99 • 44,619
York, SC 29745 • 6,412
York □, ME • 139,666
York □, NE • 14,798
York □, PA • 312,963
York □, SC • 106,720
York □, VA • 35,463
York Beach, ME 03910 • 860
York Harbor, ME 03911 • 1,400
York Haven, PA 17370 • 746
Yorkshire, NY 14173 • 850
Yorktown, IN 47396 • 3,945
Yorktown, NY 10598 • 5,400
Yorktown, TX 78164 • 2,498
Yorktown Heights, NY 10598 • 5,900
Yorktown Manor, RI 02852 • 1,300
Yorkville, IL 60560 • 3,422
Yorkville, NY 13495 • 3,115
Yorkville, OH 43971 • 1,447
Yosemite National Park, CA 95389 • 1,073
Young □, TX • 19,083
Young Harris, GA 30582 • 687
Youngstown, NY 14174 • 2,191
Youngstown, OH 44501–99 • 115,436
Youngsville, LA 70592 • 1,053
Youngsville, PA 16371 • 2,006
Youngtown, AZ 85363 • 2,254
Youngwood, PA 15697 • 3,749
Ypsilanti, MI 48197 • 24,031
Yreka, CA 96097 • 5,916
Yuba □, CA • 49,733
Yuba City, CA 95991 • 18,736
Yucaipa, CA 92399 • 20,000
Yukon, OK 73099 • 17,112
Yulee, FL 32097 • 3,168
Yuma, AZ 85364–69 • 42,481
Yuma □, AZ • 78,054
Yuma, CO 80759 • 2,824
Yuma □, CO • 9,682
Yutan, NE 68073 • 631

## Z

Zachary, LA 70791 • 7,297
Zanesville, OH 43701 • 28,655
Zapata, TX 78076 • 2,500
Zapata □, TX • 6,628
Zavala □, TX • 11,666
Zavalla, TX 75980 • 762
Zearing, IA 50278 • 630
Zebulon, GA 30295 • 995
Zebulon, NC 27597 • 2,055
Zeeland, MI 49464 • 4,764
Zeigler, IL 62999 • 1,858
Zelienople, PA 16063 • 3,502
Zephyr Cove, NV 89448 • 1,300
Zephyrhills, FL 34248–49 • 5,742
Ziebach □, SD • 2,308
Zillah, WA 98953 • 1,599
Zilwaukee, MI 48604 • 2,201
Zimmerman, MN 55398 • 1,074
Zion, IL 60099 • 17,861
Zionsville, IN 46077 • 3,948
Zolfo Springs, FL 33890 • 1,495
Zumbrota, MN 55992 • 2,129
Zuni, NM 87327 • 5,551
Zwolle, LA 71486 • 2,602